Irish Writing in the Twentieth Century

Irish Writing in the Twentieth Century

A READER

edited by
DAVID PIERCE

CORK UNIVERSITY PRESS

First published in 2000 by
Cork University Press
Cork
Ireland

British Library Cataloguing in Publication Data
A CIP catalogue record for this book is available from the British Library.

Library of Congress Cataloging-in-Publication Data

Irish writing in the twentieth century : a reader / edited by David Pierce.
       p. cm.
       Includes bibliographical references and index.
       ISBN 1-85918-258-5 (alk. paper) — ISBN 1-85918-208-9 (pbk. : alk. paper)
1. English literature—Irish authors. 2. English literature—20th
century. 3. Irish literature—Translations into English. 4.
Ireland—Literary collections. I. Pierce, David, 1947–
PR8844 .I76 2000
820.8'09417'0904—dc21

                                                                    00-056959

ISBN 1 85918 258 5 hardback
   1 85918 208 9 paperback

Typeset by Phtototype-Set Ltd, Dublin
Printed by MPG Books, Cornwall

For Alistair Stead, Richard Brown, and Pieter Bekker,
and friends in the wider Joyce community

CONTENTS

Irish Writing in the 1910s

Irish Writing in the 1920s

Irish Writing in the 1930s

Irish Writing in the 1940s

Irish Writing in the 1950s

Irish Writing in the 1960s

Irish Writing in the 1970s

CRITICAL AND DOCUMENTARY

Irish Writing in the 1980s

Irish Writing in the 1990s

IMAGINATIVE

ON A PERSONAL NOTE

Here at the beginning, you or your tutor may want to explore attitudes towards Irish writing from a personal angle. My own circumstances, caught half-way between England and Ireland, are not unique and might find an echo in your experience. As a child in the west of Ireland I found myself spending hours inside the living room at my grandmother's home in Caherbarna, Co. Clare, often looking south at the landscape and the ever-changing cloudscape and sky. My memory is now permanently scored with what resembles a primal scene, at once obvious and impenetrable. It was a laid-out landscape, ready for the painter to draw or the philosopher to admire. The fields were pieced together as if by God and not hedged in by the bitter land conflicts of the nineteenth century. In the centre of the picture is the bay of Liscannor and the resort of Lahinch, famous for its golf-links and for its mention in Percy French's 1896 song about the West Clare Railway 'Are Ye Right There, Michael?'; beyond, the magnificent and weighty slopes of Slieve Callan, where in pre-Christian times the feast of Lughnasa, a corn festival, was celebrated by lighting bonfires. To the right, there is the ruin of O'Brien's Tower, and further right in the middle distance is St Bridget's Well, a favourite stopping-off point for locals and haunt of Aran islanders on Garland Sunday. In the background of the canvas, on clear days, the contours of the Kerry Mountains, some sixty miles way, come into view. Nearby are the Cliffs of Moher, which my grandmother, unable to conceive of her locality as something to view, did not visit until she was in her seventies.

Poverty was a dull, background accompaniment but not the theme of our lives. The village in County Clare where I took my first steps in June 1948 had no running water, no electricity, and was effectively in the 'back of beyond': even today the road up to the village can be negotiated only with difficulty or in a car with a good suspension. The village had the appropriately inhospitable name of Caherbarna, or Cathair Bhearna, the gap of the homestead.[1] When I was young the townland of Caherbarna East consisted of some eleven houses all within a stone's throw of each other, but most of the families are now gone and many of the houses in ruins.[2] In retrospect, steady decline accompanied poverty, but that was not so obvious at the time. What I did vaguely sense was that my family felt dispossessed in Ireland of the Welcomes. How could it be otherwise when we had little to call our own? My grandmother's eighteen-acre farm, 200 metres above Liscannor Bay, comprised a vegetable patch, a couple of meadows, the side of a mountain and much bogland; my aunt's home, next to the shore beside the ruins of St Kilmacreehy's Church, was an agricultural labourer's cottage with less than an acre attached. In the 1905 edition of *Kelly's Directory for Ireland* there is no mention of any of the names in the family.

The most sentimental aspect to all this was that as a child and adolescent returning home to Ireland in summer from Sussex, I had no idea which powerful interest groups ran the country or why my family had been disenfranchised. I do remember going to the creamery with my uncle John Kilmartin on what I learn from Estyn Evans's *Irish Folk Ways* (1957) was a flat Scots cart which had been introduced into Ireland in the nineteenth century. The creamery can was strapped down by a coarse hay-rope, we sat on cushions of straw with legs dangling aside the two shafts, and drew over into ditches when we risked delaying the priest's Volkswagen or the hotelier's Mercedes.

But even though we were firmly excluded by circumstance from sharing the capital then being accumulated in Ireland, I always felt inside the culture, a culture I perceived even from an early age not so much in the adversarial terms of 'them and us' but as local and familial, tied to priest and parish. When I began my education proper I remember reading about Lady Gregory's visits to St Bridget's Well in search of material for her work on *Visions and Beliefs in the West of Ireland* (1920). A mile from our family home in a northerly direction is the parish of Luogh, an area chosen by Conrad Arensberg for his anthropological study *The Irish Countryman* (1937). Seven miles away is the market town of Ennistymon, the setting for Arensberg and Solon Kimball's *Family and Community in Ireland* (1940), the town where my grandmother would trek to shop, walking there and back from the anthropologist's 'rural hinterland'. Somehow I sensed that all these investigators from the academy or the Big House, even as they turned families like my own into passing objects of their investigation, were outside the culture of which I was a part. Equally, association, memory, experience have their own story to tell and an inner compulsion that undermines the work of the intellect. In reality outside and inside were reversed: charm was scarcity, the thatch leaked, the gables always in need of limewash, and the chimney open to the sky and to capricious changes in wind direction. And yet my Irish family betrayed or expressed almost no resentment. 'It's well for some' was a phrase never heard within the confines of the family. We seemed to be sufficient unto ourselves. I must have been conscious, however, at an early age that such a lifestyle was passing and worth recording, for at the heart of what I have done since has been in some sense a tribute to it.

As a child in Sussex 'Are we going home this summer?' was a question often heard. More often than not we did make the 24-hour journey, my mother and four children, each carrying one or two items of luggage; my father, who worked at Lancing Railway Carriageworks as a boilerman, would often join us later for part of the holidays. Complete with privilege tickets ensuring free passage to Dublin, we caught the train to London at around 5 o'clock in the evening, then across London by underground, and the boat-train from Paddington to Holyhead, where in the middle of the night we boarded the steamer to Dun Laoghaire, then the train into Westland Row, across Dublin by bus, train to Athenry, change for Ennis, the West Clare railway to Lahinch, then the wait for Talty the taxi-driver, and home around 5 o'clock in the evening. It was a nightmare of a journey; we were all bad travellers, invariably sea-sick, and paid more than our dues to Cathleen Ní Houlihan, romantic Ireland and her four green fields. What we looked like to others was immaterial. The first summer I spent in Ireland I was brought over in a pram. On another visit we travelled with our belongings wrapped in some twenty parcels distributed among the children. If outsiders imagined us like the Bundrens in William Faulkner's Mississippi novel *As I Lay Dying* (1931), objects of contempt, or simply the poor in transit, we felt none of it. And with no conspicuous consumption or goloshes to protect our shoes, there was certainly none of the returned Yank about us either.

It took a week or two of arriving in the west for the giddiness of the sea's waves to abate and for us to become accustomed to the broad accent of the people. Early on in our stay, as part of the welcoming celebrations, grandmother would throw a house dance, invite the neighbours and the musicians, prepare the food, arrange the furniture, and get ready the inside bedroom for guests to take tea in turns. On one legendary occasion before I was born she arranged a get-together on the evening of a dance organised by the parish priest in the local hall. The 1935 Dance Halls Act was effectively designed to enrich the church and restrain the people. All the Liscannor faithful gathered at my grandmother's house in Caherbarna much to the priest's annoyance. Not one to lick his wounds, the priest later that night forced his way into the house of music only to be rebuffed by my grandmother who somehow in the struggle managed to end up with his collar, which she humbly returned the following morning at the presbytery door.[3] There was sporadic rebellion in the family but no permanent revolution.

House dances have all but disappeared from the Irish countryside but they were at one time very common and, as we learn from a chance observation in Henry Mayhew's *London Labour and the London Poor* (1851), they also accompanied Irish emigrants abroad: 'I did not hear of any amusements popular among, or much resorted to, by the Irishmen, except dancing parties at one another's houses, where they jig and reel furiously.'[4] The view from inside the culture was of course different: you only jigged (never incidentally used as a verb) furiously when you couldn't keep time. In the corner by the door at Caherbarna, within reach of the holy water font, were positioned invited musicians for the night, three on an all-purpose kitchen-table and two or three in front on rush-seated chairs.

County Clare is known as the home of traditional music, and it possesses its own distinctive rolling ornamented style of playing, capable of great subtlety and depth of feeling. Musicians I recall coming to the house included the flute-player Autie Linnane, who had a limp, and the Killoughry brothers. Paddy Killoughry, whose photo can be seen in Nuala O'Connor's *Bringing It All Back Home* (1991), accompanied his fiddle-playing with dextrous leg movements, more so in later life; Jack was more reserved and never appeared without a hat. A young and handsome-looking John Burke, who was brought up by my grandmother at Caherbarna, is also there in my memory. He had taught himself to play the fiddle shut up in a bedroom only to take his talents across the water to the pubs off the Kilburn Road in London. There he could be found accompanying himself singing songs with opening lines such as 'Adieu, lovely Mary; I am now going to leave you'.[5] My uncle John, who never stirred from home, is also forever playing there in my memory as is an eternally youthful Denis Guerin who emigrated to New York to find work as a salaried elevator operator in an apartment block.

Long before he became an international figure in Irish traditional music circles, the flute-player Micho Russell would play at our house dances. Indeed as late as 1968 Micho played all night on his own at one of the last house dances in that part of County Clare, only stopping for some tea in the room or for a song or to beam, basking in the glory of his own people's adulation.[6] Many summers I would drive Micho, who was then in his fifties and still relatively unknown, all over the west of Ireland to visit dancers or singers or musicians he was keen on meeting and whom he had heard about on Radio Éireann. I remember how in a pub in the fishing village of Carraroe in County Galway, Micho managed to coax a celebrated dancer into performing in the wellington boots he wore for work. On another occasion in Spiddal where the Wolfe Tones, a popular Irish band at the time, were playing to a packed house under a huge currach hanging from the ceiling, Micho, husky-voiced and soft-spoken, leaned over to me slightly agitated: 'Would you ever ask them if they would mind me playing a few tunes on the stage?' Another day we visited a County Galway singer whose singing was exquisite but what I remember more was her father's interviewing of Micho. 'You mean to say you have no Irish.' Micho, not given to defending himself even though he did know Irish, shifted uneasily in front of someone whose amputated leg suggested he had seen action, possibly in the War of Independence. Several times we made a pilgrimage to see Patrick Kelly of Cree, a Clare musician who has a jig named after him and who was according to Seán Ó Riada speaking on Radio Éireann in 1962 'one of the finest fiddlers in Ireland'.[7] He was then quite elderly and would spend his mornings in bed, but he remained highly intelligent and alert, and simply by looking at someone dancing knew which dancing master had taught them. Even Micho, who was himself a brilliant musician in spite of not being able to read music, was especially attentive as Patrick showed him how to break up the rhythm of a particular reel or talked about Willie Clancy, the Crehan brothers and musicians of old or about the Redmondites marching through Miltown Malbay when he was a boy during the Great War.[8]

Periodically throughout the night of a dance, a halt would be called in the proceedings, the dancers would take a breather in the night air, water would be sprinkled on the uneven Luogh flagstones to keep the dirt from rising, and one of the guests would be encouraged to sing. At the end of a song or two the Clare half-set would start up again, reel followed by jig, by more reels, by jigs and then a hornpipe to round it off. I see it all again, me sitting on the edge of the settle bed, my eyes getting heavy with sleep. I am there taken up into the swirl of the dance, the clicking or trooping of the heels, the eyes of the dancers fixing me: 'Remember us when you come into your kingdom.' Other less romantic voices call to me down the years: 'Jasus will you mind the dresser.' 'I'm killed entirely.' 'Let me up out of this; give me some air for Christ's sake.' There in that darkened living room of my grandmother's cottage, lit only by an oil-lamp to the left of the fireplace above the hob, with the low murmuring, and the repeated entrances of strange figures from the dark with their reassuring 'God bless all here' — here was a world a young Thomas Hardy would also have recognised as he accompanied his father to house dances in Dorset in the 1840s and 1850s. It was for me a time before time began, and even today my academic work refuses to obliterate that line between the known and the half-known, as if the latter were always more important than the former and in need of protection. For what I inherited from my family was a mixed estate: a country of the mind to carry with me wherever I go and a hidden Ireland forever associated with my childhood and youth.

My Irish family were not great singers or natural musicians, but it was a great family for dancers. For her party piece my aunt Mary Haugh danced the 'The Blackbird',[9] an intricate solo dance; my mother was one of the best dancers around. Thirty years ago I was in conversation with Micho Russell's brother Packie, the concertina player who helped put Fisher Street in Doolin on the map. We were talking about all the great dancers he had played for, and chief among them I learnt was Pat Kilmartin, one of my uncles who had emigrated to England in the 1930s and worked his way across Britain harvesting until eventually finding his life's work with Laings on building sites round London. His legs deteriorated in his last years but one of his grand-daughters, who had hardly set foot outside of Reading in Berkshire, became a prize-winning Irish step dancer.

Mary Haugh, now in her seventies and the best storyteller in the family (not for nothing was she book-keeper of St Kilmacreehy graveyard), movingly recalls that era:

> As far back as I remember the old house was popular for dances, music, card-playing and story-telling. Dad (my grandfather who died in 1931) was good to tell stories and often invited to neighbouring houses to entertain them with his stories. Mummer dances, collection dances and gambles were held in the house. Dancing continued until the early hours of the morning. Tea and cake were provided and at mummer dances they had a couple of casks of Guinness; at other dances only the musicians got drink. Autie Linnane was the usual musician; he played on a concertina or tin whistle. Later, Paddy and John Killoughry and the Russells

provided the music for the big dances and the house was packed with people. Much later, John Kilmartin, John Guerin, John Burke, accompanied sometimes by the Killoughrys and Russells, entertained and were a joy to dance to. There was also step dancing while the musicians had a break and songs were sung. My earliest memories of the songs sung were by Jacky Russell singing 'The Shawl of Galway Bay' and by Martin Flanagan singing 'Eileen McMahon' and 'The Boys the County Mayo'. In the late 1940s, those great times for music and dances, I remember Mickey Guerin before he went to America singing 'The Valley of Knockanure'.

Singing was my introduction to Irish literature, and like Mary Haugh only a little prompting is needed to recall the people and the singers: Dan Considine 'The Waves of the Silvery Tide', Michael Malone the Fenian song 'Down Erin's Lovely Lea', Mary Kelly the sentimental emigration song 'Where the Shannon Water Flows'. I cannot remember a time when the words of a song were not ringing in my head: 'Revenge for Skibbereen', words from a song about the Great Famine; 'the West's Asleep, the West's Asleep', quaintly literary I remember even at the time; the rabbits in that rural idyll popularised by Christy Moore 'making holes for their homes round the cliffs of Dooneen'. The plight of emigrants always touched me. In the mid-1950s I remember being present at an American Wake, a night of music and song to celebrate and mourn the emigration of a family member to the States. It took place in a house now owned by the traditional musician Davy Spillane. I was only eight or nine at the time but remember being affected by the finality of the decision for this was the last night Tommy MacNamara's nephew would spend in Ireland, possibly, unlike today's emigrant, never to return.[10] I cannot now recall the songs that were sung that night but I remember being uneasy in case any of the phrases should apply and thereby add to his plight. Perhaps the songs were sufficiently formulaic in their phrasing and internal rhymes not to produce too many tears, as in a local song of that area 'Lovely Old Miltown':

> My countrymen I'll take my place and write a verse or two,
> And as I leave to cross the sea I'll bid my last adieu.
> Our splendid boat is now afloat and the Foyle we're sailing down,
> And as I leave my heart did grieve for lovely old Miltown.
>
> ....
>
> Amerikay lies far away, and Philadelphia Town,
> But I'll not forget the friends I left in lovely old Miltown.

By contrast, other emigration songs, such as Brian O'Higgins's 'A Stór Mo Chroí' ('Asthore Machree'), popular at American wakes at the turn of the century and recently revived through the singing of Sara and Rita Keane, have a quality which leaves singer and audience overwhelmed, unprepared for and unsoothed by the entry and course of so much emotion. There is something rather forlorn about Fr Padraig Breathnach's accompanying footnote to this song in his *Songs of the Gael* (1915): 'I hope it will turn many an intending emigrant from his or her purpose of quitting their native land.'[11]

Fighting songs were also never far away and not all of them were brassy like 'Roddy McCorley' or 'Follow Me Up to Carlow'. 'The Valley of Knockanure', for example, remains to my mind one of the best songs composed about war in the twentieth century, made even more special by the *sean nós* or old style singing of Paddy Tunney:

You may sing and speak about Easter Week
And the heroes of '98,
Of the fearless men who roamed the glen
For victory or defeat.
There were those who died on the green hillside
They were outlawed on the moor;
Not a word is said of the gallant dead
In the valley of Knockanure.

With a few light touches and traces of unmistakable irony, Bryan MacMahon sketches in something of the atmosphere of that guerrilla war when in 1919–21 groups of young men took to the hills in flying columns to fight for Irish independence against a British army that numbered over 120,000 and included the notorious unit known as the Black-and-Tans. It was a time for comradeship in arms, for high ideals, for solidarity with a local community against the stranger, for local heroes, for small-scale engagements where a blow could be struck for Ireland, the exploit retold and rewarded, possibly in a song. In *Guerrilla Days in Ireland* (1949), Tom Barry, who led the West Cork Flying Column, concentrates on military strategy and on how much force was needed to achieve particular goals. MacMahon focuses on another side to that human drama, the close links between volunteer, community and countryside, and the courage of young men who, knowing that time wasn't 'mine nor yours', sacrificed their lives for the cause.

Upon an autumn evening
These three young men sat down
To wait upon a brief dispatch
To come from Tralee town.
It wasn't long 'til Lyons came on
Saying time isn't mine nor yours
But alas it was late when they met their fate
In the valley of Knockanure.

Coursing its way beguilingly through these evocative lines and internal rhymes is a sense of Irish history which as a child I half-absorbed as a continuing story of Irish wrongs committed by the English sometime in the not-too-distant past — a past in which I, too, because of my mixed blood, was perhaps complicit.

Until I came across a recent issue of Cló Iar-Chonnachta's catalogue and their wealth of reissues on CD of what had taken me years to collect, I used to think my collection of music quite unique and impossible to gather in that form again. I had the early LPs on the Claddagh and Gael-Linn labels, Irish music on Topic and Leader, the earliest LP of the Kilfenora Céilí Band. In the mid-1960s traditional Irish music was ignored by the major recording studios. Like many of the estimated seventy million people around the world who claim Irish descent, I am prone to confusing what is common with what is personal and vice versa. I know virtually no-one these days who does not have an interesting genealogy, and many of those taking an Irish writing or Irish studies course do so because they are already involved at some level with their family's Irish roots or with the Irish situation and want to talk about it. In Britain of course it is unacceptable to talk too much about your origins unless you are 'superior'. In the States it is *de rigeur* to speak at length about one's past especially if that was a log-cabin, and my California friends cannot see how with my background I could ever want to keep quiet. But in spite of all I have written here I do not see my story as especially unique. Indeed, it might find echoes in your own experience and lead you to tell or put into words your own story. Whatever the case, here at the outset of our journey together there is something to be said for starting at the beginning.[12]

David Pierce
York, 2000

1 'Caher', or circular enclosure, is often found in place-names in the west of Ireland and is particularly associated with rocky terrain: there is a mountain on the borders of Counties Cork and Kerry named Caherbarnagh. For a recent discussion of the term 'caher' see Frank Mitchell and Michael Ryan, *Reading the Irish Landscape* (Dublin: Town House, 1997), pages 254–59.

2 This is not the whole story for since Ireland's entry into the European Union there has been an injection of money and enterprise into the village.

3 For a discussion of the forms, musical accompaniment, social context, attitude of the Church, and twentieth-century institutionalised practices concerning dancing, see Breandan Breathnach, *Dancing in Ireland* (Miltown Malbay: Dal gCais Publications, 1983).

4 Henry Mayhew, *London Labour and the London Poor*, Vol. 1, (London: Charles Griffin & Co, 1864), page 115. For other close observations on Irish immigrants in Victorian London, see Mayhew's chapter entitled 'The Street Irish'.

5 'Adieu Lovely Mary' is a traditional song given new words by Robert Dwyer Joyce. See his *Ballads of Irish Chivalry* (Dublin: Talbot, 1872).

6 For a recent discussion of the house dance and its decline, which includes material from an interview with Micho Russell, see Hazel Fairburn, 'Changing Contexts for Traditional Dance Music in Ireland: The Rise of Group Performance Practice' in *Folk Music Journal*, Vol. 6, No. 5, 1994, pages 566–599. Fairburn's first experience of traditional Irish music 'was in the context of the session', which is, as she observes, 'a relatively new context for traditional Irish music'.

7 See Seán Ó Riada, *Our Musical Heritage* (Portlaoise: Dolmen, 1982), page 57.

8 In 1994 Micho Russell was killed in a road accident, but his memory continues and in February each year there is a weekend commemorating his work. Micho's playing can be heard on the following CDs: *The Russell Family* (Ossian OSS 008), *The Limestone Rock* (GTDH 104), *The Man from Clare* (TRAD HCD 011), *Micho Russell* (Triskel TRL 1009), *Micho Russell: Traditional Music from County Clare* (Celtic Music CMCD077). For a book of the songs he sang, see Micho Russell, *Micho's Dozen: Traditional Songs From The Repertoire Of Micho Russell, Doolin, Co. Clare*. Ennistymon: Ennistymon Festival of Traditional Singing, 1994. See also *The Piper's Chair : A Collection Of Tunes And Folklore From Micho Russell* (tunes transcribed from Micho's Tin whistle-playing by Barbara Wygol ; spoken folklore and stories edited by Jenny Loui) (Cork: Ossian, 1993). For an early profile, see Breandan Breathnach, 'The Man and his Music — Micho Russell' in *Ceol: A Journal of Irish Music*, Vol. 3, No. 4, 1970, pages 98–102. See also recent video of *Ireland's Whistling Ambassador* (Penny Whistler's Press) (also available on CD: PWP CD80001), based on a concert Micho gave in Washington Square Church, New York, 23 June 1992.

9 For a discussion of 'The Blackbird' as a tune, see James R. Cowdery, *The Melodic Tradition of Ireland* (Kent, Ohio: The Kent State University Press, 1990), pages 43–77. The Blackbird was also one of Brendan Behan's party pieces.

10 Today, with the advent of cheap airfares, the situation has altered. As Dermot Bolger has rightly discerned: 'Irish writers no longer go into exile, they simply commute.' See Dermot Bolger (ed.), *Ireland in Exile: Irish Writers Abroad* (Dublin: New Island Books, 1993), page 7.

11 Fr Padraig Breathnach, *Songs of the Gael* (London: Browne and Nolan, 1915), 337. The Keane sisters' singing of 'A Stór Mo Chroí' can be heard on the CD *Once I Loved: Songs of the West of Ireland* (Claddagh Records, 4CC2).

12 For guides to Irish traditional music see in particular Fintan Vallely, *Companion to Irish Traditional Music* (1999), and the entries under Folklore and Music and under Poetry and Song in the History of Irish Literature section of the Bibliography. The titles I have found particularly helpful are: Seán Ó Riada, *Our Musical Heritage* (1982), an authoritative introduction to Irish singing and playing based on a series of programmes broadcast on Radio Éireann in 1962; Seán O Boyle, *The Irish Song Tradition* (1976), which also provides a valuable introduction to musical technique, metre and styles of singing; Nuala O'Connor, *Bringing It All Back Home* (1991), which was

based on a five-part documentary film series about Irish music and its influence abroad; Hugh Shields, *Narrative Singing in Ireland: Lays, Ballads, Come-All-Yes and Other Songs* (1993), which contains a comprehensive discography; Paddy Tunney, *The Stone Fiddle: My Way to Traditional Song* (1979), a personal record of Tunney's encounters with singers and songs and how he was affected by the advent of radio programmes in the early 1950s in Ulster; and Ciaran Carson, *Last Night's Fun: A Book About Traditional Music* (1996), an entertaining series of reflections on music, language, and social history. For a

comprehensive bibliography, see the relevant sections of James Porter, *The Traditional Music of Britain and Ireland* (1989). For an informative survey of music and literature from the nineteenth century to Brian Friel, see Harry White, 'Music and the Irish Literary Imagination' in Gerard Gillen and Harry White (eds.), *Irish Musical Studies: 3: Music and Irish Cultural History* (1995). White highlights four aspects: music as a code of remembrance, the conjunction between lyricism and history, music as the articulation of a political ideology, and music and the expression of antiquarian research.

INTRODUCTION

This *Reader* is designed to provide a core text for courses in modern Irish writing and in Irish Studies programmes. There is a need for a *Reader* which is, on the one hand, sufficiently varied and capacious for students to survey something of the field and which, on the other hand, supplies in a single volume a focus for detailed work together in class. Here in this Introduction let me draw attention to three aspects of this *Reader*: selection, arrangement, and use.

Selection

The principles governing the selection of material in this volume can be briefly identified. In terms of coverage a reader in Irish writing in the twentieth century needs to enlist the big names such as W.B. Yeats and James Joyce, George Bernard Shaw and Sean O'Casey, Elizabeth Bowen and Eavan Boland, Frank O'Connor and Sean O'Faolain, Samuel Beckett and Brian Friel, Patrick Kavanagh and Thomas Kinsella, Michael Longley and Seamus Heaney, and to embrace the major forms of twentieth-century Irish writing, represented in this instance by ten full-length plays, twenty-six short stories, forty-five extracts from novels, and nearly 170 poems. With five Nobel Prize-winners (Yeats, Shaw, Eugene O'Neill, Beckett, and Heaney), seven Irish-American Pulitzer Prize-winning writers (O'Neill, Edwin O'Connor, Galway Kinnell, Jimmy Breslin, Larry McMurtry, William Kennedy, and Frank McCourt), two Booker Prize-winning novelists (Roddy Doyle and the Irish-Australian Thomas Keneally), and scores of runners-up, modern Irish writing has an excessive quality as far as selection is concerned.[1] Equally in evidence in this *Reader* is a concern with rescuing those who have been too readily excluded from the story of modern Irish writing. Against Samuel Johnson's focussing on the 'exquisite', James Boswell in his *Life of Johnson* (1791) sets the 'middle-rate' authors, that is those writers who occupy 'different gradations of excellence'.[2] In the interests of diversity and with an eye to widening the canon of Irish literature, groups of 'middle-rate' writers have also been enrolled: 'under-appreciated' writers such as Joseph Campbell, Blanaid Salkeld, Kate O'Brien, L.A.G. Strong, Michael McLaverty, Richard Power, or Roy McFadden; popular writers such as Lee Dunne and Patrick Boyle; writers who have been neglected or fallen out of fashion such as St John Ervine, Lynn C. Doyle, or J.F. Powers; new writers such as Marina Carr and Martin McDonagh; and writers from the Irish Diaspora such as the Chicago Irish-American James T. Farrell, the New York Irish-American Betty Smith, the New Irish in America such as Eamonn Wall, the Canadian-Irish such as John Coulter and Leo Simpson, and the Irish-Australian Miles Franklin.

Writers from the Irish Diaspora are afforded more prominence than is customary in anthologies of Irish writing, especially those restricted to an island view of Ireland. Nuala O'Connor makes a telling comment in *Bringing It All Back Home* (1991): 'Being Irish outside Ireland is central to the Irish experience.'[3] As part of my non-insular or non-parochial approach, I have imported a frequently overlooked group — Irish writers in Britain such as Jim Phelan, Moy McCrory, Bill Naughton, and Ian Duhig. At the same time the *Reader* contains examples of Irish writers such as Dervla Murphy, Martin Mooney, and Robert McLiam Wilson whose work contains sharp insights into the state of Britain or English culture. Here, looking back on the twentieth century, I have seized an opportunity to locate Irish writing in a setting that does justice to Mary

Robinson's 'fifth province', that is to the seventy million Irish overseas who are first-generation Irish or who claim Irish descent. In a recent interview in *Irish America*, Elizabeth Rice Dalbey, a centenarian who emigrated to the United States from Galway in her early twenties, was asked whether she considered herself Irish or American. 'American,' she answered immediately. The interviewer persisted. 'What part of you is Irish?' he asked. 'Every bit of me,' came the reply.[4] With the coming of the Internet and of web sites with names such as 'Every Celtic Thing on the Web', there is now in existence as perhaps never before a global community confident about its Irishness and looking to foster its sense of connectedness.

Particular care has been taken to ensure other groups such as Irish-language poets and women writers are not overlooked or patronised but included as of right into the whole development of modern Irish writing. I am reminded of a complaint made in 1986 by Nuala Ní Dhomhnaill in an interview with Michael Cronin expressing her frustration with the literary scene in Ireland: 'There are the so-called "popular" poets, the poets who have made it in media terms and the also-rans and the whole thing is ridiculous. I feel that I have a double bout of it, because of being a woman and writing in Irish it's almost impossible.'[5] I prefer a student to be excited by the many textures of Irish writing and not rest content with a litany of the names of leading players. Equally, in response to a comment made by Eiléan Ní Chuilleanáin in 1992, I have tried to avoid compiling a reader which serves to 'reinforce the curriculum and promote a monolithic orthodoxy'.[6] It is for this reason I have been keen to insert, especially in the 1980s and 1990s sections, essays and articles which give a sense of an ongoing debate as well as Irish-language poems which are contentious or which exhibit an unmistakable modern sensibility.

My concern throughout is with those whose voice is rarely heard — the dispossessed — such as slum-dwellers in Britain, prisoners, or travellers and by extension dissidents and heretics such as the Modernist Jesuit priest George Tyrrell and those suffering from violations of civil liberties in areas such as divorce and censorship. Prison writings occupy a site of special interest in this *Reader*. Overshadowing all is the symbolic figure of Oscar Wilde, the person who wrote 'The Ballad of Reading Gaol' under his prison identity 'C.3.3'. Then come the political prisoners Darrell Figgis and the hunger striker Frank Gallagher in the period 1917–23; Jim Phelan, a common criminal who wrote volumes about his experiences in the 1920s and 1930s in English and Irish gaols; one-time IRA activist Brendan Behan, author of the prison play *The Quare Fellow*; Vincent Buckley's tribute to the IRA hunger striker Bobby Sands; Seamus Heaney's 1985 Amnesty poem 'From the Republic of Conscience' written for all political prisoners; and then Gerry Conlon's poignant record of his wasted years in prison, wrongly accused of the Guildford Bombings in 1984. The Irishman locked in British (and Irish) gaols is an image that haunts Irish writing in the twentieth century.

In keeping with my attempt to widen the canon, I have adopted a fluid interpretation with regard to genre and included different forms of writing: life writing or personal memoirs/reminiscences; extracts from autobiographies; private correspondence; personal testimony; critical surveys; critical essays; book reviews; interviews; travel writing/guides; cultural critiques; examples of polemical writing; sociological description; examples of reportage; political journalism; newspaper reports and articles; newspaper columns; letters to newspapers; editorials; a speech in the Senate; radio talks; extracts from prison writings; a folktale; folk-life description; humorous extracts; a war chronicle; reflective prose. With such a mixture of forms, where writing, voices, patterns, lines of argument jostle for attention, I have sought a different kind of book, for this is not an anthology straining to rank-order material or, conversely, to become what Robert Graves and Laura Riding once termed a 'composite author', but a reader at home with its divisions and differences of opinion.[7]

My intention throughout is to provide within a single volume a thoughtful, comprehensive, and pleasurable introduction to modern Irish writing and experience. Among the topics of everyday interest dealt with in the *Reader* are: family relations; childhood; death; homelessness; rituals such as Halloween, wakes, feasts, card playing; emigration and return; memory; boredom; nostalgia; masculinity; gay sexuality; sexual hunger; sexual awakening; city and country life; social class. Exploring such topics can serve to illustrate how at no stage in its recent past has Ireland *not* been undergoing profound changes.[8] This point is further underlined by the unresolved nature of polemical issues touched on in the *Reader*: the significance of the Literary Revival for later writers; the place of the Easter Rising in today's Ireland; the lessons to be drawn from history; the issue of Ireland's status as colonial or post-colonial country; the misrepresentation of Ireland; the competing claims by different interest groups to speak for Ireland; the quarrel over allegiance in the North of Ireland; the tension between the citizen and the individual; the conflict between modernity and traditional society; the effects of tourism.

'I know no civilised country, except Ireland, whose history is not familiar to its people.'[9] So complained Charles Gavan Duffy in the 1890s. A century later the complaint takes a somewhat different form. To help students who are unfamiliar with Irish history I have furnished material which contains core information about Irish history and society. Key essays and debates, informative extracts, lists of texts, historical surveys, all play a part in building up a knowledge of modern Irish history and in allaying fears about the character of 'this appallingly ancient people', a wonderfully ambivalent phrase used by the narrator in Joseph Furphy's appropriately entitled Irish-Australian novel *Such Is Life* (1903).[10] Other extracts provide a recapitulation of Irish history to strengthen familiarity with critical areas or topics such as the eighteenth-century *Aisling* (or visionary) tradition, the 1798 Rising, the Great Famine (1845–49), Thomas Davis and the *Nation* poets, Parnell and the Home Rule question. The *Reader* also includes reference to significant historical events in the twentieth century such as Easter 1916, the War of Independence (1919–21), the Irish Civil War (1922–23), Bloody Sunday 1972, the Brighton Bombing in 1984. The names of leading Irish figures in the twentieth century — Patrick Pearse, Michael Collins, Eamon de Valera, Mary Robinson — also feature. To contextualise the extracts the Appendix contains a Chronology from 1900 to 1999, and for every year I have included a handy but by no means exhaustive checklist compiled mainly from cultural, historical and political events; social legislation; mass media, including newspapers, television and films; the advent of new publishers and of new literary magazines; Nobel Prize, Pulitzer Prize and Booker Prize winners; openings of new theatres; deaths of famous writers; sporting successes; anniversaries; events in Northern Ireland since 1968.

Arrangement

This *Reader* adopts a strictly chronological approach to the material and anchors the extracts in the decade and year of their first appearance.[11] There are a number of advantages to this arrangement. Firstly, the extracts carry something of their original look and sparkle which intervening years have perhaps tarnished or extinguished.

Secondly, in time and with use such an arrangement can produce a more confident attachment towards the periodization of the extracts. Thirdly, changes can be more easily assessed and highlighted, not only social and historical changes but also, perhaps more importantly for a student of literature, changes in style and sensibility or in what Raymond Williams referred to as 'structures of feeling'.[12] Fourthly, in stressing the original contexts and reception of a particular text or play (via contemporary book reviews or early examples in print of an emerging writer), such an arrangement helps disclose a canon in formation. Finally, such a method of historicization provides a cautionary perspective on the present. It comes as a shock, for example, to read in the 1930s that Joyce was no longer read in Ireland, or that in the 1940s Irish critics feared that Irish culture was in permanent decline and would produce no more great writers.

At the start of each decade I have inserted a short extract to help with the process of orientation or adjustment. These passages, taken from texts not used in the *Reader*, are all different and designed for different purposes. The first is a dedication by Yeats to his occultist friend George Russell which conveys something of the flavour of the decade and the structure of feeling in the 1890s; the second is from a love letter by Synge the week following the *Playboy* riots and is a reminder not only of the Abbey Theatre problems but also of Synge's private life independent of what he wrote; for the 1910s I have chosen a polemical essay on the women's suffrage issue, an essay and an issue frequently overlooked in the ensuing decades. The 1920s begins with two small quotations from Darrell Figgis on war and peace and an editorial from the last issue of the feminist publication the *Irish Citizen*. At the start of the 1930s I have included a passage from a futuristic novel by Francis Stuart voicing fears for the new Ireland from the super-civilization flooding across from Europe. De Valera provides an introduction to the 1940s and to the mood of isolation then in the ascendancy. The 1950s saw more decline for rural Ireland, while in the 1960s a 'gombeen's paradise' emerged in Dublin for property developers, wittily exposed by Michael Campbell in his novel *Across the Water* (1961). An extract from Jimmy Breslin's novel *World Without End, Amen* (1973) offers a reminder of the issue of Irish or Irish-American identity-in-dissolution, an issue which is taken up by Richard Kearney in relationship not to the States but to Europe. Finally, for the 1990s I return to the position of women in Ireland, to the problems facing the woman writer, and to the question of representation. No account of the last decade of the twentieth century would be complete without reference to the 'troubles', and I have taken this opportunity to include a passage from David Park's quietly reflective novel *Stone Kingdoms* (1996). These are rough-and-ready signposts, sharp reminders of the shifts in outlook as the twentieth century unfolded for Irish writers.

Each decade is divided into two major segments: 'Critical and Documentary' and 'Imaginative'. Such an arrangement not only permits the imaginative writing to be read against the grain of other forms of writing, but it also allows it to speak to the contexts it inhabits. This format points in two different but related directions: towards deconstruction and explanation, on the one hand, and on the other, towards appreciation and celebration of a writer's work and achievement. Discursive extracts, such as critical essays, cultural critiques, book reviews, journal articles etc., have legitimate claims on the student of literature, for such material helps contextualize the imaginative extracts as well as re-presenting the literature in often new and suggestive ways. Thus Nuala Ní Dhomhnaill's complaint not only forms part of a backdrop to poems such as her 'Ceist na Teangan' (The Language Issue), but it also connects with the work of other fine Irish-language poets such as Cathal Ó Searcaigh, and with a whole discourse about language in modern Ireland potentially relevant to her point:

Douglas Hyde and de-Anglicization, Thomas MacDonagh and the presence of the Irish language in Anglo-Irish literature, Lady Gregory's interest in language and dialect, Frank O'Connor's essay on the future of Irish literature, John Montague's poem 'A Lost Tradition', or Louis de Paor's recent criticism of translations from the Irish. Equally her views on the media find echoes in other extracts reproduced in this *Reader*, as indeed does her position as a woman writer. Topics and themes are not tied to genre but find articulation in plays and polemical essays, in poems and book reviews, in short stories and travel writing. In moving between the discursive and the imaginative the student can assemble fresh insights into both the writing and the culture and discover new areas of interest in the process.

Use

To enhance its appeal also as a workbook and a resource tool for student use, the *Reader* contains a bank of carefully selected material. 'Topics and Issues' comprises lists of extracts used in the *Reader* arranged chronologically under four headings: 1. History, Politics, and Religion; 2. the City and the Country; 3. Culture and Identity; 4. the Irish Diaspora. Under the first part I have grouped: politics; religion; Irish Ireland; North of Ireland; violence. Under the second section: the city; the country; the Big House; travel writing. The third section is divided into: cultural critique; colonialism/post-colonialism; Irish language; folklore and folktales; gender and modern Irish writing; women writers; critical essays; the writer; autobiographical and personal; childhood; humour; the outsider; on the road; prison writings. The fourth section deals with writers from the Irish Diaspora. In this way I have begun the task of reconfiguration, of gathering the extracts from the *Reader* and showing how they might be compared and contrasted. Thus on the topic of gender and Irish writing, for example, there are some fifty extracts that can be referred to, including plays, verse, short stories, book reviews, critical surveys. Similarly with the issue of religion: there are over twenty extracts including expository essays, autobiographies, cultural critiques, fiction, verse, drama, travel guides. On the issue of colonialism and post-colonialism the *Reader* contains over fifty extracts and includes polemical essays, verse, newspaper articles, drama, book reviews, interviews, personal testimony, editorials, personal memoirs, short stories, extracts from fiction. The abundance of material allows the list of Topics and Issues to be supplemented and reordered in numerous ways: for instance, images of Ireland as female; spirituality; priests; pilgrimage; the dark; hunger; memory; secrecy; failure; domesticity; the global village; names and naming; topography.

More workshop material, designed for different kinds of student use, can be found in the Writing and Research section. Here I have provided some practical hints on tackling essays, a section outlining possible additional assignment topics, and a list of specific questions that might be encountered on undergraduate courses. I have also assembled an extensive Bibliography, which is envisaged as a working accompaniment to the *Reader*, to satisfy immediate and ongoing needs. The section on Anthologies of Irish Literature in English, which I have ordered chronologically and by genre, will prove especially useful as a quarry and a resource. Finally, the list of 100 books, arranged by genre into Novels, Verse, Drama and Autobiographies, is by way of a response to a question I am often asked by students keen to read more widely in the subject: which books would you recommend that I read to build up my knowledge of Irish writing. To which I normally reply: many.

1   Widespread recognition of Irish writers or writers of Irish descent is now part of our culture, as is the natural scepticism that not everything such writers produced or produce is especially or always Irish. Booker Prize Nominees and Winners include: John Banville, *The Book of Evidence* 1988; Caroline Blackwood, *Great Granny Webster* 1977; Elizabeth Bowen, *Eva Trout* 1970; Seamus Deane, *Reading in the Dark* 1996; Roddy Doyle, *The Van* 1991, *Paddy Clarke, Ha Ha Ha* 1993 [Winner]; J.G Farrell, *The Siege of Krishnapur* 1973 [Winner]; Jennifer Johnston, *Shadows on Our Skin* 1977; Molly Keane, *Good Behaviour* 1981; Thomas Keneally, *The Chant of Jimmy Blacksmith* 1972, *Gossip from the Forest* 1975, *Confederates* 1979, *Schindler's Ark* 1982 [Winner]; Thomas Kilroy, *The Big Chapel* 1971; Patrick McCabe, *The Butcher Boy* 1992; John McGahern, *Amongst Women* 1990; Brian Moore, *The Doctor's Wife* 1976, *The Colour of Blood* 1987; Julia O'Faolain, *No Country for Young Men* 1980; William Trevor, *Mrs Eckdorf in O'Neill's Hotel* 1970, *The Children of Dynmouth* 1976, *Reading Turgenev* 1991. Pulitzer Prize Winners include: Jimmy Breslin, Commentary prize for Journalism 1986; William Kennedy, *Ironweed* 1984; Galway Kinnell, *Selected Poems* 1983; Frank McCourt, *Angela's Ashes* 1997; Larry McMurtry, *Lonesome Dove* 1986; Edwin O'Connor, *The Edge of Sadness* 1962; Eugene O'Neill, *Anna Christie* 1922, *Strange Interlude* 1928.

2   James Boswell, *Life of Johnson* (ed. R.W. Chapman) (Oxford: Oxford University Press, 1980), 618. Johnson was in no mood for conversation but felt that 'there is no necessity for having poetry' and that 'it can have no value unless when exquisite in its kind'.

3   Nuala O'Connor, *Bringing It All Back Home* (London: BBC Books, 1991), 8.

4   *Irish America* May/June 1997.

5   Nuala Ní Dhomhnaill, 'Making the Millennium'. *Graph* No 1 October 1986, 5.

6   Eiléan Ní Chuilleanáin in a review of three Field Day pamphlets. *Cyphers* No 35 Spring 1992, 52.

7   Robert Graves and Laura Riding, 'True Anthologies and Popular Anthologies' (1927) in Robert Graves, The Common Asphodel: Collected Essays on Poetry 1922–49 (London: Hamish Hamilton, 1949), 183.

8   For surveys of contemporary Ireland, see John Ardagh, *Ireland and the Irish: Portrait of a Changing Society* (Harmondsworth: Penguin, 1994) or Gemma Hussey, *Ireland Today: Anatomy of a Changing State* (Harmondsworth: Penguin, 1995).

9   Charles Gavan Duffy, George Sigerson, and Douglas Hyde, *The Revival of Literature* (London: T. Fisher Unwin, 1894), 41. 'In England you encounter English history everywhere; in literature, in art, on the stage, and even in the pulpit.'

10 Joseph Furphy, *Such Is Life* (Sydney: Bulletin Newspaper Company, 1903), 73.

11 As far as possible I have tried to date material from its earliest appearance in print. I have not always been successful in this regard since poems and short stories have a habit of turning up in an earlier publication. It was not until I began trawling through *Ireland Today* (1936–8) that I discovered Michael McLaverty's story 'The Game Cock' made its first appearance in 1937 and not in his collection *The Game Cock and Other Stories* (1947). Equally, as with the text here of Yeats's 'Leda and the Swan', I have at times gathered material that first saw the light of day in earlier instalments of little magazines. A word of caution: first appearance does not automatically signify that was the year when the piece was written. Thus, 'Easter 1916' was composed in 1916 but not published until October 1920.

12 Raymond Williams, *The Long Revolution* (Harmondsworth: Pelican Books, 1975), pages 64ff. The term 'is as firm and definite as "structure" suggests ... the culture of a period ... a very wide and deep possession ... the new generation will have its own structure of feeling.' See also his remarks in *Politics and Letters: Interviews with New Left Review* (London: Verso, 1979), pages 156-159.

ABBREVIATIONS

Dinneen	Patrick S. Dinneen, *Foclóir Gaedilge Agus Bearla: An Irish-English Dictionary* (Dublin: Irish Texts Society, 1927)
P.W. Joyce	Patrick Weston Joyce, *English As We Speak It In Ireland* (1910; rpt with Introduction by Terence Dolan, Dublin: Wolfhound Press, 1979)
Share	Bernard Share, *Slanguage: A Dictionary of Slang and Colloquial English in Ireland* (Dublin: Gill & Macmillan, 1997)
QUB	Queen's University Belfast
TCD	Trinity College Dublin
UCD	University College Dublin

1890s: Shadows, Moods and Arguments

My Dear A.E.—I dedicate this book to you because, whether you think it well or ill written, you will sympathize with the sorrows and the ecstasies of its personages, perhaps even more than I do myself. Although I wrote these stories at different times and in different manners, and without any definite plan, they have but one subject, the war of spiritual with natural order; and how can I dedicate such a book to any one but to you, the one poet of modern Ireland who has moulded a spiritual ecstasy into verse? My friends in Ireland sometimes ask me when I am going to write a really national poem or romance, and by a national poem or romance I understand them to mean a poem or romance founded upon some moment of famous Irish history, and built up out of the thoughts and feelings which move the greater number of patriotic Irishmen. I on the other hand believe that poetry and romance cannot be made by the most conscientious study of famous moments and of the thoughts and feelings of others, but only by looking into that little, infinite, faltering, eternal flame that one calls one's self. If a writer wishes to interest a certain people among whom he has grown up, or fancies he has a duty towards them, he may choose for the symbols of his art their legends, their history, their beliefs, their opinions, because he has a right to choose among things less than himself but he cannot choose among the substances of art. So far, however, as this book is visionary it is Irish; for Ireland, which is still predominantly Celtic, has preserved with some less excellent things a gift of vision, which has died out among more hurried and more successful nations: no shining candelabra have prevented us from looking into the darkness, and when one looks into the darkness there is always something there.

– W.B. Yeats's Dedication to George Russell in *The Secret Rose* (1897)

DOUGLAS HYDE

from Charles Gavan Duffy, George Sigerson, and Douglas Hyde, *The Revival of Irish Literature* (1894)

Hyde's lecture, delivered to the newly formed Irish National Literary Society in Dublin on 25 November 1892, is essential reading for the student of modern Irish culture and society. His critique and diagnosis of Ireland's problems, conceived in essentially moral and racial terms, acted as a clarion call which prompted some to join the Gaelic League (founded in 1893) and learn Irish, and which prompted others such as Patrick Pearse into rethinking Hyde's message in political terms. Hyde's influence can be felt throughout the twentieth century, and not just in Ireland. The attack on West Britonism resurfaces in Joyce's *The Dead* when Miss Ivor tackles Gabriel over his lack of Irishness; the issue of Irish placenames, given a political twist, is central to Brian Friel's play *Translations* (1980); Hyde's stress on process and internal wholesale change anticipates the emphasis given by the contemporary Kenyan writer Ngugi to 'decolonizing the mind'. It is worthwhile trying to summarize Hyde's argument in this lecture, noticing the series of binary oppositions he invokes. Consider also how much of his argument remains valid today. Hyde (1860–1949) himself wrote *Casadh an tSúgáin*, a significant Irish-language play staged at the Gaiety Theatre in Dublin in 1901. See, p. 13 below, *Abhráin Grádh Chúige Connacht* (Love Songs of Connacht) for his important book of translations from Irish songs. In 1938 Hyde was elected first President of Ireland.

The Necessity for De-Anglicizing Ireland

When we speak of 'The Necessity for De-Anglicizing the Irish Nation', we mean it, not as a protest against imitating what is *best* in the English people, for that would be absurd, but rather to show the folly of neglecting what is Irish, and hastening to adopt, pell-mell, and indiscriminately, everything that is English, simply because it *is* English.

This is a question which most Irishmen will naturally look at from a National point of view, but it is one which ought also to claim the sympathies of every intelligent Unionist, and which, as I know, does claim the sympathy of many.

If we take a bird's-eye view of our island today, and compare it with what it used to be, we must be struck by the extraordinary fact that the nation which was once, as every one admits, one of the most classically learned and cultured nations in Europe, is now one of the least so; how one of the most reading and literary peoples has become one of the *least* studious and most *un*-literary, and how the present art products of one of the quickest, most sensitive, and most artistic races on earth are now only distinguished for their hideousness.

I shall endeavour to show that this failure of the Irish people in recent times has been largely brought about by the race diverging during this century from the right path, and ceasing to be Irish without becoming English. I shall attempt to show that with the bulk of the people this change took place quite recently, much more recently than most people imagine, and is, in fact, still going on. I should also like to call attention to the illogical position of men who drop their own language to speak English, of men who translate their euphonious Irish names into English monosyllables, of men who read English books, and know nothing about Gaelic literature, nevertheless protesting as a matter of sentiment that they hate the country which at every hand's turn they rush to imitate.

I wish to show you that in Anglicizing ourselves wholesale we have thrown away with a light heart the best claim which we have upon the world's recognition of us as a separate nationality. What did Mazzini say? What is Goldwin Smith never tired of declaiming? What do the *Spectator* and *Saturday Review* harp on? That we ought to be content as an integral part of the United Kingdom because we have lost the notes of nationality, our language and customs.

It has always been very curious to me how Irish sentiment sticks in this half-way house — how it continues to apparently hate the English, and at the same time continues to imitate them; how it continues to clamour for recognition as a distinct nationality, and at the same time throws away with both hands what would make it so. If Irishmen only went a little farther they would become good Englishmen in sentiment also. But — illogical as it appears — there seems not the slightest sign or probability of their taking that step. It is the curious certainty that come what may Irishmen will continue to resist English rule, even though it should be for their good, which prevents many of our nation from becoming Unionists upon the spot. It is a fact, and we must face it as a fact, that although they adopt English habits and copy England in every way, the great bulk of Irishmen and Irishwomen over the whole world are known to be filled with a dull, ever-abiding animosity against her, and — right or wrong — to grieve when she prospects, and joy when she is hurt. Such movements as Young Irelandism,[1] Fenianism,[2] Land Leagueism,[3] and Parliamentary obstruction seem always to gain their sympathy and support. It is just because there appears no earthly chance of their becoming good members of the Empire that I urge that they should not remain in the anomalous position they are in, but since they absolutely refuse to become the one thing, that they become the other; cultivate what they have rejected, and build up an Irish nation on Irish lines.

But you ask, why should we wish to make Ireland more Celtic than it is — why should we de-Anglicize it at all?

I answer because the Irish race is at present in a most anomalous position, imitating England and yet apparently hating it. How can it produce anything good in literature, art, or institutions as long as it is actuated by motives so contradictory? Besides, I believe it is our Gaelic past which, though the Irish race does not recognize it just at present, is really at the bottom of the Irish heart, and prevents us becoming citizens of the Empire, as, I think, can be easily proved.

To say that Ireland has not prospered under English rule is simply a truism; all the world admits it, England does not deny it. But the English retort is ready. You have not prospered, they say, because you would not settle down contentedly, like the Scotch, and form part of the Empire. 'Twenty years of good, resolute, grandfatherly government,' said a well-known Englishman, will solve the Irish question. He possibly made the period too short, but let us suppose this. Let us suppose for a moment — which is impossible — that there were to arise a series of Cromwells in England for the space of one hundred years, able administrators of the Empire, careful rulers of Ireland, developing to the utmost our national resources, whilst

they unremittingly stamped out every spark of national feeling, making Ireland a land of wealth and factories, whilst they extinguished every thought and every idea that was Irish, and left us, at last, after a hundred years of good government, fat, wealthy, and populous, but with all our characteristics gone, with every external that at present differentiates us from the English lost or dropped; all our Irish names of places and people turned into English names; the Irish language completely extinct; the O's and the Macs dropped; our Irish intonation changed, as far as possible by English schoolmasters into something English; our history no longer remembered or taught; the names of our rebels and martyrs blotted out; our battlefields and traditions forgotten; the fact that we were not of Saxon origin dropped out of sight and memory, and let me now put the question — How many Irishmen are there who would purchase material prosperity at such as price? It is exactly such a question as this and the answer to it that shows the difference between the English and Irish race. Nine Englishmen out of ten would jump to make the exchange, and I as firmly believe that nine Irishmen out of ten would indignantly refuse it.

And yet this awful idea of complete Anglicization, which I have here put before you in all its crudity, is, and has been, making silent inroads upon us for nearly a century.

Its inroads have been silent, because, had the Gaelic race perceived what was being done, or had they been once warned of what was taking place in their own midst, they would, I think, never have allowed it. When the picture of complete Anglicization is drawn for them in all its nakedness Irish sentimentality becomes suddenly a power and refuses to surrender its birthright.

What lies at the back of the sentiments of nationality with which the Irish millions seem so strongly leavened, what can prompt them to applaud such sentiments as:

They say the British empire owes much to Irish
    hands,
That Irish valour fixed her flag o'er many
    conquered lands;
And ask if Erin takes no pride in these her gallant
    sons,
Her Wolseleys and her Lawrences, her Wolfes and
    Wellingtons.

Ah! these were of the Empire — we yield them to
    her fame,
And ne'er in Erin's orisons are heard their alien
    name;

> But those for whom her heart beats high and
>   benedictions swell,
> They died upon the scaffold and they pined within
>   the cell.

Of course it is a very composite feeling which prompts them; but I believe that what is largely behind it is the half unconscious feeling that the race which at one time held possession of more than half Europe, which established itself in Greece, and burned infant Rome, is now — almost extirpated and absorbed elsewhere — making its last stand for independence in this island of Ireland; and do what they may the race of today cannot wholly divest itself from the mantle of its own past. Through early Irish literature, for instance, can we best form some conception of what that race really was, which, after overthrowing and trampling on the primitive peoples of half Europe, was itself forced in turn to yield its speech, manners, and independence to the victorious eagles of Rome. We alone of the nations of Western Europe escaped the claws of those birds of prey; we alone developed ourselves naturally upon our own lines outside of and free from all Roman influence; we alone were thus able to produce an early art and literature, *our* antiquities can best throw light upon the pre-Romanized inhabitants of half Europe, and — we are our father's sons.

There is really no exaggeration in all this, although Irishmen are sometimes prone to overstating as well as to forgetting. Westwood[4] himself declares that, were it not for Irishmen, these islands would possess no primitive works of art worth the mentioning; Jubainville[5] asserts that early Irish literature is that which best throws light upon the manners and customs of his own ancestors the Gauls; and Zimmer,[6] who has done so much for Celtic philology, has declared that only a spurious criticism can make an attempt to doubt about the historical character of the chief persons of our two epic cycles, that of Cuchullain[7] and of Finn. It is useless elaborating this point; and Dr Sigerson[8] has already shown in his opening lecture the debt of gratitude which in many respects Europe owes to ancient Ireland. The dim consciousness of this is one of those things which are at the back of Irish national sentiment, and our business, whether we be Unionists or Nationalists, should be to make this dim consciousness an active and potent feeling, and thus increase our sense of self-respect and of honour.

What we must endeavour to never forget is this, that the Ireland of today is the descendant of the Ireland of the seventh century, then the school of Europe and the torch of learning. It is true that Northmen made some minor settlements in it in the ninth and tenth centuries, it is true that the Normans made extensive settlements during the succeeding centuries, but none of those broke the continuity of the social life of the island. Dane and Norman drawn to the kindly Irish breast issued forth in a generation or two fully Irishized, and more Hibernian than the Hibernians themselves, and even after the Cromwellian plantation the children of numbers of the English soldiers who settled in the south and midlands, were, after forty years' residence, and after marrying Irish wives, turned into good Irishmen, and unable to speak a word of English, while several Gaelic poets of the last century have, like Father English, the most unmistakably English names. In two points only was the continuity of the Irishism of Ireland damaged. First, in the north-east of Ulster, where the Gaelic race was expelled and the land planted with aliens, whom our dear mother Erin, assimilative as she is, has hitherto found it difficult to absorb, and in the ownership of the land, eight-ninths of which belongs to people many of whom always lived, or live, abroad, and not half of whom Ireland can be said to have assimilated.

During all this time the continuation of Erin's national life centred, according to our way of looking at it, not so much in the Cromwellian or Williamite landholders who sat in College Green,[9] and governed the country, as in the mass of the people whom Dean Swift considered might be entirely neglected, and looked upon as hewers of wood and drawers of water; the men who, nevertheless, constituted the real working population, and who were living on in the hopes of better days; the men who have since made America, and have within the last ten years proved what an important factor they may be in wrecking or in building the British Empire. These are the men of whom our merchants, artisans, and farmers mostly consist, and in whose hands is today the making or marring of an Irish nation. But, alas, *quantum mutatus ab illo!*[10] What the battleaxe of the Dane, the sword of the Norman, the wile of the Saxon were unable to perform, we have accomplished ourselves. We have at last broken the continuity of Irish life, and just at the moment when the Celtic race is presumably about to largely recover possession of its own country, it finds itself deprived and stript of its Celtic characteristics, cut off from the past, yet scarcely in touch with the present. It has lost since the beginning of this century almost all that connected it with the era of Cuchullainn and of Ossian,[11] that connected it with the Christianizers of Europe, that connected it with Brian Boru[12] and the heroes of Clontarf, with the

O'Neills and O'Donnells, with Rory O'More, with the Wild Geese,[13] and even to some extent with the men of '98.[14] It has lost all that they had — language, traditions, music, genius, and ideas. Just when we should be starting to build up anew the Irish race and the Gaelic nation — as within our own recollection Greece has been built up anew — we find ourselves despoiled of the bricks of nationality. The old bricks that lasted eighteen hundred years are destroyed; we must now set to, to bake new ones, if we can, on other ground and of other clay. Imagine for a moment the restoration of a German-speaking Greece.

The bulk of the Irish race really lived in the closest contact with the traditions of the past and the national life of nearly eighteen hundred years, until the beginning of this century. Not only so, but during the whole of the dark Penal times they produced amongst themselves a most vigorous literary development. Their schoolmasters and wealthy farmers, unwearied scribes, produced innumerable manuscripts in beautiful writing, each letter separated from another as in Greek, transcripts both of the ancient literature of their sires and of the more modern literature produced by themselves. Until the beginning of the present century there was no county, no barony,[15] and, I may almost say, no townland which did not boast of an Irish poet, the people's representative of those ancient bards who died out with the extirpation of the great Milesian[16] families. The literary activity of even the eighteenth century among the Gaels was very great, not in the South alone, but also in Ulster — the number of poets it produced was something astonishing. It did not, however, produce many works in Gaelic prose, but it propagated translations of many pieces from the French, Latin, Spanish, and English. Every well-to-do farmer could read and write Irish, and many of them could understand even archaic Irish. I have myself heard persons reciting the poems of Donogha More O'Daly, Abbot of Boyle, in Roscommon, who died sixty years before Chaucer was born. To this very day the people have a word for archaic Irish, which is much the same as though Chaucer's poems were handed down amongst the English peasantry, but required a special training to understand. This training, however, nearly every one of fair education during the Penal times possessed, nor did they begin to lose their Irish training and knowledge until after the establishment of Maynooth[17] and the rise of O'Connell.[18] These two events made an end of the Gaelicism of the Gaelic race, although a great number of poets and scribes existed even down to the forties and fifties of the present century, and a few may linger on yet in remote localities. But it may

be said, roughly speaking, that the ancient Gaelic civilization died with O'Connell, largely, I am afraid, owing to his example and his neglect of inculcating the necessity of keeping alive racial customs, language, and traditions, in which with the one notable exception of our scholarly idealist, Smith O'Brien,[19] he has been followed until a year ago by almost every leader of the Irish race.

Thomas Davis and his brilliant band of Young Irelanders came just at the dividing of the line, and tried to give to Ireland a new literature in English to replace the literature which was just being discarded. It succeeded and it did not succeed. It was a most brilliant effort, but the old bark had been too recently stripped off the Irish tree, and the trunk could not take as it might have done to a fresh one. It was a new departure, and at first produced a violent effect. Yet in the long run it failed to properly leaven our peasantry who might, perhaps, have been reached upon other lines. I say they *might* have been reached upon other lines because it is quite certain that even well on into the beginning of this century, Irish poor scholars and schoolmasters used to gain the greatest favour and applause by reading out manuscripts in the people's houses at night, some of which manuscripts had an antiquity of a couple of hundred years or more behind them, and which, when they got illegible from age, were always recopied. The Irish peasantry at that time were all to some extent cultured men, and many of the better off ones were scholars and poets. What have we now left of all that? Scarcely a trace. Many of them read newspapers indeed, but who reads, much less recites, an epic poem, or chants an elegiac or even a hymn?

Wherever Irish throughout Ireland continued to be spoken, there the ancient MSS continued to be read, there the epics of Cuchullain, Conor MacNessa, Déirdre, Finn, Oscar, and Ossian continued to be told, and there poetry and music held sway. Some people may think I am exaggerating in asserting that such a state of things existed down to the present century, but it is no exaggeration. I have myself spoken with men from Cavan and Tyrone who spoke excellent Irish. Carleton's[20] stories bear witness to the prevalence of the Irish language and traditions in Ulster when he began to write. My friend Mr Lloyd has found numbers in Antrim who spoke good Irish. And, as for Leinster, my friend Mr Cleaver informed me that when he lived in Wicklow a man came by from the County Carlow in search of work who could not speak a word of English. Old 'abourers from Connacht, who used to go to reap the harvest in England and take shipping at Drogheda, told me that at that time, fifty years ago, Irish was spoken by every one round that town. I have met an old man in Wicklow, not twenty miles from Dublin, whose parents always repeated the Rosary in Irish. My friend Father O'Growney,[21] who has done and is doing so much for the Irish language and literature at Maynooth, tells me that there, within twenty miles of Dublin, are three old people who still speak Irish. O'Curry[22] found people within seven miles of Dublin city who had never heard English in their youth at all, except from the car-drivers of the great town. I gave an old man in the street who begged from me, a penny, only a few days ago, saying, '*Sin pighin agad,*' and when he answered in Irish I asked him where he was from, and he said from *Newna* (*n' Eamhain*), i.e., Navan. Last year I was in Canada and out hunting with some Red Indians, and we spent a night in the last white man's house in the last settlement on the brink of the primeval forest; and judging from a peculiarly Hibernian physiognomy that the man was Irish, I addressed him in Gaelic, and to the intense astonishment both of whites and Indians we entered into a conversation which none of them understood; and it turned out that he was from within three miles of Kilkenny, and had been forty years in that country without forgetting the language he had spoken as a child, and I, although from the centre of Connacht, understood him perfectly. When my father was a young boy in the County Leitrim, not far from Longford, he seldom heard the farm labourers and tenants speak anything but Irish amongst themselves. So much for Ulster and Leinster, but Connacht and Munster were until quite recently completely Gaelic. In fact, I may venture to say, that, up to the beginning of the present century, neither man, woman, nor child of the Gaelic race, either of high blood or low blood, existed in Ireland who did not either speak Irish or understand it. But within the last ninety years we have, with an unparalleled frivolity, deliberately thrown away our birthright and Anglicized ourselves. None of the children of those people of whom I have spoken know Irish, and the race will from henceforth be changed; for as Monsieur Jubainville says of the influence of Rome upon Gaul, England 'has definitely conquered us, she has even imposed upon us her language, that is to say, the form of our thoughts during every instant of our existence'. It is curious that those who most fear West Britainism have so eagerly consented to imposing upon the Irish race what, according to Jubainville, who in common with all the great scholars of the continent, seems to regret it very much, is 'the form of our thoughts during every instant of our existence'.

So much for the greatest stroke of all in our Anglicization, the loss of our language. I have often heard people thank God that if the English gave us nothing else they gave us at least their language. In this way they put a bold face upon the matter, and pretend that the Irish language is not worth knowing, and has no literature. But the Irish language *is* worth knowing, or why would the greatest philologists of Germany, France, and Italy be emulously studying it, and it *does* possess a literature, or why would a German savant have made the calculation that the books written in Irish between the eleventh and seventeenth centuries, and still extant, would fill a thousand octavo volumes.

I have no hesitation at all in saying that every Irish-feeling Irishman, who hates the reproach of West-Britonism, should set himself to encourage the efforts which are being made to keep alive our once great national tongue. The losing of it is our greatest blow, and the sorest stroke that the rapid Anglicization of Ireland has inflicted upon us. In order to de-Anglicize ourselves we must at once arrest the decay of the language. We must bring pressure upon our politicians not to snuff it out by their tacit discouragement merely because they do not happen themselves to understand it. We must arouse some spark of patriotic inspiration among the peasantry who still use the language, and put an end to the shameful state of the feeling — a thousand-tongued reproach to our leaders and statesmen — which makes young men and women blush and hang their heads when overheard speaking their own language.[23] Maynooth has at last come splendidly to the front, and it is now incumbent upon every clerical student to attend lectures in the Irish language and history during the first three years of his course. But in order to keep the Irish language alive where it is still spoken — which is the utmost we can at present aspire to — nothing less than a house-to-house visitation and exhortation of the people themselves will do, something — though with a very different purpose — analogous to the procedure that James Stephens[24] adopted throughout Ireland when he found her like a corpse on the dissecting table. This and some system of giving medals or badges of honour to every family who will guarantee that they have always spoken Irish amongst themselves during the year. But, unfortunately, distracted as we are and torn by contending factions, it is impossible to find either men or money to carry out this simple remedy, although to a dispassionate foreigner — to a Zeuss,[25] Jubainville, Zimmer, Kuno Meyer,[26] Windisch,[27] or Ascoli, and the rest — this is of greater importance than whether Mr Redmond[28] or Mr MacCarthy[29] lead the largest wing of the Irish party for the moment, or

Mr So-and-So succeed with his election petition. To a person taking a bird's-eye view of the situation a hundred or five hundred years hence, believe me, it will also appear of greater importance than any mere temporary wrangle, but, unhappily, our countrymen cannot be brought to see this.

We can, however, insist, and we *shall* insist if Home Rule be carried, that the Irish language, which so many foreign scholars of the first calibre find so worthy of study, shall be placed on a par with — or even above — Greek, Latin, and modern languages, in all examinations held under the Irish Government. We can also insist, and we *shall* insist, that in those baronies where the children speak Irish, Irish shall be taught, and that Irish-speaking schoolmasters, petty sessions clerks, and even magistrates be appointed in Irish-speaking districts. If all this were done, it should not be very difficult, with the aid of the foremost foreign scholars, to bring about a tone of thought which would make it disgraceful for an educated Irishman — especially of the old Celtic race, MacDermotts, O'Conors, O'Sullivans, MacCarthys, O'Neills — to be ignorant of his own language — would make it at least as disgraceful as for an educated Jew to be quite ignorant of Hebrew.

We find the decay of our language faithfully reflected in the decay of our surnames. In Celtic times a great proof of the powers of assimilation which the Irish nation possessed, was the fact that so many of the great Norman and English nobles lived like the native chiefs and took Irish names. In this way the De Bourgos of Connacht became MacWilliams, of which clan again some minor branches became MacPhilpins, MacGibbons, and MacRaymonds. The Birminghams of Connacht took the name of MacFeóiris, the Stauntons became MacAveelys, the Nangles MacCostellos; the Prendergasts of Mayo became MacMaurices, the De Courcys became MacPatricks, the Bissetts of Antrim became MacEóins, and so on. Roughly speaking, it may be said that most of the English and Norman families outside of the Pale[30] were Irish in name and manners from the beginning of the fourteenth to the middle of the seventeenth century.

In 1465 an Act was passed by the Parliament of the English Pale that all Irishmen inside the Pale should take an English name 'of one towne as Sutton, Chester, Trym, Skryne, Corke, Kinsale; or colour, as white, black, brown; or art or science, as smith or carpenter; or office, as cooke, butler; and that he and his issue shall use this name' or forfeit all his goods. A great number of the lesser families complied with this typically English ordinance; but the greater ones — the MacMurroghs, O'Tooles, O'Byrnes, O'Nolans, O'Mores, O'Ryans, O'Conor Falys, O'Kellys, &c. — refused, and never did change their names. A hundred and thirty years later we find Spenser,[31] the poet, advocating the renewal of this statute. By doing this, says Spenser, 'they shall in time learne quite to forget the Irish nation. And herewithal,' he says, 'would I also wish the O's and Macs which the heads of septs have taken to their names to be utterly forbidden and extinguished, for that the same being an ordinance (as some say) first made by O'Brien for the strengthening of the Irish, the abrogation thereof will as much enfeeble them.' It was, however, only after Aughrim and the Boyne that Irish names began to be changed in great numbers, and O'Conors to become 'Conyers', O'Reillys 'Ridleys', O'Donnells 'Daniels', O'Sullivans 'Silvans', MacCarthys 'Carters', and so on.

But it is the last sixty years that have made most havoc with our Milesian names. It seemed as if the people were possessed with a mania for changing them to something — anything at all, only to get rid of the Milesian sound. 'Why,' said O'Connell, once talking to a mass-meeting of Lord Chancellor Sugden, 'you wouldn't call a decent pig Sugden.' Yet he never uttered a word of remonstrance at the O'Lahiffs, O'Brollahans, and MacRorys becoming under his eyes Guthrys, Bradleys, and Rogerses. It is more than a little curious, and a very bad augury for the future independence of Ireland, that men of education and intelligence like Carleton the novelist, or Hardiman,[32] author of the 'History of Galway' and the 'Irish Ministrelsy', should have changed their Milesian names, one from that of O'Cairellan, who was ancient chief of Clandermot, the other from the well-known name of O'Hargadain. In Connacht alone I know scores of Gatelys, Sextons, Baldwins, Foxes, Coxes, Footes, Greenes, Keatings, who are really O'Gatlies, O'Sesnans, O'Mulligans, O'Shanahans, MacGillacullys, O'Trehys, O'Honeens, and O'Keateys. The O'Hennesys are Harringtons, the O'Kinsellaghs, Kingsleys and Tinslys, the O'Feehillys Pickleys, and so on. O'Donovan, writing in 1862, gives a list of names which had recently been changed in the neighbourhood of Cootehill, Co. Cavan. These Irish names of MacNebo, MacIntyre, MacGilroy, MacTernan, MacCorry, MacOscar, MacBrehon, O'Clery, Murtagh, O'Drum, &c., were becoming, or had become, Victory, Victoria, Callwell, Freeman, King, Nugent, Gilman, Leonard, Godwin, Goodwin, Smyth, Golderich, Golding, Masterton, Lind, Crosby, Grosby, Crosse, Corry, Cosgrove, Judge, Brabacy, Brabazon, Clarke, Clerkin, Cunningham, Drummond,

Tackit, Sexton, and Mortimer[33] — not a bad attempt at West-Britonizing for one little town!

Numbers of people, again, like Mr Davitt[34] or Mr Hennessy, drop the O and Mac which properly belong to their names; others, without actually changing them, metamorphose their names, as we have seen, into every possible form. I was told in America that the first Chauncey who ever came out there was an O'Shaughnessy, who went to, I think, Maryland, in the middle of the last century, and who had twelve sons, who called themselves Chauncey, and from whom most of or all the Chaunceys in America are descended. I know people who have translated their names within the last ten years. This vile habit is going on with almost unabated vigour, and nobody has ever raised a protest against it. Out of the many hundreds of O'Byrnes — offshoots of the great Wicklow chieftains — in the city of New York, only four have retained that name; all the rest have taken the Scotch name of Burns. I have this information from two of the remaining four, both friends of my own, and both splendid Gaelic scholars, though from opposite ends of Ireland, Donegal and Waterford. Of two brothers of whom I was lately told, though I do not know them personally, one is an O'Gara, and still condescends to remain connected with the patron of the Four Masters and a thousand years of a glorious past, whilst the other (through some etymological confusion with the word Caraim, which means 'I love') calls himself Mr Love! Another brother remains a Brehony, thus showing his descent from one of the very highest and most honourable titles in Ireland — a Brehon,[35] law-giver and poet; the other brother is John Judge. In fact, hundreds of thousands of Irishmen prefer to drop their honourable Milesian names, and call themselves Groggins or Duggan, or Higgins or Guthry, or any other beastly name, in preference to the surnames of warriors, saints, and poets; and the melancholy part of it is, that not one single word of warning or remonstrance has been raised, as far as I am aware, against this colossal cringing either by the Irish public press or public men.

With our Irish Christian names the case is nearly as bad. Where are now all the fine old Irish Christian names of both men and women which were in vogue even a hundred years ago? They have been discarded as unclean things, not because they were ugly in themselves or inharmonious, but simply because they were not English. No man is now christened by a Gaelic name, 'nor no woman neither'. Such common Irish Christian names as Conn, Cairbre, Farfeasa, Teig, Diarmuid, Kian, Cuan, Ae, Art, Mahon, Eochaidh, Fearflatha, Cathan, Rory, Coll, Lochlainn, Cathal,

Lughaidh, Turlough, Éamon, Randal, Niall, Sorley, and Conor, are now extinct or nearly so. Donough and Murrough survive in the O'Brien family. Angus, Manus, Fergal, and Felim are now hardly known. The man whom you call Diarmuid when you speak Irish, a low, pernicious, un-Irish, detestable custom, begot by slavery, propagated by cringing, and fostered by flunkeyism, forces you to call Jeremiah when you speak English, or as a concession, Darby. In like manner, the indigenous Teig is West-Britonized into Thaddeus or Thady, for no earthly reason than that both begin with a T. Donough is Denis, Cahal is Charles, Murtagh and Murough are Mortimer, Dómhnall is Daniel, Partholan, the name of the earliest colonizer of Ireland, is Bartholomew or Batty,[36] Eoghan (Owen) is frequently Eugene, and our own O'Curry, though he plucked up courage to prefix the O to his name in later life, never discarded the Eugene, which, however, is far from being a monstrosity like most of our West-Britonized names; Félim is Felix, Finghin (Finneen) is Florence, Conor is Corney, Turlough is Terence, Éamon is Edmond or Neddy, and so on. In fact, of the great wealth of Gaelic Christian names in use a century or two ago, only Owen, Brian, Cormac, and Patrick seem to have survived in general use.

Nor have our female names fared one bit better; we have discarded them even more ruthlessly than those of our men. Surely Sadhbh (Sive) is a prettier name than Sabina or Sibby, and Nóra than Onny, Honny, or Honour (so translated simply because Nóra sounds like *onóir*, the Irish for 'honour'); surely Una is prettier than Winny, which it becomes when West-Britonized. Méve, the great name of the Queen of Connacht who led the famous cattle spoiling of Cuailgne, celebrated in the greatest Irish epic,[37] is at least as pretty as Maud, which it becomes when Anglicized, and Eibhlin (Eileen) is prettier than Ellen or Elinor. Aoife (Eefy), Sighle (Sheela), Móirin (Moreen), Nuala and Fionnuala (Finnoola), are all beautiful names which were in use until quite recently. Maurya and Anya are still common, but are not indigenous Irish names at all, so that I do not mind their rejection, whilst three other very common ones, Suraha, Shinéad, and Shuwaun, sound so bad in English that I do not very much regret their being translated into Sarah, Jane, and Joan respectively; but I must put in a plea for the retention of such beautiful words as Eefee, Oona, Eileen, Méve, Sive, and Nuala. Of all the beautiful Christian names of women which were in use a century or two ago Brighid (Breed), under the ugly form of Bridget, or still worse, of Biddy, and Eiblin under the form of Eveleen, and perhaps Norah, seem to be the only survivals, and they are becoming rarer. I *do* think that the time has now come to make a vigorous protest against this continued West-Britonizing of ourselves, and that our people ought to have a word in season addressed to them by their leaders which will stop them from translating their Milesian surnames into hideous Saxon, and help to introduce Irish instead of English Christian names. As long as the Irish nation goes on as it is doing I cannot have much hope of its ultimately taking its place amongst the nations of the earth, for if it does, it will have proceeded upon different lines from every other nationality that God ever created. I hope that we shall never be satisfied either as individuals or as a society as long as the Brehonys call themselves Judges, the Clan Govern call themselves Smiths, and the O'Reardons Salmons, as long as our boys are called Dan and Jeremiah instead of Donal and Diarmuid, and our girls Honny, Winny, and Ellen instead of Nóra, Una, and Eileen.

Our topographical nomenclature too — as we may now be prepared to expect — has been also shamefully corrupted to suit English ears; but unfortunately the difficulties attendant upon a realteration of our placenames to their proper forms are very great, nor do I mean to go into this question now, for it is one so long and so difficult that it would require a lecture, or rather a series of lectures to itself. Suffice it to say, that many of the best-known names in our history and annals have become almost wholly unrecognizable, through the ignorant West-Britonizing of them. The unfortunate natives of the eighteenth century allowed all kinds of havoc to be played with even their best-known names. For example the river Feóir they allowed to be turned permanently into the Nore, which happened this way. Some Englishman, asking the name of the river, was told that it was *An Fheóir*, pronounced In n'yore, because the F when preceded by the definite article *an* is not sounded, so that in his ignorance he mistook the word Feóir for Neóir, and the name has been thus perpetuated. In the same way the great Connacht lake, Loch Corrib, is really Loch Orrib, or rather Loch Orbsen, some Englishman having mistaken the C at the end of loch for the beginning of the next word. Sometimes the Ordnance Survey people make a rough guess at the Irish name and jot down certain English letters almost on chance. Sometimes again they make an Irish word resemble an English one, as in the celebrated Tailtin in Meath, where the great gathering of the nation was held, and, which, to make sure that no national memories should stick to it, has been West-Britonized Telltown.[38] On the whole, our place names have been treated with

about the same respect as if they were the names of a savage tribe which had never before been reduced to writing, and with about the same intelligence and contempt as vulgar English squatters treat the topographical nomenclature of the Red Indians. These things are now to a certain extent stereotyped, and are difficult at this hour to change, especially where Irish names have been translated into English, like Swinford and Strokestown, or ignored as in Charleville or Midleton. But though it would take the strength and goodwill of an united nation to put our topographical nomenclature on a rational basis like that of Wales and the Scotch Highlands, there is one thing which our Society can do, and that is to insist upon pronouncing our Irish names properly. Why will a certain class of people insist upon getting as far away from the pronunciation of the natives as possible? I remember a Galway gentleman pulling me up severely for speaking of Athenree. 'It's not Athenree,' he said, 'it's called Athenrye.' Yet in saying this he simply went out of his way to mispronounce the historic name, which means the 'King's ford', and which all the natives call *-ree*, not *-rye*.[39] Another instance out of many thousands is my own market town, Ballagh-ˇa-derreen, literally, 'the way of the oak-wood'. Ballach is the same word as in the phrase *Fág a' bealach*, 'clear the way', and 'derreen' is the diminutive of Derry, an oak-wood. Yet the more 'civilized' of the population, perhaps one in fifty, offend one's ears with the frightful jargon Bálla-hád-her-een. Thus Lord Iveagh (Ee-vah) becomes Lord Ivy, and Seana-guala, the old shoulder, becomes Shanagolden, and leads you to expect a mine, or at least a furze-covered hill.

I shall not give any more examples of deliberate carelessness, ineptitude, and West-Britonizing in our Irish topography, for the instances may be numbered by thousands and thousands. I hope and trust that where it may be done without any great inconvenience a native Irish Government will be induced to provide for the restoration of our placenames on something like a rational basis.

Our music, too, has become Anglicized to an alarming extent. Not only has the national instrument, the harp — which efforts are now being made to revive in the Highlands — become extinct, but even the Irish pipes are threatened with the same fate. In place of the pipers and fiddlers who, even twenty years ago, were comparatively common, we are now in many places menaced by the German band and the barrel organ. Something should be done to keep the native pipes and the native airs amongst us still. If Ireland loses her music she loses what is, after her Gaelic language and literature, her most valuable and most characteristic possession. And she is rapidly losing it. A few years ago all our travelling fiddlers and pipers could play the old airs which were then constantly called for, the *Cúis d'á pléidh, Drinaun Dunn, Roseen Dubh, Gamhan Geal Bán, Eileen-a-roon, Shawn O'Dwyer in Glanna*, and the rest, whether gay or plaintive, which have for so many centuries entranced the Gael. But now English music-hall ballads and Scotch songs have gained an enormous place in the repertoire of the wandering minstrel, and the minstrels themselves are becoming fewer and fewer, and I fear worse and worse. It is difficult to find a remedy for this. I am afraid in this practical age to go so far as to advocate the establishment in Cork or Galway of a small institution in which young and promising pipers might be trained to play all the Irish airs and sent forth to delight our population; for I shall be told that this is not a matter for even an Irish Government to stir in, though it is certain that many a Government has lavished money on schemes less pleasant and less useful. For the present, then, I must be content with hoping that the revival of our Irish music may go hand in hand with the revival of Irish ideas and Celtic modes of thought which our Society is seeking to bring about, and that people may be brought to love the purity of *Siúbhail Siúbhail*, or the fun of the *Moddereen Ruadh* in preference to 'Get Your Hair Cut', or 'Over the Garden Wall', or, even if it is not asking too much, of 'Ta-ra-ra-boom-de-ay'.

Our games, too, were in a most grievous condition until the brave and patriotic men who started the Gaelic Athletic Association[40] took in hand their revival. I confess that the instantaneous and extraordinary success which attended their efforts when working upon national lines has filled me with more hope for the future of Ireland than everything else put together. I consider the work of the association in reviving our ancient national game of *caman*, or hurling, and Gaelic football, has done more for Ireland than all the speeches of politicians for the last five years. And it is not alone that that splendid association revived for a time with vigour our national sports, but it revived also our national recollections, and the names of the various clubs through the country have perpetuated the memory of the great and good men and martyrs of Ireland. The physique of our youth has been improved in many of our counties; they have been taught self-restraint, and how to obey their captains; they have been, in many places, weaned from standing idle in their own roads or street corners; and not least, they have been introduced to the use of a thoroughly good and Irish garb. Wherever the warm striped green jersey of the Gaelic Athletic Association was seen, there Irish manhood and Irish memories were rapidly reviving. There torn collars and ugly neckties hanging awry and far better not there at all, and dirty shirts of bad linen were banished, and our young hurlers were clad like men and Irishmen, and not in the shoddy second-hand suits of Manchester and London shop-boys. Could not this alteration be carried still further? Could we not make that jersey still more popular, and could we not, in places where both garbs are worn, use our influence against English second-hand trousers, generally dirty in front, and hanging in muddy tatters at the heels, and in favour of the cleaner worsted stockings and neat breeches which many of the older generation still wear? Why have we discarded our own comfortable frieze? Why does every man in Connemara wear home-made and home-spun tweed, while in the midland counties we have become too proud for it, though we are not too proud to buy at every fair and market the most incongruous cast-off clothes imported from English cities, and to wear them? Let us, as far as we have any influence, set our faces against this aping of English dress, and encourage our women to spin and our men to wear comfortable frieze suits of their own wool, free from shoddy and humbug. So shall we de-Anglicize Ireland to some purpose, foster a native spirit and a growth of native custom which will form the strongest barrier against English influence and be in the end the surest guarantee of Irish autonomy.

I have now mentioned a few of the principal points on which it would be desirable for us to move, with a view to de-Anglicizing ourselves; but perhaps the principal point of all I have taken for granted. That is the necessity for encouraging the use of Anglo-Irish literature instead of English books, especially instead of English periodicals. We must set our face sternly against penny dreadfuls, shilling shockers, and still more, the garbage of vulgar English weeklies like *Bow Bells* and the *Police Intelligence*. Every house should have a copy of Moore and Davis.[41] In a word, we must strive to cultivate everything that is most racial, most smacking of the soil, most Gaelic, most Irish, because in spite of the little admixture of Saxon blood in the north-east corner, this island *is* and will *ever* remain Celtic at the core, far more Celtic than most people imagine, because, as I have shown you, the names of our people are no criterion of their race. On racial lines, then, we shall best develop, following the bent of our own natures; and, in order to do this, we must create a strong feeling against West-Britonism, for it — if we give it the least chance, or show it the smallest quarter — will overwhelm us like a flood, and we shall find ourselves toiling painfully behind the English at each step following the same fashions, only six months behind the English ones; reading the same books, only months behind them; taking up the same fads, after they have become stale *there*, following *them* in our dress, literature, music, games, and ideas, only a long time after them and a vast way behind. We will become, what, I fear, we are largely at present, a nation of imitators, the Japanese of Western Europe, lost to the power of native initiative and alive only to second-hand assimilation. I do not think I am overrating this danger. We are probably at once the most assimilative and the most sensitive nation in Europe. A lady in Boston said to me that the Irish immigrants had become Americanized on the journey out before ever they landed at Castle Gardens.⁴² And when I ventured to regret it, she said, shrewdly, 'If they did not at once become Americanized they would not be Irish.' I knew fifteen Irish workmen who were working in a haggard in England give up talking Irish amongst themselves because the English farmer laughed at them. And yet O'Connell used to call us the 'finest peasantry in Europe'. Unfortunately, he took little care that we should remain so. We must teach ourselves to be less sensitive, we must teach ourselves not to be ashamed of ourselves, because the Gaelic people can never produce its best before the world as long as it remains tied to the apron-strings of another race and another island, waiting for *it* to move before it will venture to take any step itself.

In conclusion, I would earnestly appeal to every one, whether Unionist or Nationalist, who wishes to see the Irish nation produce its best — and surely whatever our politics are we all wish that — to set his face against this constant running to England for our books, literature, music, games, fashions, and ideas. I appeal to every one whatever his politics — for this is no political matter — to do his best to help the Irish race to develop in future upon Irish lines, even at the risk of encouraging national aspirations, because upon Irish lines alone can the Irish race once more become what it was of yore — one of the most original, artistic, literary, and charming peoples of Europe.

1 This was a movement in the 1840s which sought the Repeal of the Union with Great Britain. It was grouped around the *Nation*, a weekly newspaper founded and edited by Thomas Davis (1814–45). Members included Charles Gavan Duffy (1816–1903) and John Mitchel (1815–75). The Young Irelanders attempted a rising in 1848, the year of revolutions elsewhere in Europe, but without success.

2 Fenianism was an American-financed physical force movement which sought the separation of Ireland from Great Britain. Founded in 1858 the group included James Stephens (1825–1901) and John O'Leary (1830–1907). The Fenian rising of 1867 was no more than a gesture but an enduring gesture, as the influence of O'Leary on W.B. Yeats in the 1880s and 1890s suggests.

3 The Land League was founded by Michael Davitt (1846–1906) in 1879 as a militant defence by tenant farmers against unscrupulous landlords then suffering from an economic crisis occasioned by falling prices and crop failures. The Land League played a crucial role in the so-called Land War of 1879–82 when tenants were threatened with eviction. The League's agitation was used to good effect by Charles Stewart Parnell (1846–91), the leader of the Irish Parliamentary Party, in championing Home Rule for Ireland at Westminster. Hence the reference to 'Parliamentary obstruction'.

4 John O. Westwood (1805–93), entomologist and natural historian, wrote on Ireland in *Fac-Similes of the Miniatures and Ornaments of Anglo-Saxon and Irish Manuscripts* (1868).

5 Marie Henri d'Arbois de Joubainville (1827–1910), author of *The Irish Mythological Cycle and Celtic Mythology* (trans. 1903), was Professor of Celtic Literature at the Collège de France.

6 Heinrich Zimmer (1851–1910), author of *Keltische Studien* (1881) and *The Irish Element in Medieval Culture* (trans. 1891), was a German Celtic scholar and founding Professor of Celtic at Berlin in 1901.

7 One of the leading figures of Irish mythology, the Hound of Culann features prominently in the Red Branch cycle of stories. For one of his stories, see p. 95 below 'The Only Son of Aoife' in Lady Gregory, *Cuchulain of Muirthemne* (1902).

8 The lecture 'Irish Literature, Its Origins, Environment and Influence' by George Sigerson (1836–1925) was one of the three addresses included in *The Revival of Irish Literature* (1894). His major work was *Bards of the Gael and Gaul* (1897), an anthology of Irish verse in translation.

9 In the eighteenth century the Irish Parliament met at the Old Parliament house on College Green in Dublin (now the Bank of Ireland).

10 Latin: literally, how changed from him (the Hector who once came back arrayed in the armour of Achilles). Vergil, *The Aeneid*, Book 2, line 274.

11 Oisín was the son of Fionn MacCumhail (Finn Macool), a central figure in the mythological stories about the Fianna. Yeats's first book of verse was entitled *The Wanderings of Oisin* (1889).

12 Brian Boru is as much part of myth as of history. In 1002 he assumed kingship of Ireland, and at the Battle of Clontarf in 1014 he defeated the king of Leinster and the Dublin Norse, putting an end to Norse or Viking influence in Ireland.

13 The Treaty of Limerick in 1691 marked a significant defeat for the Catholic cause in Ireland, and paved the way for the Penal laws in the eighteenth century (laws which penalized Catholics in every area of social life, religious observance, and economic activity). After their defeat, the Irish Catholic nobility — 'the wild geese' as they were known — followed their leader Patrick Sarsfield to the Continent, and some of them later fought as mercenaries on the battlefields of Europe.

14   A reference to the 1798 rising against British rule in Ireland.

15   Area or parish.

16   The last group of invaders of Ireland before the advent of the historical period.

17   Maynooth College in County Kildare was established in 1795 as a seminary for training Catholic priests. During the Penal times Irish priests were educated abroad.

18   Daniel O'Connell (1775–1847) was the most important political figure in Ireland in the first half of the nineteenth century. He was central in the struggle to achieve Catholic emancipation in 1829, but he was less successful in the 1830s with his attempt to Repeal the Union. Hyde's complaint against O'Connell is that he did not do enough for Irish Ireland and should have done more to preserve Irish as a spoken language. O'Connell died in 1847 during the Great Famine, an event which marked a turning-point in the development of modern Ireland.

19   William Smith O'Brien (1803–64), a leading member of the Young Irelanders, broke with O'Connell in 1847 to form the Irish Confederation and lead a rising in 1848 against British rule in Ireland.

20   William Carleton (1794–1869), author of *Traits and Stories of the Irish Peasantry* (1830), explored the lives of ordinary people in pre- and post-Famine Ireland.

21   Father Eugene O'Growney (1863–99), Professor of Irish at Maynooth, was a prominent figure in the Irish-language revival movement of the 1890s. *Simple Lessons in Irish* (1894) became a standard primer for learning Irish.

22   Eugene O'Curry (1796–1862), Professor of Irish History and Archaeology in the Catholic University of Ireland, helped to systematize the collection of manuscript sources for studying Gaelic culture and society. He was the author of *Lectures on the Manuscript Materials of Ancient Irish History* (1861) and *On the Manners and Customs of the Ancient Irish* (1873).

23   As an instance of this, I mention the case of a young man I met on the road coming from the fair of Tuam, some ten miles away. I saluted him in Irish, and he answered me in English. 'Don't you speak Irish,' said I. 'Well, I declare to God, sir,' he said, 'my father and mother hasn't a word of English, but still, I don't speak Irish,' This was absolutely true for him. There are thousands upon thousands of houses all over Ireland today where the old people invariably use Irish in addressing the children, and the children as invariably answer in English, the children understanding Irish but not speaking it, the parents understanding their children's English but unable to use it themselves. In a great many cases, I should almost say most, the children are not conscious of the existence of two languages. I remember asking a gossoon a couple of miles west of Ballaghaderreen in the Co. Mayo, some questions in Irish and he answered them in English. At last I said to him, *'Nach labhrann tu Gaedheilg?'* (i.e., 'Don't you speak Irish?') and his answer was, 'And isn't it Irish I'm spaking?' 'No *a-chuisle*,' said I, 'it's not Irish you're speaking, but English.' 'Well then,' said he, 'that's how I spoke it ever'! He was quite unconscious that I was addressing him in one language and he answering in another. On a different occasion I spoke Irish to a little girl in a house near Kilfree Junction, Co. Sligo, into

which I went while waiting for a train. The girl answered me in Irish until her brother came in. 'Arrah now, Mary,' said he, with what was intended to be a most bitter sneer; 'and isn't that a credit to you!' And poor Mary — whom I had with difficulty persuaded to begin — immediately hung her head and changed to English. This is going on from Malin Head to Galway, and from Galway to Waterford, with the exception possibly of a few spots in Donegal and Kerry, where the people are wiser and more national. [AN]

24   The Fenian leader James Stephens (1825–1901) organized the Irish Republican Brotherhood along military lines with 'circles' and 'centres'.

25   Johann Kasper Zeuss (1806–56), a German philologist, was the author of *Grammatica Celtica* (1853).

26   Kuno Meyer (1859–1919), a leading German Celticist, taught at universities in Liverpool, Dublin, and Berlin. In 1903 he established a School of Irish Learning in Dublin.

27   Ernst Windisch (1844–1918) was a German Celticist who translated the *Táin Bó Cuailgne* (Cattle-Raid of Cooley) into German in 1905. Joyce probably consulted this edition in the Zentralbibliothek in Zurich while living there during the First World War.

28   John Redmond (1856–1918), politician, led the pro-Parnellite faction of the Irish Parliamentary Party after the fall of Parnell in 1890. He went on to become leader of the Irish Parliamentary Party in 1900 when it reunited.

29   After the fall of Parnell, Justin McCarthy (1830–1912) assumed leadership of the anti-Parnellite faction of the Irish Parliamentary Party until 1896.

30   The Pale was an area around Dublin subject to English rule. The term dates back to the fourteenth century, and the extent of the Pale varied: during the reign of Henry VIII it extended from Dublin to Dundalk and inland for some twenty miles.

31   Edmund Spenser (?1552–99), author of *The Faerie Queene* (1590–96), was given lands in County Cork after taking part in the suppression of the Desmond Rebellion. The quotation is from *A View of the Present State of Ireland* (1596; rpt. *The Works of Edmund Spenser: Spenser's Prose Works*, ed. Rudolf Gottfried, Baltimore: Johns Hopkins, 1949, lines 4859–64). *A View* provides a series of candid insights into the brutal process of Elizabethan colonization.

32   James Hardiman (1782–1855), author of *The History of the Town and County of Galway* (1820) and *Irish Minstrelsy* (1831), was appointed Librarian of University College, Galway, in 1848.

33   The following are a few instances out of hundreds of the monstrous transmographying of Gaelic names into English. The Gillespies (Giolla-Easbuig, i.e., Bishop's servant) are Archbolds or Bishops. The Mackays (Mac Aodha, i.e., son of Ae or Hugh) are Hughes. The Mac Reevys or Mac Culreevys (Mac Cúil-Riabhaigh, i.e., son of the grey poll) are Grays. The Mac Eóchagains instead of being all Gahagans or Geoghegans have — some of them — deformed their name into the monstrosity of Goggin. The Mac Feeachrys (Mac Fhiachraidh) are Vickors or even Hunters. The Mac Feehalys are often Fieldings. Mac Gilleesa (Mac Giolla Iosa, i.e., sons of Jesus' devotee) are either Gillespie or Giles. The Mac Gillamurrys (Mac Giolla-Mhuire, i.e.,

son of the Virgin's devotee) is often made Marmion, sometimes more correctly Macilmurray or Mac Ilmurry. Mac Gillamerry (Mac Giolla Meidhre, i.e., son of the servant of merriment) is Anglicized Merryman. Mac Gillaree (Mac Giolla-righ, i.e., son of the king's servant) is very often made King, but sometimes pretty correctly Mac Gilroy or Mac Ilroy — thus the Connemara people have made Kingston of the village of Ballyconry, because the *ry* or *righ* means a king. The Mac Irs, sons of Ir, earliest colonizer of Ireland, have, by some confusion with *geirr*, the genitive of *gearr*, 'short,' become Shorts or Shortalls, but sometimes, less corruptly, Kerrs. The honourable name of Mac Rannell (Mac Raghnaill) is now seldom met with in any other form than that of Reynolds. The Mac Sorarans (Mac Samhradháin, the clan or tribe name of the Mac Gaurans or Mac Governs) have become Somers, through some fancied etymology with the word *samhradh*. The Mac Sorleys (Mac Samharlaigh) are often Shirleys. The honourable and poetic race of Mac-an-bháirds (sons of the bard) are now Wards to a man. The Mac-intleevys (Mac an tsléibhe, i.e., sons of the mountain) are Levys or Dunlevys. The Macintaggarts (Mac an tsagairt, i.e., son of the priest) are now Priestmans, or occasionally, I do not know why, Segraves. The Macgintys (Mac an tsaoi, i.e., son of the sage) are very often Nobles. The Macinteers (Mac an tsaoir, i.e., son of the carpenter) instead of being made MacIntyre as the Scots always have it, are in Ireland Carpenters or Wrights, or — because *saor* means 'free' as well as Carpenter — Frees and Freemans. Many of the O'Hagans (O h-Aodhgáin) are now Fagans, and even Dickens's Fagin the Jew has not put a stop to the hideous transformation. The O'Hillans (Mac Ui Iollain, i.e., sons of Illan, a great name in Irish romance) have become Hylands or Whelans. It would be tedious to go through all the well-known names that immediately occur to one as thus suffering; suffice it to say, that the O'Heas became Hayses, the O'Queenahans, Mosses, Mossmans, and Kinahans, the O'Longans Longs, the O'Naghtens Nortons, the O'Reardons Salmons, the O'Shanahans Foxes, and so on *ad infinitum*. [AN]

34 Michael Davitt (1846–1906), leader of the Land League.

35 The Brehon (*breitheamh* is Irish for judge) legal system was the native law in Ireland until its overthrow after the Elizabethan conquest at the end of the sixteenth century.

36 It is questionable, however, whether Partholan as a modern Christian name is not itself an Irishized form of Bartholomew. [AN]

37 The reference is to the *Táin Bó Cuailgne* (Cattle-Raid of Cooley), where Medb, the queen of Connacht, sets out to capture the Brown Bull of Cooley in Ulster.

38 For more information about Tailtin, see an article by me incorporate in the 'Rules of the Gaelic Athletic Association,' recently published. [AN]

39 In Irish it is Beul-áth-an-righ contracted into B'l'áth-'n-righ, pronounced *Blawn-ree*. [AN]

40 The Gaelic Athletic Association (or G.A.A.) was founded by Michael Cusack (1847–1906) in 1884 to promote Gaelic sports.

41 Thomas Moore (1779–1852) was author of *Irish Melodies* (1807–34); Thomas Davis (1814–45) composed poems and ballads including 'A Nation Once Again', a popular song in nineteenth-century Ireland.

42 From 1855 until 1892, when Ellis Island opened, Castle Garden (sic) in the Battery in New York served as an immigration station.

DOUGLAS HYDE (trans.)
from Douglas Hyde, *Abhráin Grádh Chúige Connacht* (Love Songs of Connacht), (1893)

'This is the way with three-fourths and more of the poems in this book; there remains nothing of the people who composed them in grief and tribulation, except the songs.' This is how Hyde introduced this, the first song in his pioneering edition of Irish songs from Connacht (one of the four provinces of Ireland). In juxtaposing the Irish alongside an English translation and in providing a translation which stayed closer to the original Irish rather than to a poetic English equivalent, Hyde was putting into practice his ambition to de-Anglicize Ireland. Few English readers of this song can feel anything but excluded from a Gaelic culture which produced it. For modern spelling and a modern translation of this song see Seán Ó Tuama and Thomas Kinsella, eds., *An Duanaire 1600–1900: Poems of the Dispossessed* (1981), number 78; the Irish-language version is taken from this publication.

DÁ DTÉINNSE SIAR

Dá dtéinnse siar is aniar ní thiocfainn,
ar an gcnoc ab airde is air a sheasfainn,
's í an chraobh chumhra is túisce bhainfinn,
agus 's é mo ghrá féin is luaithe leanfainn.

Tá mo chroí chomh dubh le hairne
nó le gual dubh a dhófaí i gceárta,
nó le bonn bróige ar hallaí bána,
is tá lionn dubh mór os cionn mo gháire.

Tá mo chroí-se brúite briste
mar leac oighre ar uachtar uisce,
mar bheadh cnuasach cnó tar éis a mbriste
nó maighdean óg tar éis a cliste.

Tá mo ghrá-sa ar dhath na sméara,
's ar dhath na n-airní lá breá gréine,
ar dhath na bhfraochóg ba dhuibhe an tsléibhe,
's is minic bhí ceann dubh ar cholainn ghléigeal.

Is mithid domhsa an baile seo a fhágáil,
is géar an chloch 's is fuar an láib ann,
is ann a fuaireas guth gan éadáil
agus focal trom ó lucht an bhéadáin.

Fógraim an grá, is mairg a thug é
do mhac na mná úd ariamh nár thuig é,
mo chroí i mo lár gur fhág sé dubh é,
's ní fheicim ar an tsráid ná in áit ar bith é.

IF I WERE TO GO WEST

If I were to go west, it is from the west I would not
   come,
On the hill that was highest, 't is on it I would stand,
It is the fragrant branch I would soonest pluck,
And it is my own love I would quickest follow.

My heart is as black as a sloe,
Or as a black coal that would be burnt in a forge,
As the sole of a shoe upon white halls,
And there is great melancholy over my laugh.

My heart is bruised, broken,
Like ice upon the top of water,
As it were a cluster of nuts after their breaking,
Or a young maiden after her marrying.

My love is of the colour of the blackberries,
And the colour of the raspberry on a fine sunny day,
Of the colour of the darkest heath-berries of the
   mountain,
And often has there been a black head upon a bright
   body.

Time it is for me to leave this town,
The stone is sharp in it, and the mould is cold;
It was in it I got a voice (blame), without riches
And a heavy word from the band who back-bite.

I denounce love; woe is she who gave it
To the son of yon woman, who never understood it.
My heart in my middle, sure he has left it black,
And I do not see him on the street or in any place.

LIONEL JOHNSON
from *The United Irishman*, 7 October 1893

Lionel Johnson (1867–1902), the son of an Irish army officer, was educated at
Winchester and Oxford. Embarking on a literary career in London he joined the
Rhymers' Club, became a friend of Yeats, and discovered his Celtic roots. The disorder
of his personal life led Yeats to associate him with the Tragic Generation of the 1890s.
'Parnell' is one of Johnson's 'Irish' poems, patriotic in sentiment, Celtic in mood, and
published in the Dublin nationalist paper *The United Irishman*. The poem is dedicated
to John McGrath, whose review of Yeats's early verse in 'The Changing of "Oisin"'
made a significant impression on Yeats (see *The United Irishman*, 14 December 1895).
The figure of Parnell, who died on 6 October 1891 (commemorated as Ivy Day when a
sprig of ivy was worn in the lapel), casts a shadow over the whole life of Ireland in the

1890s and 1900s. For a survey of the effects in literature, see among others Herbert Howarth, *The Irish Writers, 1880–1940: Literature Under Parnell's Star* (1958). A description of the return of Parnell's body to Ireland can be found in Joyce's *A Portrait of the Artist as a Young Man* (1916). When Padraic Colum and Edward O'Brien compiled an anthology in 1916 entitled *Poems of the Irish Revolutionary Brotherhood* (which consisted of poems by Thomas MacDonagh, Patrick Pearse, Joseph Mary Plunkett, and Roger Casement) they framed the volume with a poem by Johnson ('Ways of War') and Yeats ('The Song of Red Hanrahan').

PARNELL
To John McGrath

The wail of Irish winds,
The cry of Irish seas:
Eternal sorrow finds
Eternal voice in these.

I cannot praise our dead,
Whom Ireland weeps so well:
Her morning light, that fled;
Her morning star, that fell.

She of the mournful eyes
Waits, and no dark clouds break:
Waits, and her strong son lies
Dead, for her holy sake.

Her heart is sorrow's home,
And hath been from of old:
An host of griefs hath come,
To make that heart their fold.

Ah, the sad autumn day,
When the last sad troop came
Swift down the ancient way,
Keening a chieftain's name!

Gray hope was there, and dread;
Anger, and love in tears:
They mourned the dear and dead,
Dirge of the ruined years.

Home to her heart she drew
The mourning company:
Old sorrows met the new,
In sad fraternity.

A mother, and forget?
Nay! all her children's fate
Ireland remembers yet,
With love insatiate.

She hears the heavy bells:
Hears, and with passionate breath
Eternally she tells
A rosary of death.

Faithful and true is she,
The mother of us all:
Faithful and true! may we
Fail her not, though we fall.

R. P. CARTON
from *The Irish Monthly*, May 1895

This relatively unknown essay by a relatively unknown critic provides a useful marker as to, firstly, the mood of the period, secondly, the unproblematic continuity between myth and history, and, thirdly, the treatment of landscape in nineteenth-century poetry. It was originally a lecture delivered in the Catholic Commercial Club in Dublin on 3 January 1895 to an Irish audience which was expected to know the range of references and allusions made by Carton.

The Associations of Scenery

In *Blackwood's Magazine* last September there appeared an article by the accomplished poet and essayist, Mr Alfred Austin, on touring in Ireland and on the varied beauties of Irish scenery. The article is written in a thoroughly genial, appreciative and laudatory spirit which one would not be inclined to expect from its title, 'That Damnable Country'. 'I came to the conclusion at last,' he says, 'that the reason why, though Ireland is more beautiful still than Britain, it is less travelled in and less talked about, is that it never produced a great poet, a great painter, or even a great novelist. I mean one who has sung or depicted the beauties of Ireland so as to excite general enthusiasm about them.' It is true that no one poet has done for Ireland what Scott did for Scotland or Wordsworth did for the English lakes. And yet I hope to show you that the criticism of Mr Austin is much too sweeping. I will admit that Irish novelists have not done as much as they might have done in the way of clustering associations round Irish places. This has arisen in great part from their having in common with many of their brethren across the water been afraid or ashamed to localize their stories in real places, but have laid their scenes either in imaginative ones or in real ones disguised under fictitious names. Here and there of course are some brilliant exceptions. The gap of Dunlo will bring before you the sad figure of hapless Eily O'Connor, and Purple Mountain is the same now as when the ponies scattered over its slopes answered to the rattle of Myles-na-Coppaleen. I must, however, respectfully decline to associate Eily with the Middle Lake or with the Colleen Bawn rock or with the caves hard by it. For scenic purposes Boucicault[1] placed Eily's cottage on the shore of the lake, magnified the caves and made them and the rock the scene of a murder only attempted. But Eily was drowned in the Flesk, and I defy anyone be he ever so murderous to have drowned her in the depth of water that flows round the rock, or anyone, be he ever so venturous, to take a header into it. In the Irish novels of Lever,[2] notably in the 'The O'Donoghue,' 'The Knight of Gwynne,' and 'Sir Brooke Fosbrooke,' he has described Irish scenery truthfully and well. So too in recent times have Rosa Mulholland,[3] Mrs Hartley,[4] and Miss Jane Barlow.[5] Unfortunately, however, the scenery for the most part is not localized. For what can be successfully done by a novelist for specific spots in Ireland I would specially point to what Miss Emily Lawless[6] has done for the scenery of Clare in 'Hurrish' and what she has done for the Islands of Arran and the Claddagh and the road to Spiddal in her very sad but beautiful and powerful story, 'Grania.'

Although no one poet, as I have said, has done for Ireland what Scott and Wordsworth did for Scotland and the English lakes, there can be found a vast body of Irish poetry, and good poetry too, associated with the scenery of Ireland and associated through that scenery with all that is best as well as all that is saddest in Irish history and Irish romance. In many of

The strains sweet foreign Spenser sung
By Mulla's shore

may be traced the influences of the scenery which suggested much of the background of the 'Fairy Queen' and 'Colin Clout's come home again.'[7] There is an Auburn in Westmeath, but Goldsmith's[8] Auburn is a picture of an English and not an Irish village. It would be wrong to deny the great and genuine and lasting services of Moore when he took up the 'Dear Harp'[9] of his country and waked its wild music to make the pulse of the patriot soldier and lover throb at the lays of their native land. I can, but I confess somewhat at a distance, join with Denis Florence MacCarthy's song of him in his glorious centenary Ode:[10]

Glory to Moore, for he has sung our story
In strains whose sweetness ne'er can pass away.

Glory to Moore, for he has sighed our sorrow
In such a wail of melody divine
That e'en from grief a passing joy we borrow
And linger long o'er each lamenting line.

Glory to Moore, that in his songs of gladness
Which neither change nor time can e'er destroy,
Though mingled oft with some faint sigh of sadness
He sings his country's rapture and its joy.

Although Moore must be ever honoured for what he did, he wanted that true poet's love for his native land which Scott felt so deeply and which alone could have enabled him to bring its charms home to the world and make them universally known. 'I am sure,' says Mr Austin in the article already referred to, 'the vale of Cashmere is not lovelier than Innisfallen and all that surrounds it, but for want of intimate affection he wrote of both in precisely the same strain and style, insensible to local colour, to local form, and to local character and in each case satisfying himself with vague dulcet adjectives and melodious generalities.' Sir Aubrey de Vere, father of the living poet and author of two splendid dramas 'Mary Tudor' and 'Julian the Apostate,' published in 1844 a little volume of poems including some sonnets which give delightful pictures of Irish scenery and especially the scenery of the Shannon and the wild coast of Clare.

But real popular Irish poetry with the genuine ring in it was to grow up later on. In the early forties a band of gifted, brilliant, cultured, and enthusiastic Irishmen undertook to found a school of Irish poetry and by it

> to wake the old weird world that sleeps
> In Irish lore.

Those were days of political as well as intellectual activity, but it is of the poetical side of the intellectual movement I mean alone to speak. These men, and their successors in the school they founded, found ready aid in the researches of their contemporaries — the antiquary and artist George Petrie, scholars like Dr Todd, Dr Reeves and John O'Donovan and later on Eugene O'Curry and Miss Margaret Stokes, whose zeal, industry and energy in all that relates to Irish art and literature is happily still unexhausted. I intend, as well as the residue of the time at my disposal will allow me, to show you what treasures of Irish poetry that school has given us instinct with Irish feeling, reviving and vivifying Irish history and Irish romance, and set at all times in real Irish scenery.

One of the band I have alluded to stands out from among his fellows, and when we are calling to mind to whom we owe this treasury, by their work, their influence and their example —

> to Thomas Davis
> Let the greater praise belong.[11]

Next to Davis, the praise is due to one who is happily still spared and who is now devoting in his honoured old age the same knowledge, energy, and whole-heartedness to the development of Irish literature which he brought to it in the days of his early man-hood. I mean, I need hardly say, Sir Charles Gavan Duffy.[12] Chief among the band associated with these in the work, I would name Samuel (afterwards Sir Samuel) Ferguson, Denis Florence MacCarthy, James Clarence Mangan,[13] John O'Hagan, and a little later Thomas D'Arcy McGee.[14]

But all these had able and willing helpers. Week after week the columns of *The Nation* newspaper teemed with Irish songs and Irish ballads by one or more of these gifted, cultured, and earnest men, and by women too, for Ellen Mary Downing and Speranza (Lady Wilde)[15] were numbered amongst *The Nation's* contributors. 'They soon,' says Duffy in his life of Davis, 'lighted up the obscure past with a sympathy

which gilded it like sunshine till the study of our annals became a passion among young Irishmen.' The work which they began with such brilliancy and success found as years went on, and down to our own days, successors to carry it on in many a stirring Irish ballad and tender love song by John Todhunter,[16] Thomas Irwin, Rosa Mulholland, Katharine Tynan,[17] W.B. Yeats, and Mr T.D. Sullivan,[18] whose fine ballad on the death of King Conor McNessa is worthy to take its place beside the best ballads of his predecessors.

Of all the poets of the school which Davis may claim to have founded, the greatest unquestionably is Ferguson. In 'The Lays of the Western Gael,' in the volume of poems published in 1880, and in 'Congal' will be found poetry, not alone thoroughly Irish in its subject and treatment, but fit to be ranked with the masterpieces of English literature. Especially has he worked up the treasures of bardic story and the chronicles of the heroic age of Ireland. He found these at his hand through the labours of those I have already mentioned, of each of whom may be said what McGee said of O'Donovan:[19]

> With gentle hand he rectified
> The errors of old bardic pride,
>   And set aright
> The story of our devious past
> And left it as it now must last
>   Full in the light.[20]

But the story as 'set aright' by the antiquary and the scholar was comparatively dull and lifeless. The noble verse of Ferguson put life into the dry bones and the misty forms of forgotten kings and heroes, and of long dead Queens become living men and women who reigned and fought and loved again in the scenes once more associated with the names.

Contemporaneously with Ferguson but labouring apart, another great Irish poet was doing in loving and lasting verse the same work for the past of Ireland. I spoke of him at length to you on the last occasion I had the honour to address you, and I will content myself now with naming Mr Aubrey de Vere,[21] whose Irish poems will be found in 'Inisfail,' 'The Legends of St Patrick,' and in the volume entitled 'The Foray of Queen Maeve and other Legends of Ireland's heroic age.'

Let me now endeavour to give some examples of what this poetry has done to give associations to Irish scenery. Say you are travelling to the north of Ireland. As the train steams out of the station at Dundalk, you may notice a hill to the left with a castle on its summit from which the hill takes its name of Castletown. On that hill stood the residence of that darling hero of

Irish romance, Cuchullin, and here, tradition has it, he was buried. Not far off, is Ardee, the scene of Cuchullin's fight with Ferdia, which is the subject of Mr de Vere's poem 'The Combat at the Ford'. Going on from Dundalk, you would soon see on the left of the train Slieve Gullion, from which Thomas Davis borrowed a *nom de plume* for his young friend, John O'Hagan, who came from the neighbouring town of Newry. At the foot of the mountain was the forge of the armourer of Slieve Gullion, the renowned Culaun. Cuchullin slew in self defence the faithful but fierce hound of the armourer and

Left an old man lonely in the world.

In compassion for Culaun's grief, Cuchullin bound himself to guard him until a dog of the hound's breed should grow up to take his place, and thus gained the name of Cuchullin 'the hound of the smith'. You will find all this vividly set out in the vigorous dramatic poem by Ferguson, 'The naming of Cuchullin', and the chapter 'Setanta and the Smith's Dog', in Mr Standish O'Grady's[22] latest work 'The Coming of Cuculain'. Go on to Armagh, associated, as it ever will be, with St Patrick. This precious association of Armagh has been beautifully dealt with by Mr de Vere in the poem in the 'Legends of St. Patrick', called 'St Patrick and the Founding of Armagh Cathedral'. But Armagh has earlier associations. About a mile and a half to the west of Armagh you will come to a circular rampart of earth enclosing some eleven acres within which are two small mounds also of earth. This is all that now remains of the palace of Emania, the fortress dwelling of the kings of Ulster with a history more or less fabulous extending from the year 330 before, to the year 336 after Christ. Here was the home of the famous Red Branch knights where they were trained in valour and feats of arms, and the name and memory of whose home is still preserved in the name of the adjoining townland Creeveroe. Here Macha, the wife of Crunn, was cruelly made to run her victorious, but fatal race against the fleet horses of Conor. Here, too, relying on the guarantee of Fergus MacRoy for their safety, came the three sons of Usnach, with Deirdre, wife of one of them; and here the three youths were treacherously murdered by the command of Conor. Here Deirdre died of grief on the body of her slaughtered husband, and here Fergus vowed his oath:

I'll take such vengeance on this traitor king
All Erin shore to shore shall ring with it,
And poetry in ages yet to come
Make tales of wonder of it for the world.

You will find these associations of Armagh enshrined in 'The Tain Quest', 'The Twins of Macha', and 'Deirdre', by Ferguson, and 'The Sons of Usna', by Mr de Vere.

From the train going further northwards you get a glimpse of the broad waters of Lough Neagh. In 'Deirdre' the ill fated party on their journey to Emania came near the lake and the legend of its origin is told by Illan thus:—

Yes, 'twas young Liban's task to watch the well
And duly close its covering lid at eve
Lest something evil there inhabiting
Should issue forth, but on an afternoon
Walking with her true lover, with a mind
That thought of nothing evil, she forgot
Well and well lid; and so the under-sea
Burst through and drowned the valley.

There is a glorious drive from Larne along the Antrim coast, turning at Cushendall into the Antrim glens and leading on through Ballycastle to the Giant's Causeway. It passes at Glenarm the entrance to Glenarm Castle, the residence of the Earls of Antrim. It was here that Randal McDonnell of Larne won the lands of Antrim and their lady in the singular fashion told in a ballad by Thomas D'Arcy McGee. She was wooed by McQuillan from Dunluce and McDonnell from Larne. She puts them to this test.

Ye both were born upon the shore,
Were bred upon the sea;
Now let me see you ply the oar
For the land you love and me.
The chief that first can reach the strand
May mount at morn and ride
And his long day's ride shall bound his land,
And I will be his bride.

The wooers accept the test, and an exciting race then begins, which is watched by the lady from the battlements of the castle. The boats at last near the shore.

Nearer, nearer on they come
Row, M'Donnell, row
For Antrim's princely castle-home,
Its lands and its lady row.
The chief that first can grasp the strand
May mount at morn and ride,
And his long day's ride shall bound his land
And she shall be his bride.

He saw his rival gain apace,
He felt the spray in his wake;

He thought of her who watched the race
More dear for her dowry's sake.
Then he drew his skein from out his sheath
And lopt off his left hand,
And, pale and fierce as a chief in death,
He hurled it on the strand.

And so he won the lady and her broad lands and at this day a Randal M'Donnell, Earl of Antrim, reigns in Glenarm Castle.

Go round to Donegal. The old Castle, the ruins of which still stand, was dismantled by Hugh Roe O'Donnell[23] previously to his journey to Spain lest it should fall into the hands of the English. Its fame and its history are commemorated in Mangan's lines on 'The ruins of Donegal Castle' and the poem 'The Haunted Castle' by McGee. If you walk to the head of a beautiful inlet of Donegal Bay you will come upon the ruins of

that Abbey
Silent by Tyrconnell's shore.

Here it was the four masters[24] laboured and produced the famous Annals

Yet I hear them in my musings,
   And I see them as I gaze,
Four meek men around the cresset
   Reading scrolls of other days
Four unwearied scribes who treasure
   Every word and every line
Saving every ancient sentence
   As if writ by hands divine.

So sings McGee who seems to have cherished a warm affection for Brother Michael O'Clery the principal master. There is an interesting memoir of O'Clery and his associates in McGee's earliest work 'The Irish writers of the 17th Century'.

You must not imagine that this poetry is confined to the north. Go almost anywhere in Ireland and you will find that it goes along with you. Baltimore for instance has been specially fortunate. The town was sacked by Algerian Pirates in 1631 and such of its inhabitants as were not slaughtered were carried off into slavery. This outrage is the subject of a fine ballad by Davis 'The Sack of Baltimore'. The town had grown up round a Castle of the O'Driscolls and Ferguson has left us a ballad telling how the O'Driscoll who was defeated at Tralee by the Anglo-Normans in 1235 obtained the name of 'The Gascon'. In Hayes's *Ballads of Ireland*[25] there is a fine anonymous ballad

telling how the pirate chief, who was supposed to have perished in one of his marauding voyages, returned to find his wife about to wed a young minstrel and how he fired the Castle, a fragment of which still stands on Sherkin Island, and how the minstrel and his intended bride perished in the conflagration.

Let me now come nearer home and find you some associations connected with our two rivers, the Liffey and the Dodder.

Not all inglorious in thy elder day
   Art thou, Moy Liffey; and the loving mind
Might round thy borders many a gracious lay
   And many a tale not unheroic find.

I will give you an example. Some amongst you, I have no doubt, know Clongowes.[26] With me it has been and will ever be associated with pleasant and grateful recollections of the happy days I spent there. Going from Sallins to Clongowes you pass close by Bodenstown where Wolfe Tone[27] is buried.

In Bodenstown Churchyard there is a green grave

wrote Davis in the poem 'Tone's Grave'. But the grave is green no longer. A monument has been raised such as the poet wished for.

A plain one, yet fit for the simple and true.

Continuing your course, you reach the Liffey at Clane, now crossed by a bridge but the river was bridgeless at the date I am about to tell of.

When glades were green where Dublin stands to-
   day
   And limpid Liffey, fresh from wood and wold,
Bridgeless and fordless, in the lonely Bay
   Sank to her rest on sands of stainless gold —[28]

Atharna the bard constructed for the use of his flocks a ford or weir of wicker work across the river which gave its ancient name to Dublin. The invasion of their pastures was resented by the Leinster people of the right bank of the Liffey. Great strifes ensued between their King Mesgedra and Conor Mac Nessa already mentioned who espoused the cause of Atharna. Conall Carnach, one of the Red Branch Knights, came to the assistance of Conor. A great battle was fought and the hosts of Mesgedra

At sunset broke before the Red-Branch swords
And, last, Mesgedra climbed his car and fled.

He was followed by Conall Carnach, and as he reached the fords of Clane, Conall came up to him and challenged him to combat. One of the arms of Mesgedra had been disabled in the battle and he agreed to accept the challenge of Conall if he would tie up one of his arms to his belt and so make the combat equal. Conall consents, binds up one of his arms accordingly and they fight. Mesgedra's sword cuts through the belt and sets the arm free. Again Conall consents to bind his arm, but for once only and again the belt is cut through by Mesgedra's sword. Mesgedra is soon slain and Conall cutting off his antagonist's head drives away in his war chariot with the ghastly trophy. He meets on his way Mesgedra's wife who falls dead at the sight of the still bleeding head of her slaughtered husband. You will find this whole incident set out with great power and descriptive beauty in Ferguson's 'Mesgedra':

> The lay, though breathing of an Irish home,
> That tells of woman-love and warrior-ruth
> And old expectancy of Christ to come.

Many amongst you, I have no doubt, have been to Bohernabreena, and in the little wooden pavilion looking down from the mountain over the plain of the Liffey have enjoyed the dinner cooked in the little monastery that used to stand beside it. Close by is Glenismole (the valley of the Thrush) the scene of Davis's ballad, 'Emmeline Talbot'. One of the most lovely walks I know near Dublin is from Bohernabreena by the upper reaches of the Dodder, tumbling in numberless cascades by banks fringed with heather and fern and bilberries and bog myrtle: and then a tramp over bare moors, bringing you out over the lonely waters of Lough Bray. But did it ever occur to any of you when in this romantic neighbourhood to inquire what Bohernabreena means? It means the road of the guest house or caravanserai. At the period of the commencement of the Christian era there appears to have been six places of the kind in Ireland, and one of them stood here. This is said to have been the scene of the death of King Conary Mor, whose reign synchronized with the close of Paganism in Ireland. Conary and his followers, with his son and brothers and foster brothers, were enjoying the hospitality of this guest house, when they were attacked by a band of pirates whose fleet

> Stay'd on the heaving ridges of the main,
> Lay off Ben-Edar.

After a long and hotly contested encounter the pirates fly but not before the king has been killed and the guest house destroyed. This incident is the subject of Ferguson's 'Conary', the best I think of all the poems he drew from bardic sources. The fight is told with Homeric power, distinctness and detail, and as you read you can hear the fierce rush of the onset and the clash of the contending weapons. The scenery of the incident is beautifully sketched in. Centuries have rolled by since Ingcel and his pirate horde and Conary and his brave companions fought that bitter fight, but the Dodder still flows by Bohernabreena as it did when those pirates dammed it up so that no water could reach the guest house, and when to quench Conary's dying thirst his brave sidesman Cecht and his little son cut their way through the surrounding hosts and brought back some water, to find that the king was dead and the pirates had fled away to their ships.

The Bay of Dublin had had its beauties sung by MacCarthy, by Lady Dufferin[29] and by R.D. Williams;[30] but I have only time to take you into one scene more. There are many beautiful spots on the Hill of Howth, and there is no place near Dublin, at all events, which teems with such rich and varied associations with our history and literature. But there is one spot in Howth pre-eminent in its beauty and pre-eminent too in its associations. It is a dell in the demesne bordered on one side by precipitous cliffs. A grassy path lies through it edged with ferns and shaded with larches and firs, and graceful silver birches, such as McWhirter so loves to paint, and then it ascends in a gentle slope to the top of the cliffs. In the latter end of May, and beginning of June, these cliffs from base to summit are all ablaze with the purple, and rose, and flame colour, and yellow and white blooms of myriads of rhododendrons, while along the right, beyond and among the ferns, is spread a great blue carpet of wild hyacinths. Near to where the path ascends the cliff, another path turns off to the right and leads you to the Cromlech of Howth. This is the tomb of Aideen, daughter of Angus of Ben Edar, and wife of Oscar, the son of Ossian. Oscar was slain at the battle of Gavra, near Tara, in Meath, and Aideen died of grief for the loss of her husband. Tradition has it that she was buried here, and that Ossian and the Fenian heroes were present at her obsequies

> They heaved the stone; they heaped the cairn;
> Said Ossian, 'In a queenly grave
> We leave her, 'mong her fields of fern,
> Between the cliff and wave.

> The cliff behind stands still and bare
> And bare above the heathery steep
> Scales the clear heaven's expanse to where
> The Danaan Druids sleep.

And all the sands that left and right
    The grassy isthmus ridge confine,
In yellow bars lie bare and bright
    Among the sparkling brine.

A clear pure air pervades the scene
    In loneliness and awe secure;
Meet spot to sepulchre a queen
    Who in her life was pure.'

These are the opening stanzas of Ferguson's beautiful poem 'Aideen's Grave'. The poem is too long for quotation here, but I know no better example of a local tradition rendered into noble verse with a true local colouring.

You are not to imagine that I have given you anything like an exhaustive catalogue of the Irish scenes associated by Irish poetry with our history and traditions. In the limits of a lecture, such as this, I could only give you a few examples, and those I have given you were selected very much at random. You will find hundreds more in the works of the various poets I have mentioned, and in the poems and ballads of other writers to be found in 'Duffy's Ballad Poetry of Ireland',[31] 'Hayes's Ballads of Ireland' in the 'Spirit of the Nation', in the 'New Spirit of the Nation', published last year in the 'New Irish Library', and in a very precious, and I fear too little known, volume 'The Romances and Ballads of Ireland', edited by the late Hercules Ellis. If you would know how this poetry can be made use of to tell the story of Ireland's heroic age, I would refer you to Lady Ferguson's charming work, 'Ireland before the Conquest.[32]

I have now come to an end of my task. I have endeavoured to show you how history and literature, and especially poetical literature, can by their associations with scenery give new and larger pleasure to travel, and even to a country ramble. I have, too, endeavoured to refute the assertion of Mr Austin to which I referred, by showing you how Irish scenery is not without the associations of Irish poetry and Irish romance to brighten and enhance its beauties. Let me hope I have done something more. Let me hope that my imperfect words this evening may induce you to work up the associations of Irish scenery for yourselves, and that you will be induced to gather the history and the traditions and the literature that centre round

The Cairn, the Dun, the Rath, the Tower, the keep
    That still proclaim,
In chronicles of clay and stone, how true, how deep,
    Was Eire's fame.

I will feel that my lecture will not have been in vain if it has the same effect on even some amongst you as the story of the spectral hero in Mr McGee's ballad had on the two brave little boys to whom he told it.

And from that night they daily read in all the quiet
    nooks
About their homes old Irish songs and new-made
    Irish books.

1   Dion Boucicault (1820–90) was the leading Irish exponent of melodrama in the nineteenth century. *Colleen Bawn* (1860), based on Gerald Griffin's (1803–40) novel *The Collegians* (1829), contained a cast which included the potentially tragic victim Eily O'Connor and the stage Irishman Myles-na-Coppaleen (Myles of the ponies) who rescues her from being murdered (in contrast to her fate in Griffin's novel). The Gap of Dunloe, Purple Mountain and the River Flesk are to be found in the district of Killarney.

2   Charles Lever (1806–72) was a leading Irish novelist in the nineteenth century. His novels include *The O'Donoghue* (1845), *The Knight of Gwynne* (1847) and *Sir Brooke Fosbrooke* (1866).

3   Rosa Mulholland (1841–1921), Belfast-born author of *Marcella Grace* (1886).

4   May Hartley (?1850–1916), Dublin-born author of *Flitters, Tatters and the Counsellor* (1879).

5   Jane Barlow (1857–1917), author of *Irish Idylls* (1892), set in the fictional Connemara village of Lisconnel.

6   Emily Lawless (1845–1913), author of *Hurrish* (1886), a novel set in County Clare about the Land War of 1879–82. *Grania*, set on the Aran Islands, was published in 1892.

7   Edmund Spenser, author of *The Faerie Queene* (1590–96) and *Colin Clouts Come Home Againe* (1595).

8   Oliver Goldsmith (1728–74), author *The Deserted Village* (1770), spent his childhood at Lissoy in County Westmeath. Lissoy is often regarded as the Auburn of the poem.

9   'Dear Harp of My Country' is the title of one of Thomas Moore's *Irish Melodies* (1807–34).

10 Denis Florence MacCarthy (1817–82) was the first Professor of English at the Catholic University of Ireland. The lines are taken from 'Moore, May 28th 1879', a centenary ode published in his *Poems* (1880).

11 These lines are from Samuel Ferguson's 'Lament for Thomas Davis'. For poetry by Ferguson (1810–86), see *Lays of the Western Gael and Other Poems* (1864), the epic poem *Congal* (1872), and *Poems* (1880). His influence on later poets, especially on Yeats, was profound.

12 Sir Charles Gavan Duffy (1816–1903) co-founded *The Nation* in 1842, took part in the abortive Rising of 1848, emigrated to Australia in 1855, became Prime Minster of Victoria in 1871, returned to Europe in 1880, was appointed first President of the Irish Literary Society in London in 1892, and established the New Irish Library to disseminate books with a nationalist appeal (which brought him into conflict with Yeats).

13 James Clarence Mangan (1803–49), author of the often quoted 'Dark Rosaleen', was an influential Irish poet.

14 Thomas D'Arcy McGee (1825–68), author, journalist and politician, escaped to North America after the 1848 Rising and in 1862 became the Canadian Minister of Agriculture.

15 Lady Wilde (1821–96), mother of Oscar, wrote under this pseudonym for *The Nation*.

16 John Todhunter (1839–1916) was a London-based poet and playwright and author of *A Sicilian Idyll* (1890).

17 Katharine Tynan (1859–1931), a friend of Yeats as a young man, became a prolific writer of both fiction and verse.

18 T.D. Sullivan (1827–1914) was the author of the unofficial national anthem of nineteenth-century Ireland 'God Save Ireland', a poem on the Manchester Fenians of 1867.

19 John O'Donovan (1806–61), Gaelic Adviser to the Ordnance Survey of 1830 and later Professor at Queen's University, Belfast. His scholarly work ranged widely in the field of cataloguing and editing of Irish manuscripts. See especially his edition of *Annála Ríoghachta Éireann: Annals of the Kingdom of Ireland by the Four Masters* (1848–51), a seventeenth-century text recording events in Ireland from antiquity to 1616, which was composed at Bundrowse in County Donegal by 'four masters'.

20 Lines are from McGee's poem 'The Dead Antiquary O'Donovan'.

21 Aubrey De Vere (1814–1902), friend of Wordsworth and Tennyson, was a leading poet in nineteenth-century Ireland. *Inisfail* was published in 1862, *The Legends of Queen Maeve* in 1882, and *Legends of St Patrick* in 1889.

22 Standish James O'Grady (1846–1928), historian and journalist, played a crucial role in the development of cultural nationalism in late nineteenth-century Ireland and was an important influence on, among others, Yeats and George Russell. *The Coming of Cuculain* was published in 1894. His *History of Ireland: The Heroic Period* (1878) is thought by some to mark the beginning of the Irish Literary Revival. Carton's debt to O'Grady is especially apparent in this passage and can be compared with the first chapter of O'Grady's *History of Ireland: Cuculain and His Contemporaries* (1880).

23 Hugh Roe O'Donnell (or Red Hugh O'Donnell) (?1571–1602), an Ulster chieftain and son-in-law of Hugh O'Neill (?1550–1616), leader of the Irish in the Elizabethan War of 1595–1603. He escaped to Catholic Spain to seek further assistance after defeat at the battle of Kinsale in 1601.

24 See note 19 above.

25 Edward Hayes, *The Ballads of Ireland* (1855).

26 Clongowes Wood College, County Kildare, an expensive Jesuit-run boarding school (where James Joyce received his early education).

27 Theobald Wolfe Tone (1763–98) was the leader of the United Irishmen who sought to break the English connection by force. He is buried at Bodenstown in County Kildare, an annual site of Republican pilgrimage.

28 Opening lines to 'Mesgedra', by Samuel Ferguson.

29 Lady Dufferin (Helen Blackwood) (1807–67) was author of 'The Lament of the Irish Emigrant'.

30 Richard D'Alton Williams (1822–62) wrote verse for *The Nation*.

31 Charles Gavan Duffy, *The Ballad Poetry of Ireland* (1845); *Spirit of the Nation* (1843); Martin MacDermot (ed.), *The New Spirit of the Nation* (1894).

32 Lady Ferguson, *Ireland Before the Conquest* (1868).

MAURICE F. EGAN
from Maurice F. Egan, *From the Land of St Lawrence* (1898)

Maurice Francis Egan (1852–1924) was born in Philadelphia and died in New York. His father was from Tipperary, while his Philadelphia mother 'looked on the Irish as a strange race capable of violating all Philadelphia conventions and of staying up until after midnight and drinking much punch on the slightest provocation!' After a successful career in journalism Egan became Professor of English first at Notre Dame and then at the Catholic University of America. Later he became President Roosevelt's Minister to Denmark. A prolific writer, he helped to edit the ten-volume edition of *Irish Literature* (general editor Justin McCarthy) (1904). For his autobiography see *Recollections of a Happy Life* (1924). There are several aspects of the following story which merit attention: sectarianism, the Irish Diaspora, Irish-American attitudes to Ireland, and style. You might begin by identifying those features which you think mark this as a story written by an Irish-American.

The Orange Lilies

When Neil Durnan's wife died, there was no lonelier man in the County Meath. His farm was in good condition. He was not, in the estimation of elderly men, old; he was healthy, and he had seen triumphant Orangemen defeated in his lifetime, over and over again. He was a very 'warm' farmer. His elder son was a Franciscan friar over in Italy; his younger had gone to America. The first was out of his world; he had never quite forgiven Friar Francis, who, after the education he had, might have been a decent parish priest at home, for joining 'the beggars', as he called the members of the great Order. The younger son, Maurice, was in America — in a place called Wisconsin. Father and son had never got on well together. They both had strong opinions; so one day, with a hundred pounds to his credit, Maurice went over the sea, and the father's heart had ached ever since, though he had not shown this in word or deed.

It was this heartache that made him look seaward. His old neighbours were gone. To the farm on his left had come a Belfast man who kept hunters, whose wife and daughters went about 'dropping pieces of pasteboard at their neighbours'.

'It's on wheels they come,' he said, 'and them calling themselves decent women, and then drop a handful of pasteboards with their names on them. And there are afternoon tays and feet champeeters and few de joys going on all the time, and him an Orange squireen[1] of a fellow, with his garden full of yellow lilies, just to spite the likes of me on the twelfth of July.'[2]

His neighbour on the right was not the less obnoxious; he had acquired poor Pat Dolan's farm, and was making it pay by means of all sort of new-fangled machinery.

'Taking the bread out of poor men's mouths,' the aggrieved Mr Durnan said; 'sure, what right has he to do *that*? Pat Dolan would have cut off his finger before he turned a man from his day's work — and *he* turned out of the farm his grandfather had before him, just because he was too kind and generous to his own people.'

The sight of the squireen's women folk, on wheels, with cardcases in their hands, was an evil thing, the farm machinery was worse, but the front garden with its orange lilies worst of all.

'And when I remarked to that woman,' says I, 'the orange lilies, saving your presence, ma'am, are symbolical of the devil himself and of all Orange haythen — what did she say in a high English voice, but "Oh, Mr Durnan, you're so old-fashioned! We must forget old feuds." And the likes of her keeping them up with their orange lilies!'

If it had not been for the enormous mastiff that guarded the Squire's house at night, he would have made short work of the masses of bloom that glowed in a hundred tints of yellow, like coiled, jewelled snakes, in the centre of his neighbour's lawn. As it was, he was helpless; the splendid flowers were a menace, a threat, a hated blot on the landscape. Finally he could endure them no more; he made a good bargain in the sale of his farm, and then a struggle began within him. Should he go to his son? — to this independent son of his, who had gone off with the portion his mother had a right to give him, refusing aught else; who had married a 'Yankee'; who — and this made Neil Durnan feel very bitter — had never asked for anything, and who — and this made the bitterness more bitter — might be better off in this world's goods than he was?

If Maurice had come to him, poor, suppliant, he would have clasped him in his arms, and killed the fatted calf, and sent out for all the purple and fine linen to be brought. If he should find Maurice with his three little children, suffering, poor, in need of help, his heart and his hand would go out to them with all the force of a strong nature. But the thought that Maurice might be 'warmer' than he, rejoicing perhaps in all those new machines which he so much detested, filled him with anger. Rumours had come to him of the prosperity of Maurice in that far-off Wisconsin; he had pretended to doubt them; he had smiled when hints of this prosperity had appeared in the letters the son wrote to his mother, but he feared they were true.

'Three sons, and one dead,' he murmured, 'and not one of them named for me. Sure, he sent word to ask me once as to the naming of his first one, but I said, "No — 'twas unbefitting that a child of his Yankee wife should be named for me." I did not mean it, but I suppose they thought I did.'

Love, which was warm at the core of the old man's heart, conquered at last, and on Sunday before he started for Queenstown,[3] he achieved a victory over himself. It was the day on which the Blue Ribbon Society went to Communion. He had a grudge against one member, whose father had been a Scotchman, and whose mother was a County Meath woman; the son called himself Scotch-Irish. He had always avoided walking in the procession next to this man, though once or twice he had been paired with him. But on this morning he took his place beside him. It was hard; but he did not wince.

'I've done *that*,' he said, when it was over, 'and now I can stand anything!'

Over the ocean, through New York and Chicago, Neil Durnan sped. He cared neither for the Brooklyn

Bridge, nor Niagara Falls, nor the great buildings in the western metropolis; he was intent on his son — full of love, full of envy, jealous as any father could be, and hoping that a cyclone or some horror might have made this proud son of his dependent on him. Of what use was the goodly sum to his credit in the bank, if Maurice had a greater sum?

He found Maurice grave, cordial, quiet; a man of consequence, and of sound judgment; he was large, handsome, red-haired — of the type of his mother. The old man's worst fears were fulfilled: the Wisconsin farm of over five hundred acres was in perfect condition. And, in this month of July, all modern appliances were in use to develop its richness.

Neil Durnan had to go to his comfortable room, to groan and almost to weep. The spectacle of his proud son's success, in which he had no hand, was like a dagger to his heart. His three grandsons were called Lewis, John, and Maurice — not one Neil among them. His son's wife was very sweet in her manner to him, 'too much of a lady, entirely,' he said. There was no denying that his grandsons were fine, affectionate little boys, well instructed in their religion. The smallest of the three was gentle, and somewhat delicate — 'like the one that died,' his mother said, softly. Neil found great consolation in this boy. He told him of the leprechauns, and of all the wonderful things that happened over in Ireland, in the old days. Still his heart was bitter; he would not pray; his beads[4] hung against the wall, untouched. His son had dared to make for himself a world of his own — and he was outside of it.

He had promised to meet his little grandson at a stream near the graveyard; the church, red brick, with a Gothic tower, was at the edge of his son's farm. In this stream grandfather and grandson fished with the gaudy flies brought from Ireland. During the long, sultry afternoons, this spot, covered by great spruce trees, was cool, and though not even a minnow bit at the elaborate flies, the two were happy. On this afternoon the little boy came, flushed and bright-eyed, carrying a bunch of orange lilies.

'For you, grandpapa!' he called out.

Neil Durnan stood like a bull at the sight of red. Then he tore the obnoxious flowers from the child's hand, threw them upon the ground, and trampled upon them. The boy opened his blue eyes, horrified, amazed, by the angry face and brutal gestures of his grandfather.

'O grandpapa!' he cried, 'how can you! They were for you; I gathered them at —'

But Neil Durnan had gone off, muttering. Everywhere he was to endure insults, and from his own kin!

'My son did this,' he said, bitterly, 'or his Yankee wife!'

He strode into the graveyard, not knowing where he was. He would leave this place; he would go at once, he resolved. And when he resolved to act in any matter, it was hard to move him. He would not say good-bye; a cold hand seemed to clutch at his heart as he thought of the tear-filled eyes of the little Maurice; but he would go — and at once.

There was a trailing mock-orange vine in his path, and as he made his next step, a tendril-coil of it caught his foot; he went down, and lay for a moment prone, in a bed of the splendid yellow-and-red flowers his heart detested. He tore them away from him, and saw that they clustered about a small stone cross; he read

> NEIL DURNAN:
> AGED TWELVE: 1896.
> MAY HE REST IN PEACE.

'Neil Durnan!' His proud son had indeed named the dead little boy for him. He forgot the yellow splendour about him, and read the name again; tears ran down his wind-reddened cheeks. He knelt for a moment; then he plucked a handful of the flowers that grew on this sacred grave, those hated flowers that dotted in a dozen places the green of the graveyard. He clasped the long leaves almost tenderly, and went back to the place where his little grandson had begun to fish, in a sober and subdued way, with the gorgeous flies.

'Here, Maurice,' he said, 'are some of the flowers you brought me just now. I know where you got them. Tell me about your little brother — Neil.' The old man's voice choked.

Maurice smiled brightly, and began to talk of the dear little brother who had died almost a year ago. And so they sat there, lovingly, the whole twelfth of July afternoon, with the orange lilies between them, symbols, not of war, but of victory.

1   A squireen was 'an Irish gentleman in a small way who apes the manners . . . of the large landed proprietors' (P.W. Joyce).
2   The twelfth of July is celebrated by Northern Irish Protestants as marking the victory at the battle of the Boyne in July 1690 by King William III (William of Orange) against the Jacobite forces who supported James II.
3   The port near Cork, now called Cobh. Dun Laoghaire was Kingstown.
4   Rosary beads. The Rosary is part of Catholic devotional practice with the focus on the Virgin Mary; it consists of a sequence of Our Father (Lord's Prayer), Hail Mary, and Glory Be To The Father.

E. Œ. SOMERVILLE and MARTIN ROSS

from E. Œ. Somerville and Martin Ross, *Some Experiences of an Irish R.M.* (1899)

Somerville and Ross was the joint pseudonym of two Anglo-Irish cousins Edith Somerville (1858–1949) and Violet Martin (1862–1915). This story is taken from their celebrated collection of witty stories *Some Experiences of an Irish R.M.* (1899), written when Martin was convalescing after a hunting accident. R.M. stands for Resident Magistrate; these magistrates, appointed by the Chief Secretary for Ireland, administered justice in rural Ireland. Two questions among others to consider: How do you respond to the use of dialect in this story? What do you think the story adds to (y)our understanding of Anglo-Irish relations?

Lisheen Races, Second-Hand

It may or may not be agreeable to have attained the age of thirty-eight, but, judging from old photographs, the privilege of being nineteen has also its drawbacks. I turned over page after page of an ancient book in which were enshrined portraits of the friends of my youth, singly, in David and Jonathan couples, and in groups in which I, as it seemed to my mature and possibly jaundiced perception, always contrived to look the most immeasurable young bounder of the lot. Our faces were fat, and yet I cannot remember ever having been considered fat in my life; we indulged in low-necked shirts, in 'Jemima' ties with diagonal stripes; we wore coats that seemed three sizes too small, and trousers that were three sizes too big; we also wore small whiskers.

I stopped at last at one of the David and Jonathan memorial portraits. Yes, here was the object of my researches; this stout and earnestly romantic youth was Leigh Kelway, and that fatuous and chubby young person seated on the arm of his chair was myself. Leigh Kelway was a young man ardently believed in by a large circle of admirers, headed by himself and seconded by me, and for some time after I had left Magdalen for Sandhurst,[1] I maintained a correspondence with him on large and abstract subjects. This phase of our friendship did not survive; I went soldiering to India, and Leigh Kelway took honours and moved suitably on into politics, as is the duty of an earnest young Radical with useful family connections and an independent income. Since then I had at intervals seen in the papers the name of the Honourable Basil Leigh Kelway mentioned as a speaker at elections, as a writer of thoughtful articles in the reviews, but we had never met, and nothing could have been less expected by me than the letter, written from Mrs Raverty's Hotel, Skebawn, in which he told me he was making a tour in Ireland with Lord Waterbury, to whom he was private secretary. Lord Waterbury was at present having a few days' fishing near Killarney, and he himself, not being a fisherman, was collecting statistics for his chief on various points connected with the Liquor Question in Ireland. He had heard that I was in the neighbourhood, and was kind enough to add that it would give him much pleasure to meet me again.

With a stir of the old enthusiasm I wrote begging him to be my guest for as long as it suited him, and the following afternoon he arrived at Shreelane. The stout young friend of my youth had changed considerably. His important nose and slightly prominent teeth remained, but his wavy hair had withdrawn intellectually from his temples; his eyes had acquired a statesmanlike absence of expression, and his neck had grown long and birdlike. It was his first visit to Ireland, as he lost no time in telling me, and he and his chief had already collected much valuable information on the subject to which they had dedicated the Easter recess. He further informed me that he thought of popularizing the subject in a novel, and therefore intended to, as he put it, 'master the brogue' before his return.

During the next few days I did my best for Leigh Kelway. I turned him loose on Father Scanlan; I showed him Mahona, our champion village, that boasts fifteen public-houses out of twenty buildings of sorts and a railway station; I took him to hear the prosecution of a publican for selling drink on a Sunday, which gave him an opportunity of studying perjury as a fine art, and of hearing a lady, on whom police suspicion justly rested, profoundly summed up by the sergeant as 'a woman who had th' appairance of having knocked at a back door'.

The net result of these experiences has not yet been given to the world by Leigh Kelway. For my own part, I had at the end of three days arrived at the conclusion that his society, when combined with a notebook and a thirst for statistics, was not what I used to find it at

Oxford. I therefore welcomed a suggestion from Mr Flurry Knox that we should accompany him to some typical country races, got up by the farmers at a place called Lisheen, some twelve miles away. It was the worst road in the district, the races of the most grossly unorthodox character; in fact, it was the very place for Leigh Kelway to collect impressions of Irish life, and in any case it was a blessed opportunity of disposing of him for the day.

In my guest's attire next morning I discerned an unbending from the role of cabinet minister towards that of sportsman; the outlines of the notebook might be traced in his breast pocket, but traversing it was the strap of a pair of field-glasses, and his light grey suit was smart enough for Goodwood.[2]

Flurry was to drive us to the races at one o'clock, and we walked to Tory Cottage by the short cut over the hill, in the sunny beauty of an April morning. Up to the present the weather had kept me in a more or less apologetic condition; anyone who has entertained a guest in the country knows the unjust weight of responsibility that rests on the shoulders of the host in the matter of climate, and Leigh Kelway, after two drenchings, had become sarcastically resigned to what I felt he regarded as my mismanagement.

Flurry took us into the house for a drink and a biscuit, to keep us going, as he said, till 'we lifted some luncheon out of the Castle Knox people at the races', and it was while we were thus engaged that the first disaster of the day occurred. The dining-room door was open, so also was the window of the little staircase just outside it, and through the window travelled sounds that told of the close proximity of the stableyard; the clattering of hoofs on cobble stones, and voices uplifted in loud conversation. Suddenly from this region there arose a screech of the laughter peculiar to kitchen flirtation, followed by the clank of a bucket, the plunging of a horse, and then an uproar of wheels and galloping hoofs. An instant afterwards Flurry's chestnut cob, in a dogcart, dashed at full gallop into view, with the reins streaming behind him, and two men in hot pursuit. Almost before I had time to realize what had happened, Flurry jumped through the half-opened window of the dining-room like a clown at a pantomime, and joined in the chase; but the cob was resolved to make the most of his chance, and went away down the drive and out of sight at a pace that distanced every one save the kennel terrier, who sped in shrieking ecstasy beside him.

'Oh merciful hour!' exclaimed a female voice behind me. Leigh Kelway and I were by this time watching the progress of events from the gravel, in company with the remainder of Flurry's household.

'The horse is desthroyed! Wasn't that the quare start he took! And all in the world I done was to slap a bucket of wather at Michael out the windy, and 'twas himself got it in place of Michael!'

'Ye'll never ate another bit, Bridgie Dunnigan,' replied the cook, with the exulting pessimism of her kind. 'The Master'll have your life!'

Both speakers shouted at the top of their voices, probably because in spirit they still followed afar the flight of the cob.

Leigh Kelway looked serious as we walked on down the drive. I almost dared to hope that a note on the degrading oppression of Irish retainers[3] was shaping itself. Before we reached the bend of the drive the rescue party was returning with the fugitive, all with the exception of the kennel terrier, looking extremely gloomy. The cob had been confronted by a wooden gate, which he had unhesitatingly taken in his stride, landing on his head on the farther side with the gate and the cart on top of him, and had arisen with a lame foreleg, a cut on his nose, and several other minor wounds.

'You'd think the brute had been fighting the cats, with all the scratches and scrapes he has on him!' said Flurry, casting a vengeful eye at Michael, 'and one shaft's broken and so is the dashboard. I haven't another horse in the place; they're all out at grass, and so there's an end of the races!'

We all three stood blankly on the hall-door steps and watched the wreck of the trap being trundled up the avenue.

'I'm very sorry you're done out of your sport,' said Flurry to Leigh Kelway, in tones of deplorable sincerity; 'perhaps, as there's nothing else to do, you'd like to see the hounds——?'

I felt for Flurry, but of the two I felt more for Leigh Kelway as he accepted this alleviation. He disliked dogs, and held the newest views on sanitation, and I knew what Flurry's kennels could smell like. I was lighting a precautionary cigarette, when we caught sight of an old man riding up the drive. Flurry stopped short.

'Hold on a minute,' he said 'here's an old chap that often brings me horses for the kennels; I must see what he wants.'

The man dismounted and approached Mr Knox, hat in hand, towing after him a gaunt and ancient mare with a big knee.

'Well, Bennett,' began Flurry, surveying the mare with his hands in his pockets, 'I'm not giving the hounds meat this month, or only very little.'

'Ah, Master Flurry,' answered Bennett, 'it's you that's pleasant! Is it give the like o' this one for the dogs to ate! She a vallable strong young mare, no more than sixteen years of age, and ye'd sooner be lookin' at her going under a side-car⁴ than eatin' your dinner.'

'There isn't as much meat on her a'd fatten a jackdaw,' said Flurry, clinking the silver in his pockets as he searched for a matchbox. 'What are you asking for her?'

The old man drew cautiously up to him.

'Master Flurry,' he said solemnly, 'I'll sell her to *your* honour for five pounds, and she'll be worth ten after you give her a month's grass.'

Flurry lit his cigarette; then he said imperturbably, 'I'll give you seven shillings for her.'

Old Barrett put on his hat in silence, and in silence buttoned his coat and took hold of the stirrup leather. Flurry remained immovable.

'Master Flurry,' said old Bennett suddenly, with tears in his voice, 'you must make it eight, sir!'

'Michael!' called out Flurry with apparent irreverence, 'run up to your father's and ask him would he lend me a loan of his side-car.'

Half an hour later we were, improbable as it may seem, on our way to Lisheen races. We were seated upon an outside-car⁵ of immemorial age, whose joints seemed to open and close again as it swung in and out of the ruts, whose tattered cushions stank of rats and mildew, whose wheels staggered and rocked like the legs of a drunken man. Between the shafts jogged the latest addition to the kennel larder, the eight-shilling⁶ mare. Flurry sat on one side, and kept her going at a rate of not less than four miles an hour; Leigh Kelway and I held on to the other.

'She'll get us as far as Lynch's anyway,' said Flurry, abandoning his first contention that she could do the whole distance, as he pulled her on to her legs after her fifteenth stumble, 'and he'll lend us some sort of a horse, if it was only a mule.'

'Do you notice that these cushions are very damp?' said Leigh Kelway to me, in a hollow undertone.

'Small blame to them if they are!' replied Flurry. 'I've no doubt that they were out under the rain all day yesterday at Mrs Hurly's funeral.'

Leigh Kelway made no reply, but he took his notebook out of his pocket and sat on it.

We arrived at Lynch's at a little past three, and were there confronted by the next disappointment of this disastrous day. The door of Lynch's farmhouse was locked, and nothing replied to our knocking except a puppy, who barked hysterically from within.

'All gone to the races,' said Flurry philosophically, picking his way round the manure heap. 'No matter, here's the filly in the shed here. I know he's had her under a car.'

An agitating ten minutes ensued, during which Leigh Kelway and I got the eight-shilling mare out of the shafts and the harness, and Flurry, with our inefficient help, crammed the young mare into them. As Flurry had stated that she had been driven before, I was bound to believe him, but the difficulty of getting the bit into her mouth was remarkable, and so also was the crab-like manner in which she sidled out of the yard, with Flurry and myself at her head, and Leigh Kelway hanging on to the back of the car to keep it from jamming in the gateway.

'Sit up on the car now,' said Flurry when we got out on to the road; 'I'll lead her on a bit. She's been ploughed anyway; one side of her mouth's as tough as a gad!'

Leigh Kelway threw away the wisp of grass with which he had been cleaning his hands and mopped his intellectual forehead; he was very silent. We both mounted the car, and Flurry, with the reins in his hand, walked beside the filly, who, with her tail clasped in, moved onward in a succession of short jerks.

'Oh, she's all right!' said Flurry, beginning to run, and dragging the filly into a trot; 'once she gets started——' Here the filly spied a pig in a neighbouring field, and despite the fact that she had probably eaten out of the same trough with it, she gave a violent side spring, and broke into a gallop.

'Now we're off!' shouted Flurry, making a jump at the car and clambering on; 'if the traces⁷ hold we'll do!'

The English language is powerless to suggest the view-halloo⁸ with which Mr Knox ended his speech, or to do more than indicate the rigid anxiety of Leigh Kelway's face as he regained his balance after the preliminary jerk, and clutched the back rail. It must be said for Lynch's filly that she did not kick; she merely fled, like a dog with a kettle tied to its tail, from the pursuing rattle and jingle behind her, with the shafts buffeting her dusty sides as the car swung to and fro. Whenever she showed any signs of slackening, Flurry loosed another yell at her that renewed her panic, and thus we precariously covered another two or three miles of our journey.

Had it not been for a large stone lying on the road, and had the filly not chosen to swerve so as to bring the wheel on top of it, I dare say we might have got to the races; but by an unfortunate coincidence both these things occurred, and when we recovered from the consequent shock, the tyre of one of the wheels had come off, and was trundling with cumbrous gaiety into the ditch. Flurry stopped the filly and began to laugh; Leigh Kelway said something startlingly unparliamentary under his breath.

'Well, it might be worse,' Flurry said consolingly as he lifted the tyre on to the car, 'we're not half a mile from a forge.'

We walked that half-mile in funereal procession behind the car; the glory had departed from the weather, and an ugly wall of cloud was rising up out of the west to meet the sun; the hills had darkened and lost colour, and the white bog cotton shivered in a cold wind that smelt of rain.

By a miracle the smith was not at the races, owing, as he explained, to his having 'the toothaches', the two facts combined producing in him a morosity only equalled by that of Leigh Kelway. The smith's sole comment on the situation was to unharness the filly, and drag her into the forge, where he tied her up. He then proceeded to whistle viciously on his fingers in the direction of a cottage, and to command, in tones of thunder, some unseen creature to bring over a couple of baskets of turf. The turf arrived in process of time, on a woman's back, and was arranged in a circle in a yard at the back of the forge. The tyre was bedded in it, and the turf was with difficulty kindled at different points.

'Ye'll not get to the races this day,' said the smith, yielding to a sardonic satisfaction; 'the turf's wet, and I haven't one to do a hand's turn for me.' He laid the wheel on the ground and lit his pipe.

Leigh Kelway looked pallidly about him over the spacious empty landscape of brown mountain slopes patched with golden furze and seamed with grey walls; I wondered if he were as hungry as I. We sat on stones opposite the smouldering ring of turf and smoked, and Flurry beguiled the smith into grim and calumnious confidences about every horse in the country. After about an hour, during which the turf went out three times, and the weather became more and more threatening, a girl with a red petticoat over her head appeared at the gate of the yard, and said to the smith:

'The horse is gone away from ye.'

'Where?' exclaimed Flurry, springing to his feet.

'I met him walking wesht the road there below, and when I thought to turn him he commenced to gallop.'

'Pulled her head out of the headstall,' said Flurry, after a rapid survey of the forge. 'She's near home by now.'

It was at this moment that the rain began; the situation could scarcely have been better stage-managed. After reviewing the position, Flurry and I decided that the only thing to do was to walk to a public-house a couple of miles farther on, feed there if possible, hire a car, and go home.

It was an uphill walk, with mild generous raindrops striking thicker and thicker on our faces; no one

talked, and the grey clouds crowded up from behind the hills like billows of steam. Leigh Kelway bore it all with egregious resignation. I cannot pretend that I was at heart sympathetic, but by virtue of being his host I felt responsible for the breakdown, for his light suit, for everything, and divined his sentiment of horror at the first sight of the public-house.

It was a long, low cottage, with a line of dripping elm-trees overshadowing it; empty cars and carts round its door, and a babel from within made it evident that the racegoers were pursuing a gradual homeward route. The shop was crammed with steaming countrymen, whose loud brawling voices, all talking together, roused my English friend to his first remark since we had left the forge.

'Surely, Yeates, we are not going into that place,' he said severely; 'those men are all drunk.'

'Ah, nothing to signify!' said Flurry, plunging in and driving his way through the throng like a plough. 'Here, Mary Kate!' he called to the girl behind the counter, 'tell your mother we want some tea and bread and butter in the room inside.'

The smell of bad tobacco and spilt porter was choking; we worked our way through it after him towards the end of the shop, intersecting at every hand discussions about the races.

'Tom was very nice. He spared his horse all along, and then he put into him——' 'Well, at Goggin's corner the third horse was before the second, but he was goin' wake in himself.' 'I tell ye the mare had the hind leg fasht in the fore.' 'Clancy was dipping in the saddle.' ''Twas a dam nice race whatever——'

We gained the inner room at last, a cheerless apartment, adorned with sacred pictures, a sewing-machine, and an array of supplementary tumblers and wineglasses; but, at all events, we had it so far to ourselves. At intervals during the next half-hour Mary Kate burst in with cups and plates, cast them on the table and disappeared, but of food there was no sign. After a further period of starvation and listening to the noise in the shop, Flurry made a sortie, and, after lengthy and unknown adventures, reappeared carrying a huge brown teapot, and driving before him Mary Kate with the remainder of the repast. The bread tasted of mice, the butter of turf-smoke, the tea of brown paper, but we had got past the critical stage. I had entered upon my third round of bread and butter when the door was flung open, and my valued acquaintance, Slipper, slightly advanced in liquor, presented himself to our gaze. His bandy legs sprawled consequentially, his nose was redder than a coal of fire, his prominent eyes rolled crookedly upon us, and his left hand swept behind him the attempt of Mary Kate to frustrate his entrance.

'Good evening to my vinerable friend, Mr Flurry Knox!' he began, in the voice of a town crier, 'and to the Honourable Major Yeates, and the English gintleman!'

This impressive opening immediately attracted an audience from the shop, and the doorway filled with grinning faces as Slipper advanced farther into the room.

'Why weren't ye at the races, Mr Flurry?' he went on, his roving eye taking a grip of us all at the same time; 'sure the Miss Bennetts and all the ladies was asking where were ye.'

'It'd take some time to tell them that,' said Flurry, with his mouth full; 'but what about the races, Slipper? Had you good sport?'

'Sport is it? Divil so pleasant an afthernoon ever you seen,' replied Slipper. He leaned against a side table, and all the glasses on it jingled. 'Does your honour know O'Driscoll?' he went on irrelevantly. 'Sure you do. He was in your honour's stable. It's what we were all sayin': it was a great pity your honour was not there, for the likin' you had to Driscoll.'

'That's thrue,' said a voice at the door.

'There wasn't one in the Barony but was gethered in it, through and fro,' continued Slipper, with a quelling glance at the interrupter; 'and there was tints for sellin' porther, and whisky as pliable as new milk, and boys goin' round the tints outside, feeling for heads with the big ends of their blackthorns, and all kinds of recreations, and the Sons of Liberty's piffler and dhrum band from Skebawn; though faith! there was more of thim runnin' to look at the races than what was playin' in it; not to mintion different occasions that the bandmasther was atin' his lunch within in the whisky tint.'

'But what about Driscoll?' said Flurry.

'Sure it's about him I'm tellin' ye,' replied Slipper, with the practised orator's watchful eye on his growing audience. ''Twas within in the same whisky tint meself was, with the bandmasther and a few of the lads, an' we buyin' a ha'porth of crackers, when I seen me brave Driscoll landin' into the tint, and a pair o' thim long boots on him; him that hadn't a shoe nor a stocking to his foot when your honour had him picking grass out o' the stones behind in your yard. "Well," says I to meself, "we'll knock some sport out of Driscoll."

'"Come here to me, acushla!" says I to him; "I suppose it's some way wake in the legs y'are," says I, "an' the docthor put them on ye the way the people wouldn't thrample ye!"

'"May the divil choke ye!" says he, pleasant enough, but I knew by the blush he had he was vexed.

'"Then I suppose 'tis a left-tenant colonel y'are," says I; "yer mother must be proud out o' ye!" says I, "an' maybe ye'll lend her a loan of thim waders when she's rinsin' your bauneen[9] in the river!" says I.

'"There'll be work out o' this!" says he, lookin' at me both sour and bitther.

'"Well indeed, I was thinkin' you were blue-moulded for want of a batin'," says I. He was for fightin' us then, but afther we had him pacificated with about a quarther of a naggin of sperrits, he told us he was goin' ridin' in a race.

'"An' what'll ye ride?" says I.

'"Owld Bocock's mare," says he.

'"Knipes!" says I, sayin' a great curse, "is it that little staggeen from the mountains; sure she's somethin' about the one age with meself," says I. "Many's the time Jamesy Geoghegan and meself used to be dhrivin' her to Macroom with pigs an' all soorts," says I; "an' is it leppin' stone walls ye want her to go now?"

'"Faith, there's walls and every vari'ty of obstacle in it," says he.

'"It'll be the best o' your play, so," says I, "to get it away home out o' this."

'"An' who'll ride her, so?" says he.

'"Let the divil ride her," says I.'

Leigh Kelway, who had been leaning back seemingly half asleep, obeyed the hypnotism of Slipper's gaze, and opened his eyes.

'That was now all the conversation that passed between himself and meself,' resumed Slipper, 'and there was no great delay afther that till they said there was a race startin' and the dickens a one at all was goin' to ride only two, Driscoll and one Clancy. With that then I seen Mr Kinahane, the Petty Sessions Clerk, goin' round clearin' the coorse, an' I gethered a few o' the neighbours, an' we walked the fields hither and over till we seen the most of th' obstackles.

'"Stand aisy now by the plantation," says I; "if they get to come as far as this, believe me ye'll see spoort," says I, "an' 'twill be a convanient spot to encourage the mare if she's anyway wake in herself," says I, cuttin' somethin' about five foot of an ash sapling out o' the plantation.

'"That's yer sort!" says Owld Bocock, that was thravellin' the race-coorse, peggin' a bit o' paper down with a thorn in front of every lep, the way Driscoll'd know the handiest place to face her at it.

'Well, I hadn't barely thrimmed the ash plant——'

'Have you any jam, Mary Kate?' interrupted Flurry, whose meal had been in no way interfered with by either the story or the highly scented crowd who had come to listen to it.

'We have no jam, only thraycle, sir,' replied the invisible Mary Kate.

'I hadn't the switch barely thrimmed,' repeated Slipper firmly, 'when I heard the people screechin', and I seen Driscoll an' Clancy comin' on, leppin' all before them, an' Owld Bocock's mare bellusin' and powderin' along, an' bedad! whatever obstacle wouldn't throw *her* down, faith, she'd throw *it* down, an' there's the thraffic they had in it.

"'I declare to me sowl," says I. "If they continue on this way there's a great chance some one o' thim'll win," says I.

"'Ye lie!" says the bandmasther, bein' a thrifle fulsome after his luncheon.

"'I do not," says I, "in regard of seein' how soople them two boys is. Ye might observe," says I, "that if they have no convanient way to sit on the saddle, they'll ride the neck o' the horse till such time as they gets an occasion to lave it," says I.

"'Arrah, shut yer mouth!" says the bandmasther; "they're puckin' out this way now, an' may the divil admire me!" says he, "but Clancy has the other bet out, and the divil such leatherin' and beltin' of Owld Bocock's mare ever you seen as what's in it!" says he.

'Well, when I seen them comin' to me, and Driscoll about the length of the plantation behind Clancy, I let a couple of bawls.

"'Skelp her, ye big brute!" says I. "What good's in ye that ye aren't able to skelp her?"'

The yell and the histrionic flourish of his stick with which Slipper delivered this incident brought down the house. Leigh Kelway was sufficiently moved to ask me in an undertone if 'skelp' was a local term.

'Well, Mr Flurry, and gintlemen,' recommenced Slipper, 'I declare to ye when Owld Bocock's mare heard thim roars she sthretched out her neck like a gandher, and when she passed me she gave a couple of grunts, and looked at me as ugly as a Christian.

"'Hah!" says I, givin' her a couple of dhraws o' th' ash plant across the butt o' the tail, the way I wouldn't blind her; "I'll make ye grunt!" says I, "I'll nourish ye!"'

'I knew well she was very frightful o' th' ash plant since the winter Tommeen Sullivan had her under a sidecar. But now, in place of havin' any obligations to me, ye'd be surprised if ye heard the blaspheemious expressions of that young boy that was ridin' her; and whether it was over-anxious he was, turnin' around the way I'd hear him cursin', or whether it was some slither or slide came to Owld Bocock's mare, I dunno, but she was bet up agin the last obstacle but two, and before ye could say "Shnipes", she was standing on her two ears beyond in th' other field! I declare to ye, on the vartue of me oath, she stood that way till she reconnoithered what side would Driscoll fall, an' she turned about then and rolled on him as cosy as if he was meadow grass!'

Slipper stopped short; the people in the doorway groaned appreciatively; Mary Kate murmured, 'The Lord save us!'

'The blood was dhruv out through his nose and ears,' continued Slipper, with a voice that indicated the cream of the narration, 'and you'd hear his bones crackin' on the ground! You'd have pitied the poor boy.'

'Good heavens!' said Leigh Kelway, sitting up very straight in his chair.

'Was he hurt, Slipper?' asked Flurry casually.

'Hurt is it?' echoed Slipper in high scorn; 'killed on the spot!' He paused to relish the effect of the *dénouement* on Leigh Kelway. 'Oh, divil so pleasant an afthernoon ever you seen; and indeed, Mr Flurry, it's what we were all sayin', it was a great pity your honour was not there for the likin' you had for Driscoll.'

As he spoke the last word there was an outburst of singing and cheering from a carload of people who had just pulled up at the door. Flurry listened, leaned back in his chair, and began to laugh.

'It scarcely strikes one as a comic incident,' said Leigh Kelway, very coldly to me; 'in fact, it seems to me that the police ought——'

'Show me Slipper!' bawled a voice in the shop; 'show me that dirty little undherlooper till I have his blood! Hadn't I the race won only for him souring the mare on me! What's that you say! I tell ye he did. He left seven slaps on her with a handle of a hay-rake——'

There was in the room in which we were sitting a second door, leading to the back yard, a door consecrated to the unobtrusive visits of so-called 'Sunday travellers'. Through it Slipper faded away like a dream, and, simultaneously, a tall young man, with a face like a red-hot potato tied up in a bandage, squeezed his way from the shop into the room.

'Well, Driscoll,' said Flurry, 'since it wasn't the teeth of the rake he left on the mare, you needn't be talking!'

Leigh Kelway looked from one to the other with a wilder expression in his eye than I had thought it capable of. I read in it a resolve to abandon Ireland to her fate.

At eight o'clock we were still waiting for the car that we had been assured should be ours directly it returned from the races. At half-past eight we had adopted the only possible course that remained, and had accepted the offers of lifts on the laden cars that were returning to Skebawn, and I presently was gratified by the spectacle of my friend Leigh Kelway wedged between a roulette table and its proprietor on one side of a car, with Driscoll and Slipper, mysteriously reconciled and excessively drunk, seated, locked in each other's arms, on the other. Flurry and I, somewhat similarly placed, followed on two other cars. I was scarcely surprised when I was informed that the melancholy white animal in the shafts of the leading car was Owld Bocock's much-enduring steeplechaser.

The night was very dark and stormy, and it is almost superfluous to say that no one carried lamps; the rain poured upon us, and through wind and wet Owld Bocock's mare set the pace that showed she knew from bitter experience what was expected from her by gentlemen who had spent the evening in a public-house; behind her the other two tired horses followed closely, incited to emulation by shouting, singing, and a liberal allowance of whip. We were a good ten miles from Skebawn, and never had the road seemed so long. For mile after mile the half-seen low walls slid past us, with occasional plunges into caverns of darkness under trees. Sometimes from a wayside cabin a dog would dash out to bark at us as we rattled by; sometimes our cavalcade swung aside to pass, with yells and counter-yells, crawling carts filled with other belated racegoers.

I was nearly wet through, even though I received considerable shelter from a Skebawn publican, who slept heavily and irrepressibly on my shoulder. Driscoll, on the leading car, had struck up an approximation of the 'Wearing of the Green'[10] when a wavering star appeared on the road ahead of us. It grew momently larger; it came towards us apace. Flurry, on the car behind me, shouted suddenly:

'That's the mail car, with one of the lamps out! Tell those fellows ahead to look out!'

But the warning fell on deaf ears.

'When laws can change the blades of grass
      From growing as they grow——'
howled five discordant voices, oblivious of the towering proximity of the star.

A Bianconi mail car is nearly three times the size of an ordinary side car, and when on a dark night it advances, Cyclops-like, with but one eye, it is difficult for even a sober driver to calculate its bulk. Above the

sounds of melody there arose the thunder of heavy wheels, the splashing trample of three big horses, then a crash and turmoil of shouts. Our cars pulled up just in time, and I tore myself from the embrace of my publican to go to Leigh Kelway's assistance.

The wing of the Bianconi had caught the wing of the smaller car, flinging Owld Bocock's mare on her side and throwing her freight headlong on top of her, the heap being surmounted by the roulette table. The driver of the mailcar unshipped his solitary lamp and turned it on the disaster. I saw that Flurry had already got hold of Leigh Kelway by the heels, and was dragging him from under the others. He struggled up hatless, muddy and gasping, with Driscoll hanging on by his neck, still singing the 'Wearing of the Green'.

A voice from the mail car said incredulously, '*Leigh Kelway!*' A spectacled face glared down upon him from under the dripping spikes of an umbrella.

It was the Right Honourable the Earl of Waterbury, Leigh Kelway's chief, returning from his fishing excursion.

Meanwhile Slipper, in the ditch, did not cease to announce that 'Divil so pleasant an afthernoon ever ye seen as what was in it!'

1   Magdalen College, Oxford; Sandhurst is the military college for training British Army officers.
2   Goodwood Races (in Sussex) are still part of the summer calendar for the wealthy.
3   Servants.
4   A common mode of horse-drawn transport in nineteenth-century Ireland. Motor cars or automobiles entered Ireland after the turn of the century.
5   A horse-drawn trap with passenger seats open to the sky.
6   40p, but worth considerably more in the 1890s (see the balance-sheet for Leopold Bloom's day in *Ulysses*, Joyce's novel of 1904).
7   Buckles or harness. Compare the expression formerly addressed to a coach- or buggy-driver: 'Drop your traces and rest awhile.'
8   The huntsman's shout on seeing the fox break cover.
9   A loose whitish jacket worn by men for work.
10 A nationalist song of defiance commemorating the 1798 Rising: 'For they're hanging men and women for the wearing of the green.'

DAVID PATRICK MORAN
from Lady Gregory (ed.), *Ideals in Ireland* (1901)

D. P. Moran (1869–1936) adopted a more thoroughgoing and single-minded attitude towards cultural nationalism than did Douglas Hyde. Through the columns of his own newspaper, *The Leader*, which he founded in 1905, he alighted on anything which suggested West Britonism, a term now decidedly more sinister than it appears in Hyde. His ideas were collected in book form in *The Philosophy of Irish Ireland* (1905). The following essay appeared in a collection of essays edited by Lady Gregory; contributors included George Russell, George Moore, Hyde, O'Grady, and Yeats (reprinted p. 38). You might like to compare it with Hyde's essay, p. 2 above, or try summarizing its argument.

The Battle of Two Civilizations

I and many others have convinced ourselves, that Ireland during this century has in many vital matters played the fool. If this view in any way soothes the conscience of the English for their own country's cruel injustices to Ireland I cannot help it. Let the truth be stated though the sky should fall. We are sick of 'Irish national' make-believes and frauds, sick of shouting nation when there is no nation; and the much-abused national consciousness of the Irish people cries for truth and light, and death to shams and impostures.

The cry of the friendly Englishman, fully responded to by the 'reasonable' Irishman, is, 'Let us know more about Irishmen, and let Irishmen know more about us; we will learn to like and understand one another.' As against this view it is absolutely clear to me, though the expression may appear to have some of the form of a 'bull',[1] that when two nations understand one another there is from that moment only one nation in it. International misunderstanding is one of the marks of nationhood. Our modern differences have largely arisen, not only because the English persisted in their attempt to bring up the Irish after their own pattern, but because the Irish, though vividly conscious of a separate national identity, did nearly their best to be English and completely failed. Where the English were dull, was in their attempt to throttle Irish civilization instead of allowing it to grow and develop in all its native vigour; and where the Irish were dull — dull beyond comprehension — was that while they with much noisy demonstration made a desperate stand for something which they called the eternal cause of Irish nationality, they did nearly their level best to turn themselves into Saxons.

Unfortunately it is difficult to get the Englishman to admit that there is any civilization in the world other than British. (And anglicized Ireland naturally enough has come roughly to that conclusion too.) This is one of his most flagrant examples of dullness. When he talks of morality, he thinks only of the British variety, of liberty, progress, good taste, and so on; he shows somewhat more intelligence on the question of manners, for here he allows himself to be haunted by the suspicion that his may after all be only second rate. He wants to anglicize the world; and everything is tainted with barbarism that is not British. This heroic state of self-conceit is perhaps natural to a vigorous but dull race that has made its mark upon the world; but it is not founded upon truth. There are other worthier things between heaven and earth than English music halls, May meetings, company promoters, and bean feasts. These may represent some of the highest points of English civilization, but there are other struggling civilizations that will have little or none of them; that may, in fact, have the hardihood to look upon most of them with contempt. The world is divided into civilizations: for several reasons I think this word is more expressive than the word nation. And surely, on the principle of liberty, which England prides herself so much upon, each civilization has as much right to look out on the world in its own way, as an individual has of holding his own views. England will not admit this. I do not blame her for attempting to spread by legitimate means, that form of civilization which, as it is her own, she not unnaturally holds to be the best; but her impatience of, and her ill-mannered contempt for, other civilizations, her denial that, if they happen to be any way weak, there is any justification whatever for their existence, makes her hated all over the world; and I fear that when a weak civilization impedes her advance, killing stands in great danger of ceasing to be murder. I think it would be a bad day for the world were one common form of civilization to embrace it all; when the individual and independent growth of separate nations was stopped. However, I cannot stay to develop this point now. I have used the word civilization instead of the word nation: the development of nationality is the natural development of a distinct civilization, and any power that kills the one, is guilty of the death of the other.

In Grattan's time[2] Irish civilization was thrown overboard; but 'Irish nationality' was stuck up on a flag of green — even the colour was new fledged — and the people were exhorted to go forward and cover themselves with glory. If I am right in equating nationality with a distinct civilization, we get now a vivid glimpse of the first great source of the insincerity — all the more insidious because unconscious — the muddled thinking, the confusion of ideas, the contradictory aims which even the most cursory observer discerns in the Ireland of to-day. Since Grattan's time every popular leader, O'Connell, Butt, Parnell, Dillon, and Redmond,[3] has perpetuated this primary contradiction. They threw over Irish civilization whilst they professed — and professed in perfect good faith — to fight for Irish nationality. What potential genius that contradiction has choked, what dishonesties and tragedies, above all what comedies, it has been responsible for, I will pass over without detailed inquiry. The Irish all this time, as they are at the present day, were absolutely different from the English. The genius of each nation was distinct. To English ideals we did not respond; English literature did not kindle our minds: we continued to be born the brightest, and continued to be reared the most stupid and helpless of peoples. There is something, be it instinct or the living subconscious tradition of an almost dead civilization, that says to nearly every Irish heart — 'Thou shalt be Irish: thou shalt not be English.' This is written plainly even over the history of the last hundred years — in every respect the most decadent century that Ireland has seen.

The propaganda of the Gaelic League[4] has effected a partial revolution in Ireland. The criticism that it has inspired has been largely destructive; the energy it has let loose decidedly constructive. Much of the perpetual flow of wholesale and largely unreasonable denunciation of England was turned from its course and directed back — where it was badly wanted — upon Irishmen themselves; much of the energy that husbanded itself in idleness until certain political reforms were granted, commenced under the new inspiration to move and bestir itself at once. It is moving with increasing velocity as the conviction gains ground, that at last Ireland has gained some kind of a footing, and can advance — somewhere.

The League found Ireland wrangling over the corpse of Parnell. When A, who shouted one cry, called himself an Irish Nationalist, and declared with many strong adjectives that B, who shouted a different cry, was a West Briton, it began gradually to dawn upon the average mind that, as there was practically no difference between A and B but a cry, 'Irish nationality' must be made of a very cloudy substance indeed. Under the inspiration of the new gospel of the Gaelic League, the common man, much to his surprise, was driven to the conclusion that A and B were, after all, a pair of ordinary, unmannerly, politicians, and nothing else. And then the light dawned upon him, that politics is not nationality, and that the nineteenth century had been for Ireland mostly a century of humbug. That, in brief, is the revolution that the Gaelic League has worked; and that revolution has fundamentally altered the Irish problem.

Until a few years ago, no one challenged the accepted view that politics was the begin-all and end-all of Irish nationality. And as politics in Ireland consisted in booing against the English Government, and as Irish nationality was politics, the English Government became logically the sole destroyer of nationality. Of course it was an utterly false and an almost fatal position for us to have taken up. All the time that we were doing our share in the killing of our nation, everything was put down to England. An infallible way to distract criticism from domestic affairs — and this can be clearly seen by observing the state of the public temper in England at the present time — is to get entangled in a foreign war. When a great struggle is on hand, domestic reformers may sing for an audience. A people who are watching their nation in death-grips with another, are in little humour for attending to the parish pumps, least of all for listening to uncomplimentary criticism. But, supposing this condition of things lasted for a hundred years, what would become of the home economy? And this has practically been the condition under which Ireland has spent the century. We have been fighting England as our only enemy, looking to her as the sole source of all our evils, as the only possible source of all our blessings, inasmuch as until we had settled with her, we could do nothing for ourselves. All the while, like Pendennis, we ourselves were our greatest enemies. As politics was nationality, every patriotic Irishman who watched his decaying nation, felt new drops of hate for England descend into his heart. Until England could be brought to her senses no progress could be made, and as the life was all the time ebbing out of the Irish nation, then ten thousand curses be upon her oppressor. This attitude flows reasonably from the first false position that politics was nationality. When Ireland was great, she sent men of learning and religion to instruct and enlighten Europe; when she was at her lowest ebb, she sent out desperadoes with infernal machines. The commandment, 'Thou shalt be Irish', was written alike upon the hearts of all.

From the great error that nationality is politics, a sea of corruption has sprung. Ireland was practically left unsubjected to wholesome native criticism, without which any collection of humanity will corrupt. If a lack of industrial energy and initiative were pointed out, the answer naturally was — 'Away, traitor. England robbed us of our industries; we can do nothing until she restores our rights.' If you said that the people drank too much — 'Well, what are the poor people to do; they are only human; wait until our rights are restored, and all that will be altered.' And so on. To find fault with your countrymen was to play into the hands of England, and act the traitor. There were enough abusing us, without Ireland's own joining in the chorus. This was the negative side of the matter: there was a positive side also. It manifestly became the policy of Irishmen to praise and bolster up their own people, and make out the most glowing account of their virtues and importance. The minor political leaders let themselves loose over the country, telling their audiences that they belonged to a great and immortal nation, that they were engaged in a noble struggle for Irish freedom, and that the eyes of the civilized world were upon them. Irish popular oratory was corrupted under these influences into one string of uncomplimentary adjectives applied to England and the English, and another string of an opposite description applied to Ireland. Thought had been squeezed out of the platform and the press, and every vestige of distinctive nationality was fast leaving the country. This was certainly a pretty pass for a quick-witted people to allow themselves to drift into. But once, I submit, that the Irish mind allowed itself to be muddled into considering politics and nationality convertible terms, the condition of things that resulted became, as an eminent Englishman might put it, 'inevitable'.

I will now attempt to trace, in broad outline, the influence which the state of things that I have referred to has had upon literary taste and literary production in Ireland, on social progress and the development of polite society, on the Irish attitude towards England and its powerful bearing upon the economic helplessness and stagnation of the country.

I think I have read somewhere that the great Duke of Marlborough knew no English history except that which he learned from Shakespeare's works. I mention this in order to point out that it takes an Englishman to get the most out of English literature, as it takes a Frenchman to get the most out of French literature. A literature steeped in the history, traditions, and genius of one nation is at the best only an imperfect tutor to the people of another nation; in fact, the common half-educated people of another nation will have none of it. The Irish nation has, this century, been brought up on English literature. Of course it never really kindled their minds or imaginations; they were driven to look at literature as a thing not understandable and above them — a position, I need scarcely say, not making for the development of self-respect or intellectual self-dependence. In most cases, when they left school they ceased to read anything but the newspapers. Of course there are many exceptions to this generalization. If an Irishman received a higher English education, and lost touch with Irish

aspirations, he practically became an Englishman; and many people with less advantages, by force of exceptional ability, got their heads above the entanglements around them and breathed something like free air. But I am talking of the common run of men who make up a nation, and not of the few exceptions. Tell me of any ordinary man in Dublin, Cork, or elsewhere, who professes an appreciation for the best products of English literature, and I will have no hesitation in informing you that he is an intellectual snob, mostly composed of affectation. Literature, to the common Irishman, is an ingenious collection of fine words which no doubt have some meaning, but which he is not going to presume to understand. A good speaker in Ireland is not a man who talks keen sense well, but one with 'the divil's flow of words'; and Irish 'oratory' has developed into the windiest thing on earth. The state of literature, and thought, and original intellectual activity of any kind had indeed dropped to a low level. The 'Irish National' literary output chiefly consisted of a few penny magazines in which the most commonplace rhymes were passed off as 'Irish' poetry, and which contained an unceasing and spirit-wearying flow of romances about '48, '98,[5] and other periods, in all of which, of course, Ireland was painted spotless white. Romances in which Irish heroes of a couple of hundred years ago, who probably never spoke a word of English in their lives, were made to prate heroics in English of the 'Seest thou yon battlements' type, were so manifestly absurd that no one but very young boys could put up with them. Thought was necessarily absent from all this literature, for assuredly the first effort of thought would be to let the light through all this make-believe that passed current as part and parcel of 'Irish national' literature. Criticism had died, and this sort of thing, along with 'oratory', was allowed to swell like soap bubbles all over the land. The Irish people dropped off reading, not from any lack of intellectual desire, but because nowhere was to be found that which would interest them. Then the great rise of cheap periodicals came about in England, and the market in Ireland was flooded with them. Ireland being a poor country, the cheapest class of periodicals only is within the popular resources, and it soon became evident that a grave evil was threatening us, and that Ireland was largely feeding on a questionable type of British reading matter. And the commandment — 'Thou shalt be Irish' — was all the while troubling Irish hearts . . .

If thought and literature dwindled away in modern Ireland, an inquiry into social life and manners presents even a more muddled and hopeless picture. It was all very well for people to say that everything would come straight when we obtained our rights from England, but in the meantime people had to do something, for what we understand in current language as 'doing nothing' is in reality a form of doing something. Even those who shouted most about Irish Parliaments and Irish Republics were swayed by the general desire, common to all aspiring men, to be gentlemen of some kind, to be socially 'superior', to reach to some point of social vantage. And in this department of Irish life we will observe the deepest muddle of all. What is a gentleman from the point of view of an English-speaking Irishman? Manifestly the same thing as a gentleman is in England. What are good breeding, good taste, etiquette, from the same man's point of view? Manifestly again the same as these things are in England. The English-speaking Irishman and the Englishman were children of one common civilization. Social advance under modern Irish conditions could therefore only lead in one way, and that way was in the direction of the English ideals. But there was still that commandment like a fallen oak across the road, barring the way — 'Thou shalt be Irish and not English.' Here was a serious question which the modern Irishman had to solve. Like many another question, he refused to face it; he merely tried to shelve it. And too often he avoided becoming an English gentleman by becoming an Irish vulgarian. Ireland had either to advance socially along English lines or along Irish lines. She refused to do the former with any thoroughness; she had cut herself completely adrift from the latter. Had Ireland developed her own civilization, the manners and etiquette of Irish society would, I think, be very formal and elegant; but as she had thrown over Irish civilization, there was nothing for her to do but imitate England with the best grace she could. But the conventions and manners of English society, owing to various local and particular reasons, as well as in consequence of the radical difference in the genius of the two peoples, she found repellent to her. Society without conventions is necessarily vulgar and chaotic, and much of the social life of Ireland was driven to prove itself Irish by kicking against convention altogether. There are various degrees in this long procession of vulgarity, and those who had least convention were perhaps less vulgar than many mean-spirited imitators of every thing they considered English and 'respectable'. You would, I believe, search the world in vain for the equals of the latter class. English conventions were known to them mostly by hearsay, and these hearsay accounts they copied with a dog-like fidelity. They cultivated English accents, they sent their children to English schools, they tucked in their skirts from

contact with the 'low Irish', and they played tennis, not because they liked it, but because it was English and 'respectable'. However, if we look charitably upon them, and keep in mind the impossible conditions under which they were compelled to live, we shall find much to say in their extenuation. Fate has revenged herself upon them, for she has decreed that all of them, from those who live in fashionable Dalkey,[6] on through the ranks of the 'gentleman farmers', down to the huxter who is making his son a doctor and his daughter a 'lady', should be known to the world under the comprehensive title of 'shoneens'.[7]

I now pass on to consider briefly the effect which the conditions of modern Ireland had upon our attitude towards England. A professed hatred of England, but not of things English, which is a different matter altogether, not illogically became part and parcel of Irish nationality. This led to more muddle. The Irish people do not hate England or any other country. As a matter of fact, the genius of our nation is far more prone to love than hate. There is no gospel of personal or national hate in our religion; we are told at our mothers' knees to love all men, including our enemies. But as England, in consequence of the situation I have attempted to sketch, became in our view the source of all our ills, was responsible not only for her own sins against us — which heaven knows are many and great — but also responsible for our own blunders and stupidity, she came in for a double dose of resentment. Whenever an Irishman contemplated anything hurtful to his national pride, a curse against England gurgled in his throat. No wonder Englishmen completely misunderstood us, and classed us as a lot of grown-up children, when Ireland swayed and writhed in a helpless entanglement herself. It was certainly difficult to deal satisfactorily with a country that had missed her own path, and had only a very muddled idea of what she wanted herself. All this light has been thrown upon Ireland by the propaganda of the Gaelic League. It has compelled us to ask ourselves the elementary question — What is Irish nationality, and what in reality do we want to see realized in Ireland? Will a few soldiers dressed in green, and a republic, absolutely foreign to the genius of the Irish people, the humiliation of England, a hundred thousand English corpses with Irish bullets or pike wounds through them, satisfy the instinct within us that says: 'Thou shalt be Irish'? These things we probably can never see, though we may try to drown our national conscience by dreaming of them. But were they possible, they were vain; for a distinct nation is a distinct civilization, and if England went down to the bottom of the sea to-morrow, that distinct civilization which we have turned our backs upon, that woof of national tradition which we have cast from us, would not be restored. Our nation cannot be resurrected merely by the weakness of England, but mainly by the strength and effort of Ireland herself. This then is the new situation that has been created — the political disabilities of Ireland remain, and the political fight must go on until they are redressed, but England stands in our mental view no longer as the sole destroyer of Irish nationality; we have learned that we ourselves have been acting like fools, that we, during this century, have been the greatest sinners against that nationality whose death we were only too anxious to lay at the door of England. The Irish nationality that has sprung merely from a misguided hatred, or affected hatred, of England has not been a brilliant success, if we judge it by its fruits. Hate, I suggest, inspires nothing but destruction. And looking over this great century during which the civilized world has made such strides, we find that Ireland, representing one of the oldest and independent civilizations, has attempted nothing and achieved nothing. She has gone back in every department where other nations have advanced. She threw away her initiative and her language, and became a mean and sulky imitator of another people whom she professed to hate. Whilst clamouring and organizing insurrections to bring about something which she called 'National Independence', she willingly cast away the main functions of independent existence, which, notwithstanding English misgovernment, she was still in a large measure free to exercise.

The baneful effect of the state of things that I have attempted to describe did not stop at literature, public opinion, and social development; it sapped the very foundations of economic advance. At the first blush it may appear a far-fetched idea that there is a strong connection between the development of a native civilization having its roots in the native language, and the production of economic wealth. English thought was, until comparatively recently, in a rather muddled state over economics; and it passes the understanding of modern man to comprehend by what mental process certain not very old theories were held by the best thinkers of those days. We have come now to see that land, though an indispensable, is by no means the main, source of modern economic wealth. Human skill in all its manifold manifestations has taken the premier place, and conditions precedent to the production of that skill are the existence of initiative and self-dependence. If you have to begin with a self-distrusting people who are afraid to rely on their own judgment, who have learnt by a long and reluctant effort to imitate a rich and highly developed people

foreign to their genius, to conceive a mean and cringing opinion of themselves, you will never get much economic initiative out of them. You will find it difficult to raise what economists call their 'standard of comfort'. Creatures may heave bricks and draw water, but it takes men to command, to think, to initiate, to organize, and to will. The first step in the acquirement of skill is a man, and if you have not a man but a sulky, imitating being to begin with, it is a poor look-out for your economic projects. For behind and above the economics of a nation is the heart of a nation. And Anglo-Ireland of to-day has no heart. It is led by a hempen cord and frightened by a shadow. The economic ills of Ireland can be traced to many diverse minor causes, but if you follow them up you arrive at the great common source — the lack of Irish heart. Ireland has not courage to say — I will wear this, or, I will not wear that. So the draper from Ballyduff goes to London — sometimes he gives out that he has been as far as Paris — and a hideous poster in three colours announces that the latest novelties and fashions from London and Paris have arrived. This sends a thrill through the households of the village. The greasy draper rubs his hands and dilates on 'the circulation of money'; and the moss on the still wheels of the village mill weeps for the native heart of other days. Ireland, because she has lost her heart, imports to-day what, on sound economic principles, she could produce for herself. She who once gave ideas to the world, begs the meanest tinsel from that world now. She is out in the cold amongst the nations, standing on a sort of nowhere, looking at a civilization which she does not understand, refuses to be absorbed into, and is unable to copy. She exports cattle, drink, and human beings; and she imports, amongst other things, men with initiative and heart. A dolt from England manages a naturally able man born of the soil, because the dolt uses his head, such as it is, and the native of the soil has lost his heart. The great modern economic tradition of Ireland is simply this — Nothing Irish succeeds! We have not even heart to amuse ourselves, and our 'humour' and our 'drama' — God save us from most of both — are imported, as well as our shoddy.[8] The tinker of thought — and modern Ireland is full of that type — has traced the ills of Ireland to everything in turn and to nothing long. His curses and complainings are ever floating over the seas; and he stands by the side of a native civilization that he has neglected almost unto death, and is never inspired to exclaim: 'It is the cause, it is the cause, my soul!'[9] In fact, he is not aware that he ever had a civilization. He frets and moans and curses as he gropes in the dark recesses between two of them. If I were autocrat of

Ireland to-morrow, and someone were to come to me and ask what I wanted most, I should have no hesitation in answering — Men. And if we are to have men, we must make the population of Ireland either thoroughgoing English or thoroughgoing Irish. No one who knows Ireland will entertain for a moment the idea that the people can be made English; the attempt has been made, and a country of sulky, dissatisfied, and self-distrusting mongrels is the result. Ireland will be nothing until she is a nation, and as a nation is a civilization, she will never accomplish anything worthy of herself until she falls back upon her own language and traditions, and, recovering there her old pride, self-respect, and initiative, develops and marches forward from thence.

I have attempted to trace the evil effects arising from our efforts to imitate England whilst the commandment 'Thou shalt be Irish' is written upon our hearts. I hope I am no quack. The influences that mould a nation are infinite, and cannot be clearly grasped by the human mind. We can only hope to trace them in the broadest outline. Of what English legislation has done to undo Ireland I have a lively appreciation, but that matter does not come within the scope of this article. I have confined myself to an inquiry into the effects of causes which it is within Ireland's power, and within her power alone, to remove. The only hope that I see for Ireland is that she may set to work to create what does not exist now, what mere political independence, a parliament in College Green,[10] or the humiliation of British arms, will not necessarily bestow — to create a nation. Abroad, during this century, wherever Irishmen have unreservedly thrown themselves in with the particular civilization of their adopted countries, they have done honour alike to themselves and their neighbours. During precious centuries Spain and France and other countries had hundreds of thousands of our bravest and our best, and well, and not without good reason, were they welcomed. The Irishman of modern times has succeeded in every land but his own. For at home is the only place where he cannot make up his mind — he will not be one thing or the other, he will not be English or Irish. Grattan, though not a great statesman, was visited with many vivid flashes of insight. The history of this century gives a new and deeper meaning to one sentence he uttered more than a hundred years ago concerning the relations of Ireland and England. 'As her equal we shall be her sincerest friend; as anything less than her equal we shall be her bitterest enemy.' Unless we are a nation we are nothing, and the growth of a civilization springing from the roots of one of the oldest in Europe, will

alone make us a nation, give us scope to grow naturally, give us something to inspire what is best in us, cultivate our national pride and self-respect, and encourage our self-dependence. Marching along that line, the hurt or humiliation of England will cease, must cease, to be our ambition; for our master-passions will be wrapped up in the construction of our own nation, not in the destruction of another. Whether an Ireland of the future, relying upon her own genius, will ever do for mankind what the old Ireland of the early centuries did with such generosity, love, and enthusiasm for Europe, is a matter for faith rather than for speculation. The prospect of such a new Ireland rising up out of the foundations of the old, with love and not hate as its inspiration, has already sent a great thrill through the land. It is a new and unlooked-for situation, full with fate, not only for Ireland, but for the world.

1   A self-contradictory expression, associated in part with Irish usage. In 1802 Maria Edgeworth and her father Richard Lovell Edgeworth wrote a famous book on the topic entitled *An Essay on Irish Bulls*, in which they defended the use of English as spoken in Ireland.

2   Henry Grattan (1746–1820) gave his name to Grattan's Parliament, a period of relative Irish autonomy from 1782 until the Act of Union in 1801. His speeches at Westminster in favour of greater Irish independence led in 1782 to the repeal of the 1720 Declaratory Act. In the same year at the Ulster Volunteers Convention in Dungannon he made his most famous speech which contained the phrases 'Spirit of Swift! Spirit of Molyneux! your genius has prevailed! Ireland is now a nation!'

3   Isaac Butt (1813–79), as MP for Limerick from 1871 until 1879, argued for Home Rule for Ireland. John Dillon (1851–1927) was a nationalist MP from 1880 until 1918. He led the anti-Parnellites from 1896 until the reunification of the Party in 1900. John Redmond (1856–1918), MP for Waterford from 1893 until 1918, was leader of Irish constitutional nationalism from 1900 until 1918.

4   Founded in 1893 by Eoin MacNeill (1867–1945) and Douglas Hyde to promote Irish language and culture.

5   The Risings of 1848 and 1798.

6   Some ten miles south of Dublin, a residential seaside town beneath the slopes of Killiney Hill. Boyhood home of George Bernard Shaw (1856–1950) and setting for Flann O'Brien's *The Dalkey Archive* (1964).

7   A would-be gentleman putting on airs (P.W. Joyce). The word combines the Irish Seán and the English John (een is a diminutive in Irish); the implication is that such Irish people, whose hearts are English, are not really Irish.

8   Woollen yarn.

9   Lines from Shakespeare's *Othello*, V. ii. 1.

10 The Irish Parliament in the eighteenth century met in what is now the Bank of Ireland in College Green, Dublin.

W. B. YEATS

from Lady Gregory (ed.), *Ideals in Ireland* (1901)

Again, the argument here is worth trying to summarize. Consider also how the three
essays by Hyde, Moran, and Yeats belong together as responses to British influence in
Ireland. What role is envisaged for literature in the construction of the new Ireland?

The Literary Movement in Ireland

I have just come to a quiet Connaught house from
seeing a little movement, in a great movement of
thought which is fashioning the dreams of the next
generation in Ireland, grow to a sudden maturity.
Certain plays, which are an expression of the most
characteristic ideals of what is sometimes called the
'Celtic movement', have been acted in Dublin before
audiences drawn from all classes and all political
sections, and described at great length in every
Nationalist newspaper. Whatever be the merit of these
plays, and that must be left to the judgment of time,
their success means, as I think, that the 'Celtic
movement', which has hitherto interested but a few
cultivated people, is about to become a part of the
thought of Ireland.

Before 1891,[1] Unionists and Nationalists were too
busy keeping one or two simple beliefs at their fullest
intensity for any complexity of thought or emotion;
and the national imagination uttered itself, with a
somewhat broken energy, in a few stories and in many
ballads about the need of unity against England, about
the martyrs who had died at the hand of England, or
about the greatness of Ireland before the coming of
England. They built up Ireland's dream of Ireland, of
an ideal country weighed down by immemorial
sorrows and served by heroes and saints, and they
taught generations of young men to love their country
with a love that was the deepest emotion they were
ever to know; but they built with the virtues and
beauties and sorrows and hopes that would move to
tears the greatest number of those eyes before whom
the modern world is but beginning to unroll itself;
and, except when some rare, personal impulse shaped
the song according to its will, they built to the formal
and conventional rhythm which would give the most
immediate pleasure to ears that had forgotten Gaelic
poetry and not learned the subtleties of English poetry.
The writers who made this literature or who shaped
its ideals, in the years before the great famine, lived at
the moment when the middle class had brought to
perfection its ideal of the good citizen, and of a
politics and a philosophy and a literature which would
help him upon his way; and they made a literature full

of the civic virtues and, in all but its unbounded
patriotism, without inconvenient ardours. They took
their style from Scott and Campbell and Macaulay,[2]
and that 'universally popular' poetry which is really
the poetry of the middle class, and from Beranger[3] and
that 'peasant poetry' which looks for its models to the
Burns of 'Highland Mary' and 'The Cottar's Saturday
Night'. Here and there a poet or a story-writer found
an older dream among the common people or in his
own mind, and made a personality for himself, and
was forgotten; for it was the desire of everybody to be
moved by the same emotions as everybody else, and
certainly one cannot blame a desire which has thrown
so great a shadow of self-sacrifice.

The fall of Parnell and the wreck of his party and of
the organizations that supported it were the symbols, if
not the causes, of a sudden change. They were
followed by movements and organizations that brought
the ideas and the ideals which are the expression of
personalities alike into politics, economics, and
literature. Those who looked for the old energies,
which were the utterance of the common will and
hope, were unable to see that a new kind of Ireland, as
full of energy as a boiling pot, was rising up amid the
wreck of the old kind, and that the national life was
finding a new utterance. This utterance was so
necessary that it seems as if the hand that broke the
ball of glass, that now lies in fragments full of a new
iridescent life, obeyed some impulse from beyond its
wild and capricious will. More books about Irish
subjects have been published in these last eight years
than in the thirty years that went before them, and
these books have the care for scholarship and the
precision of speech which had been notoriously
lacking in books on Irish subjects. An appeal to the
will, a habit of thought which measures all beliefs by
their intensity, is content with a strenuous rhetoric;
but an appeal to the intellect needs an always more
perfect knowledge, an always more malleable speech.
The new writers and the new organizations they work
through — for organizations of various kinds take the
place held by the critical press in other countries —
have awakened Irish affections among many from
whom the old rhetoric could never have got a

hearing, but they have been decried for weakening the national faith by lovers of the old rhetoric. I have seen an obscure Irish member of Parliament rise at one of those monthly meetings of the Irish Literary Society,[4] when the members of the society read sometimes their poems to one another, and ask their leave to read a poem. He did not belong to the society, but leave was given him, and he read a poem in the old manner, blaming the new critics and praising the old poems which had made him patriotic and filled his imagination with the images of the martyrs, and, as he numbered over their names, Wolfe Tone, Emmet, Owen Roe, Sarsfield,[5] his voice shook, and many were angry with the new critics.

The organizations that are making this change are the Irish Literary Society in London, the National Literary Society in Dublin, which has founded, or rather sheltered with its influence, the Irish Literary Theatre, and the Feis Ceoil Committee in Dublin, at whose annual series of concerts of Irish music singers and pipers from all parts of Ireland compete; and more important than all, the Gaelic League, which has worked for the revival of the Gaelic language with such success that it has sold fifty thousand of its Gaelic text-books in a year. All these organizations have been founded since the fall of Parnell; and all are busy in preserving, or in moulding anew and without any thought of the politics of the hour, some utterance of the national life, and in opposing the vulgar books and vulgarer songs that come to us from England. We are preparing, as we hope, for a day when Ireland will speak in Gaelic, as much as Wales speaks in Welsh, within her borders, but speak, it may be, in English to other nations of those truths which were committed to her when 'He set the borders of the nations according to His angels'; as Dionysius the Areopagite has written. Already, as I think, a new kind of romance, a new element in thought, is being moulded out of Irish life and traditions, and this element may have an importance for criticism, even should criticism forget the writers who are trying to embody it in their work, while looking each one through his own colour in the dome of many-coloured glass.

Contemporary English literature takes delight in praising England and her Empire, the master-work and dream of the middle class; and, though it may escape from this delight, it must long continue to utter the ideals of the strong and wealthy. Irish intellect has always been preoccupied with the weak and with the poor, and now it has begun to collect and describe their music and stories, and to utter anew the beliefs and hopes which they alone remember. It may never make a literature preoccupied with the circumstance of their lives, like the 'peasant poetry', whose half deliberate triviality, passionless virtue, and passionless vice has helped so many orderly lives; for a writer who wishes to write with his whole mind must knead the beliefs and hopes, which he has made his own, with the circumstance of his own life. Burns had this preoccupation, and nobody will deny that he was a great poet; but even he had the poverty of emotions and ideas of a peasantry that had lost, like the middle class into which it would have its children absorbed, the imagination that is in tradition without finding the imagination that is in books. Irish literature may prolong its first inspiration without renouncing the complexity of ideas and emotions which is the inheritance of cultivated men, for it will have learned from the discoveries of modern learning that the common people, wherever civilization has not driven its plough too deep, keep a watch over the roots of all religion and all romance. Their poetry trembles upon the verge of incoherence with a passion all but unknown among modern poets, and their sense of beauty exhausts itself in countless legends and in metaphors that seem to mirror the energies of nature.

Dr Hyde has collected many old Irish peasant love-songs, and, like all primitive poetry, they foreshadow a poetry whose intensity of emotion, or strangeness of language, has made it the poetry of little coteries. His peasant lover cries —

> It is happy for you, O blind man, who do not see much of women.
> O! if you were to see what I see, you would be sick even as I am.
> It is a pity, O God, that it was not blind I was before I saw her twisted hair.
> I always thought the blind were pitiable, until my calamity grew beyond the grief of all,
> Then though it is a pity I turned my pity into envy.
> In a loop of the loops in a loop am I.
> It is sorrow for whoever has seen her, and it is sorrow for him who does not see her every day.
> It is sorrow for him who is tied in the knot of her love, and it is sorrow for him who is loosed out of it.
> It is sorrow for him who is near her, and it is sorrow for him who is not near her.[6]

Or he cries —

> O Maurya! you are my love, and the love of my heart is your love —
> Love that is without littleness, without weakness,

Love from age till death,
Love growing out of folly,
Love that will send me close beneath the clay,
Love without a hope of the world,
Love without envy of fortune,
Love that has left me withered in captivity,
Love of my heart beyond women;
And a love such as that, it is seldom to be got from
  any man.[7]

And Lady Gregory has translated a lament, that
Raftery the wandering fiddler[8] made for a fiddler some
sixty years ago, into the simple English of the country
people of today —

The swans on the water are nine times blacker than
  a blackberry, since the man died from us that had
  pleasantness on the top of his fingers;
His two grey eyes were like the dew of the morning
  that lies on the grass;
And since he was laid in the grave, the cold is
  getting the upper hand.
There are young women, and not without reason,
  sorry and heart-broken and withered, since he
  was left at the church;
Their hair, thrown down and hanging, turned grey
  on their head.
No flower in any garden, and the leaves of the trees
  have leave to cry, and they falling on the ground;
There are no green flowers on the tops of the tufts
  since there did a boarded coffin go on Daly.

All are not like this, but the most inspired and, as I
think, the most characteristic are like this. There is a
square stone tower called Ballylee Castle,[9] a couple of
miles from where I am writing. A farmer called
Hynes, who had a beautiful daughter, Mary Hynes,
lived near it some sixty years ago; and all over the
countryside old men and old women still talk of her
beauty, and the young and old praise her with a song
made by Raftery —

O star of light, and O sun in harvest,
O amber hair, O my share of the world;
There is no good to deny it or to try and hide it,
She is the sun in the heavens who wounded my
  heart.

There was no part of Ireland I did not travel,
From the rivers to the tops of the mountains,
To the edge of Lough Greine, whose mouth is
  hidden,
And I saw no beauty but was behind hers.

It is Mary Hynes, the calm and easy woman,
Has beauty in her mind and in her face;
If a hundred clerks were gathered together
They could not write down a half of her ways.

This song, though Gaelic poetry has fallen from its old
greatness, has come out of the same dreams as the
songs and legends, as vague, it may be, as the clouds of
evening and of dawn, that became in Homer's mind
the memory and the prophecy of all the sorrows that
have beset and shall beset the journey of beauty in the
world. A very old woman who remembers Mary
Hynes said to me, and to a friend who was with me: 'I
never saw one so handsome as she was, and I never
will until I die. There were people coming from all
parts to look at her, and maybe some of them forgot
to say, "God bless her."[10] Any way, she was young
when she died, and my mother was at her funeral, and
as to whether she was taken, well, there's others have
been taken that were not handsome at all, and so it's
likely enough she might have been, for there is no one
to be seen at all that is handsome like she was.' The
spirit of Helen moves indeed among the legends that
are told about turf-fires, and among the legends of the
poor and simple everywhere. A friend of mine was
told a while ago, in a remote part of Donegal, of a
young man who saw a light before him on the road,
and found when he came near that it was from a lock
of hair in an open box. The hair was so bright that,
when he went into the stable where he slept, he put
the box into a hole in the wall and had no need of a
candle. After many wanderings he found her from
whose head it had been taken, and after many
adventures married her and reigned over a kingdom.

The peasant remembers such songs and legends, all
the more, it may be, because he has thought of little
but cows and sheep and the like in his own marriage,
for his dream has never been entangled by reality. The
beauty of women is mirrored in his mind, as the
excitement of the world is mirrored in the minds of
children, and like them he thinks nothing but the best
worth remembering. The child William Blake said to
somebody who had told him of a fine city, that he
thought no city fine that had not walls of gold and
silver. It may be that poetry is the utterance of desires
that we can only satisfy in dreams, and that if all our
dreams were satisfied there would be no more poetry.
Dreams pass from us with childhood, because we are
so often told they can never come true, and because
we are taught with so much labour to admire the paler
beauty of the world. The children of the poor and
simple learn from their unbroken religious faith, and
from their traditional beliefs, and from the hardness of

their lives, that this world is nothing, and that a spiritual world, where all dreams come true, is everything; and therefore the poor and simple are that imperfection whose perfection is genius.

The most of us think that all things, when imagined in their perfection, that all images which emotion desires in its intensity, are among the things nobody has ever seen or shall ever see; and so we are always reminding one another not to go too far from the moderation of reality. But the Irish peasant believes that the utmost he can dream was once or still is a reality by his own door. He will point to some mountain and tell you that some famous hero or beauty lived and sorrowed there, or he will tell you that Tir-nan-og, the country of the young, the old Celtic paradise — the Land of the Living Heart, as it used to be called — is all about him. An old woman close by Ballylee Castle said to a friend of mine the other day, when someone had finished a story of the poet Usheen's return from Tir-nan-og, where he had lived with his fairy mistress: 'Tir-nan-og? That place is not far from us. One time I was in the chapel of Labane, and there was a tall thin man sitting next to me, and he dressed in grey; and after the mass I asked him where he came from. "From Tir-nan-og," he said. "And where is that?" I asked him. "It's not far from you," he said. "It's near the place where you live." I remember well the look of him, and he telling me that. The priest was looking at us while we were talking together.'

There are many grotesque things near at hand, the dead doing their penance in strange shapes, and evil spirits with terrible and ugly shapes, but people of a perfect beauty are never far off; and this beauty is often, I know not how often, that heroic beauty 'which changes least from youth to age', and which has faded from modern painting and poetry before a fleeting voluptuous beauty. One old Mayo woman, who can neither read nor write, described it to me, though with grotesque comparisons. She has been long in service, and her language has not the simplicity of those who live among fields. She was standing in the window of her master's house looking out toward a mountain where Queen Maeve, the Queen of the Western Spirits,[11] is said to have been buried, when she saw 'the finest woman she ever saw' travelling right across from the mountain and straight to her. The woman had a sword by her side and a dagger lifted up in her hand, and was dressed in white, with bare arms and feet. She looked 'very strong and warry and fierce, but not wicked'; that is, not cruel, at all. The old woman had seen the Irish giant, and 'though he was a fine man, he was nothing to this woman, for he was

round, and could not have stepped out so soldierly'. She told me that she was like a certain stately lady of the neighbourhood, 'but she had no stomach on her, and was slight and broad in the shoulders, and was handsomer than anyone you ever saw now; she looked about thirty'. The old woman covered her eyes with her hands, and when she uncovered them the apparition had vanished. The neighbours were 'wild' with her for not waiting to see if there was a message, for they are sure it was Queen Maeve, who often shows herself to the pilots. I asked the old woman if she had seen others like Queen Maeve, and she said: 'Some of them have their hair down, but they look quite different, like the sleepy-looking ladies you see in the papers. Those with their hair up are like this one. The others have long white dresses, but those with their hair up have short dresses, so that you can see their legs right up to the calf.' After some careful questioning I found that they wore what appeared to be buskins. She went on: 'They are fine and dashing-looking, like the men one sees riding their horses in twos and threes on the slopes of the mountains, with their swords swinging.' She repeated over and over: 'There is no such race living now, none so fine proportioned,' or the like, and then said: 'The present queen is a nice, pleasant-looking woman, but she is not like her. What makes me think so little of the ladies is that I see none as they be,' meaning the spirits; 'when I think of her and of the ladies now, they are like little children running about, without being able to put their clothes on right. Is it the ladies? Why, I would not call them women at all!'

There are many old heroical tales about Queen Maeve, and before she was a queen she was a goddess and had her temples, and she is still the most beautiful of the beautiful. A young man among the Burren Hills of Clare told me, a couple of years ago, that he remembered an old poet who had made his poems in Irish, and had met in his youth one who had called herself Queen Maeve, and asked him if he would have money or pleasure. He said he would have pleasure, and she gave him her love for a time, and then went from him and ever after he was very sad. The young man had often heard him sing a lamentation he had made, but could only remember that it was 'very mournful', and called her 'Beauty of all Beauty'. The song may have been but a resinging of a traditional theme, but the young man believed it.

Many, perhaps most, of those that I have talked with of these things have all their earthly senses, but those who have most knowledge of these things, so much indeed that they are permitted, it is thought, to speak but broken words, are those from whom the earthly senses have fallen away. 'In every household' of the spirits even, there is 'a queen and a fool, and, maybe, the fool is the wisest of all'. This fool, who is held to wander in lonely places and to bewitch men out of the world — for the touch of the queen and of the fool give death — is the type of that old wisdom from which the good citizen and the new wisdom have led the world away, forgetting that 'the ruins of time build mansions in eternity'.[12] The poetry that comes out of the old wisdom must turn always to religion and to the law of the hidden world, while the poetry of the new wisdom must not forget politics and the law of the visible world; and between these poetries there cannot be any lasting peace. Those that follow the old wisdom must not shrink too greatly from the journey described in some verses Miss Hopper,[13] a poet of our school, has put into the mouth of Dalua, the fairy fool:

The world wears on to sundown, and love is lost or won,
But he recks not of loss or gain, the King of Ireland's son.
He follows on for ever when all your chase is done,
He follows after shadows, the King of Ireland's son.

Alone among nations, Ireland has in her written Gaelic literature, in her old love tales and battle tales, the forms in which the imagination of Europe uttered itself before Greece shaped a tumult of legend into her music of the arts; and she can discover, from the beliefs and emotions of her common people, the habit of mind that created the religion of the muses. The legends of other European countries are less numerous, and not so full of the energies from which the arts and our understanding of their sanctity arose, and the best of them have already been shaped into plays and poems. 'The Celt', as it seems, created romance, when his stories of Arthur and of the Grail became for a time almost the only inspiration of European literature, and it would not be wonderful if he should remould romance after its oldest image, now that he is recovering his possessions.

The movement of thought which has made the good citizen, or has been made by him, has surrounded us with comfort and safety, and with vulgarity and insincerity. One finds alike its energy and its weariness in churches which have substituted a system of morals for spiritual ardour; in pictures which have substituted conventionally pretty faces for the disquieting revelations of sincerity; in poets who have set the praises of those things good citizens think praiseworthy above a dangerous delight in beauty for the sake of beauty. The Romantic movement, from the times of Blake and Shelley and Keats, when it took a new form, has been battling with the thoughts of the good citizen, as moss and ivy and grass battle with some old building, crumbling its dead stone and mortar into the living greenery of earth. The disorders of a Shelley or of a Heine in their art, and in their lives that mirror their art, are but a too impetuous ardour of battle, a too swift leaping of ivy or of grass to window ledge or gable end; and the intensity and strangeness of a picture by Rossetti or of an early picture by Watts are but a sudden falling of stones. Moss and ivy and grass gather against stone and mortar in unceasing enmity, for while the old is crumbling the new is building; and the Romantic movement will never have perfect victory unless, as mystics have thought, the golden age is to come again, and men's hearts and the weather to grow gentle as time fades into eternity. Blake said that all art was a labour to bring that golden age, and we call romantic art romantic because it has made that age's light dwell in the imaginations of a little company of studious persons.

Because the greater number of persons are too busy with the work of the world to forget the light of the sun, romantic art is, as I think, about to change its manner and become more like the art of the old poets, who saw the golden age and their own age side by side like substance and shadow. Ever since Christianity turned men's minds to Judea, and learning turned them to Greece and Rome, the sanctity has dwindled from their own hills and valleys, which the legends and beliefs of fifty centuries had filled so full of it that a man could hardly plough his fields or follow his sheep upon the hillside without remembering some august story, or walking softly lest he had divine companions. When the valleys and the hills had almost become clay and stone, the good citizens plucked up their heart and took possession of the world and filled it with their little compact thoughts; and romance fled to more and more remote fairylands, and forgot that it was ever more than an old tale which nobody believes. But now we are growing interested in our own countries, and discovering that the common people in all countries that have not given themselves up to the improvements and devices of good citizens, which we call civilization, still half understand the sanctity of their hills and valleys; and at the same time a change of thought is making us half ready to believe with Ecclesiasticus, that 'all things are made double one above another', and that the forms of nature may be temporal shadows of realities.

In a little time places may begin to seem the only hieroglyphs that cannot be forgotten, and poets to remember that they will come the nearer the old poets, who had a seat at every hearth, if they mingle their own dream with a story told for centuries of some mountain that casts its shadows upon many doors, and if they understand that the beauty they celebrate is a part of the paradise men's eyes shall look upon when they close upon the world. The paradise of the Christian, as those who think more of the order of communities than of the nature of things have shaped it, is but the fulfilment of one dream; but the paradise that the common people tell of about the fire, and still half understand, is the fulfilment of all dreams, and opens its gates as gladly to the perfect lover as to the perfect saint, and only he who understands it can lift romance into prophecy and make beauty holy. Their paradise, Tir-nan-og, the Land of the Living Heart, the Grass Green Island of Apples, call it what you will, created that religion of the muses which gave the arts to the world; and those countries whose traditions are fullest of it, and of the sanctity of places, may yet remould romance till it has become a covenant between intellectual beauty and the beauty of the world. We cannot know how many these countries are until the new science of folklore and the almost new science of mythology have done their work; but Ireland, if she can awake again the but half-forgotten legends of Slieve Gullion, or of Cruachmagh, or of the hill where Maeve is buried, and make them an utterance of that desire to be at rest amid ideal perfection which is becoming conscious in the minds of poets as the good citizen wins the priests over to his side; or if she can make us believe that the beautiful things that move us to awe, white lilies among dim shadows, windy twilights over grey sands, dewy and silent places among hazel trees by still waters, are in truth, and not in phantasy alone, the symbols, or the dwellings, of immortal presences, she will have begun a change that, whether it is begun in our time or not for centuries, will some day make all lands holy lands again.

Ireland has no great wealth, no preoccupation with successful persons to turn her writers' eyes to any lesser destiny. Even the poetry which had its form and much of its matter from alien thought dwelt, as the Gaelic ballads had done before it, on ideas living in the perfection of hope, on visions of unfulfilled desire, and not on the sordid compromise of success. The popular poetry of England celebrates her victories, but the popular poetry of Ireland remembers only defeats and defeated persons. A ballad that is in every little three-penny and sixpenny ballad book asks if Ireland has no pride in her Lawrences[14] and Wellingtons, and answers that these belong to the Empire and not to Ireland, whose 'heart beats high' for men who died in exile or in prison; and this ballad is a type of all. The popular poetry, too, has made love of the earth of Ireland so much a part of her literature that it should not be a hard thing to fill it with the holiness of places. Politics are, indeed, the forge in which nations are made, and the smith has been so long busy making Ireland according to His will that she may well have some important destiny. But whether this is so or not, whether this destiny is to make her in the arts, as she is in politics, a voice of the idealism of the common people, who still remember the dawn of the world, or to give her an unforeseen history, it can but express the accidents and energies of her past, and criticism does its natural work in trying to prophesy this expression; and, even if it is mistaken, a prophecy is not always made all untrue by being unfulfilled. A few years will decide if the writers of Ireland are to shape themselves in our time for the fulfilment of this prophecy, for need and much discussion will bring a new national agreement, and the political tumult awake again.

---

1   That is, before the fall of Parnell. It was Yeats's belief that the fall of Parnell released the imagination of Ireland and enabled therefore the rise of literature to occur.
2   Thomas Campbell (1777–1844), Scottish poet, author of war poems such as 'Ye Mariners of England' and of more substantive works such as *The Pleasures of Hope* (1799) and *Gertrude of Wyoming* (1809). Thomas Babington Macaulay (1800–59) was an influential critic and historian and author of *The Lays of Ancient Rome* (1842).
3   Pierre Jean de Béranger (1780–1857) was a French lyric poet who fitted his verse to popular melodies.
4   This society, which was formed in 1892, met in London; the National Literary Society was formed in the same year and met in Dublin.
5   Robert Emmet (1778–1803) was leader of an abortive Rising in 1803. I think Owen Roe is Eoghan Rua Ó Súilleabháin (1748–84), a Gaelic poet from Kerry whose songs were sung all over the province of Munster (south west Ireland). Patrick Sarsfield (?1655–93) was leader of the Jacobite forces who defended Limerick in 1690. After the Treaty of Limerick in 1691 he led his troops to France.
6   Lines from 'Happy It Is' from Hyde's *Love Songs of Connacht* (1893). Yeats cites the literal prose translation.
7   Lines from Hyde's adaptation of 'O Maurya'.
8   Antoine Raifteараí (Anthony Raftery) (1779–1835), a blind Gaelic poet who was much admired by Yeats and Lady Gregory. For versions of this song and the one that follows, see Lady Gregory's translations in her *Poets and Dreamers* (1903).
9   Thoor Ballylee, an Anglo-Norman tower on the borders of Counties Clare and Galway, and close to Lady Gregory's Coole Park, was eventually purchased by Yeats

in 1917. Raftery's tribute to Mary Hynes is recalled by Yeats in his poem 'The Tower': 'A peasant girl commended by a song.'

10   They should have said, 'God bless her,' so that their admiration might not give the fairies power over her. [AN]

11   Medb, Queen of Connacht and wife of Ailill, features prominently in the epic of the *Táin Bó Cuailgne* (Cattle Raid of Cooley). According to legend, she is buried beneath the cairn (or stones) at the top of Knocknarea, the mountain overlooking the town of Sligo.

12   The phrase is from Blake's letter to William Hayley dated 6 May 1800. 'The Ruins of Time build Mansions in Eternity.'

13   Nora Hopper (1871–1906), author of *Ballads in Prose* (1894). The lines are from 'Daluan' (sic).

14   A reference probably to John Lawrence (1811–79), a Protestant from County Antrim, who played a leading role in the establishment of government in the Punjab, helped the British win the 1857–8 war, and was later appointed Viceroy. Lines from the ballad are quoted by Hyde on p. 3.

GEORGE RUSSELL (Æ)
from George Russell, *Imaginations and Reveries* (1899; 2nd edition, 1921)

Again try and summarize the two paths — nationality or cosmopolitanism — that are outlined here. What distinguishes Russell's position from that of his contemporaries? Alternatively, what does Russell bring to the debate about nationality?

Nationality or Cosmopolitanism

As one of those who believe that the literature of a country is for ever creating a new soul among its people, I do not like to think that literature with us must follow an inexorable law of sequence, and gain a spiritual character only after the bodily passions have grown weary and exhausted themselves. In the essay called 'The Autumn of the Body',[1] Mr Yeats seems to indicate such a sequence. Yet, whether the art of any of the writers of the decadence does really express spiritual things is open to doubt. The mood in which their work is conceived, a distempered emotion, through which no new joy quivers, seems too often to tell rather of exhausted vitality than of the ecstasy of a new life. However much, too, their art refines itself, choosing ever rarer and more exquisite forms of expression, underneath it all an intuition seems to disclose only the old wolfish lust, hiding itself beneath the golden fleece of the spirit. It is not the spirit breaking through corruption, but the life of the senses longing to shine with the light which makes saintly things beautiful: and it would put on the jewelled raiment of seraphim, retaining still a heart of clay smitten through and through with the unappeasable desire of the flesh: so Rossetti's women, who have around them all the circumstance of poetry and romantic beauty, seem through their sucked-in lips to express a thirst which could be allayed in no spiritual

paradise. Art in the decadence in our time might by symbolized as a crimson figure undergoing a dark crucifixion: the hosts of light are overcoming it, and it is dying filled with anguish and despair at a beauty it cannot attain. All these strange emotions have a profound psychological interest. I do not think because a spiritual flaw can be urged against a certain phase of life that it should remain unexpressed. The psychic maladies which attack all races when their civilization grows old must needs be understood to be dealt with: and they cannot be understood without being revealed in literature or art. But in Ireland we are not yet sick with this sickness. As psychology it concerns only the curious. Our intellectual life is in suspense. The national spirit seems to be making a last effort to assert itself in literature and to overcome cosmopolitan influences and the art of writers who express a purely personal feeling. It is true that nationality may express itself in many ways: it may not be at all evident in the subject matter, but it may be very evident in the sentiment. But a literature loosely held together by some emotional characteristics common to the writers, however great it may be, does not fulfil the purpose of a literature or art created by a number of men who have a common aim in building up an overwhelming ideal — who create, in a sense, a soul for their country, and who have a common pride in the achievement of all. The world has not seen this since the great antique civilizations of Egypt and

Greece passed away. We cannot imagine an Egyptian artist daring enough to set aside the majestic attainment of many centuries. An Egyptian boy as he grew up must have been over-awed by the national tradition, and have felt that it was not to be set aside: it was beyond his individual rivalry. The soul of Egypt incarnated in him, and, using its immemorial language and its mysterious lines, the efforts of the least workman who decorated a tomb seem to have been directed by the same hand that carved the Sphinx. This adherence to a traditional form is true of Greece, though to a less extent. Some little Tanagra terra-cottas might have been fashioned by Phidias, and in literature Ulysses and Agamemnon were not the heroes of one epic, but appeared endlessly in epic and drama. Since the Greek civilization no European nation has had an intellectual literature which was genuinely national. In the present century, leaving aside a few things in outward circumstance, there is little to distinguish the work of the best English writers or artists from that of their Continental contemporaries. Millais, Leighton, Rossetti, Turner — how different from each other, and yet they might have painted the same pictures as born Frenchmen, and it would not have excited any great surprise as a marked divergence from French art. The cosmopolitan spirit, whether for good or for evil, is hastily obliterating all distinctions. What is distinctly national in these countries is less valuable than the immense wealth of universal ideas; and the writers who use this wealth appeal to no narrow circle: the foremost writers, the Tolstois and Ibsens, are conscious of addressing a European audience.

If nationality is to justify itself in the face of all this, it must be because the country which preserves its individuality does so with the profound conviction that its peculiar ideal is nobler than that which the cosmopolitan spirit suggests — that this ideal is so precious to it that its loss would be as the loss of the soul, and that it could not be realized without an aloofness from, if not an actual indifference to, the ideals which are spreading so rapidly over Europe. Is it possible for any nationality to make such a defence of its isolation? If not, let us read Goethe, Balzac, Tolstoi, men so much greater than any we can show, try to absorb their universal wisdom, and no longer confine ourselves to local traditions. But nationality was never so strong in Ireland as at the present time. It is beginning to be felt, less as a political movement than as a spiritual force. It seems to be gathering itself together, joining men who were hostile before, in a new intellectual fellowship: and if all these could unit on fundamentals, it would be possible in a generation to create a national ideal in Ireland, or rather to let that spirit incarnate fully which began among the ancient peoples, which has haunted the hearts and whispered a dim revelation of itself through the lips of the bards and peasant story tellers.

Every Irishman forms some vague ideal of his country, born from his reading of history, or from contemporary politics, or from imaginative intuition; and this Ireland in the mind it is, not the actual Ireland, which kindles his enthusiasm. For this he works and makes sacrifices; but because it has never had any philosophical definition or a supremely beautiful statement in literature which gathered all aspirations about it, the ideal remains vague. This passionate love cannot explain itself; it cannot make another understand its devotion. To reveal Ireland in clear and beautiful light, to create the Ireland in the heart, is the province of a national literature. Other arts would add to this ideal hereafter, and social life and politics must in the end be in harmony. We are yet before our dawn, in a period comparable to Egypt before the first of her solemn temples constrained its people to an equal mystery, or to Greece before the first perfect statue had fixed an ideal of beauty which mothers dreamed of to mould their yet unborn children. We can see, however, as the ideal of Ireland grows from mind to mind, it tends to assume the character of a sacred land. The Dark Rosaleen of Mangan[2] expresses an almost religious adoration, and to a later writer it seems to be nigher to the spiritual beauty than other lands:

And still the thoughts of Ireland brood
Upon her holy quietude.

The faculty of abstracting from the land their eyes beheld another Ireland through which they wandered in dream, has always been a characteristic of the Celtic poets. This inner Ireland which the visionary eye saw was the Tirnanoge, the Country of Immortal Youth, for they peopled it only with the young and beautiful. It was the Land of the Living Heart, a tender name which showed that it had become dearer than the heart of woman, and overtopped all other dreams as the last hope of the spirit, the bosom where it would rest after it had passed from the fading shelter of the world. And sure a strange and beautiful land this Ireland is, with a mystic beauty which closes the eyes of the body as in sleep, and opens the eyes of the spirit as in dreams; and never a poet has lain on our hillsides but gentle, stately figures, with hearts shining like the sun, move through his dreams, over radiant grasses, in an enchanted world of their own: and it has become alive through every haunted rath and wood and mountain and lake, so that we can hardly think of it otherwise than as the shadow of the thought of God. The last Irish poet who has appeared shows the spiritual qualities of the first, when he writes of the grey rivers in their 'enraptured' wanderings, and when he sees in the jewelled bow which arches the heavens:

The Lord's seven spirits that shine through the rain.

This mystical view of nature, peculiar to but one English poet, Wordsworth, is a national characteristic; and much in the creation of the Ireland in the mind is already done, and only needs retelling by the new writers. More important, however, for the literature we are imagining as an offset to the cosmopolitan ideal would be the creation of heroic figures, types, whether legendary or taken from history, and enlarged to epic proportions by our writers, who would use them in common, as Cuculain, Fionn, Ossian, and Oscar were used by the generations of poets who have left us the bardic history of Ireland, wherein one would write of the battle fury of a hero, and another of a moment when his fire would turn to gentleness, and another of his love for some beauty of his time, and yet another tell how the rivalry of a spiritual beauty made him tire of love; and so from iteration and persistent dwelling on a few heroes, their imaginative images found echoes in life, and other heroes arose, continuing their tradition of chivalry.

That such types are of the highest importance, and have the most ennobling influence on a country, cannot be denied. It was this idea led Whitman to exploit himself as the typical American. He felt that what he termed a 'stock personality' was needed to elevate and harmonize the incongruous human elements in the States. English literature has always been more sympathetic with actual beings than with ideal types, and cannot help us much. A man who loves Dickens, for example, may grow to have a great tolerance for the grotesque characters which are the outcome of the social order in England, but he will not be assisted in the conception of a higher humanity: and this is true of very many English writers who lack a fundamental philosophy, and are content to take man as he seems to be for the moment, rather than as the pilgrim of eternity — as one who is flesh to-day but who may hereafter grow divine, and who may shine at last like the stars of the morning, triumphant among the sons of God.

Mr Standish O'Grady,[3] in his notable epic of Cuculain, was in our time the first to treat the Celtic tradition worthily. He has contributed one hero who awaits equal comrades, if indeed the tales of the Red Branch do not absorb the thoughts of many imaginative writers, and Cuculain remain the typical hero of the Gael, becoming to every boy who reads the story a revelation of what his own spirit is.

I know John Eglinton,[4] one of our most thoughtful writers, our first cosmopolitan, thinks that 'these ancient legends refuse to be taken out of their old environment'. But I believe that the tales which have been preserved for a hundred generations in the heart of the people must have had their power, because they had in them a core of eternal truth. Truth is not a thing of to-day or to-morrow. Beauty, heroism, and spirituality do not change like fashion, being the reflection of an unchanging spirit. The face of faces which looks at us through so many shifting shadows has never altered the form of its perfection since the face of man, made after its image, first looked back on its original:

For these red lips, with all their mournful pride,
  Troy passed away in one high funeral gleam,
    And Usna's children died.[5]

These dreams, antiquities, traditions, once actual, living, and historical, have passed from the world of sense into the world of memory and thought: and time, it seems to me, has not taken away from their power, nor made them more remote from sympathy, but has rather purified them by removing them from earth to heaven: from things which the eye can see and the ear can hear they have become what the heart ponders over, and are so much nearer, more familiar, more suitable for literary use than the day they were begotten. They have now the character of symbol, and, as symbol, are more potent than history. They have crept through veil after veil of the manifold nature of man; and now each dream, heroism, or beauty has laid itself nigh the divine power it represents, the suggestion of which made it first beloved: and they are ready for the use of the spirit, a speech of which every word has a significance beyond itself, and Deirdre is, like Helen, a symbol of eternal beauty, and Cuculain represents as much as Prometheus the heroic spirit, the redeemer in man.

In so far as these ancient traditions live in the memory of man, they are contemporary to us as much as electrical science: for the images which time brings now to our senses, before they can be used in literature, have to enter into exactly the same world of human imagination as the Celtic traditions live in. And their fitness for literary use is not there determined by their freshness but by their power of suggestion. Modern literature, where it is really literature and not book-making, grows more subjective year after year, and the mind has a wider range over time than the physical nature has. Many things live in it — empires which have never crumbled, beauty which has never perished, love whose fires have never waned: and, in this formidable competition for use in the artist's mind, to-day stands only its chance with a thousand days. To question the historical accuracy of the use of such memories is not a matter which can be rightly raised. The question is — do they express lofty things to the soul? If they do they have justified themselves.

I have written at some length on the two paths which lie before us, for we have arrived at a parting of ways. One path leads, and has already led many Irishmen, to obliterate all nationality from their work. The other path winds upward to a mountain-top of our own, which may be in the future the Mecca to which many worshippers will turn. To remain where we are as a people, indifferent to literature, to art, to ideas, wasting the precious gift of public spirit we possess so abundantly in the sordid political rivalries, without practical or ideal ends, is to justify those who have chosen the other path, and followed another star

than ours. I do not wish any one to infer from this a contempt for those who, for the last hundred years, have guided public opinion in Ireland. If they failed in one respect, it was out of a passionate sympathy for wrongs of which many are memories, thanks to them, and to them is due the creation of a force which may be turned in other directions, not without a memory of those pale sleepers to whom we may turn in thought, placing —

A kiss of fire on the dim brow of failure,
A crown upon her uncrowned head.

1   This essay, first published in the *Dublin Daily Express* in December 1898, can be found in W. B. Yeats, *Essays and Introductions* (1961).
2   A reference to James Clarence Mangan's poem 'Dark Rosaleen'.
3   See footnote 22, p. 22.
4   John Eglinton (1868–1961) was the pseudonym for W.K. Magee. Co-editor of *Dana* (1904–5), he was a prominent critic, author of *Bards and Saints* (1906), *Irish Literary Portraits* (1935), and *A Memoir of AE* (1935). His essay 'The De-Davisization of Irish Literature' (1906) is reproduced on p. 70.
5   Lines (with one missing) are from Yeats's poem 'The Rose of the World'.

JAMES CONNOLLY
from *Workers' Republic*, 22 July 1899

A clearly formulated statement on the use of violence by James Connolly (1868–1916), the revolutionary socialist who led the Irish Citizen Army into the Easter Rising seventeen years later and who was, according to Pearse writing in the besieged headquarters of the General Post Office on the Friday of Easter Week, 'the guiding brain of our resistance'. How do you respond to Connolly's argument? As a piece of historical research you might want to find out who constituted the '98 Executive Committee.

Physical Force in Irish Politics

Ireland occupies a position among the nations of the earth unique in a great variety of its aspects, but in no one particular is this singularity more marked than in the possession of what is known as a 'physical force party' — a party, that is to say, whose members are united upon no one point, and agree upon no single principle, except upon the use of physical force as the sole means of settling the dispute between the people

of this country and the governing power of Great Britain.

Other countries and other peoples have, from time to time, appealed to what the first French Revolutionists picturesquely described as the 'sacred right of insurrection', but in so appealing they acted under the inspiration of, and combated for, some great governing principle of political or social life upon which they, to a man, were in absolute agreement. The latter-day high falutin 'hillside'[1] man, on the other hand, exalts into a principle that which the revolutionists of other countries have looked upon as a weapon, and in his gatherings prohibits all discussion of those principles which formed the main strength of his proto-types elsewhere and made the successful use of that weapon possible. Our people have glided at different periods of the past century from moral force agitation, so-called, into physical force rebellion, from constitutionalism into insurrectionism, meeting in each the same failure and the same disaster and yet seem as far as ever from learning the great truth that neither method is ever likely to be successful until they first insist that a perfect agreement *upon the end to be attained* should be arrived at as a starting-point of all our efforts.

To the reader unfamiliar with Irish political history such a remark seems to savour almost of foolishness, its truth is so apparent; but to the reader acquainted with the inner workings of the political movements of this country the remark is pregnant with the deepest meaning. Every revolutionary effort in Ireland has drawn the bulk of its adherents from the ranks of the disappointed followers of defeated constitutional movements. After having exhausted their constitutional efforts in striving to secure such a modicum of political power as would justify them to their own consciences in taking a place as loyal subjects of the British Empire, they, in despair, turned to thoughts of physical force as a means of attaining their ends. Their conception of what constitutes freedom was in no sense changed or revolutionized; they still believed in the political form of freedom which had been their ideal in their constitutional days; but no longer hoping for it from the acts of the British Parliament, they swung over into the ranks of the 'physical force' men as the only means of attaining it.

The so-called physical force movement of today in like manner bases its hopes upon the disgust of the people over the failure of the Home Rule movement; it seeks to enlist the people under its banners, not so much by pointing out the base ideals of the constitutionalists or the total inadequacy of their pet measures to remedy the evils under which the people suffer, as by emphasizing the greater efficacy of physical force as a national weapon. Thus, the one test of an advanced Nationalist is, in their opinion, one who believes in physical force. It may be the persons so professing to believe are Republicans; it may be they are believers in monarchy; it may be that Home Rule would satisfy them; it may be that they despise Home Rule. No matter what their political faith may be, if only they are prepared to express belief in the saving grace of physical force, they are acclaimed as advanced Nationalists — worthy descendants of the 'the men of

'98'. The '98 Executive,[2] organized in the commencement by professed believers in the physical force doctrine, started by proclaiming its adherence to the principle of national independence 'as understood by Wolfe Tone and the United Irishmen', and in less than twelve months from doing so, deliberately rejected a similar resolution and elected on its governing body men notorious for their Royalist proclivities. As the '98 Executive represents the advanced Nationalists of Ireland, this repudiation of the Republican faith of the United Irishmen is an interesting corroboration of the truth of our statement that the advanced Nationalists of our day are utterly regardless of principle and only attach importance to methods — an instance of putting the cart before the horse, absolutely unique in its imbecility and unparalleled in the history of the world.

It may be interesting, then, to place before our readers the Socialist Republican conception of the functions and uses of physical force in a popular movement. We neither exalt it into a principle nor repudiate it as something not to be thought of. Our position towards it is that the use or non-use of force for the realization of the ideas of progress always has been and always will be determined by the attitude, not of the party of progress, but of the governing class opposed to that party. If the time should arrive when the party of progress finds its way to freedom barred by the stubborn greed of a possessing class entrenched behind the barriers of law and order; if the party of progress has indoctrinated the people at large with the new revolutionary conception of society and is therefore representative of the will of a majority of the nation; if it has exhausted all the peaceful means at its disposal for the purpose of demonstrating to the people and their enemies that the new revolutionary ideas do possess the suffrage of the majority; then, but not till then, the party which represents the revolutionary idea is justified in taking steps to assume the powers of government, and in using the weapons of force to dislodge the usurping class or government in possession, and treating its members and supporters as usurpers and rebels against the constituted authorities always have been treated. In other words, Socialists believe that the question of force is of very minor importance; the really important question is of the principles upon which is based the movement that may or may not need the use of force to realize its object.

Here, then, is the immense difference between the Socialist Republicans and our friends the physical force men. The latter, by stifling all discussions of principles, earn the passive and fleeting commendation of the unthinking multitude; the former, by insisting upon a thorough understanding of their basic principles, do not so readily attract the multitude, but do attract and hold the more thoughtful amongst them. It is the difference betwixt a mob in revolt and an army in preparation. The mob who cheer a speaker referring to the hopes of a physical force movement would, in the very hour of apparent success, be utterly disorganized and divided by the passage through the British Legislature of any trumpery Home Rule Bill. The army of class-conscious workers organizing under the banner of the Socialist Republican Party, strong in their knowledge of economic truth and firmly grounded in their revolutionary principles, would remain entirely unaffected by any such manoeuvre and, knowing it would not change their position as a subject class, would still press forward, resolute and undivided, with their faces set towards their only hope of emancipation — the complete control by the working-class democracy of *all the powers of National Government.*

Thus the policy of the Socialist Republicans is seen to be the only wise one. 'Educate that you may be free'; principles first, methods afterwards. If the advocacy of physical force failed to achieve success or even to effect an uprising when the majority were unenfranchised and the secret ballot unknown, how can it be expected to succeed now that the majority are in possession of voting power and the secret ballot safeguards the voter?

The ballot-box was given us by our masters for their purpose; let us use it for our own. Let us demonstrate at that ballot-box the strength and intelligence of the revolutionary idea; let us make the hustings a rostrum from which to promulgate our principles; let us grasp the public powers in the interest of the disinherited class; let us emulate our fathers and, like the 'true men of '98', place ourselves in line with the most advanced thought of our age, and drawing inspiration and hope from the spectacle presented by the world-wide revolt of the workers, prepare for the coming of the day when the Socialist working class of Ireland will, through its elected representatives, present its demand for freedom from the yoke of a governing master class or nation — the day on which the question of moral or physical force shall be finally decided.

1 Hillsiders was a term applied to Fenians in the late nineteenth century.
2 This was the organizing committee established to commemorate the centenary of the 1798 Rising.

ANONYMOUS
from *Irish Literary Society Gazette*, March 1899

These minutes of a meeting of the Irish Literary Society in London convey a vivid picture of Yeats's struggles to establish a new kind of Irish drama. Among those present in the audience were his father, John Butler Yeats, and his sister, Lily, D. P. Moran, Alfred Graves, the anthologist of Irish songs, author of 'Father O'Flynn', and father of Robert Graves. The English man of letters Edmund Gosse chaired the meeting and the less than enthusiastic vote of thanks was proposed by John Todhunter, author of *A Sicilian Idyll* (1890).

Lecture by Mr W. B. Yeats

A most interesting lecture on the 'Ideal Theatre', with special reference to the Irish Literary Theatre, was delivered on the evening of Saturday, April 23rd, by Mr W. B. Yeats, to the Irish Literary Society in the hall of the Society of Arts, Adelphi.

Mr Edmund Gosse presided and the members present were:– Miss Patricia Dillon, Mr J. B. Yeats, Miss Lilly Yeats, Miss S. Mitchell, Miss Fannie J. Mason, Miss A. M. O'Dwyer, Miss T. Dempsey, Mr Alfred P. Graves, Mrs A. H. Wheeler, Miss E. D. Bertram, Miss MacMahon, Mr Wm. Coates and Mrs Coates, Mr Frank MacDonagh, Miss A. Butler, Mrs E.

Aylmer Gowing, Miss F. Lynch, Miss A. Lynch, Mr E. E. Brennan, Mrs Dora Sigerson Shorter, Dr J. Todhunter, Mr F. Norreys Connell, Mrs A. Rushton, Miss E. Drury, Miss J. Buchanan, Miss C. M. Reburn, Mr A. Lucy, Mr Rickard M. J. Burke, Miss Evelyn Gleeson, Mr Nicholas P. H. Murphy, Mr J. F. McNamara, Mr Whittington Howley, Mr W. P. Ryan, Miss Katie Hayes, Miss E. T. Phelan, Mr D. P. Moran, Mr Edward Mooney, Miss N. G. Feeney, Miss E. D'Esterre-Keeling, Mr J. R. Cox and Mrs Cox, Miss G. L. Griffin, Mr J. W. Molloy, Mr Hubert J. Sweeney, Mr C. J. Kilgallin, Miss H. M. Madden, Mr D. Lehane, Mr J. MacMahon, Mr W. Boyle, Miss E. Breen, Miss Ethel Wheeler, Miss M. Hayes, Miss M. Fitzpatrick, Mr J. A. O'Sullivan, Mr P. H. MacEnery, Miss B. M. O'Reilly.

Mr Yeats said most of them were aware that they were getting up in Dublin, next month, a series of performances. From the 8th of May they would have a week, during which would be performed two plays — one by Mr Edward Martyn,[1] and one of his own. He could not ask them to listen to what he had to say if their programme simply ended with those plays, for certainly he did not wish to push his own wares. He hoped if they had the slightest welcome at all, they would go on next year and the year after, until gradually the people who cared for the particular kind of thing offered would come to hear of them. They proposed to give next year a play upon an Irish subject by the great Spanish dramatist, Calderon, translated by Denis Florence MacCarthy. They could also promise a romantic drama by Mr Standish O'Grady, whom he had for years thought to have a great dramatic capacity, and a play by Miss Fiona MacLeod. They had elected to give their plays in the Antient Concert Rooms in Dublin rather than in any big theatre. A year ago when they began inquiries they found that the expenses of the ordinary theatre would be so considerable that they could not hope to succeed unless they got the ordinary crowd of people, and unless they were able to please very much the average man. By going to a small hall they had reduced their expenses enormously, and they would be able to succeed by joining to them the exceptional man — he did not mean the man of any class or the man who read books, though he meant principally the man who reads and who loves the old Irish legends. There were a certain number of those men in Ireland, as elsewhere, and he believed they would get them in sufficient numbers and finally make the experiment pay its expenses. The scenery and costumes would be simple and inexpensive, the actors would be professional, and good actors, and he thought it would be found that their performances

would be vigorous and harmonious. Passing to the subject of the lecture proper, he said there was some hope that the ideal theatre might come about in time. First of all, they must remember that Ireland was not a country of great towns. Ireland, like ancient Greece, was a country of scattered population, and he thought that by working together with the musical festival in Dublin ('the Feis') and with the Gaelic language movement there might grow up every spring about the time of the old festival of Beltaine[2] a national, perhaps he should say a racial, festival, where they would have a sufficient number of people who were enthusiastic and sympathetic in those Celtic things to make it possible for the little theatre with its limited resources to gradually grow up to a theatre of sufficiently large resources for them all to be thinking seriously about what was the ideal theatre. The theatre of Scandinavia was the nearest approach to an ideal theatre in modern Europe. It was the only theatre whose plays were at once literary and popular. Elsewhere one never saw a literary play upon the stage unless it was old enough to be a superstition or had been produced by some Association of men of letters. It was only in the middle of this century that a rare and exceptional enthusiasm made it possible for the average Norwegian to understand great and sincere drama. Between 1840 and 1860 there arose a national literary movement in Norway founded like ours upon the old legends and the folk songs and the folk traditions of the country. Like ours, too, it had to conquer the opposition of a cosmopolitan and denationalized class. A semi-amateur theatre was founded in Bergen, under the management of Ibsen, when 23, and later on a Norwegian theatre, as it was called, was founded in Christiania under the same management. Ibsen and Bjornson, respectively vice-president and president of the Scandinavian Society, a Society with the same objects as the society he was now addressing, warred against the cosmopolitan drama, and with so much success that a famous Danish actor left the stage in disgust, and another was hissed off it. He knew well that neither Mr Martyn nor himself nor any of the writers who have promised plays could claim to be Ibsens or Bjornsons, but they might follow in the way those great men had gone, and in all humility. Heroic ideas and interest in great passions spread abroad among the mass of the people, and the only condition of the drama was at once literary and popular. The ordinary man disliked to take trouble, disliked having to think and to feel in new ways. He disliked the heroic and unadorned sincerity of a play like *Ghosts* or the *Wild Duck*, as much as he disliked the unfamiliar magnificence of plays like *Peer*

Gynt or the *Heroes of Heligoland*. But let a whole people be touched by an intensity, and they would share in the creative impulse of the poets, and every kind of great drama would spring up. Civilization unchecked by this rare and exceptional enthusiasm killed great drama by teaching people to live upon the surface, to seek easy pleasures, and to meditate little. The actor who spoke his lines like something out of the newspaper drove out that art of oratory which the stage inherited from the rhapsodists. If we were to restore drama to the stage — poetic drama, at any rate — our actors must become rhapsodists again, and keep the rhythm of the verse as the first of their endeavours. The music of a voice should seem more important than the expression of face or the movement of hands, for poetry spoken as prose, spoken without music, as the performance of Mr Swinburne's 'Loch Ryne' the other day, sounded like bad, florid prose. The conception of the drama had changed like the conception of acting. The modern drama was all action, the ancient drama was all words about action. Nothing at all happened in many of the greatest of Greek plays, and it was Hamlet's soliloquies and not his duel that were of the chief importance in the play. Even in life itself the dramatic moments were those that were inseparable from splendid and appropriate words. The object of the drama was to be a revelation of lofty and heroic life, whether in the mind of the writer alone, as with the great realists, or in the persons that move before one upon the stage, as with the Greek dramatists. It had, therefore, but a passing moment for all but a few imaginative natures. They would, therefore, do their part, according to their limited power, in building up in Ireland a dramatic tradition that would remember the purpose of drama in the world, and they threw themselves upon the national literary movement that they might have an audience. (Applause.)

Dr Todhunter, in proposing a vote of thanks to the lecturer, said that he sympathized with some of Mr Yeats's heresies. (Laughter.) He had not read Mr Martyn's work, but he had read *The Countess Kathleen*, and he considered it would be extremely difficult to put it on the stage in any way. It was not that a poetical play of the kind might not be sympathetically given by sympathetic actors; but to produce it adequately the actors would require a special training for about a year. How Mr Yeats was going to get the actors — who, he believed, were to be English and not Irish — to give perfect form to this play of *Countess Kathleen* he did not know. Mr Yeats began at the beginning of drama — that was to say, a drama which was really chiefly lyrical. He thought that was

the right way to begin such a movement; but he did not think that the purely lyrical drama was the greatest drama. With regard to the way of putting on the stage plays which were lyrical in character, he thought the great point was to give up all idea of realistic scenery. The experiment was tried at a theatre in London, when Maeterlinck's *Pelleas and Melisande* was performed with scenery of the simplest character. To him it was one of the most intensely interesting performances he had ever seen. It was done by a French company, who gave the speeches most beautifully. When he saw the same play produced at the Lyceum by Forbes Robertson with all the adjuncts of stage craft it had not for him anything like the charm of the other performance with the perfectly simple scenery.

Mr Norreys Connell seconded the vote of thanks. He did not think that Mr Yeats's idea of the theatre could ever successfully appeal to the people for support, and as a modern imitation of the old theatre it seemed impossible. (Applause.)

Mr Clement Shorter said that everyone, whatever his nationality, must wish the utmost possible success to the scheme which Mr Yeats had at heart. (Hear, hear.) It was really a matter not so much of being zealous in Ireland to produce a play which should have certain touches of Irish romance in it, but of writing in English to capture the whole English-speaking world upon lines that were strictly Irish. (Hear, hear.) The more popular Mr Yeats's plays were the greater would be the success of the Irish theatre movement, for the plays would be performed not only in Ireland, but in England, in America, and the Colonies. He did not think that mere attempts to appeal to a limited audience was the way in which Mr Yeats could render the largest and most thorough service to the country which he loved so well. (Applause.)

Miss D'Esterre-Keeling, Mr Edward Mooney and Mr H. Sweeney also joined in the discussion, and dissented from the lecturer's views.

The Chairman ventured to join issue with Mr Yeats in the illustration that he gave with regard to the Norwegian theatre. In the first place, there was an element, if he might put it so, of the fairy tale in Mr Yeats's picturesque and charming account of the birth of the Norwegian Theatre. (Laughter.) Mr Yeats represented Ibsen as sweeping away cosmopolitan drama and starting with Saga drama. As a matter of fact Ibsen during the period mentioned produced an enormous quantity of cosmopolitan plays — Danish, Swedish, and German, and even French vaudevilles and farces. It was on the basis of the practical stage and its requirements that Ibsen built up the drama which was such an extraordinary exemplification of his own individuality. If Mr Yeats represented his ideal theatre more or less on the lines of the national Norwegian theatre he must not forget the commercial play, because it was on the commercial play in the very fullest sense that the present national theatre of Norway was based. But they all knew exactly what Mr Yeats meant, and they all sympathized with him. Mr Yeats meant to call them back from the base sense of animalism and commercialism to what was noble and dignified in the art of drama. He shared with some of those who had spoken a certain scepticism as to whether the scheme suggested by Mr Yeats was really the practical mode of carrying out the idea. As to the question of chanting dramatic verse, he thought, with Dr Todhunter, that that should be confined solely to the primitive forms of lyrical drama. There was a country where it had been used from immemorial times, Persia, where the purely lyrical drama was habitually performed by actors who chanted slowly in recitative to appropriate music, and that he believed was what Mr Yeats would be glad to see. He could not conceive of a drama in which comedy did not exist. There were many things they had not got; they had not got tragedy, except bastard melodrama; but

comedy they had as purely, as exquisitely, as it had ever been except in the palmiest days of the seventeenth century. He could not but think that a people saturated with humour like the Irish would feel it to be a very imperfect thing if an ideal theatre were given them in which there was no room found for comedy. (Hear, hear, and applause.)

Mr Yeats, in returning thanks for the vote of thanks, said one of the missions of the drama was to mould and perfect national feeling. They would have no chance of success in Dublin but for national feeling. The people would be offered plays that would put before them the life, the ideals, and the legends of Ireland, and the people would come to see that which they would not find anywhere else.

A vote of thanks to the Chairman concluded the proceedings.

1   Edward Martyn (1859–1923), a Catholic landowner, was co-founder with Yeats and Lady Gregory of the Irish Literary Theatre. His play *The Heather Field* was performed with Yeats's *The Countess Cathleen* at the Antient Concert Rooms in Dublin in May 1899.
2   Bealtaine was the Celtic May festival; Samhain, the autumn festival. Yeats used both names for titles to different literary journals.

OSCAR WILDE
from C.3.3. [Oscar Wilde], *The Ballad of Reading Gaol* (1899)

The 'In Memoriam' notice at the beginning of the first edition of *The Ballad of Reading Gaol* is dedicated to C.T.W., Charles Thomas Wooldridge, a Trooper in the Royal House Guards who was hanged at Reading Gaol in July 1896 for the murder of his wife. On the title page the author's name is given as prisoner C.3.3., followed by Oscar Wilde's name in square brackets. The stark asceticism of the edition is further emphasized by printing on the right hand page only, leaving the verso blank. Gone in this extract from the poem is Wilde's lightness of mood, replaced by one more suited to his emblematic status as a homosexual Irishman in an English gaol. But he is still able to make his points and to move us by the plight of all prisoners. Here at the beginning of the *Reader* I have chosen such an extract as a reminder that imprisonment is an ongoing theme in modern Irish writing and that Oscar Fingal O'Flahertie Wills Wilde has something intelligent and awful to say about it. There is a remarkable scene in Jack Callahan's *Man's Grim Justice* (1929), a little-known autobiography about the criminal son of a Boston Irish immigrant. While serving a sentence for safe-blowing in the Connecticut State Prison at Wethersfield, Callahan watches a fellow inmate hang, accompanying him into the execution chamber, talking with the executioners while the priest heard the man's confession. For a month afterwards a distraught Callahan kept hearing Wilde's lines: 'They hanged him as a beast is hanged; / They did not even toll / A requiem that might have brought / Rest to his startled soul; / But hurriedly they took him out, / And hid him in a hole.' For another point of connection see the extract from Darrell Figgis's *A Chronicle of Jails* (1917), p. 242.

from THE BALLAD OF READING GAOL

V

I know not whether Laws be right,
  Or whether Laws be wrong;
All that we know who lie in gaol
  Is that the wall is strong;
And that each day is like a year,
  A year whose days are long.

But this I know, that every Law
  That men have made for Man,
Since first Man took his brother's life,
  And the sad world began,
But straws the wheat and saves the chaff
  With a most evil fan.

This too I know — and wise it were
  If each could know the same —
That every prison that men build
  Is built with bricks of shame,
And bound with bars lest Christ should see
  How men their brothers maim.

With bars they blur the gracious moon,
  And blind the goodly sun:
And they do well to hide their Hell,
  For in it things are done
That Son of God nor son of Man
  Ever should look upon!

The vilest deeds like poison weeds
  Bloom well in prison-air:
It is only what is good in Man
  That wastes and withers there:
Pale Anguish keeps the heavy gate,
  And the Warder is Despair.

For they starve the little frightened child
  Till it weeps both night and day:
And they scourge the weak, and flog the fool,
  And gibe the old and gray,
And some grow mad, and all grow bad,
  And none a word may say.

Each narrow cell in which we dwell
  Is a foul and dark latrine,
And the fetid breath of living Death
  Chokes up each grated screen,
And all, but Lust, is turned to dust
  In Humanity's machine.

The brackish water that we drink
  Creeps with a loathsome slime,
And the bitter bread they weigh in scales
  Is full of chalk and lime,
And Sleep will not lie down, but walks
  Wild-eyed, and cries to Time.

But though lean Hunger and green Thirst
  Like asp with adder fight,
We have little care of prison fare,
  For what chills and kills outright
Is that every stone one lifts by day
  Becomes one's heart by night.

With midnight always in one's heart,
  And twilight in one's cell,
We turn the crank, or tear the rope,
  Each in his separate Hell,
And the silence is more awful far
  Than the sound of a brazen bell.

And never a human voice comes near
  To speak a gentle word:
And the eye that watches through the door
  Is pitiless and hard:
And by all forgot, we rot and rot,
  With soul and body marred.

And thus we rust Life's iron chain
  Degraded and alone:
And some men curse, and some men weep,
  And some men make no moan:
But God's eternal Laws are kind
  And break the heart of stone.

And every human heart that breaks,
   In prison-cell or yard,
Is as that broken box that gave
   Its treasure to the Lord,
And filled the unclean leper's house
   With the scent of costliest nard.

Ah! happy they whose hearts can break
   And peace of pardon win!
How else may man make straight his plan
   And cleanse his soul from Sin?
How else but through a broken heart
   May Lord Christ enter in?

And he of the swollen purple throat,
   And the stark and staring eyes,
Waits for the holy hands that took

   The Thief to Paradise;
And a broken and a contrite heart
   The Lord will not despise.

The man in red who reads the Law
   Gave him three weeks of life,
Three little weeks in which to heal
   His soul of his soul's strife,
And cleanse from every blot of blood
   The hand that held the knife.

And with tears of blood he cleansed the hand,
   The hand that held the steel:
For only blood can wipe out blood,
   And only tears can heal:
And the crimson stain that was of Cain
   Became Christ's snow-white seal.

IRISH WRITING IN THE 1900s

It is better any day to have the row we had last night, than to have your play fizzling out in half-hearted applause. Now we'll be talked about. We're an event in the history of the Irish stage.

I have a splitting headache, and worse luck I have to go in and talk business with Lady Gregory half the day. She got an important wire from Yeats, so she came up in a hurry last night and we have to talk today. There is nothing new, only details of what we had on hand before. If I get an opportunity I think I'll tell her about us.

Dearest treasure you dont [know] how you have changed the world to me. Now that I have you I dont care twopence for what anyone else in the world may say or do. You are my whole world to me now, you that is, and the little shiney new moon, and the flowers of the earth.

My little love how I am wrapped up in you! It went to my heart to desert you last night but I could not get away from Lady Gregory. There is the quarter to eleven bell ringing! That is usually my signal to put on my shoes and start for our walk. It goes through me. Perhaps we may get a walk tomorrow, or in any case on Tuesday. Now the P.B. [*The Playboy of the Western World*] is off we are more our own masters, thank Heaven, though I have still an article to get written before Feb. 1st. I am starving God help me. Now good bye my own soul, till tomorrow. I would take this and put it into your post box, but I dont know which it is. I suppose if I wire to you tomorrow morning you could come down the quarter to two to Bray and have a little walk. I may be too busy of course or too unwell.

Goodbye again
Your old Tramp

– Synge's letter to Maire O'Neill, 27 January 1907
– from Anne Saddlemyer (ed.), *Letters to Molly: John Millington Synge to Maire O'Neill* (1971)

CRITICAL AND DOCUMENTARY

STANDISH JAMES O'GRADY
from *All Ireland Review*, 17 February 1900

In *The Crisis in Ireland* (1882) and *Toryism and Tory Democracy* (1886) O'Grady (1846–1928) called on Irish landlords to assert their power and re-establish between master and men 'the feudal feeling', but without success. In 1896 there was another period of heightened political agitation over the excessive tax burden, when, according to O'Grady in *All Ireland* (1898), the Catholic people of Ireland called on their Protestant aristocracy 'to come out from their retirement into public life and lead them in the financial war'. Here in this extract the Irish Carlyle calls on all the people of Ireland – for they are now the future, not the landlords – to awaken from the enchantment that afflicts them.

The Great Enchantment

I have been asked by a good friend and high-spirited and public-spirited fellow-countryman, to embark myself and this *All Ireland Review* in a certain political propaganda, which, I confess, seems to have everything in its favour, and which ought not to give offence to any intelligent order or interest in this country. My friend's intention is to awaken the mind of the people of Ireland — all classes — to the enormous intra-Imperial power which is ours under the Act of Union, a power which is doubled and trebled in its efficiency by the party system according to which the Empire is administered by one or other of two great parties, either of which will do wrong things for votes; and may be surely relied upon to do things right and just in themselves and conducive to the interests of the Empire in return for the enormous political support which under the Constitution, and in accordance with the Act of Union, we, at all times, are able to furnish to that Imperial British Party which will most intelligently and most sympathetically carry into effect — in legislation and administration — the purposes which we have in view. Such amongst many others, all vital or important, are reform of the incidence of international taxation, the settlement of our land question, railway reform, educational ditto, further and more extended relief to the agricultural interests, etc., etc.

The suggested propaganda would also direct the attention of our people as the possessors and inheritors of such a mighty intra-Imperial power to our Irish duties and responsibilities in the management, direction, and control of this common Anglo-Irish Empire — ours as much as any other's; perhaps more than any other's — for many reasons. The project would include, I presume, the displacement of the existing Irish Parliamentary representation, and its replacement by men of known probity, public spirit, and, perhaps, property; men, at all events, carefully and conscientiously chosen from all parts of Ireland, city and country, and from all interests, orders, and classes. The idea is admirable, but, I fear, only on paper. As for myself — some one has written, 'The passions must be held in reverence; they must not, they cannot, be excited at will.' Now, though others are made differently in this respect, I confess I could not go into politics myself save passionately, that is to say, when excited and inflamed by some matter of transcendent importance and of evident practicability. Though always a steady voter, and always forming an opinion, good or bad, about public questions as they arose, I never made but two incursions into politics in all my life. The first was in 1881 and 1882, when I thought our land question might be settled to the satisfaction of the people and without involving the destruction of our landed gentry; the other was at the end of '96, when I thought that a universal movement was on foot for a change of the incidence of Imperial taxation as it affects this country. On the first of these occasions we appointed a Committee of five eminent members of the landlord class to look after our interests, which Committee never sat and was never brought to an account for not sitting, and on the second we appointed twenty-five County Committees, not one of which ever sat. In my own county, our County Committee, which I supported by every means in my power, so far from actively concerning itself with the affairs of the country, could never manage even its own little financial relations with the business people of Kilkenny, and, down to date, has not liquidated its little debts.

Surely, we are a great people, and deserve to get on! Now, these ludicrous breaks-down, or whatever we must call them, these incredible lapses and aberrations, exhibited by a people not only as intelligent and spirited as the average, but more intelligent and spirited than the average, at the time of their occurrence only filled me with amazement and consternation. I had not then traced to its source all that folly, nor quite realized how it was the inevitable outcome and resultant of a cause operative, in different forms, through all our tragical history, nor did I connect it with a national fault, perhaps a national crime, which has checked our progress from century to century, which has brought about the destruction of aristocracy after aristocracy, and which bids fair, as I write, to involve us all in one common ruin, and leave this land free for the exploitation of tourist touts and commercial syndicates formed for the promotion of sport in waste countries. For, if things continue to go on as they are going to-day in Ireland, the bullock, which is now superseding the man, will be himself superseded by the wild beast and the wild bird which the British and American sporting plutocracy will pleasantly shoot and pleasantly pursue, sustained by a little host of Irish uniformed gillies, which, certainly, would be a rather dismal ending for this ancient and famous nation. And yet things are moving that way, steadily; sometimes, I think, inevitably.

In such a country, and dominated by such potent spells and enchantments, how can any man of understanding or self-respect take part in a political propaganda of any kind? Spells and enchantments of a kind so potent are not to be shaken off by words, no matter how eloquent. They will and can only be removed by shocks!

In the meantime I shall take no part in any propaganda, no matter how rational or promising such a propaganda may seem to be, not at least till some great tragedy, some overwhelming horror, perhaps some great deed, shall have startled this people out of the trance which now holds them, and which, sometimes, in more hopeful moments, I think, may have been laid upon them temporarily, and for reasons.

W. B. YEATS
from W. B. Yeats, *Ideas of Good and Evil* (1907)

This essay first appeared in *The Dome*, April 1900. Yeats's elusive subject matter is in part carried by his beguiling if equally elusive style. How do you think this extract belongs in a Reader in modern Irish writing?

from The Symbolism of Poetry

I

'Symbolism, as seen in the writers of our day, would have no value if it were not seen also, under one disguise or another, in every great imaginative writer,' writes Mr Arthur Symons in *The Symbolist Movement in Literature*, a subtle book which I cannot praise as I would, because it has been dedicated to me;' and he goes on to show how many profound writers have in the last few years sought for a philosophy of poetry in the doctrine of symbolism, and how even in countries where it is almost scandalous to seek for any philosophy of poetry, new writers are following them in their search. We do not know what the writers of ancient times talked of among themselves, and one bull is all that remains of Shakespeare's talk, who was on the edge of modern times; and the journalist is convinced, it seems, that they talked of wine and women and politics, but never about their art, or never quite seriously about their art. He is certain that no one, who had a philosophy of his art or a theory of how he should write, has ever made a work of art, that people have no imagination who do not write without forethought and afterthought as he writes his own articles. He says this with enthusiasm, because he has heard it at so many comfortable dinner-tables, where some one had mentioned through carelessness, or foolish zeal, a book whose difficulty had offended indolence, or a man who had not forgotten that beauty is an accusation. Those formulas and generalizations, in which a hidden sergeant has drilled the ideas of journalists and through them the ideas of all but all the modern world, have created in their turn a forgetfulness like that of soldiers in battle, so that journalists and their readers have forgotten, among many like events, that Wagner spent seven years arranging and explaining his ideas before he began his most characteristic music; that opera, and with it modern music, arose from certain talks at the house of one Giovanni Bardi of Florence; and that the Pleiade laid the foundations of modern French literature with a pamphlet. Goethe has said, 'a poet needs all philosophy, but he must keep it out of his work,' though that is not always necessary; and certainly he cannot know too much, whether about his own work, or about the procreant waters of the soul where the breath first moved, or about the waters under the earth that are the life of passing things; and almost certainly no great art, outside England, where journalists are more powerful and ideas less plentiful than elsewhere, has arisen without a great criticism, for its herald or its interpreter and protector, and it is perhaps for this reason that great art, now that vulgarity has armed itself and multiplied itself, is perhaps dead in England.

All writers, all artists of any kind, in so far as they have had any philosophical or critical power, perhaps just in so far as they have been deliberate artists at all, have had some philosophy, some criticism of their art; and it has often been this philosophy, or this criticism, that has evoked their most startling inspiration, calling into outer life some portion of the divine life, of the buried reality, which could alone extinguish in the emotions what their philosophy or their criticism would extinguish in the intellect. They have sought for no new thing, it may be, but only to understand and to copy the pure inspiration of early times, but because the divine life wars upon our outer life, and must needs change its weapons and its movements as we change ours, inspiration has come to them in beautiful startling shapes. The scientific movement brought with it a literature, which was always tending to lose itself in externalities of all kinds, in opinion, in declamation, in picturesque writing, in word-painting, or in what Mr Symons has called an attempt 'to build in brick and mortar inside the covers of a book'; and now writers have begun to dwell upon the element of evocation, of suggestion, upon what we call the symbolism in great writers.

II

In 'Symbolism in Painting'[2] I tried to describe the element of symbolism that is in pictures and sculpture, and described a little the symbolism in poetry, but did not describe at all the continuous indefinable symbolism which is the substance of all style.

There are no lines with more melancholy beauty than these by Burns —

The white moon is setting behind the white wave,
And Time is setting with me, O!

and these lines are perfectly symbolical. Take from them the whiteness of the moon and of the wave, whose relation to the setting of Time is too subtle for the intellect, and you take from them their beauty. But, when all are together, moon and wave and whiteness and setting Time and the last melancholy cry, they evoke an emotion which cannot be evoked by any other arrangement of colours and sounds and forms. We may call this metaphorical writing, but it is better to call it symbolical writing, because metaphors are not profound enough to be moving, when they are not symbols, and when they are symbols they are the most perfect, because the most subtle, outside of pure sound, and through them one can the best find out what symbols are. If one begins the reverie with any beautiful lines that one can remember, one finds they are all like those by Burns. Begin with this line by Blake —

The gay fishes on the wave when the moon sucks
    up the dew;

or these lines by Nash —

Brightness falls from the air,
Queens have died young and fair,
Dust hath closed Helen's eye;

or these lines by Shakespeare —

Timon hath made his everlasting mansion
Upon the beached verge of the salt flood;
Who once a day with his embossed froth
The turbulent surge shall cover;

or take some line that is quite simple, that gets its beauty from its place in a story, and see how it flickers with the light of the many symbols that have given the story its beauty, as a sword-blade may flicker with the light of burning towers.

All sounds, all colours, all forms, either because of their pre-ordained energies or because of long association, evoke indefinable and yet precise emotions, or, as I prefer to think, call down among us certain disembodied powers, whose footsteps over our hearts we call emotions; and when sound, and colour, and form are in a musical relation, a beautiful relation to one another, they become as it were one sound, one colour, one form, and evoke an emotion that is made out of their distinct evocations and yet is one emotion. The same relation exists between all portions of every work of art, whether it be an epic or a song, and the more perfect it is, and the more various and numerous the elements that have flowed into its perfection, the more powerful will be the emotion, the power, the god it calls among us. Because an emotion does not exist, or does not become perceptible and active among us, till it has found its expression, in colour or in sound or in form, or in all of these, and because no two modulations or arrangements of these evoke the same emotion, poets and painters and musicians, and in a less degree because their effects are momentary, day and night and cloud and shadow, are continually making and unmaking mankind. It is indeed only those things which seem useless or very feeble that have any power, and all those things that seem useful or strong, armies, moving wheels, modes of architecture, modes of government, speculations of the reason, would have been a little different if some mind long ago had not given itself to some emotion, as a woman gives herself to her lover, and shaped sounds or colours or forms, or all of these, into a musical relation, that their emotion might live in other minds. A little lyric evokes an emotion, and this emotion gathers others about it and melts into their being in the making of some great epic; and at last, needing an always less delicate body, or symbol, as it grows more powerful, it flows out, with all it has gathered, among the blind instincts of daily life, where it moves a power within powers, as one sees ring within ring in the stem of an old tree. This is maybe what Arthur O'Shaughnessy[3] meant when he made his poets say they had built Nineveh with their sighing; and I am certainly never certain, when I hear of some war, or of some religious excitement, or of some new manufacture, or of anything else that fills the ear of the world, that it has not all happened because of something that a boy piped in Thessaly. I remember once asking a seer to ask one among the gods who, as she believed, were standing about her in their symbolic bodies, what would come of a charming but seeming trivial labour of a friend, and the form answering, 'the devastation of peoples and the overwhelming of cities.' I doubt indeed if the crude circumstance of the world, which seems to create all our emotions, does more than reflect, as in multiplying mirrors, the emotions that have come to solitary men in moments of poetical contemplation; or that love itself would be more than an animal hunger but for the poet and his shadow the priest, for unless we believe that outer things are the reality, we must believe that the gross is the shadow of the subtle, that things are wise before they become foolish, and secret before they cry out in the market-place. Solitary men in moments of contemplation receive, as I think, the creative impulse from the lowest of the Nine Hierarchies, and so make and unmake mankind, and even the world itself, for does not 'the eye altering alter all'?

Our towns are copied fragments from our breast;
And all man's Babylons strive but to impart
The grandeurs of his Babylonian heart.[4]

1 *The Symbolist Movement in Literature* was first published in 1899 and was dedicated to Yeats, 'the chief representative of that movement in our country'. By 'that' Symons meant France, and by 'our' Britain and Ireland.
2 This essay was first published as an introduction to W.T. Horton, *A Book of Images* (1898).
3 Arthur O'Shaughnessy (1844–81), poet and naturalist. The reference is to his 'Ode' (better known as 'The Music Makers'), published in his volume of verse *Music and Moonlight* (1874).
4 These lines are from 'The Heart' by Francis Thompson (1859–1907).

F. P. DUNNE
from F. P. Dunne, *Mr Dooley in the Hearts of his Countrymen* (1900)

The figure of Mr Dooley first appeared in the pages of the *Chicago Times* in 1893. Its author was Finley Peter Dunne (1867–1936), 'the earliest Irish voice of genius in American literature' according to Charles Fanning in *Mr Dooley and the Chicago Irish* (1987). The Irish-American novelist James T. Farrell acknowledged his influence, as did James Joyce, who composed an anti-war poem 'Dooleysprudence' about a Mr Dooley 'the meek philosopher who doesn't care a damn / About the yellow peril or problem of Siam', who 'when he licks a postage stamp regards with smiling scorn / The face of king or emperor or snout of unicorn.' For other Dooley gems and prejudices see

F. P. Dunne, *Mr Dooley's Philosophy* (London: William Heinemann, 1900) (illustrated by William Nicholson among others). From knowledge gained in reading extracts from the 1890s you should be in a position to pick up most of Dooley's references. The constant switching between Irish, British and American politics is invigorating, a reminder that globalization was already making itself felt in 1900.

The Irishman Abroad

Mr Dooley laid down his morning paper, and looked thoughtfully at the chandeliers.

'Taaffe,' he said musingly, — 'Taaffe — where th' divvle? Th' name's familiar.'

'He lives in the Nineteenth,' said Mr McKenna. 'If I remember right, he has a boy on th' force.'

'Goowan,' said Mr Dooley, 'with ye'er nineteenth wa-ards. Th' Taaffe I mane is in Austhria. Where in all, where in all? No: yes, by gar, I have it. A-ha!

But cur-rsed be th' day,
    Whin Lord Taaffe grew faint-hearted
An' sthud not n'r cha-arged,
    But in panic depa-arted.

'D'ye mind it, — th' pome by Joyce? No, not Bill Joyce. Joyce, th' Irish pote that wrote th' pome about th' wa-ars whin me people raysisted Cromwell, while yours was carryin' turf on their backs to make fires for th' crool invader, as Finerty says whin th' sub-scriptions r-runs low. 'Tis th' same name, a good ol' Meath name in th' days gone by; an' be th' same token I have in me head that this here Count Taaffe, whether he's an austrich or a canary bur-rd now, is wan iv th' ol' fam'ly. There's manny iv thim in Europe an' all th' wurruld beside. There was Pat McMahon, th' Frinchman, that bate Looey Napoleon; an' O'Donnell, the Spanish juke; an' O'Dhriscoll an' Lynch, who do be th' whole thing down be South America, not to mention Patsy Bolivar. Ye can't go annywhere fr'm Sweden to Boolgahria without findin' a Turk settin' up beside th' king an' dalin' out th' deek with his own hand. Jawn, our people makes poor Irishmen, but good Dutchmen; an', th' more I see iv thim, th' more I says to mesilf that th' rale boney fide Irishman is no more thin a foreigner born away from home. 'Tis so.

'Look at thim, Jawn,' continued Mr Dooley, becoming eloquent. 'Whin there's battles to be won, who do they sind for? McMahon or Shurdan or Phil Kearney or Colonel Colby. Whin there's books to be wrote, who writes thim but Char-les Lever or Oliver Goldsmith or Willum Carleton? Whin there's speeches to be made, who makes thim but Edmund Burke or

Macchew P. Brady? There's not a land on th' face iv th' wurruld but th' wan where an Irishman doesn't stand with his fellow-man, or above thim. Whin th' King iv Siam wants a plisint evenin', who does he sind f'r but a lively Kerry man that can sing a song or play a good hand at spile-five? Whin th' Sultan iv Boolgahria takes tea, 'tis tin to wan th' man across fr'm him is more to home in a caubeen thin in a turban. There's Mac's an' O's in ivry capital iv Europe atin' off silver plates whin their relations is staggerin' under th' creels iv turf in th' Connaught bogs.

'Wirra, 'tis hard. Ye'd sa-ay off hand, "Why don't they do as much for their own counthry?" Light-spoken are thim that suggests th' like iv that. 'Tis asier said than done. Ye can't grow flowers in a granite block, Jawn dear, much less whin th' first shoot 'd be thrampled under foot without pity. 'Tis aisy f'r us over here, with our bellies full, to talk iv th' cowardice iv th' Irish; but what would ye have wan man iv thim do again a rig'ment? 'Tis little fightin' th' lad will want that will have to be up before sunrise to keep th' smoke curlin' fr'm th' chimbley or to patch th' rush roof to keep out th' March rain. No, faith, Jawn, there's no soil in Ireland f'r th' greatness iv th' race; an' there has been none since th' wild geese wint across th' say to France, hangin' like flies to th' side iv th' Fr-rinch ship. 'Tis only f'r women an' childher now, an' thim that can't get away. Will th' good days ever come again? says ye. Who knows!'

The Decline of National Feeling

'What ar-re ye goin' to do Patrick's Day?' asked Mr Hennessy.

'Patrick's Day?' said Mr Dooley. 'Patrick's Day? It seems to me I've heard th' name befure. Oh, ye mane th' day th' low Irish that hasn't anny votes cillybrates th' birth iv their naytional saint, who was a Fr-rinchman.'

'Ye know what I mane,' said Mr Hennessy, with rising wrath. 'Don't ye get gay with me now.'

'Well,' said Mr Dooley, 'I may cillybrate it an' I may not. I'm thinkin' iv savin' me enthusyasm f'r th' queen's birthday, whiniver it is that that blessid holiday comes ar-round. Ye see, Hinnissy, Patrick's Day is out iv fashion now. A few years ago ye'd see the President iv th' United States marchin' down Pinnsylvanya Avnoo, with the green scarf iv th' Ancient Ordher on his shoulders an' a shamrock in his hat. Now what is Mack doin'? He's settin' in his parlour, writin' letthers to th' queen, be hivins, askin' afther her health. He was fr'm th' north iv Ireland two years ago, an' not so far north ayether, — just far enough north f'r to be on good terms with Derry an' not far enough to be bad frinds with Limerick. He was raised on butthermilk an' haggis, an' he dhrank his Irish nate with a dash iv orange bitthers in it. He's been movin' steadily north since; an', if he keeps on movin', he'll go r-round th' globe, an' bring up somewhere in th' south iv England.

'An' Hinnery Cabin Lodge!¹ I used to think that Hinnery would niver die contint till he'd took th' Prince iv Wales be th' hair iv th' head, — an' 'tis little th' poor man's got, — an' dhrag him fr'm th' tower iv London to Kilmainham Jail,² an' hand him over to th' tindher mercies, as Hogan says, iv Michael Davitt. Thim was th' days whin ye'd hear Hinnery in th' Sinit, spreadin' fear to th' hear-rts iv th' British aristocracy. "Gintlemen," he says, "an' fellow-sinitors, th' time has come," he says, "whin th' eagle burrud iv freedom," he says, "lavin'," he says, "its home in th' mountains," he says, "an' circlin'," he says, "undher th' jool'd hivin," he says, "fr'm where," he says, "th' Passamaquoddy rushes into Lake Erastus K. Ropes," he says, "to where rowls th' Oregon," he says, "fr'm th' lakes to th' gulf," he says,"fr'm th' Atlantic to th' Passific where rowls th' Oregon," he says, "an' fr'm ivry American who has th' blood iv his ancesthors' hathred iv tyranny in his veins, — your ancesthors an' mine, Mr McAdoo," he says, — "there goes up a mute prayer that th' nation as wan man, fr'm Bangor, Maine, to where rowls th' Oregon, that," he says, "is full iv salmon, which is later put up in cans, but has th' same inthrest as all others in this question," he says, "that," he says, "th' descindants iv Wash'nton an'," he says, "iv Immitt,"³ he says, "will jine hands f'r to protect," he says, "th' codfisheries again th' Vandal hand iv th' British line," he says. "I therefore move ye, Mr Prisident, that it is th' sinse iv this house, if anny such there be, that Tay Pay O'Connor⁴ is a greater man thin Lord Salisberry,"⁵ he says.

'Now where's Hinnery? Where's th' bould Fenian? Where's th' moonlighter? Where's th' pikeman? Faith, he's changed his chune, an' 'tis "Sthrangers wanst, but brothers now," with him, an' "Hands acrost th' sea an' into some wan's pocket," an' "Take up th' white man's burden an' hand it to th' coons," an' "An open back dure an' a closed fr-ront dure." 'Tis th' same with all iv thim. They'se me frind Joe Choate.⁶ Where'd Joe spind

th' night? Whisper, in Windsor Castle, no less, in a night-shirt iv th' Prince iv Wales; an' the nex' mornin', whin he come downstairs, they tol' him th' rile fam'ly was late risers, but, if he wanted a good time, he cud go down an' look at th' cimit'ry! An' he done it. He went out an' wept over th' grave iv th' Father iv his Counthry. Ye'er man, George Washington, Hinnissy, was on'y th' stepfather.

'Well, glory be, th' times has changed since me frind Jawn Finerty come out iv th' House iv Riprisintatives; an', whin some wan ast him what was goin' on, he says, "Oh, nawthin' at all but some damned American business." Thim was th' days! An' what's changed thim? Well, I might be sayin' 'twas like wanst whin me cousin Mike an' a Kerry man be th' name iv Sullivan be th' gredge again a man named Doherty, that was half a Kerry man himsilf. They kept Doherty indures f'r a day, but by an' by me cousin Mike lost inthrest in th' gredge, havin' others that was newer, an' he wint over to th' ya-ards; an' Doherty an' Sullivan begin to bow to each other, an' afther a while they found that they were blood relations, an', what's closer thin that whin ye're away fr'm home, townies. An' they hooked arms, an' sthrutted up an' down th' road, as proud as imprors. An' says they, "We can lick annything in th' ward," says they. But, befure they injyed th' 'lieance f'r long, around th' corner comes me cousin Mike, with a half-brick in each hand; an' me brave Sullivan gives Doherty th' Kerry man's thrip, an' says he, "Mike," he says, "I was on'y pullin' him on to give ye a crack at him," he says. An' they desthroyed Doherty, so that he was in bed f'r a week.'

'Well, I wondher will Mike come back?' said Mr Hennessy.

'Me cousin Mike,' said Mr Dooley, 'niver missed an iliction. An' whin th' campaign opened, there wasn't a man on th' ticket, fr'm mayor to constable, that didn't claim him f'r a first cousin. There are different kinds iv hands from acrost th' sea. There are pothry hands an' rollin'-mill hands; but on'y wan kind has votes.'

---

1 Henry Cabot Lodge (1850–1924), United States Senator, a conservative party-line Republican.
2 Kilmainham Gaol in Dublin.
3 Presumably Robert Emmet, leader of the 1803 Rising.
4 T.P. O'Connor (1848–1929), a journalist and politician, known as Tay Pay. In 1902 he started his own weekly newspaper *T.P.'s Weekly*.
5 Lord Salisbury (1830–1903), Conservative leader opposed to Home Rule. He was Prime Minister on three occasions between 1885 and 1902.
6 Joseph Choate (1832–1917) was appointed U.S. Ambassador to Great Britain in 1899.

W. B. YEATS
from W. B. Yeats, *Ideas of Good and Evil* (1907)

This essay, which can be read in conjunction with 'The Symbolism of Poetry', shows Yeats's intense interest in the occult. In 1890 in London he joined the Rosicrucian Order of the Golden Dawn and became a leading member; in 1893 *The Celtic Twilight*, based on stories about the other world he collected in his native Sligo, was published; the same year saw the publication of a three-volume edition of *The Works of William Blake*, co-edited by Edwin J. Ellis and Yeats himself. In Yeats's mind, literature, especially in drama but also in the use of symbols, was close to ritual and magic.

from Magic

I

I believe in the practice and philosophy of what we have agreed to call magic, in what I must call the evocation of spirits, though I do not know what they are, in the power of creating magical illusions, in the visions of truth in the depths of the mind when the eyes are closed; and I believe in three doctrines, which have, as I think, been handed down from early times, and been the foundations of nearly all magical practices. These doctrines are —

(1) That the borders of our minds are ever shifting, and that many minds can flow into one another, as it were, and create or reveal a single mind, a single energy.

(2) That the borders of our memories are as shifting, and that our memories are a part of one great memory, the memory of Nature herself.

(3) That this great mind and great memory can be evoked by symbols.

I often think I would put this belief in magic from me if I could, for I have come to see or to imagine, in men and women, in houses, in handicrafts, in nearly all sights and sounds, a certain evil, a certain ugliness, that comes from the slow perishing through the centuries of a quality of mind that made this belief and its evidences common over the world.

VIII

I have now described that belief in magic which has set me all but unwilling among those lean and fierce minds who are at war with their time, who cannot accept the days as they pass, simply and gladly; and I look at what I have written with some alarm, for I have told more of the ancient secret than many among my fellow-students think it right to tell. I have come to believe so many strange things because of experience, that I see little reason to doubt the truth of many things that are beyond my experience; and it may be that there are beings who watch over that ancient secret, as all tradition affirms, and resent, and perhaps avenge, too fluent speech. They say in the Aran Islands that if you speak overmuch of the things of Faery your tongue becomes like a stone, and it seems to me, though doubtless naturalistic reason would call it Auto-suggestion or the like, that I have often felt my tongue become just so heavy and clumsy. More than once, too, as I wrote this very essay I have become uneasy, and have torn up some paragraph, not for any literary reason, but because some incident or some symbol that would perhaps have meant nothing to the reader, seemed, I know not why, to belong to hidden things. Yet I must write or be of no account to any cause, good or evil; I must commit what merchandise of wisdom I have to this ship of written speech, and after all, I have many a time watched it put out to sea with not less alarm when all the speech was rhyme. We who write, we who bear witness, must often hear our hearts cry out against us, complaining because of their hidden things, and I know not but he who speaks of wisdom may not sometimes in the change that is coming upon the world, have to fear the anger of the people of Faery, whose country is the heart of the world — 'The Land of the Living Heart'. Who can keep always to the little pathway between speech and silence, where one meets none but discreet revelations? And surely, at whatever risk, we must cry out that imagination is always seeking to remake the world according to the impulses and the patterns in that great Mind, and that great Memory? Can there be anything so important as to cry out that what we call romance, poetry, intellectual beauty, is the only signal that the supreme Enchanter, or some one in His councils, is speaking of what has been, and shall be again, in the consummation of time?

1901

FRANCIS A. FAHY
from Francis A. Fahy, *The Irish Language Movement* (1901)

This extract from Francis Fahy's lecture, delivered before the Irish Literary Society in London on 23 February 1901, is a reminder that for many at the time the 'Revival' meant not a literary but a language revival.

Revival

The Irish language and literature have had at all times their small body of admirers. In the dark days when Irish MSS were neglected and destroyed, Edmund Burke[1] secured for Trinity College the priceless Brehon Code going to decay in a cottage in Tipperary; O'Flaherty's *Ogygia*[2] was purchased for twenty guineas, and the great compilation of the Leabhar Breac[3] for less than £4. Henry Flood in 1791 bequeathed a large portion of his fortune to Trinity to found a permanent professorship in Irish, but the bequest was upset on a technicality. In the first forty years of the Union, various societies were started in succession to reprint the old MSS — the Gaelic, the Ossianic Society, the Archæological Society, and others. They attracted great names, published many goodly volumes, and then died out. They did not arrest the decay of the language.

In 1872 the language seemed dead. It was only mentioned in the elegies of orators or laments of poets, who spoke of the pity of it, but would not take the trouble of learning it themselves. To their credit, be it said, the school teachers were the only persons who for years took any steps to revive it.

In 1874 and '78, under the leadership of John Fleming, they petitioned the Education Commissioners' to give Results' Fees for Irish, and got it placed on the Programme, where it was, however, carefully choked with restrictions.

In '77 Father Nolan and David Comyn founded the Society for the Preservation of the Irish Language, which published three primers, but this Society being apathetic and unprogressive, the active members seceded in '80 and formed the Gaelic Union. In 1882 the *Gaelic Journal* was started. It had at first a precarious existence, five numbers appeared yearly, and it was kept alive for a time by the donations of a single Protestant clergyman, the Rev. Maxwell Close. In 1890 Father O'Growney became editor; he introduced new and popular features in the *Journal*, brought it out monthly and increased the circulation at a leap from 200 to 1,000 copies. The national conscience seemed waking at last, and Father O'Growney outlined in the *Journal* a scheme for keeping alive the language on which all the movement since has been based.

In July, '93, in a room in 9 Lower O'Connell Street,[4] the Gaelic League was formed, having for its objects: 'The preservation of Irish as the national language of Ireland, and its extension as a spoken tongue; the publication of existing Gaelic literature and the cultivation of a modern literature in Irish.'

Among the founders of the movement were Father O'Growney, Dr Douglas Hyde, John McNeill, David Comyn, O'Neill Russell, R. Gordon, and Michael Cusack, most of these old workers in the cause.

The League was distinguished from previous bodies which worked on educational lines. It appealed by local demonstration and local effort to the actual Irish-speaking people, to encourage them to keep the language alive, to stimulate them by the example of other nations to respect their tongue, and so banish their shame of it.

In October of that year was taken a step which more than any other has helped the movement to spread over the country. Archbishop Walsh, in the columns of the *Freeman*,[5] suggested to Father O'Growney that it would greatly aid students of Irish if a series of easy lessons were started with an approximate pronunciation placed after every word. These lessons appeared in the paper from week to week, and attracted thousands of learners, taking the place of all other text-books for beginners.

Irish-Speaking Districts

The field of action of the League was the Irish-speaking districts. These roughly run round the coast west and south from Donegal to Waterford, comprising the counties of Donegal, Mayo, Galway, Clare, Limerick, Kerry, Cork, and Waterford. They contain the finest scenery in Ireland. Their inhabitants are nearly as pure Gaels as can be found — in some places, like the Western Islands, wholly unmixed. They are the core of Gaeldom, mental heirs of the historic past. 'I never,' says Mr Alfred Nutt,[6] 'take up a new translation from the older Irish literature, but I am at once delighted and amazed to note the traits of resemblance in feeling, in mood, and in form between the Gael of 1,000 years ago and the Gaelic speaking peasant of to-day.' Physically — in spite of severe privations — they are among the finest specimens of the race; mentally, in spite of want of education — perhaps because of that want — they are the equals or the superiors of their English-speaking neighbours. Classed as 'illiterates', because unable to speak or write English, they are equipped with a store of folk-lore, proverbs, and legends, and endowed with an acuteness those neighbours entirely lack.

Masters of a vocabulary ten times greater than that of an English peasant, they speak their language with a fluency and accuracy which he knows nothing of and which many of the best English speakers never attain to. In respect of courtesy, reverence, or morality there is no comparison between them. Of this class of illiterates is Mrs Martin, a peasant mother of thirteen children, who (although she has never read or written a word of Irish or of English) won prizes at a recent Feis[7] for poetical talent of a very high order.

According to the 1891 Census, the number of persons who spoke Irish only, was 38,121. Irish and English, 642,053. Total close on 700,000. These figures are much below the mark. They were taken down by police — strangers in a strange land — knowing nothing and caring less whether the replies were correct or not. Such was the disregard for Irish at that time that many whose home language was Irish, and who prayed, bought, sold, and thought in Irish, and could only say 'Yes' and 'No' in English, are known to have put themselves down as English speakers. Another 200,000 at least should be fairly added for this reason, bring the proportion up to about a fifth of the population of Ireland.

To preserve the language in these retreats, to counsel, advise, exhort, stimulate the inhabitants to keep it alive, to use it constantly at home and abroad, in prayer, business, and recreation, to teach it to their children, and to spread its knowledge elsewhere throughout Ireland — this has been the main business of the League. For this it has organized local Feiseanna or meetings for Irish music, song, poetry, folk-lore, and song entirely in the Irish tongue — has appointed organizers to interview leading men in various districts, priests, teachers, town councillors, in the interest of the language — has given prizes to teachers and pupils for knowledge of Irish — has started branches everywhere with classes for study — has held public meetings and lectures to inform public opinion — has published and distributed text-books, song-books, reciters, plays, pamphlets — has collected the flotsam and jetsam of folk-lore otherwise going to decay.

It has issued the first Irish newspaper, and made it a success.

It has enlisted or produced an array of writers, the equals of any body of similar workers anywhere. Dr Douglas Hyde, poet, folklorist, historian, the leader of the language movement; the tireless Father Peter O'Leary,[8] the creator of Seadna, the first Irish dramatist, whose idiom is the very quintessence of Irish speech, and who leads one to believe that Æsop must have been originally a Gael; Father Yorke, whose lecture in Dublin blew into atoms our long accepted views of Nationality; John McNeill, master of all shades of Irish speech; Mr Flannery, our foremost philologist, who knows as much about Irish language roots as if he had been present when its seeds were first planted; Thomas Concannon, the organizer, whose speeches are revelations of the powers of Irish oratory; the pithy writers of the *Claidheamh Soluis*;[9] Conán Maol, the historian of the Boer War; Fergus Finnbeil, Cu-Uladh (whom I see here to-night), Dr O'Hickey, and Dr Henebry, sturdy fighters in the cause, besides a number of ladies like Miss Borthwick and Lady Gregory, whose presence and talents lend untold grace and support to the movement.

Already tokens of its work are manifold. There are over 300 Branches, and more people are learning Irish than actually speak it. It has gathered to its ranks recruits from all shades of politics, creeds, callings, and professions. In December last the League sold 10,000 Irish publications, and the *Simple Lessons*[10] have reached a sale of 130,000. It has done this through a handful of men with a handful of money. The League receipts for 1898 came only to £143, and since then to £1,910.

Names of streets and railway stations appear in Irish. County Councils vote money for language purposes; Irish advertisements, leaders, and stories, appear in papers. Concerts altogether of Irish songs are held. Sermons are given and public prayers offered in Irish. Plays in Irish are produced. Irish speeches are given on platforms, and one was attempted recently in Parliament. The promoters of the Irish Literary Theatre have admitted that an Irish National Literature must be in the Irish tongue. The Resident Commissioner of National Education has denounced the system of education enforced by the Board. The Irish Parliament Party have placed Irish in the forefront of their programme.

The tokens of the revival are patent to everybody and need not be further recorded.

1　Edmund Burke (1729–97), Dublin-born son of a Protestant lawyer and Catholic mother, is the famous author of *Reflections on the Revolution in France* (1790), but according to William O'Brien in *Edmund Burke as an Irishman* (1924), his is 'the greatest Irish name in the history of Civilization'. The reference to his discovering the Brehon Code is intriguing; he did discover other early manuscripts (the *Book of Leinster* and the *Book of Lecan*), but these were in Hertfordshire.

2 Roderick O'Flaherty (1629–1718) was the author of *Ogygia* (1685), a history of Ireland in Latin.

3 In English Speckled Book, an early fifteenth-century manuscript compiled by Murchadh Ó Cuindlis.

4 In Dublin.

5 *Freeman's Journal*, a Dublin newspaper.

6 Alfred Nutt (1856–1910), translator, publisher, and Celtic scholar.

7 A literature and music festival supported in particular by the Gaelic League.

8 See extract by Father O'Leary (1915) below.

9 *Claidheamh Soluis*: Or Sword of Light, a newspaper edited by Patrick Pearse.

10 Father O'Growney's Irish primer.

ARTHUR GRIFFITH
from Arthur Griffith, *The Resurrection of Hungary: A Parallel for Ireland* (1904)

Arthur Griffith (1871–1922) was an important figure in the development of modern Irish nationalism. He was the chief architect behind Sinn Féin, the political party formed in 1905 to press for Irish independence. After the Sinn Féin Rising of 1916 (it was called this in spite of it being led by the Irish Volunteers under Patrick Pearse and the Irish Citizen Army under James Connolly) he led the Irish delegation to London to negotiate the Treaty in December 1921 and was then elected the first President of Dáil Éireann in 1922. 'The Nation must depend upon itself alone' was a phrase he alighted on in his reading of Hungarian nineteenth-century history, Sinn Féin meaning ourselves or ourselves alone (the phrase was in use as a Gaelic League motto in the 1890s). Its author was Francis Deak (1803–76), a Roman Catholic country gentleman, who together with Louis Kossuth (1802–94), a Protestant barrister, was a leading figure in the Hungarian movement for independence from Austria. Griffith saw in this movement a blueprint for his own country's relationship with Britain. Here in this extract from the final pages of *The Resurrection of Hungary* Griffith draws out the lessons for Ireland and outlines a programme for achieving independence from Britain.

The Resurrection of Hungary

Count Beust, the Austrian statesman,[1] who arranged the Ausgleich with Hungary, had, twenty years later, much adverse criticism to offer on Gladstone's attempt to 'settle the Irish question'. The man who 'settled the Hungarian question' pointed out that the legislature Gladstone proposed to erect in Dublin, and which the Irish Parliamentary Party declared itself willing to accept in 'final' settlement of Ireland's claim, conferred no real power on the Irish people, and even degraded Ireland to a lower position than she at present occupies, as in exchange for an illusory 'Parliament', she was required to give up her claim to distinct nationhood. Gladstone, in introducing his Home Rule Bill,[2] had the audacity to compare it with the

Ausgleich carried out by Beust and Deak. Beust pointed out in his criticism of Gladstone that the Ausgleich rendered the Hungarian Parliament co-ordinate with the Austrian Parliament, rendered Hungary absolute mistress of her own affairs, and gave her the status in international law of a sovereign State. In Hungary the Austrian is as much a foreigner as he is in France or England, and, as in those countries, must be naturalized before he can claim the rights of citizenship. Gladstone's Bill proposed to erect a legislature in Dublin, subordinate to the Parliament of London — a legislature whose existence could be terminated in forty-eight hours if a majority of the British members of the British Parliament so desired, and this legislature was to be excluded from having any voice in questions of war and peace, foreign affairs, the army and navy, international treaties, customs dues, matters of currency, indirect taxation, etc. In return, Ireland was to resign for ever her status as a separate nationality and become a province of the Empire. There was scarce a province of the Austrian Empire whose petty Diet did not possess greater powers than Gladstone proposed to give his 'Irish Legislature', and the proposal in 1861 of the Austrians to give Hungary a Legislature with absolute power over the internal affairs of Hungary, but yet terminable in certain circumstances by the Act of the Viennese Parliament, was unanimously and contemptuously rejected by the Hungarian people. Beust, in continuing the analogy between the Hungarian and Irish questions, frankly admitted that Austria would never have conceded Hungary's demand had Hungary not made it impossible for her to refuse it by the policy she adopted and persisted in for eighteen years. England, the statesman showed, would, similarly, never concede Ireland's demands unless Ireland made it impossible for her to refuse them. There was no question of generosity or desire to do right in Austria's action. She had sworn again and again that she never would and never could admit Hungary's claims, as England has sworn again and again that it is mere midsummer madness for the Irish people to imagine she could assent to Irish independence. Swearing she would never consent, Austria consented — and England, like Austria, will consent when the Irish make it as impossible for her to combine dishonesty with profit as the Hungarians did in the case of Austria.

Count Beust admitted that the geographical position of Ireland was more favourable than the geographical position of Hungary, but he argued it as a serious weakness of her claim, that, unlike Hungary, Ireland had not a separate language and literature, and that she had, unlike Hungary, given her case away by sending members to the British Parliament, thus recognizing its authority. The first of Beust's objections was made in ignorance of Ireland, and would not, of course, be urged by him if he lived to-day. Ireland has a distinct language and literature of its own. The second is more serious, but not fatal. From the inception of *The United Irishman*[3] we have opposed the sending of Irishmen to sit in the British Parliament on two grounds: (1) That it is a recognition of the usurped authority of a foreign assembly to make laws to bind the people of Ireland, and (2) That the policy of Parliamentarianism has been materially and morally disastrous to the country. We need not labour the latter point. No measure of a beneficial nature for this country has ever been passed by the British Parliament as a result of the presence, speeches, and action of the delegation from Ireland. The five measures which are usually accepted as beneficial, passed for Ireland by that Parliament — the Catholic Emancipation Act, the Tithes Act, the Church Disestablishment Act, the Land Act of 1881 — with the supplementary Ashbourne Act — and the Local Government Act, were passed as a result of the unconscious carrying out by the people of the Hungarian policy — the policy of Passive Resistance — with occasional excursions into the domain of Active Resistance at strategic points. In one sentence the impotence of the Irish Parliamentary Party in Westminster can be exhibited. It has been there for thirty-three years — a generation — to keep it there Ireland has expended over £600,000 — and during the period of its existence the population of Ireland has decreased by 20 per cent, and the taxation of Ireland for British purposes has increased by 70 per cent. No condemnation is further needed than these figures. A man who runs his business on such lines ends in the Bankruptcy Court. A nation which persists in running its business on such lines must inevitably go smash.

The recognition of the competency of a British Parliament to make laws to bind this country, which the attendance of the Parliamentary Party at Westminster implies, is, of course, a great political mistake; but Count Beust's contention that Ireland surrendered her case when she returned men to sit in the British Parliament, goes too far. The Act of Union is illegal and unconstitutional. Acceptance of seats in the British Parliament by Irishmen cannot render this illegal enactment legal. The temporary acceptance of the Act of Union as binding has had the unfortunate result of misrepresenting the position of Ireland to the world, and of confusing the minds of her people. It has led them into a cul-de-sac, and ignorance, vanity, and selfishness on the part of their leaders prevented them admitting the truth, and retracing their steps.

O'Connell[4] had one statesmanlike idea in his latter life. It flashed across his mind to summon the Irish Parliament to meet in Dublin, and, ignoring the illegal 'Act' of Union, proceed to legislate for the country. There then existed a law known as the Convention Act, which forbade the assembly of delegates in Ireland, and the British Government attempted to counter O'Connell by its use. O'Connell sought to evade the provisions of the Act by calling his assembly the Council of Three Hundred, and the Young Irelanders, recognizing the political wisdom of the move, enthusiastically supported O'Connell — they even for the moment thought they had misjudged the Tribune in holding him to be no statesman. 'If the members be wise and brave,' said John Mitchel, 'Ireland will be saved.' The British Government was alarmed as it had not been alarmed since 1798. 'In six months,' said Lord John Russell,[5] 'the power and functions of government will be wrested from our hands, and the Lord Lieutenant will sit powerless in Dublin Castle.' The preparations for the meeting of the Council of Three Hundred proceeded apace. Thomas Davis was selected to sit for the County Down, John Mitchel for the town of Banbridge: then O'Connell discarded his own proposal. The Council of Three Hundred never met — the 'Arbitration Courts', which had been formed throughout the land to supersede the English Law Courts, were abandoned, and the English Government breathed freely again. Had Ireland been led by a statesman then, the end of the English government of Ireland was at hand. It is sixty years since, and our population has decreased by one-half. Our rights remain. The withdrawal of the Irish Parliamentary Party from the British Parliament and the summoning of the Council of Three Hundred to meet in Dublin are the initial steps for Ireland to take in the application of a National Policy.

The Council of Three Hundred should meet in Dublin during a period of the year, and initiate, discuss, and pass measures calculated to benefit the country. These measures once passed, the County Councils, Urban Councils, Poor Law Boards, and other representative bodies should, so far as they have legal powers — and the powers of the Irish County Councils and Poor Law Boards are more extensive than most Irishmen wot of — enforce them. For instance, the County Councils have power to make monetary grants and levy rates for desirable purposes. If the Council of Three Hundred pass a measure affecting the industries or agriculture of Ireland, the County Councils can by united action give the measure much of the legal force of an Act passed by the British Parliament. Let it be recollected that even under the Coercion Act, there is no violation of the law committed by 300 gentlemen meeting in Dublin and recommending the adoption of measures to the Irish people calculated to improve their condition, and that there is nothing illegal in the Irish representative bodies using their full powers to give force to these recommendations. The County Councils of Hungary formed the strongest weapon of Kossuth in the Forties and Deak in the Sixties against the Austrian Government. The County Councils of Ireland possess in some respects greater powers than the County Councils of Hungary; it needs but their united action, under the guidance of a directing mind, to render

them as potent against English misgovernment as the Hungarian Councils were against Austrian oppression. A sum of £25,000 is raised annually for the upkeep of an impotent Irish Parliamentary Party in the British Parliament. This sum should continue to be raised, but be devoted to quite a different object, to the upkeep in all the great European capitals and important commercial centres of capable and patriotic Irish men of business, whose duties would be (1) to keep Europe acquainted with the truth about the struggle in Ireland, and (2) to secure a profitable market for Irish goods and produce abroad. The Hungarians adopted this plan with a success that would seem incredible to the average Irishman. From Paris to New York Hungary established its consuls during the years of its struggles against Austria, and the efforts of these consuls trebled the export trade of Hungary during the period of their work. What Hungary did Ireland can do, but at the present time Ireland has not a direct representative of her interests in any Continental capital, and she is the only country in Europe of which that fact is true. As a consequence our export trade to the Continent is insignificant and actually decreasing.

The institution of a system of Protection for Irish industries would be one of the principal duties of the Council of Three Hundred, and one that, by the co-operation of the Irish public bodies, could be made effective. The Hungarians inaugurated and carried out such a system by means of the 'Vedegylet' association. The supersession of the English civil courts in this island, by the institution of 'Arbitration Courts', such as the Young Irelanders projected and the Hungarians established, would be a matter of no difficulty and great profit to the nation. Voluntary Arbitration Courts are legal, and their decisions have all the binding force of law when the litigants sign an agreement to abide by them. The Irish abroad, especially in America, could form a valuable auxiliary, both by rendering aid to Irish industrial enterprises and obstructing and thwarting the designs of English foreign policy, as the Hungarian exiles did from 1849 to 1867 in the case of Austria — although far less in number than the Irish abroad. It would, of course, be a principal duty of the Council of Three Hundred to keep Irishmen out of the ranks of the English armed forces. In Hungary the County Councils saw so effectively to this that the Austrian army was rendered ineffective, and went to pieces in seven days before the Prussians.

We have but roughly indicated how the policy which made Hungary what it is to-day may be applied to Ireland; where the circumstances of the countries differ, it is a work of detail to adapt the policy. For its successful working, clear-thinking, uncompromising men are required to lead. There is no doubt of the readiness of the people to follow. The people of Ireland are not less patriotic and not less intelligent than the people of Hungary — three-fourths of their misfortunes are traceable to their pusillanimous, incompetent, and sometimes corrupt leaders. An Irish Deak would have found in Ireland a support as loyal and as strong as Deak found in Hungary. But the Irish Deak never appeared, and shallow rhetoricians imposed themselves upon the people in his stead. Thus for a hundred years, with brief interruptions, Ireland has been consistently misled, and has paid for her weakness with the lives of half her people, and the loss of her fortune.

In the latter part of the eighteenth century, Ireland, by the determination and wisdom of her sons, was raised from the position of an insignificant and poverty-stricken province to the status of a nation and to a prosperity as great as that of any civilized country of her extent and population then existent. What Irishmen did in the eighteenth century, Irishmen are competent to do in the twentieth — what the

Hungarians did for Hungary, Irishmen can do for Ireland. None who reflect can doubt that, carried out with the same determination, the policy which resurrected Hungary from the tomb that Austria built for her in 1849 at Vilagos can end the usurped authority of England to rule our country.

1   Friedrich Ferdinand Beust (1809–96) was Austrian Chancellor when he negotiated the Ausgleich (compromise) of 1867 which resulted in the Austro-Hungarian Monarchy.
2   Gladstone's first Home Rule Bill for Ireland was introduced in 1886.
3   Griffith's weekly newspaper which he established in 1899 and where he printed his articles on Hungary later gathered in book form.
4   Daniel O'Connell (1775–1847), the 'Liberator', famous Irish leader whose efforts helped achieve in 1829 Catholic Emancipation and who struggled for Repeal of the Union thereafter. In 1843 he toyed with a scheme for a Council of Three Hundred but the constitutional nationalists, much to the dismay of Young Irelanders such as John Mitchel, thought better of it.
5   Russell (1792–1878) was leader of the Whig opposition in Parliament in 1841–6, and later became Prime Minister in 1846–52.

J. M. SYNGE
from *The Manchester Guardian*, 10 June 1905

In June 1905 the painter Jack B. Yeats and Synge were asked by *The Manchester Guardian* to provide a series of first-hand reports on the poor Congested Districts in the west of Ireland. They travelled widely in Mayo and Galway sending back reports as they went, Yeats providing the sketches, Synge the report. If in his plays Synge celebrates the lifestyle of the country people, here in these reports he reveals his concern with the conditions of their existence, for he took to heart a guiding principle of the Literary Revival, that it was indeed a return to the people.

From Galway to Gorumna

Some of the worst portions of the Irish congested districts — of which so much that is contradictory has been spoken and written — lie along the further north coast of Galway Bay and about the whole seaboard from Spiddal to Clifden. Some distance inland there is a line of railway, and in the bay itself a steamer passes in and out to the Aran Islands; but this particular district can only be visited thoroughly by driving or riding over some thirty or forty miles of desolate

roadway. If one takes this route from Galway one has to go a little way only to reach places and people that are fully typical of Connemara. On each side of the road one sees small square fields of oats, or potatoes, or pasture, divided by loose stone walls that are built up without mortar. Wherever there are a few cottages near the road one sees bare-footed women hurrying backwards and forwards with hampers of turf or grass slung over their backs and generally a few children running after them, and if it is a market-day, as was the case on the day of which I am going to write, one overtakes long strings of country people driving home from Galway in low carts drawn by an ass or pony. As a rule one or two men sit in front of the cart driving and smoking, with a couple of women behind them stretched out at their ease among sacks of flour or young pigs, and nearly always talking continuously in Gaelic. These men are all dressed in homespuns of the grey natural wool, and the women in deep madder-dyed petticoats and bodices, with brown shawls over their heads. One's first feeling as one comes back among these people and takes a place, so to speak, in this noisy procession of fishermen, farmers, and women, where nearly everyone is interesting and attractive, is a dread of any reform that would tend to lessen their individuality rather than any very real hope of improving their well-being. One feels then, perhaps a little later, that it is a part of the misfortune of Ireland that nearly all the characteristics which give colour and attractiveness to Irish life are bound up with a social condition that is near to penury, while in countries like Brittany the best external features of the local life — the rich embroidered dresses, for instance, or the carved furniture — are connected with a decent and comfortable social condition.

About twelve miles from Galway one reaches Spiddal, a village which lies on the borderland between the fairly prosperous districts near Galway and the barren country further to the west. Like most places of its kind, it has a double row of houses — some of them with two storeys — several public houses, with a large police barrack among them, and a little to one side a coastguard station, ending up at either side of the village with a chapel and a church. It was evening when we drove to Spiddal, and a little after sunset we walked on to a rather exposed quay where a few weather-beaten hookers were moored with many ropes. As we came down none of the crews were to be seen, but threads of turf smoke rising from the open manhole of the forecastle showed that the men were probably on board. While we were looking down on them from the pier — the tide was far out — an old grey-haired man with the inflamed eyes that are so common here from the continual itching of the turf smoke peered up through the manhole and watched us with vague curiosity. A few moments later a young man came down from a field of black earth, where he had been digging a drain, and asked the old man, in Gaelic, to throw him a spark for his pipe. The latter disappeared for a moment, then came up again with a smouldering end of a turf sod in his hand, and threw it up on the pier, where the young man caught it with a quick downward grab without burning himself, blew it into a blaze, lit his pipe with it, and

went back to his work. These people are so poor that many of them do not spend any money on matches. The spark of lighting turf is kept alive day and night on the hearth, and when a man goes out fishing or to work in the fields he usually carries a lighted sod with him, and keeps it all day buried in ashes or any dry rubbish, so that he can use it when he needs it. On our way back to the village an old woman begged from us, speaking in English, as most of the people do to anyone who is not a native. We gave her a few halfpence, and as she was moving away with an ordinary 'God save you!' I said a blessing to her in Irish to show her I knew her own language if she chose to use it. Immediately she turned back towards me and began her thanks again, this time with extraordinary profusion. 'That the blessing of God may be on you,' she said, 'on road and on ridge way, on sea and on land, on flood and on mountain in all the kingdoms of the world' — and so on, till I was too far off to hear what she was saying.

In a district like Spiddal one sees curious gradations of type, especially on Sundays and holidays, when everyone is dressed as their fancy leads them and as well as they can manage. As I watched the people coming from Mass the morning after we arrived this was curiously noticeable. The police and coastguards came first in their smartest uniforms; then the shopkeepers, dressed like the people of Dublin, but a little more grotesquely; then the more well-to-do country folk, dressed only in the local clothes I have spoken of, but the best and newest kind, while the wearers themselves looked well-fed and healthy, and a few of them, especially the girls, magnificently built; then, last of all, one saw the destitute in still the same clothes, but this time patched and threadbare and ragged, the women mostly barefooted, and both sexes pinched with hunger and the fear of it. The class that one would be most interested to see increase is that of the typical well-to-do people, but except in a few districts it is not numerous, and it is always aspiring after the dress of the shop people or tending to sink down again among the paupers.

Later in the day we drove on another long stage to the west. As before, the country we passed through was not depressing, though stony and barren as a quarry. At every cross roads we passed groups of young, healthy-looking boys and men amusing themselves with hurley or pitching, and further back on little heights, a small field's breadth from the road, there were many groups of girls sitting out by the hour, near enough to the road to see everything that was passing, yet far enough away to keep their shyness undisturbed. Their red dresses looked peculiarly beautiful among the fresh green of the grass and opening bracken, with a strip of sea behind them, and, far away, the grey cliffs of Clare. A little further on, some ten miles from Spiddal, inlets of the sea begin to run in towards the mountains, and the road turns north to avoid them across an expanse of desolate bog far more dreary than the rocks of the coast. Here one sees a few wretched sheep nibbling in places among the turf, and occasionally a few ragged people walking rapidly by the roadside. Before we stopped for the night we had reached another bay coast-line and were among stones again. Later in the evening we walked out round another small quay with the usual little band of shabby hookers, and then along a road that rose in some places a few hundred feet above the sea, and as one looked down into the little fields that lay below it they looked so small and rocky that the very thought of tillage in them seemed like the freak of an eccentric. Yet in this particular place tiny cottages, some of them without windows, swarmed by the roadside and in the 'boreens', or laneways, at either side, many of them built on a single sweep of stone with the naked living rock for their floor. A number of people were to be seen everywhere about them, the men loitering by the roadside and the women hurrying among the fields, feeding an odd calf or lamb or driving in a few ducks before the night. In one place a few boys were playing pitch with trousers buttons, and a little further on half-a-score of young men were making donkeys jump backwards and forwards over a low wall. As we came back we met two men, who came and talked to us, one of them, by his hat and dress, plainly a man who had been away from Connemara. In a little while he told us that he had been in Gloucester and Bristol working on public works, but had wearied of it and come back to his country.

'Bristol,' he said, 'is the greatest town, I think, in all England, but the work in it is hard.'

I asked him about the fishing in the neighbourhood we were in. 'Ah,' he said, 'there's little fishing in it at all, for we have no good boats. There is no one asking for boats for this place, for the shopkeepers would rather have the people idle, so that they can get them for a shilling a day to go out in their old hookers and sell turf in Aran and on the coast of Clare.' Then we talked of Aran, and he told me of people I knew there who had died or got married since I had been on the islands, and then they went on their way.

JOHN EGLINTON
from John Eglinton, *Bards and Saints* (1906)

John Eglinton, or 'Eglintoneyes' as he is called by Joyce in *Ulysses*, was arguably the most clear-headed Irish thinker of his time. Here in a Preface to a collection of early essays, which included 'The De-Davisization of Irish Literature', he set about single-handedly dismantling the framework of much that passed for nationalism and national identity. His ideas can be compared with those outlined in previous essays and extracts by Hyde, Russell, Moran, and Yeats. In retrospect, his belief that nationalism was passing away reads slightly hollow; on the other hand, it could be argued that such remarks make him our contemporary.

Preface

Whatever be thought of the literary and philological claims of the Irish language, it cannot be denied that the 'Language Movement' brings into prominence an aspect of Irish nationality of which a good many Irishmen have hitherto been content to ignore the existence. Dragged from obscurity in the hovels of the West, like the forgotten representative of some old dynasty restored by a sudden revolution, the ancient language of this country hears itself saluted as 'Our own Tongue', 'The *Irish* Language', even in the presence of that rival who has supplanted it, and who is now so securely established as the language of the country that it can afford to wink at these pretensions and even to extend municipal hospitalities to Gaelic in the decayed but still haughty capital of the Ascendancy.[1] 'Irish' Language is indeed only a title of courtesy: the ancient language of the Celt is no longer the language of Irish nationality. And in fact it never was.

A visitor commissioned to describe this country in the style and spirit of Cæsar would perhaps report that all Ireland is divided into three parts, of which the Anglo-Irish form one, the Scotch-Irish another, while the third is formed of what we may call, borrowing the phrase from Mr H.G. Wells, the peasant hinterland. These, he would probably continue, do not differ in language, institutions, or laws, but are at variance in matters of religion and history. Each of these, he might add, is concerned chiefly, as is natural, with its own interest, the northern portion being almost morosely so concerned: in fact, Presbyterian Ulster — being the only part of Ireland which really knows its own mind — hardly any longer keeps up the pretence of forming portion of an ideal Irish nation. It was with the Anglo-Irish, on the other hand, that the idea of an Irish nation originated. But the word 'nation', as adopted by Grattan and Sir Jonah Barrington,[2] sounded a little defiant and tentative; and presently, with the sudden emergence into political significance of a new and almost unsuspected Irish nationality in the time of O'Connell, the claim to nationhood died out among the Anglo-Irish. The solid word 'nation' gave place to the flimsy and doctrinaire word 'nationalism'. Yet the Anglo-Irish have never wholly lost their aspirations after nationality; with seven hundred years of history behind them, and with so many glorious names in literature and politics, they feel that they should transcend provinciality. It is this, for example, which keeps them loyal to a faded viceregal court, still gilded with a certain grace of the old *régime*; and it is to the desire to add some grace of nationality to provincial life that the cause of reviving the ancient language of the peasant hinterland makes its appeal.

No man calls himself an Irishman without some attribution of nationality to the Irish people as a whole; but it is idle to deny that the nationality which most of us have in our mind is one which has its nucleus in the Anglo-Irish population rather than in the peasant hinterland. That hinterland it was indeed the mistake of the Anglo-Irishman to ignore in the days when he arrogated to himself the lofty title of 'nation': forgetting the political lesson implied in the maxim of Mencius, 'To conquer the peasantry is the way to become the son of heaven!' He did not realize that to impart language, institutions and laws is not to impart nationality, but that it is from the peasantry that he derives nationality. And so when democratic ideas invaded Ireland at the end of the 18th century, and presently gave an independent political existence to the peasant hinterland, the political ideas of that factitious 'nation' of which Grattan was the slightly

histrionic spokesman and Sir Jonah the fitting historian, shrivelled like an unrooted plant, and the Anglo-Irishman sank into provincial apathy. All through the 19th century he has been little more than a spectator of Irish political life, abandoning to the peasant hinterland the cause of nationality, and in his dilemma between nationalism and provincialism is a butt for the sarcasm of those who, not without some justification, call their own division of the population 'Irish Ireland', and the Anglo-Irishman 'West-British'. As he stands in this uneasy situation, the first overture from the Celtic hinterland comes to him in the proposal that he should join in reinstating the ancient language of the country, and, at the risk of seeming a little ridiculous, he has felt constrained of late to give some attention to the matter. Strictly speaking, it is not for language and literature, but rather for the thews and sinews of nationality, that we should look to the peasantry: on the contrary, it is fitting that the peasantry should have the language of a superior culture imposed upon them. Where the peasantry, or the main body of a population, receives that superior culture and civilization, the product is a genuine nationality: and however defiantly both Grattan and Parnell may have vociferated that Ireland is a nation, it has never been one in this sense.

An indigenous culture, or an inner life of some kind, is that which gives individuality to a people. The true justification of the claim to nationality is nothing more or less than the discovery of the possibilities of human nature in a community of which the geographical situation is sufficiently favourable — a discovery which has never been made in Ireland. The old Celtic nationality has not made it, and for that reason has remained an outcast from the family of European nations, inheritors and preservers of the Promethean fire; nor has the nationality of the Anglo-Irish, with whom it chiefly rested to make it, as the heirs of a superior culture. All the elements of nationality exist in Ireland, yet until a discovery of this kind has connected Irish nationalism with universal and essential interests, a share in Irish national aspirations will continue to be, not the necessary mark of a good citizen, but rather, at best, a development of good nature or special circumstances. It is by a 'thought movement' rather than by a 'language movement' that Ireland will have to show that it holds the germs of true nationality.

The cry of nationalism, in the traditional sense of the word, has now, it is to be feared, a belated sound. The day of nations — those imposing entities the report of whose doings still casts a glamour over the daily papers, those Titan friends of humanity each one of which has had its peculiar part in carrying forward the human cause — the day of nations, we have begun to suspect, is passing away. The day of those institutions for which we have at present no more high-sounding names than 'local self-government', 'municipal trade', 'international arbitration', and the like, is already in progress — the period which from the point of view of the consummations of the future will perhaps appear as the democratic middle ages. We begin to demur to the romantic wars into which the touchiness of these old Titans toward one another hurries us against our interest and our will, and to feel content that they should go. Much of what is grandiose and sacrosanct will go with them, and it will rest with the smaller nations to keep alive certain graces and sentiments which belong to nationality, in a world surrendered to individualism and commonsense. The history of Ireland, if it shows any hopeful tendency, shows a tendency toward the achievement of national unity — for the first time; and it is those who have the national unity of Ireland at heart who are most likely to remain cold toward a plan for perpetuating the division of Ireland into two rival populations, having, like the Jews and the Samaritans, 'no dealings' with one another. After all it was amongst the 'lost sheep of the house of Israel' — amongst those who had lost the use of the Hebrew language — that the Jewish Messiah appeared. It was not the ancient language of the chosen people that gave expression to the most illustrious example of the fulfilment of a national dream, and it would be in keeping with the ironies of history if the fulfilment of the Gaelic dream should test the acumen of believers in a similar fashion.

The De-Davisization of Irish Literature

It has been said that during the Middle Ages great men as a rule distinguished themselves in another country than that of their birth. If this may be still said of eminent men born in Ireland, it is easy enough to understand why it should be so, in respect to men of action and administrative faculty; but that literary men and men of thought are still impelled to leave this country in order to 'find themselves' may be taken in association with a statement which is sometimes made, that Ireland has not as yet emerged properly out of the Middle Ages. To speak candidly, if cosmopolitanism be a fault, it has not always been the fault of these gifted sons of Ireland, from the time of Scotus Erigena,[3] that they have become cosmopolitan, since they, as a rule, have remembered that they were Irishmen, while the

mother-country has never had the heart to take much pride in pure intellectual achievement. The only distinctive national literary tradition, within its own coasts, acknowledged by Ireland, is mainly the creation of Thomas Davis, and had its point of departure in the anger felt by that excellent patriot when, as a young lawyer, he was brought into contact with the crass worldliness and provincialism of the official and professional classes of Dublin, to which he himself belonged. The nationalism which he was driven to adopt was not exactly, perhaps, the ideal nationalism of his 'Address to the Historical Society', with which he began his career, but suffered a little from compromise, as perhaps all ideal principles must do when practically applied. There are worldly people in every nation: a successful New York Irishman, for instance, is possibly as worldly a type as could be found; but in the nature of the case, the worldly people in Ireland were those descendants of the 'English Colony', who still monopolized the prosperity of the country. To the inert weight of provincialism and indifference to the ideal of these people, Davis gave the somewhat fallacious name of Anglicism, or Anglicization, and turned with passion to the great peasant population of Celtic Ireland, with its ancient language and history, its affiliation to the soil and geography of the country, its long-suffering under centuries of persecution, its freedom, at all events, from what he describes as 'that damned thing . . . call it Yankeeism or Englishism, which measures prosperity by exchangeable value, measures duty by gain, and limits desire to clothes, food and respectability'. It was, no doubt, a worldly time in England especially, the time of Bentham's influence and of the successes of Macaulay: and already at that time in England there had arisen in the person of a Scottish peasant, Thomas Carlyle, a prophet against worldliness, whose influence was already rousing the talent of the strongest writer whom the national cause of Ireland has yet had on its side, John Mitchel.[4] It was Davis, however, who gave a sort of religious or idealistic status to modern Irish patriotism which it has retained; for since Davis the true religion of the Irish Nationalist has been patriotism; and it remains to be decided to be decided whether this confusion of two essentially different things, idealism and patriotism, has bestowed upon Irish national literature the germs of new developments or is not rather that which must be got rid of before even the meaning of the term 'national literature' is understood.

The genius of Davis himself (who, it must be remembered, died at the age of thirty-one, after a few years of activity, and so was prevented from becoming, what perhaps he might have become to a full extent, a kind of Irish Lessing) succeeded in giving Ireland a brilliant journal, but not exactly literature. The one book of the '48 Movement — written by a kind of accident, and still (though in an exceptional way) *out* of Ireland — was the work of a man, in some respects, of a less admirable character than Davis, yet his superior in that abnormal power of spiritualized egoism which makes the writing-man. It was the lion-hearted, if somewhat wrong-headed Mitchel, who began to use a hearty directness of statement in regard to all matters which affected or interested him, which had hardly been heard in Ireland since the days of Dean Swift. In his Journal and Correspondence (or those fragments of it which are given in his Life by Dillon) as compared with the writings of Davis, we can see the difference between literature and rhetoric, which is mainly that, while rhetoric has in mind some particular audience, literature is the faithful and unbiased rendering of the individual impression. The two elements of rhetoric and literature meet in that kind of writing, designed to catch the attention of the average man in his average hours, to which, not very happily, we give the name 'journalism'; and in journalism Davis (who indeed was rather an ideal editor than what Mr T.W. Rolleston[5] has called him, 'the ideal Irishman') succeeded so well that he and his colleagues imposed the tradition of their newspaper on Irish national literature. What the Irish nationalist, as instructed by Davis, means by 'national literature', is not the interpretation of the soul of a people, still less the emancipation of the national mind by means of individual utterance, but — no doubt a very good thing — the expression of such sentiments as help to exalt an Irishman's notion of the excellence and importance of the race to which he belongs. Our friends, the Gaelic Leaguers, who hold that the English language at the best is an unsuitable vehicle of thought for Irishmen, and who have lately shown signs of ingratitude to the memory of Davis, are ready, no doubt, to accept this implied qualification of his praise, and to use it as an argument on their side; but in the *Jail Journal* of Mitchel, written far away from an audience, and in order to satisfy an overmastering need of self-expression, we do at last get literature, a book so successful in giving expression to the instincts and antipathies of Irish nationality, that, in face of it, any further talk of the inefficiency of the English language in Ireland is somewhat audacious. The literary interest of this book was at once recognized in Paris by M. Emile Montégut, who devoted to it a lengthy article in the *Revue des Deux Mondes* (Tome 10, 1855); an article which every Irishman, who wishes to 'see himself as others see him', should read. Mitchel

afterwards wrote of himself as a man who 'but once in his life [1847–8] was possessed by a great cause, whose whole life and energy converged themselves once to one focus, and were then dissipated into the general atmosphere'; but it is quite certain that so far as concerns his literary activity — for we are not here concerned with the political principles which brought him into unpleasant relations with two Governments, and very nearly with a third, and which allowed him to become the fierce champion of slavery — no other book of his has half the literary value of the *Jail Journal*, which, for many young Irish patriots, has made him the Defoe of the hulks.

There is a class of enthusiasts who pin their faith to an order of things which might have been, if something else had not happened. Thus, a goodly number hold that Christianity was an unpardonable infraction of the pagan ideal. To others, the Renaissance appears to have been the great mistake. A larger number, of course, regret the movements represented by Luther and Rousseau. English music, it is claimed, was certain of a fine career of national development, if the burly Handel had not thrown it out of its bearings. And so on. There is more to be said for the language movement, no doubt, than that it is merely the championship of one of these lost causes; one must indeed be blind not to see the poetry of this proposal to raise up around our coasts, not Bishop Berkeley's impracticable wall of brass, but a still more irrefragable if impalpable safeguard of nationality in a language bristling with difficulties to a foreigner, but within full of the kindly converse of hearts unsealed at last. It must be confessed, however, that when Anglo-Irish literature has brought us at least so far as the literary integrity and hearty directness of John Mitchel, it seems a pity if the 'Language Movement' is to transport literature in this country back again to that point where the good Davis left it, to that region, which has become now somewhat insipid, in which all private differences are sunk, and in which the Irishman has to speak in his national rather than in his human capacity. For the questions which divide household and nation against themselves, religious, political, fundamental questions, these are the questions in respect to which the literary man must have the licence of a prophet; it is these which he looks on as his peculiar region; it is these upon which literature, more than any other agency, can hope to shed some light. Literature must be free as the elements; if that is to be cosmopolitan it must be cosmopolitan. Literature, even when it is really national, is not a matter about which any nation, fortunately for its peace of mind, gives itself great concern. It proceeds quietly in the pursuit of truth and wisdom, and occasionally attracts attention to itself as an elemental force by an electric discharge of thought: whereupon follows, as a rule, one of those regrettable movements already mentioned, and the relegation of the reigning system of thought to the status of a lost cause. If the Irish nation is a literary nation it is a very wonderful nation. But no! the 'cold chain of silence'[6] will never be lifted from the soul of Ireland save by men using the homely directness of utterance, and, without much doubt, the speech of John Mitchel; and one would like to live to see the day of what might be termed, without any disrespect to Davis, the de-Davisization of Irish national literature, that is to say, the getting rid of the notion that in Ireland, a writer is to think, first and foremost, of interpreting the nationality of his country, and not simply of the burden which he has to deliver. The expression of nationality, literature cannot fail to be; and the richer, more varied and unexpected that expression the better.

1   A term that came into use at the end of the eighteenth century and which came to describe the landed Anglo-Irish interests in Ireland. Their capital was Dublin, the new Dublin laid out in the last third of the eighteenth century with fashionable squares and magnificent buildings such as the Custom House and the Four Courts.

2   For Grattan, see footnote on page 37. Sir Jonah Barrington (?1760–1834) recorded his personal views of the eighteenth-century Anglo-Irish in *Personal Sketches of His Own Time* (1827 and 1832).

3   John Scots Eriugena (?820–?880), an Irish theologian who sought an accommodation between neo-Platonic ideas and Christian theology.

4   John Mitchel (1815–75) wrote for Davis's newspaper the *Nation*, but then in 1848 founded his own more militant paper *United Irishman*. He was transported for treason-felony in 1848 to Tasmania. The one book of the '48 movement that Eglinton refers to is Mitchel's *Jail Journal, or Five Years in British Prisons* (1854).

5   T.W. Rolleston (1857–1920) was editor of *Prose Writings of Thomas Davis* (1890).

6   This phrase is from Thomas Moore's 'Dear Harp of My Country'.

FREDERICK RYAN
from Frederick Ryan, *Criticism and Courage and Other Essays* (1906)

Fred Ryan (1876–1913) is one of the more intriguing figures from this period. A friend of the pacifist and pro-feminist Francis Sheehy-Skeffington (1878–1916), Ryan was the first secretary of the Abbey Theatre, wrote an Ibsenesque play *The Laying of the Foundations* (one of the 'lost plays of the Abbey' since a part of it is missing), co-edited with John Eglinton the short-lived freethinking journal *Dana* (1904–5), edited an Egyptian nationalist newspaper in Cairo, and returned to London to edit another Egyptian nationalist newspaper owned by the Byronic anti-imperialist Wilfrid Blunt (1840–1922). Here in this extract the prescient Ryan argues for greater freedom of thought in Ireland, a country which struggled with censorship for nearly half a century after the Censorship Act of 1928.

Criticism and Courage

Whenever any attempt is made in this country to set up a platform, however modest, for the unprejudiced discussion of political and religious opinions and beliefs, it is always interesting to note the numerous and subtle arguments employed in different quarters to prove that the process of argument should not be applied to all beliefs. Some time ago I was present at a rather paradoxical discussion in a club, of which I have the honour to be a member, and which avowedly meets for the interchange of opinion. The subject under consideration was the need, as alleged, for independent thinking in Ireland; but the conclusion of the 'discussion', if it may be so summed up, was that one should have as few opinions as possible, and no expression of them at all. The futility of trying to change anyone's intimate beliefs; the impropriety and indecorum of government officials saying anything, even anonymously, in criticism of governmental practice; the propriety of teachers being obliged to resign if their opinions underwent any heterodox change, since in that case they were no longer qualified for their duties; the hardship of taking away 'sources of comfort' in the shape of theological dogmas from those who had nothing to cling to but such comforts; the arrogance of those who set themselves up as dissenters from the majority-opinion, and so forth: the changes were rung by various speakers, men and women, on all these arguments for conformity, these counsels of quiescence. Let us never do or say anything that will cause the slightest mental change in anyone, was the rule of action to be logically deduced from the argument. From this to the proposition that the life of the oyster or the tortoise is to be preferred to the life of man is only a step; and the final prescription of conformity might run: 'Let us eat, drink, and sleep, but above all, *Silence*!' It is a small part of the paradox of conformity that this precept itself was volubly elaborated, and the doctrine of not changing our neighbour's beliefs was put forward by way of changing the beliefs of those of us who stood for the morality of progressive change.

In order to clear the discussion, then, let us take the commonest subject of public contention. In the case of politics it is quite obvious that everyone is seeking to influence public opinion in favour of the policy which he thinks desirable, or in which he is personally interested. In this country, political issues are discussed vigorously enough and often acrimoniously enough, and some of those who warn us against giving pain by criticizing old traditions have themselves very little hesitation about giving pain to political opponents or ascribing their actions to base motives. It is true, of course, that the democratic side in Ireland, as elsewhere, has to bear the brunt of official and other pressure. The Government, through its extensive bureaucracy, and the Church, by its theological influence, exert an immense power which causes men to suppress their political convictions, or sub-consciously find arguments for suppressing them. What government can do in that way we see every day; the spirit of Castlereagh is not dead in Dublin Castle,[1] and the distribution of offices and favours affords an opportunity for the day-to-day repetition of the tactics by which the Act of Union was carried. As for the Church, we saw her political power during the Parnell crisis, and at present, for instance, we see her political influence exerted to press on members of Parliament and others a scheme of sectarian university 'reform',[2] for which there is little or no spontaneous public demand.

Notwithstanding these impediments and shackles, however, political discussion is comparatively free. Whenever anyone calls for a cessation of the political warfare and a 'union of all classes', we know at once that he is a reactionary, well-meaning or otherwise.

The real antithesis is not between politics and no-politics, but between good politics and bad; and part of good politics is to work for progress with as little personal ill-feeling and as much good taste as possible. In politics, then, we have little hesitation in 'disturbing the beliefs' of those who would be glad to rest in the assurance that everything was for the best in the best-governed State in the world. And when we meet benign old people who think the 'picturesque poverty' of the Irish peasant in the West is not to be disturbed as making for 'spiritual excellence', we have, most of us, little compunction in shattering the 'spiritual' dream. Political progress *must* involve change in political ideals and beliefs.

And the same falls to be said of literary and scientific discussion in the main. If a physician discovered a cure for cancer or tuberculosis, no one would dream for a moment of deterring him from publication on the ground that he might disturb the hitherto accepted view as to the origin and proper treatment of these diseases. In literature, too, criticism is free enough. Take at random any of the subjects of discussion or gossip in Ireland in the last year: Mr Yeats's plays[3] and Mr O'Brien's 'Conciliation',[4] the Sinn Féin policy,[5] and the National Exhibition — on all of these subjects we express ourselves with a commendable lack of reserve, though occasionally also with a boisterousness that, if not uniformly elevating, is at least not harmful.

The truth is that the kind of discussion which is most condemned and against which the 'arguments' mentioned at the beginning are mainly directed, is the discussion of religious ideas. Those beliefs which are supposed to be most vital and important are those which are to be least examined, and the doctrines which are held to be the most solidly established of all are thought to be the least able to bear criticism of any. No one would fear to discuss the propositions of Euclid, lest he might find them false, but most people fear to discuss their theological beliefs, lest, presumably, they might find them untenable; for, obviously, if they were certain of finding them true, they would welcome criticism. And one notes, thus, a kind of truce in Ireland between the rival Christian sects which bespeaks insincerity. The stage when Catholic and Protestant clergymen held public debates in the Rotunda on the merits of their respective creeds has long been passed. Doubtless it was realized that such encounters were more likely to make Freethinkers than converts to either Catholicism or Protestantism. And so there has set in the ignoble fashion at present in vogue of discountenancing on both sides such discussion. Catholics make little or no open attempt to convert Protestants, and, beyond one or two irresponsible agencies, Protestants make little or no attempt to convert Catholics. Whenever a zealous Protestant, thinking he is carrying light unto darkness, drops a Protestant tract in the way of Catholics, the Catholic Press raises an outcry as if some heinous offence had been committed, and the well-to-do Protestant, anxious to live on good terms with his Catholic neighbours, joins in condemning such tactics as 'bad form'. The whole phenomenon, it must be repeated, stands for insincerity, the insincerity of men who, half-conscious of the weakness of their dogmatic base, yet lack the courage to submit their beliefs to the test of examination and criticism. Men who have truth are anxious, and properly anxious, to spread it, even as men loyally desiring the truth are concerned that other men, equally sincere, should vitally differ from them. If any astronomer or physician put forward a scientific view on any aspect of his studies, he would be affected by the knowledge that other astronomers and physicians disagreed with him, and he would assuredly seek to clear the disagreement up. At the very least he would not shun the whole difficulty. Yet that is the course prescribed and pursued all round on questions of religion in Ireland. One interesting and typical incident, illustrating this, comes to my mind. Some months ago Father Sheehan delivered an address to the 'Catholic Truth Society' in Dublin. In the course of his remarks he advocated the cultivation of 'passionless' literature and the bowdlerizing of poets like Burns and Byron, and in addition referred to the large numbers of cheap rationalist publications which were now openly sold in a 'Catholic city' like Dublin, a fact which he deplored. Did he, however, recommend his hearers to peruse these books? Did he say, as one might expect a sincere and wise teacher to say: 'Read, my friends, what the best minds have to say against you if you seek loyally the truth, for until you know the best that can be said against you, you know neither your weakness nor your strength'? Not at all. Father Sheehan merely fell back on the old and shameful dictum that these were 'immoral' books, to be shunned by the faithful. And when it is mentioned that the publications in question consist mostly of cheap reprints of standard works by men like Mill, Spencer, Huxley, Darwin, Haeckel, Renan, and Matthew Arnold, the grossness of the libel may be estimated. At least Father Sheehan's creed did not deter him from blackening his neighbour's character, when that neighbour had the temerity to differ from his theology.

But that is the temper in which all such studies are met in Ireland. A cultivated ignorance, as ludicrous as it is contemptible, is the prevailing note. Read any popular journal and observe the tone of snobbish superiority to modern science and all that it stands for; so that when, as is often the case, we are warned against the 'pride of knowledge', some of us are prone to reflect that, if that be a reprehensible vanity, the pride of ignorance must be considerably worse. You will find in any newspaper you take up long accounts of the interminable laying of foundation stones of churches, of the continual opening of bazaars for ecclesiastical objects, of lugubrious addresses from prelates and priests on themes that belong to the mental atmosphere of the Middle Ages. But of anything that connects with the real intellectual life of the world outside Ireland, little or nothing is heard. When, for instance, some time ago, an article appeared on the Abbé Loisy from the pen of a French critic, a widely circulated clerical weekly editorially declared that it had never heard of Loisy and did not want to hear of him, the writer arguing, in bucolic fashion, that what did not interest him ought to interest no one else. A couple of years ago I heard a well-known Jesuit preacher, within a few months of the publication of the *Encyclopaedia Biblica* (which was itself a redaction of current continental scholarship) tell a rather high-class congregation that modern criticism had left the Bible untouched. To pretend that discoveries which tell against you do not exist, to belittle those who make them, and abuse those who publish them, and, in short, to refuse to face the intellectual battle, confident in the final victory of the truth, is the attitude of our theological guides to-day. And it is this mental and moral cowardice, for which orthodoxy is primarily responsible, that helps to keep us as a people intellectually inferior. A vital concern for truth more than for established beliefs correlates with all the other virtues that keep a nation progressive and alive.

It would, however, be idle to make light of the tremendous forces that oppose the rational discussion of such questions as I have touched upon, and which produce the corresponding insincerity. Vast vested interests of all kinds stand in the way, whereas those who follow truth loyally have a thankless task, which nothing but an inward sanction can sustain. Yet they may reflect that never yet was progress possible without intellectual change, never yet did humanity advance a step without the breaking of old traditions and the discarding of old beliefs. The true humanist will assuredly wish that such change as must be should entail as little pain as possible, since it is not pain but growth in knowledge that is desired. But some pain is inevitable, and it is in the readiness to face it that true courage lies. For a nation, certainly, it bodes ill when, as a mass, it is afraid of truth, or at least afraid of the sacrifices by which alone truth can be attained.

education in Ireland would become segregated with Catholics going to the National University and Protestants to Trinity College Dublin and Queen's University Belfast.

1   The administrative headquarters of British rule in Ireland until Irish independence in 1921.

2   In 1908 the Irish Universities Act abolished the Royal University of 1880 and provided for a National University at Dublin (with Colleges in Dublin, Cork, and Galway). In effect, as Ryan no doubt foresaw, higher

3   This is probably a reference to plays by the Abbey Theatre Company rather than to any specific play by Yeats.

4   William O'Brien (1852–1928) was an M.P. from 1883 until 1918.

5   Sinn Féin was launched as a political party by Arthur Griffith in 1905.

GEORGE A. BIRMINGHAM

from *The Fortnightly Review*, December 1907

George A. Birmingham (pseudonym of Canon James Owen Hannay) (1865–1950) was born into a Belfast Unionist family, the son of a clergyman. Educated at Trinity College Dublin he was ordained in 1892 and took up residence in Westport, County Mayo, until 1916 when he joined the British Army as a chaplain. A prolific writer, especially of fiction, he is the author of *The Northern Iron* (1907), *Spanish Gold* (1908), and *The Red Hand of Ulster* (1912). *Irishmen All* (1913), a series of portraits of Irish types with illustrations by Jack B. Yeats, reflects his inclusive sense of Irish identity; a novel *General John Regan* published the same year met with hostility from D.P. Moran and other nationalists for its satire on provincial Ireland. The following essay provides an early survey of the Irish Literary Revival.

The Literary Movement in Ireland

Ireland has enjoyed of late a large share of public attention. We have been deluged with newspaper articles and books in which the condition of the country has been discussed from almost every conceivable point of view. A powerful Government has brought to birth an unfortunate babe which everybody, Irish or English, Nationalist or Unionist, has agreed to strangle at once. There has been great talk of ecclesiastical influence; of land purchase and grazing farms; of Sinn Féiners, wild creatures whom intelligent Englishmen have agreed to consider mad though undeniably clever; of agrarian outrages here and there in Roscommon and Galway; and of many other things which no man can want to have enumerated again. But one thing has entirely escaped the notice of all observers; the fact that Ireland is producing for the first time in her history literature in the English language. And yet this is probably a more significant thing than all the political turmoil of which we hear too much.

Of course, Ireland has frequently produced great writers of English. A list of names occurs readily to the memory: Richard Steele, Oliver Goldsmith, Laurence Sterne, Edmund Burke, Maria Edgeworth, and many minor people, Parnell the Poet, Lady Morgan, Lever, Lover, Lefanu.[1] Their names are in the ordinary histories of English literature. Their works are duly chronicled. They are appreciated comfortably by cultured Englishmen, for they wrote for an English public, and followed the traditions of English letters. Once and only once in the past was there anything like a school of Irish writers making an appeal to an Irish public. Round Thomas Davis and *The Nation* newspaper in the middle of the last century there gathered an extremely brilliant band of writers. Nothing of its kind surpasses the collection of verse published under the title of *The Spirit of the Nation*. Some of the finest of these lyrics found their way to the hearts of the people, and are sung and recited still. But the merits of the Young Ireland writings were rhetorical rather than purely literary. They stir the blood and fire the passions, but we do not rejoice over them in pure satisfaction with form and style. They were meant to arouse the patriotic spirit of a nation. They were not the expression of artistic aspiration. The Young Ireland movement produced just one really great prose writer — one whose work for the sake of its excellence of literary form deserves to live — John Mitchel.[2] He was exiled from Ireland, and left behind him no literary disciples, no inheritors of his capacity for virile prose.

The Fenian movement did little for literature. John O'Leary's papers in the *Irish People* and Kickham's novels[3] are all that remain to us. They are the work of Irishmen, and were written for Ireland, but they failed to awaken the intellect of the nation. They created no school of Irish writers. The short-lived idealism of the followers of Isaac Butt[4] never got beyond politics. Parnell's leadership was entirely barren of literary inspiration. There is one lyric written by Miss Fanny Parnell.[5] There was literally nothing else except flamboyant oratory. The literary spirit of Ireland slept while men struggled with each other for land and rent; shot, hanged, boycotted, or imprisoned one another. There was no room in Ireland in those days for literature. Nobody felt nobly enough to sing well. Nobody thought calmly enough to write anything but pamphlets.

The literary intellect of Ireland slept during the Parnell epoch, but there was one Irishman who was haunted by uneasy dreams. Mr Standish O'Grady rediscovered the ancient Gaelic heroes. Himself a man with the heroic kind of soul, he wrote of heroes in an epic way. Amid the turmoil of political strife nobody grasped the spirit of his writing. The people who were passionately indignant with landlords for owning land could find no inspiration in the story of Cuculain, because it was not recorded of him that he ever shot an agent. The others, who were above all things anxious to hang an agitator, would have nothing to do with the Red Branch Knights, suspecting in a dim, vague way that such men must have been Nationalists, and therefore blackguards. Mr Standish O'Grady wrote on. His *Early Bardic History of Ireland* was followed by his *History of Ireland, Critical and Philosophical*, by *Cuculain*, *The Flight of the Eagle*, *Finn and his Companions*, *The Bog of Stars*, and other books. Mr Standish O'Grady never won great popularity. His was a nobler reward. He is the father of the Irish literary movement. From him the poets and dramatists who are writing in Ireland now drew their first inspiration. Nor do his services to Ireland stop here. By his publication of *The Library of the Nore* while he was editor of *The Kilkenny Moderator*, he gave young writers their first chance of finding a public. In his *All Ireland Review*, now, alas! dead,[6] he

steadily maintained great ways of thought, high and pure views of vexed questions, an heroic attitude of soul, which have done much to elevate and keep lofty in spirit our new literature. Yet for a long time Mr Standish O'Grady was alone, a voice in a midnight wilderness full of ravening creatures.

But the dawn came, and if we have not yet got done with the howlings of wolves, at least there is a hope that when the daylight fully comes to us they will get them away to their dens. In 1888 Miss Katharine Tynan published her first volume of verse.[7] She and another young poet, Miss Frances Wynne, who died before she had done more than give promise of good work, owed much to the wise encouragement of Father Matthew Russell, editor of *The Irish Monthly*. Here was work, not of great power or striking originality, but distinctively Irish in tone. The following year Mr Yeats published his *Wanderings of Oisin*. I can recall now the effect produced on my mind by the reading of this book. I had just left college after winning an undeserved honour degree in modern literature. I was more or less capable of appreciating English poetry. I knew Palgrave's *Golden Treasury* almost off by heart. I was totally unprepared for what I found in *The Wanderings of Oisin*. The subjects of the poems were new to me, the verse harmonies unfamiliar. It was my first introduction to the Celtic note in literature. Fortunately the book was given to me by a man whose literary judgement I trusted. I persevered with it, and bewilderment passed into admiration. I note this effect of Mr Yeats's poetry on my mind, not because it matters in the least to any one how I felt or thought, but because there are many even now to whom the new Irish literature is repellent on account of its strangeness; people who have been educated as I was to understand the English literary tradition and who find it extremely difficult to understand anything else.

With Mr Yeats's name must go that of A.E. (Mr George Russell), whose *Homeward Songs*[8] were published just after *The Wanderings of Oisin*. Mr Standish O'Grady is the father of our new literature; Mr Yeats is the most widely known of our writers; but A.E. (the pen name was adopted originally by accident) has set his distinctive mark upon Irish work. It was he more than any other who endowed it with its transcendental quality. From him comes that fondness for universal ideas, as distinguished from merely local and contemporary thought, which gives at once a depth and a vagueness to our poetry. This is no place to write of Mr Russell's other activities. He is a painter, an economist, a man of business, the editor of a brilliantly witty weekly paper. But he is a man of letters and a poet first of all. Quite possibly his later poetry has suffered from the absorption of his energies in other fields of work. It is given to few men, to no other man in Ireland, to teach political economy, paint pictures, and write mystical lyrics at the same time. It has been said that his earliest volume of verse, the *Homeward Songs*, contains his best poetry. I am not of this opinion. He seems to me to have reached the highest expression of his genius in his later books. 'The Gates of Dreamland' and 'Hope in Failure', which are to be found in *The Divine Vision*,[9] are finer than anything in the earlier book. But even if it were true that Mr Russell's earliest work is his best, his services to literature are not exhausted by his published writings. He is a man of extraordinary prodigality of mind. Ideas, the hoarded gold of others, are scattered by him with amazing profusion. There is probably no Irish writer to-day who does not owe something to the talk of Mr Russell. Round him men of different talents, striving to express themselves in different ways, gather and get courage, fresh hope, and inspiration. Time was when Irishmen of literary ability left Ireland. It was a barren land for them. It contained no public for their work. Thus Oscar Wilde, George Moore, and G.B. Shaw left Ireland to work elsewhere. Now there is no necessity for men with brains to seek sympathy out of Ireland. They can find all they want in Dublin, and the most prominent figure in this intellectual society is Mr George Russell.

Both Mr Yeats and Mr Russell are lyric poets. It is, therefore, not to be wondered at that the new Irish literature is peculiarly rich in lyric poetry. For these two are masters, and their disciples follow them. Yet, apart altogether from their influence, it is quite natural that a suddenly awakened intellectual vitality, with no literary tradition behind it, should find its expression chiefly in lyrics. Emotion is vivid. The joys and pains of life are sharply felt. The habits of reflection and analysis have not yet had time to form. A lyrical outburst is inevitable. It is characteristic, too, of a period of emotional excitement and rapturous discovery of unsuspected powers that our poets should scatter their work broadcast through the pages of newspapers and periodicals, just as Mr Russell flings ideas with reckless profusion to chance acquaintances. Very often the authors do not seem to care what happens to their poems. The work of collecting and publishing in book form Ethna Carbery's verses was only completed by pious hands after her death.[10] Miss Alice Milligan's poems have still to be sought out in all sorts of odd places.[11] No collection of Mr Rolleston's lyrics exists[12] or of Mr George Roberts's.[13] We are indebted to the enterprise of Messrs Maunsel and Co. for little volumes of Mr Thomas Keohler's verses, Miss

Ella Young's, and Mr Charles Weekes's.[14] We look to the same publishers to fulfil a promise and give us collections of the poems of Miss Eva Gore-Booth, and Mr Roberts. In a little anthology entitled *New Songs* we find gathered for us lyrics by Paudraig Colum, Susan Mitchell,[15] Seumas O'Sullivan, and others. It is interesting to notice that two papers, more than any others, have achieved a reputation for publishing really beautiful verse. *The United Irishman*, now *Sinn Féin*, and *The Celtic Christmas* are the favourite mediums of publication with our young poets. The Englishman will be struck by this fact as an instance of the unintelligible contrariness of Irish affairs, for the first of these two papers is the organ of the most vehement and extreme Nationalists, the second is the Christmas number of a weekly paper devoted to the interests of co-operative creameries, mutual credit banks and agricultural organization generally. It is as curious to find tender and graceful lyrics in the one, as it would be absurd to expect the dreams of poetical mystics in the other. In reality this is not so queer as it seems. Intellectual life, like misfortune, makes strange bedfellows. The advocates of the Sinn Féin policy and the people who are engaged in the work of agricultural organization are more mentally and spiritually awake than any other sections of Irish society. They more than others are eager for new ideas and capable of receiving them. It is quite natural that our young poets should appeal first of all to them. In the present condition of the country, the upper class stagnating in what they have inherited of the culture of two generations ago, and the bulk of the middle class either wholly impervious to ideas or fanatically devoted to some particular fad, it is inevitable that our poets should be doubtful about an appeal to the public in general. It may be hoped, however, that in the pages of the *Shanachie*[16] some of them may reach a wider public than the pages of a political paper or a Christmas number can offer.

Next to the unmistakably Irish note which predominates in this mass of lyrical poetry, the reader is struck by the direct return to the simplest aspects of human life and the most obvious beauties of nature. Along with this homeliness of subject goes the linking of the great emotions which touch the human soul in its highest moods with very humble things. Here, for example, is a poem of Paudraig Colum's called 'The Plougher', which appears in the anthology just mentioned, *New Songs*.

Sunset and silence; a man; around him earth savage,
  earth broken:
Beside him two horses, a plough!

Earth savage, earth broken, the brutes, the dawn-
man there in the sunset!
And the plough that is twin to the sword, that is
founder of cities!

'Brute-tamer, plough-maker, earth-breaker! Can'st
hear? There are ages between us!
Is it praying you are as you stand there alone in the
sunset?

'Surely our sky-born gods can be nought to you,
Earth-child and Earth-master!
Surely your thoughts are of Pan, or of Wotan or
Dana!

'Yet why give thought to the gods? Has Pan led
your brutes where they stumble?
Has Wotan put hands to the plough or Dana
numbed pain of the child-bed?

'What matter your foolish reply, O man standing
lone and bowed earthward.
Your task is a day near its close. Give thanks to the
night-giving God.'

Slowly the darkness falls, the broken lands blend
with the savage,
The brute-tamer stands by the brutes, by a head's
breadth only above them!

A head's breadth, ay, but therein is Hell's depth and
the height up to Heaven,
And the thrones of the gods, and their halls and
their chariots, purples and splendours.

The music of these verses is unfamiliar. They are
imperfect hexameters, but the author has escaped the
dreadful monotony of emphasis, which spoils almost
all attempts to render in English the rhythm of the
classical metres. Read along with this a little lyric on a
similar subject by Seosamh Mac Cathmhaoil.[17]

Go, ploughman, plough
The mearing lands,
The meadow lands,
The mountain lands:
All life is bare
Beneath your share,
All love is in your lusty hands.

Up, horses, now!
And straight and true
Let every broken furrow run:

The strength you sweat
Shall blossom yet
In golden glory to the sun.[18]

Both these poems in their cadences, the subject-
matter, and their treatment of it are highly characteristic of the new Irish lyrics. I have chosen them for
quotation rather than the work of more famous
writers, not to represent the best that has been done,
but because they are very typical of the union of what
I may call local homeliness with universal thought.

Another striking feature of our poetry is the
appearance now and then of stark ferocity, the
amazingly intense expression of the hatred of the Gael
for the stranger which underlies all Irish life. The Irish
have never forgotten that they are a conquered people.
They have never ceased to dream of a revolt against
their conquerors. The fact that Irish poets still sing
with wholehearted vehemence as Ethna Carbery did
in 'Donal Mac Seaghain na Mallacht' is a strange
comment on the attempts of English statesmen to
arrive at a compromise between the idea of a united
kingdom and the Irish conception of nationality. The
poem is an extraordinary production when one
considers that it came from the heart of a tender and
beautiful girl. The speaker, Donal, the son of John, of
the curses, replies to his mother who has been urging
him that love and pity should find some place in his
life:—

'I look on our smoking valleys,
I gaze on our wasted lands,
I stand by our grass-grown thresholds
And curse their ruffian bands.

'I curse them in dark and daylight —
I curse them the hours between
The grey dawn and shadowy night time
For the sights my eyes have seen.

'I curse them awake or sleeping,
I curse them alive or dead,
And, Oh Christ! that my words were embers
To fall on each Saxon head.'

The same note of fierceness runs through Seosamh
Mac Cathmhaoil's 'A Prophecy': —

'The loins of the Galldacht
Shall wither like grass' —
Strange words I heard said
At the fair of Dún-eas.

'A bard shall be born
Of the seed of the folk,
To break with his singing
The bond and the yoke.

'A sword, white as ashes,
Shall fall from the sky,
To rise, red as blood,
On the charge and the cry.

'Stark pipers shall blow,
Stout drummers shall beat,
And the shout of the North
Shall be heard in the street.

'The strong shall go down,
And the weak shall prevail,
And a glory shall sit
On the sign of the Gaedhal.

'Then Emer shall come
In good time by her own,
And a man of the people
Shall speak from the throne.' —

Strange words I heard said
At the fair of Dún-eas —
'The Gaedhaldacht shall live,
The Galldacht shall pass!'[19]

Next to its abundance of lyrics the most striking feature of the Irish literary movement is its drama. I leave aside plays written entirely or partly in Gaelic, though some of these, especially Dr Douglas Hyde's, display great imaginative force and dramatic feeling. The writing of plays in English for Irish audiences received a great impetus when Miss Horniman established the Abbey Theatre. But long before the National Theatre Society found a settled home plays were written and acted in Dublin, and plays like Paudraig Colum's *The Fiddler's House* and the productions of the Ulster Literary Society[20] are acted independently of the Abbey Theatre. The best known of our dramatists is Mr W. Yeats. His genius is in reality more lyrical than dramatic. The best of his plays, *The Shadowy Waters*, has strong dramatic situations, and in its latest form should be highly effective on the stage, but it claims our admiration chiefly on account of the lyrical beauty of certain passages of the dialogue. Another play of his which is rich in fine spectacular effects, *The Countless Kathleen*, has never been popular in Ireland. *The King's Threshold* gives us a great situation worked up to a moving and

heroic climax. The early days of the Irish theatre saw the production of Mr Edward Martyn's *Heather Field*, a work more purely dramatic in conception and treatment than many of the plays which have been produced. It is much to be regretted that Mr Martyn has ceased to write plays. Lady Gregory and Mr William Boyle[21] have also written plays which have been staged with good effect. By far the boldest and most original of our Irish dramatists is Mr Synge. It is unfortunate that two of his plays — *The Shadow of the Glen* and *The Playboy of the Western World* — have excited fierce controversy in Ireland. The only work of his which has been received with real popular approval is the intensely moving one-act play, *Riders to the Sea*. It is creditable to the Irish public that this play should be appreciated as it has been. It is a tragedy, not relieved but intensified by grim touches of the commonplace. It is severe and restrained, not at all what a popular audience might be expected to appreciate. It is less creditable to the Irish people that they wrangled about *The Shadow of the Glen*, and worked themselves up to actual frenzy over *The Playboy of the Western World*. Yet they were not wholly without excuse. The latter play is very difficult to understand, as difficult as Ibsen was at first to English audiences. After a while we shall get to know Mr Synge better, and pay to his genius the tribute of enthusiastic admiration which it deserves. In the meanwhile it must be his consolation that men do not become fanatics for the sake of the commonplace, and that no work without merit ever earned the distinction of columns of abuse in the daily Press, or had resolutions passed condemning it by Boards of Guardians. It is prophets, not charlatans, whom the multitude stones.

In prose literature, and especially in fiction, the Irish literary movement is comparatively weak. We have only one novelist of first-rate importance, Mr George Moore, and most of his fiction was written out of Ireland before he felt the inspiration of the new movement. His later work has, it will be generally admitted, benefited by his return to Ireland. In *Sister Teresa* there are traces of Irish influence, but *The Untilled Field*, a book more suggestive than any of the author's earlier work, contains the first fruits of his feeling for Ireland. I suppose that *The Lake*, which is Irish through and through, will be reckoned hereafter Mr George Moore's finest novel. Considering his great ability and his high literary standing, it is curious to note that Mr Moore has had almost no influence on Irish prose writing. It is perhaps possible to trace something of his spirit in Mr Synge's non-dramatic work, his *Aran Islands*, and his essays published in *The*

Shanachie and elsewhere. But Mr Synge is too virile and original a writer to be much influenced by anyone, even Mr Moore. The few other novelists whom the movement has produced have gone their own way. Miss Emily Lawless[22] cannot, either as poet or novelist, be reckoned a product of the new intellectual life of the country. Mr Shan Bullock, Miss Jane Barlow, and Mr Seumas McManus[23] have done excellent work, but our fiction falls a long way below the standard of our poetry or our drama. Good novels are the product of a mature literature, not of a movement in its infancy, and the temptation to appeal to an English, rather than a purely Irish, public is likely for many years to come to prove too strong for writers who look to earn money by their books. Miss Louise Kenny and Mr Buckley,[24] alone among our younger novelists, have struck an entirely fresh and purely Irish note in their books. Her *Red-Haired Woman* was a first effort, and was marred by a certain redundancy of style, but an atmosphere of high romance is steadily maintained, and it is likely that Miss Kenny will do much better work in future. Mr Buckley's *Cambia Carty*, published the other day, gives evidence of originality and power.

We have, besides our novelists, several writers of good prose of a distinctly Irish kind. Mr Yeats and Mr Russell — these two names meet us everywhere in the study of Irish literature — have written deeply suggestive and fascinating essays. They might both be reckoned great prose writers if they had not chosen rather to be numbered among the poets. Akin to them in spirit and form is Lady Gregory. Her name has already been mentioned as one of the Abbey Theatre dramatists, but it is on her books rather than her plays that her fame will rest. She has tried the curious experiment of using Gaelic idiom in English prose; and, dealing with purely Irish subjects, has created a style very sympathetic with her matter. She has made the ancient heroic legends live as they never did before in English.

It is necessary to mention three other detached prose writers, all of them possessed of a distinctive style, and all of them original. 'John Eglinton' (to use the writer's pseudonym) is the author of several volumes of essays. His *Pebbles from a Brook* was published by Mr Standish O'Grady as one of the volumes of *The Library of the Nore*. Other essays appeared in the short-lived periodical *Dana*, some of which have been re-published in one of the series of *Tower Press Booklets*. Mr Eglinton's prose gives the impression of being written with extreme care. It is packed with thought to such an extent as to run the risk of occasional obscurity. He will probably never find a very large public, but his readers, if few, will be

'fit,' and it is likely that his influence will be wide, working outwards through others to people whom he will fail to reach directly. Sir Horace Plunkett would probably lay no claim to be a man of letters. He writes primarily with a view to propagating his economic and social ideas, and, even with the example of Ruskin before us, it is difficult to think of political economy and sociology as having any connection with literature. But Sir Horace Plunkett has a prose style of his own. His book, *Ireland in the New Century*, is illuminated with delightful humour, and is extraordinarily lucid, so lucid that the reader is tempted by the mere simplicity of the writing to suppose that he has always been familiar with ideas which are really new to him. It is safe to say that if everybody in Ireland had not been occupied in abusing, and everybody in England in praising, the teaching of the book, the author would before this have found recognition as a writer of literary merit. If it is difficult to think of an economist as a literary man, it is still harder to give the title to a political journalist. Yet Mr Arthur Griffith pours out week after week in the columns of his paper, *Sinn Féin*, prose of a very high order of merit. He has published nothing in book form. His reputation rests so far entirely on a couple of pamphlets and his weekly articles, written as such things must be, hurriedly. He is the inheritor of John Mitchel's iron style and sledge-hammer methods. He has something also of Swift's bald simplicity of appalling statement. In all probability neither Sir Horace Plunkett nor Mr Griffith would care to write for writing's sake. They write to convert people to their ideas and ways of looking at pressing problems. All mere graces and elegances are sacrificed cheerfully by the one to the desire of being persuasive, by the other to a passion for annihilating knaves and fools. But both of them have achieved, in spite of themselves, literary distinction.

There are other names which ought to be mentioned in any complete account of Irish prose writing, Mr Rolleston, Mr Stephen Gwynn, Lord Dunsany, Miss McManus, Miss Mary Butler;[25] but enough has been said to show that as yet we have no coherent tradition of prose. Our poets and our dramatists form groups. It is possible to classify them. Our prose is like waves where cross tides meet each other at an angle and meet the wind, which do not run together or make in any one direction. Perhaps it is too soon to expect the forming of any school of Irish prose writing. A newly awakened literary spirit finds its natural expression in lyric and drama. It is only after the first raptures are over that a period of calm reflection comes and a great prose style is evolved by the labours of many writers.

1 Richard Steele (1672–1729), co-editor of *The Tatler* (1711–12); Oliver Goldsmith (1728–74), author of *The Deserted Village* (1770); Laurence Sterne (1713–68), who spent part of his childhood in Ireland, author of *Tristram Shandy* (1759–67); Edmund Burke (1729–97), author of *Reflections on the Revolution in France* (1790); Maria Edgeworth (1767–1849), author of *Castle Rackrent* (1800); Thomas Parnell (1679–1718); Lady Morgan (née Sydney Owenson) (?1776–1859), author of *The Wild Irish Girl* (1806); Charles Lever (1806–72), author of *Charles O'Malley* (1841); Samuel Lover (1797–1868), author of *Handy Andy* (1842); Sheridan Lefanu (1814–73), author of *The House by the Churchyard* (1863).

2 John Mitchel (1815–75) wrote for Davis's newspaper the *Nation*, but then in 1848 founded his own more militant paper *United Irishman*. He was transported for treason-felony in 1848 to Tasmania, and wrote about his experiences in *Jail Journal, or Five Years in British Prisons* (1854).

3 Charles Kickham (1828–82) was the author of *Sally Cavanagh* (1869) and *Knocknagow* (1873).

4 Isaac Butt (1813–79), as M.P. for Limerick from 1871 until 1879, argued for Home Rule for Ireland.

5 Fanny Parnell (1854–82), the sister of Charles Stewart Parnell, author of *Land League Songs* (1882).

6 Last issue January 1906. *All Ireland Review* began life in 1900 and was edited by Standish O'Grady in Kilkenny. See O'Grady (1900) above for example of O'Grady's style.

7 The first volume of verse by Katharine Tynan (1861–1931) was *Louise de la Vallière*, published in 1885.

8 First published in 1894.

9 First published in 1904.

10 Ethna Carbery (pseudonym of Anna MacManus) (1866–1902), author of *The Four Winds of Erin* (1902).

11 *Hero Lays* (1908) is the title of a collection of verse by Alice Milligan (1866–1953).

12 The poetry of T.W. Rolleston (1857–1920) can be found in *Sea Spray* (1909).

13 George Roberts (1873–1953) was an Irish publisher at the time, managing director of Maunsel, who earned the wrath of Joyce in 1912 for destroying the sheets of *Dubliners*.

14 Their work was published in a series entitled The Tower Press Booklets, edited by Seamas O'Sullivan and James Connolly. Thomas Keohler, *Songs of a Devotee* (1906); Ella Young, *Poems* (1906); Charles Weekes, *About Women* (1907).

15 Susan Mitchell (1866–1926) later wrote a witty volume entitled *Aids to the Immortality of Certain Persons in Ireland Charitably Administered* (1908).

16 A quarterly which ran from Summer 1906 to Winter 1907.

17 Joseph Campbell (see below for more poems).

18 This poem 'Go, Ploughman, Plough' was first published in *The Man Child* (1907).

19 This poem appeared in Campbell's *The Rushlight* (1906).

20 Birmingham cites *The Pagan* by Lewis Purcell. Maunsel and Co.

21 William Boyle (1853–1923) wrote several popular plays for the Abbey Theatre including *The Building Fund* (1905) and *The Eloquent Dempsey* (1906).

22 See footnote on page 21 for more information.

23 Shan Bullock (1865–1935), author of *The Red-Leaguers* (1904) and *The Loughsiders* (1924); Jane Barlow (1857–1917), author of *Irish Idylls* (1892), set in the fictional Connemara village of Lisconnel; for Seamas MacManus see *The Rocky Road to Dublin* (1938) below.

24 *The Red-Haired Woman*, a novel set in Thomond, was published in 1905; William Buckley was author of *Croppies Lie Down* (1903) and *Cambia Carty* (1907).

25 For Stephen Gwynn, see page 217 and Lord Dunsany, see page 267. Miss MacManus (Ethna Carbery) wrote *Passionate Hearts* (1903), a collection of stories; the largely forgotten novelist Mary Butler was author of *A Bundle of Rushes* (1899) and *The Ring of Day* (1906).

BERNARD VAUGHAN

from Bernard Vaughan, *Society, Sin and The Saviour* (1908)

Fr Vaughan (1847–1922), whose family owned property on Achill Island, was the younger brother of Cardinal Vaughan. He was born at the family estate in Herefordshire and educated at Stonyhurst. A lively preacher, Fr Vaughan was frequently invited to deliver sermons both to wealthy congregations and to the poor. According to Stanislaus Joyce, he was the model for Fr Purdon in Joyce's story 'Grace'. In a discussion with Fr Conmee in the street in *Ulysses*, Mrs Sheehy comments favourably on the sermon by Fr Vaughan she has recently heard, one that sounds not unlike the one reproduced below (it was originally given in the Church of the Immaculate Conception in Mayfair in 1907). Meanwhile, Fr Conmee, we are told, 'thought on Father Bernard Vaughan's droll eyes and cockney voice', a reference not to Fr Vaughan being a Cockney but to his skill at imitating accents. For his biography, see C.C. Martindale, S.J., *Bernard Vaughan, S.J.* (1923). See also below Stanislaus Joyce, 'The Background to "Dubliners"' (1954).

from **Christ before the People**

'His Blood be upon us and upon our children.'
— St Matt. xxvii, 25

We read that during our Lord's trial Pilate's wife sent him word to have nothing to do with that just Man, Jesus Christ; and it is likely enough that while our Lord was absent in Herod's Court, Pilate and Claudia were exchanging their views about the divine Prisoner. Perhaps it was during this conversation that Pilate was handed the sealed letter from the Tetrarch, informing him that he could come to no conclusion about the Culprit sent to his Court, and consequently that he was sending Him, with many compliments, back to a Governor whom he felt sure would make short shift with Him. Before Pilate realizes the situation, the shouts and the yells of the returning procession tell him that our Lord is actually on His way back to the Prætorium. Yes, sure enough, as Pilate can see from his balcony, there, on the western steep incline facing his palace, a veritable mob, a tangle of colour, comes swinging down like a mountain torrent let loose and meaning mischief.

Pilate, not a little disconcerted, pulls himself together, sets his teeth, and rising from his seat, steps impatiently upon the balcony where he stands with folded arms, glancing down upon the people with defiance expressed in every feature. When after a time the hissing mob has exhausted its cries, the judge makes his proposal. Being the festival season, he offers to release to them Barabbas, the murderer, or Jesus, the Christ. For a moment there is hesitation among the people, but after some parley with the chief priests and ancients, like a tornado comes the cry, 'Not this Man, but Barabbas.' 'What then,' asks the miserable compromiser, 'will you that I do to the King of the Jews?'

The Jews, having become conscious that the game is in their own hands, and that the judge is a coward, at the top of their voices scream forth exultantly their verdict, 'Crucify Him, crucify Him.' The judge timidly insists that he can find no cause in Him, but the people will not have it, declaring they have a law, 'and according to the law He ought to die, because He made Himself the Son of God.' Once more the uneasy judge holds conversation with the divine Prisoner, with the result that he makes a yet more terrible compromise, saying, 'I find no cause of death in Him. I will chastise Him therefore and let Him go.'

Here for a moment I must ask you to pause whilst I remind you of what our dear Lord endures mentally when He hears that, as no fault can be found in Him,

He is to be condemned to the lash. It is not so much the thought of being scourged in public, or even of being stripped naked in the sight of all, which is for Jesus so hard to bear, but rather that a judge, whose mission it is to hold the scales of justice, should so far forget the majesty of the law and the rights of a prisoner, that in one and the same breath he can pronounce Him to be innocent and treat Him as though guilty, inflicting on Him the most cruel and ignominious of punishments.

What a punishment! The mere anticipation of it in the Garden had forced from His human soul the cry, 'O Father, if it be possible, let it pass.' Even as we, the humble followers of the Crucified, after the lapse of so many centuries, reverently contemplate the scene of the scourging, it is difficult to understand how our divine Lord could have submitted to the agony and ignominy of it.

If the Passion can teach us nothing else, at any rate it tells us this, that none of us really knows what real love is. Is it an impulse gone mad? But come down to the courtyard of the palace where each one of you may be forced to witness the scene about to be enacted.

'Behold the Lamb of God Who taketh away the sins of the world,' in the midst of a gang of ruffians like a pack of hounds clamouring for its prey. See that broken column in the centre of the courtyard; the crowd is jostling its way there, where Jesus is to be stripped to nakedness in the sight of the surrounding multitude still crying for His Blood. And now look closer still. The Sacred Hands that have so often been raised to bless and to heal, are being actually bound by cords, drawing them upward to an iron ring which holds them rigidly in such a position that the Sacred Feet scarcely touch with their toe-tips the white pavement so soon to be dyed red with blood.

And now there rises a yell and shout from the people greeting the appearance of two strong-built soldiers who, stripped to the waist, running through their fingers the knotted cords, presently lift them to swing through the air, till down with a thud they come upon the quivering flesh of the Son of God. On they go, lash after lash, every stroke lapping the flesh and drawing blood till it is seen streaming down the Sacred Limbs, pouring itself about the ankles, while the surrounding mob is beside itself, drunk with delight. How many moments this most terrible of terrible scenes lasted I know not; but this I do know, that as it was inflicted, not with a view to punishment, but with the object of awakening pity for Jesus, the savage cruelty of it no language can describe. Perhaps some man in that throng more merciful than the rest, fearing the worst results, rushes in, cuts the rope, when Jesus falls, slipping along the pavement in a pool of warm blood.

And now, you votaries of pleasure, who proclaim so loudly that there is no such thing as sin, will most probably call upon me to have done with this realistic picture, saying, 'You are offending every canon of good taste, you are forgetting every rule of fine art. Pass from this scene of blood which blinds our sight, wounds our hearts, and stings our conscience.' But I tell you I will not have done with this picture of Jesus Christ all broken and bruised from the soles of His feet to the top of His head, lying half dead, white and ruddy in a stream of His blood, till you yourselves come to acknowledge that in the sight before you, you recognize the handiwork of your own sin. If you insist that this flagellation is meant to awaken the pity of the Jews, I declare to you it is endured by Jesus Christ to create a clean heart in you Christians; these pains are borne in the body of Christ to atone for your pleasures of the flesh. Yes, and that crown of thorns which is being so rudely pressed upon the Sacred brow is being worn in contrition for your sins of pride and vanity. Nay, the Sacred eyes are blindfolded and that mock sceptre is being placed in the gracious hand to make reparation for those sins of sight and of touch in which you have so freely indulged.

In the scene then before us I see the divine Penitent offering to Heaven an act of reparation for your vicious pleasures in the concupiscence of the flesh, in the concupiscence of the eyes, and the pride of life.

'Then the soldiers of the Governor taking Jesus into the hall gathered unto Him the whole band, and stripping Him they put a scarlet cloak about Him. And plaiting a crown of thorns they put it on His Head, and a reed in His right hand, and bowing the knee before Him they mocked Him saying, "Hail, King of the Jews," and spitting upon Him, they took the reed and struck His Head.'

Truly it is an evil and a bitter thing to offend God!

And now the scene changes. Pilate is once more standing before the people. He vainly imagines that the condition of abject misery and shame to which his cowardice has brought our dear and blessed Lord will evoke cries of awe and pity from the mob. Accordingly he orders the Prisoner under arrest to be brought forth, where with the full light of the morning sun flashing on His symbols of mock royalty all may have a good view of Him. As Jesus draws nigh Pilate addresses the mob; 'Behold!' he exclaims pleadingly, 'I bring Him forth to you that you may know I find no cause in Him.' '*Ecce Homo.*' 'Behold the Man.'

Alas! no sooner do they catch sight of our Lord with the purple rag and the mock sceptre and crown, than there rings clamorously forth through the air the people's well-schooled cry, 'Crucify Him, crucify Him.'

. . .

To us who reverently, after a lapse of nearly two thousand years, study the trial of Christ, how terribly real and actual it seems! What is so terrible about it is this, that it is being repeated over and over again with much the same result in England, in London; and, what more nearly concerns you and me, in Mayfair where we are living. Smart Society of to-day is still exclaiming with their friends the Jews, 'We will not have this Man to reign over us.' The threat held out to their consciences is still the same as that with which Pilate was menaced: 'If thou release this Man, thou art not Cæsar's friend.' And finally, as all the world knows, these fashionable votaries of pleasure to whom I refer still proclaim by the lives they lead, by the pastimes they practise, by the sensuality in which they indulge, by the luxuries in which they wallow, by the blasphemies which they utter, 'We have no king but Cæsar.' They crucify the Son of God anew by lives for which there is less excuse than there was for those of Annas, Caiaphas, Pilate, and Herod.

And it would seem from the daily record, given in social organs, of the doings of smart Society people and from what we know of the literature in which they delight, from the plays to which they resort and from the pleasures in which they revel, that their cry too is the cry which swept like a blight from the children of Israel on the first Good Friday when they howled, 'His blood be upon us, and upon our children.'

And so, as we read, 'their voices prevailed', and Pilate 'delivered Him to them to be crucified'. Then like a pack of hounds let loose upon their prey, the mob sprang upon our blessed Lord, and tearing from His bleeding wounds the insignia of mock loyalty they put His own garments on Him and led Him out to be crucified.

See Him dumb like a lamb before its shearers, while the instrument of His torture, the Cross, is laid upon His shoulder whereon so often His Mother's head had found shelter and repose.

What a sight is this! Our God Almighty reduced to the ignominy of a felon, dragging across the city of His adoption the cursed symbols of degradation and disgrace! Can nothing less than this teach man the value of suffering? Until he sees before him the Cross galling the bleeding shoulder of his Saviour, will he steadfastly refuse to take up his own and follow Him? Do we shrink so instinctively from pain that, but for this sight seen on the Via Crucis,[1] we could never bring ourselves to believe in its healing properties? It would seem indeed to be so, for no sooner does man begin to lose sight of Jesus Christ bearing His Cross than he himself begins to grow restless under the smaller one which he is called to carry after Him. And yet life itself is a cross so that the only choice that man is called upon to make is whether he will take it up and bear it onward on the right or on the left of His crucified Saviour. The choice is between Gestas and Dismas. If he uses his trials rightly, they will draw out all that is best in a man, they will purge him of sin, they will strengthen him in grace, they will elevate his thoughts beyond the realms of time and sense, they will spiritualize his life, and best of all, they will build up in him the Christ-like character, with the motto, 'Greater love than this no man hath.' Whereas if he shirks his cross and trials, if he becomes restless under the yoke, if he tries by every means in his power to rid himself of what nature so much dislikes, then will man become a mere worldling, a poor and craven creature without grit or spirit, or enterprise for Heaven. Remember the word has gone forth which shall never pass away, 'If any man will come after Me, let him deny himself, take up his cross and follow Me.'

Observe well that the Cross which our sins laid upon the shoulder of our blessed Lord was heavier than He could bear. He, the Almighty, fell under the crushing burden, and so His murderers forced one Simon of Cyrene, who was passing by, to help Him to carry it. Little did the father of Alexander and Rufus realize the privilege of his calling.

Sometimes in our better moments we are disposed to envy the honour conferred upon the man of Cyrene, and we perhaps persuade ourselves that, had we been in his position, we should have needed no forcing into that cross-bearing service. But let me ask, do our lives warrant this interpretation which so freely we put upon them? Were we as ready to help our dear and blessed Lord as we proclaim to be, perhaps we should make less of our own crosses, none too heavy for us, and certainly we should not so easily forget the words — 'Whatsoever you do to the least of My little ones, you have done it unto Me.'

Our mission in this twentieth century is to help Jesus Christ by offering service to our less favoured brothers and sisters, who are struggling under burdens heavy almost beyond endurance, along the dark and lonely lanes of penury and want. Alas! alas! and woe! woe! how blind we are, how deaf we are to the tragic scenes in our own immediate environments. Are there not tens of thousands in this city clamouring for bread, are there not thousands by the score clamouring for work, and are there not thousands by the hundred clamouring for sympathy? If only our ears were attuned to this chorus of voices beating in upon us like the wail of the wind, and the sob of the sea, we would, I feel sure, open our hands, and open our hearts, stretching forth the whole of our being to respond to the cry of humanity, pleading for help under its crushing burdens. But we are, I much fear, too self-centred, and it suits us better to lose sight of what is wanted of us here and now, to gaze in gaping wonderment across a chasm of two thousand years, marvelling at the short-sightedness of Simon of Cyrene, who failed to recognize the privilege accorded him.

We are not altogether unlike that great multitude of people and of women who 'bewailed and lamented Jesus Christ'. That mighty throng seeing His abject misery, His pitiful condition, all weary, worn, and broken, pressed about Him, following Him with tears and cries along the toilsome way to Calvary.

Look up and bend your eyes upon them. Behold! there is a pause, the procession halts, and Jesus, the Self-forgetful, turning to the crowd, so loud in the piercing cries of its lamentation, utters a word of warning good for us to remember: 'Daughters of Jerusalem, weep not over Me, but weep for yourselves and for your children.' If only the people of the city, that knew not the day of its visitation, had foreseen in prophetic vision what so soon was to befall themselves, their children, and their country, they would indeed have called out to the mountains: 'Fall upon us,' and to the hills: 'Cover us.' But instead of being occupied with the thought of their own personal guilt, and of lamenting it with purpose of amendment, they were thinking of the sin of others, and were bewailing its vengeance upon the Person of Jesus the Nazarene. It is indeed well for us to follow our Lord through every stage of His Sacred Passion with tears of sympathy and prayers of gratitude, but there is a duty more pressing still than this, and it is that of weeping over our own sins which have needed so great a redemption, and of resolving so to shun sin and the occasions of it, that we may in some measure at least make up, as St Paul puts it, what was wanting in the Passion of Christ.

If ever there was a period in the history of our country when there was occasion for weeping over it, that period is the one in which we ourselves are living. Is this England of ours a Christian land in any real and true sense? Is there not some reason for fearing that we are living in the afterglow of Christianity? Outside the Catholic Church are not the ties of Christianity being almost everywhere loosened? Is not its dogmatic teaching being almost universally ridiculed, while its moral obligations are just tossed to the winds as though worthless as the dust in our streets? Are not congresses declaring constantly that the education of our children must be free and secular, that the Word of Christ must be banished from the schools, and that not a penny of the rates and taxes should be spent on 'cramming dogmas down the throats of children'? Do we not recognize around us a spirit of discontent with all that is, with Society as at present constituted, and with religion as identified with politics, or with the State?

I will not refer to the desecration of the marriage bond, nor to the destruction of home life, nor to the prevention of child-bearing, nor to the other social and domestic horrors, which all go to prove incontestably that the Christianity of Christ is ceasing to be the leaven which alone can spiritualize now, as it spiritualized in the past, England our Fatherland.

But let me rather emphasize particularly, what still more clearly will bring home to some of you, why we have reason now more than ever to weep for ourselves and for our children. I do not mean the fact merely of the prevalence of the New Theology, in which there is little theology and nothing new, nor the promulgation of the tenets of Christian Science, in which there is neither savour of Christianity nor relish of Science, but I refer rather to the spirit of Socialism which is threatening to become in this country a cult, to its anti-militarism, and to what I must call, its anti-patriotism. Where there is loss of the true character of Christianity, there too must be wanting the true spirit of patriotism, and where there is lack of patriotism, there you will look in vain for loyalty to the throne. In many more senses than one England would seem to be on the down grade.

It would be well if we took the warning betimes, before we shall have reason to cry out to the mountains, 'Fall upon us'; and to the hills, 'Cover us.' There is, I repeat, one Name, and one only, in which we can recover ourselves and find salvation, and it is the Name of Jesus. Let us break from our frivolities and irreligion, and weeping for our past of which we have reason enough to be heartily ashamed, let us follow Him to Calvary, where, at length about noontide with the sun beating fiercely upon His gaping wounds, our dear Lord and Saviour arrives, weary with the journey, spent from want of food, athirst from loss of blood. Give Him not to drink what the soldiers offer, 'wine mingled with myrrh', but present Him from your hearts the pure wine of pure love, that it may strengthen and may comfort Him in His last hours — dying of a broken heart upon the cursèd tree. As presently we shall see, our dear and blessed Lord is suffering from a thirst which nothing but the love-stream from human hearts can slake. Let us at once respond to His gracious appeal, and plead for grace to love Him more and ever more:

> Soul of my Saviour, sanctify my breast,
> Body of Christ, be Thou my saving guest;
> Blood of my Saviour bathe me in Thy tide,
> Wash me, ye waters, gushing from His side.
> Strength and protection may His passion be,
> O dearest Jesus, hear and answer me.
> Within Thy wounds, Lord, hide and shelter me,
> That I may never, never part from Thee.
> Guard and defend me from the foe malign,
> In death's drear moment make me wholly Thine.
> Call me and bid me come to Thee on high,
> That I may praise Thee with Thy Saints for aye.

1   Latin: Way of the Cross.

IMAGINATIVE

ARTHUR CONAN DOYLE
from Arthur Conan Doyle, *The Green Flag* (1900)

Arthur Conan Doyle (1859-1930), who was educated by the Jesuits at Stonyhurst in Lancashire, had, as Owen Dudley Edwards remarks in his biographical study *The Quest for Sherlock Holmes* (1983), a 'pointedly Irish name and immediate Irish ancestry'. 'The Green Flag' focuses on the complex issue of allegiance, beginning in Ireland during the Land War of 1879–82 and moving to colonial wars in north east Africa. It was published during the Boer War, when Irishmen in the Transvaal formed two Brigades (one of them was commanded by Seán MacBride who in 1903 married Maud Gonne) and fought alongside the Boers against the British. Doyle accepts that the Irish soldiers who enlisted in the British Army were full of 'bitter hatred of the flag under which they served', but in a story full of racist imagery he brings out how they shared more with their English-speaking white oppressors than with black African Moslems.

The Green Flag

When Jack Conolly, of the Irish Shot-gun Brigade, the Rory of the Hills Inner Circle, and the extreme left wing of the Land League,[1] was incontinently shot by Sergeant Murdoch of the constabulary, in a little moonlight frolic near Kanturk, his twin-brother Dennis joined the British Army. The countryside had become too hot for him; and, as the seventy-five shillings were wanting which might have carried him to America, he took the only way handy of getting himself out of the way. Seldom has Her Majesty had a less promising recruit, for his hot Celtic blood seethed with hatred against Britain and all things British. The Sergeant, however, smiling complacently over his six feet of brawn and his forty-four-inch chest, whisked him off with a dozen other of the boys to the depot at Fermoy, whence in a few weeks they were sent on, with the spade-work kinks taken out of their backs, to the first battalion of the Royal Mallows, at the top of the roster for foreign service.

The Royal Mallows, at about that date, were as strange a lot of men as ever were paid by a great empire to fight its battles. It was the darkest hour of the land struggle, when the one side came out with crowbar and battering-ram by day, and the other with mask and with shotgun by night. Men driven from their homes and potato-patches found their way even into the service of the Government, to which it seemed to them they owed their troubles, and now and then they did wild things before they came. There were recruits in the Irish regiments who would forget to answer to their own names, so short had been their acquaintance with them. Of these the Royal Mallows had their full share; and, while they still retained their fame as being one of the smartest corps in the Army, no one knew better than their officers that they were dry-rotted with treason and with bitter hatred of the flag under which they served.

And the centre of all the disaffection was C Company, in which Dennis Conolly found himself enrolled. They were Celts, Catholics, and men of the tenant class to a man; and their whole experience of the British Government had been an inexorable landlord, and a constabulary who seemed to them to be always on the side of the rent collector. Dennis was not the only moonlighter in the ranks, nor was he alone in having an intolerable family blood-feud to harden his heart. Savagery had begotten savagery in that veiled civil war. A landlord with an iron mortgage weighing down upon him had small bowels for his tenantry. He did but take what the law allowed; and yet, with men like Jim Holan, or Patrick McQuire, or Peter Flynn, who had seen the roofs torn from their cottages and their folk huddled among their pitiable furniture upon the roadside, it was ill to argue about abstract law. What matter that in that long and bitter struggle there was many another outrage on the part of the tenant, and many another grievance on the side of the landowner! A stricken man can only feel his own wound, and the rank and file of the C Company of the Royal Mallows were sore and savage to the soul. There were low whisperings in barrack-rooms and canteens, stealthy meetings in public-house parlours, bandying of passwords from mouth to mouth, and many other signs which made their officers right glad when the order came which sent them to foreign, and better still to active, service.

For Irish regiments have before now been disaffected, and have at a distance looked upon the foe as though he might, in truth, be the friend; but when they have been put face on to him, and when their officers have dashed to the front with a wave and halloo, those rebel hearts have softened and their gallant Celtic blood has boiled with the mad joy of the fight, until the slower Britons have marvelled that they ever could have doubted the loyalty of their Irish comrades. So it would be again, according to the officers, and so it would not be if Dennis Conolly and a few others could have their way.

It was a March morning upon the eastern fringe of the Nubian desert. The sun had not yet risen; but a tinge of pink flushed up as far as the cloudless zenith, and the long strip of sea lay like a rosy ribbon across the horizon. From the coast inland stretched dreary sand-plains, dotted over with thick clumps of mimosa scrub and mottled patches of thorny bush. No tree broke the monotony of that vast desert. The dull, dusty hue of the thickets and the yellow glare of the sand were the only colours, save at one point where, from a distance, it seemed that a landslip of snow-white stones had shot itself across a low foot-hill. But as the traveller approached he saw, with a thrill, that these were no stones, but the bleaching bones of a slaughtered army. With its dull tints, its gnarled viprous bushes, its arid, barren soil, and this death streak trailed across it, it was indeed a nightmare country.

Some eight or ten miles inland the rolling plain curved upwards with a steeper slope until it ran into a line of red basaltic rock which zigzagged from north to south, heaping itself up at one point into a fantastic knoll. On the summit of this there stood upon that March morning three Arab chieftains — the Sheik Kadra of the Hadendowas, Moussa Wad Aburhegel, who led the Berber dervishes, and Hamid Wad Hussein, who had come northward with his fighting men from the land of the Baggaras. They had all three just risen from their praying-carpets, and were peering out, with fierce, high-nosed faces thrust forwards, at the stretch of country revealed by the spreading dawn.

The red rim of the sun was pushing itself now above the distant sea, and the whole coast-line stood out brilliantly yellow against the rich deep blue beyond. At one spot lay a huddle of white-walled houses, a mere splotch in the distance; while four tiny cock-boats, which lay beyond, marked the position of three of Her Majesty's ten-thousand-ton troopers and the Admiral's flagship. But it was not upon the distant town, nor upon the great vessels, nor yet upon the sinister white litter which gleamed in the plain beneath them, that the Arab chieftains gazed. Two miles from where they stood, amid the sandhills and the mimosa scrub, a great parallelogram had been marked by piled-up bushes. From the inside of this dozens of tiny blue smoke-reeks curled up into the still morning air; while there rose from it a confused deep murmur, the voices of men and the gruntings of camels blended into the same insect buzz.

'The unbelievers have cooked their morning food,' said the Baggara chief, shading his eyes with his tawny, sinewy hand. 'Truly their sleep has been but scanty; for Hamid and a hundred of his men have fired upon them since the rising of the moon.'

'So it was with these others,' answered the Sheik Kadra, pointing with his sheathed sword towards the old battlefield. 'They also had a day of little water and a night of little rest, and the heart was gone out of them ere ever the sons of the Prophet had looked them in the eyes. This blade drank deep that day, and will again before the sun has travelled from the sea to the hill.'

'And yet these are other men,' remarked the Berber dervish. 'Well, I know that Allah has placed them in the clutch of our fingers, yet it may be that they with the big hats will stand firmer than the cursed men of Egypt.'

'Pray Allah that it may be so,' cried the fierce Baggara, with a flash of his black eyes. 'It was not to chase women that I brought seven hundred men from the river to the coast. See, my brother, already they are forming their array.'

A fanfare of bugle-calls burst from the distant camp. At the same time the bank of bushes at one side had been thrown or trampled down, and the little army within began to move slowly out on to the plain. Once clear of the camp they halted, and the slant rays of the sun struck flashes from bayonet and from gun-barrel as the ranks closed up until the big pith helmets joined into a single long white ribbon. Two streaks of scarlet glowed on either side of the square, but elsewhere the fringe of fighting-men was of the dull yellow khaki tint which hardly shows against the desert sand. Inside their array was a dense mass of camels and mules bearing stores and ambulance needs. Outside a twinkling clump of cavalry was drawn up on each flank, and in front a thin scattered line of mounted infantry was already slowly advancing over the bush-strewn plain, halting on every eminence, and peering warily round as men might who have to pick their steps among the bones of those who have preceded them.

The three chieftains still lingered upon the knoll, looking down with hungry eyes and compressed lips at the dark steel-tipped patch.

'They are slower to start than the men of Egypt,' the Sheik of the Hadendowas growled in his beard.

'Slower also to go back, perchance, my brother,' murmured the dervish. 'And yet they are not many — three thousand at the most.'

'And we ten thousand, with the Prophet's grip upon our spear-hafts and his words upon our banner. See to their chieftain, how he rides upon the right and looks up at us with the glass that sees from afar! It may be that he sees this also.' The Arab shook his sword at the small clump of horsemen who had spurred out from the square.

'Lo! he beckons,' cried the dervish; 'and see those others at the corner, how they bend and heave. Ha! by the Prophet, I had thought it.'

As he spoke a little woolly puff of smoke spurted up at the corner of the square, and a seven-pound shell burst with a hard metallic smack just over their heads. The splinters knocked chips from the red rocks around them.

'Bismillah!' cried the Hadendowa; 'if the gun can carry thus far, then ours can answer to it. Ride to the left, Moussa, and tell Ben Ali to cut the skin from the Egyptians if they cannot hit yonder mark. And you, Hamid, to the right, and see that three thousand men lie close in the wady[2] that we have chosen. Let the others beat the drum and show the banner of the Prophet; for by the black stone their spears will have drunk deep ere they look upon the stars again.'

A long, straggling, boulder-strewn plateau lay on the summit of the red hills, sloping very precipitously to the plain, save at one point, where a winding gully curved downwards, its mouth choked with sand-mounds and olive-hued scrub. Along the edge of this position lay the Arab host, a motley crew of shock-headed desert clansmen, fierce predatory slave-dealers of the interior, and wild dervishes from the Upper Nile, all blent together by their common fearlessness and fanaticism. Two races were there, as wide as the poles apart, the thin-lipped, straight-haired Arab, and the thick-lipped, curly negro; yet the faith of Islam had bound them closer than a blood tie. Squatting among the rocks, or lying thickly in the shadow, they peered out at the slow-moving square beneath them, while women with water-skins and bags of dhoora fluttered from group to group, calling out to each other those fighting texts from the Koran which in the hour of battle are maddening as wine to the true believer. A score of banners waved over the ragged, valiant crew, and among them, upon desert horses and white Bishareen camels, were the Emirs and Sheiks who were to lead them against the infidels.

As the Sheik Kadra sprang into his saddle and drew his sword there was a wild whoop and a clatter of waving spears, while the one-ended war-drums burst into a dull crash like a wave upon shingle. For a moment ten thousand men were up on the rocks with brandished arms and leaping figures; the next they were under cover, again waiting sternly and silently for their chieftain's orders. The square was less than half a mile from the ridge now, and shell after shell from the seven-pound guns was pitching over it. A deep roar on the right, and then a second one showed that the Egyptian Krupps were in action. Sheik Kadra's hawk eyes saw that the shells burst far beyond the mark, and he spurred his horse along to where a knot of mounted chiefs were gathered round the two guns, which were served by their captured crews.

'How is this, Ben Ali?' he cried. 'It was not thus that the dogs fired when it was their own brothers in faith at whom they aimed!'

A chieftain reined his horse back, and thrust a blood-smeared sword into its sheath. Beside him two Egyptian artillerymen with their throats cut were sobbing out their lives upon the ground.

'Who lays the gun this time?' asked the fierce chief, glaring at the frightened gunners. 'Here, thou black-browed child of Shaitan, aim, and aim for thy life.'

It may have been chance, or it may have been skill, but the third and fourth shells burst over the square. Sheik Kadra smiled grimly and galloped back to the left, where his spearmen were streaming down into the gully. As he joined them a deep growling rose from the plain beneath, like the snarling of a sullen wild beast, and a little knot of tribesmen fell in a struggling heap, caught in the blast of lead from a Gardner. Their comrades pressed on over them, and sprang down into the ravine. From all along the crest burst the hard sharp crackle of Remington fire.

The square had slowly advanced, rippling over the low sandhills, and halting every few minutes to re-arrange its formation. Now, having made sure that there was no force of the enemy in the scrub, it changed its direction, and began to take a line parallel to the Arab position. It was too steep to assail from the front, and if they moved far enough to the right the General hoped that he might turn it. On the top of those ruddy hills lay a baronetcy for him, and a few extra hundreds in his pension, and he meant having them both that day. The Remington fire was annoying, and so were those two Krupp guns: already there were more cacolets[3] full than he cared to see. But on the whole he thought it better to hold his fire until he had more to aim at than a few hundred of fuzzy heads peeping over a razor-back ridge. He was a bulky, red-faced man, a fine whist-player, and a soldier who knew his work. His men believed in him, and he had good reason to believe in them, for he had excellent stuff under him that day. Being an ardent champion of the short-service system, he took particular care to work with veteran first battalions, and his little force was the compressed essence of an army corps.

The left front of the square was formed by four companies of the Royal Wessex, and the right by four of the Royal Mallows. On either side the other halves of the same regiments marched in quarter column of companies. Behind them, on the right, was a battalion of Guards, and on the left one of Marines, while the rear was closed in by a Rifle battalion. Two Royal Artillery seven-pound screw-guns kept pace with the square, and a dozen white-bloused sailors, under their blue-coated, tight-waisted officers, trailed their Gardner in front, turning every now and then to spit up at the draggled banners which waved over the cragged ridge. Hussars and Lancers scouted in the scrub at each side, and within moved the clump of camels, with humorous eyes and supercilious lips, their comic faces a contrast to the blood-stained men who already lay huddled in the cacolets on either side.

The square was now moving slowly on a line parallel with the rocks, stopping every few minutes to pick up wounded, and to allow the screw-guns and Gardner to make themselves felt. The men looked serious, for that spring on to the rocks of the Arab army had given them a vague glimpse of the number and ferocity of their foes; but their faces were set like stone, for they knew to a man that they must win or they must die — and die, too, in a particularly unlovely fashion. But most serious of all was the General, for he had seen that which brought a flush to his cheeks and a frown to his brow.

'I say, Stephen,' said he to his galloper, 'those Mallows seem a trifle jumpy. The right flank company bulged a bit when the niggers showed on the hill.'

'Youngest troops in the square, sir,' murmured the aide, looking at them critically through his eyeglass.

'Tell Colonel Flanagan to see to it, Stephen,' said the General; and the galloper sped upon his way. The Colonel, a fine old Celtic warrior, was over at C Company in an instant.

'How are the men, Captain Foley?'

'Never better, sir,' answered the senior captain, in the spirit that makes a Madras officer look murder if you suggest recruiting his regiment from the Punjaub.

'Stiffen them up!' cried the Colonel. As he rode away a colour-sergeant seemed to trip, and fell forward into a mimosa hush.

He made no effort to rise, but lay in a heap among the thorns.

'Sergeant O'Rooke's gone, sorr,' cried a voice.

'Never mind, lads,' said Captain Foley. 'He's died like a soldier, fighting for his Queen.'

'To hell with the Queen!' shouted a hoarse voice from the ranks.

But the roar of the Gardner and the typewriter-like clicking of the hopper burst in at the tail of the words. Captain Foley heard them, and Subalterns Grice and Murphy heard them; but there are times when a deaf ear is a gift from the gods.

'Steady, Mallows!' cried the Captain, in a pause of the grunting machine-gun. 'We have the honour of Ireland to guard this day.'

'And well we know how to guard it, Captin!' cried the same ominous voice; and there was a buzz from the length of the company.

The Captain and the two subs. came together behind the marching line.

'They seem a bit out of hand,' murmured the Captain.

'Bedad,' said the Galway boy, 'they mean to scoot like redshanks.'

'They nearly broke when the blacks showed on the hill,' said Grice.

'The first man that turns, my sword is through him,' cried Foley, loud enough to be heard by five files on either side of him. Then, in a lower voice, 'It's a bitter drop to swallow, but it's my duty to report what you think to the Chief and have a company of Jollies put behind us.' He turned away with the safety of the square upon his mind, and before he had reached his goal the square had ceased to exist.

In their march in front of what looked like a face of cliff, they had come opposite to the mouth of the gully, in which, screened by scrub and boulders, three thousand chosen dervishes, under Hamid Wad Hussein of the Baggaras, were crouching. Tat, tat, tat, went the rifles of three mounted infantrymen in front of the left shoulder of the square, and an instant later they were spurring it for their lives, crouching over the manes of their horses, and pelting over the sandhills with thirty or forty galloping chieftains at their heels. Rocks and scrub and mimosa swarmed suddenly into life. Rushing black figures came and went in the gaps of the bushes. A howl that drowned the shouts of the officers, a long quavering yell, burst from the ambuscade. Two rolling volleys from the Royal Wessex, one crash from the screw-gun firing shrapnel, and then before a second cartridge could be rammed in, a living, glistening black wave tipped with steel, had rolled over the gun, the Royal Wessex had been dashed back among the camels, and a thousand fanatics were hewing and hacking in the heart of what had been the square.

The camels and mules in the centre jammed more and more together as their leaders flinched from the rush of the tribesmen, shut out the view of the other three faces, who could only tell that the Arabs had got in by the yells upon Allah, which rose ever nearer and nearer amid the clouds of sand-dust, the struggling animals, and the dense mass of swaying, cursing men. Some of the Wessex fired back at the Arabs who had passed them, as excited Tommies will, and it is whispered among doctors that it was not always a Remington bullet which was cut from a wound that day. Some rallied in little knots, stabbing furiously with their bayonets at the rushing spearsmen. Others turned at bay with their backs against the camels, and others round the General and his staff, who, revolver in hand, had flung themselves into the heart of it. But the whole square was sidling slowly away from the gorge, pushed back by the pressure at the shattered corner.

The officers and men at the other faces were glancing nervously to their rear, uncertain what was going on, and unable to take help to their comrades without breaking the formation.

'By Jove, they've got through the Wessex!' cried Grice of the Mallows.

'The divils have hurrooshed us, Ted,' said his brother subaltern, cocking his revolver.

The ranks were breaking and crowding towards Private Conolly, all talking together as the officers peered back through the veil of dust. The sailors had run their Gardner out, and she was squirting death out of her five barrels into the flank of the rushing stream of savages.

'Oh, this bloody gun!' shouted a voice. 'She's jammed again.' The fierce metallic grunting had ceased, and her crew were straining and hauling at the breech.

'This damned vertical feed!' cried an officer. 'The spanner, Wilson, the spanner! Stand to your cutlasses, boys, or they're into us.'

His voice rose into a shriek as he ended, for a shovel-headed spear had been buried in his chest. A second wave of dervishes lapped over the hillocks, and burst upon the machine-gun and the right front of the line. The sailors were overborne in an instant, but the Mallows, with their fighting blood aflame, met the yell of the Moslem with an even wilder, fiercer cry, and dropped two hundred of them with a single point-blank volley. The howling, leaping crew swerved away to the right and dashed on into the gap which had already been made for them.

But C Company had drawn no trigger to stop that fiery rush. The men leaned moodily upon their Martinis.[4] Some had even thrown them upon the ground. Conolly was talking fiercely to those about him. Captain Foley, thrusting his way through the press, rushed up to him with a revolver in his hand.

'This is your doing, you villain!' he cried.

'If you raise your pistol, Captin, your brains will be over your coat,' said a low voice at his side.

He saw that several rifles were turned on him. The two subs. had pressed forward, and were by his side.

'What is it, then?' he cried, looking round from one fierce mutinous face to another. 'Are you Irishmen? Are you soldiers? What are you here for but to fight for your country?'

'England is no country of ours,' cried several.

'You are not fighting for England. You are fighting for Ireland, and for the Empire of which it is part.'

'A black curse on the Impire!' shouted Private McQuire, throwing down his rifle. ''Twas the Impire that backed the man that druv me on to the roadside. May me hand stiffen before I draw thrigger for it.'

'What's the Impire to us, Captain Foley, and what's the Widdy to us ayther?' cried a voice.

'Let the constabulary foight for her.'

'Ay, be God, they'd be better imployed than pullin' a poor man's thatch about his ears.'[5]

'Or shootin' his brother, as they did mine.'

'It was the Impire laid my groanin' mother by the wayside. Her son will rot before he upholds it, and ye can put that in the charge-sheet in the next coort martial.'

In vain the three officers begged, menaced, persuaded. The square was still moving, ever moving, with the same bloody fight raging in its entrails. Even while they had been speaking they had been shuffling backwards, and the useless Gardner, with her slaughtered crew, was already a good hundred yards from them. And the pace was accelerating. The mass of men, tormented and writhing, was trying, by a common instinct, to reach some clearer ground where they could re-form. Three faces were still intact, but the fourth had been caved in and badly mauled, without its comrades being able to help it. The Guards had met a fresh rush of the Hadendowas, and had blown back the tribesmen with a volley, and the Cavalry had ridden over another stream of them, as they welled out of the gully. A litter of hamstrung horses, and haggled men behind them, showed that a spearman on his face among the bushes can show some sport to the man who charges him. But, in spite of all, the square was still reeling swiftly backwards, trying to shake itself clear of this torment which clung to its heart. Would it break, or would it re-form? The lives of five regiments and the honour of the flag hung upon the answer.

Some, at least, were breaking. The C Company of the Mallows had lost all military order, and was pushing back in spite of the haggard officers, who cursed and shoved and prayed in the vain attempt to hold them. Their Captain and the subs. were elbowed and jostled, while the men crowded towards Private Conolly for their orders. The confusion had not spread, for the other companies, in the dust and smoke and turmoil, had lost touch with their mutinous comrades. Captain Foley saw that even now there might be time to avert a disaster.

'Think what you are doing, man,' he yelled, rushing towards the ringleader. 'There are a thousand Irish in the square, and they are dead men if we break.'

The words alone might have had little effect on the old moonlighter. It is possible that, in his scheming brain, he had already planned how he was to club his Irish together and lead them to the sea. But at that moment the Arabs broke through the screen of camels which had fended them off. There was a struggle, a screaming, a mule rolled over, a wounded man sprang up in a cacolet with a spear through him, and then through the narrow gap surged a stream of naked savages, mad with battle, drunk with slaughter, spotted and splashed with blood — blood dripping from their spears, their arms, their faces. Their yells, their bounds, their crouching, darting figures, the horrid energy of their spear-thrusts, made them look like a blast of fiends from the pit. And were these the Allies of Ireland? Were these the men who were to strike for her against her enemies? Conolly's soul rose up in loathing at the thought.

He was a man of firm purpose, and yet at the first sight of those howling fiends that purpose faltered, and at the second it was blown to the winds. He saw a huge coal-black negro seize a shrieking camel-driver and saw at his throat with a knife. He saw a shock-headed tribesman plunge his great spear through the back of their own little bugler from Millstreet. He saw a dozen deeds of blood — the murder of the wounded, the hacking of the unarmed — and caught, too, in a glance, the good wholesome faces of the faced-about rear rank of the Marines. The Mallows, too, had faced about, and in an instant Conolly had thrown himself into the heart of C Company, striving with the officers to form the men up with their comrades.

But the mischief had gone too far. The rank and\file had no heart in their work. They had broken before, and this last rush of murderous savages was a hard thing for broken men to stand against. They flinched from the furious faces and dripping forearms. Why should they throw away their lives for a flag for which they cared nothing? Why should their leader urge them to break, and now shriek to them to re-form? They would not re-form. They wanted to get to the sea and to safety. He flung himself among them with outstretched arms, with words of reason, with shouts, with gaspings. It was useless; the tide was beyond his control. They were shredding out into the desert with their faces set for the coast.

'Bhoys, will ye stand for this?' screamed a voice. It was so ringing, so strenuous, that the breaking Mallows glanced backwards. They were held by what they saw. Private Conolly had planted his rifle-stock downwards in a mimosa bush. From the fixed bayonet there fluttered a little green flag with the crownless harp.[6] God knows for what black mutiny, for what signal of revolt, that flag had been treasured up within Conolly's tunic! Now its green wisp stood amid the rush, while three proud regimental colours were reeling slowly backwards.

'What for the flag?' yelled the private.

'My heart's blood for it! and mine! and mine!' cried a score of voices. 'God bless it! The flag, boys — the flag!'

C Company were rallying upon it. The stragglers clutched at each other, and pointed. 'Here, McQuire, Flynn, O'Hara,' ran the shoutings. 'Close on the flag! Back to the flag!' The three standards reeled backwards, and the seething square strove for a clearer space where they could form their shattered ranks; but C Company, grim and powder-stained, choked with enemies and falling fast, still closed in on the little rebel ensign that flapped from the mimosa bush.

It was a good half-hour before the square, having disentangled itself from its difficulties and dressed its ranks, began to slowly move forwards over the ground, across which in its labour and anguish it had been driven. The long trail of Wessex men and Arabs showed but too clearly the path they had come.

'How many got into us, Stephen?' asked the General, tapping his snuff-box.

'I should put them down at a thousand or twelve hundred, sir.'

'I did not see any get out again. What the devil were the Wessex thinking about? The Guards stood well, though; so did the Mallows.'

'Colonel Flanagan reports that his front flank company was cut off, sir.'

'Why, that's the Company that was out of hand when we advanced!'

'Colonel Flanagan reports, sir, that the Company took the whole brunt of the attack, and gave the square time to re-form.'

'Tell the Hussars to ride forward, Stephen,' said the General, 'and try if they can see anything of them. There's no firing, and I fear that the Mallows will want to do some recruiting. Let the square take ground by the right, and then advance!'

But the Sheik Kadra of the Hadendowas saw from his knoll that the men with the big hats had rallied, and that they were coming back in the quiet business fashion of men whose work was before them. He took counsel with Moussa the Dervish and Hussein the Baggara, and a woestruck man was he when he learned that a third of his men were safe in the Moslem Paradise. So, having still some signs of victory to show, he gave the word, and the desert warriors flitted off unseen and unheard, even as they had come.

A red rock plateau, a few hundred spears and Remingtons, and a plain which for the second time was strewn with slaughtered men, was all that his day's fighting gave to the English General.

It was a squadron of Hussars which came first to the spot where the rebel flag had waved. A dense litter of

Arab dead marked the place. Within the flag waved no longer, but the rifle still stood in the mimosa bush, and round it, with their wounds in front, lay the Fenian private and the silent ranks of his Irishry. Sentiment is not an English failing, but the Hussar Captain raised his hilt in a salute as he rode past the blood-soaked ring.

The British General sent home dispatches to his Government, and so did the Chief of the Hadendowas to his, though the style and manner differed somewhat in each. 'The Sheik Kadra of the Hadendowa people to Mohammed Ahmed, the chosen of Allah, homage and greeting,' began the latter. 'Know by this that on the fourth day of this moon we gave battle to the Kaffirs who call themselves Inglees, having with us the chief Hussein with ten thousand of the faithful. By the blessing of Allah we have broken them, and chased them for a mile, though indeed these infidels are different from the dogs of Egypt, and have slain very many of our men. Yet we hope to smite them again ere the new moon be come, to which end I trust that thou wilt send us a thousand Dervishes from Omdurman. In token of our victory I send you by this messenger a flag which we have taken. By the colour it might well seem to have belonged to those of the true faith, but the Kaffirs gave their blood freely to save it, and so we think that, though small, it is very dear to them.'

1   See footnote on page 11.
2   A ravine or valley which is filled with water in the rainy season.
3   A military litter for carrying the wounded.
4   Here meaning rifles (Martini-Henry).
5   A reference to evictions during the Land War of 1879–82 where the story began.
6   Ireland without England, that is. 'The harp without the crown' is a phrase that appears in the Fenian song 'Down Erin's Lovely Lea'.

GEORGE RUSSELL (Æ)
from *All Ireland Review*, 6 January 1900

In its use of Celtic mythology tied to the theme of withdrawal, this poem is a fairly typical one of the period and recalls Yeats's 'Who Goes With Fergus?', a poem whose lines reverberate in Stephen Dedalus's mind in *Ulysses*. Russell's 'Farewell' is less valedictory and less warlike than it appears.

A FAREWELL TO THE HILLS

I go down from the hills half in gladness, and half with
    a pang I depart,
Where the mother with gentlest breathing made music
    on lip and in heart:
For I know that my childhood is over, a call comes out
    of the vast,
And the love that I had in the old time like beauty in
    twilight is past.

I am fired by a Danann[1] whisper of battles afar in the
    world,
And my thought is no longer of peace where the
    banners in dream are unfurled.
And I pass from the council of stars and of hills to a
    life that is new,
And I bid to you, stars, and you mountains, a
    tremulous long adieu.

I will come once again as a master who played here as
    child in my dawn;
I will enter the heart of the hills where the gods of the
    old world are gone;
And will war like the bright Hound of Ulla[2] with
    princes of earth and of sky
For my dream is to conquer the heavens and battle for
    kingship on high.

1   In pre-Christian Ireland the people of the Goddess Dana, who had defeated the Firbolgs and the Fomorii to take control of Ireland, inhabited the land before the coming of the Milesians.
2   The Hound of Ulster, that is, Cuchulain.

MOIRA O'NEILL

from Moira O'Neill, *Songs of the Glens of Antrim* (1901)

Moira O'Neill (1865–1955), whose real name was Nesta Skrine, was born in Cushendun in County Antrim. With its homely naiverty of expression, 'Corrymeela' was a very popular poem at the time and frequently anthologized.

CORRYMEELA

Over here in England I'm helpin' wi' the hay,
    An' I wisht I was in Ireland the livelong day;
Weary on the English hay, an' sorra[1] take the wheat!
    Och! Corrymeela an' the blue sky over it.

There' a deep dumb river flowin' by beyont the heavy
        trees,
    This livin' air is moithered wi' the bummin' o' the
        bees;
I wisht I'd hear the Claddagh burn go runnin' through
    the heat
    Past Corrymeela, wi' the blue sky over it.

The people that's in England is richer nor the Jews,
    There' not the smallest young gossoon[2] but thravels
    in his shoes!
I'd give the pipe between me teeth to see a barefut
    child,
    Och! Corrymeela an' the low south wind.

Here's hands so full o' money an' hearts so full o' care,
    By the luck o'love! I'd still go light for all I did go
    bare.
'God save ye, *colleen dhas*,'[3] I said: the girl she thought
    me wild.
    Far Corrymeela, an' the low south wind.

D'ye mind me now, the song at night is mortial[4] hard
    to raise,
    The girls are heavy goin' here, the boys are ill to
    plase;
When one'st I'm out this workin' hive, 'tis I'll be back
    again —
    Ay, Corrymeela, in the same soft rain.

The puff o' smoke from one ould roof before an
    English town!
    For a *shaugh*[5] wid Andy Feelan here I'd give a silver
    crown,
For a curl o' hair like Mollie's ye'll ask the like in vain,
    Sweet Corrymeela, an' the same soft rain.

1   An Irish form of sorrow, here meaning a mild expletive.
2   A young boy.
3   Irish for nice girl.
4   Presumably mortal, used here as an intensive, very.
5   A smoke of a pipe.

LADY GREGORY

from Lady Gregory, *Cuchulain of Muirthemne* (1902)

This episode is taken from a sequence of stories about Cuchulain translated into English by Lady Gregory. The language she used was based on the dialect she heard in the west of Ireland and has come to be known as Kiltartanese after the village of Kiltartan adjacent to her estate at Coole Park. The language seems eminently suited to the subject matter, capable of creating narrative interest as well as rising to poetic moments as in Cuchulain's cry against necessity. Yeats's *On Baile's Strand*, the first play produced at the Abbey Theatre when it opened in December 1904, is based on the incident described here by Lady Gregory.

The Only Son of Aoife

The time Cuchulain came back from Alban,[1] after he had learned the use of arms under Scathach, he left Aoife, the queen he had overcome in battle, with child.

And when he was leaving her, he told her what name to give the child, and he gave her a gold ring, and bade her keep it safe till the child grew to be a lad, and till his thumb would fill it; and he bade her to give it to him then, and to send him to Ireland, and he would know he was his son by that token. She promised to do so, and with that Cuchulain went back to Ireland.

It was not long after the child was born, word came to Aoife that Cuchulain had taken Emer to be his wife in Ireland. When she heard that, great jealousy came on her, and great anger, and her love for Cuchulain was turned to hatred; and she remembered her three champions that he had killed, and how he had overcome herself, and she determined in her mind that when her son would come to have the strength of a man, she would get her revenge through him. She told Conlaoch her son nothing of this, but brought him up like any king's son; and when he was come to sensible years, she put him under the teaching of Scathach, to be taught the use of arms and the art of war. He turned out as apt a scholar as his father, and it was not long before he had learnt all Scathach had to teach.

Then Aoife gave him the arms of a champion, and bade him go to Ireland, but first she laid three commands on him: the first never to give way to any living person, but to die sooner than be made turn back; the second, not to refuse a challenge from the greatest champion alive, but to fight him at all risks, even if he was sure to lose his life; the third, not to tell his name on any account, though he might be threatened with death for hiding it. She put him under *geasa*,[2] that is, under bonds, not to do these things.

Then the young man, Conlaoch, set out, and it was not long before his ship brought him to Ireland, and the place he landed at was Baile's Strand, near Dundealgan.

It chanced that at that time Conchubar, the High King, was holding court there, for it was a convenient gathering-place for his chief men, and they were settling some business that belonged to the government of that district.

When word was brought to Conchubar that there was a ship come to the strand, and a young lad in it armed as if for fighting, and armed men with him, he sent one of the chief men of his household to ask his name, and on what business he was come.

The messenger's name was Cuinaire, and he went down to the strand, and when he saw the young man he said: 'A welcome to you, young hero from the east, with the merry face. It is likely, seeing you come armed as if for fighting, you are gone astray on your journey; but as you are come to Ireland, tell me your name and what your deeds have been, and your victories in the eastern bounds of the world.'

'As to my name,' said Conlaoch, 'it is of no great account; but whatever it is, I am under bonds not to tell it to the stoutest man living.'

'It is best for you to tell it at the king's desire,' said Cuinaire, 'before you get your death through refusing it, as many a champion from Alban and from Britain has done before now.' 'If that is the order you put on us when we land here, it is I will break it,' said Conlaoch, 'and no one will obey it any longer from this out.'

So Cuinaire went back and told the king what the young lad had said. Then Conchubar said to his people: 'Who will go out into the field, and drag the name and the story out of this young man?' 'I will go,' said Conall, for his hand was never slow in fighting. And he went out, and found the lad angry and destroying, handling his arms, and they attacked one another with a great noise of swords and shouts, and they were gripped together, and fought for a while, and then Conall was overcome, and the great name and the praise that was on Conall, it was on the head of Conlaoch it was now.

Word was sent then to where Cuchulain was, in pleasant, bright-faced Dundealgan. And the messenger told him the whole story, and he said: 'Conall is lying humbled, and it is slow the help is in coming; it is a welcome there would be before the Hound.'

Cuchulain rose up then and went to where Conlaoch was, and he still handling his arms. And Cuchulain asked him his name and said: 'It would be well for you, young hero of unknown name, to loosen yourself from this knot, and not to bring down my hand upon you, for it will be hard for you to escape death.' But Conlaoch said: 'If I put you down in the fight, the way I put down your comrade, there will be a great name on me; but if I draw back now, there will be mockery on me, and it will be said I was afraid of the fight. I will never give in to any man to tell the name, or to give an account of myself. But if I was not held with a command,' he said, 'there is no man in the world I would sooner give it to than to yourself, since I saw your face. But do not think, brave champion of Ireland, that I will let you take away the fame I have won, for nothing.'

With that they fought together, and it is seldom such a battle was seen, and all wondered that the young lad could stand so well against Cuchulain.

So they fought a long while, neither getting the better of the other, but at last Cuchulain was charged so hotly by the lad that he was forced to give way, and although he had fought so many good fights, and killed so many great champions, and understood the use of arms better than any man living, he was pressed very hard.

And he called for the Gae Bulg,³ and his anger came on him, and the flames of the hero-light began to shine about his head, and by that sign Conlaoch knew him to be Cuchulain, his father. And just at that time he was aiming his spear at him, and when he knew it was Cuchulain, he threw his spear crooked that it might pass beside him. But Cuchulain threw his spear, the Gae Bulg, at him with all his might, and it struck the lad in the side and went into his body, so that he fell to the ground.

And Cuchulain said: 'Now, boy, tell your name and what you are, for it is short your life will be, for you will not live after that wound.'

And Conlaoch showed the ring that was on his hand, and he said: 'Come here where I am lying on the field, let my men from the east come round me. I am suffering for revenge. I am Conlaoch, son of the Hound, heir of dear Dundealgan; I was bound to this secret in Dun Scathach, the secret in which I have found my grief.'

And Cuchulain said: 'It is a pity your mother not to be here to see you brought down. She might have stretched out her hand to stop the spear that wounded you.' And Conlaoch said: 'My curse be on my mother, for it was she put me under bonds; it was she sent me here to try my strength against yours.' And Cuchulain said: 'My curse be on your mother, the woman that is full of treachery; it is through her harmful thoughts these tears have been brought on us.' And Conlaoch said: 'My name was never forced from my mouth till now; I never gave an account of myself to any man under the sun. But, O Cuchulain of the sharp sword, it was a pity you not to know me the time I threw the slanting spear behind you in the fight.'

And then the sorrow of death came upon Conlaoch, and Cuchulain took his sword and put it through him, sooner than leave him in the pain and the punishment he was in.

And then great trouble and anguish came on Cuchulain, and he made this complaint:

'It is a pity it is, O son of Aoife, that ever you came into the province of Ulster, that you ever met with the Hound of Cuailgne.

'If I and my fair Conlaoch were doing feats of war on the one side, the men of Ireland from sea to sea would not be equal to us together. It is no wonder I to be under grief when I see the shield and the arms of Conlaoch. A pity it is there is no one at all, a pity there are not hundreds of men on whom I could get satisfaction for his death.

'If it was the king himself had hurt your fair body, it is I would have shortened his days.

'It is well for the House of the Red Branch, and for the heads of its fair army of heroes, it was not they that killed my only son.

'It is well for Laegaire of Victories it is not from him you got your heavy pain.

'It is well for the heroes of Conall they did not join in the killing of you; it is well that travelling across the plain of Macha they did not fall in with me after such a fight.

'It is well for the tall, well-shaped Forbuide; well for Dubthach, your Black Beetle of Ulster.

'It is well for you, Cormac Conloingeas, your share of arms gave no help, that it is not from your weapons he got his wound, the hard-skinned shield or the blade.

'It is a pity it was not one on the plains of Munster, or in Leinster of the sharp blades, or at Cruachan of the rough fighters, that struck down my comely Conlaoch.

'It is a pity it was not in the country of the Cruithne, of the fierce Fians, you fell in a heavy quarrel, or in the country of the Greeks, or in some other place of the world, you died, and I could avenge you.

'Or in Spain, or in Sorcha, or in the country of the Saxons of the free armies; there would not then be this death in my heart.

'It is very well for the men of Alban it was not they that destroyed your fame; and it is well for the men of the Gall.

'Och! It is bad that it happened; my grief! it is on me is the misfortune, O Conlaoch of the Red Spear, I myself to have spilled your blood.

'I to be under defeat, without strength. It is a pity Aoife never taught you to know the power of my strength in the fight.

'It is no wonder I to be blinded after such a fight and such a defeat.

'It is no wonder I to be tired out, and without the sons of Usnach beside me.

'Without a son, without a brother, with none to come after me; without Conlaoch, without a name to keep my strength.

'To be without Naoise, without Ainnle, without Ardan; is it not with me is my fill of trouble?

'I am the father that killed his son, the fine green branch; there is no hand or shelter to help me.

'I am a raven that has no home; I am a boat going from wave to wave; I am a ship that has lost its rudder; I am the apple left on the tree; it is little I thought of falling from it; grief and sorrow will be with me from this time.'

Then Cuchulain stood up and faced all the men of Ulster. 'There is trouble on Cuchulain,' said Conchubar; 'he is after killing his own son, and if I and all my men were to go against him, by the end of the day he would destroy every man of us. Go now,' he said to Cathbad, the Druid, 'and bind him to go down to Baile's Strand, and to give three days fighting against the waves of the sea, rather than to kill us all.'

So Cathbad put an enchantment on him, and bound him to go down. And when he came to the strand, there was a great white stone before him, and

he took his sword in his right hand, and he said: 'If I had the head of the woman that sent her son to his death, I would split it as I split this stone.' And he made four quarters of the stone.

Then he fought with the waves three days and three nights, till he fell from hunger and weakness so that some men said he got his death there. But it was not there he got his death, but on the plain of Muirthemne.[4]

1   Scotland.
2   Irish for oath or injunction. A common word in Irish mythology.
3   Belly-spear, Cuchulain's special spear, originally owned by Scathach.
4   Pronounced murhevna.

W. B. YEATS
Cathleen ni Houlihan (1902)

In its fusion of the mystical and the political, *Cathleen ni Houlihan* is arguably the most political play staged in Edwardian Dublin. With Maud Gonne in the title role the play resembled a recruiting meeting that pointed almost directly towards the barricades of Easter 1916. Stephen Gwynn wondered if it was right to stage such a play 'unless one was prepared for people to go out to shoot or be shot'. And late in life in his poem 'The Man and the Echo', Yeats too wondered: 'Did that play of mine send out / Certain men the English shot?' The first person to be killed in the Easter Rising was an Abbey Theatre actor James Connolly (not to be confused with the leader of the Citizen Army).

PERSONS IN THE PLAY

Peter Gillane
Michael Gillane, *his son, going to be married*
Patrick Gillane, *a lad of twelve, Michael's brother*
Bridget Gillane, *Peter's wife*
Delia Cahel, *engaged to Michael*
The Poor Old Woman
Neighbours

Interior of a cottage close to Killala,[1] *in 1798.* BRIDGET *is standing at a table undoing a parcel.* PETER *is sitting at one side of the fire,* PATRICK *at the other.*

PETER: What is that sound I hear?
PATRICK: I don't hear anything. [*He listens.*] I hear it now. It's like cheering. [*He goes to the window and*

looks out.] I wonder what they are cheering about. I don't see anybody.
PETER: It might be a hurling.
PATRICK: There's no hurling to-day. It must be down in the town the cheering is.
BRIDGET: I suppose the boys must be having some sport of their own. Come over here, Peter, and look at Michael's wedding clothes.
PETER [*shifts his chair to table*]: Those are grand clothes, indeed.
BRIDGET: You hadn't clothes like that when you married me, and no coat to put on of a Sunday more than any other day.
PETER: That is true, indeed. We never thought a son of our own would be wearing a suit of that sort for his wedding, or have so good a place to bring a wife to.

PATRICK [*who is still at the window*]: There's an old woman coming down the road. I don't know is it here she is coming.

BRIDGET: It will be a neighbour coming to hear about Michael's wedding. Can you see who it is?

PATRICK: I think it is a stranger, but she's not coming to the house. She's turned into the gap that goes down where Maurteen and his sons are shearing sheep. [*He turns towards* BRIDGET.] Do you remember what Winny of the Cross-Roads was saying the other night about the strange woman that goes through the country whatever time there's war or trouble coming?

BRIDGET: Don't be bothering us about Winny's talk, but go and open the door for your brother. I hear him coming up the path.

PETER: I hope he has brought Delia's fortune with him safe, for fear the people might go back on the bargain and I after making it. Trouble enough I had making it.

[PATRICK *opens the door and* MICHAEL *comes in.*]

BRIDGET: What kept you, Michael? We were looking out for you this long time.

MICHAEL: I went round by the priest's house to bid him be ready to marry us to-morrow.

BRIDGET: Did he say anything?

MICHAEL: He said it was a very nice match, and that he was never better pleased to marry any two in his parish than myself and Delia Cahel.

PETER: Have you got the fortune, Michael?

MICHAEL: Here it is.

[MICHAEL *puts bag on table and goes over and leans against chimney-jamb.* BRIDGET, *who has been all this time examining the clothes, pulling the seams and trying the lining of the pockets, etc., puts the clothes on the dresser.*]

PETER [*getting up and taking the bag in his hand and turning out the money*]: Yes, I made the bargain well for you, Michael. Old John Cahel would sooner have kept a share of this a while longer. 'Let me keep the half of it until the first boy is born,' says he. 'You will not,' says I. 'Whether there is or is not a boy, the whole hundred pounds must be in Michael's hands before he brings your daughter to the house.' The wife spoke to him then, and he gave in at the end.

BRIDGET: You seem well pleased to be handling the money, Peter.

PETER: Indeed, I wish I had had the luck to get a hundred pounds, or twenty pounds itself, with the wife I married.

BRIDGET: Well, if I didn't bring much I didn't get much. What had you the day I married you but a flock of hens and you feeding them, and a few lambs and you driving them to the market at Ballina? [*She is vexed and bangs a jug on the dresser.*] If I brought no fortune I worked it out in my bones, laying down the baby, Michael that is standing there now, on a stook of straw, while I dug the potatoes, and never asking big dresses or anything but to be working.

PETER: That is true, indeed.

[*He pats her arm.*]

BRIDGET: Leave me alone now till I ready the house for the woman that is to come into it.

PETER: You are the best woman in Ireland, but money is good, too. [*He begins handling the money again and sits down.*] I never thought to see so much money within my four walls. We can do great things now we have it. We can take the ten acres of land we have the chance of since Jamsie Dempsey died, and stock it. We will go to the fair at Ballina to buy the stock. Did Delia ask any of the money for her own use, Michael?

MICHAEL: She did not, indeed. She did not seem to take much notice of it, or to look at it at all.

BRIDGET: That's no wonder. Why would she look at it when she had yourself to look at, a fine, strong young man? It is proud she must be to get you; a good steady boy that will make use of the money, and not be running through it or spending it on drink like another.

PETER: It's likely Michael himself was not thinking much of the fortune either, but of what sort the girl was to look at.

MICHAEL [*coming over towards the table*]: Well, you would like a nice comely girl to be beside you, and to go walking with you. The fortune only lasts for a while, but the woman will be there always.

PATRICK [*turning round from the window*]: They are cheering again down in the town. Maybe they are landing horses from Enniscrone. They do be cheering when the horses take the water well.

MICHAEL: There are no horses in it. Where would they be going and no fair at hand? Go down to the town, Patrick, and see what is going on.

PATRICK [*opens the door to go out, but stops for a moment on the threshold*]: Will Delia remember, do you think, to bring the greyhound pup she promised me when she would be coming to the house?

MICHAEL: She will surely.

[PATRICK *goes out, leaving the door open.*]

PETER: It will be Patrick's turn next to be looking for a fortune, but he won't find it so easy to get it and he with no place of his own.

BRIDGET: I do be thinking sometimes, now things are

going so well with us, and the Cahels such a good back to us in the district, and Delia's own uncle a priest, we might be put in the way of making Patrick a priest some day, and he so good at his books.

PETER: Time enough, time enough. You have always your head full of plans, Bridget.

BRIDGET: We will be well able to give him learning, and not to send him tramping the country like a poor scholar that lives on charity.

MICHAEL: They're not done cheering yet.

[*He goes over to the door and stands there for a moment, putting up his hand to shade his eyes.*]

BRIDGET: Do you see anything?

MICHAEL: I see an old woman coming up the path.

BRIDGET: Who is it, I wonder? It must be the strange woman Patrick saw a while ago.

MICHAEL: I don't think it's one of the neighbours anyway, but she has her cloak over her face.

BRIDGET: It might be some poor woman heard we were making ready for the wedding and came to look for her share.

PETER: I may as well put the money out of sight. There is no use leaving it out for every stranger to look at.

[*He goes over to a large box in the corner, opens it and puts the bag in and fumbles at the lock.*]

MICHAEL: There she is, father! [*An* OLD WOMAN *passes the window slowly. She looks at* MICHAEL *as she passes.*] I'd sooner a stranger not to come to the house the night before my wedding.

BRIDGET: Open the door, Michael; don't keep the poor woman waiting.

[*The* OLD WOMAN *comes in.* MICHAEL *stands aside to make way for her.*]

OLD WOMAN: God save all here!

PETER: God save you kindly!

OLD WOMAN: You have good shelter here.

PETER: You are welcome to whatever shelter we have.

BRIDGET: Sit down there by the fire and welcome.

OLD WOMAN [*warming her hands*]: There is a hard wind outside.

[*MICHAEL watches her curiously from the door. PETER comes over to the table.*]

PETER: Have you travelled far to-day?

OLD WOMAN: I have travelled far, very far; there are few have travelled so far as myself, and there's many a one that doesn't make me welcome. There was one that had strong sons I thought were friends of mine, but they were shearing their sheep, and they wouldn't listen to me.

PETER: It's a pity indeed for any person to have no place of their own.

OLD WOMAN: That's true for you indeed, and it's long I'm on the roads since I first went wandering.

BRIDGET: It is a wonder you are not worn out with so much wandering.

OLD WOMAN: Sometimes my feet are tired and my hands are quiet, but there is no quiet in my heart. When the people see me quiet, they think old age has come on me and that all the stir has gone out of me. But when the trouble is on me I must be talking to my friends.

BRIDGET: What was it put you wandering?

OLD WOMAN: Too many strangers in the house.[2]

BRIDGET: Indeed you look as if you'd had your share of trouble.

OLD WOMAN: I have had trouble indeed.

BRIDGET: What was it put the trouble on you?

OLD WOMAN: My land that was taken from me.

PETER: Was it much land they took from you?

OLD WOMAN: My four beautiful green fields.[3]

PETER [*aside to* BRIDGET]: Do you think could she be the widow Casey that was put out of her holding at Kilglass a while ago?

BRIDGET: She is not. I saw the widow Casey one time at the market in Ballina, a stout fresh woman.

PETER [*to* OLD WOMAN]: Did you hear a noise of cheering, and you coming up the hill?

OLD WOMAN: I thought I heard the noise I used to hear when my friends came to visit me.

[*She begins singing half to herself.*]

I will go cry with the woman,
For yellow-haired Donough is dead,
With a hempen rope for a neckcloth,
And a white cloth on his head, —

MICHAEL [*coming from the door*]: What is it that you are singing, ma'am?

OLD WOMAN: Singing I am about a man I knew one time, yellow-haired Donough that was hanged in Galway.

[*She goes on singing, much louder.*]

I am come to cry with you, woman,
My hair is unwound and unbound;
I remember him ploughing his field,
Turning up the red side of the ground,
And building his barn on the hill
With the good mortared stone;
O! we'd have pulled down the gallows
Had it happened in Enniscrone![4]

MICHAEL: What was it brought him to his death?

OLD WOMAN: He died for love of me: many a man has died for love of me.

PETER [*aside to* BRIDGET]: Her trouble has put her wits astray.

MICHAEL: Is it long since that song was made? Is it long since he got his death?

OLD WOMAN: Not long, not long. But there were others that died for love of me a long time ago.

MICHAEL: Were they neighbours of your own, ma'am?

OLD WOMAN: Come here beside me and I'll tell you about them. [MICHAEL *sits down beside her on the hearth.*] There was a red man of the O'Donnells from the north,[5] and a man of the O'Sullivans from the south,[6] and there was one Brian that lost his life at Clontarf by the sea,[7] and there were a great many in the west, some that died hundreds of years ago, and there are some that will die to-morrow.

MICHAEL: Is it in the west that men will die to-morrow?

OLD WOMAN: Come nearer, nearer to me.

BRIDGET: Is she right, do you think? Or is she a woman from beyond the world?

PETER: She doesn't know well what she's talking about, with the want and the trouble she has gone through.

BRIDGET: The poor thing, we should treat her well.

PETER: Give her a drink of milk and a bit of the oaten cake.

BRIDGET: Maybe we should give her something along with that, to bring her on her way. A few pence or a shilling itself, and we with so much money in the house.

PETER: Indeed I'd not begrudge it to her if we had it to spare, but if we go running through what we have, we'll soon have to break the hundred pounds, and that would be a pity.

BRIDGET: Shame on you, Peter. Give her the shilling and your blessing with it, or our own luck will go from us.

[PETER *goes to the box and takes out a shilling.*]

BRIDGET [*to the* OLD WOMAN]: Will you have a drink of milk, ma'am?

OLD WOMAN: It is not food or drink that I want.

PETER [*offering the shilling*]: Here is something for you.

OLD WOMAN: This is not what I want. It is not silver I want.

PETER: What is it you would be asking for?

OLD WOMAN: If any one would give me help he must give me himself, he must give me all.

[PETER *goes over to the table staring at the shilling in his hand in a bewildered way, and stands whispering to* BRIDGET.]

MICHAEL: Have you no one to care you in your age, ma'am?

OLD WOMAN: I have not. With all the lovers that brought me their love I never set out the bed for any.

MICHAEL: Are you lonely going the roads, ma'am?

OLD WOMAN: I have my thoughts and I have my hopes.

MICHAEL: What hopes have you to hold to?

OLD WOMAN: The hope of getting my beautiful fields back again; the hope of putting the strangers out of my house.

MICHAEL: What way will you do that, ma'am?

OLD WOMAN: I have good friends that will help me. They are gathering to help me now. I am not afraid. If they are put down to-day they will get the upper hand to-morrow. [*She gets up.*] I must be going to meet my friends. They are coming to help me and I must be there to welcome them. I must call the neighbours together to welcome them.

MICHAEL: I will go with you.

BRIDGET: It is not her friends you have to go and welcome, Michael; it is the girl coming into the house you have to welcome. You have plenty to do; it is food and drink you have to bring to the house. The woman that is coming home is not coming with empty hands; you would not have an empty house before her. [*To the* OLD WOMAN.] Maybe you don't know, ma'am, that my son is going to be married to-morrow.

OLD WOMAN: It is not a man going to his marriage that I look to for help.

PETER [*to* BRIDGET]: Who is she, do you think, at all?

BRIDGET: You did not tell us your name yet, ma'am.

OLD WOMAN: Some call me the Poor Old Woman,[8] and there are some that call me Cathleen, the daughter of Houlihan.

PETER: I think I knew some one of that name, once. Who was it, I wonder? It must have been some one I knew when I was a boy. No, no; I remember, I heard it in a song.

OLD WOMAN [*who is standing in the doorway*]: They are wondering that there were songs made for me; there have been many songs made for me. I heard one on the wind this morning.

[*Sings*]

Do not make a great keening
When the graves have been dug to-morrow.
Do not call the white-scarfed riders
To the burying that shall be to-morrow.

Do not spread food to call strangers
To the wakes that shall be to-morrow;
Do not give money for prayers
For the dead that shall die to-morrow . . .

They will have no need of prayers, they will have no need of prayers.

MICHAEL: I do not know what that song means, but tell me something I can do for you.

PETER: Come over to me, Michael.

MICHAEL: Hush, father, listen to her.

OLD WOMAN: It is a hard service they take that help me. Many that are red-cheeked now will be pale-cheeked; many that have been free to walk the hills and the bogs and the rushes will be sent to walk hard streets in far countries; many a good plan will be broken; many that have gathered money will not stay to spend it; many a child will be born and there will be no father at its christening to give it a name. They that have red cheeks will have pale cheeks for my sake, and for all that, they will think they are well paid.

[*She goes out; her voice is heard outside singing.*]

They shall be remembered for ever,
They shall be alive for ever,
They shall be speaking for ever,
The people shall hear them for ever.

BRIDGET [*to* PETER]: Look at him, Peter; he has the look of a man that has got the touch. [*Raising her voice.*] Look here, Michael, at the wedding clothes. Such grand clothes as these are! You have a right to fit them on now; it would be a pity to-morrow if they did not fit. The boys would be laughing at you. Take them, Michael, and go into the room and fit them on.

[*She puts them on his arm.*]

MICHAEL: What wedding are you talking of? What clothes will I be wearing to-morrow?

BRIDGET: These are the clothes you are going to wear when you marry Delia Cahel to-morrow.

MICHAEL: I had forgotten that.

[*He looks at the clothes and turns towards the inner room, but stops at the sound of cheering outside.*]

PETER: There is the shouting come to our own door. What is it has happened?

[*Neighbours come crowding in,* PATRICK *and* DELIA *with them.*]

PATRICK: There are ships in the Bay; the French are landing at Killala!

[PETER *takes his pipe from his mouth and his hat off, and stands up. The clothes slip from* MICHAEL'S *arm.*]

DELIA: Michael! [*He takes no notice.*] Michael! [*He turns towards her.*] Why do you look at me like a stranger?

[*She drops his arm.* BRIDGET *goes over towards her.*]

PATRICK: The boys are all hurrying down the hillside to join the French.

DELIA: Michael won't be going to join the French.

BRIDGET [*to* PETER]: Tell him not to go, Peter.

PETER: It's no use. He doesn't hear a word we're saying.

BRIDGET: Try and coax him over to the fire.

DELIA: Michael, Michael! You won't leave me! You won't join the French, and we going to be married!

[*She puts her arms about him, he turns towards her as if about to yield.*

OLD WOMAN'S *voice outside.*]

They shall be speaking for ever,
The people shall hear them for ever.

[MICHAEL *breaks away from* DELIA, *stands for a second at the door, then rushes out, following the* OLD WOMAN'S *voice.* BRIDGET *takes* DELIA, *who is crying silently, into her arms.*]

PETER [*to* PATRICK, *laying a hand on his arm*]. Did you see an old woman going down the path?

PATRICK: I did not, but I saw a young girl, and she had the walk of a queen.

1   Killala is near Ballina, on the coast of Mayo in north-west Ireland. It was here in August 1798 that a small French force under General Humbert landed as part of a more widespread Rising against British rule in Ireland. The following month, after defeating a force of yeomanry in Castlebar, Humbert was defeated at Ballinamuck in County Longford, a fictional account of which can be found below in Thomas Flanagan, *The Year of the French* (1979).

2   Meaning the English in Ireland. The phrase is quoted to good effect by Joyce in *Ulysses*.

3   This is meant in the symbolic sense, that is, Ireland's four provinces: Munster, Connacht, Leinster, and Ulster.

4   These lines were suggested to Yeats 'by some old Gaelic folk-song'.

5   For Red Hugh O'Donnell, see footnote on page 22.

6   Probably Donal O'Sullivan Beare (1560–1618), who after the Battle of Kinsale in 1601, continued to resist the English forces with the help of a Spanish contingent from the fleet of Philip III.

7   Brian Boru. See footnote on page 11 above.

8   Sometimes known by her Irish name the Shan Van Vocht. An image of Ireland, again female like Cathleen.

GEORGE MOORE
from George Moore, *The Untilled Field* (1903)

Moore's story, which is deliberately underplayed, neatly unpicks what we imagine is its direction, namely the emigrant's return to Ireland from New York. The title of the collection is taken from Shelley's 'Sonnet: England in 1819'. You might find it interesting to compare Moore's story with 'Visiting the Future' (reproduced below), a modern emigration story by the Canadian-Irish writer Leo Simpson (1976).

Home Sickness

I

He told the doctor he was due in the bar-room at eight o'clock in the morning; the bar-room was in a slum in the Bowery; and he had only been able to keep himself in health by getting up at five o'clock and going for long walks in the Central Park.

'A sea voyage is what you want,' said the doctor. 'Why not go to Ireland for two or three months? You will come back a new man.'

'I'd like to see Ireland again.'

And he began to wonder how the people at home were getting on. The doctor was right. He thanked him, and three weeks afterwards he landed in Cork.

As he sat in the railway carriage he recalled his native village — he could see it and its lake, and then the fields one by one, and the roads. He could see a large piece of rocky land — some three or four hundred acres of headland stretching out into the winding lake. Upon this headland the peasantry had been given permission to build their cabins by former owners of the Georgian house standing on the pleasant green hill. The present owners considered the village a disgrace, but the villagers paid high rents for their plots of ground, and all the manual labour that the Big House[1] required came from the village: the gardeners, the stable helpers, the house and the kitchen maids.

Bryden had been thirteen years in America, and when the train stopped at his station, he looked round to see if there were any changes in it. It was just the same blue limestone station-house as it was thirteen years ago. The platform and the sheds were the same, and there were five miles of road from the station to Duncannon. The sea voyage had done him good, but five miles were too far for him to-day; the last time he had walked the road, he had walked it in an hour and a half, carrying a heavy bundle on a stick.

He was sorry he did not feel strong enough for the walk; the evening was fine, and he would meet many people coming home from the fair, some of whom he had known in his youth, and they would tell him where he could get a clean lodging. But the carman would be able to tell him that; he called the car that was waiting at the station, and soon he was answering questions about America. But he wanted to hear of those who were still living in the old country, and after hearing the stories of many people he had forgotten, he heard that Mike Scully, who had been away in a situation for many years as a coachman in the King's County,[2] had come back and built a fine house with a concrete floor. Now there was a good loft in Mike Scully's house, and Mike would be pleased to take in a lodger.

Bryden remembered that Mike had been in a situation at the Big House; he had intended to be a jockey, but had shot up into a fine tall man, and had had to become a coachman instead. Bryden tried to recall the face, but he could only remember a straight nose, and a somewhat dusky complexion. Mike was one of the heroes of his childhood, and now his youth floated before him, and he caught glimpses of himself, something that was more than a phantom and less than a reality. Suddenly his reverie was broken: the carman pointed with his whip, and Bryden saw a tall, finely-built, middle-aged man coming through the gates, and the driver said:

'There's Mike Scully.'

Mike had forgotten Bryden even more completely than Bryden had forgotten him, and many aunts and uncles were mentioned before he began to understand.

'You've grown into a fine man, James,' he said, looking at Bryden's great width of chest. 'But you are thin in the cheeks, and you're very sallow in the cheeks too.'

'I haven't been very well lately — that is one of the reasons I have come back; but I want to see you all again.'

Bryden paid the carman, wished him 'God-speed,' and he and Mike divided the luggage between them, Mike carrying the bag and Bryden the bundle, and they walked round the lake, for the townland was at the back of the demesne; and while they walked,

James proposed to pay Mike ten shillings a week for his board and lodging.

He remembered the woods thick and well-forested; now they were windworn, the drains were choked, and the bridge leading across the lake inlet was falling away. Their way led between long fields where herds of cattle were grazing; the road was broken — Bryden wondered how the villagers drove their carts over it, and Mike told him that the landlord could not keep it in repair, and he would not allow it to be kept in repair out of the rates, for then it would be a public road, and he did not think there should be a public road through his property.

At the end of many fields they came to the village, and it looked a desolate place, even on this fine evening, and Bryden remarked that the county did not seem to be as much lived in as it used to be. It was at once strange and familiar to see the chickens in the kitchen; and, wishing to re-knit himself to the old habits, he begged of Mrs Scully not to drive them out, saying he did not mind them. Mike told his wife that Bryden was born in Duncannon, and when she heard Bryden's name she gave him her hand, after wiping it in her apron, saying he was heartily welcome, only she was afraid he would not care to sleep in a loft.

'Why wouldn't I sleep in a loft, a dry loft! You're thinking a good deal of America over here,' said he, 'but I reckon it isn't all you think it. Here you work when you like and you sit down when you like; but when you have had a touch of blood-poisoning as I had, and when you have seen young people walking with a stick, you think that there is something to be said for old Ireland.'

'Now won't you be taking a sup of milk? You'll be wanting a drink after travelling,' said Mrs Scully.

And when he had drunk the milk Mike asked him if he would like to go inside or if he would like to go for a walk.

'Maybe it is sitting down you would like to be.'

And they went into the cabin, and started to talk about the wages a man could get in America, and the long hours of work.

And after Bryden had told Mike everything about America that he thought of interest, he asked Mike about Ireland. But Mike did not seem to be able to tell him much that was of interest. They were all very poor — poorer, perhaps, than when he left them.

'I don't think anyone except myself has a five pound note to his name.'

Bryden hoped he felt sufficiently sorry for Mike. But after all Mike's life and prospects mattered little to him. He had come back in search of health; and he felt better already; the milk had done him good, and

the bacon and cabbage in the pot' sent forth a savoury odour. The Scullys were very kind, they pressed him to make a good meal; a few weeks of country air and food, they said, would give him back the health he had lost in the Bowery; and when Bryden said he was longing for a smoke, Mike said there was no better sign than that. During his long illness he had never wanted to smoke, and he was a confirmed smoker.

It was comfortable to sit by the mild peat fire watching the smoke of their pipes drifting up the chimney, and all Bryden wanted was to be let alone; he did not want to hear of anyone's misfortunes, but about nine o'clock a number of villagers came in, and their appearance was depressing. Bryden remembered one or two of them — he used to know them very well when he was a boy; their talk was as depressing as their appearance, and he could feel no interest whatever in them. He was not moved when he heard that Higgins the stone mason was dead; he was not affected when he heard that Mary Kelly, who used to go to do the laundry at the Big House, had married; he was only interested when he heard she had gone to America. No, he had not met her there; America is a big place. Then one of the peasants asked him if he remembered Patsy Carabine, who used to do the gardening at the Big House. Yes, he remembered Patsy well. Patsy was in the poor-house. He had not been able to do any work on account of his arm; his house had fallen in; he had given up his holding and gone into the poor-house. All this was very sad, and to avoid hearing any further unpleasantness, Bryden began to tell them about America. And they sat round listening to him; but all the talking was on his side; he wearied of it; and looking round the group he recognized a ragged hunchback with grey hair; twenty years ago he was a young hunchback, and, turning to him, Bryden asked him if he were doing well with his five acres.

'Ah, not much. This has been a bad season. The potatoes failed; they were watery — there is no diet in them.'

These peasants were all agreed that they could make nothing out of their farms. Their regret was that they had not gone to America when they were young; and after striving to take an interest in the fact that O'Connor had lost a mare and foal worth forty pounds Bryden began to wish himself back in the slum. When they left the house he wondered if every evening would be like the present one. Mike piled fresh sods on the fire, and he hoped it would show enough light in the loft for Bryden to undress himself by.

The cackling of some geese in the road kept him

awake, and the loneliness of the country seemed to penetrate to his bones, and to freeze the marrow in them. There was a bat in the loft — a dog howled in the distance — and then he drew the clothes over his head. Never had he been so unhappy, and the sound of Mike breathing by his wife's side in the kitchen added to his nervous terror. Then he dozed a little; and lying on his back he dreamed he was awake, and the men he had seen sitting round the fireside that evening seemed to him like spectres come out of some unknown region of morass and reedy tarn. He stretched out his hands for his clothes, determined to fly from this house, but remembering the lonely road that led to the station he fell back on his pillow. The geese still cackled, but he was too tired to be kept awake any longer. He seemed to have been asleep only a few minutes when he heard Mike calling him. Mike had come half way up the ladder and was telling him that breakfast was ready. 'What kind of breakfast will he give me?' Bryden asked himself as he pulled on his clothes. There were tea and hot griddle cakes for breakfast, and there were fresh eggs; there was sunlight in the kitchen, and he liked to hear Mike tell of the work he was going to do in the fields. Mike rented a farm of about fifteen acres, at least ten of it was grass; he grew an acre of potatoes and some corn, and some turnips for his sheep. He had a nice bit of meadow, and he took down his scythe, and as he put the whetstone in his belt Bryden noticed a second scythe, and he asked Mike if he should go down with him and help him to finish the field.

'You haven't done any mowing this many a year; I don't think you'd be of much help. You'd better go for a walk by the lake, but you may come in the afternoon if you like and help to turn the grass over.'

Bryden was afraid he would find the lake shore very lonely, but the magic of returning health is sufficient distraction for the convalescent, and the morning passed agreeably. The weather was still and sunny. He could hear the ducks in the reeds. The days dreamed themselves away, and it became his habit to go to the lake every morning. One morning he met the landlord, and they walked together, talking of the country, of what it had been, and the ruin it was slipping into. James Bryden told him that ill health had brought him back to Ireland; and the landlord lent him his boat, and Bryden rowed about the islands, and resting upon his oars he looked at the old castles, and remembered the pre-historic raiders that the landlord had told him about. He came across the stones to which the lake dwellers had tied their boats, and these signs of ancient Ireland were pleasing to Bryden in his present mood.

As well as the great lake there was a smaller lake in the bog where the villagers cut their turf. This lake was famous for its pike, and the landlord allowed Bryden to fish there, and one evening when he was looking for a frog with which to bait his line he met Margaret Dirken driving home the cows for the milking. Margaret was the herdsman's daughter, and she lived in a cottage near the Big House; but she came up to the village whenever there was a dance, and Bryden had found himself opposite to her in the reels. But until this evening he had had little opportunity of speaking to her, and he was glad to speak to someone, for the evening was lonely, and they stood talking together.

'You're getting your health again,' she said. 'You'll soon be leaving us.'

'I'm in no hurry.'

'You're grand people over there; I hear a man is paid four dollars a day for his work.'

'And how much,' said James, 'has he to pay for his food and for his clothes?'

Her cheeks were bright and her teeth small, white and beautifully even; and a woman's soul looked at Bryden out of her soft Irish eyes. He was troubled and turned aside, and catching sight of a frog looking at him out of a tuft of grass he said: —

'I have been looking for a frog to put upon my pike line.'

The frog jumped right and left, and nearly escaped in some bushes, but he caught it and returned with it in his hand.

'It is just the kind of frog a pike will like,' he said. 'Look at its great white belly and its bright yellow back.'

And without more ado he pushed the wire to which the hook was fastened through the frog's fresh body, and dragging it through the mouth he passed the hooks through the hind legs and tied the line to the end of the wire.

'I think,' said Margaret, 'I must be looking after my cows; it's time I got them home.'

'Won't you come down to the lake while I set my line?'

She thought for a moment and said: —

'No, I'll see you from here.'

He went down to the reedy tarn, and at his approach several snipe got up, and they flew above his head uttering sharp cries. His fishing-rod was a long hazel stick, and he threw the frog as far as he could into the lake. In doing this he roused some wild ducks; a mallard and two ducks got up, and they flew toward the larger lake. Margaret watched them; they flew in a line with an old castle; and they had not disappeared from view when Bryden came toward her, and he and she drove the cows home together that evening.

They had not met very often when she said, 'James, you had better not come here so often calling to me.'

'Don't you wish me to come?'

'Yes, I wish you to come well enough, but keeping company is not the custom of the country, and I don't want to be talked about.'

'Are you afraid the priest would speak against us from the altar?'

'He has spoken against keeping company, but it is not so much what the priest says, for there is no harm in talking.'

'But if you are going to be married there is no harm in walking out together.'

'Well, not so much, but marriages are made differently in these parts; there is not much courting here.'

And next day it was known in the village that James was going to marry Margaret Dirken.

His desire to excel the boys in dancing had caused a stir of gaiety in the parish, and for some time past there had been dancing in every house where there was a floor fit to dance upon; and if the cottager had no money to pay for a barrel of beer, James Bryden, who had money, sent him a barrel, so that Margaret might get her dance. She told him that they sometimes crossed over into another parish where the priest was not so averse to dancing, and James wondered. And next morning at Mass he wondered at their simple fervour. Some of them held their hands above their head as they prayed, and all this was very new and very old to James Bryden. But the obedience of these people to their priest surprised him. When he was a lad they had not been so obedient, or he had forgotten their obedience; and he listened in mixed anger and wonderment to the priest, who was scolding his parishioners, speaking to them by name, saying that he had heard there was dancing going on in their homes. Worse than that, he said he had seen boys and girls loitering about the roads, and the talk that went on was of one kind — love. He said that newspapers containing love stories were finding their way into the people's houses, stories about love, in which there was nothing elevating or ennobling. The people listened, accepting the priest's opinion without question. And their submission was pathetic. It was the submission of a primitive people clinging to religious authority, and Bryden contrasted the weakness and incompetence of the people about him with the modern restlessness and cold energy of the people he had left behind him.

One evening, as they were dancing, a knock came to the door, and the piper stopped playing, and the dancers whispered: —

'Some one has told on us; it is the priest.'

And the awe-stricken villagers crowded round the cottage fire, afraid to open the door. But the priest said that if they did not open the door he would put his shoulder to it and force it open. Bryden went towards the door, saying he would allow no one to threaten him, priest or no priest, but Margaret caught his arm and told him that if he said anything to the priest, the priest would speak against them from the altar, and they would be shunned by the neighbours. It was Mike Scully who went to the door and let the priest in, and he came in saying they were dancing their souls into hell.

'I've heard of your goings on,' he said — 'of your beer-drinking and dancing. I will not have it in my parish. If you want that sort of thing you had better go to America.'

'If that is intended for me, sir, I will go back tomorrow. Margaret can follow.'

'It isn't the dancing, it's the drinking I'm opposed to,' said the priest, turning to Bryden.

'Well, no one has drunk too much, sir,' said Bryden.

'But you'll sit here drinking all night,' and the priest's eyes went toward the corner where the women had gathered, and Bryden felt that the priest looked on the women as more dangerous than the porter. 'It's after midnight,' he said, taking out his watch.

By Bryden's watch it was only half-past eleven, and while they were arguing about the time Mrs Scully offered Bryden's umbrella to the priest, for in his hurry to stop the dancing the priest had gone out without his; and, as if to show Bryden that he bore him no ill-will, the priest accepted the loan of the umbrella, for he was thinking of the big marriage fee that Bryden would pay him.

'I shall be badly off for the umbrella to-morrow,' Bryden said, as soon as the priest was out of the house. He was going with his father-in-law to a fair. His father-in-law was learning him[4] how to buy and sell cattle. And his father-in-law was saying that the country was mending, and that a man might become rich in Ireland if he only had a little capital. Bryden had the capital, and Margaret had an uncle on the other side of the lake who would leave her all he had, that would be fifty pounds, and never in the village of Duncannon had a young couple begun life with so much prospect of success as would James Bryden and Margaret Dirken.

Some time after Christmas was spoken of as the best time for the marriage; James Bryden said that he would not be able to get his money out of America before the spring. The delay seemed to vex him, and he seemed anxious to be married, until one day he received a letter from America, from a man who had served in the bar with him. This friend wrote to ask Bryden if he were coming back. The letter was no more than a passing wish to see Bryden again. Yet Bryden stood looking at it, and everyone wondered what could be in the letter. It seemed momentous, and they hardly believed him when he said it was from a friend who wanted to know if his health were better. He tried to forget the letter, and he looked at the worn fields, divided by walls of loose stones, and a great longing came upon him.

The smell of the Bowery slum had come across the Atlantic, and had found him out in this western headland; and one night he awoke from a dream in which he was hurling some drunken customer through the open doors into the darkness. He had seen his friend in his white duck jacket throwing drink from glass into glass amid the din of voices and strange accents; he had heard the clang of money as it was swept into the till, and his sense sickened for the bar-room. But how should he tell Margaret Dirken that he could not marry her? She had built her life upon this marriage. He could not tell her that he would not marry her . . . yet he must go. He felt as if he were being hunted; the thought that he must tell Margaret that he could not marry her hunted him day after day as a weasel hunts a rabbit. Again and again he went to meet her with the intention of telling her that he did not love her, that their lives were not for one another, that it had all been a mistake, and that happily he had found out it was a mistake soon enough. But Margaret, as if she guessed what he was about to speak of, threw her arms about him and begged him to say he loved her, and that they would be married at once. He agreed that he loved her, and that they would be married at once. But he had not left her many minutes before the feeling came upon him that he could not marry her — that he must go away. The smell of the bar-room hunted him down. Was it for the sake of the money that he might make there that he wished to go back? No, it was not the money. What then? His eyes fell on the bleak country, on the little fields divided by bleak walls; he remembered the pathetic ignorance of the people, and it was these things that he could not endure. It was the priest who came to forbid the dancing. Yes, it was the priest. As he stood looking at the line of the hills the bar-room seemed by him. He heard the politicians, and the excitement of politics was in his blood again. He must go away from this place — he must get back to the bar-room. Looking up, he saw the scanty orchard, and he hated the spare road that led to the village, and he hated the little hill at the top of which the village began, and he hated more than all other places the house where he was to live with Margaret Dirken — if he married her. He could see it from where he stood — by the edge of the lake, with twenty acres of pasture land about it, for the landlord had given up part of his demesne land to them.

He caught sight of Margaret, and he called her to come through the stile.

'I have just had a letter from America.'

'About the money?' she said.

'Yes, about the money. But I shall have to go over there.'

He stood looking at her, seeking for words; and she guessed from his embarrassment that he would say to her that he must go to America before they were married.

'Do you mean, James, you will have to go at once?'

'Yes,' he said, 'at once. But I shall come back in time to be married in August. It will only mean delaying our marriage a month.'

They walked on a little way talking, and every step he took James felt that he was a step nearer the Bowery slum. And when they came to the gate Bryden said: —

'I must hasten or I shall miss the train.'

'But,' she said, 'you are not going now — you are not going to-day?'

'Yes, this morning. It is seven miles. I shall have to hurry not to miss the train.'

And then she asked him if he would ever come back.

'Yes,' he said, 'I am coming back.'

'If you are coming back, James, why not let me go with you?'

'You could not walk fast enough. We should miss the train.'

'One moment, James. Don't make me suffer; tell me the truth. You are not coming back. Your clothes — where shall I send them?'

He hurried away, hoping he would come back. He tried to think that he liked the country he was leaving, that it would be better to have a farmhouse and live there with Margaret Dirken than to serve drinks in the Bowery. He did not think he was telling her a lie when he said he was coming back. Her offer to forward his clothes touched his heart, and at the end of the road he stood and asked himself if he should go back to her. He would miss the train if he waited another minute, and he ran on. And he would have missed the train if he had not met a car. Once he was on the car he felt himself safe — the country was already behind him. The train and the boat at Cork were mere formulæ; he was already in America.

The moment he landed he felt the thrill of home that he had not found in his native village, and he wondered how it was that the smell of the bar seemed more natural than the smell of fields, and the roar of crowds more welcome than the silence of the lake's edge. He offered up a thanksgiving for his escape, and entered into negotiations for the purchase of the bar-room.

He took a wife, she bore him sons and daughters, the bar-room prospered, property came and went; he grew old, his wife died, he retired from business, and reached the age when a man begins to feel there are not many years in front of him, and that all he has had to do in life has been done. His children married, lonesomeness began to creep about him in the evening and when he looked into the fire-light, a vague, tender reverie floated up, and Margaret's soft eyes and name vivified the dusk. His wife and children passed out of mind, and it seemed to him that a memory was the only real thing he possessed, and the desire to see Margaret again grew intense. But she was an old woman, she had married, maybe she was dead. Well,

he would like to be buried in the village where he was born.

There is an unchanging, silent life within every man that none knows but himself, and his unchanging, silent life was his memory of Margaret Dirken. The bar-room was forgotten and all that concerned it and the things he saw most clearly were the green hillside, and the bog lake and the rushes about it, and the greater lake in the distance, and behind it the blue line of wandering hills.

1   A term common in Ireland to refer to the house and estate of landed gentry. By extension, the Big House novel, as evidenced in the work of Jennifer Johnston, Molly Keane, Caroline Blackwood, continues to exert an influence in modern Irish writing. Moore himself had written on the topic in *A Drama in Muslin* (1887), a novel set against the Land War.
2   Now Offaly in the province of Leinster, roughly half way between Dublin and Galway.
3   A national dish in Ireland, boiled in part together.
4   Learning is used all over Ireland for teaching.

JOSEPH FURPHY

from Joseph Furphy, *Such Is Life: Being Certain Extracts from the Diary of Tom Collins* (1903)

Such Is Life is a remarkable novel, perhaps the most remarkable to be published in the first decade of the twentieth century. This relatively unknown Australian classic, published in the same year as Synge's play *In the Shadow of the Glen*, is intermittently rediscovered but deserves a wider reading public. Joseph Furphy was born at Yarra Glen in Victoria in 1843 and worked in a variety of jobs in farming, prospecting, driving bullocks. He took up writing under the pseudonym of Tom Collins and began contributing to the *Bulletin* in 1889. *Such Is Life* was revised twice after its first submission to a publisher in 1897 and the size of the cuts suggests something of the difficulties Furphy faced with the form and ambitious nature of his project. The diary format allowed for immediacy but threatened narrative cohesion. Rory O'Halloran, a Catholic Irish immigrant from County Armagh, is the subject of Chapter 2 and here in this extract Tom ('Tammas') goes out of his way to meet him after a gap of thirteen years. Notice all the elements in Furphy's construction of this 'interior' scene: the child in Eden, the puritanical wife, the education of Rory and his writing ambitions, use of dialect, European culture and Australian explorers, the harshness of the landscape and the significance of the swagman to the narrative. For a detailed gloss on references, see Francis Devlin-Glass (et al.) *The Annotated Such Is Life* (Melbourne: Oxford University Press, 1991).

It is not in our cities or townships, it is not in our agricultural or mining areas, that the Australian attains full consciousness of his own nationality; it is in places like this, and as clearly here as at the centre of the continent. To me the monotonous variety of this interminable scrub has a charm of its own; so grave, subdued, self-centred; so alien to the genial appeal of more winsome landscape, or the assertive grandeur of mountain and gorge. To me this wayward diversity of spontaneous plant life bespeaks an unconfined, ungauged potentiality of resource; it unveils an ideographic prophecy, painted by Nature in her Impressionist mood, to be deciphered aright only by those willing to discern through the crudeness of dawn a promise of majestic day. Eucalypt, conifer, mimosa; tree, shrub, heath, in endless diversity and exuberance, yet sheltering little of animal life beyond half-specialized and belated types, anachronistic even to the Aboriginal savage. Faithfully and lovingly interpreted, what is the latent meaning of it all?

Our virgin continent! how long has she tarried her bridal day! Pause and think how she has waited in serene loneliness while the deltas of Nile, Euphrates, and Ganges expanded, inch by inch, to spacious provinces, and the Yellow Sea shallowed up with the silt of winters innumerable — waited while the primordial civilizations of Copt, Accadian, Aryan and Mongol crept out, step by step, from paleolithic silence into the uncertain record of Tradition's earliest fable — waited still through the long eras of successive empires, while the hard-won light, broadening little by little, moved westward, westward, round the circumference of the planet, at last to overtake and dominate the fixed twilight of its primitive home — waited, ageless, tireless, acquiescent, her history a blank, while the petulant moods of youth gave place to imperial purpose, stern yet beneficent — waited whilst the interminable procession of annual, lunar and diurnal alternations lapsed unrecorded into a dead Past, bequeathing no register of good or evil endeavour to the ever-living Present. The mind retires from such speculation, unsatisfied but impressed.

Gravely impressed. For this recordless land — this land of our lawful solicitude and imperative responsibility — is exempt from many a bane of territorial rather than racial impress. She is committed to no usages of petrified injustice; she is clogged by no fealty to shadowy idols, enshrined by Ignorance, and upheld by misplaced homage alone; she is cursed by no memories of fanaticism and persecution; she is innocent of hereditary national jealousy, and free from the envy of sister states.

Then think how immeasurably higher are the possibilities of a Future than the memories of any Past since history began. By comparison, the Past, though glozed beyond all semblance of truth, is a clinging heritage of canonized ignorance, brutality and baseness; a drag rather than a stimulus. And as day by day, year by year, our own fluid Present congeals into a fixed Past, we shall do well to take heed that, in time to come, our own memory may not be justly held accursed. For though history is a thing that never repeats itself — since no two historical propositions are alike — one perennial truth holds good, namely, that every social hardship or injustice may be traced back to the linked sins of aggression and submission, remote or proximate in point of time. And I, for one, will never believe the trail of the serpent to be so indelible that barefaced incongruity must dog the footsteps of civilization.

Dan O'Connell's ten-by-five paddock lay end-on to my route; his hut being about midway down the line of fence. On striking the corner of the paddock, I went through a gate, and was closing and securing it behind Bunyip and Pup, when I became aware of a stout-built, black-bearded man on a fat bay horse, approaching along the inside of the fence.

'Rory?' said I inquiringly.

'Well-to-be-shure! A ken har'ly crarit it, Tammas!' exclaimed the evergreen, grasping my proferred hand, while his face became transformed with delight.

'You're so much changed,' said I — 'so manly and sunburnt, and bearded like the patriarchs of old — that I didn't know you when I brought that wire. But I wonder how you failed to recognise me, considering that you heard my name.'

'Och, man dear! A thought ye wur farmin' in Victoria,' he replied. 'An' Collins is a purty common name, so it is; an' A didn't hear yer Chris'n name at all at all. But ye'll stap wi' me the night, an' we'll hev a graat cronia about oul' times.'

'That's just what I was looking forward to, Rory. Which way are you going now?'

'No matther, Tammas. A'll turn back wi' ye, an' we'll git home a brave while afore sundown.'

So we rode slowly side by side along the narrow clearing which extended in endless perspective down the line of fence. After giving Rory a sketch of the vicissitudes and disasters which had imparted an element of variety to the thirteen preceding years of my life, I yielded myself to the lulling influence of his own history during the same period. As you might expect, he glanced lightly over all points of real interest, and dwelt interminably on the statistics of the station — such as the percentage of lambs for each year since the stock was put on; the happily decreasing loss by dingoes; the average clip per head, and all manner of circumscribed pastoral shop.

I reined our conversation round to the future prospects and possibilities of the region wherein his lot was cast, and tried to steer it along that line. But he merely took the country as he found it, and left things at that. It had never occurred to him that a physical revolution was already in progress; that the introduction of sheep meant the ultimate extirpation of all trees and scrubs, except the inedible pine; and that the perpetual trampling of those sharp little hoofs would in time caulk the spongy, absorbent surface; so that these fluffy, scrub-clad expanses would become a country of rich and spacious plains, variegated by lakes and forests, and probably enjoying a fairly equable rainfall.

I have reason to remember that I quoted Sturt's account of the Old Man Plain as a desert solitude of the most hopeless and forbidding character. But, as I pointed out, settlement had crept over that inhospitable tract, and the Old Man Plain had become a pastoral paradise, with a possible future which no man could conjecture. Then I was going on to cite instances, within my own knowledge and memory, of permanent lakes formed in Northern Victoria, and a climate altered for the better, by mere settlement of a soil antecedently dessicated and disintegrated by idle exposure to the seasons. But I had brought round the subject of exploration; and again Rory amazed me by the extent and accuracy of his information.

Glancing from Sturt to Eyre, he firmly, yet temperately, held that the expedition carried out by this explorer along the shores of the Great Australian Bight was the ablest achievement of its kind on record; and he forthwith proceeded to substantiate his contention by a consecutive account of the difficulties met and surmounted on that journey. Also he expatiated with some severity on the slightness of public information with respect to Eyre's exploit.

He listened with kindly toleration whilst I adverted to the excellent work of more recent explorers, whose discoveries had made the Transcontinental telegraph line a feasible undertaking. But his discursive mind ricocheted off to the laying of the Transatlantic cable, in '65; and he dwelt on that epoch-marking work with such minuteness of detail, and such confident mastery of names, dates, and so forth, that I half-resented — not his disconcerting fund of information, but his modest reticence on other subjects of interest. It is a morally upsetting thing, for instance, to discover that the unassuming Londoner, to whom you have been somewhat loosely explaining the pedigrees of the British Peerage, has spent most of his life as a clerk in the Heralds' College.

But I noticed a growing uneasiness in Rory's manner, despite his efforts towards a free-and-easy cordiality. At last he said deprecatingly:

'We're about a mile aff the house now, Tammas. A must go roun' be a tank thonder, an' that manes lavin' ye yer lone. Jist go sthraight on, an' ye'll come till the horse-paddock fence, wi' a wee gate in the corner, an' the house furnent ye. An' ye might tell yourself A'll be home atoast sundown.'

He shook up his horse, and dived through the scrub at an easy trot, whilst I went on down the fence. Before I had gone three-quarters of a mile, my attention was arrested by the peculiar apple-green hue of a tall, healthy-looking pine, standing about a hundred and fifty yards from the fence. Knowing that this abnormal deviation in colour, if not forthwith inquired into, would harass me exceedingly in after years, I turned aside to inspect the tree. It was worth the trouble. The pine had been dead for years, but every leafless twig, right up to its spiry summit, was re-clothed by the dense foliage of a giant woodbine, which embraced the trunk with three clean stems, each as thick as your arm. No moralist worthy of the name could fail to find a comprehensive allegory in the tree; but I had scarcely turned away from it before my meditations were disturbed —

Ten or fifteen yards distant, under the cool shade of a large, low-growing wilga, I observed a man reclining at ease. A tall, athletic man, apparently, with a billy and water-bag beside him, and nothing more to wish for. When I caught sight of him, he was in the act of settling himself more comfortably, and adjusting his wide-brimmed hat over his face.

My first impulse was to hail him with a friendly greeting, but a scruple of punctilio made me pause. The clearing of Rory's horse-paddock was visible here and there through gaps in the scrub; even the hut was in sight from my own point of view; the sun was still a couple of hours above the horizon; and the repose of the wilga shade was more to be desired than the activity of the wood-heap. To everything there is a time and a season; and the tactical moment for weary approach to a dwelling is just when fades the glimmering landscape on the sight, and all the air a solemn stillness holds. So, after a moment's hesitation, my instinctive sense of bush etiquette caused me to turn stealthily away, and seek the wicket gate which afforded ingress to Rory's horse-paddock. But I want you to notice that this decision was preceded by a poise of option between two alternatives. Now mark what followed, for, like Falstaff's story, it is worth the marking.

• • •

As a matter of fact, I approached Rory's neat, two-roomed hut speculating as to why he had purposely left me to feel my own way. I soon formed a good rough guess. A neatly-dressed child, in a vast, white sun-bonnet, ran toward me as I came in sight, but presently paused, and returned at the same pace. On reaching the door I was met by a stern-looking woman of thirty-odd, to whom I introduced myself as an old friend of Mr O'Halloran's.

'Deed he hes plenty o' frien's,' replied the woman drily. 'Are ye gunta stap the night?'

'Well, Mr O'Halloran was kind enough to proffer his hospitality,' I replied, pulling the pack-saddle off Bunyip. 'By the way, I'm to tell you that he'll be home presently.'

'Nat a fear but he'll be home at mail-time. An' a purty house he's got fur till ax a sthranger intil.'

'Now, Mrs O'Halloran, it's the loveliest situation I've seen within a hundred miles,' I replied, as I set Cleopatra at liberty. 'And the way that the place is kept reflects the very credit upon yourself.' Moreover, both compliments were as true as they were frank.

'Dacent enough for them that's niver been used till betther. There's a dale in how a body's rairt.'

'True, Mrs O'Halloran,' I sighed. 'I'm sure you must feel it. But, my word! you can grow the right sort of children here! How old is the little girl?' My custom is to ask a mother the age of her child, and then express incredulity.

'Oul'er nor she's good. She was five on the thirteenth iv last month.'

'No, but seriously, Mrs O'Halloran?'

'A'm always sayrious about telling the thruth.' And with this retort courteous the impervious woman retired into her house, while I seated myself on the bucket stool against the wall, and proceeded to fill my pipe.

'We got six goats — pure Angoras,' remarked the little girl, approaching me with instinctive courtesy. 'We keep them for milkin'; an' Daddy shears them ivery year.'

'I noticed them coming along,' I replied. 'They're beautiful goats. And I see you've got some horses too.'

'Yis; three. We bought wan o' them chape, because he hed a sore back, fram a shearer, an' it's nat hailed up yit. Daddy rides the other wans. E-e-e! can't my Daddy ride! An' he ken grow melons, an' he ken put up shelves, an' he knows iverything!'

'Yes; your Daddy's a good man. I knew him long, long ago, when there was no you. What's your name, dear?'

'Mary.'

'She's got no name,' remarked the grim voice from the interior of the house. And the mild, apologetic glance of the child in my face completed a mental appraisement of Rory's family relations.

Half an hour passed pleasantly enough in this kind of conversation; then Rory came in sight at the wicket gate where I had entered. Mary forgot my existence in a moment, and raced toward him, opening a conversation at the top of her voice while he was still a quarter of a mile distant. When they met, he dismounted, and, placing her astride on the saddle, continued his way with the expression of a man whose cup of happiness is wastefully running over.

I had leisure to observe the child critically as she sat bareheaded beside Rory at the tea-table, glancing from time to time at me for the tribute of admiration due to each remark made by that nonpareil of men.

She was not only a strikingly beautiful child, but the stamp of child that expands into a beautiful woman. In spite of her half-Anglican lineage and Antipodean birth, there was something almost amusing in the strong racial index of her pure Irish face. The black hair and eye-brows were there, with eyes of indescribable blue; the full, shapely lips, and that delicate contour of chin which specially marks the highest type of a race which is not only non-Celtic but non-Aryan.

It is not the Celtic element that makes the Irish people a bundle of inconsistencies — clannish, yet disjunctive; ardent, yet unstable; faithful, yet perfidious; exceeding loveable for its own impulsive love, yet a broken reed to lean upon. It is not the Celt who has made Irish history an unexampled record of patience and insubordination, of devotion and treachery. The Celt, though fiery, is shrewd, sensible, and practical. It has been truly said that Western Britain is more Celtic than Eastern Ireland. But the whole Anglo-Celtic mixture is a thing of yesterday.

Before the eagle of the Tenth Legion was planted on the shore of Cantium — before the first Phœnician ship stowed tin at the Cassiterides — the Celt had inhabited the British Islands long enough to branch into distinct sub-races, and to rise from palæolithic savagery to the use of metals, the domestication of animals, and the observance of elaborate religious rites. Yet, relatively, this antique race is of last week only. For, away beyond the Celt, palæontology finds an earlier Brito-Irish people, of different origin and physical characteristics. And there is little doubt that, forced westward by Celtic invaders, of more virile type, and more capable of organization, that immemorial race is represented by the true Irish of to-day. The black hair, associated with deep-blue eyes and a skin of extreme whiteness, found abundantly in

Ireland, and amongst the offspring of Irish emigrants, are, in all probability, tokens of descent from this appallingly ancient people. The type appears occasionally in the Basque provinces, and on the Atlantic coast of Morocco, but nowhere else. Few civilized races inhabit the land where the fossil relics of their own lineal ancestors mark the furthest point of human occupancy; yet it would seem to be so with the true Irish. In what other way can this anomalous variety of the human race be accounted for? Ay, and beyond the earliest era noted by ethnography, this original Brito-Irish race must have differentiated itself from the unknown archetype, and, by mere genealogical succession, must have fixed its characteristics so tenaciously as to persist through the random admixture of conquests and colonizations during countless generations. 'God is eternal,' says a fine French apothegm, 'but man is very old.'

And very new. Mary O'Halloran was perfect Young-Australian. To describe her from after-knowledge — she was a very creature of the phenomena which had environed her own dawning intelligence. She was a child of the wilderness, a dryad among her kindred trees. The long-descended poetry of her nature made the bush vocal with pure gladness of life; endowed each tree with sympathy, respondent to her own fellowship. She had noticed the dusky aspect of the ironwood; the volumed cumuli of rich olive-green, crowning the lordly currajong; the darker shade of the wilga's massy foliage-cataract; the clearer tint of the tapering pine; the clean-spotted column of the leopard tree, creamy white on slate, from base to topmost twig. She pitied the unlovely belar, when the wind sighed through its coarse, scanty, grey-green tresses; and she loved to contemplate the silvery plumage of the two drooping myalls which, because of their rarity here, had been allowed to remain in the horse-paddock. For the last two or three springs of her vivacious existence, she had watched the deepening crimson of the quondong, amidst its thick contexture of Nile-green leaves; she had marked the unfolding bloom of the scrub, in its many-hued beauty; she had revelled in the audacious black-and-scarlet glory of the desert pea. She knew the dwelling-place of every loved companion; and, by necessity, she had her own names for them all — since her explorations were carried out on Rory's shoulders, or on his saddle, and technicalities never troubled him. To her it was a new world, and she saw that it was good. All those impressions which endear the memory of early scenes to the careworn heart were hers in their vivid present, intensified by the strong ideality of her nature, and undisturbed by other companionship, save that of her father.

This brings us to the other mark of a personality so freshly minted as to have taken no more than two impressions. Rory was her guide, philosopher, and crony. He was her overwhelming ideal of power, wisdom, and goodness; he was her help in ages past, her hope for years to come (no irreverence intended here; quite the reverse, for if true family life existed, we should better apprehend the meaning of 'Our Father, who art in heaven'); he was her Ancient of Days; her shield, and her exceeding great reward.

A new position for Rory; and he grasped it with all the avidity of a love-hungered soul. The whole current of his affections, thwarted and repulsed by the world's indifference, found lavish outlet here.

After tea, Rory took a billy and went out into the horse-paddock to milk the goats — Mary, of course, clinging to his side. I remained in the house, confiding to Mrs O'Halloran the high respect which Rory's principles and abilities had always commanded. But she was past all that; and I had to give it up. When a woman can listen with genuine contempt to the spontaneous echo of her husband's popularity, it is a sure sign that she has explored the profound depths of masculine worthlessness; and there is no known antidote to this fatal enlightenment.

Rory's next duty was to chop up a bit of firewood, and stack it beside the door. Dusk was gathering by this time; and Mrs O'Halloran called Mary to prepare her for the night, while Rory and I seated ourselves on the bucket-stool outside. Presently a lighted lamp was placed on the table, when we removed indoors. Then Mary, in a long, white garment, with her innocent face shining from the combined effects of perfect happiness and unmerciful washing, climbed on Rory's knees — not to bid him goodnight, but to compose herself to sleep.

'Time the chile was bruk aff that habit,' observed the mother, as she seated herself beside the table with some sewing.

'Let her be a child as long as she can, Mrs O'Halloran,' I remarked. 'Surely you wouldn't wish any alteration in her.'

'Nat without it was an altheration fur the bether,' replied the worthy woman. 'An' it's little hopes there is iv hur, consitherin' the way she's rairt. Did iver anybody hear o' rairin' childher' without batin' them when they want it?'

'You bate hur, an' A'll bate you!' interposed Rory, turning to bay on the most salient of the three or four pleas which had power to rouse the Old Adam in his unassertive nature.

'Well, A'm sure A was bate — ay, an' soun'ly bate — when A was lek hur; an' iv A didn't desarve it then, A desarved it other times, when A didn't git it.'

An obvious rejoinder rose to my mind, but evidently not to Rory's, for the look on his face told only of a dogged resolution to continue sinning against the light. He knew that his own contumacy in this respect would land his soul in perdition, and he deliberately let it go at that. Brave old Rory! Never does erratic man appear to such advantage as when his own intuitive moral sense rigorously overbears a conscientiousness warped by some fallacy which he still accepts as truth.

Yet the mother loved the child in her own hard, puritanical way. And, in any case, you are not competent to judge her, unless you have to work for your living, instead of finding somebody eager to support you in luxury for the pleasure of your society; unless, instead of marrying some squatter, or bank clerk, or Member of Parliament, you have inadvertently coupled yourself to a Catholic boundary man, named nothing short of Rory O'Halloran.

The embittered woman retired early, and without phrases. As she did so, I casually noticed that the bedroom was bisected by a partition, with a curtained doorway.

'Ever try your hand at literature, Rory?' I presently asked, remembering Williamson's remark.

'Well, A ken har'ly say No, an' A ken har'ly say Yis,' replied Rory, with ill-feigned humility. 'A've got a bit iv a thraytise scribbled down, furbye a wheen o' other wans on han'. A thought mebbe' — and his glance rested on the angel-face of the sleeping child — 'well, A thought mebbe it would do hur no harrum fur people till know that hur father — well — as ye might say — Nat but what she'll hev money in the bank, plaze God. But A'll lay hur down in hur wee cot now, an' A'll bring the thrifle we wur mentionin'.'

He tenderly carried the child into the first compartment of the bedroom, and, soon returning, placed before me about twenty quarto sheets of manuscript, written on both sides, in a careful, schoolboy hand. The first page was headed, *A Plea for Woman.*

'My word, Rory, this is great!' said I, after reading the first long paragraph. 'I should like to skim it over at once, to get the gist of the argument, and then read it leisurely, to enjoy the style. And that reminds me that I brought you an *Australasian.* I'll get it out of my swag, and you can read it to kill time.'

But it became evident that he couldn't fix his mind on the newspaper whilst his own literary product was under scrutiny. The latter unfolded itself as a unique example of pure deduction, aided by utter lack of discrimination in the value of evidence. It was all synthesis, and no analysis. A certain hypothesis had to be established, and it was established. The style was

directly antithetical to that curt, blunt, and simple pronouncement aimed at by innocents who deceive no one by denouncing Socialism, Trades-Unionism, &c., over the signature of 'A Working Man'. But the Essay. I am debarred from transcribing it, not only because of its length, but because —

'Rory, you must let me take a copy of this.'

'Well, Tammas, A'm glad it plazes ye; right glad, so A am; but A thought till — till —'

'Spring it on the public — so to speak?'

'Yis.'

'Well, I'll faithfully promise to keep the whole work sacred to your credit. And if ever I go into print — which is most unlikely — I'll refer to this essay in such a way as to whet public curiosity to a feather edge. Again, if anything should happen to this copy, you'll have mine to fall back upon.'

'A'll thrust ye, Tammas. God bless ye, take a copy any time afore ye go.'

The object of the essay was to prove that, at a certain epoch in the world's history, the character of woman had undergone an instantaneous transformation. And it was proved in this way:

The two greatest thinkers and most infallible authorities our race has produced are Solomon and Shakespear.

Solomon's estimate of woman is shockingly low; and there is no getting away from the truth of it. His baneful evidence has the guarantee of Holy Writ; moreover, it is fully borne out by the testimony of ancient history, sacred and profane, and by the tendency of the Greek and Roman mythologies. Examples here quoted in profusion.

The fact of woman's pre-eminent wickedness in ancient times is traceable to the eating of the apple, when Eve, being the more culpable, was justly burdened with the heavier penalty, namely, a preternatural bias toward sin in a general way.

On the other hand, Shakespear's estimate of woman is high. And justly so, since his valuation is conclusively endorsed by modern history. Examples again quoted, in convincing volume, from the women of Acts down to Mrs Chisholm and Florence Nightingale.

Now how do you bring these two apparently conflicting facts into the harmony of context? Simply by tracing the Solomon-woman forward, and the Shakespear-woman backward, to their point of intersection, and so finding the moment of transition. It is where the Virgin says:

'My soul doth magnify the Lord, and my spirit hath rejoiced in God my Saviour. For He hath regarded the low estate of His handmaiden; for, behold! from henceforth all generations shall call me blessed.'

This prophecy has not only a personal and specific fulfilment, as pointing to the speaker herself, but a transitive and general application, as referring to her sex at large. There you have it.

But no mere abstract can do justice to the sumptuous phraseology of the work, to its opulence of carefully selected adjective, or to the involved rhetoric which seemed to defeat and set at naught all your petty rules of syntax and prosody. Still less can I impart a notion of the exhaustive raking up of ancient examples and modern instances, mostly worn bright by familiarity with the popular mind, but all converging toward the conclusion striven for, and the shakiest of them accepted in childlike faith. Integrally, that essay conveyed the idea of two mighty glaciers of theory, each impelling its own moraine of facts toward a stated point of confluence — represented by a magnificent postulate — where one section, at least, of the Universal Plan would attain fulfilment, and the Eternal Unities would be so far satisfied. There was something in it that was more like an elusive glimmer of genius than an evidence of understanding, or, still less, of cleverness. Remarkable also, that, though the punctuation was deplorable, every superb polysyllable was correctly spelled. But as a monument of wasted ingenuity and industry, I have met with nothing so pathetic. A long term of self-communion in the back country will never leave a man as it found him. Outside his daily avocation, he becomes a fool or a philosopher; and, in Rory's case, the latter seemed to have been superimposed on the former.

At ten o'clock, I hunted him to bed. I had plenty of blank forms in my writing-case, and on these I took a preliminary copy of *A Plea for Woman*. This occupied about three hours. Then, not feeling sleepy, I took down one of four calico-covered books, which I had previously noticed on a corner shelf. It was my own old Shakespear, with the added interest of marginal marks, in ink of three colours, neatly ordered, and as the sand by the sea-shore innumerable. I put it back with the impression that no book had ever been better placed. The next volume was a Bible, presented by the Reverend Miles Barton, M.A., Rector of Tanderagee, County Armagh, Ireland, to his beloved parishioner, Deborah Johnson, on the occasion of her departure for Melbourne, South Australia, June 16, 1875. The third book was a fairly good dictionary, appendixed by a copious glossary of the Greek and Roman mythologies. The fourth was Vol. XII of *Macmillan's Magazine*, May to October, 1865.

Opening the latter book at random, I fell upon a sketch of Eyre's expedition along the shores of the Great Australian Bight. In another place was a contribution entitled 'A Gallery of American Presidents'. The next item of interest was an account of the Massacre of Cawnpore. And toward the end of the volume was a narrative of the Atlantic Telegraph Expedition. Of course, there were thirty or forty other articles in the book, but they were mostly strange to me, however familiar they might be to Rory.

Hopeless case! I thought, as I blew out the lamp and turned into my comfortable sofa-bed. If this morepoke's Irish love of knowledge was backed by one spark of mental enterprise, he might have half a ton of chosen literature to come and go on. And here he is, with his pristine ignorance merely dislocated.

When I woke at sunrise, Rory was kindling the fire, with the inseparable Mary squatted beside him in her nightgown. After putting on the kettle, he dressed the little girl, and helped her to wash her face. By this time, I was about; and Mary brought me a blank form, which I had dropped and overlooked the night before.

'Keep it till you learn to write, dear,' said I.

'She ken write now,' remarked Rory, with subdued exultation. 'Here, jewel,' he continued, handing her a pencil from the mantelpiece — 'write your name nately on that paper, fur Misther Collins till see.'

The child, tremulous with the ecstatic sense of responsibility, bent over her paper on the table for a full minute, then diffidently pushed it across to me; and I read, in strong Roman capitals, the inscription, MRAY, with the M containing an extra angle — being, so to speak, a letter and a half.

'Ye're wake in spellin', honey,' remarked her father merrily; 'an' the M's got an exthry knuckle on it.'

'It's right enough,' I interposed. 'Couldn't be better. Now, Mary, I'll keep this paper, and show it to you again when you're a great scholar and a great poetess. See if I don't.'

The entrance of Mrs O'Halloran cut short this nonsense; and Rory went out to milk the goats, accompanied, of course, by Mary.

After breakfast, we took our bridles and went out toward where the five horses were feeding together, the inevitable child pattering along by Rory's side.

'You have a lot to be thankful for,' I remarked.

'Blessed be His Name!' thought Rory aloud; and I continued, 'You must make up your mind to send her away to school in another four or five years.'

'Iv coorse,' replied Rory sadly.

'A convent school, mind. None of your common boarding schools for a child like Mary.'

Rory's only reply was a glance of gratitude. My stern admonition would be a moral support to him in the coming controversy.

'You mentioned some other literary work that you have on hand?' I remarked inquiringly.

'Yis; A've jotted down a few idays. Now, Tammas — where was the Garden of Aden supposed to be?'

'My word, Rory, if a man could only disclose that to the world, he would command attention. However, one theory is that it was on the lost continent of Atlantis; another, that it was in the Valley of Cashmere. There are many other localities suggested, but I think the one which meets most favour is the Isle of Kishm, in the Straits of Ormuz, at the entrance to the Persian Gulf.'

'Will ye repate that, Tammas, iv ye plaze.'

I briefly rehearsed such relevant information as I possessed, whilst Rory kidnapped the geographical names, and imprisoned them in his note-book, trusting to his memory for the rest.

'Oul' Father Finnegan, at Derryadd, useteh argie that the Garden iv Aden hed been furnent the Lake o' Killarney; an' no one dar' conthradict him,' he remarked, with a smile. 'But people larns till think fur theirselves when they're out theyre lone. An' afther consitherin' the matter over, A take this iday fur a foundation: The furst Adam was created in a sartin place; then he sinned in a sartin place. An' when the Saviour (blessed be His Name!) come fur till clane the wurrld o' the furst Adam's sin, He hed till be born where the furst Adam was created; an' He hed till die where the furbidden fruit was ait. An' A've gethered up proofs, an' proofs, an' proofs — How far is it fram Jerusalem till Bethlehem, Tammas?'

'Nearly six miles.'

'A knowed the places must be convenient. Now ye mind where the Saviour (blessed be His Name!) says, "all the blood shed on earth, fram the blood iv righteous Abel" — and so on? Well, "earth" manes "land"; an' it's all as wan as if He said, "shed on the land." An' what land? Why, the Holy Land. An' the prophets lived there when the Fall was quite racent; an' hear what they say: —'

(Here he gave me some texts of Scripture, which I afterward verified — and I would certainly advise you to do the same, if you can find a Bible. They are, Isaiah li, 3; Ezekiel xxviii, 13 — xxxi, 9-18 — xxxvi, 35; Joel ii, 3.)

'Rory, you're a marvel,' I remarked with sincerity. 'And, by the way, if there's anything in the inspiration of Art — if the Artist soars to truth by the path which no fowl knoweth — your theory may find some support in the fact that it was a usage of the Renaissance to represent the skull of Adam at the foot of the cross.'

'Ay — that!' And Rory's note-book was out again. 'Which artists, Tammas?'

'Martin Schoen — end of 15th century, for one.

Jean Limousin — 17th century — for another. Albert Dürer — beginning of 16th century — in more than one of his engravings. However, you can just hold this species of proof in reserve till I look up the subject. I won't forget.'

'God bless ye, Tammas! Would it be faysible at all at all fur ye till stap to the morrow mornin', an' ride out wi' me the day?'

'Well — yes.'

'Blessin's on ye, Tammas! Becos A've got four more idays that ye could help me with. Wan iday is about divils. A take this fur a foundation: There's sins fur till be done in the wurrld that men 'on't do; an' divils is marcifully put in the flesh an' blood fur till do them sins. "Wan iv you is a divil," says the Saviour (blessed be His Name!). "He went to his own place," says Acts — both manin' Judas. An' there's a wheen o' places where Iago spakes iv himself as a divil. An' A've got other proofs furbye, that we'll go over wan be wan. It's a mysthery, Tammas.'

'It is indeed.' Whilst replying, I was constrained to glance round at the weather; and my eye happened to fall on the creeper-laden pine, a quarter of a mile away. Suddenly a strange misgiving seized me, and I asked involuntarily, 'Do you have many swagmen calling round here?'

'Nat six in the coorse o' the year,' replied Rory, too amiable to heed the impolite change of subject. 'Las' time A seen Ward,' he continued, after a moment's pause, 'he toul' me there was a man come to the station wan mornin' airly, near blin' wi' sandy blight; an' he stapped all day in a dark skillion, an' started again at night. He was makin' fur Ivanhoe, fur till ketch the coach; but it's a sore ondhertakin' fur a blin' man till thravel the counthry his lone, at this saison o' the year. An' it's quare where sthrangers gits till. A foun' a swag on the fence a week or ten days ago, an' a man's thracks at the tank a couple o' days afther; an' the swag's there yit; an' A would think the swag an' the thracks belonged till the man wi' the sandy blight, barr'n this is nat the road till Ivanhoe.'

'My word, Rory, I wish either you or I had spoken of this when you came home last night. Never mind the horses now. Give me your bridle, and take Mary on your back.'

As we went on, I related how I had seen the man reclining under the tree; and Rory nodded forgivingly when I explained the scruple which had withheld me from making my presence known.

'He must a' come there afther ten o'clock yisterday,' observed Rory; 'or it would be mighty quare fur me till nat see him, consitherin' me eyes is iverywhere when A'm ridin' the boundhry.'

'But he wasn't near the boundary. I had turned off from the fence to see that dead pine with the big creeper on it.'

'Which pine, Tammas?'

'There it is, straight ahead — the biggest of the three that you see above the scrub. You notice it's a different colour?'

''Deed ay, so it is. A wouldn't be onaisy, Tammas; it's har'ly likely there's much wrong — but it's good to make sartin about it.'

No effort could shake off the apprehension which grew upon me as we neared the fence. But on reaching it I said briskly:

'Stay where you are, Rory; I'll be back in half a minute.' Then I crushed myself through the wires.

Fifteen or twenty paces brought me to the spot. The man had changed his position, and was now lying at full length on his back, with arms extended along his sides. His face was fully exposed — the face of a worker, in the prime of manhood, with a heavy moustache and three or four weeks' growth of beard. So much only had I noted at first glance, whilst stooping under the heavy curtain of foliage. A few steps more, and, looking down on the waxen skin of that inert figure, I instinctively uncovered my head.

The dull eyes, half-open to a light no longer intolerable, showed by their death-darkened tracery of inflamed veins how much the lone wanderer had suffered. The hands, with their strong bronze now paled to tarnished ochre, were heavily callused by manual labour, and sharply attenuated by recent hardship. The skin was cold, but the rigidity of death was yet scarcely apparent. Evidently he had not died of thirst alone, but of mere physical exhaustion, sealed by the final collapse of hope. And it seemed so strange to hear the low voices of Rory and Mary close by; to see through occasional spaces in the scrub the clear expanse of the horse-paddock, with even a glimpse of the house, all homely and peaceful in the silent sunshine. But such is life, and such is death.

Rory looked earnestly in my face as I rejoined him, and breathed one of his customary devotional ejaculations.

'Under the big wilga, just beyond that hop-bush,' said I, in an indifferent tone. 'Stay with me, Mary, dear,' I continued, taking out my note-book. 'I'll make you a picture of a horse.'

'But A'm aiger fur till see the pine wi' the big santipede on it,' objected the terrible infant.

'Nat now, darlin',' replied Rory. 'Sure we'll come an' see the pine when we've lavin's o' time; but we're in a hurry now. Stap here an' kape Misther Collins company. Daddy'll be back at wanst.'

He kissed the child, and disappeared round the hop-bush. Then she turned her unfathomable eyes reproachfully on my face, as I sat on the ground.

'A love you, Tammas, becos ye spake aisy till my Daddy. But O!' — and the little, brown fingers wreathed themselves together in the distress of her soul — 'A don't want till go to school, an' lave my Daddy his lone! An' A don't want till see that picther iv a horse; an' A 'on't lave me Daddy.'

I weakly explained that it was a matter of no great importance whether she went to school or not; and that, at worst, her Daddy could accompany her as a schoolmate. Presently Rory returned.

'Mary, jewel, jist pelt aff, lek a good chile, an' see if the wee gate's shut.' Mary shot off at full speed; and he continued gravely, 'Dhrapped aff at the dead hour o' the night, seemin'ly. God rest his sowl! O, Tammas! iv we'd only knowed!'

'Ay, or if I had only spoken to him! He must have got there yesterday morning. Likely he had heard the cocks crowing at your place before daylight, and was making for the sound, only that the light beat him, and he gave it best five minutes too soon.'

'Ah! we're poor, helpless craythurs, Tammas! But A s'pose A betther see Misther Spanker at wanst?'

'No,' I replied; 'you stay and do what you can. I'll ride back, and see Mr Spanker. How far is it to where that swag is on the fence?'

'About — well, about seven mile, as the crow flies.'

'Better have it here. Now we'll catch the horses. Come on, Mary! Take her on your back, Rory; we must hurry up now.'

I have already exceeded the legitimate exactions of my diary-record; but the rest of the story is soon told. Mr Spanker, as a Justice of Peace, took the sworn depositions of Ward, Andrews, Rory, and myself. In the man's pockets were found half-a-dozen letters, addressed to George Murdoch, Mooltunya Station, from Malmsbury, Victoria; and all were signed by his loving wife, Eliza H. Murdoch. Two of the letters acknowledged receipt of cheques; and there was another cheque (for £12 15s., if I remember rightly) in his pocket-book, with about £3 in cash. He was buried in the station cemetery, between Val English, late station storekeeper, who had poisoned himself, and Jack Drummond, shearer, who had died — presumably of heart failure — after breaking the record of the district. Such is life.

PADRAIC COLUM
from Æ (ed.), *New Songs* (1904)

Padraic Colum (1881–1972), playwright, novelist, poet, anthologist, was born in Longford the son of a workhouse manager. His plays, which include *Broken Soil* (1903), *The Land* (1905), and *Thomas Muskerry* (1910), deal with serious topics about rural Ireland in a realistic fashion. After 1914 he lived most of his life in the United States. In 'The Plougher', a poem cited in full in George A. Birmingham's essay above (1907) and worth comparing with Yeats's 'The Fisherman', Colum betrays an awareness of the problems of representing country people. Here in the following poem, which is quoted by George Russell at the end of his article 'Lessons of Revolution' in 1923 (see below), he casts a critical eye over Irish culture and its relationship with Dublin politics. The Forties in the title refers to the 1840s, a time of revolutionary activity in Ireland with the Young Irelanders pressing for the overthrow of British Rule in Ireland by force.

A PORTRAIT

(A poor scholar in the 'Forties')

My eyelids red and heavy are
With bending o'er the smouldering peat;
The Æneid now I know by heart:
I have read it in cold and heat
In loneliness and hunger-smart.
And I know Homer too, I ween,[1]
As Munster poets know Oisin.[2]

And I must walk this road that winds
'Twixt bog and bog, while east there lies
A city with its men and books
With treasures open for the wise,
Heart-words from equals, comrade-looks.
Down here they have but tale and song.
They talk Repeal[3] the whole night long.

'You teach Greek verbs and Latin nouns,'
The dreamer of Young Ireland said,
'And do not hear the muffled call,
The sword being forged, the far off tread

Of host to meet as Gael and Gall.
What good to us your wisdom store,
Your Latin verse, your Grecian lore?'

And what to me is Gael and Gall?
Less, ah far less than Latin, Greek.
I teach these by the dim rush-light,
In smoky cabins, night and week.
But what avail my teaching slight?
Years hence in rustic speech, a phrase,
As in wild earth a Grecian vase.

1 I believe.
2 Son of Finn MacCumhail. Any allusion to the Ossianic controversy associated with James MacPherson in the eighteenth century is probably not intended here.
3 The Repeal of the Act of Union (1801), Daniel O'Connell's major campaign after the Catholic Emancipation movement. The Repeal Association was formed in 1840. The Young Irelanders, dissatisfied with O'Connell's campaign, began to emerge around 1842, and in 1848, led by Smith O'Brien, John Mitchel, and Francis Meagher, they launched an abortive Rising.

EVA GORE-BOOTH
from Eva Gore-Booth, *The One and the Many* (1904)

Eva Gore-Booth (1870–1926), the sister of Constance Markievicz, was born at Lissadell in County Sligo. Abandoning her upper-class inheritance (like her sister), she moved in her early twenties to Manchester, where she worked tirelessly for the women's trade union movement, for socialism and for pacifism. 'The Little Waves of Breffny', perfectly charming in its own way, was a frequently anthologized poem and was set to music by Max Mayer.

THE LITTLE WAVES OF BREFFNY

The grand road from the mountain goes shining to the
    sea,
And there is traffic in it and many a horse and cart,
But the little roads of Cloonagh are dearer far to me,
And the little roads of Cloonagh go rambling through
    my heart.

A great storm from the ocean goes shouting o'er the
    hill,
And there is glory in it and terror on the wind,
But the haunted air of twilight is very strange and still,
And the little winds of twilight are dearer to my mind.

The great waves of the Atlantic sweep storming on
    their way,
Shining green and silver with the hidden herring
    shoal,
But the Little Waves of Breffny have drenched my
    heart in spray,
And the Little Waves of Breffny go stumbling through
    my soul.

LADY GREGORY
from Lady Gregory, *Seven Short Plays* (1909)

The following is a good example of the Abbey Theatre one-act comedy. While Yeats's
drama embodies, in a phrase from *The Secret Rose* (1897), 'the war of the spiritual with
the natural order', Lady Gregory, her ear attuned to servants and tradespeople, is more at
home with providing in her own words 'a base of realism and an apex of beauty'. Here
in *Spreading the News*, Lady Gregory celebrates small-town gossip, and even manages to
turn pinched circumstances and claustrophobia into something attractive and charming.

Spreading the News

PERSONS

Bartley Fallon	James Ryan
Mrs Fallon	Mrs Tarpey
Jack Smith	Mrs Tully
Shawn Early	*A Policeman* (Jo Muldoon)
Tim Casey	*A Removable Magistrate*

SCENE: *The outskirts of a Fair. An Apple Stall.* MRS
TARPEY *sitting at it.* MAGISTRATE *and* POLICEMAN *enter.*

MAGISTRATE: So that is the Fair Green. Cattle and
    sheep and mud. No system. What a repulsive
    sight!

POLICEMAN: That is so, indeed.

MAGISTRATE: I suppose there is a good deal of disorder
    in this place?

POLICEMAN: There is.

MAGISTRATE: Common assault?

POLICEMAN: It's common enough.

MAGISTRATE: Agrarian crime, no doubt?

POLICEMAN: That is so.

MAGISTRATE: Boycotting? Maiming of cattle? Firing
    into houses?

POLICEMAN: There was one time, and there might be
    again.

MAGISTRATE: That is bad. Does it go any farther than
    that?

POLICEMAN: Far enough, indeed.

MAGISTRATE: Homicide, then! This district has been
    shamefully neglected! I will change all that.
    When I was in the Andaman Islands,[1] my system
    never failed. Yes, yes, I will change all that. What
    has that woman on her stall?

POLICEMAN: Apples mostly — and sweets.

MAGISTRATE: Just see if there are any unlicensed goods
    underneath — spirits or the like. We had
    evasions of the salt tax in the Andaman Islands.

POLICEMAN [*sniffing cautiously and upsetting a heap of
    apples*]: I see no spirits here — or salt.

MAGISTRATE [*to* MRS TARPEY]: Do you know this town
    well, my good woman?

MRS TARPEY [*holding out some apples*]: A penny the half-
    dozen, your honour?

POLICEMAN [*shouting*]: The gentleman is asking do you
    know the town! He's the new magistrate!

MRS TARPEY [*rising and ducking*]: Do I know the town? I do, to be sure.

MAGISTRATE [*shouting*]: What is its chief business?

MRS TARPEY: Business, is it? What business would the people here have but to be minding one another's business?

MAGISTRATE: I mean what trade have they?

MRS TARPEY: Not a trade. No trade at all but to be talking.

MAGISTRATE: I shall learn nothing here.

[JAMES RYAN *comes in, pipe in mouth. Seeing* MAGISTRATE *he retreats quickly, taking pipe from mouth.*]

MAGISTRATE: The smoke from that man's pipe had a greenish look; he may be growing unlicensed tobacco at home. I wish I had brought my telescope to this district. Come to the post-office, I will telegraph for it. I found it very useful in the Andaman Islands.

[MAGISTRATE *and* POLICEMAN *go out left.*]

MRS TARPEY: Bad luck to Jo Muldoon, knocking my apples this way and that way. [*Begins arranging them.*] Showing off he was to the new magistrate.

[*Enter* BARTLEY FALLON *and* MRS FALLON.]

BARTLEY: Indeed it's a poor country and a scarce country to be living in. But I'm thinking if I went to America it's long ago the day I'd be dead!

MRS FALLON: So you might, indeed.

[*She puts her basket on a barrel and begins putting parcels in it, taking them from under her cloak.*]

BARTLEY: And it's a great expense for a poor man to be buried in America.

MRS FALLON: Never fear, Bartley Fallon, but I'll give you a good burying the day you'll die.

BARTLEY: Maybe it's yourself will be buried in the graveyard of Cloonmara before me, Mary Fallon, and I myself that will be dying unbeknownst some night, and no one a-near me. And the cat itself may be gone straying through the country, and the mice squealing over the quilt.

MRS FALLON: Leave off talking of dying. It might be twenty years you'll be living yet.

BARTLEY [*with a deep sigh*]: I'm thinking if I'll be living at the end of twenty years, it's a very old man I'll be then!

MRS TARPEY [*turns and sees them*]: Good morrow, Bartley Fallon; good morrow, Mrs Fallon. Well, Bartley, you'll find no cause for complaining to-day; they are all saying it was a good fair.

BARTLEY [*raising his voice*]: It was not a good fair, Mrs Tarpey. It was a scattered sort of a fair. If we didn't expect more, we got less. That's the way with me always; whatever I have to sell goes down and whatever I have to buy goes up. If there's ever any misfortune coming to this world, it's on myself it pitches, like a flock of crows on seed potatoes.

MRS FALLON: Leave off talking of misfortunes, and listen to Jack Smith that is coming the way, and he singing.

[*Voice of* JACK SMITH *heard singing*]:

I thought, my first love,
    There'd be but one house between you and me,
And I thought I would find
    Yourself coaxing my child on your knee.
Over the tide
    I would leap with the leap of a swan,
Till I came to the side
    Of the wife of the red-haired man!

[JACK SMITH *comes in; he is a red-haired man, and is carrying a hayfork.*]

MRS TARPEY: That should be a good song if I had my hearing.

MRS FALLON [*shouting*]: It's 'The Red-haired Man's Wife'.

MRS TARPEY: I know it well. That's the song that has a skin on it!

[*She turns her back to them and goes on arranging her apples.*]

MRS FALLON: Where's herself, Jack Smith?

JACK SMITH: She was delayed with her washing; bleaching the clothes on the hedge she is, and she daren't leave them, with all the tinkers that do be passing to the fair. It isn't to the fair I came myself, but up to the Five Acre Meadow I'm going, where I have a contract for the hay. We'll get a share of it into tramps to-day.[2] [*He lays down hayfork and lights his pipe.*]

BARTLEY: You will not get it into tramps to-day. The rain will be down on it by evening, and on myself too. It's seldom I ever started on a journey but the rain would come down on me before I'd find any place of shelter.

JACK SMITH: If it didn't itself, Bartley, it is my belief you would carry a leaky pail on your head in place of a hat, the way you'd not be without some cause of complaining.

[*A voice heard 'Go on, now, go on out o' that. Go on I say.'*]

JACK SMITH: Look at that young mare of Pat Ryan's that is backing into Shaughnessy's bullocks with the dint of the crowd! Don't be daunted, Pat, I'll give you a hand with her.

[*He goes out, leaving his hayfork.*]

MRS FALLON: It's time for ourselves to be going home. I have all I bought put in the basket. Look at there, Jack Smith's hayfork he left after him! He'll be wanting it. [*Calls.*] Jack Smith! Jack Smith! — He's gone through the crowd — hurry after him, Bartley, he'll be wanting it.

BARTLEY: I'll do that. This is no safe place to be leaving it. [*He takes up fork awkwardly and upsets the basket.*] Look at that now! If there is any basket in the fair upset, it must be our own basket!

[*He goes out to right.*]

MRS FALLON: Get out of that! It is your own fault, it is. Talk of misfortunes and misfortunes will come. Glory be! Look at my new egg-cups rolling in every part — and my two pound of sugar with the paper broke —

MRS TARPEY [*turning from stall*]: God help us, Mrs Fallon, what happened your basket?

MRS FALLON: It's himself that knocked it down, bad manners to him. [*Putting things up.*] My grand sugar that's destroyed, and he'll not drink his tea without it. I had best go back to the shop for more, much good may it do him!

[*Enter* TIM CASEY.]

TIM CASEY: Where is Bartley Fallon, Mrs Fallon? I want a word with him before he'll leave the fair. I was afraid he might have gone home by this, for he's a temperate man.

MRS FALLON: I wish he did go home! It'd be best for me if he went home straight from the fair green, or if he never came with me at all! Where is he, is it? He's gone up the road [*jerks elbow*] following Jack Smith with a hayfork.

[*She goes out to left.*]

TIM CASEY: Following Jack Smith with a hay-fork! Did ever any one hear the like of that. [*Shouts.*] Did you hear that news, Mrs Tarpey?

MRS TARPEY: I heard no news at all.

TIM CASEY: Some dispute I suppose it was that rose between Jack Smith and Bartley Fallon, and it seems Jack made off, and Bartley is following him with a hayfork!

MRS TARPEY: Is he now? Well, that was quick work! It's not ten minutes since the two of them were here, Bartley going home and Jack going to the Five Acre Meadow; and I had my apples to settle up, that Jo Muldoon of the police had scattered, and when I looked round again Jack Smith was gone, and Bartley Fallon was gone, and Mrs Fallon's basket upset, and all in it strewed upon the ground — the tea here — the two pound of sugar there — the egg-cups there — Look, now, what a great hardship the deafness puts upon me, that I didn't hear the commencement of the fight! Wait till I tell James Ryan that I see below,

he is a neighbour of Bartley's, it would be a pity if he wouldn't hear the news!

[*She goes out. Enter* SHAWN EARLY *and* MRS TULLY.]

TIM CASEY: Listen, Shawn Early! Listen, Mrs Tully, to the news! Jack Smith and Bartley Fallon had a falling out, and Jack knocked Mrs Fallon's basket into the road, and Bartley made an attack on him with a hayfork, and away with Jack, and Bartley after him. Look at the sugar here yet on the road!

SHAWN EARLY: Do you tell me so? Well, that's a queer thing, and Bartley Fallon so quiet a man!

MRS TULLY: I wouldn't wonder at all. I would never think well of a man that would have that sort of a mouldering look. It's likely he has overtaken Jack by this.

[*Enter* JAMES RYAN *and* MRS TARPEY.]

JAMES RYAN: That is great news Mrs Tarpey was telling me! I suppose that's what brought the police and the magistrate up this way. I was wondering to see them in it a while ago.

SHAWN EARLY: The police after them? Bartley Fallon must have injured Jack so. They wouldn't meddle in a fight that was only for show!

MRS TULLY: Why wouldn't he injure him? There was many a man killed with no more of a weapon than a hayfork.

JAMES RYAN: Wait till I run north as far as Kelly's bar to spread the news!

[*He goes out.*]

TIM CASEY: I'll go tell Jack Smith's first cousin that is standing there south of the church after selling his lambs.

[*Goes out.*]

MRS TULLY: I'll go telling a few of the neighbours I see beyond to the west.

[*Goes out.*]

SHAWN EARLY: I'll give word of it beyond at the east of the green.

[*Is going out when* MRS TARPEY *seizes hold of him.*]

MRS TARPEY: Stop a minute, Shawn Early, and tell me did you see red Jack Smith's wife, Kitty Keary, in any place?

SHAWN EARLY: I did. At her own house she was, drying clothes on the hedge as I passed.

MRS TARPEY: What did you say she was doing?

SHAWN EARLY [*breaking away*]: Laying out a sheet on the hedge.

[*He goes.*]

MRS TARPEY: Laying out a sheet for the dead! The Lord have mercy on us! Jack Smith dead, and his wife laying out a sheet for his burying! [*Calls out.*] Why didn't you tell me that before, Shawn Early? Isn't the deafness the great hardship? Half the world might be dead without me knowing of it or getting word of it at all! [*She sits down and rocks herself.*] O my poor Jack Smith! To be going to his work so nice and so hearty, and to be left stretched on the ground in the full light of the day!

[*Enter* TIM CASEY.]

TIM CASEY: What is it, Mrs Tarpey? What happened since?

MRS TARPEY: O my poor Jack Smith!

TIM CASEY: Did Bartley overtake him?

MRS TARPEY: O the poor man!

TIM CASEY: Is it killed he is?

MRS TARPEY: Stretched in the Five Acre Meadow!

TIM CASEY: The Lord have mercy on us! Is that a fact?

MRS TARPEY: Without the rites of the Church or a ha'porth!

TIM CASEY: Who was telling you?

MRS TARPEY: And the wife laying out a sheet for his corpse. [*Sits up and wipes her eyes.*] I suppose they'll wake him[3] the same as another?

[*Enter* MRS TULLY, SHAWN EARLY, *and* JAMES RYAN.]

MRS TULLY: There is great talk about this work in every quarter of the fair.

MRS TARPEY: Ochone! cold and dead. And myself maybe the last he was speaking to!

JAMES RYAN: The Lord save us! Is it dead he is?

TIM CASEY: Dead surely, and the wife getting provision for the wake.

SHAWN EARLY: Well, now, hadn't Bartley Fallon great venom in him?

MRS TULLY: You may be sure he had some cause. Why would he have made an end of him if he had not? [*To* MRS TARPEY, *raising her voice.*] What was it rose the dispute at all, Mrs Tarpey?

MRS TARPEY: Not a one of me knows. The last I saw of them, Jack Smith was standing there, and Bartley Fallon was standing there, quiet and easy, and he listening to 'The Red-haired Man's Wife'.

MRS TULLY: Do you hear that, Tim Casey? Do you hear that, Shawn Early and James Ryan? Bartley Fallon was here this morning listening to red Jack Smith's wife, Kitty Keary that was! Listening to her and whispering with her! It was she started the fight so!

SHAWN EARLY: She must have followed him from her own house. It is likely some person roused him.

TIM CASEY: I never knew, before, Bartley Fallon was great with[4] Jack Smith's wife.

MRS TULLY: How would you know it? Sure it's not in the streets they would be calling it. If Mrs Fallon didn't know of it, and if I that have the next

house to them didn't know of it, and if Jack Smith himself didn't know of it, it is not likely you would know of it, Tim Casey.

SHAWN EARLY: Let Bartley Fallon take charge of her from this out so, and let him provide for her. It is little pity she will get from any person in this parish.

TIM CASEY: How can he take charge of her? Sure he has a wife of his own. Sure you don't think he'd turn souper[5] and marry her in a Protestant church?

JAMES RYAN: It would be easy for him to marry her if he brought her to America.

SHAWN EARLY: With or without Kitty Keary, believe me it is for America he's making at this minute. I saw the new magistrate and Jo Muldoon of the police going into the post-office as I came up — there was hurry on them — you may be sure it was to telegraph they went, the way he'll be stopped in the docks at Queenstown![6]

MRS TULLY: It's likely Kitty Keary is gone with him, and not minding a sheet or a wake at all. The poor man, to be deserted by his own wife, and the breath hardly gone out yet from his body that is lying bloody in the field!

[*Enter* MRS FALLON.]

MRS FALLON: What is it the whole of the town is talking about? And what is it you yourselves are talking about? Is it about my man Bartley Fallon you are talking? Is it lies about him you are telling, saying that he went killing Jack Smith? My grief that ever he came into this place at all!

JAMES RYAN: Be easy now, Mrs Fallon. Sure there is no one at all in the whole fair but is sorry for you!

MRS FALLON: Sorry for me, is it? Why would anyone be sorry for me? Let you be sorry for yourselves, and that there may be shame on you for ever and at the day of judgment, for the words you are saying and the lies you are telling to take away the character of my poor man, and to take the good name off of him, and to drive him to destruction! That is what you are doing!

SHAWN EARLY: Take comfort now, Mrs Fallon. The police are not so smart as they think. Sure he might give them the slip yet, the same as Lynchehaun.[7]

MRS TULLY: If they do get him, and if they do put a rope around his neck, there is no one can say he does not deserve it!

MRS FALLON: Is that what you are saying, Bridget Tully, and is that what you think? I tell you it's too much talk you have, making yourself out to be such a great one, and to be running down every respectable person! A rope, is it? It isn't

much of a rope was needed to tie up your own furniture the day you came into Martin Tully's house, and you never bringing as much as a blanket, or a penny, or a suit of clothes with you, and I myself bringing seventy pounds and two feather beds. And now you are stiffer than a woman would have a hundred pounds! It is too much talk the whole of you have. A rope, is it? I tell you the whole of this town is full of liars and schemers that would hang you up for half a glass of whiskey. [*Turning to go.*] People they are you wouldn't believe as much as daylight from without you'd get up to have a look at it yourself. Killing Jack Smith indeed! Where are you at all, Bartley, till I bring you out of this? My nice, quiet little man! My decent comrade! He that is as kind and as harmless as an innocent beast of the field! He'll be doing no harm at all if he'll shed the blood of some of you after this day's work! That much would be no harm at all. [*Calls out.*] Bartley! Bartley Fallon! Where are you? [*Going out.*] Did anyone see Bartley Fallon?
[*All turn to look after her.*]

JAMES RYAN: It is hard for her to believe any such a thing, God help her!
[*Enter* BARTLEY FALLON *from right, carrying hayfork.*]

BARTLEY: It is what I often said to myself, if there is ever any misfortune coming to this world, it is on myself it is sure to come!
[*All turn round and face him.*]

BARTLEY: To be going about with this fork, and to find no one to take it, and no place to leave it down, and I wanting to be gone out of this. — Is that you, Shawn Early? [*Holds out fork.*] It's well I met you. You have no call to be leaving the fair for a while the way I have, and how can I go till I'm rid of this fork? Will you take it and keep it until such fine time as Jack Smith —

SHAWN EARLY [*backing*]: I will not take it, Bartley Fallon, I'm very thankful to you!

BARTLEY [*turning to apple stall*]: Look at it now, Mrs Tarpey, it was here I got it; let me thrust it in under the stall. It will lie there safe enough, and no one will take notice of it until such time as Jack Smith —

MRS TARPEY: Take your fork out of that! Is it to put trouble on me and to destroy me you want? putting it there for the police to be rooting it out maybe.
[*Thrusts him back.*]

BARTLEY: That is a very unneighbourly thing for you to do, Mrs Tarpey. Hadn't I enough care on me

with that fork before this, running up and down with it like the swinging of a clock, and afeard to lay it down in any place. I wish I never touched it or meddled with it at all!

JAMES RYAN: It is a pity, indeed, you ever did.

BARTLEY: Will you yourself take it, James Ryan? You were always a neighbourly man.

JAMES RYAN [*backing*]: There is many a thing I would do for you, Bartley Fallon, but I won't do that!

SHAWN EARLY: I tell you there is no man will give you any help or any encouragement for this day's work. If it was something agrarian now —

BARTLEY: If no one at all will take it, maybe it's best to give it up to the police.

TIM CASEY: There'd be a welcome for it with them, surely! [*Laughter.*]

MRS TULLY: And it is to the police Kitty Keary herself will be brought.

MRS TARPEY [*rocking to and fro*]: I wonder now who will take the expense of the wake for poor Jack Smith?

BARTLEY: The wake for Jack Smith!

TIM CASEY: Why wouldn't he get a wake as well as another? Would you begrudge him that much?

BARTLEY: Red Jack Smith dead! Who was telling you?

SHAWN EARLY: The whole town knows of it by this.

BARTLEY: Do they say what way did he die?

JAMES RYAN: You don't know that yourself, I suppose, Bartley Fallon? You don't know he was followed and that he was laid dead with the stab of a hayfork?

BARTLEY: The stab of a hayfork!

SHAWN EARLY: You don't know, I suppose, that the body was found in the Five Acre Meadow?

BARTLEY: The Five Acre Meadow!

TIM CASEY: It is likely you don't know that the police are after the man that did it?

BARTLEY: The man that did it!

MRS TULLY: You don't know, maybe, that he was made away with for the sake of Kitty Keary, his wife?

BARTLEY: Kitty Keary, his wife!
[*Sits down bewildered.*]

MRS. TULLY: And what have you to say now, Bartley Fallon?

BARTLEY [*crossing himself*]: I to bring that fork here, and to find that news before me! It is much if I can ever stir from this place at all, or reach as far as the road!

TIM CASEY: Look, boys, at the new magistrate, and Jo Muldoon along with him! It's best for us to quit this.

SHAWN EARLY: That is so. It is best not to be mixed in this business at all.

JAMES RYAN: Bad as he is, I wouldn't like to be an informer against any man.

[*All hurry away except* MRS TARPEY, *who remains behind her stall. Enter* MAGISTRATE *and* POLICEMAN.]

MAGISTRATE: I knew the district was in a bad state, but I did not expect to be confronted with a murder at the first fair I came to.

POLICEMAN: I am sure you did not, indeed.

MAGISTRATE: It was well I had not gone home. I caught a few words here and there that roused my suspicions.

POLICEMAN: So they would, too.

MAGISTRATE: You heard the same story from everyone you asked?

POLICEMAN: The same story — or if it was not altogether the same, anyway it was no less than the first story.

MAGISTRATE: What is that man doing? He is sitting alone with a hayfork. He has a guilty look. The murder was done with a hayfork!

POLICEMAN [*in a whisper*]: That's the very man they say did the act; Bartley Fallon himself!

MAGISTRATE: He must have found escape difficult — he is trying to brazen it out. A convict in the Andaman Islands tried the same game, but he could not escape my system! Stand aside — Don't go far — have the handcuffs ready. [*He walks up to* BARTLEY, *folds his arms, and stands before him.*] Here, my man, do you know anything of John Smith?

BARTLEY: Of John Smith! Who is he, now?

POLICEMAN: Jack Smith, sir — Red Jack Smith!

MAGISTRATE [*coming a step nearer and tapping him on the shoulder*]: Where is Jack Smith?

BARTLEY [*with a deep sigh, and shaking his head slowly*]: Where is he, indeed?

MAGISTRATE: What have you to tell?

BARTLEY: It is where he was this morning, standing in this spot, singing his share of songs — no, but lighting his pipe — scraping a match on the sole of his shoe —

MAGISTRATE: I ask you, for the third time, where is he?

BARTLEY: I wouldn't like to say that. It is a great mystery, and it is hard to say of any man, did he earn hatred or love.

MAGISTRATE: Tell me all you know.

BARTLEY: All that I know — Well, there are the three estates; there is Limbo, and there is Purgatory, and there is —

MAGISTRATE: Nonsense! This is trifling! Get to the point.

BARTLEY: Maybe you don't hold with the clergy so? That is the teaching of the clergy. Maybe you hold with the old people. It is what they do be saying, that the shadow goes wandering, and the soul is tired, and the body is taking a rest — The shadow! [*Starts up.*] I was nearly sure I saw Jack Smith not ten minutes ago at the corner of the forge, and I lost him again — Was it his ghost I saw, do you think?

MAGISTRATE [*to* POLICEMAN]: Conscience-struck! He will confess all now!

BARTLEY: His ghost to come before me! It is likely it was on account of the fork! I to have it and he to have no way to defend himself the time he met with his death!

MAGISTRATE [*to* POLICEMAN]: I must note down his words [*takes out notebook*]. [*To* BARTLEY.] I warn you that your words are being noted.

BARTLEY: If I had ha' run faster in the beginning, this terror would not be on me at the latter end! Maybe he will cast it up against me at the day of judgment — I wouldn't wonder at all at that.

MAGISTRATE [*writing*]: At the day of judgment —

BARTLEY: It was soon for his ghost to appear to me — is it coming after me always by day it will be, and stripping the clothes off in the night time? — I wouldn't wonder at all at that, being as I am an unfortunate man!

MAGISTRATE [*sternly*]: Tell me this truly. What was the motive of this crime?

BARTLEY: The motive, is it?

MAGISTRATE: Yes; the motive; the cause.

BARTLEY: I'd sooner not say that.

MAGISTRATE: You had better tell me truly. Was it money?

BARTLEY: Not at all! What did poor Jack Smith ever have in his pockets unless it might be his hands that would be in them?

MAGISTRATE: Any dispute about land?

BARTLEY [*indignantly*]: Not at all! He never was a grabber or grabbed from anyone!

MAGISTRATE: You will find it better for you if you tell me at once.

BARTLEY: I tell you I wouldn't for the whole world wish to say what it was — it is a thing I would not like to be talking about.

MAGISTRATE: There is no use in hiding it. It will be discovered in the end.

BARTLEY: Well, I suppose it will, seeing that mostly everybody knows it before. Whisper here now. I will tell no lie; where would be the use? [*Puts his hand to his mouth, and* MAGISTRATE *stoops.*] Don't be putting the blame on the parish, for such a thing was never done in the parish before — it was done for the sake of Kitty Keary, Jack Smith's wife.

MAGISTRATE [*to* POLICEMAN]: Put on the handcuffs.

We have been saved some trouble. I knew he would confess if taken in the right way.

[POLICEMAN *puts on handcuffs*.]

BARTLEY: Handcuffs now! Glory be! I always said, if there was ever any misfortune coming to this place it was on myself it would fall. I to be in handcuffs! There's no wonder at all in that.

[*Enter* MRS FALLON, *followed by the rest. She is looking back at them as she speaks.*]

MRS FALLON: Telling lies the whole of the people of this town are; telling lies, telling lies as fast as a dog will trot! Speaking against my poor respectable man! Saying he made an end of Jack Smith! My decent comrade! There is no better man and no kinder man in the whole of the five parishes! It's little annoyance he ever gave to anyone! [*Turns and sees him.*] What in the earthly world do I see before me? Bartley Fallon in charge of the police! Handcuffs on him! O Bartley, what did you do at all at all?

BARTLEY: O Mary, there has a great misfortune come upon me! It is what I always said, that if there is ever any misfortune —

MRS FALLON: What did he do at all, or is it bewitched I am?

MAGISTRATE: This man has been arrested on a charge of murder.

MRS FALLON: Whose charge is that? Don't believe them! They are all liars in this place! Give me back my man!

MAGISTRATE: It is natural you should take his part, but you have no cause of complaint against your neighbours. He has been arrested for the murder of John Smith, on his own confession.

MRS FALLON: The saints of heaven protect us! And what did he want killing Jack Smith?

MAGISTRATE: It is best you should know all. He did it on account of a love affair with the murdered man's wife.

MRS FALLON [*sitting down*]: With Jack Smith's wife! With Kitty Keary! — Ochone, the traitor!

THE CROWD: A great shame, indeed. He is a traitor, indeed.

MRS TULLY: To America he was bringing her, Mrs Fallon.

BARTLEY: What are you saying, Mary? I tell you —

MRS FALLON: Don't say a word! I won't listen to any word you'll say! [*Stops her ears.*] O, isn't he the treacherous villain? Ohone go deo![8]

BARTLEY: Be quiet till I speak! Listen to what I say!

MRS FALLON: Sitting beside me on the ass car coming to the town, so quiet and so respectable, and treachery like that in his heart!

BARTLEY: Is it your wits you have lost or is it I myself that have lost my wits?

MRS FALLON: And it's hard I earned you, slaving, slaving — and you grumbling, and sighing, and coughing, and discontented, and the priest wore out anointing you, with all the times you threatened to die!

BARTLEY: Let you be quiet till I tell you!

MRS FALLON: You to bring such a disgrace into the parish! A thing that was never heard of before!

BARTLEY: Will you shut your mouth and hear me speaking?

MRS FALLON: And if it was for any sort of a fine handsome woman, but for a little fistful of a woman like Kitty Keary, that's not four feet high hardly, and not three teeth in her head unless she got new ones! May God reward you, Bartley Fallon, for the black treachery in your heart and the wickedness in your mind, and the red blood of poor Jack Smith that is wet upon your hand!

[*Voice of* JACK SMITH *heard singing*.]

The sea shall be dry,
  The earth under mourning and ban!
Then loud shall he cry
  For the wife of the red-haired man!

BARTLEY: It's Jack Smith's voice — I never knew a ghost to sing before —. It is after myself and the fork he is coming! [*Goes back. Enter* JACK SMITH.] Let one of you give him the fork and I will be clear of him now and for eternity!

MRS TARPEY: The Lord have mercy on us! Red Jack Smith! The man that was going to be waked!

JAMES RYAN: Is it back from the grave you are come?

SHAWN EARLY: Is it alive you are, or is it dead you are?

TIM CASEY: Is it yourself at all that's in it?

MRS TULLY: Is it letting on you were to be dead?

MRS FALLON: Dead or alive, let you stop Kitty Keary, your wife, from bringing my man away with her to America!

JACK SMITH: It is what I think, the wits are gone astray on the whole of you. What would my wife want bringing Bartley Fallon to America?

MRS FALLON: To leave yourself, and to get quit of you she wants, Jack Smith, and to bring him away from myself. That's what the two of them had settled together.

JACK SMITH: I'll break the head of any man that says that! Who is it says it? [*To* TIM CASEY.] Was it you said it? [*To* SHAWN EARLY.] Was it you?

ALL TOGETHER [*backing and shaking their heads*]: It wasn't I said it!

JACK SMITH: Tell me the name of any man that said it!

ALL TOGETHER [*pointing to* BARTLEY]: It was *him* that said it!

JACK SMITH: Let me at him till I break his head!

[BARTLEY *backs in terror. Neighbours hold* JACK SMITH *back.*]

JACK SMITH [*trying to free himself*]: Let me at him! Isn't he the pleasant sort of a scarecrow for any woman to be crossing the ocean with! It's back from the docks of New York he'd be turned [*trying to rush at him again*], with a lie in his mouth and treachery in his heart, and another man's wife by his side, and he passing her off as his own! Let me at him, can't you.

[*Makes another rush, but is held back.*]

MAGISTRATE [*pointing to* JACK SMITH]: Policeman, put the handcuffs on this man. I see it all now. A case of false impersonation, a conspiracy to defeat the ends of justice. There was a case in the Andaman Islands, a murderer of the Mopsa tribe, a religious enthusiast —

POLICEMAN: So he might be, too.

MAGISTRATE: We must take both these men to the scene of the murder. We must confront them with the body of the real Jack Smith.

JACK SMITH: I'll break the head of any man that will find my dead body!

MAGISTRATE: I'll call more help from the barracks.

[*Blows* POLICEMAN'S *whistle.*]

BARTLEY: It is what I am thinking, if myself and Jack Smith are put together in the one cell for the night, the handcuffs will be taken off him, and his hands will be free, and murder will be done that time surely!

MAGISTRATE: Come on! [*They turn to the right.*]

1 In the Bay of Bengal. The Magistrate's attitude to Ireland is not unlike that expressed by Kipling when he spoke of the white man's burden.

2 A large amount of the hay trodden down (for ease of transport).

3 Where the dead person is laid out at home the night before burial. Provisions needed might include tea and cake, snuff and whiskey.

4 Intimate, closely acquainted. A common Irish expression.

5 In times of hardship Irish Catholics would sometimes convert to Protestantism in exchange for food or soup (hence souper).

6 Port in Cork Harbour (Cobh) where emigrants embarked for America.

7 Lynchehaun was an alias for James Walshe. After almost killing a woman on Achill Island he was protected by the island community but was captured and sentenced to life imprisonment. He subsequently escaped to America, and then avoided extradition proceedings because he claimed he was a political prisoner. Walshe was one of the models used by Synge in his creation of Christy Mahon in *Playboy of the Western World* (1907).

8 Irish expression. Literally alas for ever.

THE RED-HAIRED MAN'S WIFE

Spreading the News.

I thought, my first love, there'd be but one house be-tween you and me, And I thought I would find your-self coax-ing my child on your knee. O-ver the tide I would leap with the leap of a swan, Till I came to the side of the wife of the red-haired man.

G. B. SHAW
John Bull's Other Island (1904)

Shaw's devastating critique of Anglo-Irish relations, its first performance delayed to coincide with the opening of Parliament in November 1904, remains as fresh and as humorous today as it was a century ago. At the Royal Command performance on 11 March 1905 King Edward VII laughed so much that he broke the chair he was sitting on. There is of course a deeper side to trouble the confident analysis and in this play it is the figure of the visionary defrocked priest Keegan who reminds us that not everything could be accommodated by Shaw's efficient intellect. For his comments on the play's relevance and targets, see Shaw's 1906 Preface for Politicians and his 1912 Preface to the Home Rule Edition of the play. For a not dissimilar treatment of politics in provincial Ireland, see George A. Birmingham's acerbic novel *General John Regan* (1913). Shaw's interest in the alignment of orthography and the sound system of English is particularly in evidence in *John Bull's Other Island*. How do you think such an interest connects with Shaw's political concerns expressed in the play?

John Bull's Other Island

ACT I

Great George Street, Westminster, is the address of Doyle and Broadbent, civil engineers. On the threshold one reads that the firm consists of Mr Laurence Doyle and Mr Thomas Broadbent, and that their rooms are on the first floor. Most of these rooms are private; for the partners, being bachelors and bosom friends, live there; and the door marked Private, next the clerks' office, is their domestic sitting room as well as their reception room for clients. Let me describe it briefly from the point of view of a sparrow on the window sill. The outer door is in the opposite wall, close to the right hand corner. Between this door and the left hand corner is a hatstand and a table consisting of large drawing boards on trestles, with plans, rolls of tracing paper, mathematical instruments, and other draughtman's accessories on it. In the left hand wall is the fireplace, and the door of an inner room between the fireplace and our observant sparrow. Against the right hand wall is a filing cabinet, with a cupboard on it, and, nearer, a tall office desk and stool for one person. In the middle of the room a large double writing table is set across, with a chair at each end for the two partners. It is a room which no woman would tolerate, smelling of tobacco, and much in need of repapering, repainting, and recarpeting; but this is the effect of bachelor untidiness and indifference, not want of means; for nothing that DOYLE *and* BROADBENT *themselves have purchased is cheap; nor is anything they want lacking. On the walls hang a large map of South America, a pictorial advertisement of a steamship company, an impressive portrait of Gladstone, and several caricatures of Mr Balfour as a rabbit and Mr Chamberlain as a fox by Francis Carruthers Gould.*[1]

At twenty minutes to five o'clock on a summer afternoon in 1904, the room is empty. Presently the outer door is opened, and a valet comes in laden with a large Gladstone bag and a strap of rugs. He carries them into the inner room. He is a respectable valet, old enough to have lost all alacrity and acquired an air of putting up patiently with a great deal of trouble and indifferent health. The luggage belongs to BROADBENT, *who enters after the valet. He pulls off his overcoat and hangs it with his hat on the stand. Then he comes to the writing table and looks through the letters waiting there for him. He is a robust, full-blooded, energetic man in the prime of life, sometimes eager and credulous, sometimes shrewd and roguish, sometimes portentously solemn, sometimes jolly and impetuous, always buoyant and irresistible, mostly likeable, and enormously absurd in his most earnest moments. He bursts open his letters with his thumb, and glances through them, flinging the envelopes about the floor with reckless untidiness whilst he talks to the valet.*

BROADBENT [*calling*]: Hodson.

HODSON [*in the bedroom*]: Yes sir.

BROADBENT: Don't unpack. Just take out the things I've worn; and put in clean things.

HODSON [*appearing at the bedroom door*]: Yes sir. [*He turns to go back into the bedroom.*]

BROADBENT: And look here! [HODSON *turns again.*] Do you remember where I put my revolver?

HODSON: Revolver, sir! Yes sir. Mr Doyle uses it as a paperweight, sir, when he's drawing.

BROADBENT: Well, I want it packed. There's a packet of cartridges somewhere, I think. Find it and pack it as well.

HODSON: Yes sir.

BROADBENT: By the way, pack your own traps too. I shall take you with me this time.

HODSON [*hesitant*]: Is it a dangerous part you're going to, sir? Should I be expected to carry a revolver, sir?

BROADBENT: Perhaps it might be as well. I'm going to Ireland.

HODSON [*reassured*]: Yes sir.

BROADBENT: You don't feel nervous about it, I suppose?

HODSON: Not at all, sir. I'll risk it, sir.

BROADBENT: Even been in Ireland?

HODSON: No sir. I understand it's a very wet climate, sir. I'd better pack your india-rubber overalls.

BROADBENT: Do. Where's Mr Doyle?

HODSON: I'm expecting him at five, sir. He went out after lunch.

BROADBENT: Anybody been looking for me?

HODSON: A person giving the name of Haffigan has called twice today, sir.

BROADBENT: Oh, I'm sorry. Why didn't he wait? I told him to wait if I wasn't in.

HODSON: Well sir, I didn't know you expected him; so I thought it best to — to — not to encourage him, sir.

BROADBENT: Oh, he's all right. He's an Irishman, and not very particular about his appearance.

HODSON: Yes sir: I noticed that he was rather Irish.

BROADBENT: If he calls again let him come up.

HODSON: I think I saw him waiting about, sir, when you drove up. Shall I fetch him, sir?

BROADBENT: Do, Hodson.

HODSON: Yes sir. [*He makes for the outer door.*]

BROADBENT: He'll want tea. Let us have some.

HODSON [*stopping*]: I shouldn't think he drank tea, sir.

BROADBENT: Well, bring whatever you think he'd like.

HODSON: Yes sir. [*An electric bell rings.*] Here he is, sir. Saw you arrive, sir.

BROADBENT: Right. Shew him in. [HODSON *goes out.* BROADBENT *gets through the rest of his letters before* HODSON *returns with the visitor.*]

HODSON: Mr Affigan.

HAFFIGAN *is a stunted, shortnecked, smallheaded man of about 30, with a small bullet head, a red nose, and furtive eyes. He is dressed in seedy black, almost clerically, and might be a tenth-rate schoolmaster ruined by drink. He hastens to shake* BROADBENT'*s hand with a show of reckless geniality and high spirits, helped out by a rollicking stage brogue. This is perhaps a comfort to himself, as he is secretly pursued by the horrors of incipient delirium tremens.*

HAFFIGAN: Tim Haffigan, sir, at your service. The top o' the mornin' to you, Misther Broadbent.

BROADBENT [*delighted with his Irish visitor*]: Good afternoon, Mr Haffigan.

TIM: An' is it the afthernoon it is already? Begorra, what I call the mornin' is all the time a man fasts afther breakfast.

BROADBENT: Haven't you lunched?

TIM: Divil a lunch!

BROADBENT: I'm sorry I couldn't get back from Brighton in time to offer you some; but —

TIM: Not a word, sir, not a word. Sure it'll do tomorrow. Besides, I'm Irish, sir: a poor aither, but a powerful dhrinker.

BROADBENT: I was just about to ring for tea when you came. Sit down, Mr Haffigan.

TIM: Tay is a good dhrink if your nerves can stand it. Mine can't.

HAFFIGAN *sits down at the writing table, with his back to the filing cabinet.* BROADBENT *sits opposite him.* HODSON *enters empty-handed; takes two glasses, a siphon, and a tantalus from the cupboard; places them before* BROADBENT *on the writing table; looks ruthlessly at* HAFFIGAN, *who cannot meet his eye; and retires.*

BROADBENT: Try a whisky and soda.

TIM [*sobered*]: There you touch the national wakeness, sir. [*Piously.*] Not that I share it meself. I've seen too much of the mischief of it.

BROADBENT [*pouring the whisky*]: Say when.

TIM: Not too sthrong. [BROADBENT *stops and looks inquiringly at him.*] Say half-an'-half. [BROADBENT, *somewhat startled by this demand, pours a little more, and again stops and looks.*] Just a dhrain more: the lower half o' the tumbler doesn't hold a fair half. Thankya.

BROADBENT [*laughing*]: You Irishmen certainly do know how to drink. [*Pouring some whisky for himself.*] Now that's my poor English idea of a whisky and soda.

TIM: An' a very good idea it is too. Dhrink is the curse o' me unhappy counthry. I take it meself because I've a wake heart and a poor digestion; but in principle I'm a teetoatler.

BROADBENT [*suddenly solemn and strenuous*]: So am I, of course. I'm a Local Optionist[2] to the backbone. You have no idea, Mr Haffigan, of the ruin that is wrought in this country by the unholy alliance of the publicans, the bishops, the Tories, and *The Times.* We must close the public-houses at all costs [*he drinks*].

TIM: Sure I know. It's awful [*he drinks*]. I see you're a good Liberal like meself, sir.

BROADBENT: I am a lover of liberty, like every true Englishman, Mr Haffigan. My name is

Broadbent. If my name were Breitstein,[3] and I had a hooked nose and a house in Park Lane, I should carry a Union Jack handkerchief and a penny trumpet, and tax the food of the people to support the Navy League, and clamour for the destruction of the last remnants of national liberty —

TIM: Not another word. Shake hands.

BROADBENT: But I should like to explain —

TIM: Sure I know every word you're going to say before yev said it. *I* know the sort o' man yar. An' so you're thinkin' o' comin' to Ireland for a bit?

BROADBENT: Where else can I go? I am an Englishman and a Liberal; and now that South Africa has been enslaved and destroyed,[4] there is no country left to me to take an interest in but Ireland. Mind: I don't say that an Englishman has not other duties. He has a duty to Finland and a duty to Macedonia. But what sane man can deny that an Englishman's first duty is his duty to Ireland? Unfortunately, we have politicians here more unscrupulous than Bobrikoff, more bloodthirsty than Abdul the Damned; and it is under their heel that Ireland is now writhing.

TIM: Faith, they've reckoned up with poor oul Bobrikoff anyhow.

BROADBENT: Not that I defend assassination: God forbid! However strongly we may feel that the unfortunate and patriotic young man who avenged the wrongs of Finland on the Russian tyrant was perfectly right from his own point of view, yet every civilized man must regard murder with abhorrence. Not even in defence of Free Trade would I lift my hand against a political opponent, however richly he might deserve it.

TIM: I'm sure you wouldn't; and I honour you for it. You're goin' to Ireland, then, out o' sympathy: is it?

BROADBENT: I'm going to develop an estate there for the Land Development Syndicate, in which I am interested. I am convinced that all it needs to make it pay is to handle it properly, as estates are handled in England. You know the English plan, Mr Haffigan, don't you?

TIM: Bedad I do, sir. Take all you can out of Ireland and spend it in England: that's it.

BROADBENT [*not quite liking this*]: My plan, sir, will be to take a little money out of England and spend it in Ireland.

TIM: More power to your elbow! an' may your shadda never be less! for you're the broth of a boy intirely. An' how can I help you? Command me to the last dhrop o' me blood.

BROADBENT: Have you ever heard of Garden City?[5]

TIM [*doubtfully*]: D'ye mane Heav'n?

BROADBENT: Heaven! No: it's near Hitchin. If you can spare half an hour I'll go into it with you.

TIM: I tell you hwat. Gimme a prospectus. Lemmy take it home and reflect on it.

BROADBENT: You're quite right: I will. [*He gives him a copy of Ebenezer Howard's book, and several pamphlets.*] You understand that the map of the city — the circular construction — is only a suggestion.

TIM: I'll make a careful note o' that [*looking dazedly at the map*].

BROADBENT: What I say is, why not start a Garden City in Ireland?

TIM [*with enthusiasm*]: That's just what was on the tip o' me tongue to ask you. Why not? [*Defiantly.*] Tell me why not.

BROADBENT: There are difficulties. I shall overcome them; but there are difficulties. When I first arrive in Ireland I shall be hated as an Englishman. As a Protestant, I shall be denounced from every altar. My life may be in danger. Well, I am prepared to face that.

TIM: Never fear, sir. We know how to respict a brave innimy.

BROADBENT: What I really dread is misunderstanding. I think you could help me to avoid that. When I heard you speak the other evening in Bermondsey at the meeting of the National League,[6] I saw at once that you were — You won't mind my speaking frankly?

TIM: Tell me all me faults as man to man. I can stand anything but flattery.

BROADBENT: May I put it in this way? That I saw at once that you are a thorough Irishman, with all the faults and all the qualities of your race: rash and improvident but brave and good-natured; not likely to succeed in business on your own account perhaps, but eloquent, humorous, a lover of freedom, and a true follower of that great Englishman Gladstone.

TIM: Spare me blushes. I mustn't sit here to be praised to me face. But I confess to the goodnature: it's an Irish wakeness. I'd share me last shillin' with a friend.

BROADBENT: I feel sure you would, Mr Haffigan.

TIM [*impulsively*]: Damn it! Call me Tim. A man that talks about Ireland as you do may call me anything. Gimmy a howlt o' that whisky bottle [*he replenishes*].

BROADBENT [*smiling indulgently*]: Well, Tim, will you come with me and help to break the ice between me and your warm-hearted, impulsive countrymen?

TIM: Will I come to Madagascar or Cochin China wid you? Bedad I'll come to the North Pole wid you if yll pay me fare; for the divil a shillin' I have to buy a third class ticket.

BROADBENT: I've not forgotten that, Tim. We must put that little matter on a solid English footing, though the rest can be as Irish as you please. You must come as my — my — well, I hardly know what to call it. If we call you my agent, they'll shoot you. If we call you a bailiff, they'll duck you in the horsepond. I have a secretary already; and —

TIM: Then we'll call him the Home Secretary and me the Irish Secretary. Eh?

BROADBENT [*laughing industriously*]: Capital. Your Irish wit has settled the first difficulty. Now about your salary —

TIM: A salary, is it? Sure I'd do it for nothin', only me cloes ud disgrace you; and I'd be dhriven to borra money from your friends: a thing that's agin me nacher. But I won't take a penny more than a hundherd a year. [*He looks with restless cunning at* BROADBENT, *trying to guess how far he may go.*]

BROADBENT: If that will satisfy you —

TIM [*more than reassured*]: Why shouldn't it satisfy me? A hundherd a year is twelve pound a month, isn't it?

BROADBENT: No. Eight pound six and eightpence.

TIM: Oh murdher! An' I'll have to sind five timmy poor oul mother in Ireland. But no matther: I said a hundherd; and what I said I'll stick to, if I have to starve for it.

BROADBENT [*with business caution*]: Well, let us say twelve pounds for the first month. Afterwards, we shall see how we get on.

TIM: You're a gentleman, sir. Whin me mother turns up her toes, you shall take the five pounds off; for your expinses must be kep down wid a sthrong hand; an— [*He is interrupted by the arrival of* BROADBENT's *partner.*]

Mr LAURENCE DOYLE *is a man of 36, with cold grey eyes, strained nose, fine fastidious lips, critical brows, clever head, rather refined and goodlooking on the whole, but with a suggestion of thinskinnedness and dissatisfaction that contrasts strongly with* BROADBENT's *eupeptic jollity.*

He comes in as a man at home there, but on seeing the stranger shrinks at once, and is about to withdraw when BROADBENT *reassures him. He then comes forward to the table, between the two others.*

DOYLE [*retreating*]: You're engaged.

BROADBENT: Not at all, not at all. Come in. [*To* TIM.] This gentleman is a friend who lives with me here: my partner, Mr Doyle. [*To* DOYLE.] This is a new Irish friend of mine, Mr Tim Haffigan.

TIM [*rising with effusion*]: Sure it's meself that's proud to meet any friend o' Misther Broadbent's. The top o' the mornin' to you, sir! Me heart goes out teeye both. It's not often I meet two such splendid specimens iv the Anglo-Saxon race.

BROADBENT [*chuckling*]: Wrong for once, Tim. My friend Mr Doyle is a countryman of yours.

TIM *is noticeably dashed by this announcement. He draws in his horns at once, and scowls suspiciously at* DOYLE *under a vanishing mask of goodfellowship: cringing a little, too, in mere nerveless fear of him.*

DOYLE [*with cool disgust*]: Good evening. [*He retires to the fireplace, and says to* BROADBENT *in a tone which conveys the strongest possible hint to* HAFFIGAN *that he is unwelcome.*] Will you soon be disengaged?

TIM [*his brogue decaying into a common would-be genteel accent with an unexpected strain of Glasgow in it*]: I must be going. Avnmpoartnt engeegement in the west end.

BROADBENT [*rising*]: It's settled, then, that you come with me.

TIM: Ashll be verra pleased to accompany ye, sir.

BROADBENT: But how soon? Can you start tonight? From Paddington? We go by Milford Haven.[7]

TIM [*hesitating*]: Well — A'm afraid — A [DOYLE *goes abruptly into the bedroom, slamming the door and shattering the last remnant of* TIM's *nerve. The poor wretch saves himself from bursting into tears by plunging again into his role of daredevil Irishman. He rushes to* BROADBENT; *plucks at his sleeve with trembling fingers; and pours forth his entreaty with all the brogue he can muster, subduing his voice lest* DOYLE *should hear and return.*] Misther Broadbent: don't humiliate me before a fella counthryman. Look here: me cloes is up the spout. Gimmy a fypounnote — I'll pay ya nex Choosda whin me ship comes home — or you can stop it out o' me month's sallery. I'll be on the platform at Paddnton punctial an' ready. Gimmy it quick, before he comes back. You won't mind me axin, will ye?

BROADBENT: Not at all. I was about to offer you an advance for travelling expenses. [*He gives him a bank note.*]

TIM [*pocketing it*]: Thank you. I'll be there half an hour before the thrain starts. [LARRY *is heard at the bedroom door, returning.*] Whisht:[8] he's comin' back. Goodbye an' God bless ye. [*He hurries out almost crying, the £5 note and all the drink it means to him being too much for his empty stomach and overstrained nerves.*]

DOYLE [*returning*]: Where the devil did you pick up that seedy swindler? What was he doing here? [*He goes up to the table where the plans are, and makes a note on one of them, referring to his pocket book as he does so.*]

BROADBENT: There you go! Why are you so down on every Irishman you meet, especially if he's a bit shabby? Poor devil! Surely a fellow-countryman may pass you the top of the morning without offence, even if his coat is a bit shiny at the seams.

DOYLE [*contemptuously*]: The top of the morning! Did he call you the broth of a boy? [*He comes to the writing table.*]

BROADBENT [*triumphantly*]: Yes.

DOYLE: And wished you more power to your elbow?

BROADBENT: He did.

DOYLE: And that your shadow might never be less?

BROADBENT: Certainly.

DOYLE [*taking up the depleted whisky bottle and shaking his head at it*]: And he got about half a pint of whisky out of you.

BROADBENT: It did him no harm. He never turned a hair.

DOYLE: How much money did he borrow?

BROADBENT: It was not borrowing exactly. He shewed a very honourable spirit about money. I believe he would share his last shilling with a friend.

DOYLE: No doubt he would share his friend's last shilling if his friend was fool enough to let him. How much did he touch you for?

BROADBENT: Oh, nothing. An advance on his salary — for travelling expenses.

DOYLE: Salary! In Heaven's name, what for?

BROADBENT: For being my Home Secretary, as he very wittily called it.

DOYLE: I don't see the joke.

BROADBENT: You can spoil any joke by being cold blooded about it. I saw it all right when he said it. It was something — something really very amusing — about the Home Secretary and the Irish Secretary. At all events, he's evidently the very man to take with me to Ireland to break the ice for me. He can gain the confidence of the people there, and make them friendly to me. Eh? [*He seats himself on the office stool, and tilts it back so that the edge of the standing desk supports his back and prevents his toppling over.*]

DOYLE: A nice introduction, by George! Do you suppose the whole population of Ireland consists of drunken begging letter writers, or that even if

it did, they would accept one another as references?

BROADBENT: Pooh! nonsense! he's only an Irishman. Besides, you don't seriously suppose that Haffigan can humbug me, do you?

DOYLE: No: he's too lazy to take the trouble. All he has to do is to sit there and drink your whisky while you humbug yourself. However, we needn't argue about Haffigan, for two reasons. First, with your money in his pocket he will never reach Paddington: there are too many public houses on the way. Second, he's not an Irishman at all.

BROADBENT: Not an Irishman! [*He is so amazed by the statement that he straightens himself and brings the stool bolt upright.*]

DOYLE: Born in Glasgow. Never was in Ireland in his life. I know all about him.

BROADBENT: But he spoke — he behaved just like an Irishman.

DOYLE: Like an Irishman!! Man alive, don't you know that all this top-o'-the-morning and broth-of-a-boy and more-power-to-your-elbow business is got up in England to fool you, like the Albert Hall concerts of Irish music? No Irishman ever talks like that in Ireland, or ever did, or ever will. But when a thoroughly worthless Irishman comes to England, and finds the whole place full of romantic duffers like you, who will let him loaf and drink and sponge and brag as long as he flatters your sense of moral superiority by playing the fool and degrading himself and his country, he soon learns the antics that take you in. He picks them up at the theatre or the music hall. Haffigan learnt the rudiments from his father, who came from my part of Ireland. I knew his uncles, Matt and Andy Haffigan of Rosscullen.

BROADBENT [*still incredulous*]: But his brogue?

DOYLE: His brogue! A fat lot you know about brogues! I've heard you call a Dublin accent that you could hang your hat on, a brogue. Heaven help you! You don't know the difference between Connemara and Rathmines.[9] [*With violent irritation.*] Oh, damn Tim Haffigan! Let's drop the subject: he's not worth wrangling about.

BROADBENT: What's wrong with you today, Larry? Why are you so bitter?

DOYLE *looks at him perplexedly; comes slowly to the writing table; and sits down at the end next the fireplace before replying.*

DOYLE: Well: your letter completely upset me, for one thing.

BROADBENT: Why?

DOYLE: Your foreclosing this Rosscullen mortgage and

turning poor Nick Lestrange out of house and home has rather taken me aback; for I liked the old rascal when I was a boy and had the run of his park to play in. I was brought up on the property.

BROADBENT: But he wouldn't pay the interest. I had to foreclose on behalf of the Syndicate. So now I'm off to Roscullen to look after the property myself. [*He sits down at the writing table opposite* LARRY, *and adds, casually, but with an anxious glance at his partner*] You're coming with me, of course?

DOYLE [*rising nervously and recommencing his restless movements*]: That's it. That's what I dread. That's what has upset me.

BROADBENT: But don't you want to see your country again after 18 years absence? to see your people? to be in the old home again? to —

DOYLE [*interrupting him very impatiently*]: Yes, yes: I know all that as well as you do.

BROADBENT: Oh well, of course [*with a shrug*] if you take it in that way, I'm sorry.

DOYLE: Never you mind my temper: it's not meant for you, as you ought to know by this time. [*He sits down again, a little ashamed of his petulance; reflects a moment bitterly; then bursts out*] I have an instinct against going back to Ireland: an instinct so strong that I'd rather go with you to the South Pole than to Roscullen.

BROADBENT: What! Here you are, belonging to a nation with the strongest patriotism! the most inveterate homing instinct in the world! and you pretend you'd rather go anywhere than back to Ireland. You don't suppose I believe you, do you? In your heart —

DOYLE: Never mind my heart: an Irishman's heart is nothing but his imagination. How many of all those millions that have left Ireland have ever come back or wanted to come back? But what's the use of talking to you? Three verses of twaddle about the Irish emigrant 'sitting on the stile, Mary', or three hours of Irish patriotism in Bermondsey or the Scotland Division of Liverpool, go further with you than all the facts that stare you in the face. Why, man alive, look at me! You know the way I nag, and worry, and carp, and cavil, and disparage, and am never satisfied and never quiet, and try the patience of my best friends.

BROADBENT: Oh, come, Larry! do yourself justice. You're very amusing and agreeable to strangers.

DOYLE: Yes, to strangers. Perhaps if I was a bit stiffer to strangers, and a bit easier at home, like an Englishman, I'd be better company for you.

BROADBENT: We get on well enough. Of course you have the melancholy of the Keltic race —[10]

DOYLE [*bounding out of his chair*]: Good God!!!

BROADBENT [*slyly*]: — and also its habit of using strong language when there's nothing the matter.

DOYLE: Nothing the matter! When people talk about the Celtic race, I feel as if I could burn down London. That sort of rot does more harm than ten Coercion Acts. Do you suppose a man need be a Celt to feel melancholy in Rosscullen? Why, man, Ireland was peopled just as England was; and its breed was crossed by just the same invaders.

BROADBENT: True. All the capable people in Ireland are of English extraction. It has often struck me as a most remarkable circumstance that the only party in parliament which shews the genuine old English character and spirit is the Irish party. Look at its independence, its determination, its defiance of bad Governments, its sympathy with oppressed nationalities all the world over! How English!

DOYLE: Not to mention the solemnity with which it talks old-fashioned nonsense which it knows perfectly well to be a century behind the times. That's English, if you like.

BROADBENT: No, Larry, no. You are thinking of the modern hybrids that now monopolize England. Hypocrites, humbugs, Germans, Jews, Yankees, foreigners, Park Laners, cosmopolitan riffraff. Don't call them English. They don't belong to the dear old island, but to their confounded new empire; and by George! they're worthy of it; and I wish them joy of it.

DOYLE [*unmoved by this outburst*]: There! You feel better now, don't you?

BROADBENT [*defiantly*]: I do. Much better.

DOYLE: My dear Tom, you only need a touch of the Irish climate to be as big a fool as I am myself. If all my Irish blood were poured into your veins, you wouldn't turn a hair of your constitution and character. Go and marry the most English Englishwoman you can find, and then bring up your son in Rosscullen; and that son's character will be so like mine and so unlike yours that everybody will accuse me of being his father. [*With sudden anguish*] Rosscullen! oh, good Lord, Rosscullen! The dullness! the hopelessness! the ignorance! the bigotry!

BROADBENT [*matter-of-factly*]: The usual thing in the country, Larry. Just the same here.

DOYLE [*hastily*]: No, no: the climate is different. Here, if the life is dull, you can be dull too, and no great harm done. [*Going off into a passionate dream*] But your wits can't thicken in that soft moist air, on those white springy roads, in those misty rushes and brown bogs, on those hillsides of granite rocks and magenta heather. You've no such colours in the sky, no such lure in the distances, no such sadness in the evenings. Oh, the dreaming! the dreaming! the torturing, heart-scalding, never satisfying dreaming, dreaming, dreaming, dreaming! [*Savagely*] No debauchery that ever coarsened and brutalized an Englishman can take the worth and usefulness out of him like that dreaming. An Irishman's imagination never lets him alone, never convinces him, never satisfies him; but it makes him that he can't face reality nor deal with it nor handle it nor conquer it: he can only sneer at them that do, and [*bitterly, at* BROADBENT] be 'agreeable to strangers', like a good-for-nothing woman on the streets. [*Gabbling at* BROADBENT *across the table*] It's all dreaming, all imagination. He can't be religious. The inspired Churchman that teaches him the sanctity of life and the importance of conduct is sent away empty; while the poor village priest that gives him a miracle or a sentimental story of a saint, has cathedrals built for him out of the pennies of the poor. He can't be intelligently political: he dreams of what the Shan Van Vocht said in ninety-eight.[11] If you want to interest him in Ireland you've got to call the unfortunate island Kathleen ni Hoolihan and pretend she's a little old woman. It saves thinking. It saves working. It saves everything except imagination, imagination, imagination; and imagination's such a torture that you can't bear it without whisky. [*With fierce shivering self-contempt*] At last you get that you can bear nothing real at all: you'd rather starve than cook a meal; you'd rather go shabby and dirty than set your mind to take care of your clothes and wash yourself; you nag and squabble at home because your wife isn't an angel, and she despises you because you're not a hero; and you hate the whole lot round you because they're only poor slovenly useless devils like yourself. [*Dropping his voice like a man making some shameful confidence*] And all the while there goes on a horrible, senseless, mischievous laughter. When you're young, you exchange drinks with other young men; and you exchange vile stories with them; and as you're too futile to be able to help or cheer them, you chaff and sneer and taunt them for not doing the things you daren't do yourself. And all the time you laugh! laugh!

laugh! eternal derision, eternal envy, eternal folly, eternal fouling and staining and degrading, until, when you come at last to a country where men take a question seriously and give a serious answer to it, you deride them for having no sense of humour, and plume yourself on your own worthlessness as if it made you better than them.

BROADBENT [*roused to intense earnestness by* DOYLE'S *eloquence*]: Never despair, Larry. There are great possibilities for Ireland. Home Rule will work wonders under English guidance.

DOYLE [*pulled up short, his face twitching with a reluctant smile*]: Tom: why do you select my most tragic moments for your most irresistible strokes of humour?

BROADBENT: Humour! I was perfectly serious. What do you mean? Do you doubt my seriousness about Home Rule?

DOYLE: I am sure you are serious, Tom, about the English guidance.

BROADBENT [*quite reassured*]: Of course I am. Our guidance is the important thing. We English must place our capacity for government without stint at the service of nations who are less fortunately endowed in that respect; so as to allow them to develop in perfect freedom to the English level of self-government, you know. You understand me?

DOYLE: Perfectly. And Rosscullen will understand you too.

BROADBENT [*cheerfully*]: Of course it will. So that's all right. [*He pulls up his chair and settles himself comfortably to lecture* DOYLE.] Now, Larry, I've listened carefully to all you've said about Ireland; and I can see nothing whatever to prevent your coming with me. What does it all come to? Simply that you were only a young fellow when you were in Ireland. You'll find all that chaffing and drinking and not knowing what to be at in Peckham just the same as in Donnybrook. You looked at Ireland with a boy's eyes and saw only boyish things. Come back with me and look at it with a man's; and get a better opinion of your country.

DOYLE: I daresay you're partly right in that: at all events I know very well that if I had been the son of a labourer instead of the son of a country landagent, I should have struck more grit than I did. Unfortunately I'm not going back to visit the Irish nation, but to visit my father and Aunt Judy and Nora Reilly and Father Dempsey and the rest of them.

BROADBENT: Well, why not? They'll be delighted to see you, now that England has made a man of you.

DOYLE [*struck by this*]: Ah! you hit the mark there, Tom, with true British inspiration.

BROADBENT: Common sense, you mean.

DOYLE [*quickly*]: No I don't: you've no more common sense than a gander. No Englishman has any common sense, or ever had, or ever will have. You're going on a sentimental expedition for perfectly ridiculous reasons, with your head full of political nonsense that would not take in any ordinarily intelligent donkey; but you can hit me in the eye with the simple truth about myself and my father.

BROADBENT [*amazed*]: I never mentioned your father.

DOYLE [*not heeding the interruption*]: There he is in Rosscullen, a landagent who's always been in a small way because he's a Catholic, and the landlords are mostly Protestants. What with land courts reducing rents and Land Purchase Acts turning big estates into little holdings, he'd be a beggar if he hadn't taken to collecting the new purchase instalments instead of the old rents. I doubt if he's been further from home than Athenmullet for twenty years. And here am I, made a man of, as you say, by England.

BROADBENT [*apologetically*]: I assure you I never meant —

DOYLE: Oh, don't apologize: it's quite true. I daresay I've learnt something in America and a few other remote and inferior spots; but in the main it is by living with you and working in double harness with you that I have learnt to live in a real world and not in an imaginary one. I owe more to you than to any Irishman.

BROADBENT [*shaking his head with a twinkle in his eye*]: Very friendly of you, Larry, old man, but all blarney. I like blarney; but it's rot, all the same.

DOYLE: No it's not. I should never have done anything without you; though I never stop wondering at that blessed old head of yours with all its ideas in watertight compartments, and all the compartments warranted impervious to anything it doesn't suit you to understand.

BROADBENT [*invincible*]: Unmitigated rot, Larry, I assure you.

DOYLE: Well, at any rate you will admit that all my friends are either Englishmen or men of the big world that belongs to the big Powers. All the serious part of my life has been lived in that atmosphere: all the serious part of my work has been done with men of that sort. Just think of me as I am now going back to Rosscullen! to that hell of littleness and monotony! How am I to get on with a little country landagent that ekes out his 5 per cent with a little farming and a scrap of house property in the nearest country town? What am I to say to him? What is he to say to me?

BROADBENT [*scandalized*]: But you're father and son, man!

DOYLE: What difference does that make? What would you say if I proposed a visit to your father?

BROADBENT [*with filial rectitude*]: I always made a point of going to see my father regularly until his mind gave way.

DOYLE [*concerned*]: Has he gone mad? You never told me.

BROADBENT: He has joined the Tariff Reform League. He would never have done that if his mind had not been weakened. [*Beginning to declaim*] He has fallen a victim to the arts of a political charlatan who —

DOYLE [*interrupting him*]: You mean that you keep clear of your father because he differs from you about Free Trade, and you don't want to quarrel with him. Well, think of me and my father! He's a Nationalist and a Separatist. I'm a metallurgical chemist turned civil engineer. Now whatever else metallurgical chemistry may be, it's not national. It's international. And my business and yours as civil engineers is to join countries, not to separate them. The one real political conviction that our business has rubbed into us is that frontiers are hindrances and flags confounded nuisances.

BROADBENT [*still smarting under Mr Chamberlain's economic heresy*]: Only when there is a protective tariff —

DOYLE [*firmly*]: Now look here, Tom: you want to get in a speech on Free Trade; and you're not going to do it: I won't stand it. My father wants to make St George's Channel a frontier and hoist a green flag on College Green;[12] and I want to bring Galway within 3 hours of Colchester and 24 of New York. I want Ireland to be the brains and imagination of a big Commonwealth, not a Robinson Crusoe island. Then there's the religious difficulty. My Catholicism is the Catholicism of Charlemagne or Dante, qualified by a great deal of modern science and folklore which Father Dempsey would call the ravings of an Atheist. Well, my father's Catholicism is the Catholicism of Father Dempsey.

BROADBENT [*shrewdly*]: I don't want to interrupt you, Larry; but you know this is all gammon. These differences exist in all families; but the members rub on together all right. [*Suddenly relapsing into portentousness*] Of course there are some questions which touch the very foundations of morals; and on these I grant you even the closest relationships cannot excuse any compromise or laxity. For instance —

DOYLE [*impatiently springing up and walking about*]: For instance, Home Rule, South Africa, Free Trade, and putting the Church schools on the Education Rate. Well, I should differ from my father on every one of them, probably, just as I differ from you about them.

BROADBENT: Yes; but you are an Irishman; and these things are not serious to you as they are to an Englishman.

DOYLE: What! not even Home Rule!

BROADBENT [*steadfastly*]: Not even Home Rule. We owe Home Rule not to the Irish, but to our English Gladstone. No, Larry: I can't help thinking that there's something behind all this.

DOYLE [*hotly*]: What is there behind it? Do you think I'm humbugging you?

BROADBENT: Don't fly out, old chap. I only thought —

DOYLE: What did you think?

BROADBENT: Well, a moment ago I caught a name which is new to me: a Miss Nora Reilly, I think. [DOYLE *stops dead and stares at him with something like awe.*] I don't wish to be impertinent, as you know, Larry; but are you sure she has nothing to do with your reluctance to come to Ireland with me?

DOYLE [*sitting down again, vanquished*]: Thomas Broadbent: I surrender. The poor silly-clever Irishman takes off his hat to God's Englishman. The man who could in all seriousness make that recent remark of yours about Home Rule and Gladstone must be simply the champion idiot of all the world. Yet the man who could in the very next sentence sweep away all my special pleading and go straight to the heart of my motives must be a man of genius. But that the idiot and the genius should be the same man! how is that possible? [*Springing to his feet*] By Jove, I see it all now. I'll write an article about it, and send it to *Nature*.

BROADBENT [*staring at him*]: What on earth —

DOYLE: It's quite simple. You know that a caterpillar —

BROADBENT: A caterpillar!!!

DOYLE: Yes, a caterpillar. Now give your mind to what I am going to say; for it's a new and important scientific theory of the English national character. A caterpillar —

BROADBENT: Look here, Larry: don't be an ass.

DOYLE [*insisting*]: I say a caterpillar and I mean a caterpillar. You'll understand presently. A caterpillar [BROADBENT *mutters a slight protest, but does not press it*] when it gets into a tree, instinctively makes itself look exactly like a leaf; so that both its enemies and its prey may mistake it for one and think it not worth bothering about.

BROADBENT: What's that got to do with our English national character?

DOYLE: I'll tell you. The world is as full of fools as a tree is full of leaves. Well, the Englishman does what the caterpillar does. He instinctively makes himself look like a fool, and eats up all the real fools at his ease while his enemies let him alone and laugh at him for being a fool like the rest. Oh, nature is cunning! cunning! [*He sits down, lost in contemplation of his word-picture.*]

BROADBENT [*with hearty admiration*]: Now you know, Larry, that would never have occurred to me. You Irish people are amazingly clever. Of course it's all tommy rot; but it's so brilliant, you know! How the dickens do you think of such things! You really must write an article about it: they'll pay you something for it. If Nature won't have it, I can get it into Engineering for you: I know the editor.

DOYLE: Let's get back to business. I'd better tell you about Nora Reilly.

BROADBENT: No: never mind. I shouldn't have alluded to her.

DOYLE: I'd rather. Nora has a fortune.

BROADBENT [*keenly interested*]: Eh? How much?

DOYLE: Forty per annum.

BROADBENT: Forty thousand?

DOYLE: No, forty. Forty pounds.

BROADBENT [*much dashed*]: That's what you call a fortune in Rosscullen, is it?

DOYLE: A girl with a dowry of five pounds calls it a fortune in Rosscullen. What's more, £40 a year is a fortune there; and Nora Reilly enjoys a good deal of social consideration as an heiress on the strength of it. It has helped my father's household through many a tight place. My father was her father's agent. She came on a visit to us when he died, and has lived with us ever since.

BROADBENT [*attentively, beginning to suspect* LARRY *of misconduct with* NORA, *and resolving to get to the bottom of it*]: Since when? I mean how old were you when she came?

DOYLE: I was seventeen. So was she: if she'd been older she'd have had more sense than to stay with us. We were together for 18 months before I went up to Dublin to study. When I went home for

Christmas and Easter, she was there. I suppose it used to be something of an event for her; though of course I never thought of that then.

BROADBENT: Were you at all hard hit?

DOYLE: Not really. I had only two ideas at that time: first, to learn to do something; and then to get out of Ireland and have a chance of doing it. She didn't count. I was romantic about her, just as I was romantic about Byron's heroines or the old Round Tower of Roscullen;[13] but she didn't count any more than they did. I've never crossed St George's Channel since for her sake — never even landed at Queenstown and come back to London through Ireland.

BROADBENT: But did you ever say anything that would justify her in waiting for you?

DOYLE: No, never. But she is waiting for me.

BROADBENT: How do you know?

DOYLE: She writes to me — on her birthday. She used to write on mine, and send me little things as presents; but I stopped that by pretending that it was no use when I was travelling, as they got lost in the foreign post-offices. [*He pronounces post-offices with the stress on offices, instead of on post.*]

BROADBENT: You answer the letters?

DOYLE: Not very punctually. But they get acknowledged at one time or another.

BROADBENT: How do you feel when you see her handwriting?

DOYLE: Uneasy. I'd give £50 to escape a letter.

BROADBENT [*looking grave, and throwing himself back in his chair to intimate that the cross-examination is over, and the result very damaging to the witness*]: Hm!

DOYLE: What d'ye mean by Hm!

BROADBENT: Of course I know that the moral code is different in Ireland. But in England it's not considered fair to trifle with a woman's affections.

DOYLE: You mean that an Englishman would get engaged to another woman and return Nora her letters and presents with a letter to say he was unworthy of her and wished her every happiness?

BROADBENT: Well, even that would set the poor girl's mind at rest.

DOYLE: Would it? I wonder! One thing I can tell you; and that is that Nora would wait until she died of old age sooner than ask my intentions or condescend to hint at the possibility of my having any. You don't know what Irish pride is. England may have knocked a good deal of it out of me; but she's never been in England; and if I had to choose between wounding that delicacy in her and hitting her in the face, I'd hit her in the face without a moment's hesitation.

BROADBENT [*who has been nursing his knee and reflecting, apparently rather agreeably*]: You know, all this sounds rather interesting. There's the Irish charm about it. That's the worst of you: the Irish charm doesn't exist for you.

DOYLE: Oh yes it does. But it's the charm of a dream. Live in contact with dreams and you will get something of their charm: live in contact with facts and you will get something of their brutality. I wish I could find a country to live in where the facts were not brutal and the dreams not unreal.

BROADBENT [*changing his attitude and responding to* DOYLE's *earnestness with deep conviction: his elbows on the table and his hands clenched*]: Don't despair, Larry, old boy: things may look black; but there will be a great change after the next election.

DOYLE [*jumping up*]: Oh, get out, you idiot!

BROADBENT [*rising also, not a bit snubbed*]: Ha! ha! you may laugh; but we shall see. However, don't let us argue about that. Come now! you ask my advice about Miss Reilly?

DOYLE [*reddening*]: No I don't. Damn your advice! [*Softening*] Let's have it, all the same.

BROADBENT: Well, everything you tell me about her impresses me favourably. She seems to have the feelings of a lady; and though we must face the fact that in England her income would hardly maintain her in the lower middle class —

DOYLE [*interrupting*]: Now look here, Tom. That reminds me. When you go to Ireland, just drop talking about the middle class and bragging of belonging to it. In Ireland you're either a gentleman or you're not. If you want to be particularly offensive to Nora, you can call her a Papist; but if you call her a middle-class woman, Heaven help you!

BROADBENT [*irrepressible*]: Never fear. You're all descended from the ancient kings: I know that. [*Complacently*] I'm not so tactless as you think, my boy. [*Earnest again*] I expect to find Miss Reilly a perfect lady; and I strongly advise you to come and have another look at her before you make up your mind about her. By the way, have you a photograph of her?

DOYLE: Her photographs stopped at twenty-five.

BROADBENT [*saddened*]: Ah yes, I suppose so. [*With feeling, severely*] Larry: you've treated that poor girl disgracefully.

DOYLE: By George, if she only knew that two men were talking about her like this —!

BROADBENT: She wouldn't like it, would she? Of course not. We ought to be ashamed of ourselves,

LARRY. [*More and more carried away by his new fancy*] You know, I have a sort of presentiment that Miss Reilly is a very superior woman.

DOYLE [*staring hard at him*]: Oh! you have, have you?

BROADBENT: Yes I have. There is something very touching about the history of this beautiful girl.

DOYLE: Beau —! Oho! Here's a chance for Nora! and for me! [*Calling*] Hodson.

HODSON [*appearing at the bedroom door*]: Did you call, sir?

DOYLE: Pack for me too. I'm going to Ireland with Mr Broadbent.

HODSON: Right, sir. [*He retires into the bedroom.*]

BROADBENT [*clapping* DOYLE *on the shoulder*]: Thank you, old chap. Thank you.

ACT II

Rosscullen. Westward a hillside of granite rock and heather slopes upward across the prospect from south to north. A huge stone stands on it in a naturally impossible place, as if it had been tossed up there by a giant. Over the brow, in the desolate valley beyond, is a round tower. A lonely white high road trending away westward past the tower loses itself at the foot of the far mountains. It is evening; and there are great breadths of silken green in the Irish sky. The sun is setting.

A man with the face of a young saint, yet with white hair and perhaps 50 years on his back, is standing near the stone in a trance of intense melancholy, looking over the hills as if by mere intensity of gaze he could pierce the glories of the sunset and see into the streets of heaven. He is dressed in black, and is rather more clerical in appearance than most English curates are nowadays; but he does not wear the collar and waistcoat of a parish priest. He is roused from his trance by the chirp of an insect from a tuft of grass in a crevice of the stone. His face relaxes: he turns quietly, and gravely takes off his hat to the tuft, addressing the insect in a brogue which is the jocular assumption of a gentleman and not the natural speech of a peasant.

THE MAN: An' is that yourself, Misther Grasshopper? I hope I see you well this fine evenin'.

THE GRASSHOPPER [*prompt and shrill in answer*]: X.X.

THE MAN [*encouragingly*]: That's right. I suppose now you've come out to make yourself miserable be admyerin the sunset?

THE GRASSHOPPER [*sadly*]: X.X.

THE MAN: Aye, you're a thrue Irish grasshopper.

THE GRASSHOPPER [*loudly*]: X.X.X.

THE MAN: Three cheers for ould Ireland, is it? That helps you to face out the misery and the poverty and the torment, doesn't it?

THE GRASSHOPPER [*plaintively*]: X.X.

THE MAN: Ah, it's no use, me poor little friend. If you could jump as far as a kangaroo you couldn't jump away from your own heart an' its punishment. You can only look at Heaven from here: you can't reach it. There! [*pointing with his stick to the sunset*] that's the gate o' glory, isn't it?

THE GRASSHOPPER [*assenting*]: X.X.

THE MAN: Sure it's the wise grasshopper yar to know that. But tell me this, Misther Unworldly Wiseman: why does the sight of Heaven wring your heart an' mine as the sight of holy wather wrings the heart o' the divil? What wickedness have you done to bring that curse on you? Here! where are you jumpin' to? Where's your manners to go skyrocketin' like that out o' the box in the middle o' your confession [*he threatens it with his stick*]?

THE GRASSHOPPER [*penitently*]: X.

THE MAN [*lowering the stick*]: I accept your apology; but don't do it again. And now tell me one thing before I let you go home to bed. Which would you say this counthry was: hell or purgatory?

THE GRASSHOPPER: X.

THE MAN: Hell! Faith I'm afraid you're right. I wondher what you and me did when we were alive to get sent here.

THE GRASSHOPPER [*shrilly*]: X.X.

THE MAN [*nodding*]: Well, as you say, it's a delicate subject; and I won't press it on you. Now off widja.

THE GRASSHOPPER: X.X. [*It springs away.*]

THE MAN [*waving his stick*]: God speed you! [*He walks away past the stone towards the brow of the hill. Immediately a young* LABORER, *his face distorted with terror, slips round from behind the stone.*]

THE LABORER [*crossing himself repeatedly*]: Oh glory be to God! Glory be to God! Oh Holy Mother an' all the saints! Oh murdher! murdher! [*Beside himself, calling*] Fadher Keegan! Fadher Keegan!

THE MAN [*turning*]: Who's there? What's that? [*He comes back and finds the* LABORER, *who clasps his knees.*] Patsy Farrell! What are you doing here?

PATSY: Oh for the love o' God don't lave me here wi dhe grasshopper. I hard it spakin' to you. Don't let it do me any harm, Father darlint.

KEEGAN: Get up, you foolish man, get up. Are you afraid of a poor insect because I pretended it was talking to me?

PATSY: Oh, it was no pretendin', Fadher dear. Didn't it give three cheers n say it was a divil out o' hell? Oh say you'll see me safe home, Fadher; n put a blessin' on me or somethin' [*he moans with terror*].

KEEGAN: What were you doing there, Patsy, listnin? Were you spyin' on me?

PATSY: No, Fadher: on me oath an' soul I wasn't: I was waitn to meet Masther Larry n carry his luggage from the car; n I fell asleep on the grass; n you woke me talking to the grasshopper; n I hard its wicked little voice. Oh, d'ye think I'll die before the year's out, Fadher?

KEEGAN: For shame, Patsy! Is that your religion, to be afraid of a little deeshy grasshopper? Suppose it was a divil, what call have you to fear it? If I could ketch it, I'd make you take it home widja in your hat for a penance.

PATSY: Sure, if you won't let it harm me, I'm not afraid, your riverence. [*He gets up, a little reassured. He is a callow, flaxen polled, smoothfaced, downy chinned lad, fully grown but not yet fully filled out, with blue eyes and an instinctively acquired air of helplessness and silliness, indicating, not his real character, but a cunning developed by his constant dread of a hostile dominance, which he habitually tries to disarm and tempt into unmasking by pretending to be a much greater fool than he really is. Englishmen think him half-witted, which is exactly what he intends them to think. He is clad in corduroy trousers, unbuttoned waistcoat, and coarse blue striped shirt.*]

KEEGAN [*admonitorily*]: Patsy: what did I tell you about callin' me Father Keegan an' your reverence? What did Father Dempsey tell you about it?

PATSY: Yis, Fadher.

KEEGAN: Father!

PATSY [*desperately*]: Arra, hwat am I to call you? Fadher Dempsey sez you're not a priest; n we all know you're not a man; n how do we know what ud happen to us if we shewed any disrespect to you? N sure they say wanse a priest always a priest.

KEEGAN [*sternly*]: It's not for the like of you, Patsy, to go behind the instruction of your parish priest and set yourself up to judge whether your Church is right or wrong.

PATSY: Sure I know that, sir.

KEEGAN: The Church let me be its priest as long as it thought me fit for its work. When it took away my papers it meant you to know that I was only a poor madman, unfit and unworthy to take charge of the souls of the people.

PATSY: But wasn't it only because you knew more Latn than Father Dempsey that he was jealous of you?

KEEGAN [*scolding him to keep himself from smiling*]: How dar you, Patsy Farrell, put your own wicked little spites and foolishnesses into the heart of your priest? For two pins I'd tell him what you just said.

PATSY [*coaxing*]: Sure you wouldn't —

KEEGAN: Wouldn't I? God forgive you! you're little better than a heathen.

PATSY: Deedn I am, Fadher: it's me bruddher the tinsmith in Dublin you're thinkin' of. Sure he had to be a free-thinker when he larnt a thrade and went to live in the town.

KEEGAN: Well, he'll get to Heaven before you if you're not careful, Patsy. And now you listen to me, once and for all. You'll talk to me and pray for me by the name of Pether Keegan, so you will. And when you're angry and tempted to lift your hand agen the donkey or stamp your foot on the little grasshopper, remember that the donkey's Pether Keegan's brother, and the grasshopper Pether Keegan's friend. And when you're tempted to throw a stone at a sinner or a curse at a beggar, remember that Pether Keegan is a worse sinner and a worse beggar, and keep the stone and the curse for him the next time you meet him. Now say God bless you, Pether, to me before I go, just to practise you a bit.

PATSY: Sure it wouldn't be right, Fadher. I can't —

KEEGAN: Yes you can. Now out with it; or I'll put this stick into your hand an' make you hit me with it.

PATSY [*throwing himself on his knees in an ecstasy of adoration*]: Sure it's your blessin' I want, Fadher Keegan. I'll have no luck widhout it.

KEEGAN [*shocked*]: Get up out o' that, man. Don't kneel to me: I'm not a saint.

PATSY [*with intense conviction*]: Oh in throth yar, sir. [*The* GRASSHOPPER *chirps.* PATSY, *terrified, clutches at* KEEGAN'S *hands.*] Don't set it on me, Fadher: I'll do anythin' you bid me.

KEEGAN [*pulling him up*]: You bosthoon, you! Don't you see that it only whistled to tell me Miss Reilly's comin'? Look at her and pull yourself together for shame. Off widja to the road: you'll be late for the car if you don't make haste [*bustling him down the hill*]. I can see the dust of it in the gap already.

PATSY: The Lord save us! [*He goes down the hill towards the road like a haunted man.*]

NORA REILLY *comes down the hill. A slight weak woman in a pretty muslin print gown (her best), she is a figure commonplace enough to Irish eyes; but on the inhabitants of fatter-fed, crowded, hustling and bustling modern countries she makes a very different impression. The absence of any symptoms of coarseness or hardness or appetite in her, her comparative delicacy of manner and sensibility of apprehension, her fine hands and frail figure, her novel accent, with the caressing plaintive Irish melody of her speech, give her a charm which is*

*all the more effective because, being untravelled, she is
unconscious of it, and never dreams of deliberately
dramatizing and exploiting it, as the Irishwomen in
England do. For* TOM BROADBENT *therefore, an
attractive woman, whom he would even call ethereal.
To* LARRY DOYLE, *an everyday woman fit only for the
eighteenth century, helpless, useless, almost sexless, an
invalid without the excuse of disease, an incarnation of
everything in Ireland that drove him out of it. These
judgments have little value and no finality; but they are
the judgments on which her fate hangs just at present.*
KEEGAN *touches his hat to her: he does not take it off.*

NORA: Mr Keegan: I want to speak to you a minute if
you don't mind.

KEEGAN [*dropping the broad Irish vernacular of his speech to*
PATSY]: An hour if you like, Miss Reilly: you're
always welcome. Shall we sit down?

NORA: Thank you. [*They sit on the heather. She is shy
and anxious; but she comes to the point promptly
because she can think of nothing else.*] They say you
did a gradle o' travelling at one time.

KEEGAN: Well, you see I'm not a Mnooth man [*he
means that he was not a student at Maynooth
College*].[14] When I was young I admired the older
generation of priests that had been educated in
Salamanca. So when I felt sure of my vocation I
went to Salamanca. Then I walked from
Salamanca to Rome, an' sted in a monastery
there for a year. My pilgrimage to Rome taught
me that walking is a better way of travelling than
the train; so I walked from Rome to the
Sorbonne in Paris; and I wish I could have
walked from Paris to Oxford; for I was very sick
on the sea. After a year of Oxford I had to walk
to Jerusalem to walk the Oxford feeling off me.
From Jerusalem I came back to Patmos, and
spent six months at the monastery of Mount
Athos. From that I came to Ireland and settled
down as a parish priest until I went mad.

NORA [*startled*]: Oh don't say that.

KEEGAN: Why not? Don't you know the story? how I
confessed a black man and gave him absolution?
and how he put a spell on me and drove me
mad?

NORA: How can you talk such nonsense about
yourself? For shame!

KEEGAN: It's not nonsense at all: it's true — in a way.
But never mind the black man. Now that you
know what a travelled man I am, what can I do
for you? [*She hesitates and plucks nervously at the
heather. He stays her hand gently.*] Dear Miss Nora:
don't pluck the little flower. If it was a pretty
baby you wouldn't want to pull its head off and

stick it in a vawse o' water to look at. [*The*
GRASSHOPPER *chirps:* KEEGAN *turns his head and
addresses it in the vernacular.*] Be aisy, me son: she
won't spoil the swing-swong in your little three.
[*To* NORA, *resuming his urbane style*] You see I'm
quite cracked; but never mind: I'm harmless.
Now what is it?

NORA [*embarrassed*]: Oh, only idle curiosity. I wanted
to know whether you found Ireland — I mean
the country part of Ireland, of course — very
small and backwardlike when you came back to
it from Rome and Oxford and all the great cities.

KEEGAN: When I went to those great cities I saw
wonders I had never seen in Ireland. But when I
came back to Ireland I found all the wonders
there waiting for me. You see they had been there
all the time; but my eyes had never been opened
to them. I did not know what my own house was
like, because I had never been outside it.

NORA: D'ye think that's the same with everybody?

KEEGAN: With everybody who has eyes in his soul as
well as in his head.

NORA: But really and truly now, weren't the people
rather disappointing? I should think the girls
must have seemed rather coarse and dowdy after
the foreign princesses and people? But I suppose
a priest wouldn't notice that.

KEEGAN: It's a priest's business to notice everything. I
won't tell you all I noticed about women; but I'll
tell you this. The more a man knows, and the
farther he travels, the more likely he is to marry a
country girl afterwards.

NORA [*blushing with delight*]: You're joking, Mr Keegan:
I'm sure yar.

KEEGAN: My way of joking is to tell the truth. It's the
funniest joke in the world.

NORA [*incredulous*]: Galong with you!

KEEGAN [*springing up actively*]: Shall we go down to the
road and meet the car? [*She gives him her hand and
he helps her up.*] Patsy Farrell told me you were
expecting young Doyle.

NORA [*tossing her chin up at once*]: Oh, I'm not
expecting him particularly. It's a wonder he's
come back at all. After staying away eighteen
years he can harly expect us to be very anxious to
see him: can he now?

KEEGAN: Well, not anxious perhaps, but you will be
curious to see how much he's changed in all
these years.

NORA [*with a sudden bitter flush*]: I suppose that's all that
brings him back to look at us, just to see how
much we've changed. Well, he can wait and see
me be candlelight: I didn't come out to meet

him: I'm going to walk to the Round Tower [*going west across the hill*].

KEEGAN: You couldn't do better this fine evening. [*Gravely*] I'll tell him where you've gone. [*She turns as if to forbid him; but the deep understanding in his eyes makes that impossible; and she only looks at him earnestly and goes. He watches her disappear on the other side of the hill; then says*] Aye, he's come to torment you; and you're driven already to torment him. [*He shakes his head, and goes slowly away across the hill in the opposite direction, lost in thought.*]

By this time the car has arrived, and dropped three of its passengers on the high road at the foot of the hill. It is a monster jaunting car, black and dilapidated, one of the last survivors of the public vehicles known to earlier generations as Beeyankiny cars, the Irish having laid violent tongues on the name of their projector, one Bianconi, an enterprising Italian. The three passengers are the parish priest, FATHER DEMPSEY; CORNELIUS DOYLE, LARRY'S *father; and* BROADBENT, *all in overcoats and as stiff as only an Irish car could make them.*

The priest, stout and fatherly, falls far short of that finest type of countryside pastor which represents the genius of priesthood; but he is equally far above the base type in which a strongminded unscrupulous peasant uses the Church to extort money, power and privilege. He is a priest neither by vocation nor ambition, but because the life suits him. He has boundless authority over his flock, and taxes them stiffly enough to be a rich man. The old Protestant ascendency[15] *is now too broken to gall him. On the whole, an easygoing, amiable, even modest man as long as his dues are paid and his authority and dignity fully admitted.*

CORNELIUS DOYLE *is an elder of the small wiry type, with a hard-skinned, rather worried face, clean shaven except for sandy whiskers blanching into a lustreless pale yellow and quite white at the roots. His dress is that of a country-town man of business: that is, an oldish shooting suit, with elastic sided boots quite unconnected with shooting. Feeling shy with* BROADBENT, *he is hasty, which is his way of trying to appear genial.*

BROADBENT, *for reasons which will appear later, has no luggage except a field glass and a guide book. The other two have left theirs to the unfortunate* PATSY FARRELL, *who struggles up the hill after them, loaded with a sack of potatoes, a hamper, a fat goose, a colossal salmon, and several paper parcels.*

CORNELIUS *leads the way up the hill, with* BROADBENT *at his heels. The priest follows.* PATSY *lags laboriously behind.*

CORNELIUS: This is a bit of a climb, Mr Broadbent; but it's shorter than goin' round be the road.

BROADBENT [*stopping to examine the great stone*]: Just a moment, Mr Doyle: I want to look at this stone. It must be Finian's die-cast.

CORNELIUS [*in blank bewilderment*]: Hwat?

BROADBENT: Murray describes it. One of your great national heroes — I can't pronounce the name — Finian Somebody, I think.

FATHER DEMPSEY [*also perplexed, and rather scandalized*]: Is it Fin McCool you mean?

BROADBENT: I daresay it is. [*Referring to the guide book*] Murray says that a huge stone, probably of Druidic origin, is still pointed out as the die cast by Fin in his celebrated match with the devil.

CORNELIUS [*dubiously*]: Jeuce a word I ever heard of it!

FATHER DEMPSEY [*very seriously indeed, and even a little severely*]: Don't believe any such nonsense, sir. There never was any such thing. When people talk to you about Fin McCool and the like, take no notice of them. It's all idle stories and superstition.

BROADBENT [*somewhat indignantly; for to be rebuked by an Irish priest for superstition is more that he can stand*]: You don't suppose I believe it, do you?

FATHER DEMPSEY: Oh, I thought you did. D'ye see the top o' the Roun' Tower there? That's an antiquity worth lookin' at.

BROADBENT [*deeply interested*]: Have you any theory as to what the Round Towers were for?

FATHER DEMPSEY [*a little offended*]: A theory? Me! [*Theories are connected in his mind with the late Professor Tyndall,*[16] *and with scientific scepticism generally: also perhaps with the view that the Round Towers are phallic symbols.*]

CORNELIUS [*remonstrating*]: Father Dempsey is the priest of the parish, Mr Broadbent. What would he be doing with a theory?

FATHER DEMPSEY [*with gentle emphasis*]: I have a knowledge of what the Roun' Towers were, if that's what you mean. They are the forefingers of the early Church, pointing us all to God.

PATSY, *intolerably overburdened, loses his balance, and sits down involuntarily. His burdens are scattered over the hillside.* CORNELIUS *and* FATHER DEMPSEY *turn furiously on him, leaving* BROADBENT *beaming at the stone and the tower with fatuous interest.*

CORNELIUS: Oh, be the hokey, the sammin's broke in two! You schoopid ass, what d'ye mean?

FATHER DEMPSEY: Are you drunk, Patsy Farrell? Did I tell you to carry that hamper carefully or did I not?

PATSY [*rubbing the back of his head, which has almost*

dinted a slab of granite]: Sure me fut slipt. Howkn I carry three men's luggage at wanst?

FATHER DEMPSEY: You were told to leave behind what you couldn't carry, an' go back for it.

PATSY: An' whose things was I to lave behind? Hwat would your reverence think if I left your hamper behind in the wet grass; n hwat would the masther say if I left the sammin and the goose be the side o' the road for annywan to pick up?

CORNELIUS: Oh, you've a dale to say for yourself, you butther-fingered omadhaun.[17] Waitll Ant Judy sees the state o' that sammin: she'll talk to you. Here! gimmy that birdn that fish there; an' take Father Dempsey's hamper to his house for him; n then come back for the rest.

FATHER DEMPSEY: Do, Patsy. And mind you don't fall down again.

PATSY: Sure I —

CORNELIUS [*bustling him up the hill*]: Whisht! here's Ant Judy. [PATSY *goes grumbling in disgrace, with* FATHER DEMPSEY's *hamper.*]

AUNT JUDY *comes down the hill, a woman of 50, in no way remarkable, lively and busy without energy or grip, placid without tranquillity, kindly without concern for others: indeed without much concern for herself: a contented product of a narrow, strainless life. She wears her hair parted in the middle and quite smooth, with a flattened bun at the back. Her dress is a plain brown frock, with a woollen pelerine of black and aniline mauve over her shoulders, all very trim in honour of the occasion. She looks round for* LARRY; *is puzzled; then stares incredulously at* BROADBENT.

AUNT JUDY: Surely to goodness that's not you, Larry!

CORNELIUS: Arra how could he be Larry, woman alive? Larry's in no hurry home, it seems. I haven't set eyes on him. This is his friend, Mr Broadbent. Mr Broadbent: me sister Judy.

AUNT JUDY [*hospitably: going to* BROADBENT *and shaking hands heartily*]: Mr Broadbent! Fancy me taking you for Larry! Sure we haven't seen a sight of him for eighteen years, n he ony a lad when he left us.

BROADBENT: It's not Larry's fault: he was to have been here before me. He started in our motor an hour before Mr Doyle arrived, to meet us at Athenmullet, intending to get here long before me.

AUNT JUDY: Lord save us! do you think he's had n axidnt?

BROADBENT: No: he's wired to say he's had a breakdown and will come on as soon as he can. He expects to be here at about ten.

AUNT JUDY: There now! Fancy him trustn himself in a motor and we all expectn him! Just like him! he'd

never do anything like anybody else. Well, what can't be cured must be injoored. Come on in, all of you. You must be dyin' for your tea, Mr Broadbent.

BROADBENT [*with a slight start*]: Oh, I'm afraid it's too late for tea [*he looks at his watch*].

AUNT JUDY: Not a bit: we never have it airlier than this. I hope they gave you a good dinner at Athenmullet.

BROADBENT [*trying to conceal his consternation as he realizes that he is not going to get any dinner after his drive*]: Oh — er — excellent, excellent. By the way, hadn't I better see about a room at the hotel? [*They stare at him.*]

CORNELIUS: The hotel!

FATHER DEMPSEY: Hwat hotel?

AUNT JUDY: Indeedn you're not goin' to a hotel. You'll stay with us. I'd have put you into Larry's room, ony the boy's pallyass is too short for you; but we'll make a comfortable bed for you on the sofa in the parlour.

BROADBENT: You're very kind, Miss Doyle; but really I'm ashamed to give you so much trouble unnecessarily. I shan't mind the hotel in the least.

FATHER DEMPSEY: Man alive! there's no hotel in Rosscullen.

BROADBENT: No hotel! Why, the driver told me there was the finest hotel in Ireland here. [*They regard him joylessly.*]

AUNT JUDY: Arra would you mind what the like of him would tell you? Sure he'd say hwatever was the least trouble to himself and the pleasantest to you, thinkin' you might give him a thruppeny bit for himself or the like.

BROADBENT: Perhaps there's a public house.

FATHER DEMPSEY [*grimly*]: There's seventeen.

AUNT JUDY: Ah then, how could you stay at a public house? They'd have no place to put you even if it was a right place for you to go. Come! is it the sofa you're afraid of? If it is, you can have me own bed. I can sleep with Nora.

BROADBENT: Not at all, not at all: I should be only too delighted. But to upset your arrangements in this way —

CORNELIUS [*anxious to cut short the discussion, which makes him ashamed of his house; for he guesses* BROADBENT's *standard of comfort a little more accurately than his sister does*]: That's all right: it'll be no trouble at all. Hweres Nora?

AUNT JUDY: Oh, how do I know? She slipped out a little while ago: I thought she was going to meet the car.

CORNELIUS [*dissatisfied*]: It's a queer thing of her to run out o' the way at such a time.

AUNT JUDY: Sure she's a queer girl altogether. Come. Come in: come in.

FATHER DEMPSEY: I'll say good-night, Mr Broadbent. If there's anything I can do for you in this parish, let me know. [*He shakes hands with* BROADBENT.]

BROADBENT [*effusively cordial*]: Thank you, Father Dempsey. Delighted to have met you, sir.

FATHER DEMPSEY [*passing on to* AUNT JUDY]: Goodnight, Miss Doyle.

AUNT JUDY: Won't you stay to tea?

FATHER DEMPSEY: Not to-night, thank you kindly: I have business to do at home. [*He turns to go, and meets* PATSY FARRELL *returning unloaded.*] Have you left that hamper for me?

PATSY: Yis, your reverence.

FATHER DEMPSEY: That's a good lad [*going*].

PATSY [*to* AUNT JUDY]: Fadher Keegan sez —

FATHER DEMPSEY [*turning sharply on him*]: What's that you say?

PATSY [*frightened*]: Fadher Keegan —

FATHER DEMPSEY: How often have you heard me bid you call Mister Keegan in his proper name, the same as I do? Father Keegan indeed! Can't you tell the difference between your priest and any ole madman in a black coat?

PATSY: Sure I'm afraid he might put a spell on me.

FATHER DEMPSEY [*wrathfully*]: You mind what I tell you or I'll put a spell on you that'll make you lep. D'ye mind that now? [*He goes home.*]
PATSY *goes down the hill to retrieve the fish, the bird, and the sack.*

AUNT JUDY: Ah, hwy can't you hold your tongue, Patsy, before Father Dempsey?

PATSY: Well, hwat was I to do? Father Keegan bid me tell you Miss Nora was gone to the Roun' Tower.

AUNT JUDY: An' hwy couldn't you wait to tell us until Father Dempsey was gone?

PATSY: I was afeerd o' forgetn it; and then may be he'd a sent the grasshopper or the little dark looker into me at night to remind me of it. [*The dark looker is the common grey lizard, which is supposed to walk down the throats of incautious sleepers and cause them to perish in a slow decline.*]

CORNELIUS: Yah, you great gaum, you! Widjer grasshoppers and dark lookers! Here: take up them things and let me hear no more o' your foolish lip. [PATSY *obeys.*] You can take the sammin under your oxther. [*He wedges the salmon into* PATSY's *axilla.*]

PATSY: I can take the goose too, sir. Put it on me back n gimmy the neck of it in me mouth. [CORNELIUS *is about to comply thoughtlessly.*]

AUNT JUDY [*feeling that* BROADBENT's *presence demands special punctiliousness*]: For shame, Patsy! to offer to take the goose in your mouth that we have to eat after you! The master'll bring it in for you.

PATSY: Arra what would a dead goose care for me mouth? [*He takes his load up the hill.*]

CORNELIUS: Hwat's Nora doin' at the Roun' Tower?

AUNT JUDY: Oh, the Lord knows! Romancin', I suppose. Praps she thinks Larry would go there to look for her and see her safe home.

BROADBENT: Miss Reilly must not be left to wait and walk home alone at night. Shall I go for her?

AUNT JUDY [*contemptuously*]: Arra hwad ud happen to her? Hurry in now, Corny. Come, Mr Broadbent: I left the tea on the hob to draw; and it'll be black if we don't go in an' drink it.
They go up the hill. It is dusk by this time.

BROADBENT *does not fare so badly after all at* AUNT JUDY's *board. He gets not only tea and breadand-butter, but more mutton chops than he has ever conceived it possible to eat at one sitting. There is also a most filling substance called potato cake. Hardly have his fears of being starved been replaced by his first misgiving that he is eating too much and will be sorry for it tomorrow, when his appetite is revived by the production of a bottle of illicitly distilled whisky, called potcheen, which he has read and dreamed of [he calls it pottine] and is now at last to taste. His goodhumour rises almost to excitement before* CORNELIUS *shews signs of sleepiness. The contrast between* AUNT JUDY's *table service and that of the south and east coast hotels at which he spends his Fridays-to-Tuesdays when he is in London, seems to him delightfully Irish. The almost total atrophy of any sense of enjoyment in* CORNELIUS, *or even any desire for it or toleration of the possibility of life being something better than a round of sordid worries, relieved by tobacco, punch, fine mornings, and petty successes in buying and selling, passes with his guest as the whimsical affectation of a shrewd Irish humorist and incorrigible spendthrift.* AUNT JUDY *seems to him an incarnate joke. The likelihood that the joke will pall after a month or so, and is probably not apparent at any time to born Rossculleners, or that he himself unconsciously entertains* AUNT JUDY *by his fantastic English personality and English mispronunciation, does not occur to him for a moment. In the end he is so charmed, and so loth to go to bed and perhaps dream of prosaic England, that he insists on going out to smoke a cigar and look for* NORA REILLY *at the Round Tower. Not that any special insistence is needed; for the English inhibitive instinct does not seem to exist in Rosscullen. Just as* NORA's *liking to miss a meal and stay out at the Round Tower is accepted as a sufficient reason for her doing it, and for the family going to bed and leaving the door open for her, so* BROADBENT's *whim to go out for a late stroll provokes neither hospitable remonstrance nor surprise. Indeed* AUNT JUDY *wants to get rid of him whilst she makes a bed for him on the sofa. So off he goes, full fed, happy and enthusiastic, to explore the valley by moonlight.*

The Round Tower stands about half an Irish mile from Rosscullen, some fifty yards south of the road on a knoll with a circle of wild greensward on it. The road once ran over this knoll; but modern engineering has tempered the level to the Beeyankiny car by carrying the road partly round the knoll and partly through a cutting; so that the way from the road to the tower is a footpath up the embankment through furze and brambles.

On the edge of this slope, at the top of the path, NORA *is straining her eyes in the moonlight, watching for* LARRY. *At last she gives it up with a sob of impatience, and retreats to the hoary foot of the tower, where she sits down discouraged and cries a little. Then she settles herself resignedly to wait, and hums a song — not an Irish melody, but a hackneyed English drawing room ballad of the season before last — until some slight noise suggests a footstep, when she springs up eagerly and runs to the edge of the slope again. Some moments of silence and suspense follow, broken by unmistakable footsteps. She gives a little gasp as she sees a man approaching.*

NORA: Is that you, Larry? [*Frightened a little*] Who's that?

BROADBENT's *voice from below on the path*: Don't be alarmed.

NORA: Oh, what an English accent you've got!

BROADBENT [*rising into view*]: I must introduce myself —

NORA [*violently startled, retreating*]: It's not you! Who are you? What do you want?

BROADBENT [*advancing*]: I'm really so sorry to have alarmed you, Miss Reilly. My name is Broadbent. Larry's friend, you know.

NORA [*chilled*]: And has Mr Doyle not come with you?

BROADBENT: No. I've come instead. I hope I am not unwelcome.

NORA [*deeply mortified*]: I'm sorry Mr Doyle should have given you the trouble, I'm sure.

BROADBENT: You see, as a stranger and an Englishman, I thought it would be interesting to see the Round Tower by moonlight.

NORA: Oh, you came to see the tower. I thought — [*confused, trying to recover her manners*] Oh, of course. I was so startled. It's a beautiful night, isn't it?

BROADBENT: Lovely. I must explain why Larry has not come himself.

NORA: Why should he come? He's seen the tower often enough: it's no attraction to him. [*Genteelly*] An' what do you think of Ireland, Mr Broadbent? Have you ever been here before?

BROADBENT: Never.

NORA: An' how do you like it?

BROADBENT [*suddenly betraying a condition of extreme sentimentality*]: I can hardly trust myself to say how much I like it. The magic of this Irish scene, and — I really don't want to be personal, Miss Reilly; but the charm of your Irish voice —

NORA [*quite accustomed to gallantry; and attaching no seriousness whatever to it*]: Oh, get along with you, Mr Broadbent! You're breaking your heart about me already, I daresay, after seeing me for two minutes in the dark.

BROADBENT: The voice is just as beautiful in the dark you know. Besides, I've heard a great deal about you from Larry.

NORA [*with bitter indifference*]: Have you now? Well, that's a great honour, I'm sure.

BROADBENT: I have looked forward to meeting you more than to anything else in Ireland.

NORA [*ironically*]: Dear me! did you now?

BROADBENT: I did really. I wish you had taken half as much interest in me.

NORA: Oh, I was dying to see you, of course. I daresay you can imagine the sensation an Englishman like you would make among us poor Irish people.

BROADBENT: Ah, now you're chaffing me, Miss Reilly: you know you are. You mustn't chaff me. I'm very much in earnest about Ireland and everything Irish. I'm very much in earnest about you and about Larry.

NORA: Larry has nothing to do with me, Mr Broadbent.

BROADBENT: If I really thought that, Miss Reilly, I should — well, I should let myself feel that charm of which I spoke just now more deeply than I — than I —

NORA: Is it making love to me you are?

BROADBENT [*scared and much upset*]: On my word I believe I am, Miss Reilly. If you say that to me again I shan't answer for myself: all the harps of Ireland are in your voice. [*She laughs at him. He suddenly loses his head and seizes her arms, to her great indignation.*] Stop laughing: do you hear? I am in earnest: in English earnest. When I say a thing like that to a woman, I mean it. [*Releasing her and trying to recover his ordinary manner in spite of his bewildering emotion*] I beg your pardon.

NORA: How dare you touch me?

BROADBENT: There are not many things I would not dare for you. That does not sound right perhaps; but I really — [*he stops and passes his hand over his forehead, rather lost*].

NORA: I think you ought to be ashamed. I think if you were a gentleman, and me alone with you in this place at night, you would die rather than do such a thing.

BROADBENT: You mean that it's an act of treachery to Larry?

NORA: Deed I don't. What has Larry to do with it? It's an act of disrespect and rudeness to me: it shews what you take me for. You can go your way now; and I'll go mine. Good-night, Mr Broadbent.

BROADBENT: No, please, Miss Reilly. One moment. Listen to me. I'm serious: I'm desperately serious. Tell me that I'm interfering with Larry: and I'll go straight from this spot back to London and never see you again. That's on my honour: I will. Am I interfering with him?

NORA [*answering in spite of herself in a sudden spring of bitterness*]: I should think you ought to know better than me whether you're interfering with him. You've seen him oftener than I have. You know him better than I do, by this time. You've come to me quicker than he has, haven't you?

BROADBENT: I'm bound to tell you, Miss Reilly, that Larry has not arrived in Rosscullen yet. He meant to get here before me; but his car broke down; and he may not arrive until to-morrow.

NORA [*her face lighting up*]: Is that the truth?

BROADBENT: Yes: that's the truth. [*She gives a sigh of relief.*] You're glad of that?

NORA [*up in arms at once*]: Glad indeed! Why should I be glad? As we've waited eighteen years for him we can afford to wait a day longer, I should think.

BROADBENT: If you really feel like that about him, there may be a chance for another man yet. Eh?

NORA [*deeply offended*]: I suppose people are different in England, Mr Broadbent; so perhaps you don't mean any harm. In Ireland nobody'd mind what a man'd say in fun, nor take advantage of what a woman might say in answer to it. If a woman couldn't talk to a man for two minutes at their first meeting without being treated the way you're treating me, no decent woman would ever talk to a man at all.

BROADBENT: I don't understand that. I don't admit that. I am sincere; and my intentions are perfectly honourable. I think you will accept the fact that I'm an Englishman as a guarantee that I am not a man to act hastily or romantically; though I confess that your voice had such an extraordinary effect on me just now when you asked me so quaintly whether I was making love to you —

NORA [*flushing*]: I never thought —

BROADBENT [*quickly*]: Of course you didn't: I'm not so stupid as that. But I couldn't bear your laughing at the feeling it gave me. You — [*again struggling with a surge of emotion*] you don't know what I — [*he chokes for a moment and then blurts out with unnatural steadiness*] Will you be my wife?

NORA [*promptly*]: Deed I won't. The idea! [*Looking at him more carefully*] Arra, come home, Mr Broadbent; and get your senses back again. I think you're not accustomed to potcheen punch in the evening after your tea.

BROADBENT [*horrified*]: Do you mean to say that I — I — I — my God! that I appear drunk to you, Miss Reilly?

NORA [*compassionately*]: How many tumblers had you?

BROADBENT [*helplessly*]: Two.

NORA: The flavour of the turf prevented you noticing the strength of it. You'd better come home to bed.

BROADBENT [*fearfully agitated*]: But this is such a horrible doubt to put into my mind — to — to — For Heaven's sake, Miss Reilly, am I really drunk?

NORA [*soothingly*]: You'll be able to judge better in the morning. Come on now back with me, an' think no more about it. [*She takes his arm with motherly solicitude and urges him gently towards the path.*]

BROADBENT [*yielding in despair*]: I must be drunk: frightfully drunk; for your voice drove me out of my senses — [*he stumbles over a stone*]. No: on my word, on my most sacred word of honour, Miss Reilly, I tripped over that stone. It was an accident: it was indeed.

NORA: Yes, of course it was. Just take my arm, Mr Broadbent, while we're goin' down the path to the road. You'll be all right then.

BROADBENT [*submissively taking it*]: I can't sufficiently apologize, Miss Reilly, or express my sense of your kindness when I am in such a disgusting state. How could I be such a bea— [*he trips again*] damn the heather! my foot caught in it.

NORA: Steady now, steady. Come along: come. [*He is led down to the road in the character of a convicted drunkard. To him there is something divine in the sympathetic indulgence she substitutes for the angry disgust with which one of his own countrywomen would resent his supposed condition. And he has no suspicion of the fact, or of her ignorance of it, that when*] *an Englishman is sentimental he behaves very much as an Irishman does when he is drunk.*]

ACT III

Next morning BROADBENT *and* LARRY *are sitting at the ends of a breakfast table in the middle of a small grass plot before* CORNELIUS DOYLE's *house. They have finished their meal, and are buried in newspapers. Most of the crockery is crowded upon a large square black tray of japanned metal. The teapot is of brown delft ware. There is no silver; and the butter, on a dinner plate, is en bloc. The background to this breakfast is the house, a small white slated building, accessible by a half-glazed door. A person coming out into the garden by this door would find the table straight in front of him, and a gate leading to the road half way down the garden on his right; or, if he turned sharp to his left, he could pass round the end of the house through an unkempt shrubbery. The mutilated remnant of a huge plaster statue, nearly dissolved by the rains of a century, and vaguely resembling a majestic female in Roman draperies, with a wreath in her hand, stands neglected amid the laurels. Such statues, though apparently works of art, grow naturally in Irish gardens. Their germination is a mystery to the oldest inhabitants, to whose means and tastes they are totally foreign.*

There is a rustic bench, much soiled by the birds, and decorticated and split by the weather, near the little gate. At the opposite side, a basket lies unmolested because it might as well be there as anywhere else. An empty chair at the table was lately occupied by CORNELIUS, *who has finished his breakfast and gone in to the room in which he receives rents and keeps his books and cash, known in the household as 'the office'. This chair, like the two occupied by* LARRY *and* BROADBENT, *has a mahogany frame and is upholstered in black horsehair.*

LARRY rises and goes off through the shrubbery with his newspaper. HODSON *comes in through the garden gate, disconsolate.* BROADBENT, *who sits facing the gate, augurs the worst from his expression.*

BROADBENT: Have you been to the village?

HODSON: No use, sir. We'll have to get everything from London by parcel post.

BROADBENT: I hope they made you comfortable last night.

HODSON: I was no worse than you were on that sofa, sir. One expects to rough it here, sir.

BROADBENT: We shall have to look out for some other arrangement. [*Cheering up irrepressibly*] Still, it's no end of a joke. How do you like the Irish, Hodson?

HODSON: Well, sir, they're all right anywhere but in their own country. I've known lots of em in England, and generally liked em. But here, sir, I seem simply to hate em. The feeling come over me the moment we landed at Cork, sir. It's no use my pretendin', sir: I can't bear em. My mind rises up agin their ways, somehow: they rub me the wrong way all over.

BROADBENT: Oh, their faults are on the surface: at heart they are one of the finest races on earth. [HODSON *turns away, without affecting to respond to his enthusiasm.*] By the way, Hodson —

HODSON [*turning*]: Yes, sir.

BROADBENT: Did you notice anything about me last night when I came in with that lady?

HODSON [*surprised*]: No, sir.

BROADBENT: Not any — er — ? You may speak frankly.

HODSON: I didn't notice nothing, sir. What sort of thing did you mean, sir?

BROADBENT: Well — er — er — well, to put it plainly, was I drunk?

HODSON [*amazed*]: No, sir.

BROADBENT: Quite sure?

HODSON: Well, I should a said rather the opposite, sir. Usually when you've been enjoying yourself, you're a bit hearty like. Last night you seemed rather low, if anything.

BROADBENT: I certainly have no headache. Did you try the pottine, Hodson?

HODSON: I just took a mouthful, sir. It tasted of peat: oh! something horrid, sir. The people here call peat turf. Potcheen and strong porter is what they like, sir. I'm sure I don't know how they can stand it. Give me beer, I say.

BROADBENT: By the way, you told me I couldn't have porridge for breakfast; but Mr Doyle had some.

HODSON: Yes, sir. Very sorry, sir. They call it stirabout, sir: that's how it was. They know no better, sir.

BROADBENT: All right: I'll have some tomorrow.

HODSON *goes to the house. When he opens the door he finds* NORA *and* AUNT JUDY *on the threshold. He stands aside to let them pass, with the air of a well trained servant oppressed by heavy trials. Then he goes in.* BROADBENT *rises.* AUNT JUDY *goes to the table and collects the plates and cups on the tray.* NORA *goes to the back of the rustic seat and looks out at the gate with the air of a woman accustomed to have nothing to do.* LARRY *returns from the shrubbery.*

BROADBENT: Good morning, Miss Doyle.

AUNT JUDY [*thinking it absurdly late in the day for such a salutation*]: Oh, good morning. [*Before moving his plate*] Have you done?

BROADBENT: Quite, thank you. You must excuse us for

not waiting for you. The country air tempted us to get up early.

AUNT JUDY: N d'ye call this airly, God help you?

LARRY: Aunt Judy probably breakfasted about half past six.

AUNT JUDY: Whisht, you! draggin' the parlour chairs out into the gardn n givin' Mr Broadbent his death over his meals out here in the cold air. [*To* BROADBENT] Why d'ye put up with his foolishness, Mr Broadbent?

BROADBENT: I assure you I like the open air.

AUNT JUDY: Ah galong! How can you like what's not natural? I hope you slept well.

NORA: Did anything wake yup with a thump at three o'clock? I thought the house was falling. But then I'm a very light sleeper.

LARRY: I seem to recollect that one of the legs of the sofa in the parlour had a way of coming out unexpectedly eighteen years ago. Was that it, Tom?

BROADBENT [*hastily*]: Oh, it doesn't matter: I was not hurt — at least — er —

AUNT JUDY: Oh now what a shame! An' I told Patsy Farrll to put a nail in it.

BROADBENT: He did, Miss Doyle. There was a nail, certainly.

AUNT JUDY: Dear oh dear!

An oldish peasant farmer, small, leathery, peat-faced, with a deep voice and a surliness that is meant to be aggressive, and is in effect pathetic — the voice of a man of hard life and many sorrows — comes in at the gate. He is old enough to have perhaps worn a long tailed frieze coat and knee breeches in his time; but now he is dressed respectably in a black frock coat, tall hat, and pollard coloured trousers; and his face is as clean as washing can make it, though that is not saying much, as the habit is recently acquired and not yet congenial.

THE NEW-COMER [*at the gate*]: God save all here! [*He comes a little way into the garden.*]

LARRY [*patronizingly, speaking across the garden to him*]: Is that yourself, Matt Haffigan? Do you remember me?

MATTHEW [*intentionally rude and blunt*]: No. Who are you?

NORA: Oh, I'm sure you remember him, Mr Haffigan.

MATTHEW [*grudgingly admitting it*]: I suppose he'll be young Larry Doyle that was.

LARRY: Yes.

MATTHEW [*to* LARRY]: I hear you done well in America.

LARRY: Fairly well.

MATTHEW: I suppose you saw me brother Andy out dhere.

LARRY: No. It's such a big place that looking for a man there is like looking for a needle in a bundle of hay. They tell me he's a great man out there.

MATTHEW: So he is, God be praised. Where's your father?

AUNT JUDY: He's inside, in the office, Mr Haffigan, with Barney Doarn n Father Dempsey.

MATTHEW, *without wasting further words on the company, goes curtly into the house.*

LARRY [*staring after him*]: Is anything wrong with old Matt?

NORA: No. He's the same as ever. Why?

LARRY: He's not the same to me. He used to be very civil to Masther Larry: a deal too civil, I used to think. Now he's as surly and stand-off as a bear.

AUNT JUDY: Oh sure he's bought his farm in the Land Purchase.[18] He's independent now.

NORA: It's made a great change, Larry. You'd harly know the old tenants now. You'd think it was a liberty to speak t'dhem — some o' dhem. [*She goes to the table, and helps to take off the cloth, which she and* AUNT JUDY *fold up between them.*]

AUNT JUDY: I wonder what he wants to see Corny for. He hasn't been here since he paid the last of his old rent; and then he as good as threw it in Corny's face, I thought.

LARRY: No wonder! Of course they all hated us like the devil. Ugh! [*Moodily*] I've seen them in that office, telling my father what a fine boy I was, and plastering him with compliments, with your honour here and your honour there, when all the time their fingers were itching to be at his throat.

AUNT JUDY: Deedn why should they want to hurt poor Corny? It was he that got Matt the lease of his farm, and stood up for him as an industrious decent man.

BROADBENT: Was he industrious? That's remarkable, you know in an Irishman.

LARRY: Industrious! That man's industry used to make me sick, even as a boy. I tell you, an Irish peasant's industry is not human: it's worse than the industry of a coral insect. An Englishman has some sense about working: he never does more than he can help — and hard enough to get him to do that without scamping it; but an Irishman will work as if he'd die the moment he stopped. That man Matthew Haffigan and his brother Andy made a farm out of a patch of stones on the hillside: cleared it and dug it with their own naked hands and bought their first spade out of their first crop of potatoes. Talk of making two blades of wheat grow where one grew before! Those two men made a whole field of wheat grow where not even a furze bush had ever got its head up between the stones.

BROADBENT: That was magnificent, you know. Only a great race is capable of producing such men.

LARRY: Such fools, you mean! What good was it to them? The moment they'd done it, the landlord put a rent of £5 a year on them, and turned them out because they couldn't pay it.

AUNT JUDY: Why couldn't they pay as well as Billy Byrne that took it after them?

LARRY [*angrily*]: You know very well that Billy Byrne never paid it. He only offered it to get possession. He never paid it.

AUNT JUDY: That was because Andy Haffigan hurt him with a brick so that he was never the same again. Andy had to run away to America for it.

BROADBENT [*glowing with indignation*]: Who can blame him, Miss Doyle? Who can blame him?

LARRY [*impatiently*]: Oh, rubbish! What's the good of the man that's starved out of a farm murdering the man that's starved into it? Would you have done such a thing?

BROADBENT: Yes. I — I — I — I — [*stammering with fury*] I should have shot the confounded landlord, and wrung the neck of the damned agent, and blown the farm up with dynamite, and Dublin Castle[19] along with it.

LARRY: Oh yes: you'd have done great things; and a fat lot of good you'd have got out of it, too! That's an Englishman all over! make bad laws and give away all the land, and then, when your economic incompetence produces its natural and inevitable results, get virtuously indignant and kill the people that carry out your laws.

AUNT JUDY: Sure never mind him, Mr Broadbent. It doesn't matter, anyhow, because there's harly any landlords left; and therll soon be none at all.

LARRY: On the contrary, therll soon be nothing else; and the Lord help Ireland then!

AUNT JUDY: Ah, you're never satisfied, Larry. [*To* NORA] Come on, alanna, an' make the paste for the pie. We can leave them to their talk. They don't want us [*she takes up the tray and goes into the house*].

BROADBENT [*rising and gallantly protesting*]: Oh, Miss Doyle! Really, really —

NORA, *following* AUNT JUDY *with the rolled-up cloth in her hands, looks at him and strikes him dumb. He watches her until she disappears; then comes to* LARRY *and addresses him with sudden intensity.*

BROADBENT: Larry.

LARRY: What is it?

BROADBENT: I got drunk last night, and proposed to Miss Reilly.

LARRY: You hwat??? [*He screams with laughter in the falsetto Irish register unused for that purpose in England.*]

BROADBENT: What are you laughing at?

LARRY [*stopping dead*]: I don't know. That's the sort of thing an Irishman laughs at. Has she accepted you?

BROADBENT: I shall never forget that with the chivalry of her nation, though I was utterly at her mercy, she refused me.

LARRY: That was extremely improvident of her. [*Beginning to reflect*] But look here: when were you drunk? You were sober enough when you came back from the Round Tower with her.

BROADBENT: No, Larry, I was drunk, I am sorry to say. I had two tumblers of punch. She had to lead me home. You must have noticed it.

LARRY: I did not.

BROADBENT: She did.

LARRY: May I ask how long it took you to come to business? You can hardly have known her for more than a couple of hours.

BROADBENT: I am afraid it was hardly a couple of minutes. She was not here when I arrived; and I saw her for the first time at the tower.

LARRY: Well, you are a nice infant to be let loose in this country! Fancy the potcheen going to your head like that!

BROADBENT: Not to my head, I think. I have no headache; and I could speak distinctly. No: potcheen goes to the heart, not to the head. What ought I to do?

LARRY: Nothing. What need you do?

BROADBENT: There is rather a delicate moral question involved. The point is, was I drunk enough not to be morally responsible for my proposal? Or was I sober enough to be bound to repeat it now that I am undoubtedly sober?

LARRY: I should see a little more of her before deciding.

BROADBENT: No, no. That would not be right. That would not be fair. I am either under a moral obligation or I am not. I wish I knew how drunk I was.

LARRY: Well, you were evidently in a state of blithering sentimentality, anyhow.

BROADBENT: That is true, Larry: I admit it. Her voice has a most extraordinary effect on me. That Irish voice!

LARRY [*sympathetically*]: Yes, I know. When I first went to London I very nearly proposed to walk out with a waitress in an Aerated Bread shop because her Whitechapel[20] accent was so distinguished, so quaintly touching, so pretty —

BROADBENT [*angrily*]: Miss Reilly is not a waitress, is she?

LARRY: Oh, come. The waitress was a very nice girl.

BROADBENT: You think every Englishwoman an angel. You really have coarse tastes in that way, Larry. Miss Reilly is one of the finer types: a type rare in England, except perhaps in the best of the aristocracy.

LARRY: Aristocracy be blowed! Do you know what Nora eats?

BROADBENT: Eats! What do you mean?

LARRY: Breakfast: tea and bread-and-butter, with an occasional rasher, and an egg on special occasions: say on her birthday. Dinner in the middle of the day, one course and nothing else. In the evening, tea and bread-and-butter again. You compare her with your Englishwomen who wolf down from three to five meat meals a day; and naturally you find her a sylph. The difference is not a difference of type: it's the difference between the woman who eats not wisely but too well, and the woman who eats not wisely but too little.

BROADBENT [*furious*]: Larry: you — you — you disgust me. You are a damned fool. [*He sits down angrily on the rustic seat, which sustains the shock with difficulty.*]

LARRY: Steady! stead-eee! [*He laughs and seats himself on the table.*]

CORNELIUS DOYLE, FATHER DEMPSEY, BARNEY DORAN, *and* MATTHEW HAFFIGAN *come from the house.* DORAN *is a stout bodied, short armed, round-headed, red haired man on the verge of middle age, of sanguine temperament, with an enormous capacity for derisive, obscene, blasphemous, or merely cruel and senseless fun, and a violent and impetuous intolerance of other temperaments and other opinions, all this representing energy and capacity wasted and demoralized by want of sufficient training and social pressure to force it into beneficent activity and build a character with it; for* BARNEY *is by no means either stupid or weak. He is recklessly untidy as to his person; but the worst effects of his neglect are mitigated by a powdering of flour and mill dust; and his unbrushed clothes, made of a fashionable tailor's sackcloth, were evidently chosen regardless of expense for the sake of their appearance.*

MATTHEW HAFFIGAN, *ill at ease, coasts the garden shyly on the shrubbery side until he anchors near the basket, where he feels least in the way. The priest comes to the table and slaps* LARRY *on the shoulder.* LARRY, *turning quickly, and recognizing* FATHER DEMPSEY, *alights from the table and shakes the priest's hand warmly.* DORAN *comes down the garden between* FATHER DEMPSEY *and* MATT; *and* CORNELIUS, *on the other side of the table, turns to* BROADBENT, *who rises genially.*

CORNELIUS: I think we all met las' night.

DORAN: I hadn't that pleasure.

CORNELIUS: To be sure, Barney: I forgot. [*To* BROADBENT, *introducing* BARNEY] Mr Doran. He owns that fine mill you noticed from the car.

BROADBENT [*delighted with them all*]: Most happy, Mr Doran. Very pleased indeed.

DORAN, *not quite sure whether he is being courted or patronized, nods independently.*

DORAN: How's yourself, Larry?

LARRY: Finely, thank you. No need to ask you. [DORAN *grins; and they shake hands.*]

CORNELIUS: Give Father Dempsey a chair, Larry.

MATTHEW HAFFIGAN *runs to the nearest end of the table and takes the chair from it, placing it near the basket; but* LARRY *has already taken the chair from the other end and placed it in front of the table.* FATHER DEMPSEY *accepts that more central position.*

CORNELIUS: Sit down, Barney, will you; and you, Matt. DORAN *takes the chair* MATT *is still offering to the priest; and poor* MATTHEW, *outfaced by the miller, humbly turns the basket upside down and sits on it.* CORNELIUS *brings his own breakfast chair from the table and sits down on* FATHER DEMPSEY's *right.* BROADBENT *resumes his seat on the rustic bench.* LARRY *crosses to the bench and is about to sit down beside him when* BROADBENT *holds him off nervously.*

BROADBENT: Do you think it will bear two, Larry?

LARRY: Perhaps not. Don't move. I'll stand. [*He posts himself behind the bench.*]

They are all now seated, except LARRY; *and the session assumes a portentous air, as if something important were coming.*

CORNELIUS: Praps you'll explain, Father Dempsey.

FATHER DEMPSEY: No, no: go on, you: the Church has no politics.

CORNELIUS: Were yever thinkin' o' goin' into parliament at all, Larry?

LARRY: Me!

FATHER DEMPSEY [*encouragingly*]: Yes, you. Hwy not?

LARRY: I'm afraid my ideas would not be popular enough.

CORNELIUS: I don't know that. Do you, Barney?

DORAN: There's too much blatherumskite in Irish politics: a dale too much.

LARRY: But what about your present member? Is he going to retire?

CORNELIUS: No: I don't know that he is.

LARRY [*interrogatively*]: Well? then?

MATTHEW [*breaking out with surly bitterness*]: We've had enough of his foolish talk agen lanlords. Hwat call has he to talk about the lan, that never was outside of a city office in his life?

CORNELIUS: We're tired of him. He doesn't know hwere to stop. Every man can't own land; and some men must own it to employ them. It was all very well when solid men like Doran an' Matt were kep from ownin' land. But hwat man in his senses ever wanted to give land to Patsy Farrll an' dhe like o' him?

BROADBENT: But surely Irish landlordism was accountable for what Mr Haffigan suffered.

MATTHEW: Never mind hwat I suffered. I know what I suffered adhout you telling me. But did I ever ask for more dhan the farm I made wid me own hans? Tell me that, Corny Doyle, and you that knows. Was I fit for the responsibility or was I not? [*Snarling angrily at* CORNELIUS] Am I to be compared to Patsy Farrll, that doesn't harly know his right hand from his left? What did he ever suffer, I'd like to know?

CORNELIUS: That's just what I say. I wasn't comparin' you to your disadvantage.

MATTHEW [*implacable*]: Then hwat did you mane be talkin' about givin' him lan?

DORAN: Aisy, Matt, aisy. You're like a bear with a sore back.

MATTHEW [*trembling with rage*]: An' who are you, to offer to taitch me manners?

FATHER DEMPSEY [*admonitorily*]: Now, now, now, Matt! none o' dhat. How often have I told you you're ready to take offence where none is meant? You don't understand: Corny Doyle is saying just what you want to have said. [*To* CORNELIUS] Go on, Mr Doyle; and never mind him.

MATTHEW [*rising*]: Well, if me lan is to be given to Patsy and his like, I'm goin' oura dhis. I —

DORAN [*with violent impatience*]: Arra who's goin' to give you lan to Patsy, yowl fool ye?

FATHER DEMPSEY: Aisy, Barney, aisy. [*Sternly, to* MATT] I told you, Matthew Haffigan, that Corny Doyle was sayin' nothin' against you. I'm sorry your priest's word is not good enough for you. I'll go, sooner than stay to make you commit a sin against the Church. Good morning, gentlemen. [*He rises. They all rise, except* BROADBENT.]

DORAN [*to* MATT]: There! Sarve you dam well right, you cantankerous oul noodle.

MATTHEW [*appalled*]: Don't say dhat, Fadher Dempsey. I never had a thought agen you or the Holy Church. I know I'm a bit hasty when I think about the lan. I ax your pardon for it.

FATHER DEMPSEY [*resuming his seat with dignified reserve*]: Very well: I'll overlook it this time. [*He sits down. The others sit down, except* MATTHEW. FATHER DEMPSEY, *about to ask* CORNY *to proceed, remembers* MATTHEW *and turns to him, giving him just a crumb of graciousness.*] Sit down, Matt. [MATTHEW, *crushed, sits down in disgrace, and is silent, his eyes shifting piteously from one speaker to another in an intensely mistrustful effort to understand them.*] Go on, Mr Doyle. We can make allowances. Go on.

CORNELIUS: Well, you see how it is, Larry. Round about here, we've got the land at last; and we want no more Government meddlin'. We want a new class o' man in parliament: one dhat knows dhat the farmer's the real backbone o' the country, n doesn't care a snap of his fingers for the shoutn o' the riff-raff in the towns, or for the foolishness of the laborers.

DORAN: Aye; an' dhat can afford to live in London and pay his own way until Home Rule comes, instead o' wantin' subscriptions and the like.

FATHER DEMPSEY: Yes: that's a good point, Barney. When too much money goes to politics, it's the Church that has to starve for it. A member of parliament ought to be a help to the Church instead of a burden on it.

LARRY: Here's a chance for you, Tom. What do you say?

BROADBENT [*deprecatory, but important and smiling*]: Oh, I have no claim whatever to the seat. Besides, I'm a Saxon.

DORAN: A hwat?

BROADBENT: A Saxon. An Englishman.

DORAN: An Englishman. Bedad I never heard it called dhat before.

MATTHEW [*cunningly*]: If I might make so bould, Fadher, I wouldn't say but an English Prodestn mightn't have a more indepindent mind about the lan, an' be less afeerd to spake out about it dhan an Irish Catholic.

CORNELIUS: But sure Larry's as good as English: arnt you, Larry?

LARRY: You may put me out of your head, father, once for all.

CORNELIUS: Arra why?

LARRY: I have strong opinions which wouldn't suit you.

DORAN [*rallying him blatantly*]: Is it still Larry the bould Fenian?

LARRY: No: the bold Fenian is now an older and possibly foolisher man.

CORNELIUS: Hwat does it matter to us hwat your opinions are? You know that your father's bought his place here, just the same as Matt's farm n Barney's mill. All we ask now is to be let alone. You've nothin' against that, have you?

LARRY: Certainly I have. I don't believe in letting anybody or anything alone.

CORNELIUS [*losing his temper*]: Arra what d'ye mean, you young fool? Here I've got you the offer of a good seat in parliament; n you think yourself mighty smart to stand there and talk foolishness to me. Will you take it or leave it?

LARRY: Very well: I'll take it with pleasure if you'll give it to me.

CORNELIUS [*subsiding sulkily*]: Well, why couldn't you say so at once? It's a good job you've made up your mind at last.

DORAN [*suspiciously*]: Stop a bit: stop a bit.

MATTHEW [*writhing between his dissatisfaction and his fear of the priest*]: It's not because he's your son that he's to get the sate. Fadher Dempsey: wouldn't you think well to ask him what he manes about the lan?

LARRY [*coming down on MATT promptly*]: I'll tell you, Matt. I always thought it was a stupid, lazy, good-for-nothing sort of thing to leave the land in the hands of the old landlords without calling them to a strict account for the use they made of it, and the condition of the people on it. I could see for myself that they thought of nothing but what they could get out of it to spend in England; and that they mortgaged and mortgaged until hardly one of them owned his own property or could have afforded to keep it up decently if he'd wanted to. But I tell you plump and plain, Matt, that if anybody thinks things will be any better now that the land is handed over to a lot of little men like you, without calling you to account either, they're mistaken.

MATTHEW [*sullenly*]: What call have you to look down on me? I suppose you think you're everybody because your father was a land agent.

LARRY: What call have you to look down on Patsy Farrell? I suppose you think you're everybody because you own a few fields.

MATTHEW: Was Patsy Farrll ever ill used as I was ill used? Tell me dhat.

LARRY: He will be, if ever he gets into your power as you were in the power of your old landlord. Do you think, because you're poor and ignorant and half-crazy with toiling and moiling morning noon and night, that you'll be any less greedy and oppressive to them that have no land at all than old Nick Lestrange, who was an educated travelled gentleman that would not have been

tempted as hard by a hundred pounds as you'd be by five shillings? Nick was too high above Patsy Farrell to be jealous of him; but you, that are only one little step above him, would die sooner than let him come up that step; and well you know it.

MATTHEW [*black with rage, in a low growl*]: Lemmy oura dhis. [*He tries to rise; but DORAN catches his coat and drags him down again.*] I'm goin', I say. [*Raising his voice*] Leggo me coat, Barney Doran.

DORAN: Sit down, yowl omadhaun, you. [*Whispering*] Don't you want to stay an' vote agen him?

FATHER DEMPSEY [*holding up his finger*] Matt! [MATT *subsides.*] Now, now, now! come, come! Hwats all dhis about Patsy Farrll? Hwy need you fall out about him?

LARRY: Because it was by using Patsy's poverty to undersell England in the markets of the world that we drove England to ruin Ireland. And she'll ruin us again the moment we lift our heads from the dust if we trade in cheap labour; and serve us right too! If I get into parliament, I'll try to get an Act to prevent any of you from giving Patsy less than a pound a week [*they all start, hardly able to believe their ears*] or working him harder than you'd work a horse that cost you fifty guineas.

DORAN: Hwat!!!

CORNELIUS [*aghast*]: A pound a — God save us! the boy's mad.

MATTHEW, *feeling that here is something quite beyond his powers, turns openmouthed to the priest, as if looking for nothing less than the summary excommunication of LARRY.*

LARRY: How is the man to marry and live a decent life on less?

FATHER DEMPSEY: Man alive, hwere have you been living all these years? and hwat have you been dreaming of? Why, some o' dhese honest men here can't make that much out o' the land for dhemselves, much less give it to a labourer.

LARRY [*now thoroughly roused*]: Then let them make room for those who can. Is Ireland never to have a chance? First she was given to the rich; and now that they have gorged on her flesh, her bones are to be flung to the poor, that can do nothing but suck the marrow out of her. If we can't have men of honour own the land, let's have men of ability. If we can't have men with ability, let us at least have men with capital. Anybody's better than Matt, who has neither honour, nor ability, nor capital, nor anything but mere brute labour and greed in him, Heaven help him!

DORAN: Well, we're not all foostherin[21] oul doddherers

like Matt. [*Pleasantly, to the subject of this description*] Are we, Matt?

LARRY: For modern industrial purposes you might just as well be, Barney. You're all children: the big world that I belong to has gone past you and left you. Anyhow, we Irishmen were never made to be farmers; and we'll never do any good at it. We're like the Jews: the Almighty gave us brains, and bid us farm them, and leave the clay and the worms alone.

FATHER DEMPSEY [*with gentle irony*]: Oh! is it Jews you want to make of us? I must catechize you a bit meself, I think. The next thing you'll be proposing is to repeal the disestablishment of the so-called Irish Church.

LARRY: Yes, why not? [*Sensation.*]

MATTHEW [*rancorously*]: He's a turncoat.

LARRY: St Peter, the rock on which our Church was built, was crucified head downwards for being a turncoat.

FATHER DEMPSEY [*with a quiet authoritative dignity which checks* DORAN, *who is on the point of breaking out*]: That's true. You hold your tongue as befits your ignorance, Matthew Haffigan; and trust your priest to deal with this young man. Now, Larry Doyle, whatever the blessed St Peter was crucified for, it was not for being a Prodestan. Are you one?

LARRY: No. I am a Catholic intelligent enough to see that the Protestants are never more dangerous to us than when they are free from all alliances with the State. The so-called Irish Church is stronger today than ever it was.

MATTHEW: Fadher Dempsey: will you tell him dhat me mother's ant was shot and kilt dead in the sthreet o' Rosscullen be a soljer in the tithe war?[22] [*Frantically*] He wants to put the tithes on us again. He —

LARRY [*interrupting him with overbearing contempt*]: Put the tithes on you again! Did the tithes ever come off you? Was your land any dearer when you paid the tithe to the parson than it was when you paid the same money to Nick Lestrange as rent, and he handed it over to the Church Sustentation Fund? Will you always be duped by Acts of Parliament that change nothing but the necktie of the man that picks your pocket? I'll tell you what I'd do with you, Matt Haffigan: I'd make you pay tithes to your own Church. I want the Catholic Church established in Ireland: that's what I want. Do you think that I, brought up to regard myself as the son of a great and holy Church, can bear to see her begging her bread

from the ignorance and superstition of men like you? I would have her as high above worldly want as I would have her above worldly pride or ambition. Aye; and I would have Ireland compete with Rome itself for the chair of St Peter and the citadel of the Church; for Rome, in spite of all the blood of the martyrs, is pagan at heart to this day, while in Ireland the people is the Church and the Church the people.

FATHER DEMPSEY [*startled, but not at all displeased*]: Whisht, man! you're worse than mad Pether Keegan himself.

BROADBENT [*who has listened in the greatest astonishment*]: You amaze me, Larry. Who would have thought of your coming out like this! [*Solemnly*] But much as I appreciate your really brilliant eloquence, I implore you not to desert the great Liberal principle of Disestablishment.

LARRY: I am not a Liberal: Heaven forbid! A disestablished Church is the worst tyranny a nation can groan under.

BROADBENT [*making a wry face*]: Don't be paradoxical, Larry. It really gives me a pain in my stomach.

LARRY: You'll soon find out the truth of it here. Look at Father Dempsey! he is disestablished: he has nothing to hope or fear from the State; and the result is that he's the most powerful man in Rosscullen. The member for Rosscullen would shake in his shoes if Father Dempsey looked crooked at him. [FATHER DEMPSEY *smiles, by no means averse to this acknowledgment of his authority.*] Look at yourself! You would defy the established Archbishop of Canterbury ten times a day; but catch you daring to say a word that would shock a Nonconformist! not you. The Conservative party today is the only one that's not priestridden — excuse the expression, Father [FATHER DEMPSEY *nods tolerantly*] — because it's the only one that has established its Church and can prevent a clergyman becoming a bishop if he's not a Statesman as well as a Churchman.

He stops. They stare at him dumbfounded, and leave it to the priest to answer him.

FATHER DEMPSEY [*judicially*]: Young man: you'll not be the member for Rosscullen; but dheres more in your head than the comb will take out.

LARRY: I'm sorry to disappoint you, Father; but I told you it would be no use. And now I think the candidate had better retire and leave you to discuss his successor. [*He takes a newspaper from the table and goes away through the shrubbery amid dead silence, all turning to watch him until he passes out of sight round the corner of the house.*]

DORAN [*dazed*]: Hwat sort of a fella is he at all at all?

FATHER DEMPSEY: He's a clever lad: dheres the making of a man in him yet.

MATTHEW [*in consternation*]: D'ye mane to say dhat yll put him into parliament to bring back Nick Lesthrange on me, and to put tithes on me, and to rob me for the like o' Patsy Farrll, because he's Corny Doyle's son?

DORAN [*brutally*]: Arra hould your whisht: who's goin' to send him into parliament? Maybe you'd like us to send you dhere to thrate dhem to a little o' your anxiety about dhat dirty little podato patch o' yours.

MATTHEW [*plaintively*]: Am I to be towld dhis afther all me sufferins?

DORAN: Och, I'm tired o' your sufferins. We've been hearin' nothin' else ever since we was childher but sufferins. Hwen it wasn't yours it was somebody else's; and hwen it was nobody else's it was ould Irelan's. How the divil are we to live on wan anodher's sufferins?

FATHER DEMPSEY: That's a thrue word, Barney Doarn; only your tongue's a little too familiar wi dhe divil. [*To* MATT] If you'd think a little more o' the sufferins of the blessed saints, Matt, an a little less o' your own, you'd find the way shorter from your farm to heaven. [MATT *is about to reply*] Dhere now! dhats enough! we know you mean well; an' I'm not angry with you.

BROADBENT: Surely, Mr Haffigan, you can see the simple explanation of all this. My friend Larry Doyle is a most brilliant speaker; but he's a Tory: an ingrained old-fashioned Tory.

CORNELIUS: N how d'ye make dhat out, if I might ask you, Mr Broadbent?

BROADBENT [*collecting himself for a political deliverance*]: Well, you know, Mr Doyle, there's a strong dash of Toryism in the Irish character. Larry himself says that the great Duke of Wellington was the most typical Irishman that ever lived. Of course that's an absurd paradox; but still there's a great deal of truth in it. Now I am a Liberal. You know the great principles of the Liberal Party. Peace —

FATHER DEMPSEY [*piously*]: Hear! hear!

BROADBENT [*encouraged*]: Thank you. Retrenchment — [*he waits for further applause*].

MATTHEW [*timidly*]: What might rethrenchment mane now?

BROADBENT: It means an immense reduction in the burden of the rates and taxes.

MATTHEW [*respectfully approving*]: Dhats right. Dhats right, sir.

BROADBENT [*perfunctorily*]: And, of course, Reform.

CORNELIUS
FATHER DEMPSEY } [*conventionally*]: Of course.
DORAN

MATTHEW [*still suspicious*]: Hwat does Reform mane, sir? Does it mane altherin annythin dhats as it is now?

BROADBENT [*impressively*]: It means, Mr Haffigan, maintaining those reforms which have already been conferred on humanity by the Liberal Party, and trusting for future developments to the free activity of a free people on the basis of those reforms.

DORAN: Dhats right. No more meddlin'. We're all right now: all we want is to be let alone.

CORNELIUS: Hwat about Home Rule?

BROADBENT [*rising so as to address them more imposingly*]: I really cannot tell you what I feel about Home Rule without using the language of hyperbole.

DORAN: Savin' Fadher Dempsey's presence, eh?

BROADBENT [*not understanding him*]: Quite so — er — oh yes. All I can say is that as an Englishman I blush for the Union. It is the blackest stain on our national history. I look forward to the time — and it cannot be far distant, gentlemen, because Humanity is looking forward to it too, and insisting on it with no uncertain voice — I look forward to the time when an Irish legislature shall arise once more on the emerald pasture of College Green, and the Union Jack — that detestable symbol of a decadent Imperialism — be replaced by a flag as green as the island over which it waves: a flag on which we shall ask for England only a modest quartering in memory of our great party and of the immortal name of our grand old leader.

DORAN [*enthusiastically*]: Dhats the style, begob! [*He smites his knee, and winks at* MATT.]

MATTHEW: More power to you, sir!

BROADBENT: I shall leave you now, gentlemen, to your deliberations. I should like to have enlarged on the services rendered by the Liberal Party to the religious faith of the great majority of the people of Ireland; but I shall content myself with saying that in my opinion you should choose no representative who — no matter what his personal creed may be — is not an ardent supporter of freedom of conscience, and is not prepared to prove it by contributions, as lavish as his means will allow, to the great and beneficent work which you, Father Dempsey [FATHER DEMPSEY *bows*], are doing for the people of Rosscullen. Nor should the lighter, but still most important question of the sports of the people be forgotten. The local cricket club —

CORNELIUS: The hwat!

DORAN: Nobody plays bat n ball here, if dhats what you mane.

BROADBENT: Well, let us say quoits. I saw two men, I think, last night — but after all, these are questions of detail. The main thing is that your candidate, whoever he may be, shall be a man of some means, able to help the locality instead of burdening it. And if he were a countryman of my own, the moral effect on the House of Commons would be immense! tremendous! Pardon my saying these few words: nobody feels their impertinence more than I do. Good morning, gentlemen.

He turns impressively to the gate, and trots away, congratulating himself, with a little twist of his head and cock of his eye, on having done a good stroke of political business.

HAFFIGAN [*awestruck*]: Good morning, sir.

THE REST: Good morning. [*They watch him vacantly until he is out of earshot.*]

CORNELIUS: Hwat d'ye think, Father Dempsey?

FATHER DEMPSEY [*indulgently*]: Well, he hasn't much sense, God help him; but for the matter o' that, neether has our present member.

DORAN: Arra musha he's good enough for parliament: what is there to do there but gas a bit, an' chivy the Government, an' vote wi dh Irish party?

CORNELIUS [*ruminatively*]: He's the queerest Englishman I ever met. When he opened the paper dhis mornin' the first thing he saw was that an English expedition had been bet in a battle in Inja somewhere; an' he was as pleased as Punch! Larry told him that if he'd been alive when the news o' Waterloo came, he'd a died o' grief over it. Bedad I don't think he's quite right in his head.

DORAN: Divil a matther if he has plenty o' money. He'll do for us right enough.

MATTHEW [*deeply impressed by* BROADBENT, *and unable to understand their levity concerning him*]: Did you mind what he said about rethrenchment? That was very good, I thought.

FATHER DEMPSEY: You might find out from Larry, Corny, what his means are. God forgive us all! It's poor work spoiling the Egyptians, though we have good warrant for it; so I'd like to know how much spoil there is before I commit meself. [*He rises. They all rise respectfully.*]

CORNELIUS [*ruefully*]: I'd set me mind on Larry himself for the seat; but I suppose it can't be helped.

FATHER DEMPSEY [*consoling him*]: Well, the boy's young yet; an' he has a head on him. Goodbye, all. [*He goes out through the gate.*]

DORAN: I must be goin', too. [*He directs* CORNELIUS'S *attention to what is passing in the road.*] Look at me bould Englishman shakin' hans wid Fadher Dempsey for all the world like a candidate on election day. And look at Fadher Dempsey givin' him a squeeze an' a wink as much as to say It's all right, me boy. You watch him shakin' hans with me too: he's waitn for me. I'll tell him he's as good as elected. [*He goes, chuckling mischievously.*]

CORNELIUS: Come in with me, Matt. I think I'll sell you the pig after all. Come in an' wet the bargain.

MATTHEW [*instantly dropping into the old whine of the tenant*]: I'm afeerd I can't afford the price, sir. [*He follows* CORNELIUS *into the house.*]

LARRY, *newspaper still in hand, comes back through the shrubbery.* BROADBENT *returns through the gate.*

LARRY: Well? What has happened?

BROADBENT [*hugely self-satisfied*]: I think I've done the trick this time. I just gave them a bit of straight talk; and it went home. They were greatly impressed: everyone of those men believes in me and will vote for me when the question of selecting a candidate comes up. After all, whatever you say, Larry, they like an Englishman. They feel they can trust him, I suppose.

LARRY: Oh! they've transferred the honour to you, have they?

BROADBENT [*complacently*]: Well, it was a pretty obvious move, I should think. You know, these fellows have plenty of shrewdness in spite of their Irish oddity. [HODSON *comes from the house.* LARRY *sits in* DORAN'S *chair and reads.*] Oh, by the way, Hodson —

HODSON [*coming between* BROADBENT *and* LARRY]: Yes, sir?

BROADBENT: I want you to be rather particular as to how you treat the people here.

HODSON: I havnt treated any of em yet, sir. If I was to accept all the treats they offer me I shouldn't be able to stand at this present moment, sir.

BROADBENT: Oh well, don't be too stand-offish, you know, Hodson. I should like you to be popular. If it costs anything I'll make it up to you. It doesn't matter if you get a bit upset at first: they'll like you all the better for it.

HODSON: I'm sure you're very kind, sir; but it don't seem to matter to me whether they like it or not. I'm not going to stand for parliament here, sir.

BROADBENT: Well, I am. Now do you understand?

HODSON [*waking up at once*]: Oh, I beg your pardon, sir, I'm sure. I understand, sir.

CORNELIUS [*appearing at the house door with* MATT]: Patsy'll drive the pig over this evenin', Matt.

Goodbye. [*He goes back into the house.* MATT *makes for the gate.* BROADBENT *stops him.* HODSON, *pained by the derelict basket, picks it up and carries it away behind the house.*]

BROADBENT [*beaming candidatorially*]: I must thank you very particularly, Mr Haffigan, for your support this morning. I value it because I know that the real heart of a nation is the class you represent, the yeomanry.

MATTHEW [*aghast*]: The yeomanry!!!

LARRY [*looking up from his paper*]: Take care, Tom! In Rosscullen a yeoman means a sort of Orange Bashi-Bazouk.[23] In England, Matt, they call a freehold farmer a yeoman.

MATTHEW [*huffily*]: I don't need to be insthructed be you, Larry Doyle. Some people think no one knows anythin' but dhemselves. [*To* BROADBENT, *deferentially*] Of course I know a gentleman like you would not compare me to the yeomanry. Me own granfather was flogged in the sthreets of Athenmullet be them when they put a gun in the thatch of his house an' then went and found it there, bad cess to them!

BROADBENT [*with sympathetic interest*]: Then you are not the first martyr of your family, Mr Haffigan?

MATTHEW: They turned me out o' the farm I made out of the stones o' Little Rosscullen hill wid me own hands.

BROADBENT: I have heard about it; and my blood still boils at the thought. [*Calling*] Hodson —

HODSON [*behind the corner of the house*]: Yes, sir. [*He hurries forward.*]

BROADBENT: Hodson: this gentleman's sufferings should make every Englishman think. It is want of thought rather than want of heart that allows such iniquities to disgrace society.

HODSON [*prosaically*]: Yes, sir.

MATTHEW: Well, I'll be goin'. Good morning to you kindly, sir.

BROADBENT: You have some distance to go, Mr Haffigan: will you allow me to drive you home?

MATTHEW: Oh sure it'd be throublin' your honour.

BROADBENT: I insist: it will give me the greatest pleasure, I assure you. My car is in the stable: I can get it round in five minutes.

MATTHEW: Well, sir, if you wouldn't mind, we could bring the pig I've just bought from Corny —

BROADBENT [*with enthusiasm*]: Certainly, Mr Haffigan: it will be quite delightful to drive with a pig in the car: I shall feel quite like an Irishman. Hodson: stay with Mr Haffigan; and give him a hand with the pig if necessary. Come, Larry; and help me. [*He rushes away through the shrubbery.*]

LARRY [*throwing the paper ill-humouredly on the chair*]: Look here, Tom! here, I say! confound it! — [*he runs after him*].

MATTHEW [*glowering disdainfully at* HODSON, *and sitting down on* CORNELIUS's *chair as an act of social self-assertion*]: N are you the valley?

HODSON: The valley? Oh, I follow you: yes: I'm Mr Broadbent's valet.

MATTHEW: Ye have an aisy time of it: you look purty sleek. [*With suppressed ferocity*] Look at me! Do I look sleek?

HODSON [*sadly*]: I wish I 'ad your 'ealth: you look as 'ard as nails. I suffer from an excess of uric acid.

MATTHEW: Musha what sort o' disease is zhouragassid? Didjever suffer from injustice and starvation? Dhats the Irish disease. It's aisy for you to talk o' sufferin', an' you livin' on the fat o' the land wid money wrung from us.

HODSON [*suddenly dropping the well-spoken valet, and breaking out in his native cockney*]: Wots wrong with you, aold chep? Ez ennybody been doin' ennythink to you?

MATTHEW: Anythin' timmy? Didn't your English masther say that the blood biled in him to hear the way they put a rint on me for the farm I made wid me own hans, and turned me out of it to give it to Billy Byrne?

HODSON: Ow, Tom Broadbent's blad boils pretty easy over ennything that eppens aht of his aown cantry. Downt you be tiken in by my aowl men, Peddy.

MATTHEW [*indignantly*]: Paddy yourself! How dar you call me Paddy?

HODSON [*unmoved*]: You jast keep your air on and listen to me. You Awrish people are too well off: thets wots the metter with you. [*With sudden passion*] You talk of your rotten little fawm cause you mide it by chackin a few stowns dahn a ill! Well, wot prawce maw grenfawther, Oi should lawk to knaow, that fitted ap a fust clawss shop and built ap a fust clawss dripery business in Landon by sixty years work, and then was chacked aht of it on is ed at the end of is lease withaht a penny for his goodwill. You talk of evictions! you that cawnt be moved until youve ran ap ighteen months rent. Oi once ran ap four weeks in Lembeth wen Oi was aht of a job in winter. They took the door off its inges and the winder aht of its seshes on me, and gev maw wawf pnoomownia. Oi'm a widower nah. [*Between his teeth*] Gawd! when Oi think of the things we Englishmen as to pat ap with, and eah you Awrish ahlin abaht your silly little grievances, and see the wy you mike it worse for haz by the rotten wiges you'll cam over and tike and the rotten plices you'll sleep in, I jast feel that I could tike the aowl bloomin British awland and mike you a present of it, jast to let you fawnd aht wot reel awdship's lawk.

MATTHEW [*starting up, more in scandalized incredulity than in anger*]: D'ye have the face to set up England agen Ireland for injustices an' wrongs an' disthress an' sufferin'?

HODSON [*with intense disgust and contempt*]: Ow, chack it, Paddy. Cheese it. You danno wot awdship is owver eah: all you knaow is ah to ahl abaht it. You tike the biscuit at thet, you do. Oi'm a Owm Ruler, Oi em. Do you knaow woy?

MATTHEW [*equally contemptuous*]: D'ye know, yourself?

HODSON: Yus Oi do. It's because Oi wants a little attention pide to my aown cantry; and thetll never be as long as your cheps are ollerin at Westminster as if nowbody mettered but your own bloomin' selves. Send em back to ell or C'naught, as good aowld English Cramwell said.[24] I'm jast sick of Awrland. Let it gow. Cat the caible. Mike it a present to Germany to keep the aowl Kyzer busy for a wawl; and give poor aowld England a chawnce: thets wot Oi say.

MATTHEW [*full of scorn for a man so ignorant as to be unable to pronounce the word Connaught, which practically rhymes with bonnet in Ireland, though in* HODSON's *dialect it rhymes with untaught*]: Take care we don't cut the cable ourselves some day, bad scran to you![25] An' tell me dhis: have yanny Coercion Acs in England? Have yanny Removable magisthruts? Have you Dublin Castle to suppress every newspaper dhat takes the part o' your own counthry?

HODSON: We can beyive ahrselves withaht sich things.

MATTHEW: Bedad you're right. It'd ony be waste o' time to muzzle a sheep. Here! where's me pig? God forgimmy for talkin' to a poor ignorant craycher like you!

HODSON [*grinning with good-humoured malice, too convinced of his own superiority to feel his withers wrung*]: Your pig'll ev a rare doin' in that car, Peddy. Forty mawl an ahr dahn that rocky line will strawk it pretty pink, you bet.

MATTHEW [*scornfully*]: Hwy can't you tell a raisonable lie when you're about it? What horse can go forty mile an hour?

HODSON: Orse! Wy, you silly aowl rotter, it's not a orse: it's a mowtor. Do you spowse Tom Broadbent ud gow himself to fetch a orse?

MATTHEW [*in consternation*]: Holy Moses! don't tell me it's the ingine he wants to take me on.

HODSON: Wot else?

MATTHEW: Your sowl to Morris Kelly! Why didn't you tell me that before? The divil an ingine he'll get me on this day. [*His ear catches an approaching teuf-teuf.*] Oh murdher! it's comin' afther me: I hear the puff-puff of it. [*He runs away through the gate, much to* HODSON's *amusement. The noise of the motor ceases; and* HODSON, *anticipating* BROADBENT's *return, throws off the cockney and recomposes himself as a valet.* BROADBENT *and* LARRY *come through the shrubbery.* HODSON *moves aside to the gate.*]

BROADBENT: Where is Mr Haffigan? Has he gone for the pig?

HODSON: Bolted, sir. Afraid of the motor, sir.

BROADBENT [*much disappointed*]: Oh, that's very tiresome. Did he leave any message?

HODSON: He was in too great a hurry, sir. Started to run home, sir, and left his pig behind him.

BROADBENT [*eagerly*]: Left the pig! Then it's all right. The pig's the thing: the pig will win over every Irish heart to me. We'll take the pig home to Haffigan's farm in the motor: it will have a tremendous effect. Hodson!

HODSON: Yes, sir?

BROADBENT: Do you think you could collect a crowd to see the motor?

HODSON: Well, I'll try, sir.

BROADBENT: Thank you, Hodson: do.

HODSON *goes out through the gate.*

LARRY [*desperately*]: Once more, Tom, will you listen to me?

BROADBENT: Rubbish! I tell you it will be all right.

LARRY: Only this morning you confessed how surprised you were to find that the people here shewed no sense of humour.

BROADBENT [*suddenly very solemn*]: Yes: their sense of humour is in abeyance: I noticed it the moment we landed. Think of that in a country where every man is a born humorist! Think of what it means! [*Impressively*] Larry: we are in the presence of a great national grief.

LARRY: What's to grieve them?

BROADBENT: I divined it, Larry: I saw it in their faces. Ireland has never smiled since her hopes were buried in the grave of Gladstone.

LARRY: Oh, what's the use of talking to such a man? Now look here, Tom. Be serious for a moment if you can.

BROADBENT [*stupent*]: Serious! I!!!

LARRY: Yes, you. You say the Irish sense of humour is in abeyance. Well, if you drive through Rosscullen in a motor car with Haffigan's pig, it won't stay in abeyance. Now I warn you.

BROADBENT [*breezily*]: Why, so much the better! I shall enjoy the joke myself more than any of them. [*Shouting*] Hallo, Patsy Farrell, where are you?

PATSY [*appearing in the shrubbery*]: Here I am, your honour.

BROADBENT: Go and catch the pig and put it into the car: we're going to take it to Mr Haffigan's. [*He gives* LARRY *a slap on the shoulders that sends him staggering off through the gate, and follows him buoyantly, exclaiming*] Come on, you old croaker! I'll shew you how to win an Irish seat.

PATSY [*meditatively*]: Bedad, if dhat pig gets a howlt o' the handle o' the machine — [*He shakes his head ominously and drifts away to the pigsty.*]

ACT IV

The parlour in CORNELIUS DOYLE's *house. It communicates with the garden by a half glazed door. The fireplace is at the other side of the room, opposite the door and windows, the architect not having been sensitive to draughts. The table, rescued from the garden, is in the middle; and at it sits* KEEGAN, *the central figure in a rather crowded apartment.* NORA, *sitting with her back to the fire at the end of the table, is playing backgammon across its corner with him, on his left hand.* AUNT JUDY, *a little further back, sits facing the fire knitting, with her feet on the fender. A little to* KEEGAN's *right, in front of the table, and almost sitting on it, is* BARNEY DORAN. *Half a dozen friends of his, all men, are between him and the open door, supported by others outside. In the corner behind them is the sofa, of mahogany and horsehair, made up as a bed for* BROADBENT. *Against the wall behind* KEEGAN *stands a mahogany sideboard. A door leading to the interior of the house is near the fireplace, behind* AUNT JUDY. *There are chairs against the wall, one at each end of the sideboard.* KEEGAN's *hat is on the one nearest the inner door; and his stick is leaning against it. A third chair, also against the wall, is near the garden door.*

There is a strong contrast of emotional atmosphere between the two sides of the room. KEEGAN *is extraordinarily stern: no game of backgammon could possibly make a man's face so grim.* AUNT JUDY *is quietly busy.* NORA *is trying to ignore* DORAN *and attend to her game.*

On the other hand DORAN *is reeling in an ecstasy of mischievous mirth which has infected all his friends. They are screaming with laughter, doubled up, leaning on the furniture and against the walls, shouting, screeching, crying.*

AUNT JUDY [*as the noise lulls for a moment*]: Arra hold your noise, Barney. What is there to laugh at?

DORAN: It got its fut into the little hweel — [*he is overcome afresh; and the rest collapse again*].

AUNT JUDY: Ah, have some sense: you're like a parcel o' childher. Nora: hit him a thump on the back: he'll have a fit.

DORAN [*with squeezed eyes, exsufflicate with cachinnation*]: Frens, he sez to dhem outside Doolan's: I'm takin' the gintleman that pays the rint for a dhrive.

AUNT JUDY: Who did he mean be that?

DORAN: They call a pig that in England. That's their notion of a joke.

AUNT JUDY: Musha God help them if they can joke no better than that!

DORAN [*with renewed symptoms*]: Thin —

AUNT JUDY: Ah now don't be tellin it all over and settin' yourself off again, Barney.

NORA: You've told us three times, Mr Doran.

DORAN: Well but whin I think of it —!

AUNT JUDY: Then don't think of it, alanna.

DORAN: Dhere was Patsy Farrll in the back sate wi dhe pig between his knees, n me bould English boyoh in front at the machinery, n Larry Doyle in the road startin' the injine wid a bed winch. At the first puff of it the pig lep out of its skin and bled Patsy's nose wi dhe ring in its snout. [*Roars of laughter:* KEEGAN *glares at them.*] Before Broadbint knew hwere he was, the pig was up his back and over into his lap; and bedad the poor baste did credit to Corny's thrainin of it; for it put in the fourth speed wid its right crubeen[26] as if it was enthered for the Gordn Bennett.[27]

NORA [*reproachfully*]: And Larry in front of it and all! It's nothin' to laugh at, Mr Doran.

DORAN: Bedad, Miss Reilly, Larry cleared six yards sideways at wan jump if he cleared an inch; and he'd a cleared seven if Doolan's granmother hadn't cotch him in her apern widhout intindin' to. [*Immense merriment.*]

AUNT JUDY: Ah, for shame, Barney! the poor old woman! An' she was hurt before, too, when she slipped on the stairs.

DORAN: Bedad, maam, she's hurt behind now; for Larry bouled her over like a skittle. [*General delight at this typical stroke of Irish Rabelaisianism.*]

NORA: It's well Mr Doyle wasn't killed.

DORAN: Faith it wasn't o' Larry we were thinkin' jus dhen, wi dhe pig takin' the main sthreet o' Rosscullen on market day at a mile a minnit. Dh ony thing Broadbint could get at wi dhe pig in front of him was a fut brake; n the pig's tail was undher dhat; so that whin he thought he was putn non the brake he was ony squeezin' the life out o' the pig's tail. The more he put the brake on the more the pig squealed n the fasther he dhruv.

AUNT JUDY: Why couldn't he throw the pig out into the road?

DORAN: Sure he couldn't stand up to it, because he was spanchelled-like between his seat and dhat thing like a wheel on top of a stick between his knees.

AUNT JUDY: Lord have mercy on us!

NORA: I don't know how you can laugh. Do you, Mr Keegan?

KEEGAN [*grimly*]: Why not? There is danger, destruction, torment! What more do we need to make us merry? Go on, Barney: the last drops of joy are not squeezed from the story yet. Tell us again how our brother was torn asunder.

DORAN [*puzzled*]: Whose bruddher?

KEEGAN: Mine.

NORA: He means the pig, Mr Doran. You know his way.

DORAN [*rising gallantly to the occasion*]: Bedad I'm sorry for your poor bruddher, Misther Keegan; but I recommend you to thry him wid a couple o' fried eggs for your breakfast tomorrow. It was a case of Excelsior wi dhat ambitious baste; for not content wid jumpin' from the back seat into the front wan, he jumped from the front wan into the road in front of the car. And —

KEEGAN: And everybody laughed!

NORA: Don't go over that again, please, Mr Doran.

DORAN: Faith be the time the car went over the poor pig dhere was little left for me or anywan else to go over except wid a knife an fork.

AUNT JUDY: Why didn't Mr Broadbent stop the car when the pig was gone?

DORAN: Stop the car! He might as well ha thried to stop a mad bull. First it went wan way an' made fireworks o' Molly Ryan's crockery stall; an dhen it slewed round an' ripped ten fut o' wall out o' the corner o' the pound. [*With enormous enjoyment*] Begob, it just tore the town in two and sent the whole dam market to blazes. [NORA *offended, rises.*]

KEEGAN [*indignantly*]: Sir!

DORAN [*quickly*]: Savin' your presence, Miss Reilly, and Misther Keegan's. Dhere! I won't say anuddher word.

NORA: I'm surprised at you, Mr Doran. [*She sits down again.*]

DORAN [*reflectively*]: He has the divil's own luck, that Englishman, annyway; for hwen they picked him up he hadn't a scratch on him, barrn hwat the pig did to his cloes. Patsy had two fingers out o' jynt; but the smith pulled them sthraight for him. Oh, you never heard such a hullabaloo as there

was. There was Molly cryin' Me chaney, me beautyful chaney! n oul Matt shoutin' Me pig, me pig! n the polus takin' the number o' the car, n not a man in the town able to speak for laughin' —

KEEGAN [*with intense emphasis*]: It is hell: it is hell. Nowhere else could such a scene be a burst of happiness for the people.

CORNELIUS *comes in hastily from the garden, pushing his way through the little crowd.*

CORNELIUS: Whisht your laughin', boys! Here he is. [*He puts his hat on the sideboard, and goes to the fireplace, where he posts himself with his back to the chimneypiece.*]

AUNT JUDY: Remember your behaviour now.

Everybody becomes silent, solemn, concerned, sympathetic. BROADBENT *enters, soiled and disordered as to his motoring coat: immensely important and serious as to himself. He makes his way to the end of the table nearest the garden door, whilst* LARRY, *who accompanies him, throws his motoring coat on the sofa bed, and sits down, watching the proceedings.*

BROADBENT [*taking off his leather cap with dignity and placing it on the table*]: I hope you have not been anxious about me.

AUNT JUDY: Deedn we have, Mr Broadbent. It's a mercy you weren't killed.

DORAN: Kilt! It's a mercy dheres two bones of you left houldin' together. How dijjescape at all at all? Well, I never thought I'd be so glad to see you safe and sound again. Not a man in the town would say less [*murmurs of kindly assent*]. Won't you come down to Doolan's and have a dhrop o' brandy to take the shock off?

BROADBENT: You're all really too kind; but the shock has quite passed off.

DORAN [*jovially*]: Never mind. Come along all the same and tell us about it over a frenly glass.

BROADBENT: May I say how deeply I feel the kindness with which I have been overwhelmed since my accident? I can truthfully declare that I am glad it happened, because it has brought out the kindness and sympathy of the Irish character to an extent I had no conception of.

SEVERAL PRESENT: { Oh, sure you're welcome! / Sure it's only natural. / Sure you might have been kilt.

A young man, feeling that he must laugh or burst, hurries out. BARNEY *puts an iron constraint on his features.*

BROADBENT: All I can say is that I wish I could drink the health of everyone of you.

DORAN: Dhen come an' do it.

BROADBENT [*very solemnly*]: No: I am a teetotaller.

AUNT JUDY [*incredulously*]: Arra since when?

BROADBENT: Since this morning, Miss Doyle. I have had a lesson [*he looks at* NORA *significantly*] that I shall not forget. It may be that total abstinence has already saved my life; for I was astonished at the steadiness of my nerves when death stared me in the face today. So I will ask you to excuse me. [*He collects himself for a speech.*] Gentlemen: I hope the gravity of the peril through which we have all passed — for I know that the danger to the bystanders was as great as to the occupants of the car — will prove an earnest of closer and more serious relations between us in the future. We have had a somewhat agitating day: a valuable and innocent animal has lost its life: a public building has been wrecked: an aged and infirm lady has suffered an impact for which I feel personally responsible, though my old friend Mr Laurence Doyle unfortunately incurred the first effects of her very natural resentment. I greatly regret the damage to Mr Patrick Farrell's fingers; and I have of course taken care that he shall not suffer pecuniarily by his mishap. [*Murmurs of admiration at his magnanimity, and a voice* 'You're a gentleman, sir'.] I am glad to say that Patsy took it like an Irishman, and, far from expressing any vindictive feeling, declared his willingness to break all his fingers and toes for me on the same terms [*subdued applause, and* 'More power to Patsy!']. Gentlemen: I felt at home in Ireland from the first [*rising excitement among his hearers*]. In every Irish breast I have found that spirit of liberty [*A cheery voice* 'Hear Hear'], that instinctive mistrust of the Government [*A small pious voice, with intense expression,* 'God bless you, sir!'], that love of independence [*A defiant voice,* 'Thats it! Independence!'], that indignant sympathy with the cause of oppressed nationalities abroad [*A threatening growl from all: the ground-swell of patriotic passion*] and with the resolute assertion of personal rights at home, which is all but extinct in my own country. If it were legally possible I should become a naturalized Irishman; and if ever it be my good fortune to represent an Irish constituency in parliament, it shall be my first care to introduce a Bill legalizing such an operation. I believe a large section of the Liberal party would avail themselves of it. [*Momentary scepticism.*] I do. [*Convulsive cheering.*].Gentlemen: I have said enough. [*Cries of* 'Go on'.] No: I have as yet no right to address you at all on political subjects; and we must not abuse the warm-hearted Irish hospitality of Miss Doyle by turning her sitting room into a public meeting.

DORAN [*energetically*]: Three cheers for Tom Broadbent, the future member for Rosscullen!

AUNT JUDY [*waving a half knitted sock*]: Hip hip hurray!

The cheers are given with great heartiness, as it is by this time, for the more humorous spirits present, a question of vociferation or internal rupture.

BROADBENT: Thank you from the bottom of my heart, friends.

NORA [*whispering to* DORAN]: Take them away, Mr Doran [DORAN *nods*].

DORAN: Well, good evenin', Mr Broadbent; an' may you never regret the day you wint dhrivin' wid Haffigan's pig! [*They shake hands.*] Good evenin', Miss Doyle.

General handshaking, BROADBENT *shaking hands with everybody effusively. He accompanies them to the garden and can be heard outside saying Goodnight in every inflexion known to parliamentary candidates.* NORA, AUNT JUDY, KEEGAN, LARRY *and* CORNELIUS *are left in the parlour.* LARRY *goes to the threshold and watches the scene in the garden.*

NORA: It's a shame to make game of him like that. He's a gradle more good in him than Barney Doran.

CORNELIUS: It's all up with his candidature. He'll be laughed out o' the town.

LARRY [*turning quickly from the doorway*]: Oh no he won't: he's not an Irishman. He'll never know they're laughing at him; and while they're laughing he'll win the seat.

CORNELIUS: But he can't prevent the story getting about.

LARRY: He won't want to. He'll tell it himself as one of the most providential episodes in the history of England and Ireland.

AUNT JUDY: Sure he wouldn't make a fool of himself like that.

LARRY: Are you sure he's such a fool after all, Aunt Judy? Suppose you had a vote! which would you rather give it to? the man that told the story of Haffigan's pig Barney Doran's way or Broadbent's way?

AUNT JUDY: Faith I wouldn't give it to a man at all. It's a few women they want in parliament to stop their foolish blather.

BROADBENT [*bustling into the room, and taking off his damaged motoring overcoat, which he puts down on the sofa*]: Well, that's over. I must apologize for making a speech, Miss Doyle; but they like it, you know. Everything helps in electioneering.

LARRY *takes the chair near the door; draws it near the*

table; and sits astride it, with his elbows folded on the back.

AUNT JUDY: I'd no notion you were such an orator, Mr Broadbent.

BROADBENT: Oh, it's only a knack. One picks it up on the platform. It stokes up their enthusiasm.

AUNT JUDY: Oh, I forgot. You've not met Mr Keegan. Let me introjoosha.

BROADBENT [*shaking hands effusively*]: Most happy to meet you, Mr Keegan. I have heard of you, though I have not had the pleasure of shaking your hand before. And now may I ask you — for I value no man's opinion more — what you think of my chances here.

KEEGAN [*coldly*]: Your chances, sir, are excellent. You will get into parliament.

BROADBENT [*delighted*]: I hope so. I think so. [*Fluctuating*] You really think so? You are sure you are not allowing your enthusiasm for our principles to get the better of your judgment?

KEEGAN: I have no enthusiasm for your principles, sir. You will get into parliament because you want to get into it enough to be prepared to take the necessary steps to induce the people to vote for you. That is how people usually get into that fantastic assembly. ·

BROADBENT [*puzzled*]: Of course. [*Pause.*] Quite so. [*Pause.*] Er — yes. [*Buoyant again*] I think they will vote for me. Eh? Yes?

AUNT JUDY: Arra why shouldn't they? Look at the people they do vote for!

BROADBENT [*encouraged*]: That's true: that's very true. When I see the windbags, the carpet-baggers, the charlatans, the — the — the fools and ignoramuses who corrupt the multitude by their wealth, or seduce them by spouting balderdash to them, I cannot help thinking that an Englishman with no humbug about him, who will talk straight common sense and take his stand on the solid ground of principle and public duty, must win his way with men of all classes.

KEEGAN [*quietly*]: Sir: there was a time, in my ignorant youth, when I should have called you a hypocrite.

BROADBENT [*reddening*]: A hypocrite!

NORA [*hastily*]: Oh I'm sure you don't think anything of the sort, Mr Keegan.

BROADBENT [*emphatically*]: Thank you, Miss Reilly: thank you.

CORNELIUS [*gloomily*]: We all have to stretch it a bit in politics: hwats the use o' pretendin' we don't?

BROADBENT [*stiffly*]: I hope I have said or done nothing that calls for any such observation, Mr Doyle. If

there is a vice I detest — or against which my whole public life has been a protest — it is the vice of hypocrisy. I would almost rather be inconsistent than insincere.

KEEGAN: Do not be offended, sir: I know that you are quite sincere. There is a saying in the Scripture which runs — so far as the memory of an oldish man can carry the words — Let not the right side of your brain know what the left side doeth. I learnt at Oxford that this is the secret of the Englishman's strange power of making the best of both worlds.

BROADBENT: Surely the text refers to our right and left hands. I am somewhat surprised to hear a member of your Church quote so essentially Protestant a document as the Bible; but at least you might quote it accurately.

LARRY: Tom: with the best intentions you're making an ass of yourself. You don't understand Mr Keegan's peculiar vein of humour.

BROADBENT [*instantly recovering his confidence*]: Ah! it was only your delightful Irish humour, Mr Keegan. Of course, of course. How stupid of me! I'm so sorry. [*He pats* KEEGAN *consolingly on the back.*] John Bull's wits are still slow, you see. Besides, calling me a hypocrite was too big a joke to swallow all at once, you know.

KEEGAN: You must also allow for the fact that I am mad.

NORA: Ah, don't talk like that, Mr Keegan.

BROADBENT [*encouragingly*]: Not at all, not at all. Only a whimsical Irishman, eh?

LARRY: Are you really mad, Mr Keegan?

AUNT JUDY [*shocked*]: Oh, Larry, how could you ask him such a thing?

LARRY: I don't think Mr Keegan minds. [*To* KEEGAN] What's the true version of the story of that black man you confessed on his deathbed?

KEEGAN: What story have you heard about that?

LARRY: I am informed that when the devil came for the black heathen, he took off your head and turned it three times round before putting it on again; and that your head's been turned ever since.

NORA [*reproachfully*]: Larry!

KEEGAN [*blandly*]: That is not quite what occurred. [*He collects himself for a serious utterance: they attend involuntarily.*] I heard that a black man was dying, and that the people were afraid to go near him. When I went to the place I found an elderly Hindoo, who told me one of those tales of unmerited misfortune, of cruel ill luck, of relentless persecution by destiny, which sometimes wither the commonplaces of consolation on the lips of a priest. But this man did not complain of his misfortunes. They were brought upon him, he said, by sins committed in a former existence. Then without a word of comfort from me, he died with a clear-eyed resignation that my most earnest exhortations have rarely produced in a Christian, and left me sitting there by his bedside with the mystery of this world suddenly revealed to me.

BROADBENT: That is a remarkable tribute to the liberty of conscience enjoyed by the subjects of our Indian Empire.

LARRY: No doubt; but may we venture to ask what is the mystery of this world?

KEEGAN: This world, sir, is very clearly a place of torment and penance, a place where the fool flourishes and the good and wise are hated and persecuted, a place where men and women torture one another in the name of love; where children are scourged and enslaved in the name of parental duty and education; where the weak in body are poisoned and mutilated in the name of healing, and the weak in character are put to the horrible torture of imprisonment, not for hours but for years, in the name of justice. It is a place where the hardest toil is a welcome refuge from the horror and tedium of pleasure, and where charity and good works are done only for hire to ransom the souls of the spoiler and the sybarite. Now, sir, there is only one place of horror and torment known to my religion; and that place is hell. Therefore it is plain to me that this earth of ours must be hell, and that we are all here, as the Indian revealed to me — perhaps he was sent to reveal it to me — to expiate crimes committed by us in a former existence.

AUNT JUDY [awestruck]: Heaven save us, what a thing to say!

CORNELIUS [sighing]: It's a queer world: that's certain.

BROADBENT: Your idea is a very clever one, Mr Keegan: really most brilliant: I should never have thought of it. But it seems to me — if I may say so — that you are overlooking the fact that, of the evils you describe, some are absolutely necessary for the preservation of society, and others are encouraged only when the Tories are in office.

LARRY: I expect you were a Tory in a former existence; and that is why you are here.

BROADBENT [with conviction]: Never, Larry, never. But leaving politics out of the question, I find the world quite good enough for me: rather a jolly place, in fact.

KEEGAN [looking at him with quiet wonder]: You are satisfied?

BROADBENT: As a reasonable man, yes. I see no evils in the world — except, of course, natural evils — that cannot be remedied by freedom, self-government, and English institutions. I think so, not because I am an Englishman, but as a matter of common sense.

KEEGAN: You feel at home in the world, then?

BROADBENT: Of course. Don't you?

KEEGAN [from the very depths of his nature]: No.

BROADBENT [breezily]: Try phosphorus pills. I always take them when my brain is overworked. I'll give you the address in Oxford Street.

KEEGAN [enigmatically: rising]: Miss Doyle: my wandering fit has come on me: will you excuse me?

AUNT JUDY: To be sure: you know you can come in n nout as you like.

KEEGAN: We can finish the game some other time, Miss Reilly. [He goes for his hat and stick.]

NORA: No: I'm out with you [she disarranges the pieces and rises]. I was too wicked in a former existence to play backgammon with a good man like you.

AUNT JUDY [whispering to her]: Whisht, whisht, child! Don't set him back on that again.

KEEGAN [to NORA]: When I look at you, I think that perhaps Ireland is only purgatory, after all. [He passes on to the garden door.]

NORA: Galong with you!

BROADBENT [whispering to CORNELIUS]: Has he a vote?

CORNELIUS [nodding]: Yes. An' there's lotsle vote the way he tells them.

KEEGAN [at the garden door, with gentle gravity]: Good evening, Mr Broadbent. You have set me thinking. Thank you.

BROADBENT [delighted, hurrying across to him to shake hands]: No, really? You find that contact with English ideas is stimulating, eh?

KEEGAN: I am never tired of hearing you talk, Mr Broadbent.

BROADBENT [modestly remonstrating]: Oh come! come!

KEEGAN: Yes, I assure you. You are an extremely interesting man. [He goes out.]

BROADBENT [enthusiastically]: What a nice chap! What an intelligent, broadminded character, considering his cloth! By the way, I'd better have a wash. [He takes up his coat and cap, and leaves the room through the inner door.]

NORA returns to her chair and shuts up the backgammon board.

AUNT JUDY: Keegan's very queer today. He has his mad fit on him.

CORNELIUS [worried and bitter]: I wouldn't say but he's

right after all. It's a contrary world. [*To* LARRY] Why would you be such a fool as to let Broadbent take the seat in parliament from you?

LARRY [*glancing at* NORA]: He will take more than that from me before he's done here.

CORNELIUS: I wish he'd never set foot in my house, bad luck to his fat face! D'ye think he'd lend me £300 on the farm, Larry? When I'm so hard up, it seems a waste o' money not to mortgage it now it's me own.

LARRY: *I* can lend you £300 on it.

CORNELIUS: No, no; I wasn't putn in for that. When I die and leave you the farm I should like to be able to feel that it was all me own, and not half yours to start with. Now I'll take me oath Barney Doarn's going to ask Broadbent to lend him £500 on the mill to put in a new hweel; for the old one'll harly hol' together. An' Haffigan can't sleep with covetn that corner o' land at the foot of his medda that belongs to Doolan. He'll have to mortgage to buy it. I may as well be first as last. D'ye think Broadbent'd len me a little?

LARRY: I'm quite sure he will.

CORNELIUS: Is he as ready as that? Would he len me five hunderd, d'ye think?

LARRY: He'll lend you more than the land'll ever be worth to you; so for Heaven's sake be prudent.

CORNELIUS [*judicially*]: All right, all right, me son: I'll be careful. I'm goin into the office for a bit. [*He withdraws through the inner door, obviously to prepare his application to* BROADBENT.]

AUNT JUDY [*indignantly*]: As if he hadn't seen enough o' borryin when he was an agent without beginnin' borryin himself! [*She rises.*] I'll borry him, so I will. [*She puts her knitting on the table and follows him out, with a resolute air that bodes trouble for* CORNELIUS.]

LARRY *and* NORA *are left together for the first time since his arrival. She looks at him with a smile that perishes as she sees him aimlessly rocking his chair, and reflecting, evidently not about her, with his lips pursed as if he were whistling. With a catch in her throat she takes up* AUNT JUDY'*s knitting, and makes a pretence of going on with it.*]

NORA: I suppose it didn't seem very long to you.

LARRY [*starting*]: Eh? What didn't?

NORA: The eighteen years you've been away.

LARRY: Oh, that! No: it seems hardly more than a week. I've been so busy — had so little time to think.

NORA: I've had nothin' else to do but think.

LARRY: That was very bad for you. Why didn't you give it up? Why did you stay here?

NORA: Because nobody sent for me to go anywhere else, I suppose. That's why.

LARRY: Yes: one does stick frightfully in the same place, unless some external force comes and routs one out. [*He yawns slightly; but as she looks up quickly at him, he pulls himself together and rises with an air of waking up and setting to work cheerfully to make himself agreeable.*] And how have you been all this time?

NORA: Quite well, thank you.

LARRY: That's right. [*Suddenly finding that he has nothing else to say, and being ill at ease in consequence, he strolls about the room humming distractedly.*]

NORA [*struggling with her tears*]: Is that all you have to say to me, Larry?

LARRY: Well, what is there to say? You see, we know each other so well.

NORA [*a little consoled*]: Yes: of course we do. [*He does not reply.*] I wonder you came back at all.

LARRY: I couldn't help it. [*She looks up affectionately.*] Tom made me. [*She looks down again quickly to conceal the effect of this blow. He whistles another stave; then resumes*] I had a sort of dread of returning to Ireland. I felt somehow that my luck would turn if I came back. And now here I am, none the worse.

NORA: Praps it's a little dull for you.

LARRY: No: I haven't exhausted the interest of strolling about the old places and remembering and romancing about them.

NORA [*hopefully*]: Oh! You do remember the places, then?

LARRY: Of course. They have associations.

NORA [*not doubting that the associations are with her*]: I suppose so.

LARRY: M'yes. I can remember particular spots where I had long fits of thinking about the countries I meant to get to when I escaped from Ireland. America and London, and sometimes Rome and the east.

NORA [*deeply mortified*]: Was that all you used to be thinking about?

LARRY: Well, there was precious little else to think about here, my dear Nora, except sometimes at sunset, when one got maudlin and called Ireland Erin, and imagined one was remembering the days of old, and so forth. [*He whistles Let Erin Remember.*]

NORA: Did jever get a letter I wrote you last February?

LARRY: Oh yes; and I really intended to answer it. But I haven't had a moment; and I knew you wouldn't mind. You see, I am so afraid of boring you by writing about affairs you don't understand

and people you don't know! And yet what else have I to write about? I begin a letter; and then I tear it up again. The fact is, fond as we are of one another, Nora, we have so little in common — I mean of course the things one can put in a letter — that correspondence is apt to become the hardest of hard work.

NORA: Yes: it's hard for me to know anything about you if you never tell me anything.

LARRY [*pettishly*]: Nora: a man can't sit down and write his life day by day when he's tired enough with having lived it.

NORA: I'm not blaming you.

LARRY [*looking at her with some concern*]: You seem rather out of spirits. [*Going closer to her, anxiously and tenderly.*] You haven't got neuralgia, have you?

NORA: No.

LARRY [*reassured*]: I get a touch of it sometimes when I am below par. [*Absently, again strolling about*] Yes, yes. [*He gazes through the doorway at the Irish landscape, and sings, almost unconsciously, but very expressively, an air from Offenbach's Whittington.*]

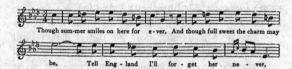

[NORA, *who has been at first touched by the tenderness of his singing, puts down her knitting at this very unexpected sentiment, and stares at him. He continues until the melody soars out of his range, when he trails off into whistling Let Erin Remember.*[28]]

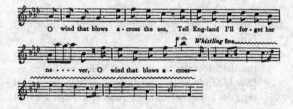

I'm afraid I'm boring you, Nora, though you're too kind to say so.

NORA: Are you wanting to get back to England already?

LARRY: Not at all. Not at all.

NORA: That's a queer song to sing to me if you're not.

LARRY: The song! Oh, it doesn't mean anything: it's by a German Jew, like most English patriotic sentiment. Never mind me, my dear: go on with your work; and don't let me bore you.

NORA [*bitterly*]: Rosscullen isn't such a lively place that I am likely to be bored by you at our first talk together after eighteen years, though you don't seem to have much to say to me after all.

LARRY: Eighteen years is a devilish long time, Nora. Now if it had been eighteen minutes, or even eighteen months, we should be able to pick up the interrupted thread, and chatter like two magpies. But as it is, I have simply nothing to say; and you seem to have less.

NORA: I — [*her tears choke her; but she keeps up appearances desperately*].

LARRY [*quite unconscious of his cruelty*]: In a week or so we shall be quite old friends again. Meanwhile, as I feel that I am not making myself particularly entertaining, I'll take myself off. Tell Tom I've gone for a stroll over the hill.

NORA: You seem very fond of Tom, as you call him.

LARRY [*the triviality going suddenly out of his voice*]: Yes: I'm fond of Tom.

NORA: Oh, well, don't let me keep you from him.

LARRY: I know quite well that my departure will be a relief. Rather a failure, this first meeting after eighteen years, eh? Well, never mind: these great sentimental events always are failures; and now the worst of it's over anyhow. [*He goes out through the garden door.*]

NORA, *left alone, struggles wildly to save herself from breaking down, and then drops her face on the table and gives way to a convulsion of crying. Her sobs shake her so that she can hear nothing; and she has no suspicion that she is no longer alone until her head and breast are raised by* BROADBENT, *who, returning newly washed and combed through the inner door, has seen her condition, first with surprise and concern, and then with an emotional disturbance that quite upsets him.*

BROADBENT: Miss Reilly. Miss Reilly. What's the matter? Don't cry: I can't stand it: you mustn't cry. [*She makes a choked effort to speak, so painful that he continues with impulsive sympathy*] No: don't try to speak: it's all right now. Have your cry out: never mind me: trust me. [*Gathering her to him, and babbling consolatorily.*] Cry on my chest: the only really comfortable place for a woman to cry is a man's chest: a real man, a real friend. A good broad chest, eh? not less than forty-two inches — no: don't fuss: never mind the conventions: we're two friends, aren't we? Come now, come, come! It's all right and comfortable and happy now, isn't it?

NORA [*through her tears*]: Let me go. I want me handkerchief.

BROADBENT [*holding her with one arm and producing a large silk handkerchief from his breast pocket*]: Here's a handkerchief. Let me [*he dabs her tears dry with it*]. Never mind your own: it's too small: it's one of those wretched little cambric handkerchiefs —

NORA [*sobbing*]: Indeed it's a common cotton one.

BROADBENT: Of course it's a common cotton one — silly little cotton one — not good enough for the dear eyes of Nora Cryna —

NORA [*spluttering into a hysterical laugh and clutching him convulsively with her fingers while she tries to stifle her laughter against his collar bone*]: Oh don't make me laugh: please don't make me laugh.

BROADBENT [*terrified*]: I didn't mean to, on my soul. What is it? What is it?

NORA: Nora Creena, Nora Creena.

BROADBENT [*patting her*]: Yes, yes, of course, Nora Creena, Nora acushla[29] [*he makes cush rhyme to plush*] —

NORA: Acushla [*she makes cush rhyme to bush*].

BROADBENT: Oh, confound the language! Nora darling — my Nora — the Nora I love —

NORA [*shocked into propriety*]: You mustn't talk like that to me.

BROADBENT [*suddenly becoming prodigiously solemn and letting her go*]: No, of course not. I don't mean it. At least I do mean it, but I know it's premature. I had no right to take advantage of your being a little upset; but I lost my self-control for a moment.

NORA [*wondering at him*]: I think you're a very kindhearted man, Mr Broadbent; but you seem to me to have no self-control at all [*she turns her face away with a keen pang of shame and adds*] no more than myself.

BROADBENT [*resolutely*]: Oh yes, I have: you should see me when I am really roused: then I have TREMENDOUS self-control. Remember: we have been alone together only once before; and then, I regret to say, I was in a disgusting state.

NORA: Ah no, Mr Broadbent: you weren't disgusting.

BROADBENT [*mercilessly*]: Yes I was: nothing can excuse it: perfectly beastly. It must have made a most unfavourable impression on you.

NORA: Oh, sure it's all right. Say no more about that.

BROADBENT: I must, Miss Reilly: it is my duty. I shall not detain you long. May I ask you to sit down. [*He indicates her chair with oppressive solemnity. She sits down wondering. He then, with the same portentous gravity, places a chair for himself near her; sits down; and proceeds to explain.*] First, Miss Reilly, may I say that I have tasted nothing of an alcoholic nature today.

NORA: It doesn't seem to make as much difference in you as it would in an Irishman, somehow.

BROADBENT: Perhaps not. Perhaps not. I never quite lose myself.

NORA [*consolingly*]: Well, anyhow, you're all right now.

BROADBENT [*fervently*]: Thank you, Miss Reilly: I am. Now we shall get along. [*Tenderly, lowering his voice*] Nora: I was in earnest last night. [NORA *moves as if to rise.*] No: one moment. You must not think I am going to press you for an answer before you have known me for 24 hours. I am a reasonable man, I hope; and I am prepared to wait as long as you like, provided you will give me some small assurance that the answer will not be unfavourable.

NORA: How could I go back from it if I did? I sometimes think you're not quite right in your head, Mr Broadbent, you say such funny things.

BROADBENT: Yes: I know I have a strong sense of humour which sometimes makes people doubt whether I am quite serious. That is why I have always thought I should like to marry an Irishwoman. She would always understand my jokes. For instance, you would understand them, eh?

NORA [*uneasily*]: Mr Broadbent: I couldn't.

BROADBENT [*soothingly*]: Wait: let me break this to you gently, Miss Reilly: hear me out. I daresay you have noticed that in speaking to you I have been putting a very strong constraint on myself, so as to avoid wounding your delicacy by too abrupt an avowal of my feelings. Well, I feel now that the time has come to be open, to be frank, to be explicit. Miss Reilly: you have inspired in me a very strong attachment. Perhaps, with a woman's intuition, you have already guessed that.

NORA [*rising distractedly*]: Why do you talk to me in that unfeeling nonsensical way?

BROADBENT [*rising also, much astonished*]: Unfeeling! Nonsensical!

NORA: Don't you know that you have said things to me that no man ought to say unless — unless — [*She suddenly breaks down again and hides her face on the table as before.*] Oh, go away from me: I won't get married at all: what is it but heartbreak and disappointment?

BROADBENT [*developing the most formidable symptoms of rage and grief*]: Do you mean to say that you are going to refuse me? that you don't care for me?

NORA [*looking at him in consternation*]: Oh, don't take it to heart, Mr Br—

BROADBENT [*flushed and almost choking*]: I don't want to be petted and blarneyed. [*With childish rage*] I love you. I want you for my wife. [*In despair*] I can't help your refusing. I'm helpless: I can do nothing. You have no right to ruin my whole life. You — [*a hysterical convulsion stops him*].

NORA [*almost awestruck*]: You're not going to cry, are you? I never thought a man could cry. Don't.

BROADBENT: I'm not crying. I — I — I leave that sort of thing to your damned sentimental Irishmen. You think I have no feeling because I am a plain unemotional Englishman, with no powers of expression.

NORA: I don't think you know the sort of man you are at all. Whatever may be the matter with you, it's not want of feeling.

BROADBENT [*hurt and petulant*]: It's you who have no feeling. You're as heartless as Larry.

NORA: What do you expect me to do? Is it to throw meself at your head the minute the word is out o' your mouth?

BROADBENT [*striking his silly head with his fists*]: Oh, what a fool! what a brute I am! It's only your Irish delicacy: of course, of course. You mean Yes. Eh? What? Yes? yes? yes?

NORA: I think you might understand that though I might choose to be an old maid, I could never marry anybody but you now.

BROADBENT [*clasping her violently to his breast, with a crow of immense relief and triumph*]: Ah, that's right, that's right: that's magnificent. I knew you would see what a first-rate thing this will be for both of us.

NORA [*incommoded and not at all enraptured by his ardour*]: You're dreadfully strong, an' a gradle too free with your strength. An' I never thought o' whether it'd be a good thing for us or not. But when you found me here that time, I let you be kind to me, and cried in your arms, because I was too wretched to think of anything but the comfort of it. An' how could I let any other man touch me after that?

BROADBENT [*moved*]: Now that's very nice of you, Nora: that's really most delicately womanly [*he kisses her hand chivalrously*].

NORA [*looking earnestly and a little doubtfully at him*]: Surely if you let one woman cry on you like that you'd never let another touch you?

BROADBENT [*conscientiously*]: One should not. One ought not, my dear girl. But the honest truth is, if a chap is at all a pleasant sort of chap, his chest becomes a fortification that has to stand many assaults: at least it is so in England.

NORA [*curtly, much disgusted*]: Then you'd better marry an Englishwoman.

BROADBENT [*making a wry face*]: No, no: the English-woman is too prosaic for my taste, too material, too much of the animated beefsteak about her.

The ideal is what I like. Now Larry's taste is just the opposite: he likes 'em solid and bouncing and rather keen about him. It's a very convenient difference; for we've never been in love with the same woman.

NORA: An d'ye mean to tell me to me face that you've ever been in love before?

BROADBENT: Lord! yes.

NORA: I'm not your first love!

BROADBENT: First love is only a little foolishness and a lot of curiosity: no really self-respecting woman would take advantage of it. No, my dear Nora: I've done with all that long ago. Love affairs always end in rows. We're not going to have any rows: we're going to have a solid four-square home: man and wife: comfort and common sense. And plenty of affection, eh? [*he puts his arm round her with confident proprietorship*.]

NORA [*coldly, trying to get away*]: I don't want any other woman's leavings.

BROADBENT [*holding her*]: Nobody asked you to, maam. I never asked any woman to marry me before.

NORA [*severely*]: Then why didn't you if you're an honourable man?

BROADBENT: Well, to tell you the truth, they were mostly married already. But never mind! there was nothing wrong. Come! don't take a mean advantage of me. After all, you must have had a fancy or two yourself, eh?

NORA [*conscience-stricken*]: Yes. I suppose I've no right to be particular.

BROADBENT [*humbly*]: I know I'm not good enough for you, Nora. But no man is, you know, when the woman is a really nice woman.

NORA: Oh, I'm no better than yourself. I may as well tell you about it.

BROADBENT: No, no: let's have no telling: much better not. *I* shan't tell you anything: don't you tell me anything. Perfect confidence in one another and no tellings: that's the way to avoid rows.

NORA: Don't think it was anything I need be ashamed of.

BROADBENT: I don't.

NORA: It was only that I'd never known anybody else that I could care for; and I was foolish enough once to think that Larry —

BROADBENT [*disposing of the idea at once*]: Larry! Oh, that wouldn't have done at all, not at all. You don't know Larry as I do, my dear. He has absolutely no capacity for enjoyment: he couldn't make any woman happy. He's as clever as be-blowed; but life's too earthly for him: he doesn't really care for anything or anybody.

NORA: I've found that out.

BROADBENT: Of course you have. No, my dear: take my word for it, you're jolly well out of that. There! [*swinging her round against his breast*] that's much more comfortable for you.

NORA [*with Irish peevishness*]: Ah, you mustn't go on like that. I don't like it.

BROADBENT [*unabashed*]: You'll acquire the taste by degrees. You mustn't mind me: it's an absolute necessity of my nature that I should have somebody to hug occasionally. Besides, it's good for you: it'll plump out your muscles and make 'em elastic and set up your figure.

NORA: Well, I'm sure! if this is English manners! Aren't you ashamed to talk about such things?

BROADBENT [*in the highest feather*]: Not a bit. By George, Nora, it's a tremendous thing to be able to enjoy oneself. Let's go off for a walk out of this stuffy little room. I want the open air to expand in. Come along. Co-o-ome along. [*He puts her arm into his and sweeps her out into the garden as an equinoctial gale might sweep a dry leaf.*]

Later in the evening, the grasshopper is again enjoying the sunset by the great stone on the hill; but this time he enjoys neither the stimulus of KEEGAN's conversation nor the pleasure of terrifying PATSY FARRELL. *He is alone until* NORA *and* BROADBENT *come up the hill arm in arm.* BROADBENT *is still breezy and confident; but she has her head averted from him and is almost in tears.*

BROADBENT [*stopping to snuff up the hillside air*]: Ah! I like this spot. I like this view. This would be a jolly good place for a hotel and a golf links. Friday to Tuesday, railway ticket and hotel all inclusive. I tell you, Nora, I'm going to develop this place. [*Looking at her*] Hallo! What's the matter? Tired?

NORA [*unable to restrain her tears*]: I'm ashamed out o' me life.

BROADBENT [*astonished*]: Ashamed! What of?

NORA: Oh, how could you drag me all round the place like that, telling everybody that we're going to be married, and introjoocing me to the lowest of the low, and letting them shake hans with me, and encouraging them to make free with us? I little thought I should live to be shaken hans with be Doolan in broad daylight in the public street of Roscullen.

BROADBENT: But, my dear, Doolan's a publican: a most influential man. By the way, I asked him if his wife would be at home tomorrow. He said she would; so you must take the motor car round and call on her.

NORA [*aghast*]: Is it me call on Doolan's wife!

BROADBENT: Yes, of course: call on all their wives. We must get a copy of the register and a supply of canvassing cards. No use calling on people who haven't votes. You'll be a great success as a canvasser, Nora: they call you the heiress; and they'll be flattered no end by your calling, especially as you've never cheapened yourself by speaking to them before — have you?

NORA [*indignantly*]: Not likely, indeed.

BROADBENT: Well, we mustn't be stiff and stand-off, you know. We must be thoroughly democratic, and patronize everybody without distinction of class. I tell you I'm a jolly lucky man, Nora Cryna. I get engaged to the most delightful woman in Ireland; and it turns out that I couldn't have done a smarter stroke of electioneering.

NORA: An' would you let me demean meself like that, just to get yourself into parliament?

BROADBENT [*buoyantly*]: Aha! Wait till you find out what an exciting game electioneering is: you'll be mad to get me in. Besides, you'd like people to say that Tom Broadbent's wife had been the making of him? that she got him into parliament? into the Cabinet, perhaps, eh?

NORA: God knows I don't grudge you me money! But to lower meself to the level of common people —

BROADBENT: To a member's wife, Nora, nobody is common provided he's on the register. Come, my dear! it's all right: do you think I'd let you do it if it wasn't? The best people do it. Everybody does it.

NORA [*who has been biting her lip and looking over the hill, disconsolate and unconvinced*]: Well, praps you know best what they do in England. They must have very little respect for themselves. I think I'll go in now. I see Larry and Mr Keegan coming up the hill; and I'm not fit to talk to them.

BROADBENT: Just wait and say something nice to Keegan. They tell me he controls nearly as many votes as Father Dempsey himself.

NORA: You little know Peter Keegan. He'd see through me as if I was a pane o' glass.

BROADBENT: Oh, he won't like it any the less for that. What really flatters a man is that you think him worth flattering. Not that I would flatter any man: don't think that. I'll just go and meet him. [*He goes down the hill with the eager forward look of a man about to greet a valued acquaintance.* NORA *dries her eyes, and turns to go as* LARRY *strolls up the hill to her.*]

LARRY: Nora. [*She turns and looks at him hardly, without*

a word. *He continues anxiously, in his most conciliatory tone.*] When I left you that time, I was just as wretched as you. I didn't rightly know what I wanted to say; and my tongue kept clacking to cover the loss I was at. Well, I've been thinking ever since; and now I know what I ought to have said. I've come back to say it.

NORA: You've come too late, then. You thought eighteen years was not long enough, and that you might keep me waiting a day longer. Well, you were mistaken. I'm engaged to your friend Mr Broadbent; and I'm done with you.

LARRY [*naïvely*]: But that was the very thing I was going to advise you to do.

NORA [*involuntarily*]: Oh you brute! to tell me that to me face!

LARRY [*nervously relapsing into his most Irish manner*]: Nora, dear, don't you understand that I'm an Irishman, and he's an Englishman. He wants you; and he grabs you. *I* want you; and I quarrel with you and have to go on wanting you.

NORA: So you may. You'd better go back to England to the animated beefsteaks you're so fond of.

LARRY [*amazed*]: Nora! [*Guessing where she got the metaphor.*] He's been talking about me, I see. Well, never mind: we must be friends, you and I. I don't want his marriage to you to be his divorce from me.

NORA: You care more for him that you ever did for me.

LARRY [*with curt sincerity*]: Yes of course I do: why should I tell you lies about it? Nora Reilly was a person of very little consequence to me or anyone else outside this miserable little hole. But Mrs Tom Broadbent will be a person of very considerable consequence indeed. Play your new part well, and there will be no more neglect, no more loneliness, no more idle regrettings and vain-hopings in the evenings by the Round Tower, but real life and real work and real cares and real joys among real people: solid English life in London, the very centre of the world. You will find your work cut out for you keeping Tom's house and entertaining Tom's friends and getting Tom into parliament; but it will be worth the effort.

NORA: You talk as if I was under an obligation to him for marrying me.

LARRY: I talk as I think. You've made a very good match, let me tell you.

NORA: Indeed! Well, some people might say he's not done so badly himself.

LARRY: If you mean that you will be a treasure to him,

he thinks so now; and you can keep him thinking so if you like.

NORA: I wasn't thinking o' meself at all.

LARRY: Were you thinking of your money, Nora?

NORA: I didn't say so.

LARRY: Your money will not pay your cook's wages in London.

NORA [*flaming up*]: If that's true — and the more shame for you to throw it in me face if it is true — at all events it'll make us independent; for if the worst comes to the worst, we can always come back here an' live on it. An' if I have to keep his house for him, at all events I can keep you out of it; for I've done with you; and I wish I'd never seen you. So goodbye to you, Mister Larry Doyle. [*She turns her back on him and goes home.*]

LARRY [*watching her as she goes*]: Goodbye. Goodbye. Oh, that's so Irish! Irish both of us to the backbone: Irish! Irish! Iri—

BROADBENT *arrives, conversing energetically with* KEEGAN.

BROADBENT: Nothing pays like a golfing hotel, if you hold the land instead of the shares, and if the furniture people stand in with you, and if you are a good man of business.

LARRY: Nora's gone home.

BROADBENT [*with conviction*]: You were right this morning, Larry. I must feed up Nora. She's weak; and it makes her fanciful. Oh, by the way, did I tell you that we're engaged?

LARRY: She told me herself.

BROADBENT [*complacently*]: She's rather full of it, as you may imagine. Poor Nora! Well, Mr Keegan, as I said, I begin to see my way here. I begin to see my way.

KEEGAN [*with a courteous inclination*]: The conquering Englishman, sir. Within 24 hours of your arrival you have carried off our only heiress, and practically secured the parliamentary seat. And you have promised me that when I come here in the evenings to meditate on my madness; to watch the shadow of the Round Tower lengthening in the sunset; to break my heart uselessly in the curtained gloaming over the dead heart and blinded soul of the island of the saints, you will comfort me with the bustle of a great hotel, and the sight of the little children carrying the golf clubs of your tourists as a preparation for the life to come.

BROADBENT [*quite touched, mutely offering him a cigar to console him, at which he smiles and shakes his head*]: Yes, Mr Keegan: you're quite right. There's poetry in everything, even [*looking absently into the cigar case*] in the most modern prosaic things, if you know how to extract it [*he extracts a cigar for himself and offers one to* LARRY, *who takes it*]. If I was to be shot for it I couldn't extract it myself; but that's where you come in, you see. [*Roguishly, waking up from his reverie and bustling* KEEGAN *goodhumouredly*] And then *I* shall wake you up a bit. That's where *I* come in: eh? d'ye see? Eh? eh? [*He pats him very pleasantly on the shoulder, half admiringly, half pityingly.*] Just so, just so. [*Coming back to business*] By the way, I believe I can do better than a light railway here. There seems to be no question now that the motor boat has come to stay. Well, look at your magnificent river there, going to waste.

KEEGAN [*closing his eyes*]:
'Silent, O Moyle, be the roar of thy waters.'[30]

BROADBENT: You know, the roar of a motor boat is quite pretty.

KEEGAN: Provided it does not drown the Angelus.

BROADBENT [*reassuringly*]: Oh no: it won't do that: not the least danger. You know, a church bell can make a devil of a noise when it likes.

KEEGAN: You have an answer for everything, sir. But your plans leave one question still unanswered: how to get butter out of a dog's throat.

BROADBENT: Eh?

KEEGAN: You cannot build your golf links and hotels in the air. For that you must own our land. And how will you drag our acres from the ferret's grip of Matthew Haffigan? How will you persuade Cornelius Doyle to forgo the pride of being a small landowner? How will Barney Doran's millrace agree with your motor boats? Will Doolan help you to get a licence for your hotel?

BROADBENT: My dear sir: to all intents and purposes the syndicate I represent already owns half Rosscullen. Doolan's is a tied house; and the brewers are in the syndicate. As to Haffigan's farm and Doran's mill and Mr Doyle's place and half a dozen others, they will be mortgaged to me before a month is out.

KEEGAN: But pardon me, you will not lend them more on their land than the land is worth; so they will be able to pay you the interest.

BROADBENT: Ah, you are a poet, Mr Keegan, not a man of business.

LARRY: We will lend every one of these men half as much again on their land as it is worth, or ever can be worth, to them.

BROADBENT: You forget, sir, that we, with our capital, our knowledge, our organization, and may I say our English business habits, can make or lose ten pounds out of land that Haffigan, with all his industry, could not make or lose ten shillings out of. Doran's mill is a superannuated folly: I shall want it for electric lighting.

LARRY: What is the use of giving land to such men? They are too small, too poor, too ignorant, too simpleminded to hold it against us: you might as well give a dukedom to a crossing sweeper.

BROADBENT: Yes, Mr Keegan: this place may have an industrial future, or it may have a residential future: I can't tell yet; but it's not going to be a future in the hands of your Dorans and Haffigans, poor devils!

KEEGAN: It may have no future at all. Have you thought of that?

BROADBENT: Oh, I'm not afraid of that. I have faith in Ireland. Great faith, Mr Keegan.

KEEGAN: And we have none: only empty enthusiasms and patriotisms, and emptier memories and regrets. Ah yes: you have some excuse for believing that if there be any future, it will be yours; for our faith seems dead, and our hearts cold and cowed. An island of dreamers who wake up in your jails, of critics and cowards whom you buy and tame for your own service, of bold rogues who help you to plunder us that they may plunder you afterwards.

BROADBENT [*a little impatient of this unbusinesslike view*]: Yes, yes; but you know you might say that of any country. The fact is, there are only two qualities in the world: efficiency and inefficiency, and only two sorts of people: the efficient and the inefficient. It don't matter whether they're English or Irish. I shall collar this place, not because I'm an Englishman and Haffigan and Co are Irishmen, but because they're duffers, and I know my way about.

KEEGAN: Have you considered what is to become of Haffigan?

LARRY: Oh, we'll employ him in some capacity or other, and probably pay him more than he makes for himself now.

BROADBENT [*dubiously*]: Do you think so? No no: Haffigan's too old. It really doesn't pay now to take on men over forty even for unskilled labour, which I suppose is all Haffigan would be good for. No: Haffigan had better go to America, or into the Union,[31] poor old chap! He's worked out, you know: you can see it.

KEEGAN: Poor lost soul, so cunningly fenced in with invisible bars!

LARRY: Haffigan doesn't matter much. He'll die presently.

BROADBENT [*shocked*]: Oh come, Larry! Don't be unfeeling. It's hard on Haffigan. It's always hard on the inefficient.

LARRY: Pah! what does it matter where an old and broken man spends his last days, or whether he has a million at the bank or only the workhouse dole? It's the young men, the able men, that matter. The real tragedy of Haffigan is the tragedy of his wasted youth, his stunted mind, his drudging over his clods and pigs until he has become a clod and a pig himself — until the soul within him has smouldered into nothing but a dull temper that hurts himself and all around him. I say let him die, and let us have no more of his like. And let young Ireland take care that it doesn't share his fate, instead of making another empty grievance of it. Let your syndicate come —

BROADBENT: Your syndicate too, old chap. You have your bit of the stock.

LARRY: Yes: mine if you like. Well, our syndicate has no conscience: it has no more regard for your Haffigans and Doolans and Dorans than it has for a gang of Chinese coolies. It will use your patriotic blatherskite and balderdash to get parliamentary powers over you as cynically as it would bait a mousetrap with toasted cheese. It will plan, and organize, and find capital while you slave like bees for it and revenge yourselves by paying politicians and penny newspapers out of your small wages to write articles and report speeches against its wickedness and tyranny, and to crack up your own Irish heroism, just as Haffigan once paid a witch a penny to put a spell on Billy Byrne's cow. In the end it will grind the nonsense out of you, and grind strength and sense into you.

BROADBENT [*out of patience*]: Why can't you say a simple thing simply, Larry, without all that Irish exaggeration and talky-talky? The syndicate is a perfectly respectable body of responsible men of good position. We'll take Ireland in hand, and by straightforward business habits teach it efficiency and self-help on sound Liberal principles. You agree with me, Mr Keegan, don't you?

KEEGAN: Sir: I may even vote for you.

BROADBENT [*sincerely moved, shaking his hand warmly*]: You shall never regret it, Mr Keegan: I give you my word for that. I shall bring money here: I shall raise wages: I shall found public institutions: a library, a Polytechnic (undenominational, of course), a gymnasium, a cricket club, perhaps an art school. I shall make a Garden city of Rosscullen: the round tower shall be thoroughly repaired and restored.

KEEGAN: And our place of torment shall be as clean and orderly as the cleanest and most orderly place I know in Ireland, which is our poetically named Mountjoy prison.[32] Well, perhaps I had better vote for an efficient devil that knows his own mind and his own business than for a foolish patriot who has no mind and no business.

BROADBENT [*stiffly*]: Devil is rather a strong expression in that connexion, Mr Keegan.

KEEGAN: Not from a man who knows that this world is hell. But since the word offends you, let me soften it, and compare you simply to an ass. [*LARRY whitens with anger.*]

BROADBENT [*reddening*]: An ass!

KEEGAN [*gently*]: You may take it without offence from a madman who calls the ass his brother — and a very honest, useful and faithful brother too. The ass, sir, is the most efficient of beasts, matter-of-fact, hardy, friendly when you treat him as a fellow-creature, stubborn when you abuse him, ridiculous only in love, which sets him braying, and in politics, which move him to roll about in the public road and raise a dust about nothing. Can you deny these qualities and habits in yourself, sir?

BROADBENT [*goodhumouredly*]: Well, yes, I'm afraid I do, you know.

KEEGAN: Then perhaps you will confess to the ass's one fault.

BROADBENT: Perhaps so: what is it?

KEEGAN: That he wastes all his virtues — his efficiency, as you call it — in doing the will of his greedy masters instead of doing the will of Heaven that is in himself. He is efficient in the service of Mammon, mighty in mischief, skilful in ruin, heroic in destruction. But he comes to browse here without knowing that the soil his hoof touches is holy ground. Ireland, sir, for good or evil, is like no other place under heaven; and no man can touch its sod or breathe its air without becoming better or worse. It produces two kinds of men in strange perfection: saints and traitors. It is called the island of the saints; but indeed in these later years it might be more fitly called the island of the traitors; for our harvest of these is the fine flower of the world's crop of infamy. But the day may come when these islands shall live by the quality of their men rather than by the abundance of their minerals; and then we shall see.

LARRY: Mr Keegan: if you are going to be sentimental

about Ireland, I shall bid you good evening. We have had enough of that, and more than enough of cleverly proving that everybody who is not an Irishman is an ass. It is neither good sense nor good manners. It will not stop the syndicate; and it will not interest young Ireland so much as my friend's gospel of efficiency.

BROADBENT: Ah, yes, yes: efficiency is the thing. I don't in the least mind your chaff, Mr Keegan; but Larry's right on the main point. The world belongs to the efficient.

KEEGAN [*with polished irony*]: I stand rebuked, gentleman. But believe me, I do every justice to the efficiency of you and your syndicate. You are both, I am told, thoroughly efficient civil engineers; and I have no doubt the golf links will be a triumph of your art. Mr Broadbent will get into parliament most efficiently, which is more than St Patrick could do if he were alive now. You may even build the hotel efficiently if you can find enough efficient masons, carpenters, and plumbers, which I rather doubt. [*Dropping his irony, and beginning to fall into the attitude of the priest rebuking sin*] When the hotel becomes insolvent [BROADBENT *takes his cigar out of his mouth, a little taken aback*] your English business habits will secure the thorough efficiency of the liquidation. You will reorganize the scheme efficiently; you will liquidate its second bankruptcy efficiently [BROADBENT *and* LARRY *look quickly at one another; for this, unless the priest is an old financial hand, must be inspiration*]; you will get rid of its original shareholders efficiently after efficiently ruining them; and you will finally profit very efficiently by getting that hotel for a few shillings in the pound. [*More and more sternly*] Besides these efficient operations, you will foreclose your mortgages most efficiently [*his rebuking forefinger goes up in spite of himself*]; you will drive Haffigan to America very efficiently; you will find a use for Barney Doran's foul mouth and bullying temper by employing him to slave-drive your labourers very efficiently; and [*low and bitter*] when at last this poor desolate countryside becomes a busy mint in which we shall all slave to make money for you, with our Polytechnic to teach us how to do it efficiently, and our library to fuddle the few imaginations your distilleries will spare, and our repaired Round Tower with admission sixpence, and refreshments and penny-in-the-slot mutoscopes to make it interesting, then no doubt your English and American shareholders will spend all

the money we make for them very efficiently in shooting and hunting, in operations for cancer and appendicitis, in gluttony and gambling; and you will devote what they save to fresh land development schemes. For four wicked centuries the world has dreamed this foolish dream of efficiency; and the end is not yet. But the end will come.

BROADBENT [*seriously*]: Too true, Mr Keegan, only too true. And most eloquently put. It reminds me of poor Ruskin: a great man, you know. I sympathize. Believe me, I'm on your side. Don't sneer, Larry: I used to read a lot of Shelley years ago. Let us be faithful to the dreams of our youth [*he wafts a wreath of cigar smoke at large across the hill*].

KEEGAN: Come, Mr Doyle! is this English sentiment so much more efficient than our Irish sentiment, after all? Mr Broadbent spends his life inefficiently admiring the thoughts of great men, and efficiently serving the cupidity of base money hunters. We spend our lives efficiently sneering at him and doing nothing. Which of us has any right to reproach the other?

BROADBENT [*coming down the hill again to* KEEGAN's *right hand*]: But you know, something must be done.

KEEGAN: Yes: when we cease to do, we cease to live. Well, what shall we do?

BROADBENT: Why, what lies to our hand.

KEEGAN: Which is the making of golf links and hotels to bring idlers to a country which workers have left in millions because it is a hungry land, a naked land, an ignorant and oppressed land.

BROADBENT: But, hang it all, the idlers will bring money from England to Ireland!

KEEGAN: Just as our idlers have for so many generations taken money from Ireland to England. Has that saved England from poverty and degradation more horrible than we have ever dreamed of? When I went to England, sir, I hated England. Now I pity it. [BROADBENT *can hardly conceive an Irishman pitying England; but as* LARRY *intervenes angrily, he gives it up and takes to the hill and his cigar again.*]

LARRY: Much good your pity will do it!

KEEGAN: In the accounts kept in heaven, Mr Doyle, a heart purified of hatred may be worth more than even a Land Development Syndicate of Anglicized Irishmen and Gladstonized Englishmen.

LARRY: Oh, in heaven, no doubt. I have never been there. Can you tell me where it is?

KEEGAN: Could you have told me this morning where hell is? Yet you know now that it is here. Do not despair of finding heaven: it may be no farther off.

LARRY [*ironically*]: On this holy ground, as you call it, eh?

KEEGAN [*with fierce intensity*]: Yes, perhaps, even on this holy ground which such Irishmen as you have turned into a Land of Derision.

BROADBENT [*coming between them*]: Take care! you will be quarrelling presently. Oh, you Irishmen, you Irishmen! Toujours Ballyhooly, eh? [LARRY, *with a shrug, half comic, half impatient, turns away up the hill, but presently strolls back on* KEEGAN's *right.* BROADBENT *adds, confidentially to* KEEGAN] Stick to the Englishman, Mr Keegan: he has a bad name here; but at least he can forgive you for being an Irishman.

KEEGAN: Sir: when you speak to me of English and Irish you forget that I am a Catholic. My country is not Ireland nor England, but the whole mighty realm of my Church. For me there are but two countries: heaven and hell; but two conditions of men: salvation and damnation. Standing here between you the Englishman, so clever in your foolishness, and this Irishman, so foolish in his cleverness, I cannot in my ignorance be sure which of you is the more deeply damned; but I should be unfaithful to my calling if I opened the gates of my heart less widely to one than to the other.

LARRY: In either case it would be an impertinence, Mr Keegan, as your approval is not of the slightest consequence to us. What use do you suppose all this drivel is to men with serious practical business in hand?

BROADBENT: I don't agree with that, Larry. I think these things cannot be said too often: they keep up the moral tone of the community. As you know, I claim the right to think for myself in religious matters: in fact, I am ready to avow myself a bit of a — of a — well, I don't care who knows it — a bit of a Unitarian; but if the Church of England contained a few men like Mr Keegan, I should certainly join it.

KEEGAN: You do me too much honour, sir. [*With priestly humility to* LARRY] Mr Doyle: I am to blame for having unintentionally set your mind somewhat on edge against me. I beg your pardon.

LARRY [*unimpressed and hostile*]: I didn't stand on ceremony with you: you needn't stand on it with me. Fine manners and fine words are cheap in Ireland: you can keep both for my friend here, who is still imposed on by them. *I* know their value.

KEEGAN: You mean you don't know their value.

LARRY [*angrily*]: I mean what I say.

KEEGAN [*turning quietly to the Englishman*]: You see, Mr Broadbent, I only make the hearts of my countrymen harder when I preach to them: the gates of hell still prevail against me. I shall wish you good evening. I am better alone, at the Round Tower, dreaming of heaven. [*He goes up the hill.*]

LARRY: Aye, that's it! there you are! dreaming! dreaming! dreaming! dreaming!

KEEGAN [*halting and turning to them for the last time*]: Every dream is a prophecy: every jest is an earnest in the womb of Time.

BROADBENT [*reflectively*]: Once, when I was a small kid, I dreamt I was in heaven. [*They both stare at him.*] It was a sort of pale blue satin place, with all the pious old ladies in our congregation sitting as if they were at a service; and there was some awful person in the study at the other side of the hall. I didn't enjoy it, you know. What is it like in your dreams?

KEEGAN: In my dreams it is a country where the State is the Church and the Church the people: three in one and one in three. It is a commonwealth in which work is play and play is life: three in one and one in three. It is a temple in which the priest is the worshipper and the worshipper the worshipped: three in one and one in three. It is a godhead in which all life is human and all humanity divine: three in one and one in three. It is, in short, the dream of a madman. [*He goes away across the hill.*]

BROADBENT [*looking after him affectionately*]: What a regular old Church and State Tory he is! He's a character: he'll be an attraction here. Really almost equal to Ruskin and Carlyle.

LARRY: Yes; and much good they did with all their talk!

BROADBENT: Oh tut, tut, Larry! They improved my mind: they raised my tone enormously. I feel sincerely obliged to Keegan: he has made me feel a better man: distinctly better. [*With sincere elevation*] I feel now as I never did before that I am right in devoting my life to the cause of Ireland. Come along and help me to choose the site for the hotel.

---

1   Gladstone was leader of the Liberal Party and Prime Minister, responsible for two Home Rule Bills in 1886 and 1893, both of which were defeated. Not to be confused with the Gladstone bag mentioned below. Arthur Balfour (1848–1930), a Conservative politician,

was Chief Secretary for Ireland from 1887 until 1891 and became Prime Minister in 1902. Joseph Chamberlain (1836–1914) resigned from the Liberal Party in 1886 in opposition to Home Rule Bill (hence telling image of fox).

2   A supporter of decisions to be taken by local community (an odd phrase but in keeping with Broadbent's character).

3   An anti-Semitic comment from 'a lover of liberty'.

4   The Boer War ended in 1902 with defeat for the Boers.

5   Garden Cities such as Letchworth (near Hitchin) in Hertfordshire combined green spaces with careful planning of housing and industrial development to enhance a sense of community. No pubs were allowed within the town centre. Ebenezer Howard (1850–1928), one of the founders of this movement, was author of *Tomorrow: A Peaceful Path to Real Reform* (1898), later reissued as *Garden Cities of Tomorrow* (1902).

6   The successor to the Land League after 1882, dominated by the Irish Parliamentary Party.

7   Port in west Wales.

8   Silence; be quiet.

9   The west of Ireland and a respectable Dublin suburb on the south side of the river.

10 Shaw has in his sights not only the contemporary Celtic Revival but also the nineteenth-century stream which fed it with its discourse about the 'Celt' and melancholy and 'the delicious sadness of its national melodies' and how English poetry got its 'turn for melancholy' from its 'Celtic source', and so on. See for example 'The Poetry of the Celtic Races' (1859) by the French critic Ernest Renan (1823–92) or Matthew Arnold's *On the Study of Celtic Literature* (1867).

11 The Poor Old Woman (image of Ireland) beckoning her sons to join the 1798 Rising (the subject of Yeats's *Cathleen ni Houlihan*).

12 In Dublin. Before the Act of Union in 1801 an Irish Parliament met in the building now owned by the Bank of Ireland opposite Trinity College.

13 Round towers, with their door some distance above the ground, their distinctive belfry and conical stone roof, are found all over Ireland. Built in the tenth-twelfth centuries, they came to symbolize Gaelic civilization and romantic Ireland. The cover of Eglinton's *Bards and Saints* and Ryan's *Criticism and Courage* (published in a series entitled Tower Press Booklets) shows a ruined round tower with ivy growing up its wall (see my *James Joyce's Ireland*).

14 Maynooth College, established in 1795 for the training of Irish priests, had the reputation of being the centre of power in Ireland. Keegan was educated abroad, outside the regime of orthodoxy imposed by Maynooth.

15 See footnote 1 on page 74.

16 John Tyndall (1820–93) was professor of natural philosophy at the Royal Institution, succeeding Michael Faraday in 1853. He helped explain science for the layman.

17 Irish for fool.

18 After the Land War of 1879–82 successive British Governments, seeing that there was no role for Irish landlordism and that land and politics needed a wedge between them, passed legislation transferring land to tenant farmers. The most famous was the Wyndham Act of 1903. In time radicalism all but disappeared from the Irish countryside.

19 Seat of British Rule in Ireland until 1921.

20 In the East End of London.

21 Fooster is hurry, fluster, great fuss (P.W. Joyce).

22 Unrest over tithes being paid to Church of Ireland came to a head in the 1830s and led to the Tithe Rent-charge Act of 1838, which converted tithe into rent. The Church of Ireland was disestablished in 1869.

23 Protestant mercenary soldier.

24 Oliver Cromwell (1599–1658) brutally crushed the Irish Catholic forces in a short campaign in 1649–50 and, with the words 'To hell or Connacht', banished Catholics to Connacht giving their land to his soldiers.

25 A mild form of bad luck to you.

26 A pig's foot.

27 The Gordon Bennett, named after an American sportsman, was an international motor car race established in 1900.

28 'Let Erin Remember the Days of Old', Thomas Moore's melody on the theme of betrayal. It includes the phrase 'the round towers of other days'. Shaw deliberately mixes words and music by Offenbach and Moore to disturb the conventional associations.

29 Irish for pulse. Cushlamochree: pulse of my heart, a common form of endearment in songs.

30 One of Thomas Moore's melodies. Fionnula, one of Lir's daughters, is transformed into a swan and condemned to wander over the rivers and lakes until Ireland's conversion to Christianity.

31 The workhouse.

32 In Dublin.

EVA GORE-BOOTH

from Eva Gore-Booth, *The Egyptian Pillar* (1906)

Emphasis on the Celtic twilight tends to obscure poems on social issues, but here is a poem by Eva Gore-Booth on a subject insufficiently addressed in modern Irish writing. Women are linked with the countryside and with nature, men with the city and the office.

WOMEN'S RIGHTS

Down by Glencar Waterfall[1]
There's no winter left at all.

Every little flower that blows
Cold and darkness overthrows.

Every little thrush that sings
Quells the wild air with brave wings.

Every little stream that runs
Holds the light of brighter suns.

But where men in office sit
Winter holds the human wit.

In the dark and dreary town
Summer's green is trampled down.

Frozen, frozen everywhere
Are the springs of thought and prayer.

Rise with us and let us go
To where the living waters flow.

Oh, whatever men may say
Ours is the wide and open way.

Oh, whatever men may dream
We have the blue air and the stream.

Men have got their towers and walls,
We have cliffs and waterfalls.

Oh, whatever men may do
Ours is the gold air and the blue.

Men have got their pomp and pride —
All the green world is on our side.

1   Near Sligo, a favourite haunt of Yeats as a boy, as his
    poem 'The Stolen Child' suggests.

J. M. SYNGE
The Playboy of the Western World (1907)

'In a good play every speech should be as fully flavoured as a nut or apple . . . In Ireland, for a few years more, we have a popular imagination that is fiery, and magnificent, and tender.' In his Preface to this play Synge focuses on his intimacy with the language and imagination of the country people, how he would listen through a chink in the floor to the talk of servant girls in the kitchen. At the time he was accused of falsely representing the country people (see Hone (1912) below for an account of the *Playboy* riots), but today audiences around the world respond to its authentic vision of a world on the point of disappearance. For a fictional account of an early (unsqueamish) production of the play, see Conal O'Riordan, *Adam of Dublin* (1920), reproduced below. The play was transferred to the big screen in 1962 by Brian Desmond Hurst.

PERSONS IN THE PLAY

CHRISTOPHER MAHON
OLD MAHON, his father, a squatter[1]
MICHAEL JAMES FLAHERTY [called MICHAEL JAMES], a
    publican
MARGARET FLAHERTY [called PEGEEN MIKE], his daughter
WIDOW QUIN, a woman of about thirty
SHAWN KEOGH, her cousin, a young farmer

PHILLY CULLEN and JIMMY FARRELL, small farmers
SARA TANSEY, SUSAN BRADY and HONOR BLAKE, village
    girls
A BELLMAN
SOME PEASANTS

*The action takes place near a village, on a wild coast of
Mayo. The first Act passes on an evening of autumn, the
other two Acts on the following day*

ACT I

Country public house or shebeen, very rough and untidy. There is a sort of counter on the right with shelves, holding many bottles and jugs, just seen above it. Empty barrels stand near the counter. At back, a little to left of counter, there is a door into the open air, then, more to the left, there is a settle with shelves above it, with more jugs, and a table beneath a window. At the left there is a large open fireplace, with turf fire, and a small door into inner room. PEGEEN, a wild-looking but fine girl, of about twenty, is writing at table. She is dressed in the usual peasant dress.

PEGEEN [*slowly as she writes*]: Six yards of stuff for to make a yellow gown. A pair of lace boots with lengthy heels on them and brassy eyes. A hat is suited for a wedding day. A fine-tooth comb. To be sent with three barrels of porter in Jimmy Farrell's creel[2] cart on the evening of the coming Fair to Mister Michael James Flaherty. With the best compliments of this season. Margaret Flaherty.

SHAWN KEOGH [*A fat and fair young man comes in as she signs, looks around awkwardly, when he sees she is alone*]: Where's himself?

PEGEEN [*without looking at him*]: He's coming. [*She directs letter*] To Mister Sheamus Mulroy, Wine and Spirit Dealer, Castlebar.

SHAWN [*uneasily*]: I didn't see him on the road.

PEGEEN: How would you see him [*licks stamp and puts it on letter*] and it dark night this half-hour gone by?

SHAWN [*turning towards door again*]: I stood a while outside wondering would I have a right to pass on or to walk in and see you, Pegeen Mike [*comes to fire*], and I could hear the cows breathing and sighing in the stillness of the air, and not a step moving any place from this gate to the bridge.

PEGEEN [*putting letter in envelope*]: It's above at the crossroads he is, meeting Philly Cullen and a couple more are going along with him to Kate Cassidy's wake.

SHAWN [*looking at her blankly*]: And he's going that length in the dark night.

PEGEEN [*impatiently*]: He is surely, and leaving me lonesome on the scruff of the hill. [*She gets up and puts envelope on dresser, then winds clock.*] Isn't it long the nights are now, Shawn Keogh, to be leaving a poor girl with her own self counting the hours to the dawn of day?

SHAWN [*with awkward humour*]: If it is, when we're wedded in a short while you'll have no call to complain, for I've little will to be walking off to wakes or weddings in the darkness of the night.

PEGEEN [*with rather scornful good humour*]: You're making mighty certain, Shaneen, that I'll wed you now.

SHAWN: Aren't we after making a good bargain, the way we're only waiting these days on Father Reilly's dispensation from the bishops, or the Court of Rome.

PEGEEN [*looking at him teasingly, washing up at dresser*]: It's a wonder, Shaneen, the Holy Father'd be taking notice of the likes of you; for if I was him I wouldn't bother with this place where you'll meet none but Red Linahan, has a squint in his eye, and Patcheen is lame in his heel, or the mad Mulrannies were driven from California and they lost in their wits. We're a queer lot these times to go troubling the Holy Father on his sacred seat.

SHAWN [*scandalized*]: If we are, we're as good this place as another, maybe, and as good these times as we were for ever.

PEGEEN [*with scorn*]: As good it is? Where now will you meet the like of Daneen Sullivan knocked the eye from a peeler;[3] or Marcus Quin, God rest him, got six months for maiming ewes, and he a great warrant to tell stories of holy Ireland till he'd have the old women shedding down tears about their feet. Where will you find the like of them, I'm saying?

SHAWN [*timidly*]: If you don't, it's a good job, maybe; for [*with peculiar emphasis on the words*] Father Reilly has small conceit to have that kind walking around and talking to the girls.

PEGEEN [*impatiently throwing water from basin out of the door*]: Stop tormenting me with Father Reilly [*imitating his voice*] when I'm asking only what way I'll pass these twelve hours of dark, and not take my death with the fear [*looking out of door*].

SHAWN [*timidly*]: Would I fetch you the Widow Quin, maybe?

PEGEEN: Is it the like of that murderer? You'll not, surely.

SHAWN [*going to her, soothingly*]: Then I'm thinking himself will stop along with you when he sees you taking on; for it'll be a long night-time with great darkness, and I'm after feeling a kind of fellow above in the furzy ditch, groaning wicked like a maddening dog, the way it's good cause you have, maybe, to be fearing now.

PEGEEN [*turning on him sharply*]: What's that? Is it a man you seen?

SHAWN [*retreating*]: I couldn't see him at all; but I heard him groaning out, and breaking his heart. It should have been a young man from his words speaking.

PEGEEN [*going after him*]: And you never went near to see was he hurted or what ailed him at all?

SHAWN: I did not, Pegeen Mike. It was a dark, lonesome place to be hearing the like of him.

PEGEEN: Well, you're a daring fellow, and if they find his corpse stretched above in the dews of dawn, what'll you say then to the peelers, or the Justice of the Peace?

SHAWN [*thunderstruck*]: I wasn't thinking of that. For the love of God, Pegeen Mike, don't let on I was speaking of him. Don't tell your father and the men is coming above; for if they heard that story they'd have great blabbing this night at the wake.

PEGEEN: I'll maybe tell them, and I'll maybe not.

SHAWN: They are coming at the door. Will you whisht, I'm saying?

PEGEEN: Whisht yourself.

She goes behind counter. MICHAEL JAMES, *fat, jovial publican, comes in followed by* PHILLY CULLEN, *who is thin and mistrusting, and* JIMMY FARRELL, *who is fat and amorous, about forty-five.*

MEN [*together*]: God bless you! The blessing of God on this place!

PEGEEN: God bless you kindly.

MICHAEL [*to men, who go to the counter*]: Sit down now, and take your rest. [*Crosses to* SHAWN *at the fire.*] And how is it you are, Shawn Keogh? Are you coming over the sands to Kate Cassidy's wake?

SHAWN: I am not, Michael James. I'm going home the short cut to my bed.

PEGEEN [*speaking across the counter*]: He's right, too, and have you no shame, Michael James, to be quitting off for the whole night, and leaving myself lonesome in the shop?

MICHAEL [*good-humouredly*]: Isn't it the same whether I go for the whole night or a part only? And I'm thinking it's a queer daughter you are if you'd have me crossing backward through the Stooks of the Dead Women, with a drop taken.

PEGEEN: If I am a queer daughter, it's a queer father'd be leaving me lonesome these twelve hours of dark, and I piling the turf with the dogs barking, and the calves mooing, and my own teeth rattling with the fear.

JIMMY [*flatteringly*]: What is there to hurt you, and you a fine, hardy girl would knock the heads of any two men in the place?

PEGEEN [*working herself up*]: Isn't there the harvest boys with their tongues red for drink, and the ten tinkers is camped in the east glen, and the thousand militia — bad cess to them! — walking idle through the land. There's lots surely to hurt me, and I won't stop alone in it, let himself do what he will.

MICHAEL: If you're that afeard, let Shawn Keogh stop along with you. It's the will of God, I'm thinking, himself should be seeing to you now. [*They all turn on* SHAWN.]

SHAWN [*in horrified confusion*]: I would and welcome, Michael James, but I'm afeard of Father Reilly; and what at all would the Holy Father and the Cardinals of Rome be saying if they heard I did the like of that?

MICHAEL [*with contempt*]: God help you! Can't you sit in by the hearth with the light lit and herself beyond in the room? You'll do that surely, for I've heard tell there's a queer fellow above, going mad or getting his death, maybe, in the gripe of the ditch, so she'd be safer this night with a person here.

SHAWN [*with plaintive despair*]: I'm afeard of Father Reilly, I'm saying. Let you not be tempting me, and we near married itself.

PHILLY [*with cold contempt*]: Lock him in the west room. He'll stay then and have no sin to be telling to the priest.

MICHAEL [*to* SHAWN, *getting between him and the door*]: Go up, now.

SHAWN [*at the top of his voice*]: Don't stop me, Michael James. Let me out of the door, I'm saying, for the love of the Almighty God. Let me out. [*Trying to dodge past him.*] Let me out of it, and may God grant you His indulgence in the hour of need.

MICHAEL [*loudly*]: Stop your noising, and sit down by the hearth. [*Gives him a push and goes to counter laughing.*]

SHAWN [*turning back, wringing his hands*]: Oh, Father Reilly, and the saints of God, where will I hide myself today? Oh, St Joseph and St Patrick and St Brigid and St James, have mercy on me now!

SHAWN *turns round, sees door clear, and makes a rush for it.*

MICHAEL [*catching him by the coat-tail*]: You'd be going, is it?

SHAWN [*screaming*]: Leave me go, Michael James, leave me go, you old Pagan, leave me go, or I'll get the curse of the priests on you, and of the scarlet-coated bishops of the Courts of Rome.

With a sudden movement he pulls himself out of his coat, and disappears out of the door, leaving his coat in MICHAEL's *hands.*

MICHAEL [*turning round, and holding up coat*]: Well, there's the coat of a Christian man. Oh, there's sainted glory this day in the lonesome west; and by the will of God I've got you a decent man, Pegeen, you'll have no call to be spying after if you've a score of young girls, maybe, weeding in your fields.

PEGEEN [*taking up the defence of her property*]: What right have you to be making game of a poor fellow for minding the priest, when it's your own the fault is, not paying a penny pot-boy to stand along with me and give me courage in the doing of my work.

She snaps the coat away from him, and goes behind counter with it.

MICHAEL [*taken aback*]: Where would I get a pot-boy? Would you have me send the bell-man[4] screaming in the streets of Castlebar?

SHAWN [*opening the door a chink and putting in his head, in a small voice*]: Michael James!

MICHAEL [*imitating him*]: What ails you?

SHAWN: The queer dying fellow's beyond looking over the ditch. He's come up, I'm thinking, stealing your hens. [*Looks over his shoulder*] God help me, he's following me now [*he runs into room*], and if he's heard what I said, he'll be having my life, and I going home lonesome in the darkness of the night.

For a perceptible moment they watch the door with curiosity. Someone coughs outside. Then CHRISTY MAHON, *a slight young man, comes in very tired and frightened and dirty.*

CHRISTY [*in a small voice*]: God save all here!

MEN: God save you kindly!

CHRISTY [*going to the counter*]: I'd trouble you for a glass of porter, woman of the house. [*He puts down coin.*]

PEGEEN [*serving him*]: You're one of the tinkers, young fellow, is beyond camped in the glen?

CHRISTY: I am not; but I'm destroyed walking.

MICHAEL [*patronizingly*]: Let you come up then to the fire. You're looking famished[5] with the cold.

CHRISTY: God reward you. [*He takes up his glass and goes a little way across to the left, then stops and looks about him.*] Is it often the polis do be coming into this place, master of the house?

MICHAEL: If you'd come in better hours, you'd have seen 'Licensed for the Sale of Beer and Spirits, to be Consumed on the Premises', written in white letters above the door, and what would the polis want spying on me, and not a decent house within four miles, the way every living Christian is a bona fide,[6] saving one widow alone?

CHRISTY [*with relief*]: It's a safe house, so.

He goes over to the fire, sighing and moaning. Then he sits down, putting his glass beside him, and begins gnawing a turnip, too miserable to feel the others staring at him with curiosity.

MICHAEL [*going after him*]: Is it yourself is fearing the polis? You're wanting, maybe?

CHRISTY: There's many wanting.

MICHAEL: Many, surely, with the broken harvest and the ended wars. [*He picks up some stockings, etc., that are near the fire, and carries them away furtively.*] It should be larceny, I'm thinking?

CHRISTY [*dolefully*]: I had it in my mind it was a different word and a bigger.

PEGEEN: There's a queer lad. Were you never slapped in school, young fellow, that you don't know the name of your deed?

CHRISTY [*bashfully*]: I'm slow at learning, a middling scholar only.

MICHAEL: If you're a dunce itself, you'd have a right to know that larceny's robbing and stealing. Is it for the like of that you're wanting?

CHRISTY [*with a flash of family pride*]: And I the son of a strong farmer [*with a sudden qualm*], God rest his soul, could have bought up the whole of your old house a while since, from the butt of his tail-pocket, and not have missed the weight of it gone.

MICHAEL [*impressed*]: If it's not stealing, it's maybe something big.

CHRISTY [*flattered*]: Aye; it's maybe something big.

JIMMY: He's a wicked-looking young fellow. Maybe he followed after a young woman on a lonesome night.

CHRISTY [*shocked*]: Oh, the saints forbid, mister; I was all times a decent lad.

PHILLY [*turning on* JIMMY]: You're a silly man, Jimmy Farrell. He said his father was a farmer a while since, and there's himself now in a poor state. Maybe the land was grabbed from him, and he did what any decent man would do.

MICHAEL [*to* CHRISTY, *mysteriously*]: Was it bailiffs?

CHRISTY: The divil a one.

MICHAEL: Agents?

CHRISTY: The divil a one.

MICHAEL: Landlords?

CHRISTY [*peevishly*]: Ah, not at all, I'm saying. You'd see the like of them stories on any little paper of a Munster town. But I'm not calling to mind any person, gentle, simple, judge or jury, did the like of me.

They all draw nearer with delighted curiosity.

PHILLY: Well, that lad's a puzzle-the-world.

JIMMY: He'd beat Dan Davies's circus, or the holy missioners making sermons on the villainy of man. Try him again, Philly.

PHILLY: Did you strike golden guineas out of solder, young fellow, or shilling coins itself?

CHRISTY: I did not, mister, not sixpence nor a farthing coin.

JIMMY: Did you marry three wives maybe? I'm told there's a sprinkling have done that among the holy Luthers of the preaching north.

CHRISTY [*shyly*]: I never married with one, let alone with a couple or three.

PHILLY: Maybe he went fighting for the Boers, the like of the man beyond, was judged to be hanged, quartered, and drawn. Were you off east, young fellow, fighting bloody wars for Kruger and the freedom of the Boers?

CHRISTY: I never left my own parish till Tuesday was a week.

PEGEEN [*coming from counter*]: He's done nothing, so. [*To* CHRISTY] If you didn't commit murder or a bad, nasty thing; or false coining, or robbery, or butchery, or the like of them, there isn't anything that would be worth your troubling for to run from now. You did nothing at all.

CHRISTY [*his feelings hurt*]: That's an unkindly thing to be saying to a poor orphaned traveller, has a prison behind him, and hanging before, and hell's gap gaping below.

PEGEEN [*with a sign to the men to be quiet*]: You're only saying it. You did nothing at all. A soft lad the like of you wouldn't slit the wind pipe of a screeching sow.

CHRISTY [*offended*]: You're not speaking the truth.

PEGEEN [*in mock rage*]: Not speaking the truth, is it? Would you have me knock the head of you with the butt of the broom?

CHRISTY [*twisting round on her with a sharp cry of horror*]: Don't strike me. I killed my poor father, Tuesday was a week, for doing the like of that.

PEGEEN [*with blank amazement*]: Is it killed your father?

CHRISTY [*subsiding*]: With the help of God I did, surely, and that the Holy Immaculate Mother may intercede for his soul.

PHILLY [*retreating with* JIMMY]: There's a daring fellow.

JIMMY: Oh, glory be to God!

MICHAEL [*with great respect*]: That was a hanging crime, mister honey. You should have had good reason for doing the like of that.

CHRISTY [*in a very reasonable tone*]: He was a dirty man, God forgive him, and he getting old and crusty, the way I couldn't put up with him at all.

PEGEEN: And you shot him dead?

CHRISTY [*shaking his head*]: I never used weapons. I've no licence, and I'm a law-fearing man.

MICHAEL: It was with a hilted knife maybe? I'm told, in the big world, it's bloody knives they use.

CHRISTY [*loudly, scandalized*]: Do you take me for a slaughter-boy?

PEGEEN: You never hanged him, the way Jimmy Farrell hanged his dog from the licence, and had it screeching and wriggling three hours at the butt of a string, and himself swearing it was a dead dog, and the peelers swearing it had life?

CHRISTY: I did not, then. I just riz the loy[7] and let fall the edge of it on the ridge of his skull, and he went down at my feet like an empty sack, and never let a grunt or groan from him at all.

MICHAEL [*making a sign to* PEGEEN *to fill* CHRISTY'S *glass*]: And what way weren't you hanged, mister? Did you bury him then?

CHRISTY [*considering*]: Aye. I buried him then. Wasn't I digging spuds in the field?

MICHAEL: And the peelers never followed after you the eleven days that you're out?

CHRISTY [*shaking his head*]: Never a one of them, and I walking forward facing hog, dog, or divil on the highway of the road.

PHILLY [*nodding wisely*]: It's only with a common weekday kind of murderer them lads would be trusting their carcass, and that man should be a great terror when his temper's roused.

MICHAEL: He should then. [*To* CHRISTY] And where was it, mister honey, that you did the deed?

CHRISTY [*looking at him with suspicion*]: Oh, a distant place, master of the house, a windy corner of high, distant hills.

PHILLY [*nodding with approval*]: He's a close man, and he's right, surely.

PEGEEN: That'd be a lad with the sense of Solomon to have for a pot-boy, Michael James, if it's the truth you're seeking one at all.

PHILLY: The peelers is fearing him, and if you'd that lad in the house there isn't one of them would come smelling around if the dogs itself were lapping poteen from the dung-pit of the yard.

JIMMY: Bravery's a treasure in a lonesome place, and a lad would kill his father, I'm thinking, would face a foxy divil with a pitchpike on the flags of hell.

PEGEEN: It's the truth they're saying, and if I'd that lad in the house, I wouldn't be fearing the loosèd khaki cut-throats, or the walking dead.

CHRISTY [*swelling with surprise and triumph*]: Well, glory be to God!

MICHAEL [*with deference*]: Would you think well to stop here and be pot-boy, mister honey, if we gave you good wages, and didn't destroy you with the weight of work?

SHAWN [*coming forward uneasily*]: That'd be a queer kind to bring into a decent, quiet household with the like of Pegeen Mike.

PEGEEN [*very sharply*]: Will you whisht? Who's speaking to you?

SHAWN [*retreating*]: A bloody-handed murderer the like of . . .

PEGEEN [*snapping at him*]: Whisht, I am saying; we'll take no fooling from your like at all. [*To* CHRISTY, *with a honeyed voice*] And you, young fellow, you'd have a right to stop, I'm thinking, for we'd do our all and utmost to content your needs.

CHRISTY [*overcome with wonder*]: And I'd be safe this place from the searching law?

MICHAEL: You would, surely. If they're not fearing you, itself, the peelers in this place is decent, drouthy poor fellows, wouldn't touch a cur dog and not give warning in the dead of night.

PEGEEN [*very kindly and persuasively*]: Let you stop a short while anyhow. Aren't you destroyed by walking with your feet in bleeding blisters, and your whole skin needing washing like a Wicklow sheep.

CHRISTY [*looking round with satisfaction*]: It's a nice room, and if it's not humbugging me you are, I'm thinking that I'll surely stay.

JIMMY [*jumps up*]: Now, by the grace of God, herself will be safe this night, with a man killed his father holding danger from the door, and let you come on, Michael James, or they'll have the best stuff drunk at the wake.

MICHAEL [*going to the door with men*]: And begging your pardon, mister, what name will we call you, for we'd like to know?

CHRISTY: Christopher Mahon.

MICHAEL: Well, God bless you, Christy, and a good rest till we meet again when the sun'll be rising to the noon of the day.

CHRISTY: God bless you all.

MEN: God bless you.

They go out, except SHAWN, who lingers at the door.

SHAWN [*to* PEGEEN]: Are you wanting me to stop along with you and keep you from harm?

PEGEEN [*gruffly*]: Didn't you say you were fearing Father Reilly?

SHAWN: There'd be no harm staying now, I'm thinking, and himself in it too.

PEGEEN: You wouldn't stay when there was need for you, and let you step off nimble this time when there's none.

SHAWN: Didn't I say it was Father Reilly . . .

PEGEEN: Go on, then, to Father Reilly [*in a jeering tone*], and let him put you in the holy brotherhoods, and leave that lad to me.

SHAWN: If I meet the Widow Quin . . .

PEGEEN: Go on, I'm saying, and don't be waking this place with your noise. [*She hustles him out and bolts door.*] That lad would wear the spirits from the saints of peace. [*Bustles about, then takes off her apron and pins it up in the window as a blind,* CHRISTY *watching her timidly. Then she comes to him and speaks with bland good humour.*] Let you stretch out now by the fire, young fellow. You should be destroyed travelling.

CHRISTY [*shyly again, drawing off his boots*]: I'm tired surely, walking wild eleven days, and waking fearful in the night.

He holds up one of his feet, feeling his blisters, and looking at them with compassion.

PEGEEN [*standing beside him, watching him with delight*]: You should have had great people in your family, I'm thinking, with the little, small feet you have, and you with a kind of a quality name, the like of what you'd find on the great powers and potentates of France and Spain.

CHRISTY [*with pride*]: We were great, surely, with wide and windy acres of rich Munster land.

PEGEEN: Wasn't I telling you, and you a fine, handsome young fellow with a noble brow?

CHRISTY [*with a flush of delighted surprise*]: Is it me?

PEGEEN: Aye. Did you never hear that from the young girls where you come from in the west or south?

CHRISTY [*with venom*]: I did not, then. Oh, they're bloody liars in the naked parish where I grew a man.

PEGEEN: If they are itself, you've heard it these days, I'm thinking, and you walking the world telling out your story to young girls or old.

CHRISTY: I've told my story no place till this night, Pegeen Mike, and it's foolish I was here, maybe, to be talking free; but you're decent people, I'm thinking, and yourself a kindly woman, the way I wasn't fearing you at all.

PEGEEN [*filling a sack with straw*]: You've said the like of that, maybe, in every cot and cabin where you've met a young girl on your way.

CHRISTY [*going over to her, gradually raising his voice*]: I've said it nowhere till this night, I'm telling you; for I've seen none the like of you the eleven long days I am walking the world, looking over a low ditch or a high ditch on my north or south, into stony, scattered fields, or scribes of bog, where you'd see young, limber girls, and fine, prancing women making laughter with the men.

PEGEEN: If you weren't destroyed travelling, you'd have as much talk and streeleen, I'm thinking, as Owen Roe O'Sullivan[8] or the poets of the Dingle Bay; and I've heard all times it's the poets are your like — fine, fiery fellows with great rages when their temper's roused.

CHRISTY [*drawing a little nearer to her*]: You've a power

of rings, God bless you, and would there be any offence if I was asking are you single now?

PEGEEN: What would I want wedding so young?

CHRISTY [*with relief*]: We're alike so.

PEGEEN [*she puts sack on settle and beats it up*]: I never killed my father. I'd be afeared to do that, except I was the like of yourself with blind rages tearing me within, for I'm thinking you should have had great tussling when the end was come.

CHRISTY [*expanding with delight at the first confidential talk he has ever had with a woman*]: We had not then. It was a hard woman was come over the hill; and if he was always a crusty kind, when he'd a hard woman setting him on, not the divil himself or his four fathers could put up with him at all.

PEGEEN [*with curiosity*]: And isn't it a great wonder that one wasn't fearing you?

CHRISTY [*very confidentially*]: Up to the day I killed my father, there wasn't a person in Ireland knew the kind I was, and I there drinking, waking, eating, sleeping, a quiet, simple poor fellow with no man giving me heed.

PEGEEN [*getting a quilt out of cupboard and putting it on the sack*]: It was the girls were giving you heed, maybe, and I'm thinking it's most conceit you'd have to be gaming with their like.

CHRISTY [*shaking his head with simplicity*]: Not the girls itself, and I won't tell you a lie. There wasn't any one heeding me in that place saving only the dumb beasts of the field.

He sits down at fire.

PEGEEN [*with disappointment*]: And I thinking you should have been living the like of a king of Norway or the eastern world.

She comes and sits beside him after placing bread and mug of milk on the table.

CHRISTY [*laughing piteously*]: The like of a king, is it? And I after toiling, moiling, digging, dodging from the dawn till dusk; with never a sight of joy or sport saving only when I'd be abroad in the dark night poaching rabbits on hills, for I was a divil to poach, God forgive me [*very naïvely*], and I near got six months for going with a dung fork and stabbing a fish.

PEGEEN: And it's that you'd call sport, is it, to be abroad in the darkness with yourself alone?

CHRISTY: I did, God help me, and there I'd be as happy as the sunshine of St Martin's Day,[9] watching the light passing the north or the patches of fog, till I'd hear a rabbit starting to screech and I'd go running in the furze. Then, when I'd my full share, I'd come walking down

where you'd see the ducks and geese stretched sleeping on the highway of the road, and before I'd pass the dunghill, I'd hear himself snoring out — a loud, lonesome snore he'd be making all times, the while he was sleeping; and he a man'd be raging all times, the while he was waking, like a gaudy officer you'd hear cursing and damning and swearing oaths.

PEGEEN: Providence and Mercy, spare us all!

CHRISTY: It's that you'd say surely if you seen him and he after drinking for weeks, rising up in the red dawn, or before it maybe, and going out into the yard as naked as an ash-tree in the moon of May, and shying clods against the visage of the stars till he'd put the fear of death into the banbhs[10] and screeching sows.

PEGEEN: I'd be well-nigh afeard of that lad myself, I'm thinking. And there was no one in it but the two of you alone?

CHRISTY: The divil a one, though he'd sons and daughters walking all great states and territories of the world, and not a one of them, to this day, but would say their seven curses on him, and they rousing up to let a cough or sneeze, maybe, in the deadness of the night.

PEGEEN [*nodding her head*]: Well, you should have been a queer lot. I never cursed my father the like of that, though I'm twenty and more years of age.

CHRISTY: Then you'd have cursed mine, I'm telling you, and he a man never gave peace to any, saving when he'd get two months or three, or be locked in the asylums for battering peelers or assaulting men [*with depression*], the way it was a bitter life he led me till I did up a Tuesday and halve his skull.

PEGEEN [*putting her hand on his shoulder*]: Well, you'll have peace in this place, Christy Mahon, and none to trouble you, and it's near time a fine lad like you should have your good share of the earth.

CHRISTY: It's time surely, and I a seemly fellow with great strength in me and bravery of . . .

Someone knocks.

CHRISTY [*clinging to* PEGEEN]: Oh, glory! it's late for knocking, and this last while I'm in terror of the peelers, and the walking dead.

Knocking again.

PEGEEN: Who's there?

VOICE [*outside*]: Me.

PEGEEN: Who's me?

VOICE: The Widow Quin.

PEGEEN [*jumping up and giving him the bread and milk*]: Go on now with your supper, and let on to be sleepy, for if she found you were such a warrant to talk, she'd be stringing gabble till the dawn of day.

He takes bread and sits shyly with his back to the door.

PEGEEN [*opening door, with temper*]: What ails you, or what is it you're wanting at this hour of the night?

WIDOW QUIN [*coming in a step and peering at* CHRISTY]: I'm after meeting Shawn Keogh and Father Reilly below, who told me of your curiosity man, and they fearing by this time he was roaring, romping on your hands with drink.

PEGEEN [*pointing to* CHRISTY]: Look now is he roaring, and he stretched out drowsy with his supper and his mug of milk. Walk down and tell that to Father Reilly and to Shaneen Keogh.

WIDOW QUIN [*coming forward*]: I'll not see them again, for I've their word to lead that lad forward to lodge with me.

PEGEEN [*in blank amazement*]: This night is it?

WIDOW QUIN [*going over*]: This night. 'It isn't fitting,' says the priesteen, 'to have his likeness lodging with an orphaned girl.' [*To* CHRISTY] God save you mister!

CHRISTY [*shyly*]: God save you kindly!

WIDOW QUIN [*looking at him with half amused curiosity*]: Well, aren't you a little smiling fellow? It should have been great and bitter torments did rouse your spirits to a deed of blood.

CHRISTY [*doubtfully*]: It should, maybe.

WIDOW QUIN: It's more than 'maybe' I'm saying, and it'd soften my heart to see you sitting so simple with your cup and cake, and you fitter to be saying your catechism than slaying your da.

PEGEEN [*at counter, washing glasses*]: There's talking when any'd see he's fit to be holding his head high with the wonders of the world. Walk on from this, for I'll not have him tormented, and he destroyed travelling since Tuesday was a week.

WIDOW QUIN [*peaceably*]: We'll be walking surely when his supper's done, and you'll find we're great company, young fellow, when it's of the like of you and me you'd hear the penny poets singing in an August Fair.

CHRISTY [*innocently*]: Did you kill your father?

PEGEEN [*contemptuously*]: She did not. She hit himself with a worn pick, and the rusted poison did corrode his blood the way he never overed it, and died after. That was a sneaky kind of murder did win small glory with the boys itself.

She crosses to CHRISTY's *left.*

WIDOW QUIN [*with good humour*]: If it didn't, maybe all knows a widow woman has buried her children and destroyed her man is a wiser comrade for a young lad than a girl, the like of you, who'd go helter-skeltering after any man would let you a wink upon the road.

PEGEEN [*breaking out into wild rage*]: And you'll say that, Widow Quin, and you gasping with the rage you had racing the hill beyond to look on his face.

WIDOW QUIN [*laughing derisively*]: Me, is it? Well, Father Reilly has cuteness to divide you now. [*She pulls* CHRISTY *up.*] There's great temptation in a man did slay his da, and we'd best be going, young fellow; so rise up and come with me.

PEGEEN [*seizing his arm*]: He'll not stir. He's pot-boy in this place, and I'll not have him stolen off and kidnapped while himself's abroad.

WIDOW QUIN: It'd be a crazy pot-boy'd lodge him in the shebeen where he works by day, so you'd have a right to come on, young fellow, till you see my little houseen, a perch off on the rising hill.

PEGEEN: Wait till morning, Christy Mahon. Wait till you lay eyes on her leaky thatch is growing more pasture for her buck goat than her square of fields, and she without a tramp itself to keep in order her place at all.

WIDOW QUIN: When you see me contriving in my little gardens, Christy Mahon, you'll swear the Lord God formed me to be living lone, and that there isn't my match in Mayo for thatching, or mowing, or shearing a sheep.

PEGEEN [*with noisy scorn*]: It's true the Lord God formed you to contrive indeed. Doesn't the world know you reared a black ram at your own breast, so that the Lord Bishop of Connaught felt the elements of a Christian, and he eating it after in a kidney stew? Doesn't the world know you've been seen shaving the foxy skipper from France for a threepenny-bit and a sop of grass tobacco would wring the liver from a mountain goat you'd meet leaping the hills?

WIDOW QUIN [*with amusement*]: Do you hear her now, young fellow? Do you hear the way she'll be rating at your own self when a week is by?

PEGEEN [*to* CHRISTY]: Don't heed her. Tell her to go on into her pigsty and not plague us here.

WIDOW QUIN: I'm going; but he'll come with me.

PEGEEN [*shaking him*]: Are you dumb, young fellow?

CHRISTY [*timidly to* WIDOW QUIN]: God increase you; but I'm pot-boy in this place, and it's here I liefer[11] stay.

PEGEEN [*triumphantly*]: Now you have heard him, and go on from this.

WIDOW QUIN [*looking round the room*]: It's lonesome this

hour crossing the hill, and if he won't come along with me, I'd have a right maybe to stop this night with yourselves. Let me stretch out on the settle,[12] Pegeen Mike; and himself can lie by the hearth.

PEGEEN [*short and fiercely*]: Faith, I won't. Quit off or I will send you now.

WIDOW QUIN [*gathering her shawl up*]: Well, it's a terror to be aged a score. [*To* CHRISTY] God bless you now, young fellow, and let you be wary, or there's right torment will await you here if you go romancing with her like, and she waiting only, as they bade me say, on a sheepskin parchment to be wed with Shawn Keogh of Killakeen.

CHRISTY [*going to* PEGEEN *as she bolts door*]: What's that she's after saying?

PEGEEN: Lies and blather, you've no call to mind. Well, isn't Shawn Keogh an impudent fellow to send up spying on me? Wait till I lay hands on him. Let him wait, I'm saying.

CHRISTY: And you're not wedding him at all?

PEGEEN: I wouldn't wed him if a bishop came walking for to join us here.

CHRISTY: That God in glory may be thanked for that.

PEGEEN: There's your bed now. I've put a quilt upon you I'm after quilting a while since with my own two hands, and you'd best stretch out now for your sleep, and may God give you a good rest till I call you in the morning when the cocks will crow.

CHRISTY [*as she goes to inner room*]: May God and Mary and St Patrick bless you and reward you for your kindly talk. [*She shuts the door behind her. He settles his bed slowly, feeling the quilt with immense satisfaction.*] Well, it's a clean bed and soft with it, and it's great luck and company I've won me in the end of time — two fine women fighting for the likes of me — till I'm thinking this night wasn't I a foolish fellow not to kill my father in the years gone by.

Curtain

ACT II

Scene as before. Brilliant morning light. CHRISTY, *looking bright and cheerful, is cleaning a girl's boots.*

CHRISTY [*to himself, counting jugs on dresser*]: Half a hundred beyond. Ten there. A score that's above. Eighty jugs. Six cups and a broken one. Two plates. A power of glasses. Bottles, a schoolmaster'd be hard set to count, and enough in them, I'm thinking, to drunken all the wealth and wisdom of the county Clare. [*He puts down the boot carefully.*] There's her boots now, nice and decent for her evening use, and isn't it grand brushes she has? [*He puts them down and goes by degrees to the looking-glass.*] Well, this'd be a fine place to be my whole life talking out with swearing Christians, in place of my old dogs and cat; and I stalking around, smoking my pipe and drinking my fill, and never a day's work but drawing a cork an odd time, or wiping a glass, or rinsing out a shiny tumbler for a decent man. [*He takes the looking-glass from the wall and puts it on the back of a chair; then sits down in front of it and begins washing his face.*] Didn't I know rightly, I was handsome, though it was the divil's own mirror we had beyond, would twist a squint across an angel's brow; and I'll be growing fine from this day, the way I'll have a soft lovely skin on me and won't be the like of the clumsy young fellows do be ploughing all times in the earth and dung. [*He starts.*] Is she coming again? [*He looks out.*] Stranger girls. God help me, where'll I hide myself away and my long neck naked to the world? [*He looks out.*] I'd best go to the room maybe till I'm dressed again.

He gathers up his coat and the looking-glass, and runs into the inner room. The door is pushed open, and SUSAN BRADY *looks in, and knocks on door.*

SUSAN: There's nobody in it. [*Knocks again.*]

NELLY [*pushing her in and following her, with* HONOR BLAKE *and* SARA TANSEY]: It'd be early for them both to be out walking the hill.

SUSAN: I'm thinking Shawn Keogh was making game of us, and there's no such man in it at all.

HONOR [*pointing to straw and quilt*]: Look at that. He's been sleeping there in the night. Well, it'll be a hard case if he's gone off now, the way we'll never set our eyes on a man killed his father, and we after rising early and destroying ourselves running fast on the hill.

NELLY: Are you thinking them's his boots?

SARAH [*taking them up*]: If they are, there should be his father's track on them. Did you never read in the papers the way murdered men do bleed and drip?

SUSAN: Is that blood there, Sara Tansey?

SARA [*smelling it*]: That's bog water, I'm thinking; but it's his own they are, surely, for I never seen the like of them for whitey mud, and red mud, and turf on them, and the fine sands of the sea. That man's been walking, I'm telling you.

She goes down right, putting on one of his boots.

SUSAN [*going to window*]: Maybe he's stolen off to Belmullet with the boots of Michael James, and you'd have a right so to follow after him, Sara Tansey, and you the one yoked the ass-cart and drove ten miles to set your eyes on the man bit the yellow lady's nostril on the northern shore. [*She looks out.*]

SARA [*running to window, with one boot on*]: Don't be talking, and we fooled today. [*Putting on the other boot*] There's a pair do fit me well and I'll be keeping them for walking to the priest, when you'd be ashamed this place, going up winter and summer with nothing worth while to confess at all.

HONOR [*who has been listening at door*]: Whisht! there's someone inside the room. [*She pushes door a chink open.*] It's a man.

SARA *kicks off boots and puts them where they were. They all stand in a line looking through chink.*

SARA: I'll call him. Mister! Mister! [*He puts in his head.*] Is Pegeen within?

CHRISTY [*coming in as meek as a mouse, with the looking-glass held behind his back*]: She's above on the cnuceen,[13] seeking the nanny goats, the way she'd have a sup of goats' milk for to colour my tea.

SARA: And asking your pardon, is it you's the man killed his father?

CHRISTY [*sidling toward the nail where the glass was hanging*]: I am, God help me!

SARA [*taking eggs she has brought*]: Then my thousand welcomes to you, and I've run up with a brace of duck's eggs for your food today. Pegeen's ducks is no use, but these are the real rich sort. Hold out your hand and you'll see it's no lie I'm telling you.

CHRISTY [*coming forward shyly, and holding out his left hand*]: They're a great and weighty size.

SUSAN: And I run up with a pat of butter, for it'd be a poor thing to have you eating your spuds dry, and you after running a great way since you did destroy your da.

CHRISTY: Thank you kindly.

HONOR: And I brought you a little cut of a cake, for you should have a thin stomach on you, and you that length walking the world.

NELLY: And I brought you a little laying pullet — boiled and all she is — was crushed at the fall of night by the curate's car. Feel the fat of the breast, mister.

CHRISTY: It's bursting, surely.

He feels it with the back of his hand, in which he holds the presents.

SARA: Will you pinch it? Is your right hand too sacred for to use at all? [*She slips round behind him.*] It's a glass he has. Well, I never seen to this day a man with a looking-glass held to his back. Them that kills their fathers is a vain lot surely. [*Girls giggle.*]

CHRISTY [*smiling innocently and piling presents on glass*]: I'm very thankful to you all today . . .

WIDOW QUIN [*coming in quietly, at door*]: Sara Tansey, Susan Brady, Honor Blake! What in glory has you here at this hour of day!

GIRLS [*giggling*]: That's the man killed his father.

WIDOW QUIN [*coming to them*]: I know well it's the man; and I'm after putting him down in the sports below for racing, leaping, pitching, and the Lord knows what.

SARA [*exuberantly*]: That's right, Widow Quin. I'll bet my dowry that he'll lick the world.

WIDOW QUIN: If you will, you'd have a right to have him fresh and nourished in place of nursing a feast. [*Taking presents*] Are you fasting or fed, young fellow?

CHRISTY: Fasting, if you please.

WIDOW QUIN [*loudly*]: Well, you're the lot. Stir up now and give him his breakfast. [*To* CHRISTY] Come here to me [*she puts him on bench beside her while the girls make tea and get his breakfast*], and let you tell us your story before Pegeen will come, in place of grinning your ears off like the moon of May.

CHRISTY [*beginning to be pleased*]: It's a long story; you'd be destroyed listening.

WIDOW QUIN: Don't be letting on to be shy, a fine, gamy, treacherous lad the like of you. Was it in your house beyond you cracked his skull?

CHRISTY [*shy but flattered*]: It was not. We were digging spuds in his cold, sloping, stony, divil's patch of a field.

WIDOW QUIN: And you went asking money of him, or making talk of getting a wife would drive him from his farm?

CHRISTY: I did not, then; but there I was, digging and digging, and 'You squinting idot,' says he, 'let you walk down now and tell the priest you'll wed the Widow Casey in a score of days.'

WIDOW QUIN: And what kind was she?

CHRISTY [*with horror*]: A walking terror from beyond the hills, and she two score and five years, and two hundred weights and five pounds in the weighing scales, with a limping leg on her, and a blinded eye, and she a woman of noted misbehaviour with the old and young.

GIRLS [*clustering round him, serving him*]: Glory be.

WIDOW QUIN: And what did he want driving you to wed with her? [*She takes a bit of the chicken.*]

CHRISTY [*eating with growing satisfaction*]: He was letting on I was wanting a protector from the harshness of the world, and he without a thought the whole while but how he'd have her hut to live in and her gold to drink.

WIDOW QUIN: There's maybe worse than a dry hearth and a widow woman and your glass at night. So you hit him then?

CHRISTY [*getting almost excited*]: I did not. 'I won't wed her,' says I, 'when all know she did suckle me for six weeks when I came into the world, and she a hag this day with a tongue on her has the crows and seabirds scattered, the way they wouldn't cast a shadow on her garden with the dread of her curse.'

WIDOW QUIN [*teasingly*]: That one should be right company.

SARA [*eagerly*]: Don't mind her. Did you kill him then?

CHRISTY: 'She's too good for the like of you,' says he, 'and go on now or I'll flatten you out like a crawling beast has passed under a dray.' 'You will not if I can help it,' says I. 'Go on,' says he, 'or I'll have the divil making garters of your limbs tonight.' 'You will not if I can help it,' says I. [*He sits up brandishing his mug.*]

SARA: You were right surely.

CHRISTY [*impressively*]: With that the sun came out between the cloud and the hill, and it shining green in my face. 'God have mercy on your soul,' says he, lifting a scythe. 'Or on your own,' says I, raising the loy.

SUSAN: That's a grand story.

HONOR: He tells it lovely.

CHRISTY [*flattered and confident, waving bone*]: He gave a drive with the scythe, and I gave a lep to the east. Then I turned around with my back to the north, and I hit a blow on the ridge of his skull, laid him stretched out, and he split to the knob of his gullet.

He raises the chicken bone to his Adam's apple.

GIRLS [*together*]: Well, you're a marvel! Oh, God bless you! You're the lad, surely!

SUSAN: I'm thinking the Lord God sent him this road to make a second husband to the Widow Quin, and she with a great yearning to be wedded, though all dread her here. Lift him on her knee, Sara Tansey.

WIDOW QUIN: Don't tease him.

SARA [*going over to dresser and counter very quickly and getting two glasses and porter*]: You're heroes, surely, and let you drink a supeen with your arms linked like the outlandish lovers in the sailor's song. [*She links their arms and gives them the glasses.*] There

now. Drink a health to the wonders of the western world, the pirates, preachers, poteen-makers, with the jobbing jockies; parching peelers, and the juries fill their stomachs selling judgments of the English law [*brandishing the bottle*].

WIDOW QUIN: That's a right toast, Sara Tansey. Now, Christy.

They drink with their arms linked, he drinking with his left hand, she with her right. As they are drinking, PEGEEN MIKE *comes in with a milk-can and stands aghast. They all spring away from* CHRISTY. *He goes down left.* WIDOW QUIN *remains seated.*

PEGEEN [*angrily to* SARA]: What is it you're wanting?

SARA [*twisting her apron*]: An ounce of tobacco.

PEGEEN: Have you tuppence?

SARA: I've forgotten my purse.

PEGEEN: Then you'd best be getting it and not be fooling us here. [*To the* WIDOW QUIN, *with more elaborate scorn.*] And what is it you're wanting. Widow Quin?

WIDOW QUIN [*insolently*]: A penn'orth of starch.

PEGEEN [*breaking out*]: And you without a white shift or a shirt in your whole family since the dying of the flood. I've no starch for the like of you, and let you walk on now to Killamuck.

WIDOW QUIN [*turning to* CHRISTY, *as she goes out with the girls*]: Well, you're mighty huffy this day, Pegeen Mike, and you, young fellow, let you not forget the sports and racing when the noon is by. [*They go out.*]

PEGEEN [*imperiously*]: Fling out that rubbish and put them cups away. [CHRISTY *tidies away in great haste.*] Shove in the bench by the wall. [*He does so.*] And hang that glass on the nail. What disturbed it at all?

CHRISTY [*very meekly*]: I was making myself decent only, and this a fine country for young lovely girls.

PEGEEN [*sharply*]: Whisht your talking of girls. [*Goes to counter on right.*]

CHRISTY: Wouldn't any wish to be decent in a place . . .

PEGEEN: Whisht, I'm saying.

CHRISTY [*looks at her face for a moment with great misgivings, then as a last effort takes up a loy, and goes towards her, with feigned assurance*]: It was with a loy the like of that I killed my father.

PEGEEN [*still sharply*]: You've told me that story six times since the dawn of day.

CHRISTY [*reproachfully*]: It's a queer thing you wouldn't care to be hearing it and them girls after walking four miles to be listening to me now.

PEGEEN [*turning round astonished*]: Four miles?

CHRISTY [*apologetically*]: Didn't himself say there were only bona fides living in the place?

PEGEEN: It's bona fides by the road they are, but that lot came over the river lepping the stones. It's not three perches when you go like that, and I was down this morning looking on the papers the post-boy does have in his bag. [*With meaning and emphasis.*] For there was great news this day, Christopher Mahon. [*She goes into room on left.*]

CHRISTY [*suspiciously*]: Is it news of my murder?

PEGEEN [*inside*]: Murder, indeed.

CHRISTY [*loudly*]: A murdered da?

PEGEEN [*coming in again and crossing right*]: There was not, but a story filled half a page of the hanging of a man. Ah, that should be a fearful end, young fellow, and it worst of all for a man destroyed his da; for the like of him would get small mercies, and when it's dead he is they'd put him in a narrow grave, with cheap sacking wrapping him round, and pour down quicklime on his head, the way you'd see a woman pouring any frish-frash from a cup.

CHRISTY [*very miserably*]: Oh, God help me. Are you thinking I'm safe? You were saying at the fall of night I was shut of jeopardy and I here with yourselves.

PEGEEN [*severely*]: You'll be shut of jeopardy no place if you go talking with a pack of wild girls the like of them do be walking abroad with the peelers, talking whispers at the fall of night.

CHRISTY [*with terror*]: And you're thinking they'd tell?

PEGEEN [*with mock sympathy*]: Who knows, God help you?

CHRISTY [*loudly*]: What joy would they have to bring hanging to the likes of me?

PEGEEN: It's queer joys they have, and who knows the thing they'd do, if it'd make the green stones cry itself to think of you swaying and swinging at the butt of a rope, and you with a fine, stout neck, God bless you! the way you'd be a half an hour, in great anguish, getting your death.

CHRISTY [*getting his boots and putting them on*]: If there's that terror of them, it'd be best, maybe, I went on wandering like Esau or Cain and Abel on the sides of Neifin or the Erris plain.[14]

PEGEEN [*beginning to play with him*]: It would, maybe, for I've heard the circuit judges this place is a heartless crew.

CHRISTY [*bitterly*]: It's more than judges this place is a heartless crew. [*Looking up at her*] And isn't it a poor thing to be starting again, and I a lonesome fellow will be looking out on women and girls the way the needy fallen spirits do be looking on the Lord?

PEGEEN: What call have you to be that lonesome when there's poor girls walking Mayo in their thousands now?

CHRISTY [*grimly*]: It's well you know what call I have. It's well you know it's a lonesome thing to be passing small towns with the lights shining sideways when the night is down, or going in strange places with a dog noising before you and a dog noising behind, or drawn to the cities where you'd hear a voice kissing and talking deep love in every shadow of the ditch, and you passing on with an empty, hungry stomach failing from your heart.

PEGEEN: I'm thinking you're an odd man, Christy Mahon. The oddest walking fellow I ever set my eyes on to this hour today.

CHRISTY: What would any be but odd men and they living lonesome in the world?

PEGEEN: I'm not odd, and I'm my whole life with my father only.

CHRISTY [*with infinite admiration*]: How would a lovely, handsome woman the like of you be lonesome when all men should be thronging around to hear the sweetness of your voice, and the little infant children should be pestering your steps, I'm thinking, and you walking the roads.

PEGEEN: I'm hard set to know what way a coaxing fellow the like of yourself should be lonesome either.

CHRISTY: Coaxing?

PEGEEN: Would you have me think a man never talked with the girls would have the words you've spoken today? It's only letting on you are to be lonesome, the way you'd get around me now.

CHRISTY: I wish to God I was letting on; but I was lonesome all times, and born lonesome, I'm thinking, as the moon of dawn. [*Going to door.*]

PEGEEN [*puzzled by his talk*]: Well, it's a story I'm not understanding at all why you'd be worse than another, Christy Mahon, and you a fine lad with the great savagery to destroy your da.

CHRISTY: It's little I'm understanding myself, saving only that my heart's scalded this day, and I going off stretching out the earth between us, the way I'll not be waking near you another dawn of the year till the two of us do arise to hope or judgment with the saints of God, and now I'd best be going with my wattle in my hand, for hanging is a poor thing [*turning to go*], and it's little welcome only is left me in this house today.

PEGEEN [*sharply*]: Christy. [*He turns round.*] Come here to me. [*He goes towards her.*] Lay down that switch and throw some sods on the fire. You're pot-boy in this place, and I'll not have you mitch off from us now.

CHRISTY: You were saying I'd be hanged if I stay.

PEGEEN [*quite kindly at last*]: I'm after going down and reading the fearful crimes of Ireland for two weeks or three, and there wasn't a word of your murder. [*Getting up and going over to the counter.*] They've likely not found the body. You're safe so with ourselves.

CHRISTY [*astonished, slowly*]: It's making game of me you were [*following her with fearful joy*], and I can stay so, working at your side, and I not lonesome from this mortal day.

PEGEEN: What's to hinder you staying, except the widow woman or the young girls would inveigle you off?

CHRISTY [*with rapture*]: And I'll have your words from this day filling my ears, and that look is come upon you meeting my two eyes, and I watching you loafing around in the warm sun, or rinsing your ankles when the night is come.

PEGEEN [*kindly, but a little embarrassed*]: I'm thinking you'll be a loyal young lad to have working around, and if you vexed me a while since with your leaguing with the girls, I wouldn't give a thraneen[15] for a lad hadn't a mighty spirit in him and a gamy heart.

SHAWN KEOGH *runs in carrying a cleeve*[16] *on his back, followed by the* WIDOW QUIN.

SHAWN [*to* PEGEEN]: I was passing below, and I seen your mountainy sheep eating cabbages in Jimmy's field. Run up or they'll be bursting surely.

PEGEEN: Oh, God mend them!

She puts a shawl over her head and runs out.

CHRISTY [*looking from one to the other. Still in high spirits*]: I'd best go to her aid maybe. I'm handy with ewes.

WIDOW QUIN [*closing the door*]: She can do that much, and there is Shaneen has long speeches for to tell you now. [*She sits down with an amused smile.*]

SHAWN [*taking something from his pocket and offering it to* CHRISTY]: Do you see that, mister?

CHRISTY [*looking at it*]: The half of a ticket to the Western States!

SHAWN [*trembling with anxiety*]: I'll give it to you and my new hat [*pulling it out of hamper*]; and my breeches with the double seat [*pulling it out*]; and my new coat is woven from the blackest shearings for three miles around [*giving him the coat*]; I'll give you the whole of them, and my

blessing, and the blessing of Father Reilly itself, maybe, if you'll quit from this and leave us in the peace we had till last night at the fall of dark.

CHRISTY [*with a new arrogance*]: And for what is it you're wanting to get shut of me?

SHAWN [*looking to the* WIDOW *for help*]: I'm a poor scholar with middling faculties to coin a lie, so I'll tell you the truth, Christy Mahon. I'm wedding with Pegeen beyond, and I don't think well of having a clever fearless man the like of you dwelling in her house.

CHRISTY [*almost pugnaciously*]: And you'd be using bribery for to banish me?

SHAWN [*in an imploring voice*]: Let you not take it badly, mister honey; isn't beyond the best place for you, where you'll have golden chains and shiny coats and you riding upon hunters with the ladies of the land.

He makes an eager sign to the WIDOW QUIN *to come to help him.*

WINDOW QUIN [*coming over*]: It's true for him, and you'd best quit off and not have that poor girl setting her mind on you, for there's Shaneen thinks she wouldn't suit you, though all is saying that she'll wed you now.

CHRISTY *beams with delight.*

SHAWN [*in terrified earnest*]: She wouldn't suit you, and she with the divil's own temper the way you'd be strangling one another in a score of days. [*He makes the movement of strangling with his hands.*] It's the like of me only that she's fit for; a quiet simple fellow wouldn't raise a hand upon her if she scratched itself.

WIDOW QUIN [*putting* SHAWN'*s hat on* CHRISTY]: Fit them clothes on you anyhow, young fellow, and he'd maybe loan them to you for the sports. [*Pushing him towards inner door.*] Fit them on and you can give your answer when you have them tried.

CHRISTY [*beaming, delighted with the clothes*]: I will then. I'd like herself to see me in them tweeds and hat.

He goes into the room and shuts the door.

SHAWN [*in great anxiety*]: He'd like herself to see them. He'll not leave us, Widow Quin. He's a score of divils in him the way it's well-nigh certain he will wed Pegeen.

WIDOW QUIN [*jeeringly*]: It's true all girls are fond of courage and do hate the like of you.

SHAWN [*walking about in desperation*]: Oh, Widow Quin, what'll I be doing now? I'd inform again him, but he'd burst from Kilmainham[17] and he'd be sure and certain to destroy me. If I wasn't so God-fearing, I'd near have courage to come behind him and run a pike into his side. Oh, it's a hard case to be an orphan and not to have your father that you're used to, and you'd easy kill and make yourself a hero in the sight of all. [*Coming up to her*] Oh, Widow Quin, will you find me some contrivance when I've promised you a ewe?

WIDOW QUIN: A ewe's a small thing, but what would you give me if I did wed him and did save you so?

SHAWN [*with astonishment*]: You?

WIDOW QUIN: Aye. Would you give me the red cow you have and the mountainy ram, and the right of way across your rye path, and a load of dung at Michaelmas,[18] and turbary[19] upon the western hill?

SHAWN [*radiant with hope*]: I would, surely, and I'd give you the wedding-ring I have, and the loan of a new suit, the way you'd have him decent on the wedding-day. I'd give you two kids for your dinner, and a gallon of poteen, and I'd call the piper on the long car to your wedding from Crossmolina or from Ballina. I'd give you . . .

WIDOW QUIN: That'll do, so, and let you whisht, for he's coming now again.

CHRISTY *comes in, very natty in the new clothes.* WIDOW QUIN *goes to him admiringly.*

WIDOW QUIN: If you seen yourself now, I'm thinking you'd be too proud to speak to at all, and it'd be a pity surely to have your like sailing from Mayo to the western world.

CHRISTY [*as proud as a peacock*]: I'm not going. If this is a poor place itself, I'll make myself contented to be lodging here.

WIDOW QUIN *makes a sign to* SHAWN *to leave them.*

SHAWN: Well, I'm going measuring the racecourse while the tide is low, so I'll leave you the garments and my blessing for the sports today. God bless you!

He wriggles out.

WIDOW QUIN [*admiring* CHRISTY]: Well, you're mighty spruce, young fellow. Sit down now while you're quiet till you talk with me.

CHRISTY [*swaggering*]: I'm going abroad on the hillside for to seek Pegeen.

WIDOW QUIN: You'll have time and plenty for to seek Pegeen, and you heard me saying at the fall of night the two of us should be great company.

CHRISTY: From this out I'll have no want of company when all sorts is bringing me their food and clothing [*he swaggers to the door, tightening his belt*], the way they'd set their eyes upon a gallant orphan cleft his father with one blow to the breeches belt. [*He opens door, then staggers back.*]

Saints of Glory! Holy angels from the throne of light!

WIDOW QUIN [*going over*]: What ails you?

CHRISTY: It's the walking spirit of my murdered da!

WIDOW QUIN [*looking out*]: Is it that tramper?

CHRISTY [*wildly*]: Where'll I hide my poor body from that ghost of hell?

The door is pushed open, and old MAHON *appears on threshold.* CHRISTY *darts in behind door.*

WIDOW QUIN [*in great amazement*]: God save you, my poor man.

MAHON [*gruffly*]: Did you see a young lad passing this way in the early morning or the fall of night?

WIDOW QUIN: You're a queer kind to walk in not saluting at all.

MAHON: Did you see the young lad?

WIDOW QUIN [*stiffly*]: What kind was he?

MAHON: An ugly young streeler[20] with a murderous gob on him, and a little switch in his hand. I met a tramper seen him coming this way at the fall of night.

WIDOW QUIN: There's harvest hundreds[21] do be passing these days for the Sligo boat. For what is it you're wanting him, my poor man?

MAHON: I want to destroy him for breaking the head on me with the clout of a loy. [*He takes off a big hat, and shows his head in a mass of bandages and plaster, with some pride.*] It was he did that, and amn't I a great wonder to think I've traced him ten days with that rent in my crown?

WIDOW QUIN [*taking his head in both hands and examining it with extreme delight*]: That was a great blow. And who hit you? A robber maybe?

MAHON: It was my own son hit me, and he the divil a robber, or anything else, but a dirty, stuttering lout.

WIDOW QUIN [*letting go his skull and wiping her hands in her apron*]: You'd best be wary of a mortified scalp, I think they call it, lepping around with that wound in the splendour of the sun. It was a bad blow, surely, and you should have vexed him fearful to make him strike that gash in his da.

MAHON: Is it me?

WIDOW QUIN [*amusing herself*]: Aye. And isn't it a great shame when the old and hardened do torment the young?

MAHON [*raging*]: Torment him, is it? And I after holding out with the patience of a martyred saint till there's nothing but destruction on, and I'm driven out in my old age with none to aid me.

WIDOW QUIN [*greatly amused*]: It's a sacred wonder the way that wickedness will spoil a man.

MAHON: My wickedness, is it? Amn't I after saying it is

himself has me destroyed, and he a liar on walls, a talker of folly, a man you'd see stretched the half of the day in the brown ferns with his belly to the sun.

WIDOW QUIN: Not working at all?

MAHON: The divil a work, or if he did itself, you'd see him raising up a haystack like the stalk of a rush, or driving our last cow till he broke her leg at the hip, and when he wasn't at that he'd be fooling over little birds he had — finches and felts — or making mugs at his own self in the bit of glass we had hung on the wall.

WIDOW QUIN [*looking at* CHRISTY]: What way was he so foolish? It was running wild after the girls maybe?

MAHON [*with a shout of derision*]: Running wild, is it? If he seen a red petticoat coming swinging over the hill, he'd be off to hide in the sticks, and you'd see him shooting out his sheep's eyes between the little twigs and the leaves, and his two ears rising like a hare looking out through a gap. Girls, indeed!

WIDOW QUIN: It was drink maybe?

MAHON: And he a poor fellow would get drunk on the smell of a pint. He'd a queer rotten stomach, I'm telling you, and when I gave him three pulls from my pipe a while since, he was taken with contortions till I had to send him in the ass-cart to the females' nurse.

WIDOW QUIN [*clasping her hands*]: Well, I never, till this day, heard tell of a man the like of that!

MAHON: I'd take a mighty oath you didn't, surely, and wasn't he the laughing joke of every female woman where four baronies meet, the way the girls would stop their weeding if they seen him coming the road to let a roar at him, and call him the loony of Mahon's?

WIDOW QUIN: I'd give the world and all to see the like of him. What kind was he?

MAHON: A small, low fellow.

WIDOW QUIN: And dark?

MAHON: Dark and dirty.

WIDOW QUIN [*considering*]: I'm thinking I seen him.

MAHON [*eagerly*]: An ugly young blackguard.

WIDOW QUIN: A hideous, fearful villain, and the spit of you.

MAHON: Which way is he fled?

WIDOW QUIN: Gone over the hills to catch a coasting steamer to the north or south.

MAHON: Could I pull up on him now?

WIDOW QUIN: If you'll cross the sands below where the tide is out, you'll be in it as soon as himself, for he had to go round ten miles by the top of the bay. [*She points to the door.*] Strike down by the head beyond and then follow on the roadway to the north and east.

MAHON *goes abruptly.*

WIDOW QUIN [*shouting after him*]: Let you give him a good vengeance when you come up with him, but don't put yourself in the power of the law, for it'd be a poor thing to see a judge in his black cap reading out his sentence on a civil warrior the like of you. [*She swings the door to and looks at* CHRISTY, *who is cowering in terror, for a moment, then she bursts into a laugh.*] Well, you're the walking Playboy of the Western World, and that's the poor man you had divided to his breeches belt.

CHRISTY [*looking out; then, to her*]: What'll Pegeen say when she hears that story? What'll she be saying to me now?

WIDOW QUIN: She'll knock the head of you, I'm thinking, and drive you from the door. God help her to be taking you for a wonder, and you a little schemer making up a story you destroyed your da.

CHRISTY [*turning to the door, nearly speechless with rage, half to himself*]: To be letting on he was dead, and coming back to his life, and following after me like an old weasel tracing a rat, and coming in here laying desolation between my own self and the fine women of Ireland, and he a kind of carcass that you'd fling upon the sea . . .

WIDOW QUIN [*more soberly*]: There's talking for a man's one only son.

CHRISTY [*breaking out*]: His one son, is it? May I meet him with one tooth and it aching, and one eye to be seeing seven and seventy divils in the twists of the road, and one old timber leg on him to limp into the scalding grave. [*Looking out*] There he is now crossing the strands, and that the Lord God would send a high wave to wash him from the world.

WIDOW QUIN [*scandalized*]: Have you no shame? [*Putting her hand on his shoulder and turning him round.*] What ails you? Near crying, is it?

CHRISTY [*in despair and grief*]: Amn't I after seeing the love-light of the star of knowledge shining from her brow, and hearing words would put you thinking of the holy Brigid speaking to the infant saints, and now she'll be turning again, and speaking hard words to me, like an old woman with a spavindy ass she'd have, urging on a hill.

WIDOW QUIN: There's poetry talk for a girl you'd see itching and scratching, and she with a stale stink of poteen on her from selling in the shop.

CHRISTY [*impatiently*]: It's her like is fitted to be handling merchandise in the heavens above, and what'll I be doing now, I ask you, and I a kind of wonder was jilted by the heavens when a day was by.

There is a distant noise of girls' voices. WIDOW QUIN *looks from window and comes to him, hurriedly.*

WIDOW QUIN: You'll be doing like myself, I'm thinking, when I did destroy my man, for I'm above many's the day, odd times in great spirits, abroad in the sunshine, darning a stocking or stitching a shift;²² and odd times again looking out on the schooners, hookers, trawlers is sailing the sea, and I thinking on the gallant hairy fellows are drifting beyond, and myself long years living alone.

CHRISTY [*interested*]: You're like me, so.

WIDOW QUIN: I am your like, and it's for that I'm taking a fancy to you, and I with my little houseen above where there'd be myself to tend you, and none to ask were you a murderer or what at all.

CHRISTY: And what would I be doing if I left Pegeen?

WIDOW QUIN: I've nice jobs you could be doing — gathering shells to make a whitewash for our hut within, building up a little goose-house, or stretching a new skin on an old curagh I have, and if my hut is far from all sides, it's there you'll meet the wisest old men, I tell you, at the corner of my wheel, and it's there yourself and me will have great times whispering and hugging . . .

VOICES [*outside, calling far away*]: Christy! Christy Mahon! Christy!

CHRISTY: Is it Pegeen Mike?

WIDOW QUIN: It's the young girls, I'm thinking, coming to bring you to the sports below, and what is it you'll have me to tell them now?

CHRISTY: Aid me to win Pegeen. It's herself only that I'm seeking now. [WIDOW QUIN *gets up and goes to window.*] Aid me for to win her, and I'll be asking God to stretch a hand to you in the hour of death, and lead you short cuts through the Meadows of Ease, and up the floor of heaven to the Footstool of the Virgin's Son.

WIDOW QUIN: There's praying!

VOICES [*nearer*]: Christy! Christy Mahon!

CHRISTY [*with agitation*]: They're coming! Will you swear to aid and save me, for the love of Christ?

WIDOW QUIN [*looks at him for a moment*]: If I aid you, will you swear to give me a right of way I want, and a mountainy ram, and a load of dung at Michaelmas, the time that you'll be master here?

CHRISTY: I will, by the elements and stars of night.

WIDOW QUIN: Then we'll not say a word of the old fellow, the way Pegeen won't know your story till the end of time.

CHRISTY: And if he chances to return again?

WIDOW QUIN: We'll swear he's a maniac, and not your da. I could take an oath I seen him raving on the sands today.

Girls run in.

SUSAN: Come on to the sports below. Pegeen says you're to come.

SARA TANSEY: The lepping's beginning, and we've a jockey's suit to fit upon you for the mule race on the sands below.

HONOR: Come on, will you?

CHRISTY: I will then if Pegeen's beyond.

SARA: She's in the boreen²³ making game of Shaneen Keogh.

CHRISTY: Then I'll be going to her now.

He runs out, followed by the girls.

WIDOW QUIN: Well, if the worst comes in the end of all, it'll be great game to see there's none to pity him but a widow woman, the like of me, has buried her children and destroyed her man.

She goes out.

Curtain

ACT III

Scene as before. Later in the day. JIMMY *comes in, slightly drunk.*

JIMMY [*calls*]: Pegeen! [*Crosses to inner door.*] Pegeen Mike! [*Comes back again into the room.*] Pegeen! [PHILLY *comes in in the same state — to* PHILLY] Did you see herself?

PHILLY: I did not; but I sent Shawn Keogh with the ass-cart for to bear him home [*trying cupboards, which are locked*]. Well, isn't he a nasty man to get into such staggers at a morning wake; and isn't herself the divil's daughter for locking, and she so fussy after that young gaffer, you might take your death with drouth and none to heed you?

JIMMY: It's little wonder she'd be fussy, and he after bringing bankrupt ruin on the roulette man, and the trick-o'-the-loop man, and breaking the nose of the cockshot-man, and winning all in the sports below, racing, lepping, dancing, and the Lord knows what! He's right luck, I'm telling you.

PHILLY: If he has, he'll be rightly hobbled yet, and he not able to say ten words without making a brag of the way he killed his father, and the great blow he hit with the loy.

JIMMY: A man can't hang by his own informing, and his father should be rotten by now.

OLD MAHON *passes window slowly.*

PHILLY: Supposing a man's digging spuds in that field with a long spade, and supposing he flings up the two halves of that skull, what'll be said then in the papers and the courts of law?

JIMMY: They'd say it was an old Dane, maybe, was drowned in the flood. [OLD MAHON *comes in and sits down near door listening.*] Did you never hear tell of the skulls they have in the city of Dublin, ranged out like blue jugs in a cabin of Connaught?

PHILLY: And you believe that?

JIMMY [*pugnaciously*]: Didn't a lad see them and he after coming from harvesting in the Liverpool boat? 'They have them there,' says he, 'making a show of the great people there was one time walking the world. White skulls and black skulls and yellow skulls, and some with full teeth, and some haven't only but one.'

PHILLY: It was no lie, maybe, for when I was a young lad there was a graveyard beyond the house with the remnants of a man who had thighs as long as your arm. He was a horrid man, I'm telling you, and there was many a fine Sunday I'd put him together for fun, and he with shiny bones, you wouldn't meet the like of these days in the cities of the world.

MAHON [*getting up*]: You wouldn't, is it? Lay your eyes on that skull, and tell me where and when there was another the like of it, is splintered only from the blow of a loy.

PHILLY: Glory be to God! And who hit you at all?

MAHON [*triumphantly*]: It was my own son hit me. Would you believe that?

JIMMY: Well, there's wonders hidden in the heart of man!

PHILLY [*suspiciously*]: And what way was it done?

MAHON [*wandering about the room*]: I'm after walking hundreds and long scores of miles, winning clean beds and the fill of my belly four times in the day, and I doing nothing but telling stories of that naked truth. [*He comes to them a little aggressively.*] Give me a supeen and I'll tell you now.

WIDOW QUIN *comes in and stands aghast behind him. He is facing* JIMMY *and* PHILLY, *who are on the left.*

JIMMY: Ask herself beyond. She's the stuff hidden in her shawl.

WIDOW QUIN [*coming to* MAHON *quickly*]: You here, is it? You didn't go far at all?

MAHON: I seen the coasting steamer passing, and I got a drouth upon me and a cramping leg, so I said: 'The divil go along with him,' and turned again. [*Looking under her shawl*] And let you give me a supeen, for I'm destroyed travelling since Tuesday was a week.

WIDOW QUIN [*getting a glass, in a cajoling tone*]: Sit down then by the fire and take your ease for a space. You've a right to be destroyed indeed, with your walking, and fighting, and facing the sun. [*Giving him poteen from a stone jar she has brought in*] There now is a drink for you, and may it be to your happiness and length of life.

MAHON [*taking glass greedily, and sitting down by fire*]: God increase you!

WIDOW QUIN [*taking men to the right stealthily*]: Do you know what? That man's raving from his wound today, for I met him a while since telling a rambling tale of a tinker had him destroyed. Then he heard of Christy's deed, and he up and says it was his son had cracked his skull. Oh, isn't madness a fright, for he'll go killing someone yet, and he thinking it's the man has struck him so?

JIMMY [*entirely convinced*]: It's a fright surely. I knew a party was kicked in the head by a red mare, and he went killing horses a great while, till he eat the insides of a clock and died after.

PHILLY [*with suspicion*]: Did he see Christy?

WIDOW QUIN: He didn't. [*With a warning gesture*] Let you not be putting him in mind of him, or you'll be likely summoned if there's murder done. [*Looking round at* MAHON] Whisht! He's listening. Wait now till you hear me taking him easy and unravelling all. [*She goes to* MAHON.] And what way are you feeling, mister? Are you in contentment now?

MAHON [*slightly emotional from his drink*]: I'm poorly only, for it's a hard story the way I'm left today, when it was I did tend him from his hour of birth, and he a dunce never reached his second book, the way he'd come from school, many's the day, with his legs lamed under him, and he blackened with his beatings like a tinker's ass. It's a hard story, I'm saying, the way some do have their next and nighest raising up a hand of murder on them, and some is lonesome getting their death with lamentation in the dead of night.

WIDOW QUIN [*not knowing what to say*]: To hear you talking so quiet, who'd know you were the same fellow we seen pass today?

MAHON: I'm the same surely. The wrack and ruin of threescore years; and it's a terror to live that length, I tell you, and to have your sons going to the dogs against you, and you wore out scolding them, and skelping them, and God knows what.

PHILLY [*to* JIMMY]: He's not raving. [*To* WIDOW QUIN] Will you ask him what kind was his son?

WIDOW QUIN [*to* MAHON, *with a peculiar look*]: Was your son that hit you a lad of one year and a score maybe, a great hand at racing and lepping and licking the world?

MAHON [*turning on her with a roar of rage*]: Didn't you hear me say he was the fool of men, the way from this out he'll know the orphan's lot, with old and young making game of him, and they swearing, raging, kicking at him like a mangy cur.

A great burst of cheering outside, some way off.

MAHON [*putting his hands to his ears*]: What in the name of God do they want roaring below?

WIDOW QUIN [*with the shade of a smile*]: They're cheering a young lad, the champion Playboy of the Western World.

More cheering.

MAHON [*going to window*]: It'd split my heart to hear them, and I with pulses in my brain-pan for a week gone by. Is it racing they are?

JIMMY [*looking from door*]: It is, then. They are mounting him for the mule race will be run upon the sands. That's the playboy on the winkered mule.

MAHON [*puzzled*]: That lad, is it? If you said it was a fool he was, I'd have laid a mighty oath he was the likeness of my wandering son. [*Uneasily, putting his hand to his head.*] Faith, I'm thinking I'll go walking for to view the race.

WIDOW QUIN [*stopping him, sharply*]: You will not. You'd best take the road to Belmullet, and not be dilly-dallying in this place where there isn't a spot you could sleep.

PHILLY [*coming forward*]: Don't mind her. Mount there on the bench and you'll have a view of the whole. They're hurrying before the tide will rise, and it'd be near over if you went down the pathway through the crags below.

MAHON [*mounts on bench,* WIDOW QUIN *beside him*]: That's a right view again the edge of the sea. They're coming now from the point. He's leading. Who is he at all?

WIDOW QUIN: He's the champion of the world, I tell you, and there isn't a ha'p'orth isn't falling lucky to his hands today.

PHILLY [*looking out, interested in the race*]: Look at that. They're pressing him now.

JIMMY: He'll win it yet.

PHILLY: Take your time, Jimmy Farrell. It's too soon to say.

WIDOW QUIN [*shouting*]: Watch him taking the gate. There's riding.

JIMMY [*cheering*]: More power to the young lad!

MAHON: He's passing the third.

JIMMY: He'll lick them yet.

WIDOW QUIN: He'd lick them if he was running races with a score itself.

MAHON: Look at the mule he has, kicking the stars.

WIDOW QUIN: There was a lep! [*Catching hold of* MAHON *in her excitement*] He's fallen? He's mounted again! Faith, he's passing them all!

JIMMY: Look at him skelping[24] her!

PHILLY: And the mountain girls hooshing him on!

JIMMY: It's the last turn! The post's cleared for them now!

MAHON: Look at the narrow place. He'll be into the bogs! [*With a yell*] Good rider! He's through it again!

JIMMY: He's neck and neck!

MAHON: Good boy to him! Flames, but he's in!

Great cheering, in which all join.

MAHON [*with hesitation*]: What's that? They're raising him up. They're coming this way. [*With a roar of rage and astonishment*]. It's Christy, by the stars of God! I'd know his way of spitting and he astride the moon.

He jumps down and makes a run for the door, but WIDOW QUIN *catches him and pulls him back.*

WIDOW QUIN: Stay quiet, will you? That's not your son. [*To* JIMMY] Stop him, or you'll get a month for the abetting of manslaughter and be fined as well.

JIMMY: I'll hold him.

MAHON [*struggling*]: Let me out! Let me out, the lot of you, till I have my vengeance on his head today.

WIDOW QUIN [*shaking him, vehemently*]: That's not your son. That's a man is going to make a marriage with the daughter of this house, a place with fine trade, with a licence, and with poteen too.

MAHON [*amazed*]: That man marrying a decent and a moneyed girl! Is it mad yous are? Is it in a crazy-house for females that I'm landed now?

WIDOW QUIN: It's mad yourself is with the blow upon your head. That lad is the wonder of the western world.

MAHON: I see it's my son.

WIDOW QUIN: You seen that you're mad. [*Cheering outside.*] Do you hear them cheering him in the zigzags of the road? Aren't you after saying that your son's a fool, and how would they be cheering a true idiot born?

MAHON [*getting distressed*]: It's maybe out of reason that that man's himself. [*Cheering again.*] There's none surely will go cheering him. Oh, I'm raving with a madness that would fright the world! [*He sits down with his hand to his head.*] There was one time I seen ten scarlet divils letting on they'd cork my spirit in a gallon can; and one time I seen rats as big as badgers sucking the lifeblood from the butt of my lug;[25] but never till this day confused that dribbling idiot with a likely man. I'm destroyed surely.

WIDOW QUIN: And who'd wonder when it's your brain-pan that is gaping now?

MAHON: Then the blight of the sacred drouth upon myself and him, for I never went mad to this day, and I not three weeks with the Limerick girls drinking myself silly and parlatic[26] from the dusk to dawn. [*To* WIDOW QUIN, *suddenly*] Is my visage astray?

WIDOW QUIN: It is, then. You're a sniggering maniac, a child could see.

MAHON [*getting up more cheerfully*]: Then I'd best be going to the union[27] beyond, there'll be a welcome before me, I tell you [*with great pride*], and I a terrible and fearful case, the way that there I was one time, screeching in a straightened waistcoat, with seven doctors writing out my sayings in a printed book. Would you believe that?

WIDOW QUIN: If you're a wonder itself, you'd best be hasty, for them lads caught a maniac one time and pelted the poor creature till he ran out, raving and foaming, and was drowned in the sea.

MAHON [*with philosophy*]: It's true mankind is the divil when your head's astray. Let me out now and I'll slip down the boreen, and not see them so.

WIDOW QUIN [*showing him out*]: That's it. Run to the right, and not a one will see.

He runs off.

PHILLY [*wisely*]: You're at some gaming, Widow Quin; but I'll walk after him and give him his dinner and a time to rest, and I'll see then if he's raving or as sane as you.

WIDOW QUIN [*annoyed*]: If you go near that lad, let you be wary of your head, I'm saying. Didn't you hear him telling he was crazed at times?

PHILLY: I heard him telling a power; and I'm thinking we'll have right sport before night will fall.

He goes out.

JIMMY: Well, Philly's a conceited and foolish man. How could that madman have his senses and his brain-pan slit? I'll go after them and see him turn on Philly now.

He goes; WIDOW QUIN *hides poteen behind counter. Then hubbub outside.*

VOICES: There you are! Good jumper! Grand lepper! Darlint boy! He's the racer! Bear him on, will you!

CHRISTY *comes in, in jockey's dress, with* PEGEEN MIKE, SARA, *and other girls and men.*

PEGEEN [*to crowd*]: Go on now, and don't destroy him, and he drenching with sweat. Go along, I'm saying, and have your tug-of-warring till he's dried his skin.

CROWD: Here's his prizes! A bagpipes! A fiddle was played by a poet in the years gone by! A flat and three-thorned blackthorn would lick the scholars out of Dublin town!

CHRISTY [*taking prizes from the men*]: Thank you kindly, the lot of you. But you'd say it was little only I did this day if you'd seen me a while since striking my one single blow.

TOWN CRIER [*outside ringing a bell*]: Take notice, last event of this day! Tug-of-warring on the green below! Come on, the lot of you! Great achievements for all Mayo men!

PEGEEN: Go on and leave him for to rest and dry. Go on, I tell you, for he'll do no more.

She bustles crowd out; WIDOW QUIN *following them.*

MEN [*going*]: Come on, then. Good luck for the while!

PEGEEN [*radiantly, wiping his face with her shawl*]: Well, you're the lad, and you'll have great times from this out when you could win that wealth of prizes, and you sweating in the heat of noon!

CHRISTY [*looking at her with delight*]: I'll have great times if I win the crowning prize I'm seeking now, and that's your promise that you'll wed me in a fortnight, when our banns is called.

PEGEEN [*backing away from him*]: You've right daring to go ask me that, when all knows you'll be starting to some girl in your own townland, when your father's rotten in four months, or five.

CHRISTY [*indignantly*]: Starting from you, is it! [*He follows her.*] I will not, then, and when the airs is warming, in four months or five, it's then yourself and me should be pacing Neifin in the dews of night, the times sweet smells do be rising, and you'd see a little, shiny new moon, maybe sinking on the hills.

PEGEEN [*looking at him playfully*]: And it's that kind of a poacher's love you'd make, Christy Mahon, on the sides of Neifin, when the night is down?

CHRISTY: It's little you'll think if my love's a poacher's, or an earl's itself, when you'll feel my two hands stretched around you, and I squeezing kisses on your puckered lips, till I'd feel a kind of pity for the Lord God is all ages sitting lonesome in His golden chair.

PEGEEN: That'll be right fun, Christy Mahon, and any girl would walk her heart out before she'd meet a young man was your like for eloquence, or talk at all.

CHRISTY [*encouraged*]: Let you wait, to hear me talking, till we're astray in Erris, when Good Friday's by, drinking a sup from a well, and making mighty kisses with our wetted mouths, or gaming in a gap of sunshine, with yourself stretched back unto your necklace, in the flowers of the earth.

PEGEEN [*in a low voice, moved by his tone*]: I'd be nice so, is it?

CHRISTY [*with rapture*]: If the mitred bishops seen you that time, they'd be the like of the holy prophets, I'm thinking, do be straining the bars of paradise to lay eyes on the Lady Helen of Troy, and she abroad, pacing back and forward, with a nosegay in her golden shawl.

PEGEEN [*with real tenderness*]: And what is it I have, Christy Mahon, to make me fitting entertainment for the like of you, that has such poet's talking, and such bravery of heart?

CHRISTY [*in a low voice*]: Isn't there the light of seven heavens in your heart alone, the way you'll be an angel's lamp to me from this out, and I abroad in the darkness, spearing salmons in the Owen or the Carrowmore?

PEGEEN: If I was your wife I'd be along with you those nights, Christy Mahon, the way you'd see I was a great hand at coaxing bailiffs, or coining funny nicknames for the stars of night.

CHRISTY: You, is it? Taking your death in the hailstones, or in the fogs of dawn.

PEGEEN: Yourself and me would shelter easy in a narrow bush [*with a qualm of dread*]; but we're only talking, maybe, for this would be a poor, thatched place to hold a fine lad is the like of you.

CHRISTY [*putting his arm round her*]: If I wasn't a good Christian, it's on my naked knees I'd be saying my prayers and paters[28] to every jackstraw you have roofing your head, and every stony pebble is paving the laneway to your door.

PEGEEN [*radiantly*]: If that's the truth I'll be burning candles from this out to the miracles of God that have brought you from the south today, and I with my gowns bought ready, the way that I can wed you, and not wait at all.

CHRISTY: It's miracles, and that's the truth. Me there toiling a long while, and walking a long while, not knowing at all I was drawing all times nearer to this holy day.

PEGEEN: And myself, a girl, was tempted often to go sailing the seas till I'd marry a Jew-man, with ten kegs of gold, and I not knowing at all there was the like of you drawing nearer, like the stars of God.

CHRISTY: And to think I'm long years hearing women talking that talk, to all bloody fools, and this the first time I've heard the like of your voice talking sweetly for my own delight.

PEGEEN: And to think it's me is talking sweetly, Christy Mahon, and I the fright of seven townlands for my biting tongue. Well, the heart's a wonder; and, I'm thinking, there won't be our like in Mayo, for gallant lovers, from this hour today. [*Drunken singing is heard outside.*] There's my father coming from the wake, and when he's had his sleep we'll tell him, for he's peaceful then.

They separate.

MICHAEL [*singing outside*]:
     The jailer and the turnkey
     They quickly ran us down,
     And brought us back as prisoners
     Once more to Cavan town
[*He comes in supported by* SHAWN.]
     There we lay bewailing
     All in a prison bound . . .

He sees CHRISTY. *Goes and shakes him drunkenly by the hand, while* PEGEEN *and* SHAWN *talk on the left.*

MICHAEL [*to* CHRISTY]: The blessing of God and the holy angels on your head, young fellow. I hear tell you're after winning all in the sports below; and wasn't it a shame I didn't bear you along with me to Kate Cassidy's wake, a fine, stout lad, the like of you, for you'd never see the match of it for flows of drink, the way when we sunk her bones at noonday in her narrow grave, there were five men, aye, and six men, stretched out retching speechless on the holy stones.

CHRISTY [*uneasily, watching* PEGEEN]: Is that the truth?

MICHAEL: It is, then; and aren't you a louty schemer to go burying your poor father unbeknownst when you'd a right to throw him on the crupper[29] of a Kerry mule and drive him westwards, like holy Joseph in the days gone by, the way we could have given him a decent burial and not have him rotting beyond, and not a Christian drinking a smart drop to the glory of his soul?

CHRISTY [*gruffly*]: It's well enough he's lying, for the likes of him.

MICHAEL [*slapping him on the back*]: Well, aren't you a hardened slayer? It'll be a poor thing for the household man where you go sniffing for a female wife; and [*pointing to* SHAWN] look beyond at that shy and decent Christian I have chosen for my daughter's hand, and I after getting the gilded dispensation this day for to wed them now.

CHRISTY: And you'll be wedding them this day, is it?

MICHAEL [*drawing himself up*]: Aye. Are you thinking, if I'm drunk itself, I'd leave my daughter living single with a little frisky rascal is the like of you?

PEGEEN [*breaking away from* SHAWN]: Is it the truth the dispensation's come?

MICHAEL [*triumphantly*]: Father Reilly's after reading it in gallous Latin, and 'It's come in the nick of time,' says he; 'so I'll wed them in a hurry, dreading that young gaffer who'd capsize the stars.'

PEGEEN [*fiercely*]: He's missed his nick of time, for it's that lad, Christy Mahon, that I'm wedding now.

MICHAEL [*loudly, with horror*]: You'd be making him a son to me, and he wet and crusted with his father's blood?

PEGEEN: Aye. Wouldn't it be a bitter thing for a girl to go marrying the like of Shaneen, and he a middling kind of a scarecrow, with no savagery or fine words in him at all?

MICHAEL [*gasping and sinking on a chair*]: Oh, aren't you a heathen daughter to go shaking the fat of my heart, and I swamped and drowned with the weight of drink? Would you have them turning on me the way that I'd be roaring to the dawn of day with the wind upon my heart? Have you not a word to aid me, Shaneen? Are you not jealous at all?

SHAWN [*in great misery*]: I'd be afeard to be jealous of a man did slay his da.

PEGEEN: Well, it'd be a poor thing to go marrying your like. I'm seeing there's a world of peril for an orphan girl, and isn't it a great blessing I didn't wed you before himself came walking from the west or south?

SHAWN: It's a queer story you'd go picking a dirty tramp up from the highways of the world.

PEGEEN [*playfully*]: And you think you're a likely beau to go straying along with the shiny Sundays of the opening year, when it's sooner on a bullock's liver you'd put a poor girl thinking than on the lily or the rose?

SHAWN: And have you no mind of my weight of passion, and the holy dispensation, and the drift of heifers I'm giving, and the golden ring?

PEGEEN: I'm thinking you're too fine for the like of me, Shawn Keogh of Killakeen, and let you go off till you'd find a radiant lady with droves of bullocks on the plains of Meath, and herself bedizened in the diamond jewelleries of Pharaoh's ma. That'd be your match, Shaneen. So God save you now!

She retreats behind CHRISTY.

SHAWN: Won't you hear me telling you . . .?

CHRISTY [*with ferocity*]: Take yourself from this, young fellow, or I'll maybe add a murder to my deeds today.

MICHAEL [*springing up with a shriek*]: Murder is it? Is it mad yous are? Would you go making murder in this place, and it piled with poteen for our drink tonight? Go on to the foreshore if it's fighting you want, where the rising tide will wash all traces from the memory of man [*pushing* SHAWN *towards* CHRISTY].

SHAWN [*shaking himself free, and getting behind* MICHAEL]: I'll not fight him, Michael James. I'd liefer live a bachelor, simmering in passions to the end of time, than face a lepping savage the like of him has descended from the Lord knows where. Strike him yourself, Michael James, or you'll lose my drift of heifers and my blue bull from Sneem.

MICHAEL: Is it me fight him, when it's father-slaying he's bred to now? [*Pushing* SHAWN] Go on, you fool, and fight him now.

SHAWN [*coming forward a little*]: Will I strike him with my hand?

MICHAEL: Take the loy is on your western side.

SHAWN: I'd be afeard of the gallows if I struck with that.

CHRISTY [*taking up the loy*]: Then I'll make you face the gallows or quit off from this.

SHAWN *flies out of the door.*

CHRISTY: Well, fine weather be after him [*going to* MICHAEL, *coaxingly*], and I'm thinking you wouldn't wish to have that quaking blackguard in your house at all. Let you give us your blessing and hear her swear her faith to me, for I'm mounted on the spring-tide of the stars of luck, the way it'll be good for any to have me in the house.

PEGEEN [*at the other side of* MICHAEL]: Bless us now, for I swear to God I'll wed him, and I'll not renege.

MICHAEL [*standing up in the centre, holding on to both of them*]: It's the will of God, I'm thinking, that all should win an easy or a cruel end, and it's the will of God that all should rear up lengthy families for the nurture of the earth. What's a single man, I ask you, eating a bit in one house and drinking a sup in another, and he with no place of his own, like an old braying jackass strayed upon the rocks? [*To* CHRISTY] It's many would be in dread to bring your like into their house for to end them, maybe, with a sudden end; but I'm a decent man of Ireland, and I liefer face the grave untimely and I seeing a score of grandsons growing up little gallant swearers by the name of God, than go peopling my bedside with puny weeds the like of what you'd breed, I'm thinking, out of Shaneen Keogh. [*He joins their hands.*] A daring fellow is the jewel of the world, and a man did split his father's middle with a single clout should have the bravery of ten, so may God and Mary and St Patrick bless you, and increase you from this mortal day.

CHRISTY and PEGEEN: Amen, O Lord!

Hubbub outside. OLD MAHON *rushes in, followed by all the crowd, and* WIDOW QUIN. *He makes a rush at* CHRISTY, *knocks him down, and begins to beat him.*

PEGEEN [*dragging back his arm*]: Stop that, will you? Who are you at all?

MAHON: His father, God forgive me!

PEGEEN [*drawing back*]: Is it rose from the dead?

MAHON: Do you think I look so easy quenched with the tap of a loy?

Beats CHRISTY *again.*

PEGEEN [*glaring at* CHRISTY]: And it's lies you told, letting on you had him slitted, and you nothing at all.

CHRISTY [*catching* MAHON's *stick*]: He's not my father. He's a raving maniac would scare the world. [*Pointing to* WIDOW QUIN] Herself knows it is true.

CROWD: You're fooling, Pegeen! The Widow Quin seen him this day, and you likely knew! You're a liar!

CHRISTY [*dumbfounded*]: It's himself was a liar, lying stretched out with an open head on him, letting on he was dead.

MAHON: Weren't you off racing the hills before I got my breath with the start I had seeing you turn on me at all?

PEGEEN: And to think of the coaxing glory we had given him, and he after doing nothing but hitting a soft blow and chasing northward in a sweat of fear. Quit off from this.

CHRISTY [*piteously*]: You've seen my doings this day, and let you save me from the old man; for why would you be in such a scorch of haste to spur me to destruction now?

PEGEEN: It's there your treachery is spurring me, till I'm hard set to think you're the one I'm after lacing in my heart-strings half an hour gone by. [*To* MAHON] Take him on from this, for I think bad the world should see me raging for a Munster liar, and the fool of men.

MAHON: Rise up now to retribution, and come on with me.

CROWD [*jeeringly*]: There's the playboy! There's the lad thought he'd rule the roost in Mayo! Slate him now, mister.

CHRISTY [*getting up in shy terror*]: What is it drives you to torment me here, when I'd asked the thunders of the might of God to blast me if I ever did hurt to any saving only that one single blow.

MAHON [*loudly*]: If you didn't, you're a poor good-for-nothing, and isn't it by the like of you the sins of the whole world are committed?

CHRISTY [*raising his hands*]: In the name of the Almighty God . . .

MAHON: Leave troubling the Lord God. Would you have Him sending down droughts, and fevers, and the old hen and the cholera morbus?

CHRISTY [*to* WIDOW QUIN]: Will you come between us and protect me now?

WIDOW QUIN: I've tried a lot, God help me, and my share is done.

CHRISTY [*looking round in desperation*]: And I must go back into my torment is it, or run off like a vagabond straying through the unions with the dust of August making mudstains in the gullet of my throat; or the winds of March blowing on me till I'd take an oath I felt them making whistles of my ribs within?

SARA: Ask Pegeen to aid you. Her like does often change.

CHRISTY: I will not, then, for there's torment in the splendour of her like, and she a girl any moon of midnight would take pride to meet, facing southwards on the heaths of Keel. But what did I want crawling forward to scorch my understanding at her flaming brow?

PEGEEN [*to* MAHON, *vehemently, fearing she will break into tears*]: Take him on from this or I'll set the young lads to destroy him here.

MAHON [*going to him, shaking his stick*]: Come on now if you wouldn't have the company to see you skelped.

PEGEEN [*half laughing, through her tears*]: That's it, now the world will see him pandied, and he an ugly liar was playing off the hero, and the fright of men.

CHRISTY [*to* MAHON, *very sharply*]: Leave me go!

CROWD: That's it. Now, Christy. If them two set fighting, it will lick the world.

MAHON [*making a grab at* CHRISTY]: Come here to me.

CHRISTY [*more threateningly*]: Leave me go, I'm saying.

MAHON: I will, maybe, when your legs is limping, and your back is blue.

CROWD: Keep it up, the two of you. I'll back the old one. Now the playboy.

CHRISTY [*in low and intense voice*]: Shut your yelling, for

if you're after making a mighty man of me this day by the power of a lie, you're setting me now to think if it's a poor thing to be lonesome it's worse, maybe, go mixing with the fools of earth.
MAHON *makes a movement towards him.*

CHRISTY [*almost shouting*]: Keep off . . . lest I do show a blow unto the lot of you would set the guardian angels winking in the clouds above.
He swings round with a sudden rapid movement and picks up a loy.

CROWD [*half frightened, half amused*]: He's going mad! Mind yourselves! Run from the idiot!

CHRISTY: If I am an idiot, I'm after hearing my voice this day saying words would raise the top-knot on a poet in a merchant's town. I've won your racing, and your lepping, and . . .

MAHON: Shut your gullet and come on with me.

CHRISTY: I'm going, but I'll stretch you first.
He runs at OLD MAHON *with the loy, chases him out of the door, followed by crowd and* WIDOW QUIN. *There is a great noise outside, then a yell, and dead silence for a moment.* CHRISTY *comes in, half dazed, and goes to fire.*

WIDOW QUIN [*coming in hurriedly, and going to him*]: They're turning again you. Come on, or you'll be hanged, indeed.

CHRISTY: I'm thinking from this out, Pegeen'll be giving me praises, the same as in the hours gone by.

WIDOW QUIN [*impatiently*]: Come by the back door. I'd think bad to have you stifled on the gallows tree.

CHRISTY [*indignantly*]: I will not, then. What good'd be my lifetime if I left Pegeen?

WIDOW QUIN: Come on, and you'll be no worse than you were last night; and you with a double murder this time to be telling to the girls.

CHRISTY: I'll not leave Pegeen Mike.

WIDOW QUIN [*impatiently*]: Isn't there the match of her in every parish public, from Binghamstown unto the plain of Meath? Come on, I tell you, and I'll find you finer sweethearts at each waning moon?

CHRISTY: It's Pegeen I'm seeking only, and what'd I care if you brought me a drift of chosen females, standing in their shifts itself, maybe, from this place to the eastern world?

SARA [*runs in, pulling off one of her petticoats*]: They're going to hang him. [*Holding out petticoat and shawl*] Fit these upon him, and let him run off to the east.

WIDOW QUIN: He's raving now; but we'll fit them on him, and I'll take him in the ferry to the Achill boat.

CHRISTY [*struggling feebly*]: Leave me go, will you? when I'm thinking of my luck today, for she will wed me surely, and I a proven hero in the end of all.
They try to fasten petticoat round him.

WIDOW QUIN: Take his left hand and we'll pull him now. Come on, young fellow.

CHRISTY [*suddenly starting up*]: You'll be taking me from her? You're jealous, is it, of her wedding me? Go on from this.
He snatches up a stool, and threatens them with it.

WIDOW QUIN [*going*]: It's in the madhouse they should put him, not in jail, at all. We'll go by the back door to call the doctor, and we'll save him so.
She goes out, with SARA, *through inner room. Men crowd in the doorway.* CHRISTY *sits down again by the fire.*

MICHAEL [*in a terrified whisper*]: Is the old lad killed surely?

PHILLY: I'm after feeling the last gasps quitting his heart.
They peer in at CHRISTY.

MICHAEL [*with a rope*]: Look at the way he is. Twist a hangman's knot on it, and slip it over his head, while he's not minding at all.

PHILLY: Let you take it, Shaneen. You're the soberest of all that's here.

SHAWN: Is it me to go near him, and he the wickedest and worst with me? Let you take it, Pegeen Mike.

PEGEEN: Come on, so.
She goes forward with the others, and they drop the double hitch over his head.

CHRISTY: What ails you?

SHAWN [*triumphantly, as they pull the rope tight on his arms*]: Come on to the peelers, till they stretch you now.

CHRISTY: Me!

MICHAEL: If we took pity on you the Lord God would, maybe, bring us ruin from the law today, so you'd best come easy, for hanging is an easy and a speedy end.

CHRISTY: I'll not stir. [*To* PEGEEN] And what is it you'll say to me, and I after doing it this time in the face of all?

PEGEEN: I'll say, a strange man is a marvel, with his mighty talk; but what's a squabble in your back yard, and the blow of a loy, have taught me that there's a great gap between a gallous story and a dirty deed. [*To men*] Take him on from this, or the lot of us will be likely put on trial for his deed today.

CHRISTY [*with horror in his voice*]: And it's yourself will send me off, to have a horny-fingered hangman hitching slip-knots at the butt of my ear.

MEN [*pulling rope*]: Come on, will you?

> *He is pulled down on the floor.*

CHRISTY [*twisting his legs round the table*]: Cut the rope, Pegeen, and I'll quit the lot of you, and live from this out, like the madman of Keel, eating muck and green weeds on the faces of the cliffs.

PEGEEN: And leave us to hang, is it, for a saucy liar, the like of you? [*To men*] Take him on, out from this.

SHAWN: Pull a twist on his neck, and squeeze him so.

PHILLY: Twist yourself. Sure he cannot hurt you, if you keep your distance from his teeth alone.

SHAWN: I'm afeard of him. [*To* PEGEEN] Lift a lighted sod, will you, and scorch his leg.

PEGEEN [*blowing the fire with a bellows*]: Leave go now, young fellow, or I'll scorch your shins.

CHRISTY: You're blowing for to torture me. [*His voice rising and growing stronger.*] That's your kind, is it? Then let the lot of you be wary, for, if I've to face the gallows, I'll have a gay march down, I tell you, and shed the blood of some of you before I die.

SHAWN [*in terror*]: Keep a good hold, Philly. Be wary, for the love of God. For I'm thinking he would liefest wreak his pains on me.

CHRISTY [*almost gaily*]: If I do lay my hands on you, it's the way you'll be at the fall of night, hanging as a scarecrow for the fowls of hell. Ah, you'll have a gallous jaunt, I'm saying, coaching out through limbo with my father's ghost.

SHAWN [*to* PEGEEN]: Make haste, will you? Oh, isn't he a holy terror, and isn't it true for Father Reilly, that all drink's a curse that has the lot of you so shaky and uncertain now?

CHRISTY: If I can wring a neck among you, I'll have a royal judgment looking on the trembling jury in the courts of law. And won't there be crying out in Mayo the day I'm stretched upon the rope, with ladies in their silks and satins snivelling in their lacy kerchiefs, and they rhyming songs and ballads on the terror of my fate?

> *He squirms round on the floor and bites* SHAWN's *leg.*

SHAWN [*shrieking*]: My leg's bit on me. He's the like of a mad dog, I'm thinking, the way that I will surely die.

CHRISTY [*delighted with himself*]: You will, then, the way you can shake out hell's flags of welcome for my coming in two weeks or three, for I'm thinking Satan hasn't many have killed their da in Kerry, and in Mayo too.

> OLD MAHON *comes in behind on all fours and looks on unnoticed.*

MEN [*to* PEGEEN]: Bring the sod, will you?

PEGEEN [*coming over*]: God help him so.

> *Burns his leg.*

CHRISTY [*kicking and screaming*]: Oh, glory be to God!

> *He kicks loose from the table, and they all drag him towards the door.*

JIMMY [*seeing* OLD MAHON]: Will you look what's come in?

> *They all drop* CHRISTY *and run left.*

CHRISTY [*scrambling on his knees face to face with* OLD MAHON]: Are you coming to be killed a third time, or what ails you now?

MAHON: For what is it they have you tied?

CHRISTY: They're taking me to the peelers to have me hanged for slaying you.

MICHAEL [*apologetically*]: It is the will of God that all should guard their little cabins from the treachery of law, and what would my daughter be doing if I was ruined or was hanged itself?

MAHON [*grimly, loosening* CHRISTY]: It's little I care if you put a bag on her back, and went picking cockles till the hour of death; but my son and myself will be going our own way, and we'll have great times from this out telling stories of the villainy of Mayo, and the fools is here. [*To* CHRISTY, *who is freed*] Come now.

CHRISTY: Go with you, is it? I will then, like a gallant captain with his heathen slave. Go on now and I'll see you from this day stewing my oatmeal and washing my spuds, for I'm master of all fights from now. [*Pushing* MAHON] Go on, I'm saying.

MAHON: Is it me?

CHRISTY: Not a word out of you. Go on from this.

MAHON [*walking out and looking back at* CHRISTY *over his shoulder*]: Glory be to God! [*With a broad smile*] I am crazy again.

> *Goes.*

CHRISTY: Ten thousand blessings upon all that's here, for you've turned me a likely gaffer[30] in the end of all, the way I'll go romancing through a romping lifetime from this hour to the dawning of the Judgment Day.

> *He goes out.*

MICHAEL: By the will of God, we'll have peace now for our drinks. Will you draw the porter, Pegeen?

SHAWN [*going up to her*]: It's a miracle Father Reilly can wed us in the end of all, and we'll have none to trouble us when his vicious bite is healed.

PEGEEN [*hitting him a box on the ear*]: Quit my sight. [*Putting her shawl over her head and breaking out into wild lamentations*] Oh, my grief, I've lost him surely. I've lost the only Playboy of the Western World.

Curtain

1   Someone without legal claim to the land he occupies.
2   A wicker frame for carrying turf in this instance.
3   A policeman. In 1829, Robert Peel (1768–1850) as Home Secretary established the London police force. Hence Peelers or in Britain, Bobbies.
4   Someone such as a town-crier employed to make public announcements in the streets.
5   A word with a wider provenance in Ireland. Here meaning distressed from cold.
6   Latin: in good faith. Here meaning there would be no need for an after-hours police search because all of Michael's customers live more than four miles away, and are hence entitled to hospitality.
7   Raised the spade. Unlike the English spade, a loy is narrow and used for making ridges or ploughing by hand or, as here, lifting potatoes. There is a sketch of a loy used in County Leitrim in E. Estyn Evans, *Irish Folk Ways* (1957).
8   See footnote 5 on page 43.
9   11 November. It was the custom to kill an animal on this feast day in readiness for winter. See Kevin Danagher, *The Year in Ireland* (1972). Sunshine in November in Ireland is always a bonus.
10   Bonnive, a sucking-pig.
11   Prefer, still in use in Ireland.
12   A settle-bed was a seat by day and a bed by night.
13   Little hill: a cnoc (knock) is a hill.
14   Neifin is more than 800 metres high, Erris a bleak moorland. Both are in County Mayo. In Douglas Hyde, *Abhráin Grádh Chúige Connacht* (Love Songs of Connacht) (1893) there is a love song entitled 'The Brow of Nefin'.
15   A traneen is Irish for a long slender grass-stalk, like a knitting-needle (P.W. Joyce).
16   A wicker basket.
17   Prison in Dublin.
18   Feast of St Michael the Archangel, 29 September.
19   Peat-bog.
20   An untidy, slovenly person.
21   Hundreds of people making their way to Britain for the harvest.
22   Underwear worn by women.
23   Narrow road or lane.
24   Hitting.
25   Ear (as in lug-hole).
26   Presumably, paralytic.
27   The workhouse.
28   Our Fathers (prayer).
29   Rump.
30   Young man, boy, young chap.

JOSEPH CAMPBELL
from Joseph Campbell, *The Gilly of Christ* (1907)

Joseph Campbell (Seosamh MacCathmaoil) (1879–1944), the mountainy singer (his *nom de plume*), who was born and educated in Belfast, was associated with the Ulster Literary Theatre and the literary magazine *Uladh*. A rescue worker in the Easter Rising, he sided with the Republicans during the Irish Civil War, was imprisoned and on his release moved to the United States. His poetry has a distinctive strain, Gaelic and Catholic with its mysticism rooted in this world.

I AM THE GILLY[1] OF CHRIST

I am the gilly of Christ,
The mate of Mary's Son;
I run the roads at seeding-time,
And when the harvest's done.

I sleep among the hills,
The heather is my bed;
I dip the termon-well[2] for drink,
And pull the sloe for bread.

No eye has ever seen me,
But shepherds hear me pass,
Singing at fall of even
Along the shadowed grass.

The beetle is my bellman,
The meadow-fire my guide,
The bee and bat my ambling nags
When I have use to ride.

All know me only the Stranger,
Who sits on the Saxons' Height:
He burned the bachach's[3] little house
On last St Brigid's Night.[4]

He sups off silver dishes,
And drinks in a golden horn,
But he will wake a wiser man
Upon the Judgment Morn!

I am the gilly of Christ,
The mate of Mary's Son;
I run the roads at seeding-time,
And when the harvest's done.

The seed I sow is lucky,
The corn I reap is red,
And whoso sings the 'Gilly's Rann'[5]
Will never cry for bread.

1   Servant. In one of the manuscripts of *A View of the Present State of Ireland* (1596), Spenser refers to 'horsboyes or guilles as they call them'.
2   A well belonging to the Church.
3   In Irish bocht is a poor person.
4   Feast of St Brigid is 1 February.
5   Irish for verse, stanza, quatrain.

LYNN DOYLE
from Lynn Doyle, *Ballygullion* (1908)

Lynn C. Doyle (pseudonym of Leslie Alexander Montgomery) (1873–1961) was born in Downpatrick in County Down and became a bank manager in Dundalk. His fictional town of Ballygullion was based on Slieve Gullion, the area between Newry and Dundalk. His humorous portrait of Irish country life, which is worth comparing with Lady Gregory's in *Spreading the News*, is carried in part through his use of Ulster dialect (which I have for the most part refrained from glossing).

The Wooden Leg

It was a black day for Michael Carlin whin he first took the notion av soldierin'. In troth, though, ye could hardly blame him; for it was all over the two things that bothers the whole men kind av us — dhrink an' the wimmen.

Michael an' Susy Bryan was coortin' sthrong for a long time, an' iverybody thought it would ha' been a match. An' a right good match it was for both av thim. Michael lived wi' his uncle, an' was sartin to get the bit av land whin the ould man died; an' Susy lived wi' an aunt on twinty-five acres av the best land in the county, that they said was her own, barrin' a life intherest the aunt had in it. The aunt got money left her at the same time, an' even if Michael an' Susy didn't come intil that in their own time — for the aunt was a tight, fresh body, not above thirty-eight or so — sure the childher were bound to fall in some day.

There niver should ha' been a match aisier to make, an' that's just what bate it. It was too simple an' complate altogether; an' the wimmen bein' the divil for pure crookedness, Susy must be carryin' on wi' wan or another, just to let Michael see he wasn't goin' to get things all his own way, till he was clane wild wi' jealousy.

Wan day as Michael was goin' in to Ballygullion fair, he happened to come on James Doran an' Susy walkin' along the road.

They were brave an' close together for a start, an' whin Susy sees Michael comin', she slithers still closer to James. James, bein' a man av spunk, didn't make much av a move away as ye may guess; so altogether they were a very lovin' lookin' couple whin Michael come near them.

Michael he niver let on, though, but just said, 'Good-mornin'' an' walked by. He niver turned his head either, or Susy niver catched him doin' it anyway, an' she turned hers brave an' often to see.

But for all that Michael took it quiet, he was badly cut; an' all that day he kept thinkin' about it, an' dhrinkin' half-wans av whiskey to dhrive the thoughts out av his head.

The more he took the angrier he got wi' Susy, till,

bein' clane beside himself wi' whiskey an' jealousy, an' happenin' to meet the Ulsther Fusiliers route-marchin' on his way home, what does he do but list. The sodgers were campin' outside av Ballygullion for two days, an' at the end av that time Michael was to join thim.

But when Michael got home, thin there was the fun. The ould uncle nearly wint mad. It was bad enough losin' Michael about the place, but that was nothin' to the disgrace av him goin' for a sodger.

There was a muttherin' av war wi' the Boers[1] at the time, an' terrible bad feelin' again England among the red-hot Nationalists; an' to list for a sodger in the British army was like turnin' your back on your politics altogether.

So ould Pether he ramped up an' down, an' cursed somethin' dhreadful, an' poor Michael sat on the dhresser very miserable lookin'; for the dhrink was dead in him be this time, an' he begin to see he'd made a fool av himself.

But if Michael's uncle was mad, it was nothin' to the rage Susy was in whin she heard av it. Susy was by way av bein' a terrible pathriot, an' used to dhress herself up av a holiday wi' a wee green hood an' a cloak wi' shamrocks embroidhered on it, for all the world like what you'd see on a Christmas card. An' mortial[2] well she looked too, wi' a handful of brown curls stickin' out on each side av as red a pair av cheeks, an' two as bright eyes as was in Ireland.

'Twas well the green suited her though; for, in troth if she'd ha' looked as well in it, there's no tellin' but she'd ha' wore orange.

Anyhow, she was clane wild wi' Michael, an' wouldn't even see him, though he hung about the house the whole two days. If she hadn't been a bit in the wrong herself, she'd maybe have come round; but that was what finished his chance entirely.

The end av it was Michael marched away wan mornin' wi' divil a wan to say 'good-bye' till him, an' wasn't heard av for more than a year.

Thin word come that he was goin' out to South Africa wi' a lot more recruits to bring up the regiment to full strength; for they'd lost heavy again the Boers. For near a year again there was no word more. An' thin a letther come for the uncle sayin' Michael had been badly wounded an' was comin' home.

For all the uncle was so mad about the soldierin' he was a kindly man at bottom, an' he made Michael welcome; though he was no manner av use till him, for wan av his legs was as stiff as a poker wi' the wound he'd got.

Wan evenin' afther Michael had been home about a couple av days, I thought I'd go down an' see him.

Whin I wint in he was sittin' before the fire wi' the game leg up on a chair before him, an' the uncle sittin' beside him talkin' very hard.

'How are ye, Michael?' sez I. 'But I needn't ask. Sure you're lookin' rightly.' An' so he was too, barrin' the leg. The soldierin' had made a man av him. He was square an' well set up lookin' about the shouldhers, an' as brown as a berry.

'Troth, Pat,' sez he, 'I've not much to boast about. I'm little betther than a cripple. An' if the uncle here hadn't taken me in, it's the beggin' I might be at.'

'Wheesht now,' sez the uncle, shufflin' on his chair — he was a terrible fidgety wee man, always on the go — 'sure you're welcome; an' if you take my advice,' sez he, 'you'll be undher a compliment to nobody very long. Not that I want to be redd av ye; but it's for your own good.'

'I'll tell ye what it is, Pat,' goes on the uncle, turnin' to me; 'I'm just advisin' him to make up to the widow beyont.'

It was on me tongue to ask Michael what about Susy, when the ould chap winks at me.

'Now that Susy's left her, an' not likely to be back, she'll jump at the chance av settlin' again,' sez he.

'An' is Susy not comin' back from her uncle Joe's?' sez I.

'No,' sez he, 'she's goin' to marry her cousin, an' they're both to keep house wi' the ould man. He's terrible lonely since the wife died.'

I stole a look at Michael, an' he was lookin' very white.

'Look here, uncle,' sez he, breakin' out suddenly, 'I'm a burden here, an' if the widow would have me I'd ask her, for I'm not carin' much who I marry; but there's no wan would have a poor cripple like me, an' well ye know it. Help me up to bed,' sez he, 'an' let Pat know the whole story. He'll not tell anybody about me that he's known from a child. If he gives in to me makin' up till any woman, when he's heard, damme, I'll marry who you like.'

So the ould fellow arms him up to bed, an' comes back to the fire. 'Look here, Pat,' sez he, 'the whole throuble's this. The lad has lost his leg above the knee, an' has got a wooden wan. Ye wouldn't notice it when he's sittin', but he can't walk barrin' on sticks yet, an' very stiff at that. That's why I tould him the crack about Susy an' the cousin. There's no chance av a young girl lookin' at him now.

'But it's different wi' the widow. Whin a widow woman gets to her time av life, an' no word av a second market, there's very little in breeches she'll not face. It's not for a lame leg she'd refuse a likely young chap like Michael.'

'Would ye not tell her 'twas a wooden wan, thin?' sez I.

'Divil a bit,' sez he, 'if I have me will. She'll niver find out till it's too late, an' thin she'll have to thole.[3] There's enough av Michael left to make as good a man as she's likely to get now, an' if he wanst gets her he's a made man. The ould hussy has bings av money, I'm tould. An' if Susy should marry the cousin, an' there is some talk av it, right enough, the aunt'll be able to buy out the place very chape. She has a life intherest in it as it is.

'The only bother wi' Michael is the leg. If him an' the widow was wanst married she'd niver tell, or if it come out she could let on she knew all the time. But if she finds out about it durin' the coortin' she'll not hould her tongue thin, an' the divil a woman he'll get at all.'

'Pether,' sez I, 'it's well ye tould me about the leg; for I know the very article for you.'

'What, Pat,' sez he; 'what do ye mane?'

'It's just this mornin',' sez I, 'I was readin' in a piece av a docthor's paper the vet brought round a linimint for the mare, about some man in Dublin that makes legs betther than the rale thing — that's if you're to believe what he sez in the advertisement.'

'But could ye walk in wan?' sez Pether.

'Walk,' sez I. 'If the man's not as big a liar as the ould fellow himself, ye could dance a hornpipe in wan. It'll carry him up the church wi' the widow anyhow,' sez I, 'an' that's all ye want.'

'Pat,' sez he, 'bring down the paper, an' if they're all you say, we'll have wan for the boy should it break me. It'll not throuble him to pay me back if he gets the widow.'

The end av it was ould Pether brings Michael round to let him send for a patent leg. An' though the price daunted him a bit, he was that sure av Michael gettin' the widow he screwed himself up to partin' wi' it.

It was no aisy job gettin' Michael to agree, for he was no way keen on the widow, an' the game leg was a fine excuse. But whin he seen how the uncle was set on the match, what could he do but give in, him bein' only a sort av pensioner in the house.

'Pat,' sez he to me, whin the uncle wasn't by, 'I've lost Susy now, an' I can't sponge here all me days. There's nothin' for it but the widow, an' I might do worse. She's a kindly wee woman, an' an ould friend av mine. But I don't like decavin' her about the leg.'

'Hould on till ye get the new wan,' sez I. 'If it's like the thing at all, ye needn't say a word. Niver mind about the decavin'. Sure all marryin' is decavin'. If she'd knowed the temper the first wan had, she'd niver ha' taken him. An' a bad temper's worse than a bad leg any day.'

'Ay, but I'm not sure it's worse than a wooden wan,' sez Michael, wi' the first smile I'd seen on his face since he come home.

Before the new leg come, Pether had the widow over for tay, an' I think he must have give her a hint that Michael was on the look out, for she was over near ivery day afther than inquirin' for his health; an' all the time she kept askin' about the bad leg, an' how soon he'd be walkin'. Michael niver would say much about it, but left ould Pether to do the talkin'. I was over wan night she was there, an' it was as good as a play to see Pether squirmin' on his chair, an' lyin' like the divil.

An' in troth I think the joke av it egged Michael on a bit; for he was mighty friendly wi' the widow before the night was over.

A couple av days afther this Pether sends up for me, an' whin I got there he runs across the kitchen an' shakes me be the hand.

'Pat,' sez he, 'you've made the boy's fortune. Look at him,' sez he, caperin' round. 'Get up an' walk, Michael.'

Up gets Michael, an' walks across the kitchen, an' faith 'twas wondherful. Barrin' a bit av a halt, you'd niver ha' known but he had two legs as sound as me own. He was greatly up wi' it himself, too.

'Would any wan know, Pat?' sez he.

'Not a mother's son,' sez I. 'I can hardly believe it meself. It's wondherful altogether. Does it work aisy?'

'There's a bit av a catch in it I was just goin' to fix whin you come in,' sez Pether. 'Sit down, Michael; an' I'll do it now.'

'Maybe you'd as well lave it alone,' sez Michael; for he knowed his uncle.

He was by way av bein' a handy man, an' always would be meddlin' at things he didn't undherstand. There was hardly a clock in the counthryside he didn't spoil, before the people found him out.

But Pether wasn't to be put off.

'Not at all,' sez he; 'I'll make it all right in a jiffey.'

So he gets Michael down on a chair at the fire, pulls up his breeches, an' begins pokin' about the knee av the patent leg wi' a screwdriver. There was a desperate lot av springs an' joints about the thing, an' I misdoubted but Pether would do it little good. An' sure enough, afther pokin' a bit, whin he thries to work the joint — 'be the holy poker,' sez he, 'she's stuck.'

An' stuck the leg was. It was bent well at the knee, but divil a bit would it go straight for all he could do, an' he tugged at it till he near pulled Michael off the chair.

'What's to be done?' sez he, afther he'd progged it for five minits. 'I'm clane bate.'

'Thry a taste av oil,' sez I.

'The very thing, Pat,' sez he; an' he reaches down a bottle av paraffin.

He put a dhrop or two in. 'Now,' sez he, 'for a good pull. That'll shift it.'

So it did. The leg straightened out wi' a snap, lit ould Pether on his back, an' the toe av it just took the wee tay-drawer that was simmerin' on the hob.

The cat an' dog was sleepin' in front av the fire; an' nayther av thim had any cause to complain av the other; for they just got the tay over thim in about equal shares. The dog run away up the house yelpin' murdher, an' the cat tears round the kitchen a couple av times, spittin' an' swearin', knocks two plates off the dhresser, an' thin out through a pane av glass.

'Holy Biddy,' sez Pether, risin' to his feet; 'there's eighteenpence gone. But niver mind, the leg's workin' again. Is it aisy, Michael?'

'It's all right, uncle,' sez Michael, walkin' up an' down the kitchen.

'I'll just put a dhrop more oil in it,' sez Pether.

'No, uncle,' sez Michael, very firm. 'Thank you, all the same, we'll just let it rest at this.'

'Maybe you're right,' sez Pether. 'It might take another thraw. Man!' sez he, 'it's doin' well. I'll dhrop over to the widow's in the mornin' an' tell her you're mendin' fast.'

Whin the widow seen Michael walkin' about wi' only a bit av a limp, she begin to set her cap at him in rale earnest. Up till then she'd been afeared he was goin' to be a lamitor[4] all his days, an' she wasn't right sure whether to face him or not. Besides, there was a pig-dealer in the neighbourhood, wan Tammas M'Gimpsey, was reported to be lookin' afther her when the word av Susy's goin' to be married come out. But afther Michael got on his feet she had no eyes for anybody but him.

About three weeks afther the patent leg come home, Pether calls up to see me.

'Pat,' sez he, 'the job's as good as done. Michael's a made man. He's goin' to ask the widow afther Mass next Sunday.'

'It's well if Susy doesn't come home before it's settled,' sez I.

'Tut,' sez Pether, 'she'd niver look at him now.'

'Ay, but she might put him off the notion av the widow,' sez I.

'Not a bit,' sez Pether. 'Sure the widow an' him's as good as trysted[5] already. Michael has a terrible notion av her now.'

I said nothin' to that, but I had an idea all the same that Michael's notion av her was little sthronger than at the first. He wasn't lookin' in big heart for a man that was goin' to be married, if it was only to a widow.

Sunday come, an' whin I sat down beside Michael an' the uncle, there was the widow right across the aisle, dhressed up to the nines.

A minit or so before the bell stopped, ould Pether give a jump an' sits well forrard in his sate. I seen him skellyin'[6] across, an' whin I looked, who should I see but Susy sittin' down beside her aunt. From the look the widow gave her I'm thinkin' she was nayther expected nor welcome.

'Pether, me man,' sez I to meself, 'your work's cut out for you now.'

An' Pether knowed that as well as me; for he aye kept edgin' furdher forrard to keep Michael from seein' Susy. Very little throuble he had; for Michael niver turned his head at all, but sat there very glum, lookin' sthraight in front av him.

All wint well till Father Connolly was just beginnin' his sermon. Michael shifted round a bit to hear him, an' his eye lights on Susy. He half riz from his sate, an' turned as white as a sheet. Sittin' down again his wooden leg slips off the wee stool he had it restin' on, an' hits the flure a brave knock. Wi' that it gives a whirr an' a bizz the same as in the kitchen at home, an' fetches the sate before us a thump ye'd have heard all over the chapel.

Ould Mrs Malone in front lepped above three inches in the air, an' dhropped her glasses, an' Father Connolly took a mortial hard look our way.

But sure lookin' at Michael was little use, for the leg was clane away wi' it, kickin' fourteen to the dozen, an' threatenin' ivery minit to break down the partition in front.

Ivery man, woman an' child in the church was standin' up, or cranin' over to see what was wrong, an' as for Father Connolly, he was near chokin' wi' the rage. The cowld sweat was runnin' down Michael's face, an' poor ould Pether was near as bad.

'Stop the cursed thing, Michael, for Hivin's sake,' sez he, in as near a whisper as he could get to bate the noise av the leg.

'I can't,' sez Michael in desperation. 'Thry an' catch it, uncle.'

So Pether stoops to get hould av it; but he missed his grip, an' the leg comes again the partition wi' a dunt that split the board for two feet.

Be this time the people was near mad wi' curiosity, an' Father Connolly had stopped in his sermon, an' was comin' down from the pulpit.

'Let me out,' sez Michael, sthrugglin' to his feet; an' out he comes, wi' the leg goin' like a flail.

The first skite[7] it kicked ould Pether's Sunday tall hat into the organ-loft. Be good luck the nixt missed Pether himself by an inch; but if it did, the third wan took me on the knee-cap, an' near desthroyed me.

Howiver, out in the aisle he gets at last, an' just that minit Father Connolly comes marchin' down it, wi' a face like a turkey-cock.

Whin Michael seen him comin' he jams the toe av the leg undher the heatin' stove, an' steadys himself as well as he could.

'An' is it you, Michael Carlin, that has been disturbin' the house av God wi' your dhrunken frolics?' sez Father Connolly. 'I might have known it. I might have known it could be none av the dacint boys av Ballygullion; but a blackguard av a soldier, that fears nayther God nor man. Lave the sacred precincts av the church, before I forget me duty as a priest,' sez he, turnin' away.

But sure enough the Ould Fellow himself was again Michael that day, for just as he dhrew the toe out to go, the leg lashes forrard an' catches Father Connolly where he didn't expect it.

Before ye could dhraw your breath the half av the congregation was on top av Michael, Tammas M'Gimpsey at the head av thim.

'Out wi' him,' sez he, 'out wi' the dirty sodger, an' tache him whether he'll kick our priest in his own church!' 'Out wi' him!' sez iverybody.

An' out they goes in a sthrugglin' crowd, Michael in the middle av thim, an' the wimmen hanging round, pullin' the skirts av men's coats, an' cryin' melia murdher.[8]

Poor Michael would ha' had a poor chance wi' them be himself, but they didn't reckon on the leg. If it did get Michael intil the throuble, manly an' well it stood to him in it.

Between the middle av the church an' the door it shifted more teeth than Docthor Cargill pulled in a year before; an' thim that only got a peeled shin or a black eye was well plazed the next day.

Be the time they got him intil the churchyard the bulk av thim was at Michael's head, an' only Tammas M'Gimpsey would face the right leg — the wooden wan, I mane — though sorrow a wan av thim knew it was wood, thin.

'Throw him in the road!' sez the men at his head.

'Put him in the river,' sez thim at his feet. They were the angriest at him, small wondher.

'Ye'll dhrown him,' sez the first party, pullin' nixt the road.

'Divil a odds, if we do,' sez Tammas M'Gimpsey, pullin' nixt the river.

At that minit the sthraps av the leg give way.

Down goes the men at Michael's head over Father Dorrian's tombstone, an' down goes Tammas M'Gimpsey wi' the leg in his hand. Whin he riz, he takes a look at Michael an' the boys lyin' on the ground in a heap, an' wan at the boot an' leg in his hand. An' thin wi' a screech like a stuck pig he over the churchyard wall, an' across the fields like a madman. He had his passage booked for Amerikay the nixt day, before he heard the leg was wood.

For the first minit or two the rest av the boys was near as much scared as Tammas; but they soon seen how the thing was; an' thin there was such a laugh riz at Ballygullion niver heard. Even thim that had broken heads an' bloody noses joined in — afther a while.

The wimmen that was hurryin' out to save Michael's life, they chimed in too, an' the only sober face I seen was the widow's. She had come out hot-foot to rescue Michael, an' near thripped over Tammas M'Gimpsey an' the leg as they both wint down.

Wan look at the leg an' another at Michael was enough for her. She stood a minit or two dumb-foundhered, an' thin down the path for the gate.

An' if the crowd laughed before, they laughed twice as much thin; for there was few didn't know about the coortin' match.

But och, och, ye would ha' been sorry for poor Michael, sittin' there in the middle av the ring av thim, the laughin'-stock av the parish. An' maybe the thought that Susy was among thim wasn't the laste av his sorrow.

In the thick av the laughin' an' jeerin' out comes Father Connolly; for somebody had tould him what had happened.

'Michael,' sez he, puttin' his hand on his head, 'Michael, me poor fellow, I miscalled ye inside. I said things to ye I shouldn't ha' said, an' things I didn't mane. But ye'll forgive me, me son, for I was angrier than a Christian man should be, let alone a priest, an' I didn't know your thrial. But keep up your heart,' sez he; 'it's not the coward that gets the knocks, an' a brave man, Michael, has no cause to be ashamed av anything. God comfort ye, Michael,' sez the ould man, turnin' away.

'An' now, boys and girls,' sez he to the rest av thim standin' round, 'go in there,' pointin' to the church, 'an' I'll see if I can't tache ye more Christian charity than to laugh at a fellow-creature's affliction. It's little betther than haythens ye are.'

It wasn't long till they were all in again, I can tell ye; all but me an' Pether.

'Uncle,' sez Michael, 'lift me up on the stone there, an' do you an' Pat lave me for a bit. Maybe you'd borrow Joe Crawley's cart from down the road an' take me home. I'm only lumber, an' the world knows it now. I've thried to decave people, an' I'm punished for it this day.'

'We'll go, Michael,' sez ould Pether. 'Pat,' sez he to me in a whisper, 'stay here an' keep an eye on the lad.'

So I tip-toes round behind Michael's back, an' plants meself on a stone a bit away, lavin' Michael sittin' there wi' his head between his hands.

Prisintly, who should comin' slippin' out av the porch but Susy. She comes right over to Michael, an' puts her hand on his shoulder.

'Michael,' sez she. Quick enough he looked up thin.

'Susy,' sez he; 'Susy, me dear, is it you?'

Maybe 'twas the words, maybe 'twas the way he said thim, but Susy's face that was glum enough before broke out in a smile like sunshine on a runnin' sthrame.

'Och, Susy,' sez poor Michael, 'don't you laugh at me too. I know I'm a mock an' a laughin'-stock — well, well, I know it; but if ye iver had a kindly thought for me, an' wanst I believe ye had, lave me to me shame, if ye can't pity me. If I did go soldierin' have I not paid the price? Och, och,' sez he, dhroppin' his head on his hands again, 'if I'd only lost me life be it. But I've lost dearer than me life, an' it's this day I know it.'

'In troth, Michael,' sez Susy, 'ye've lost me aunt right enough, if that's what ye mane. She'll niver take ye now.'

'Ye little divil ye,' sez I to myself, 'if I didn't see your face I'd think ye'd no heart, to say thim words.'

But Michael didn't see her face, an' his head dhropped lower than iver.

'I desarve it, Susy,' sez he; 'it's a hard word you're sayin', but God knows I desarve it. But me dear,' sez he, 'some day if ye should happen to think av a broken man, a man that was a burden to his friends, an' thim friends eggin' him on, ye'll maybe see some excuse for him. For all that, till I heard ye were to be married to your cousin, I niver give in. Not that I had hopes for meself. But sure till you were another man's wife, I could think av ye without sin.'

'Well, Michael,' sez Susy — the smile was still on her face, but I thought there was a glint av tears in her eye — 'I'm not goin' to marry me cousin that I know av, an' if me aunt won't have ye — an' I don't think there's much chance av it — I'll just have to take ye meself — if you'll ask me, that is,' sez she, gettin' very red.

'Susy,' sez Michael, sittin' up, 'are ye mockin' me?' 'No,' sez he, lookin' at her a minit; 'God bless your soft heart, I believe you'd do it for pity; but, child, ye don't know what you're sayin'. Is it to marry me, a cripple, an' a pauper forbye?[9] Niver,' sez he. 'I've behaved like a scoundhrel, but plaze God I'll be an honest man now. I'll love ye, Susy, till they carry out this maimed carcase av mine, but I'll niver let ye join yourself to three-quarters av a man. God bless ye again, dear,' sez he, wringin' her hand, 'an' send ye the man ye desarve.'

'Well, Michael,' sez Susy, 'I don't know what about gettin' the man I desarve, but it seems I'm not goin' to get the man I want; an' all because he's too fond av me, that's the annoyin' part av it. I didn't say what I said out av pity, though me heart's sore for your throuble, but just because I couldn't help it. I lost ye be me folly an' empty head before, an' if I'm only gettin' three-quarters av ye back I've nobody to blame but meself. An' I'd rather have that three-quarters av a man, Michael dear, than the best whole man in Ireland.'

An' thin in a minit Susy was lyin' on his breast cryin' an' croonin' over her poor boy, an' Michael strokin' her hair and sayin' niver a word. Maybe his heart was too full to spake.

It was no place for me, anyway, so I stepped quietly out be the gate.

Comin' up the road I meets ould Pether wi' the horse an' cart.

'Pat,' sez he, 'maybe this is all for the best. Ould Crawley was executor under the uncle's will, an' he tells me the farm's Susy's altogether. The aunt only got two hundhred pound an' no life intherest. So maybe Michael's well out av her, after all.'

'What?' sez I, 'the farm's Susy's? Come here, Pether,' an' I dhraws him over to the churchyard gate. 'Look at thim,' sez I. 'Wheesht now, ye ould fool. Lave thim there for a while, an' thin put thim in the cart an' let thim go home together. You an' I'll walk it. But if it wasn't that Susy's not far off bein' an angel, I'd say Michael had the divil's own luck.'

I don't well know how it come about, but whin Tammas M'Gimpsey got the notion av Amerikay in his head, he stuck till it, an' whin he wint, he tuk the widow an' the two hundred wi' him.

A fortnight afther that Susy an' Michael was married; an' now there's a lump av a gossoon runnin' about the place that thinks his daddy's the cliverest man in the country because he can stick a fork in his right leg.

The wee fellow thinks all the more av it since he thried it on himself.

---

1   The Boer War 1899–1902.
2   An obsolete form of mortal as an intensifier, meaning here terribly.
3   Endure or bear it.
4   Lamiger is a dialect word for a lame person or cripple.

5   Betrothed.
6   Squinting.
7   A blow, a sudden movement in an oblique direction.

8   Melia: Irish míle (thousand); a thousand murders.
9   Besides.

SEUMAS O'SULLIVAN

from Seumas O'Sullivan, *Verses: Sacred and Profane* (1908)

Seumas O'Sullivan (James Sullivan Starkey) (1879–1958), poet, essayist and editor of *The Dublin Magazine* from 1923 until 1958. Here are two poems published in the Tower Press Booklets Series, the second one commemorating the death of Parnell in 1891 (see Yeats's poem 'September 1913' for comparison).

A PIPER

A piper in the streets to-day,
Set up, and tuned, and started to play,
And away, away, away on the tide
Of his music we started; on every side
Doors and windows were opened wide,
And men left down their work and came,
And women with petticoats coloured like flame,
And little bare feet that were blue with cold,
Went dancing back to the age of gold,
And all the world went gay, went gay,
For half an hour in the street to-day.

GLASNEVIN, OCTOBER 9TH, 1904

They peer about his grave with curious eyes,
And for his sin they pity him, their chief,
With miserable mockery of grief;
Beyond their littleness serene he lies,
Nor heeds the insult of their sympathies,
This man pre-eminent by strong belief
In his own heart — a little while, for brief
The resting-time is when a hero dies.

Near to God's heart by greatness of thy heart,
And nearer by thy sin, O strong of will!
Send out thy spirit like a sword and kill
Their littleness; no longer dwell apart;
Send forth thy spirit like a flame, and burn
Through these a pathway for thy soul's return.

JAMES STEPHENS

from James Stephens, *Insurrections* (1909)

James Stephens (?1880–1950) was author of some of the most popular and endearing contributions to modern Irish writing. This is an example of an early poem, which has the habit of surfacing in later novels. The narrator in Bernard McLaverty's recent novel *Grace Notes* (1997) remarks that 'The Shell' 'became more and more gloomy until the last line when the mood changed and the shell was taken away from the ear.'

THE SHELL

I

And then I pressed the shell
Close to my ear,
And listened well.

And straightway, like a bell,
Came low and clear
The slow, sad, murmur of far distant seas

Whipped by an icy breeze
Upon a shore
Wind-swept and desolate.

It was a sunless strand that never bore
The footprint of a man,
Nor felt the weight

Since time began
Of any human quality or stir,
Save what the dreary winds and wave incur.

II

And in the hush of waters was the sound
Of pebbles, rolling round;
For ever rolling, with a hollow sound:

And bubbling sea-weeds, as the waters go,
Swish to and fro
Their long cold tentacles of slimy grey:

There was no day;
Nor ever came a night
Setting the stars alight

To wonder at the moon:
Was twilight only, and the frightened croon,
Smitten to whimpers, of the dreary wind

And waves that journeyed blind . . .
And then I loosed my ear — Oh, it was sweet
To hear a cart go jolting down the street.

JOSEPH CAMPBELL
from Joseph Campbell, *The Mountainy Singer* (1909)

For a fleeting moment rural Ireland comes alive in 'Night, and I Travelling'. The scene is reminiscent of Davin's story in Joyce's *A Portrait of the Artist as a Young Man* when on his return from a hurling match and missing his train Davin finds himself towards nightfall in the Ballyhoura Hills, where he knocks at a door and is offered a big mug of milk by a young woman half undressed.

I AM THE MOUNTAINY SINGER

I am the mountainy singer —
The voice of the peasant's dream,
The cry of the wind on the wooded hill,
The leap of the fish in the stream.

Quiet and love I sing —
The cairn on the mountain crest,
The cailín[1] in her lover's arms,
The child at its mother's breast.

Beauty and peace I sing —
The fire on the open hearth,
The cailleach[2] spinning at her wheel,
The plough in the broken earth.

Travail and pain I sing —
The bride on the childing bed,
The dark man labouring at his rhymes,
The ewe in the lambing shed.

Sorrow and death I sing —
The canker come on the corn,
The fisher lost in the mountain loch,
The cry at the mouth of morn.

No other life I sing,
For I am sprung of the stock
That broke the hilly land for bread,
And built the nest in the rock!

1   Irish colleen or young girl.
2   Irish for old woman.

NIGHT, AND I TRAVELLING

Night, and I travelling.
An open door by the wayside,
Throwing out a shaft of warm yellow light.
A whiff of peat smoke;
A gleam of delf on the dresser within;
A woman's voice crooning, as if to a child.
I pass on into the darkness.

IRISH WRITING IN THE 1910s

The Freeman's Journal, I notice, refers to any peaceful attempt to secure Woman Suffrage as an 'intrigue' almost in the very language in which English Tory papers refer to the passage of Home Rule, and it would appear to be no lack of desire which withholds the *Freeman* from speaking of an attempt 'to smuggle Woman Suffrage through the House of Commons'. The same paper implies that Mr Asquith's pledge to allow a free vote of the House on the amendment to the Reform Bill is worthless, since it is loaded with the unexpressed condition that he will resign if the amendment is carried. All this one must take note of, as well as the historic fact that men in the past have frequently appealed to violence when thus fobbed off on one pretence or another and denied justice. I am not a Tolstoyan, and it would be unfair and ridiculous to ask women to assume, what we all know to be untrue, that reason and justice alone sway human affairs. But when all this is allowed for, it seems perfectly clear that women have an especial interest in strengthening the forces of reason and limiting and weakening the forces of passion and violence. One would, indeed, suppose that they would much prefer to fight on the intellectual and moral field, where they are strong, rather than on the physical field, where they are weak. Civilization can only advance in proportion as we increase the sum of rational and humane behaviour in the world. The frame of mind produced by constant appeals to force is essentially reactionary. On that line we soon come to distrust reason altogether, to count only on selfish motives as worth relying on, and to believe that men are swayed only by threats and terrorism. All this every good citizen must, surely, deplore. Even if it were true, what I think is obviously and patently false, that violence now advances the suffrage cause there might be something to be said from a larger point of view for foregoing this advantage. I will not say that a victory won by persuasion is worth three won by fear. But it is indisputable that the more of persuasion and the less of fear that goes to the winning of a victory such as this, the nobler, the finer and the more fructifying will it be.

– Fred Ryan, 'The Suffrage Tangle' in *The Irish Review*, August 1912

CRITICAL AND DOCUMENTARY

REVEREND P. S. DINNEEN

from Reverend P. S. Dinneen, 'The World-Wide Empire of the Irish Race: A Plea for its Organization',
Journal of the Ivernian Society, 6 January 1910

Patrick Dinneen (an tAthair Pádraig Ó Duinnín) (1860–1934) was a Jesuit priest whose involvement in the Gaelic League led to a lifetime commitment to Irish scholarship. He is most famous for compiling *Foclóir Gaedilge Agus Béarla: An Irish-English Dictionary* (1904, later editions 1927, 1934). Here in this extract from a lecture delivered to the inaugural meeting of the Students' National Literary Society in Dublin in November 1909, he focuses on the need to strengthen the ties connecting the twenty million Irish people living outside Ireland with the five million living within its borders. In a later part of the lecture (not reproduced here) Dinneen draws attention to the four qualities shared by the Irish: oratorical genius, political genius, military genius, and religious fervour.

The World-Wide Empire of the Irish Race

I

For upwards of a hundred years a living stream of people has been flowing from our shores, and pouring itself out on the various regions of the habitable world. This stream is one of the greatest and most significant facts in the history of the modern world. About the middle of the nineteenth century it swelled in volume and increased in speed by reason of the great Famine and the Fever and the Evictions. During the sixty years that have rolled by since the Famine it has been gushing forth with unabated vigour; and though the population of this island has been reduced to one-half of what it was a little over sixty years ago, the current is to-day as strong as ever. In the fifty years between 1851 and 1901 the number of our emigrants amounted to 3,846,393. In the sixty years that have elapsed since the Famine a stream of human souls, numerically exceeding the present population of this island, has emptied itself out on foreign shores.

This fluid mass of people differed from the existing population in this, that though it frequently included whole families — father, mother and young children — it was mainly composed of the young and robust of both sexes, who had left aged and infirm parents, with younger brothers and sisters, behind. They were generally without education or experience of the world, and their minds were haunted by a bitter recollection of poverty and injustice, of landlord greed and oppression, of griping bailiffs and insolent tithe-proctors. Mournful visions of roofless houses, of families lying down to die

by the roadside, mingled with their dreams of home and saddened their memories of the past. For the most part they went forth without capital, without help, without protection. They took refuge in the United States, in Canada, in India. They settled nearer home in the industrial centres of Great Britain. In the course of the last century the vast tracts of Australia and New Zealand were opened up to them, affording a relief similar to that which the exploration of the New World afforded to the congested regions of the Old. They wandered to the Pacific Islands, they penetrated the slopes of the Himalayas, the trackless forests of Bolivia and Peru, the burning plains of Mexico, the interior of China. There is no quarter of the habitable globe which the feet of our exiles have not trodden. There is scarcely a rood of land in half the world that has not been watered by their tears and enriched by their labour.

But it was chiefly to the United States of America that their eyes were directed in that dark day when the home in which they were brought up could be looked on no longer as their own. Thither they fled when pursued by landlord rapacity, when their roof-tree was levelled to the ground by the crowbar brigade. 'You will recollect,' said John Bright,[1] addressing a Dublin audience in 1866, 'that when the ancient Hebrew Prophet prayed in his captivity he prayed with his window opened towards Jerusalem. You know that the followers of Mahommed, when they pray, turn their faces towards Mecca. When the Irish peasant asks for food and freedom and blessing, his eye follows the setting sun — the aspirations of his heart reach beyond the wide Atlantic, and in spirit he grasps hands with the great Republic of the West.' Nearly fifty years have elapsed since these words were uttered, and they are as true to-day as ever.

I wish to direct your attention to the visible results of this mighty living stream that has been flowing from our island-home for one hundred and ten years, say, since the Legislative Union was enacted, and that has been enriching the shores of distant countries with its human alluvia. I will ask you to picture in your imaginations the immense multitude of Irishmen — probably not much less than seven millions — who have left our shores as emigrants from the passing of the Act of Union until the present hour, and their descendants — to picture to yourselves that mighty host scattered over all the regions of the earth, stratified amid the teeming millions that inhabit the great cities of America, Australia, India, and Great Britain, dispersed amid the hamlets that stud the vast rich open plains of the New World and the Australasian Continent, or hidden among the vines and palms of the archipelagoes of the Indian Ocean.

It is impossible to form an exact estimate of the number now living of these seven millions and of their descendants, but we may safely assume that it amounts at least to twenty millions. These, together with the present population of our own island, make a total of twenty-five millions of the Irish race now scattered the world over. Of these it may be assumed that the number of persons of Irish birth now living beyond the seas approaches in extent the present population of this island. We have, then, outside the shores of Ireland a greater Ireland — a nation larger, more populous, richer than the parent country. It is, indeed, difficult to determine under what circumstances the descendants of our race abroad should be classed as Irish. Remoteness of descent, mixture of race-blood, weaken racial ties. Important facts such as education, the moulding of character by different laws, and even the influence of climate seriously affect the claims of a body of people originally of one stock, but now scattered wide over the earth's surface, inhabiting various regions, and living amongst and often mixing with other races, to vindicate their continuous identity as a homogeneous racial unit. But even when due allowance has been made for these influences, the truth remains that the vast mass of the descendants of our emigrants are to be considered Irish in a real sense, and may justly claim citizenship in the world-wide empire of the Gael.

The rooted affection of even those remotely sprung from Irish blood for the land of their ancestors is proverbial, and makes up in no slight degree for the weakened tie of distant descent. This affection, this attachment of the exiled Irish and of their descendants to the land of their birth or descent has given many memorable proofs of its intensity; it has manifested itself in the yearning that induces the sons and daughters of the exiles of Ireland to cross the Atlantic Ocean for the sole purpose of feasting their eyes on the spot which gave their parents birth, even when that spot is now a bleak mountain side, and when these parents, as well as all their relatives, are mouldering in foreign graves; it has manifested itself in the devotedness of the sons and daughters of small farmers and cottiers who sent home to their parents and relatives from America, between the years 1848 and 1864, thirteen millions sterling, money saved by superhuman economy directed by love of home and filial piety from the hardest-earned wages in Christendom; it has manifested itself in the significant fact that in Great Britain, in Australia, in America, and elsewhere there is a solid and steady Irish vote that politicians of all shades of opinion have to reckon with, and that those who cast it, though by no means blind to local issues, have ever before their minds the supreme interests of Ireland and of the Irish race. The bond of racial union here revealed, the identity of interest in a large spiritual and in no mean temporal domain on the part of so large, so wide extending, so rapidly growing and spreading a branch of the human family, is, if not a unique, certainly a rare phenomenon in the history of nations, and it is on such a secure and solid foundation that the world-wide empire of Gaeldom rests.

There is, perhaps, more in the ties that unite our brethren over seas with us and with each other than we can easily explain. Some explanation, however, is to be found in the untoward circumstances of their expatriation. For over half a century the great majority of Irish exiles left the shores of Ireland under circumstances calculated to arouse and foster the tenderest love of home and race, and to stamp their minds with the sad memories of a common tribulation. They were driven from the hearthstone by what has been called economic causes, evil laws directed in their deadly operation by the hand of destiny; they carried with them over seas the painful memories of outrage and injustice, of parents left behind stricken down by famine, of homes wrecked, of acres sequestered, of the tenderest ties our nature cherishes rudely rent asunder. They went forth without scrip or store into the desert, watering their path with their tears, to seek for bread in an alien land; exposed to the derision of strangers, with whom they had neither religion nor language in common. They sank in tens of thousands into nameless graves on a distant shore. The green sward covered them, as the foreign earth mingled kindly with their Irish clay; the dew of heaven refreshed the verdure that clothed the turf above them. Their offspring went forth to wander in the impenetrable woods, or by the giant rivers, or in the dusky lanes of the great cities of the West, poor, unheeded, sorrowing, unknown; with no more definite pedigree than that the tenements which their souls inhabited were of Irish clay: their bodies emaciated, their strength gone, their memories nightly haunted by vague inarticulate dreams of their name and parentage, which pursued them into their waking hours, and rendered their very existence a misery not to be endured, till earth herself, as if ashamed at their wretchedness, mercifully clasped them to her bosom in a last repose. 'I have seen,' says an eye-witness, 'in one day thirty-seven people lying on the beach crawling on the mud, and dying like fish out of water.'[2] The grave pits of Grosse Island, of Montreal, of Kingston, of Toronto, of Partridge Island, the calcareous caverns of the Atlantic, with their thousands and tens of thousands of the mouldering bodies of our kinsmen, appeal to our instincts of common racial sympathy with vivid force and pathos, and are a dearer and more glorious heritage to our race than are victorious battle-fields to more powerful and prosperous peoples. The spirit of a common brooding sorrow is calculated to keep a race, however scattered, united in the bonds of a common sympathy. Our people at home and abroad have passed through the Red Sea of a great tribulation — the traditional memories of a rooted sorrow are fresh in their hearts, and under its spell they are drawn instinctively together.

The race of the Gael at home and over seas, widely scattered though they be, assert themselves very distinctly by reason of their physical and moral characteristics. They fill such a large space in the development of some of the most important countries of the world, are growing and spreading at such a rapid rate, that we may reasonably regard them as a great empire, boundless as the world, and held together not by the force of arms, but by the irresistible attraction of mutual sympathy, and by spiritual ties whose foundations are laid in the noblest of human instincts. The empire of Gaeldom is a great spreading expanse of water, extending into many regions, welling from an island fountain, and continually augmented and kept fresh by the unfailing supply at its source. The strain of emigration is severe on the parent country in these latter years, but even in times of the greatest prosperity the outflow of our surplus population will be sufficient to keep every portion of our empire in sympathy and union with its fountain head. The significance to us of this powerful race of people — this vast empire — is becoming clearer as the modern world evolves itself. Our people abroad embrace every class of society, from the millionaire to the pauper, from the learned philosopher to the illiterate, from the highest rank in civil, military and ecclesiastical life to the most lowly; their power and influence extend to every profession, to every field of human energy; they have all the force, activity, variety, and comprehensiveness of a virtual empire, vivified and controlled by the forces of the spirit, and cemented by racial sympathy and love. It is but natural, therefore, that we should give this vast realm due attention, study its characteristics, and endeavour to strengthen and consolidate its forces.

1   English statesman and radical, supported the North in the American Civil War.
2   John Francis Maguire, *The Irish in America* (1868), 197. [AN]

PATRICK WESTON JOYCE
from P. W. Joyce, *English As We Speak It In Ireland* (1910)

Patrick Weston Joyce (1827–1914) was a prodigious Irish scholar who made significant contributions to social history, music, language, and geography. His books include *The Origin and History of Irish Names of Places* (3 vols, 1869–70), *A Social History of Ancient Ireland* (2 vols, 1907), *Old Irish Folk Music and Songs* (1909), and *English As We Speak It In Ireland* (1910). This extract not only provides a useful reminder of the language in use in Ireland but can also be returned to when analysing the language of a play such as Martin McDonagh's *The Lonesome West* (1997).

Affirming, Assenting, and Saluting

The various Irish modes of affirming, denying, &c., will be understood from the examples given in this short chapter better than from any general observations.

The Irish *ní'l lá fós é* [neel law fo-say: it isn't day yet] is often used for emphasis in asseveration, even when persons are speaking English; but in this case the saying is often turned into English. 'If the master didn't give Tim a tongue-dressing, *'tisn't day yet*' (which would be said either by day or by night): meaning he gave him a very severe scolding. 'When I saw the mad dog running at me, if I didn't get a fright, *neel-law-fo-say*.'

'I went to town yesterday in all the rain, and if I didn't get a wetting *there isn't a cottoner in Cork*': meaning I got a very great wetting. This saying is very common in Munster; and workers in cotton were numerous in Cork when it was invented.

A very usual emphatic ending to an assertion is seen in the following:— 'That horse is a splendid animal *and no mistake*.'

'*I'll engage* you visited Peggy when you were in town': i.e. I assert it without much fear of contradiction: I warrant. Much in the same sense we use *I'll go bail*:— 'I'll go bail you never got that money you lent to Tom': 'An illigant song he could sing I'll go bail' (Lever)[1]: 'You didn't meet your linnet (i.e. your girl — your sweetheart) this evening I'll go bail' (Robert Dwyer Joyce[2] in 'The Beauty of the Blossom Gate').

'I'll hold you' introduces an assertion with some emphasis: it is really elliptical: I'll hold you [a wager: but always a fictitious wager]. I'll hold you I'll finish that job by one o'clock, i.e. I'll warrant I will — you may take it from me that I will.

The phrase 'if you go to that of it' is often added on to a statement to give great emphasis, amounting almost to a sort of defiance of contradiction or opposition. 'I don't believe you could walk four miles an hour': 'Oh don't you — I could then, or five if you go to that of it': 'I don't believe that Joe Lee is half as good a hurler as his brother Phil.' 'I can tell you he is then, and a great deal better if you go to that of it.' Lowry Looby, speaking of St Swithin, says:— 'He was then, buried more than once if you go to that of it.' (Gerald Griffin:[3] *Collegians*: Munster.)

'Is it cold outside doors?' Reply, 'Aye is it,' meaning 'it is certainly.' An emphatic assertion (after the Gaelic construction) frequently heard is 'Ah then, 'tis I that wouldn't like to be in that fight.' 'Ah 'tis my mother that will be delighted.'

'What did he do to you?' 'He hit me with his stick, *so he did*, and it is a great shame, so it is.' 'I like a cup of tea at night, so I do.' In the South an expression of this kind is very often added on as a sort of clincher to give emphasis. Similar are the very usual endings as seen in these assertions:— 'He is a great old schemer, *that's what he is*': 'I spoke up to the master and showed him he was wrong — *I did begob*.'

I asked a man one day: 'Well, how is the young doctor going on in his new place?' and he replied 'Ah, how but well'; which he meant to be very emphatic: and then he went on to give particulars.

A strong denial is often expressed in the following way: 'This day will surely be wet, so don't forget your umbrella': 'What a fool I am': as much as to say, 'I should be a fool indeed to go without an umbrella to-day, and I think there's no mark of a fool about me.' 'Now Mary don't wait for the last train [from Howth] for there will be an awful crush.' 'What a fool I'd be ma'am.' 'Oh Mr Lory I thought you were gone home [from the dance] two hours ago': 'What a fool I am,' replies Lory (*Knocknagow*)[4], equivalent to 'I hadn't the least notion of making such a fool of myself while there's such fun here.' This is heard everywhere in Ireland, 'from the centre all round to the sea.'

Much akin to this is Nelly Donovan's reply to Billy Heffernan who had made some flattering remark to her:— 'Arrah now Billy what sign of a fool do you see on me?' (*Knocknagow*.)

An emphatic assertion or assent: 'Yesterday was very wet.' Reply:— 'You may say it was,' or 'you may well say that.'

'I'm greatly afeard he'll try to injure me.' Answer: — ''Tis fear *for* you' (emphasis on *for*), meaning 'you have good reason to be afeard': merely a translation of the Irish *is eagal duitse*.

'Oh I'll pay you what I owe you.' ''Tis a pity you wouldn't indeed,' says the other, a satirical reply, meaning 'of course you will and no thanks to you for that; who'd expect otherwise?'

'I am going to the fair to-morrow, as I want to buy a couple of cows.' Reply, 'I know,' as much as to say 'I see,' 'I understand.' This is one of our commonest terms of assent.

An assertion or statement introduced by the words 'to tell God's truth' is always understood to be weighty and somewhat unexpected, the introductory words being given as a guarantee of its truth:— 'Have you the rest of the money you owe me ready now James?' 'Well to tell God's truth I was not able to make it all up, but I can give you £5.'

Another guarantee of the same kind, though not quite so solemn, is 'my hand to you,' or 'I give you my hand and word.' 'My hand to you I'll never rest till the job is finished.' 'Come and hunt with me in the wood, and my hand to you we shall soon have enough of victuals for both of us.' (Clarence Mangan[5] in *Irish Penny Journal.*)

I've seen — and here's my hand to you I only say what's true —
A many a one with twice your stock not half so proud as you. (Clarence Mangan.)

'Do you know your Cathechism?' Answer, 'What would ail me not to know it?' meaning 'of course I do — 'twould be a strange thing if I didn't.' 'Do you think you can make that lock all right?' 'Ah what would ail me,' i.e., 'no doubt I can — of course I can; if I couldn't do that it would be a sure sign that something was amiss with me — that something ailed me.'

'Believe Tom and who'll believe you': a way of saying that Tom is not telling truth.

An emphatic 'yes' to a statement is often expressed in the following way:— 'This is a real wet day.' Answer, 'I believe you.' 'I think you made a good bargain with Tim about that field.' 'I believe you I did.'

A person who is offered anything he is very willing to take, or asked to do anything he is anxious to do, often answers in this way:— 'James, would you take a glass of punch?' or 'Tom, will you dance with my sister in the next round?' In either case the answer is, 'Would a duck swim?'

A weak sort of assent is often expressed in this way:— 'Will you bring Nelly's book to her when you are going home, Dan?' Answer, 'I don't mind,' or 'I don't mind if I do.'

To express unbelief in a statement or disbelief in the usefulness or effectiveness of any particular line of action, a person says 'that's all in my eye,' or ''Tis all in my eye, Betty Martin — O'; but this last is regarded as slang.

Sometimes an unusual or unexpected statement is introduced in the following manner, the introductory words being usually spoken quickly:— '*Now do you know what I'm going to tell you* — that ragged old chap has £200 in the bank.' In Derry they make it — 'Now listen to what I'm going to say.'

In some parts of the South and West and North-west, servants and others have a way of replying to directions that at first sounds strange or even disrespectful:— 'Biddy, go up please to the drawing-room and bring me down the needle and thread and stocking you will find on the table.' 'That will do

ma'am,' replies Biddy, and off she goes and brings them. But this is their way of saying 'yes ma'am,' or 'Very well ma'am.'

So also you say to the hotel-keeper:— 'Can I have breakfast please to-morrow morning at 7 o'clock?' 'That will do sir.' This reply in fact expresses the greatest respect, as much as to say, 'A word from you is quite enough.'

'I caught the thief at my potatoes.' 'No, but did you?' i.e., is it possible you did so? A very common exclamation, especially in Ulster.

'Oh man' is a common exclamation to render an assertion more emphatic, and sometimes to express surprise:— 'Oh man, you never saw such a fine race as we had.' In Ulster they duplicate it, with still the same application:— 'Oh man-o-man that's great rain.' 'Well John you'd hardly believe it, but I got £50 for my horse to-day at the fair.' Reply, 'Oh man that's a fine price.'

'Never fear' is heard constantly in many parts of Ireland as an expression of assurance:— 'Now James don't forget the sugar.' 'Never fear ma'am.' 'Ah never fear there will be plenty flowers in that garden this year.' 'You will remember to have breakfast ready at 7 o'clock.' 'Never fear sir,' meaning 'making your mind easy on the point — it will be all right.' *Never fear* is merely a translation of the equally common Irish phrase, *ná bí heagal ort.*

Most of our ordinary salutations are translations from Irish. *Go m-beannuighe Dia dhuit* is literally 'May God bless you,' or 'God bless you' which is a usual salutation in English. The commonest of all our salutes is 'God save you,' or (for a person entering a house) 'God save all here'; and the response is 'God save you kindly' (*Knocknagow*); where *kindly* means 'of a like kind,' 'in like manner,' 'similarly'. Another but less usual response to the same salutation is, 'And you too,' which is appropriate. (*Knocknagow.*) 'God save all here' is used all over Ireland except in the extreme North, where it is hardly understood.

To the ordinary salutation, 'Good-morrow,' which is heard everywhere, the usual response is 'Good-morrow kindly.' 'Morrow Wat,' said Mr Lloyd. 'Morrow kindly,' replied Wat. (*Knocknagow.*) 'The top of the morning to you' is used everywhere, North and South.

In some places if a woman throws out water at night at the kitchen door, she says first, 'Beware of the water,' lest the 'good people' might happen to be passing at the time, and one or more of them might get splashed.

A visitor coming in and finding the family at dinner:— 'Much good may it do you.'

In very old times it was a custom for workmen on completing any work and delivering it finished to give it their blessing. This blessing was called *abarta* (an old word, not used in modern Irish), and if it was omitted the workman was subject to a fine to be deducted from his hire equal to the seventh part of the cost of his feeding. (*Senchus Mór*[6] and 'Cormac's Glossary.') It was especially incumbent on women to bless the work of other women. This custom, which is more than a thousand years old, has descended to our day; for the people on coming up to persons engaged in work of any kind always say 'God bless your work,' or its equivalent original in Irish, *Go m-beannuighe Dia air bhur n-obair.* (See my *Social History of Ancient Ireland*, II, page 324.)

In modern times tradesmen have perverted this pleasing custom into a new channel not so praiseworthy. On the completion of any work, such as a building, they fix a pole with a flag on the highest point to ask the employer for his *blessing*, which means money for a drink.

1   Charles Lever (1806–72), a prolific and entertaining adventure novelist, once very popular. Author of *Charles O'Malley* (1841) and *Tom Burke of 'Ours'* (1843).
2   Robert Dwyer Joyce (1830–83) contributed verse to the *Nation* under the pseudonym of 'Feardana'. Author of 'The Men of the West' and other popular ballads. Brother of P.W. Joyce and distantly related to James Joyce.
3   For Griffin see footnote 1 on page 21.
4   Title of novel by Charles Kickham (1828–82) published in 1873.
5   For Mangan, see footnote 13 on page 21. The *Irish Penny Journal* was edited by George Petrie (1790–1866) and published in Dublin in 1840-1.
6   *Senchas Mór* (Great Tradition) is the largest collection of law texts from Gaelic Ireland, compiled probably in the eighth century. Cormac mac Cuilennáin (fl. 905) is thought to be the author of *Sanas Chormaic* (Cormac's Glossary).

JOSEPH CAMPBELL
from Joseph Campbell, *The Mearing Stones* (1911)

These two extracts are from Campbell's notebook as he travelled round Donegal. Sixteen pencil drawings accompany the prose sketches in the original.

A Ballad Singer

A ballad-singer has come into Ardara. It is late afternoon. He stands in the middle of the Diamond[1] — a sunburnt, dusty figure, a typical Ishmael and stroller of the roads. The women have come to their doors to hear him, and a benchful of police, for lack of something better to do, are laughing at him from the barrack front. The ballad he is singing is about Bonaparte and the Poor Old Woman.[2] Then he changes his tune to 'The Spanish Lady' — a Dublin street-song:

As I walked down thro' Dublin city
At the hour of twelve in the night,
Who should I spy but a Spanish lady,
Washing her feet by candlelight.

First she washed them, and then she dried them
Over a fire of amber coal:
Never in all my life did I see
A maid so neat about the sole!

Finally he gives 'I'm a Good Old Rebel,' a ballad of the type that became so popular in the Southern States of America after the Civil war:

I'm a good old rebel — that's what I am,
And for this fair land of freedom I don't care a
    damn;
I'm glad I fought agin it, I only wish we'd won,
And I don't want no one-horse pardon for anything
    I done.

I followed old Marse Robert for four years nigh
    about,
Got wounded in three places and starved at Point
    Look-Out:
I cotched the rheumatism a-campin' in the snow,
But I killed a chance[3] of Yankees, and I'd like to kill
    some moe.

Two hundred thousand Yankees is stiff in Southern
    dust,
We got two hundred thousand before they
    conquered us:

They died of Southern fever and Southern steel and
shot —
I wish it was two millions instead of what we got!

And now the war is over and I can't fight them any
more,
But I ain't a-goin' to love them — that's sartin
shor';
And I don't want no one-horse pardon for what I
was and am,
And I won't be reconstructed, and I don't care a
damn!

He howls out the verses in disjointed, unmusical
bursts. He acts with head and arms, and at places
where he is worked up to a particular frenzy he takes a
run and gives a buck-jump in the air, blissfully
unconscious, I suppose, that he is imitating the
manner in which the *ballistea*, or ancient dancing-
songs, were sung by the Romans. At the end of each
verse he breaks into a curious chanted refrain like:
'Yum tilly-yum-yum-yum-yum-yum' — and then
there are more sidlings and buck-jumps. Some of the
women throw him money, which he acknowledges by
lifting his hat grandiosely. Others of them pass
remarks, quite the reverse of complimentary, about his
voice and ragged appearance. 'Isn't it terrible he is!'
says one woman. 'Look at him with the seat out of his
trousers, and he lepping like a good one. I could
choke him, I could!' Another woman comes out of a
shop with a crying child in her arms, and shouts at
him: 'Will you go away, then? You're wakening the
childer.' 'Well, ma'am,' says he, stopping in the middle
of a verse, 'you may thank the Lord for His mercy that
you have childer to waken!' The ducks quack, the
dogs howl, the poor ballad-singer roars louder than
ever. I listen for a while, amused and interested. Then
I get tired of it, and pass on towards Bracky Bridge.

The Human Voice

The human voice — what a wonder and mystery it is!
'All power,' said Whitman, 'is folded in a great
vocalism.' I spoke to a man to-day on the roadside,
near Maghery. He was a poor, raggedy fellow, with a
gaunt, unshaven chin and wild eyes, and a couple of
barefooted children played about the mud at his feet.
He answered me in a voice that *thrilled* me — deep,
chest-full, resonant; a voice that, had he been an
educated man, might have won fame for him, as a
politician, say, or a preacher, or an actor. And voices
like his are by no means uncommon along the western
seaboard of Ireland. Men address you on the road in
that frank, human, comrade-like way of Irishmen, out
of deep lungs and ringing larynxes that bring one back
to the time when men were giants, and physique was
the rule rather than the exception. In such voices one
can imagine the Fenians to have talked one with the
other, Fionn calling to Sgeolan, and Oisin chanting
the divine fragments of song he dreamed in the
intervals of war and venery. Will Ireland ever recapture
the heroic qualities — build personality, voice, gesture
— or, as Whitman puts it: 'Litheness, majestic faces,
clear eyes' — that were hers down to a comparatively
late period, and in places have not quite died out even
yet? I believe she will.

1   In the North of Ireland towns have diamonds not
squares.
2   Usually a symbol of Ireland.
3   A lot of; cf. chance — lot (OED).

J. M. HONE
from *The Irish Book Lover*, August 1912

First published in the *Saturday Review* this article was reproduced in *The Irish Book
Lover*, an informative monthly magazine edited by J.S. Crone. Joseph Maunsel Hone
(1882–1959) was a publisher (hence Maunsel and, later, Maunsel and Roberts), critic,
and biographer. He wrote two biographies of Yeats, one in 1915, the other an
authorized one in 1942, and he also compiled a biography of George Moore published
in 1936. This extract conveys the atmosphere of the time and is a reminder of the
continuing repercussions in the wake of Synge's *Playboy*.

Yeats, Synge and *The Playboy*

The remark was once made of Oscar Wilde that he might have been Parnell's successor. Of another Irishman, who is only known to the mass as a man of letters, Mr W.B. Yeats, the biographer will probably say that an Irish leader, a Grattan[1] perhaps rather than a Parnell — an orator — was lost in a poet. That will not be strictly true, for, in fact, Mr Yeats has done much for Ireland, aside, I mean, from his actual literary achievement . . . It is not possible for an Irish writer working in Ireland to live detachedly. Synge returning home after a long absence did not realize this; the row over *The Playboy* bewildered him utterly; when he was asked what he thought of it he could only say, 'It's an extravaganza. I don't care a rap.' Mr Yeats, on the other hand, immediately found confirmation of his philosophy of Irish history, and was prepared to agree with Synge's enemies that *The Playboy*, or rather its reception in Dublin, truly raised a national issue . . . I ask myself whom we have to thank for Synge and *The Playboy of the Western World*. It happens that I can recall the first week of the production of *The Playboy* in Dublin; I can vouch for the extent and reality of the hostility it aroused. Synge, I have often thought since, might easily have been shouted into obscurity. Though he had already produced *The Well of the Saints* he was still regarded merely as one of Mr Yeats's protégés; and had the directors bent to the storm, and withdrawn *The Playboy*, it is very likely that Synge would be unknown to-day except to explorers in the by-paths of literature.

The whole situation might have been taken for intensely and merely comic. One had, for instance, a sense of delicious irrelevancy when one found the boys of Trinity College ardently supporting the management. They had, needless to say, no views either for or against the 'freedom of literature'; they had come to the Abbey for the pleasure of seeing the Papists[2] summarily dealt with by the police. When the curtain fell they used to strike up 'God save the King!'; but one night the players, lest their own political sympathies might be misconstrued, peeped out from behind the curtain and joined in the reply, 'God save Ireland,'[3] hissing their new champions.

One may laugh now when one thinks of it, but the perplexities of the position were no laughing matter for the Abbey Theatre, which had the future to think of, and seemed like, whichever way it turned, to lose its few patrons. That Mr Yeats rather underrated the determination of Synge's opponents I felt then; the subsequent career of the play has borne me out. For the time and energy he has had to spend in interpreting Synge to the Irish public, for his limitless patience in propaganda and generous labours when all seemed hopeless, Mr Yeats has never been sufficiently praised. In the upshot, Synge has not only been accepted as a national dramatist, but he has taken — wrongly, I think, though here I express a purely personal opinion — the place among modern Irish writers that previously belonged by popular consent to Yeats himself.

---

1   For Grattan, see footnote on page 37.
2   The word Papist, which has a pejorative ring to it, is not used by Catholics about themselves. Hone's social background was Protestant upper-middle-class, his politics, appropriately, Southern Unionist.
3   'God save Ireland' was the title of the song composed by T.D. Sullivan, which became the unofficial national anthem of Ireland in the nineteenth century.

GEORGE TYRRELL
from M. D. Petre, *Autobiography and Life of George Tyrrell, Vol. 1: Autobiography of George Tyrrell 1861–84* (1912)

George Tyrrell (1861–1909) is best remembered today as a leading advocate of the Catholic heresy of Modernism, a movement that sought an accommodation between Church doctrine and modern ideas of science (such as evolution) and philosophy. The movement was later condemned by Pope Pius X in his encyclical *Pascendi* (1907). Tyrrell himself was born in Dorset Street in Dublin, converted to Catholicism in 1876, was confirmed in St George's Church in Hardwick Street, and attended early Mass at the Jesuit Church in Gardiner Street. After leaving Ireland in 1879 he joined the English Jesuits but became increasingly disillusioned with systems which denied room for the individual conscience. Here in this extract he records his early attraction towards Catholicism and his bias towards the claims of interiority.

1876

My aunt Mary (Mrs John Chamney) had determined, about this time, to give up her house in Hardwick St[1] — so now we were adrift again, and my mother hesitating between two eligible sets of furnished lodgings, I gave my casting vote and all my influence in favour of those offered by a Roman Catholic lady — a certain Miss Lynch, with whom I have been in regular correspondence until quite lately, when I have had to break off all but the most necessary ties of that kind. This was my last 'home,' and this quiet, holy, unselfish little woman had more to do with my destiny than any other.

My wish to go there was simply because she was a Roman Catholic; although I did not say so and invented the reasons. This means that already, though I hardly adverted to it myself, and would have truthfully denied it if challenged, my secret deep-down wish was that even Romanism should be defensible. Here again there was no religion or faith in the wish, no love of truth as such, but only a desire that the truth might lie in a certain direction. I felt dimly that Romanism was the goal towards which High Churchism was an impeded movement; it was the unreachable centre towards which it gravitated; but though I wished it could be reached I was quite sure that its absurdities were too gross and glaring even for the ablest defender of paradox. But the danger fascinated me, and I loved to see how close I could skirt the precipice without falling over. Plainly my position was such that, so far from resisting, I would really welcome any argument or shadow of argument making for Rome; all the worst elements of my nature were on the right side; but I was not prepared to commit intellectual suicide, and as yet I never seriously believed Romanism meant anything else.

It was on March 17th, 1876, that we went to live with Miss Lynch in Eccles St. Willie,[2] having gained all that could be got at Trinity, and despairing of a fellowship falling vacant, had lately gone over to Cambridge *ad eundem gradum*,[3] to see what he could do there.

I was now pretty regular in saying my prayers from a book called the 'Altar-Manual' — always on that dreadful suppressed hypothesis which I refused to face: 'O God, if there be a God; save my soul, if I have a soul!' Not that I cared about my soul or had any sense of sin, but that I wanted to be different, to be respectable in my own eyes, to be in harmony with the system into which I had thrown my interests and energies. I was like a man who has made his fortune by a fraud and thereafter lives honestly, and gives alms from his ill-gotten goods, and tries to persuade himself he is all right morally and refuses to poke into things. Often, during the next couple of years, and occasionally, for long, long after, I would start up from my knees and say: 'Oh, this is all humbug and sham!' But then, when I faced the consequences of the admission; when I saw my air-built castle falling to pieces for lack of this foundation of cloud and darkness; when I thought of the break-up of all those interests by which I was so fascinated, to which I had so committed myself, which gave a point and meaning to my otherwise empty and meaningless life; I was driven back to my knees, and wrapped my self-wrought cloak of illusions round me more tightly than ever.

Yet I could never rest in a deliberate and approved schism between my theory and my life and conduct. It was all one thing and, as such, had to be taken or left. There might be coxcombs who could enjoy the uniform, the parade and the glory in time of peace, and forget the disagreeable contingency of war; but I was not of that sort. I wanted the real, whatever it was; and my continual disquiet was the consciousness of unreality and sham. All this might seem strange in one so untruthful as I had been and still was; but verbal untruthfulness of most kinds, and there are many, is compatible with a great dread and dislike of lying to oneself and of what may be called mental untruthfulness. By nature I always wanted to know and to understand, and that means getting behind the appearance of things and down to their reality. It is not so much a virtue as a tendency; though its violation is hardly blameless. The very style, however, of this analysis which I make of myself may perhaps tend to falsify things, by reflecting my present mind and intelligence back to those days when I was utterly incapable of diagnosing the processes of my life and thought; what is now clear was then confused; what now I see, then I felt; and mingled with all the dim reasoning and precocious rationalism there were the fancies, the instincts, the interests of the boy and the child.

I, too, had my share of the dramatic craving, and not only would have liked to, but actually did, to a great extent, make a play of religion. What prompted me to get crucifixes and Romish pictures and new prayer-books, and even more distinctively popish apparatus, which I did not for a moment approve of interiorly; what made me try sleeping on boards and using iron girdles and disciplines, and such antics, was not my truth-seeking self that I respected so far as it went, but the same instinct which, at an earlier age, made me buy a gun and a sword and dress up as a soldier. But I differed from the 'ritualist proper' in that I recognized this as childishness, and was ashamed of it and hid it away carefully from the eyes of others, and heartily despised it when I saw it in others, who confounded appearance with reality. It was like the love of toys, which I kept buried in my heart long after I was old enough to be ashamed of it.

I was as anxious to be correctly contrite for my sins as I was not to commit them at all; but only for the same reason, *sc.*[4] because contrition, like faith and every other virtue, was part of the system I had embraced; shall I hesitate to say — of the hobby I had taken up? Yet this might falsely imply that I did not believe in the real worth and seriousness of the matter. Catholicism was not a *rôle*, which I had merely assumed fictitiously; but one with which I had identified my real and inmost self — albeit, as yet, not with a clear conscience or even with mental sincerity; for I felt there was a fundamental flaw. In my manuals I found 'acts of contrition' which I wanted to mean, but did not mean. Given even a realization of God, which I had not, the thought that sin injured Him in any way, or angered Him, was utterly inconceivable; an infuriated Deity had no existence for me and therefore no terrors. Had I loved righteousness *as such*, and hated iniquity; had my will and affection been thus in unconscious agreement with God's; then I should have had implicit contrition, I should have been sorry for God's sake purely, for love of the Divine Goodness, even though the Divine personality was so dimly and doubtfully apprehended. But I was far from that stage of advance. I was sorry only that I had failed in what I wanted to do because it was part of the system, part of the personality I had determined, rightly or wrongly, to make my own. I was mortified, provoked, disappointed, discouraged; but contrite — not one bit.

I think it was in the summer of 1876 that W.M. explained to me that I ought to get confirmed; and through him I was put *en rapport* with Mr Hogan, Dr Maturin's curate, who gave me some instructions in his private room, and also advised me to attend the Sunday-school at Grangegorman — a humiliation which I bore with for the sake of Rachel. He did not suggest confession, nor was I yet prepared to go that length in my popery. I was confirmed in due course at St George's Church, somewhere about Whitsuntide; and if I was none the better for that invigorating ceremony, neither was I appreciably the worse. All that was said beforehand, as to the marvellous effects of the sacrament, not unnaturally led me to hope for some sensible results. But I did not know theologians then as I do now.

Presently I made my first Communion — fasting, for I had got that far — at Grangegorman. I had been indoctrinated with some belief in the Real Presence, and naturally expected at least as much sensible improvement in spiritual vigour as from a dose of medicine or from a square meal. I think I tried to work my feelings up to the level of the ecstatic prayers I found in the manuals for before and after receiving; and to stifle the voice of my strangled reason, calling out: 'False and unreal!' Had I listened to it I should have had to give up the whole thing and go back to the dreary chaos from which I had emerged. I wanted it all to be true; and clung to every shadow of a flimsy reason that seemed to buttress up my failing illusions. So far I can see nothing supernatural in the process; not even the persistence with which I stuck to the task of self-reformation. The interest which was the mainspring of all this movement was just such as a man might take — not in a game — but in a political or philanthropic or scientific cause, bearing on the reality of life. The very interest idled me as much, and more than did my tinkering enterprises of earlier days, which now gradually fell into abeyance; though it forced me to such reading and self-education as the subject itself involved. I regretted bitterly all the time I had lost, and recognized that, if I was to take up the clerical profession, I should have to work hard at matters only remotely bearing on my interest. Indeed my conscience twitted me very explicitly with the neglect of so plain a duty as that of working at my lessons; but the habit of idling was ingrained, nor had I enough mortification to sacrifice the present for the future, to 'leave God for God's sake,' as the ascetics say. Had I done so the passion might have died, and thus the very motive of my reform would have perished; as happens often with those who lose their religion by giving themselves to soul-absorbing labours in the cause of religion. Just once, at the beginning, I shook myself into a spasmodic industry, but it was only a spasm; though I read a great deal, and with avidity, of what was obviously and directly bearing on my interest; and my thoughts were absorbed and busied by it continually, as they used to be by my futile inventions and constructions. In this way my real mental education began, and has, roughly speaking, been carried on ever since; all my reading and study has been selected and determined by this central interest; has modified and been modified by it.

Artificial education, *ab extra*,[5] wisely begins with the remote and fundamental conditions common to many pursuits and interests; leaving it to later years to determine which shall be dominant and special, so that when that dominant interest or need manifests itself, in youth or early manhood, one may not have to do more than supply such conditions as are special and peculiar; it provides the means for a variety of possible ends; it begins with the farther and ends with the nearer knowledge. Natural self-education proceeds inversely; it first determines the end and then seeks the needful means, in that measure and no more; it begins with the nearer and ends with the farther knowledge, and proceeds altogether analytically.

If children were born with some dominating natural interest, this would be undoubtedly the best and most economical method of education; but they are not, and some, if not most, live and die without anything that could be called a central interest of their rational life, and have to be shaped passively by education and external circumstances. But if one has any kind of 'life' or dominant preoccupation from and in early years, such, I think, find the routine of artificial education irksome and impossible except so far as its connection with that 'life' is appreciated. I do not, however, think that a very strict and permanent centralization of interests is common or even desirable. A man whose interest in politics leads him to study history or economics may be permanently drawn away from his first mistress to her handmaiden; or the first love may remain only as secondary; or the secondary, remaining secondary, may acquire an independent as well as a dependent interest. The love of poetry may lead one to the love of Greek, whether as a preference or as a hobby, and not merely as a means or condition. Often the life seems ruled equally, though alternately, by several different, if not incompatible, interests; often it seems reduced to anarchy by a disorderly mob of contending interests, no one of which has been developed sufficiently to dominate in any sense at all. If I can succeed in unravelling the skein of my tangled life, I think it will be seen that the seat of government gradually shifted to what was, at first, a subordinate interest; and that, conversely, what was paramount at the beginning was eventually dethroned and pushed down to a position of dependence.

It is, in some sense, as might, *a priori*, be expected, the story of Newman[6] *à rebours*.[7] In that pure soul the presence of God in the voice of conscience was from the first — I think rather exceptionally — as self-evident as the fact of his own existence; although the outward evidence of the world's condition seemed to him to make for atheism, and to stand as a cumulative difficulty against this luminous interior intuition. I often wonder whether it was at the suggestion of some early instructor, or by some spontaneous spiritual instinct, that he was brought thus to look for God within, as the mystics do, instead of without, as is the way with savages and children, whose theology is symbolic and materialistic. To me this conception came at the end, and not at the beginning. Not merely was my earliest reason in revolt against the external, fetishistic God of the popular imagination, but when I came to hear of sacramental and supernatural indwelling I conceived it in the literal terms in which it was expressed, as the ingress of the external Deity into the soul — a notion, if possible, more unreal and more make-believe than the other — but of the natural union of the soul with God, as with the very ground of her being, I had no notion. I was too inquisitive, too eager for clearness, to accept the popular materialism; and of the spiritual truth I had learned nothing beyond words: *Foris Te quærebam et intus eras.*[8]

Newman's Catholicism was the outcome of his theism, practical and speculative; that was the firm basis on which it stood. He passed from light to fuller light, each step was prepared and established by that which preceded. I, in my dark and crooked way, almost began with Catholicism, and was forced back, in spite of myself, to theism, practical and speculative, in the effort to find a basis for a system that hung mid-air save for the scaffolding of mixed motives which made me cling to it blindly, in spite of a deep-down sense of instability. And the end of the process is that my dominant interest and strongest conviction is Theism; and dependently on this Christianity; and thirdly Catholicism, just in so far as Newman may be right; just in so far as it is the necessary implication of conscience. I sometimes think that had I, in early years, heard nothing at all about religion, I should have sooner come to the truth than was possible when my mind was blocked up with symbolic notions that I could not rightly credit, nor my instructors explain.

1   Hardwick Street is North of Rutland Square in Dublin. St George's Church is at the end of the street, and nearby is Eccles Street, occupied a little later by the Blooms.
2   His elder brother, ten years his senior, who was to die at 25, was precocious and highly intelligent.
3   Latin: for the same purpose.
4   Latin *scilicet*: namely.
5   Latin: from the outside or outset.
6   Cardinal Newman (1801–90), a leading member of the Oxford Movement, converted to Catholicism in 1845, was ordained, founded the Oratory at Birmingham, was appointed Rector of the Catholic University of Ireland in 1854, and then Cardinal in 1879. Among publications are his religious autobiography *Apologia Pro Vita Sua* (1864) and *Grammar of Assent* (1870), which is an argument in support of belief. When writing his autobiography Tyrrell had Newman as one of his models.
7   French: in reverse.
8   Latin: Outside I will seek Thee, and you will be within. A motto in a sense for Tyrrell's life.

STEPHEN GWYNN
from *The Freeman's Journal*, 25 January 1913

Stephen Gwynn (1864-1950) was a writer and politician. His work, often accompanied by illustrations by Hugh Thomson, ranged widely. He was author of *The Fair Hills of Ireland* (1906), *The Famous Cities of Ireland* (1915), *Irish Books and Irish People* (1919), and *Irish Literature and Drama* (1936). Here in this extract he comments on Irish book lovers he has known. For the record, in contrast to what is said by Gwynn, the Irish today are per head of population among the leading book-buying people in Europe.

Irish Book Lovers

Irish people are very odd about books. They are, and every Irish writer knows it to his cost, the least book buying of publics. We, who write of Ireland, labour like the peasant proprietor in his hayfield, under a wholesome cloudy sky, earning our diet of potatoes and buttermilk, though unhappily often in places where buttermilk, at least, is nohow to be come by; and we have always leisure since the day is long from dawn to sunset, for passing the time of day with our neighbours. Our occupation is effectually shielded from the glare and glamour of commercialism, and, no doubt, so much the better for our virtue. Mr Yeats has done more than any man living, perhaps than any man living or dead, to raise the fame of Ireland in the craft of letters; but heaven help Mr Yeats — heaven help any of us — if existence depended on the sale of books to the Irish public. Yet Ireland is a country of booklovers: the man for whom books are a passion and a treasure is perhaps commoner there than anywhere in the world. Let me recall some of the Irish book-lovers I have known.

A blind old man living in the steep street of a Norman-Irish town — in an old borough with memories of Gael and Gall, planter and supplanted, serf and master, monk and Cromwellian, 'Croppy' and 'Yeo,'¹ memories that he had studied, traditions that he had collected, all through a long life; and there beside him in the little sanded kitchen were stacked the volumes of his most cherished possession — all the proceedings of the Irish Parliament. Yet his days were unhappy because a careless generation disrespected his books; because his gathered hoard was scattered by the children; because even the great volumes, richly bound, were — so he feared, and not without reason — torn and abused. I was to send him a book of my editing, dealing with the scenes he knew best; he thanked me, but was half inclined to weep, forecasting the difficulties he would have in preventing its loss in the intervals between those hours when one or another might read it aloud to him. He has gone to his rest now, and may his apprenticeship as clerk to the local poor law board have qualified him for some pleasant task on that section of the Recording Angel's staff which deals with the deeds done and suffered in Ireland. Another figure rises in my mind, far away west in Connemara, in the 'next parish to America' — a retired schoolmaster having a name ancient in that region as the dawn of history, and fitly therefore a master of the Gaelic tongue and its printed records: an authority to whom scholars all over Europe referred on points of grammar, of usage, even of detailed historic fact. His tiny shelves were laden with volumes of price, gifts, many of them inscribed with illustrious names, and yet standing by others which must have been purchased at a cost that might well have seemed beyond the means of any who dwelt in that remote cottage; and all were guarded like the apples of the Hesperides. Yet for those in whom the guardian discerned a genuine love of knowledge, no dragon had to be circumvented: books and his skill in them were alike freely at command.

Richer in books, not less rich in courtesy and scholar's generosity, was one whose loss left us all impoverished — Cæsar Litton Falkiner, a true Irish bibliophile, but happily endowed with what too many of our erudite have lacked. He had the lucidus ordo,² the faculty for sifting and arranging, for selecting the relevant fact out of his store; he was a good writer as well as a good reader. Often our best book-lovers have produced some magnum opus whose bulk is crammed with a hotch-potch where shape or outline is none; and a subject like the 'History of the Irish Brigade,' fit to provide a hundred romances, becomes merely an impenetrable thicket of intertangled detail. Some such defect in architectonic quality, some such lack of binding power, robbed the world of what another Irishman might have given to it. Those of us who knew W.J. Craig knew him as a passionate devourer of books, yet least of all men a bookworm. He had drawn the very essence out of all Elizabethan and Jacobean literature. For half a lifetime he laboured, with toil like a miner's, to bring into the light a glossary of the Elizabethan English; yet for want of the simplest, almost the mechanical, aptitude of a writer's craft he never accomplished anything. These are a few names at random.

1   A reference to Croppy Boys, United Irishmen in the 1790s who cropped their hair to show their political allegiance. 'Yeo' presumably stands for Yeomen, the forces of the Crown opposed to the Croppies. Gwynn is here providing a snapshop of the history of Irish conflicts. The Irish Parliament met in the closing decades of the eighteenth century before its suppression by the Act of Union in 1801.
2   Latin: shining methodical arrangement.

ANONYMOUS
from *The Irish Book Lover*, July 1913

Here in this extract we can overhear Yeats delivering a lecture on the achievements of the Revival over a twenty-one year period, achievements in part brought about by organizations such as the Irish Literary Society in London.

Irish Literary Society: Coming of Age Celebrations

The twenty-first anniversary of the foundation of the Society was celebrated with much enthusiasm and success in the lecture theatre of University College, London, on 10th June. In the afternoon Mr W.B. Yeats — supported by Lady Gregory and Mr A.P. Graves — presided over a large gathering, when Mr T.W. Rolleston, Vice-President, delivered an address on 'Irish Thought and Art for Twenty-one Years'. The speaker, who was warmly received and loudly applauded, gave a delightful résumé of the great progress made in Ireland in Art, the Drama, Music, Literature, the Arts and Crafts, since the inception of this Society and its compeer in Dublin, the National Literary Society. Mr Yeats recalled how, in the dark winter of 1891-92,[1] Ireland, its high hopes dashed and its outlook darkened, was rent and torn with dissension. That, he felt, was an appropriate time to attempt to turn men's thoughts from the fierce field of politics to the higher realms of literature, where all could again unite on a common basis. He was told it was the wrong time, but he held it was the right, and in spite of many rebuffs succeeded, as the gathering there that day proved.

In the evening Mr A.P. Graves, the President, delivered a brilliant lecture on 'Ireland's Share in the Folk Song Revival,' tracing the influences of Irish songs in their three great varieties, from the earliest times, through Dante and Shakespeare, Beethoven and Mozart, to the present day. He was ably assisted by the famous vocalists Mr Plunket Greene and Miss Jean MacKinlay, who between them rendered some dozen songs, old and new, in illustration of the various examples cited by the lecturer, amidst great applause.

A handsome illustrated souvenir programme, with cover designed by George Morrow, was prepared for the occasion, containing a graphic account of the literary work performed by members of the Society, from the pen of Miss Eleanor Hull, in which she says: 'All that is best in Irish literary, artistic and musical London may be said to be represented in the Society; we have amongst us poets, musicians, critics, historians, dreamers and practical men. Their books, published within the years during which the Society has been in existence, would fill a small library. On our death-roll are the names of men and women who have helped to re-create what is best in the Ireland of to-day; on our roll of the living are many who are shaping the Ireland of the future'. In the words of one of the original members, 'Kindred Irish spirits have banded themselves together for thought and work in the heart of London. They have trust and energy and belief. Their Arcady is "Ireland of the four bright seas." Their muse is "Dark Rosaleen."'

1   Yeats is here referring to events after the death of Parnell in October 1891 and the split in the Irish Parliamentary Party.

GEORGE MOORE
from George Moore, *Hail and Farewell: Vale* (1914)

George Moore (1852–1933) is one of the leading modern Irish writers. Tracking his career as a writer is no easy matter. His high society novel *Drama in Muslin* (1886) concerns the plight of the landed gentry (of which he was one) at the time of Land League agitation; *Esther Waters* (1894) is a naturalist novel set in England and deals with among other things the wet nurse situation; *The Untilled Field* is a collection of stories, one of which is included in this Reader, about Ireland's unfulfilled potential; *The Lake* (1905) is a moving symbolist novel about a secret relationship between a woman parishioner and a priest. Here in this extract in silky prose from his three-volumed autobiography he paints a wickedly funny portrait of his one-time friend W.B. Yeats.

As soon as the applause died away, Yeats who had lately returned to us from the States[1] with a paunch, a huge stride, and an immense fur overcoat, rose to speak. We were surprised at the change in his appearance, and could hardly believe our ears when, instead of talking to us as he used to do about the old stories come down from generation to generation, he began to thunder like Ben Tillett himself[2] against the middle classes, stamping his feet, working himself into a great passion, and all because the middle classes did not dip their hands into their pockets and give Lane[3] the money he wanted for his exhibition. It is impossible to imagine the hatred which came into his voice when he spoke the words, 'the middle classes'; one would have thought that he was speaking against a personal foe; but there are millions in the middle classes! And we looked round asking each other with our eyes where on earth our Willie Yeats had picked up such extraordinary ideas. He could hardly have gathered in the United States the ridiculous idea that none but titled and carriage-folk can appreciate pictures. And we asked ourselves why Willie Yeats should feel himself called upon to denounce the class to which he himself belonged essentially: on one side excellent mercantile millers and shipowners, and on the other a portrait painter of rare talent.[4] With so admirable a parentage it did not seem to us necessary that a man should look back for an ancestry, and we had laughed at the story, looking upon it as *ben trovato*, that on one occasion when Yeats was crooning over AE's fire he had said that if he had his rights he would be Duke of Ormonde,[5] and that AE had answered, 'In any case, Willie, you are overlooking your father,' — a detestable remark to make to a poet in search of an ancestry; and the addition, 'Yeats, we both belong to the lower middle classes,' was in equally bad taste. AE, who is usually quick-witted, should have guessed that Yeats's belief in his lineal descent from the great Duke of Ormonde was part of his poetic equipment . . . It did not occur to us till this last minute; but AE knew that there were spoons in the Yeats family bearing the Butler crest, just as there are portraits in my family of Sir Thomas More, and he should have remembered that certain passages in *The Countess Cathleen* are clearly derivative from the spoons. He should have remembered that all the romantic poets have sought illustrious ancestry, and rightly, since romantic poetry is concerned only with nobles and castles, gonfalons and oriflammes. Villiers de l'Isle Adam believed firmly in his descent, and appeared on all public occasions with the Order of Malta pinned upon his coat; and Victor Hugo, too, had inquired out his ancestry in all the archives of Spain and France before sitting down to write *Hernani* . . . and with good reason, for with the disappearance of gonfalons and donjons it may be doubted if — My meditation was interrupted by Yeats's voice.

'We have sacrificed our lives for Art; but you, what have you done? What sacrifices have you made?' he asked, and everybody began to search his memory for the sacrifices that Yeats had made, asking himself in what prison Yeats had languished, what rags he had worn, what broken victuals he had eaten. As far as anybody could remember, he had always lived very comfortably, sitting down invariably to regular meals, and the old green cloak that was in keeping with his profession of romantic poet he had exchanged for the magnificent fur coat which distracted our attention from what he was saying, so opulently did it cover the back of the chair out of which he had risen. But, quite forgetful of the coat behind him, he continued to denounce the middle classes, throwing his arms into the air, shouting at us, and we thinking not at all of what he was saying, but of a story that had been floating about Dublin for some time. A visitor had come back from Coole[6] telling how he had discovered the poet lying on a sofa in a shady corner, a plate of strawberries on his knee, and three or four adoring ladies serving him with cream and sugar, and how the poet, after wiping his hands on a napkin, had consented to recite some verses, and the verses he recited were these:

> I said, 'A line will take us hours maybe,
> Yet if it does not seem a moment's thought
> Our stitching and unstitching has been naught.
> Better go down upon your marrow-bones
> And scrub a kitchen pavement, or break stones
> Like an old pauper in all kinds of weather;
> For to articulate sweet sounds together
> Is to work harder than all these and yet
> Be thought an idler by the noisy set
> Of bankers, schoolmasters and clergymen,
> The martyrs call the world.'[7]

The poet advanced a step or two nearer to the edge of the platform, and stamping his foot he asked again what the middle classes had done for Art, and in a towering rage (the phrase is no mere figure of speech, for he raised himself up to tremendous height) he called upon the ladies and gentlemen that had come to hear my lecture to put their hands in their pockets and give sovereigns to the stewards who were waiting at the doors to receive them, or, better still, to write large cheques. We were led to understand that by virtue of our subscriptions we should cease to belong to the middle classes, and having held out this hope to us he retired to his chair and fell back overcome into the middle of the great fur coat, and remained silent until the end of the debate.

As soon as it was over criticism began, not of my lecture, but of Yeats's speech, and on Saturday night all my friends turned in to discuss his contention that the middle classes had never done anything for Art; the very opposite seemed to AE to be the truth. He pointed out that the aristocracy had given England no great poet except Byron, whom many people did not look upon as a poet at all, and though Shelley's poetry was unquestionable, he could hardly be considered as belonging to the aristocracy, his father having been merely a Sussex baronet. All the other poets, it was urged, came from the middle classes, not only the poets, but the painters, the musicians, and the sculptors. 'Yeats's attack upon the middle classes,' somebody cried, 'is the most absurd that was ever made; the aristocracy have Byron, and the peasants have Burns, all the others belong to us.' Somebody chimed in, 'Not even the landowners have produced a poet,' and he was answered that Landor was a

considerable landed proprietor. But he was the only one. Not a single painter came out of the aristocracy. Lord Carlyle's name was mentioned; everybody laughed, and I said that the distinction of classes was purely an arbitrary one. It was agreed that if riches can poison inspiration, poverty is a stimulant, and then leaning out of his corner AE remarked that Willie Yeats's best poems were written when he was a poor boy in Sligo, a remark that fanned the flame of discussion, and the difficult question was broached why Yeats had ceased to write poetry.[8] All his best poems, AE said, were written before he went to London. Apart from the genius which he brought into the world, it was Sligo that had given his poetry a character. Everybody knew some of his verses by heart, and I took pleasure in listening to them again. The calves basking on the hillside were mentioned, the colleen going to church. 'But,' somebody cried out suddenly, 'he took his colleen to London and put paint upon her cheeks and dye upon her hair, and sent her up Piccadilly'. Another critic added that the last time he saw her she was wearing a fine hat and feathers. 'Supplied by Arthur Symons,' cried another. 'As sterile a little wanton as ever I set eyes upon,' exclaimed still another critic, 'who lives in remembrance of her beauty, saying nothing.' And the silences that Yeats's colleen had observed these many years were regretted, somewhat hypocritically I think, for, as AE says, a literary movement consists of five or six people who live in the same town and hate each other cordially. But if we were not really sorry that Yeats's inspiration was declining, we were quite genuinely interested to discover the cause of it. AE was certain that he would have written volume after volume if he had never sought a style, if he had been content to write simply; and all his utterances on the subject of style were repeated.

'He came this afternoon into the National Library,' John Eglinton said, breaking silence, 'and he told me he was collecting his writings for a complete edition, a library edition in ten or twelve volumes.'[9]

'But he is only thirty-seven.'[10]

'He said his day was over,' John Eglinton answered . . . 'and in speaking of the style of his last essay, he said: "Ah, that style! I made it myself."'

'But,' Longworth argued, 'I fail to understand how anybody can speak of a style apart from some definite work already written by him in that style. A style does not exist in one's head, it exists upon paper, and Yeats has no style, neither bad nor good, for he writes no more.'

AE thought that Yeats had discovered a style, and a very fine style indeed, and compared it to a suit of livery which a man buys before he engages a servant; the livery is made of the finest cloth, the gold lace is the very finest, the cockade can be seen from one side of the street to the other, but when the footman comes he is always too tall or too thin or too fat, so the livery is never worn.

'Excellent!' cried Gogarty,[11] 'and the livery hangs in a press upstairs, becoming gradually moth-eaten.'

AE regretted the variants; he knew them all and preferred the earlier text in every case, and when literary criticism was over we turned to the poet's own life to discover why it was that he sang no more songs for us. We had often heard him say that his poems had arisen out of one great passion, and this interesting avowal raised the no less interesting question — which produces the finer fruit, the gratified or the ungratified passion. It was clearly my turn to speak, and I told how Wesendonck had built for Wagner a pavilion at the end of his garden so that Wagner might compose the *Valkyrie*, and how at the end of every day when Wagner had finished his work, Mathilde used to come down the lawn to visit him, inspiring by degrees a great passion in him, but which, out of loyalty to Wesendonck, they resisted until the fatal day when he read her the poem of *Tristan and Isolde*. After the reading they had stood looking at each other; the poem was a magic draught. 'I am Tristan, thou art Isolde.' But it was not many days before Minna, Wagner's wife, intercepted a letter which she took to Madame Wesendonck, and the interview between the the two women was so violent that Wagner had to send his wife to Dresden, and himself retired to Venice to meditate on suicide and his setting of some verses of the well-beloved.

'Regret nothing,' he writes from Venice, 'I beseech you, regret nothing. Your kisses were the crown of my life, my recompense for many years of suffering. Regret nothing, I beseech you, regret nothing.'

Minna had no doubt as to Richard's guilt, nor have we, but the translator of the letters, Mr Ashton Ellis, and others, have preferred to regard this passion as ungratified, and it is evident that they think that the truth is not worth seeking since the drama and the music and the letters cannot now be affected thereby. 'For better or worse you have the music, you have the drama, you have the correspondence,' they declare. 'What can it matter to you whether an act purely physical happened, or failed to happen?' 'Everything,' I answer, 'for thereof I learn whether Wagner wrote out of a realized or an unrealized desire.'

As we sat round the fire I broke silence again:

'Love that has *not* been born again in the flesh crumbles like peat ash.'

And then John Eglinton's voice broke in:

'Every man is different,' and he reproached me with arguing for myself.

'The love we are considering has lasted for many years and will continue, and I know for certain that it has always been a pure love'.

'A detestable phrase, AE, for it implies that every gratified love must be impure. None except the lovers themselves know the truth.'

And from that day onwards I continued to meditate the main secret of Yeats's life, until one day we happened to meet at Broadstone Station.[12] We were going to the West; we breakfasted together in the train, and after breakfast the conversation took many turns, and we talked of her whom he had loved always, the passionate ideal of his life, and why this ideal had never become a reality to him as Mathilde had become to Richard. Was it really so? was my pressing question, and he answered me:

'I was very young at the time and was satisfied with . . .' My memory fails me, or perhaps the phrase was never finished. The words I supply, 'the spirit of sense', are merely conjectural.

'Yes, I understand, the common mistake of a boy'; and I was sorry for Yeats and for his inspiration which did not seem to have survived his youth, because it had arisen out of an ungratified desire. Hyacinths grown in a vase only bloom for a season. But if it had been otherwise? On such questions one may meditate a long while, and it was not until the train ran into Westport that I remembered my prediction when Symons had shown me *Rosa Alchemica*.

'His inspiration,' I had said, 'is at an end, for he talks about how he is going to write.' I had told Symons that I had noticed all through my life that a man may tell the subject of his poem and write it, but if he tells how he is going to write his poem he will never write it. Mallarmé projected hundreds of poems, and, like Yeats, Mallarmé was always talking about style. The word never came into Mallarmé's conversation, but, like Yeats, his belief was that the poet should have a language of his own. 'Every other art,' I remember him saying, 'has a special language — sculpture, music, painting; why shouldn't the poet have his?' He set himself to the task of inventing a language, but it was such a difficult one that it left him very little time for writing; we have but twenty sonnets and *L'après-midi d'un Faune* written in it. *Son oeuvre*[13] calls to mind a *bibelot*,[14] a carven nick-nack, wrought ivory, or jade, or bronze, and like bronze it will acquire a patina. His phrases will never grow old, for they tell us nothing; the secret meaning is so deeply embedded that generations will try to puzzle through them; and in the volume entitled *The Wind among the Reeds*[15] Yeats has written poems so difficult that even the adepts could not disentangle the sense; and since *The Wind among the Reeds* he has written a sonnet that clearly referred to a house. But to what house? AE inclined to the opinion that it referred to the House of Lords, but the poet, being written to from Ely Place, replied that the subject of his sonnet was Coole Park. Mallarmé could not be darker than this. But whereas to write a language apart was Mallarmé's sole aestheticism and one which he never abandoned after the publication of *L'après-midi d'un Faune*, Yeats advocated two languages, one which he employs himself, another which he would use if he could, but being unable to use it he counsels its use to others, and has put up a sign-post 'This way to Parnassus.'[16] It is amusing to think of Mallarmé and Yeats together; they would have got on famously until Yeats began to tell Mallarmé that the poet would learn the language he required in Le Berry.[17] Mallarmé was a subtle mind, and he would have thought the idea ingenious that a language is like a spring which rises in the highlands, trickles into a rivulet and flows into a river, and needs no filter until the river has passed through a town; he would have listened to these theories with interest, but Yeats would not have been able to persuade him to set out for Le Berry, and the journey would have been useless if he had, for Mallarmé had no ear for folk, less than Yeats himself, who has only half an ear; an exquisite ear for the beauty of folk imagination, and very little for folk idiom. Are not the ways of Nature strange? for he loves folk idiom as none has ever loved it, and few have had better opportunities of learning it than he along his uncle's wharves in Sligo Town and among the slopes of Ben Bulben, whither he went daily, interested in birds and beasts and the stories that the folk tell. As pretty a nosegay as ever was gathered he tied on those slopes; there is no prettier book of literature than *Celtic Twilight*,[18] and one of the tales, 'The Last Gleeman', must have put into Yeats's mind the idea that he has followed ever since, that the Irish people write very well when they are not trying to write that worn-out and defaced idiom which educated people speak and write, and which is known as English. And it is Yeats's belief that those amongst us who refuse to write it are forced back upon artificial speech which they create, and which is often very beautiful; the beauty of Meredith's speech, or Pater's, or Morris's, cannot be denied, but their speech, Yeats would say, lacks naturalness; it is not living speech, that is how he would phrase it, and his thoughts would go back to Michael Moran,[19] the last of the Gleemen, who, he thinks, was more fortunate than the three

great writers mentioned, for Michael wrote (it would be more correct to say he composed, for it is doubtful if he knew how to write) living speech — i.e., a speech that has never been printed. Yeats's whole aestheticism is expressed in these words, 'A speech that has never been printed.' It is printing that makes speech ugly, that is Yeats's belief, and the peasant is the only one who can give us unblunted speech. But is it not true that peasant speech limits the range of our ideas? The dropping of ideas out of literature would be a pure benefit, Yeats would say. Modern literature is dying of ideas. The literature that has come down to us is free from ideas. Ideas are the portion of vestrymen. But peasant speech is only adapted to dialogue. He might answer with Landor that Shakespeare and the best parts of Homer were written in dialogue, and it would be heartless to reply, 'But not the best part of your own works, Yeats. Your mind is as subtle as a Brahmin's, woven along and across with ideas, and you cannot catch the idiom as it flows off the lips. You are like Moses, who may not enter the Promised Land.' He would not care to answer, 'Even if what you say be true, you must admit that I have led some others there'; he would fold himself up like a pelican and dream of his disciples. He was dreaming of them before he had collected any, when I met him in the Cheshire Cheese;[20] he was ever looking for disciples and sought them in vain till he met Lady Gregory. It was a great day for Ireland the day that she came over to Tillyra. Here I must break off my narrative to give a more explicit account of Lady Gregory than the reader will find in *Ave*.

1   Yeats's first lecture tour to America was in November 1903.
2   The British Trade Union leader.
3   Hugh Lane. See footnote 2 on page 242.
4   Yeats's father John Butler Yeats (1839–1922). Yeats's maternal relations the Pollexfens were leading employers in nineteenth-century Sligo Town.
5   The family name of the Dukes of Ormonde was Butler, Yeats's middle name.
6   Coole Park, Lady Gregory's estate in the west of Ireland, where Yeats was a frequent visitor from 1897 onwards.
7   The lines are from 'Adam's Curse'.
8   The 1900s were a particularly lean period in Yeats's career as a poet. In the 1890s he wrote some sixty poems, in the 1910s nearly a hundred but in the 1900s he managed to complete only thirty or so, nearly half of which were written in 1909–10. For further information see my *Yeats's Worlds* (1995), pages 159ff.
9   The Collected Edition (8 vols) was published in 1908 by Bullen of the Shakespeare Head Press.
10   In 1903 Yeats was this age.

11 Oliver St John Gogarty (1878–1957), surgeon and writer. Friend of Joyce in 1903–04 and of Yeats in later life. Lived in Ely Place near George Moore.
12 A north Dublin terminus at this time.
13 French: his work.
14 Small curio or artistic trinket.
15 *Wind Among . . .* : Yeats's volume of verse first published in 1899.
16 Mountain in Greece sacred to the Muses. In the nineteenth century a group of French poets around Théophile Gautier dedicated to art for art's sake were called Parnassians.

17 A region of central France, a semi-arid plateau, traditionally used for cattle-rearing. Presumably a play by Moore on the unsuitability of such a background for the leading French Symbolist poet; Yeats by contrast valued the folk imagination and wild parts such as the Aran Islands.
18 Yeats's collection of stories first published in 1893.
19 Michael Moran (1794–1846) was a blind beggar who recited religious and ribald verse to passers-by in Dublin. He was known as the Last Gleeman.
20 A pub just off Fleet Street in London where members of the Rhymers' Club met in the early 1890s.

PETER O'LEARY
from An t-Athair Peadar Ó Laoghaire (Peter O'Leary), *Mo Sgéal Féin* (1915);
trans. Cyril Ó Céirín, *My Story* (1970)

Peter O'Leary (An tAthair Peadar Ó Laoghaire) (1839–1920) was brought up in an Irish-speaking part of County Cork near Macroom. After ordination to the priesthood in 1867 he served in the diocese of Cloyne. When the Gaelic League began in 1893 he devoted considerable energy to writing in Irish and later was closely involved in *The Journal of the Ivernian Society*, established in Cork in 1909. 'Materials for a Bibliography of the Very Reverend Peter Canon O'Leary 1839–1920' can be found in *Celtica*, Volume II (Dublin, 1954). The extract from his autobiography reproduced here is among the most poignant passages in this Reader, a reminder that the trauma of the Great Famine of the 1840s lived on into the twentieth century.

The Hunger

As soon as understanding comes to a child, it is usual for people to be asking him what would his vocation in life be, when he would be big. I well recall that question being put to me very often. I don't recall having any other answer to give to it but the one, solitary answer: that I would be a priest. From the beginning that much was settled in my mind and I don't recall that there was ever anything other than that. Neither do I recall when my mind first settled on my becoming a priest when I would be grown up.

I know well that people used to be making fun of the story, for it was clear to everyone that my father had nowhere near the necessary capital to set about such an undertaking. As soon as I got any sense, I also knew that he hadn't got the capital, but that did not prevent me from being steadfast in my mind about becoming a priest, whatever way this would come

about. If it were not for the blight coming on the potatoes and the bad times that came afterwards, I don't say that he would not have been able to give me the necessary amount of schooling. But the bad times turned everything upside down.

A strange thing — it was the big, strong farmers who were the first to fall! The man who had only a small farm, the grass of six or seven cows, kept his hold; the man with the big, broad, spacious farm was soon broken when the changed times came. He, who had only a little, lost only a little. Before this, there was no big rent or big demands on him. He was accustomed to living without much extravagance. It wasn't too difficult for him to tighten his belt a little bit more, and to answer the small demands on him without too much hardship. But he, who had a big farm, was accustomed to the expensive way of life. He was independent as long as his farm responded. When the change came, the returns from the farm came to a sudden stop. The loss, the extravagance, the demands were too great. It was impossible to meet them and they swept him off his feet. I well recall how I would hear the latest news and how it caused amazement: 'Oh! Did you hear? Such a person is burst! His land is up for sale. He's gone. He slipped away. His land is up!'

You would often hear 'His land is up!' — but you wouldn't hear at all that time 'His land has been taken by another person'. Nobody had any wish to take land. Things used to be very bad for those who had lost their land. They'd have neither food nor credit and there was nothing they could do but go looking for alms. They would not be long begging when they used to go into a decline and they'd die. As they were not accustomed to hunger or hardship, they couldn't stand it long when the hunger and hardship would come on them. Often, when the hunger was very severe, they'd have to rise and move out and head for the house of some neighbour (who, perhaps, would be as needy as themselves, or close to it) to see if they could get a mouthful of something to eat, which might take the frenzy of hunger off them.

One day, when I was eight years of age (I seem to remember that I was standing at the corner of the haggard), I saw a woman coming towards me up the hill. She was barefoot, walking very slowly and panting, as if she had been running. She was blowing so much, her mouth was wide open, so that I had a sight of her teeth. But the thing that amazed me altogether was her feet. Each foot was swollen so that, from the knee down, it was as big and as fat as a gallon-can. That sight took such a firm grip on my mind that it is before my eyes now, every bit as clear-cut as it was that day, although it is around three score years and five since I saw it. That woman had been fairly independent and free from adversity until the blackness had come upon the potatoes.

Another day — I can't tell if it was before or after that — I was inside in our house, standing on the hearthstone, when a boy came in the door. I saw the face that was on him and the terror that was in his two eyes, the terror of hunger. That face and those two eyes are before my mind now, as clear and as unclouded as the day I gave them the one and only look. Somebody gave him a lump of bread. He snatched the bread and turned his back to us and his face to the wall and he started right into eating it so ravenously that you would think he would choke himself. At the time I did not realize that I was so amazed by him or his voracity, but that sight has stayed in my mind, and will stay as long as I live.

I remember one evening during the period, when the people were running in and out and they talking away. In the winter, it was. The night was after falling. I heard someone saying, 'It was down by Carriginanassey I heard the shout!' 'There it is again!' said another, and they all ran out. A while afterwards, they came back in with a poor, old fellow between them. They put him standing on the floor — he was hardly able to stand. I was facing him and I had a view of his features. His mouth was wide open and his lips, upper and lower both, were drawn back, so that his teeth — the amount he had of them — were exposed. I saw the two, big, long, yellow eye-teeth in his mouth, the terror in his eyes and the confusion in his face. I can see them now as well as I could see them then. He was a neighbour. It is how the hunger drove him out to see if he could find anything to eat and the poor man went astray in the bog that was below Carriginanassey. When he found himself going astray, he became afraid that he would fall into a hole and be drowned. He stopped then and began to shout. That was a custom — there was a certain shout for the purpose — for anyone going astray. Each one knew how to send up that *liúgh*,[1] so that, when they heard it, everybody would know the meaning of it, and the people would gather and seek the person who was going astray.

There was a little stable at the head of the house. A poor person by the name of Patrick Buckley came and shelter was given to himself, his wife and two children in the stable. They stayed for some weeks there, but they had a small cabin for themselves after that. Sheila was the name of the elder of the two children. We had a serving-boy — Conor was his name — and I overheard Sheila talking to him one day.

'Con,' she said, in Gaelic.

'Coming, Sheila,' Con said.

'I have no speech now,' she said.

'*Airiú*,[2] what else have you got, Sheila?' Con said.

'English,' says she.

'*Airiú*, what English could you have?' Con said.

'Peter's English and Seáinín-Philib's English.' (Seáinín-Philib was another poor person, who lived in a cabin beside the place.)

'But surely English is speech, Sheila?'

'English speech?' she said in amazement. 'If it was, surely people would understand it!'

One day, Sheila's mother had a handful of gravel in the little broad-bottomed pot, the griddle-oven they used to call it, as she was going to bake a cake; she was scouring and scraping the inside of the griddle-oven with the gravel.

'Oh, Mam!' Sheila said, 'is it how you'll put gravel in the cake?'

'It is,' said her mother.

Out went Sheila. She saw Con.

'Oh, Con,' says she, 'What'll we do? What'll we do at all?'

'What's on you now, Sheila?' Con said.

'The grey-green gravel my mother's putting in the cake for us and I don't know how in the world we'll be able to eat it. All our teeth'll be broken. Some of the stones in the gravel are very big. Not one of us will have a tooth left in his head. It's all right for Little Jeremiah he hasn't got any teeth at all yet.'

Little Jeremiah was Sheila's small, young brother. In with Con until he'd see what Sheila's mother was doing. When he saw what the gravel was being used for, they had a great laugh.

The famine came. Sheila and her father and mother and little Jeremiah had to go down to Macroom into the poorhouse. No sooner were they inside than they were all separated from each other. The father was put among the men. The mother was put among the women. Sheila was put among the small girls. And Jeremiah was put among the very young children. The whole house, and all the poor people in it, was smothered in every kind of evil sickness, the people, almost as fast as they'd come in, falling down with a malady and — God bless the hearers! — dying as fast as the fever came on them. There used not be room for half of them in the house. The amount that would not be able to get in could only go and lay themselves on the bank of the river, on the lower side of the bridge. You would see them there every morning, after the night was over, stretched out in rows, some stirring, some quiet enough without any stir at all out of them. In a while, certain men would come and they would take those, who were not stirring, and they would put them into trucks. They would take them to a place beside Carrigastyra, where a great, wide, deep hole had been opened for them, and they would put them altogether down into the hole. They would do the same with all who had died in the house after the night.

It was not too long, after their going in and after his separation from his mother, that death came to little Jeremiah. The small body was thrown up on the truck and taken to the big hole, and it was thrown in along with the other bodies. But it was all the same to the child: long before his body was thrown in the hole, his soul was in the presence of God, in the joys of the heavens. It was not long until Sheila followed little Jeremiah. Her young body went into the hole, but her soul went up to where little Jeremiah was, in the presence of God, in the joy of the heavens, where she had solace and the company of the saints and angels,

and the company of the Virgin Mary, and speech that was better by far than 'Peter's English and Seáinín-Philib's English'.

The father and mother were asking and questioning as often as they were able about Sheila and little Jeremiah. The children were not long dead when they heard about it. All the poor people had Gaelic. The superiors hadn't got it, or else they spoke it poorly. The poor people could often get word about each other without the superiors knowing it. As soon as the father and mother found out that the pair of children had died, such a grief and a brooding came over them that they could not stay in the place. They were separated from each other, but they found the opportunity of sending word to each other. They decided to steal away from the place. The wife's name was Kit. Patrick first slipped out of the house. He waited for Kit at the top of the Road of the Whisps. In a while, he saw her coming, but she was walking very slowly. The sickness was on her. They pushed on towards Carrigastyra. They came to the place where the big hole was. They knew that the two children were down in the hole with the hundreds of other bodies. They stood beside the hole and they wept their fill. Up on Derryleigh to the east of the Caharin was the cabin in which they had been living before they went into the poorhouse. They left the big hole and they headed north-west for Derryleigh, where the cabin was. The place was six miles of a journey from them, and the night was coming, but they pushed on. The hunger was on them and the sickness on Kit. They had to walk very slowly. When they had put a couple of miles of the journey past them, Kit was forced to stop. She was not able to walk any farther. A neighbour came across them. Drink and some little bit of food was given to them, but fear would not allow anyone to give them shelter since they were only just after coming out of the poorhouse and the evil sickness was on the woman. Patrick only lifted the woman onto his back and pushed on north-westwards for the cabin.

The poor man himself was weak enough. It would have been hard on him to put the journey by him without having any load. With the load, he was often forced to stop and to leave his load down on the ditch of the road for a while. But whatever weariness was on him, he continued to put that journey by him. He did not part with his load. He reached the cabin. The cabin was cold and empty before him, without fire nor heat.

The morning after, some neighbour came to the cabin. He went inside. He saw the pair there and they both dead, and the feet of the woman in Patrick's bosom, as if he had been trying to warm them. It would seem that he had felt the weakness of death coming over Kit and her feet cold, and he put the feet into his own bosom to take the cold from them.

'He was a good, loyal, noble man!' some person might say, perhaps, 'and the deed he did was a noble one!'

It is true. But I will tell you this much. Thousands of deeds of the same kind were done in Ireland during that period, and nobody was one whit amazed at the excellence of the deeds. According to everyone, Patrick Buckley had only done a thing that any man, who was worth calling a Christian, would have done.

That little man-een, whose name was Michael O'Leary, was living in a cabin not far from that in which Patrick Buckley and his wife died. Black Michael was a nick-name they had on him. Cathleen Purcell was his wife's name. They had the full of the house of children. There wasn't as much as one word of English in themselves or in the children. The famine came hard on them. Tadhg was the name of their eldest son. He saw his father and mother growing weak with the hunger, and the youngest member of the family stretched dead in a corner of the cabin. At nightfall, he took an axe and a knife with him and out he went. He went into the cowhouse of one of the neighbours and he killed a beast. He took some of the skin from it, stripping the amount of meat he wanted to bring with him. He took away the two hind quarters and came home. They all had a good meal that night. When the hunger had been taken from them, Tadhg took out the body that was in the corner, and he made a hole out in the garden and put the body in it.

When the morning came, the people who owned the cow rose and found the cow dead out in the shed, with its two hind quarters gone. The owner went to Macroom and got a search warrant. He had an idea where the meat was brought. He and whatever law-officer he had with him came to Black Michael's cabin. The bones and some of the meat was found. Tadhg was taken prisoner and brought to Macroom and put into prison. When the time came for it, he was tried. He was sentenced without much hesitation and transported. I never heard any report since then of what happened to him afterwards nor of what end befell him.

Michael and Cathleen and those of the family who still lived left the cabin and took to the roads.

Some days after they had gone away, a neighbour was going past the cabin. He saw a hound, with something in his mouth, in the garden; the hound threw down the thing he had in his mouth and ran away. The neighbour came over and he nearly fell with the shock and the horror when he saw that it was a person's hand that the dog had in his mouth! Tadhg hadn't made the hole deep enough before he had put the body down into it.

The neighbour found a box or something of the sort. He took the rest of the body from the hole, and brought the box to the nearest graveyard and buried it. It was no cause for wonder at that time to see a person going by himself to a graveyard and a coffin with him in his cart, or on the back of two cattle if he hadn't got a horse nor a cart.

That was the way things were then, ugly and hateful and loathsome, round about the area in which I was reared. I understand that the story was exactly the same all about the whole of Ireland. And, to make matters altogether worse, it was not really by the will of God that things were so. It was that way because of the will of people. There was sent out from Ireland that year as much — no! twice as much — corn as would have nourished every person living in the country. The harbours of Ireland were full of ships and the ships full of Irish corn: they were leaving the harbours while the people were dying with the hunger throughout the land.

'Why wasn't the corn kept here?' someone will say, perhaps.

It was not kept because it had to be sold to pay the rent, it and the butter and the meat, and every other bit of produce from the land, excepting the potatoes. The blackness took away the potatoes and then there was no food left for people to eat.

Someone will say, perhaps: 'Why wasn't a law made to protect the people from the injustice that forced the people to sell the corn and not to keep anything for themselves to eat?'

I'm sorry for your want of knowledge! 'A law to protect the people,' you say? *Airiú*, if you had spoken to the gentlemen of England at that time of a law to protect the people, they would have said you were mad.

It was not at all for the protection of the people that the English made laws at that time. To crush the people down and to plunder them, to put them to death by famine and by every other kind of injustice — that's why the English made laws in those days. It is a strange story, but the English had a sort of proverb then. Here's the proverb: 'To give the tenant his rights is an injustice to the landlord.'

---

1   Irish: shout, yell.
2   Irish: but, now, really, truly (Dinneen).

JOHN HOWARD PARNELL
from John Howard Parnell, *Charles Stewart Parnell: A Memoir* (1916)

The enigma of Parnell, the national leader who hated the colour green, is added to in
this portrait of his ordinariness by his brother.

My Brother's Personality

The Man of the Moment

I think it would be fitting to give some idea, so far as I
can convey it in cold print, of my brother's appearance
and outward manner during the period of his
supremacy. I am judging, not only from my own
personal recollection, but from that of many intimate
friends who were connected with Charley at this stage
of his career.

His appearance was always a striking one. Tall and
thin (except during a period from about 1885 to 1890,
when he became rather stout), he always held himself
erect, though without stiffness, until the strain of his
serious illness and the final party split prematurely aged
him. His hair was a darkish brown, with tinges of tan
or auburn. He wore it rather long behind, curling
slightly upwards from the back of his neck. On his
entrance into Parliament in 1875 he was clean-shaven,
with the exception of side-whiskers, but by 1880 he
had grown a beard of considerable length, and a long,
somewhat drooping moustache.

His complexion was pale, but with a healthy pallor.
His white face contrasted vividly with his hair, and
accentuated the brilliancy of his dark grey eyes, with
their steady and at the same time far-away look. This,
with his long features and firm lips curving slightly
downwards, gave him a somewhat melancholy
appearance, though this was not really borne out by
his character, which was lively at times, and at all
events philosophical. It was his appearance and his
habitually reserved manner that caused many to
believe that he had no sense of humour, and never
made a joke.

This, however, was by no means the case. He was
always specially fond of quizzing me with a kind of
dry but always good-natured humour, and was fond of
making, among his intimate friends, short, pointed
jokes about men and events. This was the case even in
his later days, when he was under the full oppression
of a fight against hopeless odds.

I remember The O'Donoghue of the Glens, who
was an inseparable companion of his during the dark
days of 1890 and 1891, telling me several incidents to
that effect. On one occasion he was travelling from
Tipperary to Athlone in the course of his final
campaign of successive defeats. One of his fellow-
members, Mr Hayden, was sitting opposite to him,
and, as was not an unusual custom, had put his railway
ticket in the band of his hat. Charley looked at him
fixedly for some time, with a twinkle in his eye, and
suddenly burst forth with the remark: 'Why on earth,
Hayden, do you put your ticket in your hat like that?
Everyone must be thinking that you have just picked
up the hat as a bargain at an auction.' Poor Hayden
very shamefacedly transferred the offending ticket to
his pocket, amidst the laughter of his companions.

It was when they were being given an enthusiastic
send-off from Athlone Station that, The O'Donoghue
tells me, another little incident occurred which proved
that, even when in bad health and wearied to death
with illness, travelling, and the strain of continual
speeches, he could still appreciate the humorous side
of life. Amongst those on the crowded platform who
were wildly waving handkerchiefs, flags, and sticks,
was one young peasant woman who, having neither
handkerchief, flag nor stick to wave, and being entirely
carried away by the enthusiasm of the moment, was to
be seen wildly swinging about her unfortunate baby in
the air. Charley noticed the incident at once, and
watched this human semaphore display for a few
moments with a twinkle in his eye, which was as near
as he generally came to laughing. Then it proved too
much for him, and he laughed outright, and, turning
to his companions in the carriage, directed their
attention to this quaint expression of loyalty.

The Warmth beneath the Ice

I have spoken of his habitual coldness of manner, and
the mysterious way in which, in spite of it, or even
because of it, he used to draw all towards him, as
moths to a candle. He certainly rarely unbent in
expression, and the tone of his voice very rarely
varied. But his eyes were full of expression, and the
manner in which he accompanied an abrupt and
unalterable decision with a sudden winning smile,
which seemed to light up his whole face like a ray of
sunshine, never failed to render acceptable, and even
welcome, the curtness of the actual words he used. His
was indeed a mesmerism of manner, and neither I,
who so frequently experienced it and came under its

sway, nor any of those who were accustomed to see him daily, can actually describe it in so many words.

During this, the summit of his career, he took extreme care with regard to his dress and personal appearance. He did not often wear black, except when compelled to do so at ceremonial functions, but generally preferred tweeds of a dark shade, brown being perhaps his favourite colour. Towards green, although it was his national colour, he always had the strongest aversion, as I shall explain in a chapter devoted to his many curious superstitions. He wore rather low turned-down collars, not unlike those for which Mr Gladstone was famous, but without the long pointed ends. For tie he generally wore a cravat (blue being, I think, its usual colour), with a simple pearl or diamond pin in the centre.

In walking he held himself extremely erect, and took long, though not hurried, strides. Although I am not an exceptionally slow walker myself, I generally found it pretty hard to keep up with him when we were out together, and the more intent he happened to be upon his secret thoughts, the faster he seemed to go. To his habit of thinking deeply when walking was due the fact that he paid little attention to people or things on his way, guiding himself, it would seem, chiefly by instinct; yet, though he would appear to be entirely absorbed in his own thoughts, he would be by no means oblivious of what was being said to him, though he appeared to take no notice whatever of it. Yet he often startled one by uttering a sudden abrupt question relating to something that had been said to him some time before, which showed that he must have grasped every detail of the conversation.

When speaking in public he stood up rather stiffly, with his arms folded loosely in front of him, though very occasionally I have seen him with them clasped behind his back. This was an attitude which he had contracted in very early days. He spoke in a rather low voice, but slowly and very distinctly, making every word tell. He rarely emphasized any point, however important, by raising his voice or by gesticulating in any way with his arms. As a matter of fact, he always had a horror, even in private life, of speaking loudly. I remember an instance of this one time when we were together in Avondale.[1] We were walking down the road to the sawmills, when I noticed that some of his men working on a field near-by were taking things very easily, even for Irish labourers. I said to him: 'Why don't you call out to those fellows, Charley, and get them to hurry up? They look like being all day over that field, if they go on like that.' He replied, with a shrug of his shoulders: 'I know that; but if I wanted to make them hear I should have to shout, and I

dislike shouting.' We walked on in silence, but I believe, with his invariably retentive memory, he had something to say to them when he met them next at close quarters.

Another noticeable feature of his was what might be almost called his shyness. He had an especial dislike for the company of strangers, and, in spite of his experience, always felt nervous in the presence of crowds, frequently clenching his hands when speaking, until the blood came. He was once being entertained at a large public dinner, and a huge crowd had assembled outside the windows, the blinds of which were not drawn, in order to give the people a chance of seeing their beloved leader. He became gradually more and more uneasy under the concentrated stare of the crowd, and began to fidget in his seat and frown. Finally he called out to The O'Donoghue, who was sitting some distance off, out of sight of the crowd: 'For goodness' sake, O'Donoghue, change places with me; I can't stand those fellows staring at me any longer.'

On another occasion he and I were travelling together by train, when a number of enthusiasts followed us into the carriage. He straightened himself from his usual half-reclining position in the corner of the carriage, which he adopted when travelling, and said to me pettishly: 'Can't you get those people out of the carriage, John? they're annoying me.' I had to set about the very uncomfortable task of going up to each person and asking him whether he would mind leaving the carriage, as my brother wished to be alone.

Although he frequently told me that he felt nervous, often to a painful degree, when speaking in public, he certainly never showed any trace of it. I do not think that he felt anything like the same nervousness in delivering a speech in the House of Commons that he did in addressing a meeting of his own people. He came to the House with what he had to say cut and dried, for the English to take or leave as they pleased, and I think he thoroughly enjoyed the consternation which his speeches, which always had somewhat the nature of an ultimatum, produced among that dignified and custom-observing gathering.

In speaking to an Irish audience, however, I think he always had a deep desire for sympathy, though he disliked any noisy demonstrations of support. But he was always quite able to stand up to a hostile, and even threatening, crowd, without turning a hair.

Charley's Diet

Charley was never a heavy eater, and his state of health, which was delicate from boyhood, obliged him to be very careful as to what he took to eat.

We all got into a terribly disorganized habit as to meals during our days together at Avondale, after our father had died and our mother had gone to America. The only meal during the day at which all the family and visitors were certain of meeting was dinner, which we generally had about eight o'clock in the evening. Charley never had breakfast in the ordinary English sense, but made a sort of combined breakfast and lunch when he came down, which was usually about noon, as he was in the habit of stopping up well into the small hours of the morning. He always had some porridge and cream to start with, and a mutton chop formed the chief portion of the meal. He had toast, usually made of oatmeal bread, and very often barberry jelly, which he had been recommended, for his throat, like his chest, was always a weak spot with him. He was also very fond of tomatoes, which at that time were considered rather a luxury.

He made a good, if not heavy, breakfast, and then went right on until dinner without another sit-down meal. Afternoon tea he thoroughly despised, although I was always particularly fond of it myself; and if he felt in need of anything during the day, he contented himself with getting a glass of buttermilk from the nearest cottage or farm where he happened to be.

At dinner we very rarely had soup, but a leg of mutton with red currant jelly generally appeared, owing to its being Charley's favourite dish. He did not like salmon, but was particularly fond of trout, which were very plentiful round Avondale. Very often, when I returned just before dinner from a day's fishing, he would rap at the window as I passed, and cry out: 'Hallo, John, have you brought me any nice trout to-day?' In the same way, he very often got a special fancy for some of his favourite barberries, which he liked eating raw as well as in jelly. There was a plentiful supply of these along the road to the river quite close to the house, and he used often to say to me suddenly: 'Now, John, you might take a basket and go and pick some barberries for me.' He was very fond of potatoes cooked in their jackets, and also liked cabbage, seakale, peas, French beans, and turnips. He hardly took sweets, except rhubarb, of which he was specially fond, being in that respect the exact opposite to myself, and avoided pastry like poison, as he found it did not agree with his digestion. His cheese was, as a rule, Gruyère. He never took nuts, and practically the only form of dessert which he touched was grapes. I always lamented the fact that he did not like apples, because he not only did not eat them himself, but had all the apple-trees in the orchard cut down.

At dinner he invariably had claret; at breakfast, tea; and during the evening he occasionally took a cup of cocoa, but was not fond of coffee. He ate his meals rather quickly, and disliked talking at them, preferring apparently, as when walking or in bed, to pursue the train of his own thoughts.

While anything in the nature of a fixed timetable for meals was absolutely unknown in Avondale, his visitors were always free to have whatever they liked whenever they chose, and the result was that the dining-room saw one long succession of meals like the Mad Hatter's tea-party in *Alice in Wonderland*. As was the case with hours, he never sought to impose the nature of his meals upon his guests, or even upon his brothers and sisters. The rule at Avondale was that you could have exactly what you liked, exactly when you liked. These habits he continued right through his political life, with the exception that, if anything, his meals became more irregular as years went on. In his later days Sir Henry Thompson gradually increased the strictness of his diet, for, as I have stated, his throat and chest were always weak, and his health at the best of times was delicate.

In the early days I hardly ever remember him smoking. Later in his political days he developed a taste for cigars, though I think he never took to the pipe or cigarette. He was fond of using the smoking-room of the House of Commons, either to think out his schemes or to hold conferences with members of his party, but he by no means always smoked when he was there.

As for his amusement, outdoor sports, such as cricket, hunting, and shooting, were always his favourites when he had time to indulge in them. Chess, as I have said earlier, he knew, but did not play it exceptionally well. He was a keen billiard-player, but, as far as I can recollect, took little or no interest in cards.

As a letter-writer he confined himself to the briefest and most business-like epistles. The telegraph was his usual means of communication, and certainly the surest way of getting a reply from him, as he was rather apt to ignore the letters he received. I know that even I, when I wished to arrange to meet him, had to do so by telegram, as, if I sent on a letter in advance, he rarely took much notice of it, and I had to go and rout him out wherever he was stopping, when his invariable remark was: 'Whyever didn't you send me a telegram?'

His desire for haste showed itself even more when he was travelling. If he took a car he generally urged the driver to the utmost speed, and if he missed a train, or found that he would have to wait any appreciable time, he generally chartered a special, on several occasions travelling on the footplate of the engine. Delay in any form was, in fact, abhorrent to one of his highly-strung nervous temperament.

That is as far as I can remember of my brother's outward appearance, manner, and habits, during the time of his greatness. The details which I have given may seem trivial, taken singly, but, on the other hand, they may be of service as giving some sort of picture of the man himself.

---

1   Parnell's estate in the Wicklow Mountains, left to him by his father.

THOMAS MacDONAGH

from Thomas MacDonagh, *Literature in Ireland: Studies Irish and Anglo-Irish* (1916)

Thomas MacDonagh (1878–1916), poet, dramatist, and critic, was assistant head at Patrick Pearse's school St Enda's in Rathfarnham before taking up an appointment as lecturer in English at University College Dublin in 1911. He was co-founder of *The Irish Review* (1911–14), and became increasingly involved in nationalist politics. During the Easter Rising, along with Sean MacBride, he was Commander of the Irish Volunteers in Jacobs Biscuit factory and was a signatory to the Proclamation of the Irish Republic. Condemned to death he was executed on 3 May 1916. 'So sensitive his nature seemed, / So daring and sweet his thought.' This is how Yeats wrote about MacDonagh in 'Easter 1916', and this sweetness is in evidence in this extract.

The Irish Mode

Every syllable of a word has a vowel and may have one consonant or more. The vowel may have a short sound, as 'u' in 'nut' or a long sound, as 'o' in 'note'. A syllable may be stressed or unstressed, the stress depending on the pronunciation of the word, or, in the case of a monosyllable, on the meaning of the sentence in which it is placed. In the classical languages, which had a full inflexional system and could in consequence indicate meaning without the same use of word order that English has, we may take it that stress had no real place, either formative or combative, in the making of verse. Their metric was founded on the rhythm of long and short syllables — quantity. This system, in the case of Latin, was an adoption, but was none the less rigid. In English, metrical quantity proper does not exist, though English verse uses for a grace all the varieties of vowels, short and long, and of consonants and consonant combinations, quick and slow, light and heavy. The recurrence of stress marks the rhythm. The voice is capable of uttering, at one 'pressure', up to three syllables but not more. That is, between two stressed syllables there may be no unstressed, one unstressed or two unstressed syllables. If, as in the case

of such words as 'superfluous' or 'memorial', more than three syllables seem to be uttered at one voice-pressure, it will be found that there is either elision, as in '-uous' of 'superfluous' (if pronounced superfl'ous) or the introduction of a consonantal *yoll* sound, as in '-ial' of 'memorial' (memoryal).

English verse, then, is accentual, a rhythm of stressed and unstressed syllables. Irish verse is also accentual; but there is this occasional difference, that while what may be called central English verse, in order to emphasize the stressed, under-emphasizes the unstressed, Irish frequently allows for the clear pronunciation of several syllables between stress and stress. Such Irish verse is not rigidly governed by the law of mono-pressures; it is generally found in songs, the tunes of which have a good deal to do with drawing the metrical feet dancing out of their bars. This less pronounced hammering of the stressed syllables is more noticeable in Irish prose speech; and on account of it English as we speak it in Ireland has a much more deliberate way of pronunciation, a much more even intonation, than the English of the English. One of the ablest living English metrists, Mr T.S. Omond, complained some time ago, in a letter to the writer, that he could not make out the metre of a poem beginning with the doggerel lines:

I once spent an evening in a village
Where the people are all taken up with tillage.

An Irish reader would be content to pronounce the words as they come, to read the lines as prose reads:

I once spent an evening in a village where the people are all taken up with tillage,

not at all hurrying over or slurring 'spent', '-ening', 'taken', and not over-stressing 'in' and 'up'.

Two examples from different stages of Anglo-Irish literature will illustrate this tendency of our poetry. The reading of the first we know from its whimsical tune:

The town of Passage
Is both wide and spacious
And situated upon the sea,
'Tis neat and decent
And quite contagious
To go to Cork on a bright summer's day.[1]

The last line of this verse is always sung in such a way as to be almost spoken with rapid and even enunciation of all the syllables. The effect may be got by reading the line with little or no stress on the words, 'go', 'Cork', 'bright', 'day'. In the song this effect adds to the drollery of the words and the tune.

Very different is the well known 'Lake Isle of Innisfree' of W. B. Yeats:

I will arise and go now, and go to Innisfree,
And a small cabin build there, of clay and wattles
    made;
Nine bean rows will I have there, a hive for the
    honey bee,
And live alone in the bee-loud glade.

And I shall have some peace there, for peace comes
    dropping slow,
Dropping from the veils of the morning to where
    the cricket sings;
There midnight's all a glimmer, and noon a purple
    glow,
And evening full of the linnet's wings.

I will arise and go now, for always night and day
I hear lake water lapping with low sounds by the
    shore;
While I stand on the roadway, or on the pavements
    gray,
I hear it in the deep heart's core.

In the line

And I shall have some peace there, for peace comes
    dropping slow,

it would be as wrong to mark, as heavily stressed, the syllables 'I', 'some', 'there', as to scan it:

And I | shall have | some peace | there . . .

as some English metrists might read it.

Take the line frankly as if it were a line of prose, only with that beauty of vibration in the voice that goes with the fine grave words of poetry. (It is impossible to mark the reading by punctuation or the like.) Read it so, and you will understand the true quality of this mode in Anglo-Irish poetry. It is wrong to scan this verse, to cut off the syllables according to the measure of a rhythm that rises and falls sharply and regularly. Even with some marks to indicate that though unstressed, a syllable is slow and long:

And Í shall have sóme peace thére

the scansion is wrong. There is a recurrence in this verse, but it is not the recurrence of the foot. I have been able to take half a line to illustrate my meaning. The first three lines of each stanza have a cesura in the middle. I believe that that is the only division to make in them, and that as a rule open to exception. In general the second part of the line has a more obvious recurrence of stress than the first, as:

. . . of clay and wattles made.

Of course, as in all musical verse, there are contrasts, exceptional first half lines that run with a regular scannable rhythm, and exceptional second half lines like:

. . . with low sounds on the shore.

This general movement, changing from a slow beat to an easy rise and fall, happens constantly. I sometimes think it expresses, whether in accentual verse or quantitative, the mingled emotion of unrest and pleasure that comes with the break up of winter, with the south wind, with the thought of the shortness of life and the need to make haste to explore its good and simple joys — the desire to leave the unlovely, mingled with a vivid conception of the land of heart's desire. It is the rhythm of that fourth ode of Horace's first book. In the long lines the four solemn bars, dactyls or spondees, are followed by three light trochaic feet; and the short lines, after the unrest of one syllable taken alone, continue the movement:

> *Solvitur acris hiemps grata vice veris et Favoni, trahuntque*
>   *siccas machinæ carinas;*
> *ac neque iam stabulis gaudet pecus aut arator igni,*
>   *nec prata canis albicant pruinis.*

The system is:

$$\bar{\ }\,\smile\smile\,|\,\bar{\ }\,\smile\smile\,|\,\bar{\ }\,\smile\smile\,|\,\smile\smile\smile\,|\,\bar{\ }\,\smile\,|\,\bar{\ }\,\smile\,|\,\smile$$
$$\smile\,|\,\bar{\ }\,\smile\,|\,\bar{\ }\,\smile\smile\,|\,\bar{\ }\,\smile\,|\,\bar{\ }\,\bar{\ }$$

It would be possible to treat the second line taken above as iambic, but, considering the dactyls and trochees in the first, it must be read as trochaic.

It may be objected that owing to the utter difference between accentual and quantitative verse, it is wrong to apply these remarks to the two. I have elsewhere drawn attention to the difference, for instance, between the dactyl (quantitative) and the triple falling accentual measure of 'merrily'. This difference does not affect the similarity between the contrast of first half line and the second half life in both 'Innisfree' and this ode of Horace's. For the rest, a rhythm may be produced not only in music, in noise, in words and in other things heard, but in things seen and things felt. And not merely the words of verse express the emotion. In true poetry, as the meaning of the words comes second to their rhythm, and the rhythm expresses an emotion, it will be found that the words mean the expression of this emotion as well as the rhythm.

To read correctly Anglo-Irish poetry one must follow either Irish music or Anglo-Irish prose speech. My earliest conscious observation, and notation, so to call it, of this speech was in Cork city about ten years ago. In the house at which I stayed there were two children. One was continually looking for the other and calling all over the house. 'Is Maudie in the garden?' Jimmy would chant in a most wonderfully sweet voice, lingering on every syllable. Later I was delighted to note, when living in a little mountain lodge above Rathfarnham in County Dublin, that a blackbird which came to wake me every morning in the spring sang just the notes of Jimmy's chant — a blackbird with a Cork accent. One need not think that Jimmy was guilty of that sin of childhood never committed by the Anglo-Saxon Saint Guthlac, who 'did not imitate the various cries of birds'. Jimmy was not peculiar in his accent.

In such instances song and speech are not far apart; and Mr Yeats, for all his want of musical ear, owes, I believe, this peculiar musical quality of his early verse to that Irish chant which at once saves Irish speech from too definite a stress and from an utterance too monotonous and harsh.

At the same time one must not deduce from all this that Gaelic verse is a footless thing of sinuous windings. Nothing could be more clearly marked than most Gaelic measures. And these too have had their effect on Anglo-Irish verse. To do Mr Yeats justice, since I have quoted from him to show the serpent, I shall now quote, to show the eagle, the Musicians' song from *Deirdre:*

FIRST MUSICIAN

'Why is it,' Queen Edain said,
  'If I do but climb the stair
To the tower overhead,
  When the winds are calling there,
Or the gannets calling out,
  In waste places of the sky,
There's so much to think about,
  That I cry, that I cry?'

SECOND MUSICIAN

But her goodman answered her:
  'Love would be a thing of naught
Had not all his limbs a stir
  Born out of immoderate thought;
Were he anything by half,
  Were his measure running dry.
Lovers, if they may not laugh,
  Have to cry, have to cry.'

THREE MUSICIANS (*together*)

But is Edain worth a song
  Now the hunt begins anew?
Praise the beautiful and strong;
  Praise the redness of the yew;
Praise the blossoming apple-stem.
  But our silence had been wise.
What is all our praise to them,
  That have one another's eyes?

This poem is really syllabic, seven syllables to the line, like one species of Debhidhe[2] poems in Irish — without, of course, the arrangements of assonance. I do not know if Mr Yeats is aware of this syllabic measure; but again and again in his poems and in the poems of many contemporary Irishmen I find this tendency. Indeed I should say that the effects of our more deliberate Irish speech on our verse are these two: first, a prose intonation, not monotonous, being saved by the natural rise and fall of the voice, a remnant of the ancient pitch — a quality, as it were, of chanted speech

— and second, a tendency to give, in certain poems, generally of short riming lines, almost equal stress value to all the syllables, a tendency to make the line the metrical unit. From the first of these effects comes a more reasoning, not to say conversational tone, which disallows inversions, quaint words and turns of speech. Not conforming in our way of verse to the regular English stress rhythm we have not the same necessity as the English poets to depart from the natural word order. We have not to manufacture a rhythm in that unnatural way. I take up the first book of verse to my hand, the poems of William Drummond of Hawthornden, Ben Johnson's friend. The first poem I open, the lovely 'Phœbus Arise', does not afford good examples of poetic inversions. The lines, varying in length, go on their way freely. The last three lines are a little flat by comparison with the rest:

> The clouds bespangle with bright gold their blue;
> Here is the pleasant place,
> And everything, save Her, who all should grace.

These lines are a 'regularization' of the three that ended the poem in the earlier edition:

> The clouds with orient gold spangle their blue;
> Here is the pleasant place —
> And nothing wanting is, save She, alas!

The reasons for the changes are apparent, as is the loss of beauty. But how could the poet have conceived the fear that anyone would try to read 'spangle' with a stress on the second syllable, and to such a fear sacrificed his 'orient gold'.

The sonnet beginning 'I know that all beneath the moon decays', which follows 'Phœbus Arise' in my edition, will serve me better with examples. Lines like

> And that nought is more light than airy praise;

or

> But that, O me! I must both write and love,

would be read without difficulty and without that danger of wrong emphasis which Drummond seems to have feared.

His lines are:

> And that nought lighter is than airy praise;

and

> But that, O me! I both must write and love.

The freedom of Irish writers from these inversions and from kindred artificialities and the resultant colloquial naturalness may also, as I have suggested, have to do with the newness of the English language here, with the fact that the people, whose speech is echoed in these poems, have no literary memories in English, that we are still at the simple beginnings, that our literature is still at lyric babblings. However that may be, I am sure that the Irish writers are more direct, more modern, than such writers as Robert Bridges, Henry Newbolt and William Watson, on whom have fallen the mantles of older English writers, or at least who fill their shoes.

I go for examples to the *Oxford Book of English Verse*. I take, as I am seeking natural diction, a poem with a story and the living words of a modern man, an excellent poem, Newbolt's 'He Fell among Thieves'.

> 'Ye have robb'd,' said he, 'ye have slaughter'd and
>   made an end,
>   Take your ill-got plunder, and bury the dead,
> What will ye more of your guest and sometime
>   friend?'
>   'Blood for our blood,' they said.

The diction of this, more especially in view of the admirably direct narrative in the stanzas that follow, is stilted and wrong. That phrase, 'made an end', and the whole third line are born of pen and ink. Not so, though it is not yet common colloquial diction, is the language of Mangan's[3] version of 'O'Hussey's Ode to the Maguire' — to go back seventy years:

> Though he were even a wolf ranging the round
>   green woods,
> Though he were even a pleasant salmon in the
>   unchainable sea,
> Though he were a wild mountain eagle, he could
>   scarce bear, he,
> This sharp, sore sleet, these howling floods.
>
> Oh, mournful is my soul this night for Hugh
>   Maguire!
> Darkly as in a dream he strays! Before him and
>   behind
> Triumphs the tyrannous anger of the wounding wind,
> The wounding wind, that burns as fire!

O'Hussey is not a modern man, yet though Mangan gives him words and phrases that were scarcely ever colloquial, he gives him a natural directness that goes with emphatic speech all the world over, at all times. If this comparison be unjust, it is so rather to Mangan's bard than to the Anglo-Indian with his revolver. I have quoted these two poems for another purpose than the comparison of diction. Newbolt's poem has lines like —

He did not see the starlight on the Laspur hills,

which, contrasting with the beat of the regular lines, has something of the unstressed movement so often found in Irish poems. Here, one may take it, it comes naturally in the enumeration of scenes and sounds, as an escape and relief. Mangan's rhythms are much subtler, much deeper and more resonant; his escape, as in the second of the stanzas quoted, is from precipitate half unmeasured music to a regular tolling.

For another parallel to the passage from Newbolt I take a typical passage from a typical Irish writer of narrative poems, Alice Milligan[4]:

'If I was home at all,'
She is musing now, 'I would go that way to-night,
I would walk that way alone in the care of God,
All doors are shut and no one comes abroad
Because they think the souls are out to-night;
So in the windows they set the candles three
To let the wanderers know, "We pray for ye
And love ye yet, but would look on ye with dread
Returning from the dead."'

The inversion 'candles three' is the only forced phrase in this.

Syllabic verse, riming or assonating, develops, I think, internal rimes and the riming of monosyllables with the last syllables of long words. Of course the rules of rimes and the rest were never arbitrary. They were discovered. They are 'nature methodized'. The rimes are as accidental as anything in such a matter can be. The grace occurs first by that accident of the wind blowing where it listeth; and then, being observed, the grace is sought again. In Old Irish, syllabic verse reached great perfection. I give as an example the first stanza of a poem written by a monk, a scribe, of his cat:

Messe ocus Pangur ban
cechtar nathar fria saindan;
bith a menma-sain fri seilgg
mu menma céin im saincheirdd.[5]

It will be observed that the lines are all of seven syllables, that the first and third end in monosyllables and the second and fourth, riming with them in couplets, in words of two syllables. The constant rule in this particular kind of verse was that the second riming word should be a syllable longer than the first.

That is enough here about that wonderfully intricate thing, Gaelic versification. I leave it all the more willingly at this, as a certain over-insistence on its rarity has led many to think it is the only virtue of Gaelic poetry. That such is not the case can be seen by anyone who reads, even in unadorned prose translation, poems like the dialogue between the King and the Hermit or Finn's Song of Summer or the Lament of the Old Woman of Beare.

Next to the effects of Gaelic metre and of modern Anglo-Irish speech comes the effect of Irish music. The characteristic rhythms of Irish music are noticeable everywhere in the lyrics of the Irish Mode. In a poem like Ferguson's[6] 'Fairy Thorn' one can hear the notes of the dancing air — in the first stanza the beating of the feet to the music.

Note the different effect — the swaying with the wild sweet twist of the song — in such poems as 'The Outlaw of Loch Lene' and Ferguson's translation, 'Pasheen Finn'. I remember once hearing this latter song sung in Irish by a large number of people in the South of Ireland. The singers swayed their heads slightly in a slow, drowsy way; and the song went on through its full length, verses and chorus, without a break. When I read the poem now, the original or Ferguson's version, I find in it — read into it perhaps — that continuous swaying. In the same way my reading of 'Loch Lene' is affected by the way in which the air to the third line refuses to stop at the end, but having taken breath on the penultimate syllable hurries without a pause into the next phrase. So with a great number of Irish poems and of Anglo-Irish translations, imitations and original poems in that mode. We hear through them that music of our own. I am no exception — who can be? Here as I sit writing this on a morning of spring, in a place under the jurisdiction of the Dublin Corporation, in a garden full of flowers and thrushes, a boy is passing on the other side of my garden wall whistling a gay rambling Irish dance tune. There are words to that tune. I do not know them; but I know that, Irish or English, they have that rambling way with them. I know too that some poet who hears that tune to-day or to-morrow is likely to be so haunted by the rhythm of it that he will lay the ghost of it by singing a song to it.

The earlier Anglo-Irish poets in whose work this mode is most obvious are Mangan and Ferguson. In recent times almost everyone who has written songs and lyrics has it somewhere or other. It cannot be attributed altogether to the actual music. Several masters of it have no ear for music proper, but this, I believe, means only that while deaf to the tone of the notes they are keenly sensible of the rhythm. As Coventry Patmore has remarked, the tattoo of a knuckle upon the table will lose most, if not all, of its rhythm if transferred to a bell. 'The drum,' he says, 'gives rhythm, but the clear note of the triangle is nothing without another instrument, because it does not admit of an imagined variation.' With these tune-deaf poets the imagined variation may exist in a piece of music as in the rattle of a railway train.

The most valuable and characteristic contribution to verse made by the Anglo-Irish poets, by Moore, Mangan, Ferguson, Hyde, Yeats and all, has been a contribution of melody, a music that at once expresses and evokes emotion. In the whole body of their literature you find scarcely a true poem which, in the words of the book reviewers, treats adequately a serious subject. Of course this may be said of the purely lyric poets of all ages and countries. It is the epic and dramatic poets, to say nothing of the didactic, who write formal addresses to Light and to the Sun, who discuss at length the question of immortality, to be or not to be, the question of medicine for a mind diseased. Allusions to all these you will find in the Irish lyric — more than that, sudden illuminations, that illumination of knowledge which again is one of the marks of the true poet — *imbas forosna*.[7]

> Three things through love I see;
>   Sorrow and sin and death, —
> And my mind reminding me
>   That this doom I breathe with my breath.

> But sweeter than violin or lute
>   Is my love — and she left me behind
> I wish that all music were mute,
>   And I to all beauty were blind.

When Irish poets write the new epics of this nation and the new poetic drama of the coming years, we shall, no doubt, have plenty of those treatments of serious subjects. At present a search for the like would bring us only the moralizings of poetasters, the obvious and the devious, the things so plainly seen in our path that they do not need description or indication, or so out of the way, so far-fetched, that they recall nothing in our experience.

1   Opening lines of 'The Attractions of a Fashionable Watering-Place' by Francis Mahony (1804–66).
2   A generic form of metre in Old Irish verse. See Douglas Hyde, *A Literary History of Ireland* (1899), passim.
3   James Clarence Mangan (1803–49), a leading nineteenth-century Irish poet.
4   Alice Milligan (1866–1953), poet and dramatist, author of *Hero Lays* (1908), and considered by MacDonagh in the final issue of *The Irish Review* (September–November 1914), 'The Best Irish Poet'.
5   MacDonagh has taken his example from Douglas Hyde, *A Literary History of Ireland* (1899), 484. 'Each of us pursues his trade, / I and Pangur my comrade, / His whole fancy on the hunt, / And mine for learning ardent.' Frank O'Connor's translation of this poem and of others mentioned here can be found in his *Kings, Lords, and Commons* (1959).
6   Samuel Ferguson. See footnote 11 on page 21.
7   An incantation performed by poets/Druids in ancient Ireland. See Douglas Hyde, *A Literary History of Ireland* (1899), 84.

JAMES STEPHENS
from James Stephens, *The Insurrection in Dublin* (1916)

This is a remarkable first-hand account by James Stephens of events as they unfolded during Easter Week 1916. Its tone, while restrained, is capable of registering the significance of this moment entering 'the imagination of their race'.

Wednesday

It was three o'clock before I got to sleep last night, and during the hours machine guns and rifle fire had been continuous.

This morning the sun is shining brilliantly, and the movement in the streets possesses more of animation than it has done. The movement ends always in a knot of people, and folk go from group to group vainly seeking information, and quite content if the rumour they presently gather differs even a little from the one they have just communicated.

The first statement I heard was that the Green[1] had been taken by the military; the second that it had been re-taken; the third that it had not been taken at all. The facts at last emerged that the Green had not been occupied by the soldiers, but that the Volunteers[2] had retreated from it into a house which commanded it.

This was found to be the College of Surgeons, and from the windows and roof of this college they were sniping. A machine gun was mounted on the roof; other machine guns, however, opposed them from the roofs of the Shelbourne Hotel, the United Service Club, and the Alexandra Club. Thus a triangular duel opened between these positions across the trees of the Park.

Through the railings of the Green some rifles and bandoliers could be seen lying on the ground, as also the deserted trenches and snipers' holes. Small boys bolted in to see these sights and bolted out again with bullets quickening their feet. Small boys do not believe that people will really kill them, but small boys were killed.

The dead horse was still lying stiff and lamentable on the footpath.

This morning a gunboat came up the Liffey and helped to bombard Liberty Hall.[3] The Hall is breeched and useless. Rumour says that it was empty at the time, and that Connolly with his men had marched long before to the Post Office[4] and the Green. The same source of information relates that three thousand Volunteers came from Belfast on an excursion train and that they marched into the Post Office.

On this day only one of my men came in. He said that he had gone on the roof and had been shot at, consequently that the Volunteers held some of the covering houses. I went to the roof and remained there for half an hour. There were no shots, but the firing from the direction of Sackville Street was continuous and at times exceedingly heavy.

Today the *Irish Times* was published. It contained a new military proclamation, and a statement that the country was peaceful, and told that in Sackville Street some houses were burned to the ground.

On the outside railings a bill proclaiming martial law was posted.

Into the newspaper statement that peace reigned in the country one was inclined to read more of disquietude than of truth, and one said: Is the country so extraordinarily peaceful that it can be dismissed in three lines? There is too much peace or too much reticence, but it will be some time before we hear from outside of Dublin.

Meanwhile the sun was shining. It was a delightful day, and the streets outside and around the areas of fire were animated and even gay. In the streets of Dublin there were no morose faces to be seen. Almost everyone was smiling and attentive, and a democratic feeling was abroad, to which our city is very much a stranger; for while in private we are a social and talkative people, we have no street manners or public ease whatever. Every person spoke to every other person, and men and women mixed and talked without constraint.

Was the city for or against the Volunteers? Was it for the Volunteers, and yet against the rising? It is considered now (writing a day or two afterwards) that Dublin was entirely against the Volunteers, but on the day of which I write no such certainty could be put forward. There was a singular reticence on the subject. Men met and talked volubly, but they said nothing that indicated a personal desire or belief. They asked for and exchanged the latest news, or, rather, rumour, and while expressions were frequent of astonishment at the suddenness and completeness of the occurrence, no expression of opinion for or against was anywhere formulated.

Sometimes a man said: 'They will be beaten of course,' and, as he prophesied, the neighbour might surmise if he did so with a sad heart or a merry one, but they knew nothing and asked nothing of his views, and themselves advanced no flag.

This was among the men.

The women were less guarded, or, perhaps, knew they had less to fear. Most of the female opinion I heard was not alone unfavourable but actively and viciously hostile to the rising. This was noticeable among the best dressed class of our population; the worst dressed, indeed the female dregs of Dublin life, expressed a like antagonism, and almost in similar language. The view expressed was:

'I hope every man of them will be shot.'

And:

'They ought to be all shot.'

Shooting, indeed, was proceeding everywhere. During daylight, at least, the sound is not sinister nor depressing, and the thought that perhaps a life had exploded with that crack is not depressing either.

In the last two years of world war our ideas on death have undergone a change. It is not now the furtive thing that crawled into your bed and which you fought with pill-boxes and medicine bottles. It has become again a rider of the wind whom you may go coursing with through the fields and open places. All the morbidity is gone, and the sickness, and what remains to Death is now health and excitement. So Dublin laughed at the noise of its own bombardment, and made no moan about its dead — in the sunlight. Afterwards — in the rooms, when the night fell, and instead of silence that mechanical barking of the maxims and the whistle and screams of the rifles, the solemn roar of the heavier guns, and the red glare covering the sky. It is possible that in the night Dublin did not laugh, and that she was gay in the sunlight for no other reason than that the night was past.

On this day fighting was incessant at Mount Street Bridge. A party of Volunteers had seized three houses covering the bridge and converted these into forts. It is reported that military casualties at this point were very heavy. The Volunteers are said also to hold the South Dublin Union. The soldiers have seized Guinness's Brewery, while their opponents have seized another brewery in the neighbourhood, and between these two there is a continual fusilade.

Fighting is brisk about Ringsend and along the Canal. Dame Street was said to be held in many places by the Volunteers. I went down Dame Street, but saw no Volunteers, and did not observe any sniping from the houses. Further, as Dame Street is entirely commanded by the roofs and windows of Trinity College, it is unlikely that they should be here.

It was curious to observe this, at other times, so animated street, broad and deserted, with at the corners of side streets small knots of people watching. Seen from behind, Grattan's[5] statue in College Green seemed almost alive, and he had the air of addressing warnings and reproaches to Trinity College.

The Proclamation issued today warns all people to remain within doors until five o'clock in the morning, and after seven o'clock at night.

It is still early. There is no news of any kind, and the rumours begin to catch quickly on each other and to cancel one another out. Dublin is entirely cut off from England, and from the outside world. It is just as entirely cut off from the rest of Ireland; no news of any kind filters in to us. We are land-locked and sea-locked, but, as yet, it does not much matter.

Meantime the belief grows that the Volunteers may be able to hold out much longer than had been imagined. The idea at first among the people had been that the insurrection would be ended the morning after it had began. But today, the insurrection having lasted three days, people are ready to conceive that it may last for ever. There is almost a feeling of gratitude towards the Volunteers because they are holding out for a little while, for had they been beaten the first or second day the city would have been humiliated to the soul.

People say: 'Of course, they will be beaten.' The statement is almost a query, and they continue, 'but they are putting up a decent fight'. For being beaten does not greatly matter in Ireland, but not fighting does matter. 'They went forth always to the battle; and they always fell.' Indeed, the history of the Irish race is in that phrase.

The firing from the roofs of Trinity College became violent. I crossed Dame Street some distance up, struck down the Quays, and went along these until I reached the Ballast Office. Further than this it was not possible to go, for a step beyond the Ballast Office would have brought one into the unending stream of lead that was pouring from Trinity and other places. I was looking on O'Connell Bridge and Sackville Street, and the house facing me was Kelly's — a red-brick fishing tackle shop, one half of which was on the Quay and the other half in Sackville Street. This house was being bombarded.

I counted the report of six different machine guns which played on it. Rifles innumerable and from every sort of place were potting its windows, and at intervals of about half a minute the shells from a heavy gun lobbed in through its windows or thumped mightily against its walls.

For three hours that bombardment continued, and the walls stood in a cloud of red dust and smoke. Rifle and machine gun bullets pattered over every inch of it, and, unfailingly, the heavy gun pounded its shells through the windows.

One's heart melted at the idea that human beings were crouching inside that volcano of death, and I said to myself, 'Not even a fly can be alive in that house.'

No head showed at any window, no rifle cracked from window or roof in reply. The house was dumb, lifeless, and I thought every one of those men are dead.

It was then, and quite suddenly, that the possibility of street fighting flashed on me, and I knew there was no person in the house, and said to myself, 'They have smashed through the walls with a hatchet and are sitting in the next house, or they have long ago climbed out by the skylight and are on a roof half a block away.' Then the thought came to me — they have and hold the entire of Sackville Street down to the Post Office. Later on this proved to be the case, and I knew at this moment that Sackville Street was doomed.

I continued to watch the bombardment, but no longer with the anguish which had before torn me. Near by there were four men, and a few yards away, clustered in a laneway, there were a dozen others. An agitated girl was striding from the farther group to the one in which I was, and she addressed the men in the most obscene language which I have ever heard. She addressed them man by man, and she continued to speak and cry and scream at them with all that obstinate, angry patience of which only a woman is capable.

She cursed us all. She called down diseases on every human being in the world excepting only the men who were being bombarded. She demanded of the folk in the laneway that they should march at least into the roadway and prove that they were proud men and were not afraid of bullets. She had been herself into the danger zone. Had stood herself in the track of the guns, and had there cursed her fill for half an hour, and she desired that the men should do at least what she had done.

This girl was quite young — about nineteen years of age — and was dressed in the customary shawl and apron of her class. Her face was rather pretty, or it had that pretty slenderness and softness of outline which belong to youth. But every sentence she spoke contained half a dozen indecent words. Alas, it was only that her vocabulary was not equal to her emotions, and she did not know how to be emphatic without being obscene — it is the cause of most of the meaningless swearing one hears every day. She spoke to me for a minute, and her eyes were as soft as those of a kitten and her language was as gentle as her eyes. She wanted a match to light a cigarette, but I had none, and said that I also wanted one. In a few minutes she brought me a match, and then she recommenced her tireless weaving of six vile words into hundreds of stupid sentences.

About five o'clock the guns eased off of Kelly's.

To inexperienced eyes they did not seem to have done very much damage, but afterwards one found that although the walls were standing and apparently solid there was no inside to the house. From roof to basement the building was bare as a dog kennel. There were no floors inside, there was nothing there but blank space; and on the ground within was the tumble and rubbish that had been roof and floors and furniture. Everything inside was smashed and pulverized into scrap and dust, and the only objects that had consistency and their ancient shape were the bricks that fell when the shells struck them.

Rifle shots had begun to strike the house on the further side of the street, a jewellers' shop called Hopkins & Hopkins. The impact of these balls on the bricks was louder than the sound of the shot which immediately succeeded, and each bullet that struck brought down a shower of fine red dust from the walls. Perhaps thirty or forty shots in all were fired at Hopkins', and then, except for an odd crack, firing ceased.

During all this time there had been no reply from the Volunteers, and I thought they must be husbanding their ammunition, and so must be short of it, and that it would be only a matter of a few days before the end. All this, I said to myself, will be finished in a few days, and they will be finished; life here will recommence exactly where it left off, and except for some newly filled graves, all will be as it had been until they become a tradition and enter the imagination of their race.

I spoke to several of the people about me, and found the same willingness to exchange news that I had found elsewhere in the city, and the same reticences as regarded their private opinions. Two of them, indeed, and they were the only two I met with during the insurrection, expressed, although in measured terms, admiration for the Volunteers, and while they did not side with them they did not say anything against them. One was a labouring man, the other a gentleman. The remark of the latter was:

'I am an Irishman, and (pointing to the shells that were bursting through the windows in front of us) I hate to see that being done to other Irishmen.'

He had come from some part of the country to spend the Easter holidays in Dublin, and was unable to leave town again.

The labouring man — he was about fifty-six years of age — spoke very quietly and collectedly about the insurrection. He was a type with whom I had come very little in contact, and I was surprised to find how simple and good his speech was, and how calm his ideas. He thought labour was in this movement to a greater extent than was imagined. I mentioned that Liberty Hall had been blown up, and that the garrison had either surrendered or been killed. He replied that a gunboat had that morning come up the river and had blown Liberty Hall into smash, but, he added, there were no men in it. All the Labour Volunteers had marched with Connolly into the Post Office.

He said the Labour Volunteers might possibly number about one thousand men, but that it would be quite safe to say eight hundred, and he held that the Labour Volunteers, or the Citizens' Army, as they called themselves, had always been careful not to reveal their numbers. They had always announced that they possessed about two hundred and fifty men, and had never paraded any more than that number at any one time. Workingmen, he continued, knew that the men who marched were always different men. The police knew it, too, but they thought that the Citizens' Army was the *most deserted-from force* in the world.

The men, however, were not deserters — you don't, he said, desert a man like Connolly, and they were merely taking their turn at being drilled and disciplined. They were raised against the police who, in the big strike of two years ago,[6] had acted towards them with unparalleled savagery, and the men had determined that the police would never again find them thus disorganized.

This man believed that every member of the Citizen Army had marched with their leader.

'The men, I know,' said he, 'would not be afraid of anything, and,' he continued, 'they are in the Post Office now.'

'What chance have they?'

'None,' he replied, 'and they never said they had, and they never thought they would have any.'

'How long do you think they'll be able to hold out?'

He nodded towards the house that had been bombarded by heavy guns.

'That will root them out of it quick enough,' was his reply.

'I'm going home,' said he then, 'the people will be wondering if I'm dead or alive,' and he walked away from that sad street, as I did myself a few minutes afterwards.

1   St Stephen's Green in Dublin. Fronting the Green are the Shelbourne Hotel and the College of Surgeons. The latter was held by Volunteers under the command of Constance Markievicz; fighting was intermittent but costly.
2   The Irish Volunteers, led by Patrick Pearse, was the group that spearheaded the Easter Rising. They were assisted by James Connolly's Irish Citizen Army, established during the Great Lockout of 1913 to protect trade unionists. Each Commander was given a specific target (or 'fort') in Dublin to capture or occupy.
3   Headquarters of the Irish Citizen Army.
4   The General Post Office on Sackville Street (O'Connell Street) was to become Pearse's headquarters of the Provisional Government.
5   For Henry Grattan see footnote 2 on page 37.
6   The Great Lockout. The employers were led by William Murphy.

GEORGE BERNARD SHAW
from *The Daily News*, 10 May 1916

Not even Shaw's advocacy could save the leaders of the Rising from execution. Twelve of the insurgents had already been shot before his letter appeared on 10 May. Two more were shot on 12 May including the wounded Connolly, who was strapped to a chair and executed. By 10 May it was clear that James Stephens had misread the movement of events for it was now impossible to see a return to the status quo. As Yeats was to write (some time between May and 25 September 1916): 'A terrible beauty is born'.

The Easter Week Executions

Sir, — You say that 'so far as the leaders are concerned no voice has been raised in this country against the infliction of the punishment which has so speedily overtaken them'. As the Government shot the prisoners first and told the public about it afterwards, there was no opportunity for effective protest. But it must not be assumed that those who merely shrugged their shoulders when it was useless to remonstrate accept for one moment the view that what happened was the execution of a gang of criminals.

My own view — which I should not intrude on you had you not concluded that it does not exist — is that the men who were shot in cold blood after their capture or surrender were prisoners of war, and that it was, therefore, entirely incorrect to slaughter them. The relation of Ireland to Dublin Castle[1] is in this respect precisely that of the Balkan States to Turkey, of Belgium or the city of Lille to the Kaiser, and of the United States to Great Britain.

Until Dublin Castle is superseded by a National Parliament and Ireland voluntarily incorporated with the British Empire, as Canada, Australasia, and South Africa have been incorporated, an Irishman resorting to arms to achieve the independence of his country is doing only what Englishmen will do if it be their misfortune to be invaded and conquered by the Germans in the course of the present war.

Further, such an Irishman is as much in order morally in accepting assistance from the Germans in his struggle with England as England is in accepting the assistance of Russia in her struggle with Germany. The fact that he knows that his enemies will not respect his rights if they catch him, and that he must therefore fight with a rope round his neck, increases his risk, but adds in the same measure to his glory in the eyes of his compatriots and of the disinterested admirers of patriotism throughout the world.

It is absolutely impossible to slaughter a man in this position without making him a martyr and a hero, even though the day before the rising he may have been only a minor poet. The shot Irishmen will now take their places beside Emmet[2] and the Manchester martyrs[3] in Ireland, and beside the heros of Poland and Serbia and Belgium in Europe; and nothing in heaven or earth can prevent it.

I do not propose to argue the question: it does not admit of argument. The military authorities and the British Government must have known that they were canonizing their prisoners. But they said in their anger: 'We don't care: we will shoot them; we feel that way.' Similarly the Irish will reply: 'We knew you would: you always do; we simply tell you more or less politely how *we* feel about it.'

Perhaps I had better add that I am not a Sinn Feiner,[4] and that since those utterances of mine which provoked the American Gaels to mob my plays some years ago to the very eve of the present rising I used all my influence and literary power to discredit the Sinn Fein ideal, and in particular to insist on the duty of Ireland to throw herself with all her force on the side of the French Republic against the Hohenzollern and Hapsburg monarchies. But I remain an Irishman, and am bound to contradict any implication that I can regard as a traitor any Irishman taken in a fight for Irish independence against the British Government, which was a fair fight in everything except the enormous odds my countrymen had to face.

I may add that I think it hard that Mr Birrell, an Englishman, should be sacrificed on the tombs of the fallen Sinn Feiners. Mr Birrell and Sir Matthew Nathan[5] did what they could with their hands tied by the Army commands and Sir Edward Carson. Obviously the one thing that could have made Ireland safe from an outbreak of civil war was the impartial disarmament of the civil population, as in the sixties[6] during the Fenian scare. Failing that, it has been the merest chance that the outbreak occurred in Dublin, and was headed by Sinn Fein, provoked by a bogus Castle plot. A Popish plot, equally ingeniously simulated, might have produced the same result in Belfast, headed by the Ulster Volunteers.[7] A convincing announcement of the abandonment of Home Rule would set the National Volunteers shooting tomorrow. Why were they not all disarmed? Because the Government was afraid of Sir Edward Carson and 'the Mutineers of the Curragh', and to attempt to disarm one side without disarming the other would have been an act of open war on Irish Nationalism. The only alternative was to introduce compulsory military service, and send all the volunteers to Mesopotamia or Flanders; but this again could have been done by a national Parliament only, and the Government had postponed that. Under such circumstances, if George Washington had been Chief Secretary for Ireland, and Cavour or Carnot Under-Secretary, they could have done nothing but try their utmost to preserve goodhumor, and hope that nobody would throw a match into the gunpowder.

And this, it seems, is exactly what they very wisely did. But it should not be forgotten that all Governments of the Dublin Castle type are really in the hands of their police and permanent officials, who do very much as they please because they cannot be disowned or 'turned down' in the face of the democratic enemy. Mr Birrell, like the Kaiser or the Tsar, had not the sort of control that President Wilson or Mr Asquith enjoys. All autocracies are shams as to real public power. Ireland is governed by police inspectors, gombeen men,[8] and priests, not by Secretaries of State.

At all events, if Mr Birrell and Sir Matthew insist on their assailants explaining exactly what they should and could have done that they did not do, I shall be greatly surprised if either their critics or the gentlemen who are undertaking to replace them will venture to answer them.

1   Centre of British administration of Ireland.
2   For Robert Emmet see footnote 5 on page 43.
3   A daring rescue of Fenian prisoners in Manchester in 1867 during which a policeman was killed. Three Irishmen (Allen, Larkin and O'Brien), who became known as the Manchester Martyrs, were then apprehended and hanged for his murder. To this day in Manchester they live on in the memory of Irish Catholics.
4   Sinn Feiner: Although the Rising was led by the Irish Volunteers it almost immediately became known as the Sinn Féin Rising.
5   The Chief Secretary and Under-Secretary for Ireland, respectively, at the time of the Easter Rising.
6   1860s.
7   A Protestant force, inspired and part-financed by Edward Carson, was established in 1913 to defend Ulster against Home Rule.
8   An Irish word, always used disparagingly. Gombeen men were usurers who lent money to tenant farmers at exorbitant interest. The stories and novels of William Carleton (1794–1869) contain many portraits of such types. See also 'The Gombeen', a short poem by Joseph Campbell in *Irishry* (1911).

JAMES STEPHENS
from *Letters of James Stephens* (ed. Richard J. Finneran) (1974)

The issue of types and stereotypes and nationality often underlies Anglo-Irish critical discussion. How do you respond to Stephens's remarks in this letter to an American correspondent? Is there room today for such discourse (the typical Englishman, for example)?

Dublin 7 August 1916

Dear Mr Sherman.[1]

I have your letter of July 14th. *The Crock of Gold*[2] was published simultaneously in England and America in 1912, by the Macmillan Co. of both these countries. The American edition is the better printed; the English the better produced. I do not believe you could get a first edition easily of the English edition, the 8th edition has now been printed. As to your other question — It would require a book to answer it. Irish literature in the English tongue is yet in its infancy — a lusty infancy, but still —! Only sixty years ago the vast bulk of our population (about nine millions) spoke habitually in the Gaelic, and altho' the Gaelic has been broken as a medium of exchange a great number of our people who speak only English still think in the Gaelic mode. A great number of our Anglo-Irish writers, Lever & Lover[3] & all of that ilk, wrote English with great cleverness, but no great prose or poetry (or scarcely any) was produced in English by Irishmen. Our race had not thoroughly learned the language, or had not thoroughly learned to adapt the Irish mode to the English tongue — We have now learned it; &, outside of their real literary merit, it is for this that Yeats & Russell, Synge & Lady Gregory are remarkable — They have succeeded in freshening both the English tongue & the Irish thought. With Yeats & Russell (AE) & Standish O'Grady Anglo-Irish literature re-commences. Are the types drawn by Synge & myself true Irish types? you ask. Yes, they are true as types; but they are not *the* type. Every country is too complex to be summed up in any man's formula. In literature as in every other affair a man answers at last only for himself. Every character that he draws is a facet of himself. Synge's types are at last a synthesis of Synge, & Synge is an Irishman. My types are true to me, and I am an Irishman. I represent something that is true of my country: my types or 'creations' represent something that is true of me. If you look at the illustrations of Irish life by Jack Yeats (Willy Yeats's brother) you will see that he reproduces in line and colour the very men whom Synge reproduced in word & thought. We can all have an idea of a typical Englishman or Frenchman, for the literatures of these races have been engaged so long & so profoundly on their psychology that at last the type has emerged, not as a man, but as an understanding, a notion. In Ireland *the* type is there all right, but the destruction of the Irish language, Irish culture & tradition, the Irish 'mode' in fact, has hidden or veiled the type; so that we Irish writers must go searching for it again, & we will find it all right. These preliminary essays of the writers you have mentioned, and among whom you are pleased to include myself, are as yet no more than examinations made by the way — They are the beginning of our stock-taking. This is I believe true, that we are a good race; but our national evolution has been hindered, our traditional culture subjected to every kind of interference, so that it is a marvel it exists at all, and we have almost entirely lost the Gaelic language which is our national storehouse, & into which the Irish psychology had been precipitated. England is so strong in men, & money & culture, & yet Ireland has withstood the terrific pressure of this threefold power. That is an amazing feat, & the country which, having been impoverished in men and money & culture, could yet withstand the energetic trinity has something in it worth discovering. Has American literature been working long enough to evolve a national type, or national types. I don't believe it has. Something that is true of New York has arrived, but do you know anything that is true of America.

Yours faithfully
James Stephens

1 Philip D. Sherman (1881–1957), Associate Professor of English, Oberlin College, Ohio.
2 A popular romance by Stephens.
3 For Lever see footnote 1 on page 211; Samuel Lover (1797–1868) was an entertaining novelist, perhaps best known as author of *Handy Andy: A Tale of Irish Life* (1842). Lever and Lover were often yoked together in a disparaging fashion by Yeats and the Revivalists.

ANONYMOUS
from *The Irish Book Lover*, December and January 1916–17

A contemporary book notice of two recently published books by Yeats.

'Reveries' and 'Responsibilities'

Mr Yeats signalizes his change of publishers by the re-issue of his two latest books, one in prose the other in verse, both turned out in the elegant style that marks the output of the house of Macmillan.[1] Somehow one always regards Mr Yeats as endowed with perpetual youth, and few consider that half a century has passed over his head, so lightly does time touch him. Yet such is the fact, and now having gained fame, well deserved and not altogether undreamt of, he sits down to pen these *Reveries Over Childhood and Youth* (6s.). It is a remarkable self-revelation, and though dealing with early formative influences and boyish adventures, can hardly be called an autobiography — there isn't a date in it. He tells us of his early trials at school, trials common to all shy boys as well as misunderstood geniuses; his recollections of the artistic circles in which his father moved; his own early predilections towards Art; his associations with the stern ship-owning grandfather in his well-loved Sligo, and the mystic influences of the lake island of Innisfree. The impressions made upon him later by Prof. Dowden and John O'Leary, his affection for Charley Johnston, scion of the house of Ballykilbeg — dead ere his prime — and his antipathy towards J.F. Taylor, the orator, a specimen of whose oratory he quotes, are all set down and naught in malice. It is an interesting volume, written with all the grace and charm that marks the author's work, and will be warmly welcomed by his many admirers. We only notice one slight lapse of memory, not to be wondered at, as he admittedly 'consulted neither friend nor letter nor old newspaper.' At p. 33 he refers to 'Major Sirr, who betrayed the brothers Shears (sic), taking their children upon his knee to question them.' It was not Sirr, but John Warneford Armstrong who was guilty of that infamy. It was the author's original intention to name the book 'Memory Harbour', after the village of Rosses Point,

so we have as frontispiece a reproduction of a coloured illustration of that place by his brother Jack, and two fine portraits of the poet's parents from the brush of his father, the veteran painter. *Responsibilities* (6s.) exhibits the poet in many moods, satirical, mystical, musical. It is, in a measure, the complement of the *Reveries*, for, from the 'Introductory Rhymes', which deal with doings of his ancestors, 'traders or soldiers', old Butlers, who 'took to horse and stood beside the brackish waters of the Boyne', to that Pollexfen who 'leaped overboard after a ragged hat in Biscay Bay', to the final note, we find many personal reflections of the author on recent happenings. Thus he ventilates his opinions on those who disturbed the performance of *The Playboy*, and addresses the shade of Parnell on the treatment meted out to Sir Hugh Lane[2] by the same 'old foul mouth that slandered you'. He admits that when in September, 1913, he wrote 'Romantic Ireland's dead and gone, It's with O'Leary in the grave', he could not foresee Easter week, 1916, and the heroism of those who 'weighed so lightly what they gave'. As is his wont of recent years, Mr Yeats continues to revise and polish up his earlier work, so the volume ends with a very fine poetic version of *The Hour Glass*, first published in 1904. Taken together, it will enhance the poet's fame.

1   Macmillan became Yeats's trade publisher in 1916 and remains so until today. *Reveries Over Childhood and Youth*, the first volume of Yeats's autobiography, was published first in a limited edition by his sister's Cuala Press in 1914–5 and then by Macmillan in a trade edition in March 1916. *Responsibilities* was published by Macmillan in October 1916. The cover designs for Yeats's Macmillan editions were done by his friend T. Sturge Moore.
2   A nephew of Lady Gregory and an art collector, Hugh Lane (1875–1915) proposed to lend his collection of paintings to Dublin City if a suitable building was provided by the City Council. The 'old foul mouth' is probably a reference to the newspaper owner William Murphy, who opposed spending money on art.

DARRELL FIGGIS
from Darrell Figgis, *A Chronicle of Jails* (1917)

Darrell Figgis (pseudonym Michael Ireland) (1882–1925) was a nationalist politician and writer. Raised in an Anglo-Irish family he spent part of his childhood in India before working in London for a tea company. On his return to Ireland he became active in the nationalist movement and was involved in the Howth gun-running incident in 1914. After the split among the Volunteers in 1914 he kept to his writing. During the Easter Rising he was in Mayo but was arrested on suspicion and interned in English jails. Here he describes at firsthand some of his experiences, punctuated by the ellipsis points representing what I assume in part is the censor's cut. A compelling letter about his treatment after his arrest written by his wife Millie Figgis appeared in *New Age*, and is reproduced in Maurice Joy (ed.), *The Irish Rebellion of 1916 and Its Martyrs: Erin's Tragic Easter* (1916). For a subsequent, equally lively, account of his imprisonment see *A Second Chronicle of Jails* (1919). 'Withhold imagination from the calls / Of sensuous privilege' Figgis wrote in his long poem 'A Vision of Life', published under that title in 1909. 'Prize not thy frail self. / Strive for the larger Weal.' Perhaps the words of Duty returned to haunt the Irish writer in the English House of the Dead.

VII

At Castlebar[1] rigorous care was taken that P.J.D.[2] and I should not speak with one another. Care had been taken that we should exercise apart, and only by the accident of the shortage of staff on the Sunday had either of us been able to do more than guess at the other's presence. At Richmond Barracks[3] we were thrown together perforce, and were condemned to sleep under the one slender blanket.

In the room to which we were consigned there were already twenty-five others. The officers who took us up told me that it was known as the Leaders' Room: a description that, at that time, was . . . ominous . . . From it, De Valera had gone to his life's sentence; from it, I was told, Sean MacDiarmada had gone to his death . . . ; and there Count Plunkett had been required to answer for the consciences of his sons. And a goodly company remained there yet, from whom we received a hospitality the joviality of which gave no heed to the courtsmartial that slowly worked their way along the lists provided by a diligent officialdom. Presents from friends were permitted, under supervision; and food so obtained was put into a common commissariat, presided over by mighty Sean O'Mahony, the ruler and president of our company. From this store we were regaled without further ado, while he stood between us and the others who rose to welcome us to our fate. He would suffer none to approach us with a more immediate welcome or inquiry until we had had what we would of the hospitality it was his to dispense; and then we mixed in the company into which we had been cast.

So, for the first time I came into touch with those who had had their part in the Rising. There were some of the company on whom the burning yet remained. Most had been through a historic week, and three had been severely wounded. In all cases these were leg wounds from bullets, and two of the number had been lying on the wooden floor, covered by blankets, when we entered. Coming as I did from a part of the country where only wild, whirling rumours had reached, sound and fury of things that had and things that had not occurred, there was something of a thrill in this first touch of the actual event. One faded into insignificance beside the simplest follower that had borne the heat of the day. He would be a man of little emotion, surely, who did not feel as I did at that moment, with a touch of awe and respect kindling in his veins. It seems then to me a little thing that a man should think and labour for his country beside those who had offered dear life for her sake.

Therefore, when one of the wounded men limped up to me, claiming an acquaintance I had forgotten, I was anxious to discover from him where he had fought, and to learn some details of the fighting. He had, with high personal courage and ability, filled one of the commands in the defence of the South Dublin Union, and was not loth to tell his tale. But our conversation was overheard, and an uproar rose.

'He's going to tell about the South Dublin Union[4] again. No, no; that can't be allowed. We're tired about the South Dublin Union.' I protested that I wished to hear. 'I'm sorry, but we can't permit it. We've heard that story so often that it's not safe for us to hear it again. It's really not safe. If you let him, he'll tell it you for a week; but we can't permit it; we've our nerves to consider.'

So it was. In no way could I extract my tale, and had to remain without it.

. . .

We are sometimes derided as a people rent by divisions, but the division in this case was due to the same cause as has created nearly all our other divisions.

That cause was symbolized by the scene that was enacted that day. In no way more picturesquely could the fact of a perpetual military conquest have been staged. And when, as we marched down along the quays, most of us saw, for the first time, the havoc wrought in our capital by the guns of the conqueror, that only gave the appropriate scenery without which dramatists have agreed that the work of their artistry cannot be given to the world.

At the North Wall we were put on board a cattle boat. The cattle were herded at one end of the pens, we were being herded at the other end of the pens. When it came to my turn to be penned I was surprised to hear myself accosted by the Embarkation Officer:

'I'm B——, you know.'

'Certainly,' I replied; 'we meet again.' But I had not the dimmest notion who he was.

'I hope to be in Castlebar soon,' he said. 'I haven't been back since I went out.'

'Is that so?' I said. 'I was in Castlebar a fortnight ago. I was stopping at the jail.'

He laughed, and turned to P.J.D., who stood beside me as we awaited our turn to be penned. His manner was frank and pleasant and not at all constrained, although his penning of us was quite efficiently done. I informed him that I was not well, and asked if certain accommodation could not be found slightly more efficient than a cattle pen packed with my fellows. He promised to see what he could do, and went off. When he had gone, P.J.D. informed me that he had been a Volunteer when I was in command of the county, and had since gained some distinction in the European War. Presently he returned, and conveyed some of us to a room in the forecastle, where we had seats on which we could stretch ourselves.

When we arrived in England, however, we struck quite another atmosphere. Inquisitive crowds gathered about us who lost no opportunity of displaying their enmity and hostility. German prisoners of war might have aroused an equal curiosity, but they could not have an equal enmity. Clearly and sharply we stood out, whether we gathered on railway platforms or were marched through streets, as nation against nation, with an unbridgeable hatred between us. Any attempt on our part to meet taunt with taunt was at

. . .

; and so we were compelled to stand as the mark of contumely and the target of contempt. To be sure, that only stiffened us, and we held ourselves high and unflinchingly before the crowds. Nevertheless, there was a sickening in most of us, for Ireland was behind us and we were utterly in the stranger's power.

I had lived some years in England, and had formed many good friendships. Unlike many of my companions, England and the English were no strange things to me. Yet I came then into something utterly strange, foreign, and hostile. I could not more strangely have been led captive among the mountains of the moon, so icy was this world and such leagues apart from that which I had known.

Everything was coloured by that relation. One looked on England with new eyes, and old thoughts became startling new discoveries. Stafford lay for the most part steeped in slumber as we were marched through its streets in the morning, accompanied by a small, inquisitive crowd. It looked incredibly sleek and prosperous beside our Irish towns. The villas were sleek and comfortable; the roads were sleek and neat; the very grass beside the canal looked sleek as though nurtured with the centuries. Everything had an air of being well fed and well groomed, and quite consciously proud of the fact that it was part of a prosperous whole, where no invader's foot had trampled, where no spoliation had dared to efface the moss that had gathered for centuries on the gables, or to rough the smooth lawns. The villas might be the latest examples of modernity, yet that was the air they suggested, for they became part of something that was smooth and sleek. How different to our Irish towns, that look as though they — not the people in them, but they themselves — live a precarious day-to-day existence. Each suggests the history of their nation. One has grown sleek with prosperity, and smooth and round with the large air of the conqueror, with shores that have never known invasion. The other has been hunted from end to end by rapacious conquest; the forests that were its pride burnt away the better to root out its people; the people hunted until they lost the instinct to build for themselves permanent abodes, and, more latterly, rack-rented till they stealthily hid any small savings and kept middens before their doors, until a show of poverty from being a disguise became a habit; rising against the conqueror in a series of revolts foredoomed to failure, but triumphant in what they spoke of — a spirit still unbroken; stricken to earth again by soldiery that marched through the land; and harnessed by a network of legislative acts that intended to inhibit industry and commerce with the nations of the earth, and that succeeded in their intention. And yet there was no question of a choice between the two. For with one individuality had become smoothened away, the wheel having come full circle; with the other individuality was sharp and keen, angular it might be, but alive for the future.

H.P. and I were speaking of these things when we arrived at Stafford Jail. It was about six o'clock in the morning as we were marched through the gates and lined up outside the prison. The building looked gloomy and forbidding as it frowned down on us with its hundreds of barred windows. It had lately been used as a detention barracks; that is to say, as a prison for soldiers, the major part of the population of England having donned khaki but not having doffed their sins therewith. Therefore, it was staffed by military, who received us from our escort and marched us up the great building to the cells that had been allotted us. And once again I heard the key grate behind me.

XVIII

Reading being set deep in a valley at the confluence of two rivers, is an unhealthy town, close and sultry by summer, and damp and misty by winter. The gaol is a handsome building, erected in red brick after the manner of an old castle, with battlements and towers. One almost expected a portcullis to be lowered at the great gate; and when we were within the double gates we certainly felt as though a portcullis had been drawn after us. We stood in a small cobbled yard. Behind us was the broad wall in which the double gates were set, flanked on each side by the Governor's and the Steward's houses. Before us a flight of stone steps arose, leading to the offices, behind which was the large male prison. To the right a wall arose dividing us from the work yard; and on the left a high blind wall arose, pierced only by a single door near the wall round the jail. This was the female prison — ordinarily so, but for the time being our habitation.

Yet what astonished me most was the sight of flowers. Their presence made the cobbled yard and the precincts seem almost collegiate. In neatly kept beds about the walls they lifted their heads with a happy gaiety very strange to some of us who had known so human a touch banished from buildings more appropriately given over to the possession of flints and cinders. A few days after we were taken through the work yard behind the main prison. Here in the work hall a canteen was opened on three days in the week for the interned prisoners who now occupied the prison, but here also was the large exercise yard, and it was covered with an abundance of flowers. The familiar asphalt paths could not be seen where they threaded their way amid blossoms. In beds beneath the walls tall flowers lifted their heads, and even the graves of hanged men could not be seen beneath the blooms that covered them.

It was an amazing sight. There were not merely flowers, a sight astonishing enough in itself; there was a prodigality of flowers. Then some of us remembered the cause. One of the graves unlocked the secret. It was marked with the letters C.T.W.,[5] and the date, 1896, to whom Oscar Wilde's 'Ballad of Reading Jail' had been inscribed, and in celebration of whose passing the poem had been penned.

But neither milk-white rose nor red
    May bloom in prison-air;
The shard, the pebble, and the flint
    Are what they give us there:
For flowers have been known to heal
    A common man's despair.

So never will wine-red rose or white
    Petal by petal, fall
On that stretch of mud and sand that lies
    By the hideous prison-wall,
To tell the men who tramp the yard
    That God's Son died for all.

So Wilde had sung, not in protest, but in bitter acceptance, never dreaming that a poet's song could change the flint, the pebble, and the shard of the yard he trod. But for us who came after him with the memory of his song in our minds, the miracle had been wrought. Miracle it was, and it had been wrought in no common sort, for the great yard was a lake of leaf and bloom, and the hideous prison wall was transformed by gay figures decked in raiment that not Solomon in all his glory could outvie.

Already in the pebbled entrance yard the hand of this 'unacknowledged legislator'[6] was in evidence. We were first taken across to the office, as we arrived in batches, and our money taken from us, and our kit examined. Then we were led back through the door in the blind wall into the female prison, that had been allocated to Irish Prisoners of War. The main prison was occupied by the nations of Europe: Belgians, Germans, French, Rumanians, Russians, and indeed every degree and variety of European to the number of fourteen.

. . .

The prison actually held only twenty-two cells. There were in addition a hospital, a maternity ward, and two padded cells, one permanent and one temporary. The hospital and maternity ward consisted of two cells each, with the intervening wall removed. In each of these three men were placed (there being some little rivalry for the maternity ward), which with the use of the temporary padded cell provided for all of us. In addition to this, there was also an observation ward, on the ground floor, similarly constructed of two cells converted into one, and this was given to us as a recreation room. All these cells were on one side of the building, the other side being a blank wall, and the only light that came to the passage struggled down through skylights.

Such was the place that was to be our habitation for nearly six months, and in which we erected the structure of our communal life.

1   Figgis was taken on his arrest to the jail at Castlebar in County Mayo.
2   The editor and proprietor of *The Mayo News*.
3   In Dublin, adjacent to Kilmainham Gaol where the leaders of the Easter Rising were executed.
4   The Workhouse adjacent to the British Headquarters at the Royal Hospital. The Volunteers, under the command of Eamonn Ceannt, held out until the surrender using hand-to-hand combat.
5   Charles Thomas Wooldridge. See Wilde's poem above.
6   From Shelley's *A Defence of Poetry* (1821).

GEORGE RUSSELL (Æ)
from George Russell, *Imagination and Reveries* (1921)

Russell was the unofficial taker of the nation's pulse. In 1917 he saw his role as a peacemaker not only between Nationalist and Unionist but between those who had fought on the fields of France and those who had taken part in Easter Week. A new nation was unfolding but it had little room for voices like Russell's which sought an accommodation between politics and morality. It is worth noting that Russell's line of thinking resurfaces at the end of the century in Sebastian Barry's *The Steward of Christendom* (1995).

The New Nation

In that cycle of history which closed in 1914, but which seems now to the imagination as far sunken behind time as Babylon or Samarcand, it was customary at the festival of the Incarnation to forego our enmities for a little and allow freer play to the spiritual in our being. Since 1914 all things in the world and with us, too, in Ireland have existed in a welter of hate, but the rhythm of ancient habit cannot altogether have passed away, and now if at any time, it should be possible to blow the bugles of Heaven and recall men to that old allegiance. I do not think it would help now if I, or another, put forward arguments drawn from Irish history or economics to convince any party that they were wrong and their opponents right. I think absolute truth might be stated in respect of these things, and yet it would affect nothing in our present mood. It would not be recognized any more than Heaven, when It walked on earth in the guise of a Carpenter, was hailed by men whose minds were filled by other imaginations of that coming.

I will not argue about the past, but would ask Irishmen to consider how in future they may live together. Do they contemplate the continuance of these bitter hatreds in our own household? The war must have a *finale*. Many thousands of Irishmen will return to their country who have faced death for other ideals than those which inspire many more thousands now in Ireland and make them also fearless of death. How are these to co-exist in the same island if there is no change of heart? Each will receive passionate support from relatives, friends, and parties who uphold their action. This will be a most unhappy country if we cannot arrive at some moral agreement, as necessary as a political agreement. Partition is no settlement, because there is no geographical limitation of these passions. There is scarce a locality in Ireland where antagonisms do not gather about the thought of Ireland as in the caduceus of Mercury the twin serpents writhe about the sceptre of the god. I ask our national extremists in what mood do they propose to meet those who return, men of temper as stern as their own? Will these endure being termed traitors to Ireland? Will their friends endure it? Will those who mourn their dead endure to hear scornful speech of those they loved? That way is for us a path to Hell. The unimaginative who see only a majority in their own locality, or, perhaps, in the nation, do not realize what a powerful factor in national life are those who differ from them, and how they are upheld by a neighbouring nation which, for all its present travail, is more powerful by far than Ireland even if its people were united in purpose as the fingers of one hand.

Nor can those who hold to, and are upheld by, the Empire hope to coerce to a uniformity of feeling with themselves the millions clinging to Irish nationality. Seven centuries of repression have left that spirit unshaken, nor can it be destroyed, save by the destruction of the Irish people, because it springs from biological necessity. As well might a foolish gardener trust that his apple-tree would bring forth grapes as to dream that there could be uniformity of character and civilization between Irishmen and Englishmen. It would be a crime against life if it could be brought about and diversities of culture and civilization made impossible. We may live at peace with our neighbours when it is agreed that we must be different, and no peace is possible in the world between nations except on this understanding. But I am not now thinking of that, but of the more urgent problem how we are to live at peace with each other. I am convinced Irish enmities are perpetuated because we live by memory more than by hope, and that even now on the facts of character there is no justification for these enmities.

We have been told that there are two nations in Ireland. That may have been so in the past, but it is not true to-day. The union of Norman and Dane and Saxon and Celt which has been going on through the centuries is now completed, and there is but one powerful Irish character — not Celtic or Norman-Saxon, but a new race. We should recognize our moral identity. It was apparent before the war in the methods by which Ulstermen and Nationalists alike strove to defend or win their political objects. There is scarce an Ulsterman, whether he regards his ancestors as settlers or not, who is not allied through marriage by his forbears to the ancient race. There is in his veins the blood of the people who existed before Patrick, and he can look backward through time to the legends of the Red Branch, the Fianna and the gods as the legends of his people. It would be as difficult to find even on the Western Coast a family which has not lost in the same way its Celtic purity of race. The character of all is fed from many streams which have mingled in them and have given them a new distinctiveness. The invasions of Ireland and the Plantations, however morally unjustifiable, however cruel in method, are justified by biology. The invasion of one race by another was nature's ancient way of re-invigorating a people.

Mr Flinders Petrie, in his *Revolutions of Civilization*, has demonstrated that civilization comes in waves, that races rise to a pinnacle of power and culture, and decline from that, and fall into decadence, from which they do not emerge until there has been a crossing of races, a fresh intermingling of cultures. He showed in ancient Egypt eight such periods, and after every decline into decadence there was an invasion, the necessary precedent to a fresh ascent with reinvigorated energies. I prefer to dwell upon the final human results of this commingling of races than upon the tyrannies and conflicts which made it possible. The mixture of races has added to the elemental force of the Celtic character a more complex mentality, and has saved us from becoming, as in our island isolation we might easily have become, thin and weedy, like herds where there has been too much in-breeding. The modern Irish are a race built up from many races who have to prove themselves for the future. Their animosities, based on past history, have little justification in racial diversity to-day, for they are a new people with only superficial cultural and political differences, but with the same fundamental characteristics. It is hopeless, the dream held by some that the ancient Celtic character could absorb the new elements, become dominant once more, and be itself unchanged. It is equally hopeless to dream the Celtic element could be eliminated. We are a new people, and not the past, but the future, is to justify this new nationality.

I believe it was this powerful Irish character which stirred in Ulster before the war, leading it to adopt methods unlike the Anglo-Saxon tradition in politics. I believe that new character, far more than the spirit of the ancient race, was the ferment in the blood of those who brought about the astonishing enterprise of Easter Week. Pearse himself, for all his Gaelic culture, was sired by one of the race he fought against. He might stand in that respect as a symbol of the new race which is springing up. We are slowly realizing the vigour of the modern Irish character just becoming self-conscious of itself. I had met many men who were in the enterprise of Easter Week and listened to their speech, but they had to prove their spirit to myself and others by more than words. I listened with that half-cynical feeling which is customary with us when men advocate a cause with which we are temperamentally sympathetic, but about whose realization we are hopeless. I could not gauge the strength of the new spirit, for words do not by themselves convey the quality of power in men; and even when the reverberations from Easter Week were echoing everywhere in Ireland, for a time I, and many others, thought and felt about those who died as some pagan concourse in ancient Italy might have felt looking down upon an arena, seeing below a foam of glorious faces turned to them, the noble, undismayed, inflexible faces of martyrs, and, without understanding, have realized that this spirit was stronger than death. I believe that capacity for sacrifice, that devotion to ideals exists equally among the opponents of these men. It would have been proved in Ireland, in Ulster, if the need had arisen. It has been proved on many a battlefield of Europe. Whatever views we may hold about the relative value of National or Imperial ideals, we may recognize that there is moral equality where the sacrifice is equal. No one has more to give than life, and, when that is given, neither Nationalist nor Imperialist in Ireland can claim moral superiority for the dead champions of their causes.

And here I come to the purpose of my letter, which is to deprecate the scornful repudiation by Irishmen of other Irishmen, which is so common at present, and which helps to perpetuate our feuds. We are all one people. We are closer to each other in character than we are to any other race. The necessary preliminary to political adjustment is moral adjustment, forgiveness, and mutual understanding. I have been in council with others of my countrymen for several months, and I noticed what an obstacle it was to agreement how few, how very few, there were who had been on terms of friendly intimacy with men of all parties. There was hardly one who could have given an impartial account of the ideals and principles of his opponents. Our political differences have brought about social isolations, and there can be no understanding where there is no eagerness to meet those who differ from us, and hear the best they have to say for themselves. This letter is an appeal to Irishmen to seek out and understand their political opponents. If they come to know each other, they will come to trust each other, and will realize their kinship, and will set their faces to the future together, to build up a civilization which will justify their nationality.

I myself am Anglo-Irish, with the blood of both races in me, and when the rising of Easter Week took place all that was Irish in me was profoundly stirred, and out of that mood I wrote commemorating the dead. And then later there rose in memory the faces of others I knew who loved their country, but had died in other battles. They fought in those because they believed they would serve Ireland, and I felt these were no less my people. I could hold them also in my heart

and pay tribute to them. Because it was possible for me to do so, I think it is possible for others; and in the hope that the deeds of all may in the future be a matter of pride to the new nation I append here these verses I have written:—

TO THE MEMORY OF SOME I KNEW WHO ARE DEAD AND WHO LOVED IRELAND

Their dream had left me numb and cold,
    But yet my spirit rose in pride,
Refashioning in burnished gold
    The images of those who died,
Or were shut in the penal cell.
    Here's to you, Pearse, your dream not mine,
But yet the thought, for this you fell,
    Has turned life's water into wine.

You who have died on Eastern hills
    Or fields of France as undismayed,
Who lit with interlinkèd wills
    The long heroic barricade,
You, too, in all the dreams you had,
    Thought of some thing for Ireland done.
Was it not so, Oh, shining lad,
    What lured you, Alan Anderson?[1]

I listened to high talk from you,
    Thomas McDonagh, and it seemed
The words were idle, but they grew
    To nobleness by death redeemed.
Life cannot utter words more great
    Than life may meet by sacrifice,
High words were equalled by high fate,
    You paid the price. You paid the price.

You who have fought on fields afar,
    That other Ireland did you wrong
Who said you shadowed Ireland's star,
    Nor gave you laurel wreath nor song.
You proved by death as true as they,
    In mightier conflicts played your part,
Equal your sacrifice may weigh,
    Dear Kettle,[2] *of the generous heart.*

The hope lives on age after age,
    Earth with its beauty might be won
For labour as a heritage,
    For this has Ireland lost a son.
This hope unto a flame to fan
    Men have put life by with a smile,
Here's to you Connolly, my man,
    Who cast the last torch on the pile.

You too, had Ireland in your care,
  Who watched o'er pits of blood and mire,
From iron roots leap up in air
  Wild forests, magical, of fire;
Yet while the Nuts of Death were shed
  Your memory would ever stray
To your own isle. Oh, gallant dead —
  This wreath, Will Redmond, on your clay.

Here's to you, men I never met,
  Yet hope to meet behind the veil,
Thronged on some starry parapet,
  That looks down upon Innisfail,[3]
And sees the confluence of dreams
  That clashed together in our night,
One river, born from many streams,
  Roll in one blaze of blinding light.

December 1917

1 Alan Anderson was the son of Robert Anderson, secretary of the Irish Agricultural Organization Society (I.A.O.S.) from 1895 until 1921. A friend of Horace Plunkett, the founder of I.A.O.S., Robert became a friend of Russell. Both of them felt the loss of Alan.
2 Thomas Kettle (1880–1916), poet, economist, and political writer. A complex figure, he was both an Irish patriot and a British soldier (he was killed at the Somme). His political writings are gathered in *The Open Secret of Ireland* (1912) and *The Day's Burden* (1918).
3 Irish: island of destiny, that is, Ireland.

IMAGINATIVE

PÁDRAIC Ó CONAIRE

from Pádraic Ó Conaire, *Deoraíocht* (1910); trans. Gearailt Mac Eoin (1994)

Pádraic Ó Conaire (1882–1928) was an Irish-language novelist and short-story writer from Galway. In 1899 he went to London, joined the Gaelic League, and mixed with other Irish exiles. This extract is taken from a somewhat bleak novel he wrote in London which traces events in the life of an unemployed Irishman whose leg is amputated after being knocked down by a car. The protagonist joins a circus run by Little Yellowman which travels in the west of Ireland, and becomes part of a freak show which includes the Fat Lady (who develops an affection for him). Dissatisfaction leads him to abandon the circus and he returns to London to drift again.

Six months ago, that part of London in which I was now living was, in itself, a little Irish world. The English used to call it Little Ireland. All the people were from the province of Munster, except for the odd one. Some of them had inherited the traditions of bards and poets. All the neighbours knew each other, and not alone that, but they knew the families they had come from. They had all come from the same district in Ireland. They used to have social gatherings in the evenings, where you would find fiddlers and pipers and flute-players.

There would be a man there who could relate the contents of Keating's History of Ireland,[1] as well as a man who knew nothing about it. And if somebody were to disagree with anything the savant said, he would just go to the big trunk he had brought with him from Ireland and take out a parcel wrapped in linen. He would open the parcel and take out a large book in manuscript. And how careful he was of that book! He would then show you in black and white where you had been wrong. And when he closed the book to put it away he would look at you as if to say, 'Now what have you to say for yourself?' But he never said a word. And the daytime trade of this man who spent his evenings reading history and learning poetry was the trade of the pick and shovel.

This small population of exiles in a foreign city kept up the manners and customs of the people of the ancient Irish nation. The Irish heritage of language, music and literature which rich people at home had abandoned in their efforts to imitate the English, who would as soon have seen them at the bottom of the sea, was kept alive by these people. They understood, in their own way that a race should guard the culture which had come down to them from their ancestors and they guarded it like a precious jewel.

The adults kept up their habits, customs and language. But their sons and daughters only preserved their native characteristics, and gradually abandoned the language and a lot of its musical and literary culture. Their grandchildren lost both the language and culture, and seemed to have retained only the worst of their racial characteristics. And many, naturally, intermarried with the English. People who breed animals will tell you that when one breed is crossed with another, the offspring will inherit the worst characteristics of each. Others, however, take the opposite view.

There is probably much to be said on each side of this argument, but the first group could easily prove their case were they to make the population of this small area of London their sole object of study. When I arrived among them, there were only about forty people among them still alive of those who had come from Ireland after the Great Famine.[2] Some of them had retained a knowledge of the Irish language, its stories and sagas, and there were good musicians among them. But they belonged to the past, and their children and grandchildren were little credit to them.

One of these old men who had come over from Ireland after the Famine was my new landlord, who was known as 'Hammer'. He was given this nick-name because of his great interest in debate, and of his habit of shouting 'Another nail in the plank!' every time he believed he had won an argument. He wore an overcoat, which had belonged to his grandfather, at all seasons of the year. Even in the middle of a heat-wave, he never took off that coat. He usually carried an oak walking-stick — a heavy stick he had cut when he once went back on a week's visit to his native village.

One thing is certain. This man had never done a stroke of work since the day he set up this lodging-house. There were old people in the neighbourhood, who had known his people at home, who said that Hammer was a lazy untrustworthy fellow, just like his forbears. But nobody took any notice of them. In summer, he used to sit in his chair outdoors in a spot sheltered from the heat of the sun, and indoors in winter in a spot near the heat of the fire. Outdoors or indoors, he never took off the overcoat, nor left his stick out of his hand. Irishmen in the district who were too old to work made a habit of coming by for a

bit of debate, which would always end with, 'another nail in the plank' from Hammer.

Whether or not Hammer was lazy, his wife Brigid certainly was not. It was she who did the house-keeping. If the rooms were clean, and the beds made, it was she who cleaned and made them. If she didn't prepare meals for the two of them, they would have gone without food. If she did not wash the clothes, they would never have been washed. And, even when all these jobs were done, she would still not have finished her day's work. She could have no such luck. She was just the sort of person who worked and worked, day in, day out, week in, week out, without ever finishing. She always had the look of work about her — wet, dirty, unkempt. And all Hammer had to say to get her going was 'Isn't it little you've done since morning, Brigid?'

'If I had a proper husband,' she would say, 'he wouldn't leave all the work to me . . .' And she would go on and on without letting him put in a word.

With most people Hammer usually got the last word in any argument — 'Another nail in the plank,' except with his wife. In her case, it was always she who drove the nail in the plank, and drove it deep.

Their family had all been reared and scattered, except for one son, who was twenty-seven years old and who would never do any good. It was said that he was mentally retarded, but Brigid loved him more than any of her other sons. She never called him anything except 'the creature'[3] and because of this, there were many of the neighbours who did not know his real name, even though they had known him since birth. 'Hammer's young fellow' the locals called him. His father disliked him, or pretended to dislike him (it was said that he considered it a shame for two men in one house to be idle), and lately he had taken to calling him 'the Buckeen',[4] on account of the little steel chain he had started wearing. His mother had bought him the chain for a shilling — but that was something that Hammer knew nothing about.

It was the day the chain was bought that I first went to the house. The Big Red-haired Woman had come with me to introduce me to the family. They knew that I was coming, and that the Big Red-haired Woman had undertaken to pay them so much per week for my bed, of which, of course, I had not been told. I had been hoping that they would have given me a little credit, and that I should be able to pay them as soon as I got the job cleaning bottles, which my Red-haired Woman had arranged for me with the owner of that public house where I had first met Little Yellowman.

They gave me a hearty welcome. I should be very comfortable with them. I should have a nice clean bed

in the large room, along with six or seven others. —
'Lovely boys!' Brigid called them.

'Maybe you'd like a cup of tea now?' asked Brigid.

'We'll all have a cup,' said Hammer.

'Put the kettle on the fire,' shouted Brigid to someone in another room.

'Surely,' answered a voice.

It was a woman's voice, and I thought I recognized it. The woman came out of the room, laden with tea-things. I was engrossed in debate with Hammer on the Land Question, and did not see her at first. But she saw me, and was so startled to see me that she let all the crockery fall and smash on the floor.

When I heard the crash, I turned around, and I was now the one who was startled.

It was the Fat Lady.

1   Geoffrey Keating (c.1580–c.1644) was author of *Foras Feasa ar Éirinn* (Groundwork Knowledge of Ireland), a key work in Gaelic historiography.
2   The Great Famine of 1845–49.
3   Used here in a pitying sense, the poor creature, or poor crayther as is often heard in Ireland.
4   A young man belonging to the poorer Anglo-Irish gentry.

J. M. SYNGE
from John M. Synge, *Poems and Translations* (1911)

A group of poems which capture different moods in Synge's personality.

In Kerry

We heard the thrushes by the shore and sea,
And saw the golden stars' nativity,
Then round we went the lane by Thomas Flynn,
Across the church where bones lie out and in;
And there I asked beneath a lonely cloud
Of strange delight, with one bird singing loud,
What change you'd wrought in graveyard, rock and
    sea,
This new wild paradise to wake for me . . .
Yet knew no more than knew those merry sins
Had built this stack of thigh-bones, jaws and shins.

A Question

I asked if I got sick and died, would you
With my black funeral go walking too,
If you'd stand close to hear them talk or pray
While I'm let down in that steep bank of clay.

And, No, you said, for if you saw a crew
Of living idiots pressing round that new
Oak coffin — they alive, I dead beneath
That board — you'd rave and rend them with your
    teeth.

Prelude

Still south I went and west and south again,
Through Wicklow from the morning till the night,
And far from cities, and the sights of men,
Lived with the sunshine, and the moon's delight.

I knew the stars, the flowers, and the birds,
The grey and wintry sides of many glens,
And did but half remember human words,
In converse with the mountains, moors, and fens.

In May

In a nook
That opened south,
You and I
Lay mouth to mouth.

A snowy gull
And sooty daw
Came and looked
With many a caw;

'Such,' I said,
'Are I and you,
When you've kissed me
Black and blue!'

THE CURSE

*To a sister of an enemy of the author's who disapproved of
'The Playboy'*

Lord, confound this surly sister,
Blight her brow with blotch and blister,
Cramp her larynx, lung, and liver,
In her guts a galling give her.

Let her live to earn her dinners
In Mountjoy[1] with seedy sinners:
Lord, this judgment quickly bring,
And I'm your servant, J. M. Synge.

1 Prison in Dublin.

JOSEPH CAMPBELL

from Joseph Campbell, *Irishry* (1911)

An interior cottage scene brilliantly captured by Campbell in rhyming couplets. In
northern counties such as Donegal the handloom weaver could still be found surviving
into the twentieth century.

THE WEAVER'S FAMILY

The door lay open, and I walked in: I could hear the
　clack of a loom
And the thin sound of a woman's voice singing within
　the room.
I blessed the house, and the singer blushed redly with
　surprise:
A tall woman with ripe breasts and Spanish hair and
　eyes.
She rose shyly from the hearth and stopped her
　warping-wheel,
And three children hid in her skirts, scared from their
　evening meal.
'*Tar isteach*,'[1] she murmured in the only language she
　knew,
The Irish that's as old as earth and young as the living
　dew.
I asked her could she show me the path over the hill:

I'd lost my way in the red bog tramping from
　Columbkill.
'*Feadaim*,'[2] and she spoke a word into the inner room,
And a man came out in his bare feet, and the clack
　stopped in the loom.
He put me on the right path, and the woman with
　feet of silk
Went softly to the dresser and brought me a bowl of
　milk.
The grey sky drifted above, the sea whitened below,
And the boulder stones on Maghery strand[3] looked as
　white as snow.

1 Irish: come in.
2 Irish: I am able. (Yes I can tell you the way. A nice
　example of a reply in Irish without the use of yes.)
3 In County Donegal.

ST JOHN ERVINE

from St John G. Ervine, *Four Irish Plays* (1914)

St John Ervine (1883–1971) was born in east Belfast, emigrated to London at
seventeen, became a Fabian socialist under Shaw's influence, and returned to Ireland in
1915 to become for a short while Manager of the Abbey Theatre. After losing a leg

serving in the Great War he wrote comedies for the West End and turned his hand to biographies, reviewing and writing memoirs. *Mixed Marriage* was first performed at the Abbey Theatre in March 1911; *John Ferguson*, another fine play, was produced there in November 1915. Set midway between the Falls Road and the Shankill Road, *Mixed Marriage* provides a sober assessment of divisions within the Belfast working class. In its subject-matter, especially in the opposition it draws between love and politics, the private and the public, the home and the streets, it invites comparison with O'Casey's *Juno and the Paycock*. In his thoroughgoing commitment to a particular speech community, Ervine recalls Synge: *Mixed Marriage* also contains moments of lyrical intensity. Other contrasts suggest themselves with Yeats's *Cathleen Ni Houlihan*. I have kept the gloss to a minimum in order for the ear to become attuned to the play's distinctive accent. Here is the first of a four-act play.

Mixed Marriage

PERSONS IN THE PLAY

John Rainey
Mrs Rainey, *his wife*
Hugh Rainey ⎫
Tom Rainey ⎭ *his sons*
Michael O'Hara
Nora Murray

The scene is laid in the kitchen of a workman's home midway between the Falls Road and the Shankill Road,[1] *Belfast, in the year 19—.*

ACT I

SCENE. — *It is the evening of a warm summer day at the beginning of July. The living room of* JOHN RAINEY'S *house, by reason of the coal-fire burning in the open grate, is intolerably heated; to counteract this, the door leading to the street is partly open, and the scullery door, leading to the yard is open to its widest. Near the fireplace, above which is suspended a portrait of King William the Third*[2] *in the act of crossing the Boyne, a plain deal table, covered with dark-coloured American cloth, stands. It is laid for the evening meal. At the fire, placing a plateful of buttered toast on the fender, is* MRS RAINEY, *a slight, gentle woman, patient with the awful patience of a woman who has always submitted to her husband's will, without ever respecting him. Whilst she is completing the preparations for the meal, the street door is pushed hurriedly open and* JOHN RAINEY, *dirty from his labour, enters. He is grey-haired, but not bald; he speaks with the quick accent of one used to being obeyed.*

RAINEY: Is the tay ready?

MRS RAINEY: It'll be ready in a minute! Ye'll have to wait til Tom an' Hughie come in.

RAINEY: What are they not here fur? They haven't anny fardher nor me to come, an A'm here afore them. An' me an ould man an' all.

MRS RAINEY: Ah, now don't be puttin' yerself out. Sure, they'll be here in a minute or two. Gw'on into the scullery now an' wash yerself.

RAINEY: Has the wee boy wi' the *Tellygraph*[3] come yit?

MRS RAINEY: He'll be here in a minit. Lord bless us, ye're in a quare hurry the night.

RAINEY: He's always late, that wee lad!

MRS RAINEY: Wus there annythin' pertickler ye wur wantin' t' see in it?

RAINEY: Aye, about the strack.

MRS RAINEY: The strack! Ye're not out on strack, John?

RAINEY: Aye, we come out this avenin'.

MRS RAINEY: Aw, God help us, this is tarrible!

RAINEY: It's goan t' be a long job too, A can tell ye. The masters an' the men are determined.

MRS RAINEY: Ye nivir tould me there was goan t'be a strack.

RAINEY: Och, what wud a lock o' weemen want t'be talkin' about stracks fur. What do they know about it?

MRS RAINEY: It's on'y us that does know about it. It's us that has t' kape the heart in you while it's on.

RAINEY: Aw, now, hould yer tongue! You weemen are always down in the mouth about somethin'. Ye wud think t' hear ye talkin' we come out on strack fur the fun o' the thing. It's no joke, A can tell ye!

MRS RAINEY: It is not, indeed.

RAINEY (*taking off his coat and loosening his waistcoat*): Where's the towel?

MRS RAINEY: Behin' the scullery door.

He goes into the scullery, and the noise of great splashing is heard whilst he washes himself. A newspaper boy is heard coming down the street, crying, 'Telly-ger-ah!' He flings a paper into the little porch, utters his cry in the door, and passes on. MRS RAINEY *goes to the door and picks the paper up. As she does so, her son,* TOM, *appears in the doorway. They enter the kitchen together.*

TOM: Is that you, Ma?

MRS RAINEY: Aye, Tom! Where's Hughie?

TOM: Och, he's away after them Sinn Feiners.[4] He'll be here in a wee while. Is me da in yet?

JOHN RAINEY *appears, towelling himself vigorously.*

RAINEY: So ye're here at last, are ye? Kapin' the tay waitin'!

TOM: Och, sure, A cudden help it. A wus wi' Hughie!

RAINEY: Aye, ye're sure t'be late if ye're wi' him. Where's he?

TOM: A left him in Royal Avenue talkin' to Michael O'Hara.

RAINEY: What, thon Papish[5] fella?

TOM: Aye, they went intil the Sinn Feiners' Hall thegither. (*He sits down and takes off his boots.*) He'll not be long. (*He takes off his coat and loosens his waistcoat.*)

RAINEY: A don't like Hughie goin' after Papishes. He knows a quare lock o' them.

MRS RAINEY: Och, now, what harm is there in that? A'm sure Micky O'Hara's as nice a wee fella as ye cud wish t' meet.

RAINEY: Aw, A've nathin' agenst him, but A don't like Cathliks an' Prodesans mixin' thegither. No good ivir comes o' the like o' that.

TOM *goes into the scullery where the splashing noise is renewed.*

MRS RAINEY: They'll have to mix in heaven, John.

RAINEY: This isn't heaven.

MRS RAINEY: Indeed, that's true. What wi' stracks an' one thing an' another, it might be hell.

RAINEY: There's no peace where Cathliks an' Prodesans gits mixed up thegither. Luk at the way the Cathliks carry on on the Twelfth o' July. Ye have t' have the peelers[6] houlin' them back for fear they'd make a riot. D'ye call that respectable or dacent?

MRS RAINEY: Well, God knows, they git plenty of provokin'. What wi' them men that prache at the Custom House Steps an' yer or'nge arches an' the way the *Tellygraph* is always goin' on at them, A wonder they don't do more nor they do.

RAINEY: Aw, ye wur always one fur Cathliks!

MRS RAINEY: A belave in lavin' people alone. Come on, an' have yer tay fur dear sake. Sure ye'd go on talkin' fur a lifetime if A wus to let ye.

RAINEY: Are ye not goin' to wait fur Hughie?

MRS RAINEY: No, ye'd better have yours now: he'll have his when he comes in.

They sit down and begin the meal.

RAINEY: Dear on'y knows when that'll be, runnin' after a lock o' Socialists an' Cathliks.

MRS RAINEY: He's not runnin' after Socialists. It's Sinn Feiners he's runnin' after.

RAINEY: They're the same thing. Sinn Feiners are all Socialists. That fella Michael O'Hara, what d'ye think he said when A asked him what way o' thinkin' he was?

MRS RAINEY: A don't know, A'm sure.

RAINEY: A'm a member o' the Independent Labour Party, ses he, the I.L.P. A Socialist Society — that's what it is. Did ye ivir hear the like o' that?

MRS RAINEY: Och, A've heerd worse. A've heerd o' stracks.

RAINEY: There ye go again. What can we do? Sure, the masters is not payin' us fair, an' there's no other way o' makin' them.

TOM *re-enters the kitchen and completes his toilet in front of the small looking-glass hanging on the wall.*

Is there, Tom?

TOM: Sure, I don't know anythin' about it.

RAINEY: Naw, ye're ignorant, that's what ye are. A great big fella like you, an' don't know that yit. Ye think o' nathin but goin' up the road of an avenin' after a lot o' girls.

MRS RAINEY: Well, sure ye wur the same yerself when ye wur his age. Come on an' have yer tay, Tom.

RAINEY: The young men o' this day don't think enough. There's not one o' them knows a thing about the battle o' the Boyne. What happened on the first day o' July in the year sixteen hunderd an' ninety, will ye tell me that, now?

TOM *sits at the table.*

TOM: Aw, fur dear sake, hould yer tongue. A left school long ago.

MRS RAINEY: Mebbe some ould men lost their tempers.

RAINEY: Aye, ye can make fun, but it was the gran' day fur Englan' an' Irelan' that wus, when William o' Or'nge driv Popery out o' Irelan'.

TOM: He didden drive it far. Sure, there's plenty o' Papishes in Bilfast, an' there's more o' them in Irelan' nor Prodesans.

MRS RAINEY: A can't help thinkin' it's their country we've got.

RAINEY: Their country indeed! What d'ye think 'ud become o' us if this wur their country? There isn't a Prodesan in Irelan' wud be left alive.

MRS RAINEY: Och, now, don't tell us the like o' that, fur sure it's not true. Cathliks is jus' like wurselves, as good as we are an' as bad as we are, an' no worse. A wish to me goodness ye wudden go to the Custom House Steps if that's the soart o' nonsense they tache ye.

RAINEY: A don't nade t'be taught it — A know it.

A've read a bit in me time. Did ye ivir read the history o' Maria Monk?[7]

TOM: Sure, Hughie ses that's all lies.

RAINEY: Lies, does he call it? What does he know about it? That's what comes thrum associatin' wi Tagues.[8] He'll be disbelievin' the Bible nixt.

A knock is heard on the door, and a voice cries 'Are ye in, Mrs Rainey?'

MRS RAINEY: Aye, A am.

Enter NORA MURRAY, *a good-looking, intelligent, dark-haired girl of twenty-four.*

Och, is that yerself, Nora? Sure come on in.

NORA: Good avenin,' Mr Rainey.

RAINEY: Good avenin'.

NORA: How ir ye, Tom?

TOM: A'm bravely, thank ye, Nora.

NORA: Is Hugh in?

MRS RAINEY: He's not home yet, but he'll be here in a wee minute. Have ye had yer tay?

NORA: Aye, A have thank ye.

MRS RAINEY: Sure, ye cud take a wee drap more, cudden ye?

NORA: Aw, no, thank ye. A'm on'y after havin' it.

TOM: Gwon an' have a drap 'er that.

NORA: Och, A cud not indeed.

RAINEY: There's no good askin' her if she won't have it.

NORA: Is it true about the strack?

RAINEY: It is.

NORA: Dear-a-dear, but it's a quare pity.

RAINEY: Aw, you weemen are all the same. Ye're always lukkin' on the black side o' things, an' complainin'.

MRS RAINEY: There's nathin' but black sides to stracks.

TOM: Aw, there's a bright side, too. Ye don't have to git up so early in the mornin'.

RAINEY: Ye'll git up at the same time the morra mornin', strack or no strack. It wudden take you long t' git out o' the habit o' gettin' up early.

NORA: There'll be the quare distress in Belfast. It wus awful the last time.

RAINEY: There's always distress fur the like o' us sometime or other.

NORA: Indeed, that's true.

MRS RAINEY: There ought to be some other way o' settlin' these things nor stracks. It's wicked, that's what it is, an' it's the weemen that has to bear the worst o' it. Aw, yes, indeed it is. You men don't have to face the rent agent an' the grocer wi' no money.

RAINEY: We all have to take our share, don't we?

MRS RAINEY: Some have to take more nor their share. (*To* NORA) Are ye goan up the road wi' Hughie the night, Nora?

NORA (*somewhat embarrassed*): No, A jus' come in t'ask him about the strack.

RAINEY: Well ye've heerd about it.

NORA (*in greater confusion*): Yes, A'll jus' be goin' now.

MRS RAINEY: Fur dear sake, don't take any notis o' him. Sure, he's not beside himself the night. Jus' sit down there, an' wait till Hughie comes. He's a long time. (*She goes to the door and looks out.*) He's not in sight. Come on an' we'll walk til the head o' the street an' see if he's comin'.

NORA: Aye, A will.

NORA *and* MRS RAINEY *go out at the street door.*

RAINEY: Is Hughie goin' out wi' that girl?

TOM: Aw, he walks up the road wi' her, but sure he' done that often enough wi' other girls. He's a great boy fur girls.

RAINEY: What religion is she?

TOM (*uneasily*): A'm not sure.

RAINEY: She's got a Papish name. There's many a Fenian be the name o' Murray.

TOM: Sure, what differs does it make if she is a Cathlik. She's a brave, nice wee girl.

RAINEY: A wudden have a son o' mine marry a Cathlik fur all the wurl. A've nathin' agin the girl, but A believe in stickin' t'yer religion. A Cathlik's a Cathlik, an' a Prodesan's a Prodesan. Ye can't get over that.

TOM: Och, sure, they're all the same. Ye cudden tell the differs atween a Cathlik an' a Prodesan if ye met them in the street an' didden know what their religion wus. A'm not one fur marryin' out o' my religion meself, but A'm no bigot. Nora Murray's a fine wumman.

RAINEY: Fine or no fine, she's a Cathlik, an' A'll nivir consent til a son o' mine marryin' her.

TOM: What are ye goan t'do about the strack?

RAINEY: Do! What shud A do? Take me share in it the same's the rest o' ye? The workin' class has got t' hing thegither.

TOM: It's a tarrible pity we can't get our work done dacently. Nathin' but a lot o' fightin' an' wranglin'.

RAINEY: Ay, it's a rotten way to' git through the wurl,' fightin' over ha'pennies. Us wantin' a penny an hour more, an' the masters not willin' t' give it to us. Och, ay, it's wrong. Wrong, wrong!

Re-enter MRS RAINEY.

MRS RAINEY: Hughie's comin' down the street, now. He's got O'Hara wi' him.

RAINEY: Huh! more Cathliks! Where's that girl gone?

MRS RAINEY: A toul her t'go on an' meet them. She'll come in wi' them in a minit.

RAINEY: A'm surprised at ye encouragin' her. A Cathlik!

MRS RAINEY: Ah, fur dear sake, houl' yer wheesht. Ye've got Cathlik on the brain.

RAINEY: A'm agin mixed marriages, d'ye hear?

Enter HUGH RAINEY, MICHAEL O'HARA, *and* NORA. *Greetings, surly on the part of old* RAINEY.

MRS RAINEY: Have ye had yer tay, Michael?

HUGH: No, indeed, he hasn't, ma, an' A brought him here t' have it.

MICHAEL: Och, now, Mrs Rainey, don't put yerself til any bother. Sure, A'll git it whin A go home.

MRS RAINEY: It's no bother at all, Michael. It's on'y t'git down a cup an' sasser. Sure, there's plenty, an' yer welcome to it.

MICHAEL: It's very kind o' ye, A'm sure.

HUGH *and he sit down at the table together.* NORA *and* TOM *sit talking together on the sofa.* RAINEY *is seated before the fire reading the 'Evening Telegraph.'*

MRS RAINEY: Nora, come up here an' have a cup o' tay.

NORA: Aw, indeed a cuddent, Mrs Rainey, thank ye. A've just had it.

HUGH: Ah, come on, an' keep Michael an' me company. Sure, ye can always drink tay.

MRS RAINEY: Now, come on. We'll not take 'no' fur an answer.

RAINEY: Sure if the girl dussen want it . . .

MRS RAINEY: Aw, you go on readin' yer paper.

NORA *joins* HUGH *and* MICHAEL *at the table.*

HUGH: Da, we wur wantin' t'have a bit o' a talk wi' ye, Michael an' me, about the strack.

RAINEY: Wur ye?

HUGH: Aye, we wur. We wur thinkin' ye might give us a great dale o' help.

MICHAEL: Ye see, Mr Rainey, ye're a man that's held in great respect be the men, Cathliks an' Prodesans.

RAINEY: A've always tried t' live a straight life an' do me duty by my fellow men.

MICHAEL: Indeed, A know that quare an' well, Mr Rainey. Ye're a man that's alwis bin thought a great dale of. Well, Hugh an' me's bin talkin' this matter over, an' we've come til the conclusion that the great danger o' this strack is that the workers may get led astray be religious rancour. There's bin attempts made in that direction already.

HUGH: Ay, did ye see that bit in the *Telly* the night about Nationalists breedin' discontent among the peaceable people o' Bilfast?

RAINEY: Naw, A've not read it yit. (*Looking at the paper.*) Is this it? (HUGH *looks at the paper*). This bit.

HUGH: Ay, that. (*Reads.*) 'We feel sure that the loyal peace-abiding Protestants of this, the greatest commercial city in Ireland, will not allow themselves to be led astray by Nationalist agitators from Dublin, and that they will see that their true interests lie in the same direction as those of their employers. We should be the last to encourage religious strife, but we would remind our readers, the loyal Orangemen of Ulster, that the leaders of this strike are Roman Catholics and Home Rulers.' There's a nice thing fur ye. There's a lot o' fools in this town'll swallow that balderdash like anything.

MICHAEL: Ye see, Mr Rainey, it's a fact that the leaders are mostly Cathliks, but that dussent mane anything at all, on'y there's some people'll think that it manes that the Pope'll arrive here next week an' ordher all the Prodesans t'be slaughtered. Now, Hugh an' me thought if you wur t' come an' take a leadin' part in the strack it wud show that Cathliks an' Prodesans wus workin' han' in han' fur the same object. D'ye see?

RAINEY: Ay, A see right enough.

HUGH: D'ye agree wi' it father?

RAINEY: A'm no' sure. It wants thinkin' about.

MRS RAINEY: What thinkin' does it want to stan' thegither?

TOM: Sure ye've on'y got to go on the platform an' say we're all in the same boat.

RAINEY: What d'you know about it? You're on'y a bit o' a lad.

TOM (*sulkily*): Mebbe A know more'n some people think A do?

RAINEY: Ay, an' mebbe ye don't know s' much as ye think ye do.

MRS RAINEY: Ah, well, mebbe atween the two he knows a brave bit? Are ye ready for some more tay, Michael?

MICHAEL: Aw, sure A'm done, Mrs Rainey, thank ye.

MRS RAINEY: Och, indeed, ye're not. Sure that's no tay fur a man.

MICHAEL: Aw, now, A've done rightly, thank ye. A cudden take another drap.

MRS RAINEY: Well, A wunt coax ye, ye know.

MICHAEL: Aw, A wudden say 'no' jus' fur the sake o' bein' polite.

MRS RAINEY: Well, if ye're done, A'll jus' redd away these dishes an' things.

NORA (*rising*): Let me do it, Mrs Rainey.

MRS RAINEY: Indeed A will not. Sit down there an' rest yerself. Sure ye've bin at yer work all day.

NORA: Well, ye can let me help ye anny way?

MRS RAINEY (*smiling at her*): Well, mebbe A will. Come on intil the scullery an' we'll wash up the dishes while these men have ther crack.

MRS RAINEY *and* NORA *remove the dishes and teathings to the scullery: they pass in and out of the kitchen to the scullery, during a part of the following scene, but when all the tea-things have been removed, they remain in the scullery and the noise of dishes being washed is heard.*

RAINEY: Where is this meetin' to take place?

MICHAEL: Well, we wur thinkin' o' St Mary's Hall.

RAINEY: What!

HUGH: Sure, what does it matter where it takes place?

RAINEY: A Cathlik hall like that where Home Rulers always go?

HUGH: It's the only hall we can git. Sure, we'd take the Ulster on'y they wudden let us have it.

TOM: Ye cud have it at the Custom House Steps. Ye cud git more people there.

MICHAEL: We wur thinkin' o' that.

RAINEY: A wudden go anear St Mary's Hall.

HUGH: Wud ye go til the Steps, then?

RAINEY: Ay, A might do that.

MICHAEL: Then we'll have it there. Man, Mr Rainey, A'm quare an' glad ye're willin' till speak. It's a fine thing. Think o' it. Her's a chance t'kill bigotry and make the men o' Bilfast realize that onderneath the Cathlik an' the Prodesan there's the plain workin' man.

HUGH: Ay, that's it. They're jus' the same onderneath. They need the same food an' shelter an' clo'es, an' they suffer the same wrongs. The employers don't give a man better wages fur bein' a Prodesan or a Cathlik, do they?

RAINEY: That's true enough.

MICHAEL: A tell ye, Mr Rainey, the employers have used religion to throw dust in wur eyes. They're eggin' us on t' fight one another over religion, so's we shan't have time til think about the rotten wages they give us. They set the Cathliks agin the Prodesans, an' the Prodesans agin the Cathliks, so's ye can't git the two to work thegither for the good o' their class. Look at the way it is in the shipyards. Ye git men workin' thegither peaceably all the year til the Twelfth o' July, an' then they start batin' one another fur the love o' God. There's yourself. Ye're a very dacent, intelligent man, but ye're suspicious o' me, an' ye don't like t' see Hugh an' me so chummy as we are, an' all acause A'm a Cathlik an' you an' he are Prodesans.

RAINEY: There's a differs.

MICHAEL: On'y a very little. Look at me. A'm like yerself. A'm a workin' man. A want t' marry an' have a wife an' childher an' keep them an' me dacently, an' A want t'sarve God in the way A wus brought up. You don't want no more nor that.

TOM: Ay, indeed, that's true. People are all the same the wurl over. They jus' want t'be let alone.

HUGH: Man, da, whin A'm out wi' Mickey, A sometimes think what a fine thing it 'ud be if the workin' men o' Irelan' was to join their han's thegither an' try an' make a great country o' it. There wus a time whin Irelan' wus the islan' o' saints. By God, da, if we cud bring that time back again.

RAINEY: It's a gran' dream.

MICHAEL: To see the streets full o' happy men an' weemen again, their faces shinin' wi' the glory o' the Lord God, an' the childher runnin' about in the sun an' none o' them sick wi' hunger. Aw, if on'y we wud hould thegither an' not be led astray be people that want to keep us apart.

RAINEY: It'll nivir be.

Enter MRS RAINEY.

MICHAEL: Why not?

RAINEY: There's such a quare differs atween a Cathlik an' a Prodesan?

MRS RAINEY: Och, sure what differs does it make so long as ye act up til yer religion.

Enter NORA.

MICHAEL: That's the God's truth, Mrs Rainey. When a man's livin' at his best, it dussn't matter how much he starts differently thrum other people that's doin' the same — he gits quare an' like them in the end.

RAINEY: There's a differs.

NORA: Dear, oh, dear, are ye still wranglin' wi' one another? What ones men are fur talkin'.

MRS RAINEY (*pulling her down beside her on the sofa*): Nivir mind, dear, let them go on talkin'. It keeps them quiet.

1   The former is a working-class Catholic area, the latter Protestant. The roads run roughly parallel with each other south-west and west out of the city.

2   William of Orange defeated the Catholics under James II at the Battle of the Boyne in July 1690. Northern Irish Protestants continue to celebrate this victory on 12 July.

3   *The Belfast Telegraph*, a Protestant newspaper.

4   Sinn Feiners: Sinn Fein was founded as a political party in 1905 by Arthur Griffith. It sought an independent Ireland more through constitutional than violent means. In the North of Ireland the phrase was applied more widely to Catholic nationalists.

5   Protestant term of abuse for Catholics (after the Pope).

6   Police. See footnote on page 195.

7   Maria Monk (c.1817–45) was the author of *The Awful Disclosures of Maria Monk* (1836), disclosures allegedly about her life as a nun. She was in fact a fraud but this did not stop wide sales of the book and the fanning of anti-Catholic sentiment.

8   Another abusive word for Catholics. Normally spelt Taigs.

FRANCIS LEDWIDGE
from Francis Ledwidge, *Lyrical Poems* (1913)

Francis Ledwidge (1887–1917) came of a County Meath family who in his own words were 'ever soldiers and poets'. When he enlisted in the British Army (in the same regiment as his friend and patron Lord Dunsany) he saw little conflict of loyalties even though Pearse and Connolly were two of his heroes. On hearing the news of the Easter Rising while in Manchester, he wrote to a friend: 'MacDonagh and Pearse were two of my best friends, and now they are dead, shot by England.' This did not, however, prevent him from returning to France in December 1916. On 31 July 1917 one of Ireland's most promising poets was killed near Ypres. Here in this poem Ledwidge insists on his links with Georgian verse.

JUNE

Broom out the floor now, lay the fender by,
And plant this bee-sucked bough of woodbine there,
And let the window down. The butterfly
Floats in upon the sunbeam, and the fair
Tanned face of June, the nomad gipsy, laughs
Above her widespread wares, the while she tells
The farmers' fortunes in the fields, and quaffs
The water from the spider-peopled wells.

The hedges are all drowned in green grass seas,
And bobbing poppies flare like Elmor's light,
While siren-like the pollen-stainéd bees
Drone in the clover depths. And up the height

The cuckoo's voice is hoarse and broke with joy.
And on the lowland crops the crows make raid,
Nor fear the clappers of the farmer's boy,
Who sleeps, like drunken Noah, in the shade.

And loop this red rose in that hazel ring
That snares your little ear, for June is short
And we must joy in it and dance and sing,
And from her bounty draw her rosy worth.
Ay! soon the swallows will be flying south,
The wind wheel north to gather in the snow,
Even the roses spilt on youth's red mouth
Will soon blow down the road all roses go.

THOMAS MacDONAGH
from Thomas MacDonagh, *Lyrical Pieces* (1913)

See above p. 230 for information on MacDonagh; see below p. 272 for Francis Ledwidge's elegy on MacDonagh.

THE YELLOW BITTERN

from the Irish of Cathal Buidhe Mac Giolla Ghunna

The yellow bittern that never broke out
    In a drinking bout, might as well have drunk;
His bones are thrown on a naked stone
    Where he lived alone like a hermit monk.
O yellow bittern! I pity your lot,
    Though they say that a sot like myself is curst —
I was sober a while, but I'll drink and be wise
    For I fear I should die in the end of thirst.

It's not for the common birds that I'd mourn,
    The black-bird, the corn-crake, or the crane,
But for the bittern that's shy and apart
    And drinks in the marsh from the long bog-drain.
Oh! if I had known you were near your death,
    While my breath held out I'd have run to you,
Till a splash from the Lake of the Son of the Bird
    Your soul would have stirred and waked anew.

My darling told me to drink no more
    Or my life would o'er in a little short while;
But I told her 'tis drink gives me health and strength
    And will lengthen my road by many a mile.
You see how the bird of the long smooth neck
    Could get his death from the thirst at last —
Come, son of my soul, and drain your cup,
    You'll get no sup when your life is past.

In a wintering island by Constantine's halls
    A bittern calls from a wineless place,
And tells me that hither he cannot come
    Till the summer is here and the sunny days.
When he crosses the stream there and wings o'er the sea
    Then a fear comes to me he may fail in his flight —
Well, the milk and the ale are drunk every drop,
    And a dram won't stop our thirst this night.

W. B. YEATS
from W. B. Yeats, *Responsibilities* (1914)

A selection of poems from Yeats's middle career. 'September 1913' first appeared on 13 September 1913 in the *Irish Times* under the title 'Romance in Ireland' and with an explanatory bracket: 'On reading much of the correspondence against the Art Gallery'. Attacks on Hugh Lane's bequest to Dublin City of his collection of paintings (see footnote on page 242) had angered Yeats and Lady Gregory and prompted him to write to the press with this poem. 'Fallen Majesty', which first appeared in *Poetry* (Chicago) in December 1912, is another fine poem on Maud Gonne. 'The Cold Heaven' shows another side to Yeats, his intense interest in the occult and communicating with spirits. Here in this poem we see him attracted to the idea developed later in *A Vision* (1925) of the dead person dreaming back, compelled to live over again especially painful moments.

SEPTEMBER 1913

What need you, being come to sense,
But fumble in a greasy till
And add the halfpence to the pence
And prayer to shivering prayer, until
You have dried the marrow from the bone?
For men were born to pray and save:
Romantic Ireland's dead and gone,
It's with O'Leary[1] in the grave.

Yet they were of a different kind,
The names that stilled your childish play,
They have gone about the world like wind,
But little time had they to pray
For whom the hangman's rope was spun,
And what, God help us, could they save?
Romantic Ireland's dead and gone,
It's with O'Leary in the grave.

Was it for this the wild geese[2] spread
The grey wing upon every tide;
For this that all that blood was shed,
For this Edward Fitzgerald died,

And Robert Emmet and Wolfe Tone,[3]
All that delirium of the brave?
Romantic Ireland's dead and gone,
It's with O'Leary in the grave.

Yet could we turn the years again,
And call those exiles as they were
In all their loneliness and pain,
You'd cry, 'Some woman's yellow hair
Has maddened every mother's son':
They weighed so lightly what they gave.
But let them be, they're dead and gone,
They're with O'Leary in the grave.

FALLEN MAJESTY

Although crowds gathered once if she but showed her
    face,
And even old men's eyes grew dim, this hand alone,
Like some last courtier at a gypsy camping-place
Babbling of fallen majesty, records what's gone.

The lineaments, a heart that laughter has made sweet,
These, these remain, but I record what's gone. A crowd
Will gather, and not know it walks the very street
Whereon a thing once walked that seemed a burning cloud.

THE COLD HEAVEN

Suddenly I saw the cold and rook-delighting heaven
That seemed as though ice burned and was but the more ice,
And thereupon imagination and heart were driven
So wild that every casual thought of that and this
Vanished, and left but memories, that should be out of season
With the hot blood of youth, of love crossed long ago;
And I took all the blame out of all sense and reason,
Until I cried and trembled and rocked to and fro,

Riddled with light. Ah! when the ghost begins to quicken,
Confusion of the death-bed over, is it sent
Out naked on the roads, as the books say, and stricken
By the injustice of the skies for punishment?

1   John O'Leary (1830–1907) returned to Ireland in 1885 after a twenty-year banishment for Fenian activities and proceeded to gather round him a group of young men and women including Yeats and Maud Gonne committed to a programme of cultural nationalism. Yeats was deeply influenced by O'Leary whom he contrasted with the new breed of activists dedicated to a form of nationalism which was to exclude Yeats.
2   See footnote 13 on page 11 for more information.
3   Edward Fitzgerald (1763–98) was a United Irishman who died fighting in the 1798 Rising. Robert Emmet (1778–1803) led an abortive Rising in 1802. Wolfe Tone was the leader of the United Irishmen; see footnote on page 22 for more information.

PATRICK PEARSE

from Patrick Pearse, *Suantraide agus Goltraide* (1914)

Patrick Pearse (Pádraig Mac Piarais) (1879–1916), poet and dramatist, leader of the Easter 1916 Rising, chief signatory of the Proclamation of the Republic, President of the Provisional Government, was executed in Kilmainham Gaol on 3 May 1916. In November 1913, Pearse wrote in an article entitled 'The Coming Revolution': 'There are many things more horrible than bloodshed; and slavery is one of them.' One way to understand Pearse is to visit his house set amid the ancient stones that constitute a kind of lunar landscape at Rosmuc in Connemara, but here in this poem we also catch a glimpse of the springs of action in his austere personality.

I AM IRELAND

I am Ireland:
I am older than the Old Woman of Beare.[1]

Great my glory:
I that bore Cuchulainn the valiant.

Great my shame:
My own children that sold their mother.

I am Ireland:
I am lonelier than the Old Woman of Beare.

1   In Irish, Cailleach Beara. The Old Woman or Hag of Beare was a female divinity who gathered legends and qualities about her. She is by turns a sovereignty figure, a fertility goddess, topographical marker, symbol of wintry winds and mountain peaks, a Christian nun, and for Pearse a type of mother of the nation.

PATRICK MacGILL
from Patrick MacGill, *Children of the Dead End: The Autobiography of a Navvy* (1914)

Patrick MacGill (1891–1963), born to poverty in Glenties in County Donegal, was engaged at a hiring fair in Strabane at the age of twelve and by fourteen he was working in the potato fields of Scotland. From there he progressed to navvying jobs on the railways and in construction, 'at the end of creation' as he writes in a 1909 poem 'Down on the Dead End', where 'the sunlight is bright on the midden, with the rot of the wide world beneath'. He became a prolific writer both of fiction and of verse and took delight in bringing literature and the world into an uneasy confrontation. The navvy, as he writes in *Moleskin Joe* (1923), anticipating George Orwell's view of the underground labourer in *The Road to Wigan Pier* (1937), is 'the shunned of civilization — of which he is the pioneer'. During the Great War MacGill was a stretcher-bearer and saw at firsthand trench warfare, which he wrote about in *The Red Horizon* (1916) and *The Great Push* (1916). *Children of the Dead End* (1914) is Arthur Morrison's 1890s East-End-of-London novels transposed to Irish migratory workers in Scotland. 'De Profundis' is a modern cry of despair, and in it 'Out of the depths . . .', MacGill makes us aware of the sordid conditions under which people laboured without redemption. See 'Padding It' (p. 268) for a poem about life as a navvy. *The Irish Book Lover* (Vol. 3, No. 5, December 1912) carried a brief note on his background written by MacGill himself.

De Profundis

'I've got kitchen for my grub out of the mustard-pot of sorrow.'
— Moleskin Joe

At that time there were thousands of navvies working at Kinlochleven[1] waterworks. We spoke of waterworks, but only the contractors knew what the work was intended for. We did not know, and we did not care. We never asked questions concerning the ultimate issue of our labours, and we were not supposed to ask questions. If a man throws red muck over a wall to-day and throws it back again to-morrow, what the devil is it to him if he keeps throwing that same muck over the wall for the rest of his life, knowing not why nor wherefore, provided he gets paid sixpence an hour for his labour? There were so many tons of earth to be lifted and thrown somewhere else; we lifted them and threw them somewhere else: so many cubic yards of iron-hard rocks to be blasted and carried away; we blasted and carried them away, but never asked questions and never knew what results we were labouring to bring about. We turned the Highlands into a cinder-heap, and were as wise at the beginning as at the end of the task. Only when we completed the job, and returned to the town, did we learn from the newspapers that we had been employed on the construction of the biggest aluminium factory in the kingdom. All that we knew was that we had gutted whole mountains and hills in the operations.

We toiled on the face of the mountain, and our provisions came up on wires that stretched from the summit to the depths of the valley below. Hampers of bread, casks of beer, barrels of tinned meat and all manner of parcels followed one another up through the air day and night in endless procession, and looked for all the world like great gawky birds which still managed to fly, though deprived of their wings.

The postman came up amongst us from somewhere every day, bringing letters from Ireland, and he was always accompanied by two policemen armed with batons and revolvers. The greenhorns from Ireland wrote home and received letters now and again, but the rest of us had no friends, or if we had we never wrote to them.

Over an area of two square miles thousands of men laboured, some on the day-shift, some on the night-shift, some engaged on blasting operations, some wheeling muck, and others building dams and hewing rock facings. A sort of rude order prevailed, but apart from the two policemen who accompanied the letter-carrier on his daily rounds no other minion of the law ever came near the place. This allowed the physically strong man to exert considerable influence, and fistic arguments were constantly in progress.

Sometimes a stray clergyman, ornamented with a stainless white collar, had the impudence to visit us and tell us what we should do. These visitors were most amusing, and we enjoyed their exhortations exceedingly. Once I told one of them that if he was more in keeping with the Workman whom he represented, some of the navvies stupider than myself might endure his presence, but that no one took any heed of the apprentice who dressed better than his Divine Master. We usually chased these faddists away, and as they seldom had courage equal to their impudence, they never came near us again.

There was a graveyard in the place, and a few went there from the last shift with the red muck still on their trousers, and their long unshaven beards still on their faces. Maybe they died under a fallen rock or broken derrick jib. Once dead they were buried, and there was an end of them.

Most of the men lifted their sub. every second day, and the amount left over after procuring food was spent in the whisky store or gambling-school. Drunkenness enjoyed open freedom in Kinlochleven. I saw a man stark naked, lying dead drunk for hours on a filthy muck-pile. No one was shocked, no one was amused, and somebody stole the man's clothes. When he became sober he walked around the place clad in a blanket until he procured a pair of trousers from some considerate companion.

I never stole from a mate in Kinlochleven, for it gave me no pleasure to thieve from those who were as poor as myself; but several of my mates had no compunction in relieving me of my necessaries. My three and sixpenny keyless watch was taken from my breast pocket one night when I was asleep, and my only belt disappeared mysteriously a week later. No man in the place save Moleskin Joe ever wore braces. I had only one shirt in my possession, but there were many people in the place who never had a shirt on their backs. Sometimes when the weather was good I washed my shirt, and I lost three, one after the other, when I hung them out to dry. I did not mind that very much, knowing well that it only passed to one of my mates, who maybe needed it more than I did. If I saw one of my missing shirts afterwards I took it from the man who wore it, and if he refused to give it to me, knocked him down and took it by force. Afterwards we bore one another no ill-will. Stealing is rife in shack, on road, and in model,[2] but I have never known one of my kind to have given up a mate to the police. That is one dishonourable crime which no navvy will excuse.

As the days went on, I became more careless of myself, and I seldom washed. I became like my mates, like Moleskin, who was so fit and healthy, and who never washed from one year's end to another. Often in his old tin-pot way he remarked that a man could often be better than his surroundings, but never cleaner. 'A dirty man's the only man who washes,' he often said. When we went to bed at night we hid our clothes under the pillows, and sometimes they were gone in the morning. In the bunk beneath ours slept an Irishman named Ward, and to prevent them passing into the hands of thieves he wore all his clothes when under the blankets. But nevertheless, his boots were unlaced and stolen one night when he was asleep and drunk.

One favourite amusement of ours was the looting of provisions as they came up on the wires to the stores on the mountains. Day and night the hampers of bread and casks of beer were passing over our heads suspended in mid-air on the glistening metal strings. Sometimes the weighty barrels and cases dragged the wires downwards until their burdens rested on the shoulder of some uprising knoll. By night we sallied forth and looted all the provisions on which we could lay our hands. We rifled barrels and cases, took possession of bread, bacon, tea, and sugar, and filled our stomachs cheaply for days afterwards. The tops of fallen casks we staved in, and using our hands as cups drank of the contents until we could hold no more. Sometimes men were sent out to watch the hillocks and see that no one looted the grub and drink. These men were paid double for their work. They deserved double pay, for of their own accord they tilted the barrels and cases from their rests and kept them under their charge until we arrived. Then they helped us to dispose of the contents. Usually the watcher lay dead drunk beside his post in the morning. Of course he got his double pay.

• • •

Winter

Do you mind the nights we laboured, boys, together,
Spreadeagled at our travail on the joists,
With the pulley-wheels a-turning and the naphtha
    lamps a-burning,
And the mortar crawling upwards on the hoists,
When our hammers clanked like blazes on the facing,
When the trestles shook and staggered as we struck,
When the derricks on their pivots strained and broke
    the crank-wheel rivets
As the shattered jib sank heavy in the muck?

— From *Songs of the Dead End*

The winter was at hand. When the night drew near, a great weariness came over the face of the sun as it sank down behind the hills which had seen a million sunsets. The autumn had been mild and gentle, its breezes soft, its showers light and cool. But now, slowly and surely, the great change was taking place; a strange stillness settled softly on the lonely places. Nature waited breathless on the threshold of some great event, holding her hundred winds suspended in a fragile leash. The heather bells hung motionless on their stems, the torrents dropped silently as smoke from the scarred edges of the desolate ravines, but in this silence there lay a menace; in its supreme poise was the threat of coming danger. The crash of our hammers was an outrage, and the exploding dynamite a sacrilege against tired nature.

A great weariness settled over us; our life lacked colour, we were afraid of the silence, the dullness of the surrounding mountains weighed heavily on our souls. The sound of labour was a comfort, the thunder of our hammers went up as a threat against the vague implacable portent of the wild.

Life to me had now become dull, expressionless, stupid. Only in drink was there contentment, only in a fight was there excitement. I hated the brown earth, the slushy muck and gritty rock, but in the end hatred died out and I was almost left without passion or longing. My life now had no happiness and no great sadness. My soul was proof against sorrow as it was against joy. Happiness and woe were of no account; life was a spread of brown muck, without any relieving splash of lighter or darker colours. For all that, I had no great desire (desire was almost dead even) to go down to the Lowlands and look for a newer job. So I stayed amidst the brown muck and existed.

When I had come up my thoughts for a long while were eternally straying to Norah Ryan, but in the end she became to me little more than a memory, a frail and delightful phantom of a fleeting dream.

The coming of winter was welcome. The first nipping frost was a call to battle, and, though half afraid, most of the men were willing to accept the challenge. A few, it is true, went off to Glasgow, men old and feeble who were afraid of the coming winter.

In the fight to come the chances were against us. Rugged cabins with unplanked floors, leaking roofs, flimsy walls, through the chinks of which the winds cut like knives, meagre blankets, mouldy food, well-worn clothes, and battered bluchers were all that we possessed to aid us in the struggle. On the other hand, the winter marshalled all her forces, the wind, the hail, frost, snow, and rain, and it was against these that we had to fight, and for the coming of the opposing legions we waited tensely and almost eagerly.

But the north played a wearing game, and strove to harry us out with suspense before thundering down upon us with her cold and her storm. The change took place slowly. In a day we could hardly feel it, in a week something intangible and subtle, something which could not be defined, had crept into our lives. We felt the change, but could not localize it. Our spirits sank under the uncertainty of the waiting days, but still the wild held her hand. The bells of the heather hung from their stems languidly and motionless, stripped of all their summer charm, but lacking little of the hue of summer. Even yet the foam-flecked waters dropped over the cliffs silently as figures that move in a dream. When we gathered together and ate our midday meal, we wrapped our coats around our shoulders, whereas before we had sat down without them. When night came on we drew nearer to the hot-plate, and when we turned naked into bed we found that the blankets were colder than usual. Only thus did the change affect us for a while. Then the cold snap came suddenly and wildly.

The plaintive sunset waned into a sickly haze one evening, and when the night slipped upwards to the mountain peaks never a star came out into the vastness of the high heavens. Next morning we had to thaw the door of our shack out of the muck into which it was frozen during the night. Outside the snow had fallen heavily on the ground, and the virgin granaries of winter had been emptied on the face of the world.

Unkempt, ragged, and dispirited, we slunk to our toil, the snow falling on our shoulders and forcing its way insistently through our worn and battered bluchers. The cuttings were full of slush to the brim, and we had to grope through them with our hands until we found the jumpers and hammers at the bottom. These we held under our coats until the heat of our bodies warmed them, then we went on with our toil.

At intervals during the day the winds of the mountain put their heads together and swept a whirlstorm of snow down upon us, wetting each man to the pelt. Our tools froze until the hands that gripped them were scarred as if by red-hot spits. We shook uncertain over our toil, our sodden clothes scalding and itching the skin with every movement of the swinging hammers. Near at hand the lean derrick jibs whirled on their pivots like spectres of some ghoulish carnival, and the muck-barrows crunched backwards and forwards, all their dirt and rust hidden in woolly mantles of snow. Hither and thither the little black figures of the workers moved across the waste of whiteness like shadows on a lime-washed wall. Their breath steamed out on the air and disappeared in space like the evanescent and fragile vapour of frying mushrooms.

'On a day like this a man could hardly keep warm on the red-hot hearth of hell!' Moleskin remarked at one time, when the snow whirled around the cutting, causing us to gasp with every fiercely-taken breath.

'Ye'll have a heat on the same hearthstone some day,' answered Red Billy, who held a broken lath in one mittened hand, while he whittled away with his eternal clasp-knife.

When night came on we crouched around the hot-plate and told stories of bygone winters, when men dropped frozen stiff in the trenches where they laboured. A few tried to gamble near the door, but the wind that cut through the chinks of the walls chased them to the fire. Moleskin told the story of his first meeting with me on the Paisley toll-road, and suddenly I realized that I was growing old. It was now some years since that meeting took place, and even then I was a man, unaided and alone, fighting the great struggle of existence. I capped Moleskin's story with the account of Mick Deehan's death on the six-foot way. Afterwards the men talked loudly of many adventures. Long lonely shifts were spoken of, nights and days when the sweat turned to ice on the eyelashes, when the cold nipped to the bone and chilled the workers at their labours. One man slipped off the snow-covered gang-plank and fell like a rock forty feet through space.

'Flattened out like a jelly-fish on the groun' he was,' said Clancy, who told the story.

Red Billy, who worked on the railway line in his younger days, gave an account of Mick Cassidy's death. Mick was sent out to free the ice-locked facing points, and when they were closed by the signalman, Cassidy's hand got wedged between the blades and the rail.

'Held like a louse was Cassidy, until the train threw him clear,' concluded Billy, adding reflectively that 'he might have been saved if he had had somethin' in one hand to hack the other hand off with.'

Joe told how one Ned Farley got his legs wedged between the planks of a mason's scaffold and hung there head downwards for three hours. When Farley got relieved he was a raving madman, and died two hours afterwards. We all agreed that death was the only way out in a case like that.

Gahey told of a night's doss at the bottom of a coal slip in a railway siding. He slept there with three other people, two men and a woman. As the woman was a bad one it did not matter very much to anyone where she slept. During the night a waggon of coal was suddenly shot down the slip. Gahey got clear, leaving his thumb with the three corpses which remained behind.

'It was a bad endin', even for a woman like that,' someone said.

Outside the winds of the night scampered madly, whistling through every crevice of the shack and threatening to smash all its timbers to pieces. We bent closer over the hot-plate, and the many who could not draw near to the heat scrambled into bed and sought warmth under the meagre blankets. Suddenly the lamp went out, and a darkness crept into the corners of the dwelling, causing the figures of my mates to assume fantastic shapes in the gloom. The circle around the hot-plate drew closer, and long lean arms were stretched out towards the flames and the redness. Seldom may a man have the chance to look on hands like those of my mates. Fingers were missing from many, scraggy scars seaming along the wrists or across the palms of others told of accidents which had taken place on many precarious shifts. The faces near me were those of ghouls worn out in some unholy midnight revel. Sunken eyes glared balefully in the dim unearthly light of the fire, and as I looked at them a moment's terror settled on my soul. For a second I lived in an early age, and my mates were the cave-dwellers of an older world than mine. In the darkness, near the door, a pipe glowed brightly for a moment, then the light went suddenly out and the gloom settled again. The reaction came when Two-shift Mullholland's song, 'The Bold Navvy Man', was sung by Clancy of the Cross. We joined lustily in the chorus, and the roof shook with the thunder of our voices.

THE BOLD NAVVY MAN

I've navvied here in Scotland, I've navvied in the
   south,
Without a drink to cheer me or a crust to cross me
   mouth,
I fed when I was workin' and starved when out on
   tramp,
And the stone has been me pillow and the moon
   above me lamp.
I have drunk me share and over when I was flush with
   tin,
For the drouth without was nothin' to the drouth that
   burned within!
And where'er I've filled me billy and where'er I've
   drained me can
I've done it like a navvy, a bold navvy man.
         A bold navvy man,
         An old navvy man,
And I've done me graft and stuck it like a bold navvy
   man.

I've met a lot of women and I liked them all a spell —
They drive some men to drinkin' and also some to
  hell,
But I have never met her yet, the woman cute who
  can
Learn a trick to Old Nick or the bold navvy man,
       Oh! the sly navvy man,
         And the fly navvy man,
Sure a woman's always runnin' to the bold navvy man.

I do not care for ladies grand who are of high degree,
A winsome wench and willin', she is just the one for
  me,
Drink and love are classed as sins as mortal sins by
  some,
I'll drink and drink whene'er I can, the drouth is sure
  to come —
And I will love till lusty life runs out its mortal span,
The end of which is in the ditch for many a navvy man.
       The bold navvy man,
       The old navvy man,
Safe in a ditch with heels cocked up, so dies the navvy
  man.

I've splashed a thousand models red and raised up fiery
  Cain
From Glasgow down to Dover Pier and back that road
  again;
I've fought me man for hours on end, stark naked to
  the buff;
And me and him, we never knew when we had got
  enough.
'Twas skin and hair all flyin' round and red blood up
  and out,
And me or him could hardly tell what brought the
  fight about.—
'Tis wenches, work and fight and fun and drink
  whene'er I can
That makes the life of stress and strife as suits the
  navvy man!

'Let her go, boys; let her go now!' roared Clancy,
rising to his feet, kicking a stray frying-pan and
causing it to clatter across the shack. 'All together,
boys; damn you, all together!'

       Then hurrah! ev'ry one
       For the bold navvy man,
For fun and fight are damned all right for any navvy
  man!

Even old Sandy MacDonald joined in the chorus
with his weak and querulous voice. The winter was
touching him sharply, and he was worse off than any
of us. Along with the cold he had his wasting disease
to battle against, and God alone knew how he
managed to work along with his strong and lusty
mates on the hammer squad at Kinlochleven. Sandy
was not an old man, but what with the dry cough that
was in his throat and the shivers of cold that came over
him after a long sweaty shift, it was easily seen that he
had not many months to live in this world. He looked
like a parcel of bones covered with brown withered
parchment and set in the form of a man. How life
could remain fretting within such a frame as his was a
mystery which I could not solve. Almost beyond the
effects of heat or cold, the cold sweat came out of his
skin on the sweltering warm days, and when the
winter came along, the chilly weather hardly made
him colder than he was by nature. His cough never
kept silent; sometimes it was like the bark of a dog, at
other times it seemed as if it would carry the very
entrails out of the man. In the summer he spat blood
with it, but usually it was drier than the east wind.

At one period of his life Sandy had had a home and
a wife away down in Greenock; but in those days he
was a strong lusty fellow, fit to pull through a ten-hour
shift without turning a hair. One winter's morning he
came out from the sugar refinery, in which he worked,
steaming hot from the long night's labour, and then
the cold settled on him. Being a sober, steady-going
man, he tried to work as long as he could lift his arms,
but in the end he had to give up the job which meant
life and home to him. One by one his little bits of
things went to the pawnshop; but all the time he
struggled along bravely, trying to keep the roof-tree
over his head and his door shut against the lean spectre
of hunger. Between the four bare walls of the house
Sandy's wife died one day; and this caused the man to
break up his home.

He came to Kinlochleven at the heel of the
summer, and because he mastered his cough for a
moment when asking for a job, Red Billy Davis
started him on the jumper squad. The old ganger,
despite his swearing habits and bluntness of discourse,
was at heart a very good-natured fellow. Sandy
stopped with us for a long while and it was pitiful to
see him labouring there, his old bones creaking with
every move of his emaciated body, and the cold sweat
running off him all day. He ate very little; the tame
robin which flitted round our shack nearly picked as
much from off the floor. He had a bunk to himself at
the corner of the shack, and there he coughed out the
long sleepless hours of the night, bereft of all hope,
lacking sympathy from any soul sib to himself, and
praying for the grave which would end all his troubles.

For days at a stretch he lay supine in his bed, unable to move hand or foot, then, when a moment's relief came to him, he rose and started on his shift again, crawling out with his mates like a wounded animal.

Winter came along and Sandy got no better; he could hardly grow worse and remain alive. Life burned in him like a dying candle in a ruined house, and he waited for the end of the great martyrdom patiently. Still, when he could, he kept working day in and day out, through cold and wet and storm. Heaven knows that it was not work which he needed, but care, rest, and sympathy. All of us expressed pity for the man, and helped him in little ways, trying to make life easier for him. Moleskin usually made gruel for him, while I read the *Oban Times* to the old fellow whenever that paper came into the shack. One evening as I read something concerning the Isle of Skye Sandy burst into tears, like a homesick child.

'Man! I would like tae dee there awa' in the Isle of Skye,' he said to me in a yearning voice.

'Die, you damned old fool, you?' exclaimed Joe, who happened to come around with a pot of gruel just at that moment and overheard Sandy's remark. 'You'll not die for years yet. I never saw you lookin' so well in all your life.'

'It's all over with me, Moleskin,' said poor Sandy. 'It's a great wonder that I've stood it so long, but just now the thocht came to me that I'd like tae dee awa' back in my own place in the Isle of Skye. If I could just save as muckle siller as would take me there, I'd be content enough.'

'Some people are content with hellish little!' said Joe angrily. 'You've got to buck up, man, for there's a good time comin', though you'll never — I mean that ev'rything will come right in the end. We'll see that you get home all right, you fool, you!'

Joe was ashamed to find himself guilty of any kind impulse, and he endeavoured to hide his good intentions behind rough words. When he called Sandy an old fool Sandy's eyes sparkled, and he got into such good humour that he joined in the chorus of the 'Bold Navvy Man' when Clancy, who is now known as Clancy of the Cross, gave bellow to Mullholland's *magnum opus*.

Early on the morning of the next day, which was pay-day, Moleskin was busy at work sounding the feelings of the party towards a great scheme which he had in mind; and while waiting at the pay-office when the day's work was completed, Joe made the following speech to Red Billy's gang, all of whom, with the exception of Sandy MacDonald, were present.

'Boys, Sandy MacDonald wants to go home and die in his own place,' said Joe, weltering into his subject at once. 'He'll kick the bucket soon, for he has the look of the grave in his eyes. He only wants as much tin as will take him home, and that is not much for any man to ask, is it? So what do you say, boys, to a collection for him, a shillin' a man, or whatever you can spare? Maybe some day, when you turn respectable, one of you can say to yourself, "I once kept myself from gettin' drunk, by givin' some of my money to a man who needed it more than myself." Now, just look at him comin' across there.'

We looked in the direction of Joe's outstretched finger and saw Sandy coming towards us, his rags fluttering around him like the duds of a Michaelmas scarecrow.

'Isn't he a pitiful sight!' Moleskin went on. 'He looks like the Angel of Death out on the prowl! It's a God's charity to help a man like Sandy and make him happy as we are ourselves. We are at home here; he is not. So it is up to us to help him out of the place. Boys, listen to me!' Moleskin's voice sank into an intense whisper. 'If every damned man of you don't pay a shillin' into this collection I'll look for the man that doesn't, and I'll knuckle his ribs until he pays for booze for ev'ry man in Billy's shack, by God! I will.'

Everyone paid up decently, and on behalf of the gang I was asked to present the sum of three pounds fifteen shillings to Sandy MacDonald. Sandy began to cry like a baby when he got the money into his hands, and every man in the job called out involuntarily: 'Oh! you old fool, you!'

Pay-day was on Saturday. On Monday morning Sandy intended starting out on his journey home. All Saturday night he coughed out the long hours of the darkness, but in the morning he looked fit and well.

'You'll come through it, you fool!' said Moleskin. 'I'll be dead myself afore you.'

On the next night he went to bed early, and as we sat around the gaming table we did not hear the racking cough which had torn at the man's chest for months.

'He's getting better,' we all said.

'Feeling all right, Sandy?' I asked, as I turned into bed.

'Mon! I'm feelin' fine now,' he answered. 'I'm goin' to sleep well to-night, and I'll be fit for the journey in the morn.'

That night Sandy left us for good. When the morning came we found the poor wasted fellow lying dead in his bunk, his eyes wide open, his hands closed tightly, and the long finger-nails cutting into the flesh of the palm. The money which we gave to the man was bound up in a little leathern purse tied round his neck with a piece of string.

The man was very light and it was an easy job to carry him in the little black box and place him in his home below the red earth of Kinlochleven. The question as to what should be done with the money arose later. I suggested that it should be used in buying a little cross for Sandy's grave.

'If the dead man wants a cross he can have one,' said Moleskin Joe. And because of what he said and because it was more to our liking, we put the money up as a stake on the gaming table. Clancy won the pile, because his luck was good on the night of the game.

That is our reason for calling him Clancy of the Cross ever since.

The winter rioted on its way. Snow, rain, and wind whirled around us in the cutting, and wet us to the bone. It was a difficult feat to close our hands tightly over the hammers with which we took uncertain aim at the drill heads and jumper ends. The drill holder cowered on his seat and feared for the moment when an erring hammer might fly clear and finish his labours for ever. Hourly our tempers grew worse, each movement of the body caused annoyance and discomfort, and we quarrelled over the most trivial matters. Red Billy cursed every man in turn and all in general, until big Jim Maloney lost his temper completely and struck the ganger on the jaw with his fist, knocking him senseless into a snowdrift.

That night Maloney was handed his lying time and told to slide. He padded from Kinlochleven in the darkness, and I have never seen him since then. He must have died on the journey. No man could cross those mountains in the darkness of mid-winter and in the teeth of a snow-storm.

Some time afterwards the copy of a Glasgow newspaper, either the *Evening Times* or *News* (I now forget which), came into our shack wrapped around some provisions, and in the paper I read a paragraph concerning the discovery of a dead body on the mountains of Argyllshire. While looking after sheep a shepherd came on the corpse of a man that lay rotting in a thawing snowdrift. Around the remains a large number of half-burnt matches were picked up, and it was supposed that the poor fellow had tried to keep himself warm by their feeble flames in the last dreadful hours. Nobody identified him, but the paper stated that he was presumably a navvy who lost his way on a journey to or from the big waterworks of Kinlochleven.

As for myself, I am quite certain that it was that of big Jim Maloney. No man could survive a blizzard on the houseless hills, and big Jim Maloney never appeared in model or shack afterwards.

1   In the Scottish Highlands.
2   A large lodging-house for the poor, tramps, or, here, unskilled labourers: the working man's hotel.

LORD DUNSANY
The Poetry Review (May 1914)

Edward Lord Dunsany (1878–1957), a County Meath landowner, was educated at Eton and Sandhurst. He saw service in the Boer War, the Great War, and was shot in the face during Easter Week. When he turned to writing, his imagination was attracted to fantasy, romance, yarns, fables, tales. This poem was used by Padric Gregory as an (ironic) epilogue to *Modern Anglo-Irish Verse: An Anthology* (1914). It was reprinted in Lord Dunsany, *Fifty-One Tales* (1915).

The Assignation

Fame singing in the highways, and trifling as she sang, with sordid adventurers, passed the poet by.

And still the poet made for her little chaplets of song to deck her forehead in the Courts of Time: and still she wore instead the worthless garlands, that boisterous citizens flung to her in the ways, made out of perishable things.

And after a while whenever these garlands died the poet came to her with his chaplets of song, and still she laughed at him and wore the worthless wreaths though they always died at evening.

And one day in his bitterness the poet rebuked her

and said to her: 'Lovely Fame, even in the highways and the byways you have not forborne to laugh and shout and jest with worthless men, and I have toiled for you and dreamed of you and you mock me and pass me by.'

And Fame turned her back on him and walked away, but in departing she looked over her shoulder and smiled at him as she had not smiled before and, almost speaking in a whisper, said:

'I will meet you in the graveyard at the back of the Workhouse in a hundred years.'

PATRICK MACGILL
from Patrick MacGill, *Songs of the Dead End* (1916)

Songs of a Navvy, the forerunner of this volume of verse, was published in 1912. *Songs of the Dead End* provides another focus (see *Children of the Dead End*, p. 261) on his seven-year apprenticeship in Scotland as a 'farm-hand, drainer, tramp, hammerman, navvy, plate-layer or wrestler', as he is described in the preface. 'Padding It' deals with the idea of pacing it and makes use of a vocabulary that can fox the modern reader (some of my glosses are guesses). The revealing press opinions deliberately reproduced at the end of this book contain some gems: 'He sings of the Great Unwashed, as one who knows.' 'Rotten. MacGill's ear deserves thickening.' 'We are at a loss to understand what manner of youth he is.' 'We should like to see him devoting his undoubted powers to the task of stimulating his class to a higher ideal of life, rather than excusing their shortcomings, or laying the blame upon society.'

PADDING IT

An empty stomach, an empty sack and a long road.
            — From Moleskin's Diary[1]

Hashing it out[2] like niggers on a two and a tanner sub,[3]
Everything sunk with our uncle,[4] little to burn at the pub,
Fifty and six were our hours, and never an extra shift,
And whiles we were plunging at banker,[5] and whiles we were studying thrift —
Sewing and patching the trousers, till their parts were more than the whole,
Tailoring, cobbling, and darning, grubbed[6] on a sausage and roll —
Thrift on a fourpenny hour, a matter of nineteen bob,[7]
But we glanced askew at the gaffer, and stuck like glue to the job,
We of the soapless legion, we of the hammer and hod,
Human swine of the muck-pile, forever forgotten of God.

'Hearing of anything better?' one to another would say,
As we toiled in all moods of the weather, and cursed at the dragging day,

Winking the sweat off our lashes, shaking the wet off our hair,
Wishing to God it was raining, praying to Him it would fair.
'Curse a job in the country,' one unto one would reply,
Looking across his shoulder, to see if the boss was by —
Arrogant March came roaring down on the year, and then
A rumour spread in the model,[8] and gladdened the navvy men.

Was it the highland slogan? was it the bird of the north,
Out of its frost-rimmed eyrie that carried the message forth?
'Jackson has need of navvies, the navvies who understand
The graft of the offside reaches, to labour where God has bann'd,
Men of the sign of the moleskin who swear by the soundless pit,
Men who are eager for money and hurry in spending it.
Bluchers[9] and velvet waistcoats, and kneestraps below their knees,

The great unwashed of the model — Jackson has need
   of these.'

Then the labourer on the railway laughed at the
   engine peals,
And threw his outworn shovel beneath the flange of
   the wheels.
The hammerman at the jumper slung his hammer aside,
Lifted his lying money and silently did a slide,
The hod was thrown on the mortar, the spade was
   flung in the drain,
The grub was left on the hot-plate, and the navvies
   were out again.

All the roads of the Kingdom converged, as it were, to
   one.
Which led away to the northward under the dusk and
   dawn,
And out on the road we hurried, rugous[10] and worn
   and thin,
Our cracking joints a-staring out through our
   parchment skin,
Some of us trained from our childhood, to swab in the
   slush and muck,
Some who were new to the shovel, some who were
   down on their luck,
The prodigal son half home-sick, the jail-bird, dodger
   and thief,
The chucker-out from the gin shop, the lawyer minus
   a brief,
The green hand over from Oir'lan', the sailor tired of
   his ships,
Some with hair of silver, some with a woman's lips,
Old, anæmic, and bilious, lusty, lanky and slim,
Padding it, slowly and surely, padding it resolute, grim.

We dossed it under the heavens, watching the moon
   ashine,
And a tremor akin to palsy quivering down the spine.
We drank of the spring by the roadside using the
   hands for a cup,
Stole the fowl from the farm before the farmer was up,
We lit our fires in the darkness drumming up in the
   flame,
Primitive, rude, romantic men who were old at the
   game,
On through the palpable darkness, and on through the
   tinted dawn,
The line of moleskin and leather fitfully plodded on;
And no one faltered or weakened, and no one
   stumbled or fell,
But now and again they grumbled, saying, 'It's worse
   nor hell.'

The rain came splattering earthwards, slavering in our
   face,
But we never hinted of shelter and never slackened
   our pace,
The mornings were cool and lightsome, we never
   hurried a bit,
'Slow and easy is better than hashing and rushing[11] it.'
Ever the self-same logic, steady, sober and suave —
'The hasty horse will stumble,' 'hashing to make your
   grave,'[12]
'Easy and slow on the jumper,[13] will drive a hole for
   the blast,'
'Rome was long in the building, but the grandeur of
   Rome is past.'

You speak of the road in your verses, you picture the
   joy of it still,
You of the specs and the collars, you who are geese of
   the quill,
You pad it along with a wine-flask and your pockets
   crammed with dough,
Eat and drink at your pleasure, and write how the
   flowers grow —
If your stomach was empty as pity, your hobnails were
   down at the heels,
And a nor'-easter biting your nose off, then you
   would know how it feels,
A nail in the sole of your bluchers jagging your foot
   like a pin,
And every step on your journey was driving it further
   in,
Then, out on the great long roadway, you'd find when
   you went abroad,
The nearer you go to nature the further you go from
   God.

Through many a sleepy hamlet, and many a noisy
   town,
While eyes of loathing stared us, we who were out and
   down,
Looking aslant at the wineshop, talking as lovers talk,
Of the lure of the gentle schooner, the joy of Carroll's
   Dundalk;[14]
Sometimes bumming a pipeful, sometimes 'shooting
   the crow,'[15]
But ever onward and onward, fitfully, surely, slow,
On to the drill and the jumper, and on to the concrete
   bed,
On to the hovel and card school, the dirt-face, and
   slush ahead.

Thus was the long road followed — true is the tale I
   tell,

Ask my pals of the model — ask, they remember
   well —
Hear them tell how they tramped it, as they smoke at
   the bar and spit,
The journey to Ballachulish, for this is the song of it.

1   There is a portrait of Moleskin Joe in *Children of the Dead End* (1914). See also the tender fictional portrait of Joe in *Moleskin Joe* (1923). '*Jos his naim don be crule to him His mother*' is the note attached to the abandoned baby Joe.
2   Making do, as in hashing up food.
3   A sub of two shillings and sixpence (25p).

4   All our worldly goods pawned.
5   Betting recklessly.
6   Fed.
7   Nineteen shillings (95p). Actually 56 x 4 = 18 shillings and 8 pence.
8   Lodging-house.
9   Strong leather half-boots.
10   Wrinkled.
11   Here perhaps as in making a hash of things.
12   Here perhaps as in being mangled or destroyed by going too fast.
13   A heavy drill.
14   Carroll's cigarettes are manufactured in Dundalk in County Louth.
15   Ordering drink, having no intention of paying for it.

PATRICK PEARSE

from *Collected Works of Pádraic H. Pearse: Plays, Stories, Poems* (1916)

While awaiting his execution in Kilmainham Gaol, Pearse wrote this, his last poem. In his last letter to his mother, he explained: 'You asked me to write a little poem which would seem to be said by you about me.' There is a composure in 'The Wayfarer' as if the poet's mind were elsewhere, safe in the knowledge that he is one of the mountainy men awaiting the results of their sowing.

THE WAYFARER

The beauty of the world hath made me sad,
This beauty that will pass;
Sometimes my heart hath shaken with great joy
To see a leaping squirrel in a tree,
Or a red lady-bird upon a stalk,
Or little rabbits in a field at evening,
Lit by a slanting sun,
Or some green hill where shadows drifted by
Some quiet hill where mountainy man hath sown
And soon would reap; near to the gate of Heaven;
Or children with bare feet upon the sands
Of some ebbed sea, or playing on the streets
Of little towns in Connacht,
Things young and happy.
And then my heart hath told me:
These will pass,
Will pass and change, will die and be no more,
Things bright and green, things young and happy;
And I have gone upon my way
Sorrowful.

W. B. YEATS

from W. B. Yeats, *Michael Robartes and the Dancer* (1921)

Although Yeats's response to the most powerful event in modern Irish history was not in fact published until October 1920, the poem's intervention in Irish history has been as much a time-bomb as the event itself. Each time the names of the leaders are read aloud, we can perhaps touch something of their transformation into myth and symbol.

EASTER 1916

I have met them[1] at close of day
Coming with vivid faces
From counter or desk among grey
Eighteenth-century houses.[2]
I have passed with a nod of the head
Or polite meaningless words,
Or have lingered awhile and said
Polite meaningless words,
And thought before I had done
Of a mocking tale or a gibe
To please a companion
Around the fire at the club,
Being certain that they and I
But lived where motley is worn:
All changed, changed utterly:
A terrible beauty is born.

That woman's[3] days were spent
In ignorant good-will,
Her nights in argument
Until her voice grew shrill.
What voice more sweet than hers
When, young and beautiful,
She rode to harriers?
This man[4] had kept a school
And rode our wingèd horse;
This other[5] his helper and friend
Was coming into his force;
He might have won fame in the end,
So sensitive his nature seemed,
So daring and sweet his thought.
This other man[6] I had dreamed
A drunken, vainglorious lout.
He had done most bitter wrong
To some who are near my heart,
Yet I number him in the song;
He, too, has resigned his part
In the casual comedy;
He, too, has been changed in his turn,
Transformed utterly:
A terrible beauty is born.

Hearts with one purpose alone
Through summer and winter seem
Enchanted to a stone
To trouble the living stream.
The horse that comes from the road,
The rider, the birds that range
From cloud to tumbling cloud,
Minute by minute they change;
A shadow of cloud on the stream
Changes minute by minute;
A horse-hoof slides on the brim,
And a horse plashes within it;
The long-legged moor-hens dive,
And hens to moor-cocks call;
Minute by minute they live:
The stone's in the midst of all.

Too long a sacrifice
Can make a stone of the heart.
O when may it suffice?
That is Heaven's part, our part
To murmur name upon name,
As a mother names her child
When sleep at last has come
On limbs that had run wild.
What is it but nightfall?
No, no, not night but death;
Was it needless death after all?
For England may keep faith[7]
For all that is done and said.
We know their dream; enough
To know they dreamed and are dead;
And what if excess of love
Bewildered them till they died?
I write it out in a verse —
MacDonagh and MacBride
And Connolly and Pearse
Now and in time to be,
Wherever green is worn,
Are changed, changed utterly:
A terrible beauty is born.

September 25, 1916

1   The Easter Week rebels.
2   A reference to Dublin's architectural golden age.
3   Constance Markievicz (née Gore-Booth) (1868–1927), eldest child of Sir Henry Gore-Booth of Lissadell, County Sligo, abandoned the lifestyle of her class (riding for example) and threw herself into nationalist politics. In 1909 she organized the Irish Scout movement under the name Fianna Na h-Eireannn; during the Lockout of 1913 she helped organize a food kitchen and milk depot (an example of Yeats's 'ignorant good-will'). During the Easter Rising, she was one of the leaders tasked with securing the College of Surgeons on St Stephen's Green. Her death sentence was commuted and in 1918 she was the first woman to be elected to the House of Parliament at Westminster (she declined to take her seat).
4   Patrick Pearse. In 1907, he founded St Enda's School in Rathfarnham to give children a bilingual and Gaelic education.
5   Thomas MacDonagh.

6   Sean MacBride, who had married Maud Gonne in
    1903. The marriage proved unsuccessful and, as the
    correspondence in January 1905 between Maud and
    Yeats (and Yeats and Lady Gregory) suggests, she wanted
    to sue for divorce on account of his drunken behaviour,
    his advances toward servants, and his possible abuse of

Iseult, the daughter she had by Lucien Millevoye. For
further details see my *Yeats's Worlds*, pages 284–5.
7   At the outbreak of the Great War in 1914, all Bills at
    Westminster were frozen, including the 1913 Home
    Rule Bill which was awaiting final assent.

FRANCIS LEDWIDGE
from Francis Ledwidge, *Songs of Peace* (1917)

This is Ledwidge's elegy on his friend MacDonagh, executed in May 1916 for his part
in the Easter Rising.

THOMAS MCDONAGH

He shall not hear the bittern cry[1]
In the wild sky, where he is lain,
Nor voices of the sweeter birds
Above the wailing of the rain.

Nor shall he know when loud March blows
Thro' slanting snows her fanfare shrill,
Blowing to flame the golden cup
Of many an upset daffodil.

But when the Dark Cow[2] leaves the moor,
And pastures poor with greedy weeds,
Perhaps he'll hear her low at morn
Lifting her horn in pleasant meads.

1   The allusion here is to MacDonagh's poem 'The Yellow
    Bittern' (1913), reproduced above.
2   Image of Ireland.

JOSEPH CAMPBELL
from Joseph Campbell, *Earth of Cualann* (1917)

Two more poems from Campbell's mature period. The first contains a startling return
to earth in the last two lines; the second belongs with other contemporary war poems
about sacrifice.

EARTH OF CUALANN[1]

This grey earth is holy,
From the sun-stones of Mashóg
To the seven eyes of the rainbow
In the still water of Téa.[2]

The burning inn at the crossways,
The fian[3] tracking the boar,
The queen riding northward
With her horseboys and women —
Are the thought in your heart,
The earth under your feet.

The Revealer

Not by prayers, not by songs
Are men reborn,
But by sacrifice.

Sacrifice is the revealer:
We see all things clearly
In the glazed mirror of blood.

1   Cualann is an ancient district covering part of what is
    now County Wicklow, spreading north and north-west
    to within a short distance of Dublin.
2   Wife of Eremon, the first Milesian king, who named
    Tara after her.
3   Irish: warrior. Plural: fianna, as in Fianna Fáil.

JAMES STEPHENS
from James Stephens, *Reincarnations* (1918)

In these two poems Stephens captures something of the spirit of Gaelic Ireland, firstly
as curse, and secondly as bard. Dáibhí Ó Bruadair (?1625–98) was an Irish-language
poet who provided a running commentary on all the major events which affected
Gaelic Ireland from the Cromwellian wars of the 1640s to the Treaty of Limerick in
1691. Here in the second poem Stephens imagines himself as the bardic poet giving up
writing verse after the defeat of Limerick.

Righteous Anger

The lanky hank of a she in the inn over there
Nearly killed me for asking the loan of a glass of beer:
May the devil grip the whey-faced slut by the hair,
And beat bad manners out of her skin for a year.

That parboiled imp, with the hardest jaw you will see
On virtue's path, and a voice that would rasp the dead,
Came roaring and raging the minute she looked at me,
And threw me out of the house on the back of my
    head!

If I asked her master he'd give me a cask a day;
But she, with the beer at hand, not a gill would
    arrange!
May she marry a ghost and bear him a kitten, and may
The High King of Glory permit her to get the mange.[1]

O Bruadair

I will sing no more songs! The pride of my country I
    sang
Through forty long years of good rhyme, without any
    avail;

And no one cared even the half of the half of a hang
For the song or the singer — so, here is an end to the
    tale!

If you say, if you think, I complain, and have not got a
    cause,
Let you come to me here, let you look at the state of
    my hand!
Let you say if a goose-quill has calloused these horny
    old paws,
Or the spade that I grip on, and dig with, out there in
    the land?

When our nobles were safe and renowned and were
    rooted and tough,
Though my thought went to them and had joy in the
    fortune of those,
And pride that was proud of their pride — they gave
    little enough!
Not as much as two boots for my feet, or an old suit of
    clothes!

I ask of the Craftsman that fashioned the fly and the
    bird;
Of the Champion whose passion will lift me from
    death in a time;

Of the Spirit that melts icy hearts with the wind of a
     word,
That my people be worthy, and get, better singing
     than mine.

I had hoped to live decent, when Ireland was quit of
     her care,
As a poet or steward, perhaps, in a house of degree,

But my end of the tale is — old brogues and old
     breeches to wear!
So I'll sing no more songs for the men that care
     nothing for me.

1   A skin disease. The mange sounds worse than just
     mange.

W. B. YEATS
from W. B. Yeats, *The Wild Swans at Coole* (1919)

'The Wild Swans at Coole' was written in 1916 and first appeared in the *Little Review*
in June 1917. 'In Memory of Major Robert Gregory' was written on 14 June 1918 and
first appeared in *The English Review* in August 1918. 'An Irish Airman Foresees his
Death' was written in 1918 and first appeared in the Macmillan edition of *The Wild
Swans at Coole*. Lady Gregory's son Robert had enlisted as an airman in the British
Army and was shot down in error by an Italian pilot in January 1918. Yeats thought he
was the most accomplished man he had ever met, but in these two memorial poems he
concentrates not as much on Gregory's military prowess and bravery as on his artistic
promise and personality. Yeats maintains a certain distance in these poems as if he were
channelling his feelings through Gregory's mother. Another fine poem on Gregory,
'Reprisals', was not published in Yeats's lifetime because Lady Gregory took exception
to what she thought was its lack of sincerity. For further details see my *Yeats's Worlds*.

THE WILD SWANS AT COOLE

The trees are in their autumn beauty,
The woodland paths are dry,
Under the October twilight the water
Mirrors a still sky;
Upon the brimming water among the stones
Are nine-and-fifty swans.

The nineteenth autumn[1] has come upon me
Since I first made my count;
I saw, before I had well finished,
All suddenly mount
And scatter wheeling in great broken rings
Upon their clamorous wings.

I have looked upon those brilliant creatures,
And now my heart is sore.
All's changed since I, hearing at twilight,

The bell-beat of their wings above my head,
Trod with a lighter tread.

Unwearied still, lover by lover,
They paddle in the cold
Companionable streams or climb the air;
Their hearts have not grown old;
Passion or conquest, wander where they will,
Attend upon them still.

But now they drift on the still water,
Mysterious, beautiful;
Among what rushes will they build,
By what lake's edge or pool
Delight men's eyes when I awake some day
To find they have flown away?

IN MEMORY OF MAJOR ROBERT GREGORY

I

Now that we're almost settled in our house[2]
I'll name the friends that cannot sup with us
Beside a fire of turf in th' ancient tower,
And having talked to some late hour
Climb up the narrow winding stair to bed:
Discoverers of forgotten truth
Or mere companions of my youth,
All, all are in my thoughts to-night being dead.

II

Always we'd have the new friend meet the old
And we are hurt if either friend seem cold,
And there is salt to lengthen out the smart
In the affections of our heart,
And quarrels are blown up upon that head;
But not a friend that I would bring
This night can set us quarrelling.
For all that come into my mind are dead.

III

Lionel Johnson[3] comes the first to mind.
That loved his learning better than mankind,
Through courteous to the worst; much falling he
Brooded upon sanctity
Till all his Greek and Latin learning seemed
A long blast upon the horn that brought
A little nearer to his thought
A measureless consummation that he dreamed.

IV

And that enquiring man John Synge comes next,
That dying chose the living world for text
And never could have rested in the tomb
But that, long travelling, he had come
Towards nightfall upon certain set apart
In a most desolate stony place,
Towards nightfall upon a race
Passionate and simple like his heart.

V

And then I think of old George Pollexfen,[4]
In muscular youth well known to Mayo men
For horsemanship at meets or at racecourses,
That could have shown how pure-bred horses
And solid men, for all their passion, live
But as the outrageous stars incline
By opposition, square and trine;
Having grown sluggish and contemplative.

VI

They were my close companions many a year,
A portion of my mind and life, as it were,
And now their breathless faces seem to look
Out of some old picture-book;
I am accustomed to their lack of breath,
But not that my dear friend's dear son,
Our Sidney[5] and our perfect man,
Could share in that discourtesy of death.

VII

For all things the delighted eye now sees
Were loved by him: the old storm-broken trees
That cast their shadows upon road and bridge;
The tower set on the stream's edge;
The ford where drinking cattle make a stir
Nightly, and startled by that sound
The water-hen must change her ground;
He might have been your heartiest welcomer.

VIII

When with the Galway foxhounds he would ride
From Castle Taylor to the Roxborough[6] side
Or Esserkelly plain, few kept his pace;
At Mooneen he had leaped a place
So perilous that half the astonished meet
Had shut their eyes; and where was it
He rode a race without a bit?
And yet his mind outran the horses' feet.

IX

We dreamed that a great painter had been born
To cold Clare rock and Galway rock and thorn,
To that stern colour and that delicate line
That are our secret discipline
Wherein the gazing heart doubles her might.
Soldier, scholar, horseman, he,
And yet he had the intensity
To have published all to be a world's delight.

X

What other could so well have counselled us
In all lovely intricacies of a house
As he that practised or that understood
All work in metal or in wood,
In moulded plaster or in carven stone?
Soldier, scholar, horseman, he,
And all he did done perfectly
As though he had but that one trade alone.

XI

Some burn damp faggots, others may consume
The entire combustible world in one small room
As though dried straw, and if we turn about
The bare chimney is gone black out
Because the work had finished in that flare.
Soldier, scholar, horseman, he,
As 'twere all life's epitome.
What made us dream that he could comb grey hair?

XII

I had thought, seeing how bitter is that wind
That shakes the shutter, to have brought to mind
All those that manhood tried, or childhood loved
Or boyish intellect approved,
With some appropriate commentary on each;
Until imagination brought
A fitter welcome; but a thought
Of that late death took all my heart for speech.

AN IRISH AIRMAN FORESEES HIS DEATH

I know that I shall meet my fate
Somewhere among the clouds above;
Those that I fight I do not hate,
Those that I guard I do not love;
My country is Kiltartan Cross,
My countrymen Kiltartan's poor,
No likely end could bring them loss
Or leave them happier than before.
Nor law, nor duty bade me fight,
Nor public men, nor cheering crowds,
A lonely impulse of delight
Drove to this tumult in the clouds;
I balanced all, brought all to mind,
The years to come seemed waste of breath,
A waste of breath the years behind
In balance with this life, this death.

1   Yeats first visited Coole in 1897; he became a regular
    visitor in 1898 and a room above the library looking
    down to the lake was set aside especially for him.
2   Thoor Ballylee, which Yeats had purchased in March
    1917 perhaps with Iseult Gonne in mind. The Tower
    needed a considerable amount of repairs and it was
    nearly a year after his marriage to George Hyde-Lees in
    October 1917 that he was able to move in.

3   Yeats's friend from the Rymers' Club in the 1890s.
4   George Pollexfen (1839–1910), Yeats's maternal uncle.
    He was an accomplished jockey and had a strong interest
    in the occult, which he passed on to his nephew.
5   Philip Sidney (1554–86), the Elizabethan poet, soldier,
    and scholar, an example of Renaissance man.
6   Lady Gregory's childhood home nearby in County
    Galway.

W. B. YEATS
from W. B. Yeats, *Michael Robartes and the Dancer* (1921)

This poem, written in 1919, was Yeats's response to the profound disturbances then
taking place in world history, to what he later described as 'the growing murderousness
of the world'. The poem works at several different levels and can communicate before
it is fully understood. There are several interlocking themes or concerns: the occult,
neo-platonic ideas, and the relationship between Christianity and the occult; historical
cycles and human intervention in history; the Second Coming and modern history;
Nietzsche, heroes, and morality.

THE SECOND COMING

Turning and turning in the widening gyre[1]
The falcon cannot hear the falconer;
Things fall apart; the centre cannot hold;
Mere anarchy is loosed upon the world,

The blood-dimmed tide is loosed, and everywhere
The ceremony of innocence is drowned;
The best lack all conviction, while the worst
Are full of passionate intensity.

Surely some revelation is at hand;
Surely the Second Coming is at hand.
The Second Coming! Hardly are those words out
When a vast image out of *Spiritus Mundi*[2]
Troubles my sight: somewhere in sands of the desert
A shape with lion body and the head of a man,
A gaze blank and pitiless as the sun,
Is moving its slow thighs, while all about it
Reel shadows of the indignant desert birds.

The darkness drops again; but now I know
That twenty centuries of stony sleep
Were vexed to nightmare by a rocking cradle,
And what rough beast, its hour come round at last,
Slouches towards Bethlehem to be born?

1 Two interlocking spinning cones.
2 Latin: Soul of the world, a storehouse of images in the
  neo-platonic tradition for human beings to access.

EIMAR O'DUFFY
from Eimar O'Duffy, *The Wasted Island* (1919)

Eimar O'Duffy (1893–1935) was born in Dublin and educated at Stonyhurst in
Lancashire and at University College, Dublin. In March 1916 he was involved in an
attempt to prevent the Easter Rising and was sent to Belfast by Eoin MacNeill, the
leader of the Irish Volunteers, to try and quash the insurgency there. His first novel,
The Wasted Island, is a fictional re-creation and downbeat assessment of the years leading
up to the Easter Rising, his principal target, according to Alf MacLochlainn, being 'the
schemers who ... foisted an unwanted rebellion on the Irish Volunteers'. In this
passage towards the end of the book — one of the few moments in the novel of
heightened prose — Bernard Lascelles thinks of the waste brought about by the Rising.

Catastrophe

He was destitute of hope now and his only wish was
that death would come quickly and mercifully. He
closed his eyes, thinking of death as a pleasant restful
sinking into a warm velvet-like oblivion. He imagined
that he felt it coming to him and resigned himself to it
joyfully. But he was only falling asleep. In a short time
he was awake again, shivering with cold, and with a
throbbing pain in his head that made the pain in his
finger seem mild by contrast. He groaned in anguish
to find himself still alive. 'Buried alive!' a voice seemed
to say to him. 'Buried alive! Buried alive!': the terrible
words, beating rhythmically in his brain, made him
want to make another dash for freedom, but he found
himself too weak to rise. How his head ached! He
slept again; slept and woke alternately through several
shivering hours. While he slept he dreamed, and while
he lay awake his brain worked feverishly and
automatically. He could no more control his thoughts
than his dreams: both took possession of him and
made him their plaything. Soon he was unable to
distinguish between the dreams of his sleeping and

those of his waking, which became intermingled and
continuous like the strands of a thread or the threads of
a tangle.

He lived over again the events of the past month.
He saw Eugene fighting desperately for his life amid
fire and darkness: heard him calling for help: saw him
go down before a dozen bayonets and turn reproachful
eyes on himself standing by inactive. He saw scenes
from their life as boys: saw himself treating Eugene
always with scornful neglect: saw Eugene vainly
attempting to propitiate him and make friends: saw
again that reproachful look in his eyes. He felt himself
base, with a baseness of which he had never been
conscious before ... In the red fire-glow from his own
hearth he saw Willoughby as he had seen him their
last evening together. Then the hearth vanished and
the glow seemed to come from a burning village. He
found himself standing beside a grave in Picardy
feeling once more the flood of grief burst over him
with all the keenness of first realization.

He saw his early days of courtship with Mabel, but
they were no longer days of undiluted happiness.
Always they were strolling along a dark cedar-bordered

avenue and frequently quarrelling over some trifling difference. Then they would come round a curve and beyond it Janet would be standing, and she would say: '*I* wouldn't quarrel with you. Why did you hurt me?' Then he would start forward to go to her, but Mabel would hold him back, and Janet would disappear in the shadows. Afterwards he and Mabel would be walking together in the Dublin streets, and Musgrave's bestial face would appear out of a cloud of dust. Mabel would say: 'You like dust and all sorts of horrid things: so you can keep them,' and she would leave him and go over to Musgrave. Another time she was remonstrating with him for sacrificing their marriage to politics, and he was replying that politics was a sacred duty. Then appeared Austin Mallow[1] saying: 'Do you think we'll let ourselves be held back by you? Our minds are made up, and if you interfere we'll crush you without a thought.' And at that Mabel burst out laughing and said: 'So there's your lovely politics: and you'd sacrifice me for that!' Thereupon he showed her a picture of the island of his childish imagination, and opening his soul to her as he had never done in life unfolded to her all his hopes and projects; but at these she only laughed and said: 'That's not politics. It's only a dream.' 'Only a dream!' he replied. 'No, the world is a dream if you like, or rather a nightmare. These are the only realities.' But she merely laughed again, and in the midst of her laughter he awoke to the dark silence of the dungeon.

In this waking interval his thoughts reverted to the insurrection. What would be its results, he asked himself. What would be the fate of the rebels? Of his friends? Of himself? Death, he felt certain, would be meted out to the rebel leaders, and perhaps to the rank and file as well. He and his friends would be less fortunate: long sentences of penal servitude would be their fate: a dreary desolate prospect of wasted life sickening to contemplate. At that he gave way to a recrudescence of violent anger against the authors of the calamity and the things they had done to enforce their will. What had they achieved? In one mad week they had shattered the work of years: dead were some of the bravest hearts in Ireland: broken was the orderly, constructive, enthusiastic movement that was to have been built up until it had become the Irish nation. He gave himself up to vain regrets over his vanished hopes. And what of the future? Stephen's prophecy came back vividly to his memory. He saw the Irish people, helpless and leaderless, tortured and dragooned, and conscripted into the armies of the oppressor. He saw Ireland, plundered of wealth and manhood, lose sight at last of the light of freedom which till then had never been eclipsed. For if the

things that were done on Easter Eve can be repeated or defended, then there can be no more trust amongst Irishmen; and the country whose sons cannot trust one another can never be freed. So a despair blacker than his dungeon settled on Bernard's soul: despair for his country, despair for his friends, despair for himself. And out of his despair rose a hatred such as he had never felt before for the prime author of all these disasters: the great soulless enemy that had seized and tortured and wrecked his country and left it a wasted island of thwarted desire and lost endeavour. Over and over again, sleeping and waking, the same hatred, the same anger, the same regret, bitterness, and disillusionment turn and turn about haunted and racked his brain; over and over again the same dreams and visions flickered before his imagination, wove themselves into one vast pantomimic nightmare and left his mind a bewildered incoherent turbulence. Grinning faces made mock of him, harpies snatched feasts from him, policemen tore him from the altar just as he was about to place the wedding ring on Mabel's finger. He argued interminably with hosts of people that he knew about the same perpetual subject — Ireland and the war — tormented as much by his own fiery logic as by the stupidity of his opponents, and could never prevail. He stooped gigantically out of the clouds and watched fantastic battles raging in the island of his childish dreams. He saw the right and wrong in their quarrels with a god-like dispassionateness, and sought to intervene: vainly, for he was invisible to his pygmy creation and it was impalpable to him. Then the ten nations sprang out of the map as ten ugly little figures that came quarrelling to his feet and demanding judgment from him, which, when he gave it, they laughed to scorn and went on quarrelling. He saw Europe spread out before him like a map, with little grey lines of smoke, like the fume of a blown-out match, where the battles were: no sound, no sign of the conflict but this; but a vast and woeful wailing arose on all sides that assailed his ears in his ethereal altitude. He saw the whole world handed over to three demons wearing the faces of Sherringham, Tracy-Sidbotham,[2] and Musgrave. He saw the malevolent glee with which they took the sphere and rent it asunder and tossed it into a great fire. The fire leaped up all round him and he found himself standing in the witches' cauldron of Sackville Street; saw the city ringed round by hosts of demons led by the same infernal three. He stood in the middle of the street shouting denunciations at them, at which they shrieked with laughter. He argued and expostulated with them, and the demon whose face was Sherringham's cried: 'Of course you're right. That's why you're going to be crushed.' At that a perfect storm of hatred swept over him and he rushed headlong at the ring of ghastly faces, but even as he did so they vanished, and he found himself in a dark street gazing down on the corpse of the soldier he had killed. His eyes were fixed in a hideous stare, and even as Bernard looked into them the flame of life leaped in their depths. At that such terror came upon him as he had never experienced in life: a cold transfixing terror that paralysed every muscle in his body, glued his feet to the ground, and set every molecule in his brain in furious vibration: a freezing, devastating terror from which death itself would seem a safe and kindly refuge. He awoke with a shriek, only to plunge back again into a repetition, more tangled and fantastical than before, of the whole hideous delirium. In a few hours he went through an eternity of torment. He had lost all sense of time, all feeling of reality. Existence had become phantasmagorical.

His head ached excruciatingly and seemed ready to burst.

And then: *pitter-pitter-patter*: the scurrying of little feet. Rats? . . . Instantly he was frozen with horror. His heart stood still. A cold sweat broke forth on his brow. He felt his hair rising on his scalp. *Pitter-pitter-patter*. It was somewhere in the room, looking at him. It could see in the dark. *Pitter-pitter-patter*. Another? How many? . . . Frantically he realized his position, buried underground with this loathsome pattering horror. Shudder after shudder shook his frame. He remembered that he was weaponless, and tearing off one boot he staggered to his feet. The rats, frightened by the noise, scudded away, but he fancied they were assailing him. Their numbers sounded legion. . . . He shrieked with terror and fell . . .

In his debilitated condition the revival of a childish fear was enough to turn his mental balance, already weighted against sanity by sorrow, disillusionment, darkness and solitude. It was a madman that they found in the cell on Sunday morning — a piteous terror-distorted figure that cowered in a corner, beating the air with a boot.

1   A fictional portrait of Patrick Pearse, who is described elsewhere in the novel as a 'disease-worn fanatic'.
2   Bullies or rivals from Bernard's schooldays.

IRISH WRITING IN THE 1920s

Wherever one travelled in Ireland after Easter 1920, one saw roofless walls, stark and black, of burnt-out police barracks, loose casements rattling unheeded in the wind, sandbags piled still in the windows, through which the sky was seen, and steel, loop-holed sheeting, often twisted by fire, over friendless, deserted doors.

– Darrell Figgis, *Recollections of the Irish War* (1927)

For if the foundations of peace are ever to be laid, they will be grounded, not on Capital, nor in the chancelleries that voice Capital, nor in the wars that Capital creates, nor in the Empires expanded by Capital in its search for the raw material of men and goods, but in the Child, and the child-like of heart, in the family, and in the Social State of little nations.

– Darrell Figgis in Introduction to Seamus Burke, *The Foundations of Peace* (1920)

The future of a woman's paper in most countries is uncertain — in Ireland, at least, it is not doubtful, but the element of certainty means rather the certainty of despair and difficulty rather than the certainty of promise. Since 1912, that is for eight long and difficult years, half the time being consumed in a world war, the *Irish Citizen* has championed the cause of woman's emancipation. We began as a weekly, in 1916 became a monthly, and now, in order not to drop out entirely, we have decided to become a quarterly. Owing to increased prices of printing and postage, and owing to the extreme shortage of voluntary workers and writers for the paper, this step is necessary.

In Ireland at the present crisis we are in a state of war, and all the conditions prevailing in other countries during the late European war now apply at home. Just as then the woman's movement merged into the national movement, temporarily, at least, and women became patriots rather than feminists, and heroes' wives or widows rather than human beings, so now in Ireland the national struggle overshadows all else. We as women may sometimes regret that militarism in any form, native or foreign, has little use for women, but, however we may repine, we are compelled to acknowledge facts, even though we may hope that our cause may emerge from the struggle stronger, and reach in a few big strides the ground either partially lost or yet to be conquered. Meanwhile, we can but mark time. There can be no woman's paper without a woman's movement, without earnest and serious-minded women readers and thinkers — and these in Ireland have dwindled perceptibly of late, partly owing to the cause above mentioned, and partly because since a measure, however limited, of suffrage has been granted, women are forging out their own destiny in practical fields of endeavour.

We had recently the choice offered us of becoming the organ of a section (an important section, but yet a section) of women workers. But the experiment has not encouraged us to continue, because we feel we ought to be the organ of all women, not of a few. Then there became evident a tendency to make part of the paper a sort of 'Home Chat' affair, and that we regarded with disfavour. There are enough such papers for those who need them — the *Irish Citizen* has other interests to serve. We still believe that we have a mission and a message for Irishwomen as a purely feminist paper, and emboldened in that belief we shall carry on. It will be for our readers and supporters to help us by an increase of their support, so that when time and conditions permit we may return to our former strength.

Ask yourselves, dear readers, do I want the *Irish Citizen*? If the answer is in the affirmative, then write to us, contribute to the paper, talk about it to your friends, get us new subscribers, and make it your business to help to build up our little paper. Its life in the end depends upon each of you.

– H. S. S. (Hanna Sheehy Skeffington)
The Irish Citizen, September–December 1920

CRITICAL AND DOCUMENTARY

CONSTANCE MARKIEVICZ
from Esther Roper (ed.), *Prison Letters of Countess Markievicz* (1934)

For details on Constance Markievicz, see Yeats's 'Easter 1916' on page 271. Elected to the first Dáil Éireann (the Provisional Government considered illegal by the British Government), she was, like other ministers, the target of the British Authorities, and was eventually imprisoned in Mountjoy Gaol. In these letters to her sister Eva Gore-Booth she reveals another side to her revolutionary upper-class character.

MOUNTJOY PRISON,
DUBLIN,
December 6, 1920.

Darling, — I was delighted to get yours and paper *re* prison reform. Like most things, of course, the man who is able to start it and carry it out is the one indispensable factor, and such men are rare. Under the present system of making such appointments, it would be very unlikely that such a man would ever get the job.

You are quite right when you say things are lurid here! The Croke Park affair[1] lasted twenty minutes by my watch and there were machine-guns going. It felt like being back in the middle of Easter Week. Croke Park is quite close. It's a miracle that so few were killed.

I haven't given up the Bolshies yet: I believe that they will greatly improve conditions for the world. Of course, I agree with you in disliking the autocracy of any class, but surely if they have the sense to organize education, they can abolish class. While they are menaced by the moneyed classes of the whole world their only hope lies in the success of a strong central government: a tyranny in fact, but once the pressure is relieved, Lenin survives, and he has not lost his original ideals, we may hope. Of course, they may go mad with the idea of Empire, and go out with their armies to force the world to come under their ideas and do awful things in the name of freedom, small nationalities, etc., but even so, they have done something. The French Revolution gave France new life, though all their fine ideas ended in horrors and bloodshed and wars. The world, too, gained. Nothing else would have given courage to the underdog and put fear into the heart of the oppressor in the way it did.

I believe all the reforms at the beginning of the nineteenth century have their roots in the Terror.

I don't agree about people being sheep. I don't find

that here, except among a very small crowd indeed. Everyone wants to know, and reads and thinks and talks — especially the young. In Belfast you have the other thing — but the rest of the country is wonderfully self-controlled, patient and heroic. I have always used my influence towards decentralization, and to make people think and act independently.

How are the women doing in Italy?[2] This is being an education to them here. Their heroism and spirit of self-sacrifice is wonderful, but outside the towns they want their initiative faculties developing. There has been less physical restraint on the actions of women in Ireland than in any other country, but mentally the restrictions seem to me to be very oppressive. It is hard to understand why they took so little interest in politics as a sex, when you consider that both Catholics and Dissenters (men) laboured under all their disabilities and yet remained politicians.

I am so glad you are staying on in the sun. Do look after yourself, and whatever happens, *don't come over here.* You are *too like me* to go about safely. I loved your long letter. Any foreign gossip is interesting. You must be lonely without Esther.

'Pending Sentence.'

MOUNTJOY PRISON,
DUBLIN,
December 8, 1920.

Dearest Old Darling, — D.'s address is: Glendalough House, Annamoe, Co. Wicklow. How I would love you to see it! It's tucked away amongst the hills and lakes, behind a little village. A low, straggling house of grey stone with a porch — quite unlike the usual kind of Irish house. Some of the windows open up on the lawn, which is a steep slope down. You go up a lot of steps into the Hall, and there are lovely fir trees and woods behind the house. You climb up on to the Moor in a few minutes and look across the mountain tops. In front, the ground slopes to a mountain torrent. The place is a sun-trap, in the midst of the bleakest mountain scenery.

I was awfully interested in your bit about prisons, and I am sending you a bit of the *Irish Times* in exchange. I wonder if you'll get it. They see danger in the most extraordinary things these days.

Norah Connolly[3] has been to see me and she is full of Russian news. Glowing accounts as to organization of railways and industries, in face of almost insuperable difficulties: but says they are terribly ruthless to anyone who is 'an enemy of the Republic'. I hope they won't treat Lenin as the French treated Danton!

Do you remember my talking to you about my 'special' work, and all my difficulties and doubts? Well — I got it so under way that it goes on just as well without me. That wasn't too bad work for an untrained fool, was it?

I suppose now that I can tell you that I was tried by court-martial for 'conspiracy', and that the 'conspiracy' was the Boy Scouts![4] They have not made up their minds just what they'll do with me. I think they dislike me more than most. The whole thing is Gilbertian,[5] for we have carried on for eleven years. Anyhow, it's a fresh 'ad.' for the boys!

I am now working hard at Irish. It's awfully interesting. There are such an extraordinary number of shades of sound in it. The people must have had wonderfully subtle musical ears. I wonder how much of the history of a race lies in the language.

'Pending Sentence.'   MOUNTJOY PRISON,
DUBLIN,
December 11, 1920.

Dearest Old Darling, — Your almanack has just come. It is a joy to see all that lovely colour in the midst of this greyness. To appreciate colour, one wants to do without it for a bit.

I am so sorry that you are ill and I wish to goodness that I was with you. I learnt a lot about minding the sick when I had my two invalids in Holloway Jail,[6] and I didn't make a bad hand at it at all, in spite of the many disadvantages I was born with.

Don't bother about me here. As you know, the English ideal of modern civilization always galled me. Endless relays of exquisite food and the eternal changing of costume bored me always to tears and I prefer my own to so many people's company. To make 'conversation' to a bore through a long dinner-party is the climax of dullness. I don't mind hard beds or simple food: none of what you might call the 'externals' worry me. I have my health and I can always find a way to give my dreams a living form. So I sit and dream and build up a world of birds and butterflies and flowers from the sheen in a dew-drop or the flash of a sea-gull's wing. Everyone who has anything to do with me is considerate and kind, and the only bore is being locked up, when there is so much to be done.

I have just read the lives of Tolstoi and of Danton. I rather love the latter. The former I don't pretend to understand. He was so unbalanced, and he compromised with all his principles — like an English Trades Union leader. I am now reading *Eothen*.[7] What an oddity Lady H. Stanhope was!

Jail is the only place where one gets time to read.

I am interested in what you say about Italy. It has gone through such vicissitudes that one feels it must have learnt a good deal. Co-operation is good, but by no means a panacea. The old problem always remains: how to prevent all the money and power, etc., getting into the hands of a few, and they establishing themselves as a ruling tyrant class.

I am beginning to believe that everything must begin from the schools, and that only when all children of a nation have the same education will they have the same chances in life and learn to look after the people as a whole. Of course, education will have to be different, but now, in *England*, a few are trained to bully and rule, and the mass is brought up and educated to be fit only to be slaves. In Ireland we are not so bad, as local and family history educates the children, so our minds are more receptive and more free.

Now I've written you a long letter of rubbish and I have come to the end of my paper.

'Pending Sentence.'   MOUNTJOY PRISON,
DUBLIN,
December 15, 1920.

Dearest Old Darling, — I do wonder how you are and whether you are being looked after properly in Bordighera. I wonder where Esther is lecturing and on what. I should love to hear her.

I suppose you saw all about Cork[8] — also the explanations! It was so silly to assert that the City Hall caught fire from Patrick St. I know the city well, and a broad river and many streets lie between the two areas. An ordinary human being like myself is puzzled when the cleverest liars in the world state things that are so easily contradicted. The extraordinary policy of lying and perjury surprises me anew every day. I'd no idea people were so bad.

Italy seems to be rather lively still. I hope you won't come in for trouble. Greece makes me laugh — also Armenia. I think that they must at last have realized the capacity for lying on the part of Western politicians. I have had first-hand news of Russia. They have had a terrible lot to contend with, but they have done some wonderful reconstructive work. Of course they, the workers, were horrified with the number of executions, and thought them horribly cruel and drastic, but, comparing them to the French Terror, said that these were just, according to their own laws, and said that accusations had to be proved, and were proved, quite honestly; but that anyone proved to be acting against the interest of the new regime was remorselessly executed. Nothing approaching the orgies of appalling murders that Robespierre indulged in has occurred, although the circumstances, in many respects, are similar.

India seems to be getting pretty warm too. I see that volunteers have been 'proclaimed', according to the papers, and they don't do that for nothing. Ours were only proclaimed about a year and three months ago.

How one longs for peace! The old League of Nations is talking pompous rubbish (for the benefit of Democracy, I suppose) about the reduction of armaments, and each one of them is only intent to find out what his neighbour is going to do in the way of navies, etc., and tip his boss to go one better.

Tell me, do the Italians go in for polished brown leather boots and gaiters? The legs of the English Army of Occupation were one of the things that struck me at my court-martial. Such a lot of time must be wasted polishing them!

1 On 21 November 1920 in retaliation for the murder of fourteen Counter-Intelligence Service agents, a decision was taken to fire on a crowd at a football match in Croke Park in Dublin, which resulted in the death of twelve people and sixty wounded.
2 Eva was in Florence and the Italian riviera that autumn.
3 Wife of James Connolly, executed in May 1916.
4 Constance founded the Irish movement in 1909.
5 Ridiculous. From W.S. Gilbert (1836–1911), librettist of the Gilbert and Sullivan operas.
6 A women's prison in north London. Constance spent three Christmases in prison in 1916–18.
7 A travel book about Egypt and the Near East by Alexander William Kinglake (1809–91), published in 1844.
8 This is a reference to fires which burned part of Cork City on the night of 11 December 1920. It was unclear at the time who was responsible for the fires, the British Authorities blaming the local citizens, Corkonians blaming the Black-and-Tans as a reprisal for an ambush that took place that day outside Cork. For further details see Dorothy Macardle, *The Irish Republic* (1937). Michael Collins knew the burnings were a reprisal for the ambush at Kilmichael by Tom Barry and his flying column. See Tim Pat Coogan, *Michael Collins* (1990).

MICHAEL COLLINS
from Michael Collins, *The Path to Freedom* (1922)

Michael Collins (1890–1922), revolutionary soldier, helped negotiate the Anglo-Irish Treaty of 6 December 1921, was chairman of the Provisional Government, then Commander-in-Chief of Government forces after the outbreak of the Civil War in June 1922. He was killed in an ambush on 22 August 1922. *The Path to Freedom* was published after his death and contained his political beliefs for the new Ireland. You might want to compare this extract with the following article by George Russell. The emphasis on the healing properties of 'internal life' and 'spiritual life' is a reminder of the trauma that affected Ireland in the wake of the War of Independence and the Civil War.

Distinctive Culture

Our internal life too has become the expression of the misfit of English civilization. With all their natural intelligence, the horizon of many of our people has become bounded by the daily newspaper, the public-house, and the racecourse. English civilization made us into the stage Irishman, hardly a caricature.

They destroyed our language, all but destroyed it, and in giving us their own they cursed us so that we have become its slaves. Its words seem with us almost an end in themselves, and not as they should be, the medium for expressing our thoughts.

We have now won the first victory. We have secured the departure of the enemy who imposed upon us that by which we were debased, and by means of which he kept us in subjection. We only succeeded after we had begun to get back our Irish ways, after we had made a serious effort to speak our own language, after we had striven again to govern ourselves. We can only keep out the enemy, and all other enemies, by completing that task.

We are now free in name. The extent to which we become free in fact and secure our freedom will be the extent to which we become Gaels again. It is a hard task. The machine of the British armed force, which tried to crush us, we could see with our physical eyes. We could touch it. We could put our physical strength against it. We could see their agents in uniform and under arms. We could see their tanks and armoured cars.

But the spiritual machine which has been mutilating us, destroying our customs, and our independent life, is not so easy to discern. We have to seek it out with the eyes of our minds. We have to put against it the whole weight of our united spiritual strength. And it has become so familiar, how are we to recognize it?

We cannot, perhaps. But we can do something else. We can replace it. We can fill our minds with Gaelic ideas, and our lives with Gaelic customs, until there is no room for any other.

It is not any international association of our nation with the British nations which is going to hinder us in that task. It lies in our own hands. Upon us will rest the praise or blame of the real freedom we make for ourselves or the absence of it.

The survival of some connection with our former enemy, since it has no power to chain us, should act as a useful irritant. It should be a continual reminder of how near we came to being, indeed, a British nation. No one now has any power to make us that but ourselves alone.

We have to build up a new civilization on the foundations of the old. And it is not the leaders of the Irish people who can do it for the people. They can but point the way. They can but do their best to establish a reign of justice and of law and order which will enable the people to do it for themselves.

It is not to political leaders our people must look, but to themselves. Leaders are but individuals, and individuals are imperfect, liable to error and weakness. The strength of the nation will be the strength of the spirit of the whole people. We must have a political, economic, and social system in accordance with our national character.

It must be a system in which our material, intellectual, and spiritual needs and tastes will find expression and satisfaction. We shall then grow to be in ourselves and in what we produce, and in the villages, towns, and cities in which we live, and in our homes, an expression of the light which is within us, as now we are in nearly all those things an indication of the darkness which has enveloped us for so long.

Economically we must be democratic, as in the past. The right of all the people must be secure. The people must become again 'the guardians of their law and of their land'. Each must be free to reap the full reward of his labour. Monopoly must not be allowed to deprive anyone of that right.

Neither, through the existence of monopoly, must capital be allowed to be an evil. It must not be allowed to draw away all the fruits of labour to itself. It must fulfil its proper function of being the means by which are brought forth fresh and fuller fruits for the benefit of all.

With real democracy in our economic life, country districts would become again living centres. The people would again be co-operating in industry, and co-operating and competing in pleasure and in culture. Our countrysides would cease to be the torpid deserts they are now, giving the means of existence and nothing more.

Our Government must be democratic in more than in name. It must be the expression of the people's wishes. It must carry out for them all, and only, what is needed to be done for the people as a whole. It must not interfere with what the people can do for themselves in their own centres. We must not have State Departments headed by a politician whose only qualification is that he has climbed to a certain rung in the political ladder.

The biggest task will be the restoration of the language. How can we express our most subtle thoughts and finest feelings in a foreign tongue? Irish will scarcely be our language in this generation, not even perhaps in the next. But until we have it again on our tongues and in our minds we are not free, and we will produce no immortal literature.

Our music and our art and literature must be in the lives of the people themselves, not as in England, the luxury of the few. England has produced some historians, many great poets, and a few great artists, but they are the treasures of the cultured minority and have no place in the lives of the main body of the English people.

Our poets and artists will be inspired in the stimulating air of freedom to be something more than the mere producers of verse and painters of pictures. They will teach us, by their vision, the noble race we may become, expressed in their poetry and their pictures. They will inspire us to live as Irish men and Irish women should. They have to show us the way, and the people will then in their turn become the inspiration of the poets and artists of the future Gaelic Ireland.

Our civilization will be glorious or the reverse, according to the character of the people. And the work we produce will be the expression of what we are. Our external life has become the expression of all we have been deprived of — something shapeless, ugly, without native life. But the spark of native life is still there and can be fanned into flame.

What we have before us is the great work of building up our nation. No soft road — a hard road, but inspiring and exalting. Irish art and Irish customs must be revived, and must be carried out by the people themselves, helped by a central Government, not controlled and managed by it; helped by departments of music, art, national painting, etc., with local centres connected with them.

GEORGE RUSSELL (Æ)
from *Studies: An Irish Quarterly Review*, March 1923

Here is Russell's sober assessment of the new Ireland that emerged after the revolutionary period from 1916 until 1923: 'The mass of the people in the country continue to think as they did before the revolution.'

Lessons of a Revolution

I have found few people in Ireland deeply concerned about the ethics of civil war or revolution. The majority accept the principle that it is lawful to use physical force in support of high ideals. Their questioning is about the justice of the cause; and, if that be admitted, they seem to think the right to use physical force to secure its triumph follows in logical and unquestionable sequence. I will not discuss the morality of civil war or revolution. I remember a man, tired of ideal ethics, who cried out at a meeting many years ago: 'Let us hear no more of the good man or the bad man. Let us speak of the wise man and the foolish man.' I am like that man. I desire to question the wisdom of a policy rather than discuss the original rightness of a cause.

A policy is wise if, in operation, it secures the triumph of the ideal. It is unwise if, in destroying opposition, it does not at the same time establish in the hearts of men the lovable and desirable life for which the struggle was begun. I think few disinterested thinkers dispute the moral justice of the ideals of the Russian revolutionaries who desired to bring about such a control and use of the natural resources of their country that none would be poor or hungry or neglected. Was the policy adopted wise as

the ideal was right? Did it succeed? Could it have succeeded even if there was no blockade or foreign intervention? Lenin and Bukharin have learned wisdom. They confess to great errors. Where lay the unwisdom?

Bukharin says it lay in this, that they provoked a revolution without the technical competence to realize their ideal. On the plane of physical force they won. On the intellectual plane they were defeated. Bukharin admits that, to save the economic situation, they had to restore the control of industry to the enemies of the revolution. Intellect, science, administrative ability could not be improvised, being evolutionary products. The revolutionaries now fall back on evolution and declare their hope lies in education. They begin again in the neglected sphere of culture.

The Irish revolution, which began in Easter Week, has also triumphed solely in externals. Our spiritual, cultural, and intellectual life has not changed for the better. If anything, it has retrograded. Nothing beautiful in the mind has found freer development. In so far as anything is done efficiently, it is done by administrators, educationists, officials and guiders of industry, who maintain, so far as permitted by circumstances, the habits engendered before the war for independence. The Anglicization of the Irish mind remains unaffected. The Gaelic movement was the one movement in Ireland with a truly national character. It began its work in the soul, not on the body. It inspired a few heroes to fight; but the transfer of energy to the plane of physical conflict weakened it; and now, when there is theoretical possibility of a Gaelic State, there are not Gaels in numbers and intellect competent to take control. The mass of people in the country continue to think as they did before the revolution.

If the Republicans[1] succeeded in establishing a republic, the country would be as Anglicized as ever, because the Republic, no more than the Free State, could improvise culture, experience, intellect or administrative ability. It is practically certain that after a period of muddle — for their leaders have even less administrative experience than the Free State politicals — they would be forced like the Russians to fall back on the technical competents of the old order to prevent chaos. The Gaelic State cannot be established unless there are Gaels in multitude to administer it. The momentum of the old order carries us along in Ireland, hardly deflected a hair's breadth from the old cultural lines. It would carry us along despite the legal establishment of a republic — a purely external thing — just as that human momentum ignored the legal establishment of a Free State.

Inevitably also, after a victory brought about by the wreckage of the economic life of the people, the pre-occupation of all with the work of material reconstruction would thrust all spiritual and cultural ideals out of sight. It would give people a sense of nausea to have them discussed. The moods by which high spiritual, political or cultural ideals are appreciated are engendered in times of peace. The Free State came into being with popular feeling stagnant. Why was this? Seven years of sensation had dulled the heart and made it insensitive. If a Republic were proclaimed in Ireland next year or the year after, would there be any more exultation? I think not. Another year or two of civil conflict and the heart would have been unhappy so long that it would have become fixed in sadness. The citizens would gaze with the same apathetic dullness on Republican deputies going to Dail meetings that they now display when deputies attend the Free State assembly.

A deep mistrust exists in Ireland about the wisdom, character and intelligence of its politicals. As regards some of them this mistrust is, I believe, unjustified. In other times, these men might have won the rightly-placed confidence of the people; but they cannot, and it is not their fault, win affection or excite enthusiasm in seared and cynical hearts. Our over-long employment of physical force has prohibited the spiritual genius from manifestation among the people. It has almost become atrophied from disuse. The triumph of spiritual or cultural ideals cannot be brought about by physical force, but only by labours of the imagination and intellect. We have not laboured long enough in that field, and this is the cause of our failure in Ireland, of the moral depression, and why we seem immeasurably more distant from a spiritual nationalism than we were in 1914. We would not use the intelligence with which nature had so abundantly endowed us. We hated reading and thinking, like the old Turks. How many bookshops are there outside Dublin, Cork, and a few other towns? We have set up the machinery of self-government. The body is fashioned, but the Gaelic soul is incapable of functioning.

The champions of physical force have, I am sure, without intent, poisoned the soul of Ireland. All that was exquisite and lovable is dying. They have squandered a spirit created by poets, scholars and patriots of a different order, spending the treasure lavishly as militarists in all lands do, thinking little of what they squander save that it gives a transitory gilding to their propaganda. With what terrible images have they not populated the Irish soul as substitutes for that lovable life! The very children in the streets play at assassination, ambush and robbery. Manhood maintains in new forms the spirit of the games of youth. What future lies before the present generation? Modern psychology, after long years of research and experiment, has come to attach the utmost importance to the images in the mind. Once an image is implanted, an energy latent in the being operates through the image, as the earth gives energy to whatever seed may be flung in the clay. If these are images of health, the energy works through the image and the body becomes as the mind. If these are images of despair, the body itself grows listless. But if the images are of assassination and destruction, what follows? Thoughts and moods breed true to type, as do birds and beasts and fishes.

Where is it to end? If it be lawful for a section of the people, simply because they hold their ideal to be the highest, to use force to impose that ideal on the rest, every other group may consider itself justified in following the precedent. Why should not the proletarians in Ireland, suffering far more than middle-class nationalism has ever suffered under British rule, also use physical force to upset a social order which has never brought them physical plenty or intellectual life? Why should not Catholics or Protestants, holding sincerely to the truth of their religion, make war on those who differ from them to prevent injury to immortal souls — surely worse than injury to bodies? I could name a dozen causes all of which could be made to appear as shining in the sight of Heaven and humanity as the political idealism which is now wrecking Ireland. If politicians refuse the democratic solution of our troubles, if they insist on force, we will have proletarian wars and religious wars. Does not recent history show how easy it would be to excite such passions, how ready they are to flare up with an accompaniment of burning houses? The end of it all would be that the most ruthless militarism would conquer; and how long might it be before the tiniest flower of the soul could push up through that ice to begin a new spring in the heart?

We can establish Irish nationality only by building in the heart and the imagination. When we fight we level life to that of the primitive savage, before the imagination had built up the high poetry, arts, architecture and sciences which make civilization and distinguish race from race. We extinguish national characteristics, for there is no difference between killers in any country. They are all beasts for the time being — Russians, Germans, French, English, Irish — all the same. It is easy for a nation to break with its past in a few tragic years. The Great Famine made such a break in Irish life. The heart was too dead to grow its flowers, and beautiful traditions and customs withered with human life out of memory. The civil conflict which is devastating Ireland, if it does not end speedily, will part us from what was saved of lovable national life and character. In the Apocalypse, a spirit blows a trumpet, and a third part of life perishes. Another trumpet is blown, and the waters of life turn bitter and men die because of the bitterness. These images might stand for the tragedy which is past, and for the tragedy which is to come.

I cannot understand the faith of those who act on the belief that a nation is immortal and can survive any strain. Nations are no more immortal than individuals. The dust of the desert is over great cities whose inhabitants loved their country with no less a passion than Irish nationalists have loved theirs. Earth is dense with traditions of perished nationalities. If a nation is like a dissolute youth who impairs his vitality by excesses, it will perish as surely and by as inexorable a law of life as the debauchee. There comes a point where recovery is impossible. Something — a skeleton or larva — may survive, but not the nation with confident genius. There will always be herdsmen to look after the bullocks; but the genius of the Gael, if this conflict continues for much longer, will have vanished from its place of birth. The curious in psychology may seek to trace a flash of character here and there in some state of the new world to a possible Gaelic ancestry —

a phrase,

As in wild earth a Grecian vase.[2]

1   Those who took de Valera's side in the Civil War in 1922–23 against the Free State forces. The Republicans wanted a 32-county Ireland and no oath of allegiance to the Crown; the Free State Government, which had negotiated the Treaty with the British Government, accepted jurisdiction over 26 counties pending a Boundary Review.
2   Lines from Padraic Colum's poem 'A Poor Scholar of the Forties', first published in *Wild Earth* (1907). 'What good to us your wisdom store, / Your Latin verse, your Grecian lore?' This poem is reproduced — under a different title — on p. 117.

DANIEL CORKERY
from Daniel Corkery, *The Hidden Ireland: A Study of Gaelic Munster in the Eighteenth Century* (1924)

Here is a classic description by Daniel Corkery (1878–1964) of the *Aisling* or Jacobite visionary poem developed in Munster in the eighteenth century. Corkery shared D. P. Moran's view of Irish Ireland (see p. 31 above). In his influential critical works — *The Hidden Ireland* and *Synge and Anglo-Irish Literature* (1931) — Corkery focused on the distinguishing characteristics of Gaelic culture and on the essential link between the land and the people. Corkery's suggestive title — *The Hidden Ireland* — has a wider resonance in modern Irish writing and is worth pondering.

The Aisling

It was first the bardic schools of the previous centuries and then the Courts of Poetry, into which they declined, that had fixed the culture both of big house and cabin in the more Irish parts of the country in the eighteenth century: it was, therefore, not unnecessary to dwell a little on those institutions, since we will soon find ourselves in the presence of poets whose work is to be fully understood only in the light of that culture. That, perhaps, is the best word to use; for the literary tradition was still so strong that, in spite of the depressing poverty and hopelessness, it produced, or at least amazingly developed and perfected, a new genre in the literature. This new genre, the *Aisling*, or Vision poem, is the distinctive contribution of the period to the book of Irish literature: all the others were ancient, and had long since reached perfection. Not only was the literary tradition strong enough to do this, but it, at the same time, developed beyond what anyone could have dreamed of, the stressed metres in which those *Aisling* poems were written. The theme, as it grew, called for richer and richer music, and this it was given, lavishly, sumptuously, yet without vulgarity.

On its own account, then, the *Aisling* is worth lingering on; for in those *Aisling* poems we come on some of the best verse of the period; but it is still more worth lingering on inasmuch as in it we find intimate expression of the hidden life of the people among whom it flourished. Explicitly and implicitly it speaks to us, as with a golden mouth, of the Munster of those days.

I

Irish Ireland in the eighteenth century is not a hidden land to us merely because the older historians were either too ignorant or too disdainful to record its life: it was a hidden land in very fact. We have seen how the O'Connells[1] wished to avoid mention in Dr Smith's forthcoming account of Kerry. No more than they did the cabin-dwellers seek a place in the sun. A rush-light, and to be let alone, were all they asked. Their fathers, themselves, had suffered so much from the authorities and their laws, that an overlooked existence had now become for them a boon. This overlooked existence is to be felt in almost every poem they made for their own solacing. Those poems tell us that they were a people on whom the gates had closed. Their art-work consists of literature and music only — arts that require little or no gear. What Romain Rolland writes is surely true: 'One might even say that the plastic arts in general have need of luxury and leisure, of refined society and of a certain equilibrium in civilization in order to develop themselves fully. But when material conditions are harder, when life is bitter, starved and harassed with care, when the opportunity of outside development is withheld, then the spirit is forced back upon itself, and its external need of happiness drives it to other outlets: its expression of beauty is changed, and takes a less external character, and it seeks refuge in more intimate arts, such as poverty and music.'[2]

The mere fact, then, that the only arts they practised were poetry and music tells us that the gates were shut and the opportunity of outside development denied: and their manner of practising the arts they were confined to confirms this, if confirmation be required. In the glowing *Aisling* we find unwitting expression of the darkness that lay upon their life.

There is now no reckoning the number of *Aisling* poems written in that century. I dare to say that if we had the complete works of every Munster poet who lived at any time from the middle of the century to its close, we would find that every one of them wrote at least one such poem. Eoghan Ruadh Ó Súilleabháin[3] specialized in them; indeed, in this poet's district, Sliabh Luachra — roughly the border lands of Cork and Kerry towards Killarney — a young poet seeking admission to the brotherhood brought his *Aisling* in his hand: it was his thesis.

The *Aisling* poems were all written in stressed metres — that is, the most literary poems of the time were written in metres that the old bardic schools had despised as unliterary, if one may use such terms. The stressed metres of the untrained poets, of the wandering ballad-singers, had now displaced the syllabic metres of the bards, had become the recognized mode of the Courts of Poetry. As already hinted, these stressed metres attained their greatest development in the *Aisling* poems of the latter half of the century.

The word *Aisling* means vision; and the vision the poet always sees is the spirit of Ireland as a majestic and radiant maiden. This really is the essential feature in the *Aisling*. Of course, before the *Aisling* became recognized as a distinct genre, there were vision-poems in the language — many of them — in which the self-same spirit of Ireland appears and utters her distress and her hopes. Keating's[4] poem, 'Mo bhrón, mo cheótuirse cléibhe is croidhe' ('My sorrow, my gloomy weariness of breast and heart'), is an *Aisling* — as the editor of his poems very properly names it;[5] and the same poet's elegy on John Fitzgerald (died 1626) begins with a description of the sudden starting up of the singer, from a sleep that had overtaken him while wandering by the banks of the Slaney, to behold a gentle, bright, and timid maiden weeping silently in her distraction. In this case, however, the vision is not Erin, but Cliodhna — one of the queens of Irish faëry; in everything else this opening anticipates almost every *Aisling* poem that was to be written more than a hundred years later. When Piaras Feiritéir,[6] that gallant soldier-poet, was executed in 1653, some nameless singer made an elegy beginning: 'Do chonnac aisling ar maidin an lae ghil' ('I saw a vision on the morning of the bright day'). This vision is Erin bewailing the death of the man who had overthrown hundreds. In such poems, especially in those elegies where some such figure as Cliodhna or Erin bewails her dead, it seems to me we find the beginnings of the *Aisling* proper. The use of the word in the new technical sense may date from Aodhagán Ó Rathaille's[7] poem beginning, 'Aisling ghéar do dhearcas féin am leabaidh is mé go lagbhríoghach' (circ. 1700).

It was this poet Aodhagán Ó Rathaille, who first makes the Vision, the *Spéir-bhean* (literally, sky-woman), bewail the exile of the Pretender; it was this poet who, we may say, bound up the *Aisling* type of poem with the Jacobite cause. The *Aisling* proper is Jacobite poetry; and a typical example would run somewhat like this: The poet, weak with thinking on the woe that has overtaken the Gael, falls into a deep slumber. In his dreaming a figure of radiant beauty draws near. She is so bright, so stately, the poet imagines her one of the immortals. Is she Deirdre? or Gearnait? or is she Helen? or Venus? He questions her,

and learns that she is Erin; and her sorrow, he is told, is for her true mate who is in exile beyond the seas. This true mate is, according to the date of the composition, either the Old or the Young Pretender; and the poem ends with a promise of speedy redemption on the return of the King's son.

Now, nothing could be more unlike an *Aisling* poem, written by Eoghan Ruadh Ó Súilleabháin, say, than this meagre outline of the theme. And this we shall, perhaps, better realize, and realize also the true nature of the *Aisling* poems, if we compare these poems in general with the Jacobite poetry written in English about the same time.

1 In Chapter 1 Corkery tells the story of the visit of Dr Smith, the historian of Cork and Kerry, to the O'Connells of Derrynane. The O'Connells, an old Gaelic family, were anxious to remain unknown to the authorities for fear of losing their property which they had quietly enlarged.
2 Romain Rolland, *Some Musicians of Yesterday*. [AN]
3 Sometimes anglicized as Owen Roe O'Sullivan (1748–84), born in the Sliabh Luachra area of County Kerry.
4 Geoffrey Keating (*c*.1580–1644), Irish historian, author of *Foras Feasa ar Eirinn*, was also a considerable poet.
5 *Dánta Amhráin is Caointe Sheathrúin Céitinn*, edited by Eoin Mac Giolla Eáin, C.I. [AN]
6 Sometimes anglicized as Pierce Ferriter (?–1653).
7 Sometimes anglicized as Egan O'Rahilly (?1670–1729), born in the Sliabh Luachra area.

FRANCIS STUART and CECIL SALKELD
from *Tomorrow*, August 1924

With this striking editorial, reminiscent in its own way of Wyndham Lewis's *Blast* (1914), Francis Stuart (1902–99) and the Irish painter Cecil Salkeld announced themselves to the Irish bourgeois world. Stuart was husband of Iseult Gonne, Salkeld the son of the poet Blanaid Salkeld, but their joint initiative ended with the subsequent issue (which had to be printed in England because of censorship problems). However, their magazine made a mark for in its first issue there appeared a version of Yeats's 'Leda and the Swan' (reproduced below, p. 354). Stuart remained a controversial figure in Irish letters largely because of his stay in Berlin during the Second World War. Material from his semi-autobiographical novel *Black List Section H* (1971) is reproduced below, p. 850, as is his 1976 critique of contemporary Irish writing. See also the epigraph to the 1930s.

To All Artists and Writers

We are Catholics, but of the school of Pope Julius the Second and of the Medician Popes, who ordered Michaelangelo and Raphael to paint upon the walls of the Vatican, and upon the ceiling of the Sistine Chapel, the doctrine of the Platonic Academy of Florence, the reconciliation of Galilee and Parnassus. We proclaim Michaelangelo the most orthodox of men, because he set upon the tomb of Medici 'Dawn' and 'Night', vast forms shadowing the strength of antediluvian Patriarchs and the lust of the goat, the whole handiwork of God, even the abounding horn.

We proclaim that we can forgive the sinner, but abhor the atheist, and that we count among atheists bad writers and Bishops of all denominations. 'The Holy Spirit is an intellectual fountain', and did the Bishops believe that Holy Spirit would show itself in decoration and architecture, in daily manners and written style. What devout man can read the Pastorals of our Hierarchy without horror at a style rancid, coarse and vague, like that of the daily papers? We condemn the art and literature of modern Europe. No man can create, as did Shakespeare, Homer, Sophocles, who does not believe, with all his blood and nerve, that man's soul is immortal, for the evidence lies plain to all men that where that belief has declined, men have turned from creation to photography. We condemn, though not without sympathy, those who would escape from banal mechanism through technical investigation and experiment. We proclaim that these bring no escape, for new form comes from new subject matter, and new subject matter must flow from the human soul restored to all its courage, to all its audacity. We dismiss all demagogues and call back the soul to its ancient sovereignty, and declare that it can do whatever it please, being made, as antiquity affirmed, from the imperishable substance of the stars.

H. Stuart.
Cecil Salkeld.

W. B. YEATS
from *The Senate Speeches of W. B. Yeats* (ed. Donald R. Pearce) (1961)

Yeats was a Senator in the Upper Chamber of the new Free State from 1923 until 1928. Here in this famous speech advocating divorce he deliberately set his face against the new clericalism then in the ascendancy in the new Ireland. The Protestant people he enlists on his side include Swift, Burke, and Grattan from the eighteenth century, Emmet, the leader of an abortive Rising in 1802, and Parnell from the nineteenth century. It took another forty or fifty years for Yeats's 'iceberg' to melt.

Speech on Divorce (1925)

MR IRWIN: Is it in order for a Senator to read his speech?[1]

AN CATHAOIRLEACH:[2] It is not in order precisely, but very great latitude has been allowed always in regard to that. In fact, when dealing with a complicated question of this kind personally I think sometimes an advantage is derived from Senators sticking to their text. They are more likely to do that if they are reading from documents. I am bound to say in defence of the particular Senator that he is only reading, now and then, when quoting.

MR O'FARRELL: I think you, sir, might appeal to Senators to restrain their feelings even though they may not agree with what is said. We do not agree with it, but that is no reason why we should lose our heads.

AN CATHAOIRLEACH: Particularly so in the case of a distinguished Irishman like Senator Yeats.

DR YEATS: These are topics on which it is desirable that the use of words should be carefully weighed beforehand. That must be my excuse. It is just as much adultery according to that view as the remarriage of divorced persons is. Nor do I see why you should stop at that, for we teach in our schools and universities and print in our books many things which the Catholic Church does not approve of. Once you attempt legislation on religious grounds you open the way for every kind of intolerance and for every kind of religious persecution. I am not certain that there are not people in this country who would not urge you on to that course. I have nothing but respect for Most

Rev. Dr O'Donnell. I am told that he is a vigorous and able man, and I can say this for the speech from which I quoted, that if unwise in substance it was courteous in form. But what have I to say of the following extract from an article by Father Peter Finlay:—

> The refusal to legalize divorce is no denial of justice to any section of our people; it is no infringement of the fullest civil and religious liberty which our Constitution guarantees to all. As well say that prohibition of suttee is a denial of justice to the Hindu widow. The Hindu widow had a far clearer right to do herself to death on her husband's funeral pyre — her religion imposed it upon her as a duty — than any member of a Christian community can have to put away his wife and enter into a state of public legalized adultery. England acted justly, and in fulfilment of a plain and grave moral obligation, when she forbade suttee in India. The Irish Free State will act justly, and in fulfilment of a plain and grave moral obligation, in refusing to legalize absolute divorce and re-marriage among ourselves.

In a previous part of the essay he compares divorce with polygamy, robbery, and murder. I know little or nothing about Father Finlay's career. It may have been eminent and distinguished, but I am sure that very few members of this House will think with pleasure of following the guidance of a man who speaks with such monstrous discourtesy of a practice which has been adopted by the most civilized nations of the modern world — by Germany, England, America, France and Scandinavian countries. He must know that by every kind of statistics, by every standard except the narrowest, that those nations, because they so greatly exceed us in works, exceed us in virtue. Father Peter Finlay has been supported by an ecclesiastic of the Church of Ireland, the Bishop of Meath, who has even excelled him in invective. Perceiving, no doubt, that indissoluble marriage, which for the guilty party at least, he passionately desires, has in other countries made men and women exceedingly tolerant of certain forms of sexual immorality, he declares that every erring husband or erring wife should be treated as a robber, a forger, or a murderer. Now, there is one great difference between Father Finlay in his relation to this House and the Bishop of Meath. I think that Father Finlay may influence votes in this House, but I am sure that the Bishop of Meath has not influenced one. What is more, if the entire Protestant episcopacy in Ireland came out with a declaration on this subject, it would not influence a vote in this House. It is one of the glories of the Church in which I was born that

we have put our Bishops in their places in discussions requiring legislation. Even in those discussions involving legislation on matters of religion they count only according to their individual intelligence and knowledge. The rights of divorce, and many other rights, were won by the Protestant communities in the teeth of the most bitter opposition from their clergy. The living, changing, advancing human mind, sooner or later refuses to accept this legislation from men who base their ideas on the interpretation of doubtful texts in the Gospels. It is necessary to say, and I say it without fear of contradiction, that there is not a scholar of eminence in Europe today who considers that the Gospels are, in the strict sense of the words, historical documents. Their importance is devotional, not historical. For any ecclesiastic to advise statesmen to base legislation on a passage that may lack historical validity, is to appeal to the ignorance of the people. I am sure that the majority of those who favour the indissolubility of marriage, are under the impression that it preserves sexual morality in the country that adopts it. I think that before they are entirely certain on that point, they should study the morality of countries where marriage is indissoluble — Spain, Italy, and the South American nations. We are not proposing to take from those nations our economics, our agricultural or technical instruction, but we are proposing to take from them our marriage laws. Before doing so, I think it would be well to make some study of the effect of the marriage laws on those nations. I have gone to the authorities available, and I find that, on the whole, they have successfully suppressed much evidence of immorality. There are no reports in the newspapers of divorce proceedings. The usual number of children are born in wedlock, but I do find there is a great uncertainty as to the parentage of these children, but then, public opinion discourages curiosity on that subject, and it is a habit to discourage any inquiry into the emotional relations of men and women. Among modern communities there is a demand for happiness, which increases with education, and men and women who are held together against their will and reason soon cease to recognize any duty to one another.

You are going to have indissoluble marriage, but you are going to permit separation. You cannot help yourself there. You are going to permit young people who cannot live together, because of some intolerable wrong, to separate. You are going to invite men and women in the prime of life to accept for the rest of their existence the law of the cloisters. Do you think you are going to succeed in what the entire of Europe has failed to do for the last 2,000 years? Are you going to impose the law of the cloister on those young people? If not, you are not going to raise the morality of this country by indissoluble marriage. A great English judge, speaking out of the immensity of his experience, said that there is no cause of irregular sexual relations so potent as separation without the possibility of remarriage.

This is a question which I know to be exciting a good deal of interest. I know something of the opinions of those who will make the next generation in this country. I know it, perhaps, better than most of the members of this House, and I am going to give those young people, speaking from here, a piece of advice, though they are, perhaps, of a far less excitable temperament than I am. I urge them not to be unduly excited. There is no use quarrelling with icebergs in warm water. These questions will solve themselves. Father Peter Finlay and the Bishop of Meath will have their brief victory, but we can leave them to it.

I have said that this is a tolerant country, yet, remembering that we have in our principal streets certain monuments, I feel it necessary to say that it would be wiser if I had said this country is hesitating.

I have no doubt whatever that, when the iceberg melts it will become an exceedingly tolerant country. The monuments are on the whole encouraging. I am thinking of O'Connell, Parnell, and Nelson.[3] We never had any trouble about O'Connell. It was said about O'Connell, in his own day, that you could not throw a stick over a workhouse wall without hitting one of his children, but he believed in the indissolubility of marriage, and when he died his heart was very properly preserved in Rome. I am not quite sure whether it was in a bronze or marble urn, but it is there, and I have no doubt the art of that urn was as bad as the other art of the period. We had a good deal of trouble about Parnell when he married a woman who became thereby Mrs Parnell.

AN CATHAOIRLEACH: Do you not think we might leave the dead alone?

DR YEATS: I am passing on. I would hate to leave the dead alone. When that happened, I can remember the Irish Catholic Bishops coming out with a declaration that he had thereby doubted his offence. That is, fundamentally, the difference between us. In the opinion of every Irish Protestant gentleman in this country he did what was essential as a man of honour. Now you are going to make that essential act impossible and thereby affront an important minority of your countrymen. I am anxious to draw the attention of the Bishop of Meath to Nelson. There is a proposal to remove Nelson because he interferes with the traffic. Now, I would suggest to the Protestant Bishop of Meath that he should advocate the removal of Nelson on strictly moral grounds. We will then have the whole thing out, and discover whether the English people who teach the history of Nelson to their children, and hold it before the country as a patriotic ideal, or the Bishop of Meath represent, on the whole, public opinion. The Bishop of Meath would not, like his predecessors in Ireland eighty years ago, have given Nelson a pillar. He would have preferred to give him a gallows, because Nelson should have been either hanged or transported. I think I have not greatly wronged the dead in suggesting that we have in our midst three very salutary objects of meditation which may, perhaps, make us a little more tolerant.

I wish to close more seriously; this is a matter of very great seriousness. I think it is tragic that within three years of this country gaining its independence we should be discussing a measure which a minority of this nation considers to be grossly oppressive. I am proud to consider myself a typical man of that minority. We against whom you have done this thing are no petty people. We are one of the great stocks of Europe. We are the people of Burke; we are the people of Grattan; we are the people of Swift, the people of Emmet, the people of Parnell. We have created the most of the modern literature of this country. We have created the best of its political intelligence. Yet I do not altogether regret what has happened. I shall be able to find out, if not I, my children will be able to find out whether we have lost our stamina or not. You have defined our position and given us a popular following. If we have not lost our stamina then your victory will be brief, and your defeat final, and when it comes this nation may be transformed.

1 Owing to his defective eyesight, Yeats could not glance at his notes, but had to bring them directly to his right eye, which gave the impression of reading from his text. [AN]
2 Irish: Chairperson.
3 O'Connell, Parnell, Nelson: All have (or had in the case of Nelson until 1966) statues on O'Connell Street.

ANDREW E. MALONE
from *The Dublin Review*, July 1927

This is a conveniently short history of the Abbey Theatre by a critic who went on to
write *The Irish Drama 1896–1928* (1929).

The Coming of Age of the Irish Drama

The Abbey Theatre, Dublin, celebrated its twenty-first birthday on the 27th of December, 1925, and with that celebration the Irish Drama came of age. The theatre was opened to the public on the 27th of December, 1904, with a programme consisting of three one-act plays, two of them by Mr W.B. Yeats and one by Lady Gregory. It may be of some interest to note that on the same evening *Peter Pan* was staged for the first time in London, so that *Peter Pan* and the Irish Drama attained their majority simultaneously. Peter refused to grow up, but the Irish Drama has certainly grown and has contributed much that is of permanent worth to drama in the English language. Its first two programmes contained names that have since made history in the theatre, the names of W.B. Yeats, J.M. Synge, and Lady Gregory, and even if the Abbey Theatre had contributed nothing else to world-drama in the twenty-one years of its existence, these three names would suffice to give it a very high place in the dramatic history of its time. But it has contributed much more than these three names to the worth-while drama of its time, and it has contributed, in addition, some very remarkable acting to the stage of the English-speaking world. It has contributed a theory of acting which has done much to make the theatre a place where art and artists may be seen in combination, and it has aided very materially in bringing the drama back to literature and to life. It came into being at a very critical period in the history of contemporary drama, and its weight was thrown on the side of those who were striving in many lands to make drama an art in which there was space for brains. Of course, it has not always lived up to its own high ideals and high standards, but in its comparatively short history it has probably done more than any other theatre in the world to bring vitality into the drama and to bring the drama back into literature. No history of world-drama of the first quarter of the twentieth century can avoid giving the Irish Drama a very high, if not a dominating, position. For a little country of four millions of people this is surely a great and a notable achievement. It is all the more notable when it is remembered that before the twentieth century Ireland had no separate drama of its own.

Ireland has had a long and very distinguished connection with the drama of England. The names of such dramatists as Farquhar, Goldsmith, Sheridan, Wilde, and Shaw have only to be mentioned to make that fact obvious. It is, therefore, something of an anomaly that until the early years of the present century Ireland should not have had a drama that was distinctively national. Literature in the Irish language is often dramatic in its character, but it was never intended for presentation on the stage of a theatre. In fact, the first play in the Irish language[1] ever presented on the stage of the regular theatre was produced only in 1901 by the forerunner of the Abbey Theatre. Much of the literature in the Irish language is cast in dialogue form, and Irish folk-literature is as rich as that of any country in the world, but the very chequered history of Ireland during the centuries in which drama was being formed in Europe must be held accountable for the absence of an acted drama in Ireland. The Mysteries from which the English Drama evolved have no counterpart in Ireland, which is, perhaps, because the Guilds which produced such Mystery Plays were in Ireland dominatingly English in their membership. Against these facts may be placed some others. The tradition of the Bards lingered into the nineteenth century, keeping for the epic in Ireland the place that in other countries was taken by the drama, and that tradition preserved the individuality of the nation through the centuries of disorder. In the people there is a love of acting, as there is for oratory and fine-sounding words. In fact, it might be said that the Irish people are born actors; they can impress the world, whether the impression be worthy or the reverse. The Irishman delights in dialogue and repartee, and it is obvious that the best acting of modern English plays is to a disproportionate degree the work of Irishmen. For centuries it seemed that Irish dramatists could not produce drama in Ireland, and that they had to cross the Atlantic Ocean or the Irish Sea to find expression for their instinct for drama. It has been said that it was the mechanism of the stage that was the insurmountable obstacle to the 'dreamy Celt', but it seems more probable, in the light of recent history, that it was the absence of facilities and encouragement that for so long kept Irish authors from the stage in their own country. But it may be said: Dublin has a long and honourable history as a theatrical centre. This is so, but it was an English Dublin, a Dublin that was the capital of the English Pale, to which that record belongs. It was a Dublin which aped London and which looked to London for its drama. Dublin as the capital of a conscious, and self-conscious, Irish nation, is a comparatively new city, and it is from such national consciousness that drama, in common with other things, springs. During the greater part of the nineteenth century Ireland was interested only in its political status, and it was not until the downfall of Parnell that the mind of Ireland turned towards national culture. Then it was that the Irish theatre came into being.

It was in or about the year 1896 that Mr W.B. Yeats conceived the idea of an uncommercial theatre which would be at the same time literary and distinctively Irish. In England, France, Scandinavia, and Germany there were such theatres struggling to make the work of dramatists like Ibsen, Shaw, Strindberg and Hauptmann known to the theatre-going public. With the work of these theatres Mr Yeats was familiar, as one of his own plays had been produced by the Independent Theatre in London. His Irish project was not quite so elaborate as these experiments. It was simple to hire a small hall in Dublin for a short season every year and there produce plays of a literary and national character written by Irishmen. As Irish actors were assumed not to be available, it was arranged to bring actors from London. This project came into being under the title of 'The Irish Literary Theatre' in 1899, under the direction of W.B. Yeats, George Moore, Lady Gregory, and the late Edward Martyn. The play which was chosen to open the theatre was *The Countess Cathleen*, a play in verse by W.B. Yeats. The production of the play was greeted by an uproar, which has been many times equalled and once sur-passed in the years that have since elapsed. Suggestive propaganda was used unsparingly to influence the audiences against the play, though why it should have been used is now very difficult to understand. The play is based upon an ideal of self-sacrifice, against which it would now be thought impossible to find objection. The play has since become one of the most popular of Mr Yeats's plays, and a regular feature in the repertoire of the Abbey Theatre. During the following five years plays by Edward Martyn, Lady Gregory, George Moore, J.M. Synge, Padraic Colum, and others were produced with varying fortune and but little success.

Meanwhile a company of Irish amateur actors had been discovered by Mr George W. Russell (A.E.). It was called the 'Irish National Dramatic Company', and was being trained and directed by the brothers Frank and W.G. Fay. This company was amalgamated with the original group under the title 'Irish National Theatre Society', and provided with Irish actors the project of Mr Yeats. In the fusion the support of Edward Martyn was lost, but that of Mr George Russell (A.E.) was gained. To the brothers Fay, and to the company they collected, belongs the credit for giving to the Irish Theatre that unconventional, but natural, style of acting, which has been its distinguishing mark and which has made it famous throughout the world.

The company was still without a theatre, but that lack was shortly to be rectified. A visit by the company to London in the early part of 1904 brought its work under the notice of Miss A.E.F. Horniman, who shortly afterwards became very well known through her work at the Gaiety Theatre, Manchester, and has since been given the title Queen of Repertory by Mr Frank Vernon. Miss Horniman became so interested in the work of the Company that she provided it with a permanent home at the Abbey Theatre, and an annual subsidy for many years. The new home of the company had been made by combining an old music-hall, known as the Mechanics Theatre, with the city morgue; seating accommodation being provided for about 650 people. The right of the theatre to assume the title National has been challenged, quite a large number of people being of the opinion that it is neither Irish nor National. This section contends that such a title can be borne only by a Gaelic-speaking theatre, and such a theatre is now in its formative stages under the name of 'The Gaelic Drama League', giving frequent performances of plays in the Irish language and enjoying a small annual subsidy from the Government of the Irish Free State in common with the Abbey Theatre. The theatre thus had the distinction of being the first subsidized theatre in Great Britain or Ireland as it now has the distinction of being the only State-subsidized theatre in either island, as it receives an annual subsidy of £1,000 from the Free State Government.

The Abbey Theatre began as, and has always remained, a Repertory Theatre — that is, a theatre which is, in the words of Mr Frank Vernon, a 'permanent local theatre with a permanent company reviving good plays and producing good plays with a little more regard for their artistic values than for their immediate drawing power'. The Irish Theatre had also something more to accomplish; it had to create a National Drama. 'Our movement,' said Mr W.B. Yeats in 1902, 'is a return to the people, like the Russian movement of the early seventies, and the drama of society would but magnify a condition of life which the countryman and the artisan could but copy to their hurt. The play that is to give them a quite natural pleasure should tell them either of their own life, or of that life of poetry where every man can see his own image, because there alone does human nature escape from arbitrary conditions. Plays about drawing-rooms are written for the middle classes of great cities, for the classes who live in drawing-rooms; but if you would ennoble the man of the roads you must write about the roads, or about the people of romance, or about great historical people. We should, of course, play every kind of good play about Ireland that we can get, but romantic and historical plays, and plays about the life of artisans and country people are the best worth getting. In time, I think, we can make the poetical play a living dramatic form again, and the training our actors will get from plays of country life, with its unchanging outline, its abundant speech, its extravagance of thought, will help to establish a school of imaginative acting. . . . If we busy ourselves with poetry and the countryman, two things which have always mixed with one other in life as on the stage, we may recover, in the course of years, a lost art, which, being an imitation of nothing English, may bring our actors a secure fame and a sufficient livelihood.'[2] Since the opening of the Abbey Theatre everything that was in the mind of Mr Yeats when he wrote the words quoted has been realized. The repertoire of the Theatre has consisted in the main of plays dealing with the life of the artisan and the countryman, but it has also been rich in the poetic, the romantic, and the historical play. The plays which Mr Yeats himself contributed to the repertoire did much to bring back the verse play to the English-speaking stage. The plays of Lady Gregory brought the rural cottager on to the stage, and her folk-history plays gave the stage the great figures of Irish history as they are to the folk-mind. In John Millington Synge the Theatre had the greatest romantic comedy writer of modern times. Behind these three there is a long list of dramatists who used the life of the common people as the material for drama. There is Padraic Colum and Lennox Robinson, T.C. Murray and Lord Dunsany, St John Ervine and George Fitzmaurice, Seumas O'Kelly and Daniel Corkery, Brinsley MacNamara and Sean O'Casey, to name but a few of the dramatists whose plays have been conspicuous in the twenty-one years' record of the Theatre.

Since the opening of the Abbey Theatre the development of the drama has been rapid if not always consistent, and the development cannot be said to have been uninterrupted. The original company was dispersed in 1908 at the departure of the brothers Fay from Dublin. In 1910 Miss Horniman withdrew her subsidy, and the Theatre was compelled to become self-supporting, which it has since been, though that has been achieved only at some sacrifice of the ideals of its founders. New companies were formed, and they, too, in time succumbed to the allurements of New York or London; and a period of civil war was negotiated with no little difficulty. But the Theatre has survived all its vicissitudes, and is now the only survivor of the great days of the Repertory Theatre in England or in Ireland. But the Repertory Theatre is coming again in England; there are now Repertory Theatres in Liverpool, Birmingham, Norwich, Bristol, and many other English cities, and they are all modelled on the system of the Abbey Theatre in Dublin. The Repertory Theatre exists with the object of raising the standard of dramatic taste by giving the public a variety of good plays. It is the function of a Repertory Theatre to give facilities to local dramatists to portray the life of their own people, and to provide such local dramatists with the best models from the drama of the world. The Abbey Theatre has done all this. It has created a national drama, has raised the standard of public taste, has given audiences in Dublin opportunities of becoming familiar with masterpieces of world-drama, and has itself given to the world some masterpieces of drama and of acting. Its record is such that any theatre might be proud to own. During its twenty-one years the Abbey Theatre has produced two hundred and sixteen (216) plays by eighty-six authors. Nearly all the authors are Irish, and the large majority of the plays were produced for the first time on any stage. There were some revivals of old plays, and some translations from foreign dramatists were produced. Thus, the plays of Goldsmith and Sheridan figure in the list, as does Bernard Shaw with a dozen of his plays, including a first production of *The Shewing-up of Blanco Posnet*. Foreign drama is represented by such famous authors as Molière, Goldoni, Hauptmann, Sudermann, Strindberg, Ibsen, Maeterlinck, Tchechov, Evreinov, Sierra, and Mazaud. There is in Dublin a separate organization, The Dublin Drama League, which uses the Abbey Theatre for the production of foreign plays and plays which are considered outside the scope of the Theatre itself. This organization has produced plays by such dramatists as Toller, Andreev, Eugene O'Neill, and many others.

In 1903, while the company was still giving its performances in small halls in Dublin, there appeared among the playwrights the names of those who still dominate the Irish drama — W.B. Yeats, J.M. Synge, and Lady Gregory. That year also marked the advent of a young dramatist of great promise with the production of the first play by Padraic Colum. The great promise was, however, never fulfilled, and for many years Padraic Colum has resided in America, where he has published charming books for children, but no plays. The company had by this time established itself in the artistic life of the city, and with the introduction of the writers named, its character became definitely marked. Synge, Colum, and Lady Gregory made the 'peasant' play the speciality of the Theatre, and by the 'peasant' play it has gained its peculiar reputation. Until a few years ago very few plays dealing with the life in towns had been staged, and the Theatre came to have an exclusively rural atmosphere. This was strictly in accord with the ideals of Mr Yeats. It was also inevitable in the circumstances of Ireland, which is, even in its town life, very definitely a nation of peasants. Every aspect of rural life, and consequently the essentials of the national life, has been presented on the stage of the Abbey Theatre, often with a realism that verged upon the brutal. In 1907 the first play by George Fitzmaurice was produced. Somehow Fitzmaurice has failed to receive from the critics the attention that his work undoubtedly deserves. In 1908 the first plays of Lennox Robinson and Conal O'Riordan were produced. In 1909 the first play of Lord Dunsany was staged, and in 1910 came the first play by T.C. Murray. In 1911 St John Ervine made his first appearance on any stage. These names, with those of Seumas O'Kelly, Daniel Corkery, Brinsley MacNamara, and Sean O'Casey, constitute the more important section of the dramatists of the Abbey Theatre. The work of these dramatists accounts for more than half the number of the plays produced at the Theatre, and though the work of the remaining seventy-two dramatists is certainly not negligible, the bulk of it may be ignored without in any way depreciating the contribution of Irish dramatists to the world-drama of the twentieth century. Much of the work of the lesser dramatists consists of farce and melodrama, which is neither better nor worse than the same kind of theatrical fare in other countries.

The dramatists whose plays made the Theatre prominent have all now practically ceased to contribute to its repertoire. Synge has been dead since 1909, and only one of his plays, *The Tinker's Wedding*, remains to be produced at the Theatre. It may never be produced there, as its theme is considered to be likely to outrage the feelings of most Catholics. W.B. Yeats and Lady Gregory are still Directors of the Theatre, but it is not to be expected that anything startlingly new is likely to come from either of them in the future. Seumas O'Kelly also is dead, and Padraic Colum resides in America, and is part of the life of America, as St John Ervine and Conal O'Riordan are now part of the life of England. So the future would seem to rest with the group consisting of Lennox Robinson, T.C. Murray, George Fitzmaurice, Brinsley MacNamara, and Sean O'Casey, with possibly Lord Dunsany and Daniel Corkery. At the moment, Sean O'Casey is the great star of the Theatre, and certainly his advent is something in the nature of a Godsend after the long period of undistinguished plays which the Theatre has produced since the war. For some years little of any importance was seen on the Abbey stage, but it seems now, when the storms of politics have passed, that a revival of the great days are in prospect. Some are found to hail Sean O'Casey as the equal, if not greater, than Synge, but he has yet to prove himself equal to such distinguished comparison. Much good work may yet be expected from Lennox Robinson, who has been experimenting for some time, and whose *Crabbed Youth and Age* shows him to be a master of satirical comedy; from T.C. Murray, who has recently produced a fine play in *Autumn Fire*; from Brinsley MacNamara, who recently revealed himself as a master of rural comedy in *The Glorious Uncertainty* and *Look at the Heffernans!* The days of drab realism and the melodrama of lunacy have passed, and it is probable that satirical fantasy will form the staple of the Theatre for some time to come. How very wrong was St John Ervine when he wrote two years ago that Ireland had begun a renaissance of her own which 'speedily perished from lack of staying power'! After its twenty-one years the Irish drama is still as strong and vigorous as it was in the beginning.

At the special performance which was given to celebrate the coming-of-age of the Theatre the only thanks rendered were to 'the players, past and present'. The justice of this will be appreciated when it is remembered that the reputation of the Theatre was due as much to the acting as to the plays. The company, collected and trained by the brothers Fay, made the artistic reputation of the Theatre, and the company, of which Arthur Sinclair was the leader, made it a popular success. It is not too much to say that the acting at the Abbey Theatre has had a markedly improving effect upon the acting of the English-speaking world. The ranting and raving has given place to a naturalness which is the distinguishing mark of the Irish acting. 'More than others,' says C.E. Montague, 'they leave undone the things that ought not to be done. None of them rants or flares, trumpets or booms, or frisks about when he had better be quiet, or puts on intense looks for nothing. They seem all alike to have seized on the truth that the way to do big things in an art, as it is to get into other parts of the Kingdom of Heaven, is to become as a little child, so long as you do it without thinking all the time what an engaging child you are. Without infantilism they contrive to reach back past most of the futilities, the inexpressive apparatus of expression, that overgrow and clog the stage; they take a fresh, clear hold on their craft in its elements. They know how to let well alone; they stand still when others would "cross stage to right" to no purpose; when one of them has to be thrown up in high relief, the rest can fade into the background like mists at a dawn, or emit from their eyes an attention that fixes your eyes on the central figure more surely than the fiercest limelight that ever beat on an actor-manager. So each character is played, in a sense, by them all. . . . The actors give you the force of one character through its impression on others, as Homer expressed Helen's beauty through its effect on the aged men, and as Thackeray tells you what everyone did when Beatrix entered a playhouse.'[3] The personnel of the company has changed many times, but the character and the method of the acting have never changed. There have been variations in the quality of the acting, as might be expected, but on the whole the standard has been kept surprisingly high. Those who have seen Frank and W.G. Fay, Arthur Sinclair, J.M. Kerrigan, Fred O'Donovan, and J.A. O'Rourke, with Sara Allgood, Maire O'Neill, Maire NicShiubhlaigh, Cathleen Nesbitt, and Eileen O'Doherty, have seen some of the best acting this century has had. The present company has now reached the standard of the companies which preceded it. The acting of Miss Eileen Crowe, as Nora in *A Doll's House*, was a revelation of the resources which she can command. In Messrs M.J. Dolan and F.J. MacCormick are two actors which it would be difficult to equal, and in Barry Fitzgerald is a comedian of excellence, whose limitations as an actor are, however, easily reached. The quality of the plays and the quality of the acting are now equal to the best that the Theatre has had at any time in the past.

The plays and the acting have both received from the Directors the attention their importance deserve, and have received from critics and audiences the praise that they generally merited. There is one feature in the work of the Theatre which has received little, if any, attention, even from the Directors. That feature is staging and stage effects. Much has been written on this feature of the work of the Theatre by Mr Yeats, but beyond some experiments in the speaking of verse, and some very drab scenes by Mr Gordon Craig, nothing has yet been done to improve the art of stage

production. To the art of the theatre, as distinct from the arts of playwriting and acting, the Abbey Theatre has contributed nothing. Poverty, perhaps, is the cause of this. But when the wonderful effects of, say, the Lyric Theatre at Hammersmith, London, are borne in mind, achieved as they were by artistic instinct rather than by lavish expenditure of money, the failure of the Abbey is most marked. It is true to say that the Lyric Theatre has done more for the art of production in one year than the Abbey Theatre has done in its entire career. The absence of a producer, a 'man of the theatre', is very pronounced at the Abbey. At present three of its Directors are dramatists, the fourth is a professor of languages, added to the Directorate last year, with the subsidy from the Government of the Irish Free State. Throughout its career the Theatre has been under the direction of dramatists; never has it had the services of men like Sir Barry Jackson or Mr Nigel Playfair to attend to the production and staging of plays. So the staging has lacked distinction, it has often had the appearance of mere casualness. It is probable that this branch of theatrical work will receive more attention in the future as the financial position of the Theatre is strengthened.

To everyone interested in the theatre and the development of drama the Abbey Theatre presents a model and an inspiration. It has survived its period of experiment and of political stress, and is now secure for the future. Its repertory system has proven its worth by giving to Ireland a national drama which is worthy of the attention of the world. It has made drama possible to Irishmen at home, and has produced dramatists and actors of whom the world has taken note. Before Mr Yeats created his dream in the reality of the Abbey Theatre, Ireland had no place in the history of drama; now that has been so changed that every book on drama has a section devoted to Ireland. To all who have ideas for the development of folk-drama, too, the Abbey Theatre offers a model and a repertoire of plays that is unequalled elsewhere. Every community has its possibilities for the dramatist, but every region does not tempt the commercial theatre, and if regional drama is to be given the opportunities that its importance deserves, only the method of the Abbey Theatre, and the repertory system, will be available for guidance and inspiration. Efforts are being made in the United States, and in many parts of Great Britain, to foster national or local drama, and these efforts have been to some extent successful. So the drama is enriched by a Eugene O'Neill, a Susan Glaspell, or a Paul Green in America, and by a Stanley Houghton, a John Drinkwater, or a James Gregson in England. That is the great contribution of the repertory theatre to the life of its time. 'I am not yet convinced that, even at the present time, we have an American drama in the positive sense in which the phrase is used when we speak of . . . even the Irish drama,' said Mr Clayton Hamilton[4] in 1924. 'I say "even" in the case of Ireland, because it seems astonishing that so small a country could have produced such a great drama in so short a time. The entire population of Ireland is no more numerous than that of New York City, and nine-tenths of the Irish people have never set foot inside a theatre. . . . Yet in the short time of twenty years, the Irish have initiated, developed, and perfected a really great contribution to the drama of the world.' That is praise, indeed, coming from such a critic, but it is no less than the truth. The great dramatists of our time have all come from repertory theatres: Synge from the Abbey Theatre, Tchechov from the Art Theatre in Moscow, the Capeks from Prague, Drinkwater from Birmingham, not to mention Ibsen, Strindberg, Shaw, and Hauptmann of an earlier day. Whatever the commercial theatre will do to amuse the populace, it can do nothing to give experiments in drama any chance. For these experiments small theatres are necessary, and there must be the driving-force of enthusiastic interest in the drama and in the theatre as an institution. Great funds and elaborate organizations are unnecessary. The Abbey Theatre grew from an idea backed with energy and enthusiasm. It has grown from very small beginnings, as have other theatrical enterprises, such as the Provincetown Players in America and the Repertory Theatre in Birmingham, yet it has done more for drama than the commercial theatres of the large centres where there are many theatres but little drama. The Abbey Theatre has now entered upon its maturity, secure in the support of the Government of the Irish Free State. It is the only State-subsidized theatre in the English-speaking world. That its dramatists can still attract the attention of the outer world, the success of plays by Sean O'Casey and T.C. Murray, and the shortly to be produced play of Brinsley MacNamara, in London, stand as proof. Its acting has not declined, and it may be hoped that soon the Theatre will have several companies, some of which could go on tour in Ireland and elsewhere while one would remain at the Abbey. When this has been done the great faith and energy of Lady Gregory and W.B. Yeats will have been completely vindicated, 'and the ancient dreams come true'.

1 This was Douglas Hyde's *Casadh an tSúgáin* (Twisting of the Hay-Rope), staged at the Gaiety Theatre in Dublin in 1901.
2 From *Samhain: An Occasional Review*, October 1902. Reprinted in W.B. Yeats, *Explorations* (London: Macmillan, 1962), pages 95-6.
3 Charles Edward Montague, drama critic on *The Manchester Guardian*, wrote about Synge and the Abbey Theatre in *Dramatic Values* (London: Methuen, 1911; revised 1923).
4 See Clayton Meeker Hamilton, *Conversations on Contemporary Drama* (New York: Macmillan, 1924).

FRANK GALLAGHER
from Frank Gallagher, *Days of Fear* (1928)

Frank Gallagher (pseudonym David Hogan) (1893–1962) was a journalist, historian, and short story writer. Imprisoned in Mountjoy Jail for his political activities in 1920 he underwent a hunger strike as part of the wider struggle against the British Authorities during the War of Independence. The strike proved successful and within a week it was called off and Gallagher released. During the Civil War he took the Republican side, was imprisoned and again went on hunger strike. In 1931 he was appointed first editor of de Valera's newspaper *The Irish Press*. Here in this moving extract, studded with repeated elision points, he provides a glimpse of what surfaced in his mind as he undertook a hunger strike in 1920 for the cause of Ireland. The reference to Yeats's play *Cathleen ni Houlihan* (1902) is further testimony to the power of the imagination — including Yeats's — in the struggle for independence. For a comparative treatment of a hunger strike, this time during the Civil War period, see Peadar O'Donnell, *The Gates Flew Open* (1932).

Monday, April 12th, 1920

The clocks . . . Half-past something . . . Ssh! . . . somebody coming . . . Hear the pad of rubber boots . . . The man with the lantern . . . On the upper landing . . . He'll be here in a minute . . . That's O'Neill shouting at him:

'What the hell are you shining that thing into our eyes for? Do you think we are going to climb out of the ventilators?'

A mumbled reply . . . Here he comes . . .

'Hallo!'

'Yes.'

'What's the time?'

'Two o'clock.'

Must have slept about half an hour . . . It is quite a good poem . . .

What a fight this has become! . . . No matter how it goes now, their prison system is smashed . . . If men die, it is smashed . . . If men live on to political treatment or release, it is smashed . . . At first I thought political treatment would be better . . . Now I think it must be release. For if on any terms we remain passive in their jails, they will fill them up with thousands of us. That will be in our favour up to a certain point. It will anger the people; it will make them feel their subjection; it will keep the adventurers out of the movement, who the moment it becomes safe will swarm into it and turn it into a new Board of Erin . . . But there must come a time when thousands of arrests, with all that they mean, desolate homes, the breaking of the thrilling friendships of young men, lost positions, poverty, anxiety, hardships, loneliness — there must come a time when these things will tell upon the faith of the people and many will sigh for relief . . . for any relief . . . Yet history argues against that . . . dead against it. In the bitterest periods of oppression Ireland lived more really, more ideally than in any of the periods of peace . . .

Nations are so like men . . . In poverty and desolation they remain faithful to their souls, who would lose them in luxury. It was only in peace-times that we became corrupt and forgot or, worse, forwent our independence . . . That is true . . . But still, if we smash their prison system now, the men who, by reason of being here or in some other jail, are useless to the nation, can return to their Volunteering, to the constructive work of the Dáil, to the destructive work of many groups . . . By smashing their prison system we become free to continue the smashing in Ireland of their Empire . . . A few days' hunger in payment for such a blow is nothing . . . Even a few deaths from hunger is nothing . . .

Again, this strike draws men's minds back to the origin of things . . . A hundred men are going to prove that an Irish Republic exists, exists visibly, actively; that the independence of Ireland was declared and is as much a fact as the independence of Belgium was in 1914 . . . When the replacement of Macpherson by Greenwood, of French by Macready,[1] foreshadows 'negotiations', it is well that the national belief in the existence of the Irish Republic should be announced to England and the world, aye, and to our own people, by a hundred dead bodies . . . Compromise will be impossible over our dead bodies . . .

What a destiny to be in Mountjoy with these issues gathered around one like friends, giving comfort and strength! . . . On us, though we did not foresee that, rests the fate of the people . . . If we fail, the nation fails . . . If we succeed, Ireland becomes more than ever 'the young girl with the walk of a queen'[2] . . . Ireland? What is Ireland? . . . Land? . . . No. People? . . . No . . . Something else . . . I am not ready to die for earth or for a people . . . a people which is not very different from any other people . . . Ireland is something else . . . Ireland is the dead and the things the dead would have done . . . Ireland is the living and the things the living would die for . . . Ireland is the Spirit . . . It is the tradition of the laughing courage of men upon whose heads the pitch-cap[3] has been placed by fiends . . . It is the tradition of undefeat . . . of indomitable failure . . . of love for an ideal as strong as the love of the Apostles for Christ as He quivered upon the Cross . . . The crucifixion of Ireland is interminable and so her apostles are innumerable . . . Ireland is justice, is truth . . . That Ireland with that Christ-like spirit which God breathes into subject peoples . . . *that* Ireland I am willing to die for; I wish, I long to die for . . . To-day or to-morrow this boasting may be tested . . . I am not afraid, now . . . When these, the essential things, are clear, death has none but a beautiful meaning . . . But . . . I would prefer to die in the daytime . . . It is no harm to have a preference . . . It would be so horrible at night . . . There is the inevitable paradox in this: the weaker we become, the stronger we prove ourselves to be . . .

. . . I smell the porridge . . . The night has passed quickly . . . It will soon be daylight . . .

. . .

It is quite dark . . . All day long the people outside have been cheering and singing . . . Heard the hymn, 'Hail, Glorious St Patrick', quite distinctly . . . Thousands must have been singing it . . . From a distance girls' voices sound much more beautiful than men's . . . There is a spiritual exaltation upon the people . . . Strange what life death gives . . . It seems that only by tragedy the soul of a people may be saved . . . From the beginning of this awakening, tragedy, or the shadow of it, has been the dominant *motif* . . . The executions in 1916; Ashe's[4] death in 1917; the solemn preparations in 1918 to fight conscription to the death; the sweeping into jail of all the leaders . . . Dick Coleman's[5] death in jail . . . The General Election and the national tenseness for the militarist reply . . . Pierce McCann's[6] death in jail in 1919 . . . The beginning of the Military Terror . . . The attempt to kill Lord French[7] . . . The sack of Thurles[8] last January . . . Curfew and military law . . . The murder of the Lord Mayor of Cork[9] . . . the shock of it and the silent oath of vengeance of a nation . . . Men and women shot down in Dublin streets barely three weeks ago . . . The shadow of an Amritsar[10] upon the faces of the people . . . Volunteers stealthily oiling their rifles, counting their ammunition, stopping now and then to hold their breath and listen . . . Then, crowding on top of one another . . . Alan Bell[11] by the roadside at midday in Dublin . . . James MacCarthy in his home at midnight in Thurles . . . Thos. Dwyer[12] in his sister's arms at the Ragg . . . Easter Sunday morning with its military cordons: Easter Saturday evening with its blazing tax-collectors' offices and two hundred constabulary barracks . . . And then this . . . At first the adventure of a few men . . . Now the greatest drama of a generation . . . The players bloodless, moist, with the smell of death in them . . . An audience of white, pain-lined faces, hungry for consolation . . . A hushed, softly breathing people . . . The singing of hymns against machine-guns . . . Children calling for children, shrilly . . . The coarse, sudden bulk of a tank . . . The beautiful, delicate light of a match upon the bayonet of a soldier preparing to smoke . . . Angry words near the tin-hatted cordon . . . A blow . . . The surge forward of thousands, snarling . . . A bearded, habited priest with uplifted hand . . . A fall of voices, then silence . . . 'Hail, Mary! full of grace . . .' The feverish, thunderous knocking of an aeroplane flying low . . . 'Holy Mary, Mother of God . . .' The warning shout of a sentry . . . Mothers and fathers who entered the prison with the fire of resolution in their eyes,

leaving it with a woe in them which not even the cordon of troops can make them hide . . . They had not cried before their boys . . . Who would stop them now? . . . The respectful withdrawing of the crowd as they come . . . The whispered sympathy . . . The urgent questioning of children . . .

What a play it is! . . . Not the only actors now, these tight-skinned, clammy bodies on the prison pallets . . . The whole Nation has crowded into the cast . . . It is the world which has become the audience . . . What music could be set to this by a master? . . . beautiful music with a wail in it which would drive men mad . . .

1   Ian Macpherson, Chief Secretary for Ireland, 1918–20; Hamar Greenwood, Chief Secretary for Ireland, 1920–22; Field-Marshal French, Lord Lieutenant of Ireland, 1918–19; General Sir Nevil Macready, Commander in Chief of the British Forces in Ireland, appointed 1920.
2   Lines from Yeats's play *Cathleen ní Houlihan* (1902).
3   A cap lined with pitch (tar), used as an instrument of torture by the soldiery during the Irish rebellion of 1798 (OED).
4   Thomas Ashe (1885–1917) was arrested in 1917 after campaigning for de Valera. In prison he went on a hunger strike along with other Sinn Fein prisoners and died as a consequence.
5   Richard Coleman fought in the Easter Rising, endured two hunger strikes, and died in Usk prison in England in 1918.
6   Pierce McCann died in Gloucester prison in March 1919.
7   He was ambushed by Collins's men at Ashtown (Dublin) on 19 December 1919.
8   Thurles in County Tipperary was sacked by Crown forces on 22 January 1920 as part of a programme of reprisals.
9   Terence MacSwiney, arrested in the City Hall in Cork, was imprisoned in Brixton Jail, and died on hunger strike on 25 October 1920.
10 In April 1919 in Amritsar, centre of Sikh nationalism, the British carried out a massacre of hundreds of Indian nationalists. Gallagher here suggests the British might resort to such a policy in Ireland.
11 Alan Bell, a Resident Magistrate 'noted', according to Dorothy Macardle in *The Irish Republic* (1937), 'for his services to British Intelligence', was shot dead after being seized on a street in Dublin.
12 James McCarthy was murdered by police on 29 March 1920, Thomas Dwyer the following day.

DONN BYRNE

from Donn Byrne, *Ireland: The Rock whence I was Hewn* (1929)

Donn Byrne (1889–1928) was born in New York and raised in South Armagh and the
Glens of Antrim. After returning to the States in 1911 he took to writing fiction on
Irish themes. In this book he provides a traveller's introduction to Ireland.

Chapter 2

I suppose that to an anthropologist the smallest gesture
of a man reveals the soul within him — that is, if
anthropologists believe in a soul, which I do not know.
I have never met an anthropologist at the races. This
mind and body business is too subtle for us Irish to
see. We will stupidly go on believing that kindness is
not begotten by logic, nor heroism a product of
carbohydrates.

Assume with me, to avoid argument, that folk have
souls, and I will attempt to show you what is back of
our race. 'Fine words,' says the English proverb, 'butter
no bread.' But I distrust the ultimate wisdom of a race
which evolved that miracle of huckstering: 'Honesty is
the best policy.' 'When gentlefolk meet, compliments
are exchanged,' say the Chinese. Our '*Go manee Jeea git!*'
'God bless you,' '*Jeea is Mwirra git!*' 'God and Mary bless
you!' mean so infinitely more than 'How do you do?'

A GIVING, LOYAL PEOPLE

Even in English, our people saying good-bye to a
friend will always add, 'God bless you!' There is no
assumption of courtesy. It is there inherent.

I know of nothing more dignified than an Aran
Islander — than, indeed, any Irish peasant. When they
are young they are supple as a larch. When they are
old they have the kindness and sanity of a gnarled
apple tree. Always, your trouble is their trouble and
your joy theirs. We are a giving people.

Irish servants have a pathetic loyalty. They are often
of a carelessness which drives a sane man mad. But no
tongue-thrashing will affect them. They will say: 'Ah,
sure, himself doesn't mean a word of it! 'T is only a
gray day in his heart.' The only discipline you can use
is to forbear speaking to them for some days. This is
torture.

IRELAND'S PLACE NAMES HAVE COLOUR AND CHARM

The names folk give to places are an index to their
imaginations. In 'Valladolid' and 'Toledo', in the 'Rue

des Petits Champs', you get names like a bar of music.
All names of places meant something to their
nominators, even Poolton-cum-Seacombe and
'Bumbleby in the Wash'. But what they meant is
forgotten.

Our names are still alive in Irish speech. Aderg
means the Red Ford; Aghleim, the Horses' Leap;
Annaghgod, the Marsh of Sally Trees; Ballynagovna,
the Town of the Artificers; Ballinhoe, the Town of the
Mist; Ballin Tour, the Town of the Bleaching Green;
Bacloughadalla, the Town of the Lake of Two Swans;
Ballyderown, the Town between Two Rivers;
Ballykeen, the Pleasant Townland; Ballynabragget, the
Town of the Ale; Booleynasruhaun, the Milking Place
of the Little Streams; Breaghey, the Plain of Wolves;
Bennanilra, the Remote Place of the Eagle;
Cahirnamallaght, the Fort of Cursing; Caherapheepa,
the Fortress of the Fairy Piping; Carkfree, the District
of the Grouse; Carrigataha, the Rock of the Swarming
Bees; Clogheracullion, the Stony Place of the Holly
Bushes; Clonman, the Meadow of Fruit;
Carraghatork, the Moor of the Hawk; Derrynablaha,
the Oak Grove of the Blossoms; Drimminoweelaun,
the Ridge of the Seagulls; Gortacraghig, the Field of
Hanging; Inchbofin, the Meadow of the White Cow;
Killabrick, the Wood of the Badger; Mallyree, the
Little Hills of Heather; Moneenatieve, the Little Bog
of Rushes; Poulnaglog, the Hole of Bells, a deep hole
in Clare, where the bells of Drumcliff Abbey are
supposed to be buried; Rathnaglye, the Fortress of
Shouting; Scartnamacagh, the Thicket of the Beggars;
Scartanore, the Thicket of Gold — the Danes are
supposed to have buried much treasure in it; Slieve
Mish, the Mountain of Phantoms; Taghshinny, the
House of the Fox; Tabernadroaa, the Well of the
Druids; Tuilyval, the Hill of Honey; Vinegar Hill is a
corruption of Fidh-nagcaer, or Hill of Berries.

This quick imagination, this apt use of words,
follows us into English. Our mountainy people and
our folk of the sea still think in Gaelic, though they
have forgotten the tongue. How often have I heard
people laugh at a countryman who says, instead of 'if',
'if it's a thing that', translating the beautiful emphatic
conditional of '*Ma 's rud é*', 'If it be a fact', clumsily
into English.

Our use of prepositions is amazing and subtle. We say, 'Glory be to God! it's the fine day that's in it!' '*Ta ionn*.' And that denotes a space of time, a certain space out of the infinite, like a meteorite in the multitude of stars.

Possessions are things that are 'at you'. 'There is no silver at me,' a man will say if he is penniless. There you see the dignified human entity with possessions at his feet, but not intermingling with his personality. Any sort of suffering is 'on us'. There you have the entity, still absolute, with a load of oppression.

IRISH BULLS OFTEN REFLECT EFFORTS AT SUBTLE NUANCES OF SPEECH

Many of our 'Irish bulls', as our Saxon neighbours insist on calling them, are a result of trying to express quickly a subtle meaning in unaccustomed dress. Many others are the invention of that rogue and ruffian, the Dublin jaunting-car driver.

I heard an old Irish groom say, at a trial of races, 'If that colt could catch the other, he'd beat him!' Considering that the two-year-old was five lengths behind at the time, it was surely as ridiculous an assertion as was ever made. Everyone laughed. But I knew what he meant. The two-year-old had gameness, speed, and strength, but did not know how to use them. The boy up could not help him.

The statement of Sir Boyle Roche, that 'a man can't be in two places at the same time, barring he's a bird of the air', expresses a great deal. But all it evokes usually is the loud laugh that Oliver Goldsmith knew.

INTRICACIES OF GAELIC POETRY

This subtlety of Gaelic speech defeats its own ends rather in our poetry. What with alliteration, internal rhymes — there are usually sixteen rhymes in the Gaelic quatrain — the Irish poem is a work as intricate as chess. And one is rather amazed at the artifice than moved by the sentiment. George Fox's translation of the country poem, the 'County of Mayo', gives an idea of the heart-break underlying most Irish verse. It is a straight and somewhat facile translation:

On the deck of Patrick Lynch's boat I sit in woeful
    flight,
Through my sighing all the livelong day and
    weeping all the night,
Were it not that from my people full of sorrow
    forth I go,
By the blessed sun! 't is royally I'd sing thy praise,
    Mayo!

'Tis my grief that Patrick Laughlin is not Earl of
    Irrul still,
And that Brian Duff no longer rules as lord upon
    the hill,
And that Colonel Hugh MacGrady should be lying
    dead and low,
And I sailing, sailing swiftly from the County of
    Mayo.

An anonymous country bard, trying his hand at English, has got into that tongue a hint of the rhyme and rhythm of Gaelic in his weird poem about the Galway races:

It's there you'd see the jockeys, and they mounted
    on most stately,
The pink and blue, the red and green, the emblem
    of our nation.
When the bell was rung for starting, the horses
    seemed impatient,
Though they never stood on ground, their speed
    was so amazing.
There was half a million people there, of all
    denominations —
The Catholic, the Protestant, the Jew, the
    Prespetarian;
There was yet no animosity, no matter what
    persuasion.
But welcome and hospitality, inducing fresh
    acquaintance.

A hint of the intricate vowel rhyming of the Irish bards is in a beautiful translation by one of our two greatest poets, Douglas Hyde:

Though riders be thrown in black disgrace,
    Yet I mount for the race of my life with pride;
May I keep to the track, may I fall not back,
    And judge me, O Christ, as I ride my ride.

BLACK DESPAIR WAILS FROM IRISH PIPES

Though we have so much pleasant courtesy, yet there are black depths in us, as anyone who has listened to the Irish elbow pipes knows. The harp, with the beautiful airs of the 'Coolin' and 'The Blackthorn Bush', and those others which the poetry of Thomas Moore has made known, is nostalgic, yet often have I been thrown into the darkest of despair by the magic of the Irish pipes, the bare, desolate mountains of Connemara rising before me, and a cold wind blowing from the Pole.

Our pipe is not the Scottish pipe, but a small instrument of many keys, played on the knees with a bellows. In the 'Lament for Patrick Sarsfield', as played by old men, the shrill keen is too much for one.

And let none think all our stories are of little people, of leprechauns in red caps cobbling small shoes. The most terrible demon in Europe is the Irish Robert Artisson, who was the familiar of the dreadful Lady Alice Kyteler of Kilkenny, foulest of witches. Our Bankeentha, woman of wailing, as the banshee is properly called, is not a romantic Irish lie; neither is it a romantic fact, but a terrible one.

The stories of Garrett Oge, young Gerald, eleventh Earl of Kildare, called the Wizard Earl, are known to the Fitzgerald family to be as full of horror and as fearsome as that mystery of Glamis Castle. In a house in the Boyne Valley a skeleton climbs the wall like a huge spider. The Gormanstown foxes are too well authenticated to leave any doubt about them.

THE WORST HAUNTED HOUSE IN THE BRITISH ISLES

The worst haunted house in the British Isles is a certain castle in the heart of Ireland. The place is grim and bare, a square castle of the usual type. The top storey of the central tower is the chapel, having evidently served that purpose in time past. Often at night the place seems lit up by innumerable candles, and no member of the family or no servant will enter that room unaccompanied.

Of the ghosts, one is a monk with tonsure, who walks in at one window of the chapel and out at another. There is also a little old man in a green cutaway coat, knee breeches and buckled shoes.

But the worst ghost in the world is there, the terrible and well-known It. Here is a description of it from the lady of the house:

'I was standing one evening in the minstrels' gallery, leaning on the balustrade and looking into the hall. I felt suddenly two hands laid on my shoulders. I turned around and saw It beside me. It was human in shape and about four feet high. The eyes were like two black holes in the face and the whole figure seemed as if it were made of grey cotton-wool, while it was accompanied by a most appalling stench, such as would come from a decaying human body.'

Her health was in the balance for a long time.

It has been seen many times. The most recent victim is a clergyman, who sought to lay It. He is in St John of God's near Dublin, an asylum for the wrecked in mind.

These are facts, not to be gainsaid. The Reverend St John Seymour, as level-headed a cleric as exists, and former Inspector Neligan, of the Royal Irish Constabulary, are my authorities.

TOMÁS Ó CRIOMHTHAIN
from Tomás Ó Criomhthain, *An tOileánach* (trans. Robin Flower, *The Islandman*, 1937)

Tomás Ó Criomhthain (1856–1937) was born on the Great Blasket Island off the Dingle Peninsula in County Kerry. His extraordinary life, first published in Irish in 1929 and translated in 1937, is told in a plain style as if he were oblivious to the extraordinary nature of the life he led. The narrative shifts in this extract repay attention for we are in the presence of a culture that died in 1953 when the last remaining islanders were transferred to the mainland. How much is lost in the translation, however, is a question that remains. In his 'Cruiskeen Lawn' column in *The Irish Times* in 1941, Myles na Gopaleen (aka Flann O'Brien) mercilessly mocked Flower's 'literal', colourless translation. (Patrick Heale made a film by this name in 1938 about a Trinity medical student who finds a copy of *An tOileánach* and travels to the Blasket Islands in search of the world of the book.)

Shrovetide, 1878

Shrove[1] came early that year (1878), and the Islanders had to set about making their matches sooner than the mainlanders, you see. So one pair set out quickly. I don't think the matter of the dowry held them back very long, for there wasn't any on either side.

When this party got as far as the priest's house, and it was time for the marriage to begin, the girl couldn't be found anywhere, dead or alive, though there was a crowd hunting for her. A man from Dunquin who'd come to Ballyferriter for another marriage told them that he had met her on her way back. They sent a man on horseback to catch up with her, but, when he got to Dunquin, she had set sail for the Blasket in a boat that was going out fishing.

She hadn't been home many days when she started out again with a man she preferred to the first one. Very few people accompanied them, for they thought it rather an odd proceeding. The girl had no one with her. Though there wasn't a pin to choose between the two men, it's plain the girl had some good reason for preferring one to the other. The boy she'd jilted didn't leave his oars idle. He went as far as Tralee for a wife — the daughter of a Dunquin widow who was in service there.

I used to put up at the same farm-house in Dunquin as this young fellow, for I had one or two relations there. It happened that bad weather kept us out there after this comic wedding I've just mentioned. For I had gone to the marriage, and I was a near relation of the girl's, too, though I didn't quarrel with her for doing what she did.

Before we got a chance to go home, the beauty from Tralee was in Dunquin.

Next morning the young fellow who'd been jilted came in at the door of house where I was.

'I suppose,' he said, 'that you wouldn't care to go to Ballyferriter with me.' That's where the priest lived.

'Why do you think I wouldn't?' said I.

'O, because you've only just been there; and, besides, your relative and I didn't make a job of it together.'

'What's that to you so long as you get another wife?' said I.

'Wisha, on my baptism, maybe you're right! But I haven't got her yet,' said he.

When we got to Ballyferriter there was a great crowd there — men with a thirst, thimble-riggers,[2] and merry-makers. When the Blasket couple came up for their marriage, their own company came with them. That's the time I made the acquaintance of the girl, and I give you my word, if she'd come from Dublin itself, she wouldn't have shamed the city.

The first place we went to after the chapel was the public-house, where there was a great uproar of drinking and dancing and singing, and every other sport that serves to pass the time. When it was getting on for ten o'clock the people were beginning to scatter. You would see a man going off supported between two others, and the woman that belonged to him following behind with a lot to say.

The two wedding parties came back home the same day. They had enough provisions of every sort with them for the whole Island, and all the people of the village revelled and made merry in the two houses. I doubt whether so many Irish songs were ever sung at any two weddings as at those two. Voices were never still till high noon on the morrow in the two houses. Only the girl from Tralee sang a song or two in English. Her father-in-law danced on a table, and they had to smear it with soap for him, as a lot of people had been dancing on it before him. He was a marvellous dancer, but he'd had a drop to drink, and he hadn't been capering long when he upset, but, all the same, he recovered his stand on the floor and finished the step as prettily as I've ever seen it done.

It's still the custom in the Blasket — as it always has been — that, if any of them start on anything, all the rest are eager to follow. Some years the whole Island gets married, and for seven years after that, there won't be a single wedding. I refer to this year of which I'm talking — for not a single boy or girl was unmarried by the time Shrove was over.

One night after I'd been out — and it was pretty late on in the night, too — whom should I find in the house when I came in but windy Diarmid, and his voice was going as loud as ever I'd heard it; he was getting at the old couple, explaining what an unhandy thing it'd be for them if they spent another year without a soul to help them — 'and maybe two years,' says he; 'and I've got a proposal for you from the best girl that ever broke bread, the finest and the handsomest girl every way.'

They didn't break off the talk after I came in, and we kept it up till you'd have thought that everybody in the house was in complete agreement; though the whole affair was to be gone into again, for all the advisers were not present. Be that as it may, Diarmid went out, and he could have trodden on a shell-less egg without breaking it. He fancied that the bargain was sealed.

My sister Maura, who had been in America and who had come back home and married again, heard that Diarmid the rake had been in our house with a match on his hands, and she came to see if there was any truth in the story. We told her how things stood, and she didn't like the idea at all; she made it plain to the old couple what a responsibility anyone was taking on himself if he didn't marry near home, but made an alliance with a family that lived a long way off and wouldn't be in a position to lend a hand on a rainy day.

She had herself marked down an excellent, knowledgeable girl, whose people lived in the village, so that they could lend us a hand when we needed it, and she went on to explain the whole affair to us, like a woman reciting a litany, till she had the whole lot of us as tame as a cat.

She'd always had a great hankering after her first husband's people, and his brother's daughter it was that she'd marked down for us. The girl she had such high praise for — and she deserved it — was a sister to the man who is the King of the Blasket to-day — though he hadn't got the title of King in those days or for long after. My sister Maura, who made the match, has been in the grave since December 1923. She was eighty when she died. May her soul inherit Heaven!

A week from that day we were married — Tomás Crohan and Maura Keane — in the last week of Shrove in the year 1878. There never was a day like it in Ballyferriter. There were four public-houses there, and we spent some time in all of them until it was very late in the day. The town was packed with people, for there were a lot of other couples being married. There were five fiddlers there, one in each bar, attracting people to himself, while another of them was not in any of the houses but out in the middle of the street, and he made more than the rest, for most of the people were in the street.

We had to leave Ballyferriter at last, just when the fun was at its height, but since the great sea was before us, and there were a lot of us to take across, we had to go.

Many of the mainlanders went in with us — relations of ours. There was singing in plenty, dancing, and all sorts of amusement, and food and drink enough and to spare, till high noon on the morrow. Then the mainlanders cleared off.

It was said that there hadn't been so many marriages for fifteen years. The rest of the year was given to hard work. It was a great year for fish. They weren't catching mackerel or lobsters, but other fish which they went after in the day-time in big boats with a seine net in each boat, and the farmers of the countryside bought the catch from them.

I had been frequenting school — whenever we could get one — until I was eighteen. They had no great need of me at home for all that time, as I had a married brother in the house. His wife died and left two children. My mother looked after them till they could go by themselves. My brother went to America. Then I had to leave school, for there was only my father at home. I had left school for three years when I married, at the age of twenty-two.

Till that day I had known little of the world's responsibilities, but from that time on they came upon me. Everything I had to do with changed from that day. Marriage makes a great change in a man's life. His disposition and his view of all sorts of things alters, and, above all, it whets his appetite to be up and doing in life. As the phrase goes, I used to fancy, up till then, that food was sent from Heaven to us.

I set to work with keenness. Away I went to the strand to get seaweed for manure so that we could have more potatoes to rear pigs on. We had two cows at this time. At daybreak, stripped of everything but my drawers, with a rake to gather the weed, out I'd go up to my neck in the sea; then I had to carry it up to the top of the cliff, carry it to the field and spread it. I had no tea or sugar in those days, only milk, bread, and fish. I would be as early on hill as on strand — now off to sea, now hunting seals, another time out in the big boat with a seine net. Each of these jobs had its own time. The seal chase was pretty dangerous. At a certain period of the year men would race one another to them. On one of these days there would be a heavy swell in Poll na Baise, and a man could only make his way into that cave by turning on his side and trying to swim in, or one must go into a sea-cleft and make a shift to kill the huge seals and fetch them out through that narrow opening. I've told already how one day I nearly lost my life when the rope had broken and my uncle was drowning.

Since the day of my marriage I was always trying my best to provide for my household and get my share of everything that was going. For a long time to come my father was a great help to me in the house and out.

Ten children were born to us, but they had no good fortune, God help us! The very first of them that we christened was only seven or eight years old when he fell over the cliff and was killed. From that time on they went as quickly as they came. Two died of measles, and every epidemic that came carried off one or other of them. Donal was drowned trying to save the lady off the White Strand. I had another fine lad helping me. Before long I lost him, too.

All these things were a sore trouble to the poor mother, and she, too, was taken from me. I was never blinded altogether till then. May God spare us the light of our eyes! She left a little babe, only I had a little girl grown up to take care of her; but she, too, was only just grown up when she heard the call like the rest.

The girl who had brought her up married in Dunmore. She died, too, leaving seven children. I have only one boy left at home with me now. There is another in America. Such was the fate of my children. May God's blessing be with them — those of them that are in the grave — and with the poor woman whose heart broke for them.

1 Shrove Tuesday, the day before Lent begins, was a time when in some parts of Ireland practical jokes on bachelors took place. Shrove on the Blasket Islands and the Dingle Peninisula clearly extended over a longer period of time.
2 Cheats, professional tricksters.

IMAGINATIVE

ROBIN FLOWER
from *The Irish Book Lover*, January–February 1920

Robin Flower (1881–1946), born in Leeds and Oxford-educated, was a Gaelic scholar who became Deputy Keeper of Manuscripts in the British Museum in 1929. His long association with the Blasket Islands off the Kerry coast issued in a translation of Tomás Ó Criomhthain's *An tOileánach* (1929), a collection of verse *The Great Blasket* (1924) and a memoir *The Western Island or the Great Blasket* (1946). Here in this poem, originally published in *The Athenæum*, Flower captures (his fascination with) the poetic rhythm and phrasing of island speech.

THE GREAT BLASKET: POETS

She sat there, the strong woman,
Dark, with swift eyes alert and laughter-lighted,
And gathering that wild flock,
This on her knee, that at her side, another
Crouched hiding elfin-eyed under tossed hair;
A calf unsteady-footed
And muzzled with a stocking snuffed and blundered,
And chickens hither and thither
Pecked on the floor, fluttered on loft and settle.
'Poets? And is it poets?'

She said: 'The day has been when there were poets
Here on the Island, yonder on the mainland.
And my own father's father
Was the choice poet of the Island. Wisha!
You'ld go to the well up there to draw the water
And talk a spell, maybe, then come back to him
And he'ld have the poem for you clean and clever.
He had the wit. If only he'd had learning,
Mother of God! 'tis he would have been a poet!'

CONAL O'RIORDAN
from Conal O'Riordan, *Adam of Dublin: A Romance of Today* (1920)

Conal O'Riordan (pseudonym 'F. Norreys Connell') (1874–1948) was a playwright and novelist. He was associated with the Abbey Theatre in its early years, fought in the Great War, and returned to London to write fiction. The first of his 'Adam' series of semi-autobiographical novels is *Adam of Dublin*, a *roman-à-clef* of the Revival. Here in this extract he provides a vivid account of a 1909 (unsqueamish) production of the *Playboy* as seen through the eyes of Dublin's down-and-outs. Adam Macfadden, who at an early age 'embraced journalism' (that is, became a newspaper seller), is the son of Malachy Macfadden, an impoverished alcoholic tailor.

The Abbey Theatre

These are hungry thoughts for a strong man. He went into a tavern on the quay and ate and drank, without allowing himself to get more drunk, then he swung into the street and crossed Butt Bridge, with a notion of finding on the south side some place of entertainment other than a public-house. The music halls he tried were full, or those in charge of them said so to Mr Macfadden, perceiving him to be approaching that happy state. Attracted by a placard in Hawkins Street announcing Mr Oswald Onsin's London Company in the enormous success from the Grand Theatre, London: 'What Rot', by Oswald Onsin, 'Produced by Oswald Onsin', he lumbered to the gallery pay-box of the Theatre Royal and demanded 'sixpennyworth of your bloody rot', but the checktaker at the top of the stairs, supported by a policeman, declined to admit him, and, receiving back his money, he retired under cover of a fire of epigrams in which the name of the advertised author of the play became Mr Oscar Miyelbo. He was the more provoked because at the very bottom of the gallery steps was exhibited a most intriguing picture of a lady wearing a tall hat and pyjamas, pursued by a gentleman in a frilly nightdress. Above this picture were printed boldly the words, 'What Rot', and beneath: 'Who can stop It?' And as he gazed on it the great heart of that patriotic Irishman, Malachy Macfadden, was conscious of a feeling in common with the great heart of the British public; he would, however, have denied it.

He wandered on into Brunswick Street to see what was doing at the Queen's.[1] It was closed, so he turned back again and crossed Butt Bridge and Beresford Place. There was a crowd there, a very modest one, listening to a short man with a black moustache who addressed them from the steps of Liberty Hall,[2] using language not in Mr Macfadden's vocabulary. So Mr Macfadden just roared 'Libertymiyelbo!'[3] at him and passed on into Abbey Street. . . . There on his left hand he caught sight of yellow bills, such as those which had attracted Adam's curiosity many months before. They stood outside a building he still remembered as the Morgue.[4] He used to go there often when he was a lad, to see the coroner's jury sitting on sailors and women dragged out of the river, or murdered down the quayside as far as the North Wall. Once he had been called in as a juryman himself, as he was passing by on urgent business, going to back Father O'Flynn for the Grand National, no less, that had cost him thirty-five shillings or more, and all to sit on a blasted baby that had been dug out of a sewer under Mecklenburg Street. What fools men were! How they wasted their time and other people's money! Now the place was turned into a queer sort of theatre, not real theatre like the Queen's, where you could see a railway engine running over a policeman, or the British Army scuttling for life from a patriot in a green tie, but where they spouted like street preachers and see-sawed with their hands. He remembered once on a Bank Holiday, seeing the word, 'Kincora'[5] on the bills. He was with two other fellows who had a sup taken and they all thought Kincora must be about a lad drinking Mooney's whisky, and either getting funny on it or going grand and mad, so they all paid sixpence each and went in. But sure it was nothing of the kind. The place was as dismal as a methody chapel and not a soul scarcely in it but an old Protestant clergyman asleep in the stalls. As for the play, you couldn't make head or tail of it, except that the leading character let on to be called King Brian Boru, and talked as if he were tipsy, but he said nothing about drinking Kincora; and the whole thing being obviously a fraud, at the end of the first act they threatened to wreck the theatre unless they got their money back, and so came away and spent their sixpences on real Kincora in Marlborough Street.

But the placard now in front of him was different. That said, 'The Playboy of the Western World'. He scratched his head to think. He seemed to remember hear tell that was an immoral play, a play insulting to religion and decency, that had been hissed off the stage years ago. He was almost sure some one had told him that (perhaps it was Emily Robinson, she knew everything, the Lord have mercy on her!) when Adam was just old enough to carry the jug to the public bar. Was it possible they had the impudence to put it on the stage again after Marlborough Street[6] had declared against it? He knew he had heard of something grossly indecent in it, but he could not recall what it was, being a bit moidered by the drink and the contrariness of everything to-night . . . he was curious to know was this really the same play . . . he fumbled six coppers out of his pocket and went in.

Rotten hole the Abbey Theatre, you couldn't swing a cat in it, and yet not half full. How did they make it pay? Was it subsidized from Dublin Castle[7] to corrupt the people? The audience dotted about were mostly young men, reading books or papers, without a spark of excitement in them. They didn't seem to care if the curtain never went up. Mr Macfadden was the old enthusiastic style of playgoer: he stamped for thirteen minutes until the orchestra came in, and quieted him with familiar airs, he dozed a little until they ceased, and then stamped, like a giant refreshed, until the curtain at last rose. The play was not at all what he had been led to expect: two gentlemen and a lady in queer old clothes talked gibberish to each other as politely as if they lived in Rathmines.[8] One of them was called Robert Emmet, but he was no more like the Robert Emmet that lived in Mr Macfadden's spiritual world, than was the Brian Boru of 'Kincora' like Mr Macfadden's Brian Boru, that was done to death by Strongbow on Mud Island. The whole story might have been 'Kincora' over again, only for trifling differences in the costumes and scenery, and the presence of a queer sort of piano-organ that played 'Let Erin Remember', when there was no one near enough to lay hand or foot on it. Then Robert Emmet burst out crying because it wouldn't let him get a word in edgeways and the curtain came down.

'Is that tripe what you call "The Playboy of the Western World"?' Mr Macfadden shouted to the nearest group of young men.

They laughed shyly, and one of them, consulting his programme, answered that it was called 'An Imaginary Conversation'.[9]

'Conversationmiyelbo,' cried Mr Macfadden. 'I paid my money to see "The Playboy of the Western World", and if they can't show me that I'll take it somewhere there's a bit of fun.'

'If you wait long enough you'll see the "Playboy" all right,' they answered, and gradually sidled farther from him, not fancying his truculent tone. So he led off with his heels again and kept at it, orchestra or no orchestra, until he fell asleep and snored solidly through the first and second acts. But the clatter of the last act woke him and he gazed around resentfully.

'What the hell is all this hullabaloo?' he demanded in a voice that drowned the simulated bass of old Christy Mahon. But the actors, inured to interruption, took no notice nor halted in the wild business of the tragic farce. Mr Macfadden was enthralled: half a dozen men were holding another down that had his teeth buried in yet another's calf, and a young girl was trying to get at one or other of them with a pair of red-hot tongs. Mr Macfadden clapped his hands: he had never seen anything half so good on the stage before. A fellow in a nightshirt chasing a girl in pyjamas was poor fun compared with this. 'There's a bit of humour for you,' he called delightedly to his neighbours, who affected not to hear but huddled still farther away. Louder grew the riot on the stage, overwhelming at last even his approving voice, and he gazed spellbound, forgetful even of his injured honour. Then suddenly there was a hush: a half animal form crawled in from the back of the scene, reared up, and revealed a hairy monster of a man with a clotted bandage round his skull. Mr Macfadden gathered that he was the father of the young lad with the nippy teeth the others were holding down and the girl going to burn with the tongs. Mr Macfadden was annoyed with him as a kill-joy, and hissed and hooted, but still the actors went on acting imperturbably: no one there or in the audience took the smallest notice of him. It was maddening in itself for so big a man to be ignored. . . . But a moment later he could stand it no longer: for the young lad was no sooner released from his captors, at his father's instance, than he turned on the latter and drove him with violence off the stage.

This was the last straw. Mr Macfadden leaped on to his seat and howled at the top of his voice, 'I call the Almighty to witness that this play is a bloody scandal to good Catholics. . . . Playboymiyelbo! Playboymiyelbo!' But still the performance went on, until against his own roar he could hear the girl shrieking as though it were a personal matter between her and himself which should have the last word: 'My grief I've surely lost him now, the only playboy of the Western World!' And the curtain fell amidst applause chiefly intended to smother Mr Macfadden's language.

The audience drifted out. Mr Macfadden, shearing half a dozen of the Intelligentsia of Dublin out of his way, swept into the vestibule. He found there a very little man struggling into his overcoat. Mr Macfadden descended on him with clenched fists.

'I want to see the author of that scandalous play,' he cried.

'The first or second?' asked the little man wearily.

'The man that wrote the Playboy. That's the lad I want.'

The little man looked at a cab which stood with open door awaiting him. 'Is it urgent?' he asked.

'Urgent's the word,' returned Mr Macfadden. 'I want to knock his head off.'

'I see,' said the little man, with the condescending humility of a shop walker. 'There's no time to be lost.'

'There is not,' answered Mr Macfadden in a tone which implied that the little man's head might be found to serve his immediate purpose. 'Be quick and tell me now where I'll find him.'

'Mount Jerome,'[10] answered the little man promptly. 'Take the Harold's Cross tram from the Pillar.'[11] He stepped briskly past Mr Macfadden into his cab, and as it was moving off opened the window to add, 'You needn't be afraid of his hitting you back. But you'll want a pick-axe or you'll break your nails.'

'Is it a corpse you want me to kill, you snot?'

Mr Macfadden sprang forward to splinter the cab about its occupant's ears, but crashed in his blind rage into the lamp post to which he held, kicking it impotently. Then he dived thirstily across the road into a public-house and drank there until closing time. All caution had fallen from him when he came out. He was as bereft of reason as the bull goaded by spear and bandillero to charge the matador. Yet his soul was possessed of a notion of outrageous joy: to avenge all his manifold wrongs at one fell swoop upon the naughty world. Earlier in the evening, when comparatively sober, he had thought mainly of the wrongs he had to avenge upon his wife; then in the theatre he realized from the sight of the action upon the stage, the still greater enormity of Adam's offence; and now in the first stages of delirium tremens, a yet more provoking image rose before him: the handsome whiskered, sniggering Mr Byron O'Toole, with his fantastic claim to be a gentleman of blood and his fatal fascination for the merry wives of Marlborough Street. He would pay for presuming to patronize Mr Malachy Macfadden with his dirty custom. First of all Mr Macfadden would deal with him. Then no one could say that he swung for a woman and child and let the man who was the cause of all go free.

It wanted half an hour of midnight as he hurried, straight enough for all the drink he carried, swinging his heavy hands up Marlborough Street. There was little light in Mountjoy Court and the hall door was closed. He lit his pipe and waited, patiently smoking, until the stroke of midnight from St George's bells, when a woman opened it to come out. He gave her a confident 'God save ye', as though an inmate, and passed through, closed the door behind him and found himself in pitch darkness. By the light blown from his pipe he climbed as softly as he could the great welled, dilapidated staircase, the timber squelching under his heavy weight. Towards the top floor where, despite the improvement in his position, Mr O'Toole still modestly elected to live, the flooring was so rotten he had to strike a match to evade disaster. When reassured as to his surroundings he blew it out, waited to take his breath after the climb, and then tried the door: it was fastened, but he could see a dim light within. He tapped as gently as his iron fingers would allow. There was no answer. He tapped again, louder.

A woman's voice called faintly, as one who wishes no reply: 'Who's there?'

He said nothing but tapped again, louder.

'What do you want?' asked the timid voice.

'Mr Byron O'Toole is wanted,' he answered, hoarse with the effort to muffle his tone and struggle against the vapours bursting through his brain.

The voice came more than ever hesitantly, 'Who wants him?'

Mr Macfadden's voice took it upon itself to answer, 'Emily Robinson,' and Mr Macfadden hearing, realized that he was mad drunk and could no longer disguise it. He heard a frantic whispering inside and knew for certain that his enemy was there cornered so that he could not escape; for Malachy was not the man to be stopped by a lodging house door. . . . He spat on his hands and took a fresh grip of the door handle. The whole floor of the house trembled with his nervous rage. The voice from within came in awestruck accents. 'What are you saying about Emily Robinson? Sure isn't she dead and buried?'

'Never mind if she is that,' answered Mr Macfadden, laughing at his own humour. 'She sent me for O'Toole.'

There was a scream in the question, 'Who are you at all?'

Then he thundered through the door, 'Tell O'Toole I'm Macfadden, come to call him to my wife and Emily Robinson and Fan Tweedy, and all his other mops in hell.'

There was a scuttling inside and the sound of a window thrown open, while Macfadden's pressure threatened to start the panels of the door. The woman's voice broke forth in a despairing wail. 'Sure Mr O'Toole has never been in here this night. . . . For Christ's sake go away now.'

'Christmiyelbo!' answered Mr Macfadden, as a final challenge to his enemies, and, stepping back to throw his full weight against the door, dropped his heel in the crumbling wood, waved his mighty arms vainly to recover his balance, toppled through the broken balustrade, and fell, bounding and rebounding from side to side of the handsomely welled staircase, until he reached the hall four floors below. His ghost may rise to haunt our pages still, but his body rested there.

So perished Malachy Macfadden, a victim to his environment and the system of government that created it. We do not state his case as one of Ireland's wrongs: thousands of Macfaddens under other names smell no sweeter in London, Liverpool, Newcastle, Glasgow, or where you please, from Plymouth to Aberdeen. And our Mr Macfadden had a privilege not shared by all; for the next day Father Innocent knelt by his bier and prayed piteously to God for the soul of his poor brother. It is easy to believe that so long as there be Innocents to pray for them, the Macfaddens need not fear eternal damnation, but who is so good a Catholic as to desire the pleasure of their company in heaven?

1   The Queen's Theatre in Great Brunswick Street.
2   The headquarters of the Irish Transport and General Workers Union. They moved into the building in 1912; before that, from December 1908, business was conducted at 8 Beresford Place.
3   Adam's father's constant taunt against what he thinks is pretension. Liberty my elbow.
4   The site of the Abbey Theatre was indeed a morgue.
5   Lady Gregory's play first staged at the Abbey on 25 March 1905. Frank Fay played Brian Boru.
6   The meaning here is Dublin's drinking poor.
7   The British Authorities.
8   A respectable suburb on the south side of Dublin.
9   This was the title of O'Riordan's own one-act play produced under his pseudonym at the Abbey in May 1909.
10   The Protestant cemetery where Synge is buried.
11   Nelson's Pillar on O'Connell Street from where the trams once fanned out across the city.

JOHN O'BRIEN
from John O'Brien, *Around the Boree Log* (1921)

John O'Brien (Fr Patrick Joseph Hartigan) (1879–1952) is, according to Patrick O'Farrell, author of *The Irish in Australia* (1986), 'central to the Irish–Australian literary tradition'. As a parish priest to Irish farming communities in eastern Australia in the early years of the twentieth century he had first-hand experience of the Irish ambivalence towards both Ireland and Australia. Here in this ballad celebrating one community and both countries, he strikes a whole series of notes on a scale from nostalgia for an old way of life to accommodation with a new one. A semi-autobiographical portrait of the childhood of Fr Hartigan can be found in Phil K. Walsh's film *Around the Boree Log* (1925).

ST PATRICK'S DAY

'Tis the greatest splash of sunshine right through all
   my retrospection
On the days when fairies brought me golden dreams
   without alloy,
When I gazed across the gum-trees round about the
   old selection[1]
To the big things far beyond them, with the yearning
   of a boy.

Drab the little world we lived in; like the sheep, in
   slow procession
Down the track along the mountain, went the hours
   upon their way,
Bringing hopes and idle longings that could only find
   expression
In the riot of our bounding hearts upon St Patrick's
   Day.

There were sports in Casey's paddock, and the
   neighbours would assemble
On the flat below the homestead, where the timber
   fringed the creek;
With Australian skies above them, and Australian trees
   a-tremble
And the colours of the autumn set in hat and hair and
   cheek.

Mighty things were done at Casey's; mighty bouts
   anticipated
Made the Sunday church-door topic for a month
   ahead at least;
On the cheerless Sundays after, with misguided hope
   deflated,
We explained away our failures as we waited for the
   priest.

So when morning Mass was over, it was trot and break
  and canter
Helter-skelter down to Casey's, banging, pounding all
  the way,
And the greetings flung in Irish, and the flood of
  Celtic banter,
And the hectic flush of racial pride upon St Patrick's
  Day.

Everywhere was emerald flashing from the buggies,
  traps, and jinkers,[2]
There was green in every garment, and a splash in
  every hat,
In the bows upon the cart-whips, in the ribbons on
  the winkers,
In the wealth of woven carpet neath the gums on
  Casey's Flat.

There the new dress faced the critics, and the little
  beaded bonnet
And the feather flowing freely like a sapling in a gale;
And 'himself' inside his long black coat that bore a
  bulge upon it
Where for twelve forgotten months its weight had
  hung upon the nail;

And the 'splather' of a necktie only once a year
  paraded,
And the scarf that came from Ireland, 'ere a one of you
  were born',
And the treasured bunch of shamrock — old and
  withered now, and faded,
Blessed by every tear that stained it since the cruel
  parting morn.

Mighty things were done at Casey's. Men of solid
  reputation,
Ringing bells and giving orders, kept the programme
  moving by;
And they made you sickly conscious of your humble
  situation
When they glared upon your meanness with a cold
  official eye.

Every 'maneen' with a broken voice and backers there
  beside him,
And his socks outside his breeches, was a hero in his
  way;
Every nag around the country with a raw bush lad
  astride him
Was a racehorse with an Irish name upon St Patrick's
  Day.

Oh, the cheering that betokened those I knew so well
  competing,
With their long legs throwing slip-knots, and the look
  of men in pain —
Put me back into the reach-me-downs, and let me
  hear the greeting,
Set me loose in Casey's paddock, where I'd be a boy
  again!

Yes, 'twas good to be a pilgrim in a world that held
  such wonders,
Though eternal bad behaviour put me neath parental
  ban,
Though the staring, and the wandering, and a score of
  general blunders
Got me gaoled behind the taffrail[3] of the Old Mass
  Shandrydan.[4]

'Yerra, Johnnie, stop that gawkin'.' Is it — with the
  pulses pumping,
And the little heart high-stepping to the music of the
  drum —
Is it 'stop it', with a something in the young blood
  madly thumping
With a foreword of the purpose of the pregnant years
  to come?

Mighty things were done at Casey's. Mighty impulse
  was behind them,
'Twas the sacred spark enkindled that was burning to
  the bone;
Never yet were men more loyal to the holy ties that
  bind them,
And the love they gave their country made me
  conscious of my own.

Never yet were men more loyal. Be they met in
  thousands teeming,
Be they gathered down at Casey's with their kindred
  and their kind;
They are marching on for Ireland, with the beauteous
  vision gleaming
Of the altar-fires of Freedom in the land they left
  behind.

Not a torch was ever lighted at a tomb where
  Freedom slumbered,
But it smouldered — grimly smouldered — till the
  stone was rolled away;
When it flashed across the half-light, rallying rocket
  glares unnumbered,
Like the spangled blades of morning that bespeak the
  march of day.

Not a voice was ever lifted, but an echo never dying
Flung the slogan once repeated when the hand was on
    the gun;
Though the prophet tongue was ashes, came the
    conquering banners flying
With a dazzling watchword flashing, blazing signals in
    the sun.

Yes, the world has ever seen it in its journey down the
    ages,
Seen it writ in living scarlet in the blood that has been
    shed;
And a hand re-writes the head-line deep across the
    lurid pages,
When the stricken, fearless living meet the deathless,
    martyred dead.

Thrills a leaping thought within me, when I see a land
    around me
That has never seen the foeman's steel, nor heard the
    foeman's shot,
At whose shrine I lit the tapers, when her witching
    sweetness bound me
With an iron vow of service of a pulsing pride begot;

To that big free land I've given all the love that courses
    through me;
That her hands have rocked my cradle stirs my heart in
    every beat.
An Australian, ay, Australian — oh, the word is music
    to me,
And the craven who'd deny her would I spurn beneath
    my feet.

Thrills the thought that, did the traitor stretch a
    tainted hand to foil her,
Did I see her flag of silver stars a tattered thing and
    torn,
Did I see her trampled, breathless, neath the shod heel
    of the spoiler,
And her bleeding wounds a byword, and her name a
    thing of scorn,

There would flash the living bayonets in the strong
    hands of my brothers,
And the blood that coursed for nationhood, through
    all the years of pain,
In the veins of patriot fathers and of Little Irish
    Mothers
Would be hot as hissing lava streams to thrill the world
    again.

1   Land in Australia selected through 'free-selection'.
2   A contrivance, used in the Australian bush, consisting of two pairs of wheels, having their axle-trees joined by a long beam, under which tree-trunks are suspended by chains (OED).
3   The aftermost portion of the poop-rail of a ship (OED). Used here in a metaphoric sense for a part of the family's carriage.
4   A rickety old four-wheeled 'gazabo', mentioned by O'Brien in his poem by that name. When O'Brien was a boy it would be used for carrying hay during the week and taking the family to Mass on Sunday.

DARRELL FIGGIS
from Darrell Figgis, *The House of Success* (1922)

This novel turns on the relationship between a successful businessman interested in hard fact and making money and a son drawn from an early age to Irish nationalism and the dreams of nationhood. Against a backdrop of the decades leading up to the Easter Rising and told through the eyes of a personal clerk William Costello, the story follows the progress of Jeremiah Hare, born Diarmuid O'Hara, from poverty in Connemara to Dublin businessman. Hare's second son, born in 1895, becomes another Diarmuid O'Hara, only in his case he is driven to follow not his father but fatherland. Here in this chapter Diarmuid, now aged eighteen, reveals his commitment to the new Ireland.

Chapter 14

1

On the very heel of Jeremiah's recovered brightness followed a shadow in desperate pursuit. One night towards the end of that year Diarmuid did not return till late. It was understood he was at some meeting in the Rotunda. Late as it was when he did return, he said little when he came; he sat warming himself before the fire, wrapped in silence, looking at the flames that I, too, could see where they leapt and fell in the deep reflection of his eye. For I watched him; and the others watched him. That none of us asked for news of the night signified our recognition that this flushed, bright-eyed and silent figure among us had been, and was, unusually stirred. A little thing; yet curious; for we had been speaking together until he came, and now silence had fallen like uneasy sleep upon us.

Jeremiah was the first to leave the fireside. He did not return. I did not realize how deep a life Diarmuid lived in his father's apprehension till I learnt that Jeremiah had at that late hour telephoned the paper to discover what had taken place at the Rotunda. It was not till the following morning I myself learnt that a national military force, entitled the Irish Volunteers,[1] had been brought into being. What wonder that that figure had sat among us tense and silent, striking our comfortable speech into uneasy apprehension. We had been of our own little hour, happy in its recognition; and no doubt he had come among us conscious that he was the heir of history, his mind teeming with mighty memories, thrilled with the thought that now all baffled meanings were to take an ordered and martial purpose.

Little use to protest the wisdom of years while the youth of a nation is shaping itself into disciplined phalanxes. Jeremiah said nothing. I caught from him the appeal that I should become his mouth-piece, but I knew better than to wag a gray poll before the advance of youth. I waited before I would speak. Better to harness waters when they flow into a river than to attempt to dam them when they burst into a cataract. If Helen[2] said anything I knew nothing of it. Neither could I perceive any effect.

For the months were full of drillings, and the hours of martial text-books. And then, as the months passed, these things, too, beat themselves into the custom of our days, and one gave no more heed to them than one would to a ballad singer strayed among the faded streets of our city. One hardly turned one's head to see the martial ardour passing by.

It was the effect of that ardour on our Diarmuid O'Hara that concerned me. For it had an effect not easy to explain. He had all the high elation of a lover, but, unlike a lover, there was no visible desire to communicate any part of his rapture to us of his household. Never was there so contained a lover or so cool an elation. The distinction, however, was this, that his elation seemed to cut him off more completely from his father than his previous hostility. The result was unaccountable. When father and son had been, as it were, staring at one another hostilely all their lives, there had been a kind of understanding between them. That queer truth was now altered. A change had come. The son stared no longer at his father, for he had his eye fixed in another direction. If the two of them had circled about one another, so to speak, hitherto, that circling had been a companionship; but now that Diarmuid circled no more, the result for Jeremiah was undescribably lonely. No one could work in close intimacy with Jeremiah without feeling the new hollowness that had come into his life; a hollowness that was as if a necessary part of himself had been abstracted from his life: a hollowness to which the drillings and marchings were only a picturesque background.

That was the result of the new martial order on Jeremiah. With me the result was that my earth was in shadow because the man who for thirty years had been the lightgiver of my earth was in eclipse. This was a different matter from Diarmuid's ordering of his own life. Let him order his life as he would; that was his concern; but none of us is at liberty to order his life to the suffering of others. Diarmuid was no longer a mere boy; and I determined that here was a matter on which I could speak to him roundly.

2

I searched him out in his room, and did not trouble to wait a suitable occasion. But the door did not give to my hand. It was locked. What foolery was this, I thought; what queer bent had secretiveness now taken, if the young man could not withdraw to his own room without clicking a lock in the face of his household? I knocked vexedly, when I heard a voice asking who was without. Only when my identity was established was the key grated in the lock and I allowed to enter.

A new Diarmuid O'Hara stood before me, frowning in the waning evening light. So new and so wonderful a Diarmuid O'Hara was he that it was only by the utmost steadiness that I withheld myself from betraying my surprise. A spirit of the mountains or of the woods could not more magically have been substituted for the very human figure I had expected, than the vivid change that now for a bare moment caught my breath, and held me at the door, till he quickly closed it behind me.

He was dressed complete in a uniform of soft green. Puttees of the same colour were wound about his legs. A peaked cap was on his head, also of the same colour. The colour was well chosen, and in the warm diminished light of the evening it transfigured the mortal flesh it clothed. The toils of brown papers strewn about his bed might explain the occasion of the transformation; and the abashed scrutiny with which he faced me was his acknowledgement of that transformation; but the transformation itself surpassed its occasion and mocked its acknowledgement. Ordinarily Diarmuid was neither careful nor careless about his dress; and my eyes, accustomed to the fact of his growth to manhood, had never rested on him to note or criticize him. But now, in this new presentment of him, I saw how comely he was framed. He was of more than middle height, yet seemed not as tall as he was because of the proportion of his parts and the eager athletic balance of the whole. No uniform, be sure, made him thus; but the present uniform consummately displayed it for the first time to my eyes.

All this I saw swiftly enough. Then I recovered the purpose of my visit, feeling its hopelessness more firmly than I yet had done.

I struck straight to the heart of my theme. 'Diarmuid, you're hardly a boy any longer. Would you believe that there's a question I've had a wish to ask you for a good handful of years now? There is indeed. I've waited, as you might say, till this evening. It was little use putting it to you till now anyway. It wanted an answer that you could hardly provide till now, for you weren't old enough to find it. I wonder will you help me find it now. You see, I want to get to the heart of this difference . . . this distance . . . between you and your father. What is it, Diarmuid? We all see two people astonishingly like one another . . . in every sort of way. Only you two never seem to discover one another. I know I'm saying what will seem to you very odd, and perhaps foolish. I know you're thinking of that unhappy scene last year. But that doesn't explain anything. I want to get under that. Surely it ought not to be possible for two people, especially when they're father and son, to drift apart without some common human exchange between them.'

I had continued on, feeling deeply the futility that this uniformed figure impressed on me. At first he had been disconcerted. Now he leant against the mantel-piece looking straight at me with incredible directness and coolness.

'I don't know about drifting,' he said. 'Who said we were drifting apart? I'm damned sure father never said it.'

'I said it. I see it happening. It's now becoming worse than ever.'

'Is it drifting because he wants one sort of thing and I want another sort of thing? There's nothing sharing between us, that's all; that's not drifting apart all the same.'

The calm decision prompted me to say: 'Do you despise your father so very much, then?'

He flushed, but did not falter. 'The person that'd despise father you can put to one side. He doesn't count. Father has the whole world sorted out to his satisfaction, and that's more than you can say for most of the slobs floating about in it. But that's not to say he has it sorted out to my satisfaction. Because he knows what he wants it doesn't follow it's what I want, do you know.'

I seized upon the point he offered. 'But how do you know he didn't at one time want all you now do, and that he didn't have to surrender it as a result of hard experience?'

'I wouldn't wonder. He'd be trying to forget it then, and it would only vex him to have me reminding him. Perhaps I do remind him, and perhaps that's what all the trouble's about sometimes. I don't believe father thought there was anything especially fine about having crocks of gold. He took other people's ideas about it instead of following out his own.'

'Hm. So that's the trouble. He was all wrong, and you're all right.'

'I didn't say that. I doubt would he say it himself if he really said what he thought. Perhaps there was no other way for him but that. But we've all got to start from the beginning, haven't we?'

'And reject all experience, my dear boy?'

He nodded. 'How do we know it's going to be the same experience as before? Father doesn't expect me to wear all his old clothes, does he? Why should he expect me to wear all his old experiences?'

'Diarmuid, Diarmuid, I'm afraid you're an incurable romantic.'

A shade of annoyance crossed his face. 'That's like a literary lecture. They have all the sorts parcelled out neatly there — tragedy, comedy, farce, romance, realism, and all the rest of it. I never could make out what it meant; and I don't and won't try. We've been reading *Don Quixote*, and we're told it's comic. I think it's tragic. Some other fellow thinks it's a farce; and some other fellow romance; and some other fellow realism perhaps. But it's what goes on all the same. It's we that are different. It's what father would call a fact — only there are more facts, and other kinds of facts, do you know, than those he sees.'

'Will I tell you what I think romantic? You won't mind if I do? Well, I call a pretty uniform romantic.'

He laughed. 'Do you know, I was thinking that before you came in. I was, then. Just that.' He surveyed himself. 'I was asking myself did I care more about this blessed outfit than about Ireland.'

'Well, and what did you decide? Or didn't you decide anything?'

He frowned at me. 'I decided that I did. Still, as it's company-orders, there's no help for it, and I've got to make mine the best outfit in the company. We'd a right to dress in our ordinary clothes, like the Boers, with all the one kind of hat for uniform effect. An ugly hat would be better yet . . . say like a baker's hat. There's no denying it'd look uniform, and that's all that's wanting. No chance then to forget the facts, for there'd be no romantic feathers on that bird.'

'Tell me, how many would you get then, Diarmuid?'

'Not a great lot, I know. Not at once, anyway. It'd depend on the few how the many went, as it did evermore. I'm not such an idiot as to think you can count rightness in crowds, the way father pretends he does.' He looked at me with steady penetration, then glanced down at his uniform with a slow restrained smile. 'I'm a very fine bird in these feathers, all the same, you won't deny. They reveal my natural symmetry. There'd be no tolerating me if I took to walking abroad in them, and I'd become most unpopular with those that hadn't the same natural advantages.'

'Ah, no, no,' I protested, speaking out the heart of me. 'They'd love you. They wouldn't be able to help it.'

'Would they? You ask father would they. He knows something about facts. I believe people hate everything beautiful, unless it's at a distance. I believe they hate everything that's fine and right; and all the more because they know it's fine and right. It shews up the rottenness they live in — the rottenness they want to get content with. They'd like to drive their fist into the middle of anything beautiful, because it reminds them of too much. It's a kind of love gone mad . . . jealousy, I suppose. That's why I'm not a romantic, because I know that as surely as father does. He's right when he says folk don't like, and can't abide, a beautiful thing till it's too far away to bother them . . . safely in a book or somewhere. Where he's wrong is that he gives in to that, instead of smashing it up and

not caring.' He spoke with a great assumption of carelessness, but with real passion in his voice. Then he caught his breath, and held up a protesting hand. 'I say, I don't mean that I'm beautiful and fine, you know.'

'Though perhaps you are,' I offered him quietly.

'Though perhaps I am,' he echoed, looking ruefully at his uniform again. 'It'd be so much simpler not to be. There's a lot to be said for the baker's hat, do you know.'

There was silence between us. More than ever he had persuaded me that he bore Jeremiah's stamp, not merely in body, but in his mind also. Yet more than ever he persuaded me of the unbridgeable distance between the two. I was saddened, saddened, saddened.

'Did you ever think how like your father you are?' I asked.

He flushed with pleasure; and then instantly (visibly before my eyes) fell on his guard.

'Is that so?' He reflected. 'Then we can't meet without exposing ourselves, I suppose, and that means we must go different ways. Seems so, anyway.' Then he gave out like a rebuke, with eyes that searched commandingly into mine: 'I know if father were in want, and beaten to the world, where he'd go for help. It wouldn't be to Martin[3] he'd go. And I know who would stand by him then; and that wouldn't be Martin either. I'm not saying he wouldn't wish to, the same Martin; but . . . well, there wouldn't be anything doing.'

'That's a condition that's not likely to arise, Diarmuid. But I'm your father's old friend, and you, I like to think, are my new friend. I want . . . now, not when your father is without any other likely friend . . . to bring the two of you to an understanding before it's altogether too late.'

'I say we do understand one another, and that's just the crux. I understand him, and he understands me.'

'You think you understand him.'

'Very well, I think I understand him. What I do understand, anyway, is that he can't help wishing to destroy all that I believe is right to do, and I can't help setting out to destroy all he believes in . . . or says he believes in, because I don't think he's so sure about it himself. He's not the same as other people. There's something queer about father . . . the way he wants to baffle me, for instance.'

'There you are,' I said triumphantly. 'You see how the elements of true understanding, of love and tolerance, display themselves. Look, Diarmuid, will you come and talk with him, simply and quietly, avoiding all vexation? You're getting to be a man now . . . indeed, in many ways you are older than many men . . . and the chance may soon be lost beyond recall. Will you?'

He was plainly moved. I had never doubted his deep love for his father; and it was beyond doubt to me now. He walked up and down his room before me. Then he turned toward me. A strange expression in his eyes puzzled me.

'Now?' he asked.

'Very well; now.'

'Will I come down in this outfit, or will I take off this outfit so as to talk to him . . . which?'

I shrugged my shoulders at the hopeless alternative.

3

So there I was, more desperately than ever set between the two. Jeremiah's love for his son was more than an ordinary father's love for a son, for in Diarmuid O'Hara (as he always fully and formally called him) he loved yearningly his own youth. Diarmuid was more than a son to him; he was a passion in his blood and a dream in his mind. All his thought for life — for that life beyond life, for the perpetuation of which we all turn in our stricken years — centred in that boy. And, for his part, Diarmuid as passionately loved his father. I thought often of his words to me; and the more I thought of them the truer I saw them. Had Jeremiah fallen into poverty or other desperate need, nothing would have given the young man greater joy than to undertake his care and championship. Yet worlds were not more surely distanced by space than these two, swinging each in his own orbit, with a treasure of love of which I could discover no visible exchange.

Where there is love there is understanding, yet neither could I discover any visible exchange of that understanding. That it existed I did not doubt. Especially after Diarmuid's confident words to me I did not doubt it, for all the lack of any display of it. Not to doubt it, explained many things to me.

I noticed, for example, a quiet elation in Jeremiah these days. Even the first sight of Diarmuid in his uniform did not seem to disturb him. He even checked Helen's modulated sarcasm.

'Let him alone,' he said to her when Diarmuid had gone out. 'Urge him on, my dear, rather than check him. The faster he goes the sooner he'll turn. The farther he travels on that road the better he'll go on the other he has found; for he has his two fine feet to a safer journey now, and a better.'

'I don't know what other that might be,' she said. 'I don't see anything but drillings these times.'

'Drillings cannot last for ever, do you know.' He put his hand on her shoulder, and drew her to him. 'If you want to check him anywhere, check him in his chemistry.'

That was the cause of the quiet elation, for Diarmuid now worked indefatigably at chemistry. For Diarmuid to work indefatigably at any thing was a sign. Never could it have been an acceptance. Had I seen him labouring at trigonometry, I would have looked around for some space he expected to measure. Therefore when I saw him labouring at chemistry I was interested. It was part of Jeremiah's understanding that he also should be interested. But, while I was curious, looking about for the unexpected, Jeremiah was frankly contented.

He had cause for his content. Diarmuid was working with remarkable application. He was for all the world like a miner digging his pegged claim with eager eyes for gold. Nothing of the methodical determination he gave to his other studies was visible about this part of his chosen course. And so a new kinship was established between father and son; for when I commented on this to Jeremiah his reply was shrewd in its penetration.

'Sure,' he said. 'What would you expect else? Hasn't he just that class of a mind? He's getting down to facts now, you see. He was never one to take the outside show of the world at its face value, like most folk do. He wants to take it all to pieces, and put it together again to his own satisfaction. Facts are not what look to be facts. You must pull things to pieces, and then you find the real facts. Can't you see the way his mind's working? Because if you cannot, I can very well. He wants to get to the foundation of things, and then when he gets there he'll work them up again his own way. It's what I had to do myself when I was just where he is now. I had to find out what was, and not what looked to be; and now he has got his two feet to the same road. Sure.'

When I had surrendered hope of bringing them together, here they were, father and son, on one side and the other, speaking to me with the same voice. For when I answered Jeremiah: 'That may be; but what should he see in chemistry of all things? There's some bent in his mind, no doubt. No doubt at all about that. Diarmuid doesn't aimlessly turn up any odd thing, whatever class of a mind he may have,' — he retorted:

'Bent enough, William, my decent man. 'Tisn't only chemistry, from what I see. Chemistry's only the beginning for Diarmuid O'Hara. He's now beginning to see what I've seen for this long time, that the things that are possible for the future are different from the things that were possible for the past. Sure. Do you mind the way we used to watch Bronty[4] with his tubes and bulbs and blue flames? I thought a bit of coal was a bit of coal, and a hard fact enough; but he shewed me it wasn't a fact at all, but a whole collection of much bigger facts, dyes and poisons and medicines and the dear knows what else. There's the turning of the world inside out in that. There he was, doing with the hard world what I started to do with the people in it, turning them inside out and getting to the real people within. Not what looked to be, but what was. And do you know, when I saw that, I wished I could begin all over again, and tear the new things to pieces and put them together again in new forms and shapes . . . from this office, William, from this office. Not books, mind you, not words, but facts all the time that have been mastered and put to service. It wasn't to be, well. I had neither the time nor the chance; and it was past my day; but now, you see, Diarmuid O'Hara is setting out to do it, the way I always said he would.'

So said the father. Some days after this I deliberately created an excuse to search out the son with no other intention than to compare notes. Little I thought to be answered almost in the same words.

I constructed the scene with rare craft. It was not till I turned from his room that I stopped suddenly to say:

'You're a great man at chemistry these times. What's the cause of that? May I know?'

'Do you ask why?' he answered, with a swift glance at me, and a flicker of his lip. 'I'm not sure I rightly know. It's not only chemistry, you see. That's the beginning only, though maybe the best part of the beginning. Padraic Bronty says the future of the world will first be worked out in the laboratory; and that's right, too, though perhaps not in the way he thinks.'

'Oh, is that so? And what way does he think, and what way do you?'

'Hadn't you better ask him direct? I'm not his keeper, do you know, though he was one time thought to be mine. . . . I'm sure,' he added quickly, 'he's thinking only of Ireland, just as I'd like to . . . to make Ireland a decenter place for a fine stock.'

I looked at him blankly. 'How?' I asked. 'I don't see the connection . . . not quite.'

I wondered if he was too clear about it himself, for he hesitated, and then spoke slowly, with either great reserves of thought, or as feeling his way. 'Well, chemistry's not romance, I suppose; but with chemistry and applied physics it looks as if, if we had the proper people working at them, we could turn the world inside out all the same. And in Ireland we've got a clear field to work in, where others haven't.'

Conceive my delight at his words. 'That's the very saying of your father. Do you know that?'

'Is it? But I'm not thinking of gombeen men.[5] If England got a hold of new discoveries first she'd use them for turning everybody into slaves . . . us first and most of all, so she would. We want folk who won't be always thinking of turning them into crocks of gold, but into making Ireland the best place to live in that ever there was. If there's all in it that there seems, we might be able to pull things to pieces and make a new shape of the whole outfit. . . . I suppose you think that romantic. Maybe it is. But that's why I'm sweating at chemistry all the same.'

'I don't think anything of the kind; I'm thinking of other things altogether,' I answered.

4

Then into this happy hopefulness there came a rapid succession of events that whirled us away to entirely new issues.

Every Sunday was spent by Diarmuid drilling and route-marching. We never saw him at Mass. He cycled to early Mass at the Pro-Cathedral, and seldom returned till late. The mere physical effect on him was considerable. Helen herself was reconciled to the military order of his days when she saw the bronzed, hardy son who took shapely completeness during these summer months — though she exerted all her influence against permitting Martin to be drawn into the tide that ran about him.

When, therefore, one Sunday in late July a neighbour fluttered in to tea with news that there had been terrible happenings — guns had been run in at Howth,[6] and the Volunteers had overpowered the police, and were marching on Dublin fully armed — all our thoughts at once went to Diarmuid.

'Such things,' simmered our visitor indignantly, ridiculous, over-dressed figure that she was. 'Such defiance of all authority. I don't know what we're coming to.'

Helen gravely sympathized with her; urged her to rest herself on the couch; and finally put her to rout by never permitting the sympathy to be turned the other way. Then, when she had gone, Jeremiah burst out angrily:

'Diarmuid O'Hara's in this if it's true.'

Helen replied: 'Mrs Doran's a dear soul, but she came in to exult. I'm glad we didn't give her the chance.'

Not till Diarmuid returned was the news confirmed. He gave little satisfaction. The hour was late, and he was tired and grimly exultant. Jeremiah left the contest to Helen, wisely; but her attack wrought no change on that dusty uniform.

''Twas no use having Volunteers without arms, and

by the same token we proved to ourselves we could do things. There'll be a wonderful change from this out.' That was all the defence he would permit himself to make. 'They, and their precious orders that we mustn't sneeze till we're let,' he scoffed. 'That's a page turned over anyhow; and likely it's a new book altogether.'

Little avail to argue with such a mood, so I asked:

'Do you say that the military appeared?'

'Precious little good it did them. We fooled them up to their eyes, and by now the guns are all safe. So they went off and shot unarmed men in a crowd. About the class of thing they're fit for.'

5

I slept little that night. The following morning I read the news. The previous night we had all been tense and irritable. The only clear brain among us had been Diarmuid's; and his clarity had only irritated us by assumptions outside our knowledge. We had gone to bed with raging confused minds; and I had carried away with me the conviction, certainly of Jeremiah's hostility, and of Helen's also in milder degree. What was my surprise, therefore, to find the whole household before me buried in the daily Press. As I came in Jeremiah handed me his paper, and stood with his back to us, looking out of the window.

I read the news, and as I read, the blood in my veins was stirred. Here was a national issue as there had not been in my time. To forbid a nation the right to bear arms; to turn out military when that right was upheld; and then for that military, in revenge (it appeared) for their defeat, to shoot innocent citizens — intolerable . . . monstrous. But for my years, I would myself have enrolled among the Volunteers.

I looked up at Jeremiah, who had turned and stood over me.

'What do you think of it?' I asked him, not daring to trust myself to more.

'Bad, bad,' he said. 'Makes you feel as if you want to. . . .' His face became suddenly flushed with blood, and his hand, that hung beside me, was clenched till the skin on the knuckles was white. Then he called across the room in a voice like a challenge in battle: 'And how's Diarmuid O'Hara this morning after his wars?'

Diarmuid looked critically at his father, and laughed softly. 'I feel good,' he said.

'No wonder for you. You did well yesterday.'

Battle called across to battle from father to son. Oh, that this hour could have lasted! Torn between mood and mood, I knew not whether to rage at our

indignity or to rejoice in the understanding that had come between father and son. I was called out of my confusion by Helen's voice saying:

'Well, you had better come to breakfast, both of you.' Her voice sang with the blessed music of a heart of joy.

All that day Jeremiah was neglectful of work. I had never in my years known so complete a national unity. Irish men and women were no more men and women, but parts of a single whole annealed in a common emotion. All the ordinary differences of mood and temperament were idle breathings on the glass. And Jeremiah passed from one to another, sharing and receiving, his tall figure moving among his fellows like a beacon of war, while he surprised his grave friends by the violence of his sentiments.

That evening he returned early, and at once searched out Diarmuid.

'And how's Diarmuid O'Hara now?' he asked merrily.

'He's still good,' came the equally merry reply.

'Working away to-day? Guns all safe?'

'You may say so. We lost nineteen all told. But against that we got seven off the military.'

'Hullo! Lost on the deal? But no harm. 'Twas a good day.'

'Ay; but we gained on the cash value.'

And the two of them laughed heartily; and we all laughed. Happy hour. Then Jeremiah turned on Martin.

'And what about you, Martin?' he challenged.

'I joined up to-day.'

'Good man. Good man.'

Oh, that this hour could have lasted. Save for certain moments, that grew longer as they recurred, when Jeremiah was caught in the trammels of his life-long occupations, it continued for ten days. Father and son might have been two boys together. Scarce a cloud darkened the perfect understanding of their exchanges — an understanding too complete to require many words. Diarmuid did not search out his father as Jeremiah searched out his son, I noticed; but when they were together like called to like, and as fellows they answered one another. That was, perhaps, natural. For Diarmuid was not anything other than his habitual self, whereas Jeremiah was unlike anything I had known of him, save that he was always oddly reminiscent of himself. They did not bear their happiness apart selfishly, but bestowed it on us like sunshine, making us all happy together — gay and happy together. It was a beautiful week in my life, even while we heard the whole country stirring without.

But it was not to last. It was broken in one moment violently; and after that one moment it was as though it had never been.

One afternoon Jeremiah put down the telephone, and rose from his desk, pacing to and fro across the office in deep thought. Then he came over to my desk.

'William,' he said, and his voice was grave with care, 'we'll have to change many a thing in this office before many weeks are older. They're just after telling me from the paper that England has declared war on Germany, and that means all Europe will be putting knives into its own vitals. A serious thing for us, mind you. We'll have to heed things closely enough if we're to protect the interests of this office.'

1   The Irish Volunteers were formed in November 1913 under the leadership of Eoin MacNeill.
2   Diarmuid's mother.
3   Diarmuid's elder brother, who possessed a practical business sense.
4   In the novel Padraic Bronty, a visionary chemist who was also a nationalist, was for a time employed by Jeremiah.
5   An Irish word always used disparagingly. Gombeen men lent money to tenant farmers at exorbitant interest.
6   The Howth gun-running incident, when Erskine Childers arrived on board the *Asgard* at Howth with guns for the Irish Volunteers, took place in July 1914. The British Authorities were unable to prevent the guns being landed.

GEORGE RUSSELL (Æ)
from George Russell, *The Interpreters* (1922)

What is the relation between the politics of time and the politics of eternity? In this prose fantasy Russell explores the origins of the ideals of his generation. It is the night before they are executed for their part in a revolution, they being Lavelle (modelled on Russell himself), Brehon (Standish James O'Grady, Russell's one-time mentor), Rian (modelled in part on Yeats), and Leroy (modelled perhaps on Gogarty and Stephens). A sequel to this novel can be found in *The Avatars* (1935).

Chapter 6

'Where else,' answered Lavelle, 'but on lone earth or mountain come inspiration, and how but by divine visitations, whisperings and breathings from the dark were nations inspired? Every race, Greek, Egyptian, Hindu, or Judaean, whose culture moves us deeply, looked back to divine origins. My belief in such inspirations has, I confess, been more to me than the thoughts about the nation I have shared with others. But I do not know if I can make clear reasons for my belief in an oversoul guiding and inspiring our people. You will agree, I think, that we do not bring about revolutions because of the few people we may know personally. We do so because of the millions we do not know. And I think it is true also that we are stirred less by the ideas we make clear to ourselves than by the myriad uncomprehended ideas and forces which pour on us and through us, which are hardly intelligible to

ourselves, which we cannot rationalize, but which give us impulse, direction, and the sensation of fulness of being.'

'I guess what you mean,' said Rian. 'I rarely designed a building without imagination creating a city in harmony with it; and from this piling up of fanciful cities in the imagination comes the inspiration for the single house.'

'Do you see the buildings in your imaginary city clearly?' asked Lavelle.

'I do in part. Sometimes I can see the sun shining on architrave, carving, or pillar, casting clear-cut shadows. This I think strange and wonder how it all was born in me. I often feel a mere craftsman employed by a supernatural architect to carry out a few of his prodigal designs.'

'You believe,' Brehon asked of Lavelle, 'these intuitions about the nation have their origin in a being which has an organic life of its own, just as the half-perceived buildings of imagination with him give the sense they are really complete like a city in the heavens before he becomes aware of them?'

'Yes, I think that is a parallel. But Rian, for all his vision of cities, would find it difficult to draw in detail one after another the buildings he surmises in that architectural atmosphere around the one building he concentrates on. It is no less difficult for me to give substance to a multitude of feelings, which, if I pass them through a filter of words, will not sound like planetary murmurs, though I feel they come out of the soul of the world. I will try, however, to isolate some of these moods and interpret them. I feel it is easier now to do this because here we are, it may be, in the antechamber of death where unrealities are rare visitors. Here I find the thoughts I shared with others fade in power and the spiritual concept of nationality alone remains with me.'

'I think we shall have some light on the problem how theocratic states were born,' said Leroy. 'Lavelle is an antique.'

'It is a long history, beginning when I was a boy,' said the poet, who accepted the ironical comment of his friend with good nature. 'You remember, Rian, our holiday among the mountains? One day you wished to climb to the top of the hill, and I would not, and you went on, and for hours I was alone. But as I lay on the hillside I was no longer solitary, but smitten through and through with another being, and I knew it was the earth, and it was living, and its life was mingling with my own. Some majesty was shining on me all the day, nodding at me behind the veil of light and air, or playing hide-and-seek within the shade, or it was in me as a spirit beseeching love from my own. It seemed older than life, yet younger and nigher to me than my own boyhood. I lay there drenched in the light, and all the while imagination, as a cloud which wanders between the Earth and Heaven, was wandering between my transience and some immortal youth. I can remember that magical day. I can see the white sun blinding the sky, and light in dazzling cataracts outpoured and foam from cloud to cloud, and the earth glow beneath an ocean of light with purple shaded valleys, and lakes that mirrored back the burning air, and woods vaporous as clouds along the hills, and jutting crags, and mountains hewn in pearl, all lustrous as dream images and all remote as dream. Earth had suffused its body with its soul, and I lay on the mountain side clinging to it in a passion. When Rian came down I heard his voice beside me as from an immense distance calling me back to myself; and I was irritated by his coming, for I wanted to be alone with that spirit which had found me.'

'Oh, I know,' groaned Leroy. 'If nature catches the soul young it is lost to humanity.'

'No, no, the Earth spirit does not draw us aside from life. How could that which is father and mother of us all lead us to err from the law of our being?'

'The earth may be our mother,' retorted Leroy, 'but I am sure it is not our father. We get intellect from something beyond planets or sun.'

'Be quiet, Leroy,' said Rian, 'we will hear your reasons for revolution later. I am sure they will be the maddest of all, though Lavelle's political thinking appears to me to begin in very abstract regions.'

'No, there are the true realities,' cried the poet. 'Abstractions begin when we get away from the Earth spirit which has begotten us. Out of it have come plant, animal and man — all real things. Do plant and animal arrange their own evolution? Does the flower dream its own colour and scent? Does the bee devise its own wings or the polity of the hive? Are we less exempt from that dominion over our ways? Since I was born some wisdom, never sleeping though I slept, was in me, and cell by cell I was fashioned and woven together and over my making I had no control. We dwell in the house of the body, but its perfection and intricate life are the work of a wisdom which never relaxes dominion over a single cell. I believe that wisdom is within the soul to guide it. It is ready at every instant to declare to us the evolutionary purpose. It has planned for us a polity as it has planned for the bee the polity of the hive. We are higher than plant or animal. We can be conscious co-workers with the spirit of nature. We fall into unreal fantasy or thin abstraction when we think apart from it. We are empty as a vessel turned downward which fills itself only with air. If we think with the Earth spirit our souls become populous with beauty, for we turn the cup of our being to a spring which is always gushing.'

'The Earth spirit speaks with one voice to you on your mountain and with another voice to some solitary in a desert in Araby.'

'The Earth spirit throws itself into innumerable forms of life,' answered Lavelle. 'Did you expect it to make its children all of one pattern? For every race its own culture. Every great civilization, I think, had a deity behind it, or a divine shepherd who guided it on some plan in the cosmic imagination. "Behold," said an ancient oracle, "how the Heavens glitter with intellectual sections." These are archetypal images we follow dimly in our evolution.'

'How do you conceive of these powers as affecting civilization?'

'I believe they incarnate in the race: more in the group than in the individual; and they tend to bring about an orchestration of the genius of the race, to make manifest in time their portion of eternal beauty. So arises that unity of character which existed in the civilization of Egypt or Attica, where art, architecture, and literature were in such harmony that all that is best seems almost the creation of one myriad-minded artist.'

'But,' said the indefatigable Leroy, 'your world spirit does not merely inspire variety of civilization in Greece, Egypt, or China, it inspires individuals in the same country to work in contrary directions. How do you distinguish among varieties of national ideals those which have the divine signature from the rest? How do you thus distinguish your inspirations from those of my Dark Angel?' It was as a Dark Angel Leroy wrote his fantasies.

'It is difficult to answer you,' said Lavelle, 'and if there was a general certainty in human thought I might be regarded as foolish to risk life because of momentary illuminations. But to all of us life is a mystery, and we are like Columbus who was encouraged to venture further on the untravelled seas because he saw a single leafy branch floating on the water. We likewise dare all things if we hear a horn blown from some height of being and remember that some who lived before us reported that they too heard that horn. We have control over the work of our hands, but little over the working of the soul. But yet we must yield to it, for without it we have nothing. You or I may write something and others will say of it that there is a mastery over our art; or Rian may design a building all will applaud for its beauty; but the fountains of thought or vision are not under our control. If vision ceased suddenly with you or me, how could we regain it? If ideas did not well up spontaneously from some deep none of us would know how to trap them, so far beyond conscious life is the true begetter of thought or vision. We would appear to ourselves to have no real being but for the continuity of character of the ideas which well up within us. Because of this continuity and harmony we infer some being out of which they arise. I have come by a round-about way to answer your question. As it is by the continuity of character in our ideas we infer a soul in ourselves, so it is by continuity and harmony of inspiration in a race we distinguish those inspirations which come from the national genius from ideas which are personal. I came but slowly myself to see these distinctions, for many years passed before imagination and feeling passed into vision and I began to see in that interior light figures which enchanted

me with their beauty. These were at first mythological in character and I could not connect them with anything in the world. Then I read the history of our nation, and I was excited by that tale which began among the gods, and from history I turned to literature, and it was then I knew the forms I had seen in vision had been present to the ancestors thousands of years ago, and ever since they had been in the imagination of the poets. I felt the continuity of national inspiration, that the same light was cast upon generation after generation just as the lamp in that high window casts a steadfast glow and shape on the smoke which hurries past,' and he pointed to the ruddy coilings of smoke which flowed by a high building beyond the square.

'What do you mean when you describe forms as mythological in character?'

'There are certain figures which appear continually in our literature, spoken of as a divine folk, apparitions of light taller than human, riding on winged horses, or shining musicians circled by dazzling birds, or queens bearing branches with blossoms of light or fruit from the world of immortal youth, all moving in a divine aether. These were messengers of the gods and through these came about that marriage of Heaven and Earth in our literature which made it for long centuries seem almost the utterance of a single voice. These divine visitations have been the dominant influence in our literature so that our poets have sung of their country as the shadow of Heaven. The hills were sacred, the woods were sacred, and holy too were the lakes and rivers because of that eternal beauty which was seen behind them as the flame is seen within the lamp. Political thought with us too has been more inspired by the national culture than by the economic needs which almost completely inspire political activity elsewhere. But why should I try to convince you of the reality of national character? Has it not been noted by all who come to us? If we had not been restrained by alien power from control over our own destiny we would have manifested the national genius in a civilization of our own and it would have been moulded nearer to the divine polity. While all can see the unity of mood and character, I am perhaps alone among you here, though not alone in the nation, in believing it comes from the soul of the world. Such beliefs are perhaps above proof, though we may know the truth after to-morrow's sun has set, falling back into that fountain from which we came.'

Pages 323–346 have been removed due
to a dispute in relation to copyright

CON O'LEARY
from Con O'Leary, *The Manchester Guardian*, October 1922

Con O'Leary (1887–1958) was an English-based journalist and novelist. At one time he
worked on *The Manchester Guardian* and edited its weekly edition. Here in this short
story he provides a glimpse of ordinary Irish life in Manchester, appropriately with the
pub as centre stage.

The Snipe

The Snipe Inn, a small beerhouse somewhere between
Rochdale Road and Oldham Road, Manchester,
chucked out one manager after another with as little
ceremony as it would use towards its own 'drunks'. It is
a hardy neighbourhood, with quarrelsome vaults. But
Batt Finucane, a Tipperary man, held his ground, and
by his desire the brewery painted the front of the Snipe
a cucumber green. Batt stuck to mild beer himself,
would serve women only through a hutch in the lobby,
was friends with the police, had a way with him and a
temper that would overthrow the best man in the vault.
He had been married — but of that enough. His son
Brendan was away at school in Ireland.

Young labourers from Connaught resort (as Batt
says) the vault. They are huge men, fond of wearing
their athletic medals, and they will not be put down
by the half-breeds — men with Irish names and
English accents. To every score in these arguments
Batt says 'True' or 'There is something in that', unless
indeed his temper is out, and then the half-breeds get
the smack of it.

Batt would not like us to discuss the lobby and its
scramble of shawled women, offering jugs or coveting
gills, with so much shouting that nobody not trained
to it would know what was said. Yet they will halt
their din and will even make way for you to pass
through to the parlour. Here in the parlour it is free
for you to say what country (that is county) you come
from, how long you have been on this side, and what
you think of things in the 'old dart' now. Batt will
have a glass with you, though he will keep an eye and
an ear to the vault. He is ashamed of his trade, and if
he suspects that you are noticing things he will deplore
that vault to you.

'Decent young greenhorns come over, and in they
march to the Snipe. They'd heard tell of it in Ireland
from John or Pat. By this and by that I don't want
their custom. My poor wife's family — well, you
know. The priests should set up a sodality for them,
and a club-room with draughts and snooker and a little
game of cards.'

This will rouse Canty, a stallholder in the market,
who has unorthodox views. 'Them fellows — singing
hymns! Some of them boyos could drink the Shannon
dry. In my time every boy had to drink a pint and
walk to Goleen Cross — twenty miles maybe — when
he reached fourteen years. A nice sober country is
Ireland now; no wakes, no porter at the threshings, an
anti-treating league if you please. What's the result? I'll
tell you now — teetotallers every one of them, and
they murdering one another in their sober senses.'

This will rouse Dinny Joe, the boss's cousin, who
never says much. 'If the Volunteers[1] had given way to
drink they'd have been wiped out by their excesses —
like that!' He blows the froth off his pint.

'The drink here is like water — I mean to say in
this country, Batt,' says Jem Keeffe, the postman, who
has been a company-sergeant-major in the Munster
Fusiliers.[2] 'I seen an English corporal of mine and he
roaring drunk on the smell of Clonakilty Wrastler.'

In discussions in the Snipe temperance will get the
worst of it, despite Batt Finucane's moving description
of the crusade preached by the Irish Capuchins, who
are educating his boy. A great order, the Capuchins;
they walk about the streets in their brown habits,
nothing but sandals to their naked feet. They have
bought a gentleman's place in Cork, and fitted it up
with stained glass. (This interests Nicholas White, the
painters' delegate.)

'That's it now,' says Canty. 'All the gentry flying
from Ireland like the plague, and all their estates
turned into monasteries and convents. The marriage
rate of Ireland — what is it, somebody?'

Nobody replies. 'The birth rate's all right,' says
Dinny Joe.

'It's the destiny of our race,' says the boss, 'to
propagate the faith. I heard a missioner say the day will
come when you'll see a monastery on every Irish hill.'

The debates more often were pride of Ireland. Let it
be politics or law, racing or jockeyship, Tammany[3] or
Washington, the Church or the army — were not the
Irish always to the fore? The greatest saints, and the
Snipe gloried in them; the greatest sinners, and it saw
the genius even there. Batt would read passages from

green-backed pamphlets, or cuttings — mostly poems from the *Weekly Freeman*. Sometimes our men discussed the great boxers — Corbett, Fitzsimmons and John L. — and it was made plain that Tom Sharkey and Peter Maher would have taken the belt if they had been properly trained and fed for it. It was agreed that you could not keep the Irish down.

Across these self-satisfied lives broke the mission at St Patrick's by the Passionists, Father Bede and Father Patrick. Father Bede was a delicate little man who preached devotional sermons and took an hour to read the Mass. It was thought by the look of him that he fasted a great deal. Father Patrick was a strong, healthy, peasant-looking Irishman. He had lungs of leather and a great thump of scorn. He had a fund of menacing stories of cosmopolitan sinners who met sudden deaths, and a gentler anthology of old Irishwomen who made a beautiful passing. He insisted on rosary beads for all and on congregational singing. 'Even the corncrake testifies to his Maker.' You heard his own voice, more powerful than choir and congregation together it seemed, in the 'Hymn to St Patrick'.

Hail, glorious Saint Patrick, dear saint of our isle,
On Erin's green valleys look down in thy love!

The Snipe did justice to Father Patrick as a theologian and a pulpit orator, the foremost since Father Tom Burke.[4] Father Patrick did not know his friends or he might have been more forbearing in that devastating sermon against drink. At the close of it Batt Finucane, who always timed the sermon, did not dare to pull out his watch, but he was sure that Father Patrick preached for two hours. The publican sat with bowed head — there was a thump, thump in it — conscious that he was the scapegoat for the thirsts of all. Mrs Casey, a half-wit, turned round twice with an articulate 'Tch, tch, tch!' But even she held her breath at the passage that seemed for him alone.

He did not recall it clearly, but certain phrases were typed in his brain. 'Poisoner and plunderer . . . worse than the Crowbar brigade . . . his gilded columns, his glittering mirrors . . . instrument of poverty, vice and crime . . . thirst of Dives . . . the devil's work . . . death-bed haunted . . . curses of women and children, suicides and thieves.'

Father Patrick, wiping his brow and neck, gave out the words of the pledge, and everybody seemed to respond. 'Louder,' he cried, 'that the brewers may hear.' But Batt could only whisper the words. It flashed across his mind that he would have to leave the beer testing to his assistant now. The Snipe was deserted for once. Two brave fellows came in to play darts. The loser looked at the winner. They laughed slyly, and the loser called for two Guinness. Then came the omen. For the first time in its life the corkscrew worm jammed and would not plunge.

After an uneasy night Batt went to confession to Father Patrick, whose fury had abated: then he wrote to the Guardian of the Capuchins, where his son Brendan was now in the novitiate. They had a lay brother there, he remembered, who had been a commercial traveller in England. Father Guardian replied promptly that they were all praying for him, and they would be glad to welcome him into the community. Then Batt took his resignation to the brewery, where they pressed him very hard to change his mind. He saw the malt sifted from vat to vat, and great wells where the water came up like a flood. Last of all they took him into the testing-room and offered him champagne and stout. But he was faithful to Father Patrick.

As the effect of the mission wore off the old stalwarts crept back to the Snipe. Batt avoided the parlour, yet grew melancholy in the cellar. He fondled the old wooden mallet, so indented from tapping the 36-gallon casks. The new waste beer filter was mixing the old stuff from the drip trough lusciously with the bitter. Everything in the place was homely — the beer engine with the cream china handles, the cork drawer clamped to the counter, the green mugs, the spirit goblets, the flanged glasses (five to the quart) and the footed half-pints. He remembered great days in the Snipe — when the electric light came and the cash register, the first afternoon closing, sweepstakes he won, a char-à-banc drive. He knelt on the wooden tilter and said a prayer.

The Capuchins inquired about the matter of a wife who had died in the asylum. The circumstances might affect him, it appeared, and more particularly his son's profession. To crown the confusion Nicholas White, the painters' delegate, brought the news that the Snipe was to be painted terra-cotta for the new tenant.

'By this and by that, I'll not stand for it,' said Batt. 'I'll not stand for the eviction of my race.'

'What'll it matter to you when you'll be in the monks?' said Canty soothingly.

'What'll — where's my hat? It's not terra-cotta yet. It'll never be terra-cotta. It'll be green as I made it. It'll be Irish ground. If there's no other way I'll stop as I am. Father Patrick wouldn't forgive me, but Saint Patrick might.'

When he had gone to the brewery they 'had another', and said that Batt was a fool-rogue and Father Bede the more lasting preacher, and that Batt might now drink himself to death like the last manager.

'It is no fault for the man,' said Canty, 'to be after putting Ireland first. And what more did the best Irishman do? Or what less? Here's slauntha⁵ anyhow!'

August, 1922

1 The Irish Volunteers formed in 1913.
2 A regiment in the British Army.
3 American City Hall politics which from the 1880s onwards reflected the growing strength of Irish voters (and ensuing corruption). See Joseph Dineen's *Ward Eight* (1936) and John O'Hara's *The Last Hurrah* (1956) below.
4 Fr Tom Burke, a well-known Dominican preacher at the time.
5 Irish sláinte, health, cheers.

W. B. YEATS
from *The Dial*, January 1923

Here are two sections from the longer sequence entitled 'Meditations in Time of Civil War'. Yeats was in his Tower at Ballylee for several months in 1922 at the height of the Civil War. In October 1922 the bridge beside the Tower was blown up, the river was blocked, and the ground floor flooded. George Yeats and the servants became nervous at night and the Yeatses were pleased to leave (they returned in May 1923 when the Civil War was over). In these stanzas we see Yeats's capacity to voice the feelings of his time in some of the most memorable lines he ever wrote.

from MEDITATIONS IN TIME OF CIVIL WAR

V The Road at my Door

An affable Irregular,¹
A heavily-built Falstaffian man,
Comes cracking jokes of civil war
As though to die by gunshot were
The finest play under the sun.

A brown Lieutenant² and his men,
Half dressed in national uniform,
Stand at my door, and I complain
Of the foul weather, hail and rain,
A pear-tree broken by the storm.

I count those feathered balls of soot
The moor-hen guides upon the stream,
To silence the envy in my thought;
And turn towards my chamber, caught
In the cold snows of a dream.

VI The Stare's Nest by my Window

The bees build in the crevices
Of loosening masonry, and there

The mother birds bring grubs and flies.
My wall is loosening; honey-bees,
Come build in the empty house of the stare.³

We are closed in, and the key is turned
On our uncertainty; somewhere
A man is killed, or a house burned,
Yet no clear fact to be discerned:
Come build in the empty house of the stare.

A barricade of stone or of wood;
Some fourteen days of civil war;
Last night they trundled down the road
That dead young soldier in his blood:
Come build in the empty house of the stare.

We had fed the heart on fantasies,
The heart's grown brutal from the fare;
More substance in our enmities
Than in our love; O honey-bees,
Come build in the empty house of the stare.

1 Republican in Civil War.
2 Uniform of new Irish Free State army.
3 A starling in Ireland is sometimes called this.

DOROTHY MacARDLE
from Dorothy MacArdle, *Earth-Bound: Nine Stories of Ireland* (1924)

The following story was written by a leading Republican historian and conveys something of the mood of Ireland in the early 1920s. It takes its cue from the 1890s themes as expressed in Wilde's *The Picture of Dorian Gray* (1891), Ibsen's *When We Dead Awaken* (1900), or, closer to home, Yeats's poems and plays on beauty and politics. Dorothy MacArdle, who had been imprisoned in 1922 for Republican activities, observed in *The Irish Republic* (1937): 'Ten years after the Easter Rising, Ireland lay partitioned, impoverished, her people embittered by disappointment, divided and distraught by a half-measure of freedom and exhausted by war.' But this story, though dark, is perhaps inevitably less aware of history's dark passages to come.

The Portrait of Roisin Dhu[1]

It was a year after the artist was drowned that the loan exhibition of Hugo Blake's paintings was opened in Philadelphia by Maeve. 'Whom the gods love die young,' people said.

To remember those paintings is like remembering a dream-life spent with the Ever-living in an Ireland untrodden by men.

Except once he never painted a human face or any from of life, human or faery, yet the very light and air of them thrilled with life — it was as though he had painted life itself. There was the great 'Sliav Gullion'[2] — stony, austere, — the naked mountain against the northern sky, and to look at it was to be filled with a young, fierce hunger for heroic deeds, with the might of Cuchulain and Fionn. There was 'Loch Corrib' like a mirage from the first day of Creation — there was Una's 'Dawn' . . .

The critics, inarticulate with wonder, made meaningless phrases: 'Blake paints as a seer,' 'He paints on the astral plane.'

At the end of the room, alone on a grey wall, hung the 'Portrait of Roisin Dhu'. Before her, Irish men and women stood worshipping, the old with tears, the young with fire in their eyes. There were men whom it sent home.

Had Blake seen, anywhere on earth, others were asking, that heart-breaking, entrancing face? Knowledge of the secrets of God was in the eyes; on the lips was the memory, the endurance and the fore-knowledge of endless pain; yet from the luminous, serene face shone out a beauty that made one crave for the spaces beyond death.

No woman in the world, we said, had been Hugo's Roisin Dhu; no mortal face had troubled him when he painted that immortal dream — that ecstasy beyond

fear, that splendour beyond anguish — that wild, sweet holiness of Ireland for which men die.

Maeve, as we knew, had been his only friend. When strangers clamoured, 'Was there a woman?' she would not tell. But one evening when we were five only around Una's fire she told us the strange, incredible tale.

'I will not tell everyone for a while,' she said, 'because so few would understand, and Hugo, unless one understood to the heights and depths, might seem to have been . . . unkind. But I will tell you: There was a girl.'

'It is almost impossible to believe,' Liam said; 'It is not a human body he has painted; nor even a human soul!'

'That is true in a way,' Maeve answered, hesitating; 'I will try to make you understand.'

'He was the loneliest being I have ever known. He was a little atom of misery and rebellion when my godmother rescued him in France. She bought the child from a drunkard who was starving him almost to death. His mother, you know, was Nora Raftery, the actress; she ran away from her husband with François Raoul, taking the child, and died. Poor Blake rode over a precipice while hunting — mad with grief, and the boy was left without a friend in the world. It was I who taught him to read and write: already he could draw.

To the end he was the same passionate, lonely child. The anguish of pity and love he had had for his mother he gave to her country when he came home: he suffered unbearable 'heim-weh'[3] all the years he was studying abroad. The 'Dark Tower', as we called it, of our godmother's house on Loch Corrib was the place he loved best.

I have known no one who lived in such extremes, always, of misery or of joy. In any medium but paint he was helpless — chaotic or dumb, yet I think that his pictures came to him first not visually at all, but as intense perceptions of a *mood*. And between that moment of perception and the moment when it took form and colour in his mind he used to be like a wild creature in pain. He would prowl day and night around the region he meant to paint, waiting in a rage of impatience for the right moment of light and shadow to come, the incarnation of the soul. . . . Then, when he had found it, the blessed mood of contentment would come and he would paint, day after day, until it was done. At those times, in the evenings, he would be exhausted and friendly and grateful like a child.

For all the vehemence that you feel in his work he painted very slowly, with intense, exquisite care, like a man in love. That is indeed what he was, — in love, obliviously, with whatever spirit had enthralled his imagination at the time. And when the picture was finished and the vision gone he fell into a mood of desolation in which he wanted to die. He was very young.

I tried to scold Hugo out of those moods. I was with him in April just after he had finished his 'Loch Corrib' — you know the innocence, the angelic tranquillity in it, like the soul of a child. He would not go near the lake: 'It is nothing to me now,' he said sombrely, 'I have done with it.'

'Hugo,' I said, laughing, 'you are a vampire! The loch has given you its soul.' He answered, 'Yes: that is true; corpses are ugly things.'

For a month that empty, dead mood lasted and Hugo hated all the world. I took him to London to give him something to hate. After two days he fled back to his tower and breathed the smell of the peat and sea-wind, and the sweet, home-welcome of burning turf, and looked out on Ireland with eyes of love. The next morning he came in from a bathe in the loch with the awakened, wondering look I had longed to see and said, 'I am going to paint Roisin Dhu.' Then he went off to walk the west of Ireland seeking a woman for his need.

I was astonished and excited beyond words; he had been so contemptuous of human subjects, although I remembered, in his student days, studies for heads and hands that had made one artist whisper 'Leonardo!' under his breath.

I wondered what woman he would bring home.

They came about two weeks later, after dark, rowing over the loch, Hugo and the girl alone.

After supper, sitting over the turf fire in the round hall of the tower, Hugo told me that she was the daughter of a king.

She smiled at him, knowing that he spoke of her although she had no English at all, and I told her in

Irish what he had said. She answered gravely, 'It is true.'

I looked at her then as she moved from the window to her chair, and I felt almost afraid — her beauty was so delicate and so remote . . .

'Those red lips with all their mournful pride'[4] . . . Poems of Yeats were haunting me while I looked at her. But it was the beauty of one asleep, unaware of life or of sorrow or of love . . . the face of a woman whose light is hidden . . .

She sat in the shadowed corner, brooding, while Hugo talked. He was at his happiest, overflowing with childish delight in his achievement and with eagerness for tomorrow's sun.

Nuala was her name. The King of the Blasket Isles was her father — a superstitious, tyrannical old man. Hugo had been able to make no way with him or his sons.

'I invited one of them to come too, and take care of her,' he said, 'but they would not hear of it at all.

'The old man was as dignified as a Spanish Grandee.

'"It is not that I would be misdoubting you, honest man," says he, "but my daughter is my daughter and there is no call for her to be going abroad to the world."

'And her brothers were as obstinate:

'"'Tis not good to be put in a picture: it takes from you," they said.

'They got me into a boat by a ruse, rowed me "back to Ireland" and when they had landed me pulled off.

'"The blessing of God on your far travelling!" they called to me gravely: a hint that I would not be welcome to the island again.

'You can imagine the frenzy I was in!' he said. And I could, well. He had walked night after night on the rocks of the mainland planning some desperate thing, but one night Nuala came to him, rowed out through the darkness by some boys who braved the vengeance of the old king for her sake. He rewarded them extravagantly and brought Nuala home.

He told it all triumphantly, and Nuala looked up at him from time to time with a gentle gaze full of content and rest. But my heart sank: there was only one possible end to this; Hugo, at his best, was loving and kind and selfless — all might be well — but I knew my Hugo after work.

She slept in my room and talked to me, softly, in the dark, asking me questions about Hugo's work. 'He told me you were his sister-friend,' she said.

I told her about his childhood, his suffering and his genius: she listened and sighed.

'It is a pity of him to be so long lonely,' she said, 'but he will not be lonely any more.'

'Why, Nuala?' I asked, my heart heavy with dread for her. Her answer left me silent.

'I myself will be giving him love.'

Hugo had found a being as lost to the world as himself. How would it end for her, I wondered. She slept peacefully, but I lay long awake.

The next morning work began in the studio at the top of the tower. I gave up all thought of going home. Nuala would need me.

Hugo was working faster than usual it seemed, beginning as soon as the light was clear and never pausing until it failed. I marvelled at Nuala's endurance, but I dared not plead for her. I had wrecked a picture of Hugo's once by going into his studio while he painted: his vision fled from him at the least intrusion and I had learned to keep aloof.

Day after day, when they came down at last to rest and eat, I could measure his progress by the sombre glow of power in his eyes. I could imagine some young druid when his spells proved potent, looking like that.

But the change that came over Nuala frightened me; he was wearing her away: her face had a clear, luminous look, her eyes were large and dark; I saw an expression in them sometimes as of one gazing into an abyss of pain. The change that might come to a lovely woman in years, seemed to come to her in days: the beauty of her, as she sat in the candle-light, gazing at her own thoughts in the shadows, would still your breathing. It grew more wonderful, more tragic, from day to day.

One night after she had stolen away to bed, exhausted, while Hugo sat by the fire in a kind of trance, I forced myself to question him.

'Hugo,' I said, as lightly as I could, with my heart throbbing: 'Is it that you are in love with your Roisin Dhu?'

He looked up suddenly, with a dark fire in his eyes. 'Love,' he whispered in a voice aching with passion. He rose and threw back his head and cried out in tones like deep music —

I could plough the blue air!
  I could climb the high hills!
O, I could kneel all night in prayer
    To heal your many ills![5]

Then he sighed and went away.

Nuala's look was becoming, day by day, a look of endurance and resignation that I could not bear, as of one despairing of all human happiness yet serene.

At last I questioned him again:

'Will you be marrying your Roisin Dhu?'

He turned on me startled, with a laugh, both angry and amazed.

'What a question! What an outrageous question, Maeve!'

I was unanswered still.

When seven weeks had gone I grew gravely anxious. I feared that Nuala would die: she had the beauty you could imagine in a spirit new-awakened from death, a look of anguish and ecstasy in one . . . She was frail and spent; she scarcely spoke to me or seemed to know me; she slept always in the garden alone.

It was towards the end of June that I said to Hugo, 'You are wearing your model out.'

'I am painting her better than God created her,' he answered. Then he said, contentedly, 'I shall have done with her very soon.'

I cannot express the dread that fell on me then; I was torn with irresolution. To interfere with Hugo — to break the spell of his vision — would not only sacrifice the picture, it might destroy him. I thought his reason would not survive the laceration, the passion that would follow the shattering of that dream.

That night I found Nuala utterly changed. She came down from the studio dull-eyed and ugly and went straight to bed in my room.

Hugo told me he did not want her any more.

I rowed her out next morning across the loch: it was one of those grey, misty days when it is loveliest; the Twelve Bens[6] in the distance looked like mountains of Hy Breasail, the weeds and sedges glimmering silvery-gold . . . but she had no eyes for its beauty, no beauty of her own, no light . . . she lay drowsy and unresponsive on her cushions; her hands and face were like wax.

I would have rebelled that night, taken any risk, to make Hugo undo what he had done. She lay down to sleep under a willow by the water's edge and I went to him in the hall. He was standing by the fire and turned to me as I came in; there was a look of wondering humility in his face, as if his own achievement were a thing to worship — a thing he could not understand.

'Tomorrow!' he said: 'It will be finished in an hour: you shall see it.' Then he came and took my hands in his old, affectionate way and said:

'You have been such a good sister-friend!'

One hour more! She must endure it: I would not sacrifice him for that. But I lay awake all night oppressed with a sense of fear and cruelty and guilt.

At breakfast time there was no Hugo: he had eaten and started work. Old Kate rang the bell in the garden but Nuala did not come. My fears had vanished with the sweet air and sunshine of the early morning: larks were singing; it was mid-June: the joy of Hugo's triumph was my own joy. I went down to the willow where I had left Nuala asleep. She was lying there still; she never stirred when I touched her. She was cold.

I called no one, I ran madly up the spiral stair to Hugo's studio in the tower. Outside his door I paused: the memory of the last time I had broken in and the devastating consequences arrested me even then. I pushed the door open without a sound and stood inside, transfixed.

I looked for a moment and grew dizzy, so amazing was the thing I saw. Hugo stood by his easel: before him on the dais, glimmering in the misty silver light, stood Nuala, gazing at him, all a radiance of consummated sacrifice and sweet, unconquerable love — Nuala, as you have seen her in the portrait of Roisin Dhu.

Hugo stumbled, laid down his brush, drew his hand over his eyes, then turned and, seeing me, said, 'It is done.'

When I looked again at the dais she was gone.

I was shaken to the heart with fear. I cried out, 'Come to her! She is dead.'

He ran with me down to the water's edge.

I believe I had hoped that he would be able to waken her, but she was cold and dead, lying with wide-open eyes.

Hugo knelt down and touched her, then rose quickly and turned away: 'How unbeautiful!' he said.

I called out to him sternly, angrily, and he looked down at her again, then stooped and lifted her in his arms.

'Maeve, Maeve!' he cried then, piteously: 'Have I done this?'

He brought her home with state to the Island, told them she had been his bride and gave her such a burial as the old King's heart approved. Then he came home again to his lonely house. I left it before he came; he had told me he wanted to be alone.

I heard nothing of him for a long time and felt uneasy and afraid. After I had written many anxious letters a strange, disjointed answer came.

'She has never left me,' he wrote. 'She is waiting, near, quite near. But what can I do? This imprisoning body — this suffocating life — this burdenous mortality — this dead world.

'The picture is for you, Sister-friend, and for Ireland when you die.'

Before I could go to him the picture came and with it the news that he was drowned.

They found the boat far out on the loch.'

Maeve's face was pale when she ended: she covered her eyes for a moment with her hand.

'He had seen the hidden vision . . .' one of us said.

Nesta was looking into the fire, her dark eyes wide with foreboding.

'It is written in Destiny,' she said: 'the lovers of Roisin Dhu must die.'

1   Irish for black little rose. Title of poem by Red Hugh O'Donnell (?1571–1602), lord of Tír Chonaill, in which Hugh addresses Ireland on the subject of his love for her. In the nineteenth century, James Clarence Mangan provided a translation under the title 'My Dark Rosaleen'.
2   An area south of Newry, haunt of Cuchulain in Irish mythology.
3   German for homesickness.
4   A slight misquotation from Yeats's poem on Helen of Troy and Deirdre, 'The Rose of the World': 'Who dreamed that beauty passes like a dream? / For these red lips, with all their mournful pride . . . Troy passed away . . . And Usna's children died.'
5   Lines from Mangan's 'My Dark Rosaleen'. Again, slightly misquoted: 'I could scale the blue air, / I could plough the high hills.'
6   Mountain peaks in Connemara. Hy Breasail is an imagined Atlantis.

W. B. YEATS
from *Tomorrow*, August 1924

As an exercise in seeing something of Yeats's process of composition, this version of 'Leda and the Swan' can be compared with the final version that appeared in *The Tower* (1928). The poem first appeared in *The Dial* in June 1924 but, read against the revolutionary rhetoric of Stuart's *To-Morrow* and a puritanical new Ireland, Yeats's erotic poem can seem less reactionary than at first appears. 'Leda and the Swan' gives prominence to a theme in *The Tower* as a whole, namely Yeats's concern with gender and civilization, and with the relationship between history and violence.

LEDA AND THE SWAN

A rush, a sudden wheel, and hovering still
The bird descends, and her frail thighs are pressed
By the webbed toes, and that all-powerful bill
Has laid her helpless face upon his breast.
How can those terrified vague fingers push
The feathered glory from her loosening thighs!
All the stretched body's laid on the white rush
And feels the strange heart beating where it lies;

A shudder in the loins engenders there
The broken wall, the burning roof and tower
And Agamemnon dead.
　　Being so caught up,
So mastered by the brute blood of the air,
Did she put on his knowledge with his power
Before the indifferent beak could let her drop?

F. SCOTT FITZGERALD
from F. Scott Fitzgerald, *All the Sad Young Men* (1926)

'Absolution' is a remarkable story that can stand beside Joyce's fiction without any loss
of stature. The Joycean influence can be felt throughout, and yet the plight of the boy
remains peculiar to a world where Irish Catholicism meets the wide plains of Dakota.
For this is a story of hope where lovers lie out under the moon, where the interior
world has not been wholly occupied by the Church.

Absolution

I

There was once a priest with cold, watery eyes, who, in the still of the night, wept cold tears. He wept because the afternoons were warm and long, and he was unable to attain a complete mystical union with our Lord. Sometimes, near four o'clock, there was a rustle of Swede girls along the path by his window, and in their shrill laughter he found a terrible dissonance that made him pray aloud for the twilight to come. At twilight the laughter and the voices were quieter, but several times he had walked past Romberg's Drug Store when it was dusk and the yellow lights shone inside and the nickel taps of the soda-fountain were gleaming, and he had found the scent of cheap toilet soap desperately sweet on the air. He passed that way when he returned from hearing confessions on Saturday nights, and he grew careful to walk on the other side of the street so that the smell of the soap would float upward before it reached his nostrils as it drifted, rather like incense, towards the summer moon.

But there was no escape from the hot madness of four o'clock. From his window, as far as he could see, the Dakota wheat thronged the valley of the Red River. The wheat was terrible to look upon and the carpet pattern to which in agony he bent his eyes sent his thought brooding through grotesque labyrinths, open always to the unavoidable sun.

One afternoon when he had reached the point where the mind runs down like an old clock, his housekeeper brought into his study a beautiful, intense little boy of eleven named Rudolph Miller. The little boy sat down in a patch of sunshine, and the priest, at his walnut desk, pretended to be very busy. This was to conceal his relief that some one had come into his haunted room.

Presently he turned around and found himself staring into two enormous, staccato eyes, lit with gleaming points of cobalt light. For a moment their expression startled him — then he saw that his visitor was in a state of abject fear.

'Your mouth is trembling,' said Father Schwartz, in a haggard voice.

The little boy covered his quivering mouth with his hand.

'Are you in trouble?' asked Father Schwartz, sharply. 'Take your hand away from your mouth and tell me what's the matter.'

The boy — Father Schwartz recognized him now as the son of a parishioner, Mr Miller, the freight-agent

— moved his hand reluctantly off his mouth and became articulate in a despairing whisper.

'Father Schwartz — I've committed a terrible sin.'

'A sin against purity?'

'No, Father . . . worse.'

Father Schwartz's body jerked sharply.

'Have you killed somebody?'

'No — but I'm afraid —' the voice rose to a shrill whimper.

'Do you want to go to confession?'

The little boy shook his head miserably. Father Schwartz cleared his throat so that he could make his voice soft and say some quiet, kind thing. In this moment he should forget his own agony, and try to act like God. He repeated to himself a devotional phrase, hoping that in return God would help him to act correctly.

'Tell me what you've done,' said his new soft voice.

The little boy looked at him through his tears, and was reassured by the impression of moral resiliency which the distraught priest had created. Abandoning as much of himself as he was able to this man, Rudolph Miller began to tell his story.

'On Saturday, three days ago, my father he said I had to go to confession, because I hadn't been for a month, and the family they go every week, and I hadn't been. So I just as leave go, I didn't care. So I put it off till after supper because I was playing with a bunch of kids and father asked me if I went, and I said "no," and he took me by the neck and he said "You go now," so I said "All right," so I went over to church. And he yelled after me: "Don't come back till you go." . . .'

II
"On Saturday, Three Days Ago"

The plush curtain of the confessional rearranged its dismal creases, leaving exposed only the bottom of an old man's shoe. Behind the curtain an immortal soul was alone with God and the Reverend Adolphus Schwartz, priest of the parish. Sound began, a laboured whispering, sibilant and discreet, broken at intervals by the voice of the priest in audible question.

Rudolph Miller knelt in the pew beside the confessional and waited, straining nervously to hear, and yet not to hear what was being said within. The fact that the priest was audible alarmed him. His own turn came next, and the three or four others who waited might listen unscrupulously while he admitted his violations of the Sixth and Ninth Commandments.

Rudolph had never committed adultery, nor even coveted his neighbour's wife — but it was the confession of the associate sins that was particularly hard to contemplate. In comparison he relished the less shameful fallings away — they formed a greyish background which relieved the ebony mark of sexual offences upon his soul.

He had been covering his ears with his hands, hoping that his refusal to hear would be noticed, and a like courtesy rendered to him in turn, when a sharp movement of the penitent in the confessional made him sink his face precipitately into the crook of his elbow. Fear assumed solid form, and pressed out a lodging between his heart and his lungs. He must try now with all his might to be sorry for his sins — not because he was afraid, but because he had offended God. He must convince God that he was sorry and to do so he must first convince himself. After a tense emotional struggle he achieved a tremulous self-pity, and decided that he was now ready. If, by allowing no other thought to enter his head, he could preserve this state of emotion unimpaired until he went into that large coffin set on end, he would have survived another crisis in his religious life.

For some time, however, a demoniac notion had partially possessed him. He could go home now, before his turn came, and tell his mother that he had arrived too late, and found the priest gone. This, unfortunately, involved the risk of being caught in a lie. As an alternative he could say that he *had* gone to confession, but this meant that he must avoid communion next day, for communion taken upon an uncleansed soul would turn to poison in his mouth, and he would crumple limp and damned from the altar-rail.

Again Father Schwartz's voice became audible.

'And for your ——'

The words blurred to a husky mumble, and Rudolph got excitedly to his feet. He felt that it was impossible to go to confession this afternoon. He hesitated tensely. Then from the confessional came a tap, a creak, and a sustained rustle. The slide had fallen and the plush curtain trembled. Temptation had come to him too late. . . .

'Bless me, Father, for I have sinned. . . . I confess to Almighty God and to you, Father, that I have sinned. . . . Since my last confession it has been one month and three days. . . . I accuse myself of — taking the Name of the Lord in vain. . . .'

This was an easy sin. His curses had been but bravado — telling of them was little less than a brag.

'. . . of being mean to an old lady.'

The wan shadow moved a little on the latticed slat.

'How, my child?'

'Old lady Swenson,' Rudolph's murmur soared jubilantly. 'She got our baseball that we knocked in her window, and she wouldn't give it back, so we yelled "Twenty-three, Skidoo," at her all afternoon. Then about five o'clock she had a fit, and they had to have the doctor.'

'Go on, my child.'

'Of — of not believing I was the son of my parents.'

'What?' The interrogation was distinctly startled.

'Of not believing that I was the son of my parents.'

'Why not?'

'Oh, just pride,' answered the penitent airily.

'You mean you thought yourself too good to be the son of your parents?'

'Yes, Father.' On a less jubilant note.

'Go on.'

'Of being disobedient and calling my mother names. Of slandering people behind their back. Of smoking ——'

Rudolph had now exhausted the minor offences, and was approaching the sins it was agony to tell. He held his fingers against his face like bars as if to press out between them the shame in his heart.

'Of dirty words and immodest thoughts and desires,' he whispered very low.

'How often?'

'I don't know.'

'Once a week? Twice a week?'

'Twice a week.'

'Did you yield to these desires?'

'No, Father.'

'Were you alone when you had them?'

'No, Father. I was with two boys and a girl.'

'Don't you know, my child, that you should avoid the occasions of sin as well as the sin itself? Evil companionship leads to evil desires and evil desires to evil actions. Where were you when this happened?'

'In a barn back of ——'

'I don't want to hear any names,' interrupted the priest sharply.

'Well, it was up in the loft of this barn and this girl and — a fella, they were saying things — saying immodest things, and I stayed.'

'You should have gone — you should have told the girl to go.'

He should have gone! He could not tell Father Schwartz how his pulse had bumped in his wrist, how a strange, romantic excitement had possessed him when those curious things had been said. Perhaps, in the houses of delinquency among the dull and hard-eyed incorrigible girls can be found those for whom has burned the whitest fire.

'Have you anything else to tell me?'

'I don't think so, Father.'

Rudolph felt a great relief. Perspiration had broken out under his tight-pressed fingers.

'Have you told any lies?'

The question startled him. Like all those who habitually and instinctively lie, he had an enormous respect and awe for the truth. Something almost exterior to himself dictated a quick, hurt answer. 'Oh no, Father, I never tell lies.'

For a moment, like the commoner in the king's chair, he tasted the pride of the situation. Then as the priest began to murmur conventional admonitions he realized that in heroically denying he had told lies, he had committed a terrible sin — he had told a lie in confession.

In automatic response to Father Schwartz's 'Make an act of contrition,' he began to repeat aloud meaninglessly:

'Oh, my God, I am heartily sorry for having offended Thee. . . .'

He must fix this now — it was a bad mistake — but as his teeth shut on the last words of his prayer there was a sharp sound, and the slat was closed.

A minute later when he emerged into the twilight the relief in coming from the muggy church into an open world of wheat and sky postponed the full realization of what he had done. Instead of worrying he took a deep breath of the crisp air and began to say over and over to himself the words 'Blatchford Sarnemington, Blatchford Sarnemington!'

Blatchford Sarnemington was himself, and these words were in effect a lyric. When he became Blatchford Sarnemington a suave nobility flowed from him. Blatchford Sarnemington lived in great sweeping triumphs. When Rudolph half closed his eyes it meant that Blatchford had established dominance over him and, as he went by, there were envious mutters in the air: 'Blatchford Sarnemington! There goes Blatchford Sarnemington.'

He was Blatchford now for a while as he strutted homeward along the staggering road, but when the road braced itself in macadam in order to become the main street of Ludwig, Rudolph's exhilaration faded out and his mind cooled, and he felt the horror of his lie. God, of course, already knew of it — but Rudolph reserved a corner of his mind where he was safe from God, where he prepared the subterfuges with which he often tricked God. Hiding now in this corner he considered how he could best avoid the consequences of his mis-statement.

At all costs he must avoid communion next day. The risk of angering God to such an extent was too great. He would have to drink water 'by accident' in the morning, and thus, in accordance with a church law, render himself unfit to receive communion that day. In spite of its flimsiness this subterfuge was the most feasible that occurred to him. He accepted its risks and was concentrating on how best to put it into effect, as he turned the corner by Romberg's Drug Store and came in sight of his father's house.

III

Rudolph's father, the local freight-agent, had floated with the second wave of German and Irish stock to the Minnesota-Dakota country. Theoretically, great opportunities lay ahead of a young man of energy in that day and place, but Carl Miller had been incapable of establishing either with his superiors or his subordinates the reputation for approximate immutability which is essential to success in a hierarchic industry. Somewhat gross, he was, nevertheless, insufficiently hard-headed and unable to take fundamental relationships for granted, and this inability made him suspicious, unrestful, and continually dismayed.

His two bonds with the colourful life were his faith in the Roman Catholic Church and his mystical worship of the Empire Builder, James J. Hill. Hill was the apotheosis of that quality in which Miller himself was deficient — the sense of things, the feel of things, the hint of rain in the wind on the cheek. Miller's mind worked late on the old decisions of other men, and he had never in his life felt the balance of any single thing in his hands. His weary, sprightly, undersized body was growing old in Hill's gigantic shadow. For twenty years he had lived alone with Hill's name and God.

On Sunday morning Carl Miller awoke in the dustless quiet of six o'clock. Kneeling by the side of the bed he bent his yellow-grey hair and the full dapple bangs of his moustache into the pillow, and prayed for several minutes. Then he drew off his night-shirt — like the rest of his generation he had never been able to endure pyjamas — and clothed his thin, white, hairless body in woollen underwear.

He shaved. Silence in the other bedroom where his wife lay nervously asleep. Silence from the screened-off corner of the hall where his son's cot stood, and his son slept among his Alger books, his collection of cigar-bands, his mothy pennants — 'Cornell', 'Hamlin', and 'Greetings from Pueblo, New Mexico' — and the other possessions of his private life. From outside Miller could hear the shrill birds and the whirring movement of the poultry, and, as an undertone, the low, swelling click-a-click of the six-fifteen through train for Montana and the green coast beyond. Then as the cold water dripped from the wash-rag in his hand he raised his head suddenly — he had heard a furtive sound from the kitchen below.

He dried his razor hastily, slipped his dangling suspenders to his shoulder, and listened. Some one was walking in the kitchen, and he knew by the light footfall that it was not his wife. With his mouth faintly ajar he ran quickly down the stairs and opened the kitchen door.

Standing by the sink, with one hand on the still dripping faucet and the other clutching a full glass of water, stood his son. The boy's eyes, still heavy with sleep, met his father's with a frightened, reproachful beauty. He was barefooted, and his pyjamas were rolled up at the knees and sleeves.

For a moment they both remained motionless — Carl Miller's brow went down and his son's went up, as though they were striking a balance between the extremes of emotion which filled them. Then the bangs of the parent's moustache descended portentously until they obscured his mouth, and he gave a short glance around to see if anything had been disturbed.

The kitchen was garnished with sunlight which beat on the pans and made the smooth boards of the floor and table yellow and clean as wheat. It was the centre of the house where the fire burned and the tins fitted into tins like toys, and the steam whistled all day on a thin pastel note. Nothing was moved, nothing touched — except the faucet where beads of water still formed and dripped with a white flash into the sink below.

'What are you doing?'

'I got awful thirsty, so I thought I'd just come down and get ——'

'I thought you were going to communion.'

A look of vehement astonishment spread over his son's face.

'I forgot all about it.'

'Have you drunk any water?'

'No ——'

As the word left his mouth Rudolph knew it was the wrong answer, but the faded indignant eyes facing him had signalled up the truth before the boy's will could act. He realized, too, that he should never have come downstairs; some vague necessity for verisimilitude had made him want to leave a wet glass as evidence by the sink; the honesty of his imagination had betrayed him.

'Pour it out,' commanded his father, 'that water!'

Rudolph despairingly inverted the tumbler.

'What's the matter with you, anyways?' demanded Miller angrily.

'Nothing.'

'Did you go to confession yesterday?'

'Yes.'

'Then why were you going to drink water?'

'I don't know — I forgot.'

'Maybe you care more about being a little thirsty than you do about your religion.'

'I forgot.' Rudolph could feel the tears straining in his eyes.

'That's no answer.'

'Well, I did.'

'You better look out!' His father held to a high, persistent inquisitory note: 'If you're so forgetful that you can't remember your religion something better be done about it.'

Rudolph filled a sharp pause with:

'I can remember it all right.'

'First you begin to neglect your religion,' cried his father, fanning his own fierceness, 'the next thing you'll begin to lie and steal, and the *next* thing is the *reform* school!'

Not even this familiar threat could deepen the abyss that Rudolph saw before him. He must either tell all now, offering his body for what he knew would be a ferocious beating or else tempt the thunderbolts by receiving the Body and Blood of Christ with sacrilege upon his soul. And of the two the former seemed more terrible — it was not so much the beating he dreaded as the savage ferocity, outlet of the ineffectual man, which would lie behind it.

'Put down that glass and go upstairs and dress!' his father ordered, 'and when we get to church, before you go to communion, you better kneel down and ask God to forgive you for your carelessness.'

Some accidental emphasis in the phrasing of this command acted like a catalytic agent on the confusion and terror of Rudolph's mind. A wild, proud anger rose in him, and he dashed the tumbler passionately into the sink.

His father uttered a strained, husky sound, and sprang for him. Rudolph dodged to the side, tipped over a chair, and tried to get beyond the kitchen table. He cried out sharply when a hand grasped his pyjama shoulder, then he felt the dull impact of a fist against the side of his head, and glancing blows on the upper part of his body. As he slipped here and there in his father's grasp, dragged or lifted when he clung instinctively to an arm, aware of sharp smarts and strains, he made no sound except that he laughed hysterically several times. Then in less than a minute the blows abruptly ceased. After a lull during which Rudolph was tightly held, and during which they both trembled violently and uttered strange, truncated words, Carl Miller half dragged, half threatened his son upstairs.

'Put on your clothes!'

Rudolph was now both hysterical and cold. His head hurt him, and there was a long, shallow scratch on his neck from his father's fingernail, and he sobbed and trembled as he dressed. He was aware of his mother standing at the doorway in a wrapper, her wrinkled face compressing and squeezing and opening out into new series of wrinkles which floated and eddied from neck to brow. Despising her nervous ineffectuality and avoiding her rudely when she tried to touch his neck with witch-hazel, he made a hasty, choking toilet. Then he followed his father out of the house and along the road towards the Catholic church.

IV

They walked without speaking except when Carl Miller acknowledged automatically the existence of passers-by. Rudolph's uneven breathing alone ruffled the hot Sunday silence.

His father stopped decisively at the door of the church.

'I've decided you'd better go to confession again. Go and tell Father Schwartz what you did and ask God's pardon.'

'You lost your temper, too!' said Rudolph quickly.

Carl Miller took a step towards his son, who moved cautiously backward.

'All right, I'll go.'

'Are you going to do what I say?' cried his father in a hoarse whisper.

'All right.'

Rudolph walked into the church, and for the second time in two days entered the confessional and knelt down. The slat went up almost at once.

'I accuse myself of missing my morning prayers.'

'Is that all?'

'That's all.'

A maudlin exultation filled him. Not easily ever again would he be able to put an abstraction before the necessities of his ease and pride. An invisible line had been crossed, and he had become aware of his isolation — aware that it applied not only to those moments when he was Blatchford Sarnemington but that it applied to all his inner life. Hitherto such phenomena as 'crazy' ambitions and petty shames and fears had been but private reservations, unacknowledged before the throne of his official soul. Now he realized unconsciously that his private reservations were himself — and all the rest a garnished front and a conventional flag. The pressure of his environment had driven him into the lonely secret road of adolescence.

He knelt in the pew beside his father. Mass began. Rudolph knelt up — when he was alone he slumped his posterior back against the seat — and tasted the consciousness of a sharp, subtle revenge. Beside him his father prayed that God would forgive Rudolph, and asked also that his own outbreak of temper would be pardoned. He glanced sidewise at his son, and was relieved to see that the strained, wild look had gone from his face and that he had ceased sobbing. The Grace of God, inherent in the Sacrament, would do the rest, and perhaps after Mass everything would be better. He was proud of Rudolph in his heart, and beginning to be truly as well as formally sorry for what he had done.

Usually, the passing of the collection box was the significant point for Rudolph in the services. If, as was often the case, he had no money to drop in he would be furiously ashamed and bow his head and pretend not to see the box, lest Jeanne Brady in the pew behind should take notice and suspect an acute family poverty. But to-day he glanced coldly into it as it skimmed under his eyes, noting with casual interest the large number of pennies it contained.

When the bell rang for communion, however, he quivered. There was no reason why God should not stop his heart. During the past twelve hours he had committed a series of mortal sins increasing in gravity, and he was now to crown them all with a blasphemous sacrilege.

'Domine, non sum dignus; ut intres sub tectum meum; sed tantum dic verbo, et sanabitur anima mea. . . .'[1]

There was a rustle in the pews, and the communicants worked their ways into the aisle with downcast eyes and joined hands. Those of larger piety pressed together their finger-tips to form steeples. Among these latter was Carl Miller. Rudolph followed him towards the altar-rail and knelt down, automatically taking up the napkin under his chin. The bell rang sharply, and the priest turned from the altar with the white Host held above the chalice:

'Corpus Domini nostri Jesu Christi custodiat animam tuam in vitam æternam.'[2]

A cold sweat broke out on Rudolph's forehead as the communion began. Along the line Father Schwartz moved, and with gathering nausea Rudolph felt his heart-valves weakening at the will of God. It seemed to him that the church was darker and that a great quiet had fallen, broken only by the inarticulate mumble which announced the approach of the Creator of Heaven and Earth. He dropped his head down between his shoulders and waited for the blow.

Then he felt a sharp nudge in his side. His father was poking him to sit up, not to slump against the rail; the priest was only two places away.

'Corpus Domini nostri Jesu Christi custodiat animam tuam in vitam æternam.'

Rudolph opened his mouth. He felt the sticky wax taste of the wafer on his tongue. He remained motionless for what seemed an interminable period of time, his head still raised, the wafer undissolved in his mouth. Then again he started at the pressure of his father's elbow, and saw that the people were falling away from the altar like leaves and turning with blind downcast eyes to their pews, alone with God.

Rudolph was alone with himself, drenched with perspiration and deep in mortal sin. As he walked back to his pew the sharp taps of his cloven hoofs were loud upon the floor, and he knew that it was a dark poison he carried in his heart.

V
'Sagitta Volante in Dei'[3]

The beautiful little boy with eyes like blue stones, and lashes that sprayed open from them like flower-petals had finished telling his sin to Father Schwartz — and the square of sunshine in which he sat had moved forward an hour into the room. Rudolph had become less frightened now; once eased of the story a reaction had set in. He knew that as long as he was in the room with this priest God would not stop his heart, so he sighed and sat quietly, waiting for the priest to speak.

Father Schwartz's cold watery eyes were fixed upon the carpet pattern on which the sun had brought out the swastikas and the flat bloomless vines and the pale echoes of flowers. The hall-clock ticked insistently towards sunset, and from the ugly room and from the afternoon outside the window arose a stiff monotony, shattered now and then by the reverberate clapping of a far-away hammer on the dry air. The priest's nerves were strung thin and the beads of his rosary were crawling and squirming like snakes upon the green felt of his table top. He could not remember now what it was he should say.

Of all the things in this lost Swede town he was most aware of this little boy's eyes — the beautiful eyes, with lashes that left them reluctantly and curved back as though to meet them once more.

For a moment longer the silence persisted while Rudolph waited, and the priest struggled to remember something that was slipping farther and farther away from him, and the clock ticked in the broken house. Then Father Schwartz stared hard at the little boy and remarked in a peculiar voice:

'When a lot of people get together in the best places things go glimmering.'

Rudolph started and looked quickly at Father Schwartz's face.

'I said ——' began the priest, and paused, listening. 'Do you hear the hammer and the clock ticking and the bees? Well, that's no good. The thing is to have a lot of people in the centre of the world, wherever that happens to be. Then' — his watery eyes widened knowingly — 'things go glimmering.'

'Yes, Father,' agreed Rudolph, feeling a little frightened.

'What are you going to be when you grow up?'

'Well, I was going to be a baseball-player for a while,' answered Rudolph nervously, 'but I don't think that is a very good ambition, so I think I'll be an actor or a Navy officer.'

Again the priest stared at him.

'I see *exactly* what you mean,' he said, with a fierce air.

Rudolph had not meant anything in particular, and at the implication that he had, he became more uneasy.

'This man is crazy,' he thought, 'and I'm scared of him. He wants me to help him out some way, and I don't want to.'

'You look as if things went glimmering,' cried Father Schwartz wildly. 'Did you ever go to a party?'

'Yes, Father.'

'And did you notice that everybody was properly dressed? That's what I mean. Just as you went into the party there was a moment when everybody was properly dressed. Maybe two little girls were standing by the door and some boys were leaning over the banisters, and there were bowls around full of flowers.'

'I've been to a lot of parties,' said Rudolph, rather relieved that the conversation had taken this turn.

'Of course,' continued Father Schwartz triumphantly, 'I knew you'd agree with me. But my theory is that when a whole lot of people get together in the best places things go glimmering all the time.'

Rudolph found himself thinking of Blatchford Sarnemington.

'Please listen to me!' commanded the priest impatiently. 'Stop worrying about last Saturday. Apostasy implies an absolute damnation only on the supposition of a previous perfect faith. Does that fix it?'

Rudolph had not the faintest idea what Father Schwartz was talking about, but he nodded and the priest nodded back at him and returned to his mysterious preoccupation.

'Why,' he cried, 'they have lights now as big as stars — do you realize that? I heard of one light they had in Paris or somewhere that was as big as a star. A lot of people had it — a lot of gay people. They have all sorts of things now that you never dreamed of.'

'Look here ——' He came nearer to Rudolph, but the boy drew away, so Father Schwartz went back and sat down in his chair, his eyes dried out and hot. 'Did you ever see an amusement park?'

'No, Father.'

'Well, go and see an amusement park.' The priest waved his hand vaguely. 'It's a thing like a fair, only much more glittering. Go to one at night and stand a little way off from it in a dark place — under dark trees. You'll see a big wheel made of lights turning in the air, and a long slide shooting boats down into the water. A band playing somewhere, and a smell of peanuts — and everything will twinkle. But it won't remind you of anything, you see. It will all just hang out there in the night like a coloured balloon — like a big yellow lantern on a pole.'

Father Schwartz frowned as he suddenly thought of something.

'But don't get up close,' he warned Rudolph, 'because if you do you'll only feel the heat and the sweat and the life.'

All this talking seemed particularly strange and awful to Rudolph, because this man was a priest. He sat there, half terrified, his beautiful eyes open wide and staring at Father Schwartz. But underneath his terror he felt that his own inner convictions were confirmed. There was something ineffably gorgeous somewhere that had nothing to do with God. He no longer thought that God was angry at him about the original lie, because He must have understood that Rudolph had done it to make things finer in the confessional, brightening up the dinginess of his admissions by saying a thing radiant and proud. At the moment when he had affirmed immaculate honour a silver pennon had flapped out into the breeze somewhere and there had been the crunch of leather and the shine of silver spurs and a troop of horsemen waiting for dawn on a low green hill. The sun had made stars of light on their breastplates like the picture at home of the German cuirassiers at Sedan.

But now the priest was muttering inarticulate and heartbroken words, and the boy became wildly afraid. Horror entered suddenly in at the open window, and the atmosphere of the room changed. Father Schwartz collapsed precipitously down on his knees, and let his body settle back against a chair.

'Oh, my God!' he cried out, in a strange voice, and wilted to the floor.

Then a human oppression rose from the priest's worn clothes, and mingled with the faint smell of old food in the corners. Rudolph gave a sharp cry and ran in panic from the house — while the collapsed man lay there quite still, filling his room, filling it with voices and faces until it was crowded with echolalia,[4] and rang loud with a steady, shrill note of laughter.

Outside the window the blue sirocco trembled over the wheat, and girls with yellow hair walked sensuously along roads that bounded the fields, calling innocent, exciting things to the young men who were working in the lines between the grain. Legs were shaped under starchless gingham, and rims of the necks of dresses were warm and damp. For five hours now hot fertile life had burned in the afternoon. It

would be night in three hours, and all along the land there would be these blonde Northern girls and the tall young men from the farms lying out beside the wheat, under the moon.

1   Latin: Lord, I am not worthy to receive You. Say but the word and my soul will be healed.
2   Latin: May the body of Our Lord Jesus Christ be to us who receive it a source of eternal life.
3   Psalm 90(91) speaks of not being afraid of 'sagitta volante in die', the arrow flying in the day. 'Dei' perhaps should be 'Die', not God but day. Or perhaps Fitzgerald is playing on the arrow flying to God.
4   Meaningless repetition of sounds.

FORREST REID
from Forrest Reid, *Apostate* (1926)

Forrest Reid (1875–1947) was born in Belfast into a middle-class Presbyterian family, his mother being English, his father Irish. After a period in the tea trade Reid went up to Cambridge where he was encouraged to write by E. M. Forster. After university he lived quietly in Belfast, writing fiction as well as critical studies of Yeats and de la Mare. *Apostate*, the first of two volumes of autobiography (*Private Road*, 1940, was the second), is a journey of resistance, an entry into a dream world where the spirit of boyhood is recreated with an assured touch. In *Peter Waring* (1937), a novel dedicated to Forster, the protagonist suggests that most of his difficulties were metaphysical rather than religious. Here in this extract Reid reflects on his movement away from established religion and his cultivation of ancient Greek culture as — what I take to be — a means of assuming a homosexual identity (in the last chapter he writes more explicitly about a male friend he brought home and showed his manuscript to).

Chapter 19

Let me at this point for a moment take a glance backward, though not very far backward, as far only as the winter that preceded the summer we have now reached, the winter during which I was confirmed. It is not an important date; my confirmation possessed for me not the slightest spiritual significance, was entirely a matter of form; but it did to some extent help me to realize where I stood in relation to the religion I was called on to accept. I was no longer a child; I had reached the age of puberty, with its momentous discovery of the sexual impulse as a kind of restless goad driving the herd of dream and waking thoughts into disquieting paths. For the first time I paused, as it were, and deliberately took stock of my position.

In these chapters there have been many references to a secret world, a secret life. I now tried to examine intellectually what had hitherto reached me almost entirely through imagination. Out of fragments of the world I shared with others, out of scattered glimpses of the past, out of nature, and out of my own dreams and desires, I had built up this world which I did not and could not share; though I believed that something very like it must at one time have existed, and even felt there might be just a chance that it existed still, in some inexplicable way. Its beginnings were bound up with the first dreams I ever dreamed; in its development it led me at last to that definite revolt from Christianity which was precipitated by, and which followed immediately on, my confirmation. It was not, as I have already said, so much that I disbelieved in the Christian creed (though I did now disbelieve in it) as that temperamentally I was antagonistic to this religion, to its doctrines, its theory of life, the shadow it cast across the earth. I was antagonistic at the very hour of my final initiation into its mysteries, which took place on an evening shortly before Christmas, in Saint Thomas's Church.

Yet by the ceremony itself I was not unmoved. The place, the music, the novelty of the whole experience, produced their effect upon me. The gallery, the remoter parts of the building, remained in obscurity; the lights shone upon the centre aisle and on the chancel. Demure maidens dressed in white sat on one side of this central aisle; the boys sat on the other; while fathers, mothers, elder sisters, and aunts looked on sentimentally from the pews behind. My own thoughts were more or less distracted by the fact that I was for the first time wearing a suit with long trousers, and this distracted mood prevailed even when the moment came for me to kneel before the altar and receive the episcopal blessing. But I enjoyed this moment, and I thought the bishop was hurrying unduly. I don't quite know what I wanted him to do. To pause dramatically, perhaps, when he reached me, and pronounce a special benediction. As it was, it was all over in a few seconds. 'Defend, O Lord, this thy Child with thy heavenly grace, that he may continue thine for ever, and daily increase in thy Holy Spirit more and more, until he come unto thy everlasting kingdom.' He had passed on to the next boy without a pause; it seemed to me he was simply racing through what was by far the most attractive part of the ceremony. The moment he had removed his hands from my head my interest in the scene died, and what had been designed as the beginning of my religious life proved to be the end of it. I was sick of this slavery to what were to me no more than empty conventions, sick of professing beliefs and desires which I did not feel; and on the very next Sunday I refused point-blank to go to church any more.

I refused obstinately. Neither punishments nor persuasions moved me. They had indeed, partly on account of the form they took, a hardening effect, so that I made up my mind definitely to lead this on my own life in my own way.

Meanwhile, unguided, and more or less by chance, I had stumbled on the poetry and religion and art of the Greeks, and in this discovery seemed to find what all along I had been seeking. I hung a print of a bust of Socrates on the wall of my bedroom, with another of the Hermes of Praxiteles; and these were to be my guardians, human and divine. But I had no learning; this paganism was a subjective thing, bearing no closer relation to reality than did my imagined Greece,

which was merely a glorified reflection of my own countryside: while in my reading of Greek poetry and philosophy I was principally busy to find a confirmation of my private point of view. Certainly I seemed to find it — found an expression of thoughts and emotions and dreams that had haunted me from childhood. It was all, in truth, an emotion rather than a creed, reaching me through my senses much more than through my intellect. It was a paganism softened, orientalized, I dare say, to bring it into accord with what I desired; nevertheless, what appealed to me *was* to be found in the literature of Greece, and not elsewhere. The completed idea, the vision, was built up from the earlier dialogues of Plato, from the poets of the Palatine Anthology (Mackail's *Select Epigrams* having come by good fortune into my hands), from the fragments of Sappho, from Theocritus and the bucolic poets, from the Homeric Hymns, even from certain lyrical passages in the great dramatists. I have described it as orientalized, because a kind of romantic luxuriousness and sleepiness undoubtedly pervaded it. The landscape might be that of the world I knew best, but a hotter sun, the sun of Egypt or of Sicily, brooded upon it; and it was always summer, the summer of Theocritus, or of Giorgione's *Fête Champêtre*:

Through the apple-boughs the sighing winds go softly, and from the quivering leaves sleep seems to drip.

The crests and hollows of the mountains are asleep, and the headlands and ravines, and the leaves, and all creeping things which the black earth nourishes, and the beasts of the mountains, and the race of bees, and the monsters in the depths of the dark-gleaming sea; and there is sleep among the tribes of broad-winged birds.

Long before this, independently, I had arrived at the Greek view of nature. In wood and river and plant and animal and bird and insect it had seemed to me there was a spirit which was the same as my spirit. And here, in this poetry, every aspect of nature seemed to be perpetually passing into divinity, into the form and radiance of a god, while the human passed no less easily into tree or reed or flower. Adonis, Narcissus, Syrinx, Daphne — could I not see them with my own eyes? Could I not see Philomela flying low above the earth? Had I not, even in this land once blessed by Saint Patrick, caught a glimpse of that ill-mannered boy who, mocking the great Demeter while she drank, was straightway transformed into a lizard? The landscape was the landscape I loved best, a landscape proclaiming the vicinity of man, a landscape imbued with a human spirit that was yet somehow divine. 'At the birth of the nymphs,' I read in the *Hymn to Aphrodite*, 'there sprang up pine-trees or tall-crested oaks on the fruitful earth, flourishing and fair. . . . But when the fate of death approaches, first do the trees wither on the ground, and the bark about them moulders, and the twigs fall down, and even as the trees perish so the soul of the nymph leaves the light of the sun.' It was a world in which either everything was spirit or nothing was: and it was young, there was a freshness even in the hottest sunshine.

Sweet is the voice of the heifer, sweet her breath, sweet to lie beneath the sky in summer, by running water.

It was this mixture of homeliness with something passionate and strange that made its beauty:

As on the hills the shepherds trample the hyacinth underfoot, and the flower darkens on the ground.

Evening, you who gather all that bright morning scattered; you bring the sheep and the goat, the child back to his mother.

A mysterious and deep understanding, it seemed to me, had existed in that far-off age between man and nature, and this understanding I shared to-day, or thought I shared. There were hours when I could pass *into* nature, and feel the grass growing, and float with the clouds through the transparent air; when I could hear the low breathing of the earth, when the colour and smell of it were so close to me that I seemed to lose consciousness of any separate existence. Then, one single emotion animated all things, one heart beat throughout the universe, and the mother and all her children were united.

In this poetry I found, too, my own sense of fellowship with every scaled and furred and feathered creature. There were modern poems written to the skylark or the nightingale, or to commemorate a favourite dog perhaps; but what modern poet would write of such tiny creatures as the ant or the grasshopper?

Here beside the threshing-floor, O patient and toiling ant, I raise a memorial to you in this dry clod of earth, that the furrow and the corn of Demeter may charm you still, as you lie within your rustic tomb.

The spirit of these poems was utterly different from the spirit of any modern poetry I had read. To the Greek one bond united all mortal beings, their rights were equal, they shared the common life, for all there was the same uncertainty in the present, the same questionable future:

Earth and Birth Goddess, thou who didst bear me and thou who coverest, farewell; I have accomplished the course between you and I go, not discerning whose or who I am, or whence I came to you.

The voice of Tauros, the white dog of Melita, is 'prisoned in the silent pathways of night'. The 'poor partridge', slain by a cat, will never again ruffle his wings in the dawn: Earth is prayed to rest 'not lightly but heavily' upon him, lest his enemy drag out his remains. The shrill grasshopper 'drunk with dew' is not forgotten, though he no longer hides himself under the green leaves, 'sending forth a happy noise from his quick-fanning wings', but has been carried down to a dim lower world, to the 'dewy flowers of golden Persephone'. Somehow, to listen to his descendants whirring in the grass close by brought that old world in which he was so great a favourite very near to me. It was he who took up and prolonged the note when the string of the poet's lyre snapped, he whose evening hymn filled the house with pleasant sound, whose voice comforted the sleepless lover, whose song itself brought sleep. And the tame hare, and the favourite horse, and the swallow — all were remembered in words which had a simple gravity and affection that was no different from the affection one might feel for a child gone, too, on that same 'last road of Acheron'. One spirit, one fate, bound together all mortal children of the old Earth Mother; the lives of all were brief and perilous, their end sad and obscure. And when a voice passed into tree or plant, when the vine spoke, as in the poem of Evenus, it seemed to me in no way unnatural:

Though thou devour me down to the roots, yet still will I bear so much fruit as will serve to pour libation on thee, O goat, when thou art sacrificed.

It may be that the religious emotion is universal, finding an outlet, if not in this way, then in that; and it may be there was something of its rapture in my apprehension of nature. Certainly the Greek religions and cults and myths, of which I had so scanty and superficial a knowledge, probably misunderstanding a large part even of what I had read, were like a floating golden web that caught and held and coloured my imagination, though they had not, I dare say, really awakened what might positively be called faith. My deities were the Arcadian gods, the lesser gods, Pan and Hermes. The darker, more mystic element interwoven with the worship of Dionysus (the *truly* religious element, doubtless, with its blood-sacrifices and ecstasy, and mingled lust and madness), this was repellent to me because of the cruelty bound up with it. The deities I invoked, or evoked, were friendly, and more than half human; they were the deities of the poet and the sculptor:

> I who inherit the tossing mountain-forests of steep Cyllene, stand here guarding the pleasant playing fields, Hermes, to whom boys offer marjoram and hyacinth and fresh garlands of violets.

And I was one of those boys, though I had been born into a later age, when my offerings must be kept hidden. My gods were the protectors of the fields and orchards and flocks, who counselled the passing stranger where to rest at noon, and pointed out to him the clearest, coolest streams and wells from which to drink. Pan, who loved the rocks and woods, was associated in my mind with music, the music of leaves and running water and his own pipes; Hermes was a kind of divine playmate. These gods I loved because they had human limitations, were beautiful and strong and passionate, were neither solemn nor sad, and had morals not very different from my own. And though I somehow pictured Pan as rather old and Socratic; in spirit, in his sympathies, like Socrates, he too was young and loved to be with the young.

This adoration of youth was indeed one of the qualities of the Greek genius that most endeared it to me. I felt as I read their poetry what the Egyptian priest says in the *Timaeus*: 'O Solon, Solon, you Hellenes are never anything but children, and there is not an old man among you. . . . In mind you are all young.' And because I wanted so much these gods to be real, I felt that the earth would be almost empty without them. I would half shut my eyes, and peering through the green shadows of interlaced trees and brambles, under the streaming fire of the sun, would hypnotize myself into the belief that I could see them. And then, one day, it all very nearly came true.

It was June, and I was supposed to be working for an Intermediate examination, and had a book or two with me even on this blazing afternoon. It was hot and still. The breathless silence seemed unnatural; seemed, as I lay motionless in the tangled grass, like a bridge that reached straight back into the heart of some dim antiquity. I had a feeling of uneasiness, of unrest, though I lay so still — of longing and excitement and expectation: I had a feeling that some veil might be drawn away, that there might come to me something, some one, the Megistos Kouros perhaps, either with the winged feet of Hermes, or the thyrsus of Dionysus, or maybe only hairy-shanked Pan of the Goats. My state of mind just then was indistinguishable from that of the worshipper.

> Ἰώ, Μέγιστε Κουρε,
> Χαῖρε μοι . . . .[1]

I was certainly prepared to join in whatever rites or revels might be required. My body seemed preternaturally sensitive, my blood moved quickly, I had an extraordinary feeling of struggle, as if some power were struggling to reach me as I was trying to reach it, as if there *was* something there, something waiting, if only I could get through. At that moment I longed for a sign, some definite and direct response, with a longing that was a kind of prayer. And a strange thing happened. For though there was no wind, a little green leafy branch was snapped off from the tree above me, and fell to the ground at my hand. I drew my breath quickly; there was a drumming in my ears; I knew that the green woodland before me was going to split asunder, to swing back on either side like two great painted doors. . . . And then — then I hesitated, blundered, drew back, failed. The moment passed, was gone, and at first gradually, and then rapidly, I felt the world I had so nearly reached slipping from me, till at last there was all around me only a pleasant summer scene, through which, from the hidden river below, there rose the distant voices and laughter of a passing boating-party.

1   Greek: O Megistos Kouros (Greatest Youth), welcome me.

LIAM O'FLAHERTY
from Liam O'Flaherty, *The Tent and Other Stories* (1926)

Liam O'Flaherty (1896–1984) was born on Inishmore, the largest of the Aran Islands, saw active service in the Great War, and took the Republican side during the Civil War. Here in this disturbing short story O'Flaherty focuses on an encounter between two groups of outsiders, the (city) transient and the (country) traveller.

The Tent

A sudden squall struck the tent. White glittering hailstones struck the shabby canvas with a wild noise. The tent shook and swayed slightly forward, dangling its tattered flaps. The pole creaked as it strained. A rent appeared near the top of the pole like a silver seam in the canvas. Water immediately trickled through the seam, making a dark blob.

A tinker and his two wives were sitting on a heap of straw in the tent, looking out through the entrance at the wild moor that stretched in front of it, with a snowcapped mountain peak rising like the tip of a cone over the ridge of the moor about two miles away. The three of them were smoking cigarettes in silence.

It was evening, and they had pitched their tent for the night in a gravel pit on the side of the mountain road, crossing from one glen to another. Their donkey was tethered to the cart beside the tent.

When the squall came the tinker sat up with a start and looked at the pole. He stared at the seam in the canvas for several moments and then he nudged the two women and pointed upwards with a jerk of his nose. The women looked, but nobody spoke. After a minute or so the tinker sighed and struggled to his feet.

'I'll throw a few sacks over the top,' he said.

He picked up two brown sacks from the heap of blankets and clothes that were drying beside the brazier in the entrance and went out. The women never spoke, but kept on smoking.

The tinker kicked the donkey out of his way. The beast had stuck his hind quarters into the entrance of the tent as far as possible, in order to get the heat from the wood burning in the brazier. The donkey shrank away sideways, still chewing a wisp of the hay which the tinker had stolen from a haggard the other side of the mountain. The tinker scrambled up the bank against which the tent was pitched. The bank was covered with rank grass into which yesterday's snow had melted in muddy cakes.

The top of the tent was only about eighteen inches above the bank. Beyond the bank there was a narrow rough road, with a thick copse of pine trees on the far side, within the wired fence of a demesne, but the force of the squall was so great that it swept through the trees and struck the top of the tent as violently as if it were standing exposed on the open moor. The tinker had to lean against the wind to prevent himself being carried away. He looked into the wind with wide-open nostrils.

'It can't last,' he said, throwing the two sacks over the tent, where there was a rent in the canvas. He then took a big needle from his jacket and put a few stitches

in them.

He was about to jump down from the bank when somebody hailed him from the road. He looked up and saw a man approaching, with his head thrust forward against the wind. The tinker scowled and shrugged his shoulders. He waited until the man came up to him.

The stranger was a tall, sturdily built man, with a long face and firm jaws and great sombre dark eyes, a fighter's face. When he reached the tinker he stood erect with his feet together and his hands by his sides like a soldier. He was fairly well dressed, his face was clean and well shaved, and his hands were clean. There was a blue figure of something or other tattooed on the back of his right hand. He looked at the tinker frankly with his sombre dark eyes. Neither spoke for several moments.

'Good evening,' the stranger said.

The tinker nodded without speaking.

He was looking the stranger up and down, as if he were slightly afraid of this big, sturdy man, who was almost like a policeman or a soldier or somebody in authority. He looked at the man's boots especially. In spite of the muck of the roads, the melted snow and the hailstones, they were still fairly clean, and looked as if they were constantly polished.

'Travellin'?' he said at length.

'Eh,' said the stranger, almost aggressively. 'Oh! Yes, I'm lookin' for somewhere to shelter for the night.'

The stranger glanced at the tent slowly and then looked back to the tinker again.

'Goin' far?' said the tinker.

'Don't know,' said the stranger angrily. Then he almost shouted: 'I have no ruddy place to go to . . . only the ruddy roads.'

'All right, brother,' said the tinker, 'come on.'

He nodded towards the tent and jumped down into the pit. The stranger followed him, stepping carefully down to avoid soiling his clothes.

When he entered the tent after the tinker and saw the women, he immediately took off his cap and said: 'Good evening.' The two women took their cigarettes from their mouths, smiled and nodded their heads.

The stranger looked about him cautiously and then sat down on a box to the side of the door near the brazier. He put his hands to the blaze and rubbed them. Almost immediately a slight steam rose from his clothes. The tinker handed him a cigarette, murmuring: 'Smoke?'

The stranger accepted the cigarette, lit it, and then looked at them. None of them were looking at him, so he 'sized them up' carefully, looking at each suspiciously with his sombre dark eyes.

The tinker was sitting on a box opposite him, leaning languidly backwards from his hips, a slim, tall, graceful man, with a beautiful head poised gracefully on a brown neck, and great black lashes falling down over his half-closed eyes, just like a woman. A womanish-looking fellow, with that sensuous grace in the languid pose of his body which is found only among aristocrats and people who belong to a very small workless class, cut off from the mass of society, yet living at their expense. A young fellow with proud, contemptuous, closed lips and an arrogant expression in his slightly expanded nostrils. A silent fellow, blowing out cigarette smoke through his nostrils and gazing dreamily into the blaze of the wood fire.

The two women were just like him in texture, both of them slatterns, dirty and unkempt, but with the same proud, arrogant, contemptuous look in their beautiful brown faces. One was dark-haired and black-eyed. She had a hard expression in her face and seemed very alert. The other woman was golden-haired, with a very small head and finely-developed jaw, that stuck out level with her forehead. She was surpassingly beautiful, in spite of her ragged clothes and the foul condition of her hair, which was piled on her tiny skull in knotted heaps, uncombed. The perfect symmetry and delicacy of her limbs, her bust and her long throat that had tiny freckles in the white skin, made the stranger feel afraid of her, of her beauty and her presence in the tent.

'Tinkers,' he said to himself. 'Awful people, curse them.'

Then he turned to the tinker.

'Got any grub in the place . . . eh . . . mate?' he said brusquely, his thick lips rapping out every word firmly, like one accustomed to command inferiors. He hesitated before he added the word 'mate', obviously disinclined to put himself on a level of human intercourse with the tinker.

The tinker nodded and turned to the dark-haired woman.

'Might as well have supper now, Kitty,' he said softly.

The dark-haired woman rose immediately, and taking a blackened can that was full of water, she put it on the brazier. The stranger watched her. Then he addressed the tinker again.

'This is a hell of a way to be, eh?' he said. 'Stuck out on a mountain. Thought I'd make Roundwood tonight. How many miles is it from here?'

'Ten,' said the tinker.

'Good God!' said the stranger.

Then he laughed, and putting his hand in his breast pocket, he pulled out a half-pint bottle of whisky.

'This is all I got left,' he said, looking at the bottle.

The tinker immediately opened his eyes wide when he saw the bottle. The golden-haired woman sat up and looked at the stranger eagerly, opening her brown eyes wide and rolling her tongue in her cheek. The dark-haired woman, rummaging in a box, also turned around to look. The stranger winked an eye and smiled.

'Always welcome,' he said. 'Eh? My curse on it, anyway. Anybody got a cockscrew?'

The tinker took a knife from his pocket, pulled out a corkscrew from its side and handed it to the man. The man opened the bottle.

'Here,' he said, handing the bottle to the tinker. 'Pass it round. I suppose the women'll have a drop.'

The tinker took the bottle and whispered to the dark-haired woman. She began to pass him mugs from the box.

'Funny thing,' said the stranger, 'when a man is broke and hungry, he can get whisky, but he can't get grub. Met a man this morning in Dublin and he knew I was broke all right, but instead of asking me to have a meal, or giving me some money, he gave me that. I had it with me all along the road and I never opened it.'

He threw the end of his cigarette out of the entrance.

'Been drinkin' for three weeks, curse it,' he said.

'Are ye belongin' to these parts?' murmured the tinker, pouring out the whisky into the tin mugs.

'What's that?' said the man, again speaking angrily, as if he resented the question. Then he added: 'No. Never been here in me life before. Question of goin' into the workhouse or takin' to the roads. Got a job in Dublin yesterday. The men downed tools when they found I wasn't a member of the union. Thanks. Here's luck.'

'Good health, sir,' the women said.

The tinker nodded his head only, as he put his own mug to his lips and tasted it. The stranger drained his at a gulp.

'Ha,' he said. 'Drink up, girls. It's good stuff.'

He winked at them. They smiled and sipped their whisky.

'My name is Carney,' said the stranger to the tinker. 'What do they call you?'

'Byrne,' said the tinker. 'Tim Byrne.'

'H'm! Byrne,' said Carney. 'Wicklow's full o' Byrnes. Tinker, I suppose?'

'Yes,' murmured the tinker, blowing a cloud of cigarette smoke through his puckered lips. Carney shrugged his shoulders.

'Might as well,' he said. 'One thing is as good as another. Look at me. Sergeant-major in the army two months ago. Now I'm tramping the roads. That's boiling.'

The dark-haired woman took the can off the fire. The other woman tossed off the remains of her whisky and got to her feet to help with the meal.

Carney shifted his box back farther out of the way and watched the golden-haired woman eagerly. When she moved about her figure was so tall that she had to stoop low in order to avoid the roof of the tent. She must have been six feet in height, and she wore high-heeled shoes which made her look taller.

'There is a woman for ye,' thought Carney. 'Must be a gentleman's daughter. Lots o' these shots out of a gun in the county Wicklow. Half the population is illegitimate. Awful people, these tinkers. I suppose the two of them belong to this Tim. More like a woman than a man. Suppose he never did a stroke of work in his life.'

There was cold rabbit for supper, with tea and bread and butter. It was excellent tea, and it tasted all the sweeter on account of the storm outside which was still raging. Sitting around the brazier they could see the hailstones driving through a grey mist, sweeping the bleak black moor, and the cone-shaped peak of the mountain in the distance, with a whirling cloud of snow around it. The sky was rent here and there with a blue patch, showing through the blackness.

They ate the meal in silence. Then the women cleared it away. They didn't wash the mugs or plates, but put everything away, probably until morning. They sat down again after drawing out the straw, bed-shape, and putting the clothes on it that had been drying near the brazier.

They all seemed to be in good humour now with the whisky and the food. Even the tinker's face had grown soft, and he kept puckering up his lips in a smile. He passed round cigarettes.

'Might as well finish that bottle,' said Carney. 'Bother the mugs. We can drink outa the neck.'

'Tastes sweeter that way,' said the golden-haired woman, laughing thickly, as if she were slightly drunk. At the same time she looked at Carney with her lips open.

Carney winked at her. The tinker noticed the wink and the girl's smile.

His face clouded and he closed his lips very tightly. Carney took a deep draught and passed him the bottle. The tinker nodded his head, took the bottle and put it to his lips.

'I'll have a stretch,' said Carney. 'I'm done in. Twenty miles since morning. Eh?'

He threw himself down on the clothes beside the yellow-haired woman. She smiled and looked at the tinker. The tinker paused with the bottle to his lips and looked at her through almost closed eyes savagely. He took the bottle from his lips and bared his white teeth. The golden-haired woman laughed aloud, stretched back one arm under her head and the other stretched out towards the tinker.

'Sht,' she whistled through her teeth. 'Pass it along, Tim.'

He handed her the bottle slowly, and as he gave it to her she clutched his hand and tried to pull him to her. But he tore his hand away, got up and walked out of the tent rapidly.

Carney had noticed nothing of this. He was lying close to the woman by his side. He could feel the softness of her beautiful body and the slight undulation of her soft side as she breathed. He became overpowered with desire for her and closed his eyes, as if to shut out the consciousness of the world and of the other people in the tent. Reaching down he seized her hand and pressed it.

She answered the pressure. At the same time she turned to her companion and whispered:

'Where's he gone?'

'I dunno. Out.'

'What for?'

'Phst.'

'Give us a drop.'

'Here ye are.'

Carney heard the whispering, but he took no notice of it. He heard the golden-haired one drinking and then drawing a deep breath.

'Finished,' she said, throwing the bottle to the floor. Then she laughed softly.

'I'm going out to see where he's gone,' whispered the dark-haired one. She rose and passed out of the tent. Carney immediately turned around and tried to embrace the woman by his side. But she bared her teeth in a savage grin and pinioned his arms with a single movement.

'Didn't think I was strong,' she said, putting her face close to his and grinning at him.

He looked at her seriously, surprised and still more excited.

'What ye going to do in Roundwood?' she said.

'Lookin' for a job,' he muttered thickly.

She smiled and rolled her tongue in her cheek.

'Stay here,' she said.

He licked his lip and winked his right eye. 'With you?'

She nodded.

'What about him?' he said, nodding towards the door.

She laughed silently. 'Are ye afraid of Tim?'

He did not reply, but, making a sudden movement, he seized her around the body and pressed her to him. She did not resist, but began to laugh, and bared her teeth as she laughed. He tried to kiss her mouth, but she threw back her head and he kissed her cheek several times.

Then suddenly there was a hissing noise at the door. Carney sat up with a start. The tinker was standing in the entrance, stooping low, with his mouth open and his jaw twisted to the right, his two hands hanging loosely by his sides, with the fingers twitching. The dark-haired woman was standing behind him, peering over his shoulder. She was smiling.

Carney got to his feet, took a pace forward, and squared himself. He did not speak. The golden-haired woman uttered a loud peal of laughter and, stretching out her arms, she lay flat on the bed, giggling.

'Come out here,' hissed the tinker.

He stepped back. Carney shouted and rushed at him, jumping the brazier. The tinker stepped aside and struck Carney a terrible blow on the jaw as he passed him. Carney staggered against the bank and fell in a heap. The tinker jumped on him like a cat, striking him with his hands and feet all together. Carney roared: 'Let me up, let me up. Fair play.' But the tinker kept on beating him until at last he lay motionless at the bottom of the pit.

'Ha,' said the tinker.

Then he picked up the prone body, as lightly as if it were an empty sack, and threw it to the top of the bank.

'Be off, you —' he hissed.

Carney struggled to his feet on the top of the bank and looked at the three of them. They were all standing now in front of the tent, the two women grinning, the tinker scowling. Then he staggered on to the road, with his hands to his head.

'Goodbye, dearie,' cried the golden-haired one.

Then she screamed. Carney looked behind and saw the tinker carrying her into the tent in his arms.

''Strewth!' cried Carney, crossing himself.

Then he trudged away fearfully through the storm towards Roundwood.

''Strewth!' he cried at every two yards. ''Strewth!'

W. B. YEATS
from *The Dial*, August 1927

For the background to Yeats's visit to St Otteran's School, Waterford, in March 1926, see my *Yeats's Worlds*. For changes in Yeats's composition of the poem see Thomas Parkinson, *W. B. Yeats: The Later Poetry* (1965). In teaching this poem I have found it rewarding for students to attempt to make sense of it on their own without notes. I have rarely known this poem to fail in classroom discussion. Notice the structure of argument and the shift between stanzas VII and VIII.

AMONG SCHOOL CHILDREN

I

I walk through the long schoolroom questioning;
A kind old nun in a white hood replies;
The children learn to cipher and to sing,
To study reading books and histories,
To cut and sew, be neat in everything
In the best modern way — the children's eyes
In momentary wonder stare upon
A sixty-year-old smiling public man.

II

I dream of a Ledaean body, bent
Above a sinking fire, a tale that she
Told of a harsh reproof, or trivial event
That changed some childish day to tragedy —
Told, and it seemed that our two natures blent
Into a sphere from youthful sympathy,
Or else, to alter Plato's parable,
Into the yolk and white of the one shell.

III

And thinking of that fit of grief or rage
I look upon one child or t'other there
And wonder if she stood so at that age —
For even daughters of the swan can share
Something of every paddler's heritage —
And had that colour upon cheek or hair,
And thereupon my heart is driven wild:
She stands before me as a living child.

IV

Her present image floats into the mind —
Did Quattrocento finger fashion it
Hollow of cheek as though it drank the wind
And took a mess of shadows for its meat?
And I though never of Ledaean kind
Had pretty plumage once — enough of that,
Better to smile on all that smile, and show
There is a comfortable kind of old scarecrow.

V

What youthful mother, a shape upon her lap
Honey of generation had betrayed,
And that must sleep, shriek, struggle to escape
As recollection or the drug decide,
Would think her son, did she but see that shape
With sixty or more winters on its head,
A compensation for the pang of his birth,
Or the uncertainty of his setting forth?

VI

Plato thought nature but a spume that plays
Upon a ghostly paradigm of things;
Solider Aristotle played the taws
Upon the bottom of a king of kings;
World-famous golden-thighed Pythagoras
Fingered upon a fiddle-stick or strings
What a star sang and careless Muses heard:
Old clothes upon old sticks to scare a bird.

VII

Both nuns and mothers worship images,
But those the candles light are not as those
That animate a mother's reveries,
But keep a marble or a bronze repose.
And yet they too break hearts — O Presences
That passion, piety or affection knows,
And that all heavenly glory symbolize —
O self-born mockers of man's enterprise;

VIII

Labour is blossoming or dancing where
The body is not bruised to pleasure soul,
Nor beauty born out of its own despair,
Nor blear-eyed wisdom out of midnight oil.
O chestnut-tree, great rooted blossomer,
Are you the leaf, the blossom or the bole?
O body swayed to music, O brightening glance,
How can we know the dancer from the dance?

F. R. HIGGINS
from F. R. Higgins, *The Dark Breed* (1927)

In this poem F. R. Higgins captures something of what he imagines are the dreams of
Galway men raised on poor land in the west of Ireland.

THE DARK BREED

With those bawneen[1] men I'm one,
  In the grey dusk-fall,
Watching the Galway land
  Sink down in distress —

With dark men, talking of grass,
  By a loose stone wall,
In murmurs drifting and drifting
  To loneliness.

Over this loneliness,
   Wild riders gather their fill
Of talking on beasts and on fields
   Too lean for a plough,
Until, more grey than the grey air,
   Song drips from a still,
Through poteen,[2] reeling the dancing —
   Ebbing the grief now!

Just, bred from the cold lean rock,
   Those fellows have grown;
And only in that grey fire
   Their lonely days pass
To dreams of far clovers
   And cream-gathering heifers, alone
Under the hazels of moon-lighters,
   Clearing the grass.

Again in the darkness,
   Dull knives we may secretly grease,
And talk of blown horns on clovers
   Where graziers have lain;

But there rolls the mist,
   With sails pulling wind from the seas —
No bullion can brighten that mist,
   O brood of lost Spain.[3]

So we, with the last dark men,
   Left on the rock grass,
May brazen grey loneliness
   Over a poteen still
Or crowd on the bare chapel floor
   Hearing late Mass,[4]
To loosen that hunger
   Broken land never can fill.

1   A loose whitish jacket of home-made undyed flannel worn by men at out-door work. From Irish bán, white, with diminutive ending -een (P.W. Joyce).
2   Home-produced, illegal, whiskey.
3   The allusion here is to the legend about the remnants of the Spanish Armada breaking up on the west coast of Ireland and how the Spanish sailors intermarried and produced the characteristic dark features of people from the west of Ireland.
4   Mass later in the day at say 11.00, in contrast with early Mass at say 8.00.

W. B. YEATS
from W. B. Yeats, *The Tower* (1928)

'Sailing to Byzantium' is positioned by Yeats at the beginning of *The Tower*, a remarkable volume that deserves close attention if its overlapping themes are to be fully appreciated. Yeats, in middle age when he wrote this group of poems, tackles the theme of old age approaching, and links the Celtic myth of Tír na nÓg or Land of Youth with the contrast between the body and art, one subject to change, the other potentially eternal. He also pits the youthful enthusiasm of the young Ireland that emerged in the 1920s when nearly all the leading politicians were under forty against his own feelings of mortality (a 'crock' was how his wife described him).

SAILING TO BYZANTIUM

I

That is no country[1] for old men. The young
In one another's arms, birds in the trees
— Those dying generations — at their song,
The salmon-falls, the mackerel-crowded seas,
Fish, flesh, or fowl, commend all summer long
Whatever is begotten, born, and dies.
Caught in that sensual music all neglect
Monuments of unageing intellect.

II

An aged man is but a paltry thing,
A tattered coat upon a stick, unless
Soul clap its hands and sing, and louder sing
For every tatter in its mortal dress,
Nor is there singing school but studying
Monuments of its own magnificence;
And therefore I have sailed the seas and come
To the holy city of Byzantium.[2]

III

O sages standing in God's holy fire
As in the gold mosaic of a wall,
Come from the holy fire, perne in a gyre,[3]
And be the singing-masters of my soul.
Consume my heart away; sick with desire
And fastened to a dying animal
It knows not what it is; and gather me
Into the artifice of eternity.

IV

Once out of nature I shall never take
My bodily form from any natural thing,
But such a form as Grecian goldsmiths make
Of hammered gold and gold enamelling
To keep a drowsy Emperor awake;
Or set upon a golden bough to sing
To lords and ladies of Byzantium
Of what is past, or passing, or to come.

1   Here meaning Ireland.
2   Yeats was much taken with sixth-century Byzantine civilization, whose architecture suggested the Sacred City in the Apocalypse of St John, the closest human history came to the divine.
3   Spin in a spiral. A gyre held a special meaning for Yeats as the poem 'The Second Coming' also suggests.

THOMAS MacGREEVY
from *The Dublin Review*, January-June 1929

Thomas MacGreevy (1893–1967) was appointed Director of the National Gallery in Dublin in 1950. In the 1920s he was an art critic in Dublin and London before moving to Paris where he taught at the École Normale and became a friend of Beckett. The output of his verse is not large but it is invariably distinguished.

SEVENTH GIFT[1] OF THE HOLY GHOST

Animae suae[2]

The end of love,
Love's ultimate good,
Is the end of love . . . and
Light
On a towering wall
Yellow villages
In a vast, high, light-beaten plain,
And you
And I
Imagining

The pity we had to learn
And the terror —
The ultimate terror.

1   There are seven gifts of the Holy Ghost (which derive from *Isaiah* 11:2): wisdom, understanding, counsel, strength, knowledge, piety, fear of the Lord. The seventh therefore is fear of the Lord, but in a sense all are here present.
2   Latin: Their souls, or of his/her soul. In citing Church Latin MacGreevy makes us aware that the soul is here learning from the body's pleasures.

IRISH WRITING IN THE 1930s

I knew that there was something true in what she said. It was not only an ideal romantic Ireland that would pass away if we were beaten. Even that Ireland of which Arigho was part, of which he had wanted to take away the memory, would go too. That was the Ireland of vivid contrasts that blended into a poignant intangible atmosphere. And if those contrasts were levelled, I thought that life for us would be strained and sterilized. Left tasteless. I thought of the flowering of the Irish spring out of the cold wet bud. The Mass of Easter in a bare little church full of flowers and tawdry statues. Brigid and I walking home stirred to a depth of love beyond the physical. Everlasting. A faithfulness whose breaking would be the breaking of a precious burden. The burden and anguish and joyousness of love. And Joseph Arigho. In him there was an heroic sense, a nonsexual romanticism that thrived here and nowhere else, and which the flood would engulf too. And there was Catherine herself. In her the unique quality, that tragic sense, was more obvious. There were very many people like Arigho, like Brigid and I in Ireland, with our outlook, whose hearts were rooted in the Irish atmosphere. There were not so many Catherines. But she was the summing up, the apex of a whole side of Ireland. It too could not live outside this ark. The super-civilization that was flooding towards us through Europe would wash over us and obliterate all that. Only I did not know how we were to defend this last outpost. She seemed to know. But her ideas were impracticable and fanatical, I thought. Or were they? Were not the very things that we were to defend unpractical and tinged with fanaticism? Super-efficiency did not go with our way of life. The way of life that we were fighting to protect.

– Francis Stuart, *Pigeon Irish* (1932)

CRITICAL AND DOCUMENTARY

MARY MANNING
from *The Saturday Review of Literature*, 28 March 1931

Mary Manning (1906–) is author of *The Last Chronicles of Ballyfungus* (1978), a humorous fictional portrait of the Anglo-Irish gentry. Here is a sharp, acerbic review she wrote in her twenties for the American *Saturday Review,* giving us a snapshot of cultural life at the beginning of the 1930s (it includes an early reference to 'Mr Sam Beckett').

A Letter from Dublin

As I write a gale is blowing. Dublin Bay is agitated. The waves are rolling over the sea walls at Merrion. Seagulls scream in suburban back gardens. They cover the lake in Stephen's Green with a cloud of white wings and flash of red beaks. Sou'easterly gale; dirty weather in the channel. What are the wild waves saying? Listen and hear . . . Gaelic League calling — This is our representative Mr J.P. McGinley speaking at a meeting of the Library Association of Ireland: — 'If I had the powers of a dictator I would cast half the books into the sea. Nine-tenths of the books selected for the libraries represent the English mind, standards of taste, conduct, and morality. The talkies and radio are inimical to Irish education and must be destroyed or controlled as they are disseminating English and American ideals among the people.' Toll for the Gaelic League! Toll for McGinley and black kid gloves must be worn at the wake. He cannot stop the march of progress. No man can say to this generation — 'Thus far shalt thou go, and no further.' We must go on, over McGinley's body; though the censorship falls, though the Vatican thunder, though the Gael screams 'Back to Deirdre!' Young Ireland must fall into line with the modern world.

We are advancing. Mr Denis Johnston's expressionistic play *The Old Lady Says No* has been revived at the Gate Theatre and his *Dublin Revue*, with lyrics by the irrepressible Oliver St John Gogarty, is to be performed at Easter. Six thousand people paid to see the Russian films *Storm over Asia* and *The End of St Petersburg*. An Irish amateur film was shown in the Peacock Theatre last Autumn. Mr Yeats's latest experiment in a new dramatic form — *The Writing on the Window-pane* — was produced at the Abbey Theatre. The Gate retaliated with *Back to Methuselah* in its entirety. The Abbey answered it with Mr Lennox Robinson's modernized version of *The Critic*, which

allowed him a glorious opportunity for poking fun at the Dublin press, the Dublin critics, and the Dublin Intelligentsia. Mr Sam Beckett, now assistant French lecturer in Trinity College, has written a study of Proust which is to be published in April. An ultra-modern bookshop has been opened in Winetavern Street.

We are advancing. The Board of Censors are indefatigable in their labours for the moral welfare of the Irish reader. *The New Leader* was banned recently because it published an advertisement for contraceptives. Novels by Aldous Huxley, Somerset Maugham, Liam O'Flaherty, and Sinclair Lewis are banned because: — 'They are in their general tendency obscene.' Remote books on birth control obtain free advertisement in the fierce light of public censorship. Marie Stopes, Margaret Sanger, and even Bertrand Russell have gone the way of all flesh, while Elinor Glyn, Ethel M. Dell, and Margaret Petersen are left to carry on the good work.

We are advancing. Revengeful and unforgiving is dark Rosaleen. The Mayo County Council backed up the local library committee in their refusal to sanction the appointment of Miss Dunbar Harrison, county librarian, on the grounds that she was a Protestant, a graduate of Trinity College, and not proficient in the Irish Language. The Ministry of Local Government gave the rebels a chance to reconsider their decision, but they steadfastly adhered to it, whereupon the Local Government Board dissolved the Mayo County Council, and appointed a commissioner to administer the affairs of the County. One of the Commissioner's first duties was to appoint Miss Harrison as county librarian, and on the twelfth of January last the intrepid lady departed to take up duty in Castlebar, where she received a grand old Irish welcome in the form of a general boycott! The Mayo County Council have undoubtedly been guilty of intolerable bigotry and medievalism. It is absurd to think that a woman who has proved her efficiency in fair examination should be barred from taking up a job on such irrelevant grounds. It is intolerable to think that the religion and politics of one section, should prevent those of another from working in their own country. But by the harp of Tom Moore it would have been well for the Government to have entered into negotiations before dissolving a council which had admittedly administered its affairs efficiently! A policy of blind impartiality without tact or discrimination is worse than useless — it is dangerous. County Mayo is still a hundred years behind the times. The peasants, oppressed and ill-treated for generations, are only now beginning to assert their individuality, and when one considers that their former oppressors were persons of Miss Harrison's religion and politics one can arrive at some understanding of their state of mind. Hatred of Protestantism, landlordism, and accompanying imperialism is ingrained in them. A hundred years of smouldering resentment is only now bursting into open flame. In that wild country where Irish is native spoken; where the religion is sternly Catholic, and the peasant mind only now beginning to falter into line with twentieth century standards, tolerance is only a word. It will take years of freedom and education to weed out the inbred bitterness of generations. But we are advancing.

And in the forefront of the battle comes Peadar O'Donnell whose latest novel, *The Knife*, has been published in America under the title *There Will be Fighting*. I may say at once that O'Donnell, probably the greatest writer produced in Ireland within the last ten years, remains comparatively unknown amongst the Dublin intelligentsia, chiefly because he does not display his personality at 'First Nights', Sunday 'Evenings', and Bohemian cabarets, or flutter round the intellectual demigods. True, they read of his books in the Sunday *Observer* and other well-informed English reviews, but those who only discovered Joyce ten years after the rest of the world would hardly know anything of O'Donnell yet.

Peadar O'Donnell has published four novels dealing with different aspects of peasant life and their reaction to the national struggle. *Storm*, published about ten years ago, and now out of print, showed promise. The first few chapters describing a storm off the coast of Donegal were beautifully done, but otherwise it attracted little attention. In 1925 he ran up against O'Flaherty and showed him the MS of another novel. O'Flaherty read it, put it in an envelope, and sent it to his own publisher, Jonathan Cape, and shortly afterwards *Islanders* was published in England and acclaimed by the critics as a masterpiece of peasant life. Later it appeared in the United States under the title *The Way it Was with Them*. In 1927, while he was in gaol, the news came through to him of the death from starvation of the entire Sullivan family in Adrigoole, Co. Cork, and his third novel, written in a fury of rage and pity, was the result. *Adrigoole* remains his finest achievement up to the present. Though his latest novel, *The Knife*, marks a definite advance in technique, the propagandist has run away with the novelist. O'Donnell's best work is yet to come. He is only thirty-five, and though years of intense fighting, forty-one days hunger strike, and ceaseless revolutionary activities have left their mark on him physically, he is terrifically alive. His next novel is to be the last of a series, and then he will start work on a bigger idea — a history of Ireland from 1830, rather in the style of Kropotkin's *French Revolution*.

At the moment O'Donnell is free. I mean he has not been in the hands of the police for the last twelve months, but one never knows ... he lives in a perfectly respectable suburban quarter of Dublin. The number of Revolutionaries living in the red brick suburbs of this city are almost unbelievable. We are advancing. . . .

GEORGE RUSSELL (Æ)
from Frank O'Connor, *The Wild Bird's Nest: Poems from the Irish* (1932)

Here is George Russell's Preface to Frank O'Connor's translations from Gaelic verse. Many of his comments reflect his admiration for the work of his mentor Standish James O'Grady.

An Essay on the Character in Irish Literature

There is a character in the Irish poetry translated by Frank O'Connor which is in much of the literature in Irish, and which persists in Anglo-Irish literature in our time. I do not think this Irish character has been well understood. It arose partly out of the isolation of Ireland as an island, and partly because Ireland was never part of the ancient Roman empire. Those ancient Romans were great builders but they were also great destroyers, & they obliterated in England, France and Spain almost all traces of the culture which preceded their own. In Ireland never subject to the Latin domination there are rich survivals of a culture almost unaffected by the later European. It continued the primæval culture of imagination which was, I think, the culture of the world before the Greeks came with the beginnings of philosophy and science. People simply imagined things about the universe, and what do we not owe to that imagination which discovered above this world its heaven worlds and its god worlds, and populated them with pantheons of divinities. How dark would nature seem to us, how arid our literature and art, but for the imagination of our Graeco-Latin ancestors and their tribes of gods, nymphs, naiads, dryads, hama dryads, oreads, fauns, and satyrs. India and Persia had their own divinities; and in Ireland the imagination of the ancestors created images which are as beautiful as any to the artist mind: Angus, the Celtic Eros, a beautiful young man circled by dazzling singing birds, his messengers which he sang into the hearts of young men and girls and whose kisses brought love and death, Lug who comes over the waters on a winged horse out of the Land of Promise, Mananan the sea god with his boat, the Ocean Sweeper, Lir with his transformed children and the hosts of the Sidhe, all clear-cut, bright and beautiful to the imagination. Whatever element of truth lay in these imaginations was poetic or spiritual truth, a relation of myth and image to deep inner being. The new culture of nature begun by Aristotle culminated in modern science where truth is a relation of our thought to what is perceived by the senses, verifiable by mathematics and delicate mechanisms: and, while European thought was being disciplined by philosophy and science, Ireland outside the European system was unaffected by these and continued for long centuries the primæval culture of imagination. As it was never part of the Roman empire its own culture was not extinguished and it had not to fill the void with a culture of Graeco-Latin origins. In the Irish literature philosophy and science are absent. We never had even a great Irish theologian. Johannes Scotus Erigena, the one Irishman of intellect capable of rationalizing spiritual nature, went to Europe & became the greatest of mediæval heretics. There were few intellectual influences to deflect the Irish culture from its natural development. As with other peoples its imagination stormed the heavens. There are in Irish literature many voyages to heaven world or faery. But there was not as in Europe any rationalizing by philosophy of these heavenly adventures. Philosophy might have been a net to catch and sustain the spirit in its descent to earth and to keep it from despair at its fall. But the Irish never seem to have made any attempt to rationalize their vision. There are two poles in the literature: one where the visionary imagination rises to Ildathach the many-coloured land, while at the other pole there is a cold, hard, yet passionate realism. The Voyage of Bran and Cormac's adventure in faery were created while the imagination was at the first pole, and the Old Woman of Beare and indeed most of the poetry translated by O'Connor, were made through intensity of brooding over life. At whatever phase of the Irish imagination the poetry is composed, that is whenever it is truly poetry it has this in common, it is perfectly natural. There is hardly a trace of the philosophic mind, the mentality we see in perfection in Wordsworth's 'Ode on Intimations of Immortality' and in so much of English literature where Platonism or some other philosophical system enables the poet to interpret his experience to himself.

In Irish literature every vision is what it seems at the moment to the seer. Intuition does not penetrate to any deep of being. The alchemy of the brooding mind distils no precious knowledge. In that literature too every passion exists by itself. It is born and dies in the poet without any of the consolations of philosophy, and to this perhaps is due that mood bleak, cynical, and ironical, which pervades so much even of the love poetry. As the heavens are for ever appearing and vanishing before the mystical adventurer, so too in this world love is ever conscious of its own impermanence. It seems in its first blossoming to know how soon its petals must fall. There is so little to hold to and it goes so soon. The Old Woman of Beare cries:

I that had my day with kings
And drank deep of mead and wine,
Drink whey water with old hags,
Sitting in their rags, and pine.

Here is her counterpart in bitterness in man:

> There be three things seeking my death,
> All at my heels run wild —
> Hang them, oh God, all three,
> Devil, maggot and child!

Even in those lovely verses where Egan O'Rahilly[1] sees the magical queens go by him the vision brings him back to his sick soul. One might almost foresee in germ in the early and middle Irish poetry the cold yet passionate realism which is the dominating mood in the latest Anglo-Irish literature. The centuries have not yet brought us to the philosophic mind. I would like to speculate on the offspring of a marriage of cultures, the Irish with the European, which cannot be kept apart forever. There are intimations in the later poetry and prose of Yeats what an exciting literature might be born from that union.

Those who come after us on a later wave of time cannot realize the quickening of imagination which came to us of an earlier generation when the labour of scholars revealed to us that almost forgotten literature in Gaelic. The early sagas as raw material for the imaginative artist are, I think, equal to anything in Greek mythology. The lyric poetry is of very fine quality. The evidence is in these translations by Frank O'Connor. Many people have turned fine poetry in one language to very indifferent verse in another. But no one, I think, has ever made fine poetry out of bad originals.

The miracle of silk making out of a sow's ear is still as ever unbelievable.

1   Aodhagán Ó Rathaille (?1670–1729), Gaelic poet from County Kerry.

F. SCOTT FITZGERALD
from Andrew Turnbull (ed.), *The Letters of F. Scott Fitzgerald* (1968)

As this revealing letter to John O'Hara (1905–70) suggests, the Princeton–educated Scott Fitzgerald (1896–1940) connected his vulnerable personality with his Irishness.

> *La Paix, Rodgers' Forge*
> *Towson, Maryland*
> *July 18, 1933*

Dear O'Hara:

I am especially grateful for your letter. I am half black Irish and half old American stock with the usual exaggerated ancestral pretensions. The black Irish half of the family had the money and looked down upon the Maryland side of the family who had, and really had, that certain series of reticences and obligations that go under the poor old shattered word 'breeding' (modern form 'inhibitions'). So being born in that atmosphere of crack, wisecrack and countercrack I developed a two-cylinder inferiority complex. So if I were elected King of Scotland tomorrow after graduating from Eton, Magdalene to Guards, with an embryonic history which tied me to the Plantagenets, I would still be a parvenu. I spent my youth in alter-

nately crawling in front of the kitchen maids and insulting the great.

I suppose this is just a confession of being a Gael though I have known many Irish who have not been afflicted by this intense social self-consciousness. If you are interested in colleges, a typical gesture on my part would have been, for being at Princeton and belonging to one of its snootiest clubs, I would be capable of going to Podunk[1] on a visit and being absolutely booed and overawed by its social system, not from timidity but simply because of an inner necessity of starting my life and my self-justification over again at scratch in whatever new environment I may be thrown.

The only excuse for that burst of egotism is that you asked for it. . . .

1   A small tribe of Indians who once inhabited land near the Podunk River in Hartford, Connecticut.

'ANDREW BELIS'
from The Bookman, August 1934

Written under the pseudonym 'Andrew Belis', Samuel Beckett's review of contemporary
Irish verse is by turns splenetic, arrogant, insightful, just. Beckett's remorseless attack on
the 'twilighters', as he calls the Revival poets, stems from his modernist belief in the
need to examine not the object but the act of perception. Many of the writers referred
to in this review are mentioned or collected in this *Reader*.

Recent Irish Poetry

I propose, as rough principle of individuation in this
essay, the degree in which the younger Irish poets
evince awareness of the new thing that has happened,
or the old thing that has happened again, namely the
breakdown of the object, whether current, historical,
mythical or spook. The thermolaters[1] — and they
pullulate in Ireland — adoring the stuff of song as
incorruptible, uninjurable and unchangeable, never at
a loss to know when they are in the Presence, would
no doubt like this amended to breakdown of the
subject. It comes to the same thing — rupture of the
lines of communication.

The artist who is aware of this may state the space
that intervenes between him and the world of objects;
he may state it as no-man's-land, Hellespont or
vacuum, according as he happens to be feeling
resentful, nostalgic or merely depressed. A picture by
Mr Jack Yeats, Mr Eliot's *Waste Land*, are notable
statements of this kind. Or he may celebrate the cold
comforts of apperception. He may even record his
findings, if he is a man of great personal courage.
Those who are not aware of the rupture, or in whom
the velleity[2] of becoming so was suppressed as a
nuisance at its inception, will continue to purvey those
articles which, in Ireland at least, had ceased to be
valid even before the literary advisers to J.M. Synge
found themselves prematurely obliged to look
elsewhere for a creative hack. These are the
antiquarians, delivering with the altitudinous
complacency of the Victorian Gael the Ossianic
goods.

Thus contemporary Irish poets may be divided into
antiquarians and others, the former in the majority,
the latter kindly noticed by Mr W.B. Yeats as 'the fish
that lie gasping on the shore', suggesting that they
might at least learn to expire with an air. This
position, needless to say, is not peculiar to Ireland or
anywhere else. The issue between the conventional
and the actual never lapses, not even when the
conventional and the actual are most congruent. But it

is especially acute in Ireland, thanks to the technique
of our leading twilighters.

The device common to the poets of the Revival
and after, in the use of which even beyond the jewels
of language they are at one, is that of flight from self-
awareness, and as such might perhaps better be
described as a convenience. At the centre there is no
theme. Why not? Because the centre is simply not that
kind of girl, and no more about it. And without a
theme there can be no poem, as witness the
exclamation of Mr Yeats's 'fanatic heart': 'What, be a
singer born and lack a theme!' *(The Winding Stair)*. But
the circumference is an iridescence of themes —
Oisin, Cuchulain, Maeve, Tir-nan-og, the Táin Bo
Cuailgne, Yoga, the Crone of Beare — segment after
segment of cut-and-dried sanctity and loveliness.
There are the specialists, but no monopolies, each poet
being left perfect liberty to make his selection. The
poem of poems would embrace the sense of
confinement, the getaway, the vicissitudes of the road,
the wan bliss on the rim. But a large degree of
freedom may enter into the montage of these
components, and it is very often in virtue of this,
when the tics of mere form are in abeyance, that
attributions are to be made. Thus typically the first
may be scarcely perceptible in Mr Colum and even less
so in Mr Stephens, the second predominate in Mr
Yeats, the third be acutely dilated by Miss Pamela
Travers or the Rev. Monk Gibbon, and the fourth to
all intents and purposes discarded by Mr George
Russell who, when thoroughly galvanized by the
protracted apathies, rigidities and abstractions, enters
his heart's desire with such precipitation as positively
to protrude into the void.

What further interest can attach to such assumptions
as those on which the convention has for so long taken
its ease, namely, that the first condition of any poem is
an accredited theme, and that in self-perception there
is no theme, but at best sufficient *vis a tergo*[3] to land the
practitioner into the correct scenery, where the self is
either most happily obliterated or else so improved and
enlarged that it can be mistaken for part of the *décor*?

None but the academic. And it is in this connection that our lately founded Academy[4] may be said to meet a need and enjoy a function.

Mr W.B. Yeats, as he wove the best embroideries, so he is more alive than any of his contemporaries or scholars to the superannuation of these, and to the virtues of a verse that shall be nudist. 'There's more enterprise in going naked.' It eliminates swank — unless of course the song has something to swank about. His bequest in 'The Tower' of his pride and faith to the 'young upstanding men' has something almost second-best bed, as though he knew that they would be embarrassed to find an application for those dispositions. Yet when he speaks, in his preface to Senator Gogarty's *Wild Apples*, of the 'sense of hardship borne and chosen out of pride' as the ultimate theme of the Irish writer, it is as though he were to derive in direct descent the very latest prize canary from that fabulous bird, the mesozoic pelican, addicted, though childless, to self-eviscerations.

Mr James Stephens, in *Theme and Variations* (1930) and *Strict Joy* (1931), remains in his annexe of the tradition, where the poet appears as beauty expert:

> Yea, wonder is that he has done,
> For all that is beneath the sun
> By magic he transfigures to
> A better sound, a finer view.
>
> — *(Theme and Variations)*

Then follows the psychometricization of Plotinus, rather less of a success than that practised on Descartes by La Fontaine. When the theme, without which there can be no poem, is in itself presentable, then its transmission is a mere question of metrical adjustments; but when it is not, when it is a mournful or a miserable thing, then it must be smartened up:

> . . . Because all things transfer
> From what they seem to what they truly are
> When they are innocently brooded on —
> And so the poet makes grief beautiful.
>
> — *(Strict Joy)*

'Reverie on a Rose' is a good sample of this process — and a gloss on its innocency.

Mr Austen Clarke, having declared himself, in his *Cattle Drive in Connaught* (1925), a follower of 'that most famous juggler, Mannanaun', continues in *The Pilgrimage* (1929) to display the 'trick of tongue or two' and to remove, by means of ingenious metrical operations, 'the clapper from the bell of rhyme'. The fully licensed stock-in-trade, from Aisling to Red

Branch Bundling, is his to command. Here the need for formal justifications, more acute in Mr Clarke than in Mr Higgins, serves to screen the deeper need that must not be avowed.

Though in his *Island Blood* (1925), *The Dark Breed* (1927) and *Arable Holdings* (1933) Mr Higgins has accumulated a greater number of 'By God's' than all the other antiquarians put together, though he is less of the 'glimmering fawn' than Mr Russell and less of the lilter and lisper than Mr Colum or Mr Stephens, yet he is still victim of the centrifugal dæmon:

> Come away to this holy air . . .
> Come away to this simple lake
> And learn at the voice of a bird
> To vie with their music and make
>   New worlds in a word.
>
> — *(Island Blood)*

It is agreeable, if unreasonable, to connect this impulse, the entire Celtic drill of extraversion, with Mr Higgins's blackthorn stick, thus addressed:

> And here, as in green days you were the perch,
> You're now the prop of song . . .
>
> — *(Arable Holdings)*

His verses have what Ledwidge's had, what all modern nature poetry excepting Wordsworth's has, a good smell of dung, most refreshing after all the attar of far off, most secret and inviolate rose. And surely it is a great pity that the discernment enabling Mr Higgins to see his native land as 'an Easter Island in the Western Sea' should be so intolerant of its own company. It is symptomatic that both Mr Clarke and Mr Higgins are now taking up prose.

In *For Daws to Peck At* (1929) and *Seventeen Sonnets* (1932), the Rev. Monk Gibbon follows his secret heart far from the 'lack-luck lot'. He is the poet of children ('Chacun Son Goût'), and as such is bound to consider thought a microbe:

> 'And, though the tune's of little count
> And knowledge more than all to me,
> Who knows what music may have died
> When that small seed fell silently?
>
> — *(For Daws to Peck At)*

The sonnets, with so many definite and indefinite articles excised, recall the succinctness of the Cambridge Experimenters.

These, to whom Mr Brian O'Higgins, An Philibin and Miss Large may conveniently be annexed, are the chief of the younger antiquarians.

Mr Thomas McGreevy is best described as an independent, occupying a position intermediate between the above and the poor fish, in the sense that he neither excludes self-perception from his work nor postulates the object as inaccessible. But he knows how to wait for the thing to happen, how not to beg the fact of this 'bitch of a world' — inarticulate earth and inscrutable heaven:

I labour in a barren place,
Alone, self-conscious, frightened, blundering;
Far away, stars wheeling in space,
About my feet, earth voices whispering.
                              — *(Poems, 1934)*[5]

And when it does happen and he sees, 'far as sensitive eyesight could see', whatever happens to be dispensed, *gile na gile*[6] or empty hearths, it is the act and not the object of perception that matters. Mr McGreevy is an existentialist in verse, the Titchener[7] of the modern lyric. It is in virtue of this quality of inevitable unveiling that his poems may be called elucidations, the vision without the dip, and probably the most important contribution to post-War Irish poetry.

There is much in Mrs Blanaid Salkeld's *Hello Eternity* (1933) that is personal and moving, when not rendered blue in the face by the sonnet form. What is badly needed at the present moment is some small Malherbe of free verse to sit on the sonnet and put it out of action for two hundred years at least. Perhaps Mr Pound . . . ? Other Irish sonneteers are Mr Erik Dodds[8] (*Thirty-two Poems*, 1929) and Mr Francis Macnamara (*Marionettes*, 1909), but only in the leisure moments of a university professor and a student of social theory respectively. The influence of Rossetti is strong in Mr Macnamara. The Oxford Georgians have left their mark on Mr Dodds.

In *Man Poem* (1919) Mr Percy Usher, best known as translator of Merriman's 'Midnight Court', deals with himself and the vacuum in a manner that abides no question. One would like to see this work, before it is improved out of existence, safely between the boards.

Mr Francis Stuart is of course best known as a novelist, but he writes verse. So does Mr R.N.D. Wilson. So does Mr Leslie Yodaiken[9] when his politics let him. So I am sure do Mr Frank O'Connor and Mr Seán O'Faoláin — also best known as novelists of course. And I know that Mr Seán O'Casey does, having read a poem of his in *Time and Tide*.

In *Primordia Cæca* (1927) Mr Lyle Donaghy undertook a regular *Saison en Enfer*:

Enter again into the womb;
    be saturate with night;
    let the vain soul be satisfied.

Descend into the dark cell;
    look on the unnatured, undistinguished pulp;
    peruse the incipient page.

Retrace the way come blindly;
    from centre and cause revisited,
    draw the pure being up.

It is drawn up, but in the unfinished condition made manifest in his *Flute Over the Valley* (1931), which contains however a fine poem about a steam-roller. Some years ago Mr Donaghy published an admirable 'objectless' poem — 'The Fort' — in the *Criterion*. Another volume, *Into the Light*, is announced as impending. May it be down into the light.

Mr Geoffrey Taylor, in his *Withering of the Fig-leaf* and *It Was Not Jones*, performed a very diverting ballet away from the pundits. But I do not know that he has done anything since.

Mr Denis Devlin and Mr Brian Coffey are without question the most interesting of the youngest generation of Irish poets, but I do not propose to disoblige them by quoting from the volume of verse which they published jointly in 1930. Since then they have submitted themselves to the influences of those poets least concerned with evading the bankrupt relationship referred to at the opening of this essay — Corbière, Rimbaud, Laforgue, the *surréalistes* and Mr Eliot, perhaps also to those of Mr Pound — with results that constitute already the nucleus of a living poetic in Ireland:

Phrases twisted through other
Reasons reasons disproofs
Phrases lying low
Proving invalid that reason
With which I prove its truth
Identity obscured
Like the reflections of
One mirror in another,
Reasons reasons disproofs.

It is no disparagement of Mr Devlin to observe that this is still too much by the grace of Eluard. What matters is that it does not proceed from the *Gossoons Wunderhorn* of that Irish Romantic Arnim-Brentano combination, Sir Samuel Ferguson and Standish O'Grady, and that it admits — stupendous innovation — the existence of the author. *Es wandelt niemand ungestraft unter Palmen*[10] is peculiarly applicable to these islands, where pigeons meet with such encouragements. But it is preferable to dying of mirage.

Of Mr Niall Sheridan and Mr Donagh MacDonagh I know nothing, except that they have just published *Twenty Poems* between them; of Miss Irene Haugh, nothing, except that she has just published *The Valley of the Bells*, and that her chief concern, in the words of her *Dublin Magazine* reviewer, is God; of Mr Niall Montgomery's poetry, nothing at all.

1 Presumably, those who adjust the temperature, the parsimonious critics.
2 The mere wish.

3 Latin: kick in the rear.
4 The Irish Academy of Letters was founded by Yeats, Russell and Shaw in 1932. See Boyd (1934, p. 385) below for more information.
5 These four lines constitute the poem 'Nocturne', which was dedicated to Geoffrey England, an English soldier who died of his wounds in September 1918. The poem was first published in *The Irish Statesman* on 28 September 1928.
6 Irish: the fairest of the fair.
7 Presumably a reference to the experimental psychologist Edward Bradford Titchener, author of 'The Schema of Introspection', whose *Systematic Psychology* was published in 1929.
8 Eric (sic) Robinson Dodds, Greek scholar and later friend of MacNeice.
9 Leslie Daiken (1912–64), socialist poet and journalist.
10 German: Whoever dares to wander under palm trees won't do it with impunity.

PAT O'MARA
from Pat O'Mara, *The Autobiography of a Liverpool Irish Slummy* (1934)

Pat O'Mara dedicates the autobiography of his Liverpool years to 'all slummies'. Here in this extract he records a moment in May 1915, after the sinking of the *Lusitania* by a German submarine, when Liverpudlians turned on Germans living in their city. O'Mara himself went on to write a subsequent volume *Irish Slummy in America* (1935), which records his experiences in Baltimore as a taxi driver, the hunger he felt in the semi-slums in East and South Baltimore, and his marriage to a woman who thought for three years he was from New York. In this extract street-names form another variation on the theme of national identity.

Chapter 29

There was a new caller in our kitchen, a young soldier named Jorgensen, who boarded with his father down near the Dock Road. None of us knew anything about him, for he had enlisted in the Army at the outbreak of War straight from training school and had been preserved to this day. It seemed that one day while on leave he had met my sister and had visualized in her a respectable post-war wife.

A frail boy, he looked even more absurd in khaki than my cousin Berny. But he had a very pleasant disposition and it was easy to like him. I saw much of him during his two weeks' leave from France, and when I settled my accounts with the *Lowtyne*'s agent, we did quite a bit of 'supping up' in the pubs together — to Alice's deep chagrin. Most of it was on his money, for all I got from the *Lowtyne* trip was actual pay up to the time I landed in Liverpool — altogether

about three pounds. I felt inwardly sorry for Austin, because I believed that Alice's early life would not make her an agreeable wife for him. I think I touched on this once, but he thought otherwise, and on the day before he left for France he got a tacit promise from my mother that Alice would accept him when and if he ever returned from France.

When he was gone, I felt rather alone, for our corner now, due to the deaths of Joe, Harold and Johnny and the departure of others for France, had lost its charm. Jacko Oldham, Frankie Roza, Freddie Seegar, Jackie Sanchez, and myself were the actual members still at home. Mickey, 'the kid' from the Working Boys' Home, had drifted away in the same mysterious manner that he had come among us. Perhaps he had gone off to the colonies, as so many of the Working Boys' Home lads do — no one seemed to know. Perhaps what was chiefly responsible for breaking up the gang was the fact that we were accepted around the neighbourhood as 'men' — in lieu of real men away at the War. The old codgers, cadging from us, encouraged this vanity. So that the only time we got together was at the Saturday afternoon 'footy' game or the pitch and toss affair. For the remainder of the week, Jacko Oldham and Frankie Roza served their time in Davidson's Engineering Company in Grayson Street! Freddie Seegar, Jackie Sanchez and myself hung around the docks working whenever the whimsy struck us.

The dock cathechism went something like this:

Foreman: 'Will you go to work mate?'

Worker: 'Naw.'

Foreman: 'Will you go to a wedding?'

The hoofs of fine English draught horses beat a continuous rumble on the Dock Road as they pulled wagon load after wagon load of merchandise and munitions to and from the ships. Winches ground out all night; flashlights glared from their holds; men like Auntie Janie's husband, Mr Murray, scarcely ever ceased working.

But further in town was deep darkness and gloom and tragedy, interspersed here and there with the glowing rapture in the eyes of sooty artisans now making more money than ever before. There were few Saturday night celebrations in the streets. Flukey Alley's Flukes, Sparling Street's Negroes, and the Chinamen of Pitt Street — even into these un-British sections tragedy and gloom had seeped, for many half-caste boys had lost their lives. It was the same up the Courts, where the tragic inroads of war were worse than anywhere else. 'Wiped out' could be placed against most of the raggedy young manhood that, when war beckoned, had rushed eagerly from these cess-pools.

The Black Prince no longer paraded naked, but staggered through the streets, face eaten away with cancer. Sometimes I would stand at our door watching these hopeless creatures, scrawny children who had grown up exactly as they could have been expected to grow up — rowdies one and all, toughs or wrecks and duplicating the sordid, half-savage lives of their fathers and mothers. The money-lenders still lent their money and foistered their stinking fish upon the dupes. Mrs Golding still picked her favourite *middens*,[1] vowing now that the thing was traditional: 'Me mother before me had these middens for years. . . . There's no loiterers allowed around *these*.' A sooty couple named Bob and Leah (that's all they went by) took up where my father and mother had left off. Leah's husband had been killed in France and she married Bob with the government money the week after the news of his death. Then started another thirty years war — and they were still at it. Harris's pawnshop, despite the war

affluence (which barely affected many slummies — their ritual being, earn so much, then loaf) was doing a bigger business than ever. I met Leah coming out of the Dead House one Saturday, very gay and tipsy, and on her way to procure the services of Mr Levy, the cut-rate furniture dealer in Mill Street. 'Timmy, I wonder 'ow much 'e'll give me for the sofa and two chairs? Oo! Then me and Bob'll 'ave to sleep on the bloody floor again. . . .'

I would watch the Black Prince's son, Jimmy, as he helped his mother chop chips; I mused on his life story more than the others because it was so like my own. His head used to shake continuously and suddenly, for no apparent reason, his eyes would dilate and his mouth froth and he would subside to the pavement in the grip of a fit — his father's handiwork undoubtedly. And there was a little half-caste harlot living in Sparling Street, whom I used to see as a child in the dispensary and whom I now saw as a young woman in the same place. She was one of the many offshoots of West African Negro-Irish wife combinations. The more brazenly attractive of her mates, after working all day in Read's Tin Works up the street, would reappear of a night in Lime Street or in the dive that had taken the place of Mr Grossi's Trocadero. But not she — the darkened Courts sufficed for her. The professional witness, Kitty Daughtery, was still mooching around for 'cases' in which to give her expert evidence. The sturdy old rock, St Vincent's church, still stood, despite its economic plight, and Father Ryan's big worried face had at last assumed an aspect of quietness, for in Father Toomey's place now was a quiet, unassuming little Irish scholar, Father Dee, a professor of Theology from Dublin. This little academician — how strange he looked when, capped and gowned, I'd see him walking down Sparling Street, among all the Negroes and whites and half-caste children!

Down in the Dead House my father was up to his old tricks with a new foil — Mrs Harris. Up in the barracks, with the deaths and the general dismal effects of the War, there were few signs of any of the old activity. My grandmother, of course, sat in her rocking chair in silence, cogitating, cogitating and scowling at pro-German Lonnigan, while he gave out his latest explanation of why the Germans shelled Rheims Cathedral.[2] Perhaps my Uncle Jimmy, now acquiring a beautiful red-nose by virtue of his job on the Guinness's stout boats[3] and a nicely dyed hair by reason of something else, would drop in and buy his mother a pint; and as like as not my lugubrious Aunt Janie would drop in and (after complaining how terrible economic conditions were) duplicate his feat.

Then the dynamite hidden underneath all this was touched off. It was five o'clock one evening, and I was watching the home-coming dockers, when a newsboy came racing down from Park Lane, yelling: 'Sinking of the *Lusitania*!'[4]

The men stopped short; women peered from doorways. I joined one anxious group, poring over the fatal news. It was right — the 'Lusy', the fine boat I had left Joe Manassi and Harold May aboard not two months ago, had been torpedoed! The news was only brief — she had 'got it' in the Irish Sea bound for Liverpool 'with terrible loss,' the paper concluded. Later, another edition of the paper gave more tragic details.

My mother was shocked by the news, especially as a very good friend of hers when she worked at the Emigrant House, a steward named Alfred Gilroy, was on it. She berated me when I touched her for entrance money to the Daulby Hall. 'Here you are loafing around here and good men being sunk and shot and your poor sister and me working our hands off. . . . Here, take it!'

It took about two days for the names of the drowned among the crew to be published. They were appalling. That night Freddie Seegar and I, clad in our American tailored suits, started for a dance over Paddy's Market in St Martin's Hall. We never attended it, however. Before entering the Hall we walked around Scotland Road listening to the cries of the women whose husbands and sons had gone down in the 'Lusy' and we heard the bitter threats made against Germany and anything with a German name. We walked down Bostock Street, where practically every blind was drawn in token of a death. All these little houses were occupied by Irish coal-trimmers and firemen and sailormen on the *Lusitania*; now these men who, barely two weeks ago, had carried their bags jokingly down the street, were gone, never to return.

Some of the women, drunk, were laughing — laughing as mad people laugh when the border line had been passed. Freddie, usually a very light-hearted boy, turned to me with whitened face and said: 'Listen to all them women crying!'

On the corner of Scotland Road ominous gangs were gathering — men and women, very drunk and very angry. Something was afoot; we could sense that and, like good slummy boys, we crowded around eager to help in any disturbance. Suddenly something crashed up the road near Ben Jonson Street; followed in turn by another terrific crash of glass. We ran up the road. A pork butcher's had had its front window knocked in with a brick and a crowd of men and women were wrecking the place. A little higher up the same thing was happening — everything suggestive of Germany was being smashed to pieces.

Up the road the crowd surged, some cutting into Sawny Pope Street; others going into Ben Jonson Street; others continuing up the road. Down Scotland Road in the opposite direction the window crashing was more terrific — clear down to Byron Street. Everyone had a brick or a stick or something tucked under his or her coat or apron and there was much pilfering. The police themselves, imbued with bitterness, were the most passive guardians of law. I recall one stout little Irish sausage dealer pleading with the crowd that her husband wasn't a German; but the name was too suspicious and in the windows went and the place was wrecked.

Freddie turned to me: 'What about all the 'uns up our way? I'll bet they're having some bloody fun up there now. Let's go up there.' So we left the Scotland Road mob and took the tram up to our own South End.

Freddie had guessed correctly. As soon as the tram got near Charlie Beech's pork shop, opposite St Vincent's Church, a dense mob caused it to stop. Mr Beech had been living in Liverpool thirty odd years, but there was a faint suspicion that years ago, anticipating just such a riot, he had changed his name. His big shop was in shambles when, running from the halted tramcar, we got to it; Mr Beech and his son had made their escape.

Someone in the mob mentioned Bob Acte's sailors' boarding house in Nelson Street. Mr Acte was a retired German sailorman, now a naturalized Britisher, and married to the popular Sarah Doran, as Irish as a leprechaun. 'Ah, lave thim alone!' said a Joan of Arc who was leading the mob. 'Sarah allers hilped the church. Let's get after Yaag — that's the bloody 'un!'

So instead of Acte's we raced on to Yaag's pork butcher's in Great George's Street, most of us boys in the vanguard and anxious to be the first to crash the enemy's windows. Mr Yaag, a big, wholesome fellow, allegedly had been born in Germany, but I don't think he remembered much about it. Two of his nephews at the time were with my cousin Berny and the Eighth Irish over in France. I always liked Mr Yaag, but not quite so keenly as I liked to break his window without fear of molestation.

As we converged on the big shop, Mr Yaag, arms akimbo and thinking some urchin was fleeing from Aeroplane Joe, came out, pipe in mouth and with his usual broad smile; this vanished instantly as someone kicked him in the belly and a volley of bricks sent in the huge windows. From the sawdust floor the astounded man had the pleasure of seeing his choice sausages kicked and thrown about and the furnishings reduced to shambles. 'You'll sink the bleedin' "Lusy", will you!' yelled our Joan, waving a shillalah[5] over his prostrate form. 'I'll give you sinking the bloody "Lusy"! 'Ere, bust that up; kick that out; smash that whole bloody business!' We left Mr Yaag and Yaag, Inc., in a worse mess than Charlie Beech's.

Cook's pork butcher's in Mill Street came next. Mr Cook knew as much about Germany at the time, I think, as I did. Later investigation proved that he came from strictly Yorkshire stock and was a devoted student of Mr Kipling[6] — dashing off a bit of patriotic verse himself once in a while. But he had a pork butcher's shop, and as pork and Germany were identical terms, we left his shop in a shambles and himself stretched across the counter groaning. I began to get sick from all the free sausage I'd been eating.

When all the pork butchers (the more obvious Huns) had been satisfactorily dealt with, attention was turned to the private houses. It worked something like this. The mob would pause panting for a moment and someone would address Joan of Arc: 'You know that dirty auld man that lives in such and such a street. I think he's one of them!'

'I know he is!' someone who didn't like this particular person would agree. Then off at a gallop.

A rather pathetic case I recall was that of an aged couple who lived quietly in a house in Kent Street, just opposite St Michael's Church. Of German extraction, they had lived so long in Liverpool they looked like natives. Moreover, they had taken out naturalization papers and were drawing their support from the Parish.[7] At the moment our Joan converged on the front window with her trusty shillalah, they were in the parlour singing Lutheran hymns. In went the front window as Mrs Seymour — our Joan — screamed: 'You'll sink the bloody "Lusy", will you? Then take that! And that! And that!' We left this old house practically wrecked, but no one hit the old couple.

Our next conquest was Annie Monnigan's little shack. Annie was just as Irish as Sarah Doran, German Bob Acte's wife, but she didn't contribute as generously to St Vincent's and this made a big difference. Several reasons why Annie didn't contribute so much to the church as Sarah was that she had no sailors' boarding house, had six small children to feed, and her husband was interned.[8] But she was quite as good a Catholic as Sarah. Years ago, she had married Charlie Thomas, fresh from a German four-masted barque. As the children came, Charlie quit the sea and matriculated, like all old sailors, to dock labouring — an occupation he was at when hauled off to the German detention camp on the Isle of Man. One of our crowd, with remarkable memory, verified this — and the stampede was on. I shall never forget the hysteria of this last débâcle, with the six young children screaming and Annie, like a good colleen, fighting back and asking no quarter. After doing a sound job here, we left loudly cheering our commander-in-chief, herself now sporting a black eye, given her by the fighting Annie.

Next — of all places — was my German uncle by marriage, Chris Hazeman's house in Chesterfield Street. Long afterward I was suspected of having suggested that the expedition go there, but it wasn't true. I don't know who started it; the only thing I do confess to was that when it *was suggested*, I seconded the motion. I remembered my beautiful Aunt Lizzie and a childish bitterness against the Hazemans grew rancorous within me. Now here was an opportunity to get even! But after we wrecked the little house that Auntie Lizzie loved so well (the Hazemans had fled when they heard we were on our way up there) I was glad she was not living then, otherwise she would have received the same fate as the other Irish girls whose husbands had become suspects.

And so far on into the night our gang, along with several others equally patriotic, went through the slummy section of the town wrecking everything we tackled. Up in the North End it was the same way; the foe for the brief moment had changed from England to Germany. Many mistakes were made. Most of the slummy women already mentioned early in this book took an active part in the campaign and not a few of them dispatched themselves with signal valour. If Germany had torpedoed the *Lusitania*, we certainly had torpedoed everything German in our immediate vicinity — certainly all the pork butchers' shops. The following day all was quiet, and the police, now mindful of their jobs, started taking an inventory. All damage was carefully checked and all the victims adequately reimbursed, the cost going on the tax rate as is the way with good British justice. Our commander-in-chief, the fiery little Irishwoman, was relieved from her chip-chopping activities and given six months in Walton[9] for her valour, and only his adeptness at secreting himself behind chimney pots saved the Black Prince from going along with her. Several others got minor sentences.

There was some disguised blessings, too. Most of the wrecked butcher shops were obsolete contraptions, but when the reconstruction architects came in, newer and gaudier edifices were erected. Little fighting Annie Monnigan had always detested the little shack in

Frederick Street, so when the government offered to rebuild it according to the original plan, she threw up her hands in horror and suggested a cash settlement. Poor Charlie Beech and I were the worst sufferers. Charlie's son John dropped dead after racing with his father from the shop to his house in Aigbirth; and I got a pernicious bellyache on account of all the raw sausage I had eaten.

1   Refuse-heaps.
2   The medieval cathedral with its priceless stained glass was shelled by the Germans in 1914.

3   These boats plied between Dublin and Liverpool.
4   The *Lusitania*, a British-registered transatlantic liner, was sunk without warning off the Irish coast by a German submarine on 7 May 1915. Nearly twelve hundred people were killed including Sir Hugh Lane, the nephew of Lady Gregory, and 128 Americans (which helped turn American public opinion against Germany).
5   In Ireland, a shillelagh was a cudgel used for fighting.
6   Rudyard Kipling (1856–1936) who wrote patriotic English verse about romantic imperialism and the white man's burden.
7   Drawing relief or benefits from the local authority.
8   During the Great War many Germans or people with German surnames living in Britain were interned.
9   Walton Jail in Liverpool.

ERNEST BOYD
from *Current History*, March 1934

Ernest Boyd, literary adviser to the Talbot Press in 1917–20, emigrated to New York in 1920. His major work of literary scholarship is *Ireland's Literary Renaissance* (1916; 1922), which remains in its own way an excellent survey of the Revival. Here is another handy survey of Irish writing in the early 1930s as writers faced up to the disillusion of Ireland after Independence and to the new strident form of state censorship.

Joyce and the New Irish Writers

To many people the recent removal of the censorship ban[1] on James Joyce's *Ulysses* will seem to be the most important event in the history of contemporary Anglo-Irish literature. First published serially — until it was suppressed — in the *Little Review* of New York, then issued in Paris for limited circulation in 1922, this book has aroused, under these restricted conditions, more comment and controversy than the work of any modern Irish writer, with the possible exception of J.M. Synge's comedy, *The Playboy of the Western World*. Officially banned during all these years from both England and America, *Ulysses* has been as widely read and discussed in these two countries as if it had been on sale in every book shop. Now that it is available in its complete unexpurgated form (New York: Random House, $3.50), it is very natural that one should speculate on its reception at the hands of the general public.

Outside Ireland itself, this quintessentially Irish and local study of Dublin life has evoked somewhat extravagant enthusiasm and highly exaggerated claims for its importance. The distinguished French critic, novelist and translator, Valéry Larbaud of the *Nouvelle Revue Française*, pitched the note when he declared that, with *Ulysses*, Ireland had made her re-entry into European literature. It is true, Mr Joyce has made a daring and often valuable technical experiment, breaking new ground in English for the development of narrative prose, although the extension of the method, as exemplified in the published portions of *Work in Progress*,[2] may well give his admirers pause. But the 'European' interest of the work must of necessity be limited to its form, for its content is so local and intrinsically insignificant that few who are unfamiliar with the city of Dublin thirty years ago can possibly grasp its allusions and enter into its spirit.

Essentially *Ulysses* is a continuation of the studies of certain Dublin types first adumbrated in the superb volume of short stories, *Dubliners*, and in that fine novel, *A Portrait of the Artist as a Young Man*, neither of which excited anything like the furore in esoteric circles which greeted *Ulysses*. Much has been written about the symbolic intention of this work, of its relation to Homer's *Odyssey*, to which the plan of the three first and last chapters, with the twelve cantos of the adventures of Ulysses in the middle, is supposed to correspond. Irish criticism, on the other hand, is more impressed by its simple realism, photographic in detail and documentation, while admitting the power of Joyce's bewildering juxtaposition of the real and the imaginary, the commonplace and the fantastic. He is the first, and perhaps the last, Irish Expressionist, showing a certain kinship with the Germans Walter Hasenclever and Georg Kaiser.

To claim for this book a European significance denied to W.B. Yeats, J.M. Synge or James Stephens is to ignore its genesis in favour of mere technique, and to invest its content with a mysterious import which the actuality of the references would seem to deny. James Joyce is endowed with the wonderful, fantastic imagination which conceived the fifteenth chapter of *Ulysses*, a vision of a Dublin Brocken,[3] whose scene is the sordid underworld of that city. But he also has the defects and qualities of the French Naturalists of the Zola school, which prompt him, for example, to catalogue all the various street-car lines and to explain with the accuracy of a guide-book how the city obtains its water supply. His eroticism, too, so misleadingly advertised by the censors, will be revealed as oscillating between mocking Rabelaisian ribaldry and the contemptuous and disgusted horror of the body which makes Swift the authentic precursor of this typical expression of Irish asceticism. As Judge Woolsey says in the decision prefacing this edition, 'In spite of its unusual frankness, I do not detect anywhere the leer of the sensualist.' Thus, the hopes of a certain type of reader are fortunately doomed to disappointment.

Turning from James Joyce to the new group of writers who may be described as representing the Free State period in Anglo-Irish literature, the first fact that strikes one is the complete absence of his influence on these younger contemporaries. His own generation, and more naturally the older generation, developed along utterly different lines, so that there is little or nothing in common between him and either Yeats, AE (George Russell), Synge and Lady Gregory, or Padraic Colum, James Stephens and Lennox Robinson. So far as Joyce has influenced the writers of today, they must be sought in England or America. In Ireland his influence has been nil. Although his work is saturated with the atmosphere of his native country, and his unique theme has been himself and his native city, he has been a lifelong exile, and has very deliberately and pointedly held aloof from all those who contributed to that remarkable flowering of Irish talent, the Irish literary renaissance.

His refusal to be elected a member of the Irish Academy of Letters, which was founded in 1932, very definitely emphasized his desire to be dissociated from the intellectual life of his country. Unlike most academies, this Irish institution is essentially unacademic, having been called into existence by circumstances which make it an important event in the history of Anglo-Irish letters. Its members and associate members, numbering some thirty, include every outstanding Irish writer of today, with a very few exceptions, such as James Joyce, Sean O'Casey and Douglas Hyde. The Academy was formed primarily as a protest and protection against the encroachments of censors and politicians upon the independence and integrity of Irish literature. The roll-call of names is one of which any other country but Ireland would be proud: G.B. Shaw, W.B. Yeats, Oliver Gogarty, Lennox Robinson, Frank O'Connor, Seumas O'Sullivan, F.R. Higgins, Forrest Reid, Peadar O'Donnell, Brinsley Macnamara, Francis Stuart, St John Ervine, E.OE. Somerville, James Stephens, T.C. Murray, Austin Clarke, Sean O'Faolain, Padraic Colum, Liam O'Flaherty. To which must be added the associate members, Eugene O'Neill, Helen Waddell, J.M. Hone, L.A.G. Strong, John Eglinton, Walter Starkie, Stephen Gwynn, Shane Leslie and Lawrence of Arabia.

From the late Eighties until the signing of the treaty constituting the Irish Free State in 1921, Ireland had witnessed a progressive development of Anglo-Irish literature, which has given to the world some of the chief figures in the world of letters today. Dublin was for several decades a centre of intellectual excitement and creative activity, which culminated in 1916, the year of the Sinn Fein insurrection. Then politics held full sway and under the Free State Government literary activity declined, until the Irish writers found themselves in a position somewhat akin to that of the Russian intelligentsia under the Czars. Their czar is the censorship, which frowns upon all kinds of unorthodoxy, and derives its strength from the indifference of an apathetic peasant population to whatever indignities are imposed upon the free play of ideas. Irish literature has been driven out of Ireland, and depends exclusively on British and American support.

With the exception of Seumas O'Sullivan's quarterly *Dublin Magazine*,[4] no periodical of any literary pretentions is published in Ireland. AE's *Irish Statesman*[5] died, despite generous American help, simply because neither the government nor any group of individuals would subsidize it, and the general public ignored it. There is not a daily or weekly newspaper in the country above the level of the crudest provincial journalism. Once Irish authors were published in Ireland; today they are all on the lists of London publishers. To add intellectual insult to financial injury, the majority of the members of the academy have, at one time or another, been banned by the censorship. A list of the taboos of this inconceivable organization would make the efforts of the Boston Watch and Ward Society seem broad-minded. In the space of one year I counted more than one hundred banned books, including such universally acceptable authors as Louis Bromfield, Heinrich Mann, H.G. Wells and John Dos Passos.

Thus it can be seen that a thoroughly unacademic motive prompted Bernard Shaw and W.B. Yeats to found the Irish Academy of Letters. The wisdom of this effort at cohesion was proved by the attitude of the Irish press. The usual gibes were heard to the effect that, because they do not write in Irish, the academicians are not Irish. Mr de Valera's *Irish Press*, written almost exclusively in English, discovered that the authors were chosen 'more as a result of their success in Britain and America than because of any reflection in their published works of the real Ireland'. Opposition to the censorship, it was sapiently pointed out, is no proof of literary excellence. Contrary to the evidence, the fiction was again maintained that there are 'a philosophy of life and conduct and an appreciation of moral value' in Ireland which mark that country off from the rest of this wicked world. So far, however, no list of Irish-speaking authors writing in their mother tongue has been produced to put to shame the renegades whom the academy and the rest of the world rightly regard as the not unworthy representatives of their country's intellectual activity.

When the politicians were appealing to the intellectuals of the world for help and sympathy, they received both. Now they are bent upon stifling all manifestations of freedom of thought. As the founders expressed it, 'there is in Ireland an official censorship, possessing and actively exercising powers of suppression which may at any moment confine an Irish author to the British and American markets, and therefore make it impossible for him to live by distinctive Irish literature.'

We have now some conception of the altered conditions under which the Free State generation of Irish writers have been working, as compared with their predecessors. Like the latter, who once lived and worked in Ireland, they, too, are now scattered, and London is the exclusive scene of their publishing activities. They get their first hearing in American and English periodicals, and their champions are not Irish, but English critics. With the exception of F.R. Higgins, Austin Clarke and Sean O'Casey, they are all novelists, and for purposes of record I shall name them and their chief works: Sean O'Faolain, author of a book of short stories, *Midsummer Night Madness*, and a novel *A Nest of Gentle Folk*; Frank O'Connor, a volume of short stories entitled *Guests of the Nation*; Peadar O'Donnell, three novels published so far in America, *The Way It Was With Them*, *Adrigoole* and *There Will be Fighting*;[6] and Francis Stuart, *Pigeon Irish*, *The Coloured Dome*, *Try the Sky* and *Glory*, four novels published in America, in addition to an earlier novel and a volume of verse which are not available in this country. Liam O'Flaherty's chief works are: *Thy Neighbour's Wife*, *The Black Soul*, *The Informer*, *Mr Gilhooley*, *The Assassin*, *The House of Gold* and *The Puritan*. All are members of the Irish Academy of Letters.

Those who are familiar with the Irish literary movement will at once be struck by the preponderance of fiction, as against poetry and drama, in the two preceding generations, although the romances of Standish O'Grady were the starting point of the literary renaissance fifty years ago. Had it not been for the essays of John Eglinton, the occasional prose pieces of AE and Yeats's two volumes of stories, one might have said that during the entire period from 1880 until the war, the art of prose had been largely neglected. John Eglinton, always, at best, an occasional writer, was for many years the only author of the revival who wished to be known solely as a prosaist. Even those who wrote fiction preferred the short story to the novel, and usually contrived some even more amorphous form of narrative, held together by a loose thread. Is *The Crock of Gold*, for example, strictly speaking, a novel? Or *The Charwoman's Daughter*, for that matter? It is narrative prose; that is all that can safely be said for either of these fine works.

Of novelists in the proper sense of the word there have been very few until recently, and they did not appear to be so intimately a part of the movement as the poets and dramatists. A great deal of Irish fiction has been frank pot-boiling, even by authors of some standing in other fields, and rightly finds no mention in any history of the Irish literary renaissance. The names of Emily Lawless, Jane Barlow and Shan F. Bullock, to mention but three of more serious purpose, do not shine with the same lustre as those of their contemporaries in poetry and drama. George Moore, of course, gave us *The Lake* and *The Untilled Field* as models of Irish fiction, but we had to wait for James Joyce and Brinsley Macnamara, before there was any evidence that the Irish novel might come into its own. Daniel Corkery, who declined membership in the academy because he holds that Irishmen should write in Irish, disproved his own dictum in 1917, when his *Threshold of Quiet* appeared, a beautiful piece of work which never received the widespread recognition it deserved.

Nowadays fiction is the chief medium of the new writers, while the theatre, once the all-absorbing focus of activity, can boast of only one first-rate newcomer, Sean O'Casey. Despite the acclaim with which the present company of Abbey Players was received in the United States during its last tour, nobody familiar with the traditions of the Irish National Theatre could do other than note with regret the decline in the quality of the acting and the extraordinary banality of the new plays, all of which might have been written twenty-five years ago. Significantly, the authentic survivors of the original Abbey Players could not elicit the same applause for their fine interpretations of *Juno and the Paycock* and *The Plough and the Stars*. Mr O'Casey's latest play, *Within the Gates*, is English in characters and setting, and has likewise failed to recommend itself to a New York producer.

One point of similarity exists between the plays of Sean O'Casey and the stories of Liam O'Flaherty, Sean O'Faolain, Frank O'Connor and Peadar O'Donnell. They are all the work of the disillusioned realists of the Black and Tan period. Some of the authors took an active part in the events which they portray. Sean O'Casey fought in the Sinn Fein rebellion of 1916,[7] and Peadar O'Donnell was engaged against the Black and Tans and later, as an opponent of the treaty, he joined the Irish Republican Army in its struggle against the Free State forces, was imprisoned, escaped execution and finally jail. *There Will Be Fighting* pulsates with the realism of experience, just as *The Way It Was With Them* conveys the true note of life on one of those primitive islands which recently received such adventitious attention, when the public whim seized upon Maurice O'Sullivan's *Twenty Years A-growing*, a similar record of the Great Blasket, as if O'Donnell and Synge had never written.

Liam O'Flaherty has much of the violence, cynicism and brutal sincerity of Sean O'Casey. His Ireland, like the slums of O'Casey's Dublin, is far removed from the mysticism, the leprechauns and the fairies of the traditional Celtic twilight. He is also the most prolific of this group. His first novel, *Thy Neighbour's Wife*, appeared in 1924, and since then he has given us six novels and five volumes of short stories. Like O'Donnell, he writes out of first-hand, active experience of the Irish war, and the very titles of his books are suggestive of the fierce power of their contents. *The Assassin* is a study of political assassination. *The Informer* invokes that term of greatest opprobrium in Ireland to depict the career of a spy in revolutionary circles. *The Puritan* is a savage indictment of the type, with special reference to the peculiar manifestations of puritanism in a country where it is strangely distorted

into a form of patriotism. A greasy tragedy in mean streets, by the very simplicity of its elements, *Mr Gilhooley* has a Russian quality, a quality which is elsewhere perceptible in Liam O'Flaherty's work.

Frank O'Connor's one book of stories, *Guests of the Nation*, at once revealed his quality, and in the title story he has compressed more than others require an entire novel to relate. The eternal conflict and misunderstanding between the English and the Irish, the radical differences in their ways of thinking and feeling are dramatically expressed in this account of how some English soldiers who are being held as hostages, and have come to be the friends of their captors, having no political emotions whatever, are dismayed and horrified when they are cold-bloodedly shot in reprisals. They cannot fathom the minds of these Irishmen who, but a few hours before, were peacefully playing cards and arguing with them about matters of anything but life and death. Francis Stuart, on the other hand, differs from O'Connor and all the others by reason of a large degree of mystic fancy in his vague treatment of current conditions in Ireland. An aviator and a Republican, he is also a devoted student of St John of the Cross. His scenes are laid anywhere between Dublin and China, as befits an airman, and he is the most disembodied exponent of the modern trends in Irish fiction. Born in Australia and educated at Rugby, he lacks that autochthonous quality which gives the work of his contemporaries its distinctly Irish flavour.

The vogue for realism, so long absent from Anglo-Irish literature, tends to incense those patriotic readers who, despite the horrible evidence of 1916 and 1918–21, wish to see Ireland in terms of Yeatsian poetry rather than the realities of war and civil war. Unfortunately, these men were witnesses of that whereof they speak, and they cannot be thrust aside as libellers of their country. Much that is sordid and ugly and cruel, much that is brutal and brutalizing in Irish life has at last found expression in a literature which, whether through accident or design, has heretofore concentrated on what W.D. Howells, in a well-remembered phrase, called 'the more smiling aspects' of existence. The difference between these authentic narratives, informed by a real understanding of Irish history and psychology, will be readily seen by a glance at the substitutes for the real thing now being offered.

Shake Hands With the Devil, by Rearden Conner,[8] is a much touted example of how not to do it. Here the author merely strings together a series of violent and bloody incidents, all of which may be true to life, and presents them as a picture of the troubled years in Ireland. The inaccuracy of the local references and the impossibility of the dialect placed in the mouths of the characters are symbolic of the general distortion of the picture as a whole. These other writers do not idealize; they describe things as horrible as any in *Shake Hands With the Devil*, but absence of idealization does not mean distortion. It will be an ironical commentary on this change for the better in the direction of comprehending objectivity, if we are confronted by a spate of penny shockers, based on the calculation that Ireland provides good material for blood-and-thunder adventure stories. It does not, but it does present conditions unlike those obtaining elsewhere, and in this group of Free State authors it has found interpreters worthy of the best traditions of Ireland's literary renaissance. Despite the censorship and the dead hand of obscurantism, the creative vitality of Anglo-Irish literature has not been crushed.

1   The ban in the United States on *Ulysses* was lifted in December 1933 following a judgment in favour of the novel by Judge Woolsey.
2   The title Joyce used for the work begun in 1922–3 which became *Finnegans Wake* when published in 1939.
3   The highest peak in the Harz Mountains in central Germany. In Goethe's *Faust* the Walpurgis Night or Witches' Sabbath is set here. The fifteenth episode of *Ulysses* is the Nighttown or Circe episode.
4   The *Dublin Magazine*, among the most important literary journals published in Ireland in the twentieth century, was edited by Seumas O'Sullivan from 1923 until 1958.
5   Russell edited this from 1923 until its demise in 1930.
6   *Islanders* (1928) and *The Knife* (1930) were published in the USA under these titles.
7   A rare error on the part of Boyd.
8   *Shake Hands With the Devil* (1934) by Rearden Conner (1907–91) traces the dehumanization of an IRA commander in the War of Independence. It was made into a film in 1960.

MONK GIBBON
from Monk Gibbon, *The Seals* (1935)

Monk Gibbon (1896–1987) was a widely published man of letters, author of *Mount Ida* (1948), an autobiographical novel on the theme of love, *Inglorious Soldier* (1968), an autobiography of his life as a soldier in the Great War, and *The Masterpiece and the Man* (1959), a somewhat acerbic portrait of W. B. Yeats. Here in this extract from a book recording a seal-hunting expedition off the west coast of Ireland he provides one of the few accounts in modern Irish writing that addresses the issue of human cruelty to animals or in this case to seals.

I walk down the road with the boy and girl.

For the first time the boy indulges in a note of triumph.

'I hope they won't have forgotten about the head. I'm going to boil it down and mount the tusks in my room at Eton.'

Then he adds:

'It was hard luck your not getting one, Anne.'

'I don't mind. I'm not like you. You'd set your heart on it. I'm going to have a bag made out of part of the baby seal's skin. That will cheer me up. It's lovely and soft.'

'I hope they have finished the skinning.'

They have.

Both seals are skinned. By some grotesque irony of circumstance the big seal is lying on her back, her two

grey flippers resting across her breast like nothing so much as a corpse laid out. I wonder whether I am the only one to notice this accidental parody of human ritual. The skin is lying near. The men have gone to fetch a sack to put it in. I notice the enormous wads of protective pink and white fat, exactly like the camel fat one sees on the butchers' stalls in the poorer quarters of Cairo. No wonder that the seal remains warm-blooded in all waters, cased in such a protective thickness. The abdomen has been slit right down, and the bowels are lying half in and half out of it, a mass of pale green coils.

Near by is the carcass of the baby seal, the skin lying in a crumpled supple heap beside it, a little stained, flecked slightly with blood and sand since I last saw it.

Then I see what I had not noticed before, a third tiny gory corpse lying a little apart from the other two. When the body is tired the mind moves more slowly to its conclusions. I realize vaguely that it was not there this morning, but for a moment its significance escapes me. I wonder whether I overlooked it before, whether there had always been three, and I had stupidly been carrying about the idea that there were only two.

'But . . .'

And then it dawns on me. There had always been three. But on one of the three light had still to break, would never break now. The mother seal had been carrying her young. The slit abdomen explains the mystery.

'I didn't realize . . .'

The boy looks at me. Perhaps I have allowed some of my concern to be apparent in my face.

He laughs with that slight half-conscious brutality of which adolescence is capable.

'Oh, didn't you know? I thought you'd have noticed. She wouldn't have been as big as that unless . . .'

The little creature had been very near to birth. Its soft, tiny skin lay beside it on the wharf, white, supple, like the skin of a new-born lamb. It lacked the slightly yellowish tinge of the older baby. The clean white claws at the end of its tiny flippers were fully grown. They reminded one of the white spines of a baby hedgehog.

By one of those lightning flashes of association, I thought of my own two children, the fruit of my body, the white night-gowned small figure, swaying to and fro in its pram in front of the house, and of that other child, the child as yet unborn.

Man flatters himself when he remains indifferent to any death except the death of his own species. In those rare moments of illumination which occasionally visit us, all life appears inestimably precious, and the cessation of it in one small body as serious as its cessation in another. Such moments impinge on the mystical. They do not belong to normal consciousness. Some would call them the outcome of stretched nerves. But our reverence for man, the crown, the focus point of consciousness on this planet, is not decreased when we respect life in its other manifestations, rather the reverse.

I thought of Williamson's[1] story of the mother seal suckling her calf in the darkness of the cave while he played a penny whistle to them. And of how presently when he moved nearer to them something touched him. The mother seal had stretched out her head and licked his hand.

If seals are intelligent enough to play ball, or to bang music out on cymbals and motor horns, as I have seen them do in a circus in Copenhagen, their intelligence extends assuredly to love for their young. Parenthood, that mixture of joy and anxiety, is theirs as well as ours. The mother whose calf was clubbed to death on the shingle must have suffered most, for she had seen hope, conceptual at first, carried broodingly in the darkness of her womb, take visible form and live. Her calf had tasted something of the delight and joy of living. The cleanness and vigour of my own child's body rouses in me the same exultation that she perhaps felt when that tiny limp body first began to grow and to react to its environment. In the other case the little creature had only stirred uneasily in its sleep, and then dropped back into that darkness of un-being out of which it appeared to be on the point of rising.

Death is always overtaking life, just as life is always overtaking death; they throw the ball light-heartedly, one to the other, like two players in a game. In face of this upthrust of life, this downthrust of death, man stands at once exultant, breathless and afraid.

The men had returned with the sack and were putting in the skins, tying up the mouth ready to throw it on board.

A great and consuming loneliness seemed to invade my heart. We go through life drugged to an insensibility which we have created for ourselves. Only when love or suffering or exile or the sight of death stab us back into consciousness do we see things as they really are. It is a terrible thought, this thought that for the larger part of our lives we are blind equally to the delight and danger of living.

I looked back over the thirty-six hours which I had just lived. A fine day, sunshine, the warm friendliness of earth had roused me for a few moments into a joyous self-identification with life. A few hours' shooting, the sight of the slaughtered seals in all its crudity, had brought about a diametrically opposite realization, the feeling of man's separateness, of his enmity with nature. Each realization real, each unreal in its ephemerality.

Oneness. Separateness. The mind when it grows tired plays with generalizations like a child that has grown weary of a box of bricks and yet is unwilling to put them away. Man at one with nature, identified with it. Man separate from nature, inimical to it. I turn the thoughts over and over again, unable to escape from them.

---

1   Henry Williamson (1895–1977), a writer on country themes, best known for his *Tarka the Otter* (1927).

GEORGE C. HOMANS
from *The Saturday Review of Literature*, 17 October 1936

This review can be read in conjunction with the extract below from Joseph F. Dinneen's
Ward Eight (1936, p. 449).

Boston Irish

WARD EIGHT. By Joseph F. Dinneen. New York:
Harper & Brothers. 1936. $2.50.

For a Boston and Back Bay Yankee,[1] like the reviewer,
Ward Eight is an education. As he grew up he was
maddened by the defeats handed to his kind, Yankees,
Republicans, and therefore, he assumed, patriots, by the
Irish politicians and their following, who were, he also
assumed, corruptionists. It happened in city elections
always and in state elections more and more often, and
was only one feature of a thoroughgoing, if only half-
conscious, war between the older and the newer races.
The stock of the Puritans, in Boston at least, had
become a closed aristocracy, and like all such
aristocracies would die a more or less lingering death.
On the political front, if graft outraged the moral sense,
it was nevertheless not the important question. The Irish
and the other newcomers had feelings, ways of behaving
and of thinking unlike those of the Yankees, and on the
basis of these the Irish leaders were making a new
application of the machinery of democratic government.
Their code was not that of Sam Adams, or Daniel
Webster, or Calvin Coolidge, and with the change of
code the character of old institutions would change. But
the Back Bay Yankee never bothered to find out what
the new code was. Joseph Dinneen's book fills in the gap
in his experience. It is a story of Irish politics in the
North End of Boston since the turn of the century.

This is written in too solemn a vein. *Ward Eight* is
not a social survey report but a novel, and an absorbing one. Old Ward Eight, hemmed in by the waterfront and the markets, was the heart of the North End.
Here in these little tenements and crooked alleys had
lived in turn most of the races that were making
Massachusetts. Toward the end of the last century, the
Irish drove out the indigenous Yankees, or rather, in a
boom era the Yankees were moving out to better jobs
and better houses. Twenty years later, and for the same
reasons, the Irish were giving way to the Italians. A
man's class might almost be reckoned by how far from
the waterfront he lived.

The Boss of Ward Eight, in the novel, is Hughie
Donnelly. The Ward Boss appeared in all the big cities

of America in the time of the new immigration. The
muckrakers made him familiar. The Boss got the
people of his district jobs, kept them out of trouble
and out of jail. In return, by working on their loyalties
and on their fears he controlled their votes. The Ward
Boss could deliver the Ward. And the man with the
votes commanded the avenues to all sorts of graft.
Some of this went into his own pocket, but
maintaining his organization cost money too. The
system was a baffling mixture of government, social
service, sentiment, terrorism, and corruption.

Hughie Donnelly is the old-style politician; Big
Tim O'Flaherty is the new, who goes to high school
and college, and becomes a member of the bar. The
old man and the young fight more than once for the
control of the Ward, and the old man always wins.
When it comes to the point, Big Tim does not know
enough, is not shrewd enough to take over the job.
But Hughie never presses his victories. He knows how
to turn a defeated opponent into a loyal lieutenant,
and he can use Big Tim's energy and popularity.
Under Hughie's patronage, Big Tim goes up the
escalator. This is the story of *Ward Eight*. It is set in the
life of the Irish community: the wakes, with their loud
voices and stories as 'antidotes for unbearable grief',
the gossip that has a boy and girl engaged as soon as
they go to one dance together.

The original of Hughie Donnelly is pretty clearly
Martin Lomasney, the famous boss of the North End,
now dead, like Hughie. Bostonians can identify other
Irish politicians who appear in the Ward. Surely
Callahan with the deep and sonorous voice is now one
of our foremost humanitarians. But *Ward Eight* is no
literal reproduction of local history, under fake names.
Nor is it one which will interest only Bostonians.
Anyone who likes a vigorous novel, and a description
of how one little part of American society works, will
read *Ward Eight*.

The story ends with a twist. Hughie is dead, and
Big Tim has not been able to hold the ward
organization together. What is more, he has
determined to cut out the grafting, and he knows that
this will ruin him politically. This is not the
conventional repentance of the ageing sinner; it puts
the question raised by the system as described. How

much corruption can American democracy stand? Joseph Dinneen, in his two articles in *Harper's*, 'Murder in Massachusetts' and 'The Kingfish of Massachusetts', has already let much light in upon the realities of politics in that state.

1   For a non-Irish Bostonian from a wealthy neighbourhood. The old rich American families (the Yankees) such as the Cabots, Lowells, and Lodges built substantial houses on Beacon Hill and in the Back Bay. According to James Michael Curly (see *Ward Eight* below), the Irish dynasty began when Hugh O'Brien was elected mayor of the city in 1885.

PEADAR O'DONNELL
from *Ireland Today*, September 1936

Peadar O'Donnell (1893–1986) was a leading twentieth-century republican socialist. During the Irish Civil War he sided with the Republicans and was imprisoned by the Free State Government. During the Spanish Civil War he fought against Franco and wrote about his experiences in *Salud! An Irishman in Spain* (1937). In the 1940s he helped Sean O'Faolain edit *The Bell*. His political activity continued until his death and he involved himself in campaigns for peace and for nuclear disarmament as well as in measures to improve the conditions of people living in the west of Ireland. Here in this article, five months before George Orwell arrived in Catalonia, O'Donnell presents a wry, optimistic first-hand account of the overthrow of the brief Fascist uprising in Barcelona on the night of 19 July 1936. For a tribute on his eightieth birthday, see James Plunkett, 'O'Donnell Salud!' in *Hibernia*, 2 March 1973.

What I Saw in Spain

It is one of those exquisite ironies, which now and then become over-tones of excited moments in Ireland, that I should find myself as practically the sole voice of Green Republicanism in Ireland supporting bourgeois democracy in Spain. And the irony is not lessened by the fact that Sean Murray, Harry Midgley, Sam Hazlett, Jack Dorricott and Peadar O'Donnell alone here so far acclaim Catholic Spain against the Moors and the Spanish Foreign Legion. In that picture of Badajos with its Catholic 2,000 lined up for execution by the Moors and Legionaries, some of our principal Irish newspapers are publicists for the heathen, while this group of ours is for the Catholic masses to whose liberty these 2,000 sacrificed themselves in full gaze of the world.

I happened to be in the neighbourhood of Barcelona for a fortnight previous to the Fascist uprising, and as I had hoped to write a booklet on the changed agrarian situation since the triumph of the United Front last February, I was uncovering some of the conflicts not otherwise on view.

The situation when I left Barcelona on the Friday before the Rising was disturbing. There was much talk of a Fascist rising. The Spanish Foreign Legion was clearly won over to the Fascist. The officers' task here was easy, for the Legionaries were easily stampeded by threat of a government enquiry into their atrocities in the Austurias in 1934. The landed monopoly was mightily disturbed by the curtailment of its power over the lives of the peasantry. Quite substantial losses had been suffered by the 'landed gentry', and there was the threat that actually they might be bought out at terms they would not like. For example, in certain fruit-growing areas the landlords return of 50 per cent of the fruit was reduced to 25 per cent, and even this was mostly a purchasing rent.

The officers were drawn in large measure from this privileged class, and artillery and cavalry regiments especially were their perquisite. And it was within these officer cadres that the Fascist mutiny was hatched.

The time seemed opportune. There was evidence that the government was losing that enthusiastic backing on which it had arisen in February of this year. There was a big strike on the docks of Barcelona. A general strike was threatened on the railways. Workers were writing up on the sides of railway carriages and elsewhere, 'Don't heed the threats of the Government'. Such was the background as I saw it on the Friday.

But there was also evidence that the workers were not unaware of the dangers. For example, I was told on that Friday that many workers had been sitting up in their clubs every night since Tuesday to be in a position of readiness.

And yet in Barcelona the actual rising came as a surprise. In the small hours of Sunday morning the artillery took to the streets to get the sleeping city gripped. They arrived without incident at Place de Espagne. A detachment turned towards Sans. The alarm was raised as they entered a working-class quarter. Workers leaped to the attack. Barricades were hastily flung up. A short bloody fight followed. Soldiers who up till now had no clear idea what was afoot were guided by the attitude of the masses. They shot their officers and joined the people.

Around the Place de Catalonia, where the Fascist officers had by now more or less established themselves, a terrific street battle developed. While it was still in the balance the civil guard obeyed the government and took part with the workers. This was the beginning of the end in Barcelona. Soon the military were besieged in their barracks. By Monday afternoon they had all surrendered.

News of what was afoot in Barcelona came to the outlying villages on Sunday forenoon over the radio. You heard a call for volunteers for blood transfusions. You heard chemists being ordered to keep their shops open and receive wounded. You heard an order that all shutters were to be open and that where this was not obeyed the Government forces would fire.

In such villages as Sitges, where I was, fishermen, railway workers, tradesmen, hotel waiters gathered and set to taking control of the town. They turned up at a hall with shot-guns, Brownings, old bull-dog revolvers, and a sprinkling of rifles. They commandeered all motor cars and ordered all known Fascists to stay indoors.

Here a church was sacked in full view of the Catholic population, which did not show any impulse to interfere, although the sacking was done at noon and those doing it were less than a score of unarmed youths. When word of a Fascist advance from Saragossa came, these people rushed to throw up barricades.

I asked the local committee to permit me travel with armed workers moving thro' the country between Sitges and Barcelona. My wife and I travelled in this way thro' a great many villages. Each village had its succession of barricades, mostly bales of straw; grand barricades. The enthusiasm was tremendous.

Once in Barcelona we got a general pass — I have it as a souvenir — so that we moved about freely. Little groups herded in hotels told the weirdest stories of atrocities which they assured us had taken place in the villages thro' which we had passed. People moving around got a good deal of amusement out of the lounge stories.

I talked with a great number of deported nuns. They must have got quite a thrill when they got the British and Irish press and saw how they had been stripped and paraded. Actually they had only tame stories to tell of sorrowful expulsion, but courteous treatment.

There was no secret made in Barcelona of the fact that priests had been shot. Only just the explanation that nobody was shot, priest or layman, unless he was an active Fascist. How far scares sweep innocent people into undeserved suspicion must await cooler days.

The sight of Barcelona workers going off to free the people of Aragon from the Fascist tyranny so well established at Saragossa will remain one of the most inspiring sights I have ever seen. I recall especially one bus load of young men in their tram-workers uniform hurrying forward. And old men in editors' chairs ask us to believe that such men commit cowardly atrocities.

It is important that we all remember that the people of Spain rid themselves of the monarchy in a perfectly constitutional way in 1931. And that in 1936 they swept the Lerroux-Robles combine into obscurity in a free open election. And that it is against this democratic government that the foreign legion and the Moors are waging their war for 'Christian ideals'.

KATE O'BRIEN
from Kate O'Brien, *Farewell Spain* (1937)

Intelligence and humanity shine through every paragraph of this extract from Kate O'Brien's travel book on Spain. Published in 1937 during the Spanish Civil War and on the eve of the Second World War, *Farewell Spain* looks back to eighteenth-century grand tours such as the one parodied by Laurence Sterne in *A Sentimental Journey* (1768) (which includes reference to that medieval form of tourism, namely pilgrimages to Santiago De Compostela) and forward to an era of mass tourism, of getting away from it all. O'Brien herself was refused entry to Franco's Spain in 1947 (exception was taken to her treatment of Philip II in her novel *That Lady*) and she had to wait until a decade later before returning. Kate O'Brien (1897–1974) was a distinguished writer of fiction. Her novels include *Without My Cloak* (1931), *The Ante-Room* (1934), *Mary Lavelle* (1936), and *Pray For the Wanderer* (1938) (see p. 466 below). An extract from her travel book *My Ireland* (1962) is also included in this *Reader*. For a glowing tribute based on an interview with her the year before she died, see John Jordan, 'Kate O'Brien: First Lady of Irish Letters' in *Hibernia*, 11 May 1973. You might want to do some research on Irish writers and the Spanish Civil War, in which case see the Charles Donnelly poems below (p. 462), the poems of Thomas MacGreevy especially 'Aodh Rua Ó Domnhail', Section VI of Louis MacNeice's 'Autumn Journal', Ethel Mannin's novel *The Blossoming Bough* (1943), and contemporary Irish journals such as *Ireland Today* and *Studies*. You might extend your research to include Irish writers reflecting on the Spanish Civil War at a later date, such as Arland Ussher's comments in *Spanish Mercy* (1959) or Colm Tóibín, *Homage to Barcelona* (1990).

Adios, Turismo

Occasions of self-indulgence are rare, let moralists say what they will; and if to seek her own recollections of Spain be accounted such just now by the present writer, she must perhaps risk being regarded by others as something of a Nero.

I write indeed unashamedly as an escapist, of that which recedes and is half-remembered. For prophecy and the day ahead I have no talent and little curiosity. But death and departure attract me as man's brightest hopes have never done. So as the European *chiaroscuro*[1] in which we have all grown up becomes its own black-out and accepts its long-drawn suicide, as doom muffles folly and the courageous turn to see what life of ordeal to-morrow brings, I still look backward, self-indulgently. The morning light, even if some of us live to see it, even if it is cheerful, will be hard; if there is anything at all in human promise, in political struggle, it will be uniform and monotonous. That is what the maddened world must seek now, the justice of decent uniformity. How impossible it seems as one writes it, and how elementarily necessary! That it may come, after our deluge, must be for posterity our central hope, however obscure, however doubtful. But meanwhile if some of us can light no personal desire to see it, that impotence must be accounted understandable.

Let us fiddle who can do nothing else. And since, however the world's darkness rolls, individual life remains vivid, since faces and memories are still precious, since there is wine still to drink and the next cigarette remains an imperative pleasure, we will if we are sane pursue our constant little fads, of eating and drinking (if we have the means), of knitting, typing, or dirt-track-riding, of making pictures and money and love. For there is no help for us at all in living through this terrible day to which we have been appointed, if it takes away our egoists' courage to go on being ourselves. So, summoning mine, I write for my own comfort in a vein much over-used in the last two hundred years — but as possibly one of the last to use it, and perhaps deriving from that probability an especial satisfaction. I write as a sentimental traveller in a country long-suffering at the hands of such. But Spain must forgive the last stragglers among her foreign lovers, as she has forgiven and condescended to the first. There will be no more sentimental travellers — anywhere. Their excuse and occasion will have been removed in that day of uniformity which we are agreed is the distracted world's only hope. The tourist is already an archaism to the right-minded, who if they still go to Russia, go only to know what the second half of the century is to be, not merely in Moscow but everywhere. They go there to view experiments and models, to examine tentatives which concern and affect us all but which may yet of course be thrown away in the rising gales of nationalism before the true shape of things to come emerges. Still, accurately informative or not, these tours to Russia are not tours with the old meaning. Their impulse is newly projected. They are a gesture towards our future uniformity, not an escapist search for novelty, individualism or the past. They are the busman's holiday of sociologists and moralists, not pleasure-trips for idle pleasure-seekers.

The latter are — let us rub it in — outmoded. And eventually even the busman's holiday will be unnecessary. If European society survives its next crisis, if science, having destroyed us, permits or maybe compels us to live again, it is to a very new sort of life that these races will be beckoned back. For science, having paid the piper, will assuredly call the tune, and those of us who have never chosen to dance to her measure may be thankful that in her hour of full authority we shall be lying still, quite deaf.

There will be no point then in going out to look for a reed shaken in the wind. The woes and beauties wrought hitherto upon the map by differences of language, faith and climate will be no longer worth consideration, for — even if they are still potential — they will be controlled, patrolled by science, the international dictator, which in any case, by air-travel, radio and television will have made all possible novelties into boring fireside matters-of-fact. The world will be flat and narrow, with the Golden Horn a stone's throw from the Golden Gate and nothing unknown beyond any hill. Antarctica, where no one lives, will be a week-end joyride, and our descendants, should any records survive to catch their eyes, will marvel at our naïve interest in our neighbours, smiling to discover that once an Arab differed somewhat in his habits from a Dutchman, and a Tibetan from a Scot. Already in Spanish villages if they want to please a passing stranger, they do not sing a *cante hondo*[2] — they tune in to 'Big Ben' or Henry Hall. Science, if sane survival be indeed her aim for human life, will do well to develop such a tendency, and to follow ruthlessly all the lines that lead from it to a smooth international uniformity, trampling out the romantic differentiations through which history, or our conception of it, has led us to the twentieth-century shambles. In the reconstituted world there had better be no history. Let it start bald and be allowed to grow no hair — and no teeth. Ah, how busy science will be enforcing her new health rules! Still, she can but try. Meanwhile we wait for our old, shaggy, warted world to go off in its last fit. And we count our ill-starred blessings — the junk we have accumulated and so obstinately loved and sought to increase. Temples, palaces, cathedrals; libraries full of moonshine; pictures to proclaim dead persons, quaint legends, quainter personal conceptions; songs to praise God, or a notion we had that we called by the name of love; tombs and stained-glass windows; symphonies, sonnets, wingless victories — odds and ends of two thousand silly years in which

individualism, given its rope, contrived at last, after a lot of remarkable fuss, to hang itself. There will never again, let us hope, be two thousand years so untidy, or so vainly fruitful.

With these few words of self-depreciation — for we are all a part of our deplorable and guilty Christian era — with these few words to placate the forward marchers, the right-minded, let us draw the blinds again and invite our old cosiness. Let us praise personal memory, personal love.

Cosiness! As I write Irun[3] is burning. There is a photograph in this morning's *Times* of the little plaza with its low iron seats and clipped plane-trees — the commonplace of every Spanish town. The café at the corner is a heap of broken stones. A few men stand about dejectedly with guns. Yesterday's papers showed us women sitting on the shore at Hendaye to watch the flames rise about their houses across the estuary. This Spanish war which is being waged with all the ancient Spanish will to take or administer death on terms of ceremonious cruelty — this war is only one ulcer on an ulcered world. But the individual imagination — like the racial — is highly self-protective, and although no one with a vestige of sanity can be unaware of the universal terrors of nationalisms, dictatorships and race-antipathies, to say nothing of the comic policy of sealed lips, though no one can deny that a world unable to abolish slums, unemployment, poison gas or mine-explosions, a world at the mercy of drought, floods, strikes, manipulated markets, secret treaties, private monopolies and armament competitions, is a world abandoned to evil and its consequences — nevertheless our protective dullness is only really penetrated, our nerves only really ache when that which we have personally known, that which has touched ourselves, takes the centre of the stage awhile. So for our sins we are made, and because we are made so our sins are mountains of inhumanity. But, as Mr Salteena said about his not being a gentleman, that can't be helped now. The personal touch, sentimental individualism, has brought us to a place from which only something alien and terrible can rescue life, in destroying us who live.

Nevertheless, while China starves, Lancashire hunger-marches, educational authorities organize gas-drill for the infant class and Mussolini takes the salute from the under fours, tourists, settled in for the winter in Hampstead, Neuilly and Brooklyn, having bought new umbrellas and put their suit-cases out of sight, will mourn more than other disasters the burning of Irun. Mourn it as a sad instance which touches personal memory.

They saw it first on a wet morning in August. Never will they forget their disappointment. The night in the second-class couchettes had been hell; they had been unable to obtain coffee from over-worked, bad-tempered stewards; at Bayonne an old woman had cheated them over a purchase of pears. Now once past the bridge they would have to change trains and face a horde of Customs officers. They would be soaked to the skin. They didn't know a word of Spanish. Would anyone tell them the exact value of a peseta? Heavens, did you ever see such rain?

There was apparently nothing else to see at Irun — except just beyond the bridge, a man in black. He was standing quite still in the roadway, with his back to the train. A solid man of fifty, of respectable mien, and wearing his black overcoat slung as if it were a cape. Wearing a black beret, too. Apparently unaware of the train and indifferent to the weather.

They saw this identical man that morning, because wherever or however one enters Spain, he is the first living object that catches the eye. When your liner swings into Coruña on a warm, bright evening, he is standing among the rocks of the headland, his overcoat caped across his shoulders, his beret on his head — contemplative and solid. If you step on to the platform of Madrid's north station in the small hours, he is there, unchanged by a hair. Always you will see him a few paces south of the Bidasoa bridge.

He is in the forefront of every tourist's memory, that matter-of-fact, deliberating man.

But about Irun. In the café near the Quai d'Orsay the evening before the tourists had been excited — and perhaps a bit too informative with each other. Spain in the morning, the Spanish frontier. The Pyrenees, the sturdy Basques, Fuenterrabia, 'where Charlemagne and all his peerage fell'. The French road to Compostela. Pamplona, where Ignatius got his so significant wound. The Isle of Pheasants, where this and that forgotten parley was enacted between this and that forgotten personage. The flights to and fro of the Bourbons. Wellington's victories over Soult. The Carlist wars. The *pelota*[4] game. The terrible bullfight. Or had they better see just one? Until So-and-so, still musing on the Franks, was heard to murmur, *Dieu, que le son du cor est triste le soir, au fond des bois.*[5] Thus confounding the rest of the party and causing eyebrows to twitch exasperatingly. Was So-and-so going to prove a fearful bore throughout the trip?

Well, they got soaked to the skin. Irun is a badly organized station. Moving between the train, the customs-shed, the canteen and the other train they got very wet indeed. So did their porter, a silent, inoffensive man with light blue eyes. Not at all a Spanish type, the tourists told each other. They left Irun in discomfort, and without thinking once of Charlemagne's peerage. Indeed with no impression at all, save of the rain and the silent railway porter. He had even taken his tip in silence.

With no impression at all — and yet, though they had seen Irun often since, had walked in its *paseo*,[6] talked in its cafés, taken the tram to San Sebastian, now that it was burning they thought first of that first exasperating morning — the man in black by the bridge, the rain and silence. Odd that memory of silence — because a frontier station at the busiest hour of the day cannot be a very quiet place. And yet the tourists, recollecting by their cosy fires, remember it in an ambience of stillness, and remember a bell tolling amid soaked trees. And that was all that Spain had given them at their first stop.

The tourists sigh, stirring their beverage. For afterwards there was so much — they had become so faithfully infatuated. Being genuine sightseers. Being also of those who find life itself on any terms of chance more enriching to the heart than the most beautiful theories or experiments of living. So naturally Spain had proved their cup of tea. And now the frontier was in flames. Toledo shot to bits, Burgos a seat of war, the Guadarramas a battlefield. Ortega, the bullfighter, was shot the other day. Bombs were falling on Atocha Station, perilously near the Prado.[7] The tourists find their beverage undrinkable, and go to bed. But though depressed they believe, since that is the easier thing to do, that they will see their love again. Spaniards have taught them the allure and escape of to-morrow, and that it is another day. But in our time, how other? That is indeed a question. Still, awaiting its answer, it is something to have lived through the last and most stimulated decade in the history of tourism.

Something, personally. For internationally it appears to have been of little good, as the world to come will reflect with justice when the busy and self-denying populations — no longer nations — shall have removed from amongst them all the old sources of mutual curiosity, all pretexts for pleasure-seeking, all excuse for the indulgence of unharnessed, and therefore mischievous, dream.

Still perversely I repeat that I write in praise of personal pleasure. Though doom crack in my face I am glad to have lived before and not in the millennium. I am glad, too, to have lived so long after the period of the grand tour — for that would never have fallen to my humble lot — but to have known the bumpy blessings of the tourist cabin, the kilometric ticket, and the autobus. For idle travel as it has been cheaply and unceremoniously dispensed to my generation has assuredly been one of the deepest and most secret of all personal pleasures. Not, for me, idle travel, here, there and everywhere — my heart is narrow — but idle travel in Spain.

If it be permissible, if indeed it be not positively dangerous to quote Pater at this date, I venture here to quote these over-quoted words: 'For art comes to you proposing frankly to give nothing but the highest quality to your moments as they pass, and simply for those moments' sake.' A limiting statement, but there are those who, if they dared claim arrival at any kind of working personal truth, have found it in exactly such acceptance. Artists, whether or not they justify their classification, or even reveal at all that they carry the stigma, know themselves. They know their handicaps and, perhaps somewhat smugly, their advantages. Many of them disclaim Pater's aesthetic dictum, and can disprove it out of their own abilities and achievements while remaining incontestably artists. But for others it stands. Not that, unless they are freaks, they try to live in isolation with it, or that it yields them their whole story. But they learn, and often soberly and with regret, that it is the exaction which they most persistently understand, and they find that when it conflicts with other principles within, it overthrows them. Often wrongly or inconveniently. And the rest of us, wherever we find ourselves in the card index — are we not occasionally cross-referenced in relation to Pater's statement? Are we not visited, too, however intermittently and unrewardingly, by 'this quickened sense of life', 'multiplied consciousness' which is the daily bread of the artist? So that, troubled and deeply pleased by the visitation, we seek it uncertainly again whenever we can?

Not as a drug. The forward marchers, who read no epitaphs and find only one sermon in broken stones, must please believe that the moony junk-counting of certain others is not, as they assess it, a vice, but rather, in its manifest non-utilitarianism, a source of strength and courage, something which, breathing over us the cold air of death — that is, of eternalness and detachment — gives brief inroads of immunity against the contemporary din, whilst simultaneously suggesting that we have patience with it. For once the Aqueduct at Segovia was a racket, a busy, practical civic suggestion, and now it is by no means the worse for that, which implication is indeed the very spine of its nobility. The spine, but not the whole. For it has become a power spanning higher than a city's need of water. No need for platitudes. Either the heart lifts at the sight of it, or it does not; either that 'heightened consciousness' is induced which can give the highest

quality to a moment as it passes, or we can consider pityingly the heavy manual labour of slaves and congratulate ourselves about steel and electric power. Not that they are unworthy of our pleasure in them. It is moreover possible that two thousand years from now the soaring shell of the Empire State Building will be a nobler and more searching spectacle than it is now — if indeed such relics will be allowed to stand. Which is improbable. And as we skirt that guess let us reflect with sadness that Macaulay's New Zealander, so exciting to us all at school, will almost certainly never stand on Westminster Bridge to view the ruins of St Paul's — *(a)* because in his day no self-respecting person will see the point of such an excursion, and *(b)* because ruins will not be tolerated, for reasons of physical and mental hygiene.

What they will do for courage then, how they will electroplate their smugness and keep their idiosyncrasies of pain and irrationality from breaking through, is their secret. You and I manage, or mismanage, as we can — snatching at straws. A book, a hand, a first-rate joke; a prayer to God, or the birth of a child; an escape into solitude or a wild night out; a fit of hard work, an attack of romantic love or of marital peace; a visit to the play; a glass of good brandy or good beer. Or a trip abroad — away from it all, as we say.

Away from it all! That is a cliché of ours which for our great-grandchildren, in their uniformed world, will only have meaning when they die. One thing we can do and they will not find possible — get away from it all. That is a strength, that weakness of ours, which, unless they are indeed to be supermen, they are likely to feel the need of. When they have tidied up everything, after our dreadful picnics, and made a Utopian Home County[8] of the world — what then? Oh, Heaven pity them!

Unless gland control can pull off such a monstrous miracle as poor old Christianity never even visualized, our descendants may, I fear, discover themselves to be — if they know the word — unhappy. A happy discovery, I venture incorrigibly to believe. Happy, even if bewildering, even if irremediable — save by making ducks and drakes of the Home County. And someone may even take that retrogressive measure, since, whatever else their model citizens may be, their seed, controlled, conditioned, what-you-willed, may still be supposed to be Adam's. Or is such sentimental implication painfully outmoded?

Meanwhile we, the escapists, the wreckers, still live amid our slums and ruins, sticking to our old bearded notion that life is conditioned by something never to be caught in a test-tube. While bowing a timid knee, largely out of human respect, to our glands, as lately to our reflexes, and less lately to our complexes, we children of the long shadows of individualism still hear a murmur in the shell for which we ask no explanation from without. It has a dying fall, perhaps, but we persist in straining for it. We seek the quickened sense of life, the accidents that jab imagination, for each of us believes the life of his breast to be his own and not a unit in another man's admirable sociological plan. We are in fact hopeless cases, who insist every now and then on getting away from it all.

Hence, among other good things about to die with us, *turismo*. To each his own refuge, his own holiday. Italy has been notoriously the heart-patrie of millions. So has Greece been; so have been all the Mediterranean islands. China and the Eastern seas are far flights in search of a fluke, but many have taken them. There is Mexico too — there are Africa and empty Antarctica and the dangerous lands about the Amazon. There are Ireland and Finland and the Arabian desert — all lying in their uncertain ways fallow to idle contemplation and the deep selfish pleasure of moments as they pass — all, for various unanalysable reasons of climate, history and racial temperament, contributing in some way to that individualist excitement which brings the best quiet to the heart; all insolently suggestive of life's intractable beauty.

For some of us there has been Spain. First the Spain we imagined — a place we cannot remember now — and afterwards the Spain we found. There were many surprises in that second Spain, many shocks and longueurs, and whole stretches of time when we seemed almost as inert and out of sorts as if we were at home. But somehow we went back there and went back. We got to know it somewhat — in travellers' fashion — and as we did found ourselves caring very little whether we should ever get to know any other country even one half so well. Whenever we had any money to spend we took a train for Irun, or, if that was too dear, a boat for Santander or Coruña. And crawling into those harbours — ah, the interminable, deliberate arrivals! — we were, no matter what the superficial irritations, delighted with ourselves. Though neither harbour is in the least breath-taking, even if the sun is rioting on Coruña's *miradores*,[9] or if morning mist is pluming up from the sleepy dark hills behind Pedrosa — in the latter case, there is Alfonso XIII's ugly palace on the right — now a summer school — and many other dull vulgarities; in the former, there are some really revolting palm-trees on the quay, and nearby Sir John Moore's very ugly tomb. And in either place it is very likely to be raining cats and dogs. But we know all these things, we are old hands. Our pleasure is merely in having arrived at where we like to be. There is the middle-aged man in black, deliberating as usual and wearing his coat as if it were a cape. There are the leggy boys with sore heads, the women selling packets of burnt almonds. There are the absurd girls walking up and down in threes and fours, singing shrilly, enchanted with themselves and their absurd toilettes. And there, as always, is the tragic-eyed porter, coming forward silently to take our bags. We are back again indeed — in the country we love to be in, the land we care for uncritically, though without illusion we think, and with eyes wide open.

1   Light and shade, here with a political meaning.
2   Popular Andalusian gypsy song.
3   A Spanish Basque town on the French frontier near the Bay of Biscay. It resisted bravely Franco's bombardment during the Civil War.
4   Spanish: ballgame.
5   French: God, how the sound of the heart is sad this evening at the bottom of the woods.
6   Spanish: promenade.
7   Art Gallery in Madrid.
8   Image of home counties around London, part of the 1930s' dystopian view of a sanitized suburbia.
9   Spanish: balconies.

GRATTAN FREYER
from *Scrutiny*, March 1938

This informative survey of Ireland in 1938 appeared in *Scrutiny*, the literary and cultural magazine edited by F. R. Leavis and others in Cambridge.

A Letter from Ireland

There are two universities in Dublin. Trinity College, the elder, a contemporary foundation with Oxford and Cambridge, is residential, and poorer and cheaper than either of those. Traditionally Protestant, it now includes a large Catholic minority of students, in spite of the ban of the bishops, and has one Catholic professor. It is, in fact, the nearest thing to a national institution there is in the country, embracing North and South Catholic and Protestant, in almost representative numbers; only the opposition of the Catholic hierarchy has impeded Catholics taking a more prominent part in college affairs. In the Free State to-day there is a belief that Trinity is Protestant and therefore anti-national, but actually the leaders of the national movement have frequently been Protestants, and Connolly's Irish Citizen Army[1] was founded in rooms in Trinity College after a meeting had been turned out of the Mansion House by a Catholic Lord Mayor. There is almost as much Irish spoken to-day inside Trinity College as in University College, and it is a good deal less self-conscious.

University College is the other university in Dublin, and it is one of the three constituent colleges of the National University. These were founded after the Catholic emancipation in the last century and remain almost exclusively Catholic to-day. They are non-residential. Politically they are very much less independent of the Free State government than Trinity; Irish is compulsory. Of the two other colleges, Galway and Cork, I know nothing, except that Mr Thompson, classical fellow of King's, Cambridge, and now Professor in Birmingham, was formerly Professor of Greek through Irish in Galway; he had to write most of his text books himself in Irish, and on one occasion came up against the censorship because a sentence in the preface to one implied a belief in evolution, and also against more general opposition. He resigned after five years.

My own academic experience is limited to attending lectures in Modern Literature in Dublin. I visited the Professor of English in Trinity and ascertained that no literature since the Victorians was studied, and that the Elizabethan dramatists were studied through the medium of Lamb's *Specimens*; I asked whether he could help me to apply for a permit to import books proscribed by the Free State censor, and heard a dignified defence of the censorship. (The Censorship Act was introduced in 1929, and a list of the books banned to date may be bought for 6d.; it includes books from almost any good modern novelist: D.H. Lawrence, Dos Passos, Seán O'Faoláin, Liam O'Flaherty, Shaw, Sean O'Casey, T.F. Powys, Theodore Dreiser. Going through the list one notes that about a third of the books are genuine pornography, another third covers medical books touching on birth control, while the remainder are from authors such as those mentioned. Every quarter the list is added to.) After this, I decided not to read English in Trinity. The French, Italian and Spanish lectures in Trinity, I found progressive and interesting, and very much alive to contemporary affairs. Lectures in French and Italian which I attended at University College I found pedantic, where not dull, and the atmosphere more that of a secondary school than of a university. English, however, I believe is good in the National.

Politically, Trinity is a little more progressive than the National, but not much. The illegal I.R.A., the extremist wing of the republican movement, numbers about twenty in University College, and only two or three in Trinity; inside the universities they are not very active. Last year, a small but active socialist group was formed in Trinity, which though not recognized is also not yet banned by the Board. They held weekly meetings in college rooms and at the end of the year had about thirty members, including three or four from the National. This was in spite of attacks by prominent Catholic functionaries in Dublin on more than one occasion. Membership of the legal Communist Party last year numbered one in each university.

There are three morning and two evening daily newspapers in the Free State. Of these the *Irish Press* was founded by De Valera's party, largely on funds collected in America, to be a paper expressing all shades of opinion within the republican movement. Since then it has become gradually narrower in outlook. Soon after De Valera obtained power its columns were closed to the I.R.A., whose too radical support was found embarrassing. Immediately after the recent elections, Mrs Sheehy-Skeffington, veteran suffragette and republican, whose husband, a pacifist, was shot in 1916, was informed that owing to her public opposition to the New Constitution it was now considered anomalous that she continue to write for the paper, but this ban was very soon lifted, and seems only to have been the result of post-election pique. Then there is *Independent Newspapers*, an organization embracing the *Irish Independent,* the *Evening Herald*, the *Sunday Independent* and the *Irish Weekly Independent*. The *Irish Independent* called for the troops to fire on the strikers in 1913, for the execution of the surrendered leaders in 1916, vociferated its support of the Free State in 1922 against the Republicans (then called 'Reds'), and, immediately on the outbreak of war in Spain, championed 'the Patriots' against 'the Reds', and published the full story of Franco's triumphal entry into Madrid some time in November, 1936. Nothing is too reactionary for its support, and when the 'Irish Christian Front' was formed last year 'to combat Communism', General O'Duffy[2] and Paddy Belton found its columns ready for their fulminations. (It should be explained that 'communism' is an all embracing term of abuse in Ireland, comprising everything from De Valera leftwards; it is somewhat analogous to the use of the term 'Trotskyism' among English communists.)

The *Irish Times* is the old Protestant and Unionist paper. Crude unionism is of course a dead letter in the Free State to-day, but the *Irish Times* is still read by the sort of people who read the *Times* in England; it is a little more open to enlightened views. If it were less timid and if it cost a penny instead of twopence, it might build up a circulation on the lines of the *Manchester Guardian*. In its foreign news it is better informed than either of the two other papers, and, there being an arrangement with the London *Times*, it is well-informed on British policy. On home affairs, of course, it has not the contacts of a party organ like the *Irish Press* or the industrial ones of the *Irish Independent*. When the Spanish war started it was the only paper in the Free State to take the democratic side. The Assistant Editor was sent to Spain, and its columns were opened to controversy. Letters from prominent Catholics in Spain, Ireland and other countries, supporting the so-called 'Red' government, were published, while they were refused by the other Irish papers. But it became difficult to persist in this courageous line. Circulation began to fall, and in one or two instances at any rate (whether typical I don't know) newsagents in country districts were informed that it was sinful to display posters for the *Irish Times*.

There was an interesting sequel to the Spanish news boom in Ireland. The *Independent* had got well away with stories of the 'Patriots' advance'; the *Irish Press*, like the Vatican, had cautiously waited to see which way the cat would jump, and missed the boom. But it was in the vanguard in opening a slum campaign, and this was followed up by the *Irish Times*. This exposure of living conditions in Dublin (which are really worse than in any other town in the British Isles) takes place at intervals of about five years, and in this case it lasted for nearly three months. Of course this agitation didn't induce the government to get anything done about clearing the slums, any more than any other capitalist government has yet done anything about slums, but the exposures did to a certain extent clear the air.

They showed where the government stood, and they showed where some at any rate of the clergy stood in relation to the poorer sections of the population; undoubtedly this contributed to the big Labour gain in the recent elections.

Among periodicals, the most alive during the last year has undoubtedly been the monthly *Ireland To-day*. The editor of this is a Catholic republican, whose views waver somewhat, and the paper was intended to give expression to the multiform voice of the younger Irish generation. In providing serious regular criticism of theatre, art, music and literature, it fills a gap in Irish intellectual life, and in addition it publishes articles of widely varying merits on questions of Irish interest, and original poems and stories. Difficulty arose over the Foreign Commentary which was supposed to keep readers in touch with events abroad. This was first entrusted to Dr Owen Sheehy-Skeffington, French lecturer in Trinity, and a socialist pacifist, who provided interesting and personally informative articles on France and Spain. But when, as was inevitable, the magazine was attacked by the powers-that-be in Ireland, Dr Skeffington was the Editor. Since then, it has again been necessary to change the Foreign Commentator, but the magazine continues to be attacked in the *Irish Independent*.

The quarterly *Dublin Magazine* sometimes seems more interested in bibliographical detail than in literature, and keeps cautiously clear of politics, but often publishes interesting new work by the older generation, by W.B. Yeats, Seumas O'Sullivan (the Editor), Oliver Gogarty, and occasionally by the younger writers as well. It is predominantly Protestant.

As far as I know there is no exclusively Catholic organ to attempt serious work; in the shadow of the Irish Catholic Church, there are no T.S. Eliots, no Christopher Dawsons.

There are two good theatres in Dublin. The Abbey has fallen off a lot of late years, preserving its popularity by revivals from the 'Great Days' and modern stage-Irish plays in the Lady Gregory tradition. Two exceptions of last year must, however, be mentioned, a new play by Denis Johnston, *Blind Man's Buff*, and Paul Carroll's *Shadow and Substance*, a psychological portrayal of clashes in clerical life. Both were excellent, but it is worth remembering that Denis Johnston was only recognized by the Abbey after the Gate had made a success of his first play, which the Abbey had spurned — hence its title *The Old Lady says 'No!'*

The Gate was founded in 1928 by Michael MacLiammoir and Hilton Edwards to perform notable foreign plays as well as new Irish work outside the

Abbey tradition. Its range was therefore complementary to the Abbey, and their successes include *Faust* and Cocteau's *The Infernal Machine*, while Denis Johnston is their best original dramatist. Recently there has been an unfortunate break with their formerly generous patron, Lord Longford, and now two companies divide the year — for the first six months of the year Lord Longford's company performed good second-rate work, while Edwards and MacLiammor played in Cairo. Now these two have started their Dublin season, while Lord Longford plays first in London and then tours the Irish provinces.

To pass now from organs of opinion to writers themselves is difficult. Only a few names can be mentioned here as indicative, not representative. Of the middle generation Seán O'Faoláin, Liam O'Flaherty, and Denis Johnston seem to me the most important. O'Faoláin is, and O'Flaherty was, a Catholic. The majority of books by both writers are banned in the Free State. O'Flaherty has long since left the country to reside in England, in cynical scorn, but his last novel, *Famine*, a best-seller in Dublin before it was banned, shows a more serious and more mature attempt to grasp Irish problems than any of his previous work. O'Faoláin spends most of his time in Dublin, is a practising Catholic, though a strong anti-clerical, and is a busy and successful writer. As well as excellent novels and short stories, he contributes reviews and articles to papers in Ireland and abroad, showing a keenly critical interest in Irish life (see, for instance, his article 'The Priests and the People' in last month's *Ireland To-day* — July, 1937). Altogether he is the most optimistic of modern Irish writers. Denis Johnston after four plays, three of which are undoubtedly of exceptional interest, has left Dublin for Belfast. Though he visits Dublin frequently and in spite of his recent success at the Abbey, there seems to be an inability in this writer to come to grips with contemporary realities. He has not repeated the universal success of his first two plays *The Old Lady says 'No!'* and *The Moon in the Yellow River*, and one cannot help feeling that the curiously neurotic characters so prominent in all his plays reflect something of the philosophical *impasse* which this writer himself has reached.

Of the older writers, W.B. Yeats, of course, towers above, an international as well as a national figure. It is worth recording, however, that outside Dublin he is little known and little read in the country. His brother, Jack Yeats, the painter, is better known. Jack Yeats, a charmingly modest and very approachable figure, lives on in Dublin, observing quietly, and has of late years quite suddenly expanded his technique, to embrace a new and very interesting phase of development. An exhibition of these later, expressionist pictures was recently held in London, but they are almost unknown in Ireland, where they are not 'understood'; fortunately, his reputation survives as the Christmas card painter by which he won fame.

I suppose Æ (George Russell) was the last of W.B. Yeats's real contemporaries. A year before he died he left Dublin to live in London, worn out presumably by the persistent hostility of Irish Catholicism to his 'paganism'. The co-operative movement to which he devoted so much of his energy had achieved almost nothing.

Somewhat younger than the generation of Yeats and Æ comes the generation of *Ulysses*. James Joyce continues to live in Paris and is almost forgotten in Ireland, though any attempt to return might well be prevented by the stones of a priests' mob. *Ulysses* is not read even in Dublin. Seumas O'Sullivan has been mentioned above as editing the *Dublin Magazine*. As a Georgian and neo-Georgian poet, his output is small, but, accepting its limitations, of unusual merit. The development of Oliver St John Gogarty, character of world-wide renown, is interesting. He has lately had to give up aeroplane-flying, partly owing to very bad eyesight, but more because he had destroyed the last private plane in Ireland by hitting a sheep while landing. Although he was prominent in the fighting to establish the Free State, he is bitterly disillusioned with the logical developments of Irish nationalism. Admirer of Hitler and Mussolini, close friend of Rothermere, Yeats, and General O'Duffy, and violent anti-semite, he has recently produced a book of haphazard memoirs, *As I walked down Sackville Street*, which, in spite of careful pruning before press, seems to have tripped up over the libel laws. It has been said (presumably by Gogarty) that this book is modelled on Dante, but reversed, Paradise under the English, Purgatory under Cosgrave,[3] and Hell under de Valera. Poems also, scintillating with classical learning, flow freely from Gogarty's pen.

Sean O'Casey has not for some years resided in Ireland. As recently as 1936 there was uproar when the Abbey produced *The Silver Tassie*. Peadar O'Donnell, almost alone of the older writers, has lived continually in Ireland. A Catholic, but a fierce anti-clerical, he is still very active in the left wing of the republican movement. Recently he has produced a book on Spain *Salud!* which is politically rather incoherent, but has some brilliant descriptions of scenes he witnessed at the outbreak of war while on holiday in Catalonia.

Only the very young poets have had the courage to break away from the Celtic Twilight tradition. Denis

Devlin and Niall Montgomery have published some 'modern' poems and have also translated modern French verse (Breton and others) into Irish. I don't know Irish, but am told these translations are competent. This creative interest in language which is most typical of the National University is healthy and perhaps will prove productive.

In Irish, I don't think much literature of note has appeared since Thomas O'Crohan's *The Islandman* and Maurice O'Sullivan's *Twenty Years A-growing*. Peg Sayers's autobiography was disappointing. Censorship may be something to do with this, as the Gaeltacht writers are apt to be too vigorously pagan. I know of one lively book of experiences which was refused by Government Publications on grounds of immorality and anti-clericalism. Except officially it is difficult to get a book published in Irish; this book is now being translated into English. Opinions on the language question range in all sections of the population from uncritical enthusiasm to uncritical abuse. Most are agreed that government compulsion is not the right method, and I should say that without a radical economic change to set up industry and provide employment in the west it can never be a real success. The drain to England and the consequent commercial value of English is what is really rotting into the surviving Gaeltacht.

Politics is naturally a highly controversial subject. In a country as small as Ireland, personal and regional antagonisms play a proportionately greater part. One thing is certain: the situation is infinitely more complex and involved than a superficial view will allow. A ready-made formula, Marxist or otherwise, and particularly from an English point of view, just won't fit. For parallels we must look more towards Catholic and Latin Europe and to a country where the same anarchic individualism dominates life, such as Spain. With this reserve in mind, one may say, broadly speaking, that the change from the English to Cosgrave and from Cosgrave to de Valera has not affected the economic structure of the country. Emigration to America has stopped but the migratory emigration to England and Scotland from the whole length of the west continues. There is still substantially no employment to be found in the great majority of districts, in spite of the setting up of extravagantly subsidized industries under private ownership (boots, sugar, Shannon scheme). It has been calculated that the subsidy paid to the four sugar-beet factories would be sufficient to supply the population with imported sugar free. While this unemployment continues, no government can honestly call itself national. The changes so far since the treaty have been changes from

foreign capital to Irish capital, and from large Irish capital under Cosgrave to small Irish capital under de Valera, but the structure remains essentially the same. De Valera has set up a handful of pocket industries, heavily subsidized, for private profit, but the bankruptcy of general policy is well indicated by the introduction of the New Constitution: while in no respects is this better than the old, in several respects it is worse. There is no guarantee of rights for women, and there is a clause for limiting freedom of speech when necessary. A special position is recognized for the Roman Catholic Church in Ireland, and the property of religious orders is protected by a special guarantee. A President is to be appointed for seven years, with extended powers. All this may mean nothing, but it may be made to mean a lot on the road to the sort of dictatorship existing in Italy. Typical of the Jesuitical hair-splitting of the present government is the first clause in the Constitution: the name of the I.F.S.[4] is changed from Saorstat Eireann to Eire!

De Valera was returned after the recent elections (though with a smaller majority than was expected) partly owing to the general feeling that there was no constructive alternative, and partly owing to personal prestige. However one may dislike a certain monkishness in his person, de Valera is not corrupt. The Labour Party almost doubled its representation, but would undoubtedly have been stronger still had it taken a bold stand over home policy and over Spain. An important gain for radical opinion was the return by a large majority of Jim Larkin, veteran and uncompromising syndicalist leader, though independent of any party. There was hopeless bungling on the extreme Left. The Communist Party, which is extremely small, decided at the last moment to put up a candidate, but stood down a few days later in favour of an Independent Republican, Frank Ryan, absent in Spain, a united front candidate of the Republican Congress and the Communists. The I.R.A. were issued orders to abstain from voting, but, had the campaign for Ryan been started earlier, many of them could certainly have been won over. The I.R.A. is a terrorist and abstentionist organization with a policy vaguely resembling the anarchists, although it has points in common with the Nazi Brown-shirts before Hitler came to power. Discipline is their strong point as recent events in the North show, where twenty-eight frontier posts were destroyed simultaneously, in spite of extra vigilance on the part of an informed police. This was the occasion of the King of England's visit. The Republican Congress is a liaison formation, largely a peel-off from the I.R.A., under the leadership of Frank Ryan, Peadar O'Donnell, and George

Gilmore; policy is both nationalistic and socialistic, somewhat resembling that of the Indian Congress under Nehru.

A good deal of prominence was given in Ireland and abroad to General O'Duffy's volunteers for Spain. It is now possible to reconstruct more or less what happened. Between one thousand and two thousand men were collected, some of whom had served in the Free State army, while others had been members of the Blueshirt, or Fascist organization. They were enlisted for a period of six months' service and spent this time in Franco's Spain; though they appear to have been on active service only once (on the Guadalajara front), they suffered severely from disease, and returned home after this period with a mortality of six. Less known outside Ireland is the fact that some two hundred Irish republicans under Frank Ryan went out on the side of the democratic government. They moved into action on Christmas Day, 1936, and, as their fighting quality was high owing to previous I.R.A. training, remained constantly on active service. Mortality was very heavy, though precise figures are not yet available.

This letter makes no pretence at being comprehensive, exhaustive, or even representative. I have no knowledge of Northern Ireland. I appear to have laboured the religious question, because since 1922 this seems to have penetrated every phase of Irish life; the Orders own a large part of the land and considerable housing property, including slums; directly or indirectly they control almost all primary education and are closing up on the secondary — in one case recently a republican lay teacher was dismissed for holding views contrary to those of the clerics. The question of Catholicism or anti-clericalism is likely to be important in the future. I have mentioned facts and names which seemed to me indicative, but my choice has always been limited by my own scanty knowledge after one year's residence in Dublin.

1   A reference to James Connolly and the organization he helped found to defend the interests of workers at the time of the Dublin Lock-Out in 1913.
2   General O'Duffy (1892–1944) was leader of the Blue Shirts, an Irish fascist organization formed in the summer of 1933.
3   William Thomas Cosgrave (1880–1965) was the first President of the Executive Council from 1922 until 1932. Eamon de Valera came to power in January 1933.
4   Irish Free State. Saorstát Éireann: Irish State.

SEUMAS MacMANUS
from Seumas MacManus, *The Rocky Road to Dublin* (1938)

When Seumas MacManus (?1870–1960) emigrated to America in 1899, he took with him a store of folkloric material. A prolific writer of fiction and verse, he also compiled a popular history of Ireland, *The Story of the Irish Race* (1921). Here is a beguiling extract from his autobiography and proof if one was needed that the *púca* does indeed exist in parts of Ireland.

So They Said and Felt and Saw

A quaint and simple world, full of a beauty all its own, was that whereunto the lad was born.

All his life he regretted that his lot had not been cast in the Gaelteacht, the Gaelic-speaking territory, amongst the purely Gaelic people. Instead, his was the borderland of Gaelteacht and Galltacht — where, because of the infiltration of English and Scottish Planter descendants, the language had become English. — Still, in Gaelic idiom and a plentiful scattering of Gaelic words and phrases, this border people eked out the paucity of the *Beurla*[1] to express their feelings.

Especially by the multitudinous soft terms of endearment — *a theagair* (O Treasure), *a mhilis* (O Sweetness), *a phaiste* (O Child), *a ghradh* (O Love), *a chuisle geal mo chroidhe* (O White Pulse of my Heart), and a score of others, with which, as with diamonds to a tiara, did this fond people still brighten and beautify their converse. And though, as one entered a house here, he might salute in *Beurla*, 'God bless all here!' the return greeting was still '*Sé do bheatha!*' (May He be thy life) — '*Agus ceud fáilte romhat*' (And a hundred welcomes before thee). But if he was a long-looked for friend, whose coming brought to the hearts of the household more than ordinary joy, it was '*Ceud míle fáilte romhat*' (A hundred thousand welcomes before thee). And the parting prayer he carried with him when he left was in Gaelic, 'To God we commend thee,' 'May God send you safe,' or 'May the road rise with you.'

So Gaelic was still the spirit that the most incidental reference to the dead, invariably demanded a parenthetic prayer — 'May the heavens be his bed,' 'May God rest his soul,' — 'We hope he's with God.' With prayer the mother ended the nightly fire-raking and accompanied the morning's unearthing of 'the fire's seed'. The lighting of the candle at night brought, 'May God give us the light of Heaven.' The Christmas candle was still lighted and placed in the window-pane to shine in the night and guide wanderers, who, like Two of old, might be seeking where to lay a weary head. In Glen Ainey, then, the joy or sorrow of each was the joy or sorrow of all. In their work neighbour helped neighbour, and everyone helped the widow and orphans.

When death visited the district, all field labour was suspended till after the burial. The beggar treated with reverence, welcome, and hospitality, was always referred to as 'a poor man looking for his share' — always *his* share, never yours; for not only did they realize that the few possessions of those who did possess, were only held in trust — but also that any ragged comer to their door might be Christ himself in *shuiler*[2] guise — come to find for himself if people still remembered.

Every passing caller took part, as matter of course, in whatsoever was proceeding under the roof. If eating, he sat down to the meal; churning, he took his *brash*;[3] if the rosary was chanting, he dropped to his knees the moment he entered, joined the chorus answering the decade,[4] and when it reached his turn, led in his own decade.

The prophecies of their own great Donegal saint, Colm Cille (Dove of the Church), were on everyone's tongue, and their fulfilment hopefully and eagerly awaited — especially that part which foretold for his children the dawning of freedom's day after Éire's long, long night of suffering. Indeed, the first of the signs that were to precede that glorious event ('The seed,' said Colm, 'shall wither beneath the sod and the crops be in mourning'), behold all men had witnessed in the great potato blight! and during the Crimean war the second sign, when phenomenal prosperity gilded the land for a while ('The cow shall bring the full of her horn of money'). Succeeding signs all men awaited, and the old expected ere they died: the black pig that was to run through Barnish Mór Gap from mouth and nostrils belching fire and smoke — the three black *cuts* (assessments) that were to be levied on the land

and lifted with steel hands — the harvest that would never be reaped because Ireland, through her echoing hills, should send a call for fighting men that none dare disobey. True, before freedom was achieved a certain corn-mill in Donegal, run by a miller with two thumbs on one hand, would turn three times with human blood — yet oh! how eagerly those devoted old men questioned all *shuilers* and strollers whether in their travels they had heard of the miller's appearing!

The old-time feasts were honoured, and festivals, pagan and Christian, still celebrated. On May Day, Baal-tinne, the Druid New Year, the houses were decked with May-flowers and protecting lines of them laid along every doorstep and window-sill. On Midsummer night, bonfire night, devoted in ancient Ireland to the Druid's sun-god, huge fires leaped on every hill-top, and crowds sang, danced and made merry around, whilst torches taken from the sacred fire circled each home, its cattle-sheds and field crops, thus, for twelve month to come, averting from them all evil things.

The eve of *Samhain* (Hallow-eve) was one of the great social festivals of the year. Then there was St Bridget's eve in February with its plaiting of the rush crosses which in her name adorned and blessed the homes for the year to come. Lammas Day, first day of August, the day of the ancient god Lugh, was still one of the year's great landmarks. But, crowning all, was Christmas — of which the eve, not the day, was the time of feast and merriment.

Moreover, several festivals had their double date and honour: for, even after some centuries of the new calendar, people still observed and feasted upon Old Hallow Eve, Old Christmas Eve, Old New Year's Eve — in each case eleven days later. In the farmer's calendar, Old May Day (12th May), Old Hallow Day (12th November), and Old Lammas (12th of August), were the reckoning days — not their newer substitutes. For crop, cattle, weather reckoning, always these were used. The Lammas floods were looked for at Old Lammas. Old May-day began the farmer's year; and if he was one of the fortunate ones who could afford hired help, the half-year hiring terms began, never on May 1st and November 1st, but always on Old May-day, and Old Hallow-day.

In our *gasúr's*[5] country, the herbs of the field were, as they should be, cures for all ills. No district was there without at least one woman wise in *yarribs*,[6] who advised and compounded for the few who were troubled with complaints — and always gave gratis of her wisdom and her work. When the wise one was called, six, seven, ten miles, to a patient, the honour done her more than compensated for the trouble.

Special cures for special complaints, the rose, the whittle, the heart-fever, cancer, rabies, were secrets handed from father to eldest son in certain families. And these cures were unfailing. In both Christian and beast fairy doctors cured the mysterious ills induced by fairy power — such as heart-fever in one, and elf-shot in the other. There was in the territory a medical doctor who drew his salary and did little else; for few were ever sick enough to need him. Except of course, when they came to die; and then he was no good. For when it came a man's time to die, he just naturally stretched him out and said good-bye. A doctor was called to witness his slipping off, only by a few who were vain.

The boy's district of Glen Ainey, like every other district in Donegal — and indeed, in Ireland — was passing rich in tradition and legend. In his child days there wasn't a bird in the bush, nor an animal running on four legs but had its own story. There was hardly a bush whereon a tale did not hang, nor rock on the hillside. Every loch and every *cnoc* had its own story — tragic, poetic, romantic, dramatic — every cave, and every cairn. So, 'twas no wonder that story, story, story, filled the minds of the youth every day, and their homes every night of the year. In the Atlantic, just off the headlands which the boy could see from his own hill, lay that land of enchantment, Hy-Breasil — under the ocean, just where sea and sky met — rising up, however, and revealing itself, on rare occasions to a favoured few. Even in the lad's childhood it revealed itself to three far-drifted fishermen. The Blessed Land was to be won for Ireland — its spells to be lifted and itself recovered in its blissful reality — by a hero yet unborn, but every year expected — a saviour eagerly awaited.

Heaven still rewarded virtue in the boy's country and visited punishment on evil-doers. Instances occurred in every generation, every decade. The boy himself saw the all-powerful family of the MacCullochs wrecked, 'melt like the snow off the ditch'. Everyone knew why, even if the wild fowl had not proclaimed it. They were a Planter family living in a purely Irish locality, and though they had acres *go leor*,[7] and houses and barns crammed with full and plenty, they coveted and got the landlord to transfer to them the one little field of the Widow Meehan. On a spring day, later, when the MacCullochs were cutting turf in the Litirtraina bog, many families turf-cutting around them saw and heard a strange bird circling above the guilty ones, screaming, '*Eric! Eric!*' — which (in free translation) signifies 'Vengeance! Vengeance!' In the years immediately following, their cattle died, their crops failed, their barn burned down, one of them broke his leg, one was found dead in bed, one of

them was impaled on a pitchfork when sliding off a haycock, poverty overtook them, one went to Australia, one to Canada — and in the next generation a once great family was only a legend in Glen Ainey — remembered because of a bird's cry.

The blessed fairies, to be sure, were all around. People were still seeing them in the *gasúr*'s day. Everyone heard their music, and saw the fairy lights — on the Mount, by the Battery, on the moor between the two lochs — where they still danced and made merry during the long summer twilights and the moonlight nights. People were still being taken by them — just for a merry prank — ridden around all night, and set down unharmed by their own gable-end at break o' day. The boy knew several who had got the fairy ride — one of them Robin Porter of the Glibe — whisked all the way up to Connaught and over the tops of Cruach Padraic and Neiphin.

Lovely children were occasionally carried off by them, and fairy beings substituted. There was, for instance, the case of the strange child in Manus Mór Mac Fadyeen's cradle which everyone knew was a changeling — but of which they only got final proof the day that Doalty MacLafferty the piper left his pipes in Manus Mór's whilst he went to the hayfield where were all of the family — except It in the cradle. The pipe-music that soon began floating over the fields, the strangest and most enchanting anyone had ever listened to, drew them — as well as every worker in every field for a mile around — step by step — back to the house: and when people peeped in they beheld the 'child' in the cradle hugging the pipes like a veteran, and putting from them music that would make the hills lean to listen. When It found It was discovered, It vanished, with the pipes, and Manus Mór had an empty cradle — for which he was grateful to God — thereafter.

Everyone respected and regarded the good people highly. No one interfered with their *sciog*[8] bushes, and there was no man so sinful as to set spade or plough to the fairy rath, their pleasant green knowe on the hillside, their habitation and playground. A couple of generations before our boy's day, they had been more in evidence, had had more intercourse with human beings, and endless were the stories still told by the old people, around the firesides, of the fairy happenings in their young day.

The boy himself, as a child, knew old Máire Manachan who in her young days — when she was called the Star of Glen Ainey — encountered a fairy lover on the Alt Mór one beautiful May day. She didn't at first know that he was a fairy lover — till, as God sent it, before she let him kiss her, Father Phil, out hunting, came up with his hound Bran, and the fairy young man fled. But the particular thing which fascinated Jaimie, about Máire's adventure, was the item — which often he heard her tell: The handsome young stranger gave her to look through an emerald ring that he took off his finger — letting her get one glimpse of the fairyland he wanted to take her to, where she beheld the fairy *caman*-men playing *caman*[9] in a green vale — 'And och!' Máire would ecstatically exclaim, 'no sight on earth was ever grand to me after that!'

Thank God, evil spirits did not flourish in Donegal. One was known, but rarely did he blight the country. He was the *púca*.[10] Two generations before the boy's day he had materialized in the Glen — in Kilian. It was a dread time for the people that winter of 1829-30, when from the first full moon in November to the eve of the following St Patrick's day, the *púca's* howlings, nightly, froze the marrow in men's bones. During all that fearful winter few there were in Glen Ainey who dared stir abroad after nightfall. A very few had seen him — or it — a formless mass that lumbered toward them down the road. God and His Blessed Mother saved these men — saved their lives, that is. Their health was wrecked — or their mind. The end of the Púca Kilian (as he was and is known) was as sudden and strange as his coming. It was on St Patrick's eve of 1830 that night caught Neilis Doherty returning from the hilltop bog with a creel[11] of turf on his back. He met the Púca. Yet so sure was Neilis's faith in a protecting God that he did not throw down his creel and run. He braved the evil thing — challenged and conversed with him. Yet what was said, what passed between them, no mortal other than Neilis himself ever knew. But the Púca that night took his departure from Kilian and Glen Ainey — and was never after met or heard in the parish of Inver.

When Neilis returned home from the encounter — the creel of turf still on his back — he laid down his load and took to his bed — without saying anything — and never arose again. Within twelve months he was dead — and the secret of what passed between the Thing and himself died with him. But, after a lapse of a hundred years, the Púca Kilian is still a dread memory in the Glen.

It is wrong to say that the Púca was the only evil thing which appeared in the boy's country. The devil himself was known to have appeared — usually to someone who had done, or was about to do, wrong. He appeared to such person on a night-journey, and travelled with him step for step. He appeared to inveterate card-players — or to men returning from a card-bout where there had been cheating and swearing, hot argument and bad blood. There was one

particularly strange play of the devil with the card-players, a hundred years before the boy's day — in the neighbouring parish of the Oileigh — not only strange in itself but with a still stranger outcome.

There were in the Oileigh, then, half a dozen hard and hardened men who were notorious drinkers and card-players, wasting their time and their substance by both. The priest denounced them from the altar and they were sort of outcast. In a *shebeen* half-way between the mountains and the sea they played and drank and spent their money. The devil came to see them one Hallow night, and with them struck a bargain. He promised them all the happiness and pleasure the heart of man could wish — money in their pockets always, all the drink and all the card-playing the worst of them desired; they should lead a life of highest pleasure, with full and plenty and overflow of everything — for seven years — till All Souls' Night[12] at the seventh year's end. But on that night they should come for their final card-playing and drinking-bout in this *shebeen* of their choice, when it was to be his right to take with him the last man of them who crossed the threshold going out of the *shebeen* at midnight. To this six-to-one gamble — for such a royal stake — they gladly agreed. For seven years, then, a pleasurable life they surely led — money, cards, drink without end: and no shade or sorrow gloomed their souls till came the critical night. Honouring their bargain then, they assembled in their favourite *shebeen* for their last great bout: but as midnight neared they grew fidgety and throughout their carousing most of them couldn't help casting glances toward the door where the dread drama must soon be played. There was among them one man, Torloch Gillespie, loudest-swearing, hardest-drinking fellow of the lot, but a man of wild daring — one whom they looked to as a leader: and Torloch, when it came midnight, said to them, 'Fellows, I know what is in all your minds — No one of you wants to be the last going out of here. Every man of you is willing in his heart to murder another, in order to get out ahead of him. Now, we have been comrades for long years; we have had our pleasures together, and plenty of them, and good; and I'd be loath to see ill-feeling and treachery show now: so to prevent it I'll myself undertake to be the last man out. — Open the door, Conal O'Donnell,' he said to one man of them as the clock began striking midnight — 'Open it wide, and walk out with ye, one by one, calm and with your heads up as good men should. I'll bring up the rear.'

Conal O'Donnell opened wide the door, letting a white full moon flood the floor. One by one, calmly, steadily, they marched out — and saw, each of them as he stepped over the threshold, the Old Boy crouching by the left door-jamb, outside, readied for his grab. When five had passed, and Torloch was putting out his foot, the Fellow reached for him. But — 'You're a poor rackoner,' laughed Torloch at him — 'Can't you see another man still behind' — jerking his thumb over-shoulder to where his shadow crept after. For a moment deceived, as much by Torloch's manner as by his shadow, the Fellow, allowing Torloch to pass, grabbed — the shadow! But so mad he was for Torloch's making an idiot of him, that he held onto the shadow — and carried it off to hell with him!

The evil society broke up. The men reformed and came to their duty. But, from that night forward people shivered as Torloch Gillespie passed them by — for, no matter moonshine or sunshine, till the day of his death the man never again cast a shadow.

1   Irish for the English language.
2   Irish for wanderer, vagrant, stroller.
3   Short turn at churning the butter.
4   Ten Hail Marys of the rosary.
5   Irish: child, youngster.
6   herbs (Share).
7   Irish: plenty, enough.
8   Irish: fairy.
9   Irish: hurley.
10 Irish: pooka, hobgoblin.
11 Basket.
12 2 November.

ROBERT GIBBINGS
from Robert Gibbings, *Blue Angels and Whales* (1938)

Robert Gibbings (1889–1958), born in Cork and educated, as he remarks on the Penguin 1938 cover to *Blue Angels and Whales*, 'in the snipe bogs and trout streams of Munster', was a book-designer, artist, engraver, and travel writer. He ran the Golden Cockerell Press for nine years from 1924, was largely responsible for the establishment of the Society of Wood-engravers, and in 1938 was appointed by Allen Lane for a short while the Art Director of the Penguin Illustrated Classics series. *Blue Angels and Whales* is a record of his travels to Tahiti, Bermuda and the Red Sea, included in which is a final chapter entitled 'Leaves from My Notebook'.

from 'Leaves from My Note-book'

Taedy Murphy tells of a wake in County Cork:

'Glory be to God! He had a quiet death, he with ninety years on him, sittin' there listenin' to the wireless. Well, praise be to God! Didn't he cross over with the latest news?

'And the wake he had, with ivery wan of his children and ivery mother's son of his grandchildren, and his ould woman sittin' in the corner, and the keeners screeching, and whisky flowing, and Guinness foaming, and the poor old corpse sittin' up there with his pipe in his mouth and the cards in his hands and his ear still cocked for the wireless.

'"I've come to tell you how sorry I am," said Mrs Flanagan.

'"I didn't suppose you'd come to tell me how glad you were," murmured Mrs Doolan sadly; and there were the little children sobbing and holding on to their mothers, and half-witted Nelly screeching, and cross-eyed Mike pouring out the whisky while red-haired Dan tried to keep his wife from tearing out the eyes of her sister-in-law — engaged in an argument they were over a sow.

'The friends and the relations and them that was neither all dropped in to show their respect or, maybe, to get a free swig from the bottle. A long queue of blue-cloaked women and black-coated men stretched down the stony lane, and on the road itself was a procession of ass carts all anchored to the hedge. 'Twas early hours in the morning when the last of them were leaving.

'"Praise be to God, 'twas a grand wake! Mustn't she be the proud woman!" said Paddy O'Sullivan.

'Mrs O'Sullivan, his wife, dropped back for a last word of comfort to the widow.

'"Fifty years, was it, Mrs Doolan?" she asked.

'"Fifty years," said Mrs Doolan slowly, "and — I — niver — liked — him."'

SEAN O'CASEY
from Sean O'Casey, *I Knock at the Door* (1939)

A nicely-angled, touching moment from O'Casey's childhood. *Young Cassidy*, a film by Jack Cardiff and John Ford and released in 1965, was based on O'Casey's autobiography.

Life Is More Than Meat

Johnny didn't bother much about food or raiment. There wasn't much of either to be had, so he took what was given, and forgot to thank God.

Looking back, he could remember two suits that had come fresh to his body: one, a blue sailor suit, with gold anchor and gold stripes on the sleeve, topped with a blue velvet cap, having H.M.S Condor in gold letters round the band; and a soft tweed suit, fitted after many trials, and finally accepted from a Jew for two shillings down, and a shilling a week after, till the full price was paid. He had it on now, patched and stitched till it was tired; coaxed with care to stay together a little longer. Each touch a warning that a tear was near, with his mother nightly nursing tweedy wounds, closing them up with deft and crinkled and patient fingers. Although all its early simple pomp was gone, it hung on hard to life, a shade from the sun in the summer, a shivering shelter from the seeping rain, the biting frost, and the cold blowing blasts of the winter.

Food was rare, though there was almost always a hunk of bread to be had, but it often tasted like dust and ashes in his mouth: dust to dust and ashes to ashes. After a few years of meagre fare, anyway, his belly ceased to put up a fight, and took patiently the bread and tea and Parrish's Syrup that trickled into it; getting a start of surprise when a potato came along; and battling hastily to create a welcome whenever meat or fish came tumbling in.

How good it was for John the Baptist always to have within his reach loads of locusts and wild honey. Going about his business, and never having to bother as to where the night would fall on him. When his hat was on, his house was thatched. And the Israelites, too — look at them! Quails flutthering outa the sky, croaking out, Catch me, catch me, so that nothing had to be done but wring their necks and roast them. (Though in all fairness, and to give God His due, He sometimes flooded the bay with fish, causing poor Dublin streets to ring with the cry of, Dublin Bay herrin's, tuppence a dozen; tuppence a dozen, the Dublin Bay herrin's; which meant a daily feast of hot or cold baked herrings for a week or more for all.)

And the manna, too, dropped down from heaven for their special benefit, though it didn't keep them from grousing. Well, there was no manna dropping down on the streets of Dublin for poor boys to gather; only dung and dirt that the traffic pulverized into dust, choking the throats and cutting the eyes outa the passers-by whenever the stronger breezes blew.

Once a week, after Archie had given to the house what he had put aside to give it, Johnny and his mother set out to buy in the week's supply of tea and sugar. This meant a long journey to Lipton's in Dame Street. Before, they used to get these things in the London and Newcastle Tea Company who gave brass and bronze checks to their customers, according to the amount of tea bought, which were used, when enough had been gathered together, to buy chinaware and ironmongery. But Lipton had come, and other stores had to take a back seat.

So Johnny, furnished with a sailor's kit-bag, having large eyelet holes through which a cord ran so that the mouth could be closed, set out with his mother on a far journey for the corn and wine in Lipton's, on a cold and rainy evening.

How he hated the journey, and how tired the walking made him, for there was nothing stirring, nothing in the walk to make his feet light or lift them in a dancing step; often his mother had to tell him not to drag his feet, but to walk like an ordinary human being. Then, without knowing, he'd hang on his mother's arm till she'd cry out, oh, don't be dhraggin' outa me like that; can't you walk on the legs that God has given you? He'd take his arm away, and journey on through the wilderness of streets, shuffling his feet, and lagging a little behind.

What wouldn't he give, now, for a good topcoat, an' he goin' along Dorset Street, facin' the spittin' rain an' the penethratin' wind, whippin' in his face an' stabbin' him right through his coat an' trousers, an' tatthered shirt, making him feel numb an' sick as he dragged himself along afther his mother, protectin' himself as well as he could be holdin' the kit-bag spread out like a buckler in front of his breast.

He kept his eye on his mother ploddin' along in front of him, carryin' a basket an' an oilcan, dhressed in her faded an' thin black skirt an' cape, her shabby little bonnet tied firmly undher her chin, the jet beads in it gleamin' out of it as bright as ever; an' she steppin' it out, hell-bent for Lipton's, ignorin' all the shops that lined the way, stuffed out with all sorts of fine an' fat goods that God never meant her to have.

There were fruiterers who had piled out on the path heaps of apples an' pears from England, dates from Tunis an' Thripoli, figs from Turkey, and oranges from Spain, transported outa the sun by bullock or mule, in thrain an' boat to the wind-swept streets o' Dublin; all callin' out to be eaten; but Johnny and his mother passed heedlessly by, on their way to Samarcand and Lipton's.

Further on, they'd pass through an avenue formed be tiers on tiers of cabbages an' cauliflowers, bushels of turnips, bins of spuds, hanks of onions, an' bunches of carrots, ready to be plucked, weighed, scooped out, or handed over to anyone who needed them; but Johnny and his mother passed heedless by, turning neither to right nor left to view the kindly fruits of the earth.

Then they'd pass through an alley of butchers' benches piled high with cutlets, chops, beef for boiling, and beef for roasting; with the butchers in their blue and white overalls, bawling, buy away, buy away, new shop open; but Johnny and his mother went by unheeding, heading straight to where they had set themselves to go.

On from Dorset Street into Bolton Street, where his mother popped into a chandler's shop, and filled the can with half a gallon of oil, and her basket with quarter a stone of washing-soda, a bar of yellow soap, two candles, a penny box of Colman's starch, and some bundles of firewood, bought to fulfil what was spoken by the prophet, saying, Wash ye, make ye clean; to keep the hearth aglow; and to be a light to them that sit in darkness.

As they passed through the gauntlet of shelves and shelves of cheese, bacon, eggs, and piles of bread, made fresh from the sweet-smelling wheat, grand and golden, enough to feed five thousand, hallowed bread, bread to comfort the heart of man, bread from the earth, bread from God, on sale by the bakers, Johnny suddenly saw his mother step to the left, and hurry on, as a drunken man came staggering along the path. The man lurched in towards the shop, knocked against a tray of pigs' feet, and sent them flying all over the place.

Good God, man, what are you afther doin'! shouted the shop-boy, as he rushed over to gather them up, a crowd gathering to laugh at what had happened. Like lightning, Johnny slid a lump of bacon into the folds of his kit-bag, and snatched up an egg as he passed by, running like hell to catch up with his mother who was a little ahead. Catching his mother's arm, he cried that

he was cold, and ran her trotting along till they turned down into the dark and gloomy King's Inn Street, and he was safe and thrilled, but trembling.

Through Liffey Street they went, a street of old furniture shops, all shuttered close now, the street deserted, save for an odd straggler trudging over the straw and sodden paper that littered path and road; up the quay, across Essex Bridge, both of them bending to battle the breeze that swept up the Liffey, down Capel Street, into Dame Street, and, at last, into the warm, brightly-lighted, busy, big shop of Lipton's.

Johnny paused for a moment to look at himself in the huge mirrors panelling the walls, just inside the great door, showing him and his mother as lean, skinny-looking gazebos entering the shop.

— They'll show us up as fat as fools, goin' out, said his mother, laughing.

The shop was crowded, full of white-coated counter-jumpers handin' out tea an' sugar an' margarine as swift as hands could lay hold on them; with men in brown overalls trotting along pushing mountains of tea an' sugar in packages on little throlleys, moving silently and cunningly through the crowded shop, to fill up the vacancies on the shelves.

They waited their turn to get their seven pounds of sugar, a pound of tea for one an' six, an' a two-pound pot of Lipton's special plum an' apple jam; Johnny packing them in the kit-bag, while his mother slowly and feelingly put back sixpence change into the pocket of her skirt, strengthened with added lining to keep such treasures safe.

— Well, that'll have to provide us with whatever else we may need for the rest of the week, she murmured, lettin' the sixpence go at last when she felt it settle in the bottom of her pocket.

Johnny swung the kit-bag over his shoulder, an' he an' his ma manoeuvred to the door through the people thronging the shop; pausing to see themselves in the mirrors, looking like fat pigs, bulging cheeks, great round bellies, an' enormous bodies, showing how great the stuff was that Lipton's sold; then the pair of them plunged once more into the dark night, the spitting rain, and the biting breeze; Johnny feeling all these trials less when he remembered the egg in his pocket and the bacon in the bag.

Out in the street, moving slowly forward in the kennel, was an old grey-bearded man, with a creaking voice, singing dolefully to the busy street. The collar of his coat was pulled up, as high as it could go, and his neck and chin were sunk down in it as low as they could go to shelther them from the wind and the rain; but when high notes came, the head had to be lifted to get anywhere near them, so the thin neck rose out of its cosy nest, to sink back again when the high notes were over, and the low notes came back. Quite a number of people paused in their hurry, searched in purse or pocket to hand out a penny; and Johnny felt envious that money could be so easy earned be the cracked singin' of

Let us pause in life's pleasures, an' count its many
    fears,
While we all sup sorrow with the poor;
Here's a song that shall linger forever in our ears,
Oh, hard times, come again no more.

'Tis the song, the sigh of the weary,
Hard times, hard times, come again no more;
Many days have you lingered around my cabin
    door,
Oh, hard times, come again no more!

— Since we haven't anything to give him, it isn't fair to listen, said his mother, pulling the arm of the pausing Johnny.

When they got home again, Johnny spilled the sugar, tea, and jam out on the table. Then he put the lump of bacon and the egg right where his mother could see them when she turned round after taking off her wet things.

When she turned, she stared.

— How, in the name o' God, did those things ever creep into the kit-bag? she asked.

— I fecked[1] them, said Johnny gleefully. When the dhrunken man fell an' scatthered things, I fecked them as I passed.

— A nice thing if you'd been caught feckin' them, she said, in a frightened voice. Never, never do the like again. D'ye know, had you been nabbed, it 'ud have meant five years or more in a reformatory for you? Never do it again, Johnny. Remember what you've been taught: Take no thought for your life, what ye shall eat; nor yet for your body, what ye shall put on; for the life is more than meat, an' the body than raiment; and your heavenly Father knoweth that ye have need of all these things; so keep your hands from pickin' an' stealin', for the future; and she carefully placed the bacon and the egg in the press.

Johnny sat silent by the fire, drying his damp trousers. After a few minutes he saw his mother putting on her bonnet and cape.

— Where'r you goin' now, Ma? he asked.

— I'm goin' out to get a couple o' nice heads of cabbage, with the sixpence I've left, to go with the bacon tomorrow, she said.

1   Here meaning to steal.

PEIG SAYERS
from Peig Sayers, *Machtnamh Seana-Mhná* (1939) (trans. Séamus Ennis, *An Old Woman's Reflections*, 1962)

Peig Sayers (1873–1958) was born on the Dingle Peninsula in County Kerry and married into the Great Blasket Island. It was there she spent the greater part of her life. A natural storyteller, she relayed some 360 tales to Seósamh Ó Dálaigh, a collector for the Irish Folklore Commission (established in 1935). Unable to write Irish, she dictated her life and her stories to her son Mícheál Ó Gaoithín. *Peig*, her autobiography, appeared in 1936, and was translated by Bryan MacMahon in 1973. *Machtnamh Seana-Mhná* was first published in 1939 and translated into English in 1962. Her gifts as a storyteller are especially in evidence in the following extract.

A Milk-House in Little Island; Nance Daly and Nora Keaveney

Many an old woman in Ireland had a nicer place and more pleasant to study than this, but I prefer this lonely place to any other place in Ireland. The golden mountains of Ireland are without mist before me. The sea is pouring itself against the rocks and running up in dark ravines and caves where the seals live. We are not disturbed by the uproar and noise of the city. There is a fine hedge around us and we are inside the Summerhouse of Peace. There is no picture-house only these lovely things God created, praise for ever to Him! Every time I get the chance I give a run to get a view of these things which are most pleasant to my heart. Little Island is before me and white sheep in their fleeces grazing there where my mother remembered, when she was young, milk to be, and butter being made in plenty.

'Tis well I remember, and I looking from me on this island, listening to my father and I a little girl talking about the people who were living in Little Island at that time, and in many other places. 'Tis little I thought then that I'd be living so near to that island. But since I'm sitting here, looking over at it, see how the thoughts run far back into the years that are gone by me — to the little solitary house at the foot of the hills again. It's a little thatched house. It's where I was born and reared. There's an old ruin a bit over from it, where Maurice Scanlan was, where I spent the days of my childhood. I see, I think, Maurice himself standing in the doorway, and he giving sweets to us, after his coming from Dingle. I see, I think, my mother sitting in the corner and Nell Malone and Old Mary O'Connor, and they talking about the things they remembered in their early youth. See Kate, my brother's wife, busy about the house and myself in the corner, rocking the cradle, heeding and giving ear to my mother telling this story to the others:

'Long years after the bad times and the famine,' said she, 'much of the land of Ireland was derelict. The poor people who used to inhabit it were gone the way of truth with the hunger and want. Those of them who managed to live, and had a piece of land, had big rent to pay and the hardship of life working violently on them, and when they couldn't pay the rent they got nothing but the side of the road distressfully and their house burnt.

'As I said before, the land was derelict and there was no gain from it for the landlord. The plan he made was to put milk-houses, or *dairies* as they were called, here and there, put servants in charge of them, and put milch-cows on the land. I remember well two of them to be in Dunquin, one of them west there at the Shed and another down at the Milk Crossroads. He put another on Little Island, with a married couple minding it, a man named Richard O'Carroll and Kate Daly, or Kate from Little Island, as she was called. Kate was clever and she had good knowledge of butter and milk. She had two sisters, Brigid and Nance. It's Brigid was at the Milk Crossroads and Nance was at the Shed. There was no limit with them for minding butter and milk. None of them was married but Kate, and she had no offspring. She and her husband were living snugly with no want from the Lord. A big boat was serving them frequently. They had a nice comfortable house in Little Island, and if they hadn't a nice airly little island, it's not a day yet. There was nothing Kate lacked more than water, because there was no spring-water well in Little Island, and 'tis how Richard O'Carroll had to bring little barrels of water from the Heel of the Island. Often it wasn't calm, and the poor man would risk drowning; but long as he was succeeding, providence got a chance on him and he was drowned, may they be safe where it is told! That gave its name to the Heel since — O'Carroll's Heel it's called.

'That put an end to butter and milk and living in Little Island. Poor Kate had to leave the place and face out somewhere else to earn her living.

'As I said before, her sister, Nance, was a milk-woman at the Shed. She was a lovely young woman, and it was no wonder the young men were looking after her. Small interest Nance had in any of them but one man, that is, Young Sean O'Flaherty. He was her total share of the men of the world and she wouldn't allow any other girls to wink at him. But Young Sean wasn't so senseless after her. Over there he was living where Owen Brown's house is today. There was nobody in the house but himself and his sister, Kate. Their parents were on the way of truth for years before that and as we know they had to fend for themselves. So, when Kate got the chance she married a man from Coom named Sean Brosnahan. That left Young Sean alone and he had to marry to have a housewife. Nance thought, no wonder, that she'd be that woman — there was nothing to upset her with him. She had an overwhelming love for him and she thought that he had the same for her, but he hadn't. Love is a thing that torment and torture follows and often it's not lasting, and it's a small thing that upsets it. That's how it happened to Nance Daly.

'Shrovetide came and there was a wedding on in Flagstone Glen and there were many girls from the south parish at the wedding, and they neatly dressed in the fashion of that time. Whoever was at that wedding, Young Sean O'Flaherty was there and many a young girl was looking under her eyelashes and making honey in her heart of his good looks, because he was a proportionately-made young man, brown curly hair on him, a flush in his cheeks, and two grey eyes in his head that would make any dear girl like him.

'There was a party of the girls sitting on a seat in a lonely corner of the house, and the devil to Sean but he noticed them and went where they were. After a little talk he told one of them to sing a song, but she said she couldn't, that she never sang any song. He continued urging from one to the other until he went to the fifth girl. She took courage and she said "I'll sing a song for you, good man!" She caught him by the hand and she started on this song:

My great loss and my grief
And my visit this way,
My parents will be grieved
Asking about me of everyone.
I gave you great love
Over the boys of Ireland,
Until I'm stretched in the grave
I will not forsake your merriment.

Had I a box full of gold
And a chest full of silver,
I would give it to Sean
He's the commanding hearty.
Isn't it happy for the woman
Who will get you tied from the priest!
But my want through my heart
Is that I am for ever parted from you!

"'Forever! Forever!" said he, "What is your name, young woman? Your name, please? Tell it to me!" and he spoke very quietly, because Nance was sitting near the table and her eyes sharp peeping on him.

"'Nora Keaveney," said she, "and it's in Ventry parish my parents live."

"'You are my choice above any girl I have seen yet, and if you gave me your hand I'd have no other wife but you," said he, and he moved up to her, saying those words.

"'Have my promise and my word, if my parents agree to it."

"'All right," said Sean, and his heart was as light as a blackbird, because he had given the love of his breast to Nora at that moment. It was no wonder he had, because she was a pretty, gentle girl, with skin as white as the swan, her cheeks as red as the rose, and curly black hair on her. She was proportionately made and it would be hard to find fault with her.

'Next day Sean and a lad with him went off, and nobody knew where he was until he came back to Vicarstown with Nora Keaveney married. Then the row was on. When Nance Daly heard that her dear love was married to another woman, she nearly lost her mind. She used to be watching Nora, day and night like a cat would be watching a mouse. It was dangerous for Nora to put her head out the door, because Nance was always watching her. Poor Nora had no idea why Nance should be that way. If she had known the great love Nance had for Young Sean she

wouldn't have been so haughty as she was, coming, but nobody gave her that information.

'One day at the beginning of spring, Sean was working in the field, and when Nora had the potatoes for the dinner drained, she went out on the garden fence and called her husband aloud, but she didn't manage to make the second call when Nance had a shower of stones all around her. Barely she got her soul inside with her, because when she was standing inside on the floor Nance aimed at her with a rough stone that knocked the side out of the potato-pot beside her. The poor girl was frightened. When Sean came home he knew that Nora was not easy in her mind.

"'What's wrong with you?" said he.

"'I'm frightened alive by a woman without sense that's around there," said Nora. "I don't know who she is or what she has against me, but she's after me every day since I reached this house. And look, she has broken the potato-pot today, but I don't care in the devil, so long as it's not my head she had broken. Do you know why she's like that?"

"'It's all the same to you about her — don't pretend that you hear her, but when dinner is ready put a white rag on the gable, and I'll come home."

'Yes, the year was slipping by and if Nance was tormented, she had a kind of surrender to her enemy, Nora, because she was going to have a young child for Christmas.

'A daughter was born to Nora, and because of milk being scarce 'tis how she was buying milk in the house of White Dermot who was living down at the bridge. One morning, after the morning meal, Nora told her husband to stay and mind the baby while she'd be fetching the milk. She took a jug with her and went down the road. But Nance was not snoozing, for she saw Nora going down the road. She decided it was a good time to catch up even with her. The envy and the old love were fighting each other in her heart still, and she made out she could get some vengeance on Nora because she was the top and bottom of her heart's torment. She had a bitter hatred for her and it would be great ease of mind for her if she could get revenge on her this way or that way. On that, she followed Nora to White Dermot's house. Poor Nora was only in across the threshold when Nance was in on her heels. She had the look of anger. She was a hard strong woman and it was no wonder Nora would be afraid of her. She spoke to the woman of the house.

' "Have you milk for me today, Molly?" said she.

' "Indeed I haven't, O daughter," said Molly. "I have the last drop sent in the vessel to this good woman here."

'Nance didn't need but "I want a reason" and her

eyes lit with the flame of anger, and she said with strong, fearless voice:

'"She won't have my milk!" said she. "It's enough for her to have my dear love and the man who took my sense from me — but he won't have much good in her after me," and she shaped to fight.

'When Nora saw her with the crossing shape on her, she decided she had better stand her ground and defend herself as best in Ireland she could do. Before Nance had a chance to say "God with my soul", Nora had jumped out of herself like a wildcat, gripping her by the hair of her head. With the first twist she gave her she knocked Nance down on the floor. "Yes, girl," said she, "that's the recommendation of two people from the Big Cliff for you — whichever of us is strongest be uppermost — and as I am uppermost I'll put the mark of my limbs to be seen by everybody on you. And if you loved Young Sean O'Flaherty, he had no love for you, and I have himself and his love and his baby, and you whistle away for yourself!"

'Such wrangling and biting Moll never saw before. The flame was in her eyes looking at them. But much as Nance Daly was inclined for fight, she was as gentle as a sheep's lamb when Nora parted with her. She scraped and scratched and cut her so that there was a red brand on Nance.

'"Go now," said Nora, "and don't tell where you were, and don't look over your shoulder at me as long as you live. The lovely looks you had coming, it's different appearance you have now! But when you're healed you can give your love to somebody other than Sean O'Flaherty."

'She took the milk-jug that was on the table and little grass grew under her feet until she reached home. She suspected that Nance would follow her and split her with stones, but she didn't. She was sour enough with herself and ashamed of the mistake she had made. From that day until she left the Shed she didn't look over her shoulder at Nora Keaveney.'

The long years are gone in a gallop, and these who are in the life of my story gone too, as the mist goes with the wind. I can see today only the place where they used to live, but they draw me back on the lonely road of thoughts, and 'tis nice how Youth pays me a small visit, when I'm at tight grips with the years. I am young again, I think. There is courage and merriment in my heart. I feel the mind as strong and courageous as ever it was. But when the fine pleasant thoughts go, rust and sourness and weakness of the brain comes on me and I feel some heavy weight coming down on my heart.

Maybe the reader has youth in power. If so, he feels the heart light and secure, the laugh clean, the jump musical, the jollity and merriment, the brightness and freshness and fragrance everywhere on his way. I remember having all those little jewels myself, but see how the ugly thief age came and stole them from me! Great as the guarding is, he sneaks upon us. Nobody feels him coming.

IMAGINATIVE

FRANK O'CONNOR
from Frank O'Connor, *Guests of the Nation* (1931)

Frank O'Connor (pseudonym of Michael O'Donovan) (1903–66) was a short-story writer, novelist, and translator. Born in Cork, he left school at twelve but came under the influence of Daniel Corkery, who encouraged him to read in nationalist literature. During the Civil War he fought with the Republicans and was imprisoned in 1923. Disillusioned with guerilla warfare and with the perfidy of the participants, he began writing while finding work as a librarian. Here in this short story from a collection published in 1931, O'Connor reveals the inhuman side to the War of Independence.

The story was turned into a film by Denis Johnston in 1935.

Guests of the Nation

I

At dusk the big Englishman, Belcher, would shift his long legs out of the ashes and say, 'Well, chums, what about it?' and Noble and myself would say, 'All right, chum' (for we had picked up some of their curious expressions), and the little Englishman, Hawkins, would light the lamp and bring out the cards. Sometimes Jeremiah Donovan would come up and supervise the game and get excited over Hawkins's cards, which he always played badly, and shout at him as if he was one of our own, 'Ah, you divil, why didn't you play the tray?'[1]

But ordinarily Jeremiah was a sober and contented poor devil like the big Englishman, Belcher, and was looked up to only because he was a fair hand at documents, though he was slow even with them. He wore a small cloth hat and big gaiters over his long pants, and you seldom saw him with his hands out of his pockets. He reddened when you talked to him, tilting from toe to heel and back, and looking down all the time at his big farmer's feet. Noble and myself used to make fun of his broad accent, because we were from the town.

I couldn't at the time see the point of myself and Noble guarding Belcher and Hawkins at all, for it was my belief that you could have planted that pair down anywhere from this to Claregalway[2] and they'd have taken root there like a native weed. I never in my short experience saw two men take to the country as they did.

They were passed on to us by the Second Battalion when the search for them became too hot, and Noble and myself, being young, took over with a natural feeling of responsibility, but Hawkins made us look like fools when he showed that he knew the country better than we did.

'You're the bloke they calls Bonaparte,' he said to me. 'Mary Brigid O'Connell told me to ask you what you'd done with the pair of her brother's socks you borrowed.'

For it seemed, as they explained it, that the Second had little evenings, and some of the girls of the neighbourhood turned up, and, seeing they were such decent chaps, our fellows could not leave the two Englishmen out. Hawkins learned to dance 'The Walls of Limerick', 'The Siege of Ennis', and 'The Waves of Tory' as well as any of them, though he could not return the compliment, because our lads at that time did not dance foreign dances on principle.

So whatever privileges Belcher and Hawkins had with the Second they just took naturally with us, and after the first couple of days we gave up all pretence of keeping an eye on them. Not that they could have got far, because they had accents you could cut with a knife and wore khaki tunics and overcoats with civilian pants and boots, but I believe myself they never had any idea of escaping and were quite content to be where they were.

It was a treat to see how Belcher got off with the old woman of the house where we were staying. She was a great warrant to scold, and cranky even with us, but before ever she had a chance of giving our guests, as I may call them, a lick of her tongue, Belcher had made her his friend for life. She was breaking sticks, and Belcher, who had not been more than ten minutes in the house, jumped up and went over to her.

'Allow me, madam,' he said, smiling his queer little smile. 'Please allow me,' and he took the hatchet from her. She was too surprised to speak, and after that, Belcher would be at her heels, carrying a bucket, a basket or a load of turf. As Noble said, he got into looking before she leapt, and hot water, or any little thing she wanted, Belcher would have ready for her. For such a huge man (and though I am five foot ten myself I had to look up at him) he had an uncommon lack of speech. It took us a little while to get used to him, walking in and out like a ghost, without speaking. Especially because Hawkins talked enough for a platoon, it was strange to hear Belcher with his toes in the ashes come out with a solitary 'Excuse me, chum,' or 'That's right, chum.' His one and only passion was cards, and he was a remarkably good card-player. He could have skinned myself and Noble, but whatever we lost to him, Hawkins lost to us, and Hawkins only played with the money Belcher gave him.

Hawkins lost to us because he had too much old gab, and we probably lost to Belcher for the same reason. Hawkins and Noble argued about religion into the early hours of the morning, and Hawkins worried the life out of Noble, who had a brother a priest, with a string of questions that would puzzle a cardinal. Even in treating of holy subjects, Hawkins had a deplorable tongue. I never met a man who could mix such a variety of cursing and bad language into any argument. He was a terrible man, and a fright to argue. He never did a stroke of work, and when he had no one else to argue with, he got stuck in the old woman.

He met his match in her, for when he tried to get her to complain profanely of the drought she gave him a great comedown by blaming it entirely on Jupiter Pluvius (a deity neither Hawkins nor I had ever heard of, though Noble said that among the pagans it was believed that he had something to do with the rain). Another day he was swearing at the capitalists for starting the German war when the old lady laid down her iron, puckered up her little crab's mouth, and said: 'Mr Hawkins, you can say what you like about the war, and think you'll deceive me because I'm only a simple poor countrywoman, but I know what started the war. It was the Italian Count that stole the heathen divinity out of the temple in Japan. Believe me, Mr Hawkins, nothing but sorrow and want can follow people that disturb the hidden powers.'

A queer old girl, all right.

II

One evening we had our tea and Hawkins lit the lamp and we all sat into cards. Jeremiah Donovan came in too, and sat and watched us for a while, and it suddenly struck me that he had no great love for the two Englishmen. It came as a surprise to me, because I had noticed nothing of it before.

Late in the evening a really terrible argument blew up between Hawkins and Noble, about capitalists and priests and love of country.

'The capitalists pay the priests to tell you about the next world so that you won't notice what the bastards are up to in this,' said Hawkins.

'Nonsense, man!' said Noble, losing his temper. 'Before ever a capitalist was thought of people believed in the next world.'

Hawkins stood up as though he was preaching.

'Oh, they did, did they?' he said with a sneer. 'They believed all the things you believe — isn't that what you mean? And you believe God created Adam, and Adam created Shem, and Shem created Jehoshophat. You believe all that silly old fairytale about Eve and Eden and the apple. Well, listen to me, chum! If you're entitled to a silly belief like that, I'm entitled to my own silly belief — which is that the first thing your God created was a bleeding capitalist, with morality and Rolls-Royce complete. Am I right, chum?' he said to Belcher.

'You're right, chum,' said Belcher with a smile, and he got up from the table to stretch his long legs into the fire and stroke his moustache. So, seeing that Jeremiah Donovan was going, and that there was no knowing when the argument about religion would be over, I went out with him. We strolled down to the village together, and then he stopped, blushing and mumbling, and said I should be behind, keeping guard. I didn't like the tone he took with me, and anyway I was bored with life in the cottage, so I replied by asking him what the hell we wanted to guard them for at all.

He looked at me in surprise and said: 'I thought you knew we were keeping them as hostages.'

'Hostages?' I said.

'The enemy have prisoners belonging to us and now they're talking of shooting them,' he said. 'If they shoot our prisoners, we'll shoot theirs.'

'Shoot Belcher and Hawkins?' I said.

'What else did you think we were keeping them for?' he said.

'Wasn't it very unforeseen of you not to warn Noble and myself of that in the beginning?' I said.

'How was it?' he said. 'You might have known that much.'

'We could not know it, Jeremiah Donovan,' I said. 'How could we when they were on our hands so long?'

'The enemy have our prisoners as long and longer,' he said.

'That's not the same thing at all,' said I.

'What difference is there?' said he.

I couldn't tell him, because I knew he wouldn't understand. If it was only an old dog that you had to take to the vet's, you'd try and not get too fond of him, but Jeremiah Donovan was not a man who would ever be in danger of that.

'And when is this to be decided?' I said.

'We might hear tonight,' he said. 'Or tomorrow or the next day at latest. So if it's only hanging round that's a trouble to you, you'll be free soon enough.'

It wasn't the hanging round that was a trouble to me at all by this time. I had worse things to worry about. When I got back to the cottage the argument was still on. Hawkins was holding forth in his best style, maintaining that there was no next world, and Noble was saying that there was; but I could see that Hawkins had had the best of it.

'Do you know what, chum?' he was saying with a saucy smile. 'I think you're just as big a bleeding unbeliever as I am. You say you believe in the next world, and you know just as much about the next world as I do, which is sweet damn-all. What's heaven? You don't know. Where's heaven? You don't know. You know sweet damn-all! I ask you again, do they wear wings?'

'Very well, then,' said Noble. 'They do. Is that enough for you? They do wear wings.'

'Where do they get them, then? Who makes them? Have they a factory for wings? Have they a sort of store where you hand in your chit and take your bleeding wings?'

'You're an impossible man to argue with,' said Noble. 'Now, listen to me — ' And they were off again.

It was long after midnight when we locked up and went to bed. As I blew out the candle I told Noble. He took it very quietly. When we'd been in bed about an hour he asked if I thought we should tell the

Englishmen. I didn't, because I doubted if the English would shoot our men. Even if they did, the Brigade officers, who were always up and down to the Second Battalion and knew the Englishmen well, would hardly want to see them plugged. 'I think so too,' said Noble. 'It would be great cruelty to put the wind up them now.'

'It was very unforeseen of Jeremiah Donovan anyhow,' said I.

It was next morning that we found it so hard to face Belcher and Hawkins. We went about the house all day, scarcely saying a word. Belcher didn't seem to notice; he was stretched into the ashes as usual, with his usual look of waiting in quietness for something unforeseen to happen, but Hawkins noticed and put it down to Noble being beaten in the argument of the night before.

'Why can't you take the discussion in the proper spirit?' he said severely. 'You and your Adam and Eve! I'm a Communist, that's what I am. Communist or Anarchist, it all comes to much the same thing.' And for hours he went round the house, muttering when the fit took him. 'Adam and Eve! Adam and Eve! Nothing better to do with their time than pick bleeding apples!'

III

I don't know how we got through that day, but I was very glad when it was over, the tea things were cleared away, and Belcher said in his peaceable way: 'Well, chums, what about it?' We sat round the table and Hawkins took out the cards, and just then I heard Jeremiah Donovan's footsteps on the path and a dark presentiment crossed my mind. I rose from the table and caught him before he reached the door.

'What do you want?' I asked.

'I want those two soldier friends of yours,' he said, getting red.

'Is that the way, Jeremiah Donovan?' I asked.

'That's the way. There were four of our lads shot this morning, one of them a boy of sixteen.'

'That's bad,' I said.

At that moment Noble followed me out, and the three of us walked down the path together, talking in whispers. Feeney, the local intelligence officer, was standing by the gate.

'What are you going to do about it?' I asked Jeremiah Donovan.

'I want you and Noble to get them out; tell them they're being shifted again; that'll be the quietest way.'

'Leave me out of that,' said Noble under his breath.

Jeremiah Donovan looked at him hard.

'All right,' he said. 'You and Feeney get a few tools from the shed and dig a hole by the far end of the bog. Bonaparte and myself will be after you. Don't let anyone see you with the tools. I wouldn't like it to go beyond ourselves.'

We saw Feeney and Noble go round to the shed and went in ourselves. I left Jeremiah Donovan to do the explanations. He told them that he had orders to send them back to the Second Battalion. Hawkins let out a mouthful of curses, and you could see that though Belcher didn't say anything, he was a bit upset too. The old woman was for having them stay in spite of us, and she didn't stop advising them until Jeremiah Donovan lost his temper and turned on her. He had a nasty temper, I noticed. It was pitch-dark in the cottage by this time, but no one thought of lighting the lamp, and in the darkness the two Englishmen fetched their topcoats and said good-bye to the old woman.

'Just as a man makes a home of a bleeding place, some bastard at headquarters thinks you're too cushy and shunts you off,' said Hawkins, shaking her hand.

'A thousand thanks, madam,' said Belcher. 'A thousand thanks for everything' — as though he'd made it up.

We went round to the back of the house and down towards the bog. It was only then that Jeremiah Donovan told them. He was shaking with excitement.

'There were four of our fellows shot in Cork this morning and now you're to be shot as a reprisal.'

'What are you talking about?' snapped Hawkins. 'It's bad enough being mucked about as we are without having to put up with your funny jokes.'

'It isn't a joke,' said Donovan, 'I'm sorry, Hawkins, but it's true,' and began on the usual rigmarole about duty and how unpleasant it is. I never noticed that people who talk a lot about duty find it much of a trouble to them.

'Oh, cut it out!' said Hawkins.

'Ask Bonaparte,' said Donovan, seeing that Hawkins wasn't taking him seriously. 'Isn't it true, Bonaparte?'

'It is,' I said, and Hawkins stopped.

'Ah, for Christ's sake, chum!'

'I mean it, chum,' I said.

'You don't sound as if you meant it.'

'If he doesn't mean it, I do,' said Donovan, working himself up.

'What have you against me, Jeremiah Donovan?'

'I never said I had anything against you. But why did your people take out four of your prisoners and shoot them in cold blood?'

He took Hawkins by the arm and dragged him on, but it was impossible to make him understand that we were in earnest. I had the Smith and Wesson in my pocket and I kept fingering it and wondering what I'd do if they put up a fight for it or ran, and wishing to God they'd do one or the other. I knew if they did run for it, that I'd never fire on them. Hawkins wanted to know was Noble in it, and when we said yes, he asked us why Noble wanted to plug him. Why did any of us want to plug him? What had he done to us? Weren't we all chums? Didn't we understand him and didn't he understand us? Did we imagine for an instant that he'd shoot us for all the so-and-so officers in the so-and-so British Army?

By this time we'd reached the bog, and I was so sick I couldn't even answer him. We walked along the edge of it in the darkness, and every now and then Hawkins would call a halt and begin all over again, as if he was wound up, about our being chums, and I knew that nothing but the sight of the grave would convince him that we had to do it. And all the time I was hoping that something would happen; that they'd run for it or that Noble would take over the responsibility from me. I had the feeling that it was worse on Noble than on me.

IV

At last we saw the lantern in the distance and made towards it. Noble was carrying it, and Feeney was standing somewhere in the darkness behind him, and the picture of them so still and silent in the bogland brought it home to me that we were in earnest, and banished the last bit of hope I had.

Belcher, on recognizing Noble, said: 'Hallo, chum,' in his quiet way, but Hawkins flew at him at once, and the argument began all over again, only this time Noble had nothing to say for himself and stood with his head down, holding the lantern between his legs.

It was Jeremiah Donovan who did the answering. For the twentieth time, as though it was haunting his mind, Hawkins asked if anybody thought he'd shoot Noble.

'Yes, you would,' said Jeremiah Donovan.

'No, I wouldn't, damn you!'

'You would, because you'd know you'd be shot for not doing it.'

'I wouldn't, not if I was to be shot twenty times over. I wouldn't shoot a pal. And Belcher wouldn't — isn't that right, Belcher?'

'That's right, chum,' Belcher said, but more by way of answering the question than of joining in the argument. Belcher sounded as though whatever unforeseen thing he'd always been waiting for had come at last.

'Anyway, who says Noble would be shot if I wasn't? What do you think I'd do if I was in his place, out in the middle of a blasted bog?'

'What would you do?' asked Donovan.

'I'd go with him wherever he was going, of course. Share my last bob[3] with him and stick by him through thick and thin. No one can ever say of me that I let down a pal.'

'We've had enough of this,' said Jeremiah Donovan, cocking his revolver. 'Is there any message you want to send?'

'No, there isn't.'

'Do you want to say your prayers?'

Hawkins came out with a cold-blooded remark that even shocked me and turned on Noble again.

'Listen to me, Noble,' he said. 'You and me are chums. You can't come over to my side, so I'll come over to your side. That show you I mean what I say? Give me a rifle and I'll go along with you and the other lads.'

Nobody answered him. We knew that was no way out.

'Hear what I'm saying?' he said. 'I'm through with it. I'm a deserter or anything else you like. I don't believe in your stuff, but it's no worse than mine. That satisfy you?'

Noble raised his head, but Donovan began to speak and he lowered it again without replying.

'For the last time, have you any messages to send?' said Donovan in a cold, excited sort of voice.

'Shut up, Donovan! You don't understand me, but these lads do. They're not the sort to make a pal and kill a pal. They're not the tools of any capitalist.'

I alone of the crowd saw Donovan raise his Webley to the back of Hawkins's neck, and as he did so I shut my eyes and tried to pray. Hawkins had begun to say something else when Donovan fired, and as I opened my eyes at the bang, I saw Hawkins stagger at the knees and lie out flat at Noble's feet, slowly and as quiet as a kid falling asleep, with the lanternlight on his lean legs and bright farmer's boots. We all stood very still, watching him settle out in the last agony.

Then Belcher took out a handkerchief and began to tie it about his own eyes (in our excitement we'd forgotten to do the same for Hawkins), and, seeing it wasn't big enough, turned and asked for the loan of mine. I gave it to him and he knotted the two together and pointed with his foot at Hawkins.

'He's not quite dead,' he said. 'Better give him another.'

Sure enough, Hawkins's left knee was beginning to rise. I bent down and put my gun to his head; then, recollecting myself, I got up again. Belcher understood what was in my mind.

'Give him his first,' he said. 'I don't mind. Poor bastard, we don't know what's happening to him now.'

I knelt and fired. By this time I didn't seem to know what I was doing. Belcher, who was fumbling a bit awkwardly with the handkerchiefs, came out with a laugh as he heard the shot. It was the first time I heard him laugh and it sent a shudder down my back; it sounded so unnatural.

'Poor bugger!' he said quietly. 'And last night he was so curious about it all. It's very queer, chums, I always think. Now he knows as much about it as they'll ever let him know, and last night he was all in the dark.'

Donovan helped him to tie the handkerchiefs about his eyes. 'Thanks, chum,' he said. Donovan asked if there were any messages he wanted sent.

'No, chum,' he said. 'Not for me. If any of you would like to write to Hawkins's mother, you'll find a letter from her in his pocket. He and his mother were great chums. But my missus left me eight years ago. Went away with another fellow and took the kid with her. I like the feeling of a home, as you may have noticed, but I couldn't start another again after that.'

It was an extraordinary thing, but in those few minutes Belcher said more than in all the weeks before. It was just as if the sound of the shot had started a flood of talk in him and he could go on the whole night like that, quite happily, talking about himself. We stood around like fools now that he couldn't see us any longer. Donovan looked at Noble, and Noble shook his head. Then Donovan raised his Webley, and at that moment Belcher gave his queer laugh again. He may have thought we were talking about him, or perhaps he noticed the same thing I'd noticed and couldn't understand it.

'Excuse me, chums,' he said. 'I feel I'm talking the hell of a lot, and so silly, about my being so handy about a house and things like that. But this thing came on me suddenly. You'll forgive me, I'm sure.'

'You don't want to say a prayer?' asked Donovan.

'No, chum,' he said. 'I don't think it would help. I'm ready, and you boys want to get it over.'

'You understand that we're only doing our duty?' said Donovan.

Belcher's head was raised like a blind man's, so that you could only see his chin and the top of his nose in the lantern-light.

'I never could make out what duty was myself,' he said. 'I think you're all good lads, if that's what you mean. I'm not complaining.'

Noble, just as if he couldn't bear any more of it, raised his fist at Donovan, and in a flash Donovan raised his gun and fired. The big man went over like a sack of meal, and this time there was no need for a second shot.

I don't remember much about the burying, but that it was worse than all the rest because we had to carry them to the grave. It was all mad lonely with nothing but a patch of lantern-light between ourselves and the dark, and birds hooting and screeching all round, disturbed by the guns. Noble went through Hawkins's belongings to find the letter from his mother, and then joined his hands together. He did the same with Belcher. Then, when we'd filled in the grave, we separated from Jeremiah Donovan and Feeney and took our tools back to the shed. All the way we didn't speak a word. The kitchen was dark and cold as we'd left it, and the old woman was sitting over the hearth, saying her beads. We walked past her into the room, and Noble struck a match to light the lamp. She rose quietly and came to the doorway with all her cantankerousness gone.

'What did ye do with them?' she asked in a whisper, and Noble started so that the match went out in his hand.

'What's that?' he asked without turning round.

'I heard ye,' she said.

'What did you hear?' asked Noble.

'I heard ye. Do ye think I didn't hear ye, putting the spade back in the houseen?'[4]

Noble struck another match and this time the lamp lit for him.

'Was that what ye did to them?' she asked.

Then, by God, in the very doorway, she fell on her knees and began praying, and after looking at her for a minute or two Noble did the same by the fireplace. I pushed my way out past her and left them at it. I stood at the door, watching the stars and listening to the shrieking of the birds dying out over the bogs. It is so strange what you feel at times like that that you can't describe it. Noble said he saw everything ten times the size, as though there were nothing in the whole world but that little patch of bog with the two Englishmen stiffening into it, but with me it was as if the patch of bog where the Englishmen were was a million miles away, and even Noble and the old woman, mumbling behind me, and the birds and the bloody stars were all far away, and I was somehow very small and very lost and lonely like a child astray in the snow. And anything that happened to me afterwards, I never felt the same about again.

1   Three.
2   Some 7 miles north-east of Galway City.
3   Last shilling (about 5p).
4   Shed.

L.A.G. STRONG
from L.A.G. Strong, *The Garden* (1931)

The Garden is set in Dublin in the early years of the twentieth century. Dermot, whose family has settled in England, returns for his summers from English public school to Dublin to visit his grandfather and develops an affection for the city. Here in this extract the Great War has just broken out, drawing to a close the Edwardian summer for Strong's generation. L.A.G. Strong (1896–1958), son of Anglo-Irish parents, was born in Plymouth in Devon and, like Dermot, spent his summers in Ireland. A friend of Yeats at Oxford in the early 1920s, he went on to write fiction and verse as well as biographies of Thomas Moore and Synge and critical studies of Joyce and others. For his verse see *The Body's Imperfection* (1957, p. 706) below. For an interesting discussion between Frank O'Connor and L.A.G. Strong on the topic 'Should Provincial Writers Stay at Home?', see *The Listener*, 16 March 1938.

from Chapter 34

Dermot's public school summers passed very quickly. His last, the summer of 1914, found him preparing hard for a scholarship at Oxford. Before he came over, it had been arranged that he should go in twice a week to Trinity, to work with one of the classical tutors there. He was to have a week's grace before starting; and during this week broke out the War.

The War at first made little serious impression in Ireland. It appeared in the light of a great sporting event, and the vast majority found themselves instinctively on England's side. In a Dublin theatre, a day or so after the declaration, three parts of the audience rose to their feet at 'God Save the King'. There are those who argue that prompt and confident handling of the situation by England then could have saved much bloodshed and much bitterness: but the Government behaved as if it expected to be struck, a dangerous attitude towards animals, men, and countries. Be these things as they may, the War did not disturb the holiday season. No one had at first believed it possible. At the baths, where Dermot spent his mornings, men talked of it idly: yet no one but an Englishman foresaw the certainty. When it did break out, there was no rush to volunteer. The adventurous spirits were all busy on their own, those who loved England preparing to resist her in the North, those who disliked Ulster running guns[1] in the South. Like a boy who sees his acquaintance squabbling in a corner of the playground, they did not think the fight was serious, and looked to England to polish off her adversary inside a few weeks. News of a great naval victory, heavily placarded in the streets, confirmed this mood. Mr Gray was jubilant.

'If it's true,' he proclaimed impressively at lunch, 'it means the Germans will never dare show their faces on the sea, for dread of the British Navy.'

Unfortunately, the news was not true: but every one took the line that it well might have been, and, anyway, that it would probably be true next week: and went on as before. It was this attitude, a sort of laziness, which kept hundreds of Irishmen from running to the colours. They did not dream that it was necessary. Neither side, indeed, those for England or those against, realized for some months the meaning of what had happened.

So all went peacefully as usual, and Dermot in due course visited Trinity, and was shown to the rooms of Mr Stacpoole O'Hara. Mr Stacpoole O'Hara did not at all fit in with Dermot's idea of a famous classical scholar. He looked as if he had come to mend the gas. His face, sad and dispirited, was ornamented by a drooping and draggled moustache. He wore a bowler hat a size too big for him, which was only saved from descending over his face by his ears, stuck out at right angles with the effort of supporting it. Over his chest and stomach he wore a dirty white waistcoat, with a gold watch chain. His suit was stained and shabby, the ends of the trousers frayed, one elbow shiny, and the other through. He wore canvas shoes. Dermot could not at first believe that he had found his man: but the pencil which scored his Greek prose was authoritative enough, and it did not take a dozen sentences to show him that he was going to learn a great deal. Mr O'Hara affected a contempt for Oxford scholarship.

'I'll endeavour ta instil a little elementary accuracy inta ya,' he said, 'though maybe that'll be doing ya harm in the eyes of Oxford?'

And he proceeded to instil a great deal. Mr O'Hara had no highfalutin' notions about the classics. He approached them strictly on business. The cynical ease with which he extemporized the suavest and most admirable Latin verses confounded Dermot. Mr O'Hara would sit back, picking his teeth, and dictate a version which more than held its own with any Dermot had met. Verses were Dermot's especial line, and he left Mr O'Hara a sadder and wiser scholarship candidate. He was allowed to choose his own English, so there was no trickery about it. Mr O'Hara, who seemed to have about as much poetry in him as a louse, could hash up a convincing version of anything.

'Ah,' he said, when Dermot shyly asked the secret, 'Sure, verses is a trick': and that was all that could be got out of him.

Dermot worked hard that summer. He got up early, and sat at a queer uncomfortable little table in Granny's drawing-room. He liked his new tutor from the first, and came to feel an affection towards him. O'Hara, too, evidently liked him, for often after the hour's work he would put on his monstrous bowler and walk with him to the tram.

One afternoon, as they were going out, they met a figure which instantly reminded Dermot of a clerical Dr Johnson. Mr O'Hara stood aside, showing every symptom of the greatest respect.

'Good afternoon, Doctor,' he said.

The figure received the greeting very graciously. He peered quickly at Mr O'Hara, and quickly at Dermot.

'This is Mr Gray, a young English pupil I have,' said Mr O'Hara, with a wave of his dirty hand. Dermot was so used to the mistake, by now, that he did not bother to correct it.

The figure bowed slightly.

'How do you do,' he said grimly. Dermot stammered an answer. Susceptible always to personal quality, he realized that he was in the presence of some one very considerable indeed.

Dr Johnson looked away for a moment down the street.

'Will this war end soon?' he said abruptly.

'Ah, sure, I hope so.'

'Well' — with a glance up at the big stone front of Trinity — 'I hope you're right.'

And he passed on inside.

'Who was that?' asked Dermot, in awestruck tones.

'That,' replied Mr O'Hara, well pleased, 'is Doctor Mahaffy.'[2]

'Oh!' Dermot turned round, to stare once more after the famous figure.

When, a few days later, Mr O'Hara interrupted the course of an unseen to point out the window and say 'There goes a scholar you may have heard mentioned — Robert Yelverton Tyrrell',[3] Dermot felt that his cup was full. Of all people on the earth, scholars and writers held his passionate admiration. He had discovered Synge, and went regularly to the Abbey Theatre. Con had been the unlikely introducer to this literary pasture: he always went there to hear the dialect, and, except for this, could not at all distinguish the plays from those he saw elsewhere. It was a great disappointment to Dermot that Mr O'Hara did not share his enthusiasm.

'Did ya ever see any good thing come out of a place the like o' that?' he inquired derisively: and, 'Ah, they've learned a pretty little trick. Take any old plot of any old play, and dress it up with a bit of talk from a pub back-door.'

Dermot looked at him, more shocked than he would admit.

'I think there's more in "The Playboy of the Western World" than that,' he said.

'There is,' retorted his tutor. 'A lot of sham poetry no corner-boy would soil his tongue with.'

And Dermot, who was not yet hardened to differing in worship from those he liked, rode home in the tram hurt and dejected. He knew Mr O'Hara was wrong; he hated to be laughed at for his enthusiasm: and he felt that, by not being able to silence and out-argue him, he had let down the cause in which he believed. More than anything, he resented the unspoken suggestion that he liked the Abbey because he was an Englishman and a tourist. It was desperately hard, to get himself accepted as Irish. Even his friends at the baths all thought of him as an Englishman.

'I'll tell you what you are,' said one of them one morning, as they stood up and stretched, preparatory to swimming their length to the pier and back. 'You're a quack Irishman.'

It was not meant unkindly, but it stuck: Dermot never forgot it. He swam savagely, and beat his traducer by many yards: but the barb could not be washed out of his flesh. 'Begawrah!' Old mockeries rose up from the past. 'The quack Irishman.' These obstinate brutes wouldn't have it that any one was Irish who didn't live there all the year round, and go to school there. You might prove what you like, argue what you like, do what you like. They just grinned at you. They were like Mr O'Hara, grinning at Synge and the Abbey. A derisive grin: that was Dublin's answer to most things, whether it understood them, or, as was more likely, it had not the remotest idea what they signified. Even Con was like that: he jeered at what he could not understand. Perhaps even that was one better than Uncle Ben, who wouldn't allow that it existed. Dermot raged to himself, sitting on the draughty covered top of the tram, scowling at the big houses in their stately gardens, and the long stretch of road to Monkstown.

Though he did not know it, he, and all the world, were seeing them for the last time. Not the outward shell of them, but all that gave them meaning. The eighteen-sixties had received their death-blow. Even during the ten or twelve years Dermot had known them, they were dying. The slow pool in the river was breaking up; the eddies found themselves in the grip of the current; they and their circling lumber began to move, and were borne away. The entrapped flotsam, which in the pool seemed so solid and large, was swept into the main current, scattered, made insignificant, and disappeared. Four years more, and those big houses would be empty, staring in mournful incomprehension through their broken windows at an altered world. Old newspapers would blow about the trim drives, the orchards would be desolate and broken, the tennis lawns dishevelled patches of rank grass. The broad peace and security of an old order would be gone. When Bessie and Dermot's mother had clapped the front door of Walmer Villa after them for the last time, and faced one another on the doorstep to say good-bye, the spirit of the old times fled from its last stronghold, the little alcove in the corner where the books had been, where the dark outline of the cuckoo clock showed still upon the wall paper: the corner sacred to Tom Moore, to Dickens, and to Vousden: the corner comforted by the shade of Henry Francis Lyte, and composed by the shade of James Mongan, Barrister-at-Law. That period died. The period enshrined at Delgany survived and suffered change. 'Are ye right, there, Michael, are ye right?'[4] sang Uncle Ben: and 'When M'Carthy took the floor at Enniscorthy'. These survived: but 'The Private Still', which he also sang, was swept down the river with the years that owned it. The city Dermot had just left was to suffer change and violence. Gunfire and shells were to scar its face: Eithne was to come back ten years later, and search every stone of Middle Abbey Street to find, not the old offices, but some hint of where they stood. These tram rides in to Trinity were Dermot's last

chance to see a city which was about to disappear: 'dear old, dirty Dublin', now no more, the despair of all who lived in her, whom all that knew her regret in their hearts, while thankful for the order and cleanliness that has taken her place: the old kindly, garrulous, amusing slattern, the old witty stinking fishwife, drink-sodden, paralysed in will, driven off, battered, given a black eye, kicked out, by a young hard-eyed woman who set to work scrubbing and setting things to rights: tottering off down the quayside of men's memories, with a hiccup and a joke flung over her shoulder, disappearing into the rain and the darkness, her uncertain steps growing fainter and fainter: lovable, disgusting, butt for the sentimentality of men remembering old days, forgetting old discomforts: a tub, a target, a smell of porter: a rotten social system: ignorant, credulous, gossiping, with fits of drunken generosity: dear old dirty Dublin, staggering away to limbo down the cobbled quays. The world is well rid of her: peace to her soul.

But Dermot, clanking away towards Sandycove, knew none of this. He saw, dimly, that there were changes: he appreciated the true meaning of the alcove by the cuckoo clock: but the city he had left, a city whose spirit was expressed for him in the jeers of Mr O'Hara, seemed full of inimical health, in no wise on her deathbed. He loved Dublin, because Dublin usually meant Middle Abbey Street, the Abbey, and rides with Con. This new aspect distressed him. He did not recognize the old lady when she suddenly stuck out her tongue.

1   A reference to the Howth gun-running incident in 1914.
2   John Pentland Mahaffy (1839–1919) was a leading classicist who in 1914 became Provost of Trinity College Dublin. Wilde and Gogarty were among a generation who came under his influence.
3   Robert Yelverton Tyrrell (1844–1914), classical scholar, appointed Registrar at Trinity in 1904.
4   Humorous song by Percy French (1854–1920) about the West Clare Railway.

JOHN HEWITT
from *The Listener*, 18 May 1932

John Hewitt (1907–87), one of Ireland's leading and most prolific twentieth-century poets, was born in Belfast and educated at Queens University Belfast. His work is characterized by clarity of perception and a Presbyterian radical's conviction. He is the most articulate spokesperson for an Ulster identity that is not tied to the narrow ground (as Ulster is sometimes called). As he once remarked, he was 'by birth an Irishman of Planter stock, by profession an art gallery man, politically a man of the Left'. Here is an early poem celebrating the non-native condition of those who now live in Ireland.

IRELAND

We Irish pride ourselves as patriots
and tell the beadroll of the valiant ones
since Clontarf's[1] sunset saw the Norsemen broken . . .
Aye, and before that too we had our heroes:
but they were mighty fighters and victorious.
The later men got nothing save defeat,
hard transatlantic sidewalks or the scaffold . . .

We Irish, vainer than tense Lucifer,
are yet content with half-a-dozen turf,
and cry our adoration for a bog,
rejoicing in the rain that never ceases,
and happy to stride over the sterile acres,
or stony hills that scarcely feed a sheep.
But we are fools, I say, are ignorant fools
to waste the spirit's warmth in this cold air,
to spend our wit and love and poetry
on half-a-dozen peat and a black bog.

We are not native here or anywhere.
We were the keltic wave that broke over Europe,
and ran up this bleak beach among these stones:
but when the tide ebbed, were left stranded here
in crevices, and ledge-protected pools
that have grown salter with the drying up
of the great common flow that kept us sweet
with fresh cold draughts from deep down in the ocean.

So we are bitter, and are dying out
in terrible harshness in this lonely place,
and what we think is love for usual rock,
or old affection for our customary ledge,
is but forgotten longing for the sea
that cries far out and calls us to partake
in his great tidal movements round the earth.

1   At the Battle of Clontarf in 1014 Brian Boru became
     King of Ireland after defeating the Leinstermen and the
     Norse.

AUSTIN CLARKE
from Austin Clarke, *The Bright Temptation* (1932)

Austin Clarke (1896–1974), poet, playwright and novelist, was a prolific writer. His published work spans six decades from *The Vengeance of Fionn* (1917) to *Tiresias* (1971) and *Collected Poems* (1974). Here is an extract from a beautifully written novel set during the Viking era at a monastery on the banks of the Shannon. Aidan, a student, finds his bright temptation in the shape of Ethna, a mysterious woman he encounters while straying beyond the bounds of his school. Clarke, his sights set also on contemporary puritanical Ireland, draws on several ancient stories and imagines Aidan and Ethna perhaps travelling along the same mountain path as the legendary lovers Diarmuid and Grania.

Chapter Sixteen

'It must have been deserted many years ago.'
    'I think so too, Aidan — long, long before we were born.'
    They had wandered aimlessly around the cell, pushing their way through the rainy brambles. They stood again in front of that oratory of rough, weather-bound stone. They tried to peer under the low entrance, but it was half closed by loose rock and green tufts. The lintel and the broad jambs that supported it were of black shale. A path of narrow flagstones led from the cell, but grass or groundsel had grown between them, and the little path was almost hidden. Enclosed by a low wall of loosely piled stones was a wilderness of briar and treacherous plants.
    'There must have been a herb garden here, too.'
    Ethna stooped to pull a spray of bog-mint.
    'But the fragrance has gone.'
    Higher than their shoulders was the wilderness of fierce weeds that follow where the spade has been. There the penitential nettles were still bedded, heavy-seeded, ready with grey stings to beat down the flesh-rising which hermits fear. The humble, absolving

dockleaf was hidden, but the thistles in barbaric companies were ranked above the companionable burrs. There, there, the purple-flowered fleabane, the plant against itch, had flourished, coarse leafage of the piss-mire shrub, piss-a-beds with those gaudy tops no children pull, beggar's wort and the viper's bugloss. In that wilderness of briars, of lurking stings, frail blossoms were unsmocked. Simples that had been brought from Europe to ease, to heal, were hidden amid the fierce tenantry that triumphs over man's eviction; they were lost as gentle thoughts in the harshness of religion, they were unthriven as kindness in the celibate minds of Ireland.

'O, let us go,' said Ethna, for that loneliness had oppressed her.

They hurried along the aged flagstones. On each side, sudden and alive, the hooks of the long briars leaped at them, the treacherous nettles lay in wait, the burrs tried to follow them. Flustered and unhappy they pushed their way among stings and scratches. They leaped back from showers of raindrops, and coming through the gap in the wall found themselves outside again.

They stood there in the drizzle and the pale chill of evening. The far circle of rocks was still lighted by foam of the cataract. They heard near by the desolate sound of the waters.

'We are astray, Aidan. This is not the right glen.'

He stared at the brown stream rushing down among the rocks into the mist below.

'What are we to do?' he asked, his voice tired and troubled.

The thought of that holy glen was gone and the night was near. They turned to each other that they might find comfort in word, in look. Chill and damp they kept as near each other as they could, feeling the warmth of kindness.

'Let us go this way,' she pointed, anxious to escape from the wilderness around that lonely glen.

They walked across the green turf and came under mountain cliffs, fissured and overhanging from the mist. Great drops still clung to the pale bright fern and hart's-tongue growing above the rifts. They looked at them idly as they went by.

They came to a few small dens under the rocks. Aidan drew back, hearing a faint sound from one of them.

'It may be a fox,' she whispered. 'Often they take shelter in the hills when they are driven from the earthings.'

Great rocks, many of them more than ten feet in height, were scattered around them. They made their way among the rocks, looking here and there as if they had lost something, but did not know what it was. Their hands were chill, their faces pale in the twilight with anxiety. Suddenly Ethna hurried around a boulder close under the mountain cliff. Aidan heard her calling him; her voice was happy, excited again. He hurried forward, and met her running back to him, her cheeks glowing with excitement, her eyes bright.

'What is it?' he wondered.

'I have found a cave, a wonderful cave!' Catching his arm, she brought him around the boulder.

There, formed by a shelving slope of rock and protected by the boulder around which they had come, was a lofty narrow cave. They could see right into it, for it was not very deep. The rounded walls of the cave were bronze-coloured, its ground was strewn with dry russet bracken. There dwelt a pleasant twilight, and they looked in with awe and quiet.

Not with more surprise had holy Aeneas and his laymen come upon a cave among island hills at nightfall, and, dividing the barbecue, sat around the camp fire talking of the miracles they had known.

Ethna was the first to break that silence, for with a little cry of pleasure she hurried into the cave. He heard her bare feet rustling in the bracken. A moment later she came out smiling.

'It must have been a shelter for shepherds,' she said; 'and guess what I have found in it?'

'I don't know,' his eyes were full of wonder.

'A whole pile of bogwood and peat. We shall be able to have a fire and dry our clothes.'

She saw his bewildered face, and laughed as she searched in the inner pocket of her petticoat. She drew out a tiny fire-box of ornamented silver.

'You think of everything, Ethna,' he cried in admiration, as she opened the lid and showed him not only the little flint and steel but a leaf of dried coltsfoot.

'Hurry, bring out some of the wood. We will light our fire under the boulder.'

Happy again, he ran into the cave. He filled his arms with wood. He brought it out and piled it under the boulder.

Their heads were together, so eager they were, as she uncurled little shavings with the knife from a core of soft wood. Delicately, with skilful fingers, she set those little springes in which the spark might be caught and nourished. Lightly she prepared the tiny paths along which the first fledgling of flame would flutter. Eagerly, with bated breath, they watched, as the first spark leaped, and afraid of existence was gone. Quickly, lightly she worked, and at last the tinder had yielded. On her own sweet breath she reared that weakling, and soon it was strong. Together they led the flame, enticing it along every splinter, anxious when it feared to jump. But soon it could venture by itself, and when they heard the first crackle, saw the pleasant curl of smoke, they turned each other with joyful faces.

'It is safe now,' he cried, content to watch as she fanned it, drawing the flame together with skilful touches.

'We must have some stones to build around it,' she exclaimed. Aidan hurried around the boulder. Here, there, he found stones and came running back with them, carrying as many as he could at a time.

Ethna was in the cave, but the fire was crackling and busy. It was gossiping to itself. It was not lonely or afraid of the night.

Aidan was gazing entranced at that merry glow when she came out of the cave again. She helped him to place the stones around it. She drew the turves about the fire.

'How lovely it is!' they exclaimed together, as they watched the flame slowly conquer the smoke. When the timber was glowing and the turf had blossomed, they warmed their hands.

Ethna, like a dainty fire-keeper, busied herself about that flame, here, there, with quick touches, drawing it together until the glow was constant and secure.

They were happy, who at a stroke had defeated the mist. As they watched that merry redness they were no longer afraid of the darkness.

How often in the woods even fierce men are at peace when they are stayed by night around a camp fire! The harp begins then, and story-telling, while the flame is crossing the stile of darkness. On lonely rocks, too, clerics that have been boat-wrecked on their way to the western Paradise cower over a few twigs that the very crows have forgotten, and turn their hoods against the strange sky.

But in the little houses of Ireland, at all times the fire is served upon the earth. At night, when all are in bed, the housewife hides the seed of the fire under ash that she may find it again at dawn. When summer grows chill and every glen is closed by rain, the fire stirs under its ash, remembering the winter, and by a turn of the bellows-wheel it brings stool and bench nearer.

Small wonder that Aidan and Ethna hovered around that fire, busy as their own awakened shadows, turning to each other with little exclamations of delight. Ethna had spread out the cloak. When it was dried she turned to him.

'We must not catch cold, Aidan.' Little mists were rising from their clothes as the fire grew warmer. 'We shall have to change.'

'But what can we do?' he answered anxiously, feeling the damp sleeves of his jacket.

'You can wrap yourself in this,' she said, as she gave the cloak to him. 'See, it is quite dry inside.'

'But what will you do?'

'I am all right.' She smiled, seeing his doubting face when she turned to go into the cave.

'Do not be long,' he called, and he heard the soft sounds of her undressing inside the cave.

Aidan hesitated beside the fire and stared out at the darkening glen. One day he had strayed from Cluanmore with Declan and two other students. They had been tricking together beside the river when he had suddenly slipped from a branch. They had pulled him out before he was more than waist-deep in the water. It was a chill day with a high wind blowing, and he had to sit in his shirt for an hour while his clothes were drying on the branch.

He felt his wet jacket again, and slipped it off. He was more comfortable in his shirt-sleeves. Wrapping the cloak around him he let down his trews, which were soaking at the knees. He wound the cloak around his waist like a double kilt, and sitting down by the fire, tucked his toes in it.

The night was dark outside. He watched the shadows stirring under the boulder. He could hear no sound from the cave and he grew uneasy. Why was Ethna so long? What could she be doing? The fire was too warm, so he moved back. He made himself comfortable by leaning against the rocky side of the cave. He waited there shyly, following the coursing of the little flames.

His ear had caught a faint rustle in the bracken. He turned around quickly. His breath stopped and he gazed in astonishment at Ethna, as though she were a spirit.

Her thin arms were glimmering and white as she came through the shadows of the cave. The pale-green silk of her underdress clung without fold to her limbs and was shapen around her breasts where she had gathered it with the jewel. The silk was stayed as she walked by rich embroideries and gold hems that hid her little feet. Guarding each temple were the gold capitals of her hair, for she unfastened the thin metal fillet and combed out her curls, so that the least had not escaped. Every strand, finer than the lines a scribe interwinds or traces in coil and spirals, was shining, was lost in its own meaning. Over her bare shoulder the floating circles of her hair were hazier.

Before Aidan could speak she had come into the firelight. She was mortal again, yet lovelier than he had seen her before: flushed and restless as if she had been caught in the very phoenix-nest of light. In her hair hurried the three colours of gold, the fair and the ruddy gold, changing, encircling one another at every turn of her head. Soft shadows were busy around her, so that her cheeks were blushing, were dimpled, as she hid herself with her fingers from his gaze.

'We must eat now,' she said softly, bending over the satchel. But when they sat opposite each other she looked up again. She seemed to that poor scholar, as she leaned between the shadow and flame, to be mingling with them. Her ear glittered beneath those curls she had loosened and drawn back; her very fingernails were flashing as she ate.

She looked at him as if she would speak. Her eyes were wide, shining; they met his timidly and yet for so long a time that their hands, both half-way to their lips, stopped, hesitated and had lost the way!

He let his hand fall by his side again. There was no longer any taste in food, for his mouth was dry. Only his eyes were sure, and every sense was in them.

'I cannot eat,' he exclaimed..

'Nor I,' she murmured, her hand as idle as his. For indeed their eyes were no longer avoiding each other. Their glances, that had defeated one another all day, were at peace and had found their true resting-place. Enspelled by each other they hovered; they gazed with a steadfastness that fulfilled itself and yet was daring. Softly, softly, the discovery of their own presences by that fire drew them towards one another, so that every moment might have been the next and the moment after, the one before.

Gently as they gazed at one another, her hands had stolen out to his, and in a dream he felt that warm yet light touch, so timid it seemed to be pleading with him. In that touch he felt for the first time the joy of the human senses; pure as a tune that must return to the note from which it started, subtle as knowledge that lends itself, thought by gentle thought, to the mind, all first, rare and delicate things. That touch was so vivid yet uncertain it might have been winged, ready at the least stir to take flight.

Those young, gentle creatures were steadfast in their gaze, one with dark curls flung back and wondering lips, the other leaning forward, eager-browed, so brightly headed the night might draw her back for envy. They had found in each other the knowledge which alone could content them. Happy are they who are hidden at last in that imagination against which the dark creed of renunciation, the cruelty of middle age, is vain. Eager as light that brings back all at day and is ever delighted were they who might have seen everything anew and named it again. They were lost in that imagination which poetry alone remembers, for it is in joy that we discover ourselves.

Not more steadfastly in the western Eden, whither they had fled beyond sin, beyond the bright weathering of suns, could Connla and Adam's daughter have eyed each other than those two youngsters in that mountain cave.

The misted night had closed in. Less than the reach of a holy crook was the ring that firelight had drawn around the pair. They were filled by their gaze between flame and shadow. They did not hear any more the waterfall sounding in the darkness. They did not hear the rain that stirred newly in the night outside.

Their eyes were still with treasury, but their lips were troubled, trembling into words. Aidan was the first to break that silence, for his mind was in light. A joy swept over him that was at the same time knowledge, so that he could scarce see her as he cried:

'I love you, Ethna! I love you!'

But her voice had already mingled in his: her words had run eagerly to his words, for they awaited that moment to meet his voice.

With that sharp, sweet cry, so long delayed, her hands were clinging to his, her words were quicker. Her words would outrun his, they would hide shyly in the very camp of his love before he could surprise them.

'How can I tell you, Aidan? But I must, I must! I looked from the window at Lisnacara, I saw you on the fairgreen of our house, and I gave you my heart. And, O, darling, that instant I knew that I loved you! And I hated those men who were cruel to you, for I could not help you. But something told me that I must follow you, that I must find you.'

All, all was suddenly clear to him, for his thought had raced and outsped her thought.

'It was you, Ethna, all the time — and I did not know. You whispered to me in the wood, you freed me, you ran with me through the night. You bent over me, smiling in the darkness. I knew that you smiled though I could not see you, thinking that you were a soul from heaven.'

'It was only I, Aidan.' The whisper came faint and sweet as that night in the wood when she had freed him.

'If I had but known, Ethna . . .'

'But that night you were so weary, so dazed, I pitied you, and, and I dared not tell you, before I left. But I knew you were safe until morning.'

'And you risked all that danger for me?' he marvelled.

Her face was lifted so that shadow slanted between her brow and chin. In her eyes was racing the wild light of all those stories she had known as she bent towards him laughing.

'Aidan, dear Aidan, why should I not have hurried to the little wood of Monarua? Had not Lasara followed the lonely track of wheels so far, she found but a black ring where a camp fire had been and so was lost? Had not Grania gone farther than I when she hurried from the slope of Tara that night long ago — and were there not many braver than I?'

'And yet you came in all that darkness and rain for my sake.'

'I knew every twig, Aidan, in that wood, and my maid, who loves me and would do all for me, did she not help me to escape from the house, hurrying with me half-way down the shorter path? I ran past the hunting-mounds where often I had sat and sewn at day. I was happy when I saw the firelight in the wood, for I knew that I would find you.'

'And when I saw you first at morning, Ethna, I knew that I must follow you. But I was bewildered, I was lost in shyness.'

'I too was shy, Aidan, though I did not pretend that I was. I only knew that we must fly from the danger near us. In the hills we would be safe, we would speak to each other. But it was not the same as that night in the rain, for when I looked at you, you looked away. And I thought: "He does not care, he does not see me!" And after that I kept saying to myself, but so softly you could never hear: "He does see me, but he, too, is as shy as I am." And I told you of Diarmuid and Grania, but all the time I was thinking of you and me.'

'Ethna, Ethna, I know that I loved you all the time, even before I had ever seen you, for that night in the wood, when I heard your voice, I was suddenly happy again, and all had changed. I think I must have known you long before; I heard your voice calling me at Cluanmore. O, could that be possible?'

He was full of wonder at his own thought, but her voice was eager and triumphant.

'It must be true, Aidan, for when I saw you I knew you at once, as if indeed we had been fostered together, and I had lost and suddenly found you again. I was happy because of that, all the time. Even last night when we were in our cells, I was so happy that I could have cried. And do you remember to-day, when we came to the precipice? O, I knew then, and truly, that you loved me.'

Their eyes were full of joy and wonder as they met again, for they were stilled in that long gaze. They did not hear the waterfall sounding in the glen. They did not heed the darkness that was less than a staff's length from them. They had been suddenly surprised: they must yield silently, softly to the love-spell that was drawing them towards each other.

He saw her thin lips tremble a little as though they sought his. But the next moment he did not see them, he did not see her, for their mouths had met. So light and chill was the touching of their lips they scarce knew that they had kissed for the first time.

It was but a moment until he saw her again, but she, too, was silent, pondering, as if the chill, light touch of their lips had surprised her, too, by its strangeness.

But she had come nearer, she had rested her head upon his shoulder. Surely in each other's arms they might find what had evaded them, find a comfort that would content them; so they sighed with contentment, for they knew that in that kiss, though it had been strange and chill, they passed an invisible barrier.

'And we will always be together now, Aidan.'

They were so close that they need only speak in little murmurs, in words they could share together; so close that they could not see each other unless they stirred. But as they stared wonderingly into the fire, they might still be mingling their glances.

'And I am glad that we are lost.'

'And I too,' he exclaimed.

'And . . . Aidan.'

'O, what is it, Ethna?' he cried urgently, hearing the anxiety in her voice.

'If we had never told each other, if we had parted!'

'O, that could not be, that could not be!'

But they clung to each other, trembling at the thought.

'I would have gone back every night to the little wood at Monarua, hoping I would find you again, Aidan.'

'And I would have come back there, I know that I would have found my way there despite every danger.'

'But we will not think of that now, for we are happy, much happier than last night.'

They were silent for a long time as they watched the firelight with drowsy eyes, and the darkness outside the cave. She stirred at last from his arm.

'Aidan,' she whispered, 'are you asleep?'

'I think I almost was,' he exclaimed with a start.

'Let us cover the fire. I shall not be afraid now in the darkness,' she said softly.

Their eyes met with awe, for they suddenly knew that they were alone together in the night.

But the next moment she had left him and run to the fire. She had gone from his arms, but he was trembling with a strange excitement. In every sense of his there was left a sweetness. His eyes followed her as she stirred about the fire. He would hide her in his eyes for the darkness. But the very flame was racing his sight, it wanted to keep her too, to hide her from him. He saw the dim silk cling to her pointed breasts and slender limbs as she turned. She went down on a knee, and the glow came to her cheek; it fled to her fingers as she drew the fire into itself with a twig. She was as beautiful again as when she had come from the cave to him. His eyes were quicker, for the glow was fading, it lingered for a moment in her curls, it hid with her in darkness. She was a murmur, a rustle in that darkness.

It might have been that night in the wood when first he had been aware of a gentle presence near him. But he knew that it was Ethna; he knew that she loved him. He had but to lift his hand and in the darkness he would find her.

She was near him. She was whispering as she knelt down.

'Where are you, Aidan?'

'I am here.'

His voice was urgent. His hand had touched her bare arm in the darkness. Laughing, trembling, they had found each other again. He opened wide that cloak; heavy, dark, it had known but violence and flight. With eager fingers he spread in the night its great fold, so that in a second she was safely within and beside him.

'I am so cold,' she murmured as he leaned over to draw the cloak around her.

'You should have let me cover the fire,' he cried reproachfully.

'No, no. Put your arms around me, Aidan; I shall soon be warm again.'

She nestled like a child in his arms with a sigh of contentment. Her little feet had found his, and her very toe-nails were touching them, sharply, one by one. He thought how she had clung to him on the edge of the precipice that evening, and he was filled again with tenderness. He could scarcely believe that she was in his arms — she who had run and danced so quickly. She was still now but for that little trembling.

'I am making you cold, Aidan?'

Her voice was anxious.

'O, no.'

He would wrap her in warmth, he would give her all his own so that she should not tremble any more. He would not have cared, had he been shivering in the rain, so that she should not feel the chill of night. Tenderly, reverently he held her, that she might feel warm again. The chill was going from her cheek, and vaguely, in a dream, he felt the loveliness of warmth return, mingle, between them. He scarcely breathed as he felt a dim stirring — the rise and fall of her breasts. It was like the lost music of drowsiness to which the mind must yield, and once more his thoughts could scarcely believe it was true. She had felt that too, for she murmured sleepily:

'It is all like a dream, Aidan.'

She moved her head against his shoulder until she had made herself comfortable again. She drew his arm around her more closely so that she might really know he was there.

But even as her own arm stole around him in trust and her limbs touched his, the happiness which had filled Aidan was suddenly gone. A strange alarm filled him, for the evil from which he had escaped was coming back, and he knew instinctively that the evil was now in himself. He had heard the clerical students at Cluanmore talking among themselves at times. He had heard them tell how the hermits had to fight a terrible evil in themselves, how they plunged waist-deep into nettles, into briars, to keep their flesh from rising. This terrible change was happening to him against his will, and he was in a torment of shame. His pulse was beating fast, his brow was throbbing, perspiring. Cold shivers ran through his spine, and yet the fiery evil became worse. He was overwhelmed by secret shame and ignorance of what was attacking him.

She knew that he was miserable, for he heard her drowsy voice beside him:

'What is the matter, Aidan, are you not happy? Can you not go to sleep?'

'O, no. I am very happy.' But he knew he was lying, even as he had lied that morning at the cromlech, when she had held his chin and with cool fingers stretched back the skin from that little cut to heal it. He was lying to her again, and he hated himself.

'I am glad, for I am happy, too. Indeed I was almost asleep.'

She nestled closer to him.

'But you are burning, Aidan. You are in fever.'

She leaned over him as though she were trying to see his face. He was glad of the darkness, as he felt her palm, gentle and cooling, on his brow.

'I hope you have not caught cold!' she cried anxiously.

'No, no. I am all right, Ethna.'

His cheek was burning with shame. Her innocent alarm filled him with misery and self-reproach.

'You are quite sure?'

Her voice was still doubtful.

'Quite sure.'

He knew in the dark that she was smiling and content again.

'And you promise me you will go to sleep, Aidan?'

'I promise, Ethna.'

She had believed him, but he hated himself. She turned, and in a few minutes he knew by her gentle breathing that she was asleep. Faintly as air in a hollowed reed, he heard that gentle breathing — it was the little music of her spirit. He loved her, and only she could save him from that evil which was in him. He was not worthy of her, but he would fight that evil, and never again, now that he knew of it, would it conquer him. He would love her as she loved him. He lay staring into the darkness, making resolutions. His arm had gone to sleep, but he dared not move it lest he disturb her sleep. For hours he lay there staring into the darkness, listening to the unquiet rain outside the cave.

W. B. YEATS
from W. B. Yeats, *The Winding Stair and Other Poems* (1933)

A group of poems which convey something of Yeats's moods in old age. 'Coole Park and Ballylee, 1931', first published in *Words for Music Perhaps and Other Poems* (1932), is a moving tribute to Lady Gregory, his friend and patron for thirty years. At the end of her life Yeats spent long periods of time devoted to her care. In 'Byzantium' he takes up the theme as announced in 'Sailing to Byzantium', stung into doing so by his friend Sturge Moore's accusation that the 'goldsmith's bird in the fourth stanza is as much nature as man's body'. 'Remorse for Intemperate Speech', first published in *The Spectator* in November 1932, underlines the emotional pressure always just below the surface of Yeats's best verse. 'Crazy Jane Talks with the Bishop' is Yeats rejuvenated by salacious thoughts.

COOLE PARK AND BALLYLEE, 1931

Under my window-ledge the waters race,
Otters below and moor-hens on the top,
Run for a mile undimmed in Heaven's face
Then darkening through 'dark' Raftery's[1] 'cellar' drop,
Run underground, rise in a rocky place
In Coole[2] demesne, and there to finish up
Spread to a lake and drop into a hole.
What's water but the generated soul?

Upon the border of that lake's a wood
Now all dry sticks under a wintry sun,
And in a copse of beeches there I stood,
For Nature's pulled her tragic buskin on
And all the rant's a mirror of my mood:
At sudden thunder of the mounting swan
I turned about and looked where branches break
The glittering reaches of the flooded lake.

Another emblem there! That stormy white
But seems a concentration of the sky;
And, like the soul, it sails into the sight
And in the morning's gone, no man knows why;
And is so lovely that it sets to right
What knowledge or its lack had set awry,
So arrogantly pure, a child might think
It can be murdered with a spot of ink.

Sound of a stick upon the floor, a sound
From somebody[3] that toils from chair to chair;
Beloved books that famous hands have bound,
Old marble heads, old pictures everywhere;
Great rooms where travelled men and children found
Content or joy; a last inheritor[4]
Where none has reigned that lacked a name and fame
Or out of folly into folly came.

A spot whereon the founders lived and died
Seemed once more dear than life; ancestral trees,
Or gardens rich in memory glorified
Marriages, alliances and families,
And every bride's ambition satisfied.
Where fashion or mere fantasy decrees
We shift about — all that great glory spent —
Like some poor Arab tribesman and his tent.

We were the last romantics — chose for theme
Traditional sanctity and loveliness;
Whatever's written in what poets name
The book of the people; whatever most can bless
The mind of man or elevate a rhyme;
But all is changed, that high horse riderless,
Though mounted in that saddle Homer rode
Where the swan drifts upon a darkening flood.

BYZANTIUM

The unpurged images of day recede;
The Emperor's drunken soldiery are abed;
Night resonance recedes, night-walkers' song
After great cathedral gong;
A starlit or a moonlit dome disdains
All that man is,
All mere complexities,
The fury and the mire of human veins.

Before me floats an image, man or shade,
Shade more than man, more image than a shade;
For Hades' bobbin bound in mummy-cloth
May unwind the winding path;
A mouth that has no moisture and no breath
Breathless mouths may summon;
I hail the superhuman;
I call it death-in-life and life-in-death.

Miracle, bird or golden handiwork,
More miracle than bird or handiwork,
Planted on the star-lit golden bough,
Can like the cocks of Hades crow,
Or, by the moon embittered, scorn aloud
In glory of changeless metal
Common bird or petal
And all complexities of mire or blood.

At midnight on the Emperor's pavement flit
Flames that no faggot feeds, nor steel has lit,
Nor storm disturbs, flames begotten of flame,
Where blood-begotten spirits come
And all complexities of fury leave,
Dying into a dance,
An agony of trance,
An agony of flame that cannot singe a sleeve.

Astraddle on the dolphin's mire and blood,
Spirit after spirit! The smithies break the flood,
The golden smithies of the Emperor!
Marbles of the dancing floor
Break bitter furies of complexity,
Those images that yet
Fresh images beget,
That dolphin-torn, that gong-tormented sea.

REMORSE FOR INTEMPERATE SPEECH

I ranted to the knave and fool,
But outgrew that school,
Would transform the part,
Fit audience found, but cannot rule
My fanatic[5] heart.

I sought my betters: though in each
Fine manners, liberal speech,
Turn hatred into sport,
Nothing said or done can reach
My fanatic heart.

Out of Ireland have we come.
Great hatred, little room,
Maimed us at the start.
I carry from my mother's womb
A fanatic heart.

August 28, 1931

CRAZY JANE TALKS WITH THE BISHOP

I met the Bishop on the road
And much said he and I.
'Those breasts are flat and fallen now,
Those veins must soon be dry;
Live in a heavenly mansion,
Not in some foul sty.'

'Fair and foul are near of kin,
And fair needs foul,' I cried.
'My friends are gone, but that's a truth
Nor grave nor bed denied,
Learned in bodily lowliness
And in the heart's pride.

'A woman can be proud and stiff
When on love intent;
But Love has pitched his mansion in
The place of excrement;
For nothing can be sole or whole
That has not been rent.'

---

1 Antoine Raiftearaí (1779–1835), a blind Gaelic poet
   who was much admired by Yeats and Lady Gregory.
   Raftery had written: 'There is a strong cellar in Ballylee.'
2 Coole Park, Lady Gregory's estate, adjacent to Thoor
   Ballylee. Yeats imagines the underground stream flowing
   past his Tower emerging in the lake at Coole.
3 Lady Gregory.
4 Robert Gregory, Lady Gregory's son, killed in a flying
   accident in 1918.
5 Yeats wanted this pronounced in the older more Irish
   way with a single beat.

BLANAID SALKELD
from Blanaid Salkeld, *Hello Eternity!* (1933)

Blanaid Salkeld (1880–1959) was born in what is now Pakistan (her father was in the Indian medical service). Most of her childhood was spent in Dublin. She married an Englishman in the Indian civil service in Bombay and when she was 28 returned to Dublin where she joined the second company of actors at the Abbey Theatre. *Hello Eternity!*, a slim volume of verse, contains several gems all glistening under a well-chosen title for the volume as a whole. The rhetorical use of punctuation in 'Invitation' is especially interesting.

INVITATION

I wish to see you on an important matter. —
How important? — Infinitely so.
Come to the Zoo to see the seal with me —
One fine Sunday we could go.
What shall I do, now? . . . What shall I do, else?
I will be good, I will not look at you;
I will walk briskly with you and talk the same.
O, don't you think the fine weather and the wild
        things
Would keep even me one day without blame? . . .
I came to you with no tale of a lost kingdom,
But ignorant of honours, innocent of joy.
You kept me wondering from winter to winter:
You will not leave me for thought to destroy?
Naked to reality . . . that were a calamity;
But the seal has magic, things tragic to abolish —
Rearing his serpent bulk's grey interrogation
Up over water, for the last gold to polish;
Rolling those kindly eyes — dark, full, and loving
        eyes —
Holding bare breast to day's last illumination . . .
Dreamer Rodj, passing me — passing, and passing
        me —
Hear what I am asking you: pause to my will.
Set in desolation's cell I shall dwell after that,
Dreaming of a Sunday, and our joy in the seal.
You will agree, it is an important matter —
Most important — infinitely so:
That you see the Zoo and the seal with me?
Some fine Sunday we could go.

HERE

Because I have foresworn in your regard
My pleasant senses that could hint of sin, —
This City is our living-room wherein
You move and are not lost. High-flung and hard
The walls that gird us — for my great reward.
The rest are but love's furniture, a thin
Pretence of being. You and I are kin
To none else but each other, single-starred.

Well, you are hid. You hang your golden head,
Or to our azure ceiling lift your brow.
The soul thinks largely, free of heart and sense.
Our thoughts converse. Come here, the meal is spread;
We'll sit down to our supper-table now,
And later sleep fresh sleep of innocence.

ENCYCLOPAEDIA

Edelweiss in wild cold air at high rock ledge,
Is wrapped from harsh wind's edge —
And stores up moisture,
In woolly vesture.

Along sea's surface polished dolphin glides;
Babe dolphin slides,
Suckled at breast.
They draw calm breath —
Lean supple side
Against slant tide.

Dolphin-milk, flower-vest of wool;
Water's abyss, or dizzy steep's crag edge:
World wonderful . . .
To grow here, is a privilege.

PATRICK SLATER
from Patrick Slater, *The Yellow Briar* (1933)

The Yellow Briar was a popular Canadian-Irish novel in the 1930s. Couched as an autobiography, it tells the story of Patrick Slater who in 1847 at the age of nine was left an orphan on the streets of Toronto, his father having died on the journey from Ireland and his mother not long afterwards succumbing to plague along with 863 other poor Irish who died in Toronto that year. In this extract he recalls a lively wake he attended.

Jimmie's Speeding

The fat grey squirrel scolded me down into a sweet beulah land on that bright September morning. Everybody about the Marshall farm seemed cheerful and friendly-like. And I had my name in the family pot. Assuredly things are picking up for any Donegal lad if his share of the food comes on the table without the asking.

The log shanty the Marshall boys had put up in the fall of 1838 was now an L-shaped lean-to, in front of which stood a stout log house with a large kitchen occupying most of the ground floor, a general purpose room in which the family meals were laid. In a nook across the end of it stood a stone fireplace with pots and hooks for the cooking utensils. On the hearth glowed the embers of a fire, petted and tended with as constant a care as the sacred flame in an ancient temple. Lucifer matches[1] were things known of in 1847 — but as expensive luxuries, and not for the likes of a backwoods farmer. A dead fire in that hearth at the break of day was an awkward household incident, as provoking, indeed, to the good woman as butter that would not come in a churning. Woe's me! The day's work on the entire farm marked time waiting the slow-seeming return of a pail galloped off to a neighbour's to borrow live coals for the makings. So to this day we say to a neighbour who refuses a chair that it must be a firing he has come for.

By the kitchen window stood the spinning wheel and near at hand the reel; and, hour in and hour out, could be heard on the wide, yellow floorboards the steady tap-tap of a woman's feet as she moved backward and forward, humming softly to herself and spinning out the yarn, which, as a perfect life would be, was an even spun thread alike throughout. The outer door of the kitchen had a lower and upper section, as stable doors have to-day, a most handy wrinkle about a farm house, the lower section keeping the little children in and the pigs and poultry out; while the upper section might swing open to let freshness and sunshine in. On the inside of the door was a heavy iron latch wrought by the local smith. Fastened to it was a leather thong; and in the daytime this whang was poked out through a hole, that the door might be opened from the outside. At night, it was pulled in; and everything was snug and secure. A latch string hanging out was the token of hospitality in those days. Behind the kitchen lay two small rooms in constant use by Mr and Mrs Marshall and the small children; but one of these chambers was dolled up with wondrous feather ticks and blossomed out on the occasion of a visit as the spare bedroom that stood idle awaiting a guest. An open stairway led from the kitchen to the loft, which was partitioned into sleeping quarters.

The Marshall farm was indeed a grand place; but, somehow, I felt like a visitor there. In a home there is regular work for one to do and plenty of it. And I was just loafing. After a few days, Mr Marshall had a friendly chat with me. He told me I was a good little boy and that I was very welcome. But it would be better for me, he said, if we could find a place for me with a family who needed a boy, having none of their own, and where I would have a home to grow up in.

'You know, Patrick,' he said to me, 'your folk were Catholics, and I think you would perhaps be better living in a good Catholic family, where you would get religious instruction in the home from your own kind of people and grow up into a fine man.'

He told me he never faulted the Catholics himself, seeing his own people had once been Catholics for many hundred years. A fellow, he told me, should have a sincere faith and stick hard to it. If folk started shifting round from one faith to another they often ended by having no religion at all. And perhaps there was salt in his conversation.

He mentioned a man by the name of Martin Kelly who lived in an Irish-Catholic settlement down in Albion Township. The family were childless and hailed from County Longford. The man was a cobbler; and he had heard they were looking for a young boy. The place might suit me first rate. He would enquire further about it; and we might drive over some afternoon and see them. And the end of it was I went over to live with Martin Kelly — him with the game leg.

At Mr Kelly's place, my day's work started with the dawning; and I wrought as hard as any sinner for the living I got there.

'Hi! there, Paddy! Spring tapper! tumble too!' Martin would shout, meanwhile sprawling in comfort himself on a settle-bed[2] forninst[3] the hearth, and beating an old pan with a stick he always kept convenient to his hand. That brought me down promptly from the loft, to quicken into a blaze the smouldering embers on the hearth, and then hie away through the bush, calling: 'Co-boss! co-boss!' in search of the cows.

The Kelly house was a small log cabin standing in an acre lot on the third line of Albion, near the corner they now call Lockton. Close at hand behind the house stood the stable with a pig-sty leaning against it. From a neighbour, Martin Kelly got the grass for two cows; and it was my duty, night and morning, to bring them up from the clearing, to milk them, and then drive them back again. The cows had no fancy for the long tramp, and one morning I caught the old one, Lizzie, the sly devil, hiding on me with her neck stretched out on the ground to keep her bell from tinkling. She was a drying stripper; and the other one, the O'Leary heifer, was also slackening in her milking. I thought it would have been all right for me to take the pail down and milk the cows in the pasture; but Mrs Kelly had a strongly set notion to the contrary, she, good woman, being wishful to see all the milk they were giving. So up to the milking baween[4] I drove the Kelly cows twice daily; but I had a wooden sap-trough hidden back in the bush that helped matters out with my belly. Martin declared that bush to be infested with milk snakes that sucked the cows' teats.

'*Och hone, Machree* (Alas, my heart),' cried Mrs Kelly, 'Jimmy O'Leary's curse, it is, that is drying up the milk of the cows!'

All the day long, Martin sat by the kitchen window, bending over his last. His mouth had a deft way of gobbling handfuls of pegs with a curious clicking snap; and the quantities of snuff he took kept his nostrils as dusty as any man's at a clover thrashing. Yet I never knew him to sneeze. To his customers, Martin's breath always smelled strongly of blarney. A very agreeable man he was with the women and children who came to his place on business errands. They did be glamored with his taking ways.

'Ah! faith, Mrs Wray,' he would wheedle, squirting out a great spittle of tobacco, 'it is a grand job I'll be

making of the brogues. Dennis will be pleased with them.'

'And what will you be charging the man?' Dennis's wife would enquire.

'Well now, Mrs Wray,' Martin would confide to her after a weighty pause, 'if it were any other woman's husband, I would be charging him one and six. But seeing it is you, and a fine girl, indeed, you were — and from the Golden Vale[5] itself — faith, all I'll be charging the man is a mere nothing at all, at all — just the trifle of two bits.'

'Ah! you old devil!' the woman would cry out with a sarcastic tilt of her nose. 'None of the neighbours be knowing at all, the wonder of the world how you do be keeping a roof over your head — you do be giving away so much!'

After I had been knocking around Martin Kelly's a few days, he sent me down one afternoon on an errand to James O'Leary's farm on the next line. Mrs O'Leary was as plump as a sack of grain; and the jolly good-natured woman gave me a piece of bread with a thick spread of sugar. Her fat face puckered and cracked in a smile like a potato bust in roasting.

It was the very day after I was there that a tree fell on Mr O'Leary and killed the poor man entirely. With his sons he had been back chopping in the bush. In falling a maple the tree lodged on the limb of a large elm. The boys left it suspended thus, and went on to chop a tree standing near at hand. The thud of their next fall was so great that it shook the maple free; and it fell, crushing their father to death.

Of course, there was a wake at the O'Leary's. The wind of the news was enough for me; and, with the fall of night, I slipped over to the house of the dead to see the doings.

'*Gand e tha hawn, Pat* (how are ye Paddy)?' the widow asked me kindly as I went into the house.

'*Slanger a manugouth* (all right thank'ee),' I replied, doffing my caubeen.[6]

Then down on my knees I went before the body. My heart was fluttering like a little bird in your hand with fear Jimmie would jump out at me; but I let on to be saying my prayers.

The rough pine coffin lay lidless on a bed in the corner of the ground floor of the cabin. It was a sedate and mournful meeting. With faces long drawn out, and solemn looking as owls, the men stood lining the walls, uttering pious sighs and, betimes, scratching their polls. The women mourners sat on benches, and every few moments one of them would run her fingers through her hair and shriek out: 'Oh o o oh oh! . . . Poor Jimmie!' Her body rocked to and fro as the wail gradually died down. At the end of it she would fold her shawl again across her breast. Betimes of the wailings, the men talked of crops and kine;[7] and glancing now and again toward the body, in low guttural tones, made complimentary comments on the life, ancestry and character of the deceased. On entering the room of the dead, the mourner first knelt before the bier to say a prayer for Jimmie's soul; and then a drop of drink was taken. There was tobacco, snuff and whiskey in plenty. Pipes passed from mouth to mouth, and, in the flickering light of the candles, a haze hung in the room like the mist over a ploughed field in the plover season.

A queer little old woman came in, all bent double; and after she knelt before the body, she swallowed a tidy drop of poteen, and was given the honour of a chair. Someone thrust a freshly-filled pipe into the ashes and passed it to her.

'God and Mary bless his soul and the souls of all the dead,' she sighed; and seated in comfort at her ease, she withdrew like a turtle within the privacy of her shawl.

The woman was short and dusk like a cold winter's day; and she needed a pitch-dark night to make her good-looking. Mary Doyle went about the countryside taking care of sick folk and minding babies. She got a trifle for attending funerals because she was a special hand at keening. Devil a pinch of sorrow had she in her heart for the dead man in his going. The face of her was enough to sour a crock of cream.

The keen, which is a mournful ballad, has four feet to the line as sung in the Irish tongue; and it is only a diversion that makes an end to the number of its verses. Its general purpose is to excite pity, compassion, or hate; and to my mind it is specially effective when used to curse and blast the cruel and treacherous English. In spirit, both the keen and the wake itself are utterly and entirely pagan. And why Mother Church let such rites get mixed up with the burial of her Christian dead is beyond me. The Irish keen speaks only in terms of unqualified grief; it has a deep and hopeless melancholy at its basis; and finds no place for the joy of the blessed resurrection. In a low tone Mary Doyle began the funeral song:

Cold and silent is his bed!
Och hone!

Damp is the dew of night,
The sun brings warmth
And dries the dew,
But his heart will stay cold,
Machree!

Cold and silent is his repose!
He is gone forever.
He will return no more.
Cold and silent is his grave!
Och hone, Machree!

The keener clapped her hands and rocked her body back and forth as the dirge stretched itself out in weird and melancholy repetition. One after another the other women joined in as a chorus; and their long drawn-out, sobbing wails and piercing shrieks rent the night air. Between whiles, a pipe passed along the benches from woman to woman. The creatures were enjoying themselves immensely.

The keening died down as a fresh group of neighbours arrived and attended to their religious duties. Among them was my boss, Martin Kelly, who had enjoyed a lift getting over with his bad foot. The corpse and Martin were boys from the same parish in the old sod. Yet for years back they had never met but the din of their noise destroyed the place, and, in parting, their sticks usually shook at one another. Only recently there had been a bitter riot between them touching the price of the O'Leary heifer.

Martin rose from his knees with tears of sorrow in his eyes. There was something truly affecting as the man stood, nodding his head solemnly, looking long into the face of his dead neighbour.

'Ah me!' said Martin Kelly, 'Jimmie O'Leary was a fine man. Ah! Jimmie makes a pretty corpse!'

Then placing his rough hand on the pallid forehead, Martin sobbed out:

'Ah! cold as death is Jimmie's head!'

There are old cart-wheel tracks in every man's brain, and his thoughts slide into familiar ruts without his let or hindrance. As Martin turned sedately from the bier to take his place in the crowd, the old fire sparkled in his eyes, and, with a toss of his head, he exclaimed:

'But colder was the living heart of him!'

Pete O'Leary, the dead man's eldest son, leapt in the air like a goat. In the wink of an eye, Martin and he were hoisting their chins into each other's faces. Pete, who was a chunky young fellow, made a smart pass at Martin's jaw, but failed to make connections. Martin was an older man and a cripple; but he was slim and long bodied. Quick as a flash, he brought his skull down crack, with a vicious butt hitting Peter's face on the line where the eyebrows grow. It was a knockout puck he gave him; and down Pete went to kiss the floor boards.

Trailing his bad foot and coat along the floor, Martin shouted:

'May the devil sweep all the O'Learys together!'

Pete's wife threw her shawl off and rushed screaming to put the prick of youth into the pride of the O'Learys.

'Holy Mary! Pity my heart to be married to a good-for-nothing-at-all!' the woman exclaimed as she set upon the wounded man and belaboured him onto his feet again.

The O'Learys did then be letting manners into Martin Kelly with their sticks; and shellalaghs and wallopers came smartly into action. The women bawled themselves hoarse directing the fray, and men were running about with cracked pates, themselves roaring out they were killed entirely. A fat, little fellow on our side was giving blood like a stuck pig; but the O'Leary faction also had plenty of blood to drink. It was a roaring ruction; and everyone felt afterwards it had been highly complimentary to the corpse we were waking.

The arrival of Jimmie's cousins bearing an elegant pig hot-roasted from a spit made a sudden diversion that broke up the brawl. Four men were bearing the savoury beast on a litter; and the way of the procession was lit by lanterns made by sticking candles through broken bottoms into the necks of bottles. My heart beat like a watch with the delight of the smell of the roasted pig. I sat down on my heels, and kept a cat's eye on the victuals. Meat and drink were ordained by custom and convenient at a wake. Knives, platters, and the salt stood ready at hand to welcome to the board fatty messes that gladdened the hearts of the mourners into merry talk and stirred up cheerful music as the singers bolted the cracklings and tender meats, and sucked sweet juices out of the bones of the beast. After gorging ourselves, we wiped our hands on an old towel that was passed around; and to comfort themselves, the men had another drink anon. I curled myself up out in the stable and had forty winks.

In the heel of the evening there came from the direction of the whiskey barrel and its dipper the thumbing and squeaking of a fiddle. An old musician scraped away on one or two strings of a fiddle as battered looking as himself. His lean body swayed with his bowing; but the stamp of the man's foot made him the master of the house. Dickens a man or lass in the cabin but began shovelling away with heel and toe! It was Jimmie's daughter Molly that led the spree. What a hub-bub and a clatter! It was enough to hoist the corpse out of the coffin to hear them dancing a four-hand reel.

'Oh o o o oh! Poor Jimmie! Is he so soon forgotten?' wailed Mary Doyle, who was too old and stiff for dancing.

Faith no! Poor Jimmie was not forgotten. The coffin was fetched forward and leaned bolt upright in the chimney corner that the corpse might be observing what was going forward in his honour. The girls bobbed curtsies to the dead man as they tripped by; and some of them asked Jimmie for a dance. Every now and then, he was offered a drop of the hard stuff. During the course of the evening, Martin kneeled down before the fire to redden his baccy pipe by thrusting it into the ashes; and made final peace with his fellow countryman by sticking the stem of it into the dead man's mouth. They made a night till morning of it — what with drinking, keening, dancing and other tastes of diversion.

By the dawning, the mourners felt cold and stiff, after spending the night seeing Jimmie through the first heel of his long journey; and they were not wishful to burn up much daylight over the dead body of a man who had been called out of the way into glory. As a final mark of respect, bright and early in the morning, the coffin was hoisted on the stout shoulders of the men, who, changing off as the miles slowly went by, bore it at long last, and by the longest route, to its grave up the steep boreen at Centreville. Most willingly did the whole countryside augment the toils of their tired bodies by trailing and straggling after the bier, wailing and chanting their griefs.

During the wake, a tall young girl had sung us a keen of the Croppey Boy in the time of The Troubles, which brought tears to every eye. The deep hood of her dark-blue cloth cloak flung back on her shoulders bared the raven-black hair of a Munster peasant girl. She sobbed the boy's farewell to his old mother as he told her:

> At the siege of Ross did my father fall.
> At Gorrie, my loving brothers all.
> I'm going to Wexford to take their place
> To free my nation and my race.

Then, soft and low, she followed the tramp of his brogues to the church to make his confession to the holy father. The tune seemed to take the natural gait of its subject:

> The boy, he entered the empty hall,
> What a dismal sound makes his light footfall!
> In a silent chamber, dull and bare,
> Sat a vested priest in a lonely chair.
> The youth, he knelt to tell his sins,
> At confiteor deo, the youth begins,
> At mea culpa he struck his breast,[8]
> In broken murmurs, he tells the rest.
> 'I have no hatred against living things,

I love my country above my king.
So bless me, father, and let me go
To die if God has ordained it so.'
The priest said naught. . . .
With sparkling eye, the youth looked up.
The robes fell off, and in scarlet there
Sat a yeoman captain in a fiery glare.

Her voice rose in a wail as the keener told of the heavy-booted soldiers dragging the youth from the altar to be hanged and quartered.

A dirge like that was as a tuning fork in my youth to strike the true note of Irish feeling. In the heart of every Celt whose bare feet had trod on Irish soil there was a hatred of English rule — not of England herself, mark you, nor of the English people — but a black-hearted hatred of English rule in Ireland so sizzling hot that it scalded the blood streams. The causes of Ireland's bitterness and woes may be arguable, of course; but not with any profit by men of Irish blood whose emotions have been aroused. Nothing then is, but feeling makes it so. (Holy, jumping, suffering cats! — old John Trueman would say to that.) In my boyhood days, every emigrant ship brought to Canada the seeds of poisonous, ancient strifes; and it is the merciful providence of God that such wickedness and bigotry failed to thrive long in the sweet, virgin soil of the most tolerant country in the world. But in their short day they made an ineffaceable impression on the pioneer life of the Ontario countryside.

Revolt was endemic in Ireland throughout the last century, and English rule was maintained in the island by the constabulary and the military — ably assisted by the esculent, farinaceous tuber. The police and the garrisons cowed the spirit of the populace, and an ill-balanced diet of potato weakened the resisting power of the Irish Celt.

Yet in view of the large Celtic Irish migration into British America in those days, it must be apparent to everyone that Canada could not have survived as a British kingdom had it not been for the sincere loyalty that grew up in Irish Catholic hearts toward the struggling young country and her English queen. The truth is man is capable of a divided allegiance. He can be an Irish rebel and at the same time a loyal Canadian subject of the king. As with the saddle-bags of the Methodist circuit rider, there may be two separate compartments to the heart. In Canada, and as a Canadian, Paddy Slater never found any trouble loving both his country and his king; because in Canada, the Crown stands for nothing less than the decent and respectable public ideals of a kindly-minded and democratic people.

Of course, it was old Victoria Regina that brought this mystery to pass. For sixty odd years the great queen reigned as truly a goddess in the minds of the small children along the St Lawrence and its great feeding lakes as had the divine Mother Hathor, in old time, in the minds of the Egyptians of the Upper and Lower Nile. Regina was all powerful, and she dwelt remote as a goddess should. The queen stood for every possible sort of goodness. The children prayed for her, and in diverse ways we prayed to her. Her face may not have launched a thousand ships, but it was the face on every coin a youngster clutched in his gummy fist; and in her name, and for her honour, generations of Canadian children had a glorious holiday that ushered in the most beautiful season in the Canadian year. Her transcendent virtues may have been a myth, but as true as God's word, they firmly established a great kingdom in America, which circumstance, as you'll admit, is one of the wonders of the world. Young folk nowadays read snippy things about the old queen, but old men and women will feel what I am trying to say!

So it happened that for years Paddy Slater was a stout Tory in Canada, and, in the man's day, a great supporter was I of Old John A.[9] Yet I found on several occasions that my loyal sentiments would not stand a sea voyage. No sooner did Paddy's feet feel the cobbles of Dublin and the cry of caller herring strike his ears, than the heart of the man gave a leap like a goat, and he became an Irish patriot and rebel again. *Boie yuhd, ma vourneen! Erin go bragh!* (Victory to you, my darling! Ireland for ever!) Putting a conquered people to the sword — as the Jewish Jehovah sometimes directed — would have been a deal more kindly than crowding dispossessed peasants into rough ground like Connemara or obliging an entire subject race to live through centuries in the dire misery and carking poverty of the mud tenant hovels of Ireland. The pig, the barley, the butter and the poultry went to the towns and to England to pay the rent; whilst the Irish tenant lived on potatoes and a drop of the buttermilk. Even the year of the great famine saw a heavy export of food products from Ireland. To the great mass of the inhabitants, the British crown has always stood in Ireland for misrule and oppression.

Ireland has made an unhappy front-shop window display of British rule. However, let us thank heaven the arrogant Irish Celt has never had a chance to found an empire for himself — and disgrace us all entirely.

1 A friction match made of wood tipped with inflammable substance. In common use by the 1830s in Britain.
2 A bed that folded up into a wooden seat during the day.
3 Opposite.

4   A bawn was an enclosure where cows were milked
    (P.W. Joyce).
5   The vale extending north from Clonmel in County
    Tipperary.
6   An old shabby cap (P.W. Joyce).

7   kine: Cows.
8   I confess to God; through my fault — Latin phrases
    associated with confession.
9   John A. Macdonald, Prime Minister of Canada,
    1878–91.

JOHN O'HARA
from John O'Hara, *BUtterfield 8* (1934)

John O'Hara (1905–70) was born in the Pennsylvania coal-town of Pottsville
(Gibbsville in his novels) into a middle-class family. O'Hara, like Jimmy Malloy in the
extract which follows, was an Irish-American doctor's son, class-conscious and in some
respects non-assimilable into middle-class American society. O'Hara's fiction, always
telling in its observations of social differences, overlaps with the best traditions of
American journalism. *BUtterfield 8* is based on a New York murder and focuses on a
guilt-ridden alcoholic suicide Weston Liggett, at the centre of a café society on the
edge of things, no longer young. Here in this extract Jimmy accompanies Isobel
Stannard to a speakeasy off Broadway. A film was made of the novel in 1960 by Daniel
Mann with Elizabeth Taylor as Gloria Wandrous.

'Well, I can see why you didn't want me to see the
ending first. I never would have stayed in the theatre if
I'd seen that ending. And you wanted to see that
again? God, I hope if you ever write anything it won't
be like that.'

'I hope if I ever write anything it affects somebody
the way this affected you,' said Jimmy.

'I suppose you think that's good. I mean good
writing,' said Isabel. 'Where shall we go?'

'Are you hungry?'

'No, but I'd like a drink. One cocktail. Is that
understood?'

'Always. Always one cocktail. That's always
understood. I know a place I'd like to take you to, but
I'm a little afraid to.'

'Why, is it tough?'

'It isn't really tough. I mean it doesn't look tough,
and the people — well, you don't think you're in the
Racquet Club, but unless you know where you are, I
mean unless you're tipped off about what the place
has, what its distinction is, it's just another speakeasy,
and right now if I told you what its distinguishing
characteristic is, you wouldn't want to go there.'

'Well, then let's not go there,' she said. 'What is
peculiar about the place?'

'It's where the Chicago mob hangs out in New York.'

'Oh, well, then by all means let's go there. That is,
if it's safe.'

'Of course it's safe. Either it's safe or it isn't. They
tell me the local boys approve of this place, that is,
they sanction it, allow it to exist and do business,
because they figure there has to be one place as a sort
of hangout for members of the Chicago mobs. There's
only one real danger.'

'What's that?'

'Well, if the Chicago mobs start shooting among
themselves. So far that hasn't happened, and I don't
imagine it will. You'll see why.'

They walked down Broadway a few blocks and then
turned and walked east. When they came to a highly
polished brass sign which advertised a wigmaker,
Jimmy steered Isabel into the narrow doorway, back a
few steps and rang for the elevator. It grinded its way
down, and a sick-eyed little Negro with a uniform cap
opened the door. They got in and Jimmy said: 'Sixth
Avenue Club.'

'Yessa,' said the Negro. The elevator rose two
storeys and stopped. They got out and were standing
then right in front of a steel door, painted red, and
with a tiny door cut out in the middle. Jimmy rang the
bell and a face appeared in the tiny door.

'Yes, sir,' said the face. 'What was the name again?'

'You're new or you'd know me,' said Jimmy.

'Yes, sir, and what was the name again?'

'Malloy, for Christ's sake.'

'And what was the address, Mr Malloy?'

'Oh, nuts. Tell Luke Mr Malloy is here.'

There was a sound of chains and locks, and the door was opened. The waiter stood behind the door. 'Have to be careful who we let in, sir. You know how it is.'

It was a room with a high ceiling, a fairly long bar on one side, and in the corner on the other side was a food bar, filled with really good free lunch and with obviously expensive kitchen equipment behind the bar. Jimmy steered Isabel to the bar.

'Hello, Luke,' he said.

'Howdy do, sir,' said Luke, a huge man with a misleading pleasant face, not unlike Babe Ruth's.[1]

'Have a whiskey sour, darling. Luke mixes the best whiskey sours you've ever had.'

'I think I want a Planter's punch — all right, a whiskey sour.'

'Yours, sir?'

'Scotch and soda, please.'

Isabel looked around. The usual old rascal looking into a schooner of beer and the usual phony club licence hung above the bar mirror. Many bottles, including a bottle of Rock and Rye, another specialty of Luke's, stood on the back bar. Except for the number and variety of the bottles, and the cleanliness of the bar, it was just like any number (up to 20,000) of speakeasies[2] near to and far from Times Square. Then Isabel saw one little article that disturbed her: an 'illuminated' calendar, with a pocket for letters or bills or something, with a picture of a voluptuous dame with nothing on above the waist. The calendar still had not only all the months intact, but also a top sheet with '1931' on it. And across the front of the pocket was the invitation. 'When in Chicago Visit D'Agostino's Italian Cooking Steaks Chops At Your Service Private Dining Rooms', and the address and the telephone numbers, three of them.

By the time she had studied the calendar and understood the significance of it — what with Jimmy's advance description of the speakeasy — their drinks were served, and she began to lose the feeling that the people in the speakeasy were staring at her back. She looked around, and no one was staring at her. The place was less than half full. At one table there was a party of seven, four men and three women. One of the women was outstandingly pretty, was not a whore, was not the kind of blonde that is cast for gangster's moll in the movies, and was not anything but a very good-looking girl, with a very nice shy smile. Isabel could imagine knowing her, and then she suddenly realized why. 'Jimmy,' she said, 'that girl looks like Caroline English.'

He turned. 'Yes, she does.'

'But the other people, I've seen much worse at Coney Island,[3] or even better places than that. You wouldn't invent a story just to make an ordinary little place seem attractive, would you?'

'In the first place, no, and in the second place, no. In the first place I couldn't be bothered. In the second place I wouldn't have to. People like you make me mad, I mean people like you, people whose families have money and send them to good schools and belong to country clubs and have good cars — the upper crust, the swells. You come to a place like this and you expect to see a Warner Brothers movie, one of those gangster pictures full of old worn-out comedians and heavies that haven't had a job since the two-reel Keystone Comedies. You expect to see shooting the minute you go slumming — '

'I beg your pardon, but why are you talking about you people, you people, your kind of people, people like you. *You* belong to a country club, you went to good schools and your family at least *had* money —'

'I want to tell you something about myself that will help to explain a lot of things about me. You might as well hear it now. First of all, I am a Mick. I wear Brooks clothes[4] and I don't eat salad with a spoon and I probably could play five-goal polo in two years, but I am a Mick. Still a Mick. Now it's taken me a little time to find this out, but I have at last discovered that there are not two kinds of Irishmen. There's only one kind. I've studied enough pictures and known enough Irishmen personally to find that out.'

'What do you mean, studied enough pictures?'

'I mean this, I've looked at dozens of pictures of the best Irish families at the Dublin Horse Show and places like that, and I've put my finger over their clothes and pretended I was looking at a Knights of Columbus[5] picnic — and by God you can't tell the difference.'

'Well, why should you? They're all Irish.'

'Ah, that's exactly my point. Or at least we're getting to it. So, a while ago you say I look like James Cagney —'

'Not look like him. Remind me of him.'

'Well, there's a faint resemblance, I happen to know, because I have a brother who looks enough like Cagney to be his brother. Well, Cagney is a Mick, without any pretence of being anything else, and he is America's ideal gangster. America, being a non-Irish, anti-Catholic country, has its own idea of what a real gangster looks like, and along comes a young Mick who looks like my brother, and he fills the bill. He is the typical gangster.'

'Well, I don't see what you prove by that. I think —'

'I didn't prove anything yet. Here's the big point. You know about the Society of the Cincinnati?[6] You've heard about them?'

'Certainly.'

'Well, if I'm not mistaken I could be a member of that Society. Anyway I could be a Son of the Revolution.[7] Which is nice to know sometimes, but for the present purpose I only mention it to show that I'm pretty God damn American, and therefore my brothers and sisters are, and yet we're not American. We're Micks, we're non-assimilable, we Micks. We've been here, at least some of my family, since before the Revolution — and we produce the perfect gangster type! At least it's you American Americans' idea of a perfect gangster type, and I suppose you're right. Yes, I guess you are. The first real gangsters in this country were Irish. The Mollie Maguires.[8] Anyway, do you see what I mean by all this non-assimilable stuff?'

'Yes. I suppose I do.'

'All right. Let me go on just a few sticks more. I show a sociological fact, I prove a sociological fact in one respect at least. I suppose I could walk through Grand Central at the same time President Hoover was arriving on a train, and the Secret Service boys wouldn't collar me on sight as a public enemy. That's because I dress the way I do, and I dress the way I do because I happen to prefer these clothes to Broadway clothes or Babbitt clothes. Also, I have nice manners because my mother was a lady and manners were important to her, also to my father in a curious way, but when I was learning manners I was at an age when my mother had greater influence on me than my father, so she gets whatever credit is due me for my manners. Sober.

'Well, I am often taken for a Yale man, by Yale men. That pleases me a little, because I like Yale best of all the colleges. There's another explanation for it, unfortunately. There was a football player at Yale in 1922 and around that time who looks like me and has a name something like mine. That's not important.'

'No, except that it takes away from your point about producing public enemies, your family. You can't look like a gangster *and* a typical Yale man.'

'That's true. I have an answer for that. Let me see. Oh, yes. The people who think I am a Yale man aren't very observing about people. I'm not making that up as a smart answer. It's true. In fact, I just thought of something funny.'

'What?'

'Most men who think I'm a Yale man went to Princeton themselves.'

'Oh, come on,' she said. 'You just said —'

'All right. I know. Well, that's not important and I'm only confusing the issue. What I want to say, what I started out to explain was why I said "you people, you members of the upper crust," and so on, implying that I am not a member of it. Well, I'm *not* a member

of it, and now I never will be. If there was any chance of it it disappeared — let me see — two years ago.'

'Why two years ago? You can't say that. What happened?'

'I starved. Two years ago I went for two days one time without a thing to eat or drink except water, and part of the time without a cigarette. I was living within two blocks of this place, and I didn't have a job, didn't have any prospect of one, I couldn't write to my family, because I'd written a bad check a while before that and I was in very bad at home. I couldn't borrow from anybody, because I owed everybody money. I'd borrowed from practically everybody I knew even slightly. A dollar here, ten dollars there. I stayed in for two days because I couldn't face the people on the street. Then the nigger woman that cleaned up and made the beds in this place where I lived, she knew what was happening, and the third morning she came to work she brought me a chicken sandwich. I'll never forget it. It was on rye bread, and home-cooked chicken, not flat and white, but chunky and more tan than white. It was wrapped in newspaper. She came in and said, "Good morning, Mr Malloy. I brought you a chicken sandwich if you like it." That's all. She didn't say why she brought it, and then she went out and bought me a container of coffee and pinched a couple of cigarettes — Camels, and I smoke Luckies — from one of the other rooms. She was swell. She knew.'

'I should think she was swell enough for you to call her a coloured woman instead of a nigger.'

'Oh, balls!'

'I'm leaving.'

'Go ahead.'

'Just a Mick.'

'See? The first thing you can think of to insult me with. Go on, beat it. Waiter, will you open the door for this lady, please?'

'Aren't you coming with me?'

'Oh, I guess so. How much, Luke?'

'That'll be one-twenty,' said Luke, showing, by showing nothing on his face, that he strongly disapproved the whole thing.

Exits like the one Isabel wanted to make are somewhat less difficult to make since the repeal of Prohibition.[9] In those days you had to wait for the waiter to peer through the small door, see that everything was all right, open at least two locks, and hold the door open for you. The most successful flouncing out in indignation is done through swinging doors.

He had to ring for the elevator and wait for it in silence, they had to ride down together in silence, and find a taxi with a driver in it. There were plenty of taxis, but the hackmen were having their usual argument among themselves over the Tacna-Arica award[10] and a fare was apparently the last thing in the world that interested them. However, a cruising taxi appeared and Isabel and Jimmy got in.

'Home?' said Jimmy.

'Yes, please,' said Isabel.

Jimmy began to sing: '. . . How's your uncle? I haven't any uncle. I hope he's fine and dandy too.'

Silence.

'Four years ago this time do you know what was going on?'

'No.'

'The Snyder-Gray trial.'

Silence.

'Remember it?'

'Certainly.'

'What was Mr Snyder's first name?'

'Whose?'

'Mister *Sny*-der's.'

'It wasn't Mister Snyder. It was Ruth Snyder. Ruth Snyder, and Judd Gray.'

'There was a Mr Snyder, though. Ah yes, there was a Mr Snyder. It was he, dear Isabel, it was he who was assassinated. What was his first name?'

'Oh, how should I know? What do I care what his first name was?'

'Why are you sore at me?'

'Because you humiliated me in public, calling the waiter and asking him to take me to the door, barking at me and saying perfectly vile, vile things.'

'Humiliated you in public,' he said. 'Humiliated you in public. And you don't remember Mr Snyder's first name.'

'If you're going to talk, talk sense. Not that I care whether you talk or not.'

'I'm talking a lot of sense. You're sore at me because I humiliated you in public. What the hell does that amount to? Humiliated in public. What about the man that Ruth Snyder and Judd Gray knocked off? I'd say he was humiliated in public, plenty. Every newspaper in the country carried his name for days, column after column of humiliation, all kinds of humiliation. And yet you don't even remember his name. Humiliation my eye.'

'It isn't the same thing.'

'Yes, it is. It's exactly the same thing. If I got out of the taxi now would that be humiliating you publicly?'

'Oh, don't. It's so unnecessary.'

'Please answer my question.'

'I'd rather you didn't. Does that answer it?'

'Yes. Driver! Pull over, please, over to the curb, you dope. Here.' He gave the driver a dollar and took off his hat. 'Good-by, Isabel,' he said.

'You're being silly. You know you're being silly, don't you?'

'Not at all. I just remembered I was supposed to be covering a sermon this morning and I haven't put in at the office all day.'

'Good heavens, Jimmy! Will you call me?'

'In an hour.'

'I'll wait.'

1   Famous American baseball player.
2   Shops or bars where alcoholic liquor is sold illegally.
3   The island at the base of Manhattan. It was/is a popular venue for crowds at weekends enjoying themselves at funfairs etc.
4   Clothes for the wealthier end of the market.
5   A lay organization for the ordinary Catholic man (known also as Knights of St Columba). The Dublin Horse Show is an annual event in Dublin formerly for the Anglo-Irish and the Protestant middle class.
6   A patriotic service organization, formed in 1783 by officers of the Continental army just before they disbanded after the American Revolution. George Washington was made its national president.
7   Sons of the American Revolution was an organization formed in 1889 in New York to keep alive the spirit of those who fought in the American Revolution. It was restricted to male descendants of Revolutionary veterans.
8   A secret organization of Irishmen in the mining area of Scranton, Pennsylvania, who in the decade between 1865 and 1875 became through intimidation a dominant force in countering oppressive working and housing conditions.
9   In 1933.
10   The Tacna-Arica Controversy between Chile and Peru ran from 1883 until 1929. The southern provinces of Peru — Tacna and Arica — were ceded to Chile after the War of the Pacific in 1883. The dispute continued and in 1929 President Hoover proposed that Chile should retain Arica and return Tacna to Peru.

JAMES T. FARRELL
from James T. Farrell, *The Young Manhood of Studs Lonigan* (1934)

James T. Farrell (1904–79) was born in Chicago into a working-class Irish-American family. His early trilogy, *Studs Lonigan,* is a remarkable achievement tracing the story of Studs Lonigan from childhood through early manhood to adult life against a background of the South Side of Chicago. Here in this extract Studs watches his parents move home from what was formerly an Irish neighbourhood but is now becoming a black neighbourhood. Farrell depicts the scene with considerable skill: observing and recounting the racism of Studs's parents but avoiding judgement. The last word, together with the exclamation mark, shows an expert hand at work. The novel was turned into a film by Irving Lerner in 1960.

Chapter Twenty-Two

Studs and his father stood in the parlour and the early morning sunlight glared through the unwashed, curtainless windows. They looked around at the covered furniture. The room had an appearance of disruption.

'Bill, I'd rather let the money I made on this building go to hell, and not be moving,' Lonigan exclaimed, with wistful regret.

'Patrick, are you sure all your things are packed,' Mrs Lonigan said.

'Yes, Mother,' Lonigan said, very gently.

It seemed to Studs that his mother wiped away a tear. She turned and went towards the back of the house to ask the girls if they had all their things packed.

'Hell, there is scarcely a white man left in the neighbourhood,' Studs remarked.

'I never thought that once they started coming, they'd come so fast.'

'You know, Bill, your mother and I are gettin' old now, and, well, we sort of got used to this neighbourhood. We didn't see many of the old people, except once in a while at Church, but you know, we kind of felt that they were around. You know what I mean, they were all nearby, and they all sort of knew us, and we knew them, and you see, well, this neighbourhood was kind of like home. We sort of felt about it the same way I feel about Ireland, where I was born,' said Lonigan.

Studs didn't like the old man to let himself out like that because how could he reply? The old man and old lady were taking it hard.

'Yeah, it used to be a good neighbourhood,' said Studs.

'Well, Patrick, we're going to have a new home,' Mrs Lonigan said, returning to the parlour.

'Yes, Mary, but no home will be like this one has been to us. We made our home here, raised our children, and spent the best years of our lives here.'

'Sunday in church, I watched Father Gilhooley. Patrick, he's getting old. He's heartbroken, poor man. Here he built his beautiful church, and two years after it's built, all his parishioners are gone. He's getting old, Patrick, poor man, and he's heartbroken.'

Studs stood there, looking at nothing, feeling goofy, vague, as if he was all empty inside.

'We're all getting old, Mary; it won't be long before we're under the sod.'

'Patrick, don't talk like that, please.'

'Goddamn those niggers!' Lonigan exploded.

'I guess it was the Jew real-estate dealers who did it,' said Studs, believing that he ought to say something.

'Mary, remember that Sunday, a long time ago, when we came out here in a buggy I rented, and drove around. It was nearly all trees and woods out here then, and there wasn't many people here,' the old man said.

'Yes, Patrick, but now are you positively certain that you're not leaving anything behind?' Mrs Lonigan said.

'Nothing, Mother! And remember when we bought the building over on Wabash. That was before you were born, Bill.'

Studs walked over to the window. He saw two nigger kids twisted together, wrestling in the street. They went down squirmingly. He remembered how, coming home from St Patrick's every night, they used to wrestle and rough-house like that, and Lucy and the girls, not meaning what they said, would call them roughnecks, and then they would go at it all the harder. Funny to think that was all gone, and here he was twenty-six, actually twenty-six, and next fall, he'd be twenty-seven. He lit a cigarette.

'Out there there'll only be about ten buildings in our block, the rest's all prairie,' Lonigan said.

'It'll be nice, though,' the mother absent-mindedly exclaimed.

'Mary, you know it's not like it used to be. We're not what we used to be, and it'll be lonesome there sometimes.'

'It's a shame. This was such a beautiful neighbourhood. And such nice people. A shame,' Mrs Lonigan said.

'Well, there'll be nice people out there south, too,' said Lonigan.

'I wish they'd hurry up,' Fran said nervously, as she joined them.

'They ought to be here any minute now. The movers said they would be here at seven-thirty. Let's see now, it's seven twenty-five, no seven twenty-six,' Lonigan said.

'Well, I wish they'd come. OOOOH, I can't stand the sight or thought of this place and this neighbourhood any more. OOOH, to think of all those greasy, dirty niggers around. Every time I pass them on the street, I shudder,' Fran said.

'Yeah, they look like apes, and, God, you can smell them a mile away,' said Lonigan.

'Dad, they're coming in here, aren't they?' said Studs.

'Yeah, a shine offered the highest price for the building, so I let it go. But he paid, the black skunk.'

'And this is such a beautiful building,' Mrs Lonigan said.

'Well, they can have it, only I hate to see how this building and the neighbourhood will look in six more months,' said Lonigan.

'Yeah, I guess the damn niggers are dirty,' said Studs.

'I know it. Did you ever look out of the window of the elevated train when you go downtown and see what kind of places they live in? God Almighty, such dirt and filth,' said Lonigan.

'Sometimes, I almost think that niggers haven't got a soul,' said Mrs Lonigan.

'There's quite a few were in church last Sunday,' Lonigan said.

'Yes, and coming out, did you see how they were trying to talk to Father Gilhooley, and he trying to edge aside from them. Poor man, he's heartbroken, simply heartbroken,' said Mrs Lonigan.

'Well, well, well! How's the little fairy queen? Is she ready to move too?' Lonigan said. Loretta smiled back at her dad.

'Dad, Phil is going to come over and help us move,' she said.

'Now, that's fine of him. You know he's Jewish, and I always made it a point to never trust a Jew, but I finally am convinced that he's one white Jew, if there ever was one. And accepting the faith, well, I suppose we oughtn't to call him a Jew any more. He's on our side of the fence,' said Lonigan.

Loretta smiled.

'He's a fine boy. He's got manners, and he was willing to be an usher in the church,' said Mrs Lonigan, looking at Studs.

'Yes, Father Gilhooley, I guess, is proud he's made a convert,' said Lonigan.

'And he is so polite and thoughtful. Every time I come into the parlour when he's here, I notice that he stands up. And before he smokes in my presence, he asks my permission. I think he is a fine boy,' said Mrs Lonigan.

'Well, it's seven twenty-nine, they ought to be here,' said Lonigan.

'Martin, now you're only a boy. Don't you go trying to lift and carry any of these heavy pieces,' said the mother.

'No danger,' said Studs, smiling at Martin, who was now a tall, skinny, awkward young boy, a trifle loutish in appearance.

'I'm all right,' Martin said in a falsetto voice.

The bell rang. Loretta rushed to the buzzer and pressed it. In a moment, she came back with Rolfe, who was dressed in old clothes. He politely said hello to everyone.

'Well, Phil, we're all set,' said Lonigan.

'Yes, Mr Lonigan, I see that you are, and it's a fine day for moving too!'

'Phillip, it was awfully nice of you to come and help us,' said Mrs Lonigan.

'It wasn't any trouble, Mrs Lonigan, I was glad to help you.'

'Here, I must get you a cup of coffee,' said she.

'Please don't, Mrs Lonigan, I had my breakfast. I'm not at all hungry.'

'It won't be any trouble, and I can fix it in a jiffy,' she said, rushing out, as Phil graciously protested.

'I suppose you're glad to be moving, Mr Lonigan.'

'Well, Phillip, as I was saying, we're getting old, Mrs Lonigan and me, and we kind of felt we'd rather not live with a bunch of damn smokes.'

'Yes, I know how you feel. They ruined the neighbourhood,' said Phil.

Mrs Lonigan called him from the kitchen.

'Yes, I wish they hadn't of gotten in, and they wouldn't have, if all the property owners got together. But I'll tell you this much, they'll never get out where we are going. That's certain. It's nice out there, too.'

'Phil, Mother is calling you for your coffee,' said Fritzie.

'Hi, there, Martin. All set?' smiled Phil, turning to go out to the kitchen.

'Say, Bill, he's a good decent, clean-cut boy,' Lonigan said.

Studs nodded.

'Dad, the movers are here,' Fran called.

'Well, let's go.'

The movers commenced taking things down. Studs took a large rocker, and carried it slowly downstairs. It was tedious work. His arms and back got tired. When he set it down in the alley, he was breathless, and all pooped out. Jesus Christ, and he was only twenty-six. Goddamn it, he felt rotten. In rotten condition. He touched the soft, unnecessary flesh about his abdomen and stomach. Goddamn it!

He walked slowly back, wishing the moving was done. Upstairs, the old man, mother, and two girls were standing in the parlour.

'Well, Mother, take a last look around and say goodbye,' the old man said.

'Yes, Patrick.'

'Now, you and the girls go ahead out there.'

'No, Patrick, I'm afraid you'll forget something.'

'Not on your life.'

'I had better wait until everything is moved.'

Studs picked up a lamp. It was lighter. He carried it down towards the back. Loretta and Phil followed him. He paused at the kitchen sink, and got a drink. Turning, he noticed Loretta squeezing Phil's hand, and telling him not to hurt himself lifting anything big.

He walked downstairs with the lamp. Yeah, he was kind of sorry to be moving. So were they all. Well!

SAMUEL BECKETT
from Samuel Beckett, *Echo's Bones* (1935)

It is worth reading these lines out loud several times to see if they make sense for you. Desmond Egan wrote an elegy to Beckett on his eightieth birthday in 1986 with the same title (see p. 1037 below).

ECHO'S BONES

asylum under my tread all this day
their muffled revels as the flesh falls
breaking without fear or favour wind
the gantelope[1] of sense and nonsense run
taken by the maggots for what they are

1935

1   A military punishment in which the culprit had to run stripped to the waist between two rows of men who struck at him with a stick or knotted cord (OED). The word is now rare except in gauntlet; also contains 'antelope'.

BLANAID SALKELD
from Blanaid Salkeld, *The Fox's Covert* (1935)

Here is a section from Blanaid Salkeld's elegy on the death of her brother Padraic. There is an almost physical struggle for articulation in this poem, an exposed meditation on light and time that refuses poise and the superficialities of thought.

from THE FOX'S COVERT

XCIV

Ever I find new Lents to old fasts subsequent.
Long, I had faith:
Beyond some curtained cell the Banquet waits, for
    scent
Fires thirst. But now I say: I will no more be caught —
In august dignity of impersonal thought
Cover sense over, cloak out frowsy weathers sent
To mock the steadfast spirit. So shall truth be blent
In with my breath.

XCV

Naked wrestling with a cold angel on lone strands,
Time she forgot.
Dingily wrecked now at edge of words' drear sloblands,
Among the superficialities of thought
Her spirit shrivels. Simple solaces the tired heart sought.
Only the pride of ice in her flesh — and slow wands
Of dusk over streams that dripped down the shelving
    sands —
Clear, polyglot.

XCVI

We prize but what is lost; we pass grace sourly by —
Thought in a cloud —
And while vain scorn dries up the heart, our betters
 die.
Their noble ghosts halt by us, leisurely they halt,
To smart our lids with salt remorse. A blockish fault,
To let our gaze behind a tight slit petrify,
So the warm founts of wisdom in us frozen, die —
Sun disallowed.

XCVII

They met half-way uphill: love toiling to ascend —
He lurching back.
Love lost him? No, but like the black cat, his soft
 friend —
Incongruously at ease, the stone steps for floor,
Pillowed upon harsh lintel of his shut hall-door —
Love waits through absence, till the hand at circle's end
Lifted, makes entrance, signals her to rise, attend
Close on his track!

XCVIII

I have a plan: the day's too short for all our fun —
After the night,
If I can wake, I'll rise at one o'clock and run
And hallo to the boys across our garden wall.
Harold is my age, eight — Ted's older — Leonard's
 small,
He's only six. — 'But, Beatsi, it's pitch dark at
 one.' —
Oh, we could talk together for an hour. The sun
Soon would give light.

XCIX

On the tram-top this morning every passenger
Sounded his cough.
I too coughed. Change of the weather. The same set
 stir

Of similar machines. We are all one! I thought —
The like reactions to a cause. This way, as naught
Our dreams, our loneliness, become. Good, to aver
We are all peppered out of the one canister —
Intimate stuff.

C

You that have aristocratic senses, refined,
Fired ere the Flood —
That are sword-swift and clear-toned like her crystal
 kind —
Dared to forswear your inheritance — to efface
An image all time had been glad for, your cold race
Crowned by. But thought runs the course of the desert
 wind . . .
To misinterpret her with your parvenu mind —
Shaming high blood!

CI

As the sun takes he renders. Every blot of dew
Tumbled and scotched —
In sap and fragrance, colour, grace, hoists up anew.
Her glory was a jest, her grief a drear affair.
She could not touch his spirit — though, half unaware,
First, light of light from him, then bitterness, she drew.
The whole return — a song. It should be deep and
 true —
Gilded, tear-blotched!

CII

There is a pale calmness, its poise seems to affright
Time's to-and-fro:
So built up in serenity, storms cannot slight;
Having so sure relations to its centre — light
Flows in and out its being, and there is no night.
Made one in shadowy verse, my hearing, touch, and
 sight
Are dipped in that baptismal font, that constant bright
Stillness of snow.

TERESA DEEVY
from Teresa Deevy, *Three Plays* (1939)

Teresa Deevy (1894–1963) wrote a series of plays for the Abbey Theatre in the 1930s including *A Disciple* (1931) and *Katie Roche* (1936). There has been a revival of interest in her work in recent years. For an informative introduction, see Eileen Kearney's chapter on her in Bernice Schrank and William W. Demastes, *Irish Playwrights*

1880–1995 (1997). For an early assessment of her work see Temple Lane, 'The Dramatic Art of Teresa Deevy' in *The Dublin Magazine*, October–December 1946, pp. 35–41. *The King of Spain's Daughter* looks back to the intense world of Synge and forward to the stark landscapes of Beckett.

The King of Spain's Daughter

Characters

Peter Kinsella } *labourers*
Jim Harris

Mrs Marks, *a neighbour*
Annie Kinsella, *Peter's daughter*
Roddy Mann, *a loafer*

The action of the play takes place on a grassy road in Ireland during the dinner-hour of a day in April.

Scene: *An open space on a grassy road. At each side road-barriers with notices, 'No Traffic' and 'Road Closed'. At the back an old dilapidated wall; a small door in the centre of the wall stands open and fields can be seen beyond. County Council workers have been employed here. Two coats, a thermos flask, an old sack and a man's hat and stick have been left on a pile of stones near one of the barriers.* PETER KINSELLA, *a heavily built man of fifty, comes through the doorway. He carries a pick-axe; his overalls and boots are covered with a fine dust. He stands in the centre, looks away to the left, shading his eyes — then to the right.* JIM HARRIS *comes on, whistling. He is twenty-four, wears a cap and dusty overalls. He leaves his spade against the wall, goes to the barrier at the right side, leans on it, looking away to the right.*

JIM: Great work at the weddin' below. Miss What's-her-name getting married. The women were gathered at the wharf an hour and a half before time for send-off. (*Laughs.* PETER *nods without interest.*) Right well it looked from above, with the white launch, an' the flags flyin' an' the sun on the water. Brave and gay at the start, however 'twill go. (*Takes his thermos flask.*) Come on, man. With the noise of the sirens I didn't hear the whistle, an' I kept workin' five minutes too long. Wasn't that a terrible thing to have happen to me?
PETER: She's late with my dinner.
JIM (*dismayed*): What! didn't she come here at all?
PETER: She did not. Late — the second time in the week.
JIM: 'Tis on account of that weddin'. She'll be up now. They don't feel time or weather when they're waitin' for a bride.

PETER: I'll make her feel something . . . her father without his dinner.
JIM (*looking to the right*): Is it at the wharf she is? or the far side of the river watchin' the start?
PETER: Do I, or anyone, ever know where Annie'd be? Only sisters you have, but they'd give you more thought than that daughter of mine. Oh, she'll be sorry yet.
JIM: It is because of the day; the women can think of nothin' else; they're all the same. Molly and Dot were up at the dawn — would it be a fine day! You'd think they were guests invited. They know her by eye-sight so they'll go stand in the crowd and see how she'll look.
PETER: If I knew where to get Annie.
JIM: Annie'll be here now. They're scatterin' away off the wharf — though I can't pick her out.
PETER: And how would you? More than likely she's off with Roddy Mann. Philanderin' with the like of him — that's all she's fit for — or with any boy she can lay hold of.
JIM: If she goes on a bit aself 'tis because she must; she's made that way, she can't help it.
PETER: I'll make her help it! You're in no great hurry to have her.
JIM (*flings round on him*): You know that I am!
PETER: Why don't you marry her so? and stop her goin' on? You're in no hurry.
JIM: I want that, and you know it. How can I force the girl?
PETER: Ay, how indeed? (*Laughs contemptuously.*) Aw, you're very young.
(*Goes to the door, stands there looking out across the fields.* JIM *sits down on the stones and begins his dinner.* MRS MARKS, *a big woman of fifty-five or so, wearing a shawl and with a basket on her arm, comes to the barrier at the right. She pushes the barrier a little aside and comes on.*)
MRS MARKS: Can I pass this way? 'Twould be a short cut.
JIM: Are you a motor car, ma'am? (*Looks her up and down.*) You are not — 'tis two legs are under you. You can, and welcome.
MRS MARKS: I thought you had sense in your head, Jim Harris. (*Puts down her basket, resting it against a large stone.*) There's a terrible weight in that basket, there is.

JIM: That was a great send-off they gave the bridal pair.

MRS MARKS: It was so. I wasn't on the wharf on account of my bad knee, but I seen from above, an' I met some of them now. I'm glad she had it fine, the poor young thing.

JIM: What 'poor' is on her? Isn't it the day of her life?

MRS MARKS: You could never tell that. It might. They say he wanted the money. They say it was signed and settled before ever he seen her. Well, she'll have her red carpet and all her fine show for her poor heart to feed on. That's the way.

PETER (*coming from the door*): Fine day, ma'am.

MRS MARKS: It is indeed, thanks be to God. 'Tis a day of the earth and the sky.

JIM: With the whole month of April floatin' around.

MRS MARKS: Annie was tellin' me the bride looked like a queen.

PETER: Did you see Annie? She didn't bring me my dinner.

MRS MARKS: Oh, look at that now! a shame and a sin! She's off across the field with that Roddy Mann.

JIM (*jumps up*): I'll go call her.

PETER: Stop where you are!
(*He strides off.*)

JIM (*to* MRS MARKS): You had a right to keep that to yourself.

MRS MARKS: To leave her father without his bit! an' she romancin' around!

JIM: He'll have her life.

MRS MARKS: She earns what she gets. Why don't she settle down? She's a bold wild thing.

JIM: He treats her cruel; it don't do her any good.

MRS MARKS: And what would do her good? That Annie Kinsella will be romancin' all her life with whoever she can.

JIM: The way he treats her — it only drives her on worse.

MRS MARKS: You're too soft-hearted, Jimmy Harris. But I have a great wish for you, for the sake of your mother, God rest her soul. You'd be better to give Annie up.

JIM: Give up me life, is it?

MRS MARKS: You have two good sisters, can't you settle with them, or get a sensible girl. I'm telling you now, that one, her head is full of folly and her heart is full of wile. She'd do you no good.

JIM: You have a lot of old talk. (*Silence. Then distant cheering.*) They're not done with it yet.

MRS MARKS: I was thinking of my marriage day when I was looking at them two. It is a thought would sadden anyone.

JIM: How is that, Mrs Marks?

MRS MARKS: That's how it is; the truth is the best to be told in the end.

JIM: Haven't you Bill and Mary, and the little place? You didn't fare bad.

MRS MARKS: Bad. What have bad or good to do with it? That is outside of the question. For twenty years you're thinking of that day, an' for thirty years you're lookin' back at it. After that you don't mind — you haven't the feelin' — exceptin' maybe an odd day, like to-day. (*She takes her basket. They hear someone coming.* MRS MARKS *puts down her basket again, and waits, expectant.*) Annie . . . and you may be sure she's not alone.

(ANNIE KINSELLA *is seen in the doorway. She is about twenty. She wears a dark shawl, a red dress, black shoes and stockings — all very neat. Her hair is bright gold. With her is* RODDY MANN, *a big lounging figure, cap pulled low over his eyes.*)

ANNIE: Now, Roddy, don't come any farther. (*Low tone.* MRS MARKS *listens;* JIM *moves a little farther from the doorway.*) Give me the tin.
(RODDY *hands a tin to her.*)

RODDY: What did you promise?

ANNIE: Wait first till I tell you how she looked (*low, eager*).

RODDY: You have told me already; you have talked of nothin' else.

ANNIE: She was like what you'd dream. I think I never seen anything so grand. She was like a livin' flame passin' down by us. She was dressed in flamin' red from top to toe, and — (*puts her hand to her breast*) — here she had a diamond clasp.

RODDY: And there you have your heart. Now give us a kiss. What did you promise? Leave down the tin.
(ANNIE *puts the tin on the ground, slips her hands up about his neck and gives him a long kiss.*)

ANNIE: That will do now.

RODDY: You have my heart scalded. (*He moves off.* ANNIE *takes up the tin, wipes her mouth on her sleeve, very thoroughly, turns to wave to* RODDY. *Comes in.*)

ANNIE: Jimmy, it was like heaven. She looked that lovely. The launch was all white, and the deck covered with flowers. They had a red carpet —

JIM: You're late with his dinner.

ANNIE: Late! (*Alarmed.*) The whistle didn't go!

JIM: Ten minutes apast one.

ANNIE: He'll have my life!

MRS MARKS: An' small blame to him so! Without a bite or a sup! A man wants his dinner. He's gone down to find you.

JIM: Why couldn't you come?

ANNIE: What misfortune came over me? I am at a loss for a word. What will I do now?

MRS MARKS: Take it down to him — run.

ANNIE: He'd kill me, he'd kill me dead. I think I'll stop here till he'll come.

JIM: Here he is now.

(*All look towards the doorway.*)

MRS MARKS (*turns to* JIM): Don't be drawn into it, you. 'Twould be a mistake. Keep your eyes on the ground; 'tis the safest place. You won't see what's happening, and you won't lose your head.

PETER (*coming in*): Is she there? (*Sees* ANNIE.) Ah-h!

ANNIE (*nervous, almost perky*): I'm a bit late with the dinner; 'tis because of the weddin' I didn't hear the whistle: I didn't know it had gone one.

(*Leaves his dinner-tin on the ground, not too near him, and moves away.*)

PETER: Hand me that tin.

(ANNIE *hands it, keeping as far as possible from him.* PETER, *taking the tin, hits out at her.* ANNIE *dodges and partly escapes, but cries out;* JIM *springs forward;* MRS MARKS *catches* JIM *by the arm.*)

MRS MARKS: 'Tis a terrible misfortune for any man to take the least iota interest in a girl like that!

(*This flow stops them all.*)

JIM (*after a silence*): What do you want here, Mrs Marks?

MRS MARKS: I wouldn't be in it at all but for the sake of your mother — 'tis well she's in the grave.

PETER (*to* ANNIE): Go down there, you — (*gestures towards the barrier at the left*) — and rake up the few stones I have agen the wall.

(ANNIE *hesitates, looks at her father, at* JIM, *at* MRS MARKS.)

PETER: Do you hear what I'm saying?

ANNIE: I don't mind what'll happen; I can take care of myself.

(*Goes off,* L., *with a backward look at* JIM. JIM *would follow but for* PETER'*s forbidding look.* PETER *goes over to where the coats have been left on the stones. Takes his stick from under the coats.*)

JIM: This is the best sheltered place for takin' your dinner. You can have the sack on top of them stones.

PETER: Mind yer business.

MRS MARKS: Steady now, keep steady. Don't let us have anything happen!

JIM (*to* PETER): You have your dinner now, can't you leave her alone.

PETER: Do she belong to you? (*Pause.*) Do she? When she do you can talk.

(*Goes.*)

MRS MARKS: Supposin' you were to get a blow instead of herself — what good would that be? It might do you a grievous harm! Great cheer to see her standin' upright if yourself was lyin' low! I wouldn't stir up the embers in a man like that. (JIM *walks away from her.*) Now I'll tell you this — though I know you won't listen — if you were a man at all you'd make her marry you.

JIM: An' how can I do that?

MRS MARKS: Ah, you're too soft-hearted for any woman. 'Tis the hard man wins, and right he should. (*Confidential now.*) Annie Kinsella — when I met her down there — was tellin' me how grand the bride looked. 'She was dressed,' said she, 'in shimmerin' green from head to foot.'

JIM: What's wrong with that?

MRS MARKS: Didn't you hear her now to Roddy Mann, 'She was dressed in flamin' red from top to toe'.

JIM: So she did.

MRS MARKS: That's the count she puts on the truth! I'm only tellin' you now so's you'll harden your heart! Whatever'll come easy is what she'll say. Now — for the sake of your mother — if you marry that girl, don't believe one word she'll tell you. That's the only way you'll have peace of mind! (*A cry.* JIM *starts forward:* MRS MARKS *catches his arm.*) Be a man now! Be a man, and don't get yourself hurt!

JIM: Keep out of my way!

(*Tries to push her aside.* ANNIE, *a little dishevelled, frightened, and with her shawl trailing, runs on. She runs to the barrier at the right side, leans against it, and moans, nursing her shoulder.*)

MRS MARKS (*to* JIM): Now strengthen your heart: quiet your mind. Don't do yourself harm on anyone's account. We get what we merit, and God is good. (*Pause.*) I'll leave ye now. (*Takes her basket, does not notice that she has left a small parcel on the stone: moves off. Near the barrier she stops again, looks back at* JIM.) Don't be moved to any foolish compassion. The hard man wins.

(*Goes.* JIM *comes a little forward: sits down on an old plank, his back to* ANNIE: *takes a small notebook from his pocket, turns the pages: glances over his shoulder in* ANNIE'*s direction, slips the notebook into his pocket again: waits for* ANNIE *to come to him. After a moment she brushes aside her tears, comes over and sits down close beside him.*)

ANNIE: It was a grand sight, Jim, it was like heaven.

JIM (*catches her wrist*): He hurt you then — did he do you any harm?

ANNIE: Ah, leave that now! Let us leave that behind us. . . . The band was playing, and the flags were grand ——

JIM: 'Tis a shame you'd madden him. He'll harm you some day, and all your own fault. You won't have any life left. An' what can I do?

ANNIE: Didn't you see the launch at all?

JIM: I saw well from above.

ANNIE: You should have been on the wharf. The cheering an' the music, an' all the sun on the river, an' everyone happy ——

JIM: We'd all be happy if you'd have sense.

ANNIE: She looked lovely passin' along, her hand restin' in his, and her body swayin' beside him down the path. The arms of the two families were painted on the launch: the sun was shinin' on it: everything was white or burnin' red, but she was dressed in pale, pale gold and — (*hands to breast*) — two red flowers were crushed agen her here.

JIM (*springs up*): What lies are you tellin'? I saw her myself: she was dressed in grey; she had no flowers.

ANNIE (*gentle, bewildered*): Jimmy, what's wrong with you?

JIM: She was dressed in grey. Tell the truth!

ANNIE: It was in pale gold I saw her.

JIM (*furious*): And in shimmerin' green, an' in flamin' red, an' in milk-white when it will suit you! (*Silence.*)

ANNIE (*gets up slowly*): You are a pack of blind owls — all the lot of you! I saw what I saw! (*Turns from him.*)

JIM: But why won't you tell the truth — an' it just as easy?

ANNIE: Stop your fool talk! The truth! Burstin' in where you don't know. Oh, if I could have love!

JIM: Will you leave talkin' of love when I'm tired of askin' you'd come to the priest with me! Are we to be married ever? Are we?

ANNIE (*quietly*): Whisht, Jimmy, whisht. (*Looks off away to the right, in the direction of the river.*)

JIM: Are we? I must know.

ANNIE (*to herself*):
Then the wet windin' roads,
Brown bogs and black water,
And my thoughts on white ships
And the King of Spain's daughter.

JIM: I'm sick of that thing! Who's the King of Spain's daughter?

ANNIE: Myself.

JIM: Yourself. . . . (*A laugh.*) And the bride beyond!

ANNIE: It is myself I seen in her — sailin' out into the sun, and to adventure.

JIM: Are you going to marry me? Make up your mind. (*They hear a sound as of someone coming.*)

ANNIE: What's that? (*Frightened.*) Is he coming? Jim, he says he'll make me sign on for the factory.

JIM: The factory? in the town beyond? (*She nods.*) That you couldn't stand before?

ANNIE: I was there six months: it would be five years this time.

JIM: Five years! you couldn't do that!

ANNIE: They're only takin' them will be bound for five years. I couldn't face it. (*Falters.*) Every mornin' walkin' the road, every evenin' draggin' back so tired. He has the card: he says he'll come make me sign it now.

JIM: It was a pity you didn't bring his dinner in time!

ANNIE: It was a great misfortune for me. I am at a loss to explain it.

JIM: And I think he knew that Roddy was with you.

ANNIE: It is that decided him.

JIM: Why do you go with Roddy, and Jack?

ANNIE: It is very unfortunate that I do! . . . I would face any life — no matter what — before I'd go back to that place.

JIM: Did you kiss Roddy Mann again today?

ANNIE (*injured*): And who else was there for me to kiss?

JIM: When I left you last night, did you go back to Jack Bolger?

ANNIE: Last night . . . no, I don't think I did, last night.

JIM (*furious*): We're all the one! You have no heart.

ANNIE: So must I go to the factory? Won't you marry me now?

JIM: Annie! — won't I, is it? You know well — (*Overjoyed, but checks himself.*) Will you come with me to-night and we'll tell the priest?

ANNIE: Is it stand beside you an' you sayin' that? (*Insulted.*) The ground would open under me! Go tell him yourself, let you.

JIM: Would you go back on me then?

ANNIE: I would not.

JIM: You would not? You've changed your mind often.

ANNIE: I'll be in the chapel the day he'll name.

JIM: You will? and come with me then?

ANNIE: What else is there for me?

JIM: Annie! — (*checks himself*) — I'll tell them look out for a place so: they can get a room in the town.

ANNIE: Tell who?

JIM: Molly and Dot. 'Tis I have the house: they knew they'd have to go.

ANNIE: Well, then, they needn't. Let them stop where they are. What would I do without a woman to talk to?

JIM: I want you to myself.

ANNIE: I never heard the like! A good 'man' he'd make to begin by turnin' his two sisters on the road! And they after mindin' the place since his mother died.

JIM: Will you go back on me so?

ANNIE: Leave Molly and Dot stay where they are.

JIM: I will not.

ANNIE: What great harm would they do?

JIM: They'd be in it — spoilin' the world.

ANNIE: Spoilin' the world! I think you're crazy.

JIM: When we shut the house door I'll have no one in it but you and me.

ANNIE (*after a moment*): I think I'll stop with my father.

JIM: And go to the factory?

ANNIE: Maybe I wouldn't do either — but run away.

JIM: He'd go after you: he'd have you crippled.

ANNIE: I haven't signed yet. I might get on the soft side of him yet if I'd promise ——

JIM: What promise would you keep? (*Silence.*) I have twenty pounds saved.

ANNIE: Where did you get that?

(*Not greatly interested.* JIM *takes out his notebook, opens it.*)

JIM: Four years ago you said I had no money. I have the house now, and besides what I earn I put by two shillin's every week.

ANNIE: Two shillin's . . . you did! every week . . . since that time long ago?

JIM (*turning the pages of his notebook*): A hundred shillings . . . that was five pounds the first year . . . and another five then . . . and another . . . and this is the fourth. . . .

ANNIE (*awed*): You kept it up all along?

JIM: Did you think I'd fall tired?

ANNIE: Let me see. I didn't know you were doin' that. (*Takes the notebook, turns the pages. Silence — then*) Oh, 'tis smudged and dirty. Why couldn't you keep it clean?

(*Angered: throws the book from her. Silence.*)

JIM: Two hundred weeks, and that's all you'd care. (*Walks away.*)

ANNIE: What would you do with it?

JIM (*coming a little way back to her*): It would set us up . . . To buy a few things. I'd have to give the priest some. Then whatever you'd like for the house, and yourself, so's we could settle down right.

ANNIE: Settle down. (*A knell to her.*) I dunno could I ever get into service in a place in London?

JIM (*in fury*): If your father heard you were at the crossroad last night — or if the priest heard tell of it — dancin' on the board, an' restin' in the ditch with your cheek agen mine and your body pressed to me.

ANNIE: It is only in the dark I could do it — for when I'd see the kind you are ——

JIM (*catches her*): What's wrong with me now?

ANNIE (*holding back*): Is it *me* to go near you — me?

JIM (*crushing her to him*): What's wrong with me?

ANNIE: Jimmy! he's coming! Let go, let me go!

PETER (*coming on*): So that's what you're at! (ANNIE *tries to escape.* JIM *holds her.*) Stop there, stop there the two of you! You can let her go now. (*To* JIM. JIM *releases* ANNIE. *She stands motionless.*) Was she teasin' you?

JIM: She was.

PETER: Tauntin' you like?

JIM: She was.

PETER: I know . . . leadin' you on?

JIM: That's it.

PETER: Well, me fine lady, we'll put a stop to your fun. You can do some work now. Stay where you are! Stay there the two of you. (*Goes to where the coats have been left, takes a card and a pencil from his coat pocket. Comes over to* ANNIE.) Write your name there. (ANNIE *looks at* JIM: *he avoids her look.*) Do you hear what I say? Write your name. We'll have no more cajolin'.

(ANNIE *writes her name on the card.* PETER, *taking back the card, hits at her.* JIM *knocks aside* PETER'*s blow: they face each other angrily.*)

JIM: Can't you leave her alone!

PETER: Standin' up for her now, but you have no right! no more than to be kissin' her like you were. She don't want you. You can go your road. (*Wheels round on* ANNIE.) Will you marry him now, or go to the factory? Five years there, or your life with him?

JIM: I'm not askin' you, Annie, I wouldn't — that way.

PETER: He's backin' out now.

ANNIE (*to* JIM): I might as well have you. (*Low*) Who would I ever meet would be fit for me? Where would I ever find a way out of here?

PETER: Have ye settled it so?

JIM: We have.

PETER: You'll take her like that?

JIM: I will.

PETER: Well, I'll keep the card, fearin' she'd change. (*Puts the card in his pocket. Goes off.*)

ANNIE (*softly*): You have me ruined. It is all over now. You can go settle with the priest.

JIM: You won't ever regret it. You won't. (*But she turns away.*)

ANNIE: Go on after him now. (JIM *hesitates: goes.* ANNIE *moves over to the barrier, looks off away to the right.* MRS MARKS *comes to the barrier at the left side, shades her eyes, looking on the ground for her parcel.*)

MRS MARKS: Well — look where I left it. (*Comes on, takes the parcel she had forgotten.*) Well and indeed! my head will never spare my heels! searchin' high and low. (*Sees* JIM'*s notebook on the ground.*) What is that there?

ANNIE: That belongs to Jim Harris. (*Takes the book.*) Jim Harris and myself are getting married very soon.

MRS MARKS: What! Is he going to marry you in face of all! Well, well, you might talk your head off, or you might spare your breath — it don't make any difference!

ANNIE: Maybe I won't mind it as much as I think.

MRS MARKS: Be a good wife to him now. Don't give him the bad time you gave your poor father. Often I felt for that poor man when he wouldn't know where you'd be. (*More kindly*) You have no wish for it? (ANNIE *shakes her head*.) And there's many a girl would be boundin' with joy. Is there any other you'd liefer have? (ANNIE *shakes her head*.) Well now, well, you'll be all right. A good sensible boy. And you'll have a nice little place. Mind you keep it well — that'll give you somethin' to do. You won't feel the days slippin'. (ANNIE *moves restlessly away from her.*) Well, well, if you could get to care for him that would be a blessin' from God. It might come to you later. Sometimes it do, and more times it don't. It might come with the child.

ANNIE: I dread that.

MRS MARKS: What's that you said? Fie on you then! Did you think you needn't suffer like the rest of the world? Did you think you were put here to walk plain and easy through the gates of heaven?

ANNIE: I dread it . . . dread it.

MRS MARKS: Would you ask to get in on what others would suffer?

ANNIE (*to herself*): I couldn't bear I'd be no more than any other wife. (*Distant cheering is heard;* ANNIE *listens, looks away towards the river; flashes*) It won't be all they'll say of me: 'She married Jimmy Harris.'

MRS MARKS: And what better could they say? You have a right to be grateful. Oh, you're a wild creature!

(*But* ANNIE *is not listening; she has opened* JIM's *notebook; studies it.*)

ANNIE (*turning the page*): June . . . July . . . October . . . November . . . December . . .

MRS MARKS: Poor Jimmy Harris. . . . I hope he's doin' a wise thing.

ANNIE: February, March, April . . . June, July, August . . . October — and I was black out with him then — November, December, April, June, August —

MRS MARKS: A good, sensible boy.

ANNIE: Boy! (*She laughs exultantly.*) I think he is a man might cut your throat!

MRS MARKS: God save us all!

ANNIE: He put by two shillin's every week for two hundred weeks. I think he is a man that — supposin' he was jealous — might cut your throat.

(*Quiet, exultant, she goes.*)

MRS MARKS: The Lord preserve us! that she'd find joy in such a thought!

JOSEPH F. DINNEEN
from Joseph F. Dinneen, *Ward Eight* (1936)

Joseph F. Dinneen was the first biographer of James Michael Curley, the dominant figure in Boston politics in the first half of the twentieth century (see *The Purple Shamrock*, 1949). Dinneen's 1930s novel *Ward Eight* contains a no less sympathetic portrait of an Irish-American politician, this time modelled in part on another politician, Martin Lomasney. When Dennis and Norah O'Flaherty arrive in Boston from County Cork in 1890, the Irish part of the city is run by Hughie Donnelly. Their son Tim grows up in the shadow of Hughie and aspires to play his part among the 'Irish colony' in the extension of Tammany Hall politics and control of the City Hall. Here in this extract Tim — no longer a greenhorn from 'the old sod' (a 'far-down'), but now a 'far-up' — goes to the Jesuit-run Boston College to complete his education but finds it wanting: he is more interested in street politics and in the new wave of Italian immigrants into the city. In 'The Boston Irish', published in *The Bell* in March 1951, Francis Russell makes an appropriate mention of Dinneen's *Ward Eight*.

Chapter 12

1

He stood within the rotunda in the line of confused, perplexed entering students who asked one another questions which none among them could answer as they waited to be interviewed by the Prefect of Studies. 'Prefect' of Studies, 'Prefect' of Discipline. The word 'Prefect', Big Tim considered grave and impressive, like 'Prefect' of Police. This was one of the great moments of his life. He was about to enter college, to join the society of educated gentlemen in the hope that he might become one of them, therefore no detail of the procedure escaped his alert attention. Like hundreds of others down through the years before him, he studied from his place in line the prominent plaster plaque of Marquette[1] hanging on the wall and wondered how the priest maintained his balance standing in the flimsy canoe, and how the Indians could all paddle on the same side and keep the craft going in a straight line.

Upper classmen, sauntering through the rotunda, chatting in pairs, inspired awe and the speculative reflection that some day he might be like them. He bowed his head reverently when Jesuits passed in flowing black cassocks and white Roman collars because he had been taught so to respect them in the parochial school, but he observed that upper classmen merely nodded to them in friendly greeting and smiled.

The line dwindled, and after a time he was at the door of the Prefect's office to wait for a few minutes before he was admitted by the student attendant outside. He fingered his hat and looked down at the short, stocky priest behind the desk. His gaze focused momentarily upon his shining bald head, then dropped to the eye-glasses, prominent nose, and wide lips. The priest studied an index card form before him.

'O'Flaherty,' he said, looking up from the card.

'Yes, Father,' Big Tim answered, respectfully.

'Pretty husky, aren't you?'

'Yes, Father.'

'How much do you weigh?'

'A hundred and ninety-two.'

'Go out for football, I suppose?'

'Yes, Father, I expect to.'

The priest looked back at the card. 'You've had no Greek,' he observed, 'and you're deficient in Latin. You may have to be conditioned.' He bent over the desk, wrote upon a slip of paper, and handed it to Big Tim.

'Section F,' he said. 'The boy at the door will show you. Best of luck. Next!' Big Tim turned and walked out.

Within two weeks he was familiarly referring to the Jesuits with the time-honoured nickname 'Jebbies'. The 'Misters' and 'Fathers' among the instructors, depending upon whether they had been ordained or not, were catalogued in his mind. He began to absorb an idea of the traditions of the school, a loyal hate of 'The Cross', the despised football rival, the college in Worcester, represented to underclassmen as a prison where students were locked in with their books when curfew rang; and although he would not then admit it even to himself, he envied the students at Holy Cross because at least they enjoyed an important half of college life which he had sacrificed when he chose Boston College. They lived in dormitories and were thus forced into close association with one another. The entire student body at Boston College commuted.

He found himself wondering against his will why he had not listened to Ann Barrett; why he had been so adamant in his determination to go to Boston College. With a reasonable choice of any university offered him by the mission, he found that he had selected a glorified high school where the students came by train and street car to report every morning with their bags and books, went to section rooms resembling high-school 'home-rooms', sat at one-arm lunch chairs for lectures and instruction and followed a typical high-school routine, even to the monthly report cards. Also, it incorporated the drudgery and atmosphere of the parochial school he had left four years earlier. 'Catholic Apologetics' and 'Evidences of Religion' in boldface on a study schedule were impressive until Big Tim discovered, to his dismay, that they were synonymous with 'Catechism' in parochial grammar school. The highly praised Jesuit 'radio studiorium'[2] was convincing as outlined by the Prefect of Studies until he found that it meant tedious, tiresome, classroom drudgery and homework.

Now he saw Harvard, Yale, Dartmouth, Amherst, the colleges of New England, in a new light and from a different point of view. College life, to Big Tim, was little different from high-school life. There were none of the activities and associations common to universities where campus and dormitories kept the students together or permitted them to organize into cliques. Greek-letter and secret societies were prohibited, and even if the urge to form them existed, the confessional prevented it. The compulsion to receive regularly the sacraments of his church Big Tim accepted, unquestioning. Like the rest of the students, he got his certificate from a Father confessor every month, proving that he had attended to these duties so that he could be permitted to enter classes. There were other departures from common college practice. Instructors were never dignified with the title 'Professor'. They were addressed as 'Father' or 'Mister'.

The transition from high-school graduate to college student he found strange at first, like returning home after a long absence. Once again he was among the Irish in classrooms, but the students were not the Irish of the clan. At first he could not help but contrast the daily roll-call of the section beadle with the roll-call so familiar to his high school. 'Newbury, O'Flaherty, Palmstrom, Piston, Purdy', against 'O'Brien, O'Connell, O'Connor, O'Doherty, O'Donnell, O'Flaherty, O'Flannigan, O'Grady, O'Hara, O'Hare', and thus down through the O's to 'O'Sullivan and O'Toole'. The names of half of his section began with the letter O. His dislike of the class beadle whose duty it was to record attendance and report to the Prefect of Discipline was instinctive. On the corner the beadle would be known as a stool pigeon, and at first he felt that the Prefect of Discipline, the Sister Superior of four years before, the patrolman on the beat, and the truant officer were all vaguely similar.

'This is your college; make the most of it,' was the injunction urged upon students by all instructors. 'Don't be a two-thirty bird,' they were warned. A two-thirty bird corresponded to Harvard's untouchables. He picked up his books and belongings at that hour every day and went home and ignored the extra-curricular activities which the college provided as a substitute for social college life. Theoretically a two-thirty bird was to be shunned as one afflicted with intellectual leprosy, unmoved by the advantages and traditions of the college and unworthy of association with student gentlemen.

In place of the clubs and societies of other colleges, membership in numerous academies was open to him. The word 'academy', too, sounded impressive to Big Tim until he found that it meant a gathering of serious-minded young men with an instructor to delve more deeply into the subjects that interested them. Academy activities meant more drudgery. The 'Greek Academy' was a daily afternoon gathering of those diligent students who did not get enough Greek in class and homework and loved the language so intensely that they must gather every day to pick apart Homer, Plato, and Euripides with jolly little excursions into Greek moods and syntax. Similarly, the Latin Academy spent hours discussing advanced Cicero. Nor did the French or Spanish Academies appeal to him. Big Tim passed them by. He came to study, but, he decided, he did not care to study that seriously. All he coveted was the degree and he hoped to earn it with as little hard labour as possible.

Of all of the academies and clubs, only the Brosnahan Debating Society interested him. Here, he thought, he could learn something that would be of value to him in his chosen field. He joined promptly. The only other college organizations he joined were the men's Sodality and the League of the Sacred Heart, because joining them offered the line of least resistance. Everybody else did. At first he was fearful that the Jesuits would proselyize for recruits to the Order. He was relieved to learn that they did not and never had.

2

Ward Eight was the richest of the city in historical associations, and nothing moves a blue-blooded Bostonian more than history, ancestry, or genealogy. Longfellow memorialized the Old North Church so that it could become the sentinel of the slums. Franklin, Sam and John Adams, the patriots of another day, tramped the streets of the mount that was Ward Eight. Heroes fought and died in a massacre and were buried in Copp's Hill so that Big Tim O'Flaherty could hit their tombstones with green peppers from his bedroom window. Clipper ships had sailed to break records from the wharf where Big Tim and his gang dove and swam. An entire Irish population had moved into the ward and crowded out an entire Yankee[3] population. Ward Eight was still making its peculiar contributions to history, its recent gift a stiff drink — a Ward Eight — which symbolized its fighting red blood with a heavy dose of sweet grenadine. Another cycle was casting its shadow before it.

The O'Flahertys were regarded among the first families of Ward Eight. Dennis had been fortunate and Norah had been saving. They owned the house at the top of the hill now, and other families paid them rent. Big Tim was in college, a distinction which enhanced their position in the colony. Little Dennis was in high school; Mary was taking piano lessons from the sisters and played the organ at Sunday vespers. Michael was well along in parochial school.

The basement kitchen and the arrangement of the O'Flaherty household remained, because Dennis and Norah had become so accustomed to it that they could not bring themselves to change. Big Tim came home every night, took possession of the kitchen table after supper, and spread himself, his books and papers, over it. An elaborate gas-lamp with a flimsy, incandescent mantle had taken the place of the kerosene-lamp. When his work was done, he piled his belongings in the centre of the table and went down to the corner. He saw Sadie regularly no longer. The colony criticized his attitude toward her when they thought of it, but Big Tim was determined not to be committed.

3

Irish labour had been absorbed fast, drawn away from the docks and ditches into industry, to build tunnels and subways, to make mattresses and can tomatoes. Hard times became vague memories. John L. Sullivan's bar-room did a thriving business, a handshake with every beer, but so did all of the other saloons. The Irish were in complete control of the city government, and Hughie Donnelly, because of his peculiar position between two warring factions, held the balance of power. He dictated mayors and exacted a heavy pound of flesh. He was amassing an impressive fortune. Hughie sold his patronage over the counter and displayed it frankly as his particular merchandise. Saloon-keepers paid liberally to retain their licences and licences came as high as $2,500, depending upon the location of the saloon. He appointed bail commissioners and exacted a monthly percentage of their takings. He loaned money on mortgages and became an extensive real-estate owner. Whenever the city wanted to buy land for any purpose, if Hughie did not already own it, he became the broker through whom the deal was made and collected the commission. Usually, he bought the land first and then sold it to the city for twice his purchase price.

The demand for labour far exceeded the supply. Hughie put every available man in the ward to work and could use more. The shortage of labour became acute.

For years there had been a half-dozen Italian families in the vicinity of the spaghetti factory. Now more of them came, not to work in the spaghetti factory, but to take the menial jobs which the Irish were deserting. Hughie placed them at work as a matter of routine because he was paid so much per head by contractors to furnish them, and Irishmen were not available. For a time Hughie had ignored them. They did not fit in with his scheme of things. He could not understand them, nor make himself understood. It was difficult to incorporate them into his machine of registered voters, and Hughie's activities were now so numerous that he had little time for them.

But history repeated itself. In Genoa and Florence, Naples and Rome, steamship companies plastered posters in public places advertising the wealth and opportunity of America, and Italian labour was drawn in to fill the vacuum. Italian brawn replaced the deserting Irish brawn to load and unload and refuel ships. They hired out to stevedores, bought dories and invaded the fishing-fleets and lobster-pots. Just as the Irish had colonized in the vicinity of docks and wharves to be near their employment, so the Italians colonized in the same places.

Gradually the second army of occupation established its foothold. In less than a year both sides of the Battery along the waterfront were lined with Italian tenements. They spread out in side streets until a quarter of a mile was tenanted by them; but they were a weak minority, timid, overawed by the Irish, and elaborately grateful for such crumbs as might fall from the Irish political table. Though they were leaderless at first, inevitably the padrone among them asserted himself. In the beginning Hughie recognized him because he could speak English; and later because he could be depended upon to round up any given number of 'Eye-talians' for a specific job.

The padrone was Tony DiPisa, young, shorter than the average Irish worker, but broad-shouldered and thickset. His eyes were of such a dark brown that they appeared to be black, alive, intelligent, and crafty. Tony was in his early thirties and he was cruel and ruthless in dealing with his countrymen. From the beginning Tony disdained the rough garb of the dock and the ditch common to his people at work or at home; he appeared in neat blue serge with gaudy socks and ties, a weakness that persisted throughout the years that followed. Contractors paid Hughie for supplying labour, and the workers paid the padrone, Tony, for the privilege of working. Ultimately Hughie got around to understanding the system, and with instinctive political sense he sized up Tony and sent for him. The interview was brief.

'There's only one thing I want you to understand,' Hughie told him.

'Yes, Mr Hughie,' the Italian looked at him expectantly.

'I'm boss around here,' Hughie said.

'I understand,' the Italian answered.

No compact ever signed in the presence of regal witnesses or decorated with gold and ribbon was more binding or more religiously observed.

4

Big Tim knew every knot and strand in the awning ropes outside the corner variety store beneath the Jefferson Club; the criss-cross winding of the cord, like a figure eight over the small anchor flukes screwed into the window casing, the familiar feel of the huge knot in his hand as he hung upon it restfully like a strap-hanger, the Helmar advertisement in the window, yellowed with age and speckled with fly spots, lines of dime novels, *Buffalo Bill's Death Call*, *Frank Merriwell's Fight for Right*, their corners dog-eared and the paper-cover designs bleached by the sun; daily papers displayed on orange crates in the doorway. The gang still gathered here to cover the sidewalk with tobacco juice. Big Tim, now a junior at Boston College, still joined them nightly.

Acquiring a college education set him apart. The gang deferred to his opinions ingratiatingly, and when he was not about discussed him freely. To them he was now undoubtedly lace curtain and cut-glass. When he was among them they were restrained. He remained a court of appeal to settle disputes because he was held to know. A college education gave one, according to their view, a knowledge comparable to the Holy Trinity and judgement as infallible. None among them would voice his contempt for Big Tim in his presence. He was too big and too strong. 'Bugso' Kelliher once ventured to express his opinion of Big Tim by squirting tobacco juice upon his newly shined shoes. Bugso was treated for three weeks at the out-patient department.

Hughie shared the gang's opinion of Big Tim, and he alone could express it. Big Tim accepted his jibes in the clubroom with grim silence, but never allowed them to interfere with a shot on the pool table. The gang enjoyed it, but never openly. It was not safe. Big Tim's eyes and ears were quick. The gang code remained the same, instilled by the older bums into the younger. 'Gang!' was still the rallying cry to organize the mob in any sudden emergency. They were still Hughie's bodyguard. The raids into warehouses, docks, wharves, and railroad yards continued, but Big Tim accompanied them no longer. There was no longer a thrill for him in fouling the law. The excitement of the chase was not worth the risk.

Into this gang came Tony DiPisa, timidly at first, the pioneer Italian among the Irish. Tony was fair game, an exciting little mouse for the big cats to play with, to paw about, beat and torture, because he always came back for more. Each night Tony reported to Hughie to discover how many labourers would be needed on the morrow and to make reports for today. To reach him, Tony had to pass through the gang outside the club door. Tony was determined to become a member of this gang. It appeared to be the first step upward in a new world. His efforts were pathetic and amusing even to the colony drunkard, who tossed Tony about unmercifully for the entertainment of the gang. Tony ducked his head instinctively whenever any member of the gang approached him; and when time hung particularly heavy upon their hands, any gangster seeking diversion from the monotony would inquire: 'Where's the Ginny?'[4]

Classes, lectures, and homework prevented Big Tim from witnessing this spectacle for some time. It was always over when he arrived on the corner at night,

but the time came when the show could be put on for his benefit. Big Tim was early on the corner and Tony was late.

'Mickey' Dunn, the corner drunkard, saw Tony first. He had been waiting for him. The gang stood quietly in various poses of lassitude, awaiting his approach. As he reached the door Mickey's hand shot out and in a moment Tony's head was locked under Mickey's arm. Tony cried out in pain, gasping a pathetic, 'Please Mister!'

'Let him go,' Big Tim called to Mickey.

The gang looked at Big Tim, each one blinking in surprise, Mickey stupid and uncomprehending.

'Let him go!' Big Tim repeated.

Mickey stared, unbelieving, Tony's head still locked under his arm. This was not fair. The fun had not begun. Fired with whisky courage, Mickey's eyes blazed. 'Who says so?' he asked.

Big Tim dropped the strap-hanger's knot of the awning and walked over. Realization was beginning to dawn in Mickey's eyes. He released Tony, put up his hands to defend himself. Only one blow was struck, a crackle of bone as Big Tim's fist crashed through Mickey's guard and landed upon the point of his jaw. In a moment Mickey was an inert heap at the base of the lamp-post.

'Bring him in to Hennessey's bar, a couple of you guys,' Big Tim turned to the gang, 'and see if you can revive him.'

He returned to the rope on the awning. Mickey was removed. The gang fell back into postures as they were. Tony opened the door and went up the stairs to the club. His position in the gang was assured, guaranteed by the protection of Big Tim.

When he came down there were no thanks. Tony hurried away, but there was an expression in his eyes of gratitude and relief more eloquent than mere words. Until the day of his death Tony would be Big Tim's slave.

1   Jacques Marquette (1637–75), a French Jesuit missionary to the Ottawa and Huron Indians in what was then New France. He later helped establish the existence of a water highway from the St Lawrence River to the Gulf of Mexico.
2   *Ratio Studiorum* was a time-honoured method of teaching among the Jesuits. Radio studiorium is either a typographical error or an attempt to indicate what Big Tim thought of the curriculum and its method of delivery.
3   For more information on Irish versus Yankee in Boston, see review of *Ward Eight* by George C. Homans, p. 391 above.
4   An instrument for lifting up protective grates from store windows (Jay Robert Nash, *Dictionary of Crime*, 1992).

MILES FRANKLIN
from Miles Franklin, *All That Swagger* (1936)

When she was only sixteen, Miles Franklin (1879–1954) wrote the novel for which she is most famous — *My Brilliant Career* (1901). Born into a pioneering Irish family she was brought up in the Australian Alps in New South Wales. After a period spent as a domestic servant in Sydney and writing for the journal *Bulletin*, she moved to the United States and worked for the Womens Trade Union League. During the Great War she came to Europe and worked in slum nurseries in London. Between 1918 and 1933 she was political secretary for the National Housing Council. On her return to Australia she continued writing and publishing. *All That Swagger* is a remarkable story tracing the fortunes of Ennis-born Danny Delacy in his migration to New South Wales. Beginning at the end of the Napoleonic Wars in 1815 the story provides some telling insights into the social history of nineteenth-century Australia. Danny's warrior prowess — his swagger — is dented almost immediately he begins to establish himself in Australia when he falls from a horse and has to have his leg amputated. His wife, Johanna, who had accompanied him from Ireland, was as he tells the reader his base, the mountains his superstructure, 'his *Aisling*, his Dark Rosaleen'. His determination carries him through and he lives to see the coming of the modern world, the Boer War, and the struggle for female emancipation. Danny is captivated by the 'glory of wide horizons, sublimely empty', but, with Ireland always there in his mind, he becomes a poet without an audience. In this powerful extract Miles Franklin underlines the contribution of Irish immigrants such as Danny to the new democracy the nineteenth century bequeathed to the next.

Chapter 13

In his transition from parent of nestlings to middle-aged man maintaining his manhood among maturing sons, Delacy ran parallel with the progress of the Colony.

Rebellion had early thrown out the 'Rum Corps'[1] and burst the shell of the garde-major regime. Land grants to the favoured had ended twenty years later. The financial doldrums of the 'forties, the momentum of the golden 'fifties, more recently weathered, advanced a spirit of robust democracy.

No section of society can maintain aristocratic amenities and elegancies without a submerged race, whether slaves of another breed or the unprivileged of its own, to do the hard and menial labour. Australia began with manacled slaves, mostly misdemeanants, many of whom were bedevilled into irreclaimable outlaws by archaic officialdom and its right to prescribe the lash, but many factors operated against the continuance of this ancient social composition. Wentworth[2] and his colleagues were early leaders in its disruption. Distance from old-world authority and traditions of serfdom, and the scarcity of population of any kind from which to draft menials, coupled with inebriating opportunities for virile humanity loosed into an unspoiled continent, were defeating to class demarcation. Due to a dearth of well-bred females, the difference between freemen and emancipists was sunk in unions among the native born. Landed gentry and budding plutocracy were invigorated by marriages with the progeny of outlaws, in whose veins was some of the hardiest and most adventurous blood in the human race. Freedom and space, which in a virgin continent demanded courageous resourcefulness, sharpened wits and ingrained self-reliance in the people, and their isolation had, at its inception, an expansive influence.

Wentworth's demand for autonomy, and later the surging equality inevitable among the diversified congregations of free-men under the compulsion of gold-rush condition, smashed the aristocratic assumption in Australia and left an indelible stamp on Australian behaviour. With the passing of the earliest 'old hands' the national idiom had been democratically fixed, its spirit a fresh attempt at egalitarianism, the brothers of the Utopia to be at least as equal as blood brothers under primogeniture. Distinctive national characteristics, some of them paradoxical, were being ingrained by the force of environment.

Conditions, generally, were against the squattocracy entrenching itself as a squirearchy. The squattocracy it had to remain, with the difference between the Australian Bush and the English County so firmly marked that the Australian squatter and his missus — save in lamentable examples — have always been noted for a physical independence, a dignified ability to fend for themselves, resembling that of the higher animal world.

Thus in attacking, with single-handed hardihood, the wilderness beyond the fringe of the transplanted squirearchy, Delacy was a symbol and a portent of an Australia which still pecks at its shell a hundred years after his arrival. His practice of equality with all men was part of a continent-wide experiment, which, when Delacy was in his grave, was to flower in measures of political freedom and protection for the ordinary man which raised the personnel of the Australian working class to an unprecedented level and then left it shoaled for lack of continuing inspired leadership.

Absence of backward breeds diminished the flunkey class; the transformation of the peasant element was in part the contribution of the horse. No man can remain a peasant and go a-horse. Willy-nilly the blood saddle-horse will limber him out of his peasant characteristics. This four-footed brother cannot supply what Nature omitted, and change dunces into intellectuals, but he can lighten their bovine peculiarities.

Horses! Horses!

The whole population took to horse. Wishes were horses from the 'forties onward.

Those congenitally unsuited to excel in horseman-ship nevertheless climbed on to nags and were forbearingly carried out. Even Delacy's Chinaman used an aristocratic Nullah-Mundoey.[3] The stodginess of the yokels from Europe was swiftly massaged into something more flexible. The bumpkin was exercised towards a swagger. The galoot,[4] for good or ill, was transformed into a stockrider, a jockey, a spieler, a drover, a horse-breaker, a horse-coper, a horse-breeder — a caballero of one kind or another. He plodded no more on foot. Only derelicts walked.

The man at one with light horses may be a brave dashing gentleman at large, a cavalry officer at heel, a soulless undersized simian or any of the intermediate grades, but he ceases to be a peasant. Australia has remained a peasantless Commonwealth, a peonless community.

Cavalier qualities were heightened in the Australian by the class of horses available. He rode no mustangs with strawberry hides like those of their horned brothers, but animals with a dash of good blood. The brumby[5] of Australian beginnings was an escaped blood on one side of his family tree. Nevertheless, the dearth of menials, which forced pioneer tasks upon the

squatter, likewise saved the yokel from developing into a full-blown caballero. The Australian horseman lacked the leisure and the arena furnished with peons and flunkeys in which to develop picturesque flourish in manners and to pursue *amour* as a fine art. Comple-mentary to his responsibilities as wood-and-water joey and general rouseabout, all the pioneer women, who pulled their weight on the frontier, had to cope with toil which in Great Britain was relegated to 'general slaveys'.

The rough rider had little time for serenades and genuflexions, his lady less to accept them. That perhaps is why the Australian has been described as the world's worst lover, though he developed his own commendable qualities and habits. Australian women, though inured to hardship and deprivation, had true mateship and the large measure of marital faithfulness attendant upon monogamy enforced by conditions; the dignity of equal citizenship was early theirs.

Delacy, freeman by the accident of parentage as well as by the richer endowment of mental and spiritual independence, reared his family when the Colonies were expanding towards Commonwealth — not, however, to be consummated until fifty years later — and he reared them on horseback.

The Delacys were woven into the great days of the horse, when he was transporter in two senses, when all release, romance, adventure, travel, hung on his withers. His usage demanded ability and daring and included all the exhilarating swagger invested in furnishing the superbest of creatures in hogskin and silver. His was a high destiny which remained unchallenged for half a century.

Johanna's forebears gave their male children a horse at seven, and a sword and spear. Regardless of sex, the Australian bush child had a horse long before he was seven. Children went a-horse in the parents' arms before they could sit up. At an earlier age they rode with their undefeatable mothers to be born, for though property rights for women on the Murrumbidgee had not then advanced far beyond Brehon law,[6] the exigencies of pioneering put women on horseback. A lop-sided saddle and long robes were indispensable to constrain female limbs to spurious femininity, but were not entirely discommoding.

The Australian Alps came near to being populated in the decades succeeding the gold-rushes. Not only were there squatters, selectors[7] and fossickers.[8] Horse shooters were present to do away with thousands of horses. (Horsehair furniture was fashionable, to tickle the bare legs of children.) There were kangaroo shooters and those who slaughtered the lyre-bird. The mountains were alive with these fairy creatures. American gold-seekers of the 'fifties remained to fossick through the 'sixties, and saw the trade in their tails.

No one thought of conserving anything. Men worked to the limit, grunting with effort. Women bore children without restraint and thought it God's will. When jellied, fly-blown human backs had the sanction of society, there was no tenderness towards animals, no artistic and scientific realization that in Australia's living unique flora, fauna and avifauna were masterpieces beyond anything she can ever contribute to museums and galleries. Here was a wonder continent, a vast garden of Eden free from sin and disease, left intact by the aborigines. The aim was to rifle it, exploit it in greedy haste. People unable to project themselves beyond the ancient soul-case wrought for them by the inspired members of their race through a hundred generations in Europe were driven by their immediate needs to uproot Australia, to tame it into a semblance of familiar fields and towns. And there was abundance for all. Fire the forests, destroy them, man was merely as an ant against them. Millions of square miles of the stateliest trees in creation remained. Exterminate Menura for his tail regardless of his magic powers of mimicry. Snare and

trap the possums, the kangaroos and all the marsupial tribes, droves of them still appeared. Nemesis was not in that generation, nor the next.

That generation earned by sweat, endurance and deprivation the right to a harvest of some kind, salted with a little swagger. It lies forgotten now, while a less-inspired host of exploiteers, without hard toil, reaps where the old hands blazed the track in sturdy if ignorant hardihood.

1   In early settlement of New South Wales, spirit was used as a medium of exchange.
2   William Charles Wentworth (1793–1872) championed the cause of emancipists (liberated convicts) and in 1824 founded a newspaper the *Australian* to further his views on self-government for Australia.
3   In Australian pidgin mundoey means foot; nulla is short for nulla-nulla, an aboriginal word for club.
4   Sometimes, uncouth; here an awkward person.
5   Wild or unbroken horse.
6   The Brehon (*breitheamh* is Irish for judge) legal system was the native law in Ireland until its overthrow after the Elizabethan conquest at the end of the sixteenth century.
7   Those who acquired land in Australia through 'free-selection'.
8   Pocket-miners for gold (who used pocket knives etc.).

PATRICK KAVANAGH
from Patrick Kavanagh, *Ploughman and Other Poems* (1936)

Patrick Kavanagh (1904–67) was born in Inniskeen in County Monaghan into a family of small farmers. In 1939 he moved to Dublin, but, like William Carleton (1794–1869) a century before him, he returned to his country roots for his material. Here in the mid-1930s he celebrates the old style of life, but because he is conscious that he too is like a Crusoe figure he manages to strike a note which is personal and combative rather than sentimental and backward-looking.

INNISKEEN ROAD: JULY EVENING

The bicycles go by in twos and threes —
There's a dance in Billy Brennan's barn to-night,
And there's the half-talk code of mysteries
And the wink-and-elbow language of delight.
Half-past eight and there is not a spot
Upon a mile of road, no shadow thrown
That might turn out a man or woman, not
A footfall tapping secrecies of stone.

I have what every poet hates in spite
Of all the solemn talk of contemplation.
Oh, Alexander Selkirk[1] knew the plight
Of being king and government and nation.
A road, a mile of kingdom, I am king
Of banks and stones and every blooming thing.

1   Alexander Selkirk (1676–1721) was a Scottish sailor whose adventures were used by Defoe in *Robinson Crusoe* (1719). In 1704 after quarrelling with his captain he asked to be put ashore on Más Atierra Island where he stayed for four years and four months before being rescued.

MICHAEL McLAVERTY
from *Ireland Today*, 10 October 1937

Michael McLaverty (1904–92), born in County Monaghan, was for most of his life a primary-school teacher in Belfast before becoming headmaster of a Catholic boys' secondary school on the Falls Road. A slightly revised version of this story can be found in *The Game Cock and Other Stories* (1947).

A Game Cock

When I was young we came to Belfast and my father kept a game cock and a few hens. At the back of the street was waste ground where the hens could scrape, and my father built a shed for them in the yard and sawed a hole in the back-door, so that they could hop in and out as they took the notion. In the mornings our cock was always first out on the waste ground.

We called him Dick. He was none of your ordinary cocks. He had a pedigree as long as your arm, and his grandfather and grandmother were of Indian breed. He was lovely to look at, with his long, yellow legs, black glossy feathers in the chest and tail, and reddish streaky neck. My father would watch him for hours in the long summer evenings, smiling at the way he tore the clayey ground with his claws, coming on a large earwig, and calling the hens to share it. But one day when somebody lamed him with a stone, my father grew so sad that he couldn't take his supper.

We bought him from Jimmy Reilly, the blind man, and many an evening he came to handle him. I would be doing my school exercise at the kitchen table, my father, in his shirt sleeves, reading the paper. A knock would come to the door, and with great expectancy in his voice my father'd say: 'That's the men now; let them in, son.'

And when I opened the door, in would shuffle wee Johnny Moore leading the blind man. They'd sit on the sofa: Jimmy Reilly, hat on head, and two fists clasped round the shank of the walking stick between his legs; and Johnny Moore with a stinking clay pipe in his mouth.

As soon as they started the talk I'd put down my pen and listen to them.

'Sit up to the fire, men, and get a bit of the heat.'

'That's a snorer of a fire you've on, Mick,' would come from the blind man.

'What kind of coals is them?' says Johnny Moore, for he had my father pestered with questions.

'The best English; them's none of your Scotch slates!'

'And what's the price of them a ton?'

'They cost a good penny,' my father would answer crossly.

'And where do you get them?'

The blind man's stick would rattle on the kitchen tiles and he'd push out his lower lip, stroke his beard and shout: 'They're good coals, anyway, no matter where they're got'; and then add in his slow, natural voice, 'How's the cock, Mick?'

'He's in great fettle, Jimmy. He's jumping out of his pelt.' And he'd tell how the comb[1] was reddening and how he had chased Maguire's dunghill of a rooster from about the place. And the blind man would smile and say: 'That's the stuff! He'll soon have the walk to himself; other cocks would annoy him.'

With a lighted candle I would be sent out to the yard to lift Dick off the roost. The roosts were low so that the cock wouldn't bruise his feet when flying to the ground. He'd blink his eyes and cluck-cluck in his throat when I'd bring him into the gaslight and hand him to the blind man.

Jimmy fondled him like a woman fondling a cat. He gently stroked the neck and tail, and then stretched out one wing and then the other. 'He's in great condition. We could cut his comb and wattles any time and have him ready for Easter.' And he'd put him down on the tiles and listen to the scrape of his claws. Then he'd feel the muscles on the thighs, and stick out his beard with joy. 'There's no coldness about that fella, Mick. He has shoulders on him as broad as a bull-dog . . . Aw, my lovely fella,' feeling the limber of him as his claws pranced on the tiles. 'He'll do us credit. A hould you he'll win a main.'[2]

My father would stuff his hands in his pockets and rise off his heels. 'And you think he's doing well, Jimmy?'

'Hould yer tongue, man. I wish I was half as fit,' Jimmy would answer, his sightless eyes raised to the ceiling.

And one evening as they talked like this about the cock and forthcoming fights, Johnny Moore sneaked across to the table and gave me sums out of his head. *A rope-maker made a rope for his marrying daughter, and in the rope he made twenty knots and in each knot he put a purse, and in each purse he put seven three-penny bits and nine halfpennies. How much of a dowry did the daughter receive?*

I couldn't get the answer and he took the pipe from his mouth and laughed loudly. 'The scholars,[3] nowadays, have soft brains. You can't do it with your pencil and paper and an old man like me can do it in my head.'

My face burned as I said: 'But we don't learn them kind of sums.' He laughed so much at me that I was glad when it was time for him to lead the blind man home.

But they were soon back again; the blind man with special scissors to cut Dick's comb and wattles.[4] Jimmy handed the scissors to my father. Then he held the cock, his forefinger in its mouth and his thumb at the back of its head.

'Now,' said he, 'try and cut it with one stroke.'

When my sisters saw the chips of comb snipped off with the scissors and the blood falling on the tiles they began to cry. 'That's a sin, father! That's a sin!'

'Tush, tush,' said my father, and the blood on his sleeves. 'He doesn't feel it. It's just like getting your hair cut . . . Isn't that right, Jimmy?'

'That's right; just like getting your toenails cut.'

But when Dick clucked and shook his head with pain, my sisters cried louder and were sent out to play themselves, and I went into the scullery to gather cobwebs to stop the bleeding.

In a few days the blood had hardened and Dick was his old self again. The men came nearly every night and talked about the cock fights to be held near Toome[5] at Easter. They made plans for Dick's training and arranged how he was to be fed.

About a fortnight before the fights my father got a long box and nailed loose sacking over the front to keep it in darkness. Dick was put into this and his feathers and tail were clipped. For the first two days he got no feed so as to keep his weight down. Then we gave him hard-boiled eggs, but they didn't agree with him and made him scour.[6] The blind man recommended a strict diet of barley and barley-water: 'That's the stuff to keep his nerves strong and his blood up. A hould you it'll not scour him.'

Every morning we took him from the dark box and gave him a few runs up and down the yard. Johnny Moore had made a red-flannel bag stuffed with straw, and Dick sparred at this daily, and when he had finished my father would lift him in his arms, stroke him gently, and sponge the feet and head. Day by day the cock got very peevish, and once when he nebbed at me I gave him such a clout that brought my father running to the yard.

The night before the fight the steel spurs were tied on him to see how he would look in the pit. 'Ah, Jimmy, if you could see him,' said my father to the blind man. 'He's the picture of health.'

The blind man fingered his beard and putting a hand in his pocket, took out a few pound notes and spat on them for luck: 'Put that on him to-morrow. There's not another cock this side of the Bann[7] nor in all County Derry that could touch him.'

Even Jimmy Moore risked a few shillings; and the next morning before 5 o'clock my father wakened me to go to Toome.

It was Easter Monday and there were no trams running so early as we set off to walk to the Northern Counties Railway to catch the half-six train. The cock was in a potato-bag under my arm, and I got orders not to squeeze him, while my father carried the overcoats and a gladstone filled with things for my Granny, who lived near the place where the cocks were to fight.

The streets were deserted, and our feet echoed in the chill air. Down the Falls Road we hurried. The shop-blinds were pulled down; the tram lines shining; and no smoke coming from the chimneys. At the Public Baths my father looked at his watch and then stood out in the road to see the exact time by the Baths' clock.

'Boys-a-boys my watch is slow. We'll need to hurry.' In the excitement the cock got his neb out and pecked at me. I dropped the bag, and out jumped the cock and raced across the tramlines, the two of us after him.

'Don't excite him, son. Take him gently.'

We tried to corner him in a doorway, my father with his hand outstretched calling in his sweetest way: 'Dick, Dick, Dicky.' But as soon as he stooped to lift him, the cock dived between his legs, and raced up North Howard Street, and stood contemplating a dark-green public lavatory.

'Whisht,' said my father, holding my arm as I went to go forward. 'Whisht. If he goes in there we'll nab him.'

The cock stood, head erect, and looked up and down the bare street. Then he scraped each side of his bill on the step of the lavatory and crowed into the morning.

'Man, but that's the brazen tinker of a cock for you,' said my father, looking at his watch. And then, as if Dick were entering the hen-shed, in he walked, and in after him tiptoed my father, and out by the roofless top flew the cock with a few feathers falling from him.

I swished him off the top and he flew for all he was worth over the tram lines, down Alma Street and up on a yard-wall.

'We'll be late for the train if we don't catch him quick, and maybe the peelers[8] down on us before we know where we are.'

Up on the wall I was heaved and sat with legs astride. The cock walked away from me, and a dog in the yard yelped and jumped up the back door.

'I'm afraid, Da, I'm afraid.'

'Come down out of that and don't whinge there.'

A baby started to cry and a man looked out of a window and shouted: 'What the hell's wrong?'

'We're after a cock,' replied my father apologetically.

The man continued to lean out of the window in his shirt, and a woman yelled from the same room: 'Throw a bucket of water round them, Andy . . . A nice time of the morning to be chasing a bloody cock.'

Here and there a back-door opened and bare-footed men in their shirts and trousers came into the entry. They all chased after Dick.

'Ah, easy, easy,' said my father to a man who was swiping at Dick with a yard-brush. 'Don't hit him with that.'

By this time the cock had walked half way down the entry,[9] still keeping to the top of the yard-walls. Women shouted and dogs barked, and all the time I could hear my father saying: 'If we don't catch him quick we'll miss the train.'

'Aw,' said one man, looking at the scaldy appearance of the cock. 'Sure he's not worth botherin' about. There's not as much on him as'd set a rat-trap.'

My father kept silent about Dick's pedigree for he didn't want anyone to know about the cock-fights, and maybe have the police after us.

We had now reached the end of the entry and Dick flew off the wall and under a little hand-cart that lay in a corner. Five men bunched in after him; and screeching and scolding the cock was handed to my father.

'I can feel his heart going like a traction engine,' he said, when we were on the road again. 'He'll be bate.[10] The blind man's money and everybody's money will be lost. Lost!'

We broke into a trot, I carrying the gladstone, and my father the cock and the overcoats. Along York Street we raced, gazing up at the big clocks and watching the hands approach half-six. Sweat broke out on us and a stitch came in my side, but I said nothing as I lagged behind trying to keep pace.

We ran into the station and were just into the carriage when out went the train.

'Aw-aw-aw,' said my father, sighing out all his breath in one puff. 'I'm done. Punctured! That's a nice start for an Easter Monday!'

He took off his hard hat and pulled out a handkerchief; his bald head was speckled with sweat and the hat had made a red groove on his brow. He puffed and ah-e-e-d so many times I thought he'd faint; and I sat with my heart thumping, my shirt clammy with sweat, waiting with fear for what he'd say. But he didn't scold me.

'It was my own fault,' he said. 'I should have tied a bit of string round the neck of the bag . . . He'll be bate! He'll be bate!'

He took the spurs from his pocket and pulled the corks off the steel points. 'I might as well strap them on a jackdaw as put them on Dick this day, for he'll be tore asunder after that performance.'

As the train raced into the country we saw the land covered with a thin mist, and ploughed fields with shining furrows. The cold morning air came into the carriage; it was lovely and fresh. My father's breathing became quieter, and he even pointed out farms that would make great 'walks' for cocks. It was going to be a grand day: a foggy sun was bursting through, and crows flew around trees that were already laden with their nests.

Dick was taken from the bag and petted; and then my father stretched himself out on the seat and fell asleep. I watched the telegraph wires rising and falling, and kept a look-out for the strange birds that were cut out in the hedge near Doagh.

When we came to Toome my father tied the neck of the bag with a handkerchief and sent me on in front for fear the police might suspect something. The one-streeted village was shady and cool, the sun skimming the house-tops. Pieces of straw littered the road, and a few hens stood at the closed barrack door, their droppings on the door-step.

We passed quickly through the silent village and turned on to the long country road that led to my Granny's. Behind us the train rumbled and whistled over the bridge; and then across the still country came the dull cheer of the Bann waterfall and the wind astir in the leafing branches. Once my father told me to sit and rest myself while he crossed a few fields to a white cottage. It wasn't long until he was back again. 'I've got the stuff in my pocket that'll make him gallop . . . The boys in Lough Beg made a run of poteen for Easter.'

When we reached my Granny's she was standing at the door, a string garter fallen round her ankle, and a basin in her hand; near her my Uncle's bicycle was turned upside down and he was mending a puncture. They had great welcome for us and smiled when my father put the poteen on the table. He took tumblers from the dresser, filled one for my Granny, and in another he softened a few pieces of bread for the cock.

My Granny sat at the fire and at every sip she sighed and held the glass up to the light: 'Poor fellas, but they run great risk to make that. None of your ould treacle about the Lough Beg stuff . . . Made from the best of barley.'

As she sipped it she talked to me about my school, and the little sense my father had in his head to be bothering himself about game cocks and maybe land himself in jail; and when the car came up for him she went to the door and waved him off. 'Mind the peelers,' she shouted. 'Ye'd never know where they'd be sniffing around.'

During the day I played about the house and tormented the tethered goat, making her rise on her hind legs. I went to the well at the foot of the field and carried a bucket of water to my Granny, and she said I was a big, strong man. Later my Uncle brought me through the tumbled demesne-wall and showed me where he had slaughtered a few trees for the fire. We walked to the Big House and saw the lake covered with rushes and weeds. The Big House was in ruins and crows were nesting in the chimneys. When I asked my uncle where were all the ladies and gentlemen and the gamekeeper, he looked through the naked windows and replied: 'They took the land from the people and God cursed them.'

When we came back my Granny was standing at the door looking up and down the road wondering what was keeping my father. A few fellows coming from the cock fights passed on bicycles, and soon my father arrived. He was in great form, his face red, and his navy-blue trousers covered with clay.

The cock's comb was scratched with blood, his feathers streaky, and his eyes half shut. He was left in the byre until the tea was over. While my father was taking the tea he got up from the table and stood in the middle of the floor telling how Dick had won his fights: 'Five battles he won and gave away weight twice.'

'Take your tea, Mick, and you can tell us after,' my Granny said, her hands in her sleeves, and her feet tapping the hearth.

He would eat for a few minutes and he'd be up again: 'Be the holy frost if ye'd seen him tumbling the big Pyle cock from Derry it'd have done yer heart good. I never seen the like of it . . . Aw, he's a great battler. And look at the morning he put in on them yard-walls . . . Up and down a dozen streets he went, running and flying and crowing. And then to win his fights . . . Wait till Jimmy Reilly hears about this and the nice nest egg I have for him . . . The poteen was great stuff. A great warrior!' and he smiled in recollection.

I was glad when he was ready for home and gladder still when we were in the train where I heard the wheels rumbling and chanting . . . *They took the land from the people . . . God cursed them . . . God cursed them . . . They took the land from the people . . . God cursed them . . .*

It was dark when we reached Belfast and I carried Dick in the potato bag. We got into a tram at the station; the lights were lit and we sat downstairs. The people were staring at my father, at the clabber[11] on his boots and the wrinkles on his trousers. But he paid no heed to them. In the plate glass opposite I could see our reflections; my father was smiling with his lips together, and I knew he was thinking of the cock.

'He's very quiet, Da,' I whispered. 'The fightin' has fairly knocked the capers out of him.'

'Aw, son, he's a great warrior,' and he put his hand in his pocket and slipped me a half-crown. 'I'll get his photo took as soon as he's his old self again.'

In the kitchen I left the bag on the floor and sat on the sofa, dead tired. My father got down the olive oil to rub on Dick's legs, but when he opened the bag the cock never stirred. He took him out gently and raised his head, but it fell forward limply, and from the open mouth blood dripped to the floor.

'God-a-God, he's dead!' said my father, stretching out one of the wings. He held up the cock's head in the gaslight and looked at him. Then he put him on the table without a word and sat on a chair. For a while I said nothing, and then I asked quietly: 'What'll you do with him, Da?'

He didn't answer, but turned and looked at the cock, stretched on the table. 'Poor Dick!' he said; and I felt a lump rise in my throat.

Then he got up from the chair. 'What'll I do with him! . . . What'll I do with him! . . . I'll get him stuffed! . . . That's what I'll do!'

1   Fleshy crest on head.
2   I bet you. I'm certain. A 'main' seems to be a reference to a game of chance played with dice.
3   Children at school.
4   Fleshy part hanging from neck of bird.
5   At the top of Lough Neagh on the borders of Counties Antrim and Derry.
6   Have diarrhoea.
7   The Bann River, which acts as a divide between Antrim and Derry.
8   Police.
9   Alley, row between backs of houses.
10 Beaten.
11 Mud.

LOUIS MacNEICE
from *The Collected Poems of Louis MacNeice* (1979)

Louis MacNeice (1907–63) was brought up in the Church of Ireland Rectory at Carrickfergus. Educated at Marlborough and Oxford, he taught Classics at Birmingham University and Bedford College, London, before joining the BBC in 1941. MacNeice was part of the Macspaunday group of Thirties poets (*Mac*Neice, *Sp*ender, A*u*den, *Day* Lewis), but his Irish experience gave his work added depth. Here in this poem of even tone, written in 1937, he returns to his childhood and to his keen consciousness of social difference and to the wider historical changes then under way.

CARRICKFERGUS

I was born in Belfast between the mountain and the
    gantries
  To the hooting of lost sirens and the clang of trams:
Thence to Smoky Carrick in County Antrim
  Where the bottle-neck harbour collects the mud
    which jams

The little boats beneath the Norman castle,
  The pier shining with lumps of crystal salt;
The Scotch Quarter was a line of residential houses
  But the Irish Quarter was a slum for the blind and
    halt.

The brook ran yellow from the factory stinking of
    chlorine,
  The yarn-mill called its funeral cry at noon;
Our lights looked over the lough to the lights of
    Bangor
  Under the peacock aura of a drowning moon.

The Norman walled this town against the country
  To stop his ears to the yelping of his slave
And built a church in the form of a cross but denoting
  The list of Christ on the cross in the angle of the
    nave.

I was the rector's son, born to the anglican order,
  Banned for ever from the candles of the Irish poor;
The Chichesters[1] knelt in marble at the end of a
    transept
  With ruffs about their necks, their portion sure.

The war came and a huge camp of soldiers
  Grew from the ground in sight of our house with
    long
Dummies hanging from gibbets for bayonet practice
  And the sentry's challenge echoing all day long;

A Yorkshire terrier ran in and out by the gate-lodge
  Barred to civilians, yapping as if taking affront:
Marching at ease and singing 'Who Killed Cock
    Robin?'
  The troops went out by the lodge and off to the
    Front.

The steamer was camouflaged that took me to
    England —
  Sweat and khaki in the Carlisle train;
I thought that the war would last for ever and sugar
  Be always rationed and that never again

Would the weekly papers not have photos of sandbags
  And my governess not make bandages from moss
And people not have maps above the fireplace
  With flags on pins moving across and across —

Across the hawthorn hedge the noise of bugles,
  Flares across the night,
Somewhere on the lough was a prison ship for
    Germans,
  A cage across their sight.

I went to school in Dorset,[2] the world of parents
  Contracted into a puppet world of sons
Far from the mill girls, the smell of porter, the salt-
    mines
  And the soldiers with their guns.

---

1 A leading Ulster Protestant family.
2 Acreman House, a preparatory school.

CHARLES DONNELLY
from *Ireland Today*, January 1937, February 1937

Charles Donnelly (1914–37) was born in County Tyrone and educated for a time at University College, Dublin, until his commitment to left-wing politics took him to London in 1935 where he edited *Irish Front* with Leslie Daiken. When the Spanish Civil War began he joined the Abraham Lincoln Brigade and was killed in action (along with the English Marxist Christopher Caudwell) at the Battle of the Jarama on 27 February 1937. In these two poems he provides a thoughtful insight into the mind of a young activist. Donagh MacDonagh's fine elegy to him, 'He Is Dead and Gone, Lady . . .', appeared in *Ireland Today* (Volume 2, Number 7, July 1937), along with 'Heroic Heart', one of Donnelly's last poems written in Spain. *Pictures of Tomorrow*, a play by Martin Lynch and performed at the Lyric Theatre in Belfast in 1994, makes telling use of Donnelly, at once part of history and legend, to contrast with a disillusioned present. For more on Donnelly, see Joseph O'Connor, *Even the Olives Are Bleeding: The Life and Times of Charles Donnelly* (1992).

POEM

Between rebellion as a private study and the public
Defiance, is simple action only on which will flickers
Catlike, for spring. Whether at nerve-roots is secret
Iron, there's no diviner can tell, only the moment can
    show.
Simple and unclear moment, on a morning utterly
    different
And under circumstances different from what you'd
    expected.

Your flag is public over granite. Gulls fly above it.
Whatever the issue of the battle is, your memory
Is public, for them to pull awry with crooked hands,
Moist eyes. And village reputations will be built on
Inaccurate accounts of your campaign. You're name
    for orators,
Figure stone-struck beneath damp Dublin sky.

In a delaying action, perhaps, on hillside in remote
    parish,
Outposts correctly placed, retreat secured to wood,
    bridge mined
Against pursuit, sniper may sight you carelessly
    contoured.
Or death may follow years in strait confinement,
    where diet
Is uniform as ceremony, lacking only fruit.
Or on the barrack square before the sun casts shadow.

Name, subject of all-considered words, praise and
    blame

Irrelevant, the public talk which sounds the same on
    hollow
Tongue as true, you'll be with Parnell and with Pearse.
Name aldermen will raise a cheer with, teachers make
    reference
Oblique in class, and boys and women spin gum of
    sentiment
On qualities attributed in error.

Man, dweller in mountain huts, possessor of coloured
    mice,
Skilful in minor manual turns, patron of obscure
    subjects, of
Gaelic swordsmanship and mediaeval armoury.
The technique of the public man, the masked
    servilities are
Not for you. Master of military trade, you give
Like Raleigh, Lawrence, Childers,[1] your services but
    not yourself.

THE TOLERANCE OF CROWS

Death comes in quantity from solved
Problems on maps, well-ordered dispositions,
Angles of elevation and direction;

Comes innocent from tools children might
Love, retaining under pillows,
Innocently impales on any flesh.

And with flesh falls apart the mind
That trails thought from the mind that cuts
Thought clearly for a waiting purpose.

Progress of poison in the nerves and
Discipline's collapse is halted.
Body awaits the tolerance of crows.

1   Presumably T.E. Lawrence (1888–1935) who had just
    died. Erskine Childers (1870–1922), author of *The
    Riddle of the Sands* (1903), a minister in Dáil Éireann. He
    took the Republican side in the Civil War and refused to
    sign the Treaty then being negotiated. Later executed by
    the Free State Government in 1922.

JIM PHELAN
from Jim Phelan, *Lifer* (1938)

Information about the biography of Jim Phelan (1895–1966) is sketchy. In *New Writing*
(Issue 4, 1941) he is described as 'a young Irish writer, whose book on the prisons, *Jail
Journey*, attracted widespread attention last year. He has also written several novels,
including *Green Volcano*, a picture of Ireland in revolution, and a number of short
stories about peasant life.' He came from a family with a jail-tradition, his father, his
grandfather, and his great-grandfather all seeing the inside of prisons. His father came
from near Thurles in Tipperary; Jim grew up in Inchicore near Dublin, and was a street
kid by the age of eleven, at thirteen prowling the streets of Glasgow, and before he was
fourteen he was spending most of his time in the Liberty slum area of Dublin. After a
hold-up at a post office outside Liverpool in which a clerk was shot, he was sentenced
to life at Manchester Crown Court and thus became a 'tramp at anchor', the title of his
book published in 1954. He spent over thirteen years in prisons at Maidstone,
Dartmoor, and Parkhurst before being released some time in the late 1930s. After the
War he worked as a scriptwriter in a film company making films for the Ministry of
Information. In the second edition of *Underworld*, published in 1967, he comments on
the Great Train Robbery of 1963. He used the experience of prison and drifting as a
quarry for his writing, and, with one or two exceptions such as *Ireland-Atlantic Gateway*
(1941) (see below, p. 496), it can be said that his career as a writer is linked with his
career as a prisoner and as a tramp. In *Lifer*, a semi-autobiographical novel, he recounts
the experience of Arthur Mansell's imprisonment from the age of eighteen until his
release fifteen years later. At the beginning of the novel he is sent to Rockville where
he learns his first lessons in managing boredom and prison life.

from Chapter 2

You can see a little strip of green hill-side from the
door of the bootmakers' shop at Rockville.¹ Just a little
slope, very green, sometimes with sheep grazing, like
one of the old prints of Widdecombe Fair. The rest is
granite. Inside the shop you see nothing at first — you
just smell, half-retching with nausea, until the sense of
smell works no longer, and you can look around in the
gloom.

Four steps below ground-level, stone-floored and
damp, half-lit by small windows in thick walls, with a

cluster of bootmaker's benches at one end to
accentuate the shadows, a noise-barrage of hammering
with a vague unplaced murmur of words for accompaniment, a wooden bench where paced a warder, an
office in a corner, lighted, although it was full day, and
everywhere ghost faces, pale grey horrible twisted
faces, many of them above horrible twisted bodies (for
is not bootmaking a 'sit-down' job?) — Mansell
stopped suddenly at the bottom of the steps and
thought of Doctor Moreau's Island.

Perceptibly the hammering waned and the
muttering emerged more clearly. ''ifer. 's a lifer. 'ifer.'

The faces leered openly. Swollen tongues licked grey, swollen lips. ''s a lifer.'

'Mansell, aintcha?' a young, sly-looking warder asked. 'Lifer, eh? Well,' less mechanically, 'nevermind. Soon get used to it. Look arter yourself and you'll be all right, see? Soon get settled down. Just look arter yourself. Now,' he added briskly, in the tone of one completing an important interview, 'just go to that bloke over in the corner and he'll look arter you for the time bein'.'

Six feet high, vast arms and shoulders, a much-broken nose, greying curly wool like a negro's, little half-closed blue eyes, a wide shatter-lipped mouth with black, twisted, broken teeth, and a horrible stench of unwashed man and half-chewed tobacco — that was the 'bloke in the corner'.

'I'm Harry Colson,' he began, 'an' I'm looking arter you. You'll be *all right*, see? No one don't butt in on me, neither screws nor lags. No one'll bother you while *I'm* looking arter you, see. Me 'n you'll be *all right*, see?' Mansell held his breath and said nothing. 'Now,' went on Colson, 'just soak them soles an' beat them out, like this, see?' Mansell took his coat off and commenced to work.

'An' take yer time,' the other advised. 'No need to rush when *I'm* looking arter you. No one don't butt in on *me*. Just take yer time,' he repeated, as Mansell hammered a sole self-consciously.

Presently the young warder from the office appeared. 'Gettin' in on it all right?' he asked in friendly fashion.

'Yes, sir,' answered the lifer, and stood silent.

'Now, just take yer time,' the warder went on. 'Take yer time and settle down an' ' — he looked the boy over from head to foot with something in his eyes and mouth for which Mansell knew no name, 'an' you'll be *all* right. You'll get used to it in no time, an' Harry'll —'

'Here, you buck off an' leave Harry out of it,' interrupted Colson threateningly, and, as the warder departed with a shamefaced apologetic grin: 'No one can't butt in on me, neither screws nor lags, see?' He gripped Mansell's shoulder hard, as he repeated: 'You're all right, see?'

In the shadows the twisted faces leered, the young warder returned to his office, the warder on the bench busied himself with some numbers on a slate, and the hammering swept down over the shop again, like a dark evil-smelling cloud, hiding the mutter and whisper from the benches, as Mansell returned to his soaking and beating of soles.

Still half-dazed, he peered about him, separating the parts of the picture which had struck him as a whole.

The faces were not so horrible, he told himself — (*Yes, they were!* Was he 'gettin' used to it' already?) Ordinary faces of sick people, that was all. But why did they watch him as if they were waiting for him to do something? Why did they leer and glance away? Suddenly, for no reason, he thought of the castor-oil punishment in which a woman was heavily dosed and then dragged along the street. . . . What were they watching for?

'Three times I been bashed,' Colson's voice interrupted his thought, 'an' there ain't no one, neither screws nor lags, butts in on *me*, see?' He breathed in Mansell's face. 'Me 'n you'll get on all right, when you're settled down. Where you located?' The other stared uncomprehendingly.

'What *hall* are you in?' Colson clarified.

'Oh. 'A' hall.'

'An' is yer things all right? Anythin' you want? Gotta good bed? Kin you read? Got books? Wanta bitta stuff? Here —' As the warder on the raised bench half-ostentatiously turned his back, Mansell found himself holding between finger and thumb something like a piece of tarred rope about an inch long.

'There y'are,' said Colson, beaming a genial black-toothed twisted grin. 'Stick it in yer kisser. No need to go short when *I'm* looking arter you,' he added proudly.

Mansell slowly put the piece of tobacco in his mouth. It was so obviously regarded as a princely gift that he did not dare refuse, although the first few minutes' contact between his tongue and the strange substance produced an incredible nausea. Presently he spat, under the bench.

'Here, don't do that,' cautioned the vast figure beside him. 'You'll get pinched. Swaller it, or gob in the leather-tub when you're takin' out the soles, see? Don't worry,' he added. 'We'll teach you to take a chew — nothin' like it, in stir. Nothin' like it. You'll be all right.' And again he gripped Mansell by the shoulder, while the nearby faces leered.

There was very little to-and-fro movement in the workshop. Most of the people sat and hammered. Occasionally one shouted above the noise, 'Fall out, sir,' and made his way to lavatory, or store-bench, or office. But otherwise no one moved from his place. There was a terrible isolation about being near people who had to pretend one was not there — people one pretended not to see, even when they threw quick furtive glances that were hurriedly turned away to the boots and the hammers.

A tall, clean-faced man of twenty-five or six, with fair hair and a thin moustache, paused on his way to the office. 'You're Mansell, aren't you?' he asked civilly.

'Yes,' answered Mansell shortly.

'The Mitcham business, wasn't it?' continued the new-comer, with a sympathetic smile, and, as Mansell again shortly answered 'Yes', the other added: 'Hard luck.'

He looked almost inhumanly clean and good-looking by comparison with the sick, dirty pallor of the faces around, Mansell thought, as the stranger went on: 'Read much?'

'Yes. A lot. Or used to —' Mansell looked down at the wet soles on the bench.

'Good.' Apparently the other man had not noticed the flicker of pain in Mansell's eyes. 'Fix you up with a book or two when you get settled down. My name's Painter,' he added as he turned away, just when the warder on the observation-bench was raising his head to call out.

'Three times I been bashed, and there's no one, neither screws *nor* lags, can butt in on me, see?' came from the huge figure at his side, and Mansell wondered why he kept saying the same things over again. 'Me 'an you'll be *all right*, see?' went on the ritual, 'when you get settled down. You'll be all right when *I'm* looking arter you.'

Almost vomiting, Mansell heard the same phrases a hundred times before the hammering ceased and the order to 'Wash up' came from the man in charge. Presently the men marched outside, and shambled past a slate-and-pencil official who counted them in as an auctioneer might count sheep at a sale. Having passed him, the crowd broke up, and dispersed to the various halls or separate prisons.

Mansell, who had been in the hospital his first night, was now located in 'A' hall. He had only given a casual glance at his abode that morning, in the hurry of being taken to his new working-party. Now he looked curiously about him and sniffed. After the first shock of feeling as if he had struck the back wall of the cell with his forehead even as he stepped inside the door — after this and above everything else the cell smelt. With the curious, warm, disgustingly-not-unpleasant scent of stale humanity, it smelt. The scent seemed to be embedded in the tarred stone floor, in the lime-and-tar piebald walls, but most of all in the roll of bedding which lay where he had thrown it that morning.

The door opened, and a curious, fidgety, rabbit-looking warder appeared. He was small, with a weak, sickly ginger moustache straggling about his upper lip. The front of his tunic was very dirty with spit or food or nose-droppings, and he sniffed continually.

'Now, Mansell,' he commenced, in a diffident and apologetic tone, 'here's what you've got to do every morning. Put your mug there, your plate there, your boots there, your blankets like this and this and this —' He reeled off a myriad instructions, Mansell ceasing the attempt to follow him after the first few minutes.

'An' your beddin',' concluded the warder, 'every dinner-time you've got to put it like this.' He rolled the blankets and sheets into a weird and intricate ball, incredibly ludicrous when considered as a bed. 'That's dinner-times,' he explained, as he unrolled it again. 'Mornin's you do it like I showed you jest now. Dinner-times like this.'

'But what's it *for*?' asked the prisoner in amazement. The whole thing sounded totally unlike anything he had imagined about a prison, and he could hardly believe he was hearing correctly.

'An' your shoes is to go there,' pursued the official, as if Mansell had not spoken. 'Got all that now? 'Cause' — he was even more viciously apologetic than ever — ' 'cause you won't get away with it if it's wrong, see? An' look arter yourself on this landin',' he added, 'an' you'll be all right, see? Anyone that looks arter themselves on my landin' is *always* all right.' As he closed the door Mansell, his head spinning, leaned against the coarse built-in table and tried to separate the hackneyed, apparently meaningless phrases, which seemed to have so much significance could one but understand them.

The combination of apology and menace in the warder's gabbled litany clung to him like a smothering rag that stank. For the first time he realized that he was not in a place but in a machine, where he was to be chopped and minced and made into something else. A strange machine, wherein the knives that did the chopping were conscious, reluctant, apologetic — but chopped just the same.

Again he found himself wondering about the words that everyone seemed to use. What did they mean by 'all right'? And how did one 'look arter' oneself? Manifestly the phrases meant different things coming from different people. Further, they seemed to have various meanings when used by the same people at different times.

Suddenly there came back to him the first phrases he had heard in Rockville, 'Ecksize, Chiboo tson.' *That* was it. They used the smallest possible vocabulary, and squeezed even that out of recognition, in a crazy straining after brevity.

Again the door opened, and a hand thrust in a double-tier tin-can. On top, potatoes that stank; underneath, beans that stank; underneath all, a scrap of bacon that stank. And, strangely, the smell was the same as the smell of the walls, of the floor, of the blankets — the smell of the primal basic filth of old humanity, of the things forgotten when the oldest cities began — the smell of Rockville.

He prodded at the food with the curiously-shaped knife, forcing himself to eat. Then, finished soon, he tried to remember the warder's instructions about the blanket-ball, and commenced to make it. In vain. It was to be green-white-brown-white-brown-white-green, in alternate strips of blanket, quilt and sheet. But instead of concentrating on the work of rolling the coloured ball, he found himself wondering again and again — *why* did they want it like this?

After several failures he began to get afraid, to remember the menace of the apologetic warder's ''Cause you won't get away with it if it's wrong.' Flustered and perspiring, he managed to get the bedding into something like the required shape, and then sat down. He reached for a book and opened it, just as a bell clanged loudly and the jangle of keys told that the cells were being opened for the afternoon's work. Then he knew why they wanted the blankets rolled and unrolled insanely. You couldn't read if you were doing that. Yet no one could say you'd been made to work through the meal-hour.

He stood at his door, as everyone else seemed to be doing. There was an interval while some men went round and collected the dinner-cans, and while others collected slops in a stinking bucket. There was a little furtive moving-about besides, but for the most part 'Stand at your door' seemed to be the unwritten injunction.

Gazing about, he was irresistibly reminded of the interior of a huge ship. Four stages up, he looked down on a big rectangular place, to the sides of which clung narrow runways with iron railings. Spidery iron staircases led from runway to runway, with here and there a narrow iron bridge to complete the resemblance. Along the narrow foot-walks men were moving to and fro busily, and at the head of each ladder stood two warders, like ship's officers on the bridge.

Three cells away he saw Painter, still looking very erect and clean, smiling in his direction, and managed to smile in reply. Presently Painter quietly moved the few paces that separated them, and stood beside Mansell's door.

'Think you'd like a book or two for to-night?' he asked, and, as the other man assented eagerly, 'What d'you read? If you take my advice it'll be light stuff for the present. Light novel with nothing in it, or a book of short stories.' After a pause he went on: 'Rotten library here, but,' casually, 'I manage to get hold of a few books and can fix you up.'

---

1   The setting resembles Dartmoor in Devon, but, as Phelan remarks in his Introduction, *Lifer* is an attempt to synthesize the many prisons in England and Ireland he had seen, including Cork, Derry, Dublin, Dartmoor, Pentonville, and Parkhurst.

KATE O'BRIEN
from Kate O'Brien, *Pray for the Wanderer* (1938)

It is May 1937, on the eve of the vote on de Valera's new constitution for Ireland. Matt Costello, a writer based in England, makes his first return to Ireland after sixteen years away. As a young man in Ireland he was a nationalist, fought the Black and Tans, was imprisoned, supported Collins, but left Ireland 'having no heart for civil war'. In this extract Matt, Tom Mahoney, a lawyer, and Nell, Tom's one-time fiancée and Matt's cousin, have just returned to Tom's family in Limerick from a picnic in the country. In *The Ante-Room* (1934) Kate O'Brien tackles the Puritanism of Ireland in the era of Parnell; here she subjects to her critical eye the new Puritanism at work in de Valera's Ireland. One contemporary American reviewer in *The Saturday Review* thought the novel would not appeal to those readers 'who demand the big wow-wow strain, but persons who like to discriminate in their reading ought to like it.'

from **Chapter 2**

Dinner passed off smoothly in the big, Georgian house in King Street.[1] Aunt Hannah, Mrs Thomas Mahoney, was magnificently unwelcoming to Matt, and pointed out a number of reasons why it would have been more comfortable and suitable for him to have dined at Weir House. Tom said nothing during these speeches; merely handed Matt a glass of whisky. His mother eyed it.

'That's far too strong, Tom. Do you want to kill him? You ought to consider other people's tastes, you know. Well, now you're here we might as well dine.'

She swept across the lofty drawing-room and her guest opened the door for her.

She was a beautifully made woman, and walked as if she knew it. She had white hair, and was picturesquely dressed in amethyst foulard, with a jingling chatelaine, and a silver spectacle case hanging from her belt.

The food was good, but Mrs Mahoney did not urge it upon anyone. She ate well herself and was imperious with the servants. The dining-room in which they sat was on the first floor, behind the drawing-room. Tom's offices occupied the ground floor, and obviously the kitchen and servants' quarters must be in the basement. There was no service lift, yet dinner proceeded without a hitch in a prosperous Victorian setting. Matt marvelled. Continuity indeed! Was it still possible to ask your fellow-creatures to race up and down four flights of stairs with your roast lamb and green peas?

He also marvelled at the strength of the three personalities which shared the benefits of this archaic and smooth routine, and which yet kept so far apart from each other, were so pointedly and eccentrically themselves.

Nell seemed not as much in awe of her aunt as Tom pretended to be of his mother. Merely bored, and concealing, she hoped, her boredom from the visitor. She disagreed with Aunt Hannah as coolly as she might with anyone else, and betrayed none of the solicitude which young women sometimes give to old. Tom ate and drank, and talked rather less than seemed natural, but Matt felt that this too was merely from mild boredom, and a male habit of letting the old lady have her illusion of herself. Mrs Mahoney did most of the talking. She told Matt that his literary work was a disgrace to Ireland, and that she had never read a word of it, she was happy to say. She wondered what brought him to Mellick now, and assumed he wouldn't stay very long. She deplored Una's method of bringing up children and said that Liam's character was ruined beyond repair. She expected they had had an uncomfortable afternoon by the lake, and she decided that Leahy, her butcher, was cheating again, that this undoubtedly was Canterbury lamb, and she certainly could not recommend Matt to have any more of it.

Matt raised his brows to all this and said 'Yes?' and 'No?' But there was no conversation, and the meal was eaten in an atmosphere from which all feeling was, as it were, naturally eliminated. Matt thought that probably both Tom and Nell were too grown-up and self-sufficient to bother to pit real life against such an unreality as this old lady.

There was coffee in the drawing-room, and a lecture from Mrs Mahoney to Tom about the number of lights he switched on.

'Come on downstairs,' said Tom to Matt. 'I want to talk to you. Good night, Mother.'

'Don't be late, Tom. How will your visitor get home tonight?'

'I'll telephone Gallagher to send a driver with my car when I want it. Good night, Nell.'

The men bowed themselves out of the big drawing-room. Matt, looking back from the door, saw Nell lean forward from a sofa to pick up a book, and thought she had looked far too beautiful for the deadly evening ahead of her.

Tom used his inner office as a study. It was a tall, pleasant room with one long window. Although overfilled with books, both legal and general, it was orderly and comfortable. There were green leather arm-chairs on either side of a Georgian mantelpiece. Tom put decanters and cigars on the mahogany table desk.

'Funny to meet again as ageing clubmen,' he said.

'You haven't changed much,' said Matt. Tom had always been a heavy-shouldered and rather fleshy giant, his eyes had always been half shut and very quick, his fairish hair had always receded from his temples. He had always looked lazy, well-dressed and imperturbable.

'The change in you is marked,' he said now to Matt.

'I've learnt to be neat and tidy.'

'Yes. To keep things in their places — your heart in your boots, for instance. It used to rampage on your sleeve.'

'We were young, my dear chap.'

'And expected to be happier fellows when we should be middle-aged.'

'Aren't you?'

'Don't I look it? I never aimed at the bliss of such as your brother Will. But you're miserable. Here, have a drink.'

They drank, and lighted cigars.

'It's a miserable world,' Matt ventured.

'It always was.'

'But we didn't know it. Or we thought that we would change all that. Instead we've made it worse — all of us.'

'This cosmic conscience!'

'You find me naïve?'

'Like the "Skibbereen Eagle".[2] But if you think you're going to get away with the world situation as a reason for bitter-sweetness —'

'For a writer it's good personal reason for bitterness — I swear it. What are we to do? How can we escape from our own time? Tell me, in fact, Tom, what civilization is in the end? Is it an affair of mechanical administration, an affair of State, or is it what we used to think — the spontaneous gift of individual minds, the impeccable, free thing that only unconsciously and accidentally conditions administration?'

'I'll try to answer you out of Plato, if you like — and you know how he suspected your kind of gentry. But leave me alone with your rhetoric. Your personal life will last your own time, man! Enjoy it — and amuse us with your Stradivarius.[3] No one's asking more than that of you!'

Matt looked like a man who flings aside a thousand angry answers. Then he laughed.

'Forgive me, Tom,' he said. 'Upon my soul, you seem to be making me feel young.'

'Not young enough to play the Prince of Denmark, let us hope. What's brought you running home like this?'

'Good God! Why should I not come home?'

'Above in that field this afternoon I took a good look at you, my boyo. Your career has interested me — so I gave you the once-over, for the instruction of my Socratic soul. And do you know all that came into my head? "Man delights him not nor woman neither, Stephen said. He returns after a life of absence to that spot of earth where he was born, where he has always been, man and boy, a silent witness and there, his journey of life ended, he plants his mulberry tree in the earth. Then dies. The motion is ended. Grave-diggers bury Hamlet *père* and Hamlet *fils*. A king and a prince at last in death —".'

'Do you know *Ulysses*[4] by heart?'

'No. But I know that conversation in the library. The best conversation Ireland has done yet.'

'I'm not the Bard — and there is no Anne Hathaway here — what is it? "And in New Place a slack, dishonoured body that once was comely —"'

'The mobled queen — stretched back in the second-best bed! No such cosiness for you — that's a fact. So what are you here for? Is it time to plant the mulberry tree?'

'I don't take myself as bloody seriously as you imagine.'

'Oh yes, you do. We all take ourselves more seriously than anyone else could possibly imagine. But it's dull — your returning a mask. I was expecting a devil of a fellow — and to have the grosser parts of my education increased magnificently by meeting you again — a sophisticated dog. You were well endowed for the personal life, you always went at it pluckily enough — and your work has the ring of knowledge now. And, my God, here you turn up at thirty-seven, successful, not to say eminent — travelled, cosseted, experienced — and all you have to show for it is a civil expression of countenance, and the lovely manners of a Jesuit!'

Matt closed his eyes. Is it time to plant the mulberry tree? Oh, barrenness. Is it not enough to be in flight? The positive strength required for that makes it almost seem creative. But there whence he fled was the seed. There in that face, where roses and soft lilies blow, he had found at his most emptied moment a personal answer to contemporary negation; found that which he had long ceased to look for. And found it good and durable. His seed, his potency. In every hour with her there was vitality, and a forgetfulness of the immediate and the topical that made the writer flame with arrogant courage. No former love of his had ever thus fed talent — but rather had been withheld from tampering with it; a recreation, love, a reassurance. Never before an exaction of that part of him he held most guardedly and deeply precious — his work, which always he had fed in private, on dreams and guesses. He had wanted a wife always, but never found where he could have her the one he wanted. He had not thought that in his day a man looked for, or found, a Muse. Then she had come, and filling him with pleasure as with noonday light, had made him master again in the nick of time of his life and his ideas, had made him deaf to contemporary theorists and ideologists, had reasserted values which he had desired to find eternal, but which in his day were held for dead and evil. Into her radiant myth he had escaped from the weight and dogmatism of his time; had found his own conceptions — in every hour with her a new one. He had been amazed — but so it was. She asserted personal vision. She was — and how it had delighted her! — his Muse.

He remembered telling her the names of the Muses. She knew only a few things, having had no education, and an adult life for the most part of sharp struggle. Yet suddenly she would flash out an accurate and unlooked-for piece of knowledge. She had a flair, which derived from her own great talent, for whatever was poetic, vivid or moving. She knew the ring of good words, and a true line from a false. She knew — to a nicety that was almost suspect — the value of simplicity and non-pretentiousness. She never faked, or tried for what she was not. On the other hand, she often gave off-stage — she couldn't help it — magnificent performances of herself. 'But so do you, my darling,' she would say amusedly to that. 'You play the tormented author so beautifully, Matt, that I'm sure you'd have been a good actor.'

It was exactly two years now since they had met — at a cocktail party in Chester Square.[5] A brilliant afternoon towards the end of May. Fighting his way on to the balcony for a breath of air, he had found her and had fallen into talk with her. Exchanging names, each gravely acknowledged the renown of the other, but he admitted that he had never seen her act, and she had neither read his famous novels nor attended any of his three unlucky plays.

She was then in the first flush of absolute success. He had been abroad all the winter and had not seen those acclaimed Shakespearean performances at the Old Vic which had brought her with the spring to Shaftesbury Avenue and to perfect triumph in the leading part of a fabulously successful modern comedy. And standing now in the sun, her hat wreathed with tiny roses, her dress a pinkish cloud, blue-eyed, white-skinned and smiling, she looked, the playwright thought, exactly everything that the world desires its leading actresses to be. She looked the perfect exponent of that illusion for which men are said to have died, and without which their hearts shrivel.

He was amused at meeting such a fairy-tale. They grew confidential. She told him of childhood in Dover — not yet of the greengrocer's shop — of how religious Huguenots are, of her first tour, and her first London chance. 'I was the little, sobbing tart,' she said. 'You know the part — four lines. It's everyone's first London chance. And the play always runs five nights. That one did.' He told her about Weir House, and bicycling to school, about Dublin and the Black-and-Tans and going to prison. She was impressed by his having been in prison. 'And now here we are, famous people, drinking champagne cocktails in — in Belgravia, isn't it?' she had said, as they lifted their glasses to their triumphs, smiling at each other. Before he left the party, he had met Adam Wolfe, her husband, blond, amiable giant with a handsome face which was vaguely familiar — probably from the screen. That night, obtaining a stall with difficulty, he had gone to her play. The next day he sent roses and a note:

I was at the play last night. I shall be there again tonight — indeed I foresee that unless I watch myself I shall be there every night of the run. May I come to your dressing-room to-night to thank you for your matchless performance? And, if you have nothing else to do, will you have supper with me?

Matt Costello

A prelude like many others he had played — but he had known that here was no stale adventure in repetition. She had had supper with him, and thereafter life was re-made. The desert blossomed like the rose.

'It's a woman, of course. But surely this isn't the first one to make you run for cover? Running this direction though — that gives me pause. When the addicted wanderer makes for home —'

'I'm tired, I tell you, man! I'm sick of town,[6] and there's no quiet left in England. I wanted to see Will's kids — and to find out what Dev[7] is really doing for Cathleen Ni Houlihan's four green fields! How dated that phrase is, Tom! How old it makes us!'

'No older than we are. Then you're not talking? But there *is* a woman over there? You *are* in love?'

Matt was surprised by the manner of these questions. They were curiously deliberate.

'Keep County Court tactics out of this,' he said good-naturedly. 'I'm none of your perjuring farmers.'

'I wish to God you were — then I'd know how to make you answer straight, you twister. But the fact that you don't answer is enough. You're in love, you poor fool.'

Matt saw that the other man intended to have an answer and that therefore his best blockade was frankness.

'Yes,' he said with a cunning smile of surrender. 'Yes, I'm in love. It's a habit of mine.'

He was again surprised at the repressed explosiveness of the laugh with which Tom — wily lawyer — took his bit of comedy-playing. Evidently he had said what gave satisfaction, and he was believed. His host refilled the glasses.

'Then you won't be staying amongst us?' he said, and Matt could not exactly qualify the intonation of the query. 'You're not going to settle down and live decent, I mean. We have lots of smiling virgins, you know, whose mothers wouldn't mind —'

'Oh, don't be so sure! I write indecent books and I don't go to Mass on Sunday.'

'Ah — a lot of that could be glossed over. You're rich and famous, and you come of well-respected people. Weren't you born and bred here — God help you, child — and all your people before you? And what's all that you get on with but a lot of foolishness?

You'd soon grow out of it. Not at all, Mr Costello — no obstacle at all. A nice young wife now is the very thing for you. "Let copulation thrive." And before you can remember your last mortal sin you'll be going to Confession every Saturday.'

'Like you?'

'Like me when I marry.'

'And when will that be?'

'When there's figs on thistles.'

'You used to be — more appreciative of the sex.'

'There is a brothel in the town, in the town,' sang Tom.

'In Mellick?'

'Two, I believe. But the outsides are a fine, symbolic warning. Anyway a poor chap I know was seen going into one of them on a certain Wednesday night, and on Friday when he got his wages he got the sack. I tell you, sir, this city is going to be run on decent lines, or we're all going to know the reason why. Did you think you'd come to the land of the free?'

'I didn't. But you seem free enough — in your talk anyway.'

'Within these four walls. But I live with a couple of the female pillars of Mellick, my boy!' He waved a hand towards the ceiling.

'One of them stands a good deal from you,' said Matt.

'You mean Nell? Oh, that's a sort of game we play — I try to make her snarl at me, and she shows me she's paying no attention at all. I'm some parts of a gentleman, and so I let her win. I could easily win though — I could make a joke or two for the benefit of that light of the Legion of Mary[8] —'

'I'll believe you,' said Matt.

'Nell really is a very religious woman.' Tom said this so deliberately that Matt burst out laughing. 'No, it isn't so funny as all that,' the other went on. 'Religiosity is becoming a job in this county, you might say. A plank. A threat and a menace. A power in the land, in fact, my boy! In the Island of Saints and Scholars! Yah — it's disgusting! It's a matter of municipal policy now wearing this little button and that little badge, holding a banner here and running to make a retreat there, with Father O'Hegarty warning you kindly about this, and Father O'Hartigan rapping you over the knuckles about that, and Father O'Hanigan running off to talk to the bishop about you! Town Council stuff! Pure jobbery. "But is he a good practising Catholic, Father O'Dea?" "And are you sure he leads a moral life, Sister Mary Joseph?" And if you aren't sure, will you kindly make it your life-work to find out! My God, it's terrible! We need an Ibsen here, Matt. Is that your line? Have you returned to save your people?'

'But if it's true that religion has become a job, where do you come in? You do pretty well, I gather — and yet if you're allowed to talk like this, there must be some tolerance left!'

'Yes, there's some. We're a brainy and cynical race, you know, however they shove us around. We reserve our true opinions quite surprisingly. But we're not public-spirited. We'll be passively tolerant as long as we can, until Father O'Hanigan scares the daylights out of us with some hint that he's observing our neutrality. We're afraid of the Church — we always have been, except in sudden spurts. Her dominance has never sat naturally and humanly on us, as on the Latins. Maybe our temperament would have done better if we'd gone with the Reformation!'

'It's a wonder the house doesn't fall on you for that!'

'We've created no art in Ireland, such as the other great Catholic peoples have. A certain amount of applied art in the golden age of the monasteries; a certain amount of Romanesque architecture, apparently; a certain amount of craftsmanship — *vide*[9] the illuminators. But nothing pure, no fine art. No painters at all, by European standards. We have none yet. We don't understand painting, good, bad or indifferent. No sculptors, and none coming. Absolutely no composers of music. Although the Eternal Church, which we have served with so much passion, has been the mistress and inspirer of all these things elsewhere. It's damn queer!'

'There's the old excuse — poverty, persecution, oppression —'

'Never choked genius anywhere yet. There are no stifled geniuses, Matt. It's of the nature of the thing that if it lives it can't be held down. Talent, yes. No doubt the heel of the Saxon crushed plenty of talent — but no genius, my boy!'

'We have always inclined at least to produce good writers and good actors — and the native Irish literature has a character and strength which are downright impressive. The Bardic schools were good, Tom, and by no means naïve.'

'Granted. We can, and do, produce literature — in proportion to our population we haven't done at all badly in some of its less pure, more applied branches. Because we are cerebral — I admit that — and we're moralists and observers and mockers. That's our line — when we're not afraid of it. Words we have some mastery with. The satirical bards had, by God! But you must admit, all the same, that the language we're now digging out of the grave has left the *world* nothing. Nothing like *The Canterbury Tales*, or *The Divine Comedy*, or *Don Quixote*. No, we've only produced one native giant so far — because you can't call Swift a native — we've only got Joyce to measure against the immortals up-to-date. And his great spring seems to have dried up on him now.'

'He's banned, too.'

'Oh, but naturally. Still, there's always hope for us when we're using words. Because we're moralists, I tell you. I am. I'm typical of the race. I can read, I can talk, I can argue — but there isn't a vestige of the artist in me. We're not artists. We have no artistic exactitude or detachment, no aesthetic purity, no understanding of the isolated, clear principle which informs all greatness in fine art. And for that I'm inclined to blame some clash between our racial make-up and the Eternal Church, which scatters artists, good or bad, like daisies everywhere else. She's got hold of some material here that she can't quite make the best of, Matt! Perhaps we'd all have been more natural-like as jolly little Protestants!'

'God forbid. It's a disgusting theory. I wouldn't have missed my birth in the cradle of the Church — not for the chance of being Goethe himself!'

'Wouldn't you, then? The more fool you. He had a long, magnificent life, plenty of fun, and the most balanced mind in literary history.'

'He's welcome. I'd rather have been The Bard of Thomond.[10]

'. . . When Thady with a pack of cards
Was set in the midst of five blackguards. . . .'

Tom chanted. 'I agree with you, maybe. Protestantism is a thought too tidy for us, Matt. I don't know where our trouble lies, to tell you the God's truth!'

'Is it such a trouble, though? Look at you. You're a malcontent and a talker, and a disrespecter of persons — but here you are, peaceful and prosperous in a town that you say needs an Ibsen to wither it. How do you account for that?'

'The passive tolerance of those few who are not too much afraid of their brains and who find me amusing; the shrewdness of the farmers, who know by experience that I'm as good a lawyer as my father was, which is saying a good deal, and that in the practice of my profession I abide by the law, which I happen to know; above all, my boy, the fact that I am believed to be well-off, and my mother is known to be downright wealthy. She's mean all right, much meaner than even all her clergy-admirers guess, but she is afraid of the Church, and she thinks that eternal rest is something that you actually can't get for nothing. How much she's prepared to gamble on the purchase, her will will finally reveal — but meantime, I'm her son, and though certain clergy gentlemen don't like me — I

can quote Aquinas[11] to confound them, God help us, and they hate that like cocoa — still, I'm Mrs Mahoney's only child, I'd have you know — a bad man to quarrel with. Besides, I pay my dues, and I support the Eternal Church, which I detach with exactitude from all this new parish ignorance and darkness. I know its tremendous history and all the black sins on its aged face — and I admire it as I admire no other phenomenon of human organization. I never go to church or chapel, but I'm nothing if I'm not an upholder of the One, Holy, Catholic and Apostolical. And I bet you anything you like, Matt, that I'll die in the odour of sanctity, fortified by all the rites —'

'*Per istam sanctam unctionem*[12] . . .' said Matt.

'Yes — it's a magnificent way to say good-bye to life. I hope I'll be conscious when the moment comes.'

'But since you're supported by such an edifying faith, Tom, what is your objection to the natural piety of your cousin Nell?'

'Natural piety — that's a nice thing in a nice woman. If we'd more of it in this house, and less good works —'

'You're speaking with feeling, man!'

'My God, I always speak with feeling! But these Legions of Mary, and Catholic Actions and Knights of Saint Joseph! What are they at? The Church has been with us for two thousand years approx. — but now all of a sudden in the last ten years it's occurred to these gentry to invent it for us! Oh, I know it's customary to wave a tolerant hand and say they do good work in certain ways. Maybe they do. Maybe there are creatures so beaten and dispirited that they like to have a lot of smiling, immaculate ladies poking round in their private lives, and telling them to go here, and stay away from there and wipe off that lipstick. But the thing is wrong philosophically — this amateurish impudence is not a sane way to redeem the world! It causes an immediate discomfort in the brain — you know it does. The Church has had its eternal methods for the destitute, and for those who desire to be guided aright. They weren't broad enough or founded deeply enough in Christian Communism — but they could be expanded by an intelligent hierarchy. Expansion mightn't work, and their day may be done. But this other pious nonsense is no true palliative, I'll swear. And anyway, Nell should have more wit than to risk making a prim, interfering fool of herself!'

'But does she do that?'

'I think so. She's all for Dev, for the greatest good of the greatest number, and the end justifying the means. She despises individualism, she says, and all its cheap escapes. Cheap escapes, forsooth! She's for the law, for order and decency and obedience, and the great White Chief in Leinster House!¹³ I tell her 'tis in Russia she should be — that Stalin is waiting for her. That sets her mad. She's like the rest of the world, Matt — all she wants is to be locked up, and to have it in writing — from Dev, I suppose — that everyone else is locked up, too!'

'It's amazing! Even here!'

'Yes. It's the world disease — variations only arise from varying hereditary conditions. Here it expresses itself in an inflammation of that Jansenism¹⁴ that Maynooth¹⁵ has threatened at us for so long. Now it's ripe at last — and we're sick, like the rest of the world. But you can't argue with Nell. She knows all the answers. She's a historian, if you please, and she knew all your arguments long before you framed them. She drank in all knowledge at the feet of Professor John Marcus O'Sullivan¹⁶ — and took First Class Honours. You can't fluster Nell, who at least doesn't need whisky to talk on!' He made a comic attempt to mimic her clear, light voice.

'But why do you mind so much?'

'Mind? Do I seem to?' Tom laughed and pitched his cigar into the fireplace. 'Divil a mind, my son.' His tone changed to good-humoured musing. 'Only I sometimes suspect that her whole attitude is a put-up job, a sort of unconscious mulish come-back at me. If my guess is right, I don't like the responsibility.'

'Why should it be a come-back at you?'

'Oh, God knows! But we annoy each other. We're antipathetic, and we're obstinate. And we both have what I can only call rather exaggerated temperaments.'

'That's true.'

'We force each other to be much more ourselves than we need be. It's a peevish kind of game — but I hope it won't turn Nell into an impossible person.'

'Or you.'

'Oh, the worst it could do to me is make a drunkard of me.'

There was silence. Tom selected another cigar, clipped and lighted it with great concentration and with an expression of amusement creeping round his mouth — an expression which Matt did not understand but found vaguely insincere.

Tom blew a long whiff of smoke.

'We were once engaged to be married, Nell and I,' he said lightly.

Matt was careful to register only a mild reaction of interest.

'Indeed? And why didn't you marry?'

'Oh, it's a long time ago — temperamentally unsuited. First cousins anyway. Wouldn't have worked at all. Xanthippe and Socrates —'

'Well, if Xanthippe was one-half as beautiful, Socrates didn't have such a very bad time, my dear chap.'

'You think her beautiful?' Tom's voice was perfectly detached. 'Not many would agree with you. Una is much more admired.'

'Una's a sweet cabbage-rose — but this other has a complicated kind of beauty.'

'I suppose so. She *is* caviare to the general, certainly. In Mellick she is not particularly admired. Though she's had her share of honest-to-God suitors. There are a great many plucky men in the world.'

'Does she show signs of accepting one of them?'

'Oh, I don't know if there's anyone on the trail lately — but to my knowledge she hasn't had much use for the gentry that used to call around. It was amusing to watch sometimes. She has a deadly way of making a man feel that he hasn't quite got her attention. Brutally delicate trick.'

'Probably isn't a trick at all, but the plain truth.'

'I don't know. She's very defensive. But she ought to marry one of them. That'd put a stop to all her high-hat nonsense before it's too late. Teaching is the very worst thing for Nell. What she needs is someone to shout her down, and knock hell out of her. Marriage, in fact.'

Matt wanted more information and felt about for the best approach to it.

'I wonder why *you* became engaged to her,' he mused on a lazy tone.

'Oh, when she came tripping down from college with her M.A. diploma under her arm, she was a very, very lovely wench, my boy. It was 1926 — I was 26 and she was 22. I was very susceptible as a young fellow, Matt — you may remember? And I suddenly realized that this kid, who'd been my sister, was a beautiful woman, and by God's mercy *not* my sister. I had a great opinion of myself — and I lost no time about courting her. So we became engaged and bought the ring. And mother and various people were against it — consanguinity and all the rest. But we didn't care. We wrote off to the Pope for his kind permission. And before it came we had an almighty, glorious row, and Nell flung the ring at me and flounced off abroad for herself.'

'Well — and then what?'

'Stayed abroad for two solid years — until Una, who was worrying about her, worked my mother into believing that she simply must have Nell's assistance and companionship for her old age — and tricked Nell into coming back. And here she is.'

'And what did you say to each other when she came back?'

'What would we say? Nothing at all, man. Welcome home, Nell. How are you, Tom? Since the day she threw the ring at me we haven't mentioned our fit of youthful amorousness, I'm glad to say.'

'Why did she take up teaching?'

'More of her nonsense, that. When she came back from abroad she became interested in perfecting her Irish — spent summers in the Gaeltacht.[17] She speaks it fluently now — of course she has to for her work. She teaches world history in Irish, I'd have you know! Well, that brought her in touch with a lot of our native pedagogues, and she grew interested in education. She's a bossy character, you see. And about then her income began to shrink. They have some money, these two girls, but it's tied up in things that have dropped of late. However, there was no need for her to be anxious — she'll be well off when my mother dies — and meantime, I've always tried to make her see that any sane female would take a salary for all the time and energy mother exacts from her one way and another. But you might as well be talking to Nelson's Pillar. She decided to have a job — and her dear old *alma mater*[18] was delighted to give her one.'

'I think she's right. Damn it, you might marry any minute, and then she'd hardly desire to stay on here —'

'That's true. But why doesn't she marry herself?'

'I should think she will.'

'She's thirty-three.'

'That's not so dreadful.' Louise would be thirty-three eight months from now. Matt swerved from that thought to the distraction in hand.

'What the hell was the row about?' he asked bluntly.

Tom took a drink of whisky.

'As far as I remember,' he said slowly, and Matt reflected that such an introductory phrase must in these circumstance be a false flourish. 'As far as I remember, Matt, it was about another woman. Yes, indeed — it was. And it took place in this very room. It was a Sunday, about midday. She had just come in from Mass and was talking to me here. She was sitting on that desk, looking very gay, and I was feeling mighty pleased with myself. There were some letters on the desk that I hadn't opened — the Saturday afternoon post. I'd been out with her the day before, and she was teasing me about my slackness, so I said: "All right, boss — open them for me, and attend to them." It was all a joke, and on we went with it. She opened the damned letters, and the third one — well —'

'Well, what?'

'The third one was from a young woman whose name you might remember if I mentioned it, a decent little shop-girl with whom I had an affair for about six months when I was a law-student, and whom I got into trouble, as they say. She'd had a kid, and I supported the two of them, and everything was fine. No bones broken. She was a friendly girl, and every now and then she wrote me a silly little chummy letter to thank me about money, and say how "Tommy" was, and send his love. Well, it was one of those letters Nell opened, by God! Friendly and jocose and making everything as plain as the nose on your face.'

There was a pause, but Matt said nothing.

'That's all. The row began then. That I hadn't told her! As if I ever would, the little fool! That I could be so callous! This wretched, good-hearted, deserted girl! This poor little fatherless child! That I should dare to marry anyone else! To let her, Nell Mahoney, *cheat* another woman! The insult, the crudeness, the meanness! Oh, my dear man, the Lyceum that girl talked! The utter non-reality! The clumsy idiocy!'

'She was very young. She was in love with you. It was her first shock.'

'No one should be so young as to set up as God Almighty! Well, anyway, if she flew into a rage, faith so did I! We made a magnificent row of it, by God! And she flung the ring in my face, and swept out.' He paused and smiled at Matt, who made no comment.

'I didn't see her again that day. The next morning my mother told me with cold pleasure that she heard my engagement was broken. Una and Will never said anything. Four days later Nell had left Mellick — on her way to Italy, no less, where his Holiness was then dealing with our hasty request for his blessed dispensation to wed. *Voilà!* Old unhappy far-off things and battles long ago. We're none the worse, Nell and I. But the real joke is that a month after her departure I had another cheerful, jocose letter from the young lady in Dublin, announcing her marriage to a very decent fellow, a tobacconist. They have a large family now, and are very happy. I still occasionally get "Tommy's love" in the post.'

'Does Nell know that sequel?'

'I suppose not. I never told it to her. Have I bored you?'

'Not at all.'

'It's a ludicrously old-fashioned story — if it weren't a comedy of character it would have no value at all. But as a story of Nell, and me, I think it's illustrative.'

Matt smiled.

'You handle it like a master,' he said.

Tom looked at him with veiled sharpness, but made no answer.

Matt pondered the telling of the story. The slow, opening pace of one who gropes backward looking for something long mislaid; the quickening and lightening as the details come, the cobwebs fall; the outspoken tone of the conclusion, conveying so beautifully that now, having really exercised memory, the narrator sees the whole shape of the dead episode at last, and is willing to make it as clear as possible. Curious — because there was a kind of light, almost a patina, on these groped-for details when produced. 'It was a Sunday, about midday.' 'She was sitting on that desk.' 'She was looking very gay.' 'All right, boss — you open them.' These sentences did not seem like lumber. They had a sheen as of things cared for.

This lawyer had court-room practice in the art of making every narrative produce a specific effect, and obviously the effect aimed at here, true or false, was that this of Nell and him was an old, dead story, long dried of emotion; a curious episode with which to illustrate character, and having no relevance amid present facts. The effect had undoubtedly been produced, and might well represent the actual truth of things — very likely did. There was no sentimentality or significant reservation to be noted anywhere in the phrasing, and such facial expressions as might have suggested caution or play-acting in the narrator would arise from an inadmissible shyness, uncertainty about the correctness of telling the story — simple embarrassment in fact. As for the rather touching lights of recollection — 'she had just come in from Mass . . . she was looking very gay' — memory is random and irresponsible in every heart, Matt conceded. Some of our most vividly retained impressions seem to bear no significant relation to existent feeling.

Certainly the story threw a high light on the beautiful, bored woman upstairs — gave a picture of her young and gay and on the current of feeling. Crazily young and tiresome it revealed her, and with irrational capacities for pride and pain. Had she more or less forgotten it all? Unlikely. But Matt could not imagine her telling the story, to anyone, ever.

'Considering all things,' he said now, 'you go too near the knuckle in her presence. Why can't you let her alone? She's Puritanical, and has a perfect right to be that way if she likes. These cracks about Wordsworth's illegitimate child and so on — upon my soul, Tom, they're in bad taste when one knows your story.'

'Of course they're in bad taste. That's my point. Nell and I exaggerate each other. If she has a right to be Puritanical, all right — I have a right to be coarse. And coarse I'll be when I feel inclined. Besides — to tell you the truth I go on like that, I think, in a desperate effort to educate the foolish creature, to make her get the true, strong taste of life! A lost cause. But I'm a philanthropist, Matt, and I like to see human beings mature naturally. I like to see happiness. I like to contemplate spectacles like Una — decent human nature enjoying itself decently.'

'You don't surely think that the way to get Nell to mature into decent happiness is to madden her with what she regards as indecencies?'

'Oh, I don't madden her. She's not an innocent, you know. She's only too damn well read and aware. It's an intellectual theory she has of behaviour — that we should all behave alike, and only say what everyone wants to hear, that there are no privileges for anyone, that social duty demands certain taboos of speech and action, and that is that! I don't madden her at all nowadays. She just despises my anti-social individualism and my insistence on what she calls privilege. She despises it in you too, my boy. She has read your books, and says they are anti-social, myth-creating and unnecessary.'

'Well, I'm damned!'

'That's what Nell thinks too — though she's too highbrow to put it quite so simply.'

Silence fell again. A clock struck the quarter-past eleven. Matt felt uneasy now, and wished he were alone. Anti-social, myth-creating and unnecessary. Yes, indeed — and the gods be thanked. So might his work continue to be while the world remained the smug, dead colony of slaves he found it. Myth-creating. But his myth had vanished. Had beaten him off. Had grown common, cruel, practical, afraid. He was alone now and would always be alone — without his Muse. Without passion or hope, or any tangible sign any more that a dreamer is on the right tack. Unnecessary; of course — to everyone but himself, and in relation to those imbecile but irrepressible gambles for true fame which every artist unashamedly makes, and out of the millions of which the few immortals do in fact arise. But he was dead and tired — his gambling days were over. He had no idea on earth now of what to do or where to turn. Myth-creating. He had been debarred from that.

'I must go home,' he said.

Tom telephoned for the car.

'We must have later nights than this,' he said, 'when you begin to cheer up. You're dispirited, my boy. My God, at your age you ought to be ashamed of yourself! Have you no philosophy?'

'For two years I didn't need one.'

'That was a lucky run. Praise God.'

They walked out on to the steps. The wide Georgian street looked noble, beautifully lighted by cold arc-lamps.

'Shannon scheme?'[19]

'Yes. Good, isn't it?'

'Fine. A very creditable-looking town. Up, Dev!'

'He's up all right. Good night to you. I'll be ringing you up for another meeting.'

'Thank you. Good night, Tom.'

He was driven home swiftly, through the quiet town and along the smooth Dublin road. The night was sweet and calm, the sky was starry. Peace crushed his heart and he felt his own loneliness upon him as a drowning man must feel the weight of waves.

1   In Limerick.
2   A local newspaper based in Skibbereen, County Cork.
3   Tom had earlier taunted Matt by suggesting that as soon he left Ireland as a young man he had dropped the wild harp of Irish nationalism and begun learning to play a classical instrument.
4   Joyce's *Ulysses*. The conversation in the Library takes place in the 'Scylla and Charybdis' episode.
5   In London.
6   London, that is.
7   de Valera.
8   The Legion of Mary is a Catholic lay organization.
9   Latin: see.
10 The Limerick-born poet Michael Hogan (1832–99), author of *Lays and Legends of Thomond* (1865), was known as this.
11 St Thomas Aquinas (1225–74).
12 Latin: through this holy anointing. Prayer used for sacrament of Extreme Unction when dying person annointed with oil.
13 Home of Irish legislature on Kildare Street in Dublin.
14 Here Puritanism. Derived from Cornelis Jansen (1585–1638), Dutch Catholic theologian who advanced a form of Calvinist predestation, which was condemned as heresy by the Church.
15 Shorthand for Irish Catholic Church. Maynooth College was founded in 1795 for training Catholic priests.
16 One time Professor of History at University College Dublin.
17 Irish-speaking district.
18 Latin: life-giving mother. Old college or school.
19 The hydroelectric station at Shannon was constructed between 1925 and 1929, and proved a significant achievement.

W. B. YEATS
from W. B. Yeats, *New Poems* (1938)

You might find it helpful to compare this poem with the photograph in my *Yeats's Worlds* of the piece of lapis lazuli it refers to. The use of the word 'gay' is a reminder of Nietzsche's influence on Yeats.

LAPIS LAZULI
(For Harry Clifton)

I have heard that hysterical women say
They are sick of the palette and fiddle-bow,
Of poets that are always gay,
For everybody knows or else should know
That if nothing drastic is done
Aeroplane and Zeppelin will come out,
Pitch like King Billy bomb-balls in
Until the town lie beaten flat.

All perform their tragic play,
There struts Hamlet, there is Lear,
That's Ophelia, that Cordelia;
Yet they, should the last scene be there,
The great stage curtain about to drop,
If worthy their prominent part in the play,
Do not break up their lines to weep.
They know that Hamlet and Lear are gay;
Gaiety transfiguring all that dread.
All men have aimed at, found and lost;
Black out; Heaven blazing into the head:
Tragedy wrought to its uttermost.
Though Hamlet rambles and Lear rages,
And all the drop-scenes drop at once
Upon a hundred thousand stages,
It cannot grow by an inch or an ounce.

On their own feet they came, or on shipboard,
Camel-back, horse-back, ass-back, mule-back,
Old civilizations put to the sword.

Then they and their wisdom went to rack:
No handiwork of Callimachus,
Who handled marble as if it were bronze,
Made draperies that seemed to rise
When sea-wind swept the corner, stands;
His long lamp-chimney shaped like the stem
Of a slender palm, stood but a day;
All things fall and are built again,
And those that build them again are gay.

Two Chinamen, behind them a third,
Are carved in lapis lazuli,
Over them flies a long-legged bird,
A symbol of longevity;
The third, doubtless a serving-man,
Carries a musical instrument.

Every discoloration of the stone,
Every accidental crack or dent,
Seems a water-course or an avalanche,
Or lofty slope where it still snows
Though doubtless plum or cherry-branch
Sweetens the little half-way house
Those Chinamen climb towards, and I
Delight to imagine them seated there;
There, on the mountain and the sky,
On all the tragic scene they stare.
One asks for mournful melodies;
Accomplished fingers begin to play.
Their eyes mid many wrinkles, their eyes,
Their ancient, glittering eyes, are gay.

AUSTIN CLARKE
from Austin Clarke, *Night and Morning* (1938)

Here are two fine poems by the author of *The Bright Temptation*, one on the body as temptation, the other on the terrors of the unstable mind. 'Summer Lightning' was used by Clarke in his long poem about mental illness *Mnemosyne Lay in Dust* (1966).

THE STRAYING STUDENT

On a holy day when sails were blowing southward,
A bishop sang the Mass at Inishmore,[1]
Men took one side, their wives were on the other
But I heard the woman coming from the shore:
And wild in despair my parents cried aloud
For they saw the vision draw me to the doorway.

Long had she lived in Rome when Popes were bad,
The wealth of every age she makes her own,
Yet smiled on me in eager admiration,
And for a summer taught me all I know,
Banishing shame with her great laugh that rang
As if a pillar caught it back alone.

I learned the prouder counsel of her throat,
My mind was growing bold as light in Greece;
And when in sleep her stirring limbs were shown,
I blessed the noonday rock that knew no tree:
And for an hour the mountain was her throne,
Although her eyes were bright with mockery.

They say I was sent back from Salamanca[2]
And failed in logic, but I wrote her praise
Nine times upon a college wall in France.
She laid her hand at darkfall on my page
That I might read the heavens in a glance
And I knew every star the Moors have named.

Awake or in my sleep, I have no peace now,
Before the ball is struck, my breath has gone,
And yet I tremble lest she may deceive me
And leave me in this land, where every woman's son
Must carry his own coffin and believe,
In dread, all that the clergy teach the young.

SUMMER LIGHTNING

The heavens opened. With a scream
The blackman at his night-prayers
Had disappeared in blasphemy,

And iron beds were bared;
Day was unshuttered again,
The elements had lied,
Ashing the faces of madmen
Until God's likeness died.

Napoleon[3] took his glittering vault
To be a looking-glass.
Lord Mitchell, pale and suffering,
Fell to the ground in halves.
The cells were filling. Christopher
O'Brien, strapped in pain,
For all the rage of syphilis,
Had millions in his brain.

James Dunn leaped down the dormitory,
Thought has no stopping-place,
His bright bed was a corner shop,
Opening, closing, late.
Behind a grille, the unfrocked priest
Had told his own confession:
Accidents in every street
Rang the Angelus.

Flight beyond flight, new stories flashed
Or darkened with affliction
Until the sweet choir of Mount Argus
Was heard at every window,
Was seen in every wing. The blackman
Kept laughing at his night-prayers
For somebody in white had taken
His photograph downstairs.

When sleep has shot the bolt and bar,
And reason fails at midnight,
Dreading that every thought at last
Must stand in our own light
Forever, sinning without end:
O pity in their pride
And agony of wrong, the men
In whom God's image died.

1   The largest of the Aran Islands, off the coast of County
     Clare.
2   In the eighteenth century when the Penal Laws were in
     operation, Irish students for the priesthood were trained
     on the Continent, in France and Rome, and in the
     Spanish city of Salamanca.
3   This and the other names in this poem refer to other
     patients in the asylum.

LOUIS MacNEICE
from Louis MacNeice, *Autumn Journal* (1938)

Autumn Journal, among the best long poems in English in the twentieth century, brilliantly captures the various moods on the eve of the Second World War. In the middle of the poem MacNeice, always alive to strings that are false, rounds on his native country in a sequence which is essential reading for all those interested in the Irish Question.

SECTION XVI

Nightmare leaves fatigue:
    We envy men of action
Who sleep and wake, murder and intrigue
    Without being doubtful, without being haunted.
And I envy the intransigence of my own
    Countrymen who shoot to kill and never
See the victim's face become their own
    Or find his motive sabotage their motives.
So reading the memoirs of Maud Gonne,[1]
    Daughter of an English mother and a soldier father,
I note how a single purpose can be founded on
    A jumble of opposites:

Dublin Castle,[2] the vice-regal ball,
    The embassies of Europe,
Hatred scribbled on a wall,
    Gaols and revolvers.
And I remember, when I was little, the fear
    Bandied among the servants
That Casement[3] would land at the pier
    With a sword and a horde of rebels;
And how we used to expect, at a later date,
    When the wind blew from the west, the noise of
        shooting
Starting in the evening at eight
    In Belfast in the York Street district;
And the voodoo of the Orange bands

Drawing an iron net through darkest Ulster,
Flailing the limbo lands —
    The linen mills, the long wet grass, the ragged
        hawthorn.
And one read black where the other read white, his
    hope
    The other man's damnation:
Up the Rebels, To Hell with the Pope,
    And God Save — as you prefer — the King or
        Ireland.
The land of scholars and saints:
    Scholars and saints my eye, the land of ambush,
Purblind manifestoes, never-ending complaints,
    The born martyr and the gallant ninny;
The grocer drunk with the drum,
    The land-owner shot in his bed, the angry voices
Piercing the broken fanlight in the slum,
    The shawled woman weeping at the garish altar.
Kathaleen ni Houlihan! Why
    Must a country, like a ship or a car, be always
        female,
Mother or sweetheart? A woman passing by,
    We did but see her passing.
Passing like a patch of sun on the rainy hill
    And yet we love her for ever and hate our
        neighbour
And each one in his will
    Binds his heirs to continuance of hatred.
Drums on the haycock, drums on the harvest, black
    Drums in the night shaking the windows:
King William[4] is riding his white horse back
    To the Boyne on a banner.
Thousands of banners, thousands of white
    Horses, thousands of Williams
Waving thousands of swords and ready to fight
    Till the blue sea turns to orange.
Such was my country and I thought I was well
    Out of it, educated and domiciled in England,
Though yet her name keeps ringing like a bell
    In an under-water belfry.
Why do we like being Irish? Partly because
    It gives us a hold on the sentimental English
As members of a world that never was,
    Baptized with fairy water;
And partly because Ireland is small enough
    To be still thought of with a family feeling,
And because the waves are rough
    That split her from a more commercial culture;
And because one feels that here at least one can
    Do local work which is not at the world's mercy
And that on this tiny stage with luck a man
    Might see the end of one particular action.
It is self-deception of course;

There is no immunity in this island either;
A cart that is drawn by somebody else's horse
    And carrying goods to somebody else's market.
The bombs in the turnip sack, the sniper from the
    roof,
    Griffith, Connolly, Collins,[5] where have they
        brought us?
Ourselves alone! Let the round tower[6] stand aloof
    In a world of bursting mortar!
Let the school-children fumble their sums
    In a half-dead language;
Let the censor be busy on the books; pull down the
    Georgian slums;
    Let the games be played in Gaelic.
Let them grow beet-sugar; let them build
    A factory in every hamlet;
Let them pigeon-hole the souls of the killed
    Into sheep and goats, patriots and traitors.
And the North, where I was a boy,
    Is still the North, veneered with the grime of
        Glasgow,
Thousands of men whom nobody will employ
    Standing at the corners, coughing.
And the street-children play on the wet
    Pavement — hopscotch or marbles;
And each rich family boasts a sagging tennis-net
    On a spongy lawn beside a dripping shrubbery.
The smoking chimneys hint
    At prosperity round the corner
But they make their Ulster linen from foreign lint
    And the money that comes in goes out to make
        more money.
A city built upon mud;
    A culture built upon profit;
Free speech nipped in the bud,
    The minority always guilty.
Why should I want to go back
    To you, Ireland, my Ireland?
The blots on the page are so black
    That they cannot be covered with shamrock.
I hate your grandiose airs,
    Your sob-stuff, your laugh and your swagger,
Your assumption that everyone cares
    Who is the king of your castle.
Castles are out of date,
    The tide flows round the children's sandy fancy;
Put up what flag you like, it is too late
    To save your soul with bunting.
Odi atque amo:[7]
    Shall we cut this name on trees with a rusty dagger?
Her mountains are still blue, her rivers flow
    Bubbling over the boulders.
She is both a bore and a bitch;

Better close the horizon,
Send her no more fantasy, no more longings which
Are under a fatal tariff.
For common sense is the vogue
And she gives her children neither sense nor money
Who slouch around the world with a gesture and a
brogue
And a faggot of useless memories.

1 Maud Gonne's memoirs of her early life can be found in
The Servant of the Queen, which was published in 1938.
2 Seat of British Administration in Ireland.
3 Roger Casement (1864–1916) went to Germany in
1914 to recruit Irish prisoners of war to fight for Ireland.

On his return to Ireland in April 1916 he was
apprehended at Banna Strand in County Kerry, tried for
treason, and executed.
4 William of Orange defeated the Catholics under James II
at the Battle of the Boyne in July 1690. Northern Irish
Protestants continue to celebrate this victory on 12 July.
5 Arthur Griffith (1871–1922), James Connolly
(1868–1916), Michael Collins (1890–1922) were leading
players in the establishment of an independent Ireland.
Griffith founded Sinn Féin (Ourselves Alone) in 1905.
6 Round towers date from the period when monastic
Ireland was in the ascendancy; their ruins remain a
distinctive part of the Irish countryside, as does their
romantic associations (see *John Bull's Other Island*,
p. 126).
7 Latin: I love and hate at one and the same time.

FLANN O'BRIEN
from Flann O'Brien, *At Swim-two-birds* (1939)

Flann O'Brien (pseudonym of Brian O'Nolan; also wrote under Myles na gCopaleen)
(1911–66) was born in Strabane in County Tyrone and educated at University College,
Dublin. In 1935 he entered the Civil Service, in 1937 submitted the manuscript of *At
Swim-two-birds*, and in 1940 began his regular humorous column 'Cruiskeen Lawn' for
The Irish Times. Here in this extract O'Brien, a postmodernist before that term was
invented, shows himself the equal of Joyce in unmasking the guises of fiction.

*Further extract from my Manuscript wherein Mr Trellis
commences the writing of his story:* Propped by pillows in
his bed in the white light of an incandescent petrol
lamp, Dermot Trellis adjusted the pimples in his
forehead into a frown of deep creative import. His
pencil moved slowly across the ruled paper, leaving
words behind it of every size. He was engaged in the
creation of John Furriskey, the villain of his tale.

Extract from Press regarding Furriskey's birth: We are in
position to announce that a happy event has taken
place at the Red Swan Hotel, where the proprietor,
Mr Dermot Trellis, has succeeded in encompassing the
birth of a man called Furriskey. Stated to be doing
'very nicely', the new arrival is about five feet eight
inches in height, well built, dark, and clean-shaven.
The eyes are blue and the teeth well formed and good,
though stained somewhat by tobacco; there are two
fillings in the molars of the left upperside and a cavity
threatened in the left canine. The hair, black and of
thick quality, is worn plastered back on the head with a
straight parting from the left temple. The chest is
muscular and well-developed while the legs are straight
but rather short. He is very proficient mentally having

an unusually firm grasp of the Latin idiom and a
knowledge of Physics extending from Boyle's Law to
the Leclanche Cell and the Greasespot Photometer. He
would seem to have a special aptitude for mathematics.
In the course of a brief test conducted by our reporter,
he solved a 'cut' from an advanced chapter of Hall and
Knight's Geometry and failed to be mystified by an
intricate operation involving the calculus. His voice is
light and pleasant, although from his fingers it is
obvious that he is a heavy smoker. He is apparently not
a virgin, although it is admittedly difficult to establish
this attribute with certainty in the male.

Our Medical Correspondent writes:

The birth of a son in the Red Swan Hotel is a
fitting tribute to the zeal and perseverance of Mr
Dermot Trellis, who has won international repute in
connexion with his researches into the theory of
aestho-autogamy. The event may be said to crown the
savant's life-work as he has at last realized his dream of
producing a living mammal from an operation
involving neither fertilization nor conception.

Aestho-autogamy with one unknown quantity on
the male side, Mr Trellis told me in conversation, has

long been a commonplace. For fully five centuries in all parts of the world epileptic slavies have been pleading it in extenuation of uncalled-for fecundity. It is a very familiar phenomenon in literature. The elimination of conception and pregnancy, however, or the reduction of the processes to the same mysterious abstraction as that of the paternal factor in the commonplace case of unexplained maternity, has been the dream of every practising psycho-eugenist the world over. I am very happy to have been fortunate enough to bring a century of ceaseless experiment and endeavour to a triumphant conclusion. Much of the credit for Mr Furriskey's presence on this planet today must go to my late friend and colleague William Tracy, whose early researches furnished me with invaluable data and largely determined the direction of my experiments. The credit for the achievement of a successful act of procreation involving two unknown quantities is as much his as mine.

This graceful reference on the part of Mr Trellis to the late Mr William Tracy, the eminent writer of Western romances — his *Flower o' the Prairie* is still read — is apparently directed at the latter's gallant efforts to change the monotonous and unimaginative process by which all children are invariably born young.

Many social problems of contemporary interest, he wrote in 1909, could be readily resolved if issue could be born already matured, teethed, reared, educated, and ready to essay those competitive plums which make the Civil Service and the Banks so attractive to the younger breadwinners of today. The process of bringing up children is a tedious anachronism in these enlightened times. Those mortifying stratagems collectively known as birth-control would become a mere memory if parents and married couples could be assured that their legitimate diversion would straightway result in finished breadwinners or marriageable daughters.

He also envisaged the day when the breeding and safe deliverance of Old Age Pensioners and other aged and infirm eligible for public money would transform matrimony from the sordid struggle that it often is to an adventurous business enterprise of limitless possibilities.

It is noteworthy that Mr Tracy succeeded, after six disconcerting miscarriages, in having his own wife delivered of a middle-aged Spaniard who lived for only six weeks. A man who carried jealousy to the point of farce, the novelist insisted that his wife and the new arrival should occupy separate beds and use the bathroom at divergent times. Some amusement was elicited in literary circles by the predicament of a woman who was delivered of a son old enough to be her father but it served to deflect Mr Tracy not one tittle from his dispassionate quest for scientific truth. His acumen and pertinacity have, in fact, become legendary in the world of psycho-eugenics. Conclusion of the foregoing.

Shorthand Note of a cross-examination of Mr Trellis at a later date on the occasion of his being on trial for his life, the birth of Furriskey being the subject of the examination referred to:

In what manner was he born?

He awoke as if from sleep.

His sensations?

Bewilderment, perplexity.

Are not these terms synonymous and one as a consequence redundant?

Yes: but the terms of the inquiry postulated unsingular information.

(At this reply ten of the judges made angry noises on the counter with the butts of their stout-glasses. Judge Shanahan put his head out through a door and issued a severe warning to the witness, advising him to conduct himself and drawing his attention to the serious penalties which would be attendant on further impudence.)

His sensations? Is it not possible to be more precise?

It is. He was consumed by doubts as to his own identity, as to the nature of his body and the cast of his countenance.

In what manner did he resolve these doubts?

By the sensory perception of his ten fingers.

By feeling?

Yes.

Did you write the following: Sir Francis Thumb Drake, comma, with three inquiring midshipmen and a cabin boy, comma, he dispatched in a wrinkled Mayflower across the seas of his Braille face?

I did.

I put it to you that the passage was written by Mr Tracy and that you stole it.

No.

I put it to you that you are lying.

No.

Describe this man's conduct after he had examined his face.

He arose from his bed and examined his stomach, lower chest and legs.

What parts did he not examine?

His back, neck and head.

Can you suggest a reason for so imperfect a survey?

Yes. His vision was necessarily limited by the movement of his neck.

(At this point Judge Shanahan entered the court adjusting his dress and said: That point was exceedingly well taken. Proceed.)

Having examined his stomach, legs and lower chest, what did he do next?

He dressed.

He dressed? A suit of the latest pattern, made to measure?

No. A suit of navy-blue of the pre-War style.

With a vent behind?

Yes.

The cast-aways of your own wardrobe?

Yes.

I put it to you that your intention was purely to humiliate him.

No. By no means.

And after he was dressed in his ludicrous clothes . . . ?

He spent some time searching in his room for a looking-glass or for a surface that would enable him to ascertain the character of his countenance.

You had already hidden the glass?

No. I had forgotten to provide one.

By reason of his doubts as to his personal appearance, he suffered considerable mental anguish?

It is possible.

You could have appeared to him — by magic if necessary — and explained his identity and duties to him. Why did you not perform so obvious an errand of mercy?

I do not know.

Answer the question, please.

(At this point Judge Sweeny made an angry noise with a crack of his stout-glass on the counter and retired in a hurried petulant manner from the court.)

I suppose I fell asleep.

I see. You fell asleep.

Conclusion of the foregoing.

Biographical reminiscence, part the third: The early winter in which these matters were occupying my attention was a season of unexampled severity. The prevailing wind (according to the word of Brinsley) was from the eastern point and was not infrequently saturated with a fine chilly rain. From my bed I had perceived the sodden forms of travellers lurking behind the frosted windows of the tram-tops. Morning would come slowly, decaying to twilight in the early afternoon.

A congenital disposition predisposing me to the most common of the wasting diseases — a cousin had died in Davos — had induced in me what was perhaps a disproportionate concern for pulmonary well-being; at all events I recall that I rarely left my room for the first three months of the winter except on occasions when my domestic circumstances made it necessary for me to appear casually before my uncle attired in my grey street-coat. I was, if possible, on worse terms than ever with him, my continued failure to produce for his examination a book called *Die Harzreise* being a sore point. I cannot recall that I ever quitted the four walls of the house. Alexander, who had chosen a scheme of studies similar to my own, answered with my voice at lecture roll-calls.

It was in the New Year, in February, I think, that I discovered that my person was verminous. A growing irritation in various parts of my body led me to examine my bedclothes and the discovery of lice in large numbers was the result of my researches. I was surprised and experienced also a sense of shame. I resolved at the time to make an end of my dissolute habits and composed mentally a régime of physical regeneration which included bending exercises.

One consequence of my resolve, at any rate, was that I attended at the College every day and walked through the Green and up and down the streets, conducting conversations with my acquaintances and occasionally talking with strangers on general topics.

It was my custom to go into the main hall of the College and stand with my back to one of the steam-heating devices, my faded overcoat open and my cold hostile eyes flitting about the faces that passed before me. The younger students were much in evidence, formless and ugly in adolescence; others were older, bore themselves with assurance and wore clothing of good quality. Groups would form for the purpose of disputation and dissolve again quickly. There was much foot-shuffling, chatter and noise of a general or indeterminate character. Students emerging from the confinement of an hour's lecture would grope eagerly for their cigarettes or accept one with gratitude from a friend. Clerical students from Blackrock or Rathfarnham, black clothes and bowler hats, would file past civilly and leave the building by a door opening at the back where they were accustomed to leave the iron pedal-cycles. Young postulants or nuns would also pass, their eyes upon the floor and their fresh young faces dimmed in the twilight of their hoods, passing to a private cloakroom where they would spend the intervals between their lectures in meditation and pious practices. Occasionally there would be a burst of horse-play and a sharp cry from a student accidentally hurt. On wet days there would be an unpleasant odour of dampness, an aroma of overcoats dried by body-heat. There was a clock plainly visible but the hours were told by a liveried attendant who emerged from a small office in the wall and pealed a shrill bell similar to that utilized by auctioneers and street-criers; the bell served this purpose, that it notified professors — distant in the web of their fine thought — that their discourses should terminate.

One afternoon I saw the form of Brinsley bent in converse with a small fair-haired man who was fast acquiring a reputation in the Leinster Square district on account of the beauty of his poems and their affinity with the high-class work of another writer, Mr Pound, an American gentleman. The small man had an off-hand way with him and talked with jerks. I advanced without diffidence and learnt that his name was Donaghy. We talked together in a polished manner, utilizing with frequency words from the French language, discussing the primacy of America and Ireland in contemporary letters and commenting on the inferior work produced by writers of the English nationality. The Holy Name was often taken, I do not recollect with what advertence. Brinsley, whose education and maintenance was a charge on the rates of his native county — the product of a farthing in the pound applied for the purpose of enabling necessitous boys of promising intellect to enjoy the benefits of University learning — Brinsley said that he was prepared to give myself and Donaghy a pint of stout apiece, explaining that he had recently been paid. I rejoined that if his finances warranted such generosity, I would raise no objection, but that I (for my part) was no Rockefeller, thus utilizing a figure of speech to convey the poverty of my circumstances.

Name of figure of speech: Synecdoche (or Autonomasia).

The three of us walked slowly down to Grogan's, our three voices interplaying in scholarly disputations, our faded overcoats finely open in the glint of the winter sun.

Isn't there a queer smell off this fellow? said Brinsley, directing his inquiring face to that of Donaghy.

I sniffed at my person in mock appraisement.

You're in bad odour, said Donaghy.

Well it's not the smell of drink, I answered. What class of a smell is it?

Did you ever go into a room early in the morning, asked Brinsley, where there had been a hooley the night before, with cigars and whisky and food and crackers and women's scent? Well that's the smell. A stale spent smell.

There's a hum off yourself, I said.

We entered the tavern and ordered our dark drinks.

To convert stout into water, I said, there is a simple process. Even a child can do it, though I would not stand for giving stout to children. Is it not a pity that the art of man has not attained the secret of converting water into stout?

Donaghy gave a laugh but Brinsley restrained me from drinking by the weight of his hand upon my arm and named a proprietary brand of ale.

Did you ever taste it? he asked.

I did not, I said.

Well that crowd have the secret if you like, he said. By God I never tasted anything like it. Did *you* ever try it?

No, said Donaghy.

Keep away from it if you value your life.

Here there was a pause as we savoured the dull syrup.

We had a great feed of wine at the Inns the other night, observed Donaghy, a swell time. Wine is better than stout. Stout sticks. Wine is more grateful to the intestines, the digestive viscera, you know. Stout sticks and leaves a scum on the interior of the paunch.

Raising my glass idly to my head, I said:

If that conclusion is the result of a mental syllogism, it is fallacious, being based on licensed premises.

Two laughs in unison, these were my rewards. I frowned and drank unheedingly, savouring the dull oaten after-taste of the stout as it lingered against my palate. Brinsley tapped me sharply on the belly.

Gob you're getting a paunch, he said.

Leave my bag alone, I answered. I protected it with my hand.

We had three drinks in all in respect of each of which Brinsley paid a sixpence without regret.

The ultimate emptors: Meath County Council, rural rating authority.

The sun was gone and the evening students — many of them teachers, elderly and bald — were hurrying towards the College through the gathering dusk on foot and on pedal-cycles. We closed our coats closely about us and stood watching and talking at the corner. We went eventually to the moving pictures, the three of us, travelling to the centre of the city in the interior of a tramcar.

The emptors: Meath County Council.

Three nights later at about eight o'clock I was alone in Nassau Street, a district frequented by the prostitute class, when I perceived a ramrod in a cloth cap on the watch at the corner of Kildare Street. As I passed I saw that the man was Kelly. Large spits were about him on the path and the carriage-way. I poked him in a manner offensive to propriety and greeted his turned face with a facetious ejaculation:

How is the boy! I said.

My hard man, he answered.

I took cigarettes from my pocket and lit one for each of us, frowning. With my face averted and a hardness in my voice, I put this question in a casual manner:

Anything doing?

O God no, he said. Not at all, man. Come away for a talk somewhere.

I agreed. Purporting to be an immoral character, I accompanied him on a long walk through the environs of Irishtown, Sandymount and Sydney Parade, returning by Haddington Road and the banks of the canal.

Purpose of walk: Discovery and embracing of virgins.

We attained nothing on our walk that was relevant to the purpose thereof but we filled up the loneliness of our souls with the music of our two voices, dog-racing, betting and offences against chastity being the several subjects of our discourse. We walked many miles together on other nights on similar missions — following matrons, accosting strangers, representing to married ladies that we were their friends, and gratuitously molesting members of the public. One night we were followed in our turn by a member of the police force attired in civilian clothing. On the advice of Kelly we hid ourselves in the interior of a church until he had gone. I found that the walking was beneficial to my health.

The people who attended the College had banded themselves into many private associations, some purely cultural and some concerned with the arrangement and conduct of ball games. The cultural societies were diverse in their character and aims and measured their vitality by the number of hooligans and unprincipled persons they attracted to their deliberations. Some were devoted to English letters, some to Irish letters and some to the study and advancement of the French language.

The most important was a body that met every Saturday night for the purpose of debate and disputation; its meetings, however, were availed of by many hundreds of students for shouting, horseplay, singing and the use of words, actions and gestures contrary to the usages of Christians. The society met in an old disused lecture theatre capable of accommodating the seats of about two hundred and fifty persons. Outside the theatre there was a spacious lobby or ante-room and it was here that the rough boys would gather and make their noises. One gas-jet was the means of affording light in the lobby and when a paroxysm of fighting and roaring would be at its height, the light would be extinguished as if by a supernatural or diabolic agency and the effect of the darkness in such circumstances afforded me many moments of physical and spiritual anxiety, for it seemed to me that the majority of the persons present were possessed by unclean spirits. The lighted rectangle of the doorway to the debate-hall was regarded by many persons not only as a receptacle for the foul and discordant speeches which they addressed to it, but also for many objects of a worthless nature — for example spent cigarette ends, old shoes, the hats of friends, parcels of damp horse dung, wads of soiled sacking and discarded articles of ladies' clothing not infrequently the worse for wear. Kelly on one occasion confined articles of his landlady's small-clothes in a neatly done parcel of brown paper and sent it through a friend to the visiting chairman, who opened it *coram populo* (in the presence of the assembly), and examined the articles fastidiously as if searching among them for an explanatory note, being unable to appraise their character instantaneously for two reasons, his failing sight and his station as a bachelor.

Result of overt act mentioned: Uproar and disorder.

When I attended these meetings I maintained a position where I was not personally identified, standing quietly without a word in the darkness. Conclusion of the foregoing.

W. B. YEATS
first printed February–March 1939

'Under Ben Bulben', first printed in *The Irish Times* on 3 February 1939, within a fortnight of Yeats's death, includes the epitaph engraved on his headstone in Drumcliff churchyard. The poem used to be seen as a fitting conclusion to Yeats's poetry and was positioned accordingly, but in recent years editors, their eye on chronological accuracy, have preferred to insert the more open-ended and less pompous poem 'Politics', first printed, along with 'The Circus Animals' Desertion', in *The Atlantic Monthly* in January 1939. 'News for the Delphic Oracle' and 'The Statues' were first published in *The London Mercury* in March 1939. A remarkable group of poems in whatever order they are placed.

from UNDER BEN BULBEN

V

Irish poets, learn your trade,
Sing whatever is well made,
Scorn the sort now growing up
All out of shape from toe to top,
Their unremembering hearts and heads
Base-born products of base beds.
Sing the peasantry, and then
Hard-riding country gentlemen,
The holiness of monks, and after
Porter-drinkers' randy laughter;
Sing the lords and ladies gay
That were beaten into the clay
Through seven heroic centuries;
Cast your mind on other days
That we in coming days may be
Still the indomitable Irishry.

VI

Under bare Ben Bulben's head
In Drumcliff churchyard Yeats is laid.
An ancestor was rector there
Long years ago, a church stands near,
By the road an ancient cross.
No marble, no conventional phrase;
On limestone quarried near the spot
By his command these words are cut:

Cast a cold eye
On life, on death.
Horseman, pass by!

September 4, 1938

THE STATUES

Pythagoras planned it. Why did the people stare?
His numbers though they moved or seemed to move
In marble or in bronze, lacked character.
But boys and girls pale from the imagined love
Of solitary beds, knew what they were,
That passion could bring character enough;
And pressed at midnight in some public place
Live lips upon a plummet-measured face.

No! Greater than Pythagoras, for the men
That with a mallet or a chisel modelled these
Calculations that look but casual flesh, put down
All Asiatic vague immensities,
And not the banks of oars that swam upon
The many-headed foam at Salamis.
Europe put off that foam when Phidias
Gave women dreams and dreams their looking-glass.

One image crossed the many-headed, sat
Under the tropic shade, grew round and slow,
No Hamlet thin from eating flies, a fat
Dreamer of the Middle Ages. Empty eyeballs knew
That knowledge increases unreality, that
Mirror on mirror mirrored is all the show.
When gong and conch declare the hour to bless
Grimalkin crawls to Buddha's emptiness.

When Pearse summoned Cuchulain to his side,
What stalked through the Post Office? What intellect,
What calculation, number, measurement, replied?
We Irish, born into that ancient sect
But thrown upon this filthy modern tide
And by its formless, spawning, fury wrecked,
Climb to our proper dark, that we may trace
The lineaments of a plummet-measured face.

April 9, 1938

NEWS FOR THE DELPHIC ORACLE

I

There all the golden codgers lay,
There the silver dew,
And the great water sighed for love
And the wind sighed too.
Man-picker Niamh leant and sighed
By Oisin on the grass;
There sighed amid his choir of love
Tall Pythagoras.
Plotinus came and looked about,
The salt flakes on his breast,
And having stretched and yawned awhile
Lay sighing like the rest.

II

Straddling each a dolphin's back
And steadied by a fin
Those Innocents re-live their death,
Their wounds open again.
The ecstatic waters laugh because
Their cries are sweet and strange,
Through their ancestral patterns dance,
And the brute dolphins plunge
Until in some cliff-sheltered bay
Where wades the choir of love
Proffering its sacred laurel crowns,
They pitch their burdens off.

III

Slim adolescence that a nymph has stripped,
Peleus on Thetis stares,
Her limbs are delicate as an eyelid,
Love has blinded him with tears;
But Thetis' belly listens.
Down the mountain walls
From where Pan's cavern is
Intolerable music falls.
Foul goat-head, brutal arm appear,
Belly, shoulder, bum,
Flash fishlike; nymphs and satyrs
Copulate in the foam.

THE CIRCUS ANIMALS' DESERTION

I

I sought a theme and sought for it in vain,
I sought it daily for six weeks or so.
Maybe at last being but a broken man
I must be satisfied with my heart, although
Winter and summer till old age began
My circus animals were all on show,
Those stilted boys, that burnished chariot,
Lion and woman and the Lord knows what.

II

What can I but enumerate old themes?
First that sea-rider Oisin led by the nose
Through three enchanted islands, allegorical dreams,
Vain gaiety, vain battle, vain repose,
Themes of the embittered heart, or so it seems,
That might adorn old songs or courtly shows;
But what cared I that set him on to ride,
I, starved for the bosom of his faery bride?

And then a counter-truth filled out its play,
The Countess Cathleen was the name I gave it,
She, pity-crazed, had given her soul away
But masterful Heaven had intervened to save it.
I thought my dear must her own soul destroy
So did fanaticism and hate enslave it,
And this brought forth a dream and soon enough
This dream itself had all my thought and love.

And when the Fool and Blind Man stole the bread
Cuchulain fought the ungovernable sea;
Heart mysteries there, and yet when all is said
It was the dream itself enchanted me:
Character isolated by a deed
To engross the present and dominate memory.
Players and painted stage took all my love
And not those things that they were emblems of.

III

Those masterful images because complete
Grew in pure mind, but out of what began?
A mound of refuse or the sweepings of a street,
Old kettles, old bottles, and a broken can,
Old iron, old bones, old rags, that raving slut
Who keeps the till. Now that my ladder's gone
I must lie down where all the ladders start
In the foul rag and bone shop of the heart.

POLITICS

*'In our time the destiny of man presents its meaning
in political terms.'* — Thomas Mann

How can I, that girl standing there,
My attention fix
On Roman or on Russian
Or on Spanish politics?
Yet here's a travelled man that knows
What he talks about,

And there's a politician
That has both read and thought,
And maybe what they say is true
Of war and war's alarms,
But O that I were young again
And held her in my arms.

LOUIS MacNEICE
from *Horizon*, August-September 1939

MacNeice's short poem, taken from a longer sequence entitled 'The Closing Album', captures a turning-point in European history from which his country was largely excluded. The poem was used by Cyril Connolly to introduce *Horizon*'s 'History of the War' — see *The Golden Horizon* (1953). The title refers to Cushendun Bay in County Antrim, where MacNeice spent part of the summer of 1939 with his father who had rented a house there.

CUSHENDUN

Fuchsia and ragweed and the distant hills
Made as it were out of clouds and sea:
All night the bay is plashing and the moon
　　Marks the break of the waves.

Limestone and basalt and a whitewashed house
With passages of great stone flags
And a walled garden with plums on the wall
　　And a bird piping in the night.

Forgetfulness: brass lamps and copper jugs
And home-made bread and the smell of turf or flax
And the air a glove and the water lathering easy
　　And convolvulus in the hedge.

Only in the dark green room beside the fire
With the curtains drawn against the winds and waves
There is a little box with a well-bred voice;
　　What a place to talk of War.

August 1939

IRISH WRITING IN THE 1940s

His oratory is not at all in the Irish tradition. One searches his speeches in vain to discover any trace of the mighty eloquence of a Burke or a Grattan, the flashing wit of a Curran, the flamboyance and rollicking humour of an O'Connell, the Ciceronian periods of a Redmond, or the spell-bindery of a Jim Larkin. At his worst he is dull; at his best, he is direct, forceful, and extraordinarily effective. Nobody who listens to him when he is really roused, or on a big occasion, can fail to be impressed by a sense of his burning sincerity. Sometimes, when he broadcasts, one is given the inescapable impression of the old schoolmaster addressing a class: he becomes didactic, persuasive, patiently argumentative, or disarmingly simple. On St Patrick's Day, 1943, he went to the microphone to give his annual talk, which contained the following remarkable passage:

> The Ireland which we have dreamed of would be the home of a people who valued material wealth only as the basis of a right living, of a people who were satisfied with frugal comfort and devoted their leisure to the things of the spirit; a land whose countryside would be bright with cosy homesteads, whose fields and villages would be joyous with the sounds of industry, with the romping of sturdy children, the contests of athletic youths, the laughter of comely maidens; whose firesides would be forums for the wisdom of old age. It would, in a word, be the home of a people living the life that God desires men should live.

It takes a big man to say a thing like that, to say it without insincerity or even self-consciousness, to say it in the year 1943 in the midst of a titanic war and an over-mechanized, over-sophisticated world. Some of his listeners murmured 'Utopia!' and the Dublin cynics cried, '1066 and all that!' But if it was an Arcadian picture that he drew, de Valera was speaking to a country whose civilization is rural rather than urban, to a people whose standards of living have been moulded and simplified by centuries of persecution, spoliation and famine, to a people of whom he is one. An Englishman or a resident in a fashionable Dublin suburb might regard the sentiments expressed as hopelessly naive, but the plain people of the Irish countryside listened with respect. They realized that the ideal put before them was the dream of a man who has seen so much of the horrors of war in his own country and in other countries that he has come to believe the world's salvation may lie in a return to a simpler and healthier way of living.

– M.J. MacManus, *Eamon de Valera: A Biography* (1944)

CRITICAL AND DOCUMENTARY

JIM PHELAN
from Jim Phelan, *Jail Journal* (1940)

In the 1920s and 1930s Jim Phelan spent over thirteen years in prisons in England, first at Maidstone, then at Dartmoor, and finally at Parkhurst on the Isle of Wight. In the two-and-a-half years in Maidstone prison, he began to make notes using Pitman's shorthand with a view to turning them into stories. The germ of his *Jail Journal* was written at Parkhurst in 1928. With the exception of John Mitchel (1815–75), the Irish rebel who was transported for treason-felony in 1848 to Tasmania and who wrote *Jail Journal, or Five Years in British Prisons* (1854), and Charles Reade (1814–84), author of *It Is Never Too Late To Mend* (1856), a novel which contains scenes of prison life, Phelan felt no one had put anything real on paper about prison life. When he reviewed this book for *Horizon* in June 1940 George Orwell commented on Phelan's 'straightforward discussion of the sex life of prisons' and how the results 'make horrible reading, but genuinely horrible, and not just pornography in disguise', for 'the existing penal system simply ignores the fact that man is a sexual animal'. Here in this his 'jail journal of the nineteen thirties', as Phelan terms it, is a record made at the beginning of his stay. His interest in psychology, evident in the entries, was part of the age. Indeed, psychology's potential threat was also recognized by the authorities, for books about psychology were forbidden prisoners.

A Chiel's Amang Ye

Reepy skins mice alive with a razor-blade.

Blank licks his lips, twice, very quickly, just before he reports a man and has him punished.

Limpy the Tinker throws mess out of his window. He sent a bomb by post to a woman, says he is an anarchist but isn't. Query coprophilia or cleanliness.

Passive homosexuals love to sing at church. Active never. Query religious fervour (child-preoccupations) or grasping at only chance for exhibitionism.

The Chaplain said: 'You *do* look well, old man,' to-day, at the cell next to mine. The cell is empty.

Mudgy Morrell drops on his knees if one challenges him suddenly about anything. Three other men do this too. Query any similarity in their offences.

If an official sucks in his breath when speaking to a convict, that man's request is going to be refused.

The active homos nearly always spit a good deal, very neatly, when watching the boys.

Fair-haired slim convicts are much more likely to become 'popular' than dark stout ones of the same age. Query selection by others because of near-conformity to standard femininity?

The little growl in convict speech has never been mentioned in any book. It is very interesting and attractive. Query find the same thing in babies, later eliminated, recurrent in a reversion-environment.

Some burglars excrete on tables or floors in the houses they rob, and boast of it. Follow this up.

Mortal Sinnet, a pickpocket, confesses that he has an orgasm whenever he 'touches for' (sig. phrase) a wallet.

Three normal-bodied men, all here for raping little girls, all baby-talk and lisp if bullied.

Toddy Wayne throws mess out of his window. Laughs if questioned. Ponce. (Question other ponces.)

Everyone in 'A' hall wakes at three a.m. (Food?)

Black-thinking, the depression thought-stream, becomes severe every six days. If oftener, trouble. Query, a sensible doctor could check on that, save trouble?

Manneridge skins mice in his cell. In for pest-blackmail. Check on Reepy and others. Query any connection blackmail.

Young *souteneurs*[1] nearly always 'tan', i.e. beat, the men they have willingly allowed to have their wives or women.

Some old convicts hide fish-bones, crusts, etc., under little heaps of fluff and rubbish, in the corners of their cells, are terribly distressed if warders throw same away.

Grasses, that is convicts who give information to warders about the other convicts, are all very short, very fat men here. (Question someone who has been in another jail about the grass fraternity there.)

Food here is good, but all the men are weak. Abnormal quantity excreted subject of general comment. (Digestive juices? Gland lethargy? Jail-depression hinders assimilation or metabolism? Try get a doctor to talk.)

Touchy Cullen will strike any man who closes within three feet behind him on exercise. Several others do this too. Here is anthropophobia[2] in the raw, something I have only known previously in text-books. Query why should jail-surroundings bring this out? What happens to a poor devil with mild (and quite common) claustrophobia, when a cell-door slams behind him?

On the morning a warder wears his whistle hanging over the middle of his overcoated chest he will report someone.

About 5 per cent of convicts here begin growing little sideboard whiskers and thin wispy moustaches in their first few weeks. Appears to be gesture of protest against incipient effeminacy as many drift passive very early.

Even intelligent men make infantile sexy-drawings in jail. (The authorities know something about this which evades me. Very sensibly ignore it.)

Reepy the mouse-killer *is* a homo-blackmailer. See others.

All men over four-year limit begin to have blank eyes. (Query fantasy-thought beginning to preponderate.)

If a man standing in line draws in a long hissing breath he is being snapped back out of a day-dream, is apt to be 'insolent' to warders and be reported at such times. (One shrewd old warder 'don't never go near they while they be hissin'-like.')

Men who walk on exercise with their hands clasped behind, stooping slightly forward, are headed for nerve-breakdown and the padded cells.

Fights on parade, or struggles with warders, seem to be 'timed', period-regulated, by sex-starvation. (Query possible to find the norm-interval.)

Bad cheese at night means many insolence 'crimes' next morning.

Most of the past-seven-year-men talk to themselves, blankly.

A man who smiles too much is headed for a smash-up in a few weeks.

Most warders seem to hate a powerful-bodied convict, even if powerfully built themselves. (Just economic, query?)

'Lifers' for discharge nearly always become hysterical.

That was the kind of 'rubbish' I began to collect, and continued to glean to the last day of my confinement. Reams of it were later rejected, in the light of wider knowledge, but I felt in the beginning that *nothing* could be scrapped. Since no one, except Mitchel and, to a lesser extent, Charles Reade, had put anything real on paper.

1   A person who lives on the earnings of prostitutes under his protection, a pimp. French soutenir: to sustain, or protect.
2   Fear of human beings.

FRANK O'CONNOR
from *The Listener*, 2 January 1941

This is an engaging talk given by O'Connor at the height of the Blitz in London. Under the Emergency Powers Act all public media in Ireland were under scrutiny and O'Connor, who wanted to broadcast from Dublin, was required to travel to London in case Irish neutrality was compromised by his talk. The title of his talk, broadcast on St Stephen's Day 1940, was 'Across St George's Channel'.

An Irishman Looks at England

When I was asked some weeks ago to broadcast from London, I jumped at the chance. I didn't jump at it because I was bored or because I wanted adventure or because I was looking for copy, but because whenever I had broadcast before it was the B.B.C. that conferred the favour, and their kindness was only part of the kindness I had received whenever I went to England. When somebody who's been a good neighbour to you has trouble in his house, you do want to show, even if it's only in a small way, that you haven't forgotten his kindness. And even though London, from the quiet of a Wicklow valley, doesn't seem the sort of place you'd like to go to, I felt that this was my little chance and that if I didn't go, the chance might never recur, and that I should always be rather ashamed of myself.

That, if you like, is a sentimental attitude, and it's sentiment that makes me want to speak to you when I know well that many of you are in great trouble, and some, God help them, in grief, while here we have been having parties of mummers — 'wren-boys', we call them — going about with blackened faces, and holly-bushes with coloured streamers in their hands, knocking at the farmhouse doors and singing the Wren-Boys' Song:[1]

God bless the Master of this house
A golden chain around his neck.

Well, I think I must have been one of the very few civilians who travelled on the mail boat that day. The rest were soldiers, returning from leave, and a few doctors going back to their jobs in the industrial towns. There wasn't a woman aboard, and when they handed out the lifebelts it reminded me of the days during the last War when my father was returning to his own regiment, and my mother and I sat by the fire saying, 'He should be across by now.'

I came on deck when we got within sight of Wales. That's something I never miss if I can help it, and each time I see it, something seems to drop from me. My heart rises; I want to stand and fill my lungs with the new air. And I think most of you will understand that, because even as children we all had some house beside our own which seemed to be all we expected a house to be; where brothers and sisters weren't so horrid and tea was a real feast, and I think many of you must have felt about Boulogne or Calais all the things I feel about Holyhead. 'They order this matter better in France,' as Sterne said;[2] and I love the phrase, because I think we all do need a France, a spiritual home, where 'this matter' is always better ordered, or we at least can think it is better ordered. It is a sort of personified ideal, an extension of our own personality, that makes us live always a little above ourselves.

And this time the prospect was doubly poignant, for I knew there was trouble in that house where I had spent so many happy days, and I expected terrible changes and wondered what they could be. But in Holyhead itself there was little change. I threw a few words in Welsh to a railwayman, and of course he stopped, as I knew he would, to find out what part of Wales I came from, and when he discovered that I wasn't Welsh, what part of Wales my wife came from, because wars may rage and towns may burn but a Welshman will always expect to know every other Welshman, or at least somebody that knows him. Everything was just as before; the train went out to the minute, the attendant came round with the tea-trays, but I could scarcely keep my eyes from the country outside. There, too, there was no sign of war, but the sense of its danger had transfigured it all for me, and while half my mind devoured the landscape, the other was away wandering in the New Forest,[3] sitting by the fire in little inns, talking to lorry drivers and railwaymen.

I was travelling with an Irish soldier who was going back to his unit, and we had scarcely left Rugby before he was half out of the window, looking for searchlights and listening for gunfire, in the heartless way of professional soldiers. But he was doomed to disappointment, because when we got to Euston no 'Alert' had sounded, the station was brightly lit, there wasn't the sound of a gun, and there were taxis in plenty.

I hadn't been out of Ireland since the War,[4] and the black-out was an astonishment to me, and still more when my eyes grew accustomed to it, and I began to perceive the long hedges of little coloured crosses that are all that's left of the traffic lights. There they were in endless rows, twinkling like fairy lights in an enormous cave with the tiny yellow side-lights of cars floating between them like fireflies; the dark cliffs of the houses overhead and the stars blazing off the sky. It took my breath away, and I believe that in ten years' time young novelists will be trying to recapture the wild beauty of London in the black-out.

It was only a whisper of change. The hotel was the London I knew, with its quiet efficiency and courtesy and I could almost shut out the thought of change while I lay in a comfortable bedroom with electric fire and telephone, bedside lamp and book. Habit, reasserting itself, put me off to sleep, whispering that nothing was changed; and then came the gunfire, like somebody knocking at my door to tell me that nothing would ever be the same again. I came prepared to be frightened. I hadn't come prepared to be bewildered; and that, I am afraid, is what I was. It was like being on a see-saw; up and up triumphantly at every familiar intonation and sound; down when I was shown the air-raid shelter; up when I came downstairs to breakfast and the sun was shining brilliantly outside and the tall red buses flashing past the door, and down into despair when I opened my morning paper and my eyes fell first upon the names of those killed in action, young men of the Royal Air Force who would never again see the sunlight on the streets of London. That was the blackest moment of all.

I have rarely been so glad to see the faces of friends and to find them at least unchanged. They represent stability in a world where one becomes uncertain of everything. Until you become a good sailor, something in you kicks at every plunge of the boat and makes you ill. You can't yield yourself to it in the way a sailor does, and when I went out into the streets my heart kicked at every gap in the shop fronts. It was a comfort to go into one of those shops, and even though you couldn't concentrate on business yourself, to have others concentrate on it for you, to have business talked to you, not bombs or invasions; and when I came out into the street again it helped me to see not the gaps only but the whole streets where there were no gaps at all.

'I'd Forgotten the Air-Raid'

I saw it more clearly when the siren blew again. Everybody went on calmly about his business. We passed a street corner where they were picking up the remains of a German plane from the kerb. The body of it was already hoisted on a waiting lorry, and with its shattered propeller blades it had an astonished air, as though it didn't quite know what had happened to it. It brought back to me Fair Day in an Irish town and a newly bought calf after being hoisted on a creel with its hind legs down and its snout in the air. We rattled at the door of the shop but the occupants were still in shelter. An old lady with an indignant air rattled too and asked us why the shop wasn't open. My friend told her and her face cleared at once. 'Oh,' she said, 'I'd forgotten about the air raid.' And it was just as if she'd said, 'Oh, I thought it was something serious.' It was quite spontaneous, part of that vast normality within abnormality, and though it reassured me when I grew nervous, it made everything much harder in another way. In that atmosphere where everybody, bus-men and taxi-drivers, typists and hotel servants, went on with their jobs, where people weren't impatient or discourteous, it was almost too easy to let habit have its fling and forget there was trouble in the house. I found myself throwing myself into the job of the moment, getting the last ounce out of a conversation, storing up yarns to retail at home, and then — the downward spin of the boat, and one's heart kicked desperately against the realization that this was not the same house one had been so happy in, that these guns were not toy guns pounding off stage.

And that was how it was when I left. There were four of us at dinner together. The talk was the sort of talk I had been pining for, that I imagine whenever I get a little homesick for England. It was the talk of men fascinated by their work, by ideas, by realities; and to leave it and go out under a cloudy sky rent with flashes of light was to walk out of time into history, out of permanence into change. It was too stunning; I couldn't grasp it; I can't grasp it now.

I discovered that my train might not start at all that night, so I settled myself down in the hotel lounge. An hour later the porter called me. My train was going after all. He made no comment about it until I was leaving. Then he turned to his desk and suddenly smiled. 'Oh, we shall be all right,' he said, and for a moment I saw how pleased he was that the train really was going out, how much it meant to him that life should go on. Outside the hotel a fire was blazing in the roadway, and tiny black figures darted about it. Within the station there were hundreds of people waiting patiently for their train; I could only see their legs as the station porter guided me with his hand torch, and it was strange feeling their presence without seeing them.

When the train came in it was crowded within a few moments, but from the time it filled there might have been nobody in it. We were exposed under a raging attack while a fire blazed a few hundred yards away, but I could imagine myself on the night mail in some little wayside station in Ireland when the lights have failed and the guard and engine driver gone into the village for a drink. Just once or twice a little light bloomed up out of the wall of blackness and I saw the window of a carriage in another train and realized that over there too some hundreds of people were waiting patiently for their train to start. We remained there for hours, yet in all that time the only voice that was raised was the voice of the attendant in the sleeping-car who seemed to have it fixed in his mind that somebody was trying to travel without a sleeping-car ticket. At home there would have been a drunken man to raise a nervous laugh, or some young fellow would have started a song, but here there was nothing to break even for an instant that sense of silent, enduring, recollected life. There, at any rate, is something I shall never forget.

Things That Have Not Changed

And all the way home I kept wondering what I should say when people asked me questions. There was the heart, and the heart would remember all the gaps in the familiar skyline and want to cry out that everything was changed, but the moment one thought of it, it sounded false. It was false. Because I remembered all the places where there were no gaps, and all the people going on with their work, the waiters in the restaurants, the typists, and those hundreds of people sitting patiently in their carriages at Euston — and I wanted to say that nothing was changed.

One's impression of a nation, like one's impression of that house one knew as a child, is a distillation of hundreds of little incidents, too trifling to repeat. It is the most difficult thing in the world to generalize about; it is a perfume and one tries in vain to capture it in words. For me that perfume is compounded of many things: kindness, which is the strongest ingredient; courtesy, decency, order. Then there is a sort of simplicity; a singleness of mind and a purity of intention; a touch of knight-errantry that one loves, even though one pokes fun at it. There is last of all a mind that looks outwards on life rather than in upon itself, that doesn't exploit or dramatize itself, that does not raise its voice.

If that perfume had changed for me, I shouldn't be speaking to you now; if courtesy or candour had gone, then there would have been a real gap on the skyline. Something would have been closed forever, and I might feel that I should never again stand on the deck of the steamer at Holyhead and feel that old stirring of the heart.

But that has *not* changed, and because this is a neighbourly season, and you and I are old neighbours

and friends, I want to remind you of it. I like old festivals, old customs, old friends, and I am glad to think while I am speaking to you, of the wren-boys with their blackened faces knocking at cottage doors throughout Ireland. They are part of the permanent things of life; and it would be a sad house they didn't call on, and for the sake of old times, and that house where we have all been happy together, I want to be the wren-boy for this occasion, to knock at your door and remind you of the Wren-Boys' Song:

> God bless the master of this house,
> A golden chain around his neck;
> If he's sick or if he's sore,
> I hope that Heaven will him restore.

1   On St Stephen's Day (Boxing Day) it was customary in Ireland for boys in the village to dress up in search of the wren, visiting houses in the parish, soliciting coins or eatables. See Kevin Danaher, *The Year in Ireland: Irish Calendar Customs* (1972).
2   From the opening line of Laurence Sterne's *A Sentimental Journey Through France and Italy* (1768).
3   Ancient forest area in Hampshire, north of Southampton.
4   Since the War began that is.

LOUIS MacNEICE
from *Horizon*, February 1941

In the literary magazine *Horizon* on 12 December 1940, Cyril Connolly, the editor, complained: 'From America no traveller returns, no American letters get written, and to ask for them is like dropping pebbles down a well. This is regrettable, for *Horizon* has suspended judgement on the expatriates.' MacNeice, who had recently returned from a period of nearly twelve months spent in the United States, felt compelled to defend the decision of those such as his friend W.H. Auden who left war-torn Europe for America. (In October 1940 he stayed with Auden at 7 Middagh Street in Brooklyn Heights.)

Traveller's Return

'From America no traveller returns', so Mr Connolly wrote in his Comment in the December number of *Horizon*. Having ignored this apriori truth by landing in this country on December 9th after ten months in the U.S.A., I am surprised to find how many people ask bitterly after those other British writers who are still in America. When people over here talk about

these expatriates, more often than not their acrimony equals their ignorance. As an ex-expatriate, therefore, I am about to discuss this subject under a handicap; I have seen it from both sides of the Atlantic.

While I was in America I felt a very long way from Europe, though not so far away as I felt during the autumn of 1939 in Ireland. You cannot forget the War in America (it is the chief subject of conversation), but you cannot visualize it. I could visualize it myself so long as the 'Sitzkrieg'[1] persisted, and during that period I had no wish to return to a Chamberlain's England, where my fellow-writers were sitting around not writing. From June on I wished to return, not because I thought I could be more *useful* in England than in America, but because I wanted to see these things for myself. My chief motive thus being vulgar curiosity, my second motive was no less egotistical: I thought that if I stayed another year out of England I should have to stay out for good, having missed so much history, lost touch.

These two motives of mine seem to me valid for me, but they are not *generally* valid. If an expatriate writer is free from vulgar curiosity and does not wish to keep 'in touch' with England (and such a wish is not a moral axiom), what other reasons are there why he should return? Three possible reasons: (1) Because he could be more useful in England. (2) Because in England he would become a better writer or a better person, or both. (3) Patriotism and/or homesickness.

(1) If an expatriate writer happened, say, to be a highly skilled engineer, he might be more useful to Britain as an engineer than he would be to the U.S.A. or the world as a writer. But none of the expatriates we are discussing has any such technical qualifications; the only thing they can do particularly well is to write. Would they be useful to Britain to-day *qua* writers? Any more use, that is, than they are while they reside in America? It is more than doubtful. A writer in England now can either sink his gifts in some form of propaganda work, at which he is not necessarily better than Tom, Dick or Harry, or he can continue to survive as a free lance whom no one has time to attend to, or he can give up his profession of writing for the amateurdom of National Service. Usefulness? That is a conception which has never been commensurable with art; even the use of commercial or of propaganda art is hard to assess. Some writers of the Left in England regret that their late colleagues have not returned in order to be flaming torches. But are they, who have stayed over here, doing much flaming themselves? I will return to this point.

(2) The argument that a British-born writer by being in England now would better himself as a writer or as a person, or as both, is a good deal more plausible and may be true for certain individuals. But you cannot generalize. A minority of writers — like Malraux and Hemingway — seem to thrive *qua* writers on scenes of violence and suffering, but none of the British expatriates belongs to this minority. War again brings out in many people certain virtues — notably courage and patience and, to a less degree, generosity — which had not before been apparent, but as these virtues, with the exception of generosity, are not particularly necessary to a writer, a writer, by having them forced upon him, may become in a sense a better person while becoming an inferior, less productive or unproductive artist. If that is so — but again each case must be judged individually — his advance as a person must be balanced against his decline as an artist. On a long term view it is not axiomatic either that war improves everyone — or most people — morally, or that a writer who has become, say, courageous and patient in his life but whose art is lapsing, is in the proper (objective) sense of the word a *better* man than a writer who is not practising courage or patience, but is getting on with his job.

(3) Patriotism or homesickness? Though patriotism includes a sentimental, as it were a family, feeling for place, we can distinguish the ethical motive from the sentimental. At certain times in certain countries there has been a moral urgency to be patriotic when the actual or ideal policy of a man's nation has been a *sine qua non*[2] for his conscience. But to-day patriotism, in so far as it means subordination to a specifically national policy, is superannuated. This war, we assume, is not being fought — not by most of us — for any merely national end; we are fighting it, primarily and clearly, for our lives, and secondarily, and, alas! vaguely, for a new international order. How does this affect the expatriates? They need not at the moment fight for their lives. Will they contribute less to a new international order by living in a country where they are not nationals (a country, by the way, at least no less committed than Great Britain to internationalism)? As for homesickness, if anyone goes home because he is homesick, that is sympathetic, but it is not *ipso facto*[3] a sign of strength; it might be a sign of weakness. Just as Action at All Costs is sometimes a sign of weakness; we have heard of 'escaping to the Front'.

When I first reached England I was asked if I had read Stephen Spender's attack on the expatriates. Later I was asked if I had read his defence of them. So I got hold of his 'Letter to a Colleague in America' in *The New Statesman and Nation*, of November 16th, which both my questioners referred to. It was not stated *which* colleague he was addressing — and that makes some difference — but I received the impression that Mr Spender, while carefully conceding that 'if you can preserve the sense of the "time in London", then you are in a privileged position', was in fact suspecting the worst. His letter, especially by contrast with the press-gang attitude of others who have touched this subject, was sensitive, imaginative, and tolerant, but it struck me as inconsistent, indeed, as woolly. He writes: 'I know *as well as you must do* [italics mine] that there is no possibility of running away from a fate which affects the whole world', but later — and this time the tone implies that 'I' know it better than 'you' do — he writes that people 'cannot escape into an entirely new and less disturbing series of events, not even in Hollywood'. As he was writing to someone who was in Hollywood, and as he immediately followed this remark with aspersions on yoga and a 'philosophy of life' (presumably of the bogus Southern Californian brand), I took him to mean that his addressee *was* trying to 'escape' into an entirely new and less disturbing series of events. Mr Spender tells me he did not mean this, but there are other people who mean it and say it. And it may be true of *some* of the expatriates that they are trying to put the clock back, but it is a black lie if applied to all of them. Nor is it true of most Americans though Mr Spender implies (or doesn't he? — read it for yourself) that the whole country is backward, still living in the days before Munich.[4] We might remember too that there are people also over here — from Colney Hatch to the War Office, from the *Daily Express* to the People's Convention — whose clocks, it seems, have stopped.

Mr Spender, in his letter, made a great to-do with time and place. 'It is hardly a question,' he writes, 'of *where* you are at all, but *when*,' yet he goes on to subordinate the *when* to the *where*, at least by implication, like this: X, an English writer, is living in America, and America, because of geography, is behind the times, therefore X, *because* he is in America, is also behind the times. 'The only question worth asking,' he goes on, 'about Auden, Isherwood, Heard, Aldous Huxley, MacNeice, etc. [is] not whether they have run away on this particular occasion, but whether they think that there is a chance of escaping from this history altogether.' As Mr Spender does not answer this question, we cannot say we have been hit. Speaking for myself, I would deny that the possibility of such an escape ever occurred to me. America (I am not speaking of Hollywood, which may be a world to itself) is not a sound-proof room. Nor are Americans politically anæsthetized. If some Americans, like some Englishmen, are still pre-Munich, other Americans, like other Englishmen, were post-Munich before Munich happened. If Mr Spender *will* use this tricky time-and-place relativism he must avoid even the suggestion of downright generalizations. Anyway, to adopt his relativism for a moment, I suspect him of wishing to repeople England with pre-Munich Audens and Isherwoods. It was only before Munich that this pair attempted the rôle of the Flaming Torch (a rôle, in my opinion, to

which neither was very well suited), and it was before Munich that they wrote *On the Frontier*, their last play, their most directly political — and also their worst — work.

'But Auden and Isherwood,' people say, 'were always preaching the fight against Fascism.' So what? I had many conversations with Auden this autumn, and he still is anti-Fascist, but he is no longer in any way a 'fellow traveller'; since getting off that particular train, he had decided — as he told me in March 1939 — that it was not his job to be a crusader, that this was a thing everyone must decide for himself, but that, in his opinion, most writers falsified their work and themselves when they took a direct part in politics, and that the political end itself, however good, could not be much assisted by art or artists so falsified. Auden, that is, had repudiated propaganda.

'Well, he needn't preach or flame, but he ought at least to come back.' Why? The answer too often is jealousy or spite — 'If I am under bombs, why the hell shouldn't X be too?' But you can't conduct an argument by means of white feathers or raspberries. War makes people so illogical. *If* you disapprove of the expatriates being in America in wartime, you should have disapproved of their settling there in peace time, you should have made a row when they first took out their papers.

Some people do go so far. It is argued by extremists, most of whom have never crossed the Atlantic, that no Englishman — no English writer anyway — 'can' change countries like this; it was all right, perhaps, for Henry James and Eliot[5] to come this way, but no English writer can go that way and get away with it. This looks to me like sheer nonsense. Of course, it is hard to write where you have no 'roots', but because it is hard it may be all the more worth doing. We have had plenty of 'rooted' writing; the individual artist may have soon to dispense with 'roots' (in this narrower, local sense), just as the world must sooner or later dispense with national sovereignty. This question of roots is a question of degree: few of us believe the diehards who think you must stick to your own parish, fewer of us than formerly think that it is good for a small country like Ireland to attempt a cultural autarchy.

This reminds me; I can give myself as an example of uprootability. Born in Ireland of Irish parents, I have never felt properly 'at home' in England, yet I can write here better than in Ireland. In America I feel rather more at home than in England (America has more of Ireland in it), but I am not sure how well I could work if I settled there permanently. If I were sure on this point — as some of the expatriates are sure — it would only have been sensible of me to stay there. Many people in England, the war apart, are astonished that anyone can consider such a migration. Their astonishment is due to that anti-American prejudice which, like the corresponding anti-British prejudice among Americans, is founded on childish misconceptions and leads to a misunderstanding which is not only childish but dangerous. Dangerous especially now. If the two countries were more pervious to each other, it would not only reinvigorate the culture of both, it would ensure the existence of both. That two or three gifted English writers should be now living in the U.S.A. is at least one kind of much needed *rapprochement*.

In the long run a writer must be judged by what he writes. The British expatriates, with the exception of Isherwood, whose books have always appeared after intervals of apparent inactivity, are still at least writing. Let us look at their more recent publications.

From Los Angeles come *After Many a Summer*, by Aldous Huxley, and *The Creed of Christ*, by Gerald Heard, each of which is a logical development from its author's long-established premises and appears neither better nor worse for his change of domicile. I myself hate the Huxley novel and deplore the Heard *Weltanschauung*, but I cannot see that they would write either better or worse if they moved back to England. And I cannot see that England would gain from the physical presence of either (England can get all they can give by reading their works), whereas they, by returning, might inconvenience both themselves and us; this is no place for either the museum mind or the yogi. But it is good to know that the Heard-Huxley firm can continue in business somewhere.

In New York are Auden, George Barker, Ralph Bates. Barker has not been there long enough to publish a book, but it is probable that poetry of his kind (and it is silly to expect a war to produce mutations of kind) would not develop any better for his being in England; the chief difference is that there he may write more. Barker was never a Flaming Torch, and his sensitive, introspective, romantic, rather woozy talent is not the kind that requires a contact with mud and blood. As far as being 'of use' to his country goes, he will — paradoxically — be of more use to this country when writing as a free lance in America than when he was representing the British Council in a farcical attempt to preserve a cultural liaison with Japan.

Bates, at one time a staunch supporter of the Third International,[6] has settled in the U.S.A. and is continuing to write novels and stories which, apart from their other merits, are valuable social history.

'Well, why can't he do his social history over here? There is lots of opportunity here.' Lots of opportunity for some; you must consider Bates's background. Like many other writers of the Left, he has had to recant a policy to which he had committed himself wholeheartedly; his recantation was unusually clear-cut and courageous, but any such recantation — as can be seen from a study of ex-Fellow Travellers in England — makes it very difficult to pick up where you left off. Bates is picking up in a country which his own past — his past in England — does not obscure from him; at the same time he is making a sympathetic and intelligent study of another country, Mexico, for which his past — his past in Spain — has equipped him.

Lastly Auden, whom people over here are never tired of back-biting. London is full of silly rumours — Auden has gone yogi, neo-Brahmin, Roman Catholic; it is even alleged that he supported Willkie.[7] The accusations can be summarized under two heads: (1) Auden has got religion; (2) Auden is now just a faddist. (1) This is meant to be damning; it is not recognized, firstly, that the religious sense is something extremely valuable; secondly, that it is something which Auden has always had. What he has done recently is to concentrate and control this sense, to divorce it from what is merely private or ephemeral. (2) Auden, in a sense, has always been a faddist, and seems less of one now than formerly; in any case his fads are not the result of America. While in America he has written two books of poetry — *Another Time* and *The Double Man*. These books have their faults and lack some of the attractions of some of his earlier poems, but they are *not*, even if critics can be found to say so, reactionary or escapist or stagnating. They might be described as transitional; Auden has purged his world-view of certain ready-made, second-hand over-simplifications and is now attempting a new synthesis of his material. Considering the range of his material and considering how many writers have dropped all suggestion of synthesis, this is an attempt for which we should all be grateful.

For the expatriate there is no Categorical Imperative[8] bidding him return — or stay. Auden, for example, working eight hours a day in New York, is getting somewhere; it might well be 'wrong' for him to return. For another artist who felt he was getting nowhere it might be 'right' to return. In my own case, if I had stayed in America I do not suppose I should have felt morally guilty, though I might have felt *instinctively* so; not being on the track of a synthesis and being more attached to things than to ideas I might have felt I was only marking time in America (whereas artists of the opposite kind might be only marking time in England; war, after all, is monotonous, hostile to thought). Actually both my pleasure at being back and my regret, if I had not come, are equally unethical. Those who think it would have been selfish and irresponsible of me to stay in America might be interested to know that their opposite numbers in America thought it selfish and irresponsible of me to return to Europe. And they and their opposite numbers are both fools. The expatriates do not need anybody else to act as their *ersatz*[9] conscience: they have consciences of their own and the last word must be said by their own instinct as artists.

1   Phony war, the quiet first six months of the War until April 1940.

2   An absolute essential.
3   In itself for that reason.
4   The British Prime Minister Neville Chamberlain signed a pact with Hitler in Munich in September 1938, a pact which came to symbolize the failed policy of appeasement.
5   T.S. Eliot, the American poet who settled in England in 1914 and became a British subject in 1927.
6   The Third International was established in 1919 in the wake of the Russian Revolution of 1917.
7   Wendell Lewis Willkie (1892–1944), American industrialist and political leader who crossed the floor of the House from Democrat to Republican in protest against the New Deal.
8   The phrase is associated with the German philosopher Immanuel Kant (1724–1804). His view of the moral law was: 'Act as if the maxim from which you act were to become through your will a universal law.'
9   Substitute or surrogate.

JIM PHELAN
from Jim Phelan, *Ireland-Atlantic Gateway* (1941)

Jim Phelan described *Ireland-Atlantic Gateway* as 'the partisan statement of an anti-Nazi Irishman'. It is an unusual book, written with conviction, the argument characteristically rooted in knowledge derived from common experience peppered with anecdote and the 'commonplaces of daily conversation'. In this extract Phelan addresses the issue of Ireland's links with the United States and Australia and ends by appealing for Irish ports on the Atlantic coast to be made available for the war effort against Nazi Germany.

The Irish Empire

The simplest way to describe the American influence upon the Irish at home is to call it inverted nostalgia. British people in Canada or Italy, say, think much of 'home', often centre their thoughts on metropolitan happenings, snatch at chances for leave, return when opportunity offers and settle down in the country of their birth. The Irish did almost the exact opposite, which is amusing when one remembers their reputation for love of native land. The 'Yank', or returned American, automatically owned the village. Young men who had not been in the States were looked upon as sissified fledglings. It even reached the stage at which people *pretended* to have been in the States, for a quiet life. Sincere imitation could go no farther.[1]

Back in the States the Irish changed, much and swiftly. Bull-whacker, miner, policeman, lumberjack,

railroader, bartender — that was the Irishman until about 1869. In the big opening-up of the country that followed the westward spread of the railroads after 1869, the Irish changed, feeling more at home and having a little more security. Share-cropper, miner, clergyman, police-captain, lumberjack, saloon-owner, ward-politician — any or most of those were more likely to have a name like Donovan or Leahy than not. Then came the swift industrialization and the teeming rush of the factory towns, and Tammany Hall,[2] and fortunes in saloons and contracting. Miner, police-chief, clergyman, saloon-owner, state politician, contractor, industrial drummer, newspaperman, judge, increasingly about the turn of the century one expected to find Irish names and faces in those occupations. Only miner and clergyman (R.C.,[3] of course) would seem to be 'nationally justified'.

The intercourse between Ireland and the States was greater than ever. Steamship companies fought for the prize of the Irish trade. (In people, not in goods.) Lough Swilly and Cobh were ports for American lines. Every tiny pub in a mountain hamlet had its *Boston Globe* and its *Herald*, besides the inevitable multichrome posters of the shipping companies offering cheap fares either way. Indeed, at one time you could go from Waterford to Boston, over three thousand miles, for thirty shillings. In 1912, when the 'Curragh Mutiny'[4] took place, there was a growl from end to end of the United States which *ought to have been* heard in London, but unfortunately was not. The 1912 files of even the least pro-Irish newspapers in the States make very interesting reading.

Almost immediately after the Loyalist gun-running and the Curragh mutiny there was an Irish gun-running, followed by bloodshed. The Irish Republican Brotherhood, working with very great secrecy, organized the movement which was then called Sinn Fein and later the Irish Republic. Most of the money and the best of the propaganda came from the States. When in 1916 the rebellion boiled over, the same held good. But it was not until the years after 1919, in the struggle against the Black-and-Tans, that the full weight of Irish-American money and power was felt. Two hundred million dollars, collected openly (much of it by Eamon De Valera, the present Eire President) went into the fight against the British. The comings and goings, between Galway and New York, at a time when of course no rebel leader was allowed to be free, let alone take passage on a ship, make a vastly dramatic story. All over the United States people in every walk of life from Senator to garbageman were — not remembering but just reacting to the Big Hunger.[5]

Since 1922 the Republican organizations in America have been largely quiescent. They are extremely well organized and very numerous, besides having terrific political 'pull', something for which the Irish are almost as notorious as Right People anywhere. (Consider the names in American diplomacy, administration, state politics, the newspaper world, as an example of what a really good Big Hunger will do for a people!) Lately they have been turning anti-Nazi in a preoccupied fashion, but it would be a naïve ignorance of psychology, let alone economics, to suppose that preoccupation implied forgetfulness of Ireland at home. *Tout au contraire*.[6]

Quietly, quickly, without one wag of a flag or bang of a big drum, the far-seeing observers at the head of the Democratic Party made their reports about Eire. Quietly and without any dramatic nonsense Roosevelt sent the American food-ships to Eire last May. The first ships to brush aside with their prows the paper-waves of the Neutrality Act, be it noted. The ships

that directly and in dignified fashion contravened everything the ranchers' friends had hoped for, be it noted. The intentions of the British Government regarding Eire at that time are not known. The desires of 'We'[7] stood out like a second ace of hearts in a poker hand. 'We' wanted Eire starved into recalcitrance. The Democratic Party in America did not. In many districts the Irish *are* the Democratic Party. The ships were sent. Wisha, if that's not a wispeen o' straw sure I never saw a tempest,[8] is roughly the comment of Tipperary on the event.

There is a joke in Galway, about a hotel on the sea front, facing the Atlantic. A notice advertised it as 'To let. Apply opposite.' The strange reader looked 'opposite' and saw only the ocean. The owner lived in New York. They say New York is a suburb of Galway — 'but a little bit westerly', and that Boston, Massachusetts, is the biggest city in Ireland.

Things like that, better than argument or statistics, point to the ties between peoples. Would it be an accident, maybe, that a multi-millionaire pays Irish artists to do cartoon-strips for papers selling many millions, in which the *average* middle-class citizen (say Strube's 'Little Man' in the *Daily Express*, or Colonel Up and Mr Down) is given an unmistakably Irish phiz[9] and Irish-American friends. Or perhaps the millionaire is a bad business man? At any rate that is the kind of nation a few dozen people of the 'We' type are blindly attempting to oppose, contrary to the interests and needs of the British Government. If the Irish-Americans are anti-Nazi — what are 'We'?

The links with Australia are more emotional, being mainly religious and patriotic, which the American ties are not. Everyone knows the Aussie's joke against himself — his equivalent of the *Mayflower* story.[10] But you will not find many people claiming that their families were amongst the first settlers, nevertheless. Except the Irish. They boast about their emigration, and of course rightly, since to have been transported for life by the British about 1840-ish, from Ireland, was practically a certificate of great moral and physical courage. Anyone who has read John Mitchel's *Jail Journal*[11] will recognize the reasons for the pride.

The type-reactions of the Irish-Australian in khaki are very naïve. He is quite likely to walk up to any London journalist with an Irish name, and start to talk about Easter Week, 1916, besides showing a rosary round his neck. If tight, he will probably sing one or two of the rebel songs of 1921. The Irish in the States do not behave in that way. But then neither do the Irish in the States (yet) fight on the British side with that terrific handicraft concentration of the Australians.

It is a curious contradiction, and interesting nowadays as it was interesting in 1918, when the two groups of 'Irish Exiles' (neither of whom had ever seen Ireland, generally speaking!) got together. Perhaps it is best summed up statistically. The Irish Republican Brotherhood has not a large membership in Australia. But there is a very large number of people with Irish names, relatives 'at home', a traditional pride in a rebellious ancestry — and an automatic inclination to fight for Australia, or (as usually happens) for Britain.

No reader would be saying, 'Good; the Irish Aussies are all safe supporters, then. No need to . . .' Because only a very mean man thinks that way and generally he thinks wrong. It is a fact though that the Irish-Australians can be equated with the mass of the ordinary, quiet, unorganized Irish in Ireland. Who also fight epically, on occasion, and often in the British Army.

That is the Irish Empire. Two groups of people, one numbering many millions, with wealth and influence and a desire to aid Britain for their own sake; the other smaller, relatively even wealthier, physically superb and with a tradition of 'dropping in to lend a hand over there' which they have borrowed from their countrymen of British descent. Both 'remembering', across three generations, the small insignificant country on the Atlantic's edge. It is a big empire and a strange one. There was a time when it was matter for interest and awe but little else, what of its size and strange orientation.

But the world is getting smaller, and some of the things advanced thinkers have been saying for years, unheeded, are now the commonplaces of daily conversation. 'If one poor blackman be crushed to death on a South Sea island by a million-greedy soap company, then you and I in our daily lives cannot escape the consequences.'[12]

Time was when nations 'minded their own business', and no one cared who voted what, nor where, except in his 'own' land. Now we are seeing, slowly, that there is only one world and that anybody's business is everybody's. Victorian statesmen would have thought it ludicrous that Britons should wait with eagerness and anxiety the result of an election in a country thousands of miles away. Or that millions of Irish, in the vast Democratic Party where they bulk so big, should vote in effect for the swift succour of the 'ancient enemy'. Or that we in London should openly disclose our conviction that Democratic America ranks almost equal with the Royal Navy as a British defence. The Victorians would have called us mad; it is only getting sane that we are.

The largest solidly organized voting group in the States is the Irish. They practically *built* the Democratic Party, in the exuberance of wielding the new potent weapon of the vote. They are terrific — nobody in Britain needs telling about that nowadays. In Australia the Irish-descended make no 'nationalistic' showing. They go in the army, and fight, when there is a war, for the British, without hesitation or thought, while they boast of their rebel ancestry — and sing in Trafalgar Square the Irish Republican songs of 1920.

That is the Irish Empire, again. It is an original, not to say unique and *very* Irish way to build an empire. But it is there. Some rats would antagonize it to-day for their own ends. Some noble-minded gentlemen accidentally express their own individual dislikes in the name of the British people. (Has *anyone* forgotten the ghastly business in which one high-minded altruistic gentleman, a known former backer of Nazism, printed a deadly insult to the Americans in what was supposed to be a national work, and nearly got away with it?) Some rats in any country would do that kind of thing, too, if they were allowed. But indeed you cannot kick a man's dog, even, and then ask him to lend you a fiver. Let alone kicking his old granny and his baby and the secret toy house where he keeps his dreams.

From Blacksod[13] or Galway, America is the next stop. The dream-house where the millions of the democratic American-Irish live in spirit is nearer by vital days to the American coast than any British base. It should be used, for them and for us, now. Whoever says nay.

The Irish Empire is the friend of Britain and the enemy of Nazism at present. That is a bad thing, for Hitler and for some others. Hitler is in good hands — and sure the others only want a little watching.

---

1   It is interesting that much of the American slang now being generally used in England and elsewhere, as a result of the Hollywood influence, should have been current in Irish villages thirty or forty years ago. 'Ses you' was Irish colloquial currency when I was a boy. 'Oh, yeah?' accompanied a lift of the eyebrows in a Dublin pub about 1910. Everyone in bog-villages guessed and reckoned as far back as people can remember. [AN]

2   The control of American City Halls by in this case the Irish, and the ensuing corruption.

3   Roman Catholic.

4   The Curragh Mutiny was an incident which occurred at the time the Belfast loyalists had shown their loyalty by procuring German guns to start a rebellion. The officer in charge of the British troops at the Curragh, in Kildare, gave certain orders. Certain officers refused. 'Ulster will fight and Ulster will be Right' acquired a sinister significance thereafter. [AN]

5   The Great Famine of the 1840s became a symbol of Ireland's victim status and laid the foundations for

American sympathy for Ireland. In his use of the term Big Hunger Phelan is partly mocking conventional responses.

6 On the contrary.

7 A reference possibly to British public opinion, we in London, we his English reader.

8 Well, if that's not a small bundle of straw I've never seen a violent thunder-storm. An ungrateful comment from provincial Ireland.

9 Appearance. Short for physiognomy.

10 Once, in an English jail, I was pulling an Australian convict's leg. A real Jeff Peters person, he was a conman first and last, *but* became objurgatory when I insinuated that it ran in the family, since he belonged to an old Australian family! He indignantly denied that he was a descendant of convicts, until I pretended to be convinced, and accepted the alternative that his forebears had been transportation-warders. With that choice, he picked the hulks as his ancestral home at once. An Irish-Australian would have announced it in the first minute. [AN]

11 The account by the Young Irelander John Mitchel (1815–75) of his transportation to Van Diemen's Land (Tasmania) and ensuing experiences. The subtitle of *Jail Journal* (1854) is *Five Years in British Prisons*.

12 A reference to the South Sea Bubble and the collapse of the South Sea Company in 1720 from its unlimited expansion of credit.

13 A bay in County Mayo.

FRANK O'CONNOR
from *Horizon*, January 1942

O'Connor's article can be read as a position statement in which, now that the Yeats generation is dead, he takes stock of contemporary Irish culture and society. In a discussion reprinted in *The Listener* on 16 March 1938 between O'Connor and L.A.G. Strong on the topic 'Should Provincial Writers Stay at Home?', O'Connor had remarked: 'At one side of me is the bottomless abyss of Irish Ireland; at the other the yawning gulf of English Ireland. You know what I mean: the fellows who think Ireland is the greatest country in the world ("the greatest civilization the world has ever known was destroyed by English barbarians in the seventeenth century") and then the dear old ladies of Dunleary, to whom the mail boat is the last remaining link with civilization. Insularity and provincialism.' Here in this extract O'Connor continues the theme. Again, it is a worthwhile exercise to summarize the argument. How in fact did Irish culture avoid the dead-end anticipated by O'Connor?

The Future of Irish Literature

I

Writing about the future of Irish literature is like writing of the future of the Lancashire industrial towns — the subject is a question mark.

By Irish literature I don't, of course, mean literature written by Irishmen. People like Shaw and Elizabeth Bowen will continue to write, and to influence young men and women in Ireland, but that is not what I mean. I have no desire to be exclusive or nationalistic, because, except for reasons which have nothing to do with literature, it doesn't matter a rap whether a writer is Irish or English. A national literature is one of the luxuries of a civilized people; it is like a national opera; it permits a young man or woman growing up in Cork or Helsinki or Kalamazoo to look at the life about him through the medium of a racial outlook and philosophy, without his instantly beginning to pine for London and Paris and Rome. It is the only escape from provincialism. It was in this way that we as boys saw *The Playboy of the Western World* and felt that, after all, life in Ireland was not too bad. It was certainly not in this way that we saw *Major Barbara* with its Salvation Army and its millionaires; its young dudes and professors of Greek who were also students of comparative religion. That, if we hadn't armed ourselves against it with an overweening nationalism and racialism, would simply have made us want to get out of Ireland by the first boat. If Shaw were Irish literature, there would be no possible doubt of its future.

Irish literature, as I understand it, began with Yeats and Synge and Lady Gregory; it has continued with variations of subject and talent through a second generation. Is there to be a third, or will that sort of writing be re-absorbed into the main stream of English letters? That problem seems to be fundamental to all regional literatures. A Mistral[1] or a Synge can create one almost out of his head, but obviously it must be maintained in some other way; it must have its inspirations from without and within; the face it presents to the world and the face it presents to its own initiates; its changes of temper, its classic, romantic, realistic, philosophical periods. It must be part of the European system, not a mere folk survival, petrified in some sort of mediæval fancy dress. The death of Yeats made us all ask ourselves precisely how much of that sort of Irish literature was really left.

And first, how did it begin? It did not spring entirely out of Yeats's head. It was part of a whole national awakening when a small, defeated and embittered country began to seek the cause of its defeat in itself rather than in its external enemy. At the same time, and almost as part of it, began the attempt to revive the Irish language; the co-operative agricultural movement of Plunkett and Æ, the Labour movement led by Larkin in his eagle youth, and the Sinn Fein movement for abstention from Westminster led by Griffith. In those days there were at least half a dozen movements to which any young man of spirit could belong; all of them part of a general attack by the younger generation on the enemies within: the imitator of English ways — the provincialist; the 'gombeen man' — a very expressive Irishism for the *petit bourgeois*; and the Tammany politician who had riddled every institution with corruption. Irish literature fitted admirably into that idealistic framework; it was another force making for national dignity. 'We work to add dignity to Ireland' was Lady Gregory's favourite dictum.

But after the success of the Revolution that framework collapsed, and as happens, I suppose, after every successful revolution, Irish society began to revert to type. All the forces that had made for national dignity, that had united Catholic and Protestant, aristocrats like Constance Markievicz, Labour revolutionists like Connolly and writers like Æ, began to disintegrate rapidly, and Ireland became more than ever sectarian, utilitarian (the two nearly always go together), vulgar and provincial. In the first flush of victory a minister like Mulcahy[2] could bring over from Germany an Army Director of Music, and the Irish Government could allow an Irish engineer to plan the great Shannon Power Scheme.[3] Within a few years it would be impossible to appoint an Irish Protestant as librarian. I have seen Æ in a fury of despair raise his hands to heaven and shout curses on de Valera. 'I curse him now, as generations of Irishmen will curse him.' Æ fled the country. Every year that has passed, particularly since de Valera's rise to power, has strengthened the grip of the gombeen man, of the religious secret societies like the Knights of Columbanus; of the illiterate censorships. As I write, even a piece of sentimental Catholicism like Miss O'Brien's *Land of Spices*, which, in America, has been a colossal success among sectarian organizations, is legally outlawed in Ireland as being 'in its general tendency indecent' — it contains one brief reference to homosexuality. The Film Censor boasts that he has compelled the film renters to change the title of *I Want a Divorce* to *The Tragedy of Divorce*. One is not permitted to speak of Birth Control, and the sale of contraceptives is forbidden.

In fact, Ireland has used her new freedom to tie herself up into a sort of moral Chinese puzzle from which it seems almost impossible that she should ever extricate herself, and which young people can only contemplate with fascination and amusement. One minister is reported to have said recently when he was asked whether nothing could be done with our extraordinary broadcasting service, 'Let them listen to the B.B.C.' They do! It is part of the general breakdown of national pride that everything the Government touches is believed to be hopelessly corrupt and incompetent, that every appointment is believed to be a 'job'; and that specified and unspecified groups are supposed to be making fortunes out of the economic chaos produced by the war. That is probably a grossly exaggerated view. The significant fact about it is that there is no idealistic opposition which would enable us to measure the extent of the damage.

Even the Abbey Theatre since Yeats's death has lost all prestige. Yeats's own plays, as well as those of Synge and Lady Gregory, have been entirely dropped from the repertory. It is worth while comparing the voices. This is Lady Gregory in 1914:

> Often near midnight after the theatre had closed I have gone round the newspaper offices, asking as a favour that notices might be put in, for we could pay but for few advertisements, and it was not always thought worth while to send a critic to our plays. Often I have gone round by the stage door when the curtain was up, and come round into the auditorium by the front hall, hoping that in the darkness I might pass for a new arrival and so encourage the few scattered people in the stalls.

This is Ernest Blythe, managing director in 1941:

> It all depends whether the best plays, as you call them, played to decent audiences. As far as I'm

concerned, a play's a failure if it doesn't ultimately draw an audience. It's a miserable failure in fact. I don't think anything's so discouraging for either the actors or the playgoers as a house that's more than three-quarters empty. It doesn't do anybody any good — not even the author.

Small wonder that young men and women are fleeing the country in thousands. In the worst days of the blitz I used to meet them in the passport office; boys and girls who had cleared out of London, Birmingham and Liverpool when the raids began. Now they were shivering with fear lest the British Passport Officer might refuse to allow them back. 'Oh, anything is better than Ireland,' they said hopelessly when I drew them into conversation.

II

When O'Faolain and I began to write it was with some idea of replacing the subjective, idealistic, romantic literature of Yeats, Lady Gregory and Synge by one modelled on the Russian novelists. Superficially, there was a lot in common between the Irish and the Russian temperaments — the comparison has been overworked. And there was probably another, racial element in our choice of models. In one of his letters to Florence Farr, just published by the Cuala Press,[4] Yeats says: 'I have noticed, by the way, that the writers of this country who come from the mass of the people — or no, I should say, who come from Catholic Ireland, have more reason than fantasy. It is the other way with those who come from the leisured classes. They stand above their subject and play with it, and their writing is, as it were, a victory as well as a creation. The others, Colum and Edward Martyn, for instance, are dominated by their subject with the result that their work as a whole lacks beauty of shape, the organic quality.'

There is profound truth in this criticism, though the matter isn't quite as simple as Yeats imagined. Writers who come from Catholic Ireland do bring with them something of its anonymity; are more impersonal; more identified with their material; they tend to sentimentalize or brutalize it, and rarely does one find a Catholic Irish writer playing with his material as Synge played with his. But that is history, not destiny, as Yeats seems to have imagined. He could have seen the same thing in England of his own day; the Irishmen, Shaw and Wilde, standing above their subjects and playing with them; while Hardy and Lawrence, dominated by their subject, trudged through the mire.

But it is true that the literature of Catholic Ireland (and one needn't go beyond Joyce to prove it) is dominated by its material in a way in which the work of Synge and Yeats, derived from an abundant personality which found in the old sagas or in the wild life of the Aran Islands symbols of its own emotions, rarely was. Since Yeats's death, Irish literature has passed almost entirely into the hands of writers of Catholic Irish stock, and, as I've pointed out, since the Revolution their material has been very much under the weather.

Take, for instance, the work of Sean O'Faolain. His first novel, *A Nest of Simple Folk* (the title itself an avowed plagiarism from Turgenev), is a rich, leisurely, lyrical book about life lived at its very simplest among the peasants of County Limerick. It deals with no great events: an abortive attempt at an insurrection (lightly passed over); the transference of a family from country to country town and from country town to provincial city. It has no outstanding characters; indeed, the people he describes are scarcely articulate, yet their little pieties and follies are described with tender sympathy.

His second novel, *Bird Alone*, set in the same provincial city, is a very different kettle of fish. It is the story of a raw youth and girl whose love affair brings them into conflict with the furious piety and Puritanism of Catholic Ireland and ends in despair and suicide. The little pieties and follies are drawn once more, but now with a definitely sinister turn. The characters have begun to be articulate: to demand a fuller, richer life for themselves, but as their aspiration grows, the sense of the dead weight of his material hangs more and more heavily on the author's mind, and the book is almost choked by the feeling of anguish and claustrophobia. The nest of simple folk has raised its head out of the mud and been horrified by what it has seen.

In a play which intervenes between this and his latest novel O'Faolain seems to me to have found himself for the first time. Characteristically it is called *She Had to Do Something*. Turgenev this time is definitely off the map. It is a comedy about a Frenchwoman in just such a provincial town, and her attempts to form a society for herself and her daughter out of the tatterdemalion provincial celebrities; the 'intellectual' priesteen; the would-be small-town dandy; the poet who is giving up the job because everyone expects him to 'have a good influence'. As a play, it may not be a great success, but it is delightful entertainment. For the first time O'Faolain looks at his material through the Frenchwoman's eyes and sees how preposterous it is, and his laughter echoes right through the play. I felt when I read it in manuscript that it was the first time O'Faolain really wrote as himself, as a personality, not as an anonymous Catholic Irish writer like Colum, but throwing all ancestral pieties to the winds.

In his new novel, *Come Back to Erin*, a young revolutionary goes to America, falls in love with the middle-aged wife of his step-brother and becomes her lover. She is complex, cultured, subtle; he gawkish, puritanical; a young provincial barbarian. Irish critics profess to lament the long American interlude, but for me, as I am sure, for most other people, it is the whole book. The author of the two brief sections dealing with Ireland seems to me the old O'Faolain who is bewildered and distressed by what he describes; it is only when he reaches America that he begins again to use the full range of his powers; and there we get astonishing sureness; a broad, sweeping outline; comedy and poetry. The nest of simple folk has found its way out at last.

But what of the author? He has grown up in his own material; has learned at last to use the full range of his powers, but what the blazes can he use them on? It is quite clear that, having written the middle section of this book, he would be a fool to go back to the uncertainties of its Irish sections, except with a very different approach. It is also clear what Irish critics dislike. It is no longer regional literature; the writer has ceased to find what is most valuable to himself in Holy Ireland, and cannot translate back into its idiom what he has found outside it. Into that life a cultured Frenchwoman or American — and that means their creator — simply will not go.

III

O'Faolain's work provides the typical pattern; the rest of us the illustrations. I have just finished reading another book which drove it home to me. It is the first novel by the most remarkable of modern Irish poets, Patrick Kavanagh.[5] In it he describes the life of a country boy in a north of Ireland village which is dominated by an ignorant, good-natured old parish priest. The story begins with an attempt by a group of boys and girls to establish a village hall in which they can meet and exchange ideas. The hall is a symbol of the life they would really like to lead, but which they never can lead because the old village tyrant opposes the licensing of 'the Anti-Christ Hall', as he calls it, and there is no one strong enough to defeat him. And so we see the principal character, in love with a decent girl whom he can never meet under decent conditions, masturbating his soul away, until the girl he loves is seduced by the local Don Juan (though, except

for this once, *his* Don Juanism has never been anything but a mental exercise), while the hero settles down in comfort with a cow of a girl who has a little fortune, and the Anti-Christ Hall becomes a cattle-shed.

It is O'Faolain's second novel; my own second novel;[6] it is Gerald O'Donovan's *Father Ralph*;[7] it is *A Portrait of the Artist*; it is the novel every Irish writer who isn't a rogue or an imbecile is doomed to write when the emptiness and horror of Irish life begins to dawn on him. It raises in a peculiarly acute form the problem which Yeats merely stated, and it forces one to recognize how false is the superficial comparison with Russia of the last century. Tchekhov, the son of a slave, could write as easily of a princess as of a peasant girl or a merchant's daughter. In Ireland, the moment a writer raises his eyes from the slums and cabins, he finds nothing but a vicious and ignorant middle-class, and for aristocracy the remnants of an English garrison, alien in religion and education. From such material he finds it almost impossible to create a picture of life which, to quote Dumas's definition of the theatre, will embody 'a portrait, a judgment and an ideal'.

It is highly doubtful whether without the whole moral and philosophical background of an awakening nationality the work of Yeats, Lady Gregory and Synge would have been possible at all. Without it a realistic literature is clearly impossible. We have, I think, reached the end of a period.

IV

It is not a time for prophecies. One can say that of any stirrings from within there is no sign, but the war is far from being over, and by the time this article appears its changing fortunes may well have dissipated Mr de Valera's dream of a nonentity state entirely divorced from the rest of the world. If that happens, and Mr de Valera is obviously very much afraid it will, we shall all have to think again, but in the meantime what can the Irish writer like Patrick Kavanagh do? How is he to compose this fundamental quarrel with his material? O'Faolain's way in *Come Back to Erin* is not really a solution, nor, of course, is it intended to be. Inevitably it merely provokes the retort that, once having left it, you would be a fool to come back. That way leads to London or New York, and unless a change comes, that is where it may soon lead those of us who still hang on to Erin for choice.

Theoretically, of course, it is possible for a writer to live in a country where his books are banned, where there are no magazines to print his work, where all power is in the hands of a fanatical and corrupt middle-class, and never, never emerge from his ivory tower. But like Whitman when he saw the oak tree growing alone, 'I know I could not do it'.

The only alternative to that private world is the public platform. It is the way Spender, Day Lewis and Auden took in England, and it has always been a regret of mine that there was no corresponding movement in Ireland where the need for it was so much greater. Within the past five years there has been, so far as I know, but one play which attempted to grapple with any real problem: Collis's *Marrowbone Lane*,[8] which dealt with the Dublin slums. It was rejected by the Abbey Theatre; not, I imagine, on its merits. The only literary periodical which is generally read, *The Bell*, edited by O'Faolain, has in fifteen months of its existence steadily refused to recognize the war — it is an old dispute between myself and the editor. I am bewildered by the complete lack of relationship between Irish literature and any form of life, within or without Ireland. Blandly, sentimentally, maundering to itself, Irish literature sails off on one tack, while off on another go hand in hand Mr de Valera and the Church, the murder gangs and the Catholic secret societies. It may be argued that they are the business of publicists, not of artists, but there are no publicists, there is no public opinion, and if the artists do not fight who will? And if we don't fight, and new circumstances don't settle Mr de Valera's hash for us, what is to become of Ireland or Irish literature?

Two things must happen if Irish literature is to survive the war. One is that somehow or other a theatre must be established, since the theatre is the only art form that can directly influence opinion, particularly now that the censorship of books is acting, more or less effectively, as a gag on the novelist. Secondly, the Irish writers must be prepared to come into the open; we must have done with romanticism for the next twenty years or so and let satire have its way. Not necessarily a cruel satire, because the Bogey Man in Ireland is far less a monster than he is in industrial countries; but certainly satire; for here he has a chance which rarely comes to him in industrial countries, of smothering all opposition, quietly, good-naturedly, without a struggle.

1   Frédéric Mistral (1830–1914) was a French Provençal poet who sought to promote Provençal as a literary language.
2   General Richard Mulcahy (1886–1971) was Minister of Defence in 1923–24.
3   The hydroelectric station at Shannon was constructed between 1925 and 1929, and proved a significant achievement.
4   *Florence Farr, Bernard Shaw, W.B. Yeats* (ed. Clifford Bax) was published by the Cuala Press in 1941. The letter referred to by O'Connor is dated 6 October 1905.
5   Kavanagh's *The Green Fool* (1938).
6   *Dutch Interior* (1940).
7   First published in 1913, *Father Ralph* is a semi-autobiographical novel about a young priest's disillusionment with the Church.
8   *Marrowbone Lane* was first produced at the Gate Theatre in October 1939 and revived in 1941.

MYLES NA GCOPALEEN (FLANN O'BRIEN)
from *The Irish Times*, 2 December 1942

In 1940 Flann O'Brien began his 'Cruiskeen Lawn' column for *The Irish Times* and immediately set loose on the world a series of comic characters such as The Brother, the Plain People of Ireland, and the poets Keats and Chapman. Here in this (relatively unknown) piece that begins with a puff of a pipe he takes the reader on an opium-filled journey of the imagination to the East, only to return to the Plain People of Ireland and their prejudices against sinful foreign literature.

Cruiskeen Lawn

2nd December 1942

Puff, puff, puff.

Under the connecting feeling of tropical heat and vertical sunlights, I brought together all creatures, birds, beasts, reptiles, all trees and plants, usages and appearances, that are found in all tropical regions and assembled them together in China or Indostan. From kindred feelings, I soon brought Egypt and all her gods under the same law. I was stared at, hooted at, grinned at, chattered at, by monkeys, by parroquets, by cockatoos. I ran into pagodas; and was fixed, for centuries, at the summit, or in secret rooms; I was the idol; I was the priest; I was worshipped; I was sacrificed. I fled from the wrath of Brama through the forests of Asia; Vushnu hated me; Seeva laid wait for me. I came suddenly upon Isis and Osiris; I had done a deed, they said, which the ibis and the crocodile trembled at. I was buried, for a thousand years, in stone coffins, with mummies and sphinxes, in narrow chambers at the heart of eternal pyramids. I was kissed, with cancerous kisses, by crocodiles; and laid, confounded with all unutterable slimy things, amongst reeds and Nilotic mud.

It was the year of the split, I think, when I took to the pipe; one day since then without opium I have not lived. Could not, would not, live. Sometimes I seem to climb up and disappear amid the grotesque scenery of my own dreams; sometimes I emerge from the fumed sleep, my own nightmare incarnate.

My medical adviser (a slave to the inferior yet cognate preoccupation of laudanum) tells me that I must quit this pipe or perish. Yet my pouch today (a Kapp and Peterson job of 1918) is as well-lined as ever. My immovable leather cheeks have achieved the pattern of a comic leer. Majestic ulcerations pit my mouth. And only yesterday I gave a furtive fill to a certain high-up civil servant who has smoked away the increments of twenty golden years. He need not worry; his name and his shame are safe with me.

Believe this much. If today I was not in this mood of kingly tragedy, expressed in the great stately prose I can write so well, I would make some poor joke about the facility of descent to Avernus, and then the revocare — hic labor, hoc opium. . . .[1]

And if I did itself, damn the bit of it would you understand, dear reader, Synge Street[2] and all as you went to.

Come round the corner here for a minute out of the breeze till I light me pipe.

Quite suddenly a small dog has appeared in my mind. He is clearly the property of some deceased mandarin. His coat is clipped in the manner of the east; his waist is clipped nearly naked, fantastic pantaloons of hair are made to clothe his legs. He runs rapidly around my head, searching vainly for mice. Suddenly he has grown old. Pathetic white moustaches girdle his old jaws. He lies down.

The walls of my memory have been decorated free of charge by Mr Jack Yeats. Every night without fail there is a display of fireworks —

The Plain People of Ireland: Where?

Myself: Inside in me head.

The Plain People of Ireland: Faith there's one thing wrong with you, it's maggoty drunk you are and nothing else.

Myself: I am tangled in pale grey dreams . . . vapours . . . in my bare feet I stand on the scaly backs of pregnant crocodiles the hair of a beautiful dusky slave. . . .

The Plain People of Ireland: Aisy now, aisy there! Did you not see be the papers where there's goin' to be an end once and for all to that class of rascality . . . and licentious . . . contumalious . . . derogatory . . . dirty sinful foreign literature. Will you whist man, before you shame us all.

Myself: Eggs of the phoenix . . . ivory gobangboards . . . silver cephalopods fingered by maidens. . . .

The Plain People of Ireland: Yerrah, leave him be, himself and his pipe and his dirty books.

---

1   Latin: to recall (from exile, or a journey, or war). Hic labor, hoc opium: Latin-English: this work, that opium (opus is Latin for work).
2   A reference to the school run by the Christian Brothers on Synge Street in Dublin.

ERIC CROSS
from Eric Cross, *The Tailor and Ansty* (1942)

The model couple for the Tailor and Ansty lived near Gougane Barra in County Cork. The conversation and stories of the crippled tailor Tim Buckley and his wife Anastasia were collected by Eric Cross (1905–80) and translated into this wonderfully comic and one-time censored book. It is worth also reading O'Faolain's more sober view of the Tailor in his essay on 'Romance and Realism' (1945) on page 514 below.

Chapter Eight

'I was just thinking,' said the Tailor amidst the engrossment of poking and prodding his pipe, 'before you came in —'

'Pity you haven't something better to do,' interrupted Ansty, 'but be poking your old pipe and shm-o-o-king like a chimney and — thinking, all the day. "I was just thinking," says he, as though he had a great wonder done,' she repeats venomously.

'Hould your whist, woman! I was not talking to you. . . . What started it was a woman who walked down the road the other day while I was standing to the cow. When she saw the cow, I declare to God didn't she ask me if it was a bull or a cow —'

'A bull or a cow! Glory be! Asked if it was a bull or a cow!' echoes the chorus.

'— and she wasn't a young woman either, and she was married by the ring on her finger —'

'Married — and asked "Was it a bull or a cow?"' Ansty is stunned with amazement. The joke seems too absurd even for her. 'Hould, you divil!' she hurls at the Tailor to check his extravagance. 'It passes all belief.'

'— and she had been drinking milk all her life — and, manalive! she didn't know the difference between a bull and a cow.'

'Married and didn't know the difference between a bull and a cow,' Ansty muses, as though the Tailor's reiteration of the fact has weaned her from her former incredulity. Once or twice she repeats the statement until it is completely absorbed. Then she starts again.

'Gon rahid!' (Gan raht . . . May you have no luck.) 'That was the queer kind of marriage. What was she married to? They must have had the strange carry-on. Didn't know the difference between a bull and a cow, and married!' Whatever goes on in Ansty's imagination gives her great glee, to judge by her chuckles. Still repeating the phrase, 'Didn't know the difference between a bull and a cow', and still chuckling away to herself she goes out to the ducks and the hens.

The Tailor takes up from the interruption.

'She didn't know a bull from a cow. That is what started me thinking. Thon amon dieul!¹ but I swear that the world's gone to alabastery. It's queerer it's getting every day. Would you believe it that there are people nowadays who don't know wheat from barley and yet eat bread, and can't tell the difference between a cock and a hen and eat eggs like this one, and her — "Is it a cow or a bull?"

'It's a strange sign of the times. No wonder that the world be as it is. The more education they have the less they know. The people in the old days had no education or only very little, but they were a deal smarter and wiser than the people that is in the world today. They knew the world they lived in and didn't go round like fools, asking, "Is that a bull or a cow?" The people that is going now don't know that or anything else.

'It puzzles me what the people nowadays do learn, and what they have in their heads. We all know that they can read and write. We can all do that, and a share of the old people could do that, too. But the men haven't the bone or the strength to do much, and the women can neither cook nor breed, nor do any damn thing but cackle like hens, and make themselves look uglier every day.

'There's millions of pounds of good money spent on education, and what's the result? They don't know the difference between a bull and a cow. By the mockstick of war! it's no wonder that there is trouble in the world; and that there will be until the people get a bit of sense and a bit less education, and do a bit of thinking for themselves instead of getting everything ready-made out of books.

'For learning is like a suit of clothes. The cloth is there, but it has to be cut to the measure of every man. What fits me won't fit you, and what fits you won't fit me. Then, when the suit is made, it is mine or it's yours. The same suit won't fit the two of us. It's the same with education. The knowledge is there, like the cloth. It is there for every man. It isn't in books, but in living. We have to cut and measure and sew to suit ourselves. We have to do our own thinking.

'There have been all classes of people in here with me at different times. People who write books. People who teach in colleges and universities and such-like. But do you know, the airiest, wittiest men that ever walked into me were the men who walked the roads; men such as Jerry of the Sack, Tom Malone and Jerry Cokely — God rest his soul.

'They were the men who had the talk and the idees and the imagination. It was they who saw the world and lived in it, and were the smart and clever fellows. I'd as soon see one of those cross my doorstep as anyone, for they are always conversible, intelligent men, though people think them queer because they had their own way of living, and lived away without doing any man harm.

'It's a mystery to me that, with all this education and talk of education, it should make so many stupid people, and such people poor for living and poor in living. Thamwirrashimfaina! if a man does not use his own eyes and ears and mouth and intelligence, he may as well be dead. There's no man living can't see a new wonder every day of his life, if he keeps his eyes open and wants to see. There's no man who cannot learn every hour of the day, and be a wiser man at the end of each day until the day he dies.

'I remember years ago there was a priest in Adrigoole preached a sermon on miracles. After the sermon he was talking to a man by the name of Murphy, Tim Murphy, a half gommerish sort of a fellow.

'"Well, Tim," said the priest to him, "did you enjoy the sermon today?"

'"I did, Father," replied Tim. "It was a damn fine sermon entirely."

'"Did you understand it?" asked the priest then.

'"I did, Father. Every bloody word of it but one."

'"Oh!" said the priest. "What word was it that you did not understand?"

'"Miracle, Father. I didn't understand the meaning of the word 'miracle' – nor I don't yet!"

'The people nowadays are like Tim Murphy. They spend years at schools and colleges, and then sit still for the rest of their lives like dummies. They know nothing, and you might as well be talking to a bush at the side of the road as talking to them, for all the good you'd get out of them. Leave me alone with them. They've gone obstropelous.

'I have known men of my time, with even less education than I had myself, who went to America and made big positions for themselves, and came to be famous men. Weren't there several presidents of America who were Irishmen? But the people nowadays, with all their education, won't do that. They can't do that. They will scarcely breathe for themselves unless they get a grant from the Government.

'I remember, years ago, seeing a kind of a circus where they had a play, and all the actors were dolls. They moved and danced and walked, but all that was done with threads tied to them, and there was a fellow above who pulled the threads. That is what the people that is going nowadays seem like — dolls who won't move until the threads are pulled, and who won't speak unless the words are put into their mouths.

'Things have taken a queer turn. We used to be mad for education in the old days. We used to think that if we could read and write we were the wonder of the world, and there was nothing we could not do. All we needed was knowledge. Well, the people have knowledge. Much more than there was in the old days, but they have ended up like dolls.

'But there is a deal of difference between the knowledge you get out of a book and the wisdom that comes into your own head by living and by using yourself, and that is the difference between the old days and the present times.'

There are footsteps outside. Ansty comes in and puts down a pail of water with a clatter.

'Wisha! a married woman who didn't know the difference between a bull and a cow! No wonder the world is queer.'

There is the usual few minutes' disturbance of dust, atmosphere and continuity which Ansty's presence produces, and the Tailor fills the time in packing his pipe. Ansty disappears again on one of her thousand excursions of the day. The Tailor takes up the broken thread of talk once more.

'In my time there was no national school. Only the "fodeen",[2] the hedge school. Each pupil would pay two or three pence each week, and the master would come home with you tonight and with me tomorrow, and have his supper and bed and breakfast as part of the payment. Some of them were learned men, right scholars. Others of them could read, but were not so good at writing. Some were good at poetry, and some were good at geography.

'I was seven years of age when I went to school, and to a fodeen school. The lessons were like this. You would spell and read so much of a book. Then you would do parsing. "The" a definite article. Parsing was bloody awkward, I can tell you. It was a work of the devil himself. I was never much good at it.

'You would learn chapters of geography at home, and you would have two cards of arithmetic along with that. You would learn to write by drawing pot-hooks and hangers, until you were an expert at the game. The writing of the old people was a damned sight plainer and better-looking than the writing of the people in the world today, and that was the reason of it.

'That would be from Monday until Thursday. Friday would be repetition day, when you went through all that you had learned during the week, to see that you had it well stuck into your skull.

'For geography there would be a big map of the world or a globe, and the teacher would call out names of places and you'd find them on the map. There was hardly a fellow went to school in those days who would not be able to travel the world, they knew it so bloody well on the map, and many of them did.

'At the finish of the day you would say the Rosary and go home. The worst scholar of the day would be punished. It was a queer kind of punishment. He would have to carry home with him the skull of an old horse or donkey and carry it back the next morning. There was another custom they had in those days too. If they built a new house anywhere, they would always try to bury the skull of an old horse in the kitchen floor. I have often wondered why this was, but I have never been able to discover.

'Most of the scholars would stay only two or three years. Education was a new thing in those days, and there was plenty of work to be done. But they seem to have learned more in that time than they do with all the years they have now.

'At the time of the big emigration to America, I saw grown men, maybe twenty-three or twenty-four years of age, who were thinking of going to America going back to school to better their education. There were thirty or forty such men going with me to school when I was going.

'All the schooling was in English. There wasn't a syllable of Irish. It was against the law, and you would be beat if you used it. But the people had the Irish, and good Irish too, and they spoke it amongst themselves. Now the world has changed round, and you are paid to learn it and few people have it. It's a queer state of affairs.

'You'd start with slates and slate pencils for writing and arithmetic. They were a handy idea, for you could wipe away what you had written and you could make a devil of a noise with the pencil on the slate. There would be no copy-book for you until you had been about a year at school.

'Well, that was my education. I learned to read and write and do arithmetic, and to know the world, and to think for myself, and to know the difference between a bull and a cow. I left school when I was thirteen years of age, and I was bound to a trade in the town of Kenmare.

'Education really starts when you leave school, and some of the smartest men the world has ever known had little education. There was a man I knew who had only a poor schooling, but had used his time well all his life. One day another man came to him who had travelled the world, and they got talking. But the man who had travelled had travelled with his eyes and his ears closed, and was no wiser when he came home than when he left. He was pitying the man who had stayed at home, but he was too good for him.

'"Travel," said he. "I've travelled more of the world with the light of a penny candle than you have done in all your years of travelling."

'I was bound to a tailor. I had to pay a fee of nine pounds and have two indentures and serve for five years. It was hard work, and I had to work hard. You may be damnful sure that I did. Till ten or eleven or maybe sometimes twelve at night on two meals a day, and that a thin diet.

'It is done now, but I would not care to do it again. The worst time was at Christmas. The whole world would be wanting clothes then. You'd think that no one wore clothes at all except on Christmas Day, there was such a rush for them.

'The only holidays were Sundays and holy days. At Christmas you would be left off from Christmas Eve till the morning after St Stephen's Day. The devil a fear but you had few holidays and hard times in those days.

'Up in the morning at six, and work on until ten at least, except for the two bits of meals. And the meals, to make the most of them, did not cost above half a crown in the week. Food was very cheap then. Two loaves of bread for fourpence and a stone of sugar for one and fourpence. Not a drink, and no talk about it. You would not handle a penny from one end of the year to the other. You got nothing beyond your training and your meals and your bed.

'There was an apprentice, bound as I was bound, who had to get up and dig the potatoes and wash them and cook them for the breakfast. When they were ready he would call the master and the mistress. They would come down then and pick the best of the potatoes.

'The apprentice would get what was left in the skihogue[3] by the door, and would have to sit on the floor and eat them. That was his breakfast, and that was his table. What he left the pig got.

'Well, one morning when he was eating his breakfast this way, the sow put her head inside the door and took a bite of the potatoes out of the basket. The apprentice jumped up and took a stick and beat the sow out.

'"Blast you! Get out!" said he. "If it is the same diet we share, it shan't be at the same table."

'Such were the times. That was the way the world was going and those were the times I lived through.

'After five years you were at liberty, and you didn't give a damn. You drew your indentures and went away as journeyman.

'I stopped in Kenmare for a time with a man by the name of O'Connor, and I went from him to Killarney. I was there about four months or five. You would not stop long in one place at all. You would get very small pay in these small towns. 'Tis all that you would get would be six to eight shillings a week and be fed. The master tailor himself would get no more than ten shillings for the making of a suit.

'From Killarney I moved to Cork. When you went into a city like Cork you worked by a different system. You would be either a coat maker or a pants maker. It was all what was called "piecework", and you would make good money at it.

'You would make thirty to forty shillings a week and sometimes maybe sixty. You would get board and lodging and washing done for ten shillings a week, and good too. Yerra, manalive, the money then was worth three times as much as it is worth nowadays. Two ounces of tobacco only cost sixpence, and you would get a half-gallon of porter for eightpence.

'Cork was a great place at the time. There was a constant work. There were no factories, and no women working. Everything in those days was tailored, and there was a heap of wealthy people in Cork. Gentlemen in those days would buy as many as nine suits at a time.

'I was in Cork for some time, but after a while I thought that I might as well be seeing something of the world, so I struck away for Waterford, and that was the beginning of my travels.'

The chorus takes the stage again.

'Travels! Listen to him and his "travels". The divil a bit does he travel away from his ould box by the fire. He'll be stuck to it one of these days. "Travels"!'

1 Irish: Go to the devil.
2 Irish for sod of turf. I assume the connection in the Tailor's mind stems from scholars (pupils) taking a sod of turf with them to heat the classroom. Perhaps the word had a wider provenance; in Dineen *fód* also means knowledge, skill, meaning.
3 In Dinneen *sciobóg* means potato basket.

NESCA A. ROBB
from Nesca A. Robb, *An Ulsterwoman in England, 1924–41* (1942)

Nesca A. Robb (1905–76) was born in Ulster and was awarded a D.Phil. from Oxford in 1932. During the War years she was Advisory Officer and Registrar for the Women's Employment Federation in London. After the War she returned to Northern Ireland, wrote a biography of William of Orange (1962, 1966) and was appointed President of the Irish PEN in 1968–69. Here in this extract from her autobiography she provides a series of telling insights into London during the Blitz and into Northern Irish attitudes towards the English.

Chapter 14: Another Year

A winter less rigorous, but more prolonged than the last, has resolved itself into a cold and tardy spring; and I find myself looking back over the world-wide panorama of the war, and over the small, disjointed fragments of it that have found their way into this book. The last months of the old year and the early ones of the new have brought so swift a rush of events that we are all a little stunned by its impetuousness. For the time being the war has surged away from us, though there is no knowing for how long our respite will last. Europe lies pinioned, since the sad, heroic end of the campaign in Greece; beyond it, in Africa and Asia, battle is joined again, and we have had great victories and sharp reverses. The vicissitudes of our world are certainly absorbing to follow, if terrible to endure. The days rise full of new menace and new

uncertainty, but also not without new hope. We are still in a pretty pickle, but when one looks back on the past twelve months the wonder is not that we should have so much still to contend with, but that we are here at all and reasonably lively and pugnacious at that. Life is grim in its larger aspects and sometimes drab in its details, but it has a shilling-shockerness about it that makes it still faintly unreal. It is only a few days since Rudolf Hess landed in Scotland,[1] if not exactly like manna from heaven at least with some points of affinity between him and the beings who are first reputed to have made the descent. What the import of his coming may be is still in doubt: its sensational quality is beyond question. After this, imagination will no longer boggle at anything.

Against such a background of tragedy and melodrama, of giant treacheries and giant heroism, one's private history, with its work and recreations, its small personal and domestic concerns, seems almost ludicrously commonplace. What should such fellows as I do, crawling between heaven and earth? — writing this book, trudging home from the First Aid Post in the wind-lashed small hours of a winter day or between moon-set and dawn of a May morning? One's immediate world is still fairly normal, but the war colours and overshadows everything in it, like the sinister darkness of an eclipse spread over the earth. Sometimes, too, one walks into the conflict in the oddest ways, as I did, one foggy day in January, when I carried on a business interview to machine-gun obbligato,[2] among the battered and crater-pitted fast-nesses of the Charing Cross Road; and later drove up a Piccadilly which the damp mist and the thunder of a persistent barrage had almost emptied of people. London now, after long intervals of quiet, punctuated by a few savage raids, shows obvious marks of tribulation. Many of the 'sights' are gone irretrievably; and of those that remain there are few without a scar. Still work and life go on; and there is surprisingly much of the old gay London; theatres and concerts; pleasant clothes in the shops; pleasant, if restricted, meals in the restaurants. Spring has brought out the flower barrows heaped with tulips and narcissi, and has softened the stark ugliness of destruction. The Park, with its delicate trees and grazing sheep, lies like an expanse of cool water beneath charred shells of buildings in Park Lane and Bayswater Road. Near my house two long files of pink double cherries, now in full bloom, and looking like fluffy Renaissance angels against the blue of the May sky, screen the bare ground where those five neighbours of ours were killed last September. The city has never known more violent or abounding contrasts of beauty and horror, heroism and absurdity; or stranger minglings of pathos and comedy.

There was something oddly touching, for instance, in that episode, of last autumn's transport crisis, in which scores of provincial buses were rushed to London. One thought of them as a host of friendly monsters, grunting up through the night to the rescue of the Mother City; and every time one boarded some unfamiliar vehicle marked 'Hull' or 'Manchester' it seemed a pity that one couldn't pat the creature and offer it a bun. Then, for a taste of more romantic valour — who could be quite unmoved by the story of the fight for St Paul's during the Second Great Fire on December 29, 1940? The firemen on the roof that night were a group of young artists and architects; and there, with the copper of the dome growing with every minute more intolerably hot behind them, they stood, ringed round with flames and explosions, playing their hoses on the blaze until they had saved

the cathedral. It was not perhaps a braver deed than hundreds of others done that night and on many nights, but it had a symbolic quality that seemed to sum up all the rest.

Other cities have suffered these things too, my own among them. As we sailed down the Lough[3] in August 1939 I wondered if I should see it again, and my heart misgave me. Now, whatever my own fate may be, I know that I shall never again see it as it was. Still it is better in this war to be battered with London than to be unscathed with Paris and Rome. Even when I have grieved most over what has happened in Ulster there has been some comfort in that thought. Besides, if England is not now faced, on her Western approaches, with an Ireland in enemy hands; and if Catholic Eire is not under Nazi domination, I think they owe something of their immunity to those unaccom-modating Ulster people. If we win the battle of the Atlantic, the world will owe them something too. For the fact that Britain can dispose of some sea and air bases in Ireland, and can hold some forces there against a possible invasion of Eire, may well alter the course of the war. As for what permanent effect *this* war will have on the incredible island time alone will show. So many hopes and prophecies have already shipwrecked there that I will not add to them. I would only drop a word of warning to those — I have met a number of them — who think that the Irish question is solved because fire brigades from Eire gave their help in the air-raids on the North.[4] We have all been deeply thankful for that help, and we would do as much any day for the people of Eire if they stood in need of it; but that is quite a different thing from changing one's allegiance. There is no lack of stories of sudden gestures of courtesy between parties. One thinks — to be frivolous — of the Orangemen who lent their drums to the Hibernians so that the latter, who had lost *their* instruments while travelling, should not have their field-day spoiled; of the parish priest who lent his congregation to the rector so that the church might be packed for the Bishop's visit. Next day no doubt the worthy father gave his flock collective absolution for their attendance at a heretical service, and the Orangemen, as they carried home their drums, triumphantly rattled out 'The Boyne Water'. No doubt, in theory, you want to convert your opponent to your point of view, and will fight him shrewdly on the issue; but how little zest would be left in life if he *were* converted, how little (in your secret heart) you would respect him for his compliance. Past solutions of the Irish question, however reasoned and unanswerable, have always suffered from one crucial defect; they have left out the Irish with their inbred partisanship; their amazing capacity for self-absorption in the midst of swiftly changing international events; and all the imponderables that count for more than reason or interest. I do not say that these things can never be modified; but it is evident enough that they are still powerful and it is wishful thinking to ignore them. 'Ultimate Ireland severed from the world' is no longer a reality; but it may be a long time before Irishmen are convinced of the fact. I hope they may not have too tragic an awakening, or learn that they can no longer live unto themselves through the bitter experience of living in an invaded country.

· · ·

Of England itself what can I say? Any generalization can at best be only a 'near miss'. My own experience covers only a very limited field; yet it would be strange if no difference were perceptible between the England of to-day and the country as it was even a year ago, let alone when I knew it first.

One characteristic is at any rate still evident. English pride, like English cloth and English leather, wears well. It has had a few rude shocks and is in consequence a good deal less unthinking than it used to be, but I doubt if a morbid humility will ever be the national weakness. 'An Englishman ne'er wants his own good word,' said Defoe, in a shrewd satire on his fellow-countrymen, as apt to-day as when it was written in 1698. We have all met the newspaper article beginning: 'It is not the English way to boast,' and all know this opening gambit as the accepted introduction to an eloquent 'write up'. This immense *National* self-confidence, whose strength and weakness have been so startlingly displayed in recent history, can be quite independent of personal conceit. The individual Englishman may be either complacent or humble about himself, but to the general proposition that one Englishman is equal to any three foreigners his whole subconscious being assents, whatever his conscious mind may say; and the belief helps to make him so heedless of warnings and so doughty in battle. In the middle of last autumn, someone who could never be accused of personal complacency told me with an air of final conviction, 'I don't see that Germany has a chance'; and only the other day, after the fall of Crete, an unknown lady said to me: 'We're wonderful people.' They really are. Sometimes their sovereign assurance in so grave a pass alarms me. It makes me wonder what new blow is to be hurled against it, what volcano they have now chosen to picnic on in their leisured way. I make fun of them, but I am not really in a joking mood. The situation is

altogether too serious and too complicated; and their over-confidence has so repeatedly been their deadliest foe. I often wish they believed rather more in God and in the Devil — and rather less in themselves.

Yet can I pay them any higher compliment than to say that after two years of war spent among them, I feel more hope for this country, and even for mankind, than I did for years before the war broke out? What more can I, or anyone, say of their courage, which has won even the grudging praise of enemies not given to generosity? These years have revealed plenty of sloth and greed and of the most appalling incompetence and muddle-headedness in our midst; but they have also proved that though darkness is over the earth, the things that make men great are still alive. It may sound strange, but I think I should have felt much more at home if I had arrived for the first time in this warring England, rather than in the bewildered and bewildering society of the twenties. Here is something more akin to the small and homogeneous community of my childhood, with its basis of faith and its atmosphere of social ease, preserving, among all its faults, some of the fellowship of the Church and the loyalties of the clan. It had been ready to fight passionately — wrong-headedly if you like — for an idea; and there was a vigour about what it did and thought and felt that was intensely stimulating to live with, even if it sometimes expressed itself in narrow and repellent forms. In its own way it had a grasp of fundamentals. To-day a common danger has given the English people a feeling of solidarity and common purpose greater than anything they have had for years past. I would not of course suggest that the whole body politic has been galvanized. A good deal of the national effort still moves to the slow strains of the departmental minuet rather than to the trumps of war. Large-scale muddling is still too often evident. There are plenty of people who even now have very little idea that there is a war on. Yet, though many have suffered, it is also true that many have gained things that their peace-time life denied them. The urgencies of war have given back to the individual a lost sense of his own significance, even while he sinks his individuality in the general effort. Of late years life has often held few prospects; it has often meant work that gives little satisfaction to hand or brain or, worse still, no work at all. It has witnessed the growth of huge populations who inhabit a limbo between town and country, and lack the sense of belonging to any real community, rural or civic. People have tended to feel at once isolated and hemmed in, and to suspect that they are spending their time and labour on matters of very doubtful value. Now the day's work has acquired the dignity of a vital service, the isolated units have become part of larger groups and something essential — purpose and fellowship — have been restored to them.

For England is a perceptibly friendlier place. You notice it in trifles. People talk to you more readily and on slighter acquaintance. I am growing quite used to hearing the views and family histories of total strangers. In the bombed cities whole streets, whose inhabitants have hitherto scarcely known each other by sight, have become efficient mutual-aid societies, some of them positively fraternal. In the country districts which have most successfully handled the problems of evacuation there has been a mingling of the younger generations which may have far-reaching effects. It would be foolish to assume that even the disasters of war have removed all prejudice and suspicion between individuals or classes. The press, in its endeavours to keep our spirits up, is sometimes over-optimistic. There are still plenty of tales of the inhabitants of select rural areas talking of Londoners as it might be of lepers; and of evacuees who will not lift a finger even to help themselves if they are not going to be paid for it. All the same the mixing of all sorts and conditions of people in the army, in civil defence and other war work and in the evacuation areas should mean a clearer understanding of one another's problems, and consequently a lessening of the indifference or obstructiveness with which the post-war reformer will have to grapple.

The lady in the charming country house who is horrified because the unemployed woman spends sixpence of her dole on going to the cinema may not be at all a heartless person. She simply has not visualized — perhaps no one who has not endured it *can* visualize completely — the dingy tragedy of unemployment. If the positions were reversed, the unemployed woman might prove no more imaginative. Ignorance, want of imagination and narrow social habits have probably done more than any deliberate wickedness to produce our social ills. The fact that these have been thrust — sometimes very rudely thrust — upon the community at large may be the first real step to getting them put right. I have certainly never before heard such unanimity of opinion amongst all sorts of people on the need for reform. War is a lamentably wasteful way of stirring the public conscience, but it has been stirred enough for one to hope that it will not too readily lapse back into sleep. Indeed, if England can carry forward into peace something of the sacrificial devotion and abundant kindness that have been so common in these days, if she can find an impulse to keep them alive and

intelligence to direct them, she could well become a pattern to the world. On the international plane I think she may have to use her influence — and it should be great — in moderating the violence of loathing with which the enfranchised countries of Europe will turn against both innocent and guilty in the Axis states. Probably few outside England will be very ready to believe in the submerged and exiled good in Germany and Italy. Yet if it is to rise again someone must go on believing in it, whatever stern measures may be needed to break up Nazism. At the same time, with their admirable lack of hate, the English must guard themselves against sentimentality and not, in their haste to embrace the wronger, forget the bitter problems of the wronged, and grow too righteously indignant if they are less forthcoming. The English forgive readily because they have never, as a nation, suffered such injuries as do not merely hurt the body, but damage the soul. They find it hard to understand other temperaments — the Irish, for instance — in which resentment is a demon only to be cast out with prayer and fasting. From such knowledge as I possess, it seems to me that such a temperament is common to a good many peoples and a fruitful source of misunderstanding where England is concerned. I suppose the 'gush' that our suspicious northern eyes detected was just the easy sentiment that is the weakness of the Englishman's better nature; the kind of woolliness that loses sight of Hess's record because he has blue eyes and a curly-headed baby. The longer I live here the more I feel that a good deal of English stiffness is a thing acquired; an aristocratic tradition that has very generally imposed itself by example and education, but also a kind of carapace that the people grow because they are, like crabs and lobsters, soft inside. A long history of immunity from searing disaster and of much dazzling achievement has fostered in them both their pride and their softness; and so strangely mixed is human nature that sometimes that pride may be an element in dauntless courage, and that generosity only a factor in lazy self-deception.

1 Hess flew a plane from Germany to Scotland in May 1941 in what was possibly an attempt to negotiate a peace settlement.
2 Indispensable accompaniment (of machine-gun fire).
3 Belfast Lough.
4 German air-raids on Belfast in March and April 1941 killed 900 people.

ROBERT GREACEN
from Reginald Moore ed., *Modern Reading* No. 6 (1943)

Robert Greacen (1920–   ), poet and critic, was born in Derry and educated at Trinity College, Dublin. In 1944 he edited an anthology of Ulster writing entitled *Northern Harvest*. His early volumes of verse include *One Recent Evening* (1944) and *The Undying Day* (1948), the year he went to London to work as a teacher. Here in this article for a London magazine which carried in the same issue Michael McLaverty's 'A Game Cock', he casts a sober Northerner's eye over literary life in Ireland in the war years.

Irish Letters and the War

Since the first sweep of the flood in September 1939, the respective positions of Southern Ireland and Ulster have considerably crystallized; at the moment the former is being virtually blockaded by Great Britain to teach her good neighbourliness, while Ulster licks her air-raid wounds, feels a patriotic veteran, but most obstinately refuses to allow the Allied troops to desecrate the 'Sabbath' by opening the cinemas to them. It should be pointed out that in Ulster there is a thirty per cent minority, almost wholly Catholic, which advocates the political unity of Ireland: in Southern Ireland there is practically no vociferous opposition to the continuance of an armed neutrality, though on the whole it seems there is a fairly strong pro-British bias. In any case, the Dublin press is muzzled by an unduly strict censorship. Speaking at the Irish Book Fair on last March 28 the Editor of *The Irish Times* vigorously attacked this virtual suppression of political comment, that has reduced Editorial comment to insipid compilations from the news agencies: 'The Germans state that X has fallen, but the Russians say that X is still holding out' is the kind of thing that must be written. But despite the banning of the printed word and news-reels of the actual fighting, there is probably as much interest taken in war news in Dublin as in Belfast, and there is little doubt that Dublin runs away with cultural activity every time, quantitatively if not qualitatively.

Since the death of W.B. Yeats, there has been a struggle for literary leadership in Southern Ireland. By common consent and individual claim, he was the greatest modern Irish literary man (excluding Shaw, because of his long English residence). Propped up by the constant flow of half a century's poetry, by a rich, arrogant personality, and by his general work for culture and, in particular, the Abbey Theatre, he had many successors but no Successor: after me, the deluge. Yeats's whole outlook was based on that belief and many cultured Irishmen shared it. Of the post-Yeats generation there are few writers of distinction — Frank

O'Connor, Sean O'Faolain and F.R. Higgins (who died recently) most deserve mention. The first two are at their happiest in the short story form, in which they explore poetic realism with some success. O'Faolain is now editing *The Bell*, the foremost Dublin literary magazine; but censorship, paper shortage, that may eventually be more severe than that obtaining in Gt. Britain, fear of libel action (on which legal proceedings some impecunious artists depend for a livelihood!) and an unnatural insistence on what is considered the Gaelic tradition, combine to make it a less sound instrument of expression than it might be. The late F.R. Higgins would probably have taken the place of Yeats in a few years' time, by means of a deferred succession. He was a lyric poet of passion and beauty, unafraid of such inciting words as 'breasts' that are considered indecent by the standards of the newly-sprung morality of De Valera's Government. He had a wide canvas for his song — Jehu, Jezebel and the Nativity, the bitter beauty of his country, the agonies of sexual dissatisfaction, the recompense of beer swilling and the telling of tales. Listen to the intensity of these verses from his poem 'The Spine That Bears All Brightness':

Since Michaelmas I know they're saying that I'm a
   changeling, not a youth;
They haven't a thought of how I'm scared to madness;
   but it's gospel truth
I'm scared by love of a thoroughbred lady who lapped
   my crazy limbs in flame;
Ah, she the clergy won't defame — her name lies
   sealed within my mouth!

Of well-sprung women she's the spine that bears all
   brightness, that I swear;
I've seen the skin shine through her coat when not a
   comb could hold her hair;
And towards her hips her body seemed the unmown
   corner of a field
But there's a crop she'll never yield — yet I'll not
   wield the flail elsewhere.

Look at me now! Since she has left, beside my hearth
  I've grown
More skinned than winter till the wind can make its
  bagpipes of my bones;
Here crickets talk, but that's poor song for one who
  sought the bark of seals —
Here snipe with glint of light twist past past — hell
  blast them, my last shot is thrown.

Of Southern writers now in their thirties, Donagh MacDonagh, Patrick Kavanagh and Ewart Milne are at the top. Roughly speaking, MacDonagh and Milne may be considered 'modernist': that — a word in Ireland which damns a writer out of hand — means that their work argues acquaintance with and influence by the broad drifts in English letters from the twenties until the outburst of war. Kavanagh, both in his prose and poetry, is of the Monaghan soil — tough and vigorous as a bony field in the process of ploughing.

And so to my native Ulster. M.J. Craig, one of the new writers, puts it rather well: 'Unlike Dublin, which makes you feel that you have just arrived home again, even if you have never set foot there before, Belfast feels alien even to one, like myself, born and brought up there.'

The Englishman is usually jolted as he stands on deck, coming into Belfast Lough for the first time: he wonders if indeed these long chains of gantries and slipways can exist in Ireland. He looks for the trappings of, say, an O'Connor story, only to find as Irish a background as you would get in Wimbledon or West Bromwich. True, it is a cleaner industrialism, because it is more recent than the English; if you scratch the typical Belfastman you will find the hobnailed country fellow from Down or Tyrone beneath the umbrella and bowler of the big city. Romantic Ireland, if it existed in minds other than English, certainly does not exist in Ulster; what does exist there, I regret to say, is a ruthless efficiency and a universal distrust of progressive thought, antipathy to the Arts and an unbelievable overdose of blackmouthed Presbyterian conscience. I have lived in Ulster all my life and I know, though I confess to over-drawing the picture for emphasis. Yet it is a good place to live, for here no artist can find a niche in society for himself, that is in any way secure: he must fight his environment and break it, or go into the linen business. Louis MacNeice, for example, might have had greater depth, if less range, had he not been one of our first-class, unfinished exports.

Of Ulster writers in their thirties Michael McLaverty and W.R. Rodgers take first rank: McLaverty is a lyrical fiction writer, patently sincere, with the frank vision of childhood that films working-class life with beauty without ignoring the basic rottenness. Rodgers puts a quick fist through every door of out-worn convention, mocks and thumbs his nose at our soured civilization. Quotation is rather unfair — especially in the case of Rodgers, who carries the suitcase of technical effects right from Hopkins to Prokosch: but some readers may not know his work.

He writes of the impersonal horror of bombing:

  It is a pity distance puts
    Ten-league boots on brutality.

He is not so convincing when he becomes Audenesque:

  In cinemas we sought
    The syrupy event,
  In morning papers bought
    Our cosy sentiment.

Of writers who are just twenty or over there are several, first brought together in *The Northman*, the Belfast University magazine. It is difficult, perhaps impossible, to write dispassionately of contemporaries and friends: and, for anyone like myself it would be uncritical to pass judgment on young men who have not yet matured their respective philosophies and idioms. The names, practically unknown in this country, are Leslie Gillespie, Roy McFadden, John Gallen, and myself. The main bulk of their writing has been poetry, selections from which have appeared in *Poems From Ulster* and *Lyra*.

From this brief survey, the conclusion that emerges is this: in the neutral South, despite (or because of?) the modern traditions moulded from Yeats, Lady Gregory, J.M. Synge, James Joyce and Sean O'Casey, literary activity is slowing down in momentum and failing in urgency, while in Ulster, where all writers, Rodgers says, have been 'schooled in a backwater of literature out of sight of the running stream of contemporary verse' we have the beginning of what has proved a valuable addition to English letters. The inference is not that war, like home-brewed Guinness, would be good for the pleasant young man who inhabits the Palace Bar, now the literary centre of Dublin, as Cyril Connolly bears testimony. I give the facts and you can find the reasons, though there are two I would suggest for consideration. The first is that Ulstermen now tend to stay at home rather than migrate to England, as did St John Ervine and Robert Lynd, the second that Southern Ireland is too busy at the moment trying to work out a political and economic destiny that will preserve her ports inviolate and her people from hunger. I think it will take all of Eamon De Valera's undoubted ingenuity and skill and tact to effect that twin purpose of real, though uneasy peace and of feeding his countrymen even on bread and potatoes; and, if he does, literature or not, Southern Ireland will have done very nicely.

SEAN O'FAOLAIN
from *The Bell*, August 1945

A cool-headed look at the issue of Romance versus Realism in Ireland. In an unusual move O'Faolain manages to wrest Yeats from Romance and allocate him a place under the banner of Realism.

Romance and Realism

'Romantic Ireland's dead and gone, it's with O'Leary in the grave.' So wrote Yeats in September 1913 thinking of his old friend, John O'Leary, that picturesque and dignified link between the Irish Republican Brotherhood of the 19th century and Sinn Fein of the 20th. When he wrote the line Yeats felt the matter-of-fact hardness of the 20th century closing in on an Ireland which to him was a folk-world full of colour and mystery, ancient memories and ancient ways. As to politics, which to him meant only heroism, Paudeen with his greasy till, adding 'the halfpence to the pence and prayer to shivering prayer', seemed to have obliterated every unselfish ideal.

Within three years the Rebellion came to prove that the old fires had merely been smoored, and in September 1916 Yeats, as the voice of Ireland, acclaimed it: —

> *Now and in time to be,*
> *Wherever green is worn,*
> *Are changed, changed utterly:*
> *A terrible beauty is born.*

He lived to see the fires either smoored again or wholly smothered by the dust and destruction of Civil War, in which he took the side not of Romantic Ireland but of a hardheaded and calculating Ireland whose future he could not foresee. He became one of our first senators, and has left on record his own growing uneasiness among the bankers and the business-men. He found himself very soon in a minority on such questions as Censorship and Divorce, discovered that he was an old Liberal and that the new Conservatives were in a majority, and gradually he began to hate the Ireland they were making.

His later development is fascinating. We get a good insight into his mind in his last pamphlets, such as *On the Boiler*, and in his letters to Dorothy Wellesley;[1] those from about the summer of 1936 onward especially. We see him flare up whenever his rage or his old passions seized him, as when he defended Roger Casement's memory or when he finally became so disgusted with all post-1922 politics as to write that splendid poem 'The Statues' in which he calls Ireland back to the world of symbol and imagination. It was there that he wrote: —

> *When Pearse summoned Cuchulain to his side*
> *What stalked through the Post Office?*

Meaning that we Irish,

> *born into that ancient sect*
> *But thrown upon this filthy modern tide*
> *And by its formless, spawning fury wrecked,*

must climb again into 'our proper dark' of passion and the imagination as the boys and girls of Greece may have climbed by night to kiss some statue of Phidias that gave shape to their dreams.

He there returned to his own youth. For he always delighted in violent or heroic gesture that lifted men out of the rut of character into the fiery element he called personality, and never had much patience for the muck and ruck and pedestrian toil of everyday political endeavour. In that he showed himself a natural poetic type — though, also, a rather dangerous and not unfamiliar type of this era of ours which in growing weary of the slow machinery of democracy has been tempted to turn now to this now to that violent and spectacular avatar. It was one of Yeats's minor follies to have written some fine marching songs for General O'Duffy.[2]

Not that he ever sold himself to any narrow party-line — he was too human and intelligent and civilized behind the poetic flare. His end, rather, was that of the despairing Liberal surrounded by fountains of ideas which when analysed proved to be no more than the glitterings of brackish water. In his last years he flails both Left and Right with equal fury. He writes a cursing ballad on Cromwell whom he called the multiple Lenin of his day — the great leveller. He writes of O'Duffy's Blue Shirt movement — 'A movement called The Christian Front is gathering all the bigots together.' Or — 'A woman to whom I had sent the Casement poem writes approving of what she supposes to be my hatred of England. It has shocked me . . . I have written to my correspondent. "How can I hate England owing what I do to Shakespeare, Blake and Morris. England is the only country I cannot hate."' When *The Daily Worker*[3] attacked his friend's poem he raged: —

One reason these propagandists hate us is that we have ease and power . . . You say we must love, yes but love is not pity. It does not desire to change its object. It is a form of the eternal contemplation of what is. When I take a woman in my arms I do not want to change her. If I saw her in rags I would get her better clothes that I might resume my contemplation. But these Communists put their heads in the rags and smother.

His attitude to Ireland is that in his Casement ballads[4] he is not fighting for any country.

I am fighting in those ballads for what I have been fighting all my life, it is our Irish fight though it has nothing to do with this or that country. Bernard Shaw fights with the same object. When somebody talks of justice, who knows that justice is accompanied by secret forgery; when an archbishop wants a man to go to the communion table, when that man says he is not spiritually fit, then we Irish remember our age-old quarrel against gold-braid and ermine and that our ancestor Swift has gone where fierce indignation can lacerate his heart no more, and we go stark, staring mad . . . I am an old man now and month by month my capacity and energy must slip away so what is the use of saying that in both England and Ireland I want to stiffen the backbone of the high hearted and high minded and the sweet hearted and sweet minded so that they may no longer shrink and hedge when they face rag-merchants like ——. It is not our business to reply to this or that but to set up our love and indignation against their pity and hate.

He sums up this politics in three verses, totalling eleven lines of which the first four say it all: —

Hurrah for revolution! Let the cannon shoot,
The beggar upon horseback lashes the beggar upon foot.
Hurrah for revolution! Cannon once again.
The beggars have changed places but the lash goes on.[5]

Or when he says that in England the educated classes are politics-mad but that the mass of the people have free-minds; whereas in Ireland the educated classes have free-minds and the masses are politics-mad. But what politics! Nobody here seems to care, for instance, which side wins in Spain or anywhere else, and even as to Irish politics (he presumably means what we mean by the word, i.e. ideas not personalities) 'there is complete indifference'.

All this — I agree that I have selected, but I can only say that I have not been trying to prove anything — makes a fairly clear picture of an aristocratic intellectual poet, revolted by the end of the last phase — perhaps the dying kick — of Romantic Ireland, cursing all parties, still a nationalist in the only sense which can have any meaning for an Irish writer, i.e. one who thinks world and describes Irish, saved from Fascism by his natural humanity and liberality of mind, fearing if not actually despising the masses, full of that undefined arrogance which rounds off all in his famous testimony to Irish writers who, he says, must sing whatever is well-made, scorn the shapeless sort now growing up, sing the peasantry, country gentlemen, the holiness of monks, porter-drinkers' randy laughter, and all our lords and ladies who were beaten into the clay for seven centuries; concluding:—

Cast your mind on other days
That we in coming days may be
Still the indomitable Irishry.[6]

The romantic picture is clear; it is not simple — which is right and proper, since only *simpliste* minds and doctrinaire minds such as Party Men possess think that life or thought can be railroaded. But on one point he is both simple and clear. Romantic Ireland *had* died — for him.

As I wandered, delightedly, through his brother's[7] Exhibition in June and July at the National College of

Art — forty or fifty years of wonderful painting — I could not help thinking, excitedly, 'Dear God, was W.B. wrong after all? Can it be that this is Romantic Ireland, all of a piece, *still* living?' And for days I went around, bothered and excited, wondering if it really has died or, if it is, yet again, only smoored over? Two things sustained a persistent doubt — that no other painter, writer, or poet but this one only still sees and presents it; and the curious fact that the farther on in time one goes from the 90s and the 1900s — from those early, direct paintings of tinkers and porter-drinkers and horsecopers[8] and gypsies and peasants and sailors, the farther back one has to stand from these pictures, until at the very latest paintings of all one must stand anything up to twenty yards away, and then drop the curtains of the lashes to focus — even at that as in a glass darkly — what has evidently of late been seen by the painter only in a form of visionary longsightedness, as of a man on a mountain-top seeing — or is it remembering? — beauty at the world's rim.

But, then, one may say, all romance is a *princesse lointaine*?[9] The far-off hills are greenest. Did W.B. ever look at life close-up? Should one ever? In twilight, in memory, in age, and in exile, Ireland is at her loveliest and most indubitable. I can still think, for example, in a mood of the most nostalgic longing, how lovely my native Cork could be on one of those unsummery summer mornings of childhood, which are all the summer we ever seem to get in this tender, grey island; when the light is sifted and diffused by unbroken flocks of clouds whose shadows are so delicately moulded that one has to gaze at them for a long time before one can observe their stealthy creeping; when ever little roof is so placid in this sunless clarity that we feel hardly more awake than what we see, for those grey walls do not then show a spot of colour, and only in the memory does one know that even the hills are green — to the eye they are contused and purple as if by an injection of dark blood under the line — and all so calm and restful that one lonely cockcrow will not disturb the hooded dawn. But I know how kind our memory is, and that one does not live on monochrome and scenery, and that Cork and all such small towns have in them a life that is far from romance and prettiness.

If Jack Yeats has made this ophthalmic adjustment, and if W.B. never really was so foolish as to look things between the eyes (until the Revolution grimaced at him), have the realistic novelists of our time been wise in their insistence on ruthless close-ups? Or can one ever push back life so far that it looks pretty if it is not? There is a point beyond which one cannot retreat, a point described as having one's back to the wall. There is a point at which old values and interpretations have to be discarded, a point at which you simply throw away all your lenses and adjusting gadgets and realize that the animal has been transmogrified. In simple words it may be that no romantic world now exists — not merely in Ireland but anywhere on the face of the globe.

True — the old elements are all still there. There are still tinkers and horsecopers and sailors and porter-drinkers: but we all know that life is largely a matter of what a dramatist might call a balance of characters, and that when a new balance of the characters takes place it is no longer the old play.

I think back, for example, to the days when our generation first discovered this Romantic Ireland in the Western Gaeltacht. I think of the Festival or Pattern which is still held every Autumn in that little coom or closed valley of which Callanan[10] wrote the wonderful poem beginning:

There is a green island in lone Gougane Barra
Where Allua of songs rushes forth as an arrow
In deep-valleyed Desmond — a thousand wild fountains
Come down to that lake from their home in the mountains.

I recall the faintly blue autumn air, tinged with melancholy, studded along the roads at dusk by tinkers' fires; the smell of turfsmoke and of myrtle; the clear tinkle of the mountain streams; the linch-pin that rattles in a cart making for that hidden lake which becomes at sunset a bowl of lead in a mountain-glen; the bleating of lost sheep, like kittens in a lonely house; the long white winding roads; the huddle of porter-drinkers by the lighted inn at the lake's edge; the white cottages huddled under the scarps of the mountains; the white streaks of floodwater falling down the cliffs almost perpendicularly, silent by day, heard by night . . . It was a dramatic background to the life of our West Cork cottiers who were all that Yeats would have wished the 'folk' to be. It was like the wild, lovely, traditional Russian festival that Tchekov describes so beautifully in his story 'Easter Eve'.

By the time these lines appear I will have been down there to those mountains and back again. But it will not be the same. And will it ever be the same again? Certainly not, for our time. The balance of characters has altered too much.

To think of only one — our old friend Tailor Buckley[11] — he is now under the green sods of that little graveyard by the lake. He was never a romantic figure, not to me or to anybody. My own first contact with him was unfriendly; the local people said he was a 'Stater' (meaning that he thought us Republicans a lot of fools or playboys). I do not know whether what they said of him was true or not; my guess is that his ironical and realistic mind — a much more realistic mind than any of us had — could no more have refrained from sharp comment on our cock-eyed 'civil war' than a Shaw could. One saw, too, as well as the next man that he was a bit of a show-box; as if, Heaven help us, every Irishman isn't. There was nothing romantic or Celtic about his cottage; a bare, bald, unattractive labourer's cottage. Above all he was a satirist and satire and romance are not bedfellows. So we were under no illusions about him.

But the old man was *alive*, he was real, he was vital, he was traditional, and as Frank O'Connor said of him in a recent tribute he was above all else a gentleman — one of Yeats's natural lords who had been beaten over the centuries into our Irish clay; and his talk was the best of that sort of talk you might have heard any night in any Gaelic glen — that natural, gay, human blether which is a form of folk-art, that rollicks along with a healthy earthy bawdiness such as must be familiar to everybody in Ireland who has ever sat by a labourer's cottage fire.

Well . . . we know what happened to him. Our respectable citizens from Foxrock and Ballsbridge,[12] who were never intended to be characters in that play — least of all leading characters; they have been the butts of Gaelic humour from time immemorial — given the power and given the blessing of our new Gaelic Revivalists, took the transcript of this old man's fireside gabble, the gabble of the Gaelic hearth since the days of Bricriu or Conan Maol[13] and with their refined fingers wrote across it — '*in its general tendency indecent*'. Later, the priests made the old man take up his own copy of his own fireside talk and throw it behind the fire.

When that happened those other intrusive characters of the modern Irish comedy, the 'Gaels', never said one word in his defence. But other equally intrusive characters said many words. It will suffice to recall only one of these connoisseurs to the rostrum, a Senator named Kehoe, who assured us that he had been reading various works for the last thirty years, 'discriminately and indiscriminately', and that he had never read a finer collection of what he was pleased to call 'smut' than this Tailor's fireside chatter. 'And,' added the erudite gentleman, 'I have read all the authors from Rabelais down.' It was the same Kehoe who cried *contra mundum*:[14] — 'Authors of repute! From what point of view? From the point of view of world standards — which, mark you, are not the standards of Ireland.' He suffices because had romantic

Yeats been then alive he might have had this man as a fellow-senator.

No! Romantic Ireland was a royal play and the clowns have taken it over and destroyed it. To be sure they, too, were always there, for Senator Kehoe and his likes are no worse than the idiot who asked thirty-five years ago, 'Have you seen this awful play of Lady Gregory's *The Cowboy of the Western World*?' or the woman who said of a famous line in the same play 'the word omitted but understood was one she would blush to use even when she was alone'.[15] Nor is there any reason why we could not hear to-day what *The National Hibernian* wrote then — we hear far worse: 'Brothers and Sisters everywhere, place a little history of Ireland in the hands of each little boy and girl of the ancient race and all the Lady Gregories of the world will not be able to destroy an atom of our splendid heritage.'

What has happened is equally obvious, simple and horrible. Romantic Ireland has given way to Sentimental Ireland. Yeats adored the talk of Biddy Early[16] but he would never have been such an ass as to make a heroine of her, any more than you or I would be such an ass as to make a hero of Tailor Buckley. To him Biddy Early was but a part of a vast and elaborate complex of ideas — the depersonalizing power of the folk imagination, hatred of realism, love of personality, 'the red rose-bordered hem', Unity of Culture, Unity of Being,[17] woven with a score of other ideas into an aesthetic theory whose only test is the excellence of what he got out of it. Our intrusive characters have certainly not made a hero of Tailor Buckley: on the contrary, they have denied that he ever existed — saying, for instance, that such talk as his never goes on in our western cottages; what they have done is to sentimentalize him into a coloured postcard, which is, of course, the form of evasion practised by every nation when the national will becomes so weak that it wants to avoid every human complication and evade every human challenge. It is a thousand miles removed from Yeats's lifelong search for that image or symbol by which nations, races and men are brought to face the greatest obstacle that can be contemplated without despair — an obstacle that in rousing the will to the fullest intensity unifies them at a blow.

When the will of Ireland becomes intense again Romantic Ireland will return. When the will of the world, now barely hanging on by its finger-nails, becomes intense again romance will warm life all over the globe. For romance is not made of pretty things. As a movement, it began in France out of dissatisfaction and despair; it was heralded in England by a poet who wanted to speak the language of simple men and describe the most common and actual things; romance comes out of blood and toil and tears and sweat,

> A mound of refuse or the sweepings of a street,
> Old kettles, old bottles, and a broken can,
> Old iron, old bones, old rags, that raving slut
> Who keeps the till . . .[18]

Yeats created his lovely play *The Countess Cathleen* out of his puzzlement at a woman whose soul was being destroyed by fanaticism and hate. Baudelaire's flowers were made of evil. Villon's songs were made of rags. Chocolate-box colleens are made for money. The Sentimental Ireland is made of pound notes. The essence of both is pretence and escapism: Cathleen ni Houlihan as a pin-up girl; though the Gaelic poet, Geoffrey Keating, had a better name for her. If we wish Romantic Ireland to come again, it will only come not by closing our eyes but by opening them, indeed only by following the advice of Yeats's epitaph, cut on the limestone flag over his empty grave under Ben Bulben:—

> Cast a cold eye
> On life, on death.
> Horseman, pass by!

The hard and realist literature of our time is performing its own rôle. It keeps us looking both life and death coldly in the face until, some day, the Jacob's ladder of our vision will rise again out of this Irish clay and lift us to where we were in the days when we were not afraid to shudder at our dreams.

1   For Yeats's correspondence (from which O'Faolain cites in this article), see *Letters on Poetry from W.B. Yeats to Dorothy Wellesley* (1940). Yeats's *On the Boiler*, which contains some inflammatory remarks on race and eugenics, was published in 1939.
2   Leader of the Blue Shirts, a fascist organization. The poems O'Faolain has in mind are 'Three Marching Songs'.
3   A communist newspaper.
4   'Roger Casement' and 'The Ghost of Roger Casement', published in *New Poems* (1938).
5   Lines from 'The Great Day'.
6   I take it that 'cast' here means to cast, as the sculptor does, i.e. model, not cast back or think. [AN]
7   Jack B. Yeats, the painter.
8   Horsedealers.
9   French: distant princess.
10 'Gougane Barra' was written by Jeremiah Joseph Callanan (1795–1829).
11 See *The Tailor and Ansty* above p. 504, who lived in Gougane Barra.
12 Respectable parts of County Dublin and Dublin.
13 Bricriu was an Ulster champion from the Red Branch Cycle of stories. Conan Maol (bald) was a warrior of the Fianna.
14 Latin: against the world.
15 This refers to the Abbey Theatre's charwoman, relayed by Synge in a letter to Stephen MacKenna dated 9 April 1907. For further details, see my *Yeats's Worlds*, page 154.
16 Biddy Early (?1798–1874), a wise woman from County Clare. There is a photo of her ruined cottage at Feakle in my *Yeats's Worlds*.
17 The phrase 'red rose-bordered hem' is taken from Yeats's poem 'To Ireland in the Coming Times'. Unity of Culture and Unity of Being are terms used by Yeats in his prose writings.
18 Lines from 'The Circus Animals' Desertion'.

MICHEÁL MacLIAMMÓIR
from Micheál MacLiammóir, *All For Hecuba: An Irish Theatrical Autobiography* (1946)

In 1928 Micheál MacLiammóir (1899–1978) and Hilton Edwards (1903–82) founded the Gate Theatre in Dublin and made a contribution to modern Irish drama often overlooked by those who associate Irish drama exclusively with the Abbey Theatre. From the first season they set out their distinctively breezy stall with productions of Ibsen's *Peer Gynt*, Eugene O'Neill's *The Hairy Ape*, and Wilde's *Salome*. Here in this extract Micheál MacLiammóir recalls Denis Johnston's play *The Old Lady Says 'No!'*, which was staged in June 1929 (and revived in 1931, 1934, 1935, 1941, 1947 and 1948). For lists of their productions in the first fifty years, see Peter Luke (ed.), *Enter Certain Players: Edwards-MacLiammóir and the Gate, 1928–1978* (1978).

Reconnoitre

The second Peacock season looked an exciting one, though its financial aspect in that little place was, with our growing ambitions and hatred of tawdriness on the stage, a little rocky. Hilton and I often took a taxi because we hadn't the money for a tram, which sounds absurd if you don't know the beautiful trustfulness of Dublin taximen. They knew, like Tessie Martin, that we would pay them some day, and none of them, I hasten to add, were disappointed. In fact they were often paid sooner than they expected because on a Friday night, when we drew our small salaries, we would feel so gay at having some money in our pockets that we would decide on a taxi to the Plaza or some late-houred restaurant, and the driver would almost inevitably be one to whom we owed two or three fares. So then we would pay him altogether, and have only a little left again. People who were making money used to tell us we were crazy to work so hard for no return. 'You'll find yourselves in the soup some day,' they said, wagging their fingers. But we saw what we wanted to do and we believed that we could do it. Besides, we had discovered an amazing secretary-manager, a Mrs Isa Hughes, who seemed convinced of our ultimate success and loudly urged us forward, and also a couple of new artists — Dorothy Casey, a character actress, and Edward Lexy, whose comedy gift found its way years later on to the films. The plays, too, looked exciting, and with Coralie's help — for she is an invaluable playpicker — we had chosen them carefully.

We had done *Powers of Darkness*, *The Unknown Warrior*, Capek's *R.U.R.*, a triple bill from Galsworthy, Evreinov, and An Philbín, a delicate lyric poet, and Elmer Rice's *Adding Machine*. We produced, too, a play about a gunman called *Juggernaut*, by David Sears. It had been rejected by the Abbey but we liked it and so, it seemed, did our small but growing audience, and it gave the signal for that inevitable attack on the National Theatre by all those people in Dublin who had a grudge against it for no better reason than that it was an established institution that had had the impertinence not to fall into decay and disappear. 'The Abbey's dead,' people would say to us gleefully, knowing quite well it was nothing of the kind, and letters to the newspapers on the subject became a fashion. We at the Gate were seized upon in this campaign as a stick to beat the old traditional horse, and that we were neither flattered by this move nor willing to be so used counted little, and a few enemies were made for us in the senior theatre — a silly, distressing business it all was that should never have begun.

But as the spring days passed, paint-splashed and work-worn, into summer and the hawthorn broke into flower over the railings of Stephen's Green, a new excitement had arrived and we were too absorbed to notice anything else. Denis Johnston offered us his first play, *The Old Lady Says 'No!'*, and with it a subsidy towards its production of fifteen pounds by the Abbey. The figure sounds incredible but it is correct, and it is correct too to say that we welcomed it. More still, we welcomed the play which was altogether remarkable and precisely the sort of Irish play we had been hoping for. It was described by the author as a Romantic Play with Choral Interludes, and it dealt with an actor playing the part of Robert Emmet, the rebel leader who was executed in 1803, and with his search for Sarah Curran, for the Ireland of his imagination, and for his own self. With its majestic vocal orchestration, its deadly malice, its influence of Toller and Joyce, its dream-like atmosphere, its flashes of low comedy, its looming chaotic background of Dante's purgatory, and its Sitwellian feeling for the Irish pastorales of the nineteenth century, it read, as Hilton remarked, like a railway guide and played like *Tristan and Isolde*. It gave at least two magnificent acting parts, and the chance of a lifetime to the sort of producer Hilton was rapidly becoming, a producer who can handle choral speaking, rhythmical movement, metrical climax, and a magnificence of massed effect with the precision of a ballet-master.

I was to play the Emmet part: it remains the most musically exhilarating experience I have had on the stage, for it gives one the sense of being a soloist in some gigantic concerto, ping on the note, and away you go and keep going until the orchestra crashes about you and then is silent again for your next big attack, and all in a dazzle of green light and black, blinding shadow.

But the trouble was with the leading woman. It was not a part for Coralie, demanding as it did an Irish actress for its double role of the romantic Sarah Curran, not as yet Far from the Land for the play opens on the night of Emmet's arrest, and the blood-thirsty drab which was Denis's pleasing conception of Yeats's Cathleen Ni Houlihan, 'that Ireland for whose sake so many have lain down their lives', the old Dublin flower-woman who haunts the nightmare reaches of College Green selling, instead of flowers, her 'four beautiful green fields' which she offers at a penny a bunch.

'Oh, God, he's a terror,' I said for the twentieth time, poring over the script; 'listen to this.' And I read aloud: 'Aw, very well, very well, all me sons is again' me. But it won't be the cough'll have the stiffening of him, not if I lay a hold of him. If once I get me hands on your dirty puss I'll leave me mark on you, never fear.' Then after the boy has died for her and a government minister's wife approaches with a funeral wreath: 'Ah, come in, lady, come in; ah, he was me favourite of them all, lady, never a bitter word, never a harsh glance; ah, God, aren't ye the kindhearted government and isn't them the gorgeous flowers!'

'Oh, shut up!' said the producer, looking up from a chaotic casting list; 'who's going to play her? That's what I want to know.'

'May Craig?' I suggested.

'Abbey can't release her.'

'Shelah Richards?'

'Abbey.'

'Ria Mooney?'

'America still. Renewed her contract with Eva le Galienne.'

'Any chance of Allgood?'

'In London. It's hopeless. City the size of a flea-bite. No bloody actresses. In London you could just —'

'What about Maire O'Neill? She's the finest Irish actress —'

'Doing films at Elstree.'

'Oh, well.'

We took a tram to Lansdown Road and called on Denis. He was sitting hunched up in a chair, a colossal young man with thick coal-black hair, a long gloomy good-natured face and long gloomy good-natured feet in carpet slippers.

'Hullo.'

He got up and switched off the gramophone that was playing 'Rhapsody in Blue'.

'Now look here, Denis, we've got to find her. What are we going to do?'

'Come to supper to-morrow. You'll meet somebody you might like.' His accent, in spite of his Dublin birth and a series of universities, still reminded one of the North of Ireland. So did the brief, emphatic use of words, everything pared down to the bone.

'Is she a good actress?'

'She might be.'

'Do you know her?'

'Known her for years.'

'Irish?'

'Dublin. That's what you want, isn't it?'

'Any experience?'

'Couple of shows here. Like every one else. Then she got a few jobs. She's back from a tour with Seymour Hicks. Have some tea?'

'Hicks? That sounds like musical —'

'Well, just meet her.'

'What's her name?'

'Meriel Moore.'

And that night we met her. Very charming she looked, brown-haired and blue-eyed, cool and poised as a tight-rope walker, and with a smooth, varying contralto, long sensitive hands, and an eloquent and easy flow of speech. She talked things over with us that night, gave an audition next morning, and on the following day rehearsals for the *Old Lady* began.

We were nearly mad. All day long, until our quiet triple bill performance in the evenings came like an oasis of restful convalescence, though in reality it was strenuous enough, all day long the drum was beating. For the bulk of the action of the *Old Lady* passes in the delirium of the actor playing Robert Emmet, who has met with a blow on the head causing concussion, and Denis had introduced for his 'Choral Interlude' a host of shadows, figures of the fevered imagination of the injured man, who formed the background to many of the principal scenes. His stage directions, like Shakespeare's, were of the briefest and left unlimited scope to the producer, and Hilton had discovered a seemingly unconscious rhythm in the lines spoken by the shadows and had introduced them with a pulsation of light and the notes of a drum beaten with varying *tempi*. The effect he achieved was in performance overwhelmingly exciting, but the mastery of its technique led all of us to the threshold of sheer lunacy. One or two of the shadows dropped out exhausted, some of them wept, others departed with determined expressions and were not seen again. But most of them stuck loyally to it and, swaying their bodies, their faces gleaming with sweat, they moved silently to and fro under his beckoning hand, advancing and retreating, bending their knees and straightening their backs, revolving in circles, in semicircles, breaking up into small groups and forming big wedge-shaped battalions on the tiny stage while they whispered and shouted their lines with the fervour of negro revivalists, and all to the incessant throb-throb of the drum, while a frenzied stage-manager tried to imprison the order of their positions in the prompt-book.

Art O'Murnaghan wielded the drumsticks with untiring devotion and a rapt expression like a Druid at some sacred rite. He was an elderly saint who worshipped Angus and Lú and the ancient gods of Ireland and who had a miraculous flair for all the known arts, from the loveliest Gaelic illumination in the manner of the fifth-century monks to the making of properties, the writing of music, the research of ancient lore, the management of a stage, and the playing of character parts — his acting as Firs in our production of *The Cherry Orchard* many years later was of the rarest beauty and distinction. There he sat on these days of incessant rehearsal for the chorus of Denis Johnston's play, beating rhythmically on the drums, his thoughts in God-knew-what dim regions of mist and mistletoe, but his grey eyes faithfully fixed for the cue to stop or change the rhythm on the restless figure of Hilton, enveloped in clouds of tobacco smoke, darting backwards and forwards between stage and stalls, leaping to and fro between the players to push them into the patterns he desired, racing to the back of the auditorium to watch the effect, and beating out the time with both hands like a conductor directing an orchestra.

'Now, you Shadows,' he would shout, 'we'll go back to the third move. Hold that drum, Art. Take it easy, Meriel. Coralie, this doesn't affect you for the moment. Come and watch it with me. No, sit this side. I want to dodge about and get it from every angle. All right Art, tap tap — *pianissimo* first, please. Now — come on, you cows, it's got to start in a whisper and grow to thunder. Now . . .'

And the poor bedraggled things began all over again.

Well, it was worth it. There were thunders of applause, showers of praise and abuse, the usual accusations that the author had 'flung mud and dirt at the Irish people' — a comment neatly anticipated in the play — and one obscure but learned charge of blasphemy, not of language, but of symbolism. But Hilton and I were happy as we sat among strawberries and champagne in the house of Denis's parents after the first night, for this was the end of our shop-window days, and we knew it. Things could not go on at the Peacock for ever, but our work was growing and there was, it seemed, a place for it. Our new actress had played

beautifully and had said she wanted to remain with us. She and Coralie were perfectly balanced. Our new author had all the qualities we were seeking; he was vigorous, sensitive, and alert, and he meant what he said. What was more important still, he meant what he wrote. We went home from the party on foot, refusing lifts from a dozen people — what need to hurry to bed on a night that ought to have gone on for ever? — and walked slowly through the long brightening streets that smelt of hawthorn and wet blue slate. It was dawn by the time we stood at Tessie's door in Pembroke Street, and a cart was jolting down Fitzwilliam Square.

The play had a prolonged run and the theatre was booked out every night. That was the end of the season, and the summer sun poured out its gold on the battered, dawdling, friendly, malicious city.

Strumpet city in the sunset, Denis had made Emmet say at the end of the play:

Suckling the bastard brats of Scot, of Englishry, or
  Huguenot,
Brave sons breaking from the womb,
Wild sons fleeing from their mother,
Wistful city of savage dreamers,
So old, so sick with memories.
Old mother,
Some, they say, are damned.
But you, I think, one day shall walk the streets of
  paradise,
Head high and unashamed.
'There. Now let my epitaph be written.'

The play was launched: it might serve as a model for what we were seeking, who knew? But it had been born: the day of our anxious midwifery had dawned and died. What were we going to do now?

CATHAL O'BYRNE
from Cathal O'Byrne, *As I Roved Out: In Belfast and Districts* (1946)

The following extracts are from the newspaper column Cathal O'Byrne wrote for *Ireland's Saturday Night*. O'Byrne's distinctive leisurely Northern style enabled him to weave together a narrative from disparate material. More recently, Ciaran Carson's equally appealing *The Glass Factory* (1997) owes much to O'Byrne.

Tradition and the Falls Road

According to tradition, the old Falls road ran from its junction at Derryaghy with the 'new cut' leading to the railway halt, to the foot of High street. The story of the old road was given to me by a friend, as it was told to him by one whose people had lived for many generations in the neighbourhood of the Falls.

Beginning at Derraghy, on the old road, left-hand side coming to town, is Fair's row, in the end house of which, town side, lived Belle Steel, who kept in her house, preserved in a locked wooden box, the vestments and sacred vessels used by the priest when Mass was being said at the Mass corner up on the slope of Colin Mountain. Belle Steel was not a Catholic.

Nearer town, to the right of the steep hill that rises above the entrance to the village of Suffolk, and close to the old road, was Kilwee old church, once surrounded by a graveyard in which people were buried until well into the nineteenth century. The site of the graveyard is now a millpond. Near by is what remains of the old mansion of the McCances of Suffolk, in the farm-yard of which lay for many years the holy water font of Kilwee church until, on the McCances' leaving Suffolk House, Henry McCance sent the font to the Belfast museum, a thing he ever afterwards regretted doing, as the museum authorities did not think it worth while to acknowledge the receipt of the old font. Mr McCance often expressed the wish that he had sent it to the Catholic church at Hannahstown where it by right belonged.

Up hill and down dale, the old road winds on, past the lane that leads west to the fort of the O'Murrays and the old Catholic church and graveyard of Lambeg. Nearer town, on the left, is the square grey house built by Waddell Cunningham of slave-trading fame, and used by him as a country residence.

Callender's fort stood on what is now the Glen road, on the left going from town, where the road rises before the turn at St Teresa's church. It was a green mound, and was known to be the site of a church and graveyard, and the font belonging to it was for long kept at the little whitewashed thatched public house at Andersonstown, owned by Adam Kirkwood, and later occupied by a Mr Thomas Greer, and later still by people named Greene. In the springtime through the bottle-end panes of glass in the little windows of the place could be seen the apple trees all abloom in its tiny orchard. The word Callender is probably a corruption of the Gaelic word, Calluragh — an old graveyard.

At the making of the Glen road, in the 1840s, a cutting through Callender's fort exposed great quantities of human remains. These were seen by my informant's grandfather, who held the contract for supplying the stones that went to the making of the new road. The foundation of Callender's fort could be traced in 1846, when they measured about 114 feet by 40 feet. There is a tradition of an old corn mill being situated somewhere convenient to the cemetery — hence the name of the district. Milltown cemetery was once a brickyard and was owned by a Mr James Ross, who built and lived in the house now occupied by the Christian Brothers. Maryburn House, on the old road, was built by a Mr James Woods, linen merchant, and the district called Andersonstown was, at the time we write of, called Whitesidestown, for the reason that a little colony of people of that name had settled there. These people were prominent in '98;[1] one of them took the government side and dispossessed the others, and it is more than probable that they were of the same family as the Whitesides from Quakerstown, beyond Cave hill, whose story was once told by Mrs Pender in her lecture to the Irish Women's Association of Belfast.

The present Falls road met the old road at Maryburn lane, a little way above Milltown; it then turned across what is now the cemetery crossing in front of the industrial school and passed the workshops to the present road. A high ridge once crossed Falls road at this point, as will be seen by the deep cutting just inside the Falls park on the high ground on which the bus depot is built. To avoid this height, the road makers followed the line of least resistance by bringing the road round by the school. Lake Glen in the old days contained a lake with a crannog[2] in the centre, and the old fort in the vicinity gave its name to the townland of Ballydownfine.

Leaving the industrial school, the old road cut off a corner of the park to the high ground of the city cemetery, through Glenalina, and crossed the Whiterock road above MacRory park. A little portion of the old road still exists at this place, running between Whiterock and Dan O'Neill's loney. The old road then made its way across what is now the brickfields — some time ago I saw part of a wooden pathway unearthed here — then on by the great fort that gave its name to the Forth river, on the site of which the old cotton mill now stands. The road then passed through Springfield village, recently demolished and rebuilt, and on to Shankill.

Long ago Whiterock was known as Kill Piper's hill, and a little fort on the north side of MacRory park is said to be the fort of the pipers.

Down to near the middle of the nineteenth century the city cemetery was covered with linen cloth. It was the bleach green of the Glenalina bleach works, the proprietor of which, William Sinclair, was known as Sinclair of the Hawks. His hounds were kept at the rear of his house in Donegall place, where he also kept his hawks and his falcons, and when he rode out to Whiterock — with his falcon at his wrist — the streets of the old town were loud with the baying of his hounds and the unusual and colourful stir caused by his hawking parties.

In the olden times, the son of a family occupying a farm at Ballygomartin — his Christian names were Joseph Joy — had a vocation for the priesthood, and to gratify his desire to become a priest he travelled to Salamanca in Spain, where, not having sufficient money to carry him through his college course, he obtained an appointment as tutor to the Spanish royal family, and so was enabled to complete his studies. During his residence at the court one of the royal children was named Josephine after him.

He was ordained in Rome at the age of forty and, on his return to Ireland, was appointed parish priest of Blanchardstown, county Dublin, and the beautiful church and convent at that place are lasting memorials to his work there. This priest was a cousin of Henry Joy McCracken.

After climbing up through Springfield village, the old Falls road — it was merely a cow track in the olden time — joined the Shankill road and, passing by the old church from which the road derives its name, continued down by Bower's hill and Peter's hill to the north gate of the town, at the upper end of Goose lane, now North street, and thence into the heart of the town.

How Belfast Streets Got their Names

From its earliest hour the town seems to have suffered from, to use the jargon of the moment, an incurable 'inferiority complex'. Belfast has always 'dearly loved a lord'[4] — a foreign one, of course — and failing that, a 'lady'. It has the distinction at the moment of being able to boast that it is the only town in Ireland that has set up in its midst a statue to a German nobleman, and that statue, a life-size one, adorns the Albert Clock, the memorial erected to the memory of the husband of Queen Victoria.

The memorial clock stands in Albert square, named after the German prince, and we have also Albert street, Albert place and Albert bridge, all named after the foreign gentleman. Many other street names in Belfast, Hanover street, Moltke street, Berlin street and Danube street also suggest Teutonic affiliations. The old dock that once lay at the foot of High street was

called Hanover quay, and Prince's street is with us yet.

Mary street, Quay lane, Store lane, Weighhouse lane, Forest lane, Back lane, Mitchell's entry and Bluebell entry were all cleared away to make room for Victoria street and Albert square. We have, of course, a great Victoria street also, situated, to the confusion of strangers, in an entirely different part of the town.

Carlisle circus was named for the earl of Carlisle, who was the English viceroy in Ireland at the time the place was laid out.

We have Queen street, north Queen street, Queen's arcade, Queen's bridge, Queen's quay, Queen's road, Queen's square, Queen Victoria gardens and Queen Victoria street, all named after the English queen, Victoria. And as well as Prince's street we have Prince's court, Prince's dock. And, besides all that, we have Prince Edward park, and, of course — I had almost forgotten — the Queen's Island.

North Queen street was once called Carrickfergus road because it was the main road to that town. Crumlin road was the only road out of town to the north, and the old coach road from Ardoyne through Ligoniel was a rough and hilly way, indeed. The Antrim road is of comparatively recent formation. A country lane used to run out from the old Poor House in Clifton street to a farm and dwelling house known as Vicinage, on the site of which St Malachy's college is now built. Wolfhill is noted for being the place where the last Irish wolf was killed.

Ballymacarrett means the townland of the son of Art (O'Neill). It was densely covered with trees, and, from the old Long bridge to 'Con's water', there were only two houses. Castlereagh gets its name from the grey castle from which Con O'Neill once ruled all lower Clandeboy.

Mount Pottinger was once the residence of the Pottinger family, which gave its name to the entry off High street. A Thomas Pottinger of this family paid twenty pounds a year for all Ballymacarrett!

There was no road through the Pottinger estate in the old days; the water of the lough extended up to what is now Strandtown, and was crossed by a ford.

Arthur was a favourite name in the Donegall family, who, by the way, spell the name with two *l*'s. Hence the recurrence of the name in the street nomenclature of the town — Arthur street, Arthur lane and Arthur place. The origin of the name, Corn market, is obvious, and the great weighbridge was kept under the colonnade of the old market house. Corn market was, however, once called The Shambles, because of its many butchers' shops.

In the old days some well known localities had rather strange names, Clabber loney, Blackstaff loney and Buttermilk loney; Tay lane and Lovers' lane; Cripple row; the Gooseberry corner and Pepper Hill steps. New Lodge road was once Pinkerton's row, and McClean's fields was later known as the Chapel fields; while Lombard street was called Legg's lane; Victoria street was Cow lane, the street through which cows were driven to graze in the Point fields at the foot of Corporation street. North street was Goose lane and was named for a similar reason. Skipper street was the residence of the skippers and captains of the vessels that lay at anchor in the old dock beside it. Bridge street was so named because the principal bridge, a stone one, that covered the Farset river was situated in High street at this point. Church lane was named after the old corporation church, now St George's. Earlier it was known as Schoolhouse lane, for the reason that the first schoolhouse founded in the town by the earl of Donegall was situated in it.

Once Fountain street was called Water street, and in it were the fountains that supplied the townspeople with water. Bank lane was known as the 'Back of the river', because the open Farset river flowed down the side of it. Sugarhouse entry was named from the sugar refining industry carried on in it, and Hercules street, the old street of the butchers, was named after the landlord, Sir Hercules Langford.

Joy street was called after an ancestor of Henry Joy McCracken, and for all we know to the contrary, the name Russell street may have been given to that thoroughfare to keep green the memory of Thomas Russell, 'the man from God knows where'.[5] Marquis street was named to honour the Donegall family, but it was once called Ferguson's lane, by reason of the fact that the father of Sir Samuel Ferguson[6] — the great Irish poet, who was born in High street — had a tanyard there. Chapel lane is so called because St Mary's church, the oldest Catholic church in the city, is situated in it. Mill street gets its name from the old mill — the wheel of which was once turned by the Farset water — which stood at the north-west corner of Millfield.

Castle place, Castle market and Castle street were so called because of their proximity to the old castle of Belfast. In Castle street was set up the first fruit shop in Belfast. Mrs McTier, that delightful gossip, writes of the fact in one of her letters to her brother, Dr William Drennan, the poet:[7]

> Suggesting as agent for the soda-water sale, Grimmer, Lord Donegall's confectioner, married to his housekeeper, who has left and set up a fruit shop, the first of its kind here. It is neat, below a lounging place for men, and above lodgings. I

therefore think he is the very best person here to introduce this luxury — let the Thwaits therefore write to him their terms, directions direct to him, Castle street, Belfast. (Aug. 1804)

Barrack street was so called from the old military barracks once situated there, and Falls road means the district of the 'fals', or hedges; 'Walls' would be more accurately descriptive at the moment. From the Lagan river at Cromac to Stranmillis the country was densely covered with woods that were stocked with deer. Cromac means bending or crooked, as is the street of that name today. There were no roads between the Dublin and the Ormeau roads in the olden time, but Lord Donegall opened six footways through the forest, these were known as 'the passes', and the townspeople were permitted to make use of them to pass from one road to the other. Donegall pass is the only one remaining to remind us of that far-off time.

The name Stranmillis does not describe the district. It means the sweet or pleasant stream that the road of that name leads to, and both adjectives could once have been applied to the now very commonplace Lagan at this point. Malone road was once Magh Luan, the plain of the lambs, and goat's whey, or 'cruds and cream' could once be had at Molly Ward's cosy little inn at the first lock.

May street was named after Sir Edward May, which reclaimed all the ground along great Edward street, which, in the old days, at high tide, was covered with water. How Grattan street came to get its name I do not know, but that it was not named after the distinguished Irishman of that name we may be quite certain.[8]

• • •

'The Northern Star'

On the fourth day of January in the year 1792, the year of the French revolution, the first number of *The Northern Star* was published at Wilson's court, off High street, in the town of Belfast. While its avowed policy was to be parliamentary reform and the union of the people, from its first number its strong support was given to the Volunteer Movement, then in its infancy in Belfast.

The Northern Star had other aims also. It was to give, as Wolfe Tone said, 'a fair statement of all that passed in France, to support the emancipation of the Catholics of Ireland, and eventually, and by whatever means was found to be the most feasible, to establish in this country a republic entirely independent of England'.

The twelve proprietors of *The Northern Star* — they

were all Belfastmen and all presbyterians — entered into a partnership for twenty-two years, with a capital of £2,000 in £50 shares subscribed as follows:

Thirteen shares (£650): Samuel Neilson, woollen draper, of Waring street, corner of Sugarhouse entry;

Three shares each (£150): William Magee, printer and bookseller, William Tennent, merchant, John Rabb, clerk, John Boyle, merchant, Robert Caldwell, banker, and Henry Hazlett, merchant;

Two shares each (£100): Gilbert McIlveen, jun., linen draper, William McCleary, tanner, William Simms and Robert Simms, merchants;

One share (£50): John Hazlett, woollen draper, making in all the required £2,000.

From the first hour of its publication Samuel Neilson, of Waring street, acted as editor of *The Northern Star*, at an annual salary of £100. Neilson was, it is said, the real founder of the United Irishmen. Gaoled many times, he escaped the fate of McCracken and Russell and emigrated to America where he died, at Poughkeepsie, New York, of an apoplexy.

From its foundation, one of the principal contributors to *The Northern Star* was the Rev. James Porter, presbyterian minister of Greyabbey, county Down. The son of a farmer, he was born at Tamna Wood, Ballindrait, county Donegal. After settling in Greyabbey, as minister, writer, lecturer, politician, and inventor, he became one of the best-known men in Ulster of that day. By reason of his activities on behalf of the United Irishmen, at the outbreak of the rebellion he was promptly arrested, charged on the evidence of an informer (and on that of a man who could not identify him) with intercepting the mail, and was hanged at the rear of his own church.

The *Belfast Newsletter* of that date dismissed the incident in a few lines:

The Rev. James Porter, dissenting minister of Greyabbey, found guilty, also sentenced to be executed, on the 2nd, was put in execution yesterday at the rear of his own meeting-house at Greyabbey; head not severed.

Other contributors to the paper were William Sampson, a county Derry lawyer; the Rev. Sinclare Kelburn, minister of Rosemary street presbyterian church, who attended Henry Joy McCracken before his execution; Thomas Russell — 'the man from God

knows where' — who was then the librarian of the Linen Hall library; and the Rev. William Steele Dickson, presbyterian minister of Portaferry. The Rev. Dickson was the son of a tenant farmer of Ballycraigy, Carnmoney, in the county of Antrim. At their foundation he joined the volunteers, and later became a United Irishman, and at the planning of the rebellion he was made Adjutant-General for county Down. He was arrested but, after being kept in gaol for some time, was liberated.

Robert and William Simms, proprietors of *The Northern Star*, were also arrested. John Storey of Island Bawn, Dunadry, county Antrim, was taken captive, and a note in the *Belfast Newsletter* of 3 July 1798 tells how 'about two o'clock the court martial proceeded in the trial of John Storey, printer of Belfast, who was charged with being a rebel leader at the battle of Antrim. The prisoner, being found guilty, was hanged at the market house (Corn market) and, the head being severed from the body, was placed on a spike on the top of the market house.'

Two other men, named Dickey and Byers, were hanged and beheaded at the same time, and all three heads were allowed to remain spiked before the public gaze in Hill street for over a month, and were only taken down at the earnest request of the townspeople, on August 17 of the same year.

A paragraph appeared in the *Star* around this time telling 'that the foreman compositor was taken into custody, and a number of papers seized without any warrant to that effect. This was a most direct attack upon the freedom of the press.' And on 2 July 1798, the paper carried this announcement:

William Kean (Kane), a prisoner, charged with treason and rebellion, made his escape from confinement. A general search was immediately made throughout all the houses in town, and a notice from James Derham, colonel commandant, published, calling on all the inhabitants to assist in discovering and delivering up the said Kean, who is now concealed or harboured in some part of this town. And shall it be found hereafter that said traitor has been concealed by any person or persons, or by the knowledge or connivance of any person or persons of this town and its neighbourhood, or that they or any of them have known of the place of his concealment, and shall not have given notice thereof to the commandant of this town, such person's house will be burned and the owner thereof hanged.

But William Kean (Kane) was not discovered, and many years afterwards the daughter of Samuel Neilson, the first editor of *The Northern Star*, told the story of his escape and the arrest of her father to an American pressman, in the following words:

'Yes, I recollect when the officers came in to arrest him. I was but a very little thing then, but I knew there was something wrong. When the officers came in my father turned to them and asked: "What brings you here?" They said they had a warrant for his arrest. He told them to stand back for a minute. Then he took mother aside, and they talked to each other for some time. That was in 1797, the second time he was arrested. I don't remember when he was arrested first. The two servant girls we then had were Catholics and they used to call a spare bedroom we had for chance visitors "the priest's bedroom". One of the girls kept count, and said that twenty-six different priests had slept in that bed. You see, priests from all parts of the country used to come to see my father about Catholic emancipation, which he advocated strongly, both as editor of *The Northern Star*, publicly, and as a United Irishman, privately. That was at our house in Belfast.' (The house was one of four thatched houses next door to Sugarhouse entry in Waring street.)

'That reference to the priests,' said the venerable old lady to the pressman, 'reminds me of a good story I will tell you. When the military rabble broke into *The Northern Star* office and threw the type into the streets, and arrested the printers, there was one among them named William Kane. Of course, they were all United Irishmen, but they had proof against Kane, and I think he was tried and sentenced to death. The day before the execution he begged to be allowed to see a priest as he was a Catholic. There was a priest in the prison for treason, but he was very sick, so sick that he could not get out of bed.' (It will be remembered that Fr Phelomy O'Hamill, parish priest of old Saint Mary's, remained in Belfast gaol until he died.) 'So Willie Kane would have to go to him. But before allowing him into the priest's room they made him take off his shoes and coat, so that if he escaped he would attract attention and be arrested. "I am suffocating. Open the window,

Willie, and give me a breath of air," said the priest as the boy entered.

'It was not a regular prison — all the regular prisons were full — but a house the government had turned into a prison; so there were no bars on the window, and, his confession ended, Willie Kane climbed through it and made off for his life. But, as he had to pass a barrack, he knew that without shoes or coat he would attract attention and be arrested.

'He saw a man in a backyard and said to him: "Would you give a boy your coat and shoes to save his life?"

'"Faith an' I would," replied the man, looking at him, and suspecting what was the matter. Willie Kane put on the man's coat and shoes, and went down past the barracks whistling *Croppies lie down*.[9] He went down to the bridge and stood under it up to his neck in water until next morning, when his friends got him smuggled away on board a vessel, and finally got to America where he became a wealthy and respected citizen.'

The motto of *The Northern Star* was: 'The public will our guide: the public good our end.'

---

1   1798 and the United Irishmen Rising.
2   Lake-dwelling.
3   Henry Joy McCracken (1767–98) was a celebrated leader of the United Irishmen. A moving tribute to him can be found in Mary McNeill's *The Life and Times of Mary Ann McCracken 1770–1866* (1960).
4   The phrase was used by Byron about Thomas Moore and his fawning attitude towards the English aristocracy.
5   Thomas Russell (1767–1803), United Irishman, known by the epithet used here from a poem by Florence Wilson. He was for a time librarian at the Linen Hall Library in Belfast.
6   Sir Samuel Ferguson, (1810–86), leading Irish poet in the nineteenth century.
7   William Drennan (1754–1820), Belfast-born poet and author of 'The Wake of William Orr'.
8   Henry Grattan (1746–1820), leader of 'Grattan's Parliament', the Irish Parliament which met in the years after 1782.
9   Croppies (the word derives from style of haircut) were those who supported the aims of the United Irishmen.

PATRICK CAMPBELL
from *The Irish Times*, 12 June 1946

Patrick Campbell (1913–80) was a Dublin-born journalist who in the 1940s contributed a column for *The Irish Times* under the name 'Quidnunc' (what now). Here is a humorous sketch of Anglo-Irish relations in the post-war period, which saw an influx of English visitors to Dublin. A collection of his articles can be found in his *35 Years on the Job: The Best of Patrick Campbell, 1937–73* (1973).

An Irishman's Diary

June 12th, 1946.

You see, what happens is that this man comes in with two women and sits down on one of the sofas. He is a neat young man, wearing the tie of a fine school, and all that is wrong with him is that he doesn't seem to have been to bed for three days.

He sits down on this sofa and the two women fluff about nervously, wondering when he is going to say: 'Pray now, what will you have, Ruby and Beryl?'

It takes him some time to get round to this. He reads the evening paper peevishly. Obviously, anything is better than passing the time of day with the two pieces. In the end they say: 'Well, should we have a tiddly?'

It turns out that their conception of a tiddly is a swimming bath of mixed liquids with a slice of lemon on the top. He orders this, reluctantly.

Concerned with their problem, I lean forward, so that my face is pressed into the middle of his evening paper. I am glad that I am so close. I am able to hear his next sentence. He says: 'I'm having this one, and then I must go and get my lunch.'

Beryl and Ruby are amazed by this statement. 'Lunch?' they say.

'I must go and get my lunch,' says the young man from the fine school.

I am with Beryl and Ruby here. The time by my watch is exactly a quarter past six in the evening.

But this is our punishment, if we deserve it, for our abstention from the late war. It is our punishment that we should be seated harmlessly in our places of refreshment, and that the English visitors should come pouring in, overflowing our contemplation of the works of Thomas Davis[1] with all manner of war-created neuroses, like the need for lunch at six-fifteen p.m.

A well-known native woman, speaking for publication on this subject, said: 'Gob, Jem, do you know what it is? If another of them creatures . . .'

'Craythures,' I warned her. 'Craythures,' she said, thankfully, 'if another of them craythures comes over here and says the steaks is lovely, and it's a wonder to see cream again, I'll hit them a lash.'

'You have the wrong action,' I said severely. 'All aggressive action in this country is contained in the words: "I gev him a tip of me foot."'

Mad laughter, of course, and warnings about being a caution.

What a dreadful pity it is that we do not all speak Irish. If we all spoke Irish, the English, in search of steak and cream, with three fried eggs in the overcoat pocket as a recognition of our pleasure in seeing them here, would have to arm themselves with guide-books, in order to make their way around the town.

What I would like to see now would be a book called, *Polish Up Your Irish*.

Take, please, lightly between finger and thumb, an English visitor. He stands in need of the ability to make some communication to the natives, all native-speakers, whose only word of English lies in the sentence: 'What is there in it for me?'

All English people, of any acceptable standing, always clear their throats before speaking with the sound: 'Ech-tuel-lay.' In the same way electricians test microphones by breathing into them: 'Wan-two-tree-fower . . .'

Have we found an Irish equivalent for: 'Ech-tuel-lay?' If we have not, cancel the publication of the Irish-English guide-book.

What other phrases should be provided for the benefit of the English visitors? (It is a soft thing asking questions when you are in a position to answer them yourself.)

Let us have an Irish equivalent for these words: 'Could you put me in touch with someone who could sell me some clothing coupons? I find that the seat is out of my pinstripe.'

Next question. 'What makes you think I am prepared to pay £5 for these coupons?'

A large gap may be left now, quite safely, while the natives make terrible protestations about times being hard, and the Government going totalitarian, and the cost of living being fixed 470 per cent above the pre-war rate to suit the convenience of local manufacturers, who are receiving a subsidy to make articles that fall to pieces as they are passed across the counter.

The English visitors, perceiving the tears pouring down the native faces, ruffle through the pages of the guide book, and disinter the consolation: 'Ah, sure, do not be after upsetting yourself. It will all come right in the end.'

These questions follow. 'What, if I am in search of pleasure, shall I do with myself and my party after the public-houses close at half-past ten?'

'If I really do buy this castle in your Dingle Peninsula, how shall I pass the long winter evenings — apart from rushing around the house catching the drips from the roof in an enamel bucket — while a cloudburst vents itself upon the laurel bushes bordering the avenue?'

'Am I to take it, seeing that all my new Irish friends speak of their friends as chancers, cute hawks and cods, that as soon as I leave their company I, too, shall be pilloried by this indiscriminate malice?'

'Who are your friends, and are you loyal to them?'

'Why are you so intolerant of what appear to me to be but minor human faults?'

'What makes you think that you can hold an audience of comparative strangers by the recital of an anecdote which presents you in a favourable light, while it is perfectly obvious to any thinking listener that you have played the part, in this action, of what we spoke of at Harrow as a cad?'

'Why do you think you are so funny? Do you not know any amusing narratives about stockbrokers, Welshmen or the Italian army?'

'Do you pronounce it as — Devaleera, or Devallera?'

'Will you be kind enough to take your hand off my throat?'

---

1   The centenary of Thomas Davis (1814–45), poet and nationalist, had just been celebrated.

ARLAND USSHER
from *The Listener*, 11 September 1947

Percy Arland Ussher (1899–1980) was educated in England and returned to his family's estate at Cappoquin, County Waterford, where he began to learn Irish. In 1926 he published a translation of Brian Merriman's eighteenth-century long poem *The Midnight Court*. After moving to Dublin in 1943 he published on existentialist philosophy, on *The Face and Mind of Ireland* (1949) and on *Three Great Irishmen* (1952), that is Shaw, Yeats, and Joyce. Here in this radio talk, which raises more issues than can in fact be handled properly in the time, he focuses on contemporary thought in Ireland. The difference he draws in his closing remarks between the individual and the citizen in Ireland is an intriguing one.

The Contemporary Thought of Ireland

It must be confessed that the subject on which I have to address you is a singularly unpromising one. Indeed I may say that the thought of having to speak on the Thought of Ireland has been weighing unpleasantly on my mind. In our country, schools of philosophy do not exactly teem; one may doubt whether the idealist aesthetic of Benedetto Croce or the existentialism of Jean-Paul Sartre has aroused a flicker of interest among our intellectuals, from poets to professors. And this is to name only the two most discussed doctrines which have appeared in Europe since 1914.

Even if philosophers like Croce or Sartre were to arise in our midst, it is probable that they would remain as unheard of as would, say, a real creative writer in Irish, for philosophy like Irish is a language — a language taught and venerated in schools, but, like Irish, usually regarded as totally useless and without the least relation to real life. The one personality we have to show in this century who approached the stature of a leader of thought was the interesting and versatile George Russell; but Russell's mind hovered between Celticism and Orientalism, between Tara and Tibet, and somehow skipped Europe — where the world's thinking, hardened in the fires of action, has been chiefly carried on. Whatever may be the final assessment of A.E.'s life and work — and I am one of those who think he was over-rated during his life as he is perhaps over-neglected today — it must be said of him that his personality gave a serious and enquiring bent to all the minds it touched, and that he made Dublin during his lifetime what it has never quite been since, an intellectual capital. Our two best poets — I refer to Mr Austin Clarke and Mr Seumas O'Sullivan[1] — still carry about them some of the glory of that time, before civil war came to extinguish the Candle of Vision.[2] In a world which seems to be groping its way back to what A.E. called the Oversoul, what Aldous Huxley calls the Divine Ground, and what we may non-committally call the Values of the Contemplative Life, it is likely that George Russell will be remembered as a forerunner — a true artist philosopher, though perhaps too little of a philosopher or an artist. Such undoubtedly greater men as W.B. Yeats and George Moore, who towards the end of their lives seemed to be turning their attention to philosophy and religion, never hesitated to admit their debt to Russell. But in them one is made aware, for good and ill, as in A.E. one is not, of the escapist side of the Irish genius — even though it is an ironic escapism; an interest in ideas as a refuge from the facts rather than an interpretation of them, an attraction to the world of thought as a 'Land of Youth' for pagan myth-heroes born out of time.

This may be seen in Yeats's discovery, and misconception, of Bishop Berkeley. For Yeats saw in the Berkeleian idealism an affirmation of the anarchy of imagination, a Magna Carta for the poet's licence, a resolution of the world into a dream. But this would have horrified the devout Berkeley, who wished to turn back the anarchy and licence of atheistic philosophers by making them question their own assumptions. Berkeley was a great Irishman, who fought the sceptics of his time as Socrates fought the sophists of his, trying to establish firm foundations for knowledge; but there is a tendency among some of the Anglo-Irish to make him a *ne plus ultra*[3] in philosophy, whereas his mind was wholly 18th century and conservative. His paradox that 'Matter does not exist' is the first word and not the last word of metaphysics; as Messrs Hone and Rossi[4] have shown in their excellent 'Life', he was in reality a sturdy defender of common sense in the age of common sense. He had no suspicion of the monstrous forms which philosophic idealism would assume in the next two centuries; when he said 'To be is to be perceived' he did not foresee that the world would become

something very like a cracked looking-glass for the Yahoo, or that his idealistic tar-water[5] would be strained until nothing remained of it but pitch.

The school of Roman Catholic neo-Thomism[6] is in large measure a reaction against this cracked-looking-glass philosophy of idealism — this dream of the mind closed in upon itself — for materialism in the 19th-century sense may be said to be defunct in the present age, if we overlook America. Neo-Thomism has not yet got its Irish Maritain,[7] and can hardly yet be said to be the vital force one would expect it to be in Ireland; though it has given a direction to one or two of our better poets, like Mr Robert Farren and Mr Thomas McGreevy.[8] But in the main our writers seem to think they can preserve a virginal neutrality in this world of warring ideas, an 'art for art's sake' without even the courage of that rather ascetic doctrine. If they show the intellectual pugnacity upon which we used to pride ourselves, it is only to attack censorship or to praise Marxist Communism. I am not going to discuss here whether these attitudes are right or wrong; I would only point out that they are inconsistent with each other. One feels the lack of a synthesizing philosophy of life, one misses a realization of the anguish of the modern consciousness — such as is shown, for instance, by the French existentialists, who bravely seek to snatch a reason for living out of despair itself.

A young Frenchman said to me recently: 'We have no time to be amused.' We in Ireland, it would seem, have all the time there is to be amused; but the world no longer laughs with us, and we are somewhat in the position of the Court Jester out of court. I say this — and I immediately relent towards my fellow-countrymen; for our mental frivolity preserves us, after all, from what is the curse of most philosophy, especially in the English tongue — a portentous and bombinating seriousness. I am of the opinion that there are stray aphorisms scattered through Wilde's *Intentions* and *The Soul of Man under Socialism* which are worth most of the books of philosophy written in England during the 19th century. Even in the present paper famine, ponderous tomes issue from the presses with such titles as *Emergent Evolution* or *Religion in the Making* — to quote the linguistically barbarous heading of a work by a famous contemporary philosopher. I think we may be grateful to be saved from the present craze of evolutionary humanism in thought, as in the Victorian Age we were saved from the neo-Gothic fashion in architecture — less perhaps by our taste than by our isolation. I believe that the Irish mind is imbued with a deep innate disillusion-ment and disbelief in life, that was here even before

Christianity came to our shores and found such a quick response in our people. Though we are fond of dreams and enchantments, we play with them, and are not generally their slaves; we desire them only because we are already disenchanted with the reality. It is this which distinguishes us above all from that other great legend-loving race, the Germans — in whose sagas the Unknown is always represented by a witch or nixie, alluring, irresistible and dangerous.

The novel *Murphy*, by an expatriate Dubliner, Samuel Beckett, expresses this contradiction in a bitterly farcical form; its hero determines to become an attendant in a lunatic-asylum. He prefers the mad to the sane *because* they are mad — not because he loves madness, but because he hates the sensibly-ordered world more. As he says, he thinks of the patients 'not as banished from a system of benefits but as escaped from a colossal fiasco'. Unlike most modern novels which may be called pathological, in *Murphy* the hero's tone remains cool, reasoned and sane; even when he is most mad, the Irishman is a little of a conscious ironist and play-actor. A similar philosophy of life is expressed in Synge's beautiful play *The Well of the Saints*, in which two old people, cured of blindness, deliberately ask to be restored to the Kingdom of the Blind, because (so to speak) in that kingdom every man is a king and every woman a queen. The dream is desired *because* it is a dream — with a clear-eyed choice. This tendency of ours can seem exceedingly irritating and ostrich-like today — though, as Murphy in one place remarks, who knows what the ostrich sees in the sand? But I think nevertheless that it holds a promise for tomorrow. For whether or no the world as a whole returns to orthodox religion, it will certainly return — if it is to survive — to more sober estimates of human nature and possibilities than have been fashionable in the age which has followed the French Revolution, the age of that delirious 'Progress' which has largely been the Progress of the Rake, and of which we are already experiencing the hang-over.

More than that, if civilization is to survive it must re-discover and allow for that disabused detachment of the individual, that obstinate refusal to be involved, which I regard as a peculiarly Irish characteristic — a sense of the word 'individuality' which was largely missed during the era of political liberalism. In the more strictly philosophical field, I believe that Ireland may yet have a word to say in the 20th century, as she had through John Scotus in the 9th century and through Bishop Berkeley in the 18th — in both cases introducing a new era of thought by a daring feat of simplification. For philosophy has now to give us back, by an act of transcendental imagination, the shape and design of the external world — the world of which, through an era of analysis, she has progressively robbed and impoverished our souls; and this task demands a combination of realism and religious feeling nowhere else but here to be found, I think, among modern men. The new synthesis that I look forward to will proceed, if I am right, above all from artists; for art, as Mr Cecil Salkeld[9] once defined it in conversation with me, is 'the maximum of association with the minimum of form' — a definition which brilliantly combines modern physical and ancient metaphysical formulae for the cosmos. But in making this prophecy, I cheerfully admit, I am guided by faith — some will say by wishful thinking — rather than by reason; for Ireland at present might as well be the Gobi Desert for any tangible evidence that out of her will come a school of philosophy. But when one reflects on the impact made upon the imagination of the world by Shaw, W.B. Yeats and Joyce, it is hard to believe that Ireland has become a No-Man's-Land of the mind, or that she has grown provincial at the moment when she is, for the first time after centuries, a nation.

When intelligent visitors to our country are asked about their impressions of us, they usually pay us many kind and — we will hope — deserved compliments, but they generally end by commenting on our truly staggering indifference to events in the outer world. This shows, I think, the dangerous side of that detached spirit of which I have already emphasized the positive and hopeful side. I do not want to raise here the question of what a countryman called our 'neutrality'; in that matter we took a position I think both legitimate and dignified. But I do consider it a disgrace that freedom-loving Irishmen of intelligence could be heard to defend, as I have heard them defend, the behaviour of the German equivalent of the Black-and-Tans to the brave Catholic Poles. I hasten to leave this controversial subject; but the fact remains that a European consciousness can hardly be said to exist in Ireland. Far too many Irish people talk as if we were the pure, the uncontaminated, a race apart, shining like a good deed in a naughty world. A tight-lipped and censorious book on Voltaire appeared last year, with the *imprimatur*[10] of the President of Cork University; in it many of the Sage of Ferney's[11] best quips were held up to indignant opprobrium. This is the sort of thing that gives us that reputation for a rancid prudery formerly enjoyed chiefly by Anglo-Saxons. Sometimes one really wonders why we do not erect a statue to Oliver Cromwell, since the Puritan has become our Patron Saint.

But it would be unfair to suggest, as is sometimes suggested, that there is no constructive social and economic thought going on in Ireland; for there are some interesting trends to be noticed among both the principal religious groups — trends of which the class specifically called, or self-called, intellectuals seems to be very little aware. I may mention the interesting and provocative book on *Money* by the afore-mentioned President of Cork University, the stimulating pamphlets of the 'Towards a New Ireland' series, the books of Mr Arnold Marsh, and especially that brilliant and entertaining modernization of Berkeleian economics — the anonymous pamphlet called *The New Querist*. With the particular economic thought developed in these works — that known in England as 'The New Economics', and expounded every week by a group of gifted writers in *The New English Weekly* — I cannot deal here; nor indeed would I be competent to deal with it anywhere. But those who equally dislike complete collectivism and *laissez faire* capitalism would do better to search for the humanly-tolerable pattern of society than spend their time in bewailing the hold of religion on the popular mind. Fifty years ago, many educated people regarded religion as an obscurantist force. Today the position is changed, and the religious bodies are almost the only groups over much of the world which still stand for elementary liberties and sanities. To give one small and telling example: torture, for accidents of birth or opinion, used to be associated with the name of the Spanish Inquisition. The Spanish Inquisition looks almost like a tea-party today. From this fact people will draw varying conclusions. I am a member of no church, and my own conclusions would perhaps not be orthodox. But that it *is* a fact there can be no reasonable dispute.

I would like to add a few remarks on Contemporary Thought in the Irish language; but for the unfortunate circumstance that there is no thought whatever being produced in Irish — unless one may give that title to some of the more inspired witticisms of Myles na gCopaleen.[12] (I heard today that a young plumber was writing a poem in Irish on existentialism. If it is true, I apologize to him.) Irish is, nevertheless, no matter how often we hear assertions to the contrary, a medium very well adapted to the finer distinctions of the mind. My friend the poet and economist Francis Macnamara, who died last year, was struck by the fact

that Gaelic has two words for the concept 'good' — the one always placed before, and the other after, its noun — and similarly with the concept 'bad'. He saw in this an attempt to distinguish between the individual quality that comes from within, and the social character which is imposed from without. Most of what I have tried to say here might perhaps be expressed simply by saying that we in Ireland still prefer the *deagh-dhuine* to the *duine maith*. To translate, very inadequately — we care more for the Man than for the mere good citizen. That, maybe, is our greatest hope.

1 Seamas O'Sullivan (pseudonym of James Sullivan Starkey) (1879–1958) wrote several volumes of verse beginning with *The Twilight People* (1905). Ussher's acclaim for his verse is not widely shared. On the other hand, when he was editor of the *Dublin Magazine* from 1932 to 1958, his contribution to Irish cultural life was invaluable.
2 Russell's *Candle of Vision* (1918) was the title of a book on the mystical experience of life.
3 No greater than, the most complete, perfect, best example.
4 Joseph Hone wrote a life of Bishop Berkeley which was published in 1931; he then wrote a life of Swift with Mario Rossi and this was published in 1934.
5 A reference to Berkeley's *Siris* (1744), in which he championed the drinking of tar-water.
6 A nineteenth-century return to the work of the Medieval theologian St Thomas Aquinas, whose theology was a response to the philosophy of Aristotle rather than Plato.
7 Jacques Maritain (1882–1973), the French neo-Thomist religious thinker.
8 Robert Farren (Roibeárd Ó Faracháin) (1909–84), author of *Time's Wall Asunder* (1939) and *Rime Gentlemen, Please* (1945). For more information about McGreevy, see MacGreevy (1929), p. 371.
9 Cecil Salkeld, son of the poet Blanaid Salkeld, was an Irish painter and co-editor of *To-Morrow* (1924), p. 290.
10 *imprimatur*: Latin: let it be printed; used by Catholic Church to approve books which do not contradict Catholic teaching. Here, simply a blessing.
11 Sage of Ferney: In 1758 Voltaire purchased an estate at Ferney in France where as the 'patriarch of Ferney' he was visited by admirers of his work.
12 Brian O'Nolan or Flann O'Brien. Myles Na gCopaleen was the name he used for his columns in *The Irish Times*. See (1942) p. 503 above for an example.

JOHN V. KELLEHER
from *Irish Writing*, November 1947

Kelleher's essay is worth pondering. You might begin by outlining the strengths and weaknesses of his argument. Could this essay have been written fifty years later? Does the subsequent accumulation or expansion of Irish-American literature alter his argument? And what weight do you attach to his use of the phrase 'no suspense left'?

Irish-American Literature, and Why There isn't Any

There is an Irish family I know here in New England who had a granduncle who told the truth. His name was Dan and he was a hero, a genuine one, with four years of fighting in the American Civil War; and he was a sour, taciturn, grumpy old man, which in view of his truthfulness is what you might expect. One time one of his grandnephews — not a favourite, for he had none — got him talking about the Siege of Petersburg. 'Uncle Dan,' he said, 'you were at Petersburg, weren't you?'

'The whole bloody nine months,' said Dan.

'Did the great mine explosion take place anywhere near your part of the front?'

'Right on my goddam front,' said Dan.

'What did it look like?'

'I don't know,' said Dan, knocking out his pipe and going away for a rest. 'I wasn't there that day.'

Now, can you, gentle Irish reader, conceive of another Irish veteran of that war, who had been within six hundred miles of the scene, who would not have given his audience a complete and personalized picture of the explosion and what happened to little Paddy Keefe when the land blew up?

No. Nor can I. For a long time now I have been trying to collect materials for the great Irish-American novel, a trilogy, of course, which would tell the whole three generation story from North Cork in 1847 or 1874 to Massachusetts in 1947. I have asked literally hundreds of people. And it is well I began asking young, for there are very few left now who experienced the early part of the history. Needless to say, everybody has been most co-operative. Everyone realizes that the story must be got down before it is forgotten altogether and the Irish-Americans lose the only cultural heritage that can distinguish them from any other kind of Americans. Needless to say, the amount of fact I have found in what I have gathered borders on the microscopic.

If there were a few more Uncle Dans my hopes would be higher. Dan, it would seem, was a psychological sport, a unique eccentric, for I have met no other old Irishman or Irishwoman like him. They are not taciturn, Heaven knows, nor grumpy at all with the young people who want to hear what it was like. But they're Irish, and they tell stories. Everything comes out packaged in a story. And when you tear off the fictional wrapping, you are lucky indeed if you find a fact, or half a fact, inside. It isn't that the stories aren't good. Like all Irish stories they are very well-shaped, full of wit and sharply observed character, built around the one real folk theme, the victory of the hero through a sly and funny stratagem. But in them Uncle Mike or Daniel O'Connell[1] or The-Man-Who-Kicked-The-Dentist-Through-The-Awning are all on the same level of reality, practically in the same moment of history. Take away the stratagem and you find that though the story has seemed all along to be about something you wanted to learn — say, the methods of the Castle Garden swindlers[2] — it isn't about that at all.

I haven't heard anyone mention the Castle Garden swindlers for years. Like many another important detail in the unwritten history they have been forgotten, all but lost completely. Yet they gave many a man his first taste of America. Castle Garden, where they operated, was the old immigration depot in New York; and the swindlers were of many nationalities and were all equally mean. The old people always claimed that the Irish swindlers were the most successful and the meanest. Yet, except for an employment agency racket described in a novel written in the 1870s, I don't know how they worked, what line and bait they used, or how they won the confidence of the suspicious and frightened peasants. I really don't know anything about them except their significance. In the two stories I heard about them all the details had dropped away, leaving only an improbable yarn about how Cousin Mike or Uncle Joe swindled the swindler. The swindler himself had been reduced to a figure of fun, which he assuredly was not; and Cousin Mike swaggered across the scene 'the boy well able to look after himself', which assuredly he was not. You can depend on it that if he met with a swindler, by the time Mike got to his relatives his pockets were as empty as his pride. If I could get that story, if I could have heard Mike tell it himself, honestly, I would have the start for the novel. The story as it exists doesn't mean a damn thing, except that an Irishman hates to admit he has been made a fool of. I knew that before I could talk.

My father used to tell me I would never get what I was looking for. What I needed was the talk in the kitchens at night, when the old country friends came visiting. 'If you had the record of one night's talk, you'd have it all. But you wouldn't be able to understand most of it if you did have it.' Why, I asked; and he tried to explain how different it was from anything I could have heard at anytime after I was old enough to take notice. 'That talk vanished before the talkers. After the turn of the century it all died out; and especially after that you never heard them going off into Irish when they wanted to talk above the young folk's heads. Before ...' But he couldn't tell me what it had been like before. It was as foreign to him as to me. Probably more, for the contrast between Irish in America and Irish-American was at its sharpest in his boyhood, when all the parent generation was immigrant and the children were Americans from birth. The tangle of emotions and cultures he remembered cannot be stated simply. It was a tangle and not a dichotomy. The parents were becoming Americans (or were to become Americans: the process is sometimes as instant as physical change of phase); and the children knew Ireland only through their parents' ageing and increasingly sentimental stories. I suspect, too, that the parents were jealous of their own experience. Assimilation to American life had been a rough, painful business for them, with little free choice about it, while the children saw it as little more than a schoolyard between Dirty Micks and Hungry Yanks. As a result, the older people clung to their belief that no one could understand the story who had not been through it. After the American change of phase, they could hardly understand it themselves.

The big change — it was really the end of the story — took place around the turn of the century: say, 1905, on the average: when these American-born, American-educated children took over from the parents. They walked easily into the sort of jobs their fathers could never have dreamed of. Family incomes, with three or four of the boys working at once, shot up from eight or ten dollars a week to sixty or eighty. It was the great victory, the realization for the Irish of the American dream, as later and much more swiftly the same dream came true for the Italians, the Poles, and a dozen other immigrant nationalities. The first

result of it was that the Irish ghettos broke up. Today you will find in hardly any New England town a definite Irish quarter, though every town will have its memories of a 'Patch', a 'Kerry Acre', a 'Roscommon Gap'. At the same time Irish-American life lost its cohesion and its distinct character. The Irish began to disperse into the general American landscape: in a sense, to vanish. That process has gone a long way in the intervening forty years, less in New England than elsewhere because New England is a very small part of the United States and the Irish here are very numerous. Even here, however, the rate of amalgamation is high, and what any of us O's or Mac's can claim as truly Irish in his culture or his character is intangible and small. Old prejudices, old memories, and religion have operated to a fairly wide extent to keep the Irish apart from the Protestant Yankees, but these factors do not operate to prevent Irish-Lithuanian, Irish-Italian, Irish-Polish marriages, nor are the children of these marriages 'Irish'. Go outside New England and you will find the process gone immensely further towards completion. There is, at any rate, nothing to stop it.

The story, then, comes to its real end before 1910. Though there were plenty of families, after that, who had not yet made the grade or who were too freshly over to have gone through enough of the initiation, the results were assured, there was no suspense left. All the rest is epilogue — an epilogue that has less to do with Ireland, slow as we have been to realize it. The separation was proved in 1919, when the De Valera-Cohalan feud[3] split the Irish-American societies wide open. Today there are only a few shadows of such societies left, and their influence is a shadow of those shadows. Yet the occasion of the blow-up was ridiculously petty compared to the turmoils and scandals the Clann-na-nGael and the other Irish Independence organizations survived between 1858 and 1919. It doesn't explain it, either, to say that the organizations broke up because their object had been achieved — the Irish are not as logical as that. They broke up because they were not held together any longer by outside pressure. Given that pressure — prejudice and discrimination; given the urge it engendered to strike back hard — at England, because England was the hereditary enemy, whereas America, though at the moment it might be Purgatory, held out the promise of a Heaven; add a lot of nostalgic sentiment, some knowledge and a hell of a lot of ignorance of Irish politics; and you have the mixture that gave those organizations their driving force, their mass, their cohesion. By 1919, though they hardly knew it, they were going on old inertia. For a while it was still possible to raise money for the Cause, but the Civil War in Ireland stopped that. Now try raising a couple of hundred thousand for a grand and Irish, if unspecified, cause. Patrick Ford's 'Fenian Ram' submarine in Brooklyn Navy Yard is a monument to more than the crackpot revolutionism that thought it up. It is a monument, the only monument, to the people who subscribed the money for it out of their meagre and uncertain pay, and to the emotions that made them subscribe. People and emotions both dead now, and forgotten.

In *Ireland To-day*, in 1936, Francis Hackett described certain 'troglodyte' Irishmen you can, or could, still find here, '. . . so mummified that they seemed to me almost pre-historic. There are Irishmen driving taxi-cabs in New York who ought to be in the National Museum, like bog butter. How they do it, how they manage to feel and think and act and look like stub-ends of an extinct era is a social mystery . . . In immigrants like these there has been no new rooting, simply a persistence in folk-ways that a stubborn will has glazed over, at immense expense of spirit. Among the unemployed there are knobs and mounds of such discarded Irishmen. They could not adapt themselves, and once they leave the cluster around the historic Church their fate too often is to go to the bottom.' Hackett is quite right, of course. But one must remember that once these troglodytes would have had something more than the Church to cluster around for understanding and help. Many a family here had at least one such non-adaptor: in my time he would be a silent old man who would say nothing because nobody could understand anything he had to say. If one could reconstruct the process by which he had passed, by what degrees one can only guess, from the role of strongest link with the home village to the inevitable high and dry loneliness among grandnephews and nieces who probably did not even know the name of the village, one would have the exact index of Irish-American history. Sixty years ago a man like that might be out of place in America, but he would not be lost in America. He would have the Fenian societies, the old A.O.H.,[4] probably a dozen friends on whom he could call in the evenings for comfortable discussions of the world of Ballybeyond. By the time I might have known him even Ballybeyond was worn out. The whole congenial immigrant society in which he had sheltered was vanished away. Whatever half-pitying attention he got from the sons of his friends would be given because they too were 'Irish'. He would know damn well that they weren't. Punkauns and pishogue Yankees,[5] the whole lot of them. Till a year ago I would have passed

off the old man's deprecation of us as crankiness. But he was right.

There are a lot of Irish short stories or novels about which I used to congratulate myself that I knew exactly what they meant, because I too was 'Irish'. I felt quite familiar with Ireland, before I saw Ireland. It was an illusion, of course, produced by the fact that I had heard stories at home in the same manner and the same dialect. What I forgot was that I had the stories third hand, from my father or mother who had them from older people. The stories — they were very like some of Frank O'Connor's in *Bones of Contention*[6] — dated back to the 1860s or '70s when you could go from Cork City to any New England mill town without noticing the difference, if you squinched your eyes a bit and ignored the Yankees and the climate and anything that happened outside the 'Patch'. The town I was born in probably had the heaviest concentration of Cork and Kerry Irish in America, though by no means the largest. From the outside it might have seemed a cosmopolitan city — 53 languages were recorded there in the 1920 census — but you know the Irish won't tolerate cosmopolitanism, and the Irish ran this place.

The mills were owned from New York. The top society, what there was of it, was Yankee. Politically, the Irish were in full control. They probably made up forty per cent of the 100,000 population, and were so closely interallied that their ranks were never broken, though they were, to put it mildly, not loved by their colonials, the Wops, Turks, Frogs, Polacks, Squareheads, and other tolerated races. (There was one time the French Canadians voted *en masse* for a man named Rochefort, and then found he was from Cork!) My father used to say that the whole town was made up of Millstreet men married to Dingle women. He meant the whole of the town that mattered. At least half of the family relationships — we counted up to third cousin and if necessary allowed one or two removals — dated from the 1830s in Cork or Kerry and were uninjured by the trip across the Atlantic. In my childhood I used to hear Fermoy Irish spoken, which I'll bet few of my Fermoy contemporaries have heard. Millstreet or Dingle Irish was easy to find. The prize Irish, I was told, was from where 'you could shpit across the Blackwater'. I heard that Irish too, for the man who told me had 'often shpit that shpit'.

Now, if anyone under sixty ought to be able to write the great Irish-American novel, assuming of course enough knowledge of grammar to put the words in order, I, or any townsman of mine, ought to be able to. But I can't, as I have explained, for the reasons I have explained. I still thought I could till I went to Ireland and got up to C——, our family village in North Cork.

I had come to find one thing: if anyone remembered my great-grandfather who had stayed in C—— when the rest of the family emigrated, and who died there about 1880. It was disappointingly plain that no one did. On the other hand, the investigation was not to be abandoned for such a small failing as that. I produced genealogical evidence enough to satisfy a College of Heralds. I named the farm we had had, detailed our relationships with the other numerous families of the area, and sat back to hear the conclusions. For a couple of hours all went very well. The farm was well known and was a respectable one. The relationships had an authentic timbre. Nobody questioned my grandfather's account of who and what we were. I felt as if I were at home, playing the game of 'Tommy O'Donovan; which Tommy O'Donovan?; The Custer Street O'Donovans; which Custer Street O'Donovans — there's two'. It was a damn nice feeling. Two thousand miles and eighty years seemed the merest mist between us. The Irish are the same the world over, I was saying to myself, when the blow fell.

One of the men sensed a flaw in the evidence. 'Where did your great-grandfather marry?' he asked me.

'In B——,' I said. 'He and his brother married two sisters, O'Mahonys, from there.' I felt pretty proud of that bit of information. It brought the story back to 1832, and I could take it a step farther.

There was a strange silence. Something, plainly, had gone wrong. With a cute smile he leaned forward again. 'What did they go so far out of the parish as that for, to marry? B—— is fifteen miles and more north of here.'

'I know,' I said. And added innocently, 'What's fifteen miles?'

Fifteen miles, it turned out, was a lot. It was too far by a great deal; and it meant that there was something fishy about all the claims I had advanced on behalf of my forebears. The discussion around me became very animated, though there was a polite attempt to avoid putting the charges into definite words till they seemed proved. There were hidden reasons, however, and they had to be found.

They were found. The inquisitor challenged me with the general opinion. 'They were herdsmen,' he said. 'They were wandering up and down the country tending other people's herds; and that's how they took girls from so far out.'

Shocked, I protested. 'They had the farm at P——. They weren't herdsmen. My grandfather never said so.'

'He wouldn't say so. It was their father had the farm — and they were herdsmen. That's how they did it.'

'It', whether they did it or not, ruined my social standing in C——, and ruined it finally. I was pretty sore about it at the time. Not angry with the men of C——, who were, if anything, more kindly courteous after the dreadful decision than before, but damned angry at the assumption that eighty years of pride and honest respectability and firm Irishry in exile weighed nothing beside the possibility of a social error in 1832.

Afterwards, in a less injured mood, it occurred to me that very likely this was what my father had meant when he said, I would not have understood the talk of his parents' old friends. There must often have been very similar judgements passed in New England kitchens, in the '70s and '80s, when the local Irish Who's Who was being gone over. He had, to be sure, told me the strange case of the old lady who objected to her son's fiancée because her own (the old lady's) father had been a leaseholder, while the girl's grandfather had been a cottier 'with two rocky rack-rented acres and one cow'. That the girl's family had become more prosperous in America than her own made no difference; good blood was good blood, caste was caste. I don't suppose the old lady really expected her objection to be understood or accepted. Certainly her son would not have seen the point. He knew that his mother and his mother-in-law had worked side by side in the mills. And now to have the social grading system of rural Ireland offered him as a standard for choosing a wife!

What American could invent that sort of thing? If our hypothetical Irish-American author (me?) has to breathe his early characters to life by informing them with such attitudes and judgements as those, I'm afraid he is stuck. And all the Irish history, sociology, and anthropology in the world won't unstick him. The great book, you understand, ought to be a novel, a real one, and not one of those undisguised sociological tracts, multiple case-histories, that are passed off on us as 'serious' literature 'with a purpose'. Maybe the business could be inverted, and the book be written by an observant Irish farmer who would stoke up on American history and sociology. Any offers?

Well, let us look at some writers who have made gestures this way. We will begin with John McElgun, of whom you have no doubt heard.

If opportunities made an artist, John McElgun, author of *Annie Reilly or the Fortunes of an Irish Girl in New York* (New York: J.A. McGee, 1878), 245 pp., would be the bright star and eminence of Irish-American letters. Mr McElgun's style leaves us something to desire — he seems to have quarried his language with a pick-axe; and his thought sometimes has the consecutive direction of a Mexican jumping bean, sometimes not. Nevertheless, very plainly he knew what he was writing about. Time and again, he gives us a chunk of realism: his is the picture of the employment agency swindler I mentioned earlier. He knew Ireland; he knew Queenstown[7] and Liverpool and the passage agencies; he knew what the immigrant ships were like, what the Irish boarding houses in New York were like, what happened to the Irish who fell away from the Church. All these things he mentions. Sometimes he describes them; and when he does you want to reach out your foot across sixty-nine years and kick him solidly in the pants. Because Mr McElgun is a snob, and a double snob, true and inverted. He knows that the Irish of his time have the virtues of health, strength, sound morals, and the true religion. He says so constantly, in at least two different ways. At the same time he is ashamed because they do not also have the virtues of money, gentle breeding, secure social position, and money. Writing for God knows what expected audience, he tries to show that the Irish really have all these latter virtues, or ought by rights to have them, or soon will have them, and really, after all, don't need to have them because they have them anyway, and are just as well off without them. He cannot admit any Irish social failing, except, of course, in the case of some thick Mick who is not representative of the race and who has been seduced by the easy life of the Pennsylvania oil fields. Still, there is a lot of honesty in this author. (If there were more, his book would be an invaluable document today.) He keeps at least two toes on the ground, which sometimes gives him an incongruously equivocal air, balanced as he is on pride and shame. In the Irish boarding house, for instance, where the guests sleep three and four in a bed, 'All the floors were bare but clean, except where covered with tobacco-juice and the ashes of pipes.' You see, he can't admit that such Irish dosses were ever dirty: yet he has to note the dirt. There is a touch of the artist about old McElgun. Which is a hell of a lot more than you can say for the refined journalists and grocers' educated daughters who crashed the *Household Book of Irish Verse* and other such seven pound proofs of Irish-American culture with superior steel engravings.

McElgun romanced crudely about the facts. The journalists and the daughters wrote dishwatery appeals to Owen Roe and Red Hugh, charging them with ousting the Saxon slaves and tyrants before it was too late. McElgun had a lot of honest Irish xenophobia; he admired the Yankees, but immigrants other than Irish, particularly the 'smelly Germans', he caricatured crudely and cruelly. The Household book set, thirsting

for gentility, imitated Yankee schoolmarm poetasters with poetasteless odes and triolets to Pere Marquette,[8] the Lesser Common Song Sparrow, and the falling snow. McElgun tells us plenty, mainly because he shows himself so plainly. They only tell us why the struggling poorer Irish wrote off the lace-curtain Irish of that time as a dead loss. The trouble is that there are only a few McElguns to hundreds of the others. It is not, you see, because the Irish weren't literate that we have no Irish-American literature. It is because they wrote tripe. And not real tripe, either, like McElgun's — but imitation tripe.

There are two other writers to be considered, both very substantial. Finley Peter Dunne who wrote the Mr Dooley essays, and James T. Farrell, author of the *Studs Lonigan* trilogy and the semi-autobiographical Danny O'Neill novels, *A World I Never Made*, etc. Neither fits the bill.

Dunne's Mr Dooley is, I think, the greatest humorous character in American literature, and the wisest and most enduring. And the lesser characters, Hennessey who draws Dooley out, and Hogan and Dock O'Leary and Father Kelly whom he makes his examples of the world, are uncannily real, too. But the primary concern of the essays is philosophic, to draw the universal from the topical by stingingly moral wit. The details of Dooley's life and neighbourhood are put in only as incidental background and very stingily. If the novel I desire is ever written, the novelist will inevitably incur a tremendous debt to Dunne who recorded the speech of the immigrant generation, and who preserved half a dozen of its characters, so soundly conceived you can ring them true against any criterion. But the Dooley essays are a long way from fulfilling the rounder purposes of imaginative fiction.

Farrell, like Dunne, a Chicago man, writes of the period after the First World War, so he never comes near what I believe the essential beginning. There is no distinctive Irish-American life or thought left for him to describe. His novels are American novels with many Irish-American characters.

The significance of his work lies in his description and knowledge of the void into which whole myriads of our people have fallen, that modern, lower middle class, traditionless, urban void underlying industrially revolutionized society in Chicago, Liverpool, Paris, Milan, Dublin. The void has no national boundaries. The people in it have no essential nationality but modern barbarism. If it happens that the specimens Farrell examines are Irish-American Catholics, they could as easily be Polish-American, Italian-American, Czech-American, German-American, without his making any fundamental changes. Nor would it require a basic rewriting to set the novel outside America altogether. *Studs Lonigan*, Farrell's trilogy, can be studied with profit by any politician or priest anywhere who feels that his particular institution has faced up to its responsibilities. Studs is 'Irish', 'Catholic', 'American': these at any rate are his party labels. You know him personally, whatever your party labels are. Studs and his limbo are everywhere. Unless we fill that void with something better than propaganda, Hollywood, and defunct nationalism, we will fall into it with him, amid a universal collapse.

Again our hypothetical author must incur a debt to Chicago, for he cannot finish his story without indicating that many, many Irish families, once they broke out of the Irish slum, fell promptly into Farrell's void. They fell into it nearly naked of tradition. They neither kept their Irish traditions, which no longer seemed relevant, nor discovered the important American ones. If they carried the Church with them, as too often they did, it was to the detriment of the Church and a proof of the clergy's failure. That, of course, is not the whole epilogue to the great change of phase around 1905. Unfortunately it is too much of the epilogue. We can all examine our consciences for the fault.

I might say that the beginning of the novel is relatively easy. The story from the Famine exodus to the end of the American Civil War is given in vivid detail, splendidly composed, in Oscar Handlin's *Boston's Immigrants: 1775–1865*.[9] The Irish regimental histories, crude as they are, give us a great deal more. It is what happened to the returned Irish veteran that stumps me. Uncle Dan at the siege of Petersburg in 1864, in a regiment harmoniously made up of the survivors of Yankee and Irish outfits, can be revived as a living man. But what Dan did or thought or said or hoped, in 1870, in a mill town slum, I don't know and find hard to imagine. I hope sometime I shall know. I hope someone gets beyond the second chapter, before it is too late.

1 Daniel O'Connell (1775–1847), the 'Liberator', famous Irish leader whose efforts helped achieve in 1829 Catholic Emancipation and who struggled for Repeal of the Union thereafter.

2 Castle Garden, in the Battery park at the bottom of Manhattan, was a fort, which was in the nineteenth century an amusement park and then a centre for immigration (before Ellis Island that is); in the twentieth century it was for a time an aquarium.

3 Judge Daniel Cohalan was a United States Supreme Court Judge who helped swing sections of Irish-American opinion away from the Democratic party towards the Republicans. In 1920 on his trip to the United States de Valera sought American political and financial aid but was obstructed by Cohalan and his organization Friends of Irish Freedom. Cohalan was for self-determination for Ireland but against a republic; he also argued against a special Bond Drive for five million dollars which de Valera sought from the American people.

4 Ancient Order of Hibernians.

5 A pishogue is a charm, so a pishogue Yankee is presumably an American who sees Ireland as full of the little people. A punkawn is a talkative, self-assertive person.

6 First published in 1936.

7 Now Cobh in Cork.

8 Presumably Jacques Marquette (1637–75), the French Jesuit missionary to the Ottawa and Huron Indians in what was then New France.

9 First published in 1941.

JIM PHELAN
from Jim Phelan, *We Follow the Roads* (1949)

Jim Phelan spent part of his life when not in prison tramping the roads as a vagrant. Here in this extract he provides a sharp insight into the minds of those who spend their days 'padding it' (see Patrick MacGill's 1916 poem by this name on page 268 above). The passage also contains interesting comments on monikers, on the nicknames that attach themselves to those who follow the roads.

Drift

Fesser Teale comes down the Great North Road of England, padding it. Ten a day. A few diversions here and there, to meet a mark or make a talk. But by and large there is the same distance covered each night. Ten a day. Padding it. London 312.

Not that the distance matters. Fesser is only going along. Ten a day. And tonight it will be London 302. But the figures on the sign-post count for little.

It might well be any other road, besides the Great North, for Fesser knows them all. In the United States the road called Federal Highway 59 is just such another as this, and Fesser has padded over that one too. New York 808.

Not that he would count it. Ten a day, and tonight it could be New York 798. But Fesser would only be going along in the green.

Outside America most readers believe that all vagrants in the United States travel by railroad. In fact the great majority are padders, there as everywhere else. Why should Fesser Teale ride a train?

A moment's reflection will show that it would be folly for the ordinary tramps to go rushing across country on trains, missing their marks and losing their comfort, for nothing at the end.

The postmen, or the comets as the American tramps call them, are different. The comets are in such a way kinked that they must keep on, must eat up the miles. But they too needs must know their marks, or die on the road. The postmen's marks are more yielding, spaced farther apart, that is all.

But Fesser is no postman, was no comet in the States. Ten a day, on Federal Highway 59, he made. And tomorrow it would be New York 788, or it will be London 292, and what does it matter?

Down from Paris and striking hard south is another of them, the wide ones, the white wide slashes in the green like England's Great North or the Federal Highways of America. Marseilles 636. But that is kilometres.

It would not count for much with Fesser when he was there. Because the morrow would only show him a sign that Marseilles was 624 or some near number. And numbers come to mean nothing.

They come to mean nothing at all, on the road, whether the reckoning is of coins or kisses, meals or miles. That is part of the wisdom the road will teach, to all or nearly all who pad.

The big roads, the wide-slash highways, are the chief mark of this our civilization. Thus too were the roads across Europe, and across Britain from Kent to Holyhead, the highwater marks of the Roman Empire.

But that was in the days two thousand years ago when civilized meant living inside the Roman Empire and uncivilized meant everyone else. Times change. But the roads are the same.

The big trackways are the veins of this present way of life, and the stream of that life goes pulsing along them, in the roar and heave of haste. The tide of commerce goes by, rushing and rattling in the chase for speed that is normal now. Fesser Teale goes by too,

at ten miles a day down the Great North Road of England.

He makes few divagations, does not turn aside for many calls. Elderly clergymen, the headmaster at a school or two, a few middle-aged, scholarly people, down along the road day after day, these are the only citizens Fesser comes to meet.

Sometimes his call will be brief, sometimes protracted, and then at the end he is out again on the Great North, owning nothing and going nowhere, padding along to the next elderly clergyman or the next middle-aged student, somewhere down the road.

A man must be schooled, hard schooled, before he will choose thus to be unlike all the world. He will come from a curious mould, one who goes that way padding it, seeing only the screen of the trees as they pass, and the ever-moving surface of the road, timing his thoughts to the beat of his feet as he goes.

Banjo Patterson[1] did two hundred thousand miles in that way, counting his own footfalls all over Australia. But his nickname will tell what his interests were at night, when the day's walking was done. Tramp nicknames always pack a biography.

Oliver Goldsmith walked straight across Europe in that way, and J.M. Synge numbered his own steps for many a hundred miles before he went home to write *Riders to the Sea*. It is a species of hypnotism, the peace-walking, the pad-lulling of the road.

Walking a long road in the green, a man's thoughts take their time from the fall of his feet as he goes. To hurry is almost impossible in a case where the mind is at rest. While conversely the thinking is placid in a man who has no need for haste. To pad and plod, at ease and at random, brings always the quiet and peace we call calm of the mind. Not by folly or chance do the tramps call their progress a padding.

Marseilles 612. Or New York 778. Or London 282. They will be the numbers from yesterday. Or from tomorrow. And they mean nothing, to one who knows to go quietly, nowhere. Ten a day, and there is peace.

In a nutshell it is the difference between the young mug hurrying and the old grey tramp who goes padding it. The minds of the two men take their tune and pitch from the rhythm of the foot beats.

Turmoil and worry and fear, marked and measured by the heel-hammering of frantic haste, are in one mind, as against the other's peace and quiet certainty, the certainty and trust of a child, timed by the effortless plod of the leisurely footfalls.

So there is neither need nor urge for Fesser Teale to count the miles. Marseilles 601, or New York 768, or London 272. They are cyphers. Because Teale's is not a journey to a place but merely a contemplative going along in the green.

Contemplative is the only word. Even if the tramp be uncultured, as most are, he is perforce drawn into contemplation by the quiet untroubled rhythm of his own pad-progress. Lacking all the things life holds for the normal citizen, cut off from the daily interests of civilized men, he comes to know only the road, comes to find it all-sufficing.

Fesser is home, at any moment and every moment, whatever the sign-posts may say. He owns nothing, will have nothing, can hope for nothing. Only he goes, slowly from nowhere and slowly to the same place.

By his very deprivation of the goods life has to offer, he is placed in a field apart, where none of the ordinary hopes and fears of daily existence have any validity. Making ten miles a day, padding it effortlessly, his thoughts divorced from all the thousand urges of urban life, his total mind-energy expends itself in the mere act of being a man.

But a man on a road. A man following a road. At ten miles a day.

The tramp is a hermit who, surprisingly, moves along, and therein lies his interest for normal men. Always, everywhere, the recluse and hermit have a minor fascination for those less eccentric, those fitted to dwell amid the flashes and clashes of normality.

When the recluse is mobile, coming slowly down the road out of far places, padding slowly past towards the horizon, the interest is keener. All the way down the Great North Road, Fesser knows where to find those whose interest in one such as he will be keen. He knows his own marks. For everyone meets his own kind on the road.

So his marks know Fesser too, like him and show keen interest as he comes, slowly down out of distant nowhere and bound away for nowhere after his call. Padding that road he is an answer to many questions.

Above all, the moving milestone is an answer to that age-old query — what do men want from life? In the main, and for most, the answers to that question are brief and simple.

Men want money with which to buy for their daily needs. They want a love-life and companionship. They require a few pleasures and the admiration of a circle of friends.

Wealth and fame and the love of the opposite sex, as the psychologists say, are the mainsprings of human conduct. One of those motives is at the centre of every normal story. Every one.

To attain those things, in greater or less degree, is life. To lose or to miss them is misery and deprivation, for the vast majority of the world's people.

But the vagrant has lost and missed them in the beginning, in the days before he was a vagrant. From all the normal pulls of daily life he is immune, and the mainsprings of human conduct do not move him along his road.

What then has Fesser Teale, to move him his ten miles? Fesser will serve as the type for a thousand tramps. What has he?

For wealth he has nothing and can have nothing. So that in time he accepts an existence where wealth is not. Where by corollary the need for worry and haste, in the pursuit of money, is not either.

A coin or two for his paddincan,[2] a few cigarettes and a screw of coffee or tea — the citizen will throw a few crumbs to a robin in wintertime. The elderly clergyman or the grey-haired scholar will hand a coin to the man who pads across from horizon to horizon. There is nothing more, nor any need for more, in Fesser Teale's life.

Wealth, the psychiatrist's first mainspring, does not operate on a padding down the Great North Road.

Fame in the world, or even companionship in a circle of friends, the tramp has not either, in the ordinary way. Talk of the roads in a paddincan at night, or the shoulder-to-shoulder staring at the embers in a hearth, or the gossip of the littledrum by a fireside on the road, these are social intercourse, for the vagrant.

They are all he knows and all he can have; in time these too are accepted. The second mainspring does not work either, on the road.

In the absence of family life, of matehood, the foot-padder stands out still more clearly as different. The psychologist's third mainspring and motive, the love of women, comes hardly at all in the life of the men on the roads. It is perhaps the hallmark of the vagabond, chief evidence of his eccentricity and his deprivation, this fact that as a rule he goes solitary.

Some few, especially among the chiefs of the road, do now and then attain to the companionship of a woman like themselves. But on the roads in the United States there are four men to each woman tramp, and in England there are three. So that for the majority of the vagrants there are no women either. Especially for the postmen, who range wide and speedily, there are seldom any companions.

But the first law of life seems to be compensation. Where the world, or the intertangled forces of the universe, or the aggregate of pulls we call circumstance, deprive a living creature of some one thing, then the life force within that creature finds speedily a substitute or compensation.

If it were not true it might appear sacrilegious to say that for almost everything, for the loss of everything, the road itself can compensate Fesser Teale. That is all he has, or nearly.

Thirty-six million people die in the world every year, thirty-six millions are born. Every twenty-four hours a hundred thousand human babies come to life, begin their little circling, move in their world. Each moves to grasp, in its own time and fashion, at wealth and fame and matehood. But some grasp nothing, like Fesser.

Look at him coming down that Great North Road. London 262. Yesterday it was 272. Tomorrow it will be 252. He has covered ten miles. And he has done nothing else.

A hundred thousand children have been born since last night. Ten million machines have rumbled and flashed, making the goods of the world. A myriad pounds and dollars have changed hands.

All the thousand-odd million humans who make up our world have clutched and fought, have hoped and striven, have dreamed or struggled for wealth and fame and the love of others, during the twenty-four hours. Fesser Teale has contemplated life and has covered ten miles of the Great North Road.

Christian philosophers, and philosophers before our time, used to preach abnegation, belauded the demanding of nothing, praised contentment and self-sufficiency. But none such would count the Fesser Teales as worthy. It is only the ordinary citizen, knowing the rush and tear of the cities, who looks with sympathy on the moving hermit, on the man from the roads who has and can have nothing.

Two hundred and sixty-two miles is but a short journey, in train or car. Five hours, sometimes considerably less, will suffice for such a trip. The tramp will be twenty-six days or more on that same road. Wherefore he comes to know two things well, even if he be uncultured, as most tramps are.

He will know that road. And he will know himself. This is his compensation for all the things he has lost. It is a great compensation. And fair, strictly fair. For every man meets himself and his own kind on the road.

All the tramps come to know that law, sooner or later. Some have it taught to them, as Lumpy Fox taught me in Kells,[3] at the very beginning of their life on the roads. Some refuse to accept such a ruling, at first, and only learn after long. But all learn.

Often the nicknames bestowed in the paddincans will emphasize the fact, tell the man's history and personality in a word or two. Every tramp nickname is a packed biography. Even where a man carries only the name of a place for his moniker,[4] generally that in itself is interesting or significant.

Thus fully one-third of the nicknames or monikers are merely names of towns. Brackley Tim — there is no need for more. It is a man named Tim who may be found in Brackley. Even if one did not know he was a shuttler around that district one could almost guess. Texas Red, Towcester Dick, Stornoway Slim, a hundred thousand others, have place-names telling a story in small.

The aristocrats used to do likewise, in France and elsewhere, when a man called himself Henry of Valois or Leon da Silva!

Naturally a large number of the monikers deal with some physical peculiarity. Fatty Culver would have been so called if he had been a boy at an expensive school instead of a tramp in a paddincan.

Pegleg, Deadlight, Stumpy, Lumpy, Two-ton, Whitehead, Blackie, Red, Ginger, Snively, Wingy, One-wing, all speak for themselves. The name Slim applies to all thin men, but there is humorous emphasis in calling an extra slim tramp Split-the-wind.

All the other monikers are psychological. As a rule they are exactly descriptive of the man *as he is and not as he might seem*. Or else they describe some technical trick of his own or some personal habit. All of them are vastly shrewd.

The point is that for every type of person found in the cities a corresponding type will be found on the roads. In miniature, and diminuendo, so to speak, but the same type.

Mr John D. Rockefeller and many another, from Wall Street or the Bourse of Paris or the opulent centres of London, have shown the lengths to which the love of money, the pursuit of coins, can move a man when that mainspring alone is operative. One would not look for the type on the roads.

But every man meets his own and they are all there. Only the tramps are sharper, or less conventional, or less afraid, when it comes to naming one such. The equivalent of the million-miser is not unknown in the paddincans. And he is aptly named as a rule, after his chief love and main interest. Has not the reader met Deener Thomas at Weedon? And deener means shilling.

Often I wonder what the city people would have called those like John D. — if apt monikers were allowed in the cities.

Fumbler Kingsley was a refined and cultured tramp, now dead, who did *not* fumble or drop things. He had what a psychiatrist might call a marked inferiority complex, was quite certain to make a mess of any interview, however promising. The softest of soft marks on the road was turned into a grim, unapproachable dragon by the luckless Kingsley's awkwardness of approach. So — his life story, his personal history, in a single word. Fumbler Kingsley.

(Poor Fumbler! Right to the end, to the very end, he was a walking jest, a miracle of incompetence and ineptitude. Of all places in the world he chose to die, lying across the door so that it could not be opened, in a ladies' lavatory.)

It is quite common for a tramp to be called Sham Harry or Sham Simon, and the moniker does not by any means impugn his veracity. There is a complacent haughtiness, a placid self-satisfaction, in enormous numbers of the business men in any city. Mr Gordon Harker can play such a character to perfection. Generally the characteristics are accepted as evidence of the city man's sterling worth. But the tramps have to be keen-sighted, must needs be able to see below a man's skins. So — Sham Harry.

In the same way a vagrant may be called Colonel Bob or Flunkey Phil, although he has never been a soldier or a manservant. But in each case the moniker will be a neat psychological summing-up. Ammo, for instance, is the Spanish-gipsy word for chief.

My own nickname will have elucidated itself already. The word dollcie signifies showy, expensive, opulent. Now, I have never worn expensive clothes, nor jewellry of any kind. Neither have I ever possessed any property whatever, except a typewriter.

But of course I wanted to own all the world, and that was why I came to the road. Lumpy Fox knew, although we had only that day met for the first time, when he labelled me Dollcie Jem.

Again fairly common, and always amusing, are the monikers drawn from the (imagined) childhood of a particular vagrant. The idea is that such and such a man *must* have been such and such a child, is still that kind of person at bottom. Titty Grew, Nappie Nelson, Whiner Warwick, Bigbottle Ferguson, Suckatit, Yowler Dagges, Mamsie Pringle and above all Dadada, tell their own stories.

The remaining monikers all carry some tale of how the tramp approaches his marks. Again these are as a rule beautifully shrewd and economical to the last degree. It would need two hundred words to interpret the full meaning of the things the paddincan people will often put into a single sound.

Triangle Ted was, briefly, a make-up artist who might have made a fortune as an actor. He discovered the simple truth that he cut a most abject and humiliating figure, became an object of quick sympathy and swift charity, if he had an ugly and embarrassing triangular tear in his trousers.

So that Triangle might be seen, any night in a paddincan, carefully and skilfully marking and measuring the tears in his trousers, for the next day's meeting. Thus it goes.

Tommy Cosgrove is called Dicky Tom in the paddincans, and at first it might seem that one of his names was Richard. The reference is different, however.

Waiters and such people, who find it necessary in the way of trade to have always a clean shirt-front, often make use of a white dicky, which is a loose front that can be slipped on at a moment's notice. Anyone glancing at Cosgrove, or at a photograph of him, will note at once the clean whiteness below his beard.

The passer-by will mentally remark on the fact that the tramp is a clean and particular old fellow, trying to keep himself presentable on the road. Then a second later he will notice that the poor old man is *not* wearing a clean, white shirt-front as at first appeared. That in fact he has no shirt, and the 'dicky' is his naked chest. And then — Well, Dicky Tom's technique is generally justified. The moniker certainly is.

Thus it comes on the road. A man will be driven into self-knowledge, partly by the calm thinking that will come to one going quietly among green things. But partly also by the swift mind-searching of his fellows, their summing up of character in the word or two words of a nickname.

Fesser Teale knows himself, and can go calmly, can be certain the boys have named him aright. It would be folly, and this book would have been written thus far in vain, if the reader were to take Fesser, coming down the Great North, for a guileless and ineffectual nonentity. Of course he is not that. For such a one would die on the road. He would not make out. And he would not be called Fesser.

Every man meets his own, and Teale meets his. Elderly clergyman, middle-aged scholarly person, comfortable rural resident of intellectual pursuits, these are Fesser's marks and he approaches no others.

Mathematics he will talk, and he knows at least the names of the scholars and authors. Chess he will talk, and he knows the names and records of chess-players all over the world. More, since middle-aged scholar and elderly clergyman often play chess, then Fesser can play too, and well.

Final small touch — does not he carry a pocket chessboard, on which he will play if his temporary host be inclined. Then the white-bearded man, a scholar now and not a tramp, will beam and jubilate, in the glow of intellectual companionship, before he leaves with a coin to continue his ten a day.

He will be like the genial abstracted professor of fiction, going down that road, and at the stops with all his marks. And he will make out, whether he is on

Federal Highway 59 or the road to Marseilles or the Great North of England.

Of course he may really have been a professor of mathematics before he came down the Great North Road for the first time. But it matters nothing. Since he has found himself at last, and is a grave, reserved, recluse bachelor scholar *now*, whatever he was before.

The road will always find out what a man really wants to be, even if he does not at first know it himself. The tramps find out too, and Teale's moniker is only a paddincan way of saying professor. The tramps find out, from the road.

1   Banjo Patterson: Andrew Barton Patterson (1867–1941), author of nine volumes of verse, including some of the best Australian bush ballads, was educated in Sydney and trained for the law but spent most of his life in the newspaper industry, acquiring several county newspapers in Victoria.
2   paddincan: A lodging-house for tramps and vagrants who spend their days padding it.
3   Kells: In County Meath.
4   moniker: A tramp's name or signature. Uncertain derivation, in use in the underworld since 1859, sometimes spelt monniker, or monaker.

COLM Ó LOCHLAINN
from *The Irish Book Lover*, October 1949

A salutary reminder of the problems facing the Irish book trade at mid-century, and worth comparing with the present situation. Colm O Lochlainn made a significant contribution to the Irish book with the establishment of his publishing house, At the Sign of the Three Candles.

The Worm Turneth

Under the caption 'Pity the Publisher?' *The Listener* of 9 December, 1948 had some pertinent comments to make on the publishing business in England and America. Here are some of them: 'Within the last year or so publishers have become aware that the bottom has dropped out of publishing economics . . . it is unfortunately true that the public resistance to higher book prices is extremely stubborn . . . Publishing costs are undoubtedly very high and may not have been met by the higher prices of books. Publishers' money has to be locked up for a long time . . . Sometimes the wisest way to feed and to feast must be to encourage striving and youthful authors. They too deserve a little of our pity.'

To a large extent — allowing of course for the smaller editions an Irish publisher can risk (with the corresponding increase in production costs per copy), and the much smaller buying public he caters for — these comments apply to Ireland also. The book trade in Ireland is eighty per cent a distributing medium for English productions, and though the Irish market absorbs less than ten per cent of an English publisher's issue, the Irish bookseller enjoys the same trade terms as his English brother. No Irish publisher, without

fixing a selling price prohibitively high in comparison with the English product, can afford to give similar terms. For every thousand he can risk printing the English publisher can do five, to serve a well-organized world market.

Now the booksellers, who have built substantial business on the belief that publishers' profits never fail, are beginning to see that this belief is rapidly becoming a myth; but in spite of this realization the booksellers are taking a strong stand about the manner in which the risks and rewards of the book trade are to be shared.

Theoretically the production cost of a book is a third of the selling price and is borne by the publisher; the two-thirds remaining are divided between the publisher and bookseller — the bookseller demanding a full third, that is fifty per cent gross profit on his outlay. As he may buy the book in single copies, his financial risk is small. The publisher, out of his third, has to pay the author and advertise the book; hold and insure stock; pay for book-keeping, packing and carriage; and he cannot produce his book in small lots as needed, but only in large quantities at heavy financial risk.

The position, therefore, before the war, was that the man who made the book — the writer — received least of all, having to rest satisfied with ten per cent; the publisher who financed the book, came next, and stood to lose heavily unless the book sold well; the bookseller, who took no risk whatever, gained most — and this, whether he sold one or a hundred copies of the book. The fact that the bookseller has to pay for his shop and assistants is balanced by the publisher's office and perhaps smaller but more highly-paid staff.

Thus matters stood before the war; and thus they stand today. Yet the cost of book-production has soared in the interval. How is the increase being neutralized?

You, the fair-minded book-lover, might imagine that the astute bookseller, thinking of the well-being of the trade and his own livelihood, has turned to the publisher and said: Mac, I'll help you out — I'll accept a smaller discount!

The bookseller has turned all right, but not to the publisher; he has turned on you, the book-buyer; he makes no plea or request; he watches in silence while you hand him four half-crowns where formerly you handed three.

What is going to happen? The book-lover's inclination to buy will gradually diminish under the barrage of high prices. The author, who has to live, will turn to the well-paid fields of radio and cinema; publishers who still have money will invest it elsewhere; the bookseller will simply shorten his book-shelves and extend his stationery counter.

This might be avoided if the reader bought, as he is entitled to buy, direct from the publisher; and if the publisher decided, as he may, that the reader is, in his way, his best advertising-medium (often a miniature lending library!) and therefore entitled to some discount.

The foregoing outline may seem to be a caricature; the sober truth is that it would pay an author these days to limit his literary output to that excellently paid medium, the strip cartoon.

TOM BARRY
from Tom Barry, *Guerilla Days in Ireland* (1949)

Tom Barry (1897–1980) led the West Cork Flying Column during the War of Independence (1919–21). In *Guerilla Days in Ireland* he provides an unsentimental account of one of the first guerilla campaigns in the twentieth century against a colonial power. In this chapter entitled 'Counter-Terror' he underlines the part played by military action in a war of words. Also of interest in his account is the issue of how much violence is needed in a national liberation struggle to achieve a political objective.

Counter-Terror

While the men of the Brigade Flying Column, in conjunction with the local Companies, were pursuing, in early May, harassing tactics against the British, three more volunteers were to die for the Ireland they loved so well. On May 9, the enemy were carrying out one of their large-scale sweeps from several garrisons, when Captain Frank Hurley, of Laragh, was trapped alone in his own district by the Essex Regiment. Recognizing him they marched him towards Bandon, but Frank was never to reach that town again, for true to form the Essex butchered him on the roadside about a mile and a half from their barrack. Frank, a veteran volunteer, Captain of the Laragh Company, was a fine soldier and comrade, and had fought conspicuously with the Brigade Flying Column in many of its engagements. On that same day another Company of the Essex Regiment operating near Newcestown, a few miles from Laragh, fired on Volunteer Geoffrey Canty of Scrahane, as he sought to escape their net. Wounding him, they brought him down. There was no witness as to what happened after the Essex came up to their victim, but when local civilians came on the scene after the departure of the British, they found the dead body of the young patriot, who, not being armed, never had a fighting chance to escape. Two days later on May 11, the same Battalion of the Essex operating further to the south at Cloundreen, Kilbrittain, fired on Lieutenant Con Murphy, of Clashfluck, Timoleague. In this instance the Essex were not able to indulge their sadistic tastes for their first volleys ended the life of a good Flying Column soldier and a first-class Company officer.

The merciless murders of those men would have called for immediate counter-action, but we knew, since April 29, that the Divisional 'shoot up' of the British scheduled for May 14 was almost due. General Strickland, Cork, the British G.O.C. of the Martial Law area, had chosen to ignore the written warnings that if the executions of the I.R.A. men planned for April 28 were carried out I.R.A. counter-action would be taken against his forces. The Press of April 29 stated that British firing squads had executed in Cork on the previous day Maurice Moore, Ticknock, Cobh, Co. Cork; Thomas Mulcahy, The Island, Burnfoot, Mallow, Co. Cork; Paddy O'Sullivan, Thomas Street, Cobh, Co. Cork; and Patrick Ronayne, Burnfoot, Mallow, Co. Cork.

Already, after similar farcical courtmartials, they had executed on February 1 Con Murphy, Ballydavid, Millstreet, Co. Cork, and on February 28 six others, Sean Allen, Tipperary; John Lyons, Aghabullogue, Co. Cork; Timothy McCarthy, Fornaught, Donoughmore, Co. Cork; Thomas O'Brien, Dripsey, Co. Cork; Daniel O'Callaghan, Dripsey, Co. Cork; Patrick O'Mahony, Derry, Donoughmore, Co. Cork. And on May 4 the enemy was to drive home his contempt for our declaration of counter-action by executing in Cork another patriot, Patrick Casey, Caherally, Grange, Co. Limerick.

None of those executed men was from West Cork, and none of our volunteers was ever to be judicially executed, since the British officers in our Brigade area invariably acted as judge, jury and executioner, without bothering about the formality of a trial for suspected I.R.A. men. Yet the executions of those Irish soldiers stirred us all deeply, and although the British prisons where those men had been confined were in Cork 1 area, all other Brigades in the South were greatly concerned as to the possibility of the rescue of those doomed to death. We knew that Cork 1 had been untiring in their efforts, but we also knew that since they had rescued Donncadh Mac Neilus, a prisoner awaiting execution, from Cork Jail on November 11, 1918, the British defences of their prisons had been made well-nigh impregnable. In April, I had discussed the defences of Cork prisons with a very good friend of the I.R.A. who had the entrée to them. He was Reverend T.F. Duggan (now Very Reverend Canon Duggan, President, St Finbarr's Seminary, Farranferris, Cork), and he was prepared to take any risk to save the lives of the Irish soldiers condemned to die. Father Duggan had been a Military Chaplain in World War I and had a good grasp of technical military matters. Not being suspected by the British of I.R.A. sympathies he had many opportunities of making a study of the jail defences, and his information only confirmed the view of Cork

1 Brigade of the impossibility of rescuing the prisoners, although Father Duggan personally thought it could be effected.

The West Cork arrangements for the attack on the British on May 14 were completed in good time. At 3 p.m. on Saturday, May 14, every one of the ten garrisons in the area was to be attacked. All the arms were to be at the disposal of the hundred and twelve officers and men detailed for the attacks over an area extending about eighty miles, from Innishannon to Castletownbere. Precisely at the appointed hour the following assaults took place, and the casualties given here are those as issued by the British themselves and published in the daily Press on May 16 and 17. In this listing it will be noted that some British units gave the names of their casualties whilst others gave only the numbers, and it must be remembered also that the I.R.A. attacking parties claimed to have inflicted many more casualties than those admitted by the British.

When approaching Castletownbere, a quarter of a mile from the town, Battalion O.C. Liam O'Dwyer, Peter O'Neill and Christy O'Connell, with other riflemen, had a skirmish with an enemy patrol. The British retired into the town, but as the remainder of the garrison were then on the alert owing to the exchange of fire, the I.R.A. party could not close with them. No British casualties were announced. Three miles away, at Furious Pier, Rossmacowen, another I.R.A. party of riflemen under Michael Og O'Sullivan attacked a party of the K.O.S.B. Regiment. The British in this instance announced that four of their troops were killed and two wounded. The Press gave the names of the dead as Privates Hunter, McCullen, Chalmers and Edwards; the names of the wounded were not given. As Battalion Commandant Tom Ward's riflemen were proceeding towards the town of Bantry, they were observed by eight Black and Tan riflemen who opened fire and then retired rapidly to their barrack. Ward's men exchanged the fire and pursued the Black and Tans, but the British did not announce any casualties. Near Skibbereen, Battalion Commandant Con Connolly's men shot dead a Constable McLean and seriously wounded Constable Cooper of the Black and Tans. At Drimoleague, Company Captain Daniel O'Driscoll's men attacked Black and Tans close to their barrack, but no British casualties were announced. Liam Deasy was to have taken charge of the Dunmanway attack, but had been injured ten days previously and was unable to do so. Instead Ted O'Sullivan was brought up and he, with Paddy O'Brien, Girlough, converged with two sections of riflemen on the Square of Dunmanway to attack a lorry of enemy reported to have been at the

Square on the several preceding Saturday afternoons. Finding no enemy at the Square, the I.R.A. proceeded towards the Black and Tan barrack, but on the way there was an exchange of shots with two Black and Tans, who gained cover in a nearby house. No British casualties were announced. A party of riflemen under Battalion Commandant Jim Hurley and Vice-Commandant Tim O'Donoghue entered the town of Clonakilty and searched the streets and public-houses for enemy forces. Failing to find any they moved on to the Black and Tan barrack at MacCurtain Hill, where they exchanged fire with the Black and Tans, but failed to draw them or the British soldiers from their fortresses. Hurley's men remained for over an hour in the town before withdrawing. No British casualties were announced. At Kilbrittain, Company Captain Jackie O'Neill's riflemen fired at Black and Tans. The British announced two Black and Tans wounded. At Innishannon, Battalion Adjutant Jim O'Mahony, Captain Jack Corkery and two other riflemen shot dead a Black and Tan named Kenna a few hundred yards from his barrack door.

As I did not participate in any of the foregoing I cannot give further particulars, but as I commanded the Bandon assault on that afternoon, I can give a more detailed account of it. Bandon, the military and Black and Tan Headquarters of West Cork, had a garrison of over three times the strength of that situated in any other West Cork town. Because of the zeal of their officers and the many attacks on it, this garrison was expected to be the most alert and ready. The enemy precautions against attack were so elaborate that it would be difficult to get within shooting distance of the barrack in day-time without being observed. This made it necessary to approach Bandon by the least expected route of attack, and in such a manner as to enable us to close rapidly to within shooting range before they took up defensive positions. These circumstances indicated that the attacking party should travel to the town by motor and on a main road.

A month previously an old Ford motor car had been taken from the Essex Regiment and hidden in a field under a haystack. On May 11, it was taken from its hiding place, its hood stripped off and its windscreen removed. Six outstanding West Cork Volunteer Officers, Mick Crowley, John Lordan, Sean Lehane, Tom Kelleher, Peter Kearney and Billy O'Sullivan had been selected for the Bandon assault. Lehane was to act as driver of the car and Billy O'Sullivan to use the Lewis machine gun. The others were armed with rifles and automatics and we had also two Mills bombs. For two days before the attack,

Lehane practised driving to orders, cruise, slow, fast, turn, ditch her left or ditch her right. On the last order Sean would rush the Ford close up and parallel to the ditch indicated and halt with jammed brakes, when we would all tumble over the ditch, so gaining cover. This was our only hope should we meet enemy armoured cars on the road or in Bandon.

At noon on the 14th we arrived at Anna Hurley's of Laragh. This lady, the leader of the Cumann na mBan[1] of the Bandon district, was a sister of Frank Hurley, who had been murdered by the Essex Regiment during the previous week. She was asked to leave immediately for Bandon and to remain there until two o'clock to observe the movements of the murderers of her brother. In particular, she was to note if the enemy were strengthening any of their defences and to report back at 2.30 p.m. When Anna returned punctually she reported in detail various enemy troop movements and that the Black and Tans were very busy adding to the sandbag defences outside their barrack at the Devonshire Arms. This last news was most unwelcome, as it could be considered as indicative of the awareness of the enemy of a coming attack. Since the meeting on April 24, when those attacks were agreed on, it must have worried many that fourteen Brigade Staffs and their subordinate officers had foreknowledge of the assaults. There was always a distinct possibility that one out of the hundreds who were aware of the date and time of attack would be captured and under torture, inform. Or it could happen that some irresponsible Volunteer would mention that matter in the presence of an enemy agent. General Strickland and his officers knew the attacks were coming, because he had been officially informed that if the executions took place the I.R.A. would take counter-action against his forces but if the enemy knew of the date and time, disaster would overtake the I.R.A. in the South, as all our attacking parties would be mown down by a waiting, properly disposed enemy. On that Saturday I was of the opinion that the British knew of our coming that day, but the Bandon assault had to be attempted.

Informing the others of my suspicion that the enemy had some inkling of the proposed attack, and that it would not be wise or justifiable to risk all seven officers cramped in a small car, I asked for two to volunteer to stay behind. There was a stony silence and none of those men would drop out. Eventually an order had to be issued that the two heftiest were not to travel as they would cramp the movements of the others as well as present the easiest targets. These two were John Lordan and Tom Kelleher, but as we moved off they made a final appeal to be permitted to travel to within half a mile of Bandon, when they would go into the fields and take their chance at finding a target. The assault party in the Ford car hit the Dunmanway-Cork main road about two miles west of Bandon. Three-quarters of a mile from Bandon we halted to drop John Lordan and Tom Kelleher to scramble over the northern ditch of the road and set off across the fields for the town. Lehane drove on at about fifteen miles an hour. Billy O'Sullivan's Lewis gun rested where the hood had formerly been and he was flanked by Mick Crowley and Peter Kearney with their loaded rifles at the ready. In order that I could see better over the ditches and so detect any lurking British, I sat up on the back rest of the front seat with my feet on the cushion on which Lehane sat. A quarter of a mile from the Military barracks we spied an armed sentry at the turn of the road fifty yards ahead. He was standing up on the roadside ditch looking towards us, with his rifle and bayonet fixed at the 'at ease' position. He was as unexpected as he was unwelcome but I had time to whisper to drive on at the same speed and to take no notice. I do not know who the sentry thought we were, but immediately he saw us he jerked his rifle to the 'On Guard', then as we came to within twenty yards of him he must have accepted us as either Auxiliaries or Black and Tans as I was wearing an I.R.A. officer's tunic, and the others trench-coats, and all of us equipment. To my great relief as we came on to him he brought his rifle to the 'Slope' and as we passed he saluted smartly. I returned his salute casually and we passed on.

Our plan of attack was to drive slowly between the Essex military barracks and the Black and Tan barrack which stood about sixty yards across an open space from it. At a signal, fire was to be opened on anything in the uniform of the British armed forces standing around the two barracks. The car party was then to drive down North Main Street, across the Bridge, up South Main Street, firing at any enemy in sight. It was to retreat out the Kilbrittain road, where a mile from the town men of the Bandon Company were waiting to draw spiked harrows across the road, as soon as the Ford passed, to delay any armoured car in pursuit. Two hundred yards after passing the unexpected sentry, all this had to be changed, as within a few hundred yards of the military barracks we saw about one hundred of the Essex and a sprinkling of the Black and Tans in a field south of the road. Armed groups of troops in steel helmets stood about, with full equipment, leaning on their rifles, talking and laughing, as some others, unarmed, kicked a football around. Lehane got the order 'Slow', and as we came abreast of the enemy, 'Stop'. Sean obeyed like an

automation, and then: 'Pick out the armed gangs first. Let them have it.' The machine-gun captured at Crossbarry spluttered a drum full of ammunition at its former owners, the rifles cracked a half dozen times, and the surprised enemy let out a few yells as some dived for cover and others flattened out on the ground. As the rifles were being reloaded, Sean got the order: 'Forward and turn her.' He shot the Ford forward some distance and turned it in view of the barracks, at the windows of which some volleys were fired in an effort to delay pursuit. The car raced back past the place where we had opened fire, and out beyond the point where the sentry had been standing, but who had now vanished completely. When we had turned off the main road to the comparative safety of the by-road, Lehane broke the silence which, except for the issuing of orders, had remained unbroken since we had dropped Lordan and Kelleher. In his fine voice he started to sing:

> *We will pay them back woe for woe,*
> *Give them back blow for blow,*
> *Out and make way for the bold Fenian Men.*

Four miles from Bandon we sprinkled a tin of petrol over our reliable Ford and soon it was a blazing mass. This was necessary as it would have meant certain death for the man on whose property it might be found. Then we set out across country for Newcestown.

The British officially announced that we had killed an Essex soldier, and wounded several, including a Black and Tan. Later we were to hear that several meant seven. We thought we had hit more than eight of them, but even accepting their figures we were satisfied that we had once again shaken them up badly. The fact that five I.R.A. men could close with them in their strongest garrisoned town at three o'clock on a May day and retire unharmed, must apart from the casualties inflicted, have had a detrimental effect on the enemy morale. The reply of the British was a poor show, but judging by the report in the *Cork Examiner* on May 16 they must have become very warlike after our departure, as it stated 'the terrific machine-gun and rifle fire, lasting for over half an hour, which broke out in Bandon on Saturday afternoon, was in the general opinion an attack on the military barracks'. There was little shooting by the enemy during our attack, but apparently they must have fired wildly for over half an hour after we had retired. It was in this firing that the enemy wounded the two civilians, as most certainly there was no civilian with the unit we attacked. The manner in which Crowley, Kearney, O'Sullivan and Lehane adapted themselves, without warning, to the changed plans, and the exemplary discipline, coolness and courage were beyond praise. Sean Lehane has since died, but this fine fellow will long be remembered by those who knew him. Commandant of the Schull Battalion, a fine fighter and a grand soldier, Sean was a merry comrade with the drollest of sayings. His ready wit and fine singing voice relieved the gloom and eased the tension of many of us when the world appeared a most dreary and difficult place.

The results from other Brigades were keenly awaited as it was felt they would give a fairly good indication of the state of the organization over two Divisional areas. It must be recorded that they were in general disappointing. In his book, *On Another Man's Wound*,[2] Ernest O'Malley complained that although orders were issued nothing was done in the Second Southern Divisional area. No casualties were caused to the British and, as far as was known, no skirmishes took place in the whole of County Waterford, North Cork, West Kerry or South Kerry Brigades. The West Limerick Unit killed a Constable Bridges and wounded another Black and Tan at Drumcollogher. Kerry 1 inflicted the only casualty in the county by killing Head Constable Benson at Tralee. Cork 1 Brigade did very well. The City Battalions shot up many of the enemy posts and succeeded in killing Constables Creighton and Ryle and wounding Constables Hayes and Brackwell in Cork city. That good band of East Cork fighters killed Sergeant Coleman, Constable Comyn and Constable Thomas, wounding Constable McDonald, all of them Black and Tans, and killed one Royal Horse Artillery Gunner at East Ferry. There may have been good reasons for the failures of some of those units to effect casualties. Because events crowded in on us for the concluding six or seven weeks of the fight with the British,[3] there were more important things to attend to than to inquire from the Brigades which had failed, and as far as I know nothing was done after the Truce to clarify matters. It should be remembered, in fairness to those units, that some may not have received their orders or on that day may have been forestalled by heavy enemy offensive activity or may, indeed, have failed to contact enemy targets. One such unit was the North Cork Brigade. We had been greatly surprised that there were no reports of attacks in Liam Lynch's old area. Afterwards we learned that there was good reason for this. On the morning of May 10, extraordinary enemy activity commenced in North Cork and this was to continue for six days, during which time the North Cork I.R.A. were so hard pressed that the attacks could not be undertaken. I had a personal reason for remembering the commencement of this enemy offensive in North Cork. On the morning of May 10, two cousins of mine, Paddy O'Brien, the Column Leader in that area, and his brother, Dan, of Knockarbane, Liscarroll, and John O'Regan, Liscarroll, were surrounded by British troops at O'Donnell's, Aughrim, Liscarroll. By some miracle, Paddy, who was the most wanted man by the British in North Cork, fought his way through to safety, and it was only two hours later he learned that John O'Regan was dangerously wounded and that Dan had been captured trying to help John. Dan stood before a drumhead courtmartial on the morning of the 14th, and faced the enemy firing squad on May 16, the last of the patriot soldiers to be judicially executed in Cork by the British.

The total casualties inflicted by the West Cork Brigade were considered, in all the circumstances, as very satisfactory. The British had paid for their official and unofficial executions. The question arises as to what effect they, together with those inflicted in Cork 1, Kerry 1 and West Limerick Brigades, had on the British policy of executions. Except for the usual British Imperialist yells of 'Outrage', no official comment was made by them as to their future behaviour, but it is significant that no other I.R.A. man was executed in Cork after May 14, except Dan O'Brien already sentenced to death before our counter-attacks took place.

1   Literally, Company of Women. A female force founded in 1914 by Constance Markievicz to assist the Irish Volunteers.
2   First published in 1936. In March 1921 Ernest O'Malley (1898–1957) was appointed Commander of the Second Southern Division of the IRA.
3   The Truce was agreed on 11 July 1921.

SEAN O'CASEY
from Sean O'Casey, *Inishfallen, Fare Thee Well* (1949)

O'Casey's brilliant satirical passage from the opening of the fourth volume of his *Autobiographies* on the pretensions of Easter 1916 (including Yeats's poem).

High Road and Low Road

Things had changed, but not utterly; and no terrible beauty was to be born. Short Mass[1] was still the favourite service, and Brian Boru's[2] harp still bloomed on the bottles of beer. But the boys were home again from prison camp and prison cell. First the venial sinners from Frongoch; then the mortal sinners from Wakefield, Reading, Dartmoor, and other jails. They've had their lesson, thought the sophisticated British Authorities, and from this out they will be pure and prim. The convicts, warned by the spitting and hissing of their departure to their prisons, hoped they'd steal quietly through the city to fireside and bed; but the people had changed utterly, and thronged their streets to cheer them. The wail of the Irish ochone had changed into the roar of the Irish hurrah. Again, the felon's cap had become the noblest crown an Irish head could wear. Nothing could be too good for the boys. When one spoke, all had to remain silent. They led at all meetings, dominated committees, won at cards, got everything anyone had to give, and were everywhere forced to lay down the law on all philosophy, patriotism, foresight, prophecy, and good manners. Was he out in Easter Week? became the touchstone of Irish life. And it was those who hadn't been out themselves who roared silence at anyone venturing to send a remark into a conversation led by a lad home from a prison or a concentration camp; for the lads, themselves, were exceedingly modest about it all, and were often embarrassed by their hangers-on, who forgot that most of Dublin, willy-nilly, was out in Easter Week; that there weren't many Dublin houses without bullet-holes in them; and that casualties were heavier among those who weren't out than among those who were. So for a long time, Easter Week became the Year of One in Irish history and Irish life.

1   As opposed to High Mass or Sung Mass, which might last an hour as opposed to thirty minutes for Low Mass.
2   King of Ireland whose forces defeated the Leinstermen and the Norse at the Battle of Clontarf in 1014, even though he was killed in the same encounter.

IMAGINATIVE

EWART MILNE
from Ewart Milne, *Letter From Ireland* (1940)

Ewart Milne (1903–87) was born and educated in Dublin. He rebelled against his Anglo-Irish background and went to fight in the Spanish Civil War to be with his friend Charles Donnelly. By the time he arrived in Spain Donnelly had been killed in action and Milne returned first to London and then to Dublin. He contributed to *Ireland Today* (1936–38) and began a writing career that issued in fourteen volumes of verse. 'Thinking of Artolas', written in a thirties style which owes something to MacNeice but which consciously refuses a 'synthesis', is a meditation on the deaths of Donnelly and a German Jewish soldier called Izzy Kupchick. In 'Letter From Ireland' Milne provides an engaging reflection on Ireland's neutrality at the beginning of the Second World War and on his decision to stay in an Ireland he describes as 'calm as a storm centre'.

Thinking of Artolas[1]

Sirs and Senoras, let me tell you a story.
A story neither of long ago nor faraway
But close enough now and to you unhappily.
We will call it Going-Into-History
And you all know History is a cruel country
Where tiger terraces crouch drinking rivers waterless
And sheep immobilized by sombrero shepherds'
     piping . . .
It could be set in Estremadura or Cordova,[2]
Time crawling like inches and napoleonic wars
Dogeared in textbooks seeming the latest in
     strategy —
At least until recently. Or as Shaw[3] might have said
The life force gets going but man has his lag . . .
True. And to gain on his lag must man lose his leg,
And truncate himself, as in Estremadura?

Well, at Casada's[4] we ate ortolans[5] elsewhere we drank
     coffee.
In the Gran Via in the Colon we went into conference.
All day the starlings on the Ramblas whispered,
All day the dead air pacified the street,
Fat pigeons swaggered on the Plaza Catalunya.
It was easy enough to analyse an ortolan,[5]
Conjure pigeon into pie: translate con leche[6] . . .

But the starlings worried me, and their whispering,
I could never understand their whispering.
It weaved breathlessly up and up like the Coulin[7] —
Or like that dissonance outsoaring ecstasy, heard
Near any roadside or beside any bed, disrupting the
Lovers enlaced, singing with no sound and saying
'O the world is bright and empty'.

At Madrid we dined with the newspaper bunch.
So-and-so shouted they all called him a Fascist —
There *had* been whispers — but he didn't care
He shouted for Empire. That was all right
Empire shouted for him — one supposes, somewhere.
All day I was a method of analysis . . . Did my heart,
     Tomas,
Or your depthless eyes tell me analysis was cowardly
While Los Madrilenos[8] were barricading their old
     Madrid out?
. . . All day So-and-so the Fascist was blustering.
I analysed his quality as extreme
Scatology and efficiency walking backwards, with a
     shrug . . .
But sadly I knew the whispering starlings
Wintering would rise from the Plaza Catalunya
Before I returned.

With Jarama[9] held they brought him in, the tankist.
From his Georgian hair the blood smiled through,
And smiled on the paving and from the verandah
Smiled as it dripped and adventured below . . .
In parks they dream of penny murder non-
     intervention —
He took the hammered blow and said Salud —
All day my heart with love was helpless, all day I knew
He had gone further than I towards finding a synthesis.
With Jarama held his wound wore on, the Georgian
Who held a dawnstar and not nettles as we do —
Whisper, starlings, whisper! Be incorruptible and saying
'O the world is bright and always living'.

Sirs and Senoras, let me end my story —
I show you earth, earth formally,
And Two on guard with the junipers.
Two, Gael and Jew side by side in a trench
Gripping antique guns to flick at the grasshoppers
That zoomed overhead and the moon was rocking.
Two who came from prisonment, Gael because of
     Tone,[10]
Jew because of human love, the same for Jew as
     German —
Frail fragments both, chipped off and forgotten
     readily . . .

I set them together, Izzy Kupchick and Donnelly;
And of that date with death among the junipers
I say only, they kept it: and record the exploded
Spreadeagled mass when the moon was later
Watching the wine that baked earth was drinking.
Such my story, Sirs and Senoras. Whether you like it
Or pay a visit to your vomitorium,[11] is all one . . .
Perhaps you'll like junipers and a moon steadied,
High baked earth and night's formalism,
Remembering that History is always a cruel country
And crueller man than April.[12]

Letter from Ireland

You have asked me why I stay in this small country
Where nothing happens while perhaps the last chapter,
Europe's swan song, is being written in the
     chancelleries.
You picture me tramping Wicklow hills and among
     trees,
Producing (from thence?) word patterns and O poems
     verses —
Without the stagnating waiting for air-raids and war
     nerves . . .

You know this country? You have visited?
It is more than indigo skies than iodine rivers than the
    west!
It is not like England it is not a seat of Mars,
Though Mars indeed invaded it and divided spoil
    many times . . .
But finally left its people to divide themselves keeping
Only the balance of their division and the major
    industries.
You know all this? And you know in this half-state[13] it
    would like
Quiet now and to think about its lost state and to
    bring
Something at least to life it could call its own.

On this island then in these valleys I was born . . .
Went from . . . returned . . . went from again! It is like
    that —
It is being born and being born here: in this place;
It is not being born in England in France or
    Germany . . .
It is this place: it is the cone-shaped mountain the
Bracken in the glens the old road the gap between the
    hills;
It is the evening smelling of peat smoke smelling of rain;
It is these it is this place it is not France or England —
I might have preferred being born where you are: in
    England . . .
Often I might have preferred it: often I have thought —
Lying awake the embers crackling and in the chimney
    noises —
And I have thought this is nothing: this country
    nothing this
People always scratching nowhere where the dead are
    bodiless,
Asking the dead and the dark for a way and praying
To the empty vault of the sky for answers until death
    takes them . . .

But I cannot go beyond them I can take part
Only in whatever this country will take part: take sides
Only in whatever this country will take sides: be angry

Enough and reproach them for not taking the side not
    taken —
As it was with Spain: the side not land or country
Or religion or any of those things: the side that is
Hunger and thirst and the world lacking love and
    lacking . . .

*And for whom do they write the swan songs in the
chancelleries?*

O yes it is calm here: calm as storm centre: here
    nothing crashes . . .
The sea that tumbles into our mornings comes from
many beaches.

1   Spanish: back-to-back seats for two persons on the same
    horse.
2   Estremadura, a poor region in south-west Spain and site
    of various battles during the Peninsula War, fell to
    Franco's Nationalist forces at the outset of the Spanish
    Civil War. Cordova in the south of Spain has a Moorish
    past and a long history, much of it written before the
    thirteenth century.
3   George Bernard Shaw's Life Force is an instrument of
    Creative Evolution, the world's will, not humanity's.
    Hence the idea, the Life Force, gets going but 'man has
    his lag'.
4   I assume this was a restaurant in Barcelona. The other
    place names in this stanza are landmarks in the city of
    Barcelona.
5   A small bird, a bunting.
6   Spanish: with milk (in coffee).
7   A traditional Irish air about an Irish girl who preferred
    her Coolin (her Irish boy with flowing hair) to the
    English stranger.
8   People from Madrid.
9   Charles Donnelly died at the Battle of the Jarama on 27
    February 1937.
10 An Irishman defending freedom because of the legacy of
    the 1798 United Irishman Wolfe Tone.
11 This was originally an entry/exit to a theatre. Here also
    an emetic.
12 An echo of the first line to Eliot's *The Waste Land*.
13 A reference to the partition of Ireland. Hence 'lost state',
    the nationalist view at the time.

PATRICK KAVANAGH
from *The Great Hunger* (1942)

A section from Kavanagh's long protest poem, on the great emotional hunger in Ireland
as seen through the eyes of Patrick Maguire. The poem began life under the more
mundane title 'The Old Peasant' (see *Horizon*, January 1942).

from THE GREAT HUNGER

VII

'Now go to Mass and pray and confess your sins
And you'll have all the luck,' his mother said.
He listened to the lie that is a woman's screen
Around a conscience when soft thighs are spread.
And all the while she was setting up the lie
She trusted in Nature that never deceives.
But her son took it as literal truth.
Religion's walls expand to the push of nature.
   Morality yields
To sense — but not in little tillage fields.

Life went on like that. One summer morning
Again through a hay-field on her way to the shop —
The grass was wet and over-leaned the path —
And Agnes held her skirts sensationally up,
And not because the grass was wet either.

A man was watching her, Patrick Maguire.
She was in love with passion and its weakness
And the wet grass could never cool the fire
That radiated from her unwanted womb
In that country, in that metaphysical land
Where flesh was a thought more spiritual than music
Among the stars — out of reach of the peasant's hand.

Ah, but the priest was one of the people too —
A farmer's son — and surely he knew
The needs of a brother and sister.
Religion could not be a counter-irritant like a blister,
But the certain standard measured and known
By which man might re-make his soul though all walls
   were down
And all earth's pedestalled gods thrown.

BRYAN MacMAHON
from *The Bell*, 1943; rpt. Bryan MacMahon, *The Lion-Tamer and Other Stories* (1948)

Bryan MacMahon (1909–98) was born in Listowel in County Kerry and returned there after training to be a teacher in Dublin. His roots in rural Ireland are apparent in all his work. Here in this entertaining story, set in Montana, he reveals the ties that connect the American daughter of a Chinese father and Irish mother to the bogs of Ireland.

Yung Mari Li

Father David Neale was parish priest of Aaron, Montana (Pop. 8,104). When he was returning to Aaron, Montana (Pop. 8,104) after a six months holiday spent in his native Tarmoneerla, in County Limerick, he took with him a sod of turf. The task of selecting this sod of turf was, he found, by no means easy. He demanded of his sod that it be a typical sod; but what constitutes the typical has always been an oyster-bed of argument. Father Neale had visualized his typical sod as having an attractive texture and appearance; then, it would have to burn well in case an unbeliever in Aaron, Montana, should doubt the authenticity of the souvenir; average size was also desirable; and, *nota bene*,[1] it would have to smell well. To smell well, Father Neale repeated, almost aloud. To smell well!

He examined numerous sods from numerous bogs before he eventually selected one approximating to his definition. He learned a good deal about turf in the course of his search. Some sods, he found, are base-bred, gloomy-looking blackguards, and, with every aperture sealed to gaiety, they sit in a peasant stolidity, resigning themselves to the advent of the day when they should be re-purchased by fire. And then at the last, when they are in the midst of the conflagration, they have a habit of breaking out into the laughter of flames and revealing themselves as ill-judged honest folk. Other sods are nincompoops. They release a granular titter even at wee provocation, seem to clasp the fire eagerly, and then, if you please, have the insolence to peter out in a prolonged, slow-dying sniffle of smoke. Others are perfect in texture but are huge awkward louts of fellows in appearance: others are so small that when you look at them you say: 'These were cut by mean men with mean sleáns[2] on mean mountains!' However, Father David Neale eventually did find a sod to his entire satisfaction. It was a good human sod, satisfactory in gloss and weight, its ebon solidarity fining out to a small combustible tuft at one end. Father Neale was thoroughly satisfied with his selection and he kept tapping his right nostril to give the world some indication of his approval.

Returning to one's native place after an absence of twenty-eight years occasions major adjustments to one's mental machinery. Heigh–ho, after the inevitable drive in the trap to the station with the two yew trees, you stand at the window of a carriage and clutch your bright-ribboned breviary. There over the heads of your lugubrious kinsfolk is a normal traditional Ireland, all wolfhounds and geometric sunbursts and round towers and shamrocks. The train pulls out and you carry this precious photograph in your heart for close on thirty years and then by golly! you plump back into electric cookers and a bewildering iron alertness. It's not fair, your poor mind squeaks, when in dark prank the mahogany stool of traditional Ireland is pulled from under it. However, there had been compensations. When he did return the trees were staunch around the new houses, the cool whistle of peace was through it all, and he had nephews fit to answer his Mass, aye, and nieces big enough to turn the heel of his stocking.

From the deck of the liner he looked back at Ireland, patted his nose and said 'Good, good, good!' Taking it all in all he rather approved of this Ireland that he had not seen for twenty-eight years, so much so that a prompting from nowhere tempted him to revise certain fixed principles of his regarding the use of physical force. Then, with a sigh, he turned from the wisp of Irish shore and looked about for Irish ears into which he could empty his stock-in-trade joke of 'Come back to Aaron, Montana, Montana. . . .'

Aaron is an open town within striking distance of Montana's glacier district. Bears walk out on the black highway a few miles from Aaron. Anglers catch prodigious numbers of trout in the mountain streams. The mountains north of the town have generous selvedges of snow, rich long laps of it under the blue tops. Laps and selvedges are greedy for the sunlight seeping through the first slats of day. Whatever about Ireland that had not changed.

Back in harness, Father Neale was at first inclined to view the place with alien eyes. Gradually he eased into the old ways. He cut a few knots of procedure, he

rebuked three persons in so far as God had built him for rebuke, shied predictably at the deaths of two notable parishioners, and stolidly listened to his curate rendering a desultory parochial account over several meals. Then he made a few adjustments to a typewritten list which he kept in his desk. He struck out the names of twenty-four dead, inserted the names of thirty-three born, added the names of eight new arrivals, subtracted the names of fifteen of his flock departed and computed that the list of his flock now contained 1,126 names. Finally (as a result of the curate's rendering of account) he wrote thoughtful notes, in the space for remarks, after the names of five of his parishioners. He folded the pages sadly and carefully and replaced them in his desk. As he did so his eyes lighted on the sod of turf. His drooping spirits rose. Suddenly he grabbed his hat and went out.

He went along the Main Street to the office of *The Aaron Advertiser and Post* and made enquiries about having a poster printed. He was satisfied with the plan the printer sketched out for him. The printer himself irritated him: the man was too workaday, too nonchalant. And besides the priest fancied he saw a Methodist sniffle to the nose under the steel-rimmed spectacles. Still he found in due course that the man did his work well. Father Neale liked the type-face used in A SOD OF TURF and also the fact that that lead was dead in the optical centre of the poster. The border was sturdy and stolid; whatever qualms he had had, that solid border squashed them. His own name was, as he had intended, in no way obtrusive. He puckered a little at the word 'Lecture', but after a little thought he allowed it to pass as a subterfuge. When he passed the proof he tapped the side of his nose slowly and ponderously and said 'Good, good, good.'

At first his parishioners were disposed to be amused, but each of them retreated two steps into solemnity on finding no responding humour in the priest's face. Without vehemence he succeeded in conveying his absolute earnestness; he did it chiefly by the resolute stare in the eyes and by the set tilt of the jaw. Thus he had always tried to transfer his iron sincerity to his parishioners, mostly Irish, Irish-born and second generation, with a sprinkling of Italians and mid-Europeans. He knew that without this humourless sincerity all his plans would be defeated — all his little conspiracies to prevent the shredding of his community, each new token of which he had noted through the years with troubled eyes — the first zoot-suit[3] on a hobbledehoy[4] named O'Connor, the marriage of Sally Donegan to an Anabaptist salesman, the open rebellion of old Jim Deenihan's son.

He entrusted the task of posting the notices to his

curate, but only in the outlying portions of his parish, in Red Springs and Kanahook. The posting in Aaron he reserved for himself. One morning he strode out, the posters fingered to a careful figure of eight lest the fresh ink would kiss and blur. He called first on Charlie Meehan. Charlie became a fanatic at once. Charlie was a person of some consequence in Aaron; he owned twelve chain stores in the State and everywhere you went in Aaron you found a sly old lady on the billboards pointing to her bulging reticule and screaming, 'Meehan's for Me!' Charlie's main store was on the principal crossing of Aaron and, while the priest was softly explaining the matter to him, Charlie was away ahead of him in fierceness. Charlie had the admirable dexterity of the fat and while the priest was speaking through well-dressed lips and with round noble gestures Charlie was proving his marksmanship with accurate movements of his hands and perfectly-timed interjections such as, 'Sure! Fine! Fine! Sure!' When Charlie began to speak he did so with such concentrated vehemence that one looked everywhere for the person who was contradicting him. He manipulated his coloured words as if they were snooker-balls. In his agony he bit off the end of a cigar, looked at the cigar truculently and stowed it away quickly as if it had almost tempted him to national apostasy. 'Say, Father,' he said, 'how about lapping the old sod in a white silk scarf and putting it on the centre of my big window? Get one of the School of Art stoodents to do a pretty deckle-edged card, say? Stick ribbons and ticker-tape and arrows all around it, see? Make it kind of mysterious like! Give it the whole darned window, see? On one condition, Father. One condition, Father Neale. I gotta see the sod myself, see. And handle it myself, see. You gotta grant me that, eh? You gotta grant me that, eh?' Father Neale said, well, he hadn't figured on showing it to anyone before the night of the lecture — thought it a point of honour like — but seeing that it was Charlie Meehan and that Charlie. . . .

By noon the priest had but one poster left. Fingering it nervously, he slowed down his pace outside a jeweller's shop in Lime Avenue. The shop was discretion itself. It was painted black, and over the doorway MARY YOUNG was written in gold leaf in a rather elaborate script. The name was flanked by two scrolls bearing the legends JEWELLERY: ANTIQUES. But the priest passed the house and then his steps lost momentum. He tapped the side of his nose but he omitted the concomitant 'Good'. The tappings came slowly and thoughtfully at first but then they worked up to the crescendo of inner battle and ended with a decisive tap that was tantamount to a blow. He turned and pushed open the glass door of the jeweller's shop.

In the act of entering, one of his eyes blinked silver in the left-hand window while the other blinked brass in the right-hand window. The opening door rang a bell above his head. A German shepherd dog lying inside the door raised his jet head from the cream whorls of his chest and tilted his eyes to an angle of intelligence.

Mincing and prinking, the assistant came through the transparent glass slabs and, pouting her lips, she sweetly said 'Yes?' She had all the awareness and unctuousness of a black pullet. Father Neale raised his hat. 'Miss Young, if you please. Yes! Miss Young.' The girl bowed and turned towards a brass-studded door behind the glass trays. The door had an oblong inset of hammered glass. The door swooshed out but the return journey was baffled by its patent-closing and it whispered home with considerable dignity.

The priest was alone with the dog. It was like being alone with a Christian. Softly, very softly indeed, the priest ruffled his fingers, but the dog had abandoned him as if saying, 'I have no further interest in you: you conform to the standard of respectability this establishment demands.' The priest ceased rustling his fingers. He leaned gently against a showcase and raised his head to the ceiling. There he read an old entry in the Baptismal Registry of his church in Aaron. 'Mary Young. [Yung Mari Li.] . . . Father's name, Yung Seng Li . . . Mother's maiden name, Bridget Collins . . . hmm . . . sponsors . . . yes, yes . . . Gap of a year and a half between date of child's birth and child's baptism. Mary Young . . . Yung Mari Li.' And then the priest thought of the very last name in that typewritten list in his desk: Mary Young: and the blank after her name in the space for remarks.

Bridget Collins, the mother, he had never known. She had died previous to his appointment as Parish Priest of Aaron. But the father — wryness drew its needle across the priest's lips as he remembered Yung Seng Li and the two skirmishes he had with him perhaps fifteen years before. Father Neale still carried two tags of Confucius as scars from those little frays. And then he remembered his single encounter with Mary Young after her father's death. The girl was then twenty-five. She had heard him out, not without blandness and gentility, but afterwards there was the poise and the shrugging: 'Yes, of course . . . Baptism . . . one's time is so occupied, Father . . . one does never quite get the opportunity . . . you understand how it is. Duty . . . of course . . . duty, but one's conception of duty, even of belief, is so, shall we say personal? . . . arbitrary? Yes, yes . . . if you don't mind, the telephone. . . .'

The priest looked over the glass showcases and the silver and the brasses. The intestines of the watches are now in a workshop at the rear, he commented. A good deal of tone since the old man's time. The old man was a brass-worker but he had never quite mated his trade with that of the jeweller. His girl had succeeded. There was discretion here, even opulence. He smiled at a pair of brass snakes with tails coiled in an attractive standard and mouths gaping to receive tall tapers. He looked at the die-direct edges of the showcases; at the cut-glass; at four silver mannikins. He looked at the sleek dog.

Mary Young came out through the brass-studded black door. She bore her Oriental face before her as if it were a shield of brass embossed with a nose, a brow and a pair of eye-sockets. Her dress was the correct black. There were pearls at her throat. When she joined her defensive, her suspicious fingers, a diamond ring flashed a low warning at the priest. In the centre-parting of her black hair the skin of the scalp glowed lime-white. The hair was gathered to a spinsterish bun at the nape of the neck. Approaching him she tilted her Eastern head to remote belligerence and her ten cyclamen nails formed a purely negotiatory cradle. Without speaking she conveyed: 'At the risk of tediousness I must repeat that my attitude towards certain matters is entirely unaltered!' The priest made a quick calculation and reckoned that her age was thirty-nine.

Smiling, Father Neale raised his hat. Then replacing it, he energetically took refuge in his solitary poster. While his head was bent he resolved to play the part of an old priest whose stock reaction was benevolence. Then, the imp of his temporary embarrassment began to urge him to play his part more fully by doddering. But behind this absurd play-acting he was tremblingly alert. Yet when he raised his head, his face held the incipience of a counterfeit pastoral palsy. 'A whim of mine . . . our schools, Miss Young . . . repairing. . . . In Ireland. . . . Turf . . . peat, you know. . . . Display it . . . according as we grow older . . . primary importance.' All the while the alive eyes were seeking a cranny in her visage of beaten brass.

Mary Young grew amicable. Her eyes said 'Yes . . . yes . . . is that all? Is that all?' But when she acceded, was she eager to accede? No, no, he must not betray his eagerness to recognize her eagerness. He thanked her with a facile sliding into complete senility and fumbled his way out on to the sidewalk.

There he tossed the fiddle-face of his weakness aside. He dismissed the sham saggings of his body by the natural expedient of throwing himself upwards and outwards towards the fullness of his great frame. Now again he was a man with a task before him.

But had it all been a waste of time? How much — if

any — of her mother went to her composition? Was there even a tithe of Brigid Collins in Yung Mari Li? Or was she wholly her courteous unexpugnable Confucian father? He shrugged. He had much more to do, many people to meet, numerous letters to write.

Late that night he brought the sod out to Charlie Meehan's. Charlie had a spacious house on the fringe of the town. The house was ablaze with lights to welcome him. Charlie had allowed his kids up late to see the sod of turf. There they were whooping in the hallway. Charlie's American wife was as astute as blazes; she had reserved her role until she had observed her husband's face for a while. What she saw in his daft eyes decided her against chaffing. All through the evening she thanked her stars that she had not made the most grievous blunder of her life by falling headlong over the cliff of facetiousness. Charlie handled the sod reverently and thrust it under the nose of his eldest boy with, 'Get your nose to that, you damn Yankee, and get the smell of home!' The man was roaring; but his sorry bulwark of harshness was as thin as tissue-paper. Yet, the next morning the appearance of the wrapped sod with its panoply of streamers and arrows in Meehan's window engendered widespread hilarity. Hilarity and some fierceness. Father Neale was pleased when he heard the rumblings of this fierceness. He tapped the side of his nose and said 'Good, good, good.' By way of superfluous explanation he added to himself, 'Fierceness is cement! Fierceness is cement!'

On the night of the lecture the hall was full. Father Neale was at the door shaking hands with the Irish. His curate was busy inside. The Irish had come out of their houses — every man-jack had come out. There they were, Jack Mulcahy, Teddy Lysaght, Peter Flynn, Anthony English, Dan and Michael O'Connor, Joe Feehan, Dinny McGinley, with their wives and children, some of them with their children's children. Old Mrs Sloan (*née* Broderick) drove down from her mansion in the hills. A sprinkling of Italians came. Guiseppe Salvini was there — the richest man in town — and his gargantuan midnight glittering wife with him, waddling up the narrow pathway circling from leg to leg as a heavy box is trundled by a railway porter. Father Neale pressed Guiseppe to appear on the platform but the Italian said, 'No, the Irish to-night' and after this he telescoped ten no's.

Charlie Meehan, Tim Foley, Anthony English and young Sloan the attorney were on the platform. The wrapped sod of turf was on the table with the carafe of water beside it. Charlie and his fellows were portentous as haystacks. Then, precisely on the stroke of eight, Father Neale appeared on the platform. The people cheered. The priest looked well. He possessed the unpurchasable and wholly natural gift of ceremony.

But though it was clear that he was pleased with the size and zeal of his audience, yet some fraction of him seemed wholly not at peace within himself. Some essential lustre was absent from his lips and now and again scrawlings came out on his forehead. His tongue readied his dry lips, he walked forward and looked at the Poles, the Austrians, the Italians — and the Irish. Just then, in the pause before he began to speak, Mary Young entered the hall. Sprucely and trimly her body moved forward through the people. The minor ripple of whispering that s-s-s-ed forward and broke upon the priest's boots indicated that the woman's presence at a Catholic meeting was considered abnormal. Father Neale appraised her and then nodded to a youngster who immediately vacated his place in the front row. Mary Young graciously thanked the boy and then yielded her face up to the speaking priest.

Now, I cannot tell you with any degree of accuracy what the priest said to his people. My mouth and the priest's mouth are two different mouths. Come, now, be honest with yourself! What would *you* say about a sod of turf in Aaron, Montana? Or in any five other places, pin-pricked at random on a kid's atlas? Emotion is emotion anywhere, even in Aaron, Montana. His end and his beginning was home and the things of home. Home. Home. Home. Beyond the beloved bits of ceremony he was a baker and his people were dough. He was a potter and his people were clay. He was a sculptor and his people were stone.

When he came to the unwrapping of the sod the Irish for the most part were blatantly on the point of tears. Home. Home. Home. God dear! God dear! Home. Over the hills and the steeples and the towers and the salt water. Like the passing of a great wind every single one of them was having daybreak in his chest and a hundred cocks crowing in his heart. These poor drugged Irish were galloping like thunder at the heels of their priest.

The women were crying and they didn't give two hoots in hell who saw them either. They snuggled against husbands who had grown wondrously fierce, each man's face the hue of a cock's comb. The husbands resented such advances lest they be considered effeminate and unangrily clucked their womenfolk away. A miner who had come all the way up from Butte took his short pipe out of his mouth and said loudly, 'Wisha, Glory on you, Priesht up there!'

And then, when their emotion was at its peak, the priest, by an unpredictable flippancy, smashed the wondrous glass of their mood. This was no error on his part. It was carefully calculated.

He protested his own inadequacy to deal with his subject. If 'twere his brother Dick now or Jim Joe they could talk on turf till Tibb's Eve.[5] But he! Here he held up his milky white hands and the people gave back the guffaw he had expected. He reckoned that this breaking would now set them the communal task of gathering the fragments and setting them together again. Ultimate individual fracture, he knew, would have in any case inevitably followed.

He urged them to talk now: Charlie Meehan started off and his naturalness proved infectious. Narrowed down to the intimacy of a family group the men were soon speaking without shyness. They spoke hesitantly thus:

'Would you believe me Father, when I say I seen turf cut under the red strand of the seashore? In Ballyheigue it was and 'twas cut out at the low water mark! Cut in a great hurry too and then 'twas saved[6] on the brink of the sandhills. . . .'

'I seen a son a flamin' sleánsman and the father before him as awkward as Euclid. . . .'

'In our place we'd pelt the brúscar[7] on to the top of the reek so that it'd soak the weather. Doin' it of a windy day 'twould blind the two eyes inside your head and. . . .'

'Say! Good turf rings even when it's leaving the sleán. It squeaks under the prongs of the pike. The wax in it is sort o' slow to leave go its hoult on anything.'

'Good turf darkens on the bank within the hour. Then it glistens, man, like a pony's back. Like a pony's back and her feed thickened with linseed oil.'

'Footin' turf[8] is a job you should second to no man. Rogues footin' your turf for you mightn't stir the dead man in the heart of the grogue[9] and then. . . .'

'On the mountain in our part we'd pull the single scraw[10] from it. Up t'd walk with the little cubes of solid dark turf dangling off the grass threads. Beggin' your pardon, Father, but 'tis like nothin' on earth more than skulldraggin' a woman down a shtairs. . . .'

'Do you know what it is, but the breenshin'[11] man has a proper animal's job, as he has. . . .'

The priest was happy now. The place was crackling about him with vivid yapping. Women were eager that their husbands should be heard. No woman spoke. Instead she pulled at her husband's sleeve to make him the vehicle of her contradiction or her addition.

'An odd time the sleán'd strike a gusher.[12] A gusher, man, and then all the water in the wide world'd boil out under your boots. . . .'

'Well God be with the mornin' I so-ho-ed a hare in

a snug truppal at the butt of our reek of turf. I remember it well. 'Twas a mornin' in June and the mountain was fair drowned in clear blueness. . . .'

'I got a trálach[13] in my wrist pikin' turf of a day and I declare to the Man Above if. . . .'

'I daresay there's none among ye but found the lovely red bog-sally[14] ten sods deep in the clay. You'd find yourself nursin' it in your hand for the full round of a day. . . .'

The priest handed down the sod to be passed from hand to hand through the hall; he thought it good that each person smelled at it deeply as if to capture even one camera-click of the lost world at home.

And then when the harvest of words was almost reaped it happened. Yung Mari Li was on her feet. The Irish was out on her yellow face. Out on her face like a torch. Silence weaved through the groups. The woman's face swung from priest to people, from people to priest. And then she spoke.

'My mother was Brigid Collins from Tobbernagoneen near Knocknagoshel in the County of Kerry, Ireland. Tobbernagoneen is Irish and it means 'The Well of the Rabbits'. Miles on the land-side of Tobbernagoneen is Tournafulla which is a name as strong as a blow of a fist in the mouth for it means 'The Bleachfield of the Blood'. When my mother was a child growing up she spent all her time out on the bog. She wore a red flannel petticoat you could see two miles away. Tobbernagoneen is a townland with nothing in it but bog. My grandfather, Joseph Collins, had the grass of three hungry cows on the cutaway but he had up to sixty acres of bog. He used to let it to the farmers around at five shillings a bank for the year. I remember too my mother saying that a sleán of turf[15] is what three men would cut in the run of a day, one man cutting, one man breenshing, one man spreading. A sleán of turf worked out about thirteen rails. My grandmother, Maria Collins, used to make pillows out of the canavawn[16] that grows on the bog. I recall my mother saying that a noted fiddler called Kevin Regan was drowned in a boghole on my father's turbary.[17] My mother said that he used be heard playing 'The Job of Journeywork' there afterwards and that she and her sisters were mortally afraid to stir out after dark for fear of Kevin Regan's ghost. . . .'

Invisibly the arms of the women were out, groping about to embrace the Chinawoman. Their arms stopped short of her, repelled by the foreignness in her face. Then again the poor bewildered women sent up their arms to clutch at the garments of their priest, to pluck at him, to hook him, to ask him 'What? Why? Who? Why? Why?' And the priest was tensed and relaxed and meticulously sensitive to their pitiable queries, and hinging his face over them he chided them silently (even dangerously, lest even their clumsy breaths should knock over his lovely house of cards) and they interpreted his mouth and eyes as saying, 'This is utterly normal: utterly normal, remember. I tell you that a good deal depends on it that you should believe that this is utterly normal.' Then after the small negation, the wave of their perplexity ebbed and they were at peace. The priest appraised their acceptance and lidded up his eyes till he looked like an old hen. He began to stroke his face in thanksgiving; he put the pads of thumb and forefinger on the lids of his eyes, stroked briskly out over the cheekbones, ran them up the lip corners and vouchsafed the finger tips a minor osculation in the middle of the lips.

Afterwards the people went home through the dark.

The priest allowed five agonizing days to elapse before he called on Mary Young. As he expected, he found that she was eager to receive him. Even then, he spent five minutes lipping the tittle-tattle of the town. He skilfully avoided the topic that was a mutual urgency in them both. And then the guard of her grandeur was down. . . .

'An exclamation of my mother's,' she said: '"Reenanangel!" What does it mean?'

'King of Angels,' the priest said.

'King of Angels?'

'King of Angels! Yes, King of Angels!'

Then they both said 'King of Angels' together.

After that she was nothing but an unsure groping woman. She indicated the studded door with its rectangle of hammered glass. 'If I'm not taking up too much of your time, Father?' Then, 'Miriam!' she said, clicking the girl to her station. She put her carmine fingers on the studded door and the door shrank open. The dog saw the priest's grey head pass in, high and mighty amid the splendour of the brasses.

---

1 Normally written as abbreviation N.B. Literally, note well.

2 A sleán in a turf-spade, a slane in English.

3 Man's suit popular in 1940s, with padded shoulders and high-waisted tapering trousers (OED).

4 Clumsy, awkward youth.

5 For ever. Also never as in saying, 'You'll get your money by Tibb's Eve' (P.W. Joyce).

6 saved: Dried out.

7 Irish for crumbs or fragments; here broken bits of turf.

8 Stacking turf to dry.

9 Three or four sods of turf standing on end, supporting each other like a little pyramid on the bog to dry (P.W. Joyce).

10 A grassy sod cut from a grassy or boggy surface and often dried for firing (P.W. Joyce).

11 In Irish *brín* is happy young man.
12 Stockings with the soles cut off them (P.W. Joyce).
13 *trálach*: Irish: cramp or swelling in wrist.
14 Bog plant.

15 A way of measuring turf.
16 Bog-cotton.
17 Land where turf may be cut.

BETTY SMITH
from Betty Smith, *A Tree Grows in Brooklyn* (1943)

Betty Smith (1904–72) was born in Brooklyn and educated at the Universities of Michigan and Yale. A popular novelist, her works include *Tomorrow Will Be Better* (1948) and *Maggie — Now* (1958). She also wrote more than forty plays. Here in this extract the focus is on the father-daughter relationship. Notice the way Irishness comes to be expressed through singing ('Molly Malone' runs through the novel) and is channelled through the daughter's eyes. In its mixture of pathos and hardship *A Tree Grows in Brooklyn* belongs to its period and can be fruitfully compared with Ruth Park's novel *The Harp in the South* (1948). In 1945 it was made into a film by Elia Kazan with Dorothy Maguire as Katie and James Dunn as Johnny Nolan.

Chapter 3

Papa came home at five o'clock. By that time, the horse and wagon had been locked up in Fraber's stable, Francie had finished her book and her candy and had noted how pale and thin the late afternoon sun was on the worn fence boards. She held the sun-warmed, wind-freshened pillow to her cheek a moment before she replaced it on her cot. Papa came in singing his favourite ballad, 'Molly Malone'. He always sang it coming up the stairs so that everyone would know he was home.

In Dublin's fair city,
The girls are so pretty,
Twas there that I first met . . .

Francie, smilingly happy, had the door open before he could sing the next line.

'Where's your mother?' he asked. He *always* asked that when he came in.

'She went to the show with Sissy.'

'Oh!' He sounded disappointed. He was *always* disappointed if Katie wasn't there. 'I work at Klommer's tonight. Big wedding party.' He brushed his derby with his coat sleeve before he hung it up.

'Waiting or singing?' Francie asked.

'Both. Have I got a clean waiter's apron, Francie?'

'There's one clean but not ironed. I'll iron it for you.'

She set up the ironing board on two chairs and put the iron to heat. She got a square of thick wrinkled duck material with linen tape ties and sprinkled it. While she waited for the iron to get hot, she heated the coffee and poured him a cup. He drank it and ate the sugar bun that they had saved for him. He was very happy because he had a job that night and because it was a nice day.

'A day like this is like somebody giving you a present,' he said.

'Yes, Papa.'

'Isn't hot coffee a wonderful thing? How did people get along before it was invented?'

'I like the way it smells.'

'Where did you buy these buns?'

'Winkler's. Why?'

'They make them better every day.'

'There's some Jew bread left, a piece.'

'Fine!' He took the slice of bread and turned it over. The Union sticker was on that piece. 'Good bread, well made by Union bakers.' He pulled the sticker off. A thought struck him. 'The Union label on my apron!'

'It's right here, sewn in the seam. I'll iron it out.'

'That label is like an ornament,' he explained, 'like a rose that you wear. Look at my Waiters' Union button.' The pale green-and-white button was fastened in his lapel. He polished it with his sleeve. 'Before I joined the Union the bosses paid me what they felt like. Sometimes they paid me nothing. The tips, they said, would take care of me. Some places even charged me for the privilege of working. The tips were so big, they said, that they could sell the waiting concession. Then I joined the Union. Your mother shouldn't begrudge the dues. The Union gets me jobs where the boss has to pay me certain wages, regardless of tips. All trades should be unionized.'

'Yes, Papa.' By now, Francie was ironing away. She loved to hear him talk.

Francie thought of the Union Headquarters. One time she had gone there to bring him an apron and carfare to go to a job. She saw him sitting with some men. He wore his tuxedo all the time. It was the only suit he had. His black derby was cocked jauntily and he was smoking a cigar. He took his hat off and threw the cigar away when he saw Francie come in.

'My daughter,' he said proudly. The waiters looked at the thin child in her ragged dress and then exchanged glances. They were different from Johnny Nolan. They had regular waiter jobs during the week and picked up extra money on Saturday night jobs. Johnny had no regular job. He worked at one-night places here and there.

'I want to tell you fellows,' he said, 'that I got a couple of fine children at home and a pretty wife. And I want to tell you that I'm not good enough for them.'

'Take it easy,' said a friend and patted him on the shoulder.

Francie overheard two men outside the group talking about her father. The short man said:

'I want you to hear this fellow talk about his wife and his kids. It's rich. He's a funny duck. He brings his wages home to his wife but keeps his tips for booze. He's got a funny arrangement at McGarrity's. He turns all his tips over to him and McGarrity supplies him with drinks. He don't know whether McGarrity owes him money or whether he owes McGarrity. The system must work out pretty good for him, though. He's always carrying a load.' The men walked away.

There was a pain around Francie's heart but when she saw how the men standing around her father liked him, how they smiled and laughed at what he said and how eagerly they listened to him, the pain lessened. Those two men were exceptions. She knew that everyone loved her father.

Yes, everyone loved Johnny Nolan. He was a sweet singer of sweet songs. Since the beginning of time, everyone, especially the Irish, had loved and cared for the singer in their midst. His brother waiters really loved him. The men he worked for loved him. His wife and children loved him. He was still gay and young and handsome. His wife had not turned bitter against him and his children did not know that they were supposed to be ashamed of him.

Francie pulled her thoughts away from that day when she had visited the Union Headquarters. She listened to her father again. He was reminiscing.

'Take me. I'm nobody.' Placidly, he lit up a nickel cigar. 'My folks over from Ireland the year the potatoes gave out. Fellow ran a steamship company said he'd take my father to America — had a job waiting for him. Said he'd take the boat fare from his wages. So my father and mother came over.

'My father was like me — never held the one job long.' He smoked in silence for a while.

Francie ironed quietly. She knew that he was just thinking out loud. He did not expect her to understand. He just wanted someone to listen to him. He said practically the same things every Saturday. The rest of the week when he was drinking, he would come and go and say little. But today was Saturday. It was his day to talk.

'My folks never knew how to read or write. I only got to the sixth grade myself — had to leave school when the old man died. You kids are lucky. I'm going to see to it that you get through school.'

'Yes, Papa.'

'I was a boy of twelve then. I sang in saloons for the drunks and they threw pennies at me. Then I started working around saloons and restaurants . . . waiting on people. . . .' He was quiet awhile with his thoughts.

'I always wanted to be a real singer, the kind that comes out on the stage all dressed up. But I didn't have no education and I didn't know the first way about how to start in being a stage singer. Mind your job, my mother told me. You don't know how lucky you are to have work, she said. So I drifted into the singing waiter business. It's not steady work. I'd be better off if I was just a plain waiter. That's why I drink,' he finished up illogically.

She looked up at him as though she were going to ask a question. But she said nothing.

'I drink because I don't stand a chance and I know it. I couldn't drive a truck like other men and I couldn't get on the cops with my build. I got to sling beer and sing when I just want to sing. I drink because I got responsibilities that I can't handle.' There was another long pause. Then he whispered, 'I am not a happy man. I got a wife and children and I don't happen to be a hard-working man. I never wanted a family.'

Again that hurt around Francie's heart. He didn't want her or Neeley?

'What does a man like me want a family for? But I fell in love with Katie Rommely. Oh, I'm not blaming your mother,' he said quickly. 'If it hadn't been her, it would have been Hildy O'Dair. You know, I think your mother is still jealous of her. But when I met Katie, I said to Hildy, "You go your way and I'll go mine." So I married your mother. We had children. Your mother is a good woman, Francie. Don't you ever forget that.'

Francie knew that mama was a good woman. She *knew*. And papa said so. Then why did she like her father better than her mother? Why did she? Papa was no good. He said so himself. But she liked papa better.

'Yes, your mother works hard. I love my wife and I love my children.' Francie was happy again. 'But shouldn't a man have a better life? Maybe someday it will be that the Unions will arrange for a man to work and to have time for himself too. But that won't be in my time. Now, it's work hard all the time or be a bum . . . no in-between. When I die, nobody will remember me for long. No one will say, "He was a man who loved his family and believed in the Union." All they will say is, "Too bad. But he was nothing but a drunk no matter which way you look at it." Yes, they'll say that.'

The room was very quiet. Johnny Nolan threw his half-smoked cigar out of the unscreened window with a bitter gesture. He had a premonition that he was running his life out too fast. He looked at the little girl ironing away so quietly with her head bent over the board and he was stabbed by the soft sadness on the child's thin face.

'Listen!' He went to her and put an arm around her thin shoulders. 'If I get a lot of tips tonight, I'll put the money on a good horse that I know is running Monday. I'll put a couple of dollars on him and win ten. Then I'll put the ten on another horse I know and win a hundred. If I use my head and have any kind of luck at all, I'll run it up to five hundred.'

Pipe dreams he thought to himself, even while he was telling her about his dream winnings. But oh, how wonderful, he thought, if everything you talked about could come true! He went on talking.

'Then do you know what I'm going to do, Prima Donna?' Francie smiled happily, pleased at his using the nickname he had given her when as a baby, he swore that her crying was as varied and as tuneful as an opera singer's range.

'No. What are you going to do?'

'I'm going to take you on a trip. Just you and me, Prima Donna. We'll go way down south where the cotton blossoms blow.' He was delighted with the sentence. He said it again. 'Down where the cotton blossoms blow.' Then he remembered that the sentence was a line in a song that he knew. He

jammed his hands in his pockets, whistled, and started to do a waltz clog like Pat Rooney.[1] Then he went into the song:

> . . . *a field of snowy white.*
> *Hear the darkies singing soft and low.*
> *I long there to be, for someone waits for me,*
> *Down where the cotton blossoms blow.*

Francie kissed his cheek softly. 'Oh, Papa. I love you so much,' she whispered.

He held her tight. Again the stab-wound feeling. 'Oh, God! Oh, God!' he repeated to himself in almost unendurable agony. 'What a hell of a father I am.' But when he spoke to her again, it was quietly enough.

'All this isn't getting my apron ironed, though.'

'It's all done, Papa.' She folded it into a careful square.

'Is there any money in the house, Baby?'

She looked into the cracked cup on the shelf. 'A nickel and some pennies.'

'Would you take seven cents and go out and get me a dicky and a paper collar?'

Francie went over to the dry-goods store to get her father's Saturday night linen. A dicky was a shirt front made of stiffly starched muslin. It fastened around the neck with a collar button and the vest held it in place. It was used instead of a shirt. It was worn once and then thrown away. A paper collar was not exactly made out of paper. It was called that to differentiate it from a celluloid collar which was what poor men wore because it could be laundered simply by being wiped with a wet rag. A paper collar was made out of thin cambric stiffly starched. It could be used only once.

When Francie got back, papa had shaved, wetted his hair down, shined his shoes and put on a clean undershirt. It was unironed and had a big hole in the back but it smelled nice and clean. He stood on a chair and took down a little box from the top cupboard shelf. It contained the pearl studs that Katie had given him for a wedding present. They had cost her a month's salary. Johnny was very proud of them. No matter how hard up the Nolans were, the studs were never pawned.

Francie helped him put the studs in the dicky. He fastened the wing collar on with a golden collar button, a present that Hildy O'Dair had given him before he became engaged to Katie. He wouldn't part with that either. His tie was a piece of heavy black silk and he tied an expert bow with it. Other waiters wore readymade bows attached to elastics. But not Johnny Nolan. Other waiters wore soiled white shirts or clean shirts indifferently ironed and celluloid collars. But not Johnny. His linen was immaculate, if temporary.

He was dressed at last. His wavy blond hair gleamed and he smelled clean and fresh from washing and shaving. He put his coat on and buttoned it up jauntily. The satin lapels of the tuxedo were threadbare but who would look at that when the suit fitted him so beautifully and the crease in his trousers was so perfect? Francie looked at his well-polished black shoes and noticed how the cuffless trousers came down in the back over the heel, and what a nice break they made across his instep. No other father's pants hung just that way. Francie was proud of her father. She wrapped up his ironed apron carefully in a piece of clean paper saved for that purpose.

She walked with him to the trolley car. Women smiled at him until they noticed the little girl clinging to his hand. Johnny looked like a handsome, devil-may-care Irish boy instead of the husband of a scrubwoman and the father of two children who were always hungry.

They passed Gabriel's Hardware Store and stopped to look at the skates in the window. Mama never had time to do this. Papa talked as though he would buy Francie a pair someday. They walked to the corner. When a Graham Avenue trolley came along, he swung up on to the platform suiting his rhythm to the car's slowing down. As the car started up again, he stood on the back platform holding on to the bar while he leaned way out to wave to Francie. No man had ever looked so gallant as her father, she thought.

1   Pat Rooney: American Waltz Clog King.

JOHN HEWITT

from *Lagan* (1945); rpt. *The Collected Poems of John Hewitt* (ed. Frank Ormsby) (1991)

If anything proves Hewitt was not an alien in Northern Ireland it is this poem.

ONCE ALIEN HERE

Once alien here my fathers built their house,
claimed, drained, and gave the land the shapes of use,
and for their urgent labour grudged no more
than shuffled pennies from the hoarded store
of well rubbed words that had left their overtones
in the ripe England of the mounded downs.

The sullen Irish limping to the hills
bore with them the enchantments and the spells
that in the clans' free days hung gay and rich
on every twig of every thorny hedge,
and gave the rain-pocked stone a meaning past
the blurred engraving of the fibrous frost.

So I, because of all the buried men
in Ulster clay, because of rock and glen
and mist and cloud and quality of air
as native in my thought as any here,
who now would seek a native mode to tell
our stubborn wisdom individual,
yet lacking skill in either scale of song,
the graver English, lyric Irish tongue,
must let this rich earth so enhance the blood
with steady pulse where now is plunging mood
till thought and image may, identified,
find easy voice to utter each aright.

ROBERT FARREN

from Robert Farren, *Rime, Gentlemen, Please* (1945)

Robert Farren (Roibeárd Ó Faracháin) (1909–84), author of *Time's Wall Asunder* (1939) and *Rime, Gentlemen, Please* (1945), was a Director of the Abbey Theatre from 1940 until 1973, Controller of Programmes at RTE from 1953 until 1974. Here in this poem he expresses a legitimate complaint against the preceding generation.

FOR WHOM 'THE BELL' TOLLS

'Poetry in Ireland has declined in volume and quality.'
          Editorial in *The Bell*, February 1942

'Yeats, Moore, Joyce, Shan Bullock, MacKenna, Gregory, A.E., Higgins, have all gone. No young men are appearing.'
          Editorial in *The Bell*, November 1943

'Some time ago I had a letter from the Editor of *The Dublin Magazine* in which he told me he was publishing a good deal of the work of the Welsh poets, as the native stock was running pretty thin.'
          Pádraic Colum in
          The Saturday Review of Literature

Lord, when I come to middle days,
do not so dim the sun
that I croak then, as these croak now:
'There's no young man comes on.'

For, *how* they croak, these forty-, fifty-,
sixty-year-olds that dream

it is the native stock runs thin
and not their own bloodstream.

The tree which bore themselves — rich boughs
bent under heavy fruits! —
is spent, they say, and dies with them,
her sap sunk through the roots.

No! but the pruned tree bears, again,
her fruits ripen and round.
And, since deep roots have sunk their wells
in unexhausted ground,

through roots remounting, sap will bring
Ireland again to bud,
and the young boughs grow better crops
than the old branches could.

So, when I come to middle days,
do not so dim the sun
that I croak then, as these croak now:
'The teeming-time is done.'

VALENTIN IREMONGER
from *The Listener*, 27 June 1946

Valentin Iremonger (1918–91) was born in Sandymount, educated by the Christian Brothers, and joined the Department of Foreign Affairs. From 1964 until 1980 he was ambassador to several European countries. He was poetry editor for *Envoy* (1949–51), and his own verse was published in *Reservations* (1950), *Horan's Field and Other Reservations* (1972) and *Sandymount, Dublin* (1988). Here in this poem written in 1945 and later titled 'By the Dodder in Flood at Herbert Bridge', Iremonger presents an atmospheric view of Dublin awaiting the Hunger Moon, the store-houses empty.

POEM

In this river, flooded by recent rains,
The current sobs heavily like a girl
Watching her day anxiously warp and curl
Into scales of white foam like a dragon's mail.
Danger is on tap like oil, insolent, yet all
The olive-green pike, the brilliant-finned perch,
     behind the wall
Of weeds, where the shallows were, can cower
Grimly, counting their safety out hour by hour.

Looking across the garden toward the river, alone, I
     think
How for us, flooded by circumstance, no weedy
     margins
Offer their dubious protection, as we stand, uncertain,
With our hands hanging, by winter's brink,
Yet ours, all spring and summer, was the screwed
     concentration
On crops and fuel, preparing for this evil season,

Neither flowers nor birds tempting our attention nor
   even
Gay girls laughing in the hay-meadows, wheedling.

Silently, in late November, we in this soured land
Wait the Hunger Moon, the days closing in, rain

Gunning the windows, the wind rising, the pain
Of winter already in our numbed hands.
How will we live for the next twelve months
Is the bare question, seeing the results
Of our year's labour, turf-clamps ruined, the tempting
Harvest lost and all our store-houses empty.

ELIZABETH BOWEN
from *The Penguin New Writing*, 1944

In a note to *The Demon Lover and Other Stories* (1945), stories including 'Mysterious Kôr' which were all written between spring 1941 and late autumn 1944, Elizabeth Bowen commented: 'These are all wartime, none of them *war*, stories. There are no accounts of war action even as I knew it – for instance, air raids. Only one character – in 'Mysterious Kôr' – is a soldier; and he only appears as a homeless wanderer round a city . . . I see war (or should I say feel war?) more as a territory than as a page of history . . . In war, this feeling of slight differentiation was suspended: I felt one with, and just like, everyone else . . . Walls went down; and we felt as if we knew each other. We all lived in a state of lucid abnormality.' Angus Wilson (1913–91), the distinguished English novelist, claimed, not without justification, that 'the only two English writers who convey what life in blitzed London was like' were Henry Green and Elizabeth Bowen. He might have added with more accuracy that one of those two was Anglo-Irish. In an article in *The Listener* on 20 March 1947 Bowen describes the impact Rider Haggard's imperialist novel *She* had on her: 'But Kôr, Kôr, the enormous derelict city, whose streets the Amahagger dare not tread, is, ever, on the horizon.' And then tellingly adds: 'I saw Kôr before I saw London; I was a provincial child.'

Mysterious Kôr

Full moonlight drenched the city and searched it; there was not a niche left to stand in. The effect was remorseless: London looked like the moon's capital — shallow, cratered, extinct. It was late, but not yet midnight; now the buses had stopped the polished roads and streets in this region sent for minutes together a ghostly unbroken reflection up. The soaring new flats and the crouching old shops and houses looked equally brittle under the moon, which blazed in windows that looked its way. The futility of the black-out became laughable: from the sky, presumably, you could see every slate in the roofs, every whited kerb, every contour of the naked winter flowerbeds in the park; and the lake, with its shining twists and tree-darkened islands would be a landmark for miles, yes, miles, overhead.

However, the sky, in whose glassiness floated no clouds but only opaque balloons, remained glassy-silent. The Germans no longer came by the full moon. Something more immaterial seemed to threaten, and to be keeping people at home. This day between days, this extra tax, was perhaps more than senses and nerves could bear. People stayed indoors with a fervour that could be felt: the buildings strained with battened-down human life, but not a beam, not a voice, not a note from a radio escaped. Now and then under streets and buildings the earth rumbled: the Underground sounded loudest at this time.

Outside the now gateless gates of the park, the road coming downhill from the north-west turned south and became a street, down whose perspective the traffic lights went through their unmeaning perfor-mance of changing colour. From the promontory of pavement outside the gates you saw at once up the road and down the street: from behind where you stood, between the gateposts, appeared the lesser strangeness of grass and water and trees. At this point, at this moment, three French soldiers, directed to a hostel they could not find, stopped singing to listen derisively to the waterbirds wakened up by the moon. Next, two wardens coming off duty emerged from their post and crossed the road diagonally, each with an elbow cupped inside a slung-on tin hat. The wardens turned their faces, mauve in the moonlight, towards the Frenchmen with no expression at all. The two sets of steps died in opposite directions, and, the birds subsiding, nothing was heard or seen until, a little way down the street, a trickle of people came out of the Underground, around the anti-panic brick wall. These all disappeared quickly, in an abashed way, or as though dissolved in the street by some white acid, but for a girl and a soldier who, by their way of walking, seemed to have no destination but each other and to be not quite certain even of that. Blotted into one shadow, he tall, she little, these two proceeded towards the park. They looked in, but did not go in; they stood there debating without speaking. Then, as though a command from the street behind them had been received by their synchronized bodies, they faced round to look back the way they had come.

His look up the height of a building made his head drop back, and she saw his eyeballs glitter. She slid her hand from his sleeve, stepped to the edge of the pavement and said: 'Mysterious Kôr.'

'What is?' he said, not quite collecting himself.

'This is —

Mysterious Kôr thy walls forsaken stand,
Thy lonely towers beneath a lonely moon —
                    — this is Kôr.'

'Why,' he said, 'it's years since I've thought of that.' She said: 'I think of it all the time —

Not in the waste beyond the swamps and sand,
The fever-haunted forest and lagoon,
Mysterious Kôr thy walls —

— a completely forsaken city, as high as cliffs and as white as bones, with no history —'

'But something must once have happened: why had it been forsaken?'

'How could anyone tell you when there's nobody there?'

'Nobody there since how long?'

'Thousands of years.'

'In that case, it would have fallen down.'

'No, not Kôr,' she said with immediate authority. 'Kôr's altogether different; it's very strong; there is not a crack in it anywhere for a weed to grow in; the corners of stones and the monuments might have been cut yesterday, and the stairs and arches are built to support themselves.'

'You know all about it,' he said, looking at her.

'I know, I know all about it.'

'What, since you read that book?'

'Oh, I didn't get much from that; I just got the name. I knew that must be the right name; it's like a cry.'

'Most like the cry of a crow to me.' He reflected, then said: 'But the poem begins with "Not" — "*Not in the waste beyond the swamps and sand —*" And it goes on, as I remember, to prove Kôr's not really anywhere. When even a poem says there's no such place —'

'What it tries to say doesn't matter: I see what it makes me see. Anyhow, that was written some time ago, at that time when they thought they had got everything taped, because the whole world had been explored, even the middle of Africa. Every thing and place had been found and marked on some map; so what wasn't marked on any map couldn't be there at all. So *they* thought: that was why he wrote the poem. "*The world is disenchanted*," it goes on. That was what set me off hating civilization.'

'Well, cheer up,' he said; 'there isn't much of it left.'

'Oh, yes, I cheered up some time ago. This war shows we've by no means come to the end. If you can blow whole places out of existence, you can blow whole places into it. I don't see why not. They say we can't say what's come out since the bombing started. By the time we've come to the end, Kôr may be the one city left: the abiding city. I should laugh.'

'No, you wouldn't,' he said sharply. '*You* wouldn't — at least, I hope not. I hope you don't know what you're saying — does the moon make you funny?'

'Don't be cross about Kôr; please don't, Arthur,' she said.

'I thought girls thought about people.'

'What, these days?' she said. 'Think about people? How can anyone think about people if they've got any heart? I don't know how other girls manage: I always think about Kôr.'

'Not about me?' he said. When she did not at once answer, he turned her hand over, in anguish, inside his grasp. 'Because I'm not there when you want me — is that my fault?'

'But to think about Kôr *is* to think about you and me.'

'In that dead place?'

'No, ours — we'd be alone there.'

Tightening his thumb on her palm while he thought this over, he looked behind them, around them, above them — even up at the sky. He said finally: 'But we're alone here.'

'That is why I said "Mysterious Kôr".'

'What, you mean we're there now, that here's there, that now's then? . . . *I* don't mind,' he added, letting out as a laugh the sigh he had been holding in for some time. 'You ought to know the place, and for all I could tell you we might be anywhere: I often do have it, this funny feeling, the first minute or two when I've come up out of the Underground. Well, well: join the Army and see the world.' He nodded towards the perspective of traffic lights and said, a shade craftily: 'What are those, then?'

Having caught the quickest possible breath, she replied: 'Inexhaustible gases; they bored through to them and lit them as they came up; by changing colour they show the changing of minutes; in Kôr there is no sort of other time.'

'You've got the moon, though: that can't help making months.'

'Oh, and the sun, of course; but those two could do what they liked; we should not have to calculate when they'd come or go.'

'We might not have to,' he said, 'but I bet I should.'

'I should not mind what you did, so long as you never said, "What next?" '

'I don't know about "next", but I do know what we'd do first.'

'What, Arthur?'

'Populate Kôr.'

She said: 'I suppose it would be all right if our children were to marry each other?'

But her voice faded out; she had been reminded that they were homeless on this his first night of leave. They were, that was to say, in London without any hope of any place of their own. Pepita shared a two-roomed flatlet with a girl friend, in a by-street off the Regent's Park Road, and towards this they must make their half-hearted way. Arthur was to have the sitting-room divan, usually occupied by Pepita, while she herself had half of her girl friend's bed. There was really no room for a third, and least of all for a man, in those small rooms packed with furniture and the two girls' belongings: Pepita tried to be grateful for her friend Callie's forbearance — but how could she be, when it had not occurred to Callie that she would do better to be away tonight? She was more slow-witted than narrow-minded — but Pepita felt she owed a kind of ruin to her. Callie, not yet known to be home later than ten, would be now waiting up, in her housecoat, to welcome Arthur. That would mean three-

sided chat, drinking cocoa, then turning in: that would be that, and that would be all. That was London, this war — they were lucky to have a roof — London, full enough before the Americans came.[1] Not a place: they would even grudge you sharing a grave — that was what even married couples complained. Whereas in Kôr . . .

In Kôr . . . Like glass, the illusion shattered: a car hummed like a hornet towards them, veered, showed its scarlet tail-light, streaked away up the road. A woman edged round a front door and along the area railings timidly called her cat; meanwhile a clock near, then another set further back in the dazzling distance, set about striking midnight. Pepita, feeling Arthur release her arm with an abruptness that was the inverse of passion, shivered; whereat he asked brusquely: 'Cold? Well, which way? — we'd better be getting on.'

Callie was no longer waiting up. Hours ago she had set out the three cups and saucers, the tins of cocoa and household milk and, on the gas-ring, brought the kettle to just short of the boil. She had turned open Arthur's bed, the living-room divan, in the neat inviting way she had learnt at home — then, with a modest impulse, replaced the cover. She had, as Pepita foresaw, been wearing her cretonne housecoat, the nearest thing to a hostess gown that she had; she had already brushed her hair for the night, rebraided it, bound the braids in a coronet round her head. Both lights and the wireless had been on, to make the room both look and sound gay: all alone, she had come to that peak moment at which company should arrive — but so seldom does. From then on she felt welcome beginning to wither in her, a flower of the heart that had bloomed too early. There she had sat like an image, facing the three cold cups, on the edge of the bed to be occupied by an unknown man.

Callie's innocence and her still unsought-out state had brought her to take a proprietary pride in Arthur; this was all the stronger, perhaps, because they had not yet met. Sharing the flat with Pepita, this last year, she had been content with reflecting the heat of love. It was not, surprisingly, that Pepita seemed very happy — there were times when she was palpably on the rack, and this was not what Callie could understand. 'Surely you owe it to Arthur,' she would then say, 'to keep cheerful? So long as you love each other —' Callie's calm brow glowed — one might say that it glowed in place of her friend's; she became the guardian of that ideality which for Pepita was constantly lost to view. It was true, with the sudden prospect of Arthur's leave, things had come nearer to earth: he became a proposition, and she would have been as glad if he could have slept somewhere else. Physically shy, a brotherless virgin, Callie shrank from sharing this flat with a young man. In this flat you could hear everything: what was once a three-windowed Victorian drawing-room had been partitioned, by very thin walls, into kitchenette, living-room, Callie's bedroom. The living-room was in the centre; the two others open off it. What was once the conservatory, half a flight down, was now converted into a draughty bathroom, shared with somebody else on the girls' floor. The flat, for these days, was cheap — even so, it was Callie, earning more than Pepita, who paid the greater part of the rent: it thus became up to her, more or less, to express good will as to Arthur's making a third. 'Why, it will be lovely to have him here,' Callie said. Pepita accepted the good will without much grace — but then, had she ever much grace to spare? — she was as restlessly secretive, as self-centred, as a little half-grown black cat. Next came a puzzling moment: Pepita seemed to be hinting that Callie should fix herself up somewhere else. 'But where would I go?' Callie marvelled when this was at last borne in on her. 'You know what London's like now. And, anyway' — here she laughed, but hers was a forehead that coloured as easily as it glowed — 'it wouldn't be proper, would it, me going off and leaving just you and Arthur; I don't know what your mother would say to me. No, we may be a little squashed, but we'll make things ever so homey. I shall not mind playing gooseberry, really, dear.'

But the hominess by now was evaporating, as Pepita and Arthur still and still did not come. At half-past ten, in obedience to the rule of the house, Callie was obliged to turn off the wireless, whereupon silence out of the stepless street began seeping into the slighted room. Callie recollected the fuel target and turned off her dear little table lamp, gaily painted with spots to make it look like a toadstool, thereby leaving only the hanging light. She laid her hand on the kettle, to find it going cold again and sighed for the wasted gas if not for her wasted thought. Where are they? Cold crept up her out of the kettle; she went to bed.

Callie's bed lay along the wall under the window: she did not like sleeping so close up under glass, but the clearance that must be left for the opening of door and cupboards made this the only possible place. Now she got in and lay rigidly on the bed's inner side, under the hanging hems of the window curtains, training her limbs not to stray to what would be Pepita's half. This sharing of her bed with another body would not be the least of her sacrifice to the lovers' love; tonight would be the first night — or at least, since she was an infant — that Callie had slept

with anyone. Child of a sheltered middle-class household, she had kept physical distances all her life. Already repugnance and shyness ran through her limbs; she was preyed upon by some more obscure trouble than the expectation that she might not sleep. As to *that*, Pepita was restless; her tossings on the divan, her broken-off exclamations and blurred pleas had been heard, most nights, through the dividing wall.

Callie knew, as though from a vision, that Arthur would sleep soundly, with assurance and majesty. Did they not all say, too, that a soldier sleeps like a log? With awe she pictured, asleep, the face that she had not yet, awake, seen — Arthur's man's eyelids, cheek-bones and set mouth turned up to the darkened ceiling. Wanting to savour darkness herself, Callie reached out and put off her bedside lamp.

At once she knew that something was happening — outdoors, in the street, the whole of London, the world. An advance, an extraordinary movement was silently taking place; blue-white beams overflowed from it, silting, dropping round the edges of the muffling black-out curtains. When, starting up, she knocked a fold of the curtain, a beam like a mouse ran across her bed. A search-light, the most powerful of all time, might have been turned full and steady upon her defended window; finding flaws in the black-out stuff, it made veins and stars. Once gained by this idea of pressure she could not lie down again; she sat tautly, drawn-up knees touching her breasts, and asked herself if there were anything she should do. She parted the curtains, opened them slowly wider, looked out — and was face to face with the moon.

Below the moon, the houses opposite her window blazed back in transparent shadow; and something — was it a coin or a ring? — glittered half-way across the chalk-white street. Light marched in past her face, and she turned to see where it went: out stood the curves and garlands of the great white marble Victorian mantelpiece of the lost drawing-room; out stood, in the photographs turned her way, the thoughts with which her parents had faced the camera, and the humble puzzlement of her two dogs at home. Of silver brocade, just faintly purpled with roses, became her housecoat hanging over the chair. And the moon did more: it exonerated and beautified the lateness of the lovers' return. No wonder, she said to herself, no wonder — if this was the world they walked in, if this was whom they were with. Having drunk in the white explanation, Callie lay down again. Her half of the bed was in shadow, but she allowed one hand to lie, blanched, in what would be Pepita's place. She lay and looked at the hand until it was no longer her own.

Callie woke to the sound of Pepita's key in the latch. But no voices? What had happened? Then she heard Arthur's step. She heard his unslung equipment dropped with a weary, dull sound, and the plonk of his tin hat on a wooden chair. 'Sssh-sssh!' Pepita exclaimed, 'she *might* be asleep!'

Then at last Arthur's voice: 'But I thought you said —'

'I'm not asleep; I'm just coming!' Callie called out with rapture, leaping out from her form in shadow into the moonlight, zipping on her enchanted house-coat over her nightdress, kicking her shoes on, and pinning in place, with a trembling firmness, her plaits in their coronet round her head. Between these movements of hers she heard not another sound. Had she only dreamed they were there? Her heart beat: she stepped through the living-room, shutting her door behind her.

Pepita and Arthur stood the other side of the table; they gave the impression of being lined up. Their faces, at different levels — for Pepita's rough, dark head came only an inch above Arthur's khaki shoulder — were alike in abstention from any kind of expression, as though, spiritually, they both still refused to be here. Their features looked faint, weathered — was this the work of the moon? Pepita said at once: 'I suppose we are very late?'

'I don't wonder,' Callie said, 'on this lovely night.'

Arthur had not raised his eyes; he was looking at the three cups. Pepita now suddenly jogged his elbow, saying, 'Arthur, wake up; say something; this is Callie — well, Callie, this is Arthur, of course.'

'Why, yes of course this is Arthur,' returned Callie, whose candid eyes since she entered had not left Arthur's face. Perceiving that Arthur did not know what to do, she advanced round the table to shake hands with him. He looked up, she looked down, for the first time: she rather beheld than felt his red-brown grip on what still seemed her glove of moonlight. 'Welcome, Arthur,' she said. 'I'm so glad to meet you at last. I hope you will be comfortable in the flat.'

'It's been kind of you,' he said after consideration.

'Please do not feel that,' said Callie. 'This is Pepita's home, too, and we both hope — don't we, Pepita? — that you'll regard it as yours. Please feel free to do just as you like. I am sorry it is so small.'

'Oh, I don't know,' Arthur said, as though hypnotized; 'it seems a nice little place.'

Pepita, meanwhile, glowered and turned away.

Arthur continued to wonder, though he had once been told, how these two unalike girls had come to set up together — Pepita so small, except for her too-big head, compact of childish brusqueness and of

unchildish passion, and Callie, so sedate, waxy and tall — an unlit candle. Yes, she was like one of those candles on sale outside a church; there could be something votive even in her demeanour. She was unconscious that her good manners, those of an old-fashioned country doctor's daughter, were putting the other two at a disadvantage. He found himself touched by the grave good faith with which Callie was wearing that tartish housecoat, above which her face kept the glaze of sleep; and, as she knelt to relight the gas-ring under the kettle, he marked the strong, delicate arch of one bare foot, disappearing into the arty green shoe. Pepita was now too near him ever again to be seen as he now saw Callie — in a sense, he never *had* seen Pepita for the first time: she had not been, and still sometimes was not, his type. No, he had not thought of her twice; he had not remembered her until he began to remember her with passion. You might say he had not seen Pepita coming: their love had been a collision in the dark.

Callie, determined to get this over, knelt back and said: 'Would Arthur like to wash his hands?' When they had heard him stumble down the half-flight of stairs, she said to Pepita: 'Yes, I was so glad you had the moon.'

'Why?' said Pepita. She added: 'There was too much of it.'

'You're tired. Arthur looks tired, too.'

'How would you know? He's used to marching about. But it's all this having no place to go.'

'But, Pepita, you —'

But at this point Arthur came back: from the door he noticed the wireless, and went direct to it. 'Nothing much on now, I suppose?' he doubtfully said.

'No; you see it's past midnight; we're off the air. And, anyway, in this house they don't like the wireless late. By the same token,' went on Callie, friendly smiling, 'I'm afraid I must ask you, Arthur, to take your boots off, unless, of course, you mean to stay sitting down. The people below us —'

Pepita flung off, saying something under her breath, but Arthur, remarking, 'No, I don't mind,' both sat down and began to take off his boots. Pausing, glancing to left and right at the divan's fresh cotton spread, he said: 'It's all right is it, for me to sit on this?'

'That's my bed,' said Pepita. 'You are to sleep in it.'

Callie then made the cocoa, after which they turned in. Preliminary trips to the bathroom having been worked out, Callie was first to retire, shutting the door behind her so that Pepita and Arthur might kiss each other good night. When Pepita joined her, it was without knocking: Pepita stood still in the moon and began to tug off her clothes. Glancing with hate at the bed, she asked: 'Which side?'

'I expected you'd like the outside.'

'What are you standing about for?'

'I don't really know: as I'm inside I'd better get in first.'

'Then why not get in?'

When they had settled rigidly, side by side, Callie asked: 'Do you think Arthur's got all he wants?'

Pepita jerked her head up. 'We can't sleep in all this moon.'

'Why, you don't believe the moon does things, actually?'

'Well, it couldn't hope to make some of us *much* more screwy.'

Callie closed the curtains, then said: 'What do you mean? And — didn't you hear? — I asked if Arthur's got all he wants.'

'That's what I meant — have you got a screw loose, really?'

'Pepita, I won't stay here if you're going to be like this.'

'In that case, you had better go in with Arthur.'

'What about me?' Arthur loudly said through the wall. 'I can hear practically all you girls are saying.'

They were both startled — rather that than abashed. Arthur, alone in there, had thrown off the ligatures of his social manner: his voice held the whole authority of his sex — he was impatient, sleepy, and he belonged to no one.

'Sorry,' the girls said in unison. Then Pepita laughed soundlessly, making their bed shake, till to stop herself she bit the back of her hand, and this movement made her elbow strike Callie's cheek. 'Sorry,' she had to whisper. No answer. Pepita fingered her elbow and found, yes, it was quite true, it was wet. 'Look, shut up crying, Callie: what have I done?'

Callie rolled right round, in order to press her forehead closely under the window, into the curtains, against the wall. Her weeping continued to be soundless: now and then, unable to reach her handkerchief, she staunched her eyes with a curtain, disturbing slivers of moon. Pepita gave up marvelling, and soon slept: at least there is something in being dog-tired.

A clock struck four as Callie woke up again — but something else had made her open her swollen eyelids. Arthur, stumbling about on his padded feet, could be heard next door attempting to make no noise. Inevitably, he bumped the edge of the table. Callie sat up: by her side Pepita lay like a mummy rolled half over, in forbidding, tenacious sleep. Arthur groaned. Callie caught a breath, climbed lightly over Pepita, felt

for her torch on the mantelpiece, stopped to listen again. Arthur groaned again: Callie, with movements soundless as they were certain, opened the door and slipped through to the living-room. 'What's the matter?' she whispered. 'Are you ill?'

'No; I just got a cigarette. Did I wake you up?'

'But you groaned.'

'I'm sorry; I'd no idea.'

'But do you often?'

'I've no idea, really, I tell you,' Arthur repeated. The air of the room was dense with his presence, overhung by tobacco. He must be sitting on the edge of his bed, wrapped up in his overcoat — she could smell the coat, and each time he pulled on the cigarette his features appeared down there, in the fleeting, dull reddish glow. 'Where are you?' he said. 'Show a light.'

Her nervous touch on her torch, like a reflex to what he said, made it flicker up for a second. 'I am just by the door; Pepita's asleep; I'd better go back to bed.'

'Listen. Do you two get on each other's nerves?'

'Not till tonight,' said Callie, watching the uncertain swoops of the cigarette as he reached across to the ashtray on the edge of the table. Shifting her bare feet patiently, she added: 'You don't see us as we usually are.'

'She's a girl who shows things in funny ways — I expect she feels bad at our putting you out like this — I know I do. But then we'd got no choice, had we?'

'It is really I who am putting you out,' said Callie.

'Well, that can't be helped either, can it? You had the right to stay in your own place. If there'd been more time, we might have gone to the country, though I still don't see where we'd have gone there. It's one harder when you're not married, unless you've got the money. Smoke?'

'No, thank you. Well, if you're all right, I'll go back to bed.'

'I'm glad she's asleep — funny the way she sleeps, isn't it? You can't help wondering where she is. You haven't got a boy, have you, just at present?'

'No, I've never had one.'

'I'm not sure in one way that you're not better off. I can see there's not so much in it for a girl these days. It makes me feel cruel the way I unsettle her: I don't know how much it's me myself or how much it's something the matter that I can't help. How are any of us to know how things could have been? They forget war's not just only war; it's years out of people's lives that they've never had before and won't have again. Do you think she's fanciful?'

'Who, Pepita?'

'It's enough to make her — tonight was the pay-off. We couldn't get near any movie or any place for sitting; you had to fight into the bars, and she hates the staring in bars, and with all that milling about, every street we went, they kept on knocking her even off my arm. So then we took the tube to that park down there, but the place was as bad as daylight, let alone it was cold. We hadn't the nerve — well, that's nothing to do with you.'

'I don't mind.'

'Or else you don't understand. So we began to play — we were off in Kôr.'

'Core of what?'

'Mysterious Kôr — ghost city.'

'Where?'

'You may ask. But I could have sworn she saw it, and from the way she saw it I saw it, too. A game's a game, but what's a hallucination? You begin by laughing, then it gets in you and you can't laugh it off. I tell you, I woke up just now not knowing where I'd been; and I had to get up and feel round this table before I even knew where I was. It wasn't till then that I thought of a cigarette. Now I see why she sleeps like that, if that's where she goes.'

'But she is just as often restless; I often hear her.'

'Then she doesn't always make it. Perhaps it takes me, in some way — Well, I can't see any harm: when two people have got no place, why not want Kôr, as a start? There are no restrictions on wanting, at any rate.'

'But, oh, Arthur, can't wanting want what's human?'

He yawned. 'To be human's to be at a dead loss.' Stopping yawning, he ground out his cigarette: the china tray skidded at the edge of the table. 'Bring that light here a moment — that is, will you? I think I've messed ash all over these sheets of hers.'

Callie advanced with the torch alight, but at arm's length: now and then her thumb made the beam wobble. She watched the lit-up inside of Arthur's hand as he brushed the sheet; and once he looked up to see her white-nightgowned figure curving above and away from him, behind the arc of light. 'What's that swinging?'

'One of my plaits of hair. Shall I open the window wider?'

'What, to let the smoke out? Go on. And how's your moon?'

'Mine?' Marvelling over this, as the first sign that Arthur remembered that she was Callie, she uncovered the window, pushed up the sash, then after a minute said: 'Not so strong.'

Indeed, the moon's power over London and the imagination had now declined. The siege of light had relaxed; the search was over; the street had a look of survival and no more. Whatever had glittered there, coin or ring, was now invisible or had gone. To Callie it seemed likely that there would never be such a moon again; and on the whole she felt this was for the best. Feeling air reach in like a tired arm round her body, she dropped the curtains against it and returned to her own room.

Back by her bed, she listened: Pepita's breathing still had the regular sound of sleep. At the other side of the wall the divan creaked as Arthur stretched himself out again. Having felt ahead of her lightly, to make sure her half was empty, Callie climbed over Pepita and got in. A certain amount of warmth had travelled between the sheets from Pepita's flank, and in this Callie extended her sword-cold body: she tried to compose her limbs; even they quivered after Arthur's words in the dark, words *to* the dark. The loss of her own mysterious expectation, of her love for love, was a small thing beside the war's total of unlived lives. Suddenly Pepita flung out one hand: its back knocked Callie lightly across the face.

Pepita had now turned over and lay with her face up. The hand that had struck Callie must have lain over the other, which grasped the pyjama collar. Her eyes, in the dark, might have been either shut or open, but nothing made her frown more or less steadily: it became certain, after another moment, that Pepita's act of justice had been unconscious. She still lay, as she had lain, in an avid dream, of which Arthur had been the source, of which Arthur was not the end. With him she looked this way, that way, down the wide void pure streets, between statues, pillars and shadows, through archways and colonnades. With him she went up the stairs down which nothing but moon came; with him trod the ermine dust of the endless halls, stood on terraces, mounted the extreme tower, looked down on the statued squares, the wide, void, pure streets. He was the password, but not the answer: it was to Kôr's finality that she turned.

1   The United States entered the War on 8 December 1941.

DENIS DEVLIN
from Denis Devlin, *Lough Derg and Other Poems* (1946)

Devlin's extraordinary meditation on the two natures that have driven Europe to distraction beginning with the Greeks, through the early Christian period to Dante and the Renaissance and then on to the Irish present (and the return to North-West Europe). The movement and compression of this poem require considerable application to appreciate, but it is worth the effort. For an introduction to Devlin's verse see Brian Coffey, 'The Complete Poems of Denis Devlin' in *Irish University Review* (1963). Lough Derg is a place of pilgrimage in County Donegal. See Sean O'Faolain's short story 'Lovers of the Lake' (1957) on page 695 below for another fine meditation arising from the penitential scene.

LOUGH DERG

The poor in spirit on their rosary rounds,
The jobbers[1] with their whiskey-angered eyes,
The pink bank clerks, the tip-hat papal counts,
And drab, kind women their tonsured mockery tries,
Glad invalids on penitential feet
Walk the Lord's majesty like their village street.

With mullioned Europe shattered, this Northwest,
Rude-sainted isle would pray it whole again:
(Peasant Apollo! Troy is worn to rest.)
Europe that humanized the sacred bane
Of God's chance who yet laughed in his mind
And balanced thief and saint: were they this kind?

Low rocks, a few weasels, lake
Like a field of burnt gorse; the rooks caw;
Ours, passive, for man's gradual wisdom take
Firefly instinct dreamed out into law;
The prophets' jewelled kingdom down at heel
Fires no Augustine here. Inert, they kneel;

All is simple and symbol in their world,
The incomprehended rendered fabulous.
Sin teases life whose natural fruits withheld
Sour the deprived nor bloom for timely loss:
Clan Jansen![2] less what magnanimity leavens
Man's wept-out, fitful, magniloquent heavens

Where prayer was praise, O Lord! the Temple
    trumpets
Cascaded down Thy sunny pavilions of air,
The scroll-tongued priests, the galvanic strumpets,
All clash and stridency gloomed upon Thy stair;
The pharisees, the exalted boy their power
Sensually psalmed in Thee, their coming hour!

And to the sun, earth turned her flower of sex,
Acanthus[3] in the architects' limpid angles;
Close priests allegorized the Orphic egg's
Brood, and from the Academy, tolerant wranglers
Could hear the contemplatives of the Tragic Choir
Drain off man's sanguine, pastoral death-desire.

It was said stone dreams and animal sleeps and man
Is awake; but sleep with its drama on us bred
Animal articulate, only somnambulist can
Conscience like Cawdor give the blood its head
For the dim moors to reign through druids again.
O first geometer! tangent-feelered brain

Clearing by inches the encircled eyes,
Bolder than the peasant tiger whose autumn beauty
Sags in the expletive kill, or the sacrifice
Of dearth puffed positive in the stance of duty
With which these pilgrims would propitiate
Their fears; no leafy, medieval state

Of paschal cathedrals backed on earthy hooves
Against the craftsmen's primary-coloured skies
Whose gold was Gabriel on the patient roofs,
The parabled windows taught the dead to rise,
And Christ the Centaur, in two natures whole,
With fable and proverb joinered body and soul.

Water withers from the oars. The pilgrims blacken
Out of the boats to masticate their sin
Where Dante smelled among the stones and bracken
The door to Hell (O harder Hell where pain
Is earthed, a casuist sanctuary of guilt!).
Spirit bureaucracy on a bet built

Part by this race when monks in convents of coracles
For the Merovingian[4] centuries left their land,
Belled, fragrant; and honest in their oracles
Bespoke the grace to give without demand,
Martyrs Heaven winged nor tempted with reward.
And not ours, doughed in dogma, who never have
    dared

Will with surrogate palm distribute hope:
No better nor worse than I who, in my books,
Have angered at the stake with Bruno[5] and, by the rope
Watt Tyler[6] swung from, leagued with shifty looks
To fuse the next rebellion with the desperate
Serfs in the sane need to eat and get;

Have praised, on its thunderous canvas, the Florentine
    smile
As man took to wearing his death, his own,
Sapped crisis through cathedral branches (while
Flesh groped loud round dissenting skeleton)
In soul, reborn as body's appetite:
Now languisht back in body's amber light,

Now is consumed. O earthly paradise!
Hell is to know our natural empire used
Wrong, by mind's moulting, brute divinities.
The vanishing tiger's saved, his blood transfused.
Kent is for Jutes again and Glasgow town
Burns high enough to screen the stars and moon.

Well may they cry who have been robbed, their
    wasting
Shares in justice legally lowered until
Man his own actor, matrix, mould and casting,
Or man, God's image, sees his idol spill.
Say it was pride that did it, or virtue's brief:
To them that suffer it is no relief.

All indiscriminate, man, stone, animal
Are woken up in nightmare. What John the Blind[7]

From Patmos saw works and we speak it. Not all
The men of God nor the priests of mankind
Can mend or explain the good and broke, not one
Generous with love prove communion;

Behind the eyes the winged ascension flags,
For want of spirit by the market blurbed,
And if hands touch, such fraternity sags
Frightened this side the dykes of death disturbed
Like Aran Islands' bibulous, unclean seas:
Pietà: but the limbs ache; it is not peace.

Then to see less, look little, let hearts' hunger
Feed on water and berries. The pilgrims sing:
Life will fare well from elder to younger,
Though courage fail in a world-end, rosary ring.
Courage kills its practitioners and we live,
Nothing forgotten, nothing to forgive,

We pray to ourself. The metal moon, unspent
Virgin eternity sleeping in the mind,
Excites the form of prayer without content;
Whitethorn lightens, delicate and blind,
The negro mountain, and so, knelt on her sod,
This woman beside me murmuring *My God! My God!*

1   Dealers, traders.
2   Cornelis Jansen (1585–1638), Dutch Catholic
    theologian who advanced a form of Calvinist
    predestination, which was condemned as heresy by the
    Church. For Jansen, the body was fallen, rent, sinful.
3   A perennial herb, in Christian art a symbol of Heaven.
4   Dynasty of Frankish kings in sixth and seventh centuries.
5   Giordano Bruno (1548–1600) (Bruno of Nolan), an
    Italian Dominican burnt at the stake for heresy.
6   Leader of the English Peasants' Revolt in 1381.
7   It is thought that St John the Evangelist wrote *Revelations*
    on the island of Patmos. The epithet here is presumably
    meant to be metaphoric.

JOHN COULTER
from John Coulter, *The Blossoming Thorn* (1946)

John Coulter (1888–1980) was born in Belfast, moved to London in 1920, contributed programmes to BBC radio, edited *The New Adelphi* in 1927-30, and emigrated to Canada in the 1930s. Now considered a Canadian writer, he was deeply influenced by the Irish Literary Revival and wrote the libretto to an opera *Deirdre of the Sorrows* (1946) based on the Irish legend. In *Turf Smoke* (1945), his evocative emigration novel set in New York, the position of his protagonist Barney Cahill from Clogherbann in Ulster is given at the outset: 'In name he was an immigrant citizen of the new world, but at heart still an exile from the old.' Here in this highly-charged group of poems Coulter conveys something of the predicament of the Irish in Canada who felt caught between two worlds.

IMMIGRANT-EXILE I

It is only the charity of the slow passage of time
That can scatter at last the ambushed grief in the heart
Of the immigrant-exile unweaned from his native
    clime:
Voices and scenes that he loved, that for ever are part
Of his innermost being, mourn their betrayal and are
As weeping and wounds, an emotional gangrene, at
    the core
Of feeling and thought: he is a man with himself at war,
Sundered between a remembered real that more
And more unreal seems, and a present not yet grown
Familiar and accepted in the local aspect of reality;
And thus though in public he laughs with new friends,
    alone
He grieves, his roots still burrowing for their native clay
    Vainly, beneath will and reason, till the dark boughs
        of his mind
    Stand withered in mid-summer, spectral in an alien
        wind.

IMMIGRANT-EXILE II

These are they who stood silent by the stern-rail while
    the hills of home
Receded, washed down, far down in the wake, and
    the last beacon light
Dwindled and burned and dwindled beyond the
    hurrying foam
Till the black illimitable chasm of the Atlantic night
Engulfed them utterly, and suddenly in the windy dark
    the tears
Stoically pent behind the mask of farewell smiles
And bravery of words, flowed; these through the
    tentative years
Still wandered upon the face of the waters, retravelling
    the travelled miles,
Finding no rest for the sole of the foot but alien seas
Stretching for ever to the far horizon, from the native
    spring
Of feeling and being, severing; these were the derelict,
    these
The venturing exiles who knew not if the years should
    bring

A token wing, as once to the window of the ark the
    dove,
And the grounding of the keel at last on a new land
    to serve and love.

IMMIGRANT-EXILE III

Who turns from ancestral soil in sapling days
May strike true root in some new-chosen clime,
But the grown tree uprooted rootless stays
Shedding its withering leaves as now my rhyme
Sheds them; seeing imagination lives
And comprehends the world through symbols wrought
In the enraptured dreaming of youth, and therefrom
    gives
To all our ways a pattern of feeling and thought,
Colour and contour of mind which no more change
Than changes the hue of the eye, a natal sign
Lasting as life, I still an exile range
Through this new land, and while I claim it mine
    Do hear in my heart the contradictory call
    Of curlews on the hills of Donegal.

RHYME OF TWO WORLDS

I look upon bare trees
Under a windy sky
Yet looking see not these
But winter long gone by:

Those trees, that windy sky,
Our bleak mountain and glen
In a turf-brown country where I
Talk with the mountainy men,

Who move in a mist of dreams
Elusive as their grey eyes,
Where in the plash of streams
A lone curlew cries,

Till clamouring through that pain,
Gigantic in the sky
Comes the trans-Canada plane,
A portent, thundering by.

J. F. POWERS
from J. F. Powers, *Prince of Darkness and Other Stories* (1947)

James Farl Powers was born in Jacksonville, Illinois in 1917, and educated at Northwestern University, Chicago. *Prince of Darkness*, his first collection of stories, was followed by *The Presence of Grace* (1956) and *Look How the Fish Live* (1975). His novel *Morte D'Urban* (1962) was a winner of the National Book Award. 'Prince of Darkness', set in the American Mid-West, is a beautifully written story about the secular side to secular priests. An essay on Powers is included in Gerard Keenan, *The Professional, the Amateur and the Other Thing: Essays from 'The Honest Ulsterman'* (1995).

Prince of Darkness

I. Morning

'I should've known you'd be eating breakfast, Father. But I was at your Mass and I said to myself that must be Father Burner. Then I stayed a few minutes after Mass to make my thanksgiving.'

'Fine,' Father Burner said. 'Breakfast?'

'Had it, Father, thanking you all the same. It's the regret of my life that I can't be a daily communicant. Doctor forbids it. "Fast every day and see how long you last," he tells me. But I do make it to Mass.'

'Fine. You say you live in Father Desmond's parish?'

'Yes, Father. And sometimes I think Father Desmond does too much. All the societies to look after. Plus the Scouts and the Legion.[1] Of course Father Kells being so elderly and all . . .'

'We're all busy these days.'

'It's the poor parish priest's day that's never done, I always say, Father, not meaning to slight the ladies, God love 'em.'

Father Burner's sausage fingers, spelling his impatience over and over, worked up sweat in the folds of the napkin which he kept in view to provoke an early departure. 'About this matter you say Father Desmond thought I might be interested in —'

'The Plan, Father.' Mr Tracy lifted his seersucker trousers by the creases, crossed his shining two-tone shoes, and rolled warmly forward. 'Father . . .'

Father Burner met his look briefly. He was wary of the fatherers. A backslider he could handle, it was the old story, but a red-hot believer, especially a talkative one, could be a devilish nuisance. This kind might be driven away only by prayer and fasting, and he was not adept at either.

'I guess security's one thing we're all after.'

Father Burner grunted. Mr Tracy was too familiar to suit him. He liked his parishioners to be retiring, dumb, or frightened. There were too many references

made to the priest's hard lot. Not so many poor souls as all that passed away in the wee hours, nor was there so much bad weather to brave. Mr Tracy's heart bled for priests. That in itself was a suspicious thing in a layman. It all led up to the Plan.

'Here's the Plan, Father . . .' Father Burner watched his eye peel down to naked intimacy. Then, half listening, he gazed about the room. He hated it, too. A fabulous brown rummage of encyclopedias, world globes, maps, photographs, holy pictures, mirrors, crucifixes, tropical fish, and too much furniture. The room reproduced the world, all wonders and horrors, less land than water. From the faded precipices of the walls photographs viewed each other for the most part genially across time. Three popes, successively thinner, raised hands to bless their departed painters. The world globes simpered in the shadows, heavy-headed idiot boys, listening. A bird in a blacked-out cage scratched among its offal. An anomalous buddha peeked beyond his dusty umbilicus at the trampled figures in the rug. The fish swam on, the mirrors and encyclopedias turned in upon themselves, the earless boys heard everything and understood nothing. Father Burner put his big black shoe on a moth and sent dust flecks crowding up a shaft of sunlight to the distant ceiling.

'Say you pay in $22.67 every month, can be paid semi-annually or as you please, policy matures in twenty years and pays you $35.50 a month for twenty years or as long as you live. That's the deal for you, Father. It beats the deal Father Desmond's got, although he's got a darned good one, and I hope he keeps it up. But we've gone ahead in the last few years, Father. Utilities are sounder, bonds are more secure, and this new legislation protects you one hundred per cent.'

'You say Ed — Father Desmond — has the Plan?'

'Oh, indeed, Father.' Mr Tracy had to laugh. 'I hope you don't think I'm trying to high-pressure you, Father. It's not just a piece of business with me, the Plan.'

'No?'

'No. You see, it's more or less a pet project of mine. Hardly make a cent on it. Looking out after the fathers, you might say, so they'll maybe look out after me — spiritually. I call it heavenly life insurance.'

Slightly repelled, Father Burner nodded.

'Not a few priests that I've sold the Plan to remember me at the altar daily. I guess prayer's one thing we can all use. Anyway, it's why I take a hand in putting boys through seminary.'

With that Mr Tracy shed his shabby anonymity for Father Burner, and grew executive markings. He became the one and only Thomas Nash Tracy — T.N.T. It was impossible to read the papers and not know a few things about T.N.T. He was in small loans and insurance. His company's advertising smothered the town and country; everybody knew the slogan 'T.N.T. Spells Security.' He figured in any financial drive undertaken by the diocese, was caught by photographers in orphanages, and sat at the heavy end of the table at communion breakfasts. Hundreds of nuns, thanks to his thoughtfulness, ate capon on Christmas Day, and a few priests of the right sort received baskets of scotch. He was a B.C.L., a Big Catholic Layman, and now Father Burner could see why. Father Burner's countenance softened at this intelligence, and T.N.T. proceeded with more assurance.

'And don't call it charity, Father. Insurance, as I said, is a better name for it. I have a little money, Father, which makes it possible.' He tuned his voice down to a whisper. 'You might say I'm moderately wealthy.' He looked sharply at Father Burner, not sure of his man. 'But I'm told there isn't any crime in that.'

'I believe you need not fear for your soul on that account.'

'Glad to hear it from you, a priest, Father. Oft-times it's thrown up to me.' He came to terms with reality, smiling. 'I wasn't always so well off myself, so I can understand the temptation to knock the other fellow.'

'Fine.'

'But that's still not to say that water's not wet or that names don't hurt sometimes, whatever the bard said to the contrary.'

'What bard?'

'"Sticks and stones —"'

'Oh.'

'If this were a matter of faith and morals, Father, I'd be the one to sit back and let you do the talking. But it's a case of common sense, Father, and I think I can safely say, if you listen to me you'll not lose by it in the long run.'

'It could be.'

'May I ask you a personal question, Father?'

Father Burner searched T.N.T.'s face. 'Go ahead, Mr Tracy.'

'Do you bank, Father?'

'*Bank?* Oh, bank — no. Why?'

'Let's admit it, Father,' T.N.T. coaxed, frankly amused. 'Priests as a class are an improvident lot — our records show it — and you're no exception. But that, I think, explains the glory of the Church down through the ages.'

'The Church is divine,' Father Burner corrected. 'And the concept of poverty isn't exactly foreign to Christianity or even to the priesthood.'

'Exactly,' T.N.T. agreed, pinked. 'But think of the future, Father.'

Nowadays when Father Burner thought of the future it required a firm act of imagination. As a seminarian twenty years ago, it had all been plain: ordination, roughly ten years as a curate somewhere (he was not the kind to be sent to Rome for further study), a church of his own to follow, the fruitful years, then retirement, pastor emeritus, with assistants doing the spade work, leaving the fine touches to him, still a hearty old man very much alive. It was not an uncommon hope and, in fact, all around him it had materialized for his friends. But for him it was only a bad memory growing worse. He was the desperate assistant now, the angry functionary ageing in the outer office. One day he would wake and find himself old, as the morning finds itself covered with snow. The future had assumed the forgotten character of a dream, so that he could not be sure that he had ever truly had one.

T.N.T. talked on and Father Burner felt a mist generating on his forehead. He tore his damp hands apart and put the napkin aside. Yes, yes, it was true a priest received miserably little, but then that was the whole idea. He did not comment, dreading T.N.T.'s foaming compassion, to be spat upon with charity. Yes, as a matter of fact, it would be easier to face old age with something more to draw upon than what the ecclesiastical authorities deemed sufficient and would provide. Also, as T.N.T. pointed out, one never knew when he might come down with an expensive illness. T.N.T., despite himself, had something . . . The Plan, in itself, was not bad. He must not reject the olive branch because it came by buzzard. But still Father Burner was a little bothered by the idea of a priest feathering his nest. Why? In other problems he was never the one to take the ascetic interpretation.

'You must be between thirty-five and forty, Father.'

'I'll never see forty again.'

'I'd never believe it from anyone else. You sure don't look it, Father.'

'Maybe not. But I feel it.'

'Worries, Father. And one big one is the future, Father. You'll get to be fifty, sixty, seventy — and what have you got? — not a penny saved. You look around and say to yourself — where did it go?'

T.N.T. had the trained voice of the good and faithful servant, supple from many such dealings. And still from time to time a faint draught of contempt seemed to pass through it which had something to do with his eyes. Here, Father Burner thought, was the latest thing in simony,[2] unnecessary, inspired from without, participated in spiritlessly by the priest who must yet suffer the brunt of the blame and ultimately do the penance. Father Burner felt mysteriously purchasable. He was involved in an exchange of confidences which impoverished him mortally. In T.N.T. he sensed free will in its senility or the infinite capacity for equating evil with good — or with nothing — the same thing, only easier. Here was one more word in the history of the worm's progress, another wave on the dry flood that kept rising, the constant aggrandizement of decay. In the end it must touch the world and everything at the heart. Father Burner felt weak from a nameless loss.

'I think I can do us both a service, Father.'

'I don't say you can't.' Father Burner rose quickly. 'I'll have to think about it, Mr Tracy.'

'To be sure, Father.' He produced a glossy circular. 'Just let me leave this literature with you.'

Father Burner, leading him to the door, prevented further talk by reading the circular. It was printed in a churchy type, all purple and gold, a dummy leaf from a medieval hymnal, and entitled 'A Silver Lining in the Sky'. It was evidently meant for clergymen only, though not necessarily priests, as Father Burner could instantly see from its general tone.

'Very interesting,' he said.

'My business phone is right on the back, Father. But if you'd rather call me at my home some night —'

'No thanks, Mr Tracy.'

'Allow me to repeat, Father, this isn't just business with me.'

'I understand.' He opened the door too soon for T.N.T. 'Glad to have met you.'

'Glad to have met you, Father.'

Father Burner went back to the table. The coffee needed warming up and the butter had vanished into the toast. 'Mary,' he called. Then he heard them come gabbing into the rectory, Quinlan and his friend Keefe, also newly ordained.

They were hardly inside the dining room before he was explaining how he came to be eating breakfast so late — so late, see? — not *still*.

'You protest too much, Father,' Quinlan said. 'The Angelic Doctor' himself weighed three hundred pounds, and I'll wager he didn't get it all from prayer and fasting.'

'A pituitary condition,' Keefe interjected, faltering. 'Don't you think?'

'Yah, yah, Father, you'll wager' — Father Burner, eyes malignant, leaned on his knife, the blade bowing out bright and buttery beneath his fist — 'and I'll wager you'll be the first saint to reach heaven with a flannel mouth!' Rising from the table, he shook Keefe's hand, which was damp from his pocket, and experienced a surge of strength, the fat man's contempt and envy for the thin man. He thought he might break Keefe's hand off at the wrist without drawing a drop of blood.

Quinlan stood aside, six inches or more below them, gazing up, as at two impossibly heroic figures in a hotel mural. Reading the caption under them, he mused, 'Father Burner meets Father Keefe.'

'I've heard about you, Father,' Keefe said, plying him with a warmth beyond his means.

'Bound to be the case in a diocese as overstocked with magpies as this one.' Father Burner threw a fresh napkin at a plate. 'But be seated, Father Keefe.' Keefe, yes, he had seen him before, a nobody in a crowd, some affair . . . the K.C.[4] barbecue, the Youth Centre? No, probably not, not Keefe, who was obviously not the type, too crabbed and introversive for Catholic Action. 'I suppose,' he said, 'you've heard the latest definition of Catholic Action — the interference of the laity with the inactivity of the hierarchy.'

'Very good,' Keefe said uneasily.

Quinlan yanked off his collar and churned his neck up and down to get circulation. 'Dean in the house? No? Good.' He pitched the collar at one of the candles on the buffet for a ringer. 'That turkey we met coming out the front door — think I've seen his face somewhere.'

'Thomas Nash Tracy,' Keefe said. 'I thought you knew.'

'The prominent lay priest and usurer?'

Keefe coughed. 'They say he's done a lot of good.'

Quinlan spoke to Father Burner: 'Did you take out a policy, Father?'

'One of the sixth-graders threw a rock through his windshield,' Father Burner said. 'He was very nice about it.'

'Muldoon or Ciesniewski?'

'A new kid. Public school transfer.' Father Burner patted the napkin to his chin. 'Not that I see anything wrong with insurance.'

Quinlan laughed. 'Let Walter tell you what happened to him a few days ago. Go ahead, Walter,' he said to Keefe.

'Oh, that.' Keefe fidgeted and, seemingly against his better judgement, began. 'I had a little accident — was it Wednesday it rained so? I had the misfortune to skid into a fellow parked on Fairmount. Dented his fender.' Keefe stopped and then, as though impelled by the memory of it, went on. 'The fellow came raging out of his car at me. I thought there'd be serious trouble. Then he must have seen I was a priest, the way he calmed down, I mean. I had a funny feeling it wasn't because he was a Catholic or anything like that. As a matter of fact he wore a Masonic button.' Keefe sighed. 'I guess he saw I was a priest and ergo[5] . . . knew I'd have insurance.'

'Take nothing for your journey, neither staff, nor scrip,' Quinlan said, 'words taken from today's gospel.'

Father Burner spoke in a level tone: 'Not that I *still* see anything wrong with insurance. It's awfully easy,' he continued, hating himself for talking drivel, 'to make too much of little things.' With Quinlan around he played the conservative; among the real right-handers he was the *enfant terrible*.[6] He operated on the principle of discord at any cost. He did not know why. It was a habit. Perhaps it had something to do with being overweight.

Arranging the Dean's chair, which had arms, for himself, Quinlan sank into it, giving Keefe the Irish whisper. 'Grace, Father.'

Keefe addressed the usual words to God concerning the gifts they were about to receive. During the prayer Father Burner stopped chewing and did not reach for anything. He noted once more that Quinlan crossed himself sloppily enough to be a monsignor.

Keefe nervously cleared the entire length of his throat. 'It's a beautiful church you have here at Saint Patrick's, Father.' A lukewarm light appeared in his eyes, flickered, sputtered out, leaving them blank and blue. His endless fingers felt for his receding chin in the onslaught of silence.

'*I* have?' Father Burner turned his spoon abasingly to his bosom. '*Me?*' He jabbed at the grapefruit before him, his second, demolishing its perfect rose window. 'I don't know why it is the Irish without exception are always laying personal claim to church property. The Dean is forever saying *my* church, *my* school, *my* furnace . . .'

'I'm sorry, Father,' Keefe said, flushing. 'And I'll confess I did think he virtually built Saint Patrick's.'

'Out of the slime of the earth, I know. A common error.' With sudden, unabated displeasure Father Burner recalled how the Dean, one of the last of the old brick and mortar pastors, had built the church, school, sisters' house, and rectory, and had named the whole thing through the lavish pretence of a popular contest. Opposed bitterly by Polish, German, and Italian minorities, he had effected a compromise between their bad taste (Saint Stanislaus, Saint Boniface, Saint Anthony) and his own better judgement in the choice of Saint Patrick's.

Quinlan, snorting, blurted, 'Well, he did build it, didn't he?'

Father Burner smiled at them from the other world. 'Only, if you please, in a manner of speaking.'

'True,' Keefe murmured humbly.

'Nuts,' Quinlan said. 'It's hard for me to see God in a few buildings paid for by the funds of the faithful and put up by a mick contractor.[7] A burning bush, yes.'

Father Burner, lips parched to speak an unsummonable cruelty, settled for a smoldering aside to the kitchen. 'Mary, more eggs here.'

A stuffed moose of a woman with a tabby-cat face charged in on swollen feet. She stood wavering in shoes sliced fiercely for corns. With the back of her hand she wiped some cream from the fuzz ringing her baby-pink mouth. Her hair poked through a broken net like stunted antlers. Father Burner pointed to the empty platter.

'Eggs,' he said.

'Eggs!' she cried, tumbling her eyes like great blue dice among them. She seized up the platter and carried it whirling with grease into the kitchen.

Father Burner put aside the grapefruit. He smiled and spoke calmly. 'I'll have to let the Dean know, Father, how much you like *his* plant.'

'Do, Father. A beautiful church . . . "a poem in stone" — was it Ruskin?'

'Ruskin? *Stones of Venice*,' Father Burner grumbled. '*Sesame and Lilies*, I know . . . but I never cared for his *style*.' He passed the knife lovingly over the pancakes on his plate and watched the butter bubble at the pores. 'So much sweetness, so much light, I'm afraid, made Jack a dull boy.'

Quinlan slapped all his pockets. 'Pencil and paper, quick!'

'And yet . . .' Keefe cocked his long head, brow fretted, and complained to his upturned hands. 'Don't understand how he stayed outside the Church.' He glanced up hopefully. 'I wonder if Chesterton[8] gives us a clue.'

Father Burner, deaf to such precious speculation, said, 'In the nineteenth century Francis Thompson[9] was the only limey[10] worth his salt. It's true.' He quartered the pancakes. 'Of course, Newman.'[11]

'Hopkins[12] has some good things.'

'Good — yes, if you like jabberwocky and jebbies![13] I don't care for either.' He dispatched a look of indictment at Quinlan.

'What a pity,' Quinlan murmured, 'Oliver Wendell couldn't be at table this morning.'

'No, Father, you can have your Hopkins, you and Father Quinlan here. Include me out, as Sam Goldwyn[14] says. Poetry — I'll take my poetry the way I take my liquor, neat.'

Mary brought in the platter oozing with bacon and eggs.

'Good for you, Mary,' Quinlan said. 'I'll pray for you.'

'Thank you, Father,' Mary said.

Quinlan dipped the platter with a trace of obeisance to Father Burner.

'No thanks.'

Quinlan scooped up the coffeepot in a fearsome rush and held it high at Father Burner, his arm so atremble the lid rattled dangerously. 'Sure and will you be about having a sup of coffee now, Father?'

'Not now. And do you mind not playing the wild Irish wit so early in the day, Father?'

'That I don't. *But a relentless fate pursuing good Father Quinlan, he was thrown in among hardened clerics where but for the grace of God that saintly priest, so little understood, so much maligned . . .*' Quinlan poured two cups and passed one to Keefe. 'For yourself, Father.'

Father Burner nudged the toast to Keefe. 'Father Quinlan, that saintly priest, models his life after the Rover Boys, particularly Sam, the fun-loving one.'

Quinlan dealt himself a mighty *mea culpa*.[15]

Father Burner grimaced, the flesh rising in sweet, concentric tiers around his mouth, and said in a tone both entrusting and ennobling Keefe with his confidence, 'The syrup, if you please, Father.' Keefe passed the silver pitcher which was running at the mouth. Father Burner reimmersed the doughy remains on his plate until the butter began to float around the edges as in a moat. He felt them both watching the butter. Regretting that he had not foreseen this attraction, he cast about in his mind for something to divert them and found the morning sun coming in too strongly. He got up and pulled down the shade. He returned to his plate and settled himself in such a way that a new chapter was indicated. 'Don't believe I know where you're located, Father.'

'Saint Jerome's,' Keefe said. 'Monsignor Fiedler's.'

'One of those P.N. places, eh? Is the boss sorry he ever started it? I know some of them are.'

Keefe's lips popped apart. 'I don't quite understand.'

Quinlan prompted: 'P. N. — Perpetual Novena.'[16]

'Oh, I never heard him say.'

'You wouldn't, of course. But I know a lot of them that are.' Father Burner stuck a morsel on his fork and swirled it against the tide of syrup. 'It's a real problem

all right. I was all out for a P.N. here during the depression. Thought it might help. The Dean was against it.'

'I can tell you this,' Keefe said. 'Attendance was down from what it used to be until the casualties began to come in. Now it's going up.'

'I was just going to say the war ought to take the place of the depression.' Father Burner fell silent. 'Terrible thing, war. Hard to know what to do about it. I tried to sell the Dean the idea of a victory altar. You've seen them. Vigil lights —'

'At a dollar a throw,' Quinlan said.

'Vigil lights in the form of a V, names of the men in the service and all that. But even that, I guess — Well, like I said, I tried . . .'

'Yes, it is hard,' Keefe said.

'God, the Home, and the Flag,' Quinlan said. 'The poets don't make the wars.'

Father Burner ignored that. 'Lately, though, I can't say how I feel about P.N.'s. Admit I'm not so strong for them as I was once. Ought to be some way of terminating them, you know, but then they wouldn't be perpetual, would they?'

'No, they wouldn't,' Keefe said.

'Not *so* perpetual,' Quinlan said.

'Of course,' Father Burner continued, 'the term itself, perpetual novena, is preposterous, a solecism.[17] Possibly dispensation lies in that direction. I'm not theologian enough to say. Fortunately it's not a problem we have to decide.' He laid his knife and fork across the plate. 'Many are the consolations of the lowly curate. No decisions, no money worries.'

'We still have to count the sugar,' Quinlan said. 'And put up the card tables.'

'Reminds me,' Father Burner said earnestly. 'Father Desmond at Assumption was telling me they've got a new machine does all that.'

'Puts up card tables?' Quinlan inquired.

'Counts the collection, wraps the silver,' Father Burner explained, 'so it's all ready for the bank. Mean to mention it to the Dean, if I can catch him right.'

'I'm afraid, Father, he knows about it already.'

Father Burner regarded Quinlan sceptically. 'Does he? I suppose he's against it.'

'I heard him tell the salesman that's what he had his assistants for.'

'Assistant, Father, not assistants. You count the collection, not me. I was only thinking of you.'

'I was only quoting him, Father. *Sic*.[18] Sorry.'

'Not at all. I haven't forgotten the days I had to do it. It's a job has to be done and nothing to be ashamed of. Wouldn't you say, Father Keefe?'

'I dare say that's true.'

Quinlan, with Father Burner still molesting him with his eyes, poured out a glass of water and drank it all. 'I still think we could do with a lot less calculating. I notice the only time we get rid of the parish paper is when the new lists are published — the official standings. Of course it's a lousy sheet anyway.'

Father Burner, as editor of the paper, replied: 'Yes, yes, Father. We all know how easy it is to be wrathful or fastidious about these things — or whatever the hell it is you are. And we all know there *are* abuses. But contributing to the support of the Church is still one of her commandments.'

'Peace, Père,' Quinlan said.

'Figures don't lie.'

'Somebody was telling me just last night that figures do lie. He looked a lot like you.'

Father Burner found his cigarettes and shuffled a couple half out of the pack. He eyed Quinlan and the cigarettes as though it were as simple to discipline the one as to smoke the others. 'For some reason, Father, you're damned fond of those particular figures.'

Keefe stirred. 'Which particular figures, Fathers?'

'It's the figures put out by the Cardinal of Toledo on how many made their Easter duty last year.' Father Burner offered Keefe a cigarette. 'I discussed the whole thing with Father Quinlan last night. It's his latest thesis. Have a cigarette?'

'No, thanks,' Keefe said.

'So you don't smoke?' Father Burner looked from Keefe to Quinlan, blacklisting them together. He held the cigarette hesitantly at his lips. 'It's all right, isn't it?' He laughed and touched off the match with his thumbnail.

'His Eminence,' Quinlan said, 'reports only fifteen per cent of the women and five per cent of the men made their Easter duty last year.'

'So that's only three times as many women as men,' Father Burner said with buried gaiety. 'Certainly to be expected in any Latin country.'

'But fifteen per cent, Father! And five per cent! Just think of it!' Keefe glanced up at the ceiling and at the souvenir plates on the moulding, as though to see inscribed along with scenes from the Columbian Exposition[19] the day and hour the end of the world would begin. He finally stared deep into the goldfish tank in the window.

Father Burner ploughed up the silence, talking with a mouthful of smoke. 'All right, all right, I'll say what I said in the first place. There's something wrong with the figures. A country as overwhelmingly Catholic as Spain!' He sniffed, pursed his lips, and said, 'Pooh!'

'Yes,' Keefe said, still baulking. 'But it *is* disturbing, Father Burner.'

'Sure it's disturbing, Father Keefe. *Lots* of things *are*.'

A big, faded goldfish paused to stare through the glass at them and then with a single lob of its tail slipped into a dark green corner.

Quinlan said, 'Father Burner belongs to the school that's always seeing a great renascence of faith in the offing. The hour before dawn and all that. Tell it to Rotary[20] on Tuesday, Father.'

Father Burner countered with a frosty pink smile. 'What would I ever do without you, Father? If you're trying to say I'm a dreadful optimist, you're right and I don't mind at all. I am — and proud of it!'

Ascending to his feet, he went to the right side of the buffet, took down the card index to parishioners, and returned with it to his place. He pushed his dishes aside and began to sort out the deadheads to be called on personally by him or Quinlan. The Dean, like all pastors, he reflected, left the dirty work to the assistants. 'Why doesn't he pull them,' he snapped, tearing up a card, 'when they kick off! Can't very well forward them to the next world. Say, how many Gradys live at 909 South Vine? Here's Anna, Catherine, Clement, Gerald, Harvey, James A., James F. — which James is the one they call "Bum"?'

'James F.,' Quinlan said. 'Can't you tell from the take? The other James works.'

'John, Margaret, Matthew — that's ten, no eleven. Here's Dennis out of place. Patrick, Rita and William — fourteen of them, no birth control there, and they all give. Except Bum. Nice account otherwise. Can't we find Bum a job? What's it with him, drink?'

Now he came to Maple Street. These cards were the remains of little Father Vicci's work among the magdalens. Ann Mason, Estelle Rogers, May Miller, Billie Starr. The names had the generic ring. Great givers when they gave — Christmas, $25; Easter, $20; Propagation of the Faith, $10; Catholic University, $10 — but not much since Father Vicci was exiled to the sticks. He put Maple Street aside for a thorough sifting.

The doorbell rang. Father Burner leaned around in his chair. 'Mary.' The doorbell rang again. Father Burner bellowed. 'Mary!'

Quinlan pushed his chair away from the table. 'I'll get it.'

Father Burner blocked him. 'Oh, I'll get it! Hell of a bell! Why does he have a bell like that!' Father Burner opened the door to a middle-aged woman whose name he had forgotten or never known. 'Good morning,' he said. 'Will you step in?'

She stayed where she was and said, 'Father, it's about the servicemen's flag in church. My son Stanley — you know him —'

Father Burner, who did not know him, half nodded. 'Yes, how is Stanley?' He gazed over her shoulder at the lawn, at the dandelions turning into poppies before his eyes.

'You know he was drafted last October, Father, and I been watching that flag you got in church ever since, and it's still the same, five hundred thirty-six stars. I thought you said you put a star up for all them that's gone in the service, Father.'

Now the poppies were dandelions again. He could afford to be firm with her. 'We can't spend all our time putting up stars. Sometimes we fall behind. Besides, a lot of the boys are being discharged.'

'You mean there's just as many going in as coming out, so you don't have to change the flag?'

'Something like that.'

'I see.' He was sorry for her. They had run out of stars. He had tried to get the Dean to order some more, had even offered . . . and the Dean had said they could use up the gold ones first. When Father Burner had objected, telling him what it would mean, he had suggested that Father Burner apply for the curatorship of the armory.

'The pastor will be glad to explain how it works the next time you see him.'

'Well, Father, if that's the way it is . . .' She was fading down the steps. 'I just thought I'd ask.'

'That's right. There's no harm in asking. How's Stanley?'

'Fine, and thank you, Father, for your trouble.'

'No trouble.'

When he came back to the table they were talking about the junior clergyman's examinations which they would take for the first time next week. Father Burner interrupted, 'The Dean conducts the history end of it, you know.'

'I say!' Keefe said. 'Any idea what we can expect?'

'You have nothing to fear. Nothing.'

'Really?'

'Really. Last year, I remember, there were five questions and the last four depended on the first. So it was really only one question — if you knew it. I imagine you would've.' He paused, making Keefe ask for it.

'Perhaps you can recall the question, Father?'

'Perfectly, Father. "What event in the American history of the Church took place in 1541?"' Father Burner, slumping in his chair, smirked at Keefe pondering for likely martyrs and church legislation. He imagined him skipping among the tomes and statuary of his mind, winnowing dates and little known facts like mad, only at last to emerge dusty and downcast. Father Burner sat up with a jerk and

assaulted the table with the flat of his hand. 'Time's up. Answer: "De Soto sailed up the Mississippi."'[21]

Quinlan snorted: Keefe sat very still, incredulous, silent, utterly unable to digest the answer, finally croaking, 'How odd.' Father Burner saw in him the boy whose marks in school had always been a consolation to his parents.

'So you don't have to worry, Father. No sense in preparing for it. Take in a couple of movies instead. And cheer up! The Dean's been examining the junior clergy for twenty-five years and nobody ever passed history yet. You wouldn't want to be the first one.'

Father Burner said grace and made the sign of the cross with slow distinction. 'And, Father,' he said, standing, extending his hand to Keefe, who also rose, 'I'm glad to have met you.' He withdrew his hand before Keefe was through with it and stood against the table knocking toast crumbs onto his plate. 'Ever play any golf? No? Well, come and see us for conversation then. You don't have anything against talking, do you?'

'Well, of course, Father, I . . .'

Father Burner gave Keefe's arm a rousing clutch. 'Do that!'

'I will, Father. It's been a pleasure.'

'Speaking of pleasure,' Father Burner said, tossing Quinlan a stack of cards, 'I've picked out a few lost sheep for you to see on Maple Street, Father.'

II. Noon

He hung his best black trousers on a hanger in the closet and took down another pair, also black. He tossed them out behind him and they fell patched at the cuffs and baggy across his unmade bed. His old suede jacket, following, slid dumpily to the floor. He stood gaping in his clerical vest and undershorts, knees knocking and pimply, thinking . . . what else? His aviator's helmet. He felt all the hooks blindly in the darkness. It was not there. 'Oh, hell!' he groaned, sinking to his knees. He pawed among the old shoes and boxes and wrapping paper and string that he was always going to need. Under his golf bag he found it. So Mary had cleaned yesterday.

There was also a golf ball unknown to him, a Royal Bomber, with one small hickey in it. Father Desmond, he remembered, had received a box of Royal Bombers from a thoughtful parishioner. He stuck the helmet on his balding head to get it out of the way and took the putter from the bag. He dropped the ball at the door of the closet. Taking his own eccentric stance — a perversion of what the pro recommended and a dozen books on the subject — he putted the ball across the room at a dirty collar lying against the bookcase. A thready place in the carpet caused the ball to jump the collar and to loose a pamphlet from the top of the bookcase. He restored the pamphlet — Pius XI on 'Atheistic Communism' — and poked the ball back to the door of the closet. Then, allowing for the carpet, he drove the ball straight, *click,* through the collar, *clop.* Still had his old putting eye. And his irons had always been steady if not exactly crashing. It was his woods, the tee shots, that ruined his game. He'd give a lot to be able to hit his woods properly, not to dub his drives, if only on the first tee — where there was always a crowd (mixed).

At one time or another he had played every hole at the country club in par or less. Put all those pars and birdies together, adding in the only two eagles he'd ever had, and you had the winning round in the state open, write-ups and action shots in the papers — photo shows Rev. Ernest 'Boomer' Burner, par-shattering padre, blasting out of a trap. He needed only practice perhaps and at his earliest opportunity he would entice some of the eighth-grade boys over into the park to shag balls. He sank one more for good measure, winning a buck from Ed Desmond who would have bet against it, and put the club away.

Crossing the room for his trousers he noticed himself in the mirror with the helmet on and got a mild surprise. He scratched a little hair down from underneath the helmet to offset the egg effect. He searched his eyes in the mirror for a sign of ill health. He walked away from the mirror, as though done with it, only to wheel sharply so as to see himself as others saw him, front and profile, not wanting to catch his eye, just to see himself . . .

Out of the top drawer of the dresser he drew a clean white silk handkerchief and wiped the shine from his nose. He chased his eyes over into the corner of the mirror and saw nothing. Then, succumbing to his original intention, he knotted the handkerchief at the crown of the helmet and completed the transformation of time and place and person by humming, vibrato, 'Jeannine, I dream in lilac time,' remembering the old movie. He saw himself over his shoulder in the mirror, a sad war ace. It reminded him that his name was not Burner, but Boerner, an impediment removed at the outset of the first world war by his father. In a way he resented the old man for it. They had laughed at the seminary; the war, except as theory, hardly entered there. In perverse homage to the old Boerner, to which he now affixed a proud 'von', he dropped the fair-minded American look he had and faced the mirror sneering, scar-cheeked, and black of heart, the flying Junker who might have been.

'*Himmelkreuzdonnerwetter!*[22] When you hear the word "culture",' he snarled, hearing it come back to him in German, 'reach for your revolver!'

Reluctantly he pulled on his black trousers, falling across the bed to do so, as though felled, legs heaving up like howitzers.

He lay still for a moment, panting, and then let the innerspring mattress bounce him to his feet, a fighter coming off the ropes. He stood looking out the window, buckling his belt, and then down at the buckle, chins kneading softly with the effort, and was pleased to see that he was holding his own on the belt, still a good half inch away from last winter's high-water mark.

At the sound of high heels approaching on the front walk below, he turned firmly away from the window and considered for the first time since he posted it on the wall the prayer for priests sent him by a candle concern. 'Remember, O most compassionate God, that they are but weak and frail human beings. Stir up in them the grace of their vocation which is in them by the imposition of the Bishops' hands. Keep them close to Thee, lest the enemy prevail against them, so that they may never do anything in the slightest degree unworthy of their sublime . . .' His eyes raced through the prayer and out the window . . .

He was suddenly inspired to write another letter to the Archbishop. He sat down at his desk, slipped a piece of paper into his portable, dated it with the saint's day it was, and wrote, 'Your Excellency: Thinking my letter of some months ago may have gone amiss, or perhaps due to the press of business —' He ripped the paper from the portable and typed the same thing on a fresh sheet until he came to 'business', using instead 'affairs of the Church'. He went on to signify — it was considered all right to 'signify', but to re-signify? — that he was still of the humble opinion that he needed a change of location and had decided, since he believed himself ready for a parish of his own, a rural one might be best, all things considered (by which he meant easier to get). He, unlike some priests of urban upbringing and experience, would have no objection to the country. He begged to be graced with an early reply. That line, for all its seeming docility, was full of dynamite and ought to break the episcopal silence into which the first letter had dissolved. This was a much stronger job. He thought it better for two reasons: the Archbishop was supposed to like outspoken people, or, that being only more propaganda talked up by the sycophants, then it ought to bring a reply which would reveal once and for all his prospects. Long overdue for the routine promotion, he had a just cause. He addressed the letter and placed it in his coat. He went to the bathroom. When he came back he put on the coat, picked up the suede jacket and helmet, looked around for something he might have forgotten, a book of chances, a box of Sunday envelopes to be delivered, some copy for the printer, but there was nothing. He lit a cigarette at the door and not caring to throw the match on the floor or look for the ashtray, which was out of sight again, he dropped it in the empty holy-water font.

Downstairs he paused at the telephone in the hall, scribbled 'Airport' on the message pad, thought of crossing it out or tearing off the page, but since it was dated he let it stand and added 'Visiting the sick', signing his initials, *E.B.*

He went through the wicker basket for mail. A card from the Book-of-the-Month Club. So it was going to be another war book selection this month. Well, they knew what they could do with it. He wished the Club would wake up and select some dandies, as they had in the past. He thought of *Studs Lonigan*[23] — there was a book, the best thing since the Bible.

An oblique curve in the road: perfect, wheels parallel with the centre line. So many drivers took a curve like that way over on the other fellow's side. Father Burner touched the lighter on the dashboard to his cigarette and plunged his hams deeper into the cushions. A cloud of smoke whirled about the little Saint Christopher[24] garrotted from the ceiling. Father Burner tugged viciously at both knees, loosening the binding black cloth, easing the seat. Now that he was in open country he wanted to enjoy the scenery — God's majesty. How about a sermon that would liken the things in the landscape to the people in a church? All different, all the same, the handiwork of God. Moral: it is right and meet for rocks to be rocks, trees to be trees, pigs to be pigs, but — and here the small gesture that says so much — what did that mean that men, created in the image and likeness of God, should be? And what — He thrust the sermon out of mind, tired of it. He relaxed, as before an open fireplace, the weight of dogma off his shoulders. Then he grabbed at his knees again, cursing. Did the tailor skimp on the cloth because of the ecclesiastical discount?

A billboard inquired: 'Pimples?' Yes, he had a few, but he blamed them on the climate, the humidity. Awfully hard for a priest to transfer out of a diocese. He remembered the plan he had never gone through with. Would it work after all? Would another doctor recommend a change? Why? He would only want to know why, like the last bastard. Just a slight case of obesity, Reverend. Knew he was a non-Catholic when he said Reverend. Couldn't trust a Catholic one. Some of them were thicker than thieves with the clergy. Wouldn't want to be known as a malingerer, along with anything else.

Another billboard: 'Need Cash? See T.N.T.'

Rain. He knew it. No flying for him today. One more day between him and a pilot's licence. Thirteen hours yet and it might have been twelve. Raining so, and with no flying, the world seemed to him . . . a valley of tears. He would drive on past the airport for a hamburger. If he had known, he would have brought along one of the eighth-grade boys. They were always bragging among themselves about how many he had bought them, keeping score. One of them, the Cannon kid, had got too serious from the hamburgers. When he said he was 'contemplating the priesthood' Father Burner, wanting to spare him the terrible thing a false vocation could be, had told him to take up aviation instead. He could not forget the boy's reply: *But couldn't I be a priest like you, Father?*

On the other hand, he was glad to be out driving alone. Never had got the bang out of playing with the kids a priest in this country was supposed to. The failure of the Tom Playfair tradition. He hated most sports. Ed Desmond was a sight at a ball game. Running up and down the base lines, giving the umpires hell, busting all the buttons off his cassock. Assumption rectory smelled like a locker room from all the equipment. Poor Ed.

The rain drummed on the engine hood. The windshield wiper sliced back and forth, reminding him a little of a guillotine. Yes, if he had to, he would die for the Faith.

From here to the hamburger place it was asphalt and slicker than concrete. Careful. Slick. Asphalt. Remembered . . . Quinlan coming into his room one afternoon last winter when it was snowing — the idiot — prating:

Here were decent godless people:
Their only monument the asphalt road
And a thousand lost golf balls . . .

That was Quinlan for you, always spouting against the status quo without having anything better to offer. Told him that. Told him golfers, funny as it might seem to some people, have souls and who's to save them? John Bosco[25] worked wonders in taverns, which was not so say Father Burner thought he was a saint, but rather only that he was not too proud to meet souls halfway wherever it might be, in the confessional or on the fairways. Saint Ernest Burner, Help of Golfers, Pray for Us! (Quinlan's comeback.) Quinlan gave him a pain. Keefe, now that he knew what he was like, ditto. Non-smokers. Jansenists.[26] First fervour is false fervour. They would cool. He would not judge them, however.

He slowed down and executed a sweeping turn into the parking lot reserved for patrons of the hamburger. He honked his horn his way, three shorts and a long — victory. She would see his car or know his honk and bring out two hamburgers, medium well, onions, pickle, relish, tomato, catsup — his way.

She came out now, carrying an umbrella, holding it ostensibly more over the hamburgers than herself. He took the tray from her. She waited dumbly, her eyes at a level with his collar.

'What's to drink?'

'We got pop, milk, coffee . . .' Here she faltered, as he knew she would, washing her hands of what recurrent revelation, rather than experience, told her was to follow.

'A nice cold bottle of beer.' Delivered of the fatal words, Father Burner bit into the smoking hamburger. The woman turned sorrowfully away. He put her down again for native Protestant stock.

When she returned, sheltering the bottle under the umbrella, Father Burner had to smile at her not letting pious scruples interfere with business, another fruit of the so-called Reformation. Watch that smile, he warned himself, or she'll take it for carnal. He received the bottle from her hands. For all his familiarity with the type, he was uneasy. Her lowered eyes informed him of his guilt.

Was he immoderate? Who on earth could say? *In dubiis libertas,*[27] not? He recalled his first church supper at Saint Patrick's, a mother bringing her child to the Dean's table. She's going to be confirmed next month, Monsignor. Indeed? Then tell me, young lady, what are the seven capital sins? Pride, Covetousness . . . Lust, Anger. Uh. The child's mother, one of those tough Irish females built like a robin, worried to death, lips silently forming the other sins for her daughter. Go ahead, dear. Envy. Proceed, child. Yes, Monsignor. Uh . . . Sloth. To be sure. That's six. One more. And . . . uh. Fear of the Lord, perhaps? Meekness? Hey, Monsignor, ain't them the Divine Counsels! The Dean, smiling, looking at Father Burner's plate, covered with chicken bones, at his stomach, fighting the vest, and for a second into the child's eyes, slipping her the seventh sin. *Gluttony,* Monsignor! The Dean gave her a coin for her trouble and she stood awkwardly in front of Father Burner, lingering, twisting her gaze from his plate to his stomach, to his eyes, finally quacking, Oh Fawther!

Now he began to brood upon his failure as a priest. There was no sense in applying the consolations of an anchorite[28] to himself. He wanted to know one thing: when would he get a parish? When would he make the great metamorphosis from assistant to pastor, from mouse to rat, as the saying went? He was forty-three, four times transferred, seventeen years an ordained priest, a curate yet and only. He was the only one of his class still without a parish. The only one . . . and in his pocket, three days unopened, was another letter from his mother, kept waiting all these years, who was to have been his housekeeper. He could not bear to warm up her expectations again.

Be a chaplain? That would take him away from it all and there was the possibility of meeting a remote and glorious death carrying the Holy Eucharist to a dying soldier. It would take something like that to make him come out even, but then that, too, he knew in a corner of his heart, would be only exterior justification for him, a last bid for public approbation, a short cut to nothing. And the chaplain's job, it was whispered, could be an ordeal both ignominious and tragic. It would be just his luck to draw an assignment in a rehabilitation centre, racking pool balls and repairing ping-pong bats for the boys — the apostolic game-room attendant and toastmaster. Sure, Sarge, I'll lay you even money the Sox make it three straight in Philly[29] and spot you a run a game to boot. You win, I lose a carton of Chesters[30] — I win, you go to Mass every day for a week! Hard-headed holiness . . .

There was the painful matter of the appointment to Saint Patrick's. The Dean, an irremovable pastor, and the Archbishop had argued over funds and the cemetery association. And the Archbishop, losing though he won, took his revenge, it was rumoured, by appointing Father Burner as the Dean's assistant. It was their second encounter. In the first days of his succession, the Archbishop heard that the Dean always said a green Mass on Saint Patrick's Day, thus setting the rubrics at nought. Furious, he summoned the Dean into his presence, but stymied by the total strangeness of him and his great age, he had talked of something else. The Dean took a different view of his narrow escape, which is what the chancery office gossips called it, and now every year, on repeating the error, he would say to the uneasy nuns, 'Sure and nobody ever crashed the gates of hell for the wearing of the green.' (Otherwise it was not often he did something to delight the hearts of the professional Irish.)

In the Dean's presence Father Burner often had the sensation of confusion, a feeling that someone besides them stood listening in the room. To free himself he would say things he neither meant nor believed. The Dean would take the other side and then . . . there they were again. The Dean's position in these bouts was roughly that of the old saints famous for their faculty of smelling sins and Father Burner played the role of the one smelled. It was no contest. If the Archbishop could find no words for the Dean there was nothing he might do. He might continue to peck away at a few stray foibles behind the Dean's back. He might point out how familiar the Dean was with the Protestant clergy about town. He did. It suited his occasional orthodoxy (reserved mostly to confound his critics and others much worse, like Quinlan, whom he suspected of having him under observation for humorous purposes) to disapprove of all such questionable ties, as though the Dean were entertaining heresy, or at least felt kindly toward this new 'interfaith' nonsense so dear to the reformed Jews and fresh-water sects. It was very small game, however. And the merest brush with the Dean might bring any one of a hundred embarrassing occasions back to life, and it was easy for him to burn all over again.

When he got his darkroom rigged up in the rectory the Dean had come snooping around and inquired without staying for an answer if the making of tintypes demanded that a man shun the light to the extent Father Burner appeared to. Now and again, hearkening back to this episode, the Dean referred to him as the Prince of Darkness. It did not end there. The title caught on all over the diocese. It was not the only one he had.

In reviewing a new historical work for a national Catholic magazine, he had attempted to get back at two Jesuits he knew in town, calling attention to certain tendencies — he meant nothing so gross as 'order pride' — which, if not necessarily characteristic of any religious congregation within the Church, were still too often to be seen in any long view of history (which the book at hand did not pretend to take), and whereas the secular clergy, *per se*,[31] had much to answer for, was it not true, though certainly not through any superior virtue, nor even as a consequence of their secularity — indeed, he would be a fool to dream that such orders as those founded, for instance, by Saint Benedict, Saint Francis, and Saint Dominic (Saint Ignatius was not instanced) were without their places in the heart of the Church, even today, when perhaps . . .

Anyway 'secular' turned up once as 'circular' in the review. The local Jesuits, writing in to the magazine as a group of innocent bystanders, made many subtle plays upon the unfortunate 'circular' and its possible application to the person of the reviewer (their absolute unfamiliarity with the reviewer, they explained, enabled them indulge in such conceivably dangerous whimsey). But the direction of his

utterances, they thought, seemed clear, and they regretted more than they could say that the editors of an otherwise distinguished journal had found space for them, especially in wartime, or perhaps they did not rightly comprehend the course — was it something new? — set upon by the editors and if so . . .

So Father Burner was also known as 'the circular priest' and he had not reviewed anything since for that magazine.

The mark of the true priest was heavy on the Dean. The mark was on Quinlan; it was on Keefe. It was on every priest he could think of, including a few on the bum, and his good friend and bad companion, Father Desmond. But it was not on him, not properly. They, the others, were stained with it beyond all disguise or disfigurement — indelibly, as indeed Holy Orders by its sacramental nature must stain, for keeps in this world and the one to come. 'Thou art a priest forever.' With him, however, it was something else and less, a mask or badge which he could and did remove at will, a temporal part to be played, almost only a doctor's or lawyer's. They, the others, would be lost in any persecution. The mark would doom them. But he, if that *dies irae*[32] ever came — and it was every plump seminarian's apple-cheeked dream — could pass as the most harmless and useful of humans, a mailman, a bus rider, a husband. But would he? No. They would see. I, he would say, appearing unsought before the judging rabble, am a priest, of the order of Melchizedech. Take me. I am ready. *Deo gratias.*[33]

Father Burner got out the money to pay and honked his horn. The woman, coming for the bottle and tray, took his money without acknowledging the tip. She stood aside, the bottle held gingerly between offended fingers, final illustration of her lambishness, and watched him drive away. Father Burner, applying a cloven foot to the pedal, gave it the gas. He sensed the woman hoping in her simple heart to see him wreck the car and meet instant death in an unpostponed act of God.

Under the steadying influence of his stomach thrust against the wheel, the car proceeded while he searched himself for a cigarette. He passed a hitchhiker, saw him fade out of view in the mirror overhead, gesticulate wetly in the distance. Was the son of a gun thumbing his nose? Anticlericalism. But pray that your flight be not in the winter . . . No, wrong text: he would not run away.

The road skirted a tourist village. He wondered who stayed in those places and seemed to remember a story in one of the religious scandal sheets . . . ILLICIT LOVE in steaming red type.

A billboard cried out, 'Get in the scrap and — get in the scrap!' Some of this advertising, he thought, was pretty slick. Put out probably by big New York and Chicago agencies with crack men on their staffs, fellows who had studied at *Time*. How would it be to write advertising? He knew a few things about layout and type faces from editing the parish paper. He had read somewhere about the best men of our time being in advertising, the air corps of business. There was room for better taste in the Catholic magazines, for someone with a name in the secular field to step in and drive out the money-changers with their trusses, corn cures, non-tangle rosary beads, and crosses that glow in the dark. It was a thought.

Coming into the city limits, he glanced at his watch, but neglected to notice the time. The new gold strap got his eye. The watch itself, a priceless pyx, held the hour (time is money) sacred, like a host. He had chosen it for an ordination gift rather than the usual chalice. It took the kind of courage he had to go against the grain there.

'I'm a dirty stinker!' Father Desmond flung his arms out hard against the mattress. His fists opened on the sheet, hungry for the spikes, meek and ready. 'I'm a dirty stinker, Ernest!'

Father Burner, seated deep in a red leather chair at the sick man's bedside, crossed his legs forcefully. 'Now don't take on so, Father.'

'Don't call me "Father"!' Father Desmond's eyes fluttered open momentarily, but closed again on the reality of it all. 'I don't deserve it. I'm a disgrace to the priesthood! I am not worthy! Lord, Lord, I am not worthy!'

A nurse entered and stuck a thermometer in Father Desmond's mouth.

Father Burner smiled at the nurse. He lit a cigarette and wondered if she understood. The chart probably bore the diagnosis 'pneumonia', but if she had been a nurse very long she would know all about that. She released Father Desmond's wrist and recorded his pulse on her pad. She took the thermometer and left the room.

Father Desmond surged up in bed and flopped, turning with a wrench of the covers, on his stomach. He lay gasping like a fish out of water. Father Burner could smell it on his breath yet.

'Do you want to go to confession?'

'No! I'm not ready for it. I want to remember this time!'

'Oh, all right.' It was funny, if a little tiresome, the way the Irish could exaggerate a situation. They all had access to the same two or three emotions. They all played the same battered barrel organ handed down through generations. Dying, fighting, talking, drinking, praying . . . wakes, wars, politics, pubs, church. The fates were decimated and hamstrung among them. They loved monotony.

Father Desmond, doing the poor soul uttering his last words in italics, said: 'We make too good a thing out of confession, Ernest! Ever think of that, Ernest?' He wagged a nicotined finger. Some of his self-contempt seemed to overshoot its mark and include Father Burner.

Father Burner honked his lips — *plutt*! 'Hire a hall, Ed.'

Father Desmond clawed a rosary out from under his pillow.

Father Burner left.

He put the car in the garage. On the way to his room he passed voices in the Dean's office.

'Father Burner!' the Dean called through the door.

Father Burner stayed in the hallway, only peeping in, indicating numerous commitments elsewhere. Quinlan and Keefe were with the Dean.

'Apparently, Father, you failed to kill yourself.' Then, for Keefe, the Dean said, 'Father Burner fulfils the dream of the American hierarchy and the principle of historical localization. He's been up in his flying machine all morning.'

'I didn't go up.' Sullenness came and went in his voice. 'It rained.' He shuffled one foot, about to leave, when the Dean's left eyebrow wriggled up, warning, holding him.

'I don't believe you've had the pleasure.' The Dean gave Keefe to Father Burner. 'Father Keefe, sir, went through school with Father Quinlan — from the grades through the priesthood.' The Dean described an arc with his breviary, dripping with ribbons, to show the passing years. Father Burner nodded.

'Well?' The Dean frowned at Father Burner. 'Has the cat got your tongue, sir? Why don't you be about greeting Father O'Keefe — or Keefe, is it?'

'Keefe,' Keefe said.

Father Burner, caught in the old amber of his inadequacy, stepped over and shook Keefe's hand once.

Quinlan stood by and let the drama play itself out.

Keefe, smiling a curious mixture more anxiety than amusement, said, 'It's a pleasure, Father.'

'Same here,' Father Burner said.

'Well, good day, sirs!' The Dean cracked open his breviary and began to read, lips twitching.

Father Burner waited for them in the hall. Before he could explain that he thought too much of the Dean not to humour him and that besides the old fool was out of his head, the Dean proclaimed after them, 'The Chancery phoned, Father Burner. You will hear confessions there tonight. I suppose one of those Cathedral jokers lost his faculties.'

Yes, Father Burner knew, it was common procedure all right for the Archbishop to confer promotions by private interview, but every time a priest got called to the Cathedral it did not mean simply that. Many received sermons and it was most likely now someone was needed to hear confessions. And still Father Burner, feeling his pocket, was glad he had not remembered to mail the letter. He would not bother to speak to Quinlan and Keefe now.

III. Night

'And for your penance say five Our Fathers and five Hail Marys and pray for my intention. And now make a good act of contrition. *Misereatur tui omnipotens Deus dimissis peccatis tuis . . .*[34] Father Burner swept out into the current of the prayer, stroking strongly in Latin, while the penitent, a miserable boy coming into puberty, paddled as fast as he could along the shore in English.

Finishing first, Father Burner waited for the boy to conclude. When, breathless, he did, Father Burner anointed the air and shot a whisper, 'God bless you,' kicking the window shut with the heel of his hand, ejecting the boy, an ear of corn shucked clean, into the world again. There was nobody on the other side of the confessional, so Father Burner turned on the signal light. A big spider drowsy in his web, drugged with heat and sins, he sat waiting for the next one to be hurled into his presence by guilt ruddy ripe, as with the boy, or, as with the old ladies who come early and try to stay late, by the spiritual famine of their lives or simply the desire to tell secrets in the dark.

He held his wrist in such a way as to see the sweat gleaming in the hairs. He looked at his watch. He had been at it since seven and now it was after nine. If there were no more kneeling in his section of the Cathedral at 9:30 he could close up and have a cigarette. He was too weary to read his office, though he had the Little Hours, Vespers, and Compline still to go. It was the last minutes in the confessional that got him — the insensible end of the excursion that begins with so many sinewy sensations and good intentions to look sharp at the landscape. In the last minutes how many priests, would-be surgeons of the soul, ended as blacksmiths, hammering out absolution anyway?

A few of the Cathedral familiars still drifted around the floor. They were day and night in the shadows praying. Meeting one of them, Father Burner always wanted to get away. They were collectors of priests' blessings in a day when most priests felt ashamed to raise their hands to God outside the ceremonies. Their respect for a priest was fanatic, that of the unworldly, the martyrs, for an emissary of heaven. They were so desperately disposed to death that the manner of dying was their greatest concern. But Father Burner had an idea there were more dull pretenders than saints among them. They inspired no unearthly feelings in him, as true sanctity was supposed to, and he felt it was all right not to like them. They spoke of God, the Blessed Virgin, of miracles, cures, and visitations, as of people and items in the news, which was annoying. The Cathedral, because of its location, described by brokers as exclusive, was not so much frequented by these wretches as it would have been if more convenient to the slums. But nevertheless a few came there, like the diarrhoeic pigeons, also a scandal to the neighbourhood, and would not go away. Father Burner, from his glancing contact with them, had concluded that body odour is the real odour of sanctity.

Through the grating now Father Burner saw the young Vicar General stop a little distance up the aisle and speak to a couple of people who were possible prospects for Father Burner. 'Anyone desiring to go to confession should do so at once. In a few minutes the priests will be gone from the confessionals.' He crossed to the other side of the Cathedral.

Father Burner did not like to compare his career with the Vicar General's. The Archbishop had taken the Vicar General, a younger man than Father Burner by at least fifteen years, direct from the seminary. After a period of trial as Chancellor, he was raised to his present eminence — for reasons much pondered by the clergy and more difficult to discern than those obviously accounted for by intelligence, appearance, and, post factum,[35] the loyalty consequent upon his selection over many older and possibly abler men. It was a medieval act of preference, a slap in the face to the monsignori, a rebuke to the principle of advancement by years applied elsewhere. The Vicar General had the quality of inscrutability in an ideal measure. He did not seem at all given to gossip or conspiracy or even to that owlish secrecy peculiar to secretaries and so exasperating to others. He had possibly no enemies and certainly no intimates. In time he would be a bishop unless, as was breathed wherever the Cloth gathered over food and drink, he really was 'troubled with sanctity', which might lead to anything else, the cloister or insanity.

The Vicar General appeared at the door of Father Burner's compartment. 'The Archbishop will see you, Father, before you leave tonight.' He went up the aisle, genuflected before the main altar, opened as a gate one of the host of brass angels surrounding the sanctuary, and entered the sacristies.

Before he would let hope have its way with him, Father Burner sought to recast the expression on the Vicar General's face. He could recall nothing significant. Very probably there had been nothing to see. Then, with a rush, he permitted himself to think this was his lucky day. Already he was formulating the way he would let the news out, providing he decided not to keep it a secret for a time. He might do that. It would be delicious to go about his business until the very last minute, to savour the old aggravations and feel none of the sting, to receive the old quips and smiles with good grace and know them to be toothless. The news, once out, would fly through the diocese. Hear about Burner at Saint Pat's, Tom? Finally landed himself a parish. Yeah, I just had it from McKenna. So I guess the A.B. wasn't so sore at the Round One after all. Well, he's just ornery[36] enough to make a go of it.

Father Burner, earlier in the evening, had smoked a cigarette with one of the young priests attached to the Cathedral (a classmate of Quinlan's but not half the prig), stalling, hoping someone would come and say the Archbishop wanted to see him. When nothing happened except the usual small talk and introductions to a couple of missionaries stopping over, he had given up hope easily. He had seen the basis for his expectations as folly once more. It did not bother him after the fact was certain. He was amenable to any kind of finality. He had a light heart for a Ger — an American of German descent. And his hopes rose higher each time and with less cause. He was a ball that bounced up only. He had kept faith. And now — his just reward.

A little surprised he had not thought of her first, he admitted his mother into the new order of things. He wanted to open the letter from her, still in his coat, and late as it was send her a wire, which would do her more good than a night's sleep. He thought of himself back in her kitchen, home from the sem for the holidays, a bruiser in a tight black suit, his feet heavy on the oven door. She was fussing at the stove and he was promising her a porcelain one as big as a house after he got his parish. But he let her know, kidding on the square, that he would be running things at the rectory. It would not be the old story of the priest taking orders from his housekeeper, even if she was his mother (seminarians, from winter evenings of shooting the bull, knew only too well the pitfalls of parish life), or as with Ed Desmond a few years ago when his father was still living with him, the old man losing his marbles one by one, butting in when people came for

advice and instructions, finally coming to believe he was the one to say Mass in his son's absence — no need to get a strange priest in — and sneaking into the box to hear confessions the day before they took him away.

He would be gentle with his mother, however, even if she talked too much, as he recalled she did the last time he saw her. She was well-preserved and strong for her age and ought to be able to keep the house up. Once involved in the social life of the parish she could be a valuable agent in coping with any lay opposition, which was too often the case when a new priest took over.

He resolved to show no nervousness before the Archbishop. A trifle surprised, yes — the Archbishop must have his due — but not overly affected by good fortune. If questioned, he would display a lot of easy confidence not unaccompanied by a touch of humility, a phrase or two like 'God willing' or 'with the help of Almighty God and your prayers, Your Excellency.' He would also not forget to look the part — reliable, casual, cool, an iceberg, only the tip of his true worth showing.

At precisely 9:30 Father Burner picked up his breviary and backed out of the stall. But then there was the scuff of a foot and the tap of one of the confessional doors closing and then, to tell him the last penitent was a woman, the scent of apple blossoms. He turned off the light, saying 'Damn!' to himself, and sat down again inside. He threw back the partition and led off, 'Yes?' He placed his hand alongside his head and listened, looking down into the deeper darkness of his cassock sleeve.

'I . . .'

'Yes?' At the heart of the apple blossom another scent bloomed: gin and vermouth.

'Bless me, Father, I . . . have sinned.'

Father Burner knew this kind. They would always wait until the last moment. How they managed to get themselves into church at all, and then into the confessional, was a mystery. Sometimes liquor thawed them out. This one was evidently young, nubile. He had a feeling it was going to be adultery. He guessed it was up to him to get her under way.

'How long since your last confession?'

'I don't know . . .'

'Have you been away from the Church?'

'Yes.'

'Are you married?'

'Yes.'

'To a Catholic?'

'No.'

'Protestant?'

'No.'

'Jew?'

'No.'

'Atheist?'

'No — nothing.'

'Were you married by a priest?'

'Yes.'

'How long ago was that?'

'Four years.'

'Any children?'

'No.'

'Practise birth control?'

'Yes, sometimes.'

'Don't you know it's a crime against nature and the Church forbids it?'

'Yes.'

'Don't you know that France fell because of birth control?'

'No.'

'Well, it did. Was it your husband's fault?'

'You mean — the birth control?'

'Yes.'

'Not wholly.'

'And you've been away from the Church ever since your marriage?'

'Yes.'

'Now you see why the Church is against mixed marriages. All right, go on. What else?'

'I don't know . . .'

'Is that what you came to confess?'

'No. Yes. I'm sorry, I'm afraid that's all.'

'Do you have a problem?'

'I think that's all, Father.'

'Remember, it is your obligation, and not mine, to examine your conscience. The task of instructing persons with regard to these delicate matters — I refer to the connubial relationship — is not an easy one. Nevertheless, since there is a grave obligation imposed by God, it cannot be shirked. If you have a problem —'

'I don't have a *problem*.'

'Remember, God never commands what is impossible and so if you make use of the sacraments regularly you have every reason to be confident that you will be able to overcome this evil successfully, with His help. I hope this is all clear to you.'

'All clear.'

'Then if you are heartily sorry for your sins for your penance say the rosary daily for one week and remember it is the law of the Church that you attend Mass on Sundays and holy days and receive the sacraments at least once a year. It's better to receive them often. Ask your pastor about birth control if it's still not clear to you. Or read a Catholic book on the subject. And now make a good act of contrition . . .'

Father Burner climbed the three flights of narrow stairs. He waited a moment in silence, catching his breath. He knocked on the door and was suddenly afraid its density prevented him from being heard and that he might be found standing there like a fool or a spy. But to knock again, if heard the first time, would seem importunate.

'Come in, Father.'

At the other end of the long study the Archbishop sat behind an ebony desk. Father Burner waited before him as though expecting not to be asked to sit down. The only light in the room, a lamp on the desk, was so set that it kept the Archbishop's face in the dark, fell with a gentle sparkle upon his pectoral cross, and was absorbed all around by the fabric of the piped cloth he wore. Father Burner's eyes came to rest upon the Archbishop's freckled hand — ringed, square, and healthy.

'Be seated, Father.'

'Thank you, Your Excellency.'

'Oh, sit in this chair, Father.' There were two chairs. Father Burner changed to the soft one. He had a suspicion that in choosing the other one he had fallen into a silly trap, that it was a game the Archbishop played with his visitors: the innocent ones, seeing no issue, would take the soft chair, because handier; the guilty would go a step out of their way to take the hard one. 'I called Saint Patrick's this morning, Father, but you were . . . out.'

'I was visiting Father Desmond, Your Excellency.'

'Father Desmond . . .?'

'He's in the hospital.'

'I know. Friend of his, are you, Father?'

'No, Your Excellency. Well' — Father Burner waited for the cock to crow the third time — 'yes, I *know* the man.' At once he regretted the scriptural complexion of the words and wondered if it were possible for the Archbishop not to be thinking of the earlier betrayal.

'It was good of you to visit Father Desmond, especially since you are not close to him. I hope he is better, Father.'

'He is, Your Excellency.'

The Archbishop got up and went across the room to a cabinet. 'Will you have a little glass of wine, Father?'

'No. No, thanks, Your Excellency.' Immediately he realized it could be another trap and, if so, he was caught again.

'Then I'll have a drop . . . *solus*.' The Archbishop poured a glass and brought it back to the desk. 'A little wine for the stomach's sake, Father.'

Father Burner, not sure what he was expected to say to that, nodded gravely and said, 'Yes, Your Excellency.' He had seen that the Archbishop wore carpet slippers and that they had holes in both toes.

'But perhaps you've read Saint Bernard, Father, and recall where he says we priests remember well enough the apostolic counsel to use wine, but overlook the adjective "little".'

'I must confess I haven't read Saint Bernard lately, Your Excellency.' Father Burner believed this was somehow in his favour. 'Since seminary, in fact.'

'Not all priests, Father, have need of him. A hard saint . . . for hardened sinners. What is your estimate of Saint Paul?'

Father Burner felt familiar ground under his feet at last. There were the Pauline and Petrine factions — a futile business, he thought — but he knew where the Archbishop stood and exclaimed, 'One of the greatest —'

'Really! So many young men today consider him . . . a bore. It's always the deep-breathing ones, I notice. They say he cuts it too fine.'

'I've never thought so, Your Excellency.'

'Indeed? Well, it's a question I like to ask my priests. Perhaps you knew that.'

'No, I didn't, Your Excellency.'

'So much the better then . . . but I see you appraising the melodeon, Father. Are you musical?'

'Not at all, Your Excellency. Violin lessons as a child.' Father Burner laughed quickly, as though it were nothing.

'But you didn't go on with them?'

'No, Your Excellency.' He did not mean it to sound as sad as it came out.

'What a pity.'

'No great loss, Your Excellency.'

'You are too . . . modest, Father. But perhaps the violin was not your instrument.'

'I guess it wasn't, Your Excellency.' Father Burner laughed out too loud.

'And you have the choir at Saint Patrick's, Father?'

'Not this year, Your Excellency. Father Quinlan has it.'

'Now I recall . . .'

'Yes.' So far as he was concerned — and there were plenty of others who thought so, too — Quinlan had played hell with the choir, canning all the women, some of them members for fifteen and twenty years, a couple even longer and practically living for it, and none of them as bad as Quinlan said. The liturgical stuff that Quinlan tried to pull off was all right in monasteries, where they had the time to train for it, but in a parish it sounded stodgy to ears used to the radio and split up the activity along sexual lines, which was really old hat in the modern world. The Dean liked it though. He called it 'honest' and eulogized the men from the pulpit — not a sign that he heard how they brayed and whinnied and just gave out or failed to start — and each time it happened ladies in the congregation were sick and upset for days afterward, for he inevitably ended by attacking women, pants, cocktails, communism, cigarettes, and running around half naked. The women looked at the men in the choir, all pretty in surplices, and said to themselves they knew plenty about some of them and what they had done to some women.

'He's tried a little Gregorian,[37] hasn't he — Father Quinlan?'

'Yes, Your Excellency,' Father Burner said. 'He has.'

'Would you say it's been a success — or perhaps I should ask you first if you care for Gregorian, Father.'

'Oh, yes, Your Excellency. Very much.'

'Many, I know, don't . . . I've been told our chant sounds like a wild bull in a red barn or consumptives coughing into a bottle, but I will have it in the Cathedral, Father. Other places, I am aware, have done well with . . . light opera.'

Father Burner frowned.

'We are told the people prefer and understand it. But at the risk of seeming reactionary, a fate my office prevents me from escaping in any event, I say we spend more time listening to the voice of the people than is good for either it or us. We have been too generous with our ears, Father. We have handed over our tongues also. When they are restored to us I wonder if we shall not find our ears more itching than before and our tongues more tied than ever.'

Father Burner nodded in the affirmative.

'We are now entering the whale's tail, Father. We must go back the way we came in.' The Archbishop lifted the lid of the humidor on the desk. 'Will you smoke, Father?'

'No, thanks, Your Excellency.'

The Archbishop let the lid drop. 'Today there are few saints, fewer sinners, and everybody is already saved. We are all heroes in search of an underdog. As for villains, the classic kind with no illusions about themselves, they are . . . extinct. The very devil, for instance — where the devil is the devil today, Father?'

Father Burner, as the Archbishop continued to look at him, bit his lips for the answer, secretly injured that he should be expected to know, bewildered even as the children he toyed with in catechism.

The Archbishop smiled, but Father Burner was not sure at what — whether at him or what had been said. 'Did you see, Father, where our brother Bishop

Buckles said Hitler remains the one power on earth against the Church?'

Yes, Father Burner remembered seeing it in the paper; it was the sort of thing that kept Quinlan talking for days. 'I did, Your Excellency.'

'Alas, poor Buckles! He's a better croquet player than that.' The Archbishop's hands unclasped suddenly and fell upon his memo pad. He tore off about a week and seemed to feel better for it. His hands, with no hint of violence about them now, came together again. 'We look hard to the right and left, Father. It is rather to the centre, I think, we should look — to ourselves, the devil in us.'

Father Burner knew the cue for humility when he heard it. 'Yes, Your Excellency.'

With his chubby fingers the Archbishop made a steeple that was more like a dome. His eyes were reading the memo. 'For instance, Father, I sometimes appear at banquets — when they can't line up a good foreign correspondent — banquets at which the poor are never present and at which I am unfailingly confronted by someone exceedingly well off who is moved to inform me that "religion" is a great consolation to him. Opium, rather, I always think, perhaps wrongfully and borrowing a word from one of our late competitors, which is most imprudent of me, a bishop.'

The Archbishop opened a drawer and drew out a sheet of paper and an envelope. 'Yes, the rich have souls,' he said softly, answering an imaginary objection which happened to be Father Burner's. 'But if Christ were really with them they would not be themselves — that is to say, rich.'

'Very true, Your Excellency,' Father Burner said.

The Archbishop faced sideways to use an old typewriter. 'And likewise, lest we forget, we would not be ourselves, that is to say — what? For we square the circle beautifully in almost every country on earth. We bring neither peace nor a sword. The rich give us money. We give them consolation and make of the eye of the needle a gate. Together we try to reduce the Church, the Bride of Christ, to a streetwalker.' The Archbishop rattled the paper, Father Burner's future, into place and rolled it crookedly into the typewriter. 'Unfortunately for us, it doesn't end there. The penance will not be shared so equitably. Your Christian name, Father, is —?'

'Ernest, Your Excellency.'

The Archbishop typed several words and stopped, looking over at Father Burner. 'I can't call to mind a single Saint Ernest, Father. Can you help me?'

'There were two, I believe, Your Excellency, but Butler[38] leaves them out of his *Lives*.'

'They would be German saints, Father?'

'Yes, Your Excellency. There was one an abbot and the other an archbishop.'

'If Butler had been Irish, as the name has come to indicate, I'd say that's an Irishman for you, Father. He does not forget to include a power of Irish saints.' The Archbishop was Irish himself. Father Burner begged to differ with him, believing here was a wrong deliberately set up for him to right. 'I am not Irish myself, Your Excellency, but some of my best friends are.'

'Tut, tut, Father. Such tolerance will be the death of you.' The Archbishop, typing a few words, removed the paper, signed it and placed it in the envelope. He got up and took down a book from the shelves. He flipped it open, glanced through several pages and returned it to its place. 'No Ernests in Baring-Gould[39] either. Well, Father, it looks as if you have a clear field.'

The Archbishop came from behind the desk and Father Burner, knowing the interview was over, rose. The Archbishop handed him the envelope. Father Burner stuffed it hastily in his pocket and knelt, the really important thing, to kiss the Archbishop's ring and receive his blessing. They walked together toward the door.

'Do you care for pictures, Father?'

'Oh, yes, Your Excellency.'

The Archbishop, touching him lightly on the arm, stopped before a reproduction of Raphael's Sistine Madonna. 'There is a good peasant woman, Father, and a nice fat baby.' Father Burner nodded his appreciation. 'She could be Our Blessed Mother, Father, though I doubt it. There is no question about the baby. He is not Christ.' The Archbishop moved to another picture. 'Rembrandt had the right idea, Father. See the gentleman pushing Christ up on the cross? That is Rembrandt, a self-portrait.' Father Burner thought of some of the stories about the Archbishop, that he slept on a cot, stood in line with the people sometimes to go to confession, that he fasted on alternate days the year round. Father Burner was thankful for such men as the Archbishop. 'But here is Christ, Father.' This time it was a glassy-eyed Christ whose head lay against the rough wood of the cross he was carrying. 'That is Christ, Father. The Greek painted Our Saviour.'[40]

The Archbishop opened the door for Father Burner, saying, 'And, Father, you will please not open the envelope until after your Mass tomorrow.'

Father Burner went swiftly down the stairs. Before he got into his car he looked up at the Cathedral. He could scarcely see the cross glowing on the dome. It seemed as far away as the stars. The cross needed a brighter light or the dome ought to be painted gold and lit up like the state capitol, so people would see it. He drove a couple of blocks down the street, pulled up to the curb, opened the envelope, which had not been sealed, and read: 'You will report on August 8 to the Reverend Michael Furlong, to begin your duties on that day as his assistant. I trust that in your new appointment you will find not peace but a sword.'

1 The Legion of Mary is a Catholic lay organization.
2 Traffic in sacred things.
3 St Thomas Aquinas (1225–74).
4 Knights of Columba: A lay organization for the ordinary Catholic man.
5 Latin: therefore.
6 French: literally, terrible child.
7 Irish contractor.
8 G.K. Chesterton (1874–1936), prolific English writer, author of the Father Brown stories, converted to Catholicism in 1922.
9 Francis Thompson (1859–1907), Catholic poet, one-time opium addict, author of 'The Hound of Heaven'.
10 Derogatory word used by Americans for the English.
11 Cardinal Newman (1801–90).
12 Gerard Manley Hopkins (1844–89), English poet and Jesuit.
13 Slang for Jesuits.
14 Samuel Goldwyn (1882–1974), American film-maker.
15 Church Latin: my fault.
16 Continuous devotional service.
17 A violation of the rules of syntax.
18 Latin: thus. Used in citing a word or phrase that might be wrong or misspelt.
19 World's Columbian Exposition was a trade fair held in Chicago in 1893.
20 Rotary International, an organization for business people and professionals, founded in 1905 by a Chicago lawyer Paul Harris (1868–1947).
21 Hernando De Soto (*c*.1500–42), Spanish explorer, thought at one time to be the first European to cross the Mississippi.
22 German: Heaven confound it. The quotation is a translation thought to have originated with Hermann Goering (1893–1946) (actually by a Nazi playwright Hanns Johst).
23 Novel by James T. Farrell (extract included in Studs Lonigan).
24 Patron saint of travellers.
25 Saint John Bosco (1815–88), Italian priest, founded the Salesian Order. He was canonized in 1934.
26 Cornelius Jansen (1585–1638), Dutch Catholic theologian who advanced a form of Calvinist predestination, which was condemned as heresy by the Church.
27 Latin: freedom in uncertainty.
28 Recluse.
29 Baseball teams: Chicago White Sox (I assume, given mid-west setting for story) and Philadelphia.
30 Presumably short for Chesterfield cigarettes.
31 Latin: here, the clergy in itself or themselves.
32 Church Latin: day of wrath. Motet sung at Mass for the Dead.
33 Church Latin: Thanks be to God.
34 Church Latin: May Almighty God have mercy on you and forgive you your sins.
35 Latin: literally, after the deed or here appointment.
36 American usage meaning awkward.
37 Gregorian Chant.
38 Alban Butler (1710–73), author of *The Lives of the Fathers, Martyrs, and Principal Saints* (1756–59), often abbreviated to *Lives of the Saints*.
39 Sabine Baring-Gould (1834–1924), English clergyman, author of works on folklore and religion who also composed the hymn 'Onward Christian Soldiers'.
40 El Greco (*c*.1541–1614), Greek painter in Spain.

MÁIRTÍN Ó CADHAIN
from Máirtín Ó Cadhain, *An Braon Broghach* (1948); trans. Eoghan Ó Tuairisc, *The Road to Brightcity* (1981)

Máirtín Ó Cadhain (1906–70) was born in Connemara, trained as a teacher in Dublin, and taught in Gaeltacht schools in Galway for ten years from 1926. During the war years he was interned in the Curragh on account of his Republican sympathies. He later became a Professor of Irish at Trinity College Dublin. Here in this story he reveals some of the reasons his work as an Irish-language writer is so highly regarded. The narrative is straightforward — a woman departing for America in the period before the Great War. But inserted into the narrative are unexpected phrases, allusions, metaphors, especially the image of the departure as a funeral.

The Year 1912

— The trunk.

She said the word offhand yet there was a touch of stubbornness in her tone. She hadn't agreed to go to Brightcity with her daughter a week ago last Saturday to buy the trunk, and it irked her like a white frost the way it had been perched up on the ledge of the kitchen dresser, adored like an idol. The children having great play with it, opening it, closing it, looking it all over. She hadn't the heart to vex her daughter this final week, otherwise she would have cleared it off into the room under the bed. But tonight, though the daughter might be of a different mind and anxious to show off that expensive article to the company that had gathered, the mother had followed her own inclination at nightfall and moved the trunk into the room — it might, she said, get damaged or scratched where it was.

It was like a burnt spot or a smallpox scar on the face of life, tonight especially since she seldom had a hearty gathering under her roof. It was useful and wellmade, but that was only a chimaera, a ghost from the Otherworld come to snatch away the first conception of her womb and the spring of her daily life, just when the drinking, the high spirits, the music and merrymaking were in full spate. Seven weeks ago, before the passage-money came, she had been as much on edge awaiting it as Mairin was. That her daughter should be off to America was no surprise to her, no more than the eight sisters of her own whose going was a bitter memory still. She had been schooled by the iron necessities of life to keep a grip on her feelings and throttle her motherlove — as Eve ought to have throttled the serpent of Knowledge. It was the passage-money that had set the heather ablaze again. Flickers of affection, flashes of insight from shut-away feelings, were setting her sense and reason aglow with the knowledge that this going into exile was worse than the spoiling of a church or the wreck of a countryside . . .

But it was destiny, must be attended to. The day was agreed. Patch Thomais was gone for the sidecar. Back in the crowded kitchen the merriment had risen to a frenzy; remnants of the wreck of a people, doomed to extinction at daybreak, bringing their ritual vigil to a hurried night's-end climax of wild debauch . . .

A halfpenny candle stood on a small press by the wall in the bedroom, smeared by a breeze coming by the edge of the paper on a broken windowpane. Depth, magic, mystery of unfathomable seas, reflected by the guttering candleflame in the trunk's brass knobs. It was of pale yellow timber, the mother couldn't at once remember where she had seen that colour before — the face of a corpse after a long wake in sultry weather. And a certain distaste kept her from looking into the trunk, that same tabu which had kept her, though she had often tried, from looking at a corpse in a coffin.

— Have you everything? she asked the daughter keeping her eyes off the dimlit thing. There were all kinds of things in it — a sod of turf, a chip off the hearthstone, tresses of hair, a bunch of shamrock though it was autumn, stockings of homespun, a handful of dulse, items of clothing, papers connected with the voyage across. The daughter took her shoes, coat, hat and dress out of the trunk and laid them on the little press to put on her. During the week she had often laid them out like that but the mother had never encouraged her, and early in the night she had implored her not to put them on till morning.

The mother shut the trunk, threw the bedquilt over it. — To keep it clean. She had long feared that the daughter once she was in the American clothes would be estranged from her, alien as the trunk. Mairin was in her stocking feet and naked except for a long white shift which she had been at great pains to fix about herself that evening and which she had no intention of taking off until she had reached the house of a relative on the other side. Seeing her like that was to see a vision, the only one which had remained clearskinned and beautiful in her memory. A vision that gave bodily shape to the dear lost Tree of Life, while it made real the delicate and deceitful skin of the Knowledge-Apple — a mother's first conception, first fruit. She had so many things on the tip of her tongue to say to her, the intimacies, the affectionate things saved up in motherlove, her life-stuff, from the moment she feels the quick seed in her womb until the flush of eternity puts out the twilight of the world.

For a month now she had said many things to the daughter, scraps scattered at long intervals . . . that she couldn't care if all in the house were to go so long as Mairin stayed . . . that the whole house would miss her, herself especially . . . that of all her children she was the one who had given her the least trouble . . . that she was fine about a house. But none of all that said what she wanted to say. She felt like a servingwoman, the necklace she was putting about the young queen's neck had broken, its precious stones scattered here and there in danger of being crushed and broken. She felt as if some hostile force were filtering her speech, hindering her from letting loose the flow of talk that would ease the tight grip on her heart. She was aware she could never hope to express the things in her mind in a letter which she would have to depend on someone else to write, and in a language whose make and meaning were as unhomely to her as the make and meaning of the Ghost from the Fairymound. And a letter was a poor substitute for the living contact of speech, eyes, features. Her flowing imagination, floodtide of her love, would run thin and freeze in a niggardly writing.

She was hardly likely to see her daughter again for a very long time. Mairin would have to repay her passage, then earn the passage of one or two more of the family, as well as send a share home. It could happen that the child in her womb would set eyes on her before she did. That American coat, the graveclothes — how tell one from the other? The 'God speed her' that would be said from now on had for its undermeaning 'God have mercy on her soul'. Children often got those two expressions mixed up. And when the time came that in actual fact would change the 'God speed' into 'God have mercy', it would come without a decent laying-out and a bier to be carried, and with no passionate keen. Even the graveclothes, no mother would have them awhile to shake out the folds of them from time to time as a relief to her anguish, and there would be neither name nor surname on a rough bit of board in the churchyard by the Fiord for generations to come. The voyage — that immensity, cold and sterile — would erase the name from the genealogy of the race. She would go as the wildgeese go.[1]

But while such ideas were as a sour curd in the mother's mind, she wouldn't give in to the thought that she would never see the daughter again. Her sense and reason said no, her love, hope, determination, said yes. And it was these she listened to. Yet even if she were to see her again she knew she'd be utterly unlike the simple country girl, now nineteen years old, with a look pure as morningsun on a hillside in the Promised Land. Her lips would have been embittered by the berries from the Tree of Good and Evil. That dark weasel envy in her heart. Experience, that slimy serpent, writhing in her mind. Temper of cold steel in her countenance. The tone of her voice transformed by the spell of a harsh stepmother. Such were all returned Americans. She must reveal herself to her now, as the mother of the warriors in the cave used to reveal herself to her children when every sallying out in search of food was a matter of life and death. Reveal herself to her while her age and ignorance were still unmocked at, while there was yet no wall of disbelief between her daughter's mind and hers . . .

The money, she thought, was the best way to begin. She took a cloth purse from her bosom, took out what small change the daughter might need in Brightcity,

and gave her the purse with the rest. The daughter hung it about her neck and settled it carefully in her breast under her holy scapular.

— Look now child you take good care of it. It's likely you won't need it at all, but if you fail to find work soon it would be too much to be depending on Aunt Nora who has her own children to look after. Keep the rug tucked well round you on the vessel. Make free with no one unless it happens to be someone you know. You'll be safe as soon as you reach Nora's house. Even if you have to take small pay, don't overstrain yourself working . . . You will make a visit home after five years. Well, at least after ten years . . . It can't be but you'll have a few pence put by by then. My . . .

She had kept her spirits nicely up to that. But as soon as she thought to break the crust of speech she couldn't find a word to say but stood stockstill staring at her daughter. Hands fiddling with the folds of her apron. Blushing, tears and smiles painfully together in her cheek. Humps and wrinkles of distress coming in her forehead like keys struggling with a lock. The daughter was almost dressed by now and asked where was the small change she'd need in Brightcity? The mother had been so eager to talk that she had forgotten to get a little purse to put it in. Turning to get it she fell into such confusion she forgot the money in her fist until it fell and scattered about the floor. Her idea had been to wait till her tongue could contrive a proper speech, then to hand over the small change to the daughter as a sacred offering, embrace and kiss her . . . Instead, the sacrifice had been ripped from her hand.

Putting away the little purse the daughter felt an envelope in her pocket. — A tress of your hair, mama, she said. I thought I had put it in the trunk along with — the rest. She held the black tress between her and the candle, her blue eyes softened, became childlike. She felt an urge to say something to her mother, she didn't quite know what. Her thoughts went fumbling here and there as a stranger might among the blind holes of a bog on a dark night. The pair of them would have to be in the one bed, the light out, and a wand of moonlight through the small window to charm and set free the tongue. She looked her mother in the eyes to see if she might find encouragement there, but she remained unconscious of her mother's seething emotions, locked within, quite unable to crack the fixed and rigid mask of her features.

She put on the light and gaudy coat, then the wide-brimmed hat. Part of the preparations for her attack on life, she supposed, was to spend a long time fixing and refixing the set of the hat, though she had no idea which particular slant she wanted. She didn't realize that the size and the undulations of the hatbrim added nothing to her good looks, nor that the yellow shoes, black hat and red coat made a devil's own trinity in conflict with her fresh and delicate features. But she was ready: hat, coat, low shoes on and lady-gloves — not to be taken off again. She felt strange, surprised as a butterfly that feels for the first time that it has shed its cramped caterpillar limbs and has the endless airy spaces unimpeded to sail through on easy wings. She felt too some of the lightheaded pride of the butterfly . . .

The mother forgot until the trunk had been locked that she had forgotten to put a bit of hendirt in it, or somewhere among the daughter's clothing. But she wouldn't for the world unlock it again. She couldn't bear the daughter to make fun of her, this morning especially, accuse her of pishrogues[2] and superstition. She shook a tint of holy water on her, and while she was putting the feather back in the bottle the daughter was off out to the kitchen floor to show off her American ensemble.

The sidecar hadn't come yet. There was a swirl of dancing. Tom Neile with his back to the closed door was singing *The Three Sons* in a drunken voice drowning the music —

There's many a fine spa-a-rk young and hea-a-rty
Went over the wa-a-ter and ne-e-e-r return'd.

— Tone yourself down, said the mother to Tom, but she'd have given a deal just then to have a tune like he had in order to release the load of her love in a spilling song. The girls had gathered again about the daughter, scrutinizing her rigout, although they had been a week looking at it. They gave the mother no chance of keeping her company. They thought nothing, it seemed to her, of driving a wedge into nature, one almost as inhuman as that driven in by the immense cold sterile sea. The young women were chirruping of America. Chirruping of the life they'd have together soon in South Boston. Typical of a race whose guardian angel was the American trunk, whose guiding star was the exile ship, whose Red Sea was the Atlantic. Bidin Johnny reminded her to ask her cousin to hurry with the passage-money. Judeen Sheain told her on her life not to forget to tell Liam Pheige about the fun there was at the wake of old Cait Thaidhg.

— Take care you don't forget to tell our Sean that we have the Mountain Garth under potatoes again this year, said Sorcha Phaidin. He said when he was going that after him no one would ever again be born to the race that would attempt to sow it, it was such a hardship.

— Tell my boy, Mairin, that it won't be long till I'll be over to him, Nora Phadraig Mhurcha said in a whisper that all the girls heard.

— By cripes it won't be long till I'm knocking sparks out of the paving stones of South Boston myself, said a redhead youth whose tongue had been loosed by the drink.

— God help those that have to stay at home, said old Seamas O Currain.

The whiskey was circling again. — Here now, you ought to take a taste of it, said Peaitsin Shiubhaine who was measuring it out, heeling the glass towards Mairin with a trembling hand. He splashed some of it on her coat. — A mouthful of it will do you no harm. Devil the drop of poteen you're likely to see for the rest of your life. There was an undertone to his voice, he was remembering the five daughters of his own who were 'beyond' — one of them thirty-five years gone — and he had no hope of ever seeing them again . . . — I'll drink it myself then. Your health, Mairin, and God bring you safe to journey's end.

Neither Peaitsin nor anyone else in the gathering thought to add, — God send you safe home again. Such ignorance of the proper thing to say sparked off the mother's repressed anger. — Five years from today you'll see her back home again, she said tartly.

— God grant it, said Peaitsin and Seainin Thomais Choilm together.

— And she'll marry a monied man and stay here with us for good, laughed Citin, Mairin's aunt.

— I'll have little or nothing to show after five years, said Mairin. But maybe you'd marry me yourself, Seainin, without a sixpence?

But by this time Seainin had huddled himself back against the door and was talking like a tornado to let the mockery of the young girl pass over him.

— At all costs don't pick up an accent, said a young lad, one of her cousins, — and don't be 'guessing' all round you like Micilin Eamoinn who spent only two months beyond and came home across the fields with nothing to show for his voyage but half a guinea and a new waistcoat.

— Nor asking 'what's that, mamma?' when you see the pig.

— Anyhow, you'll send me my passage, said Mairead the next daughter to Mairin, eyes sparkling.

— And mine too, said Norin the next sister.

The mother felt a bleak touch of her own death hearing the greedy begging voices of the pair. Years of delay were being heaped on her daughter's return, as shovelfuls of earth are heaped on a coffin. And the grace of that home-coming was receding from her — as far as Judgement Day. At that moment the children she had given birth to were her greatest enemies.

She set Mairin to drink tea again though she had just stood up from it. But she wanted to come close to her again. She must break bread, make a farewell communion, weave the intimate bond of a farewell supper with her daughter. She would tell her plain and straight that she didn't believe this parting meal to be a funeral meal as far as home was concerned: there would be an Easter to come, before the Judgement. But they weren't left to themselves. Her sister Citin with her family of daughters and some of the other girls pushed up to the table by the wall and in no time had Mairin engulfed among them.

The daughter had no wish for food. Her face burned: desire, panic, wonder, an anguish of mind, all showed in her cheek. Brightcity was the farthest from home she had ever been, but she had been nurtured on American lore from infancy. South Boston, Norwood, Butte, Montana, Minnesota, California, plucked chords in her imagination more distinctly than did Dublin, Belfast, Wexford, or even places only a few miles out on the Plain beyond Brightcity. Life and her ideas of it had been shaped and defined by the fame of America, the wealth of America, the amusements of America, the agonized longing to go to America . . . And though she was lonesome now at leaving home it was a lonesomeness shot through and through with hope, delight, wonder. At last she was on the threshold of the Fairy Palace . . . Tremendous seas, masts and yardarms, blazing lights, silvertoned streets, dark people whose skin gleamed like beetles, distorting for her already the outlines of garth, mountain, rock, fiord. Her mind tonight was nothing but a ragbag to keep the castoff shreds of memory in until she might shed them as flotsam as she sailed. She was so unguarded now that she let herself be led out to dance on the stone floor, dressed as she was for America. In any case she couldn't have found it in her heart to refuse Padraigin Phaidin.

It irked her conscience that she had so long neglected him. She began to dance in a lackadaisical way, but the pulse of the music — that music to which they were beholden even in the fairyplace — excited an impulse in herself, and soon in her dappled outfit she was like a young alien deer, fullblooded, with the common young animals of the herd prancing about her, inciting her to show what she was made of, what she could do, while the elders sat around in sage contemplation. The mother was thinking that if she was ever to see her again the hard experience of life would then be a dead weight on that lust for dancing. In place of that passion of young and eager blood that wedded her limbs to the graceful movement of the stars, the thin and watery stuff of greying age would be keeping her tired bones fixed on earth.

Nevertheless the mother was closely watching, not the daughter, but Padraigin Phaidin who was dancing with her. There and then she guessed the whole story. Easy to see. Very likely the pair had never said a word of love to each other. Very likely they hadn't said a word tonight. And they were likely never to say a word in their lives. But she realized they would be married in South Boston in a year's time, in five years, ten years even . . . She was vexed. That's what lay behind Padraigin's wild dancing fit. What she had failed to say in words he was saying in dance. Body and limbs he was enacting a perfect poem, with growing zest, abandon, vigour and precision, until a lash of his nailed boot carved a spark out of the hearthstone in time with the final beat of the music. Some might put it down to intoxication, but the mother knew better. That spark was in fact a finishing touch, a final fling of the spirit in full victory. Then hardly waiting to be asked while still breathless from the dance he began with easy power to sing. And the mother forgot the daughter listening to him:

The garden's a desert, dear heart, and lonesome I be,
No fruit on the bough, no flower on the thorn,
    no leaf,
No harping is heard and no bird sings in the tree
Since the love of my heart, white branch, went
    to Cashel O'Neill.

A young spirit trying to crack the shell of a universe that shut it in, so fierce was his song. By now the mother had come to hate him. An evil being, fingering her own proper treasure . . .

Horse's hooves and the clatter of a sidecar were heard from the cart-track outside. Music and merriment ceased suddenly. Only Seainin Tolan stretched drunk against the shut door still moaning —

Ora, wora, wora,
It's on the southern side of New York quay
That I myself will land —

the only snatch of a song Seainin ever raised.

— Indeed you'd be a nice gift to America! Devil drown and extinguish you, it's a pity it isn't on some quay you are, a useless hulk, instead of here, cried a youth who could stand him no longer.

The trunk was taken from the room and set like a golden calf on the table.

— Take out that and tie it up on the sidecar, said the mother.

— It might get broken, said Mairin. Leave it alone until I'm ready to go out along with it. That trunk was her licence and authority to wear an elegant hat on her head and an ostentatious coat on her back instead of a shawl. Without the trunk her lady-outfit would be an insult to God. If she let it out of her sight for as much as a second as like as not those tricksome and showy garments would wither into rags and ashes about her body.

She turned now to say goodbye to those who hadn't the strength to accompany her as far as the king's highway. Crippled oldtimers who could barely manage to shuffle across the street; for most of them this was likely the last time they'd leave their own firesides for a social occasion. This was the first link of the chain to be jerked apart, it made her feel for the first time how hard the parting was, how merciless. Whatever about the rest of the people, she would never set eyes on these again. In spite of her distress and hurry she looked closely at each one of them so as to store up in her memory their shape and features. She kept a grip on her emotion and broke down only when she came to her grandmother at the hearth. She had as much affection for her grandmother as she had for her mother, and made more free with her. And was loved in return. Never a week went by but the old woman had laid aside a bit of her pension to give her, whatever else might be behindhand. The old creature was as speechless as if already turned to clay. In fact she almost was, for the best part of her was in the grip of 'the One with the thin hard foot', and the rest waiting on busy death to prepare her dwelling-place. Her mouth was as dry as the timber of a new-shut coffin, and except for a faint blinking of the eyelids that brought her far-off look a little closer to the here and now, Mairin would have thought that she hadn't the least notion what was going on.

— I'll never see you again, mammo, she said, her voice breaking at last in tears.

— God is good, said the mother, a shade stubborn.

Then to kiss the small children and the infant in the cradle. She felt it as a warm substantial summer after the midwinter chill. Charming her senses against the threat of the graveclothes.

The mother brought her off to the room once more. But they weren't long there till Citin and Mairead came in on them to get their shawls so as to accompany Mairin to Brightcity. The mother could have melted them. How officious they were — without them, she thought, the lump of sorrow in her throat wouldn't have hardened again. All she could say to Mairin was that she'd have good earnings; that she hoped they'd have good weather at sea; and for the life of her not to forget to have her picture taken beyond and send it home.

— My own darling girl, she said picking a speck of fluff from the shoulder of the coat and giving a hurried quirk to the hatbrim, though the daughter at once reset it her own way. And having glanced quickly round the house she was ready to go.

The sidecar went lurching down the rugged village track followed by a dense crowd, men, women and children. They had all the appearance of a sacrificial procession: the sidecar like a funeral pyre ahead, puffs of the men's tobacco-smoke hanging in the early morning air, and Mairin walking in her barbaric costume as the officiating druid.

The mother walked alongside the daughter and offered to carry her rug, but Brid Sheamais snatched it and carried it herself. She had determined to have Mairin under her own wing on this last walk, but Citin and her own Mairead thwarted her once more. Then all the young girls closed round her, some chattering and laughing, some so lonesome at her going that they hadn't the heart to say much, and others sorry that they weren't in her place or going along with her. By this time the mother had hardly any feelings of regret left so angry was she with the rabble that wished to deprive her of her daughter before she was even out of sight. She took a spleen against the sidecar too. It was moving as fast as if it was giving a corpse 'the quick trot to the graveyard'. It seemed to her that it was the trunk — perked up on the box of the car, its timber blond as an ear of corn in the rays of the virgin sun — that was pricking the horse to death's own scything speed. She hadn't a word left to say . . .

There was a mild red light from the sun just up. Field walls and piles of stone grinned bleakly. In the little pokes of fields slanting and rugged the tramped stubble was like the head of some Samson having suffered the shears of Delilah. A small sailingboat just out from harbour with a fair wind scratched a bright wake down the Fiord. Mairin looked back from the rise at Hollycliff, from then on her own house and the village houses strung around would be out of sight. Last year's new thatch joined the old black and withered roof at the ridge-strip — line of contact between the past and the time to come. And the village seemed asleep again after its brief second of action, slight as a spit in the ocean that the sailingboat might obliterate.

The sidecar halted at the end of the track. The people formed a close group in the mouth of the highway so that the mother was cut off from the daughter. Just another stray stone in the cairn, that's all she was. The same as if she was neither kith nor kin. More than ever she begrudged Citin and Mairead their going to Brightcity with Mairin. When the kissing began the women were like a gaggle of scavengers about a prey. They pushed their way rudely up to her daughter, squeezed her hand, snatched kisses one after the other like a flock of starlings on a trash-heap. The men shook hands with her, shy, laconic, seeming to say it was all one, and if it had to be done then it were best done as quickly as might be. Padraigin Phaidin did likewise, but unlike the rest of the men he gave the slightest lift to his head and the mother caught the eyes of the couple interlocked for the nick of a second.

At last it was her turn. She hadn't kissed her daughter since she was a child. But she failed to put much yearning and anguish into the kiss, though her lips hungered for her. Hadn't she kissed all and everyone? Hadn't all and everyone got ahead of herself in the kissing and hugging? The daughter's kiss was cold and insipid, the good skimmed from it by all that had been pecking at her. Her body was cold too, cold and insubstantial as a changeling from the Liss.[3]

But what quite spoiled the kiss for her was the sight of the trunk, she was unable to keep her eyes off it and it was all but whispering in her ear —

No mortal kiss will break the spell of the changeling, seduced by pleasure to wander and forget, whose dwelling is the golden web which young desires weave from the sunlight on green hills far off from the here and now.

Mairin was now on the sidecar. Mairead sitting beside her, Citin next to the driver on the other side,

Padraigin Phaidin fixing the trunk firmly between them up on the box. Damned spirits, they appeared to the mother — the accursed trunk, Mairead greedy to get her passage-money, and Padraigin Phaidin on edge to get to America and marry her daughter — three damned spirits torturing her first-born and best-beloved.

Padraigin had finished and the people were moving aside to make way for the horse. The women started in to sob, and the sobbing lifted into a loud wail of words, expressing no real anguish the mother thought, beyond voice and tears. They wouldn't leave her even the comfort of keening alone. And she shed no tear . . .

She stammered uncertainly, — I'll see you before five years are out. And couldn't raise her eyes to meet the eyes of her daughter, not if the sky fell.

The car was now moving. Sobbing the daughter whimpered, — You will. But now the mother's heart as well as her commonsense knew that she would not. Padraigin Phaidin would see her sooner and the girls of the village and her own children, even the infant then in her womb. The mother realized she was but the first of the nestlings in flight to the land of summer and joy: the wildgoose that would never again come back to its native ledge.

1   For historical meaning of this word, see footnote 13 page 11 for more information.
2   Charms.
3   Fairy-mound.

IRISH WRITING IN THE 1950s

One beautiful day followed another as in a dream. In Connemara one has a sense of being perched on the rim of the world. Dublin, that drowsy village, appears in retrospect as a roaring metropolis. It is a land of silences where nothing but the piping of larks, the mournful voices of seabirds and the splash of water is to be heard. The pointed purple-brown hills, the white cabins, the clouds passing languidly over the sky and the small black cattle are reflected sharply in the bog pools that lie still and bright as a sheet of glass. It is a land of silences, and colour. Here and there is a patch of brilliant green, a may tree or a chestnut: the rocks at the edge of the pools are festooned with shaggy golden weed: the piles of turf cut ready for the winter's burning are purple as the distant hills themselves.

It is also a land that is anything but friendly to human beings. A great deal of effort is needed to drag a living from its miserly bosom. There is little work for young men, none for girls, and away they go to England as soon as they can. The older people live as crofters, hoeing away at their potato patches and keeping a cow or two, acting as gillies to the fishermen and poaching a few salmon; and as they die off the locks are turned in the door and the small homesteads are left till they tumble down.

– Honor Tracy, *Mind You, I've Said Nothing!: Forays in the Irish Republic* (1953)

CRITICAL AND DOCUMENTARY

JOHN RYAN
from *Envoy*, February 1950

A reminder by John Ryan (1925–92), founder-editor of *Envoy* (1949–51), of the problems facing Irish publishers in the post-war period. Again, it would be worth researching the position today.

Our Irish Publishers

You have the scene arrange itself: Dublin, mid-winter, nineteen forty-nine; the wind malevolently comes up the Liffey from the Poolbeg, where the gulls squeal around the flashing light; it is raining; the sulky lip of a black cloud hangs over the Custom House as along the quays the lorries come and go.

Even in this weather, men are working here in the docks, working hard loading and unloading ships — cargoes from the Americas and the Indies are whisked away, and Ireland's produce put aboard to be carried overseas. It is the year, the era, of the Export Drive.

Our foreign trade has assumed an importance that it has never had before. 'Export' is the word that, since the war, has come to live with us, has come to face us in our newspapers at breakfast, to be with us all through the day, and to mingle with us in our relaxations in the evening. Punctually on Sunday, even, the newspapers present us with the same word.

It is a very important word to-day. It means employment; it means a reasonable standard of living; it means a fair share for each of us of the amenities of the twentieth century. And so the value of our foreign trade has increased considerably, and continues to grow.

If we turn up the Trade Statistics for December, 1947, and December, 1948, we find that in 1947 the total value of our domestic exports was almost £39 millions; in 1948, responding to the necessity for a substantial increase on that figure, our producers stepped up the value of our exports to £46 millions. A glance through the volumes in question shows that, under almost every heading, an increase was registered in the value of the goods which we sent out of the country.

But look — the value of our exports under the heading 'Books and other printed matter' fell from £289,364 in 1947 to £176,595 in 1948. These figures exclude newspapers.

The steep decline in these figures is alarming. It would seem that we are heading again for the position that obtained before the war, when the corresponding figures were:—

1936	£71,374
1937	£57,426
1938	£57,807

Obviously there is something seriously wrong with our publishing industry when figures as low as those quoted represent our total annual exports in 'Books and other printed matter'. Of course, during 1947, 1948 and the earlier part of 1949, there was a partial ban on the import of our books into Great Britain, but that fact does not account for the lowness of the figures pre-war. However, the only ban at present enforced by the British Board of Trade is on periodicals (such as *ENVOY*), which may not be imported into Britain and exposed for sale. It will be interesting, accordingly, to see whether the figures for 1949 and later 1950 will shown an improvement on the 1947 and 1948 figures. No doubt, they will, but we must remember that 'other printed matter' covers a very wide field.

It is a pity that the Trade Statistics figures are not broken down to show us the annual value of books exported. Again, it should be possible to break down the books figures further to show fiction and non-fiction. We might then have some idea of what our publishers are doing. Whatever firm figure there may be for books, however, we may take it that the greater part of it represents sales of 'pulp' fiction, i.e. the 3d. or 6d. or shilling paper-backed novels, for which there was a large market during the war, and for which there will always be an unsatisfied demand.

The vast bulk of our serious book-publishing is done from English publishing houses. One has only to look down the lists of such publishers as Macmillan, Jonathan Cape, Michael Joseph, Peter Davies, etc., to see the wealth of Irish names there — Yeats, Russell, Synge, O'Faolain, O'Connor, O'Casey, Lavin, *et al.* Practically all our writers whose names, abroad, represent Irish literature have their works produced in London. There are, of course, so far as the writers are concerned, sound financial reasons for this. If they were to depend on the ingenuity of our native publishers for their sales, there would not be much bread and butter on their tables. But the net point at issue is that so long as this position continues, and as long as our Irish publishing firms continue to allow the works of reputable writers to be published in London, there will be a loss of income and prestige to Ireland.

There is no earthly reason why Irish writers should have to turn to London for publication except the lack of enterprise and courage of our own publishers. The publishing industry in Ireland is backward and antiquated in its methods, and unless there is a change of heart on the part of the men responsible for it, the present disgraceful position must continue. We are not asking the *entrepreneurs* of the publishing world to throw their money down drains: the fact that British publishing houses carry our writers is proof that they are good sales propositions; in other words, our writers are also good business. No doubt, the Irish publisher will retort that British houses have better organizations both for bringing books to the notice of the public and for distribution, but this would seem to us to clinch the case against the initiative of Irish publishers. Problems of distribution are merely the technical problems which any business firm has to face and overcome, and provided the wares are good, the sales will be in proportion to the amount of vision and energy brought into play. A good technical school course in modern business methods would not come amiss to those in charge of our publishing houses.

The fuss raised in 1948, and during last year, by the publishers about the effect of the British ban on Irish writers was largely dishonest. By and large, our writers, with one or two exceptions, did not suffer one whit as a result of the ban. If our publishers were worried about the position at the time, it was not because their hearts were bleeding for any of our authors, but because they themselves were prevented from expanding their output for the popular fiction market which provided ready sales with a minimum of overhead expenses. It is interesting to note that their concern only grew vocal when Britain's restrictive regulations grew tighter towards the end of 1948.

We are not by any means decrying the cheap fiction production which our publishers indulge in, or any other production which they indulge in for that matter: it gives plenty of employment and it brings money into the country. But we do deplore the fact that, but for our publishers' short-sightedness, extra employment could be provided and extra money earned for us in these economically troubled times by the 'repatriation' of our foremost writers — not to speak of the prestige that would accrue to the country.

We are quite certain that our poets, novelists and play-wrights would just as readily have their productions published in Dublin, provided — and it is a very important and equitable proviso — that they got the same financial return as they get from the English publishing houses. That elusive attribute, 'prestige', will look after itself, and most honest writers are content that it should. That they gravitate to London firms is due to the fact that London publishers are willing to take on their books, and, having published them, will use all the resources of modern salesmanship to persuade the public to buy them. That 'London-consciousness' exists, and that young writers get infected with it, is entirely the fault of our unenterprising publishers. No merit attaches to the *place* of publication of a volume: worth will be recognized anyhow.

It is time, then, that our publishers reassessed their position and pulled their weight for the country's economy and prestige. It is not enough, as a Dublin firm did recently, to publish a non-Irish volume that had been brought out a few weeks previously by a well-known London firm — that is not enterprise; we doubt if it is business: it savours more of lunacy. *ENVOY* wants Irish publishers to play their fair part in the country's life, and to contribute as much to the community as they get from it. And that they get quite a lot is evidenced by the fact, made clear by a director of a leading Dublin firm recently, that every publisher's printing house in Ireland is working overtime, and has been for years, in an effort to fulfil orders.

PATRICK KAVANAGH
from *Envoy*, March 1950

Kavanagh's intervention from the touchline in the debate about culture and writing in modern Ireland.

Diary

O Come all ye tragic poets and sing a stave with me —
Give over T.S. Eliot and also W.B.
We'll sing our way through Stephen's Green where
    March has never found
In the growing grass a cadence of the verse of Ezra
    Pound.

The University girls are like tulip bulbs behind
More luxurious than ever from Holland was
    consigned,
Those bulbs will shortly break in flower — rayon, silk
    and cotton
And our verbal constipation will be totally forgotten.

Philosophy's a graveyard — only dead men analyse
The reason for existence. Come all you solemn boys
From out your dictionary world and literary gloom —
Kafka's mad, Picasso's sad in Despair's confining room.

O Come all darling poets and try to look more happy,
Forget about sexology as you gossip in the café;
Forget about the books you've read and the inbred
    verses there
Forget about the Kinsey Report[1] and take a mouthful
    of air.

The world began this morning, God-dreamt and full
    of birds,
The fashion shops were glorious with the new
    collections of words.
And Love was practising phrases in young balladry —
Ten thousand years must pass before the birth of
    Psychology.

O Come all ye gallant poets — to know it doesn't
    matter
Is Imagination's message — break out but do not scatter.
Ordinary things wear lovely wings — the peacock's
    body's common.
O Come all ye youthful poets and try to be more
    human.

This ballad may not be a complete success, though I
should not say so, for the world to a frightening extent
takes one at one's own valuation.

There is health in the barbaric simplicity of the
ballad; it compels one to say something. Most of the
verse written in this land suffers from only one thing
— the writers have nothing to say. Having something
to say is largely a mood. A man sits back in the
arrogant humility of his certainty that about those
things which are worth knowing he knows as much
and as little as any man who has ever lived. This
produces a calm mood, a still centre, which is the key
to whatever heavens of the imagination there are.

Poets are not only born, they are also made. The
nature of the true poet is such that it produces around
itself an antagonism through which he must fight.
Some men create this antagonism artificially, but they
do not become great poets. I would say that the great
poet flies from his destiny, but cannot escape it.

I have seen young men with poetic ambitions
making grand gestures, throwing over jobs, living the
'simple life', but the genuine artist is running the other
way, like Stephen Dedalus in *Ulysses*. A more perfect
example of the phoney supporter of the artist and of
the artist himself is in the characters of Haynes, the rich
Englishman, and Stephen. How dreadfully Stephen put
his foot in it when he mentioned money to Haynes.

A real patron never discusses the artist's work which
he takes for granted: he inquires how the man is living
and on what.

But come to consider this, is it not an extraordinary
piece of messianic arrogance? Why should the man who
writes verses be allowed to exist without working as
ordinary men work? Yet, it has always been a note of
the poet's life. He demands a living, and in most ages
and societies he has been granted it. There is an instinct
in mankind which recognizes the priestly nature of the
poet's function. This instinct has never been strong in
Ireland, for Ireland is a particularly cynical and
materialistic country — for all its boastings about
religion. Who, and when was, invented the romantic
Ireland? Shaw debunked it. He also caught the Dublin
version of it:— 'A certain flippant futile derision and
belittlement that confuses the noble and serious with
the base and ludicrous seems to me peculiar to Dublin.'[2]

I know it is dangerous to generalize about areas, yet
there are traditions which do count.

It would be untrue to say that Ireland does not read
as much and as seriously per head of population as any
other country. But that hardly counts at all, for with
due respects to Mr Sean O'Faolain's boast about
making his living entirely from his writing it cannot be
done by anyone who writes seriously — for Posterity
has not printed its banknotes yet.

How, for instance, would T.S. Eliot fare if he had to
live by his writings?

The sale for a book of verse runs between three
hundred and a thousand. At the height of his fame in
the late 'Thirties, Auden never sold more than eight
hundred.

In England poets live by working for the B.B.C., a
form of journalism which isn't always as bad as the

other kind. In America most of the poets who are not of independent means live by teaching in colleges.

Somebody recently mentioned the possible market for Irish-published books in the U.S. His attitude was a typical Irish one; he could only think in terms of commerce. The poet does not think in terms of commerce; he knows that his work has no commercial value. When *he* talks of money it is aside from his work.

I think I can say that the sale for Irish books in the United States is limited. It is possible that the Harp and Shamrock might sell well, or sentimental religion or melodrama, but creative work, no.

It would be interesting to know how many copies of *Ulysses* have sold in the U.S. Often a book is so famous that nobody buys it. Indeed, the irony is that several best-sellers might be written about a book that was a financial failure. An example of this was the *Quest for Corvo*, the subject of which died in a ditch. All this seems so boringly personal-pointed, intro- spective, I know; but it cannot be helped. You cannot keep the personal equation out of anything which has to do with money.

There are in this city a certain element of poetasters who engage in terrible intrigues:—

They prick the lion, Morality, with a pin,
Then glance around them grinning — Aren't we bold?
The Church is in a state at our revolt.
Tremendous counter-movements now begin.

The pigmy poets in a fearful mood
Mass on the borders of Tweedledum,
Hard words are spoken, the crowd is dumb,
Amazed at such a shocking interlude.

I was reading in a religious journal about the sex- life of the Galway male — and female.

It was the case of the 'teenagers' going to dances. A committee has been formed in many of the Galway parishes whose job it is to get the 'teenage' girls to promise not to go home with a man alone. The curate usually attends these dances where — the journal I'm quoting has the cruelty to say — he 'is the life and soul of the party'. The young men form the groups which see the young maidens home intact. A peculiar case this of the wolves being so wolverine that they must defend the young girls from the wolves.

The tribe's defence of its women was a common feature of life in my native area. Townlands often became self-determining entities. A stranger — that is a man from the next townland — found courting one of their women might be set upon and massacred. The result of it was that most of the natives were inbred and with a lot of insanity among them.

There is no use in my pretending that I was the objective philosopher looking on. Well I remember myself and another lad watching with hate and fury in our hearts that young man on a motor-bike who used to scoot over and back our road — looking for prey.

We knew he was a blackguard and we thought he might be a Protestant. Jealousy is morality's armed thug.

I have been thinking of popular journalism. Main thing is knowledge of crosswords. The use of all vulgar slang words such as 'teenage' and abbreviations such as 'congrats.' All contributors to a popular paper should have silly faces — which will be placed at the head of columns. These faces must be owned by names of nonentities. Newspapers 'written by the office boy for office boys' was the Northcliffe[3] theory and practice. There are a number of intelligent men in Dublin journalism but they haven't a chance.

At one time I used to think that because the Sunday's mental diet of the Gael was the same as the Saxon's this showed a similarity of character. Yet, one might as well say that all men are the same who smoke the same brand of cigarettes.

1 *Sexual Behavior of the Human Male* was published in 1948, followed in 1953 by *Sexual Behavior of the Human Female*.
2 From Shaw's Preface to *Immaturity* (1879; rpt London: Constable, 1931), xxxiii. The Preface was written in 1921.
3 Alfred Harmsworth (1865–1922), newspaper baron, founded the *Daily Mail* in 1896 and the *Daily Mirror* in 1903.

OLIVER ST JOHN GOGARTY
from Oliver St John Gogarty, *Rolling Down the Lea* (1950)

Gogarty's plea for the preservation of cultural reminders of Anglo-Irish culture from Swift to Yeats. If his advice had been heeded, much of the destruction of Georgian Dublin that occurred in the 1960s might have been prevented.

The Destruction Still Goes On

Ignorance and apathy are unpleasant subjects which you cannot denounce without putting yourself deliberately or unconsciously into the position of an arbiter. To ignore them makes you an accessory; nor may an Irishman by removing himself from the scene escape injury when ignorance becomes criminal, as it does when it becomes iconoclastic.

Since childhood we have heard laments for the losses of our manuscripts, our goldsmiths' work, our ancient monuments. These losses we attribute to 'the Danes'. But we abstain from any inquiry that might uncover culprits nearer home. Yet 'the Danes' did not burn Cormac's chapel;[1] nor were they the only raiders of Clonmacnoise;[2] nor were their hearts warmed by 'the memory of the lime-white mansions' their right hands had laid in ashes.

Every country has its upsurgings of the savage who is innate in humanity. Seldom have savages tried, as they did here, to justify their ruinous acts, much less attempt to vindicate the destruction of a nation's monuments by the pretence that they were objects that had to be removed from the path of Liberty; as if the liberty that arose from such licence could contribute to the culture of society. But when the 'liberty' purchased by the destruction of what was comely and cultured in this country becomes a retrograde movement and rewards barbarity and slavery, it is time that the pretenders were exposed and pilloried.

This is no easy task when a nation has been faced about and blinded to all that makes it worthy of a place on earth, when its standards have been thrown down and trampled, and pretence set up in the seat of principle — when, in a word, national life is founded on a lie.

It may be that in the breast of the savage there smoulders fear of everything that is beyond his understanding, and that when what was unapprehendable becomes familiar, fear turns into hate and envy of everything that is beyond his capacity. Culture, the cousin of wisdom, points an accusing finger at him. Therefore he obliterates its every trace. When the contempt of civilized nations makes him realize what a barbarian he is held to be, he will endeavour by vulgar shows to make the people he has outraged forget the destruction of their heritage. Beholding these puppet plays, we cannot refrain from asking how many 'Receptions' at the Vice-regal Lodge will compensate for the destruction of the records in the Record Office, 'that even the Danes spared'; or how many town houses must yet be turned into Government offices to compensate for the destruction of irreplaceable mansions of the country's greatest century. This inherent vandalism the poet Yeats foresaw when he advised his countrymen to:

> Scorn the sort now growing up
> All out of shape from toe to top,
> Their unremembering hearts and heads,
> Base-born products of base beds.[3]

A gang of ignoramuses, headed by a man who is cultureless, cheerless, songless and alien in every way to the kindly Irish, undertook to compensate the people for their ruined heritage by a series of imitation English Punch-and-Judy shows. It is as if a spoilt lay brother dressed in black were to present himself as the equivalent of an insulted hierarchy and a despoiled cathedral.

'Romantic Ireland's dead and gone.'[4]

A cuckoo has usurped the songbird's nest. The songsters are cast out to perish. The tradition is broken. The song that Finn loved to hear in Letter Lee must be heard in Ireland no more.

This is the explanation of the deliberate indifference to the nation's history and the attempted substitution of trumpery pomp for national tradition.

The destruction still goes on.

In the United States the value of monuments and ancient landmarks in the march of the nation is recognized. They are cherished. Homes of great men are known and preserved. Records of the nation's great are collected. Their statues stand. The *genius loci*[5] is honoured so that its spirit may inform the people and act as their growing inspiration through the centuries. The creative stress of those rare spirits whose lives were devoted to their fellow men is felt by all Americans in a deep and earnest mood. Britain, too, knows the worth of the example of its great sons and daughters. Whole districts are named after them. We read of the 'country' of those whose lives were spent in certain well-known parts of their native land. The houses where they dwelt are marked by entablatures. What a contrast in Ireland, where, with but very few exceptions, the birthplaces of its famous sons are unknown. How many citizens of Dublin can point out the birthplace of Swift, of Burke, or Griffith — men whose names are synonyms of human liberty? If such names cannot be associated with the spot of Irish earth their birth made sacred, what hope is there for the artists, the creators whose work made Irish culture known the world over? What hope is there for a generation whose unremembering hearts and heads are unaware of such men?

The tradition is broken.

It would seem as if the very existence of the fame of the great engendered envy and malice in the drab schemers of to-day. Not only is no effort made to preserve the names of the great, but the places that housed them or were made famous by them are razed to the ground. And the destruction still goes on apace: we read:

One of the last links that bound Dean Swift with Glasnevin has been broken. The Temple in the grounds of Delville has been demolished because it stood in the way of a roadway to a new hospital. This temple, designed and built more than two hundred years ago, had, until decay set in, a medallion of Stella painted on its walls. The Latin inscription on the façade, *Fastigia despicit urbis* (it looks down on the pinnacles of the city), is said to have been suggested by Swift himself, and likely, too, for the two senses of 'looks down' are in character.

And there is another reason for regret. The Temple, as everybody called it, was built over an arched vault in which the world-famous Drapier Letters were printed. That vault, where the remains of an old printing-press were found some years ago, has been cut in two by the new road. Near the Temple stood 'Stella's bower'. That has been partially torn down. A portion of the brick, arched roof has been cut away, probably for road-filling.

But the citizens will probably be compensated fully for such a trifling loss by the historical appearance of the President in his silk hat to open the new road to an old woman's Home and by the significance of this for the nation.

The path to the future. What is it? A pathological institute.

Delville! A name composed of parts of the names of Dr Delaney and his wife, Mary Granville. Delville, the house where the famous men of the period met — men who were not only forerunners of the Irish Literary Renaissance but helpers in the renaissance of the soul of Ireland, men who nursed it back to life and self-respect; the house where the Delaneys entertained Addison, Thomas Parnell, Stella, Dean Swift and Thomas Sheridan. An old woman's home has taken its place. It may prove to be an appropriate refuge for whatever may be left of the spirit of the nation.

And the destruction still goes on.

In his castle of Tilira near Gort in the County of Galway some years ago, that great Irishman, Edward Martyn,[6] was entertaining his literary friends, George Bernard Shaw, Arthur Symons, his cousin, George Moore, and, among others, the young Yeats. From a house a few miles away the widow of Sir William Gregory, an eminent Civil Servant, drove over to join the throng. Thus it came about that Lady Gregory was introduced to Yeats. That was the beginning of a partnership in letters which was to last for fifty years.

Lady Gregory's house, Coole Park, was one of the many houses to be found in County Galway. It was a three-storey house built of native limestone and dashed a light grey. Like Rafort, near Athenry, it was one of the smaller mansions of the country. But its woods were its principal attraction — the Seven Woods of Coole with their beautiful Gaelic names. They are worthy of a better word than mine. Let us hear Yeats recite his wonderful blank verse that names them all:

I walked among the Seven Woods of Coole,
Shan-walla, where a willow-bordered pond
Gathers the wild duck from the wintry dawn;
Shady Kyle-dortha; sunnier Kyle-na-no,
Where many hundred squirrels are as happy
As though they had been hidden by green boughs
Where old age cannot find them; Pairc-na-lee,
Where hazel and ash and privet blind the paths;
Dim Pairc-na-carraig, where the wild bees fling
Their sudden fragrances on the green air;
Dim Pairc-na-tarav, where enchanted eyes
Have seen immortal, mild, proud shadows walk;
Dim Inchy wood, that hides badger and fox —
And marten-cat, and borders that old wood
Wise Biddy Early called the wicked wood:
Seven odours, seven murmurs, seven woods.[7]

In these woods walked the men who have raised the country out of that spiritual oblivion that engulfs all parochial appendages of a great Empire. On a tree in the woods their names were cut. Here Bernard Shaw went for his constitutionals; and, happily, the years have testified their advantage to his health. Here Moore was at his most mischievous on the very few occasions he was invited to Coole Park. Strange to say, it was not George Moore but Arthur Symons who deprecated the abduction of the young Yeats by the widow Gregory. When she joined the party at Tilira, Arthur Symons warned, 'Be careful of her, Willie. She has a possessive eye.' The warning availed not. Yeats went to reside at Coole; but luckily the prognostications of Symons as to the fate of Yeats's lyricism, 'She will put an end to his poetry', proved to be unfounded. Some of the best poetry he was to write was written by Yeats during his years at Coole Park. The house was magnified by his imagination into an ideal Irish mansion full of the courtliness of a century it may not have seen at all. His imagination endowed it with the traditions of the period he most admired, that century in which the Anglo-Irish mind flowered and 'the salt of the earth', as he called them, enunciated opinions, liberal for their period and since unexcelled.

What has been done to preserve these memories? A saw-mill marks the site of Coole and its Seven Woods. The very stones and slates of the house that welcomed the great geniuses of their generation have been removed by a contractor (building materials are scarce) to build an ecclesiastical structure within the walls of the disused Galway gaol. How truly Yeats's friend, George Russell (Æ), said: 'One of the very first symptoms of the loss of the soul of a nation is the loss of the sense of beauty.'

Someone, not unmindful of the fame of Coole, bought its hall-door for five pounds ($12). From it he cut a heart-shaped piece of wood which held the knocker. This he offered to the Dublin Municipal Gallery. It was refused because, no doubt, those who conducted a gallery of Ireland's great did not want such a stultifying reminder of the many acts of vandalism against 'the noblest of the things that are gone'.

'The President has received the ex-Prime Minister at the Vice-regal Lodge.' — Daily paper.

When I consider the drabness — drab as the sodden peat in the Park[8] — and the soullessness of the present state, the paradox that puzzled me is resolved. The paradox was this: why did that efflorescence which is called the Irish Literary Renaissance manifest itself while the country was directly under British rule? The answer is that those engaged in the Irish Literary Movement drew their inspiration directly from an unbroken tradition, from the sagas, the legends and the speech of the country. There was no pretence about it. The undiluted language of the Gael was theirs. The old tongue had not been pidginized into a political shibboleth. Then, too, there was adventure in the air. Without adventure there is stagnation. The sagas had a vitalizing effect on those who listened to them. They renewed the national spirit with a love that was genuine, strong and impassioned; poets became patriots and, in turn, poets made patriots. The soul of the nation, so long silenced and alienated by the denationalizing system of education known as the Intermediate System, burst into song. The issues were clear-cut. The enemy was British domination with its universality or Imperialism, which, like a ten-cent store, was to contain everything reduced to one level (and nothing worth much) under one management or administration, an Emporium of Empire. The defence against this levelling was a return to nationalism, a recoil from Imperialism. There can be neither art nor poetry in a regime that is founded on politics which has debauched the very language of the country into ersatz Gaelic that is a confessed failure:

> Mr T. Derrig, Minister for Education, told General Mulcahy that eight essays had been received for a $500 competition in Irish on the life and works of Thomas Davis. The adjudicators did not consider that any of the essays was of sufficiently high standard to justify the award of the prizes.

And this after twenty years of compulsory Irish! There is as much spent on this attempt to spell English in Irish characters — Bus, Incoim Tax, Telephon and Phuist — as would clear the disgraceful slums of our towns and raise the standards of living to include cleanliness, health and self-respect; or to perpetuate, by the preservation of their homes, the glory of our great men.

There are certain things that may not be justly compared with one another. For instance, it is not just to compare the cost of women's imitation jewellery with the cost of demolishing slums. They are not in the same category. But the cost of a tinsel court may be compared with the cost of slum-clearing because they are under the same dispensation, and that public; and the same men have the allocation of the money. Lately, some years ago, they were endeavouring to increase their own salaries, although not one of them, according to the then Prime Minister (and he magnanimously included himself), is worth more than £1,000 ($5,000) a year.

From the ends of the earth men come, are 'received' and find a home in an Irish 'republic', where a great number of its citizens have not a home of their own.

'Will none of you blighters ever laugh?'

1 At Cashel in County Tipperary, built by Cormac MacCarthy, king of Munster, burnt in 1647 by Murrough O'Brien, Earl of Inchiquin.
2 Monastic settlement in County Offaly dating from the sixth century, plundered by Vikings and, after 1178, by England, but in the seventh century the monks at Clonmacnoise fought monks at Durrow.
3 Lines from Yeats's 'Under Ben Bulben'.
4 Line from Yeats's 'September 1913'.
5 Latin: spirit of place.
6 Edward Martyn (1859–1963), wealthy Catholic, helped co-found with Lady Gregory and Yeats the Irish Literary Theatre in 1899.
7 Opening lines from Yeats's 'The Shadowy Waters'.
8 The Phoenix Park in Dublin, where the Vice-regal Lodge once housed the Chief Secretary to Ireland (and now the President of Ireland).

GARRY HOGG
from Garry Hogg, *Turf Beneath My Feet* (1950)

The English travel writer Garry Hogg here touches on the ethical problem of
photographing Irish country people. How do you respond to his comments? It might be
worth comparing Hogg's comments with Synge's 1905 *Manchester Guardian* article above.

Turf — And A Camera

There is, they say, no finer turf than that to be found
in Connemara. They do not call it 'peat', though they
will refer to the areas where the turf is cut as 'peat-
bogs'. The men are turf-cutters; their implements are
turf-spades which are long, almost straight-shafted
tools with a narrow and very slightly concave rectangle
of bright steel having a sort of spur on one side at the
top to take the pressure of the digger's boot. On both
sides of this road running from the coast due north to
Screeb and Maam Cross the bogland is intersected by
parallel lines of a raised, hardened surface along which
the men and their donkeys and the occasional two-
wheeled carts pass to and fro, laden and empty. By the
road-side are innumerable stacks of turf in varying
stages of drying-out. They are higher by far than the
potato-clamps seen in English fields, wide at the base,
buttressed at each end and running sometimes for ten
or twenty yards alongside the road. Stacked for winter
use against the side of a cottage they will often give
the impression, seen from a certain angle, of being as
high as the thatched roof itself.

Further from the road, covering wide stretches of
the bog, are innumerable small pyramids of turves, half
a dozen or so to each pyramid, built in such a way that
the wind can pass through them to dry them. They
stand along the upper edges of bog that has been cut,
breaking the uniform levels and gentle undulations of
this saturated ground. The depth of turf among these
bogs varies greatly, but it is by no means unusual to see
three, four, five and even more 'spits' of turf, one
below the other, each clearly revealing the slanting
hollow made by the turf-cutter's spade.

When the spits have been newly cut and the vertical
edges are still oily-wet the effect is very beautiful,
particularly when the sun shines athwart the face of
the bog. Then the dark turf, nigger-brown to black,
has indistinct but regular alternating hues where sun
and shadow play hide-and-seek. The nearest parallel I
can think of is the adze-marking on old oak beams,
hard now as iron and glossy with the play of smoke
and polish in some low-ceilinged room.

There was a group of turf-cutters at work along the
road, possibly the very men who had passed me in the
two lorries. When I reached them I stopped to watch
the process. The majority of them were stacking the cut
turves into the little pyramids I have spoken of. Others
were carting the dried turves, in creels on their backs or
in rough barrows, from the small stacks towards the
bigger stacks on the road-side. They were working in
complete silence when I drew level with them, singly
and in pairs scattered over a half-acre of bog.

One man stood separate from the rest, minding an
iron pot which swung from a tripod over a turf fire by
the road-side. Round it were ranged a dozen or more
tea-cans. He had a bandaged hand which he carried
slung in the upper folds of his jacket. I asked him if the
men would mind my taking a few photographs of
what they were doing. He shook his head, so I left the
road and walked across the quaking turf towards them.
Immediately, one after another of them began to
speak. Brief remarks in a tongue I did not understand
were tossed from one to another. There were short,
unmirthful laughs. Without exception every man who
stood anywhere near me saw to it that his back was
turned to me and that he was bending over his work.
If their injured foreman had meant to indicate that
they would not mind being photographed he was
certainly mistaken. I took the hint, very ostentatiously
directed my camera at stretches of cut bog where no
men were working, and continued on my way
without looking over my shoulder at the bog I had
left.

It is difficult to know what to do about this matter
of taking photographs where people as well as landscape are involved. There is, of course, an art in the
so-called 'candid camera-work', but it is not an art I
have acquired or am ever likely to acquire. Seen from
the point of view of the 'subject' it is an offensive,
impertinent gesture on the part of the man with the
camera; yet unless all one's pictures are to be devoid of
human interest, or are to contain figures carefully
posed for effect, there seems no alternative.

In varying parts of the country the reaction of the
natives will vary surprisingly. In Bantry the Spanish

sailors clamoured to have their photographs taken; they tumbled into effective groupings without directions from me, and I am quite sure it was not simply because they hoped to receive copies of the photograph later on. The gipsies in Killorglin were the same — embarrassing in their readiness, their anxiety, to be photographed. Indeed, in Kerry generally I met with little of this shyness; but as I went further north it increased and in Connemara it was most pronounced. It is hard to make people see that you are not wanting to photograph them because you think them, so to speak, curiosities, but because they form part of the local scene and add something to it of importance.

I have been out on 'stories' with more than one professional cameraman on the staff of a weekly illustrated magazine; but though, objectively, I admire their technique, my sympathies still lie to a large extent with the folk who are dragooned, or tricked, into having photographs taken. It is all right in the towns. There, people are sophisticated; they are told the name of the magazine and know there is a sporting chance that their faces will appear in its pages. Men at any rate take the whole business as a joke. They are easy enough to handle. Not unnaturally, however, it is the countryfolk who are the problem. They don't readily answer to the same technique, though one at any rate of the cameramen I have worked with has brought to a fine art the business of mingled threat and cajolery. He has obtained pictures where I should myself have fled in fear of being lynched. After all, he is paid to succeed in this!

It may be objected that the skilled cameraman will contrive to catch his victims unawares. To a certain extent that is true. There is no doubt that the best photographs are those in which the subjects did not know till too late that they were being stalked. But it is rarely easy to take such photographs. They may sometimes be taken from a distance, but not of course when there are crowds about. The subject can then be enlarged, but that is not always satisfactory. There are gadgets on the market, I believe, for taking photographs at right angles to the subject desired, but I have not yet found one of these. I confronted that problem all the way up the west coast of Ireland, and have not solved it yet.

Ireland is perhaps a special case: the more outlandish parts of the country are more truly 'off the map' than any others in the British Isles with the exception perhaps of the islands lying off the Scottish mainland to north and west. Much later in my journey I raised the matter with an extremely intelligent farmer and his wife in County Donegal. He knew of people in the district, as it happened, who had been 'bitten'. A journalist and cameraman representing a well-known illustrated magazine had come out and spent a week and more taking photographs of their lives, their work and rare recreation; they had assured the men and women that they were doing it for their own pleasure and nothing more. The people, believing them, had co-operated to a surprising extent.

Months afterwards one member of the community, having had occasion to visit a town, had seen a copy of the magazine open at the feature on which the two men had been working. Aghast, he bought a copy and brought it back with him to look at at his leisure. No, there was no doubt about it: every angle of the little community's life — their religious exercises, their family life, their parents and grandparents, their children and grandchildren, appeared in these brazen pages. In their innocence, not knowing how curiously casual the average reader of such magazines proves to be, they imagined the whole world studying their private lives. They felt themselves stripped naked, held up as objects strange and ridiculous to the townsfolk from the big cities. It was not much more than a year or so since this had happened and the memory was still very much alive.

Children are usually all right, though not always, and they certainly make good subjects. I remember an encounter with two children that promised very well. They were approaching me along the otherwise empty road, one leading a donkey piled high with turves, the other sitting astride the load and brandishing a stick. I held out two pennies, signalled them to slow down a moment while I got them against a background I wanted, and meanwhile rapidly set my camera. But though the girl child was interested and prepared to have her picture taken, her brother, barefoot and ragged like herself, burst into tears and dashed off down the road as hard as he could pelt. Then his sister too took fright and beat the donkey and soon the three of them were no more than small black dots on a dusty road.

Yet within a couple of miles of this I came upon another child, a small boy perched high on the rump of his donkey behind its load of turf. I made the same gesture with a penny. Without replying, the boy wheeled his donkey about, retreated twenty yards or so, turned round again and approached me at a gentle walk, sitting very still on his seat until I called to him that I had taken my picture. He drew level and I offered him the penny. He looked at it soberly, then at me. He shook his head with finality, smiled happily and went on his way.

It was rarely as easy as that. There were times when I was obstinate and not to be put off. A few days later in

Connemara I rounded a corner of a winding road to find the most exquisitively sited cottage I had seen for days. Nearly all the cottages, of course, are built to the same design: single-storeyed, with the door about two-thirds of the way along the front wall, two windows to one side of it and one window to the other; small, dark, beneath overhanging thatch. But though they seem to grow out of the soil and rock on which they stand, just now and then one catches the eye as possessing a beauty of setting that makes it memorable among its fellows. It was so with this one, standing at an angle of the road, on a downward slope, screened from behind and at each end by a tree-grown bank.

Standing in her doorway was an elderly woman in the inevitable black skirt and shawl. I stopped and asked whether she would mind my photographing her cottage, and she answered that I might do so with pleasure. Having said which, she retreated through the doorway and I could see her peeping out behind one of the darkened windows.

I called her, saying I would like it so much better if she would stand for a moment in her own doorway. She would not be persuaded. Then fate played her an unkind trick. Her dog emerged and trotted quietly across the little cobbled patch in front of her door, heading for the bushes. There was a hen strutting about, too.

'The dog's after chasing your hen!' I called out excitedly.

She was out in a flash, looking to right and to left. By then the dog had vanished, but the hen was still pecking in the dirt between the cobbles, unperturbed. The woman turned inquiringly towards me, caught sight of the upraised camera, and with a shrill ejaculation swung round and headed once more for the safety of her own doorway. In that moment I got my photograph. It lacked the tranquillity of the scene I had hoped to record, but I got it. She did not emerge again until I was well down the road.

SIR CHRISTOPHER LYNCH-ROBINSON
from Sir Christopher Lynch-Robinson, *The Last of the Irish R.M.s* (1951)

Sir Christopher Lynch-Robinson (1884–1958), whose father (Sir Henry Robinson) was Head of the Irish Local Government Board and a Privy Councillor and whose mother was a descendant of the famous Lynch family from Galway, was a Resident Magistrate for the Counties of Donegal and Louth from 1912 until 1922. As the title of his autobiography suggests, he was among the last to hold such an office. Here in this extract he recounts his experience during Easter Week 1916, reproduces the Proclamation of the Republic, and compares Anglo-Irish relations to a marriage in which the woman walks out on her husband!

The First World War

Just before Easter, in 1916, my wife went to Dublin to stay with her parents who lived near mine in Foxrock, and on Easter Monday curious rumours began to spread that there was something amiss in Dublin. Nothing very definite was heard until that evening, when our District Inspector motored over from Ballyshannon[1] to tell me that he had had private word that there was an armed rising of Sinn Feiners in Dublin, that fighting was still going on, and that the City was isolated. Being alarmed about my wife's and my parents' situation, I decided to motor up early next morning, and putting the .38 Colt automatic in my

pocket — the very one which failed to secure a hit on the baboons in Pretoria — I started off by Enniskillen and Cavan, stopping at every constabulary barrack on the way to see if any of them had any definite news — which they hadn't.

It wasn't until I got to Navan in County Meath, that I learned the truth. They told me that there was an armed rising all over the country, following a landing by Roger Casement from a German submarine in the South, and that hard fighting was going on in Dublin. They thought that I'd never get through. I did not think myself that any fighting would be likely in the suburbs, so near Dunshaughlin I turned south-west, and made my way through Leixlip into the Dublin Mountains in order to by-pass the City and come down off the mountains about level with Foxrock, which was six miles due south of the capital. When I got on the high ground looking down on to the city, it was perfectly plain that there were the devil's own delights going on there. Fires were burning all over the place, some gunboat or other was lobbing shells into Liberty Hall, the Transport Workers' Union Headquarters, and one could hear the rattle of small arms and see occasional shell-bursts in the middle of the city. Along the roads there were people who had come up to watch, who all displayed strong feeling against the Sinn Feiners. 'They're as bad as the Germans, so they are . . .' destroying the people . . . murdering everyone . . .' However, I got through without any trouble and landed up at my father's house, where I found my wife and both my parents sitting out on the steps facing the lawn listening to the distant battle. The rest, of course, is history now. I stayed there several days. Everything was normal and quiet in Donegal, and as the military didn't want anyone to travel about the country roads yet, the Chief Secretary's Office[2] told me to stay where I was. Then came that amazing and sudden revulsion of popular feeling over to the side of Sinn Féin. It was caused by the execution of the rebel leaders. Here was another example of the profound difference between the Irish and the English mentalities. The English attitude was perfectly simple. The rebels were a lot of men who had led an armed revolt and stabbed England in the back whilst she was engaged in a life-and-death struggle with the Teutonic Powers; they had caused many deaths and great destruction of property. What was more natural than these men should be tried by Field General Court-Martial and pay the just penalty? The Irish did not see it in that light at all. Had ten times the number of those executed been placed against the wall and shot out of hand whilst the fighting was going on, nobody would have said a word. But when the fighting is all over, and the hot blood has cooled down, the Irish instinct is to seek the nearest public house with your late enemy and talk it over. But the English didn't; they put them all through the formality of trial by the military, and then took them out and shot them. To the English, this was merely the decent way of giving the accused a chance to defend themselves, and of refusing to take life except by proper judicial procedure. To the Irish, it was just cold-blooded, vindictive murder. The executions got on everybody's nerves; one would hear of two being shot one day, one the next, three the next, and so on, until public opinion revolted. At the popular outcry, the executions were stopped after they had shot the signatories of the Proclamation of the Irish Republic, seven others, and one man who had been

convicted of the murder of a policeman in Fermoy. Fifty-five more who had been condemned to death were reprieved and sent to prison for 'life', from which they were released shortly afterwards.

It was, therefore, largely the executions that made Sinn Féin. The whole thing was damnable; one side sincerely believed that they were fighting for the freedom of their country: the other side equally sincerely felt that they were fighting a lot of traitors and murderers who were stabbing them in the back. People did not realize in those days what we all realize now, that you cannot coerce a people who want their independence, and that if you try to do so you will only land yourself in this sort of mess. It is worth while reading the Proclamation of the Irish Republic. I am copying it from the first sheet that came off the printing press in Liberty Hall, which was saved for my father — the true-blue British die-hard — by a man in the rebel camp who liked and respected him.

The Irish Republic is entitled to, and hereby claims, the allegiance of every Irish man and Irish woman. The Republic guarantees religious and civil liberty, equal rights and equal opportunities to all its citizens, and declares its resolve to pursue the happiness and prosperity of the whole nation and of all its parts, cherishing all the children of the nation equally, and oblivious of the differences carefully fostered by an alien government, which have divided a minority from the majority in the past.

Until our arms have brought the opportune moment for the establishment of a permanent national government representative of the whole people of Ireland and elected by the suffrages of all her men and women, the provisional government, hereby constituted, will administer the civil and military affairs of the republic in trust for the people.

We place the cause of the Irish Republic under the protection of the Most High God, whose blessing we invoke upon our arms, and we pray that no one who serves that cause will dishonour it by cowardice, inhumanity or rapine. In this supreme hour the Irish nation must, by its valour and discipline and by the readiness of its children to sacrifice themselves for the common good, prove itself worthy of the august destiny to which it is called.

Signed on behalf of the Provisional Government:

THOMAS J. CLARKE.

SÉAN MACDIARMADA.   THOMAS MACDONAGH.

P. H. PEARSE.   EAMONN CEANNT.

JAMES CONNOLLY.   JOSEPH PLUNKETT.

(*Written by hand on the corner.*)

Presented to Sir H. Robinson, just run off type at Liberty Hall by an old friend.

3.5.16.   1.20 p.m.

What would the British people of to-day say to any Government of theirs that shot men for having written such a document? It is sobering to reflect that those fine lives were lost because the British people at that time had not yet attained political maturity. . . .

The Irish leaders never expected that the rising would succeed. Its purpose was to stir the people out of their political apathy by the example of their fellow-countrymen sacrificing their lives for Ireland's freedom; the leaders of the movement knew that their own lives would be forfeit, and they went into it fully aware that they would never come out of it alive. How well they succeeded in their object is now known to everyone.

It is interesting to speculate on what would have happened if previous British Governments had yielded to the demand for self-government some fifty or so years before. Unquestionably, there was always a section of Irish opinion that would never have been satisfied with anything less than a Republic. Their organization was called the Irish Republican Brotherhood, and I doubt whether anybody in official circles ever got any reliable estimate of their numbers or influence. My own belief is that the general feeling in the country was that the Irish Parliamentary Party should be given a fair chance to see what they could achieve by constitutional means, and I think that if a full measure of Dominion status had been granted twenty-five years before, quite a number of the I.R.B., and the whole of the rest of the country, would have

accepted it. In any case, once Ireland had had her own government and legislature, it would have been their business to deal with republican opposition, and in doing so, they could adopt measures which no normal English Government would dare even to consider.

At the same time, I must confess to no small amount of sympathy with those Englishmen who feel utterly bewildered by the 1916 Rising and indeed by the whole Separatist Movement. They cannot see what real grievances the Irish could possibly have to justify an open rebellion under arms, or what practical independence they want which they do not already possess, or in what respect Irish freedom is in any way inferior to that enjoyed by the English people. I think the true answer really amounts to this: that the Irish rebelled just because they felt like rebelling. The Irish body-politic's nervous system is largely feminine in character. Just as a woman will walk out on her husband, or burst into tears *à propos* of nothing at all, or smash up the new dinner service just because she feels that way, so the Irish will rise in rebellion or declare a Republic for the same reason. The English connection just irritated and annoyed them until they blew up. If any English reader cannot understand this, I venture to refer him to his wife or mother. . . .

1 In County Donegal.
2 Resident Magistrates received orders from the Chief Secretary of Ireland.

BRIAN O'NOLAN
from *Envoy*, April 1951

In April 1951, *Envoy* devoted a special issue to James Joyce and asked Brian O'Nolan (aka Flann O'Brien, Myles na Gopaleen and the Cruiskeen Lawn) to contribute something. This article is another example of Nolan's wit, here parrying the influence of a writer whose presence was a little too close for comfort.

A Bash in the Tunnel

James Joyce was an artist. He has said so himself. His was a case of Ars gratia Artist.[1] He declared that he would pursue his artistic mission even if the penalty was as long as eternity itself. This appears to be an affirment of belief in Hell, therefore of belief in Heaven and in God.

★ ★ ★

A better title for this article might be: *Was Joyce Mad?* By Hamlet, Prince of Denmark. Yet there is a reason for the present title.

★ ★ ★

Some thinkers — all Irish, all Catholic, some unlay — have confessed to discerning a resemblance between Joyce and Satan. True, resemblance, there are. Both had other names, the one Stephen Dedalus, the other Lucifer; the latter name, meaning 'Maker of Light', was to attract later the ironical gloss 'Prince of Darkness!' Both started off very well under unfaultable teachers, both were very proud, both had a fall. But they differed on one big, critical issue. Satan never denied the existence of the Almighty; indeed he acknowledged it by challenging merely His primacy. Joyce said there was no God, proving this by uttering various blasphemies and obscenities and not being instantly struck dead.

★ ★ ★

A man once said to me that he hated blasphemy, but on purely rational grounds. If there is no God, he said, the thing is stupid and unnecessary. If there is, it's dangerous.

Anatole France[2] says this better. He relates how, one morning, a notorious agnostic called on a friend who was a devout Catholic. The devout Catholic was drunk and began to pour forth appalling blasphemies. Pale and shocked, the agnostic rushed from the house. Later, a third party challenged him on this incident.

'You have been saying for years that there is no God. Why then should you be so frightened at somebody else insulting this God who doesn't exist?'

'I still say there is no God. But that fellow thinks there is. Suppose a thunderbolt was sent down to strike him dead. How did I know I wouldn't get killed as well? Wasn't I standing beside him?'

Another blasphemy, perhaps — doubting the Almighty's aim. Yet it is still true that all true blasphemers must be believers.

★ ★ ★

What is the position of the artist in Ireland?

Just after the editors had asked me to try to assemble material for this issue of *ENVOY*, I went into the Scotch House in Dublin to drink a bottle of stout and do some solitary thinking. Before any considerable thought had formed itself, a man — then a complete stranger — came, accompanied by his drink, and stood beside me: addressing me by name, he said he was surprised to see a man like myself drinking in a pub.

My pub radar screen showed up the word 'TOUCHER'. I was instantly much on my guard.

'And where do you think I should drink?' I asked. 'Pay fancy prices in a hotel?'

'Ah, no,' he said. 'I didn't mean that. But any time I feel like a good bash myself, I have it in the cars. What will you have?'

I said I would have a large one, knowing that his mysterious reply would entail lengthy elucidation.

'I needn't tell you that that crowd is a crowd of bastards,' was his prefatory exegesis.

Then he told me all. At one time his father had a pub and grocery business, situated near a large Dublin railway terminus. Every year the railway company invited tenders for the provisioning of its dining cars, and every year the father got the contract. (The narrator said he thought this was due to the territorial proximity of the house, with diminished handling and cartage charges.)

The dining cars (hereinafter known as 'the cars'), were customarily parked in remote sidings. It was the father's job to load them from time to time with costly victuals — eggs, rashers, cold turkey, and whiskey. These cars, bulging in their lonely sidings with such fabulous fare, had special locks. The father had the key, and nobody else in the world had authority to open the doors until the car was part of a train. But my informant had made it his business, he told me, to have a key too.

'At that time,' he told me, 'I had a bash once a week in the cars.'

One must here record two peculiarities of Irish railway practice. The first is a chronic inability to 'make up' trains in advance, i.e., to estimate expected passenger traffic accurately. Week after week a long-distance train is scheduled to be 5-passenger coaches and a car. Perpetually, an unexpected extra 150 passengers arrive on the departure platform unexpectedly. This means that the car must be detached, a passenger coach substituted, and the train despatched foodless and drinkless on its way.

The second peculiarity — not exclusively Irish — is the inability of personnel in charge of shunting engines to leave coaches, parked in far sidings, alone. At all costs they must be shifted.

That was the situation as my friend in the Scotch House described it. The loaded dining cars never went anywhere, in the long-distance sense. He approved of that. But they were subject to endless enshuntment. That, he said, was a bloody scandal and a waste of the taxpayers' money.

When the urge for a 'bash' came upon him, his routine was simple. Using his secret key, he secretly got into a parked and laden car very early in the morning, penetrated to the pantry, grabbed a jug of water, a glass, and a bottle of whiskey and, with this assortment of material and utensil, locked himself in the lavatory.

Reflect on that locking. So far as the whole world was concerned, the car was utterly empty. It was locked with special, unprecedented locks. Yet this man locked himself securely within those locks.

Came the dawn — and the shunters. They espied, as doth the greyhound the hare, the lonely dining car, mute, immobile, deserted. So they couple it up and drag it to another siding at Liffey Junction. It is there for five hours but ('that crowd of bastards', i.e., other shunters) it is discovered and towed over to the yards behind Westland Row Station.[3] Many hours later it is shunted on to the tail of the Wexford Express but later angrily detached owing to the unexpected arrival of extra passengers.

'And are you sitting in the lavatory drinking whiskey all the time?' I asked.

'Certainly I am,' he answered, 'what the hell do you think lavatories in trains is for? And with the knees of me trousers been wet with me own whiskey from the jerks of them shunter bastards!'

His resentment was enormous. Be it noted that the whiskey was not in fact his own whiskey, that he was that oddity, an unauthorized person.

'How long does a bash in the cars last?' I asked him.

'Ah, that depends on a lot of things,' he said. 'As you know, I never carry a watch.' (Exhibits cuffless, hairy wrist in proof.) 'Did I ever tell you about the time I had a bash in the tunnel?'

He had not — for the good reason that I had never met him before.

'I seen meself,' he said, 'once upon a time on a three-day bash. The bastards took me out of Liffey Junction down to Hazelhatch. Another crowd shifted me into Harcourt Street yards. I was having a good bash at this time, but I always try to see, for the good of me health, that a bash doesn't last more than a day and night. I know it's night outside when it's dark. If it's bright it's day. Do you follow me?'

'I think I do.'

'Well, I was about on the third bottle when this other shunter crowd come along — it was dark, about eight in the evening — and nothing would do them only bring me into the Liffey Tunnel under the Phoenix Park *and park me there*. As you know I never use a watch. If it's bright, it's day. If it's dark, it's night. Here was meself parked in the tunnel opening bottle after bottle in the dark, thinking the night was a very long one, stuck there in the tunnel. I was three-quarters way into the jigs when they pulled me out of the tunnel into Kingsbridge.[4] I was in bed for a week. Did you ever in your life hear of a greater crowd of bastards?'

'Never.'

'That was the first and last time I ever had a bash in the tunnel.'

Funny? But surely there you have the Irish artist? Sitting fully dressed, innerly locked in the toilet of a locked coach where he has no right to be, resentfully drinking somebody else's whiskey, being whisked

hither and thither by anonymous shunters, keeping fastidiously the while on the outer face of his door the simple word ENGAGED?

I think the image fits Joyce: but particularly in his manifestation of a most Irish characteristic — the transgressor's resentment with the nongressor.

★ ★ ★

A friend of mine found himself next door at dinner to a well-known savant who appears in *Ulysses*. (He shall be nameless, for he still lives.) My friend, making dutiful conversation, made mention of Joyce. The savant said that Ireland was under a deep obligation to the author of Joyce's *Irish Names of Places*.[5] My friend lengthily explained that his reference had been to a different Joyce. The savant did not quite understand, but ultimately confessed that he had heard certain rumours about the other man. It seemed that he had written some dirty books, published in Paris.

'But you are a character in one of them,' my friend incautiously remarked.

The next two hours, to the neglect of wine and cigars, were occupied with a heated statement by the savant that he was by no means a character in fiction, he was a man, furthermore he was alive and he had published books of his own.

'How can I be a character in fiction,' he demanded, 'if I am here talking to you?'

That incident may be funny, too, but its curiosity is this: Joyce spent a lifetime establishing himself as a character in fiction. Joyce created, in narcissus fascination, the ageless Stephen. Beginning with importing real characters into his books, he achieves the magnificent inversion of making them legendary and fictional. It is quite preposterous. Thousands of people believe that there once lived a man named Sherlock Holmes.

★ ★ ★

Joyce went further than Satan in rebellion.

Two characters who confess themselves based on Aquinas: Joyce and Maritain.[6]

★ ★ ★

In *Finnegan's Wake*, Joyce appears to favour the Vico[7] theory of inevitable human and recurring evolution — theocracy: aristocracy: democracy: chaos.

'A.E.' referred to the chaos of Joyce's mind.

That was wrong, for Joyce's mind was indeed very orderly. In composition he used coloured pencils to keep himself right. All his works, not excluding *Finnegan's Wake*, have a rigid classic pattern. His personal moral and family behaviours were impeccable. He seems to have deserved equally with George Moore the sneer about the latter — he never kissed, but told.

What was really abnormal about Joyce? At Clongowes he had his dose of Jesuit casuistry. Why did he substitute his home-made chaosistry?

It seems to me that Joyce emerges, through curtains of salacity and blasphemy, as a truly fear-shaken Irish Catholic, rebelling not so much against the Church but against its near-schism Irish eccentricities, its pretence that there is only one Commandment, the vulgarity of its edifices, the shallowness and stupidity of many of its ministers. His revolt, noble in itself, carried him away. He could not see the tree for the woods. But I think he meant well. We all do, anyway.

★ ★ ★

What is *Finnegan's Wake*? A treatise on the incommunicable night-mind? Or merely an example of silence, exile and punning?

★ ★ ★

I doubt whether the contents of this issue will get many of us any forrarder.

A little, perhaps. Mr Cass seems to establish that Joyce was at heart an Irish dawn-bursting romantic, an admirer of de Valera, and one one dearly wished to be recalled to Dublin as an ageing man to be crowned with a D.Litt. from the National and priest-haunted University. This is at least possible, if only because it explains the preposterous 'esthetic' affectations of his youth, which included the necessity for being rude to his dying mother. The theme here is that a heart of gold was beating under the artificial waist-coat. Amen.

★ ★ ★

The number of people invited to contribute to this issue has necessarily been limited. Yet it is curious that

none makes mention of Joyce's superber quality: his capacity for humour. Humour, the handmaid of sorrow and fear, creeps out endlessly in all Joyce's works. He uses the thing, in the same way as Shakespeare does but less formally, to attenuate the fear of those who have belief and who genuinely think that they will be in hell or in heaven shortly, and possibly very shortly. With laughs he palliates the sense of doom that is the heritage of the Irish Catholic. True humour needs this background urgency: Rabelais is funny, but his stuff cloys. His stuff lacks tragedy.

★ ★ ★

Perhaps the true fascination of Joyce lies in his secretiveness, his ambiguity (his polyguity, perhaps?), his leg-pulling, his dishonesties, his technical skill, his attraction for Americans. His works are a garden in which some of us may play. This issue of *ENVOY* claims to be merely a small bit of that garden.

★ ★ ★

But at the end, Joyce will still be in his tunnel, unabashed.

1   Art by the grace of the artist (not God or some other external agency).
2   Anatole France (1844–1924), French writer awarded Nobel Prize in 1921.
3   Now Pearse Station.
4   Now Heuston Station.
5   *The Origin and History of Irish Names of Places*, 3 vols. (1869–70) by P.W. Joyce.
6   Jacques Maritain (1882–1973), French neo-Thomist religious thinker.
7   Giovanni Battista Vico (1668–1774), Italian philosopher and historian.

ROBERT GIBBINGS
from Robert Gibbings, *Sweet Cork of Thee* (1951)

Another extract from the travel writings of Robert Gibbings, this time set on the borders of Counties Kerry and Cork. The cottage interior scene, beloved of commentators since the eighteenth century, is especially effective here.

Chapter 24

The afternoon was fine when I set out to find the source of the River Blackwater on the slopes of Knockanefune, over the Kerry border. The scent of meadow-sweet was heavy in the air, and I thought of those lines in Ethel Rolt-Wheeler's poem:

Meadow-sweet and meadow-sweet
    All the way to Tara;
Shrill of whispers in the wheat,
Bees that hum and lambs that bleat . . .
Ghosts that wear a winding-sheet . . .
    This is Royal Tara;
Hosts of ghosts the meadow-sweet
    All the way to Tara.

Tara, the throne of kings from prehistoric times to the sixth century; Tara where, if tradition is to be believed, the first law of copyright was formulated.

During the reign of Dermot son of Fergus, King of Ireland 544-65, St Columkille, Abbot of Iona, paid a visit to St Finian of Movilla in Ulster, and while there he borrowed from his host a book of psalms which he greatly admired. Fearful of refusal if he asked permission to make a copy of it, he transcribed the pages secretly. St Finian discovering this claimed the copy as his own because, he said, it had been made from his book and without his consent. There followed then a very worldly dispute between the two holy men as to the ownership of those pages, until eventually they agreed to lay their case before the king at Tara. Dermot, having heard the evidence, pronounced judgment: 'The calf, being the offspring of the cow, belongeth to the cow: so that copy, being the offspring of the book, belongeth to the book.' He thus awarded the copy to St Finian; but it is nice to know that, soon after the decision, the copy was given back to St Columkille whose kindred, the O'Donnells, treasured it for many generations. It became their *Cathach*, their 'battler', a sacred relic to be borne, sun-wise, three times round their army before battle to ensure victory, and was so used by them as late as the fifteenth century. To-day the elaborate case in which it was carried, of silver gilt, enamel, and precious stones, may be seen in the National Museum, Dublin.

My road over the mountains led me into ever-narrowing lanes until finally I stopped the car at the mouth of a bhoreen.[1] Ahead of me the first trickle of the Blackwater was 'twisting and turning like a wor-rum' through a gentle fertile valley. Here the river forms the county bounds, and the stream is so narrow that cattle grazing in Kerry can, if they so wish, change to pasturage in County Cork without as much as wetting their feet.

It was a Kerry man who said to me: 'How could you possibly write a book about a little local stream like the Lee when you have the noble Blackwater, "the Irish Rhine", that rises in Kerry, there before you?'

'Well,' I said, 'the Blackwater may rise in Kerry but it gets out of it and into Cork at the first opportunity. It is only in Cork that it achieves the full majesty of its flow.'

There has always been a friendly rivalry between the two neighbouring counties. The story goes that a young man unable to make a living on a sparse mountainside in Kerry went east to Mallow in County Cork, where the land is rich, to work for a farmer. 'It was harvest time and it was a wonderful harvest; you could hardly count the cocks they had, and they were binding them up with sugauns (straw ropes). "Well, Kerryman," said the farmer, "I suppose you never seen the like of this with your eyes before." "I am surprised at a man like you expressing yourself like that," said the Kerry man. "The sop you have in this haggard wouldn't make sugauns for my ricks."[2]

And if Kerry men are proud, the Kerry women are modest. The town of Abbeyfeale derives its name from this virtue. 'At one time there was no town there at all, only the river, and one day a woman by the name of Fial went bathing herself. She was the wife of some sort of chieftain, and 'twas a day in the middle of June, and when she came out of the water she stood in her pelt in the sun to dry herself. And while she was standing there, didn't she see a man in the distance looking at her. With that she dropped dead on the spot with shame — I dunno would a girl do it to-day — and who was the man after all but her husband. So, anyway, they called the river after her, and in the years that followed the monks came and built an abbey alongside of it, and that's how Abbeyfeale got the name.'

Below me tiny rapids were babbling between dry beaches of shingle and I was preparing to follow their course on foot, upwards, through the gorse and iris and spurge that lined their banks, when I noticed that one of the tyres of my van was flat. That meant a delay — more than a delay, for the slope and the surface of the road made it impossible to use the jack single-handed. A mist had begun to fall.

Behind the near hill I could see the smoke from a cottage. Maybe there was someone there who could help.

'Wouldn't you come in out of the wet and have a cup of tea?' said the young woman who answered my knock. 'The kettle is boiling and himself will be in directly.'

An old woman was sitting by the fire, tying a bundle of turkey quills into a brush for the hearth. Without moving from her chair she shook hands and welcomed me. The kettle was on the crane and the teapot was standing among some glowing fragments of turf at the edge of the fire. Although the floor of the room was of cement and cobbles the fire was built on bare protruding rock. The room was furnished with an old oak settle with panelled back, a table, a few chairs, and a small cupboard that held oddments of china. A staircase at the far end led to an upstairs room; a door at the back of the room opened on to stone steps set into the side of the hill. Through it I could see hens and guinea-fowl picking in the grass, almost at ceiling level.

'Shut one of them doors, Bridie,' said the old lady. In Kerry it is thought unlucky to have front and back door open at the same time, as it is also thought unlucky to go out by a different door to the one by which you entered.

There came the sound of heavy boots on the paving-stones outside and the man of the house came in. He hung a horse collar and a whip over the head of the stair rail and came towards me.

'This is my husband,' said Bridie.

'You're welcome,' he said, shaking hands. He was about thirty years of age, splendidly built, with a powerful neck set on massive shoulders.

'It's a soft evening,' I said.

'Good for the growth,' he said.

Bridie put some eggs to boil in a tin among the turfs.

'Is it yours the van is below?' asked the husband.

'It is,' I said, 'and there's a nail in the tyre.'

'That's poor employment for a nail,' he said.

'Maybe 'tis better there than in the sole of his foot,' said Bridie.

'Wouldn't Jerry fix that for him, Dan?' asked the mother.

'We'll have to lift the car,' I said. 'The jack is no use.'

'Jerry would lift the six foot of earth off the lid of his own coffin,' said Dan.

'Is he far away?' I inquired.

''Tis only two throws of a bowl before you from the cross. Slip down, Bridie, and tell him come up,' said Dan.

'Draw up and take your tea,' said Bridie, lifting the eggs out of the tin and putting them with the teapot on the table.

She went out of the door and I, also, did as I was told. Dan sat up to the table too, but the old woman stayed by the fire.

''Twas you I seen at the City on May Day,' said Dan.

'It probably was,' I said.

''Tis nothing like the old days now,' he said. 'When I was a boy you couldn't move with the crowd.'

'When I was a girl you couldn't get there with the people in squadrons on the road,' said his mother.

'And I seen you again in Kilnacrom, the Monday of the fight.'

'I missed that,' I said.

'You passed through early. 'Twas a real faction fight. There hasn't been the like for years. 'Twas some bit of old spite. Two fellows started and all the cousins and second cousins and thirty-first cousins joined in. There was twenty men a side fighting, the real old style with

sticks — cut, thrust, and parry as if they had been swords.'

'Well, isn't it a grand thing,' said his mother, 'to see the old spirit again. With them holy and blessed fights in the old days, the world was very quiet.'

'A kettle that boils over often cleans the hearth,' said Dan. 'They tell me,' he added, 'there isn't a town in the world you haven't put your foot.'

'There's plenty of them,' I said.

'And I suppose the Irish is everywhere.'

'Everywhere,' I said, 'and often in trouble.'

Then I told them of 'Tom the Divil', an Irishman who during the last century reached eminence in Samoa. Whether he was a runaway sailor or an escaped convict nobody was quite sure, but he soon achieved great influence and power on Manono and, like myself, was created a high chief of that island. Unlike myself, however, he was a great fighter and in the many local wars became the terror of the enemy. Again unlike myself, any girl he fancied was given to him immediately. When I mentioned this, Dan's eyes sparkled. His mother, still by the fire, murmured 'Oh, oh, oh!' Eventually, despite his rank — and mine — Tom's conduct became unbearable. Even his friends felt unsafe in his presence, for he liked nothing better than a fight on the village green. One evening while a number of girls engaged his attention, four young men with clubs stole upon him, and the clubs met simultaneously on his head. His last words were: 'My club! My club!'

'Didn't he have great spirit after all,' said Dan. His mother by the fire said nothing, but sighed deeply.

By this Dan and I had finished our tea, and Bridie had come back. Wouldn't I like a few more eggs? she asked.

'Pull up your chair,' said Dan, moving towards the hearth. 'A fire is a good comrade a night like this.'

'God save all here,' said a man, looking in over the half-door.

'And you too,' said Dan and his mother.

'The van's outside,' he said.

'Is it fixed, Jerry?' asked Dan.

'I put on the spare wheel,' said Jerry.

'Wouldn't you sit down a while,' said Dan. He pulled forward a chair for Jerry and then went out through the back door.

'Tell me,' I whispered to Jerry, 'how much do I owe you?'

'Yerra, don't be talking!' he replied.

Dan came back with a bottle in his hands. Bridie filled a small jug with water from a large bucket. There was no mistaking the bouquet when the cork was drawn. There was no mistaking the smoothness to the tongue when the glass was filled, or the fire in one's belly when the glass was emptied.

As Jerry said: 'Don't be talking!' You never seen the like of the dancing that happened that night. The boys came in and the girls came in. They began with puss-music[3] and they finished up with three fiddles. They sang in Irish and they sang in English, and at the end of every verse, or nearly every verse, there were cries of 'Good boy!' or 'Good girl!' 'Good! Lovely, lovely!' just as in Samoa they would call '*Malie, malie!*' meaning 'Beautiful!' If there was a pause in the music, it was only while our glasses were being refilled or while more food was put on the table. Dan sat beside

me in merry mood. His mother, still by the fire, was smiling. Bridie's eyes were flashing and her hair was flying as she swung with the music. She and Dan had only been married a few months. There was no weight of children on them yet.

1   A narrow road, boreen or bohereen. In Irish 'bóthar' is a road.
2   Hay was gathered into cocks in the fields, then transported back to the haggard adjacent to the farm-house and made into a rick. A sop is here a comment on the small amount of hay gathered.
3   Mouth music, used for entertainment and accompaniment when no musicians were available.

STANISLAUS JOYCE
from *The Listener*, 25 March 1954

Stanislaus Joyce (1884–1955), the younger brother of James Joyce, shared with his more famous relation an education at Belvedere School in Dublin and two cities, one in Ireland, the other Trieste. Trieste was the main port of the Austro-Hungarian empire before the Great War, and it was there in 1905 that Stanislaus joined his brother. Here in this extract, written at the end of his life, he reflects on the various backgrounds to *Dubliners*. *My Brother's Keeper* (1957) and *The Complete Diary of Stanislaus Joyce* (1971) are other valuable accounts of Joyce's life as a young man before he became an artist.

The Background to 'Dubliners'

Criticism of my brother's novel *Ulysses* has become almost scientific. The genuine Joyce critic examines every word under a microscope, and, it must be admitted, often obtains illuminating results, but the same method is, I think, pernicious when applied to my brother's earlier work. It is true that *Ulysses* has, and was intended by its author to have, various levels of significance, but it is quite another matter when, as I have been informed, an American critic, using a like method, arrives at a conclusion regarding *Chamber Music* which is as absurd as it is unfounded. Still another American critic finds in the short story 'The Clay' three levels of significance on which Maria is successively herself, a witch, and the Virgin Mary. Though such critics are quite at sea, they can still have the immense satisfaction of knowing that they have dived into deeper depths than the author they are criticizing ever sounded. I am in a position to state definitely that my brother had no such subtleties in mind when he wrote the story. In justice, though, I

must say that exaggerations like those I have mentioned are not typical of American criticism: on the whole, American criticism is careful, painstaking, intelligent, and highly appreciative.

Underlying Plan
The stories in *Dubliners* were not chosen haphazardly; there is an underlying plan in the book. 'The Sisters', 'Araby', and 'An Encounter' are stories of adolescent life. 'The Sisters' and 'Araby' are purely fictional, but 'An Encounter' is based on an actual incident that occurred to my brother and me when we planned and carried out a day's miching[1] together. He was about twelve and I was about ten years of age at the time, and we did not understand what kind of individual we had encountered, but our suspicions were aroused. We thought he was a 'queer juggins' — some kind of escaped lunatic — and we gave him the slip. Later my brother put him into the book as a by-product of English educational methods.

'Eveline' and 'Counterparts' are stories from the life of clerks, female and male. 'A Painful Case' and 'The

Clay' present types of celibates, male and female, but, by the way, though Maria is a virgin, she is not the Virgin Mary, and though she is a withered virgin, she is not a witch. 'Two Gallants' is a story of bachelor life, 'A Little Cloud' of married life, with the figure of a successful and impenitent bachelor in it to cause discord and cast a little cloud over married bliss. Between them 'The Boarding House' serves as a connecting link. 'After the Race', 'A Mother', 'Ivy Day in the Committee Room', 'Grace' have as backgrounds respectively sporting, musical, political, and religious life in the Irish capital, while 'The Dead', which represents festive life, serves as a kind of boisterous chorus, which is suddenly interrupted to let the book end on a note of disillusionment and resignation, though not of despair.

My brother used to show me the stories page by page as he wrote them, and when he left Dublin and finally settled down in Trieste, he used to send me the stories and invite my criticism. This continued regularly until I joined him at Trieste.

I had unintentionally some part in the stories. 'A Painful Case' is an imaginary portrait of what my brother thought I should become in middle age. The chance meeting with an unknown lady at a concert he found more or less as it is described in the story in a diary I used to keep and he used to read without troubling to ask permission. The rest is elaboration; there was no daughter at the concert, and if there was a husband I never met him. The lady, whose name I never knew, stopped me once that I remember in the street to ask me some conventional questions about my studies, and that was all. I was about eighteen then and should not have had the audacity to speak to her when I met her. Some of the traits he has borrowed from me are the hostility to socialism — my brother, for his part, in so far as he was anything politically, was a socialist — the insufferance of drunkenness, and the habit of taking notes (besides my diary) on a sheaf of papers. It was there he found the two epigrams which he used in the story. As I fancy few readers of *Dubliners* will remember them, I shall quote them. One is: Every bond is a bond to sorrow; the other reads: Love between man and man is impossible because there must not be sexual intercourse, and friendship between a man and a woman is impossible because there must be sexual intercourse. . . . Well, well! Concentrated wisdom and experience at eighteen years of age! However, the use my brother has made of them has redeemed them, and now they haunt my conscience a little less. In order to raise Mr Duffy's cultural standard he has introduced a few traits taken from his own life, such as the translation of Michael

Kramer and mention of Nietzsche, who interested me hardly at all, but he drew little from himself because he had reason not to consider himself a good type of celibate. In my diary, too, he found the conclusion for 'Counterparts'.

My brother was never in a committee room in his life. He got that background from my letters to him. I was once temporarily employed as a clerk for one of the candidates in the municipal elections in Dublin. My brother was in Paris at the time, and in my letters to him and later in conversation with him I described most of the characters that come into the story 'Ivy Day in the Committee-Room': the old caretaker, the shabby canvassers, the unfrocked priest. Instead, the poem on the death of Parnell, with which the story ends, is his own and is a very clever piece of work. It is deliberately bad, but as Mr Colum observes, in spite of the affected graces of the semi-illiterate poet who has written the poem, one is conscious of a real sorrow. He wrote the story some four or five years later in Trieste.

Parody of the 'Divina Commedia'

The second and third parts of 'Grace' and some of the dialogue as it stands he found again in my diary, but he has used another incident for the first part and changed some of the characters. There is in the story a parody of the *Divina Commedia*; in the underground lavatory, *l'Inferno*; in bed at home convalescing, *il Purgatorio*; in church listening to a sermon, *il Paradiso*. The parody in no way detracts from my brother's almost boundless admiration for the *Divina Commedia*. In fact, his admiration for it had as a consequence so fierce a contempt for Milton's 'Paradise Lost' as almost to give personal offence to the poets and men of letters in Dublin, Yeats excepted, to whom he expressed it. For the preacher of the sermon, Father Purdon, he has used the figure of Father Bernard Vaughan,[2] a very popular preacher of that time who appeared sometimes in Dublin and whose name was frequently in the newspapers. He was a Jesuit, a member of an old English family, and a cleric in search of publicity, who besides preaching from his legitimate stage, the pulpit, used to deliver short man-to-man talks from inappropriate places, such as the boxing ring before a championship match. My brother has adorned him with the name which was the old name for the street of the brothels in Dublin — Purdon Street.

Idea from a Letter

The idea for 'The Dead' was suggested also by a letter of mine to my brother when he was already in Trieste. It came about in this way. The principal singer at a Moore Centenary[3] Concert in Dublin — such was the name I remember, though 1805 was no special date in Moore's life — was a very well-known Irish baritone who lived in London, Plunket Green. As my father had sung with him in concerts when he was a young man and often used to speak of him, I went to hear him. The quality of his voice was somewhat harsh, I thought, but he could do what he liked with it. One of Moore's Irish melodies which he sang was 'The Dead'. When in the second verse of the song the dead speak, Plunket Green, instead of singing in sepulchral tones, used a plaintive pianissimo. The effect was electrifying. It reminded me of the lines of a cradle-song of Yeats':

> The angels are stooping
> Above your white bed;
> They are weary of trooping
> With the whimpering dead.

It sounded as if the dead were whimpering and jealous of the happiness of the living. My brother liked the idea and asked me to send him the song. I did so, but when he wrote the story some six or seven years later — so long it took to mature! — he preferred to use a west of Ireland ballad for the song which is the turning point of the story.

It may well seem from all this that I am laying claim to some part in my brother's work. That is not the case. A writer finds the material for his creative work everywhere — in his own experience, in something he has read or heard and reflected on, in conversation with others, in letters, even in chance words he has overheard. This quality of growth is one of the characteristics of genius, this fertility of the soil on which seed happens to fall. 'The Boarding House' was suggested by the rude and fluent remarks about his landlady and her daughter made by a little Cockney who was the English teacher in the Berlitz School at Trieste when my brother was first transferred there; the idea for 'Two Gallants' came from the mention of the relations between Porthos and the wife of a tradesman in *The Three Musketeers*, which my brother found in Ferrero's *Europa Giovane*: hence the title. Such trifles awoke a memory of Dublin in his brain; he saw the story clearly and was not at peace until he had put it on paper. In this sense *Dubliners* is as lyrical a work as *Chamber Music*.

As I shared my brother's life day by day, with brief intervals of separation, until January 1915, it was only natural that the promptings for stories should come more frequently from conversation and communication with me than with others; but in no case was it intentional on my part. For example, all the details for 'Ivy Day in the Committee Room' except the final poem, as I have said, he took from letters of mine, but it had never occurred to me that there could be a story in them — I had written in a mood of disgust and anger — and still less had it occurred to me that by writing the story dispassionately one could raise oneself above all that mean, shiftless, poverty-stricken life and regard it without hatred, even with compassion and humour.

'Ivy Day in the Committee Room' was the story in *Dubliners* that my brother preferred, yet he, too, had his doubts as to whether it could be called a story. When the manuscript of *Dubliners*, rejected by the seventh or eighth publisher, came home to roost again, and I tried to counter his disappointment, he asked me ironically:

'Do you really think that all Europe is waiting to hear the story of the municipal election in the Royal Exchange Ward in Dublin?'

'Well, if you put it that way, of course not,' I answered. 'But I think all intelligent readers are waiting to come across something that is well written.'

Dubliners was published just when the first world war broke out. My brother was in Trieste (then an Austrian port) but was allowed to go to a neutral country, Switzerland, on parole because two important people in Trieste stood surety for him. In Zurich, where he lived during the war, he at first supported himself and his family by giving lessons, and amongst his pupils he had an elderly, cultured Viennese, to whom he lent his newly published book of stories. When his pupil brought it back, my brother asked him which story he liked best. Without hesitation the Viennese answered: 'Ivy Day in the Committee Room'.

My brother was astonished. 'What on earth,' he asked, 'did you find to admire in that story?'

The Viennese laughed. 'It amused me,' said he, 'because it is so like Vienna.'

An Italian proverb says: *Tutto il mondo é paese* — the whole world is just one township.

For my part, the story which I consider the best in the collection is 'The Dead', and I am glad that my brother dictated the end of it to me, when eye trouble prevented him from writing. There is a mastery of story telling in the skill with which a crescendo of noise and jollity is gradually worked up and then suddenly silenced by the ghost of a memory that returns to blight the happiness of the living. Yet 'The Dead' is not merely a Christmas ghost story and not merely technically clever. In 'The Dead' the two polar attitudes of men towards women, that of the lover and that of the husband, are presented compassionately. It is not the eternal triangle of falsity and deception. The two men at different times in the woman's life have loved her with equal sincerity each in his way, and there is no guile in the woman. But one love is the enemy of the other, and the dead lover's romantic passion, outliving his mortal flesh, is still dominant in the woman's heart.

Towards the end of the last world war, while the Germans were still resisting on the Gothic Line, I was in Florence. Wanting to cash a small cheque on a bank in Trieste, I went to the Banca d'Italia. Over the cashier's office there was a notice to say that cheques on the north of Italy would not be accepted. Nevertheless, being hard up, I presented mine. The cashier said rather gruffly: 'Don't you see the notice?' Then, catching sight of the signature, he asked: 'Are you any relative of the writer, James Joyce?' 'His brother,' said I.

He made a sign to me to wait, and after he had dealt with the other customers — there were only a few — he began to speak to me about *Dubliners* and especially about 'The Dead'. The Italian cashier did all the talking; and he spoke with such evident enthusiasm about the humanity of the story, the pity in it, the moving beauty of it that I listened to him 'like a three years child'. And he paid the cheque.

My brother did not like the first stories, which had already appeared in a Dublin paper, and would have liked to re-write 'The Boarding House' but for a fixed objection to changing or omitting anything he had published. Moreover, he always thought that his stories could interest only Dubliners and he struggled desperately to have his book published in Dublin. He failed: 1,000 copies of *Dubliners* ready for publication in Dublin were burned at the behest of a self-authorized vigilance committee. The struggle wasted years of his life and for a while sapped his energy. He had another book of stories in mind but no wish to get on with it. It was one round to the forces behind the scenes in Irish life, but by no means the last round.

1   Playing truant from school.
2   For an example of one of his sermons, see extract above from Bernard Vaughan, *Sin, Society and Behaviour* (1908), p. 83.
3   Thomas Moore, author of *Irish Melodies* (1807–34).

HUBERT BUTLER
from *The Bell*, June 1954

Hubert Butler (1900–90) was born into an Anglo-Irish family in County Kilkenny. After graduating from Oxford he worked as a teacher in Egypt and the Balkans and travelled widely throughout the world. Butler, who was review editor for *The Bell* in the 1940s, wrote and published distinguished essays on a whole range of topics from German Catholicism to Patrick Kavanagh and the literary magazine *Envoy* (1945–51). Only toward the end of his life did Butler receive the recognition he deserved. His essays have been collected in four volumes: *Escape from the Anthill* (1985), *The Children of Drancy* (1988), *Grandmother and Wolfe Tone* (1990), and *In the Land of Nod* (1996). Always behind the writing the pressure of a European intellectual can be felt. In a famous essay 'The Children of Drancy' he explored the chain of connection set in motion by the decision of the French authorities in 1942 to ship 4,051 Jewish children to the Nazi death-camps. In the following essay his polemical sword characteristically cuts both ways.

Portrait of a Minority

We Protestants of the Irish Republic are no longer very interesting to anyone but ourselves. A generation ago we were regarded dramatically as imperialistic blood-suckers, or, by our admirers, as the last champions of civilization in an abandoned island. That is the way the Roman settler may have appeared to himself and others, when the legions had departed from Britain and he was left alone with the tribes he had dispossessed. Our brothers north of the border are still discussed in such colourful terms; as for ourselves, we merely exist and even that we do with increasing unobtrusiveness.

So we are flattered, when, as recently, an American writer, like Mr Blanshard, investigates our problems. No Irish Protestant has hitherto questioned Mr Blanshard's facts or could easily do so, for he has taken pains with his documentation. But facts, by themselves, are dispiriting things and it would be wrong if we appeared as a depressed or resentful community. A stranger would find us cheerful enough and on excellent terms with our Catholic neighbours.

Inevitably the more conscientious foreign investigator prefers newspaper files and libraries to human beings as a source of evidence. Mr Blanshard tried both and I am not surprised if he found us appallingly unsatisfactory in the witness-box. Take Mrs A., whose husband is an impoverished country gentleman; she is chatty and genial about our relations with the Catholic majority, but all her comments are marginal. Mr B., the accountant, obviously feels more deeply involved and, as a result, his replies are unconvincingly soapy and safe. On the other hand Mr C., the plasterer, has nothing to lose by candour, for he can always get a job in England. As a result his denunciations of Ireland and the Irish are frivolous and self-centred. So I do not blame our investigator if in despair he rushes to the reference library in Kildare Street[1] and feeds for the rest of his stay on statistics as dry and impersonal as he can find them.

Useful books usually result but we Irish, who had been posing for our pictures, invariably belittle them. We consider our problems too personal for charts and diagrams. And I am afraid we are mostly shockingly vague about those abstract issues, which Mr Blanshard discusses.

There is a criticism too which many Protestants as well as Catholics might level at Mr Blanshard. It was well expressed in a letter I got from a Catholic neighbour. 'We Irish are, whatever they say, a spiritual people. Has Mr Blanshard never heard of "grace"?' There is in fact in Ireland an undertone of spirituality about our most sordid sectarian wrangles. Mr Blanshard, like most Americans, believes in the panacea of good government, but our deepest discord appears to us to lie beyond the reach of legislation. It concerns impalpable things, sentiments so delicate that they seem betrayed when they are defined, loyalties which are only vulgarized by oaths and protestations. There is no orderly conflict of principle, but there are sudden gusts of noise and fury, which end as mysteriously as they began.

Mr Blanshard has made a record of these violent irruptions, but should not some Irishman also chronicle the long periods of rather hazardous calm

and contentment that intervene? Discord roars through the newspapers like an express train, blotting out the fields with dust and smoke, but in a minute or two everything looks exactly as before. There was the Tilson case, for example, in which Catholic and Protestant views about the legality of the pre-marital Ne Temere[2] pledges met with a prodigious impact; there was the case of the Master of the Galway Foxhounds, where Catholic disapproval of divorce collided with the more neutral Protestant attitude. There was Dr Noel Browne[3] and his Health Bill, when it appeared to the Protestants that the Government, responsible to the electorate only, was taking its orders from the Catholic hierarchy. There are innumerable causes celebres where the children of mixed marriages and their religious upbringing are involved.

I should not underestimate the importance of these issues or their long term effect, but they seldom interrupt the friendly relations of neighbours and there is in Ireland such a very strong tradition of 'live and let live' that in the country at least these ideological collisions are quickly forgotten. Can we congratulate ourselves on our Christian charity or is it merely that country people are slow to grasp the significance of abstract issues? Or is it that rural neighbours are not easily organized into solid blocks of opinion on religious issues?

That is so with Irish Protestants anyway. I do not like solid blocks of opinion but, in fact, there is nothing very reassuring about our Southern Protestant incapacity for congealing into aggressive or defensive blocks. It merely means that the Ulster Protestant, a more fanatical and bitter champion of the Reformation, assumes the leadership of Irish Protestant opinion. And that leadership really belongs by tradition to the Protestants of the South, the people of Swift and Berkeley, Lord Edward Fitzgerald, Smith O'Brien, Parnell, people who for a short time in the eighteenth century made Dublin a notable centre of culture and political enterprise and whose leaders often jeopardized their careers and even sacrificed their lives in the cause of an Ireland, free and united. So now our amiable inertia, our refusal to express grievances or cherish hopes about Ireland are really delaying our ultimate unity and the reconciliation of our two diversing communities.

I can imagine how exasperating we must appear to any American investigator. Let us picture him asking leading questions of that typical Irish Protestant lady, Mrs A. Though she is impecunious, she has an air of assurance based on a long inheritance of privilege of which only the tradition now remains. She is quite likely to be met in the town selling peaches to the greengrocer. She has parked her car in the wrong

place but one must admire the humour and determination with which she handles the civic guard who
comes to protest, and the easy pleasantries with which
she enlists the greengrocer on her side. She will be
ready for a talk as soon as she has delivered a large
parcel of cast-off clothes at the diocesan jumble sale.
She is flattered at being consulted but a bit wary and
inclined to think it would be better to ask the dean;
'Look why not *you*, take him the jumbles for me? That
will save me the climb up the deanery steps and give
you an opening.' But in the end she agrees to answer
some questions herself. For instance, the American has
been reading an article by Mr Frank O'Connor in
which the Irish censorship of books is ferociously
denounced. 'What do Irish Protestants think of this
violation of their sacred right to judge for themselves?'

'Well, you see, my husband and I subscribe to the
London library and no one interferes with what comes
by post. He's reading *Kon-Tiki* at present and I've got
Lord Ironside's Memoirs. And my naval nephew sent me
The Cruel Sea, though I believe it's banned. I only read
one of O'Connell's books. I thought it rather morbid.'
(I regret to say that Mrs A. is very vague about the
names of our leading Irish writers. Though Yeats, our
greatest Irish poet, was a Protestant, she is not sure
how many 'e's' there are in his name.) 'So the
censorship doesn't really affect us.'

'And then about divorce, don't you think . . .?'

'Oh, really,' she interrupts, 'what horrible people
you must think us Irish Protestants, always hankering
after divorce and nasty books! Why I don't know a
single Protestant family in the whole diocese, where
there has been a divorce. . . . Oh, yes, there's Colonel
Johnson's eldest boy, poor Eric, he got caught by a
horror in a military hospital after Dunkirk. He got a
D.S.O. you know. We were all so on his side.'

'But surely he didn't manage to get a divorce *here*,
did he?'

'Oh, dear me, no! In England, of course! And now
he's very happy on an orange farm in South Africa and
the Johnsons are charmed with the new Mrs Eric.'

'Then you do approve of divorce?'

'Well, what I say is where there are no children in
the case, far better make a fresh start than lead a cat
and dog life for ever after . . . but, look here, you'd
much better ask the dean, not me. He'll tell you it all
theologically.'

'The first Mrs Eric didn't have any children then?'

'No, mercifully not. Poor Eric couldn't afford it on
his pay, but now he's got two darling little boys.'

'Then, um . . . . er . . .' The American sees an
opening for an embarrassing but necessary question
about family restriction and a Catholic government's

veto on it, but he just cannot bring himself to ask it.
Yet no one could call Mrs A. evasive. She is as frank as
a blackbird, which hops onto a different tree when the
cat approaches, with scarcely a pause in its cheerful
twitter. Obviously, if the Irish Protestants get their
divorces and their banned books from England, then
they won't be worried by Catholic legislation on
family restriction or anything else. Only the very
disinterested will even attempt to oppose it. Otherwise
one just hops across the sea with a merry twitter,
when a difficulty arises.

So instead he asks about jobs. Do Irish Protestants
feel themselves discriminated against in the Republic?

'Well, my two are very well placed, I'm thankful to
say. Amy is in the Brussels branch of Thomas Cooks
and Arthur is in the British Consulate in Cuba. Denis
is still at school in Dublin and would have liked to
work in Ireland but the pensions are so poor and not
knowing Irish would militate against him.' Then
follows a long diatribe against compulsory Irish, which
I must be excused from repeating for I have heard it
once a month for the past twenty years; usually it pivots
on the cook, who spells jelly with a 'g', because she has
been taught through the medium. It's all perfectly true,
but, recalling that Mrs A. doesn't know how to spell
Yeats, I find it arrogant. Yet compulsory Irish *has*
become a cynical travesty of a once noble ideal. It plays
right into the hands of those who deride the Irish as a
nation of self-deceivers. And now Mrs A. is launched
on another equally beloved theme, the attempt to
suppress the coronation film in Ireland. 'The manager
of the Mayfair said he'd show it but then he got a
threatening letter and the wretched creature got cold
feet and refunded all the tickets. But thank goodness
dear old Archdeacon Potts had a bit of pluck! He
showed the film at the Diocesan Rooms. They were
packed twice over and I even saw Catholics there and
we took enough at the door to get a new bathroom for
the rectory. It's such NONSENSE. Why THEY would
give their eyes to see it too, I know. My cook has stuck
up a photograph of the Queen in her bedroom.'

All quite true doubtless but misleading. And so too
are Mrs. A.'s other views. Though all the cooks in
Ireland plastered their walls with pictures of the royal
family, the dominant sentiment of the Irish people is
anti-monarchist, anti-imperialist. Also though Mrs A.
is so little perturbed by the censorship and the other
violations of what Protestants call 'the right of private
judgment', there is an abiding Protestant resentment
against much that is enshrined in our laws. And yet
very few are sufficiently articulate to express it. There
is a very real clash of philosophies and our present
preoccupation with queens and empires merely

distracts us from the realities of our disagreement. Supposing the Queen of England became a Catholic and appealed to the Irish for support, like her predecessor James II, or supposing England became a republic (and odder things have happened in our time), there would be some confusion, no doubt, but I suspect that in the end the creeds of authority and the creeds of private judgment would run roughly along the same frontiers. Across a reconstituted barrier Irish Protestants and Irish Catholics would confront each other as before.

Mrs A. will not be very helpful on the subject of mixed marriages and *Ne Temere*. As usual she sees only the trees and no wood. 'Fortunately the two Catholic husbands in our parish are both charming. It might have been rather embarrassing for all concerned if they had to settle down here but one is in Imperial Chemicals and the other in Shell, and everything is so much easier *over there*. And *both* wives send me their subscriptions just the same for the Protestant Orphans. Even Colonel Johnson, who is on the synod, but very broadminded, says that every club has a right to make its own rules and that non-members must lump it.'

Those who argue like Colonel Johnson are usually bachelors with plenty of loopholes by which to escape from the pressure of their own arguments. Colonel Johnson has Eric but Eric has been safely remarried and, for the rest, his broadmindedness is nourished on a small house at Camberley and some queer beliefs about the Secret of the Pyramids.

But in the parish, which I know best, there are few loopholes and many children with the result that most of the families have now given one or two hostages to the community from which some centuries ago they seceded. Before the application of *Ne Temere* to Ireland hostages were exchanged *pari passu*[4] and the two communities shared in each other's lives on equal terms. Now there is no reciprocity and in those who have given all and received nothing, there is often a feeling of slow strangulation which they are forced to dissemble in case they do injury to those they love. A whole community can die without drama as though it had been struck by one of those instruments of 're-education', which leaves no external bruises.

I had hoped to say something constructive, but here I am dodging just like Mrs A. And there is no time to talk about Mr B., the accountant, or Mr C., the plasterer, though they are as Irish as she is. But, undoubtedly, Mrs A. sets the tone of Protestantism in her small local community, so that dodging and hoping for the best is no merely personal creed. It is a highly infectious habit of mind, which nothing but the reunion of Ireland is likely to cure.

There is no doubt that Salvation, if it ever comes to the A's, can only now come from across the Boyne. The whole character of Irish life might well be changed by a strong Ulster contingent in the Dáil. But the saviours are reluctant and the doomed are resigned. When questioned about Partition Mrs A. advises letting sleeping dogs lie. She has some very entertaining stories about smuggling from her married sister, who lives on the border, and she doesn't believe 'They' really *want* the border abolished 'in spite of all their shouting'. But she has no really dynamic hatred of partition, smuggling or humbug that cannot be anaesthetized by a funny anecdote. And if you were to remind her that in a United Ireland, many of the ideals which she cherishes would once more find a vigorous echo in the Dáil, she would only look bothered and begin to quote her naval nephew about submarine bases in Loch Swilly. Her intellect, like a barrage balloon that has lost its moorings, hovers uncertainly between Fishguard and Rosslare.[5] She is really more concerned that England should get the ports than that the Anglo-Irish should be able to raise their voices again in Ireland. And, while she approves of Colonel Topping and knows cousins of his in Sussex and (with reservations) of Mr Blanshard, she does not think the Colonel should ever have been invited to the Kilkenny Debate. 'It only stirs things up.'

For thirty years and more she has grown used to the Cassandra-like mournings of her hybrid race; gradually they have become less shrill and have the familiar monotony of a lullaby. They save thinking. It would only upset her to reflect that the doom which threatens the House of Atreus might be averted and all the dearly loved dirges have to be rewritten.

'The fact is,' she branches off, 'I don't really like Ulster people, though nothing could exceed the kindness of the Ballymena people to Arthur when he was stationed there. But let them mind their own business and we'll mind ours. And that's what Colonel Topping wants too!'

1 The National Library of Ireland is housed on Kildare Street in Dublin.
2 In 1908 the Catholic Church under a decree entitled *Ne Temere* declared mixed marriages between Protestant and Catholic not solemnized by the Church null and void.
3 In 1951 Noel Browne, as Minister for Health, sponsored a mother and child health bill in the Dáil. The scheme was bitterly opposed by the medical profession and the Catholic Church, the bill was withdrawn, and Browne's political career suffered accordingly.
4 Equally.
5 Ports connecting Britain and Ireland.

A. J. LEVENTHAL
from *The Dublin Magazine,* January–March 1956

Here is an early Irish reaction to a performance of Beckett's *Waiting for Godot* at the Pike Theatre in Dublin in 1956. Beckett's place in an Irish tradition continues to exercise critics.

Waiting for Godot

Waiting for Godot is at the moment of writing being produced in English, in the author's translation, both at the Criterion Theatre, London, and the Pike Theatre in this city. The London production differed from the Paris one, which was discussed in this Magazine some time ago, in so far as the stage was less bleak and that our withers were not wrung so intensely. Peter Hall, the producer, without pandering to a West End audience, trimmed ever so lightly (for there was little to offend the descendants of Mrs Grundy) the more realistic passages but there was a wide margin left for a dignified presentation — one that lives in the memory. Particularly outstanding was the performance of Peter Woodthorpe in the part of Estragon, a subtler creation than that of his fellow-in-waiting Vladimir. In contrast to the Criterion, the Pike Theatre followed the text of the author in this respect (but not in others) with pious exactitude. It was a pity they thought it necessary to issue a circular warning the public that their maiden-aunts, so to speak, might be shocked. Few are shocked nowadays by the traditional (mainly oral) terminology for certain physiological functions, and in any case such words have but a minimal part in Mr Beckett's play.

The real innovation in the Irish production lies in making the two tramps (Austin Byrne and Dermot Kelly faithfully efficient) speak with the accent of O'Casey's Joxer tempered by Myles na gCopaleen's 'Dubalin' man. It sounded strange at first and the laughs seemed to come more from the intonation than the text, but the added humour helped the audience to bear the more searing portions of the play. One is, however, not sure that this departure was justified. It seems evident that the author had in mind a universal rather than a regional application of his vision of mankind in perpetual expectation, desperately endeavouring to fill the hiatus between birth and death. There must be some significance in the fact that the names of all the characters suggest a different nationality; Estragon is French, Vladimir is Russian, Lucky is English (Irish and American too), Pozzo is Italian. On the other hand, the point might be made

that the effective use of the local idiom would also be a proof of the universal applicability of the play since its intrinsic quality would lose nothing by the change.

Mr Beckett's origin has caused the view to be widely accepted that the whole conception of *Waiting for Godot* is Irish, a fact which the original French has been unable to conceal, it is claimed. The Pike Theatre production lends support to this view, and it may well be that *Waiting for Godot* will go down in the local records as a lineal descendant of the works of the high literary kings of the Irish dramatic renascence. It is understood that there is a proposal to translate the play into Irish which would assist in bringing about a general acceptance here of this theory. Indeed later literary historians might align Mr Beckett with George Moore who, in his efforts to help in the revival of the Irish language, suggested that he might compose his work in French which could be translated into English for the convenience of the Gaelic Leaguers who would then, in their turn, have little difficulty in turning the text into Irish. If the truth were told, the Germans would have more justification in claiming Mr Beckett than they had when they took Shakespeare to their Teuton bosoms, for the song which Vladimir sings in the second act, in the original version, beginning:

Un chien vint dans l'office
Et prit une andouillette,

comes straight from the German:

Ein Hund kam in die Küche
une stahl dem Koch ein Ei.

Lucky is the character which stands out as Mr Beckett's most original creation, and much depends on the playing of the part. Jean Martin in Paris and Timothy Balison in London spoke the long automatic monologue as though it had the background of sense evident in the text. In the Dublin performance, however, Donal Donnelly smothered his words in the hysteria of his delivery. Beginning at top speed, he had nothing left for his climax when the mechanism of the record (as it were) breaks down into helpless repetition. Nigel Fitzgerald's Pozzo had the right kind of pompous self-satisfaction and ultimate, almost dignified, blinded impotence. The Pike Theatre must be congratulated on their enterprise in mounting possibly the most important drama of this century.

ELIZABETH BOWEN
from *The London Magazine*, March 1956

Elizabeth Bowen here traces the influence of London on her consciousness: the Anglo-Irish coming not the Irish going.

Coming to London — VI

All through my childhood, London had a fictitious existence for me. It loomed darkly somewhere at the other side of the water; I thought of it (when at all) as an entity, at once magnetic and dangerous. It was, from all I heard, a city into which no one ventured alone, and which was to be entered only after preparation and wary forethought. It stood for the adult, and so much so that there should be children in London seemed unimaginable — in fact that there should be people of any kind was only a secondary idea: I pictured the thing as a mass of building, a somehow impious extreme of bulk and height in whose interstices was fog. I first crossed the city when I first crossed the sea, when I was four: it must have been winter, we arrived after dark and were driven as hurriedly as possible from Euston to some other terminus in a cab. The street lamps, seeming dimmer than Dublin's, showed us to be in the continuous bottom of a chasm, among movement conveying a sense of trouble, and which one suspected rather than saw. My mother for a minute put down a window, saying, as though in extenuation, 'London has a smell of its own.' But this, like all else given off, was non-human.

I do not know when, at what later date, I came to know that the sun shone there — that is to say, there also — or when I took in that this, like some planet, also must be taken to be inhabited. If I had been an American child instead of an Anglo-Irish one, it is possible that London, from being further in the distance, would have been more clear-cut as an idea: I should have had some rational notion of it, instead of being infested by it imaginatively. As it was, it was like a hand too near my eyes. Nobody ever told me about London, or explained to me what or why it was — I was assumed, I suppose, to have been born knowing. This may have come from the Anglo-Irish ambivalence as to all things English, a blend of impatience and evasiveness, a reluctance to be pinned down to a relationship — one which, all the same, nobody could have conceived of life without. So for what seems a long time London remained partly a not quite convincing fiction, partly a symbol of ambiguity, partly an overcast physical fact. Even when my mother and I went to live in the South of England we almost never took the train to the capital. Though we knew *of* quite a number of people who lived in London, we visited only one or another aunt or my mother's godmother, to whom we glued ourselves onward from Charing Cross. My mother knew she would lose her way. For my part, each time I looked for London it had jiggled itself into a different pattern. Nothing like a picture was to be formed.

The picture, when it did form, came out of books — as I could not read easily till I was over seven, and did not begin to read novels till I was ten, it came late. It was composite, geographically wrong and intensely vivid, pieced together out of Dickens, E.F. Benson, E. Nesbit, Galsworthy, Conan Doyle and of course Compton Mackenzie. I also read many Edwardian novels in which Park Lane featured, and for some reason I saw this overhanging the Thames (really more like Riverside Drive overhanging the Hudson in New York). This envisaged London gained on me something of the obsessive hold of a daydream; it invested itself with a sensuous reality — sounds, smells, motes of physical atmosphere — so powerful as to have been equalled since by almost no experience of so-called reality. Even the weather was dramatic: fogs impenetrable, summers Mediterranean, sunsets lurid and nights gothic with pitchblack shadows. And I endowed London with extremes of fashion and wealth, alongside which lay sinister squalor. Fancy was slow to encompass the middle reaches. This romanticist's London I have never extirpated from my heart — and, like a renewed vision it does now and then, even now, reappear. Probably the magic of a city, as of a person, resides in its incapacity to be known, and the necessity therefore that it should be imagined.

Imaginative writing, fiction, was my only data for London till I was nearly twenty. Bayswater was the first region to project into my personal life, for here lived two or three of my friends at boarding-school, whom I used to visit on my way across London at the beginnings or ends of term. Theirs were the first doors I ever saw opening upon interiors — which themselves never seemed quite credible, or at any rate wholly everyday. Leaving my friends behind, I realized that their existences while apart from me were almost literally a closed book, and went back to books capable of being opened — that is, actual ones. Nothing made full sense to me that was not in print. Life seemed to promise to be intolerable without full sense, authoritative imaginative knowledge. Feeling what a book could do, and what indeed only a book *could* do, made me wish to write: I conceived of nothing else as worth doing. At the same time, what attributes were required? Could one be a writer and not a demigod? I became most anxious to be in the presence of one or two, not so much I think out of curiosity as in the hope that virtue proceeded from them. Oh to be at least in the outer precincts, whatever came of it.

In these days I cannot believe it possible that anybody should live to the age of nineteen without having encountered an author. At Folkestone a disastrous cold in the head had prevented my setting eyes on Baroness Orczy; E.V. Lucas's daughter was at my school, but when he came there I was never around. My County Cork home was eighty-five miles away from Edith Somerville's, but that was a distance, before motor cars. At last, near Limerick, at my father's wedding to my stepmother I met her magnificent brother, Stephen Gwynn[1] — talk with him confirmed me in my idea: generally, authors lived in London. So back I went, this time with intention. As a sort of disguise, I worked at the LCC[2] School of Art in Southampton Row, near which trams rushed up out of the earth. My Earls Court lodgings had the merit of being round the corner from Lilley Road, mentioned in *Sinister Street*.[3] When I moved in, theatrical autumn sunshine bathed this first part of London I was on domestic terms with, and thin blonde leaves drifted through the air. . . . The year after, I changed my locale, going to live with a great-aunt in Queen Anne's Gate. My existence there,

beautiful as it was, seemed to be missing in one dimension — unaccountably, I had not yet found Westminster in a story. It was too bad that Virginia Woolf had not by then written *Mrs Dalloway*.

The winters of 1919, '20 and '22 run together: I cannot always remember which was which. (1921, I was in Italy.) The London of then — I mean, the London I sought — could not have been kinder to that most awkward of creatures, a literary aspirant. Looking back, I fancy that there were, then, more aspirants, fewer very young authors. Not one of the great I met asked me why I was not at a university, as no doubt I should have been. At Oxford or Cambridge, I expect I should have talked about ideas; in London I was careful to keep my mouth shut, listening to talkers like a spy. Apart from schoolfriends I met again, I had not much interest in my contemporaries — I could only think about The Elect. My idea of contemporary artists was a sacerdotal one. I had read their work not only with absorption but a kind of piety; everything but their appearances was known to me. (The putting of authors' photographs on book-jackets was not then, for better or worse, in practice.) I could not wait to be where they moved and spoke.

The big orange *London Mercury* was the dominating magazine. The Poetry Bookshop was a *foyer*: upstairs, after dark, in a barnlike room, I listened to Ezra Pound reading aloud what was hypnotically unintelligible to me by the light of one candle. The beginning of my life as the greater part of it has been since was when I was asked to tea to meet Rose Macaulay at the University Women's Club: this I owed to her friend, my headmistress, Olive Willis. In youth, and I suppose always, it is kindness with a touch of imaginative genius that one rates most highly: this I had from Rose. She lit up a confidence I had never had: having written stories, I showed them to her. With her I met Naomi Royde Smith, then editing *The Saturday Westminster*: it was in those pages that a story of mine first appeared in print. But something more: there were Naomi's and Rose's memorable evening parties — Thursdays, I think. I went, supported by Mary Hope Allen. Inconceivably, I found myself in the same room as Edith Sitwell, Walter de la Mare, Aldous Huxley; and I know there were others. I remember almost unearthly electric light broken on brocade-angular folds of one poet's dress, and her benevolence (she was talking about something lost under a sofa) and the graven face and shining cavern eyes of the other. Of Aldous Huxley I was most nearly frightened, through no fault of his. But alas these images, and so many since, cast themselves on the screen as a silent film: I have a wonderful visual memory but a poor verbal one. I recall little of anything that has been at any time *said* — the sense and atmosphere of a conversation, yes, but the words no. And all things considered, this is a tragedy.

I suppose that literary London then was, as it is now, multi-cellular. That was not a thing a young provincial was likely to realize. Many of the older writers I know now, it could have been possible to meet them. In one or two cases, D.H. Lawrence, Katherine Mansfield, it was then or never: I never did meet them — but then, I hardly knew them till they were dead. My relations with London were discontinuous: for twelve years after I married I did not live there. I went to London, off and on, for a day or two at a time: strictly I think that these recollections should be called 'Going [not Coming] to London'. It was a matter of sporadic approaches, different and shifting centres of interest. I lived through the nineteen-twenties without being aware of or taking part in them: they were a placid decade of my own existence. I recall successions of parties, each of which may have stood for a further phase or a change of focus. New planets were appearing in the sky. I recall with gratitude John Strachey's 1924 literary-editorship of *The Spectator*. Cyril Connolly, whose first novel to review for *The New Statesman* had

been the first novel I had written,[4] I met at the house of Miss Ethel Sands: later, there were Cyril's and Jean's deeply enjoyable parties in the King's Road. I did not know Virginia Woolf or T.S. Eliot till I met them both at Lady Ottoline Morrell's, in Gower Street, in the early 'thirties. . . . I can give the sensations of my protracted London half-life better than I can give the facts: the scrappiness and subjective vagueness of this record are inherent in its attempt at truth. I *came* to London, with any finality, only when we came to live there, in 1935, in Regent's Park — and by then first impressions were over. The attraction of Regent's Park, the immediate sense that this place was habitable, were due to its seeming something out of (or in) a book. And throughout seventeen years, it did never wholly emerge from art. It was much as I had fancied London would be.

1   Stephen Gwynn (1865–1950) was a prolific writer of books on Ireland including *The Fair Hills of Ireland* (1906) and *Irish Literature and Drama in the English Language* (1936). Between 1906 and 1918 he was Nationalist M.P. for Galway.
2   London County Council.
3   A novel by Compton Mackenzie published in 1913–14.
4   *The Hotel* (1927).

W. R. RODGERS
from *The Listener*, 26 December 1957

William Robert Rodgers (1909–68), poet and broadcaster, was born into a Belfast Presbyterian family and ordained a minister in 1935. In 1945 he resigned from the ministry and took up a post at the BBC in London where he was responsible for a series of broadcasts on Irish writers, later published as *Irish Literary Portraits* (1972). Here in this talk he reflects on the importance of conversation and gossip to rural communities in Northern Ireland. For an affectionate character sketch of Rodgers see the essay 'At the End of His Whether' by the New Zealand-Irish writer Dan Davin in *Closing Times* (1975).

Meet, Drink, and Be Airy

There are, says the Irish triad, 'three fewnesses that are better than plenty: a fewness of fine words; a fewness of cows on grass; a fewness of good friends around good ale'. As an Ulsterman I would agree. As a people we are uncommonly sparing with words as with everything else, slow to loosen the talking-tapes or to

let ourselves go. It is our nature, if not our pride, to be withholding.

Once, at a public meeting, I was asked to devise a way of raising money for my parish. I went home and slept on the problem and in the morning I had the answer. It was very simple. In my dream I had held a Grand Charity Concert to which everybody came. I charged them one shilling to get in — but I charged them five shillings to get out. There you have the canny Ulster mind at work, ready to entertain people or ideas but guarded about letting them go again. And that goes for words, too. We have them, plenty of them, but we are slow to express them. It would take a Habeas Corpus Act to make an Ulsterman produce a full-bodied peroration. A fewness of fine words is his aim.

Yet it would be wrong to assume that, in an Ireland flowing with volubility, Ulstermen are tight-lipped Puritans writhing in the lap of luxury. Far from it. It was from my experience of a country parish in Northern Ireland that I learned how much the life of a community depends upon its talk. Cut the talk and you cut the life-line between man and man, generation and generation. I was able to observe this closely because my pastoral work involved me in talking. One of the things I liked best was careless talk, for carelessness is the gay feather in the cap of all good conversation: it is like dancing as opposed to walking.

I found that there were two kinds of careless talkers in my parish; one was the young child, the other was the old man or woman. In between were the responsible folk, the strong farmers and their wives who did the work and carried the worry of the world. 'And how's all your care?' they would say when I went to the door. 'Come on in and have a warm.' And the best chair would be dusted, the best cups brought out, and the best talk — fit for the minister — would be aired. Meet, drink, and be airy. Fond as I was of them, I would have given a lot sometimes for a bit of loose-tongued, devil-may-care conversation to break the crust of respectability. I knew that old grandpa, sitting so mum in the chimney-corner, was bursting with gossip, enough to sink a battleship, but he hadn't a chance. Everybody loves the careless prattle of a child, but the careless talk of an old man is anathema to his family. Haven't I seen them, on a summer's day, anxious to get out to the harvest field yet afraid to leave me alone with the old fellow and longing for me to go? But no. I would go on sitting there till maybe a threatening rain-cloud would pass over the sun, and, with a last despairing look at the pair of us, they would scurry off to their work.

That was what the old man was waiting for. On would go the teapot and out would pour the talk, scalding talk, scandalous talk, talk with a tooth in it; talk about bad neighbours, good old times, randy men and bandy women, feuds and fads and fancies. In no time at all half the skeletons of the countryside would be pulled out of their cupboards and made to dance for me. I would learn things that were never put down in books.

'You see,' said an old countryman to me, 'there's two kinds of education. There's the kind you have to get to live and there's the kind you have to live to get, and, to my way of thinking, you can't beat the livin'! But now, begod, it's nothing but books, books, books.' I thought of what an Oxford professor of poetry said once. 'Few revolutions,' said W.P. Ker, 'have been more important than that which cut off the old popular traditions and put modern educational textbooks in their place. People learn nothing now in the way that all generations before them learned their ballads and fairy stories. Those things may come to them by way of books. They do not come as part of their real life from the mouth of their nurse or grandmother.'

No, indeed. In our grave new world of printed words and wider screens it is the old people who are supposed to be seen and not heard. Yet the ancient world knew them as talkers and showmen and that is how I knew them in my parish. It was their sublime abandon that pleased me. They never, like younger people, sieved their facts or saved their faces. Why should they? They had done their stint of careful moralizing and were glad to let a new generation of caretakers take over. Long live the careless talkers, the old folks at home and not — as often happens today — in 'homes'.

'Word Went Round'

'The Irish,' said Walter de la Mare, speaking of the poet Yeats, 'have no sense of destination in their talk.' That is true. It is true of the poet and the peasant everywhere, for both minds work by association, not by intention; and in their conversation one thing leads aimlessly to another, much as it is doing now in this talk of mine. 'Word went round', we say in Ireland: it never goes straight.

Tell all the truth but tell it slant,
Success in circuit lies,
Too bright for our infirm delight
The truth's superb surprise.

In my parish there was no such thing as a conversational target. What you got was talk that jumped round from one topic to another, from tiddleywinks to the Trinity. As a poet this was something I knew and liked, for what is imagination but the faculty of taking off from any point and finding landing ground anywhere? It is only in cities that people will say: 'Let's get this straight,' for cities are places for planned knowledge and special skills, and city folk know the value of having a single-track mind.

A friend of mine went on an angling holiday to a country inn in the north of England. One evening he had laid out the day's catch on the hall floor when suddenly the door opened and in trooped a company of tourists. They looked at the fish. 'And what is that?' asked a woman, pointing to the largest fish. 'That, ma'am,' said my friend, 'is a salmon trout.' 'Oh,' she said, 'I never saw one of those before. What kind of fly did you use?' He told her. 'Was it,' she insisted, 'the male or female fly?' He was stumped by that. 'Describe it,' she said. So he described it and she pronounced at once that it was a female fly. 'But ma'am,' said my friend, 'you have never seen a salmon trout before and yet you know the sex of the fly that caught it?' 'Oh,' she said, 'I work in the fishing-tackle-and-fly department of a multiple London stores.' Now, that is straight specialization, fragmented skill, as one finds it in a city. But in my country parish a man might tie his own fly, catch his own fish, do a bit of poaching and perhaps be a Justice of the Peace as well. For the countryman's life is an all-round life. His skills are all-round skills — he can build a wall, sink a well, deliver a calf, grade an egg, or grow an apple. And his talk is equally rounded, as rounded as the seasons he has to deal with.

A Closed Community

A country community, then, as I saw it, is in every way a closed community, a circle of returning tasks and habits and relationships. And this has its dangers, for being deep in the circle it is difficult for the peasant mind to see beyond it in an emergency. Take this business of talk, for instance. I used to visit, in my parish, a most hospitable farmhouse where there were always lashings and leavings of talk, talk that circulated quickly from mouth to mouth till everybody in the kitchen was caught up in it. One day, after long acquaintance, I noticed that two members of the family seemed never to speak directly to each other but only, as it were, through a third party. Was I right, I wondered? I would ask. I found to my astonishment that those two people, living under one roof, had not spoken to each other for years. Long ago they had had a quarrel which had hardened into silence, and now they were unable to break the silence. It would have been a simple thing, you may say, for one of them to up and go: all that was needed was a bit of straight thinking and a removal van. But no; they remained hopelessly trapped in the circle of silence, unable to talk their way out of it.

This kind of verbal paralysis is not uncommon in the small community whether in Ireland or England, but country people fear and detest it because it threatens the very basis of their society. To cut the talk is, in the end, to cut the life-line, and this, to country-folk, is an unforgivable sin and one which invites punishment. I think of two brothers I knew, farmers, who lived together; one did the fieldwork, the other the homework; neither had spoken to the other for twenty years and more. One morning the homeworker failed to get out of bed. The fieldworker wondered why, but since no words ever passed between them there was no way of finding out: so he made the breakfast himself and fed the livestock. On the second and third and yet on the fourth day it was the same. The fieldworker was deeply worried now, and called in the doctor who found that the bedridden brother had lockjaw. He died next day. A family tragedy, yet I need hardly add that the entire countryside looked on it as a judgement of God. He who can talk and won't talk may one day not be permitted to talk.

Too Many Books Spoil the Cloth

'Only connect,'[1] said a wise man once: and any failure to connect or to communicate is quickly remarked in a country parish. 'You will notice,' said a neighbour of mine, 'that deaf people can be very cruel.' He was referring to a stone-deaf parishioner of mine who was given to making wounding remarks, not out of malice but simply because he could not hear himself, he had no sounding board. It is isolation that leads to cruelty, and few things are so isolating as deafness, nothing so humanizing as talk. In a social sense, the printed word cannot take the place of the spoken word. Too many books spoil the cloth, as any countryman will tell his parson.

To my mind the airiest talk was found in the farm kitchens round the turf fire, talk that never went straight, talk that circled the parish as the moth circles the lamp, round burning topics like birth and death and old times and strange happenings. Maybe the man of the house would tell about the six robins that fought to the death in his orchard that day, and the discussion would turn then on war, and soon we would be fighting the true and legendary battles of Ireland over again. At the end of the long night's gossip I would walk home under the stars. 'The stars, Joxer, the stars!'[2] Curious the interest that the Irishman takes in the stars. I could always get any of my parishioners to read a book or attend a talk on astronomy, though they were by no means book-lovers or lecture-goers. The stars somehow compensated them for the earthiness of their talk — they looked so aloof, so clean, so near to godliness. As the poet Yeats put it:

A starlit or a moonlit dome disdains
All that man is,
All mere complexities
The fury and the mire of human veins.[3]

All the same, I should hate to have missed the miry vein of country gossip. 'There are three great things in the world,' I heard an American poet, Robert Frost, say lately, 'there is religion, there is science, and there is gossip.'

1   The epigraph to E.M. Forster's novel *Howards End* (1910).
2   From O'Casey's *Juno and the Paycock*.
3   Lines from 'Byzantium'.

TERENCE DE VERE WHITE
from Terence de Vere White, *A Fretful Midge* (1957)

Terence de Vere White (1912–94), novelist, biographer, lawyer, and literary editor for
The Irish Times from 1961 until 1977, was an intelligent observer of Irish life. Here in
this extract from his fluently written autobiography he puts de Valera in his place.

Every summer American students come with the swallows to nest in Dublin and write theses on James Joyce. A few do as much for Yeats. Then they go home again and we forget Joyce and Yeats until the next year brings back the flight chattering and wheeling round us. When I grew up Yeats was established and renowned. Professional Dublin sneered at his pose and said his early verse was far better than his last. It had read 'Innisfree'.

Those who had read Joyce were few and far between. But there has never been any national pride in Joyce and precious little in Yeats.

The one figure that has loomed large in Irish life in my time is Mr de Valera. Others make a stir for a while, but in the end, it is de Valera and de Valera alone who overshadows the life of my generation. Since 1916, with a brief pause during the Black and Tan trouble, he has either menaced the government of the country or presided over it. If those whom the gods love die young, it has been very fortunate for Mr de Valera that all his rivals for power seem to have won such favour in Heaven. Everything has been grist to Mr de Valera's mill; but most of all he benefited by the shortness of public memory.

Arthur Griffith, Michael Collins, Kevin O'Higgins, Patrick Hogan — the four among his opponents who had the personality which political leadership requires — all died conveniently young. Erskine Childers, Mr de Valera's one distinguished associate, was put out of the way by his opponents in 1922. Sean Lemass, who is, perhaps, the ablest of Mr de Valera's followers, looked after industry, in which his chief was not particularly interested, and so kept out of Mr de Valera's path. Mr de Valera is a whole-time politician whose ideal is the restoration of the Irish language and whose vanity and hobby is mathematics.

In the early years of the Irish Free State Mr William T. Cosgrave[1] had the thankless task of keeping law and order in a country which dislikes law but likes litigation and chafes at all order except Holy Orders. Mr Cosgrave's government executed many of those who took up arms against it. The young and brave murdered, looted and burned — but these events only offended those who suffered personally. The country, as a whole, forgot and forgave them. Mr Cosgrave was never forgiven for his executions.[2] The quality which finally destroyed him was modesty. Soon after Mr de Valera took office[3] his opponents gathered together under the leadership of one whom most of them did not know, a certain General O'Duffy. With a humility as praiseworthy as it was misguided, the experienced Cosgrave stood down for this futile person who had won local celebrity as chief of police.

Mr Cosgrave was followed over the precipice by Patrick Hogan (the only man fit to succeed him at the time), Frank MacDermot and James Dillon. For Mr de Valera this spectacle must have been as encouraging as it is for a rider in a two-horse race when he sees his opponent running out of the course. Those whom the gods wish to destroy they first make mad: it almost seemed as though Heaven had a stake in Mr de Valera's fortunes. It took the Opposition fourteen years to regain the ground lost by General O'Duffy[4] and, in the meanwhile, Patrick Hogan had been killed in a motor-car accident. Unless, as some think, the Almighty precipitated the World War of 1939 for Mr de Valera's benefit, we must regard the death of Patrick Hogan as a last unmistakable intercession by Heaven on Mr de Valera's behalf.

The collapse of the Protestant ascendancy, the formation of a new civil service, a new diplomatic corps, state-sponsored industries, a national army and police force, gave an unprecedented opportunity of employment at home to those who were qualified and available to take it. While the courts continued to function, the judiciary began to wear its rue with a difference, and the local magistrates were replaced by district justices of a different political complexion to the old.

Needless to say those who followed Mr de Valera into the wilderness were deprived of the first fruits. Lawyers with the ingrained instinct for self-preservation which characterizes their profession flocked to the standard of the winning party. As a result Mr de Valera had few lawyers in his ranks — a fact which is not necessarily to be put to the discredit of the faculty — and when his time came at last, the few whom conviction, accident or desperation had brought into his camp reaped the reward of those who back a lucky long shot in preference to the favourite.

It is hard for anyone who looks at the prelatic figure of Mr de Valera to realize what passions he provoked in early days or how intensely he was, by many, disapproved of and distrusted. Until I refresh my memory by reading the history of the period I, too, find myself apt to forget the amount of trouble the country has been caused by the incredible self-sufficiency of this complicated and remarkable man. A German said of John Stuart Mill that his eminence in England was due to the flatness of the surrounding landscape: to say this of Mr de Valera would not be true because his eminence is due not to intellect or originality but to powers of will and character, a belief in the purity of his own motives, absolute self-reliance, and, above all, a sense of destiny — all this, graced by remarkable personal dignity — partly physical, partly a reflection of his own self-esteem; but so outstanding as to obliterate the impression that would otherwise be made by the dismal accents in which he discloses the workings of a mind to which incoherence lends at times an illusion of profundity. Whatever Mr de Valera may not be, as a politician he has shown genius. That Mr de Valera's mind is commonplace the record of his

writings and speeches bears ample proof; the confusion and repetitiveness of his style may have been due to a corresponding condition in his mind; or it could be attributed to the same instinct which prompts the chameleon to change its colour.

I was twenty-one when Mr de Valera first came into office. He had declared the Dail to be an unlawful body, and it was a remarkable feat of adaptation to take office under its auspices; but ever since Mr de Valera solved the problem of the Oath of Allegiance to King George it was plainly only a question of time before he formed a government. On account of this oath Mr de Valera had repudiated the Treaty and sanctioned Civil War. In 1927 an act was passed making it mandatory for parliamentary candidates to take the oath. Mr de Valera was in a dilemma. He solved it in his own way and entered the Dail. His former practice was to stand for election but not take his seat. The new law (passed after the murder of Kevin O'Higgins[5]) meant, therefore, political oblivion for Mr de Valera. This was out of the question and a solution which, had he thought of it earlier, would have saved a great deal of life and property, occurred to him in his difficulty. He explained himself to the Dail:

'Believing that "I swear" would mean an oath, I said, in my opinion, it was an oath. My view was that it was an oath. But the deputies opposite had said quite differently. They said that it was not, that it was a mere formality — they used the words long before I used them — and had no binding significance whatever, that anyone could take it, and that it meant nothing. I asked myself whether in a crisis like that I would be justified in staying outside if it were, in fact, that this thing was a mere formality. I could only find out in one way. . . . I said "I am not prepared to take an oath. I am not going to take an oath. I am prepared to put my name down in this book in order to get permission to go into the Dail, but it has no other significance." There was a testament on the table and in order that there could be no misunderstanding I went and I took the testament and put it over and said, "You must remember I am taking no oath."'[6]

In such a manner might one who was no longer a maid argue that her promotion had not impaired her chastity.

This man with a gift of leadership such as no Irishman has had since Parnell died, has dominated the country for twenty-five years. Small wonder, then, that his prestige has grown, his early truckling to violence has been forgotten, his casuistry overlooked, when no rival of comparable status has been given in place of those candidates who died so long ago.

The Irish are emotionally susceptible to personality and loyal to their leaders to an extent that the English would think mad. Disloyal the Irish have been called, but their disloyalty has been to leaders to whom they gave forced loyalty. For the sake of the craven James II, whom the English jettisoned, many Irish lost life and fortune, many became exiles for ever. In these islands only the Highlander of Scotland is capable of a similar devotion. The people who threw Churchill out of office after the war have no lesson in loyalty or gratitude to teach Ireland.

Those who have led the opposition to Mr de Valera have lacked the spark, the essence of leadership, which is undefinable and, yet, for those who have it, shines on their forehead like a star. That they tried faithfully to fulfil their bargain with England; that, within the limitations of that agreement, they pushed self-determination to its uttermost; that they governed in defiance of bullet and of bomb, of sabotage and arson; that their severities were re-enacted by the very man who denounced them; has not counted, or has

counted for less than it should, because none of them has the quality which, when a great actor has it, makes us say 'here he is' when he first appears, though we have never seen him before, and he says and does nothing to reveal himself, except to walk out on the stage.

1   William T. Cosgrave became President of the Executive Council when the Irish Free State came into formal existence on 6 December 1922.
2   Between November 1922 and May 1923 seventy-seven anti-Treaty prisoners were executed by the Free State Government.
3   In 1932.
4   In February 1933 de Valera dismissed O'Duffy as Gárda commissioner (Chief of Police); in the ensuing months O'Duffy began to organize a fascist organization the Blueshirts; in September 1933 the Blueshirts, the new Centre Party, and Cumann na nGaedheal came together to form the United Ireland party, which then became Fine Gael, with O'Duffy as leader and Cosgrave as parliamentary leader.
5   In 1927.
6   *Dáil Debates*, xli, 1101-2.[AN]

HEINRICH BÖLL
from Heinrich Böll, *Irish Journal,* trans. Leila Vennewitz (1957)

Heinrich Böll (1917–85), the great post-War German writer who had a home on Achill Island, here shows his deep understanding of Irish life as manifested in a turn of phrase. For further information, see Böll's newspaper article 'On Poetry and Poverty', written in 1965, which was reprinted in *Hibernia* on 3 November 1972, together with a tribute to Böll and a defence of his TV documentary 'Children of Éire'.

In a Manner of Speaking

When something happens to you in Germany, when you miss a train, break a leg, go bankrupt, we say: It couldn't have been any worse; whatever happens is always the worst. With the Irish it is almost the opposite: if you break a leg, miss a train, go bankrupt, they say: It could be worse; instead of a leg you might have broken your neck, instead of a train you might have missed Heaven, and instead of going bankrupt you might have lost your peace of mind, and going bankrupt is no reason at all for that. What happens is never the worst; on the contrary, what's worse never happens: if your revered and beloved grandmother

dies, your revered and beloved grandfather might have died too; if the farm burns down but the chickens are saved, the chickens might have been burned up too, and if they do burn up — well, what's worse is that you might have died yourself, and that didn't happen. And if you should die, well, you are rid of all your troubles, for to every penitent sinner the way is open to Heaven, the goal of our laborious earthly pilgrimage — after breaking legs, missing trains, surviving all manner of bankruptcies. With us — it seems to me — when something happens our sense of humour and imagination desert us; in Ireland that is just when they come into play. To persuade someone who has broken his leg, is lying in pain or hobbling around in a plaster cast, that it might have been worse is not only comforting, it is an occupation requiring poetic talents, not to mention a touch of sadism: to paint a picture of the agonies of a fractured vertebra, to demonstrate what a dislocated shoulder would be like, or a crushed skull — the man with the broken leg hobbles off much comforted, counting himself lucky to have suffered such a minor misfortune.

Thus fate has unlimited credit, and the interest is paid willingly and submissively; if the children are in bed, racked and miserable with whooping cough, in need of devoted care, you must count yourself fortunate to be on your feet and able to look after the children. Here the imagination knows no bounds. 'It could be worse' is one of the most common turns of speech, probably because only too often things are pretty bad and what's worse offers the consolation of being relative.

The twin sister of 'it could be worse' is an equally common phrase: 'I shouldn't worry' — and this among people who have every reason not to be *without* worry every minute of the day and night; a hundred years ago, during the Great Famine, with several consecutive crop failures, that great national disaster which not only had immediate devastating effects but the shock of which has been handed down through generations to this day — a hundred years ago Ireland had some seven million inhabitants, Poland probably had just as few at that time, but today Poland has more than twenty million inhabitants and Ireland scarcely four million, and Poland — God knows — has certainly not been spared by its powerful neighbours. This dwindling from seven to four million among a people with a surplus of births means a great tide of emigrants.

Parents watching their six (often eight or ten) children grow up would have reason enough to worry day and night, and no doubt they do worry, but with that submissive smile they too repeat the phrase: 'I shouldn't worry.' As yet they don't know, nor will they ever know exactly, how many of their children will populate the slums of Liverpool, London, New York, or Sydney — or whether they will be lucky. But one day the hour of farewell will come, for two out of six, for three out of eight: Sheila or Sean will go off to the bus stop, cardboard suitcase in hand, the bus will take them to the train, the train to the boat; floods of tears at bus stops, at railway stations, at the dock in Dublin or Cork in the wet, cheerless days of autumn — across the bog past abandoned houses, and not one of those who stay behind weeping knows for sure whether they will ever see Sean or Sheila again; it is a long way from Sydney to Dublin, from New York back here, and many do not even return home from London — they will get married, have children, send money home, who knows?

While almost all European countries fear a labour shortage, and many are already feeling it, here two out of six, three out of eight brothers and sisters know they will have to emigrate, so deep-rooted is the shock of the famine; from generation to generation the spectre takes its terrible toll; at times one would like to believe that this emigration is some sort of habit, a duty they take for granted — but the economic situation really does make it necessary: when Ireland became a Free State, in 1923, it not only had almost a century of industrial development to catch up with, it had also to keep pace with new developments; there are scarcely any cities, or industry, or any market for the fish. Sean and Sheila will have to emigrate.

E. ESTYN EVANS
from E. Estyn Evans, *Irish Folk Ways* (1957)

E. Estyn Evans (1905–89), born and educated in Wales, was appointed to Queen's University, Belfast, in 1928 and eventually became Professor of Geography and first Director of Irish Studies. His work ranged widely over the whole field of geography, folk life studies, archaeology, and local history. His publications include *Irish Heritage* (1942), *The Irishness of the Irish* (1985), and *Late Essays in Irish and European Culture* (1994). Here in this extract, he describes the hearth and home of country people in Ireland.

Hearth and Home

The kitchen and the hearth are the very core of the Irish house, and the turf fire burning continuously day and night, throughout the year, is the symbol both of family continuity and of hospitality towards the stranger. When it goes out, it has been said, the soul goes out of the people of the house. The fire serves not only to prepare food and dry clothes, to bring warmth and comfort to the family and to ailing animals, but also to keep the thatch dry and preserve the roof timbers, so that 'when the smoke dies out of a house, it does soon be falling down'. This is one reason for the persistence of single-storey houses open to the roof, where the turf smoke could circulate among the rafters and keep the scraws and under-thatch dry. A 'smoke', in the seventeenth century inventories and to this day among country folk, means a house. In the days before chimneys were adopted the cabins were described as oozing smoke through the thatch so that they resembled 'reeking dunghills'. It should be remembered that the brick or stone chimney flue is a relative newcomer and, as we are constantly being reminded in these days of fuel shortage, a great waster of heat. The chimneyless open fire was much more effective as a house-warmer. The turf smoke, it is true, despite the draught-regulating mechanism of the double doors, must often have been troublesome, but as we shall see the furniture was designed to keep heads low.

Dry peat burns too quickly if the draught is strong, and the fire does best at floor level, glowing on a great stone slab or on a cobbled hearth set in the mud floor. The area immediately around the fire is also paved, but the rest of the old-style kitchen is generally floored with puddled clay which takes a surprisingly well-wearing surface. The housewife will tell you that such a floor raises less dust that one of concrete, and if it tends to wear unevenly this matters little since the cooking pots and some of the furniture which is not built-in has three legs instead of four and will therefore stand firmly on an uneven floor. The rocking chair, despite New England's claim to have invented it, was surely first devised for such a floor. Lime, cowdung or ashes were sometimes added to the floor when it was being prepared, and mud scraped off the road, already well puddled, was considered an excellent floor material.[1] In Armagh, we are told, floors were made by simply digging up the ground and trampling it: 'They sometimes have a dance for that purpose, and many a match comes out of a thing of the sort.'[2] Another method was to keep a flock of sheep moving about the newly spread floor for some hours until it

was well puddled. The bottom byre-end of the old-style one-roomed farm house was cobbled, and a flagged walk led from door to door. Devices for tying up the cows were secured to or built into the bottom gable: a variety of stone and wooden fasteners may still be seen in the deserted houses of Slievemore on Achill Island. One writer humorously observes of Co. Galway that the cow had to be tethered lest she should eat the bed-straw, but that pigs and poultry were free to roam.[3] The hens spent the night on a rope or pole hung across the kitchen from eave to eave, and laid their eggs in handsome nesting-baskets of woven straw. Here we may notice a curious bit of folklore which suggests that hens were carefully looked after for superstitious reasons, as well as for their economic value and for the cockerels' time-keeping. It is said that every night the hens, when they argue among themselves before settling down, are plotting to leave Ireland and fly back to Norway, but in the end they decide to postpone the trip for another day! In Co. Limerick elaborate three-tier wooden hen-coops are sometimes seen in the kitchen, and in Co. Down I have found the sitting hen warmly ensconced in a stone-box alongside the fire. In the mud floor one may sometimes see large 'pot-holes', hollows in which the heavy iron pot is placed when the boiled potatoes are pounded for pig-food. The wooden or iron 'beetles' with which the pounding is done are as varied in shape and size as they are indispensable. Sometimes a wooden plank is set in the floor as a footing for the pot, or to give the spinning wheel a firm base. The upright churn also needs a firm footing and in the Mourne Mountains a movable granite flag was kept for this purpose. I have seen a mud floor in Co. Down with several round holes in which milk was poured for each member of a family of cats. In the Bronze-Age Orkney village of Skara Brae every hut had stone-lined holes sunk in the floor, which were thought to have been used to store limpets.[4] In archaeological excavations near Belfast I have found holes which were presumably used for storing milk-products sunk in the clay floor of an 'earth-house' (souterrain) of the Dark Ages.[5] In some old houses there is a hole near the fire, either in front or let into the wall alongside, which is used to store the ashes.

In nearly every example of prehistoric and early historic houses which have been excavated, the hearth occupies a central position, and cooking pots would have been suspended either from the roof timbers or from specially constructed supports. We knew from English travellers that this continued into recent centuries. Thus Fynes Moryson: 'the chief men in their houses make fires in the midst of the room, the smoke whereof goeth out at a hole in the top thereof.'[6] He goes on to say that the humbler clay or wattled cabins also had their fires in the middle, and in the early nineteenth century we read of houses in West Antrim where the fire, though not in the centre of the room, was 'advanced some feet from the gable wall so that the persons of the family can readily sit round it.'[7] The description given by Charles Lever of the little cabin of Owen Joyce on one of the Brannocks Islands off the west coast, even if fictional, is worth quoting because Lever was probably drawing on tradition. It reads: 'It was built in a circular form, the chimney in the middle. Certain low partitions sub-divided the space into different chambers, making the centre the common apartment of the family, where they cooked, and ate, and chatted.'[8] In the course of time, however, the fire has come to be placed against the gable or, in the central chimney house, against a partition-wall, and one cannot doubt that the general adoption of chimney flues has been the deciding factor. This innovation, slowly adopted from about the sixteenth century onwards, gave rise in time to many regional styles of chimney breast in brick and stone. I suspect that the wattled smoke canopy was the native response to the novelty of chimney flues, but I cannot find that it was adopted outside the areas of strong English influence. The substitution of peat for wood seems to have made little difference to the architecture of the hearth. When coal came to be burnt, however, the fire had to be lifted off the floor, or the hearth fire given a stronger draught by installing a built-in 'fan bellows' which forced air through a tube into the floor of the fire.

The wattled smoke canopy or brace (? breast) is still fairly common in houses with central chimney and fireside partitions, mainly in the south and east. The front of the canopy rests on a strong horizontal beam, the brace-tree, which may extend right across the kitchen from wall to wall, four or five feet out from the fire and five or six feet from the ground. Or one end of the beam may rest on a supporting jamb set under one corner of the canopy. In that case — and invariably where the front door is adjacent — there may be a draught screen of wood mud or stone — the jamb-wall — built out from the fireside and terminating in the jamb, so as to partition off the fireside. This curtain-wall is pierced by a small window known as the entry or spy-hole, through which an approaching visitor can be spied from the fireside through the open door. I have seen a few jamb-wall houses of this type in Co. Armagh where the brace-tree nevertheless continued to be the side-wall, so that the visitor had to stoop under it on entering the

house. If a door is swung on the jamb-post a small hall or internal porch is readily provided. This is characteristic of developed houses of traditional style in the Lagan Valley near Belfast, and a further refinement is to hang a mirror over the jamb-window, a looking glass replacing the plain glass of the peep hole and reflecting changing fashions. The jamb-wall, called also in Ulster the hollan-wall, is well known under that name in the south of Scotland and the north of England and may thence have reached eastern Ireland in plantation times. In Cumberland it was termed the sconce and in Lancashire the speer, which was the name of the screen which crossed the end of the halls in the Oxford colleges. James Walton tells me that in north Yorkshire the jamb post, called the witch post, is occasionally found to be covered with designs intended to protect the hearth from evil spirits. Sprigs of rowan are tied to its top for the same purpose. The partitioned hearth is characteristic of eastern and southern Ireland: it extends into the Central Lowlands but it is almost entirely lacking in the west and in the north-western province of the outshot-house to be described below. Dr Desmond McCourt tells me that he knows of two or three hybrids — having both the outshot and the partitioned hearth — in the foothills of the Sperrin Mountains, where two cultural provinces meet.

The smoke canopy varies in shape and method of construction from one region to another. The commonest type is made of laths and wattles (willow, hazel or briar), plastered with a mixture of clay and cowdung or ashes and coated with limewash. In parts of the south hay or straw ropes soaked in mud (putogs) were used, twisted between a frame of horizontal rungs and plastered over with mud or limewash. In Co. Armagh one occasionally sees a heron's wing hung on the brace: it is used for dusting the hearth. The jamb-walls — and internal walls in general — were traditionally constructed of wattle and daub, or of mud or wood. The wattle and daub construction is undoubtedly an old technique which, in the days of plentiful timber, was much more generally used in house-building. Internal partitions carried up to the roof, however, probably followed the adoption of the chimney flue, and if so this innovation must be reckoned as a contribution to privacy as well as to comfort. We note in passing that wattlework found its last traditional use in house construction in the wicker doors of the west, and in the windbreaks of the north, bundles of hazel or birch branches (wassocks) set up on the windward side of the door. The stone-built external porch must be regarded as a relatively novel addition to the traditional house style.

Wooden or stone seats are often built in near the hearth, and the wall behind the fire, protected by a flagstone or a built-up hob, usually has a keeping hole on each side of the fire. Known as boles in Antrim and coves in Cavan, these may be elaborated in Achill Island, for example, into two- or three-tier wall-dressers whose ancestry lies in the stone house tradition of the mountain country. There is an old belief that the left-hand keeping hole belongs to the woman and the right-hand one to the man of the house. Here you may see in safe keeping, on one side the woman's knitting, on the other the man's clay pipe. Stone dressers were a characteristic feature of the huts at Skara Brae,[9] where also Professor Childe found evidence that the women occupied the left side of the fire and the men the right. In the Hebridean black-houses the left-hand side of the fire was the woman's quarter.[10] Similarly in the old turf houses of the Highlands, 'the women were invariably ranged around the central fire on one side, the men on the other'.[11] It is interesting to notice that it is the Mongol usage to allot the right side of the yurt to men and the left side to women.[12] We are surely dealing with a very ancient tradition related perhaps to the ordered routine of a pastoral nomadic life. For the Mongols the right and left sides were symbolized respectively by horse and cow. In the humblest Irish farms, which lack sanitary conveniences of any kind, it is customary for the women to use the byre and the men the stable.

1   J. Binns, *The Miseries and Beauties of Ireland* (1837), 1, 112. [AN]
2   ibid., 186. [AN]
3   T. A. Finlay, 'The Economics of Carna', in *The New Ireland Review* (April, 1898). [AN]
4   V.G. Childe, *Skara Brae* (1931), 17. [AN]
5   E.E. Evans, *Ulster Journal of Archaeology*, 13 (1950), 5–27. [AN]
6   Fynes Moryson, *The Description of Ireland* (1890; originally published as *An Itinerary Written by Fynes Moryson, Gent.* (1617)), 231. [AN]
7   G.V. Sampson, *Memoir* (1814), 275. [AN]
8   Charles Lever, *The Martins of Cro' Martin* (1864), 2, ch. 31. [AN]
9   V.G. Childe, *Skara Brae*, 15. [AN]
10   A. Mitchell, *The Past in the Present* (1880), 52. [AN]
11   Hugh Miller, *My Schools and Schoolmasters* (1857), 96. [AN]
12   E.D. Chapple and C.S. Coon, *Anthropology* (1946), 539. [AN]

BRENDAN BEHAN
from Brendan Behan, *Borstal Boy* (1958)

When he was sixteen Brendan Behan (1923–64), the son of a Dublin house-painter, took part in an IRA bombing campaign in Liverpool, was apprehended by the authorities and spent three years in a borstal, followed in 1942–46 by another period in prison for political activities. *Borstal Boy* is a lively record of those years. In this extract Behan finds himself in a political discussion with an English prisoner about Robert Tressell's *The Ragged Trousered Philanthropists* (1914). As Behan points out, Tressell's real name was Noonan and his birthplace was Dublin – or at least that is what is thought, though for more information see F.C. Ball's *One of the Damned* (1973).

The foreman engineer sent for me one day and told me that he was thinking of putting me on the painters' party.

He was a squat man and built in the shape of an Oxo cube.

'I don't suppose you know that I am half Irish,' said he.

In normal circumstances I'd have said no, and what's better still, I don't give a fish's tit what he was. But he seemed a decent old skin and in any event he was giving me my detached job on the painters and I didn't want to offend him, so I just said, 'I suppose it was your ancestors were Irish.'

'My mother was Irish — she was an O'Carroll from Longford.'

'A lot of people I've met inside seem to be of Irish descent, sir.'

'It doesn't seem to interest you very much,' said he.

'Well, to tell you the truth, sir, it doesn't. When I was in Walton[1] a lot of the screws were of Irish descent — Lancashire Irish, they were, and to prove that they were as British as anyone else they were worse to me than anybody else. A Jewish fellow told me it was the same with them, only worse, as they mostly met other Jews who were judges or magistrates.'

'Well, anyway, it's something we have in common. We both had Irish mothers — can you serve Mass?'

'Yes, sure I can. But I'm excommunicated. I'm not allowed to the Sacraments.'

'You don't have to serve Mass. The present fellow goes out in a week or two and it's not always easy to get a server.'

So even the excommunicated will do, when it's not easy to get anyone else. When all fruit fails, welcome haws.

'It's a long time since I served Mass, sir.'

'I can get you the loan of a missal. You can read Latin, can't you?'

'Church Latin, I can.'

'All right, from next Wednesday — there's Mass that morning — you can start serving and, now, get in there and report to the painter-in-charge.'

The painter-in-charge was a free worker called Reub Marten. He was a small man and a local from round the district. When I reported to him he listened to my accent with uneasy amusement.

'You're not a London boy, Be-ee-hann?'

'No, I'm Irish.'

'I see. We used 'ave lots of Irish 'ere, years ago, working at 'arvest time, and pickin' taters. Funny crowd they were, they used eat taters without washin' 'em. Very 'ard to understand 'em — blowed if we could. They didn't speak English much.'

'Well, I speak English and, about washing potatoes, I never saw a lavatory without water till I came to England, and then only when I came to this part of it.'

'I dersay, Behan, I dersay,' he said and added hurriedly, 'well, now, you be agoin' up to the New Camp, and the 'ead boy there'll give you paint, and you'll go priming doors. That's putting on the paint we put on first.'

'I know; I was serving my time to the trade outside and my father's a painter, and so was my grandfather and his father and his father's father before him.'

'Well, never mind that for now, Behan; just listen to me. You'll get a pair of overalls from the Part-Worn Stores: 'ere's a chit for the officer there. I 'ave it all made out and everything. You're to wear your overalls only when you're at work, and every night you're to bring them to me and not down to your 'ouse. Do you understand that?'

'I do, Mr Marten.'

'And you'll wear your working boots every day and not your shoes. Some of the fellows seem to think that when they're on a detached job they 'ave to be "flash", as they call it, and they go wearing their shoes.'

'Right.'

'Here's the note now and hurry back here.'

I went over to the block in good humour. The day was fine, the sun shone high in the sky, and I had a detached job; there would be no more of that god-damned navvy gang, wondering every morning who you'd have to fight before the day was out.

On the way out of the engineers' yard I met Jock. He waved a note at me. 'Going over to the Part-Worn Stores?'

'I am, that,' said I.

'I'll be over with you, I'm going on the plumbers, myself. What's your bloke like? Is he a screw?'

'No, he's a free labourer.'

'I'd sooner a screw than one of these bloody swede-bashers.'[2]

'You would, if you saw the little ——t I'm with. Miserable-looking little sod with a disagreeable face.'

'My screw is all right. He was years in India and hates black men, that's all.'

'Maybe the black men weren't out of their minds about him, either.'

'Well, it seems as long as you let him go on about black men, he's all right.'

'I suppose you're right. He might as well rave there as in bed.'

'Let's go in the cawsy for a burn,[3] Paddy. No need to hurry, it's all in the boss's time.'

'We'd have a better chance of swinging the lead on the way up to the job, if we got the overalls first.'

'That won't stop us having a kip-in here, too.'

We went into the lavatory and sat smoking in opposite compartments, facing each other.

There was a bloke working cleaning up the place.

'Tell that reception to keep the nick[4] in case the screw comes,' said Jock.

I will in me ballocks, said I, in my own mind. I didn't fancy giving the bloke orders, as if we were house captains or something. 'Call him yourself there, Jock, he's over your side, I think.'

'Hey, there,' said Jock.

'Hello,' said the kid, coming down to us. He was a boy of sixteen, and he didn't seem very frit of anything for a new bloke. He stood in front of Jock with his hard brush in his hand. 'Want something, mate?'

'Yes,' said Jock, 'come in here for five minutes.'

'Sod off!' said the boy indignantly, taking up his brush to go off.

'He's only jeeing you,' said I, from behind him. 'We want you to keep an eye out there for the screw while we have a burn, and you can have the dog-ends after us.'

'I don't want your dog-ends, mate, I got some of my 'alf-ounce left, but I'll keep the nick all right.'

'Thanks,' said I.

''s all right, mate,' said he, and went on with his cleaning.

When we had finished our smoke, I smiled and thanked him for keeping the nick for us.

''s all right, mate,' said he, 'you can do the same for me some time.'

'Sure.'

The screw and his boy seemed to be in good form this day. Geordie was at the desk and shouted down the store, 'Here's old Paddy come to see us.'

The screw came down and said, easy-going and pleasant, looking at Jock, 'This an Irish invasion, Paddy?'

'No, sir. Jock here is from Glasgow.'

'Well, he would be, if he's called Jock, wouldn't he? What are you two Celts after today?'

We showed him the notes. 'So you're getting a detached job, Paddy?'

'Yes, I'm going on the painters and Jock is going on the plumbers.'

'Good-oh. Geordie, reach me down a couple of pairs of overalls for old Paddy and his china, will you?' Geordie went to a shelf. 'No, not those. There's a new lot there. Fetch 'em some of those. Only the best is good enough.' He took the notes and gave me the overalls. 'There you are, Paddy, service with a smile.'

'The blessings of God on you,' said I, 'and may the giving hand never falter.'

'When were you ordained?' asked Jock, as we went down the stairs. 'Going round blessing people like a bloody parish priest.'

'Ah, sure, that screw would take the like of that very seriously,' said I, 'and didn't he give us a new pair of overalls each?'

'Well, I didn't like his carry-on when we went in first. "What are this Paddy and Jock after?" or something, he says. I know what he's after.'

'Well, that's his business, and no skin off your nose or mine. Besides, didn't I hear you a minute ago saying to that young Reception to come in the cawsy with you?'

'Ah, but for Christ's sake, Paddy,' said Jock indignantly, 'that was only joking — everyone makes jokes like that.'

'Well, for all you or I know, sure it may be all joking about your man, too.'

'Would you catch yourself on, for Jesus' sake,' said Jock, with a scornful laugh.

'Well, they're a good pair of overalls he gave us anyway.'

'They are that — dead flash,' said Jock, going back to London talk as we got near the site.

We reported to our trades parties and put on the overalls. We met outside the painters' colour shop and walked round the job together to our places. The navvy gang looked up from their trenches and roared and shouted, and jeered us.

'We have the best of it, anyway,' said Jock.

'The divil take the begrudgers,' said I, 'we have and all.'

The work was a great deal easier than navvying and what was better, it was more interesting. I slapped into it and primed a big number of doors that afternoon. A good start is half the work, and if you get the name of an early riser you can sleep all day.

The painter over me was a thin red-haired boy from Blackpool called Tom Meadows. My pile of doors was at one end of a half-built room and he was cutting glass on a bench at the other. When we introduced ourselves and talked for a bit (he was from Andrew's and I'd never met him before, though I'd seen him round the place doing jobs on his own), he brought his bench nearer my doors, to save us the trouble of shouting down the whole length of the place.

He was a painter outside, too, A fifth-year apprentice and two years ahead of me. He'd been in the Tech in Blackpool, and did the Second Year City and Guilds examination the year I did my first. He was born in the pot, like myself, for his father and his grandfather were painters. He was a good singer like most painters, my own family included, and the first book he'd ever heard tell of was the painter's bible, *The Ragged Trousered Philanthropists* by Robert Tressall.

We had a great talk about the poor apprentice kid, 'The Walking Colour Shop', Nimrod, the old bastard of a walking foreman, and the charge-hand that was getting free drink off of most of the men so as he'd keep them on, and Slyme the craw-thumper, and Holy Joe, that scabbed it, who wouldn't join the Society, worked under the money and tried to rape Ruth, the young painter's new wife when they took him in as a lodger to help them keep their new house; we spoke of poor old Jack who was old and worn-out and got sent up the sixty-foot ladder, and was afraid to refuse in case he'd be sacked and himself and his old wife put in the workhouse, so he goes up, the poor old bastard, and falls off and gets smashed to bits, and his wife gets thrown into the workhouse, anyway.

It was our book at home, too, and when my mother was done telling us of the children of Lir and my father about Fionn Mac Cumhaill they'd come back by way of nineteen sixteen to *The Ragged Trousered Philanthropists* and on every job you'd hear painters using the names out of it for nicknames, calling their own apprentice 'The Walking Colour Shop' and, of course, every walking foreman was called Nimrod, even by painters who had never read the book, nor any other book, either.

Talking to Tom Meadows was like meeting somebody from home, not only from your own country, but from your own house and family, only better because he was more intimate than a friend without being a blood relation.

Tom took the I.R.A. very seriously and was very much against it. But he said to me that he was also against the British upper class and the Royal Family.

Jesus, it's hard pleasing you, said I in my own mind.

But I knew what he meant and agreed with him when I took time off to think about it.

He said it was the fault of the British boss class that the Irish were forced always into terrorism to get their demands, which he allowed were just and right. He was, of course, dead set against the Catholic Church, which he regarded as a tool of reaction. He said it was a disgrace to put me into Borstal among a lot of scum.

Well, fair is fair, and while I knew what he meant and it is the usual hypocrisy of the English not giving anyone political treatment and then being able to say that alone among the empires she had no political prisoners, I also knew that the I.R.A. prisoners in Dartmoor and Parkhurst were getting a bad time, with the screws putting the lags[5] up to attack them on the exercise yard — five hundred British sportsmen on to twenty of our fellows, and our fellows getting bread and water for assault when they fought back, as best they could — still, and all, I could not say that the blokes had been unfair to me, nor could I say that the Borstal screws treated me any different to anyone else.

I did not like hearing Charlie and Joe and Jock and Chewlips being called scum, but I only said, 'Ah, sure the blokes are only working-class kids the same as ourselves, Tom.'

'They're not,' said he, that indignant at the suggestion that I said in my own mind, thanks be to Jesus you're not on the bench at the Old Bailey, it'd be a poor day for the punters in the dock. 'They're not working-class blokes. They never worked in their lives and no one belonging to them ever worked. You're a worker's son, and so am I, but most of this lot, ninety per cent of them, are a lot of bloody lumpers.[6] They're reared up to thieving and stealing and living off prostitutes the same as the boss class. And they know it. If you ever heard them talking of any heroes, outside the nick, it's about the way Anthony Eden[7] dresses, or the way the Duke of Windsor ties a knot in his tie. Haven't you noticed nearly all thieves are Tories?'

I suffer from a weakness of character that I can't keep up indignation about things like that, only when there is something happening before my two eyes like a baton charge or something. And Tom was nearly frothing at the mouth like a Redemptorist preacher.

'Maybe,' said I, 'it's because all Tories are thieves.'

He laughed, and licked back some of the froth off of his jaws, and then said seriously: 'You're a couple of years younger than I am, Paddy, and I was younger than you when I came inside and I know more about these bloody lot than you do. They're a dirty degenerate lot of scum and you have nothing to do with them. When your old man was coming 'ome after 'ard day's work, theirs was putting 'is jemmy or 'is stick or whatever they call it, into 'is pocket to start 'is night's thieving. And when your Mum was sitting down to darn a few socks at the fire, theirs was loosening 'er drawers to go off down the town, on the bash. I been inside nearly three years now, and I should know them.'

I nodded my head in sympathy and went on priming my doors. If he was in three years he must be a H.M.P. bloke.[8] They didn't keep anyone else in that long. And that accounted for his giving out about the other blokes. 'I suppose you're right, Tom, when all is said and done,' said I. 'They must owe you a good many back days, here, now.'

Back days are the Friday and Saturday of the first week a painter starts work and which are not included in his first pay packet but are paid to him when he goes out.

'Reckon they do,' said Tom, 'and me 'oliday money. Well, I shouldn't grumble — it's constant employment — I can't be sacked only by 'is Majesty the King.'

He was telling me that it was H.M.P. We both laughed, and I asked him, 'You know the old saying about the skin?' 'Skin' is a slang term for painter. 'Cover me up to the First of March?'

'Should do,' said he, 'been 'earing it every winter since I was born.'

'Well, they have a song about it at home, and it goes like this:

Get me down me hacking knife, get me down me
   stock,
Get down planks and ladders, there's a big job in
   the Lock . . .

'That's the pox-hospital, and had to be done up more often than any place else, I suppose, but the old painters used to say that there was nothing poxy about the money.'

'It's a good song that, Paddy, I must get that one off you.'

'Certainly, and my old man had a recitation for the beginning of the slack season in November, and it went:

Now, Autumn leaves are falling,
    and the light is growing dim,
The painter wipes his pot clean down —
    and ——ks his brushes in!

He burst out laughing and put down his glass cutter. 'That's a right good 'un, Paddy. My old man would love to 'ear it. Your Dad and mine would get on like an 'ouse on fire.'

Well, it wasn't his old man he'd croaked anyway. He was a lonely poor old bastard, whatever way you looked at it, though everyone in the place thought he had a great time and they looked up to him more than they did to a screw when they saw him going round the place with his brushes and tools.

We sang Vera Lynn songs together, and worked away with a will. I never primed doors so quickly in my life. The pile of raw dry doors was going down and the pile of fresh, pink ones going steadily up, in time to the singing.

'You know,' said I, 'it was an Irishman that wrote *The Ragged Trousered Philanthropists.*'

'It's not an Irish name, though, is it? "Tressall."'

''Course it's not,' said I, 'it's not a person's name at all —'

'No, it's the name of a bloody — a bloody trestle, 'n't it?'

'That's it,' said I, 'his right name was Robert Noonan.'

'Well, that's Irish enough, all right. Well, I must put that in letter 'ome. That'll be summat to tell the old man. That was Tressall 'imself in the book, Frank Owen, wasn't it? He certainly knew his trade — a man with 'ands like 'is and the bloody boss — old Sludgem — couldn't whitewash a shit-'ouse wall, like all the bloody bosses — ah well, the world's changing, Paddy, you'll see.'

So on the head of that we sang the 'Red Flag', which not liking to be too conceited I did not like to

mention was written by Jim Connell — another Irishman.

In the lengthening evening we sang, with Tom singing in seconds, like a Welshman:

. . . It looked around our infant might,
When all beside looked dark as night,
It witnessed many a deed and vow,
We will not change its colour now. . . .

Then by this banner swear we all,
To bear it onward till we fall,
Come dungeons dark or gallows grim,
This song will be our parting hymn —

Then raise the scarlet standard high,
Beneath its folds we'll live or die,
Let cowards mock or traitors sneer,
We'll keep the Red Flag flying here!

'Good lad, Pat!' said Tom, more life in his face than I'd seen before.

I felt fairly good myself. 'You've a lovely way of singing seconds, Tom. Was your mother Welsh?'

'No, Paddy,' he smiled, 'I learned to sing like that in chapel, believe me or not.'

I believed him all right. 'Do you remember the hymn the young painter sings in the book?'

He put down his tools and looked over at me. 'I certainly do Paddy,' and turned his face to the window and sang, 'Work for the night is coming . . .' and I joined him, '. . . when Man's work is done.'

1   Walton Jail in Liverpool.
2   Farm worker.
3   A cawsy is a toilet or mensroom. Burn is a cigarette.
4   Keep lookout.
5   Prisoners.
6   Riverside thieves. Here more general meaning possibly intended.
7   British Foreign Secretary 1940–45 and 1951–55, then Prime Minister 1955–57.
8   His Majesty's Prisoner/Pleasure; Behan was a borstal boy, not classified as a prisoner, unlike Tom.

FRANK O'CONNOR
from *The Listener*, 23 July 1959

Frank O'Connor's advice on writing short stories. For further discussion see *The Lonely Voice* (1962), O'Connor's critical book on the short story which includes reference to the connection he draws between the genre and submerged population groups.

Writing a Story — One Man's Way

Once when I was lecturing in America and, as usual, could not think of a title for my lecture, someone advertised it as 'One Man's Way', and that seemed to me such a good title that I wanted to use it again. Because short-story writing is my job, and, as all of us who write stories will know, there is only one way to do a job and that is the way you do it yourself.

Communicate — or Bust

I am dealing here with one man's way of writing a story, and the thing this man likes best in a story is the story itself. A story begins when someone grabs you by the lapel and says: 'The most extraordinary thing happened to me yesterday.' I don't like the sort of story that begins with someone saying: 'I don't know if it's a matter of any interest to you but I'd like to describe my emotions while observing sunset last evening.' I am not saying the second man may not have important things to say, things far more important than those the first has to say, but that particular tone gives me the shivers. I like the feeling that the storyteller has something to communicate, and if he doesn't communicate it he'll bust.

The story can be anything from the latest shaggy dog story to an incident so complex that for the rest of your life you will be wondering what the meaning of it was. Let me tell you a story that has made me wonder. Once when my father and I were staying in a little seaside place in County Cork we got into conversation with a farmer whose son had emigrated to America. There he had married a North of Ireland girl, and soon after she fell very ill and was advised to go home and recuperate. Before she went to her own family she spent six weeks with her husband's family in County Cork, and they all fell in love with her. It was only when she had left that they discovered from friends in America that their son had been dead before she left America at all.

'Now, why would she do a thing like that to us?' the old farmer asked, and for years I asked myself the same question.

Sometimes a story leaves you with a question. Sometimes it answers a question that has been in your mind. I had always felt ashamed of the horrible, snobbish attitude I had adopted to my own father and mother when I was growing up — an attitude for which there was no justification. Then a couple of years ago my wife and I were out walking in the little American city where we lived and we came on my son standing at a street corner with his girl — his first girl. I was wearing an Aran Island beret which I found very comfortable in the American winters. Instantly his face grew black and her face lit up, and it was as plain as though the pair of them had said it that he was mortified by the spectacle of his degraded old father who knew no better than to wear a knitted cap in the street, and she was thrilled at the thought of a father who did not dress like every other American father.

At that moment I understood my own horrible snobbery, and realized that falling in love always means being a bit ashamed of one's own parents and a bit enthusiastic about others'. At the age of seventeen we all have ambitions to be adopted.

But before I wrote that story, or would allow any student of mine to write it, I had to see exactly what it looked like. I find it easier to see it if it is written in four lines. Four is only an ideal, of course; I don't really quarrel with five, and sometimes a difficult subject may require six. But four is the best length; four is a seed: anything more is a cutting from somebody else's garden.

Tied Hand and Foot

I mean the sort of subject that begins like this: 'Mary Martin, unmarried, aged twenty-two, is a school-teacher in Belfast. She is the daughter of respectable parents; her father being employed in the shipyards and her mother a dressmaker.' Instantly I feel tied hand and foot, by school-teaching, Belfast, ship-building and dressmaking, and have the impression that I am never going to see that subject through all the trimmings. That is why I want to see it cut to four lines, even if this involves using algebraic symbols. In that way the story I told you about the old farmer in County Cork would read something like this: 'X marries Y abroad. After Y's death, X returns home to Y's parents, but does not tell them Y is dead.'

That method looks crude, but from my point of view it has its advantages. It enables me to forget all about County Cork and farming, and the North of Ireland and the United States, even to forget the sex of the people concerned, so that I can imagine what the consequences would be if X were a man instead of a woman. It gives me freedom — freedom to try out the story in terms of any place or group of people who happen to interest me at the moment, and who may, perhaps, illustrate the subject better than those to whom it originally related.

Obviously, there are limitations to this. You could not write a story like my little 'First Confession' about a Protestant family. But I always feel that there is something wrong with the poetic quality of any short story that adheres too closely to one place or nationality or religion or profession. One of the stories of mine that I like best was told to me originally about a well-known English actor and a London girl, but I did not know anything about English actors and very little about London girls, so I set the story in Dublin, and just because I was able to do that without seriously affecting the subject, I felt it was a better story as I told it.

This necessity for freedom seems to me to hold for every aspect of storytelling. Take clergymen, for instance. When I write about clergymen I try not to think of clergymen: the same with lawyers and the same with policemen. A man's profession should be demonstrated by the circumstances of the story, and the writer's business is to get past the given circumstances, and find in the clergyman, the lawyer, or the policeman whatever it is that makes him a recognizable, individual human being and not a mere professional figure — whatever makes the clergyman have, maybe, a passion for amateur theatricals, the lawyer for roses, and makes the policeman sing in the parish choir on Sunday. That is what gives a story by Chekhov what I call 'interior perspective', so that instead of a flat surface of narrative, you get a texture like life itself, something you can walk in and out of, and move about in, and catch people in from odd angles.

Before I start the serious business of writing a story I like to sketch it out in a rough sort of way. I like to block in the general outlines and see how many sections it falls into, which scenes are necessary and which are not, and which characters it lights up most strongly. At this stage it is comparatively easy to change scenes about in order to change the lighting so as to make it fall where you want it. At a later stage it requires considerably more fortitude. Of course, a close examination of the four lines of subject should give a fair idea of what this treatment will be like, but it is surprising how often it does not.

Handling of Two Themes

Here, for example, are two themes handled by students of mine. One described how, when he was a schoolboy, his mother took him out of school one day and brought him to a suburban railway station where she pointed out to him a good-looking girl. 'Follow her wherever she goes,' said his mother. The girl got on a train, and the boy got into the same compartment. A few stops up the line she got out and he followed her off the train and down a ramp leading from an upstairs platform to the street. Below him in the street he suddenly saw his father's car and realized what his mother had made him do.

The other story was told by a student from New York. It was about the only son of a Jewish widow who kept a mean little shop in a New York slum. For close on a year the boy had been robbing the till of quarters and fifty-cent pieces to keep himself in movies and cokes. One day he came home from school to find his mother had been coshed and the till robbed by a Jewish thug. Instantly the boy wanted to call the police and report the thief, whom his mother had recognized, but his mother said in horror: 'Isn't it bad enough for poor Mrs Solomons to have a son like that without my handing him over to the police?' A little while later the boy noticed that he had stopped stealing.

Both of these were excellent themes, the second a beautiful one, but for the life of me I couldn't have said without working them out in class whether they should be told in the first person or the third. That is one of the hardest choices a young writer has to make. By using the first person you can get effects of depth and feeling that are impossible by any other method. You can see it for yourself. In the first subject: 'I saw my father's car standing below in the street' has many times the emotional effect of 'Peter saw his father's car standing below in the street'; in the second 'I stole money from my mother' is stronger than 'Isaac stole money from his mother'.

In fact, in the second subject, it seems to me so strong that I should find it hard to treat the story in any other way. If you think of it in the third person there is little to choose between the boy and Solomons, and all you can do is mark the analogy as Joyce does in 'Counterparts'. But the fact is that the boy who is really acted on in the story clearly sees the distinction; it is only gradually and almost unconsciously that he becomes aware of the analogy.

But the first subject is a much more difficult problem. You can get the same effect only by almost obliterating the whole relationship of the parents, and ignoring whatever diabolical fury there was in the mother that made her involve her innocent son in such a sordid episode. Can you afford to ignore that? Can you ignore the possibility that the father was really a decent man who was driven into devious courses by his wife's hysterical character?

This is the reason why in class I insist on this blocking out of the story, which I call a treatment. The students all hate it. They always want to begin right away with 'It was a spring evening, and under ice-cold skies the crowds were hurrying homeward along Third Avenue where the neon signs on the bars were beginning to be reflected in the exhausted eyes of office workers'. This is the sort of thing that makes me tear my hair out, because I know it is ten to one that that story should not begin on Third Avenue at all, and that whatever I may say later on about the necessity for putting it in the first or third person, somehow or other the student is going to work that story back to Third Avenue on a spring evening when the neon lights were beginning to be reflected in the exhausted eyes, etc.

Now that you know something about my shocking character, you probably have already perceived the difficulty the student has put me in. He has already surrendered his liberty for the sake of a pretty paragraph, and young writers love pretty paragraphs, so it is going to take something like a major operation to cut that pretty paragraph out and let him begin to think again about his subject. The time for fine writing comes when everything else is correct; when you know how the story should be told and whom the characters are that you want to tell it about; and the light falls not on the eyes of office workers but where you as a story-teller want it to fall — dead on the crisis, the moment after which everything changes; the moment in the first subject when the boy realizes what his mother had made him do to his father, and that in the second when the old Jewish lady says the words that will in time reveal to her son that he too is a thief.

Those of you who know something about my work will realize that even then, when you have taken every precaution against wasting your time, when everything is organized, and, according to the rules, there is nothing left for you to do but produce a perfect story, you often produce nothing of the kind. My own evidence for that comes from a story I once wrote called 'First Confession'. It is a story about a little boy who goes to confession for the first time and confesses that he had planned to kill his grandmother. I wrote the story twenty-five years ago, and it was published and I was paid for it. I should have been happy, but I was not. No sooner did I begin to re-read the story than I knew I had missed the point. It was too spread out in time.

Many years later a selection of my stories was being published, and I re-wrote the story, concentrating it into an hour. This again was published, and became so popular that I made more money out of it than I'd ever made out of a story before. You'd think that at least would have satisfied me. It didn't.

Years later, I took that story and re-wrote it in the first person because I realized it was one of those stories where it was more important to say 'I planned to kill my grandmother' than to say 'Jackie planned to kill his grandmother'. And since then, you will be glad to know, whenever I wake up at four in the morning and think of my sins, I do not any longer think of the crime I committed against Jackie in describing his first confession. The story is as finished as it is ever going to be, and, to end on a note of confidence, I would wish you to believe that if you work hard at a story over a period of twenty-five or thirty years, there is a reasonable chance that at last you will get it right.

IMAGINATIVE

EDWARD A. McCOURT
from Edward A. McCourt, *Home Is The Stranger* (1950)

Edward A. McCourt (1907–   ) was born in Ireland and went to Canada as a child. After graduating from the University of Alberta in 1932 he spent three years as a Rhodes Scholar at Oxford. In 1944 he took up an appointment at the University of Saskatchewan. *Music at the Close* (1947) is a fine novel, set at the turn of the century in the Golden West. *Home Is The Stranger* is a slow-paced meditation on a couple's destiny in migrating from rural Ulster to the plains of Canada. Norah finds the transition quite difficult, a brave new world plagued by too much imagination. Here in this chapter, at the end of the harvest, she finds a moment of peace along a moonlit road.

Chapter 9

On the prairies each day was like the day before. The sun rose at a time which Norah had always associated with the dark hours of profoundest night, and its light still coloured the lower rim of the western sky when she went to bed. The components of each day were wind and heat and sunlight, varied by rainfall which, however important it might be in terms of growth and crop-yield, was so occasional that it left the pattern almost unaffected. The routine which filled each day was as unvarying as the day itself: cooking, eating, washing dishes, house-cleaning, a futile battle against dust which seemed to filter through the very walls, tending to Phillip's innumerable wants. And once in a while a trip to town or a visit to a neighbour, these last — like the rain — so infrequent as to provide no noticeable change in the pattern of things.

The days were pleasant enough once you got used to the heat, but without savour. In the lives of the prairie folk today did not matter; everyone lived for tomorrow. Perhaps, Norah reflected, because everyone was young, if not in years then in aspiration. The men who tilled the land about Innishcoolin were heirs to the wisdom of their ancestors, a wisdom cumulative over a hundred generations, hence based on knowledge scarcely to be separated from instinct. There life moved slowly and men made no haste to the fields. In the final reckoning an hour more or an hour less did not matter. Neither did tomorrow, for tomorrow, they knew, would bring no reward greater than today's. There was a way of life in Ireland and, so Norah supposed, in all places where men worked the land of their ancestors. But there was none here in the West, only a feverish preparation for that tomorrow which, when it came, was not important in itself but only because it anticipated the day after.

Many times these days Norah thought of old William Thomas Connelly, who by favour of Uncle James lived rent-free in a thatched filthy cottage on a point of rocky land in the lower meadow where burn and river joined. For more than seventy of his eighty-odd years William Thomas Connelly had worked as labourer on land which he had never owned; he had not been twenty miles out of Innishcoolin in his life; and he had rarely, until he became eligible for the old-age pension, fingered a pound note. But he had lived a richer life than Judd McKinley or Albert Cliff; and whoever came to his cottage, whether by chance or invitation, was sure of finding good entertainment there. For in the many years of his life, outwardly years of hard work and little reward, William Thomas Connelly had learned many things that mattered. He had taken time to learn these things, because no increase of diligence in his work would have brought corresponding material reward. There were a thousand stories on his tongue that he told often and well, stories of the Little People and the Hard Times and the Trouble. And he knew a thousand songs, many of which he had often sung to Norah in a high cracked voice to his own accompaniment on a squeaky violin, songs like *The Boyne Water* and *The Protestant Boys*, and even — for in the domain of art William Thomas

Connelly recognized no religious or political boundaries — *The Soldier Boy* and *The Wearin' of the Green*. And once he had sung for Norah all the stanzas of Mangan's[1] *My Nameless One*, to an unfamiliar tune in a familiar minor key:

Roll forth my song, like the rushing river
That sweeps along to the mighty sea.
God will inspire me while I deliver
      My soul of thee!

In retrospect there was absurd incongruity between the appearance of the bard and the words of his song, but there had been none at the time of the singing.

The men she met here in the West who were so proud of their land, the women who talked of things being different meaning better, would not grow into old age as William Thomas Connelly had done, serenely and without haste. Life was physically easier here all right, but it slipped away so fast that men had no time to ripen. Judd McKinley and a million like him would to the end of their days watch the weather and hate the hail and the frost and look forward with a kind of tremulous anxiety to tomorrow, and when tomorrow came to the day after.

But Jim would never be like Judd McKinley. He didn't care enough. Not that he hadn't done his share of worrying about the weather, and with reason. But he wouldn't have to worry much longer. For now the touch of autumn was upon the earth, and across the prairies the colour patterns were changing day by day. There was nothing blatant, as she had half-expected, about the new designs. Dull grey wherever grass grew, yellow along the roadsides where masses of golden-rod bloomed, streaks of yellow in the windbreaks, green and yellow-green and light gold in the grain-fields. A yellow-golden autumn, hardly any russets and no reds at all. But yellow and gold everywhere spread out beneath a sky that seemed a lighter blue than the blue of spring or summer.

To Norah autumn was the loveliest by far of the seasons in the West which she had seen and lived through, and its loveliness brought with it an accompanying sense of tranquillity and detachment which she had not known earlier. Like the spring, autumn was a season of hard work and long hours, but there was a great difference too. For seed-time was by anticipation a time of doubt and anxiety; now the time of doubt and fear was all but past. The drought had done its worst, the threat of hail had passed with the summer, and though on three successive nights frost warnings had gone out over the radio and the temperature had hovered just above the freezing mark, the front of cold air had passed on and now the days were warm and sunny and the harvest moon rode the skies. And though the wind still blew at times, it did so with diminished violence, as if it too no longer had power to menace the fortune of men.

Around Twin Buttes the weather gods had smiled. Jim's wheat, like that of his neighbours, stood straight and high, well-filled and without blemish. He talked now of an average of twenty bushels an acre for sure, and Norah knew that he was not given to boasting. Only a few miles away — north, south and west — the picture was different. Those parts the heavy thunderstorms of the midsummer had passed by, and at least two municipalities were certain applicants for the government crop-failure bonus. And less than fifty miles to the east the grasshoppers had descended on the fields earlier in the year, leaving almost total devastation in their wake.

But whatever the catastrophes in nearby communities, Twin Buttes rejoiced in an ample harvest. And of all the crops in the neighbourhood, there was none, so Mrs McKinley told Norah, to equal Jim Armstrong's.

'You must have brought him luck,' she said, looking as if she doubted her own words. 'Before the war the place was weeds mostly. Weeds and dust drifts.'

Jim himself was exultant. 'Summer fallow is hitting fifty,' he told Norah the day he started harvest. 'We'll average around thirty all through. Four hundred acres, say a dollar and a half a bushel. Figure it out for yourself.'

Norah took pencil and paper and laboriously figured it out for herself. Twelve thousand bushels of wheat at a dollar and a half a bushel, eighteen thousand dollars. She stared at the result incredulously. Over four thousand pounds! She checked and re-checked the results, but could find no error in her calculations. Why, they were rich! She warned herself that the crop wasn't off yet, though the forecasts predicted no break in the fine weather. And expenses would be high. There would be a lot of what people called 'overhead' and she knew that farm profits were nearly all ploughed back into the land. She was not sure what 'ploughing back' meant, except that it was something which never left any money for furniture or clothes or holidays or any of the things a busy housewife looked forward to. Jim would need a lot of new machinery, of course, and there would be income tax to pay, though Judd McKinley assured Jim he had never paid a cent of income tax in his life and didn't figure to. Perhaps Jim would want even more land. Westerners, so Norah had heard or read, were chronically land-hungry.

Still, eighteen thousand dollars was a lot of money. There would surely be something left over after 'ploughing back', and the new machinery and the income tax. Presently Norah laid down her pen and began to picture the interior of the house as it would be after she had re-decorated and re-furnished it. But not for long. She could not speculate with enthusiasm for she had no trust in fortune, not even when the limited fulfilment at least of her dreams seemed assured.

It was a good time, a golden time. Jim was up and away at day-break, but now Norah was up before him, for Jim had hired Weary Rivers for the harvest, and pride would not led Norah stay in bed when there was breakfast to be got for an outsider. A foolish pride, an unworthy pride maybe, since she had permitted Jim to get his own breakfast in the spring. But not altogether pride either. She really wanted to be up early. The days were so lovely now that she hated to miss a moment of their mellow beauty. They seemed lovelier even than the days of spring, perhaps because the tinge of death was on them. Each morning now when she got out of bed and raising the blind saw the incredible dawn flame across the sky the words of the poem learned long ago and all but forgotten ran through her mind:

Look thy last on all things lovely
Every hour.[2]

It was strange how almost forgotten poems which had had no meaning for her in the old life came alive in the new. Now in the fall of the year she looked at everything with heightened feeling, knowing that she could not look for long.

Things would renew themselves, of course. The grass would grow green again and wither when the heat came; the sky would recapture the opalescent tints now faded, and across the prairie mile upon mile of grain-field would turn from black to green, to yellow, to yellow-gold; the wind would toss the standing grain into a turbulent wave-hollowed sea, and the prairie-chicken and Hungarian partridge would year after year whirr aloft in violent staccato flight. But there would be differences. Tricks of light and shade resulting from a combination of elements never to be repeated, she would not catch again. And she herself would be changed another year, so that all emotional experiences wrought through the senses would change too. Because she would never feel quite the same any more about the scarlet dawn and the tapestried sunset, or the cloud-shadows hurrying across a waving grain-field on a windy day, she looked at these things as long and often as she could.

Paradoxically, since it was the forerunner of death, autumn brought to Norah a feeling of permanence. She had seen two seasons come and go, and she had been ill at ease and unsettled all the time. The tension which exists to some degree in all rural communities between seed-time and harvest had found in her a rich breeding-place. But now she laughed at the foolish fears and fancies which had beset her in an earlier time, as on the day she had walked to the Anderson house through the rain, in a world alive with unseen inexplicable terrors, terrors which till lately had never been far away.

Now all things were changed. She felt at ease and secure when she walked across the fields, Phillip tagging at her heels, full of childish volubility, to where Jim and Weary drove the huge combine round and round the field of standing grain. She loved to watch the field contract, draw in upon itself, at last to the point of extinction. As soon as Jim saw her coming he always waved his straw hat, and his words of greeting never varied: 'Thought you were never going to get here.' Then he and Weary would sit in the shade of the combine and eat thick sandwiches greedily and in haste, and drink cup after cup of strong hot tea. Lunch over, Phillip always rode on the combine for a round, or several rounds if the field was small, until his face was thick with dust and his heart thumping with the tremendous exaltation of spirit that comes only to a small boy who feels, however mistakenly, that a mighty machine is responsive to his touch and bidding. Then back across the field, reluctantly both of them, Phillip tagging a long way behind, to the farmhouse which was no longer bleak and comfortless, although it had not changed in outward appearance from the day Norah had first seen it — the farmhouse which was home.

Glorious days, all of them! Crowded days, for Jim and Weary were hard at work from the first hour of dawn. They worked late if the dew held off, sometimes till long after dark, and went to bed at once after supper. Then Norah washed the dishes and tidied the house, so that it was often near midnight when she went to bed. Jim was always sound asleep when she went into the bedroom. She liked to look at him stretched out on his side, his face half-buried in the pillow. Always he left the blind up so that if the moon was shining the moonlight streamed in, touching everything in the room. Sometimes Norah stood in its path just before putting on her night-gown, wishing that Jim would wake up and look at her naked body silvered over with moonlight. But always, just before getting into bed, she pulled down the blind.

Saturday was the best day of all. Then Jim and Weary quit work at six o'clock no matter how fine the weather, so that supper was over by seven or earlier. As soon as supper was over, Jim helped Norah with the dishes; and while he shaved at the washstand in the shed adjoining the kitchen, Norah changed Phillip's clothes and her own. By eight they were on their way to town. At first she had felt guilty about letting Phillip stay up so late — seven was his usual bed-time — but they were always home by eleven o'clock at the latest, and Phillip could sleep undisturbed for as long as he liked on Sunday.

Partly the enjoyment of these Saturday night excursions to Twin Buttes lay in their novelty. In Innishcoolin Saturday night had been the same as any other night, except when the Orangemen paraded through the streets thumping away on their big drums and shouting 'To hell with the Pope'. But it was different in Twin Buttes and, Norah supposed, every town in the West. None of the stores closed before ten o'clock, the combined pool-room and barber-shop much later. Shopping took half an hour or so; then Norah and Phillip returned to the car, which Jim always parked in front of the Co-Op. From the car they made periodic sallies for ice-cream, and all-day suckers which, belying their name, seldom lasted more than five minutes. Jim and Weary hung about in front of the brightly-lit stores chatting with the neighbours, for on Saturday night the town was always full of farmers and their families seeking to escape for an hour or two from the relentless toil of harvest. There were, Norah believed, only two possible topics of conversation among them: the crops and the weather. The disintegration of a people, the rise of a dictator, the fall of an Empire — news that might have shaken the earth — touched Twin Buttes not at all. Not on Saturday night. Not until the harvest was safely gathered in.

It was pleasant to sit in the car and speculate about the people who passed and re-passed before you. Family groups from the country to whom Saturday night was a serious ritual, with many purchases to be made, many greetings exchanged; the young town girls, fresh-faced and with bright painted lips, who walked arm in arm up and down the length of the wooden sidewalk, stopping often to talk with the young men lounging about the store-fronts, sometimes going with them to Lee Wong's for ice-cream or cokes; the drunks who progressed with unsteady dignity along the sidewalk, never wandering far from the door of the beer-parlour in the corner hotel; the crowd that flowed in and out of the pool-room, where, through the plate-glass window, you could see figures bending over the green-baize covered tables;

and always, under a powerful naked bulb in the front of the room, a man sitting upright in the chromium-plated chair with Johnny Bates the barber ministering to his needs. Sometimes people whom Norah knew stopped to talk to her, and admire Phillip's astonishing development. 'Best country in the world for the weans,' Mrs Cliff assured her. Best country in the world for everything was what Mrs Cliff and the rest of them really meant.

Norah no longer disagreed with them wholly. For the serenity of spirit which had come to her with the autumn affected not only her attitude to the physical world about her, but to the people who inhabited it. She thought she understood them better now, and understanding dissipated resentment. They were ordinary human beings who like herself were on the defensive, not against one another but an environment which compelled them to fight or perish. You could love this strange lonely land as some men loved the sea or a beautiful mistress — or as some women loved some men, men like Brian Malory for instance — with selflessness, with passion, but never with complete trust. That was why human relationships here were so easily entered into and so slow to mature. Men had no time to cultivate one another. The pact with nature was all-demanding. Norah knew that she and Jim had been lucky this year. Most of the people around Twin Buttes had been lucky this year. But already they were beginning to talk of next year. Always their thoughts were of tomorrow because serenity was never won today.

But eighteen thousand dollars! Over four thousand pounds! And when at last, in the middle of a late September afternoon, Jim and Weary drove the big combine into the yard and stopped in front of the machine-shed where shortly the combine would be put away for the winter, Norah dared to think of how the money might be spent. But to her delight, it was Jim who first spoke of things to be bought. They were lingering over their after-supper coffee, alone, for Weary had gone off to town to celebrate the end of harvest with an orgy of beer and movie magazines, when Jim set down his cup and looked at her quizzically.

'The money's burning a hole in my pocket already,' he said. 'What are we going to do with it?'

Norah affected an air of wisdom which had nothing to do with the way she was feeling. 'I suppose you'll be wanting more land,' she said. 'And, of course, after you get what machinery you want there won't be an awful lot left. And we mustn't forget the income tax . . .'

'I told you once you'd read too many bad novels about the West,' Jim told her. 'Novels about the West

are all out of date. We've learned a lot in the last few years. We're not land-hungry any more. I'm not, anyway. If anything, I'll cut down. Maybe sell the Anderson quarter. A section is more than enough for one man to look after properly.'

'But there's the new machinery,' Norah said.

'What's the matter with the machinery I've got? Most of it was new last spring. I owe three thousand on it but I'll clean that up next week. Then a couple of thousand income tax, unless I get Judd to fill out my form for me. The rest is gravy — pure gravy.'

'But what will we do with it?' Norah said in a shaky voice. It was hard to believe that there was really money to spend, money to spend on the things which she had dreamed about but never for long, because until only a few weeks ago they had seemed wholly unattainable.

'A holiday first,' Jim said. 'To the mountains. It's late for tourists so we'll have the Rockies all to ourselves. Believe it or not there are mountains in the west, the biggest you ever saw. Afterwards we'll fix up the house. New clothes for all of us! Come winter, a fur coat for you. And not out of the catalogue either. How does it sound?'

She did not answer him at once. Her mind had leapt ahead and she was seeing the house as she wanted it: the kitchen in pale green and cream, new linoleum on the floor, cupboards everywhere, drapes for the living-room windows, a chesterfield with slim graceful lines, a rug — a real rug — on the floor. And a piano, of course, perhaps even a baby grand, and music piled high on top of it — Brahms and Debussy and Chopin and the *Pathetique* and *Appassionata*. There would be book-cases all along one wall, shelves enough to hold Jim's trunkful of favourites and her own, which she would have to buy because she hadn't been able to bring any out with her — all the Irishmen of course, Yeats and O'Casey and O'Flaherty and A.E. and the man whose name she couldn't remember who wrote about Connemara and the Western Isles. Synge, that was it. And the classics too, that she hadn't looked at since she left school but which she would read to Phillip as he grew older. Pictures, dozens of pictures. She had always liked lots of pictures on a wall. Not just a single isolated exhibit surrounded by acres of wall-paper, but good reproductions, and some by local artists too if she could find any, all framed in plain light wood.

'We'll put in electric lights,' Jim said. 'Tack on a bathroom. Outdoor plumbing in winter-time drives more women from the farm than a herd of cows.'

Norah was glad of an excuse to laugh. Jim laughed too, and Phillip joined in quickly.

'What's funny, Mummy?' he demanded, breaking off abruptly.

Norah jumped up, caught him in her arms and hugged him. 'You are, Phillip,' she said. 'Oh, Jim, it's a grand world, isn't it?'

He looked at her, smiling and proud. 'We're doing all right.'

'But, of course,' she said wisely, 'we've got to think about next year.'

Jim shook his head. 'Not too much, Norah. That's what people here have been doing since they came. I think it's wrong to be a next-year country. Sure, we'll keep a little in reserve. We can afford to. But we're going to think about now.'

Norah was pleased and surprised. Surprised because she hadn't known the way Jim was thinking. It was nice to be finding out things about a man even after you'd been married to him for over four years. But then, they had been together hardly at all.

'I'm glad, Jim,' she said. 'And you're right. We've come a long way.'

She couldn't help thinking about Brian Malory just then, Brian and Gail. She thought of them mostly with pity. Brian didn't mean anything to her now. Why, she had hardly seen him since the dance. He had never meant anything, except an antidote to dullness. Things would be different now, different always. It wasn't just because she was going to have a piano and pictures. She remembered what Jim had told her once: 'In winter we really live.' She hadn't believed him then, but it was true. She and Jim were just beginning to live now. He was young, alive again, like the Jim she had known and loved almost at first sight a long time ago, the Jim she had for so long lost sight of. She pitied Brian Malory and Gail Anderson because they had none of the things she had and could never have them. She was glad that she had let Brian kiss her, glad that she had pressed her body close to his. For she knew now that he didn't matter. No recollection of casual half-intimacy had power to move her. Jim, she was sure, felt the same way about Gail. Life was suddenly unexpectedly simplified, and fear a thing almost forgotten.

Weary came back from town about ten o'clock only slightly drunk, a bundle of magazines under his arm, a bag of candy in his pocket for Phillip. Tomorrow he would go back to his own shack — reluctantly, for he had found life with the Armstrongs pleasant. The food was good and they let him alone. Tonight he did not as usual slip at once into the little den adjoining the living-room where Norah had fixed up a bed for him.

'Figger I'll read a while,' he said. 'If you folks don't mind.'

'Read all night if you want to,' Norah said. 'We'll go to bed whenever we feel like it.'

But that wouldn't be for a while yet. Tonight she felt restless, exhilarated. She and Jim should be celebrating the end of harvest, making thank-offerings to the gods for an abundant crop. 'I know,' she said to Jim, 'let's put up an altar in the yard — a sheaf on the top of a fence-post or something — and we'll dance around it in the moonlight.'

'We could go for a walk,' Jim said.

The suggestion delighted her, all the more because it had come from Jim. 'Jim, a walk in the moonlight — a long, long walk! Hours and hours!' She threw her arms about his neck and kissed him. He picked her up and held her close, laughing while he returned her kiss.

'Maybe if we stay out till midnight we'll see the little folk dancing in the stubble,' she cried.

'Rabbits more likely,' Jim said.

But the prosaic words could not disturb her mood. She ran upstairs for her tweed coat and down again laughing all the way. 'Jim and I are going for a walk, Weary,' she said. 'A long walk. Don't wait up for us. I don't know when we'll be back.'

Weary looked at her as he usually did, bewildered. 'Walk? Where?'

'To see the fairies tossing their milk-white arms in the air and Pan chasing Diana down the road-allowance.'

She ran over to Weary and patted him lightly on the shoulder. 'Just for a walk, Weary. With my man in the moonlight. If Phillip wakes up and yells tell him Daddy and Mummy will be home soon.'

'If this was spring I could figger it out,' Weary said. 'It beats me.'

The night was calm and cloudless. The harvest moon was half-way up the sky, its light so brilliant that Norah fancied she could distinguish objects around her almost as clearly as in the day-time. By the time they reached the road she was thinking, why was I ever afraid? For even in the moonlight the world about her was familiar. Familiar and friendly now. As they walked arm in arm down the road, Jim humming a tune very softly so that it did not disturb her reflection, she thought of the afternoon when she had walked alone in the rain along this same road, her heart heavy with foreboding. Then there had been evil things crouching behind every fence-post, in every clump of weeds. All that was past now, and she would never be afraid again. There would be loneliness sometimes, for loneliness came in many forms and to all men. But she felt safe now, a feeling which she had never really known before. Not in Ireland in the old house with her father and Aunt Lucy, for there she knew, from the time she was not more than ten years old, that her father was a broken reed, and that whatever was given to her was given not as hers by right but in charity. Aunt Lucy had assumed a responsibility she could ill afford because family pride commanded. To be sustained by pride and charity instead of love — though Aunt Lucy had liked her well enough in a remote well-bred way, never forgetting that Norah's father had married beneath him — meant uncertainty and heartache; and when she was old enough to work for herself the war had come and threatened the very foundations of her existence, insecure as they already were, and even that existence itself. But all those evil times were past and now her life was secure. She was Jim's wife, Phillip's mother, and there was food and drink more than enough. And love! Love most of all. The triumph had been easy, the sense of doom banished with a snap of the fingers. 'I am the master of my fate,' she said aloud, and laughed.

'You'll frighten Pan,' Jim said.

And that was another thing that caused her heart to rejoice — the difference in Jim. Not that he had really changed, rather reverted to what he had been when she had first known him. Then she had so often been surprised by his sensitivity, his awareness of things that mattered which had its roots in instinct and owed little to formal training. In Ireland his feeling for things had nearly always been right somehow, although he could never clearly explain why he felt the way he did. He might be as ignorant as the brashest tourist about things concerning Ireland's history and traditions, but he never once offended against the canons of good taste in what he said. He had what Aunt Lucy would have called innate good breeding, the kind which did not necessarily derive from blood.

But things had been different, disappointing, all summer. Norah now knew why. It wasn't because, as she had once foolishly fancied, he was dreaming of a romantic past unrealizable in the present, of Muriel Kendall or Gail Anderson or anyone else; it was simply that no man is himself under great strain, because great strain is abnormal. But that was how men lived in the West between seed-time and harvest, beset on all sides by enemies they could not fight against: hail and frost and drought and grasshoppers; so that their essential selves tended to disappear behind an elaborate defence mechanism created to meet a sustained crisis. Jim had not been himself all summer. Now he had come back to her in his own person, and tonight she loved him in the old way. Just for a moment she wondered how she would feel now if there had been no crop. Would she

and Jim be walking light-heartedly along a moonlit road looking for Pan? But this was not the time for disturbing conjecture. In past years she had grappled with enough crises that were real to justify her present avoidance of the imaginary.

She committed herself without thought to Jim's guidance and they walked steadily down the road, still arm in arm, Jim singing snatches of old songs, Norah silent and smiling by his side. Once he stopped and turning quickly, kissed her, and she responded joyously. Then they went on again until, looking back, they could no longer see the outlines of the house, only a tiny pin-point of light which they knew shone from the living-room window. When they turned down a little-used side-road the pin-point of light disappeared and they were cut off from the world of living things, isolated in the midst of a universe of remote and lonely stars.

'Jim,' Norah said, 'it's so quiet.'

'You'd think the wind had given up,' Jim said. 'It can't bedevil us any more so it's just quit.'

'We beat it, didn't we? Beat the wind and the drought and the hail and the frost.'

He laughed out loud as if he was not quite sure of himself. 'This year,' he said. 'There are other years coming.'

'It's no good, Jim,' she said. 'Tonight I won't think of next year. Remember what you said at supper? And honestly, I don't feel this way just because we have a crop and I'm going to get a piano. It's just that . . . well . . .'

She wanted to say, 'It's because I'm walking in the moonlight with the man I love,' but that way it sounded like something out of a Tin Pan Alley lyric. Anyhow, Jim seemed to understand the way she was feeling.

'I know,' he said. 'Even if we didn't have a crop we'd still have each other and the kid.' And because of the way he said them the words did not seem trite at all.

The road-allowance along which they were walking ran alongside a low ridge, a swelling of the earth's surface hardly apparent at a distance, but which now cut off on one side their view of the prairie. It pleased Norah that she could see a long way in three directions only; for the low ridge was in its indifferent way companionable. Not, of course, as the hills of Innishcoolin were companionable, but with a vague suggestion of intimacy not to be felt in the great stretches of plain which were the common view.

Presently the ridge merged with the level prairie and ceased altogether to be. Only a few hundred yards away the deserted Anderson house stood dark and silent, its blackness accentuated by a few bright streaks of light on the roof where the moon caught in its rays some strips of un-rusted metal. Norah, seeing the house without anticipation, turned quickly away. Jim stopped and slipped his arm about her waist.

'Sort of forbidding, isn't it?'

'Sort of.'

She found the feel of his arm comforting, for she had experienced a profound sense of shock. But what she felt she could not put into words.

'Maybe I was wrong,' Jim said, 'about there being no ghosts in the West.'

'The house always makes me feel queer,' Norah said. 'I wish Gail had burned it down.'

She had told Jim what Gail said that day she found her in the house. Then Jim had said, 'Silly idea. There's a lot of good lumber in that old hulk yet.' But now, to her surprise, he was silent. In her apprehension she was prompted to tell him something else that Gail had said.

'Gail's an odd person. She doesn't think the way most people do about the land. She says the earth is hungry. Can you imagine? When it's given us eighteen thousand dollars' worth of wheat!'

'Gail has queer ideas sometimes,' Jim agreed. But that was all. No flat contradiction of Gail's words, no confirmation of what Norah wanted to believe.

'Funny thing,' Jim went on presently. 'In the Old Country I always felt, when things happened — bombing raids, things like that, I mean — that they were easier to take over there. Pain . . . . sorrow . . . .'

He spoke stumblingly, unsure of himself, and Norah knew that he was embarrassed. 'And death. Death most of all. Because over there you feel that all these things are old — ten thousand years old at least. There wasn't anything men put up with during the war that they hadn't put up with before. The agents were different, that was all. But here everything is new. And you always figure, somehow, that when you start all over again with a clean slate things will be different, easier, that the real calamities won't hit you. But it doesn't work out that way. You can't get away from pain and hardship and death, but subconsciously you think you can. And when you find out that you're wrong, it hurts.'

Norah shivered and was quiet. All the time he had been talking Jim was leading her back along the road so that the ridge had reappeared, cutting the Anderson house off from sight. Now stumblingly they crossed the shallow dry ditch of the roadside and stood in the black shadow of the ridge, an isthmus of darkness bounded on three sides by moonlight. Before Norah knew what was happening Jim had slipped the coat from her shoulders and laid it on the grass. He lifted her in his arms and kissed her lightly.

'I've never made love to you in the moonlight before,' he said.

Afterwards, she knew that she would remember this night always. Not for the uniqueness of the experience, but for its significance. Once before, when her world had literally tumbled in ruins about her and she was lost and helpless, she had cried out in her agony for the security of the flesh. And Jim had answered her. This time, when the fear was felt so obscurely that she herself was hardly aware of it, he had comforted her unasked. For what he had done was not in satisfaction of strong physical desire — his love-making had been strangely without passion — but in response to her inarticulate demand for the security of his love. She walked home by his side, quiet and subdued but inwardly triumphant. In their union the spirit and the flesh had at last been made one.

1   James Clarence Mangan (1803–49), influential Irish poet.
2   Lines from Walter de la Mare's 'Fare Well'.

SAM HANNA BELL
from Sam Hanna Bell, *December Bride* (1951)

Sam Hanna Bell (1909–90), born in Scotland into an Ulster Scots family, moved to Belfast in 1921. A features producer with BBC Northern Ireland from 1945 until 1969, in 1943 he co-founded with John Boyd and Bob Davison the socialist and non-sectarian journal *Lagan*. Later he co-edited with John Hewitt and Nesca Robb *The Arts in Ulster* (1951). He was the author of several works of fiction and *December Bride*, based in part on his own family at the turn of the century, was his first novel. Here in this extract Sarah Gomartin's relationship with the two brothers on the claustrophobic farm at Rathard on the Ards Peninsula undergoes yet another change as the local community bears down on her *ménage à trois* plus child. In 1990 *December Bride* was made into a Channel 4 film by Thaddeus O'Sullivan. When it was first published, Sean O'Faolain in a review in *The Listener* (10 January 1952) wrote: '[T]his faithful novel of Ulster life, which possibly owes something to the work of Shan Bullock, something to Hardy, and something to the growing nationalism of the Six Counties, contains some firm character-drawing, excellent natural descriptions of lakeside country, the manners and customs of the North of Ireland, the round of the seasons, the dour morality of a people as distinct from their southern fellow-countrymen as chapel is from church.'

Chapter 10

The departure of the Reverend Mr Sorleyson and his wife was hardly spoken of in Rathard. So far as Hamilton and Frank were concerned, any thought they had on the matter was one of relief, and as the Echlins had by this time completely severed themselves from Ravara Church, they did not expect a renewed effort on the part of Sorleyson's successor to interfere in the relationship between them and Sarah.

When she first heard the news, Sarah dimly associated the minister's departure with the afternoon that he had come up to the farm. But as she had already thrust the memory from her mind (in some way that she could not explain, it was associated with the memory of her mother), and because she was incapable of understanding what a disturbance the encounter had created in the more sensitive mind of the man, the news roused little interest in her, and was soon forgotten.

Isolated though they were, situated high on the hill-farm and almost sufficient to themselves, the inhabitants of Rathard were not unaware of the criticism of their conduct by the people of the townlands. The irregular *ménage* of Rathard might have been rectified by the intervention of someone with the moral authority of a clergyman. But the people knew as well as he did, that his power to bring about a more normal relationship in any home was limited to counsel and warning. And the warning was, in the last extreme, limited to such incorporeal things as the displeasure of Providence. Having no economic hold over his flock, the minister could not go beyond that.

And how potent was this warning of the displeasure of God? Men or women determined to pursue some selfish course, hardened their hearts with an ancient knowledge that the world did not behave as the clergy wanted it to do, or worse still, said it did. In a drought the peasants might flock to church with every mark of fervour to pray for rain, but they knew that when the rain did come, it would come vast, rolling, drenching the world from horizon to horizon and not seeking out, with scrupulous justice, the meadows of the pious.

For some months after the birth of the child the Echlin brothers kept as close to the farm as possible, but some traffic with their neighbours was unavoidable, and it was these few visitors to Rathard who spread the story that Sarah Gomartin was now the master as well as the mistress of the farm. They found that when they bought potatoes in the field or straw in the haggard, it was in the house they paid the money. And it was Sarah who took it.

'And are those pachels[1] of brothers going to put their hearth and bread into the fists of that creature!' cried the women in exasperation. 'Ah, fair's fair,' pleaded the storyteller. 'Fair's fair. She'll never take a penny too much, or give ye a penny less, to my knowing.'

But the women, those shapers of opinion and prejudice, would hear nothing in Sarah's favour, and the men for peace's sake, agreed that she was a shameless besom and worth the watching. Yet, among themselves, as they gathered at the crossroads, there could be detected a tickled humour at the idea of this matriarchal household set up among them, and one man expressed the opinion that if there was any truth in the old saying that 'a man maun ask his wife's leave to thrive' then the Echlins would do rightly with Martha Gomartin's girl.

While the neighbours greatly exaggerated Sarah's position in Rathard, there was no doubt that a subtle change in relationship had come about between the men and the woman. Sarah was indeed, as she had told Sorleyson, behaving with strict impartiality to the brothers, and because of this she had unobtrusively taken control of the house. Yet, she had not done it designedly.

Hamilton and Frank, for different reasons, encouraged her towards this end. For all the different, even antagonistic traits in their characters, they were both men of a fibre who did not willingly repudiate a deed whether it proved to be profitable or otherwise. Now that the child was born and the brothers realized the disrepute into which they had fallen, they felt the necessity to achieve some unity among themselves. For that, an equilibrium was necessary so they accepted Sarah's management of the economy of the farm.

It would have been unnatural if the woman had not felt some triumph at this turn of circumstance. But soon it became a matter of acceptance. It is the men and women who are unsure of themselves who are for ever triumphing over their work. But Sarah stood above, and accomplished every task with ease. She had the prudence, the physical persistence, the eternal patience of the peasant. With Hamilton, she felt a deep sense of understanding, of being cherished, but with Frank she knew that the truce was only temporary. She shared herself between them both, in body and in mind, and so disarmed the younger brother.

1   A term of abuse. In Irish *pachaille* is a swelling or bunion.

PATRICK KAVANAGH
from *Envoy*, April 1951

Kavanagh's telling satire on the burgeoning Joyce industry has more than a grain of truth.

WHO KILLED JAMES JOYCE?

Who killed James Joyce?
I, said the commentator,
I killed James Joyce
For my graduation.

What weapon was used
To slay mighty Ulysses?
The weapon that was used
Was a Harvard thesis.

How did you bury Joyce?
In a broadcast Symposium.
That's how we buried Joyce
To a tuneful encomium.

Who carried the coffin out?
Six Dublin codgers
Led into Langham Place
By W.R. Rodgers.[1]

Who said the burial prayers? —
Please do not hurt me —
Joyce was no Protestant,
Surely not Bertie?

Who killed Finnegan?
I, said a Yale-man,
I was the man who made
The corpse for the wake man.

And did you get high marks,
The Ph.D.?
I got the B.Litt.
And my master's degree.

Did you get money
For your Joycean knowledge?
I got a scholarship
To Trinity College.

I made the pilgrimage
In the Bloomsday swelter
From the Martello Tower
To the cabby's shelter.[2]

1   BBC centre in London. In 1945 W.R. Rodgers ('Bertie') took up a post at the BBC in London where he was responsible for a series of broadcasts on Irish writers, later published as *Irish Literary Portraits* (1972).
2   At Sandycove, setting for the opening of *Ulysses*. The cabman's shelter under Loop Line Bridge near the Custom House is the setting for the Eumaeus episode.

PADRAIC FALLON
from *The Dublin Magazine*, October–December 1951

Padraic Fallon's meditation on the figure of Yeats includes reference to several of Yeats's poems which I have left unglossed. Fallon's mixed attitudes to Yeats are also worth unpicking. Padraic Fallon (1905–74) was born in Athenry in County Galway but lived for most of his life in Wexford, where he earned his living in the Customs and Excise Department. His verse, which was collected posthumously, is distinguished by its engagement with the Revival and by its commitment to the present. According to his son Brian Fallon, his father is 'the great Outsider of modern Irish writing'. See Padraic Fallon, *Poems and Versions* (1983).

YEATS'S TOWER AT BALLYLEE

Is every modern nation like the Tower
Half-dead at the top?
       — *W. B. Yeats.*

A pilgrimage is one slow foot
After the other, the agony of the heart
That looks to a place that will ripen like a fruit.
Yet I arrive in a Ford car
At the Tower talking of markets and wool
And corn drowned in the stook, the country around
Rain-rotten, the wet road buzzing like a spool
And trees at their year's end
Dropping the loaded sky to the ground.
I arrive talking of heifers and wool
And am confronted by the soul
Of a man in whom man cried like a great wound.

Somewhere a man will touch his image and burn
Like a candle before it. What happened here
In this ruined place of water and drowned corn
May still be here.
The oaken door hangs open, I go in
To a desolate underground that drips;
Shadows are on the stairs, the walls are weeping
A peacock paint, where a shoe slips
I clamber into a chamber like a tomb
Or a dim woodcut by William Morris
And suddenly I know the tower is
A boy's dream and the background of his rhyme.

Here where country blood was spilt
Neither earth nor stone cries out for this is a
    dream-structure
All that the brazen Norman[1] built
To house a score of bullies in black armour
Deflected and turned to phantasy

By the boy who brooded on book and paint
Long mornings in his father's study
As mediaeval as a saint:
This is the Tower at last, its passion spent
And wearied of its own brutality
Where a boy could dream like Gabriel Rossetti;
Useless as verse and as magnificent.

I turn from the arty chimneypiece where glass
Has the pale wash of dreamy things and climb
Through a rude and navel arch, I pass
A sentry-go where no man turned a rhyme;
And the narrow stairway leads me to the place
Where he worked at the great table
Or lifted his tall height to pace
The enormous floor of his own fable;
Did he wear iron then, I wonder,
Or when the shadows stole the candle-light
Imagine himself all constellated night?
Il Penseroso[2] in the magic chamber?

Yet nothing is here but the wind in the swinging
    windows
And the roar of the flood waters far below,
Not a house in sight, the corn in rows
Drowned and the drizzle rotting in the meadows:
The earth that cares for nothing but its seasons
Of lust and fruiting and death
Worked all about him here and gave no reasons
Why any man should waste his breath
In delicate definitions of a mild
World where a man is the whole,
The individual soul
A heavenly cradle for the newborn child.

From the boy's dream to this reality
Of brutal weather and brutal stone
The Norman brought him. I come on the right day
To see for myself how earth can change a scene.

Rain and desolation, isolation
And fear in civil war can bring a man
To that harsh point in contemplation
Where soul no longer seems the sun:
In that bleak vision can man live,
Not summing up heaven and earth in measure?
Can he spend himself like a rich treasure
Where only the animal qualities survive?

Here at last he knew what opposites
War in one person. He became a man.
And the man divided into the primitive cross
Of two men in one rhythm. When the Norman
Came to the top the poet's words were blood
And what was good but a mere vision
Of arrogant foray, rape, and ride.
And then soul took its turn and with precision
Divined like an architect a house of life
Where violence had an energetic place
Only to find a holy face
Stare back serenely from the end of strife.

I climb to the wasting storey at the top.
His symbol's there where water and watery air
Soak through the plaster. The higher we clamber up
Into ourselves the greater seems the danger;
For the wider the vision then
On a desolate and more desolate world
Where the inspirations of men
Are taken by man and hurled
From shape into evil shape;
With the good and the grace gone out of them
Where indeed is there hope for men?
So every civilization tires at the top.

Around me now from this great height
Is a vision I did not seek. I have avoided it
And now I am forty-five;
And wars blow up again, the east is lit,
Towns burn, villages are bombed,
With people everywhere in flight,
Their households on a handcart, or entombed
In homes that fell about them in the night,
And dragging children homeless in the air;
A mass migration of the humble

Before some war-mad general.
O the higher we climb up the wider our despair.

This tower where the poet thought to play
Out some old romance to the end caught up
The dream and the dreamer in its brutal way
And the dream died here upon the crumbling top.
I know the terror of his vision now:
A poet dies in every poem, even
As blossom dies when fruit comes on the bough,
And world is endless time in which things happen
In endless repetition, every man
Repetitive as a pattern, no soul
But the sprawling spirit of the whole
Massing upon the careless earth like frogspawn.
Everywhere is the world. And not less here
Because the stream, dividing, moats the place.
To live a fairy tale he bought this tower
And married a woman with a pleasant face;
And built in bookshelves, cupboards, hung
His pictures up and walked around
His beehive and his acre, wrung
Some civilization from the ground:
And yet instead of rhyming country ease
As in the Eighteenth century we find
Him raving like a man gone blind
At the bloody vision that usurped his eyes.

Below me in the road two countrymen
Are talking of cattle and the price of wool,
Glad of the gossip and something held in common.
That scene would have been peaceful
An hour ago, but now I stumble down
In horror, knowing that there is no way
Of protest left to poet or to clown
That will enlarge his future by one day.
I could beat a policeman, bawl in a square, do gaol
For something silly. And what avails it? I
Step out into the drizzle of the sky
Despairingly, to talk of the price of wool.

1   Thoor Ballylee was built probably in the fourteenth
     century by the Anglo-Norman de Burgo family.
2   A reference to a line in Yeats's poem 'My House', itself a
     reference to Milton's 'Il Penseroso'.

W. R. RODGERS
from W. R. Rogers, *Europa and the Bull* (1952)

A single-minded erotic poem by an ex-Presbyterian minister.

THE NET

Quick, woman, in your net
Catch the silver I fling!
O I am deep in your debt,
Draw tight, skin-tight, the string,
And rake the silver in.
No fisher ever yet
Drew such a cunning ring.

Ah, shifty as the fin
Of any fish this flesh
That, shaken to the shin,
Now shoals into your mesh,
Bursting to be held in;
Purse-proud and pebble-hard,
Its pence like shingle showered.

Open the haul, and shake
The fill of shillings free,
Let all the satchels break
And leap about the knee
In shoals of ecstasy.
Guineas and gills will flake
At each gull-plunge of me.

Though all the Angels, and
Saint Michael at their head,
Nightly contrive to stand
On guard about your bed,
Yet none dare take a hand,
But each can only spread
His eagle-eye instead.

But I, being man, can kiss
And bed-spread-eagle too;
All flesh shall come to this,
Being less than angel is,
Yet higher far in bliss
As it entwines with you.

Come, make no sound, my sweet;
Turn down the candid lamp
And draw the equal quilt
Over our naked guilt.

SEÁN Ó RÍORDÁIN
from Seán Ó Ríordáin, *Eireaball Spideoige* (1952)

Seán Ó Ríordáin (1917–77), considered by some critics one of the finest poets writing in Irish this century, was born in Ballyvourney, County Cork, and after school became a clerk in Cork City Hall from 1936 until 1965. In 1938 he was diagnosed as suffering from pulmonary tuberculosis, and graduated, as he wittily remarked, with TB rather than with a BA. The first volume of his verse was *Eireaball Spideoige*, followed in 1964 by *Brosna* (see p. 782 below). Here, recreating a hospital ward, Ó Ríordáin reveals a playful side that conjoins the physical with the spiritual.

SIOLLABADH

Bhí banaltra in otharlann
  I ngile an tráthnóna,
Is cuisleanna i leapachaibh
  Ag preabarnaigh go tomhaiste,
Do sheas sí os gach leaba
  Agus d'fhan sí seal ag comhaireamh
Is do bhreac sí síos an mheadaracht

SYLLABLING

A nurse was in a hospital
  In the afternoon brightness
And pulses there were throbbing
  Regularly in beds;
She stood before each bed-stead
  And stayed a short while counting,
Jotting down the measure

Bhí ag siollabadh ina meoraibh,	Syllabling in each wrist;
Is do shiollaib sí go rithimeach	She syllabled herself at length
Fé dheireadh as an seomra,	Rhythmically from the ward
Is d'fhág 'na diaidh mar chlaisceadal	And left behind a chorus
Na cuisleanna ag comhaireamh:	Of pulses keeping time:
Ansin do leath an tAngelus	It was then the Angelus spread its
Im-shiollabchrith ar bheolaibh,	Syllable-shake across lips there
Ach do tháinig éag ar Amenibh	Till Amens died away
Mar chogarnach sa tseomra:	Like whispering in the ward:
Do leanadh leis an gcantaireacht	But the murmuring continued
I mainistir na feola,	In the monastery of flesh,
Na cuisleanna mar mhanachaibh	The pulses going like monks
Ag siollabadh na nónta.	Syllabling their plain-chant.

translated by Patrick Crotty

FRANK O'CONNOR
from *Irish Writing*, November 1952

Frank O'Connor's celebrated 'bifocalized' story about childhood seen through an adult's eyes.

My Œdipus Complex

Father was in the army all through the war — the first war, I mean — so, up to the age of five, I never saw much of him, and what I saw did not worry me. Sometimes I woke and there was a big figure in khaki peering down at me in the candlelight. Sometimes in the early morning I heard the slamming of the front door and the clatter of nailed boots down the cobbles of the lane. These were Father's entrances and exits. Like Santa Claus he came and went mysteriously.

In fact, I rather liked his visits, though it was an uncomfortable squeeze between Mother and him when I got into the big bed in the early morning. He smoked, which gave him a pleasant musty smell, and shaved, an operation of astounding interest. Each time he left a trail of souvenirs — model tanks and Gurkha knives with handles made of bullet cases, and German helmets and cap badges and button-sticks, and all sorts of military equipment — carefully stowed away in a long box on top of the wardrobe, in case they ever came in handy. There was a bit of the magpie about Father; he expected everything to come in handy. When his back was turned, Mother let me get a chair and rummage through his treasures. She didn't seem to think so highly of them as he did.

The war was the most peaceful period of my life. The window of my attic faced southeast. My mother had curtained it, but that had small effect. I always woke with the first light and, with all the responsibilities of the previous day melted, feeling myself rather like the sun, ready to illumine and rejoice. Life never seemed so simple and clear and full of possibilities as then. I put my feet out from under the clothes — I called them Mrs Left and Mrs Right — and invented dramatic situations for them in which they discussed the problems of the day. At least Mrs Right did; she was very demonstrative, but I hadn't the same control of Mrs Left, so she mostly contented herself with nodding agreement.

They discussed what Mother and I should do during the day, what Santa Claus should give a fellow for Christmas, and what steps should be taken to brighten the home. There was that little matter of the baby, for instance. Mother and I could never agree about that. Ours was the only house in the terrace without a new baby, and Mother said we couldn't afford one till Father came back from the war because they cost seventeen and six.[1] That showed how simple she was. The Geneys up the road had a baby, and everyone knew they couldn't afford seventeen and six. It was probably a cheap baby, and Mother wanted something really good, but I felt she was too exclusive. The Geneys' baby would have done us fine.

Having settled my plans for the day, I got up, put a chair under the attic window, and lifted the frame high enough to stick out my head. The window overlooked the front gardens of the terrace behind ours, and beyond these it looked over a deep valley to the tall, red-brick houses terraced up the opposite hillside, which were all still in shadow, while those at our side of the valley were all lit up, though with long strange shadows that made them seem unfamiliar; rigid and painted.

After that I went into Mother's room and climbed into the big bed. She woke and I began to tell her of my schemes. By this time, though I never seem to have noticed it, I was petrified in my nightshirt, and I thawed as I talked until, the last frost melted, I fell asleep beside her and woke again only when I heard her below in the kitchen, making the breakfast.

After breakfast we went into town; heard Mass at St Augustine's and said a prayer for Father, and did the shopping. If the afternoon was fine we either went for a walk in the country or a visit to Mother's great friend in the convent, Mother St Dominic. Mother had them all praying for Father, and every night, going to bed, I asked God to send him back safe from the war to us. Little, indeed, did I know what I was praying for!

One morning, I got into the big bed, and there, sure enough, was Father in his usual Santa Claus manner, but later, instead of uniform, he put on his best blue suit, and Mother was as pleased as anything. I saw nothing to be pleased about, because, out of uniform, Father was altogether less interesting, but she only beamed, and explained that our prayers had been answered, and off we went to Mass to thank God for having brought Father safely home.

The irony of it! That very day when he came in to dinner he took off his boots and put on his slippers, donned the dirty old cap he wore about the house to save him from colds, crossed his legs, and began to talk gravely to Mother, who looked anxious. Naturally, I disliked her looking anxious, because it destroyed her good looks, so I interrupted him.

'Just a moment, Larry!' she said gently.

This was only what she said when we had boring visitors, so I attached no importance to it and went on talking.

'Do be quiet, Larry!' she said impatiently. 'Don't you hear me talking to Daddy?'

This was the first time I had heard those ominous words, 'talking to Daddy', and I couldn't help feeling that if this was how God answered prayers, he couldn't listen to them very attentively.

'Why are you talking to Daddy?' I asked with as great a show of indifference as I could muster.

'Because Daddy and I have business to discuss. Now, don't interrupt again!'

In the afternoon, at Mother's request, Father took me for a walk. This time we went into town instead of out the country, and I thought at first, in my usual optimistic way, that it might be an improvement. It was nothing of the sort. Father and I had quite different notions of a walk in town. He had no proper interest in trams, ships, and horses, and the only thing that seemed to divert him was talking to fellows as old as himself. When I wanted to stop he simply went on, dragging me behind him by the hand; when he wanted to stop I had no alternative but to do the same. I noticed that it seemed to be a sign that he wanted to stop for a long time whenever he leaned against a wall. The second time I saw him do it I got wild. He seemed to be settling himself forever. I pulled him by the coat and trousers, but, unlike Mother who, if you were too persistent, got into a wax and said: 'Larry, if you don't behave yourself, I'll give you a good slap,' Father had an extraordinary capacity for amiable inattention. I sized him up and wondered would I cry, but he seemed to be too remote to be annoyed even by that. Really, it was like going for a walk with a mountain! He either ignored the wrenching and pummelling entirely, or else glanced down with a grin of amusement from his peak. I had never met anyone so absorbed in himself as he seemed.

At teatime, 'talking to Daddy' began again, complicated this time by the fact that he had an evening paper, and every few minutes he put it down and told Mother something new out of it. I felt this was foul play. Man for man, I was prepared to compete with him any time for Mother's attention, but when he had it all made up for him by other people it left me no chance. Several times I tried to change the subject without success.

'You must be quiet while Daddy is reading, Larry,' Mother said impatiently.

It was clear that she either genuinely liked talking to Father better than talking to me, or else that he had some terrible hold on her which made her afraid to admit the truth.

'Mummy,' I said that night when she was tucking me up, 'do you think if I prayed hard God would send Daddy back to the war?'

She seemed to think about that for a moment.

'No, dear,' she said with a smile. 'I don't think he would.'

'Why wouldn't he, Mummy?'

'Because there isn't a war any longer, dear.'

'But, Mummy, couldn't God make another war, if He liked?'

'He wouldn't like to, dear. It's not God who makes wars, but bad people.'

'Oh!' I said.

I was disappointed about that. I began to think that God wasn't quite what he was cracked up to be.

Next morning I woke at my usual hour, feeling like a bottle of champagne. I put out my feet and invented a long conversation in which Mrs Right talked of the trouble she had with her own father till she put him in the Home. I didn't quite know what the Home was but it sounded the right place for Father. Then I got my chair and stuck my head out of the attic window. Dawn was just breaking, with a guilty air that made me feel I had caught it in the act. My head bursting with stories and schemes, I stumbled in next door, and in the half-darkness scrambled into the big bed. There was no room at Mother's side so I had to get between her and Father. For the time being I had forgotten about him, and for several minutes I sat bolt upright, racking my brains to know what I could do with him. He was taking up more than his fair share of the bed, and I couldn't get comfortable, so I gave him several kicks that made him grunt and stretch. He made room all right, though. Mother waked and felt for me. I settled back comfortably in the warmth of the bed with my thumb in my mouth.

'Mummy!' I hummed, loudly and contentedly.

'Sssh! dear,' she whispered. 'Don't wake Daddy!'

This was a new development, which threatened to be even more serious than 'talking to Daddy'. Life without my early-morning conferences was unthinkable.

'Why?' I asked severely.

'Because poor Daddy is tired.'

This seemed to me a quite inadequate reason, and I was sickened by the sentimentality of her 'poor Daddy'. I never liked that sort of gush; it always struck me as insincere.

'Oh!' I said lightly. Then in my most winning tone: 'Do you know where I want to go with you today, Mummy?'

'No, dear,' she sighed.

'I want to go down the Glen and fish for thorny-backs with my new net, and then I want to go out to the Fox and Hounds, and —'

'Don't-wake-Daddy!' she hissed angrily, clapping her hand across my mouth.

But it was too late. He was awake, or nearly so. He grunted and reached for the matches. Then he stared incredulously at his watch.

'Like a cup of tea, dear?' asked Mother in a meek, hushed voice I had never heard her use before. It sounded almost as though she were afraid.

'Tea?' he exclaimed indignantly. 'Do you know what the time is?'

'And after that I want to go up the Rathcooney Road,' I said loudly, afraid I'd forget something in all those interruptions.

'Go to sleep at once, Larry!' she said sharply.

I began to snivel. I couldn't concentrate, the way the pair went on, and smothering my early-morning schemes was like burying a family from the cradle.

Father said nothing, but lit his pipe and sucked it, looking out into the shadows without minding Mother or me. I knew he was mad. Every time I made a remark Mother hushed me irritably. I was mortified. I felt it wasn't fair; there was even something sinister in it. Every time I had pointed out to her the waste of making two beds when we could both sleep in one, she had told me it was healthier like that, and now here was this man, this stranger, sleeping with her without the least regard for her health!

He got up early and made tea, but though he brought Mother a cup he brought none for me.

'Mummy,' I shouted, 'I want a cup of tea, too.'

'Yes, dear,' she said patiently. 'You can drink from Mummy's saucer.'

That settled it. Either Father or I would have to leave the house. I didn't want to drink from Mother's saucer; I wanted to be treated as an equal in my own home, so, just to spite her, I drank it all and left none for her. She took that quietly, too.

But that night when she was putting me to bed she said gently:

'Larry, I want you to promise me something.'

'What is it?' I asked.

'Not to come in and disturb poor Daddy in the morning. Promise?'

'Poor Daddy' again! I was becoming suspicious of everything involving that quite impossible man.

'Why?' I asked.

'Because poor Daddy is worried and tired and he doesn't sleep well.'

'Why doesn't he, Mummy?'

'Well, you know, don't you, that while he was at the war Mummy got the pennies from the Post Office?'

'From Miss MacCarthy?'

'That's right. But now, you see, Miss MacCarthy hasn't any more pennies, so Daddy must go out and find us some. You know what would happen if he couldn't?'

'No,' I said, 'tell us.'

'Well, I think we might have to go out and beg for them like the poor old woman on Fridays. We wouldn't like that, would we?'

'No,' I agreed. 'We wouldn't.'

'So you'll promise not to come in and wake him?'

'Promise.'

Mind you, I meant that. I knew pennies were a serious matter, and I was all against having to go out and beg like the old woman on Fridays. Mother laid out all my toys in a complete ring round the bed so that, whatever way I got out, I was bound to fall over one of them.

When I woke I remembered my promise all right. I got up and sat on the floor and played — for hours, it seemed to me. Then I got my chair and looked out the attic window for more hours, I wished it was time for Father to wake; I wished someone would make me a cup of tea. I didn't feel in the least like the sun; instead, I was bored and so very, very cold! I simply longed for the warmth and depth of the big featherbed.

At last I could stand it no longer. I went into the next room. As there was still no room at Mother's side I climbed over her and she woke with a start.

'Larry,' she whispered, gripping my arm very tightly, 'what did you promise?'

'But I did, Mummy,' I wailed, caught in the very act. 'I was quiet for ever so long.'

'Oh, dear, and you're perished!' she said sadly, feeling me all over. 'Now, if I let you stay will you promise not to talk?'

'But I want to talk, Mummy,' I wailed.

'That has nothing to do with it,' she said with a firmness that was new to me. 'Daddy wants to sleep. Now, do you understand that?'

I understood it only too well. I wanted to talk, he wanted to sleep — whose house was it, anyway?

'Mummy,' I said with equal firmness, 'I think it would be healthier for Daddy to sleep in his own bed.'

That seemed to stagger her, because she said nothing for a while.

'Now, once for all,' she went on, 'you're to be perfectly quiet or go back to your own bed. Which is it to be?'

The injustice of it got me down. I had convicted her out of her own mouth of inconsistency and unreasonableness, and she hadn't even attempted to reply. Full of spite, I gave Father a kick, which she didn't notice but which made him grunt and open his eyes in alarm.

'What time is it?' he asked in a panic-stricken voice, not looking at Mother but at the door, as if he saw someone there.

'It's early yet,' she replied soothingly. 'It's only the child. Go to sleep again. . . . Now, Larry,' she added, getting out of bed, 'you've wakened Daddy and you must go back.'

This time, for all her quiet air, I knew she meant it, and knew that my principal rights and privileges were as good as lost unless I asserted them at once. As she lifted me, I gave a screech, enough to wake the dead, not to mind Father. He groaned.

'That damn child! Doesn't he ever sleep?'

'It's only a habit, dear,' she said quietly, though I could see she was vexed.

'Well, it's time he got out of it,' shouted Father, beginning to heave in the bed. He suddenly gathered all the bedclothes about him, turned to the wall, and then looked back over his shoulder with nothing showing only two small, spiteful, dark eyes. The man looked very wicked.

To open the bedroom door, Mother had to let me down, and I broke free and dashed for the farthest corner, screeching. Father sat bolt upright in bed.

'Shut up, you little puppy!' he said in a choking voice.

I was so astonished that I stopped screeching. Never, never had anyone spoken to me in that tone before. I looked at him incredulously and saw his face convulsed with rage. It was only then that I fully realized how God had codded me, listening to my prayers for the safe return of this monster.

'Shut up, you!' I bawled, beside myself.

'What's that you said?' shouted Father, making a wild leap out of the bed.

'Mick! Mick!' cried Mother. 'Don't you see the child isn't used to you?'

'I see he's better fed than taught,' snarled Father, waving his arms wildly. 'He wants his bottom smacked.'

All his previous shouting was as nothing to these obscene words referring to my person. They really made my blood boil.

'Smack your own!' I screamed hysterically. 'Smack your own! Shut up! Shut up!'

At this he lost his patience and let fly at me. He did it with the lack of conviction you'd expect of a man under Mother's horrified eyes, and it ended up as a mere tap, but the sheer indignity of being struck at all by a stranger, a total stranger who had cajoled his way back from the war into our big bed as a result of my innocent intercession, made me completely dotty. I shrieked and shrieked, and danced in my bare feet, and Father, looking awkward and hairy in nothing but a short grey army shirt, glared down at me like a mountain out for murder. I think it must have been then that I realized he was jealous too. And there stood Mother in her nightdress, looking as if her heart was broken between us. I hoped she felt as she looked. It seemed to me that she deserved it all.

From that morning out my life was a hell. Father and I were enemies, open and avowed. We conducted a series of skirmishes against one another, he trying to steal my time with Mother and I his. When she was sitting on my bed, telling me a story, he took to looking for some pair of old boots which he alleged he had left behind him at the beginning of the war. While he talked to Mother I played loudly with my toys to show my total lack of concern. He created a terrible scene one evening when he came in from work and found me at his box, playing with his regimental badges, Gurkha knives and button-sticks. Mother got up and took the box from me.

'You mustn't play with Daddy's toys unless he lets you, Larry,' she said severely. 'Daddy doesn't play with yours.'

For some reason Father looked at her as if she had struck him and then turned away with a scowl.

'Those are not toys,' he growled, taking down the box again to see had I lifted anything. 'Some of those curios are very rare and valuable.'

But as time went on I saw more and more how he managed to alienate Mother and me. What made it worse was that I couldn't grasp his method or see what attraction he had for Mother. In every possible way he was less winning than I. He had a common accent and made noises at his tea. I thought for a while that it might be the newspapers she was interested in, so I made up bits of news of my own to read to her. Then I thought it might be the smoking, which I personally thought attractive, and took his pipes and went round the house dribbling into them till he caught me. I even made noises at my tea, but Mother only told me I was disgusting. It all seemed to hinge round that unhealthy habit of sleeping together, so I made a point of dropping into their bedroom and nosing round, talking to myself, so that they wouldn't know I was watching them, but they were never up to anything that I could see. In the end it beat me. It seemed to depend on being grown-up and giving people rings, and I realized I'd have to wait.

But at the same time I wanted him to see that I was only waiting, not giving up the fight. One evening when he was being particularly obnoxious, chattering away well above my head, I let him have it.

'Mummy,' I said, 'do you know what I'm going to do when I grow up?'

'No, dear,' she replied. 'What?'

'I'm going to marry you,' I said quietly.

Father gave a great guffaw out of him, but he didn't take me in. I knew it must only be pretence. And Mother, in spite of everything, was pleased. I felt she was probably relieved to know that one day Father's hold on her would be broken.

'Won't that be nice?' she said with a smile.

'It'll be very nice,' I said confidently. 'Because we're going to have lots and lots of babies.'

'That's right, dear,' she said placidly. 'I think we'll have one soon, and then you'll have plenty of company.'

I was no end pleased about that because it showed that in spite of the way she gave in to Father she still considered my wishes. Besides, it would put the Geneys in their place.

It didn't turn out like that, though. To begin with, she was very preoccupied — I supposed about where she would get the seventeen and six — and though Father took to staying out late in the evenings it did me no particular good. She stopped taking me for walks, became as touchy as blazes, and smacked me for nothing at all. Sometimes I wished I'd never mentioned the confounded baby — I seemed to have a genius for bringing calamity on myself.

And calamity it was! Sonny arrived in the most appalling hullabaloo — even that much he couldn't do without a fuss — and from the first moment I disliked him. He was a difficult child — so far as I was concerned he was always difficult — and demanded far too much attention. Mother was simply silly about him, and couldn't see when he was only showing off. As company he was worse than useless. He slept all day, and I had to go round the house on tiptoe to avoid waking him. It wasn't any longer a question of not waking Father. The slogan now was 'Don't-wake-Sonny!' I couldn't understand why the child wouldn't sleep at the proper time, so whenever Mother's back was turned I woke him. Sometimes to keep him awake I pinched him as well. Mother caught me at it one day and gave me a most unmerciful flaking.

One evening, when Father was coming in from work, I was playing trains in the front garden. I let on not to notice him; instead, I pretended to be talking to myself, and said in a loud voice: 'If another bloody baby comes into this house, I'm going out.'

Father stopped dead and looked at me over his shoulder.

'What's that you said?' he asked sternly.

'I was only talking to myself,' I replied, trying to conceal my panic. 'It's private.'

He turned and went in without a word. Mind you, I intended it as a solemn warning, but its effect was quite different. Father started being quite nice to me. I could understand that, of course. Mother was quite sickening about Sonny. Even at mealtimes she'd get up and gawk at him in the cradle with an idiotic smile, and tell Father to do the same. He was always polite about it, but he looked so puzzled you could see he didn't know what she was talking about. He complained of the way Sonny cried at night, but she only got cross and said that Sonny never cried except when there was something up with him — which was a flaming lie, because Sonny never had anything up with him, and only cried for attention. It was really painful to see how simple-minded she was. Father wasn't attractive, but he had a fine intelligence. He saw through Sonny, and now he knew that I saw through him as well.

One night I woke with a start. There was someone beside me in the bed. For one wild moment I felt sure it must be Mother, having come to her senses and left Father for good, but then I heard Sonny in convulsions in the next room, and Mother saying: 'There! There! There!' and I knew it wasn't she. It was Father. He was lying beside me, wide awake, breathing hard and apparently as mad as hell.

After a while it came to me what he was mad about. It was his turn now. After turning me out of the big bed, he had been turned out himself. Mother had no consideration now for anyone but that poisonous pup, Sonny. I couldn't help feeling sorry for Father. I had been through it all myself, and even at that age I was magnanimous. I began to stroke him down and say: 'There! There!' He wasn't exactly responsive.

'Aren't you asleep either?' he snarled.

'Ah, come on and put your arm around us, can't you?' I said, and he did, in a sort of way. Gingerly, I suppose, is how you'd describe it. He was very bony but better than nothing.

At Christmas he went out of his way to buy me a really nice model railway.

1   88p (rounded up) in decimal currency.

SAMUEL BECKETT
from Samuel Beckett, *Molloy* (1954)

It is worth listening to Jack MacGowran, one of Beckett's favourite actors, reading this passage.

I took advantage of being at the seaside to lay in a store of sucking-stones. They were pebbles but I call them stones. Yes, on this occasion I laid in a considerable store. I distributed them equally among my four pockets, and sucked them turn and turn about. This raised a problem which I first solved in the following way. I had say sixteen stones, four in each of my four pockets these being the two pockets of my trousers and the two pockets of my greatcoat. Taking a stone from the right pocket of my greatcoat, and putting it in my mouth, I replaced it in the right pocket of my greatcoat by a stone from the right pocket of my trousers, which I replaced by a stone from the left pocket of my trousers, which I replaced by a stone from the left pocket of my greatcoat, which I replaced by the stone which was in my mouth, as soon as I had finished sucking it. Thus there were still four stones in each of my four pockets, but not quite the same stones. And when the desire to suck took hold of me again, I drew again on the right pocket of my greatcoat, certain of not taking the same stone as the last time. And while I sucked it I rearranged the other stones in the way I have just described. And so on. But this solution did not satisfy me fully. For it did not escape me that, by an extraordinary hazard, the four stones circulating thus might always be the same four. In which case, far from sucking the sixteen stones turn and turn about, I was really only sucking four, always the same, turn and turn about. But I shuffled them well in my pockets, before I began to suck, and again, while I sucked, before transferring them, in the hope of obtaining a more general circulation of the stones from pocket to pocket. But this was only a makeshift that could not long content a man like me. So I began to look for something else. And the first thing I hit upon was that I might do better to transfer the stones four by four, instead of one by one, that is to say, during the sucking, to take the three stones remaining in the right pocket of my greatcoat and replace them by the four in the right pocket of my trousers, and these by the four in the left pocket of my trousers, and these by the four in the left pocket of my greatcoat, and finally these by the three from the right pocket of my greatcoat, plus the one, as soon as I had finished sucking it, which was in my mouth. Yes, it seemed to me at first that by so doing I would arrive at a better result. But on further reflection I had to change my mind and confess that the circulation of the stones four by four came to exactly the same thing as their circulation one by one. For if I was certain of finding each time, in the right pocket of my greatcoat, four stones totally different from their immediate predecessors, the possibility nevertheless remained of my always chancing on the same stone, within each group of four, and consequently of my sucking, not the sixteen turn and turn about as I wished, but in fact four only, always the same, turn and turn about. So I had to seek elsewhere than in the mode of circulation. For no matter how I caused the stones to circulate, I always ran the same risk. It was obvious that by increasing the number of my pockets I was bound to increase my chances of enjoying my stones in the way I planned, that is to say one after the other until their number was exhausted. Had I had eight pockets, for example, instead of the four I did have, then even the most diabolical hazard could not have prevented me from sucking at least eight of my sixteen stones, turn and turn about. The truth is I should have needed sixteen pockets in order to be quite easy in my mind. And for a long time I could see no other conclusion than this, that short of having sixteen pockets, each with its stone, I could never reach the goal I had set myself, short of an extraordinary hazard. And if at a pitch I could double the number of my pockets, were it only by dividing each pocket in two, with the help of a few safety-pins let us say, to quadruple them seemed to be more than I could manage. And I did not feel inclined to take all that trouble for a half-measure. For I was beginning to lose all sense of measure, after all this wrestling and wrangling, and to say, All or nothing. And if I was tempted for an instant to establish a more equitable proportion between my stones and my pockets, by reducing the former to the number of the latter, it was only for an instant. For it would have been an admission of defeat. And sitting on the shore, before the sea, the sixteen stones spread out before my eyes, I gazed at them in anger and perplexity. For just as I had difficulty in sitting on a chair, or in an arm-chair, because of my stiff leg you understand, so I had none in sitting on the ground, because of my stiff leg, for it was about this time that my good leg, good in the sense that it was not stiff, began to stiffen. I needed a prop under the ham you understand, and even under the whole length of the leg, the prop of the earth. And while I gazed thus at my stones, revolving interminable martingales[1] all equally defective, and crushing handfuls of sand, so

that the sand ran through my fingers and fell back on the strand, yes, while thus I lulled my mind and part of my body, one day suddenly it dawned on the former, dimly, that I might perhaps achieve my purpose without increasing the number of my pockets, or reducing the number of my stones, but simply by sacrificing the principle of trim. The meaning of this illumination, which suddenly began to sing within me, like a verse of Isaiah, or of Jeremiah, I did not penetrate at once, and notably the word trim, which I had never met with, in this sense, long remained obscure. Finally I seemed to grasp that this word trim could not here mean anything else, anything better, than the distribution of the sixteen stones in four groups of four, one group in each pocket, and that it was my refusal to consider any distribution other than this that had vitiated my calculations until then and rendered the problem literally insoluble. And it was on the basis of this interpretation, whether right or wrong, that I finally reached a solution, inelegant assuredly, but sound, sound. Now I am willing to believe, indeed I firmly believe, that other solutions to this problem might have been found, and indeed may still be found, no less sound, but much more elegant, than the one I shall now describe, if I can. And I believe too that had I been a little more insistent, a little more resistant, I could have found them myself. But I was tired, but I was tired, and I contented myself ingloriously with the first solution that was a solution, to this problem. But not to go over the heartbreaking stages through which I passed before I came to it, here it is, in all its hideousness. All (all!) that was necessary was to put for example, to begin with, six stones in the right pocket of my greatcoat, or supply-pocket, five in the right pocket of my trousers, and five in the left pocket of my trousers, that makes the lot, twice five ten plus six sixteen, and none, for none remained, in the left pocket of my greatcoat, which for the time being remained empty, empty of stones that is, for its usual contents remained, as well as occasional objects. For where do you think I hid my vegetable knife, my silver, my horn and the other things that I have not yet named, perhaps shall never name. Good. Now I can begin to suck. Watch me closely. I take a stone from the right pocket of my greatcoat, suck it, stop sucking it, put it in the left pocket of my greatcoat, the one empty (of stones). I take a second stone from the right pocket of my greatcoat, suck it, put it in the left pocket of my greatcoat. And so on until the right pocket of my greatcoat is empty (apart from its usual and casual contents) and the six stones I have just sucked, one after the other, are all in the left pocket of my greatcoat. Pausing then, and concentrating, so as not to make a balls of it, I transfer to the right pocket of my greatcoat, suck it, put it in the left pocket of my greatcoat, in which there are no stones left, the five stones in the right pocket of my trousers, which I replace by the five stones in the left pocket of my trousers, which I replace by the six stones in the left pocket of my greatcoat. At this stage then the left pocket of my greatcoat is again empty of stones, while the right pocket of my greatcoat is again supplied, and in the right way, that is to say with other stones than those I have just sucked. These other stones I then begin to suck, one after the other, and to transfer as I go along to the left pocket of my greatcoat, being absolutely certain, as far as one can be in an affair of this kind, that I am not sucking the same stones as a moment before, but others. And when the right pocket of my greatcoat is again empty (of stones), and the five I have just sucked are all without exception in the left pocket of my greatcoat, then I proceed to the same redistribution as a moment before, or a similar redistribution, that is to say I transfer to the right pocket of my greatcoat, now again available, the five stones in the right pocket of my trousers, which I replace by the six stones in the left pocket of my trousers, which I replace by the five stones in the left pocket of my greatcoat. And there I am ready to begin again. Do I have to go on? No, for it is clear that after the next series, of sucks and transfers, I shall be back where I started, that is to say with the first six stones back in the supply-pocket, the next five in the right pocket of my stinking old trousers and finally the last five in left pocket of same, and my sixteen stones will have been sucked once at least in impeccable succession, not one sucked twice, not one left unsucked. It is true that the next time I could scarcely hope to suck my stones in the same order as the first time and that the first, seventh and twelfth for example of the first cycle might very well be the sixth, eleventh and sixteenth respectively of the second, if the worst came to the worst. But that was a drawback I could not avoid. And if in the cycles taken together utter confusion was bound to reign, at least within each cycle taken separately I could be easy in my mind, at least as easy as one can be, in a proceeding of this kind. For in order for each cycle to be identical, as to the succession of stones in my mouth, and God knows I had set my heart on it, the only means were numbered stones or sixteen pockets. And rather than make twelve more pockets or number of stones, I preferred to make the best of the comparative peace of mind I enjoyed within each cycle taken separately. For it was not enough to number the stones, but I would have had to remember, every time I put a stone in my mouth, the number I needed and look for it in my pocket. Which would have put me off stone for ever, in a very short time. For I would never have been sure of not making a mistake, unless of course I had kept a kind of register, in which to tick off the stones one by one, as I sucked them. And of this I believed myself incapable. No, the only perfect solution would have been the sixteen pockets, symmetrically disposed, each one with its stone. Then I would have needed neither to number nor to think, but merely, as I sucked a given stone, to move on the fifteen others, each to the next pocket, a delicate business admittedly, but within my power, and to call always on the same pocket when I felt like a suck. This would have freed me from all anxiety, not only within each cycle taken separately, but also for the sum of all cycles, though they went on forever. But however imperfect my own solution was, I was pleased at having found it all alone, yes, quite pleased. And if it was perhaps less sound than I had thought in the first flush of discovery, its inelegance never diminished. And it was above all inelegant in this, to my mind, that the uneven distribution was painful to me, bodily. It is true that a kind of equilibrium was reached, at a given moment, in the early stages of each cycle, namely after the third suck and before the fourth, but it did not last long, and the rest of the time I felt the weight of the stones dragging me now to one side, now to the other. So it was something more than a principle I abandoned, when I abandoned the equal distribution, it was a bodily need. But to suck the stones in the way I have described, not haphazard, but with method, was also I think a bodily need. Here then were two incompatible bodily needs, at loggerheads. Such things happen. But deep down I didn't give a tinker's curse about being off my balance, dragged to the right hand and the left, backwards and forwards. And deep down it was all the same to me whether I sucked a different stone each time or always the same stone, until the end of time. For they all tasted exactly the same. And if I had collected sixteen, it was not in order to ballast myself in such and such a way, or to suck them turn about, but simply to have a little store, so as never to be without. But deep down I didn't give a fiddler's curse about being without, when they were all gone they would be all gone, I wouldn't be any the worse off, or hardly any. And the solution to which I rallied in the end was to throw away all the stones but one, which I kept now in one pocket, now in another, and which of course I soon lost, or threw away, or gave away, or swallowed.

1   A system in gambling which consists of doubling the stake when losing in the hope of recouping oneself. (OED)

BRENDAN BEHAN
from Brendan Behan, *The Quare Fellow* (1954)

This version of *The Quare Fellow*, a two-act play, was first performed by Joan Littlewood's Theatre Workshop at the Theatre Royal Stratford in London in May 1956. The play was turned into a film by Arthur Dreifus — shot in part in Kilmainham Jail — and released in 1962. The word quare (queer) has a wide provenance in Ireland. It is used as an intensive in Ulster: 'today is quare and hot', meaning very hot. (P.W. Joyce). More generally it is an adjective denoting something (also used of persons) odd, droll, crafty, strange. As for the underlying meaning of the play, you might begin by reflecting on the line: 'But sure, thanks to God, the Free State didn't change anything more than the badge on the warders' caps.' Here is the first act.

PERSONS IN THE PLAY

Prisoners

DUNLAVIN
NEIGHBOUR
PRISONER A. (*Hard Case*)
PRISONER B. (*The Man of Thirty*)
LIFER
THE OTHER FELLOW
MICKSER
ENGLISH VOICE
SCHOLARA ⎱
SHAYBO ⎰ (*Young Prisoners*)
PRISONER C. (*The Boy from the Island*)
PRISONER D. (*The Embezzler*)
PRISONER E. (*The Bookie*)

Warders

CHIEF WARDER
REGAN
CRIMMIN
DONELLY (*Warder 1*)
THE NEW ONE (*Warder 2*)

THE PRISONER GOVERNOR
HOLY HEALEY
THE HANGMAN
JENKINSON

ACT I

A prisoner sings: he is in one of the punishment cells.

A hungry feeling came o'er me stealing
And the mice were squealing in my prison cell,
And that old triangle
Went jingle jangle,
Along the banks of the Royal Canal.

The curtain rises.
The scene is the bottom floor or landing of a wing in a city prison, 'B.1'. The cell doors are of metal with a card giving the name, age and religion of the occupant. Two of the cells have no cards. The left of the stage leads to the circle, the administrative heart of the prison, and on the right, in the wall and at right angles to the audience, is a window, from which a view may be had of the laundry yard of the women's prison. On the wall and facing the audience is printed in large block shaded Victorian lettering the word 'SILENCE'.

PRISONER:
To begin the morning
The warder bawling
Get out of bed and clean up your cell;
And that old triangle
Went jingle jangle,
Along the banks of the Royal Canal.
A triangle is beaten, loudly and raucously. A WARDER *comes briskly and, swinging a bunch of keys, goes to the vacant cells, looks in the spyholes, takes two white cards from his pocket, and puts one on each door. Then he goes to the other doors, looks in the spyholes and unlocks them.*
Meanwhile the singer in the base punishment cells is on his third verse:
The screw was peeping
And the lag was weeping . . .[1]
But this only gets as far as the second line, for the WARDER *leans over the stairs and shouts down . . .*
WARDER: The screw is listening as well as peeping, and you'll be bloody well weeping if you don't give over your moaning. We might go down there and give you something to moan about. (*The singing stops and he turns and shouts up and down the landing.*) B. Wings: two, three and one. Stand to your doors. Come on, clean up your cells there. (*He goes off R.*)

PRISONERS A *and* B *come out of their cells, collect buckets and brushes, and start the morning's chores.* A *is a man of 40, he has done two 'laggings', a sentence of five years or more, and some preventive detention.* B *is a gentle-looking man and easy-going.*

PRISONER A: Nice day for the races.

PRISONER B: Don't think I can make it today. Too much to do in the office. Did you hear the commotion last night round in D. Wing? A reprieve must have come through.

PRISONER A: Aye, but there's two for a haircut and shave,[2] I wonder which one's been chucked?[3]

PRISONER B: Dunlavin might know; give him a call there.

PRISONER A: Dunlavin!

VOICE (*from cell*):

> There are hands that will welcome you in
> There are lips that I am burning to kiss
> There are two eyes that shine . . .

PRISONER A: Hey, Dunlavin, are you going to scrub that place of yours away?

VOICE:

> Far away where the blue shadows fall
> I will come to contentment and rest,
> And the toils of the day
> Will be all charmed away . . .

PRISONER A: Hey, Dunlavin.

DUNLAVIN *appears in the door of the cell polishing a large enamel chamber pot with a cloth. An old man, he has spent most of his life in jail. Unlike most old lags he has not become absolutely dulled from imprisonment.*

DUNLAVIN: . . . In my little grey home in the West.

PRISONER A: What do you think that is you're polishing — the Railway Cup?

DUNLAVIN: I'm shining this up for a special visitor. Healey of the Department of Justice is coming up today to inspect the cells.

PRISONER A: Will he be round again so soon?

DUNLAVIN: He's always round the day before an execution. I think he must be in the hanging and flogging section.

PRISONER B: Dunlavin, there you are, at the corner of the wing, with the joints in the hot-water pipes bringing you news from every art and part, any time you put your ear to it.

DUNLAVIN: Well? Well?

PRISONER B: Well, what was the commotion last night round in D. Wing? Did the quare fellow get a reprieve?

DUNLAVIN: Just a minute till I put back me little bit of china, and I'll return and tell all. Now which quare fellow do you mean? The fellow beat his wife to death with the silver-topped cane, that was a presentation to him from the Combined Staffs, Excess and Refunds branch of the late Great Southern Railways,[4] was reprieved, though why him any more than the other fellow is more nor I can tell.

PRISONER A: Well, I suppose they looked at it, he only killed her and left it at that. He didn't cut the corpse up afterwards with a butcher's knife.

DUNLAVIN: Yes, and then of course the other fellow used a meat-chopper. Real bog-man act. Nearly as bad as a shotgun, or getting the weed-killer mixed up in the stirabout.[5] But a man with a silver-topped cane, that's a man that's a cut above meat-choppers whichever way you look at it.

PRISONER A: Well, I suppose we can expect Silver-top round soon to start his life.

PRISONER B: Aye, we've a couple of vacancies.

PRISONER A: There's a new card up here already.

DUNLAVIN: I declare to God you're right. (*Goes to read one of the cards.*) It's not him at all, it's another fellow, doing two years, for . . . oh, the dirty beast, look what the dirty man-beast is in for. 'Clare to God,[6] putting the likes of that beside me. They must think this is the bloody sloblands.[7]

PRISONER B: There's another fellow here.

DUNLAVIN: I hope it's not another of that persuasion. (*Reads the card.*) Ah, no, it's only the murderer, thanks be to God.

The others have a read of the card and skip back to their own cells.

DUNLAVIN: You wouldn't mind old Silver-top. Killing your wife is a natural class of a thing could happen to the best of us. But this other dirty animal on me left . . .

PRISONER B: Ah well, now he's here he'll just have to do his birdlime[8] like anyone else.

DUNLAVIN: That doesn't say that he should do it in the next flowery dell to me. Robbers, thieves and murderers I can abide, but when it comes to that class of carry-on — Good night, Joe Doyle.

PRISONER A (*indicates 22*): This fellow was dead lucky.

PRISONER B: Live lucky.

PRISONER A: Two fellows waiting to be topped and he's the one that gets away. As a general rule they don't like reprieving one and topping the other.

DUNLAVIN: So as to be on the safe side, and not to be making fish of one and flesh of the other, they usually top both. Then, of course, the Minister might have said, enough is as good as a feast.

They rest on their brooms.

PRISONER B: It must be a great thing to be told at the last minute that you're not going to be topped after all. To be lying there sweating and watching. The two screws for the death watch coming on at twelve o'clock and the two going off shaking hands with you, and you go to bed, and stare up at the ceiling.

DUNLAVIN: And the two screws nod to each other across the fire to make a sup of tea, but to do it easy in case they wake you, and you turn round in the bed towards the fire and you say 'I'll take a sup as you're at it' and one of the screws says 'Ah, so you're awake, Mick. We were just wetting it; isn't it a good job you spoke up in time.'

PRISONER A: And after that, the tea is drunk and they offer you cigarettes, though the mouth is burned off you from smoking and anyway you've more than they have, you've got that many you'll be leaving them after you, and you lie down and get up, and get up and lie down, and the two screws not letting on to be minding you and not taking their eyes off you for one half-minute, and you walk up and down a little bit more . . .

PRISONER B: And they ask you would you like another game of draughts or would you sooner write a letter, and getting on to morning you hear a bell out in the city, and you ask them the time, but they won't tell.

DUNLAVIN: But they put a good face on it, and one says 'There's that old watch stopped again' and he says to the other screw 'Have you your watch, Jack?' and the other fellow makes a great joke of it, 'I'll have to take a run up as far as the North City Pawn shop and ask them to let me have a look at it.' And then the door is unlocked and everyone sweats blood, and they come in and ask your man to stand up a minute, that's if he's able, while they read him something: 'I am instructed to inform you that the Minister has, he hasn't, he has, he hasn't recommended to the President, that . . .'

PRISONER A: And the quare fellow says 'Did you say "has recommended or has not recommended . . .?" I didn't quite catch that.'

DUNLAVIN: My bloody oath but he catches it. Although I remember once in a case like now when there were two fellows to be topped over two different jobs, didn't the bloody fellow from the Prison Board, as it was then, in old Max Greeb's time, didn't he tell the wrong man he was reprieved? Your man was delighted for a few hours and then they had to go back and tell him 'Sorry, my mistake, but you're to be topped after all'?

PRISONER B: And the fellow that was reprieved, I bet he was glad.

DUNLAVIN: Of course he was glad, anyone that says that a condemned man would be better off hung than doing life, let them leave it to his own discretion. Do you know who feels it worse going out to be topped?

PRISONER A: Corkmen and Northerners . . . they've such bloody hard necks.

DUNLAVIN: I have to do me funny half-hour for Holy Healey. I'm talking serious now.

PRISONER A: All right, come on, let's have it —

DUNLAVIN: The man that feels it worst, going into that little house with the red door and the silver painted gates at the bottom of D. Wing, is a man that has been in the nick before, when some other merchant was topped; or he's heard screws or old lags in the bag shop or at exercise talking about it. A new chap that's never done anything but murder, and that only once, is usually a respectable man, such as this Silver-top here. He knows nothing about it, except the few lines that he'd see in the papers. 'Condemned man entered the hang-house at seven fifty-nine. At eight three the doctor pronounced life extinct.'

PRISONER B: That's a lot of mullarkey.[9] In the first place the doctor has his back turned after the trap goes down, and doesn't turn to face it until a screw has caught the rope and stopped it wriggling. Then they go out and lock up the shop and have their breakfast and don't come back for an hour. Then they cut your man down and the doctor slits the back of his neck to see if the bones are broken. Who's to know what happens in the hour your man is swinging there, maybe wriggling to himself in the pit.

PRISONER A: You're right there. When I was in the nick in England, there was a screw doing time, he'd been smuggling out medical reports on hangings and selling them to the Sunday papers, and he told me that one bloke had lived seventeen minutes at the end of a rope.

DUNLAVIN: I don't believe that! Seventeen minutes is a bloody long time to be hanging at the end of a rope.

PRISONER A: It was their own medical report.

PRISONER B: I'll lay odds to a make[10] that Silver-top isn't half charmed with himself if he's not going with the meat-chopper in the morning.

DUNLAVIN: You could sing that if you had an air to it.

PRISONER A: They'll have him down to reception, changed into Fry's and over here any time now.

DUNLAVIN: Him and this other jewel here. Bad an' all as Silver-top was to beat his wife's brains out, I'd as lief have him near to me as this article. Dirty beast! I won't have an hour's luck for the rest of me six months, and me hoping to touch Uncle Healey today for a letter to the Room-Keepers for when I'd go out.

PRISONER B: Eh, Dunlavin, is the Department trying to reform, reconstruct and rehabilitate you in your old age?

DUNLAVIN: Ah no, it's nothing to do with the Department. Outside his job in the Department, Uncle Healey's in some holy crowd, that does good be stealth. They never let the right hand know what the left hand doeth, as the man said. Of course they never put either hand in their pocket, so you'd never get money off them, but they can give letters to the Prisoners' Aid and the Room-Keepers. Mind you. Healey's not here today as a holy man. He'll just be fixing up the man that's getting hung in the morning, but if I can get on the right side of him, he might mix business with pleasure and give me a letter for when I get out.

PRISONER B: Now we know the cause of all the spring-cleaning.

DUNLAVIN: And a fellow in the kitchen told us they're doing a special dinner for us on account of Uncle Healey's visit.

PRISONER A: Do you mean we're getting food with our meals today?

DUNLAVIN: That's right, and I can't be standing yapping to youse. I've to hang up my holy pictures and think up a few funny remarks for him. God, what Jimmie O'Dea[11] is getting thousands for I've to do for a pair of old socks and a ticket for the Prisoners' Aid.

DUNLAVIN *goes into his cell. Two* YOUNG PRISONERS *aged about seventeen go past with sweeping brushes in front of them, singing softly in unison.*

YOUNG PRISONERS:

Only one more cell inspection
    We go out next Saturday,
Only one more cell inspection
    And we go far, far away.

PRISONER A: What brings you fellows round here this morning?

YOUNG PRISONER 1: Our screw told us to sweep all round the Juvenile Wing and then come round here and give it a bit of a going over.

PRISONER B: And have you your own wing done?

YOUNG PRISONER 2: No, but if we did our wing first, we'd miss the mots[12] hanging out the laundry. You can't see them from our wing.

PRISONER A: Just as well, maybe; you're bad enough as it is.

YOUNG PRISONER 1: But I tell you what you will see from our wing this morning. It's the carpenter bringing up the coffin for the quare fellow and leaving it over in the mortuary to have it handy for the morning. There's two orderlies besides us over in Juveniles, and we were going to toss up who'd come over here, but they're country fellows and they'd said they'd sooner see the coffin. I'd sooner pike at a good-looking mot than the best coffin in Ireland, wouldn't you, Shaybo?

YOUNG PRISONER 2: Certainly I would, and outside that, when you're over here, there's always a chance of getting a bit of education about screwing jobs, and suchlike, from experienced men. Do you think Triplex or celluloid is the best for Yale locks, sir?

YOUNG PRISONER 1: Do you carry the stick all the time, sir?

PRISONER A: If I had a stick I'd know where to put it, across your bloody . . .

YOUNG PRISONER 2: Scholara, get sweeping, here's the screw.

They drift off sweeping and singing softly.

PRISONER B: He's bringing one of 'em. Is it Silver-top or the other fellow?

PRISONER A: Silver-top. I remember him being half carried into the circle the night he was sentenced to death.

PRISONER B: He has a right spring in his step this morning then.

PRISONER A: He's not looking all that happy. Still, I suppose he hasn't got over the shock yet.

WARDER *and a prisoner come on* L. *The prisoner is in early middle age; when he speaks he has a 'good accent'. He is carrying a pillow slip which contains his sheets and other kit. The* WARDER *halts him.*

WARDER REGAN: Stand by the door with your name on it. Later on when you've seen the doctor these fellows will show you how to lay your kit. (*He goes. There is a pause, while the* PRISONERS *survey the newcomer.*)

PRISONER B: He'll bloody well cheer the place up, won't he?

LIFER: Have any of you got a cigarette?

PRISONER A: That's a good one. You're not in the condemned cell now, you know. No snout allowed here.

PRISONER B: Unless you manage to scrounge a dog-end off the remands.[13]

PRISONER A: Or pick one up in the exercise yard after a man the like of yourself that's allowed them as a special concession. Not, by God, that we picked up much after you. What did you do with your dog ends?

LIFER: Threw them in the fire.

PRISONER B: You what!

PRISONER A: How was it the other poor bastard, that's got no reprieve and is to be topped in the morning — how was it he was always able to leave a trail of butts behind him when he went off exercise?

LIFER: I've never been in prison before; how was I to know?

PRISONER A: You're a curse of God liar, my friend, you did know; for it was whispered to him by the fellows from the hospital bringing over the grub to the condemned cell. He never gave them as much as a match! And he couldn't even bring his dog-ends to the exercise yard and drop them behind for us to pick up when we came out later.

PRISONER B: I bet you're charmed with yourself that you're not going through the iron door tomorrow morning.

The LIFER *doesn't speak, but looks down at his suit.*

PRISONER A: Aye, you're better off in that old suit, bad as it is, than the wooden overcoat the quare fellow is going to get tomorrow morning.

PRISONER B: The longest you could do would be twenty years. More than likely you'll get out in half of that. Last man to finish up in the Bog, he done eleven.

LIFER: Eleven. How do you live through it?

PRISONER A: A minute at a time.

PRISONER B: You haven't got a bit of snout for him, have you? (PRISONER A *shakes his head.*) Maybe Dunlavin has. Hey, Dunlavin, have you e'er a smoke you'd give this chap? Hey, Dunlavin.

DUNLAVIN (*coming from his cell*): Yes, what is it? Anyone there the name of headache?

PRISONER B: Could you manage to give this chap something to smoke? E'er a bit of snout at all.

DUNLAVIN: There's only one brand of tobacco allowed here — 'Three Nuns'. None today, none tomorrow, and none the day after.

He goes back into his cell.

PRISONER B: Eh, Dunlavin, come back to hell out of that.

DUNLAVIN: Well, what?

PRISONER B: This poor chap after being smoking about sixty a day . . .

DUNLAVIN: Where?

PRISONER B: In the condemned cell — where else?

DUNLAVIN: Now I have you. Sure I thought you were the other fellow, and you're not, you're only the murderer. God comfort you. (*Shakes hands.*) Certainly so. (*Takes off his jacket, looks up and down*

the wing, undoes his trousers and from the depths of his combinations he produces a cigarette end, and a match, and presents them to the LIFER.) Reprieved in the small hours of this morning. Certainly so. The dead arose and appeared to many, as the man said, but you'll be getting yourself a bad name standing near that other fellow's door. This is your flowery dell, see? It has your name there on that little card. And all your particulars. Age forty-three. Religion RC.

LIFER (*reads*): Life.

DUNLAVIN: And a bloody sight better than death any day of the week.

PRISONER B: It always says that. The Governor will explain it all to you later this morning.

DUNLAVIN: Or maybe they'll get holy Uncle Healey to do it.

PRISONER B: Go into your cell and have a smoke for yourself. Bring in your kit bag. (*Passes in kit to* LIFER.) Have a quiet burn there before the screw comes round; we'll keep nick. (LIFER *closes the door of his cell.*)

DUNLAVIN: God knows I got the pick of good neighbours. Lovely people. Give me a decent murderer though, rather than the likes of this other fellow. Well, I'll go into me little place and get on with me bit of dobying[14] so as to have it all nice for Healey when he comes round. (*He goes back to his cell.*)

PRISONER B (*to* LIFER): Don't light up yet! Here's the screw coming.

PRISONER A: With the other fellow.

WARDER REGAN *and another prisoner, 'the* OTHER FELLOW', *an anxious-faced man, wearing prison clothes and carrying a kit bag, come on* L.

WARDER REGAN: Yes, this is your flowery dell. Leave in your kitbag and stand at your door and wait for the doctor. These other fellows will show you where to go when he comes.

OTHER FELLOW: Right sir. Very good, sir.

WARDER REGAN *goes, the* OTHER FELLOW *has a look round.*

PRISONER B: There's a bloke in the end cell getting himself a quiet burn. Why don't you join him before the screws get back?

The OTHER FELLOW *notices the card on* LIFER's *cell.*

OTHER FELLOW: My God! Is this what I've come to, mixing with murderers! I'd rather not, thank you, though I could do with a smoke. I'll have to spend long months here, even if I get my remission, with murderers and thieves and God knows what! You're not all murderers are you? You haven't killed anyone, have you?

PRISONER B: Not for a while, I haven't.

OTHER FELLOW: I cannot imagine any worse crime than taking a life, can you?

PRISONER B: It'd depend whose life.

OTHER FELLOW: Of course. I mean, a murderer would be justified in taking his own life, wouldn't he? 'We send him forth' says Carlisle[15] — you've heard of Carlisle haven't you? — 'We send him forth, back to the void, back to the darkness far out beyond the stars. Let him go from us.'

DUNLAVIN (*head out of the door of cell*): Oh. (*Looks at* OTHER FELLOW.) I thought it was Healey from the Department or someone giving it out of them.

PRISONER A: Looks like this man is a bit of an intellectual.

DUNLAVIN: Is that what they call it now?

LIFER: Thanks for the smoke, Mr Dunlavin.

DUNLAVIN: Not at all, sure, you're welcome, call again when you're passing. But remember the next wife you kill and you getting forty fags a day in the condemned cell, think of them as is not so fortunate as yourself and leave a few dog-ends around the exercise yard after you. Here's these noisy little gets again.

The two YOUNG PRISONERS *come round from the left, their sweeping brushes in front of them and singing their song. The* OTHER FELLOW *stands quite still at his door.*

YOUNG PRISONERS:

Only one more cell inspection
    We go out next Saturday
Only one more cell inspection
    Then we go far far away.
    (*They are sweeping near the* LIFER.)
Only one more cell inspection
    We go out next Saturday
Only one more cell . . .

LIFER: For God's sake shut up that squeaking . . .

YOUNG PRISONER 1: We've as much right to open our mouth as what you have, and you only a wet day in the place.

PRISONER B: Leave the kids alone. You don't own the place, you know. They're doing no harm. (*To the* YOUNG PRISONERS) You want to sweep this bit of floor away?

DUNLAVIN: What brings you round here so often? If you went over to the remand wings you might pick up a bit of snout or a look at the paper.

YOUNG PRISONER 1: We get a smoke and the *Mail* every day off a limey[16] on our road that's on remand. He's in over the car smuggling. But round here this morning you can see the mots from the laundry over on the female side hanging out the washing in the exercise yard. Do youse look at them? I suppose when you get old, though, you don't much bother about women.

PRISONER B: I'm thirty-six, mac.

YOUNG PRISONER 1: Ah, I thought that. Don't suppose you care if you never see a mot. There's Shaybo there and he never thinks of anything else. Do you think of anything else but women, Shaybo?

YOUNG PRISONER 2: Yes. Robbing and stealing, Scholara. You go to the window and keep an eye out for them and I'll sweep round here till you give us a call.

YOUNG PRISONER 1: Right, Shaybo, they should be nearly out now. (*Goes up and stands by window.*)

PRISONER B: I forgot about the women.

DUNLAVIN: I didn't. It's a great bit of a treat today — that and having me leg rubbed. Neighbour and I wait in for it.

YOUNG PRISONER 1 (*from the window, in a coarse whisper*): Shaybo, you can see them now.

YOUNG PRISONER 2: The blondy one from North Crumlin?

YOUNG PRISONER 1: Yes, and there's another one with her. I don't know her.

YOUNG PRISONER 2: Must be a country mot. Scholara doesn't know her. Women.

DUNLAVIN: Women.

PRISONER A: I see the blondy one waving.

YOUNG PRISONER 1: If it's all one to you, I'd like you to know that's my mot and it's me she's waving at.

PRISONER A: I'll wave you a thick ear.

DUNLAVIN: Hey, Neighbour! Where the hell is he this morning? Neighbour!

AN OLD MAN'S CREAKING VOICE: Here I am, Neighbour, here I am.

NEIGHBOUR, *a bent old man, comes from* L., *hobbling as quickly as he can on a stick.*

DUNLAVIN: Ah, you lost mass.[17]

NEIGHBOUR: What are they gone in already?

DUNLAVIN: No, but they're finished hanging up the top row of clothes. There'll be no stretching or reaching off chairs.

NEIGHBOUR: Still, thanks be to God for small mercies. They'll be out again this day week.

PRISONER A: If you lives to see it.

NEIGHBOUR: Why wouldn't I live to see it as well as what you would? This is not the nearest I was to fine women, nor are they the first good-looking ones I saw.

PRISONER A: With that old cough of yours they could easy be the last.

NEIGHBOUR: God, you're a desperate old gas bag. We remember better-looking women than ever they were, don't we, Dunlavin? Meena La Bloom, do you remember her?

DUNLAVIN: Indeed and I do; many's the seaman myself and Meena gave the hey and a do, and Mickey Finn[18] to.

NEIGHBOUR: And poor May Oblong.

DUNLAVIN: Ah, where do you leave poor May? The Lord have mercy on her, wasn't I with her one night in the digs, and there was a Member of Parliament there, and May after locking him in the back room and taking away his trousers, with him going over the north wall[19] that morning to vote for Home Rule. 'For the love of your country and mine,' he shouts under the door to May, 'give me back me trousers.' 'So I will,' says May, 'if you shove a fiver out under the door.'

NEIGHBOUR: He had the wad hid? Dirty suspicious old beast.

DUNLAVIN: That's right. He was cute enough to hide his wad somewhere, drunk and all as he was the previous night. All we got in his trousers was a locket of hair of the patriotic plumber of Dolphin's barn that swore to let his hair grow till Ireland was free.

NEIGHBOUR: Ah, poor May, God help her, she was the heart of the roll.[20]

DUNLAVIN: And when she was arrested for carrying on after the curfew, the time of the trouble,[21] she was fined for having concealed about her person two Thompson sub-machine guns. 1921 pattern, three Mills bombs, and a stick of dynamite.

NEIGHBOUR: And will you ever forget poor Lottie L'Estrange, that got had up for pushing the soldier into Spencer Dock?

DUNLAVIN: Ah, God be with the youth of us.

NEIGHBOUR: And Cork Annie, and Lady Limerick.

DUNLAVIN: And Julia Rice and the Goofy One.

NEIGHBOUR (*turns towards window*): Hey, you, move out of the way there and give us a look. Dunlavin, come up here before they go, and have a look at the blondy one.

YOUNG PRISONER 1: Go 'long, you dirty old dog. That's my mot you're speaking about. (*Shoves* NEIGHBOUR.) You old heap of dirt, to wave at a decent girl.

PRISONER A: Hey, snots, d'you think you own the bloody place?

YOUNG PRISONER 1: Would you like it, to have that dirty old eyebox looking at your mot?

PRISONER B: He's not going to eat her.

DUNLAVIN (*from behind*): No, but he'd like to.

YOUNG PRISONER 2: That's right, and Scholara is nearly married to her. At least she had a squealer[22] for him and he has to pay her money every week. Any week he's outside like, to give it, or her to get it.

YOUNG PRISONER 1 (*blows a kiss*): That's right, and I have him putting his rotten old eye on her.

OTHER FELLOW (*at his doorway*): God preserve us.

PRISONER A: Well, you don't own the bloody window. (*Shoves* YOUNG PRISONER 1 *out of the way and brings over* NEIGHBOUR.) Come on, you, if you want to see the May procession.

NEIGHBOUR: Ah, thanks, butty, your blood's worth bottling.

PRISONER A: I didn't do it on account of you, but if you let them young pups get away with too much they'd be running the place.

YOUNG PRISONER 2: Come on, Scholara, we'll mosey back. The screw will think we're lost.
They go back down the stairs, pick up their brushes, and start sweeping again and singing . . .

YOUNG PRISONER 1:
　Only one more cell inspection
　　We go out next Saturday

YOUNG PRISONER 2:
　Only one more cell inspection . . .

LIFER: Shut your bloody row, can't you?

DUNLAVIN: Shut up yourself; you're making more noise than any of them.

YOUNG PRISONER 1: Don't tell us to shut up, you bastard.

PRISONER B: Ah leave him alone; he started life this morning.

YOUNG PRISONER 1: Ah, we're sorry, mister, ain't we, Shaybo?

YOUNG PRISONER 2: God, we are. Go over and take a pike at the female yard. They hang up the clothes now and Scholara's mot is over there. You can have a look at her. Scholara won't mind, will you, Schol?

YOUNG PRISONER 1: Certainly and I won't. Not with you going to the Bog[23] to start life in a couple of days, where you won't see a woman.

YOUNG PRISONER 2: A child.

YOUNG PRISONER 1: A dog.

YOUNG PRISONER 2: A fire.

PRISONER A: Get to hell out of that round to your own wing. Wouldn't you think a man would know all that forbye[24] you telling it to him?

YOUNG PRISONER 2: We were going anyway. We've seen all we wanted to see. It wasn't to look at a lot of old men we came here, but to see mots hanging out the washing.

YOUNG PRISONER 1: And eitherways, we'll be a lot nearer the women than you'll be next Saturday night. Think of us when you're sitting locked up in the old flowery, studying the Bible, Chapter 1, verse 2, and we trucking round in chase of charver.[25]

They samba out with their brushes for partners, humming the Wedding Samba.

PRISONER A: Them young gets have too much old gab out of them altogether. I was a YP in Walton before the war[26] and I can tell you they'd be quiet boys if they got the larrying[27] we used to get.

OTHER FELLOW: And talking so disrespectfully about the Bible.

NEIGHBOUR: Belied and they needn't; many's the time the Bible was a consolation to a fellow all alone in the old cell. The lovely thin paper with a bit of mattress coir in it, if you could get a match or a bit of tinder or any class of light, was as good a smoke as ever I tasted. Am I right, Dunlavin?

DUNLAVIN: Damn the lie, Neighbour. The first twelve months I done, I smoked my way half-way through the book of Genesis and three inches of my mattress. When the Free State came in[28] we were afraid of our life they were going to change the mattresses for feather beds. And you couldn't smoke feathers, not, be God, if they were rolled in the Song of Solomon itself. But sure, thanks to God, the Free State didn't change anything more than the badge on the warders' caps.

OTHER FELLOW: Can I be into my cell for a while?

PRISONER B: Until the doctor calls you. (*Goes into his cell.*)

PRISONER A: Well, I'm going to have a rest. It's hard work doing a lagging.

LIFER: A lagging? That's penal servitude, isn't it?

DUNLAVIN: Three years or anything over.

LIFER: Three years is a long time.

DUNLAVIN: I wouldn't like to be that long hanging.

NEIGHBOUR: Is he the . . .

DUNLAVIN (*sotto voce*): Silver-top! (*Aloud.*) Started life this morning.

NEIGHBOUR: So they're not going to top you after all? Well, you're a lucky man. I worked one time in the hospital, helping the screw there, and the morning of the execution he gave me two bottles of stout to take the hood off the fellow was after being topped. I wouldn't have done it a second time for two glasses of malt, no, nor a bottle of it. I cut the hood away; his head was all twisted and his face black, but the two eyes were the worst; like a rabbit's; it was fear that had done it.

LIFER: Perhaps he didn't feel anything. How do you know?

NEIGHBOUR: I only seen him. I never had a chance of asking him. (NEIGHBOUR *goes to the murderer's door.*) Date of expiration of sentence, life. In some ways I wouldn't mind if that was my lot. What do you say?

DUNLAVIN: I don't know; it's true we're too old and bet[29] for lobbywatching and shaking down anywhere, so that you'd fall down and sleep on the pavement of a winter's night and not know but you were lying snug and comfortable in the Shelbourne.[30]

NEIGHBOUR: Only then to wake up on some lobby and the hard floorboards under you, and a lump of hard filth for your pillow, and the cold and the drink shaking you, wishing it was morning for the market pubs to open, where if you had the price of a drink you could sit in the warm anyway. Except, God look down on you, if it was Sunday.

DUNLAVIN: Ah, there's the agony. No pub open, but the bells battering your bared nerves and all you could do with the cold and the sickness was to lean over on your side and wish that God would call you.

LIFER: If I was outside my life wouldn't be like that.

NEIGHBOUR: No, but ours would.

DUNLAVIN (*quietly*): See, we're selfish, mister, like everybody else.

WARDER (*shouts off*): Medical applications and receptions. Fall in for the doctor. (LIFER *looks lost.*)

DUNLAVIN: Yes, that's you. Go up there to the top of the wing and wait till the screw tells you to go in. Neighbour, call them other fellows.

Exit LIFER.

NEIGHBOUR: Come on — the vet's here.

DUNLAVIN (*calling in to the* OTHER FELLOW): Hey, come out and get gelded.

OTHER FELLOW *and* PRISONERS A *and* B *come out of cells.*

NEIGHBOUR: You're for the doctor. Go on up there with the rest of them. Me and Dunlavin don't go up. We only wait to be rubbed.

DUNLAVIN: Don't have any chat at all with that fellow. D'you see what he's in for?

NEIGHBOUR *goes and looks. Exit* OTHER FELLOW *and* PRISONERS A *and* B.

NEIGHBOUR: What the hell does that mean?

DUNLAVIN: A bloody sex mechanic.

NEIGHBOUR: I didn't know.

DUNLAVIN: Well, you know now. I'll go in and get me chair. You can sit on it after me. It'll save you bringing yours out.

NEIGHBOUR: Well, if you go first and have a chance of a go at the spirit bottle, don't swig the bloody lot. Remember I'm for treatment too.

DUNLAVIN: Don't be such an old begrudger. He'll bring a quart bottle of it, and who could swallow that much methylated spirit in the few drops you'd get at it?

NEIGHBOUR: You could, or a bucket of it, if it was lying anywhere handy. I seen you do it, bluestone[31] and all, only buns to a bear as far as you were concerned.

DUNLAVIN: Do you remember the old doctor they had here years ago?

NEIGHBOUR: The one they used to call Crippen.[32]

DUNLAVIN: The very man. There was one day I was brought in for drinking the chat and I went to court that morning and was here in the afternoon still as drunk as Pontius Pilate. Crippen was examining me. 'When I put me hand there you cough,' and all to that effect. 'Did you ever have VD?' says he. 'I haven't got your habits,' says I to him. These fellows weren't long.

Re-enter PRISONERS A *and* B.

NEIGHBOUR: What did he give youse?

PRISONER B (*passing into cell*): Extra six ounces of bread. Says we're undernourished.

PRISONER A: Is the bar open yet?

NEIGHBOUR: Never you mind the bar. I've cruel pains in my leg that I want rubbed to take out the rheumatics, not to be jeered at, and I've had them genuine since the war.

PRISONER A: What war? The economic war?[33]

NEIGHBOUR: Ah, you maggot. It's all your fault, Dunlavin, telling them fellows we do get an odd sup out of the spirit bottle. Letting everyone know our business.

PRISONERS A *and* B *go into cells and shut the doors.*

DUNLAVIN: No sign of Holy Healey yet.

NEIGHBOUR: You're wasting your time chasing after old Healey. He told me here one day, and I trying to get myself an old overcoat out of him, that he was here only as a head man of the Department of Justice, and he couldn't do other business of any sort or size whatever, good, bad or indifferent. It's my opinion that old Healey does be half-jarred a deal of the time anyway.

DUNLAVIN: The likes of Healey would take a sup all right, but being a high-up civil servant, he wouldn't drink under his own name. You'd see the likes of Healey nourishing themselves with balls of malt, at eleven in the morning, in little back snugs round Merrion Row. The barman would lose his job if he so much as breathed their name. It'd be 'Mr H. wants a drop of water but not too much.' 'Yes, Mr O.' 'No, sir, Mr Mac wasn't in this morning.' 'Yes, Mr D. Fine morning; it will be a lovely day if it doesn't snow.' Educated drinking, you know. Even a bit of chat about God at an odd time, so as you'd think God was in another department, but not long off the Bog, and they was doing Him a good turn to be talking well about Him.

NEIGHBOUR: Here's the other two back. The MO[34] will be down to us soon.

LIFER *and* OTHER FELLOW *go into cells and shut the doors.*

DUNLAVIN: That other fellow's not looking as if this place is agreeing with him.

NEIGHBOUR: You told me a minute ago that I wasn't even to speak to him.

DUNLAVIN: Ah, when all is said and done, he's someone's rearing after all, he could be worse, he could be a screw or an official from the Department.

WARDER REGAN *comes on with a bottle marked 'methylated spirit'.*

WARDER REGAN: You're the two for rubs, for your rheumatism.

DUNLAVIN: That's right, Mr Regan sir, old and bet, sir, that's us. And the old pain is very bad with us these times, sir.

WARDER REGAN: Not so much lip, and sit down whoever is first for treatment.

DUNLAVIN: That's me, sir. Age before ignorance, as the man said. (*Sits in the chair.*)

WARDER REGAN: Rise the leg of your trousers. Which leg is it?

DUNLAVIN: The left, sir.

WARDER REGAN: That's the right leg you're showing me.

DUNLAVIN: That's what I was saying, sir. The left is worst one day and the right is bad the next. To be on the safe side, you'd have to do two of them. It's only the mercy of God I'm not a centipede, sir, with the weather that's in it.

WARDER REGAN: Is that where the pain is?

DUNLAVIN (*bending down slowly towards the bottle*): A little lower down, sir, if you please. (*Grabs the bottle and raises it to his mouth.*) Just a little lower down, sir, if it's all equal to you.

REGAN *rubs, head well bent, and* DUNLAVIN *drinks long and deeply and as quickly lowers the bottle on to the floor again, wiping his mouth and making the most frightful grimaces, for the stuff doesn't go down easy at first. He goes through the pantomime of being burnt inside for* NEIGHBOUR's *benefit and rubs his mouth with the back of his hand.*

DUNLAVIN: Ah, that's massive, sir. 'Tis you that has the healing hand. You must have desperate luck at the horses; I'd only love to be with you copying your dockets. (REGAN *turns and pours more spirit on his hands.*) Ah, that's it, sir, well into me I can feel it going. (*Reaches forward towards the bottle again, drinks.*) Ah, that's it, I can feel it going right into me. And doing me all the good in the world. (REGAN *reaches and puts more spirit on his hand and sets to rubbing again.*) That's it, sir, thorough does it; if you're going to do a thing at all you might as well do it well. (*Reaches forward for the bottle again and raises it.* NEIGHBOUR *looks across in piteous appeal to him not to drink so much, but he merely waves the bottle in elegant salute, as if to wish him good health, and takes another drink.*) May God reward you, sir, you must be the seventh son of the seventh son of one of the Lees from Limerick on your mother's side maybe. (*Drinks again.*) Ah, that's the cure for the cold of the wind and the world's neglectment.

WARDER REGAN: Right, now you.

NEIGHBOUR *comes forward.*

WARDER DONELLY (*offstage*): All present and correct, Mr Healey, sir.

DUNLAVIN: Holy Healey!

Enter WARDER DONELLY.

WARDER DONELLY: This way, Mr Healey.

WARDER REGAN: Attention! Stand by your doors.

DUNLAVIN: By the left, laugh.

WARDER DONELLY: This way.

Enter MR HEALEY, *an elegantly dressed gentleman.*

HEALEY: Good morning.

WARDER DONELLY: Any complaints?

PRISONER A: No, sir.

HEALEY: Good morning!

WARDER DONELLY: Any complaints?

OTHER FELLOW, PRISONER: No, sir.

HEALEY: Good morning all! Well, now, I'm here representing the Department of Justice, if there are any complaints now is the time to make them.

SEVERAL PRISONERS: No complaints, sir.

WARDER REGAN: All correct, sir. Two receiving medical treatment here, sir.

DUNLAVIN: Just getting the old leg rubbed, sir, Mr Healey.

HEALEY: Well, well, it almost smells like a bar.

DUNLAVIN: I'm near drunk myself on the smell of it, sir.

HEALEY: Don't let me interrupt the good work.

DUNLAVIN: Ah, the old legs. It's being out in all weathers that does it, sir. Of course we don't have that to contend with while we're here, sir.

HEALEY: Out in all weathers, I should think not indeed. Well, my man, I will be inspecting your cell amongst others in due course.

DUNLAVIN: Yes, sir.

HEALEY: It's always a credit to you, I must say that. (*He turns to* REGAN.) Incorrigible some of these old fellows, but rather amusing.

WARDER REGAN: Yes, sir.

HEALEY: It's Regan, isn't it?

WARDER REGAN: Yes, sir.

HEALEY: Ah yes, you're helping the Canon at the execution tomorrow morning, I understand.

WARDER REGAN: Well, I shall be with the condemned man, sir, seeing that he doesn't do away with himself during the night and that he goes down the hole with his neck properly broken in the morning, without making too much fuss about it.

HEALEY: A sad duty.

WARDER REGAN: Neck breaking and throttling, sir? (HEALEY *gives him a sharp look.*) You must excuse me, sir. I've seen rather a lot of it. They say familiarity breeds contempt.

HEALEY: Well, we have one consolation, Regan, the condemned man gets the priest and the sacraments, more than his victim got maybe. I venture to suggest that some of them die holier deaths than if they had finished their natural span.

WARDER REGAN: We can't advertise 'Commit a murder and die a happy death,' sir. We'd have them all at it. They take religion very seriously in this country.

HEALEY: Quite, quite so! Now, I understand you have the reprieved man over here, Regan.

WARDER REGAN: No. Twenty-six, sir.

DUNLAVIN: Just beside me, sir.

HEALEY: Ah, yes! So here we are! Here's the lucky man, eh? Well, now, the Governor will explain your position to you later in the day. Your case will be examined every five years. Meanwhile I thought you might like a holy picture to hang up in your cell. Keep a cheerful countenance, my friend. God gave you back your life and the least you can do is to thank him with every breath you draw! Right? Well, be of good heart. I will call in and see you again, that is, if duty permits. (*He moves to* DUNLAVIN'S *cell.*)

HEALEY (*at* DUNLAVIN'S *cell*): Very creditable. Hm.

DUNLAVIN: Well, to tell the truth, sir, it's a bit extra special today. You see, we heard you was here.

HEALEY: Very nice.

DUNLAVIN: Of course I do like to keep my little place as homely as I can with the little holy pictures you gave me of Blessed Martin,[35] sir.

HEALEY: I see you don't recognize the colour bar.

DUNLAVIN: The only bar I recognize, sir, is the Bridge Bar or the Beamish House the corner of Thomas Street.

HEALEY: Well, I must be off now, and I'm glad to see you're being well looked after.

DUNLAVIN: It's neither this nor that, but if you could spare a minute, sir?

HEALEY: Yes, what is it? But hurry; remember I've a lot to do today.

DUNLAVIN: It's like this, sir. I won't always be here, sir, having me leg rubbed and me bit of grub brought to me. As it says in the Bible, sir, have it yourself or be without it and put ye by for the rainy day, for thou knowest not the night thou mayest be sleeping in a lobby.

HEALEY: Yes, yes, but what is it you want?

DUNLAVIN: I've a chance of a little room up round Buckingham Street, sir, if you could only give me a letter to the Room–Keepers after I go out, for a bit of help with the rent.

HEALEY: Well, you know, when I visit the prison, I'm not here as a member of any outside organization of which I may be a member but simply as an official of the Department of Justice.

DUNLAVIN: Yes, but where else would I be likely to meet you, sir? I'd hardly bump into you in the Bridge Bar when I'd be outside, would I, sir?

HEALEY: No, no, certainly not. But you know the Society offices in the Square. See me there any Friday night, between eight and nine.

DUNLAVIN: Thank you, sir, and a bed in heaven to you, sir.

HEALEY: And the same to you. (*Goes to next cell.*)

DUNLAVIN: And many of them, and I hope we're all here this time next year (*venomously after* MR HEALEY) that it may choke you.

WARDER DONELLY *bangs on* LIFER*'s closed door, then looks in.*

WARDER DONELLY: Jesus Christ, sir. He's put the sheet up! Quick.

REGAN *and* DONELLY *go into* LIFER*'s cell. He is hanging. They cut him down.*

WARDER REGAN: Gently does it.

They lay him down in the passage and try to restore him.

HEALEY: What a dreadful business and with this other coming off tomorrow.

The prisoners crowd out of line.

WARDER DONELLY: Get back to your cells!

HEALEY: Is he still with us?

WARDER REGAN: He'll be all right in an hour or so. Better get the MO, Mr Donelly.

The triangle sounds.

WARDER DONELLY: B. Wing, two, three and one. Stand by your doors. Right, lead on. Now come on, come on, this is no holiday. Right, sir, over to you. Lead on, B.1.

WARDER REGAN *and* HEALEY *are left with the unconscious* LIFER.

HEALEY: Dear, dear. The Canon will be very upset about this.

WARDER REGAN: There's not much harm done, thank God. They don't have to put a death certificate against the receipt for his live body.

HEALEY: That doesn't seem a very nice way of looking at it, Regan.

WARDER REGAN: A lot of people mightn't consider ours a very nice job, sir.

HEALEY: Ours?

WARDER REGAN: Yes, ours, sir. Mine, the Canon's, the hangman's, and if you don't mind my saying so, yours, sir.

HEALEY: Society cannot exist without prisons, Regan. My job is to bring what help and comfort I can to these unfortunates. Really, a man with your outlook, I cannot see why you stay in the service.

WARDER REGAN: It's a soft job, sir, between hangings.

The triangle is heard. The MO comes on with two stretcher-bearers.

CURTAIN

1   Slang for prison warder and prisoner.
2   Ritual presumably before being hanged.
3   Here presumably reprieved.
4   A company which operated the railway network in the south of Ireland. At the turn of the century it operated as the Great Southern and Western Railway (GS & W). With the establishment of the Irish Free State the railway network was reorganized into two principal companies: the Great Northern Railway (for much of Ulster and Belfast-Dublin) and CIE (Córas Iompair Éireann) for the rail network in the rest of Ireland.
5   Porridge.
6   I declare to God.
7   Literally, muddy land reclaimed from water. Here place reserved for slobs, that is, for idle good-for-nothings.
8   Rhyming slang for time (in prison).
9   Slang for nonsense, variant of malarkey. Origin unknown. (OED)
10 An unusual expression, meaning presumably I'll bet against whatever you wish to choose. One meaning of 'make' historically was a halfpenny.
11 Irish comedian (1899–1965).
12 Slang word used in Ireland for woman.
13 Prisoners on remand, awaiting trial. A dog-end is the stump or butt of a cigarette.
14 Washing. From Hindi dhōb.

15 Frederick Howard, Earl of Carlisle (1748–1825), poet, playwright and Lord Lieutenant of Ireland in 1780–82.
16 Slang for Englishman.
17 Presumably lost sight of women's underwear, compared here to the Mass (also clothed in mystery).
18 A drink laced with alcohol (and possibly drugs) to render person unconscious.
19 When Irish Members of Parliament travelled to Westminster to vote they caught the boat from the North Wall in Dublin.
20 The heart of the rule, a decent person.
21 During the War of Independence (1919–21) the British authorities used the curfew to suppress opposition.
22 Child.
23 The prison at Port Laoise.
24 Without, besides.
25 Slang for sexual embrace, also copulation.
26 Young Prisoner. Walton in Liverpool. Before the war: The Second World War.
27 Possibly a form of larrikin, a street rowdy. Here meaning they suffered from too much noise. Has also association with thrashing.
28 In 1921.
29 Old and beaten.
30 Luxury hotel on St Stephen's Green in Dublin, formerly used by the Anglo-Irish in transit from their estates in Ireland to England.
31 Inferior gin or whisky.
32 Dr Crippen (1862–1910) poisoned his wife and hid her body in the coal cellar of their North London home.
33 A reference to de Valera's so-called economic war with Britain in the 1930s.
34 Medical Orderly.
35 Martin de Porres (1579–1639), born in Lima to a Spanish soldier and a freed slave from Panama. Canonized in 1962, he remains a favourite saint in Ireland.

EDWIN O'CONNOR
from Edwin O'Connor, *The Last Hurrah* (1956)

Edwin O'Connor (1918–68), the son of a doctor from Rhode Island, was educated at Notre Dame University. After time spent as a radio announcer, a coastguard in the Second World War, and a journalist, he turned to writing full-time in 1950. Death cut short an ambition to do for the Irish in America what Faulkner had done for the South. *The Last Hurrah*, about an old-style Irish-American politician, modelled in part on real Boston politicians such as James Curley and John Fitzgerald, became, according to Charles Fanning, the most popular Irish-American novel after *Studs Lonigan*. In 1958, in keeping with the last hurrah theme, it was turned into a film by John Ford with Spencer Tracy as Skeffington. Here in this extract, in discussion with his politically inexperienced nephew, Skeffington (don't miss hearing his voice) reflects on his life in politics among the Irish community. To see something of the change in Irish-American fortunes and sensibility across several decades, you might like to compare this extract with the one from *Ward Eight* (1936) on page 449 above.

'I think we might move along up to the parlor,' he said to Adam. 'I saw a priest come in as I was coming back down here: I imagine they'll be saying the Rosary any moment now. We'll join them, and then we'll go.'

Led by Skeffington, the men left the kitchen and trooped up to the parlor; there, at the door they were met by a priest. Or, more accurately, by a Monsignor; it was the Cardinal's secretary.

'Good evening, Governor,' he said pleasantly.

'Well, well,' Skeffington said, some slight surprise in his voice. 'Monsignor. This is an unexpected pleasure. Nice to see you again. Are you here as an emissary of His Eminence?'

'No, no,' the Monsignor said. 'I'm on my own tonight. Mrs Minihan is something of an old friend. When I was a boy in this part of town I used to drop in to see her fairly often. Most of the children of the neighborhood did, I think.'

'Yes,' Skeffington said thoughtfully. 'So they did. I'd almost forgotten. Poor Gert.' Then, speaking less to himself and more to the Monsignor, he said, 'Well, it's very good of you to remember and drop in now. Tell me, how's your boss these days?'

'Very well. I'll tell him I saw you, Governor.'

'Do that,' Skeffington said. 'He'll be overjoyed.'

The Monsignor smiled. 'You may be misjudging

His Eminence, Governor. It's a case of the bark being a good deal worse than the bite.'

'I wouldn't know,' Skeffington said. 'I've never been bitten. There were a few quick snaps in my direction, but I managed to avoid them. However, that's neither here nor there at the moment, I suppose; there's no reason why you should be bothered with these old-time vendettas, Monsignor. By the way, have you met my nephew, Adam Caulfield?'

The Monsignor, who would have given rather a lot to be bothered about the old-time vendettas, greeted Adam with an automatic affability, but his mind was on Skeffington. The old politician captivated his imagination; he saw him as a unique, a rich, extra-ordinary personality who contained within himself a part of local history which soon would be no more and which never again would reappear. It was a vein that called out to be tapped before it disappeared, first, from view, then even from memory; for just a moment the Monsignor thought of suggesting to Skeffington the possibility of a luncheon, a meeting, a talk. Then he thought of the Cardinal, and of the old, tough, knobby face darkening with rage and disappointment when he learned — as he surely would — of the deliberate encounter, planned by his own subordinate. It would be imprudent; worse, it would be unfair. For the time being, at least, any such meeting was impractical; a little later, perhaps . . . And so the Monsignor, nodding towards the parlor, merely said, 'I suppose we'd better go in now.'

They went in, they knelt, and the Monsignor led them in the Rosary. They recited in unison the five decades of the beads which commemorate the Sorrowful Mysteries of the Church; they prayed for the immortal soul of Aram Minihan. And as they prayed, their responses low, rhythmic, and at times not quite distinct, riding high over all other voices came one which to Adam was familiar, clear, unhesitating, and infinitely fervent. It was the voice of Delia Boylan.

The Rosary over, it was time to go. Skeffington swiftly and efficiently made the rounds, saying the necessary good-bys; then he signalled to Adam, and uncle and nephew walked towards the front door together. They had almost reached the door when Skeffington, suddenly halting, said, 'Hold on a minute. I want a word with that undertaker before we go.'

They both turned and saw the head of Johnnie Degnan, poking out of the kitchen at the far end of the hall; obviously he had been watching their departure. Skeffington beckoned, and he came running quietly to them.

'Ah, good evening, Governor,' he said, in his swift hushed tones. 'A very sad occasion. I wanted to see you before this evening, to make your acquaintance, but the pressure of my duties didn't quite allow. I'm John Degnan, Governor.'

'Glad to know you, Mr Degnan,' Skeffington said. 'As you say, it's a sad occasion. I'm happy to see you've done your best by it, however. I've been admiring your handiwork with the deceased.'

'Thank you, Governor. Thank you very much. That's nice to hear. I did my best,' the undertaker said modestly. 'I don't mind telling you, Governor, that Mr Minihan presented a very difficult case. Because of the age and the sunken cheeks and the wrinkles. I'm sure you can appreciate the difficulty of the task, Governor. Everything had to be smoothed out delicately, the youthful contours restored, and so forth.'

'Yes. Now, Mr Degnan, only one feature of your work disturbs me and that is the probable cost. You don't mind if I say that I was rather struck by the fact that the coffin, and what might be called the general deathroom décor, seem a trifle splendid for someone who was in decidedly modest circumstances?'

The undertaker smiled; it was, Adam thought, a nervous smile. 'I see what you mean, Governor,' he said swiftly. 'I appreciate that point of view. And yet I always think the family is more satisfied if the final homage, as I like to think of it, is really nice in its every aspect. Something that the deceased would have been proud of if he could have seen it.'

'Why, those are the feelings of an artist,' Skeffington said. 'They do you credit, Mr Degnan. I presume, incidentally, that you've discussed all this with Mrs Minihan?'

'Well, no. Not exactly, that is, Governor. I thought it best not to in her distraught condition. Just a few words here and there. I think you could say, more or less, that it was left to my discretion, as it so often is. I always believe in taking as many worries as possible from the shoulders of the family.'

'That's very thoughtful of you. Now then, you're a young man, Mr Degnan, but I understand you've had quite a bit of professional experience. As you might put it, you've been in charge of a good many final homages. Or as I might put it, you've buried a good many people. What would you say was the lowest price you've ever buried anyone for?'

'The lowest *price*, Governor?' The smile remained; it wavered uncertainly. 'I don't quite understand. . . . What I mean to say is, Governor, I don't believe that's anything I've ever quite figured out.'

'Try,' Skeffington urged him. 'Make a rough estimate. Would it be . . . oh, say, thirty-five dollars?'

'*Thirty-five dollars!*' The gasp of astonishment and pain broke through the modulated occupational tones;

the undertaker looked wildly at Skeffington and said, 'You couldn't *begin* to bury anyone for that price today, Governor!'

'I'll bet you could if you really tried,' Skeffington said pleasantly. 'I'll bet you could both begin and end. And just to prove my confidence in your resourcefulness, Mr Degnan, why don't you do that very thing with Mr Minihan? Let's give it a real try. I think you can do it. I'm sure the final bill won't read over thirty-five dollars. Matter of fact, I'll instruct the widow to that effect immediately.'

'But Governor, you can't be serious!' Degnan cried. The smooth round face had become agonized; the soft hands were united in front of him in a tight, beseeching clasp. He looked as if he were about to hurl himself at his persecutor's feet, and Adam, who had not until a moment ago realized just what it was that his uncle was doing, now felt a sudden pity as well as disgust for this abject little profiteer. 'The costs alone, Governor,' Degnan moaned. 'They're going up every day. I couldn't possibly do it. It's all *arranged* —'

'Fine,' Skeffington said. 'Then let it go through as arranged. But for thirty-five dollars.'

'But, *Governor* . . .'

Skeffington pulled his watch from a vest pocket and examined it with apparent surprise. 'It's later than I thought,' he said. 'Well, then, Mr Degnan, it's all settled. I'll leave the details to you. A suitable funeral conducted for thirty-five dollars, with no cutting of corners. All the normal courtesies extended, the usual paraphernalia available. I'll have a few men on hand just to see that everything goes along well. I know you'll do a grand job. In any event, I'll be sure to hear about it: my observers will give me a full report.'

The undertaker's face, which for some moments had been the color of putty, now had turned a vivid red. 'But Governor! I hope you know how eager I am to co-operate in anything you suggest. How eager I *always* am. But what you're asking is *impossible*. . . .'

'Why, that's one of the words that doesn't belong to the bright lexicon of youth,' Skeffington said reprovingly. 'I've always believed that nothing is impossible when one has youth and ambition. I hope you won't be the one to shake this treasured belief. Because if you do,' he said, regarding Degnan with a stare which its recipient suddenly found to be as unpleasant as anything he had ever experienced, 'you might shake my confidence in you. What's worse, you might even begin to shake public confidence in you. That is a bad thing to have happen to a young undertaker with dreams, Mr Degnan. You never can tell how far it might reach. It might even reach the members of the licensing board for your profession.

You never know. But we mustn't keep you from your labors any longer. I suppose you have many things to do at a time like this. Possibly even more than you'd anticipated. Good night, Mr Degnan. Glad you introduced yourself.'

They went out the door and down the steps; Degnan's anguished voice trailed them to their car. 'Thirty-five dollars!' it wailed. 'Governor, I *appeal* to you . . .'

When they were under way, Skeffington said: 'I hadn't planned on rounding your evening off in just that way. I hope you weren't too shocked by my treatment of the widow's helper.'

Adam shook his head. 'It seemed to me that the widow's helper rather had it coming. And will he do it for thirty-five dollars, do you think?'

Skeffington chuckled. 'I wouldn't be surprised,' he said dryly.

'And the sum? That puzzled me. Why exactly thirty-five dollars?'

'No particular reason. It seemed a nice round humiliating figure. I'm not very fond of these death-bed bandits.' Especially, he reflected, when they propose to enrich themselves at his expense; for rather early in the evening it had occurred to him that the funeral would necessarily be paid for from the thousand dollars he had given to the widow. 'I'd heard about this Degnan, but I'd never happened to run into him before tonight. After tonight I imagine he'll see to it that I don't run into him again. Well,' he said, shifting his position and facing his nephew more directly, 'I didn't think we'd be in there quite so long. I apologize to you. I only hope you weren't bored.'

'No, no. Far from it.' Adam thought for a moment, looking back over the evening. There were a number of questions he wanted very much to ask his uncle; the difficulty was that some of them were not so easily put. He began with one that was; he said: 'Uncle Frank, what about a man like Charlie Hennessy? I mean, what is he? What does he do?'

'He runs for office, mostly. Against me or against anybody; Charlie plays no favorites. He hasn't been very successful lately, but back about twenty years ago, Charlie was considered quite a comer. He was always a great talker and he started off with a bang. He was on the City Council, a member of the Governor's Council — not under me, I might add — and he even served a term in Congress. In those days Charlie seemed to be looking into a rosy tomorrow.'

'And the roses faded?'

'They did indeed. You see,' Skeffington said, 'they suddenly discovered two things about Charlie. First, that he was honest, and second, that he was crazy. It was the combination that killed him. Theoretically at least, an honest man can succeed in politics; and there's a considerable body of evidence to prove that a crazy man can. But a man who's both honest and crazy might just as well be a Chinese midget for all the good he'll do himself at the polls.'

Adam protested. 'But he's not a madman, surely?'

Skeffington shrugged. 'It's a nice question of definition. He's not a certifiable lunatic, if that's what you mean, but he's certainly at that stage where a man's friends begin to call him "eccentric". What his enemies call him is apt to be something else again. Politically speaking, it's my opinion that Charlie is harmless except on those rare occasions when for some mysterious reason he decides to support me; then I want to run for cover. He's a dangerous man to have in your corner. He's great on the platform, but he has a crack right down the middle, and you never know when or where he's going to take off. I remember that when he first entered the City Council we were having a big to-do about a new municipal sewage system. Danny Leary was Council President, and he had Charlie all lined up to make the big speech in favor of it. Well, it was a big speech, all right. It lasted an hour and a half; the only trouble was that somewhere in the middle of it Charlie got sidetracked into talking about the marvellous advantages of having universal, compulsory fingerprinting introduced into the city, with the FBI coming in to take the prints of everybody who was still breathing. "Not even the nuns in their convents should be exempt!" said Charlie. Naturally that made a tremendous hit with the good Sisters; poor Leary spent the next two weeks crying in convent vestibules, explaining to Mother Superiors that his own daughter was a nun, and that he himself often went to daily Mass when the weather was good. Some of us wondered, however, what all this had to do with the problem of municipal sewage, and it was just about this time I began to suspect that Charlie's political value had its limitations. It's too bad, in a way, because he's a good fellow — smart enough, and knows the local political situation from A to Z. And, as I say, he won't take a dime from anybody. Charlie's trouble is that he's not content with asking the voters to lend him their ears; halfway through the speech he starts wanting to take their pulse as well. The result is that he's the kiss of death. What was that he had with him tonight, by the way — a camera?'

Adam told him of Charlie and the self-developing camera. Skeffington listened attentively, chuckling from time to time as he heard of the photographing of John Gorman, and of the grisly potential of the camera as an instrument in the sickroom. When Adam

finished the story, which seemed to him in the retelling even more improbable than when he had witnessed it in actual development, he looked questioningly at his uncle; both men broke into laughter.

'You see how it is,' Skeffington said. 'The authentic Hennessy touch: I'd recognize it anywhere. I wonder how the patient is supposed to react when the photographer asks him for "just one more"? Sounds a little final, as if he were soon to be among the souvenirs. What else did Charlie have to say for himself?'

Adam hesitated. Then, because there was much he was still curious about, and because a note of comradeship, almost of complicity, seemed to have been established between them on this ride home, he decided to move into more doubtful waters. He said, 'Actually, he didn't talk much about himself at all. He talked mostly about you, Uncle Frank. About you and the wake.'

'Reasonable enough, under the circumstances. The wake was there, and so was I.'

'Yes. The thing was that he seemed to be saying that the conjunction had a rather peculiar effect on the wake, that it changed its character pretty drastically.'

Skeffington nodded. 'From the funereal to the political,' he said. 'And what did you think of that?' Adam hesitated again, and Skeffington gave him a look of pleasant inquiry. 'Go ahead,' he invited. 'I'll probably be able to bear it.'

'Well,' Adam said reluctantly, 'to be honest, I had something of the same thought myself a little earlier, before Charlie arrived. I had quite a talk with Mr Gorman about it.' Now that he had gone this far, further frankness seemed unavoidable; somewhat uneasily he gave his uncle the full account of what had passed between Gorman and himself. Was it a mistake? he wondered. Probably not; it occurred to him that Gorman would himself unquestionably have mentioned it in due course.

As he talked, he kept his eyes on his uncle's face: the scrutiny proved remarkably unfruitful. The heavy features registered nothing more than a polite, unchanging interest; it was impossible for Adam to tell whether his uncle was indignant, whether he was outraged, whether he was totally unaffected. Or — in a sense, even worse — whether he was simply amused. It was most disquieting . . .

He completed his explanation. Skeffington said, 'I've seldom heard of John's being so eloquent; it stands as a great tribute to your qualities as a listener. I must say he put the case for me rather well; I couldn't have done better myself. Charlie's approach, on the other hand, must have been considerably different. I imagine he probably said something to this effect.' And then, while Adam stared at him, he proceeded to duplicate Charlie's speech in astonishing detail; it seemed to Adam, remembering the original, that the reproduction was virtually word for word. Finishing, Skeffington said, 'Close enough?'

'Close enough,' Adam agreed, bewildered. 'The question is: How? You couldn't have heard it from where you were.'

'Extrasensory perception,' Skeffington said gravely. 'A man can't go far without it today.' Once again, Adam heard the familiar deep chuckle. 'Of course, there is the additional fact that Charlie's principal addresses don't change very much over the years. He has the unwillingness of the artist to tamper with the perfect production. This is one of his best, a regular party piece. Or wake piece, if you prefer. I must have heard it a hundred times. It's extremely entertaining. In addition to which,' he said casually, 'it contains more than a little truth.'

Adam looked up sharply, but his uncle seemed preoccupied in withdrawing a cigar from his vest pocket. It was long, fat, dull-greenish in color. It did not appear to be at all the same grade of cigar that had been provided in quantities for the wake.

'One over the limit,' he said cheerfully, lighting it. 'A happy shortcut to the Dark Encounter. Well, you see me refusing to be less than candid with you. I don't want to give you a misleading impression. I should add that while Charlie was telling the truth, up to a point, so was John Gorman. Actually, they were both right: Knocko's wake was and it wasn't a political rally. Given the circumstances, and,' he added, with a faintly deprecatory wave of the cigar, 'given myself, it could hardly have been anything else. You see, what you're up against here is the special local situation. To understand what happened tonight, you have to understand a little bit about that situation, and just a little bit more about my own rather peculiar position in it.'

He leaned back, relaxing against the cushions; simply, detachedly, without boast or embellishment, he began to talk about himself. It was an extraordinary procedure; just how extraordinary, Adam did not realize. For while Skeffington had long studied his city and his own relation to it, the results of these studies he had been careful to keep to himself. From the beginning of his career, he had sharply divided the private from the public side of his life. Of the many friends he had made in politics over the years, none — not Gorman, even — had been admitted to the isolated preserve of the private thought, the personal concern. His wife had been his single, ideal confidant; with her death had come a void. Because Skeffington was, literally, a family man, he had tried one day, somewhat against his better judgment, to fill this void with his son. He had talked of himself, his work, his problems and his plans, and as he talked he had gradually become aware of the look upon his son's face: that characteristic, pleasant, glazed half-smile which indicated that somewhere beneath the surface inattention struggled with incomprehension. There had been more than the look; there had been the dancing feet: they had begun an abstracted, rather complicated tapping on the floor of the study, doubtless in anticipation of their evening's work ahead. *I should have been Vernon Castle,* Skeffington had thought bitterly. He had left the room abruptly and the experiment had never been repeated.

And now, as he had one afternoon three weeks before, he talked to his nephew.

'You see,' he said, 'my position is slightly complicated because I'm not just an elected official of the city; I'm a tribal chieftain as well. It's a necessary kind of dual officeholding, you might say; without the second, I wouldn't be the first.'

'The tribe,' said Adam, 'being the Irish?'

'Exactly. I have heard them called by less winning names: minority pressure group (even though they've been the majority for half a century), immigrant voting bloc (even though many of the said immigrants have been over here for three generations). Still, I don't suppose it makes much difference what you call them; the net result's the same. I won't insult your intelligence by explaining that they're the people who put me in the mayor's chair and keep me there; I think you realize that the body of my support doesn't come from the American Indian. But as a member — at least by birth — of the tribe, you might give a thought to some of the tribal customs. They don't chew betel nut, and as far as I know the women don't beautify themselves by placing saucers in their lower lips. Although now that I come to think of it,' he said, 'that might not be a bad idea. It might reduce the potential for conversation. However, they do other things, and among them they go to wakes. And so do I.'

'Which are and are not political rallies?' Adam asked. 'Or was Knocko's case a special one?'

'Not at all special, except that the guest of honor was somewhat less popular than many of his predecessors. But of course when you speak about wakes as being political rallies, that's a little strong. You have to remember something about the history of the wake around here. When I was a boy in this city, a wake was a big occasion, and by no means a sad one. Unless, of course, it was a member of your own family that had died. Otherwise it was a social event. Some of my most vivid memories are of wakes. I remember my poor mother taking me to old Nappy Coughlin's wake. We went into the tenement, and there was Nappy, all laid out in a little coffin which was kept on ice. Embalming was a rather uncertain science in those days. It was a hot day in July and there were no screens on the parlor windows; there were flies in the room. I can still hear the ice dripping into the pans underneath the coffin, and I can still see Nappy. He had one of the old-fashioned shrouds on, and he lay stretched out stiff as a ramrod. And on his head he wore a greasy black cap, which his good wife had lovingly adjusted so that the peak was pulled down over one eye. It gave him a rather challenging look; you had the feeling that at any moment he might spring out of the coffin and offer to go four fast rounds with you. My mother was horrified at the sight, and I remember that she went directly over to the widow and told her she ought to be ashamed of herself, putting her husband in the coffin with his hat on. Whereupon the widow simply said that he'd never had it off; he'd worn it for thirty years, day and night, in bed and out. So naturally she left it on, not wanting to say good-bye to a stranger. However, when Father Conroy came in, the hat was whisked off fast enough. I can remember — it was my first wake, by the way — going into the kitchen, where somebody gave me a glass of milk and a piece of cake. And while mother was in the parlor talking with the other women, I was out there with the men, just sitting around, eating cake, and listening to them talk. I hadn't the faintest notion of what they were talking about, but it didn't matter much. I was in seventh heaven. Everybody seemed to be enjoying themselves, and I knew I was. When my mother came to get me and take me home, I left with the greatest regret; I decided I'd never had a better time. Well,' he said, 'so much for memories of happy days. I wouldn't imagine it would sound like very much to anyone who'd been brought up today.'

Adam smiled. 'It sounded like a little boy having a wonderful time for himself. Although I must say that it didn't sound very much like death. Or even a political rally, for that matter.'

'Matter of fact, it was the first political rally I'd ever been to,' Skeffington said. 'I was just too young to know it. You see, that's what all the men were talking about: politics. There was even a moment, just before I left, when Charlie McCooey himself came in: a fat man with a red face and handlebar mustache. He was the ward boss. I didn't know what that was, at the time, but I did know that the name of Charlie

McCooey commanded respect and awe. I thought he must have been some kind of god. Twenty years later this childhood illusion was blasted. I gave him the beating of his life in a fight for the leadership of the ward; the vote was four to one. In the process of doing so I discovered that the god was nothing more than a dull bully-boy with no imagination and just enough intelligence to read his way through the daily adventures of Happy Hooligan. No offense intended, incidentally, by the reference to a rival comic strip.'

'No offense received,' Adam said. 'I lack the artist's pride. Besides, I think that Happy is defunct these days.' But he spoke absently, for he was not thinking of comic strips. He had suddenly remembered, while Skeffington was talking, that once, years ago, and from a source he could not now place, he had heard a series of quite different stories about the old wakes; in these, the cake-and-milk had not figured largely. He said, 'But I had the idea from somewhere, Uncle Frank, that many of these wakes got to be pretty violent affairs. I know there was always a certain amount of drinking, but didn't some of them actually become brawls?'

Skeffington's heavy face assumed a mildly shocked expression. 'Why, I hardly know what to say,' he murmured. 'I have heard that drinking men occasionally forced their way into these gatherings, but I like to believe that they were instantly sobered by the sight of decent men and women shrinking from them in revulsion.' He glanced at his nephew, and his lips twitched just slightly. 'No,' he said, 'of course you're right. There was drinking and sometimes things got a little rough. You might not have enjoyed it very much. But it's all gone by the boards long ago, and it was the exception rather than the rule; while it may seem terrible enough from your point of view today, you might reflect on the fact that there just might have been some excuse for it. I think what you have to do,' he said, 'is to see the wakes and everything that happened at them in the light of the times. I mentioned to you the other afternoon that life wasn't exactly a picnic for our people in those days. They were a sociable people but they didn't get much chance for sociability. They were poor, they worked hard, and they didn't have much in the way of diversion. Actually, the only place people got together was at the wake. Everybody knew everybody else; when somebody died, the others went to pay their respects and also to see and talk to each other. It was all part of the pattern. They were sorry for the family of the deceased, to be sure, but while they were being sorry they took advantage of the opportunity to have a drink and a chat with the others who were being sorry, too. It was a change, an outlet for people who led back-breaking, dreary, and monotonous lives. And if, once in a while, someone took a few too many and wanted to set fire to the widow or play steam-roller in the kitchen, it was possibly deplorable but it was also slightly understandable. All in all, I've always thought the wake was a grand custom, and I still do.'

'Yes,' Adam said slowly. 'I hadn't thought of it in that light — I mean, I hadn't thought of the wake as being a kind of *relief* from grimness. And yet I guess it must have been, all right. But what about *now*, Uncle Frank? Those same conditions don't exist, do they?'

'No,' said Skeffington, 'and neither does the wake. Not in the same way, that is. It's a disappearing phenomenon, like the derby hat. As the younger people grow up, the wakes are more and more changing their character: for example, they're being held now in funeral parlors rather than in the homes. The wake will still continue in some form; after all, it takes a long time to get rid of old tribal customs. And Knocko's was a bit like some of the old wakes; that's why I wanted you to see it. And as for the political discussion, that was in the grand tradition, too. By the way, did you happen to wonder why they might have been talking politics tonight?'

'Well, I naturally thought it was because you were there. But —'

'But,' Skeffington said, interrupting with a look of some amusement, 'was I there because they were going to talk politics? Right?' It was all too remarkably right; Adam flushed and began to protest, but Skeffington said, 'A perfectly natural question. I'd be astonished if it hadn't occurred to you. The answer, by the way, is a little bit of both. I suppose I went at least partly because it was one more opportunity to keep the ball rolling. It's almost impossible for an old campaigner to avoid the occasions of sin. But whether I'd been there or not, they would have talked politics anyway. It's what interests them most. It ought to: it gave most of them everything they have. I mentioned to you the other day that the main reason I went into politics was because it was the quickest way out of the cellar and up the ladder. A good many others felt the same way. A lot of the younger men wanted a nice new dark serge suit that didn't necessarily come equipped with a chauffeur's cap. And the only way out was through politics; it was only when we gained a measure of political control that our people were able to come up for a little fresh air. They know that; they think of it as the big salvation for them; that's why they talk about it when they all get together. It's a very serious part of the business of living. And when I'm around, naturally I'm expected to talk it with them.

And I do. I may add,' he said, 'that I don't find it a hardship.'

Adam thought of one more question. 'And the family?' he said. 'The family of the deceased, I mean. Like Mrs Minihan tonight. How do they feel while all this is going on? Don't they sometimes mind, Uncle Frank?'

'I know what you mean,' Skeffington said, 'but I think you're a bit wrong there. I don't think they mind a bit. There is a contrary opinion, however. Every once in a while I see where some advanced young public servant, who still had the ring of the pot on his seat while all this was going on, publicly applauds the passing of "that cruel and barbarous custom, the wake". Whenever I see that I take down my little book and chalk up a new name in the boob section. The man who said it obviously hasn't the faintest notion of what he's talking about. He hasn't the remotest understanding of the times, the circumstances, of our people, the way they feel and the way they regard death. I've seen a good many people die around here and I'll probably see a good many more. Unless, of course,' he added, in another of those detached and faintly chilling parentheses which never failed to jolt Adam, 'I beat them to it; there's always that possibility. But I've never seen the family that thought the wake was cruel and barbarous. They expected it. They wanted it. More than that, it was good for them: it was a useful distraction, it kept them occupied, and it gave them the feeling that they weren't alone, that they had a few neighbors who cared enough to come in and see them through a bad time. And you could say, too, it was a mark of respect for the deceased: rest assured that *he* wanted his wake. I remember what happened when the Honorable Hugh Archer died. The Honorable Hugh was considerably before your time; I don't imagine you'd have heard much about him.'

'No, nothing.'

'He was a prominent Republican attorney who once refused ten thousand dollars offered to him if he'd defend a notorious criminal. The noble gesture was unprecedented in Republican circles, and immediately he became known as the Honorable. It wasn't until much later that it was discovered he had asked for twenty thousand. Well, eventually he died. He was a huge man: six foot four and weighing nearly three hundred pounds. At that time, cremation was just coming into fashion, following closely upon Mah-jongg,[1] and they whipped the Honorable Hugh out to the incinerator on the very day he died. Old Martin Canady went to the ceremony, out of a curiosity to see how the other half died, and when he came running back to me he was literally popeyed with shock. "By God, Frank!" he said. "They took the big elephant before he stopped breathin' almost and what the hell d'ye think they did with him? They put him in the oven and burned him up with the Sunday papers! When the poor man finished cookin' ye could have buried him in an ash tray! By God, Frank, I wouldn't want nothin' like that to happen to me! When I go I'm damned sure I mean to stay around the house a few days and nights so's some of the old pals can come in and have a drink and the last look! What the hell's wrong with that, now" And,' Skeffington said, 'to save my soul, I couldn't think of a blessed thing wrong with it. It's the way I want to go myself. . . . Well, here I am talking away, it's late at night, and you're probably eager to get back in your house.'

For the first time Adam noticed that the car had stopped and that they were in front of his house; they had been there, in fact, for some minutes. He said, 'Uncle Frank, thanks loads for the evening. I've had a fine time, really.' Then, because he felt that somewhere along the line his comments, however courteously they had been received by the older man, had been fairly presumptuous, he added. 'And forgive the side-line observations on wakes. I guess the trouble was that I really didn't understand very much about them.'

'Nothing wrong with your observations at all,' Skeffington said. 'To tell you the truth, I was glad you were interested enough to make them. From one point of view, they were perfectly correct. All I was concerned with doing was to show you another point of view. And I'm glad you enjoyed yourself; I was hoping you would and I thought you might. Knocko's wake is the kind of thing you might not have come across in the ordinary run of events, yet in a way I think it's far more valuable to you in understanding the whys and wherefores of the campaign and the city than attendance at any number of rallies would be. I may add that it's been pleasant for me, too: it was good to have you along. When something else comes up that I think you should take a look at, I'll give you a ring. That is, of course,' he said courteously, 'if you'd like me to.'

'Please do, Uncle Frank. And again, thanks for tonight.'

'A pleasure,' Skeffington said. 'Good night, my boy. Remember me to your wife.'

---

1   A popular game probably of Chinese origin introduced into the United States by Joseph Babcock in 1920.

EUGENE O'NEILL
from Eugene O'Neill, *Long Day's Journey into Night* (first staged 1956; written 1940)

Eugene O'Neill (1888–1953) was born in New York, the son of a famous Irish-born actor James O'Neill. After a year at Princeton he took to the seas as a seaman, contracted tuberculosis, spent time in a sanatorium, and began writing plays. In 1916 he joined the Provincetown Players, who produced his first play to be staged, *Bound East for Cardiff*. He was a prolific dramatist for whom experience (often of failure) and writing were intertwined, and in 1936 he became the first American playwright to win the Nobel Prize for Literature. *Long Day's Journey into Night*, written in 1940, was first produced posthumously in 1956 and ever since has remained a favourite with theatre-goers worldwide. The first Act is reproduced below, and for the purposes of this *Reader* you might spend time reflecting on its Irishness, beginning with some of the following: names of characters, family tensions, concept or issue of generations, images of Ireland, use of the past, Ireland *vis-à-vis* America, dream versus reality, sense of displacement.

CHARACTERS

JAMES TYRONE
MARY CAVAN TYRONE, *his wife*
JAMES TYRONE JR., *their elder son*
EDMUND TYRONE, *their younger son*
CATHLEEN, *second girl*

ACT ONE

SCENE

Living room of JAMES TYRONE'S *summer house on a morning in August, 1912.*

At rear are two double doorways with portieres. The one at right leads into a front parlor with the formally arranged, set appearance of a room rarely occupied. The other opens on a dark, windowless back parlor, never used except as a passage from living room to dining room. Against the wall between the doorways is a small bookcase, with a picture of Shakespeare above it, containing novels by Balzac, Zola, Stendhal, philosophical and sociological works by Schopenhauer, Nietzsche, Marx, Engels, Kropotkin, Max Stirner, plays by Ibsen, Shaw, Strindberg, poetry by Swinburne, Rossetti, Wilde, Ernest Dowson, Kipling, etc.

In the right wall, rear, is a screen door leading out on the porch which extends halfway around the house. Farther forward, a series of three windows looks over the front lawn to the harbor and the avenue that runs along the water front. A small wicker table and an ordinary oak desk are against the wall, flanking the windows.

In the left wall, a similar series of windows looks out on the grounds in back of the house. Beneath them is a wicker couch with cushions, its head toward rear. Farther back is a large, glassed-in bookcase with sets of Dumas, Victor Hugo, Charles Lever, three sets of Shakespeare, The World's Best Literature in fifty large volumes, Hume's History of England, Thiers' History of the Consulate and Empire, Smollett's History of England, Gibbon's Roman Empire and miscellaneous volumes of old plays, poetry, and several histories of Ireland. The astonishing thing about these sets is that all the volumes have the look of having been read and reread.

The hardwood floor is nearly covered by a rug, inoffensive in design and colour. At centre is a round table with a green shaded reading lamp, the cord plugged in one of the four sockets in the chandelier above. Around the table within reading-light range are four chairs, three of them wicker armchairs, the fourth (at right front of table) a varnished oak rocker with leather bottom.

It is around 8.30. Sunshine comes through the windows at right.

As the curtain rises, the family have just finished breakfast. MARY TYRONE *and her husband enter together from the back parlor, coming from the dining room.*

MARY *is fifty-four, about medium height. She still has a young, graceful figure, a trifle plump, but showing little evidence of middle-aged waist and hips, although she is not tightly corseted. Her face is distinctly Irish in type. It must once have been extremely pretty, and is still striking. It does not match her healthy figure but is thin and pale with the bone structure prominent. Her nose is long and straight, her mouth wide with full, sensitive lips. She uses no rouge or any sort of make-up. Her high forehead is framed by thick, pure white hair. Accentuated by her pallor and white hair, her dark brown eyes appear black. They are unusually large and beautiful, with black brows and long curling lashes.*

What strikes one immediately is her extreme nervousness. Her hands are never still. They were once beautiful hands, with long, tapering fingers, but rheumatism has knotted the joints and warped the fingers, so that now they have an ugly crippled look. One avoids looking at them, the more so because one is conscious she is sensitive about their appearance and humiliated by her inability to control the nervousness which draws attention to them.

She is dressed simply but with a sure sense of what becomes her. Her hair is arranged with fastidious care. Her voice is soft and attractive. When she is merry, there is a touch of Irish lilt in it.

Her most appealing quality is the simple, unaffected charm of a shy convent-girl youthfulness she has never lost — an innate unworldly innocence.

JAMES TYRONE *is sixty-five but looks ten years younger. About five feet eight, broad-shouldered and deep-chested, he seems taller and slenderer because of his bearing, which has a soldierly quality of head up, chest out, stomach in, shoulders squared. His face has begun to break down but he is still remarkably good looking — a big, finely shaped head, a handsome profile, deep-set light-brown eyes. His grey hair is thin with a bald spot like a monk's tonsure.*

The stamp of his profession is unmistakably on him. Not that he indulges in any of the deliberate temperamental posturings of the stage star. He is by nature and preference a simple, unpretentious man, whose inclinations are still close to his humble beginnings and his Irish farmer forebears. But the actor shows in all his unconscious habits of speech, movement and gesture. These have the quality of belonging to a studied technique. His voice is remarkably fine, resonant and flexible, and he takes great pride in it.

His clothes, assuredly, do not costume any romantic part. He wears a threadbare, ready-made, grey sack suit and shineless black shoes, a collar-less shirt with a thick white handkerchief knotted loosely around his throat. There is nothing picturesquely careless about this get-up. It is commonplace shabby. He believes in wearing his clothes to the limit of usefulness, is dressed now for gardening, and doesn't give a damn how he looks.

He has never been really sick a day in his life. He has no nerves. There is a lot of stolid, earthy peasant in him, mixed with streaks of sentimental melancholy and rare flashes of intuitive sensibility.

TYRONE*'s arm is around his wife's waist as they appear from the back parlour. Entering the living room he gives her a playful hug.*

TYRONE: You're a fine armful now, Mary, with those twenty pounds you've gained.

MARY (*Smiles affectionately*): I've gotten too fat, you mean, dear. I really ought to reduce.

TYRONE: None of that, my lady! You're just right. We'll have no talk of reducing. Is that why you ate so little breakfast?

MARY: So little? I thought I ate a lot.

TYRONE: You didn't. Not as much as I'd like to see, anyway.

MARY (*Teasingly*): Oh you! You expect everyone to eat the enormous breakfast you do. No one else in the world could without dying of indigestion.

She comes forward to stand by the right of table.

TYRONE (*Following her*): I hope I'm not as big a glutton as that sounds. (*With hearty satisfaction.*) But thank God, I've kept my appetite and I've the digestion of a young man of twenty, if I am sixty-five.

MARY: You surely have, James. No one could deny that.

She laughs and sits in the wicker armchair at right rear of table. He comes around in back of her and selects a cigar from a box on the table and cuts off the end with a little clipper. From the dining room JAMIE*'s and* EDMUND*'s voices are heard.* MARY *turns her head that way.*

Why did the boys stay in the dining room, I wonder? Cathleen must be waiting to clear the table.

TYRONE (*Jokingly but with an undercurrent of resentment*): It's a secret confab they don't want me to hear, I suppose. I'll bet they're cooking up some new scheme to touch the Old Man.

She is silent on this, keeping her head turned toward their voices. Her hands appear on the table top, moving restlessly. He lights his cigar and sits down in the rocker at right of table, which is his chair, and puffs contentedly.

There's nothing like the first after-breakfast cigar, if it's a good one, and this new lot have the right mellow flavour. They're a great bargain, too. I got them dead cheap. It was McGuire put me on to them.

MARY (*A trifle acidly*): I hope he didn't put you on to any new piece of property at the same time. His real estate bargains don't work out so well.

TYRONE (*Defensively*): I wouldn't say that, Mary. After all, he was the one who advised me to buy that place on Chestnut Street and I made a quick turnover on it for a fine profit.

MARY (*Smiles now with teasing affection*): I know. The famous one stroke of good luck. I'm sure McGuire never dreamed — (*Then she pats his hand.*) Never mind, James. I know it's a waste of breath trying to convince you you're not a cunning real estate speculator.

TYRONE (*Huffily*): I've no such idea. But land is land, and it's safer than the stocks and bonds of Wall Street swindlers. (*Then placatingly.*) But let's not argue about business this early in the morning.

A pause. The boys' voices are again heard and one of them has a fit of coughing. MARY *listens worriedly. Her fingers play nervously on the table top.*

MARY: James, it's Edmund you ought to scold for not eating enough. He hardly touched anything except coffee. He needs to eat to keep up his strength. I keep telling him that but he says he simply has no appetite. Of course, there's nothing takes away your appetite like a bad summer cold.

TYRONE: Yes, it's only natural. So don't let yourself get worried —

MARY (*Quickly*): Oh, I'm not. I know he'll be all right in a few days if he takes care of himself.

As if she wanted to dismiss the subject but can't.

But it does seem a shame he should have to be sick right now.

TYRONE: Yes, it is bad luck. (*He gives her a quick, worried look.*) But you mustn't let it upset you, Mary. Remember, you've got to take care of yourself, too.

MARY (*Quickly*): I'm not upset. There's nothing to be upset about. What makes you think I'm upset?

TYRONE: Why, nothing, except you've seemed a bit high-strung the past few days.

MARY (*Forcing a smile*): I have? Nonsense, dear. It's your imagination. (*With sudden tenseness.*) You really must not watch me all the time, James. I mean, it makes me self-conscious.

TYRONE (*Putting a hand over one of her nervously playing ones*): Now, now, Mary. That's your imagination. If I've watched you it was to admire how fat and beautiful you looked.

His voice is suddenly moved by deep feeling.

I can't tell you the deep happiness it gives me, darling, to see you as you've been since you came back to us, your dear old self again.

He leans over and kisses her cheek impulsively — then turning back adds with a constrained air.

So keep up the good work, Mary.

MARY (*Has turned her head away*): I will, dear.

She gets up restlessly and goes to the windows at right.

Thank heavens, the fog is gone.

She turns back.

I do feel out of sorts this morning. I wasn't able to get much sleep with that awful foghorn going all night long.

TYRONE: Yes, it's like having a sick whale in the back yard. It kept me awake, too.

MARY (*Affectionately amused*): Did it? You had a strange way of showing your restlessness. You were snoring so hard I couldn't tell which was the foghorn!

She comes to him, laughing, and pats his cheek playfully.

Ten foghorns couldn't disturb you. You haven't a nerve in you. You've never had.

TYRONE (*His vanity piqued — testily*): Nonsense. You always exaggerate about my snoring.

MARY: I couldn't. If you could only hear yourself once—

A burst of laughter comes from the dining room. She turns her head, smiling.

What's the joke, I wonder?

TYRONE (*Grumpily*): It's on me. I'll bet that much. It's always on the Old Man.

MARY (*Teasingly*): Yes, it's terrible the way we all pick on you, isn't it? You're so abused!

She laughs — then with a pleased, relieved air.

Well, no matter what the joke is about, it's a relief to hear Edmund laugh. He's been so down in the mouth lately.

TYRONE (*Ignoring this — resentfully*): Some joke of Jamie's, I'll wager. He's forever making sneering fun of somebody, that one.

MARY: Now don't start in on poor Jamie, dear. (*Without conviction.*) He'll turn out all right in the end, you wait and see.

TYRONE: He'd better start soon, then. He's nearly thirty-four.

MARY (*Ignoring this.*): Good heavens, are they going to stay in the dining room all day?

She goes to the back parlor doorway and calls.

Jamie! Edmund! Come in the living room and give Cathleen a chance to clear the table.

EDMUND *calls back, 'We're coming, Mama.' She goes back to the table.*

TYRONE (*Grumbling*): You'd find excuses for him no matter what he did.

MARY (*Sitting down beside him, pats his hand*): Shush.

Their sons JAMES, JR, *and* EDMUND *enter together from the back parlor. They are both grinning, still chuckling over what had caused their laughter, and as they come forward they glance at their father and their grins grow broader.*

JAMIE, *the elder, is thirty-three. He has his father's broad-shouldered, deep-chested physique, is an inch taller and weighs less, but appears shorter and stouter because he lacks* TYRONE's *bearing and graceful carriage. He also lacks his father's vitality. The signs of premature disintegration are on him. His face is still good looking, despite marks of dissipation, but it has never been handsome like* TYRONE's, *although* JAMIE *resembles him rather than his mother. He has fine brown eyes, their color midway between his father's lighter and his mother's darker ones. His hair is thinning and already there is indication of a bald spot like* TYRONE's. *His nose is unlike that of any other member of the family, pronouncedly aquiline. Combined with his habitual expression of cynicism it gives his countenance a Mephistophelian cast. But on the rare occasions when he smiles without sneering, his personality possesses the remnant of a humorous, romantic, irresponsible Irish charm — that of the beguiling ne'er-do-well, with a strain of the sentimentally poetic, attractive to women and popular with men.*

He is dressed in an old sack suit, not as shabby as TYRONE's, *and wears a collar and tie. His fair skin is sunburned a reddish, freckled tan.*

EDMUND *is ten years younger than his brother, a couple of inches taller, thin and wiry. Where* JAMIE *takes after his father, with little resemblance to his mother,* EDMUND *looks like both his parents, but is more like his mother. Her big, dark eyes are the dominant feature in his long, narrow Irish face. His mouth has the same quality of hypersensitiveness hers possesses. His high forehead is hers accentuated, with dark brown hair, sunbleached to red at the ends, brushed straight back from it. But his nose is his father's and his face in profile recalls* TYRONE's. EDMUND's *hands are noticeably like his mother's, with the same exceptionally long fingers. They even have to a minor degree the same nervousness. It is in the quality of extreme nervous sensibility that the likeness of* EDMUND *to his mother is most marked.*

He is plainly in bad health. Much thinner than he should be, his eyes appear feverish and his cheeks are sunken. His skin, in spite of being sunburned a deep brown, has a parched sallowness. He wears a shirt, collar and tie, no coat, old flannel trousers, brown sneakers.

MARY (*Turns smilingly to them, in a merry tone that is a bit forced*): I've been teasing your father about his snoring. (*To* TYRONE.) I'll leave it to the boys, James. They must have heard you. No, not you, Jamie, I could hear you down the hall almost as bad as your father. You're like him. As soon as your head touches the pillow you're off and ten foghorns couldn't wake you.

She stops abruptly, catching JAMIE*'s eyes regarding her with an uneasy, probing look. Her smile vanishes and her manner becomes self-conscious.*

Why are you staring, Jamie?

Her hands flutter up to her hair.

Is my hair coming down? It's hard for me to do it up properly now. My eyes are getting so bad and I never can find my glasses.

JAMIE (*Looks away guiltily*): Your hair's all right, Mama. I was only thinking how well you look.

TYRONE (*Heartily*): Just what I've been telling her, Jamie. She's so fat and sassy, there'll soon be no holding her.

EDMUND: Yes, you certainly look grand, Mama.

She is reassured and smiles at him lovingly. He winks with a kidding grin.

I'll back you up about Papa's snoring. Gosh, what a racket!

JAMIE: I heard him, too.

He quotes, putting on a ham-actor manner.

'The Moor, I know his trumpet.'

His mother and brother laugh.

TYRONE (*Scathingly*): If it takes my snoring to make you remember Shakespeare instead of the dope sheet on the ponies, I hope I'll keep on with it.

MARY: Now, James! You mustn't be so touchy.

JAMIE *shrugs his shoulders and sits down in the chair on her right.*

EDMUND (*Irritably*): Yes, for Pete's sake, Papa! The first thing after breakfast! Give it a rest, can't you?

He slumps down in the chair at left of table next to his brother. His father ignores him.

MARY (*Reprovingly*): Your father wasn't finding fault with you. You don't have to always take Jamie's part. You'd think you were the one ten years older.

JAMIE (*Boredly*): What's all the fuss about? Let's forget it.

TYRONE (*Contemptuously*): Yes, forget! Forget everything and face nothing! It's a convenient philosophy if you've no ambition in life except to —

MARY: James, do be quiet.

She puts an arm around his shoulder — coaxingly.

You must have gotten out of the wrong side of the bed this morning.

To the boys, changing the subject.

What were you two grinning about like Cheshire cats when you came in? What was the joke?

TYRONE (*With a painful effort to be a good sport*): Yes, let us in on it, lads. I told your mother I knew damned well it would be one on me, but never mind that, I'm used to it.

JAMIE (*Dryly*): Don't look at me. This is the Kid's story.

EDMUND (*Grins*): I meant to tell you last night, Papa, and forgot it. Yesterday when I went for a walk I dropped in at the Inn —

MARY (*Worriedly*): You shouldn't drink now, Edmund.

EDMUND (*Ignoring this*): And who do you think I met there, with a beautiful bun on, but Shaughnessy, the tenant on that farm of yours.

MARY (*Smiling*): That dreadful man! But he is funny.

TYRONE (*Scowling*): He's not so funny when you're his landlord. He's a wily Shanty Mick, that one. He could hide behind a corkscrew. What's he complaining about now, Edmund — for I'm damned sure he's complaining. I suppose he wants his rent lowered. I let him have the place for almost nothing, just to keep someone on it, and he never pays that till I threaten to evict him.

EDMUND: No, he didn't beef about anything. He was so pleased with life he even bought a drink, and that's practically unheard of. He was delighted because he'd had a fight with your friend, Harker, the Standard Oil millionaire, and won a glorious victory.

MARY (*With amused dismay*): Oh, Lord! James, you'll really have to do something —

TYRONE: Bad luck to Shaughnessy, anyway!

JAMIE (*Maliciously*): I'll bet the next time you see Harker at the Club and give him the old respectful bow, he won't see you.

EDMUND: Yes. Harker will think you're no gentleman for harboring a tenant who isn't humble in the presence of a king of America.

TYRONE: Never the mind the Socialist gabble. I don't care to listen —

MARY (*Tactfully*): Go on with your story, Edmund.

EDMUND (*Grins at his father provocatively*): Well, you remember, Papa, the ice pond on Harker's estate is right next to the farm, and you remember Shaughnessy keeps pigs. Well, it seems there's a break in the fence and the pigs have been bathing in the millionaire's ice pond, and Harker's foreman told him he was sure Shaughnessy had broken the fence on purpose to give his pigs a free wallow.

MARY (*Shocked and amused*): Good heavens!

TYRONE (*Sourly, but with a trace of admiration*): I'm sure he did, too, the dirty scallywag. It's like him.

EDMUND: So Harker came in person to rebuke Shaughnessy. (*He chuckles.*) A very bonehead play! If I needed any further proof that our ruling plutocrats, especially the ones who inherited their boodle, are not mental giants, that would clinch it.

TYRONE (*With appreciation, before he thinks*): Yes, he'd be no match for Shaughnessy.
Then he growls.
Keep your damned anarchist remarks to yourself. I won't have them in my house.
But he is full of eager anticipation.
What happened?

EDMUND: Harker had as much chance as I would with Jack Johnson. Shaughnessy got a few drinks under his belt and was waiting at the gate to welcome him. He told me he never gave Harker a chance to open his mouth. He began by shouting that he was no slave Standard Oil could trample on. He was a King of Ireland, if he had his rights, and scum was scum to him, no matter how much money it had stolen from the poor.

MARY: Oh, Lord! (*But she can't help laughing.*)

EDMUND: Then he accused Harker of making his foreman break down the fence to entice the pigs into the ice pond in order to destroy them. The poor pigs, Shaughnessy yelled, had caught their death of cold. Many of them were dying of pneumonia, and several others had been taken down with cholera from drinking the poisoned water. He told Harker he was hiring a lawyer to sue him for damages. And he wound up by saying that he had to put up with poison ivy, ticks, potato bugs, snakes and skunks on his farm, but he was an honest man who drew the line somewhere, and he'd be damned if he'd stand for a Standard Oil thief trespassing. So would Harker kindly remove his dirty feet from the premises before he sicked the dog on him. And Harker did! (*He and* JAMIE *laugh.*)

MARY (*Shocked but giggling*): Heavens, what a terrible tongue that man has!

TYRONE (*Admiringly before he thinks*): The damned old scoundrel! By God, you can't beat him!
He laughs — then stops abruptly and scowls.
The dirty blackguard! He'll get me in serious trouble yet. I hope you told him I'd be mad as hell —

EDMUND: I told him you'd be tickled to death over the great Irish victory, and so you are. Stop faking, Papa.

TYRONE: Well, I'm not tickled to death.

MARY (*Teasingly*): You are, too, James. You're simply delighted!

TYRONE: No, Mary, a joke is a joke, but —

EDMUND: I told Shaughnessy he should have reminded Harker that a Standard Oil millionaire ought to welcome the flavour of hog in his ice water as an appropriate touch.

TYRONE: The devil you did! (*Frowning.*) Keep your damned Socialist anarchist sentiments out of my affairs!

EDMUND: Shaughnessy almost wept because he hadn't thought of that one, but he said he'd include it in a letter he's writing to Harker, along with a few other insults he'd overlooked.
He and JAMIE *laugh.*

TYRONE: What are you laughing at? There's nothing funny — A fine son you are to help that blackguard get me into a lawsuit!

MARY: Now, James, don't lose your temper.

TYRONE (*Turns on* JAMIE): And you're worse than he is, encouraging him. I suppose you're regretting you weren't there to prompt Shaughnessy with a few nastier insults. You've a fine talent for that, if for nothing else.

MARY: James! There's no reason to scold Jamie.
JAMIE *is about to make some sneering remark to his father, but he shrugs his shoulders.*

EDMUND (*With sudden nervous exasperation*): Oh, for God's sake, Papa! If you're starting that stuff again, I'll beat it.
He jumps up.
I left my book upstairs, anyway.
He goes to the front parlor, saying disgustedly,
God, Papa, I should think you'd get sick of hearing yourself —
He disappears. TYRONE *looks after him angrily.*

MARY: You mustn't mind Edmund, James. Remember he isn't well.
EDMUND *can be heard coughing as he goes upstairs.*
She adds nervously.
A summer cold makes anyone irritable.

JAMIE (*Genuinely concerned*): It's not just a cold he's got. The Kid is damned sick.
His father gives him a sharp warning look but he doesn't see it.

MARY (*Turns on him resentfully*): Why do you say that? It *is* just a cold! Anyone can tell that! You always imagine things!

TYRONE (*With another warning glance at* JAMIE *— easily*): All Jamie meant was Edmund might have a touch of something else, too, which makes his cold worse.

JAMIE: Sure, Mama. That's all I meant.

TYRONE: Doctor Hardy thinks it might be a bit of malarial fever he caught when he was in the tropics. If it is, quinine will soon cure it.

MARY (*A look of contemptuous hostility flashes across her face*): Doctor Hardy! I wouldn't believe a thing he said, if he swore on a stack of Bibles! I know what doctors are. They're all alike. Anything, they don't care what, to keep you coming to them.

She stops short, overcome by a fit of acute self-consciousness as she catches their eyes fixed on her. Her hands jerk nervously to her hair. She forces a smile.

What is it? What are you looking at? Is my hair —?

TYRONE (*Puts his arm around her — with guilty heartiness, giving her a playful hug*): There's nothing wrong with your hair. The healthier and fatter you get, the vainer you become. You'll soon spend half the day primping before the mirror.

MARY (*Half reassured*): I really should have new glasses. My eyes are so bad now.

TYRONE (*With Irish blarney*): Your eyes are beautiful, and well you know it.

He gives her a kiss. Her face lights up with a charming, shy embarrassment. Suddenly and startlingly one sees in her face the girl she had once been, not a ghost of the dead, but still a living part of her.

MARY: You mustn't be so silly, James. Right in front of Jamie!

TYRONE: Oh, he's on to you, too. He knows this fuss about eyes and hair is only fishing for compliments. Eh, Jamie?

JAMIE (*His face has cleared, too, and there is an old boyish charm in his loving smile at his mother*): Yes. You can't kid us, Mama.

MARY (*Laughs and an Irish lilt comes into her voice*): Go along with both of you!

Then she speaks with a girlish gravity.

But I did truly have beautiful hair once, didn't I, James?

TYRONE: The most beautiful in the world!

MARY: It was a rare shade of reddish brown and so long it came down below my knees. You ought to remember it, too, Jamie. It wasn't until after Edmund was born that I had a single grey hair. Then it began to turn white.

The girlishness fades from her face.

TYRONE (*Quickly*): And that made it prettier than ever.

MARY (*Again embarrassed and pleased*): Will you listen to your father, Jamie — after thirty-five years of marriage! He isn't a great actor for nothing, is he? What's come over you, James? Are you pouring coals of fire on my head for teasing you about snoring? Well then, I take it all back. It must have been only the foghorn I heard.

She laughs, and they laugh with her. Then she changes to a brisk businesslike air.

But I can't stay with you any longer, even to hear compliments. I must see the cook about dinner and the day's marketing.

She gets up and sighs with humorous exaggeration.

Bridget is so lazy. And so sly. She begins telling me about her relatives so I can't get a word in edgeways and scold her. Well, I might as well get it over.

She goes to the back-parlor doorway, then turns, her face worried again.

You mustn't make Edmund work on the grounds with you, James, remember.

Again with the strange obstinate set to her face.

Not that he isn't strong enough, but he'd perspire and he might catch more cold.

She disappears through the back parlor. TYRONE turns on JAMIE condemningly.

TYRONE: You're a fine lunkhead! Haven't you any sense? The one thing to avoid is saying anything that would get her more upset over Edmund.

JAMIE (*Shrugging his shoulders*): All right. Have it your way. I think it's the wrong idea to let Mama go on kidding herself. It will only make the shock worse when she has to face it. Anyway, you can see she's deliberately fooling herself with that summer cold talk. She knows better.

TYRONE: Knows? Nobody knows yet.

JAMIE: Well, I do. I was with Edmund when he went to Doc Hardy on Monday. I heard him pull that touch of malaria stuff. He was stalling. That isn't what he thinks any more. You know it as well as I do. You talked to him when you went uptown yesterday, didn't you?

TYRONE: He couldn't say anything for sure yet. He's to phone me today before Edmund goes to him.

JAMIE (*Slowly*): He thinks it's consumption, doesn't he, Papa?

TYRONE (*Reluctantly*): He said it might be.

JAMIE (*Moved, his love for his brother coming out*): Poor kid! God damn it!

He turns on his father accusingly.

It might never have happened if you'd sent him to a real doctor when he first got sick.

TYRONE: What's the matter with Hardy? He's always been our doctor up here.

JAMIE: Everything's the matter with him! Even in this hick burg he's rated third class! He's a cheap old quack!

TYRONE: That's right! Run him down! Run down everybody! Everyone is a fake to you!

JAMIE (*Contemptuously*): Hardy only charges a dollar. That's what makes you think he's a fine doctor!

TYRONE (*Stung*): That's enough! You're not drunk now! There's no excuse —

He controls himself — a bit defensively.

If you mean I can't afford one of the fine society doctors who prey on the rich summer people —

JAMIE: Can't afford? You're one of the biggest property owners around here.

TYRONE: That doesn't mean I'm rich. It's all mortgaged —

JAMIE: Because you always buy more instead of paying off mortgages. If Edmund was a lousy acre of land you wanted, the sky would be the limit!

TYRONE: That's a lie! And your sneers against Doctor Hardy are lies! He doesn't put on frills, or have an office in a fashionable location, or drive around in an expensive automobile. That's what you pay for with those other five-dollars-to-look-at-your-tongue fellows, not their skill.

JAMIE (*With a scornful shrug of his shoulders*): Oh, all right. I'm a fool to argue. You can't change the leopard's spots.

TYRONE (*With rising anger*): No, you can't. You've taught me that lesson only too well. I've lost all hope you will ever change yours. You dare tell me what I can afford? You've never known the value of a dollar and never will! You've never saved a dollar in your life! At the end of each season you're penniless! You've thrown your salary away every week on whores and whiskey!

JAMIE: My salary! Christ!

TYRONE: It's more than you're worth, and you couldn't get that if it wasn't for me. If you weren't my son, there isn't a manager in the business who would give you a part, your reputation stinks so. As it is, I have to humble my pride and beg for you, saying you've turned over a new leaf, although I know it's a lie!

JAMIE: I never wanted to be an actor. You forced me on the stage.

TYRONE: That's a lie! You made no effort to find anything else to do. You left it to me to get you a job and I have no influence except in the theater. Forced you! You never wanted to do anything except loaf in barrooms! You'd have been content to sit back like a lazy lunk and sponge on me for the rest of your life! After all the money I'd wasted on your education, and all you did was get fired in disgrace from every college you went to!

JAMIE: Oh, for God's sake, don't drag up that ancient history!

TYRONE: It's not ancient history that you have to come home every summer to live on me.

JAMIE: I earn my board and lodging on the grounds. It saves you hiring a man.

TYRONE: Bah! You have to be driven to do even that much!

His anger ebbs into a weary complaint.

I wouldn't give a damn if you ever displayed the slightest sign of gratitude. The only thanks is to have you sneer at me for a dirty miser, sneer at my profession, sneer at every damned thing in the world — except yourself.

JAMIE (*Wryly*): That's not true, Papa. You can't hear me talking to myself, that's all.

TYRONE (*Stares at him puzzledly, then quotes mechanically*): 'Ingratitude, the vilest weed that grows'!

JAMIE: I could see that line coming! God, how many thousand times —!

He stops, bored with their quarrel, and shrugs his shoulders.

All right, Papa. I'm a bum. Anything you like, so long as it stops the argument.

TYRONE (*With indignant appeal now*): If you'd get ambition in your head instead of folly! You're young yet. You could still make your mark. You had the talent to become a fine actor! You have it still. You're my son —!

JAMIE (*Boredly*): Let's forget me. I'm not interested in the subject. Neither are you.

TYRONE *gives up.* JAMIE *goes on casually.*

What started us on this? Oh, Doc Hardy. When is he going to call you about Edmund?

TYRONE: Around lunch time.

He pauses — then defensively.

I couldn't have sent Edmund to a better doctor. Hardy's treated him whenever he was sick up here, since he was knee high. He knows his constitution as no other doctor could. It's not a question of my being miserly, as you'd like to make out.

Bitterly.

And what could the finest specialist in America do for Edmund, after he's deliberately ruined his health by the mad life he's led ever since he was fired from college? Even before that when he was in prep school, he began dissipating and playing the Broadway sport to imitate you, when he's never had your constitution to stand it. You're a healthy hulk like me — or you were at his age — but he's always been a bundle of nerves like his mother. I've warned him for years his body couldn't stand it, but he wouldn't heed me, and now it's too late.

JAMIE (*Sharply*): What do you mean, too late? You talk as if you thought —

TYRONE (*Guiltily explosive*): Don't be a damned fool! I meant nothing but what's plain to anyone! His health has broken down and he may be an invalid for a long time.

JAMIE (*Stares at his father, ignoring his explanation*): I know it's an Irish peasant idea consumption is fatal. It probably is when you live in a hovel on a bog, but over here, with modern treatment —

TYRONE: Don't I know that! What are you gabbing about, anyway? And keep your dirty tongue off Ireland, with your sneers about peasants and bogs and hovels! (*Accusingly.*) The less you say about Edmund's sickness, the better for your conscience! You're more responsible than anyone!

JAMIE (*Stung*): That's a lie! I won't stand for that, Papa!

TYRONE: It's the truth! You've been the worst influence for him. He grew up admiring you as a hero! A fine example you set him! If you ever gave him advice except in the ways of rottenness, I've never heard of it! You made him old before his time, pumping him full of what you consider worldly wisdom, when he was too young to see that your mind was so poisoned by your own failure in life, you wanted to believe every man was a knave with his soul for sale, and every woman who wasn't a whore was a fool!

JAMIE (*With a defensive air of weary indifference again*): All right. I did put Edmund wise to things, but not until I saw he'd started to raise hell, and knew he'd laugh at me if I tried the good advice, older brother stuff. All I did was make a pal of him and be absolutely frank so he'd learn from my mistakes that —

He shrugs his shoulders — cynically.

Well, that if you can't be good you can at least be careful.

His father snorts contemptuously. Suddenly JAMIE *becomes really moved.*

That's a rotten accusation, Papa. You know how much the Kid means to me, and how close we've always been — not like the usual brothers! I'd do anything for him.

TYRONE (*Impressed — mollifyingly*): I know you may have thought it was for the best, Jamie. I didn't say you did it deliberately to harm him.

JAMIE: Besides it's damned rot! I'd like to see anyone influence Edmund more than he wants to be. His quietness fools people into thinking they can do what they like with him. But he's stubborn as hell inside and what he does is what he wants to do, and to hell with anyone else! What had I to do with all the crazy stunts he's pulled in the last few years — working his way all over the map as a sailor and all that stuff. I thought that was a damned fool idea, and I told him so. You can't

imagine me getting fun out of being on the beach in South America, or living in filthy dives, drinking rotgut, can you? No, thanks! I'll stick to Broadway, and a room with a bath, and bars that serve bonded Bourbon.

TYRONE: You and Broadway! It's made you what you are!

With a touch of pride.

Whatever Edmund's done, he's had the guts to go off on his own, where he couldn't come whining to me the minute he was broke.

JAMIE (*Stung into sneering jealousy*): He's always come home broke finally, hasn't he? And what did his going away get him? Look at him now!

He is suddenly shamefaced.

Christ! That's a lousy thing to say. I don't mean that.

TYRONE (*Decides to ignore this*): He's been doing well on the paper. I was hoping he'd found the work he wants to do at last.

JAMIE (*Sneering jealously again*): A hick town rag! Whatever bull they hand you, they tell me he's a pretty bum reporter. If he weren't your son—

Ashamed again.

No, that's not true! They're glad to have him, but it's the special stuff that gets him by. Some of the poems and parodies he's written are damned good.

Grudgingly again.

Not that they'd ever get him anywhere on the big time.

Hastily.

But he's certainly made a damned good start.

TYRONE: Yes. He's made a start. You used to talk about wanting to become a newspaper man but you were never willing to start at the bottom. You expected —

JAMIE: Oh, for Christ's sake, Papa! Can't you lay off me!

TYRONE (*Stares at him — then looks away — after a pause*): It's damnable luck Edmund should be sick right now. It couldn't have come at a worse time for him.

He adds, unable to conceal an almost furtive uneasiness.

Or for your mother. It's damnable she should have this to upset her, just when she needs peace and freedom from worry. She's been so well in the two months since she came home.

His voice grows husky and trembles a little.

It's been heaven to me. This home has been a home again. But I needn't tell you, Jamie.

His son looks at him, for the first time with an understanding sympathy. It is as if suddenly a deep bond of common feeling existed between them in which their antagonisms could be forgotten.

JAMIE (*Almost gently*): I've felt the same way, Papa.

TYRONE: Yes, this time you can see how strong and sure of herself she is. She's a different woman entirely from the other times. She has control of her nerves — or she had until Edmund got sick. Now you can feel her growing tense and frightened underneath. I wish to God we could keep the truth from her, but we can't if he has to be sent to a sanatorium. What makes it worse is her father died of consumption. She worshipped him and she's never forgotten. Yes, it will be hard for her. But she can do it! She has the will power now! We must help her, Jamie, in every way we can!

JAMIE (*Moved*): Of course, Papa. (*Hesitantly.*) Outside of nerves, she seems perfectly all right this morning.

TYRONE (*With hearty confidence now*): Never better. She's full of fun and mischief.

Suddenly he frowns at JAMIE *suspiciously.*

Why do you say, seems? Why shouldn't she be all right? What the hell do you mean?

JAMIE: Don't start jumping down my throat! God, Papa, this ought to be one thing we can talk over frankly without a battle.

TYRONE: I'm sorry, Jamie. (*Tensely.*) But go on and tell me —

JAMIE: There's nothing to tell. I was all wrong. It's just that last night — Well, you know how it is, I can't forget the past. I can't help being suspicious. Any more than you can. (*Bitterly.*) That's the hell of it. And it makes it hell for Mama! She watches us watching her —

TYRONE (*Sadly*): I know. (*Tensely.*) Well, what was it? Can't you speak out?

JAMIE: Nothing, I tell you. Just my damned foolishness. Around three o'clock this morning, I woke up and heard her moving around in the spare room. Then she went to the bathroom. I pretended to be asleep. She stopped in the hall to listen, as if she wanted to make sure I was.

TYRONE (*With forced scorn*): For God's sake, is that all? She told me herself the foghorn kept her awake all night, and every night since Edmund's been sick she's been up and down, going to his room to see how he was.

JAMIE (*Eagerly*): Yes, that's right, she did stop to listen outside his room. (*Hesitantly again.*) It was her being in the spare room that scared me. I couldn't help remembering that when she starts sleeping alone in there, it has always been a sign —

TYRONE: It isn't this time! It's easily explained. Where else could she go last night to get away from my snoring?

He gives way to a burst of resentful anger.

By God, how you can live with a mind that sees nothing but the worst motives behind everything is beyond me!

JAMIE (*Stung*): Don't pull that! I've just said I was all wrong. Don't you suppose I'm as glad of that as you are!

TYRONE (*Mollifyingly*): I'm sure you are, Jamie.

A pause. His expression becomes sombre. He speaks slowly with a superstitious dread.

It would be like a curse she can't escape if worry over Edmund — It was in her long sickness after bringing him into the world that she first —

JAMIE: She didn't have anything to do with it!

TYRONE: I'm not blaming her.

JAMIE (*Bitingly*): Then who are you blaming? Edmund, for being born?

TYRONE: You damned fool! No one was to blame.

JAMIE: The bastard of a doctor was! From what Mama's said, he was another cheap quack like Hardy! You wouldn't pay for a first-rate —

TYRONE: That's a lie! (*Furiously.*) So I'm to blame! That's what you're driving at, is it? You evil-minded loafer!

JAMIE (*Warningly as he hears his mother in the dining room*): Ssh!

TYRONE *gets hastily to his feet and goes to look out the windows at right.* JAMIE *speaks with a complete change of tone.*

Well, if we're going to cut the front hedge today, we'd better go to work.

MARY *comes in from the back parlor. She gives a quick, suspicious glance from one to the other, her manner nervously self-conscious.*

TYRONE (*Turns from the window — with an actor's heartiness*): Yes, it's too fine a morning to waste indoors arguing. Take a look out the window, Mary. There's no fog in the harbor. I'm sure the spell of it we've had is over now.

MARY (*Going to him*): I hope so, dear.

To JAMIE, *forcing a smile.*

Did I actually hear you suggesting work on the front hedge, Jamie? Wonders will never cease! You must want pocket money badly.

JAMIE (*Kiddingly*): When don't I?

He winks at her, with a derisive glance at his father.

I expect a salary of at least one large iron man at the end of the week — to carouse on!

MARY (*Does not respond to his humour — her hands fluttering over the front of her dress*): What were you two arguing about?

JAMIE (*Shrugs his shoulders*): The same old stuff.

MARY: I heard you say something about a doctor, and your father accusing you of being evil-minded.

JAMIE (*Quickly*): Oh, that. I was saying again Doc Hardy isn't my idea of the world's greatest physician.

MARY (*Knows he is lying — vaguely*): Oh. No, I wouldn't say he was, either.

Changing the subject — forcing a smile.

That Bridget! I thought I'd never get away. She told me all about her second cousin on the police force in St Louis.

Then with nervous irritation.

Well, if you're going to work on the hedge why don't you go?

Hastily.

I mean, take advantage of the sunshine before the fog comes back.

Strangely, as if talking aloud to herself.

Because I know it will.

Suddenly she is self-consciously aware that they are both staring fixedly at her — flurriedly, raising her hands.

Or I should say, the rheumatism in my hands knows. It's a better weather prophet than you are, James.

She stares at her hands with fascinated repulsion.

Ugh! How ugly they are! Who'd ever believe they were once beautiful?

They stare at her with a growing dread.

TYRONE (*Takes her hands and gently pushes them down*): Now, now, Mary. None of that foolishness. They're the sweetest hands in the world.

She smiles, her face lighting up, and kisses him gratefully. He turns to his son.

Come on Jamie. Your mother's right to scold us. The way to start work is to start work. The hot sun will sweat some of that booze fat off your middle.

He opens the screen door and goes out on the porch and disappears down a flight of steps leading to the ground. JAMIE rises from his chair and, taking off his coat, goes to the door. At the door he turns back but avoids looking at her, and she does not look at him.

JAMIE (*With an awkward, uneasy tenderness*): We're all so proud of you, Mama, so darned happy.

She stiffens and stares at him with a frightened defiance. He flounders on.

But you've still got to be careful. You mustn't worry so much about Edmund. He'll be all right.

MARY (*With a stubborn, bitterly resentful look*): Of course, he'll be all right. And I don't know what you mean, warning me to be careful.

JAMIE (*Rebuffed and hurt, shrugs his shoulders*): All right, Mama. I'm sorry I spoke.

He goes out on the porch. She waits rigidly until he disappears down the steps. Then she sinks down in the chair he had occupied, her face betraying a frightened, furtive desperation, her hands roving over the table top, aimlessly moving objects around. She hears EDMUND descending the stairs in the front hall. As he nears the bottom he has a fit of coughing. She springs to her feet, as if she wanted to run away from the sound, and goes quickly to the windows at right. She is looking out, apparently calm, as he enters from the front parlor, a book in one hand. She turns to him, her lips set in a welcoming, motherly smile.

MARY: Here you are. I was just going upstairs to look for you.

EDMUND: I waited until they went out. I don't want to mix up in any arguments. I feel too rotten.

MARY (*Almost resentfully*): Oh, I'm sure you don't feel half as badly as you make out. You're such a baby. You like to get us worried so we'll make a fuss over you.

Hastily.

I'm only teasing, dear. I know how miserably uncomfortable you must be. But you feel better today, don't you?

Worriedly, taking his arm.

All the same, you've grown much too thin. You need to rest all you can. Sit down and I'll make you comfortable.

He sits down in the rocking chair and she puts a pillow behind his back.

There. How's that?

EDMUND: Grand. Thanks, Mama.

MARY (*Kisses him — tenderly*): All you need is your mother to nurse you. Big as you are, you're still the baby of the family to me, you know.

EDMUND (*Takes her hand — with deep seriousness*): Never mind me. You take care of yourself. That's all that counts.

MARY (*Evading his eyes*): But I am, dear.

Forcing a laugh.

Heavens, don't you see how fat I've grown! I'll have to have all my dresses let out.

She turns away and goes to the windows at right. She attempts a light, amused tone.

They've started clipping the hedge. Poor Jamie! How he hates working in front where everyone passing can see him. There go the Chatfields in their new Mercedes. It's a beautiful car, isn't it? Not like our secondhand Packard. Poor Jamie! He bent almost under the hedge so they wouldn't notice him. They bowed to your father and he bowed back as if he were taking a curtain call. In that filthy old suit I've tried to make him throw away.

Her voice has grown bitter.

Really, he ought to have more pride than to make such a show of himself.

EDMUND: He's right not to give a damn what anyone thinks. Jamie's a fool to care about the Chatfields. For Pete's sake, who ever heard of them outside this hick burg?

MARY (*With satisfaction*): No one. You're quite right, Edmund. Big frogs in a small puddle. It is stupid of Jamie.

She pauses, looking out the window — then with an undercurrent of lonely yearning.

Still, the Chatfields and people like them stand for something. I mean they have decent, presentable homes they don't have to be ashamed of. They have friends who entertain them and whom they entertain. They're not cut off from everyone.

She turns back from the window.

Not that I want anything to do with them. I've always hated this town and everyone in it. You know that. I never wanted to live here in the first place, but your father liked it and insisted on building this house, and I've had to come here every summer.

EDMUND: Well, it's better than spending the summer in a New York hotel, isn't it? And this town's not so bad. I like it well enough. I suppose because it's the only home we've had.

MARY: I've never felt it was my home. It was wrong from the start. Everything was done in the cheapest way. Your father would never spend the money to make it right. It's just as well we haven't any friends here. I'd be ashamed to have them step in the door. But he's never wanted family friends. He hates calling on people, or receiving them. All he likes is to hobnob with men at the Club or in a barroom. Jamie and you are the same way, but you're not to blame. You've never had a chance to meet decent people here. I know you both would have been so different if you'd been able to associate with nice girls instead of — You'd never have disgraced yourselves as you have, so that now no respectable parents will let their daughters be seen with you.

EDMUND (*Irritably*): Oh, Mama, forget it! Who cares? Jamie and I would be bored stiff. And about the Old Man, what's the use of talking? You can't change him.

MARY (*Mechanically rebuking*): Don't call your father the Old Man. You should have more respect.

Then dully.

I know it's useless to talk. But sometimes I feel so lonely.

Her lips quiver and she keeps her head turned away.

EDMUND: Anyway, you've got to be fair, Mama. It may have been all his fault in the beginning, but you know that later on, even if he'd wanted to, we couldn't have had people here —

He flounders guiltily.

I mean, you wouldn't have wanted them.

MARY (*Wincing — her lips quivering pitifully*): Don't. I can't bear having you remind me.

EDMUND: Don't take it that way! Please, Mama! I'm trying to help. Because it's bad for you to forget. The right way is to remember. So you'll always be on your guard. You know what's happened before.

Miserably.

God, Mama, you know I hate to remind you. I'm doing it because it's been so wonderful having you home the way you've been, and it would be terrible —

MARY (*Strickenly*): Please, dear. I know you mean it for the best, but —

A defensive uneasiness comes into her voice again.

I don't understand why you should suddenly say such things. What put it in your mind this morning?

EDMUND (*Evasively*): Nothing. Just because I feel rotten and blue, I suppose.

MARY: Tell me the truth. Why are you so suspicious all of a sudden?

EDMUND: I'm not.

MARY: Oh, yes you are. I can feel it. Your father and Jamie, too — particularly Jamie.

EDMUND: Now don't start imagining things, Mama.

MARY (*Her hands fluttering*): It makes it so much harder, living in this atmosphere of constant suspicion, knowing everyone is spying on me, and none of you believe in me, or trust me.

EDMUND: That's crazy, Mama. We do trust you.

MARY: If there was only some place I could go to get away for a day, or even an afternoon, some woman friend I could talk to — not about anything serious, simply laugh and gossip and forget for a while — someone besides the servants — that stupid Cathleen!

EDMUND (*Gets up worriedly and puts his arm around her*): Stop it, Mama. You're getting yourself worked up over nothing.

MARY: Your father goes out. He meets his friends in barrooms or at the Club. You and Jamie have the boys you know. You go out. But I am alone. I've always been alone.

EDMUND (*Soothingly*): Come now! You know that's a fib. One of us always stays around to keep you company, or goes with you in the automobile when you take a drive.

MARY (*Bitterly*): Because you're afraid to trust me alone!

She turns on him — sharply.

I insist you tell me why you act so differently this morning — why you felt you had to remind me —

EDMUND (*Hesitates — then blurts out guiltily*): It's stupid. It's just that I wasn't asleep when you came in my room last night. You didn't go back to your and Papa's room. You went in the spare room for the rest of the night.

MARY: Because your father's snoring was driving me crazy! For heaven's sake, haven't I often used the spare room as my bedroom? (*Bitterly.*) But I see what you thought. That was when —

EDMUND (*Too vehemently*): I didn't think anything!

MARY: So you pretended to be asleep in order to spy on me!

EDMUND: No! I did it because I knew if you found out I was feverish and couldn't sleep, it would upset you.

MARY: Jamie was pretending to be asleep, too, I'm sure, and I suppose your father —

EDMUND: Stop it, Mama!

MARY: Oh, I can't bear it, Edmund, when even you —!
Her hands flutter up to pat her hair in their aimless, distracted way. Suddenly a strange undercurrent of revengefulness comes into her voice.
It would serve all of you right if it was true!

EDMUND: Mama! Don't say that! That's the way you talk when —

MARY: Stop suspecting me! Please, dear! You hurt me! I couldn't sleep because I was thinking about you. That's the real reason! I've been so worried ever since you've been sick.
She puts her arms around him and hugs him with a frightened, protective tenderness.

EDMUND (*Soothingly*): That's foolishness. You know it's only a bad cold.

MARY: Yes, of course, I know that!

EDMUND: But listen, Mama. I want you to promise me that even if it should turn out to be something worse, you'll know I'll soon be all right again, anyway, and you won't worry yourself sick, and you'll keep on taking care of yourself —

MARY (*Frightenedly*): I won't listen when you're so silly! There's absolutely no reason to talk as if you

expected something dreadful! Of course, I promise you. I give you my sacred word of honor!
Then with a sad bitterness.
But I suppose you're remembering I've promised before on my word of honor.

EDMUND: No!

MARY (*Her bitterness receding into a resigned helplessness*): I'm not blaming you, dear. How can you help it? How can any one of us forget? (*Strangely.*) That's what makes it so hard — for all of us. We can't forget.

EDMUND (*Grabs her shoulder*): Mama! Stop it!

MARY (*Forcing a smile*): All right, dear. I didn't mean to be so gloomy. Don't mind me. Here. Let me feel your head. Why, it's nice and cool. You certainly haven't any fever now.

EDMUND: Forget! It's you —

MARY: But I'm quite all right, dear.
With a quick, strange, calculating, almost sly glance at him.
Except I naturally feel tired and nervous this morning, after such a bad night. I really ought to go upstairs and lie down until lunch time and take a nap.
He gives her an instinctive look of suspicion — then, ashamed of himself, looks quickly away. She hurries on nervously.
What are you going to do? Read here? It would be much better for you to go out in the fresh air and sunshine. But don't get overheated, remember. Be sure and wear a hat.
She stops, looking straight at him now. He avoids her eyes. There is a tense pause. Then she speaks jeeringly.
Or are you afraid to trust me alone?

EDMUND (*Tormentedly*): No! Can't you stop talking like that! I think you ought to take a nap.
He goes to the screen door — forcing a joking tone.
I'll go down and help Jamie bear up. I love to lie in the shade and watch him work.
He forces a laugh in which she makes herself join. Then he goes out on the porch and disappears down the steps. Her first reaction is one of relief. She appears to relax. She sinks down in one of the wicker armchairs at rear of table and leans her head back, closing her eyes. But suddenly she grows terribly tense again. Her eyes open and she strains forward, seized by a fit of nervous panic. She begins a desperate battle with herself. Her long fingers, warped and knotted by rheumatism, drum on the arms of the chair, driven by an insistent life of their own, without her consent.

CURTAIN

SAMUEL BECKETT
from Samuel Beckett, *Malone Dies* (1956)

The deadly funny opening to Beckett's novel *Malone Dies*.

I shall soon be quite dead at last in spite of all. Perhaps next month. Then it will be the month of April or of May. For the year is still young, a thousand little signs tell me so. Perhaps I am wrong, perhaps I shall survive Saint John the Baptist's Day and even the Fourteenth of July, festival of freedom. Indeed I would not put it past me to pant on to the Transfiguration, not to speak of the Assumption.[1] But I do not think so, I do not think I am wrong in saying that these rejoicings will take place in my absence, this year. I have that feeling, I have had it now for some days, and I credit it. But in what does it differ from those that have abused me ever since I was born? No, that is the kind of bait I do not rise to any more, my need for prettiness is gone. I could die to-day, if I wished, merely by making a little effort, if I could wish, if I could make an effort. But it is just as well to let myself die, quietly, without rushing things. Something must have changed. I will not weigh upon the balance any more, one way or the other. I shall be neutral and inert. No difficulty there. Throes are the only trouble, I must be on my guard against throes. But I am less given to them now, since coming here. Of course I still have my little fits of impatience, from time to time, I must be on my guard against them, for the next fortnight or three weeks. Without exaggeration to be sure, quietly crying and laughing, without working myself up into a state. Yes, I shall be natural at last, I shall suffer more, then less, without drawing any conclusions, I shall pay less heed to myself, I shall be neither hot nor cold any more, I shall be tepid, I shall die tepid, without enthusiasm. I shall not watch myself die, that would spoil everything. Have I watched myself live? Have I ever complained? Then why rejoice now? I am content, necessarily, but not to the point of clapping my hands. I was always content, knowing I would be repaid. There he is now, my old debtor. Shall I then fall on his neck? I shall not answer any more questions. I shall even try not to ask myself any more. While waiting I shall tell myself stories, if I can. They will not be the same kind of stories as hitherto, that is all. They will be neither beautiful nor ugly, they will be calm, there will be no ugliness or beauty or fever in them any more, they will be almost lifeless, like the teller. What was that I said? It does not matter. I look forward to their giving me great satisfaction, some satisfaction. I am satisfied, there, I have enough, I am repaid, I need nothing more. Let me say before I go any further that I forgive nobody. I wish them all an atrocious life and then the fires and ice of hell and in the execrable generations to come an honoured name. Enough for this evening.

1   Saint John the Baptist's Day: 24 June. Bastille Day: 14 July; Transfiguration: 6 August; Assumption: 15 August.

DENIS DEVLIN
from *The Sewanee Review*, October 1956

Michael Collins, Commander-in-Chief of the new Free State forces, was killed on 22 August 1922 in an ambush by Republicans at Béal-na-Bláth between Macroom and Bandon in County Cork. He was thirty-one. Here in this charged, personally engaging and composed poem Devlin returns to the significance of that moment.

The Tomb of Michael Collins

To Ignazio Silone

I

Much I remember of the death of men,
But his I most remember, most of all,
More than the familiar and forgetful
Ghosts who leave our memory too soon —
Oh, what voracious fathers bore him down!

It was all sky and heather, wet and rock,
No one was there but larks and stiff-legged hares
And flowers bloodstained. Then, Oh, our shames so massive
Only a God embraced it and the angel
Whose hurt and misty rifle shot him down.

One by one the enemy dies off;
As the sun grows old, the dead increase,
We love the more the further from we're born!
The bullet found him where the bullet ceased,
And Gael and Gall¹ went inconspicuous down.

II

There are the Four Green Fields² we loved in
  boyhood,
There are some reasons it's no loss to die for:
Even it's no loss to die for having lived;
It is inside our life the angel happens
Life, the gift that God accepts or not,

Which Michael took with hand, with harsh, grey eyes,
He was loved by women and by men,
He fought a week of Sundays and by night
He asked what happened and he knew what was —
O Lord! how right that them you love die young!

He's what I was when by the chiming river
Two loyal children long ago embraced —
But what I was is one thing, what remember
Another thing, how memory becomes knowledge —
Most I remember him, how man is courage.

And sad, Oh sad, that glen with one thin stream
He met his death in; and a farmer told me
There was but one small bird to shoot: it sang
'Better Beast and know your end, and die
Than Man with murderous angels in his head.'

III

I tell these tales — I was twelve years old that time.
Those of the past were heroes in my mind:
Edward the Bruce whose brother Robert made him
Of Ireland, King; Wolfe Tone and Silken Thomas
And Prince Red Hugh O'Donnell most of all.³

The newsboys knew and the apple and orange women
Where was his shifty lodging Tuesday night;
No one betrayed him to the foreigner,
No Protestant or Catholic broke and ran
But murmured in their heart: here was a man!

Then came that mortal day he lost and laughed at,
He knew it as he left the armoured car;
The sky held in its rain and kept its breath;
Over the Liffey and the Lee,⁴ the gulls,
They told his fortune which he knew, his death.

Walking to Vespers in my Jesuit school,
The sky was come and gone; 'O Captain, my
  Captain!'
Walt Whitman was the lesson that afternoon —
How sometimes death magnifies him who dies,
And some, though mortal, have achieved their race.

1   Gael is Irish. Gall is foreigner, carrying within it the history of Ireland's invaders from Gaul, Dane, Norman, Anglo-Norman, to the English.
2   Romantic phrase for Ireland and her four provinces.
3   Crowned king of Ireland in 1316, killed in 1318. Wolfe Tone (1763–98) was leader of the United Irishmen. Silken Thomas was the name of Thomas Fitzgerald (1513–37), tenth earl of Kildare. He staged a short-lived rebellion against Henry VIII, was caught, and hanged and quartered at Tyburn. Red Hugh O'Donnell (?1571–1602), an Ulster chieftain and son-in-law of Hugh O'Neill (?1550–1616), leader of the Irish in the Elizabethan War of 1595–1603. He escaped to Catholic Spain to seek further assistance after defeat at the battle of Kinsale in 1601.
4   The rivers that run through Dublin and Cork.

SEAN O'FAOLAIN
from Sean O'Faolain, *The Finest Stories of Sean O'Faolain* (1957)

Every line in this story resonates like a chord. Consider how it all fits together and how O'Faolain draws an intricate patterning of opposites: the Medieval experience of pilgrimage vs modern society; the demands of the body vs the aspirations of the spirit; Dublin vs the West of Ireland; illicit sex vs the claims of marriage; convention vs new life; individual vs society; living together vs living apart; masculinity vs femininity; doctor vs priest; nature vs place; scepticism vs assent. And so on. And then on reading the story again we realize that these are not so much opposites as accompaniments to a larger symphony.

Lovers of the Lake

'They might wear whites,' she had said, as she stood sipping her tea and looking down at the suburban tennis players in the square. And then, turning her head in that swift movement that always reminded him of a jackdaw: 'By the way, Bobby, will you drive me up to Lough Derg[1] next week?'

He replied amiably from the lazy deeps of her armchair.

'Certainly! What part? Killaloe? But is there a good hotel there?'

'I mean the other Lough Derg. I want to do the pilgrimage.'

For a second he looked at her in surprise and then burst into laughter; then he looked at her peeringly.

'Jenny! Are you serious?'

'Of course.'

'Do you mean that place with the island where they go around on their bare feet on sharp stones, and starve for days, and sit up all night ologroaning and ologoaning?' He got out of the chair, went over to the cigarette box on the bookshelves, and, with his back to her, said coldly, 'Are you going religious on me?'

She walked over to him swiftly, turned him about, smiled her smile that was whiter than the whites of her eyes, and lowered her head appealingly on one side. When this produced no effect she said:

'Bobby! I'm always praising you to my friends as a man who takes things as they come. So few men do. Never looking beyond the day. Doing things on the spur of the moment. It's why I like you so much. Other men are always weighing up, and considering and arguing. I've built you up as a sort of magnificent, wild, brainless tomcat. Are you going to let me down now?'

After a while he had looked at his watch and said:

'All right, then. I'll try and fix up a few days free next week. I must drop into the hospital now. But I warn you, Jenny, I've noticed this Holy Joe streak in you before. You'll do it once too often.'

She patted his cheek, kissed him sedately, said, 'You are a good boy,' and saw him out with a loving smile.

They enjoyed that swift morning drive to the Shannon's shore. He suspected nothing when she refused to join him in a drink at Carrick. Leaning on the counter they had joked with the barmaid like any husband and wife off on a motoring holiday. As they rolled smoothly around the northern shore of Lough Gill he had suddenly felt so happy that he had stroked her purple glove and winked at her. The lough was vacant under the midday sun, its vast expanse of stillness broken only by a jumping fish or by its eyelash fringe of reeds. He did not suspect anything when she sent him off to lunch by himself in Sligo, saying that she had to visit an old nun she knew in the convent. So far the journey had been to him no more than one of her caprices; until a yellow signpost marked TO BUNDORAN made them aware that her destination and their parting was near, for she said:

'What are you proposing to do until Wednesday?'

'I hadn't given it a thought.'

'Don't go off and forget all about me, darling. You know you're to pick me up on Wednesday about midday?'

After a silence he grumbled:

'You're making me feel a hell of a bastard, Jenny.'

'Why on earth?'

'All this penitential stuff is because of me, isn't it?'

'Don't be silly. It's just something I thought up all by myself out of my own clever little head.'

He drove on for several miles without speaking. She looked sideways, with amusement, at his ruddy, healthy, hockey-player face glimmering under the peak of his checked cap. The brushes at his temples were getting white. Everything about him bespoke the distinguished Dublin surgeon on holiday: his pale-green shirt, his darker-green tie, his double-breasted waistcoat, his driving gloves with the palms made of woven cord. She looked pensively towards the sea. He growled:

'I may as well tell you this much, Jenny, if you were my wife I wouldn't stand for any of this nonsense.'

So their minds had travelled to the same thought? But if she were his wife the question would never have arisen. She knew by the sudden rise of speed that he was in one of his tempers, so that when he pulled into the grass verge, switched off, and turned towards her she was not taken by surprise. A sea gull moaned high overhead. She lifted her grey eyes to his, and smiled, waiting for the attack.

'Jenny, would you mind telling me exactly what all this is about? I mean, why are you doing this fal-lal[2] at this particular time?'

'I always wanted to do this pilgrimage. So it naturally follows that I would do it sometime, doesn't it?'

'Perhaps. But why, for instance, this month and not last month?'

'The island wasn't open to pilgrims last month.'

'Why didn't you go last year instead of this year?'

'You know we went to Austria last year.'

'Why not the year before last?'

'I don't know. And stop bullying me. It is just a thing that everybody wants to do sometime. It is a special sort of Irish thing, like Lourdes, or Fatima, or Lisieux. Everybody who knows about it feels drawn to it. If you were a practising Catholic you'd understand.'

'I understand quite well,' he snapped. 'I know perfectly well that people go on pilgrimages all over the world. Spain. France. Mexico. I shouldn't be surprised if they go on them in Russia. What I am asking you is what has cropped up to produce this extra-special performance just *now*?'

'And I tell you I don't know. The impulse came over me suddenly last Sunday looking at those boys and girls playing tennis. For no reason. It just came. I said to myself, "All right, go now!" I felt that if I didn't do it on the impulse I'd never do it at all. Are you asking me for a rational explanation? I haven't got one. I'm not clever and intelligent like you, darling.'

'You're as clever as a bag of cats.'

She laughed at him.

'I do love you, Bobby, when you are cross. Like a small boy.'

'Why didn't you ask George to drive you?'

She sat up straight.

'I don't want my husband to know anything whatever about this. Please don't mention a word of it to him.'

He grinned at his small victory, considered the scythe of her jawbone, looked at the shining darkness of her hair, and restarted the car.

'All the same,' he said after a mile, 'there must be some reason. Or call it a cause if you don't like the word reason. And I'd give a lot to know what it is.'

After another mile:

'Of course, I might as well be talking to that old dolmen[3] over there as be asking a woman why she does anything. And if she knew she wouldn't tell you.'

After another mile:

'Mind you, I believe all this is just a symptom of something else. Never forget, my girl, that I'm a doctor. I'm trained to interpret symptoms. If a woman comes to me with a pain . . .'

'Oh, yes, if a woman comes to Surgeon Robert James Flannery with a pain he says to her, "Never mind, that's only a pain." My God! If a woman has a pain she has a bloody pain!'

He said quietly:

'Have you a pain?'

'Oh, do shut up! The only pain I have is in my tummy. I'm ravenous.'

'I'm sorry. Didn't they give you a good lunch at the convent?'

'I took no lunch; you have to arrive at the island fasting. That's the rule.'

'Do you mean to say you've had nothing at all to eat since breakfast?'

'I had no breakfast.'

'What will you get to eat when you arrive on the island?'

'Nothing. Or next to nothing. Everybody has to fast on the island the whole time. Sometime before night I might get a cup of black tea, or hot water with pepper and salt in it. I believe it's one of their lighthearted jokes to call it soup.'

Their speed shot up at once to sixty-five. He drove through Bundoran's siesta hour like the chariot of the Apocalypse. Nearing Ballyshannon they slowed down to a pleasant, humming fifty.

'Jenny!'

'Yes?'

'Are you tired of me?'

'Is this more of you and your symptoms?'

He stopped the car again.

'Please answer my question.'

She laid her purple-gloved hand on his clenched fist.

'Look, darling! We've known one another for six years. You know that like any good little Catholic girl I go to my duties every Easter and every Christmas. Once or twice I've told you so. You've growled and grumbled a bit, but you never made any fuss about it. What are you suddenly worrying about now?'

'Because all that was just routine. Like the French or the Italians. Good Lord, I'm not bigoted. There's no harm in going to church now and again. I do it myself on state occasions, or if I'm staying in some house where they'd be upset if I didn't. But this sort of lunacy isn't routine!'

She slewed her head swiftly away from his angry eyes. A child in a pink pinafore with shoulder frills was driving two black cows through a gap.

'It was never routine. It's the one thing I have to hang on to in an otherwise meaningless existence. No children. A husband I'm not in love with. And I can't marry you.'

She slewed back to him. He slewed away to look up the long empty road before them. He slewed back; he made as if to speak; he slewed away impatiently again.

'No?' she interpreted. 'It isn't any use, is it? It's my problem, not yours. Or if it is yours you've solved it long ago by saying it's all a lot of damned nonsense.'

'And how have you solved it?' he asked sardonically.

'Have you any cause to complain of how I've solved it? Oh, I'm not defending myself. I'm a fraud, I'm a crook, I admit it. You are more honest than I am. You don't believe in anything. But it's the truth that all I have is you and . . .'

'And what?'

'It sounds so blasphemous I can't say it.'

'Say it!'

'All I have is you, and God.'

He took out his cigarette case and took one. She took one. When he lit hers their eyes met. He said, very softly, looking up the empty road:

'Poor Jenny! I wish you'd talked like this to me before. It is, after all, as you say, your own affair. But what I can't get over is that this thing you're doing is so utterly extravagant. To go off to an island, in the middle of a lake, in the mountains, with a lot of Crawthumpers[4] of every age and sex, and no sex, and peel off your stockings and your shoes, and go limping about on your bare feet on a lot of sharp stones, and kneel in the mud, psalming and beating your breast like a criminal, and drink nothing for three days but salt water . . . it's not like you. It's a side of you I've never known before. The only possible explanation for it must be that something is happening inside in you that I've never seen happen before!'

She spread her hands in despair. He chucked away his cigarette and restarted the car. They drove on in silence. A mist began to speckle the windscreen. They turned off the main road into sunless hills, all brown as hay. The next time he glanced at her she was making

up her face; her mouth rolling the lipstick into her lips; her eyes rolling around the mirror. He said:

'You're going to have a nice picnic if the weather breaks.'

She glanced out apprehensively.

'It won't be fun.'

A sudden flog of rain lashed into the windscreen. The sky had turned its bucket upside down. He said:

'Even if it's raining do you still have to keep walking around on those damn stones?'

'Yes.'

'You'll get double pneumonia.'

'Don't worry, darling. It's called Saint Patrick's Purgatory. He will look after me.'

That remark started a squabble that lasted until they drew up beside the lake. Other cars stood about like stranded boats. Other pilgrims stood by the boat slip, waiting for the ferry, their backs hunched to the wind, their clothes ruffled like the fur of cattle. She looked out across the lough at the creeping worms of foam.

He looked about him sullenly at the waiting pilgrims, a green bus, two taxiloads of people waiting for the rain to stop. They were not his kind of people at all, and he said so.

'That,' she smiled, 'is what comes of being a surgeon. You don't meet people, you meet organs. Didn't you once tell me that when you are operating you never look at the patient's face?'

He grunted. Confused and hairy-looking clouds combed themselves on the ridges of the hills. The lake was crumpled and grey, except for those yellow worms of foam blown across it in parallel lines. To the south a cold patch of light made it all look far more dreary. She stared out towards the island and said:

'It's not at all like what I expected.'

'And what the hell did you expect? Capri?'

'I thought of an old island, with old grey ruins, and old holly trees and rhododendrons down to the water, a place where old monks would live.'

They saw tall buildings like modern hotels rising by the island's shore, an octagonal basilica big enough for a city, four or five bare, slated houses, a long shed like a ballroom. There was one tree. Another bus drew up beside them and people peered out through the wiped glass.

'Oh, God!' she groaned. 'I hope this isn't going to be like Lourdes.'

'And what, pray, is wrong with Lourdes when it's at home?'

'Commercialized. I simply can't believe that this island was the most famous pilgrimage of the Middle Ages. On the rim of the known world. It must have been like going off to Jerusalem or coming home brown from the sun with a cockle in your hat from Galilee.'

He put on a vulgar Yukon voice:

'That's gold somewhere in them thar hills. It looks to me like a damn good financial proposition for somebody.'

She glared at him. The downpour had slackened. Soon it almost ceased. Gurgles of streams. A sound of pervasive drip. From the back seat she took a small red canvas bag marked T.W.A.[5]

'You will collect me on Wednesday about noon, won't you?'

He looked at her grimly. She looked every one of her forty-one years. The skin of her neck was corrugated. In five years' time she would begin to have jowls.

'Have a good time,' he said, and slammed in the gears, and drove away.

The big, lumbering ferryboat was approaching, its prow slapping the corrugated waves. There were three men to each oar. It began to spit rain again. With about a hundred and fifty men and women, of every age and, so far as she could see, of every class, she clambered aboard. They pushed out and slowly they made the crossing, huddling together from the wind and rain. The boat nosed into its cleft and unloaded. She had a sensation of dark water, wet cement, houses, and a great number of people; and that she would have given gold for a cup of hot tea. Beyond the four or five white-washed houses — she guessed that they had been the only buildings on the island before trains and buses made the pilgrimage popular — and beyond the cement paths, she came on the remains of the natural island: a knoll, some warm grass, the tree, and the roots of the old hermits' cells across whose teeth of stone barefooted pilgrims were already treading on one another's heels. Most of these barefooted people wore mackintoshes. They not only stumbled on one another's heels; they kneeled on one another's toes and tails; for the island was crowded — she thought there must be nearly two thousand people on it. They were packed between the two modern hostels and the big church. She saw a priest in sou'wester and gum boots. A nun waiting for the new arrivals at the door of the women's hostel took her name and address, and gave her the number of her cubicle. She went upstairs to it, laid her red bag on the cot, sat beside it, unfastened her garters, took off her shoes, unpeeled her nylons, and without transition became yet another anonymous pilgrim. As she went out among the pilgrims already praying in the rain she felt only a sense of shame as if she were specially singled out under the microscope of the sky. The wet ground was cold.

A fat old woman in black, rich-breasted, grey-haired, took her kindly by the arm and said in a warm, Kerry voice: 'You're shivering, you poor creature! Hould hard now. Sure, when we have the first station done they'll be giving us the ould cup of black tay.'

And laughed at the folly of this longing for the tea. She winced when she stepped on the gritty concrete of the terrace surrounding the basilica, built out on piles over the lake. A young man smiled sympathetically, seeing that she was a delicate subject for the rigours before her: he was dressed like a clerk, with three pens in his breast pocket, and he wore a Total Abstinence badge.

'Saint's Island they call it,' he smiled. 'Some people think it should be called Divil's Island.'

She disliked his kindness — she had never in her life asked for pity from anybody, but she soon found that the island floated on kindness. Everything and everybody about her seemed to say, 'We are all sinners, wretched creatures barely worthy of mercy.' She felt the abasement of the doomed. She was among people who had surrendered all personal identity, all pride. It was like being in a concentration camp.

The fat old Kerrywoman was explaining to her what the routine was, and as she listened she realized how long her stay would really be. In prospect it had seemed so short: come on Monday afternoon, leave on Wednesday at noon; it had seemed no more than one complete day and two bits of nights. She had not foreseen that immediately after arriving she must remain out of doors until the darkness fell, walking the rounds of the stones, praying, kneeling, for about five hours. And even then she would get no respite, for she must stay awake all night praying in the basilica. It was then that she would begin the second long day, as long and slow as the night; and on the third day she would still be walking those rounds until midday. She would be without food, even when she would have left the island, until the midnight of that third day.

'Yerrah, but sure,' the old woman cackled happily, 'they say that fasting is good for the stomach.'

She began to think of 'they'. They had thought all this up. They had seen how much could be done with simple prayers. For when she began to tot up the number of paternosters and Aves that she must say she had to stop at the two thousandth. And these reiterated prayers must be said while walking on the stones, or kneeling in the mud, or standing upright with her two arms extended. This was the posture she disliked most. Every time she came to do it, her face to the lake, her arms spread, the queue listening to her renouncing her sins, she had to force herself to the posture and the words. The first time she did it, with the mist blowing into her eyes, her arms out like a crucifix, her lips said the words but her heart cursed herself for coming so unprepared, for coming at all. Before she had completed her first circuit — four times around each one of six cells — one ankle and one toe was bleeding. She was then permitted to ask for the cup of black tea. She received it sullenly, as a prisoner might receive his bread and water.

She wished after that first circuit to start again and complete a second — the six cells, and the seven other ordeals at other points of the island — and so be done for the day. But she found that 'they' had invented something else: she must merge with the whole anonymous mass of pilgrims for mass prayer in the church.

A slur of wet feet; patter of rain on leaded windows; smells of bog water and damp clothing; the thousand voices responding to the incantations. At her right a young girl of about seventeen was uttering heartfelt responses. On her left an old man in his sixties gave them out loudly. On all sides, before her, behind her, the same passionate exchange of energy, while all she felt was a crust hardening about her heart, and she thought, in despair, 'I have no more feeling than a stone!' And she thought, looking about her, that tonight this vigil would go on for hour after hour until the dark, leaded windows coloured again in the morning light. She leaned her face in her palms and whispered, 'O God, please let me out of myself!' The waves of voices beat and rumbled in her ears as in an empty shell.

She was carried out on the general sliding whispering of the bare feet into the last gleanings of the daylight to begin her second circuit. In the porch she cowered back from the rain. It was settling into a filthy night. She was thrust forward by the crowd, flowed with its force to the iron cross by the shingle's edge. She took her place in the queue and then with the night wind pasting her hair across her face she raised her arms and once again renounced the world, the flesh, and the Devil. She did four circles of the church on the gritty concrete. She circled the first cell's stones. She completed the second circle. Her prayers were become numb by now. She stumbled, muttering them, up and down the third steeply sloped cell, or bed. She was a drowned cat and one knee was bleeding. At the fourth cell she saw him.

He was standing about six yards away looking at her. He wore a white raincoat buttoned tight about his throat. His feet were bare. His hair was streaked down his forehead as if he had been swimming. She stumbled towards him and dragged him by the arm down to the edge of the boat slip.

'What are you doing here?' she cried furiously. 'Why did you follow me?'

He looked down at her calmly:

'Why shouldn't I be here?'

'Because you don't believe in it! You've just followed me to sneer at me, to mock at me! Or from sheer vulgar curiosity!'

'No,' he said, without raising his voice. 'I've come to see just what it is that you believe in. I want to know all about you. I want to know why you came here. I don't want you to do anything or have anything that I can't do or can't know. And as for believing — we all believe in something.'

Dusk was closing in on the island and the lake. She had to peer into his face to catch his expression.

'But I've know you for years and you've never shown any sign of believing in anything but microscopes and microbes and symptoms. It's absurd, you couldn't be serious about anything like this. I'm beginning to hate you!'

'Are you?' he said, so softly that she had to lean near him to hear him over the slapping of the waves against the boat slip. A slow rift in the clouds let down a star; by its light she saw his smile.

'Yes!' she cried, so loudly that he swept out a hand and gripped her by the arm. Then he took her other arm and said gently:

'I don't think you should have come here, Jenny. You're only tearing yourself to bits. There are some places where some people should never go, things some people should never try to do — however good they may be for others. I know why you came here. You feel you ought to get rid of me, but you haven't the guts to do it, so you come up here into the mountains to get your druids to work it by magic. All right! I'm going to ask them to help you.'

He laughed and let her go, giving her a slight impulse away from him.

'Ask? You will *ask*? Do you mean to tell me that you have said as much as one single, solitary prayer on this island?'

'Yes,' he said casually, 'I have.'

She scorned him.

'Are you trying to tell me, Bobby, that you are doing this pilgrimage?'

'I haven't fasted. I didn't know about that. And, anyway, I probably won't. I've got my pockets stuffed with two pounds of the best chocolates I could buy in Bundoran. I don't suppose I'll even stay up all night like the rest of you. The place is so crowded that I don't suppose anybody will notice me if I curl up in some corner of the boathouse. I heard somebody saying that people had to sleep there last night. But you never know — I might — I just might stay awake. If I do, it will remind me of going to midnight Mass with my father when I was a kid. Or going to retreats, when we used all hold up a lighted candle and renounce the Devil.

'It was a queer sensation standing up there by the lake and saying those words all over again. Do you know, I thought I'd completely forgotten them!'

'The next thing you're going to say is that you believe in the Devil! You fraud!'

'Oh, there's no trouble about believing in that old gentleman. There isn't a doctor in the world who doesn't, though he will give him another name. And on a wet night, in a place like this, you could believe in a lot of things. No, my girl, what I find it hard to believe in is the flesh and the world. They are good things. Do you think I'm ever going to believe that your body and my body are evil? And you don't either! And you are certainly never going to renounce the world, because you are tied to it hand and foot!'

'That's not true!'

His voice cut her like a whip:

'Then why do you go on living with your husband?'

She stammered feebly. He cut at her again:

'You do it because he's rich, and you like comfort, and you like being a "somebody".'

With a switch of her head she brushed past him. She did not see him again that night.

The night world turned imperceptibly. In the church, for hour after hour, the voices obstinately beat back the responses. She sank under the hum of the prayer wheel, the lust for sleep, her own despairs. Was he among the crowd? Or asleep in a corner of the boatshed? She saw his flatly domed fingers, a surgeon's hand, so strong, so sensitive. She gasped at the sensual image she had evoked.

The moon touched a black window with colour. After an age it had stolen to another. Heads drooped. Neighbours poked one another awake with a smile. Many of them had risen from the benches in order to keep themselves awake and were circling the aisles in a loose procession of slurring feet, responding as they moved. Exhaustion began to work on her mind. Objects began to disconnect, become isolated each within its own outline — now it was the pulpit, now a statue, now a crucifix. Each object took on the vividness of a hallucination. The crucifix detached itself from the wall and leaned towards her, and for a long while she saw nothing but the heavy pendent body, the staring eyes, so that when the old man at her side let his head sink over on her shoulder and then

woke up with a start she felt him no more than if they were two fishes touching in the sea. Bit by bit the incantations drew her in; sounds came from her mouth; prayers flowed between her and those troubled eyes that fixed hers. She swam into an ecstasy as rare as one of those perfect dances of her youth when she used to swing in a whirl of music, a swirl of bodies, a circling of lights, floated out of her mortal frame, alone in the arms that embraced her.

Suddenly it all exploded. One of the four respites of the night had halted the prayers. The massed pilgrims relaxed. She looked blearily about her, no longer disjunct. Her guts rumbled. She looked at the old man beside her. She smiled at him and he at her.

'My poor old knees are crucified,' he grinned.

'You should have the skirts,' she grinned back.

They were all going out to stretch in the cool, and now dry, air, or to snatch a smoke. The amber windows of the church shivered in a pool of water. A hearty-voiced young woman leaning on the balustrade lit a match for her. The match hissed into the invisible lake lapping below.

'The ould fag,' said the young woman, dragging deep on her cigarette, 'is a great comfort. 'Tis as good as a man.'

'I wonder,' she said, 'what would Saint Patrick think if he saw women smoking on his island?'

'He'd beat the living lights out of the lot of us.'

She laughed aloud. She must tell him that. . . . She began to wander through the dark crowds in search of him. He had said something that wasn't true and she would answer him. She went through the crowds down to the boat slip. He was standing there, looking out into the dark as if he had not stirred since she saw him there before midnight. For a moment she regarded him, frightened by the force of the love that gushed into her. Then she approached him.

'Well, Mr Worldly Wiseman? Enjoying your boat-house bed?'

'I'm doing the vigil,' he said smugly.

'You sound almighty pleased with yourself.'

He spoke eagerly now:

'Jenny, we mustn't quarrel. We must understand one another. And understand this place. I'm just beginning to. An island. In a remote lake. Among the mountains. Night-time. No sleep. Hunger. The conditions of the desert. I was right in what I said to you. Can't you see how the old hermits who used to live here could swim off into a trance in which nothing existed but themselves and their visions? I told you a man can renounce what he calls the Devil, but not the flesh, not the world. They thought, like you, that they could throw away the flesh and the world, but they were using the flesh to achieve one of the rarest experiences in the world! Don't you see it?'

'Experiences! The next thing you'll be talking about is symptoms.'

'Well, surely, you must have observed?' He peered at the luminous dial of his watch. 'I should say that about four o'clock we will probably begin to experience a definite sense of dissociation. After that a positive alienation . . .'

She turned furiously from him. She came back to say:

'I would much prefer, Bobby, if you would have the decency to go away in the morning. I can find my own way home. I hope we don't meet again on this island. Or out of it!'

'The magic working?' he laughed.

After that she made a deliberate effort of the mind to mean and to feel every separate word of the prayers — which is a great foolishness since prayers are not poems to be read or even understood; they are an instinct; to dance would be as wise. She thought that if she could not feel what she said how could she mean it, and so she tried to savour every word, and, from trying to mean each word, lagged behind the rest, sank into herself, and ceased to pray. After the second respite she prayed only to keep awake. As the first cold pallor of morning came into the windows her heart rose again. But the eastern hills are high here and the morning holds off stubbornly. It is the worst hour of the vigil, when the body ebbs, the prayers sink to a drone, and the night seems to have begun all over again.

At the last respite she emerged to see pale tents of blue on the hills. The slow cumulus clouds cast a sheen on the water. There is no sound. No birds sing. At this hour the pilgrims are too awed or too exhausted to speak, so that the island reverts to its ancient silence in spite of the crowds.

By the end of the last bout she was calm like the morning lake. She longed for the cup of black tea. She was unaware of her companions. She did not think of him. She was unaware of herself. She no more thought of God than a slave thinks of his master, and after she had drunk her tea she sat in the morning sun outside the women's hostel like an old blind woman who has nothing in life to wait for but sleep.

The long day expired as dimly as the vapour rising from the water. The heat became morbid. One is said to be free on this second day to converse, to think, to write, to read, to do anything at all that one pleases except the one thing everybody wants to do — to sleep. She did nothing but watch the clouds, or listen to the gentle muttering of the lake. Before noon she heard some departing pilgrims singing a hymn as the great ferryboats pushed off. She heard their voices without longing; she did not even desire food. When she met him she was without rancour.

'Still here?' she said, and when he nodded: 'Sleepy?'

'Sleepy.'

'Too many chocolates, probably.'

'I didn't eat them. I took them out of my pockets one by one as I leaned over the balustrade and guessed what centre each had — coffee, marshmallow, nut, toffee, cream — and dropped it in with a little splash to the holy fishes.'

She looked up at him gravely.

'Are you really trying to join in this pilgrimage?'

'Botching it. I'm behindhand with my rounds. I have to do five circuits between today and tomorrow. I may never get them done. Still, something is better than nothing.'

'You dear fool!'

If he had not walked away then she would have had to; such a gush of affection came over her at the thought of what he was doing, and why he was doing it — stupidly, just like a man; sceptically, just like a man; not admitting it to himself, just like a man; for all sorts of damn-fool rational reasons, just like a man; and not at all for the only reason that she knew was his real reason: because she was doing it, which meant that he loved her. She sat back, and closed her eyes, and the tears of chagrin oozed between her lids as she felt her womb stir with desire of him.

When they met again it was late afternoon.

'Done four rounds,' he said so cheerfully that he maddened her.

'It's not golf, Bobby, damn you!'

'I should jolly well think not. I may tell you my feet are in such a condition I won't be able to play golf for a week. Look!'

She did not look. She took his arm and led him to the quietest corner she could find.

'Bobby, I am going to confess something to you. I've been thinking about it all day trying to get it clear. I know now why I came here. I came because I know inside in me that some day our apple will have to fall off the tree. I'm forty. You are nearly fifty. It will have to happen. I came here because I thought it right to admit that some day, if it has to be, I am willing to give you up.'

He began to shake all over with laughter.

'What the hell are you laughing at?' she moaned.

'When women begin to reason! Listen, wasn't there a chap one time who said, "O God, please make me chaste, but not just yet"?'

'What I am saying is "now", if it has to be, if it can be, if I can make it be. I suppose,' she said wildly, 'I'm really asking for a miracle, that my husband would die, or that you'd die, or something like that that would make it all come right!'

He burst into such a peal of laughter that she looked around her apprehensively. A few people near them also happened to be laughing over something and looked at them indulgently.

'Do you realize, Bobby, that when I go to confession here I will have to tell all about us, and I will have to promise to give you up?'

'Yes, darling, and you won't mean a single word of it.'

'But I always mean it!'

He stared at her as if he were pushing curtains aside in her.

'Always? Do you mean you've been saying it for six years?'

'I mean it when I say it. Then I get weak. I can't help it, Bobby. You know that!' She saw the contempt in his eyes and began to talk rapidly, twisting her marriage ring madly around her finger. He kept staring into her eyes like a man staring down the long perspective of a railway line waiting for the engine to appear. 'So you see why there wasn't any sense in asking me yesterday why I come now and not at some other time, because with me there isn't any other time, it's always *now*, I meet you *now*, and I love you *now*, and I think it's not right *now*, and then I think, "No, not *now*," and then I say I'll give you up *now*, and I mean it every time until we meet again, and it begins all over again, and there's never any end to it until some day I can say, "Yes, I used to know him once, but not *now*," and then it will be a *now* where there won't be any other *now* any more because there'll be nothing to live for.'

The tears were leaking down her face. He sighed:

'Dear me! You have got yourself into a mess, haven't you?'

'O God, the promises and the promises! I wish the world would end tonight and we'd both die together!'

He gave her his big damp handkerchief. She wiped her eyes and blew her nose and said:

'You don't mean to go to confession, do you?'

He chuckled sourly.

'And promise? I must go and finish a round of pious golf. I'm afraid, old girl, you just want to get me into the same mess as yourself. No, thank you. You must solve your own problems in your own way, and I in mine.'

That was the last time she spoke to him that day.

She went back to the balustrade where she had smoked with the hearty girl in the early hours of the morning. She was there again. She wore a scarlet beret. She was smoking again. She began to talk, and the talk flowed from her without stop. She had fine broad shoulders, a big mobile mouth, and a pair of wild goat's eyes. After a while it became clear that the woman was beside herself with terror. She suddenly let it all out in a gush of exhaled smoke.

'Do you know why I'm hanging around here? Because I ought to go into confession and I'm in dread of it. He'll tear me alive. He'll murdher me. It's not easy for a girl like me, I can promise you!'

'You must have terrible sins to tell?' she smiled comfortingly.

'He'll slaughter me, I'm telling you.'

'What is it? Boys?'

The two goat's eyes dilated with fear and joy. Her hands shook like a drunkard's.

'I can't keep away from them. I wish to God I never came here.'

'But how silly! It's only a human thing. I'm sure half the people here have the same tale to tell. It's an old story, child, the priests are sick of hearing it.'

'Oh, don't be talking! Let me alone! I'm criminal, I tell yeh! And there are things you can't explain to a priest. My God, you can hardly explain 'em to a doctor!'

'You're married?' — looking at her ring.

'Poor Tom! I have him wore out. He took me to a doctor one time to know would anything cure me. The old foolah took me temperature and give me a book like a bus guide about when it's safe and when it isn't safe to make love, the ould eedjut! I was pregnant again before Christmas. Six years married and I have six kids; nobody could stand that gait o' going. And I'm only twenty-four. Am I to have a baby every year of my life? I'd give me right hand this minute for a double whiskey.'

'Look, you poor child! We are all in the same old ferryboat here. What about me?'

'You?'

'It's not men with me, it's worse.'

'Worse? In God's name, what's worse than men?'

The girl looked all over her, followed her arm down to her hand, to her third finger.

'One man.'

The tawny eyes swivelled back to her face and immediately understood.

'Are you very fond of him?' she asked gently, and taking the unspoken answer said, still more pityingly, 'You can't give him up?'

'It's six years now and I haven't been able to give him up.'

The girl's eyes roved sadly over the lake as if she were surveying a lake of human unhappiness. Then she threw her butt into the water and her red beret disappeared into the maw of the church porch.

She saw him twice before the dusk thickened and the day grew cold again with the early sunset. He was sitting directly opposite her before the men's hostel, smoking, staring at the ground between his legs. They sat facing one another. They were separated by their identities, joined by their love. She glimpsed him only once after that, at the hour when the sky and the hills merge, an outline passing across the lake. Soon after she had permission to go to her cubicle. Immediately she lay down she spiralled to the bottom of a deep lake of sleep.

She awoke refreshed and unburthened. She had received the island's gift: its sense of remoteness from the world, almost a sensation of the world's death. It is the source of the island's kindness. Nobody is just matter, poor to be exploited by rich, weak to be exploited by the strong; in mutual generosity each recognizes the other only as a form of soul; it is a brief, harsh Utopia of equality in nakedness. The bare feet are a symbol of that nakedness unknown in the world they have left.

The happiness to which she awoke was dimmed a little by a conversation she had with an Englishman over breakfast — the usual black tea and a piece of oaten bread. He was a city man who had arrived the day before, been up all night while she slept. He had not yet shaved; he was about sixty-two or three; small and tubby, his eyes perpetually wide and unfocusing behind pince-nez glasses.

'That's right,' he said, answering her question. 'I'm from England. Liverpool. I cross by the night boat and get here the next afternoon. Quite convenient, really. I've come here every year for the last twenty-two years, apart from the war years. I come on account of my wife.'

'Is she ill?'

'She died twenty-two years ago. No, it's not what you might think — I'm not praying for her. She was a good woman, but, well, you see, I wasn't very kind to her. I don't mean I quarrelled with her, or drank, or was unfaithful. I never gambled. I've never smoked in my life.' His hands made a faint movement that was meant to express a whole life, all the confusion and trouble of his soul. 'It's just that I wasn't kind. I didn't make her happy.'

'Isn't that,' she said, to comfort him, 'a very private feeling? I mean, it's not in the Ten Commandments that thou shalt make thy wife happy.'

He did not smile. He made the same faint movement with his fingers.

'Oh, I don't know! What's love if it doesn't do that? I mean to say, it is something godly to love another human being, isn't it? I mean, what does "godly" mean if it doesn't mean giving up everything for another? It isn't human to love, you know. It's foolish, it's a folly, a divine folly. It's beyond all reason, all limits. I didn't rise to it,' he concluded sadly.

She looked at him, and thought, 'A little fat man, a clerk in some Liverpool office all his life, married to some mousy little woman, thinking about love as if he were some sort of Greek mystic.'

'It's often,' she said lamely, 'more difficult to love one's husband, or one's wife, as the case may be, than to love one's neighbour.'

'Oh, much!' he agreed without a smile. 'Much! Much more difficult!'

At which she was overcome by the thought that inside ourselves we have no room without a secret door; no solid self that has not a ghost inside it trying to escape. If I leave Bobby I still have George. If I leave George I still have myself, and whatever I find in myself. She patted the little man's hand and left him, fearing that if she let him talk on even his one little piece of sincerity would prove to be a fantasy, and in the room that he had found behind his own room she would open other doors leading to other obsessions. He had told her something true about her own imperfection, and about the nature of love, and she wanted to share it while it was still true. But she could not find him, and there was still one more circuit to do before the ferryboat left. She did meet Goat's Eyes. The girl clutched her with tears magnifying her yellow-and-green irises and gasped joyously:

'I found a lamb of a priest. A saint anointed! He was as gentle! "What's your husband earning?" says he. "Four pounds ten[6] a week, Father," says I. "And six children?" says he. "You poor woman," says he, "you don't need to come here at all. Your Purgatory is at home." He laid all the blame on poor Tom. And, God forgive me, I let him do it. "Bring him here to me," says he, "and I'll cool him for you." God bless the poor innocent priest, I wish I knew as little about marriage as he does. But,' and here she broke into a wail, 'sure he has me ruined altogether now. He's after making me so fond of poor Tommy I think I'll never get home soon enough to go to bed with him.' And in a vast flood of tears of joy, of relief, and of fresh misery: 'I wish I was a bloomin' nun!'

It was not until they were all waiting at the ferryboat that she saw him. She managed to sit beside him in the boat. He touched her hand and winked. She smiled back at him. The bugler blew his bugle. A tardy traveller came racing out of the men's hostel. The boatload cheered him, the bugler helped him aboard with a joke about people who can't be persuaded to stop praying, and there was a general chaff about people who have a lot to pray about, and then somebody raised the parting hymn, and the rowers began to push the heavy oars, and singing they were slowly rowed across the summer lake back to the world.

They were driving back out of the hills by the road they had come, both silent. At last she could hold in her question no longer:

'Did you go, Bobby?'

Meaning: had he, after all his years of silence, of rebellion, of disbelief, made his peace with God at the price of a compact against her. He replied gently:

'Did I probe your secrets all these years?'

She took the rebuke humbly, and for several miles they drove on in silence. They were close, their shoulders touched, but between them there stood that impenetrable wall of identity that segregates every human being in a private world of self. Feeling it she realized at last that it is only in places like the lake-island that the barriers of self break down. The tubby little clerk from Liverpool had been right. Only when love desires nothing but renunciation, total surrender, does self surpass self. Everybody who ever entered the island left the world of self behind for a few hours, exchanged it for what the little man had called a divine folly. It was possible only for a few hours — unless one had the courage, or the folly, to renounce the world altogether. Then another thought came to her. In the world there might also be escape from the world.

'Do you think, Bobby, that when people are in love they can give up everything for one another?'

'No,' he said flatly. 'Except perhaps in the first raptures?'

'If I had a child I think I could sacrifice anything for it. Even my life.'

'Yes,' he agreed. 'It has been known to happen.'

And she looked at him sadly, knowing that they would never be able to marry, and even if she did that she would never have children. And yet, if they could have married, there was a lake . . .

'Do you know what I'm planning at this moment?' he asked breezily.

She asked without interest what it was.

'Well, I'm simply planning the meal we're going to eat tonight in Galway, at midnight.'

'At midnight? Then we're going on with this pilgrimage? Are we?'

'Don't *you* want to? It was your idea in the beginning.'

'All right. And what are we going to do until midnight? I've never known time to be so long.'

'I'm going to spend the day fishing behind Glencar. That will kill the hungry day. After that, until midnight, we'll take the longest possible road around Connemara. Then would you have any objections to mountain trout cooked in milk, stuffed roast kid with fresh peas and spuds in their jackets, apple pie and whipped cream, with a cool Pouilly Fuissé, a cosy 1929 claret, West of Ireland Pont l'Evêque, finishing up with Gaelic coffee and two Otards? Much more in your line, if I know anything about you, than your silly old black tea and hot salt water.'

'I admit I like the things of the flesh.'

'You live for them!'

He had said it so gently, so affectionately that, half in dismay, half with amusement, she could not help remembering Goat's Eyes, racing home as fast as the bus would carry her to make love to her Tommy. After that they hardly spoke at all, and then only of casual things such as a castle beside the road, the sun on the edging sea, a tinker's caravan, an opening view. It was early afternoon as they entered the deep valley at Glencar and he probed in second gear for an attractive length of stream, found one and started eagerly to put his rod together. He began to walk up against the dazzling bubble of water and within an hour was out of sight. She stretched herself out on a rug on the bank and fell sound asleep.

It was nearly four o'clock before she woke up, stiff and thirsty. She drank from a pool in the stream, and for an hour she sat alone by the pool, looking into its peat-brown depth, as vacantly contented as a tinker's wife to live for the moment, to let time wind and unwind everything. It was five o'clock before she saw him approaching, plodding in his flopping waders, with four trout on a rush stalk. He threw the fish at her feet and himself beside them.

'I nearly ate them raw,' he said.

'Let's cook them and eat them,' she said fiercely.

He looked at her for a moment, then got up and began to gather dry twigs, found Monday's newspaper in the car — it looked like a paper of years ago — and started the fire. She watched while he fed it. When it was big enough in its fall to have made a hot bed of embers he roasted two of the trout across the hook of his gaff, and she smelled the crisping flesh and sighed. At last he laid them, browned and crackly, on the grass by her hand. She took one by its crusted tail, smelled it, looked at him, and slung it furiously into the heart of the fire. He gave a sniff-laugh and did the same with his.

'Copy cat!' she said.

'Let's get the hell out of here,' he said, jumping up. 'Carry the kit, will you?'

She rose, collected the gear, and followed him saying:

'I feel like an Arab wife. "Carry the pack. Go here. Go there."'

They climbed out of the glens onto the flat moorland of the Easky peninsula where the evening light was a cold ochre gleaming across green bogland that was streaked with all the weedy colours of a strand at ebb. At Ballina she suggested that they should have tea.

'It will be a pleasant change of diet!' he said.

When they had found a café and she was ordering the tea he said to the waitress:

'And bring lots of hot buttered toast.'

'This,' she said, as she poured out the tea and held up the milk jug questioningly, 'is a new technique of seduction. Milk?'

'Are you having milk?'

'No.'

'No, then.'

'Some nice hot buttered toast?'

'Are you having toast?' he demanded.

'Why the bloody hell should it be up to me to decide?'

'I asked you a polite question,' he said rudely.

'No.'

'No!'

They looked at one another as they sipped the black tea like two people who are falling head over heels into hatred of one another.

'Could you possibly tell me,' he said presently, 'why I bother my head with a fool of a woman like you?'

'I can only suppose, Bobby, that it is because we are in love with one another.'

'I can only suppose so,' he growled. 'Let's get on!'

They took the longest way round he could find on the map, west into County Mayo, across between the lakes at Pontoon, over the level bogland to Castlebar. Here the mountains walled in the bogland plain with cobalt air — in the fading light the land was losing all solidity. Clouds like soapsuds rose and rose over the edges of the mountains until they glowed as if there was a fire of embers behind the blue ranges. In Castlebar he pulled up by the post office and telephoned to the hotel at Salthill for dinner and two rooms. When he came out he saw a poster in a shop window and said:

'Why don't we go to the pictures? It will kill a couple of hours.'

'By rights,' she said, 'you ought to be driving me home to Dublin.'

'If you wish me to I will.'

'Would you if I asked you?'

'Do you want me to?'

'I suppose it's rather late now, isn't it?'

'Not at all. Fast going we could be there about one o'clock. Shall we?

'It wouldn't help. George is away. I'd have to bring you in and give you something to eat, and . . . Let's go to the blasted movies!'

The film was *Charley's Aunt*. They watched its slapstick gloomily. When they came out, after nine o'clock, there was still a vestigial light in the sky. They drove on and on, westward still, prolonging the light, prolonging the drive, holding off the night's decision. Before Killary they paused at a black-faced lake, got out, and stood beside its quarried beauty. Nothing along its stony beach but a few wind-torn rushes.

'I could eat you,' he said.

She replied that only lovers and cannibals talk like that.

They dawdled past the long fiord of Killary where young people on holiday sat outside the hotel, their drinks on the trestled tables. In Clifden the street was empty, people already climbing to bed, as the lights in the upper windows showed. They branched off on the long coastal road where the sparse whitewashed cottages were whiter than the foam of waves that barely suggested sea. At another darker strand they halted, but now they saw no foam at all and divined the sea only by its invisible whispering, or when a star touched a wave. Midnight was now only an hour away.

Their headlights sent rocks and rabbits into movement. The heather streamed past them like kangaroos. It was well past eleven as they poured along the lonely land by Galway Bay. Neither of them had spoken for an hour. As they drove into Salthill there was nobody abroad. Galway was dark. Only the porch light of the hotel showed that it was alive. When he turned off the engine the only sound at first was the crinkle of contracting metal as the engine began to cool. Then to their right they heard the lisping bay. The panel button lit the dashboard clock.

'A quarter to,' he said, leaning back. She neither spoke nor stirred. 'Jenny!' he said sharply.

She turned her head slowly and by the dashboard light he saw her white smile.

'Yes, darling?'

'Worn out?' he asked, and patted her knee.

She vibrated her whole body so that the seat shook, and stretched her arms about her head, and lowering them let her head fall on his shoulder, and sighed happily, and said:

'What I want is a good long drink of anything on earth except tea.'

These homing twelve o'clockers from Lough Derg are well known in every hotel all over the west of Ireland. Revelry is the reward of penance. The porter welcomed them as if they were heroes returned from the war. As he led them to their rooms he praised them, he sympathized with them, he patted them up and he patted them down, he assured them that the ritual grill was at that moment sizzling over the fire, he proffered them hot baths, and he told them where to discover the bar. 'Ye will discover it . . .' was his phrase. The wording was exact, for the bar's gaiety was muffled by dim lighting, drawn blinds, locked doors. In the overheated room he took off his jacket and unloosed his tie. They had to win a corner of the counter, and his order was for two highballs with ice in them. Within two minutes they were at home with the crowd. The island might never have existed if the barmaid, who knew where they had come from, had not laughed: 'I suppose ye'll ate like lions?'

After supper they relished the bar once more, sipping slowly now, so refreshed that they could have started on the road again without distaste or regret. As they sipped they gradually became aware of a soft strumming and drumming near at hand, and were told that there was a dance on in the hotel next door. He raised his eyebrows to her. She laughed and nodded.

They gave it up at three o'clock and walked out into the warm-cool of the early summer morning. Gently tipsy, gently tired they walked to the little promenade. They leaned on the railing and he put his arm about her waist, and she put hers around his, and they gazed at the moon silently raking its path across the sea towards Aran. They had come, she knew, to the decisive moment. He said: 'They have a fine night for it tonight on the island.'

'A better night than we had,' she said tremulously. After another spell of wave fall and silence he said:

'Do you know what I'm thinking, Jenny? I'm thinking that I wouldn't mind going back there again next year. Maybe I might do it properly the next time?'

'The next time?' she whispered, and all her body began to dissolve and, closing her eyes, she leaned against him. He, too, closed his eyes, and all his body became as rigid as a steel girder that flutters in a storm. Slowly they opened their love-drunk eyes, and stood looking long over the brightness and blackness of the sea. Then, gently, ever so gently, with a gentleness that terrified her he said:

'Shall we go in, my sweet?'

She did not stir. She did not speak. Slowly turning to him she lifted her eyes to him pleadingly.

'No, Bobby, please, not yet.'

'Not yet?'

'Not tonight!'

He looked down at her, and drew his arms about her. They kissed passionately. She knew what that kiss implied. Their mouths parted. Hand in hand they walked slowly back to the hotel, to their separate rooms.

1   The lake for pilgrims is in County Donegal, the other one is surrounded by Counties Clare, Galway and Tipperary. Lough Derg in Donegal is a mecca for pilgrims, especially in June–August, who make their way to Station Island, the scene of St Patrick's vision of Purgatory. The pilgrimage dates from the middle of the twelfth century.

2   To behave in an affected or showy manner. (OED)

3   A cromlech or pre-Christian burial site, two stones supporting a covering stone.

4   Pejorative slang for Roman Catholics, craw being the neck or gullet.

5   Trans World Airlines.

6   £4.50.

L.A.G. STRONG

from L.A.G. Strong, *The Body's Imperfection: The Collected Poems of L.A.G. Strong* (1957)

L.A.G. Strong's work as a novelist is represented by the extract on page 419 above from *The Garden* (1931). Here are some examples of his mature verse written towards the end of his life as he seeks an accommodation with memory and the past.

RESIDUE

Fallen are breast and nostril,
Perished blood and nerve,
Even the thighbones crumble;
Nothing lasts but love.

Love that from breast and thighbone,
Nerve and nostril grew,
Evicted, undestroyed,
The flesh's residue.

RIPPLE

If you outlive me, love, by thirty years,
As, reckoned by the calendar, you should,
Long past the time of stratagems and tears,
And what is bad for love, and what is good;

When life, that was a torrent, is a pool,
Wherein serenely islanded you find
The evening luminous, the noonday cool,
And all things equidistant in your mind;

There'll come a ripple, perhaps, as something brings,
Life whiffling air, a memory of me;
A Breton toy, a duck flapping its wings
Dementedly, small fields above the sea,

A belly laugh, a line of Yeats, a kiss
No one else knew, a single tufted brow;
And, for a smiling moment, that is this,
And she is you, and long ago is now.

THE HARBOUR

A windy sunset turbulent with gulls
Over the little harbour, and my blood
Alive with you, whose image first annuls
Then marries these bright images that flood
The part-dishevelled, part-domestic hill,
Lit comfortable houses, thrashing trees,
And arrogant swift rock. Only the will
Distinguishes your image now from these
Importunate flashing voices of the skies,
Confusing sense and substance in a wild
Delirium of glory, till my eyes
And ears are one, the seer is reconciled
With what he sees, and all this tumbling flood
Of light and sound your heartbeat, breath, and blood.

Howth, September 1951

SAMUEL BECKETT
from Samuel Beckett, *Endgame* (1958)

'Withall, he seemed to me deeply Irish, with his control masking volatile swings of mood from unshakable gloom about the human condition through ferocity at any surrender to lower standards; and underlying all, the quick redeeming flash of humour, the sudden surge of generosity,' wrote John Montague in an obituary notice on Beckett in December 1989. The Irishness of *Endgame* — as indeed the Irishness of Beckett's work as a whole — remains an intriguing question. You might like to see it in the moral/personality terms that Montague suggests; others have suggested Beckett exhibits an Irish Protestant sentimentality. The play itself was written in the wake of his brother's death from cancer in August 1954. For a specifically Irish tradition of drama that places Beckett in a context that embraces Synge, Yeats, Behan and other Irish playwrights, you might begin by reading Katharine Worth, *The Irish Drama of Europe from Yeats to Beckett* (1978), Eoin O'Brien, *The Beckett Country* (1986), John P.

Harrington, *The Irish Beckett* (1991), Anthony Roche, *Contemporary Irish Drama: From Beckett to McGuiness* (1994). See also Anthony Cronin's 'Irish' biography *Samuel Beckett* (1996), which can be compared with the more authoritative 'French' biography by James Knowlson *Damned to Fame* (1996). What all this critical and biographical activity suggests is that Beckett's 'dying words' (the title of a book on Beckett by Christopher Ricks) continue to provoke critical discourse. The Irish writer, who fought in the French Resistance, therefore remains our contemporary and, like Clov with his telescope, he still has targets to observe out of the window of his theatre.

CHARACTERS

HAMM
CLOV
NAGG
NELL

Bare interior.
Grey light.
Left and right back, high up, two small windows, curtains drawn.
Front right, a door. Hanging near door, its face to wall, a picture.
Front left, touching each other, covered with an old sheet, two ashbins.
Centre, in an armchair on castors, covered with an old sheet, HAMM.
Motionless by the door, his eyes fixed on HAMM, CLOV.
Very red face.
Brief tableau.
CLOV *goes and stands under window left. Stiff, staggering walk. He looks up at window left. He turns and looks at window right. He goes and and stands under window right. He looks up at window right. He turns and looks at window left. He goes out, comes back immediately with a small step-ladder, carries it over and sets it down under window left, gets up on it, draws back curtain. He gets down, takes six steps (for example) towards window right, goes back for ladder, carries it over and sets it down under window right, gets up on it, draws back curtain. He gets down, takes three steps towards window left, goes back for ladder, carries it over and sets it down under window left, gets up on it, looks out of window. Brief laugh. He gets down, takes one step towards window right, goes back for ladder, carries it over and sets it down under window right, gets up on it, looks out of window. Brief laugh. He gets down, goes with ladder towards ashbins, halts, turns, carries back ladder and sets it down under window right, goes to ashbins, removes sheet covering them, folds it over his arm. He raises one lid, stoops and looks into bin. Brief laugh. He closes lid. Same with other bin. He goes to* HAMM, *removes sheet covering him, folds it over his arm. In a dressing-gown, a stiff toque on his head, a* large blood-stained handkerchief over his face, a whistle hanging from his neck, a rug over his knees, thick socks on his feet, HAMM *seems to be asleep.* CLOV *looks him over. Brief laugh. He goes to door, halts, turns towards auditorium.*

CLOV (*Fixed gaze, tonelessly.*): Finished, it's finished, nearly finished, it must be nearly finished. (*Pause.*) Grain upon grain, one by one, and one day, suddenly, there's a heap, a little heap, the impossible heap. (*Pause.*) I can't be punished any more. (*Pause.*) I'll go now to my kitchen, ten feet by ten feet by ten feet, and wait for him to whistle me. (*Pause.*) Nice dimensions, nice proportions, I'll lean on the table, and look at the wall, and wait for him to whistle me.
He remains a moment motionless, then goes out. He comes back immediately, goes to window right, takes up the ladder and carries it out. Pause. HAMM *stirs. He yawns under the handkerchief. He removes the handkerchief from his face. Very red face. Black glasses.*
HAMM: Me — (*He yawns.*) — to play. (*He holds the handkerchief spread out before him.*) Old stancher! (*He takes off his glasses, wipes his eyes, his face, the glasses, puts them on again, folds the handkerchief and puts it nearly in the breast-pocket of his dressing-gown. He clears his throat, joins the tips of his fingers.*) Can there be misery — (*He yawns.*) — loftier than mine? No doubt. Formerly. But now? (*Pause.*) My father? (*Pause.*) My mother? (*Pause.*) My . . . dog? (*Pause.*) Oh I am willing to believe they suffer as much as such creatures can suffer. But does that mean their sufferings equal mine? No doubt. (*Pause.*) No, all is a— (*he yawns*) —bsolute, (*proudly*) the bigger a man is the fuller he is. (*Pause. Gloomily.*) And the emptier. (*He sniffs.*) Clov! (*Pause.*) No, alone. (*Pause.*) What dreams! Those forests! (*Pause.*) Enough, it's time it ended, in the refuge too. (*Pause.*) And yet I hesitate, I hesitate to . . . to end. Yes, there it is, it's time it ended and yet I hesitate to — (*He yawns.*) — to end. (*Yawns.*) God, I'm tired, I'd be better off in

bed. (*He whistles. Enter* CLOV *immediately. He halts beside the chair.*) You pollute the air! (*Pause.*) Get me ready, I'm going to bed.

CLOV: I've just got you up.

HAMM: And what of it?

CLOV: I can't be getting you up and putting you to bed every five minutes, I have things to do.
Pause.

HAMM: Did you ever see my eyes?

CLOV: No.

HAMM: Did you never have the curiosity, while I was sleeping, to take off my glasses and look at my eyes?

CLOV: Pulling back the lids? (*Pause.*) No.

HAMM: One of these days I'll show them to you. (*Pause.*) It seems they've gone all white. (*Pause.*) What time is it?

CLOV: The same as usual.

HAMM (*Gesture towards window right.*): Have you looked?

CLOV: Yes.

HAMM: Well?

CLOV: Zero.

HAMM: It'd need to rain.

CLOV: It won't rain.
Pause.

HAMM: Apart from that, how do you feel?

CLOV: I don't complain.

HAMM: You feel normal?

CLOV (*Irritably.*): I tell you I don't complain!

HAMM: I feel a little queer. (*Pause.*) Clov!

CLOV: Yes.

HAMM: Have you not had enough?

CLOV: Yes! (*Pause.*) Of what?

HAMM: Of this . . . this . . . thing.

CLOV: I always had. (*Pause.*) Not you?

HAMM (*Gloomily.*): Then there's no reason for it to change.

CLOV: It may end. (*Pause.*) All life long the same questions, the same answers.

HAMM: Get me ready. (CLOV *does not move.*) Go and get the sheet. (CLOV *does not move.*) Clov!

CLOV: Yes.

HAMM: I'll give you nothing more to eat.

CLOV: Then we'll die.

HAMM: I'll give you just enough to keep you from dying. You'll be hungry all the time.

CLOV: Then we shan't die. (*Pause.*) I'll go and get the sheet.
He goes towards the door.

HAMM: No! (CLOV *halts.*) I'll give you one biscuit per day. (*Pause.*) One and a half. (*Pause.*) Why do you stay with me?

CLOV: Why do you keep me?

HAMM: There's no one else.

CLOV: There's nowhere else.
Pause.

HAMM: You're leaving me all the same.

CLOV: I'm trying.

HAMM: You don't love me.

CLOV: No.

HAMM: You loved me once.

CLOV: Once!

HAMM: I've made you suffer too much. (*Pause.*) Haven't I?

CLOV: It's not that.

HAMM (*Shocked.*): I haven't made you suffer too much?

CLOV: Yes!

HAMM (*Relieved.*): Ah you gave me a fright! (*Pause. Coldly.*) Forgive me. (*Pause. Louder.*) I said, Forgive me.

CLOV: I heard you. (*Pause.*) Have you bled?

HAMM: Less. (*Pause.*) Is it not time for my pain-killer?

CLOV: No.
Pause.

HAMM: How are your eyes?

CLOV: Bad.

HAMM: How are your legs?

CLOV: Bad.

HAMM: But you can move.

CLOV: Yes.

HAMM (*Violently.*): Then move! (CLOV *goes to back wall, leans against it with his forehead and hands.*) Where are you?

CLOV: Here.

HAMM: Come back! (CLOV *returns to his place beside the chair.*) Where are you?

CLOV: Here.

HAMM: Why don't you kill me?

CLOV: I don't know the combination of the larder.
Pause.

HAMM: Go and get two bicycle-wheels.

CLOV: There are no more bicycle-wheels.

HAMM: What have you done with your bicycle?

CLOV: I never had a bicycle.

HAMM: The thing is impossible.

CLOV: When there were still bicycles I wept to have one. I crawled at your feet. You told me to get out to hell. Now there are none.

HAMM: And your rounds? When you inspected my paupers. Always on foot?

CLOV: Sometimes on horse. (*The lid of one of the bins lifts and the hands of* NAGG *appear, gripping the rim. Then his head emerges. Nightcap. Very white face.* NAGG *yawns, then listens.*) I'll leave you, I have things to do.

HAMM: In your kitchen?

CLOV: Yes.

HAMM: Outside of here it's death. (*Pause.*) All right, be off. (*Exit* CLOV. *Pause.*) We're getting on.

NAGG: Me pap!

HAMM: Accursed progenitor!

NAGG: Me pap!

HAMM: The old folks at home! No decency left! Guzzle, guzzle, that's all they think of. (*He whistles. Enter* CLOV. *He halts beside the chair.*) Well! I thought you were leaving me.

CLOV: Oh not just yet, not just yet.

NAGG: Me pap!

HAMM: Give him his pap.

CLOV: There's no more pap.

HAMM (*To* NAGG): Do you hear that? There's no more pap. You'll never get any more pap.

NAGG: I want me pap!

HAMM: Give him a biscuit. (*Exit* CLOV.) Accursed fornicator! How are your stumps?

NAGG: Never mind me stumps.

Enter CLOV *with biscuit.*

CLOV: I'm back again, with the biscuit.

He gives the biscuit to NAGG *who fingers it, sniffs it.*

NAGG (*Plaintively.*): What is it?

CLOV: Spratt's medium.

NAGG (*As before.*): It's hard! I can't!

HAMM: Bottle him!

CLOV *pushes* NAGG *back into the bin, closes the lid.*

CLOV (*Returning to his place beside the chair.*): If age but knew!

HAMM: Sit on him!

CLOV: I can't sit.

HAMM: True. And I can't stand.

CLOV: So it is.

HAMM: Every man his speciality. (*Pause.*) No phone calls? (*Pause.*) Don't we laugh?

CLOV (*After reflection.*): I don't feel like it.

HAMM (*After reflection.*): Nor I. (*Pause.*) Clov!

CLOV: Yes.

HAMM: Nature has forgotten us.

CLOV: There's no more nature.

HAMM: No more nature! You exaggerate.

CLOV: In the vicinity.

HAMM: But we breathe, we change! We lose our hair, our teeth! Our bloom! Our ideals!

CLOV: Then she hasn't forgotten us.

HAMM: But you say there is none.

CLOV (*Sadly.*): No one that ever lived ever thought so crooked as we.

HAMM: We do what we can.

CLOV: We shouldn't.

Pause.

HAMM: You're a bit of all right, aren't you?

CLOV: A smithereen.

Pause.

HAMM: This is slow work. (*Pause.*) Is it not time for my painkiller?

CLOV: No. (*Pause.*) I'll leave you, I have things to do.

HAMM: In your kitchen?

CLOV: Yes.

HAMM: What, I'd like to know.

CLOV: I look at the wall.

HAMM: The wall! And what do you see on your wall? Mene, mene?[1] Naked bodies?

CLOV: I see my light dying.

HAMM: Your light dying! Listen to that! Well, it can die just as well here, *your* light. Take a look at me and then come back and tell me what you think of *your* light.

Pause.

CLOV: You shouldn't speak to me like that.

Pause.

HAMM (*Coldly.*): Forgive me. (*Pause. Louder.*) I said, Forgive me.

CLOV: I heard you.

The lid of NAGG's *bin lifts. His hands appear, gripping the rim. Then his head emerges. In his mouth the biscuit. He listens.*

HAMM: Did your seeds come up?

CLOV: No.

HAMM: Did you scratch round them to see if they had sprouted?

CLOV: They haven't sprouted.

HAMM: Perhaps it's still too early.

CLOV: If they were going to sprout they would have sprouted. (*Violently.*) They'll never sprout.

Pause. NAGG *takes biscuit in his hand.*

HAMM: This is not much fun. (*Pause.*) But that's always the way at the end of the day, isn't it, Clov?

CLOV: Always.

HAMM: It's the end of the day like any other day, isn't it, Clov?

CLOV: Looks like it.

Pause.

HAMM (*Anguished.*): What's happening, what's happening?

CLOV: Something is taking its course.

Pause.

HAMM: All right, be off. (*He leans back in his chair, remains motionless.* CLOV *does not move, heaves a great groaning sigh.* HAMM *sits up.*) I thought I told you to be off.

CLOV: I'm trying. (*He goes to the door, halts.*) Ever since I was whelped.

Exit CLOV.

HAMM: We're getting on.

> *He leans back in his chair, remains motionless.* NAGG *knocks on the lid of the other bin. Pause. He knocks harder. The lid lifts and the hands of* NELL *appear, gripping the rim. Then her head emerges. Lace cap. Very white face.*

NELL: What is it, my pet? (*Pause.*) Time for love?

NAGG: Were you asleep?

NELL: Oh no!

NAGG: Kiss me.

NELL: We can't.

NAGG: Try.

> *Their heads strain towards each other, fail to meet, fall apart again.*

NELL: Why this farce, day after day?

> *Pause.*

NAGG: I've lost me tooth.

NELL: When?

NAGG: I had it yesterday.

NELL (*Elegiac.*): Ah yesterday!

> *They turn painfully towards each other.*

NAGG: Can you see me?

NELL: Hardly. And you?

NAGG: What?

NELL: Can you see me?

NAGG: Hardly.

NELL: So much the better, so much the better.

NAGG: Don't say that. (*Pause.*) Our sight has failed.

NELL: Yes.

> *Pause. They turn away from each other.*

NAGG: Can you hear me?

NELL: Yes. And you?

NAGG: Yes. (*Pause.*) Our hearing hasn't failed.

NELL: Our what?

NAGG: Our hearing.

NELL: No. (*Pause.*) Have you anything else to say to me?

NAGG: Do you remember —

NELL: No.

NAGG: When we crashed on our tandem and lost our shanks.[2]

> *They laugh heartily.*

NELL: It was in the Ardennes.

> *They laugh less heartily.*

NAGG: On the road to Sedan. (*They laugh still less heartily.*) Are you cold?

NELL: Yes, perished. And you?

NAGG: I'm freezing. (*Pause.*) Do you want to go in?

NELL: Yes.

NAGG: Then go in. (NELL *does not move.*) Why don't you go in?

NELL: I don't know.

> *Pause.*

NAGG: Has he changed your sawdust?

NELL: It isn't sawdust. (*Pause. Wearily.*) Can you not be a little accurate, Nagg?

NAGG: Your sand then. It's not important.

NELL: It is important.

> *Pause.*

NAGG: It was sawdust once.

NELL: Once!

NAGG: And now it's sand. (*Pause.*) From the shore. (*Pause. Impatiently.*) Now it's sand he fetches from the shore.

NELL: Now it's sand.

NAGG: Has he changed yours?

NELL: No.

NAGG: Nor mine. (*Pause.*) I won't have it! (*Pause. Holding up the biscuit.*) Do you want a bit?

NELL: No. (*Pause.*) Of what?

NAGG: Biscuit. I've kept you half. (*He looks at the biscuit. Proudly.*) Three quarters. For you. Here. (*He proffers the biscuit.*) No? (*Pause.*) Do you not feel well?

HAMM (*Wearily.*): Quiet, quiet, you're keeping me awake. (*Pause.*) Talk softer. (*Pause.*) If I could sleep I might make love. I'd go into the woods. My eyes would see . . . the sky, the earth. I'd run, run, they wouldn't catch me. (*Pause.*) Nature! (*Pause.*) There's something dripping in my head. (*Pause.*) A heart, a heart in my head.

> *Pause.*

NAGG (*Soft.*): Do you hear him? A heart in his head!

> *He chuckles cautiously.*

NELL: One mustn't laugh at those things, Nagg. Why must you always laugh at them?

NAGG: Not so loud!

NELL (*Without lowering her voice.*): Nothing is funnier than unhappiness, I grant you that. But —

NAGG (*Shocked.*): Oh!

NELL: Yes, yes, it's the most comical thing in the world. And we laugh, we laugh, with a will, in the beginning. But it's always the same thing. Yes, it's like the funny story we have heard too often, we still find it funny, but we don't laugh any more. (*Pause.*) Have you anything else to say to me?

NAGG: No.

NELL: Are you quite sure? (*Pause.*) Then I'll leave you.

NAGG: Do you not want your biscuit? (*Pause.*) I'll keep it for you. (*Pause.*) I thought you were going to leave me.

NELL: I am going to leave you.

NAGG: Could you give me a scratch before you go?

NELL: No. (*Pause.*) Where?

NAGG: In the back.

NELL: No. (*Pause.*) Rub yourself against the rim.

NAGG: It's lower down. In the hollow.

NELL: What hollow?

NAGG: The hollow! (*Pause.*) Could you not? (*Pause.*) Yesterday you scratched me there.

NELL (*Elegiac.*): Ah yesterday!

NAGG: Could you not? (*Pause.*) Would you like me to scratch you? (*Pause.*) Are you crying again?

NELL: I was trying.
Pause.

HAMM: Perhaps it's a little vein.
Pause.

NAGG: What was that he said?

NELL: Perhaps it's a little vein.

NAGG: What does that mean? (*Pause.*) That means nothing. (*Pause.*) Will I tell you the story of the tailor?

NELL: No. (*Pause.*) What for?

NAGG: To cheer you up.

NELL: It's not funny.

NAGG: It always made you laugh. (*Pause.*) The first time I thought you'd die.

NELL: It was on Lake Como. (*Pause.*) One April afternoon. (*Pause.*) Can you believe it?

NAGG: What?

NELL: That we once went out rowing on Lake Como. (*Pause.*) One April afternoon.

NAGG: We had got engaged the day before.

NELL: Engaged!

NAGG: You were in such fits that we capsized. By rights we should have been drowned.

NELL: It was because I felt happy.

NAGG (*Indignant.*): It was not, it was not, it was my story and nothing else. Happy! Don't you laugh at it still? Every time I tell it. Happy!

NELL: It was deep, deep. And you could see down to the bottom. So white. So clean.

NAGG: Let me tell it again. (*Raconteur's voice.*) An Englishman, needing a pair of striped trousers in a hurry for the New Year festivities, goes to his tailor who takes his measurements. (*Tailor's voice.*) 'That's the lot, come back in four days, I'll have it ready.' Good. Four days later. (*Tailor's voice.*) 'So sorry, come back in a week, I've made a mess of the seat.' Good, that's all right, a neat seat can be very ticklish. A week later. (*Tailor's voice.*) 'Frightfully sorry, come back in ten days, I've made a hash of the crutch.' Good, can't be helped, a snug crutch is always a teaser. Ten days later. (*Tailor's voice.*) 'Dreadfully sorry, come back in a fortnight, I've made a balls of the fly.' Good, at a pinch, a smart fly is a stiff proposition. (*Pause. Normal voice.*) I never told it worse. (*Pause. Gloomy.*) I tell this story worse and worse. (*Pause.*

Raconteur's voice.) Well, to make it short, the bluebells are blowing and he ballockses the buttonholes. (*Customer's voice.*) 'God damn you to hell, Sir, no, it's indecent, there are limits! In six days, do you hear me, six days, God made the world. Yes Sir, no less Sir, the WORLD! And you are not bloody well capable of making me a pair of trousers in three months!' (*Tailor's voice, scandalized.*) 'But my dear Sir, my dear Sir, look — (*Disdainful gesture, disgustedly.*) — at the world — (*Pause.*) — and look — (*Loving gesture, proudly.*) — at my TROUSERS!'
Pause. He looks at NELL *who has remained impassive, her eyes unseeing, breaks into a high forced laugh, cuts it short, pokes his head towards* NELL, *launches his laugh again.*

HAMM: Silence!
NAGG *starts, cuts short his laugh.*

NELL: You could see down to the bottom.

HAMM (*Exasperated.*): Have you not finished? Will you never finish? (*With sudden fury.*) Will this never finish? (NAGG *disappears into his bin, closes the lid behind him.* NELL *does not move. Frenziedly.*) My kingdom for a nightman![3] (*He whistles. Enter* CLOV.) Clear away this muck! Chuck it in the sea!
CLOV *goes to bins, halts.*

NELL: So white.

HAMM: What? What's she blathering about?
CLOV *stoops, take* NELL's *hand, feels her pulse.*

NELL (*To* CLOV): Desert!
CLOV *lets go her hand, pushes her back in the bin, closes the lid.*

CLOV (*Returning to his place beside the chair.*): She has no pulse.

HAMM: What was she drivelling about?

CLOV: She told me to go away, into the desert.

HAMM: Damn busybody! Is that all?

CLOV: No.

HAMM: What else?

CLOV: I didn't understand.

HAMM: Have you bottled her?

CLOV: Yes.

HAMM: Are they both bottled?

CLOV: Yes.

HAMM: Screw down the lids. (CLOV *goes towards door.*) Time enough. (CLOV *halts.*) My anger subsides, I'd like to pee.

CLOV (*With alacrity*): I'll go and get the catheter.
He goes towards the door.

HAMM: Time enough. (CLOV *halts.*) Give me my pain-killer.

CLOV: It's too soon. (*Pause.*) It's too soon on top of your tonic, it wouldn't act.

HAMM: In the morning they brace you up and in the evening they calm you down. Unless it's the other way round. (*Pause.*) That old doctor, he's dead, naturally?

CLOV: He wasn't old.

HAMM: But he's dead?

CLOV: Naturally. (*Pause.*) *You* ask *me* that?

Pause.

HAMM: Take me for a little turn. (CLOV *goes behind the chair and pushes it forward.*) Not too fast! (CLOV *pushes chair.*) Right round the world! (CLOV *pushes chair.*) Hug the walls, then back to the centre again. (CLOV *pushes chair.*) I was right in the centre, wasn't I?

CLOV (*Pushing.*): Yes.

HAMM: We'd need a proper wheel-chair. With big wheels. Bicycle wheels! (*Pause.*) Are you hugging?

CLOV (*Pushing.*): Yes.

HAMM (*Groping for wall.*): It's a lie! Why do you lie to me?

CLOV (*Bearing closer to wall.*): There! There!

HAMM: Stop! (CLOV *stops chair close to back wall.* HAMM *lays his hand against wall.*) Old wall! (*Pause.*) Beyond is the . . . other hell. (*Pause. Violently.*) Closer! Closer! Up against!

CLOV: Take away your hand. (HAMM *withdraws his hand.* CLOV *rams chair against wall.*) There!

HAMM *leans towards wall, applies his ear to it.*

HAMM: Do you hear? (*He strikes the wall with his knuckles.*) Do you hear? Hollow bricks! (*He strikes again.*) All that's hollow! (*Pause. He straightens up. Violently.*) That's enough. Back!

CLOV: We haven't done the round.

HAMM: Back to my place! (CLOV *pushes chair back to centre.*) Is that my place?

CLOV: Yes, that's your place.

HAMM: Am I right in the centre?

CLOV: I'll measure it.

HAMM: More or less! More or less!

CLOV (*Moving chair slightly.*): There!

HAMM: I'm more or less in the centre?

CLOV: I'd say so.

HAMM: You'd say so! Put me right in the centre!

CLOV: I'll go and get the tape.

HAMM: Roughly! Roughly! (CLOV *moves chair slightly.*) Bang in the centre!

CLOV: There!

Pause.

HAMM: I feel a little too far to the left. (CLOV *moves chair slightly.*) Now I feel a little too far to the right. (CLOV *moves chair slightly.*) I feel a little too far forward. (CLOV *moves chair slightly.*) Now I feel a little too far back. (CLOV *moves chair slightly.*)

Don't stay there (*i.e. behind the chair*), you give me the shivers.

CLOV *returns to his place beside the chair.*

CLOV: If I could kill him I'd die happy.

Pause.

HAMM: What's the weather like?

CLOV: The same as usual.

HAMM: Look at the earth.

CLOV: I've looked.

HAMM: With the glass?

CLOV: No need of the glass.

HAMM: Look at it with the glass.

CLOV: I'll go and get the glass.

Exit CLOV.

HAMM: No need of the glass!

Enter CLOV *with telescope.*

CLOV: I'm back again, with the glass. (*He goes to window right, looks up at it.*) I need the steps.

HAMM: Why? Have you shrunk? (*Exit* CLOV *with telescope.*) I don't like that, I don't like that.

Enter CLOV *with ladder, but without telescope.*

CLOV: I'm back again, with the steps. (*He sets down ladder under window right, gets up on it, realizes he has not the telescope, gets down.*) I need the glass.

He goes towards the door.

HAMM (*Violently.*): But you have the glass!

CLOV (*Halting, violently.*): No I haven't the glass!

Exit CLOV.

HAMM: This is deadly.

Enter CLOV *with telescope. He goes towards ladder.*

CLOV: Things are livening up. (*He gets up on ladder, raises the telescope, lets it fall.*) I did it on purpose. (*He gets down, picks up the telescope, turns it on auditorium.*) I see . . . a multitude . . . in transports . . . of joy. (*Pause.*) That's what I call a magnifier. (*He lowers the telescope, turns towards* HAMM.) Well? Don't we laugh?

HAMM (*After reflection.*): I don't.

CLOV (*After reflection.*): Nor I. (*He gets up on ladder, turns the telescope on the without.*) Let's see. (*He looks, moving the telescope.*) Zero . . . (*He looks.*) . . . zero . . . (*He looks.*) . . . and zero.

HAMM: Nothing stirs. All is ——

CLOV: Zer ——

HAMM (*Violently.*): Wait till you're spoken to! (*Normal voice.*) All is . . . all is . . . all is what? (*Violently.*) All is what?

CLOV: What all is? In a word? Is that what you want to know? Just a moment. (*He turns the telescope on the without, looks, lowers the telescope, turns towards* HAMM.) Corpsed. (*Pause.*) Well? Content?

HAMM: Look at the sea.

CLOV: It's the same.

HAMM: Look at the ocean!
> CLOV *gets down, takes a few steps towards window left, goes back for ladder, carries it over and sets it down under window left, gets up on it, turns the telescope on the without, looks at length. He starts, lowers the telescope, examines it, turns it again on the without.*

CLOV: Never seen anything like that!

HAMM (*Anxious.*): What? A sail? A fin? Smoke?

CLOV (*Looking.*): The light is sunk.

HAMM (*Relieved.*): Pah! We all knew that.

CLOV (*Looking.*): There was a bit left.

HAMM: The base.

CLOV (*Looking.*): Yes.

HAMM: And now?

CLOV (*Looking.*): All gone.

HAMM: No gulls?

CLOV (*Looking.*): Gulls!

HAMM: And the horizon? Nothing on the horizon?

CLOV (*Lowering the telescope, turning towards* HAMM, *exasperated.*): What in God's name could there be on the horizon?
> *Pause.*

HAMM: The waves, how are the waves?

CLOV: The waves? (*He turns the telescope on the waves.*) Lead.

HAMM: And the sun?

CLOV (*Looking.*): Zero.

HAMM: But it should be sinking. Look again.

CLOV (*Looking.*): Damn the sun.

HAMM: Is it night already then?

CLOV (*Looking.*): No.

HAMM: Then what is it?

CLOV (*Looking.*): Grey. (*Lowering the telescope, turning towards* HAMM, *louder.*) Grey! (*Pause. Still louder.*) GRREY!
> *Pause. He gets down, approaches* HAMM *from behind, whispers in his ear.*

HAMM (*Starting.*): Grey! Did I hear you say grey?

CLOV: Light black. From pole to pole.

HAMM: You exaggerate. (*Pause.*) Don't stay there, you give me the shivers.
> CLOV *returns to his place beside the chair.*

CLOV: Why this farce, day after day?

HAMM: Routine. One never knows. (*Pause.*) Last night I saw inside my breast. There was a big sore.

CLOV: Pah! You saw your heart.

HAMM: No, it was living. (*Pause. Anguished.*) Clov!

CLOV: Yes.

HAMM: What's happening?

CLOV: Something is taking its course.
> *Pause.*

HAMM: Clov!

CLOV (*Impatiently.*): What is it?

HAMM: We're not beginning to . . . to . . . mean something?

CLOV: Mean something! You and I, mean something! (*Brief laugh.*) Ah that's a good one!

HAMM: I wonder. (*Pause.*) Imagine if a rational being came back to earth, wouldn't he be liable to get ideas into his head if he observed us long enough. (*Voice of rational being.*) Ah, good, now I see what it is, yes, now I understand what they're at! (CLOV *starts, drops the telescope and begins to scratch his belly with both hands. Normal voice.*) And without going so far as that, we ourselves . . . (*With emotion.*) . . . we ourselves . . . at certain moments . . . (*Vehemently.*) To think perhaps it won't all have been for nothing!

CLOV (*Anguished, scratching himself.*): I have a flea!

HAMM: A flea! Are there still fleas?

CLOV: On me there's one. (*Scratching.*) Unless it's a crablouse.

HAMM (*Very perturbed.*): But humanity might start from there all over again! Catch him, for the love of God!

CLOV: I'll go and get the powder.
> *Exit* CLOV.

HAMM: A flea! This is awful! What a day!
> *Enter* CLOV *with a sprinkling-tin.*

CLOV: I'm back again, with the insecticide.

HAMM: Let him have it!
> CLOV *loosens the top of his trousers, pulls it forward and shakes powder into the aperture. He stoops, looks, waits, starts, frenziedly shakes more powder, stoops, looks, waits.*

CLOV: The bastard!

HAMM: Did you get him?

CLOV: Looks like it. (*He drops the tin and adjusts his trousers.*) Unless he's laying doggo.

HAMM: Laying! Lying you mean. Unless he's *lying* doggo.

CLOV: Ah? One says lying? One doesn't say laying?

HAMM: Use your head, can't you. If he was laying we'd be bitched.

CLOV: Ah. (*Pause.*) What about that pee?

HAMM: I'm having it.

CLOV: Ah that's the spirit, that's the spirit!
> *Pause.*

HAMM (*With ardour.*): Let's go from here, the two of us! South! You can make a raft and the currents will carry us away, far away, to other . . . mammals!

CLOV: God forbid!

HAMM: Alone, I'll embark alone! Get working on that raft immediately. Tomorrow I'll be gone for ever.

CLOV (*Hastening towards door.*): I'll start straight away.

HAMM: Wait! (CLOV *halts.*) Will there be sharks, do you think?

CLOV: Sharks? I don't know. If there are there will be.

He goes towards door.

HAMM: Wait! (CLOV *halts.*) Is it not yet time for my pain-killer?

CLOV (*Violently.*): No!

He goes towards door.

HAMM: Wait! (CLOV *halts.*) How are your eyes?

CLOV: Bad.

HAMM: But you can see.

CLOV: All I want.

HAMM: How are your legs?

CLOV: Bad.

HAMM: But you can walk.

CLOV: I come . . . and go.

HAMM: In my house. (*Pause. With prophetic relish.*) One day you'll be blind, like me. You'll be sitting there, a speck in the void, in the dark, for ever, like me. (*Pause.*) One day you'll say to yourself, I'm tired, I'll sit down, and you'll go and sit down. Then you'll say, I'm hungry, I'll get up and get something to eat. But you won't get up. You'll say, I shouldn't have sat down, but since I have I'll sit on a little longer, then I'll get up and get something to eat. But you won't get up and you won't get anything to eat. (*Pause.*) You'll look at the wall a while, then you'll say, I'll close my eyes, perhaps have a little sleep, after that I'll feel better, and you'll close them. And when you open them again there'll be no wall any more. (*Pause.*) Infinite emptiness will be all around you, all the resurrected dead of all the ages wouldn't fill it, and there you'll be like a little bit of grit in the middle of the steppe. (*Pause.*) Yes, one day you'll know what it is, you'll be like me, except that you won't have anyone with you, because you won't have had pity on anyone and because there won't be anyone left to have pity on.

Pause.

CLOV: It's not certain. (*Pause.*) And there's one thing you forget.

HAMM: Ah?

CLOV: I can't sit down.

HAMM (*Impatiently.*): Well, you'll lie down then, what the hell! Or you'll come to a standstill, simply stop and stand still, the way you are now. One day you'll say, I'm tired, I'll stop. What does the attitude matter?

Pause.

CLOV: So you all want me to leave you.

HAMM: Naturally.

CLOV: Then I'll leave you.

HAMM: You can't leave us.

CLOV: Then I shan't leave you.

Pause.

HAMM: Why don't you finish us? (*Pause.*) I'll tell you the combination of the larder if you promise to finish me.

CLOV: I couldn't finish you.

HAMM: Then you shan't finish me.

Pause.

CLOV: I'll leave you, I have things to do.

HAMM: Do you remember when you came here?

CLOV: No. Too small, you told me.

HAMM: Do you remember your father?

CLOV (*Wearily.*): Same answer. (*Pause.*) You've asked me these questions millions of times.

HAMM: I love the old questions. (*With fervour.*) Ah the old questions, the old answers, there's nothing like them! (*Pause.*) It was I was a father to you.

CLOV: Yes. (*He looks at* HAMM *fixedly.*) You were that to me.

HAMM: My house a home for you.

CLOV: Yes. (*He looks about him.*) This was that for me.

HAMM (*Proudly.*): But for me (*Gesture towards himself.*) no father. But for Hamm (*Gesture towards surroundings.*) no home.

Pause.

CLOV: I'll leave you.

HAMM: Did you ever think of one thing?

CLOV: Never.

HAMM: That here we're down in a hole. (*Pause.*) But beyond the hills? Eh? Perhaps it's still green. Eh? (*Pause.*) Flora! Pomona! (*Ecstatically.*) Ceres! (*Pause.*) Perhaps you won't need to go very far.

CLOV: I can't go very far. (*Pause.*) I'll leave you.

HAMM: Is my dog ready?

CLOV: He lacks a leg.

HAMM: Is he silky?

CLOV: He's a kind of Pomeranian.

HAMM: Go and get him.

CLOV: He lacks a leg.

HAMM: Go and get him! (*Exit* CLOV.) We're getting on.

Enter CLOV *holding by one of its three legs a black toy dog.*

CLOV: Your dogs are here.

He hands the dog to HAMM *who feels it, fondles it.*

HAMM: He's white, isn't he?

CLOV: Nearly.

HAMM: What do you mean, nearly? Is he white or isn't he?

CLOV: He isn't.

Pause.

HAMM: You've forgotten the sex.

CLOV (*Vexed.*): But he isn't finished. The sex goes on at the end.

Pause.

HAMM: You haven't put on his ribbon.

CLOV (*Angrily.*): But he isn't finished, I tell you! First you finish your dog and then you put on his ribbon!
Pause.

HAMM: Can he stand?

CLOV: I don't know.

HAMM: Try. (*He hands the dog to* CLOV *who places it on the ground.*) Well?

CLOV: Wait!
He squats down and tries to get the dog to stand on its three legs, fails, lets it go. The dog falls on its side.

HAMM (*Impatiently.*): Well?

CLOV: He's standing.

HAMM (*Groping for the dog.*): Where? Where is he?
CLOV *holds up the dog in a standing position.*

CLOV: There.
He takes HAMM'*s hand and guides it towards the dog's head.*

HAMM (*His hand on the dog's head.*): Is he gazing at me?

CLOV: Yes.

HAMM (*Proudly.*): As if he were asking me to take him for a walk?

CLOV: If you like.

HAMM (*As before.*): Or as if he were begging me for a bone. (*He withdraws his hand.*) Leave him like that, standing there imploring me.
CLOV *straightens up. The dog falls on its side.*

CLOV: I'll leave you.

HAMM: Have you had your visions?

CLOV: Less.

HAMM: Is Mother Pegg's light on?

CLOV: Light! How could anyone's light be on?

HAMM: Extinguished!

CLOV: Naturally it's extinguished. If it's not on it's extinguished.

HAMM: No, I mean Mother Pegg.

CLOV: But naturally she's extinguished! (*Pause.*) What's the matter with you today?

HAMM: I'm taking my course. (*Pause.*) Is she buried?

CLOV: Buried! Who would have buried her?

HAMM: You.

CLOV: Me! Haven't I enough to do without burying people?

HAMM: But you'll bury me.

CLOV: No I shan't bury you.
Pause.

HAMM: She was bonny once, like a flower of the field. (*With reminiscent leer.*) And a great one for the men!

CLOV: We too were bonny — once. It's a rare thing not to have been bonny — once.
Pause.

HAMM: Go and get the gaff.
CLOV *goes to door, halts.*

CLOV: Do this, do that, and I do it. I never refuse. Why?

HAMM: You're not able to.

CLOV: Soon I won't do it any more.

HAMM: You won't be able to any more. (*Exit* CLOV.) Ah the creatures, the creatures, everything has to be explained to them.
Enter CLOV *with gaff.*

CLOV: Here's your gaff. Stick it up.
He gives the gaff to HAMM *who, wielding it like a punt-pole, tries to move his chair.*

HAMM: Did I move?

CLOV: No.
HAMM *throws down the gaff.*

HAMM: Go and get the oilcan.

CLOV: What for?

HAMM: To oil the castors.

CLOV: I oiled them yesterday.

HAMM: Yesterday! What does that mean? Yesterday!

CLOV (*Violently.*): That means that bloody awful day, long ago, before this bloody awful day. I use the words you taught me. If they don't mean anything any more, teach me others. Or let me be silent.
Pause.

HAMM: I once knew a madman who thought the end of the world had come. He was a painter — and engraver. I had a great fondness for him. I used to go and see him, in the asylum. I'd take him by the hand and drag him to the window. Look! There! All the rising corn! And there! Look! The sails of the herring fleet! All that loveliness! (*Pause.*) He'd snatch away his hand and go back into his corner. Appalled. All he had seen was ashes. (*Pause.*) He alone had been spared. (*Pause.*) Forgotten. (*Pause.*) It appears the case is . . . was not so . . . so unusual.

CLOV: A madman? When was that?

HAMM: Oh way back, way back, you weren't in the land of the living.

CLOV: God be with the days!
Pause. HAMM *raises his toque.*

HAMM: I had a great fondness for him. (*Pause. He puts on his toque again.*) He was a painter — and engraver.

CLOV: There are so many terrible things.

HAMM: No, no, there are not so many now. (*Pause.*) Clov!

CLOV: Yes.

HAMM: Do you not think this has gone on long enough?

CLOV: Yes! (*Pause.*) What?

HAMM: This . . . this . . . thing.

CLOV: I've always thought so. (*Pause.*) You not?

HAMM (*Gloomily.*): Then it's a day like any other day.

CLOV: As long as it lasts. (*Pause.*) All life long the same inanities.

Pause.

HAMM: I can't leave you.

CLOV: I know. And you can't follow me.

Pause.

HAMM: If you leave me how shall I know?

CLOV (*Briskly.*): Well you simply whistle me and if I don't come running it means I've left you.

Pause.

HAMM: You won't come and kiss me good-bye?

CLOV: Oh I shouldn't think so.

Pause.

HAMM: But you might be merely dead in your kitchen.

CLOV: The result would be the same.

HAMM: Yes, but how would I know, if you were merely dead in your kitchen?

CLOV: Well . . . sooner or later I'd start to stink.

HAMM: You stink already. The whole place stinks of corpses.

CLOV: The whole universe.

HAMM (*Angrily.*): To hell with the universe! (*Pause.*) Think of something.

CLOV: What?

HAMM: An idea, have an idea. (*Angrily.*) A bright idea!

CLOV: Ah good. (*He starts pacing to and fro, his eyes fixed on the ground, his hands behind his back. He halts.*) The pains in my legs! It's unbelievable! Soon I won't be able to think any more.

HAMM: You won't be able to leave me. (CLOV *resumes his pacing.*) What are you doing?

CLOV: Having an idea. (*He paces.*) Ah!

He halts.

HAMM: What a brain! (*Pause.*) Well?

CLOV: Wait! (*He meditates. Not very convinced.*) Yes . . . (*Pause. More convinced.*) Yes! (*He raises his head.*) I have it! I set the alarm.

Pause.

HAMM: This is perhaps not one of my bright days, but frankly —

CLOV: You whistle me. I don't come. The alarm rings. I'm gone. It doesn't ring. I'm dead.

Pause.

HAMM: Is it working? (*Pause. Impatiently.*) The alarm, is it working?

CLOV: Why wouldn't it be working?

HAMM: Because it's worked too much.

CLOV: But it's hardly worked at all.

HAMM (*Angrily.*): Then because it's worked too little!

CLOV: I'll go and see. (*Exit* CLOV. *Brief ring of alarm off. Enter* CLOV *with alarm-clock. He holds it against* HAMM*'s ear and releases alarm. They listen to it ringing to the end. Pause.*) Fit to wake the dead! Did you hear it?

HAMM: Vaguely.

CLOV: The end is terrific!

HAMM: I prefer the middle. (*Pause.*) Is it not time for my pain-killer?

CLOV: No! (*He goes to the door, turns.*) I'll leave you.

HAMM: It's time for my story. Do you want to listen to my story?

CLOV: No.

HAMM: Ask my father if he wants to listen to my story.

CLOV *goes to bins, raises the lid of* NAGG*'s, stoops, looks into it. Pause. He straightens up.*

CLOV: He's asleep.

HAMM: Wake him.

CLOV *stoops, wakes* NAGG *with the alarm. Unintelligible words.* CLOV *straightens up.*

CLOV: He doesn't want to listen to your story.

HAMM: I'll give him a bon-bon.

CLOV *stoops. As before.*

CLOV: He wants a sugar-plum.

HAMM: He'll get a sugar-plum.

CLOV *stoops. As before.*

CLOV: It's a deal. (*He goes towards door.* NAGG*'s hands appear, gripping the rim. Then the head emerges.* CLOV *reaches door, turns.*) Do you believe in the life to come?

HAMM: Mine was always that. (*Exit* CLOV.) Got him that time!

NAGG: I'm listening.

HAMM: Scoundrel! Why did you engender me?

NAGG: I didn't know.

HAMM: What? What didn't you know?

NAGG: That it'd be you. (*Pause.*) You'll give me a sugar-plum?

HAMM: After the audition.

NAGG: You swear?

HAMM: Yes.

NAGG: On what?

HAMM: My honour.

Pause. They laugh heartily.

NAGG: Two.

HAMM: One.

NAGG: One for me and one for ——

HAMM: One! Silence! (*Pause.*) Where was I? (*Pause. Gloomily.*) It's finished, we're finished. (*Pause.*) Nearly finished. (*Pause.*) There'll be no more speech. (*Pause.*) Something dripping in my head, ever since the fontannelles. (*Stifled hilarity of* NAGG.) Splash, splash, always on the same spot.

(*Pause.*) Perhaps it's a little vein. (*Pause.*) A little artery. (*Pause. More animated.*) Enough of that, it's story time, where was I? (*Pause. Narrative tone.*) The man came crawling towards me, on his belly. Pale, wonderfully pale and thin, he seemed on the point of — (*Pause. Normal tone.*) No, I've done that bit. (*Pause. Narrative tone.*) I calmly filled my pipe — the meerschaum, lit it with . . . let us say a vesta, drew a few puffs. Aah! (*Pause.*) Well, what is it *you* want? (*Pause.*) It was an extraordinarily bitter day, I remember, zero by the thermometer. But considering it was Christmas Eve there was nothing . . . extra-ordinary about that. Seasonable weather, for once in a way. (*Pause.*) Well, what ill wind blows you my way? He raised his face to me, black with mingled dirt and tears. (*Pause. Normal tone.*) That should do it. (*Narrative tone.*) No, no don't look at me, don't look at me. He dropped his eyes and mumbled something, apologies I presume. (*Pause.*) I'm a busy man, you know, the final touches, before the festivities, you know what it is. (*Pause. Forcibly.*) Come on now, what is the object of this invasion? (*Pause.*) It was a glorious bright day, I remember, fifty by the heliometer, but already the sun was sinking down into the . . . down among the dead. (*Normal tone.*) Nicely put, that. (*Narrative tone.*) Come on now, come on, present your petition and let me resume my labours. (*Pause. Normal tone.*) There's English for you. Ah well . . . (*Narrative tone.*) It was then he took the plunge. It's my little one, he said. Tsstss, a little one, that's bad. My little boy, he said, as if the sex mattered. Where did he come from? He named the hole. A good half-day, on horse. What are you insinuating? That the place is still inhabited? No no, not a soul, except himself and the child — assuming he existed. Good. I inquired about the situation at Kov, beyond the gulf. Not a sinner. Good. And you expect me to believe you have left your little one back there, all alone, and alive into the bargain? Come now! (*Pause.*) It was a howling wild day, I remember, a hundred by the anemometer. The wind was tearing up the dead pines and sweeping them . . . away. (*Pause. Normal tone.*) A bit feeble, that. (*Narrative tone.*) Come on, man, speak up, what is it you want from me, I have to put up my holly. (*Pause.*) Well to make it short it finally transpired that what he wanted from me was . . . bread for his brat. Bread? But I have no bread, it doesn't agree with me. Good. Then perhaps a little corn? (*Pause. Normal tone.*) That should do it. (*Narrative tone.*)

Corn, yes, I have corn, it's true, in my granaries. But use your head. I give you some corn, a pound, a pound and a half, you bring it back to your child and you make him — if he's still alive — a nice pot of porridge (NAGG *reacts*), a nice pot and a half of porridge, full of nourishment. Good. The colours come back into his little cheeks — perhaps. And then? (*Pause.*) I lost patience. (*Violently.*) Use your head, can't you, use your head, you're on earth, there's no cure for that! (*Pause.*) It was an exceedingly dry day, I remember, zero by the hygrometer. Ideal weather, for my lumbago. (*Pause. Violently.*) But what in God's name do you imagine? That the earth will awake in spring? That the rivers and seas will run with fish again? That there's manna in heaven still for imbeciles like you? (*Pause.*) Gradually I cooled down, sufficiently at least to ask him how long he had taken on the way. Three whole days. Good. In what condition he had left the child. Deep in sleep. (*Forcibly.*) But deep in what sleep, deep in what sleep already? (*Pause.*) Well to make it short I finally offered to take him into my service. He had touched a chord. And then I imagined already that I wasn't much longer for this world. (*He laughs. Pause.*) Well? (*Pause.*) Well? Here if you were careful you might die a nice natural death, in peace and comfort. (*Pause.*) Well? (*Pause.*) In the end he asked me would I consent to take in the child as well — if he were still alive. (*Pause.*) It was the moment I was waiting for. (*Pause.*) Would I consent to take in the child . . . (*Pause.*) I can see him still, down on his knees, his hands flat on the ground, glaring at me with his mad eyes, in defiance of my wishes. (*Pause. Normal tone.*) I'll soon have finished with this story. (*Pause.*) Unless I bring in other characters. (*Pause.*) But where would I find them? (*Pause.*) Where would I look for them? (*Pause. He whistles. Enter* CLOV.) Let us pray to God.

NAGG: Me sugar-plum!

CLOV: There's a rat in the kitchen!

HAMM: A rat! Are there still rats?

CLOV: In the kitchen there's one.

HAMM: And you haven't exterminated him?

CLOV: Half. You disturbed us.

HAMM: He can't get away?

CLOV: No.

HAMM: You'll finish him later. Let us pray to God.

CLOV: Again!

NAGG: Me sugar-plum!

HAMM: God first! (*Pause.*) Are you right?

CLOV (*Resigned.*): Off we go.

HAMM (*To* NAGG.): And you?

NAGG (*Clasping his hands, closing his eyes, in a gabble.*): Our Father which art ——

HAMM: Silence! In silence! Where are your manners? (*Pause.*) Off we go. (*Attitudes of prayer. Silence. Abandoning his attitude, discouraged.*) Well?

CLOV (*Abandoning his attitude.*): What a hope? And you?

HAMM: Sweet damn all! (*To* NAGG.) And you?

NAGG Wait! (*Pause. Abandoning his attitude.*) Nothing doing!

HAMM: The bastard! He doesn't exist!

CLOV: Not yet.

NAGG: Me sugar-plum!

HAMM: There are no more sugar-plums!
Pause.

NAGG: It's natural. After all I'm your father. It's true if it hadn't been me it would have been someone else. But that's no excuse. (*Pause.*) Turkish Delight, for example, which no longer exists, we all know that, there is nothing in the world I love more. And one day I'll ask you for some, in return for a kindness, and you'll promise it to me. One must live with the times. (*Pause.*) Whom did you call when you were a tiny boy, and were frightened, in the dark? Your mother? No. Me. We let you cry. Then we moved you out of earshot, so that we might sleep in peace. (*Pause.*) I was asleep, as happy as a king, and you woke me up to have me listen to you. It wasn't indispensable, you didn't really need to have me listen to you. Besides I didn't listen to you. (*Pause.*) I hope the day will come when you'll really need to have me listen to you, and need to hear my voice, any voice. (*Pause.*) Yes, I hope I'll live till then, to hear you calling me like when you were a tiny boy, and were frightened, in the dark, and I was your only hope. (*Pause.* NAGG *knocks on lid of* NELL's *bin. Pause.*) Nell! (*Pause. He knocks louder. Pause. Louder.*) Nell!
Pause. NAGG *sinks back into his bin, closes the lid behind him.*
Pause.

HAMM: Our revels now are ended. (*He gropes for the dog.*) The dog's gone.

CLOV: He's not a real dog, he can't go.

HAMM (*Groping*): He's not there.

CLOV: He's lain down.

HAMM: Give him up to me. (CLOV *picks up the dog and gives it to* HAMM. HAMM *holds it in his arms. Pause.* HAMM *throws away the dog.*) Dirty brute! (CLOV *begins to pick up the objects lying on the ground.*) What are you doing?

CLOV: Putting things in order. (*He straightens up. Fervently.*) I'm going to clear everything away!
He starts picking up again.

HAMM: Order!

CLOV (*Straightening up.*): I love order. It's my dream. A world where all would be silent and still and each thing in its last place, under the last dust.
He starts picking up again.

HAMM (*Exasperated.*): What in God's name do you think you are doing?

CLOV (*Straightening up.*): I'm doing my best to create a little order.

HAMM: Drop it!
CLOV *drops the objects he has picked up.*

CLOV: After all, there or elsewhere.
He goes towards door.

HAMM (*Irritably.*): What's wrong with your feet?

CLOV: My feet?

HAMM: Tramp! Tramp!

CLOV: I must have put on my boots.

HAMM: Your slippers were hurting you?
Pause.

CLOV: I'll leave you.

HAMM: No!

CLOV: What is there to keep me here?

HAMM: The dialogue. (*Pause.*) I've got on with my story. (*Pause.*) I've got on with it well. (*Pause. Irritably.*) Ask me where I've got to.

CLOV: Oh, by the way, your story?

HAMM (*Surprised.*): What story?

CLOV: The one you've been telling yourself all your . . . days.

HAMM: Ah you mean my chronicle?

CLOV: That's the one.
Pause.

HAMM (*Angrily.*): Keep going, can't you, keep going!

CLOV: You've got on with it, I hope.

HAMM (*Modestly.*): Oh not very far, not very far. (*He sighs.*) There are days like that, one isn't inspired. (*Pause.*) Nothing you can do about it, just wait for it to come. (*Pause.*) No forcing, no forcing, it's fatal. (*Pause.*) I've got on with it a little all the same. (*Pause.*) Technique, you know. (*Pause. Irritably.*) I say I've got on with it a little all the same.

CLOV (*Admiringly.*): Well I never! In spite of everything you were able to get on with it!

HAMM (*Modestly.*): Oh not very far, you know, not very far, but nevertheless, better than nothing.

CLOV: Better than nothing! Is it possible?

HAMM: I'll tell you how it goes. He comes crawling on his belly ——

CLOV: Who?

HAMM: What?

CLOV: Who do you mean, he?

HAMM: Who do I mean! Yet another.

CLOV: Ah him! I wasn't sure.

HAMM: Crawling on his belly, whining for bread for his brat. He's offered a job as gardener. Before — (CLOV *bursts out laughing.*) What is there so funny about that?

CLOV: A job as gardener!

HAMM: Is that what tickles you?

CLOV: It must be that.

HAMM: It wouldn't be the bread?

CLOV: Or the brat.

Pause.

HAMM: The whole thing is comical, I grant you that. What about having a good guffaw the two of us together?

CLOV (*After reflection.*): I couldn't guffaw again today.

HAMM (*After reflection.*): Nor I. (*Pause.*) I continue then. Before accepting with gratitude he asks if he may have his little boy with him.

CLOV: What age?

HAMM: Oh tiny.

CLOV: He would have climbed the trees.

HAMM: All the little odd jobs.

CLOV: And then he would have grown up.

HAMM: Very likely.

Pause.

CLOV: Keep going, can't you, keep going!

HAMM: That's all. I stopped there.

Pause.

CLOV: Do you see how it goes on?

HAMM: More or less.

CLOV: Will it not soon be the end?

HAMM: I'm afraid it will.

CLOV: Pah! You'll make up another.

HAMM: I don't know. (*Pause.*) I feel rather drained. (*Pause.*) The prolonged creative effort. (*Pause.*) If I could drag myself down to the sea! I'd make a pillow of sand for my head and the tide would come.

CLOV: There's no more tide.

Pause.

HAMM: Go and see is she dead.

CLOV *goes to bins, raises the lid of* NELL's, *stoops, looks into it. Pause.*

CLOV: Looks like it.

He closes the lid, straightens up. HAMM *raises his toque. Pause. He puts it on again.*

HAMM (*With his hand to his toque.*): And Nagg?

CLOV *raises lid of* NAGG's *bin, stoops, looks into it. Pause.*

CLOV: Doesn't look like it.

He closes the lid, straightens up.

HAMM (*Letting go his toque.*): What's he doing?

CLOV *raises lid of* NAGG's *bin, stoops, looks into it. Pause.*

CLOV: He's crying.

He closes the lid, straightens up.

HAMM: Then he's living. (*Pause.*) Did you ever have an instant of happiness?

CLOV: Not to my knowledge.

Pause.

HAMM: Bring me under the window. (CLOV *goes towards chair.*) I want to feel the light on my face. (CLOV *pushes chair.*) Do you remember, in the beginning, when you took me for a turn? You used to hold the chair too high. At every step you nearly tipped me out. (*With senile quaver.*) Ah great fun, we had, the two of us, great fun! (*Gloomily.*) And then we got into the way of it. (CLOV *stops the chair under window right.*) There already? (*Pause. He tilts back his head.*) Is it light?

CLOV: It isn't dark.

HAMM (*Angrily.*): I'm asking you is it light.

CLOV: Yes.

Pause.

HAMM: The curtain isn't closed?

CLOV: No.

HAMM: What window is it?

CLOV: The earth.

HAMM: I knew it! (*Angrily.*) But there's no light there! The other! (CLOV *pushes chair towards window left.*) The earth! (CLOV *stops the chair under window left.* HAMM *tilts back his head.*) That's what I call light! (*Pause.*) Feels like a ray of sunshine. (*Pause.*) No?

CLOV: No.

HAMM: It isn't a ray of sunshine I feel on my face?

CLOV: No.

Pause.

HAMM: Am I very white? (*Pause. Angrily.*) I'm asking you am I very white?

CLOV: Not more so than usual.

Pause.

HAMM: Open the window.

CLOV: What for?

HAMM: I want to hear the sea.

CLOV: You wouldn't hear it.

HAMM: Even if you opened the window?

CLOV: No.

HAMM: Then it's not worth while opening it?

CLOV: No.

HAMM (*Violently.*): Then open it! (CLOV *gets up on the ladder, opens the window. Pause.*) Have you opened it?

CLOV: Yes.

Pause.

HAMM: You swear you've opened it?

CLOV: Yes.

> *Pause.*

HAMM: Well . . . ! (*Pause.*) It must be very calm. (*Pause. Violently.*) I'm asking you is it very calm?

CLOV: Yes.

HAMM: It's because there are no more navigators. (*Pause.*) You haven't much conversation all of a sudden. Do you not feel well?

CLOV: I'm cold.

HAMM: What month are we? (*Pause.*) Close the window, we're going back. (CLOV *closes the window, gets down, pushes the chair back to its place, remains standing behind it, head bowed.*) Don't stay there, you give me the shivers! (CLOV *returns to his place beside the chair.*) Father! (*Pause. Louder.*) Father! (*Pause.*) Go and see did he hear me.

> CLOV *goes to* NAGG's *bin, raises the lid, stoops. Unintelligible words.* CLOV *straightens up.*

CLOV: Yes.

HAMM: Both times?

> CLOV *stoops. As before.*

CLOV: Once only.

HAMM: The first time or the second?

> CLOV *stoops. As before.*

CLOV: He doesn't know.

HAMM: It must have been the second.

CLOV: We'll never know.

> *He closes lid.*

HAMM: Is he still crying?

CLOV: No.

HAMM: The dead go fast. (*Pause.*) What's he doing?

CLOV: Sucking his biscuit.

HAMM: Life goes on. (CLOV *returns to his place beside the chair.*) Give me a rug, I'm freezing.

CLOV: There are no more rugs.

> *Pause.*

HAMM: Kiss me. (*Pause.*) Will you not kiss me?

CLOV: No.

HAMM: On the forehead.

CLOV: I won't kiss you anywhere.

> *Pause.*

HAMM (*Holding out his hand.*): Give me your hand at least. (*Pause.*) Will you not give me your hand?

CLOV: I won't touch you.

> *Pause.*

HAMM: Give me the dog. (CLOV *looks round for the dog.*) No!

CLOV: Do you not want your dog?

HAMM: No.

CLOV: Then I'll leave you.

HAMM (*Head bowed, absently.*): That's right.

> CLOV *goes to door, turns.*

CLOV: If I don't kill that rat he'll die.

HAMM (*As before.*): That's right. (*Exit* CLOV. *Pause.*) Me to play. (*He takes out his handkerchief, unfolds it, holds it spread out before him.*) We're getting on. (*Pause.*) You weep, and weep, for nothing, so as not to laugh, and little by little . . . you begin to grieve. (*He folds the handkerchief, puts it back in his pocket, raises his head.*) All those I might have helped. (*Pause.*) Helped! (*Pause.*) Saved. (*Pause.*) Saved! (*Pause.*) The place was crawling with them! (*Pause. Violently.*) Use your head, can't you, use your head, you're on earth, there's no cure for that! (*Pause.*) Get out of here and love one another! Lick your neighbour as yourself! (*Pause. Calmer.*) When it wasn't bread they wanted it was crumpets. (*Pause. Violently.*) Out of my sight and back to your petting parties! (*Pause.*) All that, all that! (*Pause.*) Not even a real dog! (*Calmer.*) The end is in the beginning and yet you go on. (*Pause.*) Perhaps I could go on with my story, end it and begin another. (*Pause.*) Perhaps I could throw myself out on the floor. (*He pushes himself painfully off his seat, falls back again.*) Dig my nails into the cracks and drag myself forward with my fingers. (*Pause.*) It will be the end and there I'll be, wondering what can have brought it on and wondering what can have . . . (*He hesitates.*) . . . why it was so long coming. (*Pause.*) There I'll be, in the old refuge, alone against the silence and . . . (*He hesitates.*) . . . the stillness. If I can hold my peace, and sit quiet, it will be all over with sound, and motion, all over and done with. (*Pause.*) I'll have called my father and I'll have called my . . . (*He hesitates.*) . . . my son. And even twice, or three times, in case they shouldn't have heard me, the first time, or the second. (*Pause.*) I'll say to myself, He'll come back. (*Pause.*) And then? (*Pause.*) And then? (*Pause.*) He couldn't, he has gone too far. (*Pause.*) And then? (*Pause. Very agitated.*) All kinds of fantasies! That I'm being watched! A rat! Steps! Breath held and then . . . (*He breathes out.*) Then babble, babble, words, like the solitary child who turns himself into children, two, three, so as to be together, and whisper together, in the dark. (*Pause.*) Moment upon moment, pattering down, like the millet grains of . . . (*He hesitates.*) . . . that old Greek, and all life long you wait for that to mount up to a life. (*Pause. He opens his mouth to continue, renounces.*) Ah let's get it over! (*He whistles. Enter* CLOV *with alarm-clock. He halts beside the chair.*) What? Neither gone nor dead?

CLOV: In spirit only.

HAMM: Which?

CLOV: Both.

HAMM: Gone from me you'd be dead.

CLOV: And *vice versa*.

HAMM: Outside of here it's death! (*Pause.*) And the rat?

CLOV: He's got away.

HAMM: He can't go far. (*Pause. Anxious.*) Eh?

CLOV: He doesn't need to go far.
> *Pause.*

HAMM: Is it not time for my pain-killer?

CLOV: Yes.

HAMM: Ah! At last! Give it to me! Quick!
> *Pause.*

CLOV: There's no more pain-killer.
> *Pause.*

HAMM (*Appalled.*): Good . . .! (*Pause.*) No more pain-killer!

CLOV: No more pain-killer. You'll never get any more pain-killer.
> *Pause.*

HAMM: But the little round box. It was full!

CLOV: Yes. But now it's empty.
> *Pause.* CLOV *starts to move about the room. He is looking for a place to put down the alarm-clock.*

HAMM (*Soft.*): What'll I do? (*Pause. In a scream.*) What'll I do? (CLOV *sees the picture, takes it down, stands it on the floor with its face to wall, hangs up the alarm-clock in its place.*) What are you doing?

CLOV: Winding up.

HAMM: Look at the earth.

CLOV: Again!

HAMM: Since it's calling to you.

CLOV: Is your throat sore? (*Pause.*) Would you like a lozenge? (*Pause.*) No? (*Pause.*) Pity.
> CLOV *goes, humming, towards window right, halts before it, looks up at it.*

HAMM: Don't sing.

CLOV (*Turning towards* HAMM.): One hasn't the right to sing any more?

HAMM: No.

CLOV: Then how can it end?

HAMM: You want it to end?

CLOV: I want to sing.

HAMM: I can't prevent you.
> *Pause.* CLOV *turns towards window right.*

CLOV: What did I do with that steps? (*He looks round for ladder.*) You didn't see that steps? (*He sees it.*) Ah, about time. (*He goes towards window left.*) Sometimes I wonder if I'm in my right mind. Then it passes over and I'm as lucid as before. (*He gets up on ladder, looks out of window.*) Christ, she's under water! (*He looks.*) How can that be? (*He pokes forward his head, his hand above his eyes.*)

It hasn't rained. (*He wipes the pane, looks. Pause.*) Ah what a mug I am! I'm on the wrong side! (*He gets down, takes a few steps towards window right.*) Under water! (*He goes back for ladder.*) What a mug I am! (*He carries ladder towards window right.*) Sometimes I wonder if I'm in my right senses. Then it passes off and I'm as intelligent as ever. (*He sets down ladder under window right, gets up on it, looks out of window. He turns towards* HAMM.) Any particular sector you fancy? Or merely the whole thing?

HAMM: Whole thing.

CLOV: The general effect? Just a moment.
> *He looks out of window. Pause.*

HAMM: Clov.

CLOV (*Absorbed.*): Mmm.

HAMM: Do you know what it is?

CLOV (*As before.*): Mmm.

HAMM: I was never there. (*Pause.*) Clov!

CLOV (*Turning towards* HAMM, *exasperated.*): What is it?

HAMM: I was never there.

CLOV: Lucky for you.
> *He looks out of window.*

HAMM: Absent, always. It all happened without me. I don't know what's happened. (*Pause.*) Do you know what's happened? (*Pause.*) Clov!

CLOV (*Turning towards* HAMM, *exasperated.*): Do you want me to look at this muckheap, yes or no?

HAMM: Answer me first.

CLOV: What?

HAMM: Do you know what's happened?

CLOV: When? Where?

HAMM (*Violently.*): When! What's happened! Use your head, can't you! What has happened?

CLOV: What for Christ's sake does it matter?
> *He looks out of window.*

HAMM: I don't know.
> *Pause.* CLOV *turns towards* HAMM.

CLOV (*Harshly.*): When old Mother Pegg asked you for oil for her lamp and you told her to get out to hell, you knew what was happening then, no? (*Pause.*) You know what she died of, Mother Pegg? Of darkness.

HAMM (*Feebly.*): I hadn't any.

CLOV (*As before.*): Yes, you had.
> *Pause.*

HAMM: Have you the glass?

CLOV: No, it's clear enough as it is.

HAMM: Go and get it.
> *Pause.* CLOV *casts up his eyes, brandishes his fists. He loses balance, clutches on to the ladder. He starts to get down, halts.*

CLOV: There's one thing I'll never understand. (*He gets

down.) Why I always obey you. Can you explain that to me?

HAMM: No . . . Perhaps it's compassion. (*Pause.*) A kind of great compassion. (*Pause.*) Oh you won't find it easy, you won't find it easy.

Pause. CLOV *begins to move about the room in search of the telescope.*

CLOV: I'm tired of our goings on, very tired. (*He searches.*) You're not sitting on it?

He moves the chair, looks at the place where it stood, resumes his search.

HAMM (*Anguished.*): Don't leave me there! (*Angrily* CLOV *restores the chair to its place.*) Am I right in the centre?

CLOV: You'd need a microscope to find this — (*He sees the telescope.*) Ah, about time.

He picks up the telescope, gets up on the ladder, turns the telescope on the without.

HAMM: Give me the dog.

CLOV (*Looking.*): Quiet!

HAMM (*Angrily.*): Give me the dog!

CLOV *drops the telescope, clasps his hands to his head. Pause. He gets down precipitately, looks for the dog, sees it, picks it up, hastens towards* HAMM *and strikes him on the head violently with the dog.*

CLOV: There's your dog for you!

The dog falls to the ground. Pause.

HAMM: He hit me!

CLOV: You drive me mad, I'm mad!

HAMM: If you must hit me, hit me with the axe. (*Pause.*) Or with the gaff, hit me with the gaff. Not with the dog. With the gaff. Or with the axe.

CLOV *picks up the dog and gives it to* HAMM *who takes it in his arms.*

CLOV (*Imploringly.*): Let's stop playing!

HAMM: Never! (*Pause.*) Put me in my coffin.

CLOV: There are no more coffins.

HAMM: Then let it end! (CLOV *goes towards ladder.*) With a bang! (CLOV *gets up on ladder, gets down again, looks for telescope, sees it, picks it up, gets up ladder, raises telescope.*) Of darkness! And me? Did anyone ever have pity on me?

CLOV (*Lowering the telescope, turning towards* HAMM.): What? (*Pause.*) Is it me you're referring to?

HAMM (*Angrily.*): An aside, ape! Did you never hear an aside before? (*Pause.*) I'm warming up for my last soliloquy.

CLOV: I warn you. I'm going to look at this filth since it's an order. But it's the last time. (*He turns the telescope on the without.*) Let's see. (*He moves the telescope.*) Nothing . . . nothing . . . good . . . good . . . nothing . . . goo — (*He starts, lowers the*

telescope, examines it, turns it again on the without. Pause.) Bad luck to it!

HAMM: More complications! (CLOV *gets down.*) Not an underplot, I trust.

CLOV *moves ladder nearer window, gets up on it, turns telescope on the without.*

CLOV (*Dismayed.*): Looks like a small boy!

HAMM (*Sarcastic.*): A small . . . boy!

CLOV: I'll go and see. (*He gets down, drops the telescope, goes towards door, turns.*) I'll take the gaff.

He looks for the gaff, sees it, picks it up, hastens towards door.

HAMM: No!

CLOV *halts.*

CLOV: No? A potential procreator?

HAMM: If he exists he'll die there or he'll come here. And if he doesn't . . .

Pause.

CLOV: You don't believe me? You think I'm inventing?

Pause.

HAMM: It's the end, Clov, we've come to the end. I don't need you any more.

Pause.

CLOV: Lucky for you.

He goes towards door.

HAMM: Leave me the gaff.

CLOV *gives him the gaff, goes towards door, halts, looks at alarm-clock, takes it down, looks round for a better place to put it, goes to bins, puts it on lid of* NAGG's *bin. Pause.*

CLOV: I'll leave you.

He goes towards door.

HAMM: Before you go . . . (CLOV *halts near door.*) . . . say something.

CLOV: There is nothing to say.

HAMM: A few words . . . to ponder . . . in my heart.

CLOV: Your heart!

HAMM: Yes. (*Pause. Forcibly.*) Yes! (*Pause.*) With the rest, in the end, the shadows, the murmurs, all the trouble, to end up with. (*Pause.*) Clov . . . He never spoke to me. Then, in the end, before he went, without my having asked him, he spoke to me. He said . . .

CLOV (*Despairingly.*): Ah . . .!

HAMM: Something . . . from your heart.

CLOV: My heart!

HAMM: A few words . . . from your heart.

Pause.

CLOV (*Fixed gaze, tonelessly, towards auditorium.*): They said to me, That's love, yes yes, not a doubt, now you see how —

HAMM: Articulate!

CLOV (*As before.*): How easy it is. They said to me,

That's friendship, yes yes, no question, you've found it. They said to me, Here's the place, stop, raise your head and look at all that beauty. That order! They said to me, Come now, you're not a brute beast, think upon these things and you'll see how all becomes clear. And simple! They said to me, What skilled attention they get, all these dying of their wounds.

HAMM: Enough!

CLOV (*As before.*): I say to myself — sometimes, Clov, you must learn to suffer better than that if you want them to weary of punishing you — one day. I say to myself — sometimes, Clov, you must be there better than that if you want them to let you go — one day. But I feel too old, and too far, to form new habits. Good, it'll never end, I'll never go. (*Pause.*) Then one day, suddenly, it ends, it changes, I don't understand, it dies, or it's me, I don't understand that either. I ask the words that remain — sleeping, waking, morning, evening. They have nothing to say. (*Pause.*) I open the door of the cell and go. I am so bowed I only see my feet, if I open my eyes, and between my legs a little trail of black dust. I say to myself that the earth is extinguished, though I never saw it lit. (*Pause.*) It's easy going. (*Pause.*) When I fall I'll weep for happiness.

Pause. He goes towards door.

HAMM: Clov! (CLOV *halts, without turning.*) Nothing. (CLOV *moves on.*) Clov!

CLOV *halts, without turning.*

CLOV: This is what we call making an exit.

HAMM: I'm obliged to you, Clov. For your services.

CLOV (*Turning, sharply.*): Ah pardon, it's I am obliged to you.

HAMM: It's we are obliged to each other. (*Pause.* CLOV *goes towards door.*) One thing more. (CLOV *halts.*) A last favour. (*Exit* CLOV.) Cover me with the sheet. (*Long pause.*) No? Good. (*Pause.*) Me to play. (*Pause. Wearily.*) Old endgame lost of old, play and lose and have done with losing. (*Pause. More animated.*) Let me see. (*Pause.*) Ah yes! (*He tries to move the chair, using the gaff as before. Enter* CLOV, *dressed for the road. Panama hat, tweed coat, raincoat over his arm, umbrella, bag. He halts by the door and stands there, impassive and motionless, his eyes fixed on* HAMM, *till the end.* HAMM *gives up.*) Good. (*Pause.*) Discard. (*He throws away the gaff, makes to throw away the dog, thinks better of it.*) Take it easy. (*Pause.*) And now? (*Pause.*) Raise hat. (*He raises his toque.*) Peace to our . . . arses. (*Pause.*) And put on again. (*He puts on his toque.*) Deuce. (*Pause. He takes off his glasses.*) Wipe. (*He takes out*

his handkerchief and, without unfolding it, wipes his glasses.) And put on again. (*He puts on his glasses, puts back the handkerchief in his pocket.*) We're coming. A few more squirms like that and I'll call. (*Pause.*) A little poetry. (*Pause.*) You prayed — (*Pause. He corrects himself.*) You CRIED for night; it comes — (*Pause. He corrects himself.*) It FALLS: now cry in darkness. (*He repeats, chanting.*) You cried for night; it falls: now cry in darkness. (*Pause.*) Nicely put, that. (*Pause.*) And now? (*Pause.*) Moments for nothing, now as always, time was never and time is over, reckoning closed and story ended. (*Pause. Narrative tone.*) If he could have his child with him . . . (*Pause.*) It was the moment I was waiting for. (*Pause.*) You don't want to abandon him? You want him to bloom while you are withering? Be there to solace your last million last moments? (*Pause.*) He doesn't realize, all he knows is hunger, and cold, and death to crown it all. But you! You ought to know what the earth is like, nowadays. Oh, I put him before his responsibilities! (*Pause. Normal tone.*) Well, there we are, there I am, that's enough. (*He raises the whistle to his lips, hesitates, drops it. Pause.*) Yes, truly! (*He whistles. Pause. Louder. Pause.*) Good. (*Pause.*) Father! (*Pause. Louder.*) Father! (*Pause.*) Good. (*Pause.*) We're coming. (*Pause.*) And to end up with? (*Pause.*) Discard. (*He throws away the dog. He tears the whistle from his neck.*) With my compliments. (*He throws whistle towards auditorium. Pause. He sniffs. Soft.*) Clov! (*Long pause.*) No? Good. (*He takes out the handkerchief.*) Since that's the way we're playing it . . . (*He unfolds handkerchief.*) . . . let's play it that way . . . (*He unfolds.*) . . . and speak no more about it . . . (*He finishes unfolding.*) speak no more. (*He holds the handkerchief spread out before him.*) Old stancher! (*Pause.*) You . . . remain.

Pause. He covers his face with handkerchief, lowers his arms to armrests, remains motionless.

Brief tableau.

CURTAIN

1   Intercourse, fellowship, now obsolete. (OED)
2   Shin-bones.
3   Person employed to empty cesspools. The allusion here is to Richard III: 'my kingdom for a horse'. Notice other Shakespearean references in the play such as the line from *The Tempest* 'Our revels now are ended'.

EUGENE O'NEILL
from Eugene O'Neill, *A Touch of the Poet* (first staged 1958, written 1936-9)

A Touch of the Poet, set in 1828 a few miles from Boston, provides an historical perspective on the transition from Ireland to America and on the accompanying class struggle between Catholic Irish peasant and Yankee gentleman. It is instructive comparing the first acts of this play and *Long Day's Journey Into Night*, for in structure, characterization, theme, pattern, orientation, autobiographical undertow, and attitudes to Ireland, the two plays belong together. There is a marked difference in tone, in tragic reach, and in attitudes to language-use and Hiberno-English (or brogue as it is disparagingly called in this play). If you do not know how this play unfolds you might like to provide your own version and compare it with the one O'Neill wrote. I haven't provided a gloss to the Irishisms (or Paddyisms) such as faix (faith) or av (of) since most of these can be understood in context.

CHARACTERS

MICKEY MALOY
JAMIE CREGAN
SARA MELODY
NORA MELODY
CORNELIUS MELODY
DAN ROCHE
PADDY O'DOWD
PATCH RILEY
DEBORAH (Mrs Henry Harford)
NICHOLAS GADSBY

ACT ONE

Scene. The dining-room of Melody's Tavern, in a village a few miles from Boston. The tavern is over a hundred years old. It had once been prosperous, a breakfast stop for the stagecoach, but the stage line had been discontinued and for some years now the tavern has fallen upon neglected days.

The dining-room and barroom were once a single spacious room, low-ceilinged, with heavy oak beams and panelled walls — the taproom of the tavern in its prosperous days, now divided into two rooms by a flimsy partition, the barroom being off left. The partition is painted to imitate the old panelled walls but this only makes it more of an eyesore.

At left front, two steps lead up to a closed door opening on a flight of stairs in the floor above. Farther back is the door to the bar. Between these doors hangs a large mirror. Beyond the bar door a small cabinet is fastened to the wall. At rear are four windows. Between the middle two is the street door. At right front is another door, open, giving on a hallway and the main stairway to the second floor, and leading to the kitchen. Farther front at right, there is a high schoolmaster's desk with a stool.

In the foreground are two tables. One, with four chairs, at left centre; a larger one, seating six, at right centre. At left and right rear, are two more tables, identical with the ones at right centre. All these tables are set with white tablecloths, etc., except the small ones in the foreground of left.

It is around nine in the morning of July 27, 1828. Sunlight shines in through the windows at rear.

MICKEY MALOY *sits at the table at left front, facing right. He is glancing through a newspaper.* MALOY *is twenty-six, with a sturdy physique and an amiable, cunning face, his mouth usually set in a half-leering grin.*

JAMIE CREGAN *peers around the half-open door to the bar. Seeing* MALOY, *he comes in. As obviously Irish as* MALOY, *he is middle-aged, tall, with a lantern-jawed face. There is a scar of a sabre cut over one cheekbone. He is dressed neatly but in old, worn clothes. His eyes are bloodshot, his manner sickly, but he grins as he greets* MALOY *sardonically.*

CREGAN: God bless all here — even the barkeep.

MALOY (*with an answering grin*): Top o' the mornin'.

CREGAN: Top o' me head. (*He puts his hand to his head and groans.*) Be the saints, there's a blacksmith at work on it!

MALOY: Small wonder. You'd the divil's own load when you left at two this mornin'.

CREGAN: I must have. I don't remember leaving. (*He sits at right of table.*) Faix, you're takin' it aisy.

MALOY: There's no trade this time o'day.

CREGAN: It was a great temptation, when I saw no one in the bar, to make off with a bottle. A hair av the dog is what I need, but I've divil a penny in my pantaloons.

MALOY: Have one on the house. (*He goes to the cupboard and takes out a decanter of whiskey and a glass.*)

CREGAN: Thank you kindly. Sure, the good Samaritan was a crool haythen beside you.

MALOY (*putting the decanter and glass before him*): It's the same you was drinking last night — his private dew. He keeps it here for emergencies when he don't want to go in the bar.

CREGAN (*pours out a big drink*): Lave it to Con never to be caught dry. (*Raising his glass.*) Your health and inclinations — if they're virtuous! (*He drinks and sighs with relief.*) God bless you, Whiskey, it's you can rouse the dead! Con hasn't been down yet for his morning's morning?

MALOY: No. He won't be till later.

CREGAN: It's like a miracle, me meeting him again. I came to these parts looking for work. It's only by accident I heard talk of a Con Melody and come here to see was it him. Until last night, I'd not seen hide nor hair of him since the war with the French in Spain — after the battle of Salamanca in '12. I was a corporal in the Seventh Dragoons and he was major. (*Proudly.*) I got this cut from a sabre at Talavera, bad luck to it! — serving under him. He was a captain then.

MALOY: So you told me last night.

CREGAN (*with a quick glance at him*): Did I now? I must have said more than my prayers, with the lashings¹ of whiskey in me.

MALOY (*with a grin*): More than your prayers is the truth.

CREGAN *glances at him uneasily.* MALOY *pushes the decanter towards him.*

Take another taste.

CREGAN: I don't like sponging. Sure, my credit ought to be good in this shebeen!² Ain't I his cousin?

MALOY: You're forgettin' what himself told you last night as he went up to bed. You could have all the whiskey you could pour down you, but not a penny's worth of credit. This house, he axed you to remember, only gives credit to gentlemen.

CREGAN: Divil mend him!

MALOY (*with a chuckle*): You kept thinking about his insults after he'd gone out, getting madder and madder.

CREGAN: God pity him, that's like him. He hasn't changed much. (*He pours out a drink and gulps it with a cautious look at* MALOY.) If I was mad at Con, and me blind drunk, I must have told you a power of lies.

MALOY (*winks slyly*): Maybe they wasn't lies.

CREGAN: If I said any wrong of Con Melody —

MALOY: Arrah, are you afraid I'll gab what you said to him? I won't, you can take my oath.

CREGAN (*his face clearing*): Tell me what I said and I'll tell you if it was lies.

MALOY: You said his father wasn't of the quality of Galway like he makes out, but a thievin' shebeen keeper who got rich by moneylendin' and squeezin' tenants and every manner of trick. And when he'd enough he married, and bought an estate with a pack of hounds and set up as one of the gentry. He'd hardly got settled when his wife died givin' birth to Con.

CREGAN: There's no lie there.

MALOY: You said none of the gentry would speak to auld Melody, but he had a tough hide and didn't heed them. He made up his mind he'd bring Con up a true gentlemen, so he packed him off to Dublin to school, and after that to the College with sloos of money to prove himself the equal of any gentleman's son. But Con found, while there was plenty to drink on him and borrow money, there was few didn't sneer behind his back at his pretensions.

CREGAN: That's the truth, too. But Con wiped the sneer off their mugs when he called one av thim out and put a bullet in his hip. That was his first duel. It gave his pride the taste for revenge and after that he was always lookin' for an excuse to challenge someone.

MALOY: He's done a power av boastin' about his duels, but I thought he was lyin'.

CREGAN: There's no lie in it. It was that brought disgrace on him in the end, right after he'd been promoted to major. He got caught by a Spanish noble making love to his wife, just after the battle of Salamanca, and there was a duel and Con killed him. The scandal was hushed up but Con had to resign from the army. If it wasn't for his fine record for bravery in battle, they'd have court-martialled him. (*Then guiltily.*) But I'm sayin' more than my prayers again.

MALOY: It's no news about his women. You'd think, to hear him when he's drunk, there wasn't one could resist him in Portugal and Spain.

CREGAN: If you'd seen him then, you wouldn't wonder. He was as strong as an ox, and on a thoroughbred horse, in his uniform, there wasn't a handsomer man in the army. And he had the chance he wanted in Portugal and Spain where a British officer was welcome in the gentry's houses. At home, the only women he'd known was whores. (*He adds hastily.*) Except Nora, I mean. (*Lowering his voice.*) Tell me, has he done any rampagin' wid women here?

MALOY: He hasn't. The damned Yankee gentry won't let him come near them, and he considers the few Irish around here to be scum beneath his notice. But once in a while there'll be some Yankee stops overnight wid his wife or daughter and then you'd laugh to see Con, if he thinks she's gentry, sidlin' up to her, playin' the great gentleman and makin' compliments, and then boasting afterwards he could have them in bed if he'd had a chance at it, for all their modern Yankee airs.

CREGAN: And maybe he could. If you'd known him in the auld days, you'd nivir doubt any boast he makes about fightin' and women, and gamblin' or any kind av craziness. There nivir was a madder divil.

MALOY (*lowering his voice*): Speakin' av Nora, you nivir mentioned her last night, but I know all about it without you telling me. I used to have my room here, and there's nights he's madder drunk than most when he throws it in her face he had to marry her because — Mind you, I'm not saying anything against poor Nora. A sweeter woman never lived. And I know you know all about it.

CREGAN (*reluctantly*): I do. Wasn't I raised on his estate?

MALOY: He tells her it was the priests tricked him into marrying her. He hates priests.

CREGAN: He's a liar, then. He may like to blame it on them but it's little Con Melody cared what they said. Nothing ever made him do anything, except himself. He married her because he'd fallen in love with her, but he was ashamed of her in his pride at the same time because her folks were only ignorant peasants on his estate, as poor as poor. Nora was as pretty a girl as you'd find in a year's travel, and he'd come to be bitter lonely, with no woman's company but the whores was helpin' him ruin the estate. (*He shrugs his shoulders.*) Well, anyways, he married her and then went off to the war, and left her alone in the castle to have her child, and nivir saw her again till he was sent home from Spain. Then he raised what money he still was able, and took her and Sara here to America where no one would know him.

MALOY (*thinking this over for a moment*): It's hard for me to believe he ever loved her. I've seen the way he treats her now. Well, thank you for telling me, and I take my oath I'll nivir breathe a word of it — for Nora's sake, not his.

CREGAN (*grimly*): You'd better kape quiet for fear of him, too. If he's one-half the man he was, he could bate the lights out of the two av us.

MALOY: He's strong as a bull still for all the whiskey he's drunk. (*He pushes the bottle towards* CREGAN.) Have another taste.

CREGAN *pours out a drink.*

Drink hearty.

CREGAN: Long Life.

He drinks. MALOY *puts the decanter and glass back on the cupboard. A girl's voice is heard from the hall at right.* CREGAN *jumps up — hastily.*

That's Sara, isn't it? I'll get out. She'll likely blame me for Con getting so drunk last night. I'll be back after Con is down.

He goes out. MALOY *starts to go in the bar, as if he too wanted to avoid* SARA. *Then he sits down defiantly.*

MALOY: Be damned if I'll run from her.

He takes up the paper as SARA MELODY *comes in from the hall at right.*

SARA *is twenty, an exceedingly pretty girl with a mass of black hair, fair skin with rosy cheeks and beautiful, deep-blue eyes. There is a curious blending in her of what are commonly considered aristocratic and peasant characteristics. She has a fine forehead. Her nose is thin and straight. She has small ears set close to her well-shaped head, and a slender neck. Her mouth, on the other hand, has a touch of coarseness and sensuality and her jaw is too heavy. Her figure is strong and graceful, with full, firm breasts and hips, and a slender waist. But she has large feet and broad, ugly hands with stubby fingers. Her voice is soft and musical, but her speech has at times a self-conscious, stilted quality about it, due to her restraining a tendency to lapse into brogue. Her everyday working dress is of cheap material, but she wears it in a way that gives a pleasing effect of beauty unadorned.*

SARA (*with a glance at* MALOY, *sarcastically*): I'm sorry to interrupt you when you're so busy, but have you your bar book ready for me to look over?

MALOY (*surlily*): I have. I put it on your desk.

SARA: Thank you. (*She turns her back on him, sits at the desk, takes a small account book from it, and begins checking figures.*)

MALOY (*watches her over his paper*): If it's profits you're looking for, you won't find them — not with all the drinks himself's been treating to.

She ignores this. He becomes resentful.

You've got your airs of a grand lady this morning, I see. There's no talkin' to you since you've been playin' nurse to the young Yankee upstairs.

She makes herself ignore this, too.

Well, you've had your cap set for him ever since he came to live by the lake, and now's your chance, when he's here sick and too weak to defend himself.

SARA (*turns on him — with quiet anger*): I warn you to mind your own business, Mickey, or I'll tell my father of your impudence. He'll teach you to keep your place, and God help you.

MALOY (*doesn't believe this threat but is frightened by the possibility*): Arrah, don't try to scare me. I know, you'd never carry tales to him. (*Placatingly.*) Can't you take a bit of teasing, Sara?

SARA (*turns back to her figuring*): Leave Simon out of your teasing.

MALOY: Oho, he's Simon to you, now, is he? Well, well. (*He gives her a cunning glance.*) Maybe, if you'd come down from your high horse, I could tell you some news.

SARA: You're worse than an old woman for gossip. I don't want to hear it.

MALOY: When you was upstairs at the back taking him his breakfast, there was a grand carriage with a nigger coachman stopped at the corner and a Yankee lady got out and came in here. I was sweeping and Nora was scrubbing the kitchen.

SARA *has turned to him, all attention now.*

She asked me what road would take her near the lake —

SARA (*starts*): Ah.

MALOY: So I told her, but she didn't go. She kept looking around, and said she'd like a cup of tea, and where was the waitress. I knew she must be connected someway with Harford or why would she want to go to the lake, where no one's ever lived but him. She didn't want tea at all, but only an excuse to stay.

SARA (*resentfully*): So she asked for the waitress, did she? I hope you told her I'm the owner's daughter, too.

MALOY: I did. I don't like Yankee airs any more than you. I was short with her. I said you was out for a walk, and the tavern wasn't open yet, anyway. So she went out and drove off.

SARA (*worriedly now*): I hope you didn't insult her with your bad manners. What did she look like, Mickey?

MALOY: Pretty, if you like that kind. A pale, delicate wisp of a thing with big eyes.

SARA: That fits what he's said of his mother. How old was she?

MALOY: It's hard to tell, but she's too young for his mother. I'd swear. Around thirty, I'd say. Maybe it's his sister.

SARA: He hasn't a sister.

MALOY (*grinning*): Then maybe she's an old sweetheart looking for you to scratch your eyes out.

SARA: He's never had a sweetheart.

MALOY (*mockingly*): Is that what he tells you, and you believe him? Faix, you must be in love!

SARA (*angrily*): Will you mind your own business? I'm not such a fool! (*Worried again.*) Maybe you ought

to have told her he's here sick to save her the drive in the hot sun and the walk through the woods for nothing.

MALOY: Why would I tell her, when she never mentioned him?

SARA: Yes, it's her own fault. But — Well, there's no use thinking of it now — or bothering my head about her, anyway, whoever she was.

She begins checking figures again. Her mother appears in the doorway at right.

NORA MELODY *is forty, but years of overwork and worry have made her look much older. She must have been as pretty as a girl as* SARA *is now. She still has the beautiful eyes her daughter has inherited. But she has become too worn out to take care of her appearance. Her black hair, streaked with grey, straggles in untidy wisps about her face. Her body is dumpy, with sagging breasts, and her old clothes are like a bag covering it, tied around the middle. Her red hands are knotted by rheumatism. Cracked working shoes, run down at the heel, are on her bare feet. Yet in spite of her slovenly appearance there is a spirit which shines through and makes her lovable, a simple sweetness and charm, something gentle and sad and, somehow, dauntless.*

MALOY (*jumps up to his feet, his face lighting up with affection*): God bless you, Nora, you're the one I was waitin' to see. Will you keep an eye on the bar while I run to the store for a bit av 'baccy?

SARA (*sharply*): Don't do it, Mother.

NORA (*smiles — her voice is soft, with a rich brogue*): Why wouldn't I? 'Don't do it, Mother.'

MALOY: Thank you, Nora. (*He goes to the door at rear and opens it, burning for a parting shot at* SARA.) And the back o' my hand to you, your Ladyship! (*He goes out, closing the door.*)

SARA: You shouldn't encourage his laziness. He's always looking for excuses to shirk.

NORA: Ah, nivir mind, he's a good lad. (*She lowers herself painfully on the nearest chair at the rear of the table at centre front.*) Bad cess to the rheumatism. It has me destroyed this mornin'.

SARA (*still checking figures in the book — gives her mother an impatient but at the same time worried glance. Her habitual manner towards her is one of mingled love and pity and exasperation.*) I've told you a hundred times to see the doctor.

NORA: We've no money for doctors. They're bad luck, anyway. They bring death with them. (*A pause.* NORA *sighs.*) Your father will be down soon. I've some fine fresh eggs for his breakfast.

SARA (*her face becomes hard and bitter*): He won't want them.

NORA (*defensively*): You mean he'd a drop too much

taken last night? Well, small blame to him, he hasn't seen Jamie since —

SARA: *Last* night? What night hasn't he?

NORA: Ah, don't be hard on him. (*A pause — worriedly.*) Neilan sent round a note to me about his bill. He says we'll have to settle by the end of the week or we'll get no more groceries. (*With a sigh.*) I can't blame him. How we'll manage, I dunno. There's the intrist on the mortgage due the first. But that I've saved, God be thanked.

SARA (*exasperatedly*): If you'd only let me take charge of the money.

NORA (*with a flare of spirit*): I won't. It'd mean you and himself would be at each other's throats from dawn to dark. It's bad enough between you as it is.

SARA: Why didn't you pay Neilan the end of last week? You told me you had the money put aside.

NORA: So I did. But Dickinson was tormentin' your father with his feed bill for the mare.

SARA (*angrily*): I might have known! The mare comes first, if she takes the bread out of our mouths! The grand gentleman must have his thoroughbred to ride out in state!

NORA (*defensively*): Where's the harm? She's his greatest pride. He'd be heartbroken if he had to sell her.

SARA: Oh yes, I know well he cares more for a horse than for us!

NORA: Don't be saying that. He has great love for you, even if you do be provokin' him all the time.

SARA: Great love for me! Arrah, God pity you, Mother!

NORA (*sharply*): Don't put on the brogue, now. You know how he hates to hear you. And I do, too. There's no excuse not to cure yourself. Didn't he send you to school so you could talk like a gentleman's daughter?

SARA (*resentfully but more careful of her speech*): If he did, I wasn't there long.

NORA: It was you insisted on leavin'.

SARA: Because if he hadn't the pride or love for you not to live on your slaving your heart out, I had that pride and love!

NORA (*tenderly*): I know, Acushla.[3] I know.

SARA (*with bitter scorn*): We can't afford a waitress, but he can afford to keep a thoroughbred mare to prance around on and show himself off! And he can afford a barkeep when, if he had any decency, he'd do his part and tend the bar himself.

NORA (*indignantly*): Him, a gentleman, tend bar!

SARA: A gentleman! Och, Mother, it's all right for the two of us, out of our own pride, to pretend to

the world we believe that lie, but it's crazy for you to pretend to me.

NORA (*stubbornly*): It's no lie. He *is* a gentleman. Wasn't he born rich in a castle on a grand estate and educated in college, and wasn't he an officer in the Duke of Wellington's army —

SARA: All right, Mother. You can humour his craziness, but he'll never make me pretend to him I don't know the truth.

NORA: Don't talk as if you hated him. You ought to be shamed —

SARA: I do hate him for the way he treats you. I heard him again last night, raking up the past, and blaming his ruin on his having to marry you.

NORA (*protests miserably*): It was the drink talkin', not him.

SARA (*exasperatedly*): It's you ought to be ashamed, for not having more pride! You bear all his insults as meek as a lamb! You keep on slaving for him when it's that has made you old before your time! (*Angrily.*) You can't much longer, I tell you! He's getting worse. You'll have to leave him.

NORA (*aroused*): I'll never! Howld your prate!

SARA: You'd leave him today, if you had any pride!

NORA: I've pride in my love for him! I've loved him since the day I set eyes on him, and I'll love him till the day I die! (*With a strange superior scorn.*) It's little you know of love, and you never will, for there's the same divil of pride in you that's in him, and it'll kape you from ivir givin' all of yourself, and that's what love it.

SARA: I could give all of myself if I wanted to, but —

NORA: If! Wanted to! Faix, it proves how little of love you know when you prate about ifs and want-tos. It's when you don't give a thought for all the ifs and want-tos in the world! It's when, if all the fires of hell was between you, you'd walk in them gladly to be with him, and sing with joy at your own burnin', if only his kiss was on your mouth! That's love, and I'm proud I've known the great sorrow and joy of it!

SARA (*cannot help being impressed — looks at her mother with wondering respect*): You're a strange woman, Mother. (*She kisses her impulsively.*) And a grand woman! (*Defiant again, with an arrogant toss of her head.*) I'll love — but I'll love where it'll gain me freedom and not put me in slavery for life.

NORA: There's no slavery in it when you love! (*Suddenly her exultant expression crumbles and she breaks down.*) For the love of God, don't take the pride of my love from me, Sara, for without it what am I at all but an ugly, fat woman gettin' old and sick!

SARA (*puts her arm around her — soothingly*): Hush, Mother! Don't mind me. (*Briskly, to distract her mother's mind.*) I've got to finish the bar book. Mickey can't put two and two together without making five. (*She goes to the desk and begins checking figures again.*)

NORA (*dries her eyes — after a pause she sighs worriedly*): I'm worried about your father. Father Flynn stopped me on the road yesterday and tould me I'd better warn him not to sneer at the Irish around here and call thim scum, or he'll get in trouble. Most of thim is in a rage at him because he's come out against Jackson and the Democrats and says he'll vote with the Yankees for Quincy Adams.

SARA (*contemptuously*): Faith, they can't see a joke, then, for it's a great joke to hear him shout against mob rule, like one of the Yankee gentry, when you know what he came from. And after the way the Yanks swindled him when he came here, getting him to buy this inn by telling him a new coach line was going to stop here. (*She laughs with bitter scorn.*) Oh, he's the easiest fool ever came to America! It's that I hold against him as much as anything, that when he came here the chance was before him to make himself all his lies pretended to be. He had education above most Yanks, and he had money enough to start him, and this is a country where you can rise as high as you like, and no one but the fools who envy you care what you rose from, once you've the money and the power goes with it. (*Passionately.*) Oh, if I was a man with the chance he had, there wouldn't be a dream I'd not make come true!

She looks at her mother, who is staring at the floor dejectedly and hasn't been listening. She is exasperated for a second — then she smiles pityingly.

You're a fine one to talk to, Mother. Wake up. What's worrying you now?

NORA: Father Flynn tould me again I'd be damned in hell for lettin' your father make a haythen of me and bring you up a haythen, too.

SARA (*with an arrogant toss of her head*): Let Father Flynn mind his own business, and not frighten you with fairy tales about hell.

NORA: It's true, just the same.

SARA: True, me foot! You ought to tell the good Father we aren't the ignorant shanty scum he's used to dealing with. (*She changes the subject abruptly — closing* MICKEY'*s bar book.*) There. That's done. (*She puts the book in the desk.*) I'll take a walk to the store and have a talk with Neilan. Maybe I can blarney him to let the bill go another month.

NORA (*gratefully*): Oh, you can. Sure, you can charm a bird out of a tree when you want to. But I don't like you beggin' to a Yankee. It's all right for me but I know how you hate it.

SARA (*puts her arms around her mother — tenderly*): I don't mind at all, if I can save you a bit of the worry that's killing you. (*She kisses her.*) I'll change to my Sunday dress so I can make a good impression.

NORA (*with a teasing smile*): I'm thinkin' it isn't on Neilan alone you want to make an impression. You've changed to your Sunday best a lot lately.

SARA (*coquettishly*): Aren't you the sly one! Well, maybe you're right.

NORA: How was he when you took him his breakfast?

SARA: Hungry, and that's a good sign. He had no fever last night. Oh, he's on the road to recovery now, and it won't be long before he'll be back in his cabin by the lake.

NORA: I'll never get it clear in my head what he's been doing there the past year, living like a tramp or a tinker, and him a rich gentleman's son.

SARA (*with a tender smile*): Oh, he isn't like his kind, or like anyone else at all. He's a born dreamer with a raft of great dreams, and he's very serious about them. I've told you before he wanted to get away from his father's business, where he worked for a year after he graduated from Harvard College, because he didn't like being in trade, even if it is a great company that trades with the whole world in its own ships.

NORA (*approvingly*): That's the way a true gentleman would feel —

SARA: He wanted to prove his independence by living alone in the wilds, and build his own cabin, and do all the work and support himself simply and feel one with Nature, and think great thoughts about what life means, and write a book about how the world can be changed so people won't be greedy to own money and land and get the best of each other but will be content with little and live in peace and freedom together, and it will be like heaven on earth. (*She laughs fondly — and a bit derisively.*) I can't remember all of it. It seems crazy to me, when I think of what people are like. He hasn't written any of it yet, anyway — only the notes for it. (*She smiles coquettishly.*) All he's written the last few months are love poems.

NORA: That's since you began to take long walks by the lake. (*She smiles.*) It's you are the sly one.

SARA (*laughing*): Well, why shouldn't I take walks on our own property? (*Her tone changes to a sneer.*)

The land our great gentleman was swindled into buying when he came here with grand ideas of owning an American estate! — a bit of farm land no one would work any more, and the rest all wilderness! You couldn't give it away.

NORA (*soothingly*): Hush now. (*Changing the subject.*) Well, it's easy to tell young Master Harford has a touch av the poet in him — (*She adds before she thinks.*) The same as your father.

SARA (*scornfully*): God help you, Mother! Do you think Father's a poet because he shows off reciting Lord Byron?

NORA (*with an uneasy glance at the door at left front*): Whist, now. Himself will be down at any moment. (*Changing the subject.*) I can see the Harford lad is falling in love with you.

SARA (*her face lights up triumphantly*): Falling? He's fallen head over heels. He's so timid, he hasn't told me yet, but I'll get him to soon.

NORA: I know you're in love with him.

SARA (*simply*): I am, Mother. (*She adds quickly.*) But not too much. I'll not let love make me any man's slave. I want to love him just enough so I can marry him without cheating him, or myself. (*Determinedly.*) For I'm going to marry him, Mother. It's my chance to rise in the world and nothing will keep me from it.

NORA (*admiringly*): Musha, but you've boastful talk! What about his fine Yankee family? His father'll likely cut him off without a penny if he marries a girl who's poor and Irish.

SARA: He may at first, but when I've proved what a good wife I'll be — He can't keep Simon from marrying me. I know that. Simon doesn't care what his father thinks. It's only his mother I'm afraid of. I can tell she's had great influence over him. She must be a queer creature, from all he's told me. She's very strange in her ways. She never goes out at all but stays home in their mansion, reading books, or in her garden. (*She pauses.*) Did you notice a carriage stop here this morning, Mother?

NORA (*preoccupied — uneasily*): Don't count your chickens before they're hatched. Young Harford seems a dacent lad. But maybe it's not marriage he's after.

SARA (*angrily*): I won't have you wronging him, Mother. He has no thought — (*Bitterly.*) I suppose you're bound to suspect — (*She bites her words back, ashamed.*) Forgive me, Mother. But it's wrong of you to think badly of Simon. (*She smiles.*) You don't know him. Faith, if it came to seducing, it'd be me that'd have to do it. He's that

respectful you'd think I was a holy image. It's only in his poems, and in the diary he keeps — I had a peek in it one day I went to tidy up his cabin for him. He's terribly ashamed of his sinful inclinations and the insult they are to my purity. (*She laughs tenderly.*)

NORA (*smiling, but a bit shocked*): Don't talk so bould. I don't know if it's right, you to be in his room so much, even if he is sick. There's a power av talk about the two av you already.

SARA: Let there be, for all I care! Or all Simon cares, either. When it comes to not letting others rule him, he's got a will of his own behind his gentleness. Just as behind his poetry and dreams I feel he has it in him to do anything he wants. So even if his father cuts him off, with me to help him we'll get on in the world. For I'm no fool, either.

NORA: Glory be to God, you have the fine opinion av yourself!

SARA (*laughing*): Haven't I, though! (*Then bitterly.*) I've had need to have, to hold my head up, slaving as a waitress and chambermaid so my father can get drunk every night like a gentleman!

The door at left front is slowly opened and CORNELIUS MELODY *appears in the doorway above the two steps. He and* SARA *stare at each other. She stiffens into hostility and her mouth sets in scorn. For a second his eyes water and he looks guilty. Then his face becomes expressionless. He descends the steps and bows — pleasantly.*

MELODY: Good morning, Sara.

SARA (*curtly*): Good morning. (*Then, ignoring him.*) I'm going up and change my dress, Mother. (*She goes out right.*)

CORNELIUS MELODY *is forty-five, tall, broadshouldered, deep-chested, and powerful, with long muscular arms, big feet, and large hairy hands. His heavy-boned body is still firm, erect, and soldierly. Beyond shaky nerves, it shows no effects of hard drinking. It has a bull-like, impervious strength, a tough peasant vitality. It is his face that reveals the ravages of dissipation — a ruined face, which was once extraordinarily handsome in a reckless, arrogant fashion. It is still handsome — the face of an embittered Byronic hero, with a finely chiselled nose over a domineering sensual mouth set in disdain, pale, hollow-cheeked, framed by thick, curly iron-grey hair. There is a look of wrecked distinction about it, of brooding, humiliated pride. His bloodshot grey eyes have an insulting cold stare which anticipates insult. His manner is that of a polished gentleman. Too much so. He overdoes it and one soon feels that he is overplaying a role which has become more real than his real self to him. But in spite of this, there is something formidable and impressive about him. He is dressed with foppish elegance in old, expensive, finely tailored clothes of the style worn by English aristocracy in Peninsula War days.*

MELODY (*advancing into the room — bows formally to his wife*): Good morning, Nora. (*His tone condescends. It addresses a person of inferior station.*)

NORA (*stumbles to her feet — timidly*): Good mornin', Con. I'll get your breakfast.

MELODY: No. Thank you. I want nothing now.

NORA (*coming towards him*): You look pale. Are you sick, Con, darlin'?

MELODY: No.

NORA (*puts a timid hand on his arm*): Come and sit down.

He moves his arm away with instinctive revulsion and goes to the table at centre front, and sits in the chair she had occupied. NORA hovers around him.

I'll wet a cloth in cold water to put round your head.

MELODY: No! I desire nothing — except a little peace in which to read the news. (*He picks up the paper and holds it so it hides his face from her.*)

NORA (*meekly*): I'll lave you in peace.

She starts to go to the door at right but turns to stare at him worriedly again. Keeping the paper before his face with his left hand, he reaches out with his right and pours a glass of water from the carafe on the table. Although he cannot see his wife, he is nervously conscious of her. His hand trembles so violently that when he attempts to raise the glass to his lips the water sloshes over his hand and he sets the glass back on the table with a bang. He lowers the paper and explodes nervously.

MELODY: For God's sake, stop your staring!

NORA: I — I was only thinkin' you'd feel better if you'd a bit av food in you.

MELODY: I told you once —! (*Controlling his temper.*) I am not hungry, Nora.

He raises the paper again. She sighs, her hands fiddling with her apron. A pause.

NORA (*dully*): Maybe it's a hair av the dog you're needin'.

MELODY (*as if this were something he had been waiting to hear, his expression loses some of its nervous strain. But he replies virtuously*): No, damn the liquor. Upon my conscience, I've about made up my mind I'll have no more of it. Besides, it's a bit early in the day.

NORA: If it'll give you an appetite —

MELODY: To tell the truth, my stomach is out of sorts. (*He licks his lips.*) Perhaps a drop wouldn't come amiss.

NORA gets the decanter and glass from the cupboard and sets them before him. She stands gazing at him with a resigned sadness. MELODY, his eyes on the paper, is again acutely conscious of her. His nerves cannot stand it. He throws his paper down and bursts out in bitter anger.

Well? I know what you're thinking! Why haven't you the courage to say it for once? By God, I'd have more respect for you! I hate the damned meek of this earth! By the rock of Cashel, I sometimes believe you have always deliberately encouraged me to — It's the one point of superiority you can lay claim to, isn't it?

NORA (*bewilderedly — on the verge of tears*): I don't — It's only your comfort — I can't bear to see you —

MELODY (*his expression changes and a look of real affection comes into his eyes. He reaches out a shaking hand to pat her shoulder with an odd, guilty tenderness. He says quietly and with genuine contrition*): Forgive me, Nora. That was unpardonable.

Her face lights up. Abruptly he is ashamed of being ashamed. He looks away and grabs the decanter. Despite his trembling hand he manages to pour a drink and get it to his mouth and drain it. Then he sinks back in his chair and stares at the table, waiting for the liquor to take effect. After a pause he sighs with relief.

I confess I needed that as medicine. I begin to feel more myself. (*He pours out another big drink and this time his hand is steadier, and he downs it without much difficulty. He smacks his lips.*) By the Immortal, I may have sunk to keeping an inn but at least I've a conscience in my trade. I keep liquor a gentleman can drink. (*He starts looking over the paper again — scowls at something — disdainfully, emphasizing his misquote of the line from Byron.*) 'There shall he rot — Ambition's dishonoured fool!' The paper is full of the latest swindling lies of that idol of the riffraff, Andrew Jackson. Contemptible, drunken scoundrel! But he will be the next President, I predict, for all we others can do to prevent. There is a cursed destiny in these decadent times. Everywhere the scum rises to the top. (*His eyes fasten on the date and suddenly he strikes the table with his fist.*) Today is the 27th! By God, and I would have forgotten!

NORA: Forgot what?

MELODY: The anniversary of Talavera!

NORA (*hastily*): Oh, ain't I stupid not to remember.

MELODY (*bitterly*): I had forgotten myself and no wonder. It's a far cry from this dunghill on which I rot to that glorious day when the Duke of Wellington — Lord Wellesley, then — did me the honour before all the army to commend my bravery. (*He glances around the room with loathing.*) A far cry, indeed! It would be better to forget!

NORA (*rallying him*): No, no, you mustn't. You've never missed celebratin' it and you won't today. I'll have a special dinner for you like I've always had.

MELODY (*with a quick change of manner — eagerly*): Good, Nora. I'll invite Jamie Cregan. It's a stroke of fortune he is here. He served under me at Talavera, as you know. A brave soldier, if he isn't a gentleman. You can place him on my right hand. And we'll have Patch Riley to make music, and O'Dowd and Roche. If they are rabble, they're full of droll humour at times. But put them over there. (*He points to the table at left front.*) I may tolerate their presence out of charity, but I'll not sink to dining at the same table.

NORA: I'll get your uniform from the trunk, and you'll wear it for dinner like you've done each year.

MELODY: Yes, I must confess I still welcome an excuse to wear it. It makes me feel at least the ghost of the man I was then.

NORA: You're so handsome in it still, no woman could take her eyes off you.

MELODY (*with a pleased smile*): I'm afraid you've blarney on your tongue this morning, Nora. (*Then boastfully.*) But it's true, in those days in Portugal and Spain — (*He stops a little shamefacedly, but NORA gives no sign of offence. He takes her hand and pats it gently — avoiding her eyes.*) You have the kindest heart in the world, Nora. And I — (*His voice breaks.*)

NORA (*instantly on the verge of grateful tears*): Ah, who wouldn't, Con darlin', when you — (*She brushes a hand across her eyes — hastily.*) I'll go to the store and get something tasty. (*Her face drops as she remembers.*) But, God help us, where's the money?

MELODY (*stiffens — haughtily*): Money? Since when has my credit not been good?

NORA (*hurriedly*): Don't fret, now. I'll manage.

He returns to his newspaper, disdaining further interest in money matters.

MELODY: Ha. I see work on the railroad at Baltimore is progressing. (*Lowering his paper.*) By the Eternal, if I had not been a credulous gull and let the thieving Yankees swindle me of all I had when we came here, that's how I would invest my funds now. And I'd become rich. This country, with its immense territory, cannot depend solely on creeping canal boats, as short-sighted fools would have us believe. We must have railroads. Then you will see how quickly America will become rich and great! (*His expression changes to one of bitter hatred.*) Great enough to crush England in the next war between them, which I know is inevitable! Would I could live to celebrate that victory! If I have one regret for the past — and there are few things in it that do not call for bitter regret — it is that I shed my blood for a country that thanked me with disgrace. But I will be avenged. This country — my country, now — will drive the English from the face of the earth their shameless perfidy has dishonoured!

NORA: Glory be to God for that! And we'll free Ireland!

MELODY (*contemptuously*): Ireland? What benefit would freedom be to her unless she could be freed from the Irish? (*Then irritably.*) But why do I discuss such things with you?

NORA (*humbly*): I know. I'm ignorant.

MELODY: Yet I tried my best to educate you, after we came to America — until I saw it was hopeless.

NORA: You did, surely. And I tried, too, but —

MELODY: You won't even cure yourself of that damned peasant's brogue. And your daughter is becoming as bad.

NORA: She only puts on the brogue to tease you. She can speak as fine as any lady in the land if she wants.

MELODY (*is not listening — sunk in bitter brooding*): But, in God's name, who am I to reproach anyone with anything? Why don't you tell me to examine my own conduct?

NORA: You know I'd never.

MELODY (*stares at her — again he is moved — quietly*): No. I know you would not, Nora. (*He looks away — after a pause.*) I owe you an apology for what happened last night.

NORA: Don't think of it.

MELODY (*with assumed casualness*): Faith, I'd a drink too many, talking over old times with Jamie Cregan.

NORA: I know.

MELODY: I am afraid I may have — The thought of old times — I become bitter. But you understand, it was the liqour talking, if I said anything to wound you.

NORA: I know it.

MELODY (*deeply moved, puts his arm around her*): You're a sweet, kind woman, Nora — too kind. (*He kisses her.*)

NORA (*with blissful happiness*): Ah, Con darlin', what do I care what you say when the black thoughts are on you? Sure, don't you know I love you?

MELODY (*a sudden revulsion of feeling convulses his face. He bursts out with disgust, pushing her away from him*): For God's sake, why don't you wash your hair? It turns my stomach with its stink of onions and stew!

He reaches for the decanter and shakingly pours a drink. NORA *looks as if he had struck her.*

NORA (*dully*): I do be washin' it often to plaze you. But when you're standin' over the stove all day, you can't help —

MELODY: Forgive me, Nora. Forget I said that. My nerves are on edge. You'd better leave me alone.

NORA (*her face brightening a little*): Will you ate your breakfast now? I've fine fresh eggs —

MELODY (*grasping at this chance to get rid of her — impatiently*): Yes! In a while. Fifteen minutes, say. But leave me alone now.

She goes out right. MELODY *drains his drink. Then he gets up and paces back and forth, his hands clasped behind him. The third drink begins to work and his face becomes arrogantly self-assured. He catches his reflection in the mirror on the wall at left and stops before it. He brushes a sleeve fastidiously, adjusts the set of his coat, and surveys himself.*

Thank God, I still bear the unmistakable stamp of an officer and a gentleman. And so I will remain to the end, in spite of all fate can do to crush my spirit! (*He squares his shoulders defiantly. He stares into his eyes in the glass and recites from Byron's 'Childe Harold', as if it were an incantation by which he summons pride to justify his life to himself.*)

I have not loved the World, nor the World me;
I have not flattered its rank breath, nor bowed
To its idolatries a patient knee,
Nor coined my cheek to smiles, — nor cried aloud
In worship of an echo: in the crowd
They could not deem me one of such — I stood
Among them, but not of them . . .

(*He pauses, then repeats.*)

'Among them, but not of them.' By the Eternal, that expresses it! Thank God for you, Lord Byron — poet and nobleman who made of his disdain immortal music!

SARA *appears in the doorway at right. She has changed to her Sunday dress, a becoming blue that brings out the colour of her eyes. She draws back for a moment — then stands watching him contemptuously.* MELODY *senses her presence. He starts and turns quickly away from the mirror. For a second his expression is guilty and confused, but he immediately assumes an air of gentlemanly urbanity and bows to her.*

Ah, it's you, my dear. Are you going for a morning stroll? You've a beautiful day for it. It will bring fresh roses to your cheeks.

SARA: I don't know about roses, but it will bring a blush of shame to my cheeks. I have to beg Neilan to give us another month's credit, because you made Mother pay the feed bill for your fine thoroughbred mare! (*He gives no sign he hears this. She adds scathingly.*) I hope you saw something in the mirror you could admire!

MELODY (*in a light tone*): Faith, I suppose I must have looked a vain peacock, preening himself, but you can blame the bad light in my room. One cannot make a decent toilet in that dingy hole in the wall.

SARA: You have the best room in the house, that we ought to rent to guests.

MELODY: Oh, I've no complaints. I was merely explaining my seeming vanity.

SARA: Seeming!

MELODY (*keeping his tone light*): Faith, Sara, you must have risen the wrong side of the bed this morning, but it takes two to make a quarrel and I don't feel quarrelsome. Quite the contrary. I was about to tell you how exceedingly charming and pretty you look, my dear.

SARA (*with a mocking, awkward, servant's curtsy — in broad brogue*): Oh, thank ye, yer Honour.

MELODY: Every day you resemble your mother more, as she looked when I first knew her.

SARA: Musha, but it's you have the blarneyin' tongue, God forgive you!

MELODY (*in spite of himself, this gets under his skin — angrily*): Be quiet! How dare you talk to me like a common, ignorant — You're my daughter, damn you. (*He controls himself and forces a laugh.*) A fair hit! You're a great tease, Sara. I shouldn't let you score so easily. Your mother warned me you only did it to provoke me. (*Unconsciously he reaches out for the decanter on the table — then pulls his hand back.*)

SARA (*contemptuously — without brogue now*): Go on and drink. Surely you're not ashamed before me, after all these years.

MELODY (*haughtily*): Ashamed? I don't understand you. A gentleman drinks as he pleases — provided he can hold his liquor as he should.

SARA: A gentleman!

MELODY (*pleasantly again*): I hesitated because I had made a good resolve to be abstemious today. But if you insist — (*He pours a drink — a small one — his hand quite steady now.*) To your happiness, my dear. *She stares at him scornfully. He goes on graciously.*

Will you do me the favour to sit down? I have wanted a quiet chat with you for some time. (*He holds out a chair for her at rear of the table at centre.*)

SARA (*eyes him suspiciously — then sits down*): What is it you want?

MELODY (*with a playfully paternal manner*): Your happiness, my dear, and what I wish to discuss means happiness to you, unless I have grown blind. How is our patient, young Simon Harford, this morning?

SARA (*curtly*): He's better.

MELODY: I am delighted to hear it. (*Gallantly.*) How could he help but be with such a charming nurse?

She stares at him coldly. He goes on.

Let us be frank. Young Simon is in love with you. I can see that with half an eye — and, of course, you know it. And you return his love, I surmise.

SARA: Surmise whatever you please.

MELODY: Meaning you do love him? I am glad, Sara. (*He becomes sentimentally romantic.*) Requited love is the greatest blessing life can bestow on us poor mortals and first love is the most blessed of all. As Lord Byron has it: (*He recites.*)

But sweeter still than this, than these, than all,
Is first and passionate Love — it stands alone,
Like Adam's recollection of his fall . . .

SARA (*interrupts him rudely*): Was it to listen to you recite Byron — ?

MELODY (*concealing discomfiture and resentment — pleasantly*): No. What I was leading up to is that you have my blessing, if that means anything to you. Young Harford is, I am convinced, an estimable youth. I have enjoyed my talks with him. It has been a privilege to be able to converse with a cultured gentleman again. True, he is a bit on the sober side for one so young, but by way of compensation, there is a romantic touch of the poet behind his Yankee phlegm.

SARA: It's fine you approve of him!

MELODY: In your interest I have had some enquiries made about his family.

SARA (*angered — with taunting brogue*): Have you, indade? Musha, that's cute av you! Was it auld Patch Riley, the Piper, made them? Or was it Dan Roche or Paddy O'Dowd, or some other drunken sponge —

MELODY (*as if he hadn't heard — condescendingly*): I find his people will pass muster.

SARA: Oh, do you? That's nice!

MELODY: Apparently, his father is a gentleman — that is, by Yankee standards, in so far as one in trade can lay claim to the title. But as I've become an American citizen myself, I suppose it would be downright snobbery to hold to old world standards.

SARA: Yes, wouldn't it be!

MELODY: Though it is difficult at times for my pride to remember I am no longer the master of Melody Castle and an estate of three thousand acres of as fine pasture and woodlands as you'd find in the whole United Kingdom, with my stable of hunters, an —

SARA (*bitterly*): Well, you've a beautiful thoroughbred mare now, at least — to prove you're still a gentleman!

MELODY (*stung into defiant anger*): Yes, I've the mare! And by God, I'll keep her if I have to starve myself so she may eat.

SARA: You mean, make Mother slave to keep her for you, even if she has to starve!

MELODY (*controls his anger — and ignores this*): But what was I saying? Oh, yes, young Simon's family. His father will pass muster, but it's through his mother, I believe, he comes by his really good blood. My information is, she springs from generations of well-bred gentlefolk.

SARA: It would be a great pride to her, I'm sure, to know you found her suitable.

MELODY: I suppose I may expect the young man to request an interview with me as soon as he is up and about again?

SARA: To declare his honourable intentions and ask you for my hand, is that what you mean?

MELODY: Naturally. He is a man of honour. And there are certain financial arrangements Simon's father or his legal representative will wish to discuss with me. The amount of your settlement has to be agreed upon.

SARA (*stares at him as if she could not believe her ears*): My settlement! Simon's father! God pity you — !

MELODY (*firmly*): Your settlement, certainly. You did not think, I hope, that I would give you away without a penny to your name as if you were some poverty-stricken peasant's daughter? Please remember I have my own position to maintain. Of course, it is a bit difficult at present. I am temporarily hard pressed. But perhaps a mortgage on the inn —

SARA: It's mortgaged to the hilt already, as you very well know.

MELODY: If nothing else, I can always give my note at hand for whatever amount —

SARA: You can give it, sure enough! But who'll take it?

MELODY: Between gentlemen, these matters can always be arranged.

SARA: God help you, it must be a wonderful thing to live in a fairy tale where only dreams are real to you. (*Then sharply.*) But you needn't waste your dreams worrying about my affairs. I'll thank you not to interfere. Attend to your drinking and leave me alone. (*He gives no indication that he has heard a word she has said. She stares at him and a look almost of fear comes into her eyes. She bursts out with a bitter exasperation in which there is a strong undercurrent of entreaty.*) Father! Will you never let yourself wake up — not even now when you're sober, or nearly? Is it stark mad you've gone, so you can't tell any more what's dead and a lie, and what's the living truth?

MELODY (*his face is convulsed by a spasm of pain as if something vital had been stabbed in him — with a cry of tortured appeal*): Sara! (*But instantly his pain is transformed into rage. He half rises from his chair threateningly.*) Be quiet, damn you! How dare you —

She shrinks away and rises to her feet. He forces control on himself and sinks back in his chair, his hands gripping the arms.

The street door at rear is flung open and DAN ROCHE, PADDY O'DOWD, and PATCH RILEY attempt to pile in together and get jammed for a moment in the doorway. They all have hangovers, and ROCHE is talking boisterously. DAN ROCHE is middle-aged, squat, bowlegged, with a pot belly and short arms, lumpy with muscle. His face is flat with a big mouth, protruding ears, and red-rimmed little pig's eyes. He is dressed in dirty, patched clothes. PADDY O'DOWD is thin, round-shouldered, and flat-chested, with a pimply complexion, bulgy eyes, and a droopy mouth. His manner is oily and fawning, that of a born sponger and parasite. His clothes are those of a cheap sport. PATCH RILEY is an old man with a thatch of dirty white hair. His washed-out blue eyes have a wandering, half-witted expression. His skinny body is clothed in rags and there is nothing under his tattered coat but his bare skin. His mouth is sunken in, toothless. He carries an Irish bagpipe under his arm.

ROCHE (*his back is half turned as he harangues O'DOWD and RILEY, and he does not see MELODY and SARA*): And I says, it's Andy Jackson will put you in your place, and all the slave-drivin' Yankee skinflints like you! Take your damned job, I says, and —

O'DOWD (*warningly, his eyes on MELODY*): Whist! Whist! Hold your prate!

ROCHE whirls around to face MELODY, and his aggressiveness oozes from him, changing to a hangdog apprehension. For MELODY has sprung to his feet, his eyes blazing with an anger which is increased by the glance of contempt SARA casts from him to the three men. O'DOWD avoids MELODY's eyes, busies himself in closing the door. PATCH RILEY stands gazing at

SARA *with a dreamy, admiring look, lost in a world of his own fancy, oblivious to what is going on.*

ROCHE (*placatingly*): Good mornin' to ye, Major.

O'DOWD (*fawning*): Good mornin', yer Honour.

MELODY: How dare you come tramping in here in that manner! Have you mistaken this inn for the sort of dirty shebeen you were used to in the old country where the pigs ran in and out the door?

O'DOWD: We ask pardon, yer Honour.

MELODY (*to ROCHE — an impressive menace in his tone*): You, Paddy. Didn't I forbid you ever to mention that scoundrel Jackson's name in my house or I'd horsewhip the hide off your back? (*He takes a threatening step towards him.*) Perhaps you think I cannot carry out that threat.

ROCHE (*backs away frightenedly*): No, no, Major. I forgot — Good mornin' to ye, Miss.

O'DOWD: Good mornin', Miss Sara.

She ignores them. PATCH RILEY *is still gazing at her with dreamy admiration, having heard nothing, his hat still on his head.* O'DOWD *officiously snatches it off for him — rebukingly.*

Where's your wits, Patch? Didn't yet hear his Honour?

RILEY (*unheeding — addresses SARA*): Sure it's you, God bless you, looks like a fairy princess as beautiful as a rose in the mornin' dew. I'll raise a tune for you. (*He starts to arrange his pipes.*)

SARA (*curtly*): I want none of your tunes. (*Then, seeing the look of wondering hurt in the old man's eyes, she adds kindly.*) That's sweet of you, Patch. I know you'd raise a beautiful tune, but I have to go out. Consoled, the old man smiles at her gratefully.

MELODY: Into the bar, all of you, where you belong! I told you not to use this entrance! (*With disdainful tolerance.*) I suppose it's a free drink you're after. Well, no one can say of me that I turned away anyone I knew thirsty from my door.

O'DOWD: Thank ye, yer Honour. Come along, Dan. (*He takes RILEY's arm.*) Come on, Patch.

The three go into the bar and O'DOWD *closes the door behind them.*

SARA (*in derisive brogue*): Sure, it's well trained you've got the poor retainers in your American estate to respect the master!

Then as he ignores her and casts a furtive glance at the door to the bar, running his tongue over his dry lips, she says acidly, with no trace of brogue.

Don't let me keep you from joining the gentlemen! (*She turns her back on him and goes out the street door at rear.*)

MELODY (*his face is again convulsed by a spasm of pain — pleadingly*): Sara!

NORA *enters from the hall at right, carrying a tray with toast, eggs, bacon, and tea. She arranges his breakfast on the table at front centre, bustling garrulously.*

NORA: Have I kept you waitin'? The divil was in the toast. One lot burned black as a naygur when my back was turned. But the bacon is crisp, and the eggs not too soft, the way you like them. Come and sit down now. (MELODY *does not seem to hear her. She looks at him worriedly.*) What's up with you, Con? Don't you hear me?

O'DOWD (*pokes his head in the door from the bar*): Mickey won't believe you said we could have a drink, yer Honour, unless ye tell him.

MELODY (*licking his lips*): I'm coming. (*He goes to the bar door.*)

NORA: Con! Have this in your stomach first! It'll all get cauld.

MELODY (*without turning to her — in his condescendingly polite tone*): I find I am not the least hungry, Nora. I regret your having gone to so much trouble.

He goes into the bar, closing the door behind him.
NORA *slumps on a chair at the rear of the table and stares at the breakfast with a pitiful helplessness. She begins to sob quietly.*

CURTAIN

1 Plenty. (In Share the word is dated 1829.)
2 Irish síbín. Unlicensed drinking-place.
3 Irish for pulse, a term of endearment.

JOHN HEWITT
from *New Statesman and Nation*, 16 May 1959

John Hewitt was appointed Director of the Herbert Art Gallery in Coventry in 1957. Coventry at that time was being rebuilt after being destroyed by German bombs in the Second World War.

AN IRISHMAN IN COVENTRY

A full year since, I took this eager city,
the tolerance that laced its blatant roar,
its famous steeples and its web of girders,
as image of the state hope argued for,
and scarcely flung a bitter thought behind me
on all that flaws the glory and the grace
which ribbons through the sick, guilt-clotted legend
of my creed-haunted, Godforsaken race.
My rhetoric swung round from steel's high promise
to the precision of the well-gauged tool,
tracing the logic in the vast glass headlands,
the clockwork horse, the comprehensive school.[1]

Then, sudden, by occasion's chance concerted,
in enclave of my nation, but apart,
the jigging dances and the lilting fiddle
stirred the old rage and pity in my heart.
The faces and the voices blurring round me,
the strong hands long familiar with the spade,
the whiskey-tinctured breath, the pious buttons,
called up a people endlessly betrayed
by our own weakness, by the wrongs we suffered
in that long twilight over bog and glen,
by force, by famine and by glittering fables
which gave us martyrs when we needed men,
by faith which had no charity to offer,
by poisoned memory, and by ready wit,
with poverty corroded into malice,
to hit and run and howl when it is hit.
This is our fate: eight hundred years' disaster,
crazily tangled as the Book of Kells;
the dream's distortion and the land's division,
the midnight raiders and the prison cells.
Yet like Lir's children[2] banished to the waters
our hearts still listen for the landward bells.

1 These state schools were introduced into British education in the 1950s. They allowed for the full range of ability to be taught in the same school.
2 According to legend, Lir's children were transformed into swans and forced to roam until the coming of Christianity heralded by the bell of Saint Mochaomhog. There is an account of the legend in Lady Gregory's *Gods and Fighting Men* (1904).

IRISH WRITING IN THE 1960s

'In the forty years the gifted Irish have been turned into a nation of blasted puppets. They were never so exploited! As for want, look at the children of the poor. You don't have to go far. Our thought-machine is the equal of Russia's. We have our forbidden authors too. Nothing flourishes, only the gombeen-man.'

'The who?' asked Hilda.

'Irish for usurer, me ould duck,' said Dermot, rubbing more purple on to his head in a tired way. The exhibition had reduced him.

'A gombeen's paradise they've made. Building their motels, making their films. Local players getting their five pounds a day as Black and Tans — four pounds more than the Tans got. "God, if me poor father could see me now." Ah, it makes you sick! Films, but no Abbey built as yet, of course. Not that it's any harm. The kitchen comedy has been replaced by the suburban comedy. Vile rubbish for the new middle class.'

'That's not fair,' said Dermot. 'They're doing *Private Lives* at the Gate.'

'Yes, we've a new class-tiered society now. No welfare state for us. Too Christian a notion for our spiritual leaders.'

'No classes in England, I suppose? You poor ould peasant!'

'No hunger, no rickets, at any rate. The gombeen-men have been here, you see. Out with the sawdust and in with the chromium.'

'I think it's a great improvement,' said Grania. She was enjoying herself immensely. The afternoon was turning out exactly as she had hoped.

'And in the process they've removed the wall of the Gents that was covered with the autographs of everyone who mattered when Dublin had a great cultural life.'

'You poor bloody sentimentalist! Another Gents gone.'

'It seems to me,' said Hilda bravely, 'that the country is improving itself in every way. It's coming in line with Europe. What's wrong with cleanliness and being modern? You've ceased to be an island and are looking outwards.' She lowered her high-pitched voice. 'I've noticed that two men at the bar are reading the *Daily Express* and another one is reading the *Daily Mail*.'

– Michael Campbell, *Across the Water* (1961)

CRITICAL AND DOCUMENTARY

SEAN O'FAOLAIN
from *Studies: An Irish Quarterly Review* (1962)

O'Faolain's retrospective survey has the stamp of authority, and apart from an occassional flat spot it remains one of the most accomplished half-dozen essays on modern Irish writing.

Fifty Years of Irish Writing

When the editor of *Studies* kindly invited me to write an article on the fortunes of Irish literature over the past fifty years I presumed that the main interest of anything I might have to say would lie in the fact that I am an Irish writer who was born in 1900, which implies, I suppose, that, within the limitations of my personal oddities and idiosyncrasies, what I here say cannot fail to be, at any rate to some degree, representative of the views of the generation after Yeats. In other words I am, very happily, presenting myself and my views as a type-specimen. I feel obliged to say this at the outset, to give myself full freedom of expression by making it quite clear to my readers, especially to readers outside Ireland, that some of the things I have to say must be displeasing to my host. I might otherwise seem to be taking an unfair advantage of his hospitality.

I do not propose to say much about the earlier part of the last fifty years. What was written in that period, say 1910–21, is well known and has been much discussed. It was the hey-day of the Abbey Theatre. The riots over *The Playboy* were over and the battle won — the play was now being produced without opposition, largely through the tough courage of Yeats and the gallant support of his players. Prose was flourishing — Moore, Stephens, Canon Sheehan, Somerville and Ross, lesser entertainers like George Birmingham, and, to move on a bit in years but still within the general 'period', Eimar O'Duffy, Shan Bullock, Conal O'Riordan and others. I am aware that to move on outside date-brackets is always tricky in dealing with a literary period, but, in the first place, dates and 'periods' rarely coincide in literary history. (For example, the eighteenth century period in English literature did not end with the year 1800.) And, the second, and for our purposes, more important point here is that the whole story of latter-day developments in Anglo-Irish letters is very much a story of pioneering and overlapping. (Joyce's *Dubliners*, for example, appeared in 1914 but he is alien to most of our literary traditions before him, though he was fully contemporaneous with Yeats as a young Dubliner.) Poetry, too, in the opening ten years of our chosen fifty was flourishing — Yeats, Clarke, Higgins, Campbell, Seamus O'Sullivan; though here again I am over-leaping dates, to keep the sense of period. Clarke and Higgins both were born in 1896. Clarke did not publish his first book *The Vengeance of Fionn* until 1917.

The general mood of that period, before the establishment of the Irish Free State, was romantic, nationalist, fervid, critical of others, especially of one's political opponents, whether native or foreign, but not very critical of ourselves — apart from the sort of rather superficial satire one got from plays like William Boyle's *The Eloquent Dempsey* — and it was quite uncritical in matters literary, historical and what would nowadays be called sociological. This absence of a deep-cutting critical objectivity was, I think, the great weakness of the so-called Irish Literary Movement. It made it, as some of us at the time kept on saying worriedly, without being able to do anything about it, a movement of feeling rather than of thought. As one looks back over the prose of the period one sometimes wonders whether our writers ever took off their green glasses. Exceptions will, no doubt, be offered, such as O'Duffy and O'Riordan, yet, on re-opening such novels as *The Wasted Island* or *Adam of Dublin* I, for one, still feel that nothing in them is at all as tough and clearsighted as, say, *The Real Charlotte* (Somerville and Ross) or *A Drama in Muslin*.[1] This last, and to most readers I feel sure, unexpected title, may make my point clear.

George Moore was a flippant Bohemian; the novel is not a good novel; it is melodramatic, often absurd, even penny-noveletteish; yet to what other novel of that time can one go for such a clear observation of the formative social factors behind, and responsible for, the grimness of Dublin life as depicted, but never explained — it was not his interest — by Joyce in the *Portrait* and *Ulysses*? Moore, trained by Zola and Flaubert, saw, displayed and eviscerated — an amazing feat for a man normally without an iota of responsibility in his composition — the real forces, social and economic, which had infected Ireland with the state of spiritual paralysis that so disgusted Joyce and produced in contemporary Irish writing so much verse that if not actually a form of compensatory escapism is dangerously close to it. To the Irish Literary Movement, taken by and large, the evil enemy was England, holding down and frustrating all that was lovely and worthwhile in the Holy Land of Ireland whose beauty the poets endlessly chanted. Moore, whose relations with Ireland were consistently those of *odi et amo*[2] — with at times an almost psychopathic stress on the *odi* — saw that the real source of infection was the native middle-classes, and — religion apart — all their tawdry, snobbish, and provincial, social values. Events were to support Moore's contention to the full.

This leads me to explain why, as I see things, the story of Irish writing since 1900 falls into two parts: growth and decline.

Though nobody could have observed it at the time, the causes for this decline began to operate immediately the Free State was founded, in 1921. Their effects were, however, held at bay for a time by the continuing momentum of nationalist excitement persisting after the revolution was over. Sean O'Casey's plays illustrate this. His *Juno and the Paycock* was staged in 1924, and his *The Plough and the Stars* in 1926, both of them dealing with the revolutionary period which was finished and done with. It is true that there was a theatre-riot over the latter play, but nobody attached any special significance to it. If anything one took it for a good omen. It was like the old days of the *Playboy* riots. It promised a continuity of tradition. '*Plus ça change*,'[3] we said. But we were wrong. It was not *la même chose*. There was a fundamental difference between the circumstances surrounding O'Casey and those surrounding Synge. One might build on the two riots a parable of the reasons for the later decline in Irish writing.

In the old days — to keep, for the moment, to the example of the Theatre — an élite had been in the saddle. The whole of Yeats's outlook had been aristocratic though nationalist, just as he had always been both European and Irish, as excited by the *Axel* of Villiers de l'Isle Adam as by the peasant folktales of Biddy Early.[4] He had said several times that his sort of theatre should be as hard to get into as a secret society. He liked small audiences. The poetic drama he admired could never have become popular, and in so far as the Abbey Theatre did become a popular or people's theatre, he felt that he had failed to create what he set out to create. So, he had always struggled

against the popular taste for so-called 'realistic' drama. In spite of every inevitable concession to that taste he dominated his ambiguous creation as a poet with a poet's ideals. This all began to change immediately a native government was established. The type of people who had, long ago, protested against Synge's *Playboy* had had no political power. The people who objected to O'Casey had political power. (It is to be remembered that the new Irish Government decided to subsidize the Abbey Theatre; which, at the time, seemed to us all a splendid gesture — disillusion was to come slowly with the gradual realization that when governments give money they receive influence in exchange.)

Moreover, in those 'old days' the Catholic Church had had only a limited amount of political power because the government had been an alien and non-Catholic government, and the foreign Gallio,[5] like all pro-consuls, had kept the ring with the tolerance of total indifference. Now the Church could wield almost unlimited power because the native government was composed of men who respected, loved, and feared it. It is evident that the new intellectual atmosphere depended on the sophistication, cultivation, and tolerance of both the native Government and the Church, the new élite. Unfortunately, centuries of depression had bred in both not only a passionate desire for liberty — each with its own interpretation and its own aims — but the antithesis of that natural desire. It had induced a nervy, sensitive, touchy, defensive-aggressive, on-guard mentality as a result of which patriotism became infected by chauvinism and true religious feeling by what most Irish writers after 1921 tended to call 'puritanism'. I imagine that I am describing something which happens commonly in all countries which have emerged from a revolutionary phase, and that it does not involve any special criticism of Ireland or the Irish nature. (An intellectual Jew in contemporary Palestine, an intellectual Cypriot in Cyprus, would probably nod his head in understanding and sympathy if he were to read my summary.)

The simplest illustration of what happened was the establishment of a severe Literary Censorship, in 1929. Its aim was, and its aim no doubt still is, a blending of the moral and the patriotic: the desire to protect from corruption this infant nation born out of so much hardship. Within twenty years thousands of books were banned as indecent or obscene. It will be noted that the reason for banning was not political and it was social (and religious) only in so far as books and periodicals were and still are banned if they advocate, or advertise, contraception, abortion, or the artificial insemination of humans. Within recent years this early fervour for banning has been much abated, thanks to the nomination of intelligent censors, following prolonged protests by writers and the general public. Most of the books now banned are ephemeral and their absence from the public libraries and bookshops is no loss. This may be acknowledged and welcomed as a sign of a growing sophistication in contemporary Ireland.

But there have been two particularly bad results for Irish literature; within a few years there was scarcely an Irish writer of distinction who had not, at least once, been declared the author of obscenity, and he was — and still is — denied recourse to the courts of the land in self-defence. But the worst feature of the Censorship has been that with it there arose a private censorship all over the country in the form of a witch-hunt which no librarian or bookseller could dare to resist by stocking books objected to by these un-official censors. Demos was in the saddle.[6]

To form a just picture of this new intellectual atmosphere it is essential to grasp one other point. The revolution of 1916-21 had been a social revolution. This fact lifts the history of Irish writing over the past twenty-five years out of its apparently local setting and puts it in its proper place as part of a general world-tendency. The idealists who inspired the people to rise against British rule were — as I have said — unaware of the social forces they were working with and releasing. In the nineteenth century these forces had been personified by the impoverished farming community in the Land League's fight for decent conditions of land-tenure. In our day the social forces behind the last stage of the Irish Revolution were personified by the sons and daughters of those farmers — surplus children squeezed into the towns and cities, and finding there that all the power and most of the wealth was in the hands of people of a different religion, racial origin, or political loyalty. Sean O'Casey's plays are thus an exactly true statement of the Irish Revolution whose flag, he clearly felt, should be, not the tricolour, but the plough-and-the-stars flag of the urban labouring classes.

We must, finally, understand that the class that came to power and influence was not a labouring class; the more able among them were *petit bourgeois*, middle-men, importers, small manufacturers — the modern counterpart of Moore's nineteenth century middle-classes — forming a new twentieth century middle-class to fill the vacuum created by the departure or depression of the earlier alien middle-class. These men, naturally, had had very little education and could have only a slight interest in the intellectuals' fight for liberty of expression. They were ordinary, decent, kindly, self-seeking men who had no intention of jeopardizing their new-found prosperity by gratuitous displays of moral courage. In any case, since they were rising to sudden wealth behind protective tariff-walls they had a vested interest in nationalism and even in isolationism. The upshot of it was an alliance between the Church, the new businessmen, and the politicians, all three nationalist-isolationist for, respectively, moral reasons, commercial reasons, and politico-patriotic reasons, in themselves all perfectly sound reasons. The effect on letters was not good. The intellectuals became a depressed group. Possibly they were also infected by the atmosphere around them.

For completeness let us try to look sympathetically on the other side of the picture. Ireland is not a publishing country. All but a number of books, so few that it would be an exaggeration to call them a handful, are published abroad, apart from all primary school texts and most secondary school texts. Practically all our mental food is therefore imported: good food but not native. If there is such a thing as a racial Irish quality of life it is very difficult for it to resist almost overwhelming external influences, since this local way-of-life is not equipped intellectually to support it. The intellectuals cried out for a bold, adventurous, and thoroughly modern system of popular education, but both the Church and the State feared the results. It is to be said that the Irish way-of-life, though poor, indeed impoverished as to institutions fit to represent it — e.g. publishing houses, periodicals, rich universities — is atavistically powerful, spiritually obstinate, strongly resistant, in a great many ways appealing; it represents precious and lovable qualities, and is eminently worth preservation, provided it expresses itself in achievement and not merely in emotional declaration. The intellectuals' position is that it cannot and will not preserve itself by negative methods, and that it is, in practice, now as in the past, being undermined and corrupted by a lack of moral and intellectual courage.

We can now look at Irish writing against this social, political, and religious background. First, the Theatre:

As we look back over the plays produced in the Abbey Theatre since the First World War we find that the Theatre was still lively almost up to 1932. (This suggests that the momentum of the revolutionary stimulus went on for some ten years.) The lists include first productions of plays by Lady Gregory, Brinsley MacNamara, Padraic Colum, Daniel Corkery, Shaw, Lord Dunsany, Lennox Robinson, George Shiels, Sean O'Casey, T. C. Murray, Yeats, Wilde, Rutherford Mayne, Teresa Deevy, Denis Johnston, and Paul

Vincent Carroll. Lady Gregory died in 1932. From then onward two or three plays of distinction were produced but no outstanding name is added to the list. In 1935 Yeats, who was ageing and ailing, felt that the theatre needed younger men. His friend, the poet Frederick Robert Higgins, was appointed Director; so was Frank O'Connor; and a significant name also appeared among the directors, an ex-Cabinet Minister, Mr Ernest Blythe. Mr Hugh Hunt, now producer at the Old Vic Theatre, London, was brought in as producer, and from 1935 to 1938, the combination of Higgins, O'Connor and Hunt gave the theatre a new and exciting spurt. It is of interest that in those three years the Abbey produced several non-Irish plays — including plays by Shakespeare, Flecker, Toller, Shaw, André Obey. Yeats died in 1939. O'Connor, feeling unable to cope with influences of which he disapproved, resigned in 1939. Higgins died in 1941. Mr Blythe became Managing Director. Thus, there remained on the Board, to represent old tradition, only Mr Lennox Robinson. Otherwise the bridge with the past was down.

Unless we imagine that literature exists in a vacuum we must see what sort of official influences played on the Theatre at this period. I will give two examples. In 1932 when the Abbey Theatre visited the United States the usual hyper-patriotic societies there protested against some of the plays, including O'Casey's, and at home Deputies were prompted to ask awkward questions in the Dáil. In reply to one questioner on this issue, Mr De Valera said (26 April 1933) that the Government had made indirect representations to the Abbey Theatre, and that it was hoped that if the Company visited America again plays of the kind objected to by the American-Irish would not be produced. In that year the official subsidy was reduced. In 1934 a similar angry question received a similar reply, De Valera then saying that such plays damage the good name of Ireland. Yeats stood his ground, and was attacked bitterly by the popular press.

The second significant incident occurred in 1938 when the Board of the Theatre decided that plays in the Irish language should henceforth become a regular feature of the work of the Theatre. This, I hold, was a retrograde step artistically, however laudable from the patriotic point of view, since there happened to be no Gaelic-writing playwrights worth mentioning and most of the trained actors could not speak Gaelic. The result showed itself in 1942 when the Government again intervened to ask the Theatre to take over the work of an existing company of Gaelic players called 'An Comhar Drámuíochta' (The Drama Co-operative). After this, so far as I know, no junior players were employed unless they could speak Gaelic, an accomplishment which had as much to do with acting as if they could dance the can-can. I record this incident solely to give the reader my impression of the lowering of intellectual standards after Yeats.

Let us now try to define the precise effect on the arts. Fundamentally what had happened was that a social concept of the function of literature was beginning to replace the 'individualist' concept. Compare Yeats, taking him as representative of the first twenty-five years of the Anglo-Irish revival. Yeats had loved all art that was remote and uncommon, 'distinguished and lonely'. He had seen the element of nobility in the simplest people but he had never permitted his affection for familiar life to be confused with a preoccupation with the common or the popular.[7] Thus, writing of the Theatre he had said:

> The modern author, if he be a man of genius, is a solitary, he does not know the everchanging public well enough to be its servant. He cannot learn their convention; they must learn his. All that is greatest in modern literature is soliloquy, or, at most, words addressed to a few friends.

This dislike of 'realism' had always been with him. He sought always to sublimate reality, and it was in that search for a dissolvent of the flesh that he had formed the distinction between Character, that is, the social, public, moral thing, formed by and for the purposes of organized society, and Personality, which is what appears in all the great moments of drama when this social functional thing drops away and a man's spirit burns with the 'pure gem-like flame'. So, he had found inspiration in the ancient mind of his people, but it was not a political mind, or a social mind, but a mystical memory, linking man to those ages when life was still a unity, before he became fissured by rationalism and splintered by what we nowadays call psychological analysis.

One could easily demur at much of this. The Theatre, after all, is the most sociable of all the arts. And, as I have indicated in my opening remarks, there was already too much of this withdrawal-from-life in the first period of the Irish Literary Movement. At any rate our new, ambitious, hardfaced democracy understood none of this aristocratic concept. It understood only 'realistic plays', political plays, representationalism, characterization, explanations, social comedies and tragedies. It is to the credit of some Irish playwrights resident in Ireland that they took the risks of some sort of criticism and satire, and it is to the credit of the Abbey Theatre, even in its decline, that it staged some of these plays. But what we have had even of this 'some sort of criticism and satire' has been so feeble as to extinguish the value of the terms I have used ('realistic', 'political', 'representational', 'social') to describe the sort of plays the new public wanted. Because the new audiences did not really want any of those things; they wanted those things in an *ersatz* form: plays that merely gave the illusion of being political, realistic, social, critical, and so on. They were ready to laugh at plays dealing with the surface of things. They were not ready for plays that opposed what might be called, for short, the new synthetic orthodoxy, or at any rate diverged radically from it, let alone that denied it or rejected it. No social-realistic drama — whether comic or tragic — can thrive in this atmosphere. Mr Brendan Behan, for instance, whether good, bad or indifferent, could not have broken through in Dublin. He first had to break through in London or New York.

But there are even greater and deeper dangers in the writers' battle for honesty. The danger of becoming embittered, or twisted, threatens creativity itself, and here we come to the real battle-ground of contemporary Irish writing. For the first time Irish writers have had to *think* themselves into personal release. Disillusion is also a form of revelation. There is no longer any question of dishing up local colour. (The Noble Peasant is as dead as the Noble Savage. Poems about fairies and leprechauns, about misted lakes, old symbols of national longing, are over and done with.) We need to explore Irish life with an objectivity never hitherto applied to it — and in this Joyce rather than Yeats is our inspiration. But to see clearly is not to write passionately. An artist must, in some fashion, love his material, and his material must, in some fashion, co-operate with him. It is not enough for an artist to be clinically interested in life: he must take fire from it. This has been the great rub in Ireland for some thirty years. It is not confined to Ireland. Everywhere today, as I see it, literature is facing the same problem: How to transmute into permanent forms a life that one sees critically rather than lovingly.

If this really is an universal problem, why is it so? I think it is so because writers everywhere feel that life no longer has any sense of Pattern and Destination. The argosies set out. They forget why. To give the most naïve example possible of Pattern and Destination: time was when novelists moved their men and women, with a sense of completion, towards a home and a family, in love and marriage. Countless is the number of novels and plays shaped about the thwarting of this journey. All the hypocrisy of the Victorian novel, its sentimental, evangelical piety, its

evasiveness exposed itself in this 'Destination' which everybody knows today is only a starting point, another challenge, another problem. No writer dares to play this old tune today. The result is that men of genius have been writing as the matador kills bulls, by virtuosity or by savagery — Joyce, Hemingway, Anouilh, Aymé, Bazin, Julien Green, Mailer, all the writers of the *roman nouveau*;[8] or they impose Pattern and Destination by sheer force — Lagerkvist by his symbolism, Malraux by his mysticism, Sartre by his Existentialism, Bernanos, Greene, or Mauriac by their Catholicism, the later O'Casey by his Communism. One may be lost in admiration of this forcible handling of intractable material, though one does sometimes wonder whether humanity has not emerged from their work literally man-handled, moulded to shape, intellectualized, not men but puppets. The regionalists are in the happier position. Faulkner may still find Pattern and Destination about him, or imagine he can find it.

An Irish writer might expect to find old patterns persisting in his region also. But the dilemma has here taken a particularly sardonic form. My countrymen are so satisfied with their sentimental Pattern that they have no interest in Destination. Everything having been solved they have no further to go — except to Heaven. They are frustrated by the illusory completeness of their own conventions. The novel elsewhere may be frustrated by the certainties of men lost; here it is frustrated by the certainties of men saved. We read with an excited absorption the work of Catholic novelists elsewhere — that is, novelists who work within the frame of the struggle between God and the Devil, rather than the struggle of man with material evil or impersonal misfortune — and we observe that they deal with characters who are wilful, rebellious, passionate, arrogant, conscious, persistent, reckless — men who put theology to the test of experience, either to uphold it or not as their experiences prompt. We turn, hopefully, to the potential material of Irish novels on the lines of Bernanos or Mauriac. We discover to our dismay that no error has been so great as the popular conception of the Irishman as rebellious, passionate, reckless, wilful, and so on. We are, in effect, very much in the same position as Hawthorne who just managed to squeeze one novel — and it is not really as fine a novel as the professors say; he lacked courage to push his concept of life to its end — out of equally unmalleable material, in a society where, also, sin was furtive, convention rigid, courage slight and honesty scant.

One of the most striking effects of all this on Irish letters in the period before us is the comparative failure of the modern Irish Novel. If one were to exclude Joyce — which is like saying if one were to exclude Everest — and Liam O'Flaherty how little is left! We have, of course, plenty of honourable efforts (perhaps, I might suggest, like my own efforts) but of anything like top-notchers (Joyce's *Portrait* aside) how many others would the really serious critic want to put beside, say, Elizabeth Bowen's Irish novel *The Last September* or whichever one, two or three of O'Flaherty's he would choose for this test? My explanation for this I have already given — that Irish life in our period does not supply the *dramatis personae*, ready for the hard conflicts, the readiness to take anything *jusqu'au bout*[9] in either full or at least some awareness of what is at stake, without which dramatic themes for the novel are missing. We produce spurts of spirit. They end in laughter (the great national vice and virtue) or exile.

This may be why, on the other hand, the Short Story has thriven in the meantime, and this is probably the best product of our period. The successes here have been so numerous that I need not even mention names. They have been wise to choose the smaller, yet revealing themes in the absence of the larger, more dramatic ones.

The Irish novelist who has been most persistent in mining for revolt and passion has been Liam O'Flaherty. He has found his passionate creatures in the west of Ireland and in the Revolution. His best-known novels *The Informer* (1925), *The Assassin* (1928), *The Martyr* (1932) are in the middle of our period. Each deals with the revolutionary upheaval, which was a godsend to all Irish writers until, as in the Theatre, the vein became exhausted around 1932, ten years after the Revolution ended. In that year O'Flaherty wrote *The Puritan*, a study of the new Irish rigorism, and thereafter he chose, with one exception, which was a failure, historical subjects. It is most revealing that all of O'Flaherty's work is shot through by a wild romanticism — to put it crudely, the romanticism of the Noble Savage. He had to write in this way to gear himself and his characters to action. Since he is so much a Romantic one should not expect intellectual as well as emotional rewards from his work. I regret their absence — as I do in Hemingway: it is an equally pointless regret.

I think my reader will begin to realize the difficulties of writing in a country where the policeman and the priest are in a perpetual glow of satisfaction. He must, however, also see that, to a real extent, Irish novelists have failed to solve a problem. I will illustrate this problem by quoting the comment of an intelligent American critic on his first visit to Ireland. He said: 'This seems to be a very prosperous, comfortable, well-to-do country. We do not get that picture from your writers. Why not?' His comment was not wholly fair. He ignored Emigration, to make but one point, and other things that do not immediately strike the eye. Still, I have failed to present an intelligible picture of contemporary Irish society — acquisitive, bourgeois, unsophisticated, intellectually conservative and unadventurous, rigidly controlled on every side — if the answer to that 'Why not?' is not apparent. I will underline it only by pointing out that the change-over from a stratified society — ranging from aristocrat to outcast — to a one-class society, where there are not native aristocrats and no outcasts (except the writers?), and where the hard, traditional core is in a farming population, rarely induces a fertile awareness either among people or writers. And awareness in literature is an essential. Even before the Revolution Irish writers — Joyce, Shaw, Wilde, dozens besides — felt this, in so far as our awareness was then (as they saw it) all going down the drain of politics and nationalism. They left Ireland for the more interesting life of the island next door. Unawareness itself is, it may be added, not a theme for any writer: it is a negative; it eliminates the element of self-conflict, which alone gives meaning to any theme.

One other obstacle, and of all perhaps the most difficult to surmount, has come between the Irish writer, whether poet, dramatist, or novelist, and his normal material in Irish life. It may be expressed in the words of the poet, Robert Greacen, in a poem significantly entitled 'Written on the Sense of Isolation in Contemporary Ireland'. Having called up the 'unfettered great in heart and mind who gave no inch to fate' — Swift, Burke, Sheridan, Congreve, Goldsmith, Moore and Yeats — he says:

> Yet all of these the world for subject took
> And wed the fearless thesis to their book.

We are, it would seem, only just beginning to learn how to be, as Yeats was, European though nationalist. Hitherto, Irish writers, still tuning-in, as writers always do, to the intellectual stations of the world did so almost like men in an occupied country listening to forbidden voices. The writer who had the feel of the world rose, hitherto, from his grapevine, excited by the sense of the world, then turned to his page to write as he felt . . . But with what? With whom? What characters would think and speak for him, in his poem, play, or novel? As I have said, the *dramatis personae* were otherwise engaged. Perhaps this is now changing?

I feel profoundly that Greacen's point has much to say about the last thirty years of Irish poetry. There is no loss of technical skill — if anything a far greater verbal sophistication has arrived in Irish poetry over the last thirty years than existed previously. There is no decline in receptiveness. The later work of Austin Clarke, Patrick Kavanagh, Padraic Fallon, Valentin Iremonger, Thomas Kinsella, Robert Farren, to name only a few, show poetry just as much on tiptoe, ready for flight, as it ever was. All that is lacking is not significant subject, but width of personal vision — and one rarely hears a modern idiom, a modern speech. The voltage of poetry (of any art) must do more than illuminate the local, or bring the barque of the mind happily home. Poetry is a lighthouse calling us to far seas. Clarke, for all his intense nationalism and smoored piety, often speaks with a far-echoing voice, as understandable to any part of the world as to us. I have always felt that Denis Devlin was a great loss to us: he wrote with a full response to the fullness of life everywhere. So, frequently, does Iremonger.

This need for a larger vision shows itself most poignantly in modern Irish poetry in the Irish language. Within my knowledge I am aware of only three Gaelic poets who are not utterly lost in the Gaelic Mist, trying to extract ore from long-exhausted mines, symbols worn threadbare by the first phase of the Irish Literary Movement. Those three are Máire Mhac an tSaoi (now Mrs Conor Cruise O'Brien), Tomás Tóibín, but above all the Seán O'Riordáin of *Eireball Spideóige*, a delightfully fresh-minded poet irrespective of place or language. Here, again, it is not the subject or theme (as with the novelist) which is important; it is the freedom and scope of the imagination, dealing with any subject. For where the novelist is contained by character the poet is not — he is his own character, his own subject. This O'Riordáin has instinctively grasped and is thereby liberated at once from the old trap of writing *about* Ireland.

The lesson of our time is that Irish writers cannot any longer go on writing about Ireland, or for Ireland within the narrow confines of the traditional Irish life-concept; it is too slack, too cosy, too evasive, too untense. They must, or perish as regionalists, take, as writers everywhere do, the local (since they know its detail most intimately) and universalize it, as Joyce did — as Kavanagh can do it even when he is writing about a potato-field or O'Riordáin about a hospital-nurse. It is a matter of bravely and clearsightedly accepting the tensions of one's own being, or relentlessly challenging the life about one with their sharpest questions, of looking, then, far and wide, in time and place, for others who have been in some like

conflict — a Stendhal, Balzac, Hawthorne, Forster, Joyce, Trollope, Yeats, Frost, Hardy, Lampedusa, Lorca, Cavafy, Zhivago, whoever it may be anywhere at any time who, one feels, might ironically sympathize — saying to them, 'That was how it seemed to you! Here is how it strikes me,' and seize one's pen, *for them* and one's self.

Men of genius accelerate the processes of time for their country, *if* (which is a challenging, and often the most dismaying conjecture) they can cope with their country. The problem is up to the writers themselves. Nobody outside can help them; nobody inside will help them. They will not evade it by exile — Ibsen did not, and did not wish to. (He had other reasons for his exile.) Nobody need pity them either, since by the grace of God and the savagery of Oliver Cromwell their language is now the English language and if they have anything worth saying that they can say well, the periodicals and publishers of Britain and America are waiting for them with open arms and purses. If they feel that exile is absolutely necessary, they may, alone among the writers of the small countries of the world, emigrate freely. What they have to cope with either way is complex enough. But was there ever a writer whose life and work was plain sailing? Their main worry must be that their worst enemies are impalpable and insinuating: self-pity, bitterness, sentimentality, cynicism, their own unsophistication, barren rage, even their love of country, their love of friends. (It was Ibsen who said that he had to leave Norway because friendship was too expensive: meaning that, for friendship's sake, one refrained from saying things that should be said.) It is improper for any critic to probe into these struggles. They are delicate, intimate, and fearful.

1   George Moore's novel published in 1886.
2   Latin: I hate and I love.
3   French saying: The more it changes the more it stays the same.
4   A play by the French writer Villiers de l'Isle Adam, which Yeats saw in Paris in 1894. Biddy Early (1798–1874) was a wise woman from County Clare (see my *Yeats's Worlds* for a photo of her ruined cottage).
5   Roman administrator, brother of Seneca, who refused judgement when the Jews brought Paul before him.
6   I take, at random, from my files a typical list of Banned Books as published in February 1952. Eighty-nine books were banned. The greater number included cheap American importations of a popular nature, thrillers with sexy titles on the lines of *Make Mine a Virgin*. One Irish novelist was listed, Francis Stuart, for *Good Friday's Daughter*. The list also included: John Steinbeck's *Tortilla Flat*, Anita Loos's *A Mouse is Born*, André Gide's *Les nourritures terrestres*, Carson McCuller's *Reflections in a Golden Eye*. There has been, for some years, an Appeal Board which has unbanned a small proportion of books.

They are usually out-of-print by the time they are unbanned. The Censorship Board is immune from legal action. In any case, writers have no money for prolonged action against the State. Today one still, but rarely now, finds a worthwhile book on the lists. [AN]

7   So brief a summary is inadequate even to suggest the complexity of Yeats's thought. I put the word *individualist* in inverted commas solely to indicate its inadequacy. See Yeats's attack on the popular idea of 'individualism' in his own record of his famous meeting with The Young Joyce in *The Identity of Yeats* (1954), by Richard Ellmann, p. 86 foll. [AN]

8   French: literally, new novel. New wave of French experimental novelists in the 1950s. The term was coined by Alain Robbe-Grillet in 1956.

9   French: until the end, as far as it can go.

BRIAN INGLIS
from Brian Inglis, *West Briton* (1962)

Brian Inglis (1916–91) was a journalist and broadcaster first in Dublin with *The Irish Times* and then in England with *The Spectator* and other papers. In this informative extract from his autobiography he sketches in the lifestyle of the Anglo-Irish in Ireland after 1921. His choice of title — the term is used with some relish by Miss Ivors to round on Gabriel Conroy in Joyce's 'The Dead' — is deliberately confrontational, a reminder of the old defiance that eventually died out among the southern unionists.

from Our Set

The boundaries were marked, as they are in England, by distinctions of behaviour and speech. We spoke what was later to be defined as 'U' English — though the distinction with 'non-U' would not have occurred to us, as there was no middle-class bloc to provide the indicators which later afforded Nancy Mitford[1] such amusement. Our own fun along these lines was at the expense of English boys over staying in the holidays, whose la-de-dah accents we thought comically affected; for we shared a prevailing belief that nowhere in the world was English better spoken than in Dublin. We did not have Irish accents; only an Irish lilt — often a matter of a turn of phrase, a way of speaking rather than of a different sound. Some of us would have passed for English, except under the scrutiny of a Henry Higgins.[2]

The difference between the accents of our set, and what we thought of as Irish brogues, appeared to be absolute. The gap was so great that we were hardly aware that anybody might be trying to bridge it. Dublin comedians delighted to deride the 'Rathmines[3] accent' for its intimations of social climbing; we hardly distinguished it from the adenoidal Dublin 'gutty' accents of Moore Street or the Coombe. Some of us cultivated a stage Irish accent as a pastime, the better to tell Paddy-and-Mick stories, and also because it amused us to feel we could talk to the fellows in the pub in their own language, much as some people in London society like to think they can pass themselves off as cockneys in cockney company. But for the speech of anyone in our set to have a pronounced Irish flavour was unusual. This was more commonly to be found among expatriates; especially doctors in England, who appeared to find it a social asset there, and laid it on thick.

Very young children often picked up ferocious local accents from the servants, but in Malahide[4] these did not long survive after they reached the age when they went to the Miss Aherns's junior school, an impeccably English-style establishment. A few yards from it, down the hill, was the Protestant National School, but nobody would have dreamed of sending their children to that. There must have been poor Protestant families in Malahide who sent their children there, but we had no contact with them except in connection with charitable enterprises, when some of them would join in helping to do the heavy work of preparation, discreetly effacing themselves on the actual day of the church fête, or whatever it might be.

I did not go to 'Miss Aherns' because my parents judged it wiser to send me to a boarding-school which catered specially for the children of what were called Anglo-Indian parents — the term in those days simply meant the British in India — in Bexhill.[5] To that extent I was even more anglicized than the Seamount cousins and other Malahide contemporaries who went to 'Miss Aherns' until they were nine. But after that, we were all sent to boarding-schools; and though some of these were in Ireland, they were all on the English prep. school model, and all designed with one essential purpose in mind: to prepare boys to pass the English Common Entrance (the Dragon school, to which I was sent, was far less laboriously English than most of the prep. schools around Dublin). And though at this stage an Irish school was optional, an English public school was almost obligatory. There was only one public school in the Free State, and we would have thought it degrading to be sent there: parents who had little money to spare for their children's education preferred to send them to Portora or Campbell College in Northern Ireland. But most of us were put down for an English school at birth, and sent to it as a matter of course.

And it had to be a good one. To go to one of those schools with names nobody had heard of would have been more disgraceful than not to go to a public school at all. The only recognized exceptions to this rule were boys who could not pass the Common Entrance — stupidity, provided it was set off by social standing or ability at games, was a recognized hazard — and mental deficiency. But a boy had to be very defective indeed not to be sent along with his brothers and friends to normal schools; the act of sending him to a special school would have been a confession of failure, an admission that he was not 'all there'.

For girls, the educational ladder was less rigid; they might even avoid boarding-schools altogether, as there were a few socially acceptable day schools in Dublin. But most of them were sent to English public schools for girls, returning with prissy voices to infuriate us by their conspiratorial giggling at parties.

The end product of this upbringing and education was not readily distinguishable from an Englishman. We shared the same fetishes, and the same taboos — particularly over dress. Most of the same conventions, so rigid that they could better be called compulsions, afflicted us; the bottom waistcoat button was left undone; pyjama tops were rigorously tucked into pyjama bottoms; the unforgivable solecism was a made-up tie. Clothes could be eccentric, but the oddness had to be fashionable: Oxford Bags were for a time permissible, and plus-fours almost obligatory for a golfer aspiring to get his handicap down to scratch. For anybody except the very old or the very rich, though, to dress out of fashion was a sign of crankiness — the sort of thing you would expect from a Trinity student like R.B. MacDowell, the prototype of the

absent-minded professor even in his undergraduate days; or of affectation, as with the Dublin photographer who had no lapels on his jackets and no turn-ups to his trousers. To speculate on the original reason for lapels and turn-ups was one thing; to dispense with them quite another.

With all these barricades, it was easy to cut ourselves off from what was happening around us. I did not even establish the same limited acquaintance with the new Ireland as Terence de Vere White,[6] who was growing up in Portmarnock, three miles away, the next station up on the Dublin line. White has described that childhood in *The Fretful Midge*; in some ways it resembled ours, but it was less constricted. His father was a Unionist, but as legal adviser to the Midland Great Western Railway he could not help being involved to some extent in the changes that followed 1916; his son was brought to Dublin to watch the funeral of Arthur Griffith in the early days of the civil war, and again, two weeks later, to see the funeral of Michael Collins; from which he deduces that his parents could not have been incorrigible in their anti-national prejudices. I do not recall the names of any national leader so much as being mentioned at home, except the Prime Minister, Cosgrave (usually with grudging respect) and de Valera (always with resentment); and certainly nobody would have thought of attending their funerals. Even the assassination of Kevin O'Higgins[7] made little impact; it was never mentioned.

Terence White's mother, too, was a Catholic; going with her to Mass on Sundays brought him into contact with the people of the district in a way that we Malahide Protestants never experienced. And his governess took him to Baldoyle races; only the most hardened racegoers from Malahide attended them, though Baldoyle was less than five miles away, because they were considered rough. Malahiders preferred to wait for the social occasions, Punchestown or Fairyhouse, or not to go to race meetings at all.

Still, many of the symbols White lists of the old order were much the same for both of us. *Punch*, Gilbert and Sullivan, Trinity Week, the Shelbourne Hotel, the Irish Mail at Euston, Fitzwilliam Lawn Tennis Club, Punchestown, the Prince of Wales, Horse Show Week, and Mazawattee Tea. Grandmother would have accepted these, though as she grew older she went to Dublin less often; the Trinity Week–Punchestown–Shelbourne Hotel–Horse Show side of her life, and, as a consequence, of mine, became something we only heard about, or read about in the *Tatler*, which usually had a page of pictures of some race meeting or hunt ball in Ireland.

When my mother was back from India, we used to break with the accepted order sufficiently to go to the Abbey to see one of the early O'Casey's, or the latest Lennox Robinson comedy. She had grown up into a Dublin fermenting with the new theatre of Yeats, Lady Gregory, Synge; of the brothers Fay, Sara Allgood and Maire O'Neill. The Abbey was to her a place to recapture old excitement, not simply somewhere to take English visitors who inconsiderately said they preferred to see something Irish, rather than go to the Gaiety for whatever English production happened to be on there. So I saw the Abbey players, if not at their greatest, at least when the habit of greatness was still with them: Barry Fitzgerald's *Fluther*, Sara Allgood's *Juno*; Maureen Delany's *Bessie Burgess*; F. J. McCormick's *Joxer*. Yet there was always an element of look-at-the-Irish, aren't-they-a-scream! about the performances; I enjoyed them because they were so funny. It took later companies in small back-street theatres with less gifted actors to bring tears.

Still, the Abbey is in my list of symbols; so is the Olympia pantomime. The Seamount cousins always took me to the Gaiety on Boxing Day to see the impeccably English-touring-company pantomime there, too; but it was Jimmy O'Dea (in big letters) and Noel Purcell (in small letters) at the Olympia we most enjoyed, Jimmy's Mrs Mulligan act, taking off the shawlies[8] of the Coombe; and *Dublin Opinion*, making fun of politicians whose names I hardly knew but who obviously deserved to have their legs pulled. So are the Wren Boys, on Boxing Day. They arrived soon after dawn in batches, eccentrically dressed, faces painted, and invariably began:

The wren, the wren, the king of all birds
St Stephen's day was caught in a furse
Although he's little his family's great
Te tum te tum te tum te -ate.

— the last line was usually incoherent. Then, they launched off into 'Daisy, Daisy' or something equally inappropriate; and this was comforting, as it enabled us to tell each other that the efforts to restore Irish 'culture' were obviously getting nowhere, if the village boys could think of nothing better to sing about on Boxing Day (we never called it, as the servants did, St Stephen's Day) than a bicycle made for two.

The State's effort to impose what to us was an alien culture and, worse, an alien language, was almost the only feature of life in the Free State which compelled our attention and aroused our active resentment. I was brought up on Beatrix Potter, Rider Haggard, Ballantyne and Ernest Thompson Seton: on *The Wind in the Willows*, *The Jungle Books*, and *The Just So Stories*; never an Irish tale among them, that I can recall, not even the delightful *Crock of Gold*.[9] Later, George Birmingham and Donn Byrne were the nearest we got to native authors; and as for native poets, the only Irish verse that comes back to me, apart from the lyrics of Percy French, is:

There was an old man called Barney Finnegan
Who grew whiskers on his chinnegan
The wind came out and blew them in again
Poor old Barney Finnegan

Begin again

There was an old man called Barney Finnegan
Climbed up a tree and barked his shinnegan
Tore off yards and yards of skinnegan
Poor old Barney Finnegan.

Begin again

and so on, through as many verses as we cared to improvise on the original base. Probably the work that gave us most pleasure was the *Experiences of an Irish RM*; given the inevitable difference between Malahide and Skebawn, the society portrayed by Somerville and Ross was very similar to our own. Irish literature to us was synonymous with Anglo-Irish literature — Swift, Goldsmith, Burke, Sheridan, Moore, Edgeworth, Wilde, Shaw. The Government's desire to revive what we contemptuously called 'Erse' was consequently a persistent irritant; but there was nothing that could be done to halt it. The signposts we had known all our lives were removed and replaced with new ones bearing the names of towns and villages in Irish as well as English. In some cases, the English name was abolished and an Irish one given sole rights — Queenstown became Cobh and Kingstown, Dun Laoghaire (a particularly grotesque invention, we thought at the time; it was not until many years later that, looking at an old map, I found it was simply a return to the name it had when George IV embarked there after his visit to Ireland a century before).

We continued to call it Kingstown — at least among ourselves; in public it became wiser not to, as to ask for tickets to Kingstown on, say, the No. 8 tram, was apt to bring out the clown in some conductors. 'Kingstown?' they would say, looking up at the roof of the bus, and then down at the floor, 'Kingstown? Now, where would that be? Wait a moment now: I heard of that place once . . . wasn't it in England somewhere . . . no . . .?' and then in mock desperation they would appeal to other passengers, who would tend to take their side; it could be a humiliating experience, for we were no match for them in repartee. All we safely could do was to jeer at newer words like *Telefon*, and later *Aerphort*, as they appeared; desperate expedients to bring Irish into the twentieth century — many of them, I was to find, disliked as much by friends of the language as by its detractors.

But the language continued to spread, onto lavatory entrances and into official correspondence; *A chara* replaced Dear Sir, and *Mise le meas*, Yours sincerely. The introduction of compulsory Irish in the schools caused further concern. Those of us who went to boarding schools in England were not affected; but the threat remained to anybody who might want to come back into his father's office in Dublin as a solicitor, or to become a member of the Irish Bar; as he would require some knowledge of Irish to pass the examinations. Still, at the time this seemed a long way ahead; the language was mentioned only as a subject of ridicule. Other new laws the Free State Government passed had no discernible effect. The new coins, particularly the pig and the hen, brought us in for some banter at school — but also some envy, as did the new stamps; and little inconvenience. And our elders were relieved to find the Free State's finance ministers were impeccably orthodox; they even kept income-tax lower than in England.

The emergence of the new Ireland grated mainly when it touched old sentiment. We hated to stand for the Irish National Anthem, 'The Soldiers' Song'; at private dances we always asked the band to omit it, and play God Save the King instead; and whenever God Save the King was played in public — say, to greet the English army riders at the Horse Show — we sang it so lustily that the Government eventually had to put a ban on it. We relished the story of the Irish peer who, having deserted to the Irish side, tried to keep his hat on and remain seated at the Horse Show when God Save the King had been played; the hat had been knocked off his head, and he had been lifted to his feet by some loyalist in the row behind. But though we felt malicious over this side of the Free State's activities, it was from resentment rather than fear; we were convinced it was a passing phase — that the men in power would eventually come to their senses.

Even when de Valera — de *Val*era, Grandmother called him — came into power in 1932 there was little alarm. His constitutional juggling did not make any visible difference; the Union Jack remained hanging in church, the prayers for the royal family continued; and the rector's sermon on the death of George V[10] was so moving that a formidable parishioner who had refused to take up her usual pitch in charge of the games at the

village fête, after a quarrel with him, relented on hearing it — to our annoyance, as we thought the games would be more free-and-easy without her. The economic war of the thirties might be hard on the farmers, and Grandmother found it a nuisance not to be able to buy some household goods excluded by tariffs or quota restrictions; but on the credit side, de Valera showed himself ready, like Cosgrave before him, to be firm with the I.R.A. extremists; and he made a speech at the League of Nations which had made the delegates even of the big powers sit up and take notice of him, and of Ireland . . .

For, after all, we considered ourselves Irish: not in the patronizing sense with which we thought of the Paddies and Bridies as Irish, but in the sense Shaw used the term in his preface to *John Bull's Other Island*, when he described himself as 'a genuine typical Irishman of the Danish, Norman, Cromwellian, and (of course) Scotch invasions', without a trace of the 'commercially imported Spanish strain which passes for aboriginal Irish'. Grandfather Inglis had been a Scot; and Grandfather Blood was a descendant of that Colonel Thomas Blood whose effort to steal the Crown Jewels is still (or was when I last went there) recorded in the Tower of London — though it is not there stated that he was believed to be stealing them for his master Charles II, in order to pay off some of the royal debts. Whatever the truth of this charge, Colonel Blood had certainly been rewarded with an estate in Clare; and after nearly four hundred years in Ireland his descendants might well consider themselves as Irish. We did. The English were our foes: our keenest pleasure was watching, or reading about, an English XV being trounced at Lansdowne Road.[11] We accepted unquestioningly that the Irish Guards were the most feared fighting force in the world; that Carlisle Bridge (even though it had been renamed O'Connell Bridge) was the only bridge in the world broader than it was long; that Phoenix Park was the biggest city park in the world; that Guinness's was the biggest brewery in the world — and a great many more such myths. To be Irish was something to be proud of. However little I liked the stock jokes about 'Irish temper' at school in England it would never have occurred to me to try to sink my national identity in the crowd, easy though this would have been, as I had no trace of an Irish accent. When a master shouted at me from the touchline, 'Remember Cromwell,' I felt as personally bound to set about demolishing the opposing team — though at the time I had no notion what Cromwell had done to the Irish — as if my family had been insulted, and I was being called upon to avenge them.

The Irishness of our set showed in a variety of ways, but one I particularly recall; Grandmother felt more dislike for the Black and Tans, the emergency force that had been recruited in England to put down Sinn Fein, than she did for the Sinn Feiners themselves. This dislike had been shared by many of her Unionist, a-political friends. At least with the rebels, their argument ran, you had known where you stood, whereas the Black and Tans, recruited by dubious methods — the riff-raff of demobilized regiments, the sweepings of British jails — did not know a Unionist from a Republican, and hardly bothered to try to make the distinction. 'They don't give a damn whether you're a loyal man or not,' as Adolphus Grigson complained in *The Shadow of a Gunman*; 'If you're a Republican they make you sing "God Save the King", and if you're loyal they'll make you sing "The Soldiers' Song".'

We were unaware that anybody could believe we were *not* Irish; and if we had been told that there were actually people, some of them in positions of authority in Dublin, who thought of us as alien parasites, and who made no distinction between us and the British from whom we were descended, it would have seemed a rather bad joke. But Malahide being the place it was,

nobody even hinted as much to us; or if anybody did, we were too self-satisfied to notice. And when the social structure began to disintegrate it was not because of the direct political pressures of that other Ireland, separatist in spirit; but indirectly, as a result of the new economic forces which they had encouraged, stimulating the growth of a new middle class which was not content to be pushed around by old ascendancy.

1 It was Mitford who popularized the terms U and non-U in her book *Noblesse Oblige* (1956). The terms were first used by A.C. Ross in 1954.
2 Character from Shaw's play *Pygmalion* (1914).
3 South Dublin. 'Dublin 4' address. Moore Street is central Dublin.
4 The village where Inglis grew up. Some nine miles north of Dublin.
5 On the Sussex coast in England.
6 See above (p. 628) for an extract from *A Fretful Midge* (1957).
7 He was assassinated in 1927.
8 Poor women who wear shawls.
9 By James Stephens.
10 Died in 1936.
11 A leading sporting venue in Dublin where rugby internationals are played.

FRANK O'CONNOR
from Frank O'Connor, *The Lonely Voice: A Study of the Short Story* (1962)

The Lonely Voice was based on a series of lectures O'Connor gave at Stanford University. In this extract he outlines what has become an often-quoted theory that the short story belongs to submerged population groups. Four decades on, you might like to reconsider O'Connor's thesis in the light of the subsequent history of the short story in general and of the Irish short story in particular.

In fact, the short story has never had a hero. What it has instead is a submerged population group — a bad phrase which I have had to use for want of a better. That submerged population changes its character from writer to writer, from generation to generation. It may be Gogol's officials, Turgenev's serfs, Maupassant's prostitutes, Chekhov's doctors and teachers, Sherwood Anderson's provincials, always dreaming of escape.

'Even though I die, I will in some way keep defeat from you,' she cried, and so deep was her determination that her whole body shook. Her eyes

glowed and she clenched her fists. 'If I am dead and see him becoming a meaningless drab figure like myself, I will come back,' she declared. 'I ask God now to give me that privilege. I will take any blow that may fall if but this my boy be allowed to express something for us both.' Pausing uncertainly, the woman stared about the boy's room. 'And do not let him become smart and successful either,' she added vaguely.

This is Sherwood Anderson, and Anderson writing badly for him, but it could be almost any short-story writer. What has the heroine tried to escape from? What does she want her son to escape from? 'Defeat' — what does that mean? Here it does not mean mere material squalor, though this is often characteristic of the submerged population groups. Ultimately it seems to mean defeat inflicted by a society that has no sign posts, a society that offers no goals and no answers. The submerged population is not submerged entirely by material considerations; it can also be submerged by the absence of spiritual ones, as in the priests and spoiled priests of J.F. Powers's American stories.

Always in the short story there is this sense of outlawed figures wandering about the fringes of society, superimposed sometimes on symbolic figures whom they caricature and echo — Christ, Socrates, Moses. It is not for nothing that there are famous short stories called 'Lady Macbeth of the Mtsensk District' and 'A Lear of the Steppes' and — in reverse — one called 'An Akoulina of the Irish Midlands'. As a result there is in the short story at its most characteristic something we do not often find in the novel — an intense awareness of human loneliness. Indeed, it might be truer to say that while we often read a familiar novel again for companionship, we approach the short story in a very different mood. It is more akin to the mood of Pascal's saying: *Le silence éternel de ces espaces infinis m'effraie.*[1]

I have admitted that I do not profess to understand the idea fully: it is too vast for a writer with no critical or historical training to explore by his own inner light, but there are too many indications of its general truth for me to ignore it altogether. When I first dealt with it I had merely noticed the peculiar geographical distribution of the novel and the short story. For some reason Czarist Russia and modern America seemed to be able to produce both great novels and great short stories, while England, which might be called without exaggeration the homeland of the novel, showed up badly when it came to the short story. On the other hand my own country, which had failed to produce a single novelist, had produced four or five storytellers who seemed to me to be first-rate.

I traced these differences very tentatively, but — on the whole, as I now think, correctly — to a difference

in the national attitude toward society. In America as in Czarist Russia one might describe the intellectual's attitude to society as 'It may work', in England as 'It must work', and in Ireland as 'It can't work'. A young American of our own time or a young Russian of Turgenev's might look forward with a certain amount of cynicism to a measure of success and influence; nothing but bad luck could prevent a young Englishman's achieving it, even today; while a young Irishman can still expect nothing but incomprehension, ridicule, and injustice. Which is exactly what the author of *Dubliners* got.

The reader will have noticed that I left out France, of which I know little, and Germany, which does not seem to have distinguished itself in fiction. But since those days I have seen fresh evidence accumulating that there was some truth in the distinctions I made. I have seen the Irish crowded out by Indian storytellers, and there are plenty of indications that they in their turn, having become respectable, are being outwritten by West Indians like Samuel Selvon.

Clearly, the novel and the short story, though they derive from the same sources, derive in a quite different way, and are distinct literary forms; and the difference is not so much formal (though, as we shall see, there are plenty of formal differences) as ideological. I am not, of course, suggesting that for the future the short story can be written only by Eskimos and American Indians: without going so far afield, we have plenty of submerged population groups. I am suggesting strongly that we can see in it an attitude of mind that is attracted by submerged population groups, whatever these may be at any given time — tramps, artists, lonely idealists, dreamers, and spoiled priests. The novel can still adhere to the classical concept of civilized society, of man as an animal who lives in a community, as in Jane Austen and Trollope it obviously does; but the short story remains by its very nature remote from the community — romantic, individualistic, and intransigent.

---

1   The eternal silence of these infinite spaces scares me.

KATE O'BRIEN
from Kate O'Brien, *My Ireland* (1962)

Kate O'Brien's venomous description of Dublin has more than a grain of truth. She makes Dublin in part resemble Madrid *vis-à-vis* the rest of Spain – as the unjustified centre of power, with well-heeled civil servants, and a smart set, snobbish, superior, unattractive. And for her support she turns to Joyce: 'For certainly it is not among the smart, the watchful, the authoritative ones, that a stranger would find the city that has been immortalized [by Joyce]'.

Dublin

I wonder if a capital city, seeing what its meaning and function is, could ever seem to represent humaneness, or collective peace of mind, or plain equity attempted? I believe not. A great city may, indeed must, contain secretions of these natural ideas, but being a city and therefore rich and concerned with richness, it cannot as a whole compose into an expression of the good life. And Dublin is far too small and too sociable of spirit to be able at all to hide stripes and seams of misery. The sins lie all about; and they are the world's usual sins of greed and hard-heartedness and inertia — and like all the cities of the world, she is aware of her guilt, and in common with them, of course, makes civic gestures and efforts. And we who stroll about, strangers and outsiders, inhaling the keen, bright air and the flickering gaiety of the town, are no great shakes at sociology, nor do we come visiting either from Utopia or Arcady. So we may even catch ourselves laughing quite coldly, say in beautiful, filthy York Street, as we are stung to the cynical realization that here in this small, intimate city the poor we have always with us; for it is true. And what can we do about it? After lunch at *The Russell* — and yesterday we discovered how good that can be — there is, perhaps, the Book of Kells to examine, or the Lane Collection?[1] Or we can drive out to Howth or down to Kildare to the National Stud, or go and look at that new young fellow's stained glass in Dawson Street. Or, the afternoon could pass indeed in quiet drinking and soft talk — if the stranger has a right guide, in some 'snug' near the river, mahogany and brass, and a name and address well known, it might be, to Leopold Bloom. For there is only the 'Holy Hour' of abstinence, and though that must pass quietly, with voices muted, friends need not break apart for it in Dublin, nor need glasses stand empty in every place.

It is the Top People of a period, I suppose, that give any city its dominant characteristic. No matter about the ordinary citizens, poor, or less poor, or scrupu-lously solvent — it is the Top People (a very vulgar descriptive phrase for a very vulgar social concept) who settle the tone of their city for the idly staring world. In Paris there is the *le tout Paris*, in London this *Top People* thing, in New York the Ivy League and the Social Register, and much lower down, but very influential, Café Society, the gossip column lot.

Dublin, for its size, has the most remarkably mixed set of Top People that anyone could expect to see anywhere. The place being small and having only a few 'correct' stamping grounds it is easy for the unobtrusive observer to get the form. Easy to catch, but could Balzac write it down? Ah, indeed he could. I believe he would have found much, very much, material in Dublin. I have never been a total Balzacien, because his insistence on the money-theme has crowded out passions and principles that interest me far more and that I know to be strong in certain types and in all societies. But in Dublin he would have had right of way, I think. And perhaps when I say that I explain to myself two things — why I have never been sold on Balzac, and why I have never loved, or even perhaps liked, Dublin.

Top Society is a mixum-gatherum expressing various values which have by now succeeded in imposing a peculiar, old-fashioned kind of *chic*. I mean, the elements of taste and manners are so mixed, town and country are so criss-crossed in its vogues, and the horse and horsiness achieve in Ireland so odd a poetry — a grace, an accent of design and tradition undreamt in England — that sheer originality, that is to say, innocence, shines suddenly down, one thinks, and fixes the social picture all by itself. It is stripped thus of commonplaceness — and its zigzagging pattern of what Nancy Mitford and company call U and non-U is not only delightful to analyse but suggests power, and even a kind of mystery. For taste and no-taste, education and ignorance, pursiness, bohemianism, wit, bigotry and sheer wildness, are making for better and worse a ruling caste in Dublin. This caste, which shouts about the dear, tolerant Shelbourne, for instance, on important bright mornings such as of Fairyhouse or Punchestown, is a conspired association — it is the ruling set that Dublin peculiarly required and peculiarly got. And it takes and elects its components from everything — from all walks and pursuits of life, and mixes them quite merrily and affectionately together. A ha'porth of all sorts (but only in the most metaphorical way of speaking, because nothing to be reckoned in halfpence would have brought them to this), they make a bright and versatile top decoration, effulgently *baroque*, their elements whirling needlessly and arrogantly together and apart — a great display of facile and good-natured inter-mingling between incompatibles, improbables — one might have said. But, you see, one would be wrong. For here is a society, pace-making and standard-setting, which has formed itself simply and quickly by the upside-down and, I think, accidental process of forgetting or eliminating — or letting immediate history do the forgetting — of any of the rules, taboos, snobberies, obligations, or *idées fixes* which have hitherto and in other places controlled the establishment of an upper Ten, a Brahmin caste, a Faubourg. Dublin has settled — shrewdly and sensibly enough — for an all-in Top Lot. But how can such a thing be? If from rag-picker to cardinal we are all potential leaders of society — and we are — how can any rule at all be arrived at?

Dublin has picked the simplest rule — and made it absolute. You can be anything you like within her Four Hundred — but, you must be a successful person. That is all. Successful in the plainest and commonest sense — that you make, and spend, a very great deal of hard cash in pursuit of whatever you do, and that your name is very often in the papers. That is the simple regulation which keeps the ruling class down to a very manageable, neat, proportion in Dublin; it might also seem to threaten that class with monotony, but in practice this is not so — since where every kind of creature is eligible, from duke to jockey, variety and comedy are non-stop, and easily observed from the sidelines in any decently expensive public place.

What I am trying to catch in description — present-day Dublin 'Society' — is in fact, if in microcosm, an eliminatory and absolutely simplified arrangement — illustrating, let me suggest to Proustians for their astonishment, that pathetic ultimate of levelled-up snobbery which is revealed to have come to pass in the Faubourg at the last

Guermantes reception, from which the Narrator walked away, to begin his book.

And it is notable that in consideration of this Dublin it is Proust who comes to mind — not Joyce. For certainly it is not among the smart, the watchful, the authoritative ones, that a stranger would find the city that has been immortalized. Not indeed near Cadillacs and Mercedes, minks and vicunas, not at greedily crowded auctions of 'antiques' nor in exotically shrubbed gardens of the suburbs, behind 'Spanish' gates or in 'luxury hotels' — idiotic phrase! — not at all amid this that has happened to the greedy capital, would anyone attempt to move through 'Bloomsday'. But those who know their text will know that. And if they begin with Eccles Street and Glasnevin Cemetery, and move here and there on foot and alone for awhile on a summer morning they will be safe. And while they are finding Joyce's Dublin, peaceably — in an 'ah yes!' recognitive daze — they will find Dublin itself as well. The plain, the unimagined city, the unsung. The place he used and pulled and thrust at, and then kicked aside in absentminded satisfaction when his own city was at last founded and forever built. That the tourist takes about with him safely in a heavy book — and the other, the source-place, will distract him from it constantly, and vividly, during his long walk so that he will begin to pursue and enjoy a hundred irrelevancies of the wild and witty North side, and even begin to be sorry for Joyce, the relentless, blind exile. And when long stretches back from Belvedere and over to Capel Street get him at last on to the summer-hot quays, if he is surprised by the chromium and scarlet of the Ormond Bar, he will have learnt to take it as he finds it now — and be glad of the refreshment it offers to his piety. At another time, when he is less in thirst, and far away, he will turn to the heavy book. '. . . greeting in going, past eyes and maidenhair, bronze and faint gold in deepseashadow, went Bloom, soft Bloom . . .'[2]

1   A nephew of Lady Gregory and an art collector, Hugh Lane (1875–1915) proposed to lend his collection of paintings to Dublin City if a suitable building was provided by the City Council. This was not forthcoming so he withdrew the offer and removed the paintings to London. However, in an unwitnessed codicil to his will he relented, but the National Gallery in London retained them until 1960 when an accommodation was reached between the National Gallery and the Municipal Gallery in Dublin to allow the collection to be shared by the two cities.

2   From the Sirens episode of Ulysses, an episode which begins with bronze and gold in the Ormond Hotel (see p. 335 above).

JOHN MONTAGUE

from *The Spectator*, 26 April 1963

This is a keenly felt description by John Montague (1929–   ), ever conscious of the political reality behind sociological description, of the village in County Tyrone where he grew up and the changes it was undergoing. In *The Rough Field* (1972) he transformed these memories into a poem with an epic reach, and one of these poems 'A Lost Tradition' is reproduced below (p. 853).

The Rough Field

The parish in which I was brought up lies in Tyrone, what the poet John Hewitt once called 'the heart land of Ulster'. A seventeenth-century survey, on the other hand, describes it as 'cold mountainous land', which is probably why it escaped resettling at the time of the Plantation. Across the road from the house stood the crumbling remains of stables, a halt on the old Dublin-Derry coach-road. And, with its largely Catholic population (MacRory, MacGirr, Farrel, O'Tague), Errigal Kieran could still be taken for a parish in Southern Ireland, artificially marooned. Most of the place names were pure Gaelic: Garvaghey (The Rough Field), Glencull (The Glen of the Hazels), Clogher (The Golden Stone).

But there were differences. The post-van which came down the road was still royal red, with a gold crown on either side. The postman himself was an ex-serviceman who remembered Ypres and the Somme, instead of the eighteenth day of November.[1] In school we learnt how to put out a fire in the Tower of London, or the chief industries of Manchester, but very little about Cuchulain or Connemara. And none of the farmers had enough Gaelic even to translate the names of the townlands. A dark-faced fanatical priest tried to teach us Gaelic after school hours. I thought him a fearsome bore until I greeted the last native speaker in the area after Mass one Sunday, and saw the light flood across her face.

The ordinary life of the people, however, took little stock of racial or religious differences: they were submerged in a pre-industrial farming pattern, where the important thing was 'neighbourliness'. True, there were social differences which betrayed the historical cleavage. The depressed class of farm labourers were largely Catholic, just as the majority of the stronger farmers were Protestant. There were also the sexual fantasies which emerge when, as in the American South, two cultures rub uneasily together. Pedigree bulls were mainly owned by Protestants: in fact, there was a curious legend that Catholic bulls were rarely as

potent. And when I went to fetch the local gelder it seemed oddly appropriate that he should take down his cloth-covered weapon from beside a stack of black family Bibles.

But in the seasonal tasks which pushed the wheel of the year, the criterion was skill, based on traditional practice. Turf-cutting, which began in late spring, revealed all the instinctive layers of a craft. First, there was the stripping of the bank, the rough sods being saved for the back of a fire. Then the three-man team moved in, one to cut (using the traditional *slane* or flanged spade), one to fill (grasping the wet turves in rows) and one to wheel (emptying the barrow sideways so that the turf fell uncrushed, but open to the sun, while still managing to be back for the next fill). At meal-time they sat around the basket in a circle, their hobnailed boots shining with wet, and talked of great teams of the past.

But turf-cutting was not as delicate a job as building a corn- or hay-stack. To begin with, a circle of stones and whins was laid, to 'let the air in'. Upon this the stack rose, the builder riding with it, catching and placing the sheaves, until he climbed down to complete the conical roof of thatch. One of our farmhands, slovenly enough in other matters, was regarded as a master builder: his eyes gleamed as he combed and roped his kraal of stacks. In the winter, when the thresher came, they unpeeled, in smooth slivers, like an orange.

Such tasks determined the character of the people, hard-working, frugal, escaping the traditional view of the Celt. Kitchens were generally well lit, with a dresser of shining delf along one wall, a curtained-off settle bed along another, a shotgun or fiddle resting on a third. But the centre was the great blackened tent of the hearth, where the crook swung, supporting a hierarchy of pots and pans. A three-legged stool or creepie (reserved for the very old or the very young) stood in the ingle-nook. From the fire to the dairy, with its meal bins and churns, the farmer's wife bustled, until the men came tramping in for a meal.

The hearth was also the focus of the strongest custom in Ulster farming life, the habit of dropping in, after milking-time, for a visit or *ceilidh*. One rarely knocked, one's approach being heralded by the dog's bark, the shadow crossing the window. Sometimes a worn pack of cards was produced, for a game of 'twenty-five'. Sometimes a song was called for, but the district was not rich in balladry, except for a version of the north-country 'Barbary Allen' and one or two local patriotic songs, like 'The Mountains of Pomeroy'. But the main interest of the evening was talk, seemingly casual, endless, probing.

It was at such moments that one touched the secret life of the countryside. Starting from practical details, the conversation threw a rich web of speculation over local affairs: who was 'failing fast', who was going to give birth (inside or outside the blanket), who was threatening law. Fact soon dissolved into fancy: how so-and-so had broken his leg after ploughing down a fairy thorn, how 'a b—— Special's hair'[2] had turned white because he held up a priest on his way to a dying man, how old Frank McGirk had the cure for ringworm or sprain, how Fr X had put a troublesome ghost in a bottle.

For behind the flat surface of daily life beat memories of a richer, more resonant past, half-regretted, half-feared. When I was about five I remember going to my first wake and seeing the neat row of clay pipes beside the snuff and porter. By the time I was going to secondary school my aunt had given up plaiting the rushy St Brigid's crosses which used to hang over the lintel in kitchen and byre. Even barn dances were becoming a thing of the past, though I remember one in the Fintona area a few years ago where, climbing to speak to the local fiddler, I fell straight through the loft into a nest of squealing pigs.

For a long time this older form of life survived in the remote areas, under the shadow of the mountains. But, since the war,[3] the rate of change has become relentless. The replacing of the hearth fire by a stove dealt a blow not merely to turf-cutting and breadmaking (most farmers' wives now buy theirs), but also to the practice of *ceilidh*-ing. The battery wireless was an endearingly faulty messenger from outside, but with the arrival of electric light and television the Rough Field has become a part of the twentieth century. The old coach-road is now a magnificent highway, running straight as a die through the built-up valley. The local public-house, surrounded by cars, looks like a road-house; the local shop sells ice-cream to children from the prefabricated village where the road workers and lorry drivers (formerly farm labourers) live.

But one must avoid seeing all this in a haze of Golden Age nostalgia. The last time I was back I was talking to a local farmer (of good Northumbrian origin) in his byre. Behind us the milking-machine hummed, the pan and cylinders swaying under the cow's udder. He was lamenting the decline of neighbourliness in the area, how the young had no time for anything but cars and dance halls. Then a sudden smile crossed his face, and he told how the oldest woman in the district had come down to look at his television set. 'She had a stick in either hand, and her crippled over like a hoop. She came into the kitchen — we had to pull back the dogs from her — and said she be to see the picture box. She sat in front of it, for an hour, and then she rose to go, saying that a wee man you could turn on like that would be a great comfort on a cold winter's night.'

1　A puzzle. In the slightly revised version Montague inserts 1916 before this date, so I assume it belongs to a nationalist history. Wolfe Tone, leader of the United Irishmen, died on 19 November 1798.
2　A reference to the B Specials, an Ulster Protestant part-time police force disbanded in April 1970 because of its sectarian character.
3　The Second World War.

CONOR CRUISE O'BRIEN
from A. Norman Jeffares and K.G.W. Cross (eds.), *In Excited Reverie: A Centenary Tribute to William Butler Yeats 1865–1939* (1965)

Conor Cruise O'Brien (1917–), politician, historian, writer, was one of the most remarkable intellectuals to be produced in modern Ireland. His books include *Parnell and his Party* (1957), *States of Ireland* (1972) and *The Great Melody* (1992). His essay on Yeats's politics is among the most famous essays written about the great poet, written by someone inside the culture arguing a particular line. For further discussion of Yeats's politics see my *W. B. Yeats: Critical Assessments*, 4 vols. (2000).

from **Passion and Cunning: An Essay on the Politics of W.B. Yeats**

Comment on the question of Yeats's attitude to Fascism has been bedevilled by the assumption that a great poet must be, even in politics, 'a nice guy'. If this be assumed then it follows that, as Yeats obviously was a great poet, he cannot *really* have favoured Fascism, which is obviously not a nice cause. Thus the critic or biographer is led to postulate a 'true Yeats', so that Yeats's recorded words and actions of Fascist character must have been perpetrated by some bogus person with the same name and outward appearance.[1]

If one drops the assumption, about poets having always to be nice in politics, then the puzzle disappears, and we see, I believe, that Yeats the man was as near to being a Fascist as his situation and the conditions of his own country permitted. His unstinted admiration had gone to Kevin O'Higgins,[2] the most ruthless 'strong man' of his time in Ireland, and he linked his admiration explicitly to his rejoicing at the rise of Fascism in Europe — and this at the very beginning, within a few weeks of the March on Rome. Ten years later, after Hitler had moved to the centre of the political stage in Europe, Yeats was trying to create a movement in Ireland which would be overtly Fascist in language, costume, behaviour and intent. He turned his back on this movement when it began to fail, not before. Would the irony and detachment of this phase of disillusion have lasted if a more effective Fascist leader and movement had later emerged? One may doubt it. Many in Germany who were 'disillusioned' by the failure of the Kapp *putsch* and the beer-cellar *putsch* were speedily 'reillusioned' when Hitler succeeded — and 'disillusioned' again when he lost the war.

Post-war writers, touching with embarrassment on Yeats's pro-Fascist opinions, have tended to treat these as a curious aberration of an idealistic but ill-informed poet. In fact such opinions were quite usual in the Irish Protestant middle-class to which Yeats belonged (as well as in other middle-classes), in the 'twenties and 'thirties. The *Irish Times*, spokesman of that class, aroused no protest from its readers when it hailed Hitler (4 March 1933) as 'Europe's standard bearer against Muscovite terrorism' and its references to Mussolini were as consistently admiring as those to Soviet Russia were consistently damning. But the limiting factor on the pro-Fascist tendencies of the *Irish Times* and of the Irish Protestant middle-class generally was the pull of loyalty to Britain — a factor which did not apply — or applied only with great ambivalence — in the case of Yeats. Mr T.R. Henn is

quite right when he says that Yeats was 'not alone in believing at that moment of history, that the discipline of Fascist theory might impose order upon a disintegrating world'. I cannot follow Mr Henn, however, to his conclusion that 'nothing could be further from Yeats's mind than [Fascism's] violent and suppressive practice' (*The Lonely Tower*, p. 467). 'Force, marching men' and 'the victory [in civil war] of the skilful, riding their machines as did the feudal knights their armoured horses' (*On the Boiler*),[3] surely belong to the domain of violent and suppressive practice.

Just as one school is led to claim that the pro-Fascist Yeats was not the 'true' Yeats, so another tries to believe that the Fascism to which Yeats was drawn was not a 'true' Fascism.

Several critics have assured us that he was drawn not really to Fascism, but to some idealized aristocracy of eighteenth-century stamp. 'In all fairness,' writes Dr Vivian Mercier, 'we should allow that his views were closer to Hamilton's or even to Jefferson's than they were to Mussolini's.'[4] As far as political theory is concerned this is probably correct — although the name of Swift would seem more relevant than that of Hamilton or of Jefferson. But it ignores one important reality: that Yeats was interested in contemporary politics and that he was a contemporary, not of Swift's or Jefferson's, but of Mussolini's.

He would certainly have preferred something more strictly aristocratic than Fascism, but since he was living in the twentieth century he was attracted to Fascism as the best available form of anti-democratic theory and practice. Mr Frank O'Connor, who knew him well in his last years and — politics apart — greatly admired and liked him, has told us plainly that 'he was a fascist and authoritarian, seeing in world crises only the break-up of the "damned liberalism" he hated'.[5]

George Orwell, though critical, and up to a point percipient, about Yeats's tendencies, thought that Yeats misunderstood what an authoritarian society would be like. Such a society, Orwell pointed out, 'will not be ruled by noblemen with Van Dyck faces, but by anonymous millionaires, shiny-bottomed bureaucrats and murderous gangsters'. This implies a degree of innocence in Yeats which cannot reasonably be postulated. O'Higgins and O'Duffy[6] were not 'Duke Ercole and Guidobaldo', and Yeats had considerable experience of practical politics, both in the 'nineties and in the early 'twenties. 'In the last forty years,' wrote J.M. Hone in the year of Yeats's death, 'there was never a period in which his countrymen did not regard him as a public figure.'[7] When he thought of rule by an *élite*, it was a possible *élite*, resembling in many ways the nominated members of the Senate in which he had sat. Its membership — bankers, organizers, ex-officers — would correspond roughly to what Orwell, in more emotive language, describes. Nor should it be assumed — as Orwell with his 'murderous gangsters' seems to imply — that the sensitive nature of the poet would necessarily be revolted by the methods of rule of an authoritarian state. Yeats — unlike, say, his brother, or Lady Gregory — was not, in politics, a very squeamish person. Seventy-seven executions did not repel him; on the contrary, they made him admire O'Higgins all the more. At least one of his associates of the early 'thirties might have been described as a 'murderous gangster'. And when, in 1936, Ethel Mannin appealed to him for a gesture which would have helped the German writer, Ossietzki, then in a Nazi concentration camp, Yeats refused. 'Do not,' he said, 'try to make a politician of me . . .'

It is true that neither Yeats nor anyone else during Yeats's lifetime knew what horrors Fascism would be capable of. But the many who, like Yeats, were drawn to Fascism at this time knew, and seemed to have little difficulty in accepting, or at least making allowances for, much of what had already been done and continued to be done. 'The Prussian police,' wrote the *Irish Times* in an editorial of February 1933, 'have been authorized by Herr Hitler's Minister to shoot Communists — a term which in Germany has a wide political connotation — on sight.' The same editorial which contained this information ended with the words: 'Naturally the earlier phases of this renascence are crude, but Germany is finding her feet after a long period of political ineptitude.'

Yeats read the newspapers; he also read, as Hone records, several books on Fascist Italy and Nazi Germany.[8] If, then, he was attracted to the dominant movements in these countries, and if he supported a movement in his own country whose resemblances to these Continental movements he liked to stress, it cannot be contended that he did so in ignorance of such 'crude' practices as the *Irish Times* described.

Some writers — notably Professor Donald Torchiana in his well-documented study 'W. B. Yeats, Jonathan Swift and Liberty'[9] — have insisted that, in spite of Yeats's authoritarian and Fascist leanings, he was essentially a friend of liberty. 'Both Swift and

Yeats,' Torchiana concludes, 'served human liberty.' The senses in which this is true for Yeats are important but clearly limited. He defended the liberty of the artist, consistently. In politics, true to his duality, he defended the liberty of Ireland against English domination, and the liberty of his own caste — and sometimes, by extension, of others — against clerical domination. Often these liberties overlapped, and the cause of artist and aristocrat became the same; often his resistance to 'clerical' authoritarianism (his position on the Lock-out, on divorce, on censorship) makes him appear a liberal. But his objection to clerical authoritarianism is not the liberal's objection to *all* authoritarianism. On the contrary he favours 'a despotism of the educated classes' and in the search for this, is drawn towards Fascism. It is true that Fascism was not in reality a despotism of the educated classes, but it was a form of despotism which the educated classes in the 'twenties and 'thirties showed a disposition to settle for — a disposition proportionate to the apparent threat, in their country, of Communism or 'anarchy'. In assessing Yeats's pro-Fascist opinions, there is no need to regard these as so extraordinary that he must either not have been himself, or not have known what he was about.

1   (There is a sense of course in which the poet, actually engaged in writing his poetry, is 'the true Yeats', but that is another matter.) [AN]
2   When the Irish Free State came into existence in 1922 Kevin O'Higgins (1892–1927) became Minister for Economic Affairs, then Minister for Justice and External Affairs and Vice-president of the Executive Council. A tough politician and much admired by Yeats, during the Civil War he was responsible for the execution of 77 Republicans. He was assassinated in July 1927 while on his way to Mass in Booterstown.
3   Yeats's last thoughts on eugenics and related matters can be found in *On the Boiler* (1939).
4   'To Pierce the Dark Mind', *Nation* (10 December 1960). [AN]
5   'The Old Age of a Poet', *The Bell* (February 1941). [AN]
6   General O'Duffy (1892–1944) was leader of the Blue Shirts, an Irish fascist organization formed in the summer of 1933.
7   'Yeats as a Political Philosopher', *London Mercury* (April, 1939). [AN]
8   Joseph Hone, *W.B. Yeats: 1865–1939* (London: Macmillan, 1942), p. 467. [AN]
9   *Modern Philosophy* (August 1963). [AN]

RIVERS CAREW and TIMOTHY BROWNLOW
from *The Dublin Magazine* (1965)

This editorial attempts to take the pulse of cultural life north and south of the border. The issue of Belfast v. Dublin as cultural centre of Ireland, and the early mention of Seamus Heaney and Michael Longley as new poets on the literary scene make for interesting reading from today's perspective.

Editorial

At present there are some indications that concern for the imaginative life of the community is increasing both in the Republic and in the North of Ireland. If anything, this development is more noticeable in the North than it is here. Already the theatre is more vigorous in Belfast than in Dublin, where between one Theatre Festival and the next stretches an almost waterless desert; and the recent announcement of plans for a new theatre complex for Belfast promises to widen the gap in favour of the North. A Belfast literary quarterly, *The Northern Review*, commenced publication last spring, and while the contents of its first issue were unremarkable we were impressed by the lavishness with which it was produced. A further sign of Northern activity occurred at the beginning of November, when two booklets of poems by Michael Longley and Seamus Heaney reached us. These are the first two issues in a series published under the auspices of the Festival Society, Queen's University. Seven other issues are already projected. We hope to review these booklets in future editions of *The Dublin Magazine*.

We do not mention these developments out of a chauvinistic fear of seeing Belfast making a successful bid for the position of Ireland's cultural capital; amiable rivalry provides a stimulus that should be generally welcome. Besides, Dublin still equals or is ahead of Belfast in certain respects; in music, for example, though there is some irony in the reflection that but for the assassination of President Kennedy we would probably still be waiting for the Government to recognize our sore need for a concert hall. For a long time we have had one public-spirited publisher in the Dolmen Press, and at present there is a good deal of promising literary activity. In the hope of stimulating this further, *The Dublin Magazine* intends for the future to include an essay on a living Irish writer in each issue and also, whenever suitable opportunities occur, brief articles on current events in the arts.

Apart from the possibility of taking wrong directions, however, the principal danger that literature in the Republic has to face today is less lack of talent than complacency and inactivity. We have many great achievements in the past of which to be proud, but past glories do not excuse stagnation in the present. The tree lives not only by its roots, but also by the leaves which it puts forth. It is the responsibility of those among us who are engaged in creative activities not to allow whatever gifts we have to lie fallow, nor to let them bleed to death, Dublin fashion, in a continual haemorrhage of talk. For in each generation the arts, which are the custodians of the imagination, must be renewed or they will die; and a community whose imagination is dead is dead indeed.

MICHAEL J. MURPHY
from Michael J. Murphy, 'Four Folktales About Women' in *Ulster Folklife* (1967)

The folklorist Michael Murphy collected this story from a south Armagh man who had been a pedlar and navvy in England and who was an excellent mimic of English speech. A spike is a slang word, formerly for a workhouse, now for a night shelter. For the student of literature this extract is a useful reminder of the constant need to listen to the way language is spoken.

A Long Night in the Spike

'Somewhere in England I have a son an' he's not a drops blood to me. There's not a word o' lie in what I'm goin' to tell yous. It's all down in black an' white in England wherever they keep these things written down: about me an' me son I mean.

'It was somewhere near the south of England. I was on a navvyin' job an' when it wound up I was footin' it on Shanks' mare. An' comin' on night I headed for the Spike in this town, a town something the size of Newry here. Talk about rain! The heavens opened in the evenin' an' it come down in lumps. Not a dry stitch on me when I got to the foot of the hill leadin' to the Spike on the edge of this town. It was around this time o' year too, at the fall of the leaf. Poor shelter. But wet as I was there come this unmerciful cloudburst an' I had to find what shelter I could under a tree.

'Not a sinner to be seen. I was wet, I was cold, I was wall-fallin' with hunger. An' then, in the light of the street lamp — all gas-lamps then — I seen this woman. In thon rain the light was little better than a moon behind mist. But I could see she was a tight butt of a woman with a bit of a body about her: in a coat and a big hat. She was as wet as meself an' she stood in-under the tree too.

'"It's 'rum old night," she says; an English woman. Around thirty or so, the same age as meself at the time. Then she says to me: "Are you for the Spike?"

'I said I was, and the way she asked I knew she was headin' there herself.

'Next she says, "Ever been in this Spike before, chum?"

'I said I never had, not tellin' a word o' lie, and she says: "It's not a bad one for the married blokes. When they've got the missus with them that is."

'That wasn't news to me either. Spikes is good or bad — accordin' to who runs them an' to their rules. Rules in Spikes? Aw, bedad they have rules alright, as you'll soon hear.

'The rain eased up a bit an' the two of us set off up the hill to the Spike. She walked foot for foot with me, right off the road an' up the avenue. Then she says:

"Tell you what, chum. What's wrong with you sayin' I'm your better half — your missus, you know. It'll mean better grub an' a better doss for the night for both of us. Whatcha say?"

'Well, it was six of one an' half a dozen of the other to me. I'd be on me way in the mornin' an' so would she. So I said "Fair enough." She asked me me name an' I told her: Shan McAlavey.

'There was a porter to let you in. He was asleep when we got there an' had half a mind not to let us in at all. Many a long, weary hour after I wished he hadn't. But the Englishwoman tongued him word for word an' he got out the book an' took down our names. The two of us trooped on into the body of the house. And we weren't our lone let me tell you. There was a good fire an' they gave us porridge to ate; the sort that'd run a mile on a deal board an' never leave a trace of the oatmeal. But we lapped it up an' damn glad to get it.

'I dried meself as best I could. Then she went her way to her quarters an' me to mine. I rolled into bed an' slept as snug as a bug in a rug till mornin'. Oh, a lovely bright sunny mornin' after a night of rain. Got up. Got a bite o' breakfast. Had a bit of a smoke. Stretched meself to get the life back into me bones, an' then I set off for out an' away.

'I only got as far as the door when this man stopped me; a sort of a workhouse master's-under-strapper, a big bruiser; the sort that looked as if he got his fill to ate, an' his time to take it.

'"Goin' somewhere?" says he.

'I said "Nowhere in particular": I'd make up me mind as I went along.

'"Come here, Jack," says he, and caught hold of me like a polissman. Me name as you know is Shan, not Jack; but when you have your hand in the dog's mouth the easiest way you get it out the better. He pointed to the rules hangin' on the wall. An' sure I told him that I couldn't read — an' to put me foot further in it, I told him 'twas the wife was the scholar in our family.

'So he said he'd read the rules for me. An' he did. The husband had to stay an' work a month hard for every week his wife stayed in the Spike. (Rules of the house). I began to smell a rat, but thought it better to act the greenhorn, the innocent fella that knows nothin'. An' says I to him:

'"You're a decent man, an' I can tell you come of clean an' decent people, an' isn't it you that has the learnin'. Tell her," says I, "to follow me. I'll walk easy."

'Says this big bruiser; "You're not walkin' anywhere, Jack. Not for a while anyhow. Your missus ain't walkin' either. What sort of a bloomin' man are you? Didn't you know? Your wife gave birth to a baby boy last night an' she'll be weeks here."

'You coulda knocked me down with a feather. I felt as weak as water. I lost me breath. When I got it back I started in me own mind to call her all the oul' . . . Alright, alright, I'll not say it before you good decent people. (Maybe she's dead now anyhow an' needs prayers instead.) But I says to meself: "May the divil roast her, an' double-roast me for lettin' her trap me.

Her lyin' up here an' livin' on the fat o' the land for three weeks or a month, an' me havin' to slave for her, workin' a month again every week she's here. But take it easy, McAlavey," says I to meself; "nothin's bad that couldn't be worse. You're not bet yet."

'The workhouse master's-under-strapper was turnin' over the book, an' he says to me: "No occupation down here. What are you?"

'Says I nice an' innocent: "I'm a melodeon musicianer, sir. It's the only trade I was taught to follow."

'He looked at me as much as to say you're a liar — an' he was right — an' he closed the book an' threw it down an' took me like a warder be the arm.

'"Right, Jack," says he. "Melodeon musicianer?"

'He led me out of the Spike into a big yard alongside the avenue. There was a few fellows there breakin' stones for the roads. He led me to a heap of rocks, every one the size of a table. He pointed to a sledge-hammer with a head on it bigger than many a railway waggon I've seen. And then says he to me:

'"There's the rock an' there's the sledge. Melodeon musicianer are you? Take whatever sort of music you like out of them rocks!"

'I failed away to scrapings in them three weeks, for I was out there hail, rain, blow or snow, breakin' the rocks. An' not a sign of thon targer[1] of a woman of

mine makin' a shape to leave the Spike. But this mornin' — here she comes, an' this child in her arms, an' the pair of them dickied up to the ninety-nines. An' I could see I'd have to work extra to pay for the fancy rig-out for the baby an' her too. You wouldn't get the time o' day for nothin' in thon Spike. Over three months I'd have to stay sledgin' the stones. I got as mad as forty cats in a bag. But I says to meself: "I won't gratify her to let on I know her at all." An' I started to make the sledge ring on the rocks, thinkin' she'd pass by an' wouldn't see me. But she seen me alright. When she comes abreast of where I was — what does the flamer do? She holds the baby the length of her two arms and she says:

'"Say toodle-oo to Daddy, son!" To a babby that couldn't talk mind you — Oh, a flamer! "Say toodle-oo to Daddy."

'What did I do . . . .? Sure what could I do? I could be unmannerly an' say nothin', but that'd be far off the way I was reared. An' sure it never made sense to bite your tongue for spite when you've scalded yourself drinkin' soup. So I held up me sledge like a decent Daddy should an' I shook it at them an' says I:

'"Toodle-oo, son . . . . Toodle-oo . . . . !"'

---

1. One who scolds someone, overbearing.

ANTHONY BURGESS
from *The Spectator*, 7 June 1969

The novelist Anthony Burgess (1917–93) was born in Manchester into an Irish Catholic family. He never outgrew his fascination with the Irish Catholic Joyce and always wrote with quickened interest about the culture they shared.

The Reticence of Ulysses

I write this from Malta, which has been identified by some with the island of Ogygia, where Ulysses was detained for seven years by the goddess Calypso (if Ogygia was not Malta, it must have been the subsidiary islet of Gozo). I am exiled from England for a year, so I can only imagine the pleasure with which Joyceans have been able to see the novel *Ulysses*, in its Penguin format, put forth like flowers all over England. Here in Malta we are unlikely to have this ten-shilling people's edition. The censorship is very

powerful, and it even had a nibble at one of my own blameless works, a novel praised for its eschatological content by the Jesuit periodical *The Month*. Admittedly, it was the French translation of the book that the censors pored over, there being something essentially obscene about French. But Desmond Morris, owner of one of Malta's finest mansions, found the censors intransigent over his own *The Naked Ape*, Malta being the only country of the free world unwilling to admit it.

Some of us are becoming angry with the censorship. The university librarian has complained publicly that certain technical works, needed for the department of psychology, have been impounded. The other week, *Life* magazine came to us with loving felt-pen hatching-over of certain anatomical commonplaces in photographs of a production of a Greek tragedy. The bookshops are full of Denise Robins, Malta, which got the George Cross for bravery, must be protected from *Life*, life.

This is not really my point, except in so far as Malta reminds me of England at the time when I first read *Ulysses*. I was sixteen, and I had imported the Odyssey Press edition of the work,[1] all neatly filleted and distributed over my body. The thrill of eating that forbidden fruit in my bedroom is hard to recapture now, but, callow and healthily smutty as I was, I was impressed by the essentially artistic use to which Joyce put obscenity. I am no longer precisely sure what are the boundaries of the verbally disgusting, but I think our Maltese censors might hover with their Biros over 'The snotgreen sea. The scrotumtightening sea' in the first chapter. But how apt those epithets are. Mr Bloom has, on his way home with his breakfast kidney, a vision of his ancestral lands: 'The oldest people. Wandered far away over all the earth, captivity to captivity, multiplying, dying, being born everywhere. It lay there now. Now it could bear no more. Dead: an old woman's: the grey sunken cunt of the world.' Think of an uncensorable synonym — womb, matrix? None has the hardness, the elementality, the disgust.

The Maltese search for further dirt might (since the obscene is, by definition, the disgusting) be rewarded by Mr Bloom's two-page visit to the outside jakes. He has constipation; he reads, appropriately, *Tit-Bits*. Cut out these pages, as Ezra Pound did on the first serialization of *Ulysses*, and you cut out essential symbolism. Mr Bloom is Ulysses in Ogygia, a man of the East detained in the West by singing Calypso, the wife who will later turn into Penelope. Calypso's land is full of caves, Mr Bloom is haunted by the word *metempsychosis*. The soul of man moves from body to body, which means from cave to cave, hiding from the primal or ultimate light. Zolaesque naturalism might regard an after-breakfast evacuation as something to take for granted. So might Joycean naturalism. But the dark cave of the yard-toilet is too good a symbol not to use.

The more one reads through *Ulysses*, the more one is surprised by a reticence that, granted Joyce's refusal to submit to the normal taboos of 1922 fiction, seems almost prudish. There is nothing to stop him filling Bloom's interior monologues with dirty words and erotic desiderations, but he avoids frankness for frankness's sake. The auto-erotic act that Bloom performs on the beach is symbolically suggested by a distant firework display, and even if we object to the act at all, Joyce is justified by the needs of his plot. Bloom has to enter the land of Circe, where men are turned into swine. He alone, cunning Ulysses, must be impervious to sorcery. Circe's land is, in 1904 Dublin, a street of brothels. Bloom, his erotic itch already artificially appeased, walks through it unenticed. He has put forth the white flower moly.

When, in this brothel scene, a couple of British tommies assault young Stephen, Telemachus to Ulysses-Bloom, language explodes for the first time into violent obscenity. We are shocked, and are meant to be shocked, but the shock has nothing to do with the breaking of a taboo. It is rather that, with the book's first and only incursion into physical violence (we can ignore the throwing of a biscuit-tin at Bloom by the Irish patriot who is also Polyphemus), the careful deployment of exact language has to break down. The only verbal equivalent of violence, which Joyce abhorred in life as much as in art, is mindless obscenity. Modify the obscenity, censor it, and the climax is muffled.

There is a curious irony in the fact that the victory of two highly moral books over the state's long oppression should open the gates to the indiscriminate use of literary obscenity. Neither *Lady Chatterley's Lover*[2] nor *Ulysses* is indiscriminate in its use of four-letter words. Lawrence, cut off from English usage by a long exile and perhaps protected from street-dirt by a doting mother, made the semantic error of trying to employ army language in a context of love and tenderness. But he was a puritan, and he would have been shocked by what young American authors are now free to do. Joyce had something of the tight-lipped Jesuit in him. He was a gentleman, given to the use of honorifics, distrustful of over-familiarity, far from loose-mouthed, however much he drank. He would have been disgusted to see one magazine called *Fuck You* and another called *Horseshit*.

For, as every ex-soldier knows, once you admit verbal obscenity you admit it everywhere. It becomes debased, it loses all force and, worst of all, it ceases to have much aesthetic value. A good deal of present-day 'permissive' writing admittedly does no more than record the speech of the low. I heard a boy in Brooklyn ask another what the time was. He got the reply: 'Oh, four o'clock, or some shit like that.' But, once the speech of the low has been set down, the reader automatically ignores the purely decorative obscenities: he reads them as Malays read punctuation-words like *maka*. Joyce and Lawrence were concerned with the serious, not flippant, use of obscenities: every dirty word had to tell, being transmuted into an exact technicality or else into a symbol of mindlessness.

The worst of all revolutions is that their high ideals become debased by mediocrities. Once a writer is allowed to set down freely what was formerly taboo, there will be writers who gain reputation solely from the breaking of taboos. Art is not a two-way mirror on a brothel ceiling, nor is it a cachette full of four-letter words. Art is the imposition of a pattern on the whole of life, which is only partly sex and swearing. If we are concerned with aesthetic effects, we shall get them best through reticence. Olivia Manning's *Balkan Trilogy* has no descriptions, either naturalistic or symbolic, of the sexual act, but, at a very late point in the story, the husband and wife whose story it is go into their bedroom and, a little later, come out again. The effect is far more devastating than anything in *An American Dream*.

I myself, as a practising novelist, am not altogether happy about the new freedom that the *Ulysses* and *Lady Chatterley* cases have given to the writer. I wrote my *Inside Mr Enderby* when four-letter words were still forbidden, and had to be content with locutions like 'For cough'. When I wrote *Enderby Outside*, there was no need for such orthographical squeamishness, but I kept to 'For cough'. I clung to the taboo because I enjoyed the ingenuity of getting round the taboo. I would still rather have a character call somebody a 'farkin Kant' than spell it out in the casual manner of our permissive era. Sex and the vocabulary of sex,

however metaphorical its use, seem to me too powerful and important to be thrown around like the counters of a children's game. To turn the female pudenda into a German philosopher is an act of transliteration which keeps the anatomical term pure for more serious use — like that of Joyce in Bloom's broodings over the dead lands.

I am not, of course, suggesting that the free world turn back the clock and become a sort of felt-pencilled Malta. I think merely that, having gained their freedom, writers might try sometimes to forget that they have gained it and see what can be done within the limits of a self-imposed censorship — in other words, to be like Joyce in *Ulysses*. One valuable lesson I learned when I studied orchestration was that the effect of the percussion instruments diminished with the frequency of their use, and that a gong, for instance, must only strike once if it is to be taken seriously. I fear that our post-Joyce freedom may result in both literary sex and literary obscenity becoming, like a gong on its twentieth striking, virtually inaudible. *Ulysses*, which teaches so many great artistic lessons, teaches us to give the percussion-players more rest than noise.

1   This German edition of *Ulysses* appeared in 1932, published in Hamburg and printed in Leipzig.
2   First published in Britain in an unexpurgated form in 1960.

ROY McFADDEN
from *Hibernia*, 10 October 1969

This extract and the following two extracts are from the now defunct Dublin fortnightly journal *Hibernia*. All three poets are from Northern Ireland and here give their responses to the upsurge in violence in their province. McFadden was born in 1921 and worked as a solicitor in Belfast. Author of several volumes of verse (see below pp. 992, 1036 for poems included in this *Reader*), he co-edited the literary journal *Rann* from 1948 onwards. McFadden's title plays on the red hand of Ulster, which is severed in its public display in Protestant/Loyalist areas of Northern Ireland.

The Severed Hand

The morning after the burning and the shooting was like the aftermath of the Easter Tuesday blitz. People I met were grim and despondent. Few understood. Just as, for many, the war inexplicably happened, so the

latest troubles had occurred suddenly and strangely, from the outside, like a pestilence. The Bogside, like Czechoslovakia in its day, was an unknown place.

Now there is a feeling of exhaustion as the barricades come down, as blinds did in some houses in recent weeks.

I suppose some poet could write an *Autumn Journal*[1] about the tensions and pretensions of the past twelve months. But I don't think that will happen. In 1938 poets were apprehensive. In 1969 they know. And the younger poets are knowing.

I was born in Belfast behind a barricade in a Catholic street. When I was 12 months old my family was evicted because we were Protestants. When I was 12 years old, taking a short-cut from a scout meeting through a Catholic area, I heard a boy call out to another: 'Look at the Protestant scout.'

Shortly after I got my first job, the managing clerk discovered that I wrote poetry. He said: 'I hope you're a good Orangeman.'

When the first number of *Lagan*, a somewhat highbrow literary compilation,[2] was being planned, John Boyd's household and my own had a Co-op traveller in common. Taking the order, the traveller said to me: 'Youse fellows will get yourselves into trouble.'

I tell my children that I'm half-English and less barbaric than they are. My brother, on a weekend visit from London, snorts that our mother had the misfortune to have been born in England but there's not a dram of English blood in *his* veins.

I have never liked Belfast; but I will never leave it. When I was growing up, it was an ignorant, prejudiced place, where the shawlies[3] in Cromac Street matched shawled official minds.

Now Belfast is sophisticated. It suffered education during the war. 'Whadya do here about sex,'[4] a G.I. asked an 11-year-old girl. Between sucks of her lolly, she replied: 'We have wir tay.'

Now the arts are subsidized in Northern Ireland. Poets get paid. They scramble from under distant stones to claim the dole, refusing nonetheless the courtesy of naming the alms-giver 'Northern Ireland'. Clutching the subsidy, they continue to refer glibly to 'The North of Ireland'. Every fool knows that the most northerly part of Ireland is in the south.[5] God be with the old days when I helped to produce a magazine for five years on the strength of postage stamps and postals orders. In those days poets became businessmen to remain poets. Now too many poets are businessmen.

Today, I can't write about the barricades and the petrol bombs, because I believe the present situation is contrived and secondhand. Whatever protest exists will not compel poets like me to utter a more compelling remark than: 'This is where I came in.'

I know people who want to get out. In the past, the main cause of emigration was economic. From now on, for many, it will be intellectual despair. Irresponsibility is not confined to the back streets. The press and broadcasting have surrendered objectivity for gallows-like headlines.

Far too much has been written about Ireland, now a cliché of the western world. There are more important things than Irish bores. Other countries have suffered more; have been nearer to reality. Nationality is an inherited thing, like the fading snaps in a family album. It should mean no more, no less. It was the half-Irish who created the myth of Ireland. Today it is the myth of the un-Irish that shakes the severed hand of Ulster into Frankenstein activity.

Twenty years ago a reviewer commented that I wrote about various attitudes of death in rainy Ulster. In spite of, not because of, recent events, I shall probably continue to do so. The wee boy killed in his bedroom by a stray bullet (mark the journalistic cliché: whose gun, whose hand, whose mind, whose intention?) means more to me than streets of public protest.

1 Long poem by Louis MacNeice published in 1938 which captures the mood of pre-War Europe. See MacNeice (1938) above (p. 477) for a section from this poem.
2 A literary magazine first published in 1943.
3 A colloquial word for women who wear shawls over their heads, poor women, presumably here meaning Catholics.
4 The girl thinks the question concerns the time she has tea.
5 Donegal — not one of the six counties of Northern Ireland

MICHAEL LONGLEY
from *Hibernia*, 7 November 1969

Michael Longley (1939–) was born in Belfast and worked for the Northern Ireland Arts Council. His first volume of verse was appropriately entitled *No Continuing City* and published just as this article in *Hibernia* appeared. Examples of his verse are included in the *Reader*, especially from his later work which shows him as Irish as any poet from the nationalist tradition.

Strife and the Ulster Poet

I have been asked by *Hibernia* to suggest how 'the passions now loose in the North are likely to influence, and be reflected in, the work of Northern writers'. Obviously no Ulsterman of any sensitivity is going to proceed as though nothing had happened. It's difficult to say more than that because I'm not a prophet, and because diagnosis of one's own work is dangerous, of one's colleagues' presumptuous. I can, however, point out that the recent political explosion was preceded by a flowering of the arts. This is a fact. Are the two related? Possibly.

Certainly, an outsider who wished to understand fully the present situation would do well to study Derek Mahon's remarkable poem, 'In Belfast': '. . . we keep sullen silence in light and shade, / Rehearsing our astute salvations under / The cold gaze of a sanctimonious God.' That was written about five years ago: it applies to today and tomorrow. Mahon is the most Ulster of the Ulster poets, just as Seamus Heaney is the most Irish. If in his one 'topical' piece, 'Docker', he is much less successful and penetrating than Mahon, Heaney in a poem called 'Bogland' has written what must be one of Irish poetry's profoundest attempts to define our national culture: 'Our pioneers keep striking / Inwards and downwards, / Every layer they strip / Seems camped on before.' His poetry lists things Irish, but its intensity and definitiveness are due to his making the inventory under the pressure of time and circumstance — that is, as an Ulsterman.

When I am asked to write or talk about myself, I quite naturally mention Mahon and Heaney, not because they are colleagues and close friends, but because, as Ulstermen, we share a complex and confusing culture: they help me to define myself and a culture which is for me, I think, more confusing than it is for them. They both have resource to solid hinterlands — Heaney the much publicized farm in County Derry, Mahon his working-class background and the shipyards. My parents came to Belfast from London in the Twenties. As a child I walked out of an English household on to Irish streets. I spoke with an accent which my parents considered Ulster, my friends English. We lived in a posh upper-middle-class district where all the children attended private schools. Because my father sacrificed his job to enlist in 1939, I went to a Public Elementary School where most of the children were working-class. So, although my childhood was reasonably happy and comfortable, any attitudes which at a different time and in different circumstances I might have inherited painlessly, were questioned from the start. If I add to this my growing awareness of the differences between Catholics and Protestants (which came later to me than to most because it was never a topic at home) and the uncertainties I share with many Ulstermen — the uncertainties of Irishmen carrying British passports, viewing Dublin through National Health specs[1] — I see that I have been schizophrenic on the levels of nationality, class and culture. Although it is personally uncomfortable for me to question continually my own identity, I must be pleased that one of the results has been poetry.

If my writing is seldom Irish in its subject matter, whatever virtues it may have were certainly born out of the unease of my Ulster background. I write with an Ulster accent which perhaps only Englishmen can detect. The unease has been heightened, to put it mildly, by recent events. My precarious (and, no doubt, luxurious) cultural balance has been upset. Prior to October 1968,[2] my attitude to the Ulster political scene had been ambivalent, well-laced with saving ironies. I see now that as a criticism of an unjust and, even at this late hour, dishonest regime ironies have proved pusilanimous, that in the context of lost lives and burnt-out houses they amount to an impertinence. At the same time I recognize that in the past ironies have saved me as a poet and that although fear was obviously the primary emotion behind the erection of the barricades, ironies contributed a little to their remaining in place. I accept, as I must, the criticism of the slogan 'Malone Road fiddles while the Falls Road burns',[3] the implication that the still and heartless centre of the hurricane is the civic inactivity of liberals like myself. Nevertheless, I have to insist that poetry is an act which in the broadest sense can be judged political, a normal human activity; that my own poetry, if it is any good, will be of value in Ulster more than anywhere else, despite its lack of Irish subject matter, despite my having been caught out by events. Anything I may write in the future is bound to be influenced by the recent turmoil. Whether the influence will be obvious or even recognizable, I couldn't say. I can't claim now, as I might have done a few years ago, that I myself have any longer a life which is my own entirely. However, as a poet I insist that the imagination has a life of *its* own, a life that has to be saved: if it isn't, everything else will be lost.

---

1   Spectacles manufactured for those who could not afford private opthalmic treatment.
2   When the present troubles began in earnest.
3   Malone Road is a street in Belfast synonymous with middle-class lifestyle, untouched at that time by the troubles then engulfing Catholic working-class areas such as the Falls Road.

SEAMUS HEANEY
from *Hibernia*, 21 November 1969

Heaney's tribute to the nationalist politician John Hume, who was two years his senior
at St Columb's College in Derry, contains an early formulation of Heaney's own sense
of integrity as a poet.

John Hume's Derry

The film 'John Hume's Derry' was almost irreproach-able. There may have been the occasional posed shot, too many zoom shots, too much framing of scenes through railings and burnt-out barricades, there may have been the slightest tug-o'-war between evocative, lyrical images and dispassionate, analytical commentary but these are things that had to be pointed out to me. Technical scruples apart, and ignoring the ludicrous charges of one-sidedness — did they expect John Hume to paint the sepulchre with white papers and orange art? — the film was calm, muted and melancholy where it could have been calculating, partisan and obstinate. Even Roy Bradford[1] was thrown by its tact but in the discussion loyally and irrelevantly fired the broadside of his statistical briefing.

What other politician has Hume's attentive intelligence and sympathy for his opponent? A good part of the film was in fact an investigation of Commander Anderson's Derry, done with more clearsightedness and perspective than that arrogant gentleman could be expected to appreciate. There wasn't a sneer, there wasn't a wink in the whole script. It was either perverse or paranoiac of the Unionist spokesman to say that it was 'anti-Unionist for the Southern audience'. This was clearly an attempt at honesty and revelation, an exercise that rendered introspection an education, an example indeed for the writer as well as for the documentary maker.

The ideal in politics as in writing is one of integrity; to establish a congruence between a man's public image (his speeches and actions or his writings) and his private self (his inherited emotional loyalties, his evolving ideals, his prejudices and uncertainties). I suppose most politicians fail to convince because their capacity for self-projection so far outweighs their capacity and desire for self-knowledge that they are content to save face or gain points and to hell with an achieved identity or moral delicacies. And writers may lose their public when they disappear too deeply into

the burrow of their own private worlds. In this connection, John Hume is exceptional.

His understanding of the community is his under-standing of himself. His ambition to set Derry's house in order is altruistic and whole because it is obviously the extension of an inner achievement of tolerance and concern. To call him a spokesman for the minority is only one way of putting it. He is the best consciousness of a submerged population group,[2] the questing compass-needle of another hidden Ireland. Speaking a lucid language of sociology and politics with untrammelled conscience, he comprehends the bitterness and negation of Derry without being possessed by it. By a generous effort of imagination, he has let any bad blood he may have harboured and thereby earned the right and the skill to diagnose bad blood in the community. Significantly, he used the analogy of the doctor in the argument that followed the second screening of his film; and he sat smiling indulgently at the seething and slogans of Commander Anderson, like a G.P. by the bedside of an ill-tempered hypochondriac.

There has been considerable discussion in this paper on the role (or is it the reluctance?) of the writer in the present Northern Ireland crisis, with Roy McFadden and Michael Longley uneasy at the assumption that politics should necessarily be an obvious preoccupation of the creative worker. The imagination, they rightly imply, usually operates as meditation and interpretation and not as a mode of action. Yet it seems to me that Hume has made the life-enhancing connection between vision and practice, has mated community relations with a creative imagination and engendered something like hope. His opponents' faces were grim as firemen's but there was a hint of the phoenix-flame in some of those petrol-bomb shots.

1   Ulster Unionist politician and then Minister of Development at Stormont.
2   Frank O'Connor's phrase from *The Lonely Voice* (1962) (see above p. 751).

IMAGINATIVE

EDNA O'BRIEN
from Edna O'Brien, *The Country Girls* (1960)

Here is a celebrated moment from the novel which made Edna O'Brien (1930–) an international name and a banned writer in Ireland. Caithleen Brady comes to Dublin to escape from small-town life in the west of Ireland and has an affair with a French man 'Mr Gentleman'. *The Country Girls*, the first in a trilogy of novels, was followed by *The Girl with Green Eyes* (1962) and *Girls in Their Married Bliss* (1964). The 1960s sexual revolution had begun.

It is the only time that I am thankful for being a woman, that time of evening, when I draw the curtains, take off my old clothes and prepare to go out. Minute by minute the excitement grows. I brush my hair under the light and the colours are autumn leaves in the sun. I shadow my eyelids with black stuff and am astonished by the look of mystery it gives to my eyes. I hate being a woman. Vain and shallow and superficial. Tell a woman that you love her and she'll ask you to write it down, so that she can show it to her friends. But I am happy at that time of night. I feel tender towards the world, I pet the wallpaper as if it were white rose petals flushed pink at the edges; I pick up my old, tired shoes and they are silver flowers that some man has laid outside my door. I kissed myself in the mirror and ran out of the room, happy and hurried and suitably mad.

I was late and Mr Gentleman was annoyed. He handed me an orchid that was two shades of purple — pale purple and dark. I pinned it to my cardigan.

We went to a restaurant off Grafton Street, and climbed the narrow stairs to a dark, almost dingy, little room. It had red and white striped wallpaper, and there was a black-brown portrait over the fireplace. It was in a thick gilt frame and I wasn't sure whether it was a portrait of a man or a woman, because the hair was covered with a black mop cap. We sat over near the window. It was half open, the nylon curtains blew inwards and brushed the tablecloth lightly and fanned our faces. As usual we were very shy. The curtains were white and foamy like summer clouds and he was wearing a new paisley tie.

'Your tie is nice,' I said stiffly.

'You like it?' he asked. It was agony until the first drink came and then he melted a little and smiled at me. Then the room seemed charming, with its lighted red candle in a wine bottle on the table. I shall never forget the pallor of his high cheek-bones when he bent down to pick up his napkin. He patted my knee for a second and then looked at me with one of his slow, intense, tormented looks.

'I feel hungry,' he said.

'I feel hungry,' I said. Little did he know that I ate two shop buns on my way to meet him. I loved shop buns, especially iced ones.

'For all sorts of things,' he said, as he scooped some melon with a spoon. He reminded me of the melon. Cool and cold and bloodless and refreshing. He twined his ankles round mine under the big linen tablecloth and the evening began to be perfect. Candle-grease dripped on to the cloth.

We drove home after eleven and he was pleased when I asked him in. I was ashamed of the hallway and the cheap carpet on the stairs. There was a stale, musty smell in the drawing-room when we went in first. He sat down on the sofa and I sat on a high-backed chair across the table from him. I was happy from the wine and I told him about my life and how I fell in the dance hall and went upstairs to drink minerals for the rest of the night. He was amused, but he didn't laugh outright. Always the remote, enchanting smile. I had drunk a lot and I was giddy. But the tiny remaining sober part of me watched the rest of me being happy and listened to the happy, foolish things that I said.

'Come over near me,' he asked and I came and sat very quietly beside him. I could feel him trembling.

'You're happy?' he said, tracing the outline of my face with his finger.

'Yes.'

'You're going to be happier.'

'How?'

'We're going to be together. I'm going to make love to you.' He spoke in a half whisper and kept looking, uneasily, towards the window, as if there might be someone watching us from the back garden. I went over and drew the blind, as there were no curtains in that room. I was blushing when I came back to sit down.

'Do you mind?' he asked.

'When? Now?' I clutched the front of my cardigan, and looked at him earnestly. He said that I looked appalled. I wasn't appalled really. Just nervous, and sad in some way, because the end of my girlhood was near.

'Sweetling,' he said. He put an arm round me and brought my head down on his shoulder, so that my cheek touched his neck. Some tears of mine must have trickled down inside his collar. He patted my knees with his other hand. I was excited, and warm, and violent.

'Do you know French?' he asked.

'No. I did Latin at school,' I said. Imagine talking about school at a time like that. I could have killed myself for being so juvenile.

'Well, there's a French word for it. It means . . . a . . . atmosphere. We'll go away to the right atmosphere for a few weeks.'

'Where?' I thought with horror of bacon-and-egg hotels across the central towns of Ireland with ketchup dribbles on the relish bottles and gravy stains on the check cloth. And rain outside. But I might have known that he would be more careful. He always was. Even to the extent of parking his car right outside the restaurants where we ate, so that no one would see us walking up the street to the car park.

'To Vienna,' he said and my heart did a few somersaults.

'Is it nice there?'

'It's very nice there.'

'And what will we do?'

'We'll eat and go for walks. And in the evenings we'll go up to eating places in the mountains and sit there drinking wine and looking down at the town. And then we'll go to bed.' He said it quite simply and I loved him more than I would ever love a man again.

'Is it good to go?' I asked. I just wanted him to reassure me.

'Yes. It's good. We have to get this out of our systems.' He frowned a little; and I had a vision of coming back to the same room and the same life and being without him.

'But I want you for always,' I said, imploringly. He smiled and kissed me lightly on the cheeks. Kisses like the first drops of rain. 'You'll always love me?' I asked.

'You know I don't like you to talk like that,' he said, playing with the top button of my cardigan.

'I know,' I said.

'Then why do you?' he asked, tenderly.

'Because I can't help it. Because I'd go mad if I hadn't you.'

He looked at me for a long time. That look of his which was half sexual, half mystic; and then he said my name very gently. ('Caithleen.') I could hear the bulrushes sighing when he said my name that way and I could hear the curlew too and all the lonesome sounds of Ireland.

'Caithleen. I want to whisper you something.'

'Whisper,' I said. I put my hair behind my ear and he held it there because it had a habit of falling back into its old place. He leaned over and put his mouth close to my ear and kissed it first and said: 'Show me your body. I've never seen your legs or breasts or anything. I'd like to see you.'

'And if I'm not nice then will you change your mind?' I had inherited my mother's suspiciousness.

'Don't be silly,' he said and he helped me take off my cardigan. I was trying to decide whether to take off my blouse or my skirt first.

'Don't look,' I said. It was difficult. I didn't like him to see suspenders and things. I peeled off my skirt and everything under it, and then my blouse and my cotton vest, and finally I unclasped my brassière, the black one; and I stood there shivering a little, not knowing what to do with my arms. So I put my hand up to my throat, a gesture that I often do when I am at a loss. The only place I felt warm was where my hair covered my neck and the top part of my back. I came over and sat beside him and nestled in near him for a little warmth.

'You can look now,' I said and he took his hand down from his eyes and looked shyly at my stomach and my thighs.

'Your skin is whiter than your face. I thought it would be pink,' he said and he kissed me all over.

'Now we won't be shy when we get there. We've seen one another,' he said.

'I haven't seen you.'

'Do you want to?' and I nodded. He opened his braces and let his trousers slip down around his ankles. He took off his other things and sat down quickly. He was not half so distinguished out of his coal-black suit and stiff white shirt. Something stirred in the garden or was it in the hall? I thought what horror if Joanna should burst in in her nightdress and find us like two naked fools on the green velveteen couch. And she would shout for Gustav, and the ladies next door would hear her and the police would come. I looked down slyly at his body and laughed a little. It was so ridiculous.

'What's so funny?' He was piqued that I should laugh.

'It's the colour of the pale part of my orchid,' I said and I looked over at my orchid that was still pinned to my cardigan. I touched it. Not my orchid. His. It was soft and incredibly tender, like the inside of a flower, and it stirred. It reminded me when it stirred of a little black man on top of a collecting box that shook his head every time you put a coin in the box. I told him this and he kissed me fiercely and for a long time.

'You're a bad girl,' he said.

'I like being a bad girl,' I replied, wide-eyed.

'No, not really, darling. You're sweet. The sweetest girl I ever met. My country girl with country-coloured hair,' and he buried his face in it and smelt it for a minute.

'Darling, I'm not made of iron,' he said and he stood up and drew his trousers up from around his ankles. When I got up to fetch my clothes he fondled my bottom and I knew that our week together would be beautiful.

'I'll make you a cup of tea,' I said after we had dressed ourselves and he had combed his hair with my comb.

We went out to the kitchen on tip-toe. I lit the gas and filled the kettle noiselessly by letting the water from the tap pour down the side of the kettle. The refrigerator was locked because of Herman's fits of night hunger, but I found a few old biscuits in a forgotten tin. They were soft but he ate them. After the tea he left. It was Friday so he was making the long journey down the country. On week nights he stayed in a men's club in Stephen's Green.

I stood at the door and he let down the window of the car and waved good night. He drove away without making any noise at all. I came in, put my orchid in a cup of water, and carried it upstairs to the orange box beside my bed. I was too happy to go to sleep.

PAUL SMITH
from Paul Smith, *The Countrywoman* (1962)

Paul Smith (1935–) was born in Dublin, left school when he was eight, and for his first job drove a donkey and coal cart. After a period spent travelling abroad his first novel *Esther's Altar*, set in the Dublin tenements during the Easter Rising, was published in the States in 1959 (reissued as *Come Trailing Blood* in 1977). *The Countrywoman* is also set in the Dublin slums, this time during the Irish Civil War of 1922–3. In this extract Queenie comes to tell the mother of her boyfriend Danny that she is pregnant by him. It is worth comparing Smith's handling of this scene with Sean O'Casey's in *Juno and the Paycock*. The crowded life of the tenements has a tangible quality here, and notice the way the larger conflict of the Civil War takes second place to the real dilemma facing this working-class family.

Mrs Baines had no time to wonder what Queenie Mullen wanted from her, but the sight of her standing hatless with her coat dragged loosely around her in the shadows of the hall door filled her with foreboding and made her sound cold, harsh without knowing that she did so.

'Yes, Queenie, what is it?' She stepped out into the light of the gas lamp at the corner, but Queenie drew back into the door as though afraid to be seen by anyone from the windows.

'I hope you don't mind me calling, Mrs Baines. I didn't want to go up in front of Babby an' her fella.' Her breath jerked from her in convulsive starts like the nervous rears of an animal under a fondling hand. Her face, slashed by shadows and the green glow of the gas lamp, was taut and her eyes, which had held her only

appeal until Mrs Baines spoke, leaped into a flash of arrogance.

'Musha, not at all, child!' Catapulted into a new dread, Mrs Baines spoke kindly, her eyes devouring the darkness for a complete sight of the face before her. Instinctively she was aware of a change in the girl since she had last seen her, but she could not define it nor guess its cause. She reached to draw Queenie out into the light again, but Queenie shrank back into the folds of sounds coming from the Slatterys' room, cleaving her mind through the torment of the things she must say. But, O Jesus! if they'd only stop screaming and fighting just for one lousy minute: the thought pressed Queenie up against the end of the bannister. Its square stab sank familiarly into the small of her back. Against her face, the darkness was crowded and suffocating.

'I'm in trouble.' She pushed herself away to stand at the edge of the open door. 'I'm going to have a baby,' she said out into the diffused light of the Lane.

Mrs Baines stood behind her, watching her. 'For Danny,' she said, quietly, without moving.

As though she had not spoken, Queenie said: 'For Danny. Me and Danny.' Her head snapped round. 'How'd ya know?'

How could she answer that one? Mrs Baines thought. 'You're sure?'

'What do you think I am?' Queenie's voice rose hysterically. 'What are ya tryin' to make a me? I've never been with anybody else.'

'Christ! child, I never said you had.' She took Queenie's hands. 'All I meant was are you sure you're carrying?'

'Nothing surer.' After the wry mockery, her next words could scarcely be heard. 'What am I going to do? Me ma will kill me.'

'Whisht!' Mrs Baines pressed herself against the wall. Tom Flanagan passed them on his way to the pipe, but without turning his head.

'Where'll I go?' Queenie began to cry, the sounds muffled against the hand she raised to her mouth.

'Where indeed?' Mrs Baines looked past the girl's head, across to the houses opposite. 'Do they know?'

Queenie shook her head, and Mrs Baines wondered how she had hidden her state from them and the three sisters she slept with.

'I'm not showing,' Queenie answered her thoughts. 'But it won't be long before they know. The oul' wan I work for sacked me today. She caught me being sick when I was doing out one of the rooms and said I was in the family way. I swore I wasn't and she wanted to send for Father Rex Aurealis and asked me if I'd be willing to swear the same thing to him. But I couldn't. She threw me out without a penny an' told me I needn't ask her for a reference because she won't give me one.' The tide of words stopped suddenly, then: 'She screamed out the door after me when I was going, an' said I was a whore, an' even when I was down the steps an' in the street she still screamed after me.'

'I suppose Danny knows?'

Queenie's 'Yes' was slow, almost an 'Of course.'

Tom Flanagan passed slowly back from the pipe, spilling water as he did so, but neither noticed.

'How near are you?' Mrs Baines asked through the confusion of thoughts scurrying across her mind.

Queenie hesitated. 'I'm not certain. About two, three months.'

'In that case you must be married at once.'

Queenie was startled. 'Married!' She sounded incredulous. 'How? On what?'

Mrs Baines shook her head. 'That's up to Danny.' Her voice had lost its softness. 'You don't mean to tell me he doesn't want to marry you?'

Queenie sighed into a sag against the door. 'He asked me, but I don't want him just because he feels he has to. That way no fella's worth having.'

Because Mrs Baines agreed, she didn't contradict. But Danny would be different. He was quiet and gentle and had never given her a back-answer in his life, nor had she ever seen him raise a hand to a soul, only after a lot of provocation. He would be good to his wife: this she believed, and if she hadn't, she wouldn't have wished him on the worst woman going.

'But what'll you do if you don't marry him?' she asked. 'An' what about the priest? Because don't you know that oul' wan will do as she threatened; they can't resist it.' When Queenie didn't answer, she went on. 'I couldn't let you lie up in my place, child. Not only would your mother have me life, but Father Tithe wouldn't let me give you a drink of water. He'd say I was encouraging you and leading you into sin, the way he did when Mrs Slattery tried to help Nancy O'Byrne.' She touched Queenie gently. 'Besides, pet, if not for your own sake, then the child's, you have to get married.'

Queenie looked up coldly. 'I want to get rid of it! I don't want to be saddled with a baby.'

Mrs Baines stared at the calm despair in the face turned up to her. It was an old face, with lines wide and deep drawn from each side of the nose to the mouth, the eyes not visible, only the narrow brows which met like a brand on the twin rises of the forehead.

'I went to see Mrs Ennis.' Her matter-of-fact tone contrasted with the static darkened gap of her mouth, immobile even while she spoke. 'But she won't do anything. I'm too far gone, she says.' Then suddenly she gasped out in an uneven incoherent plea what she had come to Mrs Baines for. 'But she gave me the address of a nurse in Wexford Street who'll do it. For five quid[1] down and another five when it's over.' She clutched, desperate, and pulled the woman to her until her hot breath washed over Mrs Baines's face. 'Ten quid th' oul' bitch wants, an' I haven't a farthing, I haven't a penny.'

Roughly Mrs Baines disentangled herself. 'Stop it! Stop that now an' talk sense! D'ya hear me?'

'I haven't the money.' Queenie bent to half her size, a trick Annie the Man had. 'I haven't the money.' Her voice dropped to a whinge, pinched out of her between a streel of incoherencies that stopped abruptly. 'I've got to get rid of it,' she cried. 'I've got to.' She clutched at Mrs Baines.

'Dear Jesus, will you stop it!' Mrs Baines tore herself free again, and sent Queenie staggering against the hall door which slammed against the door behind it. They heard Alexander Chance shout a complaint, accompanied by a bang as if he had flung something, and Mrs Baines held her breath, lest someone come out in search of the disturbance. No one came.

Queenie dragged herself upright. 'I'm sorry. I didn't mean to . . .' And with a young dignity, she asked. 'D'you think you could get me a lend from one of the Jew men? I'd pay you back, Mrs Baines.'

And she would, Mrs Baines knew; but she shook her head. 'Child, I couldn't get you that kind of money if my life depended on it.'

She looked away from Queenie, then out in the Lane, feeling sickened and cold and gray. She remembered that she herself had considered abortion; wasn't there every reason then why Queenie should?

'Could you try, Mrs Baines, could you?' Queenie plucked at the sleeve of her blouse.

'No, Queenie, I couldn't, an' even if I could . . .'

Queenie dropped her hands into the fog which had had its beginning earlier in the night on the Canal, and now rolled down the Lane in clouds, while through it the lights in the windows were dimmed like the dull hearts of what had been roaring fires.

'You'll have to marry Danny.' She drew Queenie down onto the bottom stair.

'I can't.'

The whisper hardly reached her. 'You can an' will. You'll go over to Father Rex Aurealis first thing in the morning an' tell him he's got to marry you.' She felt the girl's withdrawal, but held on tightly to the hands between her own and gradually felt them relax.

'I don't want to force him an' that's what I'd be doing.'

'Be sensible, child. It's right the man that fathered your child should marry you. If a marriage is anything, it's that,' she said, puzzling Queenie. 'Besides, what other decent man is going to look you straight in the eye if he knows you've had a child by somebody else? Do you think for one minute they're going to line up wanting to marry a girl like that? You'll be another Nancy O'Byrne, any man's fancy, an' the leavin's of all. If Father Rex Aurealis doesn't put you away in a home first.' She went on tiredly, 'I'm older than you, child, and know what I'm talking about. Let you be guided by me.'

'But what would we do an' where would we go?' Queenie searched the darkness for Mrs Baines's face. 'An' how would you manage without Danny?'

Aye, it was put into words before she allowed herself to think it! 'Don't fret yourself,' Mrs Baines shook her

head. 'Danny isn't keeping the teeth in my head. I'd manage, pet, as I've always managed. And as for where you'll go? Once you're married, you can come in with me till you get a place of your own.'

Queenie leaned her weight against Mrs Baines. 'What'll I tell me ma?'

'The truth. What else?'

'Nothing.' Queenie sat up. 'I didn't think you'd take it like this. I thought . . . You're very good, Mrs Baines.'

Mrs Baines sighed. 'Whisht, child.' She shivered suddenly. 'Somebody's just gone over me grave,' she said and reached forward up onto her feet again. 'You'll go over to the chapel in the morning, like a good girl?'

Queenie pulled her coat close round her. 'Yes, ma'am,' she nodded, docile, ready now to be ordered and to do as she was told. 'Will you tell Danny?' Her request was whispered as a breath in the dark of the hall.

'Aye.' Mrs Baines surveyed the girl now, standing where the light could touch her. 'I'll tell him.'

Queenie showed the trace of a smile, but there was no comfort in it, only a waiting watchfulness as though she were expecting to hear something she hadn't yet heard. But Mrs Baines had nothing more to say, at least not to Queenie.

'I'll see him at the corner on his way to work.' Queenie reached out a timid hand, roughened and hard, the calloused palm resting light and like sandpaper on Mrs Baines's forearm. 'I better go,' she said.

And when she removed her hand, Mrs Baines ran her own over the spot where Queenie's had rested.

'Good night,' she said, and darted untidily across the yard to her own hall door.

Mrs Baines stood where Queenie had left her. Her eyes roved the desolation of the squat crowded houses that at night sagged like breasts from which too many mouths have sucked. Her tongue sought the gaps where her teeth had once been and moseyed over the ones that remained like tombs standing on uneasy earth, loose and moving under the pressure of her tongue until it came to rest at last in the mouth left open to the night as she looked from the houses surrounding her to the high wall of the railway and above it to where she knew the sky must be. Denied the sight of the sky because of the fog that sealed the Lane, her eyes fell back on the gapes on the halls and windows, and on the man who was approaching her with silent footfalls. She watched him without any alarm, too wearied under the fresh burden laid on her by Queenie and Danny to care one way or the other who he was or what. She watched him touch the brim of his soft hat and drew back only when he thrust his face too close to hers, as though he wanted to make sure that her face was unknown to him.

'That's a bad night,' he said.

'It is.'

'The I.R.A. threw a bomb into a lorry-load of Free Staters[2] in O'Connell Street tonight and killed every one of them. You live here?' His voice was low and thin as he nodded towards the darkness behind her.

She nodded but said nothing, thinking of Mattie and Zena, as he stepped past her into the darkness, finding his way up and down the stairs like a bat, then emerging beside her again with an apology for troubling her.

'It's no trouble,' Mrs Baines told him.

'I wonder if you could help me?' he asked.

With the Lane's mistrust and dislike of strangers, she looked him up and down before answering. And unconsciously, her eye flickered in the direction of Annie the Man's darkened window. 'That depends on what it is you're wanting?'

Offhandedly, but without taking his eyes from her, he said, 'I was looking for Nancy O'Byrne.'

'What do you mean, you was?'

She hadn't meant to be funny, but the man grinned. 'I am.' His tone, more than the name, alerted her to a danger threatening, putting her on her guard against what as yet she could only surmise.

'You mean Cocky's daughter?' She was in control again, her voice matter-of-fact.

He nodded. 'That's what they call her.' It was hearty and false, his joviality.

'Well, you've come to the wrong house,' Mrs Baines pointed behind him. 'She lives over there.'

'Aye, I know,' he said softly. 'But she's not there now.'

'Isn't she?' Mrs Baines was all surprise.

'You know she isn't,' he replied sharply.

She glared at him. 'It isn't my business to know, or not to know!'

'Don't rise yourself, ma'am,' he said placatingly. 'I only asked a civil question.'

'Well, you may not know it, but you got a civil answer.'

'That I didn't, but we won't fall out.' He grinned. 'An' you can't help me at all at all?'

She delayed her answer, and then disguised it in a question. 'What do you want with her?' she asked.

'We want to see her, ma'am, that's all.'

'You an' the priest.' She thought he might deny this, and when he didn't she went on, 'You're from one of them homes, aren't you?'

Her manner was now answer enough for him. 'You're a great help, I must say,' he said sarcastically and turned abruptly away.

'I never intended to be,' she said after him, and remembering Mrs Kinsella's usual parting shot, she called, 'And tell that to your mother and your friends in America!'

She watched him disappear into the dark of Cocky's hall, and come out again and go into Queenie's. His soundless steps supported a bulk that glided noiseless, sinister, as he went from hall to hall in his search for the girl. She looked up at Cocky's window which was open and dark. Behind her Babby came out onto the landing and called her, claiming her from sadness and anger. 'I'm coming, child.' She turned back into the hall and began the slow ascent of the stairs. She met Nick at the door and, after bidding him goodnight, told Danny to see him down to the hall.

'Mother, what kept you?' Babby asked, as she closed the door behind them.

Mrs Baines looked to see that Neddo and Tucker Tommy were in bed asleep, then walked over to her chair and drew it as close as she could to the fire. 'I was getting a breath of air.'

'There's a cup of tea, will I pour it for you?' Babby held the teapot in her hand, and her mother nodded. As she poured, 'What did Queenie Mullen want?' she asked.

After a long sip, Mrs Baines said, 'She's going to have a baby for Danny,' and raised the cup to her lips again.

'Queenie Mullen!'

Her mother looked past her to Danny, who had come in quietly behind her.

'You're codding.' Babby looked from one to the other.

'I wish to God I was!' Mrs Baines put her cup onto the hob, and Danny sat down where he could see her sideways.

'Is it true?' Babby swung round to confront him.

He spoke across to his mother. 'I was going to tell you.'

'Sweet Jesus!' Babby said. 'As if we didn't have enough to put up with!'

'Shut up!' Danny jumped to his feet but spoke quietly, moving to place himself between his sister and his mother. 'Why don't you mind your own business?' he said, as Babby pushed herself in front of him.

'That'll do.' Mrs Baines ended the threatened flare between them just as she had done all their lives when they seemed on the very brink of a row. 'You sit down, the pair of you.'

Neither of them moved.

'Do what you're told.'

Babby, exasperated at the command, sat down, her face set in suppressed anger, bound to erupt before long.

'An' you, too.'

Without a murmur, Danny did as he was bid. 'I was going to tell you.' He spoke before she could.

'Why didn't you?' She drew her hand across her face. 'Did you think it wouldn't be necessary? Did you know Queenie was down to oul' Ennis an' out tonight looking for money for that nurse in Wexford Street?' She leaned forward. 'Did you know?'

Danny sprang to his feet; the shock of his weight upon the floor shook the room to a trembling silence. He stared his unbelief. 'No, I didn't. How would I?' His eyes snapped on his words.

'Don't you dare shout at my mother!' Babby, white-lipped, sprang up again.

'Well, she was.' Mrs Baines's glance met her son's over Babby's head. 'And it was your business to know.' She sat down suddenly, slumped in misery and disappointment, her eyes fixed in a sightless stare at a broad smut that clung to a bar on the grate, fluttering in the draft sweeping down the chimney.

'I wanted to tell you about myself and Queenie. But I didn't want to worry you about it.'

'You might have had the girl's death on your hands.' Mrs Baines uttered the weight that had lain on her since Queenie's first mention of Mrs Ennis. 'You'll have to marry Queenie, as quick as you can.'

'She doesn't want to get married.' Danny shifted on his feet awkwardly.

'She does now.' His mother proceeded to tell him what had passed between herself and Queenie, omitting nothing.

When she had finished, he asked, 'Why didn't she tell me?'

'It doesn't matter. All that does is that you should know, and you do now.' Mrs Baines looked away and Danny sat down close to her.

'We'll go to England,' he said.

'You won't have to,' Mrs Baines said quickly. 'You can stay here till you get a place of your own.'

Danny shook his head. 'What happens when he comes home?' The question was final and decisive and gave shape to the dread they lived with. 'We'll go to England the minute we're married.'

'There's nothing here, Mother,' Babby said softly. 'Sure they'd be better off in England where there's work and the chance of a living.'

Mrs Baines tore her glance from Babby, made gentle by her brother's question. She didn't want Danny to go to England, to disappear into the vastness of a country that in her ignorance she imagined to be at the other end of the world, to go where she would never see him again, as Teasey had, and Kitty. Babby stretched out a hand to her, but she moved out of its reach.

'Stay here as I said, an' maybe he ... maybe something will turn up.' But it was the unspoken fear that would not be resolved.

Danny stared at his mother as she stooped forward from her chair and began to poke at the fire, as though in its dying glow she might yet find an answer to this new trouble just arisen. Something in the stoop of her shoulders and in the white face bent beneath the weight of white hair caught Danny's attention, forced his own problems not out of mind but to one side, and impulsively he rose and went to her. She rested the poker against the hob and stayed stooping for a moment.

'Mother.'

She turned her face up to him. 'Yes, son, I know,' she said, forestalling any attempt he might make to explain why it was necessary for him to take Queenie not only from the Lane but from the country. 'If only there was something we could do.' And because she admitted the fact that there was not, she felt old suddenly, older than she had ever felt, and utterly useless.

'It's the only way,' Danny said.

Her mind spanned the years, to hear again Teasey and Kitty as in a chorus saying the same words exactly when they went from her. She shook the sound of their voices from her head, their images from her sight, her mind lingering on what she knew to be Danny's farewell to her, before she hurried to say all that she felt should be said in her desire to detain and keep him near her a little longer.

'You couldn't take that girl away in her present state. God only knows what you might be landed into in a strange country with not a soul to hand either of you a glass of water if youse were dying. Couldn't you wait until the baby is born?'

'We have to go now, Mother,' Danny said. 'Queenie's mother won't let her cross the door once she knows, and we can't come in here.'

'You can,' Mrs Baines answered desperately. She looked from Danny to Babby, reading their thoughts. 'We'd manage.'

Danny shook his head. 'No, Mother.'

She recognized the determination in his face, as he got to his feet. 'I'll get the baby.' Silence was a pressure and she went into the little room where Neddo and Tucker Tommy were asleep. Her heart was cold, and in the dark her voice was coarse: 'Not yet, Lord! Not yet!' as she took Dilsey off Babby's bed to bring her out to her own.

As she was fixing the covers round her, their voices sucked at her

'He's right,' Babby said. 'It's better for them to go now.'

Danny had stopped his pacing and stood tall and powerful before her, wanting her sanction for the decision he had made contrary to her wishes. She gazed at him across the table littered with the remains of the supper.

'Go so.' She sounded proud, dignified, even formal. 'Go with the help of God and His Blessed Mother.' But she looked gaunt, gray. 'You better go to bed,' she said.

Carefully she began to hang the clothes she had washed earlier in the evening over the line. Danny watched her, anxious for feelings he could only guess

at, and when behind her mother's back Babby signed for him to go, he said, 'Good night, Mother,' and went through the curtain to the little room.

Babby waited with her mother until there was nothing left to tidy for the morning, and as she said good night, Dilsey began to cry.

'I'll take her,' Mrs Baines said, as Babby bent to pick the baby up. She took the child in her arms, rocking it gently, and the cries subsided to the familiar pettish whinge. 'Get you to bed,' Mrs Baines said, but Babby stood for a moment looking solemnly from the baby's face to her mother's. Long after she had got into bed, she could hear slow steps pacing the other room and the mingled sounds of the mother and the child.

1 Pound in money.
2 Supporters of the Irish Free State opposed by Republicans during the Irish Civil War 1922–23.

BRIAN FRIEL
from Brian Friel, *The Saucer of Larks: Stories of Ireland* (1969)

Brian Friel (1929–) was born in Omagh, County Tyrone, and educated at St Columb's College, Derry, Maynooth, and St Joseph's College, Belfast. Friel is among the leading contemporary dramatists in Ireland but his early work as a short story writer deserves to be better known. Here in this story written in 1962, in part the basis of his later play *Aristocrats* (1979), Friel shows the future dramatist at work. Notice the skilful way he uses the tape-recorder at the centre of the action to convey both continuities and discontinuities within and between social classes and individual families.

Foundry House

When his father and mother died, Joe Brennan applied for their house, his old home, the gate lodge to Foundry House. He wrote direct to Mr Bernard (as Mr Hogan was known locally), pointing out that he was a radio-and-television mechanic in the Music Shop; that although he had never worked for Mr Hogan, his father had been an employee in the foundry for over fifty years; and that he himself had been born and reared in the gate lodge. Rita, his wife, who was more practical than he, insisted that he mention their nine children and the fact that they were living in three rooms above a launderette.

'That should influence him,' she said. 'Aren't they supposed to be one of the best Catholic families in the North of Ireland?' So, against his wishes, he added a

paragraph about his family and their inadequate accommodation, and sent off his application. Two days later, he received a reply from Mrs Hogan, written on mauve scented notepaper with fluted edges. Of course she remembered him, she said. He was the small, round-faced boy with the brown curls who used to play with her Declan. And to think that he now had nine babies of his own! Where did time go? He could collect the keys from the agent and move in as soon as he wished. There were no longer any duties attached to the position of gatekeeper, she added — not since wartime, when the authorities had taken away the great iron gates that sealed the mouth of the avenue.

'Brown curls!' Rita squealed with delight when Joe read her letter. 'Brown curls! She mustn't have seen you for twenty years or more!'

'That's all right, now,' was all Joe could say. He was

moved with relief and an odd sense of humility at his unworthiness. 'That's all right. That's all right.'

They moved into their new house at the end of summer. It was a low-set, solid stone building with a steep roof and exaggerated eaves that gave it the appearance of a gnome's house in a fairy tale. The main Derry-Belfast road ran parallel to the house, and on the other side the ground rose rapidly in a tangle of shrubs and wild rhododendron and decaying trees, through which the avenue crawled up to Foundry House at the top of the hill. The residence was not visible from the road or from any part of the town; one could only guess at its location somewhere in the green patch that lay between the new housing estate and the brassière factory. But Joe remembered from his childhood that if one stood at the door of Foundry House on a clear morning, before the smoke from the red-brick factories clouded the air, one could see through the trees and the undergrowth, past the gate lodge and the busy main road, and right down to the river below, from which the sun drew a million momentary flashes of light that danced and died in the vegetation.

For Joe, moving into the gate lodge was a home-coming; for Rita and the children, it was a changeover to a new life. There were many improvements to be made — there was no indoor toilet and no running water, the house was lit by gas only, and the windows, each made up of a score of small, diamond-shaped pieces of glass, gave little light — and Joe accepted that they were inevitable. But he found himself putting them off from day to day and from week to week. He did not have much time when he came home from work, because the evenings were getting so short. Also, he had applied to the urban council for a money grant, and they were sending along an architect soon. And he had to keep an eye on the children, who looked on the grounds as their own private part and climbed trees and lit fires in the undergrowth and played their shrieking games of hide-and-seek or cowboys-and-Indians right up to the very front of the big house itself.

'Come back here! Come back!' Joe would call after them in an urgent undertone. 'Why can't you play down below near your own house? Get away down at once with you!'

'We want to play up here, Daddy,' some of them would plead. 'There are better hiding places up here.'

'The old man, he'll soon scatter you!' Joe would say. 'Or he'll put the big dog on you. God help you then!'

'But there is no old man. Only the old woman and the maid. And there is no dog, either.'

'No Mr Bernard? Huh! Just let him catch you, and you'll know all about it. No Mr Bernard! The dog

may be gone, but Mr Bernard's not. Come on now! Play around your own door or else come into the house altogether.'

No Mr Bernard! Mr Bernard always had been, Joe thought to himself, and always would be — a large, stern-faced man with a long white beard and a heavy step and a walking stick, the same ever since he remembered him. And beside him the Great Dane, who copied his master as best he could in expression and gait — a dour, sullen animal as big as a calf and as savage as a tiger, according to the men in the foundry. And Mrs Hogan? He supposed she could be called an old woman now, too. Well over sixty, because Declan and he were of an age, and he was thirty-three himself. Yes, an old woman, or at least elderly, even though she was twenty years younger than her husband. And not Declan now, or even Master Declan, but Father Declan, a Jesuit. And then there was Claire, Miss Claire, the girl, younger than Declan by a year. Fat, blue-eyed Claire, who had blushed every time she passed the gate lodge because she knew some of the Brennans were sure to be peering out through the diamond windows. She had walked with her head to one side, as if she were listening for something, and used to trail her fingers along the boxwood that fringed both sides of the avenue. 'Such a lovely girl,' Joe's mother used to say. 'So simple and so sweet. Not like the things I see running about this town. There's something good before that child. Something very good.' And she was right. Miss Claire was now Sister Claire of the Annunciation Nuns and was out in Africa. Nor would she ever be home again. Never. Sister Claire and Father Declan — just the two of them, and both of them in religion, and the big house up above going to pieces, and no one to take over the foundry when the time would come. Everything they could want in the world, anything that money could buy, and they turned their backs on it all. Strange, Joe thought. Strange. But right, because they were the Hogans.

They were a month in the house and were seated at their tea, all eleven of them, when Mrs Hogan called on them. It was now October and there were no evenings to speak of; the rich, warm days ended abruptly in a dusk that was uneasy with cold breezes. Rita was relieved at the change in the weather, because now the children, still unsure of the impenetrable dark and the nervous movements in the undergrowth, were content to finish their games when daylight faded, and she had no difficulty in gathering them for their evening meal. Joe answered the knock at the door.

'I'm so sorry to disturb you, Mr Brennan. But I wonder could you do me a favour?'

She was a tall, ungraceful woman, with a man's

shoulders and a wasted body and long, thin feet. When she spoke, her mouth and lips worked in excessive movement.

Rita was at Joe's elbow. 'Did you not ask the woman in?' she reproved him. 'Come on inside, Mrs Hogan.'

'I'm sorry,' Joe stammered. 'I thought . . . I was about to . . .' How could he say he didn't dare?

'Thank you all the same,' Mrs Hogan said. 'But I oughtn't to have left Bernard at all. What brought me down was this. Mary — our maid, you know — she tells me that you have a tape-recording machine. She says you're in that business. I wonder could we borrow it for an afternoon? Next Sunday?'

'Certainly, Mrs Hogan. Certainly,' said Rita. 'Take it with you now. We never use it. Do we, Joe?'

'If Sunday suits you, I would like to have it then when Father Declan comes,' Mrs Hogan said. 'You see, my daughter, Claire, has sent us a tape-recording of her voice — these nuns nowadays, they're so modern — and we were hoping to have Father Declan with us when we play it. You know, a sort of family reunion, on Sunday.'

'Any time at all,' said Rita. 'Take it with you now. Go and get it, Joe, and carry it up.'

'No, no. Really. Sunday will do — Sunday afternoon. Besides, neither Bernard nor I know how to work the machine. We'll be depending on you to operate it for us, Mr Brennan.'

'And why wouldn't he?' said Rita. 'He does nothing on a Sunday afternoon, anyway. Certainly he will.'

Now that her request had been made and granted, Mrs Hogan stood irresolutely between the white gaslight in the hall and the blackness outside. Her mouth and lips still worked, although no sound came.

'Sunday then,' she said at last. 'A reunion.'

'Sunday afternoon,' said Rita. 'I'll send him up as soon as he has his dinner in him.'

'Thank you,' said Mrs Hogan. 'Thank you.' Her mouth formed an 'O', and she drew in her breath. But she snapped it shut again and turned and strode off up the avenue.

Rita closed the door and leaned against it. She doubled up with laughter. 'Lord, if you could only see your face!' she gasped between bursts.

'What do you mean, my face?'

'All scared-looking, like a child caught stealing!'

'What are you raving about?' he asked irritably.

'And she was as scared-looking as yourself.' She held her hand to her side. 'She must have been looking for the brown curls and the round face! And not a word out of you! Like a big, scared dummy!'

'Shut up,' he mumbled gruffly. 'Shut up, will you?'

Joe had never been inside Foundry House, had never spoken to Mr Bernard, and had not seen Declan since his ordination. And now, as he stood before the hall door and the evil face on the leering knocker, the only introductory remark his mind would supply him was one from his childhood: 'My daddy says here are the keys to the workshop and that he put out the fire in the office before he left.' He was still struggling to suppress this senseless memory when Father Declan opened the door.

'Ah, Joe, Joe, Joe! Come inside. Come inside. We are waiting for you. And you have the machine with you? Good man! Good man! Great! Great!'

Father Declan was fair and slight, and his gestures fluttering and birdlike. The black suit accentuated the whiteness of his hair and skin and hands.

'Straight ahead, Joe. First door to the right. You know — the breakfast room. They live there now, Father and Mother. Convenient to the kitchen, and all. And Mother tells me you are married and have a large family?'

'That's right, Father.'

'Good man! Good man! Marvellous, too. No, no, not that door, Joe; the next one. No, they don't use the drawing room any more. Too large and too expensive to heat. That's it, yes. No, no, don't knock. Just go right in. That's it. Good man! Good man!'

One minute he was behind Joe, steering him through the hallway, and the next he had sped past him and was standing in the middle of the floor of the breakfast room, his glasses flashing, his arms extended in reception. 'Good man. Here we are. Joe Brennan, Mother, with the tape recorder.'

'So kind of you, Joe,' said Mrs Hogan, emerging from behind the door. 'It's going to be quite a reunion, isn't it?'

'How many young Brennans are there?' asked Father Declan.

'Nine, Father.'

'Good! Good! Great! Great!'

'Such healthy children, too,' said Mrs Hogan. 'I've seen them playing on the avenue. And so . . . . so healthy.'

'Have a seat, Joe. Just leave the recorder there. Anywhere at all. Good man. That's it. Fine!'

'You've had your lunch, Mr Brennan?'

'Yes, thanks, Mrs Hogan. Thank you all the same.'

'What I mean is, you didn't rush off without it?'

'Lucky for you, Joe,' the priest broke in. 'Because these people, I discover, live on snacks now. Milk and bananas — that sort of thing.'

'You'll find the room cold, I'm afraid, Mr. Brennan.'

'If you have a power plug, I'll get this thing . . .'

'A power plug. A power plug. A power plug. A power plug.' The priest cracked his fingers each time he said the words and frowned in concentration.

'What about that thing there?' asked Mrs Hogan, pointing to the side of the mantelpiece.

'That's a gas bracket, Mother. No. Electric. Electric.' One white finger rested on his chin. 'An electric power plug. There must be one somewhere in the — ah! Here we are!' He dropped on his knees below the window and looked back exultantly over his shoulder. 'I just thought so. Here we are. I knew there must be one somewhere.'

'Did you find one?' asked Mrs Hogan.

'Yes, we did, didn't we, Joe? Will this do? Does your machine fit this?'

'That's grand, Father.'

'Good! Good! Then I'll go and bring Father down. He's in bed resting. Where is the tape, Mother?'

'Tape? Oh, the tape! Yes, there on the sideboard.'

'Fine! Fine! That's everything, then. Father and I will be down in a minute. Good! Good!'

'Logs,' said Mrs Hogan to herself. Then, remembering Joe, she said to him, 'We burn our own fuel. For economy.' She smiled bleakly at him and followed her son from the room.

Joe busied himself with rigging up the machine and putting the new tape in position. When he was working in someone's house, it was part of his routine to examine the pictures and photographs around the walls, to open drawers and presses, to finger ornaments and bric-à-brac. But, here in Foundry House, a modesty, a shyness, a vague deference to something long ago did not allow his eyes even to roam from the work he was engaged in. Yet he was conscious of certain aspects of the room; the ceiling was high, perhaps as high as the roof of his own house, the fireplace was of black marble, the door handle was of cut glass, and the door itself did not close properly. Above his head was a print of horses galloping across open fields; the corner of the carpet was nibbled away. His work gave him assurance.

'There you are now, Mrs Hogan,' he said when she returned with a big basket of logs. 'All you have to do is turn this knob and away she goes.'

She ignored his stiff movement to help her with her load of logs, and knelt at the fireplace until she had built up the fire. Then, rubbing her hands down her skirt, she came and stood beside him.

'What was that, Mr Brennan?'

'I was saying that all you have to do is to turn this knob here to start it going, and turn it back to stop it. Nothing at all to it.'

'Yes?' she said, thrusting her lips forward, her mind a blank.

'That's all,' said Joe. 'Right to start, left to stop. A child could work it.' He tugged at the lapels of his jacket to indicate that he was ready to leave.

'No difficulty at all,' she repeated dreamily. Then suddenly alert again. 'Here they come. You sit there, Mr Brennan, on this side of the fire, Father Declan will sit here, I will sit beside the table. A real family circle.'

'You'll want to listen to this by yourselves, Mrs Hogan. So if you don't mind . . .'

'Don't leave, Mr Brennan. You will stay, won't you? You remember Claire, our lovely Claire. You remember her, don't you? She's out in Africa, you know, and she'll never be home again. Never. Not even for a death. You'll stay, and hear her talking to us, won't you? Of course you will.' Her finger tips touched the tops of her ears. 'Claire's voice again. Talking to us. And you'll want to hear it too, won't you?'

Before he could answer, the door burst open. Mr Bernard had come down.

It took them five minutes to get from the door to the leather armchair beside the fire, and Joe was reminded of a baby being taught to walk. Father Declan came in first, backward, crouching slightly, his eyes on his father's feet and his arms outstretched and beckoning. 'Slow-ly. Slow-ly,' he said in a hypnotist's voice. 'Slow-ly. Slow-ly.' Then his father appeared. First a stick, then a hand, an arm, the curve of his stomach, then the beard, yellow and untidy, then the whole man. Since his return to the gate lodge, Joe had not thought of Mr Bernard beyond the fact that he was there. In his mind there was a twenty-year-old image that had never been adjusted, a picture which was so familiar to him that he had long since ceased to look at it. But this was not the image, this giant who had grown in height and swollen in girth instead of shrinking, this huge, monolithic figure that inched its way across the faded carpet, one mechanical step after the other, in response to a word from the black, weaving figure before him. Joe looked at his face, fleshy, trembling, coloured in dead purple and grey-black, and at the eyes, wide and staring and quick with the terror of stumbling or of falling or even of missing a syllable of the instructions from the priest. 'Lift again. Lift it. Lift it. Good. Good. Now down, down. And the right, up and up and up — yes — and now down.' The old man wore an overcoat streaked down the front with food stains, and the hands, one clutching the head of the stick, the other limp and lifeless by his side, were so big they had no contour. His breathing was a succession of rapid sighs.

Until the journey from door to armchair was completed, Mrs Hogan made fussy jobs for herself and addressed herself to no one in particular. 'The leaves are terrible this year. Simply terrible. I must get a man to sweep them up and do something with the rockery, too, because it has got out of hand altogether . . .'

'Slow-ly. Slow-ly. Left. Left. That's it . . . up yet. Yes. And down again. Down.'

'I never saw such a year for leaves. And the worst of it is the wind blows them straight up against the hall door. Only this morning, I was saying to Mary we must make a pile of them and burn them before they smother us altogether. A bonfire — that's what we'll make.'

'Now turn. Turn. Turn. That's it. Right round. Round. Round. Now back. Good. Good.'

'Your children would enjoy a bonfire, wouldn't they, Mr Brennan? Such lively children they are, too, and so healthy, so full of life. I see them, you know, from my bedroom window. Running all over the place. So lively and full of spirits.'

A crunch, a heavy thud, and Mr Bernard was seated, not upright but sideways over the arm of the chair, as he had dropped. His eyes blinked in relief at having missed disaster once more.

'Now,' said Mrs Hogan briskly, 'I think we're ready to begin, aren't we? This is Mr Brennan of the gate lodge, Daddy. He has given us the loan of his tape-recording machine and is going to work it for us. Isn't that kind of him?'

'How are you, Mr Hogan?' said Joe.

The old man did not answer, but looked across at him. Was it a sly, reproving look, Joe wondered, or was it the awkward angle of the old man's head that made it appear sly?

'Which of these knobs is it?' asked Father Declan, his fingers playing arpeggios over the recorder. ' "On." This is it, isn't it? Yes. This is it.'

'The second one is for volume, Father,' said Joe.

'Volume. Yes. I see. Well, all set?'

'Ready,' said Mrs Hogan.

'Ready, Daddy?' asked Father Declan.

'Daddy's ready,' said Mrs Hogan.

'Joe?'

'Ready,' said Joe, because that was what Mrs Hogan had said.

'Here goes then,' said Father Declan. 'Come in, Claire. We're waiting.'

The recorder purred. The soft sound of the revolving spools spread up and out until it was as heavy as the noise of distant seas. Mrs Hogan sat at the edge of her chair. Mr Bernard remained slumped as he had fallen. Father Declan stood poised as a ballet dancer before the fire. The spools gathered speed and the purring was a pounding of blood in the ears.

'It often takes a few seconds — ' Joe began.

'Quiet!' snapped Mrs Hogan. 'Quiet, boy! Quiet!'

Then the voice came and all other sound died.

'Hello, Mammy and Daddy and Father Declan. This is Sister Claire speaking to the three of you from St Joseph's Mission, Kaluga, Northern Rhodesia. I hope you are all together when this is being played back, because I am imagining you all sitting before a great big fire in the drawing room at this minute, Daddy spread out and taking his well-earned relaxation on one side, and you, Mammy, sitting on the other side, and Declan between you both. How are you all? I wish to talk to each of you in turn — to Declan first, then to you, Mammy, and last, but by no means least, to my dear daddy. Later in the recording, Reverend Mother, who is here beside me, will say a few words to you, and after that you will hear my school choir singing some Irish songs that I have taught them and some native songs they have taught me. I hope you will enjoy them.'

Joe tried to remember the voice. Then he realized that he probably had never heard Claire speak. This sounded more like reading than speaking, he thought — like a teacher reading a story to a class of infants, making her voice go up and down in pretended interest.

She addressed the priest first, and Joe looked at him — eyes closed, hands joined at the left shoulder, head to the side, feet crossed, his whole body limp and graceful as if in repose. She asked him for his prayers and thanked him for his letter last Christmas. She said that every day she got her children to pray both for him and for the success of his work, and asked him to send her the collection of Irish melodies — a blue-backed book, she said, which he would find either in the piano stool or in the glass bookcase beside the drawing-room window.

'And now you, Mammy. You did not mention your lumbago in your last letter, so I take it you are not suffering so much from it. And I hope you have found a good maid at last, because the house is much too big for you to manage all by yourself. There are many young girls around the mission here who would willingly give you a hand, but then they are too far away, aren't they? However, please God, you are now fixed up.'

She went on to ask about the gardens and the summer crop of flowers, and told of the garden she had beside the convent and of the flowers she was growing. While her daughter spoke to her, Mrs Hogan worked her mouth and lips furiously, and Joe wondered what she was saying to herself.

'And now I come to my own daddy. How are you, Daddy? I am sure you were very sorry when Prince had to be shot, you had him so long. And then the Prince before that — how long did you have him? I was telling Sister Monica here about him the other day, about the first Prince, and when I said he lived to be nineteen and a half, she just laughed in my face and said she was sure I was mistaken. But he was nineteen and a half, wasn't he? You got him on my sixth birthday, I remember, and although I never saw the second Prince — you got him after I had entered — I am quite sure he was as lovely as the first. Now, why don't you get yourself a third, Daddy? He would be company for you when you go on your rambles, and it would be nice for *you* to have him lying beside you on the office floor, the way the first Prince used to lie.'

Joe watched the old man. Mr Bernard could not move himself to face the recorder, but his eyes were on it, the large, startled eyes of a horse.

'And now, Daddy, before I talk any more to you, I am going to play a tune for you on my violin. I hope you like it. It is the "Gartan Mother's Lullaby". Do you remember it?'

She began to play. The music was tuneful but no more. The lean, tinny notes found a weakness in the tape or in the machine, because when she played the higher part of the melody, the only sound reproduced was a shrieking monotone. Joe sprang to his feet and worked at the controls but he could do nothing. The sound adjusted itself when she came to the initial melody again, and he went back to his seat.

It was then, as he turned to go back to the fire, that he noticed the old man. He had moved somehow in his armchair and was facing the recorder, staring at it. His one good hand pressed down on the sides of his chair and his body rocked backward and forward. His expression, too, had changed. The dead purple of his cheeks was now a living scarlet, and the mouth was open. Then, even as Joe watched, he suddenly levered himself upright in the chair, his face pulsating with uncontrollable emotion, the veins in his neck dilating, the mouth shaping in preparation for speech. He leaned forward, half pointing toward the recorder with one huge hand.

'*Claire!*'

The terrible cry — hoarse, breathy, almost lost in his asthmatic snortings — released Father Declan and Mrs Hogan from their concentration on the tape. They ran to him as he fell back into the chair.

Darkness had fallen by the time Joe left Foundry House. He had helped Father Declan to carry the old man upstairs to his bedroom and helped to undress

him and put him to bed. He suggested a doctor, but neither the priest nor Mrs Hogan answered him. Then he came downstairs alone and switched off the humming machine. He waited for almost an hour for the others to come down — he felt awkward about leaving without making some sort of farewell — but when neither of them came, he tiptoed out through the hall and pulled the door after him. He left the recorder behind.

The kitchen at home was chaotic. The baby was in a zinc bath before the fire, three younger children were wrestling in their pyjamas, and the five elder were eating at the table. Rita, her hair in a turban and her sleeves rolled up, stood in the middle of the floor and shouted unheeded instructions above the din. Joe's arrival drew her temper to him.

'So you came home at last! Did you have a nice afternoon with your fancy friends?'

He picked his steps between the wrestlers and sat in the corner below the humming gas jet.

'I'm speaking to you! Are you deaf?'

'I heard you,' he said. 'Yes, I had a nice afternoon.'

She sat resolutely on the opposite side of the fireplace, to show that she had done her share of the work; it was now his turn to give a hand.

'Well?' She took a cigarette from her apron pocket and lit it. The chaos around her was forgotten.

'Well, what?' he asked.

'You went up with the recorder, and what happened?'

'They were all there — the three of them.'

'Then what?'

'We played the tape through.'

'What's the house like inside?'

'It's very nice,' Joe said slowly. 'Very nice.'

She waited for him to continue. When he did not, she said, 'Did the grandeur up there frighten you, or what?'

'I was just thinking about them, that's all,' he said.

'The old man, what's he like?'

'Mr Bernard? Oh, Mr Bernard . . . he's the same as ever. Older, of course, but the same Mr Bernard.'

'And Father Declan?'

'A fine man. A fine priest. Yes, very fine.'

'Huh!' said Rita. 'It's not worth your while going out, for all the news you bring home.'

'The tape was lovely,' said Joe quickly. 'She spoke to all of them in turn — to Father Declan and then to her mother and than to Mr Bernard himself. And she played a tune on the violin for him, too.'

'Did they like it?'

'They loved it, loved it. It was a lovely recording.'

'Did she offer you anything?'

'Forced me to have tea with them, but I said no, I had to leave.'

'What room were they in?'

'The breakfast room. The drawing room was always draughty.'

'A nice room?'

'The breakfast room? Oh, lovely, lovely . . . Glass handle on the door and a beautiful carpet and beautiful pictures . . . everything. Just lovely.'

'So that's Foundry House,' said Rita, knowing that she was going to hear no gossipy details.

'That's Foundry House,' Joe echoed. 'The same as ever — no different.'

She put out her cigarette and stuck the butt behind her ear.

'They're a great family, Rita,' he said. 'A great, grand family.'

'So they are,' she said casually, stooping to lift the baby out of its bath. Its wet hands patterned her thin blouse. 'Here, Joe! A job for you. Dress this divil for bed.'

She set the baby on his knee and went to separate the wrestlers. Joe caught the child, closed his eyes, and rubbed his cheek against the infant's soft, damp skin. 'The same as ever,' he crooned into the child's ear. 'A great family. A grand family.'

PATRICK KAVANAGH
from Patrick Kavanagh, *Collected Poems* (1964)

'Raglan Road' is a perennially favourite song when shadows grow longer and regrets begin to form. Raglan Road and Grafton Street are in Dublin. The poem takes up one of the themes of his long poem 'The Great Hunger' (1942), but the mood is more lyrical. Country life is now in the past but it is momentarily revived in the ambivalence in the phrase 'not making hay'.

ON RAGLAN ROAD
(Air: The Dawning of the Day)

On Raglan Road on an autumn day I met her first
  and knew
That her dark hair would weave a snare that I might
  one day rue;
I saw the danger, yet I walked along the enchanted way,
And I said, let grief be a fallen leaf at the dawning of
  the day.

On Grafton Street in November we tripped lightly
  along the ledge
Of the deep ravine where can be seen the worth of
  passion's pledge,
The Queen of Hearts still making tarts and I not
  making hay—
O I loved too much and by such by such is happiness
  thrown away.

I gave her gifts of the mind I gave her the secret sign
  that's known
To the artists who have known the true gods of sound
  and stone
And word and tint. I did not stint for I gave her poems
  to say.
With her own name there and her own dark hair like
  clouds over fields of May.

On a quiet street where old ghosts meet I see her
  walking now
Away from me so hurriedly my reason must allow
That I had wooed not as I should a creature made of
  clay-
When the angel wooes the clay he'd lose his wings at
  the dawn of day.

CANAL BANK WALK

Leafy-with-love banks and the green waters of the canal
Pouring redemption for me, that I do
The will of God, wallow in the habitual, the banal,
Grow with nature again as before I grew.
The bright stick trapped, the breeze adding a third
Party to the couple kissing on an old seat,
And a bird gathering materials for the nest for the Word
Eloquently new and abandoned to its delirious beat.
O unworn world enrapture me, enrapture me in a web
Of fabulous grass and eternal voices by a beech,
Feed the gaping need of my senses, give me ad lib
To pray unselfconsciously with overflowing speech
For this soul needs to be honoured with a new dress
    woven
From green and blue things and arguments that cannot
    be proven.

LINES WRITTEN ON A SEAT ON THE GRAND CANAL, DUBLIN, 'ERECTED TO THE MEMORY OF MRS DERMOT O'BRIEN'

O commemorate me where there is water,
Canal water preferably, so stilly
Greeny at the heart of summer. Brother
Commemorate me thus beautifully.
Where by a lock Niagariously roars
The falls for those who sit in the tremendous silence
Of mid-July. No one will speak in prose
Who finds his way to these Parnassian islands.
A swan goes by head low with many apologies,
Fantastic light looks through the eyes of bridges —
And look! a barge comes bringing from Athy
And other far-flung towns mythologies.
O commemorate me with no hero-courageous
Tomb — just a canal-bank seat for the passer-by.

BRENDAN KENNELLY
from Brendan Kennelly, *My Dark Fathers* (1964)

Brendan Kennelly (1936–   ), a prolific contemporary poet and critic, was born in County Kerry. Among his many publications are *Cromwell* (1983) (see p. 993 for examples) and *The Book of Judas* (1991). Here in this early uncharacteristically brooding and sombre poem he returns to his roots in the west of Ireland and to the issue of guilt.

MY DARK FATHERS

My dark fathers lived the intolerable day
Committed always to the night of wrong,
Stiffened at the hearthstone, the woman lay,
Perished feet nailed to her man's breastbone.
Grim houses beckoned in the swelling gloom
Of Munster fields where the Atlantic night
Fettered the child within the pit of doom,
And everywhere a going down of light.

And yet upon the sandy Kerry shore
The woman once had danced at ebbing tide
Because she loved flute music — and still more
Because a lady wondered at the pride

Of one so humble. That was long before
The green plant withered by an evil chance;
When winds of hunger howled at every door
She heard the music dwindle and forgot the dance.

Such mercy as the wolf receives was hers
Whose dance became a rhythm in a grave,
Achieved beneath the thorny savage furze
That yellowed fiercely in a mountain cave.
Immune to pity, she, whose crime was love,
Crouched, shivered, searched the threatening sky,
Discovered ready signs, compelled to move
Her to her innocent appalling cry.

Skeletoned in darkness, my dark fathers lay
Unknown, and could not understand
The giant grief that trampled night and day,
The awful absence moping through the land.
Upon the headland, the encroaching sea
Left sand that hardened after tides of Spring,
No dancing feet disturbed its symmetry
And those who loved good music ceased to sing.

Since every moment of the clock
Accumulates to form a final name,
Since I am come of Kerry clay and rock,
I celebrate the darkness and the shame
That could compel a man to turn his face
Against the wall, withdrawn from light so strong
And undeceiving, spancelled in a place
Of unapplauding hands and broken song.

SEÁN Ó RÍORDÁIN
from Seán Ó Ríordáin, *Brosna* (1964)

Another poem by Seán Ó Ríordáin captures something of his inward struggles towards
what he once called 'the completed self'. Wine and candle offer little protection against
the night or the vulnerability of the body.

CLAUSTROPHOBIA

In aice an fhíona
Tá coinneal is sceon,
Tá dealbh mo Thiarna
D'réir dealraimh gan chomhacht,
Tá a dtiocfaidh den oíche
Mar shluaite sa chlós,
Tá rialtas na hoíche
Lasmuigh den bhfuinneoig;
Má mhúchann mo choinneal
Ar ball de m'ainneoin
Léimfidh an oíche
Isteach im scamhóig,
Sárófar m'intinn
Is ceapfar dom sceon,
Déanfar díom oíche,
Bead im dhoircheacht bheo:
  Ach má mhaireann mo choinneal
  Aon oíche amháin
  Bead im phoblacht solais
  Go dtiocfaidh an lá

CLAUSTROPHOBIA

Beside the wine
is a candle, and terror,
and the image of my Lord
with all power gone.
What remains of the night
crowds into the yard:
the night rules
outside my window.
Unless I can stop
the candle going out
night will leap
into my lungs,
mind will founder,
my terror take over,
and the night form from me
— I am living dark.
  Let the candle last
  one night, I will be
  a republic of light
  till the day comes.

translated by Thomas Kinsella

WILLIAM COTTER MURRAY
from William Cotter Murray, *Michael Joe: A Novel of Irish Life* (1965)

William Cotter Murray (1929–) was born and brought up in Miltown Malbay in
County Clare. When he was twenty he emigrated to the United States where he went
on to become a teacher-writer at Iowa University's Writers' Workshop. *Michael Joe*, his
first novel, is a slow-paced meditation on masculinity and the claustrophobia of
provincial Ireland.

That first Christmas season after his marriage Michael Joe gave up all pretence of being a family man who had suddenly been domesticated by his marriage. He had tried to fit into the role of husband, but he began to be oppressed by the evenings at home sitting listening to the wireless or reading the paper, and the early-to-bed hours, and the Sunday walks. He was flattered and pleased by the image of himself in that role, fitting into the pattern of life in Corrigbeg, the pattern of the respectably married man. Whenever he felt oppressed by the role, he simply did not think about it, and satisfied himself mainly by telling yarns about Dublin to the fellows who came in to see him in the shop.

The Whist Drive had been the first break in the routine, and the competition and being in a crowd of people made him restless again to be out and doing something exciting. Ann's pregnancy had thrilled him at first, but when he discovered what it meant in terms of his intimacy with Ann, he was irritated, angry, and then downright hostile, though he could not say why. He could not talk it over with Ann. She was impossible to talk to that way. That night he had come home drunk, he was mad enough with her and the world not to care, but to go ahead and please himself. And he had. But next day he remembered the night before with a sort of cynical anger. He faced the fact that he had practically raped his wife. From somewhere in the distant past came an accusing voice. Was that it? Was that all he was capable of? He tried not to think about what was happening. He threw himself wholeheartedly into the spirit of Christmas.

A card addressed to Mr and Mrs M.J. McCarthy came from Nell and Seamus Larkin. The message on it was brief and impersonal: 'Our best wishes for a happy and a holy Christmas: Nell and Seamus.' The card was an image of the Manger scene, with the little Child lying on a bed of golden straw in a halo of white light, the Blessed Virgin in blue bending over the crib, St Joseph, bearded and in brown, with a shepherd's crooked staff, standing behind her, and cows, donkeys and sheep peering out from the dark at the crib. A shining silver star topped off the scene.

Michael Joe always got the post in the shop from the postman. He brought the card in opened when he came in that night for supper. He threw it on the kitchen table saying to Ann: 'Here's a reminder from Mrs Seamus Larkin.'

Ann was at the range frying liver for Michael Joe's supper. He liked liver, so she tried to have it as often as she could get it fresh from Butcher Downes.

Ann turned around and glanced at the envelope on the table, and then turned back to her work. She was in her fifth month now, and the child showed plainly in a round little bulge on her thin body.

'I'll read it later, when I have time,' she said.

Michael Joe picked it up and pulled the card out of the envelope, and read the message with mock devotion and sincerity.

'Oh, that was very nice of her,' Ann said. 'And we didn't send her any. I must do that right away.'

'Do no such thing,' Michael Joe said. He tramped heavily upstairs to wash himself.

When he was gone, Ann turned around from the range and picked up the card and stared at it for a long time. She grew misty eyed at the scene in the Manger. The little Child had its tiny hands upraised to the Blessed Virgin as if crying to be taken out of the crib and nursed. Ann almost cried. She smelt the liver burning, and hurriedly lay down the card, and went back to cooking.

At supper, Mrs McCarthy sitting with them, Ann timidly asked Michael Joe why she shouldn't send a card to Nell.

'Because 'tis all a fake. And we might as well be honest if we're going to be anything.'

'All a fake?' Ann cried. 'Christmas isn't a fake. What are you saying?'

'You know nothing about *that woman*,' Michael Joe said. 'You're an innocent compared to her. She's only mocking, sending that card.'

Ann gave him a perplexed look. 'She's a nice girl. She never would do harm to no one.'

'Nice girl how-are-you,' Michael Joe said. 'You can't see beyond your nose.'

Mrs McCarthy had remained silent. She rarely spoke to Michael Joe now. Gestures of the mother and son relationship between them had vanished; they lived in the same house together, meeting but not talking and unable to tell what secret thoughts they had about one another, and were withholding.

'Yerra, whist, Michael Joe,' she said quietly. 'Let the girl's memory be in peace.'

Michael Joe gave her a quick look. 'We're all getting into the Christmas spirit, I declare,' he said. 'You changed your tune from a long time ago.'

Mrs McCarthy bowed her head. She understood. Ann did not.

'There's no harm in sending her a card to wish her a happy Christmas. What harm is in that?' Ann said.

'I don't want us to have anything to do with them two,' Michael Joe said. 'We're well rid of them.'

Ann could not understand him. She knew that he had been great once with Nell Cullen, and it was rumoured that he was almost going to marry her. She had never heard why they broke up, and she had never asked. This sudden attack on a girl she looked up to, thought of as being an ideal, someone way above herself in every way, shocked her. Michael Joe was attacking someone she thought nearly perfect. And attacking her in a tone that frightened Ann. She was getting used to the fact now, that he was not the gay, light-hearted Romeo who teased her a lot, and liked to laugh and dance. Bit by bit, little explosion after little explosion, she was getting used to the brutal side of him. Street angel, house devil. But this attack on Nell roused her. In fear and trembling she tried to fight him, to preserve her own image of the ideal woman.

'This is the Holy Season of Christmas, I'd like to remind you,' she said trying to be firm.

'Ah, balderdash,' Michael Joe said. He had come on a burned piece of liver. 'Will you ever learn to fry this damn thing right?'

'I'm trying to say something to you, Michael Joe. Will you listen.'

Michael Joe made a motion at her with his knife and fork poised, a motion half of contempt, which she ignored.

Ann was getting angry at him. She trembled, and had to lay down her own knife and fork. It was as if her emotion were too great for her body to contain it.

'If she ever did any harm to you. And I doubt it. You should forgive her. Peace on earth to men of good will. Don't you take your religion seriously at all? The little Child ... born on Christmas ... he forgave ...' She paused on the brink of incoherence.

'Ah, will you shut up. She was a whore,' Michael Joe said. He got up from the table, leaving his supper unfinished, and stomped out of the dining room.

Ann began to cry, quietly and softly, though she was nearly hysterical. It was as if she had suddenly found herself defending all womanhood, defending its highest type and ideal against the attack of a ferocious and maddened animal. A wolf. She knew somewhere inside her, with her instincts, that her defence was inadequate against the kind of attack she was faced with. There was a kind of despair in her breaking down. He had not seen. He had only used a filthy word. Thrown mud at her queen.

She cried at the table. Old Mrs McCarthy rose slowly and came around and put an arm around Ann.

'There now, a leanna.'¹ Sure he didn't mean it, at all. Stop your crying now, and don't upset yourself.'

The old mother tried to console the young, pregnant wife as best she could, knowing in her heart of hearts that there was nothing that really could be said. And her own guilt lay heavily on her.

The next day, Ann left the house late in the morning, after standing in the hall door of the house and glancing next door to make sure that Michael Joe was not in the shop door and would see her going out. She went down to P.J. Harley's and bought a very big Christmas card, a bigger and more colourful Manger scene with the words of 'Silent Night' printed on the inside. She sent it off to Nell under her own and Michael Joe's signature, and a small prayer of her own that she made up on the spot: 'May the Holy Divine Infant shine down his blessings on you and yours, and may He bring you a happy, holy, and blessed New Year.'

As she walked down the Main Street of Corrigbeg on her own, she glanced neither right nor left as she walked, and was saluted by no one. When she got home, she felt as if she had walked a hundred miles.

A few days later she had to go out again to buy a Christmas present for Michael Joe. She thought long over what kind of present she should buy him. She worked herself into a mood of forgiveness. She was willing to forget all the things he said about Nell, and the other things too. Everywhere in the town there was festivity, coloured lights and decorations in the shop windows. Toys for children. She even went so far as to decorate the window of their own kitchen with holly and ivy, and made little cups from eggshells and wrapped them in silver paper so they looked like little silver chalices. Old Mrs McCarthy helped her. Both of them together baked little goodies and cakes, and Mrs McCarthy showed Ann how to make a plum pudding for the Christmas dinner. She was completely at one with the spirit of the season, the season of the Child. It was especially sentimental this year to her, because she was carrying a child too. Often, in her private prayers, she made the mystical association between the Child Jesus and the one in her womb, and vowed that he would be dedicated to the service of Jesus and the Blessed Virgin.

In such a mood, she forgot her anger at Michael Joe, and put out of her mind any thought of bitterness or fear of what he was bringing to pass around her. She wanted to give him a present which would make him feel like she herself felt, at one with the world. And she didn't know what would accomplish that trick. Finally, she hit on a prayer book. The idea came to her almost as an inspiration. It was the very thing. She would say nothing to him, but give him the gift. He would read the prayers inside, and then feel as she herself always felt in reading prayers in her own prayer book.

On Christmas Eve, Michael Joe came in late in the afternoon with two flat boxes, and handed one to Ann and one to his mother. He was smiling broadly, and smelled of drink. 'Here ye are, the two of ye. Happy

Christmas,' was all he said. Ann told him to wait a minute. She ran upstairs, heavy though she was, and brought down the small box carefully wrapped. She gave it to him with tears in her eyes.

'What have we here, what have we here?'

He seemed to have forgotten the argument of the other night. Ann brightened. He opened the box, and he did not stop smiling when he saw the black prayer book resting in its box.

''Twas all I could think of,' Ann said.

Michael Joe gave her a kiss on the cheek. He did not take the prayer book out of the box.

'Yerra, you shouldn't have gone to the trouble for an old codger like me,' he said. 'I'm not worth it.'

His mother gave him gifts of ties and handkerchiefs, which she simply handed to him in their box, with a 'Happy Christmas'. Michael Joe took the box quickly.

'And many happy returns,' he said to her. There was an awkward silence. 'Well, I must be off out the shop. 'Twould fall down without me. Scanlon can't turn a finger right.' He left quickly, taking both boxes with him.

Ann never saw the prayer book again.

He stayed home Christmas Eve because not even Michael Joe would dare be seen out from his family on this night, unless he had a good excuse. He lit the candle in the kitchen window. And then buried himself in the paper, though he had read it from front to back already. Ann and his mother went to Confession together. Michael Joe didn't want to go. Neither of the women tried to persuade him. Ann wanted to, but she was at peace with him now, and did not want to bring on any disturbing note again.

All three of them went up in the dark to seven o'clock Mass on Christmas morning. Ann and old Mrs McCarthy, the old woman in black supported on the arm of the young woman in dark brown, went to the rails at Mass and received Holy Communion together. Michael Joe sat restlessly looking around the chapel while they were at the rails. He used neither prayer book nor rosary beads at the Mass, and did not sing the 'Silent Night' or the 'Adeste Fideles', and appeared indifferent to the Crib made of ivy and holly to the right of the main altar. Ann and Mrs McCarthy went up and knelt before the Manger scene, after Mass, while he waited sitting in his seat watching the people leave the chapel.

He was late for his first Christmas dinner as a married man. He had gone up to Blake's for a few drinks with the boys, and had not felt the time passing until he heard the clock in the kitchen strike two. He finished his pint and bought a couple of Baby Powers'[2] before he left.

When he got home, he insisted that Ann and his mother have just a little dropeen to celebrate. Ann had never touched anything stronger than a lemonade in her life. Mrs McCarthy, of late, occasionally took a drop of brandy for her heart. The good-humoured argument about whether Ann should have a drop of whisky or not helped to prevent a more serious fight over why he was late for his dinner. Finally, Ann let Michael Joe pour her a thimbleful with a lot of water in it. Mrs McCarthy took hers neat, sipping it slowly.

Michael Joe stayed in the rest of Christmas Day. Ann and Mrs McCarthy both took a rest after the dinner. He was left alone. He turned on the wireless. There was nothing but sacred music on from the BBC. He switched it off. There was no paper to read so that he could distract himself. He prowled around the house, and poked in a few cupboards. In one of them he found a book, *The Robe*, which he started to read. He gave it up. He could not go back to the time of Christ in his imagination. The story took no grip on him so he put it down. Then he went for a short walk down the back way, but it began to rain and he had to turn back.

Finally, desperate for something to do with himself, he went out to the shop and began to pore over the ledgers, making lists of his debts and his debtors. He lit a fire in the little room at the back, and eventually dozed on a chair, alone, there by the fire.

Now, alone, his mind turned back into the past, and the past was Nell. If he had felt deceived and betrayed by her in their living past, he was haunted by her now even worse, when she was no longer a living presence in the town. He didn't believe in ghosts, but whenever he closed his eyes and let himself relax, he could call her up in his mind as vividly and as fully as if she were alive before him. He did not indulge in this calling up of her image too often, or for long. A flash. She was there. He talked to her. And then he sent her away. Said no to her, rejected her again as he had in the past, and each time he said no, he knew he was being hard, bitter, and cold. Once, he thought of forgiveness. Forgive ... forgive ... forgive. He laughed. He had no idea how to go about forgiving. The idea was totally alien to him. It had no reality. It was a word he had heard, but was without substance to him. How could he forgive? What did he have to do to forgive? He did not know, now.

---

1   Irish: an leanbh, child, baby of the family. Here a term of endearment.
2   Small bottles of whiskey.

BRYAN MacMAHON
version as sung by Paddy Tunney on *Ireland Her Own* (Topic, 1966)

To my mind this is one of the best songs composed about the War of Independence in 1919–21. Listen to Paddy Tunney singing this on Topic Records and you can hear the heartbeat that accompanied Ireland in its transition from colonial rule to independence. In *Where Songs Do Thunder* (1991), Tunney writes: 'No other ballad inspired by the War of Independence evokes the pain and poignance, the pride and mórtas cine [Irish: pride of race] of a people rising from the dead to shake off the chains of bondage.' As is clear from my Introduction to the *Reader*, this song was composed much earlier than 1966.

THE VALLEY OF KNOCKANURE

You may sing and speak about Easter Week
And the heroes of '98,
Of the fearless men who roamed the glen
For victory or defeat.
There were those who died on the green hillside
They were outlawed on the moor;
Not a word is said of the gallant dead
In the valley of Knockanure.

There was Dalton, Walsh and Lyons boys,
They were young and in their pride.
In every house in every crowd
They were always side by side.
The republic bold they did uphold
Though outlawed on the moor,
And side by side they fought and died
In the valley of Knockanure.

Upon an autumn evening
These three young men sat down
To wait upon a brief dispatch
To come from Tralee town.
It wasn't long 'til Lyons came on
Saying time isn't mine nor yours
But alas it was late when they met their fate
In the valley of Knockanure.

Upon a neighbouring hillside
We listened in calm dismay,
In every house for miles around
A maiden knelt to pray.
They're closing in around them now
With rifle-fire so sure,
And Dalton's dead and Walshe is down
In the valley of Knockanure.

For they brought them hence beyond the fence
Wherein the furze did bloom,
Like brothers now they faced the foe
To meet their vengeful doom.
As Dinny spoke his voice it broke
With a passion proud and pure:
'For our land we die as we face the sky
In the valley of Knockanure.'

There they lay on the damp cold clay
Martyred for Ireland's cause
Where the cowardly clan of the Black and Tans
Has showed them England's laws.
No more they'll feel the soft breeze still
Or uplands fair and pure
For the wild geese fly where the heroes lie
In the valley of Knockanure.

When the evening sun was sinking
Beyond the Feale and Lee
The pale moon was rising
Way out beyond Tralee.
The glistening stars shone out afar
And gleamed o'er Collins moor,
And the banshee cried where the heroes died
In the valley of Knockanure.

I met with Dalton's mother
And these words to me did say:
'May the Lord have mercy on my son
Who fell in the fight today.
Could I but kiss his cold cold lips
My aching heart would cure,
And I'd gladly lay him down to rest
In the valley of Knockanure.

PATRICK BOYLE

from Patrick Boyle, *At Night All Cats Are Grey* (1966)

Patrick Boyle (1905–82) was born in Ballymoney, County Antrim, and worked all his life in the Ulster Bank, mainly in Donegal. *At Night All Cats Are Grey* was his first collection of short stories; other collections include *All Looks Yellow To The Jaundiced Eye* (1969) and *A View From Calvary* (1976). There is a rawness about Boyle's stories and at times, as in the one here, a primitive quality that is reminiscent by turns of O'Flaherty and Synge. Indeed it could be argued that the following short story is Synge without the lyricism.

Go Away, Old Man, Go Away

A sting of heat was beginning to creep into the morning sun. Like a warm hand, it clamped down on the old man's scrawny neck as if it meant to push him down into the mounds of cut turf he was so busily spreading. It wormed its way through the layers of cardigans and undershirts, it scorched his meagre shrunken buttocks, it soaked through his boots so that his scalded feet chafed against the damp wrinkled socks. Sweat trickled down his face, smarting his eyes and salting his mouth, but he worked on steadily, rolling the heaped-up sods back through his straddled legs like a terrier rooting frantically at a burrow.

Stretched ahead of him to the bog hole were rows of cut turf, lying in close-packed heaps just as they were heeled up by the barrowmen. The skin had barely formed on the spongy wet sods and often he had to ease them apart as though they were slabs of toffee. As he scrabbled and plucked and clawed, he kept up a continuous muttering grumble, punctuated by grunts of exertion.

His irritation was increased by the growling insistence of an empty stomach. Each time he stooped his guts would plunge madly around, whinnying like a horse fresh from the grass. Soon all minor grievances — his aching back, the heavy woollen drawers lacerating his fork, his scalded feet — all became blended into and seemed to increase the clamour of his empty belly. More and more frequently he paused, squatted down on his hunkers, glaring across the bog at the cottage on the roadside a few fields away. Once he saw someone come to the door and he straightened up, wiping his hands on his trousers while he waited for her to call him but she only took a look up the road and went in again.

The fowlman, he thought. I'll gamble a bob[1] that's who she's keeping an eye out for. Damn the hait[2] she cares if I died in my tracks with the hunger as long as she's there for the egg money. So help me God, I'd get more attention if I was a clucking hen. Dancing and jack-acting is all that one cares for. Oh, a nice stunner of a wife I let myself in for!

He started in, half-heartedly, to work again but soon gave it up.

'I'll not put up with it a day more,' he muttered.

He picked up his coat and started off up the deeply rutted track leading out of the bog.

By the time he reached the main road his temper had cooled and he began, as usual, looking for excuses for her. Maybe the fire had gone against her. Or she had to go for water. She was terrible sore on water, that one. Scrubbing at herself night, noon and morning. The smell of the soap trailing after her round the house till you'd nearly trip over it, it's that strong. He wrinkled his nose and sniffed. That time he had come on her, washing herself in the room. Standing there in her pelt with the pride and sleekness and grandeur shining out of her white skin like you'd see it in a blood mare. Admiring herself in the glass, no less. Posing and stroking and smirking at herself as if she were some class of a cat. My God, she could have been struck dead for less. And then rushing at him like a mad thing, spitting and cursing and slamming the door in his face. It had been that way from the start. Never letting him as much as put a hand next or near her. Cringing away from him in bed as though he was a black stranger. He sighed. Well, it wouldn't last that way for ever. She would come round some time. He would just have to take her easy and thole[3] a while longer.

He hesitated for a second on the porch, then cleared his throat and pushed in the door briskly.

'Are you aiming to starve me, girl?' he asked.

There was no one there.

The kitchen floor was unswept; the table still littered with yesterday's dishes; the fire burned down to a few coals of turf. He unhooked the kettle swinging from the crane and shook it.

'Are you within there, woman?' he roared.

He heard the bed creak and the slow reluctant steps dragging along the floor. He shook the kettle again savagely.

'Motherajaysus, are ye still in yer bed?'

She came out of the room and stopped in the doorway, yawning and scratching her head — a fine strapping piece, bubbed[4] and bottomed like a tinker woman, with oily jet-black hair, thick sensual lips and dark eyes, blurred and heavy with sleep. The dirty woollen-jumper, sweat-stained at the armpits, barely reached the rumpled partly-fastened skirt. Her bare legs were brown-blotched with the heat of the fire.

She yawned again and knuckled her eyes.

'I just threw myself on the bed a minute,' she said. 'Till the kettle would come to the boil.'

Speechless, he swung aloft the steaming kettle, as if he were exorcizing her with a smoking thurible.

She stared at him, open-mouthed.

'What are you aiming to do with that thing?' she demanded.

She darted across the room.

'Give it here, man,' she said, trying to snatch the kettle from him.

He pushed her away roughly.

'Lookat here,' he said dramatically, tilting up the kettle over the hearth so that the few remaining drops went sizzling into the fire. 'Boiled to nothing.'

The sleep had gone out of her eyes: the listlessness from her body. Her sallow face was flushed and her thick lips pouted aggressively. But though her features were distorted with rage, there was about her a curious air of satisfaction as though the very volume of her emotion brought with it some measure of bodily fulfilment.

'Is it trying to quench the fire you are?' she asked.

'Quench be damned. Wouldn't a good spit smother it?'

'Maybe if you had the trouble of lighting it, you wouldn't be so quick —'

She broke off and, stooping, commenced heaping up the glowing embers with the tongs.

'Listen here, me young tit,' he said, addressing the swaying rump-filled skirt. 'It would fit you better if you stopped home at nights instead of roaming the country. You'll have the priest naming you yet from the altar.'

The strip of white flesh below her rucked-up jumper, winking at every movement, kept ogling him slyly.

'A man at my time of life slaving and sweating like a Turk while his wife goes trapeezing around the country to every bit of a dance or a card game that's held in the parish. Sure I must be the laughing stock of half-Europe.'

His gaze travelled down to the creased hollows behind her knees.

'Letting a man off to his work without a bite to eat. Have you no shame in you?'

He moistened his flabby craving lips.

'The women . . . they're a terror . . . the same the world over . . . rising a mutiny wherever they be . . .'

He pushed out a tentative hand, but at once let it fall to his side and remained staring at her dumbly, his eyes sick and glazed with desire.

Across her shoulder she looked — taunting him with bold mocking eyes.

'Give over,' she said. 'It's the same ould tune — day in, day out. It's a wonder you took me at all, the way you go on.'

The old man struggled for speech.

'Ye-Ye-Ye-Ye're damned smart, aren't ye.'

Failing to think of any more crushing remark, he spat viciously into the heart of the fire and turned away. At the door he shouted back:

'And don't be the whole day getting me me bloody bit of breakfast.'

Outside, he squatted on the low window-sill — tired, hungry, emotionally deflated.

You common idiot, he told himself. Letting that one get the better of you with a few flirts of her backside and her stooping over the fire to give you a right view of her wherewithal. As if it wasn't sticking out like the side of a church at the best of times. Up half the night jack-acting and then basking the day long in her bed, snoring and grunting like a sow at the pigging. And across in the bog making slaughter of himself is no less a person than the boss of the house — the boss; how are you! — hugging his grinding puddings[5] with sheer starvation. The impudent trollop, slooching around half-dressed, the bare ones scalded off her with the heat of the fire and the two elders[6] swinging out of her like she was six months gone. God above, man, I don't know what you see in her.

The sun beat down on him, soaking him with listless warmth so that he sagged forward, his chin knuckle-propped, staring with drowsy cat-blinking eyes at the sweeping expanse of dun-coloured bog.

His eyes closed and the scraggy dewlap settled its folds deeper round his knuckled hands. From one nostril a green dangle of snot rattled out and in with each wheezing breath like the flickering tongue of a snake.

Her voice roused him.

'Did the fowl cart go by?'

He looked at her stupidly. Blobs of colour swayed

and danced before his eyes. His legs and the back of his neck were stiff and sore.

'Henh?' he said, rinsing the foulness from his mouth with fresh-sucked spittle.

'I suppose you fell asleep and let him pass unbeknownst. Didn't you know I had three fat pullets ready waiting for him? He'll not be here again till next week.'

He noticed she had changed her clothes, put on stockings and brushed her hair.

'Aye, so,' he said.

'Well, can't you answer me anyway? Did you see e'er a sign of the fowlman?'

'Would that be why you were toveying yerself up[7] instead of getting me me breakfast?'

'You'll get your breakfast time enough, never fret.'

'It's borne in on me that it's only when there's callers coming round the house that you take time to tidy yourself. Other times you're not so particular.'

She glowered down at him in sulky silence.

'If it's the fowlman or the post-boy or even a stinking ould tramp itself, you're into the room pulling and hauling at yourself. Wasting the day blethering to the likes of them but never a civil word for your own husband. Though God knows it's little enough to expect from you for the wheen[8] of minutes you spend at home every day.'

'Is it staying at home at the fire I'd be? Listening to you nagging and backbiting? You'd scald the heart off of a saint with that bitter ould viper's tongue of yours. I'll go out of my mind if I have to listen to much more of it.'

He rasped his hand across his stubby chin and gazed up at her with an air of patient resignation.

'That's right. That's right. I'm to blame for everything. It was me let the fire down. It was me kept you in your bed all morning. It's me hunts you out at night to the dances.'

He struck his knee with his fist.

'So-help-me-Jaysus, there was peace in this house till you come into it. I'd a right to leave you stewing in misery where you were. A bit of a tin shanty with all the winds of the world whistling through the chinks and that so-called father of yours pasted to the bed, dragging his guts up and spitting them round the floor till you could bloody near skate on it. That's what I took you from. And let you never forget it, me girl.'

He knew as he finished that he had said too much.

Two quick steps brought her standing over him, her face mottled with rage.

'Throwing the like of that up in my teeth,' she said. 'I'm as well got as the most of them, if the truth were known. There was none of this talk when you were

plastering over me to have you. Oh, you made promises then to no end! Telling me the fine easy life I'd have with all the money you'd saved. Well, it's easy to count what I've seen of it. If it weren't for a few ha'pence I get for the eggs I'd be in rags.'

She looked down contemptuously at him hunched up in misery on the window-sill.

'That your dirty money may choke you, you hungry old scaldcrow. I've a mind to pack my duds[9] and clear out of here this minute.'

He heard her go inside and then the angry clatter of roughly handled dishes. After that — silence.

His heart missed a beat. Surely to God she was never in earnest. An awful desolation swept over him, leaving him sick and trembling.

He started to rise but stopped when he heard her voice, deep and husky, singing very low as if to herself:

For an old man he is old
And an old man he is grey.

He could picture her leaning across the table, head tilted back, eyes half-closed, a cool impudent smile on her face.

And an old man's nose is damp and cold
Go away, old man, go away!

Furtively he wiped the drop off his nose with the back of his hand. The venomous targe,[10] he thought. There's no length she'll not go to bait me.

She was singing again. Louder and with a kind of a glad lilt to her voice.

But a young man he is young
And a young man he is gay
And a young man's kiss will bruise your lips
Come away, young man, come away!

So that was it, by the Lord. That was how she spent her nights. Lurking in outhouses or sprawled her length at the back of a ditch or maybe under the dry arch of a bridge. With any one of a hundred young rams from the four quarters of the universe. Giving them what *he* should have been getting. The nights she'd slip out without a word and come back hours later with two glowing coals for eyes. Her cheeks flushed, her hair tossed. 'It's a grand windy night,' she'd maybe say and sit gazing into the fire with a queer twisted smile at the corner of her lips. Thinking back on the night's doings. Feeling the moist seeking lips and the groping hands roving her body. Hearing wild, whispered words and harsh breathing and maybe the sudden step on the road to put them cowering down with their hearts pounding. Seeing the whiteness of a face looming over her, strained and vicious.

And across the fire from her is sitting . . . himself. Blind to it all.

He closed his eyes to shut out the torturing vision but his relentless imagination kept on insinuating new and ever more humiliating possibilities.

How many? In God's name how many in the parish had had her? Was there one at all he could look straight in the face and not be left wondering? Why, even that little brat she'd been on the look-out for all morning could have been . . .

He tried to thrust the thought away from him but it had taken root. Wasn't he nearly always out working when the cart called? Wouldn't he be down in the bog this minute only for she sleeping in? And wouldn't that little whelp be inside bargaining for the fowl with the whole house to himself?

The bitterness rose in his throat like a ball of puke.

It's too much, he thought. It's more than mortal man can stand.

He got to his feet and looked aimlessly about him. Something would have to be done. Things could not go on this way. Suddenly he started off towards the hen-house, muttering to himself.

'There'll be an end put to his capers.'

Unbarring the door he flung it open.

'Chook! Chook! Chook!' he called in a loud aggressive voice.

There was a flutter of startled wings and a raucous babble of excited cluckings.

He glanced over his shoulder apprehensively, then tried again, sinking his voice to a seductive whisper.

'Choooooook, chook, chook. Come on the little chookies.'

He rasped his fingers together enticingly.

They came scampering out, heads craned forward, wings tucked tight against bodies, as if they were skaters racing to reach him.

Grabbing the nearest bird by the neck, he squeezed tight with finger and thumb on its gullet. A few frantic wing flaps and he had hold of its legs, hauling on its neck like an archer bending a bow.

He flung the quivering body aside and called again.

'Chook, chook, chook. Oh, the poor wee chook-chooks.'

They stood around, eyeing him with a cagey stare, never budging an inch. Picking up a handful of gravel he shook it out on the ground.

Pushing, scrambling, they surged round him, pecking at the bare ground. This time he chose

carefully — a fine fat pullet, larded with meat. He stooped down cautiously and picked it up, one hand pinioning the wings to the body, the other nipping the squawk rising in its thrapple. Holding it up before him, he watched the gaping beak and the frantic scampering legs.

'What hurry is on you, girl?' he said. 'You'll get to the pot soon enough.'

Its neck was hard to stretch and by the time he had finished the fowl had scattered. Only one remained, picking half-heartedly at a bedded stone.

It sidled away from him, neatly avoiding his clutch. Stooping, he followed it up, his hands outspread as if to impart a blessing but it slid from under them in little mincing spurts. At the gable end of the house he caught up with it and grabbed it by the legs. The accumulation of rage that had been festering in him all morning broke out at last.

'Ye little blirt,'[11] he roared. 'I'll put manners on ye.'

He swung it up, flapping wings and squawking beak, and made pulp of it against the wall. He kept flailing away, although the bird's head was almost torn off. His face and hands were spattered with blood: the lime-washed wall red wealed. A fluffy nimbus floated over his head. In time with each welt, he ground out:

'I'll teach ye . . . to turn my house . . . into a bloody knocking shop.'

He heard her footsteps running around the house but paid no heed. It was the rough grip on his shoulder that brought him back to reality.

'What d'you think you're doing, man?' she demanded. 'Are you gone mad?'

He shook himself free and glared at her, the dead bird swinging from his hand, its head scraping the ground.

'Have you lost the use of your tongue?' she asked.

His lips moved noiselessly, seeking the right words — the bitter lacerating words. He held the limp body up, shaking it before her face.

'That'll be one less for your fancy man when he calls,' he said, throwing it down at her feet. 'And if you look beyond you'll see two more he'll be at the loss of.'

His hand was still up, thumbing over his shoulder, when she slapped his face.

The shock of the sudden blow left him dazed for a moment. He rubbed his tingling cheek, gazing at her stupidly. Then he let a roar out of him.

'Sowbitch!' he shouted and flogged the back of his fist across her mouth, feeling the rasp of his knuckles on her clenched teeth.

He stood over her, his arm drawn back threateningly.

'Ye low trollop,' he said. 'I've a right to hammer the living daylights out of ye.'

At the sight of the blood trickling from the corner of her mouth the anger died in him. They stood facing each other, so close that he could see a tiny reflected sun glittering at him from each of her eyes. There was a kind of blindness about her eyes, he thought, as though the sight in them was turned inwards. And her face too, with a queer unmindful look to it, like you'd see in the face of someone you're talking to and him listening all the time to the sound of music or great talk going on behind him.

The curious expression of her face and eyes, the glossy sheen of her freshly combed hair, the smell of scent and sweat and warm flesh sent a tepid ripple of desire through him.

'There's no rhyme or reason for a doggery the like of this,' he said. 'It's a fret to man . . . the way people gut other . . . for nothing.'

'Or next to nothing,' he added.

He put an awkward hand on her shoulder.

At once she swung in towards him, gripping him with savage arms, grinding her tensed body against him, clawing and tearing at his coat with frantic urgent fingers.

The intensity of her passion appalled him. This is awful, he thought. Outside my own house in the broad light of day.

I'm a done man if anyone sees me.

He made to push her off but his hands buried themselves in the softness of her breasts. The ache that had been coiling and twisting around inside him came back worse than ever. Crab-like his hands began exploring, finger after cautious clumsy finger, ready to shrink back at the slightest rebuff. As though calmed by his touch the convulsive shudderings died away and she lay against him inertly, breathing heavily with small pathetic gulps like a child sobbing itself to sleep. He felt the urge to comfort her — to dry her eyes and stroke her hair and say the crazy foolish things that had been shame-locked in his heart for all these years. His lacerated dignity, the turmoil of his thoughts, the pent-up torrent of his love that could be breached by the smallest, the most casual gesture of affection — all these things he pleaded through the pressure of his rough unskilful hands.

She sprang away from him, her eyes blazing, her blood-smeared face torn with hate and revulsion.

'Take your filthy hands offa me,' she screamed. 'At this age of your life to be pawing and groping at a woman! 'Tis of the grave you should be thinking, you doting old fool.'

She turned away and walked with a contemptuous swagger towards the house. Leaning against the doorjamb she watched him, her eyes spiteful: pitiless. Deliberately, in a low mocking voice, she commenced to sing:

> For an old man he is old
> And an old man he is grey
> And an old man's love is a thing of shame
> Go away, old man, go away!

For a few moments she stayed, her eyes fixed on his grimly squared shoulders and rigid stubborn back, expecting an answering jibe. When he did not rise to the bait, she turned and went in.

He stood as she had left him — stiffly erect, hands locked behind his back, his lined face expressionless but for the twitching lips.

From far across the bog a lone gull called. And called again; a tiny fretful wail as if mourning something irretrievably lost — the twinkling silver of breaking mackerel, a calm sea frosted with moonlight, the tall waves bowing their grizzled arrogant heads to the land.

The old man turned his head towards the sound, staring miserably, hopelessly, blindly ahead; the tears coursing unheeded down his ravaged face.

He heard her come to the door.

'Your breakfast's ready,' she called. And back over her shoulder as she wheeled round, 'Or maybe you've something more important to do.'

Her jibing laugh was merged in the tinkling of delf.

Again the gull mewled, a harsh discordant cackle, then rose on lazy sun-bleached wings. High overhead it flew, piping shrilly, its swaying searching neck outstretched, settling down at last in a freshly ploughed field to gorge its empty craw.

---

1   A shilling, 5p.
2   Hait is a word of encouragement given to a horse to urge it on; haith is a deformation of the word faith, a quasi-oath (OED).
3   Endure.
4   Bubs is slang for a woman's breasts.
5   Slang word meaning stomach, guts.
6   Cow's udders (P.W. Joyce).
7   Preening.
8   Few.
9   Clothes, gear, things.
10   A scolding woman (P.W. Joyce).
11   Loud-mouth (Share).

BOB SHAW
from *World's Best Science Fiction 1967*

Bob Shaw (1931–96) was born in Belfast. A graduate in mechanical engineering he went on to work in industrial relations and journalism. His prize-winning science fiction includes *Orbitsville* (1976) and *The Ragged Astronauts* (1987). Here in this short story, set in Argyll in Scotland, he gives a twist to lines from Thomas Moore's song, 'Oft in the Stilly Night'.

Light of Other Days

Leaving the village behind, we followed the heady sweeps of the road up into a land of slow glass.

I had never seen one of the farms before and at first found them slightly eerie — an effect heightened by imagination and circumstance. The car's turbine was pulling smoothly and quietly in the damp air so that we seemed to be carried over the convolutions of the road in a kind of supernatural silence. On our right the mountain sifted down into an incredibly perfect valley of timeless pine, and everywhere stood the great frames of slow glass, drinking light. An occasional flash of afternoon sunlight on their wind bracing created an illusion of movement, but in fact the frames were deserted. The rows of windows had been standing on the hillside for years, staring into the valley, and men only cleaned them in the middle of the night when their human presence would not matter to the thirsty glass.

They were fascinating, but Selina and I didn't mention the windows. I think we hated each other so much we both were reluctant to sully anything new by drawing it into the nexus of our emotions. The holiday, I had begun to realize, was a stupid idea in the first place. I had thought it would cure everything, but, of course, it didn't stop Selina being pregnant and, worse still, it didn't even stop her being angry about being pregnant.

Rationalizing our dismay over her condition, we had circulated the usual statements to the effect that we would have *liked* having children — but later on, at the proper time. Selina's pregnancy had cost us her well-paid job and with it the new house we had been negotiating and which was far beyond the reach of my income from poetry. But the real source of our annoyance was that we were face to face with the realization that people who say they want children later always mean they want children never. Our nerves were thrumming with the knowledge that we, who had thought ourselves so unique, had fallen into the same biological trap as every mindless rutting creature which ever existed.

The road took us along the southern slopes of Ben Cruachan until we began to catch glimpses of the gray Atlantic far ahead. I had just cut our speed to absorb the view better when I noticed the sign spiked to a gatepost. It said: 'SLOW GLASS — Quality High, Prices Low — J.R. Hagan.' On an impulse I stopped the car on the verge, wincing slightly as tough grasses whipped noisily at the body-work.

'Why have we stopped?' Selina's neat, smoke-silver head turned in surprise.

'Look at that sign. Let's go up and see what there is. The stuff might be reasonably priced out here.'

Selina's voice was pitched high with scorn as she refused, but I was too taken with my idea to listen. I had an illogical conviction that doing something extravagant and crazy would set us right again.

'Come on,' I said, 'the exercise might do us some good. We've been driving too long anyway.'

She shrugged in a way that hurt me and got out of the car. We walked up a path made of irregular, packed clay steps nosed with short lengths of sapling. The path curved through trees which clothed the edge of the hill and at its end we found a low farmhouse. Beyond the little stone building tall frames of slow glass gazed out towards the voice-stilling sight of Cruachan's ponderous descent towards the waters of Loch Linnhe. Most of the panes were perfectly transparent but a few were dark, like panels of polished ebony.

As we approached the house through a neat cobbled yard a tall middle-aged man in ash-coloured tweeds arose and waved to us. He had been sitting on the low rubble wall which bounded the yard, smoking a pipe and staring towards the house. At the front window of the cottage a young woman in a tangerine dress stood with a small boy in her arms, but she turned disinterestedly and moved out of sight as we drew near.

'Mr Hagan?' I guessed.

'Correct. Come to see some glass, have you? Well, you've come to the right place.' Hagan spoke crisply, with traces of the pure highland which sounds so much like Irish to the unaccustomed ear. He had one of those calmly dismayed faces one finds on elderly road-menders and philosophers.

'Yes,' I said. 'We're on holiday. We saw your sign.'

Selina, who usually has a natural fluency with strangers, said nothing. She was looking towards the now empty window with what I thought was a slightly puzzled expression.

'Up from London, are you? Well, as I said, you've come to the right place — and at the right time, too. My wife and I don't see many people this early in the season.'

I laughed. 'Does that mean we might be able to buy a little glass without mortgaging our home?'

'Look at that now,' Hagan said, smiling helplessly. 'I've thrown away any advantage I might have had in the transaction. Rose, that's my wife, says I never learn. Still, let's sit down and talk it over.' He pointed at the rubble wall then glanced doubtfully at Selina's immaculate blue skirt. 'Wait till I fetch a rug from the house.' Hagan limped quickly into the cottage, closing the door behind him.

'Perhaps it wasn't such a marvellous idea to come up here,' I whispered to Selina, 'but you might at least be pleasant to the man. I think I can smell a bargain.'

'Some hope,' she said with deliberate coarseness. 'Surely even you must have noticed that ancient dress his wife is wearing? He won't give much away to strangers.'

'Was that his wife?'

'Of course that was his wife.'

'Well, well,' I said, surprised. 'Anyway, try to be civil with him. I don't want to be embarrassed.'

Selina snorted, but she smiled whitely when Hagan reappeared and I relaxed a little. Strange how a man can love a woman and yet at the same time pray for her to fall under a train.

Hagan spread a tartan blanket on the wall and we sat down, feeling slightly self-conscious at having been translated from our city-oriented lives into a rural tableau. On the distant slate of the loch, beyond the watchful frames of slow glass, a slow-moving steamer drew a white line towards the south. The boisterous mountain air seemed almost to invade our lungs, giving us more oxygen than we required.

'Some of the glass farmers around here,' Hagan began, 'give strangers, such as yourselves, a sales talk about how beautiful the autumn is in this part of Argyll. Or it might be spring, or the winter. I don't do that — any fool knows that a place which doesn't look right in summer never looks right. What do you say?'

I nodded compliantly.

'I want you just to take a good look out towards Mull, Mr . . .'

'Garland.'

'. . . Garland. That's what you're buying if you buy my glass, and it never looks better than it does at this minute. The glass is in perfect phase, none of it is less than ten years thick — and a four-foot window will cost you two hundred pounds.'

'*Two hundred!*' Selina was shocked. 'That's as much as they charge at the Scenedow shop in Bond Street.'[1]

Hagan smiled patiently, then looked closely at me to see if I knew enough about slow glass to appreciate what he had been saying. His price had been much higher than I had hoped — but *ten years thick!* The cheap glass one found in places like the Vistaplex and Pane-orama stores usually consisted of a quarter of an inch of ordinary glass faced with a veneer of slow glass perhaps only ten or twelve months thick.

'You don't understand, darling,' I said, already determined to buy. 'This glass will last ten years and it's in phase.'

'Doesn't that only mean it keeps time?'

Hagan smiled at her again, realizing he had no further necessity to bother with me. 'Only, you say! Pardon me, Mrs Garland, but you don't seem to appreciate the miracle, the genuine honest-to-goodness miracle, of engineering precision needed to produce a piece of glass in phase. When I say the glass is ten years thick it means it takes light ten years to pass through it. In effect, each one of those panes is ten light-years thick — more than twice the distance to the nearest star — so a variation in actual thickness of only a millionth of an inch would . . .'

He stopped talking for a moment and sat quietly looking towards the house. I turned my head from the view of the loch and saw the young woman standing at the window again. Hagan's eyes were filled with a kind of greedy reverence which made me feel uncomfortable and at the same time convinced me Selina had been wrong. In my experience husbands never looked at wives that way, at least, not at their own.

The girl remained in view for a few seconds, dress glowing warmly, then moved back into the room. Suddenly I received a distinct, though inexplicable, impression she was blind. My feeling was that Selina and I were perhaps blundering through an emotional interplay as violent as our own.

'I'm sorry,' Hagan continued, 'I thought Rose was going to call me for something. Now, where was I, Mrs Garland? Ten light-years compressed into a quarter of an inch means . . .'

I ceased to listen, partly because I was already sold, partly because I had heard the story of slow glass many times before and had never yet understood the principles involved. An acquaintance with scientific training had once tried to be helpful by telling me to visualize a pane of slow glass as a hologram which did not need coherent light from a laser for the reconstitution of its visual information, and in which every photon of ordinary light passed through a spiral tunnel coiled outside the radius of capture of each atom in the glass. This gem of, to me, incomprehensibility not only told me nothing, it convinced me once again that a mind as non-technical as mine should concern itself less with causes than effects.

The most important effect, in the eyes of the average individual, was that light took a long time to pass through a sheet of slow glass. A new piece was always jet black because nothing had yet come through, but one could stand the glass beside, say, a woodland lake until the scene emerged, perhaps a year later. If the glass was then removed and installed in a dismal city flat, the flat would — for that year — appear to overlook the woodland lake. During the year it wouldn't be merely a very realistic but still picture — the water would ripple in sunlight, silent animals would come to drink, birds would cross the sky, night would follow day, season would follow season. Until one day, a year later, the beauty held in the subatomic pipelines would be exhausted and the familiar gray cityscape would reappear.

Apart from its stupendous novelty value, the commercial success of slow glass was founded on the fact that having a scenedow was the exact emotional equivalent of owning land. The meanest cave dweller could look out on misty parks — and who was to say they weren't his? A man who really owns tailored gardens and estates doesn't spend his time proving his ownership by crawling on his ground, feeling, smelling, tasting it. All he receives from the land are light patterns, and with scenedows those patterns could be taken into coal mines, submarines, prison cells.

On several occasions I have tried to write short pieces about the enchanted crystal but, to me, the theme is so ineffably poetic as to be, paradoxically, beyond the reach of poetry — mine at any rate. Besides, the best songs and verse had already been written, with prescient inspiration, by men who had died long before slow glass was discovered. I had no hope of equalling, for example, Moore with his:

Oft in the stilly night,
Ere slumber's chain has bound me,
Fond Memory brings the light
Of other days around me . . . .

It took only a few years of slow glass to develop from a scientific curiosity to a sizeable industry. And much to the astonishment of us poets — those of us who remain convinced that beauty lives though lilies die — the trappings of that industry were no different from those of any other. There were good scenedows which cost a lot of money, and there were inferior scenedows which cost rather less. The thickness, measured in years, was an important factor in the cost but there was also the question of *actual* thickness, or phase.

Even with the most sophisticated engineering techniques available thickness control was something of a hit-and-miss affair. A coarse discrepancy could mean that a pane intended to be five years thick might be five and a half, so that light which entered in summer emerged in winter; a fine discrepancy could mean that noon sunshine emerged at midnight. These incompatibilities had their peculiar charm — many night workers, for example, liked having their own private time zones — but, in general, it cost more to buy scenedows which kept closely in step with real time.

Selina still looked unconvinced when Hagan had finished speaking. She shook her head almost imperceptibly and I knew he had been using the wrong approach. Quite suddenly the pewter helmet of her hair was disturbed by a cool gust of wind, and huge clean tumbling drops of rain began to spang round us from an almost cloudless sky.

'I'll give you a cheque now,' I said abruptly, and saw Selina's green eyes triangulate angrily on my face. 'You can arrange delivery?'

'Aye, delivery's no problem,' Hagan said, getting to his feet. 'But wouldn't you rather take the glass with you?'

'Well, yes — if you don't mind.' I was shamed by his readiness to trust my scrip.

'I'll unclip a pane for you. Wait here. It won't take long to slip it into a carrying frame.' Hagan limped down the slope towards the seriate windows, through some of which the view towards Linnhe was sunny, while others were cloudy and a few pure black.

Selina drew the collar of her blouse closed at her throat. 'The least he could have done was invite us inside. There can't be so many fools passing through that he can afford to neglect them.'

I tried to ignore the insult and concentrated on writing the cheque. One of the outsize drops broke across my knuckles, splattering the pink paper.

'All right,' I said, 'let's move in under the eaves till he gets back.' You worm, I thought as I felt the whole thing go completely wrong. I just had to be a fool to marry you. A prize fool, a fool's fool — and now that you've trapped part of me inside you I'll never ever, never ever, *never ever* get away.

Feeling my stomach clench itself painfully, I ran behind Selina to the side of the cottage. Beyond the window the neat living room, with its coal fire, was empty but the child's toys were scattered on the floor. Alphabet blocks and a wheelbarrow the exact colour of freshly pared carrots. As I stared in, the boy came running from the other room and began kicking the blocks. He didn't notice me. A few moments later the young woman entered the room and lifted him, laughing easily and wholeheartedly as she swung the boy under her arm. She came to the window as she had done earlier. I smiled self-consciously, but neither she nor the child responded.

My forehead prickled icily. *Could they both be blind?* I sidled away.

Selina gave a little scream and I spun towards her.

'The rug!' she said. 'It's getting soaked.'

She ran across the yard in the rain, snatched the reddish square from the dappling wall and ran back, towards the cottage door. Something heaved convulsively in my subconscious.

'Selina,' I shouted. 'Don't open it!'

But I was too late. She had pushed open the latched wooden door and was standing, hand over mouth, looking into the cottage. I moved close to her and took the rug from her unresisting fingers.

As I was closing the door I let my eyes traverse the cottage's interior. The neat living room in which I had just seen the woman and child was, in reality, a sickening clutter of shabby furniture, old newspapers, cast-off clothing and smeared dishes. It was damp, stinking and utterly deserted. The only object I recognized from my view through the window was the little wheelbarrow, paintless and broken.

I latched the door firmly and ordered myself to forget what I had seen. Some men who live alone are good housekeepers; others just don't know how.

Selina's face was white. 'I don't understand. I don't understand it.'

'Slow glass works both ways,' I said gently. 'Light passes out of a house as well as in.'

'You mean . . . ?'

'I don't know. It isn't our business. Now steady up — Hagan's coming back with our glass.' The churning in my stomach was beginning to subside.

Hagan came into the yard carrying an oblong, plastic-covered frame. I held the cheque out to him, but he was staring at Selina's face. He seemed to know immediately that our uncomprehending fingers had rummaged through his soul. Selina avoided his gaze. She was old and ill-looking, and her eyes stared determinedly towards the nearing horizon.

'I'll take the rug from you, Mr Garland,' Hagan finally said. 'You shouldn't have troubled yourself over it.'

'No trouble. Here's the cheque.'

'Thank you.' He was still looking at Selina with a strange kind of supplication. 'It's been a pleasure to do business with you.'

'The pleasure was mine,' I said with equal, senseless formality. I picked up the heavy frame and guided Selina towards the path which led to the road. Just as we reached the head of the now slippery steps Hagan spoke again.

'Mr Garland!'

I turned unwillingly.

'It wasn't my fault,' he said steadily. 'A hit-and-run driver got them both, down on the Oban road six years ago. My boy was only seven when it happened. I'm entitled to keep something.'

I nodded wordlessly and moved down the path, holding my wife close to me, treasuring the feel of her arms locked around me. At the bend I looked back through the rain and saw Hagan sitting with squared shoulders on the wall where we had first seen him.

He was looking at the house, but I was unable to tell if there was anyone at the window.

1   Fashionable London street.

DEREK MAHON
from Derek Mahon, *Night-Crossing* (1968)

Derek Mahon (1941–), poet, critic, translator, was born in Belfast and educated at Trinity College Dublin. An accomplished poet, his imagination frequently returns to the image of community as absence. Here in this poem — perhaps the most anthologized modern Irish poem — the general sense of loss he evokes has its source in two locations — one specifically Irish and charged (Irish Civil War in 1922–3) and one more diffuse but no less unsettling (Peruvian mines, Treblinka, Pompeii).

A Disused Shed in Co. Wexford

Let them not forget us, the weak souls among the asphodels.
Seferis, *Mythistorema*, tr. Keeley and Sherrard

for J.G. Farrell

Even now there are places where a thought might
    grow —
Peruvian mines, worked out and abandoned
To a slow clock of condensation,
An echo trapped for ever, and a flutter
Of wild-flowers in the lift-shaft,
Indian compounds where the wind dances
And a door bangs with diminished confidence,
Lime crevices behind rippling rain-barrels,
Dog corners for bone burials;
And in a disused shed in Co. Wexford,

Deep in the grounds of a burnt-out hotel,
Among the bathtubs and the washbasins
A thousand mushrooms crowd to a keyhole.
This is the one star in their firmament
Or frames a star within a star.
What should they do there but desire?
So many days beyond the rhododendrons
With the world waltzing in its bowl of cloud,
They have learnt patience and silence
Listening to the rooks querulous in the high wood.

They have been waiting for us in a foetor
Of vegetable sweat since civil war days,
Since the gravel-crunching, interminable departure
Of the expropriated mycologist.
He never came back, and light since then
Is a keyhole rusting gently after rain.
Spiders have spun, flies dusted to mildew

And once a day, perhaps, they have heard
    something —
A trickle of masonry, a shout from the blue
Or a lorry changing gear at the end of the lane.

There have been deaths, the pale flesh flaking
Into the earth that nourished it;
And nightmares, born of these and the grim
Dominion of stale air and rank moisture.
Those nearest the door grow strong —
'Elbow room! Elbow room!'
The rest, dim in a twilight of crumbling
Utensils and broken pitchers, groaning
For their deliverance, have been so long
Expectant that there is left only the posture.

A half century, without visitors, in the dark —
Poor preparation for the cracking lock
And creak of hinges. Magi, moonmen,
Powdery prisoners of the old regime,
Web-throated, stalked like triffids, racked by drought
And insomnia, only the ghost of a scream
At the flash-bulb firing-squad we wake them with
Shows there is life yet in their feverish forms.
Grown beyond nature now, soft food for worms,
They lift frail heads in gravity and good faith.

They are begging us, you see, in their wordless way,
To do something, to speak on their behalf
Or at least not to close the door again.
Lost people of Treblinka and Pompeii!
'Save us, save us,' they seem to say,
'Let the god not abandon us
Who have come so far in darkness and in pain.
We too had our lives to live.
You with your light meter and relaxed itinerary,
Let not our naive labours have been in vain!'

LEE DUNNE
from Lee Dunne, *A Bed in the Sticks* (1968)

Lee Dunne (1934–   ) was born in Dublin but moved to London where he worked as a
taxi-driver and where he embarked on a writing career while waiting at taxi ranks. His
first novel, *Goodbye to the Hill* (1965), was followed by *A Bed in the Sticks* (1968), whose
opening chapter is reproduced here. Dunne's ear for popular speech is here matched by
a sixties' story-line which characteristically mixes the hard-nosed and the sentimental.
You might reflect on what this opening chapter contributes to an understanding of the
larger question of Irish identity.

1

Liverpool was a dirty hole and I was more than glad that it was only twelve hours to boat time. Roll on, I thought; just let me get out of this joint. Just let me get back to Dublin and I'll kiss the ground the minute I set foot on it.

I pushed the hamburger steak away from me; the stench of it alone was enough to turn my stomach; but I sipped the coffee. Hot or cold, weak or strong, coffee always went down very well.

The café was crowded with men. Some of them fresh-eyed, on their way to work. Others, grey lipped with grime on their faces. Just off the night shift. Night shift. God, the very thought of it sent shivers down my heart.

The normal heavy haul of everyday life could be bad enough, but, to have to work when most people were in their bed, to have to sleep through the hours when the sun was shining, seemed to me to be the end altogether.

We sat on long, hard, narrow benches, and not one of the men seemed to mind that the rough, wooden table surfaces needed a good scrub down with hot water and carbolic. They ate the bloosh[1] that was served to them and I don't think there was a miserable face in the room, apart from my own. Not that I could see my face. I just knew that if I looked half as fed up as I was feeling, I was hardly a sight for sore eyes.

It was a noisy place. Men yelling out their breakfast orders in accents familiar and strange. A lot of swearing and coughing through cigarette smoke that hovered like an umbrella above the tables. Talk spinning about my ears like the wind, fierce and funny, wild and irrational. Full of colour.

The Liverpool accent was very like my own. Adenoidal. Others. Welsh and Scottish and Irish and a few English ones that I couldn't put a name to. All talking at the same time, trying to shout each other down. Jokes, lies, soccer, dogs, rugby league, whatever that might be; darts; Jim Pike can beat the best and him throwing six-inch nails; holidays, Butlins,[2] miscarriages, piles, clap. I sipped my coffee, shaking my head, amazed at the pace of the chat and the variety of subjects under discussion at the same time.

'Hey Pat, if Ireland's such a wonderful place, what you doin' over 'ere then?' The Scouse[3] had wicked eyes, but his face didn't give a thing away.

'Hey, Taff,[4] you're the nearest. Would ye grab dat bacon butty[5] and shove it down dat bastard's trote?' The Irishman pretended to be annoyed: 'Did y'ever hear such cheek in all yer born days . . . I'll tell ye one t'ing, boyo, if it wasn't for the land of saints and scholars, dis town'd be empty except for the rats.'

'Shure 'tis maybe some day . . .' Scouse, as they called him, stood up and began to sing in a rich, not too stagey, Irish brogue.

The woman who waited on the tables slammed his breakfast down in front of him. 'Turn it up, Wilson, I aint got a bleedin' music 'all licence.'

'Some bleedin' right comedians though,' Scouse said and he slapped her rump. 'Are we right tonight, Mevanwyn?'

'Don't you Mevanwyn me, Tydfill, I'll slap a patch on your leek for you.'

'Thank Christ I'm away to ma bed.'

Scouse, already eating, gave his attention to the Scot who had spoken.

'Dinna forget to have a wee slice off the haggis afore ye go to kip, Jock.[6] If ye dinna do it, the wee wifey'll be handin' it to the milkman again.'

They all ganged up on the Scot now, laughing at Scouse's ridiculous take-off. He sat through it for a minute, his face, leather textured, stern, his eyes twinkling as he stubbed his cigarette into the saucer that served as an ashtray.

'As much sense as a laddie of two.' He turned to the man beside him. 'What can you expect from an illegitimate scouse?'

' 'Ere, watch it, thistle 'ead, I aint illegit. I've been readin' and writin' since I was six years old.'

'Oh, lovely eyes, Jock's missus has, did ye know dat, Scouse?'

'Dead right, Pat, lovely, 'specially the two on the left.'

'It'd take a wee faggot like yourself to notice, Scouse.'

' 'Ere, watch it.' The Scouse finished his tea. 'Fourteen years at sea, wasn't it, Jock? Gerron, bet you had more navy cake[7] than you had fresh air.'

'Ah, dat's awful, Scouse, talkin' about dun punchin' at the table.'

Scouse wasn't listening. He was already putting somebody else in his place. 'Oh yeh, they'll win the league all right, the bleedin' schoolboys' league.'

The man swore and Scouse laughed, his weasel face flushed from the smoke and the heat and the force of his own laughing. He looked at least thirty but he wore an Edwardian-type suit and his hair was all brushed into a duck's arse. Most of the other men were in overalls or obvious working clothes.

'Butlins,' a man at the end of the huge table was saying. 'Always go to Butlins.'

'Gerron . . . clickety-click, sixty-six, number one, Kelly's eye.' He turned to the Irishman: 'That's where the bleedin' thing went then.' The Irishman closed one eye and nodded. 'Na,' the Scouse went on. 'Jersey's the place, cheap fags, cheap booze, millions a birds all gasping for a length . . .'

'We'd a bull once that was always hopin' for a tight Jersey.'[8]

'That was your old dad, Pat, that's how he made such a bullocks of you.'

My brain reeled under it all and I know I've only remembered a fraction of what was said. It was impossible to take it all in, though I tried hard to do so.

I can see them still those men, happy as I was miserable, sitting eating and laughing in that dirty, steam-filled room, the sweat smell of old working clothes and the bodies of men somehow filling the place with life. And I felt good just for being there. A lot better anyway than I had been an hour before.

For days I'd been trying to kick the homesickness bug right out the window, but it was still there nagging away at me and I was feeling pretty miserable. I hated being that way. It was against my nature, but so far I hadn't been able to do much about it.

It was stupid and it was childish and it was all the other things, so easy to call to mind afterwards, but it was there and I was choked with myself that I couldn't shake it.

Come on, smart alec, you can do it, you can do anything. Now, don't be silly, you can't have run out of guts. Not you. If you're in a hurry to get back to Ireland, there must be a good reason.

I tried hard as I could to make myself stop and think the whole thing out, but it was no use. All I wanted to do was take a deep breath and not let go of it until I got off the boat at Dublin. I just didn't want another lungful of England inside me.

I knew all about England. It was a crocodile, a long, hungry bastard that ate up the lives of men. It was a teeming, seething mass of factories and docks and coal mines, and office blocks a mile wide and I bled a bit for every Irishman that had to spend his life in it. Everything about the place was wrong. Anyone could see that, I mean, I could see it and I'd only been in it three days.

Three days. When you're eighteen it doesn't take you long to weigh up a place. And you know that you know it all. What, at eighteen? Of course, you do, the lot. You know it all and you can see things for what they are. You wouldn't just make something out to be what it wasn't just because you didn't have the courage to face things fair and square.

It's just that I want to be in Ireland. I belong there.

Ireland. Eire. The Free State. The Republic. Kathleen Ni Houlihan. Call it what you like. Abuse her how you will. Say all the terrible, truthful things you like. It doesn't matter. Not now; least of all on that morning in nineteen-fifty. To a paddy, whether he's a bum or a bricklayer, whether he's in London, New York or Australia, Ireland continues to be home.

I spent the day wandering the streets, smiling a bit to myself every time I thought about getting on the boat. I must have noticed this and that, but hardly anything registered. It was as if I'd shut my mind off except for the boat. I wanted to go home, and that was all there was to it. I wanted to go home so badly that I couldn't think of anything else. Ireland had me by the short hairs and I didn't fight her at all. She was my mistress and I wanted to give in to her.

Somewhere in that slutwarm city of Liverpool, I did switch on for a minute or two. I stopped and looked into a shop window. A ladies' hairdresser's it was and I could see my face in the perpendicular strips of the reeded mirror that faced the street.

The pale face under the rick of dark hair. The face of a tired kid. Eighteen years old, would you eight an egg. A big drinker and a great merchant for a slice off the legs. But still a kid. Sharp as a tack most of the time, but stupid with it. Emotional enough for five people and stupid because of that. Too quick to jump the gun. Too often ready to act without taking time off to stop and think. And a bullshitter with it, blaming England for daring to exist, just because he didn't have what it took to stand on his own legs. A kid who didn't like himself all that much on that black Monday in Scouseville.

But apart from those few minutes my movements were automatic. I was like a fella who had to keep moving simply because he was afraid of his life to stand still.

I'd made a bad ricket and I knew it. No fella with half a grain of sense would have moved out the way I did. To just run away blindly with only a few quid[9] in my pocket. I felt ashamed of myself and I thanked God that Harry Redmond was over in the States. Redmond would have been mortified to think that his star pupil had laid such an egg.

How often had he pumped it into me? Always take your time. Stand back and take a drag of a butt.[10] The smoke'll calm you down, help you to use your loaf.

The way his lip used to twist when he smiled like he had the whole world in the palm of his hand. After you've weighed up the odds, you take another drag, and unless the situation is really going for you, you just let it slide.

Redmond was right, of course, and I'd always tried hard to remember whatever he said to me. I'd become a great man at feinting and weaving. Like a boxer slipping punches, waiting for the right moment to step in and clean up. But Harry wouldn't have made any allowances at all for the way I'd left home on the previous Friday night. And as for jumping on a boat at Dun Laoghaire without so much as a change of clothing . . . this, apart from being so short of dough . . . well, he would have laughed at me for a week.

I couldn't have blamed him either. The whole thing had been stupid and unnecessary. My own fault because I had misjudged Ma.

I should have known better because we had always been so close. A little time and a bit of effort to build her up, get her conditioned to the possibility that I was going to get out. Instead of which I had hit her with it, afraid that if I played it cool, she would have talked me out of it. And she might well have done so; she had always been able to stop me doing things, simply because I was afraid of hurting her.

'You've done what?' The bite in her voice had terrified me as she turned from the gas-stove to face me.

'I've taken a job in show business. I'm supposed to start on Monday week.'

'You're not going. You're not leaving that job. I won't let you be so bloody foolish.' Her eyes were full of tears from the effort she was making to control her temper, and it was the first time she had ever sworn at me.

I had tried to explain that it was something I wanted to do, but she had refused to listen. And her words, filled with anger and pain and disbelief at my stupidity, had been punches in the face. And I had finally reeled out of the flat, blinded by the tears that pumped out of me. Whisky then. Insulation against the guilt that I felt at walking out on her. And more whisky to numb the pain that I was going through every time I remembered her face and the venom in her voice when she had said: 'I'd sooner see you dead at my feet first.'

I had felt nothing by the time the old mail boat pulled away from Dun Laoghaire harbour, and I had spent an aimless weekend hitching a lift from Holyhead to Liverpool. But then it couldn't have been aimless. I mean, why Liverpool, if not just to get on another boat going back to Dublin?

My legs had been weary and I had felt drained as I walked up the gangway of the B. & I. boat.[11] The bit of life that those marvellous men in that working-men's café had injected into me, had long since evaporated, but the moment I set foot on that old packet I lost all the aches and pains. And as we pulled out of Liverpool, my feet stopped burning, my chest came up like a balloon and I wanted to sing.

That pier and that old cross-channel steamer are among the great memories of my life. And the sea, which was rough enough to make a sailor spew, was a knee-deep carpet and I was glued to the deck with

relief. And I had a glow inside like you get when you stand watching a good barman pulling a pint of stout with your name on it.

The saloon was half empty and most of the people looked so miserable that the place was like a morgue with fairy lights. Something to do with the fact that most of those who head for home on a Monday are people who have given up on England, people, who, when they've been at sea for an hour or so, begin to wonder if they shouldn't have stuck it out a bit longer. Because however bad it was; however little they had; it was almost certainly better than what they would find at home. I had started to wonder myself, but I pushed the thought away into the back of my head and went to the bar to get myself a bottle of Guinness.

'Bobbin' a bit tonight,' the barman said as he poured the stout.

I said it wasn't too bad and he accepted my offer of a drink. It wasn't that I had money to throw about or anything, but as he wasn't busy it was likely that a drink would buy me a few minutes' conversation. And I needed to talk, particularly to someone who was a total stranger.

'Miserable lot of passengers you've got.'

He swallowed half of his bottle of ale: 'Always the same Mondays. No-hopers, we call them. Goin' home, home to what? Thousands in Dublin marchin' the streets, protestin' over no work . . . bloody madness to go back to that.'

I nodded: 'Be all right if they had a job to go to.'

He snorted: 'If — that's exactly it. If me aunt had balls she'd be me uncle.'

Something behind me attracted his attention and he said: 'Don't look for a minute, but there's a mot[12] just come out of the lav.'[13] He leaned a bit closer across the bar: 'Grab an eyeful.'

I saw the girl in the mirror behind the bar and I thought for a second that I knew her. But I put this down to wishful thinking on my part. Who wouldn't want to know her, looking the way she did?

She had long, Spanish black hair, thick to her shoulders, and though her much-too-tight dress made her look a bit tarty, there was more to her than that.

The barman's eyes were popping like Belisha beacons[14] as she ordered a gin and Italian. She was bored by the attention he was giving her, but, if he noticed this, it didn't seem to bother him.

He put two cherries into her drink and he gave her a smile that went over her head. She stood and sipped the drink and I asked your man for another bottle of stout.

The look he threw at me suggested that I was seven different kinds of rat, to be dragging him away from where he stood facing her at the bar. She touched my elbow.

'Have you a match there, Dub?'[15]

Before I turned to light her cigarette, I remembered in a flash where we'd met before. She beat me to it, smiling as she said: 'The Four P's.' She spoke well, if you ignored the slight tenement twang that was in her voice.

'I was just thinking the same,' I said, holding a match to her cigarette. The Four Provinces was my favourite dance-hall in Dublin.

She inhaled and I took the Senior Service that she offered me. 'Never expected to run into you on this tub,' she remarked, as though she'd seen me the day before.

'Likewise,' I grinned, warming to the flat, matter-of-fact way she had about her. 'How's tricks, anyway?'

'Great,' she answered, her eyes coming to life. 'Come on over and sit down.'

She moved away and I smiled at the barman, who, if he didn't actually hate me, was giving a fair impression of a fella who did.

Before I sat down I placed her coat over her knees. 'Hot enough in here,' I said, and she laughed loudly, her head thrown back, and I liked her for that. I feel sorry for women who titter behind their hand in an effort to look ladylike. Little do they know, if they can't see how beautiful a woman is when she laughs in her belly.

'You home for a holiday?'

'You could say that,' she nodded, 'though it's more of a rest. I've been on the game in London.'

I tried to check my reaction, but I was a shade too late.

'I didn't think you'd be surprised.' She leaned forward, her hand on my knee. 'You wouldn't put it about?'

I shook my head: 'None of anyone's business; you needn't fret about me.'

She relaxed and sipped the rest of her drink. 'Don't know why I told you.' She shrugged: 'I had to tell somebody. Can you understand that?'

'Yeh,' I said. 'I understand exactly. We all have to tell somebody.'

'I just started asking for money,' she said, like she was thinking aloud. 'I was doing it all the time for nothing.' She grinned: 'Funny the way some girls are born easy . . .' I found myself grinning self-consciously; I didn't know what to say to that. 'God almighty, I must have been the most enthusiastic amateur in London.'

'What about your family? I mean, your mother. She doesn't know?'

'Thinks I work in a factory.' She laughed out loud again and the way most of the men in the saloon reacted, you could see that she was getting them at it. 'God, if she knew, she'd throw a blue fit. Six quid in a factory. Can't you just see me.'

Looking at her with that fantastic body I couldn't, and I wouldn't have blamed anybody for giving her three notes for a short time. She leaned over and slipped a pound note into my hand. 'Get a couple of drinks, Dub,' she said, 'and tell the quare fella where to stick his cherries.' I stood up and she gave me an old-fashioned look. 'A couple of cherries in your gin and It, and they think they can have your knickers off. Them days are over.' I smiled at her cold eyes and walked over to the bar.

'And no cherries in the gin and It.'

He put the drinks on the bar. 'You didn't waste any time, I'll say that for you.' His temper was better now, as though he was resigned to the fact that while he was stuck behind the bar he didn't have much chance of getting off his mark.

During the next hour, my brown-eyed friend told me more about herself. She was twenty-two and she'd been working the streets for three years. She had bought a house in Cricklewood,[16] she said, let out in flats through an estate agent. 'No ponces going to get their hands on my money. I've seen too much of it, girls working themselves into the bed for a load of bleedin' layabouts.'

I told her about myself, about walking out of my job the previous Friday. And about Ma and the way I'd hurt her.

'It doesn't matter,' she said, 'you're the important one. Your Ma has lived more than half of her life, yours is hardly started. . . .'

We talked and talked and she helped me more than she knew to make up my mind about taking the job with the touring company. And she planted the thought in my mind, though I didn't want to even begin to accept it, that Ma might have wanted me to stay for her own reasons. 'Irish mothers can be awful selfish,' she said. 'More than they realize.'

I had never thought of Ma as being other than the most unselfish person I had ever known. From my earliest memory of her, she had gone without so that her kids might have what little there was. And I had rarely known her complain except out of sheer worry about something or other. But the memory of our row was still fresh and I remembered that I had been amazed by her attack on me. I pulled myself up, cutting off the thought. I was looking for excuses, anything at all to lessen the guilt that I would have to carry, probably for the rest of my life.

Half an hour out of Dublin, I said I was going up on deck. 'I'll come with you, Dub.' She stopped. 'That's if you don't mind.'

'I don't mind at all, honest,' I said, delighted with her. She knew that I wasn't on the make, that I wouldn't be looking for an upright, once we got outside. That was a great thing, to be able to talk to a terrific looking bird without her automatically thinking that you wanted your corner.

It was very cold, and she snuggled into me to keep warm. I looked over the water towards Dublin, a sting in my bowels at the thought of being back. I could feel the colour riding high in my face and though the wind was cutting through me I wasn't concerned. If you feel warm in your guts, all the cold in Russia won't get to you, and my feet were hot for the taste of a Dublin street.

The Liffey stank as only she can, and I loved the smell of her. If it doesn't smell, how do you know it's not dead?

March was there, sitting on the wind. The gulls slipped before the boat, bobbing in front of my eyes like snow-flakes, and the raucous, chalk-dry cries of the birds, was the Luton Girls' Choir.

God, how different I felt. The previous Friday, I had been sick with misery once the whisky had worn off. I wanted to laugh now, make fun of myself for being such a fool. How quickly time comes to the rescue of the heart.

I thought of Liverpool, too, just a night's distance away, and I knew that it wasn't the awful place I had made it out to be. A lot of people were very happy living there. England was a great country altogether. England was all right.

My right hand clasped the rail and when the tears came, hard and fast, I cried, not caring who saw me. I was back in Dublin. Bla Cliath[17] had opened her arms to me. I was home.

There was a black man standing in the crowd on the quayside, and like everyone else he was looking up the gangplank as we filed down. He was well dressed and by the look of him well bred and educated. He waved to someone, and I thought of a road-gang in Liverpool. Men digging a trench in the street. One of them had been black. More like an African than a West Indian. And he had been in the trench, digging away with the best.

He had climbed out while I was watching and I had seen muck all over his boots. Something I'd never seen before, a black man using a shovel just like any paddy. I'd never seen the like of it. More than that, I'd never expected to see such a thing.

There were probably up to a hundred coloured people living in Ireland. Princes, aristocrats, gentlemen. The sons of people wealthy enough to send them to Trinity, or University College, or one of those places where they studied to become doctors, lawyers and what-have-you. If there was a working-class black man in Ireland, I had never seen him. In fact, I was bloody sure there wasn't one — not in the twenty-six counties, at any rate.

No wonder Ireland had no colour problem. You need the black man living around you and marrying your sister and everything before you get any problem. In Ireland the coloured people were rich visitors, intellectuals, gentle people who behaved like long-term guests. They hadn't been around long enough to get like the Irish, who wouldn't begin to resent them until this happened.

It didn't need much working out as to why only rich coloured people came to Ireland. With so many of our own men marching the streets, thousands of them tramping the city in organized protest at the unemployment situation, it was hardly likely that any foreigner was going to arrive looking for a job.

I felt a warm glow for England, where there was work for almost everybody. And I felt grateful to the English for allowing people, regardless of nationality, to go there to work. All right, so the foreigner often had to do a job that the Englishman didn't want to do, the paddy most of all. So what? It didn't seem important. Men who couldn't get a living in their own country could do all right in England if they were willing to work hard. Which, to my mind, could hardly be a bad thing.

Before I left my 'brassnail' friend — she had given me a lift to O'Connell Bridge — she made me promise to have a drink with her on the Wednesday evening. 'And don't worry if you're short of dough, I've got plenty.'

I stood and waved to her as the taxi took her away towards Thomas Street. And I hoped that her mother would receive her well, that she would be pleased to see her, and that she would never find out how her dark-eyed daughter earned her bread.

There was a rough breeze coming off the Liffey and my trousers were stiff as sails as I crossed the bridge. It was early. The city was just coming to life. A few taxis moved south. Lorries were coming off the quays, heavy loads roped tight against the wind. Bicycles bearing men and women in all directions. A newsboy at the corner by the Corinthian Cinema, to a girl wearing slacks, cycling up the quayside: 'Hello there, empty fork.' Her face, pink cold, turning to him, a cruel sneer on her mouth. 'What you have wouldn't fill it.' No answer.

It was marvellous to be back, everything about the place was great. The kick just to hear the flat,[1] yet many-sided variations, mostly adenoidal, of the Dublin accent. To inhale the city's own sweat-stench, to feel her smile as she woke up to another day.

The morning was bright, buffeting its way to life. The sun was climbing, watery and weak, fighting to establish itself against the wind-blown cloud that threatened to become a mask. It was a fairly typical Dublin March day.

1   Presumably unappetizing food.
2   Cheap sea-side holiday camps; the first one was opened in Skegness in 1936.
3   Someone from Liverpool, a Liverpudlian.
4   Welshman.
5   Bacon sandwich.
6   Someone from Scotland.
7   Homosexual encounters.
8   Play on the British island near French coast and the species of cow.
9   Pound in money
10   Inhaling the end of a cigarette.
11   British and Irish, name of a shipping company.
12   Woman.
13   Lavatory, loo, restroom.
14   Orange lights at pedestrian crossing.
15   Short for Dublin(er).
16   North London, Irish community.
17   Irish name for Dublin is Baile Átha Cliath, here shortened.

THOMAS KINSELLA
from Thomas Kinsella, *Selected Poems 1956–1968* (1968)

Thomas Kinsella (1928–), a leading poet and translator, was born in Dublin, educated by the Christian Brothers, and spent many years as writer in residence at University of Southern Illinois and Temple University. Here in this extract from a long poem he laments the loss of language and of an ancient culture which nevertheless still has the capacity to 'snuggle into the skull'. For his critical view on the loss of language, or the gapped tradition in Irish literature and culture, see his essay 'The Irish Writer' in W. B. Yeats and Thomas Kinsella, *Davis, Mangan, Ferguson?: Tradition and the Irish Writer* (1970) and 'The Divided Mind' (1971) below (p. 810).

from NIGHTWALKER

The foot of the tower. An angle where the darkness
Is complete. The parapet is empty.
A backdrop of constellations, crudely done
And mainly unfamiliar; they are arranged
To suggest a chart of the brain. Music far off.
In the part of the little harbour that can be seen
The moon is reflected in low water.
Beyond, the lamps on the terrace.
                              The music fades.
                  Snuggle into the skull.
Total darkness wanders among my bones.
Lung-tips flutter. Wavelets lap the shingle.
From the vest's darkness, smell of my body:
                              Chalk dust and flowers . . .
Faint brutality. Shoes creak in peace.
Brother Burke flattens his soutane
Against the desk.

            And the authorities
Used the National Schools to try to conquer
The Irish national spirit, at the same time
Exterminating what they called our 'jargon'
— The Irish language; in which Saint Patrick, Saint
    Bridget
And Saint Columcille taught and prayed!
Edmund Ignatius Rice founded our Order[1]
To provide schools that were national in more than
    name.
Pupils from our schools played their part,
As you know, in the fight for freedom. And you will
    be called
In your different ways — to work for the native
    language,
To show your love by working for your country.
Today there are Christian Brothers' boys

Everywhere in the Government — the present
  Taoiseach[2]
Sat where one of you is sitting now.
It wasn't long before Her Majesty[3]
Gave us the famine — the starvation, as Bernard Shaw,
A godless writer, called it more accurately.
               A hand is laid on my brow.
A voice breathes: You will ask are we struck dumb
By the unsimplifiable. Take these . . .
Bread of certainty; scalding soup of memories,
For my drowsy famine — martyrs in a dish
Of scalding tears: food of dragon men
And my own dragon half. Fierce pity!
              The Blessed Virgin smiles
From her waxed pedestal, like young Victoria;
A green snake wriggles under her heel
Beside a vase of tulips.
           Adolescents,
Celibates, we offer up our vows
To God and Ireland in Her name, grateful
That by our studies here they may not lack
Civil servants in a state of grace.
           A glass partition rattles
In the draught. Rain against the windows.
A shiver clothes the flesh
          bittersweet.
          A seamew passes over,

Whingeing:
       Eire, Eire . . . is there none
To hear? Is all lost?
               Not yet all; a while still
Your voice . . .
       Alas, I think I will dash myself
At the stones. I will become a wind on the sea
Or a wave of the sea again, or a sea sound.
At the first light of the sun I stirred on my rock;
I have seen the sun go down at the end of the world;
Now I fly across the face of the moon.
            A dying language echoes
Across a century's silence.
              It is time,
Lost soul, I turned for home.
            Sad music steals
Over the scene.
         Hesitant, cogitating, exit.

1   Founder of the Christian Brothers. Founded his first school for poor children in 1803 at Waterford; Order followed in 1820. Unlike the Jesuits, the Christian Brothers established schools for the poor and those without wealth.
2   Irish Prime Minister.
3   Queen Victoria was on the throne when the Great Famine took place.

JAMES PLUNKETT
from James Plunkett, *Strumpet City* (1969)

James Plunkett (1920–   ) was born in Dublin, left school at seventeen and worked for a time for James Larkin and his Irish Transport and General Workers' Union. He began publishing short stories in Sean O'Faolain's magazine *The Bell* and later worked in Radio Éireann as drama assistant and television producer. *Strumpet City*, a novel which deals with the years leading to the 1913 Dublin Lock-Out of workers by William Murphy and Dublin employers, was widely applauded at the time. Here in this extract Plunkett recreates the moment during the industrial dispute when the children of the desperately poor strikers were prevented from being sent to England to be cared for by English working-class families.

from Book 3, Chapter 9

The children walked in pairs with Mathews leading. He held his stick under his arm and strode purposefully. Yearling kept to the side. His job was simply to see they did not step out under the traffic. Three other men followed behind him and two more took up the rear. Yearling had counted thirty children at the beginning of their journey and threw his eyes over them at intervals during their march to count them all over again. Although nothing much was expected of him, he felt anxious and responsible. The little girl who had recited the street rhyme was talking to the child beside her, unconscious of any tension. If they attempted to use her roughly, Yearling decided, he would take a chance on violence himself.

At the Embarkation sheds they found a cordon of police waiting for them. Behind the police the demonstrators had spread out in a line across the road. Traffic was being held up and searched. There were hundreds of them. The contingent that followed the decoy had been easily spared.

Warning the children to behave, he went up front to Mathews.

'It looks rather bad,' he suggested, 'do you think we should proceed?'

'Personally, I intend to.'

'Oh. Very well.'

'But there's no obligation of any kind on you.'

'My dear Mathews,' Yearling said, 'please lead on.'

'You're quite sure?'

'Glory or the grave.'

They moved again. Yearling kept to the steady pace set by Mathews. The police parted to allow them through. Then they came up against the front ranks of their opponents, were forced to a stop and quickly surrounded. Yearling, doing his best to shield the children, was aware not of individuals but of bowler hats and moustaches in unidentifiable multitudes. Bodies pressed about him and exhaled their animal heat. The priest in charge made his slow passage towards them. He was red-faced and trembling with excitement.

'Who is in charge of these children?' he demanded. Mathews stepped forward.

'I am,' he said.

'And where are you taking them?'

'You know very well where I'm taking them,' Mathews said.

'I know where you would wish to take them,' the priest said, 'but we are here to prevent it.'

'By what right?'

'By God's right,' the priest shouted at him. There was an angry movement. The slogans were raised and began to wave wildly. 'Proselytizers,' 'Save the Children.' Someone bawled in Yearling's ear: 'Kidnapper Larkin.'

'I am not Mr Larkin,' he said.

'You're one of his tools,' the voice said. 'You're all his henchmen.'

A loud cheering distracted him and he looked around. The cabs which had set out earlier for Kingsbridge[1] were returning. They cantered in single file along the quay, their banners waving in response to those surrounding the children. At a distance behind them a group of Larkinites from Liberty Hall[2] followed. Yearling saw the police parting to let the cabs through, then closing ranks again against the Larkinites. The situation was becoming explosive. He said so to Mathews.

'These children will get hurt.'

'Hold steady,' Mathews said.

They both watched the Larkinites, who had now reached the police cordon and were parleying. An Inspector waved them back but it had no effect. The crowd about Yearling began to sing 'Faith of our Fathers'[3] once again. Almost immediately the battle between the Larkinites and the police began. The priest became excited once more.

'I command you to hand over these children,' he said to Mathews.

'Have the parents of Dublin no longer any rights?' Mathews asked.

'If you persist in refusing, I'll not be responsible for what happens.'

'But of course you'll be responsible,' Mathews said, 'and if they suffer hurt it will be your responsibility also.'

'Seize the children,' the priest shouted to his followers.

Father O'Connor, dismounting from one of the cabs, saw the mêlée about the party of children but failed to distinguish the figure of Yearling. When his attention switched to the police he found the Larkinites were breaking through. He gathered his contingent about him and began to shout instructions at them.

'Stand firm, men,' he ordered. 'Stand firm for God and His Holy Faith.'

As the Larkinites broke through the police guard he mounted the footstep of one of the cabs and waved his broken umbrella above their heads. All about him bodies heaved and tossed. Police and people struggled in several groups. He stood clear of the fighting himself but kept up a flow of encouragement for his followers. He felt no shame or hesitation. This was a battle for God.

Hands seized Yearling and pulled him away from the children he was escorting. He saw Mathews some yards ahead of him being manhandled in the same way.

'Damn you for zealots,' he shouted and began to fight back. The fury of his counter attack drove them back momentarily, but they were too many for him. They crowded about him on every side. Hands tore the lapels of his jacket, his shirt, his trouser legs. He lashed out blindly all the time until at last, exhausted, he fell to the ground. Mathews and the other men and the children had disappeared. He was alone in a circle of demonstrators. He felt blood in his mouth, explored delicately and discovered a broken tooth. Blood was running down from his forehead also, blinding one eye. He found his pocket handkerchief and tried to staunch it. He had no fear now of the faces leaning over him. A wild anger exhilarated him.

'Damn you for ignorant bigots,' he shouted at them, 'damn you for a crowd of cowardly obscurantists.'

Father O'Connor saw the police gaining control once more. The Larkinites were driven back up the quays, his own followers regrouped and began to cheer. To his left he saw the priest from Donnybrook leading the children away. The demonstrators were grouped solidly about them. He got down from the footstep and went over.

'We succeeded,' the priest said to him.

'Thanks be to God,' he answered. He searched the faces as the children passed but could find none that answered to his memory of the Fitzpatricks. For the moment at any rate they were safe. He thanked God for that too and began to push through the crowd. They gave him passage and he acknowledged grimly.

'Who have we over there?' he asked, his attention caught by a dense ring of men.

'One of the kidnappers,' a man told him. He pushed his way into the centre and recognized their prisoner with horror.

'Yearling,' he said.

Yearling had difficulty in seeing him. The blood was still blinding his right eye. He dabbed again with the handkerchief and realized who it was.

'My poor fellow,' Father O'Connor said, 'let me help you.'

'Call off your hymn howling blackguards,' Yearling demanded.

Father O'Connor motioned the crowd back.

'Let me take you home at once,' he offered, 'I have a cab just across the road.'

'No,' Yearling said, 'I intend to walk to a cab myself.'

'You're in no condition.'

'I am in excellent condition,' Yearling assured him, 'let the city look at your handiwork.'

'Please,' Father O'Connor begged, 'let me help you.'

'I don't need it.'

Yearling raised himself to his feet and tried to arrange his torn clothes. He had the appearance of a bloodied scarecrow. Father O'Connor offered his hand in assistance but Yearling stepped away. He stared at Father O'Connor.

'I see you've been on active service,' he remarked.

Father O'Connor, following Yearling's eyes, found they were fixed on his umbrella and remembered its broken handle.

'You misunderstand completely,' he said, 'let me explain.'

'You have been beating some unfortunate about the head, I suppose,' Yearling said. 'Do you regret it wasn't me?'

'Yearling, please. This is dreadful. You must listen to me.'

But Yearling turned his back. He began to limp his way towards Liberty Hall.

'Don't interfere with him,' Father O'Connor said to those around him. 'Please don't interfere with him in any way. Let him pass.'

He began to cry.

'Let him pass,' he repeated.

The priest from Donnybrook marked the occasion with an address to his followers. He reminded them that the demonstration had been unorganized and unprepared. 'It shows the love you have for the Catholic children of this city,' he told them. The great crowd cheered him. Then they formed in processional order and marched bareheaded through the streets, singing 'Hail, Glorious St Patrick'. Rashers and Hennessy watched them passing and saw Father O'Connor marching with them. They looked at each other silently.

Father O'Connor tried to join in the singing but found his thoughts pulled elsewhere. He had lost a friend for the sake of the children. He was prepared to sacrifice more. But it was hard. He offered to God the ache in his heart, the humiliation which made his cheeks burn. He offered to God also the coming loneliness and isolation.

The newspapers carried another letter from the Archbishop. It read:

Archbishop's House
Dublin
28th October 1912

Very Reverend and Dear Father,

In view of the exceptional distress resulting from the long continued and widespread deadlock in the industries of Dublin, more especially in some of those parishes that are least able from their own unaided resources to meet so grave an emergency, it occurs to me that the case is one calling for an exceptional remedy.

The children, innocent victims of the conflict, have a special claim upon us, and I think the best way of helping them is to strengthen the funds by means of which food and clothing is provided for the thousands of schoolgoing children who, even in the best of times, are in need of such assistance. Those funds, fairly adequate in ordinary times, have now been subjected to an excessive strain. In a number of cases they are practically exhausted. As usual in times of distress, the proselytizers are energetically active. If they are to be effectively combated, it must be by a combined effort, each of us doing what he can to help the poor in their hard struggle.

Although no public appeal has as yet been made, I am already in receipt of a number of subscriptions, from £25 down to 2s. 6d., sent to me by generous sympathizers, rich and poor, in England and Scotland.

It would be strange, then, if an opportunity were not afforded to the people of our own diocese to give practical expression to the sympathy which they must feel with the children suffering from hunger and from cold.

I am, therefore, asking the Parish Priests and Parochial Administrators of the various parishes, and also the heads of religious communities in charge of public churches in the diocese, to arrange for a special collection to be held in their Churches on next Sunday in aid of the fund that is now being raised.

A small Committee, consisting of some of the city clergy and some members of the St Vincent de Paul Association, will take charge of the collection of the fund, and the distribution of it in the parishes where it is needed will be in the hands of the local clergy and of the local Conferences of the Association of St Vincent de Paul.

I know that I can count upon your cordial co-operation. I ought perhaps to add that if there is any local reason why next Sunday may not be a convenient day, the collection can be held on the following Sunday. But you will kindly bear in mind that the case is one of real urgency.

I remain,
Very Rev. and Dear Father,
Your faithful servant in Christ,
✠ William
Archbishop of Dublin
Etc., etc.

P.S. The amounts received are to be sent to W.A. Ryan Esq., Treasurer, Special Committee, Council Rooms, Society of St Vincent de Paul, 25 Upper O'Connell Street, Dublin.

Yearling read it in his bed in the Nursing Home where he was recovering from a dislocated shoulder. He was enjoying the rest. Mathews had escaped with bruises which still discoloured his face. Yearling read him the letter.

'So that's what we are,' he said, 'two proselytisers, energetically active.'

'I forgot to tell you,' Mathews said, 'Mrs Rand and Mrs Montefiore have been released — on condition that they leave the country.'

'They'll miss the collection,' Yearling said.

'They can take the credit for it,' Mathews pointed out, 'and so can we. If we hadn't moved, the Hierarchy wouldn't have noticed any exceptional distress whatever. I wonder will the faithful stump up?'

When the bells of Sunday rang out above the city the collection boxes rattled in the streets and outside the church porches. The Faithful, instructed by their Archbishop, dipped into fob pocket and muff for loose change. There was exceptional distress, now officially recognized. The local clergy in consultation with laymen who were Brothers of St Vincent de Paul decided on the distribution. When their duty was done and Sunday was over they read of the arrival in the city of a large contingent of British Blacklegs. They saw nothing wrong in this, although it was designed to take the bread out of the mouths of the men and women and children they had just been collecting for. It was a crime to deport children in order to feed them, but no crime to bring in adults to see that they continued in starvation. When the workers organized a protest, the local clergy and the Brothers of St Vincent deplored mutually the grip the Atheists held on the city.

1 Kingsbridge Station, now Heuston Station.
2 Headquarters of the Irish Transport and General Workers' Union.
3 Hymn in praise of the old faith which includes the wish that England will return to it again.

RICHARD POWER
from Richard Power, *The Hungry Grass* (1969)

Richard Power (1928–70) was born in Dublin and worked in the Civil Service. He spent some time in the Aran Islands improving his Irish and wrote about his experiences in *Úll I mBarr an Ghéagáin* (1959) (*Apple on the Treetop*). *The Hungry Grass* provides a fine evocation of the last year in the life of a country parish priest Fr Tom Conroy. Here in this extract Fr Conroy enters the pulpit without a prepared script: 'Christ, what was he to say?'

The church was quiet, when at last, breathless, unshaven, unprepared, he swept out on to the altar of the chapel. A few reproachful coughs let him know they had been waiting a long time. Well, let them wait; too long had he waited on them, too long had they taken him for granted. Could he work that into the sermon? To shake them out of the trance in which they were settling themselves to 'hear' Mass? And then he faltered at the steps of the altar, when he suddenly thought, God, I've no sermon.

No sermon, not even a note. He was not an improviser; his sermons had to be assembled, built like a bridge, each pontoon fixed firmly in place as he moved steadily out from the bank behind him. Yes, like a bridge over a dark flood of water. And it had to be built in broad daylight, in the fear that at any moment he would be picked off by some unseen sniper.

Not that there was much likelihood of a sniper in Kilbride! But the feeling had always been with him. Once, coming back from a holiday he found he could not preach; the sermon just hadn't come. He never took holidays now, because he had to spend his Saturday nights walking round his parish. Saturday nights were always special. He didn't call anywhere; he knew the women were busy ironing shirts and scrubbing the necks and knees of the little ones; he knew each man was standing in his vest and trousers by the side-table, a basin steaming before him as he peered into a clouded mirror and scraped off a six-day growth of beard.

It gave him a good feeling to know that all that was going on. And so, he liked to stroll around in the dark, to look at the lights of the houses, and get 'the feel of his parish'. He knew he was preparing himself, as they were. He was building his bridge for them.

And now he had no bridge, nothing for them. He tried to pick up a few points as he rattled his way through the Gospel. It was about the confrontation of Jesus and the Jews before the Temple: 'Thou art not yet fifty years old; and hast Thou seen Abraham?' 'Amen, Amen, I say to you, before Abraham was made, I am.' Surely he could build on that? But it was going to be tough.

He took off his chasuble, folded it on the altar and came down in his white alb to the altar-rails. First, he read the announcements, the death notices, something about a meeting of the creamery committee, a notice (that must have been handed in by the Sergeant last summer and mislaid in the book) about cutting noxious weeds — thistle, ragwort and dock. Could he work that into the sermon? He had a vision of hordes of thistle, ragwort and dock converging from the

highways and byways, trampling over fields sown with faith, in their big Garda boots. Steady now, he told himself, for God's sake, concentrate.

He laid the announcement book down on the altar-rail. His arms were paining him, both arms. He reached his hands together, clasped them before him with some difficulty. He felt better with them clasped, as if he were closing some kind of circuit.

The people were watching him, no one coughing, all well above their usual level of concentration. Or were they? Hadn't they always watched him as sharply as this? Wasn't it the highlight of their week, that they looked forward to, believing in him, knowing that he would give them his best? He tightened his arms together and stiffened against the pain that ran through him, an iron hoop of pain that tightened his arms and chest. Christ, what was he to say?

A penny dropped into the candle-stand by the altar-rail and the clunk of it echoed through the church. Watch and Pray was lighting a candle. His long, shaky arm reached up to the flames on the stand, nearly level with his face. He tilted the candle to let it take light.

All Fr Conroy's frustration found vent, at last. 'Sit down,' he shouted, but the old fellow continued to stare along the line of candles, waiting for his own to take light, his face so intent, so immobile that only the shine of his eyes made it seem alive. That blind serenity enraged Fr Conroy. 'Leave the candle alone, man. And sit down.'

Watch and Pray looked up, startled, as if he had just been awakened by a voice from on high. Then he blew the candle out, dropped it back into its box and scuttled back to his seat on his crooked legs.

Where was he? Noxious weeds, seeds of faith . . . Damn it, how could he be expected to preach with clowns like that interrupting him? He glared out at the congregation, challenging them to accuse him of dereliction of duty. They sat absolutely still, eyes fixed in front of them. Maybe they weren't with him at all? Maybe they were in their usual Sunday trance? He cleared his throat and began, 'Today's Gospel, in case you didn't hear it, is about Our Lord's argument with the Jews, who refused to recognize in him the Son of God, greater than Abraham and the prophets. "If I say the truth to you," he tells them, "why do you not believe Me?" Well, why? Why was He so concerned about them? What did He want them for? Why does God want us to believe in Him?'

He stopped and looked around. Watch and Pray was murmuring the rosary to himself, fingers slipping along the beads at a great rate. The teacher was looking at his nails, comparing one hand with the other.

'There's only one answer,' he said. But what was that? He remembered something about a wager — Pascal, was it? — that it was safer to believe than to take a chance on not believing. But that couldn't be it, there must be more to it than that, Pascal wouldn't have taken such a mean way out. Surely someone else must have tackled the problem and come up with a quick answer? Yes, the quicker the better for now Watch and Pray had stopped shifting the beads; the teacher, all of them, were looking up at him with renewed interest.

His eye was caught by the big collection-box in the porch on which a couple of young fellows were leaning casually. 'Why d'ye want this church?' he asked, 'Why do ye need that article of furniture down there in the porch, which some late-comers seem to think is placed there for their comfort? Now, I've spoken to ye before about that box. 'Tis all one to me whether ye fill it or not. 'Tis not my porch, nor my church. If ye want a cracked and gutterless porch, well, that's your problem.' And then he added one of his throwaways, almost under his breath. 'Ye're well-used, God knows, to be the laughing-stock of the parishes around.'

As they stirred, some uncomfortably, some with irritation, he smiled a little, knowing that he had them to handle as he wanted. 'Not that ye need ever be ashamed of the building itself. Your great-grandfathers put it up — God only knows how they did it, two years after the Famine. It must have been a change from hearing Mass in a smoky kitchen or around a slab of rock in a corner of a field. No, they didn't do a bad job, even if it is a bit damp and has the door on the windy side. I'm just wondering whether ye would have put up anything at all.' He was really harrying them now. 'Oh, yes, ye milk yer cows and fill yer churns, ye have yer breakfast, the bowl of porridge, the eggs and bread and butter, maybe the rasher and black pudding. Ye get yer Sunday papers and see that the Russians or maybe the Yanks have sent another rocket to the moon. What do ye want a church at all for?'

They were quite still, staring up at him with real interest. Go on, man, he told himself, you're doing fine. But what was he to go on about? Christ, he thought, I'm back where I started. Only now, I've brought in churns of milk, rockets to the moon. 'All these things don't matter,' he went on, 'we have them whether we believe or not. But each one of us has the choice of something more. No one can choose for us

and all we have to go on . . .' he lifted his arms to emphasize it and the pain made him gasp, 'is that Christ said "If any man keep My word, he shall not see death forever." ' And with arms still painfully extended, he turned around to grope for the altar.

The movement took them by surprise. They stayed sitting as he drew the chasuble with trembling hands up over his head, then he heard the hurried rumble as they stood up for the Creed. They moved into it as if in relief, taking over from him even as he began the first verse.

'I believe in one God, the Father Almighty, maker of heaven and earth and of all things, visible and invisible . . .'

How had he slipped up? Not even in his first sermon had he made such a hames[1] of it. As he freewheeled through the prayer, his voice drowned by the crowd's confident sing-song, he tried to think of what he should have said, 'Everyone that is of the truth, heareth my voice?' No, not quite, but there were dozens of texts that he should have called on; not called on — they should have come to him unbidden, as they had once come. What was wrong? Why could he not lift his right arm?

The crowd was nearing the end of the Creed now, turning the corner into the straight, the finishing post within sight of them ahead,

Together with the Father and the Son He is adored
    and glorified;
He it was who spoke through the prophets.
I believe in one, holy, catholic and apostolic church.
I profess one baptism for the remission of sins.
And I look forward to the resurrection of the dead
    and the life of the world to come. Amen.

They rumbled snugly into their seats, sitting back for the Offertory, to let him get on with it. Well, he would get on with it, he just had to get on with it, accepting the wine and water from the server, keeping his hand in close to his side so that no one would know.

And get on with it he did, conscious of nothing but the effort of lifting the chalice, of breaking the bread, of extending his arms in the blessing. 'The Lord be with you.' When he left the altar at last, he felt the satisfaction of having survived, just barely survived, in spite of them all.

1   Mess.

IRISH WRITING IN THE 1970s

Throughout parts of Queens — Woodside, Sunnyside, Rockaway — and into Bay Ridge and Greenpoint in Brooklyn and up through the Inwood section of Manhattan and the Fordham section of the Bronx there are great outward signs of Irishness. A network of neighborhood travel agencies keeps the Irish Airlines waiting room at Kennedy Airport filled with people taking advantage of low-cost tours. Saloon after saloon has a shamrock on its neon sign. And once a year everybody stops and goes to the St Patrick's Day Parade on Fifth Avenue. After these things, it ends. Dermot Davey's father was born in Ireland. His mother had an uncle and aunt in Belfast. This is unusual in New York. Most people in New York with Irish names go back at least three generations before they reach Irishborn in the family. The heritage of being Irish is more a toy than a reality. A drink, a couple of wooden sayings, and a great personal pride, bordering on the hysterical, in being Irish. The bloodlines were present. But they were being thinned out by time. You could count on some help if you were Irish. But there was no way to count on the help lasting forever.

– Jimmy Breslin, *World Without End, Amen* (1973)

CRITICAL AND DOCUMENTARY

THOMAS KINSELLA
from Seán Lucy (ed.), *Irish Poets in English* (1971)

Thomas Kinsella's forthright diagnosis of the problems facing the Irish poet: the gapped tradition and the silence of the nineteenth century. For a continuation of this debate, see Peter Sirr's review of Kinsella's edition of *The New Oxford Book of Irish Verse* in *The Irish Times*, 14 June 1986.

The Divided Mind

There is no great disagreement about the term 'Anglo-Irish poetry' and what it covers: poetry written in English by Irishmen, or by someone in Ireland, or by someone with Irish connections. Some will take it in its broadest sense — as in the 1958 *Oxford Book of Irish Verse*[1] — and include Emily Bronte; others — like Russell Alspach, in his book *Irish Poetry from the English Invasion to 1798*[2] — will take a narrower view and exclude, say, Swift as being simply an English poet. The trouble is that, however we take it, the term imposes a restriction on our view of Irish poetry. It tends to stop us thinking of poetry in the Irish language. It suggests that poetry written in English in Ireland has nothing to do with our poetry in Irish; that it is instead an adjunct to English poetry — important, perhaps, but provincial or colonial.

The two languages, and their poetry, may never have had much to do with each other — may even at times have been unaware of each other's existence; and certainly our poetry in English has never been isolated from English poetry, much to the benefit of poetry in general. But the separation between the two languages was never complete, and neither was the connection between the two literatures. If we realize this we may become aware of a vital reality — one that has everything to do with the 'divided mind' of the modern Irish poet, which is my allotted subject.

A modern English poet can reasonably feel at home in the long tradition of English poetry. No matter what his preoccupations may be, he will find his forebears there, and he apparently feels free to conscript an Irish or an American poet into the tradition if that seems necessary. As he looks back, the first great objects in view might be Yeats and T.S. Eliot, then Matthew Arnold, Wordsworth, Pope — and so on through the mainstream of a tradition. An Irish poet has access to all of this through his use of the English language, but he is unlikely to feel at home in it. Or so I find in my own case. If he looks back over

his own heritage the line must begin, again, with Yeats. But then, for more than a hundred years, there is almost total poetic silence. I believe that silence, on the whole, is the real condition of Irish literature in the nineteenth century — certainly of poetry; there is nothing that approaches the ordinary literary achievement of an age. Beyond the nineteenth century there is a great cultural blur: I must exchange one language for another, my native English for eighteenth-century Irish. Yet to come on eighteenth-century Irish poetry after the dullness of the nineteenth century is to find a world suddenly full of life and voices, the voices of poets who expect to be heard and understood, and memorized. They are the almost doggerel end of Gaelic literature, but they are at home in their language and tradition; it does not occur to them to question the medium they write in. Beyond them again is Aogán Ó Rathaille, the last major poet in Irish, and beyond him the course of Irish poetry stretching back for more than a thousand years, full of riches and variety. In all of this I recognize a great inheritance and, simultaneously, a great loss. The inheritance is certainly mine but only at two enormous removes — across a century's silence and through an exchange of worlds. The greatness of the loss is measured not only by the substance of Irish literature itself, but also by the intensity with which we know it was shared; it has an air of continuity and shared history which is precisely what is missing from Irish literature, in English or Irish, in the nineteenth century and today. I recognize that I stand on one side of a great rift, and can feel the discontinuity in myself. It is a matter of people and places as well as writing — of coming from a broken and uprooted family, of being drawn to those who share my origins and finding that we cannot share our lives.

When Yeats looked back over the same stretch of time, he saw it very differently. He valued what he could in Gaelic literature and used it, as we know. But his living tradition was solely in English; and it had its high point, not its tragic last gasp, in the eighteenth century. Its literature and its human beings are specialized and cut off, an Anglo-Irish annex to the history of Ireland. He yoked together Swift, Burke, Berkeley and Goldsmith for his writers, and chose for his people a race of 'swashbucklers, horsemen, swift indifferent men'. It is English literature, not Irish, that lies behind them; and their line — as he sees it — is ending in his own time. Yeats is *in* the tradition of Irish literature; he gives it most of its body and meaning for us. But he is *isolated* in it. Early in his career, in an essay in *Ideas of Good and Evil*,[3] he wrote of the people on the Galway plains that 'One could still, if one had the genius, and had been born to Irish, write for these people plays and poems like those of Greece. Does not the greatest poetry always require a people to listen to it?' But he is partly isolated from these people: their language is not his, and therefore he cannot completely touch their lives. The separation is incomplete, but he is wounded by it. He is wounded also by the incompleteness of his identification with English poetry — indeed, by the whole historical reality that underlies these divisions. Writing in 1937, in one of his last essays, 'A General Introduction for my Work', he dramatizes his isolation, remembering the past persecutors of the Irish people: '. . . there are moments when hatred poisons my life and I accuse myself of effeminacy because I have not given it adequate expression. . . . Then I remind myself that though mine is the first English marriage I know of in the direct line, all my family names are English, and that I owe my soul to Shakespeare, to Spenser and to Blake, perhaps to William Morris, and to the English language in which I think, speak, and write, that everything I love has come to me through English; my hatred tortures me with love, my love with hate.'

For an Irish writer examining his traditional position, therefore, it doesn't seem to matter what view he chooses, or is forced to take. There can be no great difference for a writer in Irish, separated linguistically from the great majority of his fellow countrymen: what he sees and feels is division, a division so fundamental as to form a considerable part of his actual imaginative substance.

There is nothing necessarily fatal in this for poetry. It is not in itself a diminishment, something that must automatically reduce the quality of the poetic response. Yeats was in no way diminished, for example, by his 'torture'. Its nature and its cause needed to be recognized; he recognized them, and turned them into subject matter. A strong writer may benefit from the support of a living tradition, but he won't be kept from major achievement by the lack of it — though his achievement will be of a more solitary kind.

Things go harder with the weaker spirits, though they are seldom aware of their exact handicaps, and may never know what they lack in not having a full tradition — even to fight against. Such talents spring up in the usual profusion, like the poetic impulses of youth, but they are likely to grow stunted or wither away quickly, or fail in some way to grow to their full capacity, not being strong enough to drive their roots where they must for imaginative nourishment. These individual failures, by courtesy of time's cruelties, don't really matter — nothing matters but excellence. Yet taken all together, as we have the chance to see them in 'Anglo-Irish poetry' so called — a few struggling poetic souls in a bleak climate, and a host of failures — they give a certain baleful tone to our recent poetry — I mean our poetry in English since about 1800.

If we look at that poetry without sentimentality, and apply standards of poetic judgement only, what remains from the nineteenth century? My own first finding, I repeat, is dullness: a huge supply of bad verse and, amidst their own contributions to this supply, a few tentative achievements by Moore, Ferguson, Mangan and (I am sometimes tempted to feel) Allingham. From Moore: a sampler of songs and witty pieces, distinguished for their expertise and athletic lightness, but without imaginative depth, either 'serious' or 'light': 'a master in fancy', as Stopford Brooke[4] diagnoses the case . . . 'full of that power which plays with grace and brightness on the surface of Nature and man but which never penetrates . . .' Despite the extraordinary esteem in which his contemporaries held him it is close to Moore's own modest judgement on himself. Callanan . . . nothing. Thomas Davis, Thomas D'Arcy McGee, Speranza[5] . . . rhetorical fluency, savage indignation, high purpose. If pure human intensity could produce great poetry it would have done so here. But it isn't enough. The strong spirit of nationalism which seems to give their work cohesion is, for poetry, just as shallow a force as Moore's desire to 'charm' his audience. A spirit of nationalism is too simple a thing to survive for long intact — or at any rate to continue being simple — in a maturing poetic career.

From Mangan[6] . . . for the first time we are in touch with real poetry, in which from time to time the profoundest personal depths are sounded in an investigation of life, and in which language itself comes to life. Yet there are scarcely half a dozen poems that don't ask us to make allowances. For the mastery of the recurring refrain in 'Dark Rosaleen' we have to pay dearly in the exclamatory deadliness of the same device in an otherwise good poem 'The Karamanian Exile'. For the piercing images of 'Siberia', and their accurate economy, we must pay very dearly indeed in the bulk of Mangan's exotic verse, with its frivolous wastefulness. Yet I believe that those half-dozen are among our 'indispensable' poems ('Siberia', 'Dark Rosaleen', 'O'Hussey's Ode to the Maguire', 'The Lament for the Princes . . .' and perhaps 'The Nameless One'). They are the vessels of a continuous creation; their living language pours out, continually in need of refreshment to cope with the complexity of its statements, and continually finding it. But they are only the remains of a squandered future, of 'genius wasted' as Mangan himself confesses in 'The Nameless One'.

With Ferguson we are again in the presence of the real thing; his nature, against Mangan's, may seem dispassionate and slow, but it is almost as deep. And again the whole process is characterized by waste and randomness, by the funnelling away of great energies. If Mangan spent his frivolously, it seems to me that Ferguson spent his solemnly — and just as lavishly — in the service of an imposed plan. It is a great artistic temptation to impose order or purpose on one's work, and if the temptation is yielded to the price can be great. Ferguson pays the full price in his epic poems 'Congal', 'Conary' and the others, which are part of a heroic attempt to recreate Ireland's past in modern verse. Yeats has said of these historical poems that their author is 'the greatest poet Ireland has produced, because the most central and the most Celtic. . . .'[7] This bears more investigation than there is time for now — the relationships, for example, between greatness and centrality and nationality — but presumably poetic excellence was being taken for granted. I can't help suspecting, ungenerously perhaps, that it is gratitude rather than strict judgement that is involved, Yeats's gratitude to Ferguson for a great personal poetic debt. While I hesitate over Yeats's estimation of the historical poems, I think Ferguson's ballads are another matter — some of them, at least: 'The Burial of King Cormac', 'The Welshmen of Tirawley' — and the inspired 'Lament for the Death of Thomas Davis', this too one of our indispensable poems, of a simple and stubborn structure and a loose rich rhythm that equals anything by Mangan.

After these . . . One might delay a moment over names like John Todhunter or Aubrey de Vere or Alfred Percival Graves . . . but no more than a moment. A little longer over William Allingham, for a kind of passive wisdom — though it rarely comes to life in his verse, except in flashes of sudden concern, sudden power and economy, as in the eviction scene in *Laurence Bloomfield in Ireland*.[8] But then all sinks again into mood-setting and description — description in the service of nothing.

Waste is the distinguishing mark in all of these careers (as it is to mark most of our poetry so far in the twentieth century as well). If ever poets might have benefited from a living tradition these would have been among them. But they *are* heroic figures: what they are doing is what Yeats said of Ferguson — providing the 'morning' of the truly great and national literature that might come. They and all the Irish poets of the nineteenth century are in the first wave, where casualties are heaviest, and they are the ruined survivors.

Before I go further, I should return to a limiting phrase I found myself using a moment ago, when I described the major achievement of recent 'Anglo-Irish poetry' as solitary — more solitary than it might have been if it had had a living tradition to rise from. I dwell on the phrase 'solitary achievement' because, if I had to choose a single phrase to characterize *all* the good poetry of the last fifty years or more — in Ireland or anywhere else — that would probably be it. So that the 'divided mind', as a function of rootlessness, of historical or social deprivation or alienation, may not be the exclusive property of the modern Irish poet . . . One has only to say this to see that it is true — to see that 'Anglo-Irish poetry' is in a way a useful model of the whole of modern poetry. Remembering Yeats, his 'torture' and his solitude, is it not possible that we are enduring now in our lives the culmination of what he sensed in its beginnings, and endured imaginatively, in his time? The falling apart of things . . .

In the best pioneering poetry of the twentieth century, that of Yeats and Eliot and Pound, we have the first full articulation of the world as it is now becoming, the world that has replaced the essentially nineteenth-century world of sensible perfectibility. In the fifty short years since Yeats's prophetic poem 'The Second Coming', that Second Coming has been accomplished; externally, in the physical chaos of extermination and race slaughter, internally in a sense of precariousness and disorder in the spirit. The random horrors of the First World War may have begun the process, and possibly provided Yeats with his first images of basic upheaval. But it is one thing for Yeats to have foreseen such an upheaval as inevitable, in a schematic way, and even to have given body to his idea as the rough beast slouching toward the place of rebirth, destroying one state of order in the emergence of another. It is another thing to have participated in the second coming itself, even remotely, as my own generation did, coming to consciousness during the Second World War, in Ireland — to have breathed in the stench and felt the dread as the rough beast emerged out of massed human wills. It was no news that the human mind was an abyss, and that the will, just as much as the imagination, was capable of every evil. But it was something new that creatures out of Hieronymus Bosch should have materialized in the world, formally inflicting and enduring suffering beyond all reason, in obedience to a diabolic logic; it is something new to have had the orderly but insane holocausts imagined by Leonardo da Vinci set loose on the earth in an act of logical but monstrous choice. The coming to reality of these apparently fantastic images is an inner catastrophe; we have opened up another area of our selves and found something new that horrifies, but that even more intensely *disappoints*. The realization of this disappointment seems to me the most significant thing in contemporary poetry: it is the source of that feeling of precariousness which is to be found in the best poets now living.

Among the first things to go down with the destruction of the old order was the great poetic stance of Romantic isolation — isolation of the artist from a more or less unified society. After the catastrophe the poet is still isolated, of course; but so now is every man. The repeated checks to reasonable hope which the world has suffered have destroyed the cohesion of the modern social organism. The organism continues to function but the most sensitive individuals have long ago been shaken loose into disorder, conscious of a numbness and dullness in themselves, a pain of dislocation and loss. Everywhere in modern writing the stress is on personal visions of the world, in which basic things are worked out repeatedly as though for the first time.

Again, as with the special mutilations which are a part of the Irish experience, there is nothing ruinous for poetry in all of this. The poetry is in the response, and these national and general calamities have to do with the quality of the ordeal, not of the response. The ordeal is around us and in us — the ordeal of mankind and the ordeal of each man. Its qualities do not change: the same high hopes, the same disappointments, the same hideous discrepancy between what one might and what one can and does. In the private context, as the ordeal bears down on us one by one, the weight may be lightened by the experience or the ideal of love. There seems little likelihood that love — or even decency — will ever amount to much in social affairs or in the world as a whole. But that is another matter . . .

So, it appears to me that for a modern writer, Irish or not, his relation to a tradition, broken or not, is only part of the story. For any writer there is also the relationship with other literatures, with the present, with the 'human predicament', with the self. This last may be the most important of all, for certain gaps in ourselves can swallow up all the potentiality in the world. But say that we are not crippled in this way, then we inherit all the past one way or another. A writer, according to his personal scope, stands in relation to what he can use of man's total literary tradition. Eliot and Joyce could use much, Dylan Thomas very little. But Thomas's relationship with the self was — or was beginning to be — adequate for great poems. A man in his life shares more with all men than he does with any class of men — in eating, sleeping, loving, fighting, and dying; he may lack the sense of tradition, almost, and still share most of human experience.

Is there any virtue then, for literature, for poetry, in the continuity of a tradition? I believe there is not — just as its discontinuity is not necessarily a poetic calamity. A continuous tradition, like the English or French, accumulates a distinctive quality and tends to impose this on each member. Does this give a deeper feeling for the experience gathered up in the tradition, or a better understanding of it? Again, I doubt it. It is not as though literature, or national life, were a corporate, national experience — as though a nation were a single animal with one complex artistic feeler. This may be true for brief periods that have 'unity of being', like those that produced Greek or Elizabethan drama: there is probably some truth in it, ultimately, for mankind as a whole. But for the present — especially this present — it seems that every writer has to make the imaginative grasp at identity for himself; and if he can find no means in his inheritance to suit him, he will have to start from scratch.

To look at it more remotely still: pending the achievement of some total human unity of being, every writer in the modern world, since he can't be in all the literary traditions at once, is the inheritor of a gapped, discontinuous, polyglot tradition. But any tradition will do: if one function of tradition is to link us living with the significant past, this is done as well by a broken tradition as by a whole one — however painful, humanly speaking, it may be. What matters for poetry, to say it once more, is the quality of the response.

To summarize, therefore, I believe that it is a series of flaws in the responses of nineteenth-century Irish poets that makes their poetry not matter very much. I have suggested that their primary disadvantage was the lack of an available tradition — that in the traumatic exchange of one vernacular for another a vital sustaining force was lost. But underneath all that, as I have suggested also, there is the fundamental matter of the individual talent. It is the lesser talents whose art suffers by such human deprivations. Major talents are neither diminished nor set astray by these things. Yeats and Joyce take leave, with a vengeance, of the gloomy circumstances of nineteenth-century Irish literature. And we are free to do so with them, if we can.

Have we done so? What of our twentieth century so far? As to Yeats's contemporaries, my own impression is of a generation of writers entranced, understandably, by the phenomenon of Yeats among them, and themselves mainly going down in a welter of emulation and misunderstanding of his work. Among the more disappointing are Seamus O'Sullivan, Joseph Campbell, F.R. Higgins, and James Stephens (I am speaking only of his poetry). On the positive side there are distinct achievements in single poems here and there, and in the ballads in Pádraic Colum's first book of poems, *Wild Earth*.[9] In the first generation after Yeats's death there is no shortage of poetic activity, but a great deal of it is intermittent or fumbling, with much of the energy misdirected or squandered. It is a repetition, in short, of some of the characteristic shapes of the nineteenth century in Ireland, and of poor verse in general: the capering entertainer, with one eye always straying from the work to assess the effect he is making; the 'plain blunt man', confusing vigorous assertion with intensity; the serious career wasted, or gapped, in one way or another. It would be impossible to demonstrate this in a sentence or two, or to deal with the few advances — and the many throwbacks — in contemporary Irish poetry; and I am not going to try on this occasion. A good critic is really needed for that thankless task, and Ireland has not produced one yet who is able and willing. An anthology is also needed, one that will contain only good poems — nothing that is merely representative or historically important: the result could be very interesting. In the meantime it seems proper to say that two talents have risen above the general level — those of Austin Clarke and Patrick Kavanagh. Each has produced notable poems, each has established a valid individual poetic voice over the heavy reverberations of Yeats's. Not the least of their achievements is to have stood for discrimination in a poetic community that seems always in danger of falling back into self-excusing, self-congratulatory ease. When Patrick Kavanagh introduced a broadcast of *The Great Hunger*[10] some years ago, and confessed with his usual forthrightness that the work '. . . is not completely born . . . You must have technique, architecture . . .' his self-knowledge was punishing, and his self-judgement heroic. They are both a reproof to those (touching in their indiscrimination) who would still call *The Great Hunger* a great poem. To do so is a disservice not least to the set of truly fine short poems that Kavanagh wrote during the middle Fifties. We must discriminate where we can — where our best writers have shown — or we may find ourselves, again, unable to discriminate at all.

What of the future? Is there a way for a modern Irish writer to fight this danger — a danger he is more vulnerable to the more isolated he is content to be? I think there is: there is always a way. . . . It will not be found in rigid opinion or verbal gesticulation; we have had more than our share of these. But it may be found in a willingness and determination to investigate one's self and one's world, to make relentless comparisons, and to remain open at all costs to the teaching that life inflicts on us all.

1   Edited by Donagh MacDonagh and Lennox Robinson.
2   First published in 1943, revised edition 1960.
3   First published in 1903.
4   Stopford Brooke (1832–1916), born in Donegal and educated at TCD, clergyman and critic, in the 1890s he delivered an inaugural lecture to the Irish Literary Society on 'The Need and Use of Getting Irish Literature into the English Tongue'. He also co-edited *A Treasury of Irish Poetry in the English Tongue* (1900).
5   Lady Wilde, poet and mother of Oscar. In the 1840s she contributed poems to Thomas Davis's paper *Nation*.
6   James Clarence Mangan (1803–49), Irish poet, author of famous translation of 'Dark Rosaleen'. See extract from Brian Moore's *The Mangan Inheritance* (1979) on p. 909 for more on Mangan.
7   From Yeats's article 'The Poetry of Sir Samuel Ferguson' in *Dublin University Review*, November 1886.
8   First published in 1864.
9   First published in 1907.
10   First published in 1942.

JOHN JORDAN
from *Hibernia*, May 1972

John Jordan (1930–88) was a poet and critic, responsible for the revival of *Poetry Ireland* in 1963 which he edited until 1968. In the 1970s he contributed a column of literature and the arts to *Hibernia*, which at that time was a fortnightly newspaper produced in Dublin. His prose is gathered in *Blood and Stations* (1976). Here is one of his characteristic pieces on the subject of censorship.

A Censored Decade

The golden lads and lasses of Ireland '72 are at ease with Updike, Cleaver and Roth;[1] take for granted Moore and Broderick and McGahern.[2] They could scarcely conceive the situation of the young after the last war and well into the 'fifties, when they discovered, as I did, that the more important books of the more important Irish fiction writers published since the foundation of the State had been proscribed by the Censorship Board.

In fact, it would appear to have been a deliberate policy of the Board's to enforce the law with the utmost rigour against Irish writers. Looking back and remembering the adolescent exultation with which one foiled, book by book, the Board's attempt to stifle Irish writers not alone for their contemporaries but for posterity, I realize that from the carnage of the '30s purge one could build the foundations of a modern Irish library. Consider some of the books I set myself to track down in defiance of the monstrous Board between 1946 and 1950 — and I confine myself to novels: Sean O'Faolain's *Bird Alone* (1936), Frank O'Connor's *The Saint and Mary Kate* (1932), Francis Hackett's *The Green Lion* (1936), Austin Clarke's *The Bright Temptation* (1932) and *The Singing-Men at Cashel* (1936), Kate O'Brien's *Mary Lavelle* (1936) and *The Land of Spices* (1941). Of all these, so far as I know, only *The Bright Temptation* has been republished (Dolmen, 1965). Part of the cruelty done to Irish writers of an older generation has been the revocation of bans when the books themselves have been long out of print.

The attentive reader will have noticed the absence of Liam O'Flaherty's name from the short list above. But so successfully had O'Flaherty been muzzled that in the '40s my generation had only the haziest notion of his large output. His short stories, which, wrongly, I now think, were regarded as his chief glory, were all available, as were his two best known novels, *The Informer* and *Famine*. It was many years before I ever saw copies of his late '20s-early '30s novels, *Mr Gilhooley*, *House of Gold* and *Skerrett*, and then not in this country. Frank O'Connor once claimed that the English Department of a German University found it impossible to obtain a complete set of O'Flaherty in Ireland.

Irish publishing is, apparently, in a healthier condition now than at any time since Independence. One or more houses could perform an immense service for Irish letters by negotiating with the original firms and reissuing certain key books. Were I asked to submit ten titles for paperback they would be: O'Flaherty, *Skerrett*; O'Connor, *The Saint and Mary Kate*; O'Faolain, *Bird Alone* and *Come Back to Erin* (not banned, published 1940); Hackett, *The Green Lion*; O'Brien, *The Ante-Room* (not banned, published 1934) and *The Land of Spices*; Clarke, *The Singing-Men at Cashel*; Francis Stuart, *Redemption*, and Benedict Kiely, *There Was an Ancient House*. Any collection with these titles for a start would succeed both here and in America, if not in Britain. I possess only three of the titles listed. It should be noted that the first eight titles span the decade 1930-40, as crucial as any in our history, since it saw the final enactment of a bourgeois Catholic State, the one, in fact, that we now have on our hands. And it should also be noted that I have confined myself to novels: because of the prestige of O'Flaherty, O'Faolain and O'Connor, neophytes might think that Anglo-Irish literature since Independence consisted entirely of short stories. We have tended to neglect our novelists — perhaps because we have never read them.

We hear much about conservation and preservation these days, but not in the field of letters. Quite understandably, English publishers cannot be expected to keep Irish books in print indefinitely. But Irish firms might be expected to keep a record of books that have been out of print thirty, twenty or even ten years and act accordingly. And for the sake of their pockets, topically, I recommend Eimar O'Duffy's trilogy, *King Goshawk and the Birds* (1926), *The Spacious Adventures of the Man in the Street* (1928) and *Asses in Clover* (1933). O'Duffy echoes Swift but he also prefigures Flann O'Brien/Myles na Gopaleen. O'Duffy's Wheat King, Goshawk, was intended as a spectre of the twenty-first century. But he is with us already. One of his manifestations is a genial figure in a white polo-neck, beloved of the women of Ireland.

Meanwhile, I'd like to know, dear reader, what you make of my list . . .

1 American novelists.
2 Contemporary Irish novelists. Examples of the work of Brian Moore (1921–99) and John McGahern (1934–) are included in this Reader. John Broderick (1927–89) was the author of a series of novels set in the Irish Midlands as well as *London Irish* (1979) and *The Trial of Father Dillingham* (1975), set in Dublin.

CECIL KING

from Cecil King, *The Cecil King Diary, 1970–1974* (1975)

Cecil King (1901–87), a powerful newspaper magnate (Harmsworth was his middle name) who mixed in all the right circles, kept what became a famous diary during the period 1965 to 1974, a period which saw a Labour Government under Harold Wilson and a Conservative Government under Edward Heath. As can be seen from his auto-biography *Strictly Personal* (1969), King took pride in his Irish origins (between the ages of four and nineteen he lived in Dundrum in Dublin), and in a later book entitled *On Ireland* (1973) he attempted to 'explain to Englishmen why the Irish are as they are'. Here in this diary entry of a day spent in Dublin, a week before Bloody Sunday in Derry, he describes the talks he had with three leading Dublin-based journalists and commentators on the familiar topic of events in the North.

Friday, January 21st, 1972

Conor Cruise O'Brien to lunch in Dublin today — a nice man I had not met before. He is an M.P. in the Dail and sits for a North Dublin constituency. He was exceedingly pessimistic and did not seem to think there was any likely way of avoiding a blood bath. He thought Stormont[1] was finished, anyway; and he attached little importance to Paisley,[2] though he did think Paisley's mood had changed for the better. He thought the only possible course was to install direct rule by Westminster, with a council representing Catholics and Protestants in the same proportions as that of the population. The chairman would be neutral, and it was to be hoped that such a council would succeed in lowering the political temperature. The I.R.A. chiefs changed so often that it could be said they had no central authority. There had been a difference between the Official and the Provisional wings of the I.R.A. up to a year ago, but now the distinction had largely disappeared. The gunmen were youths, or very young men, without political objectives, who had acquired a taste for violence, and this was a way of working it off without too much risk.

Next I had a long talk with Gageby, the editor of the *Irish Times*. He was born in Dublin, but his family comes from Belfast and he spends most weekends in the North. He said he has travelled thousands of miles in the North in the last couple of years and has only been stopped twice, in spite of his Dublin number-plates. This does not say much for the control of traffic by the troops.

He saw no advantage in altering the line of the border; he thought Faulkner's[3] position in his own constituency a weak one; he saw no future for Stormont; he did not rate Paisley very high. Gageby

thought Hume[4] had as much influence as ever and had no reason to fear the I.R.A. (this is the opposite of what Hume told Hugh Fraser).

Neither of my informants thought a military solution of Northern Irish affairs was possible. Gageby struck me as more intelligent and better informed than O'Brien. He said that the I.R.A. had some irresponsible gunmen, but that in general they were well disciplined. He thought the only chance of an improvement would be if the British Government announced a decision to withdraw our troops from Northern Ireland and over a period to negotiate the unification of Ireland, under agreed safeguards. O'Brien thought this would encourage the gunmen and terrify the Protestants. Gageby said the problem is to convince the Protestant working man. The middle classes would now accept unification, but with high unemployment all over Ireland the proletariat would be much harder to convince. On the other hand this is the group that looks to Paisley, who is much the best demagogue in the business. Army searches are very thorough and necessarily involve tearing up the floorboards of houses they go into. In fact they partially wreck any house they search. This provokes violent hatred, not only among avowed nationalists and the working classes, but also to some degree from the better-off Catholics who were ready to put up with the O'Neill[5] and earlier regimes.

Lastly, I had a long talk with Mulcahy, editor of *Hibernia*. He is an intelligent man, a nice man and a good editor, but not a politician, and not a very practical man outside his own field. He agreed that the Army is not getting on top of the I.R.A. and could not do so. He thought there was no initiative to be expected from anyone in Northern Ireland, it must come from London. Young Cudlipp (nephew of Hugh), now on *The Times*, is here telling people that

Reggie[6] is being moved from responsibility for Ireland, and is to be replaced by a rather Junior Minister, while the real responsibility will be assumed by Ted himself.[7] Ted is already doing this with the Treasury, which must mean that the P.M.'s real work is mostly going by default.

The views of the three men I have met today differ on many points but agree on these: (1) that a military solution is not to be had; (2) that Stormont is finished; and (3) that any initiative must come from London. They all think that any course that is adopted, however successful in the long run, will cause a great deal of bitterness and disruption in the short run. They all seemed to think that much trouble is caused by the British Government's lack of a definite, consistent line of policy. They did not think Bernadette Devlin[8] important, nor that there was any danger from the Communist, anarchist, Trotsky-ite, subversive element. Though the Catholic hierarchy has lost much power in Ireland, as elsewhere, and though

Dr McQuaid, Archbishop of Dublin, has retired, there are more brave words by Lynch[9] than deeds in such matters as birth control or divorce.

1 Here meaning an independent legislative body governing Northern Ireland. Direct Rule from Westminster was introduced in July 1972.
2 Ian Paisley, co-founder of the Democratic Unionist Party in 1971.
3 Brian Faulkner, Prime Minister of Northern Ireland 1971–72.
4 John Hume, leading figure in the Social Democratic and Labour Party in Northern Ireland, founded in 1970.
5 Captain Terence O'Neill, Prime Minister of Northern Ireland 1963–69.
6 Reginald Maudling, then Home Secretary in Edward Heath's Conservative Government of 1970–74.
7 Heath.
8 Now Bernadette McAliskey, one of the leaders of People's Democracy, the group that led the campaign for civil rights in autumn 1968. Independent MP for Mid-Ulster 1969–74.
9 Jack Lynch, Irish Taoiseach 1966–73.

ROSITA SWEETMAN
from Rosita Sweetman, *'On Our Knees': Ireland 1972* (1972)

A sober assessment of Ireland in the twentieth century written by a young Dublin-based campaigning journalist and a founding member of the Irish Women's Liberation Movement. Rosita Sweetman (1947–   ) takes her cue from the socialist writings of James Connolly (1868–1916).

'Cry Irish'

In Ireland there are two acceptable reactions to a crisis. The first is to get on your knees and pray to God. The second is to go down on one knee, lift a gun and try to shoot the head off your opponent.

To be an atheist and/or a socialist is to be an outcast. The former precludes praying and the latter shooting — at least, until you've identified your real enemy.

Irish people have no philosophy. They only have attitudes. Everybody has an attitude. Taximen have some of the strongest attitudes, and anonymous old men in bars come second. Bishops and priests are also very good on attitudes. In fact, the Primate of All Ireland, Cardinal Conway, might be re-named Cardinal Dial-an-Attitude, except that he tends to

become confused he repeats his condemnations of 'violence' so often.

Violence is part and parcel of the Irish national psyche. There's the collective violence of the new bourgeoisie perpetrated on the poor. There's the psychological violence perpetrated by the Church on everybody all the time. Then there's the violence of the North — and that's a violence everyone recognizes.

At the last count there were 2,971,230 people living in the South of Ireland (the 26 Counties), and 1,525,187 living in the North (the Six Counties) — that's not counting the 15,000 British troops of course. We have a total land area of 32,595 square miles on which to disport ourselves. The furthest you can run is 302 miles, and the highest you can climb is 3,414 feet. In the South of Ireland we eat more calories per head, per day, than any other known race in the world (eat includes drink), in fact, apart from food we spend more on drink than any other single item.

The pub is the centre of Irish life. Priests like to think the Church is, but the Church is a place where men go between pubs and women go between babies. As Ireland has changed to meet the needs of the twentieth century so have her pubs. You'd be hard pushed now to find a decent pub that doesn't have leatherette seats, plastic flowers and non-stop 'muzak'. Businessmen drink in pubs at lunchtime and go back to work plastered. Poets and writers never leave pubs. Special Branch men (i.e. detectives) spend all their time in pubs watching Republicans who watch Special Branch men and every so often they all go outside for a fight.

The 'Special Branch' is a grandiose term for a rather tatty bunch of thugs in worn tweed jackets, trousers that are slack across the arse and tight at the ankle. They're quite superfluous as detectors because everybody who's anybody knows each one of them; and when Jack Lynch[1] threatened to introduce internment in the South there was almost as much consternation among 'the Branch' as among the IRA, because with 'the lads' locked up they'd have no excuse to go drinking in pubs 'detecting' Republicans.

In Ireland there are three types of Republicans. There's the Fianna Fail party which governs the country, who used to be Republicans. Then there are the Provos who are the inheritors of Fianna Fail's discarded Republicanism. Finally there are the Official Republicans[2] with a brand new style called 'Marxist Republicanism'.

Fianna Fail's Daddy, Eamon De Valera, was out in 1916 when a group of ill-fated young men got into the General Post Office in Dublin and told the Irish people that 'The Republic' had been proclaimed. The Irish people were very confused indeed but the British weren't, and after a few days fighting they captured and shot every single one of the leaders. That's when Eamon De Valera got away, and that's when the Irish people got interested. (Numerous detailed accounts of the above events are available from seventy different angles.)

The Irish really only got interested in the idea of a Republic when the British threatened to conscript the lot of them to 'fight the savage Hun'. The British had had the audacity to occupy the bulk of our land, kill our industry, deny us our faith and then expect us to go and fight their bloody wars. That was enough, and the War of Independence began, and the old maxim, 'England's difficulty is Ireland's opportunity' came into play. By 1922 the English felt they had had enough

and they told the Southern Irish they could have 26 Counties to play Republics with, but they'd hang onto the Six Counties in the North — along with the Unionists. Thus was born the first myth of modern Ireland — namely that we had a Republic.

Everyone in Ireland, or nearly everyone, was, and is, convinced that we have a Republic. They pity the poor sods up in the North who haven't, conveniently forgetting that British Imperialism has just as much a hold over Southern Ireland as over the North. In fact it's estimated that the profit flow from British business interests in the South back to Britain is $2^1/_2$ times that from the North. British capitalists own and control over 900 subsidiary factories and businesses in the South, as well as which over 65% of all Irish manufacturing industry is foreign owned.

As the Frenchman said, 'L'Irlande est une île derrière une île' — that is, Ireland is an island behind an island. The island is Britain and for 800 years Ireland has been dominated physically, economically and culturally by Britain. The proximity of the British market meant that a capitalist class never grew up in Ireland. The big businessmen found investing their surplus profit in the London Stock Exchange far more profitable and less dicey than re-investing it in a baby home market. In fact since the days when the Protestant Ascendancy[3] controlled business life in Dublin, made their quick profits here, then hot footed it back to London to invest there, London has remained the central point of the Irish economy. The Irish bourgeoisie adopted the same tactics and Ireland, for its size, has an incredibly high balance of external assets, due to these foreign investments, while remaining poor at home.

To get back to Fianna Fail. They are now termed 'The Party of Reality' — this is to show they're moving with the times. You see Fianna Fail are descended from the Republicans who went to war with their fellow countrymen over the British Treaty in 1922. The business interests won the day however and a 26 County Free State was established. (Ireland wasn't formally entitled a Republic until 1948.) For ten years Ireland was frozen in Civil War lines. The Free Staters ran the country for the benefit of grocers, big farmers and businessmen, and the Republicans led by Dev stayed outside. But Dev got fed up sitting around the hedgerows going over the horrors of the Civil War and by 1932 had formed a parliamentary party from the battered remnants of the anti-Treatyite forces. He fought and won a General Election in 1932 and came to power.

Dev was brought to power by the 'small man'. The farmers and cottiers and wee shopkeepers. Those involved in the War of Independence. They voted Dev in because he made lovely speeches about the Irish people returning to live in stone cottages, speaking mellifluous Irish and working very hard. Nobody believed him for a minute but the Irish were, and are, far more prone to adopting a philosophy known as 'The Celtic Twilights', than the hard graft the grocers advocated. Quite apart from that the austerity the Free State administration had felt necessary to impose on the people to try and turn them into good lackeys of capitalism didn't suit the Irish who thought once the British were out things would be different. As Jack Dowling, a contemporary commentator, points out, 'The Free Staters had too quickly and too smoothly taken on their neo-colonial roles to be nationally credible.' 'Parnell came down the road, he said to a cheering man: "Ireland shall get her freedom and you still break stone" ' (W.B. Yeats).[4]

Fianna Fail came to power as a populist party, but with no social or economic policy. Dev started the Economic War with Britain when he refused to continue paying land annuities and Britain replied with a boycott of Irish goods. Economic policy as outwardly displayed consisted in 'protecting' home industry, though from 1940 onwards the Government had begun to recognize the failure of a native capitalist class to develop, and semi-state, or state bodies were set up to provide the basic necessities such as travel, electricity, fuel, under the direction of the State.

In 1958 the first public recognition of Ireland's dependence on foreign capital was made when a direct state grant was given to a foreign industry to set up here. But it was Sean Lemass's Taoiseach-ship which really opened Ireland up to foreign businessmen. Lemass was the first to actually delight in the politics of international imperialism and throw out the old policies of 'green' (i.e. homegrown/ nationalistic) capitalism. Plans were drawn up to entice foreign industrialists into Mother Eire — tax free holidays, massive bonuses for buildings and equipment and above all cheap 'surplus' labour were put forward as attractions.

Since 1960, 81.8% of *all* grants paid by the State (through the Industrial Development Authority) to new industries setting up in Ireland has been to foreign owned and controlled businesses. Fianna Fail had a schizophrenic nervous breakdown from which it still suffers. The policy of protecting home industry by one party, that had been in power for more than thirty years, radically affected the ties between the Government and business interests. Sean Lemass built up a fund of repayable good will amongst the native bourgeoisie. The new men of Fianna Fail, the building

magnates, hoteliers, and factory owners, were centred in the cities. They paid to keep Fianna Fail going financially, while the old 'republican' grass roots support kept them going at the ballot box. Fianna Fail was trying to straddle its nationalistic support while accommodating the new bourgeoisie. The fact that Fianna Fail had become more bourgeois than the Free Staters, and more 'Pale' (i.e. Dublin) orientated than the British and Protestant Ascendancy, escaped many people's notice. It wasn't till this year, 1972, that Fianna Fail felt sufficiently strong to give an open mandate to capitalism at its Ard Fheis (Annual General Meeting) and to allow its cantankerous little Minister for Justice, Dessie O'Malley, declare war on all Republicans.

This then comes to the second type of Republicans in Ireland. These are the inheritors of the Republicans who fought the Civil War on Dev's side, but when Dev got into power realized he wasn't going to jeopardize his position by declaring war on Capitalism, British or Irish, or proclaim the fight for a 32 County Republic of Ireland. They remained outside parliamentary politics and in the Irish Republican Army, the IRA. Every ten years or so the IRA 'went to war'. They identified the 'problem' of Ireland as being the border between the Six and Twenty-Six Counties and the fact that Britain could still run around up North. The fact that Britain still had de facto control over the South apparently didn't enter their heads. Nor, seemingly, that the South was just as 'bourgeois' as the North. Even when Dev interned Republicans in the forties, fifties and sixties, it took the Republican Movement as a whole till 1967 to break out of pure nationalism and into Socialism. The Provisional IRA is the inheritor of pure nationalism. If Britain said tomorrow — okay, have your bloody 32 County Republic, the Provo leadership would order volunteers to lay down their arms, and would happily settle down to a gombeen Republic. (That is, a republic dominated by native businessmen acting as lackeys for British business interests.) Although the Provos leadership claims to be anti-Southern they are somewhat compromised in that they were nursed into life by the machinations of Fianna Fail, and the bulk of their money still comes from Fianna Fail businessmen. There are many radicals in the Provisional Movement who certainly wouldn't be happy with a gombeen Republic but there is no coherent political movement for them to join once the military campaign is called off, apart from the Official IRA.

This then comes to the third type of Republicans. The Official IRA. Those who sat down after the failure of yet another IRA military campaign in 1962 and tried to discover what the hell had gone wrong. Contrary to Provo propaganda the Official IRA don't go for weekly briefings to Moscow or Peking. In the main they're of working class or small farming stock, who in the last few years have been inching along the road towards a Socialist philosophy and away from the well known 'Celtic Twilights'. Their progress has been slow. Mainly because as I said earlier, in Ireland there are only two acceptable reactions to a crisis — praying or shooting, on your knees.

While the Provos go round getting down on one knee to shoot, and on two knees fairly regularly to pray, the Officials feel that until all the Irish people who are on their knees economically, socially and culturally, can be made aware of this fact, and why it is so, there's little point in either praying, or shooting.

With so much talk about praying outsiders are convinced that the Irish are a very religious people. We haven't even assimilated a smattering of Catholicism. We're basically pagans, the general trappings of Catholic Church morality has passed us by completely. True, there are hundreds of priests and nuns and brothers in Ireland. The Church controls the entire educational system, many of the hospitals, and has a stultifying almost uniform grip on the Irish psyche. The conservatism resulting from a political situation which stuck in the grooves of the 1922 situation was compounded by the conservatism of the Church. But it's a negative influence — their answer to anything new is 'Don't'.

There is very little culture left in Ireland. There's a bit of 'pure' culture left on the Western seaboard where the people speak Irish and sing songs, but apart from that we're almost purely 'Anglicized' or 'Americanized'.

There are very few people left in Ireland. There are over a million in Britain and a fine smattering of right-wing Irish in America and a few in Australia. But since 1840 the Irish have been leaving Ireland.

The one single thing that has kept Ireland going has been British Imperialism. Without it we would have sunk into the sea with a last 'ochón'[5] hundreds of years ago. But I've forgotten something — while British Imperialism has exploited us there's another thing that's kept up going — booze. To drown our sorrows, and stunt our anger, and get over our national inferiority complex, we booze morning, noon and night. If Ireland goes into the EEC[6] all the ills we've suffered from being 'an island behind an island' will be compounded. Our surplus labour will move to Munich instead of Liverpool. Our Western towns and villages will die as the small farmers are driven off the land. Our home industries will collapse with a tiny squeak under the international business conglomerates. Our almost extinguished spark of national identity, national culture, national drive, will go out with a whimper.

But then remember — 'THE GREAT ARE ONLY GREAT BECAUSE WE ARE ON OUR KNEES — LET US ARISE.'[7]

1   Irish Taoiseach 1966–73.
2   In the late 1960s and early 1970s, the IRA split into Provos (Provisional IRA) and the more left-wing Official IRA.
3   A loose term used to describe the Protestant landed interests in Ireland in the eighteenth century (the term actually emerged in the 1790s in Dublin).
4   Lines from Yeats's poem 'Parnell'.
5   Irish for wail.
6   European Economic Community (forerunner of the European Union). Ireland entered the EEC in January 1973.
7   The quotation is from the Irish labour leader Jim Larkin.

HUGH BRODY
from Hugh Brody, *Inishkillane: Change and Decline in the West of Ireland* (1973)

Inishkillane was based on a sociological study undertaken by Hugh Brody in the late 1960s. The name of the parish is invented to protect the anonymity of his informants. Brody writes: 'I have altered details of its history and played endless tricks on geography. Strictly speaking, Inishkillane does not exist. Unfortunately many hundreds of parishes very much like it do.' Here in this extract he focuses on the position of daughters in rural communities.

Family Life

The daughters in farm families are as separated from their fathers today as they always have been. And since they only very rarely consider marriage to a local man, even that corner of parental authority has been eroded which was formerly implicit in negotiations and discussions between prospective partners' fathers. A daughter still does not eat at the same time as her father. She rarely has occasion to talk to him at all. As the traditional authority and established structure of family life have weakened, so fathers have become more and more remote from their daughters. This strange distance is often accompanied by real embarrassment on the daughters' part: I have often seen a girl giggle as her father left the kitchen, as if there was something a little absurd in his demeanour which could never be expressed in front of him. Such tiny signs are not easily interpreted, but it could be that the gulf between father and daughter, based as it is on a sense of the vast difference between their preoccupations and conceptions, necessarily includes an element of awe as its counterpart. That is to say, because the father represents the traditional milieu, he is 'old-fashioned' and therefore, in the terms of a modern girl, a bit 'peculiar'; in coming from that milieu he has expected an unrelaxing respect from his children. So daughters allow distance and separation of every kind and are silent in his presence, yet titter as he leaves the room. Certainly the gulf between father and daughter is wide, and few children are emotionally able to cross it.

Between daughters and their mothers there are usually much surer bonds of sympathy. In many respects the strong relationship between mothers and daughters is continuous with the tradition. But it was the women who first felt able to leave the countryside. Mothers are even better able to sympathize with their daughters' desire to emigrate than fathers with their sons'. Moreover, the woman's role and status in the social structure have, ironically enough, given her an emotional freedom to bring the most drastic change of all to the communities. Having no part in any inheritance, the woman has always been without any material possessions. Sons inherited the house, the very cups and saucers in it, and the land. But with the inheritance went duty and responsibility: they were to keep it intact, and to maintain for generations to come the land that had for generations past been in the family. Only with considerable difficulty — as testified by a multitude of isolated bachelors living on the land — could a son, the owner and inheritor, defy his duty and neglect his responsibility. Even the last daughter, however, has been spared this tension, and has felt free to leave home without guilt.

The girls who come home to rural Ireland for their holidays often laugh and joke with their mothers about a farm woman's onerous life. But the visiting emigrant often has an ascendancy which is less charming. Ann Kenny returned to her home in Inishkillane after being away nine years in America. Her parents went by taxi from their home village to meet her off the plane at Shannon. With them they took relatives from the neighbourhood — four of Ann's cousins, an uncle, an aunt, and the ageing grandmother. It is customary for a family group to meet the returning emigrant. Ann Kenny's first words to her mother on arrival were: 'Did you have to bring half the village?' Then, on arriving back at her family home, she asked her mother to take down all the old religious pictures and calendars off the walls. Her mother complied. And Ann insisted on going out drinking in the bar in the evenings.

With the son selling cattle at the fair and a daughter out drinking in the bar, traditional family life is overthrown. And the new ascendancy of the young does not lead only to the bar or the fair, but to city life beyond them. For the most part, country girls do not go out drinking, and the fair is a periodic interruption to a long quiet year. Despite its new set of relationships, the family is much quieter and more private than ever before. The highly developed sense of privacy is outlined later. The atrophy of community life which it accompanies has already been described, and that too has altered the quality of family life on the countryside farms.

Reduction in community life and the insularity of each household has also changed the quality of marriage. Traditionally the couple on marrying entered into co-operation without much intimacy. Husband and wife were rarely alone, and always busy with their own sphere of activities. But with the contraction of these activities and the general atrophy in social conditions, marriage has come to involve much more proximity. With not much work on the land, very little social life in the villages, and rarely much rationale for visiting, husband and wife are together in the house for much of the time. A system which had evolved in a traditional society in response to very specific sets of social and economic needs could not easily support that kind of change.

Conditions of isolation and privacy require a romantic conception and prelude to marriage. Alongside the new social conditions within which marriage must now take place, a greater consciousness of urban ways and attitudes has also developed. This consciousness includes a far clearer idea of what the romance in marriage is supposed to be. Indirectly, it is from films, magazines and newspapers that the women of rural Ireland have drawn these romantic conceptions. In a situation where loneliness and isolation were beginning to abound, these ideas were sure to take a firm root, but they can not be realized in that situation. For the girls at least this means yet another displacement and potential source of anxiety. So women go to the cities to marry and raise families. To a majority of the generation of young women just leaving school and deciding their futures, the prospect of marriage in the countryside is too absurd to consider. They go to dances when they come home for visits, but mock the incompetence of the young men and do not take seriously any proposals which might entail a life in rural Ireland. These young women do not have the anxieties which seem to beset many of the young men, and they have a much clearer sense of how to appear sophisticatedly urban. They feel little duty towards traditional demands of country life, and can see no other reason for marrying locally.

Traditional family life pre-supposed a willingness on the part of young people to stay on the land. It also required a vigorous community to protect its women. Neither condition is any longer fulfilled. The authority, status, and role structure have been undermined. The women will not tolerate the demands which farm life imposes on them. For the young man who is expected to inherit the family land this new situation crates a dilemma. It has allowed the young woman a new consciousness of her predicament. Guilt-free emigration has become as natural as knowing what you want.

Today, the west room in many homes is used either as a bedroom for parents or a parlour for visitors. When it is used as a parlour the best furniture is put there with photographs of children who have emigrated. And in the newer houses, which have more rooms, there is also a small parlour leading off from the kitchen. These parlours celebrate the recent success of the family as the west room formerly symbolized the succession of generations. But the success of the family of today is indicated by pictures of the new generation making its life abroad, by signs of material prosperity imported from a very different culture: the nicely covered chair, perfect cleanliness, a small sideboard, the neat tablecloth. The parlour is rarely used by farm families. Visitors from among the tourists are led in there for tea. With so little use the parlour becomes more completely a symbol. It represents both the forces that have worked their changes on Irish family life and the absence of a generation for the future.

RICHARD HOWARD BROWN
from Richard Howard Brown, *I Am Of Ireland* (1974)

The American writer Richard Howard Brown here provides one of the most honest accounts of finding his Irish identity. The use of the word 'acquired' recalls Stephen Dedalus's reference to the English spoken by the Dean of Studies (an Englishman in Ireland) as 'an acquired speech'. Brown ends by *choosing* his Irish identity.

My introduction to being Irish was the St Patrick's morning when I was six years old and my mother pinned a doubled-over strip of green ribbon to my sweater before sending me off to school. I don't know if I actually remember it happening or merely think now that I remember because my mother told the story so many times over the years that the story and the incident are one, but as a little boy I was confused at having to wear anything so girlish as a ribbon on my sweater and even more confused by the news that I was Irish. Up to then I had considered myself Jewish because I had been born in New York.

In truth, I am only half Irish, and that half is removed by more than a hundred years from Irish soil. My father's family origins were proudly English. He was Presbyterian when he went to church, which has only been on a very few occasions that I know anything about, and largely indifferent to Ireland and things that are Irish. My mother was Catholic and that, in the days when I was born and growing up, was that.

The formation of an Irish identity, or perhaps better said, the identification of myself as Irish, was a gradual thing. It started with my Catholicism, an experience I shared with many, including those who were clearly more Irish than I. Though the Church was universal by definition, Jewish in its origins, medieval and European in its spirit and tradition, and Italian in its ultimate leadership, on the parish level, at least in the Archdiocese of New York in those days, it was easy to think of it as the special province of the Irish, if only because most of the priests and a great many of the laity bore Irish names. It was commonly understood that it had been the dedication of an immigrant Irish clergy that had established Catholicism in Protestant America, and this was reason to be grateful if you took your religion seriously, which I did, though in a very ordinary way, and to feel just that bit superior if you had any claim to being Irish yourself.

There is still today a large rectangular bronze plaque in the rear foyer of the church where I made my First Communion and Confirmation and on it are the names of all the men in the parish who had served in World War I. I remember one evening when I was in my late twenties, perhaps already thirty, reading through those names after Confession, keeping a comparative count of those that were Irish against all those that were not; pleased that there were more Irish than all the others put together. The time of that plaque is gone — was gone even when I was reading it — but I was enjoying it for what it said about the past. Those were the names of old men and most of them are dead now. I knew who some of them were when I was a little boy. Not many of them ever got to be important. They weren't the big benefactors who wrote out ten-thousand-dollar cheques to build new altars, but it is unlikely that there would have been a church there at all if it had not been for them and their kind.

The vestiges of their time and of their parents' time remain and are reaffirmed each St Patrick's Day for all the non-Irish to see and enjoy or be exasperated by. It is ironic that it should now be but one step removed from a national holiday in this Protestant land, for at bottom I'm sure it is more than just a jaunty, tuneful, good-time extravaganza. A modest celebration may suffice for Dublin, where assertion of religion and heritage is no longer necessary, but in a place like New York, a gigantic mid-city-paralysing display of bands and marchers is indulged in still.

It takes five hours and more for all those Catholic high schools and colleges, Irish county associations and church groups, nurses, policemen and firemen, military reserve units, and veterans organizations to cover forty blocks, and all along the way the sidewalks are packed with people watching. What is not understood with all the cheap 'Kiss Me, I'm Irish' buttons and the mottled green-dyed carnations is that it is also a trumpeting show of power and influence; a yearly reminder to all who are not Irish that the dumb Paddys who started out sleeping eight and ten to a room in slum cellars and were lucky to get a job hauling manure now ran the town, and what do you think of that?

I was a marcher once, on a windy cold grey day after the war. That was during my first two years of college at Iona with the Christian Brothers of Ireland. We were all in overcoats and green ties and most of us had a couple of drinks in us against the cold and because it was a holiday outing. It was eyes right and step smartly as we passed the Cardinal on the steps of the Cathedral, but the rest of the way we kidded with the girls behind the barriers along Fifth Avenue, calling out to them to meet us for beer when the parade was over.

I had been a public high school boy and marching on St Patrick's Day was a treat that first year, another new experience that set me apart from what I had been. Iona was heavily Irish in those days, a small college in New Rochelle only six years old, narrowly Catholic in the old way, its student body swollen by the G.I. Bill and far too large for its limited facilities. To me, who had not been in the war, a teen-ager still, all those Boyles and Hanrahans, Dillons, Clarys, and O'Briens, in their worn Army field jackets and old Navy pea coats, and their sixty-five dollars a month from the Government, were grown men.

They were not all Irish, of course, but I remember them as if they were. One day over coffee at the diner across from the college there was a dispute about Ireland's neutrality, which had made it possible for German submarines to lie off its coast in wait for U.S. merchant ships on which some of my fellow students had served, and I remember this fine point impressed me because I knew nothing real about Ireland, and most of what I knew about the war I had just missed going to had to do with fighter pilots and Marine landings on South Pacific islands.

Those were the days when sex meant mortal sin and each spring all of us were gathered together in the big gym for the annual spiritual retreat, and young men who'd been away in service, who had seen other men die, who would regale each other with stories of the nights they had been 'laid, re-laid, and par-laid; stewed, screwed, and tattooed' in cities and ports all over the world, looked uncomfortably at the floor when the visiting priest spoke of the body as the vessel of the Holy Spirit, a fragile, vulnerable gift from God that we so casually soiled and violated in His eyes with our lustful thoughts and impure actions.

One does not easily recover from such concepts, yet I don't think it was that I was more impressionable, a teen-ager who had never been away from home, because most of the others were from Catholic schools before the war, had been instructed since they were children by celibate models of manliness, like those Christian Brothers in their floor-length black cassocks, and knew even better than I, with only two years of parochial schooling behind me, the special intimidating nature of authority clothed in black clerical garb.

There were a few lay teachers, but the Brothers ran the college and, like school children, we all had to shuffle to our feet beside our chairs to bless ourselves and say a prayer before each class they taught. Many of the older ones spoke with brogues still, and I was told that half of them had been wanted men on the other side during the Troubles. Though I was vague then as to exactly what it was the Troubles had been, and suspected that 'half' was an exaggeration in any case, it was pleasing to think that some of these men in cassocks might have been outlaws once.

There was one we called 'Himself', a long-jawed blond man with glasses named Concannon, who used to tell us we'd all be better off if we got down on our 'benders' and said a few prayers now and again. One day he challenged a loud-mouthed veteran to go out in the hall because he was cutting up in class. That was the style of a lot of them, good guys and kidders, but willing to take you on if you got out of line.

There was a Gaelic club and a hurling club and it was the first time I had been around anything more Irish than a Holy Name Society variety show with Father Mahoney nervously singing 'Mother Macree' to end the evening. Up to then I associated being Irish with the names of the people I saw at Mass; with Bing Crosby songs; with my mother's reporting a policeman's compliment on her Irish blue eyes. This was the real thing, I thought. I enjoyed being around it and talking about it, but those Irish guys were *they* to me and whatever *I* was, I was outside it still. I never joined the Gaelic Club, or even understood what hurling was about, but I was becoming more aware that being Irish Catholic was something different, and I would draw on that time in years to come and the fact that I had been part of it would mean more to me afterward than it ever did when I was there.

I left the Brothers after my sophomore year and finished school at Syracuse, an English major with serious-minded Jews for friends. I forgot about Iona, thinking it could not compare with a big university that had so many things to do, so much to learn, and so many ways to be. I read books all the time, word by word, looking for repetitions that would provide a key, and literature became a world of hidden meanings and literary criticism was more important than the books themselves.

I talked learnedly and pretentiously about those keys and secret meanings over beer and became an honour student and went to Oxford for the summer. And I began to lose my faith but not the need for it. My depressions were monumental and weekends I got headaches because weekends meant Mass. Because it was easier to go than not to, I went, arriving late and standing in the back. Instead of a missal, I read from a small black leather-bound New Testament, underlining passages and looking for repetitions and keys that would make religion like a course in Western Culture.

I knew only two other Catholics in all my time at Syracuse, both Irish and local dayhops from the Tipperary Hill section of the city, where Irish kids had stoned the traffic light until the authorities finally yielded and placed the green light over the red. One was a bitter, pale-faced graduate student in philosophy who'd started out to be a priest, but by then was an atheist who carried a briefcase and always wore a tie and who knew all the Thomistic[1] arguments but would not believe in any God that permitted what he'd seen in war. The other, with far less hurt in him, was a boozer, a white-bucked charmer and captain of the golf team. A great one for proclaiming dirty hour if a promising girl was present, he was also given to making Latin pronouncements on the moral nature of Man.

Over the years after college I always presented myself as simply a Syracuse graduate, the product of a big university that everyone has heard about, and because of that, someone to be taken seriously. But Iona, or my memory of it, better defines me. It is not so much what it really was then, but the sense of what it was supposed to be: a collective male learning experience based on the shared premise that the Catholic Church was the one true church. If that wasn't recognized by all, it was meant to be; and if some never thought on it or took it seriously, then that was their responsibility, and their loss.

Years after that time, after I was married and had three half-grown children, after I had made money and was thought by some to be important, had known success and failure I never thought would happen, I met Brother Concannon, the one we'd called

'Himself', on a New York street corner. After so long, there was little we had to say to one another once we were past the first pleasant surprise of recognition. I asked him how the Irish Christian Brothers were doing and he shook his head and told me they had updated and restyled the Order to express a more universal mission, and that the Irish reference was no longer used. I smiled regretfully, remembering all those brogues and those reputed 'wanted men' from the time of the Troubles. Then, just as we were concluding that brief, awkward conversation, he used the words 'Praise Be To God', underlining some point amusingly in that casual way that a member of the religious will sometimes do, and I, who had left the Church, had returned to it sincerely for another decade, and then left again, who had not been to Mass in years, felt like clapping him on the shoulder and hugging him to me for speaking that way still.

★ ★ ★ ★ ★

Jack Donovan once spoke to a small meeting of visiting representatives of the Irish Government about investments or finance, and he told me he started with the remark, 'I am the only man here not born in his native land.' It was meant for a laugh, or at least to make everyone feel comfortable with the idea that here was an American who was sympathetic to Irish problems, but that was really the way Donovan had come to feel; that was the way he wanted to see himself in relation to Ireland. I don't know why it was like that for him. He was from Iowa, which is not a state I associated with Irish settlement, Anglo-Irish as I was and at least as far removed in time from Ireland.

At our first lunch the week following the seminar I told him that my connections with Ireland were actually somewhat tenuous and based on two great-grandfathers and a great-grandmother I knew nothing about. I was self-conscious about making too much of it and quite willing to dismiss it as an enthusiasm to which I was not truly entitled, but Donovan would have none of that. 'My connections are just as remote as yours if we're going to judge by time,' he told me, 'but they are anything but tenuous.'

This was in the spring of 1969, three months before the riots that burned out almost two hundred homes in the Catholic ghetto districts of the Falls Road and the Ardoyne in Belfast. There was no internment camp at Long Kesh. Bloody Sunday[2] hadn't happened yet in Derry. This was before the nightly newscasts reported the day's violence in the North and changed the placid image of Ireland promoted on radio commercials by the lilting brogues of *Aer Lingus* stewardesses and made it a country to be puzzled about, despaired over, taken seriously. You didn't often meet people like Donovan then.

I could understand someone caring about nationality, be it Irish or whatever, but not the way Donovan did when he was three generations removed and raised in the state of Iowa. I was too much aware that I had in a sense created myself as Irish to speak of Ireland the way he did. I was as entitled to be Irish as he was, but it still seemed an acquired thing to me.

It is difficult now to remember just how it started with me but I think it was a reaction to work and the respectability of fathering a family. Not work in the sense of earning one's way of life, but the fact that I had accepted the confinements of an office routine in a job I didn't like, felt guilty about being five minutes late in the morning or coming back from lunch, suited up with shined shoes every day and one winter wore a felt hat as a badge of new maturity. That was a dozen years and more before I met Donovan, long before I qualified to take a whiskey in the presence of a Prime Minister. I knew little about Ireland then but I had the romantic idea that by declaring myself an Irishman I was somehow asserting myself against the fact that I was doing well in a meaningless position; that there was a part of me that was a rebel, a free spirit and Celtic dreamer and beyond the limitations of being a young man on the rise with a new briefcase filled with office papers — as if there weren't Irish working all over New York, assiduously seeking advancement, buying insurance, riding commuter trains, and raising families in the suburbs.

It was not something I thought that much about, but it was the beginning. I toyed with it from time to time, trotted it out to sing songs with at parties, used it to kid with secretaries and impress them, played with it for fun, laying on a brogue talking with the Irish woman who had helped to raise my wife and who came out of sentiment for those days to help her with our own children when they were young. It was an easy matter. I bore no ethnic burden. Eamon Brennan, the religious friend of my late twenties, the ambitious publicist whose departure from the Church was such an occasion of crisis, told me that I wouldn't think it was such a great thing if I'd been shit-faced shanty Irish as he had, growing up and running errands after school for his father's corner grocery store in Brooklyn. He was probably right. There was no poverty identified with race in my background; no humble, balding parent with the mark of the foreign born in his speech to be ashamed of. My resentments were less precise.

To me, then, it was a way of presenting myself as different. With a name that blandly conveyed the real America, I could have been Anglo-Saxon if I wanted to. I could claim the soldiers and officers of my father's Confederate family, the surgeon who amputated four legs at the Battle of the Wilderness, the minister who in 1826 founded the Baptist Church in Clarksville, Tennessee, the distant aunt who was a niece of Thomas Jefferson. I could trace my lineage back to pre-Revolutionary War times in the Virginia Colony. I could imagine ties to the court of English kings. And I did think that way about myself sometimes. There was a period after college when I referred to some of that past occasionally, traded on it in conversations where such references came up naturally, amusingly, *pointedly*, perhaps at some party with young men in gray flannel and tattersall vests and black knit ties and girls who had come out at debutante balls. I knew such things were of little consequence. I used to make fun of those references to distinguished antecedents that appeared in announcements of weddings and engagements in the local newspaper. Still, those were the claims that went with belonging, and they were associated with well-bred Protestants who had money and status, and for a time I wanted to be like them and to have them see me that way, too. I had the right. My credentials were legitimate. But something in me finally made me say to hell with the Protestant Yalies[3] and instead, for reasons obvious to me now — reasons that were embarrassingly superficial and adolescent, and other reasons that were far more complicated, that cannot be easily understood, because they expressed something of a Catholic's mind and sense of person, an outsider's pride and resentment — I chose to be Irish.

1   From the teachings of St Thomas Aquinas (1225–74).
2   January 30, 1972.
3   From Yale University (here shorthand for WASPs).

J. P. DONLEAVY
from J. P. Donleavy, *The Unexpurgated Code: A Complete Manual of Survival & Manners* (1975)

J. P. Donleavy (1926–   ) was born in New York, the son of an Irish-born fireman. After graduating from Trinity College, Dublin, he wrote *The Ginger Man* (1955), a novel that became a best-seller. Other novels and books followed, set both in the States and in Ireland. *The Unexpurgated Code: A Complete Manual of Survival & Manners* provides a 'ruthless guide to social etiquette'.

Upon Being Told the Fatal News That You Have Only So Long to Live and That It Is Not Long

Of course this news may enrage you so much that you start throwing things, blaming and accusing everyone and generally behaving in a hostile manner. Of course this kind of antic only shows you should have been dead long ago.

If you are the nice kind of average person, moisture in the eyes is permissible but do not burst into floods of tears. This alarms others into acute apprehension concerning the moment when their turn comes. Unless death has whispered I am here, make a reasonable effort to keep going. This is often a bleak period unless you have large assets and people around you who will benefit thereby and which prospect keeps them cheerful beyond belief. However, take strong objection to any dancing joy at your sinking. Your final will and a pen handy, plus a couple of witnesses hostile to your heirs, should make the merry take heed.

Death has the remarkable aspect of looking as if it's only happening to you. Although a sad time, it does leave more room for others. This is of course no comfort if it's you it's after. Stalking your shadow down the shrinking days. The accumulative devastation this can have upon the spirit is horrendous. But life now will begin to look so good that just living seems for the first time better than money. That is if you already have money.

Although you'd much rather be doing something else than dying, you can at least now decide to die like a man or live a wee bit longer like one. The more finances you have for this purpose, the better. But do not rush out to a night club or the latest celebrity joint and scare hell out of everybody. You've had your chance, now let somebody else enjoy. Instead, gainfully occupy yourself at this time with your funeral's invitation list, the floral displays, coffin design and music. And no small satisfaction will be yours in the timely provision of your monstrous mausoleum with its splendid acoustics.

The higher your social plateau the faster news of your impending demise will travel. And reports of your final departure may come back before you've been tucked in. But even in the face of such callousness it is not chic to complain. However, in broaching the subject the more sensitive of friends will use cowboy parlance reminiscent of the rough out of doors in deference to the fighting spirit they think you want them to think you have.

'Gee Jack, I hear you're heading for the last roundup.'

It is a pleasant gesture and a reminder of your heyday haughty particularity if you can respond in a like manner.

'Well Steve, with my shooting iron indisposed and my jewels hanging pretty low, I kinda guess an easy trot to the old corral is the way I'm gonna go.'

But if Steve's jaw drops with what he thinks is a gruesomely sickly effort to keep a stiff upper lip he may attempt to soothe you with facts you know already.

'I guess it's no consolation to you that I'm going to die too Jack.'
'Well thanks Steve, yes it is a bit.'
'Well I really am, I'm with you all the way, maybe not to the grave but I mean I could get killed in the next ten minutes by accident.'
'Steve, thanks for saying that.'
'Well I really mean it, Jack. I mean look, punch me. Injure me. I could be dead if not maybe buried before you.'

Even though Jack's muscle fibre may be shot to hell, if you are Steve, the conversation should be terminated here as it could lead to your murder. Dying folk like company. And there are still those diehards who keep a gun under the pillow.

Dying

This is most stylishly done in your own lace covered bed, in your own beige walled room, in your own multi-gabled house, on your own extensive lands during late autumn when the leaves are falling.

Dismiss from your mind as an asshole anyone who tells you you can have a happy death. When father time leaves his calling card and puts his big rough hand hauntingly up your rear end, he don't know the meaning of contentment I'm telling you.

However, in spite of the attendant spiritual tremblings, do try to make an occasion out of it. Folk watching on warmly appreciate a profound if not historic remark, should you really have a damn good one up your sleeve. But beware, the body can be stubborn and right in the middle of expiring it might go on living and your inane statement on your first attempt at dying could make you look a real jerk on your second.

For the most part your last gasp will be attended by fairly contented people since most folk prefer to see you get the shove unless you're a really good cook, seamstress, wage earner or piece of arse. The exception is if you're breathing your last on a pavement or highway in any one of the better known civilized countries in the presence of total strangers. Although their curiosity may produce some pushing and shoving, their sympathy is usually of a higher quality than that of relatives.

Once it gets going, the body knows how to die and does it all by itself. When enough bad reports sneak back through the synapses, a signal rises like a bubble out of all your troubles and your pumping station closes down. As the blood stops flowing, the light in the brain dims out. However, a not unpleasant mildly sentimental phosphorescence persists. This is the soul. It steers the way as you race towards forever land, wracked with a groaning choking haunting frustration. But don't panic, there will also be sweet waves of peace overcoming you. And you'll be shouting. With echoes fading away the names you call. And you'll be lucky if one of them is socially registered. Because most will resurrect from your discarded catalogue of the bootless and unhorsed. And then you will start running. Chasing down a familiar and unfashionable street trying to catch up to those who were closest to you of all. Don't be alarmed if your legs have wings, this is, even for the most light footed, quite usual. And there will be a few folk, mostly broom carrying women in aprons, out on their stoops who look up as you flash by.

Step carefully through the parting in the tall green drapes in front of you. It is extremely bad form to register disappointment if you were expecting something more elaborate like Grand Central Station. Anyway, inside, you won't know what hit you. When you see the number of other folk standing around nearly from here to Timbuktu. Under no circumstances get on the end of any long queue you spot. But find your bearings by gently enquiring of some nearby soul. Normally booklets are issued at the curtains and it will much benefit you to read the instructions carefully. If you can't get the hang of these rely on the conduct you have learned in this life. For those of you who are not nude avoid being in any way conspicuous in your attire and ignore the rude and quite unnecessarily diabolic comments usually made to new comers. But to persistent vile lip the brief retort of 'Get stuffed' is permissible. Or in reply to simple churlishness enquire 'Who the hell buried you.'

If you are really desperate search for a person of noble mien and give him an opportunity to inject a little clarity into one's confusion.

'Excuse me, but I wonder could you help me find my place.'

'Are you to the manner dead.'

'I beg your pardon.'

'I repeat sir, are you to the manner dead.'

'You mean like one could be to the manner born.'

'Precisely.'

'To hell with that shit. I'm dead, aren't I. And that's enough for me.'

'I regret to disturb you sir, but that is not enough for us.'

This chap of sterling demeanour may just be having a bad day but make sure that the next guy you stop to ask wasn't of the previously bootless and unhorsed past whom you may have deeply elbowed in this world. And who might now relish the awe inspiring opportunity to tell you to fuck off. However, before turning left between those two large continents of crowds you see and walking for about twenty millenniums, this could be, for those of you who were expecting an afterlife of courtesy, equality and contentment, a good time to break down and cry.

BENEDICT KIELY
from Ronnie Walsh (ed.), *Sunday Miscellany* (1975)

Benedict Kiely (1919–   ) was born in County Tyrone and after graduating from University College Dublin, worked as a journalist in Dublin from 1945 until 1964 when he became a university lecturer and broadcaster. His novels include *The Cards of the Gambler* (1953), *The Captain with the Whiskers* (1963) and *Proxopera* (1978). 'The Night We Rode with Sarsfield' (1978), a short story, is included below, p. 896. His talks on Ronnie Walsh's programme *Sunday Miscellany* on RTE were always memorable. His relaxed Ulster accent seemed made for radio, and here in this example he displays his story-telling gifts to the full.

In Iowa: A Beauty Queen and a Blind Man

The longest train journey I ever made was from the city of Portland, Oregon, to the city of Des Moines, Iowa; and it took a day and a night and another day and another night and showed me some pretty interesting places: like, for example, the Red Desert of Wyoming and, on the horizon, the shiny snowy beauty of Elk Mountain where Thomas Edison went game-hunting and, possibly because of the influence on his eyes of red desert and glistening mountain, had some notable inspirations about the nature of electricity; or

like Laramie where the sand blows through the hot dry streets and it must be a hell of a job to find water for the spray-hoses to keep the suburban lawns from surrendering again to the Red Desert.

At the end of the journey I found myself at dawn in a small station in Iowa and there to meet me were two ladies: a pleasant young faculty wife from Drake University and a senior student who was, of all things, a beauty queen, was in fact the reigning Miss Iowa. Just at that season the newspapers were going clean crazy about beauty queens. Far west in Portland, Oregon, John Millington Synge would have gone blind counting queens, as he once said in a poem that he did in Glenmacnass. There were twelve spanking young fillies hot in the running, for the high-queenship of the annual Portland rose-parade. I'll quote you what one enthusiastic news-reporter wrote: 'Twelve young hearts beat faster as Rosaria awaits new Ruler: the jewelled crown of Rosaria almost as traditional now as the beauty and pageantry of Portland's fifty-eight years of rose festivals will rest upon the shining hair of a new queen.'

Another newspaper had a full-page spread of pictures under the heading: 'Beauties Love Beasts'. It showed the beautiful chosen twelve fondling cats and dogs and poodles. Yet another picture showed Miss Tan of Portland, a black beauty, heading off to Dallas, Texas, to meet in fair fight all the other Miss Tans of the U.S.A. And two nation-wide beauty competitions were coming up, one in New York, one in Miami, to pick the fairest flower of them all. In one of these competitions the Miss Iowa who met me at the station would be involved.

Then as we drove on to Des Moines over the rich rolling black soil of Iowa, the richest agricultural land in the world, I learned that the girls of Iowa had a name for good looks and also for the sort of solid sense that's supposed to be typical of the daughters of strong farmers. The pleasant young faculty wife told me that one day she went on a picnic with some of the students and listened to them discussing points of beauty. Not in beauty queens, though. Not on your life. But in heifers — Hereford as against Jersey or Frisian or Aberdeen Angus.

One of the young women talked most movingly about a cow on her home farm that had had twin calves and one calf died, and about how pathetically the cow ignored the living bawling calf in a frenzied effort to lick life into the dead one. Then when the wind blew some black Iowan dust across the picnicing place one of the young women said: 'We're losing our topsoil.' They weren't worried about their make-up. 'The girls of Iowa,' the faculty wife said, 'are for real.'

That day I had lunch in a sorority house to which Miss Iowa led me. It wasn't my first experience, foodwise — that is, of sorority houses. The house-mother presiding, the bright talkative young women, the singing of grace before meals and the entreating of the Lord for good appetites and the spirit of sisterhood: all this is an odd shadow of, or parody on, the conventual life, with the added spice to the enquiring male mind, that it's pretty certain that a fair proportion of the residents of sorority houses, in Iowa or anywhere else, do not live exactly like nuns.

After lunch, and again led by Miss Iowa who was more or less in charge of me, I walked to the lecture hall to give my first lecture, and was there welcomed in Irish by a blind man called Patrick Morrissey. When I tell you about him you'll understand why I thought immediately of Yeats, the poet, and of the legendary beauty of Mary Hynes, and of Yeats writing of the poet Raftery, as beauty's blind rambling celebrant.

For Patrick Morrissey who speaks fine Irish has never seen Ireland, nor ever will, nor ever can, and he was when I met him about seventy years of age. He has never even had a chance to visit Ireland yet. If I were a rich man there's nothing I'd like better than to do the road round Ireland with Padraig Dall. He's a scholar in several languages, and the cream of good company and can play and sing; one of my great moments in the United States was when I heard him sing with tenfold feeling and meaning the words in which Donnchadh Rua MacConmara sent the blessing of his heart from Newfoundland, the Land of the Fish, to the fair hills of Ireland: *Beir beannacht óm chroidhe go Tír na hÉireann, Bánchnoic Éireann Óigh*. Because I felt then and I still feel that blind Patrick saw Ireland better than a lot of people who live here and have the use of their eyes.

He saw it in his heart and blood and in the ancestral memory, and through readings in braille of Irish literature. He saw Donegal for instance through the novels and thus through the eyes of Peadar O'Donnell.[1] What better or clearer eyes could a man use who wanted to see Donegal? Padraig Dall had himself been responsible for having a fair share of Irish literature done into braille, so that other blind people in the States could share his vision. He had many friends among the young. Students came and read to him what he could not reach with his finger-tips and he in return gave them his music and the riches of his conversation, and if they were students of languages, his help, for as I think I've said, he was a remarkable linguist.

When I went to visit him in his apartment he was being read to by a Chicago girl of mixed Slovak and Polish ancestry. He learned his first Irish from his mother who was born in Iowa, the daughter of Irish parents. He had written prose and poems in Irish and been published in this country and in the States.

That day in his apartment he sang and we all sang and because of a blind man every person in that room could see Ireland as plain as plain could be.

---

1 Peadar O'Donnell (1893–1986), socialist activist and novelist, was born at Meenmore in County Donegal. His novels include *The Storm* (1925), *Islanders* (1928) and *Ardrigoole* (1929). 'What I Saw in Spain' from *Ireland Today* (1936) is reproduced above, p. 392.

JACK HOLLAND
from *Hibernia*, 21 March 1975

Jack Holland (1947–   ) comes from a mixed Catholic-Protestant family in Belfast and grew up in the Markets area as well as the Falls Road and Andersonstown. After graduating from Trinity College, Dublin, he became a journalist and worked for BBC Northern Ireland as well as the Insight team for the London *Sunday Times*. Later, he moved to Brooklyn where he contributed a weekly column to the *New York Irish Echo*. His valuable account of the 'Troubles' appeared in *Too Long a Sacrifice: Life and Death in Northern Ireland* (1981). Here he trains his critical eye on the so-called resurgence of poetry in the mid-1970s.

Broken Images

'Poetry is alive in Ireland today, it is winning a new and wider public, and these are the conditions in which a major poet can flourish.' So Seamus Heaney wrote nearly 12 years ago in *Hibernia*. Now, with the publication of David Marcus's anthology, *Irish Poets 1924–1974* (Pan, 75p), we have an opportunity to put Mr Heaney's optimism to the test.

On the evidence presented by *Irish Poets*, it was not well founded; at least in that Seamus Heaney's prediction of an arising major poet has not (as yet) been realized. This, however, is not altogether surprising. Very few generations are blessed with a major creative genius of any sort. But as to 'poetry being alive in Ireland today', Mr Marcus's anthology reveals only inconclusive evidence to support this more modest claim.

Undoubtedly there are many good individual poems in this selection. Such a short list would include Patrick Galvin's 'The Aunt'; Sean Lucy's 'Disappearances' and 'Game'; Brown's 'Come Softly to My Wake'; Heaney's 'Follower'; Michael Hartnett's 'For My Grandmother'; and Derek Mahon's 'A disused shed in Co. Wexford'. This handful shows a wide range of influences from other poets, from Walter de la Mare (who seems to lurk behind Mr Galvin's piece) to echoes of Auden and Day Lewis in Mahon's ambitious poem. But here the influences seem to be assimilated successfully. Elsewhere in the anthology influence stops and affectation begins. And the number of affectations is bewildering, from the meaningless metaphysics of Seamus Deane to James Simmons's rather puerile Georgianism à la mode (see 'The Prodigal Thinks of His Mother').

What this anthology reveals, in other words, is the lack of any dominating tradition in contemporary Irish poetry. Of all the poets represented, only Thomas Kinsella writes with the force of tradition behind him. Whatever we feel about the tradition, it gives him a certain consistency.

However, the corollary to this lack of tradition is more alarming. It means that, among that generation of poets born around the thirties and forties, there is no feeling of having something to fight against and change. The valuable thing about tradition of any sort is that it gives the artist, the poet, something against which he can begin by defining himself, and end by changing. But the overwhelming impression derived from reading even the best of our contemporary Irish poets is that they are satisfied with the state of the art such as it is.

In an age like ours, it is almost inevitable that one of the signs of life in a literary culture will be constant criticism, thrown up by new poets who see the need to challenge or defend previous models; the result of such activity is usually the formation of a 'movement' or school. It is in this way that modern literature has been stimulated and replenished with fresh forms, ideas, insights, and given new perspectives on the literature of the past.

As Marcus's anthology lamentably reveals, we can look in vain for such a 'movement' in Ireland today. Several years ago something like it got started up North, under the impetus of Heaney, Mahon and Longley. But even it was based more in Northern self-consciousness than in the need to break new ground or challenge old standards. This Northern self-consciousness was partly a product of a feeling of cultural inferiority in relation to 'the South'. Now, it seems hard to believe that it could ever have been felt.

The lack of such vigorous criticism and debate is a sign that — contrary to what Heaney said twelve years ago — conditions are not 'propitious'. A wider reading public has little to do with the writing of poetry. What passes for 'criticism' in Ireland today is usually the publicity hand-outs that one's friends write (see G. Dawe's recent 'review' of *The Wearing of the Black* in *Fortnight*), or the bitchiness of cliques. One way or the other, it betrays a stifling smugness out of which good poetry will not come, and against which poets will have to fight.

Such a fight has to begin with a cleaning-out job. A truly Herculean task for anyone. And the Herculean task most metaphorically appropriate is undoubtedly the cleaning of the Augean stables: but even here, Hercules has the advantage, since it is easier to shovel horseshit than to write about it.

In the meantime, *Irish Poets* gives us some indication of the state of affairs in contemporary Irish poetry. Though it shows some outstanding lapses in taste — Mr Alfred Allen's extracts from *Clashenure Skyline* must be the clumsiest enjambments ever to get into print — Mr Marcus's anthology has enough good poems in it to keep it afloat; and this in spite of the prohibitive price and lack of any first-line index.

FRANCIS STUART
from *The Irish Times*, October 1976

Francis Stuart's critique of modern Irish writing provides a challenging perspective for the student of literature.

The Soft Centre of Irish Writing

We once had some remarkable writers in our land. Yeats, Joyce, Flann O'Brien and Patrick Kavanagh make up no mean tally for so small an island. None of these, with the possible exception of Yeats, made much impact on their society. The writers who influenced this community, and were readily taken to its heart, were those who reflected, more flatteringly, its habits and thought-modes.

The relation of the imaginative artist to his society is important for both. If the truly original artist is ignored or rejected he is driven into an isolation from which his best work may spring, and the society to which he belongs is the loser. A community that prefers its more easily assimilated writers cuts itself off from one of the main sources of the vitality that preserves it from the constant encroachment of materialism and banality.

It is only those few writers capable of imagining alternative societies who can enter into a serious and mutually advantageous relationship with their own. But, being deeply critical of it, their society fears to enter into a dialogue with them, which is what serious reading involves. Instead, they take to the writers who cause hardly a ripple in the deeper recesses of their minds, and thus these receive the public acclaim. They quickly become integrated into their society and serve a civic function in the same way as do lawyers, doctors or civil servants. If one were pressed to explain their precise task, they might be said to preserve communal cultural standards and present the national identity. They are in fact performing much the same function to their society as are the members of the Writers Union to Soviet Russia, though, admittedly, without being under the same pressures to do so.

As in several other western societies, the main body of our literature plays much the same part as it does in countries such as Russia and China. It is institutional and a function of state, while it is left to a very few dissidents (at certain times and in certain communities there are none at all) to preserve the true purpose of art as an instrument for the discovery of alternative concepts and new insights.

With us soon after the appearance of *Ulysses* and a decade or so after our independence, there emerged a group of mainstream fiction writers, naturalistic, descriptive rather than probing, preoccupied with local colour and with an inherent conservatism. They were welcomed into the new political and social scene; they posed no awkward questions, imagined no alternatives, deferred gracefully to the world they and their readers had inherited. They were professional, witty, easy on tired or lazy minds, never obsessional or demanding. Their brushes with authority, as in the case of censorship, far from being any fundamental confrontation, were in the nature of family quarrels, for they shared almost all the religious, national and social assumptions of the community.

Indeed, in the thirties, looking back, there does not seem to have been a breath of effective dissent. Yeats, together with Shaw, inaugurated the Irish Academy of

Letters to combat the censoring of serious books. But, partly because the aim was a too narrow one, the Academy did not achieve it, or indeed anything else of much significance, and soon became another small institution defending establishment art and subscribing to whatever is the literary equivalent of the political tenet of not rocking the boat.

The misconception of the function of imaginative writing persists. As long as it works as a pleasant semi-intellectual pursuit for readers and writers alike, no reason is seen in a community already sufficiently disrupted and disturbed, for not preserving the fairly comfortable literary status quo, its prizes and ideals.

This falsification of standards is achieved and preserved by the simple procedure of narrowing the literary horizon. Judgement is confined to a parochial milieu, and the tone-setters never make any comparisons with the highest contemporary achievements in other countries.

All is confined in a closed cultural circle, just as in Soviet Russia where members of the Writers Union create their own complacencies and self-satisfactions, protecting themselves from what is happening outside.

This mainstream literature, wherever operative, is closely woven into the general texture of the communal mind. It deals in types or characters that are easily recognizable, rather than in unique individuals, presents situations and relationships already familiar, while giving them a whimsical, pathetic or comical twist. Once this kind of writing has cut a channel through a society, it is difficult to set up a counter-current. The few genuine artists who remain outside the literary consensus make little impact inside their community which, in the belief that it already has a native literature that it can be proud of, a decorative and pleasing adjunct to its main preoccupations, rejects what disturbs, questions, offends, angers or may even be culturally and morally subversive. These writers will first be recognized and accepted outside their communities, as were Joyce, Beckett and, to some extent, Flann O'Brien, and later be let in by their own society through, so to speak, the back door.

While pieces of soft-centred fiction like Frank O'Connor's 'Guests of the Nation' and 'First Confession' were confirming an Irish public in its new mood of complacency and satisfaction at having, as well as its own brand of government and Church, an equally national and cosy literature, the obsessive and uncompromising art of Mr Beckett was ignored. Here are the opening sentences of 'First Confession':

All the trouble began when my grandfather died, and my grandmother — my father's mother —

came to live with us. Relations in the one house are a trial at the best of times, but, to make it worse, my grandmother was a real old country-woman, and quite unsuited to the life in town. She had a fat, wrinkled old face, and, to my mother's indignation, went round the house in bare feet — the boots had her crippled, she said.

This writing — knitting would be a better word — is to the expected pattern or formula, the one then in fashion, and indeed by no means discarded today. Familiar sayings and attitudes are echoed with a nudge of humorous intent, the curtains are drawn, the fire poked, and a nice little tale with a whimsical slant is about to be told. No passion, no interior obsession, no real or outrageous comedy as in Flann O'Brien, Joyce or Mr Beckett. In contrast, here is a passage from the latters's *Molloy*. It is Moran's account of a conversation with his parish priest:

He informed me that Mrs Clement, the chemist's wife and herself a highly qualified chemist, had fallen, in her laboratory, from the top of a ladder, and broken the neck —. The neck! I cried. Of her femur, he said, can't you let me finish. He added that it was bound to happen. And I, not to be outdone, told him how worried I was about my hens, particularly my grey hen, which would neither brood or lay and for the past month and more had done nothing but sit with her arse in the dust, from morning till night. Like Job, haha, he said. I too said haha. What a joy it is to laugh, from time to time, he said . . . A brief silence ensued. What do you feed her on, he said. Corn chiefly, I said. Cooked or raw? he said. Both, I said. I added that she ate nothing anymore. Nothing! he cried. Next to nothing, I said. Animals never laugh, he said. It takes us to find that funny, I said loudly. He mused. Christ never laughed either, he said, so far as we know . . . He looked at me. Can you wonder? I said. There it is, he said. He smiled sadly. She has not the pip, I hope, he said. I said she had not, certainly not, anything he liked, but not the pip.

This, of course, is not naturalistic description. The mass of detail at the start has a different tone from the plodding, serious details of relationship in the O'Connor piece. It evokes the desultory, inconsequent kind of conversation that is universal and it doubtless causes discomfort rather than cosy reassurance in the reader who needs to feel on familiar ground.

It is imaginative writing of a kind not reached by the O'Connor group, and had it been, as part of the mainstream literature, assimilated by the reading community, it would have widened, instead of narrowing, the thought-patterns of our society.

Things may be even worse in England where since Lawrence, if one excepts Evelyn Waugh, there has been no noticeable counter-current to the main, shoddy stream, tributaries of which are hailed every Sunday in the literary supplements. As against this, intelligent English people seem more aware than we

are that the decline, however gentle, in a community, cannot be reversed by economic or social means alone. National energy, the will, not just to survive but to excel, can only be restored psychically, which is to say within the imagination.

In the past societies achieved this through their mythologies or religions. Today, it is by exposing the minds of religious orders to the shock of original writing that a community ensures its organic growth.

DENIS DONOGHUE
from *The Southern Review*, Winter 1976

Denis Donoghue (1928–   ) was born in County Carlow but grew up in Warrenpoint, a seaside resort south of Belfast. His father was a sergeant in the Royal Irish Constabulary. His undergraduate and postgraduate years were spent at University College, Dublin, and at Cambridge. A distinguished academic he was appointed Professor of Modern English and American Literature at UCD and then to the Henry James Chair at New York University. *Warrenpoint* (1990) contains a record of his early years. His critical work includes *Connoisseurs of Chaos* (1965), *Yeats* (1971), *The Arts Without Mystery* (1984) (based on the Reith lectures), and *We Irish: Essays on Irish Literature and Society* (1986). Here in this short challenging essay he takes a hard look at the Irish condition and the state of Irish letters.

Being Irish Together

Most of the towns and villages in Ireland are as peaceful as Rupert Brooke's Grantchester. Derry is safe at the moment, but it is not in its nature to be quiet for long. Belfast is ugly with fear and hatred, though it is still possible to live an unmolested life there, as Oliver Edwards does, pursuing an interest in the relation between Yeats and the German poet Dautendey. The professor of Italian at Queen's University, Belfast, has just published an important translation of Montale: it is a consolation to think of him pondering a crux of diction while the bombs wreck a bar and one assassin shoots, perhaps, another. There is a small district in South Armagh where the English queen's writ does not run and a British soldier is everyone's natural enemy. Yesterday (December 5, 1975) the secretary of state for northern Ireland announced the end of detention, formerly called internment without trial. This morning the *Irish Times* carried a photograph of a young man released from Long Kesh,[1] taking his child by the hand and walking

off into freedom: a charming picture if we could be assured that in a few days he will not take up a gun or make a bomb which will kill without prejudice men, women, Catholics, Protestants, or a child of the same age as his own. The *Irish Times* shows a decent interest in the end of detention, but like nearly everybody it has become weary of the theme and turns, with undisguised relief, to the country's economic problems, the high incidence of unemployment, and current legislation designed to prevent the Irish banks from awarding to their employees an increase of salary higher than the terms of the National Pay Agreement.

Meanwhile men and women in Ireland write verses, novels, short stories, paint pictures, sculpt, and compose string quartets. I have done none of these things and therefore speak of them with impunity: I am not in a competitive trade. It may be said that the 'troubles' in northern Ireland since 1968 have been bad for human life but good for literature: they have gained for young poets an audience which would not normally be willing to attend, and they have provided themes and occasions more demandingly intense than those which generally emerge from a comfortable society. A few poets, including Thomas Kinsella and John Montague, have responded to these occasions directly, getting the horror of it hot; but the resultant poems are hysterical rather than impassioned: it is better for a poet to let such occasions wait in silence for a while. Seamus Heaney has been wiser in his economy, approaching these violent themes indirectly, as if his poems composed not a politics but an anthropology of feeling — starting well back and deep down. One of these days the poets from the North will have to be read with an interest not chiefly topical. A reading in that spirit is perhaps premature, but I hope its day will come soon, and that Kinsella, Heaney, Mahon, Deane, Montague, and the rest will be read in the critically disinterested spirit we bring to, say, Geoffrey Hill, Roy Fisher, Charles Tomlinson, A.R. Ammons, John Ashbery, Philip Larkin, Ted Hughes.

It is true that Irish writers work under special difficulties and that they deserve the advantages of a compellingly ill wind. When Larkin writes the poems in *High Windows* he knows what he is doing, establishing his language in relation to the general body of the English language as a secure possession, mediated by Hardy, Auden, and other poets. Larkin's general body of reference is contemporary English society, dismal in many respects but well understood in terms of class and the preoccupations of class. As an economist of poetry he knows what he needs, judges precisely the moment at which his art tempts itself to archness or extravagance. Most of what he knows he has been told by his masters. But the Irish writers find it peculiarly difficult to know what they are doing: they live upon a fractured rather than an integral tradition; they do not know which voice is to be trusted. Most of them speak English, but they have a sense, just barely acknowledged, that the true voice of feeling speaks in Irish, not a dead language like Latin but a banished language, a voice in exile. English, Irish: Protestant, Catholic: Anglo-Irish, Gael: in Ireland today we do not know what to do with these fractures. Conor Cruise O'Brien[2] urges us to accept our experience as mixed and plural and to live accordingly in a spirit of tolerance. We are to repudiate the spirit of Republicanism which insists upon defining the essential Irish experience as that of driving out the English and spilling blood in this noble cause. His arguments may be found victorious at the end of the day, but meanwhile the spirit of acceptance which he espouses is attractive mainly to people who are disgusted with the Irish question and want to be rid of it; or to people who are weary, indifferent,

interested only in getting on in the world. O'Brien's words are not only despised by every nationalist and republican, but they are rejected by anyone whose sense of life demands that life be lived in conflict and stress. There are men and women who despise the concept of a plural society and who are ready to kill and be killed for the sake of national purity. O'Brien does not understand such people, or the aboriginal loyalties which mean far more to them than a contemptible liberal peace. He answers that his policy will not cause a single death: it is true. But a Republican will assert that there are things more glorious than liberal tolerance — a martyr's death, for instance. So the old rhetorical battle starts up again.

The real trouble in Ireland is that our national experience has been too limited to be true. Since the Plantation of Ulster there has been one story and one story only in Irish feeling: the English, how to get rid of them, or, failing that, to circumvent them, cajole them, twist their tails. Our categories of feeling are therefore flagrantly limited; our history has been at once intense and monotonous. We have had no industrial revolution, no factory acts, no trade union movement: hence the frail basis upon which our Labour Party exists, by contrast with the two major parties which still define themselves in terms of our civil war. A limited history, a correspondingly intimidating mythology, a fractured language, a literature of fits and starts and gestures: no continuity from one age to the next. Irish novelists, the few who survive, feel the anxiety of influence but not the incitement or the challenge of a tradition. The nineteenth-century writers whom Thomas Flanagan studied in *The Irish Novelists* do not amount to a tradition; there are novelists but there is no tradition of the novel, the force of vision, technique, and precedence available to, say, Angus Wilson when he reads George Eliot and writes *Anglo-Saxon Attitudes*. The contemporary Irish novelist looks for a tradition capable of telling him what has been done and how he ought to proceed: instead he finds Joyce, an overbearing presence. Take the story by James Plunkett in the present issue of the *Sewanee Review*. I have no information on the circumstances in which Plunkett wrote the story or the difficulties he met in writing it, but I am sure his main difficulty was the inescapable presence of Joyce's *Portrait of the Artist as a Young Man*. The price we pay for Yeats and Joyce is that each in his way gave Irish experience a memorable but narrow definition; they established it not as the ordinary but as a special case of the ordinary. Synge and the minor writers of the Irish literary revival were not strong enough to counter Yeats's incantatory rhetoric: no writer in Ireland has been strong enough to modify Joyce's sense of Irish experience in fiction. As a result the writers we particularly revere are those who encountered Yeats and Joyce and contrived to preserve minds and arts of their own. I think of Flann O'Brien who somehow deflected the blow of Joyce sufficiently to write *At Swim-Two-Birds* and *The Third Policeman*, books which could not have been written without Joyce's example but which could not have taken their definitive form if Flann O'Brien had allowed himself to be intimidated by that example. I think also of Austin Clarke's later poems, the work of a poet who languished in Yeats's shadow until, late and not a moment too soon, he swerved away from the shadow and struck out for himself.

T.S. Eliot has maintained in 'What Is a Classic?' that 'every supreme poet, classic or not, tends to exhaust the ground he cultivates, so that it must, after yielding a diminishing crop, finally be left in fallow for some generations'. I find this an ambiguous idea, but nothing in it is more significant than Eliot's assumption that we have world enough and time. Certainly there are cultures of which we feel that the question of time is not the main problem: it is possible to think of the cultures of France, England, and Greece as providing a cadence of feeling which allows for historical change and continuity. To think of Shakespeare and Milton exhausting the ground they cultivate is to respond once again to the plenitude of a literary culture in which that ground may be allowed to remain 'in fallow for some generations'. But it also exacerbates our sense of the vulnerability of those societies which cannot afford fallow years or generations.

Modern Ireland as a state rather than as a province of England is only fifty years old. The separation of North and South is arbitrary, a politician's device. We have had to concentrate in one generation the experience which more fortunate countries have been able to develop in several; and we have largely been prevented from doing so by the exorbitance of rival mythologies. So we have had to live from day to day and hand to mouth. I mention these facts to explain the impression of spasmodic achievement in Irish literature: our experience has not been sufficiently diverse, and we have had not enough time, to produce an adequate literature. Our writers are, for the most part, solitary workers: they do not find themselves as participants in an enterprise, a common pursuit. Henry James said of the solitary worker that, 'apt to make awkward experiments, he is in the nature of the case more or less of an empiric'. I take it that empiricism is work from hand to mouth. It is remarkable, and a joy, that work as fine as Clarke's *Ancient Lights* has been produced in Ireland by such an unconcerted method.

It is probably idle to posit the conditions in which good work is done. Was it necessary for Brian Moore to leave Belfast and go to Canada, then to California, for the sake of writing *Catholics*? Would Michael McLaverty have developed a more complete art by resorting to the same itinerary? It is common to have the experience and miss the meaning. Who knows? Who knows enough? Anyway it is my impression that Irish writers sense a rift between experience and meaning, but in reverse: the meaning is premature, already inscribed by a mythology they have no choice but to inherit, and the experience is too narrow to be entirely natural and representative.

1   Prison where political prisoners were held, now called The Maze.
2   In *States of Ireland* (1972), O'Brien argued for an acceptance of the dual traditions in Ireland.

SEAMUS DEANE
from *The Crane Bag*, Vol. 1, No. 1, 1977

This interview of Seamus Heaney by the poet and critic Seamus Deane (1940–) appeared in the first issue of *The Crane Bag*, an important Irish journal, co-edited by Mark Patrick Hederman and Richard Kearney, which ran from 1977 until 1985. The interview revolves around the issue of writing and politics, especially in the light of Heaney's political volume *North* which was published in 1975 (see below p. 855 for examples of poems from this volume).

Unhappy and at Home

Interview with Seamus Heaney
by Seamus Deane

DEANE: Do you believe there is a recognizably northern group of poets, recognizable, that is, in the literary as opposed to merely geographical sense? And secondly, do you believe that this can be legitimately connected with the northern troubles?

HEANEY: I think there is a recognizable group in the literary sense. This would include Simmons, Longley, Mahon, Muldoon and others; I'm not sure whether I would include you here, for I'm talking of a certain literary style which arose from the 'well made poem' cult in English writing in the late fifties and sixties. Though harking to different writers all of us in this group were harking to writers from the English cultural background. In that sense, there is a kind of tightmouthedness which might be considered 'Northern' by many in the South, but which is really the result of a particular literary apprenticeship.

DEANE: And can the emergence of this group be related in any way to the Northern crisis?

HEANEY: I think that this is a much more imponderable kind of subject. There is certainly no direct or obvious connection; but this poetry and the troubles emerged from an intensity, a root, a common emotional ground. The root of the troubles may have something in common with the root of the poetry.

DEANE: Can you give me an example?

HEANEY: Well, in my own case, the very first poems I wrote, 'Docker' and one about Carrickfergus Castle for instance, reveal this common root. The latter had William of Orange, English tourists and myself in it. A very inept sort of poem but my first attempts to speak, to make verse, faced the Northern sectarian problem. Then this went underground and I became very influenced by Hughes[1] and one part of my temperament took over: the private county Derry childhood part of myself rather than the slightly aggravated young Catholic male part.

DEANE: Speaking more generally, do you think that this fidelity of the poet to his community needs to be catered for in some political way, especially within the context of the Northern crisis, even though one would not want to be prescriptive about this?

HEANEY: I think so. But again, you can only speak from the inward side of your own notion of what it is to be a writer; and that is changing as you change; and you change in relation to the situation. Certainly, in my own writing of the last ten years it is obvious that while the mode of writing, that is, the imagery, language and general intonations of the verse, remained the same, they had to strain to face the reality of the happenings and the subterranean energies which produced these happenings.

DEANE: In view of the inevitability of facing the Northern situation, or of bearing some imprint of its experience, do you think that there are any grounds for agreeing with Conor Cruise O'Brien's view that the link between art and politics constitutes an unhealthy intersection?

HEANEY: Yes, I think he is correct. . . .

DEANE: Even though he meant this as a criticism?

HEANEY: I can only speak of myself from the notion I have of my own work. Poetry is born out of the watermarks and colourings of the self. But that self in some ways takes its spiritual pulse from the inward spiritual structure of the community to which it belongs; and the community to which I belong is Catholic and nationalist. I believe that the poet's force now, and hopefully in the future, is to maintain the efficacy of his own 'mythos', his own cultural and political colourings, rather than to serve any particular momentary strategy that his political leaders, his paramilitary organization or his own liberal self might want him to serve. I think that poetry and politics are, in different ways, an articulation, an ordering, a giving of form to inchoate pieties, prejudices, world-views, or whatever. And I think that my own poetry is a kind of slow, obstinate, papish burn, emanating from the ground I was brought up on.

DEANE: But at the same time, you'd be very anxious to refrain from taking any outright political stance in your poetry?

HEANEY: I think about that more and more since I did *North*. I always thought of the political problem — maybe because I am not really a political thinker — as being an internal Northern Ireland division. I thought along sectarian lines. Now I think that the genuine political confrontation is between Ireland and Britain. Yet it is my own sensibility and heritage of feeling which is the basis for the feeling of the poems, and I never had any strong feelings, for example, about the British army; it was always the R.U.C., the B

Specials, and so on.² Now that may have been politically shortsighted, but poetry emerges from the beat coming off images, from the aura surrounding certain words.

DEANE: Do you think that if some political stance is not adopted by you and the Northern poets at large, this refusal might lead to a dangerous strengthening of earlier notions of the autonomy of poetry and corroborate the recent English notion of the happy limitations of a 'well made poem'? And furthermore, do you feel that this disdain of poetry for all that would break its own autonomy could lead to the sponsoring of a literature which would be almost deliberately minor?

HEANEY: I think it could. . . .

DEANE: Do you think it has?

HEANEY: Most poetry is inevitably so. . . .

DEANE: But not deliberately so!

HEANEY: I think that the recent English language tradition does tend towards the 'well made poem', that is, towards the insulated and balanced statement. However, major poetry will always burst that corseted and decorous truthfulness. In so doing, it may be an unfair poetry; it will almost certainly be one-sided.

DEANE: Politically one-sided?

HEANEY: Yes. I think it has to be. As I said earlier, the poet incarnates his mythos and must affirm it. Montague's 'The Rough Field' is a poem which affirms the mythos and, in that sense, is a poem which has come to stick, to stick politically in one direction, and against many others.

DEANE: But, is not such political fidelity contradicted, in some sense, by the poet's aspiration towards an equipoise and balance of form? There is a statement by Adorno which says that the conciliatory nature of art is in direct relation to the rage which produced it. In your own case, my own feeling is that the language of much of your poetry has a good deal of violent and physical implication; and yet the poems themselves have a certain poise and balance, even sometimes to a self-conscious degree. Now do you think that the balance of poetry is something you have to achieve for the sake of art, even though it might begin in the imbalance of hatred or sectarian feeling?

HEANEY: You are touching there the very root and intimacy of the poet's act. There is a poem in *North* which is a metaphorical consideration of this. I think it is a dangerous poem to have written — a poem called 'Hercules and Antaeus'.

Hercules represents the balanced rational light while Antaeus represents the pieties of illiterate fidelity. Overall, I think that in the case of almost every Northern poet, the rational wins out too strong. This poem drifts towards an assent to Hercules, though there was a sort of nostalgia for Antaeus. . . .

DEANE: A nostalgia for Antaeus, but an assent to Hercules and rationality?

HEANEY: Yes, but I think that is wrong now.

DEANE: You mean that if rationality is to be worth the name it must confront and take account of Antaeus' bigotry, or must lift itself clear of it?

HEANEY: Yes. But this is a seesaw, an advance-retire situation. There is always the question in everybody's mind whether the rational and humanist domain which produced what we call civilization in the West should be allowed full command in the psyche, speech and utterance of Ulster.

DEANE: Do you not think that your own poetry and that of Mahon and Montague imply that this humanism, represented by Hercules, which has moulded Western civilization, is a dangerous feature because the nature of humanism is always to detach itself from that out of which it initially arises?

HEANEY: Yes, absolutely. . . .

DEANE: And do you think that the kind of humanism which Conor Cruise O'Brien sponsors is precisely that kind of humanism, totally detached from its atavisms, which, though welcome from a rational point of view, renders much of what he says either irrelevant or simply wrong. Particularly in relation to the North where bigotry is so much a part of the psyche?

HEANEY: I don't know where or what O'Brien's atavisms are. . . .

DEANE: I mean that in order to be rational O'Brien tends to renounce atavisms whereas the thing about poetry is that to survive it cannot renounce them.

Heaney: Yes, I agree partly. But I think there is a dialogue. I think the obstinate voice of rationalist humanism is important. If we lose that we lose everything too, don't we? I believe that Conor Cruise O'Brien did an utterly necessary job in rebuking all easy thoughts about the Protestant community in the North. It is to be seen in this way: 7 or 8 years ago there was tremendous sentiment for Catholics in the North, among intellectuals, politicians and ordinary people in the South. Because of his statements O'Brien is still reviled by people who held those sentiments;

yet now these people harbour sentiments which mirror O'Brien's thinking, and still they do not cede the clarity or the validity of his position.

DEANE: But surely this very clarity of O'Brien's position is just what is most objectionable. It serves to give a rational clarity to the Northern position which is untrue to the reality. In other words, is not his humanism here being used as an excuse to rid Ireland of the atavisms which gave it life even though the life itself may be in some ways brutal? Is it not a very bourgeois form of humanism?

HEANEY: O'Brien's force doesn't lie in the North. His real force and his proper ground is here in the South and I think it is entirely right that there should be some kind of clarity in southerners' thinking about the Protestant community in the North. And it is not enough for people to simply say 'ah, they're all Irishmen', when some Northerners actually spit at the word Irishman. There is in O'Brien a kind of obstinate insistence on facing up to this kind of reality, which I think is his contribution.

DEANE: To return then to the more specifically literary scene. We have already spoken of a possible Northern group of Irish poets. Could we now drop the epithet 'Northern' and say something about the movement of Irish poetry as a whole, with particular reference to its mentors, Yeats, Kavanagh or otherwise? Would you see yourself as writing in what could be recognized as a twentieth century tradition in Irish poetry? Or do you think that the poet in Ireland is forced to range eclectically for his *poetic*, and perhaps ultimately make one for himself?

HEANEY: I think we are both agreed that every tradition borrows eclectically and thereby develops and strengthens itself. However, I think we can by now speak of an Irish tradition because there is a mounting confidence in the validity and importance of our ground. If only because people are killing one another. There is a strong sense in a number of poets that the crosschannel tradition cannot deal any longer with our particular history. Discussion of what tradition means has moved from a sort of linguistic nostalgia, a puerile discourse about assonance, metres and so on, to a consideration of the politics and anthropology of our condition. I think that every poet in earnest in this country is scanning for an exemplar, Irish or otherwise, and different poets look to different people — Montague looks to David Jones, you look to Neruda, Kinsella is by now I suppose his own firm and major man. He is the poet who affirms an Irish modernity, particularly in his treatment of psychic material which is utterly Irish Catholic. In this sense he is somewhat akin to the Joyce of *Dubliners* who found a form for that unspoken world. Kinsella has found a language which is both at ease with exemplars like Joyce and Eliot, and also capable of speaking very much out of his own world and intellect and with his own voice.

DEANE: It is interesting that you name Kinsella here, for Kinsella of all poets is perhaps most interested in articulating for himself in his own work the sense that there is a specific Irish tradition in literature, one part of which is in the Gaelic language, another part of which is in the English language. Do you agree with this notion of a specifically Irish tradition? And secondly, do you think that for a poet to write he has to have the confidence that such a tradition exists or is at least possible? Or do you think one can live in a hand to mouth manner?

HEANEY: I don't think that the poet can keep living in the hand to mouth manner. I do think there is such a thing as an Irish literary tradition, using tradition here in Eliot's sense. We need only look to Kinsella's translation of the *Táin* sagas and myths which Yeats and, to some extent, Ferguson used before him, not as a picturesque manifestation of the otherness of this culture, but as an ordering structure for his own psychic materials and energies. In *The Land of the Dead*,[3] for example, he brings the ancient mythic shapes into conjunction with his disjointed, alienated and essentially artistic consciousness. In his actual writing Kinsella affirms the root and his own theorizing about tradition merely serves to nourish and clarify it.

DEANE: Are you not intent on a similar kind of enterprise to mould your own psychic disposition into a sort of cultural landscape which could be stereoscopically viewed? And are you not also, like Kinsella, obsessed with the desire that this landscape be distinctly of this culture, not in the chauvinistic sense but out of an ultimate fidelity and ultimacy which you would consider necessary for poetry if it is to achieve its validity?

HEANEY: Yes, I think I came to this notion in the writing of the *Wintering Out* collection, particularly in the place name poems: 'Anahorish', 'Broagh', and so on. I had a great sense of release as they were being written, a joy and devil-may-careness, and that convinced me that one could be faithful to the nature of the English language — for in some senses these poems are erotic mouth-music by and out of the anglo-saxon tongue — and, at the same time, be faithful to one's own non-English origin, for me that is County Derry. That glimpse is enough to convince me that this is a proper aspiration for our poetry. The difficulty is of course to repeat such experiences. I think that it was the quest for such a repetition that led me to translate *Buile Shuibhne*.[4] In this Sweeney story we have a Northern sacral king, Sweeney, who is driven out of Rasharkin in Co. Antrim. There is a sort of schizophrenia in him. On the one hand he is always whinging for his days in Rasharkin, but on the other he is celebrating his free creative imagination. Maybe here there was a presence, a fable which could lead to the discovery of feelings in myself which I could not otherwise find words for, and which would cast a dream or possibility or myth across the swirl of private feelings: an objective correlative. But one must not forget the other side of the poetic enterprise which is the arbitrariness and the innocence of the day to day poetic impulse. And again the question is how far should the mythic scheme dominate the private felicities and discoveries of the everyday occasional things. I'm speaking of the lyric impulse. The quick and the purity of the inward act has to be preserved at all costs, however essential the outward structures may be for communication, community and universal significance.

DEANE: But is there not the danger that in yielding to the private day to day impulse, the Irish poet, while writing some very felicitous poems, will ultimately feel frustrated in being unable to see his poetry as an oeuvre, belonging to a larger whole or tradition. It is my view that most poets wish they could constitute en masse some sort of thing-in-itself, which would also and at the same time be a thing in connection with other things which occurred during its generation and production. When you talk therefore of your fascination for the Sweeney saga, or of Kinsella's for the Táin cycle, or of Montague's for Gaelic lore, do you not think that it is significant that all three of you have shown interest in a poetry that is structurally epic, whereas your basic tendencies would seem to be towards the lyric? In other words, are you not in a sense looking for a tradition which would provide you with an epic impulse, not native to the modern Irish conditions but essential to your poetry?

HEANEY: Yes. But then several poets in the English tradition have nurtured me — Frost, Hopkins and Ted Hughes, for example. Yet the real strength for me has come to lie in the Irish tradition of Yeats and Kavanagh. Yeats has created a body of work which stands resonantly on its own ground and is superior, I think, to anything in the modern English tradition. On the other hand, Kavanagh challenges everything that Yeats stood for. He has, as Montague put it, liberated us into ignorance. No writer since has been free from whatever Kavanagh did to the air of consciousness. It is to do with a confidence in the deprivations of our condition. It is to do with an insouciance and trust in the clarities and cunnings of our perceptions. Yeats and Kavanagh point up the contradictions we have been talking about: the search for myths and sagas, the need for a structure and a sustaining landscape and at the same time the need to be liberated and distanced from it, the need to be open, unpredictably susceptible, lyrically opportunistic.

DEANE: Could you not say that Kavanagh is a dangerous exemplar in that he, above all others, is the one who espouses the ignorance of the day to day? And are you not now speaking of an Irish tradition with two entirely opposite dimensions, a twentieth-century day-to-day Kavanagh, and a mythological oeuvre-directed Yeats?

HEANEY: I think we must be faithful to kindred points here. On the one hand Kavanagh with his sense of 'home' and his almost extreme realization of the disobedience and peremptoriness of creative nature, on the other Yeats with his platonic rendition of 'heaven', and of what can be made of this in terms of deliberated poetic effort. You need both. *North* saw the shades of a possibility of such a union. The two halves of the book constitute two different types of utterance, each of which arose out of a necessity to shape and give palpable linguistic form to two kinds of urgency — one symbolic, one explicit. I don't know whether it succeeded, but I am pleased that it appeased and hardened out into words some complex need in me.

DEANE: You would say then that in writing *North* with this dual motivation, a certain organic form evolved which you are unhappy about when critics tend to transmogrify it into a single scheme? Is this the kind of resolution you are trying to achieve between Kavanagh and Yeats: a poetry that would be neither a matter of the day to day spontaneities alone, nor of a schematic mythologizing alone, but a matter of making the day to day become a form embedded in the day to day from which it arises?

HEANEY: That is exactly it.

DEANE: It is like what someone said of the American landscape reflecting the whole continent in its smallest portion. Is this what you are seeking in your poetry — a kind of singular universal?

HEANEY: Yes, but it is a damnable problem. The more one consciously tries to convey this imprint the more it seems to elude you. You see, the lift-off and push of the innocent creative moment can never be fully schematic. Indeed, a too conscious awareness of the experience which gave rise to a poem can very often impede its creation. The all-important thing here is the emerging authority which one senses in the poem being written, when you recognize that there are elements in the poem which are capillaries into the large brutal scheme of things, capillaries sucking the whole of the earth.

DEANE: The strange sense of unhappiness in your poetry, expressed in the now well known phrase 'lost, unhappy and at home', seems to me to have a lot to do with the particular struggle in your poetry. If happiness is being sheltered from the world then doesn't your poetry seek to acknowledge that the shelter was once there but is there no longer? Isn't your poetry trying to convey that kind of exposure which will also reveal what the shelter had been? And isn't there a sense of fear that this exposure may be intensified into a public glare so blinding that it could prevent you from recreating any longer in your poetry the sense of the lost shelter?

HEANEY: That is very true. But you have to make your own work your home. If you live as an author your reward is authority. But of course the trouble is how to be sure you are living properly.

1   Ted Hughes (1930–98), the English poet.
2   Royal Ulster Constabulary; the B Specials were an Ulster Protestant part-time police force disbanded in April 1970 because of their sectarian character.
3   *Notes for the Land of the Dead* was first published in 1972.
4   *Sweeney Astray*, published in 1983.

DONALL MacAMHLAIGH
from *The Tablet*, 18 March 1978

Donall MacAmhlaigh (1926–89) was born in Galway and emigrated to Northampton in 1951, working for most of his life as a labourer and at the same time writing a series of semi-autobiographical books in Irish. *Dialann Deoraí* appeared in 1960, and was translated by Valentin Iremonger as *The Irish Navvy* in 1964.

Britain's Irish Workers

'Britain was a revelation to the work-eager Irish who flocked here in the post-war boom.' The process of integration has gone apace since then.

The 1950s loom large in the consciousness of the Irish in Britain as a sorry decade, a period of low morale and hopelessness every bit as traumatic for us as the 1930s were for the people of Britain. True, we had no mass protest or hunger marches apart from the short-lived demonstrations of the unemployed in Dublin, and it must also be said that with the exception of our urban workless the Irish probably had a higher standard of living, food-wise, than their British counterparts, who were so cruelly betrayed by the 'land fit for heroes' promise. But there would have been protest aplenty and perhaps even bloody revolution if the safety valve of emigration to Britain had not been there, if Irish brawn, brain and diligence had not been as much in demand in post-war Britain as they were unwanted and unappreciated at home. Our elected representatives in Dail Eireann (the situation was no better in the North except for the higher dole and National Health benefits) uttered well-worn platitudes about the evil of emigration — the 'need to staunch the flow' was the favourite cliché all through the fifties, though a few politicians were callous, or perhaps just honest enough to declare that emigration was a necessary evil and that we could never hope to provide work for all our people. It is a measure, I believe, of how far we have come since then that no TD[1] who valued his career would come out with such a statement today.

The effect of the mass-exodus of the 1950s, both on

those who daily converged on the emigrant ship in Dun Laoire or elsewhere and those who remained in the rapidly-thinning countryside at home, was a wounding cynicism, a bitter sense of betrayal and a kind of shame and self-hatred born of the need to turn for your bread and butter to the old Saxon foe. The attitude of this era is epitomized for me in the reply which a Dail candidate on an election platform in Mayo was given by an embittered member of his audience: 'Arrah don't mind all your grand promises, Mick, we heard them before. Just make the suitcases a bit cheaper, that'll do us around here!' That was the motto of the many thousands who voted annually with their feet — to quote yet another cliché of the day. And those who came back a year or so later to visit their nearest and dearest with those same suitcases packed with new clothes, wearing a Burton's suit and blue gaberdine raincoat and with a well-stocked wallet of notes, saw no prospect of staying. Nor did they receive much encouragement, not even from their nearest and dearest. 'Ah sure there's nothing at all at home now, boy,' the cry went, 'what would you stay here for? Aren't they all leaving, anyone with a bit of go at all to them? This country is finished, so it is.' A Kilkenny publican put it even more bitterly to me when I was on a visit home at Easter one year: 'How is it every useless yoke can get a job in England and the best of men can get nothing here?' The feeling was everywhere, expressed by almost everyone you met, that there was no future at all for Ireland, that emigration, the low marriage-rate and unemployment would reduce us to near-disappearance; and books like *The Vanishing Irish*[2] upheld the belief. (On this side of the Irish Sea the situation was seen rather differently; the English in the main have been tolerant and appreciative — even welcoming . . . of us, but they couldn't fail to notice our arrival in ever-increasing numbers and they cracked, not wholly without malice, 'Once upon a time there was an Irishman — now there's millions of the bleeders!')

And so they went, the Irish, the very flower of the nation, the young, the strong, the productive, the comely lads and girls whom it was a crying sin to see leaving their homeland, until somewhere around 1958 the shameful figure of 60,000 per annum was reached. They went to man the buses and the hospital wards of Britain, to lay sewers and water systems, to build roads and bridges, to perform feats of labour hardly less Herculean than those performed by earlier generations of navvies and labourers in the making of the railways during the long reign of Victoria. They clustered together in great enclaves in Camden Town, Kilburn, Cricklewood (John B. Keane[3] wrote a poem about it),

in Sparkbrook in Birmingham, in Moss Side, Manchester; they invaded whole areas bringing with them a flavour and life-style of their own. In those days before the advent of the plush Irish clubs and centres, before the spread and growth of the county associations, they filled the Irish dance halls — the Galtymore, the Round Tower, the Blarney in Tottenham Court Road — and pubs like the Cock in Kilburn, the Black Cap in Camden Town, and Anty's in Manchester. They gathered outside the church gates after Mass each Sunday to exchange news of home or drank weak tea in makeshift social clubs tacked into the presbytery where provincial papers like the *Kerryman*, the *Cork Examiner*, the *Anglo-Celt* and the *Connaught Tribune* were sold along with the day-old *Irish Press* (you rarely saw the *Irish Times* or *Independent* where the ordinary working Irish assembled). Marriageable young men and women predominated in these gatherings and the speed with which, given a chance to work and earn and make their way in the world, they took on the cares and responsibilities of the married state went a long way to discredit the oft-repeated notion that there was something basically wrong with us, that the normal drive towards the creation of a home and family had somehow been drained out of the Irish by their environment and upbringing. There was some truth in the charge, of course, and there were victims aplenty of a system which many of us were fleeing from every bit as much as we fled from poverty and unemployment — the petty snobbery as damaging, every whit, as the less flexible English class structure, the misplaced zeal and greed of so many of the rural clergy, the cramping limitation on ambition and aspiration. Ireland's loss was Britain's gain, though oddly enough our foremost creative writers, preoccupied with the narrow, introspective view, found scarcely a word to say about the great national tragedy or what it was doing to Ireland, to those left behind in lonely rural parishes as well as to the young and vigorous who left. Why was no great searing novel of protest born of the era or why no great play or poem? Only journalist John Healy in his heart-rending *Nobody Shouted Stop!* wrote with bitterness, pity and love of this black chapter of modern Ireland. Perhaps our writers left Ireland too young or perhaps it is that they shared the indifference of the well-off; that they failed so singularly to say something about what was happening in those years must be a black mark against them forever.

Britain was a revelation to the work-eager Irish who flocked here during the great post-war boom, and I often wished that Englishmen, who persist in the notion that the Irish dislike them and their country, could only have heard the remarks which were commonplace when the Irish workers spoke among themselves. I say among themselves for with a stubborn loyalty the Irish never admitted to an outsider what they were forever saying to each other — that there was nothing 'back yonder', that the crowd in Dublin couldn't run a booze-up in a brewery, that Britain was the best bleddy country in the world, better even than the States where, for all the blow and big money, a man couldn't afford to fall sick. This was the 'two-face syndrome', if I may use the appropriate jargon, which lecturer Brendan Caulfield of the Lanchester Polytechnic referred to in a social study — the face we present to ourselves, the Irish here in Britain, and the face we present to outsiders.

The Irish clergy in Britain, too, were something of a revelation to us: they were of us and for us, the working people, and not aloof or demanding like a lot of the clergy at home. The priest as friend and counsellor, riding round on a bicycle often as not to visit parishioners, or organizing bingo, was something quite new to a lot of us, to countrymen and women especially, long familiar with the autocratic parish priest back home. Fr Murphy wouldn't lend the parish hall for a dance or drama or you had to get a note from Fr Kelly if you hoped to get a few months' work on some building scheme — these examples may seem extreme today but they were by no means rare. There weren't too many priests about like Fr McDyer or the founder of Muintir na Tire.[4] Here the priests played a great part in the easing in of new arrivals from Ireland, helping out at different levels. Names like Eamonn (now Bishop) Casey, Fr Paul Byrne of Shelter, Fr Dore of Kilburn ('Two Pakistanis came to me for information, they were making a survey of the Irish in London. I told them to go to hell and survey their own people. There's too many people investigating the Irish!') spring to mind at once; names too like Fr Patrick Galvin, all six-foot-four of him, who was the best advocate the Irish ever had in the east Midlands and who once, when I was out of work in the bad winter months, put his hand in his pocket and offered me a couple of quid. The clergy here played a big part in the settling in of the psychologically-battered exiles of the fifties; here in Northampton from where I write, for instance, the little pre-fabbed St Patrick's Club (still standing and in use) offered the only alternative to the pub; there was always a bite to eat at Nazareth House for the 'long-distance man' and in the prolonged big snow of 1962-1963 free meals were organized by priests of some north London parishes.

But the trauma of our uprooting persisted, more among the unskilled and the meagrely-educated than in those who came later and better equipped to succeed in business and professional life. It was reflected in many ways, in an inordinate concern with what used to be quaintly called 'our image abroad' and with what others — the English invariably! — were thinking about us. (I have always thought it significant that the English never worried too much about what *we* thought of them!) The sight of two ageing Paddies slogging it out on the pavement in front of a Kilburn public house after closing hours might have been thought to damage the precious image but there were enough of the other sort about, the sober and modestly ambitious, to ensure that the damage wasn't irreparable. As someone once remarked to Brendan Behan in Paris, we saw everything in relation to ourselves and we were often paranoically touchy; for instance when you heard of a rape or some such unsavoury crime here, some Irish person would invariably exclaim, 'Oh my God, I hope it doesn't turn out to be an Irishman!'

I find that my space is nearly gone and I have been talking nostalgically about the situation of 20 or more years ago, so just a few words to bring us up to date. The Irish in Britain are of a somewhat different composition today: a settled, largely middle-aged, largely (70 per cent according to an *Irish Post* survey) home-owning group, more fortunate in many respects — in spite of the Prevention of Terrorism Act which has given scope for considerable harassment of the innocent — than any other immigrant group. Indeed the process of integration has gone so well and so far that it would be well-nigh impossible to invoke any of the kinds of sanctions, disenfranchisement and so forth, which Mr Airey Neave[5] and other prominent people in Westminster had notions of. Integration has not meant assimilation, however, except for those who wished it so, and today as the merest glance at any copy of the London-based *Irish Post* will show, Irish culture is being lovingly fostered and passed along to a generation of children who, though born and bred here in Britain, persist in thinking themselves every bit as Irish as their cousins at home. Successive waves of Irish immigrants gave much to Britain and freely admit they got much in return; but the flood has dropped to a negligible trickle and a great many of us have even returned home. There is at least as much hope for the future in Ireland today — the sad, stricken North perhaps excepted — as there is for the future of Britain. And as someone wrote in the letters page of the *Irish Post* recently, Mrs Thatcher should not be worried about the number of Irish coming here, but rather about the number going home . . .

1 Teachtaí Dála, member of the lower House of Parliament.
2 Title of a book of essays on Ireland's declining population, edited by John A. O'Brien and published in 1954.
3 A prolific Irish writer, John B. Keane (1928–) was born in Listowel, County Kerry. Among his many popular plays are *The Field* (1965) and *Big Maggie* (1969). *Many Young Men of Twenty* (1961) is about emigration, and MacAmhlaigh may have the title song in mind here. Or it could be 'Cricklewood', the song Keane wrote for

his other emigration play *Hut 42* (1962): 'Oh, Cricklewood, Oh, Cricklewood, / You stole my heart away; / For I was young and innocent, / And you were old and grey.'
4 Irish: People of the Land, an organization founded in 1931 to promote rural life and vocationalism.
5 A Conservative politician, head of Mrs Thatcher's private office and shadow secretary of state for Northern Ireland, later murdered by the IRA in 1979 as he drove away from the underground car park at the House of Commons.

DERVLA MURPHY
from Dervla Murphy, *A Place Apart* (1978)

Dervla Murphy (1931–) was born in County Waterford and has spent her life travelling the globe. In 1963 she cycled to India, worked with Tibetan refugee children, and explored the Ethiopian highlands on foot. In *A Place Apart*, which Carlo Gébler has called 'the best modern study of Ulster', she turned her attention to a province closer to home and found herself unsettled by the rhetoric of its most vociferous preacher. As a corrective to Dervla Murphy's demonic view of him, see Ian Paisley's moving funeral oration for Esther Gibson, one of the victims of the Omagh bombing, in David McKittrick's *Lost Lives* (1999), victim number 3,606. For a sober analysis of the crisis in Northern Ireland and the political options facing the province, see John McGarry and Brendan O'Leary, *Explaining Northern Ireland: Broken Images* (1995).

The huge church was scarcely half-full when Paisley stage-managed himself into the pulpit to begin the service. The theme of his sermon was 'The Biblical Call to Arms' and the violence of his imagery was extreme. When he and the congregation had read alternate verses of Genesis 3 he picked on the fifteenth verse — 'And I will put enmity between thy seed and her seed; it shall bruise thy head and thou shalt bruise his heel' — and these words were used to 'prove' that the present state of Northern Ireland has been willed by God because until the Anti-Christ has been vanquished there can be no peace. We got the 'sharp two-edged sword' from Revelations and also Revelations 2, 9, 10, 23, 26, 27. Verse 10, I suppose, was intended to console those present who had paramilitary connections in gaol. And also, perhaps, to remind the audience that their beloved preacher had himself been cast into prison by the devil, disguised as Her Majesty's Government. Jesus evicting the money-changers from the temple came next and was used to emphasize Christ's violence. 'Christ was not a man of peace! Don't you believe it! Christ was not a namby-

pamby sentimentalist! He was no softie! Christ was a *violent* man! Violent for good! Violent to stamp out wickedness, violent for God's sake! Our battle is not against a *system* — it is against the people who uphold that system! And *we* must be violent for God's sake! We must attack the people who uphold rottenness — as Christ attacked the money-changers! Remember it's not the system we must attack but the *people* — the people who represent the Anti-Christ in our midst! Be violent for Christ's sake, to defend that faith which he himself defended with his fists!'

As I transcribe these words from my diary, where I wrote them within moments of leaving the church, I realize that some readers will have difficulty in believing that a man who pretends to be a Christian, and sits as an MP in the House of Commons, could say such things to a gathering of Belfast citizens in the year 1976.

Paisley's pulpit is in fact a small stage and while preaching he strides up and down, gesticulating, shouting, grimacing — and, on this Sunday, waving a huge Bible above his head and declaiming, 'This is not a book of peace! This is a book of war! War against Christ's enemies, against the deceits of the devil, against the snares of ecumenism! We must listen to the call to arms and not be afraid! And Christ will fight with us, as he overturned those tables, and will be proud to see us as we go forth bravely to attack for him!'

I was aware of blasphemy being committed as this demented creature paced from end to end of his pulpit-stage, flourishing the Bible and repetitively — almost hypnotically — insisting on the need to defend, to fight, to do battle, to vanquish, to conquer, to assert, to unsheath the sword, to show no mercy to the enemies of God . . . The cunning with which he used an aggressive, militaristic phraseology — all culled from the Bible — was literally blood-chilling. At a certain point it brought me out in gooseflesh though Belfast was in the middle of a heat wave. I longed then to get away, somehow to escape from this man's powerful emanations of evil. But I was afraid to move lest I might be pursued by some young man anxious to secure his salvation by putting a bullet in my irreverent back. Meanwhile everyone else was listening, rapt, and many fervent murmurs of approval greeted the various climactic exhortations. Hellfire was guaranteed for all who disregard Paisley's version of the word of God and very skilfully he presented himself as prophet, hero, saint and martyr. Occasionally there was an attempt at light relief — '*We* don't need to run jumble-sales and coffee-mornings and dandelion teas and pea-soup dinners! The Lord is providing for his chosen! Last Sunday what did the Lord provide? He provided £724.61! And for the Manse Fund an anonymous £50! And for the World Congress Chorale £566!

(These figures were also printed on the programme under the heading 'The Lord's Treasury'.) Later there was a reference to so many joints in so many ovens becoming burnt offerings if he didn't stop soon — an indication of kindly, homely humanity which had the audience in raptures. Before stopping, he told us that at 3.30 he would be preaching at Portglenone Independent Orange Service (the official Orange Order and the Free Presbyterians parted company about fifteen years ago) and that anyone who cared to attend would be most welcome. In any event, he hoped to see us all again at 7.30 p.m. when he would be back in the Martyrs' Memorial. And he announced the text for his evening sermon: 'If the Trumpet Give an Uncertain Sound, Who Shall Prepare Himself to the Battle?'

This whole horrible travesty of a Christian church service was diabolically clever. And I mean diabolically. Paisley might not convert an atheist to a belief in God but he has certainly converted me to a belief in the devil — which after all comes to the same thing. I find it hard to accept that unaided human nature has the capacity to be so evil. Although I gave up churchgoing twenty-five years ago I felt a strong urge, as I left that building, to exorcize or cleanse myself by attending some — any — really religious service. Whether Christian, Hindu or Muslim. But of course it was by then the wrong time of day; even in Belfast they knock off for Sunday lunch. In any case I had at once to find a quiet corner and make the necessary notes. But the fact that my reaction to that experience was so hysterical is a measure of Paisley's power to throw people.

IMAGINATIVE

CHRISTY BROWN
from Christy Brown, *Down All the Days* (1970)

Christy Brown (1932–81) was born with a form of paralysis which left him unable to communicate until it was discovered he was not mentally retarded. His extraordinary story was set down as *My Left Foot* (1954), which was made into a film by Jim Sheridan with Daniel Day Lewis as Christy. *Down All the Days* is a semi-autobiographical novel about life in a working-class area of Dublin (Christy Brown was at one time a neighbour of Brendan Behan's family in Dublin), reminiscent of O'Casey but with a vigour of its own. Here is a moment of celebration on the birth of a new child which is accompanied by accordion playing, singing, mayhem and rowing among the family and neighbours.

Chapter 15

A sea-lapping fringe of voices, faces, feet merging and mingling, waves breaking on a broken shore; faces revolving, flushed, serious, simpering; mouths opening and shutting, gobbling, guzzling, leering, swearing, singing, shouting, bawling, calling, emitting animal noises of weeping and laughing all under the single stark electric bulb in the jam-packed, sardine-tight, rollicking midnight house; men sitting jammed up tight against women, haunch-touching, hip-touching, calloused fingers hard on exposed silky knees; a mongrel dog nosing its way in between the erratic dancers on the floor, its tongue lolling out like a piece of red-raw liver, licking up the remains of slaughtered sandwiches; an idiot boy between his merry mother's knees reciting obscene versions of nursery rhymes to the roaring men around him who slammed pennies into his palm; a fat woman of many chins stabbing her little man to death with her eyes as he talked to a big-breasted blonde in a corner, his speaking hands hovering temptingly over the feminine promontory; Father's stringy windpipe jerking up and down as he swallowed beer in long, deep, educated gulps, standing guard over the emptying crates of stout, guarding them from the avaricious hands that reached unendingly out, like the antennae of an octopus sucking everything towards its huge black hole of a mouth; a girl of no wit bending down to retrieve her severed necklace, screaming 'Jesus!' as some eagle-eyed man swooped and twanged her suspender-belt against her leg; someone laced the idiot boy's lemonade with whiskey and he ran in and out barking and howling and frightening the dog itself, his eyes wild, his weak mouth drenched with spit. Somebody started to play the spoons.[1]

People coming in with brown parcels of beer.

'And where's herself, Paddy?'

'O still upstairs, the stitches not out yet, but that's the daughter who did such a fine job on the first grandchild.'

The faded flowered wallpaper steaming and dripping and the floor a churning mess of bashed-in bread and beer; the air popping with corks, brown foam spilling over squat green necks of bottles, knuckly wrists twisting deftly with corkscrews, bottles held rigid between knees; smooth-skinned girls with sleeves of sweaters pushed up to elbows, sitting in whispering little clusters, discussing the free antics of men and the older women, splashing gin into their minerals quickly as the quavering singers sang, the erratic dancers danced, and the waves broke and crashed louder and louder.

She lifted her petticoat over her knee
And I saw all she wanted me to see.

'None of that in a Catholic household!' roared Father, plunging his face in a tumbler of stout.

'Just for the time that's in it —'

'Somebody give us "She is Far From the Land" —'

'And she can't swim a stroke.'

'I knew you'd come out with that, Barney. Your one and only joke.'

'What about "The Fennals of Our Land"?'

'Well, what about them?'

'A fine song, a fine patriotic ballad —'

'So is "The Ould Woman Who Lived in a Shoe".'

'Sure that's not even Irish.'

'Well bejasus, if she had all them children she was Irish enough.'

People bending over the new-born member of the new generation in the carrier-cot in the corner by the fireplace, watched over by Lil the child-mother, smiling, polite, unmoving.

'A Brown if ever there was one.'

'Not at all — look at its nose —'

Father hearing this with his odd occasional adroitness of hearing even in the midst and mêlée of animated talking, jerking his head sideways, eyes piercing under scraggy brows.

'What the hell is wrong with its nose?'

'O not a thing, man dear, except that it's not a Brown nose.'

'I say it's a Brown nose, and if you say any different you're going to have a bloody red one, you oul bastard!'

'It's definitely a Brown, Da,' Lil intercepting the anger clouds tactfully, imploring with her eloquent eyes her husband to say the same, who grins and takes the eye-bulging, hair-raising new father-in-law nice and easily by the elbow.

'Any fool could see he's a Brown all over,' says Joe the deft diplomat, observing thoughtfully and with pride, 'with definite overtones of Doyle, be it said.'

Sing up once more and drink a toast
To comrades far and near.

Red Magso coming in, newly and happily deprived of life-long spouse, grimly enjoying her widowhood, on the arm of her eldest daughter, black-veiled crimson face, walking with all suitable slowness of recent bereavement, greeted and seated effusively on special armchair close to the cot of the newly-arrived, speaking in slow subdued cemetery tones, accepting the instant whiskey wanly, sipping it, to the surprise of the neighbours present who expected her to gulp it, holding her glass in a high, prominent, dainty-handed way to show she has barely touched it, the thin, anaemic, already dying daughter kneeling at the stout black-stockinged maternal knee, already fingering the black beads hanging from the matchstick neck and saying 'Mommy' instead of the usual shrill 'Ma'.

And suddenly there she was by the door in a green jumper and plaid pleated skirt, her hair caught up high on top of her head, leaving the white nape of her neck bare, laughing with a soldier, his brothers' mate; her neck swam up from the ruckered woollen polo-necked jumper curving gracefully and he remembered one burning summer day on the hot grass banks of the canal watching a swan flowing in and out among the green filigree, lifting its long drooping white neck and its black demon little eyes, watching him with frightening intensity, making him tremble strangely with the first fear of all beautiful and unknown things in the world. Her bold green gaze caught him now, swept over him coolly as a breeze, the corners of her mouth curling a little upwards in slight far-off recognition, the thrust of her breasts under the taut green wool causing a tight, painful feeling in his throat, the quick flashing movements of her long nylon-sheathed legs setting up a pounding and a drumming in his blood as she danced with her immense soldier, whose great rough hand lay on the small of her back as he held her in the dance and she laughed, shaking her hips freely against him, her red-nailed hands caressing the rough khaki of his tunic. He looked miserably down at his thin bare knees and the pain and hate that was in him then screamed out for utterance; but he only smiled bitterly to himself and at himself and looked on intently at nothing.

'That one will come to no good,' a heavy-breasted woman said shaking her head, her brass ear-rings rattling. 'Mark my words. She'll end up on the guinea side of the Green, selling it to them bloody foreign fellas that do come in on the ships from Egypt and Liverpool.'

'Her poor mother was a lovely person,' said a neighbour with terrific sorrow, nursing her dwindling glass of stout. 'She always wore lovely white blouses and her hair in a bun and never troubled a soul. O a lovely woman, and that bloody little teasy-whacker over there destroying her mother's memory!'

'The shame of it.'

'Will you look at the allegations of her! Giving them all ideas. And she's only fifteen!'

'She'll have a litter of them by the time she's twenty.'

Two well-married men close by not taking their eyes off the spinning girl now enjoying alone the cleared centre of the kitchen, keeping time to the frenzied playing of an accordion in a tango that lifted her skirt and loosened all the brown effulgence of her hair sweeping wild about her flushed ecstatic face.

'Would you, Mick?'

'Would a cat drink milk?' said Mick, heavy-lidded stare unyielding, feeling for his bottle of stout. 'Like a knife through butter.'

'For the love of Jesus I'm drownded!' bawled the earring-rattling woman as the knocked-over stout spilled over her blouse and skirt from the mesmerized fingers of Mick of the myopic stare.

'Terrible sorry, ma'am,' said Mick jumping forward, sweeping out handkerchief and dabbing at the huge stout-stained mountain of bosom. 'Me eyesight's not too good.'

'But you're feeling's all right,' screamed the woman pushing him off. 'Take your hands off me, you lustful oul demon!'

'I was only trying —'

'I know bloody well you were trying! D'you think I was born yesterday?'

'Well ma'am, to be honest, I'd say be the looks of you it's a good many yesterdays since you were born.'

The enormous breasts rose, furiously blotting out the light and the great shoulders swung as a pudding-sized fist flew and landed on Mick's craggy chin and he keeled over into the midst of screaming, laughing women who prodded and poked at him as he lay on the floor slipping and sliding as he tried to regain his feet.

'You're no man to insult a poor defenceless woman like that!' panted the injured neighbour, knotting her fists as she stood over the writhing Mick. 'Get up till I bandjax the living daylight out of you!'

'The dirty oul vomit!' yelled a younger married woman, neatly digging the fumbling man in the ribs with her high-heels as he scrambled on all fours near her chair. 'Trying to look up me clothes and me three months gone!'

'Sweet bleeding heart of Jesus!' moaned Mick, blood streaming into his eyes from a gash over his forehead.

'It's cruel hard for a poor widow woman to enjoy herself with a few kind neighbours and the body of her man still luke-warm in his grave,' spoke Red Magso dreamily as if to herself, her many-ringed hand patting the head of her kneeling daughter. 'You never miss the water till the well runs dry. Dry,' Red Magso repeated, looking around for her bottle, finding it empty, and reaching over and taking up the half-full whiskey bottle that stood on the dresser. She drank steadily, head thrown back, red-skinned throat working; she wiped her mouth with her wrist, then looked solemnly at the frightened face of her daughter who crouched at her knee. 'Would you ever go and get a man for yourself?' she suddenly shouted at the girl, pushing her away with a shove of her knee. 'You're like a bloody sticking plaster. I can't fart without you. Here's a shilling — g'wan down to the pictures — you're the spit of your oul Da, never leaving me be for one sacred second!'

'Ah, Ma!' wailed Noreen, her thin nose quivering.

'Get out of me sight for Jasus' sake child and let me enjoy meself for five minutes! O Matt me darling man!' said Red Magso addressing the ceiling with outspread arms, still holding the whiskey bottle. 'I hope you're with God in heaven tonight, but I know in me heart it's down in the quare place you are with a redhot poker up your arse and you screaming for mercy and finding none!'

'That's a shocking thing to say about your husband,' said a woman with rouged cheeks and some goldplated teeth in front.

'Whose bloody husband was he, yours or mine, Madame Starr?' asked Red Magso with rising rebellion. 'Did you have to have it every night for forty-odd years whether you wanted it or not till you couldn't call your body your own? Did you have to put up being called hoor and brasser and fornicator as he put child after child into you till you never knew what your own feet looked like with your belly always like that?' making a sweeping gesture with her hands in front of herself, her face glowing like a red lamp, the pins tumbling out of her hair, the flesh on her arms shaking as she shook them. 'Did you ever get it at all, you made-up oul bitch?' Red Magso thrust her face up close to the woman, as if challenging her to confirm or deny; the woman drew back hurriedly, tripped over out-thrust feet, and fell into a man's lap, who laughed and held her with both arms around her waist as she tried with not too much haste to get up. 'Maybe you'll get it tonight, Dolores,' Red Magso roared with great seismic heaves of deep inward mirth, putting the bottle to her lips again.

For Ireland is Ireland thro' joy and thro' tears;
hope never dies thro' the long weary years.

Father battled through and pulled Mick into the pantry to bathe his face, away from the bevy of belligerent women who cursed and shouted and giggled at the alleged attack upon their virtue and contentedly went back to their drinks and pigs' feet and gossip as the accordion player toiled bravely on, half-forgotten in a corner, a pale young man with a blue silk scarf tied around his neck and fawn-coloured bootees over which peeped violent scarlet socks.

Through a chink in the heavy flowered curtains swam the yellow lamplight outside, falling on the hair of the girl sitting with the soldier and the thunder and lightning of memory crashed down on him now and the old terrible unnameable agony that was yet delight gripped him as from his lonely perch he dared look and see again the white soft sheen of her upper leg where it parted from her black silk stocking under the cruelly careless upflung skirt as she straddled languidly on the straight-backed kitchen chair, head thrown back against the shoulder of her soldier, her throat buttercup-smooth softly swelling, her eyes half-veiled under the thick matted lashes; and his heart tumbling from its long womb-like sleep and lashed with whips of pain, told him that she was gone away from him into ways he could not follow, and nowhere in all that bewildering night and morning was there peace for him; only a terrible newness and nakedness.

'Meehawl!'[2] someone was shouting for the most popular singer in the house. 'C'mon out of that, Meehawl you oul bastard, and give us a few bars!'

'Best of order now for the singer!'

'The best of singers come from the north side of the Liffey. Me granny always said that.'

'Then your granny must've been a permanent resident up in the Gorman,' someone else countered, jumping up and waving his glass. 'The South Side forever, me boys!'

'Where the hell is Meehawl?' Father shouted, and ran and captured the bellicose balladeer from between two women and yanked him forward by the frayed cuff of the much-travelled coat he was wearing, so variegated with wrinkles and creases that it was obvious the coat also served as the man's blanket at night. He rubbed a black-nailed hand over his blade-neglected chin with a coarse rustle of sandpaper and coughed.

'Me throat is not in the best of singing order, Paddy,' he said, caressing the shiny elbow of his coat with his palm. 'It's a bit rusty on account of me practising to be a Trappist monk. I made that promise to me poor mother and she on her death-bed.'

Father retrieved the almost murdered bottle of whiskey from the huge limp hand of Red Magso as she momentarily dozed in her chair, and thrust it into the quick fist of Meehawl. 'Clear your gullet with that, man, and get on with it,' said Father, shouting a harsh 'Silence!' that brought a gradual hush over the buzzing room. Meehawl finished off the remains of the whiskey bottle, opening his eyes very wide as he drank, as if not quite believing that it was real whiskey he was consuming instead of the usual odious beverage concocted in back alleys and outsheds which his belly had come to accept as second nature. Meehawl was always a gentleman to the last and respectfully touched the peak of his non-existent hat to all the company.

'Would I be hurting the feelings of anyone present be singing a patriotic ballad?' enquired Meehawl gravely.

Father quietly picked up an empty stout bottle and waited; there came not a murmur of dissent; Meehawl at once began to sing in a voice that was ragged and torn in places but which carried an echo of former sweetness undimmed by raucous Liffey winds or the seeping chill of tenement hallways cat-haunted at dead-end of night:

Farewell to friends of Dublin Town,
I bid ye all adieu,
I cannot yet appoint the day
when I'll return to you,
I write these lines on board a ship
where the stormy billows roar
May Heaven bless our Fenian men
till I return once more.

I joined the Fenian Brotherhood
in the year of Sixty-Four
resolved to free my native land
or perish on the shore.
My friends and me we did agree
our native land to save
and raise the flag of freedom
o'er the head of Emmet's grave.

My curse attend the English spies
who did our cause betray;
I'd throw a rope around their necks
and drown them in the bay.
There was Nagle, Massey, Corydon
and Talbot — he makes four,
like demons in their thirst for gold
they're cursed forevermore.

I laid my plans and drilled my men
in dear old Skibereen
and hoped one day to meet the foe
'neath Ireland's flag of green.
I robbed no man, I spilt no blood
Yet they sent me off to jail,
because I was O'Donovan Rossa
the son of Granuaile!

Silence; then an eruption of handclapping, feet-stomping, bottles banged on wood, cries of 'Encore! Encore!' as Meehawl all meekness stood under the light, his global face shining with sweat, grasping in both hands and putting under his arms the bottles of stout that came sweeping towards him from hands that thumped his shoulder and squeezed his arm and suffering docilely the huge moist kisses that descended on him from mothering women whose tears mingled with his sweat as they recognized in him the prodigal son they might have had, the ubiquitous underdog, the worm that turned, the berated beggarman roaming the streets with flapping uppers and bleeding feet singing for his supper with the wind in his hair and the rain in his eyes, leaning over the slimy parapet looking down at his own black shadow in the serpentine river at sunset.

The smell of turf and beer and human sweat was strong in his nostrils even as he lay between the blankets on the great straw mattress upstairs in the back room, dumped there unceremoniously on the hot shoulder of Father without a whiff of warning, but far from asleep, the mercifulness of oblivion which would still for now the turmoil that was in him. His brothers were absent; he had the enormous acres of the mattress all to himself and to his own lonely imaginings. The room became a black box enclosing him on all sides; the noise of the people downstairs rang up through the floorboards beneath him, drilling monotonously into him, needles through his flesh. Faintly above it he heard the wail of his new baby brother or it might have been that of his first baby nephew, a tiny sound of protest lost in all the crashing of music and crushing of feet and the hailstone noises of voices, the hammer popping of corks; everything surged and swept over him, everything known and new, battering upon him with silence more furious than the downstairs din; and all he had ever known was nothing but an echo in a shell and only the stars seemed near. Again the sensation of being held down by chains oppressed him; the blankets felt as heavy as iron, pinning down his trembling awakening limbs, keeping him *there*, forever *there*, mute and immobile, choking the rising voices within him, numbing the rising stream of knowledge within him which was warming him now with a new and unknown and wonderful heat; tears stung his eyes and with a thrust of defiance and despair he flung off the nightclothes and tumbled out upon the cold bare boards.

He lay there for long moments, lying on his back, not feeling the cold, ravishing the stars with insatiable eyes; he heard nothing but his own heart loud with confusion, saw nothing but the jewellery spread out and shining in the black inscrutable sky burning in at him through the square windowpanes; and he breathed deep, glad that nobody was near him and he near nobody.

He crawled out upon the top landing, smelling the musty oilcloth under him. Someone stirred down in the dark depths of the hall; he edged precariously upon the uppermost stair and looked down; light from the street lamp outside the narrow space of the little squat hallway, making her hair gleam from under the broad khaki shoulder of the young soldier leaning upon her, and in a sudden lull of clamour from the kitchen he heard their rapid breathing and bated whispering exchanges; the cat-like hiss of satin.

'You're terrible heavy, aren't you?' Her hushed, amused voice. The accordion played again, the voices rang and sang, the peevish whimpering of a baby somewhere; he crawled back, blind and naked, into the darkness of his room, into the great disordered bed, under the cold blankets; and he heard in some far-off place within himself the clashing of one gate closing and the painful slow screech of another being opened.

But nobody could know, and the harsh party voices from below went on and on until he heard them no more.

1   Two spoons held in one hand used as an instrument.
2   Irish name Micheal.

J. G. FARRELL
from J. G. Farrell, *Troubles* (1970)

J. G. Farrell (1935–79) was born in Liverpool but spent much of his childhood in Ireland. His writings are dominated by the theme of the decline of the British Empire as is especially apparent in *The Siege of Krishnapur* (1971) and in this novel. In *Troubles* Major Brendan Archer returns to Ireland to marry but finds himself a witness to the last days of the Anglo-Irish as a significant force in Ireland. It is the summer of 1919 at the beginning of the War of Independence. Here in this short extract Farrell does what he does best, namely provides a double view of the Irish troubles from the wider perspective of general unrest elsewhere.

The news from Ireland was dull and dispiriting: an occasional attack on a lonely policeman or a raid for arms on some half-baked barracks. If one was not actually living in Ireland (as the lucky Major no longer was) how could one possibly take an interest when, for instance, at the same time Negroes and white men were fighting it out in the streets of Chicago? Now *that* gripped the Major's imagination much more forcibly. Unlike the Irish troubles one knew instantly which side everyone was on. In the Chicago race-riots people were using their skins like uniforms. And there were none of the devious tactics employed by the Shinners,[1] pettifogging ambushes and assassinations. In Chicago the violence was naked, a direct expression of feeling, not of some remote and dubious patriotic heritage. White men dragged Negroes off streetcars; Negroes fired rifles from housetops and alleyways; an automobile full of Negroes raced through the streets of a white district with its occupants promiscuously firing rifles. And Chicago was only a fragment of the competition that Ireland had to face. What about the dire behaviour of the Bolshevists? The gruesome murders, the rapes, the humiliations of respectable ladies and gentlemen? In late 1919 hardly a day went by without an eye-witness account of such horrors being confided to the press by some returned traveller who had managed to escape with his skin. And India: the North-West Frontier . . . Amritsar? No wonder that by the time the Major's eye had reached the news from Ireland his palate had been sated with brighter, bloodier meat. Usually he turned to the cricket to see whether Hobbs had made another century. Presently the cricket season came to an end. A rainy, discouraging autumn took its place. Soon it would be Christmas.

1   Members of Sinn Féin.

EILÉAN NÍ CHUILLEANÁIN
from *Atlantis*, No. 2, October 1970

Eiléan Ní Chuilleanáin (1942–), poet and critic, was born in Cork and now lectures at Trinity College Dublin. Her poetry volumes include *Acts and Monuments* (1972), her first collection, *The Second Voyage* (1986) and *The Magdalene Sermon* (1990). 'Early Recollections' was an impressive early poem.

EARLY RECOLLECTIONS

If I produce paralysis in verse
Where anger would be more suitable,
Could it be because my education
Left out the sight of death?
They never waked my aunt Nora in the front parlour;
Our cats hunted for mice but never
Showed us what they killed.
I was born in a war but never noticed.
My aunt Nora is still in the best of health
And her best china has not been changed or broken.
Dust has not settled on it; I noticed it first
The same year that I saw
How the colours of stones change as water
Dries off them after rain.
I know how things begin to happen
But never expect an end.

Dearest,
          if I can never write 'goodbye'
On the torn final sheet, do not
Investigate my adult life but try
Where I started. My
Childhood gave me hope
And no warnings.
I discovered the habits of moss
That secretly freezes the stone,
Rust softly biting the hinges
To keep the door always open.
I become aware of truth
Like the tide helplessly rising and falling in one place.

FRANCIS STUART
from Francis Stuart, *Black List, Section H* (1971)

Francis Stuart here recalls meeting Yeats and his wife in Merrion Square in the 1920s. The Civil War is over, and H (Stuart's protagonist) is out of prison, but still restless, as the editorial in *Tomorrow* (1924) on page 290 above suggests. Iseult Gonne (1894–1954), the daughter of Maud Gonne, had married Stuart in April 1920, but the marriage was frequently turbulent and in July 1920 Yeats was asked to provide counsel to the woman he had proposed to in 1916–17. In his autobiography *Things to Live For* (1934) Stuart writes in passing about his marriage with Iseult and their time spent in Glenmalure in the Wicklow Mountains.

Chapter 20

A few days after they'd seen Claude off, H running down the pier to keep abreast of her as she stood waving at the rail and Iseult following more slowly, Iseult suggested he accompany her to the chapel at the head of the glen on Sundays.

'Not just Sundays, Pet, I'll walk there to Mass every morning!' He resolved to make up for his backsliding.

'That's you all over, Luke, forever going to extremes.'

He admired her for the way she had tried to live up to her ideals during her cousin's visit and it inspired him to a more dedicated pursual of *his*; the trouble was he was still not sure in what these really consisted.

He started attending daily Mass, trudging the four or five miles up the mountain road and back, with the newly assimilated concept that the Mass stood in some sort of numinous relation to the Last Supper and Crucifixion as recorded in the Gospels sinking into his mind.

The idea was one that fitted easily enough into his kind of imagination. The psychology of the hours on the cross he recognized as belonging to the deepest experience. This was a familiar nightmare, the longing of exposed, tormented beings, stripped of their protective aura, for the coming of darkness. How often, for no conscious reason, had he experienced the shadow of terror in the part of him — the neurons and chromosomes? — he shared with the brute creation? He grasped instinctively the trapped beast's hope for some slight respite when darkness falls.

With His gift for taking in nuances, Christ wasn't likely to have missed a single wagging head or the spleen of the remarks of those below, solemnly reproving, contemptuous, or, especially in those addressed directly to Him, facetious: 'Give us a tip, O King of the Prophets, for Sunday's chariot race at Antioch.'

Let darkness fall. That of the time before the fiat: let there be light. This would engulf Him, His pain and humiliation, if the disaster was complete. This was the darkness that had been at the fringe of all His prayer and which He'd tried to find a path through. He had tried to shatter the treasured image that men had of themselves, of their moral judgement particularly. His presence had raised some doubt about their cherished thought processes. Now that they had Him up there, any unease and mental discomfort remaining could be erased by an orgy of righteous indignation.

Christ had held the most forward position of His time for several hours. And it would fall to the condemned, the sick-unto-death and perhaps a handful of unregarded artists to defend these areas of consciousness in the coming days as best they could.

Not that these reflections reconciled H to what he saw and heard of the functioning of the local church, and of the average priest with his stomachful of indigestible dogmatics and a half-starved mind, self-poisoned by the complementary toxins of love of authority and fear of its loss.

'Why, I'd have done it better myself, Pet!' he remarked to Iseult during an argument. 'If I was asked to compile a further instalment of the life of Jesus I'd at least have tried to follow Him in the direction He'd been going. I'd have kept His spontaneity and directness, His delight in concrete realities, and certainly wouldn't have had Him suddenly pronouncing all kind of abstract and irrelevant dogmas like His Mother's bodily Assumption into Heaven. And I'll tell you another thing, now that we're on the subject, I'd have made Him reconsider His plan to rise from the dead which, as I see it, has been the cause of all the trouble. I'd have Him forgo the Resurrection, though it would mean the loss of those wonderful incidents of recognition such as Mary Magdalen at the empty tomb, the realization, after He'd gone, that came to the two men at the inn at Emmaus as to who had been with them, and — isn't it the most touching of all reunions? — being seen and, after some doubt, recognized early one morning grilling a few fish on a fire He'd lit beside His beloved lake.

'You see, Pet, without the Resurrection there'd be no bandwagon, no grocer's scheme of reward and punishment! Just the haunting Jesus disaster to illuminate our lesser disasters.'

'No, that's too much! Some little Jew without moral values or spiritual authority; take away His teaching, His miracles, and His mother (H hadn't said anything of this sort), and that is what's left. Don't you realize it's through the Blessed Virgin that the simple and humble come to Him? When I pray it's her I see, not her face or figure, but a deep blue calm expanse like the sky just before night falls and, right across it, in even darker blue, a huge M.'

H returned to the hut leaving her sitting on the unmade bed, weighed down by her belly, surrounded by patience cards and cigarette butts, bewildered and hurt.

When an invitation came from Mrs Yeats asking them to spend a few days at the Yeats house in Dublin,[1] seeing Iseult's face brighten at the chance of some intelligent company, H didn't voice his own disinclination to have his seclusion broken again so soon.

They were given, and H was conscious of the honour, Yeats's bedroom in the tall Georgian house on Merrion Square, with reproductions of Blake's wraithlike figures on the walls: a mother and her little ones floating, upright and elegant, down the River of Life; an angel leaning precariously from her heavenly steed to gather in her arms a whimpering babe. On the outside of the door Georgie Yeats had pinned a note: 'Willie, this is now the Ruarks' room.'

'Otherwise you'd have him wandering in at any hour of the day or night,' she told them.

On the very first evening at dinner H saw that if he was to contribute to the conversation, as the poet evidently expected him to, he'd have to emerge from his own preoccupations and think up the sort of things that would interest Yeats.

As for Iseult, she was quite at home in the intellectual discussion; perhaps she should have married Yeats, but he'd have got on her nerves with his formal and deliberate ways, while H himself, idle and uncivilized, with his quiet and deceptive delinquency, still attracted her.

Yeats was talking about the newly constituted state of which he was a Senator. The whole setup hadn't come up to his expectations; he'd have liked, H saw, a role such as d'Annunzio was playing in relation to the new Mussolini government.

'Would the people you fought for have made better rulers?' he asked H, turning on him his keen glance across the table, and then unfocusing him again and dropping his head as though awaiting some revealing words.

Should H say that he hadn't fought for anybody or anything, but in pursuit of an obscure impulse of his own which had become somewhat clearer after he'd met and talked with Lane?[2] Could he explain Lane to Yeats?

'If you mean: would they also have imposed a censorship and forbidden divorce, I'm sure they would.'

H caught Mrs Yeats's eye, glowing green below her coppery hair, her bracelets jingling as she raised her long-stemmed wineglass, and it struck him that she was the one who guessed some of his real feelings.

H didn't share the sense of outrage of Yeats and his fellow intellectuals at the censorship law. It was a matter of indifference to him. The Irish censorship would catch the smaller fish but if a really big one was to swim into view it would be set on by far more ferocious foes than any Irish ones.

'If somebody somewhere writes a book which is so radical and original,' H announced, not looking at anyone in particular, 'that it would burst the present literary setup wide open, that writer will be treated with a polite contempt by the critical and academic authorities that will discourage further mention of him. He'll raise deeper, more subconscious hostility than sectarian ones and he'll be destroyed far more effectively by enlightened neglect than anything we would do to him here.'

Yeats had lifted his head and was regarding H intently.

'You believe that the artist is bound to be rejected? You equate him with the prophet?'

It was costing H a lot of nervous energy to formulate concepts for Yeats to take hold of. And, apart from that, he mustn't forget he was a nobody in the literary world addressing a Nobel Prizewinner.

'A poet may escape persecution because his vision is veiled from the literary arbiters, but the novelist who speaks more plainly is bound to scandalize them.'

H caught what he thought was an appreciative smile on Georgie Yeats's barbaric-looking, vivid, russet-tinged face in recognition of his adroit slipping out of the dilemma.

H could only contribute to this kind of talk by allowing himself to get into a state of nervous fever in which his power of invention and improvisation came to his aid.

That night, quite exhausted, he went to bed under the Samurai sword that hung over it, his thoughts madly racing. He lay awake, being anyhow miles away from sleep, and prepared some largely imaginary anecdotes embodying unexpected and original-sounding comments on the kind of things that interested Yeats.

It ended by his being carried away by his own flights of fancy and pursuing them late into the night beyond the point where they could be used in conversation to his host, quite apart from the fact that Iseult, who clung to the factual, would be sure to interrupt with, 'But, Luke, darling, whenever did all this happen?'

Example of one of these night reveries in the form of a conversation between himself and a chance acquaintance in a café in Paris, where H had never yet been:

'A votre santé, M'sieur. Ahhh! Ce n'est pas mauvais, ce "rot" ici.'[3]

Establish the locale, provide a touch of authenticity, that would compel Yeats's interest right away. 'If I were to stop a passerby out there' — H and his imaginary acquaintance were on a café terrace — 'introduce myself as an Irishman compiling a work on France and ask him who was the keeper of the French conscience, what do you suppose he'd say?'

'Depends on his political affiliations. He might well direct you to the Elysée Palace and there, after a wait, it's possible you'd be issued, Monsieur, with an answer typed on official paper, on which you'd be charged the stamp duty.'

The reference to stamped paper which H recalled having heard from Iseult was used for all official documents, he'd put in to add what he thought of as 'density'.

'And what would it say?'

'I'm not Monsieur le Président, but if you want me to hazard a guess, something to the effect that it is guarded in the works of the great writers of France, past and present.'

That would have to suffice for his little contribution to tomorrow's conversation, which he'd have to get in when Iseult wasn't there. But by now, well past midnight, it wasn't just the idea of impressing Yeats that was impelling H, but his own feverish exhaustion that made him imagine new stories to recount. He was soon involved in other even more fantastic incidents.

He saw himself in New York or San Francisco in conversation with a young woman whose husband, a university extension lecturer, whom H had been sent to interview on a subject of vital interest to Yeats, which was yet to be thought up, was unfortunately not at home. That very morning he'd taken the Studebaker and gone to summer school in a place called (just a minute) the Silver Barricades. What make of car had she said? The name, that he made her repeat, moved her lips into seductive shapes, purely American, that fascinated H.

Yeats was forgotten; he was indulging his own unprofitable night fantasies.

Yes, well, where were we? Up in the Silver Somethings with the professor of English? No, nothing to beguile himself with there. Listening to his young wife order an oven-ready chicken on the phone; then call from across the hall that she was having a quick shower but wouldn't be more than a couple of minutes. With one ear on sounds from the bathroom, H had started half-heartedly to leaf through a critical work by the professor when his hostess called again she'd be with him in a moment. She was just giving herself a rubdown with some special lotion.

'It's called Deodonus, Gift of God. Cute, isn't it? You see, we don't have air conditioning in an old place like this and the humidity clogs the skin with particles of city detritus.'

This open-fronted living, as well as the hygiene was, in H's evocation of the American scene, part of the social code and, to have left him in the dark as to what she was doing while out of his sight he imagined would have been a breach of hospitality.

What was so exhausting was that not only had H to present vividly imagined milieux of which he'd no direct knowledge, but also to remember that it all had to lead up to the significant sentence or two that, repeated across the dinner table, would come as the sort of revelation that Yeats seemed to expect of him. Not that in this particular case he wasn't being carried far beyond any such possibility, but he couldn't free himself.

There came a humming from the all-electric kitchen. Had she pressed the wrong button and, instead of turning on the infra-red roaster, shot the chicken down the outward-delivery chute, and, with the metal tag (Solidonus, Gift of the Sun) still round its leg, was it already on its way back to the department store?

In the morning H awoke red-eyed and jaded. The visit was too much for him. He tried to spend an hour or so whenever he could alone in their room with, as a respite from his imaginary American hostess, the Blessed Juliana and her 'dearworthy Lord'. But it had begun to strike him that these charming women like herself, Rose, and Angela had had rather too pleasant a time of it in their hermitages.

On one of the last evenings H came up with a view of the writer's situation that he'd been keeping in store.

'It's that he must be doubly involved.'

'Doubly involved?'

The eagle glance, the quick withdrawal, the moment of charged silence with leonine mane pushed back.

'It's the writer who's one with his work, and doesn't create it as a thing apart, as a beautiful artifice outside himself, as, say, Synge does, who says the things that now matter most.'

Had he struck a spark? The sea-green eyes, autumn colouring, and Roman nose of Georgie Yeats were in the background like an ikon. Was this the vulnerable spot? Not only had the poet failed to merge his life and his art (the classic intellectual situation, perhaps) but the style of his living was so formal and unspontaneous that it was in constant opposition to the increasingly disreputable spirit that was inspiring much of his later poetry.

1   82 Merrion Square was the Yeats house from 1922 until 1928.
2   In prison H was much influenced by Lane. When Yeats was awarded the Nobel Prize in 1923 Lane voiced his Republican opinions: 'I don't know much about the fucker . . . but to me it sounds like a sell-out, letting them hang the ribbon with the bloody medal on it round his neck. If he wrote the sort of poetry that told the truth he'd be more likely to have the other kind of noose slipped over it.'
3   Your health, sir. It's not bad, this rot (red in German) here.

JOHN MONTAGUE
from John Montague, *The Rough Field* (1972)

'The Rough Field', an article by John Montague (1929–), appeared in *The Spectator* in 1963 (see p. 755 above). Here he returns as a poet to his roots in County Tyrone in a poem that explores defeats in history and the loss of language.

A LOST TRADITION

All around, shards of a lost tradition:
From the Rough Field I went to school
In the Glens of the Hazels. Close by
Was the bishopric of the Golden Stone;[1]
The cairn of Carleton's[2] homesick poem.

Scattered over the hills, tribal
And placenames, uncultivated pearls.
No rock or ruin, dun or dolmen
But showed memory defying cruelty
Through an image-encrusted name.

The heathery gap where the Raparee,[3]
Shane Barnagh, saw his brother die —
On a summer's day the dying sun
Stained its colours to crimson:
So breaks the heart, Brish-mo-Cree.[4]

The whole landscape a manuscript
We had lost the skill to read,
A part of our past disinherited;
But fumbled, like a blind man,
Along the fingertips of instinct.

The last Gaelic speaker in the parish
When I stammered my school Irish
One Sunday after mass, crinkled
A rusty litany of praise;
Tá an Ghaedilg againn arís . . .[5]

Tír Eoghain: Land of Owen,
Province of the O'Niall;[6]
The ghostly tread of O'Hagan's
Barefoot gallowglasses marching
To merge forces in Dun Geanainn

Push southward to Kinsale!
Loudly the war-cry is swallowed
In swirls of black rain and fog
As Ulster's pride, Elizabeth's foemen,
Founder in a Munster bog.

1   The placename for Montague's home parish is
    Garvaghey, which translates into English as Rough Field.
    Glens of the Hazels is also an Englished version of an
    Irish placename Glencull. Golden Stone is Clogher, the
    little town at the foot of Knockmany.
2   William Carleton (1794–1869), author of *Traits and
    Stories of the Irish Peasantry* (1830), explored the lives of
    ordinary people in pre- and post-Famine Ireland.
3   From the Irish word for short pike. Raparees acted
    behind the Williamite lines in 1689–91.
4   Irish: breaks my heart.
5   We have the Irish again.
6   Reference to Hugh O'Neill, Earl of Tyrone
    (1540–1616), leader of the rebellion against Queen
    Elizabeth. At the Battle of Kinsale in County Cork in
    1601 his Spanish aid was destroyed and the Ulster
    rebellion at an end.

WILLIAM TREVOR
from William Trevor, *The Ballroom of Romance and Other Stories* (1972)

William Trevor (1928–) was born in Mitchelstown, County Cork, the son of a
Protestant bank official. After graduating from Trinity College Dublin he began writing
fiction, his first novel, *A Standard of Behaviour*, appearing in 1958. A prolific writer, he
was equally at home with English as with Irish subjects; his *Collected Stories* were
published in 1992. 'The Ballroom of Romance', the title story of a collection published
in 1972, has remained a favourite with readers both inside and outside Ireland. Trevor's
attitude towards his characters is always interesting to observe, never more so than in
this story of a woman caught between romance and reality.

The Ballroom of Romance

On Sundays, or on Mondays if he couldn't make it and often he couldn't, Sunday being his busy day, Canon O'Connell arrived at the farm in order to hold a private service with Bridie's father, who couldn't get about any more, having had a leg amputated after gangrene had set in. They'd had a pony and cart then and Bridie's mother had been alive: it hadn't been difficult for the two of them to help her father on to the cart in order to make the journey to Mass. But two years later the pony had gone lame and eventually had to be destroyed; not long after that her mother had died. 'Don't worry about it at all,' Canon O'Connell had said, referring to the difficulty of transporting her father to Mass. 'I'll slip up by the week, Bridie.'

The milk lorry called daily for the single churn of milk, Mr Driscoll delivered groceries and meal in his van, and took away the eggs that Bridie had collected during the week. Since Canon O'Connell had made his offer, in 1953, Bridie's father hadn't left the farm.

As well as Mass on Sundays and her weekly visits to a wayside dance-hall Bridie went shopping once every month, cycling to the town early on a Friday afternoon. She bought things for herself, material for a dress, knitting wool, stockings, a newspaper, and paper-backed Wild West novels for her father. She talked in the shops to some of the girls she'd been at school with, girls who had married shop-assistants or shop-keepers, or had become assistants themselves. Most of them had families of their own by now. 'You're lucky to be peaceful in the hills,' they said to Bridie, 'instead of stuck in a hole like this.' They had a tired look, most of them, from pregnancies and their efforts to organize and control their large families.

As she cycled back to the hills on a Friday Bridie often felt that they truly envied her her life, and she found it surprising that they should do so. If it hadn't been for her father she'd have wanted to work in the town also, in the tinned meat factory maybe, or in a shop. The town had a cinema called the Electric, and a fish-and-chip shop where people met at night, eating chips out of newspaper on the pavement outside. In the evenings, sitting in the farmhouse with her father, she often thought about the town, imagining the shop-windows lit up to display their goods and the sweet-shops still open so that people could purchase chocolates or fruit to take with them to the Electric cinema. But the town was eleven miles away, which was too far to cycle, there and back, for an evening's entertainment.

'It's a terrible thing for you, girl,' her father used to say, genuinely troubled, 'tied up to a one-legged man.'

He would sigh, heavily, hobbling back from the fields, where he managed as best he could. 'If your mother hadn't died,' he'd say, not finishing the sentence.

If her mother hadn't died her mother could have looked after him and the scant acres he owned, her mother could somehow have lifted the milk-churn on to the collection platform and attended to the few hens and the cows. 'I'd be dead without the girl to assist me,' she'd heard her father saying to Canon O'Connell, and Canon O'Connell replied that he was certainly lucky to have her.

'Amn't I as happy here as anywhere?' she'd say herself, but her father knew she was pretending and was saddened because the weight of circumstances had so harshly interfered with her life.

Although her father still called her a girl, Bridie was thirty-six. She was tall and strong: the skin of her fingers and her palms were stained, and harsh to touch. The labour they'd experienced had found its way into them, as though juices had come out of vegetation and pigment out of soil: since childhood she'd torn away the rough scotch grass that grew each spring among her father's mangolds and sugar beet; since childhood she'd harvested potatoes in August, her hands daily rooting in the ground she loosened and turned. Wind had toughened the flesh of her face, sun had browned it; her neck and nose were lean, her lips touched with early wrinkles.

But on Saturday nights Bridie forgot the scotch grass and the soil. In different dresses she cycled to the dance-hall, encouraged to make the journey by her father. 'Doesn't it do you good, girl?' he'd say, as though he imagined she begrudged herself the pleasure. 'Why wouldn't you enjoy yourself?' She'd cook him his tea and then he'd settle down with the wireless, or maybe a Wild West novel. In time, while still she danced, he'd stoke the fire up and hobble his way upstairs to bed.

The dance-hall, owned by Mr Justin Dwyer, was miles from anywhere, a lone building by the roadside with treeless boglands all around and a gravel expanse in front of it. On pink pebbled cement its title was painted in an azure blue that matched the depth of the background shade yet stood out well, unfussily proclaiming *The Ballroom of Romance*. Above these letters four coloured bulbs — in red, green, orange and mauve — were lit at appropriate times, an indication that the evening rendezvous was open for business. Only the façade of the building was pink, the other walls being a more ordinary grey. And inside, except for pink swing-doors, everything was blue.

On Saturday nights Mr Justin Dwyer, a small, thin man, unlocked the metal grid that protected his property and drew it back, creating an open mouth from which music would later pour. He helped his wife to carry crates of lemonade and packets of biscuits from their car, and then took up a position in the tiny vestibule between the drawn-back grid and the pink swing-doors. He sat at a card-table, with money and tickets spread out before him. He'd made a fortune, people said: he owned other ballrooms also.

People came on bicycles or in old motor-cars, country people like Bridie from remote hill farms and villages. People who did not often see other people met there, girls and boys, men and women. They paid Mr Dwyer and passed into his dance-hall, where shadows were cast on pale-blue walls and light from a crystal bowl was dim. The band, known as the Romantic Jazz Band, was composed of clarinet, drums and piano. The drummer sometimes sang.

Bridie had been going to the dance-hall since first she left the Presentation Nuns, before her mother's death. She didn't mind the journey, which was seven miles there and seven miles back; she'd travelled as far every day to the Presentation Nuns on the same bicycle, which had once been the property of her mother, an old Rudge purchased originally in 1936. On Sundays she cycled six miles to Mass, but she never minded either: she'd grown quite used to all that.

'How're you, Bridie?' inquired Mr Justin Dwyer when she arrived in a new scarlet dress one autumn evening in 1971. She said she was all right and in reply to Mr Dwyer's second query she said that her father was all right also. 'I'll go up one of these days,' promised Mr Dwyer, which was a promise he'd been making for twenty years.

She paid the entrance fee and passed through the pink swing-doors. The Romantic Jazz Band was playing a familiar melody of the past, 'The Destiny Waltz'. In spite of the band's title, jazz was not ever played in the ballroom: Mr Dwyer did not personally care for that kind of music, nor had he cared for various dance movements that had come and gone over the years. Jiving, rock and roll, twisting, and other such variations had all been resisted by Mr Dwyer, who believed that a ballroom should be, as much as possible, a dignified place. The Romantic Jazz Band consisted of Mr Maloney, Mr Swanton, and Dano Ryan on drums. They were three middle-aged men who drove out from the town in Mr Maloney's car, amateur performers who were employed otherwise by the tinned-meat factory, the Electricity Supply Board, and the County Council.

'How're you, Bridie?' inquired Dano Ryan as she passed him on her way to the cloakroom. He was idle for a moment with his drums, 'The Destiny Waltz' not calling for much attention from him.

'I'm all right, Dano,' she said. 'Are you fit yourself? Are the eyes better?' The week before he'd told her that he'd developed a watering of the eyes that must have been some kind of cold or other. He'd woken up with it in the morning and it had persisted until the afternoon: it was a new experience, he'd told her, adding that he'd never had a day's illness or discomfort in his life.

'I think I need glasses,' he said now, and as she passed into the cloakroom she imagined him in glasses, repairing the roads, as he was employed to do by the County Council. You hardly ever saw a road-mender with glasses, she reflected, and she wondered if all the dust that was inherent in his work had perhaps affected his eyes.

'How're you, Bridie?' a girl called Eenie Mackie said in the cloakroom, a girl who'd left the Presentation Nuns only a year ago.

'That's a lovely dress, Eenie,' Bridie said. 'Is it nylon, that?'

'Tricel actually. Drip-dry.'

Bridie took off her coat and hung it on a hook. There was a small wash-basin in the cloakroom above which hung a discoloured oval mirror. Used tissues and pieces of cotton-wool, cigarette-butts and matches covered the concrete floor. Lengths of green-painted timber partitioned off a lavatory in a corner.

'Jeez, you're looking great, Bridie,' Madge Dowding remarked, waiting for her turn at the mirror. She moved towards it as she spoke, taking off a pair of spectacles before endeavouring to apply make-up to the lashes of her eye. She stared myopically into the oval mirror, humming while the other girls became restive.

'Will you hurry up, for God's sake!' shouted Eenie Mackie. 'We're standing here all night, Madge.'

Madge Dowding was the only one who was older than Bridie. She was thirty-nine, although often she said she was younger. The girls sniggered about that, saying that Madge Dowding should accept her condition — her age and her squint and her poor complexion — and not make herself ridiculous going out after men. What man would be bothered with the like of her anyway? Madge Dowding would do better to give herself over to do Saturday-night work for the Legion of Mary: wasn't Canon O'Connell always looking for aid?

'Is that fellow there?' she asked now, moving away from the mirror. 'The guy with the long arms. Did anyone see him outside?'

'He's dancing with Cat Bolger,' one of the girls replied. 'She has herself glued to him.'

'Lover boy,' remarked Patty Byrne, and everyone laughed because the person referred to was hardly a boy any more, being over fifty it was said, a bachelor who came only occasionally to the dance-hall.

Madge Dowding left the cloakroom rapidly, not bothering to pretend she wasn't anxious about the conjunction of Cat Bolger and the man with the long arms. Two sharp spots of red had come into her cheeks, and when she stumbled in her haste the girls in the cloakroom laughed. A younger girl would have pretended to be casual.

Bridie chatted, waiting for the mirror. Some girls, not wishing to be delayed, used the mirrors of their compacts. Then in twos and threes, occasionally singly, they left the cloakroom and took their places on upright wooden chairs at one end of the dance-hall, waiting to be asked to dance. Mr Maloney, Mr Swanton and Dano Ryan played 'Harvest Moon' and 'I Wonder Who's Kissing Her Now' and 'I'll Be Around'.

Bridie danced. Her father would be falling asleep by the fire; the wireless, tuned in to Radio Eireann, would be murmuring in the background. Already he'd have listened to *Faith and Order* and *Spot the Talent*. His Wild West novel, *Three Rode Fast* by Jake Matall, would have dropped from his single knee on to the flagged floor. He would wake with a jerk as he did every night and, forgetting what night it was, might be surprised not to see her, for usually she was sitting there at the table, mending clothes or washing eggs. 'Is it time for the News?' he'd automatically say.

Dust and cigarette smoke formed a haze beneath the crystal bowl, feet thudded, girls shrieked and laughed, some of them dancing together for want of a male partner. The music was loud, the musicians had taken off their jackets. Vigorously they played a number of tunes from *State Fair* and then, more romantically, 'Just One Of Those Things'. The tempo increased for a Paul Jones,[2] after which Bridie found herself with a youth who told her he was saving up to emigrate, the nation in his opinion being finished. 'I'm up in the hills with the uncle,' he said, 'labouring fourteen hours a day. Is it any life for a young fellow?' She knew his uncle, a hill farmer whose stony acres were separated from her father's by one other farm only. 'He has me gutted with work,' the youth told her. 'Is there sense in it at all, Bridie?'

At ten o'clock there was a stir, occasioned by the arrival of three middle-aged bachelors who'd cycled over from Carey's public house. They shouted and whistled, greeting other people across the dancing area. They smelt of stout and sweat and whiskey.

Every Saturday at just this time they arrived, and, having sold them their tickets, Mr Dwyer folded up his card-table and locked the tin box that held the evening's takings: his ballroom was complete.

'How're you, Bridie?' one of the bachelors, known as Bowser Egan, inquired. Another one, Tim Daly, asked Patty Byrne how she was. 'Will we take the floor?' Eyes Horgan suggested to Madge Dowding, already pressing the front of his navy-blue suit against the net of her dress. Bridie danced with Bowser Egan, who said she was looking great.

The bachelors would never marry, the girls of the dance-hall considered: they were wedded already, to stout and whiskey and laziness, to three old mothers somewhere up in the hills. The man with the long arms didn't drink but he was the same in all other ways: he had the same look of a bachelor, a quality in his face.

'Great,' Bowser Egan said, feather-stepping in an inaccurate and inebriated manner. 'You're a great little dancer, Bridie.'

'Will you lay off that!' cried Madge Dowding, her voice shrill above the sound of the music. Eyes Horgan had slipped two fingers into the back of her dress and was now pretending they'd got there by accident. He smiled blearily, his huge red face streaming with perspiration, the eyes which gave him his nickname protuberant and bloodshot.

'Watch your step with that one,' Bowser Egan called out, laughing so that spittle sprayed on to Bridie's face. Eenie Mackie, who was also dancing near the incident, laughed also and winked at Bridie. Dano Ryan left his drums and sang. 'Oh, how I miss your gentle kiss,' he crooned, 'and long to hold you tight.'

Nobody knew the name of the man with the long arms. The only words he'd ever been known to speak in the Ballroom of Romance were the words that formed his invitation to dance. He was a shy man who stood alone when he wasn't performing on the dance-floor. He rode away on his bicycle afterwards, not saying good night to anyone.

'Cat has your man leppin' tonight,' Tim Daly remarked to Patty Byrne, for the liveliness that Cat Bolger had introduced into foxtrot and waltz was noticeable.

'I think of you only,' sang Dano Ryan. 'Only wishing, wishing you were by my side.'

Dano Ryan would have done, Bridie often thought, because he was a different kind of bachelor: he had a lonely look about him, as if he'd become tired of being on his own. Every week she thought he would have done, and during the week her mind regularly returned to that thought. Dano Ryan would have done because she felt he wouldn't mind coming to live in the farmhouse while her one-legged father was still about the place. Three could live as cheaply as two where Dano Ryan was concerned because giving up the wages he earned as a road-worker would be balanced by the saving made on what he paid for lodgings. Once, at the end of an evening, she'd pretended that there was a puncture in the back wheel of her bicycle and he'd concerned himself with it while Mr Maloney and Mr Swanton waited for him in Mr Maloney's car. He'd blown the tyre up with the car pump and had said he thought it would hold.

It was well known in the dance-hall that she fancied her chances with Dano Ryan. But it was well known also that Dano Ryan had got into a set way of life and had remained in it for quite some years. He lodged with a widow called Mrs Griffin and Mrs Griffin's mentally affected son, in a cottage on the outskirts of the town. He was said to be good to the affected child, buying him sweets and taking him out for rides on the cross-bar of his bicycle. He gave an hour or two of his time every week to the Church of Our Lady Queen of Heaven, and he was loyal to Mr Dwyer. He performed in the two other rural dance-halls that Mr Dwyer owned, rejecting advances from the town's more sophisticated dance-hall, even though it was more conveniently situated for him and the fee was more substantial than that paid by Mr Dwyer. But Mr Dwyer had discovered Dano Ryan and Dano had not forgotten it, just as Mr Maloney and Mr Swanton had not forgotten their discovery by Mr Dwyer either.

'Would we take a lemonade?' Bowser Egan suggested. 'And a packet of biscuits, Bridie?'

No alcoholic liquor was ever served in the Ballroom of Romance, the premises not being licensed for this added stimulant. Mr Dwyer in fact had never sought a licence for any of his premises, knowing that romance and alcohol were difficult commodities to mix, especially in a dignified ballroom. Behind where the girls sat on the wooden chairs Mr Dwyer's wife, a small stout woman, served the bottles of lemonade, with straws, and the biscuits and the crisps. She talked busily while doing so, mainly about the turkeys she kept. She'd once told Bridie that she thought of them as children.

'Thanks,' Bridie said, and Bowser Egan led her to the trestle table. Soon it would be the intermission: soon the three members of the band would cross the floor also for refreshment. She thought up questions to ask Dano Ryan.

When first she'd danced in the Ballroom of Romance, when she was just sixteen, Dano Ryan had been there also, four years older than she was, playing the drums for Mr Maloney as he played them now. She'd hardly noticed him then because of his not being

one of the dancers: he was part of the ballroom's scenery, like the trestle table and the lemonade bottles, and Mrs Dwyer and Mr Dwyer. The youths who'd danced with her then in their Saturday-night blue suits had later disappeared into the town, or to Dublin or Britain, leaving behind them those who became the middle-aged bachelors of the hills. There'd been a boy called Patrick Grady whom she had loved in those days. Week after week she'd ridden away from the Ballroom of Romance with the image of his face in her mind, a thin face, pale beneath black hair. It had been different, dancing with Patrick Grady, and she'd felt that he found it different dancing with her, although he'd never said so. At night she'd dreamed of him and in the daytime too, while she helped her mother in the kitchen or her father with the cows. Week by week she'd returned to the ballroom, smiling on its pink façade and dancing then in the arms of Patrick Grady. Often they'd stood together drinking lemonade, not saying anything, not knowing what to say. She knew he loved her, and she believed then that he would lead her one day from the dim, romantic ballroom, from its blueness and its pinkness and its crystal bowl of light and its music. She believed he would lead her into sunshine, to the town and the Church of Our Lady Queen of Heaven, to marriage and smiling faces. But someone else had got Patrick Grady, a girl from the town who'd never danced in the wayside ballroom. She'd scooped up Patrick Grady when he didn't have a chance.

Bridie had wept, hearing that. By night she'd lain in her bed in the farmhouse, quietly crying, the tears rolling into her hair and making the pillow damp. When she woke in the early morning the thought was still naggingly with her and it remained with her by day, replacing her daytime dreams of happiness. Someone told her later on that he'd crossed to Britain, to Wolverhampton, with the girl he'd married, and she imagined him there, in a place she wasn't able properly to visualize, labouring in a factory, his children being born and acquiring the accent of the area. The Ballroom of Romance wasn't the same without him, and when no one else stood out for her particularly over the years and when no one offered her marriage, she found herself wondering about Dano Ryan. If you couldn't have love, the next best thing was surely a decent man.

Bowser Egan hardly fell into that category, nor did Tim Daly. And it was plain to everyone that Cat Bolger and Madge Dowding were wasting their time over the man with the long arms. Madge Dowding was already a figure of fun in the ballroom, the way she ran after the bachelors; Cat Bolger would end up the same if she wasn't careful. One way or another it wasn't difficult to be a figure of fun in the ballroom, and you didn't have to be as old as Madge Dowding: a girl who'd just left the Presentation Nuns had once asked Eyes Horgan what he had in his trouser pocket and he told her it was a penknife. She'd repeated this afterwards in the cloakroom, how she'd requested Eyes Horgan not to dance so close to her because his penknife was sticking into her. 'Jeez, aren't you the right baby!' Patty Byrne had shouted delightedly: everyone had laughed, knowing that Eyes Horgan only came to the ballroom for stuff like that. He was no use to any girl.

'Two lemonades, Mrs Dwyer,' Bowser Egan said, 'and two packets of Kerry Creams. Is Kerry Creams all right, Bridie?'

She nodded, smiling. Kerry Creams would be fine, she said.

'Well, Bridie, isn't that the great outfit you have!' Mrs Dwyer remarked. 'Doesn't the red suit her, Bowser?'

By the swing-doors stood Mr Dwyer, smoking a cigarette that he held cupped in his left hand. His small eyes noted all developments. He had been aware of Madge Dowding's anxiety when Eyes Horgan had inserted two fingers into the back opening of her dress. He had looked away, not caring for the incident, but had it developed further he would have spoken to Eyes Horgan, as he had on other occasions. Some of the younger lads didn't know any better and would dance very close to their partners, who generally were too embarrassed to do anything about it, being young themselves. But that, in Mr Dwyer's opinion, was a different kettle of fish altogether because they were decent young lads who'd in no time at all be doing a steady line with a girl and would end up as he had himself with Mrs Dwyer, in the same house with her, sleeping in a bed with her, firmly married. It was the middle-aged bachelors who required the watching: they came down from the hills like mountain goats, released from their mammies and from the smell of animals and soil. Mr Dwyer continued to watch Eyes Horgan, wondering how drunk he was.

Dano Ryan's song came to an end, Mr Swanton laid down his clarinet, Mr Maloney rose from the piano. Dano Ryan wiped sweat from his face and the three men slowly moved towards Mrs Dwyer's trestle table.

'Jeez, you have powerful legs,' Eyes Horgan whispered to Madge Dowding, but Madge Dowding's attention was on the man with the long arms, who had left Cat Bolger's side and was proceeding in the direction of the men's lavatory. He never took refreshments. She moved, herself, towards the men's

lavatory, to take up a position outside it, but Eyes Horgan followed her. 'Would you take a lemonade, Madge?' he asked. He had a small bottle of whiskey on him: if they went into a corner they could add a drop of it to the lemonade. She didn't drink spirits, she reminded him, and he went away.

'Excuse me a minute,' Bowser Egan said, putting down his bottle of lemonade. He crossed the floor to the lavatory. He too, Bridie knew, would have a small bottle of whiskey on him. She watched while Dano Ryan, listening to a story Mr Maloney was telling, paused in the centre of the ballroom, his head bent to hear what was being said. He was a big man, heavily made, with black hair that was slightly touched with grey, and big hands. He laughed when Mr Maloney came to the end of his story and then bent his head again, in order to listen to a story told by Mr Swanton.

'Are you on your own, Bridie?' Cat Bolger asked, and Bridie said she was waiting for Bowser Egan. 'I think I'll have a lemonade,' Cat Bolger said.

Younger boys and girls stood with their arms still around one another, queueing up for refreshments. Boys who hadn't danced at all, being nervous because they didn't know any steps, stood in groups, smoking and making jokes. Girls who hadn't been danced with yet talked to one another, their eyes wandering. Some of them sucked at straws in lemonade bottles.

Bridie, still watching Dano Ryan, imagined him wearing the glasses he'd referred to, sitting in the farmhouse kitchen, reading one of her father's Wild West novels. She imagined the three of them eating a meal she'd prepared, fried eggs and rashers and fried potato-cakes and tea and bread and butter and jam, brown bread and soda and shop bread. She imagined Dano Ryan leaving the kitchen in the morning to go out to the fields in order to weed the mangolds, and her father hobbling off behind him, and the two men working together. She saw hay being cut, Dano Ryan with the scythe that she'd learned to use herself, her father using a rake as best he could. She saw herself, because of the extra help, being able to attend to things in the farmhouse, things she'd never had time for because of the cows and the hens and the fields. There were bedroom curtains that needed repairing where the net had ripped, and wallpaper that had become loose and needed to be stuck up with flour paste. The scullery required whitewashing.

The night he'd blown up the tyre of her bicycle she'd thought he was going to kiss her. He'd crouched on the ground in the darkness with his ear to the tyre, listening for escaping air. When he could hear none he'd straightened up and said he thought she'd be all right on the bicycle. His face had been quite close to hers and she'd smiled at him. At that moment, unfortunately, Mr Maloney had blown an impatient blast on the horn of his motor-car.

Often she'd been kissed by Bowser Egan, on the nights when he insisted on riding part of the way home with her. They had to dismount in order to push their bicycles up a hill and the first time he'd accompanied her he'd contrived to fall against her, steadying himself by putting a hand on her shoulder. The next thing she was aware of was the moist quality of his lips and the sound of his bicycle as it clattered noisily on the road. He'd suggested then, regaining his breath, that they should go into a field.

That was nine years ago. In the intervening passage of time she'd been kissed as well, in similar circumstances, by Eyes Horgan and Tim Daly. She'd gone into fields with them and permitted them to put their arms about her while heavily they breathed. At one time or another she had imagined marriage with one or other of them, seeing them in the farmhouse with her father, even though the fantasies were unlikely.

Bridie stood with Cat Bolger, knowing that it would be some time before Bowser Egan came out of the lavatory. Mr Maloney, Mr Swanton and Dano Ryan approached, Mr Maloney insisting that he would fetch three bottles of lemonade from the trestle table.

'You sang the last one beautifully,' Bridie said to Dano Ryan. 'Isn't it a beautiful song?'

Mr Swanton said it was the finest song ever written, and Cat Bolger said she preferred 'Danny Boy', which in her opinion was the finest song ever written.

'Take a suck of that,' said Mr Maloney, handing Dano Ryan and Mr Swanton bottles of lemonade. 'How's Bridie tonight? Is your father well, Bridie?'

Her father was all right, she said.

'I hear they're starting a cement factory,' said Mr Maloney. 'Did anyone hear talk of that? They're after striking some commodity in the earth that makes good cement. Ten feet down, over at Kilmalough.'

'It'll bring employment,' said Mr Swanton. 'It's employment that's necessary in this area.'

'Canon O'Connell was on about it,' Mr Maloney said. 'There's Yankee money involved.'

'Will the Yanks come over?' inquired Cat Bolger. 'Will they run it themselves, Mr Maloney?'

Mr Maloney, intent on his lemonade, didn't hear the questions and Cat Bolger didn't repeat them.

'There's stuff called Optrex,' Bridie said quietly to Dano Ryan, 'that my father took the time he had a cold in his eyes. Maybe Optrex would settle the watering, Dano.'

'Ah sure, it doesn't worry me that much —'

'It's terrible, anything wrong with the eyes. You wouldn't want to take a chance. You'd get Optrex in a chemist, Dano, and a little bowl with it so that you can bathe the eyes.'

Her father's eyes had become red-rimmed and unsightly to look at. She'd gone into Riordan's Medical Hall in the town and had explained what the trouble was, and Mr Riordan had recommended Optrex. She told this to Dano Ryan, adding that her father had had no trouble with his eyes since. Dano Ryan nodded.

'Did you hear that, Mrs Dwyer?' Mr Maloney called out. 'A cement factory for Kilmalough.'

Mrs Dwyer wagged her head, placing empty bottles in a crate. She'd heard references to the cement factory, she said: it was the best news for a long time.

'Kilmalough'll never know itself,' her husband commented, joining her in her task with the empty lemonade bottles.

''Twill bring prosperity certainly,' said Mr Swanton. 'I was saying just there, Justin, that employment's what's necessary.'

'Sure, won't the Yanks —' began Cat Bolger, but Mr Maloney interrupted her.

'The Yanks'll be in at the top, Cat, or maybe not here at all — maybe only inserting money into it. It'll be local labour entirely.'

'You'll not marry a Yank, Cat,' said Mr Swanton, loudly laughing. 'You can't catch those fellows.'

'Haven't you plenty of homemade bachelors?' suggested Mr Maloney. He laughed also, throwing away the straw he was sucking through and tipping the bottle into his mouth. Cat Bolger told him to get on with himself. She moved towards the men's lavatory and took up a position outside it, not speaking to Madge Dowding, who was still standing there.

'Keep a watch on Eyes Horgan,' Mrs Dwyer warned her husband, which was advice she gave him at this time every Saturday night, knowing that Eyes Horgan was drinking in the lavatory. When he was drunk Eyes Horgan was the most difficult of the bachelors.

'I have a drop of it left, Dano,' Bridie said quietly. 'I could bring it over on Saturday. The eye stuff.'

'Ah, don't worry yourself, Bridie —'

'No trouble at all. Honestly now —'

'Mrs Griffin has me fixed up for a test with Dr Cready. The old eyes are no worry, only when I'm reading the paper or at the pictures. Mrs Griffin says I'm only straining them due to lack of glasses.'

He looked away while he said that, and she knew at once that Mrs Griffin was arranging to marry him. She felt it instinctively: Mrs Griffin was going to marry him because she was afraid that if he moved away from her cottage, to get married to someone else, she'd find it hard to replace him with another lodger who'd be good to her affected son. He'd become a father to Mrs Griffin's affected son, to whom already he was kind. It was a natural outcome, for Mrs Griffin had all the chances, seeing him every night and morning and not having to make do with weekly encounters in a ballroom.

She thought of Patrick Grady, seeing in her mind his pale, thin face. She might be the mother of four of his children now, or seven or eight maybe. She might be living in Wolverhampton, going out to the pictures in the evenings, instead of looking after a one-legged man. If the weight of circumstances hadn't intervened she wouldn't be standing in a wayside ballroom, mourning the marriage of a road-mender she didn't love. For a moment she thought she might cry, standing there thinking of Patrick Grady in Wolverhampton. In her life, on the farm and in the house, there was no place for tears. Tears were a luxury, like flowers would be in the fields where the mangolds grew, or fresh whitewash in the scullery. It wouldn't have been fair ever to have wept in the kitchen while her father sat listening to *Spot the Talent*: her father had more right to weep, having lost a leg. He suffered in a greater way, yet he remained kind and concerned for her.

In the Ballroom of Romance she felt behind her eyes the tears that it would have been improper to release in the presence of her father. She wanted to let them go, to feel them streaming on her cheeks, to receive the sympathy of Dano Ryan and of everyone else. She wanted them all to listen to her while she told them about Patrick Grady who was now in Wolverhampton and about the death of her mother and her own life since. She wanted Dano Ryan to put his arm around her so that she could lean her head against it. She wanted him to look at her in his decent way and to stroke with his road-mender's fingers the backs of her hands. She might wake in a bed with him and imagine for a moment that he was Patrick Grady. She might bathe his eyes and pretend.

'Back to business,' said Mr Maloney, leading his band across the floor to their instruments.

'Tell your father I was asking for him,' Dano Ryan said. She smiled and she promised, as though nothing had happened, that she would tell her father that.

She danced with Tim Daly and then again with the youth who'd said he intended to emigrate. She saw Madge Dowding moving swiftly towards the man with the long arms as he came out of the lavatory, moving faster than Cat Bolger. Eyes Horgan approached Cat Bolger. Dancing with her, he spoke earnestly,

attempting to persuade her to permit him to ride part of the way home with her. He was unaware of the jealousy that was coming from her as she watched Madge Dowding holding close to her the man with the long arms while they performed a quickstep. Cat Bolger was in her thirties too.

'Get away out of that,' said Bowser Egan, cutting in on the youth who was dancing with Bridie. 'Go home to your mammy, boy.' He took her into his arms, saying again that she was looking great tonight. 'Did you hear about the cement factory?' he said. 'Isn't it great for Kilmalough?'

She agreed. She said what Mr Swanton and Mr Maloney had said: that the cement factory would bring employment to the neighbourhood.

'Will I ride home with you a bit, Bridie?' Bowser Egan suggested, and she pretended not to hear him. 'Aren't you my girl, Bridie, and always have been?' he said, a statement that made no sense at all.

His voice went on whispering at her, saying he would marry her tomorrow only his mother wouldn't permit another woman in the house. She knew what it was like herself, he reminded her, having a parent to look after: you couldn't leave them to rot, you had to honour your father and your mother.

She danced to 'The Bells Are Ringing', moving her legs in time with Bowser Egan's while over his shoulder she watched Dano Ryan softly striking one of his smaller drums. Mrs Griffin had got him even though she was nearly fifty, with no looks at all, a lumpish woman with lumpish legs and arms. Mrs Griffin had got him just as the girl had got Patrick Grady.

The music ceased, Bowser Egan held her hard against him, trying to touch her face with his. Around them, people whistled and clapped: the evening had come to an end. She walked away from Bowser Egan, knowing that not ever again would she dance in the Ballroom of Romance. She'd been a figure of fun, trying to promote a relationship with a middle-aged County Council labourer, as ridiculous as Madge Dowding dancing on beyond her time.

'I'm waiting outside for you, Cat,' Eyes Horgan called out, lighting a cigarette as he made for the swing-doors.

Already the man with the long arms — made long, so they said, from carrying rocks off his land — had left the ballroom. Others were moving briskly. Mr Dwyer was tidying the chairs.

In the cloakroom the girls put on their coats and said they'd see one another at Mass the next day. Madge Dowding hurried. 'Are you O.K., Bridie?' Patty Byrne asked and Bridie said she was. She smiled at little Patty Byrne, wondering if a day would come for the younger girl also, if one day she'd decide that she was a figure of fun in a wayside ballroom.

'Good night so,' Bridie said, leaving the cloakroom, and the girls who were still chatting there wished her good night. Outside the cloakroom she paused for a moment. Mr Dwyer was still tidying the chairs, picking up empty lemonade bottles from the floor, setting the chairs in a neat row. His wife was sweeping the floor. 'Good night, Bridie,' Mr Dwyer said. 'Good night, Bridie,' his wife said.

Extra lights had been switched on so that the Dwyers could see what they were doing. In the glare the blue walls of the ballroom seemed tatty, marked with hair-oil where men had leaned against them, inscribed with names and initials and hearts with arrows through them. The crystal bowl gave out a light that was ineffective in the glare; the bowl was broken here and there, which wasn't noticeable when the other lights weren't on.

'Good night so,' Bridie said to the Dwyers. She passed through the swing-doors and descended the three concrete steps on the gravel expanse in front of the ballroom. People were gathered on the gravel, talking in groups, standing with their bicycles. She saw Madge Dowding going off with Tim Daly. A youth rode away with a girl on the cross-bar of his bicycle. The engines of motor-cars started.

'Good night, Bridie,' Dano Ryan said.

'Good night, Dano,' she said.

She walked across the gravel towards her bicycle, hearing Mr Maloney, somewhere behind her, repeating that no matter how you looked at it the cement factory would be a great thing for Kilmalough. She heard the bang of a car-door and knew it was Mr Swanton banging the door of Mr Maloney's car because he always gave it the same loud bang. Two other doors banged as she reached her bicycle and then the engine started up and the headlights went on. She touched the two tyres of the bicycle to make certain she hadn't a puncture. The wheels of Mr Maloney's car traversed the gravel and were silent when they reached the road.

'Good night, Bridie,' someone called, and she replied, pushing her bicycle towards the road.

'Will I ride a little way with you?' Bowser Egan asked.

They rode together and when they arrived at the hill for which it was necessary to dismount she looked back and saw in the distance the four coloured bulbs that decorated the façade of the Ballroom of Romance. As she watched the lights went out, and she imagined Mr Dwyer pulling the metal grid across the front of his property and locking the two padlocks that secured it. His wife would be waiting with the evening's takings, sitting in the front of their car.

'D'you know what it is, Bridie,' said Bowser Egan, 'you were never looking better than tonight.' He took from a pocket of his suit the small bottle of whiskey he had. He uncorked it and drank some and then handed it to her. She took it and drank. 'Sure, why wouldn't you?' he said, surprised to see her drinking because she never had in his company before. It was an unpleasant taste, she considered, a taste she'd experienced only twice before, when she'd taken whiskey as a remedy for toothache. 'What harm would it do you?' Bowser Egan said as she raised the bottle again to her lips. He reached out a hand for it, though, suddenly concerned lest she should consume a greater share than he wished her to.

She watched him drinking more expertly than she had. He would always be drinking, she thought. He'd be lazy and useless, sitting in the kitchen with the *Irish Press*. He'd waste money buying a second-hand motor-car in order to drive into the town to go to the public houses on fair-days.[3]

'She's shook these days,' he said, referring to his mother. 'She'll hardly last two years, I'm thinking.' He threw the empty whiskey bottle into the ditch and lit a cigarette. They pushed their bicycles. He said:

'When she goes, Bridie, I'll sell the bloody place up. I'll sell the pigs and the whole damn one and twopence worth.' He paused in order to raise the cigarette to his lips. He drew in smoke, and exhaled it. 'With the cash that I'll get I could improve some place else, Bridie.'

They reached a gate on the left-hand side of the road and automatically they pushed their bicycles towards it and leaned them against it. He climbed over the gate into the field and she climbed after him. 'Will we sit down here, Bridie?' he said, offering the suggestion as one that had just occurred to him, as though they'd entered the field for some other purpose.

'We could improve a place like your own one,' he said, putting his right arm around her shoulders. 'Have you a kiss in you, Bridie?' He kissed her, exerting pressure with his teeth. When his mother died he would sell his farm and spend the money in the town. After that he would think of getting married because he'd have nowhere to go, because he'd want a fire to sit at and a woman to cook food for him. He kissed her again, his lips hot, the sweat on his cheeks sticking to her. 'God, you're great at kissing,' he said.

She rose, saying it was time to go, and they climbed over the gate again. 'There's nothing like a Saturday,' he said. 'Good night to you so, Bridie.'

He mounted his bicycle and rode down the hill, and she pushed hers to the top and then mounted it also. She rode through the night as on Saturday nights for years she had ridden and never would ride again because she'd reached a certain age. She would wait now and in time Bowser Egan would seek her out because his mother would have died. Her father would probably have died also by then. She would marry Bowser Egan because it would be lonesome being by herself in the farmhouse.

1   A lay organization for Catholics.
2   A country dance.
3   Market days for buying and selling of livestock.

MARY LAVIN
from Mary Lavin, *A Memory and Other Stories* (1972)

Mary Lavin (1912–96) was born in Massachusetts but returned with her Irish parents to Ireland when she was ten. Her first book of short stories, *Tales from Bective Bridge* (1943), was followed by the equally successful novel *The House in Clewe Street* (1945). She lived most of her life in Bective, County Meath, and, like the protagonist James in the following story, would have regularly caught the bus into Dublin. 'A Memory' is a fine short story, more so on a first than on subsequent readings. One baby word in the story betrays the author's American roots or connections.

A Memory

James did all right for a man on his own. An old woman from the village came in for a few hours a day and gave him a hot meal before she went home. She also got ready an evening meal needing only to be heated up. As well, she put his breakfast egg in a saucepan of water beside the paraffin stove, with a box of matches beside it in case he mislaid his own. She took care of all but one of the menial jobs of living. The one she couldn't do for him was one James hated most — cleaning out ashes from the grate in his study and lighting up the new fire for the day.

James was an early riser and firmly believed in giving the best of his brain to his work. So, the minute he was dressed he went out to the kitchen and lit the stove under the coffee pot. Then he got the ash bucket and went at the grate. When the ashes were out the rest wasn't too bad. There was kindling in the hot press and the old woman left a few split logs for getting up a quick blaze. He had the room well warmed by the time he had eaten his breakfast. His main objection to doing the grate was that he got his suit covered with ashes. He knew he ought to wear tweeds now that he was living full-time at the cottage, but he stuck obstinately to his dark suit and white collar, feeling as committed to this attire as to his single state. Both were part and parcel of his academic dedication. His work filled his life as it filled his day. He seldom had occasion to go up to the University. When he went up it was to see Myra, and then only on impulse if for some reason work went against him. This did happen periodically in spite of his devotion to it. Without warning a day would come when he'd wake up in a queer, unsettled mood that would send him prowling around the cottage, lighting up cigarette after cigarette and looking out of the window until he'd have to face the fact that he was not going to do a stroke. Inevitably the afternoon would see him with his hat and coat on, going down the road to catch the bus for Dublin — and an evening with Myra.

This morning he was in fine fettle though, when he dug the shovel into the mound of grey ash. But he was annoyed to see a volley of sparks go up the black chimney. The hearth would be hot, and the paper would catch fire before he'd have time to build his little pyre. There was more kindling in the kitchen press, but he'd have felt guilty using more than the allotted amount, thinking of the poor old creature wielding that heavy axe. He really ought to split those logs himself.

When he first got the cottage he used to enjoy that kind of thing. But after he'd been made a research professor and able to live down there all year round he came to have less and less zest for manual work. He sort of lost the knack of it. Ah well, his energies were totally expended in mental work. It would not be surprising if muscularly he got a bit soft.

James got up off his knees and brushed himself down. The fire was taking hold. The nimble flames played in and out through the dead twigs as sunlight must once have done when the sap was green. Standing watching them, James flexed his fingers. He wouldn't like to think he was no longer fit. Could his increasing aversion to physical labour be a sign of decreasing vigour? He frowned. He would not consider himself a vain man, it was simply that he'd got used to the look of himself; was accustomed to his slight, spare figure. But surely by mental activity he burned up as much fuel as any navvy or stevedore? Lunatics never had to worry about exercise either! Who ever saw a corpulent madman? He smiled. He must remember to tell that to Myra. Her laugh was always so quick and responsive although even if a second or two later she might seize on some inherently serious point in what had at first amused her. It was Myra who had first drawn his attention to this curious transference — this drawing off of energies — from the body to the brain. She herself had lost a lot of the skill in her fingers. When she was younger — or so she claimed — she'd been quite a good cook, and could sew, and that kind of thing, although frankly James couldn't imagine her being much good about the house. But when she gave up teaching and went into free-lance translation her work began to make heavy demands on her, and she too, like him, lost all inclination for physical chores. Now — or so she said — she could not bake a cake to save her life. As for sewing — well here again frankly — to him the sight of a needle in her hand would be ludicrous. In fact he knew — they both knew — that when they first met, it was her lack of domesticity that had been the essence of her appeal for him. For a woman, it was quite remarkable how strong was the intellectual climate of thought in which she lived. She had concocted a sort of cocoon of thought and wrapped herself up in it. One became aware of it immediately one stepped inside her little flat. There was another thing! The way she used the word flat to designate what was really a charming little mews house. It was behind one of the Georgian squares, and it had a beautiful little garden at the back and courtyard in front. He hadn't been calling there for very long until he understood why she referred to it as her flat. It was a word that did not have unpleasant connotations of domesticity.

Her little place had a marvellously masculine air, and yet, miraculously, Myra herself remained very feminine. She was, of course, a pretty woman, although she hated him to say this — and she didn't smoke, or drink more than a dutiful pre-dinner sherry with him, which she often forgot to finish. And there was a nice scent from her clothes, a scent at times quite disturbing. It often bothered him, and was occasionally the cause of giving her the victory in one of the really brilliant arguments that erupted so spontaneously the moment he stepped inside the door.

Yes, it was hard to believe Myra could ever have been a home-body. But if she said it was so, then it *was* so. Truth could have been her second name. With regard to her domestic failure, she had recently told him a most amusing story. He couldn't recall the actual incident, but it had certainly corroborated her theory of the transference of skill. It was — she said — as if part of her had become palsied, although at the time her choice of that word had made him wince, it was so altogether unsuitable for a woman like her, obviously now in her real prime. He'd pulled her up on that. Verbal exactitude was something they both knew to be of the utmost importance, although admittedly rarer to find in a woman than a man.

'It is a quality I'd never have looked to find in a woman, Myra,' he'd said to her on one of his first visits to the flat — perhaps his very first.

He never forgot her answer.

'It's not something I'd ever expect a man to look for in a woman,' she said. 'Thank you, James, for not jumping to the conclusion that I could not possibly possess it.'

Yes — that must have been on his first visit because he'd been startled by such quick-fire volley in reply to what had been only a casual compliment. No wonder their friendship got off to a flying start!

Thinking of the solid phalanx of years that had been built up since that evening, James felt a glow of satisfaction, and for a moment he didn't realize that the fire he was supposed to be tending had got off to a good start, and part at least of his sense of well-being was coming from its warmth stealing over him.

The flames were going up the chimney with soft nervous rushes and the edges of the logs were deckled with small sharp flames, like the teeth of a saw. He could safely leave it now and have breakfast. But just then he did remember what it was Myra had been good at when she was young. Embroidery! She had once made herself an evening dress with the bodice embroidered all over in beads. And she'd worn it! So it must have been well made. Even his sister Kay, who disliked Myra, had to concede she dressed well. Yes, she must indeed have been fairly good at sewing in her young days. Yet one day recently when she ripped her skirt in the National Library she hadn't been able to mend it.

'It wasn't funny, James,' she chided when he laughed. 'The whole front pleat was ripped. I had to borrow a needle and thread from the lavatory attendant. Fortunately I had plenty of time — so when I'd taken it off and sewed it up I decided to give it a professional touch — a finish — with a tailor's arrow. It took time but it was well done and the lavatory attendant was very impressed when I held the skirt up! But next minute when I tried to step into it I found I'd sewn the back to the front. I'd formed a sort of gusset. Can you picture it. I'd turned it into trousers!'

Poor Myra! He laughed still more.

'I tell you, it's not funny, James. And it's the same with cooking. I used at least to be able to boil an egg, whereas now — ' she shrugged her shoulders. 'You know how useless I am in the kitchen.'

She had certainly never attempted to cook a meal for him. They always went out to eat. There was a small café near the flat and they ate there. Or at least they did at the start. But when one evening they decided they didn't really want to go out — perhaps he'd had a headache, or perhaps it was a really wet night, but anyway whatever it was, Myra made no effort to — as she put it — slop up some unappetizing smather. Instead she lifted the phone, and got on to the proprietor of their little café and — as she put it — administered such a dose of coaxy-orum — she really had very amusing ways of expressing herself — that he sent around two trays of food. Two trays, mind you. That was so like her — so quick, so clever. And tactful, too. That night marked a new stage in their relationship.

They'd been seeing a lot of each other by then. He'd been calling to the flat pretty frequently and when they went out for a meal, although the little café was always nearly empty, he had naturally paid the bill each time.

'We couldn't go on like that though, James!' she'd said firmly when he'd tried to pay for the trays of food that night. And she did finally succeed in making him see that if he were to come to the flat as often as she hoped he would — and as he himself certainly hoped — it would put her under too great an obligation to have him pay for the food every time.

'Another woman would be able to run up some tasty little dish that wouldn't cost tuppence,' she said, 'but — ' she made a face '— that's out. All the same I can't let you put me under too great a compliment to you. Not every time.'

In the end they'd settled on a good compromise. They each paid for a tray.

He had had misgivings, but she rid him of them.

'What would you eat if I wasn't here, Myra?' he'd asked.

'I wouldn't have *cooked* anything, that's certain,' she said, and he didn't pursue the topic, permitting himself just one other brief enquiry.

'What do other people do, I wonder?'

This Myra dismissed with a deprecating laugh.

'I'm afraid I don't know,' she said. 'Or care! Do you?'

'Oh Myra!' In that moment he felt she elevated them both to such pure heights of integrity. 'You know I don't,' he said, and he'd laid his hand over hers as she sat beside him on the sofa.

'That makes two of us!' she said, and she drew a deep breath of contentment.

It was a rich moment. It was probably at that moment he first realized the uniquely undemanding quality of her feeling for him.

But now James saw that the fire was blazing madly. He had to put on another log or it would burn out too fast. He threw on a log and was about to leave the study when, as he passed his desk, a nervous impulse made him look to see that his papers were not disarranged, although there was no one to disturb them.

The papers, of course, were as he had left them. But then the same diabolical nervousness made him go over and pick up the manuscript. Why? He couldn't explain, except that he'd worked late the previous night and, when he did that, he was always idiotically nervous next day, as if he half expected to find the words had been mysteriously erased during the night. That had happened once! He'd got up one morning as usual, full of eagerness to take up where he thought he'd left off only to find he'd stopped in the middle of a sentence — had gone to bed defeated, leaving a most involved and complicated sentence unfinished. He'd only dreamed that he'd finished it off.

This morning, thank heavens, it was no dream. He'd finished the sentence — the whole chapter. It was the last chapter too. A little rephrasing, perhaps some rewording, and the whole thing would be ready for the typist.

Standing in the warm study with the pages of his manuscript in his hand James was further warmed by a self-congratulatory glow. This was the most ambitious thing he'd attempted so far — it was no less than an effort to trace the creative process itself back, as it were, to its source-bed. How glad he was that he'd stuck at it last night. He'd paid heavily for it by tossing around in the sheets until nearly morning. But it was worth it. His intuitions had never yielded up their meanings so fast or so easily. But suddenly his nervousness returned. He hoped to God his writing wasn't illegible? No. It was readable. And although his eye did not immediately pick up any of the particularly lucid — even felicitous — phrases that he vaguely remembered having hit upon, he'd come on them later when he was re-reading more carefully.

Pleased, James was putting down the manuscript, but on an impulse he took up the last section again. He'd bring it out to the kitchen and begin his re-reading of it while he was having his breakfast, something he never did, having a horror of foodstains on paper. It might, as it were, recharge his batteries, because in spite of his satisfaction with the way the work was going, he had to admit to a certain amount of physical lethargy, due to having gone to bed so late.

It was probably wiser in the long run to do like Myra and confine oneself to a fixed amount of work per day. Nothing would induce Myra to go beyond her pre-determined limit of two thousand words a day. Even when things were going well! It was when they were going well that paradoxically she often stopped work. Really her method of working amazed him. When she encountered difficulty she went doggedly on, worrying at a word like a dog with a bone — as she put it — in order, she explained, to avoid carrying over her frustration with it to the next day. On the other hand, when things were going well and her mind was leaping forward like a flat stone skimming the surface of a lake (her image again, not his, but good, good) *then* sometimes she stopped.

'Because then, James, I have a residue of enthusiasm to start me off next day! I'm not really a dedicated scholar like you — I need stimulus.'

She had a point. But her method wouldn't work for him. It would be mental suicide for him to tear himself away when he was excited. It was only when things got sticky he stopped. When an idea sort of seized up in his mind and he couldn't go on.

There was nothing sticky about last night though. Last night his brain buzzed with ideas. Yet now, sitting down to his egg, the page in his hand seemed oddly dull — a great hunk of abstraction. He took the top off the egg before reading on. But after a few paragraphs he looked at the numbering of the pages. Had the pages got mixed up? Here was a sentence that seemed to be in the wrong place. The whole passage made no impact. And what was this? He'd come on a line that was meaningless, absolutely meaningless — gibberish. With a sickening feeling James put down the manuscript and took a gulp of coffee. Then, by concentrating hard he could perceive — could at least form a vague idea of — what he'd been trying to get

at in this clumsy passage. At one point indeed he had more or less got it, but the chapter as a whole — ? He sat there stunned.

What had happened? Could it be that what he'd taken for creative intensity had been only nervous exhaustion? Was that it? Was Myra right? Should he have stopped earlier? Out of the question. In the excited state he'd been in, he wouldn't have slept a wink at all — even in the early hours. And what else could he have done but go to bed? A walk, perhaps? At that time of night? On a country road in the pitch dark? It was all very well for Myra — the city streets were full of people at all hours, brightly lit, and safe underfoot.

Anyway Myra probably did most of her work in the morning. He didn't really know for sure of course, except that whenever he turned up at the flat there was never any sign of papers about the place. The thought of that neat and orderly flat made him look around the cottage and suddenly he felt depressed. The old woman did her best, but she wasn't up to very much. The place could do with a rub of paint, the woodwork at least, but he certainly wasn't going to do it. He wouldn't be able. James frowned again. Why was his mind harping on this theme of fitness? He straightened up as if in protest at some accusation, but almost at once he slumped down, not caring.

He got exercise enough on the days he went to Dublin. First the walk to the bus. Then the walk at the other end, because no matter what the weather, he always walked from the bus to the flat. It was a good distance too, but it prolonged his anticipation of the evening ahead.

Ah well! He wouldn't be going today. That was certain. He gathered up his pages. He'd have to slog at this thing till he got it right. He swallowed down the last of his coffee. Back to work.

The fire at any rate was going well. It was roaring up the chimney. The sun too was pouring into the room. Away across the river in a far field cattle were lying down: a sign of good weather it was said.

Hastily, James stepped back from the window and sat down at his desk. It augured badly for his work when he was aware of the weather. Normally he couldn't have told if the day was wet or fine.

That was the odd thing about Dublin. There, the weather did matter. There he was aware of every fickle change in the sky, especially on a day like today that began with rain and later gave way to sunshine. The changes came so quick in the city. They took one by surprise, although one was alerted by a thousand small signs, whereas the sodden fields were slow to recover after the smallest shower. In Dublin the instant there was a break in the clouds, the pavements gave back an answering glint. And after that came a strange white light mingling water and sun, a light that could be perceived in the reflections under foot without raising one's eyes to the sky at all. And how fast then the paving stones dried out into pale patches. Like stepping stones, these patches acted strangely on him, putting a skip into his otherwise sober step!

Talk of the poetry of Spring. The earth's rebirth! Where was it more intoxicating than in the city, the cheeky city birds filling the air with song, and green buds breaking out on branches so black with grime it was as if iron bars had sprouted. Thinking of the city streets his feet ached to be pacing them. James glanced out again at the fields with hatred.

Damn, damn, damn. The damage was done. He'd let himself get unsettled. It would be Dublin for him today. He looked at the clock. He might even go on the early bus. Only what would he do up there all day? His interest in Dublin had dwindled to its core, and the core was Myra.

All the same, he decided to go on the early bus. 'Come on, James! Be a gay dog for once. Get the early bus. You'll find plenty to do. The bookshops! The National Library! Maybe a film? Come on. You're going whether you like it or not, old fellow.'

Catching up the poker James turned the blazing logs over to smother their flames. A pity he'd lit the fire, or rather it was a pity it couldn't be kept in till he got back. It would be nice to return to a warm house. But old Mrs Nully had a mortal dread of the cottage taking fire in his absence. James smiled thinking how she had recently asked why he didn't install central heating. In a three-roomed cottage! Now where on earth had she got that notion he wondered, as he closed the door and put the key under the mat for her. Then, as he strode off down to the road, he remembered that a son of hers had been taken on as houseman in Asigh House, and the son's wife gave a hand there at weekends. The old woman had probably been shown over the house by them before the Balfes moved into it.

The Balfes! James was nearly at the road, and involuntarily he glanced back across the river to where a fringe of fir trees in the distance marked out the small estate of Asigh. Strange to think — laughable really — that Emmy, who once had filled every cranny of his mind, should only come to mind now in a train of thought that had its starting point in a plumbing appliance!

Here James called himself to order. It was a gross exaggeration to have said — even to himself — that Emmy had ever entirely filled his mind. He'd only known her for a year, and that was the year he finished his Ph.D. He submitted the thesis at the end of the year, and his marks, plus the winning of the travelling scholarship, surely spoke for a certain detachment of mind even when he was most obsessed by her?

He glanced back again at the far trees. Emmy only stood out in his life because of the violence of his feeling for her. It was something he had never permitted himself before; and never would again. When the affair ended, it ended as completely as if she had been a little skiff upon a swiftly flowing river, which, when he'd cut the painter, was carried instantly away. For a time he'd had no way of knowing whether it had capsized or foundered. As it happened, Emmy had righted herself and come to no harm.

Again, James had to call himself to order. How cruel he made himself seem by that metaphor. Yet for years that was how he'd felt obliged to put it to himself. That was how he'd put it to Myra when he first told her about Emmy. But Myra was quick to defend him, quick to see, and quick to show him how he had acted in self-defence. His career would have been wrecked, because of course with a girl like Emmy marriage would have become inescapable. And, of course, then as now, marriage for him was out. It was never really in the picture.

Later, after Myra appeared on the scene, he came to believe that a man and woman could enter into a marriage of minds.

'But when one is young, James,' Myra said, 'one can't be expected to be both wise and foolish at the same time.'

A good saying. He'd noticed, and appreciated, the little sigh with which she accompanied her words, as if she didn't just feel *for* him but *with* him. Then she asked the question that a man might have asked.

'She married eventually I take it, this Emmy?'

'Oh good lord, yes.' How happy he was to be able to answer in the affirmative. If Emmy had not married it would have worried him all his life. But she did. And, all things considered, surprisingly soon.

'Young enough to have a family?' Myra probed, but kindly, kindly. He nodded. 'I take it,' she said then, more easily, 'I take it she married that student who —'

James interrupted '— the one she was knocking around with when I first noticed her?'

'Yes, the one that was wrestling with that window when you had to step down from the rostrum and yank it open yourself?'

Really Myra was unique. Her grasp of the smallest details of that incident, even then so far back in time, was very gratifying.

He had been conducting a tutorial and the lecture room got so stuffy he'd asked if someone would open a window? But when a big burly fellow — the footballer type — tried with no success, James strode down the classroom himself, irritably, because he half thought the fellow might be having him on to create a diversion. And when he had to lean in across a student whose chair was right under the window, he was hardly aware it was a girl, as he exerted all his strength to bring down the heavy sash. Only when the sash came down and the fresh air rushed in overhead did he find he was looking straight into the eyes of a girl — Emmy.

That was all. But during the rest of the class their eyes kept meeting. And the next day it was the same. Then he began to notice her everywhere, in the corridors, in the Main Hall, and once across the Aula Maxima at an inaugural ceremony. And she'd seen him too. He knew it. But for a long time, several weeks, there was nothing between them except this game of catch-catch with their eyes. And always, no matter how far apart they were, it was as if they had touched.

James soon found himself trembling all over when her eyes touched him. Then one day in the library she passed by his desk and he saw that a paper in her hand was shaking as if there was a breeze in the air. But there was no breeze. Still, deliberately, he delayed the moment of speaking to her because there was a kind of joy in waiting. And funnily enough when they did finally speak neither of them could afterwards remember what their first spoken words had been. They had already said so much with their eyes.

Myra's comment on this, though, was very shrewd. 'You had probably said all there was to say, James.' Again she gave that small sigh of hers that seemed to put things in proportion: to place him, and Emmy too, on the map of disenchantment where all mankind, it seems, must sojourn for a time. And indeed it was sad to think that out of the hundreds of hours that he and Emmy had spent together, wandering along the damp paths of Stephen's Green, sitting in little cafés, and standing under the lamps of Leeson Street where he was in lodgings, he could recall nothing of what was said. 'You probably spent most evenings trying out ideas for your thesis on her, poor girl.' Myra had a dry humour at times, but he had to acknowledge it was likely enough, although if so, Emmy used to listen as if she were drinking in every word.

When he'd got down at last to the actual writing of the thesis they did not meet so often. In fact he could never quite remember their last meeting either. Not even what they had said to each other at parting. Of course long before that they must have faced up to his

situation. He'd been pretty sure of getting the travelling scholarship, so it must have been an understood thing that he'd be going away for at least two years. And in the end, he left a month sooner than he'd intended. They never actually did say goodbye. He'd gone without seeing her — just left a note at her digs. And for a while he wasn't even sure if she'd got it. She'd got it all right. She wrote and thanked him. How that smarted! *Thanked* him for breaking it off with her. Years later, telling Myra, he still felt the sting of that.

Myra was marvellous though.

'Hurt pride, my dear James. Nothing more, don't let it spoil what is probably the sweetest thing in life — for all of us, men or women — our first shy, timid love.' There was a tenderness in her voice. Was she remembering some girlish experience of her own? The pang of jealousy that went through him showed how little Emmy had come to mean to him.

Myra put him at ease.

'We all go through it, James, it's only puppy love.'

'Puppy love! I was twenty-six, Myra!'

'Dear, dear James.' She smiled. 'Don't get huffy. I know quite well what age you were. You were completing your Ph.D., and you were old enough to conduct tutorials. You were not at the top of the tree, but you had begun the ascent!'

It was so exactly how he'd seen himself in those days, that he laughed. And with that laugh the pain went out of the past.

'Dear James,' she said again, 'anyone who knows you — and loves you,' she added quickly, because they tried never to skirt away from that word love, although they gave it a connotation all their own, 'anyone who loves you, James, would know that even then, where women were concerned, you'd be nothing but a lanky, bashful boy. Wait a minute!' She sprang up from the sofa. 'I'll show you what I mean.' She took down the studio photograph she'd made him get taken the day of his honorary doctorate. 'Here!' She shoved the silver frame into his hands, and going into the room where she slept, she came back with another photograph. 'You didn't know I had this one?' He saw with some chagrin that it was a blow-up from a group photograph taken on the steps of his old school at the end of his last year. 'See!' she said. 'It's the same face in both, the same ascetical features, the same look of dedication.' Then she pressed the frame end face inward, against her breast. 'Oh James, I bet Emmy was the first girl you ever looked at! My dear, it was not so much the girl as the experience itself that bowled you over.'

Emmy was not the first girl he'd looked at. In those days he was always looking at girls, but looking at them from an unbridgeable distance. When he looked at Emmy the space between them seemed to be instantly obliterated. Emmy had felt the same. That day in class her mind had been a million miles away. She was trying to make up her mind about getting engaged to the big burly fellow, the one who couldn't open the window; James could not remember his name, but he was a type that could be attractive to women. The fellow was pestering her to marry him, and the attentions of a fellow like that could have been very flattering to a girl like Emmy. She was so young. Yet, after she met *him* it was as if a fiery circle had been blazed around them, allowing no way out for either until he, James, in the end had to close his eyes and break through, not caring about the pain as long as he got outside again.

Because Myra was right. Marriage would have put an end to his academic career. For a man like him it would have been suffocating.

'Even now!' Myra said, and there was a humorous expression on her face, because of course, in their own way, he and Myra *were* married. Then, in a businesslike way, as if she were filling up a form for filing away, she asked him another question. 'What family did they have?'

'She had five or six children, I think, although she must have been about thirty by the time she married,' James couldn't help throwing his eyes up to heaven at the thought of such a household. Myra too raised her eyebrows.

'You're joking?' she said. 'Good old Balfe!' But James was staring at her, hardly able to credit she had picked up Emmy's married name. He himself had hardly registered it, the first time *he'd* heard it, so that when last summer Asigh House had been bought by people named Balfe, it simply hadn't occurred to him that it could have been Emmy and her husband until one day on the road a car passed him and the woman beside the driver reminded him oddly of her. The woman in the car was softer and plumper and her hair was looser and more untidy — well fluffier anyway — than Emmy's used to be, or so he thought, until suddenly he realized it *was* her, Emmy! She didn't recognize him though. But then she wasn't looking his way. She was looking out over the countryside through which she was passing. It was only when the car turned left at the cross-road the thought hit him, that she had married a man named Balfe, and that Balfe was the name of the people who'd bought Asigh. It was a shock. Not only because of past associations, but more because he had never expected any invasion of his privacy down here. It was his retreat, from everything and everyone. Myra — even Myra — had

never been down there. She was too sensible to suggest such a thing. And he wouldn't want her to come either.

Once when he'd fallen ill he'd lost his head and sent her a telegram, but even then she'd exercised extreme discrimination. She despatched a nurse to take care of him, arranging with the woman to phone her each evening from the village. Without once coming down, she had overseen his illness — which fortunately was not of long duration. She had of course ascertained to her satisfaction that his condition was not serious. The main thing was that she set a firm precedent for them both. It was different when he was convalescing. Then she insisted that he come up to town and stay in a small hotel near the flat, taking his evening meal with her, as on ordinary visits except — James smiled — except that she sent a taxi to fetch him, and carry him back, although the distance involved was negligible, only a block or two.

Remembering her concern for him on that occasion, James told himself that he could never thank her enough. He resolved to let her see he did not take her goodness for granted. Few women could be as self-effacing.

Yet, in all fairness to Emmy, she had certainly effaced herself fast. One might say drastically. After that one note of thanks — it jarred again that she had put it like that — he had never once heard or seen her until that day she passed him here on the road in her car. So much for his fears for his privacy. Unfounded! For days he'd half expected a courtesy call from them, but after a time he began to wonder if they were aware at all that he lived in the neighbourhood? After all, their property was three or four miles away, and the river ran between. It was just possible Emmy knew nothing of his existence. Yet somehow, he doubted it. As the crow flies he was less than two miles away. He could see their wood. And was it likely the local people would have made no mention of him? No, it was hard to escape the conclusion that Emmy might be avoiding him. Although Myra — who was never afraid of the truth — had not hesitated to say that Emmy might have forgotten him altogether!

'Somehow I find that hard to believe, Myra,' he'd said, although after he'd made the break, there had been nothing. Nothing, nothing, nothing.

But Myra was relentless.

'You may not like to believe it, James, but it could be true all the same,' she said. Then she tried to take the hurt out of her words by confessing that she herself found it dispiriting to think a relationship that had gone so deep, could be erased completely. 'I myself can't bear to think she did not recognize you that day

she passed you on the road. *She* may have changed —
you said she'd got stouter —' That wasn't the word
he'd used, but he'd let it pass — 'whereas you, James,
can hardly have changed at all, in essentials, I mean.
Your figure must be the same as when you were a
young man. I can't bear to think she didn't even
know you.'

'She wasn't looking straight at me, Myra.'

'No matter! You'd think there'd have been some
telepathy between you; some force that would *make*
her turn. Oh, I can't bear it!'

She was so earnest he had to laugh.

'It is a good job she didn't see me,' he said. Emmy
being nothing to him then, it was just as well there
should be no threat to his peace and quiet.

Such peace; such quiet. James looked around at the
sleepy countryside. The bus was very late though!
What was keeping it?

Ah, here it came. Signalling to the driver, James
stepped up quickly on to the running-board so the
man had hardly to do more than go down into first
gear before starting off again. In spite of how few
passengers there were, the windows were fogged up
and James had to clear a space on the glass with his
hand to see out. It was always a pleasant run through
the rich Meath fields, but soon the unruly countryside
gave way to neatly squared-off fields with pens and
wooden palings, where cattle were put in for the night
before being driven to the slaughter-house.

James shuddered. He was no country-man. Not by
nature anyway. He valued the country solely for the
protection it gave him from people. When he lived in
Dublin he used to work in the National Library, but as
he got older he began to feel that in the eyes of the
students and the desk-messengers, he could have
appeared eccentric. Not objectionably so, just rustling
his papers too much, and clearing his throat too
loudly; that kind of thing. He'd have been the first to
find that annoying in others when he was young. The
cottage was much better. It also served to put that little
bit of distance between him and Myra which they
both agreed was essential.

'If I lived in Dublin I'd be here at the flat every
night of the week,' he'd once said to her. 'I'm better
off down there — I suppose — stuck in the mud!'

That was an inaccurate — an unfair — description
of his little retreat, but the words had come
involuntarily to his lips which showed how he felt
about the country in general. The city streets of
Dublin were so full of life, and the people were so
dapper and alert compared with the slow-moving
country people. Every time he went up there he felt
like an old fogy — that was until he got to Myra's —

because Myra immediately gave him back a sense of
being alive. Mentally at least Myra made him feel
more alive than twenty men.

The bus had now reached O'Connell Bridge,
where James usually descended, so he got out. He
ought to have got out sooner and walked along the
Quays. One could kill a whole morning looking over
the book barrows. Now he would have to walk back
to them.

Perhaps he ought not to have come on the early
bus? It might not be so easy to pass the time. And after
browsing to his heart's content and leaning for a while
looking over the parapet on to the Liffey, it was still
only a little after 1 o'clock when he strolled back to
the centre of the city. He'd have to eat something and
that would use up another hour or more. He'd buy a
paper and sit on over his coffee.

James hadn't bargained on the lunchtime crowds
though. All the popular places were crowded, and in a
few of the better places, one look inside was enough
to send him off! These places too were invaded by the
lunchtime hordes, and the menu would cater for these
barbarians. If there should by chance happen to be a
continental dish on the menu — a goulash or a pasta
— it would nauseate him to see the little clerks
attacking it with knife and fork as if it was a mutton
chop.

At this late hour how about missing out on lunch
altogether? It never hurt to skip a meal, although,
mind you, he was peckish. How about a film? He
hadn't been in a cinema for years. And just then, as if
to settle the matter — James saw he was passing a
cinema. It was exceptionally small for a city cinema,
but without another thought he bolted inside.

Once inside, he regretted that he hadn't checked
the time of the showings. He didn't fancy sitting
through a newsreel, to say nothing of a cartoon. He
had come in just in the middle of a particularly silly
cartoon. He sat in the dark fuming. To think he'd let
himself in for this stuff. It was at least a quarter of an
hour before he realized with rage that he must have
strayed into one of the new-fangled newsreel cinemas
about which Myra had told him. For another minute
he sat staring at the screen, trying to credit the
mentality of people who voluntarily subjected
themselves to this kind of stuff. He was about to leave
and make for the street, when without warning his
eyes closed. He didn't know for how long he had
dozed off, but on waking he was really ravenous. But
wouldn't it be crazy to eat at this hour and spoil his
appetite for the meal with Myra? He could, he
supposed, go around to the flat earlier — now —
immediately? Why wait any longer? But he didn't

know at what hour Myra herself got there. All he knew was that she was always there after seven, the time he normally arrived.

But wasn't it remarkable now he came to think of it, that she *was* always there when he called. Very occasionally at the start she had let drop dates on which she had to go to some meeting or other, and he'd made a mental note of them, but as time went on she gave up these time-wasting occupations. There had been one or two occasions she had been going out, but had cancelled her arrangements immediately he came on the scene. He had protested of course, but lamely, because quite frankly it would have been frightfully disappointing to have come so far and found she really had to go out.

Good God — supposing that were to happen now? James was so scared at the possibility of such a catastrophe he determined to lose no more time but get around there quick. Just in case. He stepped out briskly.

The lane at the back of Fitzwilliam Square, where Myra had her mews, was by day a hive of small enterprises. A smell of cellulosing and sounds of welding filled the air. In one courtyard there was a little fellow who dealt in scrap-iron and he made a great din. But by early evening, the big gates closed on these businesses, the high walls made the lane a very private place, and the mews-dwellers were disturbed by no sound harsher than the late song of the birds nesting in the trees of the doctors' gardens.

Walking down the lane and listening to those sleepy bird-notes gave James greater pleasure than walking on any country road. His feet echoed so loudly in the stillness that sometimes before he rapped on her gate at all, Myra would come running out across the courtyard to admit him. A good thing that! Because otherwise he'd have had to rap with his bare knuckles; Myra had no knocker.

'You know I don't encourage callers, James,' she'd said once smiling. 'Few people ferret me out here — except you; and, of course, the tradesmen. And I know their step too! It's nearly as quiet here as in your cottage.'

'Quiet?' He'd raised his eyebrows. 'Listen to those birds; I never heard such a din!'

Liking a compliment to be oblique, she'd squeezed his arm as she drew him inside.

This evening however James was less than halfway down the lane when at the other end he saw Myra appear at the wicket gate. If she hadn't been bareheaded he'd have thought she was going out!

'Myra?' he called in some dismay.

She laughed as she came to meet him. 'I heard your footsteps,' she said. 'I told you! I always do.'

'From this distance?'

She took his arm and smiled up at him. 'That's nothing! It's a wonder I don't hear you walking down the country road to get the bus.' She matched her step with his. Normally he hated to be linked, but with Myra it seemed to denote equality, not dependence. Suddenly she unlinked her arm. 'Well, I may as well confess something,' she said more seriously. 'This evening I was listening for you. I was expecting you.'

They had reached the big wooden gate of the mews and James, glancing in through the open wicket across the courtyard, was startled to see, through the enormous window by which she had replaced the doors of the coach-house, that the little table at which they ate was indeed set up, and with places laid for two! She wasn't joking then? An unpleasant thought crossed his mind — was she expecting someone else? But reading his mind, Myra shook her head.

'Only you, James.'

'I don't understand —'

'Neither do I!' she said quickly. 'I *was* expecting you though. And I ordered our trays!' Here she wrinkled her nose in a funny way she had. 'I made the order a bit more conservative than usual. No prawns!' He understood at once. He loved prawns. 'So you see,' she continued, 'if my oracle failed, and you didn't come, the food would do for sandwiches tomorrow. As you know, I'm no use at hotting up left-overs. It smacks too much of —'

He knew. He knew.

'Too wifey,' he smiled. And she smiled. This was the word they'd ear-marked to describe a certain type of woman they both abhorred.

'You could always have fed the prawns to the cat next door,' James said. 'Whenever I'm coming he's sitting on the wall smacking his lips.'

'But James,' she said, and suddenly she stopped smiling, 'he doesn't know when you're coming — any more than me!'

'Touché,' James admitted to being caught out there. He wasn't really good at smart remarks. 'Ah well, it's a lucky cat who knows there's an even chance of a few prawns once or twice a month. That's more than most cats can count on.' Bending his head he followed her in through the wicket. 'Some cats have to put up with a steady diet of shepherd's pie and meat loaf.'

They were inside now, and he sank down on the sofa. Myra, who was still standing, shuddered.

'What would I do if you were the kind of man who *did* like shepherd's pie?' she said. 'I'm sure there are such men.' But she couldn't keep up the silly chaff. 'I think maybe I'd love you enough to try and make it' she laughed, '— if I could. I don't honestly think I'd be able. The main thing is that you are *not* that type. Let's stop fooling. Here, allow me to give you a kiss of gratitude — for being you.'

Lightly she laid her cheek against his, while he for his part took her hand and stroked it.

It was one of the more exquisite pleasures she gave him, the touch of her cool skin. His own hands had a tendency to get hot although he constantly wiped them with his handkerchief. He had always preferred being too cold to being too hot. Once or twice when he had a headache — which was not often — Myra had only to place her hand on his forehead for an instant and the throbbing ceased. This evening he didn't have a headache but all the same he liked the feel of her hand on his face.

'Do that again,' he said.

'How about fixing the drinks first?' she said.

That was his job. But he did not want to release her hand, and he made no attempt to stand up. Unfortunately just then there was a rap on the gate.

'Oh bother,' he said.

'It's only the Catering Service,' Myra said, and for a minute he didn't get the joke. She laughed then and he noticed she meant the grubby little pot-boy who brought the trays around from the café.

'Let me get them,' he said, but she had jumped up and in a minute she was back with them.

'I must tell you,' she said. 'You know the man who owns the café? Well, he gave me such a dressing-down this morning when I was ordering these.' James raised his eyebrows as he held open the door of the kitchenette to let her through. 'Just bring me the warming plate, will you please, James,' she said interrupting herself. 'I'll pop the food on it for a second while we have our little drink.' She glanced at her watch. 'Oh, it's quite early still.' She looked back at him. 'But you were a little later than usual, I think, weren't you?'

'I don't think so,' he said vaguely, as he fitted the plug of the food-warmer into the socket. 'If anything, I think I was a bit earlier. But I could be wrong. When one has time to kill it's odd how often one ends up being late in the end!'

'Time to kill?'

She looked puzzled. Then she seemed to understand. 'Oh James. You make me tired. You're so punctilious. Haven't I told you a thousand times that you don't have to be polite with me? If your bus got in early you should have come straight to the flat! Killing time indeed! Standing on ceremony, eh?'

He handed her her drink.

'You were telling me something about the proprietor of the café — that he was unpleasant about something? You weren't serious?'

'Oh that! Of course not.'

Yet for some reason he was uneasy. 'Tell me,' he said authoritatively.

Naturally, she complied. 'He was really very nice,' she said. 'He intended phoning me. He just wanted to say there was no need to wash the plates before sending them back. I'm to hand them to the messenger in the morning just as they are — and not *attempt* to wash them.' Knowing how fastidious she was, James was about to pooh-pooh the suggestion, but she forestalled him. 'I can wrap them up in the napkins, and then I won't be affronted by the sight. And I need feel under no compliment to the café — it's in their own interests as much as in mine. They have a big washing-machine — I've seen it — with a special compartment like a dentist's sterilization cabinet, and of course they couldn't be sure that a customer would wash them properly. You can imagine the cat's lick some women would give them!'

James could well imagine it. He shuddered. Myra might hate housework, but anything she undertook she did to perfection. Unexpectedly she held out her glass.

'Let's have another drink,' she said. They seldom took more than one. 'Sit down,' she commanded. 'Let's be devils for once.' This time though she sat on the sofa and swung her feet up on it so he had to sit in the chair opposite. 'There's nothing that makes the ankles ache like thinking too hard,' she said.

James didn't really understand what she meant but he laughed happily.

'Seriously!' she said. 'I am feeling tired this evening. I'm so glad you came. I think maybe I worked extra hard this morning because I was looking forward to seeing you later. Oh, I'm so glad you came, James. I would have been bitterly disappointed if you hadn't showed up.'

James felt a return of his earlier uneasiness.

'I'm afraid that premonition of yours is more than I can understand,' he said, but he spoke patiently, because she was not a woman who had to be humoured. 'As a matter of fact I never had less intention of coming to town. I'd already lit the fire in my study when I suddenly took the notion. I had to put the fire out!'

At that, Myra left down her glass and swung her feet back on to the floor.

'What time did you leave?' she asked, and an unusually crisp note in her voice took him unawares.

'I thought I told you,' he said apologetically, although there was nothing for which to apologize. 'I came on the morning bus.'

'Oh!' It was only one word, but it fell oddly on his ears. She reached for her drink again then, and swallowed it down. Somehow that too bothered him. 'Is that what you meant by having to kill time?' she asked.

'Well —' he began, not quite knowing what to say. He took up his own drink and let it down fairly fast for him.

'Oh, don't bother to explain,' she said. 'I think you will agree though it would have been a nice gesture to have lifted a phone and let me know you were in town and coming here tonight.'

'But —'

'No buts about it. You knew I'd be here waiting whether you came or not. Isn't that it?'

'Myra!'

He hardly recognized her in this new mood. Fortunately the next moment she was her old self again.

'Oh James, forgive me. It's just that you've *no* idea — simply *no* idea — how much it meant to me tonight to know in advance —' She stopped and carefully corrected herself '— to have had that curious feeling — call it instinct if you like — that you were coming. It made such a difference to my whole day. But now —' Her face clouded over, '— to think that instead of just having had a hunch about it, I could have known for certain. Oh, if only you'd been more thoughtful, James.' Sitting up straighter she looked him squarely in the eye. 'Or were you going somewhere else and changed your mind?'

What a foolish question.

'As if I ever go anywhere else!'

Her fact brightened a bit at that, but not much.

'You'll hardly believe it,' she said after a minute, 'but I could have forgiven you more easily if you had been going somewhere else, and coming here *was* an afterthought. It would have excused you more.'

Excused? What was all this about? He must have looked absolutely bewildered, because she pulled herself up.

'Oh James, please don't mind me.' She leant forward and laid a hand on his knee. 'Your visits give me such joy — I don't need to tell you that — I ought to be content with what I have. Not knowing in advance is one of the little deprivations that I just have to put up with, I suppose.'

But now James was beginning to object strongly to the way she was putting everything. He stood up. As if his doing so unnerved her, she stood up too.

'It may seem a small thing to ask from you, James, but I repeat what I said — you could have phoned me.' Then, as if that wasn't bad enough, she put it into the future tense. 'If you would only try, once in a while, to give me a ring, even from the bus depot, so I could —'

'— could what?' James couldn't help the coldness in his voice, although considering the food that was ready on the food-warmer, his question, he knew, was ungenerous. On the other hand he felt it was absolutely necessary to keep himself detached, if the evening was not to be spoiled. He forced himself to speak sternly. 'Much as I enjoy our little meals together, it's not for the food I come here, Myra. You must know that.' He very, very nearly added that in any case he paid for his own tray, but when he looked at her he saw she had read these unsaid words from his eyes. He reddened. There was an awkward silence. Yet when she spoke she ignored everything he had said and harked back to what she herself had said.

'Wouldn't it be a very small sacrifice to make, James, when one thinks of all the sacrifices I've made for you? And over so many years?' Her words, which to him were exasperating beyond belief, seemed to drown her in a torrent of self-pity. 'So many, many years,' she whispered.

It was only ten.

'You'd think it was a lifetime,' he said irritably. Her face flushed.

'What is a lifetime, James?' she asked, and when he made no reply she helped him out. 'Remember it is not the same for a woman as for a man. *You* may think of yourself as a young blade, but I . . .'

She faltered again, as well she might, and bit her lip. She wasn't going to cry, was she? James was appalled. Nothing had ever before happened that could conceivably have given rise to tears, but it was an unspoken law with them that a woman should never shed tears in public. Not just unspoken either. On one occasion years ago she herself had been quite explicit about it.

'We do cry sometimes, we women, poor weaklings that we are. But I hope I would never be foolish enough to cry in the presence of a man. And to do it to you of all people, James, would be despicable.' At the time he'd wondered why she singled him out. Did she think him more sensitive than most? He'd been about to ask when she'd given one of her witty twists to things. 'If I did, I'd have you snivelling too in no time,' she said.

Yet here she was now, for no reason at all, on the brink of tears, and apparently making no effort to fight them back.

Myra was making no effort to stem her tears because she did not know she was crying. She really did despise tears. But now it seemed to her that perhaps she'd been wrong in always hiding her feelings. Other women had the courage to cry. Even in public too. She'd seen them at parties. And recently she'd seen a woman walking along the street in broad daylight with tears running down her cheeks, not bothering to wipe them away. Thinking of such women, she wondered if she perhaps had sort of — she paused to find the right word — sort of denatured herself for James?

Denatured: it was an excellent word. She'd have liked to use it then and there but she had just enough sense left to keep it to herself for the moment. Some other time when they were talking about someone else, she would bring it out and impress him. She must not forget the word.

When Myra's thoughts returned to James she felt calmer about him. He was not unkind. He was not cruel — the opposite in fact. What had gone wrong this evening was more her fault than his. When they'd first met she had sensed deep down in him a capacity for the normal feelings of friendship and love. Yet throughout the years she had consistently deflected his feelings away from herself and consistently encouraged him to seal them off. Tonight it seemed that his emotional capacity was completely dried up. Despair overcame her. She'd never change him now. He was fixed in his faults, cemented into his barren way of life. Tears gushed into her eyes again but this time she leant her head back quickly to try and prevent them rolling down, but they brimmed over and splashed down on her hands.

'Oh James, I'm sorry,' she whispered, but she saw her apology was useless; the damage was done. Then her heart hardened. What harm? She wasn't really sorry. Not for him anyway. Oh, not for him. It was for herself she was sorry.

Grasping at a straw then, she tried to tell herself, nothing was ever too late. Perhaps tonight some lucky star had stood still in the sky over her head and forced her to be true to herself for once. James would see the real woman for a change. Oh, surely he would? And surely he would come over and put his arm around her. He would: he would. She waited.

When he did not move, and did not utter a single word, she had to look up.

'Oh no!' she cried. For what she saw in his eyes was ice. 'Oh James, have you no heart? What you have done to me is unspeakable! Yet you can't even pity me!'

James spoke at last. 'And what, Myra, what may I ask, have I done to you?'

'You have —' She stopped, and for one second she thought she'd have control enough to bite back the word, but she hadn't. 'You have denatured me,' she said.

Oh God, what had she done *now*? Clapping her hands over her mouth too late, she wondered if she could pretend to some other meaning in the words. Instead, other words gushed out, words worse and more hideous. Hearing them she herself could not understand where they came from. It was as if, out of the corners of the room she was being prompted by the voices of all the women in the world who'd ever been let down, or fancied themselves badly treated. The room vibrated with their whispers. Go on, they prompted. Tell him what you think of him. Don't let him get away with it. He has got off long enough. To stop the voices she stuck her fingers into her ears, but the voices only got louder. She had to shout them down. She saw James's lips were moving, trying to say something, but she could not hear him with all the shouting. When she finally caught a word or two of what he said she herself stopped trying to penetrate the noise. Silence fell. She saw James go limp with relief.

'What did you say? I — I didn't hear you,' she gulped.

'I said that if that's the way you feel, Myra, there's nothing for me to do but to leave.'

She stared at him. He was going over to the clothes' rack and was taking down his coat. What had got into them? How had they become involved in this vulgar scene? She had to stop him. If he went away like this would he ever come back? A man of his disposition? Could she take him back? Neither of them was of a kind to gloss over things and leave them unexplained knowing that unexplained they could erupt again — and again. Something had been brought to light that could never be forced back underground. Better all the same to let their happiness dry up if it must, than be blasted out of existence like this in one evening. Throwing out her arms she ran blindly towards him.

'James, I implore you. James! James! Don't let this happen to us.' She tried to enclose him with her arms, but somehow he evaded her and reached to take his gloves from the lid of the gramophone. Next thing she knew he'd be at the door.

'Do you realize what you're doing?' She pushed past him and ran to the door pressing her back against it, and throwing out her arms to either side. It was an outrageous gesture of crucifixion, and she knew she was acting out of character. She was making another and more frightful mistake. 'If you walk out this door, you'll never come through it again, James.'

All he did was try to push her to one side, not roughly, but not gently.

'James! Look at me!'

But what he said then was so humiliating she wanted to die.

'I am looking, Myra,' he said.

There seemed nothing left to do but hit him. She thumped at his chest with her closed fists. That made him stand back all right. She had achieved that at least! If she was not going to get a chance to undo the harm she'd done, then she'd go the whole hog and let him think the worst of her. She was ashamed to think she had been about to renege on herself. She flung out her arms again, not hysterically this time, but with passion, real, real passion. Let him see what he was up against. But whatever he thought, James said nothing. And he'd have to be the one to speak first. Myra couldn't trust herself any more.

In the end, she did have to speak. 'Say something, James,' she pleaded.

'All right,' he said then. 'Be so kind, Myra, as to tell me what you think you're gaining by this performance?' he nodded at her outstretched arms. 'This nailing of yourself to the door like a stoat!'

The look in his eyes was ugly. She let her arms fall at once and running back to the sofa flung herself face down upon it screaming and kicking her feet.

She didn't even hear the door bang after him, or the gate slam.

Outside in the air James regretted that he had not shut the door more gently, but after the coarse and brutal words he had just used it was inconsistent to worry about the small niceties of the miserable business. His ugly words echoed in his mind, and he felt defiled by them. He had an impulse to go back and apologize, if only for his language. Nothing justified that kind of thing from a man. He actually raised his hand to rap on the gate, but he let it fall, overcome by a stronger impulse — to make good his escape. But as he hurried up the lane his unuttered words too seemed base and unworthy — a mean-minded figure of speech — that could only be condoned by the fact that he had been so grievously provoked, and by the overwhelming desire that had been engendered in him to get out in the air. If Myra had not stood aside and let him pass, he'd have used brute force. All the same nothing justified the inference that he was imprisoned. Never, never had she done anything to hold him. Never had he been made captive except perhaps by the pull of her mind upon his mind. He'd always been free to come or go as he chose. If in the flat they had become somewhat closed in of late it was from expediency — from not wanting to run into stupid people. If they had gone out to restaurants or cafés nowadays some fool would be sure to blunder over and join them, reducing their evening to the series of banalities that passed for conversation with most people. No, no, the flat was never a prison. Never. It was their nest. And now he'd fallen out of the nest. Or worse still been pushed out. All of a sudden James felt frightened. Was it possible she had meant what she said? Could it be that he would never again be able to go back there? Nonsense. She was hysterical.

He stood for a minute considering again whether he should not perhaps go back? Not that he'd relish it. But perhaps he ought to do so — in the interests of the future. No, he decided. Better give her time to calm down. Another evening would be preferable. If necessary he'd be prepared to come up again tomorrow evening. Or later this same evening? That would be more sensible. He looked back. She must be in a bad state when she hadn't run out after him. Normally she'd come to the gate and stay standing in the lane until he was out of sight. Even in the rain.

James shook his head. What a pity. If she'd come to the gate he could have raised his hands or something, given some sign — the merest indication would be enough — of his forgiveness. He could have let her see he bore no rancour. But the gesture would not want to be ambiguous. Not a wave; that would be overcordial, and he didn't want her stumbling up the lane after him. No more fireworks thank you! But it would not want to appear final either. A raised hand would have been the best he could do at that time. He was going to walk on again when it occurred to him that if he'd gone back he need not have gone inside. Just a few words at the gate, but on the whole it was probably better to wait till she'd calmed down. Then he could safely take some of the blame, and help her to save face. Fortunately he did not have the vanity that, in another man, might make such a course impossible. It was good for the soul sometimes to assume blame — even wrongly. James immediately felt better, less bottled up. He walked on. But he could not rid his thoughts of the ugly business. He ought to have known that no woman on earth but was capable, at some time or another, of a lapse like Myra's. And Myra, of course, was a woman. How lacking he'd been in foresight. He'd have to go more carefully with her in future. Next time they met, although he would not try to exonerate himself from the part he'd played in the regrettable scene, at the same time it would not be right to rob her of the therapeutic effects of taking her share of the blame. He felt sure that, being fair-minded people, both of them, they would properly apportion the blame.

Anyway he resolved to put the whole thing out of his mind until after he'd eaten. To think he'd eaten nothing since morning! After he'd had some food he'd be better able to handle the situation.

James had reached the other end of the lane now and gone out under the arch into Baggot Street again. Where would he eat? He'd better head towards the centre of the city. It ought not to be as difficult as it had been at midday, although an evening meal in town could be quite expensive. He didn't want a gala-type dinner, but not some awful slop either that would sicken him. He was feeling bad. The tension had upset his stomach and he was not sure whether he was experiencing hunger pangs or physical pain. Damn Myra. If she'd been spoiling for a fight, why the devil hadn't she waited till after their meal? She'd say this was more of his male selfishness, but if they had eaten they'd have been better balanced and might not have had a row at all. What a distasteful word — the word row! Yet, that's what it was — a common row. James came to a stand again. He wouldn't think twice of marching back and banging on the gate and telling her to stop her nonsense and put the food on the table. She was probably heartbroken. But if that was the case she'd have come to the door with her face flushed and her hair in disorder. Sobered by such a distasteful picture he walked on. He could not possibly subject her to humiliation like that. It would be his duty to protect her from exposing herself further. Perhaps he'd write her a note and post it in the late-fee box at the G.P.O. before he got the bus for home. She'd have it first thing in the morning, and after a good night's sleep she might be better able to take what he had to say. He began to compose the letter.

'*Dear Myra* —' But he'd skip the beginning: that might be sticky. He'd have to give that careful thought. The rest was easy. Bits and pieces of sentences came readily to his mind — '*We must see to it that, like the accord that has always existed between us, discord too, if it should arise, must be* —'

That was the note to sound. He was beginning to feel his old self again. He probably ought to make reference to their next meeting? Not too soon — this to strike a cautionary note — but it might not be wise to let too much time pass either —

'*because, Myra, the most precious element of our friendship* —'

No, that didn't sound right. After tonight's scene, friendship didn't appear quite the right word. A new colouring had been given to their relationship by their tiff. But here James cursed under his breath. Tiff. Such a word! What next? Where were these trite words coming from? She'd rattled him all right. Damn it. Oh damn it.

James abandoned the letter for a moment when he realized he had been plunging along without regard to where he was headed. Where would he eat? There used to be a nice quiet little place in Molesworth Street, nearly opposite the National Library. It was always very crowded but with quite acceptable sorts from the library or the Arts School. He made off down Kildare Street.

When James reached the café in Molesworth Street however and saw the padlock on the area railings, he belatedly remembered it was just a coffee-shop, run by voluntary aid for some charitable organization, and only open mornings. He stood, stupidly staring at the padlock. Where would he go now? He didn't feel like traipsing all over the city. Hadn't there been talk some time ago about starting a canteen in the National Library? Had that got under way? He looked across the street. An old gentleman was waddling in the Library gate with his brief case under his arm. James strode after him.

But just as he'd got to the entrance, the blasted porter slammed the big iron gate — almost in his face. He might have had his nose broken.

'Sorry, sir. The Library is closed. Summer holidays, sir.'

'But you just let in someone! I saw that man —'

James glared after the old man who was now ambling up the steps to the reading room.

'The gentleman had a pass, sir,' the porter said. 'There's a skeleton staff on duty in the stacks and the Director always gives out a few permits to people doing important research.' The fellow was more civil now. 'It's only fair, sir. It wouldn't do, sir, would it, to refuse people whose work is —' But here he looked closer at James and, recognizing him, his civility changed into servility. 'I beg you pardon, Professor,' he said. 'I didn't recognize you, sir. I would have thought you'd have applied for a permit. Oh dear, oh dear!' The man actually wrung his hands — 'if it was even yesterday, I could have got hold of the Director on the phone, but he's gone away — out of the country too I understand.'

'Oh, that's all right,' James said, somewhat mollified by being recognized and remembered. He was sorry that he, in turn, could not recall the porter's name. 'That's all right,' he repeated. 'I wasn't going to use the library anyway. I thought they might have opened that canteen they were talking about some time back —?'

'Canteen, sir? When was that?' The fellow had clearly never heard of the project. He was looking at James as if he was Lazarus come out of the tomb.

'No matter. Good evening!' James said curtly, and he walked away. Then, although he had never before in his life succumbed to the temptation of talking to himself, now, because it was so important, he put himself a question out loud.

'Have I lost touch with Dublin?' he asked. And he had to answer simply and honestly. 'I have.' He should have known the library was always closed this month. If only there was a friend on whom he could call. But he'd lost touch with his friends too.

He looked around. There used to be a few eating places in this vicinity, or rather he could have sworn there were. It hardly seemed possible they were *all* closed down. Where on earth did people eat in Dublin nowadays? They surely didn't go to the hotels? In his day the small hotels were always given over at night to political rallies or football clubs. And the big hotels were out of the question. Not that he'd look into the cost at this stage. He stopped. If it was anywhere near time for his bus he wouldn't think twice of going straight back without eating at all.

It was all very well for Myra. She ate hardly anything anyway. He often felt that as far as food went, their meal together meant nothing to her. Setting up that damned unsteady card-table, and laying out those silly plates of hers shaped like vine leaves and too small to hold enough for a bird. They reminded him of when his sisters used to make him play babby-house.

Passing Trinity College, James saw there was still two hours to go before his bus, but it was just on the hour. There might be a bus going to Cavan? The Cavan bus passed through Garlow Cross, only a few miles from the cottage. How about taking that? He'd taken it once years ago, and although he was younger and fitter in those days, he was tempted to do it. His stomach was so empty it was almost caving in, but he doubted if he could eat anything now. He felt sickish. He might feel better after sitting in the bus. And better anything than hanging about the city.

At that moment on Aston Quay James saw the Cavan bus. It was filling up with passengers, and the conductor and driver, leaning on the parapet of the Liffey, were taking a last smoke. James was about to dash across the street, but first he dashed into a sweet shop to buy a bar of chocolate, or an apple. The sensation in his insides was like something gnawing at his guts. He got an apple and a bar of chocolate as well, but he nearly missed the bus. Very nearly. The driver was at the wheel and the engine was running. James had to put on a sprint to get across the street, and even then the driver was pulling on the big steering wheel and swivelling the huge wheels outward into the traffic before putting the bus in motion. James jumped on the step.

'Dangerous that, sir,' said the younger conductor.

'You hadn't begun to move!' James replied testily,

while he stood on the platform getting his breath back.

'Could have jerked forward sir. Just as you were stepping up!'

'You think a toss would finish me off, eh?' James said. He meant the words to be ironical, but his voice hadn't been lighthearted enough to carry off the joke.

The conductor didn't smile. 'Never does any of us any good, sir, at any age.'

James looked at him with hatred. The fellow was thin and spectacled. Probably the over-conscientious sort. Feeling no inclination to make small talk he lurched into the body of the bus, and sat down on the nearest seat. He was certainly glad to be off his feet. He hadn't noticed until now how they ached. Such a day. Little did he think setting off that it would be a case of About Turn and Quick March.

James slumped down in his seat, but when he felt the bulge of the apple in his pocket he brightened up, and was about to take it out when he was overcome by a curious awkwardness with regard to the conductor. Instead, keeping his hand buried in his pocket he broke off a piece of the chocolate and surreptitiously put it into his mouth. He would nearly have been too tired to chew the apple. He settled back on the seat and tried to doze. But now Myra's words kept coming back. They were repeating on him, like indigestion.

To think she should taunt him with how long they'd known each other? Wasn't it a good thing they'd been able to put up with each other for so long? What else but time had cemented their relationship? As she herself had once put it, very aptly, they'd invested a lot in each other. Well, as far as he was concerned she could have counted on *her* investment to the end. Wasn't it their credo that it didn't take marriage lines to bind together people of their integrity. He had not told her, not in so many words — from delicacy — but he had made provision for her in his will. He'd been rather proud of the way he'd worded the bequest too, putting in a few lines of appreciation that were, he thought, gracefully, but more important, tactfully expressed.

Oh, why had she doubted him? Few wives could be as sure of their husbands as she of him — but he had to amend this — as she *ought* to be, because clearly she had set no value on his loyalty. What was that she'd said about the deprivations she'd suffered? '*One of the many deprivations!*' Those might not have been her exact words, but that was more or less what she'd implied. What had come over her? He shook his head. Had they not agreed that theirs was the perfect solution for facing into the drearier years of ageing and decay? That dreary time was not imminent, of course, but alas it would inevitably come. The process of ageing was not attractive, and they both agreed that if they were continually together — well, really married for instance — the afflictions of age would be doubled for them. On the other hand, with the system they'd worked out, neither saw anything but what was best, and best preserved, in the other. As the grosser aspects of age became discernible, if they could not conceal them from themselves, at least they could conceal them from each other. To put it flatly, if they had been married a dozen times over, that would still be the way he'd want things to be at the end. It was disillusioning now to find she had not seen eye to eye with him on this. Worse still, she'd gone along with him and paid lip-service to his ideals while underneath she must all the time have dissented.

Suddenly James sat bolt upright. That word she used: deprivation. She couldn't have meant that he'd done her out of children? What a thought! Surely it was unlikely that she could have had a child even when they first met? What age was she then? Well, perhaps not too old but surely to God she was at an age when she couldn't have fancied putting herself in *that* condition? And what about all the cautions that were given now on the danger of late conception? How would *she* like to be saddled with a retarded child? Why, it was her who first told him about recent medical findings! And — wait a minute — that was early in their acquaintance too, if he remembered rightly. He could recall certain particulars of the conversation. They had been discussing her work, and the demands it made on her. She was, of course, aware from the first that *he* never wanted children, that he abhorred the thought of a houseful of brats, crawling everywhere, and dribbling and spitting out food. They overran a place. As for the smell of wet diapers about a house, it nauseated him. She'd pulled him up on that though.

'Not soiled diapers, James. The most slovenly woman in the world has more self-respect than to leave dirty diapers lying about. But I grant you there often is a certain odour — I've found it myself at times in the homes of my friends, and it has surprised me, I must say — but it comes from *clean* diapers hanging about to air. At worst it's the smell of steam. They have to be boiled you know.' She made a face. 'I agree with you, though. It's not my favourite brand of perfume.'

Those were her very words. If he were to be put in the dock at this moment he could swear to it. Did that sound like a woman who wanted a family? Yet tonight she had insinuated — James was so furious he

clenched his hands and dug his feet into the floor-boards as if the bus were about to hurtle over the edge of an abyss and he could put a brake on it.

Then he thought of something else: something his sister Kay had said.

It was the time Myra had had to go into hospital for a few weeks. Nothing serious, she'd said. Nothing to worry about, or so she'd told him. Just a routine tidying up job that most people — presumably she meant women — thought advisable. Naturally he'd encouraged her to get it over and done with: not to put it on the long finger. The shocking thing was how badly it had shaken her. He was appalled at how frightful she'd looked for months afterwards. Finally the doctors ordered her to take a good holiday, although it hadn't been long since her summer holidays. She hadn't gone away that summer, except for one long week-end in London, but she'd packed up her work and he'd gone up more often. But the doctor was insistent that this time she was to go away. Oddly enough, her going away had hit him harder than her going into hospital. If they could have gone away together it would have been different. That, of course, was impossible. There was no longer a spot on the globe where one mightn't run the risk of bumping into some busybody from Dublin.

'What will I do while you're away?' he'd asked.

'Why don't you come up here as usual,' she suggested, 'except you need order only one tray.'

But she over-estimated the charm of the flat for its own sake. And he told her so.

'Nonsense,' she said. 'Men are like cats and dogs; it's their habitat they value, not the occupants.'

'I'll tell you what I'll do,' he said finally. 'I'll come up the day you're coming back and I'll have a fire lit — how about that?'

'Oh James, you are a dear. It would make me so glad to be coming back.'

'I should hope you'd be glad to be coming back anyway?'

'Oh yes, but you must admit it would be extra special to be coming back to find you here — in our little nest.'

There! James slapped his knee. *That* was where he'd got the word nest. He had to hand it to her; she was very ingenious in avoiding the word 'home'. She was at her best when it came to these small subtleties other people overlooked. And the day she was due back he had fully intended to be in the flat before her, were it not for a chance encounter with his sister Kay and a remark of hers that upset him.

Kay knew all about Myra. Whether she approved of her or not James did not know: Kay and himself were too much alike to embarrass each other by confidences. That was why he found what she said that day so extraordinary.

'Very sensible of her to go away,' Kay had said, 'otherwise it takes a long time, I believe, to recover from that beastly business.' Beastly business? What did she mean? Unlike herself, Kay had gone on and on. 'Much messier than childbirth I understand. Also, I've heard, James, that it's worse for an unmarried woman —' she paused — 'I mean a childless woman.' Then feeling — as well she might — that she'd overstepped herself, she looked at her watch. 'I'll have to fly,' she said. And perhaps to try and excuse her indiscretion she resorted to something else that was rare for Kay — banality. 'It's sort of the end of the road for them, I suppose,' she said, before she hurried away leaving him confused and dismayed.

He had never bothered to ask Myra what her operation had been. He didn't see that it concerned him. At any age there were certain danger zones for a woman that had to be kept under observation. But what if it had been a hysterectomy! Was that any business of his? Medically speaking, it wasn't all that different from any other ectomy — tonsillectomy, appendectomy. What was so beastly about it? If it came to that, the most frightful mess of all was getting one's antrums cleaned out. He knew all about *that*. Anyway the whole business was outside his province. Or at least he had thought so then.

Then, then, then. But now, now it was as if he'd been asked to stand up and testify to something. It was most unfair. Myra herself had never arraigned him. Neither before nor after. Admittedly he had not given her much encouragement. But he could have sworn that she herself hadn't given a damn at the time. Ah, but — and this was the rub, the whole business could have bred resentment, could have rankled within her and gone foetid. Considered in this new light the taunts she had flung at him tonight could no longer be put down to hysteria and written off — something long festering had suppurated. He put his hand to his head. Dear God, to think she had allowed him to bask all those years in a fool's paradise!

He closed his eyes. Thank heavens he hadn't demeaned himself by going back to try and patch things up. He'd left the way open should he decide to sever the bond completely. Perhaps he ought to sever it, if only on the principle that if a person once tells you a lie, that puts an end to truth between you forever. A lie always made him feel positively sick. And God knows he felt sick enough as it was. There was a definite burning sensation now in his chest as well as his stomach. He looked around the steamy bus. Could it be the fumes of the engine that were affecting him? He'd have liked to go and stand on the platform to get some fresh air, but he hated to make himself noticeable, although the bus was now nearly empty. He stole a look at the other passengers to see if anyone was watching him. He might have been muttering to himself, or making peculiar faces. Just to see if anyone would notice he stealthily, but deliberately, made a face into the window, on which the steam acted like a backing of mercury. And sure enough the damn conductor was looking straight at him. James felt he had to give the fellow a propitiating grin, which the impudent fellow took advantage of immediately.

'Not yet, sir,' he said. 'I'll tell you when you're there!'

Officious again. Well, smart as he was, he didn't know his countryside. Clearing a space on the foggy glass, James looked out. It was getting dark outside now but the shape of the trees could still be seen against the last light in the west. The conductor was wrong! They *were* there! He jumped to his feet.

'Not yet, sir,' the blasted fellow called out again, and loudly this time for all to hear.

Ignoring him, James staggered down the bus to the boarding-platform, where, without waiting for the conductor to do it, he defiantly hit the bell to bring the bus to a stop. The fellow merely shrugged his shoulders. James threw an angry glance at him, and then, although the bus had not quite stopped, deliberately and only taking care to face the way the bus was travelling so that if he did fall it would be less dangerous, he jumped off.

Luckily he did not fall. He felt a bit shaken, as he regained his balance precariously on the dark road, he was glad to think he had spiked that conductor. He could tell he had by the smart way the fellow hit the bell again and set the bus once more in motion, that for all his solicitude on the Quays, he'd hardly have noticed if one had fallen on one's face on the road: or cared.

And Myra? If Myra were to read a report of the accident in the newspaper tomorrow, how would *she* feel? More interesting still — what would she tell her friends? Secretive as their relationship was supposed to be, James couldn't help wondering if she might not have let the truth leak out to some people. Indeed, this suspicion had lurked in his mind for some time, but he only fully faced it now.

What about those phone calls she sometimes got? Those times when she felt it necessary to plug out the phone and carry it into her bedroom? Or else talk in a lowered voice, very different from the normal way in which she'd call out 'wrong number' and bang down the receiver? Now that he thought about it, the worst give-away was when she'd let the phone ring and ring without answering it at all. It nearly drove him mad listening to that ringing.

'What will they think, Myra?' he'd cry. When she used to say the caller would think she was out, he nearly went demented altogether at her lack of logic.

'They wouldn't keep on ringing if they didn't suspect you were here,' he exploded once.

Ah! The insidiousness of her answer hadn't fully registered at the time. *Now* it did though.

'Oh, they'll understand.' That was what she'd said.

Understand what? He could only suppose she had given her friends some garbled explanation of things.

'Oh damn her! Damn her!' he said out loud again. There was no reason now why he shouldn't talk out loud or shout if he liked here on the lonely country road. 'Damn, damn,' he shouted. 'Damn, damn, damn!'

Immediately James felt uncomfortable. What if there was someone listening? A few yards ahead, to the left, there was a lighted window. But suddenly he was alerted to something odd. There should not be a light on the left. The shop at the crossroads should be on the other side. He looked around. Could that rotten little conductor have been right? Had he got off too soon? Perhaps that was why the fellow had hit that bell so smartly? To give him no time to discover his mistake?

For clearly he *had* made a mistake, and a bloody great one. He peered into the darkness. But the night was too black, he could see nothing. He had no choice but to walk on.

By the time James had passed the cottage with the lighted window, his eyes were getting more used to the dark. All the same when a rick of hay reared up to one side of the road it might have been a mountain! Where was he at all? And a few seconds later when unexpectedly the moon slipped out from behind the clouds and glinted on the tin roof of a shed in the distance it might have been the sheen of a lake for all he recognized of his whereabouts. Just then, however, he caught sight of the red tail light of the bus again. It had only disappeared because the bus had dipped into a valley. It was now climbing out of the dip again, and going up a steep hill. Ah! he knew that hill. He wasn't as far off his track as he thought. Only a quarter of a mile or so, but he shook his head. In his present state that was about enough to finish him. Still, things could have been worse.

Meanwhile a wisp of vapoury cloud had come between the moon and the earth and in a few minutes it was followed by a great black bank of cloud. Only

for a thin green streak in the west it would have been pitch dark again. This streak shed no light on his way but it acted on James like a sign, an omen.

He passed the hayrick. He passed the tin shed. But now another mass of blackness rose up to the left and came between him and the sky. It even hid the green streak this time though he was able to tell by a sudden resinous scent in the air and a curious warmth that the road was passing through a small wood. His spirits rose at once. These were the trees he could see from his cottage. Immediately, his mistake less disastrous, the distance lessened. If only that conductor could know how quickly he had got his bearings! The impudent fellow probably thought he'd left him properly stranded. And perhaps as much to spite the impudent fellow as anything else, when at that instant a daring thought entered his mind and he gave it heed. What if he were to cut diagonally across this wood? It could save him half a mile. It would actually be putting his mistake to work for him.

'What about it, James? Come on. Be a sport,' he jovially exhorted himself.

And seeing that his green banner was again faintly discernible through the dark trees, he called on it to be his lodestar, and scrambled up on the grass bank that separated the road from the wood.

James was in the wood before it came home to him that of course this must be Asigh wood — it must belong to the Balfes! No matter. Why should he let that bother him? The wood was nowhere near their house as far as he remembered its position by daylight. It was composed mostly of neglected, self-seeded trees, more scrub than timber — almost waste ground — ground that had probably deteriorated into commonage.

As he advanced into the little copse — wood was too grand a designation for it — James saw it was not as dense as it seemed from the road, or else at this point there was a pathway through it. Probably it was a short cut well known to the locals, because even in the dark, he thought he saw sodden cigarette packets on the ground, and there were toffee wrappers and orange peels lodged in the bushes. Good signs.

Further in, however, his path was unexpectedly blocked by a fallen tree. It must have been a long time lying on the ground because when he put his hand on it to climb over, it was wet and slimy. He quickly withdrew his hand in disgust. He'd have to make his way round it.

The path was not very well defined on the other side of the log. It looked as if people did not after all penetrate this far. The litter at the edge of the wood had probably been left by children. Or by lovers who only wanted to get out of sight of the road? Deeper in, the scrub was thicker, and in one place he mistook a strand of briar for barbed wire it was so tough and hard to cut through. You'd need wire clippers!

James stopped. Was it foolhardy to go on? He'd already ripped the sleeve of his suit. However the pain in his stomach gave him his answer. Nothing that would get him home quicker was foolish.

'Onward, James,' he said wearily.

And then, damn it, he came to another fallen tree. Again, he had to work his way around it. Mind you, he hadn't counted on this kind of thing. The upper branches of this tree spread out over an incredibly wide area. From having to look down, instead of up, he found that — momentarily of course — he'd lost his sense of direction. Fortunately, through the trees, he could take direction from his green banner. Fixing on it, he forged ahead.

But now there were new hazards. At least twice, tree stumps nearly tripped him, and there were now dried ruts that must have been made by timber lorries at some distant date. Lucky he didn't sprain his ankle. He took out his handkerchief and wiped his forehead. At this rate he wouldn't make very quick progress. He was beginning to ache in every limb, and when he drew a breath, a sharp pain ran through him. The pains in his stomach were indistinguishable now from all the other pains in his body. It was like the way a toothache could turn the whole of one's face into one great ache. The thought of turning back plagued him too at every step. Stubbornly, though, he resisted the thought of turning. To go on could hardly be much worse than to go back through those briars?

A second later James got a fall, a nasty fall. Without warning, a crater opened up in front of him and he went head-first into it. Another fallen tree, blown over in a storm evidently, because the great root that had been ripped out of the ground had taken clay and all with it, leaving this gaping black hole. Oh God! He picked himself up and mopped his forehead with his sleeves.

This time he had to make a wide detour. Luckily after that the wood seemed to be thinning out. He was able to walk a bit faster, and so it seemed reasonable to deduce that he might be getting near to the road at the other end. His relief was so great that perhaps that was why he did not pause to take his bearings again, and when he did look up he was shocked to see the green streak in the sky was gone. Or was it? He swung around. No, it was there, but it seemed to have veered around and was now behind him. Did that mean he was going in the wrong direction? Appalled, he leant back against a tree. His legs were giving way under him. He

would not be able to go another step without a rest. And now a new pain had struck him between the shoulders. He felt around with his foot in the darkness looking for somewhere to sit, but all he could feel were wads of soggy leaves from summers dead and gone.

Perhaps it was just as well — if he sat down he might not be able to get up again. Then the matter was taken out of his hands. He was attacked by a fit of dizziness, and his head began to reel. To save himself from falling he dropped down on one knee and braced himself with the palms of his hands against the ground. Bad as he was, the irony of his posture struck him — the sprinter, tensed for the starter's pistol! Afraid of cramp he cautiously got to his feet. And he thought of the times when, as a youngster playing hide and seek, a rag would be tied over his eyes and he would be spun around like a top, so that when the blindfold was removed, he wouldn't know which way to run.

Ah, there was the green light! But how it had narrowed! It was only a thin line now. Still, James lurched towards it. The bushes had got dense again and he was throwing himself against them, as against a crashing wave, while they for their part seemed to thrust him back. Coming to a really thick clump he gathered up enough strength to hurl himself against it, only to find that he went through it as if it was a bank of fog, and sprawled out into another clearing.

Was it the road at last? No. It would have been lighter overhead. Instead a solid mass of blackness towered over him, high as the sky. Were it not for his lifeline of light he would have despaired. As if it too might quench he feverishly fastened his eyes on it. It was not a single line any more. There were three or four lines. Oh God, no? It was a window, a window with a green blind drawn down, that let out only the outline of its light. A house? Oh God, not Balfe's? In absolute panic James turned and with the vigour of frenzy crashed back through the undergrowth in the way he had come. This time the bushes gave way freely before him, but the silence that had pressed so dank upon him was shattered at every step and he was betrayed by the snapping and breaking of twigs. When a briar caught on his sleeve it gave out a deafening rasp. Pricks from a gorse bush bit into his flesh like sparks of fire, but worse still was the prickly heat of shame that ran over his whole body.

'Damn, damn, damn,' he cried, not caring suddenly what noise he made. Why had he run like that? — Like a madman? — Using up his last store of strength? What did he care about anyone or anything if only he could get out of this place? What if it was Balfe's? It was hardly the house? Probably an outbuilding? Or the quarters of a hired hand? Why hadn't he called out?

Sweat was breaking out all over him now and he had to exert a superhuman strength not to let himself fall spent, on the ground, because if he did he'd stay there. He wouldn't be able to get up. To rest for a minute he dropped on one knee again. The pose of the athlete again! Oh, it was a pity Myra couldn't see him, he thought bitterly, but then for a moment he had a crazy feeling that the pose was for real. He found himself tensing the muscles of his face, as if at any minute a real shot would blast-off and he would spring up and dash madly down a grassy sprint-track.

It was then that a new, a terrible, an utterly unendurable pain exploded in his chest.

'God, God!' he cried. His hands under him were riveted to the ground. Had he been standing he would have been thrown. 'What is the matter with me?' he cried. And the question rang out over all the wood. Then, as another spasm went through him other questions were torn from him. Was it a heart attack? A stroke? — In abject terror, not daring to stir, he stayed crouched. 'Ah, Ah, Ahh . . .' The pain again. The pain, the pain, the pain.

'Am I dying?' he gasped, but this time it was the pain that answered, and answered so strangely James didn't understand, because it did what he did not think possible: it catapulted him to his feet, and filled him with a strength that never, never in his life had he possessed. It ran through him like a bar of iron — a stanchion that held his ribs together. He was turned into a man of iron! If he raised his arms now and thrashed about, whole trees would give way before him, and their branches, brittle as glass, would clatter to the ground. 'See Myra! See!' he cried out. So he

had lost his vigour? He'd show her! But he had taken his eyes off the light. Where was it? Had it gone out? 'I told you not to go out,' he yelled at it, and lifting his iron feet he went crashing towards where he had seen it last.

But the next minute he knew there was something wrong. Against his face he felt something wet and cold, and he was almost overpowered by the smell of rank earth and rotting leaves. If he'd fallen he hadn't felt the fall. Was he numbed? He raised his head. He'd have to get help. But when he tried to cry out no sound came.

The light? Where was it. 'Oh, don't go out,' he pleaded to it, as if it was the light of life itself, and to propitiate it, he gave it a name. 'Don't go out, Emmy,' he prayed. Then came the last and most anguished question of all. Was he raving? No, no. It was only a window. But in his head there seemed to be a dialogue of two voices, his own and another that answered derisively 'What window?' James tried to explain that it was the window in the classroom. Hadn't he opened it when the big footballer wasn't able to pull down the sash? He, James, had leant across the desk and brought it down with one strong pull. But where was the rush of sweet summer air? There was only a deathly chill. And where was Emmy?

With a last desperate effort James tried to stop his mind from stumbling and tried to fasten it on Myra. Where was *she*? She wouldn't have failed him. But she *had* failed him. Both of them had failed him. Under a weight of bitterness too great to be borne his face was pressed into the wet leaves, and when he gulped for breath, the rotted leaves were sucked into his mouth.

PATRICK GALVIN
from Patrick Galvin, *The Wood-Burners* (1973)

Patrick Galvin (1927–   ) was born in a slum area of Cork city. He left school at eleven and did various jobs before travelling to London, then to a kibbutz in Israel, and then back to England. His career as a writer includes poetry volumes such as *Christ in London* (1960) and *Man on a Porch* (1980). He has also written plays on the 'troubles' in Northern Ireland (*Nightfall to Belfast*, 1973, and *We Do It For Love*, 1975), and two volumes of autobiography (see p. 1085 below). Here in this group of poems, flushed with whimsicality, Galvin reflects on the Irish, life, death, sex, burning bodies.

THE IRISH

We are at home with death
We, the Irish
Catholic and cradle-born
Lumbered with the Faith.

Each day
A preparation for death
Each hour
A celebration of mystery.

Oh, you
Protestant and Convert
Atheist and foreign-bred
Pray for us.

That we may
Now and in time to come
Be not remembered.
Thus:

Anno Domini.

THE WOOD-BURNERS

Old women are made of wood
Blessed are the wood-burners.

The unicorns of the night have come
And the silver priests and the nuns.
We are the hunters of the dead
Holy holy in the bitter cold.

Black snow and bone crushed in the wind
The world is a ball of solid ice.

It is my thirteenth birthday
And no one writes to me.

My father is here and my stone mother
After us there will be nothing.

Christe! Christe!
Memento Mori.[1]

She lies naked in the snow
Her arms broken and her head shaved

Flowers of blood circle her feet
And her tears anoint us

White nuns open her lips
And the priests possess her

My stone mother bathes her in oil
Under torches of snow.

Christe! Christe!
Memento Mori.

After us there will be nothing
We are the wood-burners.

We drag her body to the hill
And watch it burn.

The fire eats her till noon
And then sleeps.

Only the bones remain
Damp wood under ashes of snow.

Memento Mori
I am me.

The seventh child in the last game
Iesu Christe.

BY NATURE DIFFIDENT

Not being myself to-day
I had but two requests
A glass of wine in my bed
And a naked woman.

I am by nature diffident.

My wife, loving as she is,
Was most obliging
The wine was the best that could be bought
And the sex was riveting.

She is by nature lecherous
And this is useful.

I am now eighty years of age
And flushed with whimsicality.
On odd days like to-day
I am plagued with fantasies

Like young girls running in the wind
Like living in a harem.

My wife stripped to the skin
And danced before me
A bit wide in the hips, I thought,
But deeply satisfying.

I can see now why I married her
She is more than gorgeous.

My knees ache at the joints
And my back torments me
I am not supple
And neither is my wife.

I try hard
But it's difficult to mount.

My wife takes over
She touches me with warm hands
Kisses the old root
And strokes me gently

It is an Easter Rising
Beautiful to behold.

Her breasts close to my mouth
The wine drops cover her belly
Her long hair hangs softly
Between sweating thighs.

We are in rare communion
With her riding on top.

Drawing me to her womb
Sipping honey from my pinnacle of fire.
It is my one desire
To capture Paradise.

Women are more glorious than men
I have always known it.

I am by nature diffident.

1   Church Latin: remember that you have to die, a
     reminder of death. Christe is the vocative case of
     Christus: O Christ.

JAMES SIMMONS
from James Simmons, *West Strand Visions* (1974)

'Claudy' was prompted by a bomb outrage in 1974 and is a moving tribute to the casual victims of the contemporary Northern Ireland troubles. Simmons's focus is on the essential ordinariness of ordinary life in an ordinary country town in the Sperrin Mountains, and then on the interruption to that lifestyle. The rhyming couplets are used to good effect in this song-poem, the repeated thud forcibly simulating the ending of repetition in people's lives. There was no time for last moments or final thoughts, Mrs Brown looking for her cat: 'what's strange about that?' The rhetorical question and the banality of the rhyme draw attention to the inconsequential made consequential because of the actions of the IRA bombers. The poem accumulates images of atrocity until the poet falters: 'And Christ, little Katherine Aiken is dead'.

CLAUDY
for Harry Barton, a song

The Sperrins surround it, the Faughan flows by,
at each end of Main Street the hills and the sky,
the small town of Claudy at ease in the sun
last July in the morning, a new day begun.

How peaceful and pretty if the moment could stop,
McIlhenny is straightening things in his shop,
and his wife is outside serving petrol, and then
a girl takes a cloth to a big window pane.

And McCloskey is taking the weight off his feet,
and McClelland and Miller are sweeping the street,
and, delivering milk at the Beaufort Hotel,
young Temple's enjoying his first job quite well.

And Mrs McLaughlin is scrubbing her floor,
and Artie Hone's crossing the street to a door,
and Mrs Brown, looking around for her cat,
goes off up an entry — what's strange about that?

Not much — but before she comes back to the road
that strange car parked outside her house will explode,
and all of the people I've mentioned outside
will be waiting to die or already have died.

An explosion too loud for your eardrums to bear,
and young children squealing like pigs in the square,
and all faces chalk-white and streaked with bright red,
and the glass and the dust and the terrible dead.

For an old lady's legs are ripped off, and the head
of a man's hanging open, and still he's not dead.
He is screaming for mercy, and his son stands and stares
and stares, and then suddenly, quick, disappears.

And Christ, little Katherine Aiken is dead,
and Mrs McLaughlin is pierced through the head.
Meanwhile to Dungiven the killers have gone,
and they're finding it hard to get through on the phone.

SEAMUS HEANEY
from Seamus Heaney, *North* (1975)

In 1972 Heaney moved from Belfast to Glanmore in County Wicklow, away from the
North to write about the North. Here are three poems from Heaney's most political
volume, *North*, all of them addressing whether directly or obliquely symbols of power,
attitudes to violence and revenge, and the whole issue of Northern Ireland seen
through Catholic nationalist eyes.

PUNISHMENT

I can feel the tug
of the halter at the nape
of her neck, the wind
on her naked front.

It blows her nipples
to amber beads,
it shakes the frail rigging
of her ribs.

I can see her drowned
body in the bog,
the weighing stone,
the floating rods and boughs.

Under which at first
she was a barked sapling
that is dug up
oak-bone, brain-firkin:

her shaved head
like a stubble of black corn,
her blindfold a soiled bandage,
her noose a ring

to store
the memories of love.
Little adulteress,
before they punished you

you were flaxen-haired,
undernourished, and your
tar-black face was beautiful.
My poor scapegoat,

I almost love you
but would have cast, I know,
the stones of silence.
I am the artful voyeur

of your brain's exposed
and darkened combs,
your muscles' webbing
and all your numbered bones:

I who have stood dumb
when your betraying sisters,
cauled in tar,
wept by the railings,

who would convince
in civilized outrage
yet understand the exact
and tribal, intimate revenge.

A Constable Calls

His bicycle stood at the window-sill,
The rubber cowl of a mud-splasher
Skirting the front mudguard,
Its fat black handlegrips

Heating in sunlight, the 'spud'
Of the dynamo gleaming and cocked back,
The pedal treads hanging relieved
Of the boot of the law.

His cap was upside down
On the floor, next his chair.
The line of its pressure ran like a bevel
In his slightly sweating hair.

He had unstrapped
The heavy ledger, and my father
Was making tillage returns
In acres, roods, and perches.

Arithmetic and fear.
I sat staring at the polished holster
With its buttoned flap, the braid cord
Looped into the revolver butt.

'Any other root crops?
Mangolds? Marrowstems? Anything like that?'
'No.' But was there not a line
Of turnips where the seed ran out

In the potato field? I assumed
Small guilts and sat
Imagining the black hole in the barracks.
He stood up, shifted the baton-case

Further round on his belt,
Closed the domesday book,
Fitted his cap back with two hands,
And looked at me as he said goodbye.

A shadow bobbed in the window.
He was snapping the carrier spring
Over the ledger. His boot pushed off
And the bicycle ticked, ticked, ticked.

EXPOSURE

It is December in Wicklow:
Alders dripping, birches
Inheriting the last light,
The ash tree cold to look at.

A comet that was lost
Should be visible at sunset,
Those million tons of light
Like a glimmer of haws and rose-hips,

And I sometimes see a falling star.
If I could come on meteorite!
Instead I walk through damp leaves,
Husks, the spent flukes of autumn,

Imagining a hero
On some muddy compound,
His gift like a slingstone
Whirled for the desperate.

How did I end up like this?
I often think of my friends'
Beautiful prismatic counselling
And the anvil brains of some who hate me

As I sit weighing and weighing
My responsible *tristia*.[1]
For what? For the ear? For the people?
For what is said behind-backs?

Rain comes down through the alders,
Its low conducive voices
Mutter about let-downs and erosions
And yet each drop recalls

The diamond absolutes.
I am neither internee nor informer;
An inner émigré, grown long-haired
And thoughtful; a wood-kerne[2]

Escaped from the massacre,
Taking protective colouring
From bole and bark, feeling
Every wind that blows;

Who, blowing up these sparks
For their meagre heat, have missed
The once-in-a-lifetime portent,
The comet's pulsing rose.

1   Latin: dismal surroundings. Ovid's *Tristia* contains five
    books of short poems on his exile from Rome. In
    Wicklow Heaney imagines himself as in some way in
    exile from his home in the North.
2   In the sixteenth century a kern was an Irish foot-soldier,
    a wood-kerne an Irish outlaw haunting the woods.

LEO SIMPSON
from Henry Imbleau (ed.), *The Lady and the Travelling Salesman* (1976)

Leo Simpson (1934–) was born in Limerick and emigrated to Canada in 1961. His
writing includes radio plays as well as novels and short stories. Here in 'Visiting the
Future', originally broadcast on CBC (Canadian Broadcasting Company) Anthology
under the title 'Paddy Carmody's Place', he has produced a moving story that can stand
comparison with George Moore's 'Home Sickness' (1903), reproduced on p. 103
above. And Simpson, a genuine exile, betrays little sense of Ireland as an untilled field.

Visiting the Future

The emigrant did not return with bits of glory sticking
to him, nor amid whispers of rumoured feats like John
Wayne in *The Quiet Man*; rather, he slipped through
the back door of Paddy Carmody's place, because it
was close to his house, to buy a bottle of whiskey. He
was bulky and alien in a Canadian overcoat too heavy
for the mild Irish autumn, and this was how he truly
first came home. (The other brushes had been nothing
of substance — idle, polite meetings, mildly
embarrassing for those unlucky enough to be
involved.) Now his shifting eyes met the stares, sensing
the attitudes that caused nightmares, and here and
there he saw a grotesque, a child's eyes peering from
under a balding head, or a known smile almost
encased in fat.

Joe McMahon put a hand on my shoulder first. I
didn't know it was Joe, of course, until later, and for
the moment I used no names except Declan and
Harry, who were impossible not to remember and
recognize. In fact, the nightmarish thing for me was
that they were impossible to forget. They stood a little
apart, smiling and slightly questioning, confident in
their relationship to me. When the wrapped whiskey
came I had my nose in a pint of porter, wishing I had

chosen another pub, and I left the bottle behind the
counter. One might expect that they would have
something to say to such a stranger, but they paid me
the compliment of supposing — or letting me suppose
— that my words would be more important than
theirs, and I choked on hesitant commonplaces until I
was rescued by a few hearty questions, and a failure of
interest of those on the fringes, who drifted away to
livelier conversations. It was like a gang of children
temporarily held by an untoward event.

'Where are you now?' Declan said, and the effort to
seem interested itself betrayed him. Here was a veteran
of too many returned emigrants and their overblown
tales. When I said Canada, it meant only as much as
London or Manchester. There was in them the
distance and pride of a defended integrity, and they
concealed it poorly.

Paddy Carmody's was a house before it became a
pub. It had an entrance hallway, and the kitchen had
been converted into the dispensing section of the bar.
The counter was small, since it served only as a
serving-hatch, made durably of rough painted wood.
Two barrels of porter were on tap beneath the
counter; the reserve barrels and the empties were used
as seats by the patrons of the front room — those
wishing only a quick one, and stray drinkers from

other districts. The back room, the main room of the house, was much longer, furnished with chairs and a wide bench along the wall. A piled turf fire burned in that room. The accordion player and the fiddler sat near the fire. They were talking quietly and drinking when the emigrant was brought in, their instruments nowhere visible, and they continued unheeding. No lengthy ceremonial of a mediaeval court was as formal as the behaviour of these musicians, who played before the turf fire of Paddy Carmody's every night, and whose surprise at being requested to play was as great each night as the night before. To one side sat a young guitar man, still an outsider and a novelty and the butt of jokes. He looked at the emigrant shyly, perhaps expecting support or some understanding. Harry brought another pint for the emigrant and addressed the fiddler: 'Shur, give us a tune there, now, Chris.'

'What?' Chris said. 'Shur, isn't it too early?'

'Early or late, give us a tune. Get out the old fiddle. Nine o'clock is gone.'

'Since when did you look at that old clock?'

'Will you give us a tune there, now. I'm asking you. Pat, give us a tune. I'll get one of the lads to sing.'

The modesty of those who came to sing, which was everybody in Paddy Carmody's, men and women, was so ritualized that a leader was necessary to encourage them, ensuring that no individual was missed or over-used. Harry had this part. I stood in my conspicuous clothing, too politely considerate of all, noticing the Harry who had become fixed. I remembered how he would sometimes pull down his mouth in a grimace to indicate his aloofness from a particular subject or, more frequently, from an occurrence illustrating the farce of all life, as we had diagnosed it, the madness that one could not regard seriously. That grimace had become permanent, giving Harry the manner of a 'character' such as can be found in most pubs. I thought the expression was as lightly made as formerly, and joked to change the mood, but the mouth-corners stayed down, two heavy grooves. His eyes appeared darker in colour, without light, and he was taking it seriously now.

'Give us a tune. Jim, what about a song now? Your man there will give us a song. Where's the fiddle? Get out that old fiddle, there. Shur, Paddy'll be putting us out in an hour, what's the matter with you all . . .'

'Let me have me drink in peace, will you.'

The words of the exchange were as smoothed by custom as a prayer. Harry and the musicians argued, gesturing like actors. The others were tolerant or just barely amused, but not taking much notice. Soon afterward the fiddle and accordion were reluctantly found, greeted by stray cheering and some hand-claps. A head came through the door from the front room,

peering around questingly, and the emigrant groaned and tightened his grip on his pint of porter. I wondered why he could not have waited a while longer, this guest, this memory, this awkward burden. How in the name of Jesus had I hoped to talk with him over a bottle of whiskey? There are some who make assumptions so quickly that they will never understand, nor will they be understood because of the convictions forever in readiness on their lips. He was the worst of these and, surely enough, a condescending smile, directed at the gathering, formed as he saw me. The pints of porter were like black clubs held by almost every hand there, but he delicately carried a swirl of whiskey in a stemmed glass, a foreigner's little flag. Naturally he was offered a chair in the crowded room — hospitality to a stranger, a chair beside mine — and I groaned again when he sat down, fastening his eyes on me as if nobody else existed.

'You were gone a good time for that jar, so . . .'

'Some of the boys are here. You know, Declan, Harry.'

'Oh, yes.' He added, as if sensing the deadly need behind my explanation, to mitigate his quick dismissal of them, nodding agreeably: 'The hard men.'

It wasn't enough of an explanation, but I could bear to go no deeper, now or ever. What the emigrant didn't know at this stage — a trivial ignorance in the evening's context — was that Paddy Carmody was prominent in the docker's union, and my friend with the delicately-held glass filled a high post of some kind in the steamship company. The matter was unimportant in every way — there was no strike, and no prospect of one, and no present friction. They were merely opposed in theory, and remembered. I had stood. This was the same damned abstract feeling, hatred as an abstraction, that hung over all Ireland, a plague of honour, a convenience for little politicians, a . . . 'Why don't you sit down?' he asked, swirling the whiskey, and several chairs were vacated on the spot and extended to me.

'I have to buy a round,' I said. At the counter there was an unmanageable row of pints after I made the call, and he was beside me, studying them. He said: 'Get the fellas to carry their own drinks, why don't you. Look, I'll do it for you. Hey, you fellas the drinks are here . . .' And I grasped his arm quite viciously, hurting and puzzling the blind man. I had had my pints put right into my fist. 'Go back to your seat,' the emigrant said. 'Stay there. I'll carry the drinks.' When the dispensing was done we were together again, insolubly, and a few men near us rose, in case we wanted different chairs this time.

New songs were rarely sung in the house. Usually Harry specified the song when he called the singer. The most popular were the patriotic ballads, and, of course, the love-songs. The love-songs were of lost love, most with a still mood of resignment, and not need: just recollection of the beauty in the gift, untainted by self-pity and self. During a recitation — some recitations were as worn and appreciated as the songs — the emigrant felt a tug on his sleeve and turned to find a small tubby man in a cap grinning at him. 'Terry McNamara,' the man said, sensibly identifying himself. 'How are you? How are you at all? God, it must be ages. Where are you now?'

'Terry, nice to see you,' I said, wondering dismally who Terry McNamara could have been. 'Are you drinking there?' He was noticeably drunk.

'I'm fine. Come here, till I tell you. Do you remember the play at all? The *play*? Ah, it was a fine play. In the Feile.[1] Do you remember it?'

'Well, Terry . . .' The emigrant had not been in many school plays, and he, in a rush of unfamiliar sensation, was given a clear memory of the play they brought to the Feile Dramioucta[2] in Dublin. It had been in Irish, and he groped for the title. They'd been *children* then. Even before the time with the roots of nightmares. The bunch of them eating at Clerys, stiff and well-behaved. 'I remember now, wasn't it about the cat in long waders? I was a soldier in it.'

'Puss in Boots!'

'You're right. I remember now.' The silver-painted wooden spear.

'Shur, how could you forget it? You couldn't forget a play like that at all. We went all the way to Dublin with it, and got the third prize for the whole country. We were rehearsing for months, and I'll tell you, I can remember every line, would you believe that?'

'Well, I didn't have anything to say, you see, Terry. A soldier.'

'Shur wasn't I the cat? Don't you remember at all? I was the cat in it!'

The emigrant did remember then, but the real weight of despair did not settle on him until much later, when he had the leisure to think on the scraps of happenings. That the slim, dark-haired boy, Terry, who was always thought of as a dreamer, should become an indistinguishable figure in a bar, and at ease there, was to be expected if the circumstances of Irish life, and any life, were accepted; the sharper sting was in the betrayal of expectation, that dreams could die one by one and leave only the time of dreams to remember warmly. At Paddy Carmody's place I was paying a visit to the future.

'Yes, you were the cat.'

'Wasn't it a *good* play? I mean, codding aside now?'

'The best, Terry. The very best. It should've won first prize.'

'That's the truth. I often think of it.'

'Terry, where's your drink. Let me get you a pint there.'

'Well, I won't say no, for old times.'

Although they had had little enough to say to each other in the old times, since dreams were always private. The emigrant listened to the singer when he had brought the pint, and thought that there was no other place in the world where a hollowed old man could sing with drunken sentiment of young love to an attentive audience. The faces continued to appear, recalling their earlier selves for him, and occasionally a new pint would be put in his hand. They smiled and joked, but he entertained no illusion about his importance to them. Paddy Carmody's was a permanent institution, and he was a Wednesday night phenomenon, an emigrant briefly home, a confirmer of green memories for the close friends and a curiosity for the rest. The matter of being among them was urgent only to himself. He couldn't ask their forgiveness for leaving, yet he needed the pardon and wasn't even sure how they could grant it. He understood why many returned emigrants boasted, praising the wealth and excellence of the new country, pointing to Ireland's backwardness, desperately seeking the absolution of a compliment to their wisdom in leaving home. All the emigrants lived in Tír na n-Óg,[3] bringing back predictable magic now and then, but the substance stayed behind, with the pain. No man could be successful enough in fairy places to become more than an emigrant to his friends. For me, for my homecoming, they were gathered together in one room, like a jury.

Looking at the figure of my burden squatted, waiting, on the chair, holding the whiskey as a sign proclaiming his alienness, I tried to imagine what we might have talked about. It had seemed a possible idea. We met on the street, and he was one of the few I recognized and named without hesitation. He had been as good a friend as Declan and Harry, but no better. Sitting there, he was more of a stranger to the gathering than I was, yet he had never even left the town so far as I knew. He embarrassed me by making it obvious that he was waiting, not participating. I leaned forward to suggest that he take the bottle of whiskey to the house, and wait for me there; while doing so I had my last revelation of the night, me the emigrant, and straightened again, hurt. The clock said five minutes past ten, and I had noticed each movement of the minute hand since I arrived, at nine-fifteen — but smiling all the time of course, enjoying myself greatly — and now I identified my impatience with the seated friend, who should have been as close to me as Declan and Harry, and *had* been even tonight, before he entered Paddy Carmody's. His choice of whiskey as a drink was unremarkable, though he had hardly sipped it, if he wasn't fond of the bitter porter, and my nervous dislike, the eruption, could only be directed at myself. He was a version of me if I had stayed in Ireland. That was the revelation. Oh, the changes the future works! He would be the best companion of the night for me, because we always manage to forgive ourselves, and nobody feels guilt while expecting a favourable judgement. I wondered if he knew how he had changed my feelings toward him by following me to Paddy Carmody's. I wondered what he wanted of me. 'Drink up. Have another,' I said to him, the damned outsider, detesting every movement he made, and especially the friendly smile.

'Right. Good. What do you think of this place, anyway?'

'Very busy and noisy. Dilapidated and full of life. Very Irish.'

'What about getting back to the house? Those fellas have forgotten you. You can see them another time, can't you?'

'I'll have to do that,' I said, although I knew it would be useless. My own smile was still on my face. They were, after all, honest judges. A dumpy, dirty woman in thick spectacles had begun to sing as we left, yet another song of hopeless love, piercingly beautiful.

1   Irish: festival, feast-day.
2   Drama Festival.
3   Irish: Land of Youth, mythical kingdom.

CAROLINE BLACKWOOD
from Caroline Blackwood, *Great Granny Webster* (1977)

Caroline Blackwood (1931–), daughter of the 4th Marquis of Dufferin and Ava, was born in County Down. *Great Granny Webster*, like Molly Keane's *Good Behaviour* (1979), is a black comedy on the decline of the Big House in Ireland. Here in this extract things come to a head over the cooks, the cooking, and the menus.

At the time that Tommy Redcliffe first visited Dunmartin Hall, three red-headed local girls, called the McDougal sisters, were taking turns ineptly to do the cooking. They were young and scared and highly strung, and they had never grasped the most rudimentary principles of what they were required to do down in the ramshackle unmodernized kitchen of such a palatial house. The only definite instructions they had received since their arrival was that Grandfather Dunmartin wanted several alternative menus shown to his wife every morning. My grandfather liked the feeling that he was keeping up the traditional domestic routines which his dead mother had once insisted on. He therefore wanted the menus to be written out in French.

The McDougal sisters had no experience and were hardly capable of cooking anything much more complicated than bacon and eggs. They couldn't understand a word of French and therefore the task of

writing out a series of differing menus in a foreign language was a daily torment to them. They got up at six-thirty and wasted a lot of time slowly copying out the names of various rich and refined dishes which they took from a French cookery book, often confusing the hors d'oeuvres with the entrées, for they had no idea what they were suggesting to my grandmother.

Although every day they obediently wrote out lists of pretentious courses on the stiff menu cards which were engraved with the Dunmartin coat of arms, it made not the slightest difference to them whether these cards were sent back to them covered with approving ticks or whether all their suggestions had been scratched out by the malign crayon strokes of their employer. They had very soon noticed that no one ever complained if the food they cooked had no relation to anything they had suggested to my grandmother. They found many of the procedures in this alien and sinister Anglo-Irish house baffling. They saw their job of writing out these menus as a difficult, silly, hollow formality which they would never understand the point of. When the cards were returned to them, they never bothered to look at them. They would be too preoccupied, like flustered sailors without a compass, floundering in indecision as they tried to make up their minds what they should cook for the Dunmartin dining-room. After much over-excited debate, just before lunch when the urgency of the situation forced them into action, they would nearly always agree on their favourite standbys — ham or pheasant. They preferred the latter, seeing it as an expensive and exotic food which was therefore the most suitable. They would go and get a few of these pre-cooked birds from the larder, throw them into a frying pan and then have them pompously carried by the butler to the dining-room — mahogany-coloured, rock-like objects swimming in a sauce of bacon fat.

Once when Tommy Redcliffe had caught a very bad cold, which he blamed entirely on the polar conditions prevailing in his bedroom at Dunmartin Hall, he had gone down to the kitchen to ask the McDougal sister if they would make him a drink of hot lemon and honey. He had happened to arrive just at the moment when the footman was bringing them back their menus, and he had been startled and intrigued by the hostility and contempt with which the footman treated the three young cooks.

The youngest girl greeted the footman, but he refused to answer her. He stood there in the doorway of the kitchen glaring at all the sisters, and the lid of one of his pale fastidious eyes gave an irritable nervous twitch, as if rejecting the very sight of their chapped and flaking arms, their greasy aprons, their freckled noses and frizzy ginger curls. He was immensely eager to show them that he regarded them with disgust, that he found their accent unintelligible, and saw them as no more worthy of human respect than the ill-fed scruffy fowls that pecked and squawked in the Dunmartin chicken-runs. It was obvious that he considered the sluttish way the McDougal sisters kept their kitchen as not only repugnant but dangerous. He seemed unwilling even to cross its threshold and stood there in the doorway with the nostrils of his arrogant aquiline nose flaring as if they detected some poisonous smell.

Tommy Redcliffe still vividly remembered the expression of pure revulsion with which the footman's cold pale eye had looked at all the filthy pots and pans and other cooking utensils, at the bluebottles which were settling on the butter, the wasps which were struggling in various open pots of jam. Tommy Redcliffe too was alarmed at the sight of the fuzzy grey mould that had formed on an old pudding that was lying in a china bowl on the sticky and unscrubbed kitchen table. He was shaken by the state of the unswept stone-flagged floor, on which the corpse of a mouse was rotting quietly in the corner in a mouse-trap, where everywhere there seemed to be the crunched carcases of pheasants which had been thrown, despite their sharp and choking bones, to the gun dogs and lay there littered with odd bits of withered cabbage and the peelings of potatoes and carrots.

Tommy Redcliffe doubted that the supercilious young footman would have dreamt of eating a mouthful of food which had been touched by the McDougal sisters. He suspected that the butler and the two footmen cooked their own private meals on a stove in their pantry, and that as my grandfather never bothered to check the household bills they most probably ordered themselves excellent meat from the local butcher, so that — not to mention the superb vintage wine they were always taking from the cellar — the three Englishmen fared very well.

'Take these,' the footman had suddenly snarled, throwing the menu cards on to the floor with a gesture of furious hostility and contempt. He might have been feeding some chickens with corn. He turned and strode away in his wellingtons, as if escaping from an inner region of hell.

Tommy Redcliffe noticed that the three McDougal sisters made not the slightest move to pick up the French menus. He also became aware that there were various other tattered old menu cards lying around with all the other refuse on the kitchen floor. He presumed that these were the ones that had been made out for my grandmother in the preceding week and that no one had yet got round to sweeping them up.

'Stuck-up bastard,' one of the McDougal sisters said in cheerful tones, as the black-uniformed figure of the English footman disappeared down the corridor. 'It's always a great moment to see the back of him.'

The three redheads were very friendly and maternal to Tommy Redcliffe. They sympathized with his sore throat and his swollen glands, and they scurried off to find lemons, which one of them then squeezed on a disconcertingly unclean-looking squeezer. They advised him to put a drop of whisky with it. 'Whisky takes the pain out of most things,' the least freckled-nosed of the sisters said.

Tommy Redcliffe had found them all very likeable, and he had admired the way they seemed to be able to take the footman's rudeness so lightly. He had still been keen to get out of the kitchen, for he dreaded the thought of watching them preparing their pheasants.

The three young cooks never received any criticism for the terrible meals they produced, and Tommy Redcliffe felt that this was disastrous, for it gave them the idea that everyone found their cooking satisfactory. The McDougal sisters apparently had a very hazy and inaccurate image of my grandmother. From the moment they had come to work in her house they had never set eyes on her, because their kitchen was separated by a cobbled courtyard and a labyrinthine maze of corridors from the parts of the house that she used. They had heard rumours that she was a fierce and peculiar woman, and the whole idea of her frightened them. But though they were lost and unhappy working at Dunmartin Hall, they were only too aware of the unemployment in Ulster and were anxious to please her. As my grandmother never once complained about their ludicrous cuisine, any meal that they assumed had met with her approval they liked to repeat. They had little confidence in themselves, and the reason their culinary repertoire was so small was that they considered all variation risky. Therefore they liked to reproduce almost exactly the same thing they had cooked for lunch for the Dunmartin dinner.

Although my father never grumbled about the food, he never attempted to eat it either. He smoked restlessly all through meals and shook his head irritably whenever the butler tried to serve him. He was obviously embarrassed by the cooking of the McDougal sisters, and it was clear that he felt profoundly ashamed that it was all that he was able to offer to his friend. He never mentioned it to Tommy Redcliffe, and he never tried to apologize for it, presumably because he saw it, like many other things in his family situation, as irremediable and beyond apology.

One day when the food had been so exceptionally repulsive that one of the old aunts had rushed from the Dunmartin table with a handkerchief pressed to her lips, claiming that she had been poisoned, Tommy Redcliffe had tried as tactfully as possible to suggest to his host that it might be better if he went through the daily menus himself, rather than allow the burden of choice to fall on my grandmother, when she was clearly in no state to preoccupy herself with the meals of the household. He found it astonishing that a man so apparently good-natured as my grandfather seemed content to allow such a needlessly painful and farcical daily ritual as the presentation of the French menus to continue, when alternative arrangements were so easy.

He had never thought that Grandfather Dunmartin would be upset by this common-sense suggestion. But the poor man looked so close to tears that Tommy Redcliffe felt he had been both cruel and needlessly impertinent.

'I'm afraid you are right,' Grandfather Dunmartin said. 'For a long time I've known that my poor darling wasn't really well enough to go through the menus, but I've been terrified of doing anything to upset her shaky confidence.'

He then tried to explain that my grandmother knew that, as his wife, it was her traditional right to choose the meals for the dining-room. He felt that if he was to take this little responsibility away from her, it might have a very bad psychological effect, for she would take it as a sign that she was generally considered too hopelessly incompetent to take on the most routine of the duties expected of her. 'Once she feels we don't even trust her to choose our food — how can she feel we trust her to do anything?' he asked.

He had never felt, he said, that it was the least bit important whether she looked at the menus or not. All that mattered was that she be given daily symbolic evidence that her friends and family retained respect for her as the woman who was in charge of the household. 'Meals appear anyway,' he said. 'You can't pretend that any of us are starving. The servants always produce something. That's their job . . .'

Staring with despondency and a certain bitterness at the leg of horrible fossil-like pheasant which was congealing in a pool of tepid bacon fat on his plate, Tommy Redcliffe had realized that his host felt too unhungry and too obsessed by his more disquieting concerns to care any longer what food appeared on his table. He found it comic that Grandfather Dunmartin seemed to regard the opportunity of choosing from the French menus as some important honour which he was conferring on his wife. He found it tragic that, against all evidence to the contrary, his host still managed to persist in his fantasy that this honour meant a great deal to hear.

'Oh dear!' Grandfather Dunmartin said to him. 'I suppose I'd better go through those menus for a while. I just hope to God she won't think I'm trying to insult her. I'll try to explain to her I'm only doing it temporarily until she feels more like her old self.' He said he felt sure he would manage the menus very badly. 'I'll never understand all that French. I'll probably get confused and think *crème brûlée* is a sauce you put on cauliflower! In the old days, French was something my wife never had any trouble with. Old Mrs Webster was very strict about education and always got her the best French governesses. Anyway, in lots of ways women are always much cleverer than men, don't you think?'

The day after this conversation, he told the English footman that his wife felt unwell and it was better not to bother her with the menus. He never asked to see them, and the McDougal sisters soon ceased to write out any and cooked the same kind of food that they had always cooked.

JENNIFER JOHNSTON
from Jennifer Johnston, *Shadows on Our Skin* (1977)

Jennifer Johnston (1930–), the daughter of Denis Johnston and actress and director Shelagh Richards, was born in Dublin and educated at Trinity College Dublin. A prolific novelist she made a name for herself with the Big House as a theme in novels such as *The Gates* (1973) and *How Many Miles to Babylon* (1974). Here in this novel, set in Derry, she shows skilful handling of 'troubles fiction'. Making use of a phrase in a song by Horslips as her title, Johnston explores with sensitivity the relationship between Joe Logan, on the edge of being drawn into sectarian violence, and a Protestant teacher, Kathleen, who invites him home after school.

She took her coat off and hung it on the back of the door. He sat down on the divan and looked around. There was a table covered with books and papers, an armchair, two upright chairs, a sink and a small cooker in the corner, above which were some shelves that held plates and cups and some more books. A large cupboard was half-open and bursting with clothes and suitcases and frying pans and what looked to Joe like a box overflowing with pairs of shoes. There was a heap of coloured cushions on the divan, which was covered with a brightly striped rug. There was another pop from the gas in the cooker.

'I'll have some cocoa too,' she said, emptying a bottle of milk into a saucepan.

'Why do you have a carpet on your bed?'

'Why not? You don't have to put carpets on the floor, you know. You can hang them on the walls, put them on the bed, even cut them up and make clothes of them if you want to. It's the same with most things really. You mustn't be too rigid about things. Look at every object with an open mind.'

'You could be a little mad.'

'I could,' she agreed, smiling. 'But where's the harm? The great thing is to make the most out of what you've got. What did I do with my poison?'

'There, beside the cooker.'

'Ah, yes.'

She took a deep drag and put the cigarette down in the saucer again.

'Some people believe they have nothing. Then life gets very bad.' She put two cups down side by side on the table, lining them up evenly, handles symmetrically sideways, as if it mattered.

'You have nice things.'

'Mmmm.'

'These mugs. They're nice.'

'I got them in London. There's a lot of things for buying in London, millions of people all buying, buying.'

'My brother's just come back. Did I tell you about him?'

'Oops.'

The milk rushed up the side of the saucepan and over the top on to the stove before she had time to stop it.

'Blast.'

She grabbed a cloth and mopped at the milk.

'It always does that. Even if I'm staring at it, glaring at it, willing it to behave, it does it just the same.'

She poured the milk into two mugs and stirred in the cocoa.

'Here. Take care, it's blazing.'

She threw the cloth into the sink and came and sat down beside him on the divan, cigarette and mug clutched in the same hand.

'Sorry for all that . . . you were saying something about your brother?'

'Brendan.'

'That's a nice name. I like it better than Joe.'

He blew into his cocoa and watched the rings expand out to the sides of the mug. Skin might form, he thought with distaste.

'Is it good?'

'What?'

'Brendan being home? He's been away a long time, hasn't he?'

'Yes. Ages. A couple of years. I was only a kid.'

She smiled. He felt himself blush.

'Are you pleased he's back?'

'I don't honestly know. I've hardly seen him. It'll take . . . like a while . . . you know . . .'

He paused.

'. . . to . . . to . . .'

'Come to terms.'

She leant forward and stubbed out the cigarette butt in the grate. Smoke squirmed out from under her fingers and then died. He wondered for a moment if she was a Protestant.

'Used you to like him?'

'I don't remember. That's all I remember, then he went away.'

She got up and wandered aimlessly round the room, picking things up and putting them down again. He supposed she was looking for her cigarettes.

'Mam is upset.' He threw the words after her wandering figure.

'She's afraid he'll get into trouble. Mixed up . . . you know . . . She worries a lot about that sort of thing. Like me being home from school quickly. I told you . . .'

'Yes,' she said.

She found them in the pocket of her coat, and sighed with relief. She came back and sat down again.

'She has all the worrying to do.'

'Some people quite like that, you know, Joe. They need to be worrying away all the time.'

He looked down at his cocoa, which was forming a crinkled skin across the top. 'I don't think she likes it. You know the way some people have happy faces?'

'Yes.'

'Well, she hasn't. Not even when she's watching TV. I watch her a lot. I've skin on my cocoa.'

'It won't kill you.'

'I don't like it. It makes me feel sick.'

'There's a spoon over there.' She nodded towards the sink. 'Scoop it off.'

He got up and carried his mug across the room. Outside, the almost dark sky was streaked with gold. There was a red plastic spoon on the draining board. He performed the delicate operation, dropping the skin quickly into the basin. It reminded him of a burst balloon, something else that he hated.

'She works four days a week in the Strand Café.'

'What does she do there?'

He thought for a moment.

'She performs menial tasks.'

He sat down again and sipped tentatively at his drink, hoping against hope that he hadn't left any shreds of skin behind that might touch his lips.

'That can't be very nice for her.'

'It's not. But someone has to keep the home together.' He smiled at her. 'That's what she says.'

'And your father? What does he do?'

'He's not well at all.'

'Oh.'

She put her mug on the floor and started on the cigarette-lighting business.

'My mother says he's a retired hero.' He looked at her. Her face was a serious, listening face.

'That's a sort of joke really.'

The light from the match patterned her face for a moment with orange and black. 'Wounded in the Civil War.¹ He has a bad leg . . . and his back . . . well . . . He ought to have a pension. He says the Free State government is shirking its legitimate responsibilities. He says . . . he says . . . anyway he's not at all well.'

'He must be getting on if he fought in the Civil War,' was all she said.

'Yes. He's old all right. He says . . . well, he says a lot of things, but Mammy says you shouldn't believe everything you hear. She says that a lot.'

'I can see your mother's point of view. For myself, I prefer to believe most things cautiously.'

'Are you a Protestant?'

She threw her head back and roared with laughter.

'What gives you that idea?'

He blushed.

'I hope you don't mind. I just . . . I don't know really.'

'I don't mind a bit. My mother was. So how clever you are. A positive mind-bending mind-reader.'

'I'd like to be handy with words. Like you. You are.'

'I'm sure you will be one day.'

'The cocoa's good.'

'In spite of the skin?'

He nodded.

'Have another biscuit?'

'Yes. Thanks.'

Two men ran along the street and round the corner, the metal on their heels sparking the pavement as they ran. She gave a little shiver and got up. She went over to the window and peered out and then, even though it wasn't yet dark, she pulled the curtains tight together. Keeping safety in. The safe room glowed in the warmth from the gas fire. The curtains were of some heavy brown material and her hand looked very white against them. It looked almost like a bird from where he sat watching.

'Soon the spring will come,' she said, her hand still holding together the edges of the curtains. 'Nothing ever seems so bad in the spring.'

'And then the summer,' he said.

She came over and sat down beside him again.

'I'll be gone then.'

'Oh.'

'My job was only for the year. I'll have to go then. I must say . . .'

She leant forward and blew the surface of her cocoa, blew the wrinkled skin over to one side and then took a sip.

'I didn't know you were going.'

'I have to.' She smiled to herself. 'I have a commitment elsewhere.'

'Don't you like it here?'

'I like it all right. It's not that.'

'Are you feared?'

She considered before speaking.

'I suppose so. I'm afraid of something awful happening. I don't just mean bombs and all that. You get sort of used to that in a horrible way, but something deeply awful . . . I can't explain. Words are aggravating the way they hide on you when you need them most. We must do a lot of things together, you and I, before I go. If you'd like to, that is . . .'

'That'd be O.K.'

'Good.'

She put out a hand and touched his knee.

'Drink up, there's a good boy. I wouldn't want your mother to be worried. I'll walk part of the way home with you.'

'You needn't bother.'

He felt, suddenly, that he was being treated as a child.

'No bother. I have to get my evening's supply of poison.'

He sipped slowly at his drink, not wanting to be rushed or pushed around.

'I can never correct the books without puffing away. Otherwise I give everyone terrible marks.' She laughed. 'Isn't that stupid?'

'I always get terrible marks anyway.'

'Only because you don't care. You're the sort of pupil drives teachers mad. Full of ability, but not caring a half-penny.'

For some reason she switched on the radio which was on the floor beside her. It was a fidget really, he decided, rather than a desire to hear anything. 'Now we have time to kill,' sang some young men, their voices clear, syncopated.

'Kill the shadows on our skin,
Kill the fire that burns within,

Killing time, my friend.'

Dreamtime. The words danced into Joe's mind.

'Killing time, my friend.'

Under the words the music jigged. Dreamtime. The mug drooped in his fingers.

'Mind,' she said. 'Oh, mind.'

A stream of cocoa poured on to the floor. He righted the mug with a jerk of his wrist.

'I'm sorry. I'll . . .'

'No. Don't bother. I'll do it.'

She fetched a cloth from the sink and stooped over.

'Now we have time to kill . . .' Quicker than before.

'Kill the shadows on our skin. Kill the . . .'

'Poor old time.'

She looked up at him, her face red from stooping.

'People are always killing time. Some people do nothing else all their lives . . . killing time before it kills them.' She laughed briefly. 'I think someone else must have said that before me.'

'I see the last black swan
Fly past the sun.
I wish I, too, were gone
Back home again.'

He drained the remains of his cocoa down his throat, skin and all, forcing the soft pieces down with difficulty, penance for his carelessness.

'It seems our fortunes lied . . .'

'We'd better go,' she said, rinsing the cloth under the tap.

'Despite our gain.'

'First good Saturday. Sun, you know. We'll go up in the hills. Grianan or somewhere. Would you like that?'

'I wouldn't mind.'

'Our tears fall like our pride. We cry in shame.'

'Not a very enthusiastic response.' She handed him his anorak.

'I'd like it a lot, but you probably have other things to do.'

'Now we've got time to kill . . .'

'I probably haven't. Have you ever been to Grianan?'

He shook his head.

'Well that's a date then. We'll bring hard-boiled eggs. I love hard-boiled eggs.'

'Kill the fire that burns within . . .'

She opened the door and they went out on to the landing.

'Aren't you going to turn the radio off?'

She closed the door on the voices.

'Killing time, my . . .'

'I hate going into dark lonely rooms.'

He understood.

1   1922–23.

BENEDICT KIELY
from Benedict Kiely, *A Cow in the House* (1978)

Here in this short story, which is close to autobiography and to the shanachie tradition
of oral story-telling (see his 1975 radio talk reproduced on p. 828 above), Kiely returns
to a childhood memory still indifferent to religious differences. For autobiographical
details see Kiely's *Drink to the Bird: A Memoir* (1991).

The Night We Rode with Sarsfield

That was the house where I put the gooseberries back
on the bushes by sticking them on the thorns. It wasn't
one house but two houses under one roof, a thatched
roof. Before I remember being there, I was there.

We came from the small village of Dromore to the
big town of Omagh, the county town of Tyrone, in
the spring of 1920, bad times in Ireland (Violence
upon the roads/Violence of horses[1]) particularly bad
times in the north-east corner of Ulster. There have
been any God's amount of bad times in the north-east
corner of Ulster. There were no houses going in the
big town and the nearest my father could find to his
work was three miles away in the townland of
Drumragh and under the one roof with Willy and
Jinny Norris, a Presbyterian couple, brother and sister.
They were small farmers.

That was the place then where I put the
gooseberries back on the bushes by impaling them on
the thorns. But not just yet because I wasn't twelve
months old, a good age for a man and one of the best
he's ever liable afterwards to experience: more care is
taken of him, especially by women. No, the impaling
of the gooseberries took place seven to eight years
later. For, although we were only there six or so
months until my father got a place in the town — in
the last house in a laneway overlooking the green
flowery banks of the serpentine Strule — we went on
visiting Willy and Jinny until they died, and my father
walked at their funeral and entered their church and
knelt with the congregation: a thing that Roman
Catholics were not by no means then supposed to do.
Not knelt exactly but rested the hips on the seat and
inclined the head: Ulster Presbyterians don't kneel, not
even to God above.

It was a good lasting friendship with Willy and
Jinny. There's an Irish proverb: *Níl aitheantas go
haontigheas*. Or: You don't know anybody until you've
lived in the one house with them.

Not one house, though, in this case but two houses
under one roof which may be the next best thing.

Willy and Jinny had the one funeral because one
night the house burned down — by accident.

Nowadays when you say that a house or a shop or a pub
or a factory burned down, it seems necessary to add —
by accident. Although the neighbours, living next door
in our house, did their best to rescue them and to save
the whole structure with buckets of water from the
spring-well which was down there surrounded by
gooseberry bushes, they died, Willy from suffocation,
Jinny from shock, the shock of the whole happening,
the shock of loneliness at knowing that Willy was dead
and that the long quiet evenings were over. However
sadly and roughly they left the world, they went, I
know, to a heaven of carefully kept harvest fields, and
Orange lilies in bloom on the lawn before the
farmhouse, and trees heavy with fruit, and those long
evenings spent spelling out, by the combined light of
oil-lamp and hearth fire, the contents of *The Christian
Herald*. My three sisters who were all older than me said
that that was the only literature, apart from the Bible,
they had ever seen in the house but, at that time, that
didn't mean much to me.

The place they lived in must have been the quietest
place in the world. This was the way to get there.

The Cannonhill road went up from the town in
three steps but those steps could only be taken by
Titans. Halfways up the second step or steep hill there
was on the right-hand side a tarred timber barn
behind which such of the young as fancied, and some
as didn't, used to box. My elder brother, there,
chopped one of the town's bullies, who was a head-
fighter, on the soft section of the crown of his head as
he came charging like a bull, and that cured him of
head-fighting for a long time. Every boy has an elder
brother who can box.

The barn belonged to a farmer who would leave a
team of horses standing in the field and go follow a
brass band for the length of a day. Since the town had
two brass bands, one military, one civilian, his sowing
was always dilatory and his harvests very close to
Christmas. He owned a butcher shop in the town but
he had the word, Butcher, painted out and replaced by
the word, Flesher, which some joker had told him was
more modern and polite but which a lot of people
thought wasn't exactly decent.

If you looked back from Cannonhill the prospect was really something: the whole town, spires and all, you could even see clear down into some of the streets; the winding river or rivers, the red brick of the county hospital on a hill across the valley, and beyond all that the mountains, Glenhordial where the water came from, Gortin Gap and Mullagharn and the high Sperrins. Sometime in the past, nobody knew when, there must have been a gun-emplacement on Cannonhill so as to give the place its name. Some of the local learned men talked vaguely about Oliver Cromwell but he was never next or near the place. There were, though, guns there in 1941 when a visit from the Germans seemed imminent and, indeed, they came near enough to bomb Belfast and Pennyburn in Derry City and were heard in the darkness over our town, and the whole population of Gallowshill, where I came from, took off for refuge up the three titanic steps of the Cannonhill road. It was a lovely June night, though, and everybody enjoyed themselves.

If any of those merry refugees had raced on beyond the ridge of Cannonhill they would have found themselves, Germans or no Germans, in the heart of quietness. The road goes down in easy curves through good farmland to the Drumragh River and the old graveyard where the gateway was closed with concrete and stone long before my time, and the dead sealed off forever. There's a sort of stile made out of protruding stones in the high wall and within — desolation, a fragment of a church wall that might be medieval, waist-high stagnant grass, table tombstones made anonymous by moss and lichen, a sinister hollow like a huge shellhole in the centre of the place where the dead, also anonymous, of the great famine of the 1840s were thrown coffinless, one on top of the other. A man who went to school with me used to call that hollow the navel of nothing and to explain in gruesome detail why and how the earth that once had been mounded had sunk into a hollow.

That same man ran away from home in 1938 to join the British navy. He survived the sinking of three destroyers on which he was a crew member: once, off the Faroes; once, for a change of temperature, in the Red Sea; and a third time at the Battle of Crete. It may be possible that the crew of the fourth destroyer he joined looked at him with some misgiving. A fellow townsman who had the misfortune to be in Crete as a groundsman with the RAF when the Germans were coming in low and dropping all sorts of unpleasant things to the great danger of life and limb, found a hole in the ground where he could rest unseen, and doing no harm to anybody, until he caught the next boat to Alexandria.

When he crawled into the hole who should be there but the thrice-torpedoed sailor reading *The Ulster Herald*. He said hello and went on reading. He was a cool one, and what I remember most about him is the infinite patience with which he helped me when, impelled by a passion for history, I decided to clean all the table tombstones in old Drumragh and recall from namelessness and oblivion the decent people who were buried there. It was a big project. Not surprisingly it was never completed, never even properly commenced, but it brought us one discovery: that one of the four people, all priests, buried under a stone that was flat to the ground and circled by giant yews, was a MacCathmhaoil (you could English it as Campbell or McCarvill) who had in history been known as the Sagart[2] Costarnocht because he went about without boots or socks, and who in the penal days of proscribed Catholicism[3] had said Mass in the open air at the Mass rock on Corra Duine mountain.

For that discovery our own parish priest praised us from the pulpit. He was a stern Irish republican who had been to the Irish college in Rome, had met D'Annunzio and approved of him and who always spoke of the Six Counties of north-east Ulster as *Hibernia Irredenta*.[4] He was also, as became his calling, a stern Roman Catholic, and an antiquarian, and in honour of the past and the shadow of the proscribed, barefooted priest, he had read the Mass one Sunday at the rock on Corra Duine and watched, in glory on the summit like the Lord himself, as the congregation trooped in over the mountain from the seven separate parishes.

The ground is littered with things, cluttered with memories and multiple associations. It turns out to be a long three miles from Gallowshill to the house of Willy and Jinny Norris. With my mother and my elder sisters I walked it so often, and later on with friends and long after Willy and Jinny were gone and the house a blackened ruin, the lawn a wilderness, the gooseberry bushes gone to seed, the Orange lilies extinguished — miniature suns that would never rise again in that place no more than life would ever come back to the empty mansion of Johnny Pet Wilson. That was just to the left before you turned into the Norris laneway, red-sanded, like a tunnel with high hawthorn hedges and sycamores and ash trees shining white and naked. My father had known Johnny Pet and afterwards had woven mythologies about him: a big Presbyterian farmer, the meanest and oddest man that had ever lived in those parts. When his hired men, mostly Gaelic speakers from West Donegal, once asked him for jam or treacle or syrup or, God help us, butter itself, to moisten their dry bread, he said: Do you say your prayers?

— Yes, boss.

They were puzzled.

— Do you say the Lord's prayer?

— Yes, boss.

— Well, in the Lord's prayer it says: Give us this day our daily bread. Damn the word about jam or treacle or syrup or butter.

When he bought provisions in a shop in the town he specified: So much of labouring man's bacon and so much of the good bacon.

For the hired men, the imported long-bottom American bacon. For himself, the Limerick ham.

He rose between four and five in the morning and expected his men to be already out and about. He went around with an old potato sack on his shoulders like a shawl, and followed always by a giant of a gentleman goat, stepping like a king's warhorse. The goat would attack you if you angered Johnny Pet, and when Johnny died the goat lay down and died on the same day. Their ghosts walked, it was well known, in the abandoned orchard where the apples had become half-crabs, through gaps in hedges and broken fences, and in the roofless rooms of the ruined house. Nobody had ever wanted to live there after the goat and Johnny Pet died. There were no relatives even to claim the hoarded fortune.

— If the goat had lived, my father said, he might have had the money and the place.

— The poor Donegals, my mother would say as she walked past Johnny Pet's ghost, and the ghost of the goat, on the way to see Willy and Jinny. Oh, the poor Donegals.

It was a phrase her mother had used when, from the doorstep of the farmhouse in which my mother was reared, the old lady would look west on a clear day and see the tip of the white cone of Mount Errigal, the Cock o' the North, 60 or more miles away, standing up and shining with shale over Gweedore and the Rosses of Donegal and by the edge of the open Atlantic. From that hard coast, a treeless place of diminutive fields fenced by drystone walls, of rocks, mountains, small lakes, empty moors and ocean winds the young Donegal people (both sexes) used to walk eastwards, sometimes barefoot, to hire out in the rich farms along the valley of the Strule, the Mourne and the Foyle — three fine names for different stages of the same river.

Or the young people, some of them hardly into their teens, might travel as far even as the potato fields of Fifeshire or Ayrshire. They'd stand in the streets at the hiring fairs to be eyed by the farmers, even by God to have their biceps tested to see what work was in them. The last of the hiring fairs I saw in Omagh in the early 1930s but by that time everybody was well dressed and wore boots and the institution, God be praised, was doomed. There was a big war on the way and the promise of work for all. But my mother, remembering the old days and thinking perhaps more of her own mother than of the plight of the migratory labourers, would say: The poor Donegals. Ah, the poor Donegals.

Then up the sheltered red-sanded boreen or laneway — the Gaelic word would never at that time have been used by Ulster Presbyterians — to the glory of the Orange lilies and the trim land and in the season, the trees heavy with fruit. Those gooseberries I particularly remember because one day when I raided the bushes more than somewhat, to the fearful extent of a black-paper fourteen-pound sugar-bag packed full, my sisters (elder) reproved me. In a fit of remorse I began to stick the berries back on the thorns. Later in life I found out that plucked fruit is plucked forever and that berries do not grow on thorns.

Then another day the three sisters, two of them home on holidays from Dublin, said: Sing a song for Jinny and Willy.

Some children suffer a lot when adults ask them to sing or recite. There's never really much asking about it. It's more a matter of get up and show your paces and how clever you are, like a dancing dog in a circus, or know the lash or the joys of going to bed supperless. Or sometimes it's bribery: Sing up and you'll get this or that.

Once I remember — can I ever forget it? — the reverend mother of a convent in Dublin gave me a box of chocolates because in the presence of my mother and my cousin, who was a nun, and half the community I brazenly sang:

Paddy Doyle lived in Killarney
And he loved a maid named Bessy Toole,
Her tongue I know was tipped with blarney,
But it seemed to him the golden rule.

But that was one of the exceptionally lucky days. I often wondered, too, where the reverend mother got the box of chocolates. You didn't expect to find boxes of chocolates lying around convents in those austere days. She dived the depth of her right arm for them into a sort of trousers-pocket in her habit, and the memory of them and of the way I won them ever after braced me in vigour (as the poet said) when asked to give a public performance.

— Up with you and sing, said the eldest sister.

Outside the sun shone. The lilies nodded and flashed like bronze. You could hear them. On a tailor's dummy, that Jinny had bought at an auction, Willy's bowler hat and sash were out airing for the Orange walk on the twelfth day in honour of King William and the battle of the Boyne. The sash was a lovely blue, a true blue, and the Orangemen who wore blue sashes were supposed to be teetotallers. Summer and all as it was the pyramid of peat was bright on the hearth and the kettle above it singing and swinging on the black crane, and Jinny's fresh scones were in three piles, one brown, one white, one spotted with currants and raisins, on the table and close to the coolness of the doorway.

— Sing up, said the second sister. Give us a bar.

— Nothing can stop him, said the third sister who was a cynic.

She was right. Or almost. Up I was and at it, with a song learned from another cousin, the nun's brother, who had been in 1920 in the IRA camp in the Sperrin mountains:

We're off to Dublin in the green and the blue,
Our helmets glitter in the sun,
Our bayonets flash like lightning
To the rattle of the Thompson gun.
It's the dear old flag of Ireland, boys,
That proudly waves on high,
And the password of our order is:
We'll conquer or we'll die.

The kettle sputtered and spat and boiled over. Jinny dived for it before the water could hit the ashes and raise a stink, or scald the backs of my legs where I stood shouting treason at Willy and the dummy in the bowler and the teetotaller's blue sash. It may have been a loyal Orange kettle. Willy was weeping with laughter and wiping the back of his left hand sideways across his eyes and his red moustache. In the confusion, the eldest sister, purple in the face with embarrassment, said: If you recited instead of singing. He's much better at reciting.

So I was and proud of it. Off I went into a thundering galloping poem learned by heart from the *Our Boys*, a magazine that was nothing if not patriotic and was produced in Dublin by the Irish Christian Brothers.

The night we rode with Sarsfield out from Limerick
to meet
The waggon-train that William hoped would help
in our defeat
How clearly I remember it though now my hair is
white
That clustered black and curly neath my trooper's
cap that night.

This time there was no stopping me. Anyway Willy wouldn't let them. He was enjoying himself. With the effrontery of one of those diabolical little children who have freak memories, even when they don't know what the words mean, I let them have the whole works, eight verses of eight lines each, right up to the big bang at Ballyneety on a Munster hillside at the high rock that is still called Sarsfield's Rock.

It is after the siege of Derry and the battle of the Boyne and the Jacobite disaster at the slope of Aughrim on the Galway road. The victorious Williamite armies gather round the remnants of the Jacobites locked up behind the walls of Limerick. The ammunition train, guns, and wagons of ball and powder, that will end the siege rumble on across the country. Then Sarsfield with the pick of his hard-riding men, and led by the Rapparee, Galloping Hogan, who knows every track and hillock and hollow and marsh and bush on the mountains of Silver Mine and Keeper and Slieve Felim, rides north by night and along the western bank of the big river:

'Twas silently we left the town and silently we
rode,
While o'er our heads the silent stars in silver beauty
glowed.
And silently and stealthily well led by one who
knew,
We crossed the shining Shannon at the ford of
Killaloe.

On and on from one spur of the mountains to the next, then silently swooping down on the place where, within a day's drag from the city's battered walls, the well-guarded wagons rest for the night. For the joke of it the Williamite watchword is Sarsfield:

The sleepy sentry on his rounds perhaps was musing
o'er
His happy days of childhood on the pleasant English
shore,
Perhaps was thinking of his home and wishing he
were there
When springtime makes the English land so
wonderfully fair.
At last our horses' hoofbeats and our jingling arms
he heard.
'Halt, who goes there?', the sentry cried. 'Advance
and give the word.'
'The word is Sarsfield,' cried our chief, 'and stop us
he who can,
'For Sarsfield is the word tonight and Sarsfield is the
man.'

Willy had stopped laughing, not with hostility but with excitement. This was a good story, well told. The wild riders ride with the horses' shoes back to front so that if a hostile scouting party should come on their tracks, the pursuit will be led the wrong way. The camp is captured. Below the rock a great hole is dug in the ground, the gun-powder sunk in it, the guns piled on the powder, the torch applied:

> We make a pile of captured guns and powder bags and stores,
> Then skyward in one flaming blast the great explosion roars.

All this is long long ago — even for the narrator in the poem. The hair is now grey that once clustered black and curly beneath his trooper's cap. Sarsfield, gallant Earl of Lucan, great captain of horsemen, is long dead on the plain of Landen or Neerwinden. Willy is silent, mourning all the past. Jinny by the table waits patiently to pour the tea:

> For I was one of Sarsfield's men though yet a boy in years
> I rode as one of Sarsfield's men and men were my compeers.
> They're dead the most of them, afar, yet they were Ireland's sons
> Who saved the walls of Limerick from the might of William's guns.

No more than the sleepy sentry, my sisters never recovered from the shock. They still talk about it. As for myself, on my way home past the ghosts of Johnny Pet and the gentleman goat, I had a vague feeling that the reason why the poor girls were fussing so much was because the William that Sarsfield rode to defeat must have been Willy Norris himself. That was why the poem shouldn't be recited in his house, and fair play to him. But then why had Willy laughed so much? It was all very puzzling. Happy Ulster man that I then was I knew as little about politics and the ancient war of Orange and Green as I knew about the way gooseberries grew.

It wasn't until after my recital that they found out about the black-paper fourteen-pounder of a sugar-sack stuffed full of fruit. The manufacturers don't do sacks like that any more in this country. Not even paper like that any more. It was called crib-paper, because it was used, crumpled-up and worked-over and indented here and bulged out there to simulate the rock walls of the cave of Bethlehem in Christmas cribs.

For parcelling books I was looking for some of it in Dublin the other day, to be told that the only place I'd come up with it was some unlikely manufacturing town in Lancashire.

1   A line from Yeats's poem 'Nineteen Hundred and Nineteen'.
2   Irish for priest.
3   The Treaty of Limerick in 1691 marked a significant defeat for the Catholic cause in Ireland, and paved the way for the Penal laws in the eighteenth century (laws which penalized Catholics in every area of social life, religious observance, and economic activity). Priests were not allowed to say Mass in Church and had to be educated abroad.
4   Irredentists were Italians who after 1878 sought the recovery of all Italian-speaking districts under foreign rule (such as Trieste, then under Austro-Hungarian control). In this comparison Ulster (or the Six Counties in nationalist vocabulary) should be brought under control of Hibernia or Ireland.

TESS GALLAGHER
from Tess Gallagher, *Under Stars* (1978)

Tess Gallagher (1943–) is an American poet who was married to Raymond Carver. Her poetry volumes include *Willingly* (1984), *Moon Crossing Bridge* (1992) and *Portable Kisses* (1992). Here in this poem she writes a modern ballad that in its absence of reference has the capacity to disturb as much as the 'Twa Corbies' or other ballads of old. In the fourteenth century, The Book of Ballymote, a manuscript compilation, was made by three scribes partly at Ballymote in County Sligo.

THE BALLAD OF BALLYMOTE

We stopped at her hut
on the road to Ballymote
but she did not look up
and her head was on her knee.

What is it, we asked.
As from the dreams of the dead
her voice came up.

My father, they shot him
as he looked up from his plate
and again as he stood and again
as he fell against the stove
and like a thrush his breath
bruised the room
and was gone.

A traveller would have asked directions
but saw she would not lift her face.
What is it, he asked.

My husband sits all day in a pub
and all night and I may as well

be a widow for the way he beats me
to prove he's alive.

What is it, said the traveller's wife
just come up to look.

My son's lost both eyes in a fight
to keep himself a man
and there he sits behind the door
where there is no door
and he sees by the stumps
of his hands.

And have you no daughters for comfort?

Two there are and gone to nuns
and a third to the North
with a fisherman.

What are you cooking?

Cabbage and bones, she said. Cabbage
and bones.

ROBERT CREELEY
from Robert Creeley, *Later* (1979)

In this sweet poem from a volume that includes reference to Yeats and Kavanagh, the American poet Robert Creeley (1926–) recalls a moment of discovery. Creeley, founder of *Black Mountain Review* (1954–), counted among his influences Charles Olson, William Carlos Williams, and Allen Ginsberg, but although normally viewed from an American perspective, he came to recognize and value 'being Irish'.

THERESA'S FRIENDS

From the outset charmed
by the soft, quick speech
of those men and women,
Theresa's friends — and the church

she went to, the 'other',
not the white plain Baptist
I tried to learn God in.
Or, later, in Boston the legend

of 'being Irish', the lore, the magic,
the violence, the comfortable
or uncomfortable drunkenness.
But most, that endlessly present talking,

as Mr Connealy's, the ironmonger,
sat so patient in Cronin's Bar,
and told me sad, emotional stories
with the quiet air of an elder

does talk to a younger man.
Then, when at last I was twenty-one,
my mother finally told me
indeed the name *Creeley* was Irish —

and the heavens opened, birds sang,
and the trees and the ladies spoke
with wondrous voices. The power of the glory
of poetry — was at last mine.

IAIN CRICHTON SMITH
from *Stand*, Vol. 19, No. 2, 1978

Iain Crichton Smith (1928–2000), a leading Scottish poet, was born in Glasgow but until entering university in 1945 lived on the island of Lewis. A prolific writer, he published verse in both English and Gaelic. Here in this provocative poem Smith disturbs conventional opinion and alignments in Ireland and positions himself at a genuine point of feeling between two languages and two cultures.

FOR POETS WRITING IN ENGLISH
OVER IN IRELAND

'Feeling,' they said,
'that's the important thing' —
those poets who write in English over in Ireland.

It was late.
There was dancing in the hall,
playing of pipes, of bones, of the penny whistle.

They were an island in that Irishness.
'Larkin and Dunn,'[1] they said. 'Now Dunn is open
to more of the world than aging Larkin is.

What room was Mr Bleaney in? It's like
going to any tenement and finding
any name you can think of on the door.

And you wonder a little about him but not much.'
We were sitting on the floor outside the room
where a song in Irish waltzed the Irish round.

Do the stones, the sea, seem different in Irish?
Do we walk in language, in a garment pure
as water? Or as earth just as impure?

The grave of Yeats in Sligo, Innisfree
island seen shivering on an April day.
The nuns who cycle down an Easter road.

The days are beads strung on a thin wire.
Language at Connemara is stone
and the water green as hills is running westwards.

The little children in the primary school
giggling a little at our Scottish Gaelic,
writing in chalk the Irish word for 'knife'.

To enter a different room. When did Bleaney
dance to the bones? This world is another world.
A world of a different language is a world

we find our way about in with a stick,
half-deaf half-blind, snatching a half word there,
seeing a twisted figure in a mirror,

slightly unnerved, unsure. I must go home.
To English? Gaelic? O beautiful Maud Gonne,[2]
the belling hounds spoke in what language to you?

In that tall tower[3] so finished and so clear
his international name was on the door
and who would ask who had been there before him?

I turn a page and read an Irish poem
translated into English and it says
(the poet writing of his wife who'd died):

'Half of my eyes you were, half of my hearing,
half of my walking you were, half of my side.'[4]
From what strange well are these strange words
    upspringing?

But then I see you, Yeats, inflexible will,
creator of yourself, a conscious lord,
writing in English of your own Maud Gonne.

Inside the room there's singing and there's dancing.
Another world is echoing with its own
music that's distant from the world of Larkin.

And I gaze at the three poets. They are me,
poised between two languages. They have chosen
with youth's superb confidence and decision.

'Half of my side you were, half of my seeing,
half of my walking you were, half of my hearing.'
Half of this world I am, half of this dancing.

1   Philip Larkin (1922–95), leading English poet of his generation. Mr Bleaney is one of Larkin's invented characters. Douglas Dunn (1942–), Scottish poet, a devotee of Larkin, spent several years in Hull where Larkin was Librarian at the University.
2   The champion of Irish nationalism and subject of several love poems by Yeats.
3   Yeats's Tower at Ballylee.
4   I think these are lines from an early thirteenth-century Irish poem by Muireadach O'Dalaigh entitled 'On the Death of His Wife'.

THOMAS FLANAGAN
from Thomas Flanagan, *The Year of the French* (1979)

The year is 1798, the place Ballinamuck, County Longford. The French troops under General Humbert, having landed at Killala Bay in County Mayo on 22 August, had joined forces with the United Irishmen and marched inland where they were met by the Lord Lieutenant of Ireland, Lord Cornwallis, and roundly defeated. Maria Edgeworth and her reforming father ride over from their well-managed estate at Edgeworthstown to view the battle site and are shocked by what they see. Thomas Flanagan (1923–) is an Irish-American historical novelist and critic. His fiction wears its learning with ease and conviction. Other novels include *The Tenants of Time* (1988), which recreates the period from the Fenian Rising of 1867 to the Land War of 1879–82, and *The End of the Hunt* (1995), which deals with the period from 1916 to 1922.

Ballinamuck, September 10

Two days after the battle, Richard Lovell Edgeworth, the learned and eccentric squire of Edgeworthstown, rode to the battlefield in an open carriage, accompanied by his daughter Maria, who was later to gain celebrity as the authoress of *Castle Rackrent*.[1] He was an angular, nervous man, a collection of wheels, springs, and coils across which skin had been stretched. He was dressed carelessly, his cravat loosely knotted and his hat perched on the back of his head of sandy, close-cropped hair. Maria's gown of flowered muslin and the shawl across her narrow shoulders suggested an afternoon's drive to a neighboring estate. Down the village street of Ballinamuck they rode, looking neither to left nor right,

and out upon the narrow road toward Shanmullah Hill, where the Irish had made their last stand.

Tents had been pitched upon the pastureland, and far-off figures moved among the bordering thickets. 'Who are they?' he asked, in a rasping, high-pitched voice. 'What are those people about?'

Maria too was near-sighted, but the motions of the distant figures, as she studied them, grew familiar. 'Berrying,' she said decisively. 'Those must be blackberry thickets.'

'Are they indeed? A fine task for soldiers.' He drummed his long fingers upon his kneecaps. 'A county gone to ruin, houses burned, men slit from belly to gullet at their own doors. And now they turn to berry picking.'

'It would be foolish indeed to let the berries waste upon their bushes.'

It was a splendid day. Fields, pastures, hill lay beneath a warm sky of intense blue, flecked with clouds the exact color of angelica. The bell-shaped tents lent an air of carnival. As they drove nearer, she saw that the soldiers were using their tall helmets to hold the berries. Beyond them, the reddish bog stretched toward the horizon of low hills. But her father pointed to the hill which lay near them.

'That is Shanmullah,' he said. 'The French turned here and made their stand. Climb a hill is the first thing a soldier thinks to do. Cornwallis's troops swarmed around them. A cheap sort of victory, but doubtless we shall hear it described as a great triumph.'

'What matter?' Maria said. 'The rebellion is ended. We must be thankful for that.'

'Waste,' Edgeworth said. 'Waste and mismanagement for years. I have sought by all means at my disposal to improve matters. I have spoken upon the floor of the Commons, I have published pamphlets, I have conducted a voluminous correspondence with men of learning and influence. No one heeded me.'

'Would that they had, Father,' Maria said. 'You are the cleverest man in the kingdom.'

'Not the cleverest,' Edgeworth said. 'Many are more clever. But I am the most thoughtful, the most thorough. No one heeded me. I have explained and explained at length how the children of the Irish might be educated into habits of thrift and sobriety. I have explained how this island might be transformed into a flowering garden through the reclamation of the bogs. Arthur Young[2] himself has praised me. You have read his letters.'

It was all true, she knew. She acted as his secretary. In the long evenings he dictated to her, pacing up and down in the drawing room, pausing from time to time to consult the tables of statistics which lay spread upon the long table. The dry voice, cogwheels with an engine, spun out facts, evidences, proofs, arguments, theories. Each pamphlet addressed a problem, wasteland, education, the reform of Parliament, the suppression of local superstitions, the excise, imports and exports, a more efficient system of canals. They would go out by post to English savants, learned societies, amateurs of political economy. Letters would come to Edgeworthstown in reply, flattering and deferential, 'an astonishing wealth of convincing and detailed evidence', 'a trenchant mind brought to bear upon the manifold problems of an ill-governed island', 'a true apostle of science and rationality'. Nothing happened. All waste.

At the first line of tents he halted, and shouted to three soldiers crouched about a pot hung over a low fire. One of the men looked up and answered, but he could not understand the words. 'What?' he shouted again, and the man repeated his reply, but now with a faint, derisive smile.

'What did he say, child? What did he say?'

'I doubt if he has English, Father. They are Highlanders.'

'Highlanders!' Edgeworth echoed. 'Highland Scots. Set a savage to catch a savage. Wild bare-bottomed clansmen in their first sets of trousers. I will have a seizure of the heart before this month is out and you can lay the blame before Lord Cornwallis.'

He folded his long arms across his chest and sat waiting. Presently, from the far row of tents, a young officer rode out toward the village and paused by their carriage.

'Are these your ruffians?' Edgeworth asked.

The officer looked over at the three grinning Highlanders and then back at Edgeworth. 'They are, sir. They are indeed. My ruffians. My name is Sinclair, sir.'

'I am Edgeworth of Edgeworthstown. I am a Member of Parliament and of the board of magistrates for this county.'

'An honor.' Sinclair touched his hand to his hat.

'The devil take your honor. It is your commanding officer I am looking for.'

'That would be Colonel Grant. He rode in to Carrick this morning. Perhaps I can help you.'

'Perhaps,' Edgeworth said doubtfully. 'My bailiff is a man named Hugh Laffan. He was seized up as a United Irishman and his cabin burned down around the heads of his wife and his children. He is no more a United Irishman than either of us. I want him found and I want him delivered over to me as quickly as possible.'

'You won't find him here,' Sinclair said, puzzled. 'This is a battlefield. Or it was.'

'I have been to Granard,' Edgeworth said. 'He is not there. The officer in command suggested that I try your people. I have no time to ride back and forth across the countryside.'

Sinclair shook his head. 'We had only the prisoners who were taken after the battle. They are being held in Carrick. You won't find your man with that lot. If I were you, I should try Mullingar and Longford.'

Edgeworth turned to Maria. 'Do you hear that? A man is taken up at his own door, and he may be anywhere. Longford, Mullingar, Carrick. And half a county burned down.' He turned back to Sinclair. 'The rebels burn the houses of the gentry and you burn the cabins. Between one lot of you and the other you have sought to reduce the county to a smoldering ruin.'

'I am sorry for that,' Sinclair said. 'It is what happens in a time of rebellion.'

'You are sorry for it. That is pleasant news to hear. How would you like it if I took a torch to your own shabby mountain and then told you that I was sorry?'

'I come from no shabby mountain,' Sinclair said stiffly. 'My father is a minister of God in Edinburgh.'

'Do you hear that, Maria? Mark it well. Edinburgh, the Athens of the North. And their clergymen produce cubs who go about ravaging the countryside of Ireland.'

Sinclair was becoming dimly aware that he had entered upon a conversation for which he was unprepared. 'I have never before heard of you, sir, until you just now gave me your name —'.

'Then you are an ignorant young man, and not simply a vicious one.'

'Mr Edgeworth, complaints as to the conduct of His Majesty's forces should be taken to Lord Cornwallis. It ill becomes you to give a tongue-lashing to a lieutenant who has never to his knowledge set eyes upon your estate. No cabins have been burned by this regiment, I can assure you.'

'No doubt, no doubt,' Edgeworth said testily. 'I ask your pardon in that case. What has happened in this county is a disgrace to our common humanity and it has disturbed me greatly.'

'I can understand that, sir. I took part in the battle here and it was a messy business. War is an ugly business, I am discovering. To speak plainly, I believe that I have not selected a calling suited to my nature.'

Edgeworth peered at him closely and then nodded. 'I spoke too sharply, Mr Sinclair. It is a failing of mine. I acknowledge that. I am a just man, I trust.'

'Were many taken prisoner here?' Maria asked suddenly.

Sinclair took a long time in answering her. 'Very few,' he said at last. 'About eighty.' He shifted in his saddle. 'About eighty natives. Close to nine hundred of the French.'

'I don't understand,' she said. She was a sharp-featured young woman, and she sat stiff and erect in the carriage.

Sinclair stretched out his arm and pointed. 'The rebels fell back, past that hill —'

'Yes, yes,' Edgeworth said. 'Shanmullah Hill. Things have names, Mr Sinclair, even in this county.'

'They fell back from there to the bog.'

'And there they surrendered?' Maria asked. She leaned forward now, and her near-sighted brown eyes studied him closely.

She anticipates my reply, Sinclair thought. He wished himself far away from Ballinamuck, far away from Ireland. The three Highlanders were watching them, uncomprehending.

'They were rebels,' he said. 'They were in arms against the sovereign.'

'They were indeed,' Edgeworth said. 'That is the definition of a rebel.'

'And there they surrendered?' she asked again.

Sinclair took a deep breath and expelled it slowly. 'Their surrender was not accepted. They were cut down. I — we — cut them down.'

Maria clambered to her feet, a small, graceless woman, and stretched her neck forward, toward the bog.

'I cannot see that far,' she said. 'I cannot see.'

'Oh, my dear God,' Edgeworth said softly.

'It is as well that you cannot, Miss Edgeworth. Their bodies are scattered across the bog, beyond the hedges.'

Edgeworth took off his spectacles and held them poised in the air. 'You killed them all? You took the Frenchmen prisoners but you killed the rebels?'

'Not all. Most were killed upon the bog, but some were hanged in the village. They drew lots for it. The short straws were hanged. And seventy of them were taken to Carrick. I have been sick to nausea for two days, but I helped to kill them. I took those fellows there out to the bog.'

Maria was still standing, motionless in the carriage. Her father said, 'They have been lying there for two days, like the carcasses of sheep.'

'They died rebels,' Sinclair said doggedly, his eyes upon his horse's neck. 'They died with pikes in their hands. They were a murderous crew, you know.'

'*They* were,' Maria said, with contemptuous irony. '*They* were murderous.'

Edgeworth's eyes, which had been alert and quick-moving, held bewilderment and shock. 'I will not believe this,' he said. 'I will not believe that Lord Cornwallis gave such an order.'

'General Lake's order,' Sinclair said. 'General Lake was commander in the field.'

'An island cursed by God,' Edgeworth said. The brisk, grating voice was half strangled.

'Talk to Lake,' Sinclair shouted in torment. 'Talk to Cornwallis. What good is there in talking to me?' The Highlanders were standing now, attentive to alien words, moving their eyes from Sinclair to Edgeworth and then back again.

'They are to be an example, are they?' Edgeworth asked. 'A warning to rebels. They are an example that we are as barbarous as any pikeman from Mayo or Wexford.'

'If my eyes were keener I could see them,' Maria said. 'But I can see only the bog.'

'I can see them,' Sinclair said.

'All these ancient hatreds,' Edgeworth said. 'And the people have never learned proper habits. Drinking themselves into a stupor. Groveling before their priests.'

'I know little about them,' Sinclair said. 'We came here six weeks ago. They are rather like Highlanders, I think.'

'If the bogs could be reclaimed there would be land enough for all of them,' Edgeworth said. He gestured loosely with his spectacles. Sudden sunlight glinted from the lenses. 'My pamphlets upon the matter earned the praise of Arthur Young.'

'You should look in Longford for your bailiff,' Sinclair said. 'First Longford and then Mullingar.'

Maria put her hand upon her father's arm.

'I tried to raise a company of yeomen,'[3] Edgeworth said, 'but I admitted Papists to their ranks and the government would not supply me with arms. Neighbors wrote to Dublin, warning them against me.'

'There are many Papists in the militia,' Sinclair said. 'The North Cork.'

'I know these people,' Edgeworth said. 'They are not governed by reason. All the laws and pamphlets ever written mean less to them than a poem. I have written against the dangers of poetry in this country. It is their only academy, wild words sung in taverns. Hatred breeding hatred. I have tried. No one listened to me.'

Maria sat down and took the reins from him. 'I wish you a safe return to Scotland,' she said to Sinclair.

'Not yet,' Sinclair said. 'The rebels still hold part of Mayo.'

'Hatred and intolerance,' Edgeworth said. 'Elsewhere they have been banished.'

'Not here,' Sinclair said.

Maria looked again toward the bogs. The soldiers were returning from the thickets, swinging from the straps their helmets filled with berries. She flicked the reins against the horse's rump, and the Edgeworths turned away from the bog, and rode back through the village of Ballinamuck toward the Longford road.

1   A witty Big House regional novel by Maria Edgeworth (1767–1849) published in 1800, the year that marked the passing of the Act of Union at Westminster.

2   Arthur Young (1741–1820), a leading agricultural reformer, wrote *Tour of Ireland* (1780) after his visit to Ireland in 1776–78. In 1782 Edgeworth returned to his estate to embark on a wholesale programme of improvement.

3   Earlier in 1798 Edgeworth had raised a company of yeomanry from both Catholics and Protestants, and when the Rising came he was dangerously exposed.

SEAMUS HEANEY
from Seamus Heaney, *Field Work* (1979)

'Casualty' is another poem to add to the list of fine poems about the casualties of 'the troubles'. 'The Skunk' is a love poem with a difference.

CASUALTY

I

He would drink by himself
And raise a weathered thumb
Towards the high shelf,
Calling another rum
And blackcurrant, without
Having to raise his voice,
Or order a quick stout
By a lifting of the eyes

And a discreet dumb-show
Of pulling off the top;
At closing time would go
In waders and peaked cap
Into the showery dark,
A dole-kept breadwinner
But a natural for work.
I loved his whole manner,
Sure-footed but too sly,
His deadpan sidling tact,
His fisherman's quick eye
And turned observant back.

Incomprehensible
To him, my other life.
Sometimes, on his high stool,
Too busy with his knife
At a tobacco plug[1]
And not meeting my eye,
In the pause after a slug
He mentioned poetry.
We would be on our own
And, always politic
And shy of condescension,
I would manage by some trick
To switch the talk to eels
Or lore of the horse and cart
Or the Provisionals.

But my tentative art
His turned back watches too:
He was blown to bits
Out drinking in a curfew
Others obeyed, three nights
After they shot dead
The thirteen men in Derry.[2]
PARAS THIRTEEN, the walls said,
BOGSIDE NIL. That Wednesday
Everybody held
His breath and trembled.

II

It was a day of cold
Raw silence, wind-blown
Surplice and soutane;
Rained-on, flower-laden
Coffin after coffin
Seemed to float from the door
Of the packed cathedral
Like blossoms on slow water.
The common funeral
Unrolled its swaddling band,
Lapping, tightening
Till we were braced and bound
Like brothers in a ring.

But he would not be held
At home by his own crowd
Whatever threats were phoned,
Whatever black flags waved.
I see him as he turned
In that bombed offending place,
Remorse fused with terror

In his still knowable face,
His cornered outfaced stare
Blinding in the flash.

He had gone miles away
For he drank like a fish
Nightly, naturally
Swimming towards the lure
Of warm lit-up places,
The blurred mesh and murmur
Drifting among glasses
In the gregarious smoke.
How culpable was he
That last night when he broke
Our tribe's complicity?
'Now you're supposed to be
An educated man,'
I hear him say. 'Puzzle me
The right answer to that one.'

III

I missed his funeral,
Those quiet walkers
And sideways talkers
Shoaling out of his lane
To the respectable
Purring of the hearse . . .
They move in equal pace
With the habitual
Slow consolation
Of a dawdling engine,
The line lifted, hand
Over fist, cold sunshine
On the water, the land
Banked under fog: that morning
I was taken in his boat,
The screw purling, turning
Indolent fathoms white,
I tasted freedom with him.
To get out early, haul
Steadily off the bottom,
Dispraise the catch, and smile
As you find a rhythm
Working you, slow mile by mile,
Into your proper haunt
Somewhere, well out, beyond . . .

Dawn-sniffing revenant,
Plodder through midnight rain,
Question me again.

THE SKUNK

Up, black, striped and damasked like the chasuble
At a funeral mass, the skunk's tail
Paraded the skunk. Night after night
I expected her like a visitor.
The refrigerator whinnied into silence.
My desk light softened beyond the verandah.
Small oranges loomed in the orange tree.
I began to be tense as a voyeur.

After eleven years I was composing
Love-letters again, broaching the word 'wife'
Like a stored cask, as if its slender vowel
Had mutated into the night earth and air

Of California.[3] The beautiful, useless
Tang of eucalyptus spelt your absence.
The aftermath of a mouthful of wine
Was like inhaling you off a cold pillow.

And there she was, the intent and glamorous,
Ordinary, mysterious skunk,
Mythologized, demythologized,
Snuffing the boards five feet beyond me.

It all came back to me last night, stirred
By the sootfall of your things at bedtime,
Your head-down, tail-up hunt in a bottom drawer
For the black plunge-line nightdress.

1   A compacted form of tobacco,
2   On Bloody Sunday, 28 January 1972.
3   In 1970–71 Heaney spent some time as a lecturer at the
    University of California at Berkeley.

VINCENT BUCKLEY
from Vincent Buckley, *The Pattern* (1979)

Vincent Buckley (1925–88) was an Australian critic and poet who was closely involved
in the Irish situation. His autobiographical volumes — *Cutting Green Hay* (1983)
and *Memory Ireland* (1985), an extract from which appears below on p. 928 — reflect
that involvement, as does some of his verse. Here in this extract from a prose-poem
entitled 'Gaeltacht' Buckley reflects on the Irish who emigrated to Australia, who
became both Australians and 'a separate kind of Irish'.

from **Gaeltacht**

They were from Munster, every part of Munster. But
would not talk about it: 'No, we're Australians now.'
Really, a separate kind of Irish. From them came no
cries of 'Up Tipp.'[1] or 'Rebel Cork.' They kept their
heads low, ploughing the snake-roots out of the thin-
grassed Australian soil. Yet they talked occasionally in
tongues, in a world-defying wife-hating babble, drank
Paddy, allowed a few books to insert themselves into
the dour rooms, and leave a silver snail-trace
everywhere over my childhood. Their silence was not
only lock but key, to be turned sometime in the

future, their sullenness a burden to be carried secretly
and placed back whence it came. Now the hired cars
bring us, full of effusion, to look, half-idly, at this still-
soft body-scar from which we were leeched off so long
ago. We wanted something to be proud of. This is a
point of departure, not home for us, for anyone.

1   Up Tipperary. The Irish emigrants to Australia in the
    nineteenth century were, as Robert Murray has recently
    noted, in the 'O'Connellite' tradition, accepting
    Monarchy and Empire, though without the enthusiasm
    of many Protestants. See 'Those Who came Across the
    Sea', *Quadrant*, December 1997, pages 54–6.

BRIAN MOORE
from Brian Moore, *The Mangan Inheritance* (1979)

Brian Moore (1921–99) was born in Belfast, emigrated to Canada in 1948 and then a decade later moved to the United States. His first novel was published in 1956 and I could have selected an extract from any of a dozen fluently written novels from *The Lonely Passion of Judith Hearne* (1956) to *Catholics* (1972) or *The Temptation of Eileen Hughes* (1981) or *The Statement* (1996). *The Mangan Inheritance* concerns a failed Canadian poet Jamie Mangan living in New York, on the verge of divorce from his American wife, Beatrice, who discovers in his family papers in Montreal a daguerreotype of the nineteenth-century Irish poet James Clarence Mangan. He then decides to return to Ireland and trace his family's roots to determine if he is related to the figure who is identical to him in looks. Here in this chapter Jamie learns more of his possible family identity from the local priest and then discovers more of his own identity in the arms of a local woman, Kathleen.

'Come this way,' Father Burke said, leading him out of a back door of the presbytery, through a yard which connected with a side door of the church. The priest opened the door and went into a corridor, Mangan following. The corridor led into the vestry, a room with two large oak wardrobes, some processional banners furled and stacked in a corner, a row of cupboards on top of which were a censer, a platen, and three statues in states of disrepair. On the cupboard drawers were handwritten file cards, variously marked: *altar linens, surplices, tapers, Catholic Truth Society*. There was also a desk and a chair, and on the shelf behind the desk were rows of notebooks and files. On the desk was Mangan's family Bible, surrounded by several old, legal-size ledgers, their pages marked with paper slips. One was open, with a pad on top of it. The pad was filled with notations in a small, clerkly hand. The priest turned to Mangan, his boyish features lit by a smile. 'As you'll see, I did my homework last night. Sit down there and I'll show you.'

There was only one chair. 'No, you,' Mangan said, deferentially.

'Sit,' said Father Burke, and it was an order. He took up the pad and turned back the page.

'We did pretty well,' he said. 'We've followed the fish upstream almost to the source. Now, look here.' He leaned over the ledger, his finger tracing its way along lines in faded violet ink. 'The earliest record of your family in our Drishane parish registers would be this one — the year is 1862 — the marriage of Patrick James Mangan to Kathleen Driscoll. I can trace down from this to the present time. But who was Patrick James Mangan? Well, my record shows he was baptized in Holy Cross Church, Dublin, and he was the child of a James Mangan of Dublin and Ellen O'Keefe, the

widow Boylan of Skibbereen. Now, that man, James Mangan of Dublin, that might be your man, the poet. But you'd have to check the baptismal records in Holy Cross Parish in Dublin. That way you might find out where that James Mangan was baptized. And that could tell you if he's Mangan the poet.'

'I'll do that,' Mangan said. 'I'm planning to go on to Dublin when I finish here.' He took out his notebook and wrote down the dates and names from the register, while the priest got up and produced two further registers, which he opened at marked pages.

'Now, coming down the years from that beginning in 1862, the records are all here,' the priest said. 'Whether you're related to Mangan the poet or not, you are certainly related to the Mangans who live here in Drishane. I've compared the dates in the family Bible you left with me with our records here and they tally out.

'As you can see here, the Patrick James Mangan who was married in 1862 had three sons, one born in 1872, one in 1874, and the youngest in 1875. The ten-year gap between marriage and children seems to have been because he was off serving in India. The youngest of those sons, James Patrick Mangan, would be your grandfather. There's no record here of *his* marriage, of course, because he emigrated to Montreal, as your family Bible shows. And he lived until 1952, wasn't it?'

'Yes,' Mangan said. 'I was ten when he died. I remember his funeral.'

'And the Mangans who stayed on here in Drishane were the descendants of Patrick James Mangan's oldest son, Conor James. Now, there are only two male Mangans left here, Dinny and Conor. And neither of them has married as yet.'

'So what relation would I be to Conor and Kathleen?'

'Kathleen?' the priest said.

'His sister, Conor's sister.'

'Ah, yes.' The priest bent over his ledger. 'Let's see, I'm very weak on these consanguinity things. I'll have to work it out, it will take a minute. Anyway, it's not that close.'

'That's all right,' Mangan said. 'Don't bother. I'm afraid I've put you to a lot of trouble already.'

'No, no, I found it interesting,' the priest said. 'Especially the possibility that the James Mangan of Dublin mentioned here *could* be the poet himself. The dates are more or less the same. But, as I said before, you'd have to go to Holy Cross Parish in Dublin to continue the trail.' He rose and stacked the ledgers in a pile, removing the markers. 'By the way,' he said, 'maybe you'd like to see where most of these relations of yours are buried. They're not in the churchyard here, it's too new. The old graveyard for this parish was at Dunmanus Coos. A beautiful spot. Two of the Fenian leaders, killed in '98,[1] are buried there, by the way. O'Bofey and Sean Rahilly. Which reminds me, I'm going down that way now on a sick call. I could drop you off there and pick you up on the way back.'

'Dunmanus Coos?' Mangan said. 'Isn't that down by the sea on the other side of the mountain?'

'It is, surely.'

'Well then, I'm driving in that direction myself. I'm going to stay with Conor Mangan and his sister.'

'Are you, so?' The priest put his head on one side, as though digesting this information. 'You were staying at a house belonging to Dinny Mangan, were you not?'

'Yes. But I have to move. I have my bag in the car. I thought if you were driving past the graveyard I could follow you.'

'Grand,' the priest said. He took out a key chain and, as they left the vestry, locked the door. In the yard a drizzle had started. Father Burke went back into the presbytery for his overcoat, and a few minutes later Mangan was following the priest's little car up a road outside the village, a road which intersected with a narrower road that climbed steeply up the mountainside. The rain, in the astonishing way of the country, stopped as quickly as it started and now the sky was blue as on a summer's day, the sun's heat warming the wet road in front of his car, sending up a small fog of heat mist from the road's gravel surface.

On his left, surrounded by low walls of heaped stones long overgrown with grass and broken down by trespassing cattle, was an abandoned farmhouse, its thatched roof collapsed, its cow byre lichened with weeds. And as he followed the priest's car up to the summit ridge of mountain and came to the fall of the road down the other side, he saw, below, desolate on a headland facing the sea, an older ruin, a Norman tower.

The little car ahead of him picked up speed on the descent, puttering along gaily until they reached the coastal road, which wound below the presence of mountain between a brilliant flowering of wild red fuchsia hedges. They passed a farm where a dog ran out barking, making foolhardy feints at the car wheels. An old man and then an old woman emerged from the farmhouse kitchen door, waving to the priest's car, peering in bewildered curiosity at Mangan's car, which followed. The old man wore a dark serge suit and the old woman a grey blouse, a grey apron, and a knitted black wool shawl. They were the clothes these people's parents might have worn a hundred years ago. As he passed, Mangan waved. The old man waved back.

The priest's car turned down toward the sea. As Mangan followed, he saw on a bluff just overlooking the rocky headland and the spume of wave an enclosed field of crosses and plinths, the graves overgrown and untended, the graveyard's iron gate padlocked with a rusting iron chain. The priest's car stopped outside the gate and the priest got out, his angular black-suited figure outlined like a scarecrow against the sky and the blustery wind which whipped his clothes against his body. When Mangan parked, the priest pointed to the gate. 'There's a step over there,' he said, indicating a stone ledge that jutted out of the wall to the right of the gate. 'A footstep. You can climb over. The graves of your family are down there on the right, near the sea. Just look in that general area.'

'Thanks. And thanks for all your help.'

'Not at all.' The priest's face grinned at him, eyes narrowed against the wind. 'And if you find out for sure that you're Mangan's descendant, send me a postcard, will you?'

'I will.'

'Good man, then,' the priest said, holding out his hand. 'And good luck to you.'

'Good luck,' Mangan echoed, and the priest got back into his car, waving as he drove on down the road. Within a minute he was quite alone, the other car gone as if it had never been. He looked back up at the mountain and with a start of recognition saw a small yellow speck, high up. Kathleen's caravan. Below, on lower slopes of the mountainside, were small cottages, little farms boxed in by fields surrounded by low stone walls, narrow roads intersecting, linking the dwellings with each other. But the road up to Kathleen's caravan on the mountaintop passed no other houses. The yellow speck was all alone on the summit. Mangan turned and mounted the stepping-stones on the cemetery wall, coming down on the other side, inside consecrated ground. He moved through shin-high wet grass, past gray stone plinths and lichened Celtic crosses. There was a path and he made for it, but it was long unused, its stony track infested with stinging nettles and rank yellow dandelion. He turned to the right as the priest had indicated. Above him, a shifting sky of darkening clouds came around the headland, throwing a great shadow on the graves. He stepped off the path, approaching the far corner of the graveyard, scanning names on the plinths and headstones. Almost at once, a greening stone loomed before him and he saw his name writ large.

MANGAN

PATRICK JAMES MANGAN
Departed this life
1 January 1899

There in the cloud-darkened field Mangan took out his notebook and compared the dates he had written down from the family Bible and the parish register. This was the grave of his great-grandfather. He saw again the dull young face in Conor Mangan's photograph album, the boy who had taken the Queen's shilling, served in India, and sired a Canadian Pacific Railway comptroller, at home in the drawing rooms of Montreal and New York. My great-grandfather lies here.

Light rain fell like spittle on the names of the dead. He moved on to a nearby grave and read the headstone.

FERGUS MANGAN
Erected by his loving family
1919–1972

He consulted his notebook. Fergus Mangan was the father of Conor and Kathleen. The rain, growing heavier, began to spatter his page, blurring the names and dates he had copied from the priest's ledger. He shut the notebook and put it in his pocket, moving on, searching the gravestones. But now he was down at the edge of the cemetery, the oldest part, it seemed, where most of the graves were unmarked, or recorded only by simple grassy mounds of earth. Beyond this point the graveyard sloped steeply toward the sea, so that the great sweep of Dunmanus Bay, the rocky cliff, and the ruined Norman tower far out on the headland were visible from where he stood.

He looked at the tower and thought of the broken-roofed cottage he had seen earlier, relic of emigration or famine. Abandoned, castle and cottage were co-equal in neglect, testament to the way in which this country, more than any other he had known, seemed to master time and history, rejecting men's effort to make their presence last. Ashes to ashes. He saw Beatrice walk away from him that day, her camel's-hair coat draped like a cape about her shoulders as she hurried out to meet her new lover. The rain chilled him, wept on his face. He turned back from the sea to the graves and, retracing his route along the weed-choked paths, reached the cemetery gates and climbed the stepping stones in the wall. As he reached the top of the wall and prepared to descend, a small truck came down the road, passing his parked car. There were four workmen standing up in the truck, wild-looking fellows with red, windblown complexions, dressed in old suit jackets and trousers in the Irish manner. They looked at him and he noticed that one of them at once turned away as though to hide his face. He nodded to the passing men and two of them acknowledged his greeting. Mangan stared at the one who had turned away, or the back of his serge jacket once part of a Sunday-best suit, now wetted by rains, worn with age. A stoutish fellow, he seemed, with ears which stuck out. *Why is he avoiding me?* Mangan wondered, and as the truck rattled on down the road, diminishing in perspective, the stance of the workman's back suddenly reminded him of Dinny Mangan, his visitor of last evening. It was an illusion, surely, for these men with their shovels and scythes were the County Council workmen he had seen on the roads the other day weeding ditches and trimming hedges.

The little truck rounded a bend and disappeared from sight. Within seconds, all was still again. Mangan looked up to the mountain, his eyes drawn to the yellow speck on its summit. He turned his car around and drove along the shore road until he came to one of the small intersecting roads that led toward the mountaintop. He went up this road, driving hesitantly as though he had entered a maze, his eyes searching among the jigsaw of stone walls and winding roads for the route toward that yellow speck.

He made a wrong turn. The car climbed past two small farms and ended up in the yard of a third farm, halfway up the mountainside. He backed out, pursued by barking dogs, and retraced his way to a crossroads, turning up again, always searching for the yellow speck. After another false turn he at last found himself on a lonely little road, the sort the priest, yesterday, had called a boreen. There were no farms ahead, and as he climbed ever upward, the yellow speck became the outline of the caravan, perched on the side of the road at the very ridge of summit. As he shifted down into second gear for the last climb to the top, his heart began to beat in an irregular, excited manner. Conor Mangan's little truck was not parked on the road ahead. A wisp of smoke rose from the trailer's chimney. On the clothesline, a peach-colored slip and a cotton dress danced demented in the high wind. He parked the car on the ridge of the road, opposite the opening to the field where the trailer was. He felt his hands tremble as he switched off the ignition. When he got out, he could see the small road falling away on either side of him, back toward the sea whence he had come, and on the other side toward Drishane. He went in at the entrance to the field, expecting the dog to run out at him from underneath the caravan. But no dog came. All was silent and still, with grey clouds drifting into the mountain face, swirling mistily about him as he crossed the field. The clouds moved on, clearing, and he saw that the caravan door was shut. He climbed the steps and knocked. Perhaps she had gone down to the village with her brother? He knocked again, his tension beginning to abate as he considered the chance that he might have to wait up here, alone, until someone returned. No one answered. He came down the steps and went around to the back. Here the field tilted up toward the mountain rock face, so that when he stood on tiptoe he could peer into the caravan's kitchen window. He heard a radio playing inside, very faint, a fiddle and pipe, an Irish air. 'Kathleen?' he called loudly.

But no one answered. He peered in and saw the untidy kitchen counter littered with food cartons and dirty dishes. He moved along the bank to a curtained window, and through its parted folds saw the caravan's sleeping space with two bunk beds. They were empty. He walked around the caravan, coming back to the front entrance. At that point he noticed a bicycle leaning against the low stone wall of the field in which the caravan stood. It was a large, old-fashioned man's bicycle, with a bell, a pump, a lamp, and a chain guard. The second thing Mangan noticed about this bicycle was that its owner must be a very tall man, for the distance from seat to pedal was very great. So the bicycle probably did not belong to Conor Mangan.

As he stood looking at the bicycle he heard a small growl in its vicinity and suddenly a dog which had been concealed behind the wall leaped up on top of the stones and stood, its head thrust forward, showing its teeth. It was not the dog he had seen yesterday, although all the dogs in this district seemed of the same type, piebald mongrel sheepdogs, much given to barking and menace at sight of a stranger. This dog was larger than the one which had hidden under the caravan, and watching, he realized that it would not attack him if he did not advance any farther. It saw itself as the guardian of the bicycle. 'All right, boy,' he said conciliatingly, and backed away.

The dog ceased its barking, but continued to watch him narrowly until he had retreated to the door of the caravan. It then sat down on the wall, ears pricked, studying him as though he were some errant sheep. He turned and walked out on the small road and there on the ridge summit looked down at the splendid panorama of sea, the wide sweep of bay, the headlands, like the forelegs of some enormous Sphinx, stretching out into the sea, pointing toward America. Below, on the other side of the road, he could see the rooftop of Gorteen, the Mangans' strange house, and far away in a valley the spire of Drishane church, the village rooftops clustered around it like spilled playing cards. As he stood, lulled by the beauty of the views on either side of the mountain summit, undecided whether to wait or not, he heard the dog behind him bark once. He looked back and saw the dog standing on the low stone wall, tail wagging, looking across the field to the rocky promontory behind the trailer. From the shelter of this rock came a tall old man in a shabby black serge suit, a stained old uniform cap of some sort on his head. His trouser legs were tucked tight by bicycle clips and he carried a large old leather satchel strung by a strap over his right shoulder. He was collarless and unshaven, gray-grizzled, with a high, purplish complexion. As he approached, Mangan heard his heavy boots squelch on the boggy grass of the field. He touched his forefinger to his cap in salute. 'Nice day, sir.'

'Yes, isn't it.'

'Grand, yes, grand,' the tall old man said, proceeding past Mangan, going toward the dog who stood on the wall, tail wagging frantically. Mangan looked back toward the rock face and at that moment saw Kathleen come around it, brushing mud from her jean-covered bottom. She saw him, smiled, and waved to him. 'Hello there, Jim. How are you today?'

'Fine,' he called. He looked back at the tall old man, who had picked up his bicycle and was wheeling it out onto the road. The dog, tail wagging, frisked about him in great excitement, but was ignored. The tall old man threw his leg over the crossbar and, giving himself a push, mounted the bicycle and turned down the precipitous incline toward Drishane, his fingers gripping the hand brakes to slow his progress. The dog, running ahead, scooted in a bounding gallop across the grassy ditch, keeping pace with the bicycle's rushing progress. Mangan watched it go down into a hollow, saw the old man pedal up a small rise, then disappear over another hump of road. He turned to Kathleen. 'So, you're back to see us,' she said, and smiled as though she were happy at this news. He stared at her young rounded breasts, half revealed in the unbuttoned baby-blue cardigan. What had she been doing around the other side of the mountain with that old man? 'Who was *that*?' he said, pointing off down the road where the cyclist had gone.

'Oh, that's Pat the Post,' she said. 'He had a letter for me.'

She held up a letter with an English stamp on it. 'It's from a boy I met last summer. He was here on his holidays.'

But why had they gone around the rock face, the two of them? 'Where's Con?' he asked.

'Ah, he's gone to Cork. He forgot to tell you yesterday, but he's arranged with another man to pick up a load of scrap iron down there.'

'I'm sorry I missed him.'

'Is there anything I could do?' she said.

He looked at her. 'I was wondering. I mean, you said something yesterday about being able to put me up in the house.'

'We can surely. You're very welcome. I'm sorry you missed Con, but he should be back tomorrow night. Did you bring your case with you?'

'Case?'

'Your suitcase.'

'It's in the car.'

'Then we can go down to the house directly.'

'Whatever you say.'

'We'll go down now and I'll show you your room, and you can leave your case in it. After that, we can come back here and get something to eat. The kitchen in the house is no good at all. The chimney has something wrong with it.'

As she spoke she began to walk him toward the car. 'Where's your dog?' he asked.

'Spot?' She looked around. 'I don't know. Out after rabbits, I'd say.'

In the car's front seat, sitting beside him, she leaned back, locking her hands behind her head, revealing to him the lift of her young breasts. The car went gingerly down the steep narrow road, turning in at the rusted unhinged gate. Again, he saw the tall two-storey house of gray stone, that house which would have seemed at home on the outskirts of a town as it was not here at the top of a mountain. Again, as he got out of the car, it was as though the house seemed aware of his penetration into its territory, and as he removed his bag from the back seat and walked toward

the front door, he was seized with a feeling that the place willed him to approach, yet intended to harm him. He stood waiting at the faded green door as she found the large iron key, unlocked and pushed inward, the wooden footboard clattering on the stone step.

Together they entered the dark hall. To his left was the large dining room cluttered with boxes and cartons and the shut door of the parlor containing photographs and paintings. She negotiated their way among the maze of tin cans on the floor, and they climbed a flight of uncarpeted stairs and crossed the first-floor landing, its aged, uneven boards groaning under their tread. The landing opened into a corridor similar to the one on the floor below it, on either side of which were three shut doors. Kathleen opened the first one. On entering, he was surprised at the size of the bedroom. There was a large three-sided bay window. The room was uncurtained, so that the morning entered in a gray cloudy light which glossed the furniture with a ghostly patina, turning chairs, bed, and tables into artifacts resembling sculpture. The bed was the thing he noticed, for it was very old and large, so high off the ground that it reminded him of beds he had seen in museums. The walls were unadorned with pictures, save for an oval lithograph of the Virgin Mary over the chimneypiece. There was also a large oak wardrobe, a dressing table with standing mirror, a white enamel washbasin on a marble stand, a white enamel chamber pot underneath it. The floor-boards were bare. The only ugly note in the room was a modern propane heater, which sat in the unused fireplace. He put down his bag. Kathleen went to the bed and undid the counterpane, pulling it back to show clean white sheets and pillows. 'I made it up for you last night,' she said. 'Con said you'd come.' She laughed. 'He ran into Dinny at Deegans after supper and heard that Dinny had given you the order of the boot. Is that right?'

'It is.'

'If you want hot water to shave,' she said, 'you'll have to put that little tin yoke on top of the heater. Will I leave you here now, or do you want to come back to the caravan with me?'

He turned to her. She was smiling; she stood in a mocking, provocative pose, her rich, reddish hair falling below her waist. What if he were to kiss her, as he did yesterday?

But yesterday when he had kissed her he had acted unthinkingly. Now, as he started toward her, he saw her mocking posture. Would she laugh at him? Confused, he came to a standstill.

'Well,' she said, 'are you coming or staying?'

'What?' He did not understand her.

'Are you coming up to the caravan with me or do you want to have a lie-down here and come up later?'

'I want a kiss,' he said thickly, and reached for her, taking her into his arms, his mouth blundering toward her face. Her soft lips found his, opening to his kiss, and at once her left hand slid down to his crotch, fondling his genitals. Lust clouded his mind and in an urgent clumsy lurch he pushed her back onto the high old bed. She laughed and rolled away from him, and as she did, he saw her unzip her jeans, dragging off a pair of pink bikini briefs in the process. He stared at white thighs, rounded buttocks. Her cardigan was now open all the way, so that her young breasts were exposed to him. He knelt clumsily on the bed beside her, and as he did she expertly unzipped his fly, pulled down his trousers, and, taking his member in her childish fingers, brought it to stiffness with the grasp of an expert.

He held her shoulders, beginning to slide his hands down over her breasts. Naked, she seemed even younger than in her jeans and cardigan, and now as his hands explored her, cupping her breasts, sliding down to fondle her belly and bottom, it came to him that she might be even younger than twenty. Maybe she was underage? But this prospect, while it produced in him a qualm of alarm, also elicited a shiver of illicit pleasure. As his mouth went hungrily down on her small round breast, guilt was transformed into the impure delight of the forbidden. In his fantasy he became her master, her body his to do with as he wished. But in reality he was quickly made aware that this near-child was infinitely more skilled in venery than Beatrice or any other woman he had known. It was she who — abandoned, naked, trembling yet cajoling — brought him again and again to the point of ejaculation, yet managed to prolong his pleasure. Roiling around in the bed, rearing up over her buttocks, which somehow seemed to tremble beneath him, he became aware that, without a word being said, she had divined his dream and was acting it out, playing the part of the young girl as victim, assigning to him the role of lustful tutor, older lover, occasion of her sin.

And so he spent in her and lay, breathing heavily, and she put her hand on his belly, her reddish locks spread over his thigh. She smiled up at him, her eyes so childish and innocent that he was inflamed once again to fondle her, to caress those long, slender thighs, to glut himself with kisses on her youthful breasts. And all the time, like a child doing what she had been told to do, her delicate fingers slowly kneaded his penis to full size. His face flushed, he asked her to kiss his cock, and submissively lowering

her head until all he could see below him were masses of red hair, she brought him deliciously to a second climax, an event rare enough in recent years for him to experience a sense of triumph. He laughed. He felt insatiable. He held her head against his chest and, staring out of the large window at the morning light on the cold mountain face, felt a rush of joy, and almost without thinking, as though he had composed it for the occasion, cried out one of Mangan's stanzas.[2]

'Over dews, over sands
Will I fly, for your weal:
Your holy delicate white hands
Shall girdle me with steel.
At home, in your emerald bowers,
From morning's dawn till e'en,
You'll pray for me, my flower of flowers,
My Dark Rosaleen!
My fond Rosaleen!
You'll think of me through daylight hours,
My virgin flower, my flower of flowers,
My Dark Rosaleen!'

She raised her head from his chest, tossing back her red mane of hair, smiling that smile which entranced him. 'Are you at the poetry again?' she said. 'Oh, you *are* a fillim actor, you must be.'

'No, I'm not.

'Oh, my red Rosaleen.
And one beamy smile from you
Would float like light between
My toils and me, my own, my true,
My Dark Rosaleen!
My fond Rosaleen!
Would give me life and soul anew,
A second life, a soul anew,
My Dark Rosaleen!'

'You're a gas man,' she said, twisting about in sudden girlish merriment.

'No, it's true. That's what you've given me.'

'*What* did I give you?' she asked.

He struck a pose.

'A second life, a soul anew,
My Dark Rosaleen!'

'Go on with you. Or, tell us, then, what will you give *me*? Will you give me twenty pounds? Con would kill me for telling you, but we're flat broke, the pair of us. His fault. He's spent the dole and the assistance,[3] the lot. Is is true you're rich?'

'It's true!' he shouted, his voice mad loud in the quiet room. 'I'll give you twenty pounds. I'll give you a hundred, a thousand. Come here, my red Kathleen.'

'That will be the drink talking. A thousand quid? I've never *seen* a thousand quid, let alone held it in my hand. It must be the vodka you're on, for I smell nothing.'

'I'm not drunk on drink, I'm drunk on you.' He pulled her up onto his chest, his hands sliding down along her smooth thighs. To his astonishment, his penis was again rising to the occasion. To go on fooling around with her in this high old bed seemed to him the summa of everything he wished for, and now as if she perfectly perceived each nuance of his fantasy, she turned away from him and knelt, touching her forehead to the mattress as though making obeisance to some god at the foot of the bed. In this posture her luxuriant red tresses fell away to reveal a defenseless white nape of neck as she presented her long, straight back and upraised trembling young bottom. He knelt, reaching out to caress and fondle the soft white buttocks. If happiness was this, then he wanted it never to end, unholy though it be, this joy. For she must be almost young enough to be his daughter.

'How old are you, Kathleen?' he whispered, as he handled her soft thighs.

'Nineteen,' she whispered back, submissively. 'At least I'll be nineteen at the beginning of next month. Will you still be here for my birthday?'

Eighteen. Half his age. With a moan of pleasure he penetrated her. 'I will. Of course, I will.'

1 An odd confusion of the United Irishmen (1790s) with the Fenians (1860s).
2 'Dark Rosaleen' was James Clarence Mangan's most famous poem.
3 Unemployment and social security benefit.

IRISH WRITING IN THE 1980s

What are the central issues at stake in the cultural debate? Perhaps the most dominant is the question of identity and difference. What does it mean to be Irish? Is it some unique 'essence' inherited from our ancestors? Is it a characteristic of a specific language (e.g., Gaelic) or religion (Catholic/Protestant) or ideology (nationalist/unionist)? Is it a matter of ethnic memory, genetic heritage or geographical residence? One thing is certain: the question of what it means to be Irish — who we are and where we are going to — cannot be limited to the frontiers of our island. The affirmation of a dynamic cultural identity invariably involves an exploratory dialogue with other cultures.

This is not just a feature of modern or post-modern cultures; it has always been so. And Ireland is no exception to this model of identity in dialogue with difference. Our cultural history reads like a litany of intellectual migrations which have established extensive associations between Ireland and the wider world. This is especially true of our cultural links with Europe. Those with Britain are so intimate as to require no further mention. The link with the Continent reaches back, in our literary memory, to the famous *navigatio*'s of Irish thinkers and missionaries between the seventh and tenth centuries, as recorded in the *Immram* genre of popular voyage tales and as exemplified by the expeditions abroad of figures like Eriugena, St Cilian, Columbanus, Sedulis Scottus and Clement Maelcomer who travelled throughout the Continent and were renowned for their intellectual achievements. These cultural bonds with Europe were reconfirmed after the seventeenth century when a number of Irish Colleges were established in Paris, Salamanca, Rome and Louvain for the education of Irish Catholics abroad. And this cross-fertilization of Irish and European minds was also evident in the intellectual itineraries of Irish Protestant thinkers such as Berkeley, Burke, Toland and Tone in the eighteenth century and in many of our great writers — Joyce, Beckett, Yeats, Shaw, Stephens — in our own century.

– Richard Kearney, *Across the Frontiers: Ireland in the 1990s* (1988)

CRITICAL AND DOCUMENTARY

MARY HOLLAND
from *The New Statesman*, 19 October 1984

Mary Holland (1936–), a seasoned commentator on Northern Ireland, here describes reaction to the IRA bomb at the Conservative Party Conference in October 1984. The bomb exploded at the Grand Hotel in Brighton, where Mrs Thatcher and members of her Cabinet were staying, killing five people.

Ireland Blasts Back

The most immediate lesson of last Friday's IRA attack at the Grand Hotel in Brighton is one with which, over the years, Irish politicians have become brutally familiar. One audaciously placed bomb can do more to concentrate the minds of British politicians on Northern Ireland than endless hours of patient discussion and diplomacy.

For several months now (some would say for years) the Dublin government has been trying to engage Mrs Thatcher's interest in the possibilities of much closer Anglo-Irish co-operation in dealing with the problems of the North. For most of last week, before Friday's bomb, diplomats from the Irish Embassy in London had been busy in Brighton. Their task was to canvass Conservative MPs and ministers in the hope of mustering support for some positive political response to the 'new realism' in the Republic, which has been evident since the publication of the Forum report.[1]

It was already depressingly clear, not only from the mood at the Tory Conference but with Labour in Blackpool the week before, that the miners' strike[2] had taken over British politics to an extent that displaced most other issues. One after the other, Conservative MPs, of the select band which interests itself in Northern Ireland, told me that it was now very difficult to believe that the Prime Minister would devote her mind and energy to pursuing a risky new initiative in Northern Ireland while the MacGregor-Scargill drama continued centre stage.

Whatever the IRA's own political objective in attempting to kill Mrs Thatcher and her Cabinet, their bomb certainly swept away that mood of jaded indifference to the Irish problem. The effrontery of the attack, the fact that it came so close to success has focused attention on Northern Ireland in a way that I certainly cannot remember in recent years. If anything, that interest seems to have grown rather than diminished over the past week as the general public has come to realize the full extent of the security problem which it could be facing. If, as police reports

seem to indicate, the IRA's techniques are now sufficiently sophisticated for its volunteers to be able to place undetectable bombs, designed to kill public figures, days, weeks, even months in advance the possibilities are almost too horrific to contemplate. Police all over the country must now be asking themselves who might be at risk in their areas and how far they should go to protect them.

There has been endless speculation as to why the IRA did it. The simplest and not entirely flippant answer is: because they found they were able to. Besides, the idea of wiping out the British government, or a good part of it, is one of the oldest dreams in the Irish Republican canon. Cathal Brugha, one of the IRA's most respected leaders in the War of Independence and Minister of Defence in the first Dáil, tried several times to mount such an operation. His plan, which he travelled to London to reconnoitre, was to shoot the whole government front bench from the visitors' gallery of the House of Commons.

Any active service unit operating in Britain must have as a high priority the assassination of figures prominent in public life, up to and including the Queen. These would include judges, politicians, senior members of the defence forces, almost everybody, in fact, who could be described later as part of the British war machine.

They would not now be encouraged to put the lives of innocent civilians at risk. The Harrods bomb at Christmas was judged to have been an extremely serious error and the IRA's statement that it had not been authorized was an almost unique public reproach to its own volunteers. At the moment, I understand, such a unit would be unlikely to go for members of the Labour Party. Partly this is because Labour is not in power, but also the Provisionals are keen to build support among the Left of the party. Recent issues of their newspaper, *An Phoblacht* have put considerable emphasis on Tony Benn's[3] calls for British withdrawal from Northern Ireland.

The Provisionals' own comments on the immediate purpose of the Brighton bomb have been chilling.

Even allowing for their desire to wring the maximum propaganda benefit from the incident, there seems little reason to disbelieve them. Danny Morrison has said that the IRA hoped to kill the entire cabinet. Gerry Adams has elaborated on this by saying that, if the attack had been successful, it would probably have led to the introduction of draconian security measures in the North which would have brought the whole issue to a head with considerable speed. Past experience has taught that the introduction of such measures greatly increases support for the IRA.

But these comments don't tell the whole story, nor probably even the half of it. Traditionally, operations mounted in Britain have had two objectives. One is the long-term task of sickening British public opinion so that pressure will mount for withdrawal from Ireland. But just as important as the impact that a bombing campaign might have in Britain are the effects on morale in Ireland itself and, crucially, on support in the United States. Early this month (*NS* 5 October) I wrote that the IRA's campaign would escalate — and suggested that this would be partly as a result of tensions within the Provos arising from Sinn Fein's espousal of electoral politics. Over the past few weeks Sinn Fein leaders like Gerry Adams and Danny Morrison have been absolutely explicit that they consider the continuation of a campaign of violence necessary in order to achieve the Provos' aim of British withdrawal from Northern Ireland.

What has surfaced increasingly over the past few months is the growing disenchantment within the IRA's own ranks with the amount of time and talent that has been invested in constitutional politics. The attempt to build a broad political base in the Catholic community extending beyond their own hard-core supporters has imposed considerable strains. Contrary to what some commentators have suggested, many Catholics vote for Sinn Fein in spite, and not because, of the IRA's campaign.

These Catholics desperately want some political progress which will bring peace for their families and have gauged, accurately, that the British government is most likely to be spurred into reconsidering its Northern policy by a large vote for Sinn Fein. But, as Danny Morrison has admitted, the atrocities committed by the IRA do bother Catholic voters and may cause them to withdraw their support. In order to broaden Sinn Fein's political base, the IRA has acceded to pressure to scale down its activities. The resulting drop in the statistics of violence has enabled the British to claim that the security situation is under control, a boast which has caused particular chagrin to IRA prisoners in jail.

Sinn Fein's commitment to the electoral process is also perceived as having had political effects very different from those intended by Adams and his young Turks when they first spoke of taking power with an armalite in one hand and a ballot paper in the other. Dissidents within the movement now argue, with some justification, that the main result of Sinn Fein's electoral successes has been to help the opponent they most want to defeat — John Hume's SDLP.[4]

They argue that it is only since Sinn Fein started winning elections that the British government has conceded that there is a real problem of alienation in the Catholic community in Northern Ireland. Adams's own election in Westminster, displacing the House of Commons's favourite Irishman, Gerry Fitt,[5] has been particularly effective in that regard. Critics in the IRA point to the setting up of the New Ireland Forum, the more conciliatory tone being adopted by the Unionist parties in Belfast and to closer relations between the London and Dublin governments. All these, they say, spring from the common desire to stave off the threat of Sinn Fein. This week, in the wake of the Brighton bomb, Adams has been particularly scathing about the Dublin government's insistent claim that it be given some role, as of right, to represent the interests of the Catholic minority in the North; a claim which Jim Prior[6] at least recognized as not unreasonable.

In the immediate aftermath of the bomb, Conservative politicians were insistent that the government would not be deflected by the activities of the IRA from seeking political progress in Northern Ireland; and that this would include much closer co-operation with Dublin. Two of them, Chris Patten, a Junior Minister at the Northern Ireland Office, and Michael Mates were in Dublin last weekend to give added emphasis to this view.

But already that emphasis seems to be shifting. Increasingly one hears the view expressed that Mrs Thatcher will not be able to make any moves that would involve Dublin, because these would be interpreted as concessions made under pressure from the IRA. The Prime Minister, interviewed on Monday, was less than encouraging about her hopes for any future initiative.

If, as now seems possible, the government is going into a state of funk about the fragile consensus which it seemed to have reached with Dublin, then the bomb which blasted the Grand Hotel at Brighton will have succeeded beyond the IRA's wildest dreams.

1   The New Ireland Forum report (the Forum was set up in May 1983 to canvass opinion in the Republic) suggested three possibilities for discussion: a unitary state, a federal/confederal state, joint sovereignty.

2   The Conservative Conference was held in the middle of the major industrial dispute of the Thatcher years. The all-out strike began in April 1984; in October the assets of the National Union of Mineworkers were seized; in March 1985 the miners agreed to return to work.

3   Left-wing Labour M.P., member of Wilson's Cabinet in 1966–70 and Callaghan's Government in 1975–79.
4   Social Democratic and Labour Party.
5   Leader of the SDLP when it was launched in 1970.
6   Secretary of State for Northern Ireland in 1981–84.

DERVLA MURPHY

from Dervla Murphy, *Tales from Two Cities: Travel of Another Sort* (1985)

Dervla Murphy, author of *A Place Apart* (1978) (see above p. 843), here turns her attention to the backstreets of Britain and to the condition of England. The setting for the first extract is Bradford in West Yorkshire where she was sharing a squat to see what conditions were like at first hand. Here she tackles Irish sympathizers selling papers on the street. In the second extract she has moved to the Midlands, to Handsworth, another immigrant area, and is looking for a bed-sit (one- or two-roomed flat or apartment) in an area nicknamed 'the front line'.

'Racism' and 'British Oppression in Ireland' were equally popular themes in the several Communist weeklies on sale (30p. waged, 20p. unwaged) in Bradford's city centre. With so many Red splinter-groups around I could never sort out th'other from which, but most young paper-sellers looked alike: poorly dressed and ill-nourished, with bad teeth, broken finger-nails and angry hopeless eyes. Their journals' Irish articles had predictable headlines: 'Hands off Ireland!' 'Unite to Fight the PTA!'[1] 'Irish Freedom Movement Defies Censorship!'

One afternoon I bought the TNS (*The Next Step:* Review of the Revolutionary Communist Party) from a twenty-four-year-old who had never had a job. He asked challengingly, 'D'you support Troops Out?'

'Not just at present,' I replied. 'Most Irish feel the consequences of their going could be even worse than the consequences of their staying.'

'Imperial chauvinist!' shouted the young man, clenching his free fist.

My remark that 'chauvinist' was peculiarly inappropriate provoked a tirade about the future of Ireland when 'the puppets of Westminster' (Dr FitzGerald and Mr Haughey[2]) had been overthrown, to make way for 'true patriots' (INLA[3]) who would establish a *genuinely* democratic thirty-two-county Socialist Republic.

I pointed out that few Irish will vote even for our conventional Labour Party, never mind a 'Socialist Republic'. But the young man was uninterested in reality and wittered on about 800 years of 'Protestant imperialist persecution of Catholics', overlooking the fact that 800 years ago there weren't any Protestants. He betrayed a remarkable ignorance about Ireland's past and present, yet his rage was as extreme as though he'd been born in West Belfast.[4] It was also infectious. I don't easily become enraged and it's easy to sympathize with discarded youngsters who take refuge in the fantasy world of revolution-round-the-corner. But when he called me 'a traitorous bitch' I suddenly and fiercely resented being told what to think about my own country by someone who didn't know Derry from Kerry. Losing my cool, I voiced this resentment, rather loudly — provoking further abuse which caused passers-by to swivel their eyes in our direction. It would of course be un-British actually to *turn the head* when noticing a strangers' quarrel.

I later described this encounter to a White anti-racist friend who said, 'So now you know how angry *Blacks* feel when *you* talk nonsense about *their* problems. *They* know the score, *you* don't! They're the victims of White racism, you're just an observer sitting on the fence making silly remarks!'

In certain inner-city circles my nationality was, at least initially, advantageous; and it could have been even more so had I accepted the role in which I was often automatically cast – 'IRA sympathizer'. The Provos, being near the top of League One in the world propaganda championship, have secured much support among young bottom-of-the-pilers of all races. Some of their admirers know much more than my paper-selling adversary about Irish history and politics, though naturally their informants have given them green spectacles through which to view Northern Ireland's tragedy.

At the end of a meeting with one militant Black 'community leader', who had had much to say about the usefulness of bombing campaigns to 'prove a political point', his hitherto silent companion suddenly asked me — 'Have the police called on you yet?'

To the amusement of both, I was somewhat taken aback. So the leader explained, 'You come from Ireland, you've been living in a squat-area, you've been meeting all sorts of groups like us — don't you *expect* the police to call?'

I confessed that I did not, that my career had been so dull and uneventful no police force had ever had occasion to call on me — which admission did nothing for my status in that particular group. Some people fancy that if you are not a police suspect you must be a police informer; they ignore the intermediate area occupied by most citizens.

• • •

My search for a bed-sit soon revealed the extremity of Handsworth's deprivation. What lies behind some affluent-looking, recently enveloped exteriors is not Third World destitution but a Fourth World of squalor such as I have never before encountered. The half-adoption of a Western urban life-style, by very poor Blacks and Browns living in grossly over-crowded conditions, can lead to an out-of-control degradation unknown in the worst of Third World slums. (I mean degradation as distinct from hardship.) I once lived for a fortnight in the *barriados* around Lima without seeing anything comparable to what lurks inside many Handsworth 'envelopes'. But I'll spare my readers' sensibilities by skipping the worst of it and concentrating on the comparatively innocuous livestock.

In a Pakistani-owned house three cockroach corpses lay in the lodger's sink and several live cockroaches frolicked beneath it; mini-cockroaches by Ecuadorean or Malagasy standards — scarcely an inch long — yet I felt I could do without five months of their constant companionship. In a neat and polished Black-owned house all seemed tolerable (there was a perfectly adequate el-san[5] in a garden-shed) until I noticed arcane and sinister smears on the wall above the bed. Fortunately these did not baffle me; I know a bed-bug slaughter-house when I see one. In a Sikh-owned house a spacious ground-floor room overlooking a

leafy garden seemed paradisaical and the owner and I sat on the bed to talk business. A moment later my legs began to tickle and I vaguely scratched, as one does; then they tickled much more and I glanced down to see starved fleas swarming onto my bare ankles. The Sikh, looking amused, said the room had been unoccupied for six weeks and once someone moved in the fleas would depart. This seems to me a slur on their intelligence so negotiations ceased abruptly.

Bed-sit hunting is a good way to get the feel of an area and make contacts, but after a fortnight I had had enough. Rather cravenly, I ended up in an Irish-owned pad infested only by a half-grown kitten of infinite charm and exquisite beauty who had been callously abandoned by the last tenant. When she realized that I was on her wave-length she became quite ecstatic and stood on my lap and kissed my nose whereupon I at once signed a three-month contract.

Since January I had somehow acquired an unconscionable number of books so Des and Dan volunteered to help me move to Heathfield Road. These young Irishmen owned (or at least *used*) a beat-up untaxed motor-van and lived in a Fourth World squat — a genuine squat, where four or five people shared one room, as distinct from my genteel pad. Their house was in a dangerous state of disrepair and has since been demolished; no Urban Renewal beavers could do anything for it. It was an imposing eighteen-room detached residence in a large garden bounded by beeches and flowering chestnuts; trees are Handsworth's glory — wherever you look, they seem to fill at least half the skyline. However, within this shell of Victorian affluence all was reeking, sordid disorder, presided over by a chipped statue of the Infant of Prague, a plastic bust of President Kennedy, and technicoloured pictures of the Sacred Heart of Jesus, St Patrick ankle-deep in snakes, Our Lady of Lourdes, a simpering Little Flower, Pope John Paul XXIII (also simpering), a framed 1916 Proclamation and various other symbols of popular Irish Catholicism-cum-Nationalism. Perhaps it is not as absurd as it sounds to classify the Irish as an 'ethnic minority'. The description makes no sense physically, yet in certain surroundings it can seem psychologically or temperamentally accurate.

Des, Dan and their fellow-squatters were among the many thousands of Irish youngsters who have been settling in Brum[6] during recent years – not to seek jobs, for they know none exists, but to escape from intolerable domestic situations. Contrary to popular belief, they get no more State support from the British than the Irish government, but British benefits come in a form that solves their particular problem. The DHSS[7] was paying the owner of my friends' squat directly for their board (two meals a day) and lodging, while giving them £9.50 per week in cash. At home they would have been given £30 cash and had much more spending money, since most Irish parents take only £10 a week. However, in recessed Ireland whole families are now on the dole – perhaps a still youngish father and three or four grown-up children — which soon leads to friction in cramped council houses or high-rise flats. And Irish rents are too high for a jobless youngster to move into a bed-sitter, or even a squat — hence the attraction of the British system.

We set off for the hostel accompanied by Una, a nineteen-year-old Cavan girl pregnant by one of the boys; she seemed unsure which and they seemed happy to share the credit. All three were touchingly concerned about my feckless failure to sign on for the dole. 'You're an EEC[8] citizen,' said Una, 'so you're *entitled* to it. Why throw good money away? I mean, if you're just a writer you're not really *employed*, are you? I mean, you don't have real *work*, do you?' When I pointed out that writers sometimes have to work ten hours a day, seven days a week, fifty-two weeks a year they all thought this an excellent leg-pull and roared with laughter.

Arriving at my new front door — Flat No. 3 — we couldn't open it though I did have the correct key. It would have collapsed, being half-rotten, had any one of us leant on it. But I reckoned a half-rotten door is better than none so the boys went round to the side of the house and by shoulder-standing had gained entrance to my pad within moments. The inside catch had been put on the Yale lock by someone who had then departed — presumably — through the window. Later it transpired that the previous tenant, an Englishman of mysterious provenance, had returned to help himself to all the saucepans. As I didn't plan to cook during my tenancy this was of no consequence — to me. Brigid, my landlady, naturally felt otherwise, especially as the tenant in question still owed her five weeks' rent.

Brigid had gone to some trouble to reorganize my tiny pad. A rickety wardrobe and chest-of-drawers had been moved out to the landing and replaced by a biggish desk-substitute table, standing by the sash window. I felt very happy on that June evening, writing my journal by the open window. Directly opposite, some thirty yards away, was the kitchen wing of a semi-derelict three-storey house — painted an unfortunate dried-blood-red, which took a bit of getting used to. But just to the left of that stretched a glorious expanse of woodland, an unbroken line of

beeches, limes, poplars, birches, chestnuts, ashes. Brum is to be commended for the zeal with which it cherishes — and when necessary replaces — its trees.

No. 45 had been worth waiting for; there I was at the very hub of Handsworth — or, in local terminology, 'on the front line'. (The significance of that phrase will emerge in due course.) The long Heathfield Road carries heavy commuter traffic morning and evening and is quite noisy even at night, many young Blacks being nocturnal in their habits. No. 45 is at the top end, about fifty yards from the junction with the Villa Road and the Lozells Road, and most of my immediate neighbours were young Blacks living in flats or squats. A little further down is a large Afro-Caribbean Centre, where special Saturday School classes are held, and just beyond that an enormous Nonconformist church has been converted into a Hindu temple. Within a few minutes' walk in other directions are a Vietnamese Centre, a Black Pentecostal church and the huge block of the Soho Road Sikh Gurdwara. Mirpuri families (many ex-Manningham[9]) live on various streets leading off Heathfield Road and across the Lozells Road is a considerable — though self-effacing and not very noticeable — colony of Bangladeshis. My White neighbours were OAPs[10] living in a newish but already dingy two-storey building opposite the Villa Cross pub. Handsworth is said to be the 'most multi-racial district' in all of Britain. I can believe it.

My local was the Villa Cross and the Villa Road catered for all other needs: Sikh supermarket, Gujarati newsagent, Mirpuri greengrocer, Black chemist, Sikh off-licence, Black take-away, multi-racial-staffed bank, all-White-staffed post office. It was then a grim street, always ankle-deep in litter and starkly reflecting both the poverty and the tension of this corner of Handsworth. No shop looked more than quarter-way to making a decent living and most shop windows — even tiny newsagents and pathetic cubby-holes selling cheap plastic toys — were protected by steel mesh. The mini-supermarket employed a bouncer; 'security officer' is too mild a term. He stood by the door — a squat, tough-looking elderly Black — and confiscated every customer's shopping-bag (or any other receptacle) as they entered. Although he could be quite charming, if dealing with Blacks or Browns, he positively vibrated with anti-White aggro. When I first tried to enter, he insisted that I must hand over my brief-case. It contained various vital documents (not to mention my journal, by then very fat and beyond price) so I turned away and heard him commenting loudly to no one in particular — 'Bloody suspicious old cow!' On my empty-handed return half an hour later he pounced on me again and confiscated a newly purchased electric light bulb visible in my husky pocket. Two other Blacks — male and female — sauntered all the time up and down between the meagrely stocked shelves: the Villa Road substitute for electronic surveillance devices. Not surprisingly, White customers were uncommon in that shop.

It took me less than twenty-four hours to *feel* why my pad was said to be 'on the front line'. The Villa Cross pub, the Acapulco café opposite it (at my end of the Villa Road) and nearby areas were flamboyantly 'Rasta' territory. The fact that few of the so-called Rastas were true Rastafarians need not for the moment detain us. They were universally known as such, many wore dreadlocks and Rasta hats and all smoked ganja which the dealers among them sold openly, not only in the Villa Cross and Acapulco but on the wide forecourt of the pub and along the surrounding streets. This curious situation will be considered in detail in a later chapter. Here I am concerned only with the public perception of 'the front line', the effect on the neighbourhood of this group of a few score anti-White, anti-Authority young Blacks. They scared everyone, hence the area's perceptible tension — sometimes low, sometimes high. And they angered many, by their defiant holding of the ganja-dealing 'front line' against the police. Visually and emotionally they dominated the Villa Road, Lozells Road, Heathfield Road — their influence less noticeable the further one got from the Villa Road, yet extending in a diluted form throughout Handsworth.

To me as a newcomer they seemed an unattractive segment of the variegated local population. Their mien was deliberately hostile and threatening towards the world in general but particularly towards Whites

(apart from their customers), and most particularly towards the police and all who might be considered police allies — for example, an elderly White female who clearly didn't 'belong' to Heathfield Road's squat-world yet had moved in. After 11.00 a.m., any excursion down the Villa Road involved running the gauntlet of those young men, some sitting on the low wall surrounding the Villa Cross forecourt, others hanging about on the pavement outside the Acapulco, or lounging in the doorways of the adjacent betting-office and taxi-office. By the end of my first day, during which I was to-ing and fro-ing a good deal in the course of 'home-making', I understood precisely what was meant by that term 'front-line'; it is unnerving to be the object of such concentrated animosity. Later, when I came to understand a little more about the nuances of the situation, the 'front-line' catch-phrase irritated me. Yet I could still see why those powerful Villa Road vibes aroused anxiety and antagonism among most of my non-Rasta neighbours of every colour — and mixture of colours.

1   Prevention of Terrorism Act, introduced in 1974, enables suspects to be held for seven days without being charged.
2   Both served as Irish Taoiseachs when their respective parties (Fine Gael for former, Fianna Fáil for latter) won elections in the 1980s.
3   Irish National Liberation Army.
4   Area associated with Provisional IRA influence and control.
5   A lavatory where the sludge is removed by chemical means (OED).
6   Affectionate name for Birmingham.
7   Department of Health and Social Security.
8   European Economic Community (now EU or European Union).
9   District of Bradford.
10   Old Age Pensioners.

DEREK MAHON
from *The Observer*, April 1986

'The time is coming fast, if it isn't already here, when the question, "Is so-and-so really an Irish writer?" will clear a room in seconds.' Thus begins Derek Mahon's 1974 tribute to Louis MacNeice. Here in his tribute to Beckett, which is reprinted in *Journalism: Selected Prose, 1970–1995* (1996), Mahon switches tack and makes a good case for considering the 'Parisian' Beckett Irish.

A Tribute to Beckett on his Eightieth Birthday

Everyone has his or her Beckett story, and here is mine. In the autumn of 1981 we met by appointment in the Hôtel St Jacques across the street from where he lives in Paris, and spent an hour drinking coffee. The St Jacques surprised me. A soulless, Hiltonesque place with piped muzak and revolving racks of thrillers, it seemed a far cry from what legend had led me to expect. A corner café, perhaps, where the great man would be on first-name terms with the proprietor and Jameson's Irish whiskey mysteriously available. Instead he went unrecognized, an erect, athletic figure with a cliff of white hair and a Tunisian tan, the famous gull's eyes, grey-blue behind granny glasses, an unnaturally clean tweed coat over the sweater and jeans. He was then seventy-five.

We talked in a constrained fashion about Ireland, schools, poetry, mutual friends; then I mentioned music. His wife, I knew, was an accomplished pianist, but was not he himself, as some said, a dab hand at the keyboard? He showed me his fingers, gnarled arthritic trees. No more piano playing. But now he grew animated, waxing lyrical about the benefits of age: loss of memory, of vocabulary . . . 'It's great,' he concluded, 'I've been looking forward to it all my life!' He was obviously sincere, and apparently unaware of the joke.

We parted shortly afterwards, myself slightly disappointed not to be invited back to the famous flat overlooking the exercise yard of the Santé prison. He is five years older now, and presumably five years further advanced into happy decrepitude. But the ultimate happiness, adumbrated in *Oedipus at Colonus* and rendered by Yeats as 'Never to have lived is best', has eluded him and will continue to do so; for, though he might have wished otherwise, he is alive and evidently well enough to contemplate the geriatric joys with equanimity. Indeed, he can never die, not really, not 'enough to bury'; his death would be a logical absurdity, since he was, by his own admission, 'never properly born'. It seems his 'unsuccessful abortion' took place in the Dublin suburb of Stillorgan (ha!) on Good Friday, 13 April 1906, which ghastly event we celebrated today. But let us not forget the partial nature of that birth, the fact that much remained in the womb-tomb. In this he resembles the bird in Rilke's *Elegies* which knows both the inside and the out. And indeed his apprehension of the 'real world' is painfully, if often hilariously, acute. 'Born of a wet dream and dead before morning', he might have led a happy death, but the blackest humour, if not exactly cheerfulness, keeps breaking in, for an important thing to remember about Beckett is that he is one of the funniest of modern writers, a fact often lost sight of in the sea of exposition. Ultimately, said Jacques Tati, humour is in the legs. Beckett uses words as legs, tripping over himself syntactically in a doomed effort to make himself clear: 'There are many ways in which the thing I am trying in vain to say may be tried in vain to be said.' And again: 'Let us, for once, be foolish enough not to turn tail. All have turned wisely tail, before the ultimate penury.'

What makes Beckett such a puzzle? Wherein lies the curiosity value? Why do we want to know all we can about him? The answer, I believe, lies at least partly in a widespread inability to 'place' him, both in the conventional English sense (one critic remarked of the Deirdre Bair biography, with approval it seemed, that he hadn't realized the dustbin dramatist came from such a well-to-do background) and in a sense intended by the American student who says, 'I don't know where you're coming from.' Well, as his compatriots never tire of pointing out, he is the latest, if not the last, in a series of Anglo-Irish dramatists stretching back through Shaw and Wilde to Sheridan, Goldsmith and Congreve. The name of Swift, too, is often invoked. Like them he is aphoristic ('Silence once broken can never be mended') and sometimes shocking ('The slut has yet to menstruate capable of whelping me'), but there is more Irishman to it than that.

There hangs in the Tate a picture by Jack B. Yeats, oil on canvas, entitled *Two Travellers*. The 'travellers' — 'tinkers' as they used to say — are ragged figures on a road in Connemara. Beckett's view of Jack Yeats's poet brother has always seemed sceptical at best, but he has written admiringly of the artist — himself a reticent, secretive type — and it seems evident that *Two Travellers* provided at least one point of departure for Didi and Gogo in *Waiting for Godot*. If we bear in mind that Jack Yeats collaborated extensively with Synge, and that Beckett is known to have a great fondness for *The Playboy of the Western World*, we are, I think, getting close to the truth of the matter. Beckett is not a Shaw but a Synge, not (in his plays) a ratiocinative but a demonstrative writer, one who shows but doesn't tell. To Alan Schneider, the American director, he wrote: 'If people want to have headaches among the overtones, let them. And provide their own aspirin.' The novels are different, though here too, and increasingly so, it's a matter of texture rather than incident: 'a few images on and off in the mud earth sky a few creatures in the light some still standing' (*How It Is*). This is a painterly prose without precedent in English unless one wants to reread in its strange light certain passages in Shakespeare or the opening chapters of *Wuthering Heights* and *Great Expectations*, where Pip first discerns 'the identity of things'.

Finally, though, we are back with Swift and the question of where Beckett is 'coming from'. He is coming from the Dublin Protestant middle class and, like Swift, from the Church of Ireland. Consider the Sunday text in *All That Fall*: 'The Lord upholdeth all that fall and raiseth up all those that be bowed down. (*Silence. They join in wild laughter. They move on. Wind and rain.*)' And consider too Didi's parsonical peroration in *Godot*:

> Let us not waste our time in idle discourse! Let us do something, while we have the chance! It is not every day that we are needed. Not indeed that we personally

are needed. Others would meet the case equally well, if not better. To all mankind they were addressed, those cries for help still ringing in our ears! But at this place, at this moment of time, all mankind is us, whether we like it or not . . . What are we doing here, that *is* the question. And we are blessed in this, that we happen to know the answer. Yes, in this immense confusion one thing alone is clear. We are waiting for Godot to come, or for night to fall. We have kept our appointment, and that's an end to that. We are not saints, but we have kept our appointment. How many people can boast as much?

To which, speaking for us all — the dead, the living and the unborn — Gogo replies, in a manner at once reductive and expansive (such is the Beckett paradox): 'Billions'.

PETER SIRR
from *The Irish Times*, 14 June 1986

Peter Sirr (1960–   ), author of *Marginal Zones* (1984), *Talk, Talk* (1987), and *Ways of Falling* (1991), here provides an even-handed review of Kinsella's edition of *The New Oxford Book of Irish Verse* (1986).

Poetry in Ireland from its Roots

Thomas Kinsella's anthology is one of the most ambitious literary projects to be undertaken in a long time. It is the first coherent attempt to present the entire range of Irish poetry in both languages to an English-speaking readership. It is an act of personal repossession designed to set a whole tradition squarely in front of those accustomed to think that Irish poetry begins to become acceptable for consumption with Luke Wadding or Jonathan Swift. Its almost 400 pages of text and notes cover a vast amount of material, tactfully edited to form a cohesive and convincing whole and to show the major outlines of Irish poetic culture from its beginning.

Perhaps over-compensating for the usual ignorance of Gaelic poetry, the blurb implies that the 'Irish poetic tradition' may now begin to be looked upon as a unity, and talks eagerly about the relationship between the two major bodies of poetry in this country. But what is that relationship and how, if at all, does it affect or energize the contemporary poet?

Thomas Kinsella has spoken eloquently of 'the divided mind'[1] which he feels is the condition of the modern Irish poet. The division stems from the loss of the Irish language as the major medium of expression and its significance for the poet is the discontinuous and problematic tradition bequeathed by that loss. It is, for instance, part of the problematic legacy that the Irish poet in either language is in certain vital respects closer to, say, Donne than he can ever be to Ó Rathaille[2] because Donne was a distinct forceful talent speaking in a tradition and out of a sensibility which we still receive, whereas Ó Rathaille was the voice and the archetype of a culture whose disappearance sets us at a permanent remove from his work. The real interest of this lies in the necessarily ambiguous and oblique fashion in which Gaelic tradition must communicate itself to us, and in whether those shadows might still reveal the kind of signals an acute writer can transmit.

The Gaelic tradition is one of a number of traditions available to the contemporary Irish poet, and certainly not the most important, but what a book like this does is to keep the option open for both poets and readers and perhaps, ideally, to increase the range of reference and nuance that might reasonably be expected of Irish poetry.

The anthology is divided into three 'books', the first two of which cover the bulk of the Gaelic material. The first hundred pages is taken up with translations of Gaelic poetry from the sixth to the 14th century and also includes versions from the Latin, a section of the 'Fortifications of New Ross' from the Norman French, and some anonymous Early English lyrics. Aside from the translations from the Ulster Cycle and the Fenian poems, the emphasis is predominantly Christian, ranging from the exhortations of Columbanus's 'Boat Song' through the worldliness of Sedulius Scottus to Gofraidh Fionn Ó Dálaigh's powerful parable 'A Child in Prison'.

There is a generous selection of monastic poems from the ninth century, by turns ascetic, playful and plainly celebratory and all characterized by a formal tact that is one of the most valuable features of the poetry from this period. Poem 24, the Hermit Marbán's dialogue with King Guaire, or the anonymous 'First of summer, lovely sight' are good examples of how these poets used their material.

In both we are given a spare, precise evocation of the natural world, a delighted sense of abundance in the catalogue of good things. The poems are never laboriously descriptive, the emphasis is on the quick, clean notation with economy of detail. It is, of course, a moral art — that delight is not self-sustaining but an extension of faith. But it is not all simple delight: poem three, for example, is a barbed comment on the approach of the 'Adze-heads' with their 'false' religion and a paradigm of the tension between two worlds which can crop up much later in, say, Padraigin Haicéad's furious verses written on hearing that it has been ordered 'that the Friars make no more Songs or Verses.'

Much of this poetry is of a kind that lends itself to sympathetic translation. Kinsella's versions have a certain deliberate stiffness and solidity, a lack of ornament and excess that lets the material speak for itself . . . Kinsella brings us close to the spirit but also the linguistic feel, the tough constraints of the originals. There have been many fine translations of

Gaelic poetry before, but never a project of this scope and disinterestedness. Many poets (Mangan, Ferguson, Stephens, etc.) have worked the tradition for their own ends, taking from it what best suited their own imaginative needs or, like Ferguson and particularly Mangan, admitting it to the core of their sensibility until it re-emerges as part of the personal vision. This is, of course, also partly true of Kinsella but there is a lack of clutter, a pared-down impersonality about his own gift that causes him to intrude as little as possible on the originals. Some of the examples that stood out for me were the three short lyrics which open the anthology, poem eight (the Epitaph for Cú Chuimhne) or the last two stanzas from Bláthmac Mac Con Brettan's 'Poem to Mary' with its direct, earthy note:

> . . . I will mourn
> your Son profoundly with you
> if, at some time,
> you will come to visit me.
>
> That we may talk together
> in the pity of an unstained heart,
> o head of purest faith,
> come to me, loving Mary.

Equally moving and equally plainly rendered were the lovely 'Líadan and Cuirithir' and 'Goll Mac Morna Parts from his Wife' (familiar to every Leaving Cert. student[3]). Of the slightly later material Muireadhach Albanach Ó Dálaigh's elegy for his wife shows what a powerful medium bardic poetry can be. What appeals is not any startling imagery but simply the tact, restraint and delicacy of the thing. Something of the fiercely proud spirit of the poetry is captured in the translation of Giolla Bhrighde Mac Con Midhe's dignified defence of his art, with its tight-lipped contempt for the 'clowns' who would belittle it, and managing to call up Patrick, Colum Cille and even Jesus as fellow practitioners:

> Mary's great Son will grant me
> a prize no man can give
> for a poem of my lovely craft:
> I'll have heaven, like Ó hIfearnáin!

Book Two, from the 14th to the 19th century, is essentially a selection from the 'Duanaire' material, with the addition of earlier poems (Tadhg Dall Ó hUigínn, anonymous love poetry of the *amour courtois* type[4]) and of poetry in English. Thus, for the first time between the covers of one book, poets in both languages rub shoulders: Luke Wadding with Tomás 'Láidir' Mac Coidealbhaigh, Swift with Ó Rathaille, Goldsmith with Eoghan Rua Ó Súilleabhain or Cathal Buí Mac Giolla Ghunna. There are occasional overlaps, such as Swift's rendition of Pléaraca na Ruarcach with its famous opening lines:

> O'Rourke's noble fare
> will ne'er be forgot
> By those who were there
> Or those who were not

but otherwise there is little cross-fertilization. The Gaelic poets of this period, from Ó hEoghusa to Ó Rathaille, were already locked in that long terminal lament for an order that was gradually disappearing. It might be possible to trace temperamental affinities between the author of 'An Bonnan Buí' and, say, Goldsmith, or between Ó Rathaille and Swift — both share a vein of pure anger — but the two poetries are radically different and it's not until well into the 19th century that the Gaelic voice begins to impinge, and then only partially, on poetry in English.

In terms of poetic achievement the 18th century was still dominated by Gaelic, as Kinsella's selection makes clear: Ó Rathaille, 'The Lament for Art O Leary', 'The Midnight Court'. It is the last period of that astonishing bravura, self-confidence and self-sustainment of which Gaelic poetry was always capable, and for which the occasional excellences of the folk poetry could never compensate.

The final section covers the 19th and present century. It's easy to dismiss the 19th century as a barren period, blathery and misdirected, or as Kinsella himself puts it: 'a long preparation (as it can seem) for the career of Yeats'. Yet at least two previous careers, those of Ferguson and Mangan, showed what might be possible through opening up the English language to the Gaelic voice, or at least to a dimly filtered version of it.

Both careers were flawed and uneven, but Kinsella is right to stress their importance. Ferguson impresses with his solidity and bulk but sins through dullness. Mangan is a different case. The interesting thing about Mangan is that he operated always *as a poet* in his relation to the literal translations he worked from. That relation was almost entirely a figure of his own imagination and it is his remove from the actual bone of the Gaelic tradition, rather than his fidelity to its spirit,. which animates his best lines. (Compare, for instance, the O'Hussey ode as rendered by him and by Kinsella.) The fact that he knew no Irish is a side-issue. He showed that one of the ways for a writer to

absorb the energies of a broken tradition is to give it the run of his own gift.

There are few surprises initially in the modern section: seven poems by Yeats, generous selections from Kavanagh and Clarke. It is heartening to see the still little known Padraic Fallon represented by four fine poems, by far the best of which is the late 'Painting for my Father' for which the inadequate 'haunting' is the only word. Some will feel annoyed over the omission of Coffey, McGreevy or Charles Donnelly, but Denis Devlin gets five poems, the longest an extract from 'Memoirs of a Turcoman Diplomat'. I would have preferred 'Lough Derg' or maybe 'The Colours of Love', both of them seriously flawed but containing some really excellent poetry. But Devlin was that kind of poet and even his shortest lyrics (the well-known 'Ank'hor Vat' among them) failed sadly to sustain the promise of their opening lines.

The editor himself is impressively represented by four comparatively recent poems. There are only two Irish-language poets, Sean Ó Ríordáin and Máirtín Ó Direáin (meagerly represented by the weakish 'Homage to John Millington Synge'). I found the Ó Ríordáin translations (three from 'Brosna') fine but it is inaccurate and pointless to state that he was the only poet in Irish to respond 'to the demands and opportunities of modern poetry'.

Sometimes it seems that the editor allows his thematic approach to cloud his judgement somewhat. The omissions (no Eavan Boland, Brendan Kennelly, Eiléan Ní Chuilleanáin, Paul Durcan, etc.) are annoying but so often are the inclusions. Five of Richard Murphy's six poems are from the effective but rather forced 'Battle of Aughrim' and the selection (in English) from Michael Hartnett is weak.

The anthology ends with the lame satire of the 'Chef Yeats' section of 'A Farewell to English',[5] for all too obvious thematic reasons. It would, however, be a great pity if the quirky choices from the contemporary scene — which Kinsella himself concedes were gestural rather than comprehensive — were to distract attention from the really magnificent achievement of the book as a whole.

1   See Kinsella's 1971 essay p. 810 above.
2   Leading Gaelic poet, sometimes anglicized as Egan O'Rahilly (?1670–1729), born in the Sliabh Luachra area of County Kerry.
3   Leaving Certificate, the national certificate in Ireland for pupils leaving school at eighteen.
4   French: courtly love.
5   Title of a volume of verse by Michael Hartnett published in 1975.

VINCENT BUCKLEY

from Vincent Buckley, *Memory Ireland: Insights Into the Contemporary Irish Condition* (1985)

In *Memory Ireland*, Vincent Buckley provides a very readable introduction to modern Ireland for mainly Australian readers. It is more than this, for, as Buckley explains in this piece, its hidden theme is, contrary to the conventional view, Ireland's *loss* of its own memory: 'One of the continuing tragedies of Ireland over centuries is that the conditions for sustaining corporate memory have been destroyed.' Here are the opening pages of Buckley's impressions of Ireland in the mid-1980s.

Back After Twelve Months Away

When you return to Ireland after any absence, you are caught up in immediate conversation; the Irish are instant conversationalists, whether they know you or not. If they know you, the conversational form tends to be more complex. Since it is a small country, oppressed by money worries, to some degree psychologically isolated, and amazingly homogeneous in population, the subject of conversation, after a courteous enquiry about what has been happening to yourself, is sure to be what has happened in Ireland since you were last here. You will have missed great drama, they will tell you with gleaming voices, or, it may be, great boredom, they will shrug, for sure whatever happens but the same old thing. Further, the subject of all conversations is likely to be the same, although the grace-notes will vary greatly. The theme is set by consensus, the improvisations belong to the moment.

I returned in September 1983, almost exactly a year after I had left. The air was humming with subject-matter. There were urgent trivia, such as an unusually vicious football final that had just been played (Gaelic football is relatively lacking in wanton violence, and any which occurs is worthy of comment). There was the category of the *déjà vu*, such as the new government's financial bumbling ('Ah yes, and we've got a new government since you left, Vincent'). But these were not the things which provided Subject.

There were three things that did that: the increased violence in southern cities, the dramatic increase in drug addiction, mostly heroin, and the fate of the constitutional referendum on abortion. They were certainly dramatic enough, and to the returning observer deeply revealing of some dominant forces in Irish life; to me, for example, they were connected with one another more obviously than they were to my friends who endured them, and to whom they appeared the more discrete the more dramatic they were. To me, for example, the heroin addiction

showed a vulnerability and childishness in Irish life; this was connected with the weak authoritarianism and social detachment of the Catholic bishops, and both were surely connected with the increase in violence (muggings, burglaries, hold-ups, gang warfare, political violence), which was in turn surely connected with a failure to pay full attention to the nature of violence in the north. With untrustworthy leaders, the Irish had fallen into a routinism of subdued fear, and were easy prey for violent and unexpected changes in their situation. In turn, an obscure realization of that fact made them even more depressed, if extremely lively in speech, about the continuing problems.

One of these, though not really part of the Subject, was the presence and condition of the travelling people, also called itinerants or (an older term, now both inaccurate and dismissive) tinkers. Visitors often think they are gipsies, but they are almost completely native Irish; occasionally they intermarry with English or Welsh gipsies, but although they have their own version of cant, or clan language, they are Irish, one of the products of Irish history, or, more exactly, of the history of English policy in Ireland. They camp for long periods on the roads leading into Irish cities and towns, or on small areas set aside for them inside those cities. They are bitterly resented by most of the people among whom they settle, and are always in danger of being persecuted, insulted, moved on, and having their families broken, often very brutally and abruptly. I am in no position to write about the problems thus created; what struck me in September 1983 was how numerous they had grown on the roads through the area where I stayed for part of the time. Their numbers are increasing fast, the chances of housing or otherwise settling them are shrinking even faster, and they are so much more visible, in some ways more obstructive, than they used to be. The latest estimate is 15,000, increasing by 10 per cent a year. What no one told me, although I learned it months later, was that they clustered on the roads of County Dublin because

Dublin City had driven them out; the line between these entities is not very clear except to bureaucrats.

For some time I stayed with Seamus, a taxi-driver, and Christine, his wife, a nurse, in Firhouse. The rest of the time I stayed with a poet friend near the seafront, at Merrion. In the second house some of the concerns which compose the Subject came up intermittently, but it tended to be obscured by the need for recurrent doses of wisdom and gossip. In the first house, they came up repeatedly, and in an order, with an economy, which showed them to be connected not merely in social fact but also deep in the minds of my friends.

Seamus and Christine lived on a road leading from Templeogue and Rathfarnham past the large new 'complex' of Tallaght along the south-west road through the Dublin mountains into West Wicklow and on into south Kildare.

In the year since they last had seen me, they said, some things had changed, and others became clear. As I already knew, Tallaght, place of most mysterious history and prehistory, where Parthalon and the whole of his invading people were said to have lain buried for millennia in one great mound, and where from a later date a great monastery had existed, with its precious books and texts, and its more-than-millennial central tree, for nearly the whole of Christian history in Ireland, Tallaght had spread from its village and was now an estate wasteland of nearly 100,000 people. It stretched for miles to west and north; motorways and ambitious feeder-roads sped through it, joining and diverging from each other; but some of these roads were wide, and bordered by fields, and on to their verges, and the fields, and sometimes the roads themselves, hundreds of itinerants had come, with their cars, their caravans, their outdoor kitchens, their churns of water, their clothes hung on fence and hedge, their dogs, their scrap cars and other useless metal, and above all their horses: cart horses for the most part, browsing near and straying on what, after all, were major roads. None of this was a new sight or a new concept: neither the problems which the 'travellers' had, nor those which they created, could be called new; the hostility of the people among whom they had so abruptly settled was of long standing; their own misery was still not met. Some of them had 'lived' there, or thereabouts, for years; some had been driven there; some had chosen this place. What was new was that, because no one had been able to shift them, roadways completed some time before had not yet been 'opened'; the travellers were occupying them. Nowhere are misery and anomaly more visible than Ireland; and some say that the travellers' evident misery is no more than anomaly. Whatever may be said about that, the Tallaght scene was a visible and effective sign, a mad sacrament, of governmental lack of will; for even where good purposes are followed, some final weakness of will is likely to prevent their completion. So here: you finish an important road, and are then unable to open it, because you will not find housing or fielding for a few hundred people.

Purposes in Ireland are short term, and will is mostly spasmodic, lacking in stamina. Consider, said my friends, the northern shopping. Some entrepreneur has arranged weekly bus visits to Newry, in Northern Ireland. Every week a crowded bus, filled mostly with housewives, sets off from near Tallaght to travel the sixty or seventy miles into what, after all, its occupying forces, though by no means all its occupants, call a different state (foreign country, hey, different accents, different currency, a touch of danger); the southerners would spend some hours shopping, and the bus would bring them home again. What did they shop for? Meat, groceries, petrol, booze, anything electrical. They would save the price of the bus twice or thrice over. Is that why they went? Yes, said my friends. I think there is an extra thing: the outing, the togetherness, the touch of daring. Tallaght can be drab, and even Rathfarnham broody. But who would have guessed that so many people would come to think no more of going weekly into the black north of their own country than of making day trips from Wexford to do their shopping in Bordeaux? (That's a bitter joke, reader.)

I don't grudge them: an outing is an outing, and Newry is a Catholic town which is therefore afflicted by chronic unemployment. The southern pound will do some good there. Yet it is chilling to think that in the relatively impoverished if uncomplaining south, prices should have gone so high.

In travelling to Newry, they are travelling to an area usually thought of as one of endless violence; but they are also travelling from a city, if not a locality, where violence increases every month. And they are increasingly worried by it.

The difference between Dublin and some other big cities is that many of the big robberies are political, as are the cases of kidnapping and extortion; they are standard ways of keeping buoyant the fighting funds of Republican military groups in the north. I have heard many suggestions over the years that there was some overlap between these activities (the actions of 'soldiers', as their perpetrators would see them) and the robberies organized by criminal gangs; but I have seen no investigation of this matter. It is possible that some criminals have Republican sympathies, of course.

It is now said that, where only a few years ago Dublin was divided among four criminal families, now there are ten. As well as that, there is random violence in, for example, the inner cities, among the dispossessed and often cretinized youth who, never in work, have been breathing in almost lethal quantities of lead since they were infants. So we have a combination of automatized violence, organized gang violence, and operational political violence: the whole arising from the socio-political state of Ireland, part of which is the struggle in the north.

DESMOND HOGAN

from Desmond Hogan, *The Edge of the City: A Scrapbook 1976–91* (1993)

Van Morrison, not a natural interviewee, here reveals something of himself in discussion in 1987 with the novelist and dramatist Desmond Hogan.

An Interview with Van Morrison

'I'm just channelling. That's what I do. I say it's a collective unconscious. That's what I prefer to call it. I'm channelling these ideas that are coming through me from wherever they are I don't know. I myself am not actually saying anything either way. I just get ideas coming through. It might be a line. A bit of a melody. I develop these things that come through the sub-conscious mind and put shapes on them and they become songs. And basically that's what I do. I haven't a clue what that's about myself, am trying to find out. I'm just putting down what I get and recording it.'

Van Morrison's latest album, *Poetic Champions Compose*,[1] speaks of risk, trust, entering the sun, the mystery, dancing. I'd asked him if he thought that in these grim times it might have a counter-active effect for the good.

We met in the lounge of the Shepherd's Bush Hilton. Only time I'd been in the Hilton, I told him, had been in Cairo where you could get breakfast for fifty pence.

He was a stocky figure in dark clothes. Only bright thing about his apparel was the magazine he was carrying, which he looked at when I sat down. Last person to do that to me was a member of the Gurdjieff-Ouspensky movement. I interpreted it as coming from decades of suspicion of interviewers. But it was, thankfully, a brief gesture on his part. He asked me what my angle was. I said I had none. He said that boded badly. There'd been a good interview on Radio Derry, he said.

From *Astral Weeks* to *Poetic Champions Compose* Van Morrison has retained a priestly integrity. He's been an artist in the music world who always seems to write from his inner life. I asked him how he'd retained and protected that inner space.

'You see there's two things happening, right. One thing — A — is the work itself. Basically. Writing the songs. Putting shapes on the songs. Putting down ideas for arrangements. How they should be done. Going into the studios. Developing the ideas. Developing the lines. Rewriting them. All this kind of thing. That's one thing. That process is separate from the other process which would be the B part of it. The part you're going out with, what you have to encounter business people with. You have to deal with the level they're operating on to sell this piece of what they call product. A and B are completely different and very, very much apart from one another and that's just the way it is.'

But some people mix them up?

'Exactly. What happened to me, I was early on forced into the role as producer. This role as producer put me in that situation where I was actually producing records and delivering the masters. In other words there was no middleman in between. That's put me more in the position where I'm doing what I want to do. But then when it comes to the point of selling what I've done it puts me in the other position where I have to deal with a lot more people, what they think and what they believe, which is basically the music business. I see them as being separate things. One's a creative process. The other's a selling process. You're dealing with entirely different things. The main reason that I had control is that I'm a producer. Even if I hire another producer I'm still the producer. The wave I came in on, that was a breakthrough because before that you had producers and A&R men and they were usually calling the shots. The wave I came in on, that was a breakthrough for people getting control of their work.'

But there'd obviously been very serious encroachment on him as an artist and as a human being at times I suggested.

'Also some of that encroachment taught me lessons as well. This is what you have to understand as well. Because you have to be able to deal in all angles. If you're just dealing, say, on the creative level and not bothered about how things operate when you're dealing with hardcore facts of the business world then you're sort of walking into walls. You have to be aware of that as well. What you're in is a tough business and you have to be very aware. The way I put it: I don't suffer fools gladly.'

Was that always the way?

'No that's not always been the way. To get where I am I've had to fight. It's still a fight. It's still a struggle. It's still a fight. I mean I'm not playing the same game I played twenty years ago. My particular stance at this time is that I've gone through the rock and roll stars . . . I've been a star I don't know how many times. I was a teenage star. So I went through being a teenage star. Then I went through being a twenty-year-old star. Then a singer-songwriter star. I went through that one. I found out what that was all about. I learnt my lessons and I took my blows. By the time I was twenty-seven I'd done that one. I'd gone through my second phase of being a rock star. That's what they called it in those days. But I didn't call it that. I'd already wrapped that up by the time I was twenty-eight. I started a whole new career. When I came back into the music business I started a whole new phase because I was no longer that person. I'd done that and I'd worked that out. For the past twelve years or so I've only been in it part of the time. I'm only in the music business part-time now. I finished with that whole thing then. I've run the gamut, I took the blows. I realized I've lived that out and I didn't have to do it any more.'

I said that Sartre objected to people hiding behind categories of painters, musicians, writers: their work was them and otherwise they were unlabelled human beings. Van Morrison said that was it exactly.

I asked him about the sense of light and dark in his work, like the Irish weather, the fight between the two.

'That came from having to do things . . . A lot of people say to me, well you're really lucky. I'm not lucky. At certain times I had to do certain things and that's really the way it was. I didn't have a choice. It was either A or B. I did the one thing that happened to get me through. It wasn't a matter of sitting up in an ivory tower at the time and saying, I wonder whether I want to do A or B or C. In the sixties you didn't have a choice. You were either in the van on the M1[2] going up and down the M1 doing gigs or doing nothing. When the singer-songwriter thing first appeared there wasn't a choice. You had to do that a certain way and the people that were in charge, they did things a certain way. If you wanted that you had to compromise. There was a lot of compromise and a lot of hard graft I had to do. But it got me to a point where I did have a choice.'

Sometimes in his obsession with childhood the images are amorphous — rain, sun, light; sometimes it comes up close, like black and white images in the Bill Douglas film trilogy: '. . . marching with soldier boy behind. He's much older now with hat on, drinking wine.' '. . . the kids out in the street, collecting bottle tops, gone for cigarettes and matches in the shops.' '. . . the train from Dublin up to Sandy Row,[3] throwing pennies at the bridges down below, in the rain, hail, sleet and snow.' '. . . wee Alfie at the Castle picture house on the Castlereagh Road.' '. . . whistling on the corner next door where he kept John Mack Brown's horse.'

Did he find that he, like a lot of Irish people who left Ireland, had to block out the specifics of his early life at times?

'I didn't really have a choice about any of it until I was like twenty-eight. Before that it was either put up or shut up. It was a struggle financially. I didn't even start making money until I was twenty-eight. For me that was a time I couldn't even consider looking at biography. All I did from the time I was like eighteen to twenty-seven was work. I worked my way from Belfast to New York and didn't even know I was there because it was work.'

I get the impression he goes back to Ireland much more now.

'You see there's all different levels to this. There's the personal level. Then there's the career level. I don't get into the personal level in a situation like an interview. It's mine. All I discuss in interviews, it's business, it's promotion for a record or something. Other than that I'm not available for anything else.'

Yes, but in some of his recent work, in a fairly recent song like 'Sense of Wonder', Ireland is much more up front: '. . . the man who played the saw outside the City Hall', '"O Solo Mio" by McGinsey'.

(Just then someone began banging what I thought might have been Beethoven's 'Für Elise' on the nearby piano.)

'I was actually reading a Michael Bentine book. It kept saying something about "sense of wonder". I picked up another book or something . . . something about "sense of wonder". So that went into the subconscious. I was sitting down one day and playing the guitar. "Sense of wonder . . . sense of wonder." That's my process. I remembered something about Ballystockart. I went there. That developed into a song. That's not me personally. Truman Capote called it faction. Part fact. Part fiction. You're painting on things. Part of it's fact. Part of it's fiction. That's really what I'm doing. I have to see what I'm doing in retrospect. Then I edit it. I shape it.'

Van Morrison says about 'A Sense of Wonder' that he 'ties it in with nature in Ireland'. It's about 'the vibration of nature in Ireland'. He says about what I considered his most seminal recent song, 'In the garden', from *No Guru, No Method, No Teacher* that it's about 'Christianity and nature combined'. On the album *Common One* he made a literary nature pilgrimage, to Coole Park.

'That was actually from a poem I wrote. That actual part of that song. I wrote a poem and put part of the poem in that song at that place. That's what that was. I was going to do that poem on its own and instead of doing that I put it in that part of the song. I don't even know if it was connected myself.'

On the subject of Yeats I asked him about similarities between his songs and Yeats's poems, in my mind less the mysticism than the way romanticism, allure comes to Cypress Avenue, the Castlereagh Road.

'Don't really know. You see I got that idea from someone else. It didn't really put me on the right track. Somebody wrote an article about me a while back. They were trying to say there were similarities between my songs and Yeats's poems. At the time it seemed like, you know, a good idea. Through further exploration I discovered it's not my lineage. It is in a certain way my lineage. It's a bit sort of academic. Put it that way. Even though I can get academic. My lineage would be more A.E. [George Russell]. That's more my lineage. That sort of mysticism as opposed to Yeats's mysticism.'

At one point, referring indirectly to Blake, I said I preferred to use the word religious rather than mystic.

'The thing is you have to use mysticism if you're talking on theological terms so you've got a reference point. If you say religious you could mean anything. I use mystic that way.'

His newest songs talk of the necessity of openness. Can the vulnerability of openness not be extremely dangerous? I asked him.

'I never see it that way. Open to something that's dangerous? I don't see it like that. I see it the other way. If you're closed that's more dangerous. That's dangerous, being closed.'

Yes, but he'd said he'd learnt to protect his openness.

'Not the actual creativity part. I'm talking about that other part of it which is, you know . . . I mean if you're in the Holiday Inn in the middle of nowhere on a tour on an off Sunday night or something and you're fed up you can't walk off the tour. It doesn't protect you from that. I'm talking about the openness of the creativity. The other thing I relate to, you're in a boxing ring the rest of the time. The creativity is open enough. But it's when you go out there you're out in the jungle, it's different. It's not about creativity, it's not about openness. You have to protect yourself just like you're in the ring. You've got to have gloves on there. It's a different situation.'

I talked about people I've known who'd, quoting a recent phrase of Van Morrison himself which echoed Blake, 'drunk of the fountains of innocence' and were destroyed.

'There again you see it's poems of innocence *and* experience. That's what I was talking about before. The reason I'm able to do that is that I've been able to work through that and taken the blows. It's songs of innocence *and* experience if you read the lyrics. To sing about innocence you need the experience. That's what it is. To be totally, completely innocent is absolutely useless and will get you absolutely nowhere. They will cave you in.'

I told him I'd intended to record this conversation over a tape of *Cabaret*. (The piano was banging louder than ever.) He didn't seem to find that funny. I asked him if he thought he'd stay in London. He said he didn't know.

Then I asked him what his favourite place in Ireland was.

At first he seemed either unwilling or unable to answer. Then he said: 'East Belfast.'

1   Released in 1987.
2   Motorway between (at that time) London and Birmingham.
3   Working-class Protestant area of Belfast.

BILL NAUGHTON
from Bill Naughton, *Saintly Billy: A Catholic Boyhood* (1988)

Bill Naughton (1910–92), Lancashire playwright, novelist and short-story writer, was born in Ballyhaunis, Co. Mayo, and raised as a child in Bolton, Lancashire. After leaving school at fourteen he worked as a weaver, then a coalbagger and lorry driver. His struggles to become a writer are vividly recreated in *A Roof Over Your Head* (1945), a book written in wartime London while he was a Civil Defence driver. After the war he achieved fame with *Alfie* (1966), which was turned into a film almost immediately with Michael Caine in the leading role. His Irish background accompanied him throughout his life. *One Small Boy* (1957) is a novel which begins in Ireland with his father's emigration to England and which provides a sensitive evocation of Naughton's orientation to a Lancashire mill-town. Towards the end of his life he returned to the theme in *Saintly Billy*, and in this extract it is again the differences that loom large.

from The Irish and the English

Even as a small boy I was seldom unaware of how vulnerable we Irish were. Although we had a good family sense, which was comforting, we had only a remote feeling of belonging, since we were aliens. That was a feeling I never lost. The attitude towards the Irish in those days, when Ireland was part of Great Britain, and Britain had a vast empire, was different from that of today, although more than a trace of it may remain. The Irish — like many other nations and races — were looked down upon. Nor could one blame the English, since it could hardly be otherwise. At school the huge map of the world would be spread on the blackboard, the vast British Empire marked in red, and Miss Newsham with her long cane would point out the many and various colonies, dependencies, and other possessions, and explain how on the Empire the sun could never set, since it stretched around the globe. I would watch my mates staring agog, as though asking, '*Dominion over palm and pine* — am I an' mi' mum an' dad an' mi Aunt Flo' an' our Sarah Jane included?' Even the Lancashire little-piecer,[1] undersized and underfed, working from the age of thirteen what had customarily been fifty-six hours a week in a cotton-mill — now at last reduced to forty-eight — had somehow been persuaded into considering himself a vital member, or at least a member, of the British Empire. Perhaps he was. At least I, being Irish, would have to admit an inferiority on that score, if on no other; although we were reluctant members of that same empire. Moreover, I found I was drawn to such an English boy; indeed in many ways more than I was drawn to one of my own. I respected and half-feared his cool Englishness. What made him appear superior to me and mine in the first place was that he felt himself so, and I found that a difficult thing to counter, even though it may have been assumed on dubious grounds. The Irish seemed to live in the past and the English always in the present, and that certainly put them ahead. That the Englishman was part of a society more ordered than that of the Irish could not be gainsaid: the English responded to the factory buzzer with a promptness beyond the understanding of the Irish mind, which was quite untrained to punctuality; also they were a people clearly more law-abiding and hard-working, for the Lancashire miner could leave the leisurely Irishman behind.

It was as navvies the Irish came into their own — and this difference seemed to be reflected on their faces. The Irish face — except for those of coal-miners — was ruddy and fresh, set on the broad red neck with the round cleanshaven nape, and it would be simple for anyone to pick out such a one in a crowded English street, especially so since no Irishman ever hurried. The more intelligent Irish face had a lively mobility and friendly expression, quite unlike that of the simian-featured Irishman of English cartoons; even as a small boy I felt offended by this caricature of our people. Yet it was clear that the emotional Irish expression must defer to the stolid English look, and that the swift fluty tones of the Irish lacked the authority of the strong flat English voice. Apart from these and certain racial differences, one further comparison could be made: the Irish face was free of — or possibly had not yet acquired — that certain look which industry stamps upon its subjects. There was no doubt, however, that the countenance which had grown up on familiar terms with machinery, and had acquired that particular concentrated look — a form of sophistication — was the one which would prove superior in a material or worldly sense. The face that told of outdoor labour, of familiarity with the earth, the spade, and the muck fork, must give way to the one acquainted with the spanner. Moreover, a people who have been subject to another nation for centuries need a generation or two to shake off their inadequacies and equal up (if indeed they ever can without the superior nation going down a bit).

Nor was the superiority always of a remote order: the English were a reliable people, the Englishman's word was his bond — allowing the exception of a politician — and, if he promised to see you at the Ram's Head corner at eight o'clock and lend you a pound (or more likely ten shillings), you could bet he would be there, dead on eight, without any of the Irish excuses, and the note safe in his waistcoat pocket. Nor was the Englishman deep, treacherous, or given to feuds or grudges; and, although a peaceful man, never quickly pugnacious, he would seldom duck a fight. Then there would be the calm English ritual of jackets off, and not flung down but folded up carefully, sleeves calmly rolled up, the opponents set facing each other, left fist forward, right hand on guard, and no getting the first blow in, with someone to see fair play, not a move until the call was given; the commands, *Fists only! No feet!* and *Don't hit a man when he's down!* would be followed. (I had soon discovered he might drop his guard, dodge down and grab you by the knees, and

flip you on your back in a trice.) Calls of *Play the game!* and *Play the white man!* would be made from the spectators during a fight; calls never heard, I imagine, at an Irish fight. The nature of the Celt and and that of the Anglo-Saxon were decidedly different in many respects.

'I've had Irish chaps workin' here for me for years,' I once heard a Bolton farmer say, 'the same family — come over here for the hay they do, an' I hire 'um for the month. You never saw better workers in your life; an' I'll tell you summat, they're not clockwatchers, they're gradely[2] workers — they keep gooin' till the job's done. Now at the end of the month on the Saturday night, when they're bein' paid off an' ready for gooin' off, it's always been my custom to tak' 'um to the pub an' stand 'um a pint or two. Sometimes they'll get other Irishmen from other farms about droppin' in, an' a nicer crowd o' chaps you never met — that is, until they begin findin' out they're related, an' they shake hands an' start kissin' one another. Then I'm off. For once the Irish start kissin', you can be sure that soon the fists will start — an' they get agate fightin'. Aye, as soon as I see that first kiss I make for the pub door.'

---

1   In the cotton-mills of Lancashire, a piecer was an assistant to the mule spinner, responsible for piecing together the broken threads (OED).
2   Dialect word: proper, respectable, careful.

EDWARD W. SAID
from Edward W. Said, *Nationalism, Colonialism and Literature: Yeats and Decolonization* (1988)

Here are two paragraphs from Edward Said's challenging essay on 'Yeats and Decolonization', first published as a Field Day Pamphlet. A pro-Palestinian American critic, Said sets Yeats in the context of other twentieth-century struggles for national liberation.

from **Yeats and Decolonization**

Yeats has now been almost completely assimilated to the canon as well as the discourses of modern English literature, in addition to those of European high modernism. Both of these institutions of course reckon with him as a great modern Irish poet, deeply affiliated and interacting with his native traditions, the

historical and political context of his times, and the extraordinarily complex situation of being a poet in Ireland writing in English. Nevertheless, and despite Yeats's obvious and, I would say, settled presence in Ireland, in British culture and literature and in European modernism, he does present another fascinating aspect: that of the indisputably great *national* poet who articulates the experiences, the aspirations, and the vision of a people suffering under the dominion of an off-shore power. From this perspective Yeats is a poet who belongs to a tradition not usually considered his, that of the colonial world ruled by European imperialism now — that is, during the late nineteenth and early twentieth centuries — bringing to a climactic insurrectionary stage, the massive upheaval of anti-imperialist resistance in the colonies, and of metropolitan anti-imperialist opposition that has been called the age of decolonization. If this is not a customary way of interpreting Yeats for those who know a great deal more about him as an Irish European modernist poet of immense stature than I do, then I can only say that he appears to me, and I am sure to many others in the Third World, to belong naturally to the other cultural domain, which I shall now try to characterize. If this also sheds more light on the present status of Yeats's role in post-independence Ireland, then so much the better.

. . . One feels in reading poems like 'Nineteen Hundred and Nineteen' or 'Easter 1916', and 'September 1913', not just the disappointments of life commanded by 'the greasy till' or the violence of roads and horses, of 'weasels fighting in a hole', but also of a terrible new beauty that changes utterly the old political and moral landscape. Like all the poets of

decolonization Yeats struggles to announce the contours of an 'imagined' or ideal community, crystallized not only by its sense of itself but also of its enemy. Imagined community, Benedict Anderson's fine phrase for emergent nationalism, is apt here as I have used it, so long as we are not obliged to accept his mistakenly linear periodizations of unofficial and official nationalism. In the cultural discourses of decolonization, a great many languages, histories, forms circulate. As Barbara Harlow has shown in *Resistance Literature*,[1] there are spiritual autobiographies, poems of protest, prison memoirs, didactic dramas of deliverance, but in them all is a sense of the instability of time, which has to be made and re-made by the people and its leaders. The shifts in Yeats's accounts of his great cycles invoke this instability, as does the easy commerce in his poetry between popular and formal speech, folk tale, and learned writing. The disquiet of what T.S. Eliot called the 'cunning history, [and] contrived corridors' of time — the wrong turns, the overlap, the senseless repetition, the occasionally glorious moment — furnish Yeats, as they do all the poets of decolonization with stern martial accents, heroism, and the grinding persistence of 'the uncontrollable mystery on the bestial floor'.

1   Published in 1987.

PAUL HEWSON
from Richard Kearney (ed.), *Across the Frontiers: Ireland in the 1990s, Cultural-Political-Economic*
(1988)

Here are Bono's wide-ranging thoughts on Ireland and the future. How might you develop Bono's critique of modern Ireland?

Bono: The White Nigger

How does the music of U2 relate to our being Irish? I come to this question as someone who does not know who he is. There are people out there who know who they are . . . I like to to meet these people . . . But I am not one of them. When I was growing up I didn't know where I came from . . . I didn't know if I was middle class, working class, Catholic, Protestant . . . I knew I was from Ballymun, Dublin, but I didn't know what that meant. I didn't know I was Irish until I went

to America. I never actually thought about it. One of the reasons I want to contribute to this discussion now is that I've become interested in these questions lately. But I come to it with no set point of view.

It is curious that U2 are seen as this 'Irish' thing. So much emphasis is placed on it. And we ourselves emphasize it. But if you look at the surface level of music — its obvious contents — there's maybe nothing very Irish about it. It comes from a suburban blank generation culture which I grew up in, watching cartoons on TV, Thunderbirds and Hanna Barbera and designer violence. That was the real world, concrete, grey, kicking footballs and admiring English football stars. That's the culture I came from, and that's what our music reflects, on the surface at least. It is very 'un-Irish' in the accepted sense.

However, I now realize that beneath the surface there are certain Irish characteristics to the music . . . even the choice of words. Our producer, Brian Eno, said that he thought that I was a better poet than a songwriter . . . what I think he meant by that was the sound, rhythm and colour of the words seem at times as important as the meaning. The love of language *for its own sake* and not just as a vehicle to comment on or describe events, seems to me to be very Irish — you grow up reading Joyce for God's sake or Beckett, and they seem to abuse and therefore use the English language in new and interesting ways.

With U2, people often point to a song like 'Sunday, Bloody Sunday' as an example of our Irishness, but for me it's not, and in retrospect it didn't succeed in making its point. We had this highfalutin' idea to contrast or make the connection between the blood of the crucifixion on Easter Sunday and the blood of the victims in Derry on Bloody Sunday.[1] The idea of Jesus dying to save us from death is a painful irony to both Catholic and Protestant in the light of the troubles. Anyway, now when I look at the words, all I see is a description of that day as a tragedy in the tradition of Peggy Seeger[2] or American folk: 'And the battle's yet begun / There's many lost but tell me who has won / The trenches dug within our hearts / Mothers, children, brothers, sisters torn apart.'

To me the sound and colour of the language in a song like 'A Sort of Homecoming' is more Irish: 'The wind will crack in wintertime / A lightning bomblast waltz / No spoken words . . . just a scream . . . / See the sky the burning rain, she will die and live again / Tonight, we'll build a bridge across the sea and land.' This is not American folk or blues. The words are much more influenced by poets like Heaney or Kavanagh . . . than say, Woodie Guthrie.

I used to think U2 came out of a void, a black hole; we seemed completely rootless. Though we had many influences, our version of Rock 'n' Roll didn't sound like anyone else's in the present or in the past. In '85 I met Bob Dylan for the first time backstage at Slane Castle 85. He sat there talking about the McPeake Family[3] . . . this Irish group I'd never even heard of . . . and how he used to hang around backstage at Makem & Clancy concerts[4] — yeah I said, I remember they used to be on the Late Late Show![5] . . . and then I began to listen more carefully to the bold and bald sound of Irish Folk singers . . . I recall listening to Paul

Brady kick up more of a storm with an acoustic guitar than most people could do with a rock band. I told Dylan and Van Morrison who was there at the time, that I felt we didn't belong to any tradition, it was like we were lost in space, floating over many traditions but not belonging to any one of them. It then struck us that there was a journey to be undertaken. There was something to be discovered.

We started looking back into American music, Gospel, Blues, the likes of Robert Johnson . . . John Lee Hooker. Old songs of fear and faith. As I said when we first started the band, we felt like outsiders to Rock Music but these themes were very much inside U2, they were also very Irish so even though there isn't an obvious Irishness in a song like 'Bullet The Blue Sky' (a U2 song about military interference in El Salvador), there is something Irish about the subject of oppression and also, I think, about the language I used to paint the picture: 'In the howling wind comes a stinging rain / See them driving nails into souls on the tree of pain / You plant a demon seed, you raise a flower of fire / See them burning crosses see the flames higher and higher.' I feel there is a strong link between American and Irish traditional music. So you see we found the 'Irish Thing' through the American: Gospel, Blues, Robert Johnson, Bob Dylan, these became passports home.

Though we had grown up on it, for some reason we also felt outsiders to the English Rock 'n' Roll scene. At the time it all seemed surface with nothing behind the surface. We were up there scruffy, soaked in sweat, unpoised — not concealing but revealing ourselves, what was on our minds and in our hearts. I began to realize how alien this was to the white, stiff upper lip syndrome which I still find in UK music criticism . . . They seemed to find any kind of passion hard to take, they prefer a mask of *cool* . . . unless you're black. Which is interesting, because though this passion is to me an Irish characteristic, in American blacks it's called *soul*. I was called a 'White Nigger' once by a black musician, and I took it as he meant it, as a compliment. The Irish, like the blacks, feel like outsiders. There's a feeling of being homeless, migrant, but I suppose that's what all art is — a search for identity. The images of our songs are confused, classical, biblical, American, Irish, English, but not in a negative sense. The fight, the struggle for a synthesis is what's interesting about them. The idea of an incomplete, questioning, even abandoned identity is very attractive to me.

Our journey to America eventually turned us back to where we came from. It brought up musical questions and also political questions. During Bobby

Sands' hunger strike[6] — we had money thrown onto the stage because we were Irish . . . you couldn't but be moved by the courage and conviction of this man . . . yet we struggled with the question, is this the right way? Is violence inevitable? Is it the only answer to partition in Northern Ireland? Again there was a parallel between the Irish and the blacks. In the '60s the 'Black Civil Rights Movement' led by Martin Luther King had resisted a bloody upsurge. I've read Dr King's *Strength to Love* and was inspired by his movement of aggressive but non-violent resistance. Here was a man who believed enough in his cause to give his life, but would never take a life . . . an 'armed struggle' seems cowardly in comparison. I know it's not that simple, but we must get beyond confrontation, beyond a revolution where ideas matter more than people . . . surely we are coming out of that period where we believed that just one bang of the door and it would swing open . . . it's just not like that. I mean, I'm from the South and relatively uneducated about the situation, but if war in Northern Ireland is what it means to be Irish then we must redefine Irishness. There was a time when Political thinkers could tolerate violence as a way forward, but this is a different time . . . the old ideologies of the Right and the Left — as promising a final solution — are redundant. This is the late '80s, we are only a decade away from the year 2000 — the micro-chip will dwarf the machine in its impact on our lives; multinational corporations don't need people in their workforce anymore — just people to sell to . . . we have a new problem, we need a new solution.

Even in music and art there's a changing of the guard; it's the end of the 'cold wave' and hopefully of the hardness associated with modernism, where chaos is not challenged just reflected . . . like a mirror.

There's a warmth and humanity in Irish music that I don't see in the big city music of London or New York. What kind of music will people be listening to in the 1990s? Machine music? Sophisticated noise of a New York dance club? I don't think so. I feel the music that people will be holding under their arms like holy books or treasures will be much more traditional, be it Irish, American, soul, reggae, cajun — these musics may be reinterpreted by the new technology but as we are more dehumanized, urbanized, corralled into confusion, surely we will turn to simplicity, to 'the pure drop' of Seamus Ennis,[7] the voice of Van Morrison. The anger of U2 is not cold or cynical; I hope an ambition to 'kick the darkness till it bleeds daylight' will have its place.

Maybe we Irish are misfits, travellers, never really at home, but always talking about it. I met a fisherman who told me we were like salmon: it's upriver all the time, against the odds, the river doesn't want us . . . yet we want a way home . . . but there is no home. Religious minds tell us *exile is what having eaten the apple means*, that 'home' is a spiritual condition. We in Ireland already know this, not because we've been exiles, but because hardships, be they economic or political, have forced us to be less material . . . I don't swallow the Church's idea of 'pie in the sky' when we die either! That's the worst of religion . . . accept the crap now, we'll have diamonds later. I much prefer the notion of 'Thy Kingdom Come on Earth as it is in Heaven'. Some Heaven on earth right now would be nice — they should preach that! I mean we get some glimpses of it in music, painting, the West of Ireland, Donegal, people, sex, conversation . . . a few pints, a glass of whiskey. Even if it's been a cause of bitterness and has on occasion been warped by organized religion, our Christianity, our sense of the spirit, is valuable, especially right now when a hard, empirical approach to things is beginning to give way to a more open metaphysical questioning. Belief in God does not necessarily imply a lack of belief in men.

I don't know, maybe Romantic Ireland is dead and gone.[8] If the America I love only exists in my imagination, maybe the Ireland I love is the same. Dublin, I mean, everybody gives out about Dublin and there's lots of things to give out about[9] . . . unemployment, what the planners have done to the people of Tallaght and Ballymun,[10] the architects who have defaced what was a beautiful city, these are the real vandals . . . but still we love the city . . .

I met a U2 fan in Switzerland recently who said to me: 'Jazus Bono, I can't wait to get home and throw some litter on the ground!' — I think I know what he meant.

1   28 January 1972 when thirteen people were killed by the British Army in Derry. 'Sunday Bloody Sunday' (also the title of a film by John Schlesinger) appeared on the *War* album in 1983.
2   American folk-singer, sister of Pete Seeger, she spent most of her singing career in London with the leading Scottish folk-singer Ewan MacColl.
3   Folksinging family from Belfast, well-known on the folk club circuit in the 1960s.
4   Tommy Makem and the Clancy Brothers, leading names in the folksong revival from the 1950s and 1960s.
5   A television weekly chat show on RTE since 1962.
6   In the Maze Prison in 1981, begun on 1 March, ended in death of Sands on 5 May.
7   Leading uillean piper of his generation.
8   Line taken from Yeats's poem 'September 1913'.
9   Roundly criticize.
10   Poor working-class estates on the south side of Dublin.

BILL ROLSTON
from *Race and Class*, 31 (1) 1989

> From 1969 until 1989 nearly 200 novels about 'the troubles' were published. Since then there have been many more. Bill Rolston's essay on the subject of women in this collection of novels provides a valuable starting-point for analysis. Here are his concluding remarks together with a select list of novels he compiled at that time.

from **Whores and Villains**

There are aspects of the novels which are all too accurate, regrettably, in their depiction of the oppression of women. In particular, those which set out to use the political 'troubles' as a metaphor for women's particular suffering — such as *To Stay Alive* and *Troubles* — strike close to home at numerous points. Similarly, *Dreams of Revenge* intertwines the personal and the political. The relationship between Michael and Barbara develops and disintegrates as do the Northern 'troubles'; both situations consist of a constant tension punctuated by a series of violent outbursts.

In addition, some of the novels manage to capture the way in which patriarchy is compounded by political conflict. Nora, the prisoner's wife in the novel of the same name, is trapped both by marriage and the worship of the community. Her husband is a prisoner and a hero. Consequently, 'Long Kesh kept them together; its walls, wire fences and watchtowers held them more securely than any marriage vows. Now her marriage had entered the public arena of ghetto politics and it was impossible for her to take any steps to break with him.'

But, true as these insights may be, they only tell part of the story. And it is the absence of the other parts which is the fundamental problem of these novels. There are few positive images with which to compare the women in these pages. Yet, in reality, there are *other* women with whom the women here can be compared — neither victims nor survivors, but active initiators, whether at the domestic level, in community politics or in rational and committed participation in armed struggle. Such women exist; proof of this is the delight with which they are seized on by visiting feminists eager to find evidence of women's changing role in the midst of war.[1] But they do not have fictional sisters. The peppering of the novels with occasional valuable insights into women's oppression is not enough to salvage the genre.

This is not to conclude that the novels are irretrievably woeful. Some are better than others, sometimes despite themselves. Both *Troubles* and *You're Welcome to Ulster* appear to capture well the insularity of the North's Protestant and Catholic bourgeoisies respectively, the former out of previously unchallenged authority, the latter out of fear of rocking too many boats. And class is the theme of what is perhaps the best of the novels, *The Price of Chips* — it poignantly captures the way in which the 'troubles' have been more painful for the Catholic working class than for the bourgeoisie. Similarly, in relation to women, some novels have succeeded well. *Blood Sisters*, an otherwise overly didactic story, at least has captured a debate which has possessed, and divided, the Irish women's movement, that of feminism versus republicanism. *The Streets of Derry* is excellent in conveying the fact that what women do anyway in a tight working-class community in terms of support becomes translated, in a war situation, into political action. And *Give Them Stones* is poignant in its representation of a woman whose husband turns out to have married her to take the place of his ageing mother. She has four sons and is trapped in the all-male household. After the birth of her first she thinks, 'I didn't feel any of this wonderful joy I'd read about. I felt as if somebody had kicked me up the Cave Hill and down again and I was cold and hungry and I was landed with a big son. No wee dresses and again nobody to talk to.'

Finally, it must be emphasized that, in as far as they are woeful, the novels have echoes in non-fictional representations of women in the Irish conflict. One has only to remember the British media's view of Máire Drumm, the vice-president of Sinn Féin assassinated in 1976, as 'the grandmother of hate', or of Mairead Farrell, assassinated in Gibraltar in 1988, as 'the angel of death', to realize that the fictional accounts are based on stereotypes which are well established in popular culture. The novelists are allowed more licence in using the stereotypes, but they are following a common script. Or, as Ward and McGivern put it in relation to non-fictional accounts:

> Passive victims of the troubles, viragos of the barricades, advocates of a messianic peace. Our contention is that none of these stereotypes reveal the true situation of women living in a socially deprived, war-torn, rigidly patriarchal society.[2]

1 Cf., for example, Judy Ezekiel, 'Women in Northern Ireland', *Radical America*, Vol. 14, no. 6, 1980, pp. 57-65.
2 Margaret Ward and Marie-Therese McGivern, 'Images of women in Northern Ireland', *The Crane Bag*, Vol. 4, no. 1, 1980, pp. 66-72.

References
Across the Water, Stewart Binnie, London, Alison Press, 1979
Blood Sisters, Valerie Miner, London, Women's Press, 1981
Both Your Houses, James Barlow, London, Pan, 1973
Cal, Bernard MacLaverty, Belfast, Blackstaff Press, 1983
Dreams of Revenge, Kevin Casey, Dublin, Wolfhound Press, 1987
The Extremists, Peter Leslie, London, New English Library, 1970
The Fugitives, John Broderick, London, Pan, 1976
Give Them Stones, Mary Beckett, London, Bloomsbury, 1987
Harry's Game, Gerard Seymour, London, Fontana, 1977
Hennessy, Max Franklin, London, Futura, 1975
In Connection with Kilshaw, Peter Driscoll, London, Sphere, 1975
The Killing of Yesterday's Children, M.S. Power, London, Chatto and Windus, 1985
Maureen's Ireland, Sean Patrick, USA, Author, 1986
The Minstrel Code, Walter Nelson, London, New English Library, 1980
No Time for Love, Hugo Meehan, Dingle, Brandon, 1987

The Outsider, Colin Leinster, London, New English Library, 1980
The Patriots, G.W. Target, London, Duckworth, 1974
Prayer for the Dying, Jack Higgins, London, Coronet, 1975
The Price, Peter Ransley, London, Corgi, 1984
The Price of Chips, Walter Hegarty, London, Davis-Poynter, 1973
The Prisoner's Wife, Jack Holland, London, Robert Hale, 1982
The Savage Day, Jack Higgins, London, Coronet, 1974
Shadows on Our Skin, Jennifer Johnston, London, Coronet, 1977
Silver's City, Maurice Leitch, London, Secker and Warburg, 1981
The Streets of Derry, Albert J. Countryman, Palmyra, New Jersey, Countryman Publishing, 1986
To Stay Alive, Linda Anderson, London, Bodley Head, 1974
Too Long a Sacrifice, Mildred Downey Broxon, London, Futura, 1981
Troubles, Naomi May, London, John Calder, 1976
Victims, Eugene McCabe, Dublin, Mercier, 1979
Vote to Kill, Douglas Hurd, London, Collins, 1975
The Whore Mother, Sean Herron, London, Coronet, 1975
With O'Leary in the Grave, James Carrick, London, Heinemann, 1972
You're Welcome to Ulster, Menna Gallie, London, Gollancz, 1970
[Author's Notes and References]

WILLIAM KENNEDY
from William Kennedy, *Riding the Yellow Trolley Car: Selected Non-fiction* (1993)

William Kennedy (1928–), is a leading Irish-American novelist. His home town of Albany, New York, where he began life as a journalist, is the great subject of a cycle of novels *Legs* (1975), *Billy Phelan's Greatest Game* (1978) and *Ironweed* (1983). Here in an extract from an interview conducted with Peter Quinn he reveals the extent of his Irish-American inheritance.

from Tap Dancing into Reality

QUINN: *The Ink Truck* was your first novel. It's said that there's a special relationship between authors and their first novels, a parent's pride in their firstborn. Do you feel that way about *The Ink Truck*?

KENNEDY: Yes. I love it. Some people badmouthed it after the fact, and before the fact for that matter. Actually, it sold as soon as I had finished it. It sold the first time out. I had a little problem trying to sell it before it was finished, but when it was done, my agent sent it over to Dial Press, where Ed Doctorow was the managing editor, and he bought it. Thereafter, it went out of print fairly quickly, but that's the nature of first novels. Writers who are serious about themselves don't worry about that. If you're going to cut your wrists after your first novel, you're not a writer. After the twenty-eighth novel, and nobody will buy it, well . . . But you think of Farrell.[1] He never quit. It's an admirable thing, because he was getting pleasure out of what he was doing. If there are enough people who understand that, if there are other writers getting some pleasure out of reading your twenty-eighth novel, then maybe that's enough.

QUINN: What about the influence of other writers on you? James Joyce must certainly be one of them?

KENNEDY: Yes, absolutely. I've been reading him just lately. I've read books about him, by him. There's no end to that man. He's the greatest man of letters in the twentieth century. I don't think there's a close second. If there is, it's Faulkner.

But Joyce has transcendence. Leopold Bloom is someone who is never going to die in the history of literature. Faulkner did great things. He did wonderful, wonderful things. But there's nothing like Leopold and Molly, the Blooms, in all of twentieth-century literature. I don't know where the hell you go to find their equal.

QUINN: What about the similarities between you and Joyce?

KENNEDY: Similarities? I don't aspire to similarities.

QUINN: People have compared the opening of *Ironweed* to 'The Dead' and to the 'Circe' chapter in *Ulysses*. Is there any validity to that?

KENNEDY: I wish I had heard somebody say that, but I never heard that before. Joyce is Joyce. He's by himself, and I wouldn't make any comparisons. No, it's not an attempt at conscious imitation, if that's the question.

QUINN: Your careful reconstruction of Albany, your fascination with place, certainly evokes Joyce's obsession with Dublin.

KENNEDY: That's true enough. Joyce made things easier for all of us. He prompted us to become aware of our entire heritage, including dishpans and the jakes in the back yard.

QUINN: You both are absorbed with the place where you grew up. And you both left it. Did you choose, as Joyce did, 'silence, exile and cunning', and set out to chronicle Albany at a distance? Or did you pack up all your cares and woes and only gradually come to understand your relationship to Albany?

KENNEDY: Silence was imposed on me by all my editors. My might-have-been editors. Exile came because I couldn't stay in Albany any longer and still function effectively. I had to go elsewhere. I went to Puerto Rico, which is exile under the American flag. It's as far away as you could get, and still be in the U.S.A. But cunning was not in my kit bag. I never felt that that was necessary. I was always aboveboard. I always put out my work for stomping, whatever I did. And I usually got stomped. But I never felt that it was necessary to retreat and stay home and nurse my wounds and never try again until I had a masterpiece. That was never my understanding of how to write, or how to live as a writer. Somewhere along the line I came across a phrase about 'renewing your

vulnerability'. And that seemed to me a most important thing for a writer. You renew your vulnerability. Constantly. You start out feeling so vulnerable that you're afraid the criticism will kill you. But if you're not afraid of being vulnerable, if you say, 'Go ahead, hit me again, I can take it,' you get a thick skin.

You get that as a journalist. Letters to the editor demanding 'Throw this guy in the river.' Or 'Why did you hire him to begin with? This man should be destroyed.' Or 'This is a radical', or 'This is a liberal' — or some other dirty word. You get to live with that. I remember I wrote a series of articles on the slums of Albany back in the sixties. The mail attacking me came in like you couldn't believe. I got hate calls and hate mail from grand bigots, wonderful bigots, really *creative* bigots. It didn't faze me, because I realized early on that when you get into the business of putting yourself out on the public chopping block, you have to figure you're going to get chopped at.

QUINN: With *Legs* did you set out to write an Albany cycle?

KENNEDY: No, I chose the word 'cycle' because it connotes an open-ended and related series of novels.

QUINN: Your first three novels are set in Albany in the Depression, which really seems to have captured your imagination. Why?

KENNEDY: *Legs* was 1931, and that was researched to discover that era. And once I discovered the twenties and Prohibition and the gangland world, I began to see that it had tentacles that went forward, that people I was writing about in *Legs* were going to be significant in future books I wanted to write. When I got around to writing *Billy Phelan*, which was the next one, it should have taken place in 1933, which was only two years after Diamond died, but I felt what I needed to do then was to move deeper into the Depression, into the grit of it, into the end of it, the feeling of coming out of it. I set *Billy Phelan* in 1938, which was just before the war begins and was also a political year. I manipulated history to suit myself. I made the real-life kidnapping of Dan O'Connell's[2] nephew take place five years later than it actually had, and I used the 'blackout', for instance, in *Billy Phelan*, but placed it in 1938. Dan O'Connell [Albany's political boss] 'blacked out' Governor Dewey in '42 or '43. He had the civil defence behind him when he turned off the electricity so nobody in

Albany could hear Dewey's radio speech attacking the Albany politicians.

QUINN: *Ironweed* is the latest completed part of the cycle. You said in a recent interview that it came 'like a bullet'. Is that because you had lived in that world for so long, were so familiar with it from all the research you'd done, that you already knew the characters?

KENNEDY: No. *Ironweed* was something else, and had a pre-existence in both journalism and early fiction. In that unpublished novel I wrote in Puerto Rico I created Francis Phelan, just one of several characters in a family chronicle. Then, in 1963, I wrote a series of articles on a wino couple for the *Albany Times-Union*, and I fused the fiction and nonfiction when I started to create Francis Phelan again for *Billy Phelan*. The early work was all dead at this point, which is what usually happens when you leave it in the drawer, so I began from scratch, and Francis emerged as a new and more complex character in *Billy*, so much so that I knew he should have his own book. So by the time I got to him in *Ironweed* I knew far more about the history of the city, and I was reflecting a complexity of life that I had not been able to get to in the first novels. I felt I was into higher mathematics, and that I really knew this man. And the book was written in just about seven months.

QUINN: You mentioned Farrell before. Are there any other Irish-American writers who've had an impact on your writing?

KENNEDY: Fitzgerald, if you call him an Irish-American. Actually, he was the original Yuppie. The Yuppie Irishman.

QUINN: There are similarities between *Legs* and *Gatsby*. Several critics have mentioned them.

KENNEDY: Deliberately so. *Gatsby*'s a great book, I think. And I make that comparison in homage as much as anything else. I wouldn't want anybody to think I was cavalierly using the narration of Marcus Gorman about a gangster without understanding the precedent. But I also feel that the narrator in *Gatsby* was boring as a character, and I don't think Marcus is. Fitzgerald's narrator came to life only when Fitzgerald let him stop talking about himself and allowed us to see him in action. That, very clearly, was when he leaped off the page for me.

QUINN: *Legs* and *The Great Gatsby* are both about outsiders trying to force their way into America. Is that right?

KENNEDY: Right. But you never see Gatsby doing it seriously. There are some people who have made the analogy that Diamond *is* Gatsby, but I don't think Gatsby was like Diamond. I don't think Gatsby was a gangster. I think he was just a thief. I don't think he was a killer. People said he killed a man *once*, but they said that about everybody in the twenties.

QUINN: That's the American story. The immigrant or the immigrant's son forcing his way in.

KENNEDY: The ambition was always to reach fame and fortune. Some people tried to shoot their way into it. Some survived, were acquitted, or just got rich and went straight. Big Bill Dwyer did that. He was one of the great rumrunners, and he wound up in Café Society, Palm Beach, racetracks, hobnobbing with the rich, hanging out in tuxedos. A number of Irish-Americans chose that route.

QUINN: Any other Irish-American writers besides Fitzgerald whom you value?

KENNEDY: O'Hara,[3] even though he tried to bury his Irishness and come on as a WASP clubman.[4] But his stories still have great vigor and wit. I got lost in his novels, that deluge of information that now seems the trademark of the pulp writers. Eugene O'Neill was a great favorite of mine, especially his *Iceman* and *Long Day's Journey*. Wonderful Celtic gloom and irony in those works. I liked Farrell's *Studs Lonigan* but I never wanted to write like that — the naturalism of the city. I was too interested in the dream element in life, the surreal. Flannery O'Connor[5] is terrific, now and always. I always thought Edwin O'Connor's *The Last Hurrah* was a marvellous book. I fell off the chair reading those great lines about the Curley days[6] and I could see he understood the tension between the church and politics extremely well. But I also felt he was leaving out things either to be polite to the church or to Irish society, or perhaps out of squeamishness. I felt at times that he didn't reflect Irish-American life as I knew it. I felt I had to bring in the cathouses and the gambling and the violence, for if you left those out you had only a part of Albany. The idealized Irish life of the country club and the Catholic colleges was true enough, but that didn't have anything to do with what was going on down on Broadway among all those raffish Irishmen. They were tough sons-of-bitches, dirty-minded and foul-mouthed gamblers and bigots, and also wonderful, generous, funny, curiously honest and very complex people. I felt that way of life had to be penetrated at the level of harsh reality — its wit, anger, sexuality, deviousness. It also needed to have the surreal dimension that goes with any society in which religion plays such a dominant role. Those lives are worth recording, and I'm not done with them by any means.

QUINN: Do you think, in fact, there is such a thing as an 'Irish-American literary tradition'?

KENNEDY: When we talk about Irish-American writers — or Irish-American anything — we're talking about an evolution. You can't really be negative about Finley Peter Dunne, or Farrell, or Fitzgerald, or O'Hara, or O'Connor. They all lived in a certain time and reflected that time. And for some of them, maybe, there was a sense of marginality about their background. There was an uncertainty. Certainly, in the days of Fitzgerald and O'Hara there was. The Irish were aspiring to rise in the world. You had Finley Peter Dunne satirizing those 'donkey' Irishmen in order to make them become something beyond what they could become. Everybody is a climber. Everybody is trying to come up from below. That's the first law of motion in America. Nobody wants to live in the Five Points in New York City forever. Nobody wants to live with the stereotypes that were associated with Irish thugs — the derbys and the cockeyed look, the readiness to break your ankle for a nickel or your wrist for a dime.

God knows where I am in all of this, in this evolution, but I *know* all that has come before. I know that those who came before helped to show me how to try to turn experience into literature. I know all that came before in the same way I know the Irish ascended politically to become Jack Kennedy. After Jack Kennedy, anything was possible. Goddammit, *we've* been President, and you can't hold us back anymore.

QUINN: Is there a certain defensiveness about the Irish? We know all about the lecherousness and the sinfulness but we prefer to present outsiders with the other face, the saintly side.

KENNEDY: I just got a letter from the son of the owner of a bar in Albany. You know what he told me? He said, 'Dan O'Connell told my father that he closed all the poolrooms in Albany, so how come you've got a poolroom in *Billy Phelan*?' O'Connell didn't want any poolrooms in Albany, he said, because they were corrupting influences on kids.

QUINN: As opposed to cockfights?

KENNEDY: Or as opposed to saloons? And whorehouses? Dan took tribute from them all. I don't see how you can leave all that out if you're going to talk about life in the twentieth century. Irish-American life or any kind of life.

QUINN: But haven't the Irish been blessed by a wonderful sense of guilt? Isn't that part of their Catholicism?

KENNEDY: I don't think Catholics feel that much guilt anymore. They're more and more like other Americans.

QUINN: Isn't the loss of guilt the loss of a wonderful strength? Isn't it one of the essential ingredients in the Irish-American mind, as it is in the Jewish-American mind? It's the one thing you can be sure of never losing.

KENNEDY: Well, there's always a sense of sin. I don't think we're ever going to lose that. Norman Mailer was unnecessarily worried about the loss of sin, in terms of sex, back in the sixties. He was suggesting that the only thing that makes sense is to have sex when you're sinning. Otherwise, it's no fun.

QUINN: But isn't Catholicism one of the things that makes those earthy Irishmen you write about unique? The tension created in their lives by the church?

KENNEDY: That's only part of it. You only go to church on Sundays, and maybe you talk about it the rest of the week. But politics is far more important than church, because politics is survival. You could postpone your concern about the salvation of your soul. You could always say, 'I'll get to that when I get old', and if you got a heart attack, God forbid, and died in the blossom of your youth, the chances are you would go to Purgatory.

QUINN: What about the Catholic element in your novels? One reviewer has seen in *Ironweed* a parallel between the liturgy of the Catholic church and the events of the three days the book encompasses. Is he right?

KENNEDY: Absolutely, but not for reasons of celebration and liturgy. In *Ironweed*, it was all accidental because I had already created the time frame in *Billy Phelan*.

I created it because I had to have it all happen during the pre-election period. That was the whole purpose in *Billy Phelan*. So I made the kidnapping take place in an election year. Then it moves forward into the campaign. Once I had that, I went back, and if you notice, *Billy Phelan* and *Ironweed* end on the same day. And they do that only because having created the dynamics of Billy meeting his father, the logical thing when I dealt with Francis was to see him in those post-confrontational days with Billy — to discover what it was that made him go home.

Francis Phelan wouldn't go home until he knew that Annie had never condemned or blamed him. So first come these two things: the invitation from Billy and the knowledge about Annie. They stay in his mind. He dries up. And he wants to go home. All of *Ironweed* is this tap dancing into reality, trying to figure out, 'How am I going to do it?' Talking to Helen, getting rid of Helen, walking back, putting her in the car with Finny, walking up to where he used to live, confronting that reality, going back and making some money so he could buy a turkey, and so on.

QUINN: Editors kept turning down *Ironweed* because they said it was too depressing. Nobody would want to read a novel about bums. But it's actually a very hopeful novel, isn't it? A novel about redemption? And forgiveness?

KENNEDY: 'Redemption' is the key word. That's what it's all about. It parallels the *Purgatorio*. When you talk about the liturgy or Catholic thought, you think of Dante, and eventually you think of the *Inferno*, and the *Purgatorio*, and the *Paradiso*. From the epigraph, you enter my book with Dante, and it's a journey through planes of escalation into a moment of redemption out of sin. Francis cleanses himself. It reflects something I think is profound about human behaviour. I don't look at it in the way that I used to when I was a kid, when I believed in everything, believed it was the only way to look at the world. Today I believe Catholic theology has great humanistic dimensions, great wisdom about how to achieve peace of mind in relationship to the unknown, the infinite. Maybe it's a palliative. Maybe it's one of the great lollipops of history. At the same time, it's beautiful. It's as good as I could see on the horizon. I don't need Buddhism, or Zoroastrianism — I've got Sacred Heart Church in North Albany.

QUINN: All Saints Day is taken from Irish mythology. It's based on the Celtic feast of Samhain, when the barriers between the living and the dead disappeared. Was Irish mythology a conscious part of *Ironweed*?

KENNEDY: No, it was not. I didn't know that about All Saints Day. I just grew up with it as a holy day. But I'm finding out all kinds of things about myself, things that are pushing me, nudging me into places I'm not yet fully aware of.

Much of it seems parallel to what I know about contemporary Irish life. Maybe, if there's such a thing as collective unconsciousness, then this was part of it: a kind of grip that still holds. It's really remarkable that the Irish, like the Jews, have held on so to their identity, that there was this triumphant resistance to death and genocide and their obliteration as a people. But in this case, the Irish link wasn't conscious. My consciousness as a Catholic was sufficient.

QUINN: The Irish poet Patrick Kavanagh has written that he lived in a place where literature wasn't supposed to happen. It was too conventional, supposedly. Did you ever face that stumbling block? The thought that literature happened in places grander or more exotic than Albany?

KENNEDY: Oh yes, from the very outset. I understood that Melville went to school here. I understood that Henry James touched down here, in one of his less cosmic moments. Bret Harte was born here, and left immediately. Those kind of moments, that's about as much as you used to expect out of Albany. But then I began to figure that it couldn't be all that bad, I found out that Albany was, and is, a great place. There are not all that many people who lived and died in Albany creating literature that would endure through the ages. But there was a sense of the place being valuable, and this was *tremendously* important. As soon as I began to understand this, I realized that the town was unexplored.

QUINN: Was it out of the newspaper articles you wrote about Albany that you began to sink yourself into its history? To sense its depths?

KENNEDY: No, I was writing in Puerto Rico about myself and my wife and my ancestors trying to understand it all, and then I realized I didn't understand, and that was it. That ignorance was the main drive: to come back at some point in my life, settle in and do some research in the library, and try to understand. I never expected that I would stay forever.

How can you write about a place if you don't understand what the street names mean, or who the mayor is, or what the machine was all about? I was writing from Puerto Rico at a point when I didn't really understand the political bossism in Albany. I hadn't paid sufficient attention when I was working at an Albany newspaper. I just said, 'I'm *mildly* opposed to it.' I was very self-righteous.

QUINN: One of the main components of Albany is its powerful, Democratic machine, an Irish-American machine. For the Albany Irish, you've written, 'politics was justice itself; politics was sufficient unto itself'. What did you mean by that?

KENNEDY: When I grew up, there was no sense of morality in regard to politics. If you were Irish, you were obviously a Democrat. If you were a Democrat, you were probably a Catholic. If you were a Catholic, you obviously gave allegiance to the church on the corner, and to Dan O'Connell who was a pillar of the church, inseparable from the bishop and the priests, and who was revered and prayed for. But Dan was also profiting from the whorehouses, the gambling joints, the all-night saloons and the blackout card games. He was in collusion with the grafters and the bankers, getting rich with the paving contractors.

No matter what it was in town, wherever you could make an illegal dollar, that's where the Irish were, that's where the politics were, that's where the church was, that's where the morality was. And it was all fused. You couldn't separate it because the families were so interlocked, and the goodness walked hand-in-hand with the evil. But it wasn't *viewed* as evil. It was viewed as a way to get on in the world. Objective morality didn't interest Albany. The Irish didn't care about it. They understood that *they* had been deprived and now they were not. Now they were able to get jobs. In the previous era, when the Irish were not in power, they had *not* been able to get jobs. Their families were starving, and starvation for them for them was immorality. So once they took power, O'Connell became kind of a saint. He became the man who would save your soul by putting you to work.

QUINN: Was he a Robin Hood?

KENNEDY: Of course he was a Robin Hood. Of course he was also a rascal. I don't know what the original Robin Hood was like. Maybe he has been romanticized out of existence, but there's no question that Dan O'Connell as we knew him was a Robin Hood. He certainly gave away a lot of money.

Nobody really knows how much he died with. What came out in the papers was ridiculous. A quarter of a million or so. But they would spend $200,000 in five-dollar bills every election day. He was raking it in from all quarters. All the beer drinkers in the county were adding to the party's profits, and Dan O'Connell controlled the beer. Thousands and thousands of fortunes were made in this town through politics.

QUINN: Politics was the Irish stock market?

KENNEDY: Yes, the Irish stock market. I never thought of that. That's a great phrase. You've invented something.

QUINN: Politics, then, is one of the common threads among the American-Irish? If anything united them, it was that. In Kansas City, Boston, Albany, New York, always the same story.

KENNEDY: What else could they do? They could have done other things if they had the education, but they didn't. They were the people of numbers. That was the important thing about them. They were not the people of knowledge, the people with connections to power, the people of Harvard and Wall Street. What they knew was politics. What they knew was the church. What they knew was their Irishness. What they knew was clannishness. The network was a great strength. It let Dan O'Connell hold on to the allegiance of the masses. In the face of the most vile declarations by enemies, in the face of the obvious stealing that was going on, and despite the slimy meat and the whorehouses, Dan went on and on and on.

QUINN: Albany is more than a setting for your novels. It becomes kind of a character. But do you think of yourself as a *regional* writer in the way that Flannery O'Connor thought of herself as a Southern writer?

KENNEDY: Yes and no. All regional writers are trying to capture the uniqueness of their region, obviously. And most writers who use regions are trying for universality, to speak to life outside the region. It depends, I suspect, on how well you are able to make your cosmos, however small — Milledgeville, Georgia, or Albany, New York, or Dublin, or the *Pequod* — become a center of vitality, a center of ubiquity, a center of spiritual life that will transcend any kind of limitation that geography imposes. If you never find that center, all you're doing is floating free. Until you have a Milledgeville, or unless you're a genius like Beckett, you can't coalesce your meaning. Creating life in an abstract place — that's very hard to do, you have to really have genius.

QUINN: Do you think you could move to a place, let's say to Scarsdale, stay there for two years, study the place, become familiar with its characters, and then create the same sort of magic that you've done with Albany?

KENNEDY: I don't think so. I would probably begin to impose my knowledge of Albany on Scarsdale. I tried to do that in Puerto Rico, and I couldn't do it. I didn't understand Puerto Rico that well. In those days, I could write about Puerto Rico as a reporter, but I didn't really understand the dynamics of the place, what was going on in the *soul* of Puerto Rico, in the *soul* of San Juan. When you don't have that, you don't have anything, as far as I'm concerned. You can do all the navel-gazing you want and until it's centered on a place, it seems to me that it's a vagrant pursuit, a Sunday afternoon in the park, or with the soap operas. It's an absence of significance. If you don't have the place, you don't have the dynamics of the society that exists in that place, and they're very different in Scarsdale from Albany, or San Juan, or Dublin. Georgia is not in any way equivalent to North Albany, where I grew up. No matter how Catholic Flannery O'Connor was, she's writing about a society where you have peacocks on the front porch, you have blacks and whites with active hostility toward one another, and that's not where I grew up.

QUINN: What about Ireland? Does it ever tug on your imagination? Any of the Albany cycle spinning its way back there?

KENNEDY: I've been to Ireland several times. I'll go again in quest of my ancestors, like so many other Irishmen in this country, to comprehend origin and consequences. But it's very unlikely that I will ever set a novel in Ireland because I don't know enough about the places. It's a foreign country to me. I've thought about writing about Ireland, I've been to the North, I've lived in Dublin, but I feel I don't know enough about any particular place to give me what I'd need for a novel. I'm thinking seriously about the Irish-American experience, which is not the *Irish* experience. I feel that I'd be a fraud if I went to Ireland and tried to write significantly about somebody there, when I'm not from there. I'm from Albany.

I believe that I can't be anything other than Irish-American. I know there's a division here, and a good many Irish-Americans believe they are merely American. They've lost touch with anything that smacks of Irishness as we used to know it. That's all right.

But I think if they set out to discover themselves, to wonder about why they are what they are, then they'll run into a psychological inheritance that's even more than psychological, that may also be genetic, or biopsychogenetic, who the hell knows what you call it? But there's something in us that survives and that's the result of being Irish, whether from North or South, whether Catholic or Protestant, some element of life, of consciousness, that is different from being Hispanic, or Oriental, or WASP. These traits endure. I'm just exploring what's survived in my time and place.

I don't presume that I could go back in time and find out what was going on in Belfast or Dublin before my own day, to go back as a fiction writer and reconstitute it. For me, it's a question of imagination. I don't feel I own those Irish places, but I do own Albany. It's mine. Nineteenth-century Albany is mine as well. It's a different time and in many ways a different place from what it is now, but I feel confident I can reach it.

QUINN: Do you think your fascination with place is particularly Irish?

KENNEDY: The natural world is always very important to writers. You use it wherever necessary. But it's not peculiarly Irish to have a sense of a place. For me, fiction exists, finally, in order to describe neither social conditions nor landscapes but human consciousness. Essays, documentary films, editorials in newspapers can persuade you to a political position. But nothing except great fiction can tell you what it means to be alive. Great fiction, great films, great plays, they all center in on consciousness, which always has a uniqueness about it, and that uniqueness is what a writer can give you that nobody else in the world can give you: a sense of having lived in a certain world and understood a certain place, a certain consciousness, a certain destiny, a grand unknown, all the squalor and all the glory of being alive.

And if your reduce fiction to political or social argument, or to a kind of sociological construct, you lose its real strength. When you think of Chaucer or Boccaccio, you remember the individualistic elements of their characters in the same way you remember the people in, for example, Sherwood Anderson's *Winesburg, Ohio*. They don't go bad. Great fiction doesn't go bad.

---

1   James T. Farrell, Chicago-Irish novelist, author of *Studs Lonigan* (1934) (see above p. 439).

2   Daniel Peter O'Connell (1886–1977) was the Irish boss who ensured uninterrupted Irish control of Albany from 1921 onwards. For more on O'Connell, see William Kennedy, *O Albany!* (1983).

3   John O'Hara, author of *BUtterfield 8* (1934) (see above p. 436).

4   White Anglo-Saxon Protestant.

5   Here seen in an Irish context by Kennedy.

6   *The Last Hurrah* (1956), about an old-style Irish-American politician, is modelled in part on James Curley (1874–1958), who served three times as Mayor of Boston between 1914 and 1934. See above p. 673.

EAVAN BOLAND

from Eavan Boland, *Object Lessons: The Life of the Woman and the Poet in Our Time* (1996)

Eavan Boland (1944–   ), poet and critic, was born in Dublin and educated in London, New York, and Trinity College Dublin. Here in this essay she focuses on an issue central to her work: the relationship between gender and nationalism in Ireland. At the beginning of the essay she reflects on the woman she met on Achill Island, the woman who becomes the subject of her poem 'The Achill Woman' (see p. 1165).

Outside History

Years ago I went to Achill for Easter. I was a student at Trinity then, and I had the loan of a friend's cottage. It was a one-storey stone building with two rooms and a view of sloping fields.

April was cold that year. The cottage was in sight of the Atlantic, and at night a bitter, humid wind blew across the shore. By day there was heckling sunshine, but after dark a fire was necessary. The loneliness of the place suited me. My purposes in being there were purgatorial, and I had no intention of going out and about. I had done erratically, to say the least, in my first-year exams. In token of the need to do better, I had brought with me a small, accusing volume of the court poets of the silver age. In other words, those sixteenth-century English songwriters, like Wyatt and Raleigh, whose lines appear so elegant, so offhand yet whose poems smell of the gallows.

I was there less than a week. The cottage had no water, and every evening the caretaker, an old woman who shared a cottage with her brother at the bottom of the field, would carry water up to me. I can see her still. She has a tea towel round her waist — perhaps this is one image that has become all the images I have of her — she wears an old cardigan and her hands are blushing with cold as she puts down the bucket. Sometimes we talk inside the door of the cottage. Once, I remember, we stood there as the dark grew all around us and I could see stars beginning to curve in the stream behind us.

She was the first person to talk to me about the famine. The first person, in fact, to speak to me with any force about the terrible parish of survival and death which the event had been in those regions. She kept repeating to me that they were great people, the people in the famine. *Great people.* I had never heard that before. She pointed out the beauties of the place. But they themselves, I see now, were a subtext. On the eastern side of Keel, the cliffs of Menawn rose sheer out of the water. And here was Keel itself, with its blond strand and broken stone, where the villagers in the famine, she told me, had moved closer to the shore, the better to eat the seaweed.

Memory is treacherous. It confers meanings which are not apparent at the time. I want to say that I understood this woman as emblem and instance of everything I am about to propose. Of course I did not. Yet even then I sensed a power in the encounter. I knew, without having words for it, that she came from a past which affected me. When she pointed out Keel to me that evening when the wind was brisk and cold and the light was going, when she gestured towards that shore which had stones as outlines and monuments of a desperate people, what was she pointing at? A history? A nation? Her memories or mine?

Those questions, once I began to write my own poetry, came back to haunt me. 'I have been amazed, more than once,' writes Hélène Cixous, 'by a description a woman gave me of a world all her own, which she had been secretly haunting since early childhood.' As the years passed, my amazement grew. I would see again the spring evening, the woman talking to me. Above all, I would remember how, when I finished speaking to her I went in, lit a fire, took out my book of English court poetry and memorized all over again — with no sense of irony or omission — the cadences of power and despair.

II

I have written this to probe the virulence and necessity of the idea of a nation. Not on its own and not in a vacuum, but as it intersects with a specific poetic inheritance and as that inheritance, in turn, cut across me as woman and poet. Some of these intersections are personal. Some of them may be painful to remember. Nearly all of them are elusive and difficult to describe with any degree of precision. Nevertheless, I believe these intersections, if I can observe them at all properly here, reveal something about poetry, about nationalism, about the difficulties for a woman poet within a constraining national tradition. Perhaps the argument itself is nothing more than a way of revisiting the cold lights of that western evening and the force of that woman's conversation. In any case, the questions inherent in that encounter remain with me. It could well be that they might appear, even to a sympathetic reader, too complex to admit of an answer. In other words, that an argument like mine must contain too many imponderables to admit of any practical focus.

Yet I have no difficulty in stating the central premise of my argument. It is that over a relatively short time — certainly no more than a generation or so — women have moved from being the objects of Irish poems to being the authors of them. It is a momentous transit. It is also a disruptive one. It raises questions of identity, issues of poetic motive and ethical direction which can seem almost impossibly complex. What is more, such a transit — like the slow course of a star or the shifts in a constellation — is almost invisible to the naked eye. Critics may well miss it or map it inaccurately. Yet such a transit inevitably changes our idea of measurement, of distance, of the past as well as the future. And as it does so, it changes our idea of the Irish poem, of its composition and authority, of its right to appropriate certain themes and make certain fiats. And since poetry is never local for long, that in turn widens out into further implications.

Everything I am about to argue here could be taken as local and personal, rooted in one country and one poetic inheritance, and both of them mine. Yet if the names were changed, if situations and places were transposed, the issues might well be revealed as less parochial. This is not, after all, an essay on the craft of the art. I am writing not about aesthetics but about the ethics which are altogether less visible in a poetic tradition. Who the poet is, what he or she nominates as a proper theme for poetry, what selves poets discover and confirm through this subject matter — all of this involves an ethical choice. The more volatile the material — and a wounded history, public or private, is always volatile — the more intensely ethical the choice. Poetic ethics are evident and urgent in any culture where tensions between a poet and his or her birthplace are inherited and established. Poets from such cultures might well recognize some of the issues raised here. After all, this is not the only country or the only politic where the previously passive objects of a work of art have, in a relatively short time, become the authors of it.

So it was with me. For this very reason, early on as a poet, certainly in my twenties, I realized that the Irish nation as an existing construct in Irish poetry was not available to me. I would not have been able to articulate it at that point, but at some preliminary level I already knew that the anguish and power of that woman's gesture on Achill, with its suggestive hinterland of pain, were not something I could predict or rely on in Irish poetry. There were glimpses here and there; sometimes more than that. But all too often, when I was searching for such an inclusion, what I found was a rhetoric of imagery which alienated me: a fusion of the national and the feminine which seemed to simplify both.

It was not a comfortable realization. There was nothing clear-cut about my feelings. I had tribal ambivalences and doubts, and even then I had an uneasy sense of the conflict which awaited me. On the one hand, I knew that as a poet I could not easily do without the idea of a nation. Poetry in every time draws on that reserve. On the other, I could not as a woman accept the nation formulated for me by Irish poetry and its traditions. At one point it even looked to me as if the whole thing might be made up of irreconcilable differences. At the very least it seemed to me that I was likely to remain an outsider in my own national literature, cut off from its archive, at a distance from its energy. Unless, that is, I could repossess it. This proposal is about that conflict and that repossession and about the fact that repossession itself is not a static or single act. Indeed, the argument which describes it may itself be no more than a part of it.

III

A nation. It is, in some ways, the most fragile and improbable of concepts. Yet the idea of an Ireland, resolved and healed of its wounds, is an irreducible presence in the Irish past and its literature. In one sense, of course, both the concept and its realization resist definition. It is certainly nothing conceived in what Edmund Burke calls 'the spirit of rational liberty'. When a people have been so dispossessed by event as the Irish in the eighteenth and nineteenth centuries, an extra burden falls on the very idea of a nation. What should be a political aspiration becomes a collective fantasy. The dream itself becomes freighted with invention. The Irish nation, materializing in the songs and ballads of these centuries, is a sequence of improvised images. These songs, these images, wonderful and terrible and memorable as they are, propose for a nation an impossible task: to be at once an archive of defeat and a diagram of victory.

As a child I loved these songs. As a teenager I had sought them out for some meaning, some definition. Even now, in some moods and at certain times, I can find it difficult to resist their makeshift angers. And no wonder. The best of them are written — like the lyrics of Wyatt and Raleigh — within sight of the gibbet. They breathe just free of the noose.

In one sense I was a captive audience. My childhood was spent in London. My image makers as a child, therefore, were refractions of my exile: conversations overheard, memories and visitors. I listened and absorbed. For me, as for many another exile, Ireland was my nation long before it was once again my country. That nation, then and later, was a session of images: of defeats and sacrifices, of individual defiances happening offstage. The songs enhanced the images; the images reinforced the songs. To me they were the soundings of the place I had lost: drowned treasure.

It took me years to shake off those presences. In the end, though, I did escape. My escape was assisted by the realization that these songs were effect, not cause. They were only the curators of the dream, not the inventors. In retrospect I could accuse both them and the dream of certain crucial simplifications. I made then, as I make now, a moral division between what those songs sought to accomplish and what Irish poetry must seek to achieve. The songs, with their postures and their angers, glamorized resistance, action. But the Irish experience, certainly for the purposes of poetry, was only incidentally about action and resistance. At a far deeper level — and here the Achill woman returns — it was about defeat. The coffin ships, the soup queues, those desperate villagers at the shoreline — these things had actually happened. The songs, persuasive, hypnotic, could wish them away. Poetry could not. Of course, the relation between a poem and a past is never that simple. When I met the Achill woman, I was already a poet, I thought of myself as a poet. Yet nothing that I understood about poetry enabled me to understand her better. Quite the reverse. I turned my back on her in that cold twilight and went to commit to memory the songs and artifices of the very power systems which had made her own memory such an archive of loss.

If I understand her better now, and my relation to her, it is not just because my sense of irony or history has developed over the years, although I hope they have. It is more likely because of my own experience as a poet. Inevitably any account of this carries the risk of subject codes and impressions. Yet in poetry in particular and women's writing in general, the private witness is often all there is to go on. Since my personal experience as a poet is part of my source material, it is to that I now turn.

IV

I entered Trinity to study English and Latin. Those were the early sixties, and Dublin was another world — a place for which I can still feel Henry James's 'tiger-pounce of homesickness'. In a very real sense it was a city of images and anachronisms. There were still brewery horses on Grafton Street, their rumps draped and smoking under sackcloth. In the coffee bars eggs were poached in a rolling boil and spooned onto thick, crustless toast. The lights went on at twilight; by midnight the city was full of echoes.

After the day's lectures I took a bus home from college. It was a short journey. Home was an attic flat on the near edge of a town that was just beginning to sprawl. There in the kitchen, on an oilskin tablecloth, I wrote my first real poems: derivative, formalist, gesturing poems. I was a very long way from Adrienne Rich's realization that 'instead of poems about experience, I am getting poems that are experiences'. If anything, my poems were other people's experiences. This, after all, was the heyday of the movement in Britain, and the neat stanza, the well-broken line were the very stuff of poetic identity.

Now I wonder how many young women poets taught themselves — in rooms like that, with a blank discipline — to write the poem that was in the air, rather than the one within their experience? How many faltered, as I did, not for lack of answers but for lack of questions. 'It will be a long time still, I think,' wrote Virginia Woolf, 'before a woman can sit down to write a book without finding a phantom to be slain, a rock to be dashed against.'

But for now let me invent a shift of time. I am turning down those streets which echo after midnight. I am climbing the stairs of a coffee bar which stays open late. I know what I will find. Here is the salt-glazed mug on a tabletop which is as scarred as a desk in a country school. Here is the window with its view of an empty street, of lamplight and iron. And there, in the corner, is my younger self.

I draw up a chair, I sit down opposite her. I begin to talk — no, to harangue her. Why, I say, do you do it? Why do you go back to that attic flat, night after night, to write in forms explored and sealed by Englishmen hundreds of years ago? You are Irish. You are a woman. Why do you keep these things at the periphery of the poem? Why do you not move them to the centre, where they belong?

But the woman who looks back at me is uncomprehending. If she answers at all, it will be with the rhetoric of a callow apprenticeship: that the poem is pure process, that the technical encounter is the one which guarantees all others. She will speak about the dissonance of the line and the necessity for the stanza. And so on. And so on.

'*For what* is the poet responsible?' asks Allen Tate.

'He is responsible for the virtue proper to him as a poet, for his special *arête*: for the mastery of a disciplined language which will not shun the full report of the reality conveyed to him by his awareness.'

She is a long way, that young woman — with her gleaming cup and her movement jargon — from the full report of anything. In her lack of any sense of implication or complication, she might as well be a scientist in the thirties, bombarding uranium with neutrons.

If I try now to analyse why such a dialogue would be a waste of time, I come up with several reasons. One of them is that it would take years for me to see, let alone comprehend, certain realities. Not until the oilskin tablecloth was well folded and the sprawling town had become a rapacious city, and the attic flat was a house in the suburbs, could I accept the fact that I was a woman and a poet in a culture which had the greatest difficulty associating the two ideas. 'A woman must often take a critical stance towards her social, historical and cultural position in order to experience her own quest,' writes the American poet and feminist Rachel Blau de Plessis. 'Poems of the self's growth, or of self-knowledge may often include or be preceded by a questioning of major social prescriptions about the shape women's experience should take.' In years to come I would never be sure whether my poems had generated the questions or the questions had facilitated the poems. All that lay ahead. 'No poet,' says Eliot, 'no artist of any kind, has his complete meaning alone.' In the meantime, I existed whether I liked it or not in a mesh, a web, a labyrinth of associations. Of poems past and present. Contemporary poems. Irish poems.

V

Irish poetry was predominantly male. Here or there you found a small eloquence, like 'After Aughrim' by Emily Lawless.[1] Now and again, in discussion, you heard a woman's name. But the lived vocation, the craft witnessed by a human life — that was missing. And I missed it. Not in the beginning, perhaps. But later, when perceptions of womanhood began to redirect my own work, what I regretted was the absence of an expressed poetic life which would have dignified and revealed mine. The influence of absences should not be underestimated. Isolation itself can have a powerful effect in the life of a young writer. 'I'm talking about real influence now,' says Raymond Carver. 'I'm talking about the moon and the tide.'

I turned to the work of Irish male poets. After all, I thought of myself as an Irish poet. I wanted to locate myself within the Irish poetic tradition. The dangers

and stresses in my own themes gave me an added incentive to discover a context for them. But what I found dismayed me.

The majority of Irish male poets depended on women as motifs in their poetry. They moved easily, deftly, as if by right among images of women in which I did not believe and of which I could not approve. The women in their poems were often passive, decorative, raised to emblematic status. This was especially true where the woman and the idea of the nation were mixed: where the nation became a woman and the woman took on a national posture.

The trouble was these images did good service as ornaments. In fact, they had a wide acceptance as ornaments by readers of Irish poetry. Women in such poems were frequently referred to approvingly as mythic, emblematic. But to me these passive and simplified women seemed a corruption. Moreover, the transaction they urged on the reader, to accept them as mere decoration, seemed to compound the corruption. For they were not decorations, they were not ornaments. However distorted these images, they had their roots in a suffered truth.

What had happened? How had the women of our past — the women of a long struggle and a terrible survival — undergone such a transformation? How had they suffered Irish history and rooted themselves in the speech and memory of the Achill woman, only to re-emerge in Irish poetry as fictive queens and national sibyls?

The more I thought about it, the more uneasy I became. The wrath and grief of Irish history seemed to me, as it did to many, one of our true possessions. Women were part of that wrath, had endured that grief. It seemed to me a species of human insult that at the end of all, in certain Irish poems, they should become elements of style rather than aspects of truth.

The association of the feminine and the national — and the consequent simplification of both — are not, of course, a monopoly of Irish poetry. 'All my life,' writes Charles de Gaulle, 'I have thought about France in a certain way. The emotional side of me tends to imagine France like the princess in the fairy tale, or the Madonna of the Frescoes.' De Gaulle's words point up the power of nationhood to edit the reality of womanhood. Once the idea of a nation influences the perception of a woman, then that woman is suddenly and inevitably simplified. She can no longer have complex feelings and aspirations. She becomes the passive projection of a national idea.

Irish poems simplified women most at the point of intersection between womanhood and Irishness. The further the Irish poem drew away from the idea of

Ireland, the more real and persuasive became the images of women. Once the pendulum swung back, the simplifications started again. The idea of the defeated nation's being reborn as a triumphant woman was central to a certain kind of Irish poem. Dark Rosaleen. Cathleen ni Houlihan. The nation as woman; the woman as national muse.

The more I looked at it, the more it seemed to me that in relation to the idea of a nation many, if not most, Irish male poets had taken the soft option. The irony was that few Irish poets were nationalists. By and large, they had eschewed the fervour and crudity of that ideal. But long after they had rejected the politics of Irish nationalism, they continued to deploy the emblems and enchantments of its culture. It was the culture, not the politics, which informed Irish poetry: not the harsh awakenings but the old dreams.

In all of this I did not blame nationalism. Nationalism seemed to me inevitable in the Irish context, a necessary hallucination within Joyce's nightmare of history. I did blame Irish poets. Long after it was necessary, Irish poetry had continued to trade in the exhausted fictions of the nation, had allowed those fictions to edit ideas of womanhood and modes of remembrance. Some of the poetry produced by such simplifications was, of course, difficult to argue with. It was difficult to deny that something was gained by poems which used the imagery and emblem of the national muse. Something was gained, certainly, but only at an aesthetic level. While what was lost occurred at the deepest, most ethical level, and what was lost was what I valued. Not just the details of a past. Not just the hungers, the angers. These, however terrible, remain local. But the truth these details witness — human truths of survival and humiliation — these also were suppressed along with the details. Gone was the suggestion of any complicated human suffering. Instead you had the hollow victories, the passive images, the rhyming queens.

I knew that the women of the Irish past were defeated. I knew it instinctively long before the Achill woman pointed down the hill to the Keel shoreline. What I objected to was that Irish poetry should defeat them twice.

'I have not written day after day,' says Camus, 'because I desire the world to be covered with Greek statues and masterpieces. The man who has such a desire does exist in me. But I have written so much because I cannot keep from being drawn toward everyday life, toward those, whoever they may be, who are humiliated. They need to hope and, if all keep silent, they will be forever deprived of hope and we with them.'

This argument originates in some part from my own need to locate myself in a powerful literary tradition in which until then, or so it seemed to me, I had been an element of design rather than an agent of change. But even as a young poet, and certainly by the time my work confronted me with some of these questions, I had already had a vivid, human witness of the stresses which a national literature can impose on a poet. I had already seen the damage it could do.

VI

I remember the Dublin of the sixties almost more vividly than the city which usurped it. I remember its grace and emptiness and the old hotels with their chintzes and Sheffield trays. In one of these I had tea with Padraic Colum. I find it hard to be exact about the year, somewhere around the middle sixties. But I have no difficulty at all about the season. It was winter. We sat on a sofa by the window overlooking the street. The lamps were on, and a fine rain was being glamorized as it fell past their cowls.

Colum was then in his eighties. He had come from his native Longford in the early years of the century to a Dublin fermenting with political and literary change. Yeats admired his 1907 volume of poetry, *Wild Earth*. He felt the Ireland Colum proposed fitted neatly into his own ideas. 'It is unbeautiful Ireland,' Yeats writes, 'he will contrast finely with our Western dialect-makers.'

In old photographs Colum looks the part: curly-headed, dark, winsome. In every way he was a godsend to the Irish Revival. Nobody would actually have used the term *peasant poet*. But then nobody would have needed to. Such things were understood.

The devil, they say, casts no shadow. But that folk image applies to more than evil. There are writers in every country who begin in the morning of promise but by the evening, mysteriously, have cast no shadow and left no mark. Colum is one of them. For some reason, although he was eminently placed to deal with the energies of his own culture, he failed to do so. His musical, tender, hopeful imagination glanced off the barbaric griefs of the nineteenth century. It is no good fudging the issue. Very few of his poems now look persuasive on the page. All that heritage which should have been his — rage robbed of language, suffering denied its dignity — somehow eluded him. When he met it at all, it was with a borrowed sophistication.

Now in old age he struggled for a living. He transited stoically between Dublin and New York, giving readings, writing articles. He remained open and approachable. No doubt for this reason, I asked him what he really thought of Yeats. He paused for a moment. His voice had a distinctive, treble resonance. When he answered, it was high and emphatic. 'Yeats hurt me,' he said. 'He expected too much of me.'

I have never been quiet sure what Colum meant. What I understand by his words may be different from their intent. But I see his relation with the Irish Revival as governed by corrupt laws of supply and demand. He could be tolerated only if he read the signals right and acquiesced in his role as a peasant poet. He did not, and he could not. To be an accomplice in such a distortion required a calculation he never possessed. But the fact that he was screen-tested for it suggests how relentless the idea of Irishness in Irish poetry has been.

Colum exemplified something else to me. Here also was a poet who had been asked to make the journey, in one working lifetime, from being the object of Irish poems to being their author. He too, as an image, had been unacceptably simplified in all those poems about the land and the tenantry. So that — if he was to realize his identity — not only must he move from image to image maker, he must also undo the simplifications of the first by his force and command of the second. I suspect he found the imaginative stresses of that transit beyond his comprehension, let alone his strength. And so something terrible happened to him. He wrote Irish poetry as if he were still the object of it. He wrote with the passivity and simplification of his own reflection looking back at him from poems, plays and novels in which the so-called Irish peasant was a son of the earth, a cipher of the national cause. He had the worst of both worlds.

VII

Like Colum, Francis Ledwidge was born at the sharp end of history. He was an Irish poet who fought as a British soldier, a writer in a radical situation who used a conservative idiom to support it, and Ledwidge's short life was full of contradiction. He was in his early twenties when he died in the First World War.

Despite his own marginal and pressured position, Ledwidge used the conventional language of romantic nationalism. Not always; perhaps not often. But his poem on the death of the leaders of the Easter Rising, 'The Blackbirds',[2] is a case in point. It is, in a small way, a celebrated poem, and I have certainly not chosen it because it represents careless or shoddy work. Far from it. It is a skilful poem, adroit and quick in its rhythms, with an underlying sweetness of tone. For all that, it provides an example of a gifted poet who did not resist the contemporary orthodoxy. Perhaps he might have had he lived longer and learned more. As it

was, Ledwidge surrendered easily to the idioms of the Irish Revival. This in turn meant that he could avail himself of a number of approved stereotypes and, chief among them, the easy blend of feminine and national. Even here he could exercise a choice although, it must be said, a limited one. He could have had the Young Queen or the Old Mother. As it happens, he chose the Poor Old Woman. But we are in no doubt what he means:

THE BLACKBIRDS

I heard the Poor Old Woman say
'At break of day the fowler came,
And took my blackbirds from their songs
Who loved me well thro' shame and blame.

'No more from lovely distances
Their songs shall bless me mile from mile,
Nor to white Ashbourne call me down
To wear my crown another while.

'With bended flowers the angels mark
For the skylark the place they lie.
From there its little family
Shall dip their wings first in the sky.

'And when the first surprise of flight
Sweet songs excite, from the far dawn
Shall there come blackbirds, loud with love,
Sweet echoes of the singers gone.

'But in the lonely hush of eve
Weeping I grieve the silent bills'
I heard the Poor Old Woman say
In Derry of the little hills.

I am not sure this poem would pass muster now. There are too many sugary phrases — 'loud with love' and 'shame and blame' — evoking the very worst of Georgian poetry. But Ledwidge was young, and the impulse for the poem was historical. The 1916 leaders were dead. He was at a foreign front. The poem takes on an extra resonance if it is read as a concealed elegy for his own loyalties.

What is more interesting is how, in his attempt to make the feminine stand in for the national, he has simplified the woman in the poem almost out of existence. She is in no sense the poor old woman of the colloquial expression. There are no vulnerabilities here, no human complexities. She is a Poor Old Woman in capital letters. A mouthpiece. A sign.

Therefore, the poem divides into two parts: one vital, one inert. The subject of the poem appears to be the woman. But appearances deceive. She is merely the object, the pretext. The real subject is the blackbirds. They are the animated substance of the piece. They call from 'lovely distances'; their 'sweet songs' 'excite' and 'bless'. Whatever imaginative power the lyric has, it comes from these birds. Like all effective images, the blackbirds have a life outside the poem. They take their literal shape from the birds we know, and to these they return an emblematic force. They continue to be vital once the poem is over.

The woman, on the other hand, is a diagram. By the time the poem is over, she has become a dehumanized ornament. When her speaking part finishes, she goes out of the piece and out of our memory. At best she has been the engine of the action, a convenient frame for the proposition.

The question worth asking is whether this fusion of national and feminine, this interpretation of one by the other are inevitable. It was after all common practice in Irish poetry: Mangan's 'Dark Rosaleen' comes immediately to mind. In fact, the custom and the practice reached back, past the songs and simplifications of the nineteenth century, into the bardic tradition itself. Daniel Corkery refers to this in his analysis of the Aisling convention in *The Hidden Ireland*.[3] 'The vision the poet sees,' he writes there, 'is always the spirit of Ireland as a majestic and radiant maiden.'

So many male Irish poets — the later Yeats seems to me a rare exception — have feminized the national and nationalized the feminine that from time to time it has seemed there is no other option. But an Irish writer who turned away from such usages suggests that there was, in fact, another and more subversive choice.

In the opening pages of *Ulysses* Joyce describes an old woman. She climbs the steps to the Martello tower, darkening its doorway. She is, in fact, the daily milkwoman. But no sooner had she started to pour a quart of milk into Stephen's measure than she begins to shimmer and dissolve into legendary images: 'Silk of the kine and poor old woman, names given her in old times. A wandering crone, lowly form of an immortal serving her conqueror and her gay betrayer, their common cuckquean, a messenger from the secret morning. To serve or to upbraid, whether he could not tell: but scorned to beg her favour.'

The same phrase as Ledwidge uses — poor old woman — is included here. But whereas Ledwidge uses it with a straight face, Joyce dazzles it with irony. By reference and inference, he shows himself to be intent on breaking the traditional association of Ireland with ideas of womanhood and tragic motherhood. After all, these simplifications are part and parcel of what he, Joyce, has painfully rejected. They are some of the reason he is in exile from the mythos of his own country. Now by cunning inflations, by disproportions of language, he takes his revenge. He holds at a glittering, manageable distance a whole tendency in national thought and expression; and dismisses it. But then Joyce is a poetic moralist. Much of *Ulysses*, after all, is invested in Dedalus's search for the ethical shadow of his own aesthetic longings. He has a difficult journey ahead of him. And Joyce has no intention of letting him be waylaid, so early in the book, by the very self-deceptions he has created him to resolve.

VIII

It is easy, and intellectually seductive, for a woman artist to walk away from the idea of a nation. There has been, and there must continue to be, a great deal of debate about the energies and myths women writers should bring with them into a new age. 'Start again' has been the cry of some of the best feminist poets. 'Wipe clean the slate, start afresh.' It is a cry with force and justice behind it. And it is a potent idea: to begin in a new world, clearing the desert as it were, making it blossom, even making the rain.

In any new dispensation the idea of a nation must seem an expendable construct. After all, it has never admitted women. Its flags and songs and battle cries, even its poetry, as I've suggested, make use of feminine imagery. But that is all. The true voice and vision of women are routinely excluded.

Then why did I not walk away? Simply because I was not free to. For all my quarrels with the concept, and no doubt partly because of them, I needed to find and repossess that idea at some level of repose. Like the swimmer in Adrienne Rich's poem 'Diving into the Wreck', I needed to find out 'the damage that was done and the treasures that prevail'. I knew the idea was flawed. But if it was flawed, it was also one of the vital human constructs of a place in which, like Leopold Bloom, I was born. More important, as a friend and feminist scholar said to me, we ourselves are constructed by the construct. I might be the author of my poems; I was not the author of my past. However crude the diagram, the idea of a nation remained the rough graphic of an ordeal. In some subterranean way I felt myself to be part of that ordeal; its fragmentations extended into mine.

'I am an invisible man . . .' begins the Prologue of Ralph Ellison's *Invisible Man*.[4] 'I am invisible, understand, simply because people refuse to see me. Like the bodiless heads you see sometimes in circus sideshows, it is as though I have been surrounded by mirrors of hard, distorting glass. When they approach me they see only my surroundings, themselves, or figments of their imagination — indeed, everything and anything except me.'

In an important sense, Ellison's words applied to the sort of Irish poem which availed of that old, potent blurring of feminine and national. In such poems not only was the real woman behind the image not explored, she was never even seen. It was a subtle mechanism, subtle and corrupt. And it was linked, I believed, to a wider sequence of things not seen.

A society, a nation, a literary heritage are always in danger of making up their communicable heritage from their visible elements. Women, as it happens, are not especially visible in Ireland. This came to me early and with personal force. I realized when I published a poem that what was seen of me, what drew approval, if it was forthcoming at all, was the poet. The woman, by and large, was invisible. It was an unsettling discovery. Yet I came to believe that my invisibility as a woman was a disguised grace. It had the power to draw me, I sensed, towards realities like the Achill woman. It made clear to me that what she and I shared, apart from those fragile moments of talk, was the danger of being edited out of our own literature by conventional tribalisms.

Marginality within a tradition, however painful, confers certain advantages. It allows the writer clear eyes and a quick critical sense. Above all, the years of marginality suggest to such a writer — and I am speaking of myself now — the real potential of subversion. I wanted to relocate myself within the Irish poetic tradition. I felt the need to do so. I thought of myself as an Irish poet, although I was fairly sure it was not a category that readily suggested itself in connection with my work. A woman poet is rarely regarded as an automatic part of a national poetic tradition, and for the reasons I have already stated. She is too deeply woven into the passive texture of that tradition, too intimate a part of its imagery, to be allowed her freedom. She may know, as an artist, that she is now the maker of the poems and not merely the subject of them. The critique is slow to catch up. There has been a growing tendency in the last few years for academics and critics in this country to discuss women's poetry as a subculture, to keep it quarantined from the main body of poetry. I thought it vital that women poets such as myself should establish a discourse with the idea of the nation. I felt sure that the most effective way to do this was by subverting the previous terms of that discourse. Rather than accept the nation as it appeared in Irish poetry, with its queens and muses, I felt the time had come to rework those images by exploring the emblematic relation between my own feminine experience and a national past.

The truths of womanhood and the defeats of a nation? An improbable intersection? At first sight perhaps. Yet the idea of it opened doors in my mind which had hitherto been closed fast. I began to think there was indeed a connection, that my womanhood and my nationhood were meshed and linked at some root. It was not just that I had a womanly feeling for those women who waited with handcarts, went into the sour stomach of ships and even — according to terrible legend — eyed their baby's haunches speculatively in the hungers of the 1840s. It was more than that. I was excited by the idea that if there really was an emblematic relation between the defeats of womanhood and the suffering of a nation, I need only prove the first in order to reveal the second. If so, then Irishness and womanhood, those tormenting fragments of my youth, could at last stand in for each other. Out of a painful apprenticeship and an ethical dusk, the laws of metaphor beckoned me.

I was not alone. 'Where women write strongly as women,' says Alicia Ostriker, the American poet and critic, in her book *Stealing the Language*,[5] 'it is clear their intention is to subvert the life and literature they inherit.' This was not only true of contemporary women poets. In the terrible years between 1935 and 1940 the Russian poet Anna Akhmatova composed 'Requiem'.[6] It was written for her only son, Lev Gumilev, who at the start of the Stalinist terror had been arrested, released, rearrested. Then, like so many others, he disappeared into the silence of a Leningrad prison. For days, months, years Akhmatova queued outside. The 'Epilogue to the Requiem' refers to that experience. What is compelling and instructive is the connection it makes between her womanhood and her sense of a nation as a community of grief. The country she wishes to belong to, to be commemorated by is the one revealed to her by her suffering.

And if ever in this country they should want
To build me a monument

I consent to that honour
But only on condition that they

Erect it not on the sea-shore where I was born:
My last links with that were broken long ago,

Nor by the stump in the Royal Gardens
Where an inconsolable young shade is seeking me

But here, where I stood for three hundred hours
And where they never, never opened the doors for me

Lest in blessed death I should ever forget
The grinding scream of the Black Marias,

The hideous clanging gate, the old
Woman wailing like a wounded beast.

(Translation D.M. Thomas)

IX

I want to summarize this argument. At the same time I am concerned that in the process it may take on a false symmetry. I have, after all, been describing ideas and impressions as if they were events. I have been proposing thoughts and perceptions in a way they did not and could not occur. I have given hard shapes and definite outlines to feelings which were far more hesitant.

The reality was different. Exact definitions do not happen in the real life of a poet, and certainly not in mine. I have written here about the need to repossess the idea of a nation. But there was nothing assured or automatic about it. 'It is not in the darkness of belief that I desire you,' says Richard Rowan at the end of Joyce's *Exiles*, 'but in restless, living, wounding doubt.' I had the additional doubts of a writer who knows that a great deal of her literary tradition has been made up in ignorance of her very existence, that its momentum has been predicated on simplifications of its complexity. Yet I still wished to enter that tradition, although I knew my angle of entry must be oblique. None of it was easy. I reached tentative havens after figurative storms. I came to understand what Mallarmé meant when he wrote: 'Each newly acquired truth was born only at the expense of an impression that flamed up and then burned itself out, so that its particular darkness could be isolated.'

My particular darkness as an Irish poet has been the subject of this piece. But there were checks and balances. I was, as I have said, a woman in a literary tradition which simplified them. I was also a poet lacking the precedent and example of previous Irish women poets. These were the givens of my working life. But if these circumstances displaced my sense of relation to the Irish past in Irish poetry, they also forced me into a perception of the advantages of being able to move, with almost surreal inevitability, from being within the poem to being its maker. A hundred years ago I might have been a motif in a poem. Now I could have a complex self within my own poem. Part of that process entailed being a privileged witness to forces of reaction in Irish poetry.

Some of these I have named. The tendency to fuse the national and the feminine, to make the image of the woman the pretext of a romantic nationalism — these have been weaknesses in Irish poetry. These simplifications isolated and estranged me as a young poet. They also made it clearer to me that my own discourse must be subversive. In other words, that I must be vigilant to write of my own womanhood — whether it was revealed to me in the shape of a child or a woman from Achill — in such a way that I never colluded with the simplified images of women in Irish poetry.

When I was young, all this was comfortless. I took to heart the responsibility of making my own critique, even if for years it consisted of little more than accusing Irish poetry in my own mind of deficient ethics. Even now I make no apology for such a critique. I believe it is still necessary. Those simplified women, those conventional reflexes and reflexive feminizations of the national experience, those static, passive, ornamental figures do no credit to a poetic tradition which has been, in other respects, radical and innovative, capable of both latitude and compassion.

But there is more to it. As a young poet I would not have felt so threatened and estranged if the issue had merely been the demands a national program makes on a country's poetry. The real issue went deeper. When I read those simplifications of women, I felt there was an underlying fault in Irish poetry, almost a geological weakness. All good poetry depends on an ethical relation between imagination and image. Images are not ornaments; they are truths. When I read about Cathleen ni Houlihan or the Old Woman of the Roads or Dark Rosaleen, I felt that a necessary ethical relation was in danger of being violated over and over again, that a merely ornamental relation between imagination and image was being handed on from poet to poet, from generation to generation, was becoming orthodox poetic practice. It was the violation, even more than the simplification, which alienated me.

No poetic imagination can afford to regard an image as a temporary aesthetic manoeuvre. Once the image is distorted, the truth is demeaned. That was the heart of it all as far as I was concerned. In availing themselves of the old convention, in using and reusing women as icons and figments, Irish poets were not just dealing with emblems. They were also evading the real women of an actual past, women whose silence their poetry should have broken. In so doing, they ran the risk of turning a terrible witness into an empty decoration.

Writers, if they are wise, do not make their home in any comfort within a national tradition. However vigilant the writer, however enlightened the climate, the dangers persist. So too do the obligations. There is a recurring temptation for any nation, and for any writer who operates within its field of force, to make an ornament of the past, to turn the losses to victories and to restate humiliations as triumphs. In every age language holds out narcosis and amnesia for this purpose. But such triumphs in the end are unsustaining and may, in fact, be corrupt.

If a poet does not tell the truth about time, his or her work will not survive it. Past or present, there is a human dimension to time, human voices within it and human griefs ordained by it. Our present will become the past of other men and women. We depend on them to remember it with the complexity with which it was suffered. As others, once, depended on us.

1   Emily Lawless (1854–1913), novelist and poet, author of *Hurrish* (1886), a Land League novel, and *With the Wild Geese* (1902), a collection of verse from which 'After Aughrim' is taken.

2   From Francis Ledwidge, *Songs of Peace* (1917).

3   See extract above on p. 288 from Daniel Corkery, *The Hidden Ireland: A Study of Gaelic Munster in the Eighteenth Century* (1924).

4   First published in 1952.

5   Subtitled 'The Emergence of Women's Poetry in America', and first published in 1986.

6   Published in Anna Akhmatova, *Requiem and Poem Without a Hero* (1976).

JOHN GREGORY DUNNE
from John Gregory Dunne, *Harp* (1989)

John Gregory Dunne (1932–), American novelist and writer, was born in Connecticut but has lived most of his life in southern California. His famous novel *True Confessions* was published in 1977, followed in 1994 by *Playland*. With its echo of Vardaman's 'I am a fish' from William Faulkner's *As I Lay Dying* (1931), 'I am a harp' is an unsentimental view of Irish-America and worth juxtaposing with Richard Brown's more pious tribute in *I Am of Ireland* (1974; see above p. 822). Later in the autobiography, when Dunne eventually set foot on Irish soil for the first time, *The Irish Times* ran a headline 'Dublin Man Jailed for Buggery of Student, 17', it was raining, and his spirits only lifted when he saw a chain-store truck with the lettering 'If Dunne Can't Do It, It Can't Be Dunne'.

I am a harp, that is my history, Irish and Catholic, from steerage to suburbia in three generations. The Kennedys defined a certain kind of Irish: Don't get mad, get even, was the commandment to which they swore allegiance — Irish to be sure, but gentrified. I am cut from a rougher bolt of Irish cloth: Get mad *and* get even is the motto on the standard I fly. I call myself a harp because I like the sound of the word — it is short, sharp and abusive. Christopher Isherwood once told me that he preferred being called a faggot to being called gay; words like faggot and kike and nigger, Christopher said, were simple and unequivocal, and the person who called himself the one that fit defined his attitude toward the world.

In the New England where I grew up, being Irish and Catholic meant being a social outcast. This was in the years before John Kennedy was elected president in 1960, an event that, difficult as it is to believe now, offered to certain sections of New England a kind of absolution for having a tainted ethnic and religious pedigree. With a distaste not allayed by my years, I still call Hartford Protestants 'Yanks'; WASP belongs to the sanitized diction of pop anthropology. The Irish Catholics of my parents' generation did not know Protestants. They did not know Jews, let alone blacks. In a surfeit of Yank good humour, Whetten Road in West Hartford, where the richest Jewish families lived, was called, by Protestant gentry and upwardly mobile harps alike, Kikes Peak. When my wife and I were married, in the mid-1960s, my mother gave a reception for us in Hartford. There were 125 people present; 124 were Irish Catholics; the 125th was my wife, who was an Episcopalian and — worse — a Californian.

In this Irish diaspora, there was a whole set of unwritten rules, a survival kit, as it were, for the interloper in the Yank jungle. Paramount among the rules was the injunction 'Don't make waves'. Aunt Harriet would tell me not to make waves, and my mother, especially after my father died, she a widow charged with the upbringing of six children, five still to be educated. Don't make waves meant know your place, don't stand out so that the Yanks could see you, don't let your pretensions become a focus of Yank merriment and mockery. Not making waves offered the possibility of Yank acceptance. Yank norms were the approved norms; risk-taking in areas beyond the traditional ways of making a living invited disapproval; risk-taking made waves. 'It never hurts to have a friend in court,' was another diaspora aphorism; it was of course implicit that the friend was a Yank, who would be judicious if waves were not made. To those who chose to wander outside the established Irish pecking order, it was asked, 'What's so good about you?' It never seemed to occur to the diaspora Irish that playing the Yanks' game only encouraged a servant mentality, one laced with a sour envy, and worse, one

that made lives of caution and contented mediocrity attractive.

My parents' generation of course did not see it that way. My mother was only forty-eight when my father died (actually forty-nine; until her last illness she always took one year off her age, a white lie she did not admit until she prepared to meet her maker), and I don't think it ever occurred to her to remarry; widowhood, the widow business, was part of God's plan, and to interfere was blasphemy. She was a hard woman with whom to argue the social logic that gave order to her life, tough and smart, but born and forever a daughter of the diaspora. She had a sharp temper and a sharper tongue, and when I was a child she could deliver a sudden stinging slap on the face that effectively stamped out adolescent rebellion. Into my early middle age, she would listen to some heresy I would put forth, and when I finished, she would pause, collect her thoughts, and finally, inevitably, curtail argument with the same four words, 'Your breath is bad,' a response that even as I remember it can still infuriate. 'What's the matter with the good old middle?' she liked to ask when some social risk was in order, and it would pain me to hear her say it. If she ever read a word I wrote, she was circumspect about mentioning it. A writer made waves, and I wrote about the Irish and sex, and those were subjects that in her mind did not just make waves, they made a fucking typhoon.

AIDAN HIGGINS
from Aidan Higgins, *Helsingør Station & Other Departures* (1989)

Aidan Higgins here does to a turn the year of his birth.

1927: Earliest Misgivings; the March of the Cadavers

Is it the sole, that strange denizen of the deep, a lurker on sea-beds, that (out of curiosity about the hook) *catches itself*? Unless I am confusing sole with plaice, or monk, or flounder.

Be that as it may, I was born on the third day of March in the year 1927 in the old Barony of Salt in the County Kildare in the Province of Leinster, of

lapsed Catholic parents since deceased, under the watery astrological sign of Pisces.

A fresh westerly airstream covered most areas while a frontal trough of low pressure remained stationary over Ireland but seemed about ready to move eastward.

Conceived at the tail-end of an early June day, in the Year of Grace 1926, I was expelled the following March 3rd, passing over into 1927 puffing and choking with mouth half open, the cold without being so intense, wellnigh irresistible the compulsion to sink back into the warmer uterine depths with a bubbling groan.

Hearing faraway music, moody themes from the good-times-gone: Albinoni's now-famous *Adagio* or a Debussy *Arabesque* played on the harp. Not yet the wild nocturnal bagpipe music and the night wind tipping the pans of the weighing-scales as they filled with rainwater on the bedroom windowsill of a bungalow in Emor Street just off the South Circular Road in the so-called Liberties in the city of Dublin. This would be in the late seventies when I was the ill-dressed recipient of a most welcome cheque for $7,000 from the American-Irish Foundation — Kennedy bad-conscience money paid out on sole condition that I reside for ten months in my erstwhile homeland, which I had not been in a position to afford since leaving it twenty-five years before.

A group of young lady harpists from New York, all of surpassing comeliness, were entertaining the American ambassador, Mr Shannon, and his lovely wife and their selected guests after lunch in the US representative's fine residence in the Phoenix Park. A herd of grazing deer was visible through the elegant long windows as Ambassador Shannon, bald as a coot though a decade younger than the shabby recipient, handed over a sealed envelope. Held in close-up for Irish television viewers to admire, it was seen to be clearly addressed to Seamus Heaney, the previous year's winner.

I had just turned fifty.

All this by way of preamble. Nothing is too clear, of its nature, least of all the limpidities of language, the particles of which must be 'clear as sand'. The strange phosphorus of life, nameless under the old mis-appellation.

I tell you a thing. I could tell it otherwise. A few pictures emerge into the light from the shadows within me. I consider them. Quite often they fail to please me. I call them 'pictures' but you, kind readers, ideal readers suffering from an ideal insomnia,[1] must know otherwise. What I mean to convey is: *movements from the past*.

So, putting as bold a face on it as I could under the circumstances, out I crawled yelling blue bloody murder, roughly handled by a wet-nurse from Cavan.

Why, there are days when we do not know ourselves, when we do not properly belong to ourselves, as children know to their cost. Assailed by mysterious sundowns and gory red endings of days: the extraordinary clarity of the nocturnal firmament burning above the little pier on Annaghvaughan and the unmilked cattle bawling in descent. Then out went the candle and we were left darkling. Breathe in, breathe out. In the memory of old men it's always

June. But were the summers of my childhood as sunny as I seem to recall?

In that Year of Our Lord nineteen hundred and twenty-seven, Coole Park was taken over by the Land and Forestry Commission in Co. Galway. In America, at Bridgewater Penitentiary, Sacco and Vanzetti walked to the electric chair. Flying out over the Atlantic in the dark, the intrepid Colonel Lindbergh landed near Paris in the dark. In Berlin the ageing lecher Frank Harris was lecturing on Shakespeare. Kevin O'Higgins, our first diplomat, returning home from Mass, was murdered outside his own front gate.[2] In a public ward of St Patrick Dun's Hospital in Dublin, the Countess Markievicz died of peritonitis. Long insane and widowed sixty years, the Empress Carlotta passed quietly away quietly in Belgium.

The lost *mediodesorientado*[3] Hugo von Hofmannstahl died in Vienna. In Paris the long-demented Baroness Elsa von Freytag-Loringhoven gassed herself, the baron having taken his own life just before the outbreak of the Great War. In Paris the American novelist Djuna Barnes with her lover Thelma Wood, the silverpoint artist from Missouri, were looking after the richly left Natalie Clifford Barney's garden in the rue Jacob, a patch of earth that had formerly belonged to Racine. Tea and special little cakes were served up there in the temple dating from just before the French Revolution; tall Thelma the infected carrier of the past, the born *somnambule*,[4] the bitch of all time, turning up as 'Robin Vote' in the 1936 novel *Nightwood*; Djuna Barnes was 'Nora Flood'. Their anguished avatars were quarrelling in the apartment with the wooden horse and heavy liturgical decorations, the ill-fitting purple dress and shapeless Napoleonic hat, on the fifth floor of number 9 rue St-Romain, going out to get thoroughly pickled at the Flore.

It was the year that Alice Prin (Kiki of Montparnasse), the mistress of Man Ray the Dada artist and photographer, had an exhibition of her paintings at Galerie du Sacre du Printemps.

While from Kenosha, a town on Lake Michigan on the Wisconsin shore, Richard Ives Welles was committed by his father into Kankee State Institution for the Insane. Stuttering Dick had been the laughing-stock of the Kenosha cornerboys. In Cuba that summer his precociously gifted younger brother George Orson was on vacation with his guardian, the shifty Dr Bernstein.

All this occurred in 1927, the year of the long count in the Dempsey–Tunney world heavyweight fight, the year when de Valera began the even longer *völkisch* reign of Fianna Fáil. Hand in glove with the cultural nationalism proper to those peerless warriors of yore: our own élite dead long gone to their reward, the Fianna Eireann.

In 1927, a year after the first staging of Sean O'Casey's play *The Plough and the Stars*, the playwright married Eileen Reynolds, a pretty actress twenty-three years younger than himself.

Do you hear me now?

Are we not all somebody's rearings in the wretched bric-à-brac and rigmarole of history, of which our life may be assigned some part, however minor, if only as passive bystander?

In that Year of Grace 1927, Sylvia Townsend Warner's novel *Mr Fortune's Maggot* came out in London. Vipers appear, earthworms engender, forward turnips rot and toads crawl forth every year in March. 'It is the period *just before oneself*, the period of which in earliest days one knew the actual survivors, that really lays a strong hand upon one's heart.' I must have read it somewhere.

In 1927 young Clarence Malcolm Lowry was homeward bound aboard the SS *Pyrrhus* from the Far East with a mixed cargo of wild beasts and crawling reptiles, an elephant, five black panthers, ten snakes, a wild boar, all trapped in the Straits Settlements and now consigned to lifelong captivity in the Dublin zoo, to be cared for by Superintendent Flood. Where presently, shivering all over like a dog, I would be lifted up by my nanny, in order to offer a banana to Lowry's elephant, or rather to a long, feeling, prehensile trunk that blew on me a gust of wildness, unknown terrain, swamps, a scorching sun. Taken by Nanny to see the wild animals, I was struck by the untamed sulphurous stink of the lion house, hardly less by the rude monkey house, the elephant house, the giraffe house. Cracked semi-human voices spoke out from the fidgety macaws in the parrot house, their plumage the colour of fire and blood, of red rage trapped in a hothouse, humming, lurid, obscene. These fraught excursions to the grey city with its own peculiar and (for me) disturbing smells would always end with a spell of vomiting.

'The lad's over-excited,' my parents agreed.

Henry Williamson's *Tarka the Otter* was published in 1927, to be read aloud to me by my mother some years later. Joseph-Napoléon Primoli died that year. Between receiving the Nobel Prize in 1925 and publishing *The Intelligent Woman's Guide to Socialism and Capitalism*, the spry septuagenarian and vegetarian George Bernard Shaw, social reformer and patron of the Life Force, dogmatic busybody and former vestryman and borough councillor who had several times raised the question of women's toilets for St Pancras and tried to organize a

crematorium there, had turned seventy-one. Instantly recognizable everywhere thanks to his tweedy knickerbockers and long argumentative beard, he had been around since 1856, seemingly the same frail Elderly Protestant Irish Gent all his natural life. He had twenty-three more useful years of postcard-writing to total strangers, when not pottering about the garden at Ayot St Lawrence. Captious, he had an answer for everything, liked to put philosophers in their place, dined on raw vegetables, milk, hardboiled eggs. He wanted to dazzle, to confound.

In the same year America drew up secret military plans for war against Great Britain. Against Winter, chess grandmaster Capa made insolent moves standing up, hardly bothering to sit down and think.

Legend had it that grandmaster Paul Morphy died in his bath surrounded by women's shoes. It was not long before Alekhine gave up alcohol, switched to milk and trounced Dr Max Euwe (1901–81) to hold the world chess title for the next two years, a decade before *Guernica*. In Trinity College, Dublin, a Bachelor of Arts degree was conferred upon Samuel Barclay Beckett.

In 1927 King Ferdinand I of Romania, the second Hohenzollern king, died of cancer of the bowel in Bucharest. Abel Gance's epic movie *Napoléon* was released; the talkies began in Hollywood. Micheál MacLiammóir left the Slade and joined the touring company of his brother-in-law, Anew MacMaster. In Dublin the O'Nolan family, formerly of Tyrone, moved from Herbert Place to Blackrock. Virginia Woolf's novel *To the Lighthouse* was published by the Hogarth Press. Hammond of Gloucestershire scored a thousand runs in May, at Southampton against Hampshire.

On August 6th a London insurance clerk called Edward Harry ('Ed') Temme swam the freezing English Channel from Cap Grisnez to Lydden Spout, using the trudgeon stroke. Helen Wills Moody won the ladies' singles in the first of her record eight victories at Wimbledon. Anne Yeats, W.B.'s little daughter, put a squeaky cushion on a chair for Lady Gregory to sit upon; Her Ladyship was not amused.

It was the year of '*la generación de 1927*'[5] in Madrid, with Lorca, Alberti, Altolaguirre, Cernude, José Bergamin and Pedro Garfias meeting to talk and foment dissension in the Café Gijon, the Granje del Henar, the Café Castilla, the Fornos, Kutz, Café de la Montaña, Café Pombo where Raymon de la Serna held court every Saturday night; Buñuel, Dali and Pepin Bello were in the Casa de Leonor, a brothel on the Calle de la Reine.

In the spring of that year, V.S. Pritchett had set out from London to walk across western Spain from

Badajoz to León, a hundred-mile hike in heavy winter tweeds, on foot and alone. In Berlin the shifty Brecht, a lifelong womanizer, parted company with Marianne Brecht, née Zoll, to take up with his future wife Helene Weigel. Gunter Grass was born in Danzig, hereinafter Gdansk, Poland.

In 1927 T.S. Eliot was received into the Anglo-Catholic faith at St Stephen's church opposite the Russian Orthodox Church in Exile, not far from the Round Pond in Kensington where W.B. Yeats as a boy had sailed his fancy toy yacht.

In June of that year the Woolfs had witnessed an eclipse of the sun from a moor in north Yorkshire ('The earth was dead,' Virginia recorded in her diary). The next eclipse would be in 1999.

In that year Buckminster Fuller, the Harvard man who had invented the geodesic dome, gave up earning a living, stopped talking for two years. Ernst Lubitsch made *In Old Heidelberg*, a silent movie version of Romberg's operetta *The Student Prince*. Hollywood films were shown in the stables off the cobbled courtyard at Oakley Park. My younger brother and I sucked bull's-eyes and marvelled at the G-men. The villagers craned forward on kitchen chairs, guffawed at Leon Errol.

In 1933, when I would have turned six, the Liffey flooded the village up as far as Marley Abbey. The flood came out through the open forge door and the houses seemed all set to sail away.

March 3rd in Basho's day was the Festival of the Dolls in sixteenth-century Japan: *hina matsuri*, sometimes called the Festival of Pearl Blossoms. Or simply Girls' Festival, which would suit me fine, backing into the strange withdrawn world of the fish. The Piscean twilight world of the deep fish lost, or just gone astray in the head. Is this why the light still enchants me, the hidden observer remaining a prey to the most giddy kind of guilt? But now, classic-lovers, it's diddley-diddley time once again.

Fifty was Basho's age when with failing health he began that long last marathon hike into south Japan in 1694. He was six years junior to Jane Bowles — if you'd kindly be good enough to move on three centuries — when she died in a hospital in Málaga, capital of sorrow. In a snail-bar near the brothel quarter the shabby ghost of Terry Butler of Shanganagh, never so shabby in life, failed to recognize me, darkened by tramping in the Sierra Almijara.

Who am I? Am I or am I not the same person I have always taken myself to be? In that case, who am I? Is the silence significant or just lack of something to say?

Is that significant? Speak up, but kindly confine yourself to essentials; write on one side of the paper only.

Where am I? Where was I then? What do you do when memory begins to go? I spend much of the time looking back into the past. It is no longer there. It has moved. Where to?

The city certainly had changed. The Grafton Picture House was closed, turned into a bingo arcade, the ghosts in the toilet departed, the commissionaire Mr Shakespear dead. It was still raining in that most mournful thoroughfare called Aungier Street, on the offices of Fanagan the undertaker, the busiest man in Dublin.

Meanwhile, then, up in his fine new residence in Rathfarnham,[6] Senator William Butler Yeats, impaled upon a fine idea, was just looking at his yellow canaries and saw symbols streaming. Moving to his writing-desk in a dream he seated himself, drew out his day-book, wrote in his distinguished calligraphy: 'I am a crowd. I am a lonely man. I am nothing.' Whereupon all the canaries started singing.

He did not care to name his enemies as such when corresponding with fine ladies, Irish and English, but designated them thus: The Wolf Dog, The Harp, The Shamrock, The Tower. And (rather finely) Verdis-Green Sectaries.

Senator Willie was his father's son and no two ways about it. The correspondence with his father is nothing less than heart-warming, and not something you expect in such close blood connections. James Joyce was still working on the scaffolding of the *Wake* in sinful Paris. Mr Beckett had just written: 'The sun shone, having no alternative, on the nothing new.'[7] The sharp-faced student Brian Ó Nuallain was refusing to learn bad Irish from his professor, Douglas Hyde, later to be President of Ireland; he whom David Thomson saw crawling on all fours across a drawing-room with a bar of chocolate protruding from his mouth below the walrus moustache, challenging some well-brought-up little colleens to take a bite; he too perhaps impaled upon a dream.

In Kinsale great hauls of mackerel were taken; three fishgirls sea-salting and packing per barrel, cutting and stowing the catch for the cooper to come and tack down the barrels which were then rolled along the pier.

The Wall Street Crash was imminent.

1 Joyce's characterization of readers of *Finnegans Wake* (120:13–14).
2 Kevin O'Higgins (1892–1927) was Minister for Economic Affairs, then Minister for Justice and External

Affairs and Vice-president of the Executive Council in the first Irish Government. A tough politician and much admired by Yeats, during the Civil War he was responsible for the execution of seventy-seven Republicans. He was assassinated in July 1927 while on his way to Mass in Booterstown.

3   Spanish: half-disoriented.

4   French: somnambulist, sleepwalker.

5   Spanish: the generation of 1927, a play on the generation of '98, the Spanish literary and cultural movement of the first two decades of the twentieth century which had a lasting impact.

6   In fact Yeats did not move to Rathfarnham until July 1932, and by that stage he had ceased being an Irish Senator.

7   Opening line of Beckett's novel *Murphy* (1938).

IMAGINATIVE

PAUL MULDOON

from Paul Muldoon, *Why Brownlee Left* (1980)

Paul Muldoon (1955–) was raised near Moy, Co. Tyrone, and educated at Queen's University, Belfast. After working with BBC Northern Ireland as a radio producer Muldoon taught at Columbia and Princeton Universities in the United States. His distinguished career as a poet began with the publication of *New Weather* (1973) and *Mules* (1977). Here is an intriguing short poem that can be used as an ice-breaker at the beginning of a course in class.

IRELAND

The Volkswagen parked in the gap,
But gently ticking over.
You wonder if it's lovers
And not men hurrying back
Across two fields and a river.

MARY BECKETT

from Mary Beckett, *A Belfast Woman* (1980)

Mary Beckett (1926–) was born in Belfast, educated at St Mary's Training College and taught in Ardoyne until her marriage in 1956 when she moved to Dublin. Six of her early stories can be found in *The Bell* in 1951–54. *A Belfast Woman*, her first book of short stories, was followed by a second collection, *A Literary Woman*, in 1990. Here in this short story she uses an engagingly naive narrator to recreate the history of sectarianism in her native city.

A Belfast Woman

I mind well the day the threatening letter came. It was a bright morning, and warm, and I remember thinking while I was dressing myself that it would be nice if the Troubles were over so that a body could just enjoy the feel of a good day. When I came down the stairs the hall was dark but I could see the letter lying face down. I lifted it and just my name was on the envelope, 'Mrs Harrison' in red felt pen. I knew what it was. There was a page of an exercise book inside with 'Get out or we'll burn you out' all in red with bad printing and smeared. I just went in and sat at the kitchen table with the note in front of me. I never made myself a cup of tea even. It was a shock, though God knows I shouldn't have been surprised.

One of the first things I remember in my life was wakening up with my mother screaming downstairs when we were burned out in 1921. I ran down in my nightgown and my mother was standing in the middle of the kitchen with her hands up to her face screaming and screaming, and the curtains were on fire and my father was pulling them down and stamping on them with the flames catching the oilcloth on the floor. Then he shouted, 'Sadie, the children,' and she stopped screaming and said, 'Oh, God, Michael, the children,' and she ran upstairs and came down with the baby in one arm and Joey under the other, and my father took Joey in his arms and me by the hand and we ran out along the street. It was a warm summer night and the fires were crackling all over the place and the street was covered with broken glass. It wasn't until we got into my grandmother's house that anybody noticed that I had nothing on but my nightie and nothing on my feet and they were cut. It was all burned, everything they had. My mother used to say she didn't save as much as a needle and thread. I wasn't able to sleep for weeks, afraid I'd be wakened by that screaming.

We stayed in my grandmother's house until 1935 and my grandmother was dead by that time and my father too, for he got T.B.[1] like many another then. He used to say, 'When you have no house and no job sure what use are you?' and then he'd get fits of coughing. In 1935 when we got the letter threatening to burn us out I said to my mother, 'We'll gather our things and we'll go.' So we did, and like all the rest of them in our street we went up to Glenard to the new houses. When we showed our 'Get out or we'll burn you out' note they gave us a house and we'd enough out to get things fixed up. We got new jobs in another mill, my mother and Patsy and me. Only my mother never liked it there. She always said the air was too strong for her. It was cold right enough, up close to the mountains. But when I was getting married to William, and his aunt who was a Protestant gave him the key of her house in this street, my mother was in a terrible state — 'Don't go into that Protestant street, Mary, or you'll be a sorry girl' — and she said we could live with her. But I didn't want William to pine like my poor father, so here we came and not a day's trouble until the note came.

Mind you, the second night we were here there was trouble in the Catholic streets across the road. We heard shots first and then the kind of rumbling, roaring noises of all the people out on the streets. I wanted to get up and run out and see what was wrong, but William held on to me in bed and he said, 'They don't run out on the street here. They stay in.' And it was true. They did. I was scared lying listening to the noise the way I never was when I was out with my neighbours. It turned out some poor young lad had stayed at home when he should have gone back to the British Army and they sent the police for him. He got out of the back window and ran down the entry and the police ran after him and shot him dead. They said their gun went off by accident but the people said they beat him up. When I went over the next day I saw him laid out in the wee room off the kitchen and his face had all big yellowy-greenish blotches on it. I never mentioned it to my new neighbours and they never mentioned it to me.

I couldn't complain about them. They were good decent people. They didn't come into the house for a chat or a loan of tea or milk or sugar like the neighbours in Glenard or North Queen Street but they were ready to help at any time. I didn't know the men much because they had work so they didn't stand around the corners the way I was used to. But when Liam was born they all helped and said what a fine baby he was. He was too. Nine pounds with black hair and so strong he could lift his head and look round at a week old. They were always remarking on his mottled skin — purply kind of measles when he'd be up out of the pram — and said it was the sign of a very strong baby. At that time I had never seen a baby with any other colour of skin — I suppose Catholic babies had to be strong to get by. But when Eileen was born a year and ten months later she was different. She had beautiful creamy skin. She was plump and perfect and I loved her more than Liam, God forgive me, and more than William and more than anybody in the world and I wanted everything to be right for her. I thought to myself, *If I was a Protestant now we'd have just the two and no more and I'd be able to look after them and do well for them.* So I didn't act fair with William at all.

Then I started having trouble. I looked as if I was expecting again and my stomach was hard and round but I had bleeding and I could feel no life so I was afraid. I went to the doctor and he said, 'No, Mrs Harrison, you're not pregnant. There is something here we shall have to look into.' And I said, 'Is it serious, doctor?', and he said, 'I can't tell you that, can I, until you go into hospital and have it investigated,' and I said, 'Do you mean an operation?' and he said, 'I do, Mrs Harrison.' I came home saying to myself, *It's cancer and who will rear my Eileen and Liam?* I remembered hearing it said that once they put the knife into you, you were dead in six months, so I made up my mind I'd have no operation and I'd last out as long as I could. Every year I was able to look after them would be a year gained and the bigger they were the better they'd be able to do without me. But oh dear, it was terrible hard on everybody. I told William and my mother and Patsy there was nothing at all the matter with me but they knew to look at me it wasn't true. I was really wan and I was so tired I was ready to drop. I'd sit down by the fire at night when the children were in bed and my eyes would close, and if I opened them I'd see William staring at me with such a tortured look on his face I'd have to close them again so that I wouldn't go and lean my head against him and tell him the whole thing. I knew if I did that he'd make me go back to the doctor and I'd be done for. At times I'd see against my closed eyes the white long roots of the cancer growing all over my inside and I'd remember the first time William brought me to see his father in the country.

He had a fine labourer's cottage for he was a Protestant and was head ploughman to some rich farmer down there. He was a good man. William's mother was a Catholic and she died when William was a wee boy but they brought him up a Catholic because it had been promised. He was cross-looking though, and I was a bit nervous of him. He had his garden all planted in rows and squares and he was digging clods in one corner and breaking them up fine and I could see all the long white roots and threads he was shaking the mud out of and he turned to us and he said, 'Sitfast and scutch! Sitfast and scutch![2] They're the plague of my life. No matter how much I weed there's more in the morning.' I told him about my grandfather and the big elderberry tree that grew behind the wee house he'd got in the country when he was burned out in Lisburn. It wasn't there when he went into the house and when he noticed it first it was only a wee bit of a bush but it grew so quickly it blocked out all the light from his back window. Then one summer it was covered with black slimy kind of flies so he cut it down to the stump, but it started growing again straightaway. One day when my father took Patsy and Joey and me down to visit him he had dug all round the stump and he was trying to pull it out with a rope. He told my father to pull with him. My father tried but then he leaned against the wall with his face pale and covered with sweat. My grandfather said, 'Are you finished, Michael?' and my father said, 'I'm clean done,' and my grandfather said, 'God help us all,' and brought us into the house and gave us lemonade. It was just after that my father went into the sanatorium and my mother was all the time

bringing him bottles of lemonade. At the funeral I asked my grandfather if he got the stump out and he didn't know for a minute what I was talking about. Then he said, 'No, no. Indeed the rope's still lying out there. I must bring it in or it'll rot.' I never saw him again, never saw the wee house either. My mother never was one for the country.

She wasn't old herself when she died — not that much over fifty, but she looked an old woman. She wore a shawl at times and not many did that anymore. She was always fussing about my health and me going to the doctor but I managed fine without. I didn't look much. I had this swollen stomach and I got into the way of hiding it with my arms. But every year I got through I'd say to myself, wasn't I right to stick it out? When the war finished and the free health came, everybody thought I'd get myself seen to, and my mother was at me that she'd mind Liam and Eileen. Of course there were no more children but I kept those two lovely. There was no Protestant child better fed or better dressed than those two, and I always warned them to fight with nobody, never to get into trouble. If any of the children started to shout at them about being Catholics or Fenians or Teagues[3] they were just to walk away, not to run, mind you, but just walk home. And Liam was the best boy ever. He wasn't great at his lessons but the masters said how pleasant and good he was. Eileen was inclined to be a bit bold and that was the cause of the only terrible thing I ever did. I can't believe even now how I came to do it. It was the week after my mother had died.

I blamed myself for what happened to my mother. I should have seen in time that she wasn't well and made her mind herself and she'd have lasted better. She came into my house one day with her shawl on and I was going to say I wished she'd wear a coat and not have my neighbours passing remarks, but she hung the shawl up on the back of the door and she looked poorly. She said she'd had a terrible pain in her chest and she had been to the doctor and he'd told her it was her heart. She was to rest and take tablets. She had other wee tablets to put under her tongue if she got a pain and she was not to go up hills. She looked so bad I put her to bed in the wee room off the kitchen. She never got up again. She had tense crushing pains and the tablets did no good. Sometimes the sip of Lourdes water helped her.[4] The doctor said he could do nothing for her unless she went into hospital and she wouldn't hear of that. 'Ah no, no. I'm just done, that's all.' Every now and again she'd say this would never have happened if she hadn't been burned out of her home down near the docks and had to go half roads up the mountains with all the hills and the air too strong for her. 'And your father wouldn't ever have got consumption if he hadn't had to move in with my mother and spend his days at the street corner. You wouldn't remember it, Mary. You were too small,' she'd say and I never contradicted her, 'but we hadn't left as much as a needle and thread. The whole block went up. Nothing left.' She was buried from our house even though she kept saying she must go home. She had a horror of my Protestant neighbours even though she liked well enough the ones she met. But at her funeral, better kinder decenter neighbours you could not get. When it was over, all I could so was shiver inside myself as if my shelter had been taken away. William was good to me, always good to me, but I had to keep a bit of myself to myself with him. My mother never looked for anything from me. I'd tell her what I needed to tell her and she'd listen but she never interfered. And she was as proud of Liam and Eileen as I was. I'd see the way she looked at them.

The week after she died Eileen came home from school crying. She was ten years of age and she didn't often cry. She showed me the mark on her legs where the head teacher had hit her with a cane. A big red mark it was, right across the back of her legs. And she had lovely skin on her legs, lovely creamy skin. When I think of it I can still see that mark. I didn't ask her what happened. I just lifted my mother's shawl from where it was still hanging on the back of the kitchen door and I flung it round me and ran down to the school. I knocked on the door and she opened it herself, the head teacher, because most of the school had gone home. She took one look at me and ran away into a classroom. I went after her. She ran into another room off it and banged the door. My arm stuck in through the glass panel and I pulled it out with a big deep cut from my wrist to my elbow. She didn't come out of the door and I never spoke to her at all. There were a couple of other teachers over a bit and a few children about but I couldn't say anything to anybody and they just stood. To stop the blood pouring so much I held my arm up out of my mother's shawl as I went back up the street. There was a woman standing at her door near the top of the street. She was generally at her door knitting, that woman. She had very clever children and some of them did well. One got to be a teacher; another was in the post office, which is about as far as a clever poor Catholic can get. She asked me what happened but when I couldn't answer she said, 'You'd need to get to the hospital, missus, I'll get my coat and go with you.' I didn't want to go to any hospital. I just wanted to go home and wash off all the blood but my head was spinning so I let myself be helped on the bus. They

stitched it up and wanted me to stay in for the night but I was terrified they'd operate on me just when I was managing so well. I insisted I couldn't because the children were on their own and Mrs O'Reilly came with me right to the end of my own street. 'If your neighbours ask what happened, just tell them you fell off the bus,' she told me. 'You don't want them knowing all about your business.' I've heard she was from the west of Ireland.

When I went into the kitchen I was ready to drop but Eileen started screaming and crying and saying how ashamed of me she was and that she'd never go back to school again. Liam made me a cup of tea and stood looking worried at me. When William came in from work he helped me to bed and was kind and good but I could see by the cut of his mouth that he was shocked and offended at me. It took a long time to heal and the scar will never leave me. The story went around the parish in different ways. Some said I hit the teacher. Some said she knifed me. I was too ashamed ever to explain.

Eileen never was touched in school after that, though, and when she left she learned shorthand and typing and got an office job. She grew up lovely, and I used to think, watching her going out in the morning in the best of clothes with her hair shining, that she could have gone anywhere and done herself credit. She wasn't contented living where we did. At first I didn't understand what she wanted. I thought she wanted a better house in a better district. I didn't know how we could manage it but I made up my mind it would have to be done. I went for walks up round the avenues where there were detached houses with gardens and when I saw an empty house I'd peer in through the windows. Then one day a woman from the parish, who worked cleaning one of those houses, saw me and asked me in because the people of the house were out all day. Seeing it furnished with good solid shining furniture I knew we'd never manage it. In the sitting room there was an old-fashioned copper canopy over the fire and when I looked into it I could see the whole room reflected smaller like a fairy tale with flowers and books and pictures and plates on the wall. I knew it wasn't for us. How could I go in and out there? William and Liam wouldn't look right in their working clothes. Only Eileen would fit in. I was a bit sad but relieved because at no time could I see where the money would have come from. I told her that night when she came in but she looked at me puzzled. 'But that wasn't what I meant, Mammy,' she said. 'I have to get away from everything here. There's no life for me here. I'm thinking of going to Canada.' That was before any trouble at all here. People now would say that was in the good times when you could get in a bus and go round the shops or into the pictures[5] and nothing would have happened by the time you came home except that the slack would have burned down a bit on the fire.

Off she went anyway and got a job and wrote now and again telling us how well off she was. In no time at all she was married and was sending photographs, first of this lovely bungalow and then of her two wee girls with the paddling pool in her garden or at their swing when they were a bit bigger. I was glad she was doing so well. It was the kind of life I had reared her for and dreamed of for her, only I wished she and her children were not so far away. I kept inviting her home for a visit but I knew it would cost far too much money. Only I thought if she was homesick it would help her to know we wanted to see her too. Once the troubles came I stopped asking her.

Liam at that time was getting on well too. He was always such a nice pleasant big fellow that a plumber in the next street to ours asked him to join in his business at putting in fireplaces and hot-water pipes. Liam put in a lovely fireplace for me with a copper canopy like the one I'd seen years before and built me a bathroom and hot water and put in a sink unit for me till I was far better off than any of my neighbours, even though a lot of them had their houses very nice too. They were able to get paint from the shipyard[6] of course, and marble slabs and nice bits of mahogany. He got married to a nice wee girl from the Bone and they got a house up in one of the nice streets in Ardoyne — up the far end in what they call now a mixed area.[7] It's all gone, poor Liam's good way of living. When that street of houses up there was put on fire in 1972 his wife Gemma insisted on coming back to the Bone and squatting in an empty house. They did their best to fix it up but it's old and dark. Then when the murders got bad his partner asked him not to come back to work anymore because he'd been threatened for working with a Catholic. I was raging when Liam told me, raging about what a coward the plumber was, but then as Liam said, you can't blame a man for not wanting to be murdered. So there he is — no work and no house and a timid wife and a family of lovely wee children. He had plenty to put up with. But where else could I go when I got the note? I sat looking round my shining kitchen and the note said, 'Get out or we'll burn you out,' and where could I go for help but to Liam?

Still I was glad William was dead before it happened. He would have been so annoyed. He felt so ashamed when the Protestants did something nasty. I could swallow my own shame every time the I.R.A. disgraced us. I lived with it the same as I lived with the memory of my own disgrace when I went for the teacher and ripped my arm. But William had always been such a good upright man, he could never understand wickedness. Even the way he died showed it. He was a carter all his days, always in steady work, but for a while before he died they were saying to him that nobody had horses anymore and they were changing to a lorry. He could never drive a lorry. He was afraid he'd be on the dole. It wasn't the money he was worrying about, for I kept telling him it would make little difference to us — just the two of us, what did it matter? It was his pride that was upset. For years there was a big notice up on a corner shop at the bottom of the Oldpark Road. It said, 'Drivers, dismount. Don't overload your horses going up the hill.' He used to remark on it. It irked him if he didn't obey it. So one day in March when there was an east wind he collapsed on the hill and died the next day in hospital with the same disease as my mother.

There was a young doctor in the hospital asked me did I need a tranquillizer or a sleeping tablet or something to get over the shock. I told him no, that I never took any tablets, that I had had cancer when I was in my twenties and that I was still alive in my fifties with never a day in bed. He was curious and he asked me questions and then he said, 'Mrs Harrison, of course I can't be absolutely sure, but I'd say it was most unlikely you had cancer. Maybe you needed a job done on your womb. Maybe you even needed your womb removed but I would be very, very surprised if you had cancer. You wouldn't be here now if you had.' So I went in and knelt down at William's side. He still had that strained, worried look, even then. All I could think was: *Poor William. Poor William. Poor, poor, poor William.*

It wasn't that I was lonely without him for I'd kept him at a distance for a long time, but the days had no shape to them. I could have my breakfast, dinner, and tea whatever time I liked or I needn't have them at all. For a while I didn't bother cooking for myself, just ate tea and bread. Then Liam's wife, Gemma, said the butcher told her that I hadn't darkened his door since William died and that if I wouldn't cook for myself I'd have to come and have my dinner with them. So I thought to myself I wasn't being sensible and I'd only be a nuisance to them if I got sick, so I fixed everything to the clock as if there was no such thing as eternity. Until that morning the note came and then I just sat; I didn't know how long I stayed. I felt heavy, not able to move. Then I thought maybe Liam could get somebody with a van to take out my furniture and I could think later where to go. I took my rosary beads from under my pillow and my handbag with my money and my pension book and Eileen's letters and the photographs of her children and I shut the door behind me. There wasn't a soul in the street but there was nothing odd about that. You'll always know you're in a Protestant street if it's deserted. When I went across the road to get to Liam's house there were children playing and men at the corner and women standing at the doors in the sun and a squad of nervous-looking soldiers down at the other end.

Liam wasn't in but Gemma and the children were. The breakfast table wasn't cleared and Gemma was feeding the youngest. When he finished she stood him up on her lap and he reached over her shoulder trying to reach the shiny new handle Liam had put on the door. He was sturdy and happy and he had a warm smell of milk and baby powder. I wanted to hold him but I was afraid of putting her out of her routine. Sometimes I wonder if she has a routine — compared to the way I reared mine. Nothing was allowed to interrupt their feeding times and sleeping times. Maybe I was wrong and I'll never know what way Eileen managed hers. I would have liked to do the dishes too but I was afraid it might look like criticizing. After a wee while chatting Gemma got up to put the child in his pram and make us a cup of tea. 'You don't look great, Granny,' she said. 'Are you minding yourself at all?' I opened my bag and showed her the note.

She screamed and put her hands up to her face and the baby was startled and cried and bounced up and down in his pram with his arms up to be lifted. I said, 'Don't scream, Gemma. Don't ever scream, do you hear me?' and I unstrapped the baby and hugged him. She stared at me, surprised, and it stopped her.

'You'll have to come and stay here,' she said. 'We'll fit you in.' She gave a kind of a look round and I could see her thinking where on earth she could fit me in. Still, where could I go?

'All I wanted was for Liam to get a van and take out my stuff,' I explained. 'Maybe my sister Patsy would have more room than you.'

She took the baby and gave me my cup of tea. 'You'll come here,' she said. 'You'll count this your home and we'll be glad to have you.' She was a good kind girl, Gemma, and when Liam came in he was the same, only anxious to make me welcome, and he went off to get the van.

After a while Gemma said, 'Write to Eileen straightaway. She's the one you should be living with anyway — not all alone over yonder. All her money and her grand house. She's the one should have you.'

I laughed but it hurt me a bit to hear it said. 'What would I do in Eileen's grand house in Canada? How would I fit in?'

And Gemma said, 'You could keep her house all shining. She'd use you for that. Where would you see the like of your own house for polish! You'd do great for Eileen.' I looked round her own few bits and pieces — no look on anything, and a pile of children's clothes on the floor waiting to be washed and the children running in and out and knocking things over. Mary, my wee godchild, came and stood leaning against my knees, sucking her thumb. She was wearing one of the dresses I make for them. In the spring when I was fitting it on her I was noticing how beautiful her skin was with little pinprick freckles on the pink and white and I was thinking, *When she's so lovely what must Eileen's children be like?* Then she turned her head and looked at me and her eyes were full of love — for me! I couldn't get over it. Since then sometimes she'd just hold my hand. When Liam came back I said, 'Liam, I'm going home. I'm sorry about the bother. I just got frightened but you can cancel the van. I'm going home and I'm staying home. I've a Protestant house to the right of me and a Protestant house to the left of me. They'll not burn me out.' They argued with me and they were a bit upset but I knew they were relieved and I stuck to it.

Liam insisted on going back to the house with me, although since the murders started I had never let him come down my side of the road. There was a Land-Rover with soldiers in it not far from my door and no flames, no smoke. But when I opened the door, such a mess. There was water spouting out of a broken pipe in the wall where they had pulled out my sink. The Sacred Heart statue and the wee red lamp[8] were broken on the floor. My copper canopy was all dinged. The table had big hatchet marks on it. The cover on the couch was ripped and the stuffing pulled out. And filth. For months I thought I could get the smell of that filth. I wouldn't let Liam turn off the water until I had it washed away. We cleaned up a bit but Liam said he'd have to get help before he could do much and not to touch the electric because the water had got into it. He had been very quiet so I jumped when he shouted at the soldiers once he went out the door. They drove up very slowly and he was shouting and waving his arms and calling them names. One of them looked into the house and started to laugh. Liam yelled at him about me being a widow woman living alone and that they were here to protect me, but one of them said, 'You've got it wrong. We're here to wipe out the I.R.A.'

'Oh, Liam,' I said, 'go home. Go home before harm befalls you,' and he shook his fist at the soldiers and shouted, 'I'm going now but I'll be back and I won't be on my own then. Just look out. I'm warning you.'

He turned and ran off down the street and the soldier turned and looked after him and I thought he was lifting up his gun and I grabbed at his arm and the gun went off into the air and I begged, 'Don't shoot at him. Oh, don't shoot him.'

He said, 'Missus, I have no intention . . .' and then I fell against the wall and when I came to they were making me drink whiskey out of a bottle. It made me cough and splutter but it brought me round. They weren't bad to me, I must admit. When I was on my feet they corked up the bottle and put it back in the Land-Rover and drove off. Not one of my neighbours came out and all evening when I worked at tidying up, and all night when I sat up to keep watch, not one of them knocked at my door.

Next day Liam brought back two other lads and they fixed up the electricity and the water. It took a while to get everything decent again but they were in and out every day, sometimes three or four of them, and it never cost me a penny. Then a queer thing happened. My neighbours began moving out. The woman next door told me out of the side of her mouth that they had all been threatened. I didn't understand how a whole Protestant area could be threatened but out they all went. Of course I know they can always get newer better houses when they ask for them and indeed there was a lot of shooting and wrecking on the front of the road, but still I often wondered what was the truth of it. Maybe I'm better off not knowing. As they left, Catholics from across the road moved in — mostly older people — and I have good friends among them although it took us a while to get used to each other. I didn't take easy to people expecting to open my door and walk in at any hour of the day. They thought I was a bit stiff. I have no time for long chats and I never liked gossip. But Mrs Mulvenna, next door now, has a son in Australia — farther away than my Eileen and I think sons are even worse at writing home. I listen to her and I feel for her and I show her my photographs. I didn't tell her when Eileen wrote about how ashamed she was of us all and how she didn't like to let on she was Irish. I see talk like that in the papers too. It's not right to put the blame on poor powerless people. The most of us never did anything but stay quiet and put up with things the way they were. And we never taught our children to hate the others nor filled their heads with their wrongs the way it's said we did. When all the young people thought they could fix everything with marches and meetings I said it wouldn't work and they laughed at me. 'All you old ones are awful bitter,' they said and they jeered when Hannah in the shop and I were warning them, 'It'll all lead to shooting and burning and murder.'

Still, last November a man came round here trying to sell venetian blinds. Some of the houses have them but I said no, I liked to see out. I pointed to the sunset behind Divis — bits of red and yellow in the sky and a sort of mist all down the mountain that made it nearly see-through. The man looked at it for a minute and then he said, 'Do you know Belfast has the most beautiful sunsets in the whole world?' I said I didn't because I'd never been anyplace else to look at sunsets and he said, 'They tell me Belfast has the best and do you know why? It's because of all the smoke and dirt and dust and pollution. And it seems to me,' he said, 'it seems to me that if the dirt and dust and smoke and pollution of Belfast just with the help of the sun can make a sky like that, then there's hope for all of us.' He nodded and winked and touched his hat and went off and I went in and sat down at the table. And thinking of it I started to laugh, for it's true. There is hope for all of us. Well, anyway, if you don't die you live through it, day in, day out.

1   Tuberculosis.
2   The plants restharrow and creeping crowfoot; scutch is a type of grass.
3   Abusive names used by Protestants about Catholics.
4   A place of Catholic pilgrimage in south-west France. The waters are thought to provide cures for illness.
5   See a film.
6   Harland and Woolf, the leading Belfast shipyard, employed a workforce almost entirely Protestant.
7   Where Catholics and Protestants lived, not segregated.
8   A lamp burns continuously in front of the statue of the Sacred Heart.

JOHN McGAHERN
from John McGahern, *High Ground* (1985)

John McGahern (1934–   ), one of Ireland's leading fiction writers, lives near Mohill in County Leitrim. Son of a police sergeant in Cootehill, Co. Cavan, McGahern in his fiction from *The Barracks* (1963) onwards affords a telling insight into Irish masculinity.

'Gold Watch', among the best stories in this *Reader*, belongs to the same period of writing as *Amongst Women* (1990) and covers territory which McGahern has been exploring for some considerable time.

Gold Watch

It was in Grafton Street[1] we met, aimlessly strolling in one of the lazy lovely Saturday mornings in spring, the week of work over, the weekend still as fresh as the bunch of anemones that seemed the only purchase in her cane shopping basket.

'What a lovely surprise,' I said.

I was about to take her hand when a man with an armload of parcels parted us as she was shifting the basket to her other hand, and we withdrew out of the pushing crowds into the comparative quiet of Harry Street. We had not met since we had graduated in the same law class from University College five years before. I had heard she'd become engaged to the medical student she used to knock around with, and had gone into private practice down the country, perhaps, waiting for him to graduate.

'Are you up for the weekend or on holiday or what?' I asked.

'No. I work here now.' She named a big firm that specialized in tax law. 'I felt I needed a change.'

She was wearing a beautiful suit, the colour of oatmeal, the narrow skirt slit from the knee. The long gold hair of her student days was drawn tightly into a neat bun at the back.

'You look different but as beautiful as ever,' I said. 'I thought you'd be married by now.'

'And do you still go home every summer?' she countered, perhaps out of confusion.

'It doesn't seem as if I'll ever break that bad habit.'

We had coffee in Bewley's[2] — the scent of the roasting beans blowing through the vents out on to Grafton Street forever mixed with the memory of that morning — and we went on to spend the whole idle day together until she laughingly and firmly returned my first hesitant kiss; and it was she who silenced my even more fumbled offer of marriage several weeks later. 'No,' she said. 'I don't want to be married. But we can move in together and see how it goes. If it doesn't turn out well we can split and there'll be no bitterness.'

And it was she who found the flat in Hume Street, on the top floor of one of those old Georgian houses in off the Green,[3] within walking distance of both our places of work. There was extraordinary peace and loveliness in those first weeks together that I will always link with those high-ceilinged rooms — the

eager rush of excitement I felt as I left the office at the end of the day; the lingering in the streets to buy some offering of flowers or fruit or wine or a bowl and once one copper pan; and then rushing up the stairs to call her name, the emptiness of those same rooms when I'd find she hadn't got home yet.

'Why are we so happy?' I would ask.

'Don't worry it,' she always said, and sealed my lips with a touch.

That early summer we drove down one weekend to the small town in Kilkenny[4] where she had grown up, and above her father's bakery we slept in separate rooms. That Sunday a whole stream of relatives — aunts, cousins, two uncles, with trains of children — kept arriving at the house. Word had gone out, and they had plainly come to look me over. This brought the tension between herself and her schoolteacher mother into open quarrel late that evening after dinner. Her father sat with me in the front room, cautiously kind, sipping whiskey as we measured each careful cliché, listening to the quarrel slow and rise and crack in the far-off kitchen. I had found the sense of comfort and space charming for a while, but by the time we left I, too, was beginning to find the small town claustrophobic.

'Unfortunately the best part of these visits is always the leaving,' she said as we drove away. 'After a while away you're lured into thinking that the next time will somehow be different, but it never is.'

'Wait — wait until you see my place. Then you may well think differently. At least your crowd made an effort. And your father is a nice man.'

'And yet you keep going back to the old place?'

'That's true. That's something in my own nature. I have to face that now. It's just easier for me to go back than to cut. That way I don't feel any guilt. I don't feel anything.'

I knew myself too well. There was more caution than any love or charity in my habitual going home. It was unattractive and it had been learned in the bitter school of my ungiving father. I would fall into no guilt, and I was already fast outwearing him. For a time, it seemed, I could outstare the one eye of nature.

I had even waited for love, if love this was; for it was happiness such as I had never known.

'You see, I waited long enough for you,' I said as we drove away from her Kilkenny town. 'I hope I can keep you now.'

'If it wasn't me it would be some other. My mother will never understand that. You might as well say I waited long enough for you.'

The visit we made to my father, some weeks later, quickly turned to disaster far worse than I had at the very worst envisaged. I saw him watch us as I got out of the car to open the iron gate under the yew, but instead of coming out to greet us he withdrew into the shadows of the hallway. It was my stepmother, Rose, who came out to the car when we both got out and were opening the small garden gate. We had to follow her smiles and trills of speech all the way into the kitchen to find my father, who was seated in the car chair, and he did not rise to take our hands.

After a lunch that was silent, in spite of several shuttlecocks of speech Rose tried to keep in the air, he said as he took his hat from the sill, 'I want to ask you about these walnuts,' and I followed him out into the fields. The mock orange was in blossom, and it was where the mock orange stood out from the clump of egg bushes that he turned suddenly and said, 'What age is your intended? She looks well on her way to forty.'

'She's the same age as I am,' I said blankly. I could hardly think, caught between the shock and pure amazement.

'I don't believe it,' he said.

'You don't have to, but we were in the same class at university.' I turned away.

Walking with her in the same field close to the mock orange tree late that evening, I said, 'Do you know what my father said to me?'

'No,' she said happily. 'But from what I've seen I don't think anything will surprise me.'

'We were walking just here,' I began, and repeated what he'd said. When I saw her go still and pale I knew I should not have spoken.

'He said I look close to forty,' she repeated. 'I have to get out of this place.'

'Stay this one night,' I begged. 'It's late now. We'd have to stay in a hotel. It'd be making it into too big of a production. You don't ever have to come back again, if you don't want to, but stay the night. It'll be easier.'

'I'll not want to come back,' she said as she agreed to see out this one night.

'But why do you think he said it?' I asked her later when we were both quiet, sitting on a wall at the end of the Big Meadow, watching the shadows of the evening deepen between the beeches, putting off the time when we'd have to go into the house, not unlike two grown children.

'Is there any doubt? Out of simple hatred. There's no living with that kind of hatred.'

'We'll leave first thing in the morning,' I promised.

'And why did you,' she asked, tickling my throat with a blade of ryegrass, 'say I was, if anything, too beautiful?'

'Because it's true. It makes you public and it's harder to live naturally. You live in too many eyes — in envy or confusion or even simple admiration, it's all the same. I think it makes it harder to live luckily.'

'But it gives you many advantages.'

'If you make use of those advantages, you're drawn even deeper in. And of course I'm afraid it'll attract people who'll try to steal you from me.'

'That won't happen.' She laughed. She'd recovered all her natural good spirits. 'And now I suppose we better go in and face the ogre. We have to do it sooner or later and it's getting chilly.'

My father tried to be very charming when we went in, but there was a false heartiness in the voice that made clear that it grew out of no well-meaning. He felt he'd lost ground, and was now trying to recover it far too quickly. Using silence and politeness like a single weapon, we refused to be drawn in; and when pressed to stay the next morning, we said unequivocally that we had to get back. Except for one summer when I went to work in England, the summer my father married Rose, I had always gone home to help at the hay; and after I entered the civil service I was able to arrange holidays so that they fell around haytime. They had come to depend on me, and I liked the work. My father had never forgiven me for taking my chance to go to university. He had wanted me to stay at home to work the land. I had always fought his need to turn my refusal into betrayal. And by going home each summer I felt I was affirming that the great betrayal was not mine but nature's own.

I had arranged the holidays to fall at haytime that year as I had all the years before I met her, but since he'd turned to me at the mock orange tree I was no longer sure I had to go. I was no longer free, since in everything but name our life together seemed growing into marriage. It might even make him happy for a time if he could call it my betrayal.

'I don't know what to do,' I confessed to her a week before I was due to take holidays. 'They've come to depend on me for the hay. Everything else they can manage themselves. I know they'll expect me.'

'What do you want to do?'

'I suppose I'd prefer to go home — that's if you don't mind.'

'Why do you prefer?'

'I like working at the hay. You come back to the city feeling fit and well.'

'Is that the real reason?'

'No. It's something that might even be called sinister. I've gone home for so long that I'd like to see it through. I don't want to be blamed for finishing it, though it'll finish soon, with or without me. But this way I don't have to think about it.'

'Maybe it would be kinder, then, to do just that, and take the blame.'

'It probably would be kinder, but kindness died between us so long ago that it doesn't enter into it.'

'So there was some kindness?'

'When I was younger,' I had to smile. 'He looked on it as weakness. I suspect he couldn't deal with it. Anyhow it always redoubled his fury. He was kind, too, in fits, when he was feeling good about things. That was even more unacceptable. And that phrase from the Bible is true that after enough suffering a kind of iron enters the soul. It's very far from commendable, but now I do want to see it through.'

'Well, then go,' she said. 'I don't understand it but I can see you want to go. Being new, the earliest I can get holidays will be September.'

We had pasta and two bottles of red wine at the flat the evening before I was to leave for the hay, and with talking we were almost late for our walk in the Green. We liked to walk there every good evening before turning home for the night.

The bells were fairly clamouring from all corners, rooting vagrants and lovers from the shrubbery, as we passed through the half-closed gates. Two women at the pond's edge were hurriedly feeding the ducks bread from a plastic bag. We crossed the bridge where the Japanese cherry leaned, down among the empty benches round the paths and flowerbeds within their low railings. The deckchairs had been gathered in, the sprinklers turned off. There was about the Green always at this hour some of the melancholy of the beach at the close of holiday. The gate we had entered was already locked. The attendant was rattling an enormous bunch of keys at the one through which we had to leave.

'You know,' she said, 'I'd like to be married before long. I hadn't thought it would make much difference to me, but, oddly, now I want to be married.'

'I hope it's to me,' I said.

'You haven't asked me.'

I could feel her laughter as she held my arm close.

'I'm asking now.'

I made a flourish of removing a non-existent hat. 'Will you marry me?'

'I will.'

'When?'

'Before the year is out.'

'Would you like to go for a drink to celebrate, then?'

'I always like any excuse to celebrate.' She was biting her lip. 'Where will you take me?'

'The Shelbourne.[5] It's our local. It'll be quiet.'

I thought of the aggressive boot thrown after the bridal car, the marbles suddenly rattling in the hub caps of the honeymoon car, the metal smeared with oil so that the thrown boxes of confetti would stick, the legs of the comic pyjamas hilariously sewn up. We would avoid all that. We had promised one another the simplest wedding.

'We live in a lucky time,' she said and raised her glass, her calm, grey, intelligent eyes shining. 'We wouldn't have been allowed to do it this way even a decade ago. Will you tell your father that we're to be married?'

'I don't know. Probably not unless it comes up. And you?'

'I'd better. As it is, Mother will probably be furious that it is not going to be a big splash.'

'I'm so grateful for these months together. That we were able to drift into marriage without that drowning plunge when you see your whole life in a flash. What will you do while I'm away?'

'I'll pine,' she teased. 'I might even try to decorate the flat out of simple desperation. There's a play at the Abbey that I want to see. There are some good restaurants in the city if I get too depressed. And in the meantime, have a wonderful time with your father and poor Rose in the nineteenth century at the bloody hay.'

'Oh, for the Lord's sake,' I said and rose to leave. Outside she was still laughing so provocatively that I drew her towards me.

The next morning on the train home I heard a transistor[6] far down the carriage promise a prolonged spell of good weather. Meadows were being mowed all along the line, and I saw men testing handfuls of hay in the breeze as they waited for the sun to burn the dew off the fallen swards. It was weather people prayed for at this time.

I walked the three miles from the station. Meadows were down all along the road, some already saved, in stacked bales.[7] The scent of cut grass was everywhere. As I drew close to the stone house in its trees I could hardly wait to see if the Big Meadow was down beyond the row of beech trees. When I lived here I'd felt this same excitement as the train rattled across the bridges into the city or when I approached the first sight of the ocean. Now that I lived in a city on the sea the excitement had been gradually transferred home.

Before I reached the gate I could tell by the emptiness beyond the beeches that the Big Meadow had been cut. Rose and my father were in the house. They were waiting in high excitement.

'Everything's ready for you,' Rose said as she shook my hand, and through the window I saw my old clothes outside in the sun draped across the back of a chair.

'As soon as you get a bite you can jump in your old duds,' my father said. 'I knocked the Big Meadow yesterday. All's ready for go.'

Rose had washed my old clothes before hanging them outside to air. When I changed into them they were still warm from the sun, and they had that lovely clean feel that worn clothes after washing have. Within an hour we were working the machines.

The machines had taken much of the uncertainty and slavery from haymaking, but there was still the anxiety of rain. Each cloud that drifted into the blue above us we watched as apprehensively across the sky as if it were an enemy ship, and we seemed as tired at the end of every day as we were before we had the machines, eating late in silence, waking from listless watching of the television only when the weather forecast showed; and afterwards it was an effort to drag feet to our rooms where the bed lit with moonlight showed like heaven, and sleep was as instant as it was dreamless.

And it was into the stupor of such an evening that the gold watch fell. We were slumped in front of the television set. Rose had been working outside in the front garden, came in and put the tea kettle on the ring, and started to take folded sheets from the linen closet. Without warning, the gold watch spilled out on to the floor. She'd pulled it from the closet with one of the sheets. The pale face was upwards in the poor light. I bent to pick it up. The glass had not broken. 'It's lucky it no longer goes,' Rose breathed.

'Well, if it did you'd soon take good care of that.' My father rose angrily from the rocking chair.

'It just pulled out with the sheets,' Rose said. 'I was running into it everywhere round the house. I put it in with the sheets so that it'd be out of the way.'

'I'm sure you had it well planned. Give us this day our daily crash. Tell me this: would you sleep at night if you didn't manage to smash or break something during the day?' He'd been frightened out of light sleep in the chair. He was intent on avenging his fright.

'Why did the watch stop?' I asked.

I turned the cold gold in my hand. *Elgin* was the one word on the white face. The delicate hands were of blue steel. All through my childhood it had shone.

'Can there be two reasons why it stopped?' His anger veered towards me now. 'It stopped because it got broke.'

'Why can't it be fixed?' I ignored the anger.

'Poor Taylor in the town doesn't take in watches anymore,' Rose answered. 'And the last time it stopped we sent it to Sligo. Sligo even sent it to Dublin but it was sent back. A part that holds the balance wheel is broke. What they told us is, that they've stopped making parts for those watches. They have to be specially handmade. They said that the quality of the gold wasn't high enough to justify that expense. That it was only gold plated. I don't suppose it'll ever go again. I put it in with the sheets to have it out of the way. I was running into it everywhere.'

'Well, if it wasn't fixed before, you must certainly have fixed it for good and forever this time.' My father would not let go.

His hand trembled on the arm of the rocking chair, the same hand that would draw out the gold watch long ago as the first strokes of the Angelus[8] came to us over the heather and pale wheaten sedge of Gloria Bog:[9] 'Twenty minutes late, no more than usual. . . . One of these years Jimmy Lynch will startle himself and the whole countryside by ringing the Angelus at exactly twelve. . . . Only in Ireland is there right time and wrong time. In other countries there is just time.' We'd stand and stretch our backs, aching from scattering the turf, and wait for him to lift his straw hat.

Waiting with him under the yew, suitcases round our feet, for the bus that took us each year to the sea at Strandhill[10] after the hay was in and the turf home; and to quiet us he'd take the watch out and let it lie in his open palm, where we'd follow the small second hand low down on the face endlessly circling until the bus came into sight at the top of Doherty's Hill. How clearly everything sang now set free by the distance of the years, with what heaviness the actual scenes and days had weighed.

'If the watch isn't going to be fixed, then, I might as well have it.' I was amazed at the calm sound of my own words. The watch had come to him from his father. Through all the long years of childhood I had assumed that one day he would pass it on to me. Then all weakness would be gone. I would possess its power. Once in a generous fit he even promised it to me, but he did not keep that promise. Unfairly, perhaps, I expected him to give it to me when I graduated, when I passed into the civil service, when I won my first promotion, but he did not. I had forgotten about it until it had spilled out of the folded sheets on to the floor.

I saw a look pass between my father and stepmother before he said, 'What good would it be to you?'

'No good. Just a keepsake. I'll get you a good new watch in its place. I often see watches in the duty-free airports.' My work often took me outside the country.

'I don't need a watch,' he said, and pulled himself up from his chair.

Rose cast me a furtive look, much the same look that had passed a few moments before between her and my father. 'Maybe your father wants to keep the watch,' it pleaded, but I ignored it.

'Didn't the watch once belong to your father?' I asked as he shuffled toward his room, but the only answer he made was to turn and yawn back before continuing the slow, exaggerated shuffle toward his room.

When the train pulled into Amiens Street Station,[11] to my delight I saw her outside the ticket barrier, in the same tweed suit she'd worn the Saturday morning we met in Grafton Street. I could tell that she'd been to the hairdresser, but there were specks of white paint on her hands.

'Did you tell them that we're to be married?' she asked as we left the station.

'No.'

'Why not?'

'It never came up. And you, did you write home?'

'No. In fact, I drove down last weekend and told them.'

'How did they take it?'

'They seemed glad. You seemed to have made a good impression.' She smiled. 'As I guessed, Mother is quite annoyed that it's not going to be a big do.'

'You won't change our plans because of that.'

'Of course not. She's not much given to change herself, except to changing other people so that they fit in with her ideas.'

'This fell my way at last,' I said and showed her the silent watch. 'I've always wanted it. If we believed in signs it would seem life is falling into our hands at last.'

'And not before our time, I think I can risk adding.'

We were married that October by a Franciscan in their church on the quay, with two vergers as witnesses, and we drank far too much wine at lunch afterwards in a new restaurant that had opened in Lincoln Court; staggering home in the late afternoon, I saw some people in the street smile at my attempt to lift her across the step. We did not even hear the bells closing the Green.

It was dark when we woke, and she said, 'I have something for you,' taking a small, wrapped package from the bedside table.

'You know we promised not to give presents,' I said.

'I know but this is different. Open it. Anyhow, you said you didn't believe in signs.'

It was the gold watch. I held it to my ear. It was running perfectly. The small second hand was circling endlessly low down on the face. The blue hands pointed to past midnight.

'Did it cost much?'

'No. Very little, but that's not your business.'

'I thought the parts had to be specially made.'

'That wasn't true. They probably never even asked.'

'You shouldn't have bothered.'

'Now I'm hoping to see you wear it,' she laughed.

I did not wear it. I left it on the mantel. The gold and white face and delicate blue hands looked very beautiful to me on the white marble. It gave me a curious pleasure mixed with guilt to wind it and watch it run; and the following spring, coming from a conference in Ottawa, I bought an expensive modern watch in the duty-free shop of Montreal Airport. It was guaranteed for five years, and was shockproof, dustproof, waterproof.

'What do you think of it?' I asked her when I returned to Dublin. 'I bought it for my father.'

'Well, it's no beauty, but my mother would certainly approve of it. It's what she'd describe as *serviceable*.'

'It was expensive enough.'

'It looks expensive. You'll bring it when you go down for the hay?'

'It'll probably be my last summer with them at the hay,' I said apologetically. 'Won't you change your mind and come down with me?'

She shook her head. 'He'd probably say I look fifty now.' She was as strong-willed as the schoolteacher mother she disliked, and I did not press. She was with child and looked calm and lovely.

'What'll they do about the hay when they no longer have you to help them?' she said.

'What does anybody do? Do without me. Stop. Get it done by contract. They have plenty of money. It'll just be the end of something that has gone on for a very long time.'

'That it certainly has.'

I came by train at the same time in July as I'd come every summer, the excitement I'd always felt tainted with melancholy that it'd probably be the last summer I would come. I had not even a wish to see it to its natural end anymore. I had come because it seemed less violent to come than to stay away, and I had the good new modern watch to hand over in place of the old gold. The night before, at dinner, we had talked about buying a house with a garden out near the strand in Sandymount.[12] Any melancholy I was feeling lasted only until I came in sight of the house.

All the meadows had been cut and saved, the bales stacked in groups of five or six and roofed with green grass. The Big Meadow beyond the beeches was completely clean, the bales having been taken in. Though I had come intending to make it my last summer at the hay, I now felt a keen outrage that it had been ended without me. Rose and my father were nowhere to be seen.

'What happened?' I asked when I found them at last, weeding the potato ridge one side of the orchard.

'The winter feeding got too much for us,' my father said. 'We decided to let the meadows. Gillespie took them. He cut early – two weeks ago.'

'Why didn't you tell me?'

My father and Rose exchanged looks, and my father spoke as if he was delivering a prepared statement.

'We didn't like to. And anyhow we thought you'd want to come, hay or no hay. It's more normal to come for a rest instead of just to kill yourself at the old hay. And indeed there's plenty else for you to do if you have a mind to do it. I've taken up the garden again myself.'

'Anyhow, I've brought these.' I handed Rose the box of chocolates and bottle of scent, and gave my father the watch.

'What's this for?' He had always disliked receiving presents.

'It's the watch I told you I'd get in place of the old watch.'

'I don't need a watch.'

'I got it anyhow. What do you think of it?'

'It's ugly,' he said, turning it over.

'It was expensive enough.' I named the price. 'And that was duty free.'

'They must have seen you coming, then.'

'No. It's guaranteed for five years. It's dustproof, shockproof, waterproof.'

'The old gold watch — do you still have that?' He changed after silence.

'Of course.'

'Did you ever get it working?'

'No,' I lied. 'But it's sort of nice to have.'

'That doesn't make much sense to me.'

'Well, you'll find that the new watch is working well anyway.'

'What use have I for time here anymore?' he said, but I saw him start to wind and examine the new watch, and he was wearing it at breakfast the next morning. He seemed to want it to be seen as he buttered toast and reached across for milk and sugar.

'What did you want to get up so early for?' he said to me. 'You should have lain in and taken a good rest when you had the chance.'

'What will you be doing today?' I asked.

'Not much. A bit of fooling around. I might get spray ready for the potatoes.'

'It'd be an ideal day for hay,' I said, looking out the window on the fields. The morning was as blue and cool as the plums still touched with dew down by the hayshed. There was a white spider webbing over the grass. I took a book and headed towards the shelter of the beeches in the Big Meadow, for, when the sun would eventually beat through, the day would be uncomfortably hot.

It was a poor attempt at reading. Halfway down each page I'd find I had lost every thread and was staring blankly at the words. I thought at first that the trees and green and those few wisps of cloud, hazy and calm in the emerging blue, brought the tension of past exams and summers too close to the book I held in my hand, but then I found myself stirring uncomfortably in my suit — missing my old loose clothes, the smell of diesel in the meadow, the blades of grass shivering as they fell, the long teeth of the raker kicking the hay into rows, all the jangle and bustle and busyness of the meadows.

I heard the clear blows of a hammer on stone. My father was sledging stones that had fallen from the archway where once the workmen's bell had hung. Some of the stones had been part of the arch and were quite beautiful. There seemed no point in breaking them up. I moved closer, taking care to stay hidden in the shade of the beeches.

As the sledge rose, the watch glittered on my father's wrist. I followed it down, saw the shudder that ran through his arms as the metal met the stone. A watch was always removed from the wrist before such violent work. I waited. In this heat he could not keep up such work for long. He brought the sledge down again and again, the watch glittering, the shock shuddering through his arms. When he stopped, before he wiped the sweat away, he put the watch to his ear and listened intently. What I'd guessed was certain now. From the irritable way he threw the sledge aside, it was clear that the watch was still running.

That afternoon I helped him fill the tar barrel with water for spraying the potatoes, though he made it clear he didn't want help. When he put the bag of blue stone into the barrel to steep, he thrust the watch deep into the water before my eyes.

'I'm going back to Dublin tomorrow,' I said.

'I thought you were coming for two weeks. You always stayed two weeks before.'

'There's no need for me now.'

'It's your holidays now. You're as well off here as by the sea. It's as much of a change and far cheaper.'

'I meant to tell you before, and should have but didn't. I am married now.'

'Tell me more news,' he said with an attempt at cool

surprise, but I saw by his eyes that he already knew. 'We heard but we didn't like to believe it. It's a bit late in the day for formal engagements, never mind invitations. I suppose we weren't important enough to be invited.'

'There was no one at the wedding but ourselves. We invited no one, neither her people or mine.'

'Well, I suppose it was cheaper that way,' he agreed sarcastically.

'When will you spray?'

'I'll spray tomorrow,' he said, and we left the blue stone to steep in the barrel of water.

With relief, I noticed he was no longer wearing the watch, but the feeling of unease was so great in the house that after dinner I went outside. It was a perfect moonlit night, the empty fields and beech trees and walls in clear yellow outline. The night seemed so full of serenity that it brought the very ache of longing for all of life to reflect its moonlit calm: but I knew too well it neither was nor could be. It was a dream of death.

I went idly toward the orchard, and as I passed the tar barrel I saw a thin fishing line hanging from a part of the low yew branch down into the barrel. I heard the ticking even before the wrist watch came up tied to the end of the line. What shocked me was that I felt neither surprise nor shock.

I felt the bag that we'd left to steep earlier in the water. The blue stone had all melted down. It was a barrel of pure poison, ready for spraying.

I listened to the ticking of the watch on the end of the line in silence before letting it drop back into the barrel. The poison had already eaten into the casing of the watch. The shining rim and back were no longer smooth. It could hardly run much past morning.

The night was so still that the shadows of the beeches did not waver on the moonlit grass, seemed fixed like a leaf in rock. On the white marble the gold watch must now be lying face upwards in this same light, silent or running. The ticking of the watch

down in the barrel was so completely muffled by the spray that only by imagination could it be heard. A bird moved in some high branch, but afterward the silence was so deep it began to hurt, and the longing grew for the bird or anything to stir again.

I stood in that moonlit silence as if waiting for some word or truth, but none came, none ever came; and I grew amused at that part of myself that still expected something, standing like a fool out there in all that moonlit silence, when only what *was* increased or diminished as it changed, became only what is, becoming again what *was* even faster than the small second hand endlessly circling in the poison.

Suddenly, the lights in the house went out. Rose had gone to join my father in bed. Before going into the house this last night to my room, I drew the watch up again out of the barrel by the line and listened to it tick, now purely amused by the expectation it renewed — that if I continued to listen to the ticking some word or truth might come. And when I finally lowered the watch back down into the poison, I did it so carefully that no ripple or splash disturbed the quiet, and time, hardly surprisingly, was still running; time that did not have to run to any conclusion.

1 Main shopping street in Dublin.
2 Famous restaurant (chain).
3 St Stephen's Green.
4 In County Kilkenny, that is.
5 The Shelbourne Hotel on St Stephen's Green.
6 Transistor radio.
7 Saving hay is the phrase used in Ireland for the process of harvesting the hay. Saved carries the connotation of saved from the bad weather.
8 A form of prayers said at midday and 6 p.m. when church bells ring out the Angelus across Catholic Ireland.
9 A turf-bog with this name.
10 In County Sligo.
11 In Dublin.
12 Four miles south of the centre of Dublin.

DESMOND EGAN
from *Aquarius*, No. 12, 1980

Desmond Egan (1936–   ), poet, publisher and classics teacher, founded the Goldsmith Press in 1972 which published several volumes of his own verse (with illustrations) including *Midland* (1973), *Siege* (1976), and *Woodcutter* (1978). His poetry deliberately resists, yet calls out for, incorporation into a critical vocabulary. 'Unique' appeared in Egan's 1983 collection *Seeing Double*.

UNIQUE

A man's a genius just for being himself — Kavanagh

this blinking digital watch i bought secondhand
it has an alarm which must go off though i never need
    it
and as you'd guess my zipped sweater
has christmas written all over it
my clothes are an anthology of others' tastes
casuals for example a present too and slightly on the
    big side
though their unambitious lack of polish is my
    contribution
this navy poloneck shirt and come to think of jacket
were given to me at various stages for nothing

even the football style socks are not my property
but the jeans? bought by me all right from a nice
    Indian girl
with a diamond in her cheek at an upstairs market in
    London

all the rest even underwear like my ideas
philosophy if you like more or less received
used as this '74 Fiat

so now
why do you think you like me?

BRIAN FRIEL
from Brian Friel, *Translations* (1980)

Brian Friel's *Translations* received its première in Derry in October 1980. The play marked the launch of Field Day, a theatrical company founded by Friel and the actor Stephen Rea, who were later joined by Seamus Deane, David Hammond, Tom Paulin and Seamus Heaney. In a survey of Field Day five years on in *The Linen Hall Review* in Summer 1985, John Gray suggested *Translations* was especially suited to a Derry launch pad, a city then undergoing 'an explosion of civic pride, and a company presenting itself in a physical sense on the communal frontier'. According to Friel, in Ireland 'everything is immediately perceived as political and the artist is burdened instantly with politicization'. Set in pre-Famine Ireland at a time when the map of Ireland was being redrawn by an Ordnance Survey, *Translations* is Friel's attempt to negotiate — or, rather, reflect on — this difficult terrain between past and present (and future), culture and politics, language and identity, Ireland and Britain. In his concern with a conceptual language and in his suggestive arrangement of interlocking themes, Friel is arguably the most distinguished living Irish playwright and all his plays from *Philadelphia, Here I Come!* (1964) and *The Freedom of the City* (1973) to *Dancing at Lughnasa* (1990) and *Molly Sweeney* (1994) repay close study. The setting for *Translations* is a hedge school in the 1830s, the decade that saw the building of the first National Schools and the increasing control of the State. It is an Irish-speaking district and English sappers have arrived in the area to conduct an Ordnance Survey. English is the language of the play and the audience are asked to imagine that the Irish characters speak to each other in Irish. The opening scene is devoted to language learning — Latin, English, and even speech itself. Sarah is learning to speak; Máire is learning English to enable her to emigrate to America; the drunken schoolmaster Hugh laments the loss of Gaelic civilization; Hugh's son Manus, who is in love with Máire, is suspicious of the newly arrived English sappers, one of whom, Lieutenant Yolland, strikes up a relationship with a responsive Máire. During the course of the first act, Hugh's other son Owen, after a six years' absence, returns as an Irish intermediary for the English. Act Two, the extract which follows, constitutes the central section of the play.

The action takes place in a hedge-school[1] in the townland of Baile Beag/Ballybeg, an Irish-speaking community in County Donegal.

ACT ONE   An afternoon in late August 1833.
ACT TWO   A few days later.
ACT THREE   The evening of the following day.

Act Two

SCENE ONE

The sappers have already mapped most of the area. YOLLAND's *official task, which* OWEN *is now doing, is to take each of the Gaelic names — every hill, stream, rock, even every patch of ground which possessed its own distinctive Irish name — and Anglicize it, either by changing it into its approximate English sound or by translating it into English words. For example, a Gaelic name like Cnoc Ban could become Knockban or — directly translated — Fair Hill. These new standardized names were entered into the Name-Book, and when the news maps appeared they contained all these new Anglicized names.* OWEN's *official function as translator is to pronounce each name in Irish and then provide the English translation.*

The hot weather continues. It is late afternoon some days later.

Stage right: an improvised clothes-line strung between the shafts of the cart and a nail in the wall; on it are some shirts and socks.

A large map — one of the new blank maps — is spread out on the floor. OWEN *is on his hands and knees, consulting it. He is totally engrossed in his task which he pursues with great energy and efficiency.*

YOLLAND's *hesitancy has vanished — he is at home here now. He is sitting on the floor, his long legs stretched out before him, his back resting against a creel, his eyes closed. His mind is elsewhere. One of the reference books — a church registry — lies open on his lap.*

Around them are various reference books, the Name-Book, a bottle of poteen, some cups etc.

OWEN *completes an entry in the Name-Book and returns to the map on the floor.*

OWEN: Now. Where have we got to? Yes — the point where that stream enters the sea — that tiny little beach there. George!

YOLLAND: Yes. I'm listening. What do you call it? Say the Irish name again?

OWEN: Bun na hAbhann.

YOLLAND: Again.

OWEN: Bun na hAbhann.

YOLLAND: Bun na hAbhann.

OWEN: That's terrible, George.

YOLLAND: I know. I'm sorry. Say it again.

OWEN: Bun na hAbhann.

YOLLAND: Bun na hAbhann.

OWEN: That's better. Bun is the Irish word for bottom. And Abha means river. So it's literally the mouth of the river.

YOLLAND: Let's leave it alone. There's no English equivalent for a sound like that.

OWEN: What is it called in the church registry?

(*Only now does* YOLLAND *open his eyes.*)

YOLLAND: Let's see . . . Banowen.

OWEN: That's wrong. (*Consults text.*) The list of freeholders calls it Owenmore — that's completely wrong: Owenmore's the big river at the west end of the parish. (*Another text.*) And in the grand jury lists it's called — God! — Binhone! — wherever they got that. I suppose we could Anglicize it to Bunowen; but somehow that's neither fish nor flesh.

(YOLLAND *closes his eyes again.*)

YOLLAND: I give up.

OWEN (*At map*): Back to first principles. What are we trying to do?

YOLLAND: Good question.

OWEN: We are trying to denominate and at the same time describe that tiny area of soggy, rocky, sandy ground where that little stream enters the sea, an area known locally as Bun na hAbhann . . . Burnfoot! What about Burnfoot?

YOLLAND (*Indifferently*): Good, Roland. Burnfoot's good.

OWEN: George, my name isn't . . .

YOLLAND: B-u-r-n-f-o-o-t?

OWEN: I suppose so. What do you think?

YOLLAND: Yes.

OWEN: Are you happy with that?

YOLLAND: Yes.

OWEN: Burnfoot it is then. (*He makes the entry into the Name-Book.*) Bun na hAbhann — B-u-r-n-

YOLLAND: You're becoming very skilled at this.

OWEN: We're not moving fast enough.

YOLLAND (*Opens eyes again*): Lancey lectured me again last night.

OWEN: When does he finish here?

YOLLAND: The sappers are pulling out at the end of the week. The trouble is, the maps they've completed can't be printed without these names. So London screams at Lancey and Lancey screams at me. But I wasn't intimidated.

(MANUS *emerges from upstairs and descends.*)

'I'm sorry, sir,' I said, 'but certain tasks demand their own tempo. You cannot rename a whole country overnight.' Your Irish air has made me bold. (*To* MANUS.) Do you want us to leave?

MANUS: Time enough. Class won't begin for another half-hour.

YOLLAND: Sorry — sorry?

OWEN: Can't you speak English?

(MANUS *gathers the things off the clothes-line.* OWEN *returns to the map.*)

OWEN: We now come across that beach . . .

YOLLAND: Tra — that's the Irish for beach. (*To* MANUS.) I'm picking up the odd word, Manus.

MANUS: So.

OWEN: . . . on past Burnfoot; and there's nothing around here that has any name that I know of until we come down here to the south end, just about here . . . and there should be a ridge of rocks there . . . Have the sappers marked it? They have. Look, George.

YOLLAND: Where are we?

OWEN: There.

YOLLAND: I'm lost.

OWEN: Here. And the name of that ridge is Druim Dubh. Put English on that, Lieutenant.

YOLLAND: Say it again.

OWEN: Druim Dubh.

YOLLAND: Dubh means black.

OWEN: Yes.

YOLLAND: And Druim means . . . what? a fort?

OWEN: We met it yesterday in Druim Luachra.

YOLLAND: A ridge! The Black Ridge (*To* MANUS.) You see, Manus?

OWEN: We'll have you fluent at the Irish before the summer's over.

YOLLAND: Oh I wish I were.

(*To* MANUS *as he crosses to go back upstairs.*) We got a crate of oranges from Dublin today. I'll send some up to you.

MANUS: Thanks. (*To* OWEN.) Better hide that bottle. Father's just up and he'd be better without it.

OWEN: Can't you speak English before your man?

MANUS: Why?

OWEN: Out of courtesy.

MANUS: Doesn't he want to learn Irish? (*To* YOLLAND.) Don't you want to learn Irish?

YOLLAND: Sorry — sorry? I — I —

MANUS: I understand the Lanceys perfectly but people like you puzzle me.

OWEN: Manus, for God's sake!

MANUS (*Still to* YOLLAND): How's the work going?

YOLLAND: The work? — the work? Oh, it's — it's staggering along — I think — (*To* OWEN.) — isn't it? But we'd be lost without Roland.

MANUS (*Leaving*): I'm sure. But there are always the Rolands, aren't there? (*He goes upstairs and exits.*)

YOLLAND: What was that he said? — something about Lancey, was it?

OWEN: He said we should hide that bottle before Father gets his hands on it.

YOLLAND: Ah.

OWEN: He's always trying to protect him.

YOLLAND: Was he lame from birth?

OWEN: An accident when he was a baby: Father fell across his cradle. That's why Manus feels so responsible for him.

YOLLAND: Why doesn't he marry?

OWEN: Can't afford to, I suppose.

YOLLAND: Hasn't he a salary?

OWEN: What salary? All he gets is the odd shilling Father throws him — and that's seldom enough. I got out in time, didn't I?

(YOLLAND *is pouring a drink.*)

Easy with that stuff — it'll hit you suddenly.

YOLLAND: I like it.

OWEN: Let's get back to the job. Druim Dubh — what's it called in the jury lists? (*Consults texts.*)

YOLLAND: Some people here resent us.

OWEN: Dramduff — wrong as usual.

YOLLAND: I was passing a little girl yesterday and she spat at me.

OWEN: And it's Drimdoo here. What's it called in the registry?

YOLLAND: Do you know the Donnelly twins?

OWEN: Who?

YOLLAND: The Donnelly twins.

OWEN: Yes. Best fishermen about here. What about them?

YOLLAND: Lancey's looking for them.

OWEN: What for?

YOLLAND: He wants them for questioning.

OWEN: Probably stolen somebody's nets. Dramduffy! Nobody ever called it Dramduffy. Take your pick of those three.

YOLLAND: My head's addled. Let's take a rest. Do you want a drink?

OWEN: Thanks. Now, every Dubh we've come across we've changed to Duff. So if we're to be consistent, I suppose Druim Dubh has to become Dromduff.

(YOLLAND *is now looking out the window.*)

You can see the end of the ridge from where you're standing. But D-r-u-m or D-r-o-m? (*Name-Book*) Do you remember — which did we agree on for Druim Luachra?

YOLLAND: That house immediately above where we're camped —

OWEN: Mm?

YOLLAND: The house where Maire lives.

OWEN: Maire? Oh, Maire Chatach.

YOLLAND: What does that mean?

OWEN: Curly-haired; the whole family are called the Catachs. What about it?

YOLLAND: I hear music coming from that house almost every night.

OWEN: Why don't you drop in?

YOLLAND: Could I?

OWEN: Why not? We used D-r-o-m then. So we've got to call it D-r-o-m-d-u-f-f — alright?

YOLLAND: Go back up to where the new school is being built and just say the names again for me, would you?

OWEN: That's a good idea. Poolkerry, Ballybeg —

YOLLAND: No, no; as they still are — in your own language.

OWEN: Poll na gCaorach,

(YOLLAND *repeats the names silently after him.*)

Baile Beag, Ceann Balor, Lis Maol, Machaire Buidhe, Baile na gGall, Carraig na Ri, Mullach Dearg —

YOLLAND: Do you think I could live here?

OWEN: What are you talking about?

YOLLAND: Settle down here — live here.

OWEN: Come on, George.

YOLLAND: I mean it.

OWEN: Live on what? Potatoes? Buttermilk?

YOLLAND: It's really heavenly.

OWEN: For God's sake! The first hot summer in fifty years and you think it's Eden. Don't be such a bloody romantic. You wouldn't survive a mild winter here.

YOLLAND: Do you think not? Maybe you're right.

(DOALTY *enters in a rush.*)

DOALTY: Hi, boys, is Manus about?

OWEN: He's upstairs. Give him a shout.

DOALTY: Manus!

The cattle's going mad in that heat — Cripes, running wild all over the place.

(*To* YOLLAND.) How are you doing, skipper?

(MANUS *appears.*)

YOLLAND: Thank you for — I — I'm very grateful to you for —

DOALTY: Wasting your time. I don't know a word

you're saying. Hi, Manus, there's two bucks down the road there asking for you.

MANUS (*Descending*): Who are they?

DOALTY: Never clapped eyes on them. They want to talk to you.

MANUS: What about?

DOALTY: They wouldn't say. Come on. The bloody beasts'll end up in Loch an Iubhair if they're not capped. Good luck, boys!

(DOALTY *rushes off.* MANUS *follows him.*)

OWEN: Good luck! What were you thanking Doalty for?

YOLLAND: I was washing outside my tent this morning and he was passing with a scythe across his shoulder and he came up to me and pointed to the long grass and then cut a pathway round my tent and from the tent down to the road — so that my feet won't get wet with the dew. Wasn't that kind of him? And I have no words to thank him . . . I suppose you're right: I suppose I couldn't live here . . . Just before Doalty came up to me this morning, I was thinking that at that moment I might have been in Bombay instead of Ballybeg. You see, my father was at his wits end with me and finally he got me a job with the East India Company — some kind of a clerkship. This was ten, eleven months ago. So I set off for London. Unfortunately I — I — I missed the boat. Literally. And since I couldn't face Father and hadn't enough money to hang about until the next sailing, I joined the Army. And they stuck me into the Engineers and posted me to Dublin. And Dublin sent me here. And while I was washing this morning and looking across the Tra Bhan, I was thinking how very, very lucky I am to be here and not in Bombay.

OWEN: Do you believe in fate?

YOLLAND: Lancey's so like my father. I was watching him last night. He met every group of sappers as they reported in. He checked the field kitchens. He examined the horses. He inspected every single report — even examining the texture of the paper and commenting on the neatness of the handwriting. The perfect colonial servant: not only must the job be done — it must be done with excellence. Father has that drive, too; that dedication; that indefatigable energy. He builds roads — hopping from one end of the Empire to the other. Can't sit still for five minutes. He says himself the longest time he ever sat still was the night before Waterloo when they were waiting for Wellington to make up his mind to attack.

OWEN: What age is he?

YOLLAND: Born in 1789 — the very day the Bastille fell. I've often thought maybe that gave his whole life its character. Do you think it could? He inherited a new world the day he was born — the Year One. Ancient time was at an end. The world had cast off its old skin. There were no longer any frontiers to man's potential. Possibilities were endless and exciting. He still believes that. The Apocalypse is just about to happen . . . I'm afraid I'm a great disappointment to him. I've neither his energy, nor his coherence, nor his belief. Do I believe in fate? The day I arrived in Ballybeg — no, Baile Beag — the moment you brought me in here, I had a curious sensation. It's difficult to describe. It was a momentary sense of discovery; no — not quite a sense of discovery — a sense of recognition, of confirmation of something I half knew instinctively; as if I had stepped . . .

OWEN: Back into ancient time?

YOLLAND: No, no. It wasn't an awareness of *direction* being changed but of experience being of a totally different order. I had moved into a consciousness that wasn't striving nor agitated, but at its ease and with its own conviction and assurance. And when I heard Jimmy Jack and your father swopping stories about Apollo and Cuchulainn and Paris and Ferdia — as if they lived down the road — it was then that I thought — I knew — perhaps I could live here . . . (*Now embarrassed.*) Where's the pot-een?

OWEN: Poteen.

YOLLAND: Poteen — poteen — poteen. Even if I did speak Irish I'd always be an outsider here, wouldn't I? I may learn the password but the language of the tribe will always elude me, won't it? The private core will always be . . . hermetic, won't it?

OWEN: You can learn to decode us.

(HUGH *emerges from upstairs and descends. He is dressed for the road. Today he is physically and mentally jaunty and alert — almost self-consciously jaunty and alert. Indeed, as the scene progresses, one has the sense that he is deliberately parodying himself. The moment* HUGH *gets to the bottom of the steps* YOLLAND *leaps respectfully to his feet.*)

HUGH (*As he descends*):
Quantumvis cursum longum fessumque moratur
Sol, sacro tandem carmine vesper adest.
I dabble in verse, Lieutenant, after the style of Ovid.
(*To* OWEN.) A drop of that to fortify me.

YOLLAND: You'll have to translate it for me.

HUGH: Let's see —
No matter how long the sun may linger on his long and weary journey
At length evening comes with its sacred song.

YOLLAND: Very nice, sir.

HUGH: English succeeds in making it sound . . . plebeian.

OWEN: Where are you off to, Father?

HUGH: An *expeditio,* with three purposes. Purpose A: to acquire a testimonial from our parish priest — (*To* YOLLAND.) a worthy man but barely literate; and since he'll ask me to write it myself, how in all modesty can I do myself justice? (*To* OWEN) Where did this (*Drink*) come from?

OWEN: Anna na mBreag's.

HUGH (*To* YOLLAND): In that case address yourself to it with circumspection.
(*And* HUGH *instantly tosses the drink back in one gulp and grimaces.*)
Aaaaaaagh!
(*Holds out his glass for a refill.*)
Anna na mBreag means Anna of the Lies. And Purpose B: to talk to the builders of the new school about the kind of living accommodation I will require there. I have lived too long like a journeyman tailor.

YOLLAND: Some years ago we lived fairly close to a poet — well, about three miles away.

HUGH: His name?

YOLLAND: Wordsworth — William Wordsworth.

HUGH: Did he speak of me to you?

YOLLAND: Actually I never talked to him. I just saw him out walking — in the distance.

HUGH: Wordsworth? . . . no. I'm afraid we're not familiar with your literature, Lieutenant. We feel closer to the warm Mediterranean. We tend to overlook your island.

YOLLAND: I'm learning to speak Irish, sir.

HUGH: Good.

YOLLAND: Roland's teaching me.

HUGH: Splendid.

YOLLAND: I mean — I feel so cut off from the people here. And I was trying to explain a few minutes ago how remarkable a community this is. To meet people like yourself and Jimmy Jack who actually converse in Greek and Latin. And your place names — what was the one we came across this morning? — Termon, from Terminus, the god of boundaries. It — it — it's really astonishing.

HUGH: We like to think we endure around truths immemorially posited.

YOLLAND: And your Gaelic literature — you're a poet yourself —

HUGH: Only in Latin, I'm afraid.

YOLLAND: I understand it's enormously rich and ornate.

HUGH: Indeed, Lieutenant. A rich language. A rich literature. You'll find, sir, that certain cultures expend on their vocabularies and syntax acquisitive energies and ostentations entirely lacking in their material lives. I suppose you could call us a spiritual people.

OWEN (*Not unkindly; more out of embarrassment before* YOLLAND): Will you stop that nonsense, Father.

HUGH: Nonsense? What nonsense?

OWEN: Do you know where the priest lives?

HUGH: At Lis na Muc, over near . . .

OWEN: No, he doesn't. Lis na Muc, the Fort of the Pigs, has become Swinefort. (*Now turning the pages of the Name-Book — a page per name.*) And to get to Swinefort you pass through Greencastle and Fair Head and Strandhill and Gort and Whiteplains. And the new school isn't at Poll na gCaorach — it's at Sheepsrock. Will you be able to find your way?

(HUGH *pours himself another drink. Then.*)

HUGH: Yes, it is a rich language, Lieutenant, full of the mythologies of fantasy and hope and self-deception — a syntax opulent with tomorrows. It is our response to mud cabins and a diet of potatoes; our only method of replying to . . . inevitabilities.

(*To* OWEN.) Can you give me the loan of half-a-crown? I'll repay you out of the subscriptions I'm collecting for the publication of my new book. (*To* YOLLAND.) It is entitled: 'The Pentaglot Preceptor or Elementary Institute of the English, Greek, Hebrew, Latin and Irish Languages; Particularly Calculated for the Instruction of Such Ladies and Gentlemen as may Wish to Learn without the Help of a Master'.

YOLLAND (*Laughs*): That's a wonderful title!

HUGH: Between ourselves — the best part of the enterprise. Nor do I, in fact, speak Hebrew. And that last phrase — 'without the Help of a Master' — that was written before the new national school was thrust upon me — do you think I ought to drop it now? After all you don't dispose of the cow just because it has produced a magnificent calf, do you?

YOLLAND: You certainly do not.

HUGH: The phrase goes. And I'm interrupting work of moment. (*He goes to the door and stops there.*)

To return briefly to that other matter, Lieutenant. I understand your sense of exclusion, of being cut off from a life here; and I trust you will find access to us with my son's help. But remember that words are signals, counters. They are not immortal. And it can happen — to use an image you'll understand — it can happen that a civilization can be imprisoned in a linguistic contour which no longer matches the landscape of . . . fact.

Gentlemen. (*He leaves.*)

OWEN: 'An *expeditio* with three purposes': the children laugh at him: he always promises three points and he never gets beyond A and B.

YOLLAND: He's an astute man.

OWEN: He's bloody pompous.

YOLLAND: But so astute.

OWEN: And he drinks too much. Is it astute not to be able to adjust for survival? Enduring around truths immemorially posited — hah!

YOLLAND: He knows what's happening.

OWEN: What is happening?

YOLLAND: I'm not sure. But I'm concerned about my part in it. It's an eviction of sorts.

OWEN: We're making a six-inch map of the country. Is there something sinister in that?

YOLLAND: Not in . . .

OWEN: And we're taking place-names that are riddled with confusion and . . .

YOLLAND: Who's confused? Are the people confused?

OWEN: . . . and we're standardizing those names as accurately and as sensitively as we can.

YOLLAND: Something is being eroded.

OWEN: Back to the romance again. Alright! Fine! Fine! Look where we've got to. (*He drops on his hands and knees and stabs a finger at the map.*) We've come to this crossroads. Come here and look at it, man! Look at it! And we call that crossroads Tobair Vree. And why do we call it Tobair Vree? I'll tell you why. Tobair means a well. But what does Vree mean? It's a corruption of Brian — (*Gaelic pronunciation.*) Brian — an erosion of Tobair Bhriain. Because a hundred-and-fifty years ago there used to be a well there, not at the crossroads, mind you — that would be too simple — but in a field close to the crossroads. And an old man called Brian, whose face was disfigured by an enormous growth, got it into his head that the water in that well was blessed; and every day for seven months he went there and bathed his face in it. But the growth didn't go away; and one morning Brian was found drowned in that well. And ever since that crossroads is known as Tobair Vree — even though that well has long since dried up. I know the story because my grandfather told it to me.

But ask Doalty — or Maire — or Bridget — even my father — even Manus — why it's called Tobair Vree; and do you think they'll know? I know they don't know. So the question I put to you, Lieutenant, is this: What do we do with a name like that? Do we scrap Tobair Vree altogether and call it — what? — The Cross? Crossroads? Or do we keep piety with a man long dead, long forgotten, his name 'eroded' beyond recognition, whose trivial little story nobody in the parish remembers?

YOLLAND: Except you.

OWEN: I've left here.

YOLLAND: You remember it.

OWEN: I'm asking you: what do we write in the Name-Book?

YOLLAND: Tobair Vree.

OWEN: Even though the well is a hundred yards from the actual crossroads — and there's no well anyway — and what the hell does Vree mean?

YOLLAND: Tobair Vree.

OWEN: That's what you want?

YOLLAND: Yes.

OWEN: You're certain?

YOLLAND: Yes.

OWEN: Fine. Fine. That's what you'll get.

YOLLAND: That's what you want, too, Roland.
    (*Pause*)

OWEN (*Explodes*): George! For God's sake! *My name is not Roland!*

YOLLAND: What?

OWEN (*Softly*): My name is Owen.
    (*Pause*)

YOLLAND: Not Roland?

OWEN: Owen.

YOLLAND: You mean to say —?

OWEN: Owen.

YOLLAND: But I've been —

OWEN: O–w–e–n.

YOLLAND: Where did Roland come from?

OWEN: I don't know.

YOLLAND: It was never Roland?

OWEN: Never.

YOLLAND: O my God!
    (*Pause. They stare at one another. Then the absurdity of the situation strikes them suddenly. They explode with laughter.* OWEN *pours drinks. As they roll about their lines overlap.*)

YOLLAND: Why didn't you tell me?

OWEN: Do I look like a Roland?

YOLLAND: Spell Owen again.

OWEN: I was getting fond of Roland.

YOLLAND: O my God!

OWEN: O–w–e–n.

YOLLAND: What'll we write —

OWEN: — in the Name-Book?!

YOLLAND: R–o–w–e–n!

OWEN: Or what about Ol-

YOLLAND: Ol- what?

OWEN: Oland!
    (*And again they explode,*
    MANUS *enters. He is very elated.*)

MANUS: What's the celebration?

OWEN: A christening!

YOLLAND: A baptism!

OWEN: A hundred christenings!

YOLLAND: A thousand baptisms! Welcome to Eden!

OWEN: Eden's right! We name a thing and — bang! — it leaps into existence!

YOLLAND: Each name a perfect equation with its roots.

OWEN: A perfect congruence with its reality.
    (*To* MANUS) Take a drink.

YOLLAND: Poteen — beautiful.

OWEN: Lying Anna's poteen.

YOLLAND: Anna na mBreag's poteen.

OWEN: Excellent, George.

YOLLAND: I'll decode you yet.

OWEN (*Offers drink*): Manus?

MANUS: Not if that's what it does to you.

OWEN: You're right. Steady — steady — sober up — sober up.

YOLLAND: Sober as a judge, Owen.
    (MANUS *moves beside* OWEN.)

MANUS: I've got good news! Where's Father?

OWEN: He's gone out. What's the good news?

MANUS: I've been offered a job.

OWEN: Where? (*Now aware of* YOLLAND.) Come on, man — speak in English.

MANUS: For the benefit of the colonist?

OWEN: He's a decent man.

MANUS: Aren't they all at some level?

OWEN: Please.
    (MANUS *shrugs.*)
    He's been offered a job.

YOLLAND: Where?

OWEN: Well — tell us!

MANUS: I've just had a meeting with two men from Inis Meadhon. They want me to go there and start a hedge-school. They're giving me a free house, free turf, and free milk; a rood of standing corn; twelve drills of potatoes; and — (*He stops.*)

OWEN: And what?

MANUS: A salary of £42 a year!

OWEN: Manus, that's wonderful!

MANUS: You're talking to a man of substance.

OWEN: I'm delighted.

YOLLAND: Where's Inis Meadhon?

OWEN: An island south of here. And they came looking for you?

MANUS: Well, I mean to say . . .

(OWEN *punches* MANUS.)

OWEN: Aaaaagh! This calls for a real celebration.

YOLLAND: Congratulations.

MANUS: Thank you.

OWEN: Where are you, Anna?

YOLLAND: When do you start?

MANUS: Next Monday.

OWEN: We'll stay with you when we're there. (*To* YOLLAND.) How long will it be before we reach Inis Meadhon?

YOLLAND: How far south is it?

MANUS: About fifty miles.

YOLLAND: Could we make it by December?

OWEN: We'll have Christmas together. (*Sings*) 'Christmas Day on Inis Meadhon . . .'

YOLLAND (*Toast*): I hope you're very content there, Manus.

MANUS: Thank you.

(YOLLAND *holds out his hand.* MANUS *takes it. They shake warmly.*)

OWEN (*Toast*): Manus.

MANUS (*Toast*): To Inis Meadhon. (*He drinks quickly and turns to leave.*)

OWEN: Hold on — hold on — refills coming up.

MANUS: I've got to go.

OWEN: Come on, man; this is an occasion. Where are you rushing to?

MANUS: I've got to tell Maire.

(MAIRE *enters with her can of milk.*)

MAIRE: You've got to tell Maire what?

OWEN: He's got a job!

MAIRE: Manus?

OWEN: He's been invited to start a hedge-school in Inis Meadhon.

MAIRE: Where?

MANUS: Inis Meadhon — the island! They're giving me £42 a year and . . .

OWEN: A house, fuel, milk, potatoes, corn, pupils, what-not!

MANUS: I start on Monday.

OWEN: You'll take a drink. Isn't it great?

MANUS: I want to talk to you for . . .

MAIRE: There's your milk. I need the can back.

(MANUS *takes the can and runs up the steps.*)

MANUS (*As he goes*): How will you like living on an island?

OWEN: You know George, don't you?

MAIRE: We wave to each other across the fields.

YOLLAND: Sorry – sorry?

OWEN: She says you wave to each other across the fields.

YOLLAND: Yes, we do; oh yes, indeed we do.

MAIRE: What's he saying?

OWEN: He says you wave to each other across the fields.

MAIRE: That's right. So we do.

YOLLAND: What's she saying?

OWEN: Nothing — nothing — nothing.

(*To* MAIRE.) What's the news?

(MAIRE *moves away, touching the text books with her toe.*)

MAIRE: Not a thing. You're busy, the two of you.

OWEN: We think we are.

MAIRE: I heard the Fiddler O'Shea's about. There's some talk of a dance tomorrow night.

OWEN: Where will it be?

MAIRE: Maybe over the road. Maybe at Tobair Vree.

YOLLAND: Tobair Vree!

MAIRE: Yes.

YOLLAND: Tobair Vree! Tobair Vree!

MAIRE: Does he know where I'm saying?

OWEN: Not a word.

MAIRE: Tell him then.

OWEN: Tell him what?

MAIRE: About the dance.

OWEN: Maire says there may be a dance tomorrow night.

YOLLAND (*To* OWEN): Yes? May I come?

(*To* MAIRE) Would anybody object if I came?

MAIRE (*To* OWEN): What's he saying?

OWEN (*To* YOLLAND): Who would object?

MAIRE (*To* OWEN): Did you tell him?

YOLLAND (*To* MAIRE): Sorry – sorry?

OWEN (*To* MAIRE): He says may he come?

MAIRE (*To* YOLLAND): That's up to you.

YOLLAND (*To* OWEN): What does she say?

OWEN (*To* YOLLAND) She says —

YOLLAND (*To* MAIRE): What – what?

MAIRE (*To* OWEN): Well?

YOLLAND (*To* OWEN): Sorry – sorry?

OWEN (*To* YOLLAND): Will you go?

YOLLAND (*To* MAIRE): Yes, yes, if I may.

MAIRE (*To* OWEN): What does he say?

YOLLAND (*To* OWEN): What is she saying?

OWEN: O for God's sake!

(*To* MANUS *who is descending with the empty can.*) You take on this job, Manus.

MANUS: I'll walk you up to the house. Is your mother at home? I want to talk to her.

MAIRE: What's the rush? (*To* OWEN.) Didn't you offer me a drink?

OWEN: Will you risk Anna na mBreag?

MAIRE: Why not?

> (YOLLAND *is suddenly intoxicated. He leaps up on a stool, raises his glass and shouts.*)

YOLLAND: Anna na mBreag! Baile Beag! Inis Meadham! Bombay! Tobair Vree! Eden! And poteen — correct, Owen?

OWEN: Perfect.

YOLLAND: And bloody marvellous stuff it is, too. I love it! Bloody, bloody, bloody marvellous!

> (*Simultaneously with his final 'bloody marvellous' bring up very loud the introductory music of the reel. Then immediately go to black. Retain the music throughout the very brief interval.*)

SCENE TWO

The following night.
This scene may be played in the schoolroom, but it would be preferable to lose — by lighting — as much of the schoolroom as possible, and to play the scene down front in a vaguely 'outside' area.
The music rises to a crescendo. Then in the distance we hear MAIRE *and* YOLLAND *approach — laughing and running. They run on, hand-in-hand. They have just left the dance. Fade the music to distant background. Then after a time it is lost and replaced by guitar music.*
MAIRE *and* YOLLAND *are now down front, still holding hands and excited by their sudden and impetuous escape from the dance.*

MAIRE: O my God, that leap across the ditch nearly killed me.

YOLLAND: I could scarcely keep up with you.

MAIRE: Wait till I get my breath back.

YOLLAND: We must have looked as if we were being chased.

> (*They now realize they are alone and holding hands — the beginnings of embarrassment. The hands disengage. They begin to drift apart. Pause.*)

MAIRE: Manus'll wonder where I've got to.

YOLLAND: I wonder did anyone notice us leave.

> (*Pause. Slightly further apart.*)

MAIRE: The grass must be wet. My feet are soaking.

YOLLAND: Your feet must be wet. The grass is soaking.

> (*Another pause. Another few paces apart. They are now a long distance from one another.*)

YOLLAND (*Indicating himself*): George.

> (MAIRE *nods: Yes – yes. Then*)

MAIRE: Lieutenant George.

YOLLAND: Don't call me that. I never think of myself as Lieutenant.

MAIRE: What – what?

YOLLAND: Sorry — sorry? (*He points to himself again.*) George.

> (MAIRE *nods*: Yes – yes. *Then points to herself.*)

MAIRE: Maire.

YOLLAND: Yes, I know you're Maire. Of course I know you're Maire. I mean I've been watching you night and day for the past . . .

MAIRE (*Eagerly*) :What – what?

YOLLAND (*Points*): Maire. (*Points*) George. (*Points back*) Maire and George.

> (MAIRE *nods: Yes – yes – yes.*)

I — I — I —

MAIRE: Say anything at all. I love the sound of your speech.

YOLLAND (*Eagerly*): Sorry – sorry?

> (*In acute frustration he looks around, hoping for some inspiration that will provide him with communicative means. Now he has a thought: he tries raising his voice and articulating in a staccato style and with equal and absurd emphasis on each word.*)

Every-morning-I-see-you-feeding-brown-hens-and-giving-meal-to-black-calf — (*The futility of it.*) — O my God.

> (MAIRE *smiles. She moves towards him. She will try to communicate in Latin.*)

MAIRE: *Tu es centurio in — in — in exercitu Britannico —*[2]

YOLLAND: Yes – yes? Go on — go on — say anything at all — I love the sound of your speech.

MAIRE: *— et es in castris quae — quae — quae sunt in agro —* (*The futility of it.*) — O my God.

> (YOLLAND *smiles. He moves towards her.*
> *Now for her English words.*) George — water.

YOLLAND: 'Water'? Water! Oh yes — water — water — very good — water — good — good.

MAIRE: Fire.

YOLLAND: Fire — indeed — wonderful — fire, fire, fire — splendid — splendid!

MAIRE: Ah . . . ah . . .

YOLLAND: Yes? Go on.

MAIRE: Earth.

YOLLAND: 'Earth'?

MAIRE: Earth. Earth.

> (YOLLAND *still does not understand.*
> MAIRE *stoops down and picks up a handful of clay. Holding it out*) Earth.

YOLLAND: Earth! Of course — earth! Earth. Earth. Good Lord, Maire, your English is perfect!

MAIRE (*Eagerly*): What – what?

YOLLAND: Perfect English. English perfect.

MAIRE: George —

YOLLAND: That's beautiful — oh that's really beautiful.

MAIRE: George —

YOLLAND: Say it again — say it again —

MAIRE: Shhh. (*She holds her hand up for silence — she is trying to remember her one line of English. Now she remembers it and she delivers the line as if English were her language — easily, fluidly, conversationally.*) George, in Norfolk we besport ourselves around the maypoll.

YOLLAND: Good God, do you? That's where my mother comes from — Norfolk. Norwich actually. Not exactly Norwich town but a small village called Little Walsingham close beside it. But in our own village of Winfarthing we have a maypole too and every year on the first of May — (*He stops abruptly, only now realizing. He stares at her. She in turn misunderstands his excitement.*)

MAIRE (*To herself*): Mother of God, my Aunt Mary wouldn't have taught me something dirty, would she?

(*Pause.*)

YOLLAND *extends his hand to* MAIRE. *She turns away from him and moves slowly across the stage.*)

YOLLAND: Maire.

(*She still moves away.*)

YOLLAND: Maire Chatach.

(*She still moves away.*)

YOLLAND: Bun na hAbhann? (*He says the name softly, almost privately, very tentatively, as if he were searching for a sound she might respond to. He tries again.*) Druim Dubh?

(MAIRE *stops. She is listening.* YOLLAND *is encouraged.*)

Poll na gCaorach. Lis Maol.

(MAIRE *turns towards him.*)

Lis na nGall.

MAIRE: Lis na nGradh.

(*They are now facing each other and begin moving — almost imperceptibly — towards one another.*)

MAIRE: Carraig an Phoill.

YOLLAND: Carraig na Ri. Loch na nEan.

MAIRE: Loch an Iubhair. Machaire Buidhe.

YOLLAND: Machaire Mor. Cnoc na Mona.

MAIRE: Cnoc na nGabhar.

YOLLAND: Mullach.

MAIRE: Port.

YOLLAND: Tor.

MAIRE: Lag. (*She holds out her hands to* YOLLAND. *He takes them. Each now speaks almost to himself/herself.*)

YOLLAND: I wish to God you could understand me.

MAIRE: Soft hands; a gentleman's hands.

YOLLAND: Because if you could understand me I could tell you how I spend my days either thinking of you or gazing up at your house in the hope that you'll appear even for a second.

MAIRE: Every evening you walk by yourself along the Tra Bhan and every morning you wash yourself in front of your tent.

YOLLAND: I would tell you how beautiful you are, curly-headed Maire. I would so like to tell you how beautiful you are.

MAIRE: Your arms are long and thin and the skin on your shoulders is very white.

YOLLAND: I would tell you . . .

MAIRE: Don't stop — I know what you're saying.

YOLLAND: I would tell you how I want to be here — to live here — always — with you — always, always.

MAIRE: 'Always'? What is that word — 'always'?

YOLLAND: Yes – yes; always.

MAIRE: You're trembling.

YOLLAND: Yes, I'm trembling because of you.

MAIRE: I'm trembling, too. (*She holds his face in her hand.*)

YOLLAND: I've made up my mind . . .

MAIRE: Shhhh.

YOLLAND: I'm not going to leave here . . .

MAIRE: Shhh — listen to me. I want you, too, soldier.

YOLLAND: Don't stop — I know what you're saying.

MAIRE: I want to live with you — anywhere — anywhere at all — always — always.

YOLLAND: 'Always'? What is that word — 'always'?

MAIRE: Take me away with you, George.

(*Pause.*

Suddenly they kiss.

SARAH *enters. She sees them. She stands shocked, staring at them. Her mouth works. Then almost to herself.*)

SARAH: Manus . . . Manus!

(SARAH *runs off.*

Music to crescendo.)

---

1   From the end of the seventeenth century until the Great Famine hedge-schools provided education for Catholics forbidden under the Penal laws to have their own schools. The hedge-schools, which gained their name from their construction in the shelter of hedges, were kept secretly. Schoolmasters were appointed often by a committee; the teaching, often associated with pedantry, was aimed at adults or grown children, among whom were poor scholars sometimes from other parts of the country intent on becoming schoolmasters themselves or priests. There are portraits of pre-Famine hedge-schools in William Carleton's *Traits and Stories of the Irish Peasantry* (1830).

2   Latin: You are a soldier in the British army.

MOLLY KEANE
from Molly Keane, *Good Behaviour* (1981)

Molly Keane (1904–96) was born into an Anglo-Irish family in County Kildare. Her first novel, *The Knight of the Cheerful Countenance*, was published in 1926 under her pseudonym M.J. Farrell. *Good Behaviour*, which traces the decline of an Anglo-Irish family in the years around the Great War, was her first novel to appear under her own name. The story is beautifully told through Aroon, the innocent narrator, and in this chapter she misses all the signs (and *double entendres*) of her father's liaison with the Crowhurst twins.

Chapter 18

At luncheon Papa decided for me. He said: 'Got to go to the Wine Cellars. And the car's not her burning best either. Care to come along in case she stops with me? We'll get her sharpened up while we're busy in the Cellars.'

'So long as we don't have to go to tea with the Crowhurst girls.'

The girls lived near the Wine Cellars and he had often been known to call in and bask for an hour in their acidulated adoration. I can only suppose the girls and their lives were like a comic strip to Papa. He followed their activities, some of them rather shady; it was a game, laughing at their contrivances. Their bitter, nipped tongues kept him guessing at what they might say next. He liked to nose out their small scandalous escapades — nothing like love affairs, poor things, of course not, more likely a sharpish bit of horse dealing. One of their pleasures was not telling. It put an edge on everything they did or said. Poor unhappy things. Much as I pitied and faintly despised them, they had the knack of making me feel I was lolling helplessly through an objectless, boring life. I never wanted to see them, or listen to them, or even to eat any of the delightful food they produced from air, or sea, or garden.

Papa, I knew, felt very differently about their ways of overriding poverty, rejecting its limitations. He was fascinated by all they had taught themselves about horses, and never tired of analysing the curious theories they accepted from that wild tinker fellow they employed as a part-time groom. He could charm warts, or go up to any horse, where another dare not lay his hand. Besides being so knowledgeable on horses and horse lore, they knew the cures for all the diseases from which dogs could suffer. They despised vets. Even when one of their viperous miniature dachshunds was in hideous whelping difficulties, they used their own clever fingers, and an hour after achieving a safe delivery for their darling they would be sitting on a sofa at their petit point,[1] their hands as elegantly and carefully employed as those of any ancestress. They were very well born and never forgot it.

Today I could sense Papa making his way wordlessly towards a cup of tea with Nod and Blink; it was a delayed action. At the garage he ordered work on the car which must take hours to accomplish. At the Wine Cellars we stayed a long time ordering good things in the dark drift of smells in the grocery department. After that came the real matter of the visit, wines and their years and qualities, their prices unimportant when compared with the delights Papa was accumulating.

When, at half past four, I heard him ask for a bottle of Gordon's gin, a bottle of Noilly Prat, 'and, of course, a lemon,' I knew we were bound for tea with the Crowhurst girls, bringing a little present with us. 'Calling for this lot later,' he indicated his purchases.

The elder of the two gentlemanly old gnomes who owned the Wine Cellars was ushering us out. 'And if it would be convenient, Major,' he said, laughing a little, 'we were wondering could you let us have something on account.'

'Of course, of course — what a terrible pair you are. Why haven't you sent it in long ago?'

'We did, Major. Excuse us, but we have it furnished a few little times now.' It was an extreme apology and he accepted it, royally.

'That's right.' He hobbled away, very lame, still talking. 'Times are awful, always are awful, send it in again *at once*, do you hear me? Don't delay, never delay, and I'll let you have a cheque by return of post.'

Out in the sunny street he was soon walking more soundly, heading for the Crowhursts without any unnecessary explanations to me. I went along beside him, the gin under one arm, the vermouth under the other, the lemon in my handbag.

'Can you manage, darling, bless you? Poor things, they do need it so.' He put me on his own level, while they sank to the position of being simply pitiable.

I was less able to pity them as we clicked open the neat iron gate, painted by themselves, and walked towards the house, past groupings of electric blue hydrangeas. 'How do they do it?' Papa paused to admire. 'And they won't tell a soul.' His admiration of the cruel electric blue and the girls' secrecy was equal. Round the corner of the little Regency house, a blazing autumn border caught his eye. 'Good girls, good girls,' he murmured, 'redhot pokers — my favourites.'

Blink opened their door to us. She was close-lipped and elegant and nearly thirty. I thought the twins hopelessly aged. 'How awfully kind,' she said to Papa, taking the gin away from me. Then: 'Oh, Aroon,' as if she only now saw I was there.

The hall, where we delayed, was that of a small country gentleman. Leather-covered sticks and hunting whips lay on an oak chest. A series of good prints hung on the walls. A water dish marked DOG and a trug of clean garden tools and powerful secateurs stood together in a corner.

In the drawingroom, where dachshunds lay like a nest of serpents in a round, well-cushioned basket, tea was laid for four. The position of the teatray commanded a splendid view of the blazing border, where huge, meaty dahlias (fit flesh for cannibals I always think) were divided, and given added value, by fish-shaped drifts of Michaelmas daisies, and grey-blue pools of agapanthus lilies. Blink looked away from her border with affected indifference, giving Papa time to admire and wonder at its perfection. Presently Nod (Papa's favourite one) came in with a trayful of beautiful food.

'We heard you were in the Wine Cellars,' she said unaffectedly, 'so we hoped you would come to tea.'

'You made all these sandwiches just on the chance?' Papa said gratefully. 'Just for us? Good girls.'

'Well, Blink and I could have finished them for dinner —' they never talked about supper — 'the more we eat, the thinner we grow.' She looked at me as if she were going to apologize for an unfortunate remark, and under her veiled glance I felt my bosoms and bottom swelling up through my head. I was so conscious of their size and presence they could have toppled me off my legs.

We had China tea out of thin, shallow cups, and I found the fish pâté sandwiches irresistible. The dachshunds crawled out of their basket to join in the pickings, and one of them almost took my hand off when I gave her a tiny piece of buttered scone.

'*Please* don't feed the brutes,' Nod said gently. Then with chill command: 'Basket, girls, to your basket.' They slunk away, remorseful and vindictive. 'The postman won't come here any more,' she told Papa

with great amusement. 'They've bitten him twice now and one bite festered. Blink's making a letter-box for the gate.'

'Big enough to take garden catalogues and the *Times*.' Blink spoke seriously of her project. 'They gave me a lovely old brass slit or slot at the post office, and I picked up a beautiful piece of teak on the beach — just the thing.'

'You'll make a job of it,' Papa said, approvingly. 'You should use copper nails.'

Now and then they spoke to me politely and handed me plates of food or filled up my tiny cup. But I knew their joint unjealous interest focused entirely on Papa. Tea over, Papa provided us each with a cigarette from his never-empty case. 'I knew I meant to ask you something,' he said to Nod. 'How's Fred Astaire's leg?'

'I'm afraid he's finished,' she said.

'Oh, that's a great pity. Best hunter in the country. Shall I go and put my hand on it?' There was nothing he liked more than fiddling round lame horses. Now there would be an hour of suggestion and counter-suggestion. When I got up to follow them out of the room Blink spoke unhurriedly from behind the teatray.

'You've seen darling Fred often enough, dear fellow, wouldn't you rather look at Heidi's puppies? They're very sweet.'

'Shouldn't we call Papa?' I said, after a lingering examination of Heidi's litter. 'The garage will be shut soon.'

'Oh yes, if you must. Nod's so upset about Fred Astaire, let's give them a few minutes while I get hold of some glasses.'

Blink took another ten minutes to find and polish the right glasses, and the only knife suitable for paring zest from a lemon. In the drawingroom, where we carried the tray of drinks, she said: 'Oh, wouldn't it be nice if we cleared away tea? Could you feed Heidi while I tidy it up?'

'No,' I said, 'you feed Heidi, let me do this.'

'You can't really be afraid of her; she's so gentle.' She left me blushing with rage as I piled up the doll-size cups and plates.

'Oh,' Nod said, coming in with Papa, 'that awful Blink — she always finds someone else to do her work.' She spoke with indulgent approval.

'You want to watch it,' Papa said. 'Aroon's champion cup smasher.' Nod took the tray from me immediately and carried it away. 'I don't know about you, sweetheart,' Papa said, when she had gone, 'but I need a drink. Martinis for us all — sort of — no ice.' When the girls came back he was paring lemon peel.

'Perfect blade,' he said, 'worth anything.' He pinched the peel into their glasses and handed them with grave concern that the drinks should be absolutely as they liked them. They might have been glamorous women. He was far too kind, I thought. After two powerful martinis Papa roused himself out of a pleasant lull to say to Blink: 'I haven't seen your letter-box yet, have I?'

'Oh, *Papa*.' Kindness was one thing, but this was silly. 'The garage will be shut. We can't walk home.'

'No,' he agreed, 'of course not. The old leg, you know. Look — you nip down to the garage, child, and bring the car up here, if you'll be so sweet. I'll be waiting at the gate.' 'I'll be waiting at the gate' — the words had a dying fall, a promise to me alone, the chosen companion.

At the garage, the owner was ready to tell me that nothing whatever had been done about the car. It was more than one afternoon's work and an expensive job. Would the Major call at his convenience to discuss it, and would I remind him about the account?

'The Major will call on his way home,' I said. 'Will you be here?'

'I will, if there's any chance he'll call.' He sounded as though he doubted the likelihood. I felt he ought to have said 'the Major,' not 'he.'

Of course there was no one waiting at the gate. I had hardly expected it. Papa wasn't in the drawing-room either. Nod was snuggled down on the sofa with five dachshunds and her petit-point. She glanced up as I came in. 'I expect they'll be here soon,' she said, settling down again.

Presently they came, walking slowly together over the perfect grass, almost more brilliant than the awful border around which it curved, neat and level as water. Papa stopped and stooped (always a job for him) to pick something out of the grass. 'Look what I've found,' he said when they came in, as unhurriedly as though it had been three o'clock. 'Plantain in the lawn. It's disgraceful. I am shocked.'

They did not deny the plantain. 'Have a drink,' they suggested amiably.

'I'm not sure if Aroon will allow it.' He looked at me remorsefully. 'And what about the car, pet? All right?'

'Not all right,' I said. 'He's done exactly nothing and he wants you to call and see him this evening.' All the ease and pleasure went from Papa's face and attitude. Suddenly he was a tired, middle-aged, worried gentleman, with bags under his eyes, licking his lips uncertainly. A gentleman on a stick, gaiety spent, his son dead — a thought to be escaped: Hubert's horrible death[2] never confronted.

'I'm awfully tired,' he said. 'Take me home. We're going to be late for dinner and I ordered a soufflé. Why did I? Let's be off, darling. No, I don't *want* it,' he refused the offered drink rather crossly, then picked up the glass. 'Oh, you *are* naughty,'' he said to the girl who gave it to him.

On the path to the gate the girls' pigeons were carrying on as if it were Trafalgar Square. 'You forgot their feed,' Nod accused Blink. 'How could you?' Fantails and birds with heads like Pekinese dogs circled them, cuddling into their shoulders, toppling over red feet on the path. It was a Walter Crane picture — a picture of two lives of innocent content and industry, full of birds and flowers and dogs, not to mention dear old horses and minute tapestry works.

'Well, we made their day,' Papa said. 'I suppose that's something. You drive. Why are you turning round?'

'The garage,' I reminded him. 'The wine.'

'No, no, no. Not tonight. First things first. Let's get home to dinner.'

1   Needlework.
2   In the Great War.

JOHN BANVILLE
from John Banville, *Kepler* (1981)

John Banville (1945–   ) was born in Wexford and educated by the Christian Brothers. In 1988 he became literary editor at *The Irish Times*. *Kepler* is one a series of novels exploring the imaginative life of great scientists from the past that began with *Doctor Copernicus* (1976). Here in this extract Kepler takes a leap forward in his understanding of the harmony of the universe.

He was after the eternal laws that govern the harmony of the world. Through awful thickets, in darkest night, he stalked his fabulous prey. Only the stealthiest of hunters had been vouchsafed a shot at it, and he, grossly armed with the blunderbuss of his defective mathematics, what chance had he? crowded round by capering clowns hallooing and howling and banging their bells whose names were Paternity, and Responsibility, and Domestgoddamnedicity. Yet O, he had seen it once, briefly, that mythic bird, a speck, no more than a speck, soaring at an immense height. It was not to be forgotten, that glimpse.

The 19th of July, 1595, at 27 minutes precisely past 11 in the morning: that was the moment. He was then, if his calculations were accurate, 23 years, 6 months, 3 weeks, 1 day, 20 hours and 57 minutes, give or take a few tens of seconds, old.

Afterwards he spent much time poring over these figures, searching out hidden significances. The set of date and time, added together, gave a product 1,652. Nothing there that he could see. Combining the integers of that total he got 14, which was twice 7, the mystical number. Or perhaps it was simply that 1652 was to be the year of his death. He would be eighty-one. (He laughed: with his health?) He turned to the second set, his age on that momentous July day. These figures were hardly more promising. Combined, not counting the year, they made a quantity whose only significance seemed to be that it was divisible by 5, leaving him the product 22, the age at which he had left Tübingen. Well, that was not much. But if he halved 22 and subtracted 5 (that 5 again!), he got 6, and it was at six that he had been taken by his mother to the top of Gallows Hill to view the comet of 1577. And 5, what did that busy 5 signify? Why, it was the number of the intervals between the planets, the number of notes in the arpeggio of the spheres, the five-tone scale of the world's music! . . . if his calculations were accurate.

He had been working for six months on what was to become the *Mysterium cosmographicum*, his first book. His circumstances were easier then. He was still unmarried, had not yet even heard Barbara's name, and was living at the Stiftsschule in a room that was cramped and cold, but his own. Astronomy at first had been a pastime merely, an extension of the mathematical games he had liked to play as a student at Tübingen. As time went on, and his hopes for his new life in Graz turned sour, this exalted playing more and more obsessed him. It was a thing apart, a realm of order to set against the ramshackle real world in which he was imprisoned. For Graz was a kind of prison. Here in this town, which they were pleased to call a city, the Styrian capital, ruled over by narrow-minded merchants and a papist prince, Johannes Kepler's spirit was in chains, his talents manacled, his great speculative gift strapped upon the rack of school-mastering — right! yes! laughing and snarling, mocking himself — endungeoned, by God! He was twenty-three.

It was a pretty enough town. He was impressed when first he glimpsed it, the river, the spires, the castle-crowned hill, all blurred and bright under a shower of April rain. There seemed a largeness here, a generosity, which he fancied he could see even in the breadth and balance of the buildings, so different from the beetling architecture of his native Württemberg towns. The people too appeared different. They were promenaders much given to public discourse and dispute, and Johannes was reminded that he had come a long way from home, that he was almost in Italy. But it was all an illusion. Presently, when he had examined more closely the teeming streets, he realized that the filth and the stench, the cripples and beggars and berserks, were the same here as anywhere else. True, they were Protestant loonies, it was Protestant filth, and a Protestant heaven those spires sought, hence the wider air hereabout: but the Archduke was a rabid Catholic, and the place was crawling with Jesuits, and even then at the Stiftsschule there was talk of disestablishment and closure.

He, who had been such a brilliant student, detested teaching. In his classes he experienced a weird frustration. The lessons he had to expound were always, always just somewhere off to the side of what really interested him, so that he was forever holding himself in check, as a boatman presses a skiff against the run of the river. The effort exhausted him, left him sweating and dazed. Frequently the rudder gave way, and he was swept off helplessly on the flood of his enthusiasm, while his poor dull students stood abandoned on the receding bank, waving weakly.

The Stiftsschule was run in the manner of a military academy. Any master who did not beat blood out of his boys was considered lax. (Johannes did his best, but on the one occasion when he could not avoid administering a flogging his victim was a great grinning fellow almost as old as he, and a head taller.) The standard of learning was high, sustained by the committee of supervisors and its phalanx of inspectors. Johannes greatly feared the inspectors. They dropped in on classes unannounced, often in pairs, and listened in silence from the back, while his handful of pupils sat with arms folded, hugging themselves, and gazed at him, gleefully attentive, waiting for him to make a fool of himself. Mostly he obliged, twitching and stammering as he wrestled with the tangled threads of his discourse.

'You must try to be calm,' Rector Papius told him. 'You tend to rush at things, I think, forgetting perhaps that your students do not have your quickness of mind. They cannot follow you, they become confused, and then they complain to me, or . . .' he smiled '. . . or their fathers do.'

'I know, I know,' Johannes said, looking at his hands. They sat in the rector's room overlooking the central courtyard of the school. It was raining. There was wind in the chimney, and balls of smoke rolled out of the fireplace and hung in the air around them, making his eyes sting. 'I talk too quickly, and say things before I have had time to consider my words. Sometimes in the middle of a class I change my mind and begin to speak of some other subject, or realize that what I have been saying is imprecise and begin all over again to explain the matter in more detail.' He shut his mouth, squirming; he was making it worse. Dr Papius frowned at the fire. 'You see, Herr Rector, it is my *cupiditas speculandi*[1] that leads me astray.'

'Yes,' the older man said mildly, scratching his chin, 'there is in you perhaps too much . . . passion. But I would not wish to see a young man suppress his natural enthusiasm. Perhaps, Master Kepler, you were not meant for teaching?'

Johannes looked up in alarm, but the rector was regarding him only with concern, and a touch of amusement. He was a gentle, somewhat scattered person, a scholar and physician; no doubt he knew what it was to stand all day in class wishing to be elsewhere. He had always shown kindness to this strange little man from Tübingen, who at first had so appalled the more stately members of the staff with his frightful manners and disconcerting blend of friendliness, excitability and arrogance. Papius had more than once defended him to the supervisors.

'I am not a good teacher,' Johannes mumbled, 'I know. My gifts lie in other directions.'

'Ah yes,' said the rector, coughing; 'your astronomy.' He peered at the inspectors' report on the desk before him. 'You teach *that* well, it seems?'

'But I have no students!'

'Not your fault — Pastor Zimmermann himself says here that astronomy is not everyone's meat. He recommends that you be put to teaching arithmetic and Latin rhetoric in the upper school, until we can find more pupils eager to become astronomers.'

Johannes understood that he was being laughed at, albeit gently.

'They are ignorant barbarians!' he cried suddenly, and a log fell out of the fire. 'All they care for is hunting and warring and looking for fat dowries for their heirs. They hate and despise philosophy and philosophers. They they they — they do not *deserve* . . .' He broke off, pale with rage and alarm. These mad outbursts must stop.

Rector Papius smiled the ghost of a smile. 'The inspectors?'

'The . . .?'

'I understood you to be describing our good Pastor Zimmermann and his fellow inspectors. It was of them we were speaking.'

Johannes put a hand to his brow. 'I — I meant of course those who will not send their sons for proper instruction.'

'Ah. But I think, you know, there are many among our noble families, and among the merchants also, who would consider astronomy *not* a proper subject for their sons to study. They burn at the stake poor wretches who have had less dealings with the moon than you do in your classes. I am not defending this benighted attitude to your science, you understand, but only drawing it to your attention, as it is my —'

'But —'

'— As it is my *duty* to do.'

They sat and eyed each other, Johannes sullen, the rector apologetically firm. Grey rain wept on the window, the smoke billowed. Johannes sighed. 'You see, Herr Rector, I cannot —'

'But try, will you, Master Kepler: try?'

He tried, he tried, but how could he be calm? His brain teemed. A chaos of ideas and images churned within him. In class he fell silent more and more frequently, standing stock still, deaf to the sniggering of this students, like a crazed hierophant. He traipsed the streets in a daze, and more than once was nearly run down by horses. He wondered if he were ill. Yet it was more as if he were . . . in love! In love, that is, not with any individual object, but generally. The notion, when he hit on it, made him laugh.

At the beginning of 1595 he received a sign, if not from God himself then from a lesser deity surely, one of those whose task is to encourage the elect of this world. His post at the Stiftsschule carried with it the title of calendar maker for the province of Styria. The previous autumn, for a fee of twenty florins from the public coffers, he had drawn up an astrological calendar for the coming year, predicting great cold and an invasion by the Turks. In January there was such a frost that shepherds in the Alpine farms froze to death on the hillsides, while on the first day of the new year the Turk launched a campaign which, it was said, left the whole country from Neustadt to Vienna devastated. Johannes was charmed with this prompt vindication of his powers (and secretly astonished). O a sign, yes, surely. He set to work in earnest on the cosmic mystery.

He had not the solution, yet; he was still posing the questions. The first of these was: Why are there just six planets in the solar system? Why not five, or seven, or a thousand for that matter? No one, so far as he knew, had ever thought to ask it before. It became for him the fundamental mystery. Even the formulation of such a question struck him as a singular achievement.

He was a Copernican. At Tübingen his teacher Michael Mästlin had introduced him to that Polish master's world system. There was for Kepler something almost holy, something redemptive almost, in that vision of an ordered clockwork of sun-centred spheres. And yet he saw, from the beginning, that there was a defect, a basic flaw in it which had forced Copernicus into all manner of small tricks and evasions. For while the *idea* of the system, as outlined in the first part of *De revolutionibus*, was self-evidently an eternal truth, there was in the working out of the theory an ever increasing accumulation of paraphernalia — the epicycles, the equant point, all that — necessitated surely by some awful original accident. It was as if the master had let fall from trembling hands his marvellous model of the world's working, and on the ground it had picked up in its spokes and the fine-spun wire of its frame bits of dirt and dead leaves and the dried husks of worn-out concepts.

Copernicus was dead fifty years, but now for Johannes he rose again, a mournful angel that must be wrestled with before he could press on to found his own system. He might sneer at the epicycles and the equant point, but they were not to be discarded easily. The Canon from Ermland had been, he suspected, a greater mathematician than ever Styria's calendar maker would be. Johannes raged against his own inadequacies. He might know there was a defect, and a grave one, in the Copernican system, but it was a different matter to find it. Nights he would start awake thinking he had heard the old man his adversary laughing at him, goading him.

And then he made a discovery. He realized that it was not so much in what he *had* done that Copernicus had erred: his sin had been one of omission. The great man, Johannes now understood, had been concerned only to see the nature of things demonstrated, not explained. Dissatisfied with the Ptolemaic conception of the world, Copernicus had devised a better, a more elegant system, which yet, for all its seeming radicalism, was intended only, in the schoolman's phrase, to save the phenomena, to set up a model which need not be empirically true, but only plausible according to the observations.

Then had Copernicus believed that his system was a picture of reality, or had he been satisfied that it agreed, more or less, with appearances? Or did the question arise? There was no sustained music in that old man's world, only chance airs and fragments, broken harmonies, scribbled cadences. It would be Kepler's task to draw it together, to make it sing. For truth was the missing music. He lifted his eyes to the bleak light of winter in the window and hugged himself. Was it not wonderful, the logic of things? Troubled by an inelegance in the Ptolemaic system, Copernicus had erected his great monument to the sun, in which there was embedded the flaw, the pearl, for Johannes Kepler to find.

But the world had not been created in order that it should sing. God was not frivolous. From the start he held to this, that the song was incidental, arising naturally from the harmonious relation of things. Truth itself was, in a way, incidental. Harmony was all. (Something wrong, something wrong! but he ignored it.) And harmony, as Pythagoras had shown, was the product of mathematics. Therefore the harmony of the spheres must conform to a mathematical pattern. That such a pattern existed Johannes had no doubt. It was his principal axiom that nothing in the world was created by God without a plan the basis of which is to be found in geometrical quantities. And man is godlike precisely, and only, because he can think in terms that mirror the divine pattern. He had written: The mind grasps a matter so much the more correctly the closer it approaches pure quantities as its source. Therefore his method for the task of identifying the cosmic design must be, like the design itself, founded in geometry.

Spring came to Graz and, as always, took him by surprise. He looked out one day and there it was in the flushed air, a quickening, a sense of vast sudden swooping, as if the earth had hurtled into a narrowing bend of space. The city sparkled, giving off light from throbbing window panes and polished stone, from blue and gold pools of rain in the muddied streets. Johannes kept much indoors. It disturbed him, how closely the season matched his present mood of restlessness and obscure longing. The Shrovetide carnival milled under his window unheeded, except when a comic bugle blast or the drunken singing of revellers shattered his concentration, and he bared his teeth in a soundless snarl.

Perhaps he was wrong, perhaps the world was not an ordered construct governed by immutable laws? Perhaps God, after all, like the creatures of his making, prefers the temporal to the eternal, the makeshift to the perfected, the toy bugles and bravos of misrule to the music of the spheres. But no, no, despite these doubts, no: his God was above all a god of order. The world works by geometry, for geometry is the earthly paradigm of divine thought.

Late into the nights he laboured, and stumbled through his days in a trance. Summer came. He had been working without cease for six months, and all he had achieved, if achievement it could be called, was the conviction that it was not with the planets themselves, their positions and velocities, that he must chiefly deal, but with the intervals between their orbits. The values for these distances were those set out by Copernicus, which were not much more reliable than Ptolemy's, but he had to assume, for his sanity's sake, that they were sound enough for his purpose. Time and time over he combined and recombined them, searching for the relation which they hid. Why are there just six planets? That was a question, yes. But a profounder asking was, why are there just these distances between them? He waited, listening for the whirr of wings. On that ordinary morning in July came the answering angel. He was in class. The day was warm and bright. A fly buzzed in the tall window, a rhomb of sunlight lay at his feet. His students, stunned with boredom, gazed over his head out of glazed eyes. He was demonstrating a theorem out of Euclid — afterwards, try as he might, he could not remember which — and had prepared on the blackboard an equilateral triangle. He took up the big wooden compass, and immediately, as it always contrived to do, the monstrous thing bit him. With his wounded thumb in his mouth he turned to the easel and began to trace two circles, one within the triangle touching it on three sides, the second circumscribed and intersecting the vertices. He stepped back, into that box of dusty sunlight, and blinked, and suddenly something, his heart perhaps, dropped and bounced, like an athlete performing a miraculous feat upon a trampoline, and he thought, with rapturous inconsequence: I shall live forever. The ratio of the outer to the inner circle was identical with that of the orbits of Saturn and Jupiter, the furthermost planets, and here, within these circles, determining that ratio, was inscribed an equilateral triangle, the fundamental figure in geometry. Put therefore between the orbits of Jupiter and Mars a square, between Mars and earth a pentagon, between earth and Venus a . . . Yes. O yes. The diagram, the easel, the very walls of the room dissolved to a shimmering liquid, and young Master Kepler's lucky pupils were treated to the rare and gratifying spectacle of a teacher swabbing tears from his eyes and trumpeting juicily into a dirty handkerchief.

1   Latin: passion for speculating.

MEDBH McGUCKIAN
from Medbh McGuckian, *The Flower Master* (1982)

Medbh McGuckian (1950–   ) was born in Belfast and educated at Queens University, Belfast. She is among the best known of contemporary women poets in Ireland, and her volumes include *Venus and the Rain* (1984), *On Ballycastle Beach* (1988), *Marconi's Cottage* (1992) and *Captain Lavender* (1994). The following poem is a fine example of the way McGuckian shifts the ground of her argument and beckons the reader into a physically alive but essentially interior landscape. Probably no two readers will agree on what this poem means: postmodernist play, female identity-in-construction, Lawrentian nature/power poem, a Wallace Stevens poem rearranging perception/experience.

THE FLOWER MASTER

Like foxgloves in the school of the grass moon
We come to terms with shade, with the principle
Of enfolding space. Our scissors in brocade,
We learn the coolness of straight edges, how
To stroke gently the necks of daffodils
And make them throw their heads back to the sun.
We slip the thready stems of violets, delay
The loveliness of the hibiscus dawn with quiet ovals,
Spirals of feverfew like water splashing,

The papery legacies of bluebells. We do
Sea-fans with sea-lavender, moon-arrangements
Roughly for the festival of moon-viewing.

This black container calls for sloes, sweet
Sultan, dainty nipplewort, in honour
Of a special guest, who summoned to the
Tea ceremony, must stoop to our low doorway,
Our fontanelle, the trout's dimpled feet.

PAUL MULDOON
from Paul Muldoon, *Quoof* (1983)

'Quoof' is another good example of Muldoon's playful sensibility and is not easy to paraphrase.

QUOOF

How often have I carried our family word
for the hot water bottle
to a strange bed,
as my father would juggle a red-hot half-brick
in an old sock
to his childhood settle.[1]
I have taken it into so many lovely heads
or laid it between us like a sword.

An hotel room in New York City
with a girl who spoke hardly any English,
my hand on her breast
like the smouldering one-off spoor of the yeti
or some other shy beast
that has yet to enter the language.

1   A settle-bed was a seat by day and a bed by night.

PAUL DURCAN
from Paul Durcan, *Jumping the Tracks with Angela* (1983)

Another delightfully seditious poem which takes its cue from the cobblestones that
grace the quads at Trinity College, Dublin.

TRINITY COLLEGE DUBLIN, 1983

I don't think you know what *cobblestones* are . . .
I think that it is just that you like the sound of the words.
Look, do you see that girl over there in the blue jacket?
The tall girl . . . yes . . . in the red slippers?
With the small bloke in the long black overcoat?
Do you know that in her life — she's about
     twenty-seven —
She has made love about nine hundred times?
Whereas he to whom she is talking

— He's about forty-three —
He has made love about five — maybe ten — times.
The reason that he is lying flat on his back on the
     ground
And that she is standing with one foot on his forehead
Is that he's nuts about her and she's not altogether
     quite sane about him.
That's what *cobblestones* are for; that's what *cobblestones*
are.

ROY McFADDEN
from John Boyd (ed.), *The Selected Roy McFadden* (1983)

Roy McFadden, author of 'The Severed Hand' (1969) (see above p. 763), was born in 1921 and worked as a solicitor in Belfast. Author of several volumes of verse including *The Heart's Townland* (1947), *A Watching Brief* (1978) and *Letters to the Hinterland* (1986) (see below pp. 992, 1036), he co-edited the literary journal *Rann* from 1948 onwards. There is a recent interview with McFadden in *Irish Studies Review*, 17, Winter 1996–97. Here in this poem we watch a solicitor at work transforming the language of the law into the language of literature.

CONVEYANCER

I remember your saying
That among our acquaintances
There was scarcely a reader who
Was not ambitiously, however covertly,
    A writer also; who
Read just for love without a vested interest too.

I omitted to mention
The withdrawn conveyancer
Who, throughout my apprentice years,
Taciturn in his tent of blue tobacco smoke,
    Probed at ancient roots
Of title in shrinking lease and wizened fee farm grant.

Compulsively weeding
Through recitals and convenants,
He examined the drift of a field
Towards a ramification of streets and sites with red
        boundaries,
    Down to the last demise,
Where a brisker narration begins new chapters of lives
        and deaths.

You could say it was factual,
A sort of biography
Of properties shaping a town;
And their people coming and going, appurtenant, in a
        word,
    Till they claimed the ultimate word,
Unanswerable at the end, in the form of the probated
        will.

Or again, alternatively,
That his reading was really romance;
For the parchment pages proclaim
A myth of ownership for ever-and-a-day,
    Whose hereditaments
Are sanctioned by yellowing skin mortgaged to
        truculent time.

JULIE O'CALLAGHAN
from Julie O'Callaghan, *Edible Anecdotes* (1983)

Julie O'Callaghan (1954–   ) was born in Chicago and now lives in Dublin. A writer of poetry for children, she has also composed verse for adults: see for example *Edible Anecdotes* (1983) and *What's What* (1991). Here she takes a swipe at the expression of a certain form of Irish-American relations.

A Tourist Comments on the Land of His Forefathers

Take Dublin for instance:
what is it anyway?
You walk across O'Connell Bridge,
little kids begging — gives the place atmosphere;
ya look around through a flea-bitten crowd
and wonder why they stay here.
Their cousins in Milwaukee write,
saying *come on over* — *we'll fix ya up*.
But no, it's safer going to ceilis and mass,
please God-ing and making themselves believe that
Grafton Street is elegant and an ice-cream cone
in summer is high adventure.

As for me, I got some great shots of the place
and as soon as I get back to the U S of A
I'll put them right where they belong:
first in the projector shining on our living-room wall
and then in a bright yellow Kodak box
next to all the others in my sock drawer.
No offence meant.

BRENDAN KENNELLY
from Brendan Kennelly, *Cromwell* (1983)

Cromwell by Brendan Kennelly, author of 'My Dark Fathers' (1964) (see above p. 781),
is a remarkable sequence of poems on the seventeenth-century English statesman who
entered into the Irish psyche not as the military genius and inspirer of Parliamentary
opposition to the Monarchy but as the cruel slayer of the native Irish. Here in this
selection taken from different parts of the sequence Kennelly — to make what I take to
be a larger point — plays havoc with pious and tragic readings of Irish history.

MAGIC

Oliver Cromwell's first season as
Manager of Drogheda[1] United was not
Impressive. A bit of a calamit-
y, in fact. 'Get rid of Cromwell' howled
The Drogheda fans, 'Send him to Home Farm,
Athlone, St Pats, Bohemians, U.C.D.[2]
The bastard has brought nothing but harm
To our side. Fling him into the sea!'
Oliver was hauled up before the Board
And asked to account for his performance
Or lack of it. Oliver kept his head.
'We'll top the table yet, I give you my word,
Deep winter approaches, keep your patience,
I'll work magic under floodlights' Oliver said.

WINE

William of Orange[3] barged into the room
In *Sunnyside* where Cromwell was resting
After chasing a fox from Mitchelstown
To Caherciveen, in vain. 'What's cooking?'
Barked Oliver, 'Why horse in here like that?
My bones are coming asunder after that chase
And the bloody fox escaped. Too much art
For these Irish hounds. But, William, what's this
Distress I see written across your face?'
'Oliver' sweated William 'I'm back from the Boyne
Where I drank deep draughts from victory's cup.
And yet, doubt chews my heart, I must confess.'

'Why should it?' queried Oliver.

       'Where's the wine?'
Croaked William, 'I think I've fucked things up!'

A BIT OF A SWAP

When the Pope came to Ireland, William of Orange
Was chosen by the two Houses of Government
To talk to the Pontiff on a wide range
Of subjects. William was subtle and blunt,
The right mix for a man who'd cope with the Pope.

'Holy Father' smiled William, mustering his
    intellectual forces,
'My chief concern is Irish industry. I hope
You'll like my suggestion about thoroughbred horses.
I understand you have a deep interest in bulls[4]
And own, in fact, some choice Italian herds.
Swap bulls for horses, that's what I propose.'

The Pontiff ruminated: 'My child, your sales
In horses are about to soar. My word
On that. As for my bulls to you, who knows?'

'THEREFORE, I SMILE'

'Under it all' Oliver said, 'The problem was simple.
How could I make Ireland work?
The Irish hate work, not knowing what it means.
I do. Work exists. It is inevitable and stark,
A dull, fierce necessity. Later ages may consider it
Superfluous but my glimpses of this world were true.
I looked, I saw, I considered, I did what
Was necessary. To live is to work. To be is to do.

Put a man in a field
A soldier fighting a wall
A wife in bed
A whore in a street
A king on a throne

Someone must dig a grave for the dead
And the dead must rot.

Even dead flesh works in the earth
But not the Irish, Buff,[5] not you, not your countrymen.
They will prattle, argue, drink, yarn, but not
Work. Someone had to teach them

Not to idle their lives away.
I taught them to do things my way.
Against their will
I gave them a style.
I tendered them the terrible gift of my name,
Knowing they would make songs about me
Echoing curses soaked in verbal bile
Twisted poems and stories
To make me an excuse for what they
Would fail to do, to be, being themselves.

I am Oliver Cromwell still.

Therefore, I smile.'

A RUNNING BATTLE

What are they doing now? I imagine Oliver
Buying a Dodge, setting up as a taxi-driver
Shunting three dozen farmers to Listowel Races.
I see Ed Spenser, father of all our graces
In verse, enshrined as a knife-minded auctioneer
Addicted to Woodbines[6] and Kilkenny beer,
Selling Parish Priests' shiny furniture
To fox-eyed housewives and van-driving tinkers.
William of Orange is polishing pianos
In convents and other delicate territories,
His nose purple from sipping turpentine.
Little island is Big, Big Island is little.
I never knew a love that wasn't a running battle
Most of the time. I'm a friend of these ghosts. They're
    mine.

1   In September 1649 Oliver Cromwell laid siege to the
     town, and after its fall he proceeded to slaughter 2,000
     of the 3,000 garrison (most of whom were Catholic
     refugees from the English Civil War).
2   University College Dublin, here a football team.
3   William of Orange defeated the Catholics under James II
     at the Battle of the Boyne in July 1690, a generation
     after Cromwell's victories.
4   A play on Papal Bulls (edicts) and possibly on Irish bulls
     (self-contradictory expression).
5   Buffún, a character from the Irish tradition who acts as a
     foil for the figure of Oliver Cromwell.
6   Cheap brand of untipped cigarettes.

WILLIAM KENNEDY
from William Kennedy, *Ironweed* (1983)

Here is the opening to William Kennedy's famous novel which was turned into a film
by Hector Babenco with Jack Nicholson as Francis Phelan. From the opening sentence
the reader is aware that Kennedy is no ordinary writer but one peculiarly gifted to
express a whole chapter in the history of Irish immigration.

from **Chapter 1**

Riding up the winding road of Saint Agnes Cemetery in the back of the rattling old truck, Francis Phelan became aware that the dead, even more than the living, settled down in neighbourhoods. The truck was suddenly surrounded by fields of monuments and cenotaphs of kindred design and striking size, all guarding the privileged dead. But the truck moved on and the limits of mere privilege became visible, for here now came the acres of truly prestigious death: illustrious men and women, captains of life without their diamonds, furs, carriages, and limousines, but buried in pomp and glory, vaulted in great tombs built like heavenly safe deposit boxes, or parts of the Acropolis. And ah yes, here too, inevitably, came the flowing masses, row upon row of them under simple headstones and simpler crosses. Here was the neighbourhood of the Phelans.

Francis's mother twitched nervously in her grave as the truck carried him nearer to her; and Francis's father lit his pipe, smiled at his wife's discomfort, and looking out from his own bit of sod to catch a glimpse of how much his son had changed since the train accident.

Francis's father smoked roots of grass that died in the periodic droughts afflicting the cemetery. He stored the root essence in his pockets until it was brittle to the touch, then pulverized it between his fingers and packed his pipe. Francis's mother wove crosses from the dead dandelions and other deep-rooted weeds; careful to preserve their fullest length, she wove them while they were still in the green stage of death, then ate them with an insatiable revulsion.

'Look at that tomb,' Francis said to his companion. 'Ain't that somethin'? That's Arthur T. Grogan. I saw him around Albany when I was a kid. He owned all the electricity in town.'

'He ain't got much of it now,' Rudy said.

'Don't bet on it,' Francis said. 'Them kind of guys hang on to a good thing.'

The advancing dust of Arthur T. Grogan, restless in its simulated Parthenon, grew luminous from Francis's memory of a vital day long gone. The truck rolled on up the hill.

FARRELL, said one roadside gravestone. KENNEDY, said another. DAUGHERTY, MCILHENNY, BRUNELLE, MCDONALD, MALONE, DWYER, and WALSH, said others. PHELAN, said two small ones.

Francis saw the pair of Phelan stones and turned his eyes elsewhere, fearful that his infant son, Gerald, might be under one of them. He had not confronted Gerald directly since the day he let the child slip out of its diaper. He would not confront him now. He avoided the Phelan headstones on the presumptive grounds that they belonged to another family entirely. And he was correct. These graves held two brawny young Phelan brothers, canalers both, and both skewered by the same whiskey bottle in 1884, dumped into the Erie Canal in front of The Black Rag Saloon in Watervliet, and then pushed under and drowned with a long stick. The brothers looked at Francis's clothes, his ragged brown twill suit jacket, black baggy pants, and filthy fireman's blue shirt, and felt a kinship with him that owed nothing to blood ties. His shoes were as worn as the brogans they both had been wearing on the last day of their lives. The brothers read also in Francis's face the familiar scars of alcoholic desolation, which both had developed in their graves. For both had been deeply drunk and vulnerable when the cutthroat Muggins killed them in tandem and took all their money: forty-eight cents. We died for pennies, the brothers said in their silent, dead-drunken way to Francis, who bounced past them in the back of the truck, staring at the emboldening white clouds that clotted the sky so richly at midmorning. From the heat of the sun Francis felt a flow of juices in his body, which he interpreted as a gift of strength from the sky.

'A little chilly,' he said, 'but it's gonna be a nice day.'

'If it don't puke,' said Rudy.

'You goddamn cuckoo bird, you don't talk about the weather that way. You got a nice day, take it. Why you wanna talk about the sky pukin' on us?'

'My mother was a full-blooded Cherokee,' Rudy said.

'You're a liar. Your old lady was a Mex, that's why you got them high cheekbones. Indian I don't buy.'

'She come off the reservation in Skokie, Illinois, went down to Chicago, and got a job sellin' peanuts at Wrigley Field.'

'They ain't got any Indians in Illinois. I never seen one damn Indian all the time I was out there.'

'They keep to themselves,' Rudy said.

The truck passed the last inhabited section of the cemetery and moved toward a hill where raw earth was being loosened by five men with pickaxes and shovels. The driver parked and unhitched the tailgate, and Francis and Rudy leaped down. The two then joined the other five in loading the truck with the fresh dirt. Rudy mumbled aloud as he shovelled: 'I'm workin' it out.'

'What the hell you workin' out now?' Francis asked.

'The worms,' Rudy said. 'How many worms you get in a truckload of dirt.'

'You countin' 'em?'

'Hundred and eight so far,' said Rudy.

'Dizzy bedbug,' said Francis.

When the truck was fully loaded Francis and Rudy climbed atop the dirt and the driver rode them to a slope where a score of graves of the freshly dead sent up the smell of sweet putrescence, the incense of unearned mortality and interrupted dreams. The driver, who seemed inured to such odours, parked as close to the new graves as possible and Rudy and Francis then carried shovelfuls of dirt to the dead while the driver dozed in the truck. Some of the dead had been buried two or three months, and yet their coffins were still burrowing deeper into the rain-softened earth. The gravid weight of the days they had lived was now seeking its equivalent level in firstborn death, creating a rectangular hollow on the surface of each grave. Some of the coffins seemed to be on their way to middle earth. None of the graves were yet marked with headstones, but a few were decorated with an American flag on a small stick, or bunches of faded cloth flowers in clay pots. Rudy and Francis filled in one hollow, then another. Dead gladiolas, still vaguely yellow in their brown stage of death, drooped in a basket at the head of the grave of Louis (Daddy Big) Dugan, the Albany pool hustler who had died only a week or so ago from inhaling his own vomit. Daddy Big, trying futilely to memorize anew the fading memories of how he used to apply topspin and reverse English to the cue ball, recognized Franny Phelan, even though he had not seen him in twenty years.

'I wonder who's under this one,' Francis said.

'Probably some Catholic,' Rudy said.

'Of course it's some Catholic, you birdbrain, it's a Catholic cemetery.'

'They let Protestants in sometimes,' Rudy said.

'They do like hell.'

'Sometimes they let Jews in too. And Indians.'

Daddy Big remembered the shape of Franny's mouth from the first day he saw him playing ball for Albany at Chadwick Park. Daddy Big sat down front in the bleachers[1] behind the third-base line and watched Franny on the hot corner, watched him climb into the bleachers after a foul pop fly that would have hit Daddy Big right in the chest if Franny hadn't stood on his own ear to make the catch. Daddy Big saw Franny smile after making it, and even though his teeth were almost gone now, Franny smiled that same familiar way as he scattered fresh dirt on Daddy Big's grave.

Your son Billy saved my life, Daddy Big told Francis. Turned me upside down and kept me from chokin' to death on the street when I got sick. I died anyway, later. But it was nice of him, and I wish I could take back some of the lousy things I said to him. And let me personally give you a piece of advice. Never inhale your own vomit.

Francis did not need Daddy Big's advice. He did not get sick from alcohol the way Daddy Big had. Francis knew how to drink. He drank all the time and he did not vomit. He drank anything that contained alcohol, anything, and he could always walk, and he could talk as well as any man alive about what was on his mind. Alcohol did put Francis to sleep, finally, but on his own terms. When he'd had enough and everybody else was passed out, he'd just put his head down and curl up like an old dog, then put his hands between his legs to protect what was left of the jewels, and he'd cork off. After a little sleep he'd wake up and go out for more drink. That's how he did it when he was drinking. Now he wasn't drinking. He hadn't had a drink for two days and he felt a little bit of all right. Strong, even. He'd stopped drinking because he'd run out of money, and that coincided with Helen not feeling all that terrific and Francis wanting to take care of her. Also he had wanted to be sober when he went to court for registering twenty-one times to vote. He went to court but not to trial. His attorney, Marcus Gorman, a wizard, found a mistake in the date on the papers that detailed the charges against Francis, and the case was thrown out. Marcus charged people five hundred dollars usually, but he only charged Francis fifty because Martin Daugherty, the newspaper columnist, one of Francis's old neighbours, asked him to go easy. Francis didn't even have the fifty when it came time to pay. He'd drunk it all up. Yet Marcus demanded it.

'But I ain't got it,' Francis said.

'Then go to work and get it,' said Marcus. 'I get paid for what I do.'

'Nobody'll put me to work,' Francis said. 'I'm a bum.'

'I'll get you some day work up at the cemetery,' Marcus said.

And he did. Marcus played bridge with the bishop and knew all the Catholic hotshots. Some hotshot ran Saint Agnes Cemetery in Menands. Francis slept in the weeds on Dongan Avenue below the bridge and woke up about seven o'clock this morning, then went up to the mission on Madison Avenue to get coffee. Helen wasn't there. She was truly gone. He didn't know where she was and nobody had seen her. They said she'd been hanging around the mission last night, but then went away. Francis had fought with her earlier over money and she just walked off someplace, who the hell knows where?

Francis had coffee and bread with the bums who'd dried out, and other bums passin' through, and the preacher there watchin' everybody and playin' grabass with their souls. Never mind my soul, was Francis's line. Just pass the coffee. Then he stood out front killin' time and pickin' his teeth with a matchbook cover. And here came Rudy.

Rudy was sober too for a change and his grey hair was combed and trimmed. His moustache was clipped and he wore white suede shoes, even though it was October, what the hell, he's just a bum, and a white shirt, and a crease in his pants. Francis, no lace in one of his shoes, hair matted and uncut, smelling his own body stink and ashamed of it for the first time in memory, felt deprived.

'You're lookin' good there, bum,' Francis said.

'I been in the hospital.'

'What for?'

'Cancer.'

'No shit. Cancer?'

'He says to me you're gonna die in six months. I says I'm gonna wine myself to death. He says it don't make any difference if you wined or dined, you're

goin'. Goin' out of this world with a cancer. The stomach, it's like pits, you know what I mean? I said I'd like to make it to fifty. The doc says you'll never make it. I said all right, what's the difference?'

'Too bad, grandma. You got a jug?'

'I got a dollar.'

'Jesus, we're in business,' Francis said.

But then he remembered his debt to Marcus Gorman.

'Listen, bum,' he said, 'you wanna go to work with me and make a few bucks? We can get a couple of jugs and a flop tonight. Gonna be cold. Look at that sky.'

'Work where?'

'The cemetery. Shovelin' dirt.'

'The cemetery. Why not? I oughta get used to it. What're they payin'?'

'Who the hell knows?'

'I mean they payin' money, or they give you a free grave when you croak?'

'If it ain't money, forget it,' Francis said. 'I ain't shovelin' out my own grave.'

1 Benches for spectators, open to the sky.

BERNARD Mac LAVERTY
from Bernard Mac Laverty, *Cal* (1983)

Bernard Mac Laverty (1942–), novelist and short-story writer, was born in Belfast and worked as a laboratory technician before taking a degree at Queen's University, Belfast. His novels include *Lamb* (1980) and *Grace Notes* (1997). *Cal* is a fine tender novel which was made into a film in 1984 by Pat O'Connor with John Lynch and Helen Mirren in the leading roles. Cahal (Cal) McCluskey, from the only Catholic family on a Protestant estate, suffers loyalist intimidation, drifts into petty crime and then into assisting in a sectarian murder. His victim turns out to be the husband of Marcella, who works in a local library and with whom Cal is in love (he conceals from her his role in the murder as their relationship develops). In this extract Cal goes over in his mind the murder and tries without success to wash away his guilt.

from **Chapter 2**

The next morning, feeling drained rather than restored by his shallow sleep, Cal stood at the corner, as always, waiting for Cyril Dunlop. He did not like this being at the same place at the same time. Every day Catholics were being shot dead for no apparent reason, as the police said. Were they *so* stupid? It wasn't the thought

of being killed that frightened him, it was the fear that he would lose his dignity if they tortured him. Men had been castrated before they were killed — one bloke had had his head put between the jaws of a vice and the vice tightened until his skull cracked; and a Catholic butcher was murdered and hung up on a meat hook in his own shop like a side of beef. They were the actions of men with sick minds.

He kept moving his eyes, scanning the road both ways, expecting to see two blokes on a motorbike. They would slow down and draw level, then the guy on the pillion would point something at him and Cal would be dead. Once that first week he did see two people on a motorbike and he stepped closer to the wall but it roared past. If it happened this morning he would be ready for them. Then he thought of reaching into his inside pocket, taking out the paper bag, unfolding it, removing the gun, releasing the safety catch and aiming it. Then firing. Cal smiled. His killers would be in Belfast having a cup of tea by that time if they had anything above second gear. If somebody wanted to get you they would get you. Having a gun was no help.

Dunlop's car came along and pulled in to the side. Cal got in.

'I didn't expect you see you today,' said Cyril.

'You heard then?'

'It was all over the town. What happened? Was it accidental?'

Cal laughed at his question.

'We were burned out.'

Cyril shook his head in disbelief and pursed his mouth.

'I'll have to admit, Cal, there's bad bastards on both sides.'

'Thanks.'

Cal was conscious of the hardness of the gun pressing into the left side of his chest. If they were stopped and searched this morning, what would the police make of it? A staunch Orangeman and a Republican with a gun in the same car. Then he remembered with relief that Cyril Dunlop was never stopped. When they recognized him they waved him on. It was funny, Cal thought, how Protestants were 'staunch' and Catholics were 'fervent'.

All that day he spent mucking out the byre again and carrying in winter feed. Dunlop told him that now the cattle were in most of the time this had to be done every day. Cal worked on his own and the noise of the beasts was a comfort to him. They snuffled and breathed, chewed and ground their teeth. One would occasionally low for no reason at all. He wondered why children were taught that a cow said 'moo'. It was the last word to describe the kind of nasal moan that they made. They had such white eyelashes, such huge eyes that they turned on him when he came near. Cal talked to them as he worked among their skidding, hoofed feet. The task of mucking out was so mindless that he had too much time to think. He wondered if anything could be salvaged from his bedroom. The guitar was certainly a goner — and all his tapes. His tape deck might still work. He felt sorry for Shamie, losing all the things he had gathered over a lifetime. But in a way for himself it could be a clean start. Like burning a wound to cleanse it.

At lunchtime he took a walk to the derelict cottage. He made sure that nobody was around and went into the glass porch. He had brought a small iron bar with him, but he didn't need it because when he tugged at the padlock it snapped open in his hand. He drew the bolt back and stepped quickly inside. The room to the right was filled with a pyramid of mouldering furniture with chair legs sticking out at all angles. There were tins of paint piled in one corner and someone had cleaned brushes with different colours on the wall. On the shelf by the door there was a bottle of purple meths with a label 'Not to be taken'. Someone had added in Biro 'seriously'. The room to the left was empty but had lino covering the floor. Two panes of the window were broken and someone had nailed a square of hardboard over the bottom of the frame. He pulled back a corner of the lino and with the crowbar eased up a floorboard. The nails screeched dryly as he put his whole weight on it. Give me a big enough lever and I'll move the world. He tucked the paper bag containing the gun under the floor and jumped on the board to flatten it.

That afternoon he told Dunlop that he would not need transport. He had a mate who was picking him up and that same mate would leave him out in the mornings. Dunlop shrugged. He seemed disgruntled that Cal was no longer dependent on him.

'O.K., if that's the way you want it,' he said.

At six he passed Cal sheltering from the wind and rain at the gable wall.

'He's always late,' said Cal.

After Dunlop's car had turned on to the main road Cal headed down the lane. About a mile and a half farther along the Toome road was a pub, the Stray Inn, and he walked to it to pass the time until dark. He sat in the warmth sipping a pint and spoke to no one. When he saw the lights come on in the car park, Cal set off back to Morton's farm. He got to the cottage, opened the door and went in. By now it was completely black and he moved slowly, waving his arms in front of him like antennae. He located the sideboard in the hall, went into the empty room and hunkered down on the floor. 'I'm squatting,' he thought, smiling in the dark. He had planned this whole thing very badly. He should have got himself a torch and something to sleep on. Tomorrow he could get them. When he was in the kitchen for a tea break in the afternoon he had nicked a couple of rolls from the breadbin. There had been a pile of them so two wouldn't be missed. The coat pocket of his jacket swung heavily with a can of beer — the last of six he had bought himself on Tuesday. He chugged open the ring-pull and the beer hissed in the dark. He covered the foam with his mouth to stop it spilling. He ate the rolls slowly to make them last and kept some of the beer for later. His eyes were becoming used to the dark and when he struck a match to light his cigarette it briefly lit up the room like daylight. He smoked while walking up and down, his feet crunching over fragmented glass.

From the back window he could see the Morton farmhouse and he was close enough to the lane to hear the Anglia drive past. He watched but only saw an instant of her framed in the light of the doorway as she went in. He leaned his forehead against the window. In the total darkness he was sensitive to minute changes of light and aware immediately a lamp went on upstairs in the farmhouse. He looked up. Marcella came to the window and with a gesture like a priestess pulled the heavy curtains together. At least now he knew which was her bedroom.

He thought of himself as a menial at the gate-lodge to the house of his mistress. If his guitar had not broken he could have stood beneath her window and serenaded her. Again he smiled sourly in the darkness. Then gradually as the evening dragged by, minute by slow minute, he became depressed. He thought of himself as a monk in his cell not only deprived of light and comfort but, in the mood he was in, deprived of God. He had ceased to believe in the one thing that dignified his suffering. Matt Talbot[1] lived with chains embedded in him for the love of God. What if he had not believed in God and yet had continued with his pain? What if he had suffered for another person? To suffer for something which didn't exist, that was like Ireland. People were dying every day, men and women were being crippled and turned into vegetables in the name of Ireland. An Ireland which never was and never would be. It was the people of Ulster who were heroic, caught between the jaws of two opposing ideals trying to grind each other out of existence.

His sin clawed at him, demanding attention. He fought it for as long as he could but there was little to distract him except the cold. In the pitch darkness his eyes, with nothing to do, naturally turned inside himself. Tired of pacing, he lay down on the floor with his knees to his chest for warmth. He lay inert on broken glass, his eyes open to the night, and saw again the terrible thing that he had done.

It was almost a year ago to the day that he had called for Crilly in the van. He had felt sick in his stomach because when Crilly had met him in the street earlier he had said that this was the big one. They drove to the town hall to a dance. The band was tuning up and there were two or three girls, embarrassed by being early, standing in the darkness at the back of the hall. The place was so empty Cal could hear doors closing.

Crilly and he had gone to the bar and then retired to a corner with their drinks.

'Well, what's the big one?'

'A cop — the Police Reserve.'

'What about him?'

'We do him — that's what.'

The muscles of Cal's stomach went rigid and he felt his palms sweaty. He rubbed his hands slowly together.

'Is he coming here?'

'No. We'll be seen here. We'll do it, then come back.'

'I see.'

'"Where were you last night?" Answer: "At a dance." Boom-boom.'

Cal bought two more pints.

'Don't worry, Cal. This guy is the greatest bastard unhung. Skeffington says that we've got to squeeze the Police Reserve and the U.D.R.[2] Maybe put people off joining them. So he picked this guy, this real turd who lives outside Magherafelt. And tonight we do him.' Cal said nothing. He cleaned the condensation from the outside of his pint with one finger. 'He planted a gun on two totally innocent guys about a month ago,' Crilly went on. 'They are up in Crumlin Road jail now. Not only that, but he had his mates give them a kicking to end all kickings and said that they had resisted arrest. He knew them too — two Catholic lads from the town — the big fucker.'

'I'm just driving,' said Cal.

'That's all we're asking you to do.'

After his second pint Crilly warned him that he could have no more. They shouldn't be drinking at all before a job. Cal had to drive straight. The band began to play and gradually the hall filled. Crilly bought a half bottle of whiskey over the counter and slipped it into his pocket. They danced with three girls each — 'Someone who knows you well,' said Crilly. Cal was incapable of conversation with any of them. During a fast number the keys in his pocket chinked and he thought they might give him away.

Crilly looked at his watch and said that he had some hardware to pick up and he would see him in the car park in fifteen minutes.

'By that time you should have wheels for us.'

Cal loathed Crilly's Hollywood turn of phrase. On nights like this Crilly thought he was in the big picture. Cal gritted his jaw and followed him. They had the date in purple ink stamped on the backs of their hands so they could come back in again.

'I feel like a library book,' said Crilly, going down the stairs.

'Don't be stupid,' said Cal. 'They closed ages ago.' He felt guilty making a laugh but he was nervous.

Cal slipped on a pair of thin leather gloves and walked around the dark end of the car park. There were two Cortinas among the ranks of cars. He tried the doors of one and they were locked. In the other, a red one, he noticed that the lock button of the back door was up. He was in and quickly over into the front seat. He pulled the string of Ford keys from his pocket and began to work through them systematically. Crilly had got them from a bloke in a garage in return for not burning it down. 'He was a good mate of mine, anyway,' he'd said. Eight keys tried and still no luck. The eleventh key clicked and the starter fired. He was expecting it so much that the sudden noise made him jump. He turned on the lights and edged the car out between the others and down the aisle. When the attendant waved a casual goodnight Cal made sure he was looking the other way. He parked, waiting for Crilly, the engine running. He should have gone to the lavatory after two pints. He rubbed his stomach and belched quietly. Nerves gave him wind. It was ten minutes before Crilly appeared from a side street with a Spar carrier bag. When he got into the car Cal smelt petrol but didn't say anything.

'Nice one, Cal,' he said, looking round him. 'Enough juice?'

'Three-quarters.'

They drove on to the main Magherafelt road. Crilly navigated and checked his gun at the same time. The tiny clicking of bullets set Cal's teeth on edge.

'I love the weight of an automatic,' Crilly said. 'You wee beauty.' He held it up for Cal to see. 'The only thing is, they're liable to jam.'

Cal did not look at it but kept his eyes on the road. Undipped headlights glared in his driving mirror and he slowed down. With relief he saw the car pass him and its tail lights draw away. Crilly slipped the gun into his pocket. From the other pocket he took the half bottle and opened it with a tearing click. He tilted it to his mouth and after swallowing gasped.

'Oh fuck — that's good stuff. Left here.'

Cal had missed the turn and had to reverse back to it. His voice was thin and tight.

'You didn't give me enough warning. Keep your eyes on the road.'

'Oh-ho. Cal's nervous. Getting jumpy, eh?'

Crilly gave him plenty of warning for the farm lane on the right. Cal slowed and the car bumped and swayed through the potholes. They passed a dilapidated cottage on the right and then pulled into a farmyard. It was a big cream house. Dogs in an outhouse somewhere started up a frantic barking. Crilly took another swig from his bottle.

'Keep her running, Cal. This won't take long.'

Cal pulled the car up close to the front door and Crilly got out. Cal waited. He badly needed a piss. He held on tight to the steering wheel. He ran his fingers round the back of it. For some reason it reminded him of the ridges on the roof of his mouth. He curled his tongue and touched them with its tip, counting. Five or six. Like the hard sand of the sea-shore. He wanted a cigarette but he knew it would be in his way if they had to take off fast. The idling engine missed a beat and Cal touched the accelerator lightly to keep it going. The thought of a stall at this stage made him weak.

He didn't hear the bell when Crilly pressed the button. It was dark but there was a light somewhere in the house. Cal tried to burp. The beer and his nerves combined to make him feel he had swallowed lead. He didn't want to watch but he felt compelled to. He tried to get beneath the wind by swallowing air but just managed to belch the pockets of air which he had swallowed. A light came on in the hall, lighting up the area of the front door. Cal felt his bladder on the point of bursting. Crilly waited, one hand in his pocket. The net curtain twitched, then the door opened. Still the dogs kept up their incessant barking.

Cal saw the man smile. Then he looked confused. Crilly pulled the gun from his pocket and the man froze. He was in carpet slippers. Crilly shot him twice in the chest. The gun sounded unreal — like a child's cap gun. The man very slowly genuflected. He shouted as if he'd been punched in the stomach.

'Mar- cell- a.'

It was a kind of animal roar. Cal heard a click and Crilly saying fuck. With both hands he snapped the gun and cleared the jam.

'Marcella,' the man roared again. Then Crilly fired a shot through his head, the gun only inches from it. Stuff came out on the wallpaper behind him. Crilly fired three more shots up the hallway then turned and ran. He jumped into the car shouting,

'Go like fuck.'

Cal heard the tyres scream as they sprayed muck and stones before they finally gripped. He swung at the gateway, going too fast in first gear. The car slewed sideways in the mud and thumped off the cement gatepost with a metallic clang.

'Keep her going, keep her going,' screamed Crilly.

Cal bounced the car into the lane and drove at speed. He did not stop at the turn on to the main road but blazed out, hoping there was nothing coming.

'What did I tell you,' shouted Crilly, 'the fuckin' thing jammed.'

Cal felt sick. He wanted to let all his functions go at once.

'This wee bastard puts his head round the corner of the hall. So I let him have it too.'

'Who?'

'I don't know who he was. But he was too nosey for his own good.'

They did the return journey in half the time. Crilly talked non-stop, dressing-room talk, none of which Cal heard, and finished his half bottle which he put in the Spar bag. He directed Cal to park behind some sheds on wasteground. They got out and Crilly took a can from the bag and poured it over the upholstery of the car.

'Have you got a match?'

Cal gave him a box of matches and could wait no longer. He opened his trousers and urinated in a gush against the side of a corrugated-iron shed. It drummed like stampeding animals. Crilly struck a match and threw it on the seat. The match went out and he cursed. He struck another one. Cal's stream seemed endless and he pushed to get it out quicker. This time the car exploded with a dull whumph — blue at first, turning to yellow flame. Crilly started to run.

'Jesus, will you come on.'

Cal still had not finished but he stopped his stream and zipped himself up at the run. On the street they stopped running, Crilly saying it was too suspicious.

'You go back to the dance. I'll get rid of these,' he said.

Cal climbed the stairs to the hall with his knees trembling. He wanted to burst out crying like a child. He held out his hand to the man sitting at the entrance table to show him his stamp. His hand was shaking badly. He went to the lavatory to finish emptying his bladder and saw himself chalk-white in the mirror. He felt physically sick looking at himself and yet he continued to stare, his hands holding the sides of the wash-basin. But he did not vomit.

He went into the hall and straight to the bar. The place was hot now and smelt of sweat and perfume. It throbbed with noise. The band in matching powder-blue uniforms were moving in unison.

'I see a face,' sang the vocalist, 'a smiling face . . .'

Cal could feel the pulse of the maple floor in his feet. He ordered a large whiskey and drank it straight off and ordered another one. There was a mirror behind the bar so he eased himself off the stool and found a corner. He saw Crilly barging his way through the crowd. He winked at Cal when he came up.

'O.K., kid?'

Cal nodded.

'Right, we've got to dance. Be seen.'

He took Cal by the arm and thrust him towards a group of girls. Cal stopped in front of one with ginger hair and pale eyelashes. He asked her to dance by holding out his hand to her. She came with him on to the floor. The tempo had slowed and everybody seemed to be doing old-fashioned ballroom dancing. Cal put one hand on her back and held her fingers with his other hand. She was not fat but he felt the indentation her bra strap made in her back. She danced, afraid to meet his eyes, staring into the distance humming the tune. She was warm to the touch and her hand was damp. Cal guided her inexpertly round the floor, conscious of the living movement of her body under his hand. He saw the man genuflect again, his heel coming away from his slipper, the astonishment in his eyes. Marcella. The name roared in his ears, drowning out the band. The ginger girl was chewing gum, not constantly or he would have noticed it before now, but occasionally she would move it around her mouth, give a few chews and then rest. She had a dark mole beneath her chin with a tiny blonde hair curling from it. The quick whiskeys made him unsure of his feet. It was the first dance of a set of three but when the band stopped the girl gave a quick chew.

'Thanks,' she said and walked off the floor back to her friends. In the bar he flinched seeing a woman raising a tomato juice to her mouth. Crilly was still on the floor, his shoulders swaying, both hands low on his partner's back. He was talking furiously. Cal waited until Crilly danced to the edge of the floor and shouted to him.

'I'm away home.'

He did not wait for a reply but shouldered and elbowed his way towards the door in such a way that people looked after him in annoyance. He felt that he had a brand stamped in blood in the middle of his forehead which would take him the rest of his life to purge.

---

1   Matt Talbot (1856–1925), born into a labouring family in Dublin, became an ascetic after a youth spent in heavy drinking.
2   Ulster Defence Regiment, a British Army regiment which recruited locally in Ulster.

SEAMUS HEANEY
from Seamus Heaney, *Station Island* (1984)

Here is a section from *Station Island*, a long sequence modelled on Dante's *Purgatorio* in which Heaney comes upon the figure of James Joyce. The title refers to the site of pilgrimage at Lough Derg in County Donegal. See Denis Devlin's 'Lough Derg' (1946) and Sean O'Faolain's short story 'Lovers of the Lake' (1957) above for other fine meditations arising from the penitential scene.

XII

Like a convalescent, I took the hand
stretched down from the jetty, sensed again
an alien comfort as I stepped on ground

to find the helping hand still gripping mine,
fish-cold and bony, but whether to guide
or to be guided I could not be certain

for the tall man in step at my side
seemed blind, though he walked straight as a rush
upon his ash plant, his eyes fixed straight ahead.

Then I knew him in the flesh
out there on the tarmac among the cars,
wintered hard and sharp as a blackthorn bush.

His voice eddying with the vowels of all rivers
came back to me, though he did not speak yet,
a voice like a prosecutor's or a singer's,

cunning, narcotic, mimic, definite
as a steel nib's downstroke, quick and clean,
and suddenly he hit a litter basket

with his stick, saying, 'Your obligation
is not discharged by any common rite.
What you must do must be done on your own

so get back in harness. The main thing is to write
for the joy of it. Cultivate a work-lust
that imagines its haven like your hands at night

dreaming the sun in the sunspot of a breast.
You are fasted now, light-headed, dangerous.
Take off from here. And don't be so earnest,

let others wear the sackcloth and the ashes.
Let go, let fly, forget.
You've listened long enough. Now strike your note.'

It was as if I had stepped free into space
alone with nothing that I had not known
already. Raindrops blew in my face

as I came to. 'Old father, mother's son,
there is a moment in Stephen's diary
for April the thirteenth, a revelation

set among my stars — that one entry
has been a sort of password in my ears,
the collect of a new epiphany,[1]

the Feast of the Holy Tundish.'[2] 'Who cares,'
he jeered, 'any more? The English language
belongs to us. You are raking at dead fires,

a waste of time for somebody your age.
That subject people stuff is a cod's game,
infantile, like your peasant pilgrimage.

You lose more of yourself than you redeem
doing the decent thing. Keep at a tangent.
When they make the circle wide, it's time to swim

out on your own and fill the element
with signatures on your own frequency,
echo soundings, searches, probes, allurements,

elver-gleams[3] in the dark of the whole sea.'
The shower broke in a cloudburst, the tarmac
fumed and sizzled. As he moved off quickly

the downpour loosed its screens round his straight walk.

---

1   Collect here is presumably a reference to the Collect said before the Epistle at Mass and containing a short dedicated prayer; epiphany is Joyce's special word for a moment of revelation in a narrative, but it also derives from the Feast of the Epiphany.

2   A reference to the scene in *A Portrait of the Artist as a Young Man* when Stephen tackles the Director of Studies (an English Jesuit) over his use of the word funnel, which as Stephen reminds him is called 'tundish' in Ireland.

3   An elver is an eel, often a conger eel.

TESS GALLAGHER
from Tess Gallagher, *Willingly* (1984)

This strange poem, intensely physical yet also suggestive metaphorically, perhaps offers itself as a study of gender and taboo, or perhaps in the context of Ireland gender and nationalism. See 'The Ballad of Ballymote (p. 900) for another poem by Gallagher.

EACH BIRD WALKING

Not while, but long after he had told me,
I thought of him, washing his mother, his
bending over the bed and taking back
the covers. There was a basin of water
and he dipped a washrag in and
out of the basin, the rag
dripping a little onto the sheet as he
turned from the bedside to the nightstand
and back, there being no place

on her body he shouldn't touch because
he had to and she helped him, moving
the little she could, lifting so he could
wipe under her arms, a dipping motion
in the hollow. Then working up from
the feet, around the ankles, over the
knees. And this last, opening

her thighs and running the rag firmly
and with the cleaning through
up through her crotch, between the lips
over the V of thin hairs —

as though he were a mother
who had the excuse of cleaning to touch
with love and indifference
the secret parts of her child, to graze
the sleepy sexlessness in its waiting
to find out what to do for the sake
of the body, for the sake of what only
the body can do for itself.

So his hand, softly at the place
of his birth-light. And she, eyes deepened
and closed in the dim room.
And because he told me her death as
important to his being with her,
I could love him another way. Not
of the body alone, or of its making,
but carried in the white spires of trembling
until what spirit, what breath we were
was shaken from us. Small then,
the word *holy*.

He turned her on her stomach
and washed the blades of her shoulders, the
small of her back. 'That's good,' she said,
'That's enough.'

On our lips that morning, the tart juice
of our mothers, so strong in remembrance, no
asking, no giving, and what you said, this
being the end of our loving, so as not to hurt
the closer one to you, make me look
to see what was left of us
with our sex taken away. 'Tell me,' I said
'something you can't forget.' Then the story of
your mother, and when you finished
I said, 'That's good, that's enough.'

PAUL DURCAN
from Paul Durcan, *The Berlin Wall Café* (1985)

Paul Durcan's humorous imagination here alights on an everyday scene and shakes it free of prejudice.

BEWLEY'S ORIENTAL CAFÉ, WESTMORELAND STREET

When she asked me to keep an eye on her things
I told her I'd be glad to keep an eye on her things.
While she breakdanced off to the ladies' loo
I concentrated on keeping an eye on her things.
What are you doing? — a Security Guard growled,
His moustache gnawing at the beak of his peaked cap.
When I told him that a young woman whom I did
    not know
Had asked me to keep an eye on her things, he barked:
Instead of keeping an eye on the things
Of a young woman whom you do not know,
Keep an eye on your own things.
I put my two hands on his hips and squeezed him:
Look — for me the equivalent of the Easter Rising
Is to be accosted by a woman whom I do not know
And asked by her to keep an eye on her things;
On her medieval backpack and on her spaceage
    Walkman;
Calm down and cast aside your peaked cap
And take down your trousers and take off your shoes
And I will keep an eye on your things also.

Do we not cherish all the children of the nation equally?
That woman does not know the joy she has given me
By asking me if I would keep an eye on her things;
I feel as if I am on a Dart[1] to Bray,
Keeping an eye on her things;
More radical than being on the pig's back,
Keeping an eye on nothing.
The Security Guard made a heap on the floor
Of his pants and shoes,
Sailing his peaked cap across the café like a frisbee.
His moustache sipped at a glass of milk.
It is as chivalrous as it is transcendental
To be sitting in Bewley's Oriental Café
With a naked Security Guard,
Keeping an eye on his things
And on old ladies
With thousands of loaves of brown bread under their
    palaeolithic oxters.

1 Dublin Bay Area Rapid Transport system (train that runs
  from Bray to Howth).

VAN MORRISON
from Van Morrison, *A Sense of Wonder* (1985)

Van Morrison is the proverbial legend in his own lifetime: on the wall of the house in East Belfast where he was born there is already a plaque to his name (which Morrison wanted removed). His Irish quality needs little insisting on. 'Days Like This' has become part of the peace movement in Northern Ireland and was sung by 60,000 people during President Clinton's visit to Belfast in 1996. Ironically, but also in a strange way in keeping, Morrison is one of the few Irish writers to make England resemble a land of mystery. As he says in 'Summertime in England', a song that links geography, poetry, drugs, and Arthurian legend in a visionary embrace, 'Can you feel the light in England?' Where Morrison is most himself is in his double insistence on a mystical basis to life and on there being no mystery to what he himself does. 'A Sense of Wonder' is a remarkable song about his working-class upbringing that works on several different levels: a series of memories, teenage friendships, youth culture, a city's familiar landmarks and 'characters', topographical street references, a Wordsworthian walk through nature, a Blakean hymn to transfiguration and visionary life. For a tribute to Van Morrison by a contemporary Irish power, see Paul Durcan, 'The Drumshanbo Hustler: A Celebration of Van Morrison', in *Magill,* May 1988, a version of which can be found on the Internet (see Van home page). See also interview with Desmond Hogan (p. 930).

A SENSE OF WONDER

I walked in my greatcoat
Down through the days of the leaves.
No before after, yes after before
We are shining our light into the days of blooming
    wonder
In the eternal presence, in the presence of the flame.

Didn't I come to bring you a sense of wonder
Didn't I come to lift your fiery vision bright
Didn't I come to bring you a sense of wonder in the
    flame.

On and on and on and on we kept singing our song
Over Newtownards and Comber, Gransha and the
    Ballystockart Road.
With Boffyflow and Spike
I said I could describe the leaves for Samuel and
    Felicity
Rich, red browny, half burnt orange and green.

Didn't I come to bring you a sense of wonder
Didn't I come to lift your fiery vision bright
Didn't I come to bring you a sense of wonder in the
    flame.

It's easy to describe the leaves in the Autumn
And it's oh so easy in the Spring
But down through January and February it's a very
    different thing.

On and on and on, through the winter of our
    discontent.
When the wind blows up the collar and the ears are
    frostbitten too
I said I could describe the leaves for Samuel and what
    it means to you and me
You may call my love Sophia, but I call my love
    Philosophy.

Didn't I come to bring you a sense of wonder
Didn't I come to lift your fiery vision bright
Didn't I come to bring you a sense of wonder in the
    flame.

Wee Alfie at the Castle Picturehouse on the
    Castlereagh Road.
Whistling on the corner next door where he kept
    Johnny Mack Brown's horse.
O Solo Mio by McGimpsey and the man who played
    the saw outside the city hall.
Pastie suppers down at Davy's chipper
Gravy rings, barmbracks Wagon wheels, snowballs.

MALCOLM LYNCH
from Malcolm Lynch, *The Streets of Ancoats* (1985)

Malcolm Lynch was born in Ancoats, Manchester, the setting for his semi-autobiographical novel *The Streets of Ancoats*. In the late 1920s Ancoats, where Irish and Italian immigrants had settled, was one of the worst slums in Europe. Lynch had a varied career which included writing episodes for television soap operas and acting as editor for *Coronation Street* for a year. Here in this extract he recreates a classroom scene in which English Catholic saints are forced to compete with an Irish popular imagination.

The cuckoo is a pretty bird,
She singeth as she flies;
She bringeth us good weather,
She telleth us no lies.
Cuckoo! Cuckoo!
Cuckoo! Cuckoo!

The singing came from the hall. The sky was as dull as dishwater, and lights were being lit. The class waited for Mr Beaumont; they guessed he was walking in the cellar playground to smoke a cigarette. Somebody had once seen him doing it; but it was no use writing a secret letter to the headmaster because the headmaster also took turns in smoking in the cellar. It seemed a waste of time putting cigarette smoke in the air when it was already full of stinks from the gasworks, the rubber works and the chemical factory; there was enough to occupy Mr Beaumont's lungs. And of course the injustice of it all was that he caned any child he caught smoking in the cellar or the lavatories.

When he returned to the classroom, he took a piece of chalk, breathed on it, and wrote, 'Anselm. Lanfranc. Becket.' on the board.

'What have those three names got in common? Hands up!' No hands went up, and Mr Beaumont looked around the class. 'My word, I have got a lot of smartly dressed pupils in here today.' This was true, for nearly half the class was better dressed than it had ever been before. This annoyed Kevin, for he was usually the best-dressed kid in class; true, most of his clothes came from the middens but his mother spent half the nights washing and patching and darning them, just like his dad spent a lot of time on the last, cobbling away at old boots for him. He was peeved that many of the kids he disliked most were smartly dressed, even though a lot of their clothes didn't fit. It was something he'd have to punish Arthur for; after all, Arthur existed to be punished by him.

'Right,' said Mr Beaumont. 'Then who's the first victim? Arthur, how about you? Anselm, Lanfranc and Becket?'

'They all play for United,' whispered Kevin behind the back of his hand.

'They all play —'

Kevin realized Arthur would get the strap for being funny. It might be going too far; anyway, Arthur wasn't too well dressed for he had a bit of shirt sticking out through a hole in his trousers. 'Canterbury!' he whispered, a little louder than before.

'They all play for Canterbury, sir,' Arthur answered, though with a puzzled sort of frown which gave the impression he wasn't sure the answer was correct.

Mr Beaumont strode between the desks. 'Kevin, on your feet. Hold your hand out!' he shouted, and Kevin received one mighty whack — slash — across his palm with the ruler. 'As Arthur is presumably your pal, at least according to one of his compositions, I'm sure you won't mind taking his punishment for him.'

'I'll bloody kill you when I get you outside,' Kevin whispered to Arthur as Mr Beaumont walked back to the blackboard.

'In 1093, Anselm was made Archbishop of Canterbury,' said Mr Beaumont, writing 1093 against Anselm. And then he smiled to himself. 'I'm sure I don't know how any of you will become good plumbers or streetsweepers or window-cleaners, or whatever you'll become, without knowing that little piece of information.'

The singing in the hall stopped, and another song was started. Mr Beaumont listened to it.

> *In Manchester, this famous town,*
> *What great improvements have been made, sirs;*
> *In fifty years 'tis mighty grown*
> *All owing to success in trade, sirs.*
> *For see the mighty buildings rising,*
> *To all beholders how surprising;*
> *The plough and harrow are now forgot, sirs;*
> *'Tis coal and cotton that now we've got, sirs.*
> *Sing heigh-ho, sing hey-down gaily,*
> *Manchester's improving daily.*

'Aye,' whispered Kevin to Arthur, 'specially since they've built the new shit-house in All Saints.'

'Hands up those who are proud of this city?' Mr Beaumont asked.

'Not me,' said Jimmy Cathcart from the back. 'There's too many blooming immigrants. They should go back to where they come from, sir.'

'In 1800,' began Mr Beaumont, 'the first city treasurer was Charles Brandt, a German immigrant. He found the money to build drains and roads and put gas lighting in the streets. Later, when Manchester was without money because of its support of Abraham Lincoln in the Civil War, a group of German immigrants got together and helped finance the University of Manchester; they caused it to be built. So the Germans might justifiably call this a German city. The thousands of Italians have filled the drab streets with music and colour; they've opened restaurants; they might say this is an Italian city. Walk up Cheetham Hill Road any night and if you look down into every cellar you will see Russian and Polish Jews sewing garments, sometimes all through the night, on their sewing-machines. Might they not consider this to be a Jewish town —'

'Please, sir,' interrupted Kevin, 'what about us micks?'

'The Irish have been coming to Manchester for three hundred years. Their muscles and tenacity built the first railway station in the world, in this town. Against impossible odds of marshes and swamps they put the first ever railway line from here to Liverpool for Stephenson's Rocket to pull passengers on. Right now, they're building a magnificent library in Peter's Square, where Peterloo[1] took place. In the Great War, which isn't all that long ago, the Manchester Regiment was recruited almost exclusively from the Ancoats Irish — yes, the Ancoats Irish. So the Irish may claim this as an Irish town. Things are changing. Ancoats won't always be the murky ghetto it is today; and those changes, when they come, will have been brought about by the sons and daughters of the immigrants. Yes, Manchester's improving daily.' Mr Beaumont threw his chalk in a good-natured way at a boy in the back row. 'And that's probably a better history lesson than Anselm, Lanfranc and Becket.'

1   The famous massacre at Peterloo in 1819.

ERIC VISSER and ANTOINETTE HENSEY
from Mary Coughlan, *Under the Influence* (1986)

Mary Coughlan's singing of this song captures a mood of antipathy and disillusionment especially evident among the young.

MY LAND IS TOO GREEN

My land is bogged down in religious tradition,
We nod our heads in humble submission.
One foot at the door, a hand in your pocket,
We export our problems for foreign solutions.

My land is naive, too scared of the devil,
Holier than thou with eyes up to heaven,
And when nobody looks we tear strips off our
    neighbour,
Have a good laugh at it all in the end.

Shrouded in mist the outlook's appalling,
Pressure is rising and temperature's falling,
Sunny spells and scattered showers,
And still it rains for hours and hours.

And as the floods rise we'll drown our sorrows,
Tossing them back like there is tomorrow,
And in the end we'll sit or stand,
And piss it back into the bog-holes of Ireland again.

My land is too fond of incurable scheming
The promises given are nothing but dreaming
We all love a rogue we'll make him our leader
But every few years it's right back to zero

My land is too poor and underdeveloped,
We talk round our problems for hours on end,
And then we decide there's two sides to the story
And have a good laugh at it all in the end.

Shrouded in mist the outlook's appalling,
Pressure is rising and temperature's falling,
Sunny spells and scattered showers.
And still it rains for hours and hours.

And as the floods rise we'll drown our sorrows,
Tossing them back like there is tomorrow,
And in the end we'll sit or stand,
And piss it back into the bog-holes of Ireland again.

TOM MURPHY
Conversations on a Homecoming (1985)

Tom Murphy (1935–   ) was born in Tuam, Co. Galway, left school at fifteen, took up a teaching scholarship, and was for a time a metalwork teacher. *Whistle in the Dark* (1960) was rejected by the Abbey but it had a successful run in London, the city he emigrated to in the 1960s. When he returned to Ireland in 1970 his plays met with increasing success, especially *The Gigli Concert* (1983) and *Bailegangaire* (1985). *Conversations on a Homecoming*, which is in part a rewriting of a 1972 play *The White House*, was first performed by the Druid Theatre Company in April 1985. Murphy's depiction of modern Ireland is at once disturbing and disconsolate, a systematic closing off of every valve, lyrical impulse, or escape route.

Time and place: The early 1970s
A pub in a town in east Galway

A forgotten-looking place, a run-down pub. Faded printing on a window or on a panel over the door: The White House. The place is in need of decoration, the clock is stopped, stocks on the shelves are sparse, there is a picture of John F. Kennedy . . . A partition has been erected to divide the room in two, a public bar (not seen) and the lounge which is the main acting area.

The lights come up on ANNE. *She is seventeen, standing behind the counter, motionless, staring blankly out the window, her expression simple and grave. A tapping on the counter in the public bar; it is repeated before she reacts and moves off to serve a customer.*

TOM is hunched in his overcoat, seated at a table, sipping from a half-pint glass of Guinness, reading a newspaper; his feet resting on the rung of another chair give him a posture that is almost foetal. He is in his late thirties.

JUNIOR is entering front door and hallway. He pauses in door to investigate momentarily the sound of a car pulling into the car park. JUNIOR is thirty-one, more casually dressed than the others (a duffel coat and a good heavy pullover), a contented, unaffected man; a big — though simple — sense of humour; an enviable capacity to enjoy himself. En route to the counter:

JUNIOR: Well, bolix![1]
TOM (*mildly*): Oh? (*And continues with his newspaper.*)
JUNIOR (*at the counter, poking his head around the end of the partition*): Well, Anne! How yeh, Johnny! (*Exaggerated nasal brogue.*) We'll have fhrost!
Chuckling voice, off, in reaction: We will, a dhiabhail![2]
JUNIOR (*To* TOM): He didn't come in yet?
TOM: Was that him?
JUNIOR: No. What are you having, boy?
TOM: Pint.
JUNIOR: Two pints, Anne. (*To* TOM.) Liam Brady pulling into the car park. Well, Anne! Are you well?
ANNE (*almost silently; smiles*): Fine.
LIAM entering, car keys swinging, about the same age as JUNIOR; well-dressed and groomed: expensive, heavy pinstripe, double-breasted suit, a newspaper neatly folded sticking out of his pocket for effect. He is a farmer, an estate agent, a travel agent, he owns property . . . he affects a slight American accent; a bit stupid and insensitive — seemingly the requisites of success.
LIAM: Hi! (*TOM merely glances up.*) Hi, Junie!
JUNIOR: How yeh!
LIAM: What's bringing ye in here?
JUNIOR: Michael Ridge is home from America.
LIAM: Hi, Anne! (*Craning over the bar to see if there is anyone in the public bar.*)

JUNIOR: We'll get all the news. What are you having?
LIAM (*indecisive*): Ahm . . .
JUNIOR: It's all the same to me.
LIAM: Had me a few shots earlier. Pint.
JUNIOR: Three pints, Anne.
LIAM joins TOM, takes out his newspaper, is not interested in it, is replacing/arranging it in his pocket again.
TOM: Give us a look at that. What time is it?
LIAM: It's nearly eight.
TOM (*disinterestedly*): And what has *you* in here?
LIAM: Oh!
JUNIOR: Thanks, Anne. (*Takes first pint to table.*) There's only Johnny Quinn in the public bar.
Off, the town clock chiming eight.
LIAM: That town clock is fast.
JUNIOR: He was taking his mother or something out the country to see relations. I lent him the car.
TOM: I thought he said he might be here sooner.
JUNIOR: No. He said he'd hardly make it before eight. A reunion, wuw! We'll get all the news.
LIAM: He didn't bring a bus home with him then?
JUNIOR: No — Thanks, Anne — I lent him the car. (*Taking the other two pints to the table; quietly.*) He was anxious to see JJ too.
LIAM: JJ was up in Daly's earlier. On another batter.[3] Getting mighty opstreperous, fellas, mighty maudlin.
TOM: Are they singing up in Daly's? (*To himself.*) The cowboys.
JUNIOR (*suddenly*): I'm not staying out late tonight.
TOM: What? (*Chucks LIAM's paper aside.*) And who's asking yeh?
They have been waiting for their pints to 'settle'. Off, the church clock is chiming eight.
LIAM (*a major triumph for his watch*): There, the church clock, eight!
TOM: Another discrepancy between Church and State.
LIAM: What?
TOM: Nothing. Good luck!
JUNIOR: Luck, boy!
LIAM: Good luck, fellas!
JUNIOR (*appreciative gasp after a long draught*): Aah, Jasus! (*And starts to sing absently to himself.*) 'They were only a bunch of violets, violets so blue / Fresh and fair and dainty, they sparkled like the dew / Fresh and fair and dainty, they sparkled like the dew / But I'll not forget old Ireland / Far from the old folks at home.'
During this, MISSUS has come down the stairs (which are at the end of the hall), gone into the public bar — a greeting, off, to Johnny — and now reappears behind the counter in the lounge. She is in her early fifties,

carelessly dressed (a dirty house-coat); a worried, slow-moving drudge of a woman, senses a bit numbed by life, but trying to keep the place together.

MISSUS: Aa, the boys!

JUNIOR: Hello, Missus! (*And continues another jumbled verse of the song to himself.*)

MISSUS: Yas.

LIAM: How do, Mrs Kilkelly!

MISSUS: And Liam.

She beckons ANNE, *whispers something to her and* ANNE *goes about collecting her coat to go on an errand.*

LIAM: The partition is holding up well?

MISSUS: Yas, thanks. Yas, Liam.

(*Smiles/drools at* LIAM, *and she exits to public bar.*) Cold enough, Johnny?

JUNIOR (*to himself*): We'll have fhrost.

TOM: Shh!

TOM *has been listening to a car pulling into the car park.*

ANNE *is pulling on her overcoat, going out front door when she bumps into* MICHAEL *who is entering.*

MICHAEL: Oops!

ANNE: Sorry.

MICHAEL: Sorry.

A backward glance from ANNE *at him as she exits.* MICHAEL *pauses for a brief moment to muster himself before going into the lounge. He is the same age as* TOM; *defensively inclined towards the supercilious, false panache to hide his failure.*

MICHAEL: Hello there!

JUNIOR: Hah, here he is! —

TOM: Oh, look in! —

LIAM: The man himself! —

MICHAEL: Gee! Gee! Lots of changes round here! —

TOM: Don't start that game now — How yeh, you're welcome, how yeh! —

LIAM (*pushing awkwardly through them, nearly spilling* JUNIOR*'s pint*): Well, howdy, Mick! —

JUNIOR (*protecting his pint*): Jasus, the cowboy! (LIAM) —

MICHAEL: Liam! And how are you?

LIAM: Good to see yeh, well good to see yeh! —

TOM: That's a fancy-lookin' suit you have on. —

MICHAEL: What's fancy about it? —

TOM: Nothing —

LIAM: You look just great! —

TOM (*shaking hands*): Well? How yeh, you're welcome, how yeh?

MICHAEL: Not too bad.

JUNIOR: Not three bad, what're you having, boy?

TOM: Oh, a brandy, a brandy, a brandy for the emigrant, don't yeh know well? —

LIAM: Pull up a pew, fella —

MICHAEL: I'll have a pint, Junie.

JUNIOR: Fair play to yeh. (*Going to counter.*) Missus!

TOM: Well!

MICHAEL: How are you?

TOM: I'm alright.

JUNIOR (*impatient at counter*): Missus!

TOM: You're lookin' well.

MICHAEL: Can't help it. You know?

TOM: I suppose you can't.

JUNIOR (*to* MISSUS *who has entered behind counter*): A pint, please.

LIAM: A holiday, Mick?

MICHAEL: Ah . . . . yeh.

LIAM *nods in that solemn provincial way, eyes fixed on* MICHAEL *in ignorant assessment.*

And how are things with you, Liam?

LIAM: Fightin' fit, fella.

MICHAEL: The farming, the rates collecting, the —

TOM: Oh and sure he's an auctioneer too now.

MICHAEL: Yeh?

LIAM: Estate agent, Mick.

TOM: Took out his diploma after intensive and in-depth study last year.

JUNIOR (*from counter*): M15 AA!

MICHAEL: What?

TOM: Junior's sense of humour.

LIAM: MIAA, Mick.

JUNIOR: Letters after his name and the car he drives doesn't need a clutch!

MICHAEL: So business is good then?

LIAM: Property-wise, this country, A-one, Mick. This country, Mick, last refuge in Europe.

MICHAEL: Good begod, I came to the right place then!

JUNIOR: Thanks, Missus. (*He is waiting for his change.*)

TOM: You haven't much of an accent?

MICHAEL (*British accent*): Only for the stage.

TOM (*British accent*): Yes, yes, good show, jolly good, right chaps, it's up to us, we're going through. John Mills![4]

MICHAEL: Aw, he's making better ones now.

TOM: Is he?

JUNIOR: Thanks, Missus.

MISSUS (*retreating off, fingering her dirty house-coat*): Aa, Michael.

We see her a few moment later reappear from the public bar into the hallway and going upstairs.

MICHAEL: How's your mother, Tom?

TOM: Oh, she's fine.

MICHAEL: And the school?

TOM: Fine. The headmaster might drop dead any day now —

JUNIOR (*setting pint in front of* MICHAEL): Now, boy —

TOM: And my subsequent rise in station and salary will make all the difference.

MICHAEL: Thanks, Junie.

TOM: What brought you back?

MICHAEL (*evasive*): Oh, before I forget them — (*He gives car keys to* JUNIOR.) Thanks.

JUNIOR: Not at all, boy.

TOM: Hmm? At this time of year.

JUNIOR: Jasus, you weren't home for . . .

TOM: Must be ten years.

JUNIOR: That race week. (*He starts to laugh.*)

TOM: Aw Jay, that Galway race week!

    They start to laugh.

JUNIOR: Aw Jasus, d'yeh remember your man?

TOM: Aw God, yes, your man!

JUNIOR: Aw Jasus, Jasus! (JUNIOR's *laugh usually incorporates 'Jasus'.*)

TOM: The cut of him!

JUNIOR: Aw Jasus, Jasus!

LIAM: Who?

JUNIOR: D'yeh remember?

MICHAEL: I do.

JUNIOR: But do yeh? — Jasus, Jasus!

LIAM: Who was this?

JUNIOR: Do yeh, do yeh, remember him?

MICHAEL (*laughing*): I do!

JUNIOR: Jasus, Jasus!

    JUNIOR's *laugh is infectious, all laughing. Ritual toast again.*

MICHAEL: Good luck, Junie!

JUNIOR: Good luck phatever (*whatever*)!

TOM: Good luck!

LIAM: Good luck, fellas!

    They drink.

MICHAEL: Is JJ around?

TOM: No. But what brought you back?

    MICHAEL *glances at him, unsure.*

    So sudden. This time of the year.

JUNIOR: Nos-talgia!

MICHAEL: Something like that.

TOM: What?

MICHAEL (*forces a laugh*): The White House, our refuge, our wellsprings of hope and aspiration. (*Mimicking JJ/Kennedy.*) Let the word go forth from this time and place to friend and foe alike that the torch has been passed to a new generation![5]

LIAM: JJ doing his Kennedy bit, is it? Making speeches. (*Dismissive.*) JJ.

MICHAEL (*to* LIAM): We virtually built this place with JJ. Right, Tom?

JUNIOR: Jasus we did!

MICHAEL: Night after night, while you were wasting all those years away at university.

JUNIOR: Jasus, we did — And sank pints!

TOM (*to* JUNIOR): Sure you were only a boy.

MICHAEL: You wrote your rightest poems here.

TOM (*laughing at himself*): I did — and read them!

MICHAEL: You wrote that speech — JJ's inaugural — for our opening. (*JJ/Kennedy voice again.*) Friends, all this, our cultural centre, has been a co-sponsorial job from design to décor. Mark its line, its adornment.

TOM: I never said 'mark' —

MICHAEL: Its atmosphere derives from no attribute of wild wisdom, vestige of native cunning, or selfish motive. The day of the dinosaur is gone forever, and with it the troglodytian attitude incarcerated in the cave whence it came —

TOM: Troglodytical —

MICHAEL: And as I look around me, I know that some of us will be departing —

JUNIOR: To ride the waves or drown in them!

MICHAEL: That's it Junie —

JUNIOR (*pleased with himself*): As the fella says —

MICHAEL: To seek the new ideas. And some of us will remain, custodians of this, *our* White House, to keep the metaphorical doors of thought, hope, generosity, expression, aspiration open. So that all will find — the denizen of this hamlet, the traveller in his frequent returnings — a place of fulfilment, or a refuge if need be. Something like that. You wrote that.

TOM (*chuckling*): I suppose I did. Sure we'd all have been departing, riding the waves, if we paid heed to poor auld JJ.

LIAM *laughs.*

But you didn't tell us. What brought you back?

MICHAEL: I told you. Lost horizons.

TOM: Wha! (*First wonderings: Can he be serious?*)

MICHAEL: No.

TOM: Hmm?

MICHAEL: No, you'd be surprised at how dicked-up one can get — I mean, how meaningless things can become for one — occasionally of course — away from one's — you know.

TOM: I suppose 'one' can. (*Awkward moment's pause.*) But you're looking well.

MICHAEL: Can't help it.

LIAM (*eyes all the time fastened on* MICHAEL): It could be a good stand for a fella, Mick? This place, properly handled.

MICHAEL (*joking*): You didn't consider taking up the gun and marching on the North?

JUNIOR: We thought about it.

MICHAEL *laughs.*

Serious.

MICHAEL: What?

JUNIOR: We did.

LIAM: We nearly did.

JUNIOR: Serious.

LIAM: Shoot us a few Prods.[6]

> MICHAEL *looks at* TOM.

TOM: It's very bad up there.

MICHAEL: I know. I've been reading, but.

LIAM: We nearly did, one night.

TOM: The way the Catholics are being treated.

MICHAEL (*trying to conceal his disbelief*): Yeh?

LIAM: A geezer up there in the papers one evening talking about coming down here and burning us all to the ground.

JUNIOR: We knew where to lay our hands on a few guns.

LIAM: Well, I'm telling you, when I read that!

MICHAEL: Guns!?

JUNIOR: We did. He (TOM) did.

MICHAEL (*laughs in disbelief*): You did, Tom?

TOM (*frowning*): What?

LIAM (*boasting*): I was awful drunk that night. I was awful sick — Did ye see me?

MICHAEL (*because* TOM *is still frowning*): No, I believe — I believe things are pretty bad alright, but, a baby and all now, Junie?

JUNIOR: Oh, oh!

MICHAEL: And how is Peggy, Tom?

TOM: Fine.

MICHAEL: Yeh? She's okay?

TOM: Fine. I sent her word we'd be in here.

MICHAEL: Any signs of ye doing it yet as the saying goes?

TOM: Aren't we engaged, isn't that enough?

JUNIOR: Jasus, ten years engaged!

TOM (*mock belligerence*): Well, isn't it better than nothing!

JUNIOR (*laughing*): Aw Jasus, Jasus!

LIAM: But he's bought the site, Mick.

TOM: And isn't it doubled in value now!

LIAM: Trebled, trebled, fella!

JUNIOR: Jasus, ten years engaged!

TOM: D'yeh hear Sonny?

JUNIOR: Jasus, Jasus!

TOM: Napkin-head, procreation hope!

JUNIOR: What does that mean, sir?

TOM: Dick!

> *They laugh.*
> *During this last,* MISSUS *has come down the stairs, along hallway and is entering lounge, now minus her dirty house-coat, wearing her best cardigan.*

MISSUS: Aa, the boys! And Liam. You're welcome, Michael.

MICHAEL: Hello, Missus!

MISSUS: Welcome, yas, now.

MICHAEL: You're looking well.

MISSUS: Oh now, pulling the divil by the tail. Isn't that the way, boys? But your mother is delighted, yas, the surprise of your visit. I was talking to her for a minute this morning in the post office and she was telling me. Now.

MICHAEL: We were just saying we had some great times here, what?

MISSUS: Yas, but Liam is the boy that's doing well. Waiting for the right girl. And poor Tom waiting on you there this hour.

TOM: I am indeed, Missus, the hound!

MISSUS: Aa, sure he doesn't mean that at all. Usen't we call the two of you the twins one time? Always together, always together. D'ye know now.

JUNIOR (*quietly*): Yas, the twins.

MISSUS: Yas, the twins. Aa, I think Junior is a bit of a rogue.

TOM: A blackguard, Missus.

MISSUS: Aa, no joking. D'ye know now. A nice wife and a baby and a home of his own to go into. The way everyone should be.

JUNIOR (*to* TOM): Now!

MISSUS: Isn't that right, Liam?

LIAM: That is c'rrect, Mrs Kilkelly.

MISSUS: A nice sensible girl, and not be roaming the world.

JUNIOR (*to* MICHAEL): Now!

MICHAEL: How is JJ?

MISSUS: Oh JJ is — very well, thank you.

MICHAEL: The time of our lives putting this place together, we were just saying. Do you remember the night — Where's the painting of the nude?

MISSUS: Yas, but you're doing well, your mother was saying, and are you alright there now, boys?

JUNIOR: Well, you might start filling another round. (*To* TOM.) *Your* round.

MISSUS: Certainly. (*Going back to the bar.*) Nice to see you all again.

JUNIOR: She's desperate slow on the aul pints.

> MICHAEL *is still looking after her, shaken by the transformation that has come over her.*

MICHAEL: She was the first lady. But where is JJ?

TOM: Sure the man is dyin'.

MICHAEL: What!

TOM: Drinkin' himself to death, don't be talking.

LIAM: That's where she sent the young one, out looking for him.

MICHAEL: Did you tell him I'd be here? (JUNIOR *nods.*) And?

JUNIOR: He isn't together at all: he's on a batter.

MICHAEL: But you told him?

> JUNIOR *nods.*

LIAM: He's probably gone into Galway or some place by now.

MICHAEL: But he'll show up?

TOM: You won't see him for a week. What about yourself?

LIAM (*pleasure of the anticipation on his face*): I'll have the selling of this place before long.

TOM: What about yourself?

MICHAEL: What?

LIAM: Gals.

JUNIOR: 'Gals'. Jasus, you have more of an American accent than him!

TOM: There was a rumour some time back you were married.

MICHAEL: No.

TOM: What?

MICHAEL: Free love.

TOM: Oh God!

MICHAEL: Who was the bird I bumped into at the door?

JUNIOR: Fair play to yeh!

MICHAEL: A young one.

LIAM: You never lost it, Mickeen!

MICHAEL: As a matter of fact I did. Plenty of it, too much of it over there.

TOM: What about our new bank clerk for him, Junie?

JUNIOR: Grrrrrah, Josephine!

TOM: We have a right one for yeh.

LIAM (*to himself*): Dirty aul' thing.

JUNIOR: She stays here and all: a quick nip up the stairs on your way out tonight and 'wham, bang, alikazam!'

TOM: The most ridiculous whore of all times.

JUNIOR: No bra.

LIAM: Dirty aul' thing.

MICHAEL: Why so ridiculous?

TOM: A bank clerk, a bank clerk! A girl in her position!

JUNIOR (*whispering*): And they say she wears no knickers either. Ich bin ein Berliner![7]

TOM (*frowning*): What were you going to say?

MICHAEL: No, but this young one at the door, that wasn't her.

LIAM: Who?

MICHAEL: A blue coat, fair, about eighteen.

JUNIOR: Anne. (*It doesn't register with* MICHAEL.)

TOM: Anne, Annette.

JUNIOR: Missus's daughter —

TOM: JJ's daughter.

MICHAEL (*brightening*): Well-well!

JUNIOR: She's turning out nice on me word.

MICHAEL: Annette. JJ's daughter. I bumped into her at the door and I got the whiff of soap, sort of schoolgirl kind of soap, and —

TOM: It took you back?

MICHAEL: It did.

TOM: Tck!

MICHAEL: No, there's a distinctive kind of aroma off —

TOM: Gee, aroma! It'd be great to be young again.

MICHAEL: You're a bogman, Ryan.

TOM: I've no sensitivity alright.

They are chuckling. JUNIOR *draining his glass as* MISSUS *arrives with one pint which she puts before* LIAM.

MISSUS: Now, Liam. The other three are coming, boys. (*Returning to bar.*)

MICHAEL: Well, news!

Short pause; all thinking.

JUNIOR: Molloy's dog got killed by a tractor last month.

TOM: Did you hear Stephen Riley died?

MICHAEL: No!

TOM *nods.*

Hoppy?

TOM: Yeh, with the limp.

MICHAEL: Well did he?

TOM: He did.

JUNIOR: D'yeh remember the Christmas he split the wife with the crucifix? (*They laugh. Solemnly.*) The Lord have mercy on him.

They burst into irreverent laughter.

TOM: And of course you know Larry, Larry O'Kelly got transferred?

MICHAEL: Yeh. I was looking around for his painting of the nude.

JUNIOR: Transferred, and *Bridget Reclining* with him.

MICHAEL: It used to hang there.

TOM: JJ defying Church and State hanging a nude.

JUNIOR: And the priest, Father Connolly — remember? — up and down here, hotfoot about the nude.

TOM: That wasn't why —

JUNIOR (*taking fresh pint that was set before* LIAM): Here, cowboy, gimme that pint and I'll be working away on it.

MICHAEL: And JJ. 'I do not speak for the Church on public matters, Father, and the Church is not going to speak for me!'

JUNIOR: Good luck!

MICHAEL: And JJ sent Father Connolly packing.

TOM: He didn't.

MICHAEL: He did.

JUNIOR (*after appreciative draught*): Aaa, Jasus!

MICHAEL: 'When long-held power leads men towards arrogance, art reminds them of their limitations!'

JUNIOR: Father Connolly called it a dirty picture.

TOM *and* MICHAEL *speaking simultaneously*:

TOM: He didn't!

MICHAEL: 'When long-held power narrows men's minds, art, poetry, music cleanses —'

TOM: He called it a *bad* picture —

MICHAEL: As far as you're concerned then, Father —

JUNIOR: } 'Art galleries —'
MICHAEL: } 'Art galleries —'

    MICHAEL *and* JUNIOR *laugh.*

MICHAEL: 'As far as you are concerned then, Father, art galleries all over the world are filled with dirty pictures?'

TOM (*playing Fr Connolly*): 'Please, please — Boys! — please don't talk to me about art galleries. Holy Moses, I've visited hundreds of them. You see, boys, I am a man who has travelled the world —'

MICHAEL: 'I heard you spent a few years in Nigeria, but remember you're not talking to the Blacks now!'

    JUNIOR *collects the other three pints, paying* MISSUS.

MISSUS: } Now, boys, yas.
JUNIOR: } 'You're not talking to the Blacks now.'

TOM: Aw but do ye see? The arrogance and condescension which you impute to Fr Connolly's remarks were only too evident in our swinging liberal JJ's statements.

MICHAEL: What does that mean?

JUNIOR: That's what I was going to say.

    TOM *waives the question.*

LIAM: Good luck, fellas!

TOM: The reason, the *real* reason, behind Fr Connolly's visits had nothing to do with the painting.

MICHAEL: He wanted JJ to take it down.

TOM: That was the *ostensible* reason. The real reason was to tell JJ to behave himself like a good boy, to *warn* him.

JUNIOR: And JJ *didn't* take it down — fair play to him.

MICHAEL: To *warn* him?

TOM: A token glance at the nude, a few token remarks about art galleries or something, and 'Haw-haw-haw, you are a son-of-a-bachelor, John-John.' The real reason. 'You see, John-John, pub, club, art-centre, whatever it is you are running here, people are growing concerned. And particularly since your trade to date seems to be in the young. Already there have been complaints, indeed visits to the presbytery from worried parents and other concerned parties.'

JUNIOR: The opposition, Paddy Joe Daly, and the other wise publicans.

TOM: 'One native son, a guileless youth it appears, is about to leave a respectable clerkship which I had a hand in getting him myself —'

MICHAEL: He never spoke for me! —

TOM: 'And a widowed mother —'

MICHAEL: My mother never went near —

TOM: 'To go off to Dublin to become — of all things! — an actor.'

MICHAEL: Maybe your mother did —

TOM: 'While another is suddenly contemplating leaving a secure pensionable position. Think of it! A teacher! The first from the generations of plebs to which he belongs to make such breakthrough — to the professions! And going off without prospects, John-John, to God knows where!'

JUNIOR: To become a writer.

TOM: 'Others — youths!' —

JUNIOR: Taking to hard liquor — Wuw!

TOM: 'And all, it would appear, being influenced by something called the *vision* of a Johnny-come-lately.'

LIAM: That's right, fellas, JJ was a blow-in, a cute buff-sham from back there Caherlistrane-side.

TOM: 'Too far too fast for us, John-John.'

MICHAEL: And that was the warning?

TOM (*silent 'No'*): 'I think — John — you would be well advised to leave the decision-making to the parents and their spiritual advisors as to what is best for their children. I know you have it in you to take careful account of what I have said and the *security* of wiser steps.'

MICHAEL: That sounds more like a threat.

TOM: 'Holy Moses, Michael — John-John — we don't threaten anyone. We don't have to. We, the poor conservatives — troglodytes, if you will — have seen these little phases come and go. All we have to do is wait.'

    MICHAEL *laughs. Then ritual toast:*

MICHAEL: Good luck!

TOM: 'God bless you.'

JUNIOR: Luck!

LIAM: Good luck, fellas!

MICHAEL: But he might show up.

    TOM *shakes his head.*

    Aw, you'd never know.

    TOM *throws his head back at* MICHAEL's *romantic hope springing eternal.*

LIAM: Strangers wanting to run the town.

MICHAEL: There was never anything like it before. And where did that lousy partition come out of?

    TOM *and* JUNIOR — *with no great interest* — *notice the partition for the first time.*

LIAM: No decent heating in the place. The place was mighty cold without that.

MICHAEL: And how is Silver Strand?

LIAM: Oh! Oh!

JUNIOR: Tell him.

LIAM: Aw no, fellas!

JUNIOR: Tell him! The place is crawling with priests and police since the bishop's niece got poled back there last year — Tell him.

LIAM: Well. Well. I shifted this Judy at a dance in Seapoint and wheeled her back to the Strand, and we were coorting away there nicely — No! No! A fair coort mind! I hadn't even bothered to let back the seats of the auld jalop. But next thing — suddenly — my heart was in my mouth. Tap-tap-tap at the window, and it was all fogged up. A big policeman with a flashlamp. What are yeh doin' there, says he. Kneckin', fella, says I. Well, says he — Well, says he, stick your neck now back in your trousers and hump off.

They laugh.

JUNIOR: Tell him about Dooley.

TOM: Aw wait'll I tell yeh.

JUNIOR: Yeh remember Dooley?

MICHAEL: The librarian is it?

TOM: Shiny boots —

JUNIOR: Holy Harry —

TOM: First Mass, Communion, a pillar of the community. Well, it's all an act. He hates it all: Church, State, everything.

JUNIOR: Jasus, Jasus, Jasus . . .

TOM: Stall it a minute now. The headmaster sent me down to organize some kind of library service with him for the school and we got talking. And d'yeh know his great secret rebellion against it all? Called me down to the shelf like this. *The Life Story of the Little Flower*[8] filed under horticulture. Well laugh when I saw it? I nearly died. And giggling away to himself. The malice! I never enjoyed anything so much. (*Laughter subsiding.*) Well yourself?

MICHAEL: Oh, having a great time. You know?

TOM: *News! News!*

MICHAEL: Well, I was with this buddy of mine one night and we picked up these two chicks in a bar.

LIAM: Yeh? —

JUNIOR: Yeh?

MICHAEL: Well. It was coming to closing time anyway and they're clearing the glasses away, see, and one of the barmen — just like that — grabbed the glass out of one of the chick's hands —

LIAM: Yeh? —

JUNIOR: Yeh?

MICHAEL: And this buddy of mine — and he's only a little guy — took a swing at the barman, and the barman — and not at my buddy — but a swing at the chick. So I took a swing at the barman. Me! You know?

TOM: Missed.

MICHAEL: Yeh. And then, the most marvellous choreographed movement, three more barmen vaulting over the counter and —

TOM: You all ended up on your arses outside.

MICHAEL: Yeh, and then —

TOM: You all had to go back meekly for your overcoats . . . You told us ten years ago!

MICHAEL: . . . Well, I was at this party the other night and I don't know what came over me, but I did something crazy.

TOM: Yeh?

LIAM: Yeh? —

JUNIOR: Yeh? —

TOM: Yeh?

MICHAEL (*evasive*): No, forget that. But, ah, forget that, I was in the Village[9] — you know? — one of those Village bars there recently and —

TOM: No, the party the other night — you did something crazy — What were you going to say?

MICHAEL: Ah, that was nothing. But, one of those Village bars, and, and, listening to these two weirdos. One of them proving that Moses was in fact a stonecutter.

LIAM: Proving it?

MICHAEL: Proving it: dates, figures, blisters, the lot. And the other fella —

LIAM: The Ten Commandments?!

MICHAEL: The other fella trying to get in with his own thesis, 'Yeah, man, I dig, man, but do you believe Jesus Christ committed suicide?'

TOM: They're daft alright.

MICHAEL: It was very funny.

LIAM: And no one around to give one of them a box?

MICHAEL: It was very funny.

JUNIOR: Moses up the mountain chiselling away on the quiet behind a cloud.

MICHAEL: It was very funny, Junie.

JUNIOR: That's a good one.

But the general feeling is that it is not such a good one.

LIAM: But you're faring out well over there, Mick?

MICHAEL: Yep.

LIAM: Hah?

MICHAEL: Oh, pretty good. I'm — I'm up for this part in a film, actually. And that tele a while back. And there's a possibility of a part in a stage play, but we don't know yet.

TOM: 'We'? Who?

MICHAEL: My agent.

TOM: Oh, *you* have an agent?

MICHAEL: I had an agent the last time I was home, what's wrong with an agent?

TOM: I didn't say there was anything.

MICHAEL: Everyone has an agent.

JUNIOR: Begobs I haven't.

MICHAEL: I'd say averaging ten — eleven grand over the past two/three years. That's not bad.

JUNIOR: Not bad he says and the few quid a week my auld fella gives me.

MICHAEL: What? Well, it's not bad. It's not good either. I know guys making fifty — a hundred grand a year.

JUNIOR: I know fellas making nothing.

TOM: So what? What are you telling us for?

MICHAEL: Well, I wouldn't have made it clerking around here.

TOM: You wouldn't.

JUNIOR: Or teaching.

TOM: What are you laughing at? — You wouldn't, you can say that again.

JUNIOR (*laughing*): You could sing that, sir!

TOM: Tck, Jack!

JUNIOR (*guffawing*): As the bishop said to the actress!

TOM: Shut up, you eejit!

JUNIOR (*continues laughing/singing*): 'Sure no letter I'll be wearin', for soon will I be sailing —'[10] (*To* MICHAEL.) Hey, did you bring any home with yeh?

Laughing subsiding.

MICHAEL: But I was in this place the other night.

TOM: The party, is it?

MICHAEL: No. Yes. But there was a guy there anyway —

TOM: Who?

MICHAEL: No, wait'll you hear this one, Tom. A fella, some nut, I didn't know him.

TOM: Yeh?

LIAM: Yeh? —

JUNIOR: Yeh? —

TOM: Yeh?

MICHAEL: Well, he went a bit berserk anyway.

JUNIOR: Beresk!

TOM: Shh!

MICHAEL: Well. He took off his clothes. (*He looks at them, unsure, his vulnerability showing; he is talking about himself.*) Well, he took off his clothes. Well, bollocks naked, jumping on tables and chairs, and then he started to shout 'No! No! This isn't it at all! This kind of — life — isn't it at all! Listen! Listen to me! Listen! I have something to tell you all!'

TOM: Making his protest.

MICHAEL: Yeh.

TOM: Yeh?

MICHAEL: Something to tell them all.

TOM: Yeh?

MICHAEL: Whatever — message — he had, for the world. But the words wouldn't come for him anyway. And (*Moment's pause; then, simply.*) Well. Then he tried to set himself on fire. (*He averts his eyes.*)

LIAM: Women there, Mick?

MICHAEL: Yeh. (*Mustering himself again.*) Ah, it wasn't anything serious — I mean, a party, a weirdo job. They were only laughing at him.

TOM: Yeh?

MICHAEL: Well, that's it. (*Forces a laugh.*) They calmed him down — put out the flames, what?

TOM: Yeh?

LIAM: Yeh?

MICHAEL: Oh yes! (*Trying to laugh.*) But then, then, one of the women took off *her* clothes and started cheering 'Up the Irish, up the IRA!'

TOM (*quietly*): His protest really foiled.

MICHAEL: Yeh.

LIAM: He was *Irish*?

MICHAEL: What?

JUNIOR: But what was up with him?

LIAM: He was *Irish*?

MICHAEL: Yeh.

JUNIOR: But what was up with him?

MICHAEL: I don't know. Maybe someone put something in his drink or — There were all sorts of things going round — I mean, we, *we* were only laughing at him.

LIAM: Did you know him, Mick?

MICHAEL: I mean, I was drunk out of my skull myself.

TOM: Yeh?

MICHAEL: Well, that's it. Then he started crying, put on his clothes, I suppose, and left. I thought it was a good one.

LIAM: Did you know him, Mick?

TOM: Well that's a good one.

Exchange glances with JUNIOR.

JUNIOR: 'Tis.

MICHAEL: I thought it was a good one.

LIAM: Did he pull the quare one?[11]

MICHAEL: What?

LIAM: The one that took off her clothes.

MICHAEL (*extreme reaction*): Aw for Jesus' sake, Liam!

LIAM: I was only joking.

TOM: Well that's a good one.

JUNIOR: 'Tis.

MICHAEL (*he goes to the counter*): We need another round.

PEGGY *has entered the front door and hallway. Now poking her head in lounge doorway. She is forty.*

PEGGY: Hello, did he arrive, is he here, did he come? Ary how yeh, Ridge, y'auld eejit yeh, you're as beautiful as ever, janeymack[12] you're looking delicious, you're as welcome as the flowers in May!

MICHAEL: Peggy!

PEGGY: Look at you — gorgeous — and the suit!

MICHAEL: You're looking well.

PEGGY: Oh flattery, flattery! Holding my own —

MISSUS (*appearing for a moment to see who has arrived*): Aaa —

PEGGY: How long are you home for?

MICHAEL: Oh —

MISSUS: Peggy —

PEGGY: How long? — Hello, Missus —

MICHAEL: Well —

PEGGY: A few weeks?

MICHAEL: Yeh. Well, we'll see.

PEGGY: Well you're a sight for sore eyes, you didn't change a bit, he's looking tip-top, isn't he?

TOM: Will you sit down —

PEGGY: Bejaneymack tonight, you're looking smashing!

TOM: Will you sit down and don't be making a show of yourself!

She sticks out her tongue at TOM, *pokes a finger in his ribs and sits on the arm of his chair, stroking his hair.*

TOM *making private world-weary faces to himself.*

PEGGY: When did you arrive?

MICHAEL: Last night.

PEGGY: Aa, did yeh?

MICHAEL: What are you having, Peggy?

PEGGY: Well, I'm going to have a gin and tonic in honour of yourself if his Nibs will allow me.

MICHAEL: Will we switch to shorts?

TOM: Oh? The Yank.

JUNIOR: The returned wank as the fella says!

MICHAEL (*calls*): The same again Missus, please!

TOM (*mock belligerently — as is his style*): I'll have a whiskey! —

JUNIOR: I'll stick to the pint —

LIAM: And a shot o' malt for me, Mike.

MICHAEL: Gin and tonic, Missus, three Scotch and a pint.

TOM: Irish!

MICHAEL: What?

TOM: Irish! Irish!

LIAM: And an Irish for me, Mike. Nothing but.

MICHAEL: One Scotch, Missus.

MISSUS: Thanks, thanks, alright, Michael.

PEGGY: Well.

Short silence.

LIAM: 'Around the fire one winter's night the farmer's rosy children sat.'

TOM: Oh?

PEGGY: It's nice to see us all together again, isn't it, it's like old times?

TOM: Isn't there a chair over there for yeh!

JUNIOR (*vacating his chair*): Here, a girleen.

PEGGY (*tongue out at* TOM, *a finger in his ribs*): Sourpuss! (*And takes* JUNIOR'*s chair.*)

JUNIOR (*belches*): Better out than your eye!

PEGGY: But tell us who you met over there, tell us all about the stars.

MICHAEL: Oh! (*Shrugs.*)

TOM *sighs.*

PEGGY: Did you meet what's-his-name?

TOM (*to himself*): Tck!

MICHAEL: You meet them all different times.

TOM (*to himself*): Do yeh?

MICHAEL: Peter O'Toole.

PEGGY: Aa go on.

JUNIOR (*impressed*): Did yeh, did yeh though?

LIAM: Old Lawrence himself.

MICHAEL: Jack Lemmon.

PEGGY: And the other fella, the long fella?

MICHAEL: No.

JUNIOR: Did you ever meet —

MICHAEL: Paul Newman, Al Pacino.

PEGGY: Louis Jordan?

MICHAEL: Who?

TOM: Hopalong Cassidy. (*To* JUNIOR) Give us a cigarette.

JUNIOR: That big one, the Redgrave one — Veronica, is it?

TOM (*irritably*): Vanessa.

JUNIOR: Fine bird — Oosh! Big.

TOM: You must be a very popular fella over there, Michael.

JUNIOR: You must be a very familiar fella over there, sir.

TOM (*groans*): Isn't this awful?

JUNIOR: Jealousy will get you nowhere, Ryan.

TOM: D'yeh hear Jack, D'yeh hear Sonny, off-to-Palestine head. Palestine, was it, or the Congo, was it, Junie, you were going to a few years ago?

JUNIOR: You were the one always talking about travelling — JJ arranging things for you — you were the one was meant to be off doing the great things.

TOM: I never mentioned the Palestine Police Force.

JUNIOR (*laughing — as is the case with the others through the following*): I got married.

TOM: And look at the cut of you!

JUNIOR: Nice home, nice baba, nice wife, Gloria — (*Singing.*) Oosh, she has a lovely bottom — set of teeth.

TOM: Ah but sure, what harm, your children will travel, your son will.

JUNIOR: He won't be a schoolmaster anyway.

TOM: An architect in Canada.

PEGGY (*laughing shrilly*): Oh yes, he was telling us one night!

TOM (*philosophical sniff*): But d'yeh see what I mean, the way the people are here; passing the buck. Twenty-seven years of age —

JUNIOR: Thirty-one —

TOM: And he's talking about what a five-month old son is going to do.

JUNIOR: Trotsky!

TOM: Now! That's smiling Jack the Palestine Policeman!

JUNIOR: Now! The great writer; did ye read his great socialist piece in *Boy's Own*?

TOM: Did you mend many carburettors today?

JUNIOR: Did yous give many slaps today?

He drains his glass; MISSUS *is approaching with a tray of drinks. She serves* LIAM *first as usual.*

MISSUS: Now, yas, that's the boy, Liam.

JUNIOR: Off to write his great book.

LIAM: Thank you, Mrs Kilkelly.

JUNIOR: But he had the first page wrote — the dedication, 'In gratitude to J.J. Kilkelly'.

TOM *reacts to this but bides his time.*

LIAM: A nation of drop-outs as that professor said on the Late Late Show.[13]

MISSUS: When will be seeing you on television, Michael, we do be watching?

MICHAEL: Well, it's a question of whether the things I'm in are sold to here or —

But MISSUS *is already on her way back to the bar.*

MISSUS: Your pint is on the way, Junior.

JUNIOR: No hurry, Missus. (*Sighs, lamenting into his empty glass.*)

TOM: I never dedicated anything to anyone.

JUNIOR: You never wrote anything.

TOM: And I certainly never thought of dedicating anything to JJ.

JUNIOR: Off to travel round the world to gain experience, and look at him, lazier than Luke O'Brien's dog that has to lean up against the wall to bark.

Big laugh.

PEGGY: Well, cheers, Michael!

MICHAEL: Good health, Peggy!

JUNIOR: Cathaoireacha! (*Cheers*)

PEGGY (*to* MICHAEL): You're a tonic.

LIAM: Good luck, fellas!

PEGGY: You're just what we needed.

JUNIOR (*again to his glass*): Yas.

PEGGY: But tell us all.

MICHAEL: Oh. You know?

PEGGY: Aa go on now, tell us all.

TOM *groans.*

What's up with you tonight?

TOM: 'Tell us all.' What does that mean?

PEGGY *looks away, hurt.*

LIAM: The sooner you two mavericks get hitched, the better.

TOM: Did you hear the definition of the gentleman farmer? A fella who bulls his own cows.

LIAM (*through the laughter*): Ryan! . . . Ryan! One good heifer any day is worth two months of a teacher's salary pound for pound.

TOM: Sterling or avoirdupois, Liam?

Off, the town clock ringing nine.

MISSUS *approaching with* JUNIOR's *pint.*

LIAM: Ryan! Ryan! I made four hundred and twenty-eight pounds on a single deal last week.

TOM: At a puffed up auction.

JUNIOR: God bless yeh, Missus.

LIAM: What?

TOM: Nothing. Good man.

MISSUS: Now.

MICHAEL *has risen to pay for the round but* LIAM *is now awkwardly on his feet, bumping into* JUNIOR, *in his haste.*

LIAM: No! No! It's my round! I'm getting this! —

JUNIOR (*protecting his pint*): Jasus! —

MICHAEL: This one is mine, Liam —

LIAM: No! No! Don't take anyone's money!

TOM: He's getting carried away.

LIAM: My round, fella! —

MISSUS: Sure it's alright, Liam. —

LIAM (*to* MICHEAL): I've a question for you in a minute

MISSUS: Sure it's —

LIAM: No! And have one yourself, Mrs Kilkelly.

MISSUS: No thanks, Liam, you're too good. (*Returning to bar.*)

LIAM: As a matter of fact my salary last year was — Well, it was in excess — greatly in excess of any figure you mentioned, boy. How much tax did you pay last year?

TOM: Sit down! —

LIAM: How much? —

JUNIOR: Sit *down*! —

LIAM: For a little comparison, boy —

TOM: Sit down outa that! —

JUNIOR: For Jasus' sake! Good luck who stood!

MISSUS *returning with change for* LIAM.

MISSUS: Now, Liam. That's the man.

PEGGY: How's the lodger, Missus?

JUNIOR: Josephine, wuw!

MISSUS *laughs, catering for them.*

PEGGY (*aside to* MICHAEL): Were they telling you about the one?

MISSUS: Aa but she's nice.

JUNIOR: Very good-natured they say.

MISSUS: But talking to the lads and her tea waiting on her in there this two hours. (*Wandering out to front door.*) That's who I am waiting for now. (*Alone in front door.*) D'ye know now. (*Where she remains for some moments.*)

Off, the church clock is chiming nine.

PEGGY: The place is gone to hell, isn't it?

MICHAEL: I don't know. Not irreparably. But *who* put up that partition? This was all one room. Remember, Tom, one of your socialist ideas to JJ? We were all very impressed: that there should be no public bar, no divisions or class distinctions.

LIAM: What d'yeh mean, not irreparably, fella?

MICHAEL (*not listening*): What? Get rid of that (*partition*) and see the space we'd have.

LIAM: I wouldn't like to be the fella to inherit the debts of this place.

MICHAEL: What are you on about all evening, Liam?

LIAM: You're not fond of America, Mick?

MICHAEL: This was our roots, Liam. This was to be our continuing cultural cradle: 'Let the word go forth from this time and place —' What? We could do it again! Wake up, wake up, boys and girls! — 'with a constant flow of good ideas.'

TOM *laughs/snorts at* MICHAEL's *romanticism.* What?

JUNIOR: We could!

TOM: Oh God, two of ye!

MICHAEL: But doesn't it seem a pity?

LIAM: That's okay, Mick —

MICHAEL: Well, doesn't it?

TOM: Create another pub?

MICHAEL: It was more than a pub.

TOM: Our culture, as indeed our nationalism, has always had the profoundest connections with the pub.

LIAM: That's okay, fella. I'm keeping my eye on it quietly. I've the customer already on my books that it suits.

PEGGY: Now. And poor Missus has other ideas. She thinks she has him earmarked for Anne.

LIAM (*cockily — and he is drunker than the others*): I'm in no hurry for any Anne, or any other Anne (*To* MICHAEL.) And, fella — fella! — that partition, out of the goodness of my pocket and my heart. Without obligation.

MICHAEL *looks at* TOM. TOM *has been waiting for him.*

TOM (*blandly*): Yeh?

LIAM (*laughs*): Unless, of course, you or your agent or your dollars would like me to handle the purchase for you. (*Sings in celebration to himself.*) 'Put the blanket on the ground!' (*And drinks.*)

MICHAEL *looks at* TOM *again.*

TOM (*smiles blandly*): The torch has been passed to a new generation.

JUNIOR (*has been puzzling over a song to himself*): 'The Sheep with their little lambs, passed me by on the road' — How does that begin?

TOM (*still smiling blandly, cynically at* MICHAEL): Hmm?

JUNIOR: That was JJ's song.

MICHAEL: But. (*Drinks.*) No, but Annette, come to think of it now, she looks like JJ.

PEGGY: Aa did you meet her? Isn't she a dote?

TOM: That's an extraordinary observation, Michael, seeing you didn't recognize her when you saw her.

MICHAEL: Aw, she does, does, looks like JJ.

PEGGY: But what has you home at this awful time of the year?

TOM: Hope, refuge, to drink from his wellsprings, the romantic in his fancy suit.

MICHAEL: It'd be no harm if you smartened yourself up a bit.

TOM (*going to counter*): You'll have to do better than that. Missus! Give us a packet of cigarettes. Ten Carrolls.

JUNIOR (*still trying to work it out*): 'The sheep with their little lambs passed me on the road.'

MICHAEL: What's your news, Peggy, they told me nothing.

PEGGY: Did they tell you we have a new priest?

MICHAEL: No. What's he like?

TOM: Ridiculous. Jesus, the last fella was bad, Fr Connolly was a snob, but at least that's something: this fella is an eejit.

PEGGY: For as much as you see of the church to know what he is.

TOM: Ah, but I went to check him out. My dear brethren — This was his sermon one Sunday. (*A warning to* PEGGY.) Don't interrupt me now! A maan (*man*) wan time, wan place, somewhere, that kept leaving the church before the maas (*Mass*) was ended, and continued this maalpractice though repeatedly warned about it. An' wan Sunday, my dear brethren, wasn't he sloping outa the church wance again, an' just as he was stepping outside didn't he look up at the clock to see what time 'twas, and d'yeh know what happened to him — d'ye know what happened to him! The church clock fell off the tower on top of him. Now! Killed stone dead.

PEGGY: Oh that's exaggerated, love.

TOM: Ridiculous. In this day and age! And the young ones are worse, falling over backwards, arse over elbow, to talk about sex to show how progressive they are. Sex: progressive — Jesus! — Ridiculous — Smoke? (*To* JUNIOR.)

PEGGY: You never see any good in the Church.

TOM: Aa but I do, love. Look at Liam there, and he's a regular churchgoer. And think of how the marriage figures all over the country would have slumped again only for all the young nuns jumping over the wall and the young priests waiting for them outside with their cassocks lifted.

PEGGY: Oh that's not right.

TOM: Ridiculous. Tell us something, Ridge, anything, something interesting, for God's sake.

PEGGY: . . . You got quiet or something, Michael. Tell us how are all the girls treating you? Oh, there was a rumour some time back — Wasn't there, love? — that you were married?

MICHAEL: No.

PEGGY: What?

MICHAEL: I answered that one.

PEGGY: What?

MICHAEL: Well, there was a girl — some time back. I knew her quite well — intimately — know what I mean? She was working in this night club, and this guy starts chatting her up, charming her, et cetera.

LIAM: Yeh?

JUNIOR: Big bird?

MICHAEL: But this guy, he had a few bucks anyway, a yacht and all that, and he was trying to persuade her go off on a trip with him.

JUNIOR: Yi-yi!

MICHAEL: That's the point. Eventually she did, the two of them alone on the boat for three weeks and he never tried to make her, never laid a hand on her. And she committed suicide.

TOM: Ary Ridge!

MICHAEL: I thought that would be your reaction.

LIAM: What?

TOM: Tck!

PEGGY (*smiling/frowning*): Did she drown herself or what Michael?

LIAM: A good boot in the arse she wanted.

MICHAEL: He was a sadist or something.

JUNIOR: He was a gomey[14] if you ask me.

TOM: And what's to signify in that story?

MICHAEL: I knew her. She was — a friend. And I knew him.

TOM (*rising*): Ridiculous country. The luck is on me I never left here. (*Calls.*) You might as well start filling the acthoring man's round, Missus!

MICHAEL: Better make them doubles!

TOM: Oh?

MICHAEL: Some people need the stimulation.
       TOM *laughs and exits to the Gents.*

PEGGY: But you must go into a lot of queer places over there?

MICHAEL: Maybe they'd only be *queer* to people from round here.

MISSUS: Doubles, Michael?

MICHAEL: Yes! Why not!

PEGGY: Oh, did they tell you they nearly marched on the North one night?

MISSUS: And a pint for you, Junior?

JUNIOR: Aye-aye, Missus!

PEGGY: Did they tell you?

LIAM: You're not a political animal, Mike?

MICHAEL: Excuse me, Liam, but no one round here ever called me Mick, Mike or Mickeen, okay?
       LIAM *nods, gravely bovine.*
       MICHAEL *offering cigarettes around.*
       PEGGY *accepts one unconsciously.*
       JUNIOR *singing snatches of 'All in the April Evening'.*

PEGGY: But you're getting on well over there?

MICHAEL: Strugglin'. Smoke, Junie?

PEGGY: Aa go on, but are —

JUNIOR: Thanks boy —

PEGGY: But are yeh getting on well though?

MICHAEL: Yep.

LIAM: Never use 'em.

PEGGY: But seriously, are you? (*He is lighting her cigarette.*)

MICHAEL: Yes.

JUNIOR: ⎱ 'The sheep with their little lambs . . .'

PEGGY: ⎰ Oh I didn't want this at all.
       (*But she puffs away at it.*) But do yeh like it all the time?

MICHAEL (*irritably*): Yes, Peggy, it's marvellous.

PEGGY: I see.

MICHAEL: And how are things with you?

PEGGY: Oh now.

MICHAEL: What?

PEGGY: Oh indeed —

MICHAEL: Yes?

PEGGY: Oh now, don't ask me.

MICHAEL: You gave up the dressmaking, didn't you?

PEGGY: Well, yeh know, around here.

MICHAEL: And the singing?

PEGGY: What singing? (*Remembering, laughing shrilly.*) Oh yes! JJ and his classical music, and he having me up to the nuns taking singing lessons. Wasn't I the eejit? And wait'll I tell yeh. (*Whispering.*) I had a crush on him. That slob. And he old enough to be my father. I'm not saying anything, it was all in innocence. And Sister Jerome, the singing teacher, tone deaf.

JUNIOR: ⎱ 'Passed me by on the road.'
MICHAEL: ⎰ Who was the slob?

PEGGY: JJ! Wait'll Tom comes back. (*He'll tell you.*)

MICHAEL: So, you're minding the house with your mother?

PEGGY: Oh but I do a morning or two a week, now and again, bookkeeping for the vet.

MICHAEL: And how is that old friend of yours, Helen Collins?

PEGGY: Isn't she married? Sure you must have known — She's producing like mad. Well, three and one on the way, as they say. But she's let herself go to hell — Hasn't she, Junie? — I'm meant to look like her daughter and she's ten months younger than me.

MICHAEL: I see.

PEGGY: But sure you must have known, wasn't she an old flame of yours? (*She pauses for only the briefest moment not wanting to acknowledge the thought that he has been getting at her.*) Oh but they're hopefully going to open a tourist office here next year — isn't that right, Liam? — and I'm in the running for it (*A smile at* LIAM.) if I know the right people. (*Then smiling bravely, a glance at* MICHAEL, *then averts her eyes.* MICHAEL *feeling ashamed of himself, looks at her empty glass and his own.*)

MICHAEL: That's — That's great. Hang on.
He goes to the counter and returns with his own and PEGGY'*s drink.*

LIAM: An' so was Beethoven, fellas. Stone deaf.

MICHAEL (*toasting* PEGGY): The best! Those curtains are yours.

PEGGY: And I was up all night finishing them. And never got paid.

MICHAEL: We didn't want to get paid.

PEGGY (*impulsively, she throws her arms around him*): Ary, yeh daft and romantic, it's lovely to see yeh! Oh gosh-golly, this is gone out again.
MICHAEL relights her cigarette.
MISSUS approaching with TOM'*s and* LIAM'*s drinks.*

MISSUS: I'll clear a few of these glasses out of yer way now.

JUNIOR: And the pint, Missus?

MISSUS: That's coming, Junior.
JUNIOR sighs to himself.

PEGGY: And d'yeh know? I could whistle the whole of the Sixth Symphony from beginning to end.

TOM (*returning from Gents*): They're daft alright.

PEGGY: Stop now, we were having a lovely time while you were out.

TOM: But do you yourself take questions like that seriously now?

PEGGY: Cheers, Michael!

MICHAEL: Cheers!

LIAM: Luck, fellas!

TOM: Michael?

MICHAEL: Questions like what?

LIAM: Questions like did Jesus Ch — Did you-know-who commit suicide.

TOM: And questions of the immoral and unethical behaviour of not screwing a bird on a boat.
MISSUS returning to the bar.
And, as Liam so delicately put it, for the proprietress's and my fiancée's sensitivities no doubt, questions like do you believe did you-know-who commit suicide.

MICHAEL: What's up with you?

TOM (*philosophical sniff*): Aw now.

JUNIOR (*to himself*): Aw fuck this! — Missus! — (*Striding to the bar, frustrated by his empty glass.*) Give me a drop of the hard tack too, and as well as the pint you're filling *now* you might start filling *another* pint for whoever is buying the next round.

MICHAEL: What's up with you?

TOM: Aw now.

PEGGY: You've changed, Michael.

MICHAEL: *I've* changed?

PEGGY: You used to be a grand shy lad with just the odd old, yeh know, flourish.

TOM: And supercilious with it.

MICHAEL: Well, I never nearly marched on the North, and I never thought a bank clerk is any more ridiculous for what she does than anybody else, and I never thought the jackboot in the arse was the cure for everything, and I never thought —

LIAM: Hold it, fella —

MICHAEL: That you (TOM) did either —

LIAM: Right there, fella —

MICHAEL: And to think of it! —

LIAM: Fella!

MICHAEL: We were going to change all this!

LIAM: Fella!

TOM: You're missing the point —

MICHAEL: In this very room! And now it's bollocks talk about Protestants —

TOM: No one said anything about —

MICHAEL: The great anti-cleric (TOM) nearly going off to fight a Holy War!

TOM: No one said anything about —

LIAM: A minority Catholic group being oppressed! —

MICHAEL: You must be very unhappy in your lives —

TOM: Nothing to do with clerics —

LIAM: Fella! —

TOM: It's your ridiculous attitude —

LIAM: Brave Irish Catholic men and women —

MICHAEL: Everything seems ridiculous to you —

TOM: Women and sex orgies and some myth in your mind about JJ —

LIAM: Because — because a discriminating majority —

MICHAEL: You're really into 1917 —

TOM: What's all this talk about JJ? —

LIAM: A discriminating and — And! — gerrymandering majority! —

MICHAEL: Back to the stuck-in-the-mud-festering ignorance! —

TOM: 'Wellsprings and lost horizons!' —

MICHAEL: Yes! —

LIAM: A gerrymandering! —

MICHAEL: Lost horizons! —

LIAM: Fella, fella! A gerrymandering majority! —

TOM: Never arriving at reality —

LIAM: You can't deny it, you can't deny it — And! —

TOM: All mixed up —

LIAM: And! Racial memory, boy! —

TOM: Stop, Liam —

LIAM: Deny that one, boy! —

TOM: Stop, Liam! —

LIAM: Cause you can't deny it! — And! — And! — You can't deny it! —

TOM: Stop! —

LIAM: Cause — cause! — Fella! — Fella! —

TOM: Stop-stop-stop!

LIAM: You can't deny it!

TOM: Stop, will you, Liam! — Stop! — Forget that.

LIAM: I will not forget it! (*Forgetting it.*) I will not forget it.

TOM: You and your kind with your rose-coloured lights that you can switch on and off so easily. You don't want reality.

MICHAEL: Well, if yours is the reality.

TOM: Oh?

MICHAEL: Reality is always about poverty, is it?

TOM: No, it's always about flowers. Look, excuse me, Michael —
But LIAM *is off again.*

LIAM: And there's a thing called Truth, fella — you may not have heard of it. And Faith, fella. And Truth and Faith and Faith and Truth inex — inextricably — inextricably — bound. And-And! — cultural heritage — you may not (have) heard of it — No border, boy! And cultural heritage inex-inextricably bound with our Faith and Hope and Hope and Faith and *Truth*! And some of us, and some of us, at least, cherish and — cherish and — and — are not supercilious, boy, with it — about it. Fella! I will not forget it! Last refuge in Europe.

TOM: Fine, Liam. Rest yourself now.

JUNIOR (*in answer to a glance from* LIAM): Well spoken, boy.

TOM: Look, excuse me, Michael, but what is the point, the real issue of what we are discussing!

MICHAEL: Well, maybe I have changed, because my enjoyment in life comes from other things than recognizing my own petty malice in others.

TOM: Is that the point?

MICHAEL: A simple matter — and it's not a dream — of getting together and doing what we did before.

TOM: Is that the point? To do what we did before? And tell me, what did we do before?

MICHAEL: To do what we did before!

TOM (*to himself*): Jesus! Extraordinary how the daft romantics look back at things.

MICHAEL: Why is everyone calling me a romantic?

TOM: It's more polite.

MICHAEL: You would never have made the statements you are making tonight a few years ago.

LIAM: I'd reckon, fella, that proves he ain't static.

MICHAEL: It depends on which direction he went.

LIAM: I'd reckon, fella, that you are all — (*washed-up*).

TOM: No. Hold on. I think you're serious, Michael, hmm? I think he's serious. I think we have *another* leader. Another true progressive on our hands at last, lads. Another white fuckin' liberal.

PEGGY: Shh, love!

TOM: Home to re-inspire us, take a look at our problems, shake us out of our lethargy, stop us vegetating, show us where we went wrong —

MICHAEL: You're choosing the words —

TOM: Show us that we're not forgotten, bringing his new suicidal fuckin' Christ with him!

PEGGY: Love —

MICHAEL: Vegetating, lethargy, forgotten —

TOM: And most surprisingly, I think the poor hoor — like his illustrious predecessor — does not know where he is himself.

MICHAEL (*laughs*): I've been having a great time —

TOM: No! — No! —

MICHAEL: Marvellous time!

TOM: You're too depressed, Jack, too much on the defensive Jack —

MICHAEL: Marvellous! But cheers anyway, Jack, cheers!

TOM: The point, Michael, the real point and issue for you, Michael — D'yeh want to hear? You came home to stay, to *die*, Michael.

LIAM: Correct.

TOM: And fair enough, do that, but be warned, we don't want another JJ.

MICHAEL (*laugh/smile is gone*): I never mentioned I had any intention of staying home.

LIAM: Correct.

MICHAEL: What do you know about JJ?

LIAM: Enough, fella. But leave it to me. I'll rescue this place shortly.

MICHAEL: You spent so much of your time away as a student, the story was they were going to build a house for you in the university.

TOM: Michael.

MICHAEL: And you know nothing about JJ either.

TOM: I'm marking your card for you. JJ is a slob.

MICHAEL: He —

TOM: A slob —

MICHAEL: Isn't.

TOM: Is, was, always will be. A slob. He's probably crying and slobbering on somebody's shoulder now this minute, somewhere around Galway. Missus in there treats him as if he were a child.

JUNIOR (*angrily, rising*): And what else can the woman do?

TOM: I'm just telling him.

JUNIOR (*exits to Gents*): Jesus!

MICHAEL: Why?

TOM: Why what?

MICHAEL: Why are you telling me — and glorying in it?

TOM: JJ is a *dangerous* and weak slob. He limped back from England, about 1960. England was finished for him. He could not face it again. I hope this is not ringing too many bells for you personally. And he would have died from drink, or *other* things, but for the fact that the John F. Kennedy show had started on the road round about then, and some auld women in the town pointed out doesn't he look like John F. Kennedy. And JJ hopped up on that American-wrapped band-wagon of so-called idealism —

MICHAEL: He had his own idealism.

TOM: Until he began to think he *was* John F. Kennedy.

MICHAEL: And, in a way, he was.

TOM: And Danny O'Toole up the road thinks he's Robert Mitchum and he only five feet two?

MICHAEL: He re-energized this whole town.

TOM: And Danny O'Toole is winning the west for us? Then people started to look at our new slob-hero afresh. People like Missus in there — she pinned her hopes on him — and, he quickly hopped up on her too. And, so, became the possessor of her premises, which we, and others, put together for him, restyled at his dictates into a Camelot, i.e., a thriving business for selling pints.

MICHAEL: No —

TOM: Alright, selling pints was a secondary consideration. Like all camelot-pub owners he

would have welcomed a clientele of teetotallers. His real purpose of course was to foster the arts, to give new life to broken dreams and the — horn — of immortality, nightly, to mortal men . . . But then came the fall.

MICHAEL: The assassination.

TOM: Of whom?

MICHAEL: Kennedy.

TOM: Oh, I thought for a minute there you were talking about *our* president, JJ.

MICHAEL: Well.

TOM: What?

MICHAEL: Well, as I heard it, after Kennedy's death, the *character*-assassination of JJ started in earnest.

TOM: No.

MICHAEL: Well, as you said yourself earlier, the priest's visits, other people's visits and the people the priest represented.

TOM: No. After Kennedy's assassination, the grief, yes. We all experienced it. But is grief a life-long profession?

MICHAEL: A lot of people feared and hated JJ in this town.

TOM: Feared? No. Never.

MICHAEL: Well, even on the evidence of tonight one could easily get the impression that this town could have had a few things — just a few, Tom? — to do with 'our' president's fall.

TOM: No! Look, he hopped up on the load of American straw and he had so little going for him that when that load of straw went up in smoke, JJ went up with it. Oh yes, they *hated* him — Why wouldn't they: Puppetry, mimicry, rhetoric! What had he to offer anyone? Where were the facts, the definitions?

MICHAEL: Why are you getting so excited?

TOM: I'm not getting excited. He-fed-people's-fantasies. That all he did. Fed — people's — fantasies.

MICHAEL: People are afraid of realizing themselves.

TOM: Look, look, look — lookit! (*To himself.*) Shit!

MICHAEL: They fear that.

TOM: Realizing themselves? Like you did! Look! — Lookit! — leaving aside the superficial fact that he looked like John F. Kennedy — somewhere around the left ball — he could just as easily have thought he was John McCormack or Pope John.[15] He had so little going for him and we are such a ridiculous race that even our choice of assumed images is quite arbitrary.

MICHAEL: Are you finished?

TOM: The only mercy in the whole business, as I see it, is that he did not in fact think he was John McCormack.

LIAM: Man, Tomeen!

MICHAEL: JJ's respect, opinion and esteem for you —'

TOM: To thine own self be true? God we're a glorious people alright.

LIAM: C'rrect.

LIAM has risen and is going to Gents.

TOM: Look, don't fret yourself about not seeing him tonight —

MICHAEL: I haven't given up on seeing him tonight.

TOM (*groans*): Aw Lord! There are plenty of JJs about. (*Pointing at* LIAM *who is exiting to Gents.*) I prefer *that*.

MICHAEL: You won't listen to my interpretation?

PEGGY: Aa, lads —

TOM: By all means — if you have one.

MICHAEL: JJ's opinion of you —

TOM: And if it's a sensible one.

MICHAEL: The *esteem* he held you in, always, way above the rest of us —

TOM: Ah-ah-ah-ah! Don't try that one. Remember where you are now. It's clear from the way you've been talking all night that the — innocence — naiveté of New York has softened your head, but remember you're talking to the people of a little town in the west of Ireland now: a little more sophisticated than that for us, Michael.

MICHAEL: JJ and his wife, his first wife, were walking along a street, and —

TOM: In England?

MICHAEL: Yes.

PEGGY: Lads.

TOM: Just making sure I'm following facts.

MICHAEL: And a car came along, the steering was perfect, the driver was sober, but the driver was some poor unhappy bitter little prick who wanted to kill someone, anyone, and he drove the car up on the footpath and knocked JJ's wife over, and she died in hospital three months later.

TOM: Yes.

MICHAEL: And that's what you describe as the *limp* JJ came into this town with?

TOM: Yes?

MICHAEL: What do you mean 'yes'?

TOM: Yes, I heard that story, and I'm sorry for him — if it's true.

MICHAEL: What?

TOM: No-no-no. Like, there are a lot of things we heard and believed some years ago, but we're a little older now.

MICHAEL: A man — after a tragedy like that —

TOM: More interesting stories are emerging about JJ's past.

MICHAEL: To pull himself together after a tragedy like that and start afresh.

TOM: Look, I don't recall anybody ever reading any headlines about that tragic and dramatic event.

PEGGY: He made it up, Michael.

TOM (*to* PEGGY): Keep out of it. And people are now of the opinion that JJ was never married before, that there was no first wife, that there was only a bird, and there was no —

MICHAEL: Jesus, you're exceeding yourself! What's happened to you?

TOM: Alright, there *was* an accident! — and you can drag your own limp into it and your own grandmother as well — but it does not change the fact of the point we are *now* discussing, which is that JJ is, was, always will be a slob. Now, can-you-contradict-me?

MICHAEL: I like him.

TOM: A-a-a-w! Back to the flowers. How nice, how fey, how easy for you! 'I like him.' And the way he upset and thwarted and wilfully and irresponsibly inflated and abused people. When I think of it. 'Together let us explore the stars.' Jesus!

JUNIOR comes out of the Gents: his hand up for attention: he had got the first line of the song.

JUNIOR: I've got it! 'All in the April evening.'

TOM (*to himself*): And left them high and dry.

PEGGY (*catering to him*): And bills outstanding all over the country, love, didn't he?

An angry grimace/gesture from TOM: *he does not want her comments.* JUNIOR — *this is not his game — goes to the bar and stays there for some moments.*

JUNIOR: Missus! Throw us out that other pint.

TOM: God, we're a glorious people alright. Half of us, gullible eejits, people like yourself, ready to believe in anything. And the other half of us —

MICHAEL: People like yourself, ready to believe nothing.

TOM: People like yourself — people like yourself — ready to believe, get excited, follow to the death any old bollocks with a borrowed image, any old JJ who has read a book on American politics or business methods. Jesus, images: fuckin' neon shadows!

PEGGY: Love.

MICHAEL: And the other half of us ready to believe in nothing.

TOM: No! You don't understand! Never the sound, decent, honest-to-God man for us. Never again in this world, for us, or for anyone else.

JUNIOR joins them.

JUNIOR: Good luck, fellas.

Silence.

MICHAEL (*quietly*): He nearly made it.

TOM: 'Nearly'? I thought you were knocking us for that word a few minutes ago.

MICHAEL: He was great.

TOM: In what way? When? — How? — Where? — Convince me! — Tell me!

MICHAEL: He hadn't got over the first knock when the second happened.

TOM: Isn't that my proof, isn't that the test of a man? Sure all you're mentioning is his — dubious — misfortunes and some kind of hypothetical potential. What did he achieve? What was he talking about?

MICHAEL: I don't know what he was talking about but wasn't he right?

TOM: Tck! . . . That's fine, you don't know, that concludes the matter.

MICHAEL: Did you believe too much in him?

TOM: Now, I like that. You're coming up to our standards after all.

MICHAEL: Do you feel he let you down personally or what?

TOM: The gentle romantic has his subtly nasty side.

MICHAEL: Did you hope too much in him? — Was he your only lifeline?

TOM: No, I didn't hope too much in him, and I never ran messages for him or fell flat on my face for him.

MICHAEL: He didn't ask you to —

TOM: Bloody sure he didn't.

MICHAEL: Because you were the — doyen? — of his group.

TOM: I wouldn't have minded him — succeeding — but I had him taped from the start.

JUNIOR (*warning that* MISSUS *has appeared*): Yas, enough dialectics as the fella said.

But MISSUS *has come outside the bar-counter to intercept* LIAM *who is entering from the Gents and slip him a drink on the house and have a fawning word with him.*

TOM: I can see you're not the wide-eyed boy who left here —

MICHAEL: Thanks —

TOM: But since you have nothing to offer but a few distorted memories, and a few personal tricks on the burning monk caper, I'm marking your card. You've come home to stay, die, whatever — and you're welcome — but save us the bullshit. We've had that from your predecessor. We won't put up with it again. Don't try to emulate him, no re-energizing, cultural cradles or stirring that old pot. Now I know you have it in you to take careful account of what I've said, and the *security* — Michael! — of wiser steps.

MICHAEL: Are you threatening me?

TOM: Holy Moses, Michael! — Me twin! — We don't threaten anyone. We don't have to! All we have to do — all we have ever had to do — is wait! (*He laughs.*) We leave it at that? God bless you.

MICHAEL: I'm not sure what I came home for, but I think I'm finding out.

LIAM *and* MISSUS *joining them.*

LIAM: Leave that matter to me, Mrs Kilkelly.

MISSUS: Better looking this man (LIAM) is getting every day, isn't he? D'ye know now. Yas. You didn't bring a blondie home with you, Michael?

MICHAEL: There are dark-haired girls in America too, Missus.

MISSUS: Musha, God help them. Be careful of them American ladies, a mac (*son*).

MICHAEL (*pointedly looking about*): How's business, Missus?

MISSUS: Oh, well, now, the off-season. Isn't that it, Liam?

LIAM: That is c'rrect, Mrs Kilkelly.

MISSUS: And things'll be picking up for us soon. Now.

MICHAEL: What you should do is get in a few of the natives telling funny stories for the tourists, and singing. And when things get going you could move out with the family and live in the henhouse for the season.

MISSUS: Isn't that what they're doing, some of them, living with the hens, to make room for tourists. And some of them, Michael —

MICHAEL: Yes, I didn't pay you for the last round.

MICHAEL *is standing, a roll of money ostentatiously in his hand.* MISSUS *feels offended by his cutting her short.*

MISSUS: Five pounds and sixty-nine new pence. Yas, your mother is delighted; I was talking to her for a minute this morning in the post office and she drawing out a wad of money. (*All get the implications of her remark. She gives* MICHAEL *change out of her cardigan pocket.*) Thanks, Michael. That's the woman with the money.

JUNIOR: Looking for a girl he is, Missus, wasn't he admiring the daughter?

MISSUS: Aa, Annette.

PEGGY: Aa, she's a dote! What's she going to do, Missus?

JUNIOR: I bet she wants to be an air hostess.

MISSUS: The cute Junior: how did you know that now?

JUNIOR: Oh-oh!

MISSUS: No. We were thinking of the bank. (*A glance at* LIAM.) Well, for the meanwhile, that is.

JUNIOR: Speak of an angel!

PEGGY: Oh hello, Anne!

ANNE (*silently*): Hello!

    ANNE *has come in. She moves aside with* MISSUS *to report briefly in a whisper — little more than a shake of her head. (She has not found her father.)* MISSUS *contains a sigh.*

PEGGY: The lovely coat! (ANNE's)

MISSUS: And any sign of Josephine?

ANNE: She's up in Daly's lounge. She said she had a sandwich and not to bother with her tea.

MISSUS: Alright.

    MISSUS *wanders off, out to the front door, sighs out at the night, then exits upstairs. And, meanwhile,* ANNE *is taking off her coat and moving to attend the bar.*

TOM: Anne! Come 'ere a minute. D'yeh know our acthoring man, Michael Ridge?

MICHAEL: D'yeh not remember me?

    She has a natural shyness but it does not efface an interest she has in him.

    Hmm?

ANNE: I do.

MICHAEL: What?

ANNE: I remember you here with Daddy.

MICHAEL: How is he?

ANNE: Not so good. (*She looks up at him, gravely, simply, for his reaction. He nods, simply, his understanding. Then she smiles.*) You're welcome home. (*And they shake hands.*)

TOM: Gee, kid, you were only so high when I saw you last.

MICHAEL: Is it Anne or Annette?

    She shrugs: her gesture meaning that the choice is his.

    Anne.

    She nods, smiles, a silent 'okay'.

    You're finished school?

ANNE: Three months time.

MICHAEL: And you won't be sorry.

ANNE: No. (*And she laughs.*)

PEGGY: Dreadful people, the nuns. Dreadful. Sister Bartholomew is the worst, don't you think, Anne?

ANNE: Isn't she dead?

PEGGY (*laughing shrilly*): Oh God yes, I forgot! I'm awful. But they're dreadful tyrants.

    ANNE *is already moving away.*

MICHAEL: Will you come back and join us?

ANNE (*a toss of her head, smiling back at him*): I might.

TOM: Is it Anne or Annette, Michael?

MICHAEL: And she *is* like JJ. Well, things are looking up!

JUNIOR: Will we go up and have a few in Paddy Joe Daly's?

MICHAEL: The opposition, the enemy? No! We're grand here now.

JUNIOR: We'll introduce you to Josephine —

TOM: } Grrrah!

JUNIOR: } Grrrah!

PEGGY: But were they telling you about the one? And the hair? And the walk?

MICHAEL: Red hair? Frizzed out? I saw her crossing the street near the bank when I was driving my mother today.

PEGGY: The most ridiculous thing that ever hit this town — isn't she, love?

MICHAEL: I was wondering who she was. She's a fine-looking bird.

JUNIOR (*his appreciation again for large ladies*): She's big.

PEGGY: Excuse me —

JUNIOR: No bother there, sham.

MICHAEL: No! Anne! Hope!

TOM: God!

PEGGY: Excuse me! That girl (*Josephine*) is fine looking?

MICHAEL: Hmm?

PEGGY: I'm disappointed in you, Michael.

LIAM: Dirty aul' thing.

JUNIOR: I hear she fancies you, cowboy.

PEGGY (*at* MICHAEL): Tck!

MICHAEL: What?

PEGGY: Your taste. That girl.

MICHAEL: I'm not interested in her.

TOM: Gee, tough luck on Josephine.

PEGGY (*neurotically*): She's a disgusting girl, she's stupid — Did you see her neck?

MICHAEL: I only said —

PEGGY: Of course you didn't. Everyone is talking about her, she won't last long here. She wouldn't even be kept in this place only for it's up to its eyes in debt.

TOM: What's up with yeh?

PEGGY: Every man in the town, married and single, around her, like — like terriers.

TOM: What's up with yeh?

PEGGY: Ary I get sick of this marvellous stuff. Everything is *marvellous* with Ridge.

MICHAEL: I only said —

PEGGY: Everything is *marvellous* —

MICHAEL: Alright she isn't marvellous —

PEGGY: Everything *is marvellous* —

TOM: What are ye — what's —

MICHAEL: But she's good-looking, good legs.

PEGGY: Everything is *marvellous* —

JUNIOR: Jugs (*tits*) —

MICHAEL: She has a good job —

JUNIOR: Bottom —

PEGGY: Will she keep it — Will she keep it? —

MICHAEL: Sexy-looking —

PEGGY: I don't agree, I don't agree! —

TOM: Wait a minute —

PEGGY: I don't agree! —

TOM: Hold on a minute —

PEGGY: Why should I agree? —

TOM: What are ye talking about! —

LIAM: She's a dirty aul' thing!

TOM (*silencing them*): What-are-ye-on-about! (*To* PEGGY.) And what are you squealin' about?

PEGGY (*laughs suddenly, shrilly*): Ary shut up the lot of ye!

TOM: Are you finished? She's ridiculous alright.

PEGGY: Of course, she is —

TOM: And you're worse! The whole town is filled with — pookies.

LIAM: Strangers comin' in to run the town, fellas.

TOM (*groans to himself, then*): Anne! Annette! Missus! Where are they? Pint, gin, tonic, Scotch, two Irish! (*He feels* MICHAEL's *eyes on him.*) Yeh?

MICHAEL: Why don't you leave?

TOM: But I might lose my religion.

PEGGY: What's he (MICHAEL) saying?

MICHAEL: You can still get out.

TOM: But what of my unfinished work here? My feverish social writings. Whose red pen would in merit and logic stand up to the passionate lucidity of Fr. O'Mara's sermons? Would you take my place, take me from my great vocation, and send me off to be setting myself on fire in the great adventure of the New World?

MICHAEL: There's still time.

PEGGY: What's he saying?

TOM: I've always taken my responsibilities seriously.

PEGGY: Of course you have, love.

TOM *is rolling his head in reaction to her.*

MICHAEL: What responsibilities for Christ's —

TOM: My mother, Jack, for Christ's sake, and my father, Jack, for Christ's sake. You enquired about my mother's health earlier but, for some strange reason or other, not my father's. Well, I can assure you they're both still alive — (*To* LIAM.) Don't be making wild-life faces at me, cowboy, I've got the goods on you!

LIAM: Didn't say a thing, fella.

Off, the town clock chiming ten.

MICHAEL: Do you know what he said about you one evening?

TOM: Who? (*Closes his eyes; he doesn't want to know.*) Oh yes, our president.

MICHAEL: That if you didn't break out of it, none of us would.

TOM (*continues with eyes shut*): Break out of what?

MICHAEL: This.

TOM: Are you speaking geographically?

MICHAEL: Not necessarily. This talk all evening, and what it seems to represent?

TOM: What does it represent?

MICHAEL: You'd think the sixties never happened.

TOM: What did the sixties represent?

MICHAEL: Not this.

TOM: You haven't answered-a-single-question-all-night. You, too, are a great dealer in the abstract.

MICHAEL: The social movements of the minority's groups in the sixties, in towns, villages and cities, was the rising culture.

TOM: And *is* this the *rising* culture, begod?

ANNE *arrives with a tray of drinks.*

ANNE: Scotch, Michael? —

TOM: Ah, God bless yeh, Anne! Because, despite the current swing to the right of the majorities, and the crusades of the christian fundamentalist majorities, promoting medieval notions of morality and reality, begod —

JUNIOR: ⎱Thanks, girl —

TOM: ⎰We the creative minorities are still here, begod, thank God, swinging to the left, while they're swinging to the right. But we, the swinging-to-the-lefters will see those swinging-to-the-righters go swinging to their decline and disintegration. For! — And! — As you say! — Even though we are the minority, it is always out of the creative cultural minority, it is always out of the creative cultural minority *groups* that change irrevocable comes about! — Begod! What do you think of that? (*To* MICHAEL.) Happy? He's not happy still — begod! And why would he? I left out the big one! (*He is searching his pockets for money for the round.*)

LIAM: Good luck, fellas!

TOM: Because — fellas! — despite us, the representatives of the rising cultural minorities afore-mentioned, what is going on now, this minute, ablow in Paddy Joe Daly's? 'Put th' fuckin' blanket on the ground.' (*They laugh.*) But Paddy Joe Daly is not the enemy. He may personify it, the bullets in his bandy legs may symbolize it, the antics of his lump of a wife may dramatize it. But no — No! — the real enemy — the big one! — that we shall overcome, is the country-and-western system itself. Unyielding, uncompromising, in its drive for total sentimentality. A sentimentality I say that would have us all an unholy herd of Sierra Sues, sad-eyed inquisitors, sentimental Nazis, fascists, sectarianists, black-and-blue shirted nationalists, with spurs a-jinglin', all ridin' down the trail to Oranmore. Aw great, I knew I'd make ye all happy.

They laugh.

JUNIOR: Aw, Jasus, the twins! (*He slips the money for the round to* ANNE.)

MICHAEL: Do you ever go for rambles down to Woodlawn like we used to, Anne?

ANNE: Sometimes.

And she moves off to answer a tapping on the counter in the public bar — a toss of her head and a smile back at MICHAEL.

JUNIOR: The two of ye together might make up one decent man.

TOM: Well, whatever about me, I don't know what reason you had to hang around here, Sonny.

JUNIOR: We've had the complimenting stage, let that be an end to the insulting stage, and we'll get on to the singing stage. (*Singing.*) 'All in the April evening' —

TOM: And your father won't leave you the garage. One of the young brothers will have that.

JUNIOR (*smile disappears*): They can have it so they can.

TOM: They will.

LIAM: And that's the belief in the town.

JUNIOR (*back in form*): No! No! They're all off, the whole seven of them, to join the Palestine Police Force next week. Wuw! Jasus, Jasus . . .! Come on, Peggy, you're the singer here. 'All in the —'

PEGGY: Oh stop, Junior.

JUNIOR: Come on, that one, JJ's song —

PEGGY: I don't know when I sang last.

JUNIOR: 'All in the April evening, April airs —'

PEGGY: Stop, Junie. No. No —

JUNIOR: } 'The sheep with their little lambs —' Come on!

PEGGY: } No, no, no, no, no —

JUNIOR: } Come on, come on —

PEGGY: } No, no, no, no, no —

LIAM (*about to sing*): Fellas!

PEGGY: Alright, so.

PEGGY is standing up; she sings the first line of 'All in the April Evening'; then giggling, fixing herself into the pose of the amateur contralto at the wedding, and singing deliberately off key and 'poshly' distorting the words.

'All in the April evening, April airs were abroad.' — No, wait a minute . . . 'This is my lovely dee. This is thee dee I shall remember the dee' — Christina Jordan, did you ever hear her? — 'I'll remember, I'll remember —!' The cheek of her, not a note right in her head — 'I'll remember, I'll remember —' Jeeney, the eejit!' (*And she sits abruptly, hands over her mouth, giggling.*)

LIAM: Fellas!

TOM *exits to the Gents.*

(*Fancies himself as a cowboy singer.*) 'There's a bridle hanging on the wall / There's a saddle in a lonely stall / You ask me why my tear drops fall / It's that bridle hanging on the wall / And that pony for my guide I used to ride down the trail watching the moon beam low-ow —' (*The others stifling their laughter at him.*)

MICHAEL *and* JUNIOR, *through the song.*

MICHAEL: I need a drop more water for this one.

JUNIOR: One voice! One voice!

MICHAEL *joins* ANNE *at the bar.*

LIAM: 'And the pony for my guide I used to ride down the trail / he's gone where the good ponies go-oh / There's a bridle hanging on the wall . . .' (*etc.*)

JUNIOR: Lovely hurlin', cowboy!

PEGGY: Smashin', Liam!

LIAM: I must mosey to the john again, fellas. Watch that latchyco, Anne! 'You ask me why my tear drops fall —'

TOM *entering as* LIAM *exits.*

TOM: And *your* sisters or young brother will have the farm.

LIAM: Sure, fella. (*Exits, returns a moment later in response to* TOM's '*Hey!*'.)

TOM: Hey! This eejit, this bollocks, with his auctioneering and tax-collecting and travel-agenting and property dealing and general greedy unprincipled poncing, and Sunday night dancing — Mr successful-swinging-Ireland-In-The-Seventies! — and he's still — Jesus! — watching the few acres of bog at home, still — Jesus! — caught up in the few acres of bog around the house at home.

LIAM: What — what would you say, fella, if I said it was mine already?

TOM: I'd say, fella, that you're a liar.

LIAM: Well, it is mine.

TOM: As the bishop said to the actress.

LIAM: By deed — by deed! — The deeds are signed over to me.

PEGGY: But why suddenly all this talk tonight?

LIAM: And my young brother is studying to be a doctor.

TOM: Weren't *you* studying to be a doctor?

LIAM: Oh, d'yeh hear him now?

TOM: And quietly, it was a fortuitous outcome for the sick and the ailing that you never made it.

LIAM: D'yeh hear him now — Tro'sky!

TOM: And even if the young brother proves less thick than you, haven't the two spinster sisters a claim on the place?

LIAM: By deed —

PEGGY: But why —

TOM: No — No deed! Because your attempts, and the details of your attempts, and the details of the failure of your attempts to unseat them and evict them off the nine-and-a-half acre O'Brady estate are widely discussed and reported upon — in this town.

LIAM: I'm setting up my sisters in an antique shop.

JUNIOR (*quietly*): That's the place for them.

TOM: And, quietly, and with little or no respect, I don't think either of them, in their advanced post-state of nubility, has much prospects of the bed.

LIAM: Oh d'yeh hear — I take exception to that remark!

TOM: Take what you like. Give us a drop of water here too for this one, Anne. So, the next time you see someone driving around in a Merc[16] just think of him.

ANNE *arrives to add water to* TOM's *drink.*

LIAM: Why don't you get married?

TOM: Why don't yeh yourself? (*To* ANNE.) That's fine. (*He is rooting in his pockets again for further coins to pay for the last round.*)

LIAM: Afraid of his Mammy and Daddy. And, d'ye know, he has to hand over his paypacket to his Mammy, intact, every week, into her hand.

TOM: I get paid by cheque, Liam — monthly. (*To* ANNE.) Just a sec.

ANNE: It's paid for —

TOM: Just a sec —

LIAM: Then cheque, countersigned, it has to be handed over to Mammy.

PEGGY: Aa, change the subject, lads —

ANNE: Junie paid for it.

JUNIOR: Sure poor auld Liam couldn't go bringing a woman into a house where there's three of them already —

PEGGY (*offering* TOM *two pounds*): Here, love —

TOM (*to* ANNE): What?

JUNIOR: Jasus, they'd ate each other.

TOM (*to* LIAM): You are the worst of the worst type of a ponce of a modern fuckin' gombeen man,[17] that's all that's to be said about it! (*To* ANNE.) What?

ANNE: It's paid for, Tom.

LIAM: There's an answer for that one too.

TOM: Yes, Liam.

JUNIOR: It's paid for, it's okay —

LIAM (*only just containing his drunken fury*): My birthright!

TOM   ⎫ (*to* JUNIOR): What? —
PEGGY ⎭ Here, loveen —

TOM   ⎫ (*to* PEGGY): What? —
LIAM   ⎭ That's no argument! —

TOM   ⎫ (*to* LIAM): What?
JUNIOR ⎭ It's okay, it's paid for —

TOM: What?

LIAM: The eldest son, fella!

TOM (*to* LIAM): What are you talking about? (*To* ANNE.) And who asked anyone to pay for it? (*To himself.*) Tck! — Look — Jesus! — (*To* LIAM.) Look, don't talk to me about argument — Look — lookit, don't talk to me at all! (*To* PEGGY.) Will-you-put-that (*money*) — away! (*To* LIAM.) You're only a fuckin' bunch of keys! (*To* ANNE.) Bring us another round!

ANNE *returns to bar.*

PEGGY: Why don't you drive up and bring Gloria down. Do, Junie.

JUNIOR: Oh-oh.

PEGGY: Aa go on, good lad, do, do.

JUNIOR: Won't I be seeing her later!

LIAM: I'll squeeze your head for you some night, Ryan.

TOM: Good man. My round is coming, is it, Anne?

LIAM: Cause I hate ye all — and all belongin' to ye!

He sweeps up his newspaper, then wrong-foots himself in his indecision as to whether to leave or not, remembers he has a stake in the place and exits to the Gents.

JUNIOR: Once you go once you're knackered for the evening.

MICHAEL *laughing with* JUNIOR, *then* TOM *starts to chuckle and he joins* MICHAEL *and* ANNE *at the counter.*

ANNE: But he's a lovely dancer though.

TOM, MICHAEL, JUNIOR *laughing again.* ANNE *joining in.*

TOM: Now: the new generation: 'you ask me why my tear drops fall, it's that pony hangin' on the wall'. *Excepting* PEGGY *they are laughing again. And* JUNIOR *is now rising to go to the Gents.*

JUNIOR: Jasus, Jasus — (*To* PEGGY.) Excuse me, the call of the wild, the enemy within — you have a great pair of kidneys, Ridge! Shake hands with the devil, wuw!

And he has exited to the Gents.

PEGGY *now continues self-consciously isolated at the table, her back to the others. And they have all but forgotten her.* TOM's *mood is now pacificatory.*

ANNE: What part are you in, Michael?

MICHAEL: Well, I'm not working, obviously at the moment, but —

TOM: What part of America she's asking, eejit.

MICHAEL *looks at him:* TOM *gestures/shrugs that no malice is intended.*

MICHAEL: New York.

ANNE: What's it like?

MICHAEL: Well, it's not too bad at all. Were you ever in the States?

ANNE: No, but I was in London last summer. Two of us went over and we stayed with some friends of daddy's.

MICHAEL: Did you? Did he arrange it for you?

ANNE: Yes.

PEGGY (*isolated*): Indeed I was there myself for a few months once.
 Nobody is listening to her.

ANNE: We went to a place — I said I was eighteen — and got a job in an ice-cream factory.

PEGGY: I was putting the tops on polish tins.
 ANNE *has set up the other round.*

TOM: Make that a double for your man (MICHAEL) and mine the same and tell your mother to put it on the slate.

MICHAEL: I'll get it.

TOM: Don't be so extravagant with your mother's money. (*Then gestures/shrugs again to* MICHAEL'*s reaction; no malice intended; and showing* MICHAEL *the few coins in his hand.*) Look at the way I am myself.

ANNE: And will I make the others doubles?

TOM: Are yeh coddin' me!

MICHAEL: What would you say to a stroll down to Woodlawn tomorrow, Anne?
 She nods. This forthright reply, the immediate success of his proposition surprises and stops him for a moment.

ANNE: Fine.

MICHAEL: What?

ANNE: That'd be lovely . . . What time?
 He gestures: what time would suit her?
 Four?

MICHAEL (*nods*): . . . Where shall I . . . ? (*meet you*).

ANNE: The Bridge.

MICHAEL: Ah! The Bridge.
 LIAM *comes in and stands away from them, aloof, sulking.* MICHAEL *has started singing/performing — perhaps Rex Harrison/James Cagney style — for* ANNE.

MICHAEL: 'At seventeen he falls in love quite madly with eyes of tender blue.'

TOM (*to* LIAM): There's a drink there for you, bollocks.

MICHAEL: 'At twenty-four, he gets it rather badly with eyes of different hue.'

TOM (*to* ANNE): Give him (LIAM) that.

MICHAEL: 'At thirty-five, you'll find him flirting sadly with two, or three, or more.'

TOM (*edging him further away from the others*): Come over here a minute.

MICHAEL: 'When he fancies he is past love' —

TOM: This is nonsense, this caper all evening.

MICHAEL: 'It is then he meets his last love —'

TOM: Don't mind that. Hmm?

MICHAEL: Well, what's up with you?

TOM: Nothing. What's up with you?

MICHAEL: Not a thing.

TOM: Well then. Good luck!

MICHAEL: Good luck!
 They toast each other. Short pause; they can't think of anything to say.

MICHAEL (*in* ANNE'*s direction*): 'And he loves her as he's never loved before.'

TOM: I can't help it . . . I can't feel anything about anything anymore.

MICHAEL: I know.

TOM: What?

MICHAEL: I know what you mean.

TOM: You're the only friend I have . . . Wha'?

MICHAEL: Mutual.

TOM: Say something.

MICHAEL (*quietly*): Yahoo?

TOM: Did JJ admire me?

MICHAEL: Yeh.

TOM: But what good is that? I don't think he understood my — (*sighs*) — situation. Isn't that what people want? What? A true and honest account of the situation first. What? A bit of clarity and sanity. Definition. Facts. Wha'? . . . Did he admire me?

MICHAEL: Yeh.

TOM: More than the others, you said.

MICHAEL: Bigger expectations (*shrugs*) — I suppose.

TOM: What? . . . Will I tell you something: What? Will I? Will I tell you something confidential? What? Will I? I never lost an argument in my life. What? What d'yeh think of that? What? Isn't that something? . . . But you're doing well.

MICHAEL: No.

TOM: No! You are!

MICHAEL: Setting myself on fire.

TOM: You're doing well, you're doing well, someone has to be doing well, and we're all delighted, we are, we are, we really are . . . The only friend I have, bollocks, with your cigarette holder in your top pocket. (MICHAEL'*s hand guiltily to his top pocket,* TOM, *intensely, drunkenly.*) Why didn't yeh use it, why didn't yeh use it?

MICHAEL: Just one of them filter things.

TOM: But why didn't yeh use it? D'yeh see what I mean? . . . (*Genuinely pained.*) I try. I can't help it.

PEGGY (*rising, approaching, smiling bravely*): What are the men talking about? I know well; the women are always left out of the juicy things.

TOM (*frowning to himself*): What?

PEGGY: Cheers!

TOM: What?

MICHAEL: Cheers, Peggy.

PEGGY: Do you ever meet anyone from round here over there, Michael?

MICHAEL: Oh, I met Casey.

PEGGY: Aa did yeh, Joe? D'yeh hear that, love? How's he getting on?

MICHAEL: Fine. Getting the dollars regular every week, hot and cold water in his room, and paying no income tax.

PEGGY: Indeed we heard the opposite —

TOM: Hold it a second, Peg —

PEGGY: Someone who saw him over there —

TOM: A minute, Peg —

PEGGY: No shirt, an old pullover, no heels to his shoes.

TOM: Why do you always reduce everything?

PEGGY: . . . Well it was you told me.

Off, the town clock ringing eleven.

MICHAEL: One for the road, Anne. (*Extricating himself from* TOM *and* PEGGY.)

JUNIOR (*off, and entering*): 'Oi, oi, oi, Delilah, phy, phy, phy, Delilah —' (*He surveys the room.*) Jasus, I was at better parties in the Mercy Convent!

MICHAEL (*kicking cigarette holder across the room*): I don't give a damn! A walk in the woods, a breath of fresh air! — Right Anne?

She laughs, nods.

JUNIOR: Into the net, Seaneen!

LIAM (*glowering; a warning*): Watch it! (*The cigarette holder flying past him.*)

JUNIOR: Keep the faith, cowboy! I'll sing a hymn to Mary, he says, the mother of them all! (*Sings.*) 'I'll sing a hymn' —

MICHAEL: No, nice and quiet, Junie. (*Sings.*) 'I'll sing a hymn to Mary . . .'

JUNIOR: ⎱ 'The mother of my God . . .'

MICHAEL: ⎰ 'The mother of my God, the virgin of all virgins —'

LIAM (ANNE *has brought a drink to him*): Nothing for me. (*He spills the drink* TOM *bought him and the one that has just arrived on the floor and continues brooding.*)

JUNIOR (*singing*): 'The virgin of all virgins of God's own dearly son!'

MICHAEL: 'Of David's royal blood.'

JUNIOR: 'Of David's royal blood.'

MICHAEL: Nice and quiet, Junie (*They sing together,* ANNE *singing with them:*) 'Oh teach me Holy Mary a loving song to frame / When wicked men blaspheme thee / I'll love and bless Thy name / Oh Lily of the Valley . . .' (*Etc., until it is stopped by* TOM*'s attack on* PEGGY.)

TOM (*through the above, muttering*): Ugliness, ugliness, ugliness. (*He becomes aware of* PEGGY.) What are you looking at?

PEGGY *has been casting hopeful glances at him. She does not reply,* MICHAEL, JUNIOR *and* ANNE *continue softly — under the following:*

TOM (*to* PEGGY): Do even *you* admire me? My feverish social writings.

PEGGY: It's late, love.

TOM: My generous warm humour.

PEGGY: I'd like to go home, love.

TOM: What?

PEGGY: I don't feel well, love.

TOM: Well, go! Who's stopping yeh? My God, you walk up and down from your own house twenty times a day with your short little legs! No one will molest you! We're all mice!

She hurries from the room, stops in the front doorway, can't leave, her life invested in TOM *— and hangs in the doorway crying. Off, the church clock ringing eleven.*

MICHAEL (*about to follow* PEGGY): Ah Jesus, sham.

TOM (*stops him with his voice*): Hey! (*Then:*) Ugliness, ugliness, ugliness!

ANNE: She's not feeling well.

TOM (*stopping* MICHAEL *again with his voice and warning him not to interfere*): Hey! Gentlemen! Jim! My extravagant adventurous spirit. And the warm wild humour of Liam over there. And all those men of prudence and endeavour who would sell the little we have left of charm, character, kindness and madness to any old bidder with a pound, a dollar, a mark or a yen. And all those honest and honourable men who campaign for the right party and collect taxes on the chapel road. And all those honest and honourable men who are cutting down the trees for making — Easter-egg boxes!

MICHAEL: That's more like it!

TOM: Is it? (*Stopping* MICHAEL *again from going out to* PEGGY.) Hey!

JUNIOR (*quietly to* MICHAEL): Leave it so.

MICHAEL: Let us remember that civility is not a sign of weakness —

TOM (*mimics Kennedy*): 'And that sincerity is always subject to proof.' You all love speeches, rhetoric, crap, speeches. Right! 'I know you all, and will a while uphold the unyoked humour of your idleness.'[18] I was always a better actor than you, better at everything than anyone round here. 'Yet herein will I imitate the sun who doth permit the base contagious clouds to smother up his beauty from the world!'

MICHAEL: 'But when he please again to be himself —'

TOM: *That!* '*That* when he please again to be himself, being wanted, he may be more wondered at, by breaking through the foul and ugly mists of vapour that seem to strangle him, tangle him, bangle him . . .'

VOICE (*off*): Goodnight to ye now.

JUNIOR: Good luck, Johnny!

ANNE: Good night, Johnny!

MICHAEL: Deoch an dorais, Tom, come on.

TOM (*quietly: going — now docilely — to bar with* MICHAEL): 'And when this loose behaviour I throw off, by how much better than my word I am, my reformation glittering o'er my faults shall show more goodly and attract more eyes than this which hath no foil to set it off.'

Through this last section, PEGGY *is in the doorway — she has had her head to the wall, crying — now listening, hoping someone will come out to her. She starts to sing — at first tentatively, like someone making noises to attract attention to herself. Then progressively, going into herself, singing essentially for herself; quietly, looking out at the night, her back to us, the sound representing her loneliness, the gentle desperation of her situation, and the memory of a decade ago. Her song creates a stillness over them all.*

PEGGY: 'All in the April evening, April airs were abroad / The sheep with their little lambs passed me by on the road / The sheep with their little lambs passed me by on the road / All in the April evening I thought on the lamb of God.'

At the conclusion of the song, MISSUS *coming down the stairs.* PEGGY *instinctively moving out of the doorway to stand outside the pub.*

TOM (*quietly*): 'I'll so offend to make offence a skill, redeeming time when men think least I will.'

MISSUS *comes in to collect a broom.*

MISSUS: Come on now, boys, it's gone the time.

TOM: One for the road, Missus.

MISSUS (*returning to the public bar*): And Johnny Quinn is half-way home the back way to his bed by now.

JUNIOR: Well, that's it.

LIAM: Well, that's not it! (*He rattles a chair: his statement of challenge to fight.*) I can quote more Shakespeare than any man here! (*He glances at each of them in turn, culminating with* TOM.)

MISSUS (*off*): Drink up now boys!

LIAM: 'And still they marvelled and the wonder grew, that one *big* head could carry all he knew.'

TOM (*eyes closed*): Shakespeare?

LIAM: No. Goldsmith.

JUNIOR: Well said, boy.

LIAM: *The Deserted Village*, fella.

MISSUS (*off*): Finish up now, boys!

LIAM: Ryan! The village schoolmaster . . . The f-f-f- . . . The f-f-f- . . . Ryan!

LIAM *breathing heavily through his nose, jaws set, fists clenched.* TOM, *still with eyes closed, arms limply at his sides, turns to* LIAM, *nods, prepared to be hit, perhaps wanting to be hit.*

The village schoolmaster.

TOM *eyes closed, nods again.* LIAM *unsure as to whether or not he is being mocked, glancing at the others . . . then suddenly grabs* TOM's *hand and shakes it.*

MISSUS (*coming in with broom which she gives to* ANNE): And the guards are on the prowl these nights.

TOM (*to* LIAM): So, are we quits?

LIAM: Okay, fella.

TOM (*glancing at* MICHAEL): But we're not quite through.

PEGGY *comes in timidly, gets her coat, hopeful glances at* TOM.

They all speak at once:

MICHAEL: We're going to start again with a constant flow of good ideas. 'Let the word go forth . . .'

TOM (*by way of apology to* PEGGY): Just . . . a bit of Shakespeare.

MICHAEL: 'From this time and place, to friend and foe alike, that the torch has been passed to a new generation.'

MISSUS: Come on now, boys, come on.

JUNIOR: Well I must be getting home anyway to Gloria — Oosh!

MICHAEL: 'Let every nation know, whether it wishes us good or ill, that we shall pay any price, bear any burden, endure any hardship, to ensure the success and the survival of liberty.'

MISSUS (*to* LIAM): Call again during the week, Liam — why wouldn't ye — and have a nice bite of tea with us. And thanks, the good boy, Liam. Drink up now, boys, and haven't ye all night tomorrow night, and thanks, thank ye all now. Yas. And safe home. D'ye know now.

She has switched off the lights in the lounge — (the spill of light from the hallway and from the public bar now light the lounge) — and she is on her way along the hallway, upstairs, counting the money from her cardigan pockets. ANNE *is about to exit with the broom and some dirty glasses to public bar.*

MICHAEL: Goodnight, princess, till it be morrow!

ANNE: Goodnight. (*And exits to public bar.*)

They are pulling on their coats, etc. in silence. JUNIOR *scrutinizing the table for any drink that might have been left unfinished.*

MICHAEL: But it wasn't a bad night.

JUNIOR: It wasn't a bad auld night alright. (*And eager for further confirmation of this.*) Wha'?

LIAM (*muttering*): I wouldn't advise anyone to go messing with my plans.

MICHAEL: And I'll be wheeling Annette tomorrow.

TOM: Good man.

LIAM (*muttering*): I know a thing or two about you, Ridge.

PEGGY: What's he muttering about?

MICHAEL (*singing quietly*): 'Sure no letter I'll be mailin' ' —

LIAM: It's not right.

MICHAEL: 'For soon will I be sailin' ' —

PEGGY: Brrah! Come on, loveen, I'm perished.

TOM (*sudden thought*): Wait a minute.

MICHAEL: 'And I'll bless the ship that takes me —'

TOM: It's not right alright —

MICHAEL: 'To my dear auld Erin's shore —'

TOM: Michael. Anne.

MICHAEL: ⎫ 'There I'll settle down forever —'

TOM: ⎬ Serious — Michael — Don't start messin'.

MICHAEL: ⎭ What?

LIAM: Don't start messin' fella. Invested time and money. My — our territory. Right, Tom? Junie?

MICHAEL (*laughs*): 'There's a pretty spot in Ireland —'

TOM: Michael. Are you listening?

MICHAEL: It's not a jiggy-jig job. JJ's daughter. A walk in the wood, a breath of fresh air. (*He looks at their serious faces.*) You know it's nothing else.

TOM: We don't.

LIAM: We don't, fella. A word to Mrs Kilkelly — or to Anne herself.

TOM: So cop on.

MICHAEL: Who?

TOM: You.

LIAM: You, fella. Don't infringe.

MICHAEL *looks incredulously at* TOM.

TOM (*shrugs/blandly*): Liam's territory. Right Liam, you nearly have it sold, right? Good. Even if they don't know it. Better for Missus, Anne, better for — Put a bomb under it if you like — better for everyone. Reality. So that's okay. And we'll fix you up with the gammy one tomorrow. Josephine. Right, Junie?

JUNIOR (*has enough of them*): I'm off. Jasus, I only meant to have the two pints. (*To* MICHAEL.) D'yeh want a lift? (*To* TOM *and* PEGGY.) D'ye want a lift? Okay, see ye.

He goes off, puffing a tuneless whistle and a few moments later we hear him drive away.

PEGGY: Oh come on, loveen, your mother will have your life.

TOM: Don't be silly!

LIAM: So that's okay then, Tom?

TOM (*quietly but firmly*): Yeh.

LIAM: Okay, fellas, God bless.

He exits.

TOM: . . . . I hope he remembers he has no clutch in his car or he'll be all night looking for it.

LIAM'*s car starting up and driving away.*

Come on, we'll walk you home.

MICHAEL: I'm dead sober. And I'm certainly not as confused as I was.

TOM (*pacificatory*): Ary! You're only an eejit, Ridge.

MICHAEL *nods.*

PEGGY: Y'are.

MICHAEL *nods.*

TOM (*mock gruffness*): Y'are!

MICHAEL: But I know what I came home for.

TOM: Come on, we'll walk yeh down.

MICHAEL: No. I'm okay.

TOM: Give us a shout tomorrow.

PEGGY: Night-night, Michael.

TOM: We didn't get a chance to have a right talk.

PEGGY: God bless, take care.

TOM: Good luck, sham.

MICHAEL: Good luck.

TOM *and* PEGGY *have left.*

TOM (*off*): Give us a shout tomorrow!

PEGGY (*off*): 'Bye-'bye, Michael!

TOM (*off*): Will yeh?

PEGGY (*off*): 'Bye-'bye, Michael!

TOM (*off*): Will yeh?

PEGGY (*off*): 'Bye-'bye!

MICHAEL *continues standing there. He looks up and around at the room. He finishes his drink and is about to leave.*

MISSUS (*off*): Leave the light on in the hall, Annette, in case.

The light is switched off in the public bar and ANNE *enters and discovers* MICHAEL. *Her simple grave expression.*

MICHAEL (*whispers*): I have to go in the morning.

ANNE (*silently*): What?

MICHAEL: Have to go in the morning. (*He smiles, shrugs.*) They've probably cut down the rest of the wood by now, anyway.

ANNE: There's still the stream.

MICHAEL: Yeh. But I have to go. Tell JJ I'm sorry I didn't see him. Tell him . . . (*He wants to add something but cannot find the words yet.*) . . . Tell him I love him.

She nods, she smiles, she knows. He waits for another moment to admire her, then he walks off. ANNE *continues in the window as at the beginning of the play, smiling her gentle hope out at the night.*

1   A milder form of bollocks.
2   Irish: devil.
3   Drinking spree.
4   A British actor who often played the hero in Second World War movies.
5   Lines from Kennedy's inauguration speech in 1961.
6   Disparaging term for Protestants.
7   German: I too am a Berliner. Kennedy's famous remark on his visit to Berlin.
8   On account of her special devotion and piety, St Theresa of Lisieux (1873–97) acquired the epithet Little Flower of Jesus.
9   Greenwich Village in New York.
10 From the sentimental emigration song 'Where the River Shannon Flows'.
11 Strange one.
12 An expression of surprise, release of emotion.
13 A weekly television show on RTE, running since 1962.
14 A simple-minded fellow, from Irish gamal.
15 Famous Irish tenor. Pope John XXIII.
16 Mercedes.
17 An Irish word, always used disparagingly. Gombeen men were usurers who lent money to tenant farmers at exorbitant interest.
18 Lines from Shakespeare's *Henry IV*, Part One, Scene Two.

SEAMUS HEANEY
from Seamus Heaney, *From the Republic of Conscience* (1985)

This poem was written by Heaney in response to an invitation by Amnesty International and published on Human Rights Day, 10 December 1985.

FROM THE REPUBLIC OF CONSCIENCE

I

When I landed in the republic of conscience
it was so noiseless when the engines stopped
I could hear a curlew high above the runway.

At immigration the clerk was an old man
who produced a wallet from his homespun coat
and showed me a photograph of my grandfather.

The woman in customs asked me to declare
the words of our traditional cures and charms
to heal dumbness and avert the evil eye.

No porter. No interpreter. No taxi.
You carried what you had to and very soon
your symptoms of creeping privilege disappeared.

II

Fog is a dreaded omen there but lightning
spells universal good and parents hang
swaddled infants in trees during thunderstorms.

Salt is their precious mineral. And seashells
are held to the ear during births and funerals.
The base of all inks and pigments is seawater.

Their sacred symbol is a stylized boat.
The sail is an ear, the mast a sloping pen,
the hull a mouth-shape, the keel an open eye.

At their inauguration, public leaders
must swear to uphold unwritten law and weep
to atone for their presumption to hold office —

and to affirm their faith that all life sprang
from salt in tears which the sky-god wept
after he dreamt his solitude was endless.

III

I came back from that frugal republic
with my two arms the one length, the customs woman
having insisted my allowance was myself.

The old man rose and gazed into my face
and said that was official recognition
that I was now a dual citizen.

He therefore desired me when I got home
to consider myself a representative
and to speak on their behalf in my own tongue.

Their embassies, he said, were everywhere
but operated independently
and no ambassador would ever be relieved.

PADRAIC FIACC
from Padraic Fiacc, *Missa Terribilis* (1986)

Padraic Fiacc (pseudonym of Patrick O'Connor) (1924–   ) was born in Belfast and after emigrating with his family to New York returned to Belfast in 1946. He has published several volumes of verse including *Woe to the Boy* (1957), *Odour of Blood* (1973) and *Nights in the Bad Place* (1977). *Missa Terribilis*, a sequence of profoundly disquieting poems on what Fiacc would see as war in Northern Ireland, makes use of the prayers and liturgy of the Mass, only here it is terribilis, dreadful, fearful. One poem entitled 'The British Connection' contains for its subtitle 'a litany of terror'. Another poem compares the victim of a sectarian murder with the crucified Christ. 'Tears / A *Lacrimosa*' recalls all the powerful Passion Week images of weeping now applied to those moments of extreme suffering caused by the 'troubles'. (The Latin word 'lachrymosa' appears in the motet sung at the Mass for the Dead 'Dies Irae, Dies Illa'.)

THE BRITISH CONNECTION
a litany of terror

In Belfast, Europe, your man
Met the Military come to raid
The house: 'Over my dead body
Sir,' he said, brandishing
A real-life sword from some
Old half-forgotten war . . .

And youths with real bows and arrows
And coppers and marbles good as bullets
And old time thrupenny bits and stones
Screws, bolts, nuts (Belfast confetti),[1]

And kitchen knives, pokers, Guinness tins
And nail-bombs down by the Shore Road

And guns under the harbour wharf
And bullets in the docker's tea tin
And gelignite in the tool shed
And grenades in the scullery larder
And weedkiller and sugar
And acid in the French letter

And sodium chlorate and nitrates
In the suburban garage
In the boot of the car
And guns in the oven grill
And guns in the spinster's shift

And ammunition and more, more
Guns in the broken-down rusted
Merry-go-round in the scrapyard —

Almost as many hard-on
Guns as there are Union Jacks.

ENEMY ENCOUNTER
For Lilac

Dumping (left over from the autumn)
Dead leaves, near a culvert
I come on a British Army soldier
With a rifle and a radio,
Perched hiding. He has red hair.

He is young enough to be my weenie
-bopper daughter's boyfriend.

He is like a lonely little winter robin.

We are that close to each other, I
Can nearly hear his heart beating.

I say something bland to make him grin,
But his glass eyes look past my side
-whiskers down the Shore Road street.

I am an Irishman, and he is afraid
That I have come to kill him.

CRUCIFIXUS

Odour of blood when Christ was slain
Made all Platonic tolerance vain
And vain all Doric discipline.
                                    — W.B. Yeats[2]

I

Dandering home from work at mid
-night, they tripped him up on a ramp,
Asked him if he were a 'Catholic' . . .

A wee bit soft in the head he was,
The last person in the world you'd want
To hurt: His arms and legs, broken,

His genitals roasted with a ship
-yard worker's blowlamp.

II

In all the stories that the Christian Brothers
Tell you of Christ He never screamed
Like this. Surely this is not the way

To show a 'manly bearing' —
Screaming for them to *'Please Stop!'* —
And then, later, like screaming for death!

When they made Him wash the stab
Wounds at the sink, they kept on
Hammering Him with the pick

-axe handle, then they pulled
Christ's trousers down, threatening to
'cut off His balls!' Poor boy Christ, for when

They finally got round to finishing Him off
by shooting Him in the back of the head,

'The poor Fenian fucker was already dead!'

TEARS/A *LACRIMOSA*
For Geraldine

I   UNISEX

After the bombing the British soldier
Looks up into the barbed-wire Irish
Twilight. His unflinching, open eyes
Deaden, yet involuntarily flood
With the colour of tea —
Drenches his combat jacket sleeve.

Now he is hugging,
Now he is giving
His male love
To a screaming fellow being he does
Not know if it is a man or a woman.

II   RAPE OF THE CHILD

Nine years of age, on the bus, like a baby
Inside of her crying, crying,
Like the length of a lifetime journey . . .

Not that she 'lost' her penny
But that is was 'stolen'.

The conductor said 'Quit blurtin' love!
Didn't I let you on without the penny?
Is a penny worth the blurtin' for?'

But nobody can stop the long thin crying

For nobody saw her the day that the men
Were that busy holding back the women
They forgot about the kids,

The day she ran up the street along
To the pub still smouldering like peat:
Somebody younger than nine years of age
Watching them dig from the wreckage.

III   LULLABY

When the ricocheting bullet bites into
The young child wanted to walk
In her mother's high heels to push
The doll's pram, she
Gives out a funny little 'oooh!'

And lets the blood spill
All over her bright new bib . . .

No pallbearers are needed.

The young father is able himself to carry
The immaculate white coffin, but
Stains it with a dirty-faced boy's
Fist-smudged tears, then suddenly cries
Out like a man being tortured by water.

1   See explanation by Ciaran Carson in *The Star Factory*
    (1997) (below p. 1155).
2   Lines from Yeats's poem 'Two Songs from a Play', the
    play being *Resurrection* (1927).

ROY McFADDEN
from Roy McFadden, *Letters to the Hinterland* (1986)

Two more poems from the pen of Roy McFadden, the first on ageing, the second on times past. In a recent interview, McFadden remarked: 'I imagine my poems will survive for those who prefer to read rather than be read at.'

SURVIVOR

In early summer snatched
Into whatever alien element
Or separate dream, she could
Given a voice declare
That all those unpermitted years,
Extended to others, have edged away like a dream,
Leaving only a pared phrase, a glance's glint
And flurried lipless cries
Sifted by weeds short of the open shore.

Tidying her hair,
One who survived declared
It was another world
It was as if
Some other had performed her part;
Or more as if
She'd found a letter written long ago
Purporting to be hers:
Or even more as if
She'd come upon a shiny photograph
Of once-upon-a-time, and cried
Alas for a slip of a girl with her winning smile.

THE ASTORIA

Outlandish frontager,
Confronting thoroughfare
With unabashed bucolic innocence,
Its old glass signalling
Back to the sparking trams;
Decades of privet, cemetery paths,
A tepid greenhouse, couped red wheelbarrows:

Shorn from the hinterland,
It mimed suburban ways;
Rubbed shoulders with the shops and houses, paid

Its taxes, and observed
The early-closing day;
But stoically, if absentmindedly,
It kept its *thereness* like a stranded tree.

Abruptly it was gone.
You noticed first the lack
Of glass, then took in all the emptiness
Where bushes along the paths
Had made a natural maze.
Laid out along the slope the apple-trees
Were statues in a morgue, dead, falsified.

Hoarding and scaffolding
Thwarted a sneak preview.
But nobody was moved to entertain
A plea for pleasance when
That local Eden changed
Into a hothouse for exotic love,
Lettuce supplanted by a let's-pretend.

Sixpenny patrons, we
Embraced in the back-stalls
Sophistication and unnatural warmth;
Inhaled America
And Ealing's England,[1] but
Translated them to Ballyhackamore,
Ecumenists in the vernacular.

Now *it's* succinctly gone,
The skyline engineered
To prop a concrete coffin. In your mind,
Circle and stalls line up
To join old greenery
Vegetating in the hinterland,
Where yesterday perhaps is still today.

1   Ealing was once the home of the British film industry.

DESMOND EGAN
from *The Irish Times*, April 1986

Desmond Egan's fine elegy to Beckett recalls Beckett's own poem with this title (see p. 442 above). Egan once wrote: 'Must we accept the common perception of him as "Ireland's best-known atheist" and one whose work lacks a religious dimension?' 'Echo's Bones' appeared in *Elegies* (1996).

ECHO'S BONES
(For Sam Beckett on his eightieth birthday)

what have we to do with this hotel
its glass and boutiques and revolving chrome
and black waiter looking for a tip?

where we are sitting again at *doubles* of coffee
conferring like exiles *between the years*
your voice as gently Dublin as Yeats's
and nimbler than hands fallen
like my father's into age

austere and kindly — a monk on his day out
ready to consider any topic for a change
even writers! Joyce and that death mask[1] —
Auden's verse about which we share doubts —
meeting Patrick Kavanagh in Paris —
the fifteen minutes you sat *post-prandium*[2]
when neither you nor Pound uttered a word —
the Paris exhibitions? one shrug
puts them further off than Ireland
(and who could imagine you anyway
stalking peering with a catalogue?)
Company[3] with your own father's 'loved trusted face'
calling to you out of the Forty Foot waves[4] . . .

Marijuana in Ballymahon[5] — *there's a poem for you!*

and you still surprise me now as you
lean across the marble top with ravelled face
and blue eyes that make us responsible
to quote from *Watt*[6] those lines

'of the empty heart
of the empty hands
of the dark mind stumbling
through barren lands . . .'

and my mind knots again in loneliness
and we are no longer in a coffee bar but somewhere
in the outer space of your words
that almost intolerable silence where
we must try to hang onto some kind of dignity
out in the blinding dark you never shirked

later an embrace and you step off firmly
into streets gone eighty years old
God bless now Desmond

— and you Sam our navigator our valiant necessary
wanderer to the edges of this interpreted world

God bless

1 In the early 1980s Beckett was angered to learn that Joyce's death-mask had been put up for sale at Sotheby's, a death-mask which had been bequeathed to the James Joyce Museum at the Martello Tower in Sandycove.
2 Latin: After lunch.
3 First published in English in 1979.
4 A place for bathing below the Martello Tower at Sandycove reserved for men. In *Company* Beckett recalls how he was taught to swim here by his father.
5 Ballymahon, in County Longford, was Oliver Goldsmith's last home in Ireland.
6 Beckett's novel, first published in 1953.

STEWART PARKER
from Stewart Parker, *Three Plays For Ireland: Northern Star, Heavenly Bodies, Pentecost* (1989)

Stewart Parker (1941–88) was born in Protestant East Belfast and educated at Queen's University, Belfast. His career as a playwright began with *Spokesong* (1974) and included radio plays and a remarkable trilogy of 'history plays' which concludes with *Pentecost*.

Northern Star (1984) deals with Henry Joy McCracken, the United Irishman; *Heavenly Bodies* (1986) with the nineteenth-century Irish dramatist Dion Boucicault, and *Pentecost*, first performed in September 1987 by the Field Day Theatre Company in Derry, with the Loyalist Workers' Strike of May 1974. In Parker's own words, the plays form a triptych 'hinged together in a continuing comedy of errors', which is true, but this does not do justice to the sense of tragedy or to the visionary quality especially evident in *Pentecost*.

Pentecost (1987)

ACT I

[*The time is 1974*]
[*The place is Belfast*]
[*The play takes place in the downstairs back part of a respectable working-class 'parlour' house, built in the early years of this century. There is a kitchen with a fireplace, a rocking chair, a sofa, a dining table. On one side a doorway leads into the scullery, with its flagstone floor and its old cast-iron range for cooking on and its 'jawbox' of a sink. At the far end of the scullery another door leads into the pantry, which we can't see*]
[*The large kitchen window looks out on the back yard, which is very narrow, with high, whitewashed walls topped by lines of broken glass. The yard door is heavily bolted, even though its worn ribs are showing through*]
[*On the other side of the kitchen is the door leading into the hall and thence to the rest of the house. There is an under-stairs cupboard by this door*]
[*There is a single electric light with conical shade hanging from the middle of the ceiling in kitchen and scullery both; but there are also working gas mantles in the walls*]
[*Everything is real except the proportions. The rooms are narrow, but the walls climb up and disappear into the shadows above the stage. The kitchen in particular is cluttered, almost suffocated, with the furnishings and bric-a-brac of the first half of the century, all the original fixtures and fittings still being in place. But in spite of now being shabby, musty, threadbare, it has all clearly been the object of a desperate, lifelong struggle for cleanliness, tidiness, orderliness — godliness*]
[*The people are* MARIAN, LENNY *and* PETER, *who are all 33;* RUTH, *who is 29; and* LILY MATTHEWS, *who is 74.*]

SCENE ONE

[*A night in February*]
[LENNY *is seated on the kitchen sofa, playing 'I Can't Get Started' on his trombone. His tape machine is on*

the table, providing the rhythm-section backing. He is wearing his overcoat and hat: it's very cold, there is no fire in the grate. Only the single electric lights are on*]
[MARIAN *enters from the hall, also in her overcoat. She switches off* LENNY's *backing track. His trombone peters out*]

MARIAN: Did you make tea?
LENNY: The gas is off.
     [MARIAN *has moved on into the kitchen, and is peering into a teapot on the top of the range*]
MARIAN: What's this?
LENNY: That's old. So. What do you reckon?
MARIAN: There's a cup sitting here with milk and sugar in it. Christ.
LENNY: I told you. I haven't touched a thing.
MARIAN: She must have brewed this up just before it happened.
LENNY: No such thing.
MARIAN: She never got a chance to pour it out.
LENNY: The ambulancemen, is all it would have been.
MARIAN: It's stone cold.
LENNY: The ambulancemen at the door, is all it possibly could have been.
     [MARIAN *turns her full attention on him for the first time*]
MARIAN: I see. They prepared a nice pot of tea, prior to removing the corpse.
LENNY: She walked out of here, in her Sunday hat and coat and best handbag, is what I'm saying, under her own steam, into the ambulance, it was in the hospital she died . . .
MARIAN: When?
LENNY: How do I know, under the anaesthetic.
MARIAN: When?
LENNY: Why?
MARIAN: I'm asking you when.
LENNY: What does it matter, Wednesday sometime . . .
MARIAN: Christ.
LENNY: Meaning what?
MARIAN: Why is her family not here?
LENNY: No surviving relatives, I told you. There wasn't even anybody at the funeral.
MARIAN: So. I wonder how they manage in a case like that.

LENNY: My Great-Aunt Rosaleen owned the whole terrace, it was all in her will, I told . . .

MARIAN: Holding a funeral when there's nobody at it, I mean.

LENNY: Very good, Marian. Right, well, let's see. The wee butcher from the shop on the front of the road was there, her churchgoing cronies, a few oul' dolls who used to live next door when there used to be a door next door, no family is actually of course what I was saying, okay? Me, I was there. Standing foundered in Dundonald at half nine this morning, being tonguelashed by the Free Presbyterian notion of a requiem mass, that was it. Just what *is* this?

MARIAN: You haven't exactly let the grass grow.

LENNY: Just how is this, whenever I start the evening doing you a favour, ten minutes into it and suddenly I'm a heartless creep, dishonouring the dead, I never once clapped eyes on the woman!

MARIAN: Well you've sure as hell inherited the woman.

LENNY: The house, I've inherited the house, by law it has to come to me once the sitting tenant's dead, you think I ever wanted this? — I thought you'd maybe appreciate the chance, before there's any sort of an auction, you could have the pick of all this for your shop, you were never off my back about being careless with money, okay, great stuff, go ahead and take advantage of it.

MARIAN: You haven't lost your knack of feeling put-upon, I see.

LENNY [*Leaping up*]: Forget I ever mentioned it, Marian.

MARIAN: Sit down. Here. Stick this in your gub. [*Producing a half-bottle of brandy from her shoulder-bag*] What was her name?

LENNY: Matthews. Mrs Alfred George Matthews.

MARIAN [*A toast*]: God love you, Mrs Matthews.

LENNY: Lily to her friends.

MARIAN: Nice house, Lily, you kept it lovely. [*She swigs and passes the bottle to* LENNY, *who finally decides to accept it*]

LENNY: Responsibilities, who needs them.

MARIAN: Property used to be theft, in your book.

LENNY: What are you supposed to do? It was my mother insisted I go to the funeral. 'That wee woman lived her whole life in that house, it's your responsibility now, the least you can do is honour her memory' — what memory? None of us even once met her. If she'd known her rent was going straight to the Legion of Mary,[1] she'd have dropped dead years ago. The last thing she'd ever have asked for was me mooching round her graveside, did it never strike you that funerals and weddings are much of a muchness in this country?

MARIAN: Certainly. Our wedding was exactly like a funeral.

LENNY: There's just one way to tell the difference. Nobody takes photographs at a funeral.

MARIAN: Apart from the Special Branch. [*She has wandered back into the kitchen and is examining a row of mugs displayed on a shelf*] Look at this. Queen Victoria's Diamond Jubilee, the wedding of Queen Mary, the Coronation of Lizzie the Second, 1953 — that must be the most modern item in the house. Most of the furniture's Edwardian, there's a Regency dressing table upstairs that must have come down through her grandparents.

LENNY: Is it all worth much? What do you reckon? [MARIAN *deliberates, moving about amongst the furniture*]

MARIAN: As I remember it — what was the word you most detested in the whole of the English language — 'antiques'.

LENNY: Yeah. Well. You felt much the same way about 'trombone'.

MARIAN: I didn't feel that different about 'antiques' as a matter of fact.

LENNY: Antiques have been your whole livelihood.

MARIAN: It's been my trade, I don't have to love it.

LENNY: You always loved it.

MARIAN: Things, individually crafted, well-cared-for, those I love, not the business, you never could grasp that. Old and beautiful things.

LENNY: The sash my father wore.[2]

MARIAN: Up yours too. I've sold the shop. If you want to know. [LENNY *is thunderstruck*]

LENNY: You've done what?

MARIAN: For an amazingly good price, when you consider the state the city's in, but then it's what I'm good at, isn't it, as you're at pains to point out, trading, buying and selling. I don't have to love it. Just get on with it. Survival. It's one bloody useful knack, knowing the value of things to people, what they'll pay, what they think they're worth. The things, that is. The people of course are not worth shit. I didn't have to love them either. You and I tend to diverge on that point, you having all that deep-seated compassion, for anything that snuffles into your shoulder . . .

LENNY: Hold on a minute!

MARIAN: In my case the embattled bourgeoisie of Belfast was one long procession of avaricious gobshites — hell-bent on overloading their lounge cabinets and their display units with any bauble or knick-knack, so long as it looked like it cost more than it did, so long as it was showy enough to advertise their grandeur, and their fashionable taste and stylishness, not to mention their absolutely bottomless vulgarity, it was bad enough before the shooting-match started, it's grotesque at this point, I couldn't handle any more of it.

LENNY: Why Marian did it not maybe, I mean how come you never . . . ?

MARIAN: Besides I didn't have you to feed and clothe any more, so who needs it? Do you ever actually earn money these days?

LENNY: What do you imagine you're going to do?

MARIAN: You can't possibly get paid for playing that thing.

LENNY: Why did you bother coming here to look at this at all?

MARIAN: I need a house.

LENNY: You what? What do you mean, a house? You're not thinking of starting up as an estate agent?

MARIAN: I need a house. To live in.

LENNY: You've got a flat to live in.

MARIAN: I've put it on the market.

LENNY: Marian . . . Exactly what's going on with you?

MARIAN: Have you had this place valued?

LENNY: Of course I haven't had it bloody valued, the woman was only buried this morning!

MARIAN: I'll buy it from you. Wholesale. House and contents, jut the way they stand at the minute. The lock, the stock and the barrel. I'll pay you the going price. Whatever the valuation is. We can go and see your solicitor uncle first thing in the morning.

[*In the time that it takes for* LENNY *to get to grips with this bizarre motion, the soft booming of two distant explosions is heard*]

LENNY: What kind of game are we playing here?

MARIAN: Trading, buying and selling. The one I'm so good at.

LENNY: God. The years I've spent wondering what you'd hit me with next . . .

MARIAN: I want the house. No joke.

LENNY: Talk sense!

MARIAN: You haven't lost your belief in the free spirit, surely, the unencumbered impulse. The pure spontaneous gesture. All that life-embracing bollocks that I so conspicuously lacked, well here's me right now acting like mad on impulse, Lenny, free-spirited as all get out, so what exactly are we waiting for?

LENNY: The name of the game, for a start.

MARIAN: Who cares, imagine whatever takes your fancy, maybe I've noticed a Gainsborough lying behind the mangle,[3] check it out. So long as we have a deal.

LENNY: A deal, Marian — is what we don't actually have. You and me.

MARIAN: Don't start that.

LENNY: Still don't have, not since a year ago last May.

MARIAN: Business is all I'm here to talk . . .

LENNY: So fine, you want to buy this hovel for reasons as yet unexplained, that can certainly be arranged — providing we're agreeing to a brand new deal. Namely. The house is yours as stated, terms agreed. In return for a divorce.

MARIAN: We are divorced, as good as.

LENNY: I'm talking about your signature on a petition.

MARIAN: What difference does it make?

LENNY: It makes it official, it makes it binding, it makes it definite.

MARIAN: Not in the one and only place where it actually means something . . .

LENNY: The church? — the church is beneath my notice, it's beneath contempt, if the church won't recognize my divorce, that's fine, great. Because I don't recognize its existence. Because out here in the real world, Marian, we've been conducting separate lives in separate houses for one year ten months, where's the point, it's only suspended animation, I can't keep on like this, let's pull the plug and have done with it. I can't see what your difficulty is. [*She is silent*] There's nobody else I'm planning to marry, if that's what you're thinking. There's nobody else full stop. It's got nothing to do with anybody else. [*She remains silent*] We have no children, we have no mortgage, there's no argument over an estate, you were the one who made all the money anyway, you've got it all, what's your problem? What are you holding out for? We're never going to get together again, not in a million years, you can't stand me, less than ever, why prolong it? Let's get shot of it. What's your objection?

[MARIAN *remains silent for a moment longer, then turns abruptly towards him*]

MARIAN: Okay. Tomorrow morning. Your uncle can take care of that along with the house.

[LENNY *is gobsmacked*]

LENNY: Well. I'd rather it wasn't actually my Uncle Phelim. I mean, I don't mind, if you want to talk about it . . .

MARIAN: You've said all there is. I agree.

LENNY: I mean, I'm not trying to force you into a

corner. It's something we need to feel the same way about.

MARIAN: It's settled. We're doing it.

LENNY: Ach, for Jesus' sake come off it, Marian, you can't possibly live in this gaff,[4] it's the last house on the road left inhabited! — the very road itself is scheduled to vanish off the map, it's the middle of a redevelopment zone, not to mention the minor detail that it's slap bang in the firing line, the Prods are all up in that estate, [*Gesturing towards the back of the house*] the Taigs are right in front of us,[5] anyway look at it — it's reeking of damp, there's five different layers of wallpaper hanging off the walls, she was still using gas lamps in half the rooms, nothing to cook on apart from that ancient range, brown lino everywhere and rooms bunged up with junk, there's probably rats, mice and badgers in the belfry, it's riddled with rot and it's dingy, dank and absolutely freezing!

MARIAN: Perfect. I'll take it.

[*She sweeps out into the hall to take another look around.* LENNY *is left staring after her, entirely at a loss for further words. He punches his cassette player on the table and the backing track is heard again. He picks up his trombone and plays along to it*]

[*The lights fade slowly to blackout*]

[*End of Scene One*]

SCENE TWO

[*A night in April*]

[*The gaslight comes up on* MARIAN *standing in the scullery, making herself a cup of coffee. She is wearing a sweater and skirt. She has lit the kitchen fire as well as the gas mantles*]

[*She carries her coffee into the kitchen and pauses to take a sip of it, gazing into the fire, the flames glimmering over her face*]

[*She sets the coffee down on the table, fetches the half-bottle of brandy from her shoulder bag and unscrews the top*]

MARIAN: Begging your pardon, Lily Matthews. I'm sure no sup ever passed your lips. Show a little mercy. Some of us are made of weaker stuff.

[*She pours a shot of brandy into the coffee, and then carries both over to the rocking chair, sits herself down and rocks a little*]

Pleased to make your acquaintance, by the way.

[*Holding up the coffee and taking a swig, as in a mock toast, and then setting down the coffee on the floor — which causes her to notice a raffia basket tucked in beside the chair. She picks it up, takes the lid off, lifts*

out a piece of unfinished knitting still on the needles]

So. What was this going to be?

[*She finds the pattern in the basket*]

Aha. A woolly bedjacket — by God you certainly need one in that bedroom. I might just finish it off for you. If you're sure you don't object to me wearing it, that is.

[*She rocks a little more*]

I've got to make some plans for you and me, Lily Matthews.

[*A low distant rumble of explosions is heard*]

[LILY MATTHEWS, *in Sunday coat and hat and best handbag, appears in the shadowy doorway leading from the pantry*]

LILY: I don't want you in my house.

[MARIAN *keeps her eyes on the knitting pattern: on guard but not entirely frightened, aware that her mind is playing tricks on her*]

MARIAN: You needn't try to scare me, Lily.

LILY: Don't you 'Lily' me. I don't want you in here, breathing strong drink and profanity, and your husband deserted.

MARIAN: Maybe you'd prefer him.

LILY: I want no truck with any of you's, stay you with your own and let me rest easy with mine.

MARIAN: Take a look — your things are in safe hands.

LILY: The hands of an idolater!

MARIAN: I've changed nothing. I've brought nothing with me. See? No sacred hearts, no holy water, not even a statue of yer woman — everything still in its place the way you left it, the way you wanted it.

LILY: You're here. With all that's in you. [*Entering the kitchen*] This house was my life.

MARIAN: I know it was.

LILY: You know nothing about it. You'd be singing on the other side of your face if my Alfie was here.

MARIAN [*Closing her eyes*]: There's nobody here. Nobody.

LILY: It was Alfie Matthews found this house, it was him that first put down the deposit, moved the pair of us into it within a week of them building it — the year of nineteen and eighteen — and me a bride at eighteen years of age . . . Alfie had come back, that's why. Back from Passchendaele. Hellfire Corner. Back from the dead. Him and Jackie Midgely, the only two from Hope Street, out of the twelve that went. All in the one week, married and moved in, he wouldn't wait . . . not after what he's seen . . . this house was his life, same as mine. He never left it, not for a night. Except the once, to try and find work, in the Depression. That and the day they carried him to his grave. You have no right to be in here.

MARIAN [*Raising the brandy*]: Alfie Matthews, God rest him. [*Swigs*] No doubt he was fond of a drop himself.

LILY: My man would take a stout like any other, of a Friday night, what harm in that? He never lifted his hand to me, not once, in forty-one years of marriage, no matter what amount of drink was on him.

MARIAN: Must have died in '59, then.

LILY: He never harmed a living soul . . .

MARIAN: Fifteen years left on your own.

LILY: Every pipe in this house was laid by his hands, the plumbing, the gas, gas fitting was his trade, every pipe had to be put back and it was him put them back . . . after your crowd burnt it down round us.

MARIAN: I don't want to hear this.

LILY: Three years we'd been in this street.

MARIAN: No end to reprisals, is there . . .

LILY: Three years of sacrificing for every little stick we possessed, all that we'd managed to scrape together, destroyed in the one night, it's a mercy we even lived through it, me crouched in there, in that pantry, crying out for the Lord Jesus to deliver us, Alfie out in the yard trying to block up the back door, but they come over the wall and bate him senseless to the ground and on into this very kitchen roaring and rampaging like the cruel heathens they were, smashing through those gas mantles with their clubs and cudgels till the whole house went up. I was trapped in that pantry for a solid hour, [*She moves back towards the pantry door*] Alfie lying bleeding in the yard, if it hadn't been for the fire brigade lads moving in as fast as they did, I wouldn't be here now.

MARIAN: You're not here now.

LILY: Smoke and ashes, scorched walls, water flooded everywhere . . . my beautiful house . . . there was sky showing through a part of the rafters . . . every wee thing we'd saved up for ruined in the one night. By a pack of Fenian savages!

MARIAN: It was probably nothing personal, Lily.

LILY: Stay you away from where you're not welcome.

MARIAN: I have a problem with that, you see . . . seeing as the place where I'm least welcome of all is the inside of my own skull . . . so there's something we can agree on at least, Lily. I don't like me either.

[*From offstage comes the sound of urgent hammering at the front door.* MARIAN *looks out into the hall, tense*]

MARIAN: Is this maybe a return bout — your mob calling round to take care of me? What do you think?

[*She turns her head back, but* LILY *has melted away into the shadows of the pantry*]

[*The hammering is heard again*]

[MARIAN *moves out into the hall and calls*]

MARIAN: Who's there, please?

RUTH [*Offstage*]: It's me, Marian. It's Ruth.

MARIAN: Ruth, is that you? Hang on a minute.

[*She exits, and we hear her opening the front door off*]

MARIAN [*Off*]: Come on in, what are you doing down here at this hour?

RUTH [*Off*]: I wasn't sure of the house.

MARIAN: Go ahead.

[*We hear the front door being closed*]

[RUTH *appears in the kitchen doorway, dressed in a long white raincoat, with a scarf wound tightly round her neck and a bandanna on her head, worn low over the eyes*]

RUTH: None of them seem to be working the lamps. Out there.

MARIAN: They've stripped all the timers out of them, for the bombs.

RUTH: Yes. They do actually do that.

MARIAN: How did you track me down here, Ruth?

RUTH: I'm sorry, Marian.

MARIAN: I was only wondering.

RUTH: I suppose your idea is to sell all these old things.

MARIAN: Sit down.

RUTH: Nice big fire. [*She moves to it but doesn't sit down*] It was just, earlier today, bumping into Lenny, are you really going to live down here, it's all a bit . . . all . . .

MARIAN: You need a drink?

RUTH: It's quite hard, getting here. That fire's quite warm.

[*She yawns*]

MARIAN: You might as well tell me about it, Ruth.

RUTH: I was just wondering, I know it's rather late to be asking, I would have phoned only you haven't got one, I did actually phone, at the flat, and the shop, not knowing, but anyway — if there was any chance, you could maybe put me up for the night, Marian.

MARIAN: What has he done to you this time?

[RUTH *moves around, looking evasively out into the kitchen and the yard*]

RUTH: I have decided, actually. To leave — David.

MARIAN: Take your coat off.

RUTH: It was, rather sudden. I'll need to get, you know . . . get my things, tomorrow. It was just, tonight, I couldn't think, where else . . . he might try . . . [*Yawns*] . . . he wouldn't know . . . down here's the last place he'd think.

MARIAN: Just sit down. [*Guiding her into the rocking*

chair] Ruth — there's blood seeping through this, I'm going to take it off . . .

RUTH: No, no leave it, it's nothing, I just gave my head a crack . . .

MARIAN: I'm taking it off, Ruth.

RUTH [*Clinging to the bandanna*]: . . . getting out of the car it was, just a bump, honest . . .

MARIAN [*Sharply*]: Let go! [*She begins to undo the bandanna*]

RUTH: Oh, no, it's not, it's not . . . oh, no, no, oh no, oh no, no no no no no no . . . [*It has developed into an uncontrollable cry, her whole body rocking back and forward*] . . . oh no . . . no . . . NO!

MARIAN [*As she struggles with the bandanna*]: All right, Ruth. It's okay. You're all right now.

[*She gets the bandanna off to reveal a livid, glistening, purplish-red weal slantwise across* RUTH's *forehead, and her hair wet with blood*]

RUTH: No . . . No . . . NO!

MARIAN [*Holding her hands*]: It's all over. You're safe now. You're safe here. Easy, now. Hold on, Ruth. I'm just going to get something for that wound.

[*She runs out to the bathroom*]

[RUTH *begins to quieten*]

[MARIAN *returns, clutching* LILY MATTHEWS's *old-fashioned wooden first-aid box. She takes out lint and antiseptic and proceeds to clean* RUTH's *wounds during the continuing dialogue*]

MARIAN: Okay. This should sort you out. It looks to me like Army Surplus from the Dardanelles campaign. Definitely guaranteed to separate the women from the girls. [*As she swabs the wound*] Does that hurt?

RUTH [*Nodding*]: Unh.

MARIAN: Terrific. What in God's name did he hit you with? The lawnmower or what?

RUTH: The, the . . . truncheon . . .

MARIAN [*Stopping work*]: His police truncheon? He took that to you?

[RUTH *starts to sob again a little*]

MARIAN: All right, all right, as you were. We'll have to get this X-rayed, there could easily be concussion . . .

RUTH: There's no . . . no . . .

MARIAN: Is your sight blurred?

RUTH: No. Never fainted.

MARIAN: Well. We'll see about that in the morning. I'll put you in Lily's bed tonight, I can kip down here. It's a lot warmer anyhow.

RUTH: I'm — sorry.

MARIAN: Lily's our hostess here, in case you're wondering. Lily Matthews. It's her house. All her gear. I haven't touched anything, I don't want anything tidied up or touched, Ruth, that's the one stipulation I have to make, about you staying here.

RUTH: Is she not . . . dead?

MARIAN: She was the same age as the century. Born 1900. Married 1918. Dispossessed — for the first time anyway — 1921.

RUTH: How do you know?

MARIAN: I've started going through her belongings. Her whole life's here, all intact. Her husband died in 1959. She changed not a single detail from then till the day she died herself, two months ago. [*Finishing her ministrations*] There. That should keep you healthy for a bit longer. How does it feel?

RUTH: Okay.

MARIAN: Yeah, like a bandaged migraine. Time for that drink now. [*Producing brandy*] For me, I mean. Not that you can't join me if you absolutely insist on it.

[*She takes a swig, hands it to* RUTH *who pours a capful and drinks it from the cap*]

[*They stare into the fire for a bit*]

RUTH: Remember your flat. Magdala Street. Calling round. Always the big fire. Out would come the bottle.

MARIAN: Rough cider in those days, girl. [*Picking up the brandy bottle*] That's the one thing that's tangibly improved. In the intervening decade.

[*She swigs. They stare into the fire*]

RUTH: We haven't done — all that well, have we.

MARIAN: Speak for yourself.

RUTH: Sorry.

MARIAN: Joke.

[RUTH *consciously rallies herself for the next bit*]

RUTH: I know what you think of David . . .

MARIAN: Don't talk to me about it.

RUTH: Please, Marian.

MARIAN: You said you'd left him. Sound move. Stick to it. He's behind you now. Receding over the horizon. Bye-bye David. There he goes. Good riddance.

RUTH: The way you did with Lenny, I suppose.

MARIAN: Lenny played that godawful noise, on that trombone of his, half the night, it was enough to give you a splitting headache, certainly — however, he never actually smashed me across the skull with it.

RUTH: You can't even begin to imagine the pressure the police are under . . .

MARIAN: I don't want to get into it, Ruth.

RUTH: I'm not making excuses for him.

MARIAN: He's a policeman, who strikes his wife, about

the head, with his own truncheon, there are no excuses.

RUTH: I know that.

MARIAN: No imaginable excuses, I'm talking fractured skulls, brain damage, haemorrhages — he could have killed you!

RUTH: He's not a bad person, Marian, honest to God, his nerves are frayed away to nothing . . .

MARIAN: Forget it.

RUTH: They never know the minute, he's had three good mates killed in his own station, and a fourth one blinded, it's the waiting around all day that gets to him, all the threats and the hatred and no outlet, he comes home coiled up like a spring, he's frightened of his life, it's all pent up inside him . . . Christ, I'm no better, sitting at home, waiting to hear the worst . . . I caught my sleeve on one of his swimming trophies — Waterford crystal it was — it smashed to bits in the hearth . . . I just stared down stupid at the pieces like a child who knows it's in for a thumping ... it was a sort of blinding crunch and a flash of light, I was lying behind the sofa then and I could feel my hair getting wet . . . twice more he hit me . . . but I had my arms up by then . . . the phone started to ring, I think that saved me, not that he answered it, it sort of half brought him round, he just stared down at me and said, 'that's you sorted out', and then he threw the truncheon into a corner and went into the hall for his coat and I heard the front door slamming. He hadn't even had his dinner. So I got up and cleaned myself off — I knew then I had to go, get away — I didn't want to be there when he got back, not this time — I really knew this time I couldn't live with him anymore — how can you love somebody once you're actually in fear of your life of him — I don't blame him, Marian, but I can't stay with him, I can't stand being so scared . . . I'm sorry.

[MARIAN *is staring into the fire.* RUTH *pours herself another capful of brandy*]

RUTH: God. Look at us. Magdala Street.

MARIAN: Scarcely.

RUTH: All over again. Isn't it?

MARIAN: Not exactly.

RUTH: All those nights, landing in on you . . . boyfriends usually, it was . . .

MARIAN: One boyfriend, it was.

RUTH: If it wasn't the shorthand and typing course. Oh well.

MARIAN: He was clouting you even then, Ruth.

RUTH: It was forever me crying my eyes out anyhow.

MARIAN: Even as the boyfriend he was at it.

RUTH: Always some thing or another.

MARIAN: He started it then. He started it right at the beginning. Before the troubles were ever heard of, well before he joined the police, this has nothing to do with the police. He was handing you out a regular hiding, even then, that was what brought you crying to me, night in night out, only you never owned up to it, you covered up for the bastard till you had your first miscarriage for which he was to blame . . .

RUTH: It's not true!

MARIAN: The lies you've told for the sake of that sadistic pig . . .

RUTH: Who are you . . . ?

MARIAN: Ten years of it.

RUTH: What have you got to show?

MARIAN: I said I didn't want to get into it.

RUTH: He's no pig, he's a human being!

MARIAN: All right. Enough.

RUTH: We had fights, everybody has fights, maybe you didn't, married to that pathetic piss-artist . . .

MARIAN: You want to stay here?

RUTH: Lenny Harrigan was a gutless dropout fit-for-nothing from the day and hour you met him, my David's out there on those streets day and night risking his life to protect other people . . .

MARIAN: He's done a really impressive job for you.

RUTH: If you're so very superior, Marian, what exactly are you doing here, sitting here, in a condemned slum, at one in the morning, completely alone, sitting here staring into that fire, drinking on your own, if you know so much more, just show us what it is, the secret of your massive fucking success, because the rest of us would love to know, what it is we're doing, patronizing and protecting your antiques business and your husband who abandoned his law degree and has been sponging off the state ever since and his daddy the Catholic barrister who makes a fat living out of finding loopholes in the law for Republican mass murderers to slip through, and your intellectual I.R.A. friends who're busy liberating us from our legs and our brains and our children, just tell us . . . who in hell you are . . . to sit in judgement, all the time . . .

MARIAN: You want to stay here?

RUTH: I'm sorry.

MARIAN: You still want to stay?

RUTH: I'm like . . . something wild . . .

MARIAN: Because ground rules are needed here. There are things to bear in mind here. Such as. This is the third time you've left David and come running to me.

RUTH: Marian, don't be angry. I'm really sorry, honest to God . . .

MARIAN: The previous two times you went back to him. I'm beginning to feel like the other woman. With all the aggravation and no sex.

RUTH: I won't be going back again.

MARIAN: Where will you live?

RUTH: I — plan to find a flat.

MARIAN: Tomorrow? [RUTH *hesitates*] You can't live here.

RUTH: No, of course, it was just for tonight, I couldn't think where else . . . I mean, if it's a problem . . .

MARIAN: It's a problem. [*She sustains her level stare at* RUTH, *who looks away*] I'm hardly going to throw you out on the street, am I. Tomorrow you find a flat.

RUTH: I said. Look, I could easily sleep in the front parlour, that way I'd be no trouble at all . . .

MARIAN: You're not sleeping in Lily's parlour, she has the dust sheets on still. You'll be in her bedroom.

RUTH: Thank you.

MARIAN: Concerning the other matters, Ruth — the heavy burden of my antiques business which you feel that you've been carrying . . .

RUTH: Please, Marian . . .

MARIAN: The shop has in fact been taken over by Tom Feeney, the gallery owner, who has impeccably Protestant credentials as of course you well know. Lenny, just for the record, hasn't actually had to draw the dole since receiving an annuity from the same maiden aunt who left him this house in her will, the two friends I had who joined the Republican movement are no longer friends, on account of one being dead and the other being a pious fool who's now in Long Kesh[6] and deserves to stay there, Lenny isn't entirely my husband since we're halfway through a divorce, and I can hardly be held responsible for his da who, amongst other things, was always avid to achieve purchase on my inner thigh over the Christmas period . . .

RUTH: I remember.

MARIAN: Generally speaking, Ruth, in regard to these ground rules, whereas you may be a girlhood friend, you're nobody's probation officer, and if I choose to drink brandy in front of a fire in a house eloquent with the history of this city at a time of the night when I feel most sensate, that's a choice I'm making out of my own free will under my own control for my own pleasure which is a private decision not subject to invasion by anyone whatsoever . . .

[*The sound of someone opening and coming through the front door is heard from offstage*]

RUTH: O my God!

MARIAN [*Leaping up*]: Quiet!

[*She grabs a poker from the fireplace and positions herself by the kitchen door, on the non-opening side*]

[*The door is flung open — concealing* MARIAN *from view altogether — and* LENNY *enters, precipitously, since he is carrying two bulging holdalls and has his trombone case under one arm*]

LENNY: Ruth? — how did you get here? What happened to your head?

[MARIAN *reveals herself by pushing the door shut.* LENNY *registers the poker*]

Have you two been fighting each other?

MARIAN: What's this all about?

LENNY: Who did you imagine I was?

MARIAN: What are these bags?

LENNY: I've been totally burgled. The entire place, stripped clean. I was out playing at a gig. My house is like a bomb site. Well — nearly.

MARIAN: You're not planning on staying here?

LENNY: It's really very kind of you to sympathize, Marian — but I expect I'll get over it in time.

RUTH: Did you notify the police?

LENNY: Usual formalities. They are a bit otherwise engaged — hardly news to you.

MARIAN: Ruth's already staying tonight.

LENNY: Fine. Lovely. A few more arrivals and we can throw a party.

MARIAN: There's nowhere for you to sleep.

LENNY: Marian — I could begin to feel a trifle testy at your demeanour.

RUTH: I'll make us some tea. [*She hurries out of the hostilities into the scullery, and proceeds to put the kettle on*]

LENNY: I get home after midnight to find that everything of value I possess has been stolen, right down to the brass bed, which is particularly inconvenient since I normally use it for sleeping on . . .

MARIAN: There's plenty of beds in your parents' house.

LENNY: What the hell do you think you're doing here anyway?

MARIAN: Looking for a quiet life, quaint as that may sound to you.

LENNY: Who said you could move in, the house doesn't belong to you, not yet.

MARIAN: We've exchanged contracts.

LENNY: We haven't completed!

MARIAN: Don't start on the legalese, we've both agreed I'm buying the house, so I'm living here now and I don't want you poking your head round the door any time the fancy takes you.

LENNY: What do you imagine this is, some clever ploy to worm my way back in beneath your panty-hose, forget it — not interested.

MARIAN: Not on offer if you were.

LENNY: Good, that's a relief. So. You and your friend want to camp out overnight in my house, is that it?

MARIAN: Fuck off.

LENNY: Well, you're most welcome to, yes, certainly. First up makes breakfast. [*Calling through the door*] Find everything you need there, Ruth?

RUTH: Thanks, Lenny, yes.

LENNY: Great stuff. [*Sotto voce to* MARIAN] What's Desdemona doing here exactly?

MARIAN: Another refugee.

LENNY: Did he give her that head?

MARIAN: She's left him.

LENNY: Not again. He'll be the next one through the door, then. Just like old times, really.

MARIAN: Not in any respect whatsoever.

LENNY: Where's she sleeping?

MARIAN: Lily's bed.

LENNY: You?

MARIAN: In front of this fire.

LENNY: The top bedroom for me then.

MARIAN: The bedding's damp.

LENNY [*Picking up one of the holdalls*]: Sleeping bag.

MARIAN: Thoughtful of the burglars to leave you that.

LENNY: It's yours, actually. It was under the stairs.

MARIAN: Great. I can use it for in here. [*Takes the holdall, unzips it, removes the sleeping bag*]

LENNY: Just bear in mind, Marian — I can have you evicted from this house. If I had a mind to do it, I could still call off the sale.

MARIAN: I've moved in. I'm here to stay. Try it.

LENNY: You know — I was left in bits after you walked out on me. Except for enormous relief about one thing. Which I've never stopped thanking God for. I didn't have to attempt to understand you any more.

MARIAN: Well, I'm run ragged, Lenny. From understanding you through and through.

RUTH [*Calling through to them*]: Tea's nearly ready!

LENNY: Scrub it, Ruth. I think you'll find the milk's all curdled.

[*He picks up his luggage and exits upstairs*]

RUTH: Will I use these mugs?

MARIAN: No. Leave them.

RUTH: Where are the cups?

MARIAN: I don't want any tea. You can use the kettle for a hot water bottle. You're going to need one, in that bedroom.

RUTH: Right-o.

[*She looks around the scullery for it, then returns to the kitchen door in a helpless kind of way*]

MARIAN: It's on the back of the door.

[RUTH *mutely fetches it*]

[MARIAN *has sat down again in the rocking chair and is staring into the fire. From upstairs, the sound of* LENNY *playing his trombone starts up: loud and up-tempo. She looks slowly up at the ceiling, at the sound*]

[*The lights fade to blackout*]

[*End of Scene Two*]

SCENE THREE

[*The night of Sunday, May 19th*]

[*The kitchen and scullery are dark and deserted*]

[*The sound of half a dozen drunken youths running up the back entry, shouting and whistling, is heard from off. A beer bottle sails over the yard wall and smashes harmlessly on the floor of the yard. Then silence returns. Until the front door can be heard opening and two slightly drunk men* (LENNY *and* PETER) *coming into the hall*]

LENNY [*Offstage*]: Easy on.

PETER [*Offstage*]: Bloody blind man's bluff . . .

LENNY: Sshh . . . [*Calling out*] Fear not, ladies, it's reinforcements. You can put the poker away!

[*Sound of* PETER *laughing and then stumbling*]

LENNY: Watch the bottles, for God's sake . . .

PETER: Well, get some lights on . . .

[*The kitchen door is thrust open, to reveal* LENNY *carrying a cardboard box full of beer cans, and bottles of spirits. He gropes round for the light switch with his free hand, makes contact, and the electric light comes on*]

LENNY: What do you know, we're in luck, head. Double luck. The electricity is on and the housemother is absent. We've got power without responsibility.

[PETER *has followed him into the room, carrying a travel bag and a bulky paper sack, like a small bag of cement. His style is 1974 casual chic*]

PETER: My drinking arm's gone dead with the weight of this stuff.

[*He dumps the heavy sack down along with his travel bag*]

LENNY: What did you have to hump that muck across the water[7] for anyhow?

PETER: It's muesli. Grain and nuts, honey, dried fruit . . .

LENNY: It has been heard of here, you know, you don't actually have to define it.

PETER: Didn't want to use up your food supplies.

LENNY: You've brought about three stone of it.

PETER: It's very nutritious, I figured I could live on it, if the strike[8] goes on indefinitely, do you think it might?

LENNY: You need milk.

PETER: This is true.

LENNY: You can't eat it without milk. Is what I'm saying.

PETER: Ah, holy God, they haven't stopped the milk, have they.

LENNY: Peter, use the loaf — protest strike by loyalist workers, right? Electricity cuts. No petrol supplies. No animal foodstuffs. Barricades all over the city turning back the traffic. Three quarters of all cows are Protestant. What chance has the milk got?

PETER [*Who has been holding out his right arm, wincing*]: Pins and needles.

[LENNY *opens a can of beer from the box*]

LENNY: Here. Try it left-handed. As they say in the Marriage Guidance Council.

PETER: Do they?

LENNY: More or less.

PETER: Well, you should know. Cheers.

LENNY: And welcome home to you, old fruit.

[*They drink*]

PETER: Do I sound very English?

LENNY: Yeah, but only when you talk.

PETER: Don't you just love it — the sly dig, the dry remark, how painfully I've missed it. The authentic Lilliputian wit. [*Moving round, surveying the rooms*] And this is the inheritance?

LENNY: It's the best I can do for you tonight.

PETER: An ethnic little gem, though. What? Set this load down in a choicer part of Birmingham, a treasure trove is what you'd have, my son, a highly des. res.[9] in need of minor gentrification.

LENNY: You're welcome to ship the whole lot back with you, I can't believe you managed to get over here. Or why.

PETER: I did have to hang about most of the night, it's true — waiting for the blasted ferry to make up its mind to sail from Heysham.[10]

LENNY: There can only have been you on it.

PETER: Well, aside from a coach party of foreign travel agents, and a young soldier's wife.

LENNY: No doubt you took care of her.

PETER: Once she got her horrible kids to sleep. It was the travel agents who were really in need of looking after, though. Wholesale shitlessness.

LENNY: How did you get the booze?

PETER: Bribed the barman.

LENNY: Jesus. See you, head? People like you lead a charmed life. If I hadn't just chanced to sneak across town this evening . . . you do realize it's mob law here at the minute?

PETER: I've been watching it all week. The BBC have adapted it for television, you know.

LENNY: I haven't been living in my own place for nearly a month, since the burglary, I hadn't even set foot in it in the last four days, since the strike got heavy — it was a pure fluke, showing up there tonight, just in time to bump into you. Anybody but you could have been in a tightish corner.

PETER: I placed my faith in the Ulster Sunday. I believed in my heart, brother — even if the Protestant blackshirts had finally staged a putsch, they would still remember the seventh day and keep it holy. Not to mention rainy, bleak, doom-laden, and utterly devoid of human life. Sure enough. I was able to roam at will around the mean streets — apart from the occasional catcall, and comment of a personal nature.

LENNY: You didn't want to miss all the stir, I suppose.

PETER: It sounds to me like the big picture. The '74 Uprising. The Great Loyalist Insurrection. Historic days in Lilliput.

LENNY: Sure, every bloody day in the week's historic, in this place.

PETER: Anyway, I was due a trip home. It's been three years.

LENNY: You're not going to go on calling it Lilliput the whole time?

PETER: What, this teeny weeny wee province of ours and its little people, all the angry munchkins, with their midget brains, this festering pimple on the vast white flabby bum of western Europe, what would *you* call it?

LENNY: I call it home.

PETER: You do realize — the rest of the world has crossed the street, long since, passed on by — on account of having fully-grown twentieth-century problems to be getting on with — the continued existence of the planet, say, or the survival of the species?

LENNY: So is that what they fight about in Birmingham?

PETER: What am I hearing? For God's sake don't tell me you've turned into a proud wee Ulsterman?

LENNY: Coals to Newcastle, okay? Coals of fire, in this case, you get them heaped on your head here every time you turn round. The last thing I need is you landing in and dumping another load on me.

PETER: Only the truth. Crass insensitivity. Craven apologies. Not another slur against the dear wee darling homeland shall pass these lips.

LENNY: It's the arsehole of hell, who's arguing. No future in it. Whatsoever. Once this Prod agitation is over, I'm off out, I've definitely had enough, I know what you're going to say.

PETER: All right — but apart from that . . .

LENNY: What? Apart from what?

PETER: Apart from the fact that you've said it all a dozen times before . . .

LENNY: Dammit, Peter, I knew that's what you were going to say!

PETER: I wasn't going to say it, you asked me to say it.

LENNY: I'm serious. I mean it.

PETER: All right.

LENNY: Things have changed. Is what I'm saying.

PETER: All right. Always assuming it ever will be over, of course.

LENNY: What? The strike? 'Course it will.

PETER: Strike? This is no strike. [*Paisleyite*[11] *voice*] This is a constitutional stoppage!

LENNY: God save us, Doctor, that sounds agonizing, is there nothing you could prescribe that would shift it?

PETER: I mean, what if they do take over, for keeps? They'll throw all you Fenian rebels into the Gulag — make you earn your supplementary benefit sewing mailbags.

LENNY: What makes you think you'd be let off?

PETER: Me, I'm one of the elect — my daddy's even a minister of the true faith.

LENNY: You're joking, he's a Methodist. Out on the barricades there, that counts as dangerous left-wing subversion. Your da's ecumenical!

PETER: All right, keep your voice down.

LENNY: Anyhow, with that hair and those jeans, and the way you talk — not to mention the muesli —

PETER: All right, all right, I've got the gag.

LENNY: Never you fret, head, it'll be over within the week.

PETER: Somebody on the boat was saying they'd declared a state of emergency.

LENNY: Meaning the army's finally going to be ordered to break it. The English have just been hanging on as usual, waiting for reason and moderation and fair play to break out suddenly — you know — just like it always does in the Houses of Parliament.

PETER [*Parliamentary braying*]: Heah heah, heah heah heah . . .

LENNY [*Joining in*]: Heah heah heah . . . [*Laughs*]

. . . yeah, right. So anyhow. You still like it over there?

PETER: It's a lot bigger.

LENNY: Well. This is it. [*A gap has opened in the banter*]

PETER: And how about you? You're actually going to attempt the great escape this time?

LENNY: Nothing to keep me here now. Apart from three hundred-odd street barricades, and thousands of hooded men with clubs.

[*The front door being opened is heard from off*]

PETER: Is that Marian?

LENNY: Look, just remember what I told you, right?

PETER: I'm cool.

LENNY: Leave her to me.

PETER: All yours.

[*They are all tensed up in anticipation of the onslaught*]

[*The door from the hall opens, and* RUTH *enters, carrying a heavy bale of peat briquettes in one hand, and a Bible in the other. She is dressed in her Sunday best*]

RUTH: Sorry . . .

LENNY: Ah, Ruth. It's you.

RUTH: Look what Marian's mother gave us. For the fire.

LENNY: Did Marian come back with you?

RUTH: She's just parking her car. Up behind our church. There's a car park there.

LENNY: Good thinking.

RUTH: It's bit safer.

PETER: I'm glad to hear those old buildings are being put to some practical use.

RUTH: It's the Church of God, it was only built last year.

LENNY: By the way, Ruth, this here is a friend of mine from student days, Peter Irwin. [*To the latter*] This is Ruth Macalester.

RUTH [*As she sets the bale of peat down in the hearth*]: How'd you do.

PETER: Fancy a beer?

RUTH: I have to change, excuse me.

[*She exits, up the stairs*]

PETER: Protestant nookie, in the house, why wasn't I informed.

LENNY: She was supposed to be moving to her ma's this morning.

PETER: Not a bad arse on her.

LENNY: Forget it, she's one of Marian's lame ducks.

PETER: Not the cop's wife again?

LENNY: She left him three weeks ago, serious GBH.[12] She's been holed up here ever since.

PETER: My God, so you've been besieged, all this time, with not just one but two frigid cows — lucky I turned up, head. You're in serious need of reinforcements.

LENNY: Listen. Go easy with Marian.

PETER: What? I haven't even clapped eyes on her yet.

LENNY: I know how to handle her, it's just, when she sees you here — she's definitely going to cut up rough.

PETER: Sure. Yeah. Marian and me were never exactly a mutual admiration society.

LENNY: It's not that, it's the state she's in . . . totally obsessive, don't ask me what the story is . . . some weird syndrome, you know how it is with women. I'm just thankful she's finally agreed to a divorce.

PETER: Would it still be losing the kid, maybe?

LENNY: That? — oh, she took that in her stride . . . didn't she . . . no problem. Anyhow. It's five years now.

PETER: Can't be.

LENNY: Near as dammit. August '69.

PETER: A vintage month.

LENNY: The marriage started to go dead too, from then on.

PETER: Bound to. The pair of you had never intended to hitch up in the first place. Not until the pregnancy.

LENNY: Yeah, but let me tell you a funny story. When the sprog was born — Christopher, to give him his due and proper name — the bunched-up fingers and feet, like tight fat buds, flailing away at us . . . when he was there between us on the bed, all crinkled-up and livid . . . something out of order happened. Between Marian and me. We sort of fell in love. With each other. At least I know I did, she would sneer at all that now, don't ever let me catch you breathing a word of this . . .

PETER: Swear.

LENNY: . . . I'd stake my life on it, if you really want to know, so there we were. Married lovers, the way it's always supposed to be in the booklets. It wasn't exactly a pleasure trip, there was very little sleep, money was tight, we didn't get out a lot. It's the one time so far I've ever felt one hundred per cent alive. For five months. That was how long it lasted . . . that was how long the sprog lasted. At that point he checked out, he'd seen enough. Maybe it was the prospect of having me as a da, you could hardly blame him . . . she came down in the morning . . . the cot was still, no more fury . . . just a tiny silent shrivelled-up rickle of bones and skin. She came and woke me. She took it in her stride. I picked him up . . . you didn't know this. Any of it. He was my son.

She was my wife.

[PETER *is left at a loss for a few moments. Then he fetches a can of beer from the box, opens it and offers it to* LENNY. LENNY *takes it and drinks deep*]

[*The sound of somebody coming in from the street is heard from off. After a moment,* MARIAN *enters from the hall, in church-going clothes also, carrying a bag of dry foods*]

MARIAN: My God.

PETER: Hello there, Marian.

MARIAN: The lulu's back in town. How did you get here?

PETER: Oh, you know — the spirit moved me.

MARIAN: So how long has the spirit dumped you here for?

PETER: That's really up to the Ulster Worker's Council.

MARIAN: Hang on a minute. You went off and qualified as a property surveyor. Is that right?

PETER: It's what pays the rent.

MARIAN: I imagine it does. You need a place to stay?

LENNY: In actual point of fact . . .

MARIAN: Here's an offer. You can have the boxroom upstairs for a week. In return for doing me a professional full-scale written structural survey of the house.

PETER: What for?

MARIAN: What do you say?

PETER: If you like.

MARIAN: I've got some people coming from the National Trust on Thursday, that's when you have to do it by. Deal?

PETER: Fine.

MARIAN: Very good, Peter, glad you managed back.

[*She moves on into the kitchen to unload her bag*]

LENNY: Hold it just a minute. What has the National Trust got to do with anything?

MARIAN: Very little, in your case.

PETER [*To* MARIAN]: Is the survey meant to be shown to them or something?

MARIAN: Given to them.

PETER: Why on earth?

MARIAN: Because I'm making them an offer too. To take over this house as a National Trust property.

LENNY: Take over — here? This?

[*It's too much for him, he lets out a bellow of incredulous laughter*]

[PETER *grimaces at him to be quiet and moves to the kitchen door*]

PETER [*To* MARIAN]: Is it really — their style, though? Marian? Would you say? The National Trust?

MARIAN: Not yet, it isn't.

PETER: I mean, it certainly does have plenty of atmosphere . . .

LENNY: God knows, fish could nearly swim in it.

PETER: It's just, you know — all those Castle Coole and Castleward types of places . . .

LENNY: It's all those fully upholstered la-di-da lady baritones, Jesus wept, can you imagine them in here, selling postcards of the outside bog and knitted tea cosies?

MARIAN: I'm glad I'm keeping you entertained.

PETER: Where on earth did you get the idea, Marian?

MARIAN: Lily Matthews lived here. 1900 to 1974. This house was her whole life. She never threw anything away. I've started cataloguing it all. Every last thimble and shirt stud, every grocery bill and cigarette card and rationing coupon, every document of her and Alfie's life together.

[*She scoops up some documents from a shoe box on the sideboard*]

Look at this — the dismissal from his gasfitting job in 1931. They were able to manage through the Depression by finding a lodger to take in — that's his rent book there. Alan Ferris. He was an English airman. His photograph's here. The three of them together.

[*She carefully scrutinizes the photograph*]

PETER: Right. Yeah. Though, there must be thousands of houses like this . . . thousands of people, like that. It's very touching, absolutely — but it's nothing special, though. Is it?

MARIAN: You think not? So why should Lily Matthews' home and hearth be less special than Lord Castlereagh's or the Earl of Enniskillen's? A whole way of life, a whole culture, the only difference being that this home speaks for a far greater community of experience in this country than some transplanted feeble-minded aristocrat's ever could, have you looked at it, properly?

PETER: Haven't had a chance yet.

MARIAN: Never mind what you learnt as a student architect, this is what design and building and history mean, to the people of this city, go ahead. Look around it. Just don't touch anything, I've changed nothing. Lenny, show him where the boxroom is.

LENNY: Why can't he sleep in the front parlour?

MARIAN: It's a front parlour, that's why.

LENNY: Exactly. Instead of being a boxroom.

PETER: Why don't I just take my gear upstairs, while I'm at it. [*Picking up his travel bag and making an exit out the hall door and up the stairs*]

LENNY [*To* MARIAN]: The National Trust . . . you're not actually serious?

MARIAN: No more refugees. There are three too many as it is.

LENNY [*Gesturing towards the bag*]: Help yourself to the muesli.

[*He exits in pursuit of* PETER]

[MARIAN *closes the door behind them. She crosses to the rocking chair, sits down in it, and stares into the empty grate*]

[*From the far distance, the sound of two lambeg drums*[13] *head-to-head starts up*]

[LILY MATTHEWS *appears from the pantry. She comes right into the kitchen, to behind the rocking chair. She looks to be in late middle age now, but wearing a pretty print dress from the early thirties with a pinafore over it, and her hair drawn up in a bun*]

LILY: You needn't bother getting settled. You'll have no peace in this house, nor good fortune neither.

MARIAN: What kind of fortune did you have, Lily?

LILY: Four of you's now, in on me, tramping your filth all over my good floors.

MARIAN: We'll have it back to ourselves, you and me, soon enough. Back to rights.

LILY: You've been to your Mass again, I can smell it off you.

MARIAN: Something I've been meaning to ask you . . .

LILY: Why did you come here? What possessed you to move in on me?

MARIAN: Fifteen years, all on your own. The neighbours leaving one by one, blind houses blocked up behind them, the street gradually silenced. Shut up in here. The loneliness of it.

LILY: I had my own people round me, never wanted for anything.

MARIAN: I've been lonely myself, you see.

LILY: Never wanted company . . .

MARIAN: Five years now.

LILY: Quite content on my own, thank you.

MARIAN: That's why.

LILY: Up until you turned up. Four of you's now, in on me.

MARIAN: Company like that only makes you lonelier, you think I don't understand that, you think I want them here either?

LILY: Don't you imagine you can find favour with me, dear, when you couldn't even make a decent life with your own husband, your own sort.

MARIAN: That's the dress you were wearing in that photograph.

LILY: Stay you out of my private belongings!

MARIAN: In the name of Jesus I'm trying to preserve them!

LILY: Don't you dare blaspheme in my kitchen!

MARIAN: Sorry, I'm sorry . . .

LILY: Nobody asked your help and it's not wanted.

MARIAN: It's not help that I'm offering ... it's help that

I'm looking for. Is that not obvious?

[LILY *begins to sing*]

LILY: Oh, God our help in ages past . . .

MARIAN: Don't fight me, Lily, . . .

LILY [*Continuing to sing over* MARIAN's *lines*]:
Our hope for years to come . . .

MARIAN: I need you, we have got to make this work, you and me . . .

LILY [*Singing on regardless*]:
Our shelter from the stormy blast,
And our eternal home!

MARIAN: You think you're haunting me, don't you. But you see it's me that's actually haunting you. I'm not going to go away. There's no curse or hymn that can exorcize me. So you might as well just give me your blessing and make your peace with me, Lily.

LILY: You'll have no peace in this house.

MARIAN: Why had you not wee 'uns? You weren't able, was that it?

LILY: Never had a day's sickness in my life, there was nothing the matter with me or mine.

MARIAN: So it was Alfie, then?

LILY: That's no business of yours or of your like, my Alfie was a good man, he would have made a loving father, if the Good Lord didn't see fit to send us a little one, so be it, he giveth and he taketh away, blessed be the name of the Lord. Anyway, I haven't noticed you bringing up any youngsters.

MARIAN: No. The Lord didn't do too well by me either. In that respect.

LILY: What right does a hussy like you have, to question God's will? Why would he bless the fruit of your womb more than mine, look at this place, you have it like a pigsty . . . are there not enough runty litters running the streets, whelped by your kind, reared with a half-brick in their fists, and the backsides hanging out of their trousers?

[MARIAN *has reached into the raffia basket tucked in by the side of the rocking chair*]

MARIAN: It was just that I found this.

[*She takes out and holds up a 1930's child's christening gown, trimmed with lace and ribbons*]

LILY: [*Terrified*] The devil . . .

MARIAN: Folded up.

LILY: The devil is in this house . . .

MARIAN: Wrapped in tissue.

LILY: The Antichrist is in our midst!

MARIAN: Hidden amongst your underwear.

[LILY *backs away into the scullery*]

LILY: Oh, Lord Jesus, send the devil out of this room,

let your servant now depart in peace . . . [*She is melting into the shadows once again*]

[RUTH *comes in from the hall*]

RUTH: Is he away?

MARIAN: What? Who?

RUTH: The friend of Lenny's. Peter.

MARIAN: He's staying here.

RUTH [*Seeing the christening robe*]: Och, look, isn't that the loveliest thing . . . was it hers? I thought there were no children?

MARIAN: Maybe she lived in hope. Like you and me.

RUTH: Not me, Marian. Not now.

MARIAN: You're not even thirty. There's a whole life to come.

RUTH: They don't think . . . after I lost the third one . . . they told me that . . . it mightn't . . .

MARIAN: It's a childless house. Barren. Why else would I feel so much at home.

RUTH: What do you know about it, yours was alive, at least you had it at your breast, for a while at least, you knew what it was, oh Jesus if only I'd been able to keep just one of them, to hold it back to make it grow, we'd be all right, all different, if I can't have a child I won't live!

MARIAN: Christopher would have been five in August. Starting school. If he hadn't gone. Left me. Given up the ghost in me. My own soul, left for dead. He was our future, you see. Future, at a time like this . . . what could it possibly mean — a future? In a place like this?

[*She looks down at* LILY's *unused christening robe.* RUTH *goes to her, kneels by her, embraces her*]

[*The light fades to blackout, on the grief of the three women*]

[*End of Scene Three*]

ACT 2

SCENE FOUR

[*The night of Saturday, May 25th*]

[*The house is in darkness*]

[*Over the theatre P.A., we hear the opening of a broadcast to the nation being given by the Prime Minister, Harold Wilson*]

BROADCAST TAPE: As this holiday weekend begins, Northern Ireland faces the gravest crisis in her history. It is a crisis equally for all of us who live on this side of the water. What we are seeing in Northern Ireland is not just an industrial strike. It has nothing to do with wages. It has nothing to do with jobs — except to imperil jobs. It is a deliberate and calculated attempt to use every undemocratic and unparliamentary means for the purpose of bringing down the whole constitution of Northern Ireland so as to set up there a sectarian and undemocratic state . . .

[RUTH *has come into the kitchen from the hall, with a lighted candle in one hand and a transistor radio in the other. The sound of the broadcast from her radio overlaps with and soon takes over from the theatre P.A.*]

RADIO: . . . We recognize that behind this situation lie many genuine and deeply held fears. I have to say that these fears are unfounded. That they are being deliberately fostered by people in search of power.

[PETER *has followed* RUTH *into the kitchen, carrying a lighted oil lamp. She has set her candle down on the mantelpiece and the radio on the table, and has sat down to listen. He places the oil lamp on the sideboard, and also sits down to listen*]

RADIO: The people on this side of the water — British parents — have seen their sons vilified and spat upon and murdered. British taxpayers have seen the taxes they have poured out, almost without regard to cost — over three hundred million pounds a year this year with the cost of the Army operation on top of that — going into Northern Ireland. They see property destroyed by evil violence and are asked to pick up the bill for rebuilding it. Yet people who benefit from all this now viciously defy Westminster, purporting to act as though they were an elected government; people who spend their lives sponging on Westminster and British democracy and then systematically assault democratic methods. Who do these people think they are?

[RUTH *springs up in a fury and switches the radio off*]

PETER: Hey.

RUTH: How dare he?

PETER: He hasn't finished.

RUTH: How dare he say that to us? — *us* — spongers!

PETER: What's the odds?

RUTH: We worked hard for everything we have and hold, we're British taxpayers just the same as they are!

PETER: He's talking about the seizing of power!

RUTH: This city was full of life, full of industry, built by our people, they made it into a capital city, to be proud of . . .

PETER: All right.

RUTH: Everything we have and hold, for five long years now we've watched it rent asunder, pulverized into rubble by the real spongers, cruel and murderous bastards . . .

PETER: All right!

RUTH: How long are we supposed to grin and bear it?

PETER: I haven't noticed much grinning.

RUTH: We've had enough, far more than enough.

PETER: So this is your idea of a solution?

RUTH: Something had to be done!

PETER: No food, no light, no heat, the bullet-heads in charge?

RUTH: That smug wee English shite with his weaselly voice, what right has he to lecture us, he'll soon know his driver, the same boyo . . .

PETER: He isn't here, Ruthie child, he's five hundred-odd miles in that direction, over the sea, fully fed and comfortable, this is being done to us, the people here, self-inflicted, is this what you want? — the apemen in charge, shops without food to sell, garages without petrol, people penned into their own homes, cold hungry and terrified, there's a mile-long queue of doctors and nurses and social workers, and lawyers, up at Hawthornden Road, queuing up to beg for a special pass to get them through the barricades to their patients and clients, and from who? — from the wee hard men who can barely sign their name to their special bloody passes, from shipyard Bible-thumpers, unemployed binmen, petty crooks and extortionists, pigbrain mobsters and thugs, they've seized control over all of us, they're now ordering the sewage workers out, the raw sewage is about to come flooding down those streets out there, and it won't be the English who die of typhoid, Ruth, this is not what we call a protest movement, this is what is historically known as root and branch fascism . . .

RUTH: Just shut up and listen for a minute!

PETER: We're at the mercy of actual real-life fascist jackboot rule!

RUTH: Use your ears, just listen. Out there. Right? Nothing. No gunplay. No bombs. How long is it — how long, since you could go to sleep at night, without that? Of course you wouldn't know, would you.

PETER: What does that prove?

RUTH: The I.R.A. have been stopped in their tracks at last.

PETER: For Christ's sake, they're on hold, that's all, you're doing it all for them, alienate the Brits, that broadcast was like music to their ears, are you deaf, blind and entirely thick?

RUTH: Don't you condescend to me . . .

PETER: Can you not see, this whole tribe, so-called Protestants, we both of us grew up in it, all that endless mindless marching, they've been marching away with the lambegs blattering and the banners flying straight up a dead-end one-way blind alley, self-destroying, the head's eating the tail now, it's a lingering tribal suicide going on out there, there was no need for any of it, they held all the cards, they only needed to be marginally generous, how did I get into this, I apologize for what I called you, I got carried away, fear no doubt, funny isn't it . . . it's not as if I'm unfamiliar with tense situations. Six years ago, I was standing in a human chain encircling a building. It was in America . . . a university. Black students had seized the building and smuggled in guns, the police were lined up in their hundreds, ready to storm it. Me and a fewscore of other white liberals had put our bodies in between, holding hands with each other, armed blacks behind us and armed cops in front . . . it was scary as hell, but there was playacting involved too, a big American psychodrama, the college president and the blacks' leader were up on a stage together at the end, hugging each other, I don't quite see that happening here. God, I'm hungry. Do you want some muesli?

[*He goes to the sack and spoons some into a bowl*]

RUTH: You don't know what's been happening here. What the people have gone through. How could you. You got out.

PETER: Why are the police not intervening, this is wholesale lawlessness . . . why are the Army standing aside, watching people being roughed up, vehicles being hijacked, shops being looted, doing sod-all about it? Who's supposed to be in charge?

RUTH: They can't take on an entire community. You don't know your own people, not any more. This strike is theirs. They're completely behind it now. Nationalist rebels have been imposed as executive ministers, ruling over them, against their will . . .

PETER: Do us a favour . . .

RUTH: They won't be coerced. They won't be dictated to. All they're proving is what your sort was always chanting — the power lies with the people. Only in this case it's your own people. You have no notion how they feel, you opted out. You lost touch. You see it all like the English now, 'a plague on both their houses' . . . easy to say when it isn't your own house that's in mortal danger.

PETER: I haven't exactly noticed you manning the barricades.

RUTH: There's no shortage of volunteers.

PETER: And this is what your husband makes of it all?

RUTH: My husband and I are separated.

PETER: He hasn't tracked you down yet, then?

RUTH: I wrote. Told him — not to bother.

[*She bites her lip, fighting back the tears*]

PETER: That's the stuff. [*Proffering the bowl of muesli*] Have some of this.

RUTH: No thanks.

PETER [*Pouring milk on the muesli*]: Just the powdered milk, I'm afraid. Go ahead. [*She shakes her head*] Sure? [*He shovels a spoonful into his mouth, munches it*] It's not bad at all, actually. [*He takes another spoonful*] Aaggh! [*He clutches his jaw in pain, thrusting the muesli bowl aside*]

RUTH: What's up?

PETER: Bugger it.

RUTH: Broken filling?

PETER: All I need.

RUTH: It's those wee black things. [*Looking in the bowl*] Lenny says it's buckshot.

PETER: They're seeds.

RUTH: Do you want an aspirin? He says he read it on the packaging . . .

PETER: Buck*wheat*!

RUTH: How did you find such a big bag of that stuff?

PETER: American couple, downstairs. Made it up for me.

RUTH: You mean in Birmingham?

PETER: They have a health-food shop. Under my flat.

RUTH: It's tasteless muck, isn't it.

PETER: Well, it hasn't been fried sodden, in rancid lard, if that's what you mean. So it scarcely counts as fit to eat at all, in this wee province of ours.

RUTH: You don't think very much of us, do you.

PETER: Why can I never remember it, until the minute I set foot . . . that ache in the arse, whatever the direct opposite of homesickness is. Exilephilia. The desperate nagging pain of longing to be far, far away.

RUTH: In Birmingham, you mean? Do you really like it there?

PETER: It's a lot bigger.

RUTH: It's where all the roads are, isn't it.

[*She goes into the kitchen and fetches him a glass of water and two aspirin*]

Here. Take these.

PETER [*Taking the glass*]: What are we supposed to do when they turn this stuff off?

RUTH: I've already filled up every receptacle in the house.

PETER: Amazing . . .

RUTH: We'll get by fine. Sooner or later the English will cave in, they have to. They'll disband the executive.

PETER: Out of the whole four of us — you're the only one who's really coping with all this.

RUTH: I just like having things to do. Looking after people. At school I always wanted to be a nurse, really bad . . .

PETER: The uniform would suit you.

RUTH: Only trouble being, it's the sort of thing you need a good stomach for.

PETER: Looks terrific from here.

RUTH: No, I mean, you know what I mean, not the uniform. Blood and things. Not my strong point. I've always been quite well organized, though.

PETER: Lucky somebody is, in this house.

RUTH: Is it really bad? The tooth?

PETER: A slight throb, that's all. Sorry I blew a fuse earlier.

RUTH: Don't mention it.

PETER: Kiss and make up, then.

RUTH: That's right.

PETER: I've been meaning to ask you, how did you and Marian come to be friends?

RUTH: The swimming.

PETER: What swimming?

RUTH: We both swam for our schools, we got selected for the Northern Ireland youth squad. We went away to Scotland and Holland. She was nearly seventeen. I was only thirteen, I wasn't like you, I was desperately homesick, it used to be the buses and trams that set me off the worst — the funny colour of them, I cried my eyes out over that. Honest to God, the things you feel. I'm no different, even now. Anyhow. It was Marian looked after me, she was like a big sister. We just somehow stayed friends, from that day to this.

PETER: It must be the swimming that keeps your figure so lithe.

RUTH: Oh, I don't compete now . . . not since my marriage . . . just for the club occasionally . . . you see, David, my husband, he was a real championship swimmer, I met him then too.

PETER: Lucky fellow.

RUTH: Not in his book.

PETER: You must have been spoilt for choice, with your looks.

RUTH: Oh, yes. Fighting them off.

PETER: Bet you were.

RUTH: Some hope.

PETER: You're quite remarkable, Ruth. In my book, that is.

RUTH: Not me.

PETER: Can I ask you something?

RUTH: Up to you.

PETER: It may seem a bit presumptuous.

RUTH: What is it?

PETER: Supposing we really were to kiss and make up?

RUTH: What sort of a question's that . . .

[*He's kissing her. Slowly and tentatively, she begins to respond*]

[*He guides her to the sofa, sits her down, lifts her legs on to the sofa so that she is lying with her knees bent, and him kneeling by her. He kisses her again, gently nudging her skirt up over her knees and caressing her thighs*]

[*The sound of* LENNY's *solo trombone suddenly blares out from upstairs.* RUTH *thrusts* PETER *aside and sits up*]

RUTH: What's he doing here?

PETER: They were both supposed to be searching for the car.

RUTH: He must have been dossing up there this whole time, he could easy have been in on us!

[*She is hurriedly pulling down her skirt and sitting up straight*]

PETER: Easy, it's all right, we'll go into the front parlour.

RUTH: We can't do that, not in there.

PETER: There's a lock on the door.

RUTH: Lily always kept it special!

PETER: It's a room, that's all. It's privacy.

RUTH: Marian would kill me!

PETER: Ruth, it's our business. It's strictly between us. Our secret. You and me.

[*Strokes her hair, gently kisses her again. Then he takes the candle and leads her by the hand, out the hall door and towards the forbidden pleasures of the front parlour*]

[LENNY's *trombone continues for a while from upstairs*]

[*There is a sudden hammering from outside the backyard door.* MARIAN's *voice is heard shouting* 'Lenny! Lenny! Hello! Down here! Open up!']

[*The trombone music stops and* LENNY *is heard thundering down the stairs: he appears rushing in from the hall carrying a torch, and continues straight through the kitchen to the scullery door, which he unlocks and opens, and thence down the yard to the yard door which he unbolts and flings back — to reveal* MARIAN, *in the light of the torch, mud-spattered with her coat ripped, and scratch marks on her face*]

[*She makes straight for the kitchen to wash her face and hands, while he re-bolts and re-locks the two doors*]

LENNY: Are you hurt bad?

MARIAN: Scratched a bit, but not as much as my car is.

LENNY: You found it?

MARIAN: It's the centrepiece of the barricade at the entrance to the estate up there.

LENNY: I suppose it's where we should have looked first.

MARIAN: There wasn't anybody about, I tried to drive it away.

LENNY: Chrissake, Marian, that was totally asking for it!

MARIAN: They knew me instantly on sight of course — 'that fenian hoor of a squatter' — that's what they actually think we are — squatters.

LENNY: Right.

MARIAN: It's quite funny, actually.

LENNY: That's it. We're moving out.

MARIAN: It was all women — shrieking and squealing and scrabbing at me, is that your radio? [*She has just spotted it on the table*]

LENNY: We can camp out in my place . . .

MARIAN: I thought I told you to keep it out of here. [*Thrusting the radio into his midriff*]

LENNY: Where's Ruth and Peter? [*Registering the radio*] Whose is this?

MARIAN: Yeah, take him and her with you both. If you walk across town you should have no problems.

LENNY: We'll leave together, all four of us.

MARIAN: I'm the one who lives here, if you recall. I'm going nowhere, I've only just got home.

LENNY: Marian, we're not talking personal issues, not any longer. This right here is Nazi Belfast now, and it's us playing the Jews.

MARIAN: God, but you're simple. People, cast adrift, in hysterics . . . spare me your vision of the Third Reich in Ballyhackamore.

LENNY: Look at yourself. Look at the news. It's nearly two weeks now, the animals have taken over the zoo, it's all poised on the verge of a massive pogrom, we're sitting here like a row of ducks in a shooting gallery.

[MARIAN *has been getting out a big church candle from a drawer and lighting it, to supplement the light from the camping lamp left behind by* RUTH *and* PETER]

MARIAN: Sounds to me like you haven't got a minute to lose.

LENNY: Right, okay. I'm withdrawing the house from sale.

MARIAN: Ruth's car is still sitting up there, untouched, up in the churchyard, if you want to try using that. You better go and get your gear together, there's a good boy.

LENNY: The contracts are off. Null and void.

MARIAN: Yes, well away you and explain all that to your Uncle Phelim, if you can track him down in his underground bunker, it's somewhere up Fortwilliam way, isn't that right?

LENNY: What exactly do you envisage happening here — the National Trust turning up in riot gear and storming the house to rescue you?

MARIAN: I'm seeing this through. That's all. On my own terms. For Jesus' sake just leave me in peace, the whole shower of you, I'm sick of your filth and mess and noise and bickering, in every last corner of the house, I've had enough.

LENNY: Marian . . .

MARIAN: You find a refuge, you find a task for your life, and then wholesale panic breaks out, and they all come crowding in the door, her and you and that trend-worshipping narcissist . . .

LENNY: It's beside the point, you're in terrible danger, we've all got to get out of here. The last thing I ever intended or needed, me and you under the same roof, it was another one of his lame jokes, [*Gesturing skywards*] okay, we move out, we go our separate ways to our respective families. I don't like to see you in the state you're in. You're just not fit to be left on your own.

[MARIAN *slowly turns on him*]

MARIAN: What are you getting at?

LENNY: I'm talking about what's going on!

MARIAN: Such as?

LENNY: What have we been having this entire conversation about?

MARIAN: You consider that I'm cracking up?

LENNY: When did I say that?

MARIAN: Not fit to be alone?

LENNY: In this house, that's all!

MARIAN: It wouldn't maybe have occurred to you, it wouldn't maybe have penetrated even that dim featherweight brain — that being on my own is the one thing I am fit for?

LENNY: Okay . . .

MARIAN: That being on my own is precisely what I bought this house for, the reason I sold my business and my flat, the reason I reconciled myself to meeting you for an evening to look this place over?

LENNY: Okay, okay, but it's all changed — out there!

MARIAN: It's all changed in here, Lenny. For five weeks you've been living with me again. It took me three years to break out of our marriage, and now for the past five weeks you've been living with me again, here in the house, the very place I chose as a refuge. So even if you do believe that I'm cracking up . . .

LENNY: I never said you were cracking up . . .

MARIAN: . . . it's conceivably not actually a psychiatrist that I need . . .

LENNY: Who said you needed a psychiatrist?

MARIAN: You've always been very ready with that solution in the past.

LENNY: For pity's sake, Marian . . .

MARIAN: It may just be that all I need is to get the three spineless parasites, with whom I'm presently saddled, off my back — or maybe your uncle the psychiatrist would consider such a desire irrational?

LENNY: Quit it, will you, just scrub it, it's the same old trick all over, putting words into my mouth to avoid facing your own reality . . .

MARIAN: Don't start the usual bloody put-upon whinge, I'm not one of your doting maiden aunts, I can see clean through it, you can't face up to emotion in any shape or form . . .

LENNY: Here it comes.

MARIAN: Feeling. Passion. This. [*Jabbing at her heart*] Every time I stubbed my toe or smashed a tumbler and swore loudly, you were offering to turn me over to your uncle the psychiatrist, it's beyond your capability, grown-up anger, pain, commitment, love — have you never considered that if one of us needs treatment it might be you?

LENNY: I never know how you do this, I start off trying to help you, and within ten minutes I'm a villain, I'm a deviant, I'm the one in need of help, in the name of God just face reality!

MARIAN: Which reality did you have in mind?

LENNY: Your own, Marian, your own reality, you've been talking to yourself, you've been counting spoons, you've been babbling in tongues in the middle of the night!

[*Too late he realizes the blunder. Now that she has successfully accomplished it,* MARIAN *relaxes*]

MARIAN: Thanks, Lenny. Very much. I thought we were never going to get to it.

LENNY: Well, what are we *supposed* to think?

MARIAN: Don't think, Lenny. Don't think anything at all. Don't even try. It doesn't agree with you. Here's what we're doing. I'm staying here with my tongues — and you're going home with your trombone. That way we're all quits. Okay?

LENNY: I don't know why I waste my time. You'd think I'd know better by now.

[*He retires, out the hall door and back up the stairs*]
[MARIAN *closes the door after him*]
[LILY MATTHEWS *immediately appears from the shadows of the pantry. She is wearing the print dress now without the pinafore over it, and her hair is down: we can see in her the ghost of her 33-year-old self*]

LILY: Nice way to treat your own husband.

MARIAN: Lenny's no husband of anybody's. Never was, never will be.

LILY: In the eyes of God he's your man still.

MARIAN: God's eyes were put out, Lily, did you not hear.

LILY: What sort of talk is that?

MARIAN: The old boy. Blinded. He only exists in the dark now.

LILY: Have you drink taken?

MARIAN: We're his guide dogs now. Dragging him round from pillar to post. Half of us in rut, and the other half rabid. Without us, he can't survive. But without him, without him, to love, honour and obey . . . it's just a dog's life for us. So far as I can see.

LILY: Is this the sort of blasphemous babble the priests are filling your heads with now?

MARIAN: What makes you think I'm a Catholic?

LILY: I suppose that's your idea of amusement. Sacrilege and mockery.

MARIAN: You're out in your figure today, I see. Where did you get that dress from, anyway?

LILY: Mind your own business.

MARIAN: The height of the Depression. Alfie two years jobless . . . it was Alan Ferris bought it for you, wasn't it.

LILY: What if it was, he was a good lodger and a good friend to us.

MARIAN: The English airman. Stores and maintenance, Sydenham aerodrome.

LILY: It was only him spied it, that was the reason. Hanging in Price's window. He egged me on to try it on for size, it was my birthday, that was why. Before I know where I am, he's the money out and paid across the counter, and me walking out of the shop still wearing it. When he was in one of those daft oul' moods of his, he could charm the birds down out of the trees.

MARIAN: Crêpe-de-chine.

LILY: I never owned anything like that in my life before, the sheer clean feel of it all over you . . .

MARIAN: Did you go dancing?

LILY: I was a married woman of thirty-three, catch yourself on.[14]

MARIAN: You went to Groomsport,[15] though.

LILY: Who told you that?

MARIAN: I'm thirty-three as well, Lily.

LILY: What of it?

MARIAN: Did you make a day of it?

LILY: No, we did not, his skin was very fair, he burnt easy, he didn't like the sand. It was only an evening dander along the front. The sun was setting over the lough, hanging out of the sky like a big swollen blood orange. The water all glistening with the redness of it and the sky and the hills on fire with it. Like what you'd see after a war, maybe . . . it took your breath away, it was a real picture, but it was frightening. That's what I thought anyhow.

MARIAN: Did you say it?

LILY: He laughed. Nothing frightened him.

MARIAN: Why would it.

LILY: We stood there and looked, at the water, and the air. He'd come from across the water, you see. Flown across, through the air. I'd never even been on the water, let alone up in the air, couldn't imagine it. I wanted to. It was frightening, but. We just stood there and looked, in the cool of the evening, drinking it in.

MARIAN: I could do with an evening in Groomsport myself, just at the minute.

[She sits down in the rocking chair]

LILY: All we did was stand and look across the water.

MARIAN: That was the moment when it hit you, though. You already could tell that he wanted you. That was the moment you realized that you were going to give yourself . . . all of yourself, whatever he wanted to do to you, that same evening . . .

LILY: Keep you your guttersnipe mind to yourself, what do you know about my life, over forty years ago!

MARIAN: Only what I've read, Lily.

[She reaches into the raffia basket which is tucked in beside the rocking chair, and takes out an old and disintegrating leather-bound padlocked diary]

LILY: How did you get hold of that?

MARIAN: Under the cellar stairs wasn't the ideal place for it. There's dampness there. Mildew. Rust. The lock has rusted away, look.

[She holds up the diary and it swings open, the lock coming adrift]

LILY: Leave that be, that's private property, don't you dare touch that!

MARIAN: You wanted it read, Lily, you must have.

LILY: No!

MARIAN: Why else hide it? Why write it? You wanted somebody to know. It's just turned out to be me, that's all.

LILY: Why can't you mind your own business, what right have you to go poking and prying into a body's private life . . .

MARIAN: What about the life of your baby?

LILY: My baby was strong . . . he was well happed-up[16] . . .

MARIAN: You abandoned him.

LILY: I entrusted him to the care of the Lord!

MARIAN: You left him lying in the porch of a Baptist church!

LILY: A well-off congregation, it was for the best . . . moneyed people . . . some pair of them would take him in, adopt him as their own, what did you want me to do, he had a better chance there than the orphanage or the hospital . . .

MARIAN: He would have had his best chance right here, being reared by you and Alfie.

LILY: My Alfie would have struck the pair of us down dead. He was capable of it, he knew it too, he told me the day we moved in here, never make me lose my temper . . . he never found out, about the child, that was the one mercy, he was away that whole year tramping all over England, looking for work with Jackie Midgely. Nobody ever knew but me, my own mother was dead by then with the T.B., I was inclined towards stoutness then anyway . . . one day it just arrived . . . on that floor, five hours I lay there . . . I delivered it myself. By the time Alfie come home again, the whole thing was over and done, as though it had never been . . . he had no inkling of any of it, from then till his dying day.

MARIAN: You and Alan Ferris. On the front parlour sofa. He'd no inkling of that?

LILY: Oh, sweet God in heaven forgive me!

MARIAN: Alfie was impotent, wasn't he. A souvenir of Passchendaele, maybe. Scarcely the first nor the last to come back from the dead in that condition.

LILY: I sinned against my own flesh in lust and fornication, I had to desert my own baby, nobody ever knew only the Lord our God knew and His eye was on me all right, burning into the very soul of me, He alone was witness to the torment that I've suffered every living hour in this house where the very walls and doors cry out against me, there was never anybody to tell the knife that went through me a dozen dozen times a day, minding how I left my child, walking away from him, leaving him bundled up there in that wooden box, nobody to help me, only me here in this house, gnawing and tearing away at my own heart and lights, day in day out . . . until I was all consumed by my own wickedness, on the inside, nothing left but the shell of me, for appearance's sake . . . still and all. At least I never let myself down — never cracked. Never surrendered. Not one inch. I went to my grave a respectable woman, Mrs Alfred George Matthews, I never betrayed him. That was the way I atoned, you see. I done him proud. He never knew any reason to be ashamed of me, or doubt my loyalty. From the day we met till the day I went to my grave.

MARIAN: You loved Alan Ferris, Lily. These things can't be helped. He introduced you to the body's actual passion. The English airman. Then he flew away.

LILY: Alan . . . he came from across the water you see . . . there was a picture in my Bible, at Sunday school, the fair-skinned archangel standing at the gates of heaven, that was what he looked like . . . only he was a dark angel. Angel of death. Agent of Satan. He swept me up, high up, took me up into the sky . . . and then he dropped me. Left me. Flew home. Left me falling. Falling.

[MARIAN *takes* LILY'*s hand and holds it against her own heart*]

MARIAN: Forgive me, Lily.

[*Lights fade to blackout*]

[*End of Scene Four*]

SCENE FIVE

[*The early hours of Sunday, June 2nd*]

[MARIAN *is asleep on the sofa in the dark kitchen. There is glimmering of distant bonfires in the night sky above the yard, and the faint sounds of an Orange band playing and of a mob celebrating*]

[*Gradually this is overtaken by the din of a military helicopter approaching and hovering low over the house*]

[PETER *appears outside, dragging himself up on the top of the yard wall, having climbed up from a dustbin in the alley on the far side. He has a banjo case slung across his back*]

[*He is suddenly caught in the blinding searchlight of the hovering helicopter. He shields his eyes from the light with an arm*]

[MARIAN, *awakened by this, goes to the window.* PETER *drops down into the yard and makes for the scullery door.* MARIAN *goes to it and lets him in. The searchlight switches off and the helicopter moves away*]

[MARIAN *is lighting the gas mantles as* PETER *talks*]

PETER: Couldn't get back into the street . . . just young bloods drunk, dozens of them, hooligan types, I was carrying a couple of bottles, you see, they probably thought it was whiskey or something, they'd a shock in store, it was my father's elderberry wine. You wouldn't exactly want to die for it, Christ . . . I'm all slashed on that wall. At least I managed to hang on to my old banjo. Cold, isn't it. Sorry to disturb you. I hadn't expected, what with the strike being over, I see the gas supply has returned anyway . . .

MARIAN: Not to mention the Army.

PETER: What? Oh, right, right, the chopper, yeah, I was actually bloody glad, as a matter of fact, it showing up, at least it got them off my back . . .

MARIAN: There's a glimmer of life in that fire. Hoke it out and throw those sticks on it.

[*She exits to the bathroom to fetch the first-aid kit.* PETER, *alone and shivering, goes to the press where the remains of the drink are stored and takes a swig of vodka*]

[RUTH *rushes in, in her nightdress*]

RUTH: Marian says you were attacked . . .

PETER: I'm fine.

RUTH: You poor love, you're all cut . . .

[PETER *thrusts his bloodstained hand in front of her face*]

PETER: Oh yeah, the red hand.[17] Makes you puke, doesn't it. Blood and things.

[*He turns away from her and tends to the fire*]

RUTH: I'm only trying to be your friend, Peter.

[MARIAN *returns with* LILY'*s first-aid box*]

PETER: I'll let you both get back to sleep then.

MARIAN: Sit down.

PETER: I'll just go and get myself cleaned up . . . [*But she has firmly planted him in the chair and is starting to swab the cuts on his hands*] . . . ah. Well. Thanks. Funny time for this, isn't it. They're all celebrating, out there. My crowd and hers, I mean. The end of being forced to share the top table with a few Popeheads, they're beside themselves with the glorious deliverance of it, the executive forced to resign, you'd think they'd given birth, actually created something for once, instead of battering it to death, yet again, the only kind of victory they ever credit, holding the good old fort, stamping the life out of anything that starts to creep forward, even my reverend father and mother were quietly crowing over it, in the same way she is of course, [*At* RUTH] with a proper air of restrained well-balanced smugness . . .

RUTH: Stop it!

PETER: What odds, they're all one, under the skin, all at one with those vicious little buggers, out there, who put their toecaps into me . . . [*He suddenly breaks down but immediately swallows it back*] . . . sorry, I don't know . . .

MARIAN: It's this stuff, it shows no mercy.

PETER: I don't, I don't know why it matters, why I care, I don't know, what the fuck I have to come back here for, what I expect, what it is I think I'll find here, whatever it is I think I'm missing . . .

[LENNY *comes in from the hall, returning from a gig, in his street clothes, and carrying his trombone*]

LENNY: What's going on, then?

RUTH: Peter got roughed up.

[*She brushes out past him*]

LENNY [*To* PETER]: I thought you were visiting your parents?

PETER: Correct.

LENNY: What happened?

PETER: Who knows — my mother just suddenly went for my hands with a broken bottle.

LENNY: Your mother's a justice of the peace!

[MARIAN *is finishing cleaning the cuts on* PETER'*s hands and putting plaster on them*]

PETER [*To* MARIAN]: Did he ever tell you how close we came to preventing the entire Ulster conflict from getting off the ground?

MARIAN: Bound to have.

LENNY: You're not referring to McManus, I hope?

MARIAN: Bound to be.

[RUTH *re-enters wearing a dressing gown*]

PETER: There was a spaceman we all knew, as students, you see, Ruth — a wild mad bugger called Vincent Moog McManus, he stayed on indefinitely as a research student in Chemistry. [LENNY *has retreated to the kitchen to fetch himself a scrap of food*] He spent most of his time in the lab synthesizing LSD — the drug, that is — and I'm not talking in spoonfuls, he had rows of big sweety jars lined along his kitchen shelves, chocolate eclairs, liquorice comfits, you name it, all fully primed. This was high-class stuff, before anybody here had even heard tell of it, Moog was a bona-fide visionary. So one hot night, pinhead here and me and Moog were tripped out in my garden, beatific, except there'd been the early riots, the initial killings, the first stirrings of the reawakening of the Protestant dragon and the Catholic dragon, and the three of us felt a messianic impulse, to slay these ancient monsters, we felt summoned, as a holy trinity of the new age, father son and holy ghost, Moog being the ghost and me the messiah, but it was Godhead here who came up with the redemption — why not take the total stash of acid in Moog's sweety jars, transport it up to the Mourne Mountains, and dump it into the Silent Valley reservoir? The entire Belfast water supply was in that lovely man-made lake. We could turn on the population, comprehensively, with one simple transcendental gesture, that would be it, the doors of perception flung wide, wholesale mind-shift, no more bigotry and hatred, a city full of spaced-out contemplatives like the three of us. So off I went and filched the keys of my mother's Austin Princess, and we loaded it up with the sweety jars and headed for the hills. We actually got as far as Dundrum . . . before negative signals began to filter through even to us, scrambled brains and all, we hadn't seen the news, not for days, that was the basic flaw. The Silent Valley reservoir had been blown up by the U.V.F.[18] Belfast was dry. The Mourne Mountains were swarming like an anthill with the security forces. We got searched three times on the way home . . . Moog said he was a supplier for his family's confectionery business, it was true in a way, not that it made any odds, they wouldn't have known the drug if we'd force-fed them on it, we were entirely beside the point, am I right, head? What the hell. At least we tried. How many can say as much.

[LENNY *has registered the banjo*]

LENNY: Is that your old five-string?

PETER: Haven't played it in five years.

LENNY: How's the tuning?

PETER: You tell me.

[LENNY *removes the banjo from its case and quietly tunes it up during the ensuing dialogue*]

PETER: So anyway, there you go. That's my bedtime story. Time for you three girls to kiss and tell. Seeing as we're all up and about. What do you say, Marian? How about dishing the real dirt on Orange Lily Matthews, you must have dug up some scandal by this time.

MARIAN: I found a used condom behind the parlour sofa. [*An awkward moment all round*] The pair of you might have cleaned up behind you, at least.

PETER: I don't think much of that, as a story.

RUTH: I really am sorry, Marian . . .

MARIAN: I'll give you a story. Lily sat in that parlour, right through the Blitz. Alfie was a fire warden, out most nights — she promised him she'd stay down in the cellar during the air-raids, instead of which she sat up in that front parlour, in the blackout, the pitch dark, listening to the war in the air . . . the bombers and the fighters, the ack-ack and the shells falling, falling and exploding . . . she stretched out on that self-same sofa, where Alan Ferris had stretched her out seven years earlier and pleasured her till her ears sang with a whole wild uncontainable babble . . .

PETER: Holy shit, tell us more.

LENNY: Quiet.

MARIAN: She lay down in the dark on her own now, and pictured him, up there, burning a hole through the sky, a dark angel, and her ears roared now with the rage of a wholesale slaughter, pounding the ground under her and the air all round her, armageddon, random and blind, pulverizing her whole body until she once more came and came again, and she composed herself to die there, waiting for the chosen bomb to fall on her and cleanse her terrible sinfulness and shame . . . the street next to this one was totally flattened one night. The parlour windows came in on her, but Lily wasn't even scratched. The skies cleared. The war ended. And there she still was — unscathed. She interpreted this as her punishment. She had been condemned to life. A life sentence.

[*They are all reduced to silence, staring into the fire*]

LENNY: I wonder what it was like here. Before Christianity.

RUTH: What are you going to do with the house, Marian?

MARIAN: Live in it.

PETER: National Trust permitting, you mean.

MARIAN: That was a wrong impulse. A mistaken idea. It would only have been perpetuating a crime . . . condemning her to life indefinitely. I'm clearing most of this out. Keeping just the basics. Fixing it up. What this house needs most is air and light.

[*She starts building up the fire with turf*]

PETER: Exactly what I say. Minor gentrification. [*To* LENNY] As for you, head, you appear to be saying nothing.

LENNY: What of it?

PETER: It's your turn for the story.

LENNY [*Offering him the banjo*]: Here, you're in tune now.

PETER: You play it, I think I've lost my touch. [*Holding up his hands*] Give us a talking blues.

[LENNY *fools around on the banjo for a moment*]

LENNY: There was something happened to me last summer — as it happens — last August, down near Kinsale. [*He sets the banjo aside*] There's a Dutch guy with a pub there, runs a lot of jazz nights. This particular night went on till half-six in the morning, the sun was hanging out, I was ready for a look at the ocean, so was the lady vocalist. She was a strange woman, half gipsy, from Sligo or somewhere weird like that, totally wrecked on everything on offer, which was plenty . . . so. We stumbled down to this cove, a lovely horseshoe of sand, except her and me couldn't handle any more bright lights, so we collapsed on to a sheltered bit of grass behind some boulders. And your woman starts crooning. [*Sings*] 'Just a closer walk with thee . . .' lying there splayed out in the warm singing away . . . and she begins to peel her clothes off. Nothing to do with me — she was stretched out

flat with her eyes closed — but before too long, she's entirely bare, the voice floating in the early breeze, [*Sings*] 'Grant it Jesus if you please . . .' and I'm hunkered down beside her, with a swollen mouth from playing all night, staring out at the glittery water, stunned all over, the way you are. And then, into my line of vision — there comes this sight, at first I thought I was hallucinating, it was a gaggle of nuns, real nuns, in the whole gear, which they were busy stripping off, over their heads. There was a dozen or more of them. It was a nuns' swimming party. Underneath their habits, they had these interlock jobs, sort of vests and baggy long johns. I suppose they reckoned at that hour there'd be nobody to see them. So down they pelted into the sea, frisking around and frolicking like nine-year-olds, the noise of it — while your woman is meanwhile stretched out starkers beside me, singing this deep-throated heartfelt version of 'Just a Closer Walk With Thee' . . . entirely oblivious . . . and the nuns are splashing each other, and giggling and screaming, and flinging themselves about in the golden light, with the wet interlock clinging to their excited bodies — and it doesn't take a lot to see that the nuns are experiencing their sex and the vocalist her spirit. And for a crazy few seconds I all but sprinted down to the nuns to churn my body into theirs, in the surf foam, and then bring them all back to the lady vocalist, for a session of great spirituals . . . and maybe that's how it was . . . what it was like here. Before Christianity. Is what I'm saying.

RUTH: You don't even know Christianity. You think it's only denial, but that's wrong. It's meant to be love and celebration. You don't even know what day it is now, the meaning of it.

PETER: You tell them, Ruthie child. Pentecost Sunday.

LENNY: So what? [*He has turned away from this to his trombone, which he takes out and cleans and puts together*]

RUTH: The day our Lord's apostles were inspired by the Holy Spirit. 'And when the day of Pentecost was fully come, they were all with one accord in one place. And suddenly there came a sound from heaven as of a rushing mighty wind, and it filled all the house where they were sitting. And there appeared unto them cloven tongues like as of fire, and it sat upon each of them. And they were all filled with the Holy Ghost, and began to speak with other tongues, as the Spirit gave them utterance.'

[*She retreats into herself again*]

PETER: You can't stop there. It's your story, you have to finish it.

RUTH: I don't remember it all.

PETER: 'And they were all amazed, and were in doubt, saying to one another, What meaneth this? . . .'

RUTH: 'Others mocking said, These men are full of new wine . . .'

PETER: 'But Peter, standing up with the eleven, lifted up his voice and said unto them: Ye men of Judea and all ye that dwell at Jerusalem, let this be known unto you and hearken to my words: For these are not drunken as ye suppose, seeing it is but the third hour of the day . . .'

RUTH: [*Squaring up to him, as it turns into a contest*] 'But this is that which was spoken by the prophet Joel: And it shall come to pass in the last days, saith God, I will pour out of my spirit upon all flesh: and your sons and your daughters shall prophesy, and your young men shall see visions, and your old men shall dream dreams. And on my servants and on my handmaidens I will pour out in those days of my spirit; and they shall prophesy . . .'

PETER: 'And I will shew wonders in heaven above, and signs in the earth beneath; blood and fire, and vapour of smoke; the sun shall be turned into darkness, and the moon into blood, before that great and notable day of the Lord come . . .'

RUTH: 'And it shall come to pass, that whosoever shall call on the name of the Lord shall be saved.'

PETER: The old familiar payoff! — but it hasn't entirely held up, Ruthie. I mean they're never done calling on the name of the Lord in this wee province of ours, so it ought to be the most saved place on God's earth instead of the most absolutely godforsaken, not so?

RUTH: Some of us love this province.

PETER: By God you do and with a vengeance, and you've finally loved it to death, Ruth, stone dead and in its grave and we're all sitting here at the wake. Take a long hard look. Because our whole wee family's here, gathered together round the hearth, our *holy* family — Marian the mother at the head, the holy virgin, shielding us from all harm, keeping faithful little Ruthie safe from her night fears, the funny-coloured buses and the psychopathic Christian spouse . . .

RUTH: Leave you David out of this, you're not worth a hair of his head!

PETER: We're certainly not in any doubt that you'll be going back to him.

RUTH: He's up in Purdysburn Hospital, if you must know.

MARIAN: What happened?

RUTH: He's had a breakdown. Smashed his own two hands to a pulp before they could restrain him.

MARIAN: You never told me, Ruth.

RUTH: I went to visit him. Told him it was over. He's accepted it. He knows I won't be going back.

PETER: Why not? I thought you were hell-bent on being a nurse.

LENNY: All right, enough! No more.

MARIAN: Leave him. Let him get rid of it.

PETER: You see how she forgives the one stray sheep, the prodigal, we're such an Irish little family, the strong saintly suffering ma and the shiftless clown of a da here, no damn use to man or beast, hunched up against the wall, hands in empty pockets, jiggling his limp thing like a dead hen's thrapple[19] . . .

LENNY: No more of this shit tonight . . .

[PETER *grabs hold of him*]

PETER: Pentecost is upon us, head, so where's the fire on your tongue? Or is there maybe not a fizzle left in any part of you at all?

LENNY: Not like you, I suppose, dicking your way round the Brummie[20] discos every night of the week . . .

PETER: You're never going to leave here, face it, your life's locked in and the key surrendered . . .

LENNY: I'll live whatever life I choose, and I'll live it here, what's it to you, you think you're any further on? You seriously think I'd want what you have? I live like a prince compared to you, I live for my real friends, for good crack, I'm a musician, I live for what I play!

PETER: On that? [*The trombone*] Play on that? You want to know what playing on that is? Farting into the wind.

[LENNY, *with a sudden spasm of rage, dislodges* PETER'*s grip on him, flings him across the table, and then turns away in self-disgust*]

PETER [*Winded, picking himself up*]: Of course . . . we're null and void as a holy family, aren't we . . . missing our most important member . . . the Prince of Peace Himself. [*Pulling himself painfully into a seat*] Can you see him? Here? Can you see him? Dandering down Royal Avenue? Dropping into a Council meeting at the City Hall? The Son of Man . . . in the middle of the marching ranks of the Ulster zealots, watching at the elbow of the holy Catholic Nationalist zealot as he puts a pistol to a man's knee, to a man's brains, to a man's balls, the Son of God in the polling booth, observing the votes being cast in support of that, suffering the little children with murder festering in their hearts, what would Jesus Holy Christ do with us all here, would you say?

LENNY: I'll tell you exactly what he'd so, he'd close down every church and chapel, temple and tabernacle in the whole island, put them to the torch, burn them into rubble, turf the congregations out priests and pastors face first, and drive them up into the mountains, up to the boniest, bleakest stretches of the Sperrins and the Mournes, and he'd flay them into the rock, until the Christianity was scourged out of the very marrows of their bones, he'd expunge religion once and for all from off the face of this country, until the people could discover no mercy except in each other, no belief except to believe in each other, no forgiveness but what the other would forgive, until they cried out in the dark for each other and embraced their own humanity . . . that's the only redemption he'd offer them. Never mind believing in Jesus Christ. That's the point at which Jesus Christ might just begin to believe in us.

PETER: Why would he come near the place, let's face it, he's already been crucified once. He's already been once in hell.

LENNY: The Church invented hell. They've just used this town to show us what they mean.

MARIAN: They. They. You think you can both shuffle it off, so easily, with your righteous anger, let me tell you, you're not even in the same league as I am for righteous anger, I've supped on precious little else for five years past, it changes nothing. Forget the church. Forget the priests and pastors. There is some kind of christ, in every one of us. [PETER *and* LENNY *turn their faces against this language*] Each of us either honours him, or denies him and violates him, what we do to him is done to ourselves. I had a child once.

LENNY: No. Marian . . .

MARIAN: I called him Christopher. Because he was a kind of Christ to me, he brought love with him . . . the truth and the life. He was a future. Until one day I found him dead. I thought like you for a long time. He chose death in the cot rather than life in this town, in these times, it was their fault, they had done it to me, I hated them. Hated life. It was all a lie, of course. The cause and effect were in me, in him too, [*At* LENNY] we were mortal after all, we were human, had to be, we couldn't bear one another, couldn't tolerate ourselves, the child was only a fallible mortal the same as us, that was all that he was telling us. I felt him as a raw scar across my own spirit, stinging me, every minute, every hour, everything defaced by it . . . until I was blaming

him, for all the pain, he was one of them too. They. I denied him. The christ in him. Which he had entrusted to my care, the ghost of him that I do still carry, as I carried his little body. The christ in him absorbed into the christ in me. We have got to love that in ourselves. In ourselves first and then in them. That's the only future there is.

[*She has been on her feet during this, and is close to the sofa where* LENNY *is sitting, hunched up, close to tears now. Privately and unobtrusively, he touches her hand*]

Personally, I want to live now. I want this house to live. We have committed sacrilege enough on life, in this place, in these times. We don't just owe it to ourselves, we owe it to our dead too . . . our innocent dead. They're not our masters, they're only our creditors, for the life they never knew. We owe them at least that — the fullest life for which they could ever have hoped, we carry those ghosts within us, to betray those hopes is the real sin against the christ, and I for one cannot commit it one day longer.

[*The sky above the backyard has been growing light*]

[LENNY, *overwhelmed by what* MARIAN *has said, picks up his trombone and goes out to the backyard. He sits down on the window ledge*]

[RUTH, *at the table, opens her Bible at the second chapter of the Acts of the Apostles. She reads from it*]

RUTH: 'Therefore did my heart rejoice, and my tongue was glad; moreover also my flesh shall rest in hope: Because thou wilt not leave my soul in hell, neither wilt thou suffer thine Holy One to see corruption. Thou hast made known to me the ways of life; thou shalt make me full of joy with thy countenance.'

[*During this,* LENNY *has started to play a very slow and soulful version of 'Just a Closer Walk with Thee'*]

[*After some time,* PETER *picks up his banjo from where it has been left lying, close to him. Tentatively, he starts to pick out an accompaniment to the tune*]

[RUTH *reaches across and opens the window*]

[*As the music swells, the lights fade, very slowly, to blackout*]

[*The End*]

---

1   A Catholic lay organization.
2   Title of a Loyalist Orange song.
3   A machine for wringing out wet clothes.
4   A low class of theatre, a public place of amusement.
5   Slang terms for Protestants and Catholics.
6   High-security prison for political prisoners, now known as the Maze prison.

7 From Britain, the mainland.
8 The Ulster Workers' Council strike in May 1974. The UWC was a body of loyalist trade unionists who brought down the power-sharing executive of Brian Faulkner and Gerry Fitt, leaders respectively of the Unionist Party and the Social Democratic and Labour Party.
9 Desirable residence.
10 A port in Lancashire which used to run daily sailings to Belfast.
11 Supporter of Ian Paisley.
12 Grievous bodily harm.
13 Big drums used by Protestants during the marching season and associated by Catholics with intimidation.
14 Catch on is listen, use your head.
15 In County Down.
16 Wrapped up with clothes.
17 Also a symbol of the Protestant red hand of Ulster.
18 Ulster Volunteer Force, a Protestant paramilitary organization.
19 Scottish dialect word for throat.
20 Affectionate name for Birmingham.

CIARAN CARSON
from Ciaran Carson, *The Irish For No* (1987)

Ciaran Carson (1948–) was born in Belfast and after graduating from Quenns University, Belfast worked for the Arts Council in Northern Ireland. *The Irish For No* (there is no single word as in English) was warmly received and was followed by the equally interesting volumes *Belfast Confetti* (1989) and *Opera Et Cetera* (1996) (see below). For the original meaning of Belfast confetti, see the extract from *The Star Factory* (1997) (p. 1155 below).

BELFAST CONFETTI

Suddenly as the riot squad moved in, it was raining
                                        exclamation marks,
Nuts, bolts, nails, car-keys. A fount of broken type.
                                        And the explosion
Itself — an asterisk on the map. This hyphenated line,
                                        a burst of rapid fire . . .
I was trying to complete a sentence in my head, but it
                                        kept stuttering,
All the alleyways and side-streets blocked with stops
                                        and colons.

I know this labyrinth so well — Balaclava, Raglan,
        Inkerman, Odessa Street —
Why can't I escape? Every move is punctuated.
        Crimea Street. Dead end again.
A Saracen, Kremlin-2 mesh. Makrolon face-shields.
        Walkie-talkies. What is
My name? Where am I coming from? Where am I
        going? A fusillade of question-marks.

EAVAN BOLAND
from Eavan Boland, *The Journey* (1987)

Three poems by Eavan Boland on the theme of displacement. 'Mise Eire' (I am Ireland) is a defiant reply to Pearse's poem 'I Am Ireland' (reproduced above p. 260). The phrase 'a kind of scar' is used as the title of a pamphlet published in 1989 which addresses the position of women/woman in the Irish national tradition. The second poem offers a reflection on emigration, on the way those who were once put out the back now have a role to play inside the house of Ireland. The third poem, 'Tirade for the Lyric Muse', a tirade for not against, considers another form of displacement, that of the woman poet *vis-à-vis* the (female) muse.

MISE EIRE

I won't go back to it —

my nation displaced
into old dactyls,
oaths made
by the animal tallows
of the candle —

land of the Gulf Stream,
the small farm,
the scalded memory,
the songs
that bandage up the history,
the words
that make a rhythm of the crime

where time is time past.
A palsy of regrets.
No. I won't go back.
My roots are brutal:

I am the woman —
a sloven's mix
of silk at the wrists,
a sort of dove-strut
in the precincts of the garrison —

who practises
the quick frictions,
the rictus of delight
and gets cambric for it,
rice-coloured silks.

I am the woman
in the gansy-coat
on board the 'Mary Belle',
in the huddling cold,

holding her half-dead baby to her
as the wind shifts East
and North over the dirty
waters of the wharf

mingling the immigrant
guttural with the vowels
of homesickness who neither
knows nor cares that

a new language
is a kind of scar
and heals after a while
into a passable imitation
of what went before.

THE EMIGRANT IRISH

Like oil lamps we put them out the back,

of our houses, of our minds. We had lights
better than, newer than and then

a time came, this time and now
we need them. Their dread, makeshift example.

They would have thrived on our necessities.
What they survived we could not even live.
By their lights now it is time to
imagine how they stood there, what they stood with,
that their possessions may become our power.

Cardboard. Iron. Their hardships parcelled in them.
Patience. Fortitude. Long-suffering
in the bruise-coloured dusk of the New World.

And all the old songs. And nothing to lose.

TIRADE FOR THE LYRIC MUSE

You're propped and swabbed and bedded.
I could weep.
There's a stench of snipped flesh
and tubed blood.
I've come to see if beauty is skin deep.

Mongrel features.
Tainted lint and cotton.
Sutures from the lip to ear to brow.
They've patched your wrinkles
and replaced your youth.
It may be beauty
but it isn't truth.

You are the victim of a perfect crime.
You have no sense of time.
You never had.
You never dreamed he could be so cruel.
Which is why you lie back
shocked in cambric,
slacked in bandages
and blubbing gruel.
My white python writhing your renewal!

I loved you once.
It seemed so right, and neat.
The moon, the month, the flower, the kiss —
there wasn't anything that wouldn't fit.

The ends were easy
and the means were short
when you and I were lyric and elect.
Shall I tell you what we overlooked?

You in this bed.
You with your snout,
your seams, your stitches
and your sutured youth.
You,
you with your smocked mouth
are what your songs left out.

We still have time.
Look in the glass.
Time is the flaw.
Truth is the crystal.

We have been sisters
in the crime.
Let us be sisters
in the physic.

Listen.
Bend your darned head.
Turn your good ear.
Share my music.

SEÁN Ó TUAMA
from Seán Ó Tuama, *An Bás i dTír na nÓg* (1988)

Seán Ó Tuama (1926–   ), author of 'Twentieth Century Poetry in Irish' (1991) (see
p. 1092), is also a fine Irish-language poet whose volumes include *Saol Fó Thoinn*
(1978) and *An Bás I dTír na nÓg* (1988). Here in this poem he controversially pays
homage to the violence that created the Irish Free State.

ABAIR DO PHAIDIR
*(an tan a rinne polaiteoirí tréas ar
náisiúntóirí na hÉireann)*

Abair do phaidir (más cuimhin leat í),
ná bac an té adéarfaidh leat
nach cóir gach lá guí ar son
ár muintire a dhein foréigean
nuair ab éigean dóibh.

Anseo ar ché na Gaillimhe
i measc seantán is tithe stórais,
i measc fo-éadaí ag síleadh súlaigh,
tá greanta ar sheanchloch tréigthe an scríbhinn:
'guigh ar son anam uasal x
a fuair bás ar son na saoirse.'
Ná múch anois ionat an phaidir
a líonann ort aniar-aduaidh.

Dhein x foréigean, ní foláir —
agus dhein fir a pháirte roimhe:
dheineadar, le binb,
pící a ropadh
piléir a ghreadadh
cnámha a bhriseadh
scornaigh a ghearradh,

SAY A PRAYER
*(at a time when Irish politicians broke
faith with their ancestors)*

Say a prayer (if you remember any)
don't mind all those who tell us
it is politically incorrect to pray
for those before us who took to violence
when only violence was on offer.

On this derelict Galway quayside
in the jumble of sheds and buildings
under the drip from a line of clothes
you will find a worn slab engraved:
'Pray for the noble soul of X
who died in the fight for freedom.'
Clear a way for that insistent prayer
which takes you a little by surprise.

X was, no doubt, a violent man,
violent, too, his people.
With deadly purpose
they stuck with pikes,
blasted with shot,
smashed bones,
severed throats,

is súile boga a phiocadh
as a log sa chloigeann —
   d'fhonn teacht slán.

Abair do phaidir go simplí nádúrtha
ar son daoine a bhí iad féin nádúrtha
is a chleacht foréigean de réir a ngnáis.
Iarr ar an Dia is ansa leat
ná fágfaí iad anois ar crochadh
gan ómós ná aithint choiteann
i measc fo-éadaí is fallaí gruama
de dheascaibh tréas na bpolaiteoirí . . .
Is barbair bhunaidh iad aon chine
ná tugann an t-ómós is dual
don saghas foréigin is dual ómós
ó tháinig ann don duine.

Abair do phaidir, fiú más í
do phaidir, um a' dtaca seo,
do dheor.

and gouged soft eyes
from the sockets —
all to survive.

Say your prayer, intimately, naturally,
for people who themselves were naturally
violent in the political correctness of their age.
Plead with the God you cherish
not to leave them drifting there
unrecognized, despised,
between dank walls and dripping clothes
because our politicians abandon them.
It is against all nature to deny
homage to that violence
which has been honoured
since we became human.

Say your prayer — even if
you find your prayers
have turned to tears.

PHILIP CHEVRON
from The Pogues, *If I Should Fall From Grace* (1988)

This is one of the great Irish songs of emigration, but, unlike many such songs, 'Thousands Are Sailing' is concerned less with the fate of the individual and more with the collective 'we', the impersonal 'you', the lonely 'I'. In thus mixing the pronouns Chevron captures something of the common fate awaiting those at the bottom of society's ladder. He dwells not on those who became the lace-curtain Irish but on those who were dealt a poor hand by a country which at the same time voted an Irishman in the shape of JFK into the Oval Office. The song is full of disturbing mood swings: the brief élan of walking down Broadway (in the death of afternoon) and following in the footsteps of the larger-than-life figure of the fifties Irish dramatist Brendan Behan; the emigrant's tears in the empty room; the expectancy of a new life which could bring what in the emigration songs was called 'fortune' but is now ominously linked by Chevron with the lottery; the slight desperation of 'But we dance', well captured by Shane MacGowan on the CD. But the rhythm and refrain keep going and we find ourselves singing along to words that in the end trip us up.

THOUSANDS ARE SAILING

The Island it is silent now
But the ghosts still haunt the waves
And the torch lights up a famished man
Who fortune could not save

Did you work upon the railroad
Did you rid the streets of crime
Were your dollars from the White House
Were they from the five and dime

Did the old songs taunt or cheer you
And did they still make you cry
Did you count the months and years
Or did your teardrops quickly dry

Ah No, says he 'twas not to be
On a coffin ship I came here
And I never even got so far
That they could change my name

Thousands are sailing
Across the Western Ocean
To a land of opportunity
That some of them will never see
Fortune prevailing
Across the Western Ocean
Their bellies full
And their spirits free
They'll break the chains of poverty
And they'll dance

In Manhattan's desert twilight
In the death of afternoon
We stepped hand in hand on Broadway
Like the first men on the moon

And 'The Blackbird' broke the silence
As you whistled it so sweet
And in Brendan Behan's footsteps
I danced up and down the street

Then we said goodnight to Broadway
Giving it our best regards
Tipped our hats to Mister Cohen
Dear old Times Square's favourite bard

Then we raised a glass to JFK
And a dozen more besides
When I got back to my empty room
I suppose I must have cried

Thousand are sailing
Again across the ocean
Where the hand of opportunity
Draws tickets in a lottery
Postcards we're mailing
Of sky-blue skies and oceans
From rooms the daylight never sees
Where lights don't glow on Christmas trees
But we dance to the music
And we dance

Thousands are sailing
Across the Western Ocean
Where the hand of opportunity
Draws tickets in a lottery

Where e'er we go, we celebrate
The land that makes us refugees
From fear of Priests with empty plates
From guilt and weeping effigies
And we dance

MARY GORDON
from Mary Gordon, *The Other Side* (1989)

The American writer Mary Gordon (1949–   ) was born on Long Island and educated at Barnard College. She is a Catholic by upbringing — her father was a Jew — and in 'Father Chuck: A Reading of *Going My Way* and *The Bells of St Mary's*, or Why Priests Made Us Crazy' (see *South Atlantic Quarterly* 93: 3 Summer 1994) she describes the effect such films had on Catholic culture in New York. Her career as a writer of fiction began with *Final Payments* (1978) and continued with *The Company of Women* (1980) and *Men and Angels* (1985). In *The Other Side* she returns to her Irish roots in a family saga involving four generations of the MacNamara family, the first members of whom, Vincent and Ellen, emigrated to the States in the early years of the twentieth century. Here in this extract memories of Ireland are juxtaposed with the reality as their grandchildren Camille (Cam) and Daniel reminisce about the past.

from **Chapter 1**

'It's only a matter of time,' Theresa says. 'I think we should start packing things up gradually, the things they never use. They won't notice and we can keep on top of it, not have some huge mess all at once.'

'We're not going to do that, Theresa,' Cam says. 'It's their house. He's coming back today. He'll be here living in it.'

'It's ridiculous, him rattling around this house like that.'

Marilyn and Dan listen to them, standing in the doorway of Ellen's room. They watch everyone fall into place: Cam and Theresa fixed at the center, the antagonists; Sheilah in back of her mother urging injury; Ray and his son, John, outside the circle, knowing no act of theirs can have weight. Marilyn hangs behind Dan a little, waiting for him to walk between the two antagonists, to fool them, to distract them, sing, tell a joke, make a remark on the weather, anything to make them stop.

'I thought we were going for a walk,' Dan says to Cam.

Cam walks out of the house ahead of him and bangs the screen door. He can see the line of it, starting with Ellen, hating herself, refusing to love her daughters, stealing him from his mother, taking Cam from Magdalene; he sees John and Sheilah in their mother's blackened house. And he and Marilyn, always a little desperate: We'll fix it, wait a minute, we'll do something; it will be all right.

He knows he has to make something move in Cam, Cam's anger is like a foreign power that can colonize their lives. When she's angry (she is never angry at him), the look of the world changes for him, as if a war had happened. The peaceful streets where you could live a modest, public life have been demolished; where there were cafés, churches, simple houses there is rubble: you sit on the bombed-out site searching in the wreck for the familiar things.

'Look around at all this,' he says, pointing to the new houses. 'Look how it's changed.'

He knows that, even angry, she can be interested in the world.

'I mind,' he says, 'You wouldn't think I'd mind, considering we weren't happy here. You'd think I'd like it all wiped out.'

He knows she has begun to listen, but he hasn't got her yet. The engine of her anger still runs, he can hear it; it slows down but doesn't stop. She knows he's trying to distract her; she can feel his effort.

'I guess that's the oldest story in the book, right, talking about the neighborhood going downhill? They probably said it in the Stone Age — "Look at those assholes, iron" — and in the Middle Ages, "Who wants those goddamn spices from the East?"'

She pities him. She sees him floundering, desperately trying to be interesting, to make her laugh so that she'll give it up, this anger that she treasures, that she doesn't want to give up, that she enjoys hoarding, fingering. Its sharpness creates borders she can understand: a skeleton, a frame. Pleasant to feel that bone, that wood, like lying down and feeling the jutting pelvis, like touching rafters, beams, before the ornamental camouflage is once and for all in place. She can know who she is in the world if she is somebody's antagonist; to be Theresa's enemy, therefore *not Theresa* in the world, satisfies her, gives her certainty and hope. But Dan is drowning in his efforts to make her stop; what gives her certainty and hope brings him anxiety and displacement. She won't do that to him. She'll give it up for him, this anger, desirable to her, valuable as medicine or wealth.

'Do you remember that magazine with house plans in it?' she says.

He remembers it; it was a magazine Vincent brought home for them, made up of photographs of houses with blueprints of the houses beneath. He thinks of them poring over it as children, looking for something. What? The book itself enchanted them. They loved the shiny pages, heavier than those of ordinary magazines, the photographs of new-built houses among trees that in themselves looked modern, unencumbered trees, trees without sad histories, trees that would give the right amount of shade, but wouldn't, for a moment, cut off from the wonderful and lucky family who lived among them even an inch of light. The man outside the house, the father, wore a plaid shirt, smoked a pipe; the mother wore a Fair Isle sweater. He forgets the children, their faces, what they wore. The children, boy and girl, were not important: it was those young parents. Those young parents who had nothing at all to do with Europe. He and Cam got the magazine in 1949. He remembers: she was eight and he was six. Europe seemed to him still covered over by a cloud of danger and shame, the War, the ruined streets, children hidden for years in basements. Europe was Ireland, which Ellen called a bog, a backwater, a filthy hole. She mocked the rich first-generation greenhorns who took their families back home. To see what? she would say. The cattle shitting in the streets, right up to your door, the children with their teeth rotted out of their heads, the beautiful thatched cottages swept only once a year, the tinkers carrying their filthy babies in their filthy blankets? Oh, this beautiful thing, Ellen would say, through furious cruel teeth, we loved it so, that's why we couldn't wait to leave. And when his grandfather would send into the air a nice memory, rising like a balloon to give them pleasure, when he would say: The greenness of the grass, the goodness of the milk, the lovely bread, the songs, the smell of the peat fire, she would raise the hammer of her scorn. She would begin to talk in a false brogue. 'Yes, Dad,' she'd say, ''tis little enough ye knew of it. You left at fifteen and lucky for you. 'Twas a lovely life you had. Breaking your back on the farm that went all to your brother, then apprenticed out at twelve. 'Twas what ye wanted for yer children, wasn't it. The lovely bread, the lovely singsongs by the peat fire. Everybody slaving till they died or wore out. 'Twas wonderful. If only I could have it back, my carefree youth.' And she would flap and dance and invent a song. 'My carefree youth / The cowshit and the toothless mother / And the starving tinkers out to steal me blind / Back, back to the auld sod of my dreams.'

Dan would see his grandfather pretend to laugh, or genuinely laugh, for Ellen could do that, she could make her husband laugh, and when her wit was cruel and meant to draw fresh blood he would go quiet. She could see that she had hurt him, and she would regret, but not apologize.

So that was Europe: the War, the Ireland he could not make a clear picture of. Was it the green country of his grandfather, or the hard, filthy place that she spoke of? He'd travelled to France and Italy, to Spain with Sharon, long before he went to Ireland. He'd gone only two years ago, with Cam and with the girls.

Cam and Darci loved it. But for him, the country was a sign: they could never be happy, any of them, coming from people like the Irish. Unhappiness was bred into the bone, a message in the blood, a code of weakness. The sickle-cell anemia of the Irish: they had to thwart joy in their lives. You saw it everywhere in Irish history; they wouldn't allow themselves to prosper. They didn't believe in prosperity. Perhaps, he thought, they were right not to.

He saw it everywhere he went in Ireland, the proof of the Irish temperament, the doomed service of the ideal, the blatant disregard of present pleasure. He could see it in their politics, their architecture, in the layout of their living rooms, their towns. He compared the way the Irish lived with what he'd seen in France and Italy. In Ireland, there were no glimpses of shocking, reassuring brightness: a plate with overlarge, loud-colored flowers, a milk jug in the shape of a bird's head, a rectangular pillow in a dark, primary shade, a fountain, just for nothing, in the center of a town, the trees extravagantly leaved, the chestnut, and

the willow. It was fine for Cam and Darci to bend over laughing at the decor of their Bed and Breakfasts, but for him it was a dreadful talisman. It seemed that in every dining room of every B & B in Ireland, even in those that took in only three or four paying guests, there was an inexplicable presence: a tableau of animals that appeared from a distance to be the work of a skilled taxidermist, but upon a closer look (and Cam and Darci planned their mornings around the opportunities to get a closer look) turned out to be plastic animals frozen in deadly attitudes, about to swoop or perch or use their talons, beneath a sheet of Plexiglas.

He understood the Irish. They were a colonized nation and had taken from their colonizers all their symbols of prosperity and of success. The English gave them their model, and like the colonized everywhere, they learned their lesson only halfway: they learned the wrong half. They copied from the English the jarring printed carpets and the half-glass doors that closed as if they kept out someone dangerous or insane. And, fearful of their reputation as slatterns (fatal to the tourist industry), they put dust-resistant covers on their furniture, and on their mattresses quickly drying nylon sheets. They seemed, Dan thought, to have been taken up by an obsession with concealment, or protection, by impermeable plastic. On the graves were arrangements of plastic flowers, in what looked like plastic cake dishes, the kind churchgoing women would use to transport their layer cakes to the bake sale or the parish tea. He watched the furious, the desperate, the anxiety-filled cleaning of the Irish women who had taken paying guests. He saw that there was nothing natural about their cleaning, nothing learned in childhood, practiced over the years. The cruel, expensive vacuum cleaners (*Just doing a bit of Hoovering, so*) set the rhythm of the day for these genuinely nice women and their families. A few hours of frantic activities: the breakfasts, the cleaning up. Then the long day of waiting, like unsure lovers, for the rented car, with its Americans, its Germans, for someone to come out and say, 'How much?' The tourists didn't say, as they should have, 'How much for the family beds?' For Dan had seen how they had done it — the Americans, the Germans, the English, by their holidaying — turned the children from their beds. He'd awakened in the night and found the children sleeping in their sleeping bags on the sitting-room floor in front of fireplaces that sometimes held peat, but more often facsimiles of peat in neon-colored plastic. How nice they were, how friendly, these children and their mothers. The fathers you never saw: they drove away quite early in the mornings, or they were outside with the cows all day; they came back for a silent dinner; they went back out then to the pub. Sometimes if you were at the same pub as one of these men in the evenings he would smile, embarrassed, for he knew and you knew: his wife was making money off your need for shelter and a bed.

The towns displayed their own kind of blindness, not mistaken and mislearned, like the distressing ugliness of the private houses, but a willed, blunt disregard for beauty, a blank, punitive, ungenerous self-presentation, a reproach to ornament, to prideful style. The towns were built for commerce, and stripped down for it. They had been market towns once, cattle had been brought from the surrounding areas into the large central square. He saw the trees brutally pollarded, the unwelcoming pebble-dash faces of the houses, the thin sills painted dull blue or prison-green. Some curse of money-changing, money-making, had come down upon these towns. They stood for commerce, but with none of its excitement: no goods flashing, bright stuff disappearing, then appearing once again. No, what Dan could see was that this was the idea of 'the town' thought up by people whose genius was rural. Real life was in the countryside. And the country was miraculous.

So they had both been right, his grandmother, his grandfather. Ellen, brought up in town, had seen the bleak, commercial greed; his grandfather had seen the land's beauty. Dan had wanted to see what they both had seen. So they had driven south to Cork and found Vincent's village, Dromnia, lush and gentle, a female landscape full of hidden brooks and noble trees. And they had gone north, to the west of Clare, and had found Tulla, Ellen's town. A steep-streeted town with mute, gray sooty houses all connected, as if they'd all been poured from the same batch of concrete, all at once. They'd found her father's pub.

Darci and Cam, who loved pub life (Darci was, to her great joy, served her first drink in Tulla, a shandy, beer and lemonade), were adopted lovingly by Ellen's town. 'Can you imagine, this one is the granddaughter of Ellen Costelloe.' No one remembered Ellen; they couldn't have; no one they met was old enough; they pretended that they did. It was a kind pretense; Dan didn't mind. But in the stones of the streets, in the blank cement faces of the houses, Dan felt the child Ellen's misery, imagined her a little girl living above the pub noise, the men's sickness, the dark small rooms. For he could feel it when he walked into the rooms she knew. He saw the countryside around the town, brief fertile patches, taken over soon by brown grass and the gorse the farmers cursed. Everyone but tourists cursed it. He understood. He couldn't sing

and joke like Cam and Darci; he was happy to take Staci home to the room, to read while she made perfect sketches of the hillsides and the furniture and wrote brief, numerous, and uninforming letters to her friends back home.

He felt they were his people, the Irish, and he pitied and admired them. He enjoyed them, but he felt that, like him, they had no idea how to live.

He takes Cam's arm as they walk down their childhood street. They look across the street; their eyes fall on the same sight; they are thinking the same thing. Some children, young teenagers they must be, thirteen at most, are getting on the bus for Jamaica. Cam and Dan know from the way they're dressed (uneasily) and standing (tentatively, as if they are afraid someone will come along and tell them they have no right to be there) that these children will take the subway at Jamaica and get off in midtown Manhattan. The City. They travel only from borough to borough but it is as if they travel to another continent. They are leaving home.

Dan says: 'Remember when you took me into the museum. It was so exciting. I felt like you were taking me in a covered wagon.'

Cam isn't listening. They are about to pass by 163 Linwood Avenue, where Cam lives with her mother and Bob. Cam's eye is on Magdalene's window, facing out onto the street. Dan sees Cam's mouth go tense. He knows she won't suggest that they go in. It occurs to him that in all his life he hasn't been in that house more than twenty times. *That* house. It was a place that you got out of, quickly, into the fresh air, to the city, or to Vincent and Ellen's, or away somewhere in your car. Cam never wanted him in that house; he never particularly wanted to be there. There was something dangerous about it: infected, forbidden. Magdalene ruled there, making Cam behave her worst.

Cam sees that the drapes of her mother's room are drawn. It makes her furious; she'd like to bang open the doors of the house, run up the stairs, open the curtains, and say, 'Mother, it's the middle of the day. How about letting the sunshine in.'

She knows it's a bad sign, the drawn curtains. She wonders how much time she has before she'll have to go into the house and find out, once and for all, whether Magdalene will do it. Whether she'll walk out of her room, onto the street, back to her parents' house. To be there for her father.

Cam expects the worst. She doesn't want to think about it now. She takes Dan's arm and steers him forcefully around the corner, as if he were a stranger, as if he didn't know where they were.

ROBERT McLIAM WILSON
from Robert McLiam Wilson, *Ripley Bogle* (1989)

Robert McLiam Wilson (1964–   ), was born in Belfast and educated at Cambridge, which he left before taking his degree. The jobs he has performed include refuse-collector, bartender, bodyguard, kilt salesman. In 1991–94 he was writer-in-residence at the University of Ulster at Coleraine. His other novels include *Manfred's Pain* (1992) and *Eureka Street* (1997) (see below p. 1233). *The Dispossessed* (1992) is a documentary account with photographs by Donovan Wylie of poverty in Thatcherite Britain. There is an engaging power behind Wilson's writing, particularly when the topic, as here, is about those excluded from life's feast.

It suddenly comes to me that I am hungry. Well, perhaps 'hungry' is not quite the right word. Bowelwitheringly fucking ravenous might well be a more just and measured phrase to describe what I am currently experiencing. All right, so I'm a young man and, no doubt, prone to the overstatement of youth but this is the real thing. This is the actual, veritable item. Hunger is hitting me hard. Hunger is tickling me with a crowbar and Hunger is enjoying it. Have I already mentioned the fact that I haven't eaten in more than three days! Big deal, you'll be saying, I've had worse than that! Well — four days ago I hadn't eaten for five days and I grew so fucking desperate that I picked a half-eaten hamburger out of a litter bin, cleaned the grit off and wolfed it down with relish. (The enjoyment kind not the condiment kind.) How about that, then? Eh? I bet you wish you hadn't opened your mouth now. (N.B. I was so ashamed and disgusted that I almost immediately boked it all up again and haven't tried it since.)

Anyway, back to my present little pangs. I think I've done pretty well up to now. I've suffered in something close to silence. Which is big of me (and uncharacteristic). Your actual attenuation is a weird and many-faceted thing. It goes in stages. (I've never actually gone more than a fortnight without food so my expertise is of necessity limited. Any more extensive and I'd be blind or mad or dead.)

First, you ache dully for a day or so. Your abdomen is swollen and taut, you belch prodigiously and seem to have more saliva than you know what to do with. We all know that hunger. Between-meal hunger, fast-hunger, travel-hunger, diet-hunger even. It's a doddle. Easypeasy. Just not a problem. Then you hit a nice upward curve of comfort and strength. As your brain chews over the last of its glucose, your wits are sharpened, your mind clears. Your thoughts and words are airy, dashing, pyrotechnic in scope and beauty. You write poems, play probability and find three separate cures for cancer.

This is good. This is fun. But then Agony sticks a knobbly great pole up your arse and waves it around in your already stretching abdomen. Half a day of festive screeching and this passes . . . thankfully. Not stopping for a moment, you move onto another plateau of tranquillity. You are unaccountably happy. Not even the dullard intrusion of encroaching brain death can disturb this new serenity. You know and welcome all. Macrocosm and microcosm. You have a great aerial breadth of wisdom and reparation. You are the Hunger Philosopher with the seer's bowl of vision and sagacity. God comes and speaks to you.

Agony interrupts and rapes you violently. Thirty minutes later you give birth to a combine harvester with blades a-spinning and you cough up what looks like your major intestine. It slithers away to a new life in the sun before you can catch it.

And just as you think you've had it, just as you think you're all finally fucked-up, the calm comes again. It's a slow calm now. A coma-calm. Time stretches and you foray into Hippyland. Perception and intelligence take a little holiday somewhere out of the way and you wallow in feeble peace. You don't care very much about what happens to you at this point and you may well find yourself trying to sleep on motorways, etc. just about now. Don't worry though, with the state that you're in you need all the carelessness you can jolly well muster.

Whoops! But what's this? Why, stap me vitals, it's old Agony again! He is truly pissed off now and desires to do you harm. He starts off with a spot of resolute bowelboiling before going to work on your stomach wall with a brillo pad. In a moment of inspiration, he ties your pancreas to your bladder with a cheesewire. You crumple and stay that way. Your legs drop off and when you essay to put them back, they don't seem to fit. You improvise and fall over.

It passes. You wouldn't think so but it does.

Having reduced options, your brain decides on a

little scrambling. Neurons collide and tumble against your throbbing skullbone. You come over all esoteric. Phantasmagoria is the name of the game now and suddenly Kafka seems like P.G. Wodehouse. The Devil comes to call as a fetchingly giant spider with suppurating boils and diarrhoea sweat. His monstrous, quivering maw pouts invitingly at you as he squats in his own shimmering, steaming obscenity. Aroused now, he snogs with you for a while before lunching on your lungs and liver . . .

Et cetera . . .

Bad, eh?

Actually, the thing about starvation that most people don't realize is that if you ignore your hunger it sulks and goes away. Up to a point. After a while, of course,

you die. You really, truly die. I mean, don't try it — it's not much fun.

Wow, that helped! I feel a lot better for that. The vacant claxon of my gut has hushed its noise. For this relief much thanks.

Well, that's just about it for Hunger. Apart, of course, from the terrible endocrinal, subchemical mess it gets your poor old body into. This we can imagine. Who needs to know that? With Hunger such a permanent and stalwart companion, I prefer to ward it off with the extremes of optimism and ignorance. What you don't know *can* actually hurt you quite prodigiously but what you've never *had*, you never do miss. Or, more precisely, what you haven't eaten, you can't chuck up. Anyhow, hunger's horrible but here to stay.

IRISH WRITING IN THE 1990s

One of the arguments I had heard against Boland was that she could not possibly represent Irish women because she had not shared the experience of the majority of them. I mentioned this, and she smiled widely, as though she had heard it too often. With marked disdain for the idea she said, 'No poet has ever represented a people. Poets represent themselves and the private obsessive world out of which they make the poem. I make zero claims to do anything but give the view I have of the time I live in, the obstructions I've found, and the freedoms I've gained. And that is representative of nobody, and if I had a mainstream background that connected me to the majority of the people in any country I would find it extraordinarily arrogant, dangerous, and inappropriate to claim that I represented them. I'm not a politician, I'm a poet. Poets subvert representation. They do not make a sort of stand on things. And to make them an index of a community has never worked. Yeats is not representative and is still being attacked in this country for his Anglo-Irish background. I want to be absolutely fair about this. I don't want to cheapen that argument or glamorize that argument or say I'm an individual and I'm being falsely represented as someone who is not representative. Perhaps a country that has a bardic tradition has a hunger for the representative poet, but the Irish community has an extremely disreputable history in its transactions with its artists. Its requirements that the artist be representative kept James Joyce out of the bookshops in this country until 1969. You still couldn't get *Ulysses* in the bookshops in the early sixties, and that is because they felt that this man with his obscene view of the lived life in his time was not representative of the Irish people. The claims of the Irish people have usually been suspect, and they have led to the most Draconian censorship laws outside of the political tyranny.'

– Rosemary Mahoney, *Whoredom in Kimmage: Irish Women Coming of Age* (1993)

Two days after Michael Stone attacks the mourners at the funeral of the IRA unit shot in Gibraltar I pass a paint-daubed wall. 'It only takes one Stone to kill three Taigs,' it says. Soon the same celebratory slogan is everywhere and suddenly it feels as if we are spiralling out of control, no longer just some monotonous side-show, each new burst of savagery reaching out to taint any life it chooses. The whole city tenses, the tight little lines of streets I pass each day, spokes on a wheel which rolls inexorably towards its fate. As always it is unspoken, but you feel it in your stomach, see it in the eyes of the policeman who checks your licence, hear it in the staff-room conversations which avoid its every mention. And always the hovering helicopter, watching, waiting, the sound of its engine throbbing at first like a migraine, then gradually absorbed into the consciousness until it is no longer heard.

– David Park, *Stone Kingdoms* (1996)

CRITICAL AND DOCUMENTARY

EDNA LONGLEY
from *From Cathleen to Anorexia: The Breakdown of Irelands* (1990)

Edna Longley (1940–   ), Professor of English at QUB and a leading critic in Ireland, is author of *Poetry in the Wars* (1986), *Louis MacNeice* (1988), and *The Living Stream: Literature and Revisionism in Ireland* (1994). In this famous controversial essay, writing to the moment, she attacks some of the sacred cows of nationalism. At the end of the essay she includes a list of texts cited.

Northern Ireland has been called a 'failed political entity'. I think it's time to admit that both parts of Ireland are failed conceptual entities. That is, the ideas which created them and the ideologies which sustained them have withered at the root. If 'Northern Ireland' has visibly broken down, the 'Republic' as once conceived has invisibly broken down. And since 1968 each has helped to expose the inner contradictions of the other.

In his poem 'Aisling', written near the time of the hunger strikes, Paul Muldoon asks whether Ireland should be symbolized, not by a radiant and abundant goddess, but by the disease anorexia:

> Was she Aurora, or the goddess Flora,
> Artemidora, or Venus bright,
> or anorexia, who left
> a lemon stain on my flannel sheet?

In blaming the hunger-strikers' emaciation on their idealized cause, the poem equates that cause with a form of physical and psychic breakdown. 'Anorexia' is thus Cathleen Ní Houlihan in a terminal condition. Anorexic patients pursue an unreal self-image — in practice, a death-wish. Similarly, the nationalist dream may have declined into a destructive neurosis.

Feminists question any exploitation of the female body for symbolic or abstract purposes. So perhaps Anorexia should, rather, personify Irish women themselves: starved and repressed by patriarchies like unionism, Catholicism, Protestantism, nationalism. But here we come up against a difficulty. Not all Irish women resist these patriarchies. And for some, mainly from the North, Cathleen flourishes abundantly still. The Northern women's movement has been divided and retarded; while the Southern movement, preoccupied with church-and-state, has largely avoided 'nation'. Eavan Boland's feminist poem 'Mise Éire' (I am Ireland) destabilizes Mise but not Éire. There is some reluctance, partly for fear of further division, to reopen the ever-problematic, ever-central issue of 'nationalism and feminism'. Later I will ask whether they are compatible. For the moment, I offer the reluctance as symptomatic.

This pamphlet will mainly focus on the ideological breakdown of nationalism because its breakdown is more complex and less obvious. Nationalism and unionism are not in fact the same kind of ideology, nor do they function in the same manner. So they differ in their modes of collapse as in their modes of construction. Unionism since the first Home Rule Bill has always been reactive: a coalition of sects, interests, loyalties and incoherent hatreds in the face of a perceived common emergency. No totalizing philosophy covers the whole coalition, even if religious and secular alarm fuse on its fundamentalist wing. Orangeism and Paisleyism maintain a select tribal memory-bank of historical persecutions, in which emblematic events (1641, 1690)[1] are reinforced by biblical parallels. But this has never developed into a comprehensive symbolic system. You can't personify unionism. 'Orange Lil' is not the whole story.

As a separatist movement, nationalism had to put together a more elaborate ideological package and make more absolute claims. Also, like Polish nationalism, it is informed by Catholic theological habits. When the SDLP[2] and Sinn Féin deny any sectarian component in their politics, these very habits blind them to the seamless join between Catholicism and nationalism, a join which is a matter of form as much as content. Nationalism thinks of unionism as heresy — hence past failures to analyse or understand it. And to come up against the church on *ne temere*[3] or integrated education is to be as chillingly excluded as when one meets the guardians of the republican grail.

Lapsed nationalists are, therefore, more liable than lapsed unionists to suffer from metaphysical angst. One example is Richard Kearney's compulsion to redefine the platonic Republic. Other southern writers and intellectuals strangely complain that 'Ireland does not exist'. This seems less an empirical judgement than a state of unconscious mourning for a god, a goddess, a symbolic future that failed. Two other post-nationalist reactions are revisionism and cynicism. But there has to be *some* reaction. Nationalism was internalized as God, nature and family. So it can leave painful withdrawal symptoms as it recedes.

Unionism does not linger like bog-mist in unsuspected crannies. For better or worse, you generally know it's there. Unionism exposes its contradictions in public: in the gap between its interior monologues and what it can get the rest of the world to believe. All ideologies work through unconscious assumptions as well as conscious creeds. But the unionist unconscious, in both its secular and religious versions, has never been open to outsiders, whereas the reflexes of the nationalist unconscious have been widely accepted as norms. The situation in the North is not helped by the tendency of nationalist Ireland to swallow or re-import its own dated propaganda. Patrick Kavanagh once said (with regard to the popularity of *The Quiet Man* in Dublin): 'the only place now where phoney ould Oireland is tolerated is in Ireland itself'. Unfortunately, he underestimated an export market which continues to boom. When flattered by Irish-American sentiment or left-wing 'Brit guilt', nationalism becomes less disposed to self-criticism and forgets its inner malaise.

Literature plays a part in all this too. (We import some starry-eyed lit crit from the USA.) Now and then I will use contemporary writing as an index of the double ideological breakdown in Ireland. There are good historical reasons why Irish nationalism so often reads like bad poetry and Ulster unionism like bad prose. Cathleen of course has been muse as well as goddess. Eoin MacNeill[4] tried to lower the political temperature before the Rising by sending round a circular which plainly stated: 'What we call our country is not a poetical abstraction . . . there is no such person as Cathleen Ní Houlihan . . . who is calling upon us to serve her.' Ulster Protestantism, which prides itself on plain statement, has been slow to evolve a self-critical prose tradition, let alone qualifying clauses. Thus from the 1920s most writers had no option but to constitute themselves an opposition to the ideological clamps holding both Irish entities together. In my lifetime, these clamps have distorted ethics, politics, social and personal relations, the lives of women, education, what passes here for religion, and our whole understanding of Irish culture.

Literature remains the primary place where language changes, where anorexic categories are exposed. This is no less the case in Ireland than in Eastern Europe.

Irish, Irisher, Irishest

'Irishness' is the most inclusive category for Irish Nationalist ideology — and also the most insidious. In the last paragraph of *Modern Ireland*, Roy Foster criticizes the recurring theme of 'being "more" or "less" Irish than one's neighbours; Irishness as a scale or spectrum rather than a simple national or residential qualification; at worst, Irishness as a matter of aggressively displayed credentials'. Last Easter, Cardinal O'Fiaich proved how this theme persists in the collective unconscious. 'Many Protestants,' he said, 'love Ireland as devoutly as *any* Catholic does' (my italics). He then recited the litany of patriot Prods (Tone, Emmet, etc.) usually produced in support of such statements. It sometimes seems as if Protestants have to die for Ireland before being allowed to live here.

The Cardinal meant his remarks kindly. But in so deliberately including Protestants, he excluded them. He fed the belief that Protestants have to work their passage to Irishness. Catholics, on the other hand, are born loving the country, knowing by instinct its entire history and literature, and generally 'kinned by hieroglyphic peat' (Seamus Heaney). This nonsense, out of date in the Republic, is widely swallowed by both sides in the North. But Ulster Irishness, like Ulster Britishness, is a state neither of nature nor of grace. It is enforced and reinforced by socialization, often by simplifications and stereotypes. In *Ripley Bogle*[5] Robert McLiam Wilson satirizes the conditioning processes of the North:

> I learnt a great many things on my first day at school. I discovered that I lived in Belfast and that Belfast lived in Ireland and that this combination meant that I was Irish. The grim young bint we were loaded with was very fervent on this point. She stressed with some vigour that no matter what anyone else were to call us, our names would always be Irish . . . [she] told us that the occasional Misguided Soul would try to call us British but that of all things to call us — this was the wrongest. No matter how the Misguided Souls cajoled, insisted or pleaded, our names would remain Irish to the core, whatever that meant . . . in the spirit of compromise (ever with me even then), I dubbed myself 'Ripley Irish British Bogle'.

Roy Foster would replace the competing indoctrinations with 'a more relaxed and inclusive definition of Irishness, and a less constricted view of Irish history'. Who would not agree? Yet when he developed this idea in his lecture 'Varieties of Irishness', the Unionist David Trimble felt political pressures in the very term 'Irishness', however far its elastic might stretch. Of course Unionists can be equally paranoid about being called Irish and not being called Irish (as Jews in pre-war Poland resented the alternatives of assimilation and expulsion). But this seeming paradox is in fact an accurate response to the rhetorical tactics famously admitted by Senator Michael Hayes in 1939: 'We have had a habit, when it suited a particular case, of saying they were Irish, and when it did not suit a particular case of saying they were British.'

One way of circumventing an elaborate quadrille, in which the dancers contrive never to meet on the same ground, might be to accelerate the separation between political Irishness and culture in Ireland. Culture in Ireland is a range of practices, expressions, traditions, by no means homogeneously spread nor purely confined to the island. Political Irishness, on the other hand, is the ideology of identity ('Irish to the core') mainly packaged by the Gaelic League, which, twined with Catholicism, served to bind the new state. In the Republic the strings of this package have got looser and looser, and much of its substance has leaked out. In the North, Sinn Féin still tries to deliver a fossilized and belated version. There, whether embraced or resisted, Irishness endures as an absolute abstract noun. When threatened by that absolute, Unionists reach for the security-blanket of Britain or Ulster. Meanwhile, they are happy enough with relative or adjectival usages: Northern Irish, Irish Protestant, even Irish Unionist. In these usages, Ireland stands for the country, not the nation, and 'Erin's Orange lily' feels at home. The often-put question 'Are you British or Irish?' is strictly meaningless, since 'Irish' does double duty as an allegiance and as an 'ethno-cultural', description. 'British' is only an allegiance, an umbrella for English, Scots, Welsh and some Northern Irish. Allegiance has cultural effects, and culture influences allegiance. Yet 'Britishness' is not opposite to 'Irishness': it is the affiliation whereby Ulster Protestants seek to maintain those aspects of their identity which are threatened by political Irishness.

Perhaps their reactions might seem less paranoid after we have visited the political unconscious of Alban Maginness, SDLP Councillor in Belfast. Here he is replying to an article by John Wilson Foster in which Foster contends that 'Northern Protestants have been excluded by the Nationalist majority in Ireland from being Irish'. Maginness says:

Curiously, in some non-political situations, the Northern Protestant, which Foster unapologetically claims to be, concedes, asserts or even claims Irishness . . . the train loads of rugby supporters from Belfast to Lansdowne Road[6] . . . bear witness to [it]. A tired and over-worked example some might say, but it does raise the question, why can't this 'sporting' patriotism be translated into political patriotism?

My understanding of modern Irish history is that the majority culture was and still is inclusive, not exclusive and has an almost missionary zeal to persuade if not cajole Northern Protestants into realizing or owning up to their innate Irishness . . . why this absurd denial of Irishness?

Studies, Winter, 1988

The above manifests a deep confusion between cultural and political Irishness. Maginness's rugby example should indeed be laid to rest since the only group not heading for Lansdowne Road are Ulster Catholics. The culture of sport is heavily politicized in the North, keeping talent from the great games of rugby and hurling. And surely Maginness answers his own questions when he finds Irish Protestants, Irish unionists relaxed about their affiliations to this country — a different matter from patriotic acceptance of the Republic — when the political heat is turned off. (People constantly generalize about 'Ireland' when they mean the Republic.)

Maginness might also compare his own feelings whenever unionism proposes to 'include' him, or professes 'missionary zeal' about persuading him to own up to his innate Britishness. And what exactly should Foster be *apologizing* for?

As unionists shy away from cultural areas that seem appropriated by nationalists, so nationalists assume that cultural 'Irishness', very narrowly defined, functions as a prelude to the political variety. A *cúpla focal*[7] on the lips, a twiddle on the fiddle, and 'from their full and genial hearts/An Irish feeling [will] burst'. Labhrás Ó Murchú actually told the New Ireland Forum[8] that 'any unionist who is exposed to the *Tobar an Dúchais*[9] will come up with a much more legitimate status for himself than the status that was contrived'. (This is the same man who decided that traditional Irish music opposed abortion.) The celebrated dulcimer-player John Rea was an Orangeman who, although always friendly toward Catholic fellow-musicians, called them 'them' to the end of his days. False hopes and fears are invested in 'the convert syndrome'. This encompasses the Protestant Gaeilgeoir[10] as well as the Protestant patriot. Unfortunately, all converts impress the congregation they join a lot more than the one they have left. (They may also be subtly patronized as heretics who have seen the light.) A type of Aran-knit Ulster Protestant is particularly misleading in this respect, and has no battalions at his (or her) back. But even if East Belfast was teeming with potential Douglas Hydes,[11] it doesn't follow that the language leads to the nation. After all, Samuel Ferguson[12] set out to show that Gaelic literature is not the exclusive property of Catholics and nationalists. Mutterings to this effect have even been heard from the vicinity of the UDA.[13]

What about literature in English written by Irish people? Does it belong to the nation, the country, the island, these islands, the world? Patrick Kavanagh knew he was on dangerous ground when he claimed that 'the writers of Ireland [are] no longer Corkery and O'Connor and the others but Auden and George Barker':

> Saying this is liable to make one the worst in the world, for a national literature, being based on a convention, not born of the unpredictable individual and his problems, is a vulnerable racket and is protected by fierce wild men.

John Banville has been able to say more coolly that 'there is no such thing as an Irish national literature, only Irish writers engaged in the practice of writing'. Yet when progressive cultural thinkers in the Republic dwell on the Europeanism or Atlanticism of Irish writing, they sometimes forget that its Irishness has been shelved rather than interrogated. For naive readers some Irish writers and texts are still more Irish than others. And, thanks to the Irish Literary Revival, the canon retains a vaguely nationalist aura, abroad if not always at home.

This is ironical, given that some literary critics have problems with Yeats's English literary connections, and with his latter-day cult of the Anglo-Irish Ascendancy. But if Yeats's Protestant and English affiliations were more sympathetically regarded, it might illuminate the role of the North in Ireland's literary culture. Still quoted is AE's dictum: 'Unionism in Ireland has produced no literature.' This, like Irishness and Britishness, involves a false alternative whereby anything written by Irish people can be turned to the glory of nationalism. Meanwhile, Protestant cultural expression is caricatured as drums and banners (not that the interest of these should be overlooked). Such perceptions reproduce an image foisted by political Irishness on to political Protestantism (and sometimes internalized by it). This image excludes the dual Irish-British context, and what Protestants actually write, paint and perform, whatever their political allegiances.

In 1985 Gerald Dawe and I edited a collection of critical essays entitled *Across a Roaring Hill: The Protestant Imagination in Modern Ireland*. To some, the category appeared sectarian (whereas 'Irish' would have been taken for granted). One reviewer (Declan Kiberd) assumed that we had a hidden unionist agenda; another (Enoch Powell) assumed that we belonged to the nationalist conspiracy. Brendan Kennelly quoted an acquaintance who reacted to the book's title by declaring that 'Protestants have no imagination at all'. This stereotype partly results from the inhibition of artistic expression within Scottish and Ulster Calvinism. But instead of putting down that culture with reference to 'the wonderfully rich Irish literary tradition etc.' it should be understood in its own terms. Again, the relation of all Irish writing to Protestantism and Catholicism, an issue masked by homogenizing 'Irishness', should be opened up — as should relations between Irish and English literature after 1922.

So I think that 'Irishness' with its totalitarian tinge, ought to be abandoned rather than made more inclusive. To include/exclude the Ulster Prods involves another false alternative (cf. Senator Hayes) with underlying nationalist assumptions. 1798 is no more practical use to us than 1916. Charles Haughey[14] may have pragmatically modified his views since he made his opening speech to the Forum. Yet, in his psychic alarm, he identified the real agenda: 'The belief has been canvassed that we would have to jettison almost the entire ethos on which the independence movement was built and that Irish identity has to be sacrificed to facilitate the achievement of Irish unity.' In fact, some such sacrifice may be necessary for the sake of peace let alone unity as once dreamed. But cultural change and changing awareness of culture, in the Republic and even in the North, have already exposed political Irishness (the 'ethos on which the independence movement was built') as now more a prison than a liberation.

Northern nationalists and southern revisionists

When nationalism achieves its object it 'begins to die'. So said Seán O'Faoláin in 1951. This means that the relation between southern and northern nationalism is one of uneven development. The southern state was gradually born into evolution, while northern nationalism (like unionism) froze in an archaic posture. It stayed bent on realizing what revisionism now seems wantonly to discard. But perhaps northern nationalists, nearly as anachronistic in Dublin as the unionists in London, will have to accept that the southern clock cannot be stopped or wound back.

As Clare O'Halloran shows in *Partition and the Limits of Irish Nationalism*, between northern and southern nationalists there lies a distance not only of time but experience, a distance usually disguised by rhetorical togetherness. She quotes John A. Costello on the adversarial imperative that gives northern nationalism its distinctive shape: 'they have to fight their fight up there as a minority, and every piece of Protestant bitterness in the North has its counterpart, both politically and in a religious sense, in the hearts and in the actions of a northern Catholic. We in the South have got to recognize that we cannot understand that problem or appreciate it to the full.' That applies whether you are shocked by the atavisms of the North, or whether you don't want the North to rock the (relatively) secure southern boat.

The affair of Conor Cruise O'Brien, Garret FitzGerald, Senator John A. Murphy and the SDLP was a tremor produced by the largely unexamined relation between northern and southern nationalist consciousness. This relation rarely reaches the political surface, because there is assumed to be not relation but identity: identity of perception, interest, objective, context, historical moment. In this case tensions surfaced over SDLP attitudes to the RUC. Yet the emotional temperature of the row, particularly the reflex to execrate O'Brien and protect Hume, soared above its occasion. That signalled psychic alarm: the alarm-bells that ring whenever northern nationalism and southern revisionism touch.

In fact to deny any split or breakdown within the Irish nationalist psyche is to deny well-attested trauma. The South's long neglect of northern nationalists (documented by O'Halloran) breeds guilty over-compensation — which does not necessarily heal underlying resentments. (Go back, Austin Currie.) But Senator Murphy's hostilities, like O'Brien's certitudes, may be unwise in trying to break a taboo with a crowbar. Meanwhile slagging the South goes down well in West Belfast,[15] and opinion in the Republic swings between indifference and feverish identification. The latter, however, is mostly roused by events which concern 'British justice' (the Gibraltar killings)[16] and thus recall shared experience before 1922. In my view such philosophical and political incoherence serves neither side in the north, and retards the Republic's maturation into being part of the solution rather than central to the problem. It might advance the Hillsborough Accord[17] if psychic separation were promoted not only between Britain and the unionists, but also between the Irish Government and northern nationalists.

Even *Irish Times* editorials can regress towards political infancy when championing the SDLP: 'the SDLP and Provisionals may share, in part, a mistily defined political objective — the unification of Ireland. That is not an illegitimate objective: indeed it is a noble and attractive ideal' (22 April 1989). The last twenty years have seen the nemesis of misty definitions and attractive ideals. As for 'noble' (an adjective generally reserved for the male sex), in a fit of crazed ecumenism Bishop Cahal Daly recently maintained that unionism and nationalism were *both* 'noble aspirations'. It would be preferable to downgrade nationalism to the ignoble status traditionally enjoyed by unionism, rather than cling to the notion that a 'good' or 'real' nationalism exists in some zone uncontaminated by the Provos. We could also give 'aspirations' a rest. Fintan O'Toole has argued (*The Irish Times*, 20 April 1989) that Section 31 permits physical-force Republicanism to function as the id of the body politic. It subsists at an unconscious level where it cannot be interrogated. And if Sinn Féin remains below interrogation, the SDLP (a political party after all) remains above it. Thus southern nationalism cedes control over its own redefinition. The very structure of the New Ireland Forum, in asserting the unity of the nationalist family, excluded agonizing reappraisal of other unitary principles. Nevertheless, *de facto* reappraisal takes place all the time: at the level of economic necessity, historical revisionism, cultural change, the cycles of shock and weariness over the northern war.

Literature makes a good barometer of asymmetric consciousness in Ireland. As a literary critic who sometimes notices distinctive elements in northern writing, I have been suspected equally of partisanship and partitionism. This looks like another over-anxious unitary reflex. It is absurd to contend that Northern Ireland and the Republic have had identical socio-political experiences since 1922, or since 1968. And if we believe that literature is (up to a point) conditioned by society, and criticizes society, we should not sacrifice any insights it can offer. For instance, I have certainly learned more about the culture of the North from Medbh McGuckian's or Seamus Heaney's poetry (even after his move to Dublin), and that of the Republic from Paul Durcan's or Thomas McCarthy's.[18]

Durcan's visionary radicalism, for instance, criticizes a particular *status quo*. Unlike the majority of southern poets, he broaches the North. But he does so from outside the territory, without inhabiting its tensions as do the imaginations of Muldoon or Heaney. And Durcan's special focus is to open up the Republic's implication in the war. Thus long before Enniskillen he wrote the satirical 'National Day of Mourning for

Twelve Protestants'. Life slowly catches up with art. Durcan's poetry neither renounces its own cultural roots nor overlooks loyalist terror. But he concentrates on the spiritual failings of the society he knows and for which he feels responsible. So, generally, do other writers North and South. An exception that proves the rule may be recent fiction and drama from the Southern border counties, which contains two-way perspectives from a neglected limbo and source of light. But the Republic's writers are distinctively obsessed with secularism, sexuality, socialism, versions of feminism, and other libertarian themes. Literature and theatre seem to be mounting a communal psychodrama that releases what the official political culture won't admit.

Field Day is often perceived as speaking for Ireland. The company has indeed sometimes sponsored pluralism: in staging Stewart Parker's *Pentecost*, in publishing a pamphlet by Unionist Robert McCartney. But the pamphlet-topics so far chosen give a northern nationalist priority to cultural and political 'decolonization'. The latest trio was written by foreign literary critics better acquainted with general theories of colonialism than with Ireland after 1922. For Edward Said and Terry Eagleton, all 'the Irish people' are still engaged in a single national struggle. Reviewing the pamphlets (*Fortnight* no 271), Colm Tóibín found a time-warp in Field Day's own perceptions: 'the social and cultural revolution of the 1960s has left the artists in the Field Day group singularly unmoved . . . They write as though nothing had ever changed: their Ireland is distinctly pre-decimal. Thus England is the problem and the enemy (and the dramatic other).' Field Day's latest production *Saint Oscar*[19] looked out of date in Dublin because it was an instance of the re-imported nationalist propaganda I mentioned earlier. Its author, Eagleton again, used Wilde to present a timeless thesis about imperialist oppression. Field Day's eagerness to collude with the hoary stereotypes of the English hard Left seems significant.

Common to Friel's drama and the critical writings of Seamus Deane is a powerful sense of Palestinian dispossession. The alienation of Friel's Ballybeg is utterly different from the post-nationalist alienation of Tom Murphy's *Bailegangaire*. When speaking of Ireland's literary and political traditions, Deane repeatedly uses the terms 'crisis' and 'discontinuity'. These conditions he generalizes to cover the total past and this total island now. But his perceptions cannot be divorced from the recent history of Derry with its lost hinterland. (The other side of this bleak coin is the siege-haunted Derry Protestant.) The same affiliation

may show itself in Deane's intellectual resistance to the 'mystique of Irishness' concocted by Yeats on the one hand, Corkery on the other. Perhaps his otherwise rather extreme (and contradictory) desire for 'new writing, new politics, unblemished by Irishness, but securely Irish' (*Heroic Styles*) reflects, and aspires to redress, the exclusion of northern nationalists from the self-images and cultural definitions that became operational in the new state. Certainly, critics associated with Field Day approach the Irish Literary Revival both as a colonial manifestation, and as a present hegemony (not a receding phase in literary history). They question the Revival's cultural power as revisionists question the political power of 1916. As for Corkery, Tom Garvin argues that Munster, remote from *both* Ulster communities, played a disproportionate part in theorizing the revolution (see *Nationalist Revolutionaries in Ireland 1858–1928*). Perhaps that explains the tiff between John A. Murphy and Nell McCafferty.

Whatever its other purposes and qualities, the Field Day project for 'a comprehensive anthology' of Irish literature ('what writing in this country has been') shows a desire to influence definitions. Within the literary sphere it seeks to piece together a broken past, to go back behind all deforming colonization, to return to origins (550 AD), and thus to clarify 'Irish reality' so that we can start again. In contrast, revisionism seeks to break down a monolithic idea of the past, to go back behind the revolution's ideology, to return to origins in 1922 and understand them more empirically. In my view the former project risks the dangerous fantasy that loss and breakdown can be retrieved. Rather than start a new literary and political clock, I think we should try to tell the time accurately.

• • •

Women and nationalism

I have compared Irish nationalism to bad poetry. In bad poems the relations between word, image and life break down. Political images, like political language (from which they are never quite distinct), eventually exhaust themselves or prove incapable of renewal. I think this happens at the juncture where the image women-Ireland-muse meets contemporary Irish women. There, I believe, the breakdown of nationalist ideology becomes particularly clear.

In the film *Mother Ireland* (Derry Film and Video) Nell McCafferty regrets that the Committee for the Liberation of Irish Women, to avert a potential split, decided not to talk about the North. She would now welcome general debate on topics like 'Feminism and physical force'. While I might hope for a different outcome than she does, I agree that the issue of women and nationalism cannot be dodged for ever. Southern women too are implicated in this issue, although they may neither know it nor wish it. Even on her death-bed Cathleen-Anorexia exerts a residual power over the image and self-images of all Irish women. Both at home and abroad, she still confers status on selected kinds of Irish woman-ness (not, for instance, the Rhonda Paisley kind). The absurd 'Irish' edition of *Spare Rib* (August 1989), of which more anon, is a case in point.

Of course the Ulster Protestant community, though dragged forward faster by Westminster legislation, is as traditionally patriarchal as Catholic nationalism. This tribe too has its cult of male chieftains: Carson, Moses, the Big Man (compare Dev, the Pope, the Boss). And the whole country abounds in Ancient Orders of Hibernian Male-Bonding: lodges, brotherhoods, priesthoods, hierarchies, sodalities, knights, Fitzwilliam Tennis Club, Field Day Theatre Company. But at least unionism does not appropriate the image of woman or hide its aggressions behind our skirts. Nor does it — as a reactive ideology — seek ideological mergers. A unionist feminist might be these things separately, though genuine feminism would erode her Unionism. A nationalist/republican feminist, less readily regarded as a contradiction in terms, claims that her ideologies coincide. And in so doing she tries to hijack Irish feminism.

Terry Eagleton (in *Nationalism: Irony and Commitment*) develops an analogy between nationalism and feminism as responses to 'oppression'. He argues that nationalism must not prematurely sell its soul to revisionism and pluralism, just as feminism — until women have been truly liberated — must not sell its soul to 'a troubling and subverting of all sexual strait-jacketing'. As I will indicate later, with respect to the history of women and nationalism, strait-jackets tend to remain in place after the revolution unless their removal has been intrinsic to the revolution. Eagleton does not recognize that Catholic nationalism has often been as great an oppressor of Irish people, Irish women, as British imperialism or Ulster unionism. Perhaps the equivalent of advanced feminist 'troubling and subverting' is precisely what our nationalist and unionist patriarchal strait-jackets need.

Subversions occur wherever Protestants and Catholics in Ulster evade the binary ideological trap. But we need help from the Republic. I was surprised that Eavan Boland's LIP pamphlet, *A Kind of Scar: The Woman Poet in a National Tradition*, ignored the extent to which the North has destabilized the 'nation'.

Boland holds to unitary assumptions about 'a society, a nation, a literary heritage'. Troubled about 'the woman poet', she takes the 'national tradition' for granted — and perhaps thereby misses a source of her trouble. Because *A Kind of Scar* activates only one pole of its dialectic, it does not evolve the radical aesthetic it promises. By not asking why 'as a poet I could not easily do without the idea of a nation', Boland fails to challenge an idea of Irish poetry which is narrow as well as patriarchal. She refers to 'marginality *within* a tradition' (my italics) and regrets that 'the Irish nation as an existing construct in Irish poetry was not available to me', without considering how that construct itself, both inside and outside poetry, has marginalized and scarred many Irish women and men.

Earlier I suggested that to over-stress the independence of Irish literature from English literature (and vice versa) distorts literary history and does not help contemporary politics. Boland, it seems to me, feels unnecessarily guilty for (as an apprentice poet) having read 'English court poetry' on Achill, and having imitated the English 'Movement' mode of the early sixties. To whom, to what avatar, to what icon is she apologizing?

In fact, it is to Mother Ireland herself. Although Boland criticizes male poets for having made woman a silent object in their visionary odes (to 'Dark Rosaleen. Cathleen Ni Houlihan. The nation as woman: the woman as national muse'), she insists: 'in all this I did not blame nationalism'. Because she does not blame nationalism, her alternative Muse turns out to be the twin sister of Dark Rosaleen etc.: 'the truths of womanhood and the defeats of a nation. An improbable intersection?' No, as Conor Cruise O'Brien said in a similar context, 'a dangerous intersection'. Boland's new muse, supposedly based on the varied historical experience of Irish women, looks remarkably like the sean bhean bhocht.[20] Her pamphlet begins by invoking an old Achill woman who speaks of the Famine. The 'real women of an actual past' are subsumed into a single emblematic victim-figure: 'the women of a long struggle and a terrible survival', 'the wrath and grief of Irish history'. By not questioning the nation, Boland recycles the literary cliché from which she desires to escape.

Boland notes that 'the later Yeats' is a rare exception among poets who 'have feminized the national and nationalized the feminine'. There are good reasons why this should be so. Yeats's early play *Cathleen Ni Houlihan* helped to propagate the feminine mystique of Irish nationalism. During the three years after 1916, in such poems as 'On a Political Prisoner' and the much misunderstood 'A Prayer for my Daughter', he broke the icon his poetry had gilded. That is, he questioned Cathleen as then incarnated by Constance Markievicz and Maud Gonne MacBride.

In 'A Prayer for my Daughter' Yeats criticizes Ireland/Gonne for her 'opinionated mind'. By 'opinion' he always means dogmatic nationalism. So he is revising his image of woman-Ireland-muse, and divining Anorexia in Gonne 'choked with hate':

> Have I not seen the loveliest woman born
> Out of the mouth of Plenty's horn,
> Because of her opinionated mind
> Barter that horn and every good
> By quiet natures understood
> For an old bellows full of angry wind?

That 'old bellows' is already full of destructive clichés. Yeats may be patriarchal in the female qualities he values above ideological rigidity: 'natural kindness', 'heart-revealing intimacy', 'courtesy', 'rootedness'. But it might be argued that at least he replaces the aisling of nationalist male fantasy with a model for the Irish future that draws on (some of) women's own qualities — the 'womanly times' for which Ian McEwan has called.

However, Gonne, Markievicz and Maeve the warrior-queen have enjoyed a new lease of life in northern republican ideology. Perhaps feminists too readily assume that it's *always* a good thing when passive versions of women are transformed into active ones. Both have political uses.

Two passive images are the vulnerable virgin and the mourning mother: images that link Cathleen with Mary. They project the self-image of Catholic nationalism as innocent victim, equally oppressed at all historical periods. (Is there a subconscious admission that Irish men victimize women?) This assigns to Britain the perpetual role of male bully and rapist. In Seamus Heaney's 'Ocean's Love to Ireland': 'The ruined maid complains in Irish.' In the mid-1970s Heaney could still symbolize the northern conflict as 'a struggle between the cults and devotees of a god and a goddess'; between 'an indigenous territorial numen, a tutelar of the whole island, call her Mother Ireland, Cathleen Ni Houlihan . . . the Shan Van Vocht, whatever' and 'a new male cult whose founding fathers were Cromwell, William of Orange and Edward Carson'. To characterize Irish nationalism (only constructed in the nineteenth century) as archetypally female both gives it mythic pedigree and exonerates it from aggressive and oppressive intent. Its patriarchal elements also disappear. Here, perhaps, we glimpse the poetic unconscious of northern nationalism. At the same time, Heaney's mouldering 'Bog Queen' in *North* may indirectly represent the cult of Cathleen as a death-cult. The book contains an unresolved tension between two Muses: a symbolic mummified or mummifying woman (not yet Anorexia) and the warmly creative, life-giving aunt who bakes scones in the poem 'Sunlight'.

While Virgin-Ireland gets raped and pitied, Mother Ireland translates pity into a call to arms and vengeance. She resembles the white-feather-bestowing 'Little Mother' in First-World-War recruiting. Traditionally, it is *her* sons whom Mother Ireland recruits and whose *manhood* she tests. More recently, some of her daughters have also become 'freedom-fighters'. In *Mother Ireland* Bernadette Devlin and Mairead Farrell differed in their attitudes to the personification. Devlin felt that Mother Ireland had empowered her as a strong woman; Farrell said: 'Mother Ireland, get off our backs.' But did she? Is there not collusion between all feminine nationalist images, between Queen Maeve and Mother Ireland, between the feminine-pathetic and the feminine-heroic? The latter too disguises or softens aggression: the looks and dress of Gonne and Markievicz were propaganda-assets. On the cover of the biased *Only The Rivers Run Free: Northern Ireland: The Women's War* a glamorous young paramilitary woman fronts a desperate-looking Sean Bhean.

Such images of Irish women are among those selectively approved by Anorexia. The cover of *Spare Rib* (August 1989) features another: a West Belfast Mother Courage with child in pram, smoke and flames behind her, and insets of a British soldier and 'Stop Strip Searches'. Of course there are many courageous working-class mothers on the Falls — ditto on the Shankill. But does it help them if this magazine distorts the profile of Irish women to include no police or UDR widows; no non-aligned social-workers, doctors or teachers; no members of the DUP; no Belfast or Dublin yuppies; no Southern feminists; no TDs? There are also articles with titles like 'Britain's War on Ireland' and 'Irish in Britain — Living in the Belly of the Beast' (an interesting variation on rape-images: cannibalism? Jonah and the whale?). And a literary section, among other poetic sentimentalities, reprints Susan Langstaff Mitchell's 'To the Daughters of Erin': 'Rise from your knees, O daughters rise! / Our mother still is young and fair . . . Heroes shall leap from every hill . . . The red blood burns in Ireland still'. (Feminism, where are you?) *Spare Rib* has certainly provided the most ludicrous instance yet of the British Left's anachronistic and self-righteous pieties on Ireland. But it's up to Irish women themselves to expose the loaded terms in a statement like: 'In the *Six Counties Irish* women experience *oppression* both as women and as members of a *colonized people*' (my italics). I attended a 'Time To Go' conference in London which offered a seminar on 'Ireland in Feminism'. I think Feminism in Ireland should have something to say about that.

During the Irish revolution nationalist women discovered — though not all acknowledged or cared — that their oppression as women did not end with the Dawning of the Day. The briefly eulogized 'Dáil Girl . . . wielding a cudgel in one hand and a revolver in the other' soon gave way to Dev's ideal of 'life within the home'. Nor had the Dáil girl necessarily taken up her cudgel for Feminism. As a general rule: the more Republican, the less Feminist. The ultra-nationalism of the six women deputies who opposed the Treaty was, in Margaret Ward's words, governed by the 'ghosts of dead sons, husbands and brothers'. Theirs were 'opinionated minds' with no — female? — capacity for compromise, and they set a pattern for the limited participation of women in the Free State/Republic's political life: almost invariably licensed by male relatives, by dynastic privilege. Rosemary Cullen Owens in *Smashing Times* (less romantic than Ward's *Unmanageable Revolutionaries*) brings out the tension between nationalism and suffragism: 'From 1914 onwards, with Home Rule on the statute book, it was the growing separatist movement which created the greatest obstacle to a united women's movement.'

Sinn Féin women (the only women quoted in *Spare Rib*) have recently adopted some feminist ideas. But they cling, like their elder sisters, to the prospective goodwill of republican men, and to the fallacy that: 'there can't be women's liberation until there's national liberation'. Devlin in *Spare Rib* seems significantly wary of 'the gospel according to the holy writ of feminism'. What a woman 'needs to know is that we, her sisters, will catch her if she stumbles, help her find the questions — the answers she must find herself'. Who are 'we, her sisters'? And what kind of élitism lurks in Devlin's assertion (in *Mother Ireland*) that 'the best young feminist women today are those who have come through the experience of the Republican movement'?

While admiring the bonding that tough circum-stances beget, and perceiving these circumstances as tragic, I do not accept that either the supportiveness of the ghetto or the essential survival-strategy in Armagh Gaol affords a model for Irish women in general. The basis of such bonding is tribal rather than sisterly. It remains true that the vast majority of Republican

women come from traditionally Republican families — recruited by and for a patriarchal unit. The Irish women's movement, instead of walking away or vaguely empathizing, might examine the role of nationalist conditioning in all this: the ideological forces which played a part in sending out Mairéad Farrell to be shot.

Contrary to Nell McCafferty, I think that 'feminism and physical force' is self-evidently a contradiction in terms. Years ago a member of the Irish Women's Franchise League said: 'It is our conviction feminism and militarism are natural born enemies and cannot flourish in the same soil.' Militarism, that touch of Madame Defarge, gives the Sinn Féin sisterhood its faintly chilling aura. In *The Demon Lover: On the Sexuality of Terrorism*, Robin Morgan argues that revolutionary terrorism inevitably involves a death-cult. It enacts the quest of the male hero who already 'lives as a dead man'. She asks: 'Why is manhood always perceived as the too-high price of peace?' and notes that when men take over any movement: 'what once aimed for a humanistic triumph now aims for a purist defeat. Martyrdom'. The same syndrome can be detected in Protestant anticipations of Armageddon, apocalypse, their last stand (the ghosts of religious wars walk on both sides). Morgan's conclusion mirrors the Irish nationalist historical pattern: 'The rebel woman in a male-defined state-that-would-be is merely acting out another version of the party woman running for office in the state-that-is.' Unionist party-women have been equally acquiescent in militarism.

Cathleen-Anorexia encourages women to join a male death-cult which has a particularly masochistic martyrology. This cult's rituals deny the 'connectivity' which Morgan sees as the 'genius' of feminist thought: 'In its rejection of the static, this capacity is witty and protean, like the dance of nature itself . . . It is therefore a volatile capacity — dangerous to every imaginable status quo, because of its insistence on *noticing*. Such a noticing involves both attentiveness and recognition, and is in fact a philosophical and activist technique for being in the world, as well as for changing the world.' In 'Easter 1916' Yeats understands that 'Too long a sacrifice / Can make a stone of the heart', and contrasts that stone with 'the living stream'. Surely the chill, the stone, the self-destructiveness at the heart of Irish nationalism shows up in its abuse of women and their gifts of life.

Conclusion: after Anorexia

I have argued that nationalism and unionism in Ireland are dying ideologies, death-cult ideologies. Yet these ideologies are also masks for an intensely local territorial struggle. Ulster's territorial imperative has produced a politics which pivots on male refusal to give an inch. John Hewitt characterizes the Protestant people as 'stubborn'; Seamus Heaney characterizes the Catholic people as 'obstinate'.

But this polarized macho politics travesties the North's cultural complexity. In the report on *Cultural Traditions in Northern Ireland* Brian Turner emphasizes how the thriving local studies movement has 'challenged the "two traditions" terminology'. And Anthony Buckley in 'Collecting Ulster's Culture: Are There Really Two Traditions?', illustrates ways in which culture has been caricatured for the purpose of 'asserting group identities'. A more negative term for this is 'cultural defence'. In fact insecurities underlie the self-assertive rhetorics of both unionism and nationalism. Cultural defence is the reflex of frontier-regions where communities fear extinction or absorption. It explains, for instance, the Catholic Church's not-an-inch attitude to integrated education. And it explains unionism's perennial paranoia about the Irish language (only now to be properly supported and thus depoliticized).

That the Free State's Gaelicization policy attracted more unionist jeers than did Rome Rule indicates fears of ethnic exclusion (and also the counter-productiveness of nationalist ideology). Yet Gaelicization, which attempted an *impossible* separation of Irishness from Britishness, was itself a form of cultural defence. Its errors are reproduced today by Sinn Féin's cultural self-ghettoization. There is a sad element of barren triumphalism in the West Belfast festival.

Locked into dying ideologies, a territorial imperative and cultural defence, Northern Irish people do not immediately hold all the keys to their own salvation. One key is held by the Republic and Britain; another by a slow process of education.

Firstly, only the Republic and Britain together can defuse the mutual fear of their client communities. This should involve the Republic honestly re-examining its own nationalism; making its constitutional claim as inoperative in theory as it is in practice; and adopting the same hands-off stance as the UK government. (John Hume's argument that the British have thereby left matters up to the people of Ireland should be resisted.) Advance depends on an intricately engineered four-wheel drive which engages all parties to the dispute, and which encourages momentum within the North.

Secondly, without education in the broadest sense we cannot loosen the grip of Anorexia, of ideological rigor mortis. Progress will not only stem from official or institutional sources — Education for Mutual Understanding, Co-operation North, putting Cultural Traditions on the curriculum etc. — it occurs wherever people work together practically and constructively. Yet, as with the Irish language, we also need more formal means to dismantle the frameworks of cultural defence.

One pilot-model is the local studies movement. This, at the micro-level, breaks down monolithic versions of nationalist and unionist history. It also maximizes the strength rather than the weakness of Ulster's territorial imperative: attachment to place. Local studies promote the 'noticing' that Robin Morgan values. Many Unionists (the DUP[21] wing) refuse to notice the ground under their own feet, the very territory they claim. Since 1922 they have often imported an anxious, ersatz and self-mutilating Englishness to stand in for Britishness and fend off Irishness. The Campaign for Equal Citizenship (for getting British parties to organize in Northern Ireland) is a recent instance of unionists staring across the water and trying to walk on it. Really, they are motivated by political sulks and cultural defence in the wake of the Anglo–Irish Agreement. Unionist attempts to base themselves in London, like the SDLP inclination to identify with Dublin, show the vital importance of the regionalist concept. Some local councils now lead the way in power-sharing, as local studies do in culture-sharing.

Another model — which gives the lie to equations of the regional with the provincial — is Northern writing, especially since the early 1960s. At the start of this pamphlet I called literature the primary place where language changes and anorexic categories are exposed (not always a conscious process). Writers born into an over-determined, over-defined environment, into a tension between political simplicities and cultural complexity, have felt impelled to redefine: to explore and criticize language, images, categories, stereotypes, myths. Northern writing does not fit the binary shapes cut out by nationalism and unionism. It trellises the harsh girders with a myriad details. It overspills borders and manifests a web of affiliation that stretches beyond any heartland — to the rest of Ireland, Britain, Europe. But the range of styles, histories, myths and influences perhaps could only enter the imagination in this unique zone of 'problems and cleavages' (John Hewitt's phrase). All the 'cultural traditions' count somewhere; nor are the political divisions discounted.

There is a third model in women's groups whose generally pragmatic priorities have theoretical implications. These groups exemplify how we learn and teach by doing. Recently, when the sectarianism of that male-dominated mayhem, Belfast City Council, blocked a grant to the Falls Road Women's Centre, their indignation was shared by the Women's Centre on the Shankill.

The image of the web is female, feminist, 'connective' — as contrasted with male polarization. So is the ability to inhabit a range of relations rather than a single allegiance. The term 'identity' has been coarsened in Ulster politics to signify two ideological package-deals immemorially on offer. To admit to more varied, mixed, fluid and relational kinds of identity would advance nobody's territorial claim. It would undermine cultural defences. It would subvert the male pride that keeps up the double frontier-siege. All this would be on the side of life — like noticing, redefining and again redefining, doing.

Bernard Crick argues:

> While nationalisms are real and authentic in these islands, yet none are as self-sufficient as their adepts claim. In Northern Ireland most people are, in fact, torn in two directions: 'torn', that is, while their political leaders will not recognize that people can, with dignity, face in two directions culturally at once, and refuse to invent political institutions to match. In the world before nation-states such dualities and pluralities were common enough, as in some other border-areas today.
>
> *Irish Review*, 5, Autumn 1988

Both Irish nationalism and Ulster unionism must accept the reality of the North as a frontier-region, a cultural corridor, a zone where Ireland and Britain permeate one another. The Republic should cease to talk about 'accommodating diversity' and face up to duality. This would actually help the North to relax into a less dualistic sense of its own identity: to function, under whatever administrative format, as a shared region of these islands. At which point there will definitely be no such person as Cathleen Ní Houlihan.

References and further reading

Boland, Eavan. *A Kind of Scar: The Woman Poet in a National Tradition.* Dublin: Attic Press (LiP Pamphlet), 1989

Buckley, Anthony. *In the Use of Tradition.* Alan Gailey (ed.) Cultra: Ulster Folk and Transport Museum, 1988

Dawe, Gerald, and Edna Longley (eds.). *Across a Roaring Hill: The Protestant Imagination in Modern Ireland.* Belfast: Blackstaff, 1985

Eagleton, Terry. *Nationalism: Irony and Commitment.* Derry: Field Day Pamphlet No. 13, 1988

Foster, Roy. *Modern Ireland 1600-1972.* London: Allen Lane: The Penguin Press, 1988

Garvin, Tom. *Nationalist Revolutionaries in Ireland 1858-1928.* Oxford: Clarendon Press, 1987

Kearney, Richard. *Across the Frontiers: Ireland in the 1990s.* Dublin: Wolfhound Press, 1989

Morgan, Robin. *The Demon Lover: On the Sexuality of Terrorism.* London: Methuen, 1989

O'Halloran, Clare. *Partition and the Limits of Irish Nationalism: An Ideology Under Stress.* Dublin: Gill and Macmillan, 1987

Owens, Rosemary Cullen. *Smashing Times: A History of the Irish Women's Suffrage Movement, 1889-1922.* Dublin: Attic Press, 1984

Said, Edward. *Yeats and Decolonisation.* Derry: Field Day Pamphlet No. 15, 1988

Turner, Brian. Local Studies Section in *Cultural Traditions in Northern Ireland.* Belfast: Queen's University Institute of Irish Studies, 1989

Ward, Margaret. *Unmanageable Revolutionaries.* Dingle: Brandon Press/London: Pluto Press, 1983

1   1641: Irish rebellion by Catholic Gaelic Irish against English domination of Ireland. 1690: William of Orange defeated the Catholics under James II at the Battle of the Boyne in July 1690.

2   Social Democratic and Labour Party, a nationalist party in Northern Ireland, led by John Hume.

3   In 1908 the Catholic Church under a decree entitled *Ne Temere* declared mixed marriages between Protestant and Catholic not solemnized by the Church null and void.

4   Leader of the Irish Volunteers. In March/April 1916 he tried to prevent the Easter Rising and sent Eimar O'Duffy to Belfast to quash the insurgency there.

5   First published in 1989.

6   Sports stadium in Dublin, venue for international rugby union.

7   Irish: couple of words.

8   The New Ireland Forum report (the Forum was set up in May 1983 to canvass opinion in the Republic) suggested three possibilities for discussion: a unitary state, a federal/confederal state, joint sovereignty.

9   Irish: fountainhead of tradition.

10 Irish: Irish-speaker.

11 Douglas Hyde: Founder of the Gaelic League in the 1890s.

12 Leading Irish poet in nineteenth century, author of *Lays of the Western Gael and Other Poems* (1864), the epic poem *Congal* (1872), and *Poems* (1880).

13 Ulster Defence Association, Protestant paramilitary organization.

14 Irish Taoiseach at the time.

15 Republican stronghold.

16 Controversial killing of three members of the IRA in Gibraltar in 1988.

17 Anglo-Irish Agreement signed at Hillsborough in November 1985 between Prime Minister Thatcher and Garret Fitzgerald, the Irish Taoiseach.

18 Thomas McCarthy: Author of *The Sorrow Garden* (1981), which includes a sequence of poems on de Valera, and *The Non-Aligned Storyteller* (1984).

19 First performed in 1989.

20 Irish: poor old woman, traditional image of Ireland, the Shan Van Vocht.

21 Democratic Unionist Party.

PATRICK GALVIN

from Patrick Galvin, *Song For A Poor Boy: A Cork Childhood* (1990)

Patrick Galvin's autobiography provides a memorable picture of life in a poor area of Cork. Here is the scene he recreates after the death of his mother, a moment of revelation for the boy as he adjusts to the changed relationship with his father and learns of his uncle's part in the Easter Rising.

Chapter 29

On an evening shortly after my mother's death, my father knelt on the floor of the bedroom they had shared throughout their married life and prayed for her soul. Her photograph stood on the table beside the bed. Her shoes, recently polished, lay under the bed, and her black shawl still hung from a nail behind the bedroom door.

When my father had finished praying for my mother, he rose to his feet and stood for a moment looking down at the white mourning-sheet now stretched across the bed. He had made the bed. He had swept the floor and moved all his personal belongings into a small room at the rear of the house. Nothing more remained to be done. My mother was dead. My father left the room, locked the door securely behind him and never entered the bedroom again.

Six months later, my father moved his belongings from the room at the rear of the house into the kitchen. He locked the back door, slept near the kitchen fire and, like his mother before him, refused to leave the house.

'It will see me out,' he said. 'We were married here. She died here. It will see me out.'

He sat by the fire, close to the bed, his personal belongings scattered about him.

'She left the rosary beads to you,' he continued. 'I don't know why. Sure you don't believe in anything.'

'I'd still like to have them,' I said.

'They're hanging on the wall. You can have that tin whistle, too. I don't play it anymore.'

'I'm sorry to hear that.'

'Nothing to be sorry about. Everything goes in the end.'

He reached up and removed the tin whistle from its place above the mantelpiece. It was covered in dust.

'I haven't cleaned it. I haven't cleaned anything in here. Mrs Barratt comes in sometimes, but you know what she's like.'

He handed me the tin whistle and moved closer to the fire. On the dresser beside him, his photograph, framed in gilt, was also covered in dust.

'You can have that, if you want to,' he said. 'There's nothing else I can give you.'

His image smiled through the dust on the photograph and, in his British Army uniform, he looked brave and soldierly.

'India blest me,' he said. 'Did I tell you that? Reached down to my soul and blest me. Your mother didn't understand that.'

'She married you.'

'We married each other,' he said and lapsed into silence.

Presently, he rose to his feet and moved over to the sideboard. He opened the drawer and removed a small box with a broken hinge. He raised the lid and stared down at the medal resting inside.

'You'd better have that, too,' he said. 'It belonged to her brother.'

'I didn't know she had a brother,' I said. 'What happened to him?'

My father looked at me for a moment and handed me the box. 'He died in jail,' he said. 'What else would you expect?'

He turned away, moved over to the bed and sat on the edge of it. I read the inscription on the medal: *Seachtain Na Cásca*[1] — 'Politics,' he said. 'Politics and remembrance. They bleed us dry.'

'You had the two days,' I said.

'Yes. We had the two days. And I'm grateful for that. Maybe we'll have two more in the next world. I pray we do. But you don't believe in things like that, do you?'

'I'll hang on to the medal,' I said.

'And the other things? The photograph, the rosary beads and my tin whistle?'

'Those, too.'

'You're odd,' he said. 'I said that on the day you were born. You haven't changed. Your mother was the same. Odd as bedamned — and a champion of lost causes.'

'You were some champion yourself,' I said.

'Yes, wasn't I? Some champion. And I washed my face in the Ganges. Not many can say that.'

'Not many.'

He lowered his head, covered his face with his hands and remained there for a little while, waiting for the dark.

1   Easter Week.

GERRY CONLON
from Gerry Conlon, *Proved Innocent* (1990)

Gerry Conlon (1964-   ) was brought up on the Falls Road in Belfast, ran away to London as a teenager, returned home, and then moved back and forth over a number of years between England and Belfast, drifting in and out of petty crime, working on building sites. *Proved Innocent*, which was made into a film by Jim Sheridan, *In the Name of the Father*, is Conlon's wrenching account of what happened when he became one of the Guildford Four, wrongly accused of planting IRA bombs outside two pubs in Guildford in 1974 which killed five people. His autobiography, none of which can be read with an easy conscience by those who believe in British justice, contains a record of the fifteen years he spent in prison before being released in 1989. Here in this chapter Conlon recalls his first days in Wandsworth at the start of his sentence.

Wandsworth

The Category A van crossed London Bridge and drove south-west through Elephant and Castle. We didn't know where we were going because that's the policy: Category A prisoners on the move are never told their destination. I prayed it would be Brixton. I accepted I would never again sit in the comparative comfort of a remand wing, but at least in Brixton I would be near to my father.

The prison convoy trundled down Kennington Park Road until it reached the Oval cricket ground. So far so good. But now, instead of branching left down Brixton Road, we kept straight on towards Clapham and that was it — it wasn't Brixton. I saw Paul[1] mouth the name the same moment I thought it: Wandsworth. Anybody who'd even done a day's remand knew that the two hardest prisons in the system were Manchester's Strangeways and London's Wandsworth. Both were militant strongholds of the Prison Officers' Association, and in both the POA had the final say in everything that happened. It was in these places the system preferred to incarcerate all the toughest cons.

We arrived in the courtyard and Paul and I were taken out. The A van did not stay long, but immediately drove away with Paddy[2] still inside. I later found out he went to the Scrubs.

I was apprehensive as two screws marched me into the reception area. As an already convicted man, Paul had been kept here all through the trial, so for him there was no formality. He picked up his box with his prison clothes, changed and was whisked off within a matter of minutes. I was left standing at the desk.

There were cons[3] sitting around on benches, probably waiting to be processed, but they made a nice little audience for the pantomime the screws now put on. Your man handed over my Category A book to the reception screw, who was sitting behind a sort of

lectern, like you might read a text from in chapel. He never looked up, he just said, 'Empty your pockets, Irish bastard.'

I was frightened and just froze. So now he did look at me, a look of loathing.

'I said empty your fucking pockets.'

I took out a two-ounce tin of tobacco, two packets of cigarettes and a box of matches and put them on the desk. He picked up the tin and, holding it far from his face like it contained excrement, prized it open. Then he poured its contents into the waste-paper basket beside him and replaced the tin on the table. Next he picked up the cigarettes and very deliberately crushed them, wringing the packets between his hands. These, too, he dropped into the bin.

'Get your clothes off.'

I undressed and he made me stand there in front of him while he wrote down all my details very slowly. After a while his nostrils started flaring. He yelled out of the side of his mouth: 'Fill a bath for this bastard. He needs a wash.'

One of the cons started giggling and I could hear water rushing into a bath somewhere near as they took my fingerprints. Then a towel was slung at me and four screws marched me through to the bathroom. It was a big old enamel bathtub, full almost up to the brim.

'There's your bath, get in.'

I put my foot over to the side and into the water. It did not just feel cold, it felt somewhere close to freezing. I snatched out my foot and looked at them. But they snapped, 'Get in that fucking bath and wash yourself.'

I set my teeth, eased my body into the cold water and started rubbing my skin miserably with a bar of disgusting prison soap. The four screws stood over me laughing and joking about it. By the time they let me out my teeth were chattering.

The clothing scene was reminiscent of Winchester,[4] but far worse. The underpants were like a pair of Stanley Matthews's[5] old football shorts, and there was a long cream-coloured vest and a shirt. The shirt was obviously built for the Incredible Hulk, it had at least a size 19 collar. If the wind had caught me inside it I'd have been blown over the wall. I wrapped myself in this tent and reached for the trousers.

I had at the time a slim waist of only twenty-eight inches. These trousers were thirty-eights. I rolled up the bottoms and stuffed the huge excess of shirt-tails into the top, but it made no difference. I rolled the waistband over until it looked like I had a punctured lifebelt round my waist. But the trousers still hung loosely round my hips. If I took a few steps they began to slide towards the floor.

Finally I was given shoes two sizes too big and a denim jacket and returned to the desk. There was no question of me marching now, I shuffled along. The cons and the screws thought it was hilarious. I got my cell card (a red card, as I was a Catholic, which I had to hang on my door) and was loaded up with the kit: bedding roll, basin, plates, plastic knife, fork and spoon, jug and cup, pot.

'Come on.'

As always, it was one screw in front and one behind. I followed the one in front as best I could, but after twenty yards I had to stop, put down the bundle and hitch up the trousers. Then I went on, trying to hold on to the trousers as well as the kit. So I started dropping things. We made another twenty yards like this until the leading screw unlocked a gate and we were inside a wing.

There were cons milling around everywhere on the floor of the wing, and we had to weave our way through them. At first they were laughing and pointing at this Charlie Chaplin character as I tried to balance my bundle and keep my trousers up at the same time. But then it turned nasty: one of them recognized me.

'That's that murdering IRA bastard.'

There was pandemonium. They were shrieking insults at me, dancing in front of me and yelling abuse, and I was shuffling along in this ridiculous way. Somehow I got down that wing, literally having to hold myself together.

There's a spot in Wandsworth known as the Centre, a circular hall acting like a hub from which the wings radiate. I didn't know it, but the floor of this Centre is kept shined up at all times for visitors and it's an absolute taboo to walk into the middle of this polished floor. So now we were in the Centre and the screw just said, 'Straight on.'

So I wandered straight across the middle, hardly able to see where I was going with this bundle in front of me, and the screw just screamed at me, 'GET OFF THE CENTRE, YOU FUCKING BASTARD!'

I didn't know what he meant. He'd said 'straight on'. So I stood there, revolving stupidly, trying to see what the trouble was. The screw leaped across and yanked me towards the edge of the floor.

'You never, ever, EVER walk across the floor, stupid git. That floor is sacred. You walk round the edge, always round the edge, got it?'

I just nodded my head, wishing this sacred floor would open up and I could disappear into it. I didn't dare speak in case I burst into tears.

'OK. Now go on, that way.'

Then I was taken straight into the punishment block on E Wing.

I shouldn't have been on the block at Wandsworth at all if two Irish prisoners, Gerry Hunter of the Birmingham Six and another called Mick Sheehan, hadn't been attacked in one of the workshops by another prisoner. The governor then decided it wasn't safe for prisoners convicted of IRA offences to mix with other men on the Category A block. So he simply put us in solitary confinement on the punishment block.

I was put in the cell about five o'clock. I dumped my kit and looked around. There wasn't much to see, just another dirty, dingy, stinking cell, the same filthy grime in the corners, the same graffiti, the same spilled food on the floor, the same smears of blood on the walls.

I was tired and drained, but not sleepy. Slowly I made up my bed and got out my radio and listened to what they were saying about us on the news. We were the headline story, the longest sentences ever handed out for murder, all that. They brought me some kind of watery stew which I couldn't eat. I only had a piece of bread and jam. Then I returned the radio to a football commentary, Real Madrid against Derby County. I lay down and tried to concentrate on the match, anything to distract me.

Then they put my lights out, and it was only seven o'clock. I shivered, still cold from the bath but also from delayed shock. I was listening, trying to listen, to the commentator's voice, but it was so unreal. I got to bed and lay there with the radio on trying not to think.

I was woken by the heavy toe of a screw's boot kicking the door.

'Get out of bed, you Irish bastard. And make sure you make the bed after you.'

It was still dark outside and the floor was cold as ice. I was making the bed when the screw opened me up.

'Slop out, one trip.'

This meant I had to carry everything together, pot, basin, water-jug. I did it clumsily under the eyes of the screw, spilling water on the floor.

After breakfast they came in and made me rip the bedclothes off my bed. I was handed a sheet of paper with a diagram on it, showing exactly how to fold them and how to place them on the mattress: sheet, blanket, sheet, blanket, pillowcase, bedspread. It had to be done in that precise way and I spent the next half hour all thumbs, struggling to fold each sheet and blanket correctly.

Then I used up some time looking out the window, a view with nothing much to see — grey prison buildings and a grey sky — but a view I would soon know in every minute detail, brick by brick, slate by slate. Suddenly the door came flying open and a new voice barked at me.

'Name and number to the Governor.'

It was the chief prison officer, on governor's rounds, and I stepped down and started towards the door to meet him. Suddenly the governor himself swept around the corner and into the cell. The only thing I had time to register was his belly. It stuck out in front of him, as if artificially inflated, and now he came in so quickly I couldn't get out of the way. So I cannoned off this hard, massive stomach and was knocked backwards into the cell. He glowered down at me.

'You little bastard, Conlon. You didn't get the right sentence yesterday. You should have hanged, you know that?'

I shrank back. This enormous figure frightened the daylights out of me, otherwise I might have laughed. If you could have found the plug in him and pulled it out I swear he'd have gone up — 'zzzzzz' — away into the sky like a punctured balloon. Instead he swivelled on his heel and marched out.

I had already been wondering which cell Paul Hill was in, but by dinner time it already made no difference. I was told he'd gone that morning, moved to another prison. I didn't see him again for two years. I did see Gerry Hunter, though. He was collecting his dinner and he looked terribly nervous, like a rabbit that had a car's headlights shone in its eyes. He seemed half frozen by fear. We just nodded heads to each other and went back in with our dinners.

I saw Gerry Hunter again on exercise, though that afternoon I went out first on my own. I must try to describe this ordeal. The exercise yard was a small triangular space bounded by the block, the Catholic chapel, and D Wing where all the other long-term

prisoners were. It was probably only about ten yards from one end to the other, with a small ditch or dry moat running around the edge at the foot of the buildings, then grass within that and a circle of paving stones in the middle. It was claustrophobic to be in there, like I was walking around at the bottom of a well, so terribly aware of these clown's clothes I was wearing, and all these windows above with men's faces peering down.

Ten minutes later they brought out Mick Sheehan and Gerry Hunter, looking as nervous as I felt. The screws on exercise appeared completely terrifying, quite deliberately hoping to look something like the Waffen SS. The highly polished peaks of their caps came down at a steep angle over their eyes, they wore black leather gloves and would watch us in silence, never moving, never speaking except to bark an order. They made us walk in a circle five yards apart, and wouldn't let us talk.

Suddenly I heard a voice calling down from one of the windows.

'Irish scumbags.'

Then another: 'You should have been hung.'

Something fell and bounced off the grass into the little moat. I saw it was a PP9 battery[6] and it hadn't fallen, it was thrown.

'Hey, Conlon! Only twenty-nine years, three hundred and sixty-four days to go.'

Another missile came down. It was a jam jar. It smashed in the moat and when I looked I saw they had filled it with shit. Loads of batteries, bottles, jars filled with shit and urine, rained down on us.

I turned to the screws.

'Hey! Can't you see what's happening?'

But they stood motionless staring straight ahead, smirking a little. We had to keep walking.

This was exercise. It normally lasted an hour, every day.

In the next fifteen years, I was to spend a total of just over three years in solitary confinement. Unless you have experienced it, it is a difficult thing to explain or describe — the loneliness, isolation and vulnerability. Your cell is a bubble of silence, where the only noises are the ones you make yourself. If you have a radio it soon shrinks into a background buzz, because you spend so much time listening to the beat of your own thoughts. It's like being walled in a tomb.

You pace the cell, walk up and down quickly at first, then more slowly, measuring out the steps. Seventeen and a half feet from window to door, nine and a half feet from wall to wall. You read and read the tiny names scribbled on the walls, you talk to those names, have dialogues with them, give them faces and imagine the crimes they must have committed to get themselves in here. Some of them, though, must have been innocent like you . . . Emotionally, I was in an absolute muddle. It was probably the hardest jigsaw puzzle that anybody could ever put together. I didn't understand the emotional state I was in, that I was in trauma. Confusion, an identity crisis — everything. Profound guilt was the hardest to come to terms with because I knew I had played a major part in my own downfall by signing statements and accepting total responsibility for what happened to my father. Trying to come to terms with those things at my age was too great to handle. And always self-pity is lying in wait, to descend on you without warning, making you cry to yourself, 'Why me?'

Self-pity and silence are the two enemies. You go to the window because it's a source of sounds. You can hear prisoners talking dimly, distantly, over in D Wing. You strain to catch what they're saying, as if you could take part in the chat. But you can't, it's too far. In the morning there's the sound of the sparrows, and prisoners throwing stale bread out to them. They chirp to each other and even from that you're feeling excluded.

If you're not at the window you're at the door, ear pressed to the crack, trying to eavesdrop, to catch the sound of what people are saying, to catch what's happening and remind yourself you're part of a larger system. There are other people in other cells going through the same thing you're going through. You try to hang on to that. They haven't just locked *you*, 462779 Gerry Conlon, up in this box, dropped the key down a grating somewhere and forgotten you. They haven't kept this place as a living burial chamber just for you.

And then, for long periods, your brain shuts down and you just sit looking at the wall. Then you stop noticing time go by, which can be the most frightening thing of all.

That night after tea at seven, just like the night before, my light went off. I looked out the window and saw other lights still blazing in D Wing, so I knew this was special treatment: longer hours of darkness for the Irish bastards on the block. I put myself to bed and tried to sleep.

I lay there thinking about our trial — what went wrong, whether, how and when it could ever be put right. I wondered if Paddy Maguire's[7] belief in British justice had been dented at all by the verdict. And I thought of my father, who came over to England to help me and got caught up in this foul, shameful mess. He was coming up for his own trial in three months' time but, after what happened to us, what hope could he have?

These were the thoughts dragging miserably through my head when, suddenly, the cell door swung open. A screw stood there framed by the light.

'Get up, Conlon. Visitors.'

1   Paul Hill, one of the Guildford Four.
2   Paddy Armstrong, another of the Guildford Four.
3   Convicts.
4   Prison where Conlon was held on remand from December 1974 until March 1975.
5   Famous footballer, played for Blackpool 1947–61 at a time when long shorts were the norm.
6   Batteries were used in planting bombs.
7   The Maguire Seven, including Gerry's uncle Paddy Maguire and Gerry's father, were (wrongly) implicated in the Guildford Bomb and found guilty of possessing nitroglycerine in March 1976. By that time Paddy Maguire's belief in British justice (he had served in the British Army and had become in Gerry's word 'Anglicized') had disappeared. There is an interview with Annie Maguire who spent ten years in prison in Rita Wall (ed.), *Leading Lives: Irish Women in Britain* (1991). For the moving story of her own arrest and imprisonment see Anne Maguire, *Why Me? One Woman's Fight for Justice and Dignity* (1990).

GERALD DAWE
from *The Irish Review*, Autumn 1990

Gerald Dawe (1952–   ), poet and critic, was born in Belfast into a Protestant family and now lectures at TCD. His poetry includes *Sheltering Places* (1978) and *Sunday School* (1991), his criticism *Against Piety* (1995). Taking his cue from O'Faolain's 'Fifty Years of Irish Writing' (1962), Dawe here provides a sharp analysis of the state of contemporary poetry in Ireland.

Anecdotes over a Jar

The lesson of our time is that Irish writers cannot any longer go on writing about Ireland, or for Ireland within the narrow confines of the traditional Irish life-concept; it is too slack, too evasive, too untense.

Seán Ó Faoláin, 'Fifty Years of Irish Writing',[1]
Studies, 1962

I was in Holland in 1981 with Richard Murphy,[2] on a reading tour, and in Amsterdam we were separately interviewed. The keen radio interviewer wanted me to talk about 'vio-lence' and 'pol-it-ic-al repression' and later on, in a taxi, I heard my own voice, with estranged *gravitas*,[3] struggling to answer him. It was obvious that the good Dutch radio man had clear ideas about Ireland and wanted to have them confirmed in double-quick time before moving on to the next item — William Burroughs, if I am not mistaken, who was sitting in a marble-like pool of silence, cane-in-hand and Trilby hat, like a spectral clerk of works.

It was my first experience of the weight of assumption and expectation which bears upon the two words 'Irish Poet'. Five years later, in a packed hotel in Sydney, for the city's Poetry Festival, the sign on the door revealed 'Irish Poet' reading along with Les Murray and Tom Murphy. Through the steamy night, lots of people milled in and out but, half-way through my stint, a (drunken) voice came from the back of the hall: 'You're not following in the footsteps of Heaney.' This question, complaint or statement (I was never sure which), was patently true since I stood reading my own poems and they had little to do with Seamus Heaney's. But I understood and sympathized with what the man meant.

Probably an expatriate, here he was amongst a mixed bunch of 'ex-pats' of all kinds and on stage was this poet, from Ireland mark you, reading poems *not* about the Ireland he knew, or thought he knew: Ó Faoláin's 'traditional life-concept'. And, if you weren't insulted, the poet was actually talking about Edward Carson,[4] for Christ's sake, and little towns in the north no one ever heard of. What he was hearing simply did not *fit* and he was having none of it.

Another quirky illustration might be sufficient to indicate the weight of expectation that lies upon this notion of the Irish poet, whether at home or abroad. It is a fascinating subject in itself since its powerful influence, particularly *via* the States, has rarely been touched upon by critics of writing from Ireland.

Quite recently, I met an EC[5] literary journalist accompanied by an avid Irish intellectual trend-spotter.

In the brief exchange, I was asked for an opinion on several questions: about 'the loss of Irish', colonial history, identity crises, and the role of women writers in modern Ireland. This menu of issues, of which I had personally little experience, amounted to an agenda and it became crystal-clear that *poetry* had very little to do with it except to serve as a springboard for someone else's flights of fancy. Irish poets were influenced by Irish poets and Irish history, O.K. Game, set and match. As for Europe . . .?

When I muttered something about coming from a Protestant background in Belfast and living in the west of Ireland, a professional smile glazed over what remained of their time. Critical comment on that background, indeed, on any sense of alternative influences, arguments or literary ideals, went out the window, *pronto*. May as well talk about green blackbirds.

Three random experiences. But behind them there are other conversations and impressions which illustrate the kind of busy and processed responses poets in Ireland must resist in their work if they are to remain truly themselves as artists. There is, and probably always has been, a shifting agenda of themes and issues which 'Irish' literature is seen as addressing. In the 1970s, for instance, it was 'The North'; in the 1980s it was 'Women' and 'Regionalist Writing', and speculatively, the 1990s could well see the received wisdom switch back to 'The South' again.

These crude generalizations are nevertheless influential both in a popular sense and in strict terms of criticism (i.e. what gets written about) as they underpin certain kinds of public space and esteem (i.e. recognition) in which the individual poet lives and writes.

The story goes that Ireland is coming down with poets. Certainly, it is much *easier* to have a poem or collection of poetry published in Ireland today than it was, say, twenty years ago. This is a 'good thing' but what it really means in artistic and critical terms is another matter. All too easily, the books go unheeded in the literary pages of the newspapers and the few literary journals cannot hope to keep pace. Giving readings is more important than reading and the undiscriminating media happily obliterate the work of art in a haze of well-meaning publicity surrounding this writer or that and their ability to make themselves and/or their writing 'accessible', 'controversial' and so forth. Where is the artistic daring, one asks, as the poem evaporates? Literary standards are equated with *élitism* or derided as academic when really it is 'period styles' that should be criticized — outdated or hackneyed themes; stale language; flat rhetoric; predictable feelings. Could there be, for instance, an equivalent version of Alvarez's *New Poetry*,[6] the publication of which in the mid-1960s (with the brilliant Jackson Pollock *Convergence* as cover) challenged so many imaginations and critical sensibilities, both old and new? Or of Donald Hall's updated version of Michael Roberts's *Faber Book of Modern Verse* whose presence on 'A' level courses throughout Britain and Northern Ireland during the late 1960s enlightened an entire generation of poets and readers in a handful of years, along with the marvellous BBC Radio school programmes on poetry accompanied by their extraordinary texts? By comparison with these, the *Penguin Book of Contemporary British* (or *Irish*) *Poetry*[7] seems a fairly tame affair, yet the late 1970s and 1980s really mark an epoch in which poets and poetry became *sexy*, an acceptable career-move with its own structure of blandishments, self-promotion and sales-pitch at a time, ironically, of economic recession, political meanness and cultural bonanza. Is there a poet of the 1990s for whom one will wait as one did in the 1970s for Derek Mahon's *Lives* or *The Snow Party*? If there are such names, the territory around them is much more hotly disputed than seemed either natural or decent in the late '60s and '70s to at least one reader of poetry.

But to go back to that term 'academic'. As someone who flits between two worlds — of trying to live as a writer and also help keep a roof over my family's heads through teaching — the extent to which the life of the intelligence is belittled in Ireland often in support of the imagination never fails to surprise me. Indeed ignorance of the poetic traditions of writing is sometimes seen as a guarantee and index of artistic integrity. This perverse and deeply damaging notion is related to the persistent, bathetic belief in the poetic 'personality' as a hero.

The problem is the basic uncertainty about the *value* of contemporary literary work whereas the public role and social occasion of its expression are more eagerly assimilated in the Irish literary culture. This avoids the awkward, time-consuming business of assessing, questioning, considering and vindicating artistic worth which becomes a matter of anecdotes over a jar.

As in our politics, personality is inflated with meaning and thence to the ghastly patronage of 'the character'. It is amazing, too, how many writers, including younger ones, seem to connive at this recognition. The main thrust of our generalizations about art, writing and the imagination (all such vague, abstract words in comparison with the homely 'saying' of a poem) reflect this unease. For in some deep-seated

fashion poets in Ireland must not take their work seriously. The point of recognition is to be perceived *as a writer*, somewhere between priest (vocation) and vagabond (dislocation) — reverence and piety — but the cost this exacts as regards reality is colossal. This is where the myth of the 'Irish Poet' intercedes, bolstered very often by archaic ideas and misconceptions about the country as a whole. For example, Irish writers are *not*, generally speaking, badly done by; their work *is* published relatively easily; there *are* various venues, festivals, art-centres, magazines, television and radio programmes interested in promoting and conferring reputations on people as poets. The Arts Councils *do* fork out bursaries and other monies. Aosdána[8] pays people to concentrate upon their writing. UK and US reading circuits, publishers, universities and so on, *are* receptive to Irish poets. In other words, as poets we do not actually suffer directly from repression, political violence, the loss of our language . . .

Yet for all that there *is* the sense of claustrophobia, of a kind of repressiveness bedded in the culture and internalized by those writers conscious of their 'privileged' position within Irish society and troubled by both sets of circumstances. Familiarity may well breed a contempt of sorts when there is not sufficient *critical* respect given to the art of poetry. And there is, too, the business of just how independent writers in Ireland can be, given the close ties between the writing establishment, the state and the commercial world.

Who is looking at the effects and influences of this liaison upon standards in the arts? Does it lead to conformity or artistic compromise with a view to what gets bought, read or produced? Who are the people in Ireland entrusted with promoting standards in the literary or visual arts? What do we know of them; what are their qualifications in fulfilling such creative, editorial or judgemental roles?

Great hatred, little room?[9] Not quite — more like anxiety, that verges on neurosis, surrounding the social and political orthodoxies and conformism of a culture which is still morally and artistically unsure of itself. It is a culture, moreover, which is contradictorily ambivalent about its *need* for recognition from other cultures, particularly English and American, and peculiarly conscious of having to live up to *their* expectations of what it is, along with the sort of things we are meant to write about it.

I think of Seán Ó Faoláin again, of his isolation too, and a further passage from 'Fifty Years of Irish Writing' which opened these notes, where, with a characteristic flourish, he remarked:

It is a matter of bravely and clearsightedly accepting the tensions of one's own being, or relentlessly challenging the life about one with their sharpest questions, of looking, then, far and wide, in time and place, for others who have been in some like conflict ... saying to them, 'That was how it seemed to you! Here is how it strikes me,' and seize one's pen, *for them* and one's self.

1   This essay is reproduced above p. 740.
2   Author of *Sailing to an Island* (1963), *The Battle of Aughrim* (1968) and *High Island* (1974), all fine collections

3   Latin: seriousness.
4   Leader of the Ulster Unionist Party in 1912 and leader of the Ulster Volunteer Force in 1914, implacably opposed to Home Rule.
5   European Community.
6   Published in 1962 by Penguin.
7   Edited by Blake Morrison and Andrew Motion, published in 1982.
8   An organization established in 1983 by the Arts Council in Ireland to honour and support writers, artists, and musicians.
9   Phrases from Yeats's poem 'Remorse for Intemporate Speech'.

SEÁN Ó TUAMA
from *Krino*, 11, Summer 1991 (trans. A. Mac Póilín)

Seán Ó Tuama (1926–), poet, playwright and critic, here provides a useful survey of contemporary Irish verse. This is an expanded English-language version of his Introduction to *Coiscéim na hAoise Seo* (1990), an anthology of twentieth-century Irish-language poetry recently published by Coiscéim.

Twentieth–Century Poetry in Irish

Irish was the language of the mass of the Irish people for some two thousand years up to the middle of the nineteenth century. Only in the second half of that century, following three hundred years of planned military, economic and cultural pressures, did English become the dominant vernacular of the country. By this time also literature in English began to replace literature in Irish as the national literature of Ireland. The nineteenth century then is the century when literature in Irish, for the first time since recorded history, lost its status and dynamism.

Between the years 1880 and 1921 an extraordinary national resurgence took place. With the founding of an Irish Free-State in 1921 the Irish language gained new status, and since that time the number of people who declare themselves to have a reasonable knowledge of Irish continues to grow. There are now more than a million people in the Republic, out of a population of over three million, who claim to be able to read and/or speak Irish at a moderate level of competence. That figure, of course, must greatly exaggerate the number of people who, in fact, do communicate — even sporadically — with other people through the medium of Irish. On the other

hand only a quarter of the population report themselves as having no knowledge of Irish. Moreover the level of claimed Irish language competence is found uniformly throughout the greater part of the country. Even in Dublin, where in Joyce's time not more than a few thousand people would claim knowledge of Irish, the figure now stands at more than a quarter of a million.

Favourable statistics regarding competence, and still more favourable statistics regarding attitudinal support, are not good indicators, however, of the position of Irish as an everyday spoken language in the country as a whole. Indeed Irish is rarely heard as a normal spoken language, a language of daily routines, except in the minute Gaeltacht[1] areas, in which the number of Irish speakers continues to decline catastrophically: in fact the numbers have declined since 1921 at approximately the same rate as they declined in the nineteenth century under British rule. In these areas there are now no monoglot speakers; English as well as Irish is used in everyday affairs. A certain stabilization in the linguistic position in the Gaeltacht may have been achieved in recent years with the establishment of a vital community radio (and the promise of a television station), as well as a successful programme of industrialization. The next twenty years will finally reveal whether the last traditional Irish-speaking communities in Ireland are going to survive. As it is, the picture is very black indeed: only 1-2% of the population of Ireland, some 35,000-60,000 people, speak Irish as a community language today in the Gaeltacht areas.

Viewed against this general linguistic and cultural background, modern poetry in Irish is quite a remarkable phenomenon. For so disadvantaged a language, the amount and quality of verse produced is astonishing. Rarely, in a short period of years, does any language, even the most flourishing, produce a significant concentration of poets with substantial creative talent. It is all the more surprising then that in this century so many talented poets are writing in a language that has been in danger of extinction since the middle of the 19th century. From this anthology it is evident that we consider three, at least, of these poets, Máirtín Ó Direáin, Seán Ó Ríordáin and Nuala Ní Dhomhnaill,[2] to have gifts of a very high order.

Máirtín Ó Direáin is undoubtedly the stylist *par excellence* among modern Irish writers. From both the living language of the Gaeltacht and literary sources he has forged an elegant and polished mode of speech: everything he has written bears the seal of a master-stylist. Ó Direáin was the first Irish poet to speak in a recognizable contemporary voice to the generation which came after the founding of the State. His early work was an innocent lyric celebration of traditional life and values: a challenging bitterness — and a newly developed hard-edged style — protesting against how modern materialist, urban society has reneged on these values, surfaced later. His best poetry from beginning to end grows from his naïve vision of life in his native Aran Islands. There is a tendency towards sentimentality throughout his work, however, not only in idealizing the lost paradise of his youth — a tendency common in the work of many artists — but in idealizing the entire life of his Aran island as Paradise. This prevents him from dealing at a deeper level with that world, or any other world, or indeed with himself: he has been unable to take a major leap into the dark, into the dark of Aran, or his own personal dark. As a result, his work as a whole lacks incisive insights and a certain substantiality. Despite this, however, there are among his work some of the most delicate and appealing lyrics in modern Irish.

On the other hand, Seán Ó Ríordáin has agonized unendingly — sometimes even humorously — about his own personal dilemmas of faith and conscience. His entire work reflects his struggle to try to understand his own frustrations and half-hidden insights about the world and himself. This gives his poetry an overwhelming sense of search: at times a restless and agonized search, sometimes a witty intellectual search that can lean too much, perhaps, in the direction of philosophic theorizing. Though he did not compose nearly as much as Ó Direáin, there is substance and fine craftmanship in his work, particularly in a series of dark, beautifully crafted lyrics, full of a unique imagery. In these, the poet is often overwhelmed by a kind of terror, the terror of a sick and isolated individual who senses that the evil forces of the mad-house of this world are set to destroy him. These poems of sickness, death, loneliness and frustration bear an overwhelming taste of the abyss to which he obviously fears he will be consigned. In the conflict between the poet's chaotic feelings and the rigid dogmatic society in which he lived, we come on some of the most authentic insights available to us into postwar Ireland. In developing these insights Ó Ríordáin has integrated fundamental aspects of European Catholic or post-Catholic sensibility with Irish tradition in a new way. His work, the greater part of which is not yet adequately translated, is not in any noticeable way influenced by Yeats or by any other Irish poet writing in English; and, of English-language poets, only the modern, consciously Christian writers, Hopkins and Eliot, have left their mark. He is best read with some of the classic European poets Baudelaire, Rilke or Ponge. Above all other writers of Irish, Ó Ríordáin has brought modern literature in Irish back into the mainstream European tradition.

Nuala Ní Dhomhnaill may still be at an early stage of her development, but already she has produced an opus which confirms her as one of the major poets of this century. Her poetry published to date is evidence of an overflowing feminine nature, yet is not in any conscious way a plea for women's rights or a proclamation of the freedom of modern woman. Freedom for her is the freedom to express her own turbulent psyche. Her need for the life of the senses — children and lovers, flora and fauna — is evident throughout her work. There is a rich diversity, an immediacy, and a daring honesty in all her verse. She explores folktales and mythological concepts in a remarkable effort to comprehend her own contemporary femininity, which she finds both highly attractive and highly repellent. Although she does not have the same sense of style Ó Direáin has, or Seán Ó Ríordáin's wrought craftmanship, her sweeping grasp of this explosive misshapen world — life as it is rather than as it was or could be — can be clearly seen in her poetry.

Each of these three poets has a particular personal sensibility out of which special insights emanate, and each can *create* these insights through their art (as opposed to 'reporting' them: I am thinking here of Ó Ríordáin's use of the word 'insint' in the famous preface to *Eireaball Spideoige*).

The first attempts to establish a 'modern' poetry in Irish were made at the end of the 19th century. Poets then, and for a long period after that, had one major obstacle to overcome that is no longer a problem for contemporary poets. After the disastrous decline of the language and literature for a hundred years prior to this, no-one knew exactly where or how to begin. There was no living tradition of poetry, or any recognized masters to help nourish a contemporary voice. For a long time previously, the only contemporary masters had been English poets; the nearest living tradition in Irish was the debased tradition of the 18th century. Pádraig Pearse clearly identified the problem in 1905: 'the predicament of the poets has been that, until now, they have had only two models: the fettered, complicated, superficial 18th century model, and the English language model, which had itself colonized the spirit of poetry'.

Pearse was entirely correct, and he was himself, perhaps, the only poet of his generation to escape, to some degree, both dangers. He managed, as a result, to fuse his own sensibility with the spirit of his time in a handful of vibrant lyrics. Although his corpus of poetry is tiny, no other poet among the pioneers of the literary revival at the beginning of the century could by any stretch of the imagination be called a modern poet.

Some sense of the spirit of his times was also captured by L. S. Gogan,[3] a poet who, of all those who wrote between the founding of the State and the Second World War, has received the least recognition. Gogan was unusual in expressing his own sophisticated, urban mind by drawing on the poetic tradition of the 18th century, that very tradition most other good poets avoided. This, and Dinneen's Dictionary, left its mark on his language, which was often eccentric and over-literary. The reader sometimes feels of this poet what Ben Johnson said of Spenser: 'he writ no language'. Spenser, however, wrote poetry that still lives — and I have no doubt that some of L. S. Gogan's lyrics will also live. Even in an 18th century idiom, he still could successfully set a personal love-event in a wood painted by Corot ('Fantais Coille'), or portray a common canal barge in a manner that shows the influence of modern Impressionism ('Liobharn Stáit'). The latter poem may be, indeed, one of the most accomplished poems written in modern Irish.

There is stronger evidence still from the work of the generation of poets which emerged during the second stage of the literary revival (1939–*c.* 1970) that the poetic muse, however personal, is closely connected in some way with contemporary feeling. Ó Direáin's poetry speaks to us not only of his own personal longing for the old ways of life on Aran, but also of the longing of all of those of his contemporaries who were concerned by the death of an old culture. Ó Ríordáin's poetry is a mirror, not only for his own troubled spirit as he faces eternity, but also for the turbulent doubting of the whole post-war generation. If 'Ceathrúintí Mháire Ní Ogáin' is an account by Máire Mhac an tSaoi[4] of a particular love-affair, it is evident that it also grows out of that same general turbulence. And in 'Aifreann no Marbh' by Eoghan Ó Tuairisc,[5] we have a highly-skilled description by a multi-talented writer of the greatest day of shame for his contemporaries: 'the day of the blasphemy against the sun', the dropping of the nuclear bomb on Hiroshima.

Neither Pearse nor Gogan provided a model which the post-war generation of poets (1939–70) could use to nourish their own contemporary voices. Every poet had to begin a personal search for language and verse forms that would be suitable for his or her stylistic needs. Folk-songs, looser accented forms of syllabic models (Pearse, it is true, had already tried this), versions of incantory 'keening' verse, and so on, were all tried. Free verse forms — often based on the songs and verses of Gaeltacht people — tend to be the most common. Máirtín Ó Direáin and Seán Ó Ríordáin were the most successful in forging their own voice from all this experimentation, and so they are the most imitated. Masters were, at last, available to the younger Irish poets, masters from whom they could learn or against whom they could react.

Máire Mhac an tSaoi does not seem to have widely influenced the poets who came after her. Though she was not herself born in an Irish-speaking area, she made a more determined effort than any other poet to tie her muse to the traditional voice of the Gaeltacht. This brings a tremendous richness of language to her entire work. One can see, however, in her best lyrics, lyrics that are often concerned with moments of love and companionship, that her passionate sensibility is most evident when she restrains her remarkable eloquence, cuts back on traditional flourishes.

Most of the poets writing today belong, one could say, to the third phase (*c.* 1970–) of the literary revival. This generation deals more than did any previous generation with the modern world, life as it is lived in cities and towns throughout Ireland. As Irish spreads, particularly in the cities, the psychological barriers that existed not so long ago between Irish and English speakers become less clear. Therefore, though many young poets appreciate the richness of the language of the Gaeltacht, they often prefer to create an idiom which identifies more closely with their own daily experiences, even if that idiom tends to show the influence of English. Though some of them are concerned about the threat to the language, or the waning of the ancient culture, they, ultimately, are more committed to celebrating or expressing their own humanity: humanity as it is rather than humanity as other people think it should be. They tend to ignore dogma, or at least any authoritarian traditional mode of thinking; and though the language in which they compose is that of a tiny minority even in Ireland, they wish to see themselves as ordinary Irish people partaking in a common culture at the end of the 20th century. It is little wonder, therefore, that they take an interest — sometimes over-selfconsciously — in all the distinctive features of that culture from pop-music to haiku.

It is little wonder either, in this age of feminism, that the voice of women poets is to be heard with more openness and assurance than ever before in Irish. Besides Nuala Ní Domhnaill, two of these, Biddy Jenkinson[6] and Aine Ní Ghlinn, have a rare poetic integrity. They each skilfully express a completely individual sensibility in a manner that will ensure, I think, that their work will gain increased recognition in the future.

If one poet more than another can be identified with this new poetic wave in Irish poetry it is Michael Davitt. The poetry journal *Innti* which he and his friends founded in 1970 has deeply influenced the attitudes of young poets, as much as *Comhar*[7] did for the previous generation. Not only that, but he has himself composed distinctive poetry — poetry which is a strange amalgam of violence and humanity — and has developed a poetic idiom with which Irish speakers, from modern suburban Ireland especially, can identify.

Many readers of poetry first discovered in *Innti*, not only Davitt and the young female poets I have mentioned, but also the work of many other fine writers, some of whom are represented in this anthology: Conleth Ellis, Tomás Mac Síomóin, Michael Hartnett,[8] Caitlín Maude, Derry O'Sullivan, Mícheál Ó Cuaig, Liam Ó Muirthile, Cathal Ó Searcaigh. I cannot attempt here to assess individually the work of these poets, except to make a brief reference to Michael Hartnett, who has written both in English and Irish. His poetry in Irish overflows

with a magical native lyric quality; indeed his poetic voice is more lucid, more natural perhaps, in his Irish poems than those in English, so that he was probably wise to turn away from English composition for a while. However, despite the naturalness of the poetic voice he found for himself when he turned from English composition, and however attractive the lyrical quality he developed in his work, he often finds it difficult to achieve definitive expression of his subject matter through the medium of Irish.

It appears that the new generation of poets found little difficulty knowing where or how they would start writing poetry. Their path had been cleared already, so that the increase in the number of poets writing today in comparison to twenty years ago is phenomenal. It was recently calculated in Ciarán Ó Coigligh's anthology *An Fhilíocht Chomhaimseartha* that at least 94 original books of verse had been published in the ten years between 1975 and 1985. It is likely that not even a half of that number of books of verse appeared in the previous 75 years of this century. It should be noted that some of the work being published is not of a particularly high quality, but on the other hand it should also be noted that the general standard of writing has improved dramatically. A high standard of writing does not itself, of course, ensure poetic talent. One cannot ignore the possibility that some of our writers of verse would express themselves more effectively were they to turn to prose.

As it is however, the fact that so many fine poets are writing in Irish must be seen as a remarkable phenomenon, as is the way modern Irish writing can successfully draw on a two thousand year old literary tradition to deal in a unique manner with modern sensibility.

1   Irish-speaking districts, mainly along the western seaboard.
2   Máirtín Ó Direáin (1910–88) was born on the Aran Islands and worked in the Civil Service in Dublin from 1938 onwards. His volume of verse *Rogha Dánta* (1949) is highly acclaimed. Seán Ó Ríordáin (1916–77) was born in Ballyvorney in a Gaelic-speaking part of West Cork. He worked for Cork Corporation and produced his first volume of verse *Eireaball Spideoige* in 1952, followed in 1964 by *Brosna*. Nuala Ní Dhomhnaill (1952–) was born in Lancashire and raised in an Irish-speaking area of Ventry in Kerry. She was educated at University College Cork where she was influenced by the *Innti* group of poets. Examples of all their work can be found in this *Reader*.
3   Liam Gogan (1891–1979) was born in Dublin and educated at UCD. Interned after the Easter Rising he eventually found work again at the National Museum of Ireland in 1922. He began publication of his verse with *Nua-Dhánta* (1919) and continued with *Dánta agus Duanóga* (1929).

4   Máire Mhac an tSaoi (1922–) was born in Dublin but spent periods of her childhood in the Gaeltacht in County Kerry. Her verse can be found in *Margadh na Saoire* (1956) and *Codladh an Ghaiscígh* (1973).

5   Eoghan Ó Tuairisc (1919–82), novelist, translator, and poet. *Dialann sa Díseart* (1981) was a volume of verse produced with Rita Kelly.

6   Her collections of verse include *Báisteadh Gintlí* (1987) and *Uiscí Beatha* (1988).

7   A monthly literary journal founded in 1942, which published the work of the leading Irish-language writers of the time.

8   Michael Hartnett (1941–99), poet and translator, was born in County Limerick where he returned to live in 1974. *A Farewell to English* (1975) signalled a new direction in his writing career, an ambition to publish only in Irish. *Inchicore Haiku* (1985) marked a return to writing in English.

THOMAS KENEALLY
from Thomas Keneally, *Now And In Time To Be* (1991)

The Australian writer Thomas Keneally (1935–), author of *Schindler's Ark* (1982), trained for the priesthood for a number of years but was never ordained. An early novel *Three Cheers for the Paraclete* (1968), a study of a Catholic priest caught between obedience and speaking out, anticipates certain later themes also present in *A River Town* (1995), where a young Irish immigrant, Tim Shea, recklessly opposes a call to support the British Army in the Boer War. Here in this travel book Keneally returns to the spot where his grandparents emigrated from Ireland. With his title taken from Yeats's poem 'Easter 1916', Keneally sets out to write a book about Ireland that is by turns anecdotal, informative, and frequently insightful. For his full-length study of the Irish diaspora in the nineteenth century, see *The Great Shame: A Story of the Irish in the Old World and the New* (1998).

Chapter 1

I was alone on the cliffs near the fishing village of Ballycotton, Cork. Ballycotton is that kind of fishing port, a *Ryan's Daughter*[1] kind of port, even though it is on the wrong coastline for that, the Cork coastline and not the Dingle Peninsula in Kerry. Ballycotton is a stereotype of the Irish fishing village. Steep streets where Irish families of modest means might spend a week every summer in some tidy guesthouse called the 'Aisling'. A high sea wall raised like a muscular forearm against the ocean, and — though not quite the currachs[2] of Aran — risky-looking fishing boats, rowboats in one or two cases, in others rickety trawlers equipped with radar, nosing out to make free of the sea. An off-harbour island, a peril-to-shipping one with a heavy surf and a lighthouse on its bare, green apex.

Ballycotton fronts a glowering sea, spotlit only here and there by light through the sort of clouds which aren't going to let anyone declare an unambiguous day.

My reason for starting here is that this is the sea my grandparents took to when they — separately —

chose to launch themselves on the longest journey of the Irish diaspora — Cork to Australia. These were the cliffs — between here and Cobh — they last saw, and only then if the weather was good. I don't know the answer to any of these questions: did they look back on them from the deck of whatever class they sailed in with a frightful grief, or with a mix of wistfulness and exaltation? Was their young blood really geared up for the longest possible dosage of sea then available to them? Did they think they'd be back to the dear, familiar sights and faces so often invoked in songs of emigration?

I'm sayin' farewell to the land of my birth
 And the homes that I know so well,
And the mountains grand of my own native land,
 I'm biddin' them all adieu . . .[3]

On the other hand, were they pleased to see the last of it: the tribalism, the recurrent want, the contumely of being one of Britain's sub-races? Or did they harbour both sets of feelings? In any event, these cliffs were the last they would ever see of Cork or Ireland.

In the North Coast Licensing Court held at Kempsey, New South Wales, Australia, in May 1889, Timothy Thomas Keneally, who has worked well and more or less soberly for a wagon transport company since his arrival in this relatively remote coastal town three hundred miles north of Sydney, applies for the licence of the Pelican Island Hotel. Pelican Island itself is set on a beautiful flood-prone river called the Macleay. Some of the people who drink there are warders from the local Trial Bay prison. This is an experimental gaol, a model prison set on an exquisite beach on the Pacific coast, where prisoners are to be redeemed by building a breakwater. The other customers he hopes for will be dairy farmers and fishermen.

He isn't given the licence outright, he is awarded it provisionally. His affianced, the Licensing Court is told, Kate McKenna of County Clare, is on her way from Cork to Sydney aboard the ship *Woodburn*. When she arrives and marries Timothy, he will be declared licensee in full.

The marriage takes place at Pelican Island in August, 1889. Kate is only five feet tall, but has a reputation as a no-nonsense, fight-a-tiger-with-a-twig woman. Some might call her a virago. She bears nine children, the youngest my father, eighty-three years old as I write. He would marry a New South Wales country girl, my mother, whose ancestors came from Donegal.

As usual for the grown children of immigrants, he knows little of Kate's motives for travelling such a distance to marry a man she had courted in Ireland. A village scandal, though that seems unlikely? Love? The glory of a pub licence in such a far place? (They called the pub The Harp of Erin, and my father — their youngest child — would always be nicknamed Harper, according to the Australian habit of shortening everything and turning it into a nickname.)

Was she tormented by the last sight of these cliffs across the spotlit sea south of Cobh? Again, her Australian children never asked that question. They seemed to presume that the cooking of their dinner in Pelican Island and, later, in Kempsey, New South Wales, was the one possible destiny on earth open to her.

Now for the first time we encounter a phrase which will recur frequently in this book: *Without being too sentimental . . .* Sentiment is the malaise of the returning pilgrim of Irish connection. The sensible native Irish are offended by it. Nonetheless, *without being too sentimental*, I have to say that the loss in some senses must have been a grievous one for her. For what does cause someone from so far away, both in terms of geography and blood descent, to come to Ireland and feel at once a sense of wistful and ecstatic recognition. Is it a matter of grandparental propaganda, murmured in the ear of childhood? Is it things forgotten but absorbed into the fibre?

We people of the diaspora, whether from Australia or Michigan or the plains of Canada, get back here, returning ghosts, utterly confused and in need of guidance; and we see a place like Ballycotton, and recognize it straight away as a never but always known place.

Up on the cliff at Ballycotton then, I notice a girl is reading the *Irish Times* on the doorstep of a house. The name of this cliff house is, according to its gate post, 'Ardanna'. The opposing gate post whimsically translates it thus: 'Annaville'. While the girl reads, another somewhat older woman emerges and speaks to her. She folds the paper and rises from the steps. She has the oval face of which I have heard people say, 'That's a Cork face.' My grandmother possessed it too and gave it to me and my younger daughter Jane. It is sometimes referred to as 'a potato-face', unjustly, since it can be handsome, especially on the young. The girl follows the woman inside and I can see her through the window joining still another youngish woman and a similarly youngish man. They all sit to tea with their backs to the sea.

The question is, why is this that girl's place, the place where she goes in to tea? Why did my grandmother have to travel so far to find the place where her tea was taken?

Kate, variously Kenna, McKenna, lies now in the outer perimeter of Ireland's cure of souls, on a hill in West Kempsey, New South Wales, Australia, looking west to a smoke-blue tangle of hills which she spent all her married life regarding. I have her to thank for my first pair of sandshoes, for my immutably Irish way of saying *theatre* (the-ay-tah) and my dumpling genes. In acquittal of these debts, I decide sentimentally that I should at least be her eyes in Erin of the Harp.

For her sake I had been to Mass in the town of Cloyne. 'Let us pray for the repose of the soul of . . .'

The officiating priest had the same tendency as her to drop aitches not from the front of words but from the back. 'Mont' for month, 'catedral' for cathedral, 'fait' for faith. As an Irish priest should, he seemed to have plenty of homely parables. 'Remember when the new furniture came in, and people couldn't wait to get rid of the old. But then, after a while, people saw the new, mass-produced stuff was shoddy and began to seek the old again. It had enduring value. So it is with the old dogmas we dropped for the sake of the new, flashy, shoddy ones.

'People say, "I'm not a religious person. Could you be saying a prayer for me?" That's' (pronounced grandmother-wise, *dat's*) 'like trying to do a line with a girl and saying to a friend, "Would you be going up to that girl and doing a line for me?"'

Then, at my first Irish Mass, he declared Ireland very worldly. Dangerously secular. Irish clerics the world over always say 'secular' if they want to disapprove of something. Yet, it was hard to believe it of those plain Irish faces in the Cloyne parish church, across from the hurling field with its statue of the great hurler Christy Ring not yet dry from the overnight, autumn storms. Maybe it is true that Ireland's getting worldlier in the strictest theological sense. Yet, in a fundamental sense, it isn't of this world. There is a knowledge legible in those Irish faces in the pews that divine forces will make a mockery of too much cleverness. There is a modesty of hope there, based on the concept that perfection is not meant for the vale of tears. As an American waiting in line for breakfast in

Dublin said, 'I suppose if they had all this better organized, they wouldn't be the Irish.' The kingdom is not of this world, and slickness is a tool of the Devil.

That is a philosophic awareness that shapes the life of this island, particularly the Republic's life. But it is there in the average Loyalist Protestant in the North too. The two working classes, who hate each other too much up there, are united in a resistance to the idea that they should become lickety-split model workers, like the Germans or Japanese who are so frequently held up to them as models. Ireland, and Irish history, have made them the one being after all, though they don't know it.

But I get ahead of myself.

1   A film by David Lean made on the Dingle Peninsula in the west of Ireland, released in 1970.
2   Hollowed-out, flat-bottomed boats used by Aran Islanders for fishing and transport.
3   Lines from emigration song 'Shores of Amerikay'.

BRENDAN KENNELLY
from Brendan Kennelly, *Journey Into Joy: Selected Prose* (1994)

There are few better surveys of Irish poetry after Yeats than the following by Brendan Kennelly. It contains a wealth of information and leads for the student new to the subject, and I have left the footnotes much as they appear in the original. Several of the poems mentioned by Kennelly are reproduced in this *Reader*.

Irish Poetry Since Yeats

1

Whenever one or two figures seem dominant in a country's poetry, several others are writing in a different but not equally acclaimed or recognized way. When Yeats was at the height of his powers towards the end of his life, an anthology, *Goodbye, Twilight*,[1] was published containing the work of poets who saw themselves as writing a very different kind of poetry from that of Yeats and other distinguished Celtic Twilighters. In 1993, Gabriel Fitzmaurice edited an anthology, *Irish Poetry Now: Other Voices*[2] which, he holds, contains a kind of poetry different from and interesting as the mainstream of contemporary verse in Ireland. Such oppositions, such alternatives, are a healthy sign; they lessen the likelihood that readers may fall into attitudes of lazy categorization; and they

suggest that the scene is more vigorous, varied and complex than we had hitherto realized. Further, they create the possibility that poets in scrupulous opposition to each other may produce better work. There should be fewer cosy coteries, more fierce and intelligent opposition. That's the stuff of which genuine friendship between poets is made.

Yeats's Cuala Press published Patrick Kavanagh's long poem *The Great Hunger* in 1942. Kavanagh went on to denounce Yeats as being 'protected by ritual' in his poem, 'An Insult';[3] he also criticized him severely in several essays. This was Kavanagh's way of distancing himself from Yeats. He went on to explain and express his own vision, a vision which in the end has, ironically, some remarkable similarities to Yeats's. Kavanagh called it 'comedy';[4] Yeats called it 'tragic joy'.[5] Kavanagh's castigating references to Yeats and others helped him to create for himself that space, that freedom from other poets' work (even as they are deeply aware of it) that most poets need. Poets' vicious denunciations of the work of others can be forms of self-liberation.

Creating space is always a problem, particularly, perhaps, in the congested Irish scene. Poets such as Samuel Beckett, Denis Devlin, Brian Coffey and Thomas MacGreevy created this cultural space for themselves in ways which indicate that their poetry is not widely read today. (Why should it be? — some purists will ask.) Much of Beckett's poetry is knotted and ironic; it often transmits the sense of a man muttering to himself in no particular method or order; yet it gives the reader the feeling that he's listening to a private monologue, labyrinthine and tortuous at certain times, at others, comic and self-mocking. It is at once inviting and offputting, like a nutty conversationalist with a kindly countenance. It is particularly striking when read aloud, as indeed all poetry should be, if subtleties of rhythm are to be properly grasped.

Traces of Beckett's oddly fascinating qualities are to be found in the work of contemporary poets such as Tom McIntyre and Hugh Maxton. Paul Durcan's ability to write like a comic Hamlet suggests that he has listened to Beckett at some stage. He has also listened to Kavanagh's call for a comic poetry which, in its spirit of self-criticism allied to criticism of society, brings Swift to mind and reminds poets everywhere that they must avoid becoming pompous or pretentious. Most of the reservations about Yeats's work which I hear expressed here and there throughout Ireland and other places centre on his tendency towards rhetorical pomposity. This tendency may be due to his compulsion to mythologize and dramatize everyone, including himself. His aesthetic compels him to be always at the centre of the poem's action, determined not to fall apart. Beckett and Kavanagh, in their different ways, reject the inflated feelings consequent on dramatic mythologizing, Kavanagh especially denouncing Yeats's 'myth of Ireland as a spiritual entity'[6] and proceeding in a defiant and convincing manner to write about the most ordinary situations, events, people: the life of a street, the 'undying difference in the corner of a field',[7] cubicles and wash-basins in a chest hospital, the canal in Dublin, bogs and small 'incurious'[8] hills in Monaghan, pubs, coffee-shops, mundane aspects of life as he saw it about him. All this, however, was coloured by an intense inner life, a religious conviction that 'God is in the bits and pieces of Everyday'.[9] The result is a delightful body of poetry in which the mundane is transfigured by the mystical, and the mystical is earthed in the mundane.

This religious streak in Irish poetry goes back to older poetry in the Irish language and is present, in muted and varied ways, in contemporary poetry. Denis Devlin, deeply influenced by the work of European writers (he translated a considerable amount of French poetry), produced a body of religious verse which grows more fascinating the more one reads it. Compare his poem 'Lough Derg' with poems by Kavanagh and Seamus Heaney on the same topic[10] and it becomes possible to appreciate the varied effects of his deliberate, resonant syntax, his long, evocative lines, his meditative rhythms, his ability to think things through. There is in Devlin a readiness to experiment with language and rhythm that is not very common in Irish poetry which, if I may generalize, tends to be formally conservative and rather cautious in its choices of themes. For such a rebel race, eloquently so, Irish poets can be comically, sadly conservative. Poetry should be adventurous and daring, even offensive at times. It *has* to be, if it is serious in its self-scrutiny and in its response to the abundant casual corruptions and abuses in society, not forgetting the wriggling evils in oneself. The exploration of a deep religious impulse goes hand in hand with the compulsion to satirize its abuses and abusers. This is true of Kavanagh; it is also true of Austin Clarke whose work, helpfully edited by Hugh Maxton in a recent Penguin edition,[11] satirizes the hypocrisies and abuses that abound in Irish life even as churches on Sundays bulge with the faithful. Clarke had a lot of courage, and in his satire one can see the outrage suffered by a person who knows what a genuine religious impulse is, and how such an impulse is so often flouted and maimed in a 'religious' society. So Clarke wrote himself into a corner of articulate indignation and rage until, towards the end of his life, he began to write a more 'cheerful' verse. In a note on the Tiresias myth he mentions Tennyson's Victorian respectability and T.S. Eliot's puritan gloom in their treatment of this figure; he then stresses his own 'cheerful' view of the Tiresias drama, and goes on to offer us a sparkling poem.[12] Like Yeats and Kavanagh, like O'Casey in drama, like Joyce in the novel, Clarke's work slowly and tortuously approaches a climax of joy and celebration. I find it honest and convincing because he has brooded on the injustices, abuses, forms of ignorance and prejudice (can they be separated?) inherent in Irish life and yet, in the end, he flies in the face of squalor with poetry that is playful, amusing and sexually exuberant. I find a similar exuberance in the work of Medbh McGuckian. I'm not saying that she has been directly influenced by Clarke; but influence in poetry is a strangely arbitrary, insidious, floating affair; Clarke helped to create a climate of spontaneity and freedom; poets all through the island have breathed that air. McGuckian is a complex writer, her language has a kind of wild freedom in it that suggests she has coped firmly with conflicts in herself. The writing of poetry is a lifelong bid for freedom from many forces, people, ideas and influences that the poet must be concerned with until, by sheer constant grappling with these forces, people, ideas and influences, he/she liberates himself/herself from their intimidating pressure. Sustained imaginative, sexual sympathy has, in Irish poetry, proved crucial in this liberation. Crazy Jane helps to deliver Yeats. I suspect Molly Bloom did much the same thing for James Joyce. Austin Clarke's lifelong preoccupation with women in his work helped to create that late, cheerful poetry. In the imagination, there's a deep connection between feminization and freedom. It took Clarke a lifetime to achieve this. Medbh McGuckian, a young woman, electrifies her poetry with this freedom. So, in a different way, does Nuala Ní Dhomhnaill whose writing has an added comic-mythological dimension which, allied to her sexual realism, makes her poetry both colourful and penetrating. Some of these young Irish women poets are more relaxed and free, though no less disciplined in their approach to writing, than most of their male equivalents manage to be after sixty or seventy solemn years on this earth that somehow tolerates every conceivable kind of poet and poetry.

Why is poetry so often considered high-falutin by 'ordinary', intelligent people? I think it has to do, to a considerable extent, with a certain male pomposity and self-regard which exudes an almost incredible sense of the incomparable value of the poet himself, created and sustained by himself, the great untouchable, the victim who also happens to be an unquestionable master. This attitude of severed élitism has gone unchallenged for too long. It is the stance of men who love looking uptight and 'serious', sensitive and manageably oppressed by just about everyone else. That look of special agony is crucial. It could make the poetry itself more interesting. On the whole, the women poets of Ireland have little or no time for this carefully publicized pain. They suffer their confusions alone; they deliver their clarities to the reading, listening public with style, frequently with humour. Women poets have done a great deal to humanize and normalize people's experience of poetry in Ireland: when Mary O'Donnell's poetry programme on radio is compared with Austin Clarke's,[13] you know the difference between poetry that is enjoyed and poetry that is endured. I have genuine admiration for Clarke's work; it is daring and tenacious; but his presentation of poetry on radio was pretentious, sloppy and effete. O'Donnell's is direct, crisp, deeply satisfying.

It is important to say this because poetry, no matter how disturbing, should be enjoyed in its full range without pretence or manipulation on the poet's part.

There are many women poets in Ireland now, in both Irish and English, whose work has brought a new wave of excitement into Irish writing. Eavan Boland's work in such books as *The War Horse*, *In Her Own Image*, *Night Feed*, *The Journey*, *Outside History* and *In a Time of Violence*[14] shows a powerful, questioning intelligence. Time and again, she places herself not only outside history but also outside mythology, as created and narrated by men, in an attempt to gain a perspective from which she can witness the places and roles of women in history, myth, in town and country, at home and in public. She is, in fact, making her own myth.

> I am Chardin's woman
> edged in reflected light,
> hardened by
> the need to be ordinary.[15]

Like McGuckian and Ní Dhomhnaill, Boland has pondered her situation in depth and at length. She is a superb craftswoman, her poems time and time again exploring complex ideas and situations in lucid, sensuous language. She could be even more hard-hitting; her intellectual stance, her impassioned sense of inquiry and her ability to see different sides of any problem or situation justify the use of more direct mind-blows to Irish society. She is one of the most exciting writers in Ireland today. The rage of time itself is a force in her poetry.

The rage of time. The rage of history. The rage of women. The rage of the oppressed, of the poor against the rich, of the deprived against the privileged, of the uneducated against the educated, of the powerless against the empowered. How much of this rage has been confronted and expressed by Irish poets? Undoubtedly, some of it has. Yeats, Clarke, Kavanagh, MacNeice in 'Autumn Journal', Eavan Boland, Anne Hartigan have expressed rage. Yeats more than any, it must be admitted.

> You think it horrible that lust and rage
> Should dance attention upon my old age . . .[16]

There is rage in some of Seamus Heaney's work and in a number of Thomas Kinsella's powerfully concentrated poems. James Simmons expresses rage in some of his poems and songs. But where is there a close, passionate statement or evocation of the rage that is making murder a daily event in the North of Ireland? And how close do Irish poets look at *the kinds of responses* from people to these events? How closely *connected* are Irish poets to what is actually going on? How interested are they? Who speaks out? Which poets express the different viewpoints? Is there something offensive to most poets in the notion of taking sides? Patrick Galvin certainly doesn't think so. In a shockingly candid poem entitled 'Letter to a British Soldier on Irish Soil', he concludes:

Go home, Soldier
Before we send you home
Dead.[17]

That's the conclusion to a rather fiercely Nationalist poem. Is there a similar Unionist poem? Should there be? Should the war be kept out of poetry? Out of criticism? Or is poetry expected not to 'take sides' but to stay on the sidelines, silent, sensitive, agonized, properly inarticulate, as the savage game is played according to its own murderous rules?

How daring are Irish poets prepared to be? If we live in a murderous society should not our poetry reflect that fact? Does it? Or do poets create and cherish their own partitions?

It may be, of course, that murder is of limited interest, even when it is the expression of some ancient, entangled religious hatred or of a prejudice at once so remote in time and so vile in its current intensity that any coherent human understanding of it is no longer possible. Life in Ireland can be like that. Who battered the epileptic to death and dumped the body in a playground for children to discover?

2

There are certain words in Ireland that glint, quiver and stick in people's minds like the thin blades of knives. 'Partition' is one such word. The political-territorial partition of Ireland intensified further divisions among Catholics and Protestants, Nationalists and Unionists. Partition begets partition and endows certain words with a virulent significance. The word 'North', title of Seamus Heaney's strongest collection, contains an entire history in itself which, the moment the book is opened and the poems begin to be read, throws light and shadows over practically every line. Heaney makes an admirable effort to be detached from 'the Northern problem', 'the Northern tragedy', but Heaney's words, attitudes, his tight, slit-eyed rhythms show him as a Northern Catholic of rural origin with appropriate political sympathies. And why not?

If partition creates partition, labels create labels: Catholic, Protestant, Unionist, Nationalist, Pan-Nationalist. Can an Irish poet escape being labelled? One understands why Joyce, wishing to escape Ireland's labelling congestion, its ruthless 'I know you no matter what you do or say or write' intimacy, saw himself sitting on a cloud over the city of Dublin, paring his fingernails in a show of indifference. But cloud-squatting is not a popular posture among Irish poets; and the few souls on the island who aspire to the name of 'critic' are usually loaded with labels when they come to 'evaluate' a book of poems. Nevertheless, there are a few critics who try to rise above the label-tyranny.

The Northern poet (I'm starting to use my own little labels now!) enjoys the advantage of being both Irish and British. This can be ignored or exploited at will. A Catholic Northern poet can be seen as a victim deserving sympathy everywhere he or she goes; but if he writes savage poems like Patrick Galvin he won't be much heard of. The old question recurs: how daring are poets prepared to be? A choice of theme is a measure of courage. Courage, the no-warning bombing of one's own cosy limits, is one of the hallmarks of verse alive.

And there is indeed considerable courage in Heaney's poetry, in the poetry of Derek Mahon, Michael Longley, Seamus Deane, James Simmons, Medbh McGuckian, Frank Ormsby, Ciaran Carson and Paul Muldoon. The first thing one must say about these, and other Northern writers, is that they are darned good poets, some of whose poems hit you right between the eyes and force you to think anew about the Northern problem and other matters. And these forceful poems are not always *directly* about that problem; yet violence sweeps into Simmons's poems about love and marriage as well as ballads such as 'Claudy' (which *is* a direct violence-poem);[18] Longley's versions of the Greek poets as well as poems like 'Wounds' and 'The Ice-Cream Man';[19] Mahon's bleak, ironic meditations on loneliness, on being lost; and Muldoon's atrocity-haunted, witty creations. An older poet like John Montague has a lot to say about life in Northern Ireland but the fact that he has lived away from it for so many years, doing his own bit of cloud-squatting here and there throughout the world, gives his poetry an air of rather sad, travelled wisdom which makes it calmer, though not less urgent, than the work of younger poets. This calm, detached note in Montague's verse, creating space for compassionate meditation on suffering and emotional entrapment, is deeply attractive. A similar calm concern marks the work of another Northern poet, Gerald Dawe, whose essays on contemporary poetry are pithy, incisive and illuminating.[20]

If a sharp-minded anthology were made from the work of these poets, it would be a forceful, haunting book. A sort of history of our times and crimes.

Poetry will not solve the Northern problem, but when the terrorists, murderers and assassins decide to call it a day (as they finally will, when it suits them), poetry will have written its own history of the horrors. Even the youngsters, the schoolboys and schoolgirls of Belfast and other places are writing poems in response to the Troubles. A Belfast childhood darkened by terrorism involves us all, even the resolutely complacent middle-classes of the Irish Republic where interest in the North and its distresses could hardly be slighter. Partition is a line dividing suffering from unawareness. And unawareness can be very 'superior'. 'Honestly, darling, have you ever heard of such barbarism?'

And yet the North *must* somehow infiltrate the consciousness of Southern poets (another wee label!). To what degree such infiltration occurs is anybody's guess. There's not much evidence of it in most of the poetry written in the South. Partition is a line beyond which certain imaginations refuse to go.

The critic Edna Longley has tried to cross such lines, such boundaries. There's a visionary quality in some of her criticism which, wittily bitter and insistent, makes many people, including poets, stop and think about the implications of their conscious and unconscious prejudices.

Violence is a form of publicity. The sensationalism that accompanies terrorism may transfer itself to the poetry arising from that violence, giving it a disproportionate prominence, causing the work of quieter poets to be overlooked.

There are three poets of another generation whose work must constantly be brought to mind, particularly in the South: Louis MacNeice, W.R. Rodgers and John Hewitt. The influence of MacNeice, particularly, on poets both North and South, is far-reaching. 'Why do you never sing?' some tone-deaf, ignorant Southern poet said to him once. 'Why do you never think?' replied MacNeice. MacNeice's brief reply constitutes one of the most telling criticisms I know of poetry written in Ireland.

This Southern ignorance takes many forms and is especially strong in Dublin. It springs from what can only be called a deliberately *willed* partition — the line drawn between Dublin and the rest of Ireland. A Southern singer, Donagh MacDonagh, son of the executed 1916 leader, Thomas MacDonagh, a far more gifted poet than his endlessly judgemental son, has a poem called 'Dublin Made Me', a manifesto of that ignorance proclaiming itself as loyalty which is a solid basis for partition. Dublin alone is worthwhile;

every other part of Ireland, North, West and South, is dismissed for various 'reasons'. The curious thing about this poem is that it applies not only to poetry, but to many other aspects of culture and living. Dublin *is* a very attractive city; MacDonagh's response to that attractiveness is ignorant and dismissive.

Dublin made me and no little town
With the country closing in on its streets
The cattle walking proudly on its pavements
The jobbers the gombeenmen and the cheats

Devouring the fair-day between them
A public-house to half a hundred men
And the teacher, the solicitor and the bank-clerk
In the hotel bar drinking for ten.

Dublin made me, not the secret poteen still,
The raw and hungry hills of the West
The lean road flung over profitless bog
Where only a snipe could nest,

Where the sea takes its tithe of every boat.
Bawneen and curragh have no allegiance of mine,
Nor the cute self-deceiving talkers of the South
Who look to the East for a sign.

The soft and dreary midlands with their tame canals
Wallow between sea and sea, remote from adventure,
And Northward a far and fortified province
Crouches under the lash of arid censure.

I disclaim all fertile meadows, all tilled land
The evil that grows from it and the good,
But the Dublin of old statues, this arrogant city,
Stirs proudly and secretly in my blood.[21]

The troglodytic attitudes in that poem still exist but not at all, I would say, to the same degree. MacDonagh was a prime specimen of the most close-minded class in Dublin, probably in the Republic, the Catholic middle class; and many of the best poets in Dublin today come from a very different Dublin. The Dublin of Paula Meehan's poetry is startlingly different from that of MacDonagh; Meehan's is humane, troubled, compassionate, funny, eager to reach out and touch other aspects of life. A similar openness appears in the poetry of Dermot Bolger and Michael O'Loughlin. Bolger, a publisher as well as poet, and an accomplished novelist and dramatist, brought 'invisible Dublin' into the light, gave a forum to poets who would almost certainly not otherwise have been heard. Bolger has always campaigned against partitioning ignorance, one of the most powerful forces in Irish life, a force that is frequently obvious, but just as frequently subtle and even stylish in its sinister workings. It is, for example, quietly rampant in our educational system, especially at University level.

Dublin continues to produce many fine poets. Thomas Kinsella has written incisively about Dublin, using various parts of the city as a means of exploring his own dark, complex vision. Gerald Smyth's images of Dublin life are snappy and penetrating as well as reflective. And Michael Hartnett's *Inchicore Haiku*[22] contains unforgettable pictures of Dublin. Some of Paul Durcan's most outrageously vivid poems are set in Dublin; and Macdara Woods charts his Dublin in a spirit of patient affirmation. Woods wrote the introduction to *Collected Poems* of John Jordan,[23] a book containing much wisdom and wit concerning Dublin and its people. In the elegance of its phrasing, in the sharp intelligence of its perceptions, Jordan's work brings to mind the graceful poetry of Val Iremonger. Iremonger's poems about Dublin, particularly those about Sandymount and its people, are full of crisp images that linger in the memory. 'Elizabeth, frigidly stretched,/On a spring day surprised us.'[24] So do Iremonger's poems.

Micheal O'Siadhail's *Hail! Madam Jazz*[25] shows a shrewd observer of Dublin life at work in thoughtful, well-made poems. O'Siadhail, like these other younger poets, writes with open heart and sharp intelligence about the uncertainties of living in a capital city that is both ancient and modern.

The poetry emerging from any city is an acute guide to the tolerance of that city's people. By that criterion, Dublin today is a growingly tolerant city. In spite of its increasing crime rate, its many social problems such as poverty, AIDS, drugs, unemployment on an alarming scale, Dublin life is marked, on the whole, by decency, humour and intelligence. The more critical poetry is, the more these qualities tend to emerge. The more savage poetry is, the more humanizing its effects. Individual sentimentality is an insult to society, a gross offence to readers. Students in schools and universities should be encouraged to write this kind of cutting, critical poetry so that their vision of their own society may be less clouded, less deceptive. Poets like Meehan and Bolger, Theo Dorgan and Michael Hartnett produce a sharply critical poetry that does much to limit the damaging effects of both the obvious and subtle forms of divisiveness. The poetry that battles against partitionism will open the hearts and minds of people who read it or hear it properly spoken or read at public poetry-readings.

Probably the deepest partition in Irish life is the sexual divide between men and women. The Catholic Church established and exploited this partition for its own ends. Austin Clarke is probably our most combative anti-partitionist in this area; he fought for the dignity of women in his poems. Today, the women poets of Ireland are still fighting that deepest of all partitions. Some fight it with satirical wit, like Rita Ann Higgins, Julie O'Callaghan, and Rosemarie Rowley; others, like Anne Hartigan and Moya Cannon, in steely, defiant poems; others, like Eavan Boland and Eiléan Ní Chuilleanáin, with formidable intelligence; and others still, like Paula Meehan and Katie Donovan, with a spirit at once critical and magnanimous. There are many striking individual differences between these poets but they all have one thing in common: a defiant, dignified sense of creating their own forms of independence. These forms are the forms of their poems. Sinéad O'Connor's full-page poem, 'I am Sinéad O'Connor', in *The Irish Times* in the summer of 1993[26] was an impassioned statement of that independence and her need for it. The poem drove some people hopping mad; it compelled others to state their admiration in public. Poetry by Irish women will, I believe, elicit such strong responses in the future.

And yet this partition remains widespread and profoundly rooted. Some of its most devoted practitioners don't even know they're promoting and sustaining it. This is the deepest single cultural/ emotional/spiritual partition in Ireland. The act of exploring it will produce a more humane poetry from men and women, and ultimately from these young poets in schools, colleges, universities, and from outside these institutions, too. Poetry is the deepest kind of education there is, a conscious, structured, logical, inspiring illumination of the various darknesses in us all. Poetry which is fully alive is always on a threshold, making fresh assaults on ignorance, intolerance and evil so that concepts and practices of tolerance may be endlessly refreshed and re-invigorated, even as intense, rhythmical language is enjoyed and reflected on. This is especially true in Ireland, a society always in danger of succumbing to that paralysis so feared and yet so ruthlessly explored by Joyce; a society, too, permanently menaced by the 'great hatred, little room'[27] noted by Yeats. Paralysis, hatred, poverty, intolerance, cynicism, begrudgery, bored indifference and, most of all, that horrible, effective half-heartedness with its workable lethargy, its viable apathy, its slithery key to 'success' — these should be the targets of poets and poetry. Of poetry, above all. If our society is to be fully alive, self-questioning and realizing its potential, poetry must be ruthless and brave. In this small country, where news of terrorism's latest atrocities is served with breakfast, the need for such poetry is deep indeed.

Other forms of partition involve the relative subjugation, or at least quietly pushing into the background, of some genuinely interesting poets. Anthony Cronin is one such. A social critic of remarkable range and depth, a distinguished biographer and literary historian, an independent-minded critic of literature, he is also a poet whose work spans several generations of Irish life and writing. Yet his poems are scarcely available. He is a victim of that aggressive lazy-mindedness that stems from partition. He is not easily labelled; therefore, let's not mention him just now. Later, perhaps.

Curious how, in the swirling pool of poetry-politics, some poets become the victims of critical clichés and labels while others profit from the same mindless method. And it's curious, too, how Cronin, a prominent public figure (he was cultural advisor to the former Taoiseach, C.J. Haughey), seems to be penalized for this. The current Minister for the Arts, Michael D. Higgins, is a poet of some substance. It is to be hoped that his public prominence won't diminish this fact or, more likely, lead to a cartooning of it. Bad criticism is a form of caricature, a systematic misrepresentation of a poet's real worth. This malignant approach is rife in Ireland: Brendan Behan was 'a great bloody character' but he is largely unread. I wonder how true this is of Flann O'Brien, Patrick Kavanagh and others. The stage Irishman is not an English but an Irish creation. What it means is this: 'I want you, the writer, to be colourfully unreal so that I won't have to listen to what your work has to say. Entertain me so that I may laugh you out of existence and into absurdity.'

One of the odd consequences of partition is the emphasis it throws on the figure of the loner in poetry, the man or woman outside the cliques or mutually back-slapping groups that pop up here and there in a climate of acclaim for each other. John Ennis is a good example of the loner. Quiet, undemonstrative, tucked unobtrusively away 'somewhere in the provinces' (he lives and works in Waterford) he writes an adventurous poetry with a strong narrative pulse. Similarly interesting figures are Mary O'Donnell, Robert Greacen, Fred Johnston, Robert O'Donoghue, Rory Brennan, Seán Dunne, Gerard Fanning, Ciaran O'Driscoll, John F. Deane, Francis Harvey, Desmond Egan, Dennis O'Driscoll, Michael Coady, Peter Sirr, Peter Fallon and the versatile Desmond O'Grady. Over the years, these poets have worked hard to produce their highly individual and very readable verse.

Another loner is Padraic Fallon. He was so during his lifetime; he remains that sort of figure today. Up until recently when a summer-school began to bring attention to his work at last, Fallon was a poet you simply had to go in search of. His work is complex, richly-wrought in a self-conscious way, musical, meditative, absorbing a lot of influences from the Classical to the Gaelic.

One of the most gifted loner-figures is Richard Murphy. Murphy has never been labelled. What higher praise can an Irish poet be given? In this century, his narrative poems are among the most thrilling of their kind.[28]

But there are other loners. I'm thinking of poets who, instead of becoming embroiled in Ireland's local squabbles, write and work in different parts of the world. Bernard O'Donoghue, Eamon Grennan, Peter McDonald, Greg Delanty, James Liddy, Matthew Sweeney are, literally, outsiders whose work reflects that fact. Ireland is an island washed, in the eyes of many exiles, by nostalgic seas. None of the poets I've mentioned has been a victim of this nostalgia. Each, in his different way, is creating a poetry free of Ireland's turmoil but true to his own experience in the broader world. In that broader world, these poets are relatively free of the partitions that both inhibit and stimulate poets living in Ireland.

3

In the context of what I've tried to present in the second part of this essay, the poetry of personal relationships may tend to be overlooked; but right across the entire spectrum of contemporary Irish poetry, a keen scrutiny of such relationships occurs. Poetry is a solitary art and no amount of engagement with public issues can alter that fact. The number of intense, individual energies in Irish poetry now is impressive, and the style of each of these poets may be savoured for reasons peculiar to each writer. Each poet's moulding of his/her own language is ultimately the most revealing aspect of the work.

A poet's relationship with language is one of the deepest there is. The kind of English spoken and written in Ireland has a twist to it. It can be Janus-faced, crooked, indirect, poisonously comic, inflated, often pretending to a false sophistication, haunted by the Irish language, resenting or cherishing that influence. The English of Dublin is very different from that of Belfast or Cork or Galway. Even within these places there are different Englishes. In poetry, one English is as effective as another, depending on how imaginatively, passionately, skilfully it is used. When these qualities are present it doesn't matter what town, village, city, region or prison a poet is from; the necessary bridge between writer and reader is created. I should point out here, being aware of the approaches of some other poets, that I consider such bridges 'necessary'. An unshared poetry might as well be an unwritten poetry. The silence of the unread poem accuses us all.

Part of the problem of writing an essay entitled 'Irish Poetry Since Yeats' is the fact that each one of an impressive number of poets thinks that he or she is the best Irish poet since Yeats. The rest of the good souls know it. It's an odd business. It's a comical, rubbishy business, full of raised and unraised hackles. I suppose this kind of labelling is inevitable; critics go in for it, too; but if it stimulates somebody to produce better work, well, fair enough! The main problem would appear to be to keep on motoring. Egotism, no matter how deluded, can be the petrol that keeps the poetry-machine ticking over. The *sources* of poetry may be ludicrous, tragic, lonely, self-deceiving, bullying, vile in one way or another; the poetry itself may bring a keen and echoing pleasure.

The important thing for Irish poetry now is to be open to all kinds of influences from cultures all over the world. I know no good study of the effects of insularity on Irish writing, on Irish criticism. Insularity is both a state of severance and a state of self-containment. It can lead to the most inflated view of one's self and the most distorted views of others. Insularity is a shocking revelation of the implications and consequences of the big fish in the small pond situation. It can be a source of the most atrocious smugness and totally believed-in self-delusion. Insularity can be a method of cutting out of one's life the challenging forms of comparison and contrast that help us towards some kind of sane evaluation of who we are, what we are, and what we do. The seas that perpetually wash the shores of Ireland can help to fortify this sad state of affairs. 'Thank God we're surrounded by water' as the song says.

But an intelligent, vigilant, outward-looking insularity, not obsessed with self-protection, open to comparison, learning from contrast, welcoming challenge, developing the sense of proportion, eager to experience *difference* in whatever shape or form, can be a healthy, productive state for a poet. At some fundamental level, there's an ongoing conflict between the cautious, delusive, strong form of insularity, and the open, risk-taking, learning, adventurous kind. I believe this is a challenge that faces many English poets and critics also. It is a complex matter. Closed insularity is often connected with what people take to be love of place, language, rituals, local culture. The open brand challenges this love, its very nature and

implications. When love is questioned the battle is bound to be furious.

Part of the problem with Irish poetry is the failure to find a proper balance between these two emotional/cultural/spiritual conditions. This failure to find a balance helps to explain the vicious antagonisms within the Irish poetry scene; the creators of beauty can be a malignant lot, at times. If there is an answer, it must be somewhere in the willingness to open up, to question the function of the seas, to look ever more closely at oneself, the land, its people.

This openness to otherness has implications of a purely thematic and technical kind for poetry. The strangest and most disturbing forms of otherness, often eruptively violent, reside in the self. Equally important is the otherness in thought, feeling, values, beliefs one finds throughout the world. Only in his or her own loneliness can the poet's bridges be created. That bleak need for connection, root of most poetry, is founded in the confrontation of that fact. There are many factors in Irish life working against this confrontation. The significant poets are those who insist on it.

This openness brings in themes that minds largely shaped by closed insularity will find distasteful, ugly, vulgar or simply wrong-headed. I experienced a fair amount of this kind of talk after the publication of *The Book of Judas*.[29] I received letters from friends telling me I was 'a disgrace' and 'a traitor'. I also received letters from strangers saying that the poem had helped them to understand problems in their own lives and in society. I mention this simply to illustrate what happens when poetry ventures into 'forbidden territory' or explores the state of the outcast, the lost, the damned. Irish life shivers and burns with little hells. There are little heavens too. And countless, tacky little purgatories. They should all be explored. Therefore, poetry will be 'offensive' or 'outrageous', as you will, as readers will. Readers read poetry and are in turn read by it. This is one further reason why poetry in Ireland should be more and more open and experimental. It's as if this experimentation at every level is part of a battle against stagnation, half-heartedness, closed insularity, rigid judgementalism, ready prejudice, cosy certainties, unexpressed angers, active hatreds, fear. Fear above all, perhaps. Poetry is a battle against these horrors, even as it is often, surprisingly, rooted in them. This recognition has been made by many poets writing in Ireland today. It helps to account for the vigour and variety of the poetry they produce. It is up to the poets themselves to discover and take measures against the reasons that help to account for its shortcomings. This always involves a necessary return to the hurts and honesty of that solitude where poetry begins and ends and then again, true to its own resilient spirit in a world that usually ignores it and always needs it, begins.

Some Irish poets have been influenced by Yeats but Irish poetry on the whole has been surprisingly unintimidated by the range and magnitude of his achievement. This may be because his vision of Irish society ('Sing the peasantry and then/Hard-riding country gentlemen')[30] is so silly, so irrelevant to life in contemporary Ireland, that his verse can be appreciated as something quite apart from his vision of the country. Besides, the deepest, most far-reaching aspect of Yeats's achievement must always inspire poets everywhere. Poetry is hard work. Yeats's real meaning for poets can be put simply: 'Work hard at exploring the abyss of yourself and at clarifying your discoveries.'

Poetry is trouble. Much of it springs from emotional trouble. Writing it can be nightmarish though words are fun; dangerous too. To read poetry properly, in a state of concentrated, fluent attention, is almost impossible, frequently leaving the reader with a sense of dissatisfaction, even uncouthness. Reading poetry aloud can be a painful exercise in personal absurdity. Some souls find it consoling and enlightening. But trouble is the name of the game. Poets are addicted to this trouble.

Ireland is a post-colonial island. Trouble. Thousands of years old and still struggling to be born. I'm a post-colonial scribbler with vast resources of ignorance, prejudice, misunderstanding and self-deception. An English poet said to me last year, 'You don't write English, Brendan, you write an Irish version of my language. I don't know whether it's rhetorical or real.' I think I know what she meant. On the other hand, it does no harm to feel homeless in a language, does it? A language, like any house, can be a source of homely smugness.

The problem is to be at home in the sense of home-lessness, to risk rhetoric, to overcome embarrassment, to forgive oneself for follies leaping from brain to tongue to pen, to be candid, to try to achieve a light-filled laughter, to make the trouble lilt and sing and plant a look of amazement on the face of a youngster who is convinced that poetry is crap he has to endure for examinations which he must 'pass' or 'fail', hideous words. Keats and Milton and Yeats and Eliot make life bloody hard for some people doing the Leaving Certificate. Poetry is trouble. 'Christ in heaven' a young man exploded to me some years ago. ''Twas a great pity Keats didn't shoot that fuckin' Nightingale!'

I'd be a fool to try to predict the likely course of Irish poetry. I hope it develops more of a sense of humour, of comic selfmockery, thereby admitting its own seriousness and limitations. Our beautiful world is a horror-pit; how can our poetry not be comic? The kind of poetry envisaged here would involve a properly savage and sustained act of self-criticism. I hope this poetry reaches out to more and more people without compromising its seriousness or concealing its limitations. I hope it tackles the trouble that walks the streets, teaches in the schools, preaches in the churches, judges in the courts, festers or prospers in prison ('universities of crime' as one prisoner remarked to me), adores the music and songs of U2 and Sinéad O'Connor, speculates on the Stock Exchange, lives with AIDS, is sexually abused, sexually abuses, becomes anorexic, is unemployed, perhaps hopelessly so, condemns or praises the IRA and the UVF, begs in the streets of Dublin and talks to itself endlessly, lips moving with an eloquent, steady desperation that suggests nobody is listening or will ever listen.

I hope the troublesome art and craft will turn all this trouble into a thoughtful word-music that will, even for a brief while, make sense to whoever reads or listens. I hope it will give some people the courage to sit alone and listen to their own neglected voices. I hope it will make them remember and prepare. But most of all I hope it will bring them joy, sharp and deep, the kind of joy that often co-exists with deepened feelings of sadness or pain. More than anything else, poetry is a celebration of certain hard-won clarities arising from trouble and confusion. In today's world, these clarities can be won only by a poetry that is open, experimental and so serious it doesn't give a hoot about anything except what it dreams it believes it is struggling to suggest or say.

1   *Goodbye Twilight: Songs of the Struggle in Ireland*, edited by Leslie H. Daiken (London: Lawrence & Wishart, 1936).
2   (Dublin: Wolfhound Press, 1993).
3   *Collected Poems* (London: MacGibbon and Kee, 1964), p. 185; see also 'Yeats', *The Complete Poems*, edited by Peter Kavanagh (Newbridge: Goldsmith Press, 1984), pp. 348-49.
4   For example, 'Signposts', *Collected Prose* (London: Martin, Brian & O'Keefe, 1973), p. 25; also 'Author's Note', *Collected Poems*, p. xiv.
5   W.B. Yeats, 'The Gyres', *Collected Poems* (London: Macmillan, 1958), p. 337.
6   Patrick Kavanagh, 'From Monaghan to Grand Canal', *Collected Prose*, p. 228.
7   'Why Sorrow?', *The Complete Poems*, p. 180.
8   'Shancoduff', *The Complete Poems*, p. 13.
9   *The Great Hunger*, *The Complete Poems*, p. 88.
10 Denis Devlin, 'Lough Derg', *Collected Poems*, edited by J.C.C. Mays (Dublin: Dedalus Press, 1989); Patrick Kavanagh, 'Lough Derg', *The Complete Poems*; Seamus

Heaney, 'Station Island', *Station Island* (London: Faber and Faber, 1984).

11 *Selected Poems*, edited by W.J. McCormack (pseudonym Hugh Maxton) (Harmondsworth: Penguin Books, 1992); first published in 1991, edited by Hugh Maxton (Dublin: Lilliput Press).

12 'Tiresias', *Selected Poems*, pp. 168-88; 'Note', p. 267. Poem appeared in 1971.

13 Mary O'Donnell's weekly programme on poetry is entitled *Along the Backwater*, series started on 4 October 1992. Austin Clarke's weekly programme was entitled *Poetry* and broadcast between the late 1940s [1948] and the mid-1960s.

14 *The War Horse* (London: Gollancz, 1975, and Dublin: Arlen House, 1980); *In Her Own Image* (Dublin: Arlen House, 1980); *Night Feed* (Dublin: Arlen House, and London: Marion Boyars, 1982); *The Journey* (Dublin: Gallery Press, 1982); *Outside History* (Manchester: Carcanet, 1990); *In a Time of Violence* (Manchester: Carcanet, 1994).

15 'Self-Portrait on a Summer Evening', *Selected Poems* (Manchester: Carcanet, 1989), p. 73.

16 W.B. Yeats, 'The Spur', *Collected Poems*, p. 359.

17 First collected in *Between Innocence and Peace: Favourite Poems of Ireland*, edited by Brendan Kennelly (Cork and Dublin: Mercier Press, 1993), p. 205 [Patrick Galvin informed Kennelly that the poem first appeared in a limited edition published by the small American hand press Red Hanrahan Press, 1971].

18 *Poems 1956-1986* (Dublin: Gallery Press, and Newcastle upon Tyne: Bloodaxe Books, 1986).

19 'Wounds', *Poems 1963-1983* (Edinburgh: Salamander Press, and Dublin: Gallery Press, 1985); 'The Ice-Cream Man' appears in *Gorse Fires* (London: Secker & Warburg, 1991).

20 For example, *How's the Poetry Going? Literary Politics & Ireland Today* (Belfast: Lagan Press, 1991), and *A Real Life Elsewhere* (Belfast: Lagan Press, 1993).

21 Donagh MacDonagh, *The Hungry Grass* (London: Faber and Faber, 1947), p. 19.

22 (Dublin: Raven Arts Press, 1985).

23 Edited by Hugh McFadden, introduction by Macdara Woods (Dublin: Dedalus Press, 1991).

24 'This Houre Her Vigil', *Sandymount, Dublin: New and Selected Poems* (Dublin: Dedalus Press, 1988), p. 15. The poem was originally written in 1943.

25 *Hail! Madam Jazz: New and Selected Poems* (Newcastle upon Tyne: Bloodaxe Books, 1992).

26 *The Irish Times*, 10 June, 1993, p. 9.

27 W.B. Yeats, 'Remorse for Intemperate Speech', *Collected Poems*, p. 288.

28 For example, 'The Last Galway Hooker', 'The Cleggan Disaster', and *The Battle of Aughrim, New Selected Poems* (London: Faber and Faber, 1989), pp. 19-23; 31-41; 45-79.

29 (Newcastle upon Tyne: Bloodaxe Books, 1991).

30 'Under Ben Bulben', *Collected Poems*, p. 400.

COLIN GRAHAM
from *Irish Studies Review*, No. 13, Winter 1995/6

In *Irish Studies Review*, No. 8, Autumn 1994, Colin Graham advanced a thesis in an article entitled 'Post-Nationalism/Post-Colonialism: Reading Irish Culture'. Two issues later Gerry Smyth outlined his response in 'The Past, the Post, and the Utterly Changed: Intellectual Responsibility and Irish Cultural Criticism'. In issue 13, Winter 1995/6, Graham replied with the following article. For further analysis of Irish culture by Colin Graham, see his recent study written with Richard Kirkland, *Ireland and Cultural Theory: The Mechanics of Authenticity* (1999). Footnotes are as in original.

Rejoinder
The Irish 'Post-'? A reply to Gerry Smyth

In the period of colonization when it is not contested by armed resistance, when the sum total of nervous stimuli overstep a certain threshold, the defensive attitudes of the natives give way and they find themselves crowding the mental hospitals.[1]

In a recent article in *ISR*, Gerry Smyth speculated on the course of Irish cultural criticism in recent years and more specifically on where the trends he identified might lead in a post-ceasefire Ireland.[2] It seems to be Smyth's conviction that the conflicting varieties of critical methodologies available in Irish criticism are all in danger of impotence if or when the situation in Northern Ireland reaches a dénouement, partly because they are in some degree conceptually dependent on a perpetual 'Troubles'. I want to pick up some of the general strands of Smyth's argument and, more specifically, to reply to some of the comments and criticisms he made about my own position on post-colonial theory in the Irish context and its relationship to the concept of nation.[3]

The notion that critical methodologies employed in reading Ireland are fatally balanced on the process rather than the outcome of the 'Troubles' is initially an attractive one. Certainly nationalism and revisionism, for different reasons, have found themselves inevitably made contingent upon events in Northern Ireland. But it may be a mistake to assume that because they have been drawn towards continual engagement with the conflict they will be silenced by its 'ending'. Nationalism is already contorting itself into various post-nationalisms which have their own problems (not exclusively linked to the 'Troubles'); and, additionally, its very nature is surely to be perpetually tempted to set against post-nationalism (or establish within it) an ideological core resistant to change. And if revisionism's weakest liberal ethical strand has been at best capable of uttering only 'the horror, the horror', it can rely on its 'work', its methodological scholarliness, in the unlikely event that revisionists should feel an impulse towards entire political disengagement (a concept that only revisionists could hold).

The fate of revisionism or nationalism becomes enmeshed in Smyth's article with what he initially describes as 'theory' and what immediately becomes post-colonial theory, an assumption which is revealing about the extent to which Irish cultural criticism has been theorized at all:

The dates of the 'Troubles' coincide interestingly with another crisis which has been taking place in British and Irish intellectual formations generally, and in the institutions of higher education specifically. 'Theory' deserves its scare quotes every bit as much as 'Troubles', because of its uncertain status both as description and practice.[4]

Perhaps the reasons for sliding 'theory' into post-colonialism become clearer here: this is a pleasing parallel but it covers an error in chronology, since 'theory' may have 'begun' in 1968, but post-colonialism, as Smyth himself points out, can only look back to specifically academic origins in Said's *Orientalism* in 1978. Even then it took some years for the discipline to filter into institutional practice, and the main writings of Bhabha and Spivak, for example, are of the mid- to late-80s. Indeed Bhabha's work remained unpublished in book form until late 1994.

But this is a matter of chronology. What is more important is Smyth's assertion that 'theory'/post-colonialism in an Irish context is as dependent on the continuation of the 'Troubles' as its counterpart methodologies. In one sense it is possible to agree with Smyth: the 'cessation of hostilities' may indeed present post-colonial theory in an Irish context with problems, but these are the reverse of how Smyth sees them. Post-colonial theory, used in its most sophisticated and 'current' form, has the ability and potential to comprehend the complex and the hybrid in Irish culture. Used in a form derived from Bhabha and Spivak, for example, it is beholden upon post-colonial theory to look beyond the safe simplicities and binarisms which paradoxically constitute its initial conceptual basis — indeed contemporary post-colonial theory thrives best on a continual overturning of the settled, the accepted and the critically dominant. The problem in the Irish context is that post-colonialism has been applied and understood patchily — it still wavers between a revamped theoretical nationalism and the matrix provided by its use of notions of the subaltern and the hybrid, its readings of gender and desire, and its critiques of nation and ethnicity. Given this ambiguous state of post-colonial theory it is possible that future post-colonial readings of Ireland could reify at the very point when further and crucial movement is needed, becoming a retro-fashion used to sell nationalist nostalgia.

In writing the article to which Smyth responded, I was attempting to set out a version of post-colonial theory which had a conceptual rigour, primarily by contrasting the possibilities of post-colonialism against the shortcomings and inconsistencies of post-nationalism. I want now to answer some of Smyth's specific criticism and questions about what I said, before moving on to the wider issues of intellectual responsibility which he links to the theories he discusses.

Smyth describes the post-colonialism I formulated as being 'specifically deployed *against* the concept of nation, denying its validity if not at times its very existence'.[5] The first part of this criticism may be just an overstatement, the second is misleading. My conviction that post-colonial theory has begun to turn its attention to the deficiencies of the concept of 'nation' is not a revelation, or even a contemporary diagnosis, in terms of post-colonial theory. Guha's *Subaltern Studies* project, interrogating the course and practice of Indian nationalism before and after Independence, dates from 1982, and still continues.[6] One might say that 'even' Said, who has in some ways been left behind by much post-colonial thinking, has begun to examine how this difference with nationalism fits with his theoretical beliefs and political convictions.[7] But, as I suggested in my article, one can go back to the very origins of anti-colonial critical thought in Frantz Fanon to uncover a deep suspicion about the nature of nationalism, the ideological restrictions it implies and the effects of its political power. From Fanon's *The Wretched of the Earth* the chapter usually anthologized is 'On National Culture', enticingly subtitled 'Reciprocal Bases of National Culture and the Fight for Freedom'. However, Fanon only begins his discussion of the uses of 'National Culture' in anti-colonial struggle after a chapter entitled 'The Pitfalls of National Consciousness', in which he says:

> National consciousness, instead of being the all-embracing crystallization of the innermost hopes of the whole people, instead of being the immediate and most obvious result of the mobilization of the people, will be in any case only an empty shell, a crude and fragile travesty of what might have been.[8]

The recognition that post-colonialism meets the concept of 'nation' at some point, does not therefore tie the two concepts together irredeemably. This historical proximity puts post-colonial theory in a unique position as regards nationalism, comprehending its aims and ideologies yet able to step outside them in order to see their limitations, restrictions and incapacities. In this, post-colonialism can differ from revisionism's critique of nationalism in that it can avoid creating what Luke Gibbons calls 'the spectre of nationalism conjured up by revisionism . . . a spirit of the nation whose very lack of substance makes it all the more easy to exorcize'.[9] Post-colonial theory does not need to construct its own version of nationalism; it has been with nationalism and partially arises from it, and yet it need not, as I said in my article, be 'continually drawn into defending the post-colonial nation as an ethically and politically proper outcome of the wrong of colonization.' Only if we allow our understanding of colonization and imperialism to be irrevocably constructed as phenomena played out in terms of 'nations' is this the case; post-colonial theory needs to recognize this as a significant temptation in the Irish context and as a disabling dead end.[10]

Post-colonialism's advantage over nationalism is that it has been able to move on with integrity to examine issues of class, gender and marginality which the 'nation' and its narratives cannot prioritize. Smyth himself makes this point and examines Gibbons's essay in *The Field Day Anthology* as a typical example of a revision of nationalism from within.[11] Gibbons reads against the grain of the argumentative traits of revisionism by suggesting that revisionism constructs monoliths of nationalism while nationalism in Ireland is in fact diverse, disputed and historically in flux.

Gibbons's argument is compelling, for against an ideological and partially abstract critique it sets an historically exacting and precise version of differences within the formulation of 'nation' within Ireland. Gibbons cites, for example, misreadings of MacDonagh and shifts of perspective following the election of Lemass as significant moments. And he is thus able to establish that Irish nationalism is *not* just Moran's or Corkery's Irish Ireland transmuted into de Valera's Ireland. This is a vital complication of the cultural vocabulary of criticism of Ireland, and one that is often lacking in cultural criticism, if not historical criticism — it also suggests that nationalism is being historically homogenized by its debate with revisionism. Any post-colonial theory of Ireland must be prepared to accept the varieties of nationalism which have competed in Irish culture. The attention which post-colonial theory pays to factors which disrupt, undermine and speak back to monolithic cultural structures surely makes this possible, not only in terms of gender and class, but in the competing ways in which notions of ethnicity and authenticity are constructed. Yet the argument that post-colonial theory should have with the construction and praxis of the concept of 'nation' in Ireland is not ultimately materially altered by the knowledge of nationalism that Gibbons gives us. As Bhabha points out, there is 'a particular ambivalence [which] haunts the idea of nation, the language of those who write of it and the lives of those who live it', and, making a similar point to Gibbons, 'the cultural temporality of the nation inscribes a much more transitional social reality.'[12] 'Nation' can and should be *read* as fragile, opaque and fractured, by recognizing that its call for coherence is built on the double-voice of 'affiliation' and 'exclusion', and using 'theory' to widen the gaps in the '*in-between* spaces'.[13] The danger is that in critically reading the ideology of nation as ambivalent (or more benignly, diverse) we come to believe that the nation recognizes itself as such. Post-colonial theory must look at nationalism through its ideological histories and be aware of both its bases for construction and its claims to liberation. This would lead post-colonial theory in an Irish context to critically examine the 'failings' of nationalism — to interrogate the ironies of the fact (even if Smyth sees it as a truism) that Irish nationalist ideologies developed 'against' versions of Englishness in peculiarly dependent ways, and to be able to read without 'affiliation' the places of race, gender and ethnicity in Irish nationalism. To use post-colonial theory 'against' the nation in this way is the very opposite of 'denying its existence'. (Indeed to see this as reading 'against' to the point of denial seems to be close to a perfect example of the affiliation/exclusion binarism central to nation — not being national is not to be non-national, it is to be violently anti-national.) Post-colonial theory still places ultimate importance on the nation as the cultural dynamic of colonialism/post-colonialism; but it stops celebrating the nation and seeks to demystify the 'pathos of authenticity' which nation demands.[14]

This is to make post-colonial theory into something of an unrealized manifesto for Irish criticism, and I am very conscious of the weaknesses of such postulating. The position I am outlining is largely unmanifested in actual readings of Irish culture, and some of the other disagreements Smyth has with my position partly arise from the untested nature of what I have said about post-colonial theory. One specific point on which I would wish to focus relates specifically to what post-colonial theory will see in Irish culture when it applies the theoretical assumptions I have suggested. Smyth comments on the last sentence of my article which talks of post-colonial theory 'moving towards a notion of Irish culture which views the dialogic hybridity of "Irishness" in empowered ways'. Smyth says:

A commendable ideal, as no doubt all would agree; indeed, this formulation is not far removed from [Gerry] Adams's rhetoric, borrowed from the Proclamation of 1916, which promised to pursue the happiness and prosperity of the whole nation and all of its parts and to cherish 'all children of the nation equally'.[15]

Crucial, here, are assumptions about the role and provenance of the intellectual utterance in an Irish context, and I will return to this below. But Smyth is seriously misreading the very nature of post-colonial theory's use of terms such as 'dialogic' and 'hybridity' if he sees them as synonymous with the kinds of malign liberalized discourse used by politicians who wish to say little. Adams may hide behind the Proclamation; post-colonial theory could only poke, pull and undermine its fabric. The notion of cultural dialogism is not critical-theory-speak for dialogue, talking or 'getting on'. Dialogism (derived from Bakhtin) describes relationships (cultural, linguistic or otherwise) in which two entities are bound together in a process and in which they are mutually defining. Nowhere is equality implied or expected — heterogeneity can be misread as a United Colours of Bakhtin, but that was never Bakhtin's intention, and it need not be inevitable contemporary cultural criticism. In an Irish context, cultural dialogism could only describe the meta-relationship of Ireland with Britain in a way that relied upon a knowledge of the

desperate imbalance of power in that 'dialogue' (hence the awkward but significant phrase 'empowered ways' in my original piece).

'Hybridity' is then an outcome of this dialogic process, describing both the cultural products of colonialism as they fit in the context of the 'dialogic' and examining the rifts within the self-seeking solidities of 'Irishness' and 'Englishness'. Robert Young compellingly describes this notion of hybridity in a general way:

[The] conflictual structures generated by [the] imbalances of power [in culture] are consistently articulated through points of tension and forms of difference that are then superimposed upon each other: class, gender and race are circulated promiscuously and crossed with each other, transformed into mutually defining metaphors that mutate within intricate webs of surreptitious cultural values that are then internalized by those whom they define. Culture has always carried these antagonistic forms of inner dissonance within it: even 'Englishness' has always been riven by its own alterity.[16]

As Young stresses, to use the concept of hybridity and the dialogics which produce it is to read culture as 'conflictual', 'imbalanced', 'antagonistic' and 'dissonant'; hybridity does not allow cultural products which do no fit the categories of 'Irish' or 'English' to float in a disowned space. Rather it sees culture within the colonial relationship as always necessarily producing artefacts and events which are 'riven' internally and externally — 'a commendable ideal, as all would no doubt agree'? It is hard to see a consensus emerging for such methodology (as Smyth's article proves).

This brings me to the aspect of Smyth's article which is most unsettling and least clear in the specific context of post-colonial theory and in the wider sense of the relationship of the Irish critic with the 'nation'. Early in his essay Smyth says, 'The age of the organic intellectual is over, and contemporary commentators are no longer capable of making Yeatsian interventions in "the living stream".'[17] A debatable point, but one that I can partially accept. However, Smyth, in the conviction that I was 'denying' the existence of nationalism (which he has unhelpfully converged with 'nation'), later says:

But nationalism, for good or bad, *did* happen; it *did* win the hearts and minds of a large section of the population of the island. If one important part of the critic's intellectual responsibility is to invent possible futures, another is to respect the integrity of the past, even those pasts which we consider flawed or detrimental to our aims. Graham's concept of a post-colonial criticism totally inimical to nationalism is an unrealistic sacrifice of history to theory.[18]

My initial question must be, if the organic intellectual is dead in the sense that Smyth describes, where does this 'responsibility' originate? The assumption that I have an intellectual obligation towards nationalism (even if it is 'bad') just because *it was or is there* seems to me to be bizarre, and certainly no basis upon which to carry out intellectual activity of any sort. The whole passage in fact is peculiarly at odds both with Smyth's initial description of the loss of intellectual influence and the scepticism he expresses about the rhetorical 'cover' of dialogic hybridity. Indeed, if I am in an unwitting and unholy rhetorical alliance with Gerry Adams, a phrase such as 'the hearts and minds of a large section of the population of the island' might have been ghost-written by John Hume.

Defining the role of the intellectual is one of the most tortuous ventures that the 'intellectual' can undertake, and Smyth, at the end of his article, makes some very lucid and challenging comments. But it is desperately unclear where he sees 'responsibility' beginning and ending, and to whom it is owed. Edward Said gets himself into similar contortions on the subject, but the set of characteristics he sees as useful for an intellectual are at least appealing: 'Least of all should an intellectual be there to make his/her audience feel good: the whole point is to be embarrassing, contrary, even unpleasant.'[19]

It is still my conviction that the advantage post-colonial theory offers the critic in an Irish context is the opportunity not to be a hostage to the 'audience' which is a discourse of the nation. Smyth says that 'the status of post-colonial criticism is uncertain and its relationship with indigenous initiatives troubled'.[20] I entirely agree, but this is the very nature of post-colonial theory and it is its inherent value for Irish Studies. Post-colonialism is at its best when troubled and troubling — it is a continually changing, self-criticizing theory which does not allow itself or its subject to settle into complacent patterns. Maybe this makes it the ultimate critical 'industry', to use Smyth's word, and perhaps post-colonial theory evolved with a ready knowledge of how to preserve itself. But it is partly the very non-indigenous nature of post-colonialism which guarantees its continual and fruitful application to the Irish situation. Because it is not

dependent on Ireland for its impetus there is no reason why that impetus should decline when the political situation changes. The theory has already acknowledged and coped with the ends of militaristic hostilities in other contexts; it is capable of reading the aftermath and the residue. Where revisionism, nationalism, unionism, liberalism may be shaken by the aftershocks of peace, post-colonial theory holds power and lack of power, violence and hiatus, identity and crisis equally well within its critical remit. And while an Irish post-colonial theory could never deny the 'existence' of the nation, it has the capacity to challenge both the nation's claims to authenticate culture, and its claims to the sort of intellectual 'respect' to which Smyth accedes.

1   Frantz Fanon, *The Wretched of the Earth* (1961; Penguin, 1990), p. 201.
2   G. Smyth, 'The Past, the Post, and the Utterly Changed: Intellectual Responsibility and Irish Cultural Criticism', *Irish Studies Review*, vol. 10 (1995), pp. 25-9.
3   Smyth writes specifically about my article, 'Post-Nationalism/Post-Colonialism: Reading Irish Culture', *Irish Studies Review*, vol. 8 (1994), pp. 35-7.
4   Smyth, 'The Past, the Post, and the Utterly Changed', p. 27.
5   Smyth, 'The Past, the Post, and the Utterly Changed', p. 27.
6   See Ranajit Guha (ed.), *Subaltern Studies*, vol. I (Oxford University Press, 1982).
7   See, for example, E.W. Said, *Representations of the Intellectual: The 1993 Reith Lectures* (Vintage, 1994), especially chapter II 'Holding Nations and Traditions at Bay'; Said's *Culture and Imperialism* (Chatto & Windus, 1993) in parts reflects similar concerns.
8   Fanon, *The Wretched of the Earth*, p. 119.
9   L. Gibbons, 'Challenging the Canon: Revisionism and Cultural Criticism', *The Field Day Anthology of Irish Writing*, vol. III (Faber, 1991), p. 568.
10 Perhaps paradigmatic in this type of reading is Homi Bhabha's 'DessemiNation: time narrative, and the margins of the modern nation,' *Nations and Nationalism*, ed. H.K. Bhabha (Routledge, 1990), pp. 291–322.
11 L. Gibbons, 'Challenging the Canon: Revisionism and Cultural Criticism'.
12 Bhabha, 'Introduction: Narrating the Nation', *Nations and Nationalism*, p. 1.
13 Bhabha, 'Introduction: Narrating the Nation', p. 4.
14 'Authenticity' can be said to lie at the basis of many national claims to 'affiliation'. Jacob Golomb paraphrases Heidegger's socialized notion of authenticity thus: 'One is historically authentic when one creates one's own history by utilizing and recreating one's past and the past of one's people, projecting then with anticipatory resoluteness towards one's future. If "resoluteness constitutes the loyalty of existence to its own Self" [Heidegger], authenticity is the loyalty of one's own self to its past, heritage and ethos.' J. Golomb, *In Search of Authenticity: From Kierkegaard to Camus* (Routledge, 1995), p. 117.

15 Smyth, 'The Past, the Post and the Utterly Changed',
    p. 28 (Smyth's emphasis).
16 R.J.C. Young, *Colonial Desire: Hybridity in Theory,
    Culture and Race* (Routledge, 1995), p. xii.
17 Smyth, 'The Past, the Post, and the Utterly Changed',
    p. 25.

18 Smyth, 'The Past, the Post, and the Utterly Changed',
    p. 28.
19 Said, *Representations of the Intellectual*, pp. 9–10.
20 Smyth, 'The Past, the Post, and the Utterly Changed',
    p. 27.

PHILIP HOBSBAUM

from *The Honest Ulsterman*, No. 97, Spring 1994

Philip Hobsbaum (1932–), poet and critic, here recalls meetings of a writers' group
he established at Queen's University, Belfast, in 1963 when he was teaching there. The
sessions proved an important platform for future writers where they learnt
encouragement, group identity, and the obligation to revise.

The Belfast Group

The Belfast Group was an ad-hoc association of writers
loosely connected with Queen's University. It met eight
times each term, week by week, on a weeknight. The
idea was that each person would contribute a number of
poems, or a short story, or part of a novel, or part of a
play. These were duplicated and circulated so as to reach
those attending before the meeting at which the item in
question was to feature. Each meeting consisted of the
author reading out the item or items he or she had contributed, and each reading was followed by a discussion.
Because each person had before him or her a copy of the
work read, it meant that the discussion could be specific
and closely related to the text. The discussion would
take about an hour. Then there would be a break during
which coffee was served. After the break, there would be
a second half, when each of those present would in turn
read out poems or a prose piece that they had brought
along. This could be something written by a classic
author, or a modern, or indeed something composed by
the reader.

The Group ran under my aegis from October 1963
to March 1966. This duration covered eight terms,
during which twenty-eight different contributors read
out scripts and had them discussed. There were sixty-
four scripts in all. Seamus Heaney, a recent graduate,
produced seven scripts and consequently read at seven
meetings. So did the short story writer, John Bond,
then an undergraduate. Michael Longley, whom I had
met through his wife Edna, a colleague of mine,
produced four scripts. So did Stewart Parker, a
research student of mine who was studying non-

realistic drama. Four scripts apiece also were
contributed by Bernard MacLaverty, who was then a
laboratory assistant in the Queen's Medical Faculty;
and by Hugh T. Bredin, a research student in
philosophy who at that period shared a flat with
Seamus Heaney. The Professor of Spanish, Arthur
Terry, produced three scripts; so did Maurice
Gallagher, a student who wrote short stories; so did
Joan Newmann, a civil servant whom I had met
through classes at the Adult Education Department.
And I produced three scripts, all of them sheafs of
poems, myself.

As this list of names suggests, the Group was fairly
eclectic. In particular, I had little idea of the ground I
was breaking when I invited people from both
communities, Catholic and Protestant, or from no
community at all, to take part. These people might
have met one another if there had been no Group, but
that seems unlikely. In any case, the fortuitous
encounter can be a fruitful outcome of relatively
informal proceedings such as these were.

Membership was at the invitation of the Chairman.
He based his decisions on his apprehension not only of
the quality of the writer, but also on that writer's
promise. A few of the participants, notably Heaney
and Longley, had already published some work.
Creativity was in the air, north and south of the
Border. There was *Poetry Ireland*, a literary magazine
based in Dublin. There was the Queen's University
Festival. Also, a number of writers who did not attend
the Group were nevertheless friendly with one or
another of the participants. And there was a highly
positive radio programme, *The Arts in Ulster*.

The number of writers who emerged from the Group to become professional may not seem large, but it is certainly striking. In addition to those participants already named, Norman Dugdale, Robert Sullivan and James Simmons have made names for themselves in one sphere or another. Though the ability of the star attractions may seem to be agreed now, the matter was not so obvious thirty years ago. Seamus Heaney had been thought by the University staff to be a relatively slight figure in comparison with the other first-class students. One of my colleagues in the English Department at Queen's spoke of Stewart Parker, novelist and poet as well as later an original playwright, as 'nothing out of the ordinary'.

Behind these meetings was the concept that writing — including one's own writing — could be discussed. Also implicit was the concept of apprenticeship. Not, I have to say, apprenticeship to myself as guru, but rather that of learning one's trade; seeking to master a technique. Essentially, people learned from one another.

From the first, Seamus Heaney was dedicated as writer, as participant, and as a keen but sympathetic critic of the scripts of others. An early success of his — so far as those present in the Group were concerned — was the poem 'Digging'. It begins:

Between my finger and my thumb
The squat pen rests; snug as a gun.

Beneath my window, a rich rasping sound
When the spade sinks clean into gravelly ground:
My father, digging. I look down

Till his straining rump among the flowerbeds
Bends low, comes up twenty years away
Stooping in rhythm through potato drills
Where he was digging . . .

(I quote, here as elsewhere, from the actual Group sheet.)

Perhaps it doesn't take too much discernment to see that here already was an accomplished writer. The analogy between literary labour and agricultural labour remains poignant, possibly because there is a kind of apology in the atmosphere. That snugness of the sedentary poet appears a little guilty before the straining and stooping of the man digging. At the same time, the poet has the power of conjuration. It can be seen in the transition marked by the phrase 'twenty years *away*'. There we have the incipient distinction of the poet Heaney was to become. A lesser author would have written 'twenty years *ago*'.

There was no one school of thought in the Belfast Group. For all his similarity to Heaney in age and enthusiasm, Michael Longley was a highly contrasted voice. Urbane, urban, literary as it was, I admired his poem 'Dr Johnson on the Hebrides'. It shows a bulky townsman trudging through the mists of the Western Isles. The poem draws a degree of attention to its highly deliberate tone:

The Hebridean gales, mere sycophants,
So many loyal Boswells at his heel —
Yet the farflung outposts of experience
In the end outdo a Roman wall . . .

The Longleys, Michael and Edna, seem to have felt that I was rather hard on them. At the time it seemed to me that Michael's literariness, demonstrated here, rather got in the way of his experience. Even so, I persuaded the publishing firm of Macmillan to overturn their original decision against accepting his first book, *No Continuing City*, and the firm has since thanked me for my intervention.

The inhibition, it appears now, was not literariness *per se* so much as a reliance on rhyme. The rhymes in themselves cannot be faulted, and the craft of the early poems seems on the surface to be most assured. But there has been a break-through, at a time well advanced in this poet's working life, with the remarkable collection *Gorse Fires*. This seems to me qualitatively superior to any of the previous books, and it cannot be a coincidence that the poems in *Gorse Fires* are unrhymed. There must have been in the past some inhibiting pressure that was later removed. Longley can now take his place alongside his distinguished contemporaries and near-contemporaries, both in the Group and outside it.

The Group mainly existed to encourage writers in future endeavours. But some poets used it as a means of revision. James Simmons had a rather artless piece on an early sheet, 'On Gardens':

I want a walled garden's protective peace,
With many bushes, tall flowers and trees,
A wooden well-aired bower in a simple design,
With a watertight roof and a dry seat, to be
   mine . . .

This lurches along quite charmingly. But there is an effect of each line having to be wound up at the beginning, the rhythm running down as it reaches the end, with an awkward pause as the rhythm is wound up again for the beginning of the next line. There is in a later version a wholesale tidying up, a revision presumably prompted directly by a Group discussion.

This is the beginning of the text as it appears in Simmons's first book, *Late but in Earnest*:

A garden I might get lost in, with old trees,
Surrounded by high walls to protect my peace:
In the middle a rainproof shelter, where fresh air
Could enter, with room for a solid wicker
　　chair . . .

This tendency to use the Group as a means of revision was not general. The action of reading aloud a text of one's own to a selection of acquaintances gives the sense of having an audience. It is an audience, moreover, that exists before writers, critics and the public at large have had a chance to clapperclaw the offering. The writer therefore has an opportunity to find out how and where to pitch his or her voice.

Prose was as important as verse at the various Group meetings. An early story by Bernard MacLaverty, 'Jim Scroggy', was applauded at the time and has retained its vivacity. The story has never been printed so far as I know, but I have read it aloud to audiences in places as diverse as Warsaw and Urbana, Illinois, and it never fails to seize attention. The following excerpt is from the third section of the story:

The whole breed of them is as odd as mare's pish. Firewatcher stood close to the bar holding lightly onto his black pint. Beside him listening attentively, while laughing at him and with him, stood a young man who worked for the Electricity Board. The barman vigorously polishing glasses came over to them.

　　Who's that you're giving off about, now Firewatcher?

　　It's them Scroggys.

　　You mean Jim and Martha. What about them?

　　Well this young fellah was asking me about them and I'm just putting him in the picture. Odd as mare's pish. At least they are now. Didn't always used to be, mind you. I remember the time Jim was doing well for himself — owned the half of the townland. Then he went odd about ten years ago — all of a sudden. He was getting old, but that wasn't the reason at all. Nor was it the drink, nor women, nor nothing that I can think of. Just something inside a man grows odd, and it spreads from him to his wife to his work and now he does damn all except hump about that house of his, never speaking nor working. Oh he does alright for money though, he hires out the land for grazing. Doesn't have to work just sits on his odd ass and collects . . .

The ear for speech, and the authority, is already there. Colloquialism is settled in the text, not imposed upon it. Consider the idiosyncratic use of that word 'odd', which echoes through the rest of Firewatcher's talking. Notice the touch of the master storyteller, which invites one to read on: to find out about the oddness of the Scroggys, to discover what happens next. A discerning reader could have expected the emergence of the great popular figure MacLaverty has become, with his novels *Lamb* and *Cal*, and the evocative films made of these novels.

The short story, however, is a difficult medium from one point of view. Publishers fight shy of taking on collections, and media for the transmission of individual stories are few. It may have been an aura of discouragement well beyond the Group that caused such promising voices as John Bond, Paul Smyth and Hugh Bredin to fall into silence, though Bredin has certainly expressed himself in conceptual prose, as a philosopher.

For me, Stewart Parker was a star from the very beginning, in prose fiction as in other genres. It is good to think that an Irish publisher has promised to bring out his early novel, *The Tribulations of ST Toile*. This chronicles, with the blackest of black humour, the goings-on at a school which appears to be entirely populated by cripples and defectives. Stewart Parker died of cancer in 1990. But 'his words wing on — as live words will'. This early work remained unknown, except to members of the Group, until recently. However, Parker became famous as the author of some breathtakingly original plays, including *Spokesong*, *Iris in the Traffic*, *Ruby in the Rain*, and *The Kamikaze Ground Staff Annual Reunion*.

It may be felt that ideology was absent from the Group. The procedure was, indeed, formalist. That was not because individuals were devoid of political stance but because concentration tended to be upon the 'how' — the 'how' of communication. Such a concern may be sidelined now, when all too much criticism is a summary of what the critic takes to be the author's ideas. As often as not the summary is followed by condemnation of such texts as do not follow the critic's party line, be that feminism, Marxism or nationalism. It seems to me that aesthetic value and linguistic texture cannot be set aside in such a fashion.

The Group was a form of educational process. One could protest that, out of the twenty-eight people who actually proferred sheets, only eight to ten made some kind of name in literature. But surely we all benefited by looking attentively at texts of our time, and hearing them intensively discussed. Such a process necessarily influences one's mode of reading, and shapes one's thinking for a long time to come.

AIDAN HIGGINS
from Aidan Higgins, *Donkey's Years: Memories of a Life as Story Told* (1995)

In perhaps the finest single sentence produced by a modern Irish writer, Aidan Higgins here recalls the collection of impressions that constituted his childhood.

The Great Flood

I recall: Aladdin paraffin lamps and anthracite and coke and Bird's Custard and sago and tadpoles (pollywoggles) wriggling in the pond at the edge of the Crooked Meadow and cruel hare-coursing and blooding of hounds and the baying of the pack after foxes and twists of hardboiled sweeties in paper bags, a pennyworth and tuppenceworth, and Findlater's men carrying in a week's supplies and being checked by the cook and Wild Woodbines in open packets of five for tuppence halfpenny old currency with farthings in the change and the mad dog frothing at the mouth running in mad circles in humpy commonage near Oakley Park one lovely summer's day returning from the village with fags and brother Bun and I feeling sick and giddy from the first tobacco and the PP's[1] alarming *Diktat* from the pulpit on Sunday and pea-picking for Mumu in the garden and the Bogey Man lurking in the cellar with the arrowheads and the mouldy masks and looking for mushrooms in Mangan's long field with Mumu and the Dodo early one morning in summer and the stink of ammonia in the convent class and the damp poor clothes in the hanging cupboard and the musty smell of nuns and the rustle of their habits and the small turf fire dying in the narrow grate when Sister Rumold prepared us for First Holy Communion and told us, 'You must prepare yourself to receive Our Lord' and the hot smell of the big girls and the provenance of sin — a writhing serpent impaled on the Patriarch's crozier and St Brigid the patroness blushing scarlet up on her pedestal and St Patrick watching with his curly beard — and the purple-shrouded statues at Passion Week[2] and the whispering in the dim confessional and Crunchies[3] in golden foil wrappings and chocolate whirls with whipped cream centres that the Dote and I called Dev's[4] Snots and then Bull's Eyes and Peggy's Leg and liquorice twists and fizzy sherbets and stirabout with cream and brown sugar in the dark after early Mass and servants churning in the chilly dairy and butter pats in the tub and bluebottles buzzing against the larder screen and a snipe rotting on a hook and the cat-stink behind the mangle and the sheets airing on the stiffened hillocks of the frozen bleach-green and the tracks of the hare in the snow and lowing cows calving and calves on spindle legs suckling their mothers and mares foaling and stallions mounting with flared nostrils and sows farrowing and ewes lambing and the baldy priest in the awful brown wig saying mass below us at Straffan and the polychrome Christ bleeding with one arm missing at the scourging in the Stations of the Cross that stuck out in little polychrome grottos from the nave and the nun with pinched bloodless lips genuflecting and extinguishing candles with a long snuffer and the lovely by-road by the Liffey to Odlums' and the May procession between the cypress trees along the convent avenue and the gravel biting into my bare knees and I thinking only of the cold roast with lots of salt and the ruffled nun walking against the wind and ruddyfaced Sister Rumold nodding her wimple — like the scuffed lining of a shallow Jacob's biscuit tin or glacé fruit packings — and leaning forward from her highbacked chair in the Holy Faith Convent waitingroom and genteelly offering Mumu a Zube from a little oval box sprung open in her white speckled hand and my mother in her blandest grandest way (with fur coat thrown open so that the nun could get an eyeful of her expensive Switzer's[5] dress) saying how important education was and the wimple nodding like mad for Sister Rumold couldn't agree more, for the youngest (aged four) and myself (aged six) the middle child were to be taken under her wing the following Monday in the class of Second Infants and Lizzy Bolger had painted her mouth with the reddest lipstick and seemed to be bleeding from the mouth and was coaxing, 'Gizzakiss, ah g'wan!' and the big girls were tittering in the playground and the men were playing Pitch & Toss after Mass above Killadoon front gate and the hay-bogies were grinding along the Naas-Celbridge road and the steamroller belching smoke and stinking of tar and twenty Collegiate College girls in slate-gray uniforms were rounding Brady's corner and two teachers with long forbidding Protestant horse-faces pacing along in front and their shadows flitting along the wall and myself in great embarrassment cycling rapidly by and Satan dining at Castletown (narrated dramatically by the Keegans as if they had been present, carrying in steaming dishes) and the PP sweating and called in after the Vicar couldn't shift His Nibs who sat there sneering and then the PP showed him the crucifix and told him to go about his business and the

PP himself sweated seven shirts and died but Satan had gone straight through the floor in a puff of black smoke, leaving a cracked mirror behind as a memento as you can see to this day; all that I recall of those grand times that can never return.

1 Parish priest.
2 The week before Easter when all the statues in the church were covered with purple cloth.
3 A brand of chocolate.
4 Presumably after De Valera.
5 Fashionable department store on Grafton Street, Dublin.

TIM ROBINSON
from Tim Robinson, *Stones of Aran: Labyrinth* (1995)

Tim Robinson (1935–) was born and raised in Yorkshire. After studying mathematics at Cambridge he worked as a teacher and artist in Istanbul, Vienna, and London. In 1972 he moved to the Aran Islands to write and make maps. He has written two companion volumes about the Aran Islands, *Stones of Aran: Pilgrimage* (1986) and *Stones of Aran: Labyrinth* (1995). Robinson's writing has been much admired and this passage is typical of the author's capacity to move effortlessly between different genres.

Among the Thorns

Certain areas of Aran are so heavy with the presence of the past that to linger in them leaves one as enriched and as drained as can the contemplation of a work of art. The fields that tumble down the hillside west of Mainistir village have this quality, and also a faintly disquieting atmosphere of their own I have often tried to characterize more exactly than by the words that first present themselves: *siógach*,[1] *unheimlich*,[2] spooky. These fields are small, crooked, interlinked by gaps in odd sequences, full of little stone-ricks and the thicketed mounds of collapsed stone huts. The thresholds of the gaps are worn into hollows, the gullies are bridged here and there by stones thrown down so casually or so long ago that it is difficult to be sure they are not accidental assemblages. The age of such places is more palpable than are the many centuries archaeology attaches to certain identifiable combinations of stones — the chapels and beehive huts and ring-forts — for in fact all the stones here look not only as if they have been disposed and redisposed many times but as if their present order is very old. And since the land is less used than it was a couple of generations ago, it is true that these stones have not been disturbed for a long time; the one or two men I see making their familiar twice-daily way to the cow at milking-time have been doing so for fifty or seventy years, and their sons and grandsons will not be following them. Briars invade from neglected corners; the hazel bushes, in which one occasionally notices obliquely truncated stems where rods were cut years ago, are spreading out

of the dells, for nobody comes for hazel-rods now. In fact no one apart from those old men visits these out-of-the-way corners at all. The stiles and stepping-stones that help them over the walls and clefts are so clearly intended only for the toe and heel of the men who made them that, when I use them in scrambling from field to field looking for clocháns or wild-flowers, I feel as if I had crept into someone's house and am trying the armchairs, peeping into the books. This sense of intruding on a privacy makes one move quietly, furtively. On a silent summer afternoon, when one parts the bracken closing some tiny pathway, and suddenly a thousand bluebottles go up, one starts guiltily. Here one is in intimate contact with a world withdrawn into the past. Seeing it revealed thus in its obsessional, finicky, obsolete ways is touching, and at the same time illicitly exciting. If there is haunting here, it is not that some returned frequenter of these fields is peering into our time, but that I myself am trespassing back through gaps in walls of the past.

This world protects itself with prickles, spikes, barbs. The Eochaill people's land on the terraces running westwards from the old village of Mainistir is called An Sceach Mhór, the big thorn, probably from an old hawthorn under which a holy woman lies, a sleeping spiritual beauty. The brambles around St Asurnaí's grave and holy well, the inner sanctum of this thorny locality, are almost impenetrable, but the ruin of her little oratory nearby is welcoming, though few come there, as it is eremitically withdrawn from notice. A finger-post by the coast-road directs one to it along a path that absolves one from insensitive intrusion. It leads first across a few fields, or more accurately *creagáin*, patches of rock patched with grass, patches of grass patched with rock, and in spring splashed with primroses, celandines and daisies. Low blackthorn bushes lie along the walls, their dark, glossy twigs foaming with creamy blossom in April when they are still leafless. The hawthorns rooted in fissures of the pavement have been dwarfed by the prevailing wind into hummocks with their eastward rims spreading out on the ground; these limestone-warmed fringes flower earlier than the rest, so that the hunchbacked bushes trail lace-trimmed robes. Sharp eyes might notice that these grotesque, perfumed exquisites sometimes wear tiny rings on their crooked fingers. Looking closely one sees that these are bands of minute brownish granules, the eggs of the lackey moth. When they hatch out the caterpillars spin themselves a communal web of silk that gradually envelopes several twigs. They take the sun on this web, twenty or thirty of them lying curved together in a velvet mat. After a shower, with a few raindrops glistening among their delicate blue-grey and orange stripes, the colony looks like a piece of barbaric jewellery, but when one bends to look at the gorgeous thing it stirs, breaks up, and creeps piecemeal into its foul tent.

Farther up the hillside the bushes are higher, and in late summer are hung with heavy festoons of honeysuckle, each blossom a seduction of claret and oyster-satin. The path becomes almost a tunnel through the scented foliage where it climbs the first scarp. Look at the ground here: thousands of limpet- and winkle-shells are spilling out of it, detritus of long-gone generations' ascetic and monotonous feasts. Such shell-middens are found all along the spring-line here. The narrow terrace above is what the islanders called *sean-talamh*, old land; fertile and well-watered, it never had to be reclaimed from the rock, or at least not in any period known to oral lore. The little oratory stands here, in the shelter of an ivy-covered cliff-face, above which are stonier reaches of the hillside.

Teampall Asurnaí is tiny — just sixteen feet by twelve — craggily built, dumpy. Its side-walls are three feet thick and bulge like the sides of a boat. The gables stand to just above head-height; in the east one, above the altar, is the base of a narrow window-light, and at the south-east corner a projecting stone which would have supported the barge of the roof. The Office of Public Works, statutorily charged with the dis-enchantment of Ireland, has treated this chapel with a lighter hand than usual, and wild flowers still flourish within and without. A plot of ground over a field-wall a few yards to the east, which used to be impregnably briary, has recently been cleared, revealing two prone cross-slabs and a broken quern-stone. To the west, in

the next field, are the low remains of three-foot-thick walls outlining a rectangular building. The topmost stone of a window-light lies on one of these walls, which if it is from Teampall Asurnaí shows that it had a narrow slit window with an ogival point — fifteenth-century work, much later than the rest of the church. Under the cliff behind the church is a good spring. The cliff itself is full of interest. The gleaming, shadowy face of the clay band from which the water oozes at the foot of the scarp is covered with golden saxifrage, as if with layer upon layer of burnished thumb-prints; this, and Tobar Chiaráin further east and under the same scarp, are virtually the only places in Aran I have seen the plant. A flight of small rough steps has been cut into the rock-face for bringing water up to the pastures above. Just to the west a natural recess in a bulge of the cliff has been closed up with stones to make a little sheep-fold; it is called Scailp Pháidín Uí Uiginn, Paddy Wiggins's cleft, from a man who lived in it once after being thrown out of home by his wife. The wrinkled crag over it looks like a face, or an Arcimboldo painting of a cliff that looks like a face, a likeness of the disconsolate Wiggins himself perhaps.

When O'Donovan[3] saw this chapel in 1839, there was 'a small apartment adjoining the east gable called St Soorney's Bed, in which people sleep expecting to be cured of diseases, and about 20 paces to the east . . . a holy well called Bullaun na Surnaighe'. However, there is little trace of the apartment now, and whatever rites took place here have long been neglected. The *bullán*, presumably one of those stones with a hollow originally used as mortars, often found near monastic sites and regarded as holy wells, must have been in the little grave plot. But the Bullán Asurnaí and Leaba Asurnaí known to the villagers of today are on the terrace below the chapel, about a hundred yards away to the north-west. From above it is easy to see a hawthorn tree taller than the rest which marks the spot, but it is still not easy to get there, for the obsessively detailed subdivision of the land makes every traverse into a succession of moves on a Lewis Carroll chess-board, and rampant growth turns every fence into a quandary. A faint path runs down the hill on the further side of the next field-wall west of the sheep-pen, crossing the low, mounded remains of walls much more ancient even than the ivy-knotted antiquities that serve today, and ends in a field where a large glacial boulder sits on a little hummock. The well and the 'bed' or grave are within a few yards of this landmark, and yet one may fail to find either, for the place has nodded off in a torpor of neglect. Massive moss-covered walls and heaps of stone, the remains of another wall long-removed, have been welded together by the overgrowth into a little oval precinct around the grave, the entrance to which, disguised by nettles, is in the south-east corner of the next field to the west. The grave is obliterated by thorns (as de Sade wanted his to be), and is indicated only by a slim finger of stone sticking up through the brambles, about three feet high, with the faintest suggestion of a cross rubbed into one face. Although it has not been the object of a *turas* or pilgrimage for generations now, with imagination one can make out the trodden path of the 'rounds' about the knot of briars. Another gap in the circle of mouldering stone opens westwards into a small pasture, and the 'well', a granite bullaun-stone usually holding a bit of rainwater, lies half hidden by leafage on the left of this entrance. Above it is the big thorn-tree, bent like an old woman; perhaps this is not the original holy bush, which the 1898 map marks a little farther west, but simply the oldest surviving tree in the vicinity, and therefore inheritor of the title.

The stories I have collected about this fane are various, odd, and tantalizing. The bullaun, of course, never goes dry even in the droughtiest weather. People from Connemara used to come here to be baptized — 'but that was back in the pagan times'. The field by the bullaun has good soil — it is under a scarp with a clay-band at its foot — but it has never been dug; its owner once decided to set potatoes in it, and came with a load of sea-weed on his horse, but the horse refused to carry it into the field. Finally (and this is true; I heard it in Evelyn's shop in Eochaill village), somewhere the cult of St Asurnaí still lives, for in 1978 a young Australian came enquiring for the place, spent a day trying to find it and got terribly scratched, but failed to obtain what he had been told to bring home, two pounds of thorns from St Asurnaí's bush.

What recluse lies here, though, after what purifying or stultifying life? St Asurnaí is supposed to be the nun to whom a church is dedicated at Drumacoo in south Galway, but according to Fr Killeen the latter's right name was Sarnait. O'Donovan suggests the church is actually called Teampall na Surnaighe, the church of the vigils. In Archbishop O'Cadhla's list of Aran churches we have:

The church called *Tempull-Assurnuidhe*, which is said to be dedicated to St Assurnidhe (or, perhaps, Esserninus), and this church is held in the greatest veneration among the islanders.

Esserninus was one of St Patrick's bishops sent to Ireland in 438, long before the foundation of Cill Éinne, and nothing connects him with Aran. If the matter was obscure when the archbishop wrote three hundred and fifty years ago, it seems likely to remain so. I will scratch myself no longer on the thorny question.

Turning away from the saint's grave, my eyes adjusted to shadows, I look deeper into the bushes, searching under them for the modest heaven of flowers to be found on the dark earth: the damp lilac silk tags of wood-sorrel in summer, or sanicle with its little spherical clouds of minute flowers like puffs of hoar-frost; in the very early days of spring often nothing but celandines. In such a place I once saw a single yellow celandine blossom, its eight glossy petals sharply separate and spread as if it were straining to grasp as much definition for itself as possible out of its penumbral bower. It hypnotized my memory, so that I had to return the next day with a camera. But then I saw that the dim perspective of twigs I was looking through was as precise in its enmeshed tonalities and interpenetrating articulations as the star of hermetic knowledge shining in its depths. No camera could encompass this microcosm, and I came away with renewed respect for the eye, leaving the flower to the perverse purity of self-perfection.

1   Irish: fairy-like.
2   German: weird, uncanny.
3   John O'Donovan (1806–61), Gaelic Adviser to the Ordnance Survey of 1830, and later Professor at Queen's University, Belfast. He was George Petrie's principal colleague, and for a decade from 1834 travelled round Ireland recording place-names, local history and folklore and describing antiquities. A forerunner, that is, of Robinson himself.

AILBHE SMYTH
from *Critical Survey*, Vol. 8, No. 2, 1996

Ailbhe Smyth here provides a very useful survey and critique of Irish identity from the position and perspective of a woman and a woman writer. The essay speaks for itself and footnotes are as in the original. You might follow up some of the references for yourself.

Declining identities (lit. and fig.)

1 SOUNDING

We are sick of reacting to Catholicism, to anti-women laws in Ireland, to constantly being cornered and attacked about feminism, to being seen as 'the Other'. We are fed up trying to survive, only survive, instead of finding a space for all of us to thrive in. (Louise Walsh)[1]

In 1992, two Irish artists, Louise Walsh and Pauline Cummins, collaborated in a remarkable installation, 'Sounding the Depths', at the Irish Museum of Modern Art. Through a complex and sophisticated weave of 'cool' media, including photography, video, lighting and sound, the artists explore the hotly contested terrain of women's bodies, 'shrieking in delight', tongues reaching out, liquefying, teeth clamped, biting, parting, bellies opening, stretching into mouths superimposed on torsos revealed, exposed, hands pulling apart, prising open. The images are searing red — 'red is the loudest colour, and the most secret' — deliberately personal and defiantly public, passionate, sexual, sensuous, reckless in their openness, drowning historical silences in a fiery river of energy refusing to be contained any longer:

The mouth becomes wide and starts things a-moving, giving a voice to the body, locating the wound, tight and sealed though it is — closing up all that needs to be said . . . [T]he open, vulnerable mouth/hole in our belly [enables us] to shout, to roar with laughter, grief and joy and finally, to be whole, healed and open. (Louise Walsh, p. 6)

These visual, visible, visceral soundings come from the depths of the silence imposed on women by a culture which has colonized, contained and controlled women's bodies, women's sexuality, with particular ferocity and tenacity.

I love to use Virginia Woolf's words 'as a woman I have no country', but I like to say, 'as a woman my body is my country'. I used this paraphrase during the dreadful anti-abortion campaign in 1983. When we were being told what we could or could not do with our bodies, our country was being invaded. (Pauline Cummins, p. 6)

In a culture where, as Eavan Boland has argued, the land and the nation and the feminine figure all come together,[2] the statement, or question, of national identity is problematic for women, historically and emblematically denied the power to shape its meaning. This may not matter (although I think it should) where national identity is a confident assumption, not a question or an open wound. But that is not the case in Ireland. Louise Walsh and Pauline Cummins are not alone in seeking a space in which Irish women may thrive. That space is being found, constructed, created in many ways by many women in Ireland — activists and politicians, educators and thinkers, artists and writers.[3] And whether we think it should or it should not, making that space involves negotiating, or re-negotiating, the questionable terrain of Irishness. For we do, women as much as men, have a country, although the ways in which we may inhabit and inflect it — culturally, socially, politically — are not the same.

There is a great need for feminists in the North and in the South to have much more dialogue, to think creatively about the possibilities of the future, to imagine what a new Ireland could mean for us and to build on the many gains for women that we have achieved, North and South. (Clare Hackett)[4]

Soundings have reverberations: the question is, do we hear them? Or what might change if we were to listen?

We won't shut up. We'll not be silenced. We'll find the strength to open up. (Louise Walsh, p. 6)

2 MEANING

While not precisely up for grabs (we have our pride), Irish identity in the 1990s has become something of a commodity on an open market. It's a multipurpose product with fluctuating values depending on how much we're looking for, whom we're dealing with — EU, UK, USA, UN, global corporations — and what we're trading in — a President-Stateswoman, rock bands, or 'peace-keeping' soldiers.

Of course, the currency of Irish identity has been changing with no subtlety at all since the 1950s, becoming more flexible and eclectic. I choose not to call that flexible eclecticism 'postmodern' because, while I don't know exactly what the word means (does anyone?), it appears to be used (*inter* much *alia*) to connote meaninglessness, even in respect of 'Irishness':

Postmodern culture takes the form of an incoherent and meaningless pastiche of temporally instan-taneous and disjointed experiences of images and surfaces which the decentered subject is left up to his/her own devices to deal with. (Kieran Keohane)[5]

Whatever it is or may be in the process of becoming, the evidence of my own eyes and ears tells me that the Irish Identity business has by no means crashed, or slumped into meaninglessness or temporal instantaneity. *Au contraire*, it seems to be on the biggest roll of its heretofore necessarily mono-directional life. Eclecticism is not the same as meaninglessness. It is (among other meaningful meanings) defined as 'broad not exclusive' (*Shorter Oxford Dictionary*). This, I want to suggest, is a primary aspect of the new *possibility* of 'Irishness'. It is no longer owned and commodified by an élite ruling group (however disenfranchised they claimed to have been by colonial history), no longer exclusively riveted on the interminable struggle for freedom (a struggle, let us remind ourselves, not at all the exclusive experience of the Irish), no longer represented by the cultural trinity of Yeats, Joyce and Beckett. (Their, and other, hegemonic meanings of Irishness were in any case always plural and typically in contradiction with one another, if not actively incompatible.) Neither the problematic nature of 'One-ness' nor the ubiquitousness of contradiction was discovered by postmodernists, although (Columbus-like) they have appropriated them unto themselves:

I'd like to see a Kevin McAleer
on Derrida. There is an unthinkable
tonnage of paper recording the turnout
of words required by the system
to gain this and that advantage —
letters after the name, tenure,
head of the faculty, head of
thinking and so on. Think
of the phoniness, Come on Kevin.

(Eithne Strong)[6]

But don't misunderstand me: because I challenge the usefulness of postmodernism as some kind of explanation of the reprocessing of 'Irishness', it does not follow that I reject that process. My point is that 'Irishness' is being invested with new and different meanings which we would do very well to attend to, in socially and politically meaningful ways. In my view, we need all the flexibility and eclecticism — or pluralism, to put it in more explicitly political terms — we can get. 'Incoherence', or the abandonment of 'sense-making', is neither a necessary nor a desirable

corollary of new kinds of openness. *Come on Kevin* (or Kieran).

Over the past few years, thinking about the political and creative work of Irish women, and about how the one is imbricated in the other, it has seemed to me that the terms — the reverberations — of 'Irishness' are being radically altered by this work (to say nothing of the small matter of the ways in which people live their lives), although usually without the *bona fides* 'required by the system' for the seriousness of its (far from homogenous) challenge to be valued as real, hard currency. For Irish women's work, economically, politically, socially, culturally still has far less value accruing to it than that of Irish men.[7]

I was interested in circles and their tongue-like bodies — I was intrigued by their shell hardness, and their inner softness, and the choices we all have about when to be open or closed. (Pauline Cummins, p. 6)

I am interested in how the hard shell of 'Irishness' is being prised apart and opened up by the work of Irish women, although in an almost imperceptible process, since the editors of 'Irishness' so rarely trouble to note its occurrence. For it seems to me that we are dealing now with new contradictions, and new possibilities. I want to know what they mean, and whether, perhaps, we need to deal in the currency of 'Irishness' at all:

The taciturn clams break their silence to say
'Dig us out if you need to
position the steel,
raise the concrete walls,
but, when your shell is complete,
remember that your life,
no less than ours,
is measured by the tides of the sea
and is unspeakably fragile'

(Moya Cannon)[8]

3   DECLINING
To decline: v. trans.
(1) to turn aside (lit. and fig.): not to consent or engage in, practise or do; not to accept (something offered); to refuse or object to the jurisdiction of.
(2) To inflect or recite in order the cases; to recite in definite order.

(*Shorter Oxford Dictionary*)

Of course, there is no rule stipulating that we must proceed in terms of definitions. But since I am considering how and why Irish identity may be (being) (differently) declined by women, it seems only fair to offer a definition of my own. That is now done. I shall return to the declining business from time to time.

Identity, however, I shall not define, precisely because I want to focus on what it means for Irish women (not, please note, just 'women in Ireland', for there is a difference, although we do not always attend to it: the diaspora also defines) to contest what we have inherited from a version of the history of this place, this island, this *entity*. For such it is, however divided, and by many borders (both lit. and fig.), which that history has declined to record.

> Before me from that high watershed the west
> expands to reach a sixty mile horizon.
> Headland on headland bands grey sea with grey.
> But when I slowly turn to search the east
> the inland hills have hazed a white retreat.
>
> Years and damage march their motes through air.
>
> (Catherine Byron)[9]

I am keeping 'identity' in parentheses, as befits a contested meaning, because parentheses are 'an interlude; interval; hiatus' (*Shorter Oxford Dictionary*), which is exactly where, it seems to me, this question of identity should be located for the present. I mean, to be sure, the question of national identity, Irish identity, 'Irishness'. In the context, the qualification is surely redundant, because although identity is not indeed singular and is always, at some level, tacit or otherwise, specified and modified — *personal identity, collective identity, class identity, racial identity, ethnic identity, religious identity, sexual identity, political identity, social identity, gender identity* — in this place, this island, this *entity*, the only identity (or sense of identity) allowed pride of place in public discourse is *national identity*: all other senses must be contained within that conflation, or denied. However much we may argue about the meaning of Irish national identity, we rarely question its right to *be* the dominant meaning. Irish first, and all the rest comes after and sometimes not at all.

> I bagged it and debagged it
> I got it in my sights
> Sniffed it
> Tracked it
> I selected it.
> Chose it.
> Distinguished it.
> Examined it.
> Tested it.

> Held it.
> Weighed it.
> Balanced it.
> Judged it.
> Accepted it.
> Took it.
> Made room for it.
> Received it.
> Handled it.
> Fondled it.
> Presented it.
> Paid a price for it.
> I managed it.
> I carried it.
> I took care of it.
> Ferried it.
> Lugged it.
> Unloaded it.
> Delivered it.
> Herded it.
> Stripped it.
> Exposed it.
> Arranged it.
> Sorted it.
> Shelved it.
> Relegated it.
> Displayed it.
> Transformed it.
> Incorporated it.
> Accomplished it.
> Achieved it.
> Consumed.
>
> (Mairead Byrne)[10]

Identity (I'll come to the plural in a moment), the need to know 'who we are' or 'what we are' (and I'll return to that 'we' along with the plural), is a problem which will not go away, or which we cannot leave alone. Identity is like a scab: we cannot resist constantly pulling and picking at it, as if to see what lies beneath its surface. We come back to it again and again, defining it, stating it, restating it, debating it, as if the pulling and the picking can uncover its eternal and essential truth.

> The material mark of a wound,
> a wound in the process of healing,
> healing too has a physical reality,
> a past, a present, a future
> imperfect.

To pluralize identity is, to be sure, progress of a kind: we acknowledge (or more properly, 'it is acknowledged', since 'we' remain unqualified), that identity is not a given, not *one* thing but rather a series of things, each with its own depth beneath the surface, its own history, its own truth. Pluralizing identity does not automatically reduce the risk of eternalizing and essentializing, does not necessarily lessen the acuteness of our anxiety about it, does not make our pulling and picking less obsessive, but it does mean that it is no longer assumed to be the same for all. The plural allows for variations on the theme. But they are only variations: the theme remains the same — and *forte*, marching its motes through the air we breathe, the lives we live. In Ireland, identity is still construed as being centrally about *national identity*: how we speak it, how we live it, how we are and are not 'taking it' like a woman, like a man, like a Unionist or a Nationalist or a Catholic or (by implication) a Protestant — although, indeed, separately, never in combination. Whatever we are, one day at a time, we must be that thing first and foremost in terms of some collective, national consensual label. Circular synonymity or synonymous circularity: nationality *is* identity *is* nationality. No getting away from it. However much we are questioning what it is, exactly, the central point of reference stays the same.[11] Remains in place, as nation:

> My national badge, my passport (which does not belong to me, but to the State) identifies me, the bearer, as Irish first and foremost and only then as 'F', a Dubliner, and an academic. That is all you know and all you need to know, apparently. Thus am I identified (but to whom does that identity belong?).

> Terse reduction of a particular life to such general and, in their generality, meaningless terms: certainly questionable.

Do such obsessions and reductive conflations afflict only the Irish? Are 'we' unique in this? No, of course not. The more insecure we are, the more beleaguered we believe ourselves to be, the more historically, politically, socially, culturally, linguistically or physically precarious our position, the more we have been excluded or marginalized from or within dominant groups, the more likely we are to vociferously 'claim' an identity as a collectivity. And that, I think, is as relevant (although variously expressed) for ethnicity, class, religion, sexuality and gender as for nationality. Politically and strategically, 'having' an identity (whoever it 'belongs' to) appears to be a precondition of self-determination and independence, whatever the context.

There are positive dimensions to the desire to 'claim' and to 'have' an identity, not the least of which is that because identity always defines itself as difference from some other (more powerful or hegemonic) identity (Irish is different from British, black from white, women from men, homosexuality from heterosexuality, the 'third' world from the first, south from north, east from west and so on), the very act of claiming calls into question the credentials of the more powerful group — its moral right, so to speak, to impose its 'identity' as valid for all, its right to shape past, present and future, 'our' world, 'our' lives, 'our' tongues, 'our' visions. The problem, as we know, is that the two parts of the shell — whatever logic or morality may say — are hierarchically sealed into *unequal* difference.

Whatever it *might* be, however it is now being re-theorized (by postmodernists, whoever they are), '*equal* difference' remains, for all practical purposes, an abstraction, a political and social reality yet to be realized. Difference, in the world we live in every day, and not the place we go to in our theories and our articles, is not about plural equalities. It is about *some* people's equality — and *some* people's inequality:

> Some people know what it is like,
> [. . . . . . .]
>
> to be second hand
> to be second class
> to be no class
> to be looked down on
> to be walked on
> to be pissed on
> to be shat on
>
> and other people don't
>
> (Rita Ann Higgins)[12]

Establishing Irishness, for example and for cogent historical reasons, has involved dis-establishing Britishness. Being 'Irish' is about *not* being British: in shorthand, it is (or used to be) about dis-allowing foreign games.[13]

> The game is up. It's over.
> We're not playing with you anymore.

Declining an imposed identity (and no matter why or how or by whom it has been imposed) implies some level of understanding (and dislike) of that identity. It necessarily involves a consciousness and, no doubt to a variable degree, an articulate analysis of what it is that is to be opposed, and why.

> As anyone who tries will discover, it is immeasurably easier to define what one is not rather than the opposite. (Margo Harkin, film-maker)

That process is an interesting and, I think, important one precisely because it names the hegemonic identity as particular, as site-specific. Disposing of an imposed identity historicizes it, de-naturalizes and de-universalizes that identity:

> My main interest is the human condition. My work is a reflection of my own observations, memories, emotions and opinions. I simply wish to express how one woman in Belfast feels.
>
> What you are is not what I am or want to be, and you better believe that what you are is not the universal human condition. (Rita Duffy)[14]

It pressurizes the more powerful group to acknowledge its own identity as question, because questioned:

> If I define my Irishness as significantly different from your Britishness, it behoves you to think about your Britishness and what (else) it differs from. If 'I and We' are oppositional, are *you* any different?
>
> (Although as the man said, or was it 'our' Taoiseach in a moment of truth, 'You women are all the same').[15]

Of course, no powerful group will do this willingly: contest its own certainties, disturb its own foundations. Opposition will be — is — resisted. Both consciously and unconsciously. And resistance comes in many forms — denial and suppression of difference chief among them, often in the most subtle ways:

> I am not forbidden to speak, but you are forbidden to hear. There are some things you are not allowed to know. (Maud Casey)

The act (which is never singular in fact) of claiming an identity *in* difference or *through* opposition to some other identity demonstrates (a) the limits of (any) identity and (b) its fictional quality.

> I have been surrounded all my life by images of a culture which values highly physical beauty and wholeness, a culture which denies difference. My

identity as a woman with a disability is one that is strong, sensual, sexual, fluid, flexible and political. Reclaiming and redefining my body and its politics continues to be an extraordinary learning experience. I am just beginning to define for myself, my difference, my sense of wholeness and to welcome it deeply and intensely. (Mary Duffy)[16]

Identities, in essence and in contradiction, are made, not born. They are, as we well know, constructs, inventions, imaginations, stories we are told or tell ourselves about ourselves. But 'fictions of identity are no less powerful for being fictions',[17] and stories do, after all, make our lives livable. This is as true for the new, oppositional, emergent identity as it is for that of the dominant group — be it British, or white or heterosexual or male or, as is the case in this particular case, all of these in powerful combination. It is, again, no bad thing to know about limits and fictions.

> Yes, father, I will have more tea
> and sit here quiet in this room of my childhood
> and watch while the flames flicker
> the story of our distance on the wall.
>
> (Paula Meehan)[18]

For there is also danger in 'claiming' an identity. The danger — and it is an entirely ironic one — lies in that, the more a group *needs* an identity to realize its independence, the more vociferously we 'claim' it, the more successfully we 'have' it, the more likely we are to believe in it, once and for all of 'us' and for all time. Identities don't come cheap, even on the 1990s open market. We want a return on our centuries of investment, which means no betrayals, no withdrawals, no refusals. However emergent, I think we construct that new identity according to the same principles as the old — the reject. The new is also structured along lines of inclusion and exclusion, with its 'in' groups and 'out' groups, margins and centres. It too will have its limits, which it similarly and equally may decline to recognize. It too will have its fictions — of myth and tradition, memory and history, language and culture, symbol and image — to give it shape, substance and power.

> For you'd think to listen to her she'd never heard
> that discretion is the better part, that our names are writ
> in water, that the greenest stick will wizen:
> even if every slubberdegullion once had a dream-vision

in which she appeared as his own true lover,
those days are just as truly over.
And I bet Old Gummy Granny
has taken none of this on board because of her
    uncanny
knack of hearing only what confirms
her own sense of herself, her honey-nubile form
and the red rose, proud rose or canker
tucked behind her ear, in the head-band of her
    blinkers.

(Nuala Ní Dhomhnaill)[19]

The new identity is not necessarily more generous than the old. Rather the contrary: the insecurity of its very newness constantly producing and reproducing the need for reassurance, for protection against attack, whether from within or without. Cohesiveness becomes an absolute imperative even when what is to be adhered to is a flimsy thing. There can be no cracks, no fissures, no vulnerability in the face presented to the 'other', 'outside' force from whom we differ. Even less will this new identity accept being undermined from within: dissenters are not easily tolerated, if they are tolerated at all. Even to question is perceived as betrayal.

What's the age of consent for being Irish? [. . .] I mean, I don't seem to remember ever being consulted [. . .] All that cultural baggage foisted [. . .] absolutely foisted, upon us without a by-your-leave. [. . .] And what happens when you try and refuse it or leave it behind? Everybody freaks out as if you've dumped a baby in a carrier bag at the airport. (Emma Donoghue)[20]

Identity has a double mission: it is about both reinforcing difference and enforcing sameness:

We are unique and unified in our uniqueness.

The danger with an identity rooted in notions of uniqueness and sameness (and I am really not sure that there can be any other kind) is that it must inevitably collide with *other* identities rooted in uniqueness and sameness. The peaceful coexistence of multiplicity and contradiction, if it is possible, does not appear to be a practice. Identities do not easily coalesce with one another.

So what are we to do? When our theories and articles provide no solutions, no solace for daily living, no stories we can live by, no truths we can live for?

My time, she said, has never been my own.
I have so much to do
and do again tomorrow.

Between all of you
I am exhausted, she said,
I will take time off and go away.

So she built an igloo in her head
and found it cold
but private.

She often goes there now
but still hears the lean wolves howling
far across the tundra.

(Joan McBreen)[21]

4 IDENTIFYING

More than once, I have been warned against the risk of falling into a reactionary and essentialist trap in focusing (more than once) on the business of collective identity. I also know perfectly well that having the leisure to explore it is a luxury enjoyed — or an obsession compulsively indulged — principally by intellectuals, who are (as a collective entity) remarkably adept at exempting ourselves from the conditions and limitations we observe in or impose upon others. Although, actually and politically, I am specifically concerned about *who* a collective identity collects and who is left — dispersed and dismissed — somewhere on a bleak and lonely ledge. I make no bones about it: I think identity *is* an issue for those who have never had it or who are struggling to emerge from a (straight) jacket that most definitely does not fit, even while it shapes and moulds and stifles:

I live with these half dead, half alive people, waiting for the cease-fire, longing to be released with them, from this eternal waiting. (Pauline Cummins)[22]

It is a matter of the devil and the deep green sea.

So I am ambivalent about identity: wary of its limits and constraints, yet unwilling to abandon it entirely in favour of — what? The return of the heroes, herding the natives into multinational markets? What guarantees have I — or 'we', all parenthetical as we must remain — that *you* will stop *your* games if I stop mine? I cannot/will not subscribe to an historical, monolithic lie, which collective identities tell to and about those who dissent or do not fit. Neither do I (quite — yet — maybe never) believe enough in the will of the powerful to desist from creating all before them, god-like, in their own image. Why would they desist? What's in it for them? Virtue has never been a seriously countenanced reward. Still less do I trust the political efficacy of the (postmodern) notion of a multiplicity of endlessly open-ended, contradictory, constantly forming and re-forming local and fragmentary meanings. Or meaninglessness.

> On the morning of leave-taking,
> TV AM announced 'A man was shot dead last night
> In Mag-here-a on the shores of Lough Nee.'
> Ahogill, Aghadowey, Magherafelt —
> The sticky place names of the North
> Get caught in an English throat.
> Old meaningless conjectures
> Woven out of lost tongues,
> Evolving Irish-Anglo non-senses.
> They call us British.
> Stamp out our language,
> Undermine our culture,
> Swallow our pride.
>
> (Cherry Smyth)[23]

I am therefore in at least three minds about identity in general and (Irish) national identity in particular:

(1) It is difficult not to have it at all (although easy enough to say others shouldn't indulge or bother if you already have one anyway).

(2) Which begs the (related) question of whether or not we really need one. We argue that it is politically useful, even vital, for you can't begin to resist oppression entirely on your own. *Knowing* it's oppression requires more than one, who think (at least roughly) the same. So we do need one (at least). Still, I am acutely mindful that 'who am I?' is not the same question as 'what is to be done?' and that the first is never a reliable and effective substitute for the second, even though we may be seduced into believing that it is. I actually do need to know who I am/We are at this moment, in this place, in order (precisely) to set about turning this place into something else. I/We need *provisional* certainties and agreements, which may enable provisional connections.

> We'll glean a common language
> to describe our differing fates:
> you'll be fugitive forever
>
> (Paula Meehan, p. 26)

(3) If we have to have it, because we cannot not and because we need it, can it then be so constructed,

imagined, created that it will allow for variations, versions, commodiously accommodating 'we who are many and do not want to be the same' (Adrienne Rich), we who are different yet together in the one space? I mean, can it be made not in one image but in many and still be 'an identity'? Is it possible to realize the rhetoric of 'unity in difference and diversity', to mobilize it, acting with our differences, not in spite of them? Can identity avoid *super*-imposing and become *com*-posing?

I don't know for sure, but I do know that 'we' are not united in or by our Irishness, although we have been forced to cement over the cracks which would appear if honesty and straight talking prevailed. Which I think, in my more optimistic moments, they are (at last, and tentatively) beginning to do.

> myth is the wound we leave
> in the time we have
>
> (Eavan Boland)[24]

The 'we' is of course the great lie. Being born in the same place does not make us the same, although I think it may connect us. Same birthplace does not mean same birthright, same past or present or future; certainly and self-evidently does not mean same class, same politics, same religion, same race, same sex. And whether we think these ought to be or ought not to be significant factors, the reality is that they are. Our histories and experiences 'within the nation', and betwixt and between it, are unequal and different, yet 'our' national identity does not allow or acknowledge this. Its confusions are not the result of openness and generosity, rather the unthinking reverse.

5 IMAGINING

To 'have' an identity is not automatically to be free, and most certainly Irish identity has functioned as a confinement for women. But is history always 'to be between us and our heroes', us and our lives, us and our different truths?

Historically, Irish identity has been imagined in the heroic mode, simultaneously full of bravado and glory, and marked by martyrdom and sacrifice (which of course work perfectly in combination). In fact and in deed, it has only been realized by sacrificing the differences within, in the 'collective' interest of the 'common' good. But who exactly has been paying the price at which the supposedly 'common' good is achieved? And are they prepared to go on paying it, to go on being sacrificed?

Our Lady, dispossessed
on some Alpen ice-cap
would not look out of place
in ski-pants, zipping
down virgin slopes
to the sound of music

But wait for her second
coming round the mountain —
the icon-shattering thaw
Our immaculate image, white-iced
and frosted for two thousand years,
might melt to nothing more divine
than a seething woman, cheated
out of sex and a son in his prime.

(Ruth Hooley)[25]

I heed the warning now, even though I don't have the answers. If I did, if we did, I think they would vastly complicate this question of identity — mine and yours and even ours, as may be. Perhaps this is the most, and the best, that I at least can hope for: that it become complicated beyond blind belief and unthinking acceptance.

Our voices are lighter
Must we speak louder
Must we shout?
Our tongues have been tied
Cleft to our palate
Have been cut out
Listen

We are learning our language
Foreign to our ears
We are sounding out
We are on an adventure
There is no turning back
Listen . . .

(Ann Le Marquand Hartigan)[26]

I don't have the answers. But I do hear voices and see visions. Yet, I would put it to you, I am not mad.

I listen to what women are saying and I look at what women are doing, because I am one, because it is a revelation, because it is a delight, because that pleasure has been so long denied, because it is provoking. (But why should I explain and justify? The powerful never do.)

We are sometimes fat, thin, heavy-breasted, flat-chested, high-hipped. We are sometimes droopy with lust and drowsy with love. We are fast, we are

tight, we are so loose the wind could blow a hole in our fannies. But the shape of us is not important. We love sex, we go wild for it at times, but you'd never guess by what they've said, now would you? (Evelyn Conlon)[27]

What I see and what I hear — what is there — is not at all singular. It is about declining to be an unvarying symbol, once and for all; declining to be 'outside history' or politics or citizenship; declining to be an instrument, used in the 'collective' interest of the dominant group; declining to be chaste, passive and invisible; declining to be Mother Ireland, the fertile source, the rich terrain, from which the 'nation', vampire-like, draws its sustenance, bleeding the blood of real women dry; declining to be idealized or romanticized; declining to be 'made immobile by oppression', choosing instead to be 'made active because of it' (Pauline Cummins);[28] declining to be sacrificed in the name of the father or of anything else:

I shall never look
into those eyes again on this earth,
and he knows before he dies
that I have chosen
finally not to be butchered.

(Rita Kelly)[29]

I see and hear Irish women speaking previously 'unspoken truths',[30] to ourselves at this time and in this place, including its diaspora, and to all who would listen and look, see and hear. For these soundings have reverberations which will not disappear. When you think about it, women do not, after all, have much of a stake in Irish national identity. Women have nothing to lose but our silence by testing the veracity of its borders, by declining it differently, or even altogether.

I am Ireland and I'm sick
I'm sick of this tidy house where I exist
that reminds me of nothing
not of the past / not of the future
I'm sick of depression
I'm sick of shame
I'm sick of poverty
I'm sick of politeness
I'm sick of looking over my shoulder
I'm sick of standing by the shore/
waiting for some prince to come on the tide
[. . . . . . .]
I am Ireland /
and I'm not waiting anymore.

(Maighread Medbh)[31]

I see and hear women learning how to thrive in this space, exposing the lie of sameness, inflecting and reciting identity as plural possibilities, not singular destiny; wilfully contradicting the statements, the icons and images which made us out to be *one* thing, which we have never been and will never be. The same.

Deliberately personal and defiantly public. Not all women, but enough to complicate the issue.

And who are you
Come to that?
All of you
out there
out of the spotlight —
out for a night's entertainment,
smiles upturned so politely;
asking me
why I have to be —
so raw
and deliberately
personal?

(Mary Dorcey)[32]

1   Pauline Cummins and Louise Walsh, *Sounding the Depths: A Collaborative Installation* (catalogue; Dublin: Irish Museum of Modern Art, 1992), p. 5.

2   See Eavan Boland, *A Kind of Scar: The Woman Poet in a National Tradition* (LiP pamphlet; Dublin: Attic Press, 1989), and 'Outside History', *Object Lessons: The Life of the Woman and the Poet in Our Time* (New York and London: W. W. Norton & Company, 1995).

3   For a sense of the range of Irish women's contemporary social, political and cultural concerns and activities, see A. Smyth (ed.), *Wildish Things: An Anthology of New Irish Women's Writing* (Dublin: Attic Press, 1989); *Canadian Journal of Irish Studies*, 18:1 (July, 1992), special issue *Women and Irish Politics*, edited by C. St Peter and R. Marken; A. Smyth (ed.), *Irish Women's Studies Reader* (Dublin: Attic Press, 1993); *Journal of Women's History*, 6:4-7:1 (Winter-Spring 1995), special double issue on Irish women, edited by J. Hoff and M. Coulter; *Feminist Review*, 50 (Summer 1995), special issue *The Irish Issue: The British Question*, edited by F. R. Collective, M. Hickman and A. Smyth.

4   Clare Hackett, 'Self-determination: The Republican Feminist Agenda', *Feminist Review*, 50 (Summer 1995), p. 115.

5   Kieran Keohane, 'Unifying the Fragmented Imaginary of the Young Immigrant: Making a Home in the Post-Modern with the Pogues', *Irish Review*, 9 (Autumn 1990), p. 73.

6   Eithne Strong, 'Thinking of Kevin McAleer, Derrida and Hogan Shea', in *Spatial Nosing: New and Selected Poems* (Galway: Salmon Press, 1993), p. 117.

7   The *Field Day Anthology of Irish Writing* (sic) is a fiasco in point. Mind you, it is now considered impolite and unfair to dwell on it, since its (numerous) editors have atoned for their sins of ignorance, denial, erasure and contempt by apologizing publicly and altogether prettily by commissioning an after-the-furore thought: a fourth women-edited volume. To each his or her own, but less, and later, to her than to him.

8   Moya Cannon, 'Foundations', *Oar* (Galway: Salmon Press, 1990), p. 45.

9   Catherine Byron, 'Border Country', *Settlements* (Durham: Taxus Press, 1985), p. 45.

10 Mairead Byrne, 'Hunting', *Seneca Review*, 23:1/2 (1993), p. 43.

11 The catalyst for the present article was a series of short articles by 'prominent' Irish men and women on the theme *Mise Eire* ('I am Ireland'), published by *The Irish Times* during April-May 1993. None of the commissioned pieces explored the dynamics of gender and national identity.

12 Rita Ann Higgins, 'Some People', *Witch in the Bushes* (Galway: Salmon Press, 1988), p. 59.

13 Until very recently, Gaelic Athletic Association (GAA) rules prohibited members from playing 'foreign' games such as soccer and rugby. Badminton or squash were not mentioned.

14 Rita Duffy, in *Women on Women: An Exhibition of Paintings, Walldrawings and Installation* (catalogue, Belfast: Fenderesky Art Gallery, 1986).

15 Albert Reynolds, former Irish Taoiseach, is reputed to have made this remark, in Dáil Éireann in 1993.

16 Mary Duffy, in *Irish Art: Pauline Cummins, Mary Duffy and Alanna O'Kelly* (Dublin: Women Artists' Action Group, 1987).

17 Diana Fuss, *Essentially Speaking: Feminism, Nature and Difference* (New York and London: Routledge, 1989), p. 104.

18 Paula Meehan, 'Return and no Blame', *The Man Who Was Marked by Winter* (Oldcastle: The Gallery Press, 1991), p. 23.

19 Nuala Ní Dhomhnaill, 'Cathleen', *The Astrakhan Cloak: Poems in Irish by Nuala Ní Dhomhnaill with Translations into English by Paul Muldoon* (Oldcastle: The Gallery Press, 1992), p. 38.

20 Emma Donoghue, 'Going Back', *Alternative Loves: Irish Gay and Lesbian Stories*, edited by D. Marcus with a Foreword by A. Smyth (Dublin: Martello Press, 1994), p. 212.

21 Joan McBreen, 'The Woman and the Igloo', *The Wind Beyond the Wall* (Brownsville: Story Line Press, 1991), p. 27.

22 Pauline Cummins, text accompanying *Unearthed* (sculpture), in *Art Beyond Barriers* (catalogue: Bonn: Frauen Museum, 1989), p. 120.

23 Cherry Smyth, 'Coming Home', *Feminist Review*, 50 (Summer 1995), p. 20.

24 Eavan Boland, 'The Making of an Irish Goddess', *Outside History* (Manchester: Carcanet Press, 1990), p. 31.

25 Ruth Hooley, 'Cut the Cake', cited in J. McCurry, '"Our Lady Dispossessed": Female Ulster Poets and Sexual Politics', *Colby Quarterly*, 27:1 (March 1991), p. 5.

26 Anne Le Marquand Hartigan, 'Occupied Country', *Women's Studies International Forum*, 11:4 (1988), special issue *Feminism in Ireland*, edited by A. Smyth, p. 315.

27 Evelyn Conlon, 'Taking Scarlet as a Real Colour', in *Taking Scarlet as a Real Colour and Other Stories* (Belfast: Blackstaff Press, 1993), p. 171.

28 Pauline Cummins, in *Sounding the Depths*, p. 8.

29 Rita Kelly, 'The Patriarch', *Fare Well/Beir Beannacht: Poems in English and Irish* (Dublin: Attic Press, 1990), p. 27.

30 *Unspoken Truths* was the title of an exhibition of the work of Dublin-based Irish women, shown in the Irish Museum of Modern Art in 1993 in the context of

IMMA's innovative Educational and Community Arts programme.

31 Maighread Medbh, 'Easter 1991', *Feminist Review*, 44 (Summer 1993), p. 58.

32 Mary Dorcey, 'Deliberately Personal', *Moving Into the Space Cleared by Our Mothers* (Galway: Salmon Press, 1991), p. 22.

EAMONN WALL
from *Éire-Ireland*, Winter 1996, Vol. XXX, No. 4

Eamonn Wall was born in Enniscorthy, County Wexford, in 1955, and emigrated from Ireland to the United States in 1982. His verse can be found in *Dyckman-200th Street* (1994) and *Iron Mountain Road* (1997). Here is a first-hand illuminating account of contemporary emigration to America by the New Irish.

Exile, Attitude, and the Sin-É Café: Notes on the 'New Irish'

In his foreword to his 1993 anthology *Ireland in Exile: Irish Writers Abroad*,[1] which features the work of writers in their twenties and thirties, Dermot Bolger notes that the terms '*exile* and *departure* suggest an out-dated degree of permanency' and that 'Irish writers no longer go into exile, they simply commute'. Furthermore, Bolger states that a problem he encountered while editing *Ireland in Exile* 'was remembering who was now back [in Ireland] and who was away.' Clearly, the Irish diaspora isn't what it used to be.

I belong to that generation of Irish people, born in the 1950s and 1960s, who got Irish emigration rolling again. We left Ireland *en masse* — our exact numbers are in dispute — and, as Dermot Bolger's anthology indicates, we can be located in every pocket of the earth. In the United States, we are referred to as the 'New Irish'. I commute between exile and Ireland, but it's an expensive business. I often wish I were another person: if that were the case, I wouldn't always have be saving up my money to go 'home' and neglecting all the other fascinating parts of the world. Commuting makes assimilation impossible.

Before coming to the United States, I worked as a teacher primarily: my purpose in coming here was to attend graduate school, and experience America first-hand. This essay will provide notes on poetry, music, and the Sin-É Café in the East Village, which was the centre of expatriate artistic activity when I lived in New

York. But I'll also look back to Ireland to see how those of my generation who have remained at home have reacted to the loss of their neighbours and friends, their brothers and sisters, and I'll try to describe the 'attitude' that renewed emigration has planted in the hearts and minds of my generation. An 'attitude' is that edge to a person which indicates an undefined degree of dissatisfaction — if you know teenagers, you know what I mean. As for becoming an exile, well that's just something I sort of fell into. I didn't actually decide in some rational manner that I was going to stay in the United States, I just realized at some point that I was staying, since the work was here. Just like one of Donall Mac Amhlaigh's navvies,[2] I am happy to follow the work, and am happy with my lot.

But first, let's look for a minute at emigration itself and at the type of person who ended up drinking coffee or Rolling Rocks and eating pie, while listening to poets read or musicians play at the Sin-É Café on St Mark's Place in the East Village in the early 1990s. Perhaps he or she has emerged from the following mould. In his introduction to *Ireland in Exile*, the novelist Joseph O'Connor[3] describes candidly and bitterly the appearance in University College, Dublin, of a photographer from the Industrial Development Authority who had been 'commissioned to take pictures for an advertisement that would persuade rich foreign capitalists to open factories all over the Irish countryside'. The resulting photograph and its legend THE REPUBLIC OF IRELAND: WE'RE THE YOUNG EUROPEANS is familiar to all of us who have entered

Ireland in recent years. I see it in Dublin Airport at the end of the walkway when I emerge bleary-eyed from the plane.

Why does O'Connor adopt such a bitter and ironic tone? It's because most of these educated people whose faces appear in this photograph — all personally known to O'Connor — have emigrated from Ireland because they have, in common with many other university graduates, been unable to find satisfactory work or opportunities. O'Connor believed that his future, and that of his contemporaries, was in Ireland, but this lie which had been planted in the optimistic Sixties and early Seventies was exploded by the recession which followed its blooming. O'Connor believes that the collapse of this dream of a bright future has devastated an innocent generation reared on the notion that the bad old days were over, and that emigration was finished. His representation of the feelings of his generation and mine is powerful:

You might be coming home for Christmas, or a family celebration, or a funeral, or to see a friend. Or you might be just coming back to Ireland because you're so lonely and freaked-out where you are that you can't stick it anymore, and you need a break, and you'd sell your granny to be back in the pub at home by nine o'clock on a Friday night, having fun and telling stories.

And there it is, this IDA[4] poster, illuminated at the end of the corridor that leads from the airbridge gates to the arrivals terminal: the ghostly faces of those beautiful Young Europeans. It always seems poignant as any ancient Ulster saga to me, this pantheon of departed heroes, so hopeful and innocent, frozen in their brief moment of optimism.

O'Connor's words are angry but telling. By describing the unfulfilled promises a whole generation of young Irish are fleeing from and the feelings of loss and bitterness engendered by this, O'Connor is indicating just why so many of the New Irish in North America, Ireland, and elsewhere have 'attitudes'. How could it be otherwise?

Joseph O'Connor is an eloquent spokesperson for his disaffected, Ryanair, generation. I suppose the most notorious manifestation of this Irish 'attitude' to date was Sinéad O'Connor's tearing up of the Pope's picture during her appearance on 'Saturday Night Live'. In the last few years we have seen the effective dismantling of church and state in Ireland by a busy media staffed in large part by members of a lost generation, like Joseph O'Connor, who have seen

family and friends lost into exile. The failures of political will and imagination in Ireland are represented subtly in Colm Tóibín's *The Heather Blazing*[5] and with sledgehammer-like force in Dermot Bolger's harrowing and ironically titled *The Journey Home*.[6] Irish writers of this generation, living at home and abroad, or commuting, have come to explore, what Adrienne Rich has called in a different but parallel context, 'the wreck'.

I came to explore the wreck.
The words are purposes.
The words are maps.
I came to see the damage that was done
and the treasures that prevail.

Although we are the commuters Dermot Bolger calls us, we still carry the same heavy emotional baggage which Irish exiles have always carried with them. Those of us, and I place myself in this group, who enjoy living in the United States are not immune from being drowned in the feelings O'Connor so eloquently describes. All of us, at home and abroad, in our edgy ways are concerned with locating internal and external 'damage' and 'treasures'.

Emigration, for me, although it's the subject of much political debate, is fundamentally a personal matter. I remember one day a few years ago sitting with my father on the beach at Ardamine, County Wexford, after we had spent a long time swimming together, when he asked me if I intended to stay in America. After I answered 'Yes', he looked silently at the sea for a long time before replying, 'This wasn't supposed to happen. We worked hard and we believed that emigration was over, but here it is starting all over again. What went wrong?' There are no easy answers to this: for us Irish, emigration is both a welcome safety-net and a curse.

What is a fact is that everyone emerges changed from the experience, and fathers like mine, who believed in the great new day of Modern Ireland, have been forced to accept that things haven't worked out as planned. If some sons and daughters are confused by unfamiliar terrain, their parents are devastated by the empty bedrooms in their homes, by the silence at the dinner tables, and by the photos on the mantelpieces of the grandchildren they rarely see. By emigrating I have become a part of history and politics, which doesn't always sit well with me. Joseph O'Connor reminds me of my father to the extent that both believed in a future and were disappointed.

There's difficulty all round, but the old-fashioned American wakes are a thing of the past because, as

Dermot Bolger reminds us, we don't emigrate, we commute. As writers, we are not forgotten at home since Irish publishers support our efforts, and we are not unwelcome in the United States either, as the Irish-American community has shown in its efforts to win visas for us. But I believe we write our stories, poems, plays, and novels for an audience in Ireland, to remind the people that we may be gone, but are not silent. The fact that so many Irish writers live in clusters on the United States' East coast and in London has forced, in the words of Helena Mulkerns, 'the Irish literary scene to extend its parameters to include them'.[7] Added pieces to this complex puzzle have been the decisions by a variety of American writers to take up semi- or permanent residence in Ireland — Jean Valentine, Jessie Lendennie,[8] James McCourt, Richard Tillinghast, to name just a few. Patrick Kavanagh spoke of the parochial and provincial: perhaps an appropriate binary notion for the future will be the parochial and international.

One day while waiting in the express checkout line in the Grand Union near Dyckman Street in Inwood, I started talking to the man behind me in the queue who, it happened, had emigrated from Ireland forty-five years previously, and had never returned. This kind of emigrant no longer exists. Did he hate Ireland so much that he was happy to be away from it and couldn't be bothered returning? I remembered the relief I felt, and still do, at not having to face the prospect of permanent residence in Ireland. Similar feelings are brilliantly articulated by Rosita Boland in a poem celebrating her arrival in Australia: 'The Korean taxi-driver / Had never heard of Ireland / and I felt thrillingly rootless.'[9]

It is in part because so many of us New Irish are able to feel what Boland feels one minute and O'Connor feels the next that we have developed hard edges, or 'attitudes'. What has been interesting to me has been discovering similar points of view expressed in the work of such writers as Bharati Mukherjee and Sandra Cisneros about their own cultures and divided loyalties. Given that the movement of peoples from country to country is likely to increase rather than diminish in the future, it is certain that this pot-pourri of alienation and excitement which one finds in contemporary writing is likely to continue to be vital in the writing of the future.

I spent many days wandering around Inwood on the way to or from the shops or park with my kids in tow, and, because I had kids with me, people thought I was OK and would talk to me. Almost all of those elderly, Irish-born people I spoke with expressed a great gratitude for the opportunity they'd received to live and work in the United States. None of them expressed such sentiments as those that appear in John Montague's poem about his mother's feelings of estrangement: '. . . my mother's memories / of America; / a muddy cup / she refused to drink.'[10] Yet, we know from the work that writers as various as Mary Gordon, Michael Stephens, and Pete Hamill[11] have produced that some wounds may have been merely covered over with Band-Aids. At the same time, it is rare to hear the New Irish declare how grateful they are for the opportunity to work in the United States: they know they have earned the right to play a part in the international economy. The New Irish drink deeply of America, but retain their edge.

The New Irish have spawned artists in all fields and the work that has been produced to date, although it speaks primarily to an Irish-based audience, should be accessible to all Americans since no part of contemporary American life is immune to the effects of migration. These recent exiles have not bought into the ancient culture of emigration, but have fallen backwards into it, updating and transforming it in the process. But here a distinction should be considered, if not insisted upon. When I think of these artists, I am concerned with people who did not arrive in the United States with artistic identities in place, but who came here to begin, or continue, the process of gaining and developing identities as poets, novelists, musicians, or painters. Some Irish writers who arrived before the current wave have ignored the immigrant experience altogether — they have not felt it, or have been moved by living in the United States, and it has had little or no effect on their themes or forms — whereas other writers have been absolutely energized by their experience of America — Brian Moore, Eavan Boland, James Liddy, Eamon Grennan.[12] But the raw New Irish are very much engaged with American culture and none are afraid of it, having spent their childhoods in the Sixties and Seventies growing up on it. They haven't come to the United States to reap the rewards for their artistic endeavours, but to learn the artist's ropes on American, not native, soil.

What one finds in the poetry written by commuters is a mixture of alienation and excitement. These exiles of Erin may be better educated and may use more sophisticated forms and language than their predecessors from earlier generations, who created melodies and lyrics, but they frequently share common sentiments and a sense of loss. The young Irish certainly know that when they leave school or college they will enter a global economy and that they are as likely — in fact, much more likely — to be able to find work in Frankfurt, Chicago, or London as they are in Dublin or Cork. However, even though each and every one of them knows this, and understands that emigration is a way of life for Irish people, they are often still overwhelmed by feelings of loss when they settle down away from Ireland. And the poetry and music produced by the voices of this new generation, my own included, frequently express such feelings. Take for example these lines from 'Fault', a Sara Berkeley poem describing California:

I was not built for
the dull rumble of the valley air,
the great steel birds
that fly with a dark gray
whine, grazing the sky.[13]

The speaker in this poem — the 'I' — is as much at odds with California as the 'she', the fault which might destroy the state. Take away the twentieth-century *topoi*, and Berkeley's poem could just as easily be referring to those exiles who'd arrived in France and Spain in the wake of the Nine Years' War.

A similar line of thinking can be found in many of Greg Delanty's[14] poems written since he came to the United States: 'Perhaps now I understand the meaning of home / for I'm in a place, but it is not in me.' The final lines of this poem suggest that the New Irish, instead of being able to trade the unemployment and unhappiness of home for the wealth and freedoms of the New World, have fallen into the ancient core of exile, and are repeating the lives lived out by their predecessors. Frequently, as in 'Home from Home', the theme is exile, the tone sorrowful:

I'll introduce you to all & sundry
even to those who are dead & gone,
or just gone, unable to make home at home.
When time is called we'll stagger from this poem.[15]

What is interesting, though, is that when Delanty celebrates American life, as he does in the final poems of *Southward*, he abandons the closed forms which characterize his poems set in Ireland, and the poems which describe his feelings of separation and alienation from home, and adopts open American poetic forms to celebrate America:

Beneath the green fountain
of a palm tree
a duck loiters on one leg
with wings in white pockets . . .
I blaze, blessed
by the brilliance of them all.

To be able to write convincingly about America, contemporary Irish poets must be able to partly unlearn what they have picked up in Ireland, and produce newer hybrid forms which are part-Irish and part-American. For the New Irish who have sought their artistic voices in the United States, their facility at being able to absorb American influences and styles has been crucial to their success, as is evidenced by the work of writers as diverse as Greg Delanty, Sara Berkeley, Nuala Archer, Gerard Donovan, Helena Mulkerns, and Colum McCann.[16] Perhaps the perfectly formed artistic work combines the precise closed forms employed by many Irish poets with the open forms of American poets — perfection lies somewhere between Derek Mahon and Anne Waldman![17] That such old themes as exile and loss are being recorded using new forms represents an important development in Irish writing. A generation of exiles, expatriates, commuters is writing its own story as it goes along — a quilt, or tapestry, or documentary is being created minute by minute.

The meeting and performance place for many of the Irish exiles based in New York is the Sin-É Café in the East Village. It has been such a remarkable financial and cultural success that it's become a kind of icon of an age and is even written up in *The New Yorker*'s 'Rock and Folk' section, which suggests the extent to which those who have been a part of this scene have made waves in the cultural marketplace. Previously, Irish expatriate artists involved themselves in American artistic and cultural movements and undergrounds. What has happened at the Sin-É is that the sassy New Irish have created their own cultural movement, one which is part Irish, part East Village, and which is unashamedly ethnic and multicultural. The Sin-É has more in common with the Nuyorican Café than it does with the uptown Irish American Historical Society. Of course, it was founded as a café, not as a cultural society; however, it has drawn in artists and given them stages on which to perform. The Sin-É is a postmodern, downtown, *fin de siècle*, Gaelic Park with attitude.

If you have heard all the good words about the Sin-É and you go there with your head full of wonders, your heart may drop when you walk in the door, but as *The New Yorker* notes,

Don't be misled by the sleepy, hole-in-the-wall atmosphere of this bohemian Irish cafe, or by the fact that the place has no stage. While patrons have been writing in their journals, rolling cigarettes, or lingering over their Rolling Rocks, some pretty fine musicians have turned up and tuned up: Sinéad O'Connor, Marianne Faithfull, and Luka Bloom.[18]

The relaxed ambience of the Sin-É is in keeping with the anti-establishment mood of Shane Doyle, its creator, and his patrons. The readings and sessions, often put together by the writer, journalist, United Nations translator Helena Mulkerns, reflect this predominant zeitgeist. In my last years in New York, I attended some remarkable readings and heard some great music there: readings by poets Nuala Ní Dhomhnaill and Rita Ann Higgins, and novelist Colm Tóibín spring to mind. One afternoon while I was sipping a coffee, I looked up and saw Mike Scott of the Waterboys — one of my all-time heroes — sitting across the room. I pointed him out to my kids, who were hard at work on their sodas, but they didn't believe that he was *really* the man who sang 'Fisherman's Blues'. They reckoned I was joking. Helena Mulkerns's most elaborate organizational feat was her 'Bloomsday in the East Village' on June 16, 1991. This cabaret reading and performance of *Ulysses* had a cast of forty or fifty people — it was often difficult to tell who was in the cast and who was in the audience — and went on riotously for twelve hours. The odyssey began in the Sin-É before proceeding to other East Village hostelries. People are still talking about it, but not about my off-off-off Broadway début as an 'actor' in that extravaganza.

I was enormously grateful that the Sin-É was there when I lived in New York: it was exciting to come downtown on the A Train from Inwood and walk across St Mark's to listen, read, and drink, to be involved in a great adventure. The Sin-É is a vibrant emotional and artistic home-away-from-home, which bridges the divide between two countries, and which provides writers, painters, and musicians with a meeting place. Such venues are vital since they act as magnets for developing artists and give them the stepping-stones, exposure, and confidence they need. It was great that is existed while I was there; great that it was Irish; great that it was so casual; and great — and significant socially and historically — that Irish people could move at such ease, be right at home in the East Village. The New Irish looked like everyone else downtown — well, maybe not everybody, but you know what I mean. The distance in cultural terms between St Mark's and Temple Bar[19] has grown so small that it's no longer worth calculating. Perhaps, as a result of its recent sale and renovation, the greatest days of the Sin-É are over, but there are also now other cafés — Anseo and The Scratcher are two — in the neighbourhood which have grown up under Sin-É's influence and which provide a similar kind of ambience. Also of note now has been the appearance of the first three issues of *Here's Me Bus*, edited by

Martin Mahoney and Colin Lacey, which is full of the words and art of the New Irish, and which is heavy with attitude.

The healthy clash between present and past and the subsequent merging of forms and genres is exuberantly manifested in the CDs and live performances of Black 47. I heard them first in the Sin-É and later in Paddy Reilly's at 28th and Second Avenue. Into their traditional Irish core are mixed layers of reggae, rap, hip-hop, new wave, and the result is a dynamic hybrid — a music which is simultaneously Irish and urban American. Larry Kirwin, Black 47's principal writer, is much more tuned in to the America of the margins than he is to the central cultural matrix. Because the centre didn't hold at home, because the exiles feel marginalized, they are inclined to gravitate toward the comfort of the margins in search of those who share their concerns. But there is always the sense in America that the margins possess the energy for change and are rising with the tide. He is not alone in this among Irish artists: U2's *Rattle & Hum* and Roddy Doyle's *The Commitments* are homages to African-American music and culture, Paul Muldoon has gravitated toward Native America, and Eavan Boland has found kindred spirits among American feminists. Intense contact with America has had a huge influence on what and how these people have written: the contact has empowered them. But they have gone to the margins, away from the centre and from traditional Irish-America. Immigrants, in a political climate in which the political right and some elements of the centre and left seek to marginalize and expel them, will continue to gravitate toward the invisibility and warmth of the margin.

Larry Kirwin's songs describe and celebrate the lives of the New Irish in New York, and they, like their subjects, are full of hope, failure and ambivalence. His typical protagonist seeks self-definition, and this is done by poking fun at those who lack style, at least as he defines it:

We got a gig in the Village Pub
But the regulars there all said that we sucked
Then Big John Flynn, said 'oh, no no
You'll be causin' a riot if I don't let you go'

Then a flintstone from the Phoenix gave us a call
But when he heard the beat, he was quite appalled
'D'yez not know nothin' by Christy Moore?'
The next thing you'll be wantin' is Danny Boy![20]

And Kirwin's Irish exile is one of the commuters Dermot Bolger describes; however, a commuter is caught in the Catch-22 situation of being able to visit Ireland, but not stay:

> Sit down by the fire, put your feet on the grate
> Spend the night reminiscin' 'til the hour grows late
> Always remember at the end of the day
> You can always go home — you just can't stay.[21]

Of course, it is by no means certain that the returned exile wants to remain at home for longer than a couple of weeks.

On the back cover of *Ireland in Exile* is a photograph which defines the attitude I've been discussing: a young man with an odd fade-like haircut has his back to the camera. One hand is placed behind his back and presented to the camera: he is giving the two-fingered salute. Against whom is this salute directed? It's directed at everybody and nobody, at Ireland, the United States, and the rest of the world: it's full of significance, and it's infantile. After a lull, Irish immigration to the United States has resumed. A wave of New Irish have arrived and set up camps, and begun the process of defining in their own words what it means to be Irish women and men who live in America at the end of the twentieth century.

— *Creighton University*

1 First published in 1993.
2 Donall MacAmhlaigh's *Dialann Deorai* appeared in 1960, translated by Valentin Iremonger as *The Irish Navvy* in 1964. See also 'Britain's Irish Workers' (1978) p. 840 above.
3 Joseph O'Connor (1963–) was born in Dublin, lived in London for a time and returned to Ireland in 1993. He is author of *The Secret World of the Irish Male* (1994), a series of reflections on Irish culture and its icons from James Joyce to Daniel O'Donnell, as well as the wittily observant *Sweet Liberty: Travels in Irish America* (1996).
4 Industrial Development Authority.
5 First published in 1993.
6 First published in 1990.
7 Helena Mulkerns, 'Emigrants Catch the Bus', *The Irish Times Weekend Supplement*, December 16, 1995, p. 2.
8 Publisher of Salmon Books, important poetry outlet.
9 Rosita Boland, 'Arriving', in *Ireland in Exile*.
10 John Montague, *The Dead Kingdom* (1984).
11 Contemporary American authors who write on Irish themes. For Gordon, see *The Other Side* (1989). Hamill is author of *The Gift* (1973) and *Loving Women: A Novel of the Fifties* (1989). Extracts from both authors appear in this *Reader*.
12 James Liddy (1934–), a celebrated poet, was born in Dublin and educated at UCD. His published volumes of poetry include *Esau, My Kingdom for a Drink* (1962) and *Art Is Not for Grown-Ups* (1990). In 1976 he took up an appointment at the University of Wisconsin-Milwaukee. Eamon Grennan (1941–) has taught at Vassar College. His verse includes *Wildly for Days* (1983), *What Light There Is* (1987) and *As If It Matters* (1991).
13 Sara Berkeley, *Facts about Water: New and Selected Poems* (Dublin: New Island Books, 1994), p. 76.
14 Greg Delanty (1958–) was born in Cork and has lectured in Vermont and New Hampshire. His published work includes *Southward* (1992) and *American Wake* (1994). See below pp. 1224, 1263.
15 Greg Delanty, *Southward* (Baton Rouge: Louisiana State University Press, 1992), p. 16.
16 Nuala Archer, poet and anthologist, was born to Irish parents in Rochester, New York. Gerard Donovan was born in Wexford and teaches at Suffolk Community College on Long Island. His published volumes of verse include *Columbus Rides Again* (1992) and *Kings and Bicycles* (1995). Helena Mulkerns was born in Dublin and now lives in New York where she has worked as a freelance journalist. Colum McCann was born in Dublin in 1966 and lives in the United States; his short story collection *Fishing the Sloe-Black River* was published in 1994, followed in 1995 by a novel *Songdogs*.
17 Anne Waldman (1945–), American poet, friend of Allen Ginsberg, author of *Fast Speaking Woman and Other Chants* (1975).
18 'Rock and Folk', *The New Yorker* (February 7, 1994), p. 18.
19 In Dublin, hub of activity, especially for the young.
20 Larry Kirwin, 'Rockin' the Bronx', in Black 47, *Fire of Freedom* (New York: SBK Records, 1993).
21 Larry Kirwin, 'American Wake', in Black 47, *Home of the Brave* (New York: SBK Records, 1994).

COLM TÓIBÍN

from the *London Review of Books*, 18 April 1996

Colm Tóibín (1955–), a journalist and novelist, was born in County Wexford and educated at UCD. His novels include *The South* (1990), *The Heather Blazing* (1993) and *The Story of the Night* (1996), an impressive novel set in Argentina after the Falklands War. His most recent novel, *The Blackwater Lightship* (1999), was shortlisted for the Booker Prize. Here in this review of *Inventing Ireland* (1995), a book which has become a standard work in modern Irish criticism, Tóibín takes issue with Declan Kiberd's analysis of modern Irish writing.

Playboys of the GPO

'The most important thing we have done is that we have made a modern art, taking our traditional art as a basis, adorning it with new material, solving contemporary problems with a national spirit,' the Catalan architect Josep Puig i Cadafalch wrote in 1903. By the turn of the century, the national spirit had taken over most cultural activities in Catalonia, so that art, architecture and the Catalan language had become more powerful weapons in politics than resentment about Madrid's handling of foreign or economic policy. The architects who worked on the new apartment blocks and public buildings in Barcelona between 1880 and 1910 began to play with a dual mandate, not merely innovative but Catalan as well, in an effort to create a national spirit in their buildings. They used the most modern methods available: in 1888 Domènech i Montaner used unadorned brick and industrial iron for his café-restaurant in the Parc de la Ciutadella; 16 years later he used a steel frame for his concert hall, El Palau de la Música Catalana, making it the first curtain-wall building in Spain and one of the first in the world. Both buildings sought to establish the progressive nature of the Catalan enterprise, but both are also laden with medieval motifs, reminders of former greatness, of the time before 1492 and the beginning of Castilian imperialism. Like most turn-of-the-century buildings in Barcelona they used Gothic and Romanesque references, spiky shapes, cave-like entrances, floral motifs in wrought iron, coloured glass or ceramic tiles, ornate sculpture, conveying both craft and opulence. They were intensely political buildings, and both Domènech i Montaner and Puig i Cadafalch became leading politicians — Domènech i Montaner was one of the founders of the Lliga de Catalunya in 1887. Both were elected to the Cortes in Madrid to represent the Catalan cause.

I spent a year in Barcelona at the end of the Eighties, looking at these buildings, reading about these architects and thinking about their efforts to construct a nation. Sometimes, as I sat in the Biblioteca de Catalunya in the 14th-century hospital building, I had to blink to make sure that I was not in the National Library in Dublin. Some of the connections between Catalonia and Ireland during this period of nation-inventing were obvious: the Catalans founded a political party in the early Twenties called Nosaltres Sols, a direct translation of Sinn Fein — Ourselves Alone. There were poems in Catalan on the death of Terence MacSwiney on hunger strike in 1921. A stirring poem had been written in Catalan in 1848 which inspired a generation of nationalists; in the same year in Ireland Thomas Davis wrote the song 'A Nation Once Again'. Both Catalan and Irish politicians could, and still can, play tricks with the arithmetic of the Cortes in Madrid and the Mother of Parliaments in Westminster.

But it was the general shape and atmosphere of Catalan cultural politics between 1890 and 1910 which constantly reminded me of Ireland. The foundation of the Barça football club, and its role in creating waves of Catalan emotion, was close to that of the Gaelic Athletic Association in Ireland, founded in the same period. The fetishization of certain parts of the landscape — Montseny, for example, or the Canigó — bore a great resemblance to the sanctity of the Aran Islands and the Blasket Islands in Ireland. The attempt by Yeats and Lady Gregory and Douglas Hyde to surround the Gaelic past with holiness had loud echoes in the efforts by Catalan architects and artists, from Gaudí to Miró, to establish the Romanesque tradition as quintessentially Catalan while the rest of Spain was Moorish. And the attempt, too, by Yeats and Synge, and indeed Joyce, to embrace modernity and Europe as a way of keeping England at bay was close to Domènech's use of iron and steel and modern systems while Spain slept. There were echoes, too, between the careers of Joyce and Picasso, who found all this rhetoric and invention too much for them, who viewed Dublin and Barcelona respectively as centres of paralysis, and who got the hell out as early as they could. And other echoes between the careers of the visionaries Yeats and Gaudí, one of whom embraced magic and the other extreme Catholicism, in a fraught political and emotional climate where everything from the self to the nation was open to invention.

Declan Kiberd tries in this vast, wide-ranging book to find various contexts in which the literature of the Irish Renaissance can be placed.

> To write a deliberately new style, whether Hiberno-English or Whitmanian slang, was to seize power for new voices in literature . . . Since there were no clear protocols for a national poet, Yeats and Whitman were compelled to charm an audience into being by the very tone of their own voices, assuming a people in order to prove that they were really there.

Whitman and Emerson's efforts to invent America are regularly placed beside the efforts of Yeats and his friends to invent Ireland. Kiberd looks for Indian and African models for the Irish experience, so that figures such as Tagore and Rushdie, Naipaul and Achebe, Fanon and Nandy float on the surface of these pages.

Kiberd loves playing with paradoxes, oppositions and juxtapositions. Whenever the word 'periphery' appears in this book, it will almost certainly, by the next sentence, have become the 'centre', and the past the future ('The past is the only certifiable future we have,' Kiberd quotes Carlos Fuentes as saying), just as women will become men and vice versa (this is a major theme), Protestants will become Catholics and vice versa (one chapter is called 'Protholics and Cathestants') and, of course, England will become Ireland (Chapter 1 is entitled 'A New England Called Ireland?'). This results in a good deal of fine writing and exciting analysis, but the playing with fixity is, at times, a mask for some very old-fashioned views on Irish nationalism and Irish history.

Kiberd tells us that Clontarf in Dublin is 'the site of a famous victory by which the Irish had terminated Viking power in Europe'. There is a good reason why there is no footnote here: there is no evidence for this statement. It is the sort of thing which was included in school history books up to the Sixties, but even using the term 'the Irish' here is misleading.

In a book so concerned with flux and non-binary systems, such phrases fall with a dull thud. Later, without explanation or justification, Kiberd uses the phrase 'occupied Ireland' about Ireland in 1907. This is a phrase which might appear now and again in IRA propaganda, but it cannot be thrown casually into a book full of sophisticated distinctions. Elsewhere, Kiberd refers to the Dublin of *Ulysses* as 'an occupied city'. It is hard not to feel that it was occupied by Leopold and Molly Bloom, Stephen Dedalus, Buck Mulligan and others too numerous to mention. Later, he writes: 'After all, one of the first policies formulated by the Norman occupiers was to erase Gaelic culture.' Once again, there is no footnote, no explanation. A few hundred pages earlier, through the medium of Joyce, he had acknowledged that 'the Irish' had roots all over the place (he lists Scandinavia, Normandy, Spain, England): how come the Normans, then, were 'occupiers'?

These dull thuds are important because they give us a sense of the political baseline from which Kiberd is serving. He sets out to explore the origins of Irish national identity, how a number of writers and intellectuals imagined a country, how the country came unto being and how we are destined to live there, in a place created by imagination and rhetoric and eccentric dreams. He writes with reverence about the central figures in this drama — Yeats, Douglas Hyde, Lady Gregory, Patrick Pearse — and, perhaps

more significantly, manages to recruit figures such as Wilde, Joyce and Beckett, placing them posthumously in the pantheon of postcolonial writers who, by revolting into style, created a nation. He wants everyone who put pen to paper in Ireland in these years to lie down in the bed of nation-building, and he is clever enough, much of the time, to make his characters seem grander and more important, rather than cut down to size, because of their close involvement with Holy Mother Ireland.

Some texts were created, you feel, so that Kiberd could play his game with them. It is tempting to think that Shaw wrote *John Bull's Other Island* and Brian Friel wrote *Translations* with Kiberd watching over them, egging them on. Both plays are full of the paradoxes proposed by England in Ireland and Ireland in England. The drama comes from the identity games which colonized and colonizer will play, the masks they will put on, the misunderstandings they will have. In both plays, Ireland and England are imaginary properties.

Kiberd is fascinated by the questions that Oscar Wilde's presence in London raised about Ireland and England.

Wilde's entire literary career constituted an ironic comment on the tendency of Victorian Englishmen to attribute to the Irish those emotions which they had repressed within themselves. His essays on Ireland question the assumption that, just because the English are one thing, the Irish must be its opposite. The man who believed that truth in art is that whose opposite is also true was quick to point out that every good man has the element of the woman in him, just as every sensitive Irishman must have a secret Englishman within himself — and vice versa.

It is useful for Kiberd to read Wilde in terms of Anglo-Irish tensions, and to see him ultimately as a martyr for the cause, a cross between St Sebastian and Kevin Barry,[1] which is how Stephen Rea made him appear in Terry Eagleton's play *St Oscar*.[2] Kiberd's reading remains tentative and convincing, but he is forced to leave a great deal out, such as Wilde's homosexuality.

In taking only the aspects of Wilde and Shaw which fit with his theme, Kiberd comes close to distorting their careers and concerns, but when he comes to Yeats, he is more comfortable, and has more material to use. Yeats is the book's presiding spirit. He is the one who really invented Ireland, and Kiberd delights in the attention he paid to the self while he did this, at the same time as running a theatre, reinventing a national literature, dabbling in magic, calling up the ghosts of the Gaelic past and spending a good deal of time in London.

Yeats offered a sort of grandeur to the class which had attended O'Connell's monster meetings and relished Parnell's mockery of the British Parliamentary system. 'Rereading England,' Kiberd writes, 'the artists learned to rewrite Ireland, and so enabled an Irish Renaissance. In its critical thinking, it was largely a product of artists rather than academics.' Kiberd does not deduce much from that, but the invention of Ireland by Yeats and his friends seems to me to have had some dire consequences for the citizens of Ireland, for the people who occupy the country. In this invention it was possible by using poems and plays, rather than pamphlets and economic argument, to create a vague consensus and a rhetoric of classlessness: a nation rather than a set of clashing interests. By establishing that 'Ireland' existed as an entity, it was easier for governments after Independence to indulge in constant nationalist rhetoric and self-justification while hundreds of thousands emigrated. Ireland is free, who dares complain? In Catalonia the nationalists viewed the loss of the colony of Cuba as a disaster, and had no difficulty opposing anarchism and socialism and, indeed, demands for wage increases as anti-national.

Kiberd tells the story of Ireland's move towards independence with skill and serious analysis, from Douglas Hyde's speech on 'The Necessity for De-Anglicizing Ireland' in November 1892, when there were only six books in print in the Irish language, through the founding of the Abbey Theatre, the first productions of Synge, the writings of Pearse, up to the 1916 Rising. Kiberd likes to deal with the Irish Revival at its most noble and idealistic; that is part of the reason, I assume, for this book. Thus he can write: 'The Gaelic obscurantist, the anti-intellectual priest and the propagandist politician were all as inimical to the revivalist ideal as were the empire men or the shallow cosmopolitans.' This may be the case, but it is likely that all three in the first list enjoyed some aspects of the Revival, and took advantage of it whenever they could.

Kiberd manages most of the time to repel the attacks of Joyce and O'Casey on the invention of Ireland. O'Casey is no use to him: he had no interest in Anglo-Irish paradoxes, he lived in a real rather than an imagined Ireland and he wrote accordingly. 'O'Casey's code,' Kiberd writes, 'scarcely moved beyond a sentimentalization of victims, and this in turn led him to a profound distrust of anyone who makes an idea the basis of an action.' He wants

O'Casey's plays to contain 'the essential criticism of the code' to which they 'finally adhere'.

Kiberd quotes from Joyce's story 'A Mother': 'When the Irish Revival began to be appreciable, Mrs Kearney determined to take advantage of her daughter's name and brought an Irish teacher to the house . . . People said that [her daughter] was very clever at music and a very nice girl, and, moreover, that she was a believer in the language movement. Mrs Kearney was well content with this.' *Ulysses*, Kiberd later writes, 'is one of the first major literary utterances in the modern period by an artist who spoke for a newly liberated people'. I take it he means here that *Ulysses* appeared in 1922, the same year as the foundation of the Irish Free State. Were Mrs Kearney and her daughter, I wonder, part of the 'newly liberated people'? It is hard to think of a phrase less apposite for the transfer of power.

The battle for the soul of Joyce has become almost as intense in recent years as the battle for the GPO in Easter Week. Seamus Deane and Kiberd, both of whom have edited Penguin editions of Joyce's fiction, have made efforts to dragoon him into the soldiers of destiny. In his essay on Joyce in *The Field Day Anthology of Irish Writing*, Deane wrote that Joyce 'remained, at one level, an anti-clerical Irish nationalist with socialist leanings, close to Fenianism and even closer to the position of Michael Davitt'. In *Inventing Ireland*, Kiberd writes: 'Yet into his own exile Joyce took with him the ancient Gaelic notion that only in literature can the consciousness of the people be glimpsed.' Again, there is no footnote. Joyce, he writes, 'attempted in *Ulysses* to unleash a plurality of voices which would together sound the notes that moved beyond nationalism to liberation'. There is much evidence both in the few newspaper articles which Joyce wrote in Italian and in his fiction that he viewed Irish nationalism and the whole business of inventing Ireland as a sour joke. Phrases like 'beyond nationalism to liberation' or 'a newly liberated people' would have been given short shrift in the pages of *Ulysses*.

For Joyce, the idea of England, or Britain, as a mainland was an even sourer joke than Irish nationalism. He himself, rather than any society or nation, was the centre, in a way that no writer from an imperial power could ever be. He knew two sets of tricks; he knew, as Kiberd puts it, 'that fantasy, untouched by any sense of reality, is only a decadent escapism, while reality, unchallenged by any element of fantasy, is a merely squalid realism'. But he was not a political idealist, and the Ireland he invented was not the Ireland of the Revival, or of Pearse and Yeats, and he cannot be treated as part of the same tradition, just as he cannot be treated as apolitical.

We come then to the 1916 Rising, famed in song and story. In a few sentences on pages 329 and 330 Kiberd becomes very brave, and writes that 'the Rising and *Ulysses* can be interpreted in rather similar ways: as attempts to achieve, in the areas of politics and literature, the blessings of modernity and the liquidation of its costs'. But they cannot be interpreted in the same way at all. Literary critics writing about history and politics often mistake them for texts, and this is the real problem with Kiberd's book and, indeed, with the Ireland that was invented — this both gives the book its importance and explains a great deal about Ireland. Not enough distinction is made between what was imagined and what happened, between the rhetoric of Pearse (which happened, but is unreal) and the characters of O'Casey (who never happened but are, none the less, real).

'By 1913,' Kiberd writes, 'Pearse had endowed Synge with the saintliness of his own putative sacrifice — to be made three years later for the work of art called Ireland.' In his chapter on the Rising and the playboys of the GPO, he quotes Yeats:

When Pearse summoned Cuchulain to his side,
What stalked through the Post Office? What
    intellect,
What calculation, number, measurement replied?

'And the answer,' according to Kiberd, 'was in due time: India, Egypt, Nigeria and so on.'

The old schoolbook version of the Rising was that all the efforts of cultural nationalism led to it, and that it resulted in independence. But nobody much accepts this version any more. It is not accepted, for example, in Joe Lee's *Ireland: Politics and Society 1912–1986* or Roy Foster's *Modern Ireland*. Cultural nationalism did not lead to the Rising, though it may have been in part responsible for it; the executions after the Rising certainly inflamed public opinion, but not as much perhaps as the threat of conscription. Also, the myth of the Rising was easy to spread in the years afterwards when all the leaders but one — de Valera — were dead, and Yeats was ready to publish his poem 'Easter 1916'.

'They must have been the gentlest revolutionaries in history,' Kiberd writes. But no one holding a gun is gentle, as O'Casey makes clear. Kiberd is prepared to accept the old schoolbook version, and prepared to castigate Roy Foster for his tentative version of the events and patronize him thereafter as a patriotic Southern Irish Protestant 'who believes that the most useful service which he can perform for his people is the devaluation of a nationalism, some of whose disciples are still willing to kill and be killed in its defence'. (I notice that he does not patronize Joe Lee in this way; could it be because he is not a Protestant?) But this is hardly the point; the point is how we approach the Rising: with Kiberd, who views it as part of a grand narrative, as though history had been written by Flaubert, or with Foster, who is wary about the myths surrounding the central moments in Irish history and seeks to examine the past using merely the available evidence.

No one is dispassionate. Kiberd is not a historian, but this does not dent his confidence in sticking to the story we all read in the schoolbooks, which he is the last to believe. Yet, as in all the other sections of the book, there are questions he asks and points he makes about the relationship between literature and history which take your breath away and make you want to tell him to come home all is forgiven: 'To creative artists may have fallen the task of explaining what no historian has fully illuminated — the reason why the English came to regard the Irish as inferior and barbarous, on the one hand, and, on the other, poetic and magical.'

The debate about 1916 continues to haunt us in the Republic for good reasons, best explained by the poet Michael O'Loughlin: 'It is, I believe, almost impossible for anyone of my generation to think about 1916 as an actual event in history, discrete and autonomous. The way in which 1916 had been presented to us was an important process in our understanding of the nature of our society, and of ourselves. For my generation' — O'Loughlin was born in 1958 — 'the events of Easter 1966 were crucial, so much so that I think it is almost possible to speak of a generation of '66.'

In 1966 the state celebrated the 50th anniversary of the Rising with enormous gusto, with marches in which schools took part and rousing speeches and an emotional television series called *Insurrection*, broadcast nightly. But once the North broke and the IRA campaign recommenced, the state's attitude changed. 'In an act of astonishing political opportunism,' O'Loughlin wrote, '1916 was revised. By 1976, and the 60th celebrations, a different tune was being played. For people of my generation, who were and who are, in an important sense, neither Republican nor non-Republican, this was a lesson they would never forget. To see history so swiftly rewritten was to realize that what was called history was in fact a façade behind which politicians manoeuvred for power.'

The rebels, Kiberd writes with approval, 'staged the Rising as street theatre'. Pearse 'saw that, in a traditionalist society, it is vitally necessary to gift-wrap the gospel of the future in the packaging of the past. This Connolly also did when he presented socialism as a return to the Celtic system whereby a chief held land in the common name of all the people. Joyce adopted a similar tactic when he concealed the subversive narrative of *Ulysses* beneath the cover of one of Europe's oldest stories, *The Odyssey*.' Kiberd is prepared to treat the Rising in the terms in which some of its leaders sought to present it. But it was not a text: it involved the burning of buildings, the execution of prisoners, the shooting of soldiers, the murder of civilians. And it also used the idea of theatre and text — Kiberd calls it a performance — to create a cult of violence. I loathe everything about it, every single moment of it. And the stuff about 'the Celtic system whereby a chief held land in the common name of all the people' is pure nonsense.

In 1991, on the occasion of the 75th anniversary of the Rising, there were calls to retransmit *Insurrection*, but the television station refused on the basis that it was too inflammatory. There were a few half-hearted public ceremonies, presided over by the Taoiseach, but hardly anyone attended. However, the Government sponsored a scheme called the Flaming Door in which Irish writers were invited to read their work during Easter in appropriate places such as the GPO or the jail where the leaders had been executed. When in doubt, they brought in the artists.

We have to live here and face the idea that our state was built on these dreams and texts, on this violence. It is easy to be in a rage with the cult of the Rising, but then Kiberd ends a chapter with the following: 'In the aftermath of the Rising, as the poetry and prose of the rebel leaders were widely circulated among a sympathetic American audience, H.G. Wells, John Galsworthy and Arnold Bennett published essays critical of them in the United States. The poets' crazy dream was to be countered by some of the leading practitioners of modern English prose.' I realize when I read this passage that if I had a choice between the ambiguous heritage left by Pearse and Yeats and the unambiguous legacy of Wells, Galsworthy and Bennett, I am happier on this side — the Irish side — of the Irish Sea: it is hard to imagine how you would get through the day with the dryness of the other heritage. But I still hate the Rising, and Kiberd's chapter on it has not helped me. I was the only writer, as far as I am aware, who refused the invitation to take part in the Flaming Door. I left the country for Easter Week 1991.

Once Yeats's career has come to an end — and Kiberd has much of interest to say about it — it is difficult to see where *Inventing Ireland* can go. It is depressing to watch him treating de Valera as a text:

'De Valera's pastoral politics owed much to Thomas Jefferson, sharing his hope of having things both ways, of avoiding the savagery of absolute, untamed nature, and also the desiccation of great modern cities.' He goes on to write about the ideal Ireland of the nationalists as 'a political version of literary modernism which compensated for all that was lost in the consumer society by emphasizing the complexity, beauty and quality of many traditions. It was in this sense that the cultural values promoted by Yeats and Synge could be both very new and very old, evoking Adam and a perpetual Last Judgment.' He reads Ireland in the Thirties, with its rampant emigration, poverty and class division, as though it were Yeats's *Last Poems*. He refuses to deal with the grubbiness of Irish politics after Independence, reading it as though it were a medieval illuminated manuscript rather than a politics rife with opportunism, hypocrisy and failure.

Ireland continued and continues to be invented by writers, mainly these days by Brian Friel and Seamus Heaney. Most other writers, however, do not inhabit a universe shaped by Ireland's relationship to its past or to England, thus it is difficult for Kiberd to have much to say about John Banville or Tom Murphy or Derek Mahon. And there are other writers, such as John McGahern, to whom these old dreams and inventions mean nothing at all, or those who found or find them worthy merely of jokes and asides, such as Flann O'Brien or Paul Muldoon. Inventing Ireland, in the sense that Yeats invented Ireland, has stopped; writers now invent other sorts of Ireland, and it is not necessary to read their work politically.

Is Beckett, then, the one who got away? Kiberd has him 'deeply moved' sixty years later by his memory of watching Dublin burning in 1916. He deals here with Beckett and his relationship to the Gaelic, rather than the nationalist, tradition, placing the origin of his interest in language and silence in the death of the Irish language. ('It will be dead in time, just like our own poor dear Gaelic, there is that to be said,' says Mrs Rooney in *All that Fall*.) One can presume that Murphy wanted his ashes flushed down the toilet of the Abbey Theatre, because Beckett thought that this was a good joke — the building in which Ireland had been so intensely invented he viewed with amusement, even scorn perhaps. But Kiberd is having none of this. He wants to make Beckett's tramps stand for much more than tramps: he wants them to be cast-out Gaelic poets. He wants the idea of 'A voice comes to one in the dark' in 'Company' to reflect the habit of Gaelic poets who composed in the dark. But the dark here surely has to be a real, literal dark without any literary resonance or echo. A dark from which the

Irish heritage, like all heritage, has been stripped away, the dark before death, the darkness that is death. To find an Irish origin for 'Company' is to take all its power away.

Yet Kiberd here, as in much of the book, manages to keep his interpretation intriguing; his analysis is constantly full of fancy footwork. Also, he is right when he writes:

> The voices which Beckett heard and committed to paper for the rest of his life as an artist were unambiguously Irish. Occasionally, they bore faint Wildean echoes, as in the inversion of a famous quotation or proverb, but more often they were austere, controlled, pared back. The promise of Yeats and Joyce to take revivalist rhetoric and wring its neck was being brought to a strict conclusion.

It is not easy to bring Kiberd's project to a strict conclusion. He is not good at dealing with matters which do not fit into his grand plan. He alludes several times to the Gaelic writers from the Blasket Islands, but he does not deal with the fact that, surviving at the very heart of 'the nation', they had no time for it, they were too interested in the world. In a way, it is that tradition, the attempt to describe the known world through attention to detail, the placing of a small community at the centre of the universe, which has survived and flourished in Ireland. It belongs to a book called 'Not Inventing Ireland' in which Joyce and O'Casey and the writers of the Blasket Islands lead to Kavanagh and McGahern, with Beckett and Banville nearby; in which writers ignored the idea of Ireland and concentrated on communities or formal questions and made the whole idea of Irish nationalism a sick joke or a burden or a lie. The idea that we all inhabit both an invented and a non-invented Ireland may help explain why people emigrate from here whenever there is an economic crisis.

In his final chapter Kiberd takes issue with *Ireland: Politics and Society 1912–1986*, in which Joe Lee makes clear that Ireland's economic performance after the British withdrawal was worse than under the British. Lee compares the Irish performance with that of other countries of a similar size, such as Denmark, which, Kiberd says, 'did not undergo the long nightmare of colonial expropriation and misrule'. Nor were these countries dreamed into existence by a mixture of poetry and violence. Kiberd blames colonization for bad economic performance, but it is just as likely that the way in which Ireland was invented, with so much emphasis on the Gaelic past and foreign occupation and so little on how people lived and what they wanted, meant that economic performance would never be a priority for an Irish government.

This book is a complex and fascinating account of a golden age in Irish writing, or a version of the way self-delusion, fanaticism and rhetoric can capture the soul of a small, fragile place and make it into the nation from which we are still trying to awake. As always, it depends on your politics.

1 Kevin Barry (1902–20) was an IRA volunteer, who was captured after taking part in a raid for arms in which six soldiers were killed. He was hanged in Mountjoy jail on 1 November 1920 and became a folk hero made popular by a song with his name in the title.
2 First performed in 1989.

LOUIS DE PAOR
from *Poetry Ireland Review*, Number 51, Autumn 1996

In this article, based on a talk he gave at the Féderation Intérnationale des Traducteurs Conference in Melbourne, Australia, in February 1996, Louis de Paor raises some awkward questions about the imbalance between English and Irish.

Disappearing Language: Translations from the Irish

The history of translation from Irish to English is characterized from the outset by the unequal relationship between the two languages, a product of sustained colonial pressure to undermine the authority of a separate Gaelic culture whose independence is guaranteed by the irredeemable otherness of its language. That connection between culture and politics which motivated colonial efforts to silence Irish is evident in Edmund Spenser's remark that 'the speech being Irish, the heart must needs be Irish'. Following the political destruction of an independent Gaelic Ireland at the Battle of Kinsale in 1601 and the subsequent dispersal of the native Irish aristocracy Sir John Davies anticipated a disintegration of Irish cultural separateness confirmed by the silence of their language: 'We may conceive and hope that the next generation will in tongue and heart and every way else become English; so that there will be no difference or distinction but the Irish Sea between us.'

In fact it took almost another three hundred years of conquest during which time the language was systematically cut off from economic, social and political status to achieve the final degradation of Irish. The great 'famines' of the 1840s which devastated the Irish-speaking peasant class reinforced the colonial connection between ignorance, poverty and back-wardness and the traditional patterns of the language itself which seemed to prolong the powerlessness of those who spoke it. For Irish-speakers themselves as much as for colonial imperialists the language had now become in Matthew Arnold's formulation the 'badge of the beaten race, the property of the vanquished'. Within a generation the language shift from Irish to English, the ultimate translation, had been virtually completed.

From the beginning then, translation from Irish to English is as much an act of obliteration and annihilation as it is one of discovery and exchange. Translation begins in earnest in the late eighteenth century as a politically ascendant Anglo-Irish class attempts to reconcile its own conflicting loyalties by aligning itself culturally with a disappearing Gaelic tradition while maintaining its political commitment to English rule. Antiquarian interest increases as the cultural authority of Irish is forcibly diminished and the language becomes, according to Seamus Deane, the 'symbol of a lost culture rather than a reminder of a rebellious one'. The gradual recuperation and appro-priation of material from a supposedly 'lost' tradition by philologists, antiquarians and others in the eighteenth and nineteenth centuries is part of a process of political assimilation at the same time that it is a sincere gesture of cultural deference. In translation the English text pays homage to an invisible but certainly not dead Gaelic tradition. As it celebrates, it conceals, or at best embalms, the language in which the work, poem or story was originally created.

If the English words represent a nostalgic gesture towards a Gaelic tradition which on occasion remains unsighted for both readers and translators, they point finally to themselves rather than directing the reader back to the original material in Irish. The English translation then replaces the Irish while appearing to replicate it, insisting it has redeemed the original while suggesting itself as a legitimate substitute.

Another aspect of the interaction between Irish and English which indicates the imbalance of power that makes translation so problematic is the borrowing or infiltration of one language from or by the other. The intrusion of English words in seventeenth century Irish poetry shows the extent to which colonial distribution of power is evident in the collision of two languages. The strange words which disrupt the progress of familiar Irish verse patterns proclaim the powerlessness of Irish while, at the same time, they affirm the colonial structures that uphold the authority of English. The foreign words which force themselves on the Irish without any attempt at accommodation or possibility of translation replicate those structures of legal and military power which will eventually reduce the indigenous language to political impotence — Exchequer, Court of Wards, King's Bench, Assizes, pistol, carbine, firelock, conquest, transplant, transport, Jamaica.

The English language of abuse interrupts Éamon an Dúna's 'Mo lá leóin go deo go n-éagad'. The violent prejudice of colonial attitudes is unmistakeable in 'Shoot him, kill him, strip him, tear him. / A Tory, hack him, hang him, rebel / a rogue, a thief, a priest, a papist'. The threatening force of the English words is founded on the superior military strength of those who utter them and their irruption into the Irish text indicates the helplessness of Irish in responding to the argot of absolute authority. By contrast the Irish words which are gradually absorbed into official English are entirely unthreatening, confirming the unequal distribution of power between the two languages. The stage-Irish whimsy of smithereens, galore, wisha, omadhaun, leprechaun — not to mention spurious Gaelicisms such as 'begorrah and begob' — prove the quaint charm of a language strategically removed from social status and political power. In the exchange between languages blarney is the Irish counter to the authority of English.

To a greater or lesser extent these historical inequalities are still evident in the uneasy process of translation from Irish to English. Although up to a million people have claimed in recent census returns that they speak Irish, estimates of the number of native speakers vary between twenty and eighty thousand out of a total population of 3.5–5 million people. Prior to the Great Famine Irish was one of the one hundred most widely spoken of the world's five thousand or more languages. The diminishing number of speakers rather than any reduction in the resources of the language itself has continued the imbalance imposed by colonialism. In literature English is now the language of status and prestige and writing in Irish for most of the twentieth century has been invisible except where it has been assimilated through translation into the mainstream English language tradition. It is as though English were a mark of distinction, a category of excellence, and to be translated from Irish an achievement, a granting of aesthetic value and critical approval. The exclusion of writers such as Seán Ó Ríordáin and Máirtín Ó Cadhain, whose work is not easily rendered into English, from most anthologies of Irish writing as indeed from scholarly analysis indicated the colonial arrogance and critical wrongheadedness of such a myopic approach to literature. It might also explain the ambivalence and suspicion, and in some cases the outright hostility, of Irish language writers to the business of translation.

Biddy Jenkinson,[1] one of the finest contemporary Irish poets, has reacted against the continuing colonial force of English which insists that writing in Irish only becomes visible and worthy of critical attention when it has been made available in English by prohibiting translation of her work in Ireland: 'It is a small rude gesture to those who think that everything can be harvested and stored without loss in an English-speaking Ireland.' Her gesture is also a tactical reaction to the ongoing capacity of English translation to assimilate and finally supplant the Irish, silencing that which it is apparently giving voice to, consigning to the realms of the unliving what it is supposedly rescuing from extinction: 'If I were a corncrake I would feel no need to have my skin cured, my tarsi injected with formalin so that I could fill a museum shelf in a world that saw no need for my kind. There are others with more generous souls and I take a certain malicious pleasure in seeing some of them sweep in to take centre stage often enough in places where they were being offered a token spot in the wings.' Despite the sincerity of the translator the imbalance of power between the two languages ensures that English commands the page while Irish looks on from the margins, its prompting for the most part unheard by the audience.

The work of Brian O'Nolan, novelist, controversialist and linguistic subversive can be read as a sustained onslaught on the authority of English. His relentlessly literal approach to translation begins as a satire on the Kiltartanese of Lady Gregory and Synge which proposes the mouth-music of an invented Hiberno-English dialect as an appropriate register for the adequate rendering of Irish in English and finishes as a rigorous questioning of the colonial attitudes implied in supposedly faithful translation. He pours scorn on Robin Flower's 'mistranslation' of Tomás Ó Criomhthain's *An tOileánach*, 'the superbest of all books' according to O'Nolan: 'A greater parcel of bosh and bunk than Flower's *Islandman* has rarely been imposed on the unsuspecting public. Not only was it a mistranslation but it gives a wholly wrong impression, hiding inside its covers of opulent tweed.' While Flower avoids the faithless charm of Hiberno-English in attempting to render what he calls the 'colloquial simplicity of the original' — 'rouge,' he says, 'is no substitute for a natural complexion' — his 'plain straightforward English' gives no sense of the perfectly wrought tightlipped classicism of Ó Criomhthain's Irish. The exaggerated literalness of O'Nolan's own mock translation of *The Islandman* parodies the bad faith of so-called faithful translation which suggests that bad English, hilarious and unthreatening in its unintended gaucherie, is an accurate rendering of the otherness of Irish:

> It was a day in Dingle and Paddy James, my sister's man, in company with me and us in the direction of each other in the running of the day. A time after that my brother Paddy moved towards me from being over there in Ameriky. There was great surprise on me he is coming from being over there the second time, because the two sons who were at him were strong hefty ones at that time.

Here as elsewhere in his work O'Nolan's mimicry is remorseless, pushing the parody of literal translation beyond clumsiness to suggest that an utterly faithful translation will be literally incomprehensible in the target language. The near unreadability of his English sends the reader back to the Irish to make sense of a language which has been made incomprehensibly foreign to the familiar patterns of standard English in deference to the irreducible and finally unutterable otherness of Irish. In doing so he has drawn attention to the suppression of difference which is required to accommodate Irish to the alien structure of English. Even in what purport to be faithful and literal translations, he suggests the material has been tailored not only to the grammatical patterns of English but also to the cultural expectations of an audience which has been persuaded that funny and peculiarly bad English is a true representation of the unfamiliar strangeness of Irish. In his column in *The Irish Times* O'Nolan frequently drew attention to the seemingly endless polyguity of apparently simple Irish words which finally defeat the most well-meaning and rigorous attempts at translation.

His linguistic subversion is evident again in a virtuoso demonstration which proves that a sentence in Irish which appears to mean:

It is entirely a new thing that a symphony concert should be held in conjunction with a Gaelic choir.

might be rendered with equal conviction in English as:

It is longitudinally a strong anxiety that a wise and vigorous ancient Irish ale should be in moderato time at once with an unsophisticated troop.

Only by deferring to the authority of the original can it be established whether the semantic space between the Irish text and the English copy has been loaded with sense or nonsense. It is precisely that authority which needs to be continually reasserted against the colonial power of English to obliterate Irish in the process of translation. Yet the mistaken belief persists that the proper arena of Irish is the 'backward' 'primitive' world of pre-modern peasant culture with its 'archaic' rituals of folk custom and belief and that the modern urban industrial world remains firmly within the Pale beyond its reach. There may be forty words for seaweed in Irish and any number of quaint distinctions between different categories of other-worldly creatures but the language of computer technology and urban industry, the contemporary argot of power and authority, must remain in quarantine on its borders lest it contaminate the essential purity of Irish as a fossilized relic of antiquity. The patronizing and misplaced concern that patterns of traditional usage be neither disturbed nor corrupted in the process of modernizing the language may be the latest colonial strategy for keeping Irish in its place at a remove from the structures of power and authority which would ensure its survival as a living language. While writers such as Ó Ríordáin, Ó Cadhain and Ó Tuairisc and more recently Michael Davitt,[2] Liam Ó Muirthile, Séamus Mac Annaidh and others prove the enduring capacity of Irish to accommodate new areas of experience without compromising its integrity, the response to the work of Davitt and Nuala Ní Dhomhnaill, the two finest contemporary poets in Irish in translation, indicates the lingering force of cultural colonialism as it affects the presentation and reception of Irish material in English.

Davitt is, perhaps, the most experimental poet in Irish and his work continues to surprise and sometimes shock readers by its appropriation into Irish of aspects of contemporary urban reality which had been previously considered the exclusive preserve of English. In translation that element of innovation is almost completely absent as what was exotic in Irish appears familiar and consequently uninventive in English. In the case of Nuala Ní Dhomhnaill whose work is steeped in folklore and mythology the process is reversed. Elements of Nuala's work which are entirely traditional in Irish appear exotic and foreign in English. That which challenges readers' expectations in English is often what most conforms to traditional practice in Irish. While not suggesting there is a deliberate misreading of either poet's work in translation I would argue that the critical response to their work in English has been skewed by the colonial history of interaction between the two languages which has privileged English in the familiar modern industrial world while continuing the marginalization of Irish by consigning it to the exotic and unfamiliar pre-modern rural world.

In multicultural Australia the colonial imbalance of power between competing languages is confirmed in some areas while being totally subverted in others. The absence of languages other than English in literary journals and newspapers suggests that, in Australia, as in Ireland despite the multilingual nature of the society, English is in itself a mark of excellence, and translation into English not only an aesthetic achievement but an absolute requirement for artistic legitimacy. On the other hand bilingual publishing in Australia reverses the equation of power which induces even Irish-speaking readers in Ireland to turn their backs on the original text and accept in its place the forgery on the facing page. In Australia the familiarity of the English encourages the reader to look back to the original in the expectation of finding some foothold there to further understanding. Paradoxically the unreadability of the Irish, and its impenetrability to the uninitiated, increases the authority of the original by urging the reader to question the status of the English copy and heightening his awareness of the distance between the familiar words on one side of the page and their origin in the strange indecipherable formations on the other.

The response to my own work in translation directly contradicts the response to the same poems among Irish readers, by favouring those which draw more on traditional rural images and beliefs, over others which articulate aspects of contemporary suburban living in Ireland or Australia. While this response would seem to confirm the colonial compartmentalization of languages, I have found the reaction to English versions of my poems in Australia curiously liberating. Nuala Ní Dhomhnaill has pointed out that we're all dirt farmers if you dig back a couple of generations. However the determination of writers in Irish to refute colonial misrepresentations by proving the adaptability of Irish to the contemporary urban situation may have caused some of us at least to neglect or even deny crucial aspects of our own identity, an altogether unexpected consequence of our anti-colonial stance. Aspects of early Irish mythology, of folk tradition and belief as well as elements of my own family history which I had felt were irreconcilable with my own sense of myself as a thoroughly modern urban dweller, a chauvinistic townie in fact, have gradually extended my sense of belonging in the entire history and geography of Ireland rather than being confined to the immediate here and now which I had felt was my proper place.

In translating then for an Australian audience, the boundaries of my own identity and the limits of the language I write have been extended to include elements which the post-colonial conflict between the traditional and the modern might otherwise have consigned to silence. Translation, which in Ireland has often been more effective as a gag than as a second voice bridging the immense distance between languages, has not only made my voice audible, albeit at very low volume in Australia — it has extended considerably the range of sounds and their echoes across time and space which I can now hear in my own language.

1 Her collections of verse include *Báisteadh Gintlí* (1987) and *Uisá Beatha* (1988).
2 Michael Davitt (1950–) was born in Cork and educated at University College Cork where he founded the literary journal *Innti* in 1970. His first collection of verse *Gleann ar Ghleann* was published in 1982, followed by *Bligeard* (1983) and *An Tosta Scagadh* (1993).

FINTAN O'TOOLE
from *Granta*, Spring 1996

There are few better antidotes to the sentimental picture of Ireland than this essay on Tony O'Reilly by Fintan O'Toole. Indeed, of all the extracts in this *Reader*, this essay provides arguably the best introduction to contemporary Irish culture. O'Toole traces the web of interconnections between business, politics, sport, and ownership of the media, and he shows how Ireland is united as an island, united, that is, to a global economic system. In a devastating critique he also underlines how his subject has made 'a nonsense of history and indeed of geography'. For other work by O'Toole, see *Meanwhile, Back at the Ranch* (1995), *The Ex-Isle of Erin* (1998), *The Lie of the Land* (1998), and *The Irish Times Book of the Century* (1999). O'Toole, who is on the staff of *The Irish Times*, has also written on Tom Murphy and Sebastian Barry, as well as an acclaimed biography of Richard Brinsley Sheridan.

Brand Leader

On the morning last December that Tony O'Reilly spoke at a conference in Belfast, his own newspaper the *Irish Independent* ran two full pages about the event. One of them was dominated by a stark black-and-white advertisement. At its centre was a map of Ireland. Around the map was the distinctive triple-bordered shape of a label familiar to devotees of tomato ketchup and baked beans. Within the borders were five large letters spelling HEINZ. There was nothing else — no slogan, no exhortation: just this strange map of a small island in the Atlantic. Inside the jagged contours of its coastline, this country had no political boundaries, no features, no landmarks of history, none of the resonant names or contested zones of a place emerging from a dark and tangled past. It was a clear, uncomplicated space, a brand image, a label that could be stuck on a billion sauce bottles.

As he rose to speak that morning in the Europa Hotel, against a backdrop of cobalt blue emblazoned with the logo of Independent Newspapers and an abstract painting of the globe, Tony O'Reilly seemed the perfect citizen of an Ireland that had escaped from itself. He had been introduced as the Irish head of a multinational company, H. J. Heinz, with expected sales this year of nine billion dollars, as a man who 'encapsulates perfectly' the theme of the conference —

global economics. And that image had been driven home by his own newspapers over many years. His *Sunday Independent* once devoted an eight-page colour supplement to him, headlined A MAN FOR ALL CONTINENTS, with no fewer than seventeen photographs of the proprietor: Tony O'Reilly with Henry Kissinger, Tony O'Reilly with Margaret Thatcher, Tony O'Reilly with Valéry Giscard D'Estaing, Tony O'Reilly with Robert Mugabe, Tony O'Reilly stepping off his corporate jet, Tony O'Reilly with his beautiful first wife and six beautiful children.

In Belfast that morning he laid out the colour supplement of his own personality for the admiring gaze of his audience, every inch the smiling public man, at ease in the way that only someone who has been a star since he was barely out of school can be. A rugby international at the age of eighteen, he still has the height and bearing of a sportsman, even if the smooth beauty of his youth has now become rugged, its effect more imposing than dazzling. Because he seems to take his own air of authority for granted, he can afford to be charming, even gossipy, knowing that nobody will take advantage of the sense of intimacy he creates.

He is a man for whom there is no clear distinction between the private and the public self, a man whose acquaintances all remark on the fact that almost every meal in one of his houses in Pittsburgh or in Ireland seems to be a public event, shared with friends, contacts, associates: people who are, for one reason or another, being wooed. One former colleague remembers the brilliant mixture of private charm and public purpose: 'I found him big, expansive, talkative. He tells funny stories; he's charming; he makes you feel that his wealth, his big house and his ambience are yours to enjoy, that you're being given privileged and undivided access to it all. You need that kind of charm and loquaciousness and those gifts in business and in public life, and he's got them in abundance. You find yourself with a sense of intimacy with him in your conversation, because he's indiscreet, and he speaks in a mischievous way about people he knows, so you feel quite close to him. And then you hear that if any of his staff fail to call him "Doctor O'Reilly", he hangs them up by their heels and pours boiling pitch down the front of their trousers.'

The contradiction is present even in his name. He is universally known as Tony, except in his own newspapers, where he is always referred to as 'Dr A. J. F. O'Reilly', the doctorate being a Ph.D in food marketing awarded by the University of Bradford in 1980 for a thesis he submitted on the launch of Kerrygold butter, his first great business coup. Yet in reality Tony and Dr A. J. F. are indistinguishable in the persona of a man with whom the whole world is on intimate terms.

Even in front of his formal audience in Belfast, he presented that same package of public and private, knowing that the details of his own career had already acquired the aura of legend. Many of his listeners could have rattled off its milestones. The birth of Anthony John Francis O'Reilly in Dublin on 7 May 1936 as the first and only child of an apparently respectable middle-class couple, his mother a housewife, his father a customs official. His education at a fee-paying Jesuit school, followed by a law degree at University College Dublin. His glorious rugby career in which he played twenty-nine times for Ireland. His membership from the age of nineteen of the British Lions, the all-star touring team made up of the best rugby players from Ireland, England, Scotland and Wales, and the swashbuckling tours of South Africa, New Zealand and Australia through which he made a name for himself on three continents. The sure-footedness with which he bartered that sporting fame into an equally dazzling corporate career, first as a managing director of the Irish state dairy and sugar companies, then on to his present pinnacle as chairman, president and chief operating officer of H. J. Heinz, and chairman and controlling shareholder of Independent Newspapers in Dublin and a range of other Irish-based companies. His first marriage to Susan Cameron, an Australian with whom he had six children, including triplets. His second marriage to Chryss Goulandris, a member of a hugely wealthy Greek shipping dynasty which has become an important ally in his business ventures. His Georgian mansion, stud farm and estate at Castlemartin in County Kildare, Ireland, and his other homes in Dublin, West Cork, Pittsburgh (where Heinz has its headquarters) and the Bahamas. His foundation of the Ireland Fund, a multinational charitable trust that funds projects in both parts of Ireland.

He littered his speech in Belfast with anecdotes drawn from most of these chapters of his own legend, reminding his audience that he was himself his own message. And all the time his own story was made to seem a parable of globalization, of a man rising from a specific time and place into a great network of worldwide power. Even his jokes were global — flow charts parodying management styles in China, Britain, Italy, Saudi Arabia, Latin America, Ireland and the United States appearing on the screen beside him as he performed his accomplished warm-up act.

In the face of this tour of far horizons, the petty details of Irish history, so recently strewn in the shape of twisted metal and torn flesh on the streets outside the hotel, dissolved into insignificance. Facing an audience of besuited businessmen drawn from both sides of the Irish border and both sides of the Protestant-Catholic divide, he felt confident enough to tease them with a small political joke. His lecture, he announced, would be called 'The island of Ireland — united'. He paused just long enough to hear the strain in the room, the jerk of raw nerves being touched by the cruel point of politics. And then, his craggy face broken by a small smile, he picked up his sentence: '. . . to a global economic system.'

After the jokes, he started to talk about history. He explained to the members of his audience, with the help of slides, and as if they didn't know this, that we are at the end of the twentieth century. The century, he said, is a triptych. In the first panel are two brutal world wars. In the second is a forty-five-year period of geopolitical equilibrium and dramatic economic growth. And in the third, 'here we are', in a new age of 'capital ruthlessly seeking the best rate of return', of 'the emergence of the global consumer'. The twentieth century, he said, was dominated by ideological competition, but the twenty-first will belong to commercial competition.

The slide showing now was made up of a large picture of O'Reilly's friend Nelson Mandela and a smaller one of Yitzhak Rabin and Yasser Arafat shaking hands, with the caption 'The Collapse of Communism and the Promise of Peace'. It looked like the end of history, and he mentioned that Francis Fukuyama wrote a book of that name after the demolition of the Berlin Wall.

For Tony O'Reilly, the great symbolic event of the last decade was not so much the fall of the Wall as the opening of the first McDonald's in Moscow. It was, he has said, not just a new product launch; it was 'a social and cultural event of international proportions'. While others were thinking about the peace dividend at the end of the cold war or about the triumph of democracy, he was thinking about the beginning of global marketing and the arrival of the new, placeless consumer, belonging to a world where allegiances to brand names have replaced the more dangerous and visceral loyalties of history and geography.

He looks and sounds like a man who has made a nonsense of history and indeed of geography. His deep voice carries an Irish accent that has been levelled out by a quarter of a century in America so that it seems to echo with only the faintest undertone of time and place. His easy mimicry, the way he slips, in his jokes, into perfectly tuned Belfast or Dublin, or English or American accents, serves merely to emphasize the neutrality of his own voice, to draw attention to the fact that local inflections are something he can put on or take off at will. And everything he said that morning in Belfast seemed to suggest that he really believes that history is over, that the business of the world, now and for evermore, is business.

But something — perhaps the fact that he was speaking in a hotel that was known until recently, in spite of the antiseptic internationalism of its decor, as the most bombed building in Europe — seemed suddenly to make him doubtful. History did not really end, he mused. It 'emerged from the permafrost of communism. Theological nationalism is re-emerging.' It was an anomalous moment of doubt and it passed quickly. He moved on to talk with his usual certainty about the scarce and demanding nature of capital, about the need to get governments off the back of business, about the beneficial effects of the North American Free Trade Agreement in allowing Heinz to keep wages down. But somehow, the moment lingered as an undercurrent of fear. Even Tony O'Reilly can't mention theological nationalism in Belfast without reminding his audience that there are other forces in the world besides global competition. And even he knows, from his own life, something about those forces.

Had any of the businessmen at that conference in Belfast been present in November 1982 at a function in the Abbey Theatre in Dublin to honour the novelist Peadar O'Donnell, they would have been amazed to find Tony O'Reilly not merely present but more or less running the show. O'Donnell embodied in many ways a past that few of them would have wanted to recognize. As well as being a distinguished writer, he was also the last surviving member of the executive of the old Irish Republican Army. He was a Marxist radical, a fiery trade union organizer and professional agitator. And he was, for five years in the 1940s, Tony O'Reilly's mentor. When O'Reilly started his tribute to O'Donnell by declaring that the old man had 'almost reared me', many of those present thought at first that it was another of O'Reilly's jokes, that the punchline would be coming soon.

There was no punchline. O'Donnell's nephew and namesake was O'Reilly's best friend at school, and the two boys spent all their summers in O'Donnell's big house in the countryside near Dungloe in County Donegal. 'Peadar was Uncle Peadar to me,' O'Reilly told his audience, 'and his wife was Auntie Lil . . . I remember Peadar's glittering conversation, and the notion that we were both interested in Marx: he in Karl, I in Groucho.' The predictable joke, intended to dismiss the strangeness of this icon of multinational capitalism adopting a communist uncle, could not hide the vestiges of rapture in the memory of golden times: 'I learned how to fish there, how to row and how to drink altar wine.' Those, he recalled, were 'sunlit days, and both glittering and glamorous as well'. For once he had nothing clever to say, no pronouncements to make. For once he allowed the distance between the president of Heinz and a certain kind of Irish past to stretch over a terrain not of triumph but of loss.

O'Donnell was just one of three veterans of Ireland's bloody wars who helped to shape O'Reilly's early life, and the memory of the other two was less golden. When he was born in 1936, in a state still struggling to emerge from the bloody circumstances of its birth, Tony O'Reilly was named after his mother's brother, Tony O'Connor, who was always to be his favourite uncle. Uncle Tony was a man who had seen history at first-hand. In the savage civil war that followed the Anglo-Irish treaty of 1921, fought between those who accepted the establishment of an Irish Free State within the British Empire and those who wanted to hold out for a republic, the O'Connors took the Free State side. Tony O'Connor himself joined the Free State army when it was established, and he later wrote that before he was twenty he had killed at least a dozen fellow Irishmen in the wild country-road skirmishes that constituted the civil war, rising in the process to the rank of sergeant.

He survived the war but he was always haunted by the memory of a day in January 1923 in Athlone, where he had grown up and played as a child with a 'tall, slender and dark-haired' boy. For more than fifty years, he carried with him the secret of what had happened to that boy. In 1975, when O'Reilly had ascended beyond the internecine hatreds of a small nation and was already president and chief executive of H. J. Heinz, he let the secret out.

O'Reilly had by then reached a point from which he could look back on Irish history, with all its entanglements, as a joke. In 1970, for instance, when he was managing director of Heinz UK, he had made an extraordinary comeback, after an absence of fifteen years, to play rugby for Ireland against England at Twickenham. In the programme for the match, he wrote a burlesque of Anglo-Irish history in which even the massacres of Cromwell could be laughed about: 'To the English it is a game of rugger — to the Irish a historical pageant, the continuation of centuries of loose rucks, crooked into the scrum, and bad refereeing, including a particularly nasty period when England were strong up front and had Oliver Cromwell at fly-half, "a very mean fella with the boot

and elbow and distinctly anti-clerical when he got you on the ground", as a decaying Irish wing-forward was heard to remark.'

For O'Connor, though, history was not a game, but a personal burden, a story he would like to forget but was compelled to remember. Even then, it was too painful to be told bluntly and was wrapped in a thin layer of fiction, as a novel called *He's Somewhere In There*. Its status was deliberately confused in a foreword confessing that the story, in spite of its fictional form, was 'a factual account of the Western Sector during the Irish Civil War'.

If the line between fact and fiction is unclear, so too is that between history and news. The memories of bloody death that came spilling out between the covers of the book had an awful familiarity in 1975, in the middle of the worst period of sectarian murder in the Northern Ireland conflict. The sense of violence as a cycle, an inescapable undertow, even 'a way of life', is continually present in Tony O'Connor's memory.

What he used the novel to recount was his own betrayal of his friend Johnny, the boy he used to play with in Athlone. He and Johnny were neighbours and best friends. Johnny joined the IRA and, when the truce with the British was declared, emerged from the underground as a glamorous hero. Wanting to be like him, O'Connor joined the new national army. As soon as he was in, the army split, and Johnny disappeared into the diehard faction, leaving O'Connor behind, caught in a nightmare of carnage.

After seven months of war, his comrades brought in six captured republicans, Johnny among them, and decided to shoot them. O'Connor was forced to watch as his friend was killed, afraid to speak or to plead: 'Through a mist of tears I tried hard to restrain, I looked over at Johnny with the life gone out of him. Those gay eyes would smile no more, and he would be buried in a lost grave thirty yards from the handball alley where we had played so often.'

He was haunted ever afterwards, not just by the deed, but by its secrecy: 'Only those involved would know they were gone. There would be no listings in daily orders, no newspaper reports. It could be months or years before relations heard what had happened to their rebel husbands or sons. Talk was dangerous, and the men who were unlucky enough to form part of any firing party were always given separate, speedy postings to various camps around the country. Even then, one careless slip would result in them being trailed and a bullet-ridden body found in a ditch.'

When Johnny's mother came to ask about her son, O'Connor said nothing, but fifty years on, he reflected that Johnny would remain: 'Forever and forgotten, like those with him will be forgotten. They fought for a cause that failed, and how it failed! And they will be forgotten because Ireland, in its own shame, cannot afford to remember them.'

By the time the book appeared, O'Reilly already controlled Independent Newspapers, the largest newspaper group in Ireland. The book's oblique commentary on news — on the force of facts that do not appear in the newspapers, on the way today's news headlines are yesterday's dark secrets, on the things that societies cannot afford to remember and speak about — must have struck O'Reilly with peculiar force. All the more so because he had his own intimate secrets of subterfuge and betrayal to protect.

In March 1987 Tony O'Reilly handed over a piece of England to Margaret Thatcher. Having bought Cape Cornwall, a mile of English coastline, he presented it to Mrs Thatcher at a public ceremony, remarking that it was especially piquant that an Irishman should be presenting the title deeds to a piece of 'English land' to a British prime minister, and that he did so with a special sense of privilege. It was an odd but telling moment, a half-comic, half-serious reversal of those poignant end-of-empire scenes such as the surrender of Dublin Castle to Michael Collins in 1922 or the handing over of Irish ports to Eamon de Valera in 1939, when O'Reilly was a small child. It was an act of historic cheek, but also an act of great confidence, a public sign that here was an Irishman who didn't have to watch out for himself in England.

This confidence was new among Irishmen. A story that exemplifies older attitudes happened one night in the Second World War. Brendan Bracken, the British minister for information, was introduced at the Ritz to Major-General Emmet Dalton, like Tony O'Connor a veteran of the Irish civil war. It was ostensibly an encounter between a successful Englishman and an Irishman who had taken arms against England. When he had stood, successfully, as Tory candidate for North Paddington in 1929, Bracken had himself described in the local papers as being 'of Anglo-Irish stock . . . born in Bedfordshire nearly thirty years ago. He has residences in North Street, Westminster, and in Bedfordshire, Scotland and Ireland. He graduated from Oxford University.' He was, in other words, exactly the sort of person who might own, as he did, a controlling interest in the *Economist* and the *Financial Times.*

But Dalton recognized Bracken and said to Lord Milton, who was introducing them, 'Brendan and I know one another of old. We were schoolmates in Dublin.' Bracken tried to look puzzled. How could a wealthy Bedfordshire man of Anglo-Irish stock have been to school with a lower-middle-class Irish rebel? Dalton became angry. 'If you don't remember me, Brendan,' he said, 'I bloody well remember you and those corduroy trousers which you wore day in day out until you stank to high heaven. The smell is not out of my nostrils yet.'

Bracken was the most spectacular example of what an Irishman once had to do if he wanted to be an English press baron. Brought up Catholic and Irish in Dublin, the son of a Fenian revolutionary, he reinvented himself as an English toff. When he first arrived in England, he pretended to be Australian. He stayed in Oxford for a while, so that he could subsequently pass himself off as a graduate of Balliol. And he acquired for himself a set of impeccably Tory and imperialist views, impressing Winston Churchill as a soulmate and indispensable ally.

The problem with such a feat of camouflage was that it entailed a constant risk of exposure. The power involved in being the owner of newspapers was limited by the possibility of being a victim of newspapers. In 1944 Lord Beaverbrook sent a reporter to Ireland to uncover Bracken's true background. Bracken used his powers as minister for information to excise from the *Evening Standard* references to his father's record as an Irish rebel. Even so, there were always people like Dalton who knew him when his trousers stank.

When, in a dawn raid in early 1994, O'Reilly bought twenty-five per cent of Newspaper Publishing, publishers of the London *Independent* and *Independent on Sunday*, he became the first Irishman since Bracken to own a large chunk of an English media group. As a keen reader of English history, he knew enough about his predecessor to recognize the similarities between himself and Bracken. Like Bracken, O'Reilly came from a family with a history of Irish nationalist connections. Like him, he grew up in the Catholic middle-class suburbs of north Dublin. Like him, he was educated by Irish Jesuits. And like Bracken, he idolized Churchill.

Bracken's connection with Churchill was so strong that there were false but widespread rumours that he was the prime minister's natural son. O'Reilly's connection was second-hand. Churchill was his 'great hero', and he quoted him regularly in his speeches. 'His life to me,' O'Reilly once told the BBC, 'was and continues to be an inspiration.' Asked what he had taken from Churchill, he replied, 'I think he was a very selfish man. He believed he was the epicentre of all that was happening. He was . . . a truly conceited man. He felt he was very important, and I suppose that is one of the principal criteria of success — to believe in yourself so strongly that you are the epicentre of all that is happening.'

O'Reilly could have turned into a milder version of Bracken. The rugby writer Terry Maclean, covering the Lions rugby tour of New Zealand in 1959, noted O'Reilly's attitude to those English members of the side who came from upper-class backgrounds. It was, he wrote, 'a strange regard, almost amounting to envy, for those fortunate folk who move through the world with a lordly calm based upon a secure place in the scheme of things.' His idolization of Churchill, his avid reading of biographies of other British prime ministers such as Disraeli and Gladstone, his lord-of-the-manor posturing at his Castlemartin estate, all bear witness to that strange regard. When the band played 'Land of Hope and Glory' as he entered the village hall in Kilcullen, near Castlemartin, for his fiftieth birthday party, it was not an entirely inappropriate anthem.

But O'Reilly never had the opportunity that Bracken had to reinvent himself. His rugby career made him a star before he was twenty, a visible international symbol of Ireland. Disguise, even had he wanted it, was impossible for a red-haired boy in a green shirt, ducking and weaving before cheering crowds. And besides, O'Reilly had darker, more intimate secrets to conceal than Brendan Bracken ever had. Disguise invites revelation, and early in his career, O'Reilly was vulnerable to revelations.

When he was seventeen, O'Reilly discovered that he was not, as he had always believed, an only child. In his last year at school, one of the priests who taught him took him aside and told him that his parents were not married, that his father had another wife and other children — three half-sisters and a half-brother whom he had never seen. The priest may have told him all of this because he wanted to spare him the shock of later revelations, or he may have been concerned that Tony was considering, as most bright Irish boys did at some stage, entering the priesthood. An illegitimate child could not be a priest.

That rule reflected a wider prejudice in an overwhelmingly Catholic society obsessed with sexual purity. The Irish state made it explicit in law that illegitimate children were second class. The Legitimacy Act of 1931, passed just five years before O'Reilly was born, allowed that a child born out of wedlock might inherit its mother's property if she died without making a will, but it refused to grant any such rights of succession to the estate of a child's natural father who would be, after all, much more likely to have money.

Only in 1964 did Irish law give statutory expression to the notion that an unmarried woman had the right to be regarded as the guardian of her child. Even then, the stigma of illegitimacy retained the sanction of law. Not until 1987 was the legal concept of illegitimacy abolished in Ireland. Well past the age of fifty, O'Reilly, as well as being the richest man in Ireland, was also, secretly, a second-class Irishman.

O'Reilly's position was in one sense less shameful than that of the child of an ordinary unmarried mother: he was cherished and recognized by both his natural parents. But in another sense it was more darkly secretive. For most illegitimate children, the sin was acknowledged and open, the shame explicit. There was, at least, little else to be revealed. But for him, his public identity was a subterfuge. His parents pretended to be married and concealed the existence of a whole other family. His cupboard contained not a skeleton, but several living reminders of what was being hidden: his half-siblings. Not only was the existence of his father's other family a secret, but so was the fact that he himself knew about it. He told neither his father nor his mother that he shared their private knowledge until the early 1970s. For twenty more years after that, until he allowed his official biographer Ivan Fallon to reveal the truth, he watched as every profile of him in a magazine or newspaper around the world repeated the official lie that he was an only child.

One can never know how much one's inner life is shaped by social circumstances, and no one else can ever guess. But it is hard to avoid the belief that something of his anomalous origins must be present in what Tony O'Reilly has become. It may be there in his obsessive, driven hunger for success: this is a man who, already one of the highest paid managers in America, used his spare time to build a private industrial empire and to pursue the dream of becoming a global media mogul. It may be there in his attitude to Ireland, the peculiar mixture of distance from a society and intimate knowledge of its workings that belongs to a secret outsider who looks like the ultimate insider. And it must be there in the overwhelming desire to control news, to have power over image and information.

If the Ireland that Tony O'Reilly grew up in had had any of the tabloid newspapers that he now controls — newspapers such as the *Sunday World* or the Irish edition of the British *Daily Star* (a tabloid which he controls jointly with Express Newspapers in London and which is further downmarket than Murdoch's *Sun*) — they would certainly have revealed his secrets. Rugby had made him a glamorous public figure, fair game for prurient curiosity. If, at any time in his youth, his family background had been revealed, it would have caused not just personal hurt but probably fatal damage to his public career. His success depended on media reticence, on the maintenance of a clear distinction between the private realm and the public.

In 1962, for example, when O'Reilly was head of the Irish Milk Marketing Board, and his car hit a cyclist as he was driving back from a rugby match, he was able to arrange through his father's contacts with the local hospital and the local newspaper to have the incident kept quiet, and no newspaper reported it, even though he was one of the best-known men in Ireland. In the most intimate way imaginable, he learned the meaning of news. He learned that the ability to control what can and cannot be said about you is an indispensable form of power. For such a man, the ownership of newspapers would always be more than a business.

None of this has had any discernible effect on his attitude to news values, and his tabloid papers have been no better, if no worse, than those belonging to Rupert Murdoch, whom he affects to regard as a barbarian at the gates. He publicly defended the *Sunday World*, for instance, when some Independent Newspapers shareholders attacked it at the company's annual general meeting. One of them complained particularly about an article about female bus conductors in Dublin, then a new phenomenon and an important test case for women in traditionally male roles, which appeared under the headline RANDY CLIPPIES. It was, the shareholder said, 'a cheap and scurrilous attack on the sexual morality of an easily identified small group of women in this city.' O'Reilly told him, though, that 'just because of the somewhat prurient nature of some of its publications', there was no reason why the *Sunday World* should not be part of Independent Newspapers. 'In many cases,' he remarked, 'we try to lead public taste, but in most we follow it.'

In April 1993, the *Sunday Independent* ran what purported to be an interview with Bishop Eamon Casey, who had fled Ireland after admitting that he was the father of a child. Had it ever taken place, the interview would have been a worldwide scoop. But in fact, as the paper subsequently admitted, it had not taken place. O'Reilly, when asked about this, merely said that he was 'out of the country' when the story ran and that he had not read it or been briefed by his executives about it before it appeared. He wasn't, he said, involved in making editorial decisions 'in that way'.

But he is certainly involved in other ways. In 1973, he bought control of Independent Newspapers in Dublin for just one million pounds. The company now has assets of five hundred million pounds and effectively controls businesses worth a billion. Slowly at first and then quite suddenly, Independent Newspapers has expanded beyond Ireland and into Britain, France, Portugal, Mexico, South Africa, Australia and New Zealand. Since the beginning of 1994, Independent has acquired sixty per cent of the Argus group, South Africa's largest newspaper chain; forty-three per cent of Newspaper Publishing in Britain; fifty-five per cent of Australian Provincial Newspapers; twenty-five per cent of Irish Press Newspapers in Ireland; and forty-four per cent of Wilson and Horton, the largest newspaper group in New Zealand. It also has extensive interests in cable television in Ireland; radio and television in Australia; and outdoor advertising in Portugal, France and Mexico. And it is clear that O'Reilly intends to expand his empire: he tried to buy the Fairfax group in Australia in 1991 but lost out to Conrad Black, and has made little secret of his interest in both the Mirror and Express groups in Britain.

'I have never sought to exercise any personal political power in the newspapers,' he has always claimed. Guarantees of editorial independence were an important part of his failed bid for the Fairfax group, and of his attempt to gain control of Newspaper Publishing in Britain. But he does hold a three-day strategy meeting every year which his editors as well as his managers are expected to attend. And he talks on the phone every day to Independent's deputy chairman, John Meagher.

When Independent Newspapers tried to gain a majority shareholding in the Irish *Sunday Tribune*, O'Reilly had to convince the Competition Authority there that the company would not limit the newspaper's editorial independence. The authority was shown a quotation from O'Reilly, inspired by the style book of the *Washington Post*, of which he was then a director, in which he stated that 'In a world where the ownership of newspapers is increasingly concentrated amongst a smaller group of names . . . the newspaper's duty is to its readers and to the public at large and not to the private interests of the owner.' The Authority was also told that Independent Newspapers had agreed an editorial charter for the *Tribune* guaranteeing editorial independence. But it was unconvinced by either of these submissions. Nobody seriously doubts that O'Reilly's influence, however passive, is pervasive.

In refusing him permission to take a majority stake in the *Sunday Tribune*, the Competition Authority pointed out that his proposal for an editorial charter would have little real effect: 'There would not seem to be a possibility . . . that an editor could be completely independent of the proprietor of the paper, and it seems unlikely that this could ever be properly established. At the end of the day, the editor is constrained by commercial and financial considerations, which can be conclusive. The editor may exercise self-censorship, deliberately or unconsciously. There may be direct interference by the proprietor, or influence may be imposed in more subtle ways, and an editor may take heed of the proprietor for fear of losing his job.' In fact, in early 1994, Independent's two directors on the *Tribune* board supported a successful motion to sack the paper's editor Vincent Browne, who had attacked the *Sunday Independent* in print over the Bishop Casey affair.

In spite of such concerns, Tony O'Reilly has now reached a position in Ireland where, as the Competition Authority expressed it in 1995 in another report on his dealings — this time his investments in the rival *Irish Press* group — 'the possibility cannot be ruled out that in a relatively short period of time, the only remaining Irish newspapers will be those owned in whole or in part by Independent Newspapers plc.' The authority found, in this instance, that O'Reilly's investment in another Dublin daily, the *Irish Press*, which closed in 1995, was made to prevent it being taken over by another newspaper group 'which might be expected to compete more vigorously in the market for newspapers and newspaper advertising'. The rhetoric of free-market competition that trips so easily off O'Reilly's lips is somewhat undermined by the authority's finding that his *Irish Press* investment 'amounts to an abuse of a dominant position' in the market place.

The complex relationship between politics, money and the control of newspapers that O'Reilly embodies is best illustrated in the hysteria over oil exploration off the coast of Ireland in the 1980s. While the national debt rose beyond twenty billion pounds, and the rate of unemployment went beyond twenty per cent, while all the country's dreams of prosperous modernity turned sour, ordinary people in rural Ireland started to see statues of the Virgin moving, waving, weeping, floating. But while the doctors and dentists, the solicitors and small businessmen of the cities sneered at them, they too looked to their own icon to perform a miracle. Instead of prayers and candles, they turned for salvation to O'Reilly.

Such was the charisma, the allure, the sheer magic of O'Reilly's name, that at his call Irish investors poured fifty million pounds into five deep holes in the Atlantic seabed off the coast of County Waterford,

into which O'Reilly himself put five million pounds of his own money. The oil crisis of 1979 had sent the Irish economy into a downward spiral, and people believed that O'Reilly would find oil under the sea and save the nation. When Atlantic Resources, O'Reilly's oil company, made its shares available on the Dublin stock market in April 1981 there were, as all the newspapers agreed, unprecedented scenes of mayhem. Throughout the mid-1980s there were bouts of hysterical exultation and suicidal depression as the price of shares in Atlantic Resources fluctuated wildly. The prices of the shares depended on speculation in the newspapers, and O'Reilly owned many of them.

There was more than money at stake. Oil would save Ireland from debt and allow it to take its place in the Reagan-Thatcher revolution. Thatcher, O'Reilly said, had used the revenues from North Sea oil to 'purchase the silence of the non-working classes' — meaning the unemployed. If he too struck oil, it would 'enable us to pay the bill, as it has enabled Mrs Thatcher to pay the bill while she put into effect the structural changes that are going on in Britain'.

The oil rush could not be disentangled from O'Reilly's position as the largest owner of newspapers in Ireland. In a rare moment of genuine indiscretion, he told *Forbes* magazine in September 1983 that his geologist had chosen six blocks of seabed for exploration. 'Since I own thirty-five per cent of the newspapers in Ireland I have close contact with the politicians. I got the blocks he [his geologist] wanted.'

Even after he got those blocks, however, O'Reilly became increasingly impatient with what he saw as the restrictive terms imposed by the Irish government in its exploration licences. Garret FitzGerald, who headed that government for most of the period, had been a friend of O'Reilly's since the early 1960s, but he felt the effects of O'Reilly's anger.

O'Reilly had supported FitzGerald's liberal, mildly social-democrat politics, and, according to FitzGerald, 'once he acquired Independent Newspapers, he remained very supportive'. In 1982 when Charles Haughey was in power and there were allegations that his government was interfering with the independence of the police, FitzGerald 'was in touch with' O'Reilly 'over the political situation'. 'In talking to him over that period it was kind of on the assumption that he had some degree of influence over the newspapers, I suppose,' Fitzgerald recalls. 'I certainly would have been seeking his assistance in terms of the papers at that time. If I was ringing him, it wasn't just for a general chat.

'When we were in government, he remained supportive to a degree, but towards the end there's no doubt that the *Independent* swung somewhat, and I think the oil thing was a major factor. He felt that the terms we were imposing for oil were too tough and he wanted them changed. The pressure was expressed rationally enough in terms of the need to modify the terms. I didn't feel there was improper pressure. But I felt as time went on he was getting more and more frustrated and he was allowing this to influence his overall judgement. He became irritable and angry. And I didn't think he was very helpful to us afterwards as a result.'

There is a sense in which Tony O'Reilly has always been in the media, even when he was not yet in the newspaper business. He is a self-made man, a folk hero of capitalism who has built a personal fortune of five hundred million pounds from a standing start. But he is a hero of capitalism's unheroic age. His genius is not for making or inventing things, but for buying cheap and selling hard.

Though he heads a great industrial enterprise, his interest is not really in manufacturing at all. In 1986, for instance, he threatened, somewhat rhetorically, to take Heinz out of manufacturing altogether, to buy its food products from factories that could produce them cheaply, and to concentrate instead on selling brands and tastes. He is part of an age of capitalism in which the idea of the entrepreneur as inventor is long past. As a multinational manager, he does two things — he cuts costs and he buys companies. One of his most famous ideas at Heinz was to remove the back label from ketchup bottles, saving four million dollars a year. He has never pretended to be interested in developing new things to sell. He told New York journalists in 1978 that 'The best way to get into new product development is to steal the other guy's ideas. You buy the company.' This is essentially what he does.

Having bought or made the products, he turns them into images. In the last financial year Heinz sold eight billion dollars' worth of food. To do so, it spent $1.7 billion, nearly a quarter of what it earned from sales, on advertising and marketing.

His gift is not so much for thinking up ideas as for selling them. As early as 1966 he was saying things like 'the greatest supermarket in the world is in the United Kingdom housewife's mind.' He sells into the supermarket of the mind, stocking its shelves with images and desires. He has come to believe deeply in the magic of brands, in brand names as a replacement for politics and religion. 'Truly great brands,' he told the British Council of Shopping Centres in 1990, 'are far more than just labels for products; they are symbols that encapsulate the desires of consumers; they are

standards held aloft under which the masses congregate.'

His first and most enduring feat of marketing was to turn Ireland itself into a desirable brand. In 1962, when he was twenty-six, he was appointed general manager of Bord Bainne, the Irish milk marketing board. The appointment of a dashing, young sportsman to such a post was itself heavily symbolic. The nationalist dream of economic and cultural self-sufficiency had finally collapsed under the weight of mass emigration. Fianna Fáil, the ruling nationalist party, had abandoned protectionism and invited American multinational companies to invest in Ireland and engineer a belated industrial revolution in a country that was still overwhelmingly rural and traditional.

The atmosphere was not unlike that of Eastern Europe after the fall of communism. O'Reilly's appointment coincided with a number of other signals of change: the IRA's temporary abandonment of a violent campaign for a United Ireland, the inauguration of an Irish television service, Ireland's application to join the EEC. The *taoiseach* (prime minister) Sean Lemass gave a speech urging older company directors to 'consider whether they have not outlived their usefulness and decide to pass their responsibilities over to younger men'. O'Reilly, the most spectacular example of what Lemass desired, was thus himself a kind of symbol, the image of a new Ireland. And this, throughout the rest of his career, is what he has tried to be.

It is this desire that lies behind his refusal to be happy even with his spectacular success at Heinz. Being the bean baron is all very well, but he actually sees himself as very much more than an exemplar of the American corporate dream. He wants to be, at the same time, the embodiment of an Ireland different to that of his adoptive uncle Peadar O'Donnell and his real uncle Tony O'Connor. He wants to be a new Irish brand name, a standard held aloft under which the masses of Irish around the world can congregate; to be, in his own words, 'a representative of the hopes and dreams and aspirations of the Irish around the globe', the man who 'planted the flag of the New Ireland abroad in various forms — Independent Newspapers, capitalism, entrepreneurial spirit, managerial competence . . . The New Ireland which sees we have a right not just to be colonized, but to go to other countries and to harvest and prosper there.'

His position in Bord Bainne was a job of considerable political and economic importance: nearly a third of the Irish workforce was employed in agriculture, and O'Reilly's actions directly affected about half a million people from a population of less than three million. What he did was to invent a symbol of a new Ireland, a symbol of Irish agriculture that could be marketed firstly in Britain and then around the world. The product was simple — Irish butter — and he did nothing to change it. It was the name he put on the wrapping that turned it into money: Kerrygold, a name that had, as the marketing reports put it, 'a definite Irish sound, with overtones of richness and purity'.

In Ireland, the name was nonsensical since Kerry was associated with stony mountains, not green pastures. But soon Irish people too were buying Kerrygold. The golden wrapping, the sonorous name, turned slabs of butter into desirable objects. The allure of the image, the magic of brands, had been released into an emerging Ireland, and O'Reilly was the conjurer.

The old history, the old Ireland, could not be transformed so easily, though. Moving on from Bord Bainne after his triumph with Kerrygold, he was appointed by the Irish government to head an even bigger state enterprise, the Irish Sugar Company. He replaced the third veteran of the nationalist struggle, and of the civil war, to play a part in O'Reilly's career: General Michael Costello.

In the official summary of his career prepared by O'Reilly's press agent, all the many companies in which he has played a leading role are listed — except one. H. J. Heinz is there of course, as are Independent Newspapers, his investment conglomerate Fitzwilton, Waterford Wedgwood, the minerals and oil company Arcon, Bord Bainne and the Irish Sugar Company. The only exception is Erin Foods. It is easy to understand the omission: Erin is a sensitive subject. But it is hard to understand O'Reilly's career unless you know what happened there.

Costello was a veteran of the old IRA, a protégé of Michael Collins, who promoted him from private to colonel commandant at the age of eighteen after a particularly daring operation during the civil war, in which he took the Free State side. Afterwards he became a general, then the head of the Irish Sugar Company, a large nationalized industry that processed sugar beet. He brought with him the charisma of history and a military attention to detail. More importantly, he applied to the job the idealism of the first generation of nationalist revolutionaries: a deep belief in cooperative effort, in self-reliance and in public service. He came to hate O'Reilly, and, with time, the feeling became mutual.

Costello was fiercely anti-communist, but he was also, almost as passionately, anti-capitalist. He saw 'cooperation' as the 'only alternative to the communist collective or the amalgamation of small farms to form large capitalistic enterprises'. And he tried to create an aggressively commercial but socially progressive food processing industry in rural Ireland by setting up a company called Erin Foods (Erin means simply Ireland, and the symbolism was intentional — Costello saw the company as a national metaphor) as a subsidiary of Irish Sugar. A team of young scientists in Irish Sugar had developed a new freeze-drying technology, which meant that prepared vegetables could be packed, stored outside a fridge (still a rare enough appliance in Ireland then) and reconstituted simply by pouring boiling water over them. Costello intended to use it to sell the produce of Irish agricultural cooperatives and state-owned factories, first to Irish cities and then to the huge British market. To do this he would have to take on the dominant companies in the British processed food market — among them Heinz.

One of Costello's most important allies was an extraordinary Catholic priest, James McDyer. A radical socialist in clerical clothing, McDyer had founded a rural commune in a poor and remote part of County Donegal called Glencolumbkille, and with the encouragement and support of O'Reilly's adoptive 'uncle' Peadar O'Donnell, he persuaded Costello to site one of his vegetable processing factories there. Costello, as Brendan Halligan, a young economist with Erin in the 1960s, recalls, 'dreamed of creating a network of factories, to bring about the stabilization of population in rural areas. He was motivated by old-fashioned nationalism — wanting to develop the economy, seeing resources lying unused and being extremely angry about that, and seeing the depopulation of large parts of the country. He embarked on the Erin dream without the civil service in the Department of Finance or the political establishment really understanding what he was at. When he got to a certain point and he was investing a lot of money which they regarded as losses, they began to understand.' And when they understood what he was doing, they moved to stop him.

In December 1966, Costello left Irish Sugar and Erin Foods and recommended, in his letter of resignation, that 'someone be found who believes that food processing can be run as the Department of Finance wants it run.' That someone was Tony O'Reilly. He was given the job by the leading Fianna Fáil politicians Jack Lynch and Charles Haughey, and by the Department of Finance, which had long distrusted Costello's tendency to put social objectives on the same plane as commercial ones. Officially,

O'Reilly was said to be continuing Costello's work, with a brief 'to build the marketing structure that would enable a big expansion to take place in the export drive'. The government assured parliament that 'Erin Foods is now engaged in a vigorous development of the UK market and an expansion of their existing range of products.' In fact, his job was to cut back the operation, stop Erin from competing with private enterprise and tidy up its chaotic books.

Within a month O'Reilly was in touch with Heinz, one of Erin's competitors, to offer a deal. The two companies would merge. Erin would supply Heinz with raw vegetables for processing, and would itself sell Heinz products in Ireland. The Erin offices in Britain would close, and its sales force would be sacked. Two Heinz executives would sit on the Erin board. As for Peadar O'Donnell and James McDyer, they would have to realize that, as O'Reilly later told his official biographer, 'You just can't grow vegetables competitively on the hillsides of Donegal.' O'Reilly and Haughey, now Minister for Finance, discussed the deal on a winter holiday together in the Canaries, and a new company, Heinz-Erin, was formed. Soon after, O'Reilly addressed the workers and small farmers of Glencolumbkille and warned them that they must 'appreciate that the international market place is the supreme discipline in their activities. Heinz-Erin provides such a challenge.'

To Costello, the deal was 'a give-away'. He maintained until his death in 1986 that Erin 'had Heinz beaten as competitors', and that 'Heinz certainly got more out of the deal than Erin Foods, even to the extent of buying Irish vegetables in bulk and shipping them out to factories in Britain where they provide employment which could be better provided here.' He revealed that Heinz had already offered a merger while he was in charge, and that he had rejected it — 'Heinz was simply like other foreign firms, looking for something for nothing, or something for very little, anyway. In fact they got something for nothing. Nobody had anything to gain in this country, but naturally enough the people who delivered to Heinz had a lot to gain.'

For Tony O'Reilly, the deal was the beginning of his global career. Less than two years after he joined Irish Sugar and Erin, O'Reilly was negotiating a job with Heinz and in May 1969 became managing director of Heinz UK. Two years after that he was in Pittsburgh as senior vice-president and by 1973 he was president and chief operating officer of Heinz worldwide.

Erin meanwhile went into permanent decline. The merger with Heinz was a commercial failure, and

O'Reilly left the company in poor shape. It stumbled on for years as an agency for Heinz in Ireland. In 1990, Heinz, of which O'Reilly was now chairman, president and chief executive, announced abruptly that it was planning to remove the sale and marketing of its products in Ireland from Erin Foods. Erin's chief executive told the press 'I'm extremely disappointed in Tony O'Reilly. I thought Tony had more loyalty to the business.' O'Reilly was unavailable for comment, even to his own newspapers.

When Tony O'Reilly moved to Heinz he made a profound statement about the nature of power in the late twentieth century. He could at that stage have launched a political career that would almost certainly have taken him all the way to the office of *taoiseach*. In the late 1960s, O'Reilly himself was offered political power by both of Ireland's major political parties. The Fianna Fáil *taoiseach* Jack Lynch, who had sponsored him from the start, told him that if he refused the Heinz job, he would make him minister for agriculture in his cabinet. But the rival Fine Gael party also asked him to stand in the 1969 general election. The offer was made by Garret FitzGerald, who says that 'I had the authority of the party to talk to him. I wasn't authorized, so far as I can recall, to say to him that he would be a minister, but he obviously would have had a good prospect of ministerial office given his abilities. But then he got the offer of the Heinz job in England. And he said to me, "Garret, if I get the Heinz job I can make a hundred thousand pounds clear in five years and come back and enter full-time into politics."'

Given a choice between running a multinational company and running a small European country, however, he chose the former. He had seen that once Ireland opened itself up to American multinationals, the idea of national sovereignty, of state control, had become untenable. Years later, when idealistic nationalists came to power in Africa, first Robert Mugabe in Zimbabwe, then Nelson Mandela in South Africa, he would point out to them that they could not run their own economies, that economic nationalism was dead, that they would have to come to terms with the power of scarce and demanding capital.

Shortly after Mugabe was installed in power in Harare, on a Marxist and nationalist platform, O'Reilly went to see him to try to persuade him to allow Heinz to open a plant there. 'We had both been educated by Irish Jesuits,' he later recalled, 'and through this common kinship, we discussed the notion, the model of economic nationalism . . . I was trying to teach him about the limits of economic nationalism.' His arguments about the nature and limits of political power were persuasive — Heinz and the Zimbabwean state established a profitable joint venture, Olivine, making cooking oil and marketing Heinz products.

Equally, in defiance of the fact that he had boasted as late as 1988 that, were he still playing rugby, he would play in South Africa regardless of UN sanctions, and that he would have 'immediate access' to old rugby comrades such as General Magnus Malan, now indicted for murder for his involvement in the establishment of death squads, he quickly established a friendship with Nelson Mandela after the latter's release from prison. Mandela spent Christmas 1993 in O'Reilly's holiday home on the island of Nassau. He too came to accept the limits of political power, among them the necessity to allow a foreign businessman such as O'Reilly to take over his country's largest newspaper group.

Fine Gael and Fianna Fáil were the political heirs of the two sides in the Irish civil war. The fact that both wanted O'Reilly was a sign of how far he had succeeded in creating a persona that transcended history, that seemed finally to lay all the ghosts of the past. In his bright, charming, efficient persona lay the promise of an end to history, of a politics that would be about management, not ideology. But the paradox of that image is that on the one hand it seemed to offer a new Ireland but on the other it embodied an embrace of the global economy in which no Ireland, new or old, could really matter.

From time to time, the idea of a political career for O'Reilly has resurfaced. In 1980 Garret FitzGerald authorized a fresh approach to O'Reilly, testing whether he would agree to stand in the next election. He 'quite possibly' would have appointed him to the cabinet. 'At that stage, he would have had a reasonable expectation of office, if he was going to divert his whole career from where he was. And he would have been very dynamic I'm sure.' But Ireland was now too small a stage. And FitzGerald was subsequently relieved that O'Reilly did not take up his offer: 'He has perhaps come to feel that Tony O'Reilly's interest is Ireland's interest, is the world's interest, the way people do when they get to his stage.'

In 1979 O'Reilly speculated that he might seek to be appointed as a Commissioner of the European Community though 'not in the near term'. In 1988 he fuelled speculation that he would be appointed US Secretary of Commerce by George Bush, for whom he had served as a fund-raiser. But at the same time as he was musing in public on what he might do with the job, he was also making it clear that politicians, even members of the Washington cabinet, have too

little power to satisfy him. Unlike Silvio Berlusconi who used his control of large sections of the Italian media to gain political power, O'Reilly has a sharp sense that the global business tycoon and the global media mogul have more power than politicians do. He is also the first person fully to understand that the corporate manager and the media magnate can now be one and the same.

This, more than anything else, is what makes him a representative figure of life at the end of the twentieth century. He belongs to the era of post-industrial capitalism in which a product and its image, commodities and the media through which they are sold, have become virtually indistinguishable. It is an era in which, in O'Reilly's own words, 'the communications revolution and the convergence of cultures have set the stage for truly global marketing.' And in this era the relationship between business and news is that of a closed circle. The mass media obliterate the distinctions of aspiration and taste inherent in national cultures. This in turn allows the same company to sell the same product in the same packaging everywhere in the world: 'Television will further homogenize the cultures of the developed world. It will in turn generate the cosmopolitan aspirations best satisfied by global brands. The capacity for transnational production is available . . . The final step in the process will be mass communication. And the technology of satellite and cable television will make that possible.' When that happens, the news in the broadest sense will be not just a report of what happens, but an agent for making it happen.

Recently, when Tony O'Reilly took over Waterford Wedgwood, he commissioned market research in the United States, the main market for Waterford Crystal. Its object was to answer one question — did the consumers of crystal know that Waterford is in Ireland? If they did, the workers in the factory had some power. They could remain, as they had been for many years, a radical elite in the Irish workforce, knowing that since Waterford crystal had to come from Waterford, their product was proof against global forces, against the ruthless mobility of capital. If on the other hand they did not, Waterford crystal could just as well come from Poland or the Czech Republic, where it could be made much more cheaply. Waterford would, in economic terms, have ceased to be a place and become a brand. It would be possible to do with crystal what the company intends to do with linen this year, selling on the US market cloth produced in China, Belgium and the Philippines under the Waterford brand name. The answer that the research provided was that very few American consumers associated Waterford with Ireland. It was the news that O'Reilly wanted to hear: that the process of branding Ireland that he had begun more than thirty years before had now reached the point where a part of the country had become, finally, no more than a brand, a name without a face, a placeless image, freed at last from history.

CIARAN CARSON
from Ciaran Carson, *The Star Factory* (1997)

The Star Factory is described on the jacket as 'a shaggy-dog story delivered without once drawing breath: a risky, nerve-wracking, extraordinary performance'. Ciaran Carson takes his cue from Cathal O'Byrne, *As I Roved Out: In Belfast and Districts* (1946) (see p. 521 above), and, like a little piecer in a cotton-mill, he has collected the broken threads of his native city and restitched them into a beautiful patchwork quilt. For Carson's equally engaging book on Irish traditional music, see *Last Night's Fun: A Book About Traditional Music* (1996).

Brickle Bridge

Most of Belfast is built of brick. Brick is riot-friendly, especially when broken into halves, more easily to fit the hand. It then became a *hicker*, in Belfast dialect, a thing to be *chucked*, or thrown: these words might be related, since Chambers cites one usage of *chuck* as 'a small pebble or stone'; *hicker* might derive from *hack*, 'a bank for drying bricks'. The hicker is one ingredient of the ammunition *Belfast confetti*, which originally referred to a not-so-welcome shower of shipyard-workers' bolts and rivets, and later, by extension, to any ad hoc compendium of hand-launched missiles, which might include slates, buckets, iron railings, jam-jars, ball-bearings, and coal, as well as the usual assortment of small bombs contained by coffee-jars or milk-bottles; once I saw formes and clichés of type, looted from Ticard's the printers in Durham Street, being fired at the army. Another great element was the *kidney-paver*, a small human-organ-shaped cobblestone which fitted to the hand as if preordained by geological authority. Kidney-pavers are now completely extinct, since the civic authority which put them there in the first place tore them up one by one from their matrices, and replaced their habitat with concrete. Then the street would be occupied with military-mortar cement-mixers and a team of sappers in mismatching uniforms of greasy serge suits, a pair of whom would tamp parallels along the wet concrete street with a plank set on edge, two sets of rocking-horse handles attached to its ends. For a day and a night, or more, the street would be a no-go zone, demarcated by the serial monocular glow of red bull's-eye oil-lamps hooked onto wooden rails between saw-horses, as the aromatic burning oil you sniffed was cut by acrid coke-smoke from the watchman's brazier that had red holes punched in it. Nevertheless, some boys would not be deterred by this prospect, and would dare each other to leave their matrix footprints in the Hollywood Boulevard wet concrete.

Ticard's the printers lay near the Protestant vs. Catholic fault line of the aforementioned Boyne or Brickle Bridge, and here the 'Battle of the Brickfields' would be regularly re-enacted. On both sides of this divide, its denizens were known to have knocked down the back-yard walls of their own dwellings in order to provide themselves with cross-community ammunition.

Herein lie some interesting etymological meanders: according to Dinneen,[1] the Irish for 'The Battle of the Boyne' is *Briseadh na Bóinne*, i.e., the breaking of the Boyne; and brick has its root in *break*, allied to the flaw in Irish linen known as a *brack*. Chambers' *brickle*, 'apt to break, troublesome', is appropriate in the context, and *brock*, whether it refers to food-scraps, broken down stuff, or to the animal, is also relevant; and the badger is a *brockit* beast, as he lends his distinctive fur coat to the concept of variegation, especially in black and white. To me, all these bricky words sound like Irish *breac*, speckled, which extends to mean, in the verb *breacaim*, 'to cover a paper with writing'. Cuneiform-covered clay tablets of Babylon occur to me, as I inscribe these words in a Challenge A4 feint-ruled notebook with a red-inked Japanese Zebra 'Zeb-rolle' 0.5 pen that bleeds through a little to the other side of the page, giving it a speckly effect. This is not a serious problem, since I write the main text on the recto, using the preceding verso as a scribble pad for notions I might use in the future, or for possible revisions: for instance, I've just scrawled *Lilliput Laundry*, possibly to remind myself of its bizarre Ulster-pawky-humorous nomenclature, or of the classic SF film *The Incredible Shrinking Man*, or primarily, perhaps, of those indelible pencils used to label laundry and school-uniform name-tags. You sucked the point of the pencil to make it work,

empurpling your tongue with gentian violet, and the DNA of your spit was engraved in the letters of your name, and it was possible that future scientists might make an identifiable schoolboy clone of you.

1   Patrick Dinneen, author of *Foclóir Gaeilge Agus Béarla: An Irish-English Dictionary* (1904, later editions 1927, 1934).

TERRY EAGLETON

from Terry Eagleton, *Crazy John and the Bishop and Other Essays on Irish Culture* (1998)

Terry Eagleton's interventions in recent Irish critical debates have been lively and telling; see, for example, *Heathcliff and the Great Hunger* (1995) and *Scholars and Rebels* (1999). Here, in concluding remarks to an essay on revisionism, he attempts to shift conventional lines of argument onto a new plane.

from Revisionism Revisited

There is one particular way in which revisionism seems oblivious to its own historical conditions, an oblivion which is a common characteristic of ideological thought. This is the fact that it clearly belongs to the more general cultural milieu we call postmodernism, while seeming for the most part quite unaware of it. Since revisionists generally know more about Lyons than Lyotard, they appear unable to place themselves in broader cultural terms. But their nervousness of grand narratives, their preference for pragmatic explanations rather than big ideas, their embarrassment with the ethical, their emphasis on regionality, complexity, ambiguity, on plurality rather than monocausality, on heterogeneity and discontinuity, on the role of sheer happenstance in historical affairs: all of this places them firmly within the postmodern camp whether they know it or not, which for the most part they do not. What a remarkable coincidence, then, that the values and methods which for revisionists are determined simply by the requirements of disinterested academic scholarship, and which must therefore claim a timeless validity, should also turn out to be the reach-me-down pieties of a highly specific cultural movement which rejects the whole notion of disinterested judgement as a political fiction! Indeed much of the programme of academic Irish studies today is silently set by a postmodern agenda,

with some interesting political effects. Nationalism, for example, is not much in favour because it is 'essentialist', whereas feminism is firmly on the agenda because it is not. The truth is that some nationalism is anti-essentialist whereas some feminism is essentialist; but one should not allow such minor considerations to interfere with one's comfortingly clear-cut oppositions. Nationalism is also upbraided for cutting across and concealing other kinds of social division; but then some feminist and ethnic theory can do this too, and for its own purposes quite properly so. The concept of ethnicity is much to the fore in such studies — there are, believe it or not, still essays tumbling from the press on the racialization of the Celt in Matthew Arnold — since the Irish are of course ethnic. Ethnic for whom, and how many ethnicities there are on the island, are questions worth raising. Ethnic, to be sure, for radical American academia, which thus categorizes the much-vaunted 'other' of Irishness in highly *American* terms, terms relevant to its own internal politics, with a touch of the very intellectual colonialism it is most at pains to disown.

Or take the fact that postmodernists, like liberal humanists, are notorious for their scepticism of the concept of social class, a scepticism apparently not shared by Liverpool dockers or Chicano grape-pickers. Social class today is a much less sexy notion than gender or ethnicity, a prejudice which may then determine the way one views such social formations as the Anglo-Irish

Ascendancy. If one wishes to deflect a nationalist or socialist critique of them, it is always possible to repress their exploitative role as a landowning or urban class and redefine them rather more glamorously as an ethnic minority, hounded out of existence by a bellicose Celticism. Or take the fact that postmodernism tends to be naïvely enthused by margins and majorities as such, suspecting consensus and solidarity as inherently authoritarian. This, need one point out, is an utterly formalistic prejudice: not all minorities are to be applauded (neo-Nazis? ley line buffs?), and the solidarity which brought down apartheid was not an oppressive one. Applied to Ireland, however, such profoundly questionable theoretical assumptions will generate some well-nigh automatic political consequences. Since the Ascendancy formed a minority, one is likely to feel the kind of sympathy for these poor abused gentlefolk that one might otherwise reserve for, say, the Caribbean community in Britain, even though that community does not own almost all the land in the country it inhabits, as the Anglo-Irish governing class once did. But these minor differences need not be unduly inflated. Those who persist in reproaching the Ascendancy can then be accused of ethnic prejudice rather than socialist principle. Just the same can be said of those who criticize the Northern Unionists; it all depends on whether you are thinking of them as an ethnic or cultural minority or a politically dominant formation. In a postmodern age, the former is rather more visible than the latter, so that theoretical fashions give birth to loaded political judgements. The Northern nationalists are a minority too, but from a postmodern viewpoint adhere to the distinctly uncool policy of wishing to join a majority to the south of them. It is hard to see them as aberrant, any more than one can view the Home Counties as aberrant, and aberrancy for postmodern thought is an index of authenticity.

Postmodernism, as I have argued elsewhere,[1] is also a brand of culturalism, which habitually overestimates the centrality of cultural matters. In this way, too, it licenses certain readings of Irish politics while suppressing others. 'Culture' has been foregrounded as a topic in our time partly because of the growing importance of ethnic minorities in the west consequent on the globalization of capital, but also because it has become for the first time in history a major force of material production in its own right. It is also a natural stomping-ground of intellectuals, who can find outlets in this field which are denied to them by the political deadlocks of our time, and can thus act as a form of theoretical displacement as well as of political enrichment. But the politics of culture are by no means innocent. One can make rational choices between

forms of politics, but not for the most part between forms of cultures, so that to redefine the political in cultural terms — to call Orange marches a celebration of one's cultural heritage, for example — is to render one's politics far less vulnerable to critique. Even some of the South African Boers, architects of apartheid, are now claiming privileged status as a dispossessed cultural minority, in what must surely be the ultimate postmodern irony. For a sufficiently woolly-minded Irish liberal, there need be no massive difference in principle between the Unionists and travelling people. Both, viewed from a perspective long enough to obscure the question of power, can be seen as distinct cultural groupings out to defend their unique inheritance. The conflation of culture and politics is in the service of a particular politics, in postmodern thought in general and in Ireland in particular. To view the conflict in the North as primarily one between alternative 'cultural traditions' fits well with postmodern culturalism in general, and so sounds reasonably persuasive; it is just that it also happens to be false.

What is at stake in Irish intellectual debate is in fact much less a conflict between tradition and modernity, than one between modernity and postmodernity. The clash between Irish nationalists and Irish revisionists is a reproduction *in parvo*[2] of a more global altercation between those for whom modernity is still alive if unwell, and those who believe themselves to be confidently posterior to it. The political discourse of modernity is one of rights, justice, oppression, solidarity, universality, exploitation, emancipation. Nationalism, along with liberalism and socialism, belongs with this world-view. The political language of postmodernity is one of identity, marginality, locality, difference, otherness, diversity, desire. With some important qualifications, revisionism is part of this milieu. There are those for whom the former language is now effectively bankrupt, and there are those for whom the second way of speaking is no more than a disastrous displacement of the first, one consequent on the failure of that discourse to realize itself politically in our time. There are others, yet again, who acknowledge the extreme tension between these different registers, but regard them as ultimately compatible and indeed urgently in need of one another. Within Ireland, the best aspects of what might be called the Field Day case have tried to do exactly this — to argue that genuine identity, true difference and authentic pluralism can finally be established only on the basis of political justice and emancipation. Political justice is essential so that men and women can be free to explore what they wish to become, and confirm one another's autonomy in this regard; but if the language of difference and identity is abstracted from this material context, it will end up short-circuiting the very political conditions necessary for its realization. There is, on the other hand, a real danger that the drive to autonomy, equality and emancipation will ride roughshod over a need to acknowledge difference and otherness here and now. Cusped as we are between modernity and post-modernity, there is no satisfying theoretical resolution of these questions historically available to us. Right now, the two registers in question are bound to remain to some degree incommensurable, which is to say that nationalists and revisionists will doubtless carry on talking past one another while purporting to be conducting a dialogue.

It may well be, then, that only 'history' will ultimately resolve these matters, and not just the history of Ireland. The coming century is indeed likely to be dominated by a battle between north and south, but on the globe as a whole rather than in Ireland in particular. As the post-colonial nations of the south affirm their rights to autonomy, they are likely to run into headlong conflict with a north whose 'advanced' economic system forms an obstacle to their well-being, and which is already armed to the teeth against their encroachments. It might then become apparent that it is this system above all which is conservatively restricting human freedom, and the post-colonial world which is in the van of human development. In that case, what now seems the latest thing to some Irish liberal modernizers will be shown up in its true reactionary colours, while the Irish colonial history some of them find so acutely embarrassing can be read as prefiguring the shape of the future. The country will then have to decide whether to continue to cast its fortunes with a global capitalism which for many in the impoverished world has overstayed its welcome, thus becoming, so to speak, a good deal too traditionalist, or whether it should draw upon the resources of its own history of dispossession in order to align itself with the coming epoch. The situation would then be reversed: the revisionists would then be those who were prepared to make that forward-looking commitment, while the traditionalists would be those reluctant to let go of the benefits of a Western modernity whose praises they now sing, but which would then already be in the process of being surpassed.

1   See *The Illusions of Postmodernism* (Oxford, 1996).
2   Latin: in miniature.

MICHAEL PATRICK MACDONALD
from Michael Patrick MacDonald, *All Souls: A Family Story from Southie* (1999)

The tough south side of Boston is the setting for this recent Irish-American auto-biography. In it Michael MacDonald tells the traumatic story of his family, his accordion-playing mother, the deaths of four of his siblings, the clashes in the 1970s and 1980s between the Irish and the Blacks over integration and bussing, and the advent of drugs into that community. In this episode he recreates the scene at the wake of his elder brother Frankie (who died in 1984 aged twenty-four). A prize boxer, Frankie had been the family's success-story, but he comes to a grim end when, having agreed to take the place of another brother in an armoured car heist, he is wounded and then strangled by his partners in case he should inform on them. As is evident in Edwin O'Connor's *The Last Hurrah* (1956) reproduced above on page 673, wakes are the 'tribal' occasions when a sense of Irishness brings Irish emigrants together, but in this story the family are living through an explosion where cocaine has replaced snuff as the form of solidarity.

from Chapter 8

The lines went around the block and up the hill, to Jackie O'Brien's Funeral Parlor. Of all Southie's wakes, this was the most people I'd ever seen come to pay respects, and I was proud to be from a neighborhood that cared so much about my brother. But I still wasn't going to believe Frankie was in that casket until I saw him, even though his body had been identified, and even though I'd seen Kevin at the house with baby

Katie since the death. At first I was sure that it must have been Kevin who'd been killed robbing the Wells Fargo armored car. Frankie? Robbing a bank truck? Kevin maybe, but not Frank. I didn't want Kevin to have been the one shot down in the afternoon ambush; I just wanted to know the truth. Now I knew Kevin was alive, but I still wanted to see if it was Frankie in the casket. I know Ma was thinking the same thing, and that's why she fell apart when she finally saw her favorite son, the shell of her favorite son, laid out with his huge boxing fists folded and wrapped in Rosary beads. Ma knocked over the people in her way to climb on top of the casket, and she put her arms around Frankie's neck, pulling him up and out of the box. It took Johnnie and four muscled gangsters to tear Ma away from her Frankie. The casket wheeled a few feet, with the strength of Ma's grip. The O'Briens had to send everyone into the other room so that they could reassemble Frank's limbs and straighten out the purple satin robe he was being buried in.

Before the wake, Kevin had run around making the arrangements for Frankie, and everyone agreed that he should be buried in his Golden Gloves championship robe. The rest was the usual for Southie's buried children: Rosary beads, Irish flags, and shamrock trinkets collected from the annual St Paddy's Day parade. But Frankie's purple robe made him look like royalty. Grandpa didn't get it, though. In a room packed to capacity with people telling stories about Frankie's boxing matches, and re-enacting them with slow motion blows to the air, Grandpa walked up to Frankie's body and held his hand. The room got quieter. Grandpa turned around and said to himself, in the loudest of Irish whispers, 'That's an awful fuckin' shame! A handsome man like that being buried in an old bathrobe.' Ma cracked up laughing then. The whole family did. Later that night Grandpa said to Ma, 'I only wish I'd known him better.'

All types streamed in to pay their respects: young kids; local priests we'd never seen in the neighborhood before; all of Old Colony; Jimmy Kelly, who was now city councillor of South Boston; teenagers Frank had trained in the ring, like Joey Degrandis and 'Little Red' Shea; and the gangsters. Then there were a few suspicious-looking characters, definitely outsiders, who Ma later said introduced themselves as detectives.

It was a good thing we had the breakthrough apartment, with the two joined living rooms, because after the wake the house turned into a full-on disco. It was our Old Colony version of a real Irish wake. 'A good send-off' is what they called it that night. People danced in one living room, then went into the other living room where Frank's corner men had laid out mountains of free cocaine, then they went back to the other living room to dance some more. Then the trips back to the coke table got more frequent, and soon some of the neighbors weren't leaving the table at all, and were looking at that cocaine as if the mountain was going to disappear. The house was packed. Ma came out of the back room where she'd been hiding out for a while. She was all smiles but looked a little dizzy. Tommy Cronin said, 'Try some — c'mon, Helen, it'll make you feel better.' Ma replied, 'Well, I'm willing to try anything at this point.' Ma did a line and then she was dancing too. Kevin made sure I knew I was welcome to the coke. I'd tried it a few times before, but I didn't like the feeling it gave me of being out of control, desperate for more. And I especially couldn't imagine doing drugs with my family. Ma got me out of it saying, 'Mike's never touched drugs, he's too quiet, he thinks too much. I never had to worry about that one,' she added. I didn't pass judgment on anyone else taking coke that night, though, and was even willing to let Ma try it if that might numb a pain I couldn't even begin to imagine. I chose to get shitfaced drunk for the heavy weight of sadness I was feeling, sneaking to my stash of whiskey in the back room.

She was doing a line and offered the rolled-up hundred-dollar bill to Mrs O'Connor, Okie's mother. She looked at Joe, then right in front of the boys she said, 'That's the shit that killed my son.' Mrs O'Connor had had a couple of years to figure that one out; but we hadn't started to make the connection between Frank's death and the mountains of white powder that Whitey was bringing into the neighborhood from his Colombian connections in Florida.

I don't know how we made it to the funeral in the morning, after about an hour of sleep. My head was pounding as I sat in an aisle next to Frankie's casket. I thought we might have to catch Ma as she walked slowly up to the altar, holding onto any church fixtures she could grab. Ma had written a song that she wanted to read. I knew it was important to her to show she could still 'hold her head high' in front of everyone:

You've broken down my prison walls,
You've melted the bars,
You've raised up my soul,
So that I could see your stars.
My honky-tonk ways are past and now gone,
And my cold heart now has hope,
With each dawn . . .

'That's a shameful poem altogether,' Grandpa muttered as Ma continued reading slowly, 'some kind of country-and-western song about prison.' But we found out later that Grandpa actually kept the poem, scrawled onto wrinkled notebook paper, in his top drawer along with his precious novenas to saints, and letters to him from his own mother from when he'd left Ireland, never to see her again. Although it broke my heart to see our fun-loving hell-raising mother all dressed in black and reading about her dead son, I don't remember much about that funeral. But I do remember that Frankie's casket weighed an awful lot. Frankie was like a rock. My head was pounding, and I couldn't believe that he was really lying there inside the Irish flag-draped box, never again to play with Seamus and Stevie, never again to drive Ma to breakfast or to the cemetery, never again to be seen by any of us.

That night Ma was standing in the kitchen, looking out the back window. She usually looked out the front window, but I figured she probably didn't want to do that now, and see Frankie's empty-looking apartment across the street. 'Frick . . . ah . . . frack . . . n . . . pfft.' Ma looked fine — she was smiling — but she was talking gibberish. She forced some real words out of her mouth slowly, but said she couldn't feel her left arm. I told her to lie on the couch and I called Mary, who said Ma was probably having a stroke. Ma insisted she was just tired and refused to go to the hospital that night, no matter how much I begged. I was relieved to see her awake later that night. She got up around midnight, flicked on the kitchen light, and started pummeling the ground with her bare hands, killing cockroaches with a vengeance.

The next morning, with the funeral over, and Frankie buried, and the crowds gone, I opened my eyes and looked up from my mattress on the parlor floor to find Ma crying and clawing at the curtains, trying to tear them down to get a better view of Frankie's apartment. We'd always been able to see him in his kitchen window, cooking or shadow boxing, and Ma was looking for him once more. But he wasn't there. His kitchen light bulb was still on, shining dimly onto yellow cement walls and open cabinets. Ma saw that I was awake but just fell to her knees at the window, looking for Frankie, and saying over and over, 'He was such a beautiful kid, he was such a beautiful fuckin' kid.' Her wailing went right through me. I cried inside, but Ma couldn't hold her pain in any longer. It all spilled out that morning, and I could hardly bear to see it.

DAVID McKITTRICK, SEAMUS KELTERS, BRIAN FEENEY and CHRIS THORNTON

from *Lost Lives: The Stories of the Men, Women and Children who Died as a Result of the Northern Ireland Troubles* (1999)

The recent Northern Ireland troubles, which began in earnest in October 1968, lasted for over thirty years and at the time this was published had claimed the lives of some 3,636. *Lost Lives* is a remarkable testimony to the lives of those killed during that period. The entries prompt a range of responses, none of which can be readily absorbed by the reader: despair and hopelessness in the face of so much bitterness, 'hope against history' as Jack Holland entitles his book of the Ulster conflict published in 1999, comfort of sorts for the knowledge that most of the bullets had names on them, sympathy for the families of victims, gratitude for living elsewhere. Samantha McFarland and Lorraine Wilson were two of the victims of the Omagh Bombing in August 1998. The accounts of the twenty-nine people who died in what was perhaps the worst single incident of the troubles have a cumulative effect that leaves the reader emotionally drained as if he or she were in a blacked-out theatre witnessing a tragedy on stage. These two young women, one a schoolgirl of fifteen, the other a seventeen-year-old student, were helping out at a local charity shop that fateful Saturday afternoon. When asked to evacuate the shop because of a bomb warning they wandered into the centre of the explosion. There was terrible added irony in that the Oxfam shop was not damaged in the blast. The other entry I have chosen from *Lost Lives* is also instructive in its own way; it concerns the reformed killer who after his term of imprisonment turns on himself, never having come to terms with the sectarian murder he had committed sixteen years before.

3618. August 15, 1998
Samantha McFarland, Tyrone
Civilian, Protestant, 17, student, shop worker
From Hospital Road, Omagh, she was killed with her best friend Lorraine Wilson. When the Oxfam shop where they worked was evacuated they went to the point where the bomb exploded. Having left the shop the two girls met Samantha McFarland's brother nearby. She told him she did not want to move too far away because she had the keys of the premises. The Oxfam shop was not damaged in the explosion. The McFarland family waited through the night at the leisure centre until 5.30 a.m. when they were told that the 17-year-old was dead. The mothers of the dead teenagers took on the Oxfam voluntary work as a tribute to the girls.

A former pupil at Omagh High School and a GCE A-level student at Strabane College, Samantha McFarland was working as a volunteer at the shop one day a week for six weeks over the summer period. Another volunteer worker lost her brother, Fred White, and her nephew, Bryan White. Messages of sympathy arrived from Oxfam offices around the world. Samantha McFarland was also a voluntary worker in a Barnardo's shop in the town. Brian McCrory, a brother of the deputy manager at the Barnardo's shop, was also killed.

The funeral service, which was attended by David Trimble, was at the Church of the Holy Trinity, Lislimnaghan, where Samantha McFarland had been confirmed five years earlier. At the service the Rev. Derek Quinn described her as 'a wonderful young girl', and added: 'There will be people who have been terribly maimed returning to the community, children who have lost limbs who will be around for the next 60 years. They will be the visible signs for generations to come. And there are people who have seen things no one should see, including children who have seen their friends blown to pieces.'

The minister continued: 'We gather here to thank God for the life of Samantha McFarland, and to say to her parents and the other members of the family circle and to her many friends, we share in your loss.' Reporters and photographers wept as they stood outside the church during the service. The cortège then went to Roselawn Crematorium in Belfast.

See also: Breda Devine (3598), Lorraine Wilson (3619).

———

3619. August 15, 1998
Lorraine Wilson, Tyrone
Civilian, Protestant, 15, schoolgirl
Lorraine Wilson, who came from Camowen Bungalows, Omagh, had a sister and two brothers. She was working with Samantha McFarland in the charity shop run by Oxfam when it was evacuated. Her 20-year-old brother unsuccessfully searched the town and the hospital wards and corridors looking for her. It was 11 a.m. on Sunday, 21 hours after the explosion, when her parents received confirmation that their daughter was dead. The whole family went to the mortuary.

'Her body was left as it was found so it was very tough having to identify her but the whole family was there. She had a face full of shrapnel,' said her father. The family had spent the night in the town's leisure centre with other relatives and friends. Her father said: 'We reared an angel to 15 and now she has been taken away from us.' Lorraine had just earned her first pay packet for a week of summer work in her sister's café. 'I told her to save half of it but she spent none of it,' her father said. 'She never got the chance to spend it.'

The cortège passed through the centre of Omagh and passed the site of the explosion on the journey to Cappagh Parish Church for the funeral service. Pupils from Omagh High School formed a guard of honour as the coffin, draped with pink and white flowers, was carried into the church by her father and brothers.

The bishop of Derry, Dr James Mehaffey, told the congregation: 'The dark cloud of evil is being penetrated by numerous acts of love and goodness which are happening all around us.' The Rev. Derek Quinn said Lorraine Wilson had died helping others in what was often a cruel and uncaring world. A pupil from Omagh High School sang Elton John's song 'Candle in the Wind' before Lorraine Wilson's coffin was followed by her family to the adjoining graveyard, where she was buried wearing her mother's wedding dress.

See also: Breda Devine (3598), Samantha McFarland (3618).

3628. September 25, 1998
Billy Giles, East Belfast
Civilian, 42, single, prisoners' welfare worker

Billy Giles took his own life by hanging himself after serving a 15-year sentence for the UVF killing of a Catholic man, Michael Fay, in 1982. In a television interview shortly before his death, he said he had 'never felt a whole person again' since the day of the killing. Michael Fay had been on his way to visit his daughter at the Ulster Hospital at Dundonald when he was abducted and shot. A statement issued under the UVF's cover name of Protestant Action Force said he had been shot in retaliation for the IRA killing of UVF Shankill Butchers leader Lenny Murphy four days earlier.

Billy Giles was one of a number of men jailed in connection with the Fay murder. He came from a family with a strong military tradition, his father and three brothers all serving with the army. While in prison he graduated from the Open University.

In 1993 he gave an interview while on pre-release parole from prison. He said there was a strong mood of optimism among loyalist inmates of the Maze prison about the prospects for peace, adding: 'My own opinion is that it is over. My view of killing is that there is nothing worth killing for. What we have here, we have to make the best of and get on with life. The only way to get around things is to talk. You have to be fair.' He admitted he would not know what to say if he met Michael Fay's family: 'I would not like to face them. I just could not say enough.'

In 1998, following his release from prison, he gave what many regarded as a particularly compelling interview to reporter Peter Taylor which was screened in the three-part BBC series *Loyalists* in February and March 1999. In the interview he said of the 1980s: 'My whole mentality at that time would be preparing for war. Protestants were fearful of what was going to happen, that there was going to be an uprising, that they were all going to be slaughtered.'

He said of Michael Fay, whom he described as a workmate and a friend: 'The target was a Catholic man, guy the same age as myself. It didn't matter who it was, to me it didn't matter. Everything went out the window. My whole being up until that time was away, that's how it affected me personally. What would have been classed before as a decent young man certainly turned into this. That's the effect the environment I was living in had on me. It turned me into a killer.

'When it happened it felt to me that somebody had reached down inside me and ripped my insides out. It felt like somebody had just put their hand down in through my head and just ripped the insides out of me. I was empty. I felt empty. You hear a bang and it's too late. It's too late then. You've went somewhere you've never been before and it's not a very nice place and you can't stop it, it's too late then.' He was asked by Peter Taylor, 'Did you ever come back from that place?' Billy Giles replied, 'No, no, never felt a whole person again. I lost something that day I don't think I'll ever get back.'

He later hanged himself. He said in a suicide note: 'I was a victim too. Please let our next generation live normal lives, tell them of our mistakes and admit to them our regrets. I've decided to bring this to an end now. I'm tired.'

See also: Lenny Murphy (2483), Michael Fay (2486).

IMAGINATIVE

NUALA NÍ DHOMHNAILL
from Nuala Ní Dhomhnaill, *Pharaoh's Daughter* (1990)

Nuala Ní Dhomhnaill (1952–) was born in Lancashire and raised in an Irish-speaking area of West Kerry. She was educated at University College Cork where she was influenced by the *Innti* group of poets. Her *Selected Poems/Rogha Dánta* (1986) with translations by Michael Hartnett was highly acclaimed as were her following volumes *Pharaoh's Daughter* (1990) and *The Astrakhan Cloak* (1992). Here are two poems suggesting the range of her imagination.

AN BHEAN MHÍDHÍLIS

Do phioc sé suas mé
ag an gcúntúirt
is tar éis beagáinín cainte
do thairg deoch dom
nár eitíos uaidh
is do shuíomair síos
ag comhrá.
Chuamair ó dheoch go deoch
is ó *joke* go *joke*
is do bhíos-sa sna trithí aige
ach dá mhéid a bhíos ólta
ní dúrt leis go rabhas pósta.

Dúirt sé go raibh carr aige
is ar theastaigh síob abhaile uaim
is ní fada ar an mbóthar
nó gur bhuail an teidhe é.
Do tharraing sé isteach ag *lay-by*
chun gurbh fhusaide mé a phógadh.
Bhí málaí plaisteacha ar na sceacha
is bruscar ag gabháilt lastuas dóibh
is nuair a leag sé a lámh idir mo cheathrúna
ní dúrt leis go rabhas pósta.

Bhí sé cleachtaithe deaslámhach
ag oscailt chnaipí íochtair mo ghúna,
ag lapadáil go barr mo stocaí
is an cneas bog os a gcionnsan
is nuair a bhraith sé
nach raibh bríste orm
nach air a tháinig giúmar
is cé thógfadh orm ag an nóiméad sin
ná dúrt leis go rabhas pósta.

Do bhain sé do a threabhsar
leis an éirí a bhuail air
is do shleamhnaigh sall im shuíochánsa
is do tharraing sé anuas air mé
is nuair a shuíos síos air go cúramach
is gur mharcaíos thar an sprioc é
ba é an chloch ba shia im phaidrín
a rá leis go rabhas pósta.

Bhí mus úr a cholainne
mar ghairdín i ndiaidh báistí
is bhí a chraiceann chomh slim
chomh síodúil sin lem chneas féin
agus is mór an abairt sin
is nuair a bhíos ag tabhairt
pléisiúrtha dho
d'fhéach sé sa dá shúil orm
is fuaireas mothú pabhair is tuisceana
nár bhraitheas ó táim pósta.

THE UNFAITHFUL WIFE

He started coming on to me
at the spirit-grocer's warped and wonky counter
and after a preliminary spot of banter
offered to buy me a glass of porter;
I wasn't one to demur
and in no time at all we were talking
the hind leg off a donkey.
A quick succession of snorts and snifters
and his relentless repartee
had me splitting my sides with laughter.
However much the drink had loosened my tongue
I never let on I was married.

He would ask if he could leave me home
in his famous motoring-car,
though we hadn't gone very far down that road
when he was overtaken by desire.
He pulled in to a lay-by
the better to heap me with kisses.
There were plastic bags bursting with rubbish
stacked against the bushes.
Even as he slipped his hand between my thighs
I never let on I was married.

He was so handy,
too, when it came to unbuttoning my dress
and working his way past my stocking-tops
to the soft skin just above.
When it dawned on him
that I wasn't wearing panties
things were definitely on the up and up
and it hardly seemed the appropriate moment
to let on I was married.

By this time he had dropped his trousers
and, with his proper little charlie,
manoeuvred himself into the passenger-seat
and drew me down until, ever so gingerly,
I might mount.
As I rode him past the winning-post
nothing could have been further from my mind
than to let on I was married.

For his body was every bit as sweet
as a garden after a shower
and his skin was as sheer-delicate as my own
— which is saying rather a lot —
while the way he looked me straight in the eye
as he took such great delight
gave me a sense of power and the kind of insight
I'd not had since I was married.

Bhí boladh lofa ós na clathacha
is dramhaíl ag bun na gcrann
is bhí an port féarach taobh liom
breac le cac gadhar na gcomharsan
is nuair a thráigh ar an éirí air
tháinig aithis is ceann faoi air
is nár dhomh ba mhaith an mhaise ansan
ná dúrt leis go rabhas pósta.

Do bhuaileas suas an casán
lem scol amhráin is lem phort feadaíle
is níor ligeas orm le héinne
an eachtra a bhí laistiar díom
is má chastar orm arís é
i ndioscó nó i dteach tábhairne
ar ghrá oinigh nó réitigh
ní admhód riamh bheith pósta.

An ndéanfása?

There was this all-pervasive smell
from the refuse-sacks lying under the hedge
while the green, grassy slope beyond
was littered with dog-shit.
Now, as the groundswell of passion
began to subside,
he himself had a hang-dog, coy expression
that made me think it was just as well
I never let on I was married.

As I marched up my own garden-path
I kicked up a little dust.
I burst into song and whistled a tune
and vowed not to breathe a word
to a soul about what I'd done.
And if, by chance, I run into him again
at a disco or in some shebeen[1]
the only honourable course — the only decent
    thing —
would be to keep faith and not betray his trust
by letting on I was married.

Don't you think?

(trans. Paul Muldoon)

Ceist na Teangan

Cuirim mo dhóchas ar snámh
i mbáidín teangan
faoi mar a leagfá naíonán
i gcliabhán
a bheadh fite fuaite
de dhuilleoga feileastraim
is bitiúman agus pic
bheith cuimilte lena thóin

ansan é a leagadh síos
i measc na ngiolcach
is coigeal na mban sí
le taobh na habhann,
féachaint n'fheadaráis
cá dtabharfaidh an sruth é,
féachaint, dála Mhaoise,
an bhfóirfidh iníon Fharoinn?

The Language Issue

I place my hope on the water
in this little boat
of the language, the way a body might put
an infant

in a basket of intertwined
iris leaves,
its underside proofed
with bitumen and pitch,

then set the whole thing down amidst
the sedge
and bulrushes by the edge
of a river

only to have it borne hither and thither,
not knowing where it might end up;
in the lap, perhaps,
of some Pharaoh's daughter.

(trans. Paul Muldoon)

1   An unlicensed public-house or alehouse where spirits are
    sold on the sly (P.W. Joyce).

EAVAN BOLAND
from Eavan Boland, *Outside History* (1990)

This poem can be read in conjunction with Boland's essay 'Outside History' (1989), reproduced above on page 946.

THE ACHILL WOMAN

She came up the hill carrying water.
She wore a half-buttoned, wool cardigan,
a tea-towel round her waist.

She pushed the hair out of her eyes with
her free hand and put the bucket down.

The zinc-music of the handle on the rim
tuned the evening. An Easter moon rose.
In the next-door field a stream was
a fluid sunset; and then, stars.

I remember the cold rosiness of her hands.
She bent down and blew on them like broth.
And round her waist, on a white background,
in coarse, woven letters, the words 'glass cloth'.

And she was nearly finished for the day.
And I was all talk, raw from college —
week-ending at a friend's cottage
with one suitcase and the set text
of the Court poets of the Silver Age.

We stayed putting down time until
the evening turned cold without warning.
She said goodnight and started down the hill.

The grass changed from lavender to black.
The trees turned back to cold outlines.
You could taste frost

but nothing now can change the way I went
indoors, chilled by the wind
and made a fire
and took down my book
and opened it and failed to comprehend

the harmonies of servitude,
the grace music gives to flattery
and language borrows from ambition —

and how I fell asleep
oblivious to

the planets clouding over in the skies,
the slow decline of the Spring moon,
the songs crying out their ironies.

MOY McCRORY
from Moy McCrory, *Those Sailing Ships of his Boyhood Dreams* (1991)

Moy McCrory (1953–   ), writer of short stories and children's books, comes from Liverpool, and since 1987 has been tutor in Irish Literature at Birkbeck College, in London. In 'A Well Travelled Woman' she re-creates the special effect Lourdes has on English and Irish Catholics. In 1858 a peasant girl Bernadette Subirous had a vision of the Virgin Mary, and thereafter Lourdes in south-west France became a place of Catholic pilgrimage. Annual pilgrimages are made and thousands come to witness the torchlight processions with the stretcher-bearers given a special place since the waters are thought to provide a cure for illness. Here in this story Moy McCroy strikes the right balance between sympathy and humour and in the figure of Aunt Mairead (who would not have liked to have stayed in the hotel with the name Immaculate Conception — just to be on the safe side) she has touched a chord familiar to Catholics in Britain and Ireland.

A Well Travelled Woman

My Aunt Mairead's most cherished possession was kept inside a little buff carton printed with the words 'Stereoscope Pour Positifs'. It was a black hollow box-shaped piece of equipment with two peepholes at one end and a piece of clear film at the other.

When you put the special slides in the back and looked through the lens your sight went funny for a bit because the slides, which were all black and white shots of Lourdes, were made up of two identical photographs, and your eyes would dance between one and the other. But if you held the stereoscope still for a few seconds, the picture settled. As it merged into one image, a wonderful thing happened. People began to stand out.

There were three dimensions in that funny little viewer. The pictures became rounded until Lourdes was no longer a flat memory but a real world. If you put a hand out you would touch the faces of those attending benediction.

I half expected someone to move and duck behind a column in the photograph taken outside the Church of the Rosary. There were pictures of people who queued, eternally patient, to fill bottles with water from taps in the grotto. In one an old woman leans her elbow on a wall and her head is turned to speak to another behind her. I always wondered what she said. Did she know her photograph had been taken?

Great leather wheelchairs rested in the sun and the Red Cross wore funny hats like nuns. That was the Lourdes of my Aunt Mairead where she had been moved deeply by everything she saw.

'You can't beat the torchlight procession,' she'd say, staring into space. 'The Lady Day March in May's not a patch on it. Can you imagine it now? It stretches back for miles. Hundreds of souls each carrying a flickering candle, each praying for a miracle and not a Protestant in sight.'

Aunt Mairead was the most exotic person I knew. She had crossed the channel and seen another world. It took her two years to save up the money, paying every week into the Pilgrimage Fund when Ron McCarthy came round with his little red ledger on a Thursday evening. But she was determined. Ever since she was a girl she longed to travel abroad and she dreamed about visiting Lourdes, the most famous of all shrines to the Virgin.

She was genuinely religious. It was a good thing because her faith must have been sorely tested by the rigours of the journey. Her friends had seen her off an able-bodied person, but by all accounts she was so ill at the other end that she had to be taken from the train on a stretcher by the Red Cross. She must have been shocked by the length of the journey for nothing could have prepared her for that. Any sea journey was torture to Mairead at the best of times, but to find that she had to board yet another train for the longest part of the route after surviving the boat must have been as much as she could endure. The cramped conditions and the heat in carriage class caused her to faint repeatedly. On arrival her appearance must have been terrible because the brancardiers, who were waiting for an invalid train on the next platform and were used to transporting the sick and dying to and from the grotto, suggested that she be taken to a hospice instead of the hotel. She remained for three days in a paupers' ward, because the parish had only taken out minimum insurance.

Later, she said that she was too dispirited to care, but as her malaise subsided she began to feel frustrated. This was Lourdes the Wonderful and she was missing it. She managed to persuade a kind-hearted nun to push her out to the grotto, where she was left all afternoon like an overgrown baby in the sun.

The sight of all the serious invalids made her feel cowardly and she determined to rejoin her group now that her strength had returned. She was bothered about her suitcase which she had been separated from. Before they left, Father O'Flynn had said they might find some of the customs quite different and had warned them to keep an eye on their handbags. She had a good lace mantilla in her case among other things and was anxious to check that her black strap shoes were still where she'd packed them. This accomplished she insisted on going with the pilgrim group to the evening service so that she could give thanks.

She had seen enough of the inside of strange corridors and rooms to last her a lifetime. She had scrimped and saved just to be there and she wanted to be out in it, seeing, hearing, and grateful for the faculties in a place full of those who could do neither. She wanted to move around freely. All she had managed since her arrival was sitting among the dying for an afternoon, unable to get her wheelchair to reverse.

Martha Kilhooley, who carried the pennant for the Legion of Mary in the May procession, was impressed by my aunt's determination to attend the service.

'You couldn't have kept her back,' she used to say in years to come. 'Just up from her sick bed, and wouldn't stay in the hotel, but she'd have to be out at mass giving thanks to Our Blessed Mother.'

On Saturday afternoons they would take tea together and swop memories. Martha had been to Lourdes eight times and was known as The Continental because she was always telling the neighbours there was nothing like travel to give a person an education.

'Indeed the young women now isn't like that. All

they're concerned about is having a good time. I remember telling Mairead, Now only if you're up to it, I said. God knows how you've suffered just to be here. There's no sin in you staying comfortable in the hotel room. You can pray just as well from there, I said, but she'd have none of it.'

Neither Martha nor my aunt ever married. Their ideal man was a cross between someone with the selflessness of a missionary priest and Saint Francis of Assisi, because he was kind to animals. There can't have been many round our way who measured up.

But on Saturday afternoons over tea and shop-bought cakes in Martha Kilhooley's parlour they let the stereoscope transport them into another world. It was a strange one where much of the population was sick or dying, but where there was always an abundance of willing helpers. Where there were more nuns and priests per square foot than any other place in the world. And the language was softly spoken.

'Entry, that's a French word,' Aunt Mairead told me. 'And when they give you something you say Mercy, as if they might be going to kill you.' She giggled at the illogicality of foreigners.

'When you've travelled like me,' The Continental said, 'you get to know how to treat them. Sure, they're no different from us, there are good foreigners, like there are bad ones of your own.'

'San Ferry Ann,' the breadman told me. 'That's French.'

'French letters,' his delivery boy said and was given a clip round the ear. But The Continental had learned to speak it, she could say the entire Hail Mary.

'Oh go on Martha,' Mairead would entreat her. 'It makes it seem so . . . oh I don't know, foreign.' And brushing away the last crumbs from her second slice of almond gâteau The Continental would clear her throat and begin.

'Je Vous salue Marie, pleine de grace.'[1] Her voice would sweep and fall theatrically.

They held fast to the miracle of Lourdes, even when some who had been on pilgrimage began to doubt openly that it had ever worked.

'Remember Jack Traynor!' they were fond of telling those of little faith. But those who doubted said there were often other reasons for cures. And weren't some of those illnesses odd anyway? Who knows if someone's really blind or not, the sceptics said.

But Jack Traynor had been crippled and he walked down the platform at Lime Street Station.[2]

Explain that.

The Continental had a pamphlet from the Catholic Truth Society. She'd wave it in their faces if they dared to challenge her.

'Look at this,' she said. '*I Met a Miracle: The Story of Jack Traynor*. Eleven and three halfpence. They can get their own copies. They make me sick, these knowalls.'

It was in the papers, years ago. The *Liverpool Post* gave it headline space. LOURDES PILGRIMS RETURN. PARALYSED MAN ABLE TO WALK.

The reporters had been waiting. The man had sent a telegram to his wife. 'Am better,' it said.

EXTRAORDINARY SCENES WERE WITNESSED AT LIME STREET STATION ON SATURDAY NIGHT WHEN 400 PILGRIMS, FORMING PART OF THE GREAT LANCASHIRE CONTINGENT WHO LEFT FOR LOURDES EIGHT DAYS AGO, ARRIVED BACK.

'I WAS UP BY SAINT GEORGE'S WHEN I SAW CROWDS OF PEOPLE, AND POLICEMEN WITH BATONS PUSHING THEM,' A BYSTANDER SAYS.

Mairead could rattle off the press stories that accompanied the event, even though the man himself was dead before she went on her pilgrimage.

For some reason his miracle was never accredited, the medical report was never received by the diocese. But Jack Traynor was their hero, as Saint Bernadette was their saint.

'He's living proof of God's mercy,' Mairead said.

'I thought he died years ago,' my father said.

'He was living proof while he was alive,' my mother shouted, 'which is more than you are.'

But miracles or not, Mairead fell in love with Lourdes. When she spoke about it I could smell the candles burning in the grotto, feel the cool evening air as she felt it on her stroll back to the hotel.

She remembered the narrow streets crowded with establishments with religious sounding names: The Golgotha, The Vatican, The Angelus, Our Lady of the Sorrows, even The Hotel of the Immaculate Conception, which she would not have liked to stay in, just to be on the safe side. And the hundreds of souvenir shops selling medals and cheap tin and plaster statues of the Virgin. There must have been hundreds of strings of rosary beads which shopkeepers hung over sticks to catch the sun like so many brightly coloured baubles, as the traders vied with each other for business in prayer cards and wax candles.

'Every day I lit a candle in the grotto. The heat from thousands of them was incredible. And my small prayer was there among them.'

That was the only time in her life that she had owned a bathing suit, which she bought specially thinking she would need one to take the waters in the holy spring. Bathing in Lourdes was something she knew she must do, it was an essential part of the pilgrimage.

Mairead was terrified of water. She would not even take her shoes off at the seaside. But it was more like taking a bath, than a swim, the experienced pilgrims told her. Her party had all been while she was ill, but Father O'Flynn fixed it so that she could join another group. There were always steady queues of people waiting to get into the baths. Mairead couldn't bring herself to look at them, and told Father O'Flynn that if she was causing too much trouble she didn't mind missing, because she could always wash her feet under the taps outside the shrine, and she would be just as satisfied with that.

'The bath is essential to the Lourdes experience, my child. It wouldn't be fair for you to come all this way and miss it,' and he smiled kindly at her generosity of spirit.

It was not as public as she feared. There was a changing room with cubicles and she left her clothes on a peg. They made her leave her bathing suit there as well and volunteers handed her a plain cotton shift, which was still wet from the previous bather. Getting into that was the most difficult part and she felt so peculiar that she was glad to be among strangers.

The volunteers pointed her towards three stone steps which led into the grey bath. The water was completely still and she could not see the bottom, or guess how deep it might be. She had been told that they frowned on total immersion because it held up the proceedings, so trusting it would not cover her head, she stepped out into freezing water. It came up to her hips and before she knew where she was, she was struggling to walk through it with the borrowed robe billowing around her. The volunteers shouted something she didn't understand. They indicated that she ought to sit or kneel and one raced out on the bit of duckboard by the side and pushed her shoulder down. Water took her breath away as it covered her chest. And then she could not say what happened, she must have slipped, because a film of ice seemed to cover her face. It numbed her cheeks. Her one great fear was of drowning. She had never put her ears under water in her life and now she was hearing those odd water sounds as everything was swallowed by the liquid which was swallowing her.

Rouoo, rouoo, rouoo, deep-voiced water said. The green sentences were stretched thinly until they broke into single letters, which sucked water like drinking straws through their hollow-tubed legs. Full up, they became swollen and deadly white like tubercular milk bottles on the doorstep at home. But home was a long way away and the letters regrouped into senseless foreign words. Rouoo, rouoo, rouoo.

Water trickled through her ears into her head. She felt it fill up her mind and seep through her skin turning her veins to water, and she was floating in the rouoo, rouoo, rouoo, drowning in its forgetful, faithless

embrace. She must breathe, she must reach the surface.

Water broke around her. A volunteer pulled her upright and she gasped and shuddered. She must have had her head under for barely seconds, but the watery clock ticking in the belly of the holy spring said otherwise. It had moved its heavy, waterlogged fingers and its sonorous ticking said rouoo, rouoo, rouoo.

The timepiece pulsed its hours through the green ripples and she coughed, afraid that she would make a fool of herself. The volunteer rushed her out of the public bath and held up a tiny picture of Our Lady of Lourdes for her to kiss. She had done it. For ever after she would recommend Lourdes as opposed to any other holy water. She kept a bottle on top of the piano and would bless herself regularly with the substance of her triumph over evil. For she knew now what lurked under calm lakes. Her particular devil was green and wet, a shell-covered, misshapen thing that wrecked ships and counted time backwards. That afternoon was to remain with her all her life.

'You mustn't dry yourself after. You just have to get dressed as best you can.'

She remembered that everything stuck to her. Her stockings twisted and creased round her ankles. Elastic snapped back away from her. She had put her slip on and without thinking started to rub it round over her front, before she realized. 'You just have to let the water dry on you.'

'It's torture entirely,' Martha Killhooley agreed, 'the miracle is we don't all come back with pneumonia.' And they would both laugh. But Mairead said that for the rest of the day her body did tingle, and she had a wonderful sense of relief. But after that she could never imagine why anybody should go swimming by way of recreation.

She had a lovely glittering rosary of red glass beads which turned greeny-blue in the light. On the central medal before the crucifix, was a scene depicting Bernadette when she first saw Aquero, as the peasant's daughter referred to the Lady in their local dialect. On the reverse side was a glass window with the words 'Eau de Lourdes' punched in the metal surround and a clear liquid sealed inside.

'Just think, she was only fourteen when she saw Her first. She could hardly write her name.'

'Lots of saints were stupid,' my father said. 'God sometimes chooses fools to do his business because they're without sin.'

'We could do with less cleverness round here, and a bit more goodness,' my mother would snap back. 'The simple faith of children was good enough for Christ and it's good enough for me.'

Aunt Mairead's faith may have been simple but she was none the less a realist. She returned home knowing that it was one thing to be Bernadette Soubirous in the nineteenth century, and live in picturesque poverty with a father that hauled dirty linen for a hospital, but it was quite another to be unemployed in Liverpool with a father who delivered coal on the back of a wagon. She knew what romance was. It illuminated a drab life — like the brightly coloured beads of so many rosaries taken up by the faithful on feastdays to Our Lady.

Sometimes on Saturday afternoons she and The Continental would sing 'Bring flowers of the fairest', and could not prevent themselves from weeping, especially at the words, 'Lilies of the valley', for they were Mary's special flowers. They were the flowers she carried when she first appeared to Bernadette. I had a head-dress made out of plastic ones, only they had begun to yellow like the net veil I wore on Lady Day when the junior school walked in procession. But these sung lilies were beautiful, defied description and made grown women cry.

Then I would long to live in Lourdes, and go to the torchlight procession every night. I could get a room in a pension, and live just by the grotto. I would earn my living teaching English.

'That's your sister's fault. She's been filling her head up with daft ideas again,' my father said.

But it was a wonderful vision, of escape and other-worldliness. And there was no laughter like Aunt Mairead's. No one ever matched her, for happiness which was infectious or for sorrow which left you desolate.

She and Martha would cry over newspaper stories. Their favourite was the one about Sparkle the little black and white mongrel who got run over. There was a photograph of the owner looking sadly at the camera while holding the dead body of Sparkle who looked as if he was sleeping. The owner must have considered the newsworthy potential of his pet even as it breathed its last. But Aunt Mairead trusted in the man's decency. She cut the story out and kept it folded between the pages of a book.

'Look at the little dog, looking at him as if to say "Why did you tell me it was safe to cross when it wasn't? Why did you say it was all right?"'

IT WILL BE ON MY CONSCIENCE FOR EVER, GRIEF STRICKEN OWNER SAYS.

'Wouldn't you feel awful if it was you?' Martha Kilhooley used to say, and they would sit over their tea feeling awful.

The obedience of the dog was what touched them most.

'Such a trusting little thing.'

'Poor Sparkle.'

'You have to trust God,' Aunt Mairead said. 'They wanted Bernadette put away in an asylum for incurables, but she kept on. She wouldn't take back what she'd seen.'

'Would you, Mairead?' The Continental asked her.

'Oh, I don't know. I've never had a vision.'

'I wonder what it's like, you know, seeing someone?' And they would imagine themselves, holding out against the ignorance of others. Alone in our street full of infidels and the ungodly, my Aunt Mairead and The Continental lit candles in their stark bedrooms. And watched each other growing old.

They counted themselves lucky, they had seen the sick and the dying lined up on leather stretchers for the last hope of the hopeless, waiting patiently at the hospital of faith for a cure defying medical science.

Mairead had been shocked by the sight of so much flesh exposed to the air, bandages removed, ready for the priest's touch, for another blessing, for the holy waters, for the intercession of the faithful, for prayers, hymns, for all the despair of the suffering in this world, and for Aquero's offer, 'I don't promise to make you happy in this world, but in the next.'

Lourdes displayed the most barbarous acts of nature and she agonized at the workings of her God and prayed. Here they were granted a respite from despair, if only for as long as the holy waters took to chill leaving them sodden and chastened. A minute of hope in a lifetime of abandon. And the promise of the next, not this world, but the next. And she understood and lit her yellow candles.

She wanted me to have the stereoscope when she died. Her shaking hands had scrawled my name on the buff carton, just to be on the safe side. She'd been adamant that the simple amusement, the 'child's toy' as my father called it, be left with someone who valued it and in my early enthusiasm I had shown myself to be a worthy custodian.

It came, packed carefully between two eggboxes with different coloured scraps of tissue paper that she'd saved. It was secured by an elastic armband of the type men once wore to keep their shirt cuffs straight, a respectable item that was no longer fashionable and circled the two halves of the eggbox like a mourner's dark ribbon. This was her greatest treasure.

As I looked through the slides, I found faces I remembered. The images of Lourdes were exactly as I'd seen them years ago. Inside the box, time had been arrested. I recognized the same people in the close-up shots, the procession, the blessing of the sick. It was familiar. But for the first time, I noticed how silent it had become now that Mairead was no longer there to fill up the background with noises, arguing and discussing with her friend about what they remembered. Now, with her dead, nobody spoke, there was no chant of prayers outside the basilica at the open air service, no gush of excitement at the appearance of a bishop, and the hollow baths were still.

A piece of paper fell out of the box. It was a handbill advertising the funicular railway. I opened it out.

DON'T LEAVE LOURDES AND THE PYRENEES, it warned in large blue letters, WITHOUT ASCENDING THE PIC DU JER. It promised an unrivalled view over the French and Spanish Pyrenees. WHEN BOOKING, INSIST UPON FUNICULAIRE DU PIC DU JER. SEE THE BASILICA AND SANCTUARIES. MAGNIFICENT PROSPECT OVER LOURDES.

And for a moment the silence broke. Mairead would have been shrieking with excitement. She was scared of heights. The old wooden train must have shook and thumped as it crawled upwards. And when she looked out, Lourdes would be shrinking. Below, thousands of humans scuttled round in meaningless patterns. For Mairead there was still an all-loving God.

That was comforting to think. Someone who could pick out individuals, could recognize a single soul in the heaving mass of humanity, and know them precisely, down to the last groove and swirl of their thumbprint.

Down below, she had seen dark shapes converging into solid wedges — a narrow strip wending its way along the river possibly. The world that day must have felt blue-peaked and enormous.

The train rattled and banged. Lourdes grew smaller. The pain congregating in clusters, faded. The sky opened and the air was clear and sweet, rising over the presence of suffering. Higher, higher, and beyond to where there was perfection and purity. The place where every prayer ascended, every mouthing of belief since the dawn of thought, every word rose here and swelled the sky, reaching a deafening plateau of noise and brilliance, which climbed still further up, up and beyond, until it joined the vastness of Mairead's faith.

1　French: Hail, Mary, full of grace (the opening phrase of the Hail Mary).
2　In Liverpool.

MAURA DOOLEY
from Maura Dooley, *Explaining Magnetism* (1991)

Maura Dooley (1957–), English-born poet and literary organizer, is author of *Ivy Leaves and Arrow* (1986), *Turbulence* (1988), and *Knowing a Bone* (1996). Her family connections with Ireland are now remote but still in evidence as this poem suggests.

SECOND GENERATION

There's just no fuchsia in it, my Dad would joke,
but my dreams are hedged with red and purple,
seal-lined, damp under blue mountains, caught like a
　　burr
on this country's old coat that I try to shrug around me.

It's one long past of never having a future,
taking the slow boat to a better land,
needing to fill stomachs with something more than
　　prayer,
shedding a language, watching the shore grow small.

We want the tongue they took such care to lose,
to feel its shuffling sadness in our mouths,
we want to feel this greenness like a skin,
to scratch it when it itches, watch it heal.

Wearing the Claddagh ring, hoping its two hands
would hold, not tear, this tiny heart,
could I slip in there to watch the sea shift
or cut some warmth out of a peaty soil?

No Siege of Ennis[1] in the Irish Club,
no convent childhood, shamrock through the post,[2]
can net us back across that narrow passage
nor make this town a place we can call home.

1　An Irish country dance, a favourite dance at Irish Clubs in Britain.
2　It was the custom for shamrock to be sent from Ireland to members of the family living abroad in Britain to wear on St Patrick's Day.

MICHAEL LONGLEY
from Michael Longley, *Gorse Fires* (1991)

Michael Longley's poetry from *Gorse Fires* onwards commands particular attention.
Here he presents two versions of death, one his own, the other a free translation from
Homer's *Odyssey*, given a special twist by its resonance against the 'troubles' of his
native province.

DETOUR

I want my funeral to include this detour
Down the single street of a small market town,
On either side of the procession such names
As Philbin, O'Malley, MacNamara, Keane.
A reverent pause to let a herd of milkers pass
Will bring me face to face with grubby parsnips,
Cauliflowers that glitter after a sunshower,
Then hay rakes, broom handles, gas cylinders.
Reflected in the slow sequence of shop windows
I shall be part of the action when his wife
Draining the potatoes into a steamy sink
Calls to the butcher to get ready for dinner
And the publican descends to change a barrel.
From behind the one locked door for miles around
I shall prolong a detailed conversation
With the man in the concrete telephone kiosk
About where my funeral might be going next.

THE BUTCHERS

When he had made sure there were no survivors in his
  house
And that all the suitors were dead, heaped in blood
  and dust
Like fish that fishermen with fine-meshed nets have
  hauled
Up gasping for salt water, evaporating in the sunshine,
Odysseus, spattered with muck and like a lion
  dripping blood
From his chest and cheeks after devouring a farmer's
  bullock,
Ordered the disloyal housemaids to sponge down the
  armchairs
And tables, while Telemachos, the oxherd and the
  swineherd

Scraped the floor with shovels, and then between the
  portico
And the roundhouse stretched a hawser[1] and hanged
  the women
So none touched the ground with her toes, like long-
  winged thrushes
Or doves trapped in a mist-net across the thicket
  where they roost,
Their heads bobbing in a row, their feet twitching but
  not for long,
And when they had dragged Melanthios's corpse into
  the haggard
And cut off his nose and ears and cock and balls, a
  dog's dinner,
Odysseus, seeing the need for whitewash and
  disinfectant,
Fumigated the house and the outhouses, so that
  Hermes
Like a clergyman might wave the supernatural baton
With which he resurrects or hypnotizes those he
  chooses,
And waken and round up the suitors' souls, and the
  housemaids',
Like bats gibbering in the nooks of their mysterious
  cave
When out of the clusters that dangle from the rocky
  ceiling
One of them drops and squeaks, so their souls were
  batsqueaks
As they flittered after Hermes, their deliverer, who led
  them
Along the clammy sheughs,[2] then past the oceanic
  streams
And the white rock, the sun's gatepost in that dreamy
  region,
Until they came to a bog-meadow full of bog-asphodels
Where the residents are ghosts or images of the dead.

1   A large rope or cable.
2   Ditches, furrows.

VINCENT BUCKLEY

from Vincent Buckley, 'Hunger Strike', *Last Poems* (1991)

Bobby Sands (1954–81), IRA prisoner, began a hunger strike on 1 March 1981 in the Maze Prison in support of the right to political status; it ended with his death on 5 May. Nine other prisoners died on hunger strike during this same campaign by the IRA, but the British Government at the time remained unmoved. For an extended discussion by Buckley of Bobby Sands, see his *Memory Ireland* (1985). Buckley imagines Sands as a modern-day warrior, his weapons the sticks of his forearms and the electric pain of his body. An anthology of writings by Sands can be found in *Skylark, Sing Your Lonely Song* (1982).

BOBBY SANDS: ONE[1]

Now he is laid on the sheepskin rug
so that his bones will not burn him,
pads are put on his heels
against the bedsores. He is blind
and deaf. The pain they told him of
jolts its thin current
into every movement. His teeth
protrude like the bones of a dead man.
He is dying for his word. *Geronimo.*

They would not let him alone.
Day and night they came and went
stirring his pallid shadow,
interpreters of his dying.

Day and night he hung on the wire,
his curled body outlasting them
till they fell silent; 'he was the piper
walking in the front of battle'.

Then, he died in a clean place,
crooked, on the waterbed, the Pope's
crucifix proudly beside him, his mind
open as a galaxy.
Le dur desir de durer[2]
saw him buried as Geronimo.

1   This is an extract from the poem 'Hunger Strike'.
2   French: the strong desire to endure.

MÁIRE BRADSHAW

from Máire Bradshaw, *high time for all the marys* (1991)

Máire Bradshaw wrote this poem to commemorate the occasion when President Mary Robinson received the Freedom of the City of Cork on 23 February 1991. The poem captures the celebratory mood and plays with the placenames and landmarks of the city such as St Finbarr's Cathedral and St Anne's Church Shandon.

HIGH TIME FOR ALL THE MARYS

I

anna lee[1]
is dressed
in black
tonight
wearing a
halter neckline
rucked in

velvet and gold
a swan
pinned
here and there
for decoration

a sailor's fancy
she'll dance
'til the sun rises
on dawn square
and better value

mr dunne
cuts his disco lights
to off —

chaperoned by quays
locked by bridges
north to south
poverty and class
out for a night —

II

old women darn —
holy spires
needle the
dark sky

finbarr's golden angel
wings akimbo
ready to box
the ears
of drunks
and lovers
pausing
on their way
to barrack street
for chips . . .

voices ring out
in shandon
the belfry
silent for once —
pigeons of peace
taking their ease —

III

in rte[2]
— an angelus[3] pause —
a different angel
declaring unto
yet another mary . . .
a woman is lifting
up her skirt
ready for a jig

she's rolling up
her sleeves
a washload of dreams
ready for ironing

a medb[4]
of the táin
she is taking

the brown bull
through silver bells
and cockle shells
to the park . . .
young men and women
first to vote
owing no favours
cheer —
and 'here's to you
mrs robinson'[5]

IV

for certain
women are up
off their knees

all at once
being a housewife —
a housekeeper
or pushing a trolly
in dawn square

has a certain
air about it
a moment
when mrs nobody
becomes mrs somebody
head and tail
at high doh
stepping lightly

anna lee and
anna livia plurabelle
the kissing cousins[6]
at high tide
and high time
for all the marys . . .

1   A poetic name for the River Lee, which flows through
    Cork. Anna Livia Plurabelle is a poetic name for the
    River Liffey used by Joyce in *Finnegans Wake*.
2   Radio Telefis Eireann.
3   A form of prayers said at midday and 6 p.m. when
    church bells ring out the Angelus across Catholic
    Ireland. The Angelus contains the following exchange
    between the Archangel Gabriel and the Virgin Mary:
    'Behold the handmaid of the Lord. Be it done unto me
    according to Thy word.' Hence the association by the
    poet between the two Marys.
4   The reference in this stanza is to the *Táin Bó Cuailgne*
    (Cattle-Raid of Cooley), where Medb, the queen of
    Connacht, sets out to capture the Brown Bull of
    Cuailgne in Ulster.
5   A refrain from a Simon and Garfunkel song.
6   Echo of a line in an Elvis song.

IAN DUHIG
from Ian Duhig, *The Bradford Count* (1991)

Born in London of Irish Catholic parents, Ian Duhig now lives in Leeds. For fifteen years he helped to run a hostel for the homeless in York. His verse is distinguished by its popular appeal, its humorous turns, and its engagement with telling, often little-known incidents or episodes of history. Here in this poem he makes use of Patrick Dinneen's *Irish-English Dictionary* to play on the phrase 'from the Irish'.

FROM THE IRISH

According to Dinneen, a Gael unsurpassed
in lexicographical enterprise, the Irish
for moon means the white circle in a slice
of half-boiled potato or turnip. A star
is the mark on the forehead of a beast
and the sun is the bottom of a lake, or well.

Well, if I say to you your face
is like a slice of half-boiled turnip,
your hair is the colour of a lake's bottom
and at the centre of each of your eyes
is the mark of the beast, it is because
I want to love you properly, according to Dinneen.

NUALA NÍ DHOMHNAILL
from Nuala Ní Dhomhnaill, *The Astrakhan Cloak* (1992)

Nuala Ní Dhomhnaill here takes liberties with the most potent modern female symbol of Ireland. Paul Muldoon takes further liberties with Nuala Ní Dhomhnaill's liberties.

CAITLÍN

Ní fhéadfá í a thabhairt in aon áit leat,
do thabharfadh sí náire is aithis duit.
Díreach toisc go raibh sí an-mhór ina *vamp*
thiar ins na fichidí, is gur dhamhas sí an Searlastan
le tonntracha méiríneacha ina gruaig dhualach
    thrilseánach;
gur phabhsae gléigeal í thiar i naoi déag sé déag,
go bhfacthas fornocht i gConnachta í, mar áille na
    háille,
is ag taisteal bhóithre na Mumhan, mar ghile na gile;
go raibh sí beo bocht, gan locht,
a píob mar an eala, ag teacht taobh leis an dtoinn
is a héadan mar shneachta,

ní théann aon stad uirthi ach ag maíomh
as na seanlaethanta, nuair a bhíodh sí ag ionsaí

CATHLEEN

You can't take her out for a night on the town
without her either showing you up or badly letting
    you down:
just because she made the Twenties roar
with her Black and Tan Bottom — O Terpsichore[1] —
and her hair in a permanent wave;
just because she was a lily grave
in nineteen sixteen; just because she once was spotted
quite naked in Cannought, of beauties most beautied,
or tramping the roads of Moonstare,[2] brightest of the
    bright;
just because she was poor, without blemish or blight,
high-stepping it by the ocean with her famous swan's
    prow
and a fresh fall of snow on her broadest of broad
    brows —

because of all that she never stops bending your ear
about the good old days of yore

na dúthaí is an drúcht ar a bróga,
maidin Domhnaigh is í ag dul go hEochaill
nó ar an mbóthar cothrom idir Corcaigh agus Dúghlas.
Na rudaí iontacha a dúirt an Paorach fúithi
is é mar mhaor ar an loing. Is dúirt daoine eile
go mbeadh an Éirne ina tuilte tréana, is go réabfaí
cnoic. Murab ionann is anois nuair atá sí ina baintreach
  tréith
go raibh sí an tráth san ina maighdean mhómhar,
  chaoin, shéimh
is díreach a dóthain céille aici chun fanacht i gcónaí
ar an dtaobh thall den dteorainn ina mbítear de shíor.

Ba dhóig leat le héisteacht léi nár chuala
sí riamh gur binn béal ina thost, is nach mbíonn
in aon ní ach seal, go gcríonnann an tslat le haois
is fiú dá mba dhóigh le gach spreasán an uair úd
go mba leannán aige féin í, go bhfuil na laethanta san
  thart.
Cuirfidh mé geall síos leat nár chuala sí leis
mar tá sé de mhórbhua aici agus de dheis
gan aon ní a chloisint ach an rud a 'riúnaíonn í féin.
Tá mil ar an ógbhean aici, dar léi, agus rós breá
ina héadan. Is í an sampla í is fearr ar m'aithne
de bhodhaire Uí Laoghaire.

when she crept through the country in her dewy high
  heels
of a Sunday morning, say, on the road to Youghal
or that level stretch between Cork and Douglas.
There was your man Power's ridiculous
suggestion when he was the ship's captain, not to speak
of the Erne running red[3] with abundance and
  mountain-peaks
laid low. She who is now a widowed old woman
was a modest maiden, meek and mild, but with
  enough gumption
at least to keep to her own
side of the ghostly demarcation, the eternal buffer-
  zone.

For you'd think to listen to her she'd never heard
that discretion is the better part, that our names are
  writ
in water, that the greenest stick will wizen:
even if every slubberdegullion[4] once had a dream-vision
in which she appeared as his own true lover,
those days are just as truly over.
And I bet Old Gummy Granny[5]
has taken none of this on board because of her
  uncanny
knack of hearing only what confirms
her own sense of herself, her honey-nubile form
and the red nose, proud rose or canker
tucked behind her ear, in the head-band of her blinkers.

(trans. Paul Muldoon)

1 Female muse of dancing.
2 A play on Connacht and Munster.
3 An echo of Mangan's line from 'Dark Rosaleen'. Other phrases and echoes can be heard in this poem.
4 A worthless sloven.
5 A caricature of the Poor Old Woman, Kathleen ni Houlihan, appears under this name in the Nighttown episode of Joyce's *Ulysses*.

PATRICK McCABE
from Patrick McCabe, *The Butcher Boy* (1992)

Patrick McCabe (1955–) was born in Clones, County Monaghan, and moved to London to become a teacher. *The Butcher Boy*, which was turned into the play *Frank Pig Says Hello*, provides a disturbing insight into the brutalized mind of a deprived adolescent in 1960s' provincial Ireland. Francie Brady, son of an alcoholic father and a mother driven mad by despair, takes out his resentment on the mother of his one-time school friend Philip Nugent. In this scene he breaks into the Nugent house and re-enacts a series of imaginary conversations before Mrs Nugent arrives home.

I think it was him looking at me with them sad eyes that made me get up and say that was a good laugh but I think it's about time I was back at the farmyard what do you say Mrs Nugent? But she said nothing only stood there twisting a clothes peg and saying please stop this please! Right you be now Mrs Nooge I said and hopskipped down the lane, I'll call back another day I said and I did.

And the reason I did that was because when I got to thinking about it back in the house I thought what am I worrying about Philip Nugent's sad eyes for? I had probably imagined it, he might even have been putting it on. The more I thought about it the more I said yes that's right he was just putting it on. Philip Nugent, I said to myself, you are a crafty devil, the way they say it in the comics. That old Philip Nugent, the trickster! So a couple of days later, back I went except this time I made sure they weren't in. I waited until I saw the car heading off down the lane I knew they were going to visit Buttsy up the mountains.

In I went through the back window hello Francie welcome to Nugents! Oh hello there nobody I said.

Dant-a dan! Welcome to Nugents Mr Francie Brady! Thank you I said, thank you very much. It gives me great pleasure to be here standing on these black and white tiles in the scullery, Mrs Nugent. Oh no not at all Francis we're delighted to have you. Now you must meet everyone. This is my husband and this is my son Philip but of course you know him. Except that really there'd be no fear of Mrs Nugent saying any of that she'd be on the phone to the sergeant straight away but oh no she wouldn't for she was up the mountains drinking tin mugs of tea with carrot-head Buttsy the brother in a cottage that stank of turf-smoke and horsedung. But Nugents didn't smell like that. Oh no. It smelt of freshly baked scones, that's what it smelt of. Scones just taken out of the oven that very minute. I went on the hunt for them but I could find them nowhere. I think it was just the smell of old baking days that had stuck to the place and she hadn't been making scones at all. No matter. Sniff sniff. Polish too there was plenty of that. Mrs Nugent polished everything till you could see your face in it. The kitchen table, the floor. You name it if you looked at it you were in it. You had to hand it to Mrs Nugent when it came to the polishing. Flies? Oh no, not in Mrs Nugents! And any cakes there were were all under lock and key where Mr Fly and his cronies couldn't get at them. You could see them in the glass case under plastic domes and there was a three-tiered stand with two pink ones and a half-eaten birthday cake on it. Those flies they must have been

driven daft — looking in at them beautiful cakes and not being able to get at them. I was myself so I knew what they must have felt like. I could have broken it open but I didn't want to spoil it they looked so good in there. I'd say she made all them herself. There was a photo on the wall of Mrs Nugent lying on the grass in a park somewhere. What came into my mind was that I never knew that Mrs Nugent had been young once as young as me. For a long time I thought she had been born the same age as she was now but of course that was stupid. In that photo she was about five. She was lying there with a big gap between her teeth and freckles all over her face like Buttsy. Hee hee she was saying to the camera. Good old Mrs Baby Nooge I thought. How many years ago was that I wondered. Could have been a hundred for all I knew. Mr Nugent's briefcase was sitting in the corner and his tweed overcoat was hanging up behind the door. I helped myself to some bread and jam and turned on the television. What was on only Voyage to The Bottom of The Sea, Admiral Nelson and his submarine gang they were getting a bad doing off a giant octopus that was hiding inside a cave where they couldn't get at him. He was a cute bastard sending out these big curling tentacles with suckers on them knocking the sub against rocks upside down and everything. All you could see was these two eyes shining away in the darkness of the cave as much as to say I have you now Mr smart alec navy men, let's see you work your way out of this one. *Dive! Dive!* snapped the admiral into a microphone but she wouldn't go down. The music was going mad. *Kill the bastard!* I shouted, I was getting excited too, *harpoon him that'll shut him up!* But the admiral wasn't as stupid as the octopus thought he was. *Right that's it all systems are go!* and the next thing these depth charges start hitting the octopus smack between the eyes boom and the squeals of him then. Pop pop out go the two eyes like lights and the tentacles flapping around like wasted elastic and the sub away up to the surface with the whole crew cheering and the admiral wiping the sweat off his face smiling OK everybody that's enough back to work. Then beep beep goes the echo sounder and away off they go happy as Larry and back to normal. Fair play to you admiral, I said, that shut him up. And it sure did, the octopus was lying at the back of the cave like a busted cushion and it would be a long time before he was suckering or tentacling again. I made myself a big mug of tea and another doorstep of bread and jam to celebrate. It was hard to beat it sitting there eating and enjoying myself. It was a grand day outside. There were a few skittery bits of cloud lying about the sky but they didn't care if they ever got anywhere. Birds, crows mostly, hanging about Nugents window sill to see what they could see. Well well look who's in there Francie Brady. He's not supposed to be in there. Hey crows I said, fuck off and that shifted them. Ah this is the life I said I wonder have we any cheese or pickle. We certainly had — there it was in the brown jar in the fridge! And did it taste nice! It certainly did! Make no mistake — I would definitely be staying at Nugents Hotel on my next trip to town.

When I had finished my snack I went upstairs to see if I could find Philip's room. No problem. Comics and a big sucker arrow lying on the bed, dunk went the arrow into the back of the door and dangled there. Then I opened the wardrobe and what did I find only Philip's school uniform the one he wore at private school in England. There it was, the navy blue cap with the crest and the braided blazer with the silver buttons. There was a pair of grey trousers with a razor crease and black polished shoes could you see your face in them you certainly could. I thought to myself, this could be a good laugh and so I put it on. I looked at myself in the mirror. I say Frawncis would you be a sport and wun down to the tuck shop for meah pleath? I did a twirl and said abtholootely old boy. I say boy what is your name pleath? Oo, I said, my name ith Philip Nuahgent!

Then I went round the house like Philip. I walked like him and everything. Mrs Nugent called up the stairs to me are you up there Philip? I said I was and she told me to come down for my tea. Down I came and she had made me a big feed of rashers and eggs and tea and the whole lot. What were you at upstairs Philip dear she said. Oh I was playing with my chemistry set mother I said. I hope you're not making any stink bombs she said. Oh no mother I said, I wouldn't do that — it's naughty! Mr Nugent lowered his spectacles and looked at me over the top of the paper. That's correct son, indeed it is. I'm glad to hear you saying that. Well it thrilled me no end to hear Mr Nooge saying that. Then when I looked again he was back reading his paper.

I felt good about all this. When I was finished I said I was going back upstairs to finish my experiments but I didn't, I waltzed around the landing singing one of the *Emerald Gems* to myself O the days of the Kerry Dances O the ring of the piper's tune! and then into Mr and Mrs Nugent's room. I lay on the bed and sighed. Then I heard Philip Nugent's voice. But it was different now, all soft and calm. He said: You know what he's doing here don't you mother? He wants to be one of us. He wants his name to be Francis Nugent. That's what he's wanted all along! We know that — don't we mother?

Mrs Nugent was standing over me. Yes, Philip, she said. I know that. I've known it for a long time.

Then slowly she unbuttoned her blouse and took out her breast.

Then she said: This is for you Francis.

She put her hand behind my head and firmly pressed my face forward. Philip was still at the bottom of the bed smiling. I cried out: *Ma! It's not true!* Mrs Nugent shook her head and said: *I'm sorry Francis it's too late for all that now. You should have thought of that when you made up your mind to come and live with us!*

I thought I was going to choke on the fat, lukewarm flesh.

No!

I drew out and tried to catch Nugent on the side of the face.

I heeled over the dressing table and the mirror broke into pieces. Mrs Nugent stumbled backwards with her breast hanging. Now Philip I said and laughed. Philip had changed his tune now he was back to *please Francie*. I said: Are you talking to me Mr Pig?

When he didn't answer I said: Did you not hear me Philip Pig? Hmm?

He was twisting his fingers and so was his mother.

Or maybe you didn't know you were a pig. Is that it? Well then, I'll have to teach you. I'll make sure you won't forget again in a hurry. You too Mrs Nugent! Come on now! Come on now come on now and none of your nonsense. That was a good laugh, I said it just like the master in the school. Right today we are going to do pigs. I want you all to stick out your faces and scrunch up your noses just like snouts. That's very good Philip. I found a lipstick in one of the drawers and I wrote in big letters across the wallpaper PHILIP IS A PIG. Now, I said, isn't that good? Yes Francie said Philip. And now you Mrs Nugent. I don't think you're putting enough effort into it. Down you get now and no slacking. So Mrs Nugent got down and she looked every inch the best pig in the farmyard with the pink rump cocked in the air. Mrs Nugent, I said, astonished, that is absolutely wonderful! Thank you Francie said Mrs Nugent. So that was the pig school. I told them I didn't want to catch them walking upright anymore and if I did they would be in *very* serious trouble. Do you understand Philip? Yes he said. And you too Mrs Nugent. It's your responsibility as a sow to see that Philip behaves as a good pig should. I'm leaving it up to you. She nodded. Then we went over it one more time I got them to say it after me. I am a pig said Philip. I am a sow said Mrs Nooge. Just to recap then I said. What do pigs do? They eat pig nuts said Philip. Yes that's very good I said but what else do they do? They run around the farmyard Philip said. Yes indeed they do but what else? I tossed the lipstick up and down in my hand. Any takers at the back? Yes Mrs Nugent? They give us rashers! Yes that's very true but it's not the answer I'm looking for. I waited for a long time but I could see the answer wasn't going to come. No, I said, the answer I'm looking for is — *they do poo!* Yes, pigs are forever doing poo all over the farmyard, they have the poor farmer's heart broken. They'll tell you that pigs are the cleanest animals going. Don't believe a word of it. Ask any farmer! Yes, pigs are poo animals I'm afraid and they simply will cover the place in it no matter what you do. So then, who's going to be the best pig in the pig school and show us what we're talking about then, hmm? Come on now, any takers? Oh now surely you can do better than that! That's very disappointing, nobody at all! Well I'm afraid I'll just have to volunteer someone. Right come on up here Philip and show the class. That's the boy. Good lad Philip. Watch carefully now everyone. Philip got red as a beetroot and twisted up his face as he went to work. Now, class! What would you call someone that does that? Not a boy at all — a pig! Say it everyone! Come on! Pig! Pig! Pig!

That's very good. Come on now Philip you can try even harder!

What do you think Mrs Nugent? Isn't Philip a credit?

At first Mrs Nugent was shy about what he was doing but when she saw the great effort he was making she said she was proud of him. And so you should be I said. Harder, Philip, harder!

He went at it then for all he was worth and then there it sat proud as punch on the carpet of the bedroom, the best poo ever.

It really was a big one, shaped like a submarine, tapered at the end so your hole won't close with a bang, studded with currants with a little question mark of steam curling upwards.

Well done, Philip, I cried, you did it! I clapped him on the back and we all stood round admiring it. It was like a rocket that had just made it back from space and we were waiting for a little brown astronaut to open a door in the side and step out waving. Philip, I said, congratulations! I was beaming with pride at Philip's performance. I wouldn't have believed he had it in him. Philip was proud as punch too. I turned to the class. Boys, I said, who's the best pig in the whole pig school? Can you tell me? Philip they all cried without a moment's hesitation. Hip hip hooray. Clap clap the class lifted the roof. Very good easy now steady I said. Now it's time for Mrs Nugent to show us how well she can perform. Can she do poo as well as her son

Philip? We'll soon find out! Are you ready Mrs Nugent? I was waiting for her to say yes Francis indeed I am then away she'd go hoisting up her nightdress and scrunching up her red face trying to beat Philip but I'm afraid that wasn't what happened at all.

Mrs Nugent was there all right but she wasn't in her nightdress. She was wearing her day clothes and carrying a bag of stuff she had brought back from Buttsy's.

Her mouth was hanging open and she was crying again pointing to the broken mirror and the writing on the blackboard I mean wall. I looked at Philip he was white as a ghost too what was wrong with him now, hadn't he got the prize for the pig poo what more did he want? But Mr Nugent said he was in charge now. *I'll deal with this!*, he said in his Maltan Ready Rubbed[1] voice. Philip and Mrs Nugent went downstairs and then there was only me and him. He looked good Mr Nugent you had to say that for him. His hair was neatly combed across his high forehead in a jaunty wave and he had shiny leather patches on the sleeves of his jacket. He sported a pioneer pin too — that was a metal badge the Sacred Heart gave to you and it meant you were saying: *I've never taken a drink in my life and I have no intention of ever taking one either!* He stared me right in the eye he didn't flinch once. He didn't even raise his voice. He said: You won't get away with it this time! This time I'll see to it you're put where you belong. And you'll clean up *that* before you leave here with the police and the walls too for my wife's not going to do it. You've put her through enough. Well, that Mr Nugent, I thought. How was I supposed to run a proper pig school with these kind of interruptions? Mm? That's what I want to know I said. But not to Mr Nooge to myself. What I said to him was: Tell me Mr Nugent how's Buttsy getting along? He didn't answer me so I just went on talking away to him about all sorts of other stuff. He was standing with his back to the door in case I might make a run for it. But I couldn't be bothered running anywhere. The rocket had cooled now and the tail of steam was gone. I was thinking about the small astronaut appearing out of the door saluting with a grin on his face reporting for duty *sir* when this smack hits me right on the side of the face and there's the sergeant standing there rubbing his knuckles and saying: *Don't, don't!* Or you'll be the sorry man. Don't don't what was he talking about don't what? You'll clean it up, he seethed, make no mistake about that. Of course I'd clean it up if he wanted me to I don't know what he was getting all hot and bothered about. I brought it off down the garden in a bit of newspaper and broke it up with a stick behind the nettles. I was whistling. If there was a small astronaut inside it he'd had it now. Mrs Nugent was still crying when I left but Mr Nooge put his arm around her and led her inside. When the silent films are over sometimes this hand comes out of nowhere and hangs up a sign with THE END on it. That's what it was like when we were driving away in the car. The Nooges' house standing there and the hand hanging up the sign on the doorknob as phut phut off we went.

So that was the end of Nugents, for the time being anyway.

1   A brand of pipe tobacco.

MARTIN MOONEY
from Martin Mooney, *Grub* (1993)

Martin Mooney (1964–   ) was born in Belfast and educated at Queen's University, Belfast. After working in pubs in north London he returned to Belfast to write. *Grub*, the young Irish expatriate adrift in London, his four-letter name disturbingly akin to Ted Hughes's Crow, is his first volume of verse.

IN THE PARLOUR

'Every connection is a revelation.
People I pierced and tethered secretly
always dreaded the giveaway clink:
now that's all out in the open. Look
in the portfolio, towards the back,
for a picture of the man whose penis
has been sliced lengthwise, the two
halves of the glans like segments
of dusty purple fruit, pinned by metal.
You can't see it but the gold
ends in an anus-ring. That's his wife,
the skinhead aphrodite overleaf,
her clitoris bound to her nipples,
nose and navel, as if she thinks
the insurrectionary body might break up
and break away, escape from itself
into a Balkans of erogenous zones . . .
In the last photograph they stand
face to face, chin to brow, the space
between them bright with chains.
Leaning backwards, they hold each other up.'

GATE 49

If air's the poet's element each poem's a landing,
sometimes an effortless, perfect touchdown,

more often endangered and delayed. Circling
above Heathrow, peering out at landmarks

I recognized from TV and the tourist circuit,
I rehearsed my sonnet for the Special Branch,

all names and addresses. In my pocket
a sheaf of directions mapped a mock-epic.

My ears still rang as I was questioned:
'What is the purpose of your journey?

'Where will you be staying? And who with?'
I might have answered: self-imposed exile;

terra firma; with the other Irish losers —
unlikely though. They let me through

and onto the tube, where the green suburbs
led to the worming maze below the city

and to Victoria Station, the concourse
a huddle of rucksacks and beggars

like a scene from a famine or a lost war.
'Any spare change . . . homeless . . . hungry . . .'

The voices were always over my shoulder.
After each landing, the interrogation.

MADONNA AND CHILD

I bump into Grub on the Embankment,
sharing a flat pint bottle
of watered-down cough mixture
with a derelict Irishwoman.
He coughs and hawks a greeting.
She screeches 'Up the Ra',[1]
and wrecks their nest
of cardboard and newspaper.

I recognise her woollen overcoat
and the thin summer frock
worn under a back number
of the *Irish News*.[2] Her plastic bag
says Stewarts, not Safeways.
When Grub leers and snuggles close
he's enjoying my confusion:
she could be his granny or his lover.

'I was looking for my mother,'
he says. 'A last resort . . .
I haven't seen her since I was nine,
so for all anyone knows
this could be a family reunion.'
He licks the cracked brown leatherette
stretched over her cheekbones
and a cord of spittle links them for a second.

1   IRA, pronounced without the 'I'.
2   Belfast newspaper sympathetic to nationalist opinion.

GEORGE McWHIRTER
from George McWhirter, *A Staircase for All Souls: The British Columbia Suite* (1993)

George McWhirter (1939–   ) was born in the Shankill Road area of Belfast and educated at QUB and the University of British Columbia. After spending a year in Spain in 1965–66 he returned to Canada, taught in high school and then became a Creative Writing professor at the University of British Columbia. 'At Spanish Banks', a lyrical evocation of being born again on the other side, is taken from a longer sequence entitled 'Summary Weather' published in the same volume.

AT SPANISH BANKS

I

Through fog, like a long needle
Thrust through burning wool;
Through fog, the long grey neck
Of the heron, drawn.

Through grey skies
Into greyer twilight,
We remember the Christmas cardigans
Flaming on our fathers' chests.
And the tears
Sparked in our mothers' eyes
Still claw,

Liquid red,
            Like thorn trees
Brim with haw.

Below Black Mountain, the fires banked
In the dead kitchen-houses
Smoke, leaking through

The hills of slack,
Damped-down, glistening
Like nightfall.

Heart fire
Hidden in the hearth,

Sucking on the same air
That carried us, emigrant souls

Through fog
Over the grey blooms of chimney smoke.

II

Through a fog of incense
Will the taper of prayer be drawn,
Pale heron
Burning through our Lady of Perpetual Help,
Or amid the bricks of First Presbyterian Churches

Will our names be blotted with salt water,
Washed out of common register:
Disbelievers, who could not cross the threshold
Of another faith?

Who will tell our children
How we crossed over,
How we died the once
And have no other where to go
Above this fir-clad paradise?

How we bubbled through,
In our coracles

And boats,
Like blisters of quicksilver
On the great grey mirror of the waters,

Or flew, Gaels
On the rising gale,
And were made over,
                    Fresh as air?

What shall we name the craft
Our souls sailed on
In that great fly-past,
Squadron of talkers, walkers
On air?

How we flew in
Throughout the history of this country
Like birds,

Strutting round the tablecloths,
More loyal than any to those picnic places

On Dominion Days.[1]

After this new life,
Do we deserve another
Laid by,
One more island,
Tucked under cloud
Beyond Vancouver's?

III

Here we came,
The most West of that ancient West,
To the farthest compass point
Of the personality. The red flame of our heart-blood,
Forged in the hearth of hardships — the clans
And calamities, our tribal tempers
Cooled only in extremities,

These peninsulas fingering
The ice and isolation.

The trans-oceanic shudder
On the tide of souls
Out of little Ulster;

The weight,
The watershed of two seas
On its shoulder.

We rose
In weather-buoyant, dirty fair
As gulls;
                    We escaped
Ginger as foxes through the whins;

Crowded
Dark as crows,

Or sermons
By Redemptorists

At the World's End. Glided down
In our black Sunday voices.

Offended all the light
And gingham
Laid out on the lawns.

Can our clean Canadian children
With their clear Canadian talk

Ever wash
Their fathers and their mothers
Clean of tar and travel?

We watch them from our windows

Stride into their cars
And pass on, clear
As water into water,
The stream
Into the river.

IV

A daughter said,
Examining the screen
And the demonstration,
The thousands flocked

At that City Hall;[2]
The rifle butt of that man's chin
Jabbing, his face
Opened wide to let it out,

The black mouth on that Ulsterman.
Who yelled:

'Never, never! We are British.
We are British, and British
We will stay!'

And those of us —

The ten times ten Irelands
Landed here,
What are we now —

Brutish little birds
Across this great water?

Canadian,

Content
In a nearly nameless nation?

'Look, a crazy countryful
Of my Daddy and my Mummy,'

A daughter said to the image of us
In that grey mirror.

But do they know we are the dead
And born again
On the other side
Of these solemn waters?

We sleep
Listening to their voices
Washed clean of dangers.

And the consolation of this,
In the smouldering grey light;
Our admiration at
The great, grey careful birds
Lifting this country
Back out of the sea,
Laying us
To crawl,
Fledgling,
In its infinite nest of trees.

1   1 July, a day celebrating the uniting in 1867 of Upper
    and Lower Canada, New Brunswick, and Nova Scotia in
    the Dominion of Canada.
2   In Belfast.

HARRY CLIFTON
from Harry Clifton, *At The Grave Of Silone: An Abruzzo Sequence* (1993)

Harry Clifton (1952–) was born in Dublin, educated at UCD and has worked
abroad in Africa and Thailand, Italy and London. *The Deserted Route* (1992) contains a
selection of his poetry, 1973–88. 'Where We Live' is an unsentimental acceptance of
the uninvited guests who accompany us wherever we live.

WHERE WE LIVE

Where we live no longer matters
If it ever did, the difference
Between North and East, South and West,
Belfast Central, or Budapest,
Currency changed, like innocence,
For the life that was going to be ours.

Let us admit it. There are powers
No border can contain.
They sit with us, the uninvited guests,
Wherever our table is laid,
Accepting a second coffee,
Awaiting the end of the story.

They were in ourselves
From the beginning. Dark and placeless,
Asian suns, or the greys of Ulster,
Meant nothing to them. Your skies, my skies,
Everywhere in between
Was a place they could work unseen.

Here, they can rest a while
In our latest exile. Groundless,
Taking root anywhere,
Living on thin Italian air,
Our house is their house,
With the bats and the swallows,

Demons and angels, ghosting
The warm red sandstone
Of borrowed quarters. Leave us alone!
Wherever life is an open question
They have beaten us to it
Already, come into their own.

They are the lightnings
That transfigure us, our troubles —
Homeless, the ancient weather
That travels inside us
And breaks out, here or there,
The days we despair of each other.

CATHAL Ó SEARCAIGH
from Cathal Ó Searcaigh, *Homecoming/An Bealach 'na Bhaile* (1993)

Cathal Ó Searcaigh (1956–   ), Irish-speaking gay poet and playwright, was born near
Ghort an Choirce (Gortahork) in a Gaelic-speaking part of Donegal and was educated
in Limerick and at Maynooth. After working in London and Dublin he returned to his
small hill farm at the foot of Mount Errigal in Donegal where he found, as he says in
one of his poems, 'a fresh dimension'. In an interview with Liz Curtis in *Fortnight* in
April 1996, Ó Searcaigh affirmed that 'Irish is the language of my emotions. English is
a language I have learned.'

COR ÚR

Ciúnaíonn tú chugam as ceo na maidine
mus na raideoige ar d'fhallaing fraoigh,
do ghéaga ina srutháin gheala ag sní
thart orm go lúcháireach, géaga
a fháiltíonn romham le fuiseoga.

Féachann tú orm anois go glé
le lochanna móra maorga do shúl
Loch an Ghainimh ar deis, Loch Altáin ar clé,
gach ceann acu soiléir, lán den spéir
agus snua an tsamhraidh ar a ngruanna.

A FRESH DIMENSION

Like silence you come from the morning mist,
musk of bog-myrtle on your heather cloak,
your limbs — bright streams lapping joyfully
around me, limbs
that welcome me with skylarks.

You see me truly
in the majestic lakes of your eyes —
Loch an Ghainimh on the right, Loch Altán on the left,
both plainly visible, full of sky,
the complexion of summer on their cheeks.

Agus scaoileann tú uait le haer an tsléibhe
crios atá déanta as ceo bruithne na Bealtaine
scaoileann tú uait é, a rún mo chléibhe,
ionas go bhfeicim anois ina n-iomláine
críocha ionúine do cholainne

ó Log Dhroim na Gréine go hAlt na hUillinne
ón Mhalaidh Rua go Mín na hUchta,
thíos agus thuas, a chorp na háilleachta
gach cuar agus cuas, gach ball gréine,
gach ball seirce a bhí imithe i ndíchuimhne

ó bhí mé go deireanach i do chuideachta.
Tím iad arís, a chroí, na niamhrachtaí
a dhearmadaigh mé i ndíbliú na cathrach.
Ó ná ceadaigh domh imeacht arís ar fán:
clutharaigh anseo mé idir chabhsaí geala do chos,
deonaigh cor úr a chur i mo dhán.

And you loosen to the mountain air
your girdle of the hazy heat of May;
you loosen it, my love,
that I may wholly see
the beloved boundaries of your body

from Log Dhroim na Gréine to Alt na hUillinne,
from the Malaidh Rua to Mín na hUchta,
below and above, body most beautiful,
every hollow and curve, every sunspot,
every love-spot I'd forgotten

since last I was with you.
I see them again, love, the resplendence
I'd forgotten in the misery of the city.
Oh! don't let me stray again:
Shelter me here between the bright causeway of your
    legs,
add a fresh dimension to my poem.

(trans. Gabriel Fitzmaurice)

EOIN McNAMEE
from Eoin McNamee, *Resurrection Man* (1994)

Eoin McNamee (1961–) was born in Kilkeel, County Down, and educated at
Trinity College, Dublin. After spending a year in New York as a waiter he returned to
Ireland to write. *Resurrection Man*, a novel set in Belfast about a Protestant paramilitary
group, is a disturbing example of 'troubles' fiction, uncompromising in tone, graphic in
detail, where the city becomes 'a diagram of violence'. Here is a scene from an early
part of the novel in which a Catholic is picked up off the street, tortured and then
murdered. In the past, a resurrection man was a person who exhumed dead bodies to
sell to anatomists, a corpse-stealer. In this story the phrase takes on another meaning: a
person who kills others and forces them to await their resurrection, as it were.

Chapter 4

Sometimes Victor would take Big Ivan and Willie
Lambe on a night-time tour. It was a game he liked to
play. He would sit in the back of the car with his eyes
closed and tell them where they were. They argued
about how he did it. Big Ivan said it was the sense of
smell. Bread from the Ormeau bakery, hot solder near
the shipyard, the hundred yards stink from the
gasworks. Big Ivan reckoned that he mapped the city
with smells, moving along them like a surveyor along
sightlines. Willie thought of pigeons homing.

Migrations moving to some enchanted and magnetic
imperative.

Driving in and around the Shankill his recitations
became more ambitious. He knew the inhabitants of
every house and would tell their histories, give details
of women's lives lived on the intricate margins of
promiscuity. This was the bit that Willie liked. Victor
always had a ride on his arm. He told them about the
forty-five-year-old schoolteacher who waited for him
dressed as a widow. Or Sawn-off, the sixteen-year-old
with inverted nipples. Big Ivan was haunted by this
idea. He tried to imagine the nipped ends. It was part

of the imagery of women which scared him. Part of hosiery, bra sizes, the language of B-cup, D-cup, something he couldn't cope with. He thought about women's ironic conversations in changing rooms. Terrifying dialogues carried out over the lingerie counter in Anderson and Macauley's department store. Fifteen denier. Sheer.

Sometimes when they stopped the car outside the Pot Luck or Maxies Victor would stay in the back seat, his lips moving. It was an inventory of the city, a naming of parts. Baden-Powell Street, Centurion Street. Lonely places along the river. Buildings scheduled for demolition. Car parks. Quiet residential areas ideal for assassination. Isolated gospel halls. Textures of brick, rain, memory.

Joining the UVF[1] put him in touch with Big Ivan, Willie and others. Onionhead Graham. Hacksaw McGrath. He learned about serious money. First of all just going into shops and taking things. He learned that he didn't have to threaten. Shopkeepers were glad to hand over goods. He was relieving them of hidden fears, split-second images of wives and children being confronted by masked men. Then he started going on to building sites and offering protection. He believed they would sleep better by paying him. No-warning bombs were frequent. People were being gunned down in the street. He was offering them a place in random events and always made a point of calling at the same time every week. He was the means by which they could align themselves to unpredictable violence.

With his first real money he bought a black Ford Capri from Robinson's showrooms. Robinson gave him the nod when it came in. Here's a 007 for Victor he said, a fucking Bondmobile. He hinted at lethal extras, hidden blades, machine-guns behind the headlights. He was a gifted salesman and knew what Victor wanted. He regarded car showrooms as centres of subliminal knowledge. People lowered their voices instinctively. The lighting was austere and respectful. The cars were tended daily by mechanics in white overalls. He would open the car door and invite the customer to enter the interior with its smell of imitation leather, polish and warm plastic. He wanted them to feel dazed and exalted. He picked out the Capri for Victor because it had suggestions of power and generosity. It implied little margin for error, lives on the edge.

Victor was in Maxies the night they got John McGinn. They had picked him up earlier on the Crumlin Road. Maxies was to be the Romper Room. The name was taken from a children's television programme where the presenter looked through a magic mirror and saw children sitting at home. You sent in your name and address if you wanted to be seen through the mirror. The magic mirror had no glass. It was thought to contain secrets of longevity. It gave you access to the afterlife.

'What's your name?'

'John.'

'John fucking who?'

'John McGinn.'

'Through the magic mirror today we can see John McGinn. Hello John. We'll call you Johnnie. Do your friends call you Johnnie? We're your friends.'

We share your sense of bewilderment. Your intense loneliness. You were in a hurry walking down the Crumlin Road. You were going to work, to a night class, to meet a woman in a bar. We can hear her crying because you didn't turn up. We share her sadness. We will be a comfort to her.

'Over to you Victor.'

'Fucking butterfingers.'

'Hey, he near broke my foot. He's got something hard in there.'

'It's his fucking skull.'

'He levitated. I swear to God he levitated over the bar. He's a magician or something.'

'Here's a message for the fucking Pope.'

Billy McClure was the first to use the Romper Room. He was familiar with forms of initiation. He had convictions for paedophilia and knew that complicity was everything. It was a question of maintaining a ceremonial pace with pauses and intervals for reflection. There had to be a big group of participants. Twenty or thirty was good, particularly if they were close-knit. That way you could involve whole communities. You implicated wives and children, unborn generations. The reluctant were pressed forward and congratulated afterwards.

'Good man, Billy.'

'I seen teeth coming out. I definitely seen teeth. There's them on the floor over there.'

'You can come around our place give the wife one of them digs any time, Billy.'

There were long pauses for drinking. Men crowded round the bar eager to buy rounds for the whole company. The victim was ignored. He lay on the ground between the poker machine and the pool table. There was blood on the ground, bits of scalp. Victor would wander over with a drink in his hand, stir McGinn with his boot and stare blankly at him as if he were a specimen of extinction.

Later Victor would see that these events had formal structure. The men settled down after the first round of drinks. They took their jackets off and precision became important. A whole range of sounds could be extracted from the victim. The third stage came around 3 a.m. No one spoke. The men's breathing was laboured. It was 3 a.m., hour of mile-deep disappointments. Futility and exhaustion began to set in.

At 4 a.m. Victor took McGinn into the toilets where he cut his throat.

1   Protestant paramilitary organization, the Ulster Volunteer Force.

MARINA CARR
from Marina Carr, *The Mai* (first performed 1994)

Marina Carr (1964–   ) was born in Offaly and educated at UCD. *The Mai*, a memory play in two Acts, has similarities with Friel's *Dancing at Lughnasa* (1990), but in terms of theme and mood is reminiscent of Eugene O'Neill. Here is the first Act; as an exercise in composition you might consider writing the second Act yourself.

Characters

THE MAI, age 40
MILLIE, her daughter, age 16 and 30
GRANDMA FRAOCHLÁN, age 100
ROBERT, The Mai's husband, age 42
BECK, her sister, age 37
CONNIE, her sister, age 38
JULIE, her aunt, age 75
AGNES, her aunt, age 61

Time

Act One, Summer 1979
Act Two, one year later

ACT ONE

A room with a huge bay window. Sounds of swans and geese, off. MILLIE *is standing at the window* (NOTE: MILLIE *remains onstage throughout the play*). *Enter* ROBERT. *In one arm he has a travel bag, in the other a cello case. He looks around, examines the room in amazement, opens the double doors upstage, sees a music stand, turns aside thinking, and brings the bag and cello case into the room. He closes the door.*

THE MAI *passes the window, turns to look out on Owl Lake, hears a cello note, freezes — it stops — and decides she is dreaming. She enters the room, wearing a summer dress and carrying an armful of books. She places the books on the bookshelf, a few here, a few there. Drawn to the window, she looks out at the lake, waiting, watching. She places a few more books, then moves again to the window.*

A low cello note floats across the room. THE MAI — *startled — freezes, listens; the cello plays, melodic, romantic, beautiful.* THE MAI *moves to the double doors. She slides them across to reveal* ROBERT *engrossed in his playing. She listens, wanting to interrupt, yet also not. Now the piece finishes. Silence. For the first time* ROBERT *looks at her, cello bow in his hand.*

ROBERT: Well — well — well.
    He taps her shoulder, hip bone, ankle, on each of the 'Wells'.
THE MAI: Just look at you.
ROBERT: You're as beautiful as ever.
THE MAI: Am I?
    Now he plays the cello bow across her breasts. THE MAI *laughs.*
    Softer.
ROBERT: Like this? Hmm?
THE MAI: Yeah.
ROBERT (*He waves the bow around the room*): What's all this?
THE MAI: I built it.
ROBERT: All by yourself? How?
THE MAI: Just did.
ROBERT: And Owl Lake, my God, it's incredible.

THE MAI: You'll see it better in the morning.

ROBERT: In the morning. Will I? How did you know I'd come back?

THE MAI: Don't know — just knew.

ROBERT lifts THE MAI and carries her to a chair by the bay window, taking a bag from his belongings en route. He takes a scarf from the bag and ties it around her neck. It's lovely.

ROBERT (*He produces perfume, tears the wrapper, and sprays it all over her*): It's the one you wear, isn't it, or have you changed?

THE MAI: It's the one I wear.

ROBERT: And these (*flowers*) are for you.

He produces a bottle of whiskey and a cigar.

And this is for you (*whiskey*) and I'll have a shot as well.

THE MAI goes to the drinks cabinet, pours the whiskeys. MILLIE moves forward, looks at ROBERT, looks at THE MAI.

Now let me see, is it Orla or Millie?

THE MAI: Millie.

ROBERT: Millie.

THE MAI: She's sixteen now.

ROBERT: I bought sweets for the children — but I suppose you're too big for sweets.

THE MAI: She's not too big for sweets yet.

ROBERT places a box of sweets in MILLIE's hands.

MILLIE: Where were you?

ROBERT: Here — there —

MILLIE: Everywhere. We were here all the time and in the old house.

ROBERT: I know you were.

MILLIE: Mom, will I get the others?

THE MAI: Not yet, in a little while.

MILLIE: Your jumper's lovely.

THE MAI: You'd better hide it or she'll have it on her.

ROBERT (*He takes off the jumper*): Here, put it on. (*He puts it on her*)

THE MAI: It's lovely on you — have a spray of perfume. And don't tell the others yet. I want it to be a surprise for them.

ROBERT and THE MAI exit hand in hand to the bedroom. MILLIE looks after them, moves around cleaning up, goes to the study, sounds a note on the cello, listens, looks out on Owl Lake.

MILLIE: When I was eleven The Mai sent me into the butcher's to buy a needle and thread. It was the day Robert left us. No explanations, no goodbyes, he just got into his car with his cello and drove away. So The Mai and I went into town and sat in the Bluebell Hotel where The Mai downed six Paddys and red and I had six lemon-and-limes. Then The Mai turned to me with her sunglasses on, though it was the middle of winter, she turned to me and said, Millie, would you ever run up to the butcher's and get me a needle and thread. Now at eleven I knew enough to know that needles and thread were bought in the drapery, but I thought maybe it was a special kind of thread The Mai wanted and because of the day that was in it I decided not to argue with her. So up I went to the butcher's and asked for a needle and a spool of thread and of course they didn't have any. Back I went to the Bluebell, sat beside The Mai and said rather gruffly, Mom, they don't sell needles and thread in the butcher's. Do they not, sweetheart? The Mai whispered and started to cry. Are you all right, Mom? I said. I'm grand, she said. Go up there and order me a Paddy and red. When I came back with the drinks The Mai said, Don't you worry about a thing, Millie, your Dad'll come back and we will have the best of lives.

Lights change. It's later that evening. Enter THE MAI in a slip, wildly happy. She collects a bottle of whiskey off the cabinet and moves across to the window.

THE MAI: Look at the swans taking flight, Millie, aren't they beautiful?

And she drifts off.

MILLIE: The Mai set about looking for that magic thread that would stitch us together again and she found it at Owl Lake, the most coveted site in the county. It was Sam Brady who sold the site to The Mai. For years he'd refused all offers, offers from hoteliers, publicans, restaurateurs, rich industrialists, Yanks, and then he turned round and gave it to The Mai for a song. When asked by irate locals why he'd sold it to The Mai, a blow-in, Sam merely answered, *Highest Bidder!*

And so the new house was built and, once she had it the way she wanted, The Mai sat in front of this big window here, her chin moonward, a frown on her forehead, as if she were pulsing messages to some remote star which would ricochet and lance Robert wherever he was, her eyes closed tightly, her temples throbbing as her lips formed two words noiselessly. Come home — come home.

Light change. Daytime. The cello bursts into song, wild, buoyant, practising. A huge currach oar moves across the window with a red flag on it. CONNIE appears, stares in the window, nosey. She bangs the oar in her nosiness.

GRANDMA F (*Off*): Would ya watch where ya're goin'!

CONNIE (*Shouts back*): Would you ever stop givin' orders from the car!

GRANDMA F (*Grumbling*): Shoulda carried ih meself!

CONNIE: Ara dry up! Millie, how are you? Give us a hand with this, will you? Would it go through the window?

MILLIE *opens the window.*

THE MAI: Ah you've arrived.

CONNIE: Hello Mai.

THE MAI: Easy, easy, mind the window.

GRANDMA F (*Off*): Mind me oar!

CONNIE: God give me patience with that one! Nearly got us killed, her and her bloody oar.

THE MAI: Leave it outside, we'll sort it out later.

CONNIE: She'll nag us till it's in the bed beside her.

THE MAI: Ara for God's sake, she's not sleepin' with it now!

CONNIE: Don't even ask! How are ya, *a stóir?*[1]

THE MAI: Toppin', and yourself?

CONNIE: The house is amazing, Mai, beautiful.

She hears the cello.

So he's here?

THE MAI: Yeah, isn't it wonderful?

CONNIE: Here, try it up this way.

GRANDMA FRAOCHLÁN *enters, leaning on* MILLIE.

GRANDMA F: Show! Did ya do any damage ta ih?

CONNIE: It's fine! Would you move out of the way or you'll be knocked down!

GRANDMA F: Ah Mai, great ta see ya, *a chroí.*[2]

THE MAI: You've poor Connie moidered. (*She kisses* GRANDMA FRAOCHLÁN) Could we not put it in the garage?

GRANDMA F: Well then ya can puh me in tha garage along wud ih.

CONNIE: That's the place for ya!

GRANDMA F (*Nods towards the study*): An' whin did he arrive?

CONNIE: There! I have it! Millie, run round and catch it!

GRANDMA F: Aisy, aisy, go aisy an ih!

CONNIE: Would you ever! Honest ta God, you'd put years on me!

GRANDMA F: Sorry, *a stóir,* buh it's all I've left of him now. Why didn't ya build a bigger winda, Mai?

CONNIE: I've never seen one bigger! Ya needn't be turnin' on The Mai now! We had to saw through the banister to get it into our house.

GRANDMA F: Every time I move, ye have a hullabaloo abouh me oar!

CONNIE: Go in! Go in! Before I throw ya in the lake. We have it! We have it. (*The oar is finally in*)

GRANDMA F: Me bags, where are tha?

CONNIE: I've only two hands, Jesus!

THE MAI: How's Derek?

CONNIE: Askin' for you, the kids too.

GRANDMA F: I feel a bih wake, need a piece a chocolah. Connie, where's me chocolah?

CONNIE: Comin'! Comin'!

She goes off. THE MAI *leads* GRANDMA FRAOCHLÁN *in.*

GRANDMA F: Ya couldn'ta chose a nicer place, Mai, on'y —

THE MAI: Only what?

GRANDMA F: Well's noh tha sea, is ih? Why didn't ya move back ta Connemara like ya said ya would?

THE MAI: Ah I wouldn't get Principalship of another school so easy.

GRANDMA F: Ya'd be employed anawhere. Ya built this house for him, didn't ya?

THE MAI: And for myself and for the children.

GRANDMA F: Ya survived this long withouh him, why'a ya bringin' all this an ya'arself agin?

CONNIE *enters with bags.*

CONNIE: There you go.

GRANDMA F: Where's th'other bag?

CONNIE: Millie must've brought it in.

GRANDMA F: And me pinsion walleh, where's thah?

CONNIE: How'd I know! Where'd you put it?

GRANDMA F: Gev ih ta you.

CONNIE: Did you? When — (*She looks in handbag*) — Oh, right, there you go.

GRANDMA F: Chocolah.

CONNIE: Which bag is it in?

GRANDMA F: Can't amimber, look in all a thim.

CONNIE *glares at her.*

THE MAI: Here. I have chocolate bought in for you.

GRANDMA F (*Taking the chocolate*): And where's tha hundert pound tha President gev me for me birta?

CONNIE *raises her hands in exasperation.*

Well, where is ih?

CONNIE (*Growls*): You spent it!

GRANDMA F: Did I? Whin?

CONNIE: Last week.

GRANDMA F: On whah?

CONNIE: On tobacco and pipes and chocolate and snuff and cigarettes and the Lord knows what!

GRANDMA F: Thah's arrigh' so. Did I buy anathin' for you?

CONNIE: No, you didn't.

GRANDMA F: Very thoughtless a me, it's th'auld memory. Sorry, Connie.

CONNIE (*Lighting a cigarette, relieved the transfer is nearly over*): Ara I don't want anything.

THE MAI *and* CONNIE *exit.* CONNIE *beckons* THE MAI, *wants to see around the house.*

GRANDMA F: Millie, a glass a mulberry wine there ta puh manners an tha ghosts.

MILLIE (*Gives her a glass*): Grandma Fraochlán?

GRANDMA F (*Dreamily, eating chocolate and drinking wine*): Hah, lovey?

MILLIE: The name alone evokes a thousand memories in me. She was known as the Spanish beauty though she was born and bred on Inis Fraochlán, north of 'Bofin.[3] She was the result of a brief tryst between an ageing island spinster and a Spanish or Moroccan sailor — no one is quite sure — who was never heard of or seen since the night of her conception. There were many stories about him as there are about those who appear briefly in our lives and change them forever. Whoever he was, he left Grandma Fraochlán his dark skin and a yearning for all that was exotic and unattainable.

THE MAI *enters*.

GRANDMA F (*Looking around*): I don't know abouh all this, Mai.

THE MAI: You're just like the rest of that Connemara click, always hoping that things will turn out for the worst! Well they won't! Because Robert is back and he's here for good and that's all I care about.

GRANDMA F: I won't open me mouh agin!

THE MAI: Ah now don't be like that. You know I'm delighted to have you here. Grandma Fraochlán, you don't realize how awful it's been these last few years, and now I have the chance of being happy again and I can't bear anyone to say anything that'll take that away.

GRANDMA F: Ya shouldn't think like thah, Mai. Ya're strong, ya must be, look ah all ya done this last few years. Anaway, how is he?

THE MAI: Never seen him more alive. You'd never think we were married seventeen years. I feel like a bride all over again.

GRANDMA F: An' ya look like wan too. Ya're th' image a Ellen, God rest her.

THE MAI: Am I?

CONNIE *enters*.

GRANDMA F: More an' more every day. Ellen goh all tha brains an' all tha beauhy a my loh, just like you did ouha Ellen's loh.

CONNIE: And I suppose Beck and myself are scarecrows.

GRANDMA F (*Ignoring her*): In me darkest hour I often wisht thah God had taken wan a th'others an' left me Ellen. Isn't thah an awful wish from tha mouth of a mother?

CONNIE: You should be struck down.

GRANDMA F: An' she was so proud a her three little girls — Mai, Connie an' Beck. Didn't she pick lovely names for ye ah a time in Connemara whin everywan was called Máire or Bridgín or Cait. Oh she was way ahead a her time —

CONNIE: Ah don't start.

GRANDMA F: Won scholarships an' prizes inta tha best schools an' colleges i' tha country —

CONNIE: We know! We know! (*Raconteur voice*) She was the only woman in her class doing Medicine the year she entered the Dublin university, and she did it all be herself, I had nothin' in those days —

GRANDMA F: Shame on ya mockin' ya'ar own mother! And thin thah summer in Dublin, halfway through her college degree, an a wild nigh' a drink an' divilment, me darlin' girl goh pregnant be a brickie.

CONNIE: Ara give over!

GRANDMA F (*Lost in memory*): Oh Lord, nineteen years a age, she had ta marry him, whah else could she do, ih was nineteen-thirty-eight.

A few mock tears from CONNIE.

Ya'd want ta show a bih more respect.

CONNIE: I've run out of respect.

THE MAI: We know all this, Grandma Fraochlán.

GRANDMA F: Thin heed ih! Ya're too like her for my peace a mind!

CONNIE (*Listening to cello, looking around*): Well I don't know how you did it, Mai, it's a mansion — I mean Derek and I are on very good incomes and we'd never attempt something like this. Has he written anything worth talking about these last few years?

THE MAI: He has. Loads.

CONNIE: That's all very well but what're ye goin' to do for bread and butter.

THE MAI: He's going back teaching in the college in the autumn.

CONNIE: I thought he walked out of there after Julie's Michael gettin' him the job an' all.

THE MAI: Well, he's sorted it out, they're delighted to have him.

GRANDMA F (*Who has been dreaming and muttering to herself during the above exchanges*): Would ya say I'll go ta heaven, Mai?

THE MAI: Why wouldn't you, if there's such a place.

GRANDMA F: If indeed, buh seriously now d'ya think I'm paradise material or am I wan a Lucifer's wicked auld childer?

THE MAI (*Laughs*): Paradise material definitely.

GRANDMA F: I bin havin' woeful drames lately. I keep dramin' I'm in hell an' I'm tha on'y wan there apart from Satan himself —

CONNIE: He'd be well matched.

GRANDMA F: An' through a glass ceilin' I can see everywan I ever cared abouh, up beyant in heaven, an' d'ya know tha worst part a tha drame is Satan an' meself gets an like a house an fire. We're there laughin' an' skitterin' like two schoolgirls. Isn't thah a frigh'?

THE MAI: Ara it's only a dream. Any word from Beck?

CONNIE: She rang last week. Have you heard from her?

THE MAI: Not in months.

CONNIE: She's in great form, met a new man.

GRANDMA F: Another wan.

CONNIE: This time she said it's for real.

GRANDMA F: That's whah she said tha last time an' tha time before. Whah does he do?

CONNIE: I told you I didn't ask her.

GRANDMA F: Well whah does his father do or did ya noh think a askin' thah aither?

THE MAI: These things don't matter anymore.

GRANDMA F: I remember tha first time I met tha nine-fingered fisherman. Is mise Tomás, scipéir, mac scipéara,[4] he said. I knew where he was comin' from, wan sentence, wan glance a his blue eyes an' me heart was in his fist.

THE MAI: Has she any plans to come home?

CONNIE: You know Beck. Well I'd better be off.

THE MAI: Have something to eat first. I've dinner made for you.

CONNIE: I can't, Mai, I've a hundred and one things to do and Derek's expecting me, but thanks anyway.

GRANDMA F (*Who has been muttering to herself*): Buh ih doesn't mahher — I'm proud a Beck, proud a Connie an' proud a Tha Mai. Three great women! (*A bit tipsy, gets up to embrace them*)

THE MAI: Sit down, *a stóir.*

GRANDMA F: Mighy women tha loh a ye!

CONNIE: She's off!

GRANDMA F: If Ellen could see ye now! D'ya think she'd be happy wud tha way I rared ye? I'm so proud a ye! (*Swinging her glass, she spills the wine*)

THE MAI: Mind the wine!

CONNIE: Jesus, The Mai's new rug!

GRANDMA FRAOCHLÁN *pays no heed, continues swinging the glass.*
Bye, *a stóir.*
She kisses GRANDMA FRAOCHLÁN. *Exits.*

GRANDMA F (*In full flight, ignores* CONNIE's *exit*): An' I'm proud a Beck too, though she's flittin' from wan country ta tha next wud noh a stitch an her back nor a shillin' in her purse. Doesn't mahher. I'm proud. Mighy proud.

THE MAI *and* CONNIE *drift off during this. We see* THE MAI *waving* CONNIE *off.*

MILLIE: Grandma Fraochlán became a little sentimental after a few glasses of mulberry wine, and after a few more she began to call up the ghosts and

would wrestle with them until sleep finally overtook her. These ghosts were as numerous as they were colourful. One of her favourite buddies from the ghost department was the Sultan of Spain.

GRANDMA F (*Incensed*): Now Sultan! You give me wan good reason why women can't own harems full a men whin ih is quihe obvious thah men owns harems full a women! G'wan! I'm listenin'! G'wan! Answer me thah! An' cuh ouh thah desert swagger! (*She listens earnestly, then with growing annoyance*) Seafóid[5] Sultan! Nowhere in tha holy books does ih say thah! (*Listens*) I'll geh upseh if I want ta! G'wan! Off wud ya'arself! There's no gettin' through ta you! Don't know why I even waste me time wud ya! Off! An' God help tha harem thah has ta puh up wud ya!

MILLIE: And she'd banish him back to his tent in the desert or to his palace in Morocco or his villa in Spain or to the exotic ghost section of her ancient and fantastical memory.

GRANDMA F (*Putting on lipstick*): Thah you, Tomás?

MILLIE: A more intimate ghost was the nine-fingered fisherman, Grandma Fraochlán's beloved husband, who was drowned in a fishing accident some sixty years ago.

GRANDMA F (*Holds up lipstick*): Remember ya bough' ih for me — 1918 ah tha Cleggan fair — still have ih — Why wouldn't I? Remember tha Cleggan fair, me nine-fingered fisherman, we wint across from Fraochlán in tha currach, me thirty-eighth birta, a glorious day — (*Listens, laughs softly*) I knew ya'd remember, ya'd goh me a boult a red cloth an' I'd made a dress an' a sash for me hair. Remember, Tomás, remember, an' ya toult me I was tha Queen a th'ocean an' thah natin' mahherd in tha wide worlt on'y me. An' we danced ah tha Cleggan fair an' ya whispert in me ear — sweet natin's — sweet natin's.

GRANDMA FRAOCHLÁN *dances with the air; cello provides music, Irish with a flavour of Eastern. Let her dance a while. The music stops.* GRANDMA FRAOCHLÁN *stands there lost in memory.* ROBERT *enters.*

ROBERT: You OK there, Grandma Fraochlán?

GRANDMA F (*Wiping off lipstick*): Grand, grand.

ROBERT: Settling in all right?

GRANDMA F (*Sharply*): Are you?

ROBERT (*Smiles*): Yes, it's lovely here.

GRANDMA F (*Looking at him, the Mirada Fuerte*):[6] I think ya on'y cem back because ya couldn't find anathin' behher elsewhere an' ya'll be gone as soon as ya think ya've found somethin' behher —

ROBERT: You don't know the whole story and I'd advise you not to be —

GRANDMA F: I know enough! Ya didn't see her strugglin' wud thim youngsters, all yours — in case ya've forgotten — scrimpin' an' scrapin' ta get this house built an' whin everythin's laid an, you appear an tha doorstep wud a bunch a flowers. Ah! (*Gesture of dismissal*)

ROBERT: People change.

GRANDMA F: I'm noh an this planeh wan hundert year withouh learnin' a thing or two. People don't change, Robert, tha don't change ah all!

ROBERT: Well maybe if you and the rest of The Mai's family weren't livin' in our ear —

GRANDMA F: I'm here as an invihed guest in Tha Mai's new house an' I'll lave whin Tha Mai axes me ta lave an' noh before!

ROBERT: Grandma Fraochlán, I don't want to fight with you.

GRANDMA F: Why couldn't ya a just lave her alone? Ya come back here an' fill tha girl's head wud all sourts a foolish hope. Ya'ar own father left ya'ar mother, didn't he?

ROBERT: He never left her! He went to America for a few years. It was after the War, he had to get work, but he came back, didn't he!

GRANDMA F: An' thousands sted, war or no war, or brung their wives an' childer wud em. Buh noh you, no, an' noh ya'ar father, an' sure as I'm sittin' here, ya'll noh be stoppin' long, because we can't help repeatin', Robert, we repeah an' we repeah, th'orchestration may be different but tha tune is allas tha same.

ROBERT *exits*. GRANDMA FRAOCHLÁN *dozes. Light changes.* BECK *enters with a gift.*

BECK: Now you're not to tell anyone.

GRANDMA F: I won't, I won't, whah is ih?

BECK: The Mai'd kill me if she ever found out.

GRANDMA FRAOCHLÁN *opens the gift.*

Happy birthday, Grandma Fraochlán.

GRANDMA F: An opium pipe. Glory be, Beck, ya didn't!

BECK: Didn't I tell you I would.

GRANDMA F: I haven't seen wan a these in — in —

BECK: Is it the right kind?

GRANDMA F: Sure ih is. (*She takes a puff to test it*) There's greah pullin' in thah — Now did ya geh anathin' ta puh in ih?

BECK: Course I did. We'll have a wee smoke later on down in your room.

GRANDMA F (*Still examining it*): Wud tha windas open, aye. We couldn't have wan now, could we?

BECK (*A look around*): What ya think? (A *devilish smile* from GRANDMA FRAOCHLÁN) Come on.

GRANDMA F: Ya're th'original angel, Beck, th'original angel.

They exit. *Evening. Lights up on* THE MAI *and* ROBERT. *He plays a piece for her. She listens.*

ROBERT (*Finishing*): Well?

THE MAI: It's very dark.

ROBERT: You're not crazy about it.

THE MAI: No, it's beautiful but —

ROBERT: But what?

THE MAI: I thought you'd write something lighter — happier — that's all.

ROBERT: Maybe next time I will.

THE MAI: Why'd you come back?

ROBERT: Why'd I come back? Difficult one — it's not so great out there, Mai.

THE MAI: Is it not?

ROBERT: No.

THE MAI: And I thought you came back for me.

ROBERT: I think maybe I did — you really want to know what brought me back?

THE MAI: Yeah I do.

ROBERT: I dreamt that you were dead and my cello case was your coffin and a carriage drawn by two black swans takes you away from me over a dark expanse of water and I ran after this strange hearse shouting, Mai, Mai, and it seemed as if you could hear my voice on the moon, and I'm running, running, running over water, trees, mountains, though I've long lost sight of the carriage and of you — And I wake, pack my bags, take the next plane home.

THE MAI: So you've come back to bury me, that what you're sayin'?

ROBERT: Why do you always have to look for the bleakest meaning in everything?

THE MAI: It's usually the right one.

ROBERT: Not everything has to be final and tragic, Mai, not everything. And dreaming about death always means something else. Dreams aren't that vulgar, they're coy, elusive things. They have to be, the amount of times I've dreamt about you dying, and here you are healthy as a trout.

THE MAI: And just how many times have you dreamt of me dying?

ROBERT: I don't remember.

THE MAI: That many?

ROBERT: Don't tell me you haven't dreamt about me dying?

THE MAI: Once — only once — Was the night before we got married —

ROBERT: Yeah —

THE MAI: Remember Grandma Fraochlán had put you sleeping in the kitchen in front of the range?

ROBERT: Yeah —

THE MAI: And I was in the back room with Connie and Beck?

ROBERT: Yeah — And you crept out to me when the whole house was asleep.

THE MAI: Yeah — And we drank all Grandma Fraochlán's mulberry wine.

ROBERT: Yeah — And we had to whisper so we wouldn't wake the old crone.

THE MAI: Yeah —

ROBERT (*Looking at her*): So, your dream.

THE MAI: I dreamt it was the end of the world and before my eyes an old woman puts a knife through your heart and you die on the grey pavement, and for some reason I find this hilarious though I also know your loss will be terrible. Then the scene changes and I'm a child walking up a golden river and everything is bright and startling. At the bend in the river I see you coming towards me whistling through two leaves of grass — you're a child too — and as you come nearer I smile and wave, so happy to see you, and you pass me saying, Not yet, not yet, not for thousands and thousands of years. And I turn to look after you and you're gone and the river is gone and away in the distance I see a black cavern and I know it leads to nowhere and I start walking that way because I know I'll find you there.

ROBERT: That's an awful fuckin' dream to tell anyone.

THE MAI: Well, y'asked me to tell you.

ROBERT: The night before we got married?

THE MAI: Yeah — remember it like it was yesterday.

A pause. They look at one another. Hold a while.

ROBERT: Mai, I've finished nothing this past five years — nothing I'm proud of.

THE MAI: Have you not?

ROBERT: I need you around me —

THE MAI: So you came back for your work?

ROBERT: No. Not only — All those years I was away, not a day went by I didn't think of you, not a day someone or something didn't remind me of you. When I'd sit down to play, I'd play for you, imagining you were there in the room with me.

THE MAI: I used to talk to you all the time.

ROBERT: I used to hear you.

THE MAI: Used you?

He looks at her, plays her toes with his cello bow.

ROBERT: Don't you know you are and were and always will be the only one? Don't you know, no matter what the hurtling years may do to us?

He hands her tickets.

THE MAI: Tickets — For Paris — Both of us?

ROBERT: And why not?

THE MAI: I've never been to Paris.

ROBERT: I know. C'mon, let's go into town for dinner.

MILLIE: Can I go with ye?

ROBERT: Ah? (*He defers to* THE MAI)

THE MAI: Some other evening.

MILLIE: Tch!

ROBERT: Poor Millie's bored.

MILLIE: Well I am! There's nothin' to do round here except chase tractors or listen to Grandma Fraochlán blatherin' about the nine-fingered fisherman.

ROBERT: I'll take you in tomorrow for a surprise.

ROBERT *and* THE MAI *go out.*

MILLIE (*Watching them depart*): Maybe we did go into town the following day, I don't remember. It is beyond me now to imagine how we would've spent that day, where we would've gone, what we would've talked about, because when we meet now, which isn't often and always by chance, we shout and roar till we're exhausted or in tears or both, and then crawl away to lick our wounds already gathering venom for the next bout. We usually start with the high language. He'll fling the Fourth Commandment at me, *HONOUR THY FATHER!* And I'll hiss back, a father has to be honourable before he can be honoured, or some facetious rubbish like that. And we'll pace ourselves like professionals, all the way to the last round, to the language of the gutter, where he'll call me a fuckin' cunt and I'll call him an ignorant bollix! We're well matched, neither ever gives an inch, we can't, it's life and death as we see it. And that's why I cannot remember that excursion into town if it ever occurred. What I do remember, however, is one morning a year and a half later when Robert and I drove into town to buy a blue nightgown and a blue bedjacket for The Mai's waking. Still reeling from the terrible events of that weekend, we walked through The Midland drapery, the floorboards creaking, the other shoppers falling silent and turning away, they knew why we were there and what we'd come for, afraid to look yet needing to see, not wanting to move too closely lest they breathed in the damaged air of Owl Lake that hung about us like a wayward halo. No shroud for The Mai. It was her wish. In one of those throwaway conversations which only become significant with time, The Mai had said she wanted to be buried in blue. So here we were in a daze fingering sky blues, indigo blues, navy blues, lilac blues, night blues, finally settling on a watery blue silk affair. Business done, we moved down the aisle towards the door. A little boy, escaping his mother, ran from the side, banged off Robert and sent him backwards into a display stand. About him on the floor, packets of needles and spools of thread all the colours of the rainbow.

Daylight, sunshine, cello music, sound of children playing off. BECK *enters in swimming togs and a bathrobe, screeching and yelping from the lake.*

Enter THE MAI *with a boy's trousers, sewing them.*

BECK: Well that's the end of my swimming for another summer. (*She pours a drink*) Will you have one?

THE MAI: When I've finished this (*sewing*).

BECK (*Goes to window, waves at the children*): You're so lucky to have them all. I don't suppose I'll ever have a child now.

THE MAI: You're still young enough.

BECK: Mai, I'm thirty-seven.

THE MAI: Wasn't St Elizabeth ninety-two when she had John the Baptist?

BECK: You never take no for an answer, do you?

THE MAI: And didn't the Duchess have Grandma Fraochlán when she was forty-five and didn't Aunt Julie have Barclay when she was forty-three?

BECK: And didn't she make a right job of him! No, I won't have any now. I suppose there has to be one spinster in every generation.

THE MAI: Honest to God, Beck, you'd swear you were on your last legs. Tell me more about this Wesley fella?

BECK: Not much to tell.

THE MAI: Don't be so cagey, you know I'm dyin' to hear.

BECK: He's fifty-three and he thought I was thirty. He was married once before and he has two teenage sons who I got on better with than Wesley. I like being around young people, Mai — anyway Wesley was jealous, he was like a big baby sulkin' in the background but I didn't care. Brian, the older one, used to take me surfing and on my thirty-seventh birthday, thirty-first to them, he drove down from his college, a whole hundred miles, just to give me a birthday present. Of course Wesley couldn't handle this at all.

THE MAI: Poor Wesley.

BECK: Yeah — he wasn't really my sort, too educated for me, though I must say I've always been attracted to educated men, probably because of my own dismal academic record.

THE MAI: You could've gone on and studied if you'd wanted.

BECK: Not at all, I'm thick. Always was.

THE MAI: You were never thick.

BECK: Five *Es* in my Leaving Cert.[7]

THE MAI: Will you see him when you go back?

BECK: Mai, I'm married to him.

THE MAI: You're not!

BECK: In a registry office five months ago, don't ask me why.

THE MAI: Ah, why didn't you tell us?

BECK: Because I'm getting a divorce.

THE MAI: Ah you're not, Beck. Listen, congratulations anyway. (*Gets up to kiss her*)

BECK: Ara would you stop! Now don't say a word to anyone. The last thing I need is the Connemara click in on top of me.

THE MAI: I won't open me mouth. Was it a lovely ceremony?

BECK: It was, it was wonderful.

THE MAI: I would've gone. Why didn't you invite me, Beck? Do you have any photos?

BECK: I burnt them all.

THE MAI: Ah you didn't, what happened?

BECK: The only reason he married me was because he was afraid of getting old and being left alone.

THE MAI: Is that what he said?

BECK: No, of course that's not what he said. He made it seem like he was doing me a favour.

THE MAI: Well it's not exactly Tristan and Isolde —

BECK: Don't get me wrong, he was kind, kind enough until one night I got a little drunk and believed myself to be a lot closer to him than I actually was and I told him I wasn't thirty-one and that I wasn't in fact a qualified teacher but a low-down waitress.

THE MAI: Ah, Beck, why did you have to tell him all those lies in the first place?

BECK: Mai, you don't know what it's like out there when you're nothing and you have nothing, because you've always shone, always, you've always been somebody's favourite or somebody's star pupil or somebody's wife, or somebody's mother or somebody's teacher. Imagine a place where you are none of those things.

THE MAI: It hasn't always been easy for me, Beck.

BECK: You don't know what you're talking about.

THE MAI: You didn't see me after Robert left me! What a struggle it was. You never wrote or phoned and Connie never came to see me, and yet the pair of ye kept in contact all the time, and now you sit in my new house and tell me I don't know what it's like.

BECK: I never knew what to write, Mai. You know I'm useless in a crisis.

THE MAI: You don't have to be. That's the easy option. You've an awful lot to offer anyone, if you'd just believe in yourself.

BECK: The truth is, Mai, I've damn all to offer anyone. I can barely stay alive myself without getting involved in your hopeless affairs with Robert.

THE MAI: He's my husband and he's back and I love him, so don't you freeway in here and tell me it's hopeless.

BECK: Well it is, and Connie says so too.

THE MAI: Well why doesn't she say it to my face? I never see Connie anymore. Anytime I suggest we meet she's busy. I'm fed up of it, Beck.

BECK: Well that's between Connie and yourself, none of my business.

THE MAI: Ye're thick as thieves, always were.

BECK: You had Grandma Fraochlán, we had one another.

THE MAI: That's no explanation. That's childhood. We had no choice then.

BECK: And we've had none since! Wesley said I had the deportment of a serving girl — low voice, head down, don't interrupt anyone.

THE MAI: It's a very cruel thing to say to anyone.

BECK: Well it's the truth, isn't it!

THE MAI: It's not how I would've described you or how anyone who cared for you would.

BECK: Doesn't matter. It's over now anyway.

THE MAI: You won't go back to him?

BECK: I never give second chances, Mai. Don't believe in them. Anyway I knew it wouldn't last.

THE MAI: Then why did you marry him?

BECK: Ah I don't know.

THE MAI: You don't know?

BECK (*Exploding*): I told you I was thick! I don't know! Maybe because everything I touch turns to shite! Now will you stop asking me all these questions!

THE MAI: I'm sorry, Beck — I didn't mean to —

BECK: Don't apologize! I'm the one who's sorry. I've no right to take it out on you. I'm just a bit under the weather these days. I'm thirty-seven years of age, Mai, and what've I got to show for it? Nothing. Absolutely nothing!

THE MAI: You're still young, Beck. Why don't you do some kind of course here, get a job, settle down?

BECK: I don't see the point, Mai. I can't think of any good reasons to do anything ever again. (*Drinks*) THE MAI *and* BECK *exit.*

MILLIE: Needless to say, within days the story of Beck's liaison had travelled through the family like wildfire. None of The Mai's doing. No, Beck herself felt the need to tell everyone that she had been married, however briefly. I think maybe to raise herself a little in everyone's estimation.

JULIE *and* AGNES *appear in fur coats, with similar handbags, outside the window, peering in, nosing around.*

AGNES (*Looking around furtively*): Well, what do you think?

JULIE: A lot of money's been spent here. I wonder where they got it from.

AGNES: Everythin's on credit these days. Would you look at the size of that window?

JULIE (*Peering in the window*): An ordinary house wouldn't do them. No, The Mai'd have to do the bigshot thing. I'd say they haven't two pennies to rub together. Is it my eyesight or is that a Persian rug?

AGNES (*Taking out glasses*): Show. It is. It is.

JULIE (*Taking glasses off* AGNES, *looking through them*): Not a mock one?

AGNES: Show. (*Taking glasses back*) The genuine article.

JULIE: They don't fall off the trees.

AGNES: You can be sure of that, oh but isn't the view magnificent?

JULIE: They could've bought a picture of a view.
They pass across the window.

MILLIE: Two of The Mai's aunts, bastions of the Connemara click, decided not to take the prospect of a divorcée in the family lying down. So they arrived one lovely autumn day armed with novenas, scapulars and leaflets on the horrors of premarital sex which they distributed amongst us children along with crisp twenty-pound notes. Births, marriages and deaths were their forte and by Christ, if they had anything to do with it, Beck would stay married even if it was to a tree.

JULIE *and* AGNES *enter, disarmed of their furs, but not their handbags which go everywhere with them.*

THE MAI (*Off*): Make ye'erselves at home, I'll be in in a minute.

AGNES: Well that was lovely.

JULIE: It was. I wonder how much the site cost.

AGNES: What is it? Half an acre? You wouldn't get much change out of eight grand, not with a view like that.

JULIE: Eight grand! Where did The Mai get hold of money like that with all those young ones?

AGNES: They're a fine healthy clatter.

JULIE: And she's manners on them. I'll say that for The Mai, she's a bit of *slacht*[8] on that brood.

AGNES: They've all plenty to say for themselves.

JULIE: Maybe a bit too much to say, and the posh accents of them. Must be the schools she's sendin' them to. They didn't learn to speak like that around here.

AGNES: That's for sure.

JULIE: Still, they set to the washin' up and not a gig or a protest out a one of them.

AGNES: And Robert there helpin' to serve up the dinner.

JULIE: Thanks be to the Lord Jesus, though it might be just for show.

AGNES: No, I was watching him, he knew where everything was and what needed to be done.

JULIE: Thanks be to God he's back, one less to worry about. I wonder where he really was all that time.

AGNES: Wasn't he in America?

JULIE: You can be sure that's only the tip of the iceberg; strange crowd, tell you nothin'.

AGNES: What'll we say to Beck?

JULIE: We'll play it by ear. I wish to God she'd take that peroxide out of her hair.

AGNES: She's a holy show in those tight black pants.

JULIE: I hope to God she's not pregnant.

AGNES: Glory be, I never thought of that.

JULIE (*Proud she's thought of it*): Oh you have to think of everything.

AGNES: She'd never have it.

JULIE: God forbid! A divorcée with a child, born after the divorce.

AGNES: She'd never go for an (*Whisper*) abortion, would she?

JULIE: We'll find out if she's pregnant first and, if she is, with the luck of God she'll miscarry.

AGNES: Poor little Beck, she was always so nervous.

JULIE: A jittery little thing from the outset, all that opium Ellen took and Grandma Fraochlán feedin' it to her.

AGNES: It's up to us, Julie, to see that she's all right.

JULIE: It is indeed. And isn't Grandma Fraochlán looking well?

AGNES: She looks very stooped to me.

JULIE: Not at all, she'll have to be shot. Here they are now. Go easy for a while, we'll have a bit of a chit-chat first.

(*Cute wink to* AGNES)

AGNES (*Cute wink back*): I'll wait for you to start.

JULIE: Grand. (*One more cute wink*)

GRANDMA FRAOCHLÁN *enters on* BECK's *arm, followed by* THE MAI.

THE MAI: Ye'll have a glass of sherry.

JULIE: Not at all, we're grand.

THE MAI *offers one to* AGNES. AGNES *looks at* JULIE *who is busy looking at* BECK's *belly*. AGNES *accepts*.

GRANDMA F (*Filling her pipe*): Still teetotallin', Julie?

JULIE: When you give up the pipe I'll hit the bottle.

GRANDMA F: You'll never drink this side a Paradise so. I'd hate ta die an' never've tasted sweet wine, wouldn't you, Beck?

JULIE: You're looking great, Beck.

BECK: I'm pushin on, Aunt Julie.

AGNES: None of us are spring chickens any longer.

JULIE (*To* GRANDMA FRAOCHLÁN): I see you're still on the mulberry wine.

GRANDMA F: An' I'll be an ih as long as I can swalla.

JULIE: You know it's against your doctor's orders. Mai, why're you letting her drink mulberrry wine?

THE MAI: Ara it does her no harm and she enjoys it.

JULIE: She wouldn't be allowed it in my house.

GRANDMA F: Precisela why I never stay in your house, Julie, *a stóir*.

THE MAI: Now Grandma Fraochlán, don't start a row. Remember you promised.

JULIE: You were told no tobacco and no alcohol. I can't see why you can't obey two simple rules.

GRANDMA F: Tha Lord puh grapes an' tabacca plants an th'earth so his people could get plastered ah every available opportunihy.

JULIE: Ah there's no talkin' to you.

AGNES: You're very quiet there, Beck.

THE MAI: Have a whiskey, love, you're on your holidays.

AGNES: Honestly, Mai, you get more and more like Ellen every day.

THE MAI: Grandma Fraochlán's always sayin' that.

JULIE: It's true and you've the same voice.

AGNES: The very same. She'd be sixty now, a year younger than me.

JULIE: It was shameful what happened to Ellen.

AGNES: It couldn't be helped.

JULIE: I'll never understand how a young woman in the whole of her health dies in childbirth in the best nursing home in Galway.

GRANDMA F: She was worn ouh from all thim miscarriages and pregnancies.

JULIE: Twenty-seven years of age. You should've looked after her better, Grandma Fraochlán.

GRANDMA F: So ih was all my fault, was ih?

JULIE: I'm not saying it was.

GRANDMA F: Thin whah are ya sayin'?

JULIE: Nothin', only I remember a few nights before she got married, she appeared on my doorstep, three months pregnant with The Mai there, and she begged me to take her in until the child was born and she wanted me to go and talk to you and make you see that she didn't have to marry him.

GRANDMA F: An' why didn't ya!

JULIE: If it was now I'd mow ya down!

GRANDMA F: We're all wonderful after th'event, Julie, tha mebbe if we done this an' tha mebbe if we done thah! Why didn't ya come an' make me see an' why sih here an' tell me a lifetime too late?

JULIE: Because I knew it would be pointless.

GRANDMA F: Well thah's wan knife ya've buried in me an' ya're noh here two hours. Where's tha next wan?

AGNES (*Peacemaker*): What's Australia like, Beck?

BECK: Oh it's beautiful.

AGNES: Did you travel much around it?

BECK: Yeah, I was all over.

AGNES: And did you meet any aborigines?

BECK: Several.

AGNES: And what're they like?

BECK: Well they're like ourselves, I suppose.

JULIE: Indeed'n they are not! They live in caves, don't they, and they're black, black as ravens with teeth of snow. Sure didn't I see them on the telly!

BECK: Most of them live in houses now. Only a few still live in caves.

AGNES: And did you see the ones in the caves?

JULIE: Wouldn't be my style at all!

BECK: I did, I went on a camping holiday in the outback last summer.

JULIE (*Time for the jugular*): Was that where you met your husband?

BECK: No, I met him in Sydney.

AGNES (*Dreamy*): In Sydney, Australia.

JULIE: And when are we going to meet him?

GRANDMA F: Ye're noh. Tha Mai toult y'all abouh ih an tha telephone.

AGNES: You're not really getting a (*Whisper*) divorce, are you, sweetheart?

BECK: I'm afraid I am.

AGNES: Don't worry, don't worry.

JULIE: None of ours ever got a divorce!

BECK: It just didn't work out, Aunt Julie. I tried. I really did.

JULIE: What's all this talk about working out. In my day you got married and whether it worked out or it didn't was by the way.

GRANDMA F: I didn't bring ya up ta think like thah, Julie!

JULIE: You didn't bring me up at all. I brought myself up and all the others. You were at the window pinin' for the nine-fingered fisherman!

THE MAI: Ah there's no need to be shoutin' now, Julie.

JULIE: Sorry, I'm only tryin' to help Beck.

AGNES: And what'll you do now, sweetheart?

JULIE: I don't like your carry on one bit, young lady! All this hoorin' around for years and finally someone marries you and you walk out on him. And I suppose you'll be back hoorin' around before we can bat an eyelid!

GRANDMA F: Ara, cop onta ya'arself,[9] Julie! This is th'age a freedom, isn't thah righ', Beck?

JULIE: I still call it hoorin' around!

GRANDMA F: Mebbe a bih a hoorin' around would a done ya'arself no harm; might take thah self-righteous *straois*[10] off ya'ar puss!

JULIE: You watch your dirty Arab tongue!

THE MAI: Go easy, the pair of ye!

GRANDMA F: I'm half Spanish, half Moroccan for ya'ar infor —

JULIE: Oh it's half Moroccan this time, is it! Last time it was three-quarters Tunisian!

GRANDMA F: I toult ya, y'eejit! Me greah grandfather was Tunisian! I'm on'y quarter Tunisian, half Moroccan an' half Spanish!

JULIE: That makes five quarters! How many quarters in a whole?

GRANDMA F: A good kick up yours is whah you need! Don't ya dare come tha schoolteacher wud me, ya little faggot ya!

THE MAI: Oh Jesus!

JULIE: No thanks to you I became a schoolteacher. If you had your way I'd still be out there on Fraochlán scrawbin' the seaweed off the rocks. Anyway it's all rubbish about the Tunisian and the Moroccan. You don't know where you came from!

AGNES: This'll get us nowhere.

THE MAI: Wouldn't ya think ye could be civil to one another at this stage of ye'er lives. (*Points finger to* GRANDMA FRAOCHLÁN) And you promised you'd behave yourself.

GRANDMA F: Sorry, Mai, sorry. It's a swanky auhum day, isna, Julie?

JULIE: You haven't changed one bit, always fillin' our heads with stories and more stories —

AGNES: Ah, Julie, leave it.

JULIE: Whose side are you on?

AGNES: I'm not on any side. And sure who knows but you'll marry a decent man yet, Beck. (*A glare from* JULIE) After the (*Whisper*) divorce, I mean.

BECK: I think I'll end up like yourself, Aunt Agnes, without a man or a care in the world.

GRANDMA F: Ya'll pilla a fine man yeh, Beck, don't mind ana a thim.

JULIE: Are you still talking about sex at your age?

GRANDMA F: Well I wasn't particularly, buh now thah ya mention ih, whah else is there ta talk abouh ah any age? Ya're born, y'ave sex, an' thin ya die. An' if ya're wan a thim lucky few whom tha gods has blesst, tha will send ta ya a lover wud whom ya will partake a thah most rare an' sublime love there is ta partake a an this wild an' lonely planeh. I have bin wan a them privileged few an' I know a no higher love in this worlt or tha next.

THE MAI: You make our men seem like nothing.

GRANDMA F: I on'y talk abouh me own.

JULIE: Well maybe you should talk about him less, seeing as he left ya penniless with seven offspring.

GRANDMA F: He didn't lave me. He was taken from me. He was given ta me an' he was taken from me, somethin' you would never understand, you who was seduced be ledgers an' balance sheets, installed in a house wud a slate roof an' an auhomobile be a walkin' cheque book who counted his thingamagigs as he cem —

JULIE: You're a vicious auld witch!

THE MAI: Grandma Fraochlán, that's enough! I mean it!

GRANDMA F: Sorry, Mai, sorry, Julie, sorry, *a stóir*, it's me filthy foreign tongue. Julie, I calt y'after tha sunshine though ya were a child a winter, me on'y winter birth, me first born, greahest love abounding in ya'ar makin'. Mebbe parents as is lovers is noh parents ah all, noh enough love left over. Did we fail ya, *a stóir*?

JULIE: You're the same, still the same, a dagger in one hand, a flower in the other — Well it doesn't wash with me anymore. (*Getting upset*)

THE MAI: Ah come on now, Julie.

BECK (*To* GRANDMA FRAOCHLÁN): Come on, you and I'll go for a lie down.

JULIE: Sorry, she provokes me.

GRANDMA F (*Being led away by* BECK *and* AGNES): Me pipe! I'm noh sittin' beyant in tha room till thah wan's gone, sans me pipe!

AGNES: I have it, I have it.

GRANDMA F: An' me mulberry wine.

AGNES: Yes, yes.

GRANDMA F: Ya blem me for everthin'! Y'allas have, an' y'allas will!

JULIE: Ara whisht, Mom, or you'll drive me mad!
The three of them exit.
She takes it out of me everytime.

THE MAI: Ah she's not the worst.

JULIE: I'm sorry for fightin' in your new house, Mai —

THE MAI: Ara for God's sake.

JULIE: And don't hold it against me that I don't get on with her.

THE MAI: Of course I won't.

JULIE: A lot of things happened, Mai, long before you were born and I'm not just talkin' about Ellen.

THE MAI: Julie, none of us are perfect.

JULIE: I'm not talkin' about perfection. You didn't know her as a young woman. She was fiery, flighty. She had little or no time for her children except to tear strips off us when we got in her way. All her energy went into my father and he thought she was an angel. And then when she was left with all of us and pregnant with Ellen,

she was a madwoman. Mai, I'm not makin' it up. She spent one half of the day in the back room pullin' on an opium pipe, a relic from her unknown father, and the other half rantin' and ravin' at us or starin' out the window at the sea.

THE MAI: Did she? She must've been heartbroken.

JULIE: I know, I know. Several nights I dragged her from the cliffs, goin' to throw herself in, howlin' she couldn't live without the nine-fingered fisherman, opiumed up to the eyeballs. She was so unhappy, Mai, and she made our lives hell.

THE MAI: It must have been terrible for you.

JULIE: And then Ellen, she was brilliant, that girl was going places but there was something in Grandma Fraochlán that must stop it, and she did. She made that child marry that innocent. He wasn't Ellen's steam at all and he only married her because Grandma Fraochlán saw he did. He married her and then he left her on Fraochlán to rot. Came home every summer, left her with another pregnancy. And she belittled your father all the time to Ellen, till Ellen grew to hate him and looked down on him. He couldn't write or spell very well and Grandma Fraochlán would mock his letters until finally Ellen stopped writing to him. And at the same time she filled the girl's head with all sorts of impossible hope, always talkin' about the time she was in college, and how brilliant she was, and maybe in a few years she'd go back and study. And it only filled Ellen with more longing and made her feel that what she had lost was all the greater. And do you know the worst, the worst of it all, Ellen adored her and looked up to her and believed everything she said, and that's what killed her, not childbirth, no, her spirit was broken.

THE MAI: Are you serious?

JULIE: Well that's what I saw. Just be careful with Robert, don't let her interfere, she doesn't realize the influence she has over all of us. I'm seventy-five years of age, Mai, and I'm still not over my childhood. It's not fair they should teach us desperation so young or if they do they should never mention hope. Now where's my coat? Oh, I almost forgot, here's a little something. (*She produces an envelope from breast*)

THE MAI: I wouldn't dream of taking it.

JULIE (*She puts it into* THE MAI's *dress, and produces another envelope from her other breast*): And that's for Beck. Don't let on I gave it to her. I can't be seen to be supportin' a divorcée.

THE MAI: There's no sense to this —

JULIE: He wasn't an aborigine, was he?

THE MAI: Who?

JULIE: Beck's husband?

THE MAI (*Controls a titter of amusement*): No — aah — he wasn't.

JULIE: Not that I've anythin' against them. It's just these mixed marriages rarely work. There's plenty more (*Indicating envelope*) where that came from, so don't ever be stuck. I know you've had it rough.

JULIE *and* THE MAI *exit.*

MILLIE: Owl Lake comes from the Irish, *loch cailleach oíche,* Lake of the Night Hag or Pool of the Dark Witch. The legend goes that Coillte, daughter of the mountain god, Bloom, fell in love with Bláth, Lord of all the flowers. So away she bounded like a young deer, across her father's mountain, down through Croc's Valley of Stone, over the dark witch's boglands till she came to Bláth's domain. There he lay, under an oak tree, playing his pipes, a crown of forget-me-nots in his ebony hair. And so they lived freely through the spring and summer, sleeping on beds of leaves and grass, drinking soups of nettle and rosehip, dressing in acorn and poppy. One evening approaching autumn Bláth told Coillte that soon he must go and live with the dark witch of the bog, that he would return in the spring, and the next morning he was gone. Coillte followed him and found him ensconced in the dark witch's lair. He would not speak to her, look at her, touch her, and heartbroken Coillte lay down outside the dark witch's lair and cried a lake of tears that stretched for miles around. One night, seizing a long awaited opportunity, the dark witch pushed Coillte into her lake of tears. When spring came round again Bláth was released from the dark witch's spell and he went in search of Coillte, only to be told that she had dissolved in a lake of tears. Sam Brady told me that when the geese are restless or the swans suddenly take flight, it's because they hear Bláth's pipes among the reeds, still playing for Coillte.

Ghostly light on the window. ROBERT *stands there with* THE MAI's *body in his arms, utterly still.* MILLIE *watches them a minute. Ghostly effect.*

A tremor runs through me when I recall the legend of Owl Lake. I knew that story as a child. So did The Mai and Robert. But we were unaffected by it and in our blindness moved along with it like sleepwalkers along a precipice and all around gods and mortals called out for us to change our course and, not listening, we walked on and on.

Lights down.

1 Irish: Darling, love, dear.
2 Irish: My dear.
3 Presumably, Inishbofin, off the Connemara coast.
4 Irish: It is Thomas, skipper, son of a skipper.
5 Irish: Nonsense.
6 Spanish: strong look.
7 Leaving Certificate, the national certificate in Ireland for pupils leaving school at 18, A being the top mark.
8 Irish: finish, polish.
9 Get yourself some streetwise knowledge (Share).
10 Irish: grin.

PAUL MULDOON
from Paul Muldoon, *The Prince of the Quotidian* (1994)

Paul Muldoon's playful juxtaposition of Irish writers and phrases from their work, *una mezcla,* as the Spaniards would say.

AFTER TWO DAYS GRADING PAPERS
FROM THE SEMINAR I TAUGHT

After two days grading papers from the seminar I taught
on Swift, Yeats, Sterne,
Joyce, and Beckett,
I break my sword across my iron knee:
in the long sonata of *The Dead*
ceremony's a name[1] for the rich horn —

these images fresh images beget —
and custom for the hardy laurel tree;
for the gravel[2] was thrown up against the window-
pane
not by Michael Furey but the Dean
who stepped on to an outward-bound tram[3]

and embarked on *Immram Curaig Mael Duin*,[4]
while the Butler that withstood beside the brackish
  Boyne[5]
was one James Butler, Corporal Trim.[6]

1 This line and the following two lines are phrases from
   Yeats's verse.
2 From Joyce's story 'The Dead'.
3 Swift is the Dean, and it was Fr Conmee who stepped
   on to an outward-bound tram in 'Wandering Rocks' in
   Ulysses.
4 Voyage of Máel Dúin's Boat, an immram or voyage tale
   dating from the 8th or 9th century.
5 Yeats's middle name was Butler. The phrase 'brackish
   Boyne' is an echo of Yeats's phrase in 'Pardon Old
   Fathers' about one of his Butler ancestors fighting
   'Beside the brackish waters of the Boyne' against James
   and the Irish.
6 A character in Sterne's *Tristram Shandy* (1759–68).

TOM PAULIN
from Tom Paulin, *Walking A Line* (1994)

The broadcaster, poet and critic Tom Paulin was born in Leeds in 1949 and grew up in
Belfast. Here are two poems set or, rather, staged in Belfast, the first about sounds of
conscience as he is awoken in his parents' flat by a British Army helicopter on patrol,
the second about an innocent 'pumpkin' vision for his city, free at last of civic angst. A
Bildungsroman is a traditional novel of education, where the hero/heroine comes to
understand the realm of necessity in social life; 'sans souci' is without worry, care-free.

51 SANS SOUCI PARK

I wake early in their new flat
— my parents' flat off the Malone Road
wake to an unremitting a constant sound
six inches above the roof
— a batty churgle
a frantic mishmash
that's the entirely usual noise
of an army helicopter
— usual but this time worse
than ho-ho normal
because a gong is sounding
inside my head already
you sinned with drink dong!
you sinned with drink bong!
so an armed flying machine
is way inside my head
inside a strange new room
just four doors up the street
they lived in my mum and dad
for over thirty years
and a voice thrashing in the wilderness
an unstill enormous voice
is offering me this wisdom
action's a solid bash
narrative a straight line
try writing to the moment
as it wimples like a burn
baby it's NOW!

A BELFAST *BILDUNGSROMAN*

'And suddenly there came a sound from heaven as of a rushing
mighty wind and it filled all the house where they were sitting.'

As if I could write it out forever and ever
and me and the city be growing up always
pitching each fiction story or play
into that unscripted unwritten palm house
where the lord mayor ex-rigger plumber retired doffer
need never run out of gas or get stopped at a road block
for now the library shelves are chockablock with our
  consonants
and this great wee nest's packed with scaldies and egg
  sodas
we're being televised like wildlife *The Quaint the Cute*
  and the Feral
goes out on all channels 24 hours of the day
while up in the sky there's this huge transparent
  balloon
saying BELFAST DERRY it gets tighter and tighter
till it looks like bursting
                              who's stuffed on hot air?
who's been shooting their mouth off? can you tell us?
but the play is as innocent as seakale and needn't
  answer
for myself I want to lie on the ground like a humid
  pumpkin
— innocent postliterate no longer dirigible
my tiny cargo of civic angst floating down the lough
toward *that great and notable day* when the curtain goes up
on a stagestruck city soughing like a full house

SEBASTIAN BARRY
from Sebastian Barry, *Plays: 1* (1997)

Sebastian Barry was born in Dublin in 1955 and educated at TCD. He is the author of a number of plays including *Prayers of Sherkin* (1990) and *The Only True History of Lizzie Finn* (1995) as well as novels and collections of verse. *The Steward of Christendom* is a memory play which focuses on the plight of the Catholic loyalist reduced to history's margins in the period from the Dublin Lock-Out of 1913 to the emergence of the Irish Free State in 1922, as Ireland turned to new leaders in the shape of James Larkin and Michael Collins. The central figure is the tragic Thomas Dunne, a superintendent in the Dublin Metropolitan Police, and loyal to the Queen. In the constant criss-crossing in Thomas's disordered mind between Dublin and County Wicklow, history and setting also meet in a fruitful exchange. 'My father was the steward of Humewood, and I was the steward of Christendom.' Father and son are servants of the old power, in one case the landlord class and in the other that of a Queen who is identified by Thomas in mystical terms spreading her mantle of light and civilization across her Empire. Quite naturally, the new Ireland that came to birth in 1922 had little room for those Irish who fought in the Great War and sacrificed their lives or for those West Britons who upheld British law and order in Ireland; seventy years later, as is evident in the work of Sebastian Barry, the tide has turned and a place is now being made for what might now be termed in retrospect disloyal subjects. For Barry's continuing preoccupation with this theme of Irish men in British uniform, see his novel *The Whereabouts of Eneas McNulty* (1998). His latest harrowing play *Our Lady of Sligo* (1998), set in Jervis Street Hospital, Dublin, in 1953, again draws on his family history to emphasize the failures of post-independence Ireland. 'Ireland, where is that country? Where are those lives that lay in store for us, in store like rich warm grain?'

The Steward of Christendom (1995)

CHARACTERS

THOMAS DUNNE, *early to mid seventies at the time of the play, 1932*

SMITH, *fiftyish*

MRS O'DEA, *likewise or older*

RECRUIT, *eighteen*

WILLIE DUNNE, *Thomas's son, born late 1890s, died in the First World War, thirteen or so as he appears in the play to Thomas, his voice not yet broken*

ANNIE DUNNE, *Thomas's middle daughter, bowed back, about twenty in 1922, thirtyish 1932*

MAUD DUNNE, *Thomas's eldest daughter, early twenties in 1922*

DOLLY DUNNE, *Thomas's youngest daughter, about seventeen in 1922*

MATT KIRWAN, *Maud's suitor and husband, mid to late twenties in 1922, mid to late thirties in 1932*

The play is set in the county home in Baltinglass, County Wicklow, in about 1932.

ACT ONE

Circa 1932. THOMAS's *bare room in the county home*[1] *in Baltinglass.*[2] *A toiling music-hall music distantly. A poor table, an iron bed with a thin mattress and yellowing sheets. A grey blanket, a three-legged stool. A poor patch of morning light across* THOMAS, *a solitary man of seventy-five, in the bed. His accent is south-west Wicklow, with his words clear.*

THOMAS: Da Da, Ma Ma, Ba Ba, Ba Ba. Clover, clover in my mouth, clover honey-smelling, clover smelling of Ma Ma's neck, and Ma Ma's soft breast when she opens her floating blouse, and Da Da's bright boots in the grasses, amid the wild clover, and the clover again, and me the Ba Ba set in the waving grasses, and the smell of honey, and the farmhands going away like an army of redcoats but without the coats, up away up the headland with their scythes, and every bit of the sun likes to run along the scythes and laugh along the blades, now there are a score of shining scythes, dipping and signalling from the backs of the men.

A sharp banging on the door.

SMITH: Wakey, wakey!

THOMAS: Who is there?

SMITH: Black Jim. Black Jim in the morning.

THOMAS: Oh, don't come in, Black Jim, with your blackthorn stick raised high.

SMITH: It's Black Jim.

THOMAS: But don't you come in. There's no need. Is it Da Da?

SMITH: It's Black Jim, and he must come in.

THOMAS: There's no need. Thomas sleepy sleepy, beddy bye. Is it Da Da? (*No answer. More distantly on other doors there's a banging and the same 'Wakey, wakey' receding.*) Da Da comes in, Da Da comes in, Tom no sleepy, Tom no sleepy. Tom you sleep, says Da Da, or you get big stick. And when little Tom no sleepy sleep, big stick comes in and hitting Tom Tommy, but now the polished boots are gone, and the dark has closed over the fields, and the smell of the clover is damped down now by summer cold, and the dress of Ma Ma hangs on the chair, and her face is pressed into the goosey pillow, and all is silence in the wooden world of the house, except the tread of the Da Da, a-worrying, a-worrying, except the fall of the big stick, cut from the blackthorn tree in the hushed deeps of winter. Da Da is golden, golden, golden, nothing that Da Da do takes away the sheen and the swoon of gold.

He bestirs himself, wipes his big hands on his face vigorously, gets out of bed with good strength. He is big-framed but diminished by age, in a not-too-clean set of long johns.

You bloody mad old man. Gabbling and affrighting yourself in the dark. Baltinglass, Baltinglass, that's where you are. For your own good, safe from harm. Like the milking cow taken down from the sloping field when the frost begins to sit on her tail. When her shit is frosty.

Snug in the byre. (*He sits on the stool and leans in to the table as if pressing his face against the cow.*) Come to it, Daisy now, give your milk. Go on. (*Slaps a leg.*) Ah, Daisy, Daisy, sweet, give it up, for Thomas. Oh. (*As if getting a jet into the bucket.*) Oh, oh. (*Happily.*) Aye. (*Catching himself, stopping.*) The county home in Baltinglass, that's where you're situated. Seventy-five summers on your head and mad as a stone mason. Safe, safe, safety, safe, safe, safety, mad as a barking stone mason. Because you were not civil to your daughter, no, you were not. You were ranting, you were raving, and so they put you where you were safe. Like a dog that won't work without using his teeth, like a dog under sentence. But please do not talk to Black Jim, Thomas, please do not, there's the manny. Because he is not there. (*Singing.*) There was an old woman that lived in the wood, willa, willa, wallya.³

His own silence.

Da Da?

MRS O'DEA, *the seamstress, a small plump woman in an ill-made dress and a white apron with big pockets full of tape and needles and oddments of black cloth, opens the door with her key and comes in.*

MRS O'DEA (*a local accent*): Will you let me measure you today, Mr Dunne?

THOMAS: What for indeed?

MRS O'DEA: You can't wear those drawers forever.

THOMAS: I won't need to, Mrs O'Dea, I won't live forever.

MRS O'DEA: And what will you do when summer's gone? How can you bear to wear rags?

THOMAS: I rarely go out, you see.

MRS O'DEA: Look at the state of yourself. You're like something in a music-hall. Mrs Forbes, the Boneless Wonder, or some such.

THOMAS: This is a madhouse, it suits me to look like a madman while I'm here.

MRS O'DEA: If you allow me measure you, I'll make up a fine suit for you, as good as my own attire.

THOMAS: With that black cloth you use for all the poor men?

MRS O'DEA: Yes and indeed, it must be black, by regulation of the board.

THOMAS: If you had a bit of gold or suchlike for the thread, something to perk the suit up, why then, Mrs O'Dea, I would let you measure me.

MRS O'DEA: Gold thread? I have none of that, Mr Dunne.

THOMAS: That's my bargain. Take it or leave it.

MRS O'DEA: Would a yellow do?

THOMAS: Yes, yes.

MRS O'DEA: You're not afraid of looking like a big goose?

THOMAS: I go out but rarely. If I look like a goose, few will see me. (*As an inspiration.*) I won't venture out at Christmas!

MRS O'DEA (*taking our her measuring tape*): Have you fleas?

THOMAS: No, madam.

MRS O'DEA (*calling out the door*): Mr Smith! (*To* THOMAS.) You won't mind Mr Smith washing you, just a little.

THOMAS (*anxiously*): Don't let Black Jim in here. Don't let him, for I've no sugar lumps. It's only sugar lumps appeases him.

MRS O'DEA: He must wash you, Mr Dunne. It's just Mr Smith. You smell like a piece of pork left out of the dripping press, man dear.

SMITH, *about fifty, balding, with the cheerfulness about him of the powerful orderly, comes in with a basin.*

SMITH: Raise 'em.

THOMAS (*backing away*): The blackthorn stick hurts Tommy Tom. Sugar lumps, sugar lumps!

MRS O'DEA: Take off your old long johns, and be easy in yourself. It's only a sponging.

THOMAS (*trying to hold his clothes fast*): Tum tum tum, bum bum bum.

SMITH *roughly unbuttons the long johns and pulls them off,* THOMAS *miserably covering himself.*

SMITH: I'd a mind once to join my brother on the Hudson river.[4] He has a whole flensing business there, flourishing. Would that I had joined Jack, I say, when I have to wash down an old bugger like you. I would rather flense whales,[5] and that's a stinking task, I'm told.

THOMAS (*smiling red-faced at* MRS O'DEA): Da Da.

MRS O'DEA (SMITH *beginning to sponge*): Good man yourself, Mr Dunne.

THOMAS (*weeping*): Da Da, Ma Ma, Ba Ba.

MRS O'DEA: My, my, that's a fine chest you have on you, Mr Dunne. What was your work formerly? I know you've told me often enough.

THOMAS (*proudly enough*): I was a policeman.

MRS O'DEA: You had the chest for it.

THOMAS: I had, madam.

SMITH (*sponging*): Dublin Metropolitan Police, weren't you, boyo? In your braid. The DMP, that are no more. Oh, la-di-da. Look at you.

THOMAS (*smiling oddly*): La-di-da.

SMITH (*sponging*): Castle Catholic[6] bugger that you were. But you're just an old bastard in here with no one to sponge you but Smith.

THOMAS: Black Jim no like Tommy Tom. No like Tommy Tom.

SMITH: Chief superintendent, this big gobshite was, Mrs O'Dea, that killed four good men and true in O'Connell Street in the days of the lock-out.[7] Larkin. Hah? His men it was struck down the strikers. (*A gentle hit with the dry cloth.*) Baton-charging. A big loyal Catholic gobshite killing poor hungry Irishmen. If you weren't an old madman we'd flay you.

MRS O'DEA: That's fine, Mr Smith, leave him be. Can't you see you terrorize him? That's him scrubbed.

SMITH (*going off with the basin*): Excusing my language.

MRS O'DEA: Can you put on your own clothes, Mr Dunne?

THOMAS: I can, madam.

MRS O'DEA: Is it true you gave your previous suit to a man in the walking meadow?

THOMAS: It is. (*Dressing.*)

MRS O'DEA: Why would you do a thing like that, and go in those rags yourself? Was the man you gave it to cold?

THOMAS: No. He was hungry.

MRS O'DEA: There's no eating in a suit, man dear.

THOMAS: I was out a-walking in the lunatics' meadow, and Patrick O'Brien asked me for the suit. He was in former times the finest thrower of the bullet in Kiltegan. Do you know what a bullet is? It is a ball of granite whittled down in an evening by a boy. I could tell you tales of Patrick O'Brien and the bullet, on the roads there round about. All the men of the village milling there, raging to win fame at the bulleting if God shone the light of luck on them, the thrower slowly slowly raising the bullet, slowly dipping it, then away, with a great fling of the arm, down the road with it, and well beyond the next corner if he could. And if the bullet touched the grassy marge, a terrible groan would issue from the man and his supporters. And the young boys red in the face from ambition and desire. Patrick O'Brien, a tall yellow streak of a man now, that thinks he is a dog. A dog, Mrs O'Dea. When he asked for the suit, I couldn't refuse him, for memory of his great skill. They were evenings any human person would remember.

MRS O'DEA (*measuring him now with the tape, putting up his arms and so on as necessary*): What did he want with your suit?

THOMAS: To eat, he said. To bury it and eat it, piecemeal, as the spirit took him.

MRS O'DEA: You gave your good suit to a poor madman to be eaten?

THOMAS: I was glad to give it to him. Though indeed truly, it was one of Harrison's suits, and the last of my finery from the old days. A nice civilian suit, made by Harrison, in North Great George's Street, years ago.

MRS O'DEA: I can't believe that you gave away a suit like that. A lovely bespoke suit.

THOMAS: Why not? Amn't I a lunatic myself?

MRS O'DEA (*sensibly*): Well, there must be a year's eating in a man's suit. You won't need to give him the new one.

THOMAS: No, but it won't be much to me all the same, if it has no gold in it. The boy that sings to me betimes wears gold, and I have a hankering now for a suit with a touch of gold. There was never enough gold in that uniform. If I had made commissioner I might have had gold, but that wasn't a task for a Catholic, you understand, in the way of things, in those days.

MRS O'DEA: You must have been a fine policeman, if they made you all of a chief superintendent.

THOMAS: Maybe so. But, to tell you the truth, I was forty-five years in the DMP when they did so, and promotion was really a matter of service. Not that they would put a fool to such a task, when you think of the terrible responsibility of it. I had three hundred men in B Division, and kept all the great streets and squares of Dublin orderly and safe, and was proud, proud to do it well.

MRS O'DEA: I am sure you did, Mr Dunne, because you carry yourself well yet. You mustn't mind Mr Smith. He's younger than yourself and one of his brothers was shot in the twenties, so he tells me.

THOMAS: The DMP was never armed, not like the Royal Irish Constabulary. The RIC could go to war. That's why we were taken off the streets during that rebellion at Easter time, that they make so much of now. We were mostly country men, and Catholics to boot, and we loved our King and we loved our country. They never put those Black and Tans among us, because we were a force that belonged to Dublin and her streets. We did our best and followed our orders. Go out to Mount Jerome some day, in the city of Dublin, and see the old monument to the DMP men killed in the line of duty. Just ordinary country men keen to do well. And when the new government came in, they treated us badly. Our pensions were in disarray. Some said we had been traitors to Ireland. Though we sat in Dublin Castle all through twenty-two and tried to protect the city while the whole world was at each other's throats. While the most dreadful and heinous murders took place in the fields of Ireland. With nothing but our batons and our

pride. Maybe we weren't much. You're thinking, of course he would speak well for his crowd. Yes, I'll speak well for them. We were part of a vanished world, and I don't know what's been put in our place. I'd like to see them clear Sackville Street[8] of an illegal gathering without breaking a few heads. There was a proclamation posted the week before that meeting. It was my proper duty to clear the thoroughfare. There was no one killed that day that I know of, there were scores of my men in Jervis Street and the like, with head wounds. I'm sorry Smith's brother was killed. I'm sorry for all the poor souls killed these last years. Let them come and kill me if they wish. But I know my own story of what happened, and I am content with it.

MRS O'DEA: Mercy, Mr Dunne, I didn't mean to prompt a declaration. You're all in a sweat, man. The sooner you have a new suit, the better.

THOMAS: But I tell you, there's other things I regret, and I regret them sorely, things of my own doing, and damn history.

MRS O'DEA: We all have our regrets, man dear. Do calm yourself.

THOMAS: I regret that day with my daughter Annie and the sword, when we were home and snug in Kiltegan at last.

MRS O'DEA: There, there, man dear. We'll see if we can't keep the next suit on you, when you go a-walking in the lunatics' meadow, as you call it. It's just the exercise field, you know, the walking meadow. It will have plenty of yellow in it.

THOMAS (*differently, head down*): I suppose it is very sad about Patrick O'Brien. I suppose.

MRS O'DEA: I have all your measurements now, Mr Dunne. And a fine big-boned gentleman you are. (*Looking at his bare feet.*) What became of your shoes, but?

MRS O'DEA *and* THOMAS (*after a moment, as one*): Patrick O'Brien!

MRS O'DEA: Maybe there's a pair of decent shoes about in the cupboards, that someone has left.

THOMAS: Coffin shoes, you mean, I expect. Oh, I don't mind a dead man's shoes. And a nice suit, yes, that I can wear in my own coffin, to match, with yellow thread.

MRS O'DEA: Not yet, Mr Dunne, not by a long chalk. (*Going out.*) I'll do my best for you. (*Locking the door.*)

THOMAS (*alone, in an old summer light*): When the rain of autumn started that year, my mother and me went down into the valley by the green road. Myself trotting beside her in my boyish joy. We passed the witch's farm, where the witch crossed the fields in her dirty dress to milk her bloodied cow, that gave her bloodied milk, a thing to fear because she used the same well as ourselves, and washed her bucket there before drawing water. My father was the steward of Humewood and she should have feared to hurt our well, but you cannot withstand the mad. Well, we passed the nodding bell-flowers that I delighted to burst, and ventured out on to the Baltinglass road, to beg a perch for our bums on a cart. (*Sitting up on the bedstead.*) For my father would not let my mother take the pony and trap, because he said the high lamps made too great a show of pride, and we were proud people enough without having to show it. Not that he didn't drive the trap himself when he needed it. But we were soon in the old metropolis of Baltinglass, a place of size and wonder to a boy. (*Pulling out his ragged socks from under the mattress.*) There we purchased a pair of lace-up boots. A pair of lace-up boots which banished bare feet, which I was soon able to lace and tighten for myself of a morning, when the air in the bedroom was chill as a well, and the icy cock crowed in the frosty yard, and Thomas Dunne was young and mightily shod. (*Looking down at his feet.*) And Dolly my daughter later polished my policeman's boots, and Annie and Maud brought me my clothes brushed and starched in the mornings, as the castle of soldiers and constables woke. When my poor wife was dead those many years, and Little Ship Street stirred with the milkman's cart. And the sun herself brought gold to the river's back. (*He looks at the locked door.*) If they lock that door how can my daughters come to rescue me? (*He holds out a hand and takes it with his other hand, and shakes.*) How do you do? How do you do? (*Very pleased.*) How do you do? (*Holds out his arms, embraces someone.*) How do you do? (*Gently.*) How do you do? Oh, how do you do?

Music. After a little white, SMITH *enters with a cracked bowl with a steam of stew off it. He hands* THOMAS *a big spoon which* THOMAS *holds obediently.*

SMITH: You look just like an old saint there, Mr Dunne, an old saint there, with your spoon. You may think me a rough sort of man but I know my saints. I see a picture of St Jerome with a spoon like that and a bowl like that. (THOMAS *sits to eat.*) Eat away, man. You should see the cauldron of that stuff the cooks have made. The kitchens are in a fog. Seven lambs went into it, they say. Isn't it good stuff? (*Friendly.*) What's it

your name is again, your first name? I've so many to remember.

THOMAS: Thomas. They named me Thomas long ago for my great-great-grandfather the first steward of Humewood, the big place in Kiltegan, the main concern. Though all his own days they called him White Meg on account of his fierce white beard. He'd stride up the old street from his house to the great gates and say nothing to no one. White Meg. But Thomas it was, was his name.

SMITH: With your spoon. St Thomas! When I brought Mrs O'Dea her cocoa in at five, she had you all cut out and hung up on a hook with the other inhabitants, and the breeze was blowing you softly from the crack in the pane. She's a keen seamstress. St Thomas. Do you like the stew?

THOMAS (*expansively*): Of all the dishes in the world I may say I relish mostly a stew.

SMITH: You, St Thomas, that knew kings and broke Larkin. Stew.

THOMAS (*alerted*): Put a piece of lamb in it at the bottom, for the men that are working, and let the child eat off the top of it. The child's spoon is a shallow spoon. Parsnips. The secret of stew on our hillside was just a scrape of crab apple in it — just a scrape. But then we'd fierce crab apples. And not to curse while it was cooking. And not to spit while it was cooling.

SMITH: What was the name of the patriot was killed years past in Thomas Street outside the church of St Thomas, in the city of Dublin?

THOMAS (*thinking, innocently*): Thomas Street wasn't in my division. But Emmet, was it, you mean? Robert Emmet?[9]

SMITH: That's the one. They hung him there and the people cried out against the soldiers and the peelers, and after they dragged his body over the parade ground till it was bleeding and broken in its bones, and then they got a loyal butcher to cut him into four pieces. He was dead then.

THOMAS: I should think.

SMITH: That's what they did to him, those official men, and a fine Protestant gentleman at that.

THOMAS (*pleasantly*): It's as well to throw a bit of rosemary across it too, if you have rosemary. Rosemary smells good when the land gets hot. Across the stew. Rosemary. Thyme would do either, if you've none. When you put in the spuds. Or lavender maybe. Did you ever try clover? A child will eat clover when he is set down on the meadow to sit. The bee's favourite. A cow makes fine milk from a field of clover. So put in rosemary, if you have it. Ah, fresh spuds, turned out of the blessed earth like — for all the world like newborn pups. (*Laughing.*)

SMITH: I suppose you held the day of Emmet's death as a festive day. A victory day. I suppose you did. I suppose you were all very queer indeed up there in the Castle. I'm thinking too of the days when they used to put the pitch caps on the priests when they catched them, like they were only dogs, and behind the thick walls of the city hall all the English fellas would be laughing at the screams of the priests, while their brains boiled. I'm thinking of all that. I suppose you never put a pitch cap[10] on anyone. They weren't in fashion in your time. A pity. It must have been a great sight, all the same.

THOMAS (*eating rapidly*): Good stew, good stew. Wicklow lambs.

SMITH (*looking at him*): St Thomas, isn't it?

THOMAS (*smiling*): St Thomas.

SMITH *goes off with the empty bowl.*

I loved her for as long as she lived, I loved her as much as I loved Cissy my wife, and maybe more, or differently. When she died it was difficult to go from her to the men that came after her, Edward and George, they were good men but it was not the same. When I was a young recruit it used to frighten me how much I loved her. Because she had built everything up and made it strong, and made it shipshape. The great world that she owned was shipshape as a ship. All the harbours of the earth were trim with their granite piers, the ships were shining and strong. The trains went sleekly through the fields, and her mark was everywhere, Ireland, Africa, the Canadas, every blessed place. And men like me were there to make everything peaceable, to keep order in her kingdoms. She was our pride. Among her emblems was the gold harp, the same harp we wore on our helmets. We were secure, as if for eternity the orderly milk-drays would come up the streets in the morning, and her influence would reach everywhere, like the salt sea pouring up into the fresh waters of the Liffey. Ireland was hers for eternity, order was everywhere, if we could but honour her example. She loved her Prince. I loved my wife. The world was a wedding of loyalty, of steward to Queen, she was the very flower and perfecter of Christendom. Even as the simple man I was I could love her fiercely. Victoria.

The RECRUIT, *a young man of eighteen or so comes on. He has obviously made a great effort to smarten*

himself *for this meeting. He is tall and broad, and stoops a little as he takes off his hat.*

Good morning, son. How are you?

RECRUIT: Oh, most pleasant, sir, most pleasant.

THOMAS: You had a good journey up from your home place?

RECRUIT: It didn't take a feather out of me, sir.

THOMAS: Good man. What age are you?

RECRUIT: Eighteen, sir, this November past.

THOMAS: Height?

RECRUIT: Six foot three, sir, in my winter socks.

THOMAS: Well, you look a very fine man indeed. You were never in trouble yourself, son?

RECRUIT: Oh, no, sir.

THOMAS: And did you serve in the Great War? I don't suppose you could have.

RECRUIT: No, sir. I was too young.

THOMAS: Of course. A soldier doesn't always make a good policeman. There's too much — sorrow — in a soldier. You're a drinking man?

RECRUIT: I'll drink a glass of porter, with my father.

THOMAS: Very good. I've read your father's letter. And I want to tell you, we are going to give you a go at it. I have a big book in my office within, bound in gold, that has the name of every DMP man that has ever served the crown. Do you wish for your own name to be added in due course?

RECRUIT: Oh — indeed and I do, sir. Most fervently.

THOMAS: I hope you will do well, son. These are troubled times, and men like yourself are sorely needed. I will be watching your progress — watching, you understand, in a fatherly way. Do your best.

RECRUIT: I will, sir. Thank you, sir!

THOMAS (*taking his hand*): I was a young recruit myself once. I know what this means to you.

RECRUIT: The world, sir, it means the world.

THOMAS: Good man. I'll write to your father in Longford. Take this now as a token of our good faith. (*Handing him the spoon.*)

RECRUIT: Thank you, sir, thank you.

The RECRUIT *shadows away.* THOMAS *kneels at the end of his bed and grips the metal tightly.*

THOMAS: I must not speak to shadows. When you see the shadows, Thomas, you must not speak. Sleep in the afternoon, that's the ticket. How did I get myself into this pickle, is it age just? I know I did what Annie said I did, but was it really me, and not some old disreputable creature that isn't me? When it was over, I knew suddenly in the car coming here what had happened, but at the time, at the time, I knew nothing, or I knew something else. And it was the gap between the two things that caused me to cry out in the car, the pain of it, the pain of it, the fright of it, and no one in the world to look at me again in a manner that would suggest that Thomas Dunne is still human, still himself. Everything is as clear as a glass. I can remember how lovely Cissy was the day we were married, and that smile she gave me when the priest was finished, how she looked up at me in front of all our people, her face shining, astonishing me. You don't expect to see love like that. And that's a long time ago. And I can remember, now, the last day with Annie, and how I was feeling that day, and I can see myself there in the kitchen, and I know how mad I was. And I am ashamed. I am ashamed. I am ashamed. (*After a while of breathing like a runner.*) Hail Mary, full of Grace, the Lord is with thee, blessed art Thou amongst women, and blessed is the fruit of thy womb. (*He gets stuck, bangs his head with his right palm.*) — Jesus. Holy Mary, mother of. Holy Mary, mother of. I remember, I do remember. Hail Mary full of grace the Lord is with me blessed art Thou amongst women and blessed is the fruit of Thy womb Jesus holy Mary Mother of . . . of . . . of God! Of God! (*Climbs into bed.*) Robert Emmet. (*Pulls the sheet over his face.*) Robert Emmet. (*Spits the t's so the sheet blows up from his lips.*) Robert Emmet. (*After a moment.*) Sleep, sleep, that's the ticket.

His son, WILLIE, *neat and round, comes in and sits on the end of his bed and sings to him Schubert's Ave Maria. At the end,* THOMAS *looks over the sheet.* WILLIE *wears his army uniform.*

Hello, child. Are you warm?

WILLIE: It's cold in the mud, Father.

THOMAS: I know child. I'm so sorry.

Sunlight grows slowly over the scene, banishing WILLIE. *The imagined stir and calling of the Castle below.* THOMAS *is at ease suddenly. His middle daughter,* ANNIE, *in a light cotton dress of the early twenties, a bow in her spine, carries on a white shirt, which illumines like a lantern when she crosses the windowlight. There's an old music.*

ANNIE: Now, Papa — there's the best-ironed shirt in Christendom.

THOMAS: Thank you, dear.

ANNIE: It took the best part of an hour to heat the hearth, to heat the iron. There's enough starch in the breast to bolster Jericho.

THOMAS: Thank you, dear.

ANNIE: If Dolly had ironed it, you'd look at it more intently.

THOMAS: I am looking at it, Annie. Or I would, if it weren't so blinding white.

ANNIE: And it isn't that white, Papa. And you've things on your mind today, I know. A black day.

THOMAS: I expect it is.

ANNIE: Why Collins of all people to give the Castle to? Couldn't they find a gentleman?

THOMAS: He is the head of the new government, Annie.

ANNIE: Government! We know what sort of men they are. Coming in here to the likes of you. Whose son gave his life for Ireland.

THOMAS (*coming over to her, kindly*): Will gave his life to save Europe, Annie, which isn't the same thing.

ANNIE: I miss Willie, Papa. I miss him. We need him today.

THOMAS: I blame myself. There was no need for him to go off, except, he hadn't the height to be a policeman. The army were glad to take him. I blame myself.

ANNIE: Will was proud, Papa, proud to be in the Rifles. It was his life.

THOMAS: It was the death of him. You cannot lose a son without blaming yourself. But that's all history now, Annie.

MAUD, *his eldest, a very plain woman with black hair, dressed heavily for the bright day, carries on his dress uniform, struggling to balance the ceremonial sword.*

Let me help you.

MAUD: It's all right, Papa, I'll plonk it on the bed.

THOMAS: Where's Dolly?

MAUD: Polishing the boots. I hate to see a woman spit. Lord, Lord, she's a spitter, when it's Papa's old shoes. And she was away out this morning, I know not why, all secretive.

ANNIE: Away out this morning? She didn't touch her bed all night. Up at that dance at the Rotunda. She should be whipped.

MAUD: And did you say she could go to that dance?

ANNIE: I didn't say she could take all night to walk home.

THOMAS: Thoughtful daughters you are, to be helping me so. How did you get the creases so firm?

MAUD: I slept on them. In as much as I slept. I cannot sleep these times.

THOMAS: I could meet the emperor of the world with those creases.

ANNIE: You'll have to make do with Michael Collins.

MAUD: Oh, don't start that old story, Annie. We've had enough of it now, God knows.

ANNIE: I was only saying.

MAUD: Well, don't be only saying. Go and stir the teapot, can't you, and give over the politics.

ANNIE: I was only saying.

MAUD: You're only always only saying, and you have

me stark wide-eyed in the bed all night, worrying and turning and fretting, and a great headache pounding away, because you can leave nothing alone, Annie, till you have us all miserable and mad with concern.

THOMAS: Now, girls, think of your mother. Would she want you to be talking like this?

MAUD: No, Papa, of course not. She would not.

ANNIE: Mam? What do you know about Mam, if I may ask?

MAUD: Don't I see her often when I sleep? Don't I see her blue polka-dot dress, yes, and her bending down to me and making me laugh?

ANNIE: That's only ould stuff Willie told us.

MAUD: Oh, Annie, Annie, I was four years old, you were only two!

THOMAS: Daughters, daughters — what a terrible thing to be arguing about!

ANNIE: Oh, a thing indeed.

MAUD (*after a little*): I'm sorry, Annie.

ANNIE: That's all right, girl. It's not your fault Collins is a criminal.

MAUD: I'll be dead, that's it! I'll be dead by day's end. I can't take everything in! My head's bursting with Papa and Michael Collins and I don't know what . . .

DOLLY, *holding out the polished boots carefully from her dress, starts across to* THOMAS, *smiling.* THOMAS's *face lights like a lamp.*

THOMAS: Oh, Dolly, Dolly, Dolly!

Before she reaches him, an intrusion of darkness, the scattering of his daughters. THOMAS *roars, with pain and confusion. He lifts his arms and roars. He beats the bed. He hits the table. He roars.* SMITH *unlocks the door and hurries in, brandishing a pacifier. It looks like a baton.*

SMITH: What the hell is all the shouting? You have the pauper lunatics in a swelter! Crying and banging their heads, and laughing like fairground mechanicals, and spitting, and cutting themselves with items. (*Looking back out.*) Mrs O'Dea, Mrs O'Dea — try and sort those screamers!

MRS O'DEA (*off*): I will, I will!

SMITH: Even the long ward of old dames with their dead brains, have some of them opened their eyes and are weeping to be woken, with your bloody shouting. Do you want to go in with them, old man? After I beat you!

THOMAS (*hurrying back into his bed*): I only shouted the one time. It must have been the moon woke them. (*Drawing the sheet high.*) My daughter Annie gives you the shillings for the room, Black Jim.

SMITH: She can give all the shillings she likes. She won't know where we throw you.

THOMAS: Don't put Thomas with the poor dribblers. I've seen them. I've seen that terrible long ward of women, belonging to no one at all, no one to pay shillings for them. Don't put me there.

SMITH: Then show me silence. (*Striking the end of the bed.*)

THOMAS: Don't strike there. My son sits there.

SMITH: You are a violent, stupid man, Mr Dunne, and I want silence out of you!

THOMAS (*a finger to his lips*): Silence.

SMITH *goes, banging the door, locking it harshly.* (*Pulling up the sheet.*) Robert Emmet.

ANNIE *has slipped over to his bed.*

ANNIE: Papa.

THOMAS (*looking out again*): I must be silent, child.

ANNIE: Papa, please will you tell me.

THOMAS: What, child?

ANNIE: Why is my back bowed, Papa?

THOMAS: Why, child, because of your polio.

ANNIE: Why, Papa?

THOMAS: I don't know, Annie. Because it afflicts some and leaves others clear. I don't know.

ANNIE: Will I ever have a husband, Papa?

THOMAS: I do hope so.

ANNIE: I think a woman with such a back will not find a husband.

THOMAS: She might.

ANNIE: I see the prams going by in Stephen's Green, glistening big prams, and I look in when the nannies are polite, and I look in, and I see the babies, with their round faces, and their smells of milk and clean linen, and their heat, and Papa —

THOMAS: Yes, child?

ANNIE: They all look like my babies.

ANNIE *goes,* THOMAS *looks after her, then covers his face again. A country music. He sleeps, he sleeps. The moon, the emblem of lunacy, appears overhead, pauses there faintly, fades again. It is a very delicate, strange sleep. The calling of a cock distantly, birdsong, the cock louder. An arm of sunlight creeps into the room and across* THOMAS's *covered face. His hand creeps out and his fingers wave in the light. He pulls down the sheet and the noises cease. He listens. Imitates the cock softly.*

THOMAS: The cock crows in the morning yard, banishing all night fears. No person, that has not woken to the crowing of a familiar cock, can know how tender that cry is evermore, stirring the child out into the fresh fingers of sunlight, into the ever-widening armfuls of sunlight. How stray the child looks in the yard, bare feet on the old pack-stones in the clay, all his people have come out in their own vanished times, as small as him, surrounded by the quiet byres just wakening now, the noses of the calves wet in the closed dark, the sitting hens in the coop anxious to be released, out away from the night fear of foxes, so they may lay their eggs beyond finding in the hayshed and the hawthorn bushes. Only the boy knows their terrible tricks. He inserts an arm into the known places and feels the warm eggs, smells them happily in his brown palms, and searches out the newest places of the hens in the deepest bowers of the straw. He carries them back in to his Ma Ma, folded in his gansey, with the glow of pride about him as big as the sun. Then he goes back out into the yard while the eggs are boiling, or put aside carefully for the cake, and tries to read the story of the day in the huge pages of the clouds. And he sees the milking cow driven up on to the top field where the summer grass is rich and moist, and how well he knows the wild garden there of meadowsweet, where the dragonfly is hard as pencil. And the boy's Ma Ma is calling him, and he goes, and there is no greater morning, no morning in his life of greater importance.

SMITH *enters with a newspaper. He fetches out* THOMAS's *po. It's empty.*

SMITH: I hope you're not blocking up like some of the old fellas.

THOMAS: A deserted house needs no gutter. Is that my newspaper?

SMITH: It is. (*Throws it to him.* THOMAS *opens it.*) Can you not order a decent newspaper?

THOMAS: *Irish Times* suits me.

SMITH: It's all fools on horseback.

THOMAS: Not so much. I'm trying to keep up on the activities, if I may call them that, of a certain Hinky Dink Kenna, who runs the first ward in Chicago. I tell you, you'd have to call him a criminal here. Himself and Bath-house John Coughlan. Villains. If they had never left Ireland, I'd have had to lock them up in Mountjoy. But you can do what you like in America, or so it seems.

SMITH: Is that right? And what do they get up to, those two?

THOMAS: Oh, they're in the liquor trade, you might say. It makes powerful reading.

MRS O'DEA *comes in with big flaps of black cloth —* THOMAS's *suit in its unsewn parts.*

SMITH: He hasn't washed himself.

MRS O'DEA: Didn't you wash him yesterday? Do you want to rub him out? Come on up, Mr Dunne, and let me pin these to you for a look at it.

SMITH: Can't you see he's reading.

THOMAS (*getting out of bed*): Oh, I've time for reading. In my retirement.

He stands for the fitting. MRS O'DEA *begins to pin the sections of the suit to his long johns.*

MRS O'DEA: You're the cleanest man in Baltinglass.

THOMAS *seems agitated, looking down at the sections.* What's the matter, Mr Dunne?

THOMAS: That's just the old black stuff.

MRS O'DEA: And what if it is?

THOMAS (*so* SMITH *won't hear*): Didn't we discuss yellow?

MRS O'DEA: Yellow thread, Mr Dunne. I can only stitch the sections together with yellow. The trustees buy us in the black cloth from Antrim.

THOMAS: But it's fierce, foul stuff, isn't it?

SMITH: I'll leave you to it, Mrs O'Dea. I'll be over in the Monkey Ward, sluicing them out, if you need me. Be good, Mr Dunne. (*Goes.*)

MRS O'DEA (*taking a bobbin from her apron*): Look it, isn't that the bee's knees? That's from my own sewing box, that Mr O'Dea gave me in the old days. I can't do fairer than that.

THOMAS: Oh, it's very sunny.

MRS O'DEA: Now. (*Pinning again.*) It'll do beautifully. Can't your daughter bring you in clothes, if you don't like mine?

THOMAS: I wouldn't go bothering her. All my daughters are good, considerate women. We looked after each other, in that fled time, when their mother was dead.

MRS O'DEA: I'm sorry, Mr Dunne. And how did she die?

THOMAS: They never failed their father, their Papa, in that fled time. You should have seen them when they were little. Three little terrors going round with the knicks to their knees.

MRS O'DEA (*pricking him by mistake*): Oh, sorry. And where are your other daughters, Mr Dunne, these days?

THOMAS: We stood under the hawthorn, while the bees broke their hearts at the bell-flowers, because the fringes of darkness had closed them.

MRS O'DEA: Who did, Mr Dunne?

THOMAS: My wife Cissy and myself. Cecilia. In courting days. Old courting days.

MRS O'DEA: And what did she die of, did you say? (*Pricking.*)

THOMAS: Nothing at all. Her farm was Lathaleer, her father's farm. The most beautiful piece of land. He was woodsman and keeper at Humewood, but he was a most dexterous farmer. The Cullens of Lathaleer. What a match she was for me! A strong, straight-backed, sensible person that loved old steps and tunes. She'd rather learn a new step than boil turnips, old Cullen said to me — but it wasn't so. What does a father know? King Edward himself praised her hair, when we were presented in nineteen-three. A thorough mole-black devious hair she had.

MRS O'DEA: I'm sure. And didn't you do well by her, rising so high, and everything?

THOMAS: Our happiest days were when I was only an inspector in Dalkey village. We lived there in a house called Polly Villa. There was precious little villainy in Dalkey. Three girls she bore there, three girls. And the boy already, before we came.

MRS O'DEA: You have a son too? You have a lot.

THOMAS: No. No, he didn't come back from France that time. He wrote me a lovely letter.

MRS O'DEA (*after a little*): And King Edward praised your wife's hair. Fancy.

THOMAS: Aye — All the ladies loved him. Of course, he was old in that time. But a true king.

MRS O'DEA (*finished with the fitting, unpinning him again*): What would you say about King De Valera?

THOMAS: I would say very little about him, in that I wouldn't know much to say. Of course, I see a bit about him in the papers.

MRS O'DEA: As much a foreigner as the King of England ever was, Mr O'Dea used to say, when he was overground. Mr O'Dea was a pundit, I'm afraid.

THOMAS: He wants to buy the Irish ports back from Mr Churchill. I think that's a great pity. A man that loves his King might still have gone to live in Crosshaven or Cobh,[11] and called himself loyal and true. But soon there'll be nowhere in Ireland where such hearts may rest.

MRS O'DEA: You're as well to keep up with the news, Mr Dunne.

THOMAS: I had an admiration for the other man though, the general that was shot, I forget his name.

MRS O'DEA (*ready to go*): Who was that?

THOMAS: I forget. I remember the shock of sorrow when he was killed. I remember Annie and me crying in the old parlour of our quarters in the Castle. A curiosity. I met him, you see, the one time. He was very courteous and praised Wicklow and said a few things to me than rather eased my heart, at the time. But they shot him.

MRS O'DEA (*going*): They shot a lot of people. Was it Collins?

THOMAS: I don't know, I forget. I remember the sorrow but not the name. Maybe that was the name.

MRS O'DEA: I may have left a few pins in you, Mr Dunne, so don't go dancing about unduly.

THOMAS: Dancing? I never danced in my life. I was a tree at a dance.

MRS O'DEA *goes off.* THOMAS *discovers a pin and holds it up.*

Where are your other daughters, Mr Dunne, these days? (*After a little, moving the pin about like a tiny sword.*) The barracks of Ireland filled with new faces. And all the proud regiments gone, the Dublin Rifles and the Dublin Fusiliers. All the lovely uniforms. All the long traditions, broken up and flung out, like so many morning eggs on to the dung heap. Where are your other daughters, Mr Dunne, these days? Dolly of the hats. Annie told me the name of the place. Somewhere in America. What was the name?

The light of their parlour in the Castle. ANNIE *comes on with a big bundle of socks to sort. She sits on the three-legged stool. The socks are all the same. She looks in the socks for holes by thrusting her right hand into each of them, sorts the good from the bad.*

ANNIE: There's a terrible queer sort of a quietness settled over this Castle. How Papa expects to hang on here now till September. The city will be rubble, rubble by September.

MAUD *follows on looking pale and alarmed.*

MAUD: Have you seen that Dolly?

ANNIE: No.

MAUD: I can't keep a hoult on her at all these days.

ANNIE: She'll be down the town, as usual.

MAUD: How can she go shopping in times like these?

ANNIE: What's civil unrest to Dolly and her shopping?

MAUD (*feeling the back of her head*): Oh, dear.

ANNIE: What is it, Maud?

MAUD: Nothing, nothing at all.

ANNIE: Maud, what is it now?

MAUD: I have an ache here, Annie, at the base of the skull, do you think it might be something deadly?

ANNIE: I never knew a one to worry like you do, girl.

MAUD: Do you want to feel it? Is there a lump?

ANNIE: Don't come near me with your head! It's nothing. It's called a headache. Any normal person would accept that it's a headache. Girl, sometimes I don't wonder if you mightn't be seriously astray in your wits, girl.

MAUD: Oh, don't say that, Annie.

ANNIE: Am I not allowed sort the darning in peace?

DOLLY *comes in to them, wearing a neat outfit. She looks subdued.*

What's happened you, Dolly?

MAUD: I was all over the yards looking for you, Dolly, where on earth do you get to, these days?

DOLLY: I was down at the North Wall[12] with the Galligan sisters.

MAUD: At the North Wall?

ANNIE: What were you doing there, Dolly?

DOLLY: Mary Galligan was going out with one of the Tommies,[13] and he and his troop were heading off home today, so we went down to see them off.

ANNIE (*sorting away*): Well, well, I don't know, Dolly, if you aren't the biggest fool in Christendom.

DOLLY: No, I'm no fool. They were nice lads. There was a good crowd down there, and the Tommies were in high spirits, singing and so on. It was very joyful.

MAUD: You've to keep your skirts long these times, Dolly. You're not to be seen waving to soldiers.

DOLLY: They're going from Ireland and they'll never be back, why shouldn't we say goodbye? Do you know every barracks in Ireland has lost its officers and men? Regiments that protected us in the war, who went out and left thousands behind in France. Willie's own regiment is to be disbanded, and that's almost entirely Dublin lads.

ANNIE: Dolly, why are you so surprised? Haven't we known for the last six months that Ireland is to be destroyed? I don't know why it's such news to you. Haven't you listened? Haven't you seen your father's face? Haven't you felt for him, Dolly?

DOLLY: It's different when you see it.

ANNIE: You're a fool, Dolly.

DOLLY: I'm no fool.

ANNIE *picks up in one hand the good socks and in the other the ones needing mending — they look like two woolly hands themselves.*

And I'll tell you. Coming home in the tram, up the docks road, Mary Galligan was crying, and we were talking kindly to her, and trying to comfort her, and I don't know what we said exactly, but this woman, a middle-aged woman, quite well-to-do, she rises up and stands beside us like a long streak of misery, staring at us. And she struck Mary Galligan on the cheek, so as she left the marks of her hand there. And she would have attacked me too, but that the conductor came down and spoke to the woman. And she said we were Jezebels and should have our heads shaved and be whipped, for following the Tommies. And the conductor looked at her, and hadn't he served in France himself, as one of the Volunteers, oh, it was painful, the way she looked back at him, as if he were a viper, or a traitor. The depth of foolishness in her. A man that had risked himself, like Willie, but that had reached home at last.

DOLLY *crying.* ANNIE *gets up and puts her arms around her, still holding the socks.*

ANNIE: Things will sort themselves out, Dolly dear.

DOLLY: If she had shot us it wouldn't have been so bad.

ANNIE: Things will sort themselves out.

MAUD *feeling the back of her head again, confused.* We'll put on our aprons and get the tea. We'll go on ourselves as if we were living in paradise. (*The three go out.*)

THOMAS: Their father's face. Their father's face.

He puts his hands over his face. MATT, *a youngish man in a hat, his shirt sleeves held by metal circlets, sets up his easel centrestage. Sunlight gathers about him, clearing the sense of* THOMAS's *room. Rooks. A suggestion of meadow grass.* MATT *holds a square of cut-out cardboard to the view, deciding on a composition. He wipes at his face.*

MATT: Midges! The artist's bane!

THOMAS *approaches him, a little wildly.*

THOMAS: Patrick O'Brien, Patrick O'Brien, wherever did you bury my suit, man dear? They are tormenting me with dark cloth, and I hope you will give it back to me, despite your great prowess and fame, as a bulleter.

MATT: It isn't who you think, Thomas. It is Matt Kirwin that married your daughter Maud.

THOMAS (*astonished*): Oh — is it? (*After a moment.*) You have a strong look of Patrick about you. Except I see now, you are not on all fours, as I would expect. Are you a hero too?

MATT (*kindly*): How are you getting on, Thomas?

THOMAS: How does it come that you are here in the walking meadow? I only ask, as I am used to seeing people hither and thither and yon. (*Feeling his arms for solidity.*) Have you lost your wits also?

MATT: Maybe so, but I have brought Annie over in the Ford. We're over there in Kiltegan for a week or two with the little boys. I thought I might capture a water-colour while I waited.

THOMAS: You might, like a man might capture a butterfly. You haven't started your capturing.

MATT: In a minute, when I decide the view I want. The painting itself will only take a moment.

THOMAS: They're all choice views. Where's Maud then?

MATT: She stayed in Dublin this time.

THOMAS: It isn't the melancholy?

MATT: I don't know what it is. She has certainly kept to her bed of recent months. Has she been right since the second boy came? I don't know.

THOMAS: Her mother was always very jolly. I don't know where she gets it from.

MATT: The sea air of Howth will cure all that, in time,

the sea air, the quieter nature of life there in Howth, and the boys. She does love to see the boys, and they are most dignified and splendid boys.

THOMAS: You say? (*Warmly.*) Well, Matt (*taking* MATT's *hand*), how are you? (*Oddly.*) How do you do?

MATT: We're going along fine. I'm teaching in the technical school in Irishtown — for my sins. And painting for myself when I can. I have done a great deal of work on the Great South Wall, in my lunchtimes. The Poolbeg Lighthouse? But we couldn't get by at all without Annie. She keeps everything going.

THOMAS: Yes, yes, she told me you had one of your drawings printed up in a book, didn't you, yes, of the Bailey Lighthouse I think she said. You will be a great expert soon on lighthouses.

MATT (*pleased*): It was little enough.

THOMAS: Ah, Matthew, it is good to see you. You're looking so well. I forget, you know, I forget how much I like you. And the boys, the two grand boys, will I see them today? Are they in the Ford?

MATT: No, Thomas. They're so little still, and this is such a strange spot, for children, and, you know, they were a bit upset the last time. The elder boy has read his *Oliver Twist* and you were all mixed up in his mind with Fagan. Do you remember, at the end of the book, when the child is brought in to see Fagan before Fagan is hanged?

THOMAS: Hanged? No.

MATT: Maud was worried that . . .

THOMAS: Certainly, certainly. You must excuse my long johns. I lost my suit only recently. As a matter of fact, it must be buried around here somewhere. Well, no matter, they'll make me another, and then maybe you will bring my grandsons again to see me? Or you could fetch me over to Kiltegan in the Ford if they were afraid of this place. I'd be very quiet for you in the Ford.

MATT: Of course, Thomas.

THOMAS: I know I look a sight. And that won't do for such fine boys. I only saw them those few times, but, I think it is the smell of children that gets in upon you. You long for it then. And the roundness of them, and the love they show you. It could be anywhere about here, my suit. But I'm having a touch of gold put into the new one — well, yellow, anyhow.

MATT: You'll find Annie in your room if you go up, I'll be bound. She thought you were inside, you know.

THOMAS: Yellow thread, you know?

MATT: All right.

THOMAS: Matt, I don't like to ask Annie, to bother her, but do you think there's any great likelihood of my getting away from here at all in the coming times?

MATT: I don't know rightly, Thomas.

THOMAS: Of course, of course. It is quite a pleasant station. You see all the country air we have. Not like the city. The city would ruin a man's health. Though it has its beauties. Do you know, I used at one time to be a policeman? Do you know I used at one time be Chief Superintendent of B Division? With responsibility for the Castle herself? It was I cleared all the vermin out of Yorke Street, that time, the fancy men from the Curragh and all their girls — it *was* me, wasn't it, Matt? I held that post? You must bring the boys to Kiltegan as often as you can.

MATT: Well, we do, Thomas. You have a fine vista here, look. (*Having him look into the cardboard framer.*) You do, what with those oaks, and the field of wheat beyond.

THOMAS (*peering, after a moment*): It's only grass just.

MATT: Oh, is it grass?

THOMAS: Paint away, Matthew.

MATT: Thank you.

The light of THOMAS's *room again finds* ANNIE, *more spinsterish now, strong, bony, simply dressed, with her handbag and a brown paper bag. She looks anxious.* THOMAS *goes to her with a great smile, raising his arms.*

THOMAS (*searching in his mind for her name*): Dolly — Maud — Annie!

ANNIE: Papa.

THOMAS (*his arms collapsing slowly*): What has happened to you, Annie? You look very different to how you were just this morning.

ANNIE: What happened to your clothes, Papa?

THOMAS: I don't know, Dolly.

ANNIE: Annie, it is.

THOMAS: Annie. I don't know. I think I heard there was a bit of thievery going on, but I don't think there's any truth in it. Nothing for the magistrate. I'll deal with it. You know Mr Collins is to take over the Castle in January. I'll need all my clothes done over like new.

ANNIE: No, Papa. That was all years ago. In bygone times. You are in Baltinglass County Home, Papa.

THOMAS: I know. And I tell myself, so I won't forget. I had it written down somewhere, but I lost the bit of paper. What is it about the old head? Give me the name of any street in Dublin and I'll name every lane, alleyway, road, terrace and street around it. I could knit you the whole thing with names, and if you forgot a few places, and found a hole there in your memory, I could darn it for you. I am in effect a sort of Dublin Street Directory. But when it comes to the brass tacks of things, everyday matters, as, for instance, where in the name of God I am, well, daughter dear, I'm not so quick then. But look, girl, what Annie gave me. (*Going to his mattress and fetching a book out.*) A wonderful strange story about a boy on the Mississippi. And his friend. They are lost in a cave together, the two boys, and the poor bit of a greasy candle they have is burning lower and lower, and the demons of the dark are surely approaching . . . I feel I know that cave. Do you see, Dolly? I can see it when I put my hands over my face. Like this. Yes, there she is, the mighty Mississippi, going along like Godly pewter. And those poor boys, Huckleberry and Tom, and the yellow walls of the cave, and the big drips of water. Oh, Dolly, and the old granite bathing place at Vico Rock. And there's the terrible suck-up of water when Davy Byrnes the newspaper vendor takes his dive, the fattest man in Ireland, and there's Annie, all decked out in her first communion regalia like a princess, oh, mercy, and there's the moon over a bay that reputable people have compared to Naples — Sorrento, Vico, beautiful Italian names living the life of Reilly in old Killiney and Dalkey. On a summer's night, you were born, Dolly, deep in the fresh dark, just when the need for candles failed. Oh, Dolly.

ANNIE (*trying to calm him*): I gave you the book about the Mississippi, Papa. It's a book you loved in your youth, so you always said.

THOMAS (*gripping her arm a bit roughly*): Where is Maud, where is she, that she doesn't come in to me?

ANNIE: She's taken refuge, taken refuge you might say, in her own difficulties.

THOMAS: Is that right? And Dolly, where is Dolly?

ANNIE: Gone out into the wide world, Papa. Would you blame her?

THOMAS: Blame her? (*Formal again.*) How do you do? How is Maud? How are the boys? No, no, I know all that. Don't tell me. I won't waste your time, never you fear. How are you? That's the important thing to establish. That's how people go on among themselves, family people. Is there any word from Dolly in America? Annie, Annie, where is she in America?

ANNIE: Ohio, Papa?

THOMAS: Ohio, Ohio! That's the place. Ah, I was tormented trying to think of the word. Ohio. Dolly in Ohio. I must write it down. Do you have a dragonfly — a pencil?

ANNIE: No, Papa, I don't. This room is so bare and dark, for all the shillings I give them. I hope they give you your paper. It's all I can manage, Papa, out of your pension. It is a very miserly pension. Matt makes up the rest of it for us. And he has a pittance.

THOMAS: Don't I have a beautiful pension for my forty-five years of service?

ANNIE: No, Papa, you don't.

THOMAS: I think I should have.

ANNIE: Look, Papa, what I brought for you. (*She pulls a bunch of heather from the bag.*)

THOMAS: Oh, Lord, Lord. (*Smelling it in his hands tenderly.*) From the hills above Kiltegan. How the heat of the day makes the heather raise its smell to the grateful native. The peace, the deep peace in the evening as we stared, you and me, into the last lingering flames running across the ashen turf, and the ghostly tiredness in us after slaving about the place all day.

ANNIE: When was that, Papa?

THOMAS: Those three years in Kiltegan, Annie, when you and me were left to amuse ourselves as we could, Annie. You remember?

ANNIE: I do, Papa, I remember the three years well enough. With you sinking lower and lower in your chair beside that fire, and muttering about this and that, and the way you had been abandoned, you wouldn't treat a dog like that, you said, muttering, muttering, till I was driven mad. And all the work of the dairy and the byre and the hens to do. It was like living with Hannibal in Abyssinia, when Hannibal was a leader no more.

THOMAS: Who? Where? But didn't the Cullens of Lathaleer come visiting like royalty in their high trap, and the Dunnes of Feddin, and the Cullens of Kelsha?

ANNIE: No, Papa, they did not, not after you drove them away with insult and passing remarks.

THOMAS: I never did. We lived there like, like . . .

ANNIE: Like, like the dead, Papa.

THOMAS (*angry*): All right. So there were demons in the high wood, and the screams of the lost from the byres, and the foul eggs in the rotting hay, and every pitchfork in the barn was sharp, glinting sharp, for you to thrust into my breast.

ANNIE: Papa, Papa, calm and ease, calm and ease.

THOMAS: Oh, fearsome, fearsome, fearsome. Can I see my grandsons?

ANNIE (*holding on to her father*): Papa, Papa. Your grandsons are afraid of you.

THOMAS: Afraid? Filthy, filthy.

ANNIE: Papa, Papa. How many miles to Babylon?

THOMAS: (*smiling*) Babylon.

ANNIE: Three score and ten. Remember, Papa, remember?

THOMAS: Will I be there by candlelight?

ANNIE: Sure, and back again.

THOMAS: Candlelight. Oh, yes, yes. (*Weeping.*) Yes. (*Smiling.*) Yes.

ANNIE: How many times in that last year in Kiltegan did I have to sing you the songs to calm your fears?

THOMAS: Was it so many?

ANNIE: Many, many, many. Three score and ten, Papa.

THOMAS (*after a long breath*): My father was the steward of Humewood, and I was the steward of Christendom. Look at me.

ANNIE: Papa, we've all to grow old.

THOMAS (*patting her back with his right hand, like a child*): Oh, yes. Oh, yes.

ANNIE *goes quietly.* THOMAS *sits on the stool slowly. The door ajar.*

Candlelight. (*After a little.*) A bit of starch for a new shirt, a bit of spit for my shoes, I could set out for Kiltegan as an ordinary man and see those shining boys. (*After a little.*) No. (*After a little.*) And take them up and smell their hair and kiss their noses and make them do that laughter they have in them. (*After a little.*) No. (*After a little.*) Dear Lord, put the recruits back in their barracks in Fitzgibbon Street, put the stout hearts back into Christendom's Castle, and troop the colours once more for Princess and Prince, for Queen and for King, for Chief Secretary and Lord Lieutenant, for Viceroy and Commander-in-Chief. (*After a little.*) But you cannot. (*After a little.*) Put the song back in the mouth of the beggar, the tune back in the pennywhistle, the rat-tat-tat of the tattoo back in the parade ground, stirring up our hearts. (*After a little.*) But you cannot. (*After a little.*) — Gone. The hearth of Kiltegan. How many miles to Kiltegan, Nineveh and Babylon? The sun amiable in the yard and the moon in the oaks after darkness. The rabbitman stepping out of the woods at dusk with a stick of dangling snags and a dark greeting. — Gone. (*After a little, quietly.*) Candlelight. I walked out through the grounds of Loreto College as far as the sea. The midwife

had bade me to go. I was a man of fifty. Rhododendrons. All night she had strained in the bed, she was like a person pinned by a fallen rock, waving her arms and legs and groaning, and shouting. Her shouts escaped from Polly Villa and ran up the road to the station and down the road to the village in darkness. I was becoming distressed myself, so the midwife bade me go. Willie, Maud and Annie had been difficult for her too, because she was small, small and thin and hard-working. Cullen's daughter. And she was like a sort of dancer in the bed, but stuck in the dance. King Edward himself praised her hair, it was mole-black, though there are no moles in Ireland. Out at sea, the lighthouse was hard at work too, warning the mail-packet and the night fishermen. I thought of all the nuns asleep up in the college, asleep in their quiet rooms, the sea asleep herself at the foot of the cliff. And I thought, I would do anything for that woman of mine behind me in the house, where we had done all our talking and laughing and our quarrelling. But my mind was in a peculiar state. I thought of all the Sunday roasts she had made, all piled up somewhat in eternity, a measure of her expertise. And I thought of how much her daughters and her son loved her, and depended on her for every sort of information, and how stupid and silent I was with my son. How she made the world possible and hopeful for him and the two girls. (*Sits on bed.*) I started to tremble, it was a moment in your life when daily things pass away from you, when all your concerns seem to vanish, and you are allowed by God a little space of clarity and grace. When you see that God himself is in your wife and in your children, and they hold in trust for you your own measure of goodness. And in the manner of your treatment of them lies your own salvation. I went back to the house with a lighter heart, a simpler man than the one who had set out. And the house was quiet. It was as if it were itself asleep, the very bricks, living and asleep with a quiet heartbeat. (*Holding the pillow.*) Suddenly I was terribly afeared that my new child was dead, I don't know why. You expect its cries, you long for its cries. I pushed open my front door and hurried down into the back room. The midwife was over by the window, with a little bundle. And Cissy was lying quiet, still, at ease. The midwife came over immediately and placed her bundle in my arms. It was like holding a three-pound bag of loose corn. (*The pillow.*) And there was a little face in the midst of the linen, a little wrinkled face, with red skin, and two big round eyes seeming to look up at me. I pledged all my heart and life to that face, all my blood and strength to that face, all the usefulness of my days to that face. And that was Dolly. And that was just as the need for candlelight fails, and the early riser needs no candle for his task.

Music. Dark after a few moments.

ACT TWO

THOMAS's *room as before,* MAUD *holding his sword in readiness.* ANNIE *near.* DOLLY *looking at* THOMAS *with the polished shoes just on. He wears his dress uniform, the helmet as yet on the table.*

THOMAS: Oh, Dolly, Dolly, Dolly.

DOLLY: Will they do, Papa?

THOMAS: They're beautiful shoes now.

DOLLY: This whole day reminds me of when I was twelve, and there were snipers on the roofs above the music-hall, and me and Annie and Maud would be crawling along the sandbags outside the gates, trying to get in home from the shops. And laughing. And the soldiers at the gates laughing too.

ANNIE: That poor lieutenant didn't laugh when they put a bullet in his head.

MAUD: And you were only ten then, Miss Dolly, and as wild as a tenement cat.

DOLLY: Will it be like that today?

THOMAS: No, sweet, that's all done with now. This is an act of peace.

ANNIE: My foot.

THOMAS (*putting an arm about* DOLLY): Mr Collins and a small staff will come in, and we'll all meet like gentlemen.

ANNIE: Ha.

THOMAS: And he will take command of the place, in effect. Don't you worry, Dolly, don't you worry.

DOLLY: And what time is the meeting, Papa?

THOMAS: Shortly. The chief secretary wanted to meet at six but Collins sent in a note to say he wasn't a blackbird.

ANNIE: Blackguard more like.

DOLLY: You are sure no one will try to shoot you?

THOMAS: Why would they want to shoot me?

ANNIE: They would hardly have offered Papa a position in their new police force if they wanted to shoot him.

DOLLY: Did they, Papa? Oh, and will you take up that offer, Papa? It would be exciting.

THOMAS: We'll be Wicklow people again by year's end. Look at your father, Dolly. I am sixty-six years old! I am too old for new things. Indeed, I wish I were a younger man again, and I could kiss your noses, like when you were babies, and make you scream with delight.

MAUD: Papa! Come along, Papa, and we'll get your sword on you.

MAUD *and* ANNIE *attach the sword to its belt.*

THOMAS: A man with three such daughters, three beautiful daughters, will never be entirely worthless. This January morning is the start of peace, and we may enjoy that peace till September, and then be gone — gone like shadows of an old dispensation.

DOLLY: A girl of eighteen is never a shadow, Papa.

THOMAS: Today is — what do you call it — symbolical. (MAUD *doing the last buttons on the jacket.*) Like those banners in the Chapel Royal for every lord lieutenant that has ruled Ireland. It's a mighty symbolical sort of a day, after all these dark years. I'll be worn out. I'll be practising now. (*Taking* DOLLY's *hand.*) Good man, Joe, good man, Harry — that's the constables, because they're young too, Dolly, and will be greatly affected. Oh, big country hands, with rural grips! I'll have crushed fingers, like a visiting king.

ANNIE: And well, Papa, you are a king, more than some of those other scallywags.

THOMAS: That is the whole crux of the matter. I am not a king. I am the servant of a king. I am only one of the stewards of his Irish city.

ANNIE: Collins is no king either, begging your pardon. With a tally of carnage, intrigue and disloyalty that would shame a tinker. And that King, for all his moustaches and skill on horseback, has betrayed us.

MAUD: Annie, Annie, be quiet while Papa goes out. It isn't Papa's fault.

THOMAS: I served that King, Annie, and that will suffice me. I hope I guarded his possession well, and helped the people through a terrible time. And now that story is over and I am over with it, and content. I don't grieve.

MAUD: Of course you don't. Won't we have the great days soon in Kiltegan?

THOMAS: But won't Dolly miss the fashions and the shops and the to-do of the town?

ANNIE (*before* DOLLY *can answer*): I'll miss nothing. If they want to destroy everything, let them do so without us. It will be whins and waste everywhere, with bits of stones sticking up that were once Parliament, Castle and Cathedral. And people going round like scarecrows and worse. And Cuckoo Lane and Red Cow Lane and all those places just gaps with rubbish in them.

MAUD: Annie, you're giving me a powerful headache.

ANNIE: The like of Collins and his murdering men won't hold this place together. They haven't the grace or the style for it. So you needn't mourn your shops and hats and haircuts, Dolly Dunne — they won't be there.

THOMAS: Will I tell Mr Collins you said so, Annie?

MAUD: You'll miss the show if you don't go now, Papa. You don't want to be running over the square to them and sweating in your finery.

THOMAS: Am I shipshape?

MAUD: Shipshape as a ship.

DOLLY: Wait, don't let the king go! (*Hurrying out for something.*)

THOMAS: Where's she off to now?

ANNIE: Who can say where Dolly goes.

MAUD: Poor Dolly — I do feel sorry for her.

ANNIE: Why for Dolly? Feel sorry for yourself, woman.

DOLLY (*coming back with a buttonhole*): I got this for you last night, Papa.

ANNIE: On that dangerous trek back from the dance at the Rotunda . . .

DOLLY (*looking at* ANNIE): Fresh up from the country.

ANNIE: I hope you can wear a buttonhole today? It seems frivolous.

THOMAS: Put it in for me, Dolly. A white rose! Now I'm ready for them.

DOLLY (*catching sight of the heather on the table*): Oh, but, Papa, you'd flowers already — maybe you meant to wear a bit of this?

ANNIE: It isn't there at all yet. Just mere hints of flowers. That heather was born in the snow.

MAUD (*smelling it*): That heather was born in the snow, right enough, Annie.

ANNIE (*drawn to the heather, as are* THOMAS *and* DOLLY): It came up on the Wicklow train. Sometimes you find you need a hint of home.

DOLLY: Born in the snow, like a lamb.

THOMAS: That's from the hill beside the sloping field. I know that colour. (*Smelling, all of them smelling.*) It smells like God's breath, it does.

MAUD: We won't mind going home to such riches.

THOMAS: It is the very honeyed lord of a smell, so it is.
THOMAS *goes out the door happily. The daughters scatter. Then the noise of a ruckus in the corridor.*

SMITH (*off*): Where are you wandering to? (*After a little.*) Where are you heading, old man?

THOMAS (*off*): What are you saying to me, constable? — Get back from me!

SMITH (*off*): Mrs O'Dea, Mrs O'Dea! Lie in there against the wall, you scarecrow, you. Mrs O'Dea! Come up, come up!

MRS O'DEA (*off*): Oh, I'm hurrying, I'm hurrying . . .
MRS O'DEA *steps into the room.*

THOMAS (*off*): But I have to go and meet Collins!

SMITH (*off*): Collins is stone dead.
THOMAS, *in his long johns again, propelled in by* SMITH.

THOMAS: Where are you putting me? This isn't our quarters!

SMITH: Who was it left his door open? He might have gone raving up the main street of Baltinglass.

MRS O'DEA: I don't know. It must have been his daughter.

THOMAS: What have you done with my daughters? (*Pushing* SMITH.) Get back from me, you blackguard. By Christ, assaulting a policeman. That's the Joy for you, you scoundrel.

SMITH (*drawing out the pacifier*): Right, boy, I did warn you. Now you'll get it. (*Raising the implement.*) Mrs O'Dea, fetch the jacket off the hook in the corridor. (MRS O'DEA *goes out.*) You'll see the suit she has for you now, Thomas Dunne.

THOMAS: You'll see the suit, Tomassy Tom. You'll see the suit.
THOMAS *escapes from him, leaps the bed like a youth.*

SMITH: Jesus of Nazareth. (SMITH *goes after him,* THOMAS *ducks around to the stool,* MRS O'DEA *brings in the strait-jacket.*)

THOMAS: Nicks, nicks.

SMITH: He's claiming nicks off the three-legged stool.
SMITH *strides to* THOMAS *and strikes him with the pacifier, expertly enough.*
Why couldn't I go with my brother flensing whales?

THOMAS (*wriggling*): You think I haven't had worse? See this thumb? See the purple scar there? My own Da Da did that, with a sheath knife. What do you think of that? (SMITH *struggles to place the jacket on him.*) Do you want to see my back? I've a mark there was done with a cooper's band, and on a Sunday too. But he loved me.

MRS O'DEA: Lie up on your bed, Mr Dunne. (*To* SMITH.) He'll be worn out in a minute. I have your suit ready, Mr Dunne, will I bring it up to you? He'll be good now, Mr Smith.

THOMAS (*lying on the bed awkwardly, bound*): Give it to Patrick O'Brien that excelled mightily at the bulleting. He'll eat it piecemeal like a dog. (MRS O'DEA *and* SMITH *go out, and lock the door.*)

We're all here, the gang of us, all the heroes of my youth, in these rooms, crying and imagining, or strung out like poor paste pearls of people along the rows of the graveyard. Lizzie Moran and Dorothy Cullen I saw there, two beauties of Lathaleer, and Hannigan that killed his mother, under a whinbush. And the five daughters of Joseph Quinn, the five of them, much to my amazement, side by side in five short graves. All of them lost their wits and died, Black Jim. If I could lead those poor souls back across the meadows and the white lanes to the hearths and niches of their youth, and fill the farms with them again, with their hopes and dreams, by God ... I am a tired old man and I'll have terrible aches forthwith. Let him hit. What else has he, but hitting? Does he know why the calf is stupid? No. There he is in his ignorance, hitting. Let him hit. (*After a little.*) My two bonny grandsons would cure me. (*After a little.*) It's a cold wind that blows without forgiveness, as the song says.

There's a sort of darkness in the room now, with a seep of lights. WILLIE *stands in the corner, quietly, singing softly.*

My poor son ... When I was a small child, smaller than yourself, my Ma Ma brought me home a red fire engine from Baltinglass. It was wrapped in the newspaper and hid in the hayshed for the Christmas. But I knew every nook and cranny of the hayshed, and I soon had it found, and the paper off it. And quite shortly I had invented a grand game, where I stood one foot on the engine and propelled myself across the yard. I kept falling and falling, tearing and scumming my clothes, but no matter, the game was a splendid game. And my mother she came out for something, maybe to fling the grains at the hens in that evening time, and she saw me skating on the engine and she looked at me. She looked with a terrible long face, and I looked down and there was the lovely engine all scratched and bent, and the wheel half-rubbed off it. So she took the toy quietly from under my foot, and marched over to the dunghill and shoved it in deep with her bare hands, tearing at the rubbish there and the layers of dung. So I sought out her favourite laying hen and put a yard-bucket over it, and it wasn't found for a week, by which time the Christmas was over and the poor hen's wits had gone astray from hunger and darkness and inertia. Nor did it ever lay eggs again that quickened with chicks. And that was a black time between my Ma Ma and me. (*After a little.*) You were six when your Mam died, Willie. Hardly enough time to be at war with her, the way a son might. She was very attached to you. Her son. She had a special way of talking about you, a special music in her voice. And she was proud of your singing, and knew you could make a go of it, in the halls, if you wished. I wanted to kill her when she said that. But at six you sang like a linnet, true enough. (*After a little.*) I didn't do as well as she did, with you. I was sorry you never reached six feet. I was a fool. What big loud talking fools are fathers sometimes. Why do we not love our sons simply and be done with it? She did. I would kill, or I would do a great thing, just to see you once more, in the flesh. All I got back was your uniform, with the mud only half-washed out of it. Why do they send the uniforms to the fathers and the mothers? I put it over my head and cried for a night, like an owl in a tree. I cried for a night with your uniform over my head, and no one saw me.

MRS O'DEA *unlocks the door and comes in with the new suit, a rough black suit that she has joined with her yellow thread. She brings it to his bedside, dispelling* WILLIE.

MRS O'DEA: Look at the lovely thread I used in it, just like you asked. Do you think you are quiet now?

THOMAS: Yes.

MRS O'DEA *starts to untie him,* SMITH *comes in with a bowl of food, puts it on the table.*

MRS O'DEA (*To* SMITH): Help me get him into bed. He'll lie quiet. (*To* THOMAS.) Take off the long johns too, I'll wash them for you. (SMITH *pulls down the top. The two wounds from the beating are revealed on* THOMAS's *chest.*) We should put something on those weals.

SMITH: He's only scratched. Let the sleep heal him. He'll spring up in the morning, gabbling as always, crazy as ever. God knows I can't deal with him now, I have a fancy dress to go to in the town.

MRS O'DEA: Well, I can't wash a man, Mr Smith.

SMITH: He doesn't need washing. He's barely marked.

MRS O'DEA: Won't you at least wash his hands, they're all black from the floor. And I suppose his feet are as bad.

SMITH: He may be St Thomas, Mrs O'Dea, but I'm not Jesus Christ, to be washing his hands and feet.

MRS O'DEA: What is he talking about, Mr Dunne?

SMITH: I have to collect my costume at six, Mrs O'Dea, off the Dublin train.

MRS O'DEA: Tuck yourself up, Mr Dunne, and have a rest.

They go out. ANNIE *and* DOLLY *come on in mid-conversation.*

DOLLY: Where is my husband to come from, if we're to go back to Wicklow? I'm not marrying a farmer.

ANNIE: Oh, are you not, Dolly? Isn't it pleasant to pick and choose? What farmer would take a woman like me, and I might have had a sailor once for a husband if I'd been let. So you're not the only one with difficulties, though you always think you are. That's the way of the pretty.

DOLLY: You couldn't go marrying a sailor, Annie. You never see a sailor. They're always away — sailing.

ANNIE: And our father humiliated by renegades. Collins!

DOLLY: They didn't humiliate him, Annie, indeed, not at all. I'm sure it was all very polite. I think the truth is, Papa is delighted to be going back to Kiltegan, where he can have us all about him, slaving for him, and being his good girls, and never never marrying.

ANNIE: Dolly, that's poor wickedness.

DOLLY: I know.

ANNIE: He's desolated to be going back.

DOLLY: I don't believe he is. Or he'd have taken the new post in the whatever you call them. The Civic Guard.

ANNIE: You don't think they were offering him Chief Superintendent?

DOLLY: So. Let him be a superintendent again, and stay in Dublin, where a person can buy a decent hat. There's nothing in Baltinglass but soda-bread and eggs.

ANNIE: There's your father struggling to put a brave face on this day, which is no doubt the death of all good things for this country, and you're worrying about hats.

DOLLY: Hats are more dependable than countries.

ANNIE: You're a nonsensical girl, Dolly. Why don't you go away somewhere with yourself, if you don't want to go back to Wicklow?

DOLLY: I might!

ANNIE: You will not!

DOLLY: Aren't you just after telling me to?

ANNIE: Dolly, don't dream of going and leaving me alone in Wicklow!

DOLLY: For you to be giving out to me, like I was a little girl, and telling me I mustn't think of hats?

ANNIE (*seriously*): Dolly, Dolly, you wouldn't go?

DOLLY: Why not?

ANNIE (*almost shaking her*): Dolly, I'm serious, say you wouldn't. (*After a little.*) Say you wouldn't.

DOLLY: All right, all right, I wouldn't! I wouldn't. I wouldn't, Annie, dear.

ANNIE *nods at her fiercely. They go off.*

THOMAS (*from the bed*): I could scarce get over the sight of him. He was a black-haired handsome man, but with the big face and body of a boxer. He would have made a tremendous policeman in other days. He looked to me like Jack Dempsey, one of those prize-fighting men we admired. I would have been proud to have him as my son. When he walked he was sort of dancing, light on his pins, like a good bulleter. Like Patrick O'Brien himself. He looked like he might give Patrick O'Brien a good challenge for his money on some evening road somewhere, hoisting that ball of granite. He had glamour about him, like a man that goes about with the fit-ups,[14] or one of those picture stars that came on the big ship from New York, to visit us, and there'd be crowds in the streets like for royalty, and it would be a fierce job to keep them held back. Big American men and women, twice the size of any Irish person. And some of them Irish too, but fed those many years on beef and wild turkeys. He was like that, Mr Collins. I felt rough near him, that cold morning, rough, secretly. There never was enough gold in that uniform, never. I thought too as I looked at him of my father, as if Collins could have been my son and could have been my father. I had risen as high as a Catholic could go, and there wasn't enough braid, in the upshot. I remembered my father's anger when I failed at my schooling, and how he said he'd put me into the police, with the other fools of Ireland. I knew that by then most of the men in my division were for Collins, that they would have followed him wherever he wished, if he had called them. And for an instant, as the Castle was signed over to him, I felt a shadow of that loyalty pass across my heart. But I closed my heart instantly against it. We were to have peace. On behalf of the Crown the chief secretary wished him well. And indeed it was peaceful, that moment. The savagery and ruin that soon followed broke my heart again and again and again. My streets and squares became places for murder and fire. All that spring and summer, as now and then some brave boy spat at me in the streets, I could not hold back the tide of ruin. It was a personal matter. We had restored order in the days of Larkin. One morning I met a man in St Stephen's Green. He was looking at a youngster thrown half-in under a bush. No more than eighteen. The man himself was one of that army of ordinary, middle-class Irishmen with firm views and moustaches. He was apoplectic. We looked at each other. The birds were singing pleasantly, the early sun was up. 'My grandsons,' he said, 'will be feral[15] in this garden — mark my words.'

DOLLY, MAUD *and* ANNIE *come on and move* THOMAS's *table out a little and start to half-set it. There's a knock, and* MATT *appears.*

ANNIE: Who are you? What do you want?

DOLLY: Who is that, Annie?

ANNIE: What do you want here?

MATT: My name's Matthew Kirwin, ma'am. I was asked to supper by Maud Dunne.

ANNIE: By Maud Dunne?

MAUD (*coming over*): Oh, hello, Mr Kirwin. How kind of you to come.

ANNIE: How kind of him to come?

MAUD: Come in, Mr Kirwin, and meet my sisters. This is Dolly.

DOLLY: How do you do?

MAUD: And this is Annie.

ANNIE: Yes, this is Annie. And who is this, Maud?

MAUD: My friend, Annie, Mr Matthew Kirwin.

ANNIE: Since when do you have friends, Maud, coming to supper?

MAUD: I suppose I can have friends just as soon as Dolly? I suppose I can.

ANNIE: And have you known Mr Kirwin long, Maud?

MAUD: We have an acquaintance. Mr Kirwin was painting in Stephen's Green last Saturday, and I happened to look over his shoulder at what he was doing, and as a matter of fact he was quite cross with me, weren't you, Mr Kirwin, for doing so, and we fell to talking then, and I explained my interest in the old masters . . .

ANNIE: Your interest in the old masters?

MAUD: Yes, Annie. And we both agreed that the newer type of painters were all mad, and I invited him to supper.

ANNIE (*almost pushing him back*): I'm sorry, Mr Kirwin, but you'll have to go.

MAUD: Annie Dunne!

ANNIE: I don't know how you got past the gates, but there are to be no strangers coming in here. (*Pushing him elegantly.*)

MATT: If it isn't convenient . . .

ANNIE: It isn't even desirable, Mr Kirwin.

MAUD: Annie, lay your hands off that man, he is my artist that I found in Stephen's Green.

ANNIE: And do you go out into the street, these times, Maud, and shake hands with everyone you see, and ask them to supper, if they are not doing anything better that night?

MAUD: I do not, Annie Dunne.

ANNIE: What do you know about a man like this, with the leisure to be painting in daylight . . .

MATT: It was my day off, Miss Dunne . . .

ANNIE: And with a foreign accent . . .

MATT: I'm from Cork city . . .

ANNIE: And who may be the greatest rogue or the greatest saint that ever came out of — Cork city . . .

MAUD: You are not my mother, Annie, in fact I am older and wiser than you . . .

DOLLY: Let him stay till Papa comes, Annie, and if Papa says he is all right, we can have him to supper. It would be lovely to have friends to supper again. Let's, Annie.

ANNIE: And if he is an assassin?

DOLLY: He's just a young man like any other young man.

ANNIE: So are assassins. No, it cannot be. (*Pushing him more vigorously.*) Out with you, Mr Kirwin.

MAUD: Leave him be, oh, Annie, leave him be! (*She seems faint now, her legs buckling under her.*) Leave my artist be . . .

DOLLY *tries to hold her up.*

DOLLY: Help me, please.

MATT *holds her too.*

ANNIE: Let go of her, let go of her!

MAUD *falls to the ground.*

DOLLY: Oh, Annie, look what you've done now. Now we're the assassins, and Maud is killed.

The banging of a door below.

ANNIE: That's Papa. Papa always bangs the lower door for us, Mr Kirwin, because he has a house of girls. Now you'll get your supper!

MATT: I assure you, Miss Dunne . . .

THOMAS *comes from the bed and stops by them. He doesn't speak.* MAUD *opens her eyes, looks at him, gets up.* DOLLY *goes and kisses her father.*

DOLLY: What is it, Papa? You look so pale.

MAUD: Do you have a chill, Papa?

MATT (*to* ANNIE): I'll go, I'll go . . .

ANNIE (*not hearing him*): Are you all right, Papa?

THOMAS (*after a little*): The city is full of death. (*After a little, crying.*) The city is full of death.

ANNIE (*hissing, to* MAUD): Look at the state Papa is in — it's no night for a visitor.

THOMAS: How do you do, how do you do.

MAUD (*to* MATT): By the pillar,[16] Saturday noon.

MATT *nods and goes.*

THOMAS: Do I smell a stew, a real stew? Is that the aroma of lamb, bless me?

ANNIE: It is, Papa.

THOMAS: Where did you get lamb, Annie?

ANNIE: The Dunnes of Feddin sent it up. It's Wicklow lamb.

THOMAS: Wicklow. It is — Elysium. It is paradise . . . We'll be happy there, girls . . .

ANNIE: We will, Papa. We'll fetch the supper, Papa.

But they go out taking the things from the table with them. The door unlocks behind THOMAS, *and* SMITH *enters with a basin and a bottle of ointment. He is dressed like a cowboy complete with six-shooters.* THOMAS *stares at him.*

THOMAS: Black Jim!

SMITH: Ah, never let it be said I left you alone with those cuts. Come here and sit, if you will. (THOMAS *obediently goes to the stool.* SMITH *puts down the bowl and begins to tend to* THOMAS.) What's got into me? There's a lovely party going on in the town.

THOMAS: I could be a man war-wounded.

SMITH: You could. Or the outcome of a punch-up in a western saloon.

THOMAS (*laughing*): You think so?

SMITH (*posing with the ointment*): Do I not remind you of anyone in this get-up?

THOMAS (*trying*): No.

SMITH: Maybe you never fancied the pictures, did you?

THOMAS: I went the odd time to the magic lanthorn show.

SMITH: You couldn't guess then who I am, besides being Mr Smith, I mean?

THOMAS: Black Jim?

SMITH: Gary Cooper, Gary Cooper. Ah, you're no use.

THOMAS: Gary Cooper? Is that the Coopers of Rathdangan?

SMITH (*putting on the ointment*): *Lilac Time.* Did you never catch that? You haven't lived. Of course, it wasn't a cowboy as such. *Redemption* was a hell of a good cowboy.

THOMAS: No man is beyond redemption, my Ma Ma said, when he let the dog live.

SMITH: Who, Thomas? If men were beyond redemption, Thomas, what would we do in Ireland for Presidents?

THOMAS: That's a fair question. (*Laughing.*)

SMITH (*doing a cowboy*): You dirty dog, you dirty dog. (*After a little.*) Did you go to the war, Thomas?

THOMAS: Me? No — I was too old. My son was with the Dublin Rifles.

SMITH: Oh, I think I knew that. He was the boy that was killed.

THOMAS: He was that boy.

SMITH: I had a first cousin in it. A lot of men went out.

THOMAS: Did he come home?

SMITH: Not at all. They sent the uniform.

THOMAS: That's right, they do. I've only a letter from him, that's all I have in the world of him.

SMITH: Written from the battlefield?

THOMAS: Oh, aye, from the trenches themselves.

SMITH: I'd be very interested to see that letter.

THOMAS: Would you, Mr Smith? Of course. I have it somewhere, stuck in Annie's book. Will I get it?

SMITH: Do, get it, man, and we'll have a read of it. Why not?

THOMAS (*fetching the letter*): Do you not want to get to your fancy dress?

SMITH: The party can wait. (*Taking the old letter.*) It looks old enough.

THOMAS: Well, it's coming up to twenty years now.

SMITH (*opening it carefully*): It's an historical document.

THOMAS (*laughing*): Oh, aye. Historical.

SMITH (*reading*): He has a good hand at the writing, anyhow. (*Reading.*)

THOMAS (*nudging his knee*): Would you not . . .

SMITH: Read it aloud? You want me to?

THOMAS: I do. I would greatly like that.

SMITH: Fair enough. Okay. (*Settling himself to read it, clearing his voice, a little self-conscious.*) Of course, I don't read aloud much, so . . . (THOMAS *smiles.*) Right. — My dearest Papa, Here I am writing to you in the midst of all these troubles. We are three weeks now in the one spot and we all feel we are dug in here for an eternity. The shells going over have become familiar to us, and my friend the first lieutenant from Leitrim, Barney Miles, has given our regular rats names. Our first idea was to thump them with spades because they eat the corpses up on the field but surely there has been enough death. We have not got it as bad as some companies, because our position is raised, and we get drainage, but all the same we know what real mud is by now. We have had some miracles, in that last week deep in the night one of our men was thrown back over the rampart wounded, by what hands we do not know. Another man was sent out with a dispatch and on his way back found a big sow thrashing in the mud. He would have taken her on with him for chops except she was twice his weight and not keen. It made us remember that all hereabout was once farms, houses and farms and grass and stock, and surely the farmer in you would weep, Papa, to see the changes. I hope you don't mind my letter going on. It gives me great comfort to write to my father. You will probably think I am raving a bit, and ranting, but nevertheless, since I am so far distant, I tell myself you will be interested to get news of me here. I wish I could tell you that I am a hero, but truth to tell, there are few opportunities for valour, in the way we all imagined when we set out. I have not seen the enemy. Sometimes in the dark and still of the night-times I see lights over where their position is, and on the stillest evenings you can just hear their voices. Sometimes they sing! Sometimes we sing, low and quiet, we have quite a repertoire now of risky songs, that you wouldn't approve at all. But it is a grand thing that we can still use our voices, and when I sing I think of home, and my sisters, and my father, and hope and know that my mother is watching over me here. God keep you all safe, because we have been told of the ruckus at home, and some of the country men are as much upset by that as they would be by their present emergency. I know you are in the front line there, Papa, so keep yourself safe for my return, when Maud will cook the fatted calf! The plain truth is, Papa, this is a strange war and a strange time, and my whole wish is to be home with you all in Dublin, and to abide by your wishes, whatever they be. I wish to be a more dutiful son because, Papa, in the mire of this wasteland, you stand before my eyes as the finest man I know, and in my dreams you comfort me, and keep my spirits lifted. Your son, Willie.

THOMAS (*after a little, while* SMITH *folds the letter and gives it back to him*): In my dreams you comfort me . . .

SMITH: That's a beautiful letter, Mr Dunne. A memento. A keepsake.

THOMAS *nods his head, thinking.*

(*Getting up to go.*) Good man, good man. (*Goes, locks the door.*)

THOMAS *puts away his letter and climbs into bed. After a little* DOLLY *enters and goes to his bedside, with a big ticket in her hand.* THOMAS *looks at her, takes the ticket, reads it, looks at her.*

DOLLY: You aren't angry, Papa? It took all my courage to buy it, every ounce I had, you can't imagine. (*After a little.*) You are wondering how I could afford it? It was quite expensive, but it's only steerage. I had to sell Mam's bracelet that I was given, the ruby one you gave me, and I've to work for an agency the first two years, as a domestic, in Cleveland, Ohio.

THOMAS (*after a little*): Is it because she died on us? She was mortally sorry to die. She died as the need for candlelight failed. She would have adored you, even as she gave her life for you.

DOLLY: Papa, don't be angry with me, please, I could not bear it, it took all my courage.

THOMAS: Why would you go, Dolly, that is loved by us all, and young men going crazy over you here, and queueing up to marry you?

DOLLY: They're not, Papa. I want to be liked and loved, but people are cold towards me, Papa.

THOMAS: Why would they be, Dolly?

DOLLY: Because — because of you, Papa, I suppose.

THOMAS: It will pass, Dolly. In Wicklow we will be among our own people.

DOLLY: I don't want to be like the Dunnes of Feddin, three wild women with unkempt hair and slits on the backs of their hands from ploughing. You're old, Papa, it's not the same for you.

THOMAS (*smiling, giving back the ticket*): Yes, I am old.

DOLLY: I didn't mean to say that, Papa. I knew you would be angry with me, I prayed you wouldn't be.

THOMAS: Come here to me. (*He embraces her.*) How could I be angry with you? It's a poor look-out if I am angry with my own baby because she is afraid.

DOLLY: I didn't want to hurt you, Papa.

THOMAS: Papa is strong enough for all these things.

DOLLY: You'll take care, Papa, and write to me, about all the goings-on in Kiltegan?

THOMAS: I will of course. (*The lock turns in the door,* DOLLY *breaks from him, goes.*) I will of course!

MRS O'DEA *pops in and places a pair of black shoes by his bed.*

MRS O'DEA: I'm just putting these here for you. I found you shoes at last, to go with the beautiful suit. I didn't mean to disturb you. You're the neatest sleeper I ever did meet, Mr Dunne. Never a ruffle in the sheets, just a long warm nest where your body lies.

THOMAS: That's about the height of it.

MRS O'DEA: Oh, you're a man for a bit of philosophy, I know.

THOMAS: Whose shoes were they, Mrs O'Dea?

MRS O'DEA: Let's see now. They were Patrick O'Brien's, Mr Dunne.

THOMAS (*after a moment*): You must take them for another man. I'd never fill them.

MRS O'DEA: But what if your grandsons come to see you and you've nothing to put on your feet?

THOMAS: There's no chance of that now.

MRS O'DEA (*taking up the bowl of food*): It's stone cold and you ate nothing. (*Going.*) Didn't I make you a beautiful suit?

She goes, locks the door. ANNIE *comes on with one of his big socks to darn and sits on the stool and works on the darning.* THOMAS *dons* MRS O'DEA's *suit.*

ANNIE: Three days now, Papa.

THOMAS: Three days, Annie. And we'll be set up in the old house again. We'll get that dairy going again first thing, a good scrub-down with the carbolic.

ANNIE: Yes.

THOMAS: And I'll have our milking cow fetched over from Feddin, and the Dunnes of Feddin can hire someone else's fields, because we'll need them presently.

ANNIE: We will.

THOMAS: And we'll be dog tired every night from the wealth of work, and be proud. And we have eight Rhode Island Reds[17] and a crowing cock, that they are keeping for me in Lathaleer. And they're looking out for a pony, they say they know a fair-minded tinker will sell us something apt, and two hours at the most with a pot of polish will have those high lamps on the old trap gleaming. And we will cut a fine figure, you and I, Annie, Thomas Dunne and his daughter, throughout Kiltegan, Feddin and Kelsha.

ANNIE: We'll enjoy ourselves.

THOMAS: And I'll lime the whole place. The house will be blinding white. We'll have red geraniums on the sills like the very dark conscience of summer or we're not Christians at all.

ANNIE: And Maud to visit, and we'll be peering at her, you know? (*Winking.*)

THOMAS: And letters from Dolly, in the meantime, till she wishes to come home.

A knocking. The RECRUIT, *now a constable, comes on.* ANNIE *goes to him. The* CONSTABLE *whispers in her ear.* ANNIE *comes back to* THOMAS.

ANNIE: It's one of the constables, Papa. He wants a word with you privately.

THOMAS *goes over to him. The* CONSTABLE *whispers to him.* THOMAS *at length pats the man briefly on the arm. The* CONSTABLE *goes.* THOMAS *returns slowly to* ANNIE.
What, Papa?

THOMAS: They have killed Collins in Cork.

ANNIE (*after a little*): We'll be doubly glad to be going home now, and free of it all, Papa.

THOMAS *can say nothing.*
Doubly glad.

A country music, and the wide ash-glow of a fire in the grate.

THOMAS (*to himself*): She died as many persons do, at the death of candlelight, as the birds begin to sing. She was a child again at the end, as if she was back again years ago in Lathaleer, and talking to her father, Cullen the coppicer. I stood by her bed, holding Dolly in my arms like a three-

pound bag of loose corn, and Cissy spoke to me as if I were her own father. But our account was clear. (*Calling.*) Annie! When I went out that day to stop Larkin in Sackville Street, all the world of my youth, the world of Ireland that I knew, was still in place, loyal, united and true. I had three lovely daughters, and a little son as glad as a rose. And I had risen as high as Catholic could in the Dublin Metropolitan Police. And we were drawn up, ready to dispel them. (*Sits in near fire.*) Annie!

ANNIE: Yes, Papa?

THOMAS: Bring my sword, would you?

ANNIE: No, Papa, I'm not bringing your sword.

THOMAS: There's fellas roaming the countryside seeking out the maiming of this man and the death of that man, old scores must be settled, they're whispering and conspiring in the dark.

ANNIE: There's nothing and no one out there, Papa.

THOMAS: But there is. I can smell them. Dark boys in black suits bought off the back of carts in county fairs, with old guns that might as soon blow off their own fingers when they fire. They won't get us. You must bring the sword.

ANNIE: There's nothing but your own fears. Go in to your bed and pull the blankets over your face and get a sleep, Papa.

THOMAS: And lose my last daughter to ruffians and murderers?

ANNIE: You have the respect of the district, Papa.

THOMAS: And what about that filthy mass of men that came up the yard last week and rattled our latch, and shouted in at me, while you were away at the well?

ANNIE: It was only a crowd of tinkers, Papa, that thought you were a woman alone, and wanted to frighten you. They took two churns from the shed and a length of rope because you wouldn't go out to them.

THOMAS: I didn't dare breathe, I didn't dare breathe. I held fast to the fire.

ANNIE: Papa, you know country life better than me, but you are not suited to it, I think.

A soughing in the maples outside.

THOMAS: There's them breathing now. Fetch the sword!

The soughing. THOMAS *bolts from the stool and gets the sword, comes back and stands in the middle of the room holding it high.*
Come in now to us, and see what you'll get!

ANNIE: Papa, Papa, please. (*She tries to hold him and take the sword.*) If you'll be quiet, I'll make us another pot of tea and then we can go to our rest.

THOMAS (*breaking from her*): I must strike, I must strike.

(*He goes about hitting at whatever he can, table and stool and such.*) Look at them running about like rats! Annie, there's rats come in, down the chimney! (*Striking the floor.*) Look at them, they're too quick for me!

ANNIE: There's no rats in my house! (*She covers her face with her hands.*) It's a clean house.

THOMAS (*raving*): What a to-do and a turmoil it is, with all their heroes lying in state about the city! They're bringing him up tonight to lie in state in the Pro-cathedral! Collins! We'll be doubly glad to be going home, now, she said! Because of you, Papa, I suppose, says Dolly. Says Dolly, says Dolly, says Dolly, says Dolly . . .

ANNIE: Papa! Stop it!

He does. He stands still where he is, the sword loose in his grip. He breathes heavily. He sinks to his knees, offers ANNIE *the sword.*

THOMAS: Please, child . . .

ANNIE: What now?

THOMAS: I am quiet now, Annie. I ask you a simple favour.

ANNIE: What favour, Papa?

THOMAS: Take the sword, Annie, and raise it up like a slash-hook, and bring it down on top of me like I was brambles, with all your might.

ANNIE *looks at him. She goes to him and pulls the sword roughly from him. Maybe she considers using it for a moment. She goes, taking the sword with her.* THOMAS *stares after her. He closes his eyes and cries like a child. The fire fades away, and the colder light of his room in the Baltinglass home returns.* WILLIE *comes, his uniform flecked with gold.*

THOMAS (*head down*): Da Da, Ma Ma, Ba Ba . . . (*After a little, seeing his son.*) Oh, Willie . . . (*Humorously.*) The great appear great because we are on our knees.[18] Let us rise.

WILLIE *holds a hand to help him get up.* THOMAS *is surprised to find it solid enough when he takes it.*

Oh, Willie . . .

WILLIE *brings him over to the bed and helps him get in.*

It's all topsy-turvy, Willie. (*After a little.*) Sure, Willie, I think the last order I gave to the men was to be sure and salute Mr Collins's coffin as it went by . . . (*After a little.*) One time, Willie, and it was Christmastime too, and I was a young fellow in Kiltegan, our dog Shep went missing for some days, as dogs in winter will. I was maybe ten or eleven, and I loved that Shep, and feared he was gone forever. We had got him as a young dog that had been beaten somewhere, and broken, till he reached our haven, and uncoiled,

and learned to bark like a baby learns to laugh, and he shone at his work.

WILLIE *gets up on the bed besides his father.*

One morning early after a fall of snow I went out to break the ice on the rain-barrel to plash my face, and I saw his tracks in the snow going up the sloping field, high to the fringes of the wood, and I was greatly afeared, because there were drops of blood now and then as he went, little smears of it on the cleanly snow. So I followed him up, sinking here and there in the drifts, well used to it, well used to it, and on a piece of field we called the upper garden, because it was flat there and you could see across to Baltinglass and some said even to Shillelagh and the dark woods of Coollattin, I found our dog there with the carcass of a ewe well-eaten, only the hindquarters remaining. I saw my father's blue sign on the wool and knew the worst. For a dog that would kill a sheep would die himself. So in my innocence I went down to my father and told him and he instructed me, as was right and proper, to go back up with a rope and lead Shep down so the killing could take place. The loss of a ewe was a disaster, a disaster, there'd be pounds of money gone into her. But I loved the dog so sorely, I hesitated when I had the rope tied about him, and at length led him off further up the hill, across the little stand of scrubby pines, and on into the low woods dark with snow and moss. And we went through by a snaking path I knew, till we got to the other side, where there was a simple man living, that made his living from the rabbits, and maybe had need of a watchful dog. But he wouldn't take a dog that had killed, though he was a tender man enough, and it behoved me to retrace my steps back into the woods, now moving along but slowly, and the dog sort of dragging behind, as if he knew well his misdeed and his fate. And I stopped in the centre of the trees, and do you know my young legs would not go forward, they would not proceed, try as I might, and there I was all that afternoon and night with the dog and the hazels. How is it that the drear of winter didn't eat my bones and murder me for my foolishness? Love of the dog kept me standing there, as only a child can stand, without moving, thinking, the poor dog whimpering with the cold. About five o'clock I went on, because I heard calling over the hill, here and there, and I could see black figures with lights moving and calling, calling out to me and the dog to come home. We came down the sloping field with the neighbours about us, them not saying a word, maybe marvelling at me, thinking I had been dead, and the torches and lamps making everything crazy with light, the old crab apple enlarging to the size of the field, its branches wild like arms. Down at last into the yard we came, the dog skulking on the rope just the same as the day he had arrived to us, and my father came out from the house in his big clothes. All brown with clothes and hair. It was as if I had never seen him before, never looked at him in his entirety, from head to toe. And I knew then that the dog and me were for slaughter. My feet carried me on to where he stood, immortal you would say in the door. And he put his right hand on the back of my head, and pulled me to him so that my cheek rested against the buckle of his belt. And he raised his own face to the brightening sky and praised someone, in a crushed voice, God maybe, for my safety, and stroked my hair. And the dog's crime was never spoken of, but that he lived till he died. And I would call that the mercy of fathers, when the love that lies in them deeply like the glittering face of a well is betrayed by an emergency, and the child sees at last that he is loved, loved and needed and not to be lived without, and greatly.

He sleeps. WILLIE *lies in close to him. Sleeps. Music. Dark.*

1 A home run by the local authority formerly for the mentally ill but now also for geriatric patients.
2 A town in County Wicklow on the River Slaney.
3 From a gruesome song about infanticide entitled 'Weila Waila' (sung by The Dubliners).
4 In New York.
5 Whale skinning.
6 Someone who supported the British presence in Ireland (the headquarters of the British Administration was based in Dublin Castle).
7 The Dublin Lock-Out of workers in 1913; Jim Larkin was leader of the Irish Transport and General Workers' Union which resisted the Lock-Out.
8 Now O'Connell Street, Dublin
9 Leader of an abortive Rising in 1803.
10 A cap lined with pitch (tar) and placed by the British military on the heads of rebels during the 1798 Rising as a form of torture.
11 The port for Cork. Its name was changed to Queenstown in 1849 after Queen Victoria's visit; in 1922 it reverted to Cobh.
12 Dublin quayside from where sailings for Britain depart.
13 British soldiers.
14 Fit-up companies of travelling theatre performers.
15 Wild beasts.
16 Nelson's Pillar on O'Connell Street.
17 A species of hen.
18 Larkin's words spoken in 1912.

MICHAEL LONGLEY
from Michael Longley, *The Ghost Orchid* (1995)

Two more poems by Michael Longley, before and after, the first on female sexuality, the second on male withdrawal. A Sheela-Na-Gig is a carving of a female figure emphasizing the sexual attributes. Such carvings are found all over Ireland on both secular and religious buildings. In the second poem Longley insists on a contemporary reading by the title he uses.

SHEELA-NA-GIG

She pulls her vulva apart for everyone to look at,
Not just for me, a stonemason deflowering stone.
She behaves thus above the church door at Kilnaboy

Where the orchids have borrowed her cunty petals.
A proper libation would be sperm and rainwater.
Ivy grows over her forehead, wall-rue at her feet.

CEASEFIRE

I

Put in mind of his own father and moved to tears
Achilles took him by the hand and pushed the old king
Gently away, but Priam curled up at his feet and
Wept with him until their sadness filled the building

II

Taking Hector's corpse into his own hands Achilles
Made sure it was washed and, for the old king's sake,
Laid out in uniform, ready for Priam to carry
Wrapped like a present home to Troy at daybreak.

III

When they had eaten together, it pleased them both
To stare at each other's beauty as lovers might,
Achilles built like a god, Priam good-looking still
And full of conversation, who earlier had sighed:

IV

'I get down on my knees and do what must be done
And kiss Achilles' hand, the killer of my son.'

GREG DELANTY
from Greg Delanty, *American Wake* (1995)

Greg Delanty (1958–   ) was born in Cork and lives in Burlington, Vermont, where he teaches at St Michael's College. Among his collections of verse are *Cast in the Fire* (1986), *Southward* (1992), *American Wake* (1995), and *The Hellbox* (1998). With Nuala Ní Dhomhnaill he edited *Jumping Off Shadows: Selected Contemporary Irish Poetry* (1995). The *Irish Literary Supplement*, Spring 1999, contains an informative interview with the poet in which he refers to his upbringing, his first paid employment in the Eagle Printing Company where his father was foreman, his exiled status, and the effect of living in America on his writing. Delanty's verse provides an insight into the complex fate of being Irish-American, not least in being neglected at home. In his recent interview his pain can be heard as he levels the charge: 'It is curious that the Irish in Ireland don't want to really hear, acknowledge, or take the Fifth province into account as much as they let on. For instance, "Ireland and the Diaspora" was the theme of the Frankfurt Book Fair of 1996. There were over fifty writers invited from the island of Ireland to articulate this and not one actual emigrant who was articulating this state was invited.' The word for province in Irish means a division; here in 'The Fifth Province' Delanty is referring to the Irish outside the four provinces of Ireland, the province, as it were, of the emigrant. Ellis Island, the entry point for millions of American immigrants in the past, was renovated in 1990 and opened as a museum.

THE FIFTH PROVINCE

Meeting in a café, we shun the cliché of a pub.
  Your sometime Jackeen accent is decaffed
like our coffee, insisting you're still a Dub.
  You kid about being half & halfed.
The people populating your dreams are now
  American, though the country they're set in
is always the Ireland within a soft Dublin.

In the country of sleep the voiceless citizens
  trapped in my regime of dreams are Irish,
but they're all the unlikely green denizens
  of an island that's as mysterious
as the volcano, bird or sheep islands
  that Brendan with his homesick crew,
  bound for the Promised Land, bumped into.

Last night I combed sleep's shore for its name.
    A familiar adze-crowned man appeared
waving his crook's question mark, nursing a flame
    on a hill and impatiently declaring in weird
pidgin Irish that the fifth province is
    not Meath or the Hy Brasil of the mind.
    It is this island where all exiles naturally land.

ON THE RENOVATION OF ELLIS ISLAND

What is even worse than if the walls wept
like a mythical character trapped in wood

or stone is that the walls give off nothing:
nothing of all those who were chalk-branded
for a limp, bedraggled look or vacant brow;
nothing of the man who thought Liberty
wore a crown of thorns; nothing of boys
who believed that each foot of anyone
who wore pointed shoes had only one toe;
nothing of mothers clutching tattered shawls
& belt-strapped cases like Old World beliefs;
nothing of petticoated women who turned flapper . . .
Surely if we stripped the coats of fresh paint
as anxiously as those women undid petticoats,
walls would weep, but for nothing now, for ever.

RODDY DOYLE
from Roddy Doyle, *The Woman Who Walked Into Doors* (1996)

A chapter from Roddy Doyle's novel told from the perspective of a battered wife. Here she reflects on missing the 1980s and surviving. The novel caused a minor stir at the time, partly because of the gender issue and Doyle taking it upon himself to speak for this group of women.

Chapter 27

It's all a mess — there's no order or sequence. I have dates, a beginning and an end, but the years in between won't fall into place. I know when I met him, I know our wedding day, I know the day I threw him out, the day he died. I have other dates — births, my father's death, communions, confirmations, other deaths. I can put them in a list down a page, but they're the only guide I have.

I missed the 80s. I haven't a clue. It's just a mush. I hear a song on the radio from the 60s or 70s and I can remember something that happened to me; it has nothing to do with liking the song. Song Sung Blue — I'm doing my homework, listening to Radio Luxemburg, the chart show on Monday night, with Carmel and Denise. I'm drawing a map of Ireland, the rivers of Ireland. My blue marker is nearly wasted and I haven't got to Ulster yet. Lily The Pink — I'm sitting on my mother's knee, watching my Uncle Martin singing Delilah; I have a toothache. Somebody else sang Lily The Pink before or after him; I can't remember who — one of my cousins. All The Young Dudes — I'm watching Charlo washing himself at the

sink. He still has some of his summer tan. But I don't know any songs from the 80s; they mean nothing — and the radio was on all the time. What did I do in the 80s? I walked into doors. I got up off the floor. I became an alcoholic. I discovered that I was poor, that I'd no right to the hope I'd started out with. I was going nowhere, straight there. Trapped in a house that would never be mine. With a husband who fed on my pain. Watching my children going nowhere with me; the cruellest thing of the lot. No hope to give them. They saw him throw me across the kitchen. They saw him put a knife to my throat. Their father; my husband.

— I do.

I was their future. That was what they saw. The grown-up world. Violence, fat and an empty fridge. A bottle of gin but no meat. Black eyes, no teeth; a lump in the corner. Do your homework, say your prayers, brush your teeth, say please and thank you — and you'll end up like me.

I never gave up.

Carmel told me to go. Fill a bag, get the kids and go. Anywhere, her house, a refuge; go. She kept at me; I hated her for it. It was none of her business. She promised the police and barring orders. She was standing on me, making it worse, rubbing it in. There was nothing wrong. He'd be fine. He'd get a job and everything would go back to normal. He loved me. She just didn't like him; she was jealous. I was cruel to her. I shut the door on her. I threw things at her. (But she was there all the time. She was there when I wanted her. I've never thanked her.) I wouldn't go. I'd get to the door. I'd open it. No further.

The hidings, the poverty, the pain and the robbery. I never gave up. I always got up off the floor. I always borrowed a tenner till Thursday. There were always Christmas presents, birthday presents. They always had a Christmas tree. There was always some sort of food. I got between them and him. I guarded the fridge. I made ends meet.

I never gave up.

I'm here.

I picked myself up. I washed the blood off my face. I put on the kettle.

I came close. I wanted to die. I lay on the floor and felt death under it. It was warm and I wanted it. I never wanted to get up. I was broken; I wanted to melt. I didn't know who I was. All I knew was the pain.

But I got up. I always got up. I had children. I had a husband. I limped around the rooms, tucking the children up in their beds. I hung out the washing with a broken finger. I ate sugar and drank gin. I made

sandwiches for their lunches; thin slivers of ham around the edges to hide the nothing in the middle. I hid. I hid the pain, the bruises and the poverty. The front door stayed shut. I went mad if one of the kids left it open. A knock on the door terrified me. I'd been seen, I'd been caught. I was guilty.

He beat me brainless and I felt guilty. He left me without money and I was guilty. I wouldn't let the kids into the kitchen after teatime, I couldn't let them near the cornflakes — and I was to blame. They went wild, they went hungry and it was my fault. I couldn't think. I could invent a family meal with an egg and four slices of stale bread but I couldn't think properly. I couldn't put a shape on anything. I kept falling apart.

The floor was warm and sticky. It was easier to stay there. It was nice. The blood hardened. It didn't want me to move. It wanted me to stay on the floor.

But I got up. Always, eventually. I'd remember who I was. I'd remember the time of day; I had things to do, things to look after. I'd mop the floor and start again. That was my life. Getting hit, waiting to get hit, recovering; forgetting. Starting all over again. There was no time, a beginning or an end. I can't say how many times he beat me. It was one beating; it went on forever. I know for how long: seventeen years. One stinking, miserable, gooed lump of days. Daylight and darkness. Pain and the fear of it. Darkness and daylight, over and over; world without end. Until I saw him looking at Nicola.

DEREK MAHON
from Derek Mahon, *The Hudson Letter* (1995)

Derek Mahon here provides not only further proof that he is among the most intelligent poets writing in English but also a word of caution to those tempted to complete the sentence beginning 'Irish identity is . . .'

III GLOBAL VILLAGE[1]

The reader need only . . . separate in his own thoughts the being of a sensible thing from its being perceived.

— George Berkeley,
The Principles of Human Knowledge

This morning, from beyond abandoned piers
where the great liners docked in former years,
a fog-horn echoes in deserted sheds

known to Hart Crane,[2] and in our vigilant beds.
No liners now, nothing but ice and sleet,
a late flame flickering on Brodsky St.
News-time in the global village — Bosnia, famine, drought,
whole nations, races, evicted even yet,
rape victim and blind beggar at the gate —
the images forming which will be screened tonight
on CNN and *The McNeil-Lehrer News Hour*,
the sense of being right there on the spot
— a sense I get right here that Gansevoort

has no 'existence, natural or real, apart
from its being perceived by the understanding'.[3] Not
that I seriously doubt the reality of the Hudson Bar
and Diner; but the skills of Venturi, Thompson,
    Rowse
that can make post-modern a 19th-century warehouse
and those of Hollywood *film noir* have combined
to create virtual realities in the mind
so the real thing tells us what we already know:
American Gothic. Obviously I don't mean
to pen yet one more craven European
paean to the States, nor would you expect me to,
not being a yuppie in a pinstripe suit
but an Irish Bohemian even as you are too
though far from the original 'Ballroom of Romance',[4]
far too from your posh convent school in France.
Out here, in the clear existential light,
I miss the half-tones I'm accustomed to:
an amateur immigrant, sure I like the corny
humanism and car-stickers — 'I ♥ NY'[5]
— and yet remain sardonic and un-*chic*,
an undesirable 'resident alien' on this shore,

a face in the crowd in this 'off-shore boutique'
inscribed with the ubiquitous comic-strip blob-speak
— LOVE ONE ANOTHER, RESIST INSIPID RHYME —
exposed in thunderstorms, as once before,
and hoping to draw some voltage one more time
or at least not die of spiritual cowardice.
'After so many deaths I live and write'
cried, once, Geo. Herbert[6] in his Wiltshire plot:
does lightning ever strike in the same place twice?

1   This is an extract from a longer poem 'Hudson Letter'.
2   Hart Crane (1899–1932), American poet, author of *The Bridge* (1930), a sequence of poems in praise of Brooklyn Bridge in New York.
3   A phrase from Berkeley's *The Principles of Human Knowledge* (1710). His famous phrase was *esse est percipi* (being is being perceived), that there is no existence of matter independent of perception.
4   Presumably a reference to William Trevor's story by that name (see above p. 854), 1950s provincial Ireland.
5   In the Gallery Press edition the heart is coloured red.
6   George Herbert (1593–1633), English metaphysical poet, an expert, like Mahon, in the use of conceits.

DERMOT HEALY
from Dermot Healy, *The Bend For Home* (1996)

Dermot Healy (1947–) was born in Finea, County Westmeath. Founding editor of *Force 10*, a community arts journal, he is also the accomplished author of *Banished Misfortune* (1982), a collection of short stories, and a fine ambitious novel *A Goat's Song* (1994). Here in this fictional memoir, which includes at one point a reference to a priest devoting an entire sermon to Beckett's *Waiting for Godot*, he re-creates the experience of growing up in small-town Ireland.

from Chapter 32

In an ironic piece some time ago in The Irishman's Diary in the *Irish Times*, Kevin Myers wrote that out beyond where I live in north Sligo every few years Hy Brazil, like another Atlantis, rises. This was news to me. I have not seen it yet, but I think of it this morning, rising out of the sea like a whale, or resting gently on the bottom of the ocean, waiting for the next time.

I think of Hy Brazil as I sit in the living room with a terrible hangover, my mother asleep in her armchair, Nancy asleep in my room, Maisie perched by the radio in the dining room, the central heating going up into a whine. Lack of sleep after spending the night on cushions on the floor has made me start to hallucinate.

If I close my eyes I think I can see Hy Brazil, a little beyond Inishmurray Island, not exactly land, not even someplace eternal, but a place imagined by people long before me that I must imagine in my turn. Imagination hands on a duty to those who come after. So it is with Hy Brazil.

So it is with Hy Brazil. Because it doesn't exist we wish it into being because someone else did in another age. Like a star that appears say once every two hundred years, you watch for Hy Brazil every seven years but in truth it has no definite orbit, no mathematics can accurately predict its appearance at a definite hour on a definite day. But you want to be there when it happens. Even if it never happened. Even if it never existed, you wish it into being. You wish for the language to recover it from the void.

I don't have any books to hand here in Cootehill in County Cavan that tell me who the imaginary folk were who inhabited Hy Brazil, how they arrived there, whether it is like Tír na nÓg. Are they ageless folk who live there? Is it an island inhabited by heroes? Shape-changers? Is it where suicides go? Or has it been long deserted, and rises out of the sea as a reminder to us of another civilization that has long disappeared off the face of the earth. Did the inhabitants do wrong that the island sank? Did a catastrophe greet them because of some terrible evil doing?

Is Hy Brazil the place we go to after we die? I don't know, so I make up my own Hy Brazil.

But the minute I start imagining it, my mind refuses Hy Brazil. The language won't budge. Instead I think of trivial things, irritations, domestic affairs; a dream of the previous night where an old lover, with astounding familiarity, visited, and a book that I can't finish writing presented itself. Nursing. Drinking. How the smell of my mother's waste made me retch as I cleaned her this morning.

But I suppose those who dreamed up Hy Brazil must have also known these irritations and mood swings. Mythology is full of sordidness. The fears of the storytellers are exaggerated in the tales. The

unbelievable takes on a human presence. What has happened repeatedly turns into a ritual. What has not happened turns into a mystery. The island is peopled with our uncertainties. Peace is only allowed a certain passage of time before terror intrudes again.

So that is how it must be on Hy Brazil for those who live there, and how it must have been for the makers of Hy Brazil, the ones that dreamed it up and make it sink and make it rise.

It's not the island that rises out of the sea but the observer out of the torpor of everyday. And on Hy Brazil I imagine there is someone looking back at us, wishing that they might begin again, be trapped once more among all that human and domestic trivia. Someone out there would probably like to swap places with me, they'd like to hear human voices again, listen to human despair and laughter, wake to a new day.

By thinking of Hy Brazil I get homesick for my cottage in Sligo. I sit there thinking of the cottage in the same way I used think of Finea before sleep. I go up the road that was taken away in the storm. The asses roar. The sea is thumping the rocks. Beside me my mother sleeps with a cooing sound. She — despite infirmity, spasms and weakness — is on her own Hy Brazil. Next door Maisie calls for green grapes. On the TV, 7000 people gather in the Shankill Road in Belfast to mourn nine out of ten killed in an explosion in a fishmonger's shop.

The tenth they will not mourn.

He planted the bomb.

RITA ANN HIGGINS
from Rita Ann Higgins, *Higher Purchase* (1996)

Rita Ann Higgins (1955–), one of eleven children, was born in Galway, left school at fourteen and began writing poetry in her late twenties. *Goddess on the Mervue Bus* (1986) was her first volume, followed by several more volumes including *Philomena's Revenge* (1992) and *Sunny Side Plucked: New and Selected Poems* (1996). Here in this poem she plays with the overworked, critical discourse and imagery of maps and borders.

REMAPPING THE BORDERS

In Texas
after the conference
they put on a céilí,
nearly everyone danced,
a few of us Margarita'd.

In jig time
everyone knew everyone.
After the Siege of Ennis[1]
a woman asked me,
'Could you see my stocking belt
as I did the swing?'

I was taken aback.

Me, thigh, knee, no,
I saw nothing.
I saw no knee
no luscious thigh
no slither belt,
with lace embroidered border
that was hardly a border at all.

I was looking for the worm in my glass.

I thought about her after,
when I was high above St Louis.
I'm glad I didn't see
her silk white thighs

her red satin suspender belt
with black embroidered border
that was hardly a border at all.

I swear to you
I saw nothing,
not even the worm
lying on his back
waiting to penetrate my tongue.

1 An Irish country dance, a favourite dance at Irish Clubs
   in Britain (and at conferences in America).

SEAMUS DEANE
from Seamus Deane, *Reading in the Dark* (1996)

Seamus Deane (1940–), critic, poet, and now novelist, was born in Derry and educated at QUB and Cambridge. A director of Field Day, he went on to become the General Editor of *The Field Day Anthology of Irish Literature* (1991). *Reading in the Dark*, a poignant novel re-creating the guilt and secrets of family life in the late 1940s and early 1950s, was shortlisted for the Booker Prize in 1996. In an interview with Helen Meany in *The Irish Times*, Deane explained: 'It's not a memoir. It's a conflation of about three or four families' histories, but a good deal of it I directly experienced. The fundamental story about Eddie, and, in fact, all the disappearance, is family history.' Here in this chapter we watch the boy watching his mother lose her mind, haunted by the memory that Eddie, her brother-in-law, was shot in April 1922 as an informer on the orders of her father. For an epigraph to the novel Deane makes use of lines from 'She Moved Through the Fair': 'The people were saying no two were e'er wed / But one had a sorrow that never was said.'

Mother

May 1953

My mother moved as though there were pounds of pressure bearing down on her; and when she sat, it was as though the pressure reversed itself and began to build up inside her and feint at her mouth or her hands, making them twitch. I knew now, or thought I knew, what it was, especially when I watched her eyes follow my father with such fear and pity that I wondered he didn't stop dead and realize there was something wrong, something she wanted to be

forgiven for. I couldn't tell him if she didn't. I couldn't even let her know that I knew. It would make her more frightened, more depressed. I longed to find some way to give her release, but could think of nothing; every set of words that came to my mouth felt lethal. I would come in to find her at the turn of the stairs, looking out the lobby window, still haunted, but now with a real ghost crouched in the air around her. She would come down with me, her heart jackhammering, and her breath quick, to stand at the range and adjust the saucepans in which dinner simmered, her face in a rictus of crying, but without tears.

She was always on the stairs, usually at the lobby window, looking out, whispering to herself, sometimes crying out an incoherent noise. Once, when I came up, she turned to me, her eyes wet.

'Burning. It's burning. All out there, burning.'

She flapped her hand at the field beyond the window. Then she turned away again, her mouth working like a muscle in her still face.

It was always like that. Even at night, we would be wakened by voices and come downstairs to find her sobbing in the backyard, freezing in her nightdress, resisting my father's attempts to lead her back in.

'What is it, love?' he would ask.

'Burning; it's all burning,' she would cry, dragging her hand away from him and going a few steps away, her arms clasped round herself, staring towards the sky.

'Come to bed; you'll get your death of cold; c'mon now, there's a love.'

But she would shake her head and keep staring beyond, her face shiny with tears.

Everyone would be awake, huddled at the back door, watching them both in the yard: he with his raincoat over his pyjamas, she slippery in the light and dark, moving always towards the blackness beyond the range of the kitchen light. Then, always, when he reached her down there near the yard wall, there was a murmuring and a sobbing, and his arm would black out her shoulders as it went round her. And they would come up towards us, she with her head bent, all of us retreating into the kitchen, out to the foot of the stairs in the hall, as he led her to the fold-out bed and persuaded her to lie down. I could see her shiver as the blankets were drawn over her and he came to shoo us up the stairs to bed, his face heavy and graven, the stubble visible on his cheeks.

'What does she mean?' I would ask him. 'What's burning? What's the matter with her?'

'It's a kind of sleepwalking,' he would say, 'dreaming. She's upset; but don't worry, she'll come round and be all right.'

'What's got her upset?'

'It's losing her father. And it's brought Una[1] — losing Una — back in on her too.'

We were all frightened. Also, I was ashamed. When I saw her wandering around the house, touching the walls, tracing out the scrolls of varnish on the sitting-room door with her finger, or climbing wearily up the stairs to gaze out of the window, my cheeks burnt and the semi-darkness seemed to be full of eyes. She was going out from us, becoming strange, becoming possessed, and I didn't want anyone else outside the family to know or notice.

Besides, I always had the feeling that there was someone else who had died, someone besides Una, or my mother's father or mother, or Eddie, someone I knew of, someone secret for whom hope had long been lost. And it had something to do with my father. Something made worse by his having told us about Eddie being an informer. I could understand, but only in part. There was something missing. My mother's grieving was so inconsolable, I thought it must be for a lost soul, someone woven into the fires of hell the way gas was into a flame. I used to sit beside her at the grate and watch the coal burn. After a piece started to smoke heavily, there would be the tiniest hiss as the flame took. She would see me watching.

'See that?' she'd say. 'The pain is terrible. The flame is you, and you are the flame. But there's still a difference. That's the pain. Burning.'

Then she would weep again. Sometimes she'd let me hold her hand as she cried. Sometimes she'd brush my hand away and sit rigid, with only the tears moving on her face until she was wet under the chin and the skin in the valley of her throat looked liquid.

The doctor came and gave her pills and medicines. She'd take them and become calmer, but her grief just collected under the drugs like a thrombosis. When it took over, overcoming the drugs, her body shook and her eyes glimmered with tears that rarely flowed but shone there, dammed up in her tear-ducts, dangerous. She was in such pain she could not cry, only wish that she could. I could touch her, run my finger over the curve of her forearm, rub my thumb against the inside of her wrist with its thick blue vein, and she would seem to feel nothing. 'This is my mother,' I would say to myself. 'This is my mother.' I dreamt of a magic syringe that I could push up into the inside skin of her arm and withdraw, black with grief, and keep plunging it and withdrawing it, over and over, until it came out clear, and I would look up in her face and see her smiling and see her eyes full of that merriment I thought I remembered. Her hair was cold. Her skin was stretched glossy on her bones and tightening with wrinkles. 'Oh, Jesus,' my father would say under his breath, the holy name hissing in his mouth like snakes in a pit, 'Oh, Jesus, Jesus, where have you gone, love?' He tilted her chin very gently to lift her face to the evening light, and she would respond with the tiniest of uninterested smiles. As he withdrew his hand, and she lowered her face again, I thought — he thought — that she said, 'Burning, burning,' but it was really only a noise she made, and all her noises had come to sound in our ears like that word, and when my father sigh-heaved himself out of the chair, making my nose sting with all the salty, chalky smells of the docks that were folded into the wrinkles of his dungarees, he too sounded as if he were saying that word even though his voice was just a hum in his throat. I'd put my hands down inside my socks, as far as my ankles, and grip the bones and tighten myself up for a while before I could walk away from her tilted face and her quietly folded hands and the troubling chill of her black-grey hair.

Liam and I played football in the backyard, our movements quick and loud with the panic we both felt. If we fought, we did so in the same high-edged way, striking clean blows, no wrestling or snarling about. The sky sloped up into the sun and down into the stars, and she went on, scarcely moving, haunted and burning, audibly, inaudibly.

Then, at last, the real crying began, a lethal sobbing that ran its fright through us like an epidemic. Sundays were the worst. We'd come back from Mass, all spruced up, my sisters fresh and ingeminated in their light-green tweed coats, my brothers and I self-conscious in shirts and ties, with our hair sticking up at odd angles because of Liam's advice that we should soak it in a mix of sugar and water 'to make it sit still'.

Father was a stride before us as we went into the hall, for he could hear her sobbing, a sound that moved and wavered in phases, a stripping-off of unbearably tight panics that only found more — tighter ones — within. I wanted to run away, to flee across Meenan's Park past the Sunday football games, past the crouching players of marbles, and the children on swings with their legs out stiff, past the card-players squatting on the broken slabs of the air-raid shelters in a pale blue trance of smoke, and on into the shuttered Lecky Road, up the long hill to Bishop Street, down Abercorn Road to the river and over the bridge into the safety of really foreign territory, the estrangement of Protestants with their bibles and the ache of the railway line curving away towards Coleraine, Portstewart, Belfast. But I also wanted to run into the maw of the sobbing, to throw my arms wide to receive it, to shout into it, to make it come at me in words, words, words and no more of this ceaseless noise, its animality, its broken inflection of my mother. Instead, I stood there and looked at her while my father pottered helplessly about her and everyone came over and touched her, petted her, stroked her hair, let tears roll on their cheeks. Eilis knelt in front of her and squeezed her, face against her stomach, but my mother's arms hung helplessly down by her sides, and her semi-brushed hair fell sideways across her streaming face. The hairbrush lay in the corner of the kitchen where she must have thrown it. I picked it up and tugged at the strands of her hair caught in the wire bristles, winding them round my fingers, feeling them

soften on my skin as though the tightness were easing off them into me. I felt it travelling inside, looking for a resting place, a nest to live in and flourish, finding it in the cat's cradle of my stomach and accumulating there.

She cried for weeks, then months. A summer passed in a nausea of light, and we took turns at the cooking and shopping, we all did odd jobs for extra shillings round the area — collecting scrap metal, rags, jamjars, and selling them to a dealer on the Lecky Road. His shed was always dark, mounded with piles of the stuff. In the yard behind, a cart always sat with its shafts in the air, their tips catching light. Everything else was mauve dark, and all the smells of the place came with him as he approached to look at what we had brought. He wore a begrimed raincoat, belted, with its collar turned up in all weathers. His hair was wild and wiry, his trousers ragged; but his shoes were always clean. When he gave us the coins, they chinked into our hands but they had no brightness, so dirty were they. We would wash them in suds at the sink and feel we had revealed their true value when they came up glistening brown, yellow, silver. I always felt better-paid when I put the clean coins on the mantelpiece, or showed them to my mother. She sometimes took them and put them in her apron pocket and said, 'That's grand. You're good children. Good wee'uns.' But when one of us would ask her later for the money to buy food, she would look puzzled, and we would have to fish them out of her pocket and show them to her. That often made her weep again. I was glad when the darker weather came again. It was more appropriate, especially when the wind drove the rain at a sharp slant into me as I ran from the grocer's with a stone of potatoes, carrots, onions and a round of country butter, heavy with salt, bumping against my legs in the cloth shopping-bag. When the snow came, I fractured my arm in a spill from a sleigh that crashed into the wall at the end of the street. My mother would ask me to take the clumsy plaster-of-Paris casing out of the sling and she would caress it as though she could reach the arm inside. It felt strange to hear and see her hand move on the plaster and not feel anything except its light pressure and an itch writhing in ringworm patterns inside.

'Paradise was not far away when I died,' she said one day — a Tuesday in February — into clear air, when my father was washing the dishes, and Deirdre and I were drying and putting them away. It made me smile, that remark. The blue willow-pattern plate I was holding was light and burnished as I stacked it on the shelf. I knew for the first time, in a real way, that she had been in love. Her voice was clear and young; sure enough, when I stepped into the kitchen from the scullery to look at her, she was smiling to herself. I looked towards my father, but he was staring into the sudsy water, his thick arms plunged in and still. Deirdre batted her eyelids at me, signalling her own amusement. Then, some weeks later, one Friday in April, when Mother was folding sheets at the ironing-board, she said in the same voice, 'Not far. I could see the rim of it.' This was her new conversation. Connected remarks separated by days, weeks, months, but always in her new voice. I knew she was getting stranger; she was telling herself a story that only appeared now and again in her speech.

She talked mostly to the younger children, Gerard, Eamon, Deirdre. Sometimes she would hold Gerard's little round flaxen head close to her breast and bend down to say things in her new voice into his shy face, things that enthralled and mystified me. 'To go halfway round the globe and never speak again. The poor coward. The lonely soul.' I listened, envying him. I had the impression she was talking to him and to the others in little confidential bursts, but was leaving my father, Eilis, Liam and me out of it. Once, when I had taken the back off the wireless and was trying to get it to work again, she leaned over and clicked her finger-nail against one of the valves. It gave a hoarse ping and lit briefly before fading. A remark hung in the air between us, expanding in a bubble of light, but she said nothing. I left the wireless's entrails scattered on the table and took a rubber ball from the drawer. Since my arm fracture, I had been told to rebuild the wasted muscles by squeezing this ball, in, out, in, out, as often as possible. I stood there squeezing it and looking at her until my forearm was tired. She talked about this and that, evasively. How cruel she was! I longed for her to talk in her new voice to me, and she felt my longing and she resisted it. I went upstairs and sat on the bed in the cold bedroom and looked at the picture of the Sacred Heart and thought I understood how Jesus felt, him with his breast open and the pierced blood-dripping muscle emblazoned there. I still had the ball in my hand. I lobbed it against the glass of the picture, scoring a bull's-eye on the heart, and caught it on the first bounce. Her voice came up to me, young and clear in its inflection, but I didn't catch the words. I lay on the bed and wept. She had been in love with someone else, not quite my father. That's what she was telling, and not telling, him. And she was telling me. Most of all, she was telling herself. A great lamentation of seagulls filled the air as a storm came up from the harbour and the room seemed to lift into the sky with their rising shadows.

One day, it must have been the following winter, she went to the shelf where the round white boxes of pills were kept, and brought them in the lap of her apron over to me. She asked me to open the boxes and empty them out on to a saucer. I did. Then, she asked me to throw them into the fire. I did that too. They lay there in coloured specks, darkening into nothing. Then she brought out five medicine bottles, red, blue, yellow, two of them clear. She took a jug from the press and emptied them all in, one on top of the other. She asked me to smell it. I bent over and inhaled.

'Slime,' she said, nodding at me. 'Chemical slime. Putrid. It makes me sick. Sick even to think I ever took it. Look what it did to my teeth.' She showed me how her teeth had rotted. Then she went out to the scullery and poured it all down the sink. She came in and smiled at me, but her white smile was ruined now, had been for some time, and her breath was bad.

'I'm better now, son. But I'll never be as I was. You poor child. My poor family.'

She hugged my head to her breast. She still smelt of medicine and I could feel her older, as though her breath were shallower than it had once been. I held her for a moment, ashamed of the shame I had been feeling. But I never felt less like asking anything. That night, for the first time in weeks, she made dinner and even talked about Hallowe'en and Christmas. By All Souls' Night she had false teeth, and her smile was white again. But when I saw her smile, then and ever afterwards, I could hear her voice, creased with sorrow, saying, 'Burning, burning,' and I would look for the other voice, young and clear, lying in its crypt behind it. But it slept there and remained sleeping, behind her false white smile.

Her startling illness aged them both. My father's physical strength was still immense, but I sensed that he now began to feel it useless. Sometimes, when he came up the back lane from work, two or three of us would be standing on the backyard wall. As he came alongside, we would jump towards him. He would catch us one by one and swing us on to his shoulders, duck through the gate and then plant us back on the wall as though we weighed nothing. But once, after my mother's illness was over, when we jumped, he caught us — Eilis first, then Deirdre, then Gerard, then Eamon — but before Liam or I could jump, he let them slither gently down to the ground and waved us off.

'Not tonight, children. You're too many for me.'

I watched him go up the yard, leaving a trail of children behind him, and held tight to the clothes-line post as I teetered on the rounded wall-top. Liam was standing on his hands on the wall beside me, trying to keep his legs straight.

'He's far shook, that man, far shook,' he said upside down. I remember thinking how strange his mouth was when he spoke in that position. Then he somersaulted off into the lane, landing on his feet. 'As you'd expect,' he added.

I nodded, but I hadn't expected it at all, not this fast, at least not until he said it. I slid off the wall carefully, as though from a great height, and felt grateful for the solidity of the black loam of the lane under my boots. But even that solidity weakened as I moved to the gate and saw, through the kitchen window, her smiling her false teeth at him as they talked.

1   His sister who had died of meningitis.

ROBERT McLIAM WILSON
from Robert McLiam Wilson, *Eureka Street* (1996)

Eureka Street is a story of contemporary Belfast spanning the ceasefires of 1994–96. The focus is on a disaffected group of young Protestants, surrounded by Belfast hatreds but keenly alive to the tragi-comic fate of Northern Ireland which threatens to deprive them of a voice. Here in this scene the group meet up at a yuppie-bar on the Dublin Road only to discover a poetry reading given by a Catholic poet (who sounds not unlike Seamus Heaney).

from **Chapter 8**

When I got to the bar where I was meeting the boys, I was horrified. There was a sign over the door.

'An Evening of Irish Poetry Tonight 8 p.m.,' it said.

'Oh, fuck,' I replied.

Obviously there were no bouncers that night. What hordes would they be fighting off? I stood on the doorstep and pondered. Could any solitude be worse than this? I was amazed that Chuckie would attend such a gathering. I mean, Slat, Septic and the rest of us were basically yobbish, vulgar and sad but we could claim some form of brush with education, with literature. Chuckie, however, was moronically ill-informed. I suspected Max's hand in this.

Inside, I found that my suspicions were correct and I also found, to my meagre delight, that Aoirghe was with them. I walked up to them. I patted Chuckie's arm, said hello to Max and was greeting the fearsome Aoirghe when I unfortunately coughed.

Her eyes narrowed. 'Are you taking the piss again?'

'Jesus!' I choked. 'I just coughed. Gimme a break.'

Her eyes narrowed more (how could she see anything like that?). 'Yeah, and I got your message. Thanks very much, it was charming.' She hissed the last word.

I blushed and coughed again. 'Whoops, sorry. Sorry about the message. I was pissed about getting nosy calls from Amnesty.'

She turned to Max and started some chat with her. I shrugged my shoulders at Chuckie, smiled amiably at him and grabbed him viciously by the balls.

'Ow.'

'I don't fucking believe it, Chuckie. How come you didn't tell me she was going to be here?' I gave his pebbles another twist. 'Hmm?'

'Fuck, Jake. Let go. It wasn't my fault.'

I released him.

Slat, Septic and Donal arrived. We stood in a bunch waiting for the wimp who couldn't stand the pressure of resisting buying the first round.

'Look,' Chuckie whispered to me, 'she's just staying for the poetry. After that, she's fucking off with one of the poets.'

My relief was tempered with a qualm of jealousy. That moment scared me badly. I shook my head and cleared my mind. I held my hand in front of my face and counted my fingers. I was OK.

'What's wrong with you?' asked Chuckie.

'Never mind that. What the fuck are you doing at a poetry reading?'

Chuckie looked slightly miffed at my surprise. Septic muffled a laugh. 'It was Aoirghe's idea. One of the guys reading is a councillor for Just Us. He wrote a book when he was in the Maze.'

'Oh, great.'

'One of them's famous,' said Chuckie consolingly. 'Shauny . . . Shinny . . . Shamie . . .'

'Sugar Ray Leonard?' suggested Septic.

'No.' Chuckie struggled on manfully, 'Shilly . . . Shally . . .'

'Shague Ghinthoss,' shouted Max.

'Even better,' I complained.

Shague Ghinthoss was an inappropriately famous poet who looked like Santa Claus and wrote about frogs, hedges and long-handled spades. He was a vaguely anti-English Catholic from Tyrone but the English loved him. They had a real appetite for hearing what a bunch of fuckers they were. I liked that about the English.

Max sloped over with a book. Aoirghe trailed along reluctantly behind her. Max smiled. 'It's the launch of this new book. It's supposed to be very good.' She passed it to me.

'According to whom?' I asked grammatically.

Chuckie coughed and old Aoirghe looked ready to tell me. I dipped into the book to avoid her eye.

'Of course,' she put in acidly, 'I wouldn't expect you to be sympathetic to any writers belonging to the Movement but even you couldn't deny Shague Ghinthoss's reputation.'

'Is that right?'

'There's a beautiful one of his on the first page,' said Max brightly. 'It was good of a writer of his repute to endorse a book like this, don't you think?'

'I bet I can recite it without reading it.'

Chuckie looked impressed at this — sometimes satire passed him by. Aoirghe bristled. I passed the book to Deasely, open at the first page. Donal adopted a pedagogical expression.

I cleared my throat.

The blah blah under the brown blah of the blah
    blah hedges.
I blahhed her blah with the heft of my spade
The wet blah blahhed along the lines of the country
    with all the blah of the blah blah blackberries.

I stopped. There was no applause. Deasely looked at me severely. He tutted. 'You left out the fifth blah, Jackson. Go to the back of the class and buy me a beer.'

He chucked the book back to Aoirghe. She looked like she was pissing blood. 'Jesus, Jackson. Your friends are near as bad as you. Do you boys go to asshole support groups at weekends?'

It was a bad, bad evening. Before the reading started we were reluctantly — on both sides — introduced to a number of Aoirghe's friends and associates. To do her justice, they weren't all extremist republicans. There was a man who taught Television-watching Skills at the University of Ulster. There was an old

college chum of hers, a man with a Theory of everything. He had a Theory of Poetry. He had a Theory of Parties. A Theory of History. A Theory of Haircuts. He told me all of them. He did not include a Theory of How Not To Be Boring.

Then the reading commenced. We stood still while a series of twats in poetic clothes (a varying costume, always expressing equal measures of nonconformity, sensitivity and sexual menace) drivelled on about the flowers, the birds, the hedges, the berries, the spades, the earth, the sky and the sea. Whatever you said about Shague Ghinthoss's reputation, he definitely had one. All these tossers bore his mark. Unlike Ghinthoss, none of these boys was from the country. They were all pale-faced city boys and most obviously had never seen any of the hedges, berries or spades about which they wrote so passionately.

It was clear, in addition, that these were all nationalist hedges, republican berries, unProtestant flowers and extremely Irish spades. These subtleties were dashed, however, when the penultimate poet did his stuff. This unprepossessing john, we were told, had had his work translated from the original Gaelic into Russian but not into English. He was to read one of his poems in Irish and some guy would translate into English. (I should point out that I had seen this poet at the bar, showing a fine grasp of idiomatic English when he was trying to chat up one of the bar girls — though, admittedly, he seemed to have some difficulty in understanding the phrase, 'Fuck off, you ugly twat.')

This man read, haltingly but confidently, a poem entitled 'Poem to a British Soldier About to Die'. It was hard enough to follow the text in detail, what with the simultaneous translation and the fact that it was crap, but the sentiments were apparent enough. The poem told the young British soldier (about to die) why he was about to die, why it was his fault, how it had been his fault for eight hundred years and would probably be his fault for another eight hundred, why the man who was going to shoot him was a fine Irishman who loved his children and never beat his wife and believed firmly in democracy and freedom for all, regardless of race or creed, and why such beliefs gave him no option but to murder the young British soldier (about to die).

There was silence after he finished. I waited for the boos and catcalls. How foolish. It wasn't until a few seconds into the cheers and whoops that I realized that everybody loved it. Weren't there any Protestants here? I looked over at Chuckie but he was blithe. He hadn't even been listening, a condition he shared with many of his faithmates.

The fat poet milked the applause. Some of the other scribes joined him on the podium. The rapture sounded as though it would never end. These culture vultures were frenzied in their acclaim. After a time the hubbub died down. The chubby humanist waited for total silence, then leaned close to the microphone.

'*Tiocfaidh ar La*,'[1] he bellowed.

Chuckie jumped in his skin. 'What?' he squeaked.

Thankfully, no one heard him in the resumption of the tumult.

It went on. It was as bad as could be. The great man, Ghinthoss, got up and read. He read about hedges, the lanes and the bogs. He covered rural topography in detail. It felt like a geography field trip. In a startling departure, he read a poem about a vicious Protestant murder of a nice Catholic. There were no spades in this poem, and only one hedge, but by this time the crowd were whipped into such a sectarian passion they would have lauded him if he'd picked his nose with any amount of rhythm or even in a particularly Irish manner.

He milked it all. Then he took some questions. I'm not saying they were entirely facile but their content was mostly eugenic. These people gathered close together, snug in their verse, their culture, they had one question. Why can't Protestants do this? they asked themselves. What's wrong with those funny people? Why aren't they spiritual like us?

Ghinthoss was grandly forgiving. He seemed to think it was not all the Protestants' fault. Given a million or so years of Catholic supremacy, Protestant brows might lift, they might start with a few uneasy grunts, invent the wheel and wear bearskins. If we were kind, the poor dumb brutes might be able to manage a few domestic poetic tasks in a century or so.

'Mr Ghinthoss,' I asked in a pause (oh, I didn't want to, I couldn't help myself, I bit my tongue, I put my hands over my mouth but it just would come out), 'Mr Ghinthoss,' I enquired, 'could you tell us, whether, great poet that you are, whether . . . whether your dick reaches your arse yet?'

I was always good at public speaking.

As I was being thrown out I arranged to meet the others. They wanted to go to Lavery's — I was being lifted in the air by two ten-foot revolutionaries at that point so I couldn't debate the venue.

I checked myself out in the bathroom of a hamburger joint nearby. A graze on my forehead, a cut on my lip. Oh, my poor fucking face. It was getting boring, this Jake-beating thing, it was happening every day. I used to be so pretty. I used to be so tough.

1   Irish: Our day will come, a republican slogan.

CIARAN CARSON
from Ciaran Carson, *Opera Et Cetera* (1996)

Three more entertaining poems by Ciaran Carson on words and action.

O

The tea-cup stain on the white damask table-cloth was
   not quite perfect. Never-
Theless, I'd set my cup exactly on it, like it was a stain-
   remover.

I sipped the rim with palatable lip. I drank the
   steaming liquor up.
My granny then would read my future from the tea-
   leaves' leavings in the cup.

I stared into enormous china *O* and saw its every
   centrifugal flaw,

The tiny bobbles glazed in its interior of Delphic
   oracle. I yawned

Into its incandescent blaze of vowel like the cool of
   dudes in black fedoras
At high noon; trigger-fingered, shadowless, they
   walked beneath sombreros.

They stopped me inadvertently and asked for my
   identity. I did not know
Until the mouth of a gun was pressed against my
   forehead, and I felt its *O*.

JACTA EST ALEA[1]

It was one of those puzzling necks of the wood where
  the South was in the North, the way
The double cross in a jigsaw loops into its matrix,
  like the border was a *clef*

With arbitrary teeth indented in it. Here, it cut clean
  across the plastic
Lounge of The Half-Way House; my heart lay in
  the Republic

While my head was in the Six, or so I was inclined.
  You know that drinker's
Angle, elbow-propped, knuckles to his brow like one
  of the Great Thinkers?

He's staring at my throat in the Power's[2] mirror,
  debating whether
He should open up a lexicon with me: the price of
  beer or steers, the weather.

We end up talking about talk. We stagger on the
                                              frontier.
He is pro. I am con.
Siamese-like, drunken, inextricable, we wade
  into the Rubicon.

TANGO

It's all long steps and pauses, where the woman uses
  the man as a crutch;
Ironically, it is unlikely that it comes from the Latin
  verb 'to touch'.

It is not the foxtrot nor the frug, still less the polka-dot
  or rigadoon;
Zapateado, tarantella, rhumba, mambo, allemande, it's
                                                    not.
It is a swoon

Of music, castanetted by the clicking silver buttons
  of the square bandoneon,
Which is its instrument, bass-and-treble toned
  like the chameleon:

Beautiful gloomy levity of camouflage, like when
  the girl's bolero
Creaks against the moustachioed starched shirt, as he
  struts and pansies in torero

Mode. He leans into her quickstep jitterbug. Her legs
  are all akimbo.
As he shimmies lower, lower, entering the possibility
  of limbo.

1   Latin: The die has been cast. Caesar's remark when he
    came to the Rubicon.
2   A brand of whiskey.

MICHAEL O'LOUGHLIN
from Michael O'Loughlin, *Another Nation: New and Selected Poems* (1996)

Michael O'Loughlin (1958–   ) here levels with the ancient Irish mythological figure
given a new lease of life by the Irish Literary Revival. See Tóibín (above p. 1133) for
O'Loughlin's views on Easter 1916/1966.

CUCHULAINN

If I lived in this place for a thousand years
I could never construe you, Cuchulainn.
Your name is a fossil, a petrified tree
Your name means less than nothing.
Less than Librium, or Burton's Biscuits
Or Phoenix Audio-Visual Systems —
I have never heard it whispered

By the wind in the telegraph wires
Or seen it scrawled on the wall
At the back of the children's playground.
Your name means less than nothing
To the housewife adrift in the Shopping Centre
At eleven-fifteen on a Tuesday morning
With the wind blowing fragments of concrete

Into eyes already battered and bruised
By four tightening walls
In a flat in a tower-block
Named after an Irish Patriot
Who died with your name on his lips.

But watching TV the other night
I began to construe you, Cuchulainn;

You came on like some corny revenant
In a black-and-white made for TV
American Sci-Fi serial.
An obvious Martian in human disguise
You stomped about in big boots
With a face perpetually puzzled and strained
And your deep voice booms full of capital letters:
What Is This Thing You Earthlings Speak Of

TIMOTHY O'GRADY
from Timothy O'Grady and Steven Pyke, *I Could Read the Sky* (1997)

Timothy O'Grady was born and educated in Chicago. He is co-author with Kenneth Griffith of *Curious Journey: An Oral History of Ireland's Unfinished Revolution* (1982). *Motherland* (1989) was his first novel. *I Could Read the Sky*, indebted in its own way to the work of John Berger and enriched by Steve Pyke's black and white photographs, is an intensely lyrical novel on the fate which befell many Irish emigrants to Britain: a search for meaning across very different cultures. For background reading you might refer at this point to Donall MacAmhlaigh's 'Britain's Irish Workers' (1978) (see p. 840). You might also find it instructive to compare the sense of realism and tragedy in O'Grady's novel with extracts from Patrick MacGill's *Children of the Dead End* (1914) and his poem 'Padding It' (1916) (see p. 268). Here in the following passage the narrator has been hospitalized following an accident on a building site and struggles to recover his ability to play the accordion again. Camden Town in North London has a large Irish population.

Chapter 25

I've finished the tea and swallowed the pills the nurse brought me in the little paper cup. She stretches up in her white uniform to draw the curtain and tells us all that we should go to sleep. The new man beside me does as he is told and the old boy across is asleep already. It is two-thirty on a Monday afternoon. I have clean pyjamas, clean sheets and a clean face. I am sitting up in the bed with my hands folded across my lap and my eyes wide open staring at a spot on the wall opposite. I'm awake like I've had a bucket of sea water thrown over me.

Into the room, carrying a box of chocolates, steps my mother's Uncle John. He makes straight for me and sits down at the end of my bed. I don't know how I built him the way I did but he is a fine man, a lean islander's face, the blue eyes full of sea and sky, the lines around his eyes and mouth receiving his laughter. What way was he when the men in masks found him in the room in Northampton? He has a jacket on Roscoe would have liked and a gold ring. The flat cap is new and sits on his knee. There are men on the Kilburn High Road you can only see unfinished buildings in their eyes. You cannot see the city in his face. You see the sea. You see him with his hand on the till of a boat cutting through water. He looks right just the way the house does when I think of it set into the side of the green hill in Labasheeda. But while the lines smile his mouth can't, for a scar curves like a turning centipede from the left corner of his nose, down onto his lip and into his mouth. This part of him cannot move.

'When I first left I lived in New York,' he says. 'I found a patch of grass in among the buildings and the concrete and on Sundays I would go there and sit in it. It was just like the grass on the rise of Tullaherin.' He laughs and gives my leg a squeeze through the covers like I know all about the bitterness of this joke.

He starts with the two houses on Tullaherin and moves in a sweep across the townland. He tells me the colours of the doors the day he left. He tells me what fields had the finest animals. He tells me about him who could throw heavy stones the furthest, made the best thatch, could ride a horse standing on its back, lift and carry a curragh on his own, shout loudest, sing sweetest, drink deepest, charm women. He told me about her that reared children that could run fast, had the loveliest hair, moved with the lightest step, said words in French, argued with the priest, remembered the generations, made the sweetest butter.

'I read a book once,' he says. 'I read many one time. The thing about a book is that the man who is writing it brings all the lives from all the different places and makes them flow together in the same stream. As they move down towards the end it's like they have loops and holes and shapes that all fit together just nicely so that they're just one big piece really. You can look back and see how all of them got where they are. That's the time the writer brings the book to an end and there's no seeing past it. I'd like to meet the man who wrote a book like that so I could ask him where he got those lives. I never met anything like that in all my time. I look back and I see a big field full of mud, people and animals sliding and me sliding with them. There's no end. There's just times when some are standing and some are fallen.'

He tells me then he's heard about the music I make with the accordion and I want so badly to play for him to keep him there. He fades in and out like a radio losing its signal.

He leaves the chocolates down beside the bed, and he stands up. He places his large warm hand on my brow and makes a cross like a priest giving ashes before Lent. 'Those people from home, any that remember me tell them I was asking. We're the same, you and me. Tell them we forgive them and they should forgive us.'

He goes then, the bitter laugh he means for me breaking and falling behind him like a ring of smoke.

Chapter 26

The spade feels heavy in my hand. On the scaffolding I fear a fall. When there's crack I step away with shame at the way the words are so slow and broken in my mouth. The accordion is the worst. It has so many buttons and I cannot find or remember them all.

They have me sweeping. I sweep dust and shavings of wood and food that falls to the ground. When I am doing this work I have in my mind only the picture of myself with the broom in my hand. I could stuff a saddle. From this there is no hiding.

I wait with the others in the early morning darkness along the railings in Camden Town. They are all in their coats leaning over, smoking cigarettes. Men who would live in your ear in a bar hold back from speech. They look serious. They look like they could be looking down into a river watching a swimming race. We wait for the Animal to come and pick the gang. When he steps down from the van he will take his coat off even in winter for he wants everyone there to see his arms. From the back he looks like a turf stack and from the front he's a fright. He's a scar like a trench running down from his eye, the eyes two halfpennies. In the centre is the nose. It's like a big potato breaking up through the ground. It bends one way, then another and then back as it goes from the bridge to the tip. Many's the man waiting on the railings would like to be the man who broke it for him. The mouth curves around his face like a dog's. You have to watch him. You could be talking with him in a bar in a peaceful way about greyhounds or the price of drink and he'd rear up on you. He could break the pint glass on the edge of the table and bring it right up to your eye. When he walks his hands face backwards. His right arm swings like a weight at the end of a chain. Men from Connemara inspired by their hatred took him into the toilet in the Spotted Dog in Willesden and broke it over a knee.

I wait there mornings for work with Francie and Martin and the others. Most always I get it even if it's only sweeping. Ivan came with us when we first went down, a scarf and woollen hat on him and the donkey jacket so big he was like a clothes peg holding up a tent. When the Animal stepped from the van and saw him he knew he could have sport. 'And what can you do, man of straw?' he said. The voice would just cut you. 'I can dig,' says Ivan. 'You couldn't dig the shite from your own arse,' says the Animal. He leans over with the two hands on his knees and lets out a roar. Anyone he spots not laughing doesn't work that day. 'I'm going to work on the buses,' says Ivan to us.

I sit alone in the room with the accordion and try to get the feel of it. I lift it up and down like you would a baby to try to get the right sense of its weight. I move my fingers over the buttons. I play tunes Da tried to teach Joe when he was a child. On a Saturday afternoon with Francie at the bookie's I sit on the edge of the bed and I try to play 'She Moves Through the Fair'. My finger slips from a button and I get a flat sound like the call of a goose. I start again. The notes which are so full of this yearning hold just right until they move and fade into those that follow. I know then that you play not for what you can give anyone or for what they will think of you but only for the sake of the tune itself. It goes to the point where it seems it can get away from me but doesn't. I can hold it in. I hold it as though in a dance. This is the time when no one can touch you. I am just like this when I hear Francie. 'Jesus Christ, will you ever stop?' he says. He's standing in the centre of the room with a look on him like a thirsty man begging for coins in the street. 'The sadness of it,' he says, and he goes back out.

MARY O'MALLEY
from Mary O'Malley, *The Knife in the Wave* (1997)

Mary O'Malley, poet and broadcaster, was educated at University College, Galway, and worked in London for two years and in Portugal for eight. She now lives in the Moycullen Gaeltacht in County Galway. Here, in a poem dedicated to her daughter on her eleventh birthday, she celebrates the coming of spring and the feast of St Brigid, the most important female saint after the Virgin Mary in the Irish calendar.

THE LIGHTCATCHERS

for Maeve on her eleventh birthday

i

St Brigid's Day[1] comes storming in,
I make my act of faith in Spring.
The mystery of planting — what grows
In bleak or lush places is on us.
A courgette swells from orange flowers
And the untilled rock yields sea thrift.

We reaped the wind and you came,
Child of hibiscus and cinnamon.
No statue from a cold museum
You spark and shine through every room
In the house. Home is the husk.
Soon you will shuck it off to go dancing.

Look how for centuries we nourished sons,
Buried the girl children, bound their feet.
Did we think it would make no difference?
As we slouch towards the millennium
The portents are all for the world ending.
Soldiers are sprouting along every border.
They are tumbling
Out of their mothers' wombs with guns.

Something has changed.
You are eleven this Saint Brigid's Day.
Last year's party girls in coloured dresses
Are swirling over our honey timbered floor,
A carousel of lightcatchers
Tinkling like Christmas chimes.
This year they will be more faceted still.
The music slows.

ii

I hang a cross of fresh rushes.
There is a stretching under the ground,
A reaching for the sun.
Brid, open your throat and bless them!
Let this treasury of minded daughters
Planted as sapphires
Ripen across the continents into rubies.

1   1 February. In Irish homes a St Brigid Cross, made in the shape of a cross with rushes, can often be seen hanging on a wall.

MARTIN McDONAGH

from Martin McDonagh, *The Lonesome West* (1997)

Martin McDonagh was born in London of Irish parents. *The Lonesome West* belongs with *The Beauty of Leenane* and *A Skull in Connemara* to a trilogy of plays entitled *The Leenane Trilogy*. McDonagh, along with Conor McPherson, author of the highly acclaimed play *The Weir*, is among the most exciting of the new Irish dramatists. In plays such as *The Cripple of Inishmaan* (1996) and *The Leenane Trilogy* (1997) he revisits the world of Synge and discovers equally strong story-lines, characters, and language, but now the charm has all but disappeared, postmodernism has taken hold, and Lady Gregory's 'apex of beauty' has been supplanted by a 'base of realism'. Or at least that is one view. For it can be equally argued that McDonagh's humour empties the base of realism, overturns the misplaced heroic ideals of the Revival, and returns us to language and the destructive charm of Irish speech, 'as fully flavoured as a nut or apple' (to quote from Synge's Preface to *Playboy*). In the opening scene of *The Lonesome West* two brothers return from their father's funeral and continue their feuding . . .

SCENE ONE

The kitchen/living-room of an old farmhouse in Leenane, Galway. Front door far right, table with two chairs down right, an old fireplace in the centre of the back wall, tattered armchairs to its right and left. Door to COLEMAN's *room in the left back wall. Door to* VALENE's *room far left. A long row of dusty, plastic Catholic figurines, each marked with a black 'V', line a shelf on the back wall, above which hangs a double-barrelled shotgun and above that a large crucifix. A food cupboard on the wall left, a chest of drawers towards the right, upon which rests a framed photo of a black dog. As the play begins it is day.* COLEMAN, *dressed in black, having just attended a funeral, enters, undoing his tie. He takes a biscuit tin out of a cupboard, tears off the Sellotape that binds its lid and takes out from it a bottle of poteen, also marked with a 'V'.* FATHER WELSH, *a thirty-five-year-old priest, enters just behind him.*

WELSH: I'll leave the door for Valene.

COLEMAN: Be doing what you like.

He pours two glasses as WELSH *sits at the table.*
You'll have a drink with me you will?

WELSH: I will, Coleman, so.

COLEMAN (*quietly*): A dumb fecking question that was.

WELSH: Eh?

COLEMAN: I said a dumb fecking question that was.

WELSH: Why, now?

COLEMAN gives WELSH *his drink without answering and sits at the table also.*

WELSH: Don't be swearing today of all days anyway, Coleman.

COLEMAN: I'll be swearing if I want to be swearing.

WELSH: After us only burying your dad, I'm saying.

COLEMAN: Oh aye, right enough, sure you know best, oh aye.

WELSH (*Pause*): Not a bad turnout anyways.

COLEMAN: A pack of vultures only coming nosing.

WELSH: Come on now, Coleman. They came to pay their last respects.

COLEMAN: Did seven of them, so, not come up asking where the booze-up after was to be held, and Maryjohnny then 'Will ye be having vol-au-vents?' There'll be no vol-au-vents had in this house for the likes of them. Not while Valene holds the purse-strings anyways. If it was me held the purse-strings I'd say aye, come around for yourselves, even if ye are vultures, but I don't hold the purse-strings. Valene holds the purse-strings.

WELSH: Valene does be a biteen tight with his money.

COLEMAN: A biteen? He'd steal the shite out of a burning pig, and this is his poteen too, so if he comes in shouting the odds tell him you asked me outright for it. Say you sure enough demanded. That won't be hard to believe.

WELSH: Like an alcoholic you paint me as half the time.

COLEMAN: Well that isn't a big job of painting. A bent child with no paint could paint you as an alcoholic. There's no great effort needed in that.

WELSH: I never touched the stuff before I came to this parish. This parish would drive you to drink.

COLEMAN: I suppose it would, only some people don't need as much of a drive as others. Some need only a short walk.

WELSH: I'm no alcoholic, Coleman. I like a drink is all.

COLEMAN: Oh aye, and I believe you too. (*Pause.*) Vol-au-vents, feck. The white-haired oul ghoulish fecking whore. She's owed me the price of a pint since nineteen-seventy-fecking-seven. It's always tomorrow with that bitch. I don't care if she does have Alzheimer's. If I had a vol-au-vent I'd shove it up her arse.

WELSH: That's not a nice thing to be saying about a . . .

COLEMAN: I don't care if it is or it isn't.

WELSH (*pause*): This house, isn't it going to be awful lonesome now with ye're dad gone?

COLEMAN: No.

WELSH: Ah it'll be a biteen lonesome I'm sure.

COLEMAN: If you're saying it'll be a biteen lonesome maybe it *will* be a biteen lonesome. I'll believe it if you're forcing it down me throat and sure aren't you the world's authority on lonesome?

WELSH: Are there no lasses on the horizon for ye, now ye're free and easy? Oh I'll bet there's hundreds.

COLEMAN: Only your mammy.

WELSH: It's a beautiful mood today you're in. (*Pause.*) Were you never in love with a girl, so, Coleman?

COLEMAN: I was in love with a girl one time, aye, not that it's any of your fecking business. At tech this was. Alison O'Hoolihan. This gorgeous red hair on her. But she got a pencil stuck in the back of her gob one day. She was sucking it the pointy-end inwards. She must've gotten a nudge. That was the end of me and Alison O'Hoolihan.

WELSH: Did she die, Coleman?

COLEMAN: She didn't die, no. I wish she had, the bitch. No, she got engaged to the bastarding doctor who wrenched the pencil out for her. Anybody could've done that job. It didn't need a doctor. I have no luck.

Pause. WELSH *drinks some more.* VALENE *enters with a carrier bag out of which he takes some new figurines and arranges them on the shelf.* COLEMAN *watches.*

VALENE: Fibreglass.

COLEMAN (*Pause*): Feck fibreglass.

VALENE: No, feck you instead of feck fibreglass.

COLEMAN: No, feck you two times instead of feck fibreglass . . .

WELSH: Hey now!! (*Pause.*) Jesus!

VALENE: He started it.

WELSH (*Pause*): Tom Hanlon I see he's back. I was speaking to him at the funeral. Did Tom know ye're dad?

COLEMAN: Slightly he knew dad. He arrested him five or six times for screaming at nuns.

WELSH: I remember hearing tell of that. That was an odd crime.

COLEMAN: Not that odd.

WELSH: Ah come on, now, it is.

COLEMAN: Oh if you say it is, Walsh, I suppose it is.

VALENE: I do hate them fecking Hanlons.

WELSH: Why now, Val?

VALENE: Why, is it? Didn't their Mairtin hack the ears off of poor Lassie, let him fecking bleed to death?

COLEMAN: You've no evidence at all it was Mairtin hacked the ears off of Lassie.

VALENE: Didn't he go bragging about it to Blind Billy Pender?

COLEMAN: That's only hearsay evidence. You wouldn't get that evidence to stand up in a court of law. Not from a blind boy anyways.

VALENE: I'd expect you to be agin me. Full well I'd expect it.

COLEMAN: That dog did nothing but bark anyways.

VALENE: Well barking doesn't deserve ears chopped off, Coleman. That's what dogs are supposed to do is bark, if you didn't know.

COLEMAN: Not at that rate of barking. They're meant to ease up now and then. That dog was going for the world's fecking barking record.

WELSH: And there's plenty enough hate in the world as it is, Valene Connor, without you adding to it over a dead dog.

VALENE: Nobody'll notice a biteen more hate, so, if there's plenty enough hate in the world.

WELSH: A nice attitude that is for a . . .

VALENE: Feck off and sling your sermons at Maureen Folan and Mick Dowd, so, if it's nice attitudes you're after, Walsh. Wouldn't that be more in your fecking line?

WELSH *bows his head and pours himself another drink.*

COLEMAN: That shut the fecker up.

VALENE: It did. You see how quick he is to . . . That's my fecking poteen now! What's the . . . eh?

COLEMAN: He did come in pegging orders for a drink, now. What was I supposed to say to him, him just sticking dad in the ground for us?

VALENE: Your own you could've given him so.

COLEMAN: And wasn't I about to 'til I up and discovered me cupboard was bare.

VALENE: Bare again, was it?

COLEMAN: Bare as a bald fella's arse.

VALENE: Never unbare are your cupboards.

COLEMAN: I suppose they're not now, but isn't that life?

WELSH: And there's no such word as unbare.

VALENE *stares at* WELSH *sternly.*

COLEMAN (*laughing*): He's right!

VALENE: Picking me up on me vocabulary is it, Welsh?

COLEMAN: It is, aye.

WELSH: I'm not now. I'm only codding ya, Val.

VALENE: And shaking the hands of Mick and Maureen weren't you, too, I saw you at the grave there, and passing chit-chat among ye . . .

WELSH: I was passing no chit-chat . . .

VALENE: A great parish it is you run, one of them murdered his missus, an axe through her head, the other her mammy, a poker took her brains out, and it's only chit-chatting it is you be with them? Oh aye.

WELSH: What can I do, sure, if the courts and the polis . . .

VALENE: Courts and the polis me arse. I heard the fella you represent was of a higher authority than the courts and the fecking polis.

WELSH (*sadly*): I heard the same thing, sure. I must've heard wrong. It seems like God has no jurisdiction in this town. No jurisdiction at all.

VALENE *takes his bottle, mumbling, and pours himself a drink. Pause.*

COLEMAN: That's a great word, I think.

VALENE: What word?

COLEMAN: Jurisdiction. I like J-words.

VALENE: Jurisdiction's too Yankee-sounding for me. They never stop saying it on *Hill Street Blues*.

COLEMAN: It's better than unbare anyways.

VALENE: Don't you be starting with me again, ya feck.

COLEMAN: I will do what I wish, Mr Figurine-man.

VALENE: Leave me figurines out of it.

COLEMAN: How many more do ya fecking need?

VALENE: Lots more! No, lots and lots more!

COLEMAN: Oh aye.

VALENE: And where's me felt-tip pen, too, so I'll be giving them me 'V'?

COLEMAN: I don't know where your fecking felt-tip pen is.

VALENE: Well you had it doing beards in me *Woman's Own* yesterday!

COLEMAN: Aye, and you wrenched it from me near tore me hand off.

VALENE: Is all you deserved . . .

COLEMAN: You probably went hiding it then.

On these words, VALENE *instantly remembers where his pen is and exits to his room. Pause.*

He's forever hiding things that fella.

WELSH: I'm a terrible priest, so I am. I can never be defending God when people go saying things agin him, and, sure, isn't that the main qualification for being a priest?

COLEMAN: Ah there be a lot worse priests than you, Father, I'm sure. The only thing with you is you're a bit too weedy and you're a terror for the drink and you have doubts about Catholicism. Apart from that you're a fine priest. Number one you don't go abusing poor gasurs,[1] so, sure, doesn't that give you a head-start over half the priests in Ireland?

WELSH: That's no comfort at all, and them figures are overexaggerated anyways. I'm a terrible priest, and I run a terrible parish, and that's the end of the matter. Two murderers I have on me books, and I can't get either of the beggars to confess to it. About betting on the horses and impure thoughts is all them bastards ever confess.

COLEMAN: Em, only I don't think you should be telling me what people be confessing, Father. You can be excommunicated for that I think. I saw it in a film with Montgomery Clift.

WELSH: Do ya see? I'm shite sure.

COLEMAN: Too hard on yourself is all you are, and it's only pure gossip that Mick and Maureen murdered anybody, and nothing but gossip. Mick's missus was a pure drink-driving accident is unfortunate but could've happened to anybody . . .

WELSH: With the scythe hanging out of her forehead, now, Coleman?

COLEMAN: A pure drink-driving, and Maureen's mam only fell down a big hill and Maureen's mam was never steady on her feet.

WELSH: And was even less steady with the brains pouring out of her, a poker swipe.

COLEMAN: She had a bad hip and everybody knew, and if it's at anybody you should be pegging murder accusations, isn't it me? Shot me dad's head off him, point blank range.

WELSH: Aye, but an accident that was, and you had a witness . . .

COLEMAN: Is what I'm saying. And if Valene hadn't happened to be there to see me tripping and the gun falling, wouldn't the town be saying I put the barrel bang up agin him, blew the head off him on purpose? It's only because poor Mick and Maureen had no witnesses is why all them gobshites do go gossiping about them.

VALENE *returns with his pen and starts drawing 'V's on the new figurines.*

WELSH: See? You do see the good in people, Coleman. That's what I'm supposed to do, but I don't. I'm always at the head of the queue to be pegging the first stone.

VALENE: He's not having another fecking crisis of faith?

COLEMAN: He is.

VALENE: He never stops, this fella.

WELSH: Aye, because I have nothing to offer me parish at all.

COLEMAN: Sure haven't you just coached the under-twelves football to the Connaught semifinals yere first year trying?

WELSH: Ah the under-twelves football isn't enough to restore your faith in the priesthood, Coleman, and we're a bunch of foulers anyway.

COLEMAN: Ye aren't. Ye're skilful.

WELSH: Ten red cards in four games, Coleman. That's a world's record in girls' football. That'd be a record in boys' football. One of the lasses from St Angela's she's still in hospital after meeting us.

COLEMAN: If she wasn't up for the job she shouldn't've been on the field of play.

WELSH: Them poor lasses used to go off crying. Oh a great coach I am, oh aye.

COLEMAN: Sissy whining bitches is all them little feckers are.

A rap on the front door, then GIRLEEN, *a pretty girl of seventeen, puts her head round it.*

GIRLEEN: Are ye in need?

VALENE: Come in for yourself, Girleen. I'll be taking a couple of bottles off ya, aye. I'll get me money.

VALENE exits to his room as GIRLEEN *enters, taking two bottles of poteen out of her bag.*

GIRLEEN: Coleman. Father Welsh Walsh Welsh . . .

WELSH: Welsh.

GIRLEEN: Welsh. I know. Don't be picking me up. How is all?

COLEMAN: We've just stuck our dad in the ground.

GIRLEEN: Grand, grand. I met the postman on the road with a letter for Valene.

She lays an official-looking envelope on table.

That postman fancies me, d'you know? I think he'd like to be getting into me knickers, in fact I'm sure of it.

COLEMAN: Him and the rest of Galway, Girleen.

WELSH *puts his head in his hands at this talk.*

GIRLEEN: Galway minimum. The EC[2] more like. Well, a fella won't be getting into my knickers on a postman's wages. I'll tell you that, now.

COLEMAN: Are you charging for entry so, Girleen?

GIRLEEN: I'm tinkering with the idea, Coleman. Why, are you interested? It'll take more than a pint and a bag of Taytos,[3] mind.

COLEMAN: I have a three-pound postal order somewhere I never used.

GIRLEEN: That's nearer the mark, now. (*To* WELSH.) What kind of wages do priests be on, Father?

WELSH: Will you stop now?! Will you stop?! Isn't it enough for a girl going round flogging poteen, not to go talking of whoring herself on top of it?!

GIRLEEN: Ah, we're only codding you, Father.

She fluffs her fingers through WELSH's *hair. He brushes her off.*

(*To* COLEMAN.) He's not having another crisis of faith is he? That's twelve this week. We should report him to Jesus.

WELSH *moans into his hands.* GIRLEEN *giggles slightly.*
VALENE *enters and pays* GIRLEEN.

VALENE: Two bottles, Girleen.

GIRLEEN: Two bottles it is. You've a letter there.

COLEMAN: Buy me a bottle, Valene. I'll owe ya.

VALENE (*opening letter*): Buy you a bottle me arse.

COLEMAN: Do ya see this fella?

GIRLEEN: You've diddled me out of a pound, Valene.

VALENE *pays up as if expecting it.*

VALENE: It was worth a go.

GIRLEEN: You're the king of stink-scum fecking filth-bastards you, ya bitch-feck, Valene.

WELSH: Don't be swearing like that now, Girleen . . .

GIRLEEN: Ah me hairy arse, Father.

VALENE (*re letter*): Yes! It's here! It's here! Me cheque! And look how much too!

VALENE *holds the cheque up in front of* COLEMAN's *face.*

COLEMAN: I see how much.

VALENE: Do ya see?

COLEMAN: I see now, and out of me face take it.

VALENE (*holding it closer*): Do ya see how much, now?

COLEMAN: I see now.

VALENE: And all to me. Is it a closer look you do need?

COLEMAN: Out of me face take that thing now.

VALENE: But maybe it's closer you need to be looking now . . .

VALENE *rubs the cheque in* COLEMAN's *face.* COLEMAN *jumps up and grabs* VALENE *by the neck.* VALENE *grabs him in the same way.* GIRLEEN *laughs as they struggle together.* WELSH *darts drunkenly across and breaks the two apart.*

WELSH: Be stopping, now! What's the matter with ye?

WELSH *gets accidentally kicked as the brothers part. He winces.*

COLEMAN: I'm sorry, Father. I was aiming at that feck.

WELSH: Hurt that did! Bang on me fecking shin.

GIRLEEN: You'll know now how the lasses at St Angela's be feeling.

WELSH: What's the matter with ye at all, sure?

VALENE: He started it.

WELSH: Two brothers laying into each other the same day their father was buried! I've never heard the like.

GIRLEEN: It's all because you're such a terrible priest to them, Father.

WELSH *glares at her. She looks away, smiling.*

GIRLEEN: I'm only codding you, Father.

WELSH: What kind of a town is this at all? Brothers fighting and lasses peddling booze and two fecking murderers on the loose?

GIRLEEN: And me pregnant on top of it. (*Pause.*) I'm not really.

WELSH *looks at her and them sadly, moving somewhat drunkenly to the door.*

WELSH: Don't be fighting any more, now, ye's two. (*Exits.*)

GIRLEEN: Father Walsh Welsh has no sense of humour. I'll walk him the road home for himself, and see he doesn't get hit be a cow like the last time.

COLEMAN: See you so, Girleen.

VALENE: See you so, Girleen. (GIRLEEN *exits. Pause.*) That fella, eh?

COLEMAN (*in agreement*): Eh? That fella.

VALENE: Jeez. Eh? If he found out you blew the head off dad on purpose, he'd probably get three times as maudlin.

COLEMAN: He takes things too much to heart does that fella.

VALENE: Way too much to heart.
Blackout.

SCENE TWO

Evening. Against the back wall and blocking out the fireplace is now situated a large, new, orange stove with a big 'V' scrawled on its front. COLEMAN, *in glasses, sits in the armchair left, reading* Woman's Own, *a glass of poteen beside him.* VALENE *enters, carrying a bag. Slowly, deliberately, he places a hand on the stove in a number of places in case it's been used recently.* COLEMAN *snorts in disgust at him.*

VALENE: I'm checking.

COLEMAN: I can see you're checking.

VALENE: I like to have a little check with you around.

COLEMAN: That's what you do best is check.

VALENE: Just a biteen of a check, like. D'you know what I mean? In *my* opinion, like.

COLEMAN: I wouldn't touch your stove if you shoved a kettle up me arse.

VALENE: Is right, my stove.

COLEMAN: If you fecking paid me I wouldn't touch your stove.

VALENE: Well I won't be fecking paying you to touch me stove.

COLEMAN: I know well you won't, you tight-fisted feck.

VALENE: And *my* stove is right. Did *you* pay the three hundred? Did *you* get the gas fixed up? No. Who did? Me. My money. Was it your money? No, it was my money.

COLEMAN: I know well it was your money.

VALENE: If you'd made a contribution I'd've said go ahead and use me stove, but you didn't, so I won't.

COLEMAN: We don't even need a stove.

VALENE: You may not need a stove, but I need a stove.

COLEMAN: You never fecking eat, sure!

VALENE: I'll start! Aye, by Christ I'll start. (*Pause.*) This stove is mine, them figurines are mine, this gun, them chairs, that table's mine. What else? This floor, them cupboards, everything in this fecking house is mine, and you don't go touching, boy. Not without me express permission.

COLEMAN: It'll be hard not to touch your fecking floor, now.

VALENE: Not without me express . . .

COLEMAN: Unless I go fecking levitating.

VALENE: Not without me express . . .

COLEMAN: Like them darkies.

VALENE (*angrily*): Not without me express fecking permission I'm saying!

COLEMAN: Your express permission, oh aye.

VALENE: To *me* all this was left. To me and me alone.

COLEMAN: Twasn't left but twas *awarded*.

VALENE: Me and me alone.

COLEMAN: Awarded it was.

VALENE: And you don't go touching. (*Pause.*) What darkies?

COLEMAN: Eh?

VALENE: What darkies go levitating?

COLEMAN: Them darkies. On them carpets. Them levitating darkies.

VALENE: Them's Pakies. Not darkies at all!

COLEMAN: The same differ!

VALENE: Not at all the same differ! Them's Paki-men, same as whistle at the snakes.

COLEMAN: It seems like you're the expert on Paki-men!

VALENE: I *am* the expert on Paki-men!

COLEMAN: You probably go falling in love with Paki-men too, so! Oh I'm sure.

VALENE: Leave falling in love out of it.

COLEMAN: What did you get shopping, Mister 'I-want-to-marry-a-Paki-man'?

VALENE: What did I get shopping, is it?
VALENE *takes two figurines out of his bag and arranges them delicately on the shelf.*

COLEMAN: Ah for feck's sake . . .

VALENE: Don't be cursing now, Coleman. Not in front of the saints. Against God that is.
He takes eight packets of Taytos out of the bag and lays them on the table.
And some Taytos I got.

COLEMAN: Be getting McCoys if you're getting crisps.

VALENE: I'll be getting what I li . . .

COLEMAN: Ya fecking cheapskate.

VALENE (*Pause. Glaring*): I'm not getting some crisps taste exactly the same, cost double, Coleman.

COLEMAN: They don't taste the same and they have grooves.

VALENE: They do taste the same and feck grooves.

COLEMAN: Taytos are dried fecking filth and everybody knows they are.

VALENE: The crisp expert now I'm listening to. What matter if they're dried fecking filth? They're seventeen p., and whose crisps are they anyways? They're my crisps.

COLEMAN: They're your crisps.

VALENE: My crisps and my crisps alone.

COLEMAN: Or get Ripples.

VALENE: Ripples me arse and I don't see you digging in your . . . what's this?

VALENE picks up COLEMAN's glass and sniffs it.

COLEMAN: What's wha?

VALENE: This.

COLEMAN: Me own.

VALENE: Your own your arse. You've no money to be getting your own.

COLEMAN: I do have.

VALENE: From where?

COLEMAN: Am I being interrogated now?

VALENE: You are.

COLEMAN: Feck ya so.

VALENE takes his poteen out of his biscuit tin to check if any is missing. COLEMAN puts the magazine aside, takes his glasses off and sits at the table.

VALENE: You've been at this.

COLEMAN: I haven't at all been at that.

VALENE: It seems very . . . reduced.

COLEMAN: Reduced me arse. I wouldn't be at yours if you shoved a fecking . . .

VALENE (*sipping it, uncertain*): You've topped it up with water.

COLEMAN: Be believing what you wish. I never touched your poteen.

VALENE: Where would you get money for . . . Me house insurance?! Oh you fecker . . . !

VALENE desperately finds and examines his insurance book.

COLEMAN: I paid in your house insurance.

VALENE: This isn't Duffy's signature.

COLEMAN: It is Duffy's signature. Doesn't it say 'Duffy'?

VALENE: You paid it?

COLEMAN: Aye.

VALENE: Why?

COLEMAN: Oh to do you a favour, after all the favours you've done me over the years. Oh aye.

VALENE: It's easy enough to check.

COLEMAN: It *is* easy enough to check, and check ahead, ya feck. Check until you're blue in the face.
Confused, VALENE puts the book away.
It's not only money can buy you booze. No. Sex appeal it is too.

VALENE: Sex appeal? You? Your sex appeal wouldn't buy the phlegm off a dead frog.

COLEMAN: You have your own opinion and you're well entitled to it. Girleen's of the opposite opinion.

VALENE: Girleen? Me arse.

COLEMAN: Is true.

VALENE: Eh?

COLEMAN: I said let me have a bottle on tick and I'll be giving you a big kiss, now. She said 'If you let me be touching you below, sure you can have a bottle for nothing.' The deal was struck then and there.

VALENE: Girleen wouldn't touch you below if you bought her a pony, let alone giving poteen away on top of it.

COLEMAN: I can only be telling the God's honest truth, and how else would I be getting poteen for free?

VALENE (*unsure*): Me arse. (*Pause.*) Eh? (*Pause.*) Girleen's pretty. (*Pause.*) Girleen's awful pretty. (*Pause.*) Why would Girleen be touching you below?

COLEMAN: Mature men it is Girleen likes.

VALENE: I don't believe you at all.

COLEMAN: Don't so.

VALENE (*Pause*): What did it feel like?

COLEMAN: What did what feel like?

VALENE: The touching below.

COLEMAN: Em, nice enough now.

VALENE (*unsure*): I don't believe you at all. (*Pause.*) No, I don't believe you at all.

COLEMAN opens and starts eating a packet of VALENE's crisps.

VALENE: Girleen wouldn't be touching you below. Never in the world would Girleen be touching y . . . (*Stunned.*) Who said you could go eating me crisps?!

COLEMAN: Nobody said.

VALENE: In front of me?!

COLEMAN: I decided of me own accord.

VALENE: You'll be paying me seventeen p. of your own accord so! And right now you'll be paying me!

COLEMAN: Right now, is it?

VALENE: It is!

COLEMAN: The money you have stashed?

VALENE: And if you don't pay up it's a batter I'll be giving you.

COLEMAN: A batter from you? I'd be as scared of a batter from a worm.

VALENE: Seventeen p. I'm saying!

Pause. COLEMAN slowly takes a coin out of his pocket and, without looking at it, slams it down on the table. VALENE looks at the coin.

That's ten.

COLEMAN looks at the coin, takes out another one and slams that down also.

COLEMAN: You can keep the change.

VALENE: I can keep the change, can I?

He pockets the coins, takes out three p., opens one of COLEMAN's *hands and places the money in it.*

I'm in no need of charity.

He turns away. Still sitting, COLEMAN *throws the coins hard at the back of* VALENE's *head.*

Ya fecker ya!! Come on so!

COLEMAN *jumps up, knocking his chair over.*

COLEMAN: Come on so, is it?

VALENE: Pegging good money at me?!

COLEMAN: It is. And be picking that money up now, for your oul piggy-bank, ya little virgin fecking gayboy ya . . .

The two grapple, fall to the floor and roll around scuffling. WELSH *enters through the front door, slightly drunk.*

WELSH: Hey ye's two! Ye's two! (*Pause. Loudly.*) Ye's two!

COLEMAN (*irritated*): Wha?

WELSH: Tom Hanlon's just killed himself.

VALENE: Eh?

WELSH: Tom Hanlon's just killed himself.

VALENE (*Pause*): Let go o' me neck, you.

COLEMAN: Let go o' me arm so.

The two slowly let go of each other and stand up, as WELSH *sits at the table, stunned.*

WELSH: He walked out into the lake from the oul jetty there. Aye, and kept walking. His body's on the shingle. His father had to haul me drunk out of Rory's to say a prayer o'er him, and me staggering.

VALENE: Tom Hanlon? Jeez. Sure I was only talking to Tom a day ago there. The funeral.

WELSH: A child seen him. Seen him sitting on the bench on the jetty, a pint with him, looking out across the lake to the mountains there. And when his pint was done he got up and started walking, the clothes still on him, and didn't stop walking. No. 'Til the poor head of him was under. And even then he didn't stop.

COLEMAN (*Pause*): Ah I never liked that Tom fecking Hanlon. He was always full of himself, same as all fecking coppers . . .

WELSH (*angrily*): The poor man's not even cold yet, Coleman Connor. Do you have to be talking that way about him?

COLEMAN: I do, or if I'm not to be a hypocrite anyways I do.

VALENE: It's hypocrites now. Do you see this fella, Father? Ate a bag of me crisps just now without a by your leave . . .

COLEMAN: I paid you for them crisps . . .

VALENE: Then says he's not a hypocrite.

COLEMAN: I paid thruppence over the odds for them crisps, and how does eating crisps make you a hypocrite anyways?

VALENE: It just does. And interfering with a schoolgirl on top of it is another crime, Father.

COLEMAN: I interfered with no schoolgirl. I was interfered with be a schoolgirl.

VALENE: The same differ!

WELSH: What schoolgirl's this, now?

COLEMAN: Girleen this schoolgirl is. This afternoon there she came up and a fine oul time we had, oh aye.

WELSH: Girleen? Sure Girleen's been helping me wash the strips for the under-twelves football all day, never left me sight.

Embarrassed, COLEMAN *gets up and moves towards his room.* VALENE *blocks his way.*

VALENE: Aha! Aha! Now who's the virgin fecking gayboy, eh? Now who's the virgin fecking gayboy?

COLEMAN: Out of me way, now.

VALENE: *Now,* eh?

COLEMAN: Out of me way I'm saying.

VALENE: I knew well!

COLEMAN: Are you moving or am I moving ya?

VALENE: *Now* did I know well? Eh?

COLEMAN: Eh?

VALENE: Eh?

WELSH: Coleman, come back now. We . . .

COLEMAN: And you can shut your fecking gob too, Welsh or Walsh or whatever your fecking name is, ya priest! You don't go catching Coleman Connor out on lies and expect to be . . . and be expecting to . . . to be . . .

COLEMAN *enters his room, slamming its door.*

VALENE: You're a stuttering oul ass, so you are! 'To be . . . to be . . . to be . . .' (*To* WELSH) Eh?

As VALENE *turns back to* WELSH, COLEMAN *dashes out, kicks the stove and dashes back to his room.* VALENE *trying and failing to catch him.*

Ya fecker, ya!

He checks the stove for damage.

Me good fecking stove! If there's any damage done to this stove it'll be you'll be paying for it, ya feck! Did you see that, Father? Isn't that man mad? (*Pause.*) Do ya like me new stove, Father? Isn't it a good one?

COLEMAN (*off*): Do ya see that 'V' on his stove, Father? Do you think it's a V for Valene? It isn't. It's a V for Virgin, it is.

VALENE: Oh is it now . . . ?

COLEMAN (*off*): V for virgin it is, uh-huh.

VALENE: When you're the king of the virgins?

COLEMAN (*off*): Valene the Virgin that V stands for.

VALENE: The fecking king of them you are! And don't be listening at doors!

COLEMAN (*off*): I'll be doing what I wish.

VALENE *checks stove again.* WELSH *is on the verge of tears.*

VALENE (*re stove*): No, I think it's okay, now . . .

WELSH: You see, I come in to ye . . . and ye're fighting. Fair enough, now, that's all ye two ever do is fight. Ye'll never be changed. It's enough times I've tried . . .

VALENE: Are you crying, Father, or is it a bit of a cold you do have? Ah it's a cold . . .

WELSH: It's crying I am.

VALENE: Well I've never seen the like.

WELSH: Cos I come in, and I tell ya a fella's just gone and killed himself, a fella ye went to school with . . . a fella ye grew up with . . . a fella never had a bad word to say about anybody and did his best to be serving the community every day of his life . . . and I tell you he's killed himself be drowning, is a horrible way to die, and not only do ye not bat an eye . . . not only do ye not bat an eye but ye go arguing about crisps and stoves then!

VALENE: I batted an eye.

WELSH: I didn't notice that eye batted!

VALENE: I batted a big eye.

WELSH: Well I didn't notice it, now!

VALENE (*Pause*): But isn't it a nice stove, Father?

WELSH *puts his head in his hands.* VALENE *goes to the stove.*

VALENE: Only a day I've had it fixed up. You can still smell as clean as it is. Coleman's forbid to touch it at all because Coleman didn't contribute a penny towards it, for Coleman doesn't *have* a penny to contribute towards it. (*Picks up the three p.*) He has three pee, but three p. won't go too far towards a stove. Not too far at all. He threw this three p. at me head earlier, d'you know? (*In realization, angrily.*) And if he has no money and he wasn't interfered with, where the feck was it that poteen did come from?! Coleman . . . !

WELSH (*Screams*): Valene, you fecking fecker ya!!

VALENE: Wha? Oh, aye, poor Thomas.

VALENE *nods in phoney empathy.*

WELSH (*Pause. Sadly, standing*): I came up to get ye to come to the lake with me, to be dragging poor Tom's body home for himself. Will ye be helping now?

VALENE: I will be, Father. I will be.

WELSH (*Pause*): Feck. Two murders and a suicide now. Two murders and a fecking suicide . . .

WELSH *exits, shaking his head.*

VALENE (*calling out*): Sure, not your fault was it, Father. Don't you be getting maudlin again! (*Pause.*) Coleman? I'm off down . . .

COLEMAN (*off*): I heard.

VALENE: Are ya coming so?

COLEMAN (*off*): Not at all am I coming. To go humping a dead policeman about the country? A dead policeman used to laugh at me press-ups in PE? I don't fecking think so, now.

VALENE: You forever bear a grudge, you. Ah anyways it's good strong men Father Walsh does need helping him, not virgin fecking gayboys couldn't pay a drunk monkey to go interfering with him.

VALENE *quickly exits.* COLEMAN *storms into the room to find him gone. He goes to the door and idles there, thinking, looking around the room. His gaze falls on the stove. He picks up some matches and opens the stove door.*

COLEMAN: A virgin fecking gayboy, is it? Shall we be having gas mark ten for no reason at all, now? We shall, d'you know?

He lights the stove, turns it up, closes its door and exits to his room. He returns a few seconds later and looks around the room.

For no reason at all, is it?

He takes a large oven-proof bowl out of a cupboard, places all of the figurines from the shelf into the bowl and puts the bowl inside the stove, closing its door afterwards.

Now we'll be seeing who's a virgin gayboy couldn't pay a monkey to interfere with him. I'll say we'll fecking see.

He pulls on his jacket, brushes his unkempt hair for two seconds with a manky comb, and exits through the front door. Blackout.

SCENE THREE

A few hours later. VALENE *and* WELSH *enter, slightly drunk.* VALENE *takes his poteen out of his tin and pours himself a glass.* WELSH *eyes it a little.*

VALENE: That was an awful business, eh?

WELSH: Terrible. Just terrible, now. And I couldn't say a thing to them. Not a thing.

VALENE: What could be said to them, sure? The only thing they wanted to hear was 'Your son isn't dead at all', and that wouldn't have worked. Not with him lying in their front room, dripping.

WELSH: Did you ever hear such crying, Valene?

VALENE: You could've filled a lake with the tears that family cried. Or a russaway at minimum.

WELSH (*Pause*): A wha?

VALENE: A russaway. One of them russaways.

WELSH: Reservoir?

VALENE: Russaway, aye, and their Mairtin crying with the best of them. I've never seen Mairtin crying as hard. I suppose that's all you deserve for chopping the ears off a poor dog.

WELSH: I suppose if it's your only brother you lose you do cry hard.

VALENE: I wouldn't cry hard if I lost me only brother. I'd buy a big cake and have a crowd round.

WELSH: Ah Valene, now. If it's your own brother you can't get on with, how can we ever hope for peace in the world . . . ?

VALENE: Peace me arse and don't keep going on, you. You always do whine on this oul subject when you're drunk.

VALENE *sits at the table with drink and bottle.*

WELSH (*Pause*): A lonesome oul lake that is for a fella to go killing himself in. It makes me sad just to think of it. To think of poor Tom sitting alone there, alone with his thoughts, the cold lake in front of him, and him weighing up what's best, a life full of the loneliness that took him there but a life full of good points too. Every life has good points, even if it's only . . . seeing rivers, or going travelling, or watching football on the telly . . .

VALENE (*nodding*): Football, aye . . .

WELSH: Or the hopes of being loved. And Thomas weighing all that up on the one hand, then weighing up a death in cold water on the other, and choosing the water. And first it strikes you as dumb, and a waste, 'You were thirty-eight years old, you had health and friends, there was plenty worse off fecks than you in the world, Tom Hanlon' . . .

VALENE: The girl born with no lips in Norway.

WELSH: I didn't hear about her.

VALENE: There was this girl in Norway, and she was born with no lips at all.

WELSH: Uh-huh. But then you say if the world's such a decent place worth staying in, where were his friends when he needed them in this decent world? When he needed them most, to say 'Come away from there, ya daft, we'd miss ya, you're worthwhile, as dumb as you are.' Where were his friends then? Where was I then? Sitting pissed on me own in a pub. (*Pause.*) Rotting in hell now, Tom Hanlon is. According to the Catholic Church anyways he is, the same as every suicide. No remorse. No mercy on him.

VALENE: Is that right now? Every suicide you're saying?

WELSH: According to us mob it's right anyways.

VALENE: Well I didn't know that. That's a turn-up for the books. (*Pause.*) So the fella from *Alias Smith and Jones*, he'd be in hell?

WELSH: I don't know the fella from *Alias Smith and Jones.*

VALENE: Not the blond one, now, the other one.

WELSH: I don't know the fella.

VALENE: He killed himself, and at the height of his fame.

WELSH: Well if he killed himself, aye, he'll be in hell too. (*Pause.*) It's great it is. You can kill a dozen fellas, you can kill two dozen fellas. So long as you're sorry after you can still get into heaven. But if it's yourself you go murdering, no. Straight to hell.

VALENE: That sounds awful harsh. (*Pause.*) So Tom'll be in hell now, he will? Jeez. (*Pause.*) I wonder if he's met the fella from *Alias Smith and Jones* yet? Ah, that fella must be old be now. Tom probably wouldn't even recognize him. That's if he saw *Alias Smith and Jones* at all. I only saw it in England. It mightn't've been on telly here at all.

WELSH (*sighing*): You wouldn't be sparing a drop of that poteen would ya, Valene? I've an awful thirst . . .

VALENE: Ah, Father, I have only a drop left and I need that for meself . . .

WELSH: You've half the bottle, sure . . .

VALENE: And if I had some I'd spare it, but I don't, and should priests be going drinking anyways? No they shouldn't, or anyways not on the night . . .

WELSH: Thou shouldst share and share alike the Bible says. Or somewhere it says . . .

VALENE: Not on the night you let one of your poor flock go murdering himself you shouldn't, is what me sentence was going to be.

WELSH: Well was that a nice thing to be saying?! Do I need that, now?!

VALENE (*mumbling*): Don't go trying to go cadging a poor fella's drink off him so, the wages you're on.

VALENE *gets up, puts the bottle back in his biscuit tin and carefully sellotapes the lid up, humming as he does so.*

WELSH: Is there a funny smell off of your house tonight, Val, now?

VALENE: If you're going criticizing the smell of me house you can be off now, so you can.

WELSH: Like of plastic, now?

VALENE: Cadging me booze and then saying me house smells. That's the best yet, that is.

WELSH (*Pause*): At least Coleman came down to help us with poor Thomas after all, even if he was late. But that was awful wrong of him to go asking Tom's poor mam if she'd be doing vol-au-vents after.

VALENE: That was awful near the mark.

WELSH: And her sitting there crying, and him nudging her then, and again and again 'Will ye be having vol-au-vents, Missus, will ye?'

VALENE: If he was drunk you could excuse it, but he

wasn't. It was just out of spite. (*Laughing.*) Although it was funny, now.

WELSH: Where is he anyways? I thought he was walking the road with us.

VALENE: He'd stopped to do up his shoelaces a way back. (*Pause. In realization.*) Coleman *has* no shoelaces. He has only loafers. (*Pause.*) Where have all me Virgin Marys gone?!

He leans in over the stove, placing his hands on its top, to see if the figurines have fallen down the back. The searing heat from the stove burns his hands and he pulls them away, yelping.

(*Hysterical.*) Wha?! Wha?!

WELSH: What is it, Valene? Did you go leaving your stove on?

Stunned, VALENE *opens the stove door with a towel. Smoke billows out. He takes the steaming bowl of molten plastic out, sickened, places it on the table and delicately picks up one of the half-melted figurines with the towel.*

All your figurines are melted, Valene.

VALENE (*staggering backwards*): I'll kill the feck! I'll kill the feck!

WELSH: I'll be betting it was Coleman, Valene.

VALENE: That's all there is to it! I'll kill the feck!

VALENE *pulls the shotgun off the wall and marches around the room in a daze, as* WELSH *jumps up and tries to calm him.*

WELSH: Oh Valene now! Put that gun down!

VALENE: I'll blow the head off him! The fecking head off him I'll blow! I tell him not to touch me stove and I tell him not to touch me figurines and what does he do? He cooks me figurines in me stove! (*Looking into bowl.*) That one was blessed be the Pope! That one was given me mammy be Yanks! And they're all gone! All of them! They're all just the fecking heads and bobbing around!

WELSH: You can't go shooting your brother o'er inanimate objects, Valene! Give me that gun, now.

VALENE: Inanimate objects? Me figurines of the saints? And you call yoursel' a priest? No wonder you're the laughing stock of the Catholic Church in Ireland. And that takes some fecking doing, boy.

WELSH: Give it me now, I'm saying. Your own flesh and blood this is you're talking of murdering.

VALENE: Me own flesh and blood is right, and why not? If he's allowed to murder his own flesh and blood and get away with it, why shouldn't I be?

WELSH: What are you talking about, now? Coleman shooting your dad was a pure accident and you know well.

VALENE: A pure accident me arse! You're the only fecker in Leenane believes that shooting was an accident. Didn't dad make a jibe about Coleman's

hairstyle, and didn't Coleman dash out, pull him back be the hair and blow the poor skulleen out his head, the same as he'd been promising to do since the age of eight and da trod on his Scalectrix, broke it in two . . .

COLEMAN *enters through the front door.*

COLEMAN: Well I did love that Scalectrix. It had glow in the dark headlamps.

VALENE *turns and points the gun at* COLEMAN. WELSH *backs off moaning, hands to his head.* COLEMAN *nonchalantly idles to the table and sits down.*

WELSH: It can't be true! It can't be true!

COLEMAN: Look at that fella gone pure white . . .

VALENE: No, shut up you! Don't be coming in mouthing after your fecking crimes . . .

WELSH: Tell me you didn't shoot your dad on purpose, Coleman. Please, now . . .

VALENE: This isn't about our fecking dad! This is about me fecking figurines!

COLEMAN: Do you see this fella's priorities?

VALENE: Melting figurines is against God outright!

WELSH: So is shooting your dad in the head, sure!

VALENE: And on gas mark ten!

WELSH: Tell me, Coleman, tell me, please. Tell me you didn't shoot your dad there on purpose. Oh tell me, now . . .

COLEMAN: Will you calm down, you? (*Pause.*) Of course I shot me dad on purpose.

WELSH *starts groaning again.*

COLEMAN: I don't take criticizing from nobody. 'Me hair's like a drunken child's.' I'd only just combed me hair and there was nothing wrong with it! And I know well shooting your dad in the head is against God, but there's some insults that can never be excused.

VALENE: And cooking figurines is against God on top of it, if they're Virgin Mary figurines anyways.

COLEMAN: Is true enough, be the fella with the gun, and I'll tell you another thing that's against God, before this fella puts a bullet in me . . . (*To* WELSH.) Hey moany, are you listening . . . ?

WELSH: I'm listening, I'm listening, I'm listening . . .

COLEMAN: I'll tell you another thing that's against God. Sitting your brother in a chair, with his dad's brains dripping down him, and promising to tell everyone it was nothing but an accident . . .

VALENE: Shut up now, ya feck . . .

COLEMAN: So long as there and then you sign over everything your dad went and left you in his will . . .

WELSH: No . . . no . . . no . . .

COLEMAN: His house and his land and his tables and his chairs and his bit of money to go frittering away on shitey-arsed ovens you only got to torment me, ya feck . . .

WELSH: No, now . . . no . . .

VALENE: Be saying goodbye to the world, you, fecker!

COLEMAN: And fecking Taytos then, the worst crisps in the world . . .

VALENE cocks the gun that's up against COLEMAN's head.

WELSH: No, Valene, no!

VALENE: I said say goodbye to the world, ya feck.

COLEMAN: Goodbye to the world, ya feck.

VALENE pulls the trigger. There is a hollow click. He pulls the trigger again. Another click. A third time, and another click, as COLEMAN reaches in his pocket and takes out two shotgun cartridges.

COLEMAN: Do you think I'm fecking stupid, now? (*To* WELSH.) Did you see that, Father? My own brother going shooting me in the head.

VALENE: Give me them fecking bullets, now.

COLEMAN: No.

VALENE: Give me them bullets I'm saying.

COLEMAN: I won't.

VALENE: Give me them fecking . . .

VALENE tries to wrench the bullets out of COLEMAN's clenched fist, COLEMAN laughing as he does so. VALENE grabs COLEMAN by the neck and they fall to the floor, grappling, rolling around the place. WELSH stares at the two of them dumbstruck, horrified. He catches sight of the bowl of steaming plastic beside him and, almost blankly, as the grappling continues, clenches his fists and slowly lowers them into the burning liquid, holding them under. Through clenched teeth and without breathing, WELSH manages to withhold his screaming for about ten or fifteen seconds until, still holding his fists under, he lets rip with a horrifying high-pitched wail lasting about ten seconds, during which VALENE and COLEMAN stop fighting, stand, and try to help him . . .

VALENE: Father Walsh, now . . .

COLEMAN: Father Walsh, Father Walsh . . .

WELSH pulls his fists out of the bowl, red raw, stifles his screams again, looks over the shocked VALENE and COLEMAN in despair and torment, smashes the bowl off the table and dashes out through the front door, his fists clutched to his chest in pain.

WELSH (*exiting, screaming*): Me name's *Welsh*!!!

VALENE and COLEMAN stare after him a moment or two.

COLEMAN: Sure that fella's pure mad.

VALENE: He's outright mad.

COLEMAN: He's a lube.[4] (*Gesturing at bowl.*) Will he be expecting us to clear his mess up?

VALENE puts his head out the front door and calls out.

VALENE: Will you be expecting us to clear your mess up, you?

COLEMAN (*Pause*): What did he say?

VALENE: He was gone.

COLEMAN: A lube and nothing but a lube. (*Pause.*) Ah it's your fecking floor. You clean it up.

VALENE: You wha?!

COLEMAN: Do you see me nice bullets, Valene?

COLEMAN rattles his two bullets in VALENE's face, then exits to his room.

VALENE: Ya fecking . . . !

COLEMAN's door slams shut. VALENE grimaces, pauses, scratches his balls blankly and sniffs his fingers. Pause. Blackout.

Interval.

SCENE FOUR

A plain bench on a lakeside jetty at night, on which WELSH sits with a pint, his hands lightly bandaged. GIRLEEN comes over and sits down beside him.

WELSH: Girleen.

GIRLEEN: Father. What are ya up to?

WELSH: Just sitting here, now.

GIRLEEN: Oh aye, aye. (*Pause.*) That was a nice sermon at Thomas's today, Father.

WELSH: I didn't see you there, did I?

GIRLEEN: I was at the back a ways. (*Pause.*) Almost made me go crying, them words did.

WELSH: You crying? I've never in all the years heard of you going crying, Girleen. Not at funerals, not at weddings. You didn't even cry when Holland knocked us out of the fecking World Cup.

GIRLEEN: Now and then on me now I go crying, over different things . . .

WELSH: That Packie fecking Bonner. He couldn't save a shot from a fecking cow.

WELSH sips his pint.

GIRLEEN: I'd be saying you've had a few now, Father?

WELSH: Don't you be starting on me now. On top of everybody else.

GIRLEEN: I wasn't starting on ya.

WELSH: Not today of all days.

GIRLEEN: I wasn't starting at all on ya. I do tease you sometimes but that's all I do do.

WELSH: Sometimes, is it? All the time, more like, the same as everybody round here.

GIRLEEN: I do only tease you now and again, and only to camouflage the mad passion I have deep within me for ya . . .

WELSH gives her a dirty look. She smiles.

GIRLEEN: No, I'm only joking now, Father.

WELSH: Do ya see?!

GIRLEEN: Ah be taking a joke will ya, Father? It's only

cos you're so high-horse and up yourself that you make such an easy target.

WELSH: I'm not so high-horse and up meself.

GIRLEEN: All right you're not so.

WELSH (*Pause*): *Am* I so high-horse and up meself?

GIRLEEN: No, now. Well, no more than most priests.

WELSH: Maybe I am high-horse so. Maybe that's why I don't fit into this town. Although I'd have to have killed half me fecking relatives to fit into this town. Jeez. I thought Leenane was a nice place when first I turned up here, but no. Turns out it's the murder capital of fecking Europe. Did *you* know Coleman had killed his dad on purpose?

GIRLEEN (*lowers head, embarrassed*): I think I did hear a rumour somewhere along the line . . .

WELSH: A fecking rumour? And you didn't bat an eye or go reporting it?

GIRLEEN: Sure I'm no fecking stool-pigeon and Coleman's dad was always a grumpy oul feck. He did kick me cat Eamonn there once.

WELSH: A fella deserves to die, so, for kicking a cat?

GIRLEEN (*shrugs*): It depends on the fella. And the cat. But there'd be a lot less cats kicked in Ireland, I'll tell ya, if the fella could rest-assured he'd be shot in the head after.

WELSH: You have no morals at all, it seems, Girleen.

GIRLEEN: I have plenty of morals only I don't keep whining on about them like some fellas.

WELSH (*Pause*): Val and Coleman'll kill each other someday if somebody doesn't do something to stop them. It won't be me who stops them anyways. It'll be someone with guts for the job.

He takes out a letter and passes it to GIRLEEN.

I've written them a little lettereen here, Girleen, would you give it to them next time you see them?

GIRLEEN: Won't you be seeing them soon enough yourself?

WELSH: I won't be. I'm leaving Leenane tonight.

GIRLEEN: Leaving for where?

WELSH: Anywhere. Wherever they send me. Anywhere but here.

GIRLEEN: But why, Father?

WELSH: Ah lots of different reasons, now, but the three slaughterings and one suicide amongst me congregation didn't help.

GIRLEEN: But none of that was your fault, Father.

WELSH: Oh no?

GIRLEEN: And don't you have the under-twelves semifinal tomorrow morning to be coaching?

WELSH: Them bitches have never listened to me advice before. I don't see why they should go starting now. Nobody ever listens to my advice. Nobody ever listens to me at all.

GIRLEEN: I listen to you.

WELSH (*sarcastic*): Ar that's great comfort.

GIRLEEN *bows her head, hurt.*

WELSH: And you don't listen to me either. How many times have I told you to stop flogging your dad's booze about town, and still you don't?

GIRLEEN: Ah it's just 'til I save up a few bob, Father, I'm doing that flogging.

WELSH: A few bob for what? To go skittering it away the clubs in Carraroe, and drunk schoolboys pawing at ya.

GIRLEEN: Not at all, Father. I do save it to buy a few nice things out me mam's Freeman's catalogue.[5] They do have an array of . . .

WELSH: To go buying shite, aye. Well I wish I did have as tough problems in my life as you do in yours, Girleen. It does sound like life's a constant torment for ya.

GIRLEEN *stands up and wrenches* WELSH's *head back by the hair.*

GIRLEEN: If anybody else went talking to me that sarcastic I'd punch them in the fecking eye for them, only if I punched you in the fecking eye you'd probably go crying like a fecking girl!

WELSH: I never asked you to come sitting beside me.

GIRLEEN: Well I didn't know there was a law against sitting beside ya, although I wish there fecking was one now.

GIRLEEN *releases him and starts walking away.*

WELSH: I'm sorry for being sarcastic to you, Girleen, about your mam's catalogue and whatnot. I am.

GIRLEEN *stops, pauses, and idles back to the bench.*

GIRLEEN: It's okay.

WELSH: It's only that I'm feeling a bit . . . I don't know . . .

GIRLEEN (*sitting beside him*): Maudlin.

WELSH: Maudlin. Maudlin is right.

GIRLEEN: Maudlin and lonesome. The maudlin and lonesome Father Walsh. *Welsh.* (*Pause.*) I'm sorry, Father.

WELSH: Nobody ever remembers.

GIRLEEN: It's just Walsh is so close to Welsh, Father.

WELSH: I know it is. I know it is.

GIRLEEN: What's your first name, Father?

WELSH (*Pause*): Roderick.

GIRLEEN *stifles laughter.* WELSH *smiles.*

GIRLEEN: Roderick? (*Pause.*) Roderick's a horrible name, Father.

WELSH: I know, and thanks for saying so, Girleen, but you're just trying to boost me spirits now, aren't ya?

GIRLEEN: I'm just being nice to ya now.

WELSH: What kind of a name's Girleen for a girl anyways? What's your proper first name?

GIRLEEN (*cringing*): Mary.

WELSH (*laughing*): Mary? And you go laughing at Roderick then?

GIRLEEN: Mary's the name of the mammy of Our Lord, did you ever hear tell of it?

WELSH: I heard of it somewhere along the line.

GIRLEEN: It's the reason she never got anywhere for herself. Fecking Mary.

WELSH: *You'll* be getting somewhere for yourself, Girleen.

GIRLEEN: D'ya think so, now?

WELSH: As tough a get as you are? Going threatening to thump priests? Of course.

GIRLEEN *brushes the hair out of* WELSH's *eyes.*

GIRLEEN: I wouldn't have gone thumping you, now, Father.

She gently slaps his cheek.

Maybe a decent slapeen, now.

WELSH *smiles and faces front.* GIRLEEN *looks at him, then away, embarrassed.*

WELSH (*Pause*): No, I just came out to have a think about Thomas before I go on me way. Say a little prayer for him.

GIRLEEN: It's tonight you're going?

WELSH: It's tonight, aye. I said to meself I'll stay for Tom's funeral, then that'll be the end of it.

GIRLEEN: But that's awful quick. No one'll have a chance to wish you goodbye, Father.

WELSH: Goodbye, aye, and good riddance to the back of me.

GIRLEEN: Not at all.

WELSH: No?

GIRLEEN: No.

Pause. WELSH *nods, unconvinced, and drinks again.*

Will you write to me from where you're going and be giving me your new address, Father?

WELSH: I'll try, Girleen, aye.

GIRLEEN: Just so's we can say hello now and then, now.

WELSH: Aye, I'll try.

As he speaks, GIRLEEN *manages to stifle tears without him noticing.*

This is where he walked in from, d'you know? Poor Tom. Look at as cold and bleak as it is. Do you think it took courage or stupidity for him to walk in, Girleen?

GIRLEEN: Courage.

WELSH: The same as that.

GIRLEEN: And Guinness.

WELSH (*laughing*): The same as that. (*Pause.*) Look at as sad and as quiet and still.

GIRLEEN: It's more than Thomas has killed himself here down the years, d'you know, Father? Three other fellas walked in here, me mam was telling me.

WELSH: Is that right now?

GIRLEEN: Years and years ago this is. Maybe even famine times.

WELSH: Drowned themselves?

GIRLEEN: This is where they all come.

WELSH: We should be scared of their ghosts so but we're not scared. Why's that?

GIRLEEN: You're not scared because you're pissed to the gills. I'm not scared because . . . I don't know why. One, because you're here, and two, because . . . I don't know. I don't be scared of cemeteries at night either. The opposite of that, I do *like* cemeteries at night.

WELSH: Why, now? Because you're a morbid oul tough?

GIRLEEN (*embarrassed throughout*): Not at all. I'm not a tough. It's because . . . even if you're sad or something, or lonely or something, you're still better off than them lost in the ground or in the lake, because . . . at least you've got the *chance* of being happy, and even if it's a real little chance, it's more than them dead ones have. And it's not that you're saying 'Hah, I'm better than ye', no, because in the long run it might end up that you have a worse life than ever they had and you'd've been better off as dead as them, there and then. But at least when you're still here there's the *possibility* of happiness, and it's like them dead ones know that, and they're happy for you to have it. They say 'Good luck to ya.' (*Quietly.*) Is the way I see it anyways.

WELSH: You have a million thoughts going on at the back of them big brown eyes of yours.

GIRLEEN: I never knew you did ever notice me big brown eyes. Aren't they gorgeous, now?

WELSH: You'll grow up to be a mighty fine woman one day, Girleen, God bless you.

WELSH *drinks again.*

GIRLEEN (*quietly, sadly*): One day, aye. (*Pause.*) I'll be carrying on the road home for meself now, Father. Will you be staying or will you be walking with me?

WELSH: I'll be staying a biteen longer for meself, Girleen. I'll be saying that prayer for poor Thomas, now.

GIRLEEN: It's goodbye for a while so.

WELSH: It is.

GIRLEEN *kisses his cheek and they hug.* GIRLEEN *stands.*

WELSH: You'll remember to be giving that letter to Valene and Coleman, now, Girleen?

GIRLEEN: I will. What's in it, Father? It does sound very mysterious. It wouldn't be packed full of condoms for them, would it?

WELSH: It wouldn't at all, now!

GIRLEEN: Cos, you know, Valene and Coleman'd get no use out of them, unless they went using them on a hen.

WELSH: Girleen, now . . .

GIRLEEN: And it'd need to be a blind hen.

WELSH: You do have a terrible mouth on ya.

GIRLEEN: Aye, all the better to . . . no, I won't be finishing that sentence. Did you hear tell of Valene's new hobby, Father? He's been roaming the entirety of Connemara picking up new figurines of the saints for himself, but only ceramic and china ones won't go melting away on him. Thirty-seven of them at last count he has, and only to go tormenting poor Coleman.

WELSH: Them two, they're just odd.

GIRLEEN: They *are* odd. They're the kings of odd. (*Pause.*) See you so, Father.

WELSH: See you so, Girleen. Or Mary, is it?

GIRLEEN: If you let me know where you get to I'll write with how the under-twelves get on tomorrow. It may be in the *Tribune* anyways. Under 'Girl decapitated in football match'.

WELSH *nods, half smiles.* GIRLEEN *idles away.*

WELSH: Girleen, now? Thanks for coming sitting next to me. It's meant something to me, it has.

GIRLEEN: Any time, Father. Any time.

GIRLEEN *exits.* WELSH *stares out front again.*

WELSH (*quietly*): No, not any time, Girleen. Not any time.

WELSH *finishes his pint, puts the glass down, blesses himself and sits there quietly a moment, thinking. Blackout.*

SCENE FIVE

Stage in darkness apart from WELSH, *who recites his letter rapidly.*

WELSH: Dear Valene and Coleman, it is Father Welsh here. I am leaving Leenane for good tonight and I wanted to be saying a few words to you, but I won't be preaching at you for why would I be? It has never worked in the past and it won't work now. All I want to do is be pleading with you as a fella concerned about ye and ye're lives, both in this world and the next, and the next won't be too long away for ye's if ye keep going on as mad as ye fecking have been. Coleman, I will not be speaking here about your murdering of your dad, although obviously it does concern me, both as a priest and as a person with even the vaguest moral sense, but that is a matter for your own conscience, although I hope some day you will realize what you have done and go seeking forgiveness for it, because let me tell you this, getting your hairstyle insulted is no just cause to go murdering someone, in fact it's the worst cause I did ever hear. But I will leave it at that although the same goes for you, Valene, for your part in your dad's murdering, and don't go saying you had no part because you did have a part and a big part. Going lying that it was an accident just to get your father's money is just as dark a deed as Coleman's deed, if not more dark, for Coleman's deed was done out of temper and spite, whereas your deed was done out of being nothing but a money-grubbing fecking miser with no heart at all, but I said I would not be preaching at you and I have lost me thread anyways so I will stop preaching at you and be starting a new paragraph. (*Pause.*) Like I said, I am leaving tonight, but I have been thinking about ye non-stop since the night I did scald me hands there at ye'res. Every time the pain does go through them hands I do think about ye, and let me tell you this. I would take that pain and pain a thousand times worse, and bear it with a smile, if only I could restore to ye the love for each other as brothers ye do so woefully lack, that must have been there some day. Didn't as gasurs ye love each other? Or as young men, now? Where did it all go on ye? Don't ye ever think about it? What I think I think what ye've done is bury it deep down in ye, under a rack of grudges and hate and sniping like a pair of fecking oul women. Ye two are like a pair of fecking oul women, so ye are, arging over fecking Taytos and stoves and figurines, is an arse-brained argument. But I do think that ye're love is still there under all of that, in fact I'd go betting everything that's dear to me on it, and may I rot in hell for ever if I'm wrong. All it is is ye've lived in each other's pockets the entire of ye're lives, and a sad and lonesome existence it has been, with no women to enter the picture for either of ye to calm ye down, or anyways not many women or the wrong sort of women, and what's happened the bitterness has gone building up and building up without check, the daily grudges and faults and moans and baby-crimes against each other ye can never seem to step back from and see the love there underneath and forgive each other for. Now, what the point of me letter is, couldn't ye do something about it? Couldn't the both of ye, now, go stepping back and be making a listeen of all the things about the other that do get on ye're nerves, and the wrongs the other has done all down through the years that you still hold against him, and be reading them lists out, and be discussing them openly, and be taking a deep breath then and be forgiving each other them wrongs, no matter what they may be? Would that be so awful hard, now? It would for ye two, I know, but couldn't ye just be trying it, now? And if it doesn't work it doesn't work, but at least ye could say ye'd tried and would ye be any worse off? And if ye wouldn't be doing it for yourselves, wouldn't ye be doing it for me, now? For a friend of ye'res, who cares about ye, who doesn't want to see ye blowing the brains out of each other, who never achieved anything as a priest in Leenane, in fact the opposite, and who'd see ye two becoming true brothers again as the greatest achievement of his whole time here. Sure it would be bordering on the miraculous. I might be canonized after. (*Pause.*) Valene and Coleman, I'm betting everything on ye. I know for sure there's love there somewheres, it's just a case of ye stepping back and looking for it. I'd be willing to bet me own soul that that love is there, and I know well the odds are stacked against me. They're probably 64,000 to one be this time, but I'd go betting on ye's still, for despite everything, despite ye're murder and ye're mayhem and ye're miserliness that'd tear the teeth out of broken goats, I have faith in ye. You wouldn't be letting me down now, would ye? Yours sincerely, and yours with the love of Christ now, Roderick Welsh.

Pause. WELSH *shivers slightly. Blackout.*

SCENE SIX

VALENE'*s house. Shotgun back on wall, over shelf full of new ceramic figurines, all marked with a 'V'.* COLEMAN, *in glasses, sits in the armchair left, glass of poteen beside him, perusing another women's magazine.* VALENE *enters carrying a bag and places his hand on the stove in a number of places. Irritated,* COLEMAN *tries to ignore him.*

VALENE: I'm checking. (*Pause.*) It's good to have a little check. (*Pause.*) I think it is, d'you know? (*Pause.*) Just a *little* check. D'you know what I mean, like? *After a while more of this,* VALENE *takes some new ceramic figurines out of his bag, which he arranges with the others on the shelf.*

COLEMAN: Ah for . . .

VALENE: Eh?

COLEMAN: Eh?

VALENE: Now then, eh?

COLEMAN: Uh-huh?

VALENE: Eh? Nice, I think. Eh? What do *you* think, Coleman?

COLEMAN: I think you can go feck yourself.

VALENE: No, not feck meself at all, now. Or over to the left a biteen would they look better? Hmm, we'll put the new St Martin⁶ over here, so it balances out with the other St Martin over there, so's we have one darkie saint on either side, so it balances out symmetrical, like. (*Pause.*) I'm a great one for shelf arranging I am. It is a skill I did never know I had. (*Pause.*) Forty-six figurines now. I'm sure to be getting into heaven with this many figurines in me house.

VALENE *finds his pen and marks up the new figurines.*

COLEMAN (*Pause*): There's a poor girl born in Norway here with no lips.

VALENE (*Pause*): That's old news that lip girl is.

COLEMAN: That girl'll never be getting kissed. Not with the bare gums on her flapping.

VALENE: She's the exact same as you, so, if she'll never be getting kissed, and you've no excuse. You've the full complement of lips.

COLEMAN: I suppose a million girls you've kissed in your time. Oh aye.

VALENE: Nearer two million.

COLEMAN: Two million, aye. And all of them aunties when you was twelve.

VALENE: Not aunties at all. Proper women.

COLEMAN: Me brother Valentine does be living in his own little dream-world, with the sparrows and the fairies and the hairy little men. Puw-ooh! And the daisy people.

VALENE (*Pause*): I hope that's not my poteen.

COLEMAN: It's not at all your poteen.

VALENE: Uh-huh? (*Pause.*) Did you hear the news?

COLEMAN: I did. Isn't it awful?

VALENE: It's a disgrace. It's an outright disgrace, and nothing but. You can't go sending off an entire girl's football team, sure.

COLEMAN: Not in a semi-fecking-final anyways.

VALENE: Not at any time, sure. If you have to send people off you send them off one at a time, for their individual offences. You don't go slinging the lot of them off wholesale, and only seven minutes in, so they go crying home to their mammys.

COLEMAN: St Josephine's have only got through be default, and nothing but default. If they had any honour they'd not take their place in the final at all and be giving it to us.

VALENE: I hope they lose the final.

COLEMAN: The same as that, *I* hope they lose the final. Sure, with their goalie in a coma they're bound to.

VALENE: No, their goalie came out of her coma a while ago there. Intensive care is all she's in now.

COLEMAN: She was fecking feigning? Getting us expelled from all competitions for no reason at all? I hope she relapses into her coma and dies.

VALENE: The same as that, *I* hope she lapses into her coma and dies. (*Pause.*) Look at us, we're in agreement.

COLEMAN: We are, I suppose.

VALENE: We can agree sometimes.

He snatches the magazine out of COLEMAN's *hands.*

Except don't go reading me magazines, I've told you, 'til I've finished reading them.

He sits at the table and flips through the magazine without reading it. COLEMAN *fumes.*

COLEMAN (*standing*): And don't go . . . don't go tearing them out of me fecking hands, near tore the fingers off me!

VALENE: Have these fingers you (*V-sign.*) and take them to bed with ya.

COLEMAN: You're not even reading that *Take a Break.*

VALENE: I *am* reading this *Take a Break,* or anyways I'm glancing through this *Take a Break* at me own pace, as a fella's free to do if it's with his own money he goes buying his *Take a Break.*

COLEMAN: Only women's magazines is all you ever go reading. Sure without doubt it's a fecking gayboy you must be.

VALENE: There's a lad here in Bosnia and not only has he no arms but his mammy's just died. (*Mumbles as he reads, then:*) Ah they're only after fecking money, the same as ever.

COLEMAN: And no fear of you sending that poor no-armed boy any money, ah no.

VALENE: They've probably only got him to put his arms behind his back, just to cod ya.

COLEMAN: It's any excuse for you.

VALENE: And I bet his mammy's fine.

COLEMAN (*Pause*): Get *Bella* if you're getting magazines. *Take a Break*'s nothing but quizzes.

VALENE: There's a coupon here for Honey Nut Loops.

VALENE *starts carefully tearing out the coupon at the same time as* COLEMAN *quietly takes some Taytos out of a cupboard.*

COLEMAN: Quizzes and deformed orphans. (*Pause.*) Em, would you let me be having a bag of Taytos, Val? I'm hungry a biteen.

VALENE (*looking up. Pause*): Are you being serious, now?

COLEMAN: G'wan. I'll owe you for them.

VALENE: Put that bag back, now.

COLEMAN: I'll owe you for them, I'm saying. You can put them on the same bill you've put your melted figurines.

VALENE: Put them . . . put them . . . What are you

doing, now? Put them Taytos back, I said.

COLEMAN: Valene, listen to me . . .

VALENE: No . . .

COLEMAN: I'm hungry and I need some Taytos. Didn't I wait 'til you came back in to ask you, now, and only because I'm honest . . .

VALENE: And you've asked me and I've said no. Slinging insults at me Taytos the other week I remember is all you were. I see the boot's on the other foot now.

COLEMAN: I've asked polite, now, Valene, and feck boots. Three times I've asked polite.

VALENE: I know well you've asked polite, Coleman. You've asked awful polite. And what I'm saying to ya, ya can't have any of me fecking Taytos, now!

COLEMAN: Is that your final word on the subject?

VALENE: It *is* me final word on the subject.

COLEMAN (*Pause*): I won't have any of your Taytos so. (*Pause.*) I'll just crush them to skitter.

He crushes the crisps to pulp and tosses the packet at VALENE. VALENE *darts up and around the table to get at* COLEMAN, *during which time* COLEMAN *grabs two more packets from the cupboard and holds them up, one in each hand, threatening to crush them also.*

Back off!

VALENE *stops dead in his tracks.*

COLEMAN: Back off or they'll be getting it the same!

VALENE (*scared*): Be leaving me crisps now, Coleman.

COLEMAN: Be leaving them, is it? When all I wanted was to go buying one of them and would've paid the full whack, but oh no.

VALENE (*tearfully, choking*): That's a waste of good food that is, Coleman.

COLEMAN: Good food, is it?

VALENE: There's Bosnians'd be happy to have them Taytos.

COLEMAN *opens one of the bags and starts eating just as the front door bangs open and* GIRLEEN *enters, face blotchy, letter in hand.*

COLEMAN: They *are* good food, d'you know?

GIRLEEN (*in shock throughout*): Have ye heard the news, now?

COLEMAN: What news, Girleen? The under-twelves . . .?

Seeing COLEMAN *distracted,* VALENE *dives for his neck, trying to get the crisps off him at the same time. They drag each other to the floor, rolling and scuffling,* COLEMAN *purposely mashing up the crisps any chance he gets.* GIRLEEN *stares at them a while, then quietly takes a butcher's knife out of one of the drawers, goes over to them, pulls* COLEMAN's *head back by the hair and puts the knife to his neck.*

VALENE: Leave Coleman alone, Girleen. What are you doing, now?

GIRLEEN: I'm breaking ye up.

COLEMAN (*scared*): We're broke up.

VALENE (*scared*): We're broke up.

> *Once the two are separated,* GIRLEEN *lets* COLEMAN *go and puts the letter on the table, sadly.*

GIRLEEN: There's a letter there Father Welsh wrote ye.

VALENE: What does that feck want writing to us?

COLEMAN: Going moaning again, I'll bet.

> VALENE *picks the letter up,* COLEMAN *pulls it off him,* VALENE *pulls it back. They stand reading it together,* COLEMAN *getting bored after a few seconds.* GIRLEEN *takes out a heart pendant on a chain and looks at it.*

GIRLEEN: I read it already on ye, coming over. All about the two of ye loving each other as brothers it is.

COLEMAN (*stifling laughter*): Wha?

VALENE: Father Walsh Welsh's leaving, it looks like.

COLEMAN: Is it full of moaning, Valene? It is.

VALENE: And nothing but moaning. (*Mimicking.*) 'Getting your hairstyle insulted is no just cause to go murdering someone, in fact it's the worst cause I did ever hear.'

COLEMAN (*laughing*): That was a funny voice.

GIRLEEN: I did order him this heart on a chain out of me mam's Freeman's catalogue. Only this morning it came. I asked him to be writing me with his new address last night, so I could send it on to him. I'd've never've got up the courage to be giving it him to his face. I'd've blushed the heart out of me. Four months I've been saving up to buy it him. All me poteen money. (*Crying.*) All me poteen money gone. I should've skittered it away on the boys in Carraroe, and not go pinning me hopes on a feck I knew full well I'd never have.

> GIRLEEN *cuts the chain in two with the knife.*

COLEMAN: Don't be cutting your good chain there, Girleen.

VALENE: Be leaving your chaineen there now, Girleen. That chain looks worth something.

> GIRLEEN *tosses the chain in a corner.*

GIRLEEN (*sniffling*): Have you read the letter there, now?

VALENE: I have. A pile of oul bull.

GIRLEEN: I read it to see if he mentioned me. Not a word.

COLEMAN: Just shite is it, Valene? It's not worth reading?

VALENE: Not at all.

COLEMAN: I'll leave it so, for I've no time for letters. I've never seen the sense in them. They're just writing.

GIRLEEN: I did like the bit about him betting his soul on ye. Didn't ye like that bit?

> VALENE *picks up the broken chain.*

VALENE: I don't think I understood that bit.

GIRLEEN (*pause*): Father Welsh drowned himself in the lake last night, same place as Tom Hanlon. They dragged his body out this morning. His soul in hell he's talking about, that only ye can save for him. (*Pause.*) You notice he never asked me to go saving his soul. I'd've liked to've saved his soul. I'd've been honoured, but no. (*Crying.*) Only mad drunken pig-shite feck-brained thicks he goes asking.

> *Shocked,* COLEMAN *reads the letter.* GIRLEEN *goes to the door.* VALENE *offers the pendant out to her.*

VALENE: Your heart, Girleen, be keeping it for yourself.

GIRLEEN (*crying*): Feck me heart. Feck it to hell. Toss it into fecking skitter's the best place for that fecking heart. (*Exiting.*) Not even a word to me!

> *After* GIRLEEN *exits,* VALENE *sits in an armchair, looking at the chain.* COLEMAN *finishes reading the letter, leaves it on the table and sits in the opposite armchair.*

VALENE: Did you read it?

COLEMAN: I did.

VALENE (*Pause*): Isn't it sad about him?

COLEMAN: It *is* sad. Very sad.

VALENE (*Pause*): Will we be trying for ourselves? To get along, now?

COLEMAN: We will.

VALENE: There's no harm in trying.

COLEMAN: No harm at all, sure.

VALENE (*Pause*): Poor Father Welsh Walsh Welsh.

COLEMAN: Welsh.

VALENE: Welsh. (*Pause.*) I wonder why he did it?

COLEMAN: I suppose he must've been upset o'er something.

VALENE: I suppose. (*Pause.*) This is a pricey chain. (*Pause.*) We'll be giving it back to her next time we see her. She's only shocked now.

COLEMAN: Aye. She's not in her right mind at all. She did hurt me hair when she tugged at it too, d'you know?

VALENE: It did look like it hurt.

COLEMAN: It did hurt.

VALENE (*Pause*): Father Welsh going topping himself does put arging o'er Taytos into perspective anyways.

COLEMAN: It does.

VALENE: Eh?

COLEMAN: It does.

VALENE: Aye. Awful perspective. Awful perspective.

COLEMAN (*Pause*): Did you see 'Roderick' his name is?

VALENE (*snorts*): I did.

COLEMAN (*Pause. Seriously*): We shouldn't laugh.

> VALENE *nods. Both pull serious faces. Blackout.*

SCENE SEVEN

Room tidier. WELSH's *letter pinned to the foot of the crucifix.* VALENE *and* COLEMAN *enter dressed in black, having just attended* WELSH's *funeral,* COLEMAN *carrying a small plastic bag full of sausage rolls and vol-au-vents. He sits at the table.* VALENE *opens his poteen biscuit tin.*

VALENE: That's that, then.

COLEMAN: That's that, aye. That's Father Welsh gone.

VALENE: A good do.

COLEMAN: Aye. It's often a good do when it's a priest they're sticking away.

COLEMAN *empties his bag onto table.*

VALENE: You didn't have to go nabbing a whole bagful, now, Coleman.

COLEMAN: Didn't they offer, sure?

VALENE: But a whole bagful, I'm saying.

COLEMAN: It'd have only gone to waste, and sure a bagful won't be going very far between us.

VALENE: Between us?

COLEMAN: Of course between us.

VALENE: Ohh.

They both eat a little.

These are nice vol-au-vents.

COLEMAN: They *are* nice vol-au-vents.

VALENE: You can't say the Catholic Church doesn't know how to make a nice vol-au-vent, now.

COLEMAN: It's their best feature. And their sausage rolls aren't bad either, although they probably only buy them in.

VALENE (*Pause*): Em, would you be having a glass of poteen with me, Coleman?

COLEMAN (*shocked*): I would, now. If you can spare a drop, like.

VALENE: I can easy spare a drop.

VALENE *pours two glasses, one bigger than the other, thinks about it, then gives* COLEMAN *the bigger.*

COLEMAN: Thank you, Valene. Sure we have our own little feasteen now.

VALENE: We do.

COLEMAN: D'you remember when as gasurs we did used to put the blankets o'er the gap between our beds and hide under them like a tent it was o'er us, and go having a feasteen of oul jammy sandwiches then?

VALENE: That was you and Mick Dowd used to go camping in the gap between our beds. You'd never let me be in with yous at all. Ye used to step on me head if I tried to climb into that camp with you. I still remember it.

COLEMAN: Mick Dowd, was it? I don't remember that at all, now. I did think it was you.

VALENE: Half me childhood you spent stepping on me head, and for no reason. And d'you remember when you pinned me down and sat across me on me birthday and let the stringy spit dribble out your gob and let down and down it dribble 'til it landed in me eye then?

COLEMAN: I remember it well, Valene, and I'll tell you this. I did mean to suck that spit back up just before it got to your eye, but what happened I lost control o'er it.

VALENE: And on me birthday.

COLEMAN (*Pause*): I do apologize for dribbling in your eye and I do apologize for stepping on your head, Valene. On Father Welsh's soul I apologize.

VALENE: I do accept your apology so.

COLEMAN: Although plenty of times as a gasur I remember you dropping stones on me head while I was asleep and big stones.

VALENE: Only in retaliation them stones ever was.

COLEMAN: Retaliation or not. Waking up to stones dropped on ya is awful frightening for a small child. And retaliation doesn't count anyways if it's a week later. It's only then and there retaliation does apply.

VALENE: I do apologize for dropping stones on you so. (*Pause.*) For your brain never did recover from them injuries, did it, Coleman?

COLEMAN *stares at* VALENE *a second, then smiles.* VALENE *smiles also.*

VALENE: This is a great oul game, this is, apologizing. Father Welsh wasn't too far wrong.

COLEMAN: I hope Father Welsh isn't in hell at all. I hope he's in heaven.

VALENE: *I* hope he's in heaven.

COLEMAN: Or purgatory at worst.

VALENE: Although if he's in hell at least he'll have Tom Hanlon to speak to.

COLEMAN: So it won't be as if he doesn't know anybody.

VALENE: Aye. And the fella off *Alias Smith and Jones.*

COLEMAN: Is the fella off *Alias Smith and Jones* in hell?

VALENE: He is. Father Welsh was telling me.

COLEMAN: The blond one.

VALENE: No, the other one.

COLEMAN: He was good, the other one.

VALENE: He was the best one.

COLEMAN: It's always the best ones go to hell. Me, probably straight to heaven I'll go, even though I blew the head off poor dad. So long as I go confessing to it anyways. That's the good thing about being Catholic. You can shoot your dad in the head and it doesn't even matter at all.

VALENE: Well it matters a little bit.

COLEMAN: It matters a little bit but not a big bit.

VALENE (*Pause*): Did you see Girleen crying her eyes out, the funeral?

COLEMAN: I did.

VALENE: Poor Girleen. And her man two times has had to drag her screaming from the lake at night, did you hear, there where Father Walsh jumped, and her just standing there, staring.

COLEMAN: She must've liked Father Welsh or something.

VALENE: I suppose she must've. (*Taking out* GIRLEEN's *chain.*) She wouldn't take her chaineen back at all. She wouldn't hear tell of it. I'll put it up here with his letter to us.

He attaches the chain to the cross, so the heart rests on the letter, which he gently smoothes out.

It's the mental they'll be putting Girleen in before long if she carries on.

COLEMAN: Sure it's only a matter of time.

VALENE: Isn't that sad?

COLEMAN: Awful sad. (*Pause. Shrugging.*) Ah well.

He eats another vol-au-vent. VALENE *remembers something, fishes in the pockets of his jacket, takes out two ceramic figurines, places them on the shelf, uncaps his pen almost automatically, thinks better of marking them as before, and puts the pen away.*

I think I'm getting to like vol-au-vents now. I think I'm developing a taste for them. We ought to go to more funerals.

VALENE: They do have them at weddings too.

COLEMAN: Do they? Who'll next be getting married round here so? Girleen I would used to have said, as pretty as she is, only she'll probably have topped herself before ever she gets married.

VALENE: *Me* probably'll be the next one getting married, as handsome as I am. Did you see today all the young nuns eyeing me?

COLEMAN: Who'd go marrying you, sure? Even that no-lipped girl in Norway'd turn you down.

VALENE (*Pause. Angrily*): See, I'm stepping back now . . . I'm stepping back, like Father Walsh said and I'm forgiving ya, insulting me.

COLEMAN (*sincerely*): Oh . . . oh, I'm sorry now, Valene. I'm sorry. It just slipped out on me without thinking.

VALENE: No harm done so, if only an accident it was.

COLEMAN: It *was* an accident. Although remember you did insult me there earlier, saying I was brain-damaged be stones as a gasur, and I didn't even pull you up on it.

VALENE: I apologize for saying you was brain-damaged as a gasur so.

COLEMAN: No apology was necessary, Valene, and I have saved you the last vol-au-venteen on top of it.

VALENE: You have that last vol-au-vent, Coleman. I'm not overly keen on vol-au-vents.

COLEMAN *nods in thanks and eats the vol-au-vent.*

VALENE: Weren't them young nuns lovely today now, Coleman?

COLEMAN: They was lovely nuns.

VALENE: They must've known Father Welsh from nun college or something.

COLEMAN: I'd like to touch them nuns both upstairs and downstairs, so I would. Except for the fat one on the end.

VALENE: She was a horror and she knew.

COLEMAN: If dad was there today he'd've just gone screaming at them nuns.

VALENE: Why *did* dad used to go screaming at nuns, Coleman?

COLEMAN: I don't have an idea at all why he used to scream at nuns. He must've had a bad experience with nuns as a child.

VALENE: If you hadn't blown the brains out of dad we could ask him outright.

COLEMAN *stares at him sternly.*

VALENE: No, I'm not saying anything, now. I'm calm, I've stepped back, and I'm saying this quietly and without any spite at all, but you know well that that wasn't right, Coleman, shooting dad in the head on us. In your heart anyways you know.

COLEMAN (*Pause*): I *do* know it wasn't right. Not only in me heart but in me head and in me everywhere. I was wrong for shooting dad. I was dead wrong. And I'm sorry for it.

VALENE: And I'm sorry for sitting you down and making you sign your life away, Coleman. It was the only way at the time I could think of punishing ya. Well, I could've let you go to jail but I didn't want you going to jail and it wasn't out of miserliness that I stopped you going to jail. It was more out of I didn't want all on me own to be left here. I'd've missed ya. (*Pause.*) From this day on . . . from this day on, this house and everything in this house is half yours again, Coleman.

Touched, COLEMAN *offers his hand out and they shake, embarrassed. Pause.*

Is there any other confessions we have to get off our chests, now we're at it?

COLEMAN: There must be millions. (*Pause.*) Crushing your crisps to skitter, Valene, I'm sorry for.

VALENE: I forgive you for it. (*Pause.*) Do you remember that holiday in Lettermullen as gasurs we had, and you left your cowboy stagecoach out in the rain that night and next morning it was gone and mam and dad said 'Oh it must've been hijacked be Indians'. It wasn't hijacked be Indians. I'd got up early and pegged it in the sea.

COLEMAN (*Pause*): I did love that cowboy stagecoach.

VALENE: I know you did, and I'm sorry for it.

COLEMAN (*Pause*): That string of gob I dribbled on you on your birthday. I didn't try to suck it back up at all. I wanted it to hit your eye and I was glad. (*Pause.*) And I'm sorry for it.

VALENE: Okay. (*Pause.*) Maureen Folan did once ask me to ask you if you wanted to see a film at the Claddagh Palace with her, and she'd've driven ye and paid for dinner too, and from the tone of her voice it sounded like you'd've been on a promise after, but I never passed the message onto ya, out of nothing but pure spite.

COLEMAN: Sure that's no great loss, Valene. Maureen Folan looks like a thin-lipped ghost, with the hairstyle of a frightened red ape.

VALENE: But on a promise you'd've been.

COLEMAN: On a promise or no. That was nothing at all to go confessing. Okay, it's my go. I'm winning.

VALENE: What d'you mean, you're winning?

COLEMAN (*thinking*): Do you remember your Ker-Plunk game?

VALENE: I *do* remember me Ker-Plunk game.

COLEMAN: It wasn't Liam Hanlon stole all them marbles out of your Ker-Plunk game at all, it was me.

VALENE: What did you want me Ker-Plunk marbles for?

COLEMAN: I went slinging them at the swans in Galway. I had a great time.

VALENE: That ruined me Ker-Plunk. You can't play Ker-Plunk without marbles. And, sure, that was *both* of ours Ker-Plunk. That was just cutting off your nose to spite your face, Coleman.

COLEMAN: I know it was and I'm sorry, Valene. Your go now. (*Pause.*) You're too slow. D'you remember when we had them backward children staying for B & B, and they threw half your *Spiderman* comics in on the fire? They didn't. D'you know who did? I did. I only blamed them cos they were too daft to arg.

VALENE: They was good *Spiderman* comics, Coleman. Spiderman went fighting Doctor Octopus in them comics.

COLEMAN: And I'm sorry for it. Your go. (*Pause.*) You're too slow . . .

VALENE: Hey . . . !

COLEMAN: D'you remember when Pato Dooley beat the skitter out of you when he was twelve and you was twenty, and you never knew the reason why? I knew the reason why. I did tell him you'd called his dead mammy a hairy whore.

VALENE: With a fecking chisel that Pato Dooley beat me up that day! Almost had me fecking eye out!

COLEMAN: I think Pato must've liked his mammy or something. (*Pause.*) I'm awful sorry for it, Valene. COLEMAN *burps lazily.*

VALENE: You do sound it!

COLEMAN: Shall I be having another go?

VALENE: I did pour a cup of piss in a pint of lager you drank one time, Coleman. Aye, and d'you know what, now? You couldn't even tell the differ.

COLEMAN (*Pause*): When was this, now?

VALENE: When you was seventeen, this was. D'you remember that month you were laid up in hospital with bacterial tonsilitis. Around then it was. (*Pause.*) And I'm sorry for it, Coleman.

COLEMAN: I do take your poteen out its box each week, drink the half of it and fill the rest back up with water. Ten years this has been going on. You haven't tasted full-strength poteen since nineteen eighty-fecking-three.

VALENE (*drinks. Pause*): But you're sorry for it.

COLEMAN: I suppose I'm sorry for it, aye. (*Mumbling.*) Making me go drinking piss, and not just anybody's piss but *your* fecking piss . . .

VALENE (*angrily*): But you're sorry for it, you're saying?!

COLEMAN: I'm sorry for it, aye! I'm fecking sorry for it! Haven't I said?!

VALENE: That's okay, so, if you're sorry for it, although you don't sound fecking sorry for it.

COLEMAN: You can kiss me fecking arse so, Valene, if you don't . . . I'm taking a step back now, so I am. (*Pause.*) I'm sorry for watering your poteen down all these years, Valene. I am, now.

VALENE: Good-oh. (*Pause.*) Is it your go now or is it mine?

COLEMAN: I think it might be your go, Valene.

VALENE: Thank you, Coleman. D'you remember when Alison O'Hoolihan went sucking that pencil in the playground that time, and ye were to go dancing the next day, but somebody nudged that pencil and it got stuck in her tonsils on her, and be the time she got out of hospital she was engaged to the doctor who wrenched it out for her and wouldn't be giving you a fecking sniffeen. Do you remember, now?

COLEMAN: I do remember.

VALENE: That was me nudged that pencil, and it wasn't an accident at all. Pure jealous I was.

Pause. COLEMAN *throws his sausage rolls in* VALENE's *face and dives over the table for his neck.* VALENE *dodges the attack.*

And I'm sorry for it! I'm sorry for it! (*Pointing at letter.*) Father Welsh! Father Welsh!

VALENE *fends* COLEMAN *off. They stand staring at each other,* COLEMAN *seething.*

COLEMAN: Eh?!!

VALENE: Eh?

COLEMAN: I did fecking love Alison O'Hoolihan! We may've been married today if it hadn't been for that fecking pencil!

VALENE: What was she doing sucking it the pointy end inwards anyways? She was looking for trouble!

COLEMAN: And she fecking found it with you! That pencil could've killed Alison O'Hoolihan!

VALENE: And I'm sorry for it, I said. What are you doing pegging good sausage rolls at me? Them sausage rolls cost money. You were supposed to have taken a step back and went calming yourself, but you didn't, you just flew off the handle. Father Welsh's soul'll be roasting now because of you.

COLEMAN: Leave Father Welsh's soul out of it. This is about you sticking pencils down poor girls' gobs on them.

VALENE: That pencil is water under a bridge and I've apologized whole-hearted for that pencil. (*Sits down.*) And she had boss-eyes anyways.

COLEMAN: She didn't have boss-eyes! She had nice eyes!

VALENE: Well there was something funny about them.

COLEMAN: She had nice brown eyes.

VALENE: Oh aye. (*Pause.*) Well it's your go now, Coleman. Try and top that one for yourself. Heh.

COLEMAN: Try and top that one, is it?

VALENE: It is.

COLEMAN *thinks for a moment, smiles slightly, then sits back down.*

COLEMAN: I've taken a step back now.

VALENE: I can see you've taken a step back.

COLEMAN: I'm pure calm now. It does be good to get things off your chest.

VALENE: It *does* be good. I'm glad that pencil-nudging's off me chest. I can sleep nights now.

COLEMAN: Is it a relief to ya?

VALENE: It *is* a relief to me. (*Pause.*) What have you got cooking up?

COLEMAN: I have one and I'm terrible sorry for it. Oh terrible sorry I am.

VALENE: It won't be near as good as me pencilling poor boss-eyed Alison, whatever it is.

COLEMAN: Ah I suppose you're right, now. My one's only a weeny oul one. D'you remember you always thought it was Mairtin Hanlon snipped the ears off of poor Lassie, now?

VALENE (*confidently*): I don't believe you at all. You're only making it up now, see.

COLEMAN: It wasn't wee Mairtin at all. D'you know who it was, now?

VALENE: Me arse was it you. You'll have to be doing better than that, now, Coleman.

COLEMAN: To the brookeen I dragged him, me scissors in hand, and him whimpering his fat gob off 'til the deed was done and he dropped down dead with not a fecking peep out of that whiny fecking dog.

VALENE: D'you see, it doesn't hurt me at all when you go making up lies. You don't understand the rules, Coleman. It does have to be true, else it's just plain daft. You can't go claiming credit for snipping the ears off a dog when you didn't lay a finger on that dog's ears, and the fecking world knows.

COLEMAN (*Pause*): Is it evidence, so, you're after?

VALENE: It *is* evidence I'm after, aye. Go bring me evidence you did cut the ears off me dog. And be quick with that evidence.

COLEMAN: I won't be quick at all. I will take me time.

He slowly gets up and ambles to his room, closing its door behind him. VALENE *waits patiently, giving a worried laugh. After a ten-second pause,* COLEMAN *ambles back on, carrying a slightly wet brown paper bag. He pauses at the table a moment for dramatic effect, slowly opens the bag, pulls out a dog's big fluffy black ear, lays it on top of* VALENE's *head, takes out the second ear, pauses, places that on* VALENE's *head also, puts the empty bag down on the table, smoothes it out, then sits down in the armchair left.* VALENE *has been staring out into space all the while, dumbstruck. He tilts his head so that the ears fall down onto the table, and he stares at them a while.* COLEMAN *picks up* VALENE's *felt-tip pen, brings it over and lays it on the table.*

COLEMAN: There's your little peneen, now, Val. Why don't you mark them dog's ears with your V, so we'll be remembering who they belong to.

He sits back down in the armchair.

And do you want to hear something else, Valene? I'm sorry for cutting off them dog's ears. With all me fecking heart I'm sorry, oh aye, because I've tooken a step back now, look at me . . .

He half-laughs through his nose. VALENE *gets up, stares blankly at* COLEMAN *a moment, goes to the cupboard right and, with his back to* COLEMAN, *pulls the butcher's knife out of it. In the same brief second* COLEMAN *stands, pulls the shotgun down from above the stove and sits down with it.* VALENE *turns, knife ready. The gun is pointed directly at him.* VALENE *wilts slightly, thinks about it a moment, regains his courage and his anger, and slowly approaches* COLEMAN, *raising the knife.*

COLEMAN (*surprised, slightly scared*): What are you doing, now, Valene?

VALENE (*blankly*): Oh not a thing am I doing, Coleman, other than killing ya.

COLEMAN: Be putting that knife back in that drawer, you.

VALENE: No, I'll be putting it in the head of you, now.

COLEMAN: Don't you see me gun?

VALENE: Me poor fecking Lassie, who never hurt a flea.

VALENE *has gotten all the way up to* COLEMAN, *so that the barrel of the gun is touching his chest. He raises the knife to its highest point.*

COLEMAN: What are you doing, now? Stop it.

VALENE: I'll stop it, all right . . .

COLEMAN: Father Welsh's soul, Valene. Father Wel . . .

VALENE: Father Welsh's soul me fecking arse! Father Welsh's soul didn't come into play when you hacked me dog's ears off him and kept them in a bag!

COLEMAN: Ar that was a year ago. How does that apply?

VALENE: Be saying goodbye to the world, you, ya feck!

COLEMAN: *You'll* have to be saying goodbye to the world too, so, because I'll be bringing you with me.

VALENE: Do I look like I mind that at all, now?

COLEMAN (*Pause*): Er er, wait wait wait, now . . .

VALENE: Wha . . . ?

COLEMAN: Look at me gun. Look at me gun where it's going, do ya see . . . ?

COLEMAN *slides the gun away and down from* VALENE'*s chest 'til it points directly at the door of the stove.*

VALENE (*Pause*): Be pointing that gun away from me stove, now.

COLEMAN: I won't be. Stab away, now. It's your stove it'll be'll be going with me instead of ya.

VALENE: Leave . . . what . . . ? That was a three-hundred-pound stove now, Coleman . . .

COLEMAN: I know well it was.

VALENE: Be leaving it alone. That's just being sly, that is.

COLEMAN: Be backing off you with that knife, you sissy-arse.

VALENE (*tearfully*): You're not a man at all, pointing guns at stoves.

COLEMAN: I don't care if I am or I'm not. Be backing off, I said.

VALENE: You're just a . . . you're just a . . .

COLEMAN: Eh?

VALENE: Eh?

COLEMAN: Eh?

VALENE: You're not a man at all, you.

COLEMAN: Be backing away now, you, cry-baby. Be taking a step back for yourself. Eheh.

VALENE (*Pause*): I'm backing away now, so I am.

COLEMAN: That'd be the best thing, aye.

VALENE *slowly retreats, lays the knife on the table and sits down there sadly, gently stroking his dog's ears.* COLEMAN *is still pointing the gun at the stove door. He shakes his head slightly.*

COLEMAN: I can't believe you raised a knife to me. No, I can't believe you raised a knife to your own brother.

VALENE: You raised a knife to me own dog and raised a gun to our own father, did a lot more damage than a fecking knife, now.

COLEMAN: No, I can't believe it. I can't believe you raised a knife to me.

VALENE: Stop going on about raising a knife, and be pointing that gun away from me fecking stove, now, in case it does go off be accident.

COLEMAN: Be accident, is it?

VALENE: Is the safety catch on that gun, now?

COLEMAN: The safety catch, is it?

VALENE: Aye, the safety catch! The safety catch! Is it ten million times I have to be repeating meself?

COLEMAN: The safety catch, uh-huh . . .

He jumps to his feet, points the gun down at the stove and fires, blowing the right-hand side apart. VALENE *falls to his knees in horror, his face in his hands.* COLEMAN *cocks the gun again and blows the left-hand side apart also, then nonchalantly sits back down.*

No, the safety catch isn't on at all, Valene. Would you believe it?

Pause. VALENE *is still kneeling there, dumbstruck.*

And I'll tell you another thing . . .

He suddenly jumps up again and, holding the shotgun by the barrel, starts smashing it violently into the figurines, shattering them to pieces and sending them flying around the room until not a single one remains standing. VALENE *screams throughout. After* COLEMAN *has finished he sits again, the gun across his lap.* VALENE *is still kneeling. Pause.*

And don't go making out that you didn't deserve it, because we both know full well that you did.

VALENE (*numbly*): You've broken all me figurines, Coleman.

COLEMAN: I have. Did you see me?

VALENE: And you've blown me stove to buggery.

COLEMAN: This is a great gun for blowing holes in things.

VALENE (*standing*): And now you do have no bullets left in that great gun.

He lazily picks the knife back up and approaches COLEMAN. *But as he does so* COLEMAN *opens the barrel of the gun, tosses away the spent cartridges, fishes in his pocket, comes out with a clenched fist that may or may not contain another cartridge, shows the fist to* VALENE . . .

There's no bullet in that hand! There's no bullet in that hand!

. . . *and loads, or pretends to load, the bullet into the gun, without* VALENE *or the audience at any time knowing if there is a bullet or not.* COLEMAN *snaps the barrel shut and lazily points it at* VALENE'*s head.*

There was no bullet in that hand, Coleman! No bullet at all!

COLEMAN: Maybe there wasn't, now. Maybe it's pretending I am. Be taking a pop for yourself.

VALENE: I *will* be taking a pop for meself.

COLEMAN: And then we'll see.

VALENE: There was no bullet in that hand at all. (*Tense pause.*) And even if there was, you didn't go shooting me before. Why would you shoot me now?

COLEMAN: Maybe I just wanted you to see your oul stove shot and your figurines clobbered before you went dying, to give you something to be thinking about.

VALENE (*Pause*): There was no bullet in that hand.
COLEMAN *cocks the gun. Long, long pause.*

VALENE: I want to kill you, Coleman.

COLEMAN: Ar, don't be saying that, now, Val.

VALENE (*sadly*): It's true, Coleman. I want to kill you.

COLEMAN (*Pause*): Try so.
Pause. VALENE *turns the knife around and around in his hand, staring at* COLEMAN *all the while, until his head finally droops and he returns the knife to the drawer.* COLEMAN *uncocks the gun, stands, and lays it down on the table, staying near it.* VALENE *idles to the stove and touches the letter pinned above it.*

VALENE: Father Welsh is burning in hell, now, because of our fighting.

COLEMAN: Well, did we ask him to go betting his soul on us? No. And, sure, it's pure against the rules for priests to go betting anyways, neverminding with them kinds of stakes. Sure a fiver would've been overdoing it on us, let alone his soul. And what's wrong with fighting anyways? I do like a good fight. It does show you care, fighting does. That's what oul sissy Welsh doesn't understand. Don't you like a good fight?

VALENE: I *do* like a good fight, the same as that. Although I don't like having me dog murdered on me, and me fecking dad murdered on me.

COLEMAN: And I'm sorry for your dog and dad, Valene. I *am* sorry. Truly I'm sorry. And nothing to do with Father Welsh's letter is this at all. From me own heart this is. The same goes for your stove and your poor figurines too. Look at them. That was pure temper, that was. Although, admit it, you asked for that stove and them figurines.

VALENE: You never fecking stop, you. (*Pause.*) *Are* you sorry, Coleman?

COLEMAN: I am, Valene.

VALENE (*Pause*): Maybe Father Walsh's Welsh's soul'll be all right so.

COLEMAN: Maybe it will, now. Maybe it will.

VALENE: He wasn't such a bad fella.

COLEMAN: He wasn't.

VALENE: He wasn't a great fella, but he wasn't a bad fella.

COLEMAN: Aye. (*Pause.*) He was a *middling* fella.

VALENE: He was a *middling* fella.

COLEMAN (*Pause*): I'm going out for a drink for meself. Will you be coming with me?

VALENE: Aye, in a minute now I'll come.
COLEMAN *goes to the front door.* VALENE *looks over the smashed figurines sadly.*

COLEMAN: I'll help you be clearing your figurines up when I get back, Valene. Maybe we can glue some of them together. Do you still have your superglue?

VALENE: I do have me superglue, although I think the top's gone hard.

COLEMAN: Aye, that's the trouble with superglue.

VALENE: Ah, the house insurance'll cover me figurines anyways. As well as me stove.

COLEMAN: Oh . . .

VALENE (*Pause*): What, oh?

COLEMAN: Do you remember a couple of weeks ago there when you asked me did I go stealing your insurance money and I said no, I paid it in for you?

VALENE: I do remember.

COLEMAN (*Pause*): I didn't pay it in at all. I pocketed the lot of it, pissed it up a wall.
VALENE, *seething, darts for the knife drawer.* COLEMAN *dashes out through the front door, slamming it behind him.* VALENE *tosses the knife away, darts back to the gun and brings it to the door.* COLEMAN *is long gone. Gun in hand,* VALENE *stands there, shaking with rage, almost in tears. After a while he begins to calm down, taking deep breaths. He looks down at the gun in his hands a moment, then gently opens the barrel to see if* COLEMAN *had really loaded it earlier. He had.* VALENE *takes the cartridge out.*

VALENE: He'd've fecking shot me too. He'd've shot his own fecking brother! On top of his dad! On top of me stove!
He tosses the gun and cartridge away, rips FATHER WELSH's *letter off the cross, knocking* GIRLEEN's *chain onto the floor, brings the letter back to the table and takes out a box of matches.*

And you, you whiny fecking priest. Do I need your soul hovering o'er me the rest of me fecking life? How could anybody be getting on with that feck?
He strikes a match and lights the letter, which he glances over as he holds up. After a couple of seconds, the letter barely singed, VALENE *blows the flames out and looks at it on the table, sighing.*

(*Quietly.*) I'm too fecking kind-hearted is my fecking trouble.

He returns to the cross and pins the chain and letter back onto it, smoothing the letter out. He puts on his jacket, checks it for loose change and goes to the front door.

Well I won't be buying the fecker a pint anyways. I'll tell you that for nothing, Father Welsh Walsh Welsh.

VALENE *glances back at the letter a second, sadly, looks down at the floor, then exits. Lights fade, with one light lingering on the crucifix and letter a half second longer than the others.*

1   Irish: youngsters, boys.
2   The European Community.
3   Crisps.
4   Mad.
5   A mail order catalogue.
6   St Martin de Porres, a South American black saint held in special esteem in Ireland.

GREG DELANTY
from Greg Delanty, *The Hellbox* (1998)

Another poem by Greg Delanty where, drawing on his family's involvement in the printing business, he plays with the image of reversal, an image especially suitable for the Irish emigrant.

THE PRINTER'S DEVIL
to the Cork CND[1] Office

My father led me round the compositors' room
and forecast comps were for the hellbox
as they set up in reverse words.
He showed me how to space the words between
lines, fix leads and distribute in.

One Christmas he boxed me a printer's set
like the one I use now to stamp cards envelopes
Compliments of this boxed Hotel
to that, jabbing as your appears to set
the upside-down, backward aright.

But I haven't the skill to make out demons,
or the knack of stacking the characters
to publicize the right way
round and I keep stumbling between the lines.

1   Campaign for Nuclear Disarmament.

PAUL DURCAN
from Paul Durcan, *Greetings to Our Friends in Brazil* (1999)

Paul Durcan provides an appropriate note on which to end. With Máire Bradshaw's poem in mind (p. 1172), high time yet again for all the Marys.

THE MARY ROBINSON YEARS

The just shall flourish like the palm tree
Psalm 91:13

I

In November 1990 Mary Robinson lit a candle in her
    window
For all the exiles of the Irish diaspora.
Seven years later Mary threw her farewell party
In the Copacabana Palace Hotel
On the seafront in Rio — a gem of art deco;
Her husband Nick being an architectural historian
Has a professional interest in art deco
And in any case that's where Mary happened to be
And she thought it would be an agreeable idea
If we all flew out to Rio to join her —
Bride and Luke and Barbara and Enda and Ann and all
    the gang.

It was a fireworks night in Rio.
All the men as well all the ladies
Came in smart, casual attire.
The best of champagne, wine, rum.
Motivated conversation
Bejewelled with serious
Humour of the right kind.
Fernando Henrique
Attended with Ruthie.

That the party had helicoptered
Over Corcovado —
The Statue of Christ the King
Far below us on its hill top
Overseeing Rio and the sea —
Ignited theological controversy
A propos liberation theology;
The nexus, if any,
Between inequality
And the Ascension into Heaven;
What Leonardo Boff called
'The aerodynamics of injustice'.
Amidst the rocks of his own laughter
The curly, grey, apostle-like Boff cried out:
'Bearded in my own den —
Danton amongst the Robespierres!'

The only other jarring note
Was that although
I was seated opposite Mary
I could not get a word in.
In fact, I could not
Make eye contact with Mary.
If I didn't know Mary

I might have thought
She was snubbing me.
But then suddenly at the end
She caught my eye:
'Black eye, Paul?'
I blushed puce.
'No, no, no, no —'
I cried, rubbing the red
Bruise under my right eye —
'That's my birthmark.
Keeps getting me into deep water!'

II

It was a palmy night
Outside the Copacabana Palace Hotel.
The most stunning woman I have ever set eyes on in
    my life —
Six foot tall, mulatto, red hair down to her hips —
Stepped right up to me,
Whipped up her T-shirt
To show me her incredible breasts,
Whipped it down again.

She said: 'Don't faint, darling.
I'm a transvestite and
You won't believe this but
I'm from Tipperary.'
I said: 'Oh!
Whereabouts in Tipperary
Are you from?'
'Killenaule' — she smiled — 'Killenaule.'
I said: 'What are you doing in Copacabana?'
'My night off' — she smiled — 'my night off!
I'm an NGO relief aid worker.
Faith and good works and all that.
The Gospel according to Saint Matthew.'
She added: 'What are you doing here?'
I said: 'I'm a friend of Mary Robinson's.'
She said: 'Oh you're not!
Only a friend?'

She turned her smouldering spine on me
And strode off into the night of Rio,
The gigantic, ocean waves of the South Atlantic
Breaking in rainbows of fireworks behind her.
It was midnight, September 1, 1997 —
High time to get down on my knees
And to light a candle in the sand,
Cupping a flame in my hand.

Only a friend
Cupping a flame in my hand.

TOPICS AND ISSUES

1. **HISTORY, POLITICS, AND RELIGION**
2. **THE CITY AND THE COUNTRY**
3. **CULTURE AND IDENTITY**
4. **THE IRISH DIASPORA**

1. HISTORY, POLITICS, AND RELIGION

The Presence of History
Some questions worth asking:
- Why so much attention to history in Irish writing?
- How much history does a student of Irish literature need to know about Irish history?
- What kinds of history are invoked in modern Irish writing? (Pre-modern, Elizabethan, eighteenth-century, nineteenth-century, the Famine, the nationalist high-points, the War of Independence, the Civil War, the Second World War, the fifties, the emergence of the new Ireland.)
- How much does modern Irish writing alter our view of modern Irish history?
- History as death, or death as history. The dead and death. Wakes. The walking dead. Shades and shadows. The living and the dead.
- To what extent is history in modern Irish writing essentially about the future not the past?

The Presence of Politics
- Try to decide what you are looking for in discussing the politics of a particular text. There are at least three different approaches to this question: are you trying to locate the political context of a text? Are you attempting to identify the explicit political message a text contains? Are you offering a political reading of a past text? You might also consider the political responsibility on the part of the reader, a politics of reading.
- Often the politics of a text is unmissable. The author makes his or her point abundantly plain for the reader. This is especially the case with critical or cultural essays or articles. With imaginative texts it is sometimes not easy discerning a political viewpoint.
- From the following extracts select a group and consider how they treat or express their political concerns. Which do you find more convincing and why? Which kind of politics is rarely explored or touched on by Irish writers? The environment? Social class? Position of women?

- Gather together a selection of extracts from different decades. How does the politics or political position alter? How much remains the same?
- At what point does politics come into play in Irish writing? And how is this different from texts by writers in other cultures? What is the driving force behind these writers? Is it that modern Ireland is becoming ordinary, the cry of the heart against necessity?

The Presence of Religion
- The portrayal of priests is a good place to start. Again, select a number of texts and see how they can be compared.
- Conscience and sexuality. Adolescence. Again, another fertile area for Irish writers.
- The occult has a particular fascination for Irish writers such as Yeats. How is this reflected in his writings?
- Spirituality and spiritual devotion have also a very strong appeal.
- Catholics and Protestants: what other groups are represented in modern Irish writing? Think of the Presbyterian background of John Hewitt for example.
- Where does a writer like Beckett belong? To religion?
- Forrest Reid's *Apostate* is a secular autobiography. Have you found other examples from your reading?
- Northern Irish, whether Catholic or Protestant, are moral, Southern Irish are devout. Do you agree?

Politics
Extracts:
Lionel Johnson, 'Parnell' (1893) [verse]
D.P. Moran, 'The Battle of Two Civilizations' (1899) [cultural critique]
James Connolly, 'Physical Force in Irish Politics' (1899) [position statement]
Standish James O'Grady, 'The Great Enchantment' (1900) [political analysis]
Arthur Conan Doyle, 'The Green Flag' (1900) [short story]
W.B. Yeats, *Cathleen ni Houlihan* (1902) [nationalist drama]
Arthur Griffith, *The Resurrection of Hungary* (1904) [political writing]
G.B. Shaw, *John Bull's Other Island* (1904) [drama]

Padraic Colum, 'A Poor Scholar of the Forties' (1904) [verse]

Frederick Ryan, *Criticism and Courage* (1906) [polemical essay]

Seumas O'Sullivan, 'Glasnevin, October 9th, 1904' (1908) [verse]

Reverend P.S. Dinneen, 'The World-wide Empire of the Irish Race' (1910) [lecture]

St John Ervine, *Mixed Marriage* (1911) [drama]

John Howard Parnell, *Charles Stewart Parnell* (1916) [memoir]

James Stephens, *The Insurrection in Dublin* (1916) [reportage]

George Bernard Shaw, 'The Easter Week Executions' (1916) [letter to newspaper]

W.B. Yeats, 'Easter 1916' (written 1916) [verse]

George Russell (Æ), *Imagination and Reveries* (1917) [personal statement, poem]

Darrel Figgis, *A Chronicle of Jails* (1917) [prison chronicle]

Eimar O'Duffy, *The Wasted Island* (1919) [fiction]

Darrell Figgis, *The House of Success* (1922) [fiction]

Michael Collins, *The Path to Freedom* (1922) [political writing]

George Russell (Æ), 'Lessons of Revolution' (1923) [cultural critique]

Francis Stuart, *Tomorrow* (1924) [editorial]

Dorothy Macardle, 'The Portrait of Roisin Dhu' (1924) [short story]

W.B. Yeats, 'Speech on Divorce' (1925) [speech in Senate]

Frank O'Connor, 'Guests of the Nation' (1931) [short story]

Pat O'Mara, *The Autobiography of a Liverpool Irish Slummy* (1934) [autobiography]

Joseph F. Dinneen, *Ward Eight* (1936) [fiction]

Peadar O'Donnell, 'What I Saw in Spain' (1936) [reportage]

Charles Donnelly, 'Poem', 'The Tolerance of Crows' (1937) [verse]

Louis MacNeice, *Autumn Journal* (1938) [verse]

Jim Phelan, *Ireland-Atlantic Gateway* (1941) [polemical argument]

Sean O'Faolain, 'Romance and Realism' (1945) [editorial]

John Hewitt, 'Once Alien Here' (1945) [verse]

Tom Barry, *Guerilla Days in Ireland* (1949) [war chronicle]

Sir Christopher Lynch-Robinson, *The Last of the Irish R.M.s* (1951) [personal memoir]

Edwin O'Connor, *The Last Hurrah* (1956) [fiction]

Denis Devlin, 'The Tomb of Michael Collins' (1956) [verse]

Terence de Vere White, *A Fretful Midge* (1957) [personal reminiscence]

John Montague, 'The Rough Field' (1963) [reflective essay]

Conor Cruise O'Brien, 'Passion and Cunning' (1965) [polemical essay]

James Plunkett, *Strumpet City* (1969) [fiction]

J.G. Farrell, *Troubles* (1970) [historical fiction]

Cecil King, *The Cecil King Diary 1970-1974* (1972: 1975) [diary entries]

Rosita Sweetman, *'On Our Knees': Ireland 1972* (1972) [polemical writing]

John Jordan, 'A Censored Decade' (1972) [polemical column]

James Simmons, 'Claudy' (1974) [song]

Seamus Heaney, *North* (1975) [verse]

Dervla Murphy, *A Place Apart* (1978) [reportage]

Mary Beckett, 'A Belfast Woman' (1980) [short story]

Brian Friel, *Translations* (1981) [drama]

Brendan Kennelly, *Cromwell* (1983) [verse]

Mary Holland, 'Ireland Blasts Back' (1984) [journalistic analysis]

Dervla Murphy, *Tales from Two Cities* (1985) [reportage]

Vincent Buckley, *Memory Ireland* (1985) [polemical essay]

Eric A. Visser and Antoinette Hensey 'My Land is too Green' (1986) [song]

Padraic Fiacc, *Missa Terribilis* (1986) [verse]

Ciaran Carson, 'Belfast Confetti' (1987) [verse]

Stewart Parker, *Pentecost* (1987) [drama]

Edward Said, 'Yeats and Decolonization' (1988) [polemical essay]

Bill Rolston, 'Mothers, Whores and Villains' (1989) [critical survey]

Maire Bradshaw, 'high time for all the marys' (1991) [verse]

Vincent Buckley, 'Hunger-Strike: Bobby Sands: One' (1991) [verse]

Philip Hobsbaum, 'The Belfast Group' (1994) [literary reflections]

Eoin McNamee, *Resurrection Man* (1994) [fiction]

Sebastian Barry, *The Steward of Christendom* (1995) [drama]

Colm Tóibín, 'Playboys of the GPO' (1996) [book review]

Robert McLiam Wilson, *Eureka Street* (1996) [fiction]

Terry Eagleton, *Crazy John and the Bishop* (1998) [polemical essay]

Fintan O'Toole, 'Brand Leader' (1996) [polemical essay]

Religion
Extracts:
W.B. Yeats, 'Magic' (1901) [expository essay]

Joseph Campbell, 'I am the Gilly of Christ' (1907) [verse]

Bernard Vaughan, *Sin, Society and Behaviour* (1908) [sermon]

St John Ervine, *Mixed Marriage* (1911) [drama]

George Tyrrell, *Autobiography and Life of George Tyrrell* (1912) [autobiography]

W.B. Yeats, 'The Second Coming' (1921) [verse]

F. Scott Fitzgerald, 'Absolution' (1924) [short story]

Forrest Reid, *Apostate* (1926) [autobiography]

Thomas MacGreevy, 'Seventh Gift of the Holy Ghost' (1929) [verse]

Austin Clarke, *The Bright Temptation* (1932) [fiction]

Denis Devlin, 'Lough Derg' (1946) [verse]

J.F. Powers, 'Prince of Darkness' (1947) [short story]

Seán Ó Ríordáin, 'Siollabadh' (Syllabling) (1952) [verse]

Sean O'Faolain, 'Lovers of the Lake' (1957) [short story]

Michael J. Murphy (ed), 'A Long Night in the Spike' (1967) [modern folktale]

Richard Power, *The Hungry Grass* (1969) [fiction]

Patrick Galvin, 'The Irish' (1973) [verse]

Dervla Murphy, *A Place Apart* (1978) [reportage/sermon]

Padraic Fiacc, *Missa Terribilis* (1986) [verse]

Desmond Hogan, 'Interview with Van Morrison' (1987) [interview]

Stewart Parker, *Pentecost* (1987) [drama]

Moy McCrory, 'A Well Travelled Woman' (1991) [short story]

Martin McDonagh, *The Lonesome West* (1997) [drama]

Irish Ireland

Extracts:

Douglas Hyde trans., 'Dá Dtéinnse Siar' (If I Were to Go West) (1893) [verse]

D.P. Moran, 'The Battle of Two Civilizations' (1899) [cultural critique]

Lady Gregory, *Cuchulain of Muirthemne* (1902) [ancient mythological story]

Reverend P.S. Dinneen, 'The World-wide Empire of the Irish Race' (1909) [lecture]

Patrick Pearse, 'Mise Éire / I Am Ireland' (1914) [verse]

Peter O'Leary, *My Story* (1915) [personal reminiscence]

Thomas MacDonagh, *Literature in Ireland* (1916) [critical essay]

James Stephens, 'Righteous Anger', 'O'Bruadair' (1918) [verse]

Robin Flower, 'The Great Blasket: Poets' (1920) [verse]

Daniel Corkery, 'The Aisling' (1924) [critical survey]

F.R. Higgins, 'The Dark Breed' (1927) [verse]

Austin Clarke, *The Bright Temptation* (1932) [fiction]

Tomás Ó Criomhthain, *An tOileánach* (*The Islandman*) (1929) [personal memoir]

George Russell (Æ), 'An Essay on the Character in Irish Literature' (1932) [cultural critique]

Seamas MacManus, *The Rocky Road to Dublin* (1938) [personal memoir]

Peig Sayers, *An Old Woman's Reflections* (1939 [1962]) [personal reminiscence]

Eric Cross, *The Tailor and Ansty* (1942) [personal memoir]

Máirtín Ó Cadhain, 'The Year 1912' (1948) [short story in Gaelic]

Seán Ó Ríordáin, 'Siollabadh' (Syllabling) (1952) [verse]

John Montague, 'The Rough Field' (1963) [reflective essay]

Seán Ó Ríordáin, 'Claustrophobia' (1964) [verse]

Brendan Kennelly, 'My Dark Fathers' (1964) [verse]

Michael J. Murphy (ed.), 'A Long Night in the Spike' (1967) [modern folktale]

Thomas Kinsella, 'The Divided Mind' (1971) [radio lecture]

John Montague, 'A Lost Tradition' (1972) [verse]

Patrick Galvin, 'The Irish' (1973) [verse]

Vincent Buckley, 'The Gaeltacht' (1979) [prose-poem]

Brian Friel, *Translations* (1981) [drama]

Iain Crichton Smith, 'For Poets Writing In English Over In Ireland' (1984) [verse]

Peter Sirr, 'Poetry in Ireland from its Roots' (1986) [book review]

Nuala Ní Dhomhnaill, 'An Bhean Mhídhílis' (The Unfaithful Wife), 'Ceist na Teangan' (The Language Issue) (1990) [verse]

Seán Ó Tuama, 'Twentieth Century Poetry in Irish' (1991) [critical survey]

Ian Duhig, 'From the Irish' (1991) [verse]

Nuala Ní Dhomhnaill, 'Caitlín' (Cathleen) (1992) [verse]

Dermot Healy, *The Bend For Home* (1996) [fictional memoir]

Louis de Paor, 'Disappearing Language' (1996) [polemical essay]

Seán Ó Tuama, 'Abair do Phaidir' (Say a Prayer) (1997) [verse]

Michael O'Loughlin, 'Cuchulainn' (1997) [verse]

Ciaran Carson, *The Star Factory* (1997) [reflective prose]

Martin McDonagh, *The Lonesome West* (1997) [drama]

North of Ireland

Extracts:

Lynn Doyle, 'The Wooden Leg' (1908) [short story]

St John Ervine, *Mixed Marriage* (1911) [drama]

W.B. Yeats, 'Speech on Divorce' (1925) [speech in Senate]

John Hewitt, 'Ireland' (1932) [verse]

Louis MacNeice, 'Carrickfergus' (1937) [verse]

Michael McLaverty, 'The Game Cock' (1937) [short story]

Louis MacNeice, 'Cushendun' (1939) [verse]

Nesca A. Robb, *An Ulsterwoman in England 1924-1941* (1942) [personal testimony]

John Hewitt, 'Once Alien Here' (1945) [verse]

Cathal O'Byrne, *As I Roved Out* (1946) [newspaper articles]

Sam Hanna Bell, *December Bride* (1951) [fiction]

W.R. Rodgers, 'Meet, Drink, and Be Airy' (1957) [radio talk]

Brian Friel, 'Foundry House' (1962) [short story]

John Montague, 'The Rough Field' (1963) [reflective essay]

Rivers Carew and Timothy Brownlow, 'Editorial, *The Dublin Magazine*' (1965) [editorial]

Roy McFadden, 'The Severed Hand' (1969) [personal testimony]

Michael Longley, 'Strife and the Ulster Poet' (1969) [contemporary observation]

Seamus Heaney, 'John Hume's Derry' (1969) [personal testimony]

John Montague, 'A Lost Tradition' (1972) [verse]

Rosita Sweetman, *'On Our Knees': Ireland 1972* (1972) [polemical writing]

James Simmons, 'Claudy' (1974) [verse]

Cecil King, *The Cecil King Diary 1970-1974* (1975) [diary entries]

Seamus Heaney, *North* (1975) [verse]

Jack Holland, 'Broken Images' (1975) [cultural critique]

Jennifer Johnston, *Shadows on Our Skin* (1977) [fiction]

Caroline Blackwood, *Great Granny Webster* (1977) [fiction]

Dervla Murphy, *A Place Apart* (1978) [reportage]

Benedict Kiely, 'The Night We Rode With Sarsfield' (1978) [short story]

Seamus Heaney, 'Casualty', 'The Skunk' (1979) [verse]

Mary Beckett, 'A Belfast Woman' (1980) [short story]

Paul Muldoon, 'Ireland' (1980) [verse]

Brian Friel, *Translations* (1981) [drama]

Roy McFadden, 'Conveyancer' (1983) [verse]

Bernard MacLaverty, *Cal* (1983) [fiction]

Paul Muldoon, 'Quoof' (1983) [verse]

Mary Holland, 'Ireland Blasts Back' (1984) [journalistic analysis]

Vincent Buckley, *Memory Ireland* (1985) [polemical essay]

Van Morrison, 'A Sense of Wonder' (1985) [song]

Padraic Fiacc, *Missa Terribilis* (1986) [verse]

Roy McFadden, 'Survivor', 'The Astoria' (1986) [verse]

Ciaran Carson, 'Belfast Confetti' (1987) [verse]

Stewart Parker, *Pentecost* (1987) [drama]

Edna Longley, 'From Cathleen to Anorexia' (1990) [polemical essay]

Michael Longley, 'The Butchers' (1991) [verse]

Vincent Buckley, 'Hunger–Strike: Bobby Sands: One' (1991) [verse]

Harry Clifton, 'Where We Live' (1993) [verse]

Colin Graham, 'Rejoinder: The Irish 'Post-'? A Reply to Gerry Smyth' (1994) [polemical essay]

Eoin McNamee, *Resurrection Man* (1994) [fiction]

Philip Hobsbaum, 'The Belfast Group' (1994) [literary reflections]

Michael Longley, 'Ceasefire' (1995) [verse]

Seamus Deane, *Reading in the Dark* (1996) [fiction]

Bill Rolston, 'Mothers, Whores and Villains' (1989) [critical survey]

Dermot Healy, *The Bend For Home* (1996) [fictional memoir]

Robert McLiam Wilson, *Eureka Street* (1996) [fiction]

Ciaran Carson, *The Star Factory* (1997) [reflective prose]

David McKittrick et al., *Lost Lives* (1999) [documentary record]

Violence

This is a topic in itself as the following extracts suggest. Attitudes to violence are worth exploring both for their variety and for their emotional intensity.

Extracts:

Lionel Johnson, 'Parnell' (1893) [verse]

James Connolly, 'Physical Force in Irish Politics' (1899) [position statement]

Oscar Wilde, 'The Ballad of Reading Gaol' (1899) [verse]

Arthur Conan Doyle, 'The Green Flag' (1900) [short story]

W.B. Yeats, *Cathleen ni Houlihan* (1902) [nationalist drama]

W.B. Yeats, 'Easter 1916' (1920) (written 1916) [verse]

Darrel Figgis, *A Chronicle of Jails* (1917) [prison chronicle]

Eimar O'Duffy, *The Wasted Island* (1919) [fiction]

W.B. Yeats, 'The Second Coming' (1921) [verse]

W.B. Yeats, 'Leda and the Swan' (1924) [verse]

Dorothy Macardle, 'The Portrait of Roisin Dhu' (1924) [short story]

W.B. Yeats, 'Sailing to Byzantium', 'Meditations in Time of Civil War' (1928) [verse]

Frank O'Connor, 'Guests of the Nation' (1931) [short story]

Pat O'Mara, *The Autobiography of a Liverpool Irish Slummy* (1934) [autobiography]

Monk Gibbon, *The Seals* (1935) [reflective prose]

Tom Barry, *Guerilla Days in Ireland* (1949) [war chronicle]

Brendan Behan, *The Quare Fellow* (1954) [drama]

Denis Devlin, 'The Tomb of Michael Collins' (1956) [verse]

Conor Cruise O'Brien, 'Passion and Cunning' (1965) [polemical essay]

Bryan MacMahon, 'The Valley of Knockanure' (1966) [song]

Roy McFadden, 'The Severed Hand' (1969) [personal testimony]

Michael Longley, 'Strife and the Ulster Poet' (1969) [contemporary observation]

Seamus Heaney, 'John Hume's Derry' (1969) [personal testimony]

J.G. Farrell, *Troubles* (1970) [historical fiction]

Rosita Sweetman, *'On Our Knees': Ireland 1972* (1972) [polemical writing]

Seamus Heaney, *North* (1975) [verse]

Jennifer Johnston, *Shadows on Our Skin* (1977) [fiction]

Thomas Flanagan, *The Year of the French* (1979) [historical fiction]

Seamus Heaney, 'Casualty', 'The Skunk' (1979) [verse]

Mary Beckett, 'A Belfast Woman' (1980) [short story]

Bernard MacLaverty, *Cal* (1983)

Mary Holland, 'Ireland Blasts Back' (1984) [journalistic analysis]

Padraic Fiacc, *Missa Terribilis* (1986) [verse]

Stewart Parker, *Pentecost* (1987) [drama]

Ciaran Carson, 'Belfast Confetti' (1987) [verse]

Seán Ó Tuama, 'Abair do Phaidir' (Say a Prayer) [verse]

Edward Said, 'Yeats and Decolonization' (1988) [polemical essay]

Bill Rolston, 'Mothers, Whores and Villains' (1989) [critical survey]

Gerry Conlon, *Proved Innocent* (1990) [prison record]

Michael Longley, 'The Butchers' (1991) [verse]

Vincent Buckley, 'Hunger-Strike: Bobby Sands: One' (1991) [verse]

Patrick McCabe, *The Butcher Boy* (1992) [fiction]

Eoin McNamee, *Resurrection Man* (1994) [fiction]

Michael Longley, 'Ceasefire' (1995) [verse]

Roddy Doyle, *The Woman Who Walked Into Doors* (1996) [fiction]

Seamus Deane, *Reading in the Dark* (1996) [fiction]

Dermot Healy, *The Bend For Home* (1996) [fictional memoir]

Ciaran Carson, *The Star Factory* (1997) [reflective prose]

Michael MacDonald, *All Souls* (1999) [autobiography]

David McKittrick et al., *Lost Lives* (1999) [documentary record]

2. THE CITY AND THE COUNTRY

Some thoughts:

- Attachment to a local place, to the parish, is a characteristic feature of Irish writing, ancient and modern. Kate O'Brien's Mellick, Brian Friel's Ballybeg, Frank O'Connor's Cork. The sense of return (and of leaving).
- Pastoral vision from Colum to Hewitt to Kavanagh to Heaney is pervasive.
- The country is also a place to escape from. Claustrophobia. Compare George Moore story with Leo Simpson's story.
- Changing attitudes towards the city. From Joyce's Edwardian Dublin to Roddy Doyle's contemporary working-class estates.
- The contrast between the citizen and the individual is often pronounced in modern Irish writing. Individual in touch with the cosmos, the citizen with the mundane.
- Parish, village, market town, county town, provincial city, regional capital, European capital. Which is best reflected in modern Irish writing?
- Landscape: how is this different from nature?

The City
Extracts:

Pádraic Ó Conaire, *Deoraíocht* (Exile) (1910) [fiction]

St John Ervine, *Mixed Marriage* (1911) [drama]

James Stephens, *The Insurrection in Dublin* (1916) [reportage]

Conal O'Riordan, *Adam of Dublin* (1920) [fiction]

Darrell Figgis, *The House of Success* (1922) [fiction]

James Joyce, *Ulysses* (1922) [fiction]

L.A.G. Strong, *The Garden* (1931) [fiction]

James T. Farrell, *The Young Manhood of Studs Lonigan* (1934) [fiction]

Joseph F. Dinneen, *Ward Eight* (1936) [fiction]

Louis MacNeice, 'Dublin' (1939) [verse]

Nesca A. Robb, *An Ulsterwoman in England 1924-1941* (1942) [personal testimony]

Betty Smith, *A Tree Grows In Brooklyn* (1943) [fiction]

Elizabeth Bowen, 'Mysterious Kôr' (1944) [short story]

Cathal O'Byrne, *As I Roved Out* (1946) [newspaper articles]

Edna O'Brien, *The Country Girls* (1960) [fiction]

Paul Smith, *The Countrywoman* (1962) [fiction]

Patrick Kavanagh, *Collected Poems* (1964) [verse]

Patrick Boyle, 'Go Away, Old Man, Go Away' (1966) [short story]

Lee Dunne, *A Bed in the Sticks* (1968) [fiction]

James Plunkett, *Strumpet City* (1969) [fiction]

Donall MacAmhlaigh, 'Britain's Irish Workers' (1978) [journalistic article]

Mary Beckett, 'A Belfast Woman' (1980) [short story]

William Kennedy, *Ironweed* (1983) [fiction]

Julie O'Callaghan, 'A Tourist Comments on the Land of his Forefathers' (1983) [verse]

Paul Durcan, 'Bewley's Oriental Café, Westmoreland Street' (1985) [verse]

Dervla Murphy, *Tales from Two Cities* (1985) [reportage]

Malcolm Lynch, *The Streets of Ancoats* (1985) [autobiographical fiction]

Van Morrison, 'A Sense of Wonder' (1985) [song]

Ciaran Carson, 'Belfast Confetti' (1987) [verse]

Robert McLiam Wilson, *Ripley Bogle* (1989) [fiction]

Eamonn Wall, 'Exile, Attitude, and the Sin-É Café: Notes on the "New Irish"' (1996) [personal observation]

Roddy Doyle, *The Woman Who Walked Into Doors* (1996) [fiction]

Robert McLiam Wilson, *Eureka Street* (1996) [fiction]

Ciaran Carson, *The Star Factory* (1997) [reflective prose]

Timothy O'Grady, *I Could Read the Sky* (1997) [fictional photographic portrait]

Michael MacDonald, *All Souls* (1999) [autobiography]

The country
Extracts:

R.P. Carton, 'The Associations of Scenery' (1895) [lecture]

Joseph Furphy, *Such Is Life* (1903) [fiction]

J.M. Synge, 'From Galway to Gorumna' (1905) [reportage]

E. Œ. Somerville and Martin Ross, 'Lisheen Races, Second-Hand' (1899) [short story]

George Moore, 'Home Sickness' (1903) [short story]

Padraic Colum, 'The Plougher' (1904; see Birmingham, 1907) [verse]

Lady Gregory, *Spreading the News* (1904) [one-act Abbey play]

J.M. Synge, *The Playboy of the Western World* (1907) [drama]

Lynn Doyle, 'The Wooden Leg' (1908) [short story]

Joseph Campbell, 'I am the Mountainy Singer', 'Night, and I Travelling' (1909) [verse]

Joseph Campbell, 'The Weaver's Family' (1911) [verse]

J.M. Synge, 'In Kerry' (1911) [verse]

Francis Ledwidge, 'June' (1913) [verse]

Peter O'Leary, *My Story* (1915) [personal reminiscence]

Francis Ledwidge, 'Thomas McDonagh' (1917) [verse]

Robin Flower, 'The Great Blasket: Poets' (1920) [verse]

Liam O'Flaherty, 'The Tent' (1926) [short story]

Thomás Ó Criomhthain, *An tOileánach* (*The Islandman*) (1929) [personal memoir]

Teresa Deevy, *The King of Spain's Daughter* (1935) [drama]

Patrick Kavanagh, 'Inniskeen Road: July Evening' (1936) [verse]

Michael McLaverty, 'The Game Cock' (1937) [short story]

Seamas MacManus, *The Rocky Road to Dublin* (1938) [personal memoir]

Peig Sayers, *Machtnamh Seana Mhná* (1939) [personal reminiscence]

Eric Cross, *The Tailor and Ansty* (1942) [personal memoir]

Patrick Kavanagh, Section VII *The Great Hunger* (1942) [verse]

Máirtín Ó Cadhain, 'The Year 1912' (1948) [short story in Gaelic]

Garry Hogg, *Turf Beneath My Feet* (1950) [travel writing]

Sam Hanna Bell, *December Bride* (1951) [fiction]

Padraic Fallon, 'Yeats's Tower at Ballylee' (1951) [verse]

Robert Gibbings, *Sweet Cork Of Thee* (1951) [travel writing]

E. Estyn Evans, *Irish Folk Ways* (1957) [folk life description]

Sean O'Faolain, 'Lovers of the Lake' (1957) [short story]

John Montague, 'The Rough Field' (1963) [reflective essay]

Brendan Kennelly, 'My Dark Fathers' (1964) [verse]

William Cotter Murray, *Michael Joe* (1965) [fiction]

Michael J. Murphy (ed), 'A Long Night in the Spike' (1967) [modern folktale]

Derek Mahon, 'A Disused Shed in County Wexford' (1968) [verse]

Richard Power, *The Hungry Grass* (1969) [fiction]

Mary Lavin, 'A Memory' (1972) [short story]

John Montague, 'A Lost Tradition' (1972) [verse]

William Trevor, 'The Ballroom of Romance' (1972) [short story]

Hugh Brody, *Inishkillane* (1973) [sociological portrait]

Benedict Kiely, 'The Night We Rode With Sarsfield' (1978) [short story]

John McGahern, 'Gold Watch' (1980) [short story]

Tom Murphy, *Conversations On A Homecoming* (1985) [drama]

Michael Longley, 'Detour' (1991) [verse]

Tim Robinson, *Stones of Aran: Labyrinth* (1995) [writing the Aran Islands]

Mary O'Malley, 'The Lightcatchers' (1997) [verse]

Martin McDonagh, *The Lonesome West* (1997) [drama]

The Big House

I could have made more of this in the *Reader*. What other texts might you include? How does the Big House tradition in Ireland compare with that in England?

Extracts:

E. Œ. Somerville and Martin Ross, 'Lisheen Races, Second-Hand' (1899) [short story]

John Howard Parnell, *Charles Stewart Parnell* (1916) [memoir]

L.A.G. Strong, *The Garden* (1931) [fiction]

W.B. Yeats, 'Coole and Ballylee, 1931' (1933) [verse]

Caroline Blackwood, *Great Granny Webster* (1977) [fiction]

Molly Keane, *Good Behaviour* (1981) [fiction]

Travel Writing

An enjoyable topic and one worth adding to from your own reading. If you write about this topic try to establish an argument or test an hypothesis. Avoid the temptation to think this is an easy topic.

Extracts:

Joseph Furphy, *Such Is Life* (1903) [fiction]

Donn Byrne, *Ireland* (1929) [travel writing]

Kate O'Brien, *Farewell Spain* (1937) [travel writing]

Garry Hogg, *Turf Beneath My Feet* (1950) [travel writing]

Robert Gibbings, *Sweet Cork Of Thee* (1951) [travel writing]

Heinrich Böll, *Irish Journal* (1957) [reflections]

Kate O'Brien, *My Ireland* (1962) [travel writing]

Dervla Murphy, *A Place Apart* (1978) [reportage]

Julie O'Callaghan, 'A Tourist Comments on the Land of his Forefathers' (1983) [verse]

Thomas Keneally, *Now And In Time To Be* (1991) [travel writing]

Tim Robinson, *Stones of Aran: Labyrinth* (1995) [writing the Aran Islands]

Derek Mahon, 'The Hudson Letter: Global Village' (1995) [verse]

3. CULTURE AND IDENTITY

Cultural Critique

This section is a good place to start for students on Irish Studies programmes. Again, you might begin by grouping material under specific headings: publishing, death, marriage, ritual, censorship, race, tourism, globalisation, and so on.

Extracts:

Douglas Hyde, 'The Necessity for De-Anglicizing Ireland' (1892) [lecture]

D.P. Moran, 'The Battle of Two Civilizations' (1899) [cultural critique]

W.B. Yeats, 'The Literary Movement in Ireland' (1899) [cultural critique]

George Russell (Æ), 'Nationality or Cosmopolitanism' (1899) [position statement]

Standish James O'Grady, 'The Great Enchantment' (1900) [political analysis]

Padraic Colum, 'A Poor Scholar of the Forties' (1904) [verse]

John Eglinton, 'The De-Davisisation of Irish Literature' (1906) [cultural critique]

Frederick Ryan, *Criticism and Courage* (1906) [polemical essay]

Reverend P.S. Dinneen, 'The World-wide Empire of the Irish Race' (1909) [lecture]

St John Ervine, *Mixed Marriage* (1911) [drama]

Stephen Gwynn, 'Irish Book Lovers' (1913) [newspaper article]

George Russell (Æ), *The Interpreters* (1922) [prose fantasy]

George Russell (Æ), 'Lessons of Revolution' (1923) [cultural critique]

Francis Stuart, *Tomorrow* (1924) [editorial]

Mary Manning, 'A Letter from Dublin' (1931) [cultural survey]

George Russell (Æ), 'An Essay on the Character in Irish Literature' (1932) [cultural critique]

Monk Gibbon, *The Seals* (1935) [reflective prose]

Frank O'Connor, 'An Irishman Looks at England' (1941) [radio talk]

Frank O'Connor, 'The Future of Irish Literature' (1942) [cultural critique]

Sean O'Faolain, 'Romance and Realism' (1945) [cultural critique]

Arland Ussher, 'The Contemporary Thought of Ireland' (1947) [radio talk]

Oliver St John Gogarty, *Rolling Down the Lea* (1950) [polemical essay]

John Ryan, 'Our Irish Publishers' (1950) [editorial]

Sean O'Faolain, 'Fifty Years of Irish Writing' (1962) [critical survey]

Heinrich Böll, *Irish Journal* (1957) [reflections]

W.R. Rodgers, 'Meet, Drink, and Be Airy' (1957)
[radio talk]

Samuel Beckett, *Endgame* (1958) [drama]

Frank O'Connor, *The Lonely Voice* (1962) [critical
argument]

Rivers Carew and Timothy Brownlow, 'Editorial, *The
Dublin Magazine* ' (1965) [editorial]

Conor Cruise O'Brien, 'Passion and Cunning' (1965)
[polemical essay]

John Jordan, 'A Censored Decade' (1972) [cultural
critique]

Hugh Brody, *Inishkillane* (1973) [sociological portrait]

Jack Holland, 'Broken Images' (1975) [cultural critique]

Denis Donoghue, 'Being Irish Together' (1976)
[polemical essay]

Donall MacAmhlaigh, 'Britain's Irish Workers' (1978)
[journalistic article]

Brendan Kennelly, *Cromwell* (1983) [verse]

Julie O'Callaghan, 'A Tourist Comments on the Land
of his Forefathers' (1983) [verse]

Tom Murphy, *Conversations On A Homecoming* (1985)
[drama]

Philip Chevron, 'Thousands are Sailing' (1988) [song]

Paul Hewson, 'Bono: The White Nigger' (1988)
[personal testimony]

Bill Rolston, 'Mothers, Whores and Villains' (1989)
[critical survey]

Eavan Boland, 'Outside History' (1989) [cultural
critique]

Maire Bradshaw, 'high time for all the marys' (1991)
[verse]

Gerald Dawe, 'Anecdotes Over A Jar' (1991) [cultural
critique]

Martin Mooney, *Grub* (1993) [verse]

Philip Hobsbaum, 'The Belfast Group' (1994) [literary
reflections]

Derek Mahon, 'The Hudson Letter: Global Village'
(1995) [verse]

Robert McLiam Wilson, *Eureka Street* (1996) [fiction]

Michael O'Loughlin, 'Cuchulainn' (1996) [verse]

Fintan O'Toole, 'Brand Leader' (1996) [polemical
essay]

Martin McDonagh, *The Lonesome West* (1997) [drama]

Terry Eagleton, *Crazy John and the Bishop* (1998)
[polemical essay]

Colonialism/Post-colonialism

Notes:
- The relevance or otherwise of this axis for
understanding modern Irish writing.
- The connection between modern Irish writing
and post-colonial theory. Ireland as a proving-

ground or as a complication, a strange country.
Shaw's *John Bull's Other Island*.
- Post-nationalism versus post-colonialism.
- The contribution of Northern writers to this debate.
- The changing nature and interpretation of Irish
identity.
- The Irish diaspora. Attitudes of Irish writers to
Britain and Europe. Ties of Irish-American and
Irish-Australian writers to Ireland.

Extracts:

Lionel Johnson, 'Parnell' (1893) [verse]

Maurice F. Egan, 'The Orange Lilies' (1898) [short
story]

D.P. Moran, 'The Battle of Two Civilizations' (1899)
[cultural critique]

W.B. Yeats, 'The Literary Movement in Ireland' (1899)
[cultural critique]

Arthur Conan Doyle, 'The Green Flag' (1900) [short
story]

E. Œ. Somerville and Martin Ross, 'Lisheen Races,
Second-Hand' (1899) [short story]

W.B. Yeats, *Cathleen ni Houlihan* (1902) [nationalist
drama]

Joseph Furphy, *Such Is Life* (1903) [fiction]

Arthur Griffith, *The Resurrection of Hungary* (1904)
[political writing]

G.B. Shaw, *John Bull's Other Island* (1904) [drama]

Frederick Ryan, *Criticism and Courage* (1906)
[polemical essay]

Reverend P.S. Dinneen, 'The World-wide Empire of
the Irish Race' (1909) [lecture]

John Howard Parnell, *Charles Stewart Parnell : A
Memoir* (1916) [memoir]

George Bernard Shaw, 'The Easter Week Executions'
(1916) [letter to newspaper]

George Russell (Æ), 'The New Nation' (1917)
[personal statement, poem]

John O'Brien, 'St Patrick's Day' (1921) [verse]

George Russell (Æ), 'Lessons of Revolution' (1923)
[cultural critique]

Francis Stuart, *Tomorrow* (1924) [editorial]

Louis MacNeice, *Autumn Journal* (1938) [verse]

Sean O'Faolain, 'Romance and Realism' (1945)
[editorial]

Nesca A. Robb, *An Ulsterwoman in England 1924-1941*
(1942) [personal testimony]

John V. Kelleher, 'Irish-American Literature, And
Why There Isn't Any' (1947) [polemical essay]

Tom Barry, *Guerilla Days in Ireland* (1949) [war chronicle]

Conor Cruise O'Brien, 'Passion and Cunning' (1965)
[polemical essay]

J.G. Farrell, *Troubles* (1970) [historical fiction]

Richard Howard Brown, *I Am Of Ireland* (1974) [personal memoirs]

Rosita Sweetman, *'On Our Knees': Ireland 1972* (1972) [polemical writing]

Cecil King, *The Cecil King Diary 1970-1974* (1972: 1975) [diary entries]

Seamus Deane, 'Unhappy and At Home: Interview with Seamus Heaney' (1977) [interview]

Donall MacAmhlaigh, 'Britain's Irish Workers' (1978) [journalistic article]

Brian Moore, *The Mangan Inheritance* (1979) [fiction]

Vincent Buckley, 'The Gaeltacht' (1979) [prose-poem]

Brian Friel, *Translations* (1981) [drama]

Brendan Kennelly, *Cromwell* (1983) [verse]

Mary Holland, 'Ireland Blasts Back' (1984) [journalistic analysis]

Vincent Buckley, *Memory Ireland* (1985) [polemical essay]

Tom Murphy, *Conversations On A Homecoming* (1985)

Malcolm Lynch, *The Streets of Ancoats* (1985) [autobiographical fiction]

Paul Hewson, 'Bono: The White Nigger' (1988) [personal testimony]

Patrick Galvin, *Song For A Poor Boy* (1990) [autobiography]

Vincent Buckley, 'Hunger-Strike: Bobby Sands: One' (1991) [verse]

Gerald Dawe, 'Anecdotes Over A Jar' (1991) [cultural critique]

Nuala Ní Dhomhnaill, 'Caitlín' (Cathleen) (1992) [verse]

Colin Graham, 'Rejoinder: The Irish 'Post-'? A Reply to Gerry Smyth' (1994) [polemical essay]

Philip Hobsbaum, 'The Belfast Group' (1994) [literary reflections]

Derek Mahon, 'The Hudson Letter: Global Village' (1995) [verse]

Sebastian Barry, *The Steward of Christendom* (1995) [drama]

Rita Anne Higgins, 'Remapping the Borders' (1996) [verse]

Colm Tóibín, 'Playboys of the GPO' (1996) [book review]

Robert McLiam Wilson, *Eureka Street* (1996) [fiction]

Louis de Paor, 'Disappearing Language' (1996) [polemical essay]

Michael O'Loughlin, 'Cuchulainn' (1996) [verse]

Martin McDonagh, *The Lonesome West* (1997) [drama]

Irish Language

Extracts:

Francis Fahy, *The Irish Language Movement* (1901) [lecture]

Lady Gregory, *Cuchulain of Muirthemne* (1902) [ancient mythological story]

Reverend P.S. Dinneen, 'The World-wide Empire of the Irish Race' (1909) [lecture]

P.W. Joyce, *English As We Speak It In Ireland* (1910) [linguistic description]

Peter O'Leary, *My Story* (1915) [personal reminiscence]

Thomas MacDonagh, *Literature in Ireland* (1916) [critical essay]

Robin Flower, 'The Great Blasket: Poets' (1920) [verse]

Tomás Ó Criomhthain, *An tOileánach* (*The Islandman*) (1929) [personal memoir]

George Russell (Æ), 'An Essay on the Character in Irish Literature' (1932) [cultural critique]

Peig Sayers, *Machtnamh Seana Mhná* (1939) [personal reminiscence]

Máirtín Ó Cadhain, 'The Year 1912' (1948) [short story in Gaelic]

Seán Ó Ríordáin, 'Siollabadh' (Syllabling) (1952) [verse]

Thomas Kinsella, 'The Divided Mind' (1971) [radio lecture]

Benedict Kiely, 'In Iowa: A Beauty Queen and a Blind Man' (1975) [radio talk]

Vincent Buckley, 'The Gaeltacht' (1979) [prose-poem]

Brian Friel, *Translations* (1981) [drama]

Iain Crichton Smith, 'For Poets Writing In English Over In Ireland' (1984) [verse]

Peter Sirr, 'Poetry in Ireland from its Roots' (1986) [book review]

Seán Ó Tuama, 'Twentieth Century Poetry in Irish' (1991) [critical survey]

Nuala Ní Dhomhnaill, 'An Bhean Mhídhílis' (The Unfaithful Wife), 'Ceist na Teangan' (The Language Issue) (1990) [verse]

Nuala Ní Dhomhnaill, 'Caitlín' (Cathleen) (1992) [verse]

Cathal Ó Searcaigh, *Homecoming/An Bealach 'na Bhaile* (1993) [verse]

Dermot Healy, *The Bend For Home* (1996) [fictional memoir]

Louis de Paor, 'Disappearing Language' (1996) [polemical essay]

Ciaran Carson, *The Star Factory* (1997) [reflective prose]

Seán Ó Tuama, 'Abair do Phaidir' (Say a Prayer) (1997) [verse]

Folklore and Folk Tales

Extracts:

Lady Gregory, *Cuchulain of Muirthemne* (1902) [ancient mythological story]

Lord Dunsany, 'The Assignation' (1914) [modern tale]

George Russell (Æ), 'An Essay On The Character In Irish Literature' (1932) [cultural critique]

Cathal O'Byrne, *As I Roved Out: In Belfast and Districts* (1946) [newspaper articles]

E. Estyn Evans, *Irish Folk Ways* (1957) [folk life description]

Michael J. Murphy (ed.), 'A Long Night in the Spike' (1967) [modern folktale]

Tim Robinson, *Stones of Aran: Labyrinth* (1995) [writing the Aran Islands]

Michael O'Loughlin, 'Cuchulainn' (1996) [verse]

Dermot Healy, *The Bend for Home* (1996) [fictional memoir]

Mary O'Malley, 'The Lightcatchers' (1997) [verse]

Gender and modern Irish writing

Some thoughts:

- Cathleen Ní Houlihan. The representation of Ireland as female. From Yeats to Ní Dhomhnaill.
- Rites of passage in male autobiographical writing. From darkness to light, from experience to articulation. Guilt. Jansenism and the body.
- The issue of taboo and transgression in modern Irish writing. Joyce, McGahern, Edna O'Brien.
- The links with male violence as in *Butcher Boy* and *Resurrection Man*.
- Domesticity and women's writing. Eavan Boland.
- Sexuality and desire.
- Gay sexuality. Wilde to Cathal Ó Searcaigh.
- Honesty and evasion. Paul Smith.
- Censorship. What was censored? Is what was censored Ireland's repressed unconscious? If so what does it look like? Or how does it relate to the conscious part?

Extracts:

Lady Gregory, *Cuchulain of Muirthemne* (1902) [ancient mythological story]

W.B. Yeats, *Cathleen ni Houlihan* (1902) [nationalist drama]

G.B. Shaw, *John Bull's Other Island* (1904) [drama]

Eva Gore-Booth, 'Womens Rights' (1906) [verse]

J.M. Synge, *The Playboy of the Western World* (1907) [drama]

J.M. Synge, *Poems and Translations* (1911) [verse]

St John Ervine, *Mixed Marriage* (1911) [drama]

W.B. Yeats, 'Fallen Majesty' (1914) [verse]

James Joyce, Penelope episode from *Ulysses* (1922) [fiction]

F. Scott Fitzgerald, 'Absolution' (1924) [short story]

Austin Clarke, *The Bright Temptation* (1932) [fiction]

Blanaid Salkeld, *Hello Eternity!* (1933) [verse]

W.B. Yeats, 'Crazy Jane Talks with the Bishop', 'After Long Silence' (1933) [verse]

Teresa Deevy, *The King of Spain's Daughter* (1935) [drama]

Miles Franklin, *All That Swagger* (1936) [fiction]

Austin Clarke, 'The Straying Student' (1938) [verse]

Patrick Kavanagh, *The Great Hunger* (1942) [verse]

Bryan MacMahon, 'Yung Mari Li' (1943) [short story]

Edward A. McCourt, *Home Is The Stranger* (1950) [fiction]

Sam Hanna Bell, *December Bride* (1951) [fiction]

W.R. Rodgers, 'The Net' (1952) [verse]

Frank O'Connor, 'My Oedipus Complex' (1952) [short story]

Sean O'Faolain, 'Lovers of the Lake' (1957) [short story]

Michael J. Murphy (ed.), 'A Long Night in the Spike' (1967) [modern folktale]

Edna O'Brien, *The Country Girls* (1960) [fiction]

Paul Smith, *The Countrywoman* (1962) [fiction]

William Cotter Murray, *Michael Joe* (1965) [fiction]

Patrick Boyle, 'Go Away, Old Man, Go Away' (1966) [short story]

Lee Dunne, *A Bed in the Sticks* (1968) [fiction]

Mary Lavin, 'A Memory' (1972) [short story]

William Trevor, 'The Ballroom of Romance' (1972) [short story]

Patrick Galvin, *The Wood-Burners* (1973) [verse]

Seamus Heaney, 'The Skunk' (1979) [verse]

Brian Moore, *The Mangan Inheritance* (1979) [fiction]

John McGahern, 'Gold Watch' (1980) [short story]

Molly Keane, *Good Behaviour* (1981) [fiction]

Paul Durcan, 'Trinity College Dublin, 1983' (1983) [verse]

Bill Rolston, 'Mothers, Whores and Villains' (1989) [critical survey]

Edna Longley, 'From Cathleen to Anorexia' (1990) [polemical essay]

Maire Bradshaw, 'high time for all the marys' (1991) [verse]

Nuala Ní Dhomhnaill, 'An Bhean Mhídhílis' (The Unfaithful Wife), 'Ceist na Teangan' (The Language Issue) (1990) [verse]

Patrick McCabe, *The Butcher Boy* (1992) [fiction]

Nuala Ní Dhomhnaill, 'Caitlín' (Cathleen) (1992) [verse]

Martin Mooney, 'In the Parlour' (1993) [verse]

Cathal Ó Searcaigh, *Homecoming/An Bealach 'na Bhaile* (1993) [verse]

Marina Carr, *The Mai* (1994) [drama]

Michael Longley, 'Sheela-Na-Gig' (1995) [verse]

Ailbhe Smyth, 'Declining Identities (lit. and fig.)' (1996) [polemical essay]

Colm Tóibín, 'Playboys of the GPO' (1996) [book review]

Mary O'Malley, 'The Lightcatchers' (1997) [verse]

Women Writers
Extracts:

Lady Gregory, *Cuchulain of Muirthemne* (1902) [ancient mythological story]

E. Œ. Somerville and Martin Ross, 'Lisheen Races, Second-Hand' (1899) [short story]

Lady Gregory, *Spreading the News* (1904) [one-act Abbey play]

Eva Gore-Booth, 'Womens Rights' (1906) [verse]

Dorothy Macardle, 'The Portrait of Roisin Dhu' (1924) [short story]

Blanaid Salkeld, *Hello Eternity!* (1933) [verse]

Teresa Deevy, *The King of Spain's Daughter* (1935) [drama]

Blanaid Salkeld, *The Fox's Covert* (1935)

Miles Franklin, *All That Swagger* (1936) [fiction]

Kate O'Brien, *Farewell Spain* (1937) [travel writing]

Kate O'Brien, *Pray for the Wanderer* (1938) [fiction]

Peig Sayers, *Machtnamh Seana Mhná* (1939) [personal reminiscence]

Nesca A. Robb, *An Ulsterwoman in England 1924-1941* (1942) [personal testimony]

Elizabeth Bowen, 'Mysterious Kôr' (1944) [short story]

Betty Smith, *A Tree Grows In Brooklyn* (1943) [fiction]

Elizabeth Bowen, 'Coming to London' (1956) [personal reminiscence]

Kate O'Brien, *My Ireland* (1962) [travel writing]

Edna O'Brien, *The Country Girls* (1960) [fiction]

Eiléan Ní Chuilleanáin, 'Early Recollections' (1970) [verse]

Rosita Sweetman, *'On Our Knees': Ireland 1972* (1972) [polemical writing]

Mary Lavin, 'A Memory' (1972) [short story]

Jennifer Johnston, *Shadows on Our Skin* (1977) [fiction]

Caroline Blackwood, *Great Granny Webster* (1977) [fiction]

Tess Gallagher, 'The Ballad of Ballymote' (1978) [verse]

Dervla Murphy, *A Place Apart* (1978) [reportage]

Mary Beckett, 'A Belfast Woman' (1980) [short story]

Molly Keane, *Good Behaviour* (1981) [fiction]

Medbh McGuckian, 'The Flower Master' (1982) [verse]

Julie O'Callaghan, 'A Tourist Comments on the Land of his Forefathers' (1983) [verse]

Tess Gallagher, 'Each Bird Walking' (1984) [verse]

Mary Holland, 'Ireland Blasts Back' (1984) [journalistic analysis]

Dervla Murphy, *Tales from Two Cities* (1985) [reportage]

Mary Gordon, *The Other Side* (1989) [fiction]

Eavan Boland, 'Outside History' (1989) [cultural critique]

Eavan Boland, 'The Achill Woman' (1990) [verse]

Edna Longley, 'From Cathleen to Anorexia' (1990) [polemical essay]

Nuala Ní Dhomhnaill, 'An Bhean Mhídhílis' (The Unfaithful Wife), 'Ceist na Teangan' (The Language Issue) (1990) [verse]

Maire Bradshaw, 'high time for all the marys' (1991) [verse]

Maura Dooley, 'Second Generation' (1991)[verse]

Moy McCrory, 'A Well Travelled Woman' (1991) [short story]

Nuala Ní Dhomhnaill, 'Caitlín' (Cathleen) (1992) [verse]

Eavan Boland, 'The Singers' (1994) [verse]

Marina Carr, *The Mai* (1994) [drama]

Rita Anne Higgins, 'Remapping the Borders' (1996) [verse]

Ailbhe Smyth, 'Declining Identities (lit. and fig.)' (1996) [polemical essay]

Critical Essays
Extracts:

W.B. Yeats, 'The Symbolism of Poetry ' (1900) [critical essay]

George A. Birmingham, 'The Literary Movement in Ireland' (1907) [critical survey]

Thomas MacDonagh, *Literature in Ireland* (1916) [critical essay]

Daniel Corkery, 'The Aisling' (1924) [critical survey]

Andrew E. Malone, 'The Coming of Age of the Irish Drama' (1927) [critical survey]

'Andrew Belis' (Samuel Beckett), 'Recent Irish Poetry' (1934) [critical essay]

Ernest Boyd, 'Joyce and the New Irish Writers' (1934) [critical survey]

Grattan Freyer, 'A Letter From Ireland' (1938) [cultural survey]

Brian Nolan, 'A Bash in the Tunnel' (1951) [editorial note]

Sean O'Faolain, 'Fifty Years of Irish Writing' (1962) [critical survey]

Frank O'Connor, *The Lonely Voice* (1962) [critical argument]

Anthony Burgess, 'The Reticence of "Ulysses"' (1969) [critical essay]

Thomas Kinsella, 'The Divided Mind' (1971) [lecture on Radio Eireann]

Sean O'Casey, *I Knock at the Door* (1939) [autobiography]

Betty Smith, *A Tree Grows In Brooklyn* (1943) [fiction]

Frank O'Connor, 'My Oedipus Complex' (1952) [short story]

Bob Shaw, 'Light of Other Days' (1967) [science fiction story]

Eiléan Ní Chuilleanáin, 'Early Recollections' (1970) [verse]

Christy Brown, *Down All the Days* (1970) [autobiographical fiction]

Jennifer Johnston, *Shadows on Our Skin* (1977) [fiction]

Benedict Kiely, 'The Night We Rode With Sarsfield' (1978) [short story]

Malcolm Lynch, *The Streets of Ancoats* (1985) [autobiographical fiction]

Padraic Fiacc, 'Tears/A *Lacrimosa*' (1986) [verse]

Roy McFadden, 'Survivor' (1986) [verse]

Bill Naughton, *Saintly Billy* (1988) [autobiography]

Eavan Boland, 'The Achill Woman' (1990) [verse]

Patrick Galvin, *Song For A Poor Boy* (1990) [autobiography]

Patrick McCabe, *The Butcher Boy* (1992) [fiction]

Seamus Deane, *Reading in the Dark* (1996) [fiction]

Humour
Extracts:

F.P. Dunne, *Mr. Dooley In the Hearts of His Countrymen* (1900) [humorous essays]

E. Œ. Somerville and Martin Ross, 'Lisheen Races, Second-Hand' (1899) [short story]

G.B. Shaw, *John Bull's Other Island* (1904) [drama]

Lynn Doyle, 'The Wooden Leg' (1908) [short story]

Robert Gibbings, *Blue Angels and Whales* (1938) [humorous notebook entry]

Flann O'Brien, *At Swim-Two-Birds* (1939) [fiction]

Flann O'Brien, 'Cruiskeen Lawn' (1942) [newspaper column]

Patrick Campbell, 'An Irishman's Diary' (1946) [newspaper column]

Samuel Beckett, *Molloy* (1954) [fiction]

Samuel Beckett, *Endgame* (1958) [drama]

J.P. Donleavy, *The Unexpurgated Code* (1976) [humorous articles]

Brendan Kennelly, *Cromwell* (1983)

Malcolm Lynch, *The Streets of Ancoats* (1985) [autobiographical fiction]

Paul Durcan, 'Bewley's Oriental Café, Westmoreland Street' (1985) [verse]

The Outsider
Notes:
- The outsider defined by reference to the insider. Writers on a scale from inside to outside community. Changing attitudes in Ireland towards Yeats, once an outsider but now a culural icon (which is also an outsider). Interest of writers in outsiders. Synge's Christy Mahon and Joyce's Bloom for example. Modern Irish writing as the work of outsiders. Francis Stuart, 'The Soft Centre of Irish Writing': a useful starting-point.
- The outsider and language. Irish language. P.W. Joyce, Montague.
- Garry Hogg's discussion of photographing country people. Compare with Synge's *Guardian* article. See also Kate O'Brien on Spain and tourism.
- Tribalism and the North. Catholic writers' sense of community. Contrast Heaney's possessive imagination with MacNeice and Mahon. Would this 'line' confirm certain stereotypes criticised by Edna Longley and Robert McLiam Wilson.
- The Big House. The Anglo-Irish, Protestant middle class in the new Ireland.
- The Church defining those outside. The place of interiority and the sense of alienation.
- Gossip. *Spreading the News*.
- Tramps. MacGill to Jim Phelan to *Ripley Bogle*.
- Beckett. On and on.

On the Road
Extracts:

Michael J. Murphy (ed.), 'A Long Night in the Spike' (1967) [modern folktale]

Patrick MacGill, 'Padding It' (1916) [verse]

Jim Phelan, *We Follow the Roads* (1949) [sociological description/personal memoir]

Desmond Hogan , 'Interview with Van Morrison' (1987) [interview]

Robert McLiam Wilson, *Ripley Bogle* (1989) [fiction]

Martin Mooney, 'Madonna and Child' (1993) [verse]

Prison Writings
Extracts:

Oscar Wilde, 'The Ballad of Reading Gaol' (1899) [verse]

Patrick Pearse, 'The Wayfarer' (1917) [verse]

Darrel Figgis, *A Chronicle of Jails* (1917) [prison chronicle]

Constance Markievicz, 'December 1920' [letters from prison]

Frank Gallagher, *Days of Fear* (1928) [diary entries]

Jim Phelan, *Lifer* (1938) [fiction]

Jim Phelan, *Jail Journal* (1940) [prison notebook]

Brendan Behan, *The Quare Fellow* (1954) [drama]

Brendan Behan, *Borstal Boy* (1958) [prison autobiography]

Seamus Heaney, 'From the Republic of Conscience' (1985) [verse]

Gerry Conlon, *Proved Innocent* (1990) [prison record]
Vincent Buckley, 'Hunger-Strike: Bobby Sands: One'
    (1991) [verse]

4. THE IRISH DIASPORA

Irish Writers in Britain
Extracts:
Lionel Johnson, 'Parnell' (1893) [verse]
Anon., 'Irish Literary Theatre: Lecture by Mr W.B.
    Yeats' (1899) [minutes of meeting]
Oscar Wilde, 'The Ballad of Reading Gaol' (1899)
    [verse]
Arthur Conan Doyle, 'The Green Flag' (1900) [short
    story]
Francis Fahy, *The Irish Language Movement* (1901)
    [lecture]
G.B. Shaw, *John Bull's Other Island* (1904) [drama]
Pádraic Ó Conaire, *Deoraíocht* (Exile) (1910) [fiction]
Patrick MacGill, *Children of the Dead End* (1914)
    [fiction]
Patrick MacGill, 'Padding It' (1916) [verse]
Con O'Leary, 'The Snipe' (1922) [short story]
L.A.G. Strong, *The Garden* (1931) [fiction]
Pat O'Mara, *The Autobiography of a Liverpool Irish
    Slummy* (1934) [autobiography]
Louis MacNeice, 'The Sunlight on the Garden' (1937)
    [verse]
Jim Phelan, *Lifer* (1938) [fiction]
Louis MacNeice, 'Cushendun' (1939) [verse]
Jim Phelan, *Jail Journal* (1940) [prison notebook]
Frank O'Connor, 'An Irishman Looks at England'
    (1941) [radio talk]
Jim Phelan, *Ireland-Atlantic Gateway* (1941) [polemical
    argument]
Nesca A. Robb, *An Ulsterwoman in England 1924-1941*
    (1942) [personal testimony]
Elizabeth Bowen, 'Mysterious Kôr' (1944) [short story]
Jim Phelan, *We Follow the Roads* (1949) [sociological
    description/personal memoir]
Elizabeth Bowen, 'Coming to London' (1956)
    [personal reminiscence]
John Hewitt, 'An Irishman in Coventry' (1959) [verse]
Lee Dunne, *A Bed in the Sticks* (1968) [fiction]
Anthony Burgess, 'The Reticence of "Ulysses"'
    (1969) [critical essay]
Caroline Blackwood, *Great Granny Webster* (1977)
    [fiction]
Donall MacAmhlaigh, 'Britain's Irish Workers' (1978)
    [journalistic article]
Mary Holland, 'Ireland Blasts Back' (1984)
    [journalistic analysis]

Malcolm Lynch, *The Streets of Ancoats* (1985)
    [autobiographical fiction]
Dervla Murphy, *Tales from Two Cities* (1985)
    [reportage]
Bill Naughton, *Saintly Billy* (1988) [autobiography]
Robert McLiam Wilson, *Ripley Bogle* (1989) [fiction]
Moy McCrory, 'A Well Travelled Woman' (1991)
    [short story]
Maura Dooley, 'Second Generation' (1991) [verse]
Ian Duhig, 'From the Irish' (1991) [verse]
Martin Mooney, *Grub* (1993) [verse]
Martin McDonagh, *The Lonesome West* (1997) [drama]
Timothy O'Grady, *I Could Read the Sky* (1997)
    [fictionalized photographic portrait]

Irish-American Writers
Extracts:
Maurice F. Egan, 'The Orange Lilies' (1898) [short
    story]
F.P. Dunne, *Mr. Dooley In the Hearts of His Countrymen*
    (1900) [humorous essays]
F. Scott Fitzgerald, 'Absolution' (1924) [short story]
John O'Hara, *BUtterfield 8* (1934) [fiction]
F. Scott Fitzgerald, 'Letter to John O'Hara' (1933)
    [private correspondence]
Ernest Boyd, 'Joyce and the New Irish Writers' (1934)
    [critical survey]
James T. Farrell, *The Young Manhood of Studs Lonigan*
    (1934) [fiction]
Joseph F. Dinneen, *Ward Eight* (1936) [fiction]
George C. Homans, 'Boston Irish' (1936) [book
    review]
Betty Smith, *A Tree Grows In Brooklyn* (1943) [fiction]
J.F. Powers, 'Prince of Darkness' (1947) [short story]
John V. Kelleher, 'Irish-American Literature, And
    Why There Isn't Any' (1947) [polemical essay]
Edwin O'Connor, *The Last Hurrah* (1956) [fiction]
Eugene O'Neill, *Long Day's Journey Into Night* (1956;
    written 1940) [drama]
Eugene O'Neill, *A Touch of the Poet*, Act One (1958;
    written 1936-9) [drama]
Richard Howard Brown, *I Am Of Ireland* (1974)
    [personal memoirs]
J.P. Donleavy, *The Unexpurgated Code* (1976)
    [humorous articles]
Robert Creeley, 'Theresa's Friends' (1978) [verse]
Tess Gallagher, 'The Ballad of Ballymote' (1978)
    [verse]
Thomas Flanagan, *The Year of the French* (1979)
    [historical fiction]
William Kennedy, *Ironweed* (1983) [fiction]
Julie O'Callaghan, 'A Tourist Comments on the Land
    of his Forefathers' (1983) [verse]

Tess Gallagher, 'Each Bird Walking' (1984) [verse]

John Gregory Dunne, *Harp* (1989) [autobiography]

Mary Gordon, *The Other Side* (1989) [fiction]

William Kennedy, *Riding the Yellow Trolley Car: Selected Nonfiction* (1993) [interview]

Eamonn Wall, 'Exile, Attitude, and the Sin-É Café: Notes on the "New Irish"' (1996) [personal observation]

Michael MacDonald, *All Souls* (1999) [autobiography]

Canadian-Irish Writers
Extracts:

Patrick Slater, *The Yellow Briar* (1933) [fiction]

John Coulter, 'Immigrant Exile I, II, III', 'Rhyme of Two Worlds' (1946) [verse]

Edward A. McCourt, *Home Is The Stranger* (1950) [fiction]

Leo Simpson, 'Visiting the Future' (1976) [short story]

Brian Moore, *The Mangan Inheritance* (1979) [fiction]

George McWhirter, 'At Spanish Banks' (1993) [verse]

Irish–Australian Writers
Extracts:

Joseph Furphy, *Such Is Life* (1903) [fiction]

John O'Brien, 'St Patrick's Day' (1921) [verse]

Miles Franklin, *All That Swagger* (1936) [fiction]

Vincent Buckley, 'The Gaeltacht' (1979) [prose-poem]

Vincent Buckley, *Memory Ireland* (1985) [polemical essay]

Vincent Buckley, 'Hunger-Strike: Bobby Sands: One' (1991) [verse]

Thomas Keneally, *Now And In Time To Be* (1991) [travel writing]

Return
In one respect, every extract in the *Reader* could come under this heading.
Extracts:

Moira O'Neill, 'Corrymeela' (1901) [verse]

George Moore, 'Home Sickness' (1903) [short story]

John O'Brien, 'St Patrick's Day' (1921) [verse]

Miles Franklin, *All That Swagger* (1936) [fiction]

Louis MacNeice, 'Carrickfergus' (1937), 'The Sunlight on the Garden' (1937) [verse]

Seamas MacManus, *The Rocky Road to Dublin* (1938) [personal memoir]

Louis MacNeice, *Autumn Journal* (1938) [verse]

Kate O'Brien, *Pray for the Wanderer* (1938) [fiction]

Louis MacNeice, 'Traveller's Return' (1941) [personal testimony]

John Hewitt, 'Once Alien Here' (1945) [verse]

John Coulter, 'Immigrant Exile I, II, III', 'Rhyme of Two Worlds' (1946) [verse]

Edward A. McCourt, *Home Is The Stranger* (1950) [fiction]

L.A.G. Strong, 'The Harbour' (1957) [verse]

Heinrich Böll, *Irish Journal* (1957) [reflections]

Brian Friel, 'Foundry House' (1962) [short story]

Lee Dunne, *A Bed in the Sticks* (1968) [fiction]

Leo Simpson, 'Visiting the Future' (1976) [short story]

Caroline Blackwood, *Great Granny Webster* (1977) [fiction]

Robert Creeley, 'Theresa's Friends' (1978) [verse]

Donall MacAmhlaigh, 'Britain's Irish Workers' (1978) [journalistic article]

Brian Moore, *The Mangan Inheritance* (1979) [fiction]

Tom Murphy, *Conversations On A Homecoming* (1985) [drama]

Roy McFadden, 'Survivor', 'The Astoria' (1986) [verse]

Patrick Galvin, *Song For A Poor Boy* (1990) [autobiography]

Maura Dooley, 'Second Generation' (1991) [verse]

Harry Clifton, 'Where We Live' (1993) [verse]

George McWhirter, 'At Spanish Banks' (1993) [verse]

Eamonn Wall, 'Exile, Attitude, and the Sin-É Café: Notes on the "New Irish"' (1996) [personal observation]

WRITING AND RESEARCH

WRITING

I often recommend to my students if they are faced with a 2,000 word (or seven-page) assignment the following regime or method of approach:

1. Select a topic or a particular question.

2. A week or so before you have to submit your assignment, place on your desk a large A3 sheet of paper to jot down thoughts as they come to you.

3. Then begin gathering your thoughts and see if you can order them.

4. Aim for around 10-12 main points. These will then constitute the basis of your paragraphs.

5. List your paragraphs and then write the actual topic sentence for each paragraph on a sheet of A4. Re-arrange the order accordingly.

6. Write your essay on the basis of supporting the topic sentence of each paragraph.

7. Leave for a day or two and come back to edit.

8. Leave time at end before running off (I am assuming you're working with a wordprocessor) for any problems with printer etc.

In other words I see writing not so much in terms of burning the midnight oil (Yeats's 'blear-eyed wisdom'), but rather as occupying three distinct moments: preparation, writing proper, editing. If you have found your writing a problem or your grades not reflecting your true ability, you might want to try the method outlined here.

EXAMPLES OF TOPICS YOU MIGHT WANT TO CONSIDER

General topics

If you don't want something that sounds too prescriptive, you might like to consider some of the following suggestions.

1. Look again at the titles listed in the Chronology. Because the Chronology separates out various forms of writing, texts can be read synchronically (across a decade for example) or diachronically (by genre through time as it were). You might want to investigate how a group of texts published at the same time tackle a similar theme or in what other ways they belong together.

2. Or you might take a different approach and do some research into texts within a particular genre. Autobiographies, for example, provide a rich seam for the student of modern Irish writing. Read a selection of the autobiographies (say three or four) and see if you can begin to notice common themes, or how they tackle particular moments (rites of passage for example or a death in the family), or how a public history enters the text. Is history offstage or central to the autobiography? In what ways does the autobiography you are reading tell you something about the period it is set in or the period when it was written? Think too about structural considerations. How does the autobiography begin and end? What are its salient features? Is there a theme or pattern running through the book?

3. The historical novel is another area you might like to explore. There are many novels listed in the Chronology that belong to this particular genre. Begin gathering information. Try drawing up a list of novels, their date of publication, the period dealt with. To get you thinking see the list reproduced below from James Cahalan, *Great Hatred, Little Room: The Irish Historical Novel* (1983). Thomas Flanagan's *The Year of the French* deals with the 1798 Rising, Liam O'Flaherty's *Famine* with the Great Famine of the 1840s, James Plunkett's *Strumpet City* with the Dublin working class and poor in the years leading up to the Great Lock-Out in 1913. Read some more historical novels and add to the list accordingly. In addition, draw up a series of questions that you want to answer. What events or historical figures are writers at a given period drawn to? To give your study a sharper focus, you might like to consider this in relation to novels written in the 1930s say. I am thinking here of the rise of the Irish bourgeoisie in the nineteenth century and how this is portrayed in the work of Sean O'Faolain's *A Nest of Simple Folk* (1933) or Kate O'Brien's *Without My Cloak* (1931). How do historical novelists portray their chosen period? A related question is: How adequately or otherwise

Author and title	Date	Period dealt with	Years of retrospect
J. Banim, *The Boyne Water*	1820	c. 1685–95	137
M. Banim, *The Croppy*	1828	1798	30
J. Banim, *The Last Baron of Crana*	1830	c. 1690–1720	140
J. Banim, *The Conformists*	1830	c. 1750–60	80
Le Fanu, *Torlough O'Brien*	1847	c. 1689–91	158
Carleton, *Redmond Count O'Hanlon*	1862	c. 1696–1700	192
O'Grady, *Ulrick The Ready*	1896	c. 1598–1602	298
O'Grady, *The Flight of The Eagle*	1897	c. 1587–91	310
Buckley, *Croppies Lie Down*	1903	1798	105
O'Faolain, *A Nest Of Simple Folk*	1933	1854–1916	79
MacManus, *Candle For The Proud*	1934	c. 1740–50	194
MacManus, *Stand And Give Challenge*	1936	c. 1750–70	186
O'Flaherty, *Famine*	1937	c. 1845–49	92
MacManus, *Men Withering*	1939	c. 1770–98	169
O'Flaherty, *Land*	1946	c. 1880–85	64
O'Flaherty, *Insurrection*	1950	1916	34
Macken, *Seek The Fair Land*	1959	c. 1649–55	310
Ó Tuairisc, *L'Attaque*	1962	1798	164
Macken, *The Silent People*	1962	c. 1826–47	136
Macken, *The Scorching Wind*	1964	c. 1916–22	48
Murdoch, *The Red and The Green*	1965	1916	49
Plunkett, *Strumpet City*	1969	1907–14	62
Dillon, *Across The Bitter Sea*	1973	1851–1916	122
Dillon, *Blood Relations*	1977	c. 1916–24	61
Flanagan, *The Year of the French*	1979	1798	181

do historical novelists portray their chosen period? In what ways (if at all) do they complicate a known story or a familiar picture? Another ideological tack would be to inquire into how historical novels reflect the period in which they were written.

4. In the Bibliography I have begun collecting titles to anthologies of verse, short stories, plays. I have for many years been collecting anthologies of Irish writing and thought at one time I might be able to provide an exhaustive list, but it proved beyond me. There are several tasks you might like to perform here. You might begin by looking at the general discussion on anthologies, the issue of coverage, and possible research activity, in a chapter entitled 'The Woman Author: Lost and Found' in Mary Eagleton's *Working with Feminist Criticism* (1996). How might some of the questions raised by Eagleton apply to Irish writing? The issue of publishing and marketing Irish writers is always a live issue. Who's selling what to whom through whom? What groups of writers are pushed to the foreground? Who gets left out? Think too about the

point made by Eiléan Ní Chuilleanáin in that anthologies 'reinforce the curriculum and promote a monolithic orthodoxy' (*Cyphers* 35 Spring 1992). It is worth undertaking some detailed work in this area. Resist the temptation to be satisfied with the easy position, as for example that the commercial world has its own values, hostile to literature. Perhaps take a viewpoint that you want to support in some way by evidence, as for example that women writers are regularly ignored in anthologies, or that the British market has played a crucial if detrimental role in what's published in Ireland. How might you go about proving your case? Compare and contrast the governing principles behind a selection of anthologies. Which poems or authors are regularly selected? Take an anthology of verse from five different decades and identify major differences and similarities. Why do you think there are so many anthologies of Irish verse?

5. Little magazines. As is apparent from this *Reader*, the first appearance of a particular work in modern Irish writing frequently came via little magazines.

You might like to do some research into these literary journals. Take one specific title and begin by tracing its career and development. Outline its primary concerns, its attitude towards modern writing, its bias towards writers and which forms of writing. The first issue often includes a mission statement (such as *Atlantis* in 1970) and these can be compared with what the magazine in fact achieved. Some of these magazines have indexes (some now available on the Web) and these should be consulted to save time. Some such as the early years of *The Crane Bag* were later reprinted in book form.

6. Creative writing. Use a particular extract as the starting-point for your own imaginative writing. Ask your tutor for guidance. See if you can secure a publishing outlet for your effort.

Specific topics

Below are a series of more specific questions to help you collect your thoughts on modern Irish writing. You might be interested in working your way through some of them.

1. 'Every culture invents its future by reinventing its past.' To what extent is this true of modern Irish writing?

2. Critically explore the portrayal of Irish identity in one or more texts from this *Reader*.

3. Write an essay exploring attitudes to violence.

4. Compare and contrast the depiction of masculinity.

5. 'His language, so familiar and so foreign, will always be for me an acquired speech. I have not made or accepted its words. My voice holds them at bay. My soul frets in the shadow of his language (Joyce's *A Portrait*). In what ways is language an issue in modern Irish writing? Discuss with reference to one or two writers.

6. Compare and contrast two writers in their contribution to the Irish comic tradition.

7. 'The Revivalist project was to renew the link with tradition in order to rescue Ireland from spiritual homelessness and colonial dependency.' Discuss with reference to one or more writers studied.

8. Write an essay exploring the evocation of childhood in the work of one or more writers in this *Reader*.

9. Critically explore the response of Irish writers to the recent 'troubles' in the North of Ireland? Discuss with reference to one or two writers.

10. 'Irish culture, now, and for the last one hundred years, has been preoccupied with the question of continuity, and this at a time when it seems that the idea of continuity and the related one of community are cracking up irremediably.' Discuss with particular reference to one or more writers.

11. 'The emotional climate of the Irish short story is one where passion and encounter are matters of fleeting privacies, where disillusionment dogs individual hope and disappointment enforces bitter submission.' Critically examine three short stories in the light of this remark.

12. Analyse the role and treatment of the father in one or more texts studied in this *Reader*.

13. 'The notion that Irishness is simply an amalgam of Nationalist, Catholic and rural concerns cannot be supported by even the most cursory reading of contemporary Irish poetry.' Discuss with detailed reference to the work of one or more writers studied.

14. Assess the relationship between writing and politics in one or more extracts from this *Reader*.

15. 'The personification of Ireland as a woman . . . is a function of the patriarchal opposition between male Culture and female Nature, which defines women as the passive and silent embodiments of matter.' Evaluate the representation of women in one or more studied in the light of this remark.

16. 'The ability to engage with the day-to-day experiences of a community is simultaneously the greatest strength and the defining limitation of much twentieth-century Irish writing.' Discuss.

17. 'A sixty-year-old smiling public man' (Yeats's view of himself in 'Among School Children'). Analyse the tension between private and public history in one or more extracts studied.

18. 'Irish writers give us access to the minutiae of the everyday in order to expose the processes by which place becomes a facet of identity.' Critically examine the relationship of place and identity in one or more works studied in the light of this remark.

19. Examine the ways in which writers have constructed a distinctively Irish idiom in one or more texts studied.

20. 'Far from debunking the myth of the West, many modern writers seem to have striven to maintain the fiction that the West of Ireland is the sole location of authentically Irish values and beliefs.' Discuss.

21. 'The modern literature of Ireland, and indeed all that stir of thought which prepared for the Anglo-Irish war, began when Parnell fell from power in 1891.' Assess the ways in which the fall of Parnell may be said to inform Irish literature of the early twentieth century. (This is a large topic, perhaps best answered as a long project.)

22. Critically explore the role that literature has played in the development (or otherwise) of an Irish national identity.

23. How do modern Irish writers make use of songs in their work?

24. 'Out of Ireland have we come. / Great hatred, little room, / Maimed us at the start. / I carry from my mother's womb / A fanatic heart.' To what extent can Yeats's lines from 'Remorse for Intemperate Speech' be applied to contemporary Irish writing?

25. What strategies have Irish writers adopted in their work to counter the presence of Britain in Ireland?

26. Critically explore the relationship between gender and nationality in any two extracts from this *Reader*.

27. Write an essay critically exploring the theme of dispossession in modern Irish literature.

28. Compare and contrast the evocation of rural Ireland in a selection of poems and/or short stories.

29. 'At the heart of modern Irish drama is a conflict or tension between modernity and traditional society.' Discuss with specific reference to two plays from this *Reader*.

30. Write an essay exploring your first impressions of the 'Penelope' extract from *Ulysses*.

31. Write an essay exploring the contribution of modern Irish writing to the development of modernism.

32. Write an essay exploring the visual impact of modern Irish writing. (Take two or more texts for comparison.)

33. Re-read the extracts from *Ulysses* in this *Reader* and write an essay either on the theme of faithfulness *or* on the incorporation of the past into the present.

34. 'It is not the literal past, the "facts" of history, that shape us, but the images of the past embodied in language' (Friel's *Translations*). Discuss with reference to two or more writers selected from this *Reader*.

35. Outline what you consider to be some characteristic tensions in modern Irish writing.

36. 'Any country developing culturally as rapidly as Ireland is bound to produce interesting writing' (*Irish Times* commentator in 1996). Discuss.

37. Trace some responses in modern Irish writing to Matthew Arnold's feminization of the Celt.

38. 'We Irish writers are more concerned with defining our Irishness than with pursuing it' (Friel). Discuss.

39. 'Beckett, despite his background and early devotion to Joyce, is at once the least and yet the most intensely Irish of writers, redefining as much as confirming what it means to be a modern Irish writer.' Discuss.

40. What contribution can or does Irish writing make to an understanding of postcolonial theory?

41. Write an assignment exploring the depiction of father-son or mother-daughter relationships in any two texts from modern Irish literature.

42. 'It is one of the findings of Ireland's dual tradition

that an empire is a passing thing, but that a colony is not' (Kinsella). Discuss.

43. 'Irishness is a form of anti-art. A way of posing as a poet without actually being one' (Kavanagh). Discuss.

44. 'Can we as women write the slave blood out of ourselves? To live in Ireland is to have a continual, urgent presentiment of what those words mean' (Eavan Boland, 1982). Discuss.

45. 'One of the continuing tragedies of Ireland over centuries is that the conditions for sustaining corporate memory have been destroyed' (Vincent Buckley). Discuss.

46. 'It is only those few writers capable of imagining alternative societies who can enter into a serious and mutually advantageous relationship with their own.' Discuss.

47. 'Lost, unhappy, and at home.' In what ways is Heaney's fate shared by other Irish writers? You may restrict your answer to one particular writer.

48. 'The first-rate writers of Ireland, the Joyces, Synges and O'Caseys, side-stepped the cliché of the all-powerful Irish mother and resolved to examine the deeper underlying problem of the inadequate Irish male' (Declan Kiberd). Discuss.

49. 'The religious instinct is a permanent feature of Irish writing and seems designed to sharpen the sense of the here and now' (Robert Welch). Discuss.

50. To what extent or in what ways do writers from the Irish diaspora belong to the tradition of Irish literature?

CHRONOLOGY

The Chronology is designed to provide a handy but by no means exhaustive checklist of some of the more important publications and events in Irish writing in the twentieth century. In addition, under the Miscellaneous column I have included films and CDs, as well as biographies and critical works of note. Against each year I have indicated one or two events from the political or social arenas to give an idea of the flavour of the period. After 1970 I have devoted more space to the unfolding of events in Northern Ireland, but my primary focus has been on what happened on the cultural front, on the practical contexts and material conditions under which Irish writing has taken place: the establishment of new theatres, developments in the publishing world, founding of new journals, the promotion of awards and outlets for Irish writers, changes in the media, censorship, and so on. For more authoritative guides to Irish history, see among others, J. J. Lee, *Ireland 1912-1985: Politics and Society* (1989); Jonathan Bardon, *A History of Ulster* (1992); S. J. Connolly, *The Oxford Companion to Irish History* (1998); David Fitzpatrick, *The Two Irelands 1912-1939* (1998) (which includes a chronology). For a chronology of 'The Troubles' see Paul Bew and Gordon Gillespie, *Northern Ireland: A Chronology of the Troubles 1968-1999* (1999). *The Irish Times Book of the Century* by Fintan O'Toole (1999) provides the ideal accompaniment to the chronology below and will help not only in giving you a taste of Irish history but also in filling in and clarifying many of the contexts, gaps and shorthand notes.

Fiction	Poetry	Drama	Autobiography	Miscellaneous

1900: Boer War. Queen Victoria's visit to Dublin. D.P. Moran launches *The Leader*. First issue of *All Ireland Review*, edited by Standish O'Grady in Kilkenny.

Fiction	Poetry	Drama	Autobiography	Miscellaneous
Arthur Conan Doyle, *The Green Flag*	T.W. Rolleston and Stopford Brooke, *Treasury of Irish Poetry*			Finley Peter Dunne, *Mr Dooley's Philosophy*
Canon Sheehan, *My New Curate*				

1901: Death of Queen Victoria.

Fiction	Poetry	Drama	Autobiography	Miscellaneous
	Moira O'Neill, *Songs of the Glens of Antrim*	An Craoibhín Aoibhinn (Douglas Hyde), *Casadh an tSúgáin*		Lady Gregory ed., *Ideals in Ireland*

1902: End of Boer War. Dun Emer Press (later the Cuala Press) founded by Yeats's sisters. Ulster Literary Theatre founded by Bulmer Hobson and David Parkhill. T.P. O'Connor launches *T.P.'s Weekly*. *Ireland's Own* founded by Edward O'Cullen.

Fiction	Poetry	Drama	Autobiography	Miscellaneous
		W.B. Yeats, *Cathleen ni Houlihan*		John Eglinton, 'The De-Davisisation of Irish Literature'
				Lady Gregory, *Cuchulain of Muirthemne*

1903: Wyndham Land Act. Patrick Pearse edits *An Claidheamh Soluis* (Sword of Light). Irish Folk Song Society founded under inspiration of A.P. Graves and Charlotte Fox.

Fiction	Poetry	Drama	Autobiography	Miscellaneous
Shan Bullock, *The Squireen*	W.B. Yeats, *In the Seven Woods*	John Millington Synge, *In the Shadow of the Glen*		Lady Gregory, *Poets and Dreamers*

Fiction	Poetry	Drama	Autobiography	Miscellaneous
Joseph Furphy, *Such Is Life*				Francis O'Neill, *The Music of Ireland*
George Moore, *The Untilled Field*				Katharine Tynan Hinkson ed., *The Cabinet of Irish Literature*, 4 vols

1904: Launch of *Dana: A Magazine of Independent Thought,* edited by Fred Ryan and John Eglinton. Abbey Theatre founded. First issue of the *Journal of the Irish Folk Song Society*, edited by Charlotte Fox.

Fiction	Poetry	Drama	Autobiography	Miscellaneous
	Eva Gore-Booth, *The One and the Many*	Lady Gregory, *Spreading the News*		Fr Dinneen, *Foclóir Gaedhilge agus Béarla: An Irish-English Dictionary*
	Æ (George Russell) ed., *New Songs*	George Bernard Shaw, *John Bull's Other Island*		Arthur Griffith, *The Resurrection of Hungary*
		John Millington Synge, *Riders to the Sea*		Justin McCarthy ed., *Irish Literature,* 10 vols
		W.B. Yeats, *On Baile's Strand*		Horace Plunkett, *Ireland in the New Century*

1905: Arthur Griffith founds Sinn Féin. *Irish Independent* established by William Murphy. Maunsel & Company founded by George Roberts, Stephen Gwynn and Joseph Maunsel Hone. *Uladh*, a Belfast literary magazine, founded, edited by G.M. Reynolds.

Fiction	Poetry	Drama	Autobiography	Miscellaneous
George Moore, *The Lake*	James Joyce, 'The Holy Office'	Padraic Colum, *The Land*		D.P. Moran, *The Philosophy of Irish Ireland*
Canon Sheehan, *Glenanaar*	Oscar Wilde, *De Profundis*	George Bernard Shaw, *Man and Superman* and *Major Barbara*		
		John Millington Synge, *The Well of the Saints*		

1906: First issue of Griffith's *Sinn Féin.*

Fiction	Poetry	Drama	Autobiography	Miscellaneous
		William Boyle, *The Eloquent Dempsey*		John Eglinton, *Bards and Saints*
		Lady Gregory, *The Gaol Gate*		Frederick Ryan, *Criticism and Courage and Other Essays*
				The Story of the Kelly Gang (Australian film)

Fiction	Poetry	Drama	Autobiography	Miscellaneous

1907: *Playboy* riots at Abbey Theatre. Belfast Dock Strike. *Ne Temere* Papal Decree.

Fiction	Poetry	Drama	Autobiography	Miscellaneous
George A. Birmingham, *The Northern Iron*	Joseph Campbell, *The Gilly of Chris*	George Fitzmaurice, *The Country Dressmaker*		William Bulfin, *Rambles in Eirinn*
Canon Sheehan, *Lisheen*	James Joyce, *Chamber Music*	Lady Gregory, *The Rising of the Moon*		John Millington Synge, *The Aran Islands*
		John Millington Synge, *The Playboy of the Western World*		
		W.B. Yeats, *Deirdre*		

1908: Old Age Pensions Act. National University of Ireland established. The Municipal Gallery of Modern Art opens in Dublin. Shaw's *Blanco Posnet* staged at the Abbey amid controversy over government censorship. Cork Dramatic Society founded by Daniel Corkery and Terence MacSwiney. Irish Women's Franchise League founded by Hannah and Francis Sheehy-Skeffington.

Fiction	Poetry	Drama	Autobiography	Miscellaneous
George A. Birmingham, *Spanish Gold*		George Fitzmaurice, *The Pie-Dish*		Susan Mitchell, *Aids to the Immortality of Certain Persons in Ireland Charitably Administered*
		Lady Gregory, *The Workhouse Ward*		
		Lennox Robinson, *The Clancy Name*		W.B. Yeats, *Collected Works*

1909: First issue of the *Irish Booklover*, edited by J.S. Crone. Irish Transport and General Workers' Union founded in Dublin under leadership of Jim Larkin. The Volta (first cinema in Ireland) opens in Dublin.

Fiction	Poetry	Drama	Autobiography	Miscellaneous
	Joseph Campbell, *The Mountainy Singer*	Lady Gregory, *Seven Short Plays*		Jane Barlow, *Irish Ways*
	James Stephens, *Insurrections*	Seamus O'Kelly, *The Shuiler's Child*		P.W. Joyce, *Old Irish Folk Music and Songs*
		George Bernard Shaw, *The Shewing-up of Blanco Posnet*		

1910: Irish made compulsory matriculation subject for National University. Liberal victory at General Election.

Fiction	Poetry	Drama	Autobiography	Miscellaneous
Pádraic Ó Conaire, *Deoraíocht* (Exile)	W.B. Yeats, *The Green Helmet and Other Poems*	Padraic Colum, *Thomas Muskerry*		James Connolly, *Labour in Irish History*
		T.C. Murray, *Birthright*		P.W. Joyce, *English as We Speak It in Ireland*

1911: Home Rule Bill introduced into House of Commons. Agitation in North against Home Rule. *The Irish Review* launched by Padraic Colum, Thomas MacDonagh, James Stephens, and David Houston.

Fiction	Poetry	Drama	Autobiography	Miscellaneous
	J.M. Synge, *Poems and Translations*	St John Ervine, *Mixed Marriage*	William Butler, *An Autobiography*	George A. Birmingham, *The Lighter Side of Irish Life*

Fiction	Poetry	Drama	Autobiography	Miscellaneous
		Lady Gregory, *The Deliverer*	George Moore, *Hail and Farewell* (1911–14)	Joseph Campbell, *The Mearing Stones*

1912: Third Home Rule Bill and Ulster Rebellion. Ulster Volunteers formed. Sinking of the *Titanic* (built in Belfast). *Irish Citizen* founded and edited by the Sheehy Skeffingtons and others.

Fiction	Poetry	Drama	Autobiography	Miscellaneous
George A. Birmingham, *The Red Hand of Ulster*	Seamas O'Sullivan, *Collected Poems*	T.C. Murray, *Maurice Harte*		W.P. Ryan, *The Pope's Green Island*
James Stephens, *The Charwoman's Daughter* and *The Crock of Gold*		George Bernard Shaw, *Pygmalion*		

1913: Third Home Rule Bill passed in Commons, rejected in Lords. The Great Lockout in Dublin led by William Martin Murphy. Irish Volunteers formed. Irish Citizen Army founded by James Connolly.

Fiction	Poetry	Drama	Autobiography	Miscellaneous
George A. Birmingham, *General John Regan*	Joseph Campbell, *Irishry*	George Fitzmaurice, *The Magic Glasses*	Katharine Tynan, *Twenty-Five Years*	George A. Birmingham, *Irishmen All*
Alexander Irvine, *My Lady of the Chimney Corner*	Patrick MacGill, *Songs of the Dead End*	Seamas O'Kelly, *The Bribe*		
Gerald O'Donovan, *Father Ralph*	George Russell, *Collected Poems*			

1914: Third Home Rule Bill gets its third reading and is passed in August but is then suspended because of outbreak of Great War. The Irish Theatre launched by Edward Martyn, Thomas MacDonagh, and Joseph Mary Plunkett. Gun-running by Ulster Volunteers. Irish Volunteers land guns at Howth. Launch of Gaelic Athletic Association of New York.

Fiction	Poetry	Drama	Autobiography	Miscellaneous
James Joyce, *Dubliners*	Christopher Brennan, *Poems 1913*	Lord Dunsany, *Five Plays*	Wilfrid Scawen Blunt, *My Diaries*	*A Long, Long Way to Tipperary* (Australian film by George Dean)
Patrick MacGill, *Children of the Dead End*	Patrick Pearse, *Suantraide agus Goltraide (Songs of Sleep and Sorrow)*	George Fitzmaurice, *Five Plays*		
Gerald O'Donovan, *Waiting*	W.B. Yeats, *Responsibilities*			

1915: Sinking of the *Lusitania*. Body of Fenian veteran Jeremiah O'Donovan Rossa returned to Ireland.

Fiction	Poetry	Drama	Autobiography	Miscellaneous
Lord Dunsany, *Fifty-One Tales*	Francis Ledwidge, *Songs of the Field*	St John Ervine, *John Ferguson*	Peter O'Leary, *Mo Sgéal Féin (My Story)*	Stephen J. Brown, *Ireland in Fiction*
	James Stephens, *Songs from the Clay*		W.B. Yeats, *Reveries Over Childhood and Youth*	Stephen Gwynn, *The Famous Cities of Ireland*

Fiction	Poetry	Drama	Autobiography	Miscellaneous

1916: Easter Rising, followed by executions of its leaders. Battle of the Somme. Trial and execution of Roger Casement.

Fiction	Poetry	Drama	Autobiography	Miscellaneous
Daniel Corkery, *A Munster Twilight*	Padraic Colum, *Wild Earth*	Lennox Robinson, *The White-headed Boy*		E.A. Boyd, *Ireland's Literary Renaissance*
James Joyce, *A Portrait of the Artist as a Young Man*	Katharine Tynan, *The Holy War*			Shane Leslie, *The End of the Chapter*
				Thomas MacDonagh, *Literature in Ireland*
George Moore, *The Brook Kerith*				George Russell, *The National Being*
				James Stephens, *The Insurrection in Dublin*

1917: De Valera elected President of Sinn Féin and Irish Volunteers. America enters the War. Russian Revolution.

Fiction	Poetry	Drama	Autobiography	Miscellaneous
Daniel Corkery, *The Threshold of Quiet*	Austin Clarke, *The Vengeance of Fionn*			Darrell Figgis, *A Chronicle of Jails*
	Francis Ledwidge, *Songs of Peace*			Seamas O'Sullivan, *Mud and Purple*
	Patrick MacGill, *Soldier Songs*			Patrick Pearse, *Complete Works*
	W.B. Yeats, *The Wild Swans at Coole* (Cuala Press)			

1918: Extension of the Franchise to include women. Agitation in Ireland against conscription. 'German plot' held against Irish leaders. Armistice in November marks end of Great War. Sinn Féin electoral triumph.

Fiction	Poetry	Drama	Autobiography	Miscellaneous
Lynn Doyle, *Ballygullion*	Eimar O'Duffy, *A Lay of the Liffey*	James Joyce, *Exiles*		George Russell, *The Candle of Vision*
Brinsley MacNamara, *The Valley of the Squinting Windows*	James Stephens, *Reincarnations*	Lennox Robinson, *The Lost Leader*		
		Katharine Tynan, *Herb O'Grace*		
William O'Brien, *When We Were Boys*				

1919: Dáil Éireann established. War of Independence 1919-21. Dublin Drama League founded by Robinson, Yeats, and Stephens.

Fiction	Poetry	Drama	Autobiography	Miscellaneous
Eimar O'Duffy, *The Wasted Island*	Francis Ledwidge, *Complete Poems*			Darrell Figgis, *A Second Chronicle of Jails*
Seamus O'Kelly, *The Golden Barque and the Weaver's Grave*				Sean O'Casey, *The Story of the Irish Citizen Army*

Fiction	Poetry	Drama	Autobiography	Miscellaneous

1920: Anti-Catholic riots in Belfast. Terence MacSwiney, Lord Mayor of Cork, dies on hunger strike in Brixton Prison. Thirteen men killed by IRA in Dublin, eleven of whom were British intelligence officers; reprisal killing of twelve people at football match in Croke Park by Auxiliaries. Government of Ireland Act divides Ireland in two.

Fiction	Poetry	Drama	Autobiography	Miscellaneous
Daniel Corkery, *The Hounds of Banba*				Lady Gregory, *Visions and Beliefs in the West of Ireland*
F. Scott Fitzgerald, *This Side of Paradise*				
Brinsley MacNamara, *The Clanking of Chains*				
Séamus Ó Grianna, *Mo Dhá Róisín*				
Conal O'Riordan, *Adam of Dublin*				

1921: Intensification of War of Independence leads to Anglo-Irish Treaty in December.

Fiction	Poetry	Drama	Autobiography	Miscellaneous
George Moore, *Héloïse and Abelard*	John O'Brien, *Around the Boree Log*	George Bernard Shaw, *Heartbreak House*		Seamas MacManus, *The Story of the Irish Race*
Gerald O'Donovan, *Vocations*	L.A.G. Strong, *Dublin Days*	George Shiels, *Bedmates*		
	W.B. Yeats, *Michael Robartes and the Dancer*	W.B. Yeats, *Four Plays for Dancers*		

1922: Civil War 1922-23. New Senate meets. RUC officially established. Eugene O'Neill wins Pulitzer Prize with *Anna Christie*.

Fiction	Poetry	Drama	Autobiography	Miscellaneous
Darrell Figgis, *The House of Success*	W.B. Yeats, *Later Poems*	Lennox Robinson, *Crabbed Youth and Age*		
James Joyce, *Ulysses*				
George Russell, *The Interpreters*				

1923: Continuing internment of republicans. Censorship of films introduced under Free State Law. W.B. Yeats wins Nobel Prize. *Dublin Magazine* founded by Seamas O'Sullivan. George Russell assumes editorship of *The Irish Statesman*.

Fiction	Poetry	Drama	Autobiography	Miscellaneous
Con O'Leary, *An Exile's Bundle*	Oliver St John Gogarty, *An Offering of Swans*	Brinsley MacNamara, *The Glorious Uncertainty*	Frank Harris, *My Life and Loves* (1923-1930)	George Russell, 'The Lessons of Revolution'
		Sean O'Casey, *The Shadow of a Gunman*		
		George Bernard Shaw, *Saint Joan, Back to Methusaleh*		

Fiction	Poetry	Drama	Autobiography	Miscellaneous

1924: Boundary Commission meets. BBC establishes a broadcasting station in Belfast. *Tomorrow*, edited by Francis Stuart and Cecil Salkeld, launched.

Fiction	Poetry	Drama	Autobiography	Miscellaneous
Shan F. Bullock, *The Loughsiders*	F.R. Higgins, *Salt Air*	T.C. Murray, *Autumn Fire*	William Orpen, *Old Ireland and Myself*	Daniel Corkery, *The Hidden Ireland*
F. Scott Fitzgerald, 'Absolution'		Sean O'Casey, *Juno and the 'Paycock'*		
Dorothy Macardle, *Earth-Bound*				
Liam O'Flaherty, *Spring Sowing* and *The Black Soul*				
Séamus Ó Grianna, *Caisleáin Óir* (Castles of Gold)				

1925: Divorce proposals rejected by Senate. George Bernard Shaw wins Nobel Prize for Literature.

Fiction	Poetry	Drama	Autobiography	Miscellaneous
Donn Byrne, *Hangman's House*			Walter McDonald, *Reminiscences of a Maynooth Professor*	W.B. Yeats, *A Vision*
S.R. Lysaght, *My Tower in Desmond*				
Liam O'Flaherty, *The Informer*				
Edith Somerville, *The Big House at Inver*				

1926: De Valera founds Fianna Fáil. Radió Éireann begins broadcasting.

Fiction	Poetry	Drama	Autobiography	Miscellaneous
Eimar O'Duffy, *King Goshawk and the Birds*	T.F. O'Rahilly, ed., *Dánta Grádha*	Brinsley MacNamara, *Look at the Heffernans!*	Forrest Reid, *Apostate*	Harold Speakman, *Here's Ireland*
Liam O'Flaherty, *The Tent* and *Mr Gilhooley*		Sean O'Casey, *The Plough and the Stars*	W.B. Yeats, *Autobiographies*	
Maurice Walsh, *The Key Above The Door*		Lennox Robinson, *The Big House*		

1927: An Taibhdhearc, an Irish-language theatre founded by Séamus Ó Beirn, opens in Galway. *Béaloideas*, journal of the Folklore of Ireland Society, launched, edited by Séamus Ó Duilearga (James Delargy). Quota Press founded by Dora Kennedy. Electricity Supply Board established. Kevin O'Higgins, Minister of Justice, assassinated.

Fiction	Poetry	Drama	Autobiography	Miscellaneous
Peadar O'Donnell, *Islanders*	F.R. Higgins, *The Dark Breed*			
	James Joyce, *Pomes Penyeach*			

Fiction	Poetry	Drama	Autobiography	Miscellaneous

1928: Gate Theatre opens under direction of Micheál Mac Liammóir and Hilton Edwards. Abbey Theatre rejects O'Casey's *The Silver Tassie*. Eugene O'Neill wins Pulitzer Prize with *Strange Interlude*. *Irish Post* newspaper launched in New York by Charles Connolly.

Fiction	Poetry	Drama	Autobiography	Miscellaneous
Norah Hoult, *Poor Women*	W.B. Yeats, *The Tower*	Sean O'Casey, *The Silver Tassie*	Frank Gallagher, *Days of Fear*	John S. Crone, *A Concise Dictionary of Irish Biography*
James Joyce, *Anna Livia Plurabelle*				
Liam O'Flaherty, *The Assassin*				
James Stephens, *Etched in Moonlight*				
Maurice Walsh, *While Rivers Run*				

1929: Censorship of Publications Act. Shannon hydro–electric scheme begins.

Fiction	Poetry	Drama	Autobiography	Miscellaneous
Elizabeth Bowen, *The Last September*	Austin Clarke, *Pilgrimage and Other Poems*	Denis Johnston, *The Old Lady Says 'No!'*	P.L. Dickinson, *The Dublin of Yesterday*	Samuel Beckett et al., *Our Exagmination Round the Factification for Incamination of Work in Progess*
Seosamh Mac Grianna, *An Grá agus An Ghruaim*			Tomás Ó Criomhthain (O'Crohan), *An An tOileánach* (The Islandman)	
Brinsley MacNamara, *The Various Lives of Marcus Igoe*				Donn Byrne, *Ireland: The Rock Whence I Was Hewn*
Henry Handel Richardson, *Ultima Thule*				*The Informer* (film by Arthur Robison)
Peadar O'Donnell, *Adrigoole*				

1930: Free State elected to League of Nations.

Fiction	Poetry	Drama	Autobiography	Miscellaneous
Peadar O'Donnell, *The Knife*	Brian Coffey with Denis Devlin, *Poems*	Austin Clarke, *The Flame*	Liam O'Flaherty, *Two Years*	*Song of My Heart* (film by Frank Borzage with John McCormack)
Henry Handel Richardson, *The Fortunes of Richard Mahony*				
L.A.G. Strong, *Northern Lights*				

1931: First number of the *Irish Press* (de Valera's newspaper). Muintir na Tíre (People of the land) founded by Fr John Hayes.

Fiction	Poetry	Drama	Autobiography	Miscellaneous
Kate O'Brien, *Without My Cloak*		Denis Johnston, *The Moon in Yellow River*	Shan F. Bullock, *After Sixty Years*	Daniel Corkery, *Synge and Anglo-Irish Literature*

Fiction	Poetry	Drama	Autobiography	Miscellaneous
Frank O'Connor, *Guests of the Nation*		Lennox Robinson, *The Far-off Hills*		*Public Enemy* (Cagney film)
Liam O'Flaherty, *The Puritan*		W.B. Yeats, *The Dreaming of the Bones*		
L.A.G. Strong, *The Garden*				

1932: Fianna Fáil, led by de Valera, wins general election (in power until 1948). Irish Academy of Letters founded by Yeats, Russell and Shaw. Eucharistic Congress in Dublin.

Fiction	Poetry	Drama	Autobiography	Miscellaneous
Joyce Cary, *Aissa Saved*	Frank O'Connor, *The Wild Bird's Nest: Poems from the Irish*	Teresa Deevy, *Temporal Powers*	Peadar O'Donnell, *The Gates Flew Open*	
Austin Clarke, *The Bright Temptation*				
Frank O'Connor, *The Saint and Mary Kate*				
Sean O'Faolain, *Midsummer Night Madness*				
Liam O'Flaherty, *Skerrett*				

1933: Fine Gael party formed. The Blueshirts are banned.

Fiction	Poetry	Drama	Autobiography	Miscellaneous
Lord Dunsany, *The Curse of the Wise Woman*	Blanaid Salkeld, *Hello, Eternity!*	Brinsley MacNamara, *Margaret Gillan*	Maurice O'Sullivan, *Fiche Blian ag Fás (Twenty Years A-Growing)*	
George Russell, *The Avatars*	W.B. Yeats, *The Winding Stair*	Eugene O'Neill, *Days Without End*		
Patrick Slater, *The Yellow Briar*		Lennox Robinson, *Drama At Inish*		

1934: Lord Craigavon refers to Northern Ireland as 'a Protestant Parliament and a Protestant State'.

Fiction	Poetry	Drama	Autobiography	Miscellaneous
Samuel Beckett, *More Pricks than Kicks*	Thomas MacGreevy, *Poems*	Rutherford Mayne, *Bridgehead*	Liam O'Flaherty, *Shame the Devil*	'Andrew Belis' (Samuel Beckett), 'Recent Irish Poetry'
Molly Keane, *Devoted Ladies*		W.B. Yeats, *The Words Upon the Window Pane*	Pat O'Mara, *The Autobiography of a Liverpool Irish Slummy*	Robert Flaherty's film *Man of Aran*
Patricia Lynch, *The Turf Cutter's Donkey*				Esther Roper, ed., *Prison Letters of Countess Markievicz*
Kate O'Brien, *The Ante-Room*				
Sean O'Faolain, *A Nest of Simple Folk*				
John O'Hara, *BUtterfield 8*				

Fiction	Poetry	Drama	Autobiography	Miscellaneous

1935: Irish Folklore Commission established. Public Dance Halls Act. Sale of contraceptives prohibited.

Fiction	Poetry	Drama	Autobiography	Miscellaneous
James T. Farrell, *Studs Lonigan: A Trilogy*	Samuel Beckett, *Echo's Bones*	Teresa Deevy, *The King of Spain's Daughter*		John Eglinton, *Irish Literary Portraits*
Nora Hoult, *Holy Ireland*	Louis MacNeice, *Poems*			Monk Gibbon, *The Seals*
John O'Hara, *Appointment in Samara*				*The Informer* (film by John Ford)

1936: Spanish Civil War prompts support for both sides in Ireland. Eugene O'Neill receives Nobel Prize. *Ireland To-Day* launched, edited by Michael O'Donovan (Frank O'Connor).

Fiction	Poetry	Drama	Autobiography	Miscellaneous
Joyce Cary, *The African Witch*	Patrick Kavanagh, *Ploughman and Other Poems*	Teresa Deevy, *Katie Roche*	Peig Sayers, *Peig*	*The Plough and the Stars* (film by John Ford with Barry Fitzgerald as Fluther)
Joseph F. Dinneen, *Ward Eight*		Eugene O'Neill, *A Touch of the Poet* (first performed 1958)		
Miles Franklin, *All That Swagger*				
Kate O'Brien, *Mary Lavelle*				
Frank O'Connor, *Bones of Contention*				
Sean O'Faolain, *Bird Alone*				

1937: De Valera's new constitution approved.

Fiction	Poetry	Drama	Autobiography	Miscellaneous
Olivia Manning, *The Wind Changes*	Denis Devlin, *Intercessions*	Paul Vincent Carroll, *Shadow and Substance*	Oliver St John Gogarty, *As I Was Going Down Sackville Street*	Conrad Arensberg, *The Irish Countryman*
Liam O'Flaherty, *Famine* and *The Short Stories of Liam O'Flaherty*			Maud Wynne, *One Man and His Family*	Kate O'Brien, *Farewell Spain*
Forrest Reid, *Peter Waring*				Robert Lloyd Praeger, *The Way that I Went*

1938: End of economic war between Britain and Ireland. Douglas Hyde becomes first President of Éire (holds office until 1945). First issue of *Hibernia*. Ulster Group Theatre founded by Joseph Tomelty and others. Dublin Verse-Speaking Society founded by Austin Clarke and Robert Farren. Munich crisis.

Fiction	Poetry	Drama	Autobiography	Miscellaneous
Samuel Beckett, *Murphy*	Austin Clarke, *Night and Morning*	W.B. Yeats, *Purgatory*	Patrick Kavanagh, *The Green Fool*	Robert Gibbings, *Blue Angels and Whales*
Elizabeth Bowen, *The Death of the Heart*	W.B. Yeats, *New Poems*		Seamas MacManus, *The Rocky Road to Dublin*	Sean O'Faolain, *King of the Beggars*
Joyce Cary, *Castle Corner*				

Fiction	Poetry	Drama	Autobiography	Miscellaneous
Kate O'Brien, *Pray for the Wanderer*			Maud Gonne MacBride, *A Servant of the Queen*	*Angels with Dirty Faces* (Cagney film)
Jim Phelan, *Lifer*				*In Old Chicago* (film by Edwin Curtis with Spencer Tracy as Fr Tim Mullin)
Jack B. Yeats, *The Charmed Life*				

1939: Death of W.B. Yeats. IRA explosions in Coventry. Ireland neutral in Second World War.

Fiction	Poetry	Drama	Autobiography	Miscellaneous
Joyce Cary, *Mister Johnson*	Louis MacNeice, *Autumn Journal*		Patrick Gallagher, *My Story*	Una Ellis-Fermor, *The Irish Dramatic Movement*
James Joyce, *Finnegans Wake*			Sean O'Casey, *I Knock at the Door*	Colm Ó Lochlainn, *Irish Street Ballads*
Michael McLaverty, *Call My Brother Back*			Peig Sayers, *Machtnamh Seana-Mhná*	
Flann O'Brien, *At-Swim-Two-Birds*				

1940: Battle of Britain. Sean O'Faolain founds *The Bell* magazine. Eugene O'Neill writes *Long Day's Journey into Night.*

Fiction	Poetry	Drama	Autobiography	Miscellaneous
Frank O'Connor, *Dutch Interior*	F.R. Higgins, *The Gap of Brightness*	Sean O'Casey, *The Star Turns Red*	John Lavery, *The Life of a Painter*	
	Ewart Milne, *Letter from Ireland*	George Shiels, *The Rugged Path*	Seosamh Mac Grianna, *Mo Bhealach Féin*	
	W.R. Rodgers, *Awake! and Other Poems*			
	W.B. Yeats, *Last Poems*			

1941: January: Death of James Joyce in Zurich. March/April: German air-raids on Belfast. First Irish Book Fair.

Fiction	Poetry	Drama	Autobiography	Miscellaneous
Michael McLaverty, *Lost Fields*			Enid Starkie, *A Lady's Child*	Flann O'Brien, *An Béal Bocht (The Poor Mouth)*
Flann O'Brien *An Béal Bocht*				
Kate O'Brien, *The Land of Spices*				
L.A.G. Strong, *The Bay*				

1942: Rationing introduced. *Comhar*, Irish language monthly, begins publication.

Fiction	Poetry	Drama	Autobiography	Miscellaneous
Mary Lavin, *Tales from Bective Bridge*	Patrick Kavanagh, *The Great Hunger*	Austin Clarke, *As The Crow Flies* (radio play)	Nesca A. Robb, *An Ulsterwoman in England, 1924-1941*	Eric Cross, *The Tailor and Ansty*
Francis MacManus, *Watergate*	Máirtín Ó Direáin, *Coinnle Geala*	Sean O'Casey, *Red Roses For Me*		Joseph Hone, *W.B. Yeats: 1865-1939*

Fiction	Poetry	Drama	Autobiography	Miscellaneous
Jack B. Yeats, *Ah Well*	Jack B. Yeats, *La La Noo*		Lennox Robinson, *Curtain Up*	Sean O'Sullivan, *A Handbook of Irish Folklore*

1943: Fianna Fáil wins general election. *Inniu*, Irish-language newspaper, begins publication. Sir Basil Brooke becomes Prime Minister of Northern Ireland.

Fiction	Poetry	Drama	Autobiography	Miscellaneous
Charles B. Driscoll, *Kansas Irish*	Máirtín Ó Direáin, *Dánta Aniar*	M.J. Molloy, *The Old Road*		
Francis MacManus, *The Greatest of These*		Eugene O'Neill, *A Moon for the Misbegotten*		
Ethel Mannin, *The Blossoming Bough*				
Betty Smith, *A Tree Grows in Brooklyn*				

1944: Paris liberated. The Mercier Press founded by John M. Feehan. Lyric Theatre Company founded by Austin Clarke and Roibeárd Ó Faracháin (Robert Farren).

Fiction	Poetry	Drama	Autobiography	Miscellaneous
Joyce Cary, *The Horse's Mouth*	Louis MacNeice, *Springboard*		R.H. Henderson, *An Ulsterman in Africa*	*Going My Way* (film by Leo McCarey with Bing Crosby as Fr Chuck O'Malley)
James Joyce, *Stephen Hero*				
Frank O'Connor, *Crab Apple Jelly*				
Helen Wilson, *Moonshine*				
Jack B. Yeats, *And To You Also*				

1945: End of Second World War. Labour victory in UK general election. Sáirséal agus Dill, Irish-language publishers, founded by Seán Ó hÉigeartaigh and Brid Ní Mhaoileoin. Arts Theatre Studio in Belfast founded by Hubert and Dorothy Wilmot.

Fiction	Poetry	Drama	Autobiography	Miscellaneous
John Coulter, *Turf Smoke*	Bryan Merriman, *The Midnight Court* (trans. Frank O'Connor)	Sean O'Casey *The Purple Dust*		*The Bells of St Mary's* (film by Leo McCarey with Bing Crosby)
Robert Gibbings, *Lovely Is the Lee*				
Mary Lavin, *The House in Clew Street*				

1946: Soviet Union opposes Ireland's application to join United Nations.

Fiction	Poetry	Drama	Autobiography	Miscellaneous
Elizabeth Bowen, *Ivy Gripped the Steps*	Denis Devlin, *Lough Derg and Other Poems*	Donagh MacDonagh, *Happy as Larry*	Lady Gregory, *Journals 1916-1930*	Cathal O'Byrne, *As I Roved Out*
John Coulter, *The Blossoming Thorn*		Micheál MacLiammóir, *Ill Met By Moonlight*	Micheál MacLiammóir, *All For Hecuba*	

Fiction	Poetry	Drama	Autobiography	Miscellaneous
Mervyn Wall, *The Unfortunate Fursey*		Louis MacNeice, *The Dark Tower and other Radio Scripts*		
		Joseph Tomelty, *Right Again, Barnum*		

1947: Coal rationing in Dublin. First issue of *Irish Writing*, edited by David Marcus and Terence Smith.

Fiction	Poetry	Drama	Autobiography	Miscellaneous
Michael McLaverty, *The Game Cock and Other Stories*	Patrick Kavanagh, *Soul for Sale*		Mary Colum, *Life and Dream*	Ethel Mannin, *Connemara Journal*
Séamus Ó Néill, *Tonn Tile*				*Odd Man Out* (film by Carol Reed)
J.F. Powers, *Prince of Darkness And Other Stories*				Sean O'Faolain, *The Irish*

1948: Coalition government formed under John A. Costello. Republic of Ireland declared. Last trams in Dublin. *Poetry Ireland* founded by David Marcus. *Rann*, a quarterly of Ulster verse, launched, edited by Roy McFadden and Barbara Edwards. First issue of *Feasta*, journal of the Gaelic League.

Fiction	Poetry	Drama	Autobiography	Miscellaneous
Patrick Kavanagh, *Tarry Flynn*		M.J. Molloy, *The King of Friday's Men*	Monk Gibbon, *Mount Ida*	Roibeárd Ó Faracháin, *The Course of Irish Verse in English*
Bryan MacMahon, *The Lion-Tamer and Other Stories*		Joseph Tomelty, *All Souls' Night*		
Máirtín Ó Cadhain, *Cré na Cille* and *An Braon Broghach*				
Ruth Park, *A Harp in the South*				
Betty Smith, *Tomorrow Will Be Better*				
Francis Stuart, *A Pillar of Cloud*				

1949: Ireland leaves the Commonwealth. Northern Ireland Labour Party commits itself to working with the British Labour Partry. Ireland Act at Westminster guarantees status of Northern Ireland. First issue of *Envoy*, edited by John Ryan.

Fiction	Poetry	Drama	Autobiography	Miscellaneous
Elizabeth Bowen, *The Heat of the Day*	Denis Devlin, *Exile*		Sean O'Casey, *Inishfallen, Fare Thee Well*	Tom Barry, *Guerilla Days in Ireland*
Joyce Cary, *A Fearful Joy*	Louis MacNeice, *Collected Poems*		Jim Phelan, *We Follow the Roads*	
Dan Davin, *Roads From Home*	Máirtín Ó Direáin, *Rogha Dánta*			

Fiction	Poetry	Drama	Autobiography	Miscellaneous

1950: Death of George Bernard Shaw. Industrial Development Authority (IDA) Act passed.

Fiction	Poetry	Drama	Autobiography	Miscellaneous
Walter Macken, *Rain on the Wind*	Valentin Iremonger, *Reservations*	Seamus Byrne, *Design for a Headstone*	Oliver St John Gogarty, *Rolling Down the Lea*	Garry Hogg, *Turf Beneath My Feet*
Edward A. McCourt, *Home is the Stranger*		Padraic Fallon, *Diarmuid and Grainne* (radio play)		
Henry Morton Robinson, *The Cardinal*				

1951: De Valera elected Taoiseach. The Dolmen Press founded by Liam Miller. *Envoy* founded by John Ryan. First national Fleá Cheoil (music festival) held in Mullingar. Comhaltas Ceoltóiri Éireann formed. Lyric Players Theatre founded by Mary and Pearse O'Malley. Noel Browne's Mother and Child Scheme defeated. Free Presbyterian Church of Ulster established by Ian Paisley. Abbey Theatre burns down.

Fiction	Poetry	Drama	Autobiography	Miscellaneous
Samuel Beckett, *Molloy* (in French)	Oliver St John Gogarty, *Collected Poems*		Paul Henry, *An Irish Portrait*	Patrick Campbell, *Life in Thin Slices*
Sam Hanna Bell, *December Bride*			Sir Christopher Lynch-Robinson, *The Last of the Irish R.M.s*	Austin Clarke, *Poetry in Modern Ireland*
				Robert Gibbings, *Sweet Cork of Thee*
				Lennox Robinson, *Ireland's Abbey Theatre: A History, 1899-1951*

1952: Brief run of *Kavanagh's Weekly*.

Fiction	Poetry	Drama	Autobiography	Miscellaneous
Mervyn Wall, *Leaves for the Burning*	Seán Ó Ríordáin, *Eireaball Spideoige*	Samuel Beckett, *En attendant Godot*		Maurice Craig, *Dublin 1660-1860*
	W.R. Rodgers, *Europa and the Bull*			Michael MacManus, *Adventures of an Irish Bookman*
				The Quiet Man (film by John Ford)

1953: Gael-Linn established to promote Irish language. Pike Theatre opens in Dublin, founded by Alan Simpson and Carolyn Swift. Final evacuation of Great Blasket Island. Alfred Chester Beatty Library opens in Dublin.

Fiction	Poetry	Drama	Autobiography	Miscellaneous
Samuel Beckett, *Watt* and *Malone meurt* (in French)	Austin Clarke, *Ancient Lights*	Louis D'Alton, *This Other Eden*	Denis Johnston, *Nine Rivers From Jordan*	*The Devil's Playground* (Australian film by Fred Schepisi)
Benedict Kiely, *Cards of the Gambler*	Padraic Colum, *Collected Poems*	Padraic Fallon, *The Vision of Mac Conglinne*		
Frank O'Connor, *The Stories of Frank O'Connor*		M.J. Molloy, *The Wood of the Whispering*		

Fiction	Poetry	Drama	Autobiography	Miscellaneous

1954: Costello becomes Taoiseach in second inter-party government.

Fiction	Poetry	Drama	Autobiography	Miscellaneous
Samuel Beckett, *Molloy*		Samuel Beckett, *Waiting for Godot*	Sean O'Casey, *Sunset and Evening Star*	John O'Brien ed., *The Vanishing Irish*
		Brendan Behan, *The Quare Fellow*	Christy Brown, *My Left Foot*	Jim Phelan, *Tramp at Anchor*
		Joseph Tomelty, *Is the Priest at Home?*		Allan Wade, ed., *The Letters of W.B. Yeats*

1955: Ireland admitted to the United Nations. First television service begins in Northern Ireland. Bord Fáilte Éireann (Irish Tourist Board) established.

Fiction	Poetry	Drama	Autobiography	Miscellaneous
J.P. Donleavy, *The Ginger Man*	Austin Clarke, *Ancient Lights*	Sean O'Casey, *The Bishop's Bonfire*		
Janet MacNeill, *A Child in the House*				
Brian Moore, *Judith Hearne* (republished in 1956 as *The Lonely Passion of Judith Hearne*)				
John O'Hara, *Ten North Frederick*				
James Plunkett, *The Trusting and the Maimed*				

1956: Balance of payments crisis. Roinn na Gaeltachta (Department of the Gaeltacht) established to support the Irish-speaking regions of Ireland. IRA Border campaign 1956-62. Ronnie Delaney wins gold medal in Melbourne Olympics.

Fiction	Poetry	Drama	Autobiography	Miscellaneous
Janet McNeill, *Tea at Four O'Clock*	Thomas Kinsella, *Poems*	Eugene O'Neill, *Long Day's Journey into Night*		Honor Tracy, *Mind You, I've Said Nothing*
Edwin O'Connor, *The Last Hurrah*				

1957: IRA attack on Brookeborough police barracks in Northern Ireland. Dublin Theatre Festival inaugurated. *Threshold* founded by Mary O'Malley. Tennessee Williams's play *The Rose Tattoo* breaches law and director imprisoned.

Fiction	Poetry	Drama	Autobiography	Miscellaneous
Bill Naughton, *One Small Boy*	Máirtín Ó Direáin, *Ó Mórna agus Dánta Eile*	Samuel Beckett, *All That Fall* and *Endgame*	James Michael Curley, *I'd Do It Again*	Heinrich Böll, *Irish Journal*
Sean O'Faolain, *The Finest Stories of Sean O'Faolain*	L.A.G. Strong, *The Body's Imperfection*	Eugene O'Neill, *A Touch of the Poet*	Mary McCarthy, *Memories of a Catholic Girlhood*	E. Estyn Evans, *Irish Folk Ways*
				The Rising of the Moon (film by John Ford)

Fiction	Poetry	Drama	Autobiography	Miscellaneous

1958: Aer Lingus begins flights to the USA. Ardmore Film Studios founded. Kilkenny Design Workshops begin.

Fiction	Poetry	Drama	Autobiography	Miscellaneous
Samuel Beckett, *Malone Dies* and *The Unnamable*	Thomas Kinsella, *Another September*	Samuel Beckett, *Krapp's Last Tape*	Brendan Behan, *Borstal Boy*	Stanislaus Joyce, *My Brother's Keeper*
Brian Moore, *The Feast of Lupercal*	John Montague, *Forms of Exile*	Brendan Behan, *The Hostage*		*A Night to Remember* (film by Roy Baker)
				Anne O'Neill–Barna, *Himself and I*

1959: De Valera elected President (until 1973). Seán Lemass becomes Taoiseach.

Fiction	Poetry	Drama	Autobiography	Miscellaneous
Walter Macken, *Seek the Fair Land*		John B. Keane, *Sive*	Risteard de Paor, *Úll i mBarr an Ghéagáin*	Mary Durack, *Kings in Grass Castles*
		Sean O'Casey, *The Drums of Father Ned*	Terence de Vere White, *The Fretful Midge*	Richard Ellmann, *James Joyce*
				Mise Éire (film with music score by Seán Ó Riada)
				Shake Hands with the Devil (film by Michael Anderson)

1960: Radio Telefís Éireann (RTÉ) established by Broadcasting Authority Act. John F. Kennedy elected United States President. Yeats Summer School begins. First issue of the *Kilkenny Magazine*, edited by James Delahunty.

Fiction	Poetry	Drama	Autobiography	Miscellaneous
Dónal Mac Amlaigh, *Dialann Deoraí (An Irish Navvy)*	Patrick Kavanagh, *Come Dance With Kitty Stobling*	Micheál Mac Liammóir, *The Importance of Being Oscar*	C. Day Lewis, *The Buried Day*	*A Terrible Beauty* (film by Tay Garnett)
Brian Moore, *The Luck of Ginger Coffey*		Bryan MacMahon, *Song of the Anvil*	Robert Harbinson, *No Surrender* and *Song of Erne*	
Edna O'Brien, *The Country Girls*		Sam Thompson, *Over the Bridge*		
Elizabeth O'Connor, *The Irishman*				

1961: RTÉ begins TV transmission. Ceoltóirí Chualann founded by Seán Ó Riada. John Ryan edits new series of *The Dublin Magazine*.

Fiction	Poetry	Drama	Autobiography	Miscellaneous
Michael Campbell, *Across the Water*	Austin Clarke, *Later Poems*	Samuel Beckett, *Happy Days*	Robert Harbison, *Up Spake the Cabin Boy*	*The Singer Not the Song* (film by Roy Baker)
Edwin O'Connor, *The Edge of Sadness*	John Montague, *Poisoned Lands*	Bryan MacMahon, *The Honey Spike*	Frank O'Connor, *An Only Child*	
	Seán Ó Tuama, *Faoileán na Beatha*	Tom Murphy, *A Whistle in the Dark*	Máirtín Ó Direáin, *Feamainn Bhealtaine* (May Seaweed)	

Fiction	Poetry	Drama	Autobiography	Miscellaneous

1962: Ireland becomes a member of the first UN Security Council. Second Vatican Council meets. First showing on RTÉ of *The Late Late Show*, presented by Gay Byrne. Edwin O'Connor wins Pulitzer Prize with *The Edge of Sadness*. *Poetry Ireland* edited by John Jordan.

Fiction	Poetry	Drama	Autobiography	Miscellaneous
Brian Friel, *The Saucer of Larks*	Thomas Kinsella, *Downstream*	Hugh Leonard, *Stephen D.*	Austin Clarke, *Twice Round the Black Church*	Brian Inglis, *West Briton*
Walter Macken, *The Silent People*				Vivian Mercier, *The Irish Comic Tradition*
J.F. Powers, *Morte D'Urban*				Kate O'Brien, *My Ireland*
Paul Smith, *The Countrywoman*				Frank O'Connor, *The Lonely Voice*
				Cecil Woodham-Smith, *The Great Hunger*

1963: Death of Pope John XXIII. Kennedy visits Ireland in June, assassinated in November. First issue of *Arena* edited by James Liddy and Liam O'Connor.

Fiction	Poetry	Drama	Autobiography	Miscellaneous
Michael Farrell, *Thy Tears Might Cease*	Austin Clarke, *Flight to Africa*	John B. Keane, *The Man from Clare*	Robert Harbinson, *The Protégé*	
John McGahern, *The Barracks*	Richard Murphy, *Sailing to an Island*			
	Máirtín Ó Direáin, *Ar Ré Dhearóil*			

1964: Arkle wins Cheltenham Gold Cup (and does so the following two years). *The Dublin Magazine* relaunched under Rivers Carew and Timothy Brownlow.

Fiction	Poetry	Drama	Autobiography	Miscellaneous
Anthony Cronin, *The Life of Riley*	Denis Devlin, *Collected Poems*	Brian Friel, *Philadelphia Here I Come*	Sean O'Faolain, *Vive Moi!*	The Chieftains' first album (Claddagh Records)
Walter Macken, *The Scorching Wind*	Patrick Kavanagh, *Collected Poems*			Anthony Cronin, *The Life of Riley*
Janet McNeill, *The Maiden Dinosaur*	Brendan Kennelly, *My Dark Fathers*			*Girl with Green Eyes* (film by Desmond David)
John Montague, *Death of a Chieftain*	Sean Ó Ríordáin, *Brosna*			*The Luck of Ginger Coffey* (film by Irvin Kershner)
Flann O'Brien, *The Dalkey Archive*				
William Trevor, *The Old Boys*				

1965: W.B. Yeats Centenary. Seán Lemass, Irish Taoiseach, meets Terence O'Neil, Prime Minister of Northern Ireland.

Fiction	Poetry	Drama	Autobiography	Miscellaneous
John McGahern, *The Dark*		John B. Keane, *The Field*	Louis MacNeice, *The Strings Are False*	*I Was Happy Here* (film by Desmond Davis)

Fiction	Poetry	Drama	Autobiography	Miscellaneous
Brian Moore, *The Emperor of Ice-Cream*				Conor Cruise O'Brien, 'Passion and Cunning'
Iris Murdoch, *The Red and the Green*				
William Cotter Murray, *Michael Joe*				

1966: Fiftieth Anniversary of Easter Rising. Nelson's Pillar in Dublin destroyed by explosion. New Abbey Theatre opens. De Valera is President for second term. Jack Lynch elected Taoiseach.

Fiction	Poetry	Drama	Autobiography	Miscellaneous
Patrick Boyle, *Like Any Other Man*	Austin Clarke, *Mnemosyne Lay in Dust*		Seamus Murphy, *Stone Mad*	
Aidan Higgins, *Langrishe, Go Down*	Seamus Heaney, *Death of a Naturalist*			
Edwin O'Connor, *All In the Family*				
Bob Shaw, *Light of Other Days*				

1967: Northern Ireland Civil Rights Association formed. New University of Ulster opens. Merriman Summer School established. David Marcus edits New Irish Writing for *The Irish Press*.

Fiction	Poetry	Drama	Autobiography	Miscellaneous
Flann O'Brien, *The Third Policeman*	Eavan Boland, *New Territory*			The Dubliners, *Seven Drunken Nights* (album)
Patrick Kavanagh, *Collected Prose*	John Montague, *A Chosen Light*			Frank O'Connor, *The Backward Look*
				Ulysses (film by Joseph Strick)

1968: Clash between Civil Rights protestors and police in Derry (October). *The Honest Ulsterman* founded by James Simmons. Publishers Gill & Macmillan join forces.

Fiction	Poetry	Drama	Autobiography	Miscellaneous
Lee Dunne, *A Bed in the Sticks*	John Hewitt, *Collected Poems*	Thomas Murphy, *Famine*	Monk Gibbon, *Inglorious Soldier*	Van Morrison, *Astral Weeks* (album)
Thomas Keneally, *Three Cheers For the Paraclete*	Thomas Kinsella, *Nightwalker and Other Poems*		Frank O'Connor, *My Father's Son*	*The Bofors Gun* (film by Jack Gold)
Brian Moore, *I am Mary Dunne*	Derek Mahon, *Night-Crossing*			*The Rocky Road to Dublin* (documentary film by Peter Lennon)

1969: People's Democracy march ambushed by militant Protestants at Burntollet. British troops move into Northern Ireland in August. Samuel Beckett wins Nobel Prize. Income tax abolished for writers and artists in the Irish Republic. First issue of *Lace Curtain* edited by Michael Smith and Trevor Joyce.

Fiction	Poetry	Drama	Autobiography	Miscellaneous
W.A. Ballanger, *The Green Grassy Slopes*	Seamus Heaney, *Door Into the Dark*	Samuel Beckett, *Breath*		

Fiction	Poetry	Drama	Autobiography	Miscellaneous
Elizabeth Bowen, *Eva Trout*	Michael Longley, *No Continuing City*	Tom Kilroy, *The Death and Resurrection of Mr Roche*		
Patrick Boyle, *All Looks Yellow to the Jaundiced Eye*				
Beatrice Coogan, *The Big Wind*				
James Plunkett, *Strumpet City*				
Richard Power, *The Hungry Grass*				

1970: Social Democratic and Labour Party (SDLP) founded in the North. Split between Provisional and Official IRA. Provisionals embark on campaign of violence. *Irish University Review* begins publication under editorship of Maurice Harmon. First issue of *Atlantis*, edited by Seamus Deane, Derek Mahon, Hugh Maxton, Augustine Martin, and Michael Gill. Gallery Press founded by Peter Fallon. *Innti*, an Irish-language magazine, founded by Michael Davitt and other students at University College, Cork. Commission on the Status of Women established.

Fiction	Poetry	Drama	Autobiography	Miscellaneous
John Banville, *Long Lankin*	John Montague, *Tides*	Brian Friel, *Crystal and Fox*	Christy Brown, *Down All the Days*	*The Molly Maguires* (film by Martin Ritt)
Elizabeth Cullinan, *House of Gold*				*Ryan's Daughter* (film by David Lean)
Dan Davin, *Not Here, Not Now*				
J.G. Farrell, *Troubles*				
John McGahern, *Nightlines*				
William Trevor, *Mrs Eckdork in O'Neill's Hotel*				

1971: First British soldier killed in Northern Ireland (February). Brian Faulkner elected leader of Unionist Party. Women's Liberation Movement holds its first meeting in Dublin. Internment without trial introduced in August. The Blackstaff Press founded by Diane and Jim Gracey. Irish National Ballet formed.

Fiction	Poetry	Drama	Autobiography	Miscellaneous
Thomas Kilroy, *The Big Chapel*	Seán Ó Ríordáin, *Línte Liombo*	John Boyd, *The Flats*		
Mary Lavin, *Collected Stories*		Tom Murphy, *The Morning After Optimism*		
Francis Stuart, *Black List/Section H*				

Fiction	Poetry	Drama	Autobiography	Miscellaneous

1972: Bloody Sunday in Derry (30 January). British Embassy in Dublin burned (January). Direct Rule introduced in North (March). Launch of Radio Na Gaeltachta (Irish-language radio service). *Siamsa Tíre*, a National Folk Theatre, established at Tralee. *The Journal of Irish Literature* founded by Robert Hogan. Lille Centre of Irish Studies founded.

Fiction	Poetry	Drama	Autobiography	Miscellaneous
Jennifer Johnston, *The Captains and the Kings*	Seamus Heaney, *Wintering Out*	Wilson John Haire, *Within Two Shadows*	W. B. Yeats, *Memoirs*	Horslips, *Happy to Meet, Sorry to Part* (debut album)
Mary Lavin, *A Memory and Other Stories*	Thomas Kinsella, *Notes from the Land of the Dead and Other Poems*			Conor Cruise O'Brien, *States of Ireland*
Brian Moore, *Catholics*	Derek Mahon, *Lives*			Rosita Sweetman, *'On Our Knees': Ireland 1972*
William Trevor, *The Ballroom of Romance and Other Stories*	John Montague, *The Rough Field*			
	Eiléan Ní Chuilleanáin, *Acts and Monuments*			

1973: Ireland enters EEC (European Economic Community). Liam Cosgrave becomes Taoiseach in coalition government. Meeting between British and Irish governments and power-sharing Executive meet at Sunningdale.

Fiction	Poetry	Drama	Autobiography	Miscellaneous
John Banville, *Birchwood*	Patrick Galvin, *The Wood-Burners*	Brian Friel, *The Freedom of the City*		Hugh Brody, *Inishkillane*
Jimmy Breslin, *World Without End, Amen*	Michael Longley, *An Exploded View*	Patrick Galvin, *Nightfall to Belfast*		
Eilís Dillon, *Across the Bitter Sea*	Paul Muldoon, *New Weather*	Hugh Leonard, *Da*		
Peter Hamill, *The Gift*				

1974: IRA bombs kill 21 people in Birmingham. Loyalist bomb kills 25 people in Dublin. Ulster Workers' Council strike. Power-sharing Executive resigns. IRA bomb in Guildford kills four members of British Army. Seán MacBride wins Nobel Peace Prize. Collapse of Irish University Press. O'Brien Press founded by Michael O'Brien. Arlen Press founded by Catherine Rose. Wolfhound Press founded by Seamus Cashman. First issue of *Scríobh*.

Fiction	Poetry	Drama	Autobiography	Miscellaneous
Maeve Brennan, *Christmas Eve*	Padraic Fallon, *Poems*	Ron Blair, *The Christian Brothers*	Robert Harbinson, *Songs Out of Oriel*	Richard Howard Brown, *I Am Of Ireland*
Jennifer Johnston, *How Many Miles to Babylon*	Padraic Fiacc, ed., *The Wearing of the Black*	David Rudkin, *Ashes*	David Thomson, *Woodbrook*	
Dónal Mac Amlaigh, *Schnitzer Ó Sé*	Thomas Kinsella, *One*			
	Richard Murphy, *High Island*			

Fiction	Poetry	Drama	Autobiography	Miscellaneous

1975: Balcombe Street siege. Druid Theatre Company founded in Galway by Garry Hynes, Mick Lally, and Marie Mullen. Death of de Valera. Appletree Press established by John Murphy. First issue of *Cyphers* edited by Leland Bardwell, Eiléan Ní Chuilleanáin, Pearse Hutchinson, and Macdara Woods.

Fiction	Poetry	Drama	Autobiography	Miscellaneous
William Kennedy, *Legs*	Paul Durcan, *O Westport in the Light of Asia Minor*	Margaretta D'Arcy and John Arden, *The Non-Stop Connolly Show*		*Barry Lyndon* (film by Stanley Kubrick)
Brian Moore, *The Great Victorian Collection*	Robert Greacen, *A Garland for Captain Fox*	Brian Friel, *Volunteers* and *Living Quarters*		J.P. Donleavy, *The Unexpurgated Code*
	Michael Hartnett, *A Farewell to English*	Patrick Galvin, *We Do It For Love*		Cecil King, *The Cecil King Diary 1970-1974*
	Seamus Heaney, *North*			John Ryan, *Remembering How We Stood: Bohemian Dublin at the Mid-Century*
	Derek Mahon, *The Snow Party*			
	John Montague, *A Slow Dance*			
	Eiléan Ní Chuilleanáin, *Site of Ambush*			

1976: Jack Lynch becomes Taoiseach. Assassination of Christopher Ewart–Biggs, British Ambassador to Ireland. *Books Ireland* founded by Jeremy Addis. Irish Book Fair.

Fiction	Poetry	Drama	Autobiography	Miscellaneous
John Banville, *Dr Copernicus*	Paul Durcan, *Teresa's Bar*	Thomas Murphy, *The Sanctuary Lamp*		Anthony Cronin, *Dead As Doornails*
Eugene McCabe, *Victims*	Thomas Kinsella, *A Technical Supplement*			Eamon Kelly, *In My Father's Time*
Brian Moore, *The Doctor's Wife*	Michael Longley, *Man Lying On A Wall*			Edna O'Brien, *Mother Ireland*
Breandan Ó hÉithir, *Lig Sinn i gCathú* (Lead us into Temptation)	James Simmons, *Judy Garland and the Cold War*			
William Trevor, *The Children of Dynmouth*				
Leon Uris, *Trinity*.				

1977: First issue of *The Crane Bag* under editorship of Mark Hederman and Richard Kearney. Employment Equality Act.

Fiction	Poetry	Drama	Autobiography	Miscellaneous
Caroline Blackwood, *Great Granny Webster*	Paul Muldoon, *Mules*	Bill Morrison, *Flying Birds*		*The Heritage of Ireland* (RTÉ series)
Kevin Casey, *Dreams of Revenge*	Eiléan Ní Chuilleanáin, *The Second Voyage*			*A Portrait of the Artist as a Young Man* (film by Joseph Strick)

Fiction	Poetry	Drama	Autobiography	Miscellaneous
John Gregory Dunne, *True Confessions*				
Jennifer Johnston, *Shadows on Our Skin*				
Colleen McCullough, *The Thorn Birds*				
Francis Stuart, *A Hole in the Head*				

1978: Well Woman Clinic opens in Dublin and is picketed. Bord na Gaeilge established.

Fiction	Poetry	Drama	Autobiography	Miscellaneous
Mary Gordon, *Final Payments*	John Hewitt, *The Rain Dance*			*The Irishman* (Australian film by Donald Crombie)
Benedict Kiely, *A Cow in the House*	John Montague, *The Great Cloak*			Benedict Kiely, *All The Way to Bantry Bay*
Eugene McCabe, *Heritage*				Dervla Murphy, *A Place Apart*
Patrick McGinley, *Bogmail*				Eiléan Ní Chuilleanáin, *Cork*
Mary Manning, *The Last Chronicles of Ballyfungus*				*On A Paving Stone Mounted* (film by Thaddeus O'Sullivan)

1979: Lord Mountbatten murdered by IRA. Visit of Pope John Paul II to Ireland. Charles Haughey becomes Taoiseach. *Poetry Ireland*, the National Poetry Society, founded by John F. Deane. Raven Arts Press founded by Dermot Bolger.

Fiction	Poetry	Drama	Autobiography	Miscellaneous
Anthony Cronin, *Identity Papers*	Vincent Buckley, *The Pattern*	Brian Friel, *Faith Healer* and *Aristocrats*	C.S. Andrews, *Dublin Made Me*	Paddy Tunney, *The Stone Fiddle* (album)
Thomas Flanagan, *The Year of the French*	Robert Creeley, *Later*		Hugh Leonard, *Home Before Night*	
Jennifer Johnston, *The Old Jest*	Seamus Heaney, *Field Work*			
John McGahern, *The Pornographer*				
Brian Moore, *The Mangan Inheritance*				
Gilbert Sorrentino, *Mulligan Stew*				
E.V. Thompson, *The Music Makers*				

Fiction	Poetry	Drama	Autobiography	Miscellaneous

1980: Hunger Strikes by republicans in Maze Prison. Field Day Theatre Company founded by Brian Friel and Stephen Rea.

Fiction	Poetry	Drama	Autobiography	Miscellaneous
Mary Beckett, *A Belfast Woman*	Eavan Boland, *In Her Own Image*	Brian Friel, *Translations*		Shaun Davey, *The Brendan Voyage* (album)
Ita Daly, *The Lady with the Red Shoes*	Thomas Kinsella, *Poems 1956-73*			Michael Viney, *Another Life*
Benedict Kiely, *The State of Ireland*	Paul Muldoon, *Why Brownlee Left*			
Julia O'Faolain, *No Country for Young Men*	Máirtín Ó Direáin, *Dánta 1939-1979*			
	Tom Paulin, *The Strange Museum*			
	James Simmons, *Constantly Singing*			
	Eithne Strong, *FLESH ... the Greatest Sin*			

1981: Garrett FitzGerald forms coalition government. Death of Bobby Sands on hunger strike. A Sense of Ireland exhibition in London. Aosdána, an affiliation of artists, established by An Chomhairle Ealaíon/The Arts Council of Ireland. Salmon Books founded by Jessie Lendennie.

Fiction	Poetry	Drama	Autobiography	Miscellaneous
John Banville, *Kepler*	Nuala Ní Dhomhnaill, *An Dealg Droighin*	Margaretta D'Arcy, *Tell Them Everything*		Patrick Campbell, *Rambles Round Donegal*
Andrew M. Greeley, *The Cardinal Sins*	Seán Ó Tuama and Thomas Kinsella (eds), *An Duanaire 1600-1900: Poems of the Dispossessed*	Patrick Shea, *Voices and the Sound of Drums*		Tom Corkery, *Tom Corkery's Dublin*
Jennifer Johnston, *The Christmas Tree*				*Maeve* (film by Pat Murphy and John Davies)
Molly Keane, *Good Behaviour*				
Maurice Leitch, *Silver's City*				
Brian Moore, *The Temptation of Eileen Hughes*				

1982: Charles Haughey returns to power. Brandon Books co-founded by Steve MacDonough and Bernie Goggin. Minister for the Arts appointed for first time since Independence. James Joyce centenary year. First issue of *Theatre Ireland*.

Fiction	Poetry	Drama	Autobiography	Miscellaneous
Michael Mullen, *Kelly*	Anthony Cronin, *New and Selected Poems*	Martin Lynch, *The Interrogation of Ambrose Fogarty*		*Angel* (film by Neil Jordan)
William Trevor, *Beyond the Pale*	John Hewitt, *Mosaic*			*Is There One Who Understands Me* (Seán Ó Mórdha film on James Joyce)

Fiction	Poetry	Drama	Autobiography	Miscellaneous
	Wes Magee, *A Dark Age*			
	Derek Mahon, *The Hunt By Night*			

1983: Gerry Adams elected MP for West Belfast. In a referendum Ireland votes against abortion. *Sunday Tribune* begins publication.

Fiction	Poetry	Drama	Autobiography	Miscellaneous
Clare Boylan, *Holy Pictures*	Paul Durcan, *Jumping the Train Tracks with Angela*	Tom MacIntyre, *The Great Hunger*	Bobby Sands, *One Day in My Life*	*Ascendancy* (film by Edward Bennett)
Joe Flaherty, *Tin Wife*		Thomas Murphy, *Gigli Concert*		Samuel Beckett, *Disjecta*
William Kennedy, *Ironweed*	Brendan Kennelly, *Cromwell*			Mary Durack, *Sons in the Saddle*
Patrick McGinley, *Foggage*	Paul Muldoon, *Quoof*			U2, 'Sunday Bloody Sunday' (song)
Bernard MacLaverty, *Cal*	Tom Paulin, *Liberty Tree*			Van Morrison, *Inarticulate Speech of the Heart* (album)
Dorothy Nelson, *In Night's City*				
William Trevor, *Fools of Fortune*				

1984: President Reagan visits Ireland. IRA bomb nearly kills Prime Minister Margaret. Thatcher. Lilliput Press founded by Antony Farrell. Attic Press founded by Roisín Conroy, Mary Paul Keane and Ailbhe Smyth. *Linen Hall Review* established by John Gray and Paul Campbell. *Anois* supersedes *Inniu*. William Kennedy wins Pulitzer Prize with *Ironweed*.

Fiction	Poetry	Drama	Autobiography	Miscellaneous
Desmond Hogan, *A Curious Street*	Seamus Heaney, *Station Island*	Stewart Parker, *Northern Star*	Bernard Smith, *The Boy Adeodatus*	Tom Paulin, *Ireland and the English Crisis*
Sam Keery, *The Last Romantic out of Belfast*	John Montague, *The Dead Kingdom*			
	Nuala Ní Dhomhnaill, *Féar Suaithinseach*			
	Iain Crichton Smith, *The Exiles*			

1985: Anglo-Irish Agreement. Irish-language publishers Cló Iar-Chonnachta founded by Mícheál Ó Conghaile.

Fiction	Poetry	Drama	Autobiography	Miscellaneous
Malcolm Lynch, *The Streets of Ancoats*	Paul Durcan, *The Berlin Wall Café*	Anne Devlin, *Ourselves Alone*		Vincent Buckley, *Memory Ireland*
John McGahern, *High Ground*		Frank McGuinness, *Observe the Sons of Ulster Marching Towards the Somme*		Hubert Butler, *Escape from the Anthill*
Patrick McGinley, *The Trick of the Ga Bolga*				Frank McDonald, *The Destruction of Dublin*

Fiction	Poetry	Drama	Autobiography	Miscellaneous
Frances Molloy, *No Mate For the Magpie*		Thomas Murphy, *Conversations on a Homecoming* and *Bailegangaire*		Dervla Murphy, *Tales from Two Cities*
Diarmuid Ó Súilleabháin, *Uain Bheo*		Graham Reid, *Ties of Blood* (TV series)		Tim Robinson, *Stones of Aran: Pilgrimage*
				Van Morrison, *A Sense of Wonder* (album)

1986: In a referendum Ireland votes against divorce. Irish Writers' Union founded by Jack Harte. Progressive Democratic Party founded by Des O'Malley and other former Fianna Fáil TDs. Larry McMurtry wins Pulitzer prize with *Lonesome Dove. Krino* founded by Gerald Dawe and Jonathan Williams.

Fiction	Poetry	Drama	Autobiography	Miscellaneous
Linda Anderson, *Cuckoo*	Eavan Boland, *The Journey and other Poems*	Stewart Parker, *Heavenly Bodies*	Deborah Tall, *The Island of the White Cow*	*Eh Joe* (film by Alan Gilsenan)
John Banville, *Mefisto*	Padraic Fiacc, *Missa Terribilis*			The Pogues, *If I Should Fall From Grace* (album)
Jimmy Breslin, *Table Money*				
Thomas Kilroy, *Double Cross*	Roy McFadden, *Letters to the Hinterland*			
Dónal MacAmhlaigh, *Deoraithe* (Exiles)				

1987: Charles Haughey returns as Taoiseach. Irish Writers' Centre founded by Jack Harte. Stephen Roche wins Tour de France.

Fiction	Poetry	Drama	Autobiography	Miscellaneous
Mary Beckett, *Give Them Stones*	Ciaran Carson, *The Irish for No*	Michael Harding, *Strawboys*		*The Lonely Passion of Judith Hearne* (film by Jack Clayton)
Maud Casey, *Over the Water*	Paul Durcan, *Going Home to Russia*	Stewart Parker, *Pentecost*		U2, *The Joshua Tree* (album)
Jennifer Johnston, *Fool's Sanctuary*	Seamus Heaney, *The Haw Lantern*			
Brian Moore, *The Colour of Blood*	Paul Muldoon, *Meeting the British*			

1988: Gibraltar shootings of three unarmed members of the IRA.

Fiction	Poetry	Drama	Autobiography	Miscellaneous
John Banville, *The Book of Evidence*	Paul Durcan, *Jesus and Angela*	Brian Friel, *Making History*	Bill Naughton, *Saintly Billy*	Van Morrison, *Irish Heartbeat* (album)
Roddy Doyle, *The Commitments*	Medbh McGuckian, *On Ballycastle Beach*	Frank McGuinness, *Carthaginians*	Alice Taylor, *To School Through the Fields*	Edward Said, *Nationalism, Colonialism and Literature: Yeats and Decolonization*
Thomas Flanagan, *The Tenants of Time*		Billy Roche, *A Handful of Stars*		

Fiction	Poetry	Drama	Autobiography	Miscellaneous
Eilís Ní Dhuibhne, *Blood and Water*				
Breandan Ó hÉithir, *Sionnach ar mo Dhuán*				
Glenn Paterson, *Burning Your Own*				

1989: Pat Finucane, Belfast solicitor, shot dead. Legal Separation Bill approved in Dáil. Guildford Four released from prison. Limerick becomes a university city. Samuel Beckett dies.

Fiction	Poetry	Drama	Autobiography	Miscellaneous
Shane Connaughton, *A Border Station*	Ciaran Carson, *Belfast Confetti*	Dermot Bolger, *The Lament for Arthur O'Leary*	Paddy Doyle, *The God Squad*	*My Left Foot* (film by Jim Sheridan)
Mary Gordon, *The Other Side*	Eiléan Ní Chuilleanáin, *The Magdalene Sermon*	Terry Eagleton, *Saint Oscar*	John Gregory Dunne, *Harp*	
Danny Morrison, *West Belfast*		Michael Harding, *Una Pooka*	Desmond Egan, *A Song for My Father*	
Patrick O'Flaherty, *Priest of God*		Billy Roche, *Poor Beast in the Rain*	Aidan Higgins, *Helsingør Station and Other Departures*	
Timothy O'Grady, *Motherland*				
Robert McLiam Wilson, *Ripley Bogle*				

1990: Mary Robinson elected President of Ireland. Ireland's soccer team reach quarter-finals of World Cup in Italy.

Fiction	Poetry	Drama	Autobiography	Miscellaneous
Dermot Bolger, *The Journey Home*	Eavan Boland, *Outside History*	Sebastian Barry, *Prayers of Sherkin*	Gerry Conlon, *Proved Innocent*	*December Bride* (film by Thaddeus O'Sullivan)
Roddy Doyle, *The Snapper*	Paul Durcan, *Daddy, Daddy*	Dermot Bolger, *High Germany* and *The Holy Ground* and *Blinded by Light*	Patrick Galvin, *Song For A Poor Boy: A Cork Childhood*	P.J. Kavanagh, *Finding Connections*
Hugo Hamilton, *Surrogate City*	Brendan Kennelly, *A Time for Voices: Selected Poems 1960-1990*	Brian Friel, *Dancing at Lughnasa*		Sinéad O'Connor, *I Do Not Want What I Haven't Got* (album)
John McGahern, *Amongst Women*				
Brian Moore, *Lies of Silence*	Roy McFadden, *After Seymour's Funeral*	Seamus Heaney, *The Cure at Troy*		
Eilís Ní Dhuibhne, *The Bray House*	Nuala Ní Dhomhnaill, *Pharoah's Daughter*	Graham Reid, *The Closed Door*		

1991: Birmingham Six released. Dublin Writers' Museum opens.

Fiction	Poetry	Drama	Autobiography	Miscellaneous
Paddy Doyle, *The Van*	Vincent Buckley, *Last Poems*	Billy Roche, *Belfry*		*The Commitments* (film by Alan Parker)
Anne Enright, *The Portable Virgin*	Maura Dooley, *Explaining Magnetism*			Gerald Dawe, *How's The Poetry Going*

Fiction	Poetry	Drama	Autobiography	Miscellaneous
Nina Fitzpatrick, *Fables of the Irish Intelligentsia*	Seamus Heaney, *Seeing Things*			*The Field Day Anthology of Irish Writing*
Moy McCrory, *Those Sailing Ships of his Boyhood Dreams*	John Hewitt, *The Collected Poems of John Hewitt*			Thomas Keneally, *Now And In Time To Be*
Eilís Ní Dhuíbhne, *Eating Women Is Not Recommended*	Brendan Kennelly, *The Book of Judas*			U2, *Achtung Baby* (album)
Joseph O'Connor, *True Believers*	Michael Longley, *Gorse Fires*			
William Trevor, *Reading Turgenev*				

1992: Haughey resigns over phone tapping of journalists allegations in 1982. Girl of fourteen ('X' case) prevented from travelling to Britain for an abortion after being raped. Poll on abortion sees a third in favour. Maastricht Treaty receives 69 per cent approval. November general election sees women TDs increase from twelve to twenty (out of 166). Dr Eamonn Casey, RC Bishop of Galway, resigns in disgrace and leaves Ireland. Michael Carruth wins boxing gold medal at Barcelona Olympics. Irish spend £23 per head on books; 41 per cent of books purchased are published in Ireland. Raven Arts Press reformed into New Island Books.

Fiction	Poetry	Drama	Autobiography	Miscellaneous
Clare Boylan, *Home Rule*	Nuala Ní Dhomhnaill, *The Astrakhan Cloak*	Sebastian Barry, *White Woman Street*	Mary Costello, *Titanic Town*	*The Crying Game* (film by Neil Jordan)
Eugene McCabe, *Death and Nightingales*		Bernard Farrell, *Forty-four Sycamore*	Denis Donoghue, *Warrenpoint*	Bryan MacMahon, *The Master*
Patrick McCabe, *The Butcher Boy*			Brian Keenan, *An Evil Cradling*	
Carl Aidan Mathews, *Lipstick on the Host*				
Glenn Patterson, *Fat Lad*				
Colm Tóibín, *The Heather Blazing*				

1993: Albert Reynolds re-elected Taoiseach. IRA bombs in Warrington and city of London. Downing Street Declaration. Irish President meets Queen of England. Department of Arts, Culture and the Gaeltacht established. Second Commission on the Status of Women reports. Roddy Doyle wins Booker Prize with *Paddy Clarke, Ha Ha Ha*.

Fiction	Poetry	Drama	Autobiography	Miscellaneous
Roddy Doyle, *Paddy Clarke, Ha Ha Ha*	Gabriel Fitzmaurice, *The Space Between*			Cranberries, *Everyone Else Is Doing It, So Why Can't We* (debut album)
Martin Flanagan, *Going Away*	Medbh McGuckian, *The Flower Master and Other Poems*			Desmond Hogan, *The Edge of the City*

Fiction	Poetry	Drama	Autobiography	Miscellaneous
Brian Moore, *No Other Life*	Martin Mooney, *Grub*			*In the Name of the Father* (film by Jim Sheridan)
Jane Urquhart, *Away*	Cathal Ó Searcaigh, *Homecoming / An Bealach 'na Bhaile*			William Kennedy, *Riding the Yellow Trolley Car*
				Patrick O'Farrell, *The Irish in Australia* (rev. ed.)
				Van Morrison, *Too Long in Exile* (album)

1994: IRA ceasefire. Taoiseach Albert Reynolds resigns over High Court's handling of case of Brendan Smyth, a paedophile priest.

Fiction	Poetry	Drama	Autobiography	Miscellaneous
Michael Collins, *The Life and Times of a Teaboy*	Eavan Boland, *In A Time Of Violence* and *Night Feed*	Marina Carr, *The Mai*	Pete Hamill, *A Drinking Life*	Brendan Kennelly, *Journey Into Joy*
Nina Fitzpatrick, *The Loves of Faustyna*	Paul Muldoon, *The Prince of the Quotidian*	Teresa Deevy, *Katie Roche* (revived)	Annie Maguire, *Why Me?*	Kerby Miller and Paul Wagner, *Out of Ireland* (US TV documentary)
Thomas Flanagan, *The End of the Hunt*		Brian Friel, *Molly Sweeney*		
Charles Foran, *Kitchen Music*		Martin Lynch, *Pictures of Tomorrow*		The Saw Doctors, *All The Way From Tuam* (album)
Dermot Healy, *A Goat's Song*				*Words Upon the Window Pane* (film by Mary McGuckian)
Patrick McGinley, *The Lost Soldier's Song*				
Eoin McNamee, *Resurrection Man*				
Edna O'Brien, *The House of Splendid Isolation*				
Robert Welch, *The Kilcolman Notebook*				

1995: Taoiseach John Bruton and Prime Minister John Major launch Framework Document. Confrontation at Drumcree during marching season in the North. David Trimble elected leader of Unionist Party. In a referendum on divorce Ireland votes narrowly in favour. Seamus Heaney receives Nobel Prize.

Fiction	Poetry	Drama	Autobiography	Miscellaneous
Emma Donoghue, *Hood*	Ciaran Carson, *Letters from the Alphabet*	Sebastian Barry, *The Steward of Christendom*	Aidan Higgins, *Donkey's Years*	Dermot Healy, *The Bend For Home*

Fiction	Poetry	Drama	Autobiography	Miscellaneous
Anne Enright, *The Wig My Father Wore*	James Liddy, *Collected Poems*	Tom Murphy, *She Stoops to Folly*	Paddy Joe Hill and Gerard Hunt, *Forever Lost, Forever Gone*	Declan Kiberd, *Inventing Ireland*
Jennifer Johnston, *The Illusionist*	Michael Longley, *The Ghost Orchid*			*Nothing Personal* (film by Thaddeus O'Sullivan)
Thomas Keneally, *A River Town*	Derek Mahon, *The Hudson Letter*		Thomas Keneally, *Homebush Boy*	
Patrick McCabe, *The Dead School*				Fintan O'Toole, *Meanwhile Back at the Ranch: The Politics of Irish Beef*
Kate O'Riordan, *Involved*				Séan Ó Tuama, *Repossessions*
James Ryan, *Home From England*				Tim Robinson, *Stones of Aran: Labyrinth*
Pádraig Standún, *Stigmata*				

1996: IRA renew campaign of violence with bombs in London and Manchester. All-Party talks revived under chairmanship of US Senator George Mitchell. Child–abuse allegations made against Goldenbridge Orphanage in 1950s. Theme of Frankfurt Book Fair: Ireland and Its Diaspora. Murder of Veronica Guerin, Dublin journalist.

Fiction	Poetry	Drama	Autobiography	Miscellaneous
Mary Rose Callaghan, *Emigrant Dreams*	Eavan Boland, *Collected Poems*	Marina Carr, *Portia Coughlan*	Frank McCourt, *Angela's Ashes*	Eavan Boland, *Object Lessons*
Seamus Deane, *Reading in the Dark*	Ciaran Carson, *Opera Et Cetera*	Martin McDonagh, *The Beauty Queen of Leenane*		Anthony Cronin, *Samuel Beckett: The Last Modernist*
Roddy Doyle, *The Woman Who Walked Into Doors*	Maura Dooley, *Kissing A Bone*	Enda Walshe, *Disco Pigs*		James Knowlson, *Damned to Fame: The Life of Samuel Beckett*
Deirdre Madden, *One By One In The Darkness*	Seamus Heaney, *The Spirit Level*			Joseph O'Connor, *Sweet Liberty: Travels in Irish America*
Brian Moore, *The Statement*	Rita Ann Higgins, *Higher Purchase*			Nuala O'Faolain, *Are You Somebody?*
Edna O'Brien, *Down By The River*	Paul Muldoon, *New Selected Poems 1968-1994*			The Saw Doctors, *World of Good* (album)
Colm Tóibín, *The Story of the Night*	Michael O'Loughlin, *Another Nation: New and Selected Poems*			Michael Viney, *A Year's Turning*
Robert McLiam Wilson, *Eureka Street*				*Michael Collins* (film by Neil Jordan)

Fiction	Poetry	Drama	Autobiography	Miscellaneous

1997: Bertie Ahern succeeds John Bruton as Taoiseach. IRA new ceasefire. Mary McAleese elected President of Ireland. Frank McCourt wins Pulitzer Prize with *Angela's Ashes*.

Fiction	Poetry	Drama	Autobiography	Miscellaneous
John Banville, *The Untouchable*	Derek Mahon, *The Yellow Book*	Brian Friel, *Give Me Your Answer Do!*	Robert Greacen, *The Sash My Father Wore*	Roy Foster, *W.B. Yeats: A Life* Vol. 1
Dermot Bolger et al., *Finbar's Hotel*	Mary O'Malley, *The Knife in the Wave*	Martin McDonagh, *The Lonesome West*	Cal McCrystal, *Reflections on a Quiet Rebel*	Fintan O'Toole, *The Ex-Isle of Erin*
Dermot Bolger, *Father's Music*	Seán Ó Tuama, *Rogha Dánta/Death in the Land of Youth*	Frank McGuinness, *Mutabilitie*		Ciaran Carson, *The Star Factory*
Anthony Glavin, *Nighthawk Alley*	Matthew Sweeney, *The Bridal Suite*	Conor McPherson, *The Weir*		
Bernard MacLaverty, *Grace Notes*	Eamonn Wall, *Iron Mountain Road*			
Danny Morrison, *The Wrong Man*				
Timothy O'Grady and Steve Pyke, *I Could Read the Sky*				
Deirdre Purcell, *Love Like Hate Adore*				

1998: Northern Ireland Peace talks given renewed emphasis. An agreement reached on Good Friday is confirmed in a Referendum in May and elections held for new Assembly in June. Omagh bomb kills twenty-nine people. Stand-off at Drumcree by Orangemen. John Hume and David Trimble receive Nobel Prize for Peace. On 16 June a global reading of *Ulysses* takes place on the Internet for the first time.

Fiction	Poetry	Drama	Autobiography	Miscellaneous
Sebastian Barry, *The Whereabouts of Eneas McNulty*	Medbh McGuckian, *Shelmalier*	Sebastian Barry *Our Lady of Sligo*	George O'Brien, *Dancehall Days*	*The Boxer* (Jim Sheridan film)
Carlo Gébler, *How To Murder a Man*	Paul Muldoon, *Hay*		Richard White, *Remembering Ahanagran*	*Butcher Boy* (Neil Jordan film)
Patrick Kavanagh, *Gaff Topsails*	Seamus Heaney, *Opened Ground*			
Maurice Leitch, *The Smoke King*	Eavan Boland, *The Lost Land*			
Patrick McCabe, *Breakfast on Pluto*	Aidan Matthews, *According to the Small Hours*			
Colum McCann, *This Side of Brightness*				
William Trevor, *Death in Summer*				
Jennifer Johnston, *Two Moons*				

Fiction	Poetry	Drama	Autobiography	Miscellaneous

1999: Launch of the Euro. Rosemary Nelson, prominent lawyer, murdered in Lurgan, Co. Armagh. Ireland in record exchequer surplus. RTÉ documentary 'States of Fear' uncovers widespread abuse of children in care from 1940s on. Flood Committee Hearings on payments to politicians. New British and Irish initiatives on Good Friday Agreement. Scottish and Welsh Assemblies open in Edinburgh and Cardiff. Assembly meets in Belfast, then suspended.

Fiction	Poetry	Drama	Autobiography	Miscellaneous
Maeve Brennan, *The Springs of Affection*	Paul Durcan, *Greetings to Our Friends in Brazil*		Peter Sheridan, *44: A Dublin Memoir*	McKittrick et al., *Lost Lives*
Roddy Doyle, *A Star Called Henry*	Seamus Heaney, *Beowulf*		Michael MacDonald *All Souls*	
Colm Tóibín, *The Blackwater Lightship*	John Montague, *Smashing the Piano*			
	Nuala Ní Dhomhnaill, *The Water Horse*			

2000: Renewed attempts at reviving Assembly at Stormont meet with success.

100 RECOMMENDED BOOKS

Some students like a sense of challenge and they may find the following list of titles helpful as a way of building up their knowledge of Irish literature The titles are arranged alphabetically by genre in author order.

Journals and Autobiographies

Brendan Behan, *Borstal Boy* (1958)
Christy Brown, My *Left Foot* (1954)
Austin Clarke, *Twice Round the Black Church* (1962)
Anthony Cronin, *Dead As Doornails* (1976)
Oliver St John Gogarty, *As I Was Going Down Sackville Street* (1937)
Lady Gregory, *Lady Gregory's Journals,* Volume One (1978)
Brian Inglis, *West Briton* (1962)
Hugh Leonard, *Home Before Night* (1979)
Maud Gonne MacBride, *A Servant of the Queen* (1938)
Seamas MacManus, *The Rocky Road to Dublin* (1938)
Frank McCourt, *Angela's Ashes* (1996)
George Moore, *Hail and Farewell* (1911–14)
Sean O'Casey, *Autobiographies,* 2 Volumes (1963)
Frank O'Connor, *An Only Child* (1962)
Sean O'Faolain, *Vive Moi!* (rev. ed. 1993)
Maurice O'Sullivan, *Twenty Years A-Growing* (1933)
Terence De Vere White, *A Fretful Midge* (1959)
William Butler Yeats, *Autobiographies* (1955)

Short Stories and Folk Tales

Elizabeth Bowen, *The Collected Stories of Elizabeth Bowen* (1982)
Lady Gregory, *Cuchulain of Muirthemne* (1902)
James Joyce, *Dubliners* (1914)
Mary Lavin, *Selected Stories* (1981)
John McGahern, *The Collected Stories* (1992)
Michael McLaverty, *Collected Short Stories* (1978)
George Moore, *The Untilled Field* (1903)
Frank O'Connor, *The Stories Of Frank O'Connor* (1953)
Sean O'Faolain, *Stories of Sean O'Faolain* (1970)
Liam O'Flaherty, *The Short Stories of Liam O'Flaherty* (1937)
Seán O'Sullivan (ed. and trans.), *Folktales of Ireland* (1966)
Edith Somerville and Violet Ross, *Some Experiences of an Irish R.M.* (1899)
William Trevor, *The Stories of William Trevor* (1983)

Novels

Samuel Beckett, *Malone Dies* (1951)
Elizabeth Bowen, *The Last September* (1929)
Christy Brown, *Down All the Days* (1970)

Seamus Deane, *Reading in the Dark* (1996)
Roddy Doyle, *The Barrytown Trilogy* (1992)
James T. Farrell, *Studs Lonigan* (1935)
Thomas Flanagan, *The Year of the French* (1978)
Aidan Higgins, *Langrishe, Go Down* (1966)
Joseph Furphy, *Such Is Life* (1903)
Jennifer Johnston, *Shadows on Our Skin* (1979)
James Joyce, *A Portrait of the Artist as a Young Man* (1916)
Molly Keane, *Good Behaviour* (1981)
John McGahern, *Amongst Women* (1990)
Patrick MacGill, *Lanty Hanlon* (1912)
Patrick McCabe, *The Butcher Boy* (1992)
Edward A. McCourt, *Home Is The Stranger* (1950)
Bernard MacLaverty, *Cal* (1983)
Brian Moore, *The Mangan Inheritance* (1979)
George Moore, *The Lake* (1905)
Flann O'Brien, *At Swim-Two-Birds* (1939)
Kate O'Brien, *Mary Lavelle* (1936)
Edwin O'Connor, *The Last Hurrah* (1956)
Liam O'Flaherty, *Famine* (1937)
Richard Power, *The Hungry Grass* (1969)
James Stephens, *Crock of Gold* (1912)
Francis Stuart, *BlackList, Section H* (1971)
William Trevor, *Fools of Fortune* (1983)
Robert McLiam Wilson, *Eureka Street* (1997)

Drama

Samuel Beckett, *After the Fall* (1957)
Marina Carr, *The Mai* (1994)
Padraic Colum, *The Land* (1905)
St John Ervine, *Mixed Marriage* (1911)
Brian Friel, *Translations* (1980) and *Dancing at Lughnasa* (1990)
Lady Gregory, *Seven Short Plays* (1909)
Denis Johnston, *The Old Lady Says 'No'!* (1928)
Martin McDonagh, *The Beauty Queen of Leenane* (1996)
Frank McGuinness, *Observe the Sons of Ulster Marching Towards the Somme* (1986)
Tom Murphy, *Conversations on a Homecoming* (1985)
Sean O'Casey, *Juno and the Paycock* (1924)
Eugene O'Neill, *Long Day's Journey Into Night* (1956)
Stewart Parker, *Pentecost* (1987)
George Bernard Shaw, *John Bull's Other Island* (1904)
John Millington Synge, *The Playboy of the Western World* (1907)
William Butler Yeats, *Cathleen ni Houlihan* (1902)

Poetry and Song

Eavan Boland, *Collected Poems* (1995)
Ciaran Carson, *Belfast Confetti* (1989)

Austin Clarke, *Collected Poems* (1974)

Seamus Heaney, *New Selected Poems 1966-1987* (1990)

Denis Devlin, *Collected Poems* (1964)

Paul Durcan, A *Snail In My Prime: New and Selected Poems* (1993)

Padraic Fiacc, *Missa Terribilis* (1985)

John Hewitt, *Collected Poems* (1991)

Patrick Kavanagh, *Collected Poems* (1964)

Thomas Kinsella, *Collected Poems* (1996)

Francis Ledwidge, *The Complete Poems* (1974)

Michael Longley, *Gorse Fires* (1991) and *The Ghost Orchid* (1995)

Derek Mahon, *Selected Poems* (1993)

Roy McFadden, *Letters to the Hinterland* (1986)

John Montague, *Selected Poems* (1982)

Paul Muldoon, *New Selected Poems 1968-1994* (1996)

Nuala Ní Dhomhnaill, *Pharaoh's Daughter* (1990)

Colm Ó Lochlainn, *The Complete Irish Street Ballads* (1984)

Cathal Ó Searcaigh, *Homecoming/An Bealach 'na Bhaile* (1993)

Donal O'Sullivan, *Songs of the Irish* (1960)

James Simmons, *Poems 1956-1986* (1986)

William Butler Yeats, *Collected Poems* (1950)

SELECT LIST OF AUTHORS

Writers included in this *Reader* are marked with an asterisk.

*Banville, John (1945–), novelist.
Bardwell, Leland (1928–), poet and novelist.
Barlow, Jane (1857–1917), poet and novelist.
*Barry, Sebastian (1955–), playwright, poet, and novelist.
*Barry, Tom (1897-1980), guerrilla leader.
*Beckett, Mary (1926–), novelist, short story writer.
*Beckett, Samuel (1906–89), novelist, playwright.
*Behan, Brendan (1923–64), playwright and novelist.
Behan, Dominic (1928–), songwriter.
*Bell, Sam Hanna (1909–90), novelist, short story writer.
Berkeley, Sara (1967–), poet and short story writer.
Binchy, Maeve (1940–), novelist and short story writer.
*Birmingham, George (pseudonym of Canon James Owen Hannay) (1865–1950), novelist and playwright.
*Blackwood, Caroline (1931–), novelist.
Blair, Ron (1942–), Australian playwright and novelist.
*Boland, Eavan (1944–), poet.
Bolger, Dermot (1959-), novelist and playwright.
*Böll, Heinrich (1917–87), German novelist and writer.
*Bono (Paul Hewson) (1960–), singer and writer.
*Bowen, Elizabeth (1899–1973), novelist and short story writer.
*Boyd, Ernest (1887–1946), literary critic and journalist.
Boylan, Clare (1948–), novelist.
*Boyle, Patrick (1905–82), novelist and short story writer.
Boyle, William (1853–1923), playwright.
Brennan, Christopher (1870–1932), Australian poet.
*Breslin, Jimmy (1930–), American novelist.
Broderick, John (1927–89), novelist.
*Brody, Hugh (1943–), sociologist and writer.
*Brown, Christy (1932-1981), novelist and poet.
*Buckley, Vincent (1925–88), Australian critic and poet.
Bullock, Shan F. (1865–1935), novelist.
*Burgess, Anthony (1917–93), novelist, composer, critic.
*Butler, Hubert (1900–90), man of letters.
Byrne, Donn (1889–1928), novelist and short story writer.
Callaghan, Mary Rose (1944–), novelist and critic.

*Campbell, Joseph (1879–1944), poet.
*Campbell, Patrick (1913–80), journalist and broadcaster.
*Carbery, Ethna (1866–1911), poet and short story writer.
*Carew, Rivers (1935–), editor.
*Carr, Marina (1964–), playwright.
Carroll, Paul Vincent (1900–68), playwright.
*Carson, Ciaran (1948–), poet.
Cary, Joyce (1888–1957), novelist.
Casey, Kevin (1940–), novelist.
Casey, Philip (1950–), poet, playwright, and novelist.
*Clarke, Austin (1896–1974), poet, playwright, novelist.
*Clifton, Harry (1952–), poet.
*Coffey, Brian (1905–95), poet.
*Colum, Mary (1887–1957), critic.
*Colum, Padraic (1881–1972), poet, playwright, novelist, short story writer, biographer.
*Conlon, Gerry (1964–), prisoner.
Conner, Rearden (1907–91), novelist.
*Corkery, Daniel (1878–1964), critic, short story writer.
*Coulter, John (1888–1980), Canadian playwright, novelist, short story writer, poet.
Cousins, James H. (1873–1956), poet and playwright.
Cronin, Anthony (1928–), poet, critic, novelist, biographer.
*Cross, Eric (1905–80), memorialist.
Cullinan, Elizabeth (1933–), American novelist.
D'Alton, Louis (1900–51), playwright and novelist.
D'Arcy, Margaretta (1934–), playwright and producer.
Davin, Dan (1913–90), New Zealand novelist and critic.
Davitt, Michael (1950–), poet and critic.
*Dawe, Gerald (1952–), critic and poet.
Day Lewis, Cecil (1904–72), Anglo-Irish poet and critic.
Deane, John F. (1943–), poet.
*Deane, Seamus (1940–), poet, critic, and novelist.
*Deevy, Teresa (1894–1963), playwright.
*Delanty, Greg (1958–), poet and critic.
Devlin, Anne (1951–), playwright and short story writer.
*Devlin, Denis (1908–59), poet.
Devlin, Polly (1941–), writer.
Dillon, Eilis (1920–94), novelist and children's writer.

*Dinneen, Patrick (an tAthair Pádraig Ó Duinnín) (1860–1934), lexicographer.

*Dinneen, Joseph (1897–), American biographer and novelist.

*Donleavy, J.P. (1926–), American novelist and writer.

*Donnelly, Charles (1914–37), poet.

*Donoghue, Denis (1928–), critic.

Donoghue, Emma (1969–), novelist.

*Dooley, Maura (1957–), English poet.

Dorgan, Theo (1953–), critic and poet.

*Doyle, Arthur Conan (1859–1930), British fiction writer.

*Doyle, Lynn C. (pseudonym of Leslie Montgomery) (1873–1961), short story writer.

*Doyle, Roddy (1958–), novelist.

Dowden, Edward (1843–1913), critic.

Driscoll, Charles B. (1885–1951), American novelist.

Duggan, Eileen (?1894–1972), New Zealand poet.

*Dunne, Finley Peter (1867–1936), American journalist and humorist.

*Dunne, John Gregory (1932–), American novelist.

*Dunne, Lee (1934–), novelist and scriptwriter.

*Dunsany, Lord (1878–1957), short story writer and playwright.

Durack, Mary (1913–), Australian writer.

*Durcan, Paul (1944–), poet.

*Eagleton, Terry (1943–), critic and playwright.

*Egan, Desmond (1936–), poet.

*Egan, Maurice Francis (1852–1924), American novelist and writer.

*Eglinton, John (pseudonym of William K.Magee) (1868–1961), critic.

Ennis, John (1944–), poet.

Enright, Anne (1962–), novelist and short story writer.

*Ervine, St John (1883–1971), playwright and critic.

*Fahy, Francis (1854–1935), songwriter.

*Fallon, Padraic (1905–74), poet and playwright.

*Fallon, Peter (1951–), poet and publisher.

Farrell, Bernard (1939–), playwright.

*Farrell, James T. (1904–79), American novelist.

Farrell, Michael (1899–1962), novelist.

*Fiacc, Padraic (1924–), poet.

*Figgis, Darrell (pseudonym Michael Ireland) (1882–1925), novelist, political journalist, poet.

*Fitzgerald, F. Scott (1896–1940), American novelist and short story writer.

Fitzmaurice, Gabriel (1952–), poet and critic.

Fitzmaurice, George (1877–1963), playwright.

*Flanagan, Thomas (1923–), American historical novelist and critic.

*Flower, Robin (1881–1946), poet and translator.

Foley, Michael (1947–), novelist and poet.

*Franklin, Miles (1879–1954), Australian novelist.

*Friel, Brian (1929–), playwright and short story writer.

*Furphy, Joseph (pseudonym of Tom Collins) (1843–1912), Australian novelist.

*Gallagher, Frank (1898–1962), newspaper editor and writer.

*Gallagher, Tess (1943–), American poet.

*Galvin, Patrick (1927–), poet and playwright.

Gébler, Carlo (1954–), novelist, short story writer, journalist.

*Gibbings, Robert (1889–1958), wood-engraver, book designer, travel writer.

*Gibbon, Monk (1896–1987), poet and critic.

Gill, Brendan (1914–), American novelist.

Glavin, Anthony (1946–), American fiction writer.

*Gogarty, Oliver St John (1878–1957), poet and writer.

*Gordon, Mary (1949–), American novelist.

*Gore-Booth, Eva (1870–1926), poet.

*Greacen, Robert (1920–), poet and critic.

Greeley, Andrew M. (1928–), American novelist.

*Gregory, Lady Augusta (1852–1932), playwright and folklorist.

*Griffith, Arthur (1871–1922), journalist and politician.

Gwynn, Stephen (1864–1950), travel writer, poet, biographer, critic.

Hackett, Francis (1883–1962), novelist and critic.

Hamill, Peter (1935–), American novelist.

Hamilton, Hugo (1953–), novelist.

*Hartnett, Michael (1941–99), bi-lingual poet.

*Healy, Dermot (1947–), novelist and short story writer.

*Heaney, Seamus (1939–), poet and critic.

Henn, Thomas Rice (1901–74), critic.

*Hewitt, John (1907–87), poet.

*Higgins, Aidan (1927–), novelist and short story writer.

*Higgins, Frederick Robert (1896–1941), poet.

*Higgins, Rita Ann (1955–), poet.

*Hobsbaum, Philip (1932–), British poet and critic.

*Hogan, Desmond (1950–), novelist and writer.

*Holland, Jack (1947–), journalist and writer.

*Holland, Mary (1936–), newspaper journalist.

Holloway, Joseph (1861–1944), diarist.

*Hone, Joseph (1882–1959), biographer.

Hoult, Nora (1898–1984), novelist and short story writer.

Hutchinson, Pearse (1927–), Irish-language poet.

*Hyde, Douglas (An Craoibhin Aoibhinn) (1860–1949), poet and translator.

*Inglis, Brian (1916–91), journalist and broadcaster.

*Iremonger, Valentin (1918–91), poet.

Jeffares, A. Norman (1920–), biographer and critic.

*Johnson, Lionel (1867–1902), British poet.

Johnston, Denis (1901–84), playwright.

Johnston, Fred (1951–), poet and critic.

*Johnston, Jennifer (1930–), novelist.

*Jordan, John (1930–88), poet and critic.

Jordan, Neil (1951–), short story writer, screenplay writer, film director.

*Joyce, James (1882–1941), novelist and short story writer, poet and playwright.

*Joyce, Patrick Weston (1827–1914), musicologist, historian, linguist, and geographer.

*Joyce, Stanislaus (1884–1955), biographer and diarist.

*Kavanagh, Patrick (1904–67), poet and novelist.

Keane, John B. (1928–), playwright and fiction writer.

*Keane, Molly (1905–96), novelist and playwright.

Kearney, Peadar (1883–1942), songwriter.

*Kearney, Richard (1954–), critic and novelist.

*Kelleher, John V. (1916–), American critic.

*Keneally, Thomas (1935–), Australian novelist.

Kennedy, Jimmy (1902–84), songwriter.

*Kennedy, William (1928–), American novelist.

*Kennelly, Brendan (1936–), poet.

*Kettle, Thomas (1880–1916), critic and essayist.

*Kiely, Benedict (1919–), novelist, critic and short story writer.

Kilroy, Thomas (1934–), playwright and novelist.

*King, Cecil (1901–87), newspaper magnate and writer.

Kinnell, Galway (1927–), American poet.

*Kinsella, Thomas (1928–), poet and translator.

Laverty, Maura (1907–66), novelist and playwright.

*Lavery, John (1856–1941), artist.

*Lavin, Mary (1912–96), novelist and short story writer.

Lawless, Emily (1845–1913), novelist and poet.

*Ledwidge, Francis (1887–1917), poet.

Leitch, Maurice (1933–), novelist.

Leland, Mary (1941–), novelist and journalist.

Leonard, Hugh (1926–), playwright.

Leslie, Shane (1885–1971), man of letters.

Letts, Winifred (1882–1972), poet, playwright, and novelist.

*Leventhal, A.J. (1896–1979), critic.

Liddy, James (1934–), poet.

Lingard, Joan (1932–), Scottish children's writer.

Longford, Lord (1902–61), playwright and politician.

*Longley, Edna (1940–), critic.

*Longley, Michael (1939–), poet.

Lynch, Brian (1945–), poet, translator, and writer.

Lynch, Thomas (1948–), American poet and undertaker.

*Lynch-Robinson, Sir Christopher (1884–1958), Resident Magistrate.

Lynd, Robert (1879–1949), essayist and journalist.

Macken, Walter (1915–67), playwright and novelist.

Madden, Deirdre (1960–), poet

*Mahon, Derek (1941–), poet.

*Malone, Andrew E. (1890–1939), critic.

Malloy, Frances (1947–91), novelist.

Mannin, Ethel (1900–84), novelist.

*Manning, Mary (1906–), novelist and playwright.

Manning, Olivia (1908–80), novelist.

*Markievicz, Constance (née Gore-Booth) (1868–1927), revolutionary.

Martyn, Edward (1859–1923), playwright.

Mathews, Carl Aidan (1956–), novelist, short story writer, and poet.

Mayne, Rutherford (1878–1967), playwright.

*Mac Amlaigh, Dónal (1926–89), Irish-language novelist.

*Macardle, Dorothy (1899–1958), playwright, novelist and historian.

McCabe, Eugene (1930–), playwright, novelist, and scriptwriter.

*McCabe, Patrick (1955–), novelist.

McCarthy, Mary (1912–89), American writer and critic.

McCormack, William J. (pseudonym Hugh Maxton) (1947–), critic and poet.

*McCourt, Edward. A. (1907–), Canadian novelist.

*McCrory, Moy (1953–), Liverpool novelist and short story writer.

MacDonagh, Donagh (1912–68), poet and playwright.

*MacDonagh, Thomas (1878–1916), poet and critic.

*McDonagh, Martin (1970–), dramatist from London.

*McFadden, Roy (1921–), poet.

*McGahern, John (1934–), novelist and short story writer.

*MacGill, Patrick (1891–1963), novelist and poet.

McGinley, Patrick (1937–), novelist.

McGrath, Eamonn (1929–), novelist.

*MacGreevy, Thomas (1893–1967), poet and critic.

Mac Grianna, Seosamh (1901–90), Irish-language novelist.

*McGuckian, Medbh (1950–), poet.

McGuinness, Frank (1953–), playwright.

MacIntyre, Tom (1931–), playwright.

*MacLaverty, Bernard (1942–), novelist and short story writer.

*McLaverty, Michael (1907–92), novelist and short story writer.

*MacMahon, Bryan (1909–98), novelist, short story writer, playwright.

MacManus, Francis (1909–65), novelist.

*MacManus, Seamas (1869–1960), poet, songwriter, novelist and critic.

MacNamara, Brinsley (1890–1963), novelist, short story writer, and playwright.

*McNamee, Eoin (1961–), novelist.

*MacNeice, Louis (1907–63), poet and critic.

McNeill, Janet (1907–), novelist.

McSorley, Edward (1902–66), American novelist.

*McWhirter, George (1939–), Canadian poet.

Meehan, Paula (1955–), poet.

Milligan, Alice (1865–1953), poet and playwright.

*Milne, Ewart (1903–87), poet.

Molloy, M.J. (1917–94), playwright.

*Montague, John (1929–), poet.

*Mooney, Martin (1964–), poet.

*Moore, Brian (1921–99), Canadian novelist.

*Moore, George (1852–1933), novelist and short story writer.

*Moran, David Patrick (1869–1936), journalist and essayist.

*Morrison, Van (1945–), songwriter and singer.

*Muldoon, Paul (1951–), poet.

Mulholland, Rosa (1841–1921), novelist.

Mulkerns, Val (1925–), novelist and short story writer.

Murdoch, Iris (1919–99), novelist.

*Murphy, Dervla (1931–), travel writer.

*Murphy, Michael (1913–96), folklorist.

Murphy, Richard (1927–), poet.

Murphy, Seamus (1907–75), stonemason.

*Murphy, Thomas (1935–), playwright.

Murray, T.C. (1873–1959), playwright.

*Naughton, Bill (1910–92), Lancashire playwright, novelist and short story writer.

*Ní Chuilleanáin, Eiléan (1942–), poet and critic.

Ní Dhuibhne, Eilis (1954–), novelist and short story writer.

*Ní Dhomhnaill, Nuala (1952–), Irish-language poet.

*O'Brien, Conor Cruise O'Brien (1917–), critic and historian.

*O'Brien, Edna (1930–), novelist and short story writer.

*O'Brien, John (pseudonym of Rev P.J. Hartigan) (1878-1952), Australian poet.

*O'Brien, Kate (1897–1974), novelist, playwright, travel writer.

O'Brien, Kate Cruise (1948–), novelist and short story writer.

O'Brien, William (1852–1928), political journalist and novelist.

*Ó Cadhain, Máirtín (1906–70), Irish-language novelist and short story writer.

*O'Callaghan, Julie (1954–) (Irish poet born in United States).

*O'Casey, Sean (1880–1964), playwright.

Ó Conaire, Pádraic (1882–1928), Irish-language novelist and short-story writer.

*O'Connor, Edwin (1918–68), American novelist and short-story writer.

O'Connor, Elizabeth (1913–), Australian novelist.

*O'Connor, Frank (1903–66), short story writer critic, and translator.

O'Connor, Ulick (1928–), writer and critic.

*Ó Criomhthain, Tomás (Thomas O'Crohan) (1856–1937), Irish-language writer.

Ó Direáin, Máirtín (1910–88), Irish-language poet.

*O'Donnell, Peadar (1893–1986), novelist and political writer.

O'Donoghue, David James (1866–1917), biographer and critic.

O'Donovan, Gerald (1871–1942), novelist.

O'Driscoll, Dennis (1954–), poet and critic.

*O'Duffy, Eimar (1893–1935), novelist.

O'Faolain, Julia (1932–), novelist and short story writer.

*O'Faolain, Sean (1900–90), novelist, short story writer, and critic.

*O Faracháin, Roibeárd (Robert Farren) (1909–84), poet and critic.

*O'Flaherty, Liam (1896–1984), novelist and short story writer.

O'Flaherty, Patrick (1939–), Canadian novelist and short story writer.

Ó Floinn, Criostóir (1927–), bi-lingual playwright, poet, short story writer.

O'Grady, Desmond (1935–), poet.

*O'Grady, Standish James (1846–1928), historian, novelist and journalist.

*O'Hara, John (1905–70), American novelist and short story writer.

Ó hEithir, Breandan (1930–90), Irish-language novelist.

O'Higgins, Brian (1882–1949), poet, songwriter and novelist.

O'Kelly, Seumas (c.1875–1918), novelist, playwright and short story writer.

*Ó Laoghaire, Peadar (1839–1916), Irish-language fiction writer.

*O'Leary, Con (1887–1958), English-based journalist and short story writer.

*O'Loughlin, Michael (1958–), poet.

*O'Mara, Pat (1901–), English writer.

Ó Muirthile, Liam (1950–), Irish-language poet and journalist.

*O'Neill, Eugene (1888-1953), American dramatist.

*O'Neill, Moira (pseudonym of Nesta Skrene)
(1865–1955), poet.

*O'Nolan, Brian ('Flann O'Brien') (1911–66),
novelist and journalist.

*Ó Ríordáin, Seán (1916–77), Irish-language poet.

*O'Riordan, Conal ('F. Norreys Connell')
(1874–1948), novelist and playwright.

*Ó Searcaigh, Cathal (1956–   ), Irish-language poet.

Ó Siadhail, Mícheál (1947–   ), bilingual poet and
educator.

*Ó Suilleabháin, Muiris (Maurice O'Sullivan)
(1904–50), Irish-language writer.

*O'Sullivan, Seumas (pseudonym of James Sullivan
Starkey) (1879–1958), poet.

*O'Toole, Fintan (1958–   ), journalist and critic.

*Ó Tuama, Seán (1926–   ), Irish-language poet,
playwright and critic.

Ó Tuairisc, Eoghan (1919–82), bilingual poet and
novelist.

Palmer, Vance (1885–1959), Australian novelist and
playwright.

*Parker, Stewart (1941–88), playwright.

*Patterson, Glen (1961–   ), novelist.

*Paulin, Tom (1949–   ), poet and critic.

*Pearse, Patrick (1879–1916), poet and short story
writer.

*Phelan, Jim (1895–1966), novelist and short story
writer.

*Plunkett, James (1920–   ), novelist and short story
writer.

*Power, Richard (1928–70), novelist.

*Powers, J.F. (1917–99), American novelist and short-
story writer.

*Reid, Forrest (1875–1947), novelist.

Reid, Graham (1945–   ), playwright.

*Richardson, Henry Handel (pseudonym of Ethel
F.L. Robertson) (1870–1946), Australian novelist.

*Robb, Nesca (1905–76), writer.

Robinson, Lennox (1886–1958), playwright.

*Robinson, Tim (1935–   ), English writer, travel
writer and mapmaker.

Roche, Billy (1949–   ), playwright.

*Rodgers, W.R. (1909–69), poet and critic.

Rolleston, T.W. (1857–1920), man of letters.

Ros, Amanda McKittrick (1860–1939), novelist.

Rosenstock, Gabriel (1949–   ), Irish-language poet
and translator.

*Russell, George ('Æ') (1876–1935), poet, novelist,
critic.

*Ryan, Frederick (1876–1913), essayist and
playwright.

*Ryan, James (1962–   ), novelist.

*Ryan, John (1925–92), editor and writer.

*Said, Edward (1935–   ), Palestinian critic.

*Salkeld, Blanaid (1880–1959), poet.

*Shaw, Bob (1931–96), science fiction writer.

*Shaw, George Bernard (1856–1950), playwright.

Sheehan, Canon (1852–1913), novelist.

Shiels, George (1886–1949), playwright.

Shorter, Dora Sigerson (1866–1918), poet.

Sigerson, George (1836–1925), man of letters.

*Simmons, James (1933–   ), poet.

*Simpson, Leo (1934–   ), Canadian novelist,
playwright and short story writer

*Sirr, Peter (1960–   ), poet.

Skeffington, Francis Sheehy (1878–1916), writer.

Smith, Bernard (1916–   ), Australian art critic and
cultural historian.

*Smith, Betty (1904–72), American novelist and
playwright..

*Smith, Iain Crichton (1928–   ), Scottish poet and
writer.

*Smith, Paul (1935–   ), novelist.

Smith, Sydney Bernard (1936–   ), poet and playwright.

Smithson, Annie (1873–1948), novelist.

*Somerville, Edith (1858–1949) and Martin Ross (real
name Violet Martin) (1862–1915), novelists and
short story writers.

Standún, Padráig (1944–   ), Irish-language novelist.

Starkie, Walter (1894–1976), author.

*Stephens, James (1880 or 1882–1950), poet, novelist
and short story writer.

Stoker, Bram (1847–1912), novelist.

Strong, Eithne (1923–   ), poet and fiction writer.

*Strong, L.A.G. (1896–1958), novelist, poet and critic.

*Stuart, Francis (1902–   ), novelist and poet.

Sullivan, T.D. (1827–1914), journalist, poet, and
songwriter.

Sweeney, Matthew (1952–   ), poet.

*Sweetman, Rosita (1947–   ), journalist.

*Synge, John Millington (1871–1909), playwright and
poet.

*Thomson, David (1914–   ), British writer.

Thomson, Hugh (1860–1920), book illustrator.

Titley, Alan (1947–   ), Irish-language novelist,
translator and critic.

Todhunter, John (1839–1916), poet and playwright.

*Tóibín, Colm (1955–   ), novelist and critic.

Tomelty, Joseph (1911–95), playwright and novelist.

*Tracy, Honor (1913–87), English novelist and writer.

*Trevor, William (1928–   ), novelist and short story
writer.

Tynan, Katharine (1861–1931), poet and novelist.

*Tyrrell, George (1861–1909), Jesuit priest and heretic.

Uris, Leon (1924–   ), American novelist.

Urquhart, Jane (1949–   ), Canadian novelist.

*Ussher, Arland (1899–1980), critic.

*Vaughan, Bernard (1847–1922), English Jesuit and sermon-writer.

Waddell, Helen (1889–1965), writer and scholar.

*Wall, Eamonn (1955–   ), poet and critic.

Wall, Mervyn (1908–   ), novelist.

Walsh, Maurice (1879–1964), novelist.

Walshe, Dolores (1949–   ), novelist and dramatist.

*White, Terence de Vere (1912–94), novelist and critic.

White, William (1920–80), novelist and playwright.

*Wilde, Oscar (1854–1900), playwright, poet, short story writer.

Wilson, Helen (1874–1957), New Zealand novelist.

*Wilson, Robert McLiam (1964–   ), novelist.

Woods, Macdara (1942–   ), poet and editor.

Yeats, Jack B. (1871–1957), painter, playwright and novelist.

*Yeats, William Butler (1865–1939), poet, playwright, critic, and writer of short stories.

BIBLIOGRAPHY

GENERAL BIBLIOGRAPHICAL WORKS

Annotated Bibliography for English Studies. Lisse, Exton, Abingdon, Tokyo: Swets & Zeitlinger, 1996– .

Baumgarten, R. *Bibliography of Irish Linguistics and Literature, 1942-71*. Dublin: Dublin Institute of Advanced Studies, 1986.

Best, Richard. *Bibliography of Irish Philology and Printed Literature*. 1913; rpt. New York and London: Johnson, 1970.

———— *Bibliography of Irish Philology and Manuscript Literature Publications 1913-1941*. Dublin: Institute for Advanced Studies, 1942.

Blessing, Patrick J. 'Irish' entry. *Harvard Encyclopedia of American Ethnic Groups*. ed. Stephan Thernstrom. Cambridge, Mass.: Harvard University Press, 1980, 524–45.

Brady, Ann. *Women in Ireland: An Annotated Bibliography*. Westport, Conn.: Greenwood, 1988.

Brown, Stephen J. *A Guide to Books on Ireland*. Dublin: Hodges Figgis, 1912.

———— *Ireland in Fiction: A Guide to Irish Novels, Tales, Romances and Folklore*. 2nd edn 1919; repr. Shannon: Irish University Press, 1969.

Brown, Stephen J. and Desmond Clarke. *Ireland in Fiction: A Guide to Irish Novels, Tales, Romances and Folklore*. Cork: Royal Carbery, 1985.

Doloughan, Phyllis E. *Ulster Poetry: A Checklist of Published Collections, 1960-1980*. Belfast: Queen's University, 1983.

Doughan, David and Denise Sanchez. *Feminist Periodicals, 1855-1984: An Annotated Critical Bibliography of British, Irish, Commonwealth, and International Titles*. New York: New York University Press, 1987.

Duetsch, Richard R. *Northern Ireland 1921-1974: A Select Bibliography*. New York and London: Garland, 1975.

Eager, Alan. *A Guide to Irish Bibliographical Material*. London: London Library Association, 1964; enlarged second edition, 1980.

Finneran, Richard. *Anglo-Irish Literature: A Review of Research*. New York: Modern Language Association, 1976.

———— *Recent Research on Anglo-Irish Writers*. New York: Modern Language Association, 1983.

Gonzalez, Alexander, ed. *Modern Irish Writers: A Bio-Critical Sourcebook*. London: Aldwych Press, 1997.

Harmon, Maurice. *Modern Irish Literature, 1800-1967; A Reader's Guide*. Chester Springs, Pa: Dufour Editions, 1968.

———— *Select Bibliography for the Study of Anglo-Irish Literature and Its Backgrounds: An Irish Studies Handbook*. Dublin: Wolfhound Press, 1977.

Hayes, Richard J. *Manuscript Sources for the History of Irish Civilisation*, 11 vols. Boston: G.K. Hall, 1965; First Supplement, 3 vols. 1979.

———— *Sources for the History of Irish Civilisation: Articles in Irish Periodicals*, 9 vols. Boston: G.K.Hall, 1970.

Holzapfel, Rudi. *An Index of Contributors to the 'Dublin Magazine'*. Dublin: Museum Bookshop, 1966.

Irish Music Handbook. Dublin Castle: Music Network, 1996.

Irish Publishing Record. (Published annually) Dublin: National Library of Ireland.

Jones, Maldwyn. 'Scotch-Irish' entry. *Harvard Encyclopedia of American Ethnic Groups*. ed. Stephan Thernstrom. Cambridge, Mass.: Harvard University Press, 1980, 895–908.

Kersnowski, Frank L., C. W. Spinks, and Laird Loomis. *A Bibliography of Modern Irish and Anglo-Irish Literature*. San Antonio, Tex.: Trinity University Press, 1976.

Kosok, H. 'Anthologies of Anglo-Irish Literature: 1772-1986: A Checklist.' *Irish University Review*, vol. 18, no. 2 (Autumn 1988), 251–62.

McVeagh, John. *Irish Travel Writing: A Bibliography*. Dublin: Wolfhound, 1996.

Mikhail, E.H. *A Bibliography of Modern Irish Drama 1899-1970*. Introd. by William A. Armstrong. London: Macmillan, 1972.

———— *An Annotated Bibliography of Modern Anglo-Irish Drama*. Troy, New York: Whitston, 1981.

Miller, Liam. *Dolmen XXV: An Illustrated Bibliography of the Dolmen Press, 1951-1976*. Dublin: Dolmen Editions; Atlantic Highlands, N.J.: distributed by Humanities Press, 1976.

Nilsen, Don L.F. *Humor in Irish Literature: A Reference Guide*. Westport, Conn.: Greenwood Press, 1996.

Northern Ireland Political Literature 1973-74. (microfiche) Dublin: Irish Microforms, 1976.

Northern Ireland Political Literature 1966-1985. (microfiche) Belfast: Linen Hall Library, 1989.

Ó Cearnaigh, Seán. *Scríbhneóirí na Gaeilge, 1945-1995*. Baile Atha Cliath: Comhar Teoranta, 1995.

Ó Danachair, Caoimhín. *A Bibliography of Irish Ethnology and Folk Tradition*. Cork and Dublin: Mercier, 1978.

O'Malley, William T. *Anglo-Irish Literature: A Bibliography of Dissertations, 1873-1989*. New York: Greenwood Press, 1990.

Oram, Hugh. *The Newspaper Book: A History of Newspapers in Ireland 1649-1983*. Dublin: MO Books, 1983.

Political Literature of Northern Ireland, 1968-1972 : The Linenhall Library Collection Of Underground And Extreme Opinion Ephemera. (microfiche) Dublin: Irish University Press, 1974.

Porter, James. *The Traditional Music of Britain and Ireland. A Select Bibliography and Research Guide*. New York & London: Garland, 1989.

Rockett, Kevin, ed. *The Irish Filmography: Fiction Films, 1896-1996*. Dublin: Red Mountain Press, 1996.

Schaeffer, Deborah L. *Irish Folk Music: A Selected Discography*. New York and London: Greenwood, 1989.

Schrank, Bernice and William W. Demastes eds., *Irish Playwrights, 1880-1995: A Research and Production Sourcebook*. Westport, Conn.: Greenwood Press, 1997.

Shannon, Michael Owen. *Irish Republic*. Oxford: Clio Press, 1986.

_____ *Northern Ireland*. Oxford: Clio Press, 1991.

Shields, Hugh. *A Short Bibliography of Irish Folk Song*. Dublin: Folk Music Society of Ireland, 1985.

Warmer, Alan. *A Guide to Anglo-Irish Literature*. Dublin: Gill and Macmillan; New York: St Martin's Press, 1981.

Weekes, Ann Owens. *Unveiling Treasures: The Attic Guide to the Published Works of Irish Women Literary Writers: Drama, Fiction, Poetry*. Dublin: Attic Press, 1993.

ARCHIVES AND LIBRARIES

Alden, John Eliot. *Bibliographica Hibernica; Additions and Corrections to Wing*. Charlottesville Bibliographical Society of the University of Virginia, 1955.

Blessing, Patrick. *The Irish in America: A Guide to the Literature and the Manuscript Collections*. Washington, D.C.: Catholic University of America, 1992.

Bloomfield, B.C. (assisted by Karen Potts). *A Directory of Rare Books and Special Collections in the United Kingdom and the Republic of Ireland*. 2nd ed. London: Library Association Publishing, 1997.

Cambridge University Library. *Bradshaw Irish Collection: A Catalogue of the Bradshaw Collection of Irish Books in the University Library, Cambridge*. Cambridge: Printed for the University Library and to be had of B. Quaritch, 1916.

Colby College, Maine. *James Augustine Healy Collection of Nineteenth and Twentieth Century Irish Literature*. Compiled and edited by Cheryl Abbott and J. Fraser Cocks, III. Waterville, Me.: Colby College, 1978.

De Brún, Pádraig and Máire Herbert. *Catalogue of Irish Manuscripts in Cambridge Libraries*. Cambridge: Cambridge University Press, 1986.

Downs, Robert B. and Robert Bingham. *British and Irish Library Resources: A Bibliographical Guide*. rev. ed. London: Marshall, 1981.

Eleuterio-Comer, Susan K. *Irish American Material Culture: A Directory Of Collections, Sites, and Festivals in the United States and Canada*. New York: Greenwood Press, 1988.

Foster, Jane and Julia Sheppard. *British Archives: A Guide to Archive Resources in the United Kingdom*. Basingstoke: Macmillan, 1995.

Helferty, Seamus and Raymond Refausse. *Directory of Irish Archives*. Dublin: Irish Academic Press, 1993.

de Jubainville, Henry d'Arbois (Henry). *Essai d'un catalogue de la littérature épique de l'Irlande. Précédé d'une étude sur les manuscrits en langue irlandais conservés dans les Iles britanniques et sur le continent*. Nieuwkoop: B. de Graaf, 1969.

O'Neill, Robert K. *Guide to the Libraries and Archives of Ulster*. Ulster Historical Foundation, 1996.

_____ *Ulster Libraries: Archives, Museums and Ancestral Heritage Centres*. Ulster Historical Foundation, 1997.

Royal Irish Academy. *Catalogue of Irish Mss. in the Royal Irish Academy* (microform). Cork: Munster Microfilming, 1988.

Trinity College, Dublin. *Catalogue of the Irish Manuscripts in the Library of Trinity College, Dublin*. Compiled by T.K. Abbott and E.J. Gwynn. Dublin: Hodges, Figgis, 1921.

Weaver, Jack W. and DeeGee Lester. *Immigrants from Great Britain and Ireland: A Guide to Archival and Manuscript Sources in North America*. Westport, Conn.: Greenwood Press, 1986.

ANTHOLOGIES OF IRISH LITERATURE IN ENGLISH (arranged chronologically)

1. General

Read, Charles Anderson, ed. *The Cabinet of Irish Literature,* 4 vols. London, 1879-80; rev. and enl. edn by Katharine Tynan Hinkson, 4 vols. London: Gresham, 1902.

Pearson, P.M., ed. *Pearson's Irish Reciter and Reader*. London: C.A. Pearson, 1904.

McCarthy, Justin, et al., eds. *Irish Literature*. 10 vols. Deluxe Edition. Philadelphia: John D. Morris and

Company; Regular Edition. New York: P.F. Collier and Son, 1904.

Russell, Diarmuid, ed. *The Portable Irish Reader*. New York: Viking Press, 1946.

Greacen, Robert. *Irish Harvest: An Anthology of Prose and Poetry*. Dublin: New Frontiers Press, 1946.

Mercier, Vivian and David Greene, eds. *1000 Years of Irish Prose: The Literary Revival*. New York: Devin Adair, 1952.

Greene, David H. ed. *An Anthology of Irish Literature*. New York: Modern Library, 1954.

O'Connor, Frank, ed. *A Book of Ireland*. London: Collins, 1959.

Clune, Anne. *Readings in Anglo-Irish Literature*. Dublin: Academy Press, 1979.

Tremayne, Peter, ed. (ill. by Jeannette Dunne). *Irish Masters of Fantasy: An Anthology*. Portmarnock, Co. Dublin: Wolfhound Press, 1979.

Fallon, Padraic and Sean Golden, eds. *Soft Day: A Miscellany of Contemporary Irish Writing*. Notre Dame: University of Notre Dame Press, 1980.

Freyer, Grattan, ed. *A Prose and Verse Anthology of Modern Irish Writing*. Dublin: Irish Humanities Centre, 1980.

O'Farrell, Padraic. *The Bedside Book of West of Ireland*. Dublin: Mercier Press, 1981.

Murphy, Maureen O'Rourke and James MacKillop, eds. *Irish Literature: A Reader*. New York: Syracuse University Press, 1987.

Greeley, Andrew M. *The Irish*: (photographs by Andrew M. Greeley along with poems, proverbs, and blessings). Chicago, Ill.: Contemporary Books, 1990.

Deane, Seamus, general editor. *The Field Day Anthology of Irish Writing, 3 vols*. Derry: Field Day Publications, 1991.

Rice, Adrian, ed. *Signals: An Anthology of Poetry and Prose*. Newry: Abbey Press, 1997.

Craig, Patricia. *The Oxford Book of Ireland*. Oxford: Oxford University Press, 1998.

Bolger, Dermot, ed. *The New Picador Book of Irish Fiction*. London: Picador, 2000.

2. Drama

Barnet, Sylvan, Morton Berman, and William Burton, eds. *The Genius of the Irish Theater*. New York: Mentor, 1960.

Owens, Coilin D. and Radner, Joan N. *Irish Drama, 1900-1980*. Washington D.C.: Catholic University of America, 1990.

Harrington, John P., *Modern Irish Drama*. New York and London: W.W. Norton, 1991.

Herr, Cheryl, ed. *For the Land They Loved: Irish Political Melodramas, 1890-1925*. Syracuse: Syracuse University Press, 1991.

Great Irish Plays. New York: Gramercy Books, 1995.

Fitz-Simon, Christopher and Sanford Sternlicht, eds. *New Plays from the Abbey Theatre 1993-1995*. Syracuse, New York: Syracuse University Press, 1997.

3. Folklore

Hyde, Douglas. *Beside the Fire, a Collection of Irish Gaelic Folk Stories* with additional notes by Alfred Nutt. London: Nutt, 1890.

O'Connor, Barry, *Turf-Fire Stories & Fairy Tales of Ireland*. New York: Kennedy, 1890.

Batten, John D., ed. *Celtic Fairy Tales*. London: Nutt, 1892.

O'Grady, Standish Hayes, ed. and trans. *Silva Gadelica (I.-XXXI.): a collection of tales in Irish with extracts illustrating persons and places*. London: Williams and Norgate, 1892.

Larminie, William, ed. *West Irish Folk-Tales and Romances*. London: E. Stock, 1893.

Curtin, Jeremiah, ed. *Tales of the Fairies and of the Ghost World, Collected from Oral Tradition in South-West Munster*. Boston: Little, Brown, 1895.

McManus, Seamus. *In Chimney Corners, Merry Tales of Irish Folklore*. New York: McClure, 1899.

Gregory, Lady Augusta. *Cuchulain of Muirthemne: The Story of the Men of the Red Branch of Ulster*. London: John Murray, 1902.

Gregory, Lady Augusta. *Gods and Fighting Men: The Story of the Tuatha De Danaan and the Fianna of Ireland*. London: John Murray, 1904.

Gregory, Lady Augusta. *A Book of Saints and Wonders*. Dundrum: Dun Emer Press, 1906; London: John Murray, 1907.

Gregory, Lady Augusa. *The Kiltartan Wonder Book*. Dublin: Maunsel, 1910.

Rolleston, T. W. *The High Deeds of Finn, and Other Bardic Romances*. New York: Thomas Y. Crowell, 1910.

Gregory, Lady Augusta. *Visions and Beliefs in the West of Ireland*. 1920; Gerrards Cross: Colin Smythe; New York: Oxford University Press, 1970.

Stephens, James. *Irish Fairy Tales*. New York: Macmillan, 1923.

Leamy, Edmund. *Irish Fairy Tales*. Dublin: M.H. Gill & Son, 1926.

Murphy, Gerard. *Tales from Ireland*. Dublin: Browne & Nolan, 1947.

Colum, Padraic, ed. *A Treasury of Irish Folklore: The Stories, Traditions, Legends, Humour, Wisdom, Ballads and Songs of the Irish People*. New York: Crown, 1954.

Campbell, J. J., *Legends of Ireland*. London: Batsford, 1955.

Ó Duilearga, Seamus, ed. *Irish Folk-Tales* (collected by Jeremiah Curtin). Dublin: Talbot, 1956.

Kiernan, Thomas J., ed. *The White Hound of the Mountain and Other Irish Folk Tales*. New York: Devin-Adair, 1962.

O'Faolain, Eileen, *Children of the Salmon and Other Irish Folktales*. Boston: Little, Brown, 1965.

O'Sullivan, Sean. *Folktales of Ireland*. London: Routledge and Kegan Paul; Chicago: University of Chicago Press, 1966.

Berry, James. *Tales of the West of Ireland* (ed. Gertrude M. Horgan). Dublin: Dolmen; London: Oxford University Press, 1966.

Danaher, Kevin (Caoimhín Ó Danachair). *Folktales of the Irish Countryside*. Cork: Mercier Press, 1967.

Crofton Croker, T. and Sigerson Clifford. *Legends of Kerry*. Tralee: Geraldine Press, 1972.

McGarry, Mary, ed. *Great Folk Tales of Ireland*. London: Muller, 1972.

Daiken, Leslie, ed. *Out Goes She: Dublin Street Rhymes*. Dublin: Dolmen, 1973.

McGarry, Mary, ed. *Great Fairy Tales of* Ireland. London: Wolfe, 1973.

Murphy, Michael J. *Now You're Talking . . . Folk Tales from The North of Ireland*. Belfast: Blackstaff, 1975.

Murphy, Michael J. *Mountainy Crack: Tales of Slieve Gullioners*. Belfast: Blackstaff, 1976.

O'Sullivan, Sean. *Legends from Ireland*. London: B. T. Batsford, 1977.

Gmelch, George and Ben Kroup, *To Shorten the Road: Traveller Folktales from Ireland*. Dublin: The O'Brien Press, 1978.

Kelly, Eamon. *The Rub of the Relic*. Dublin and Cork: Mercier Press, 1978.

Ó Cathain, Seamas. *The Bedside Book of Irish Folklore*. Dublin and Cork: Mercier Press, 1980.

Ó Cathain, Seamas. *Irish Life and Lore*. Cork: Mercier Press, 1982.

Lenihan, Edmund, ed. *Long Ago by Shannon Side*. Dublin and Cork: Mercier Press, 1982.

Scott, Michael, *Irish Folk and Fairy Tales*, 2 vols. London: Sphere Books, 1983.

Glassie, Henry, ed. *Irish Folk Tales*. 1985; Harmondsworth: Penguin, 1987.

Heaney, Marie. *Over Nine Waves: A Book of Irish Legends*. London: Faber, 1994.

O'Farrell, Padraic. *Irish Fairy Tales*. Dublin: Gill and Macmillan, 1997.

4. Poetry and Song

Hyde, Douglas, trans. *Abhráin Grádh Chúige* Connacht (Love Songs of Connacht). Dublin: Gill; London: T. Fisher Unwin, 1893.

Graves, Alfred Perceval. *The Irish Song Book*. London: T. Fisher Unwin, 1895.

MacDermott, Martin. *Songs and Ballads of Young Ireland*. London: Downey & Co., 1896.

Moffat, Alfred. *The Minstrelsy of Ireland*. London: Augener & Co., 1897.

Sigerson, George, ed. *Bards of the Gael and Gall*. London: T. Fisher Unwin, 1897.

Brooke, Stopford and T. W. Rolleston, eds. *A Treasury of Irish Poetry in the English Tongue*. London: Smith Elder, 1900.

Gregory, *Lady Augusta. Poets and Dreamers: Studies and Translations from the Irish*. Dublin: Hodges, Figgis, 1903.

Gregory, Lady, *Poets and Dreamers: Studies and Translations from the Irish*. London: Murray, 1903.

Æ, ed. *New Songs: A Lyric Selection*. Dublin: O'Donoghue, 1904.

Leahy, A.H., trans., *Heroic Romances of Ireland*, 2 vols. London: Nutt, 1905.

Hyde, Douglas, ed. *Abhráin Diadha Chúige Connacht (Religious Songs of Connacht)*. Dublin: M.H. Gill; London: Fisher Unwin, 1906.

A Little Garland of Celtic Verse. 2nd edn. Portland, Me: T.B. Mosher, 1907.

Sigerson, George, ed. *Bards of the Gael and Gall*. London: T. Fisher Unwin 1897; rev. edn 1907.

Cooke, John, ed. *The Dublin Book of Irish Verse 1728-1909*. Dublin: Hodges, Figgis & Co.; London: Henry Frowde, Oxford University Press, 1909.

Joyce, P.W. *Old Irish Folk Music and Songs*. 1909; repr. New York: Cooper Square, 1965.

Hughes, Herbert. *Irish Country Songs*, 4 vols. London: Boosey & Hawkes, 1909–36.

Gregory, Padraic, ed. *Modern Anglo-Irish Verse: An Anthology, Selected from the Work of Living Irish Poets*. London: David Nutt, 1914.

Levins, Anna Frances, ed. *Freedom! The Battle Cry of Ireland: A Chain Of Patriotic Poems Proving The Unswerving Devotion Of The Irish Race To The Cause Of Liberty*. New York: Levins, 1916.

Gregory, Lady. *The Kiltartan Poetry Book: Translations from the Irish*. London: Putnam, 1918.

Breathnach, Rev P., ed. *Songs of the Gael: A Collection of Anglo-Irish Songs and Ballads Wedded to Old Traditional Irish Airs*. Dublin: Browne, 1922.

Colum, Padraic, ed. *An Anthology of Irish Verse*. 1922; repr. New York: Liveright, 1974.

Robinson, Lennox, ed. *A Golden Treasury of Irish Verse.* London: Macmillan, 1925.

O'Connor, Frank. *The Wild Bird's Nest: Poems from the Irish*. Dublin: Cuala, 1932.

Broadsides: A Collection Of Old And New Songs. Dublin: Cuala Press, 1935-7.

Fitzhenry, Edna C., ed. *Nineteen-Sixteen: An Anthology*. Dublin: Browne & Nolan; London: Harrap, 1935.

Daiken, Leslie H., ed. *Good-bye Twilight: Songs of the Struggle in Ireland*. London: Lawrence & Wishart, 1936.

Yeats, William Butler, *The Oxford Book of Modern Verse*. Oxford: Clarendon Press, 1936.

O'Faolain, Sean, ed. *The Silver Branch: A Collection of the Best Old Irish Lyrics*. London: Jonathan Cape, 1938.

O'Lochlainn, Colm. *Irish Street Ballads*. Dublin: Three Candles, 1939.

Daiken, Leslie, ed. *They Go, The Irish: A Miscellany of War-time Writing*. London: Nicholson and Watson, 1944.

Hoagland, Kathleen. *1000 Years of Irish Poetry*. New York: Devin Adair, 1947.

Colum, Padraic, ed. *An Anthology of Irish Verse*. New York: Liveright, 1948.

Taylor, G., ed. *Irish Poets of the Nineteenth Century*. London: Routledge and Kegan Paul, 1951.

Knott, E. *Irish Syllabic Poetry 1200-1600*. 2nd edn, Dublin: Institute for Advanced Studies, 1957.

MacDonagh, Donagh and Lennox Robinson, eds. *The Oxford Book of Irish Verse, XVIIth Century-XXth Century*. Oxford: Clarendon Press, 1958.

O'Sullivan, Donal, ed. *Songs of the Irish: An Anthology of Irish Folk Music and Poetry with English Verse Translations*. Dublin: Browne & Nolan, 1960.

Carroll, D., ed. *New Poets of Ireland*. Denver: Alan Swallow, 1963.

Behan, Dominic, ed. *Ireland Sings: An Anthology Of Modern And Ancient Irish Songs And Ballads*. London: Essex Music, 1965.

Garrity, Devin A., ed. *The Mentor Book of Irish Poetry*. New York: Mentor, 1965.

Wannan, Bill, ed. *The Wearing of the Green: The Lore, Literature, Legend and Balladry of the Irish in Australia*. Melbourne: Lansdowne, 1965.

Cleary, James Mansfield, ed. *Proud Are We Irish: Irish Culture And History As Dramatized In Verse And Song*. Chicago: Quadrangle Books, 1966.

Lucy, Sean, ed. *Love Poems of the Irish*. Cork: Mercier Press, 1967.

Healy, James, ed. *The Mercier Book of Old Irish Ballads* 4 vols. Cork: The Mercier Press, 1967.

Zimmerman, Georges-Denis. *Songs Of Irish Rebellion: Political Street Ballads and Rebel Songs 1780-1900*. Dublin: Allen Figgis, 1967.

Lucy, Seán, ed. *Five Irish Poets*. Cork: Mercier Press, 1970.

Simmons, James, ed. *New Poems from Ulster*. Coleraine: New University of Ulster, 1971.

Robson, Jeremy, ed. *The Young British Poets*. London: Chatto and Windus, 1971.

Heaney, Seamus, ed. *Soundings '72: An Annual Anthology of New Irish Poetry*. Belfast: Blackstaff, 1972.

Mahon, Derek, ed. *The Sphere Book of Modern Irish Poetry*. London: Sphere Books, 1972.

Egan, Desmond and Michael Hartnett, eds. *Choice: An Anthology of Irish Poetry Selected by the Poets Themselves with a Comment on their Choice*. Dublin: Goldsmith Press, 1973.

Fiacc, Padraic, ed. *The Wearing of the Black: An Anthology of Contemporary Ulster Poetry*. Belfast: Blackstaff Press, 1974.

Simmons, James, ed. *Ten Irish Poets: An Anthology of Poems*. Cheadle: Carcanet, 1974.

Montague, John, ed. *The Faber Book of Irish Verse*. London: Faber and Faber, 1974, 1978; retitled *The Book of Irish Verse*. New York, 1976.

Hewitt, John, ed. *Rhyming Weavers and Other Country Poets of Antrim and Down*. Belfast: Blackstaff, 1974.

Marcus, David, ed. *Irish Poets 1924-1974*. London: Pan Books, 1975.

Healy, James N., ed. *Love Songs of the Irish* . Dublin and Cork: Mercier Press, 1977.

O'Canainn, Tomas. *Songs of Cork*. Skerries, Co. Dublin: Gilbert Dalton, 1978.

Hammond, David. *Songs of Belfast*. Skerries, Co. Dublin: Gilbert Dalton, 1978.

Meek, Bill. *Songs of the Irish in America*. Skerries, Co. Dublin: Gilbert Dalton, 1978.

Harmon, Maurice, ed. *Irish Poetry After Yeats: Seven Poets*. Dublin: Wolfhound, 1978.

O Boyle, Cathal. *Songs of County Down*. Skerries, Co. Dublin: Gilbert Dalton, 1979.

McDonnell, John. *Songs of Struggle and Protest*. Skerries, Co. Dublin: Gilbert Dalton, 1979.

Ormsby, Frank, ed. *Poets from the North of Ireland*. Belfast: Blackstaff Press, 1979.

Kennelly, Brendan, ed. *The Penguin Book of Irish Verse*. Harmondsworth: Penguin, 1979.

Moulden, John, ed. *Songs of the People: Selections from the Sam Henry Collection, Pt 1*. Belfast: Blackstaff, 1979.

Muldoon, Paul, ed. *The Scrake of Dawn: Poems by Young People from Northern Ireland*. Belfast: Blackstaff, 1979.

Bradley, A., ed. *Contemporary Irish Poetry: An Anthology*. Berkeley: University of California Press, 1980.

Harmon, Maurice, ed. *Irish Poetry After Yeats: Seven Poets*. Dublin: Wolfhound, 1981.

Fallon, Padraic and Sean Golden, eds. *Soft Day: A Miscellany of Contemporary Irish Writing*. Notre Dame and Dublin: University of Notre Dame Press, 1981.

Ó Tuama, Seán and Thomas Kinsella, eds. *An Duanaire 1600-1900: Poems of the Dispossessed*. Portlaoise: Dolmen, 1981.

Bauerle, Ruth, ed. *The James Joyce Songbook*. New York: Garland, 1982.

Dawe, Gerald, ed. *The Younger Irish Poets*. Belfast: Blackstaff Press, 1982.

Shields, Hugh. *Shamrock, Rose and Thistle: Folk Singing in North Derry*. Belfast: Blackstaff Press, 1982.

Smith, Michael, ed. *Irish Poetry, the Thirties Generation*. Dublin: Raven Arts in association with New Writers Press, 1983.

O'Hara, Mary. *A Song for Ireland*. London: Michael Joseph, 1983.

Dunne, Sean, ed. *Poets of Munster*. Dingle: Brandon, 1985.

O'Rourke, Brian. *Blas Meala: A Sip from the Honeypot: Gaelic Folksongs with English Translations*. Dublin: Irish Academic Press, 1985.

Bolger, Dermot. *An Tonn Gheal: The Bright Wave*. Dublin: Raven Arts Press, 1985.

Barry, Sebastian, ed. *Inherited Boundaries: Younger Poets from the Republic of Ireland*. Mountrath: Dolmen, 1986.

Kinsella, Thomas, ed. *The New Oxford Book of Irish Verse*. Oxford, N.Y.: Oxford University Press, 1986.

Monaghan, Patricia, ed. *Unlacing Ten Irish American Women Poets*. Fairbanks, Alaska: Fireweed Press, 1987.

Ormsby, Frank, ed. *The Long Embrace: Twentieth Century Irish Love Poems*. Belfast: Blackstaff, 1987.

Kelly, A.A., ed. *Pillars of the House: An Anthology of Verse by Irish Women from 1690 to the Present*. Dublin: Wolfhound, 1987.

Bradley, Anthony, ed. *Contemporary Irish Poetry*. New edition. Berkeley: University of California Press, 1988.

Leyden, Maurice, ed. *Belfast: City of Song*. Dingle: Brandon, 1989.

Lampe, David, ed. *The Legend of Being Irish: A Collection of Irish-American Poetry*. New York: White Pine Press, 1989.

Fallon, Peter and Derek Mahon, eds. *The Penguin Book of Contemporary Irish Verse*. Harmondsworth: Penguin, 1990.

Fitzmaurice, Gabriel and Declan Kiberd, eds. *An Crann Faoi Bhláth: The Flowering Tree: Contemporary Irish Poetry With Verse Translations*. Dublin: Wolfhound, 1991.

Conway, Sheelagh, *The Faraway Hills Are Green: Voices of Irish Women in Canada*. Toronto: Women's Press, 1992.

Deane, John, ed. *The Cold Heaven: Irish Religious Poetry of Faith and Doubt*. Dublin: Wolfhound, 1991.

Ormsby, Frank, ed. *A Rage For Order: Poetry of The Northern Ireland Troubles*. Belfast: Blackstaff, 1992.

Davitt, Michael and Iain MacDhomhnaill, eds. *Sruth ma Maoile: Modern Gaelic Poetry from Scotland and Ireland*. Edinburgh: Canongate; Baile Atha Cliath: Coisceim, 1993.

Fitzmaurice, Gabriel, ed. *Irish Poetry Now: Other Voices*. Dublin: Wolfhound, 1993.

Moulden, John. *Thousands are Sailing: A Brief Song History of Irish Emigration*. Portrush: Ulstersongs, 1994.

Crotty, Patrick, ed. *Modern Irish Poetry: An Anthology*. Belfast: Blackstaff, 1995.

Donovan, Katie and Brendan Kennelly, eds. *Dublines*. Newcastle Upon Tyne: Bloodaxe, 1995.

Robertson, Fleur, ed. *Remembered Kisses: An Illustrated Anthology of Irish Love Poetry*. Dublin: Gill & Macmillan, 1997.

O'Brien, Sean. *The Firebox: Poetry in Britain and Ireland after 1945*. London: Picador, 1998.

Caddel, Richard and Peter Quartermain, *Other: British and Irish Poetry since 1970*. Hanover and London: Wesleyan University Press, 1999.

McCormack, W.J., ed. *Ferocious Humanism: An Anthology of Irish Poetry from before Swift to after Yeats*. London: J.M. Dent, 2000.

Ó Cróinín, Dáibhi, *The Songs of Elizabeth Cronin: Irish Traditional Singer*. Dublin: Fourt Courts, 2000.

5. Short Story

Mercier, Vivian ed. *Great Irish Short Stories*. New York: Dell, 1964.

Marcus, David, ed. *Modern Irish Love Stories*. London: Pan, 1974.

Vor, William, ed. *Paddy No More: Modern Irish Short Stories*. Dublin: Wolfhound, 1978.

Marcus, David, ed. *Best Irish Short Stories*. London: Elek, 1978.

Hone, Joseph, ed. *Irish Ghost Stories*. London: Hamish Hamilton, 1978.

Morrissey, Una, ed. *Great Irish Love Stories*. Cork and Dublin: Mercier, 1978.

Vorm, William, ed. *Paddy No More: Modern Irish Short Stories*. Dublin: Wolfhound, 1978.

Barr, Fiona, ed. *The Wall Reader and Other Stories*. Dublin: Arlen House, 1979.

Forkner, Ben, ed. (preface by Anthony Burgess). *Modern Irish Short Stories*. Harmondsworth: Penguin, 1980.

Marcus, David, ed. *The Bodley Head Book of Irish Short Stories*. London: Bodley Head, 1980.

Martin, Augustine, ed. *Forgiveness: Ireland's Best Contemporary Short Stories*. Peterborough: Ryan, 1989.

DeSalvo, Louise, Kathleen Walsh D'Arcy and Katherine Hogan, eds. *Territories of the Voice: Contemporary Stories by Irish Women Writers*. Boston: Beacon Press, 1989.

Gonzalez, Alexander, ed. *Short Stories from the Irish Renaissance: An Anthology*. Troy, New York: Whitston, 1992.

Marcus, David, ed. *State of the Art: Short Stories by New Irish Writers*. London: Sceptre, 1992.

Bolger, Dermot, ed. *The Picador Book of Contemporary Irish Fiction*. London and Basingstoke: Picador, 1993.

McCarthy, John, ed. *More Stories from the Great Irish Writers*. Cork and Dublin: Mercier Press, 1994.

Parker, Michael, ed. *The Hurt World: Short Stories of the Troubles*. Belfast: Blackstaff, 1995.

Quinlivan, Valerie, ed. *Writing from Ireland*. Cambridge: Cambridge University Press, 1995.

Marcus, David, ed. *Writer's Week: Award-Winning Short Stories 1973-1994*. Dublin: Marino, 1995.

Marcus, David, ed. *The Phoenix Book of Irish Short Stories 1996*. London: Phoenix, 1996.

Marcus, David, ed. *The Phoenix Book of Irish Short Stories 1997*. London: Phoenix, 1997.

Titley, Alan, ed. *Fourfront: Short Stories from the Irish*. Indreabhán, Co. Gaillimhe: Cló Iar Chonnachta, 1998.

6. Miscellaneous

Saul, George Brandon, ed. *Age of Yeats: Irish Literature*. New York, New York: Dell Publishing Company, 1964.

Marcus, David, ed. *New Irish Writing 1: An Anthology from 'The Irish Press' Series*. Dublin: Dolmen Press, 1970.

McMahon, Sean, ed. *The Best from the Bell*. Dublin: The O'Brien Press, 1978.

Ingraham, L. Vernon, ed. *Literature from the Irish Literary Revival: An Anthology*. Washington, D.C.: University Press of America, 1982.

Ormsby, Frank, ed. *Northern Windows: An Anthology of Ulster Autobiography*. Belfast: Blackstaff Press, 1987.

Carroll, James, ed. *Modern Irish-American Fiction: A Reader*. Syracuse, New York: Syracuse University Press, 1989.

O'Brien, Anthony, ed. *On the Counterscarp: Limerick Writing 1961-1991*. Introd. Michael Hartnett. Galway: Salmon, 1991.

Ó hEithir, Breandán and Ruairí, eds. *An Aran Reader*. Dublin: Lilliput Press, 1991.

Share, Bernard, ed. *Far Green Fields: Fifteen Hundred Years of Irish Travel Writing*. Belfast: Blackstaff, 1992.

Craig, Patricia, ed. *The Rattle of the North: An Anthology of Ulster Prose*. Belfast: Blackstaff Press, 1992.

Carola, Leslie Conron, ed. *The Irish: A Treasury of Art and Literature*. Hugh Lauter Levin Associates, Inc, New York: Distributed by Macmillan Publishing Company, 1993.

Keane, Molly and Sally Phipps, *Molly Keane's Ireland: An Anthology*. London: HarperCollins, 1993.

Monaghan, Patricia, ed. *The Next Parish Over: A Collection of Irish-American Writing*. Minneapolis: New Rivers Press, 1993.

Dunne, Seán, ed. *The Cork Anthology*. Cork: Cork University Press, 1993.

MacAnna, Ferdia, ed. *An Anthology of Irish Comic Writing*. London: Michael Joseph, 1995.

Murphy, Lizz, ed. *Wee Girls*. Melbourne: Spinifex, 1996.

Marcus, David, ed. *The Irish Eros: Irish Short Stories & Poems on Sexual Themes*. Dublin: Gill & Macmillan, 1996.

Ryan, Louise. *Irish Feminism and the Vote: An Anthology of the Irish Citizen Newspaper, 1912-1920*. Dublin: Folens, 1996.

Flanagan, Laurence, ed. *Irish Women's Letters*. Sutton: Far Thrupp, 1997.

Lenox-Conyngham, Melosina, ed. *Diaries of Ireland: An Anthology, 1590-1987*. Dublin: Lilliput, 1998.

Simion, D., ed. *Argus: Journal Literature and Arts Selection 1996-1998*. Cavan: Millennium Three Press, 1998.

Craig, Patricia, ed. *The Belfast Anthology*. Belfast: Blackstaff, 1999.

HISTORY OF IRISH LITERATURE IN ENGLISH

1. General Works

Browne, Ray Broadus, William John Roscelli and Richard Loftus, eds. *The Celtic Cross: Studies in Irish Culture and Literature*. West Lafayette, Indiana: Purdue University Studies, 1964.

Cahalan, James M. *Modern Irish Literature and Culture: A Chronology*. New York: G.K. Hall; Toronto: Maxwell Macmillan, 1993.

Cairns, David and Shaun Richards, *Writing Ireland: Colonialism, Nationalism and Culture*. Manchester: Manchester University Press, 1988.

Carpenter, Andrew, ed. *Place, Personality and the Irish Writer*. Gerrards Cross and New York: Colin Smythe, 1977.

Deane, Seamus. *A Short History of Irish Literature*. London: Hutchinson, 1986.

Eagleton, Terry. *Heathcliff and the Great Hunger*. London: Verso, 1995.

_____ *Crazy John and the Bishop*. Cork: Cork University Press, 1998.

Eyler, Audrey S. and Robert F. Garrat, eds. *Uses of the Past: Essays on Irish Culture*. Newark: University of Delaware Press, 1988.

Farrell, James T. *On Irish Themes*. ed. Dennis Flynn. Philadelphia: University of Pennsylvania Press, 1982.

Flower, Robin. *The Irish Tradition*. Oxford: Clarendon, 1947.

Gwynn, Stephen. *Irish Literature and Drama*. New York, 1936.

Hyde, Douglas. *A Literary History of Ireland*. London, 1899; rev. edn. London: Benn, 1967; 1980.

Innes, C.L. *Woman and Nation in Irish Literature and Society 1880-1935*. London: Harveter Wheatsheaf, 1993.

Johnson, Toni O'Brien and David Cairns, *Gender in Irish Writing*. Milton Keynes: Open University Press, 1991.

Kearney, Richard. *Transitions: Narratives in Modern Irish Culture*. Manchester: Manchester University Press, 1988.

Longley, Edna. *The Living Stream: Literature and Revisionism in Ireland*. Newcastle: Bloodaxe Books, 1994.

MacDonagh, Thomas. *Literature in Ireland: Studies Irish and Anglo-Irish*. Dublin: Talbot, 1916.

McHugh, Roger and Maurice Harmon, *Short History of Anglo-Irish Literature: From its Origins to the Present Day*. Dublin: Wolfhound Press; New York: Barnes and Noble, 1982.

McKillop, James, ed. *Contemporary Irish Cinema: From 'The Quiet Man' to 'Dancing at Lughnasa'*. New York: Syracuse University Press, 1999.

Mercier, Vivian. *The Irish Comic Tradition*. New York: Oxford University Press, 1969.

Ní Chuilleanáin, Eiléan, ed. *Irish Women: Image and Achievement*. Dublin: Arlen House, 1985.

O'Connor, Frank. *The Backward Look: A Survey of Irish Literature*. London: Macmillan, 1967.

Ó Tuama, Seán. *Repossessions: Selected Essays on the Irish Literary Heritage*. Cork: Cork University Press, 1995.

Paulin, Tom. *Ireland and the English Crisis*. Newcastle: Bloodaxe Books, 1984.

Ronsley, Joseph, ed. *Myth and Reality in Irish Literature*. Waterloo, Ontario: Wilfred Laurier University Press, 1977.

Skelton, Robin and David R. Clark, eds. *Irish Renaissance: A Gathering of Essays, Memoirs, and Letters from 'The Massachusetts Review'*. Dublin: Dolmen Press, 1965.

Todd, Loreto. *The Language of Irish Literature*. Basingstoke: Macmillan, 1989.

Trevor, William. *A Writer's Ireland: Landscape in Literature*. London and New York: Thames and Hudson, 1984.

Vance, Norman. *Irish Literature: A Social History*. Oxford: Blackwell, 1990.

2. Drama and Theatre

Bell, S.H. *The Theatre in Ulster: A Survey of the Dramatic Movement in Ulster from 1902 to the Present Day*. Dublin: Gill and Macmillan, 1972.

Duggan, George Chester. *The Stage Irishman: A History of the Irish Play and Stage Characters from Earliest Times*. Dublin and Cork: Talbot Press, 1937.

Edwards, Philip. *Threshold of a Nation: A Study in English and Irish Drama*. Cambridge: Cambridge University Press, 1979.

Ellis-Fermor, Una. *The Irish Dramatic Movement*. 1939; rev. edn. London: Methuen, 1954.

Etherton, Michael. *Contemporary Irish Dramatists*. Basingstoke: Macmillan, 1989.

Gregory, Augusta. *Our Irish Theatre*. 1914; enlarged edn. Gerrards Cross: Colin Smythe, 1973.

Grene, Nicholas. *The Politics of Irish Drama: Plays in Context from Boucicault to Friel*. Cambridge: Cambridge University Press, 1999.

Griffiths, Trevor R. and Margaret Llewellyn-Jones, eds. *British and Irish Women Dramatists Since 1958: A Critical Handbook*. Buckingham: Open University Press, 1993.

Hogan, Robert. *After the Irish Renaissance: A Critical History of Irish Drama Since 'The Plough and the Stars'*. Minneapolis: University of Minnesota Press, 1967; London: Macmillan, 1968.

Hogan, Robert and James Kilroy, *The Modern Irish Drama: A Documentary History*, vols. 1-6. Dublin: Dolmen Press, 1975-9.

Hunt, Hugh. *The Abbey, Ireland's National Theatre, 1904-1979*. Dublin: Gill and Macmillan, 1979.

King, Kimball. *Ten Modern Irish Playwrights: A Comprehensive Annotated Bibliography*. New York: Garland Press, 1979.

Malone, Andrew. *The Irish Drama 1896-1928*. London: Constable, 1929.

Maxwell, D.E.S. *A Critical History of Modern Irish Drama: 1891-1980*. Cambridge: Cambridge University Press, 1984.

Mikhail, E.H. *A Bibliography of Modern Irish Drama 1899-1970*. (Introd. by William A. Armstrong). London: Macmillan, 1972.

_____ *A Research Guide to Modern Irish Dramatists*. Troy, New York: Whitston, 1979.

Murray, Christopher. *Twentieth-Century Irish Drama: Mirror Up to Nature*. Manchester: Manchester University Press, 1997.

Robinson, Lennox. *Ireland's Abbey Theatre: A History 1899-1951*. London: Sidgwick and Jackson, 1951.

Robinson, Lennox, ed. *The Irish Theatre*. London: Macmillan, 1939.

Roche, Anthony. *Contemporary Irish Drama*. Dublin: Gill and Macmillan, 1994.

Schrank, Bernice and William W. Dernastes, *Irish Playwrights 1880-1995: A Research and Production Sourcebook*. Westport: Greenwood, 1997.

Worth, Katharine. *The Irish Drama of Europe from Yeats to Beckett*. London: The Athlone Press, 1978.

3. Folklore

Ellis, Peter Berresford. *A Dictionary of Irish Mythology*. London: Constable, 1987.

Glassie, Henry. *Passing the Time in Ballymenone: Folklore and History of an Ulster Community*. Dublin: O'Brien Press; Philadelphia: University of Pennsylvania Press, 1982.

Ó Danachair, C. *A Bibliography of Irish Ethnology and Folk Tradition*. Dublin and Cork: Mercier Press, 1978.

Ó Suilleabháin, Seán. *A Handbook of Irish Folklore*. Dublin: Educational Company, 1942; repr. Detroit: Singing Tree Press, 1970.

O'Sullivan, Donal. *Irish Folk Music and Song*. Dublin: At the Sign of the Three Candles, 1952.

Vallely, Fintan. *Companion to Irish Traditional Music*. Cork: Cork University Press, 1999.

4. Novel

Cahalan, James M. *Great Hatred, Little Room: The Irish Historical Novel*. New York: Syracuse University Press, 1983.

_____ *The Irish Novel: A Critical History*. Boston: Twayne Publishers, 1988.

Flanagan, Thomas. *The Irish Novelists, 1800-1850*. New York: Columbia University Press, 1959.

Foster, John Wilson. *Forces and Themes in Ulster Fiction*. Dublin: Gill and Macmillan, 1974.

_____ *Fictions of the Irish Literary Revival: A Changeling Art*. Dublin: Gill and Macmillan, 1987.

Kiely, Benedict. *Modern Irish Fiction: A Critique*. Dublin: Golden Eagle Books, 1950.

Martin, Augustine, ed. *The Genius of Irish Prose*. Cork: Mercier, 1984.

Murphy, James H., *Catholic Fiction and Social Reality in Ireland, 1873-1922*. Westport: Greenwood, 1997.

Rafroidi, Patrick and Maurice Harmon, eds. *The Irish Novel in Our Time*. Lille: Publications de l'Université de Lille III, 1976.

Rafroidi, Patrick and Terence Brown, eds. *The Irish Short Story*. Gerrards Cross: Colin Smythe, 1979.

5. Poetry and Song

Alspach, R.K. *Irish Poetry from the English Invasion to 1798*. Philadelphia, 1943; 2nd rev. edn, University of Pennsylvania Press, 1960.

Andrews, Elmer, ed. *Contemporary Irish Poetry: A Collection of Critical Essays*. Gerrards Cross: Colin Smythe, 1989.

Brown, Terence. *Northern Voices: Poets from Ulster*. Dublin: Gill and Macmillan, 1975.

Caball, Marc. *Poets and Politics: Reaction and Continuity in Irish Poetry*. Cork: Cork University Press, 1998.

Corcoran, Neil, ed. *The Chosen Ground: Essays on the Contemporary Poetry of Northern Ireland*. Bridgend, Glamorgan: Seren Books; Chester Springs, Pa.: Dufour Editions, 1991.

Coughlan, Patricia and Alex Davis, eds. *Modernism and Ireland: The Poetry of the 1930s*. Cork: Cork University Press, 1995.

Dawe, Gerald. *How's The Poetry Going?: Literary Politics & Ireland Today*. 2nd ed. Belfast: Lagan Press, 1993.

_____ *Against Piety: Essays in Irish Poetry*. Belfast: Lagan Press, 1995.

Dunn, Douglas, ed. *Two Decades of Irish Writing*. Manchester: Manchester University Press, 1975.

Garratt, Robert F. *Modern Irish Poetry: Tradition and Continuity from Yeats to Heaney*. Berkeley: University of California Press, 1986.

Haberstroh, Patricia Boyle. *Women Creating Women: Contemporary Irish Women Poets*. Dublin: Attic Press, 1996.

Johnston, Dillon. *Irish Poetry After Joyce*. Dublin/Notre Dame: University of Notre Dame Press, 1985.

Kinsella, Thomas. *The Dual Tradition: An Essay on Poetry and Politics in Ireland*. Manchester: Carcanet, 1995.

Loftus, Richard. *Nationalism in Modern Anglo-Irish Poetry*. Madison and Milwaukee: University of Wisconsin Press, 1969.

Longley, Edna. *Poetry in the Wars*. Newcastle: Bloodaxe Books, 1986.

Lucy, Sean, ed. *Irish Poets in English*. Cork and Dublin: Mercier, 1972.

Matthews, Steven. *Irish Poetry: Politics, History, Negotiation*. Basingstoke: Macmillan, 1997.

O'Boyle, Sean. *The Irish Song Tradition*. Toronto: Macmillan, 1977.

O'Brien, Sean. *The Deregulated Muse: Essays on Contemporary British and Irish Poetry*. Newcastle: Bloodaxe, 1998.

Tunney, Paddy. *Where Songs do Thunder: Travels in Traditional Song*. Belfast: Appletree, 1991.

Wills, Clair. *Improprieties: Politics and Sexuality in Northern Irish Poetry*. Oxford: Clarendon Press, 1993.

6. Short Story

Avererill, Deborah M. *The Irish Short Story from George Moore to Frank O'Connor*. Lanham, Md: University Press of America, 1982.

Kilroy, James F., ed. *The Irish Short Story: A Critical History*. Boston, Mass: Twayne, 1984.

Rafroidi, Patrick and Terence Brown, *The Irish Short Story*. Gerrards Cross: Colin Smythe, 1979.

Thompson, Richard J. *Everlasting Voices: Aspects of the Modern Irish Short Story*. Troy, NY: Whitston, 1989.

7. Twentieth Century

Bielenberg, Andy, ed. *The Irish Diaspora*. Harlow: Longman, 2000.

Boyd, Ernest. *Ireland's Literary Renaissance*. New York: Alfred Knopf, 1916; rev. edn, 1922.

Bradley, Anthony and Maryann Valiulis, eds. *Gender and Sexuality in Modern Ireland*. Amherst: University of Massachusetts Press, 1997.

Brown, Malcolm. *The Politics of Irish Literature: From Thomas Davis to W.B. Yeats*. London: George Allen & Unwin, 1972.

Brown, Terence. *Ireland: A Social and Cultural History 1922-79*. London: Fontana, 1981.

Connolly, P., ed. *Literature and the Changing Ireland*. Gerrard's Cross: Colin Smythe, 1982.

Corcoran, Neil. *After Yeats and Joyce: Reading Modern Irish Literature*. Oxford and New York: Oxford University Press, 1997.

Corkery, Daniel. *Synge and Anglo-Irish Literature*. Cork: Cork University Press, 1931.

Costello, Peter. *The Heart Grown Brutal: The Irish Revolution in Literature from Parnell to the Death of Yeats, 1891-1939*. Dublin: Gill and Macmillan, 1977.

Cronin, Anthony. *Heritage Now: Irish Literature in the English Language*. Dingle: Brandon Press, 1982; New York: St Martin's Press, 1983.

Curtin, Chris, Hastings Donnan and Thomas M. Wilson. *Irish Urban Cultures*. Belfast: Institute of Irish Studies, 1993.

Dawe, Gerald and Edna Longley, eds. *Across a Roaring Hill: The Protestant Imagination in Modern Ireland*. Belfast, 1985.

Deane, Seamus. *Celtic Revivals: Essays in Modern Irish Literature, 1880-1980*. London: Faber and Faber, 1985.

Devine, Kathleen. *Modern Irish Writers and the Wars*. Gerrards Cross: Colin Smythe, 1998.

Donovan, Katie. *Irish Women Writers: Marginalised By Whom?* Finglas, Dublin: Raven Arts Press, 1988.

Duytschaever, Joris and Geert Lernout, eds. *History and Violence in Anglo-Irish Literature*, Amsterdam: Rodopi, 1988.

Fallis, Richard. *The Irish Renaissance: An Introduction to Anglo-Irish Literature*. New York: Syracuse University Press, 1977; Dublin: Gill and Macmillan, 1978.

Fallon, Brian. *An Age of Innocence: Irish Culture 1930-1960*. Dublin: Gill and Macmillan, 1999.

Graham, Colin. *Deconstructing Ireland: Identity, Theory, Culture*. Edinburgh: Edinburgh University Press, 2000.

Grant, Patrick. *Breaking Enmities: Religion, Literature and Culture in Northern Ireland, 1967-97*. London: Macmillan; New York: St Martin's Press, 2000.

Harmon, Maurice, ed. *The Irish Writer and the City*. Gerrards Cross: Colin Smythe; Totowa, New Jersey: Barnes and Noble, 1984.

Herr, Cheryl Temple, *Critical Regionalism and Cultural Studies: From Ireland to the American Midwest*. Miami: Florida University Press, 1996.

Howarth, Herbert. *The Irish Writers, 1880-1940*. London: Rockliff, 1958.

Kain, Richard. *Dublin in the Age of William Butler Yeats and James Joyce*. Norman: University of Oklahoma Press, 1962.

Kenner, Hugh. *A Colder Eye: The Modern Irish Writers*. London: Allen Lane, 1983.

Kiely, Benedict. *A Raid into Dark Corners and Other Essays*. Cork: Cork University Press, 1999.

Kosok, Heinz, ed. *Studies in Anglo-Irish Literature*. Bonn: Bouvier Verlag, 1983.

Lloyd, David. *Ireland After History*. Cork: Cork University Press, 1999.

Lyons, F.S.L. *Culture and Anarchy in Ireland 1890-1939*. Oxford: Clarendon Press, 1979.

MacRaild, Donald M. *Irish Migrants in Modern Britain 1750-1922*. London: Macmillan, 1999.

Mahony, Christina Hunt. *Contemporary Irish Literature*. Basingstoke: Macmillan, 1998.

McCormack, William J. *From Burke to Beckett: Ascendancy, Tradition and Betrayal in Literary History*. Cork: Cork University Press, 1994.

McGarry, John and Brendan O'Leary. *Explaining Northern Ireland: Broken Images*. Oxford: Blackwell, 1995.

Mercier, Vivian. *Modern Irish Literature: Sources and Founders*. ed. Eilis Dillon. Oxford: Clarendon Press; New York: Oxford University Press, 1994.

Miller, David, ed. *Rethinking Northern Ireland: Culture, Ideology and Colonialism.* London and New York: Longmans, 1995.

O'Connor, Ulick. *Celtic Dawn: A Portrait of the Irish Literary Renaissance.* London: Hamilton, 1984.

O'Leary, Philip. *The Prose Literature of the Gaelic Revival 1881-1921: Ideology and Innovation.* Pennsylvania: Pennsylvania State University Press, 1994.

Paulin, Tom. *Ireland and the English Crisis.* Newcastle: Bloodaxe, 1984.

Pelaschiar, Laura. *Writing the North: The Contemporary Novel in Northern Ireland.* Trieste: Edizioni Parnaso, 1998.

Porter, Raymond and J. D. Brophy, eds. *Modern Irish Literature: Essays In Honour of William York Tindall.* New York: Iona College and Twayne, 1972.

Rafroidi, Patrick and Maurice Harmon, eds. *The Irish Novel in Our Time.* Lille: Publications de l'Université de Lille III, 1976.

Smyth, Gerry. *Decolonisation and Criticism: The Construction of Irish Literature.* London: Pluto, 1998.

Somerville-Large, Peter. *Irish Voices: 50 Years of Irish Life 1916-1966.* London: Chatto and Windus, 1999.

Tracy, Robert. *The Unappeasable Host: Studies in Irish Identities.* Dublin: UCD Press, 1998.

Watson, George J. *Irish Identity and the Literary Revival: Synge, Yeats, Joyce and O'Casey.* 1979; repr. Washington DC: Catholic University of America, 1995.

Welch, Robert. *Changing States: Transformations in Modern Irish Writing.* London and New York, Routledge, 1993.

8. Irish-American Literature

Braham, David. *Irish American Theater.* New York: Garland, 1994.

Callahan, Bob, ed. *The Big Book of American Irish Culture.* New York: Viking Press, 1987.

Casey, Daniel J. and Robert E. Rhodes, eds. *Irish-American Fiction: Essays in Criticism.* New York: AMS Press, 1979.

Edwards, Owen Dudley. 'The American Image of Ireland: A Study of Its Early Phases.' *Perspectives in American History,* IV (1970): 199-282.

Fanning, Charles. *The Woman of the House: Some Themes in Irish-American Fiction.* Boston, MA: Irish Studies Program, Northeastern University, 1985.

_____ ed. *The Exiles of Erin: Nineteenth-Century Irish-American Fiction.* Notre Dame: University of Notre Dame Press, 1987.

_____ *The Irish Voice in America: 250 Years of Irish-American Fiction.* 2nd ed. Lexington, Kentucky: University of Kentucky Press, 2000.

Fine, David. *The City, the Immigrant, and American Fiction.* Metuchen, N.J.: Scarecrow Press, 1977.

Greene, David. 'Literary Interactions.' *Irish Times* (Supplement: 'The Irish-American Link') 15 March 1976: xii.

Griffin, William D. *The Irish in America 550-1972, A Chronology and Fact Book.* Dobbs Ferry, New York: Oceana Publications, 1973.

A Guide to Irish Studies in the United States. Rev. 3rd ed. Hempstead, N.Y.: ACIS, Hofstra University, 1982.

Harrington, John P. *The Irish Play on the New York Stage 1874-1966.* Kentucky: University Press of Kentucky, 1997.

Kelleher, John V. 'Irish American Literature and Why There Isn't Any.' *Irish Writing* (Cork), November 1947: 71-81.

McCaffrey, Lawrence J. *The Irish Diaspora in America.* 1976. Washington: Catholic University of America Press, 1984.

_____ *Textures of Irish America.* New York: Syracuse University Press, 1994.

Meagher, Timothy J., ed. *From Paddy to Studs: Irish-American Communities in the Turn of the Century Era, 1880-1920.* New York: Greenwood Press, 1986.

Metress, Seamus P. *The Irish-American Experience: A Guide to the Literature.* Washington, D.C.: University Press of America, 1981.

Miller, Kerby A. *Emigrants and Exiles: Ireland and the Irish Exodus to North America.* New York and Oxford: Oxford University Press, 1985.

_____ *Out of Ireland: The Story of Irish Emigration to America.* Washington, D.C.: Elliott and Clark, 1994.

O'Hanlon, Ray. *The New Irish Americans.* Dublin: Roberts Rinehart, 1998.

Sloan, Barry. *The Pioneers of Anglo-Irish Fiction, 1800-1850.* Gerrards Cross: Colin Smythe; Totowa, N.J.: Barnes and Noble, 1987.

White, James A. *The Era of Good Intentions: A Survey of American Catholics Writing Between the Years 1880-1915.* New York: Arno Press, 1978.

Wittke, Carl. *The Irish in America.* 1956. New York: Russell & Russell, 1970.

9. Canadian-Irish Literature

Fitzgerald, Margaret E. and Joseph A. King. *The Uncounted Irish in Canada and the United States.* Toronto: P.D. Meany Publishers, 1991.

Mangan, James J., ed. *Gerald Keegan's Famine Diary: Journey to a New World.* Original text published as: 'Summer of Sorrow', in the second set of Robert Sellar, *Gleaner Tales* (1895). Dublin: Wolfhound Press, 1992.

10. Irish–Australian Literature

Buckley, Vincent. *Cutting Green Hay: Friendships, Movements and Cultural Conflicts in Australia's Great Decades*. Ringwood, Victoria: Penguin, 1983.

Kiernan, Colm. *Australia and Ireland 1788-1988: Bicentenary Essays*. Dublin: Gill and Macmillan, 1986.

MacDonagh, Oliver and W.F. Mandle, eds. *Irish-Australian Studies: Papers Delivered at the Fifth Irish-Australian Conference*. Canberra: Australian National University, 1989.

O'Farrell, Patrick. *The Irish In Australia*. Kensington, NSW: New South Wales University Press, 1986.

Wannan, Bill. *The Wearing of the Green: The Lore, Literature, Legend, and Balladry of the Irish in Australia*. Melbourne: Lansdowne, 1965.

LITERARY THEORY AND CRITICISM

Ryan, Frank L. ed. *Irish Literary Criticism, 1900-1970*. Lexington, Mass: Ginn Press, 1985.

ENCYCLOPEDIAS AND DICTIONARIES OF LITERATURE

Boylan, Henry. *A Dictionary of Irish Biography*. Dublin: Gill and Macmillan, 1978; second edition 1987; New York: St Martin's Press, 1988.

Brady, Anne M. and Brian Cleeve, *A Biographical Dictionary of Irish Writers*. Mullingar: Lilliput Press, 1985.

Cahill, Susan and Thomas. *A Literary Guide to Ireland*. Dublin: Wolfhound, 1979.

Cleeve, B. *Dictionary of Irish Writers*, 3 vols. Cork: Mercier Press, 1967-71.

Crone, John S. *A Concise Dictionary of Irish Biography*. Dublin: Talbot Press, 1928.

Daiches, David, ed. *The Penguin Companion to English Literature*. Harmondsworth: Penguin; New York, McGraw-Hill, 1971.

Eagle, Dorothy and Hilary Carnell, eds. revised by Dorothy Eagle. *The Oxford Illustrated Literary Guide to Great Britain and Ireland*. Oxford and New York: Oxford University Press, 1985.

Hamilton, Ian, ed. *The Oxford Companion to Twentieth-Century Poetry*. Oxford and New York: Oxford University Press, 1994.

Hogan, Robert, editor-in-chief. *The Macmillan Dictionary of Irish Literature*. London: Macmillan, 1980.

————— *Dictionary of Irish Literature*, 2 vols. Westport, Conn.: Greenwood, 1996.

Irish Theatre Handbook. Dublin: New Island Books, 1998

McCormack, W.J. *The Blackwell Companion to Modern Irish Culture*. Oxford: Blackwell, 1999.

McRedmond, Louis, ed. *Modern Irish Lives: Dictionary of Twentieth-century Irish Biography*. Dublin: Gill and Macmillan, 1998.

Meally, Victor. *Encyclopaedia of Ireland*. Dublin: Allen Figgis; New York and Toronto: McGraw Hill, 1971.

O'Donoghue, D.J. *The Poets of Ireland: A Biographical and Bibliographical Dictionary*. Dublin: Hodges Figgis, 1912; repr. Detroit: Gale Information Guide Library, 1968.

Sheehan, Sean. *Dictionary of Irish Quotations*. Cork: Mercier, 1993.

Welch, Robert, ed. (assistant editor, Bruce Stewart). *The Oxford Companion to Irish Literature*. Oxford and New York: Clarendon Press, 1996.

ACKNOWLEDGEMENTS

I would like here to record my gratitude to the following individuals whose advice I have sought in assembling this *Reader*: Pieter Bekker, Terry Eagleton, John Wyse Jackson, Jim McCord, Harry Marten, Peter Mills, Alistair Stead, Mel Tuohey (who died before this project was completed).

My students in York should also be thanked for suffering my various enthusiasms, and my College too for kindly releasing me from a substantial number of teaching duties for the period of a year while I was working on this *Reader*.

Cork University Press sought the advice of some twelve readers, whose valuable comments have been incorporated into this *Reader*. I mention by name the identity of those I know: Peter de Voogd and Jörg Rademacher. Thank you to all these individuals.

I should also like to record a debt of gratitude to the Librarians and staff at the following libraries: the British Library, Cambridge University Library, the Brotherton Library Leeds, the Morrell University Library York, the University of Warwick Library, the University of Toronto Library, and my own College Library. Libraries on the internet should also be thanked here but the list would occupy several pages, but let me say I have benefited enormously from the James Hardiman Library Galway, the Libraries at University College Dublin, University College Cork, Socrates at Stanford, Melvyl California, and the Library of Congress.

A *Reader* such as this depends on the labours of others and I would like to here mention in particular those books which have been my constant companion: Robert Welch (ed.), *The Oxford Companion to Irish Literature* (1996) (rarely wrong); Robert Hogan (ed.), *The Macmillan Dictionary of Irish Literature* (1980) and his *Dictionary of Irish Literature* 2 vols. (1996); Seamus Deane (general editor), *The Field Day Anthology of Irish Writing* 3 vols. (1991); Patrick Crotty (ed.), *Modern Irish Poetry: An Anthology* (1995); Charles Fanning, *The Irish Voice in America: Irish-American Fiction From the 1760s to the 1980s* (1990); Patrick O'Farrell, *The Irish in Australia* (1986).

To all the authors who gave permission for me to use their work in this *Reader* (see below for formal acknowledgements): thank you. I hope this *Reader* will find new readers of your work.

The *Reader* you have in your hand would not have materialised without the courage of Sara Wilbourne, Editor and Publisher at Cork University Press, to pursue a suggestion I made at the Frankfurt Book Fair in October 1996. I have always wanted to publish with an Irish publisher, and it has been a pleasure to work with her team at Cork.

As ever, my chief debt is to Mary Eagleton and Matthew Eagleton-Pierce, cheerful co-opted co-workers in the field that has occupied me now for more than thirty years.

David Pierce

The editor and publishers wish to thank the many writers and publishers whose work is featured in this *Reader*. The publishers have made every effort possible to trace copyright holders but will undertake to rectify any omissions or misrepresentations in future reprints.

Banville, John, from *Kepler* (Secker and Warburg, London, 1981)

Barry, Tom, from *Guerrilla Days in Ireland* (The Irish Press, Dublin, 1949)

Barry, Sebastian, from *Plays: 1* (London, Methuen, 1997)

Beckett, Mary, from *A Belfast Woman* (Poolbeg, Dublin; William Morrow, New York, 1980)

Beckett, Samuel, from *Echo's Bones* (Europa Press, London, 1935); from *Molloy* (trans. Patrick Bowles

and author) (Merlin/Olympia, Paris, 1954); from
Malone Dies (Grove Press, New York, 1956);
Endgame (Faber and Faber, London, 1958)

Behan, Brendan, from *Borstal Boy* (London:
Hutchinson, 1958); from *The Quare Fellow* (1954;
London, Methuen, 1977)

Bell, Sam Hanna, from *December Bride* (1951; reprinted
Blackstaff, Belfast, 1982)

Birmingham, George A., from *The Fortnightly Review*,
Vol. 82, No. 392, December, 1907

Blackwood, Caroline, from *Great Granny Webster*
(1977; reprinted Palm Books, London, 1993)

Eavan Boland, from *Object Lessons: The Life of the
Woman and Poet in Our Time* (The Carcanet Press
Limited, Manchester, 1995); from *Outside History*
(The Carcanet Press, Manchester, 1990); from
Collected Poems (The Carcanet Press, Manchester,
1995); all copyright Eavan Boland, reproduced by
permission of W.W. Norton and Co. Inc.

Boll, Heinrich (1957) from *Irish Journal* (trans. Leila
Vennewitz) (McGraw-Hill Inc., New York, 1971)

Bowen, Elizabeth, from *The Penguin New Writing*,
No. 20, 1944; from *The London Magazine* Vol. 3,
No. 3, March 1956; all copyright Elizabeth Bowen,
reproduced by permission of Curtis Brown Ltd

Boyd, Ernest, from *Current History*, March 1934,
Vol. XXXIX, No. 6

Boyle, Patrick, from *At Night All Cats Are Grey*
(MacGibbon and Kee, London, 1966)

Bradshaw, Maire, from *high time for all the marys* (1991,
courtesy of the author)

Brody, Hugh, from *Inishkillane: Change and Decline in
the West of Ireland* (Penguin, Harmondsworth,
1973, courtesy Faber and Faber, London)

Brown, Christy, from *Down All the Days* (1970;
reprinted, Minerva, London, 1990)

Brown, Richard Howard, from *I Am Of Ireland*
(Harper and Row, New York, 1974)

Byrne, Donn, from *Ireland: The Rock Whence I Was
Hewn* (Sampson Low, Marston, London, 1929)

Buckley, Vincent, from *The Pattern* (Dolmen, Dublin,
1979); from *Memory Ireland: Insights into the
Contemporary Irish Condition* (Penguin, Australia,
1985); from *Last Poems* (Penguin, Victoria, 1991)

Burgess, Anthony, from *The Spectator*, 7 June 1969,
copyright estate of Anthony Burgess

Butler, Hubert, from *The Bell*, June 1954

Campbell, Joseph, from *The Gilly of Christ* (Maunsel,
Dublin, 1907); from *The Mountainy Singer*
(Maunsel, Dublin, 1909); from *The Mearing Stones*
(Maunsel, Dublin, 1911); from *Irishry* (Maunsel,
Dublin, 1911); from *Earth of Cualann* (Maunsel,
Dublin and London, 1917)

Campbell, Patrick, from *The Irish Times*, 12 June 1946

Carew, Rivers and Timothy Brownlow, from *The
Dublin Magazine*, Autumn/Winter 1965, Vol. 4,
Nos 3/4

Carson, Ciaran, from *The Irish For No* (Gallery Press,
Oldcastle, 1987); from *The Star Factory* (Granta,
London, 1997); from *Opera Et Cetera* (Bloodaxe,
Newcastle upon Tyne; The Gallery Press, Dublin,
1996)

Carton, R P., from *The Irish Monthly*, Vol. 23,
No. 263, May 1895

Chuilleanáin, Eiléan Ní, from *Atlantis*, No. 2,
October, 1970

Clarke, Austin, from *The Bright Temptation* (Dolmen,
Dublin, 1965); from *Night and Morning* (Orwell,
Dublin, 1938)

Clifton, Harry, from *At the Grave of Silone: An Abruzzo
Sequence* (The Honest Ulsterman, Belfast, 1993)

Collins, Michael, from *The Path to Freedom* (Talbot,
Dublin and T. Fisher Unwin, London, 1922)

Colum, Padraic, from Æ (ed.) *New Songs*
(O'Donoghue, Dublin and A H Bullen, London,
1904), courtesy the estate of Padraic Colum

Connolly, James, from *Workers Republic*, 22 July 1899

Conlon, Gerry, from *Proved Innocent* (1990, reprinted
Penguin, Harmondsworth, 1991)

Corkery, Daniel, from *The Hidden Ireland: A Study of
Gaelic Munster in the Eighteenth Century* (1924,
reprinted Gill & Macmillan, Dublin, 1970)

Coulter, John, from *The Blossoming Thorn* (Ryerson,
Toronto, 1946)

Creeley, Robert, from *Later* (Marion Boyars Publishers
Ltd., London, 1978); copyright Robert Creeley,
reprinted by permission of New Directions
Publishing Corp.

Cross, Eric, from *The Tailor and Ansty* (1942: reprinted
Mercier, Cork, 1970)

Dawe, Gerald, from *The Irish Review*, Autumn 1990.

Deane, Seamus, from *The Crane Bag*, Vol. 1, No. 1,
1977; from *Reading in the Dark* (Jonathan Cape,
London, 1996)

Deevy, Teresa, from *Three Plays* (Macmillan Press Ltd.,
London, 1939)

Delanty, Greg, from *American Wake* (Belfast, Blackstaff,
1995); from *The Hellbox* (Oxford University Press,
1998), by kind permission of the author.

De Paor, Louis, from *Poetry Ireland Review*, No. 51,
Autumn 1996

Devlin, Denis, from *Lough Derg and Other Poems*
(Dedalus Press, Dublin, 1946); from *The Southern
Review*, LXIV 4 (October 1956) with kind
permission of The Dedalus Press, Dublin.

Dhomhnaill, Nuala Ní, 'An Bhean Mhidhilis'/The

Unfaithful Wife (trans. Paul Muldroon) and 'Ceist na Teangan'/The Language Issue (trans. Paul Muldoon) from *Pharaoh's Daughter* (Gallery Press, Oldcastle, 1990). 'Caitlin' (trans. Paul Muldoon) from *The Astrakhan Cloak* (Gallery Press, Oldcastle, 1992)

Dinneen, Joseph F., from *Ward Eight* (Harper & Brothers, New York and London, 1936)

Dinneen, Rev. P.S., from *Journal of the Ivernian Society*, Vol. II, No. 6 January 1910

Donleavy, J.P., from *The Unexpurgated Code: A Complete Manual of Survival and Manners* (1975: reprinted Penguin, Harmondsworth, 1976)

Donnelly, Charles, from *Ireland Today* Vol. 2, No. 1, January 1937/Vol. 2, No. 2, February 1937

Donoghue, Denis, from *Southern Review*, Vol. LXXXIV, No. 1, Winter 1976

Dooley, Maura, from *Explaining Magnetism* (Bloodaxe, Newcastle upon Tyne, 1991); from *Kissing A Bone* (Bloodaxe, Newcastle upon Tyne, 1996)

Doyle, Sir Arthur Conan, from *The Green Flag* (Smith, Elder, London, 1900)

Doyle, Lynn, from *Ballygullion* (1908. reprinted Maunsel, Dublin, 1918)

Doyle, Roddy, from *The Woman Who Walked into Doors* (Jonathan Cape, London, 1996)

Dunne, F.P., from *Mr Dooley in the Hearts of His Countrymen* (Grant Richards, London, 1900)

Dunne, John Gregory, from *Harp* (Simon and Schuster, New York, 1989)

Dunne, Lee, from *A Bed in the Sticks* (Hutchinson, London, 1968)

Dunsany, Lord, from *The Poetry Review* May 1914, Vol. IV, No. 5.

Durcan, Paul, from *Jumping the Tracks with Angela* (Raven Arts, Dublin and Carcanet Press Limited, Manchester); from *The Berlin Wall Cafe* (Blackstaff Press, Belfast, 1985); from *Greetings to Our Friends in Brazil* (London: Harvill, 1999) all reproduced by permission of the author

Egan, Desmond, from *Aquarius*, No. 12, 1980; from *A Song for My Father* (Peterloo Poets, Calstock, Cornall; The Kavanagh Press, Newbridge, Ireland, 1989), reproduced by kind permission of the author

Egan, Maurice F., from *From the Land of St Lawrence* (1898), reprinted William J. O'Neill Daunt and Alice Furlong (eds) *Irish Literature Volume III* (PF Collier, New York, 1904)

Eglinton, John, from *Bards and Saints* (Maunsel, Dublin, 1906)

Evans, E Estyn., from *Irish Folk Ways* (Routledge and Kegan Paul, 1957)

Fahy, Francis, from *The Irish Language Movement* (Gaelic League, London, 1901)

Fallon, Padraic, from *The Dublin Magazine*, Vol. 26, No. 4, October-December 1951

Farrell, James T., from *The Young Manhood of Studs Lonigan* (1934: reprinted in *Studs Lonigan: A Trilogy* (Vanguard Press, New York, 1935)

Farrell, J.G., from *Troubles* (Cape, London, 1970, courtesy Rodgers, Coleridge and White)

Farren, Robert, from *Rime, Gentleman, Please* (Sheed & Ward, London, 1945)

Fiace, Padraic, from *Missa Terribilis* (Blackstaff Press, Belfast, 1986, reprinted by kind permission of the author)

Figgis, Darrell, from *A Chronicle of Jails* (The Talbot Press, Dublin, 1917)

Figgis, Darrell, from *The House of Success* (Gael Co-operative Publishing Society, Dublin, 1922)

Fitzgerald, F. Scott, from *All The Sad Young Men* (1926) reprinted *The Bodley Head Scott Fitzgerald Volume 5 Short Stories*, Malcom Cowley (ed.) (The Bodley Head, London, 1963); from Andrew Turnbull, *The Letters of F. Scott Fitzgerald* (Penguin Books, Harmondsworth, 1968)

Flanagan, Thomas, from *The Year of the French* (1979: Arrow Books, London, 1980)

Flower, Robin, from *The Irish Book Lover*, January-February 1920, Vol. XI, No. 6 & 7

Franklin, Miles, from *All That Swagger* (Angus and Robertson, Sydney, 1936)

Freyer, Grattan, from *Scrutiny* March 1938, Vol. VI, No. 4

Friel, Brian, from *The Saucer of Larks: Stories of Ireland* (Arrow Books, London, 1969); from *Translations* (Faber and Faber Limited, London, 1981)

Furphy, Joseph, from *Such Is Life: Being Certain Extracts from the Diary of Tom Collins* (Bulletin Newspaper Company, Sydney, 1903)

Gallagher, Frank, from *Days of Fear* (John Murray, London, 1928)

Gallagher, Tess, from *Under Stairs* (Graywolf Press, Port Townsend, Washington, 1978); from *Willingly* (Graywolf Press, Port Townsend, Washington, 1984)

Galvin, Patrick, from *The Wood-Burners* (New Writers' Press, Dublin, 1973); from *Song for a Poor Boy: A Cork Childhood* (Raven Arts Press, Dublin, 1990)

Gibbings, Robert, from *Blue Angels and Whales* (Penguin Books, Harmondsworth, 1938); from *Sweet Cork of Thee* (J. M. Dent, London, 1941), all copyright Laurence Pollinger Limited and the estate of Robert Gibbings

Gibbon, Monk, from *The Seals* (1935: reprinted Allen Figgis, Dublin, 1970)

Gogarty, Oliver St John, from *Rolling Down the Lea*

(Constable, London, 1950)

Gopaleen, Myles na (Flann O'Brien), from *The Irish Times*, 2 December 1942

Gordon, Mary, from *The Other Side* (Viking Penguin, New York, 1989)

Gore-Booth, Eva, from *The One and the Many* (1904, reprinted *Poems of Eva Gore-Booth*, Longmans Green, London, 1929); from *The Egyptian Pillar* (1906, reprinted *The Poems of Eva Gore-Booth*, Longmans Green, London, 1929)

Graham, Colin, from *Irish Studies Review*, No. 8, Autumn 1994

Greacen, Robert, from Reginald Moore (ed.) *Modern Reading*, No. 4, 1943

Gregory, Lady, from *Cuchulain of Muirthemne* (John Murray, London, 1902)

Gregory, Lady, from *Seven Short Plays* (Maunsel, Dublin, 1909)

Griffith, Arthur, from *The Resurrection of Hungary: A Parallel for Ireland* (Whelan, Dublin, 1904, 1918)

Gwynn, Stephen, from *Freeman's Journal*, 25 January 1913

Healy, Dermot, from *The Bend for Home*. First published in 1996 by The Harvill Press © Dermot Healy, 1996. Reproduced by permission of The Harvill Press.

Heaney, Seamus, from *Hibernia* 21 November 1969; from *North* (Faber and Faber, London, 1975); from *Field Work* (Faber and Faber, London, 1979); from *Station Island* (Faber and Faber Limited, London, 1984); from *From the Republic of Conscience* (Produced by Peter Fallon for Amnesty International (Irish Section) 1985); all reproduced by kind permission of the author.

Hewitt, John, from *The Listener*, 18 May 1932; from *Lagan*, No. 3 (1945); from *New Statesman and Nation*, 16 May 1959; all reprinted in *The Collected Poems of John Hewitt*, Frank Ormsby (ed.) (Blackstaff, Belfast, 1991)

Hewson, Paul, from Richard Kearney (ed) *Across the Frontiers: Ireland in the 1990s Cultural-Political-Economic* (Wolfhound, Dublin, 1988)

Higgins, Aidan, from *Helsingor Station and Other Departures* (Secker and Warburg, London, 1989); from *Donkey's Years: Memories of a Life as Story Told* (Secker and Warburg, London, 1995)

Higgins, F.R., from *The Dark Breed* (Macmillan Press Ltd, London, 1927)

Higgins, Rita Anne, from *Higher Purchase* (Salmon Poetry, Cliffs of Moher, 1996)

Hobsbaum, Philip, from *The Honest Ulsterman*, No. 97, Spring 1994

Hogan, Desmond, from *The Edge of the City: A Scrapbook 1976-91* (Faber and Faber, London 1993; courtesy Rodgers, Coleridge and White)

Hogg, Garry, from *Turf Beneath My Feet* (Museum Press, London, 1950)

Holland, Jack, from *Hibernia*, 21 March 1975

Holland, Mary, from *The New Statesman*, 19 October 1984

Homans, George C., from *The Saturday Review of Literature*, 17 October 1936

Hone, J. M., from *The Irish Book Lover*, August 1912, Vol. IV, No. 1

Hyde, Douglas, from Charles Gavan Duffy, George Sigerson and Douglas Hyde, *The Revival of Irish Literature* (T. Fisher Unwin, London, 1894); *Abhráin Gradh Chúige Connacht (Love Songs of Connacht)* (T. Fisher Unwin, London and Gill & Son, Dublin, 1893)

Inglis, Brian, *West Briton*, reproduced with permission of Curtis Brown Ltd, London, on behalf of the Estate of Brian Inglis. Copyright Brian Inglis 1962.

Iremonger, Valentin, from *The Listener*, 27 June 1946

Johnson, Lionel, from *United Irishman*, 7 October 1893, reprinted Iain Fletcher (ed.) *The Complete Poems of Lionel Johnson* (The Unicorn Press, London, 1953)

Johnston, Jennifer, from *Shadows on Our Skin* (1977, reprinted Penguin, Harmondsworth, 1991)

Jordan, John, from *Hibernia*, 1972

Joyce, James, from *Ulysses* (Paris, Shakespeare and Co., 1922); edition used here: Danis Rose (ed.) *Ulysses: A Reader's Edition* (London: Picador, 1997), by kind permission of editor.

Joyce, Patrick Weston, from *English As We Speak It In Ireland* (1910, reprinted Wolfhound, Portmarnock, 1979)

Joyce, Stanislaus, from *The Listener*, 25 March 1954

Kavanagh, Patrick, from *Ploughman and Other Poems* (Macmillan Press Ltd, London, 1936); from *The Great Hunger* (1942; reprinted Patrick Kavanagh Collected Poems MacGibbon and Kee, London, 1964); from *Envoy* Vol 1, No. 4, March 1950; from *Envoy*, Vol. 5, No. 17, April 1951; reprinted with the permission of the Trustees of the Estate of the late Katharine B. Kavanagh, through the Jonathan Williams Literary Agency

Keane, Molly, from *Good Behaviour* (Virago, London, 1981, David Higham Associates)

Kelleher, John V., from *Irish Writing*, No. 3, November 1947

Keneally, Thomas, from *Now And In Time To Be* (1991, reprinted Flamingo, London, 1992)

Kennedy, William, from *Riding the Yellow Trolley Car: Selected Nonfiction* (Penguin, Harmondsworth, 1993: New York Writers' Institute); from *Ironweed*

(Viking, New York, 1983)

Kennelly, Brendan, from *My Dark Fathers* (New Square Publications, Dublin, 1964), reprinted in *A Time for Voices: Selected Poems 1960-1990* (Bloodaxe, Newcastle-upon-Tyne, 1990); from *Cromwell* (1983, reprinted Bloodaxe, Newcastle upon Tyne, 1987); from *Journey Into Joy: Selected Prose* Ake Persson (ed.) (Bloodaxe, Newcastle upon Tyne, 1994)

Kiely, Benedict, from Ronnie Walsh (ed.), *Sunday Miscellany* (Gill & Macmillan, Dublin, 1975); *A Cow in the House* (Gollancz, London, 1978)

King, Cecil, from *The Cecil King Diary 1970-1974* (Jonathan Cape, London, 1975)

Kinsella, Thomas, from *Selected Poems 1956-1968* (Dolmen, Dublin, 1973); from Sean Lucy (ed.) *Irish Poets in English* (Mercier Press, Cork, 1973)

Lavin, Mary, from *A Memory and Other Stories* (Houghton Mifflin, Boston, and Constable, London, 1972)

Ledwidge, Francis, from *Lyrical Poems* (*Irish Review*, Dublin, 1913); from *Songs of Praise* (Herbert Jenkins, London, 1917)

Leventhal, A.J., from *The Dublin Review*, January-March 1956

Longley, Edna, *From Cathleen to Anorexia: The Breakdown of Irelands* (LIP pamphlet, 1990, Attic Press, Dublin)

Longley, Michael, from *Hibernia* 7 November 1969; from *Gorse Fires* (Secker and Warburg, London, 1991); from *The Ghost Orchid* (Cape, London, 1995)

Lynch, Malcolm, from *The Streets of Ancoats* (Constable, London, 1985)

Lynch-Robinson, Sir Christopher, from *The Last of the Irish R.M.s* (Cassell, London, 1951)

MacAmhlaigh, Donall, from *The Tablet*, 18 March 1978

Macardle, Dorothy, from *Earth Bound: Nine Stories of Ireland* (The Harrigan Press, Worcester, Mass. 1924)

MacDonagh, Thomas, from *Literature in Ireland: Studies Irish and Anglo Irish* (T. Fisher Unwin, London, 1916); from *Lyrical Pieces* (*Irish Review*, Dublin, 1913)

MacDonald, Michael Patrick, *All Souls: A Family Story from Southie* (Beacon Press, Boston, 1999)

MacGill, Patrick, from *Children of the Dead End* (1914; reprinted Caliban, London, 1983); from *Songs of the Dead* (Year Book, London, 1916)

MacGreevy, Thomas, from *The Dublin Review*, January-June 1929

MacLaverty, Bernard, from *Cal* (1983, reprinted Penguin, Harmondsworth, 1984)

MacLiammóir, Micheál, from *All For Hecula: An Irish Theatrical Autobiography* (Methuen, London, 1946)

MacMahon, Bryan, from *The Bell*, Vol. 8, No. 2, 1943

MacManus, Seamas, from *The Rocky Road to Dublin* (1938, reprinted Devin-Adair, New York, 1947)

MacNeice, Louis, from *Autumn Journal* (1938) reprinted in *The Collected Poems of Louis MacNeice*, E. R. Dodds (ed.) (Faber and Faber, London, 1979, courtesy David Higham Associates); from *Horizon*, Vol. II, No. 14, February 1941; from *Horizon*, Vol. 1, No. 1, January 1940

Mahon, Derek, from *Night Crossing* (OUP, 1968); from *The Hudson Letter* (The Gallery Press, Oldcastle, 1995); from *Journalism: Selected Prose 1970-1995* (The Gallery Press, Oldcastle, 1996)

Malone, Andrew, from *The Dublin Review*, July 1927, No. 362

Manning, Mary, from *The Saturday Review of Literature*, 28 March 1931

Markievicz, Constance, from Esther Roper (ed.) *Prison Letters of Countess Markievicz* (Longmans Green, London, 1934)

McCabe, Patrick, from *The Butcher Boy* (Pan, London, 1992)

McCourt, Edward A., from *Home is the Stranger* (Macmillan, Toronto, 1950)

McCrory, Moy, from *Those Sailing Ships of his Boyhood Dreams* (Jonathan Cape, London, 1991)

McDonagh, Martin, from *The Lonesome West* (Methuen, London, 1997)

McFadden, Roy, from *Hibernia*, 10 October 1969; from John Boyd (ed.) *The Selected Roy McFadden* (Blackstaff, Belfast, 1983); from *Letters to the Hinterland* (The Dedalus Press, Dublin, 1986)

McGahern, John, from *High Ground* (Faber and Faber, London, 1985)

McGuckian, Medbh, from *The Flower Master* (OUP, Oxford and New York, 1982)

McLiam Wilson, Robert, from *Ripley Bogle* (1989; reprinted Minerva, London, 1997; copyright André Deutsch Ltd on behalf of the author); from *Eureka Street* (1996; reprinted Minerva, London, 1997)

McLaverty, Michael, from *Ireland Today*, Vol. 2., No. 10, October 1937

McNamee, Eoin, from *Resurrection Man* (Macmillan Press Ltd., London and Basingstoke, 1994)

McWhirter, George, from *A Staircase for All Souls: The British Columbia Suite* (Oolichan Books, Lantzville, BC., 1993; with kind permission of the author)

Milne, Ewart, from *Letter From Ireland* (The Gayfield Press, 1940)

Montague, John, from *The Spectator*, 26 April 1963; 'The Rough Field' copyright © John Montague

1963, reproduced by permission of PFD on behalf of John Montague; 'A Lost Tradition' from *The Rough Field* (Dolmen, Dublin, 1972) copyright © John Montague 1972, reproduced by permission of PFD on behalf of John Montague

Mooney, Martin, from *Grub* (Blackstaff, Belfast, 1993)

Moore, Brian, from *The Mangan Inheritance* (1979: reprinted Penguin Harmondsworth, 1980), copyright Brian Moore 1979 reproduced by permission of Curtis Brown Ltd

Moore, George, from *The Untilled Field* (T. Fisher Unwin, London, 1903); from *Hail and Farewell: Vale* (William Heinemann, London, 1914)

Moran, David Patrick, from Lady Gregory (ed.) *Ideals in Ireland* (Unicorn, London, 1901)

Morrison, Van, *A Sense of Wonder*, 1985

Muldoon, Paul, from *Why Brownlee Left* (Faber and Faber, London, 1980); from *Quoof* (Faber and Faber, London, 1983); from *The Prince of the Quotidian* (The Gallery Press, Oldcastle, 1994)

Murphy, Dervla, from *A Place Apart* (1978; reprinted Penguin, Harmondsworth, 1979); from *Tales from Two Cities: Travels of Another Sort* (Penguin, Harmondsworth, 1987)

Murphy, Michael J., from *Ulster Folklife*, Vol. 13, 1967

Murphy, Tom, *Conversations On A Homecoming* (1985, reprinted Methuen, London, 1988)

Murray, William Cotter, from *Michael Joe: A Novel of Irish Life* (Appleton Century, New York, 1965)

Nolan, Brian, from *Envoy*, Vol. 5, no. 17, April 1951

O'Brien, Conor Cruise, from *In Excited Reverie: A Centenary Tribute to William Butler Yeats 1865-1939* (Macmillan Press Ltd, London, 1965)

O'Brien, Edna, from *The Country Girls* (Hutchinson, London, 1960) courtesy of Duncan Heath Associates, London and the author

O'Brien, Flann, from *At Swim-Two-Birds* (1939: reprinted Penguin, Harmondsworth, 1967)

O'Brien, John, from *Around the Boree Log* (1921; reprinted The Mercier Press, Cork and Dublin, 1988)

O'Brien, Kate, from *Farewell Spain* (1937: reprinted Virago, London, 1985); from *Pray for the Wanderer* (1938, reprinted Penguin, Harmondsworth, 1951); from *My Ireland* (Batsford, London, 1962)

O'Cadhain, Mairtin, from *An Braon Broghach* (1948), (trans. Eoghan Ó Tuairisc, *The Road to Bright City*) (Poolbeg, Dublin, 1981)

O'Callaghan, Julie, from *Edible Anecdotes* (Dolmen, Dublin, 1983)

O'Casey, Sean, from *I Knock at the Door* (Macmillan Press Limited, London, 1939); from *Inishfallen: Fare Thee Well* (Macmillan Press Limited, London, 1949)

Ó Conaire, Padraic, from *Deoraíocht* (1910); trans. Gearailt Mac Eoin (Cló Iar-Chonnachta, Conamara, 1994)

O'Connor, Edwin, from *The Last Hurrah* (Little Brown, Boston, 1956)

O'Connor, Frank, from *Guests of the Nation* (Macmillan Press Ltd., London, 1931); from *The Listener*, 2 January 1941; from *Horizon*, Vol. 5, No. 25, January 1942; from *The Listener*, 23 July 1959; from *Irish Writing* November 20-21, 1952, reprinted in *The Stories of Frank O'Connor* (Hamish Hamilton, London, 1953); from *The Lonely Voice: A Study of the Short Story* (Macmillan Press Ltd., London, 1963)

Ó Criomhthain, Tomás, from *An tOileánach* (trans. Robin Flower, *The Islandman*) (1929; reprinted OUP, Oxford, 1978)

O'Donnell, Peadar, from *Ireland Today*, Vol. 1, no. 4, September 1936

O'Duffy, Eimar, from *The Wasted Island* (Martin Lester, Dublin, 1919)

O'Faolain, Sean, from *The Bell*, August 1945, Vol. X, No. 5; from *The Finest Stories of Sean O'Faolain* (1957: reprinted Bantam, New York, 1965); from *Studies: An Irish Quarterly Review*, Spring 1962

O'Flaherty, Liam, from *The Tent and Other Stories* (Jonathan Cape, London and Harcourt Brace Inc., 1926)

O'Grady, Standish James, from *All Ireland Review*, 17 February 1900

O'Hara, John, from *BUtterfield 8* (Harcourt Brace Inc., New York, 1934)

O'Leary, Con, from *The Manchester Guardian*, October 1922

O'Leary, Peter, from *Mo Sgéal Fein;* trans. Cyril Ó *My Story* (Mercier Press, Cork, 1970, reproduced by kind permission of Kit Ó Céirín)

O'Lochlainn, Colm, from *Irish Book Lover*, October 1949, Vol. XXXI, No. 3

O'Loughlin, Michael, from *Another Nation: New and Selected Poems* (Arc Publications, Todmorden: New Island Books, Dundrum, 1996)

O'Malley, Mary, from *The Knife in the Wave* (Salmon Poetry, Cliffs of Moher, 1997)

O'Mara, Pat, from *The Autobiography of a Liverpool Irish Slummy* (Martin Hopkinson, London, 1934)

O'Neill, Eugene, from *Long Day's Journey Into Night* written 1940, first staged 1956, © 1955 Carollotta Monterey O'Neill; from *A Touch of the Poet* written 1936-39 (Royal National Theatre, London and Nick Heron, 1993)

O'Neill, Moira, from *Songs of the Glens of Antrim* (William Blackwood, Edinburgh and London, 1901)

Ó Ríordáin, Seán, from *Eireaball Spideoige* (1952),

trans. Patrick Crotty in Patrick Crotty (ed.) *Modern Irish Poetry: An Anthology* (Blackstaff, Belfast, 1995); from *Brosna* (trans. Thomas Kinsella) (Baile Atha Cliath, 1964)

O'Riordan, Conal, from *Adam of Dublin: A Romance of Today* (W. Collins, London, 1920)

O'Sullivan, Seumas, from *Verses: Sacred and Profane* (Maunsel, Dublin, 1908)

O'Toole, Fintan, from *Granta*, Spring, 1996

Ó Tuama, Seán, from *Rogha Dánta Death in the Land of Youth* (Cork University Press, Cork, 1997); from *Krino*, 11 Summer 1991 (trans. A. MacPóilín)

Parker, Stewart, from *Three Plays for Ireland: Northern Star, Heavenly Bodies* (Oberon Books, Oldcastle, 1989)

Parnell, John Howard, from *Charles Stewart Parnell: A Memoir* (Constable, London, 1916)

Paulin, Tom from *Walking a Line* (London: Faber and Faber, 1994)

Pearse, Patrick, from *Suantraide agus Goltraide* (1914) reprinted *Collected Works of Padraic H. Pearse: Plays, Stories and Poems* (Maunsel, Dublin and London, 1917)

Phelan, Jim, from *Lifer* (Peter Davies, London, 1938); from *Jail Journal* (Secker & Warburg, London, 1940); from *Ireland-Atlantic Gateway* (John Lane, The Bodley Head, London, 1941); *We Follow the Roads* (Phoenix House, London, 1949)

Plunkett, James, from *Strumpet City* (Hutchinson, London, 1969; copyright © James Plunkett 1969) by permission of PFD on behalf of James Plunkett

Power, Richard, from *The Hungry Grass* (The Bodley Head, London, 1969)

Powers, J.F., from *Prince of Darkness and Other Stories* (1947: reprinted Vintage, New York, 1979)

Reid, Forrest, from *Apostate* (Constable, London, 1926)

Robb, Nesca A., from *An Ulsterwoman in England 1924-1941* (Cambridge University Press, Cambridge, 1942)

Robinson, Tim, from *Stones of Aran: Labyrinth* (1995, reprinted Penguin, Harmondsworth, 1997)

Rodgers, W.R., from *The Listener*, 26 December 1957, copyright Campbell Thomson & McLaughlin Ltd on behalf of Lucy Rodgers Cohen

Rolston, Bill, from *Race and Class* 31(1) 1989

Russell, George, from *Imagination and Reveries* (Maunsel and Roberts, London and Dublin, 1921); from *All Ireland Review*, 6 January 1900; from *Studies: An Irish Quarterly Review*, Vol. XII, No. 45, March 1923; from *The Interpreters* (Macmillan Press Ltd., London, 1922); from Frank O'Connor *The Wild Bird's Nest: Poems from the Irish* (Cuala Press, Dublin, 1932)

Ryan, Frederick, from *Criticism and Courage and Other Essays* (Maunsel, Dublin, 1906)

Ryan, John, from *Envoy* Vol. 1 February 1950

Said, Edward, from *Nationalism, Colonialism and Literature: Yeats and Decolonization* (Field Day, Derry, 1988)

Salkeld, Blanaid, from *Hello Eternity* (Elkin Mathews and Marrot, London, 1933); from *The Fox's Covert* (J. M. Dent & Sons, London, 1935, copyright Phoenix House)

Shaw, G. B., *John Bull's Other Island* (1904; London: Constable, 1907)

Simpson, Leo, from *The Lady and the Travelling Salesman*, Henry Imbleau (ed.), (University of Ottawa Press, Ottawa, 1976)

Sirr, Peter, from *The Irish Times*, 14 June 1986

Slater, Patrick, from *The Yellow Briar* (1933; reprinted Macmillan, Toronto, 1941)

Smith, Iain Crichton, from *The Exiles* (Raven Arts Press, Dublin, 1984; Carcanet, Manchester, 1984)

Somerville and Ross, from *Some Experiences of an Irish R.M.* (Longmans, Green, London, 1899)

Shaw, G.B., from *The Daily News* (London), 10 May 1916

Simmons, James, from *West Strand Visions* (1974)

Smith, Betty, from *A Tree Grows in Brooklyn* (Harper and Brothers, New York, 1943)

Smith, Paul, from *The Countrywoman* (1962; reprinted Pan, London, 1987)

Smyth, Ailbhe, from *Critical Survey* Vol. 8, no. 2, 1996

Stephens, James, from *Insurrections* (Maunsel, Dublin, 1909); from *The Insurrection in Dublin* (1916, reprinted Scepter, Dublin, 1965); from *Letters of James Stephens*, Richard J. Finneran (ed.) (Macmillan Press Ltd., London, 1974); from *Reincarnations* (Macmillan Press Ltd, London, 1918)

Strong, L.A.G., from *The Garden* (1931; reprinted Methuen, London, 1945); from *The Body's Imperfection: The Collected Poems of L.A.G. Strong* (Methuen, London, 1957)

Stuart, Francis and Cecil Salkeld, from *Tomorrow*, Vol. 1, No. 1, August 1924

Stuart, Francis, from *The Irish Times*, October 1976; from *Black List Section H* (1971; reprinted Penguin, Harmondsworth, 1982)

Sweetman, Rosita, from *On Our Knees: Ireland 1972* (Pan, London, 1972)

Synge, J.M., from *The Manchester Guardian*, 10 June 1905; *The Playboy of the Western World* (1907); from *Poems and Translations* (Maunsel, Dublin, 1911)

Tóibín, Colm, from *London Review of Books*, 18 April 1996

Trevor, William, from *The Ballroom of Romance and Other Stories* (The Bodley Head, London, 1972)

Tyrrell, George, from M.D. Petre, *Autobiography and Life of George Tyrrell, Vol. 1, Autobiography of George Tyrrell 1861-1884* (Edward Arnold, London, 1912)

Vaughan, Bernard, from *Sin, Society and Behaviour* (London, 1908)

Visser, E. and Hensey, A. 'My Land is too Green' from Mary Coughlan, *Under the Influence* (1986), courtesy MCD

Wall, Eamonn, from *Eire-Ireland*, Winter 1996, Vol. XXX, No. 4; copyright © 1996 Irish American Cultural Institute, 1 Lackawanna Place, Morristown, NJ 07960. Reproduced by permission of the publisher.

White, Terence de Vere, *A Fretful Midge* (Routledge and Kegan Paul, 1957)

Wilde, Oscar, from *The Ballad of Reading Gaol* (Leonard Smithers, London, 1899)

Yeats, W.B., from Lady Gregory (ed.) *Ideals in Ireland* (Unicorn, London, 1901); *Ideas of Good and Evil* (A.H. Bullen, London and Maunsel, Dublin, 1907); *Cathleen ni Houlihan* (1902); from *Responsibilities* (Macmillan Press Ltd., London, 1914); from *Michael Robartes and the Dancer* (Macmillan Press Ltd., London, 1921); from *The Wild Swans at Coole* (Macmillan Press Ltd., London, 1919); from *The Senate Speeches of W.B. Yeats*, Donald R. Pearce (ed.) (Faber and Faber Ltd, London, 1961); from *The Dial* January 1923; from *Tomorrow*, Vol. 1, No. 1, August 1924; from *The Winding Stair and Other Poems* (Macmillan Press Ltd., London, 1933); from *New Poems* (1938); all reprinted by permission of A.P. Watt Ltd on behalf of Michael B. Yeats and courtesy Simon & Schuster Inc., New York

INDEX OF AUTHOR NAMES